PHILI|

STREE
Lo

www.philips-maps.co.uk
First published in 2000 by Philip's,
a division of Octopus Publishing Group Ltd.
www.octopusbooks.co.uk
Endeavour House, 189 Shaftesbury Avenue
London WC2H 8JG
An Hachette UK Company
www.hachette.co.uk
Fourth edition 2010
First impression 2010
ISBN 978-1-84907-060-7 (pocket spiral)
ISBN 978-1-84907-061-4 (pocket paperback)
LONDA
© Philip's 2010

Ordnance Survey®

This product includes mapping data licensed
from Ordnance Survey® with the permission
of the Controller of Her Majesty's Stationery
Office. © Crown copyright 2010. All rights
reserved. Licence number 100011710.

Data for the speed cameras supplied by
PocketGPSWorld.com Ltd

Post Office is a trade mark of Post Office Ltd in
the UK and other countries.

Printed and bound in China

Contents

II **Key to map pages**

IV Administrative and Postcode boundaries

VI **Route planning**

XXIV **Key to map symbols**

1 **Street maps**

228 **Keys to enlarged map pages and symbols**

229 **Enlarged street maps**

271 **Index**

477 **List of numbered locations**

498 West End theatres and cinemas

500 Central London buses

502 Local rail and London Underground

Digital Data

The exceptionally high-quality mapping found in this atlas is available as digital data in
TIFF format, which is easily convertible to other bitmapped (raster) image formats. The
index is also available in digital form as a standard database table. It contains all the
details found in the printed index together with the National Grid reference for the map
square in which each entry is named.

For further information and to discuss your requirements, please contact
philips@mapsinternational.co.uk

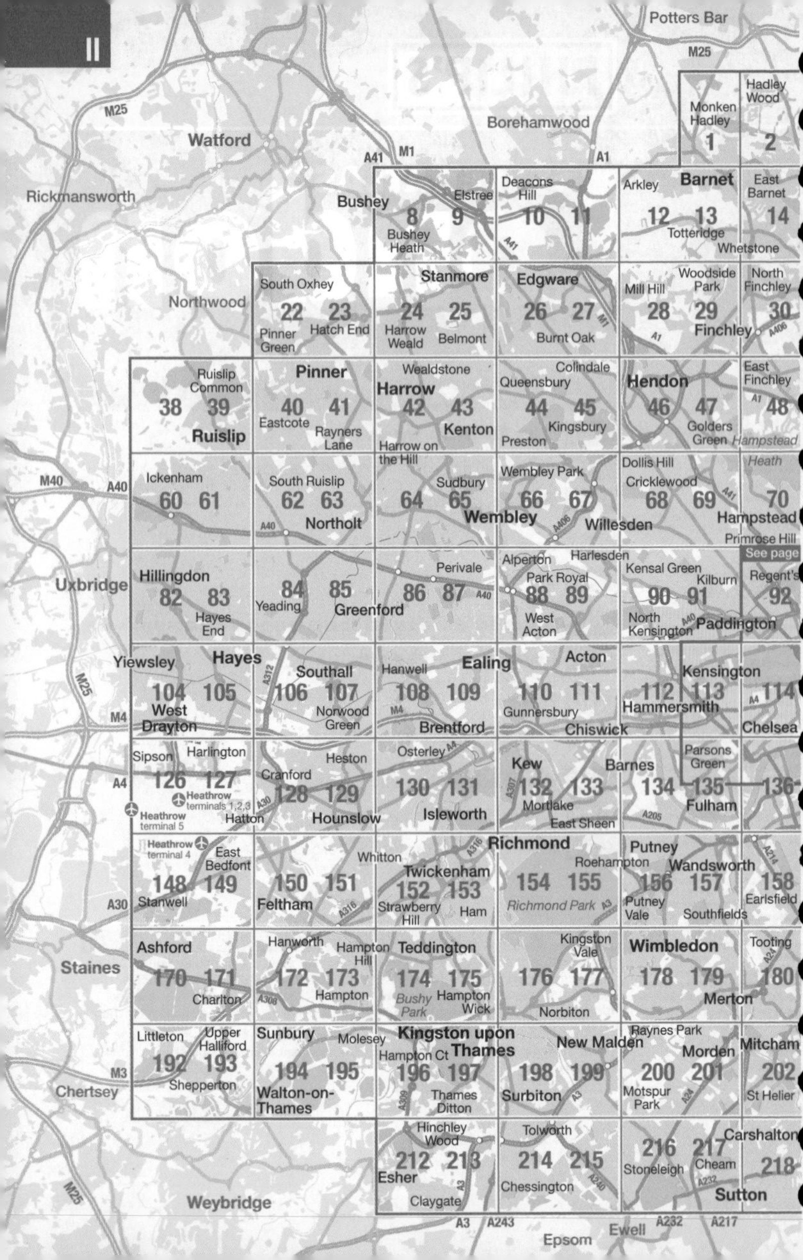

Potters Bar

M25

Monken Hadley **1** | Hadley Wood **2**

Watford

A41 | M1

Borehamwood

A1

Rickmansworth

M40 | M25

Bushey **8** | Elstree **9** | Deacons Hill **10** | **11**

Bushey Heath

Arkley | **Barnet** | East Barnet

12 **13** | **14**

Totteridge | Whetstone

Northwood

South Oxhey **22** **23** | **Stanmore 24** **25** | Edgware **26** **27** | Mill Hill **28** | Woodside Park **29** | North Finchley **30**

Pinner Green | Hatch End | Harrow Weald | Belmont | Burnt Oak | **Finchley** | A1 | A406

Ruislip Common **38** **39** | **Pinner 40** **41** | Wealdstone **Harrow 42** **43** | Colindale Queensbury **44** **45** | **Hendon 46** **47** | Golders Green | East Finchley **48**

Ruislip | Eastcote | Rayners Lane | Kenton | Kingsbury | A1 | Hampstead

Harrow on the Hill | Preston | *Heath*

Ickenham **60** **61** | South Ruislip **62** **63** | Sudbury **64** **65** | Wembley Park **66** **67** | Dollis Hill Cricklewood **68** **69** | **70**

Northolt | **Wembley** | Willesden | Hampstead

A40 | A406 | Primrose Hill

Hillingdon **82** **83** | **84** **85** | Perivale **86** **87** | Alperton Harlesden **88** **89** | Kensal Green **90** **91** | Regent's | *See page* **92**

Uxbridge | Hayes End | Yeading | **Greenford** | Park Royal | Kilburn

A40 | West Acton | North Kensington | A40 | **Paddington**

Yiewsley **Hayes** | Southall **106** **107** | Hanwell **108** **109** | **Ealing 110** **111** | Acton | **Kensington 112** **113** | **114**

104 **105** | Norwood Green | M4 | | M4

West Drayton | Gunnersbury | **Hammersmith** | Chelsea

M4 | Brentford | Chiswick

Sipson Harlington **126** **127** | Cranford Heston **128** **129** | Osterley **130** **131** | Kew **132** **133** | Barnes **134** **135** | Parsons Green **136**

A4 | Heathrow terminals 1,2,3 | Hatton | **Hounslow** | **Isleworth** | Mortlake | East Sheen | **Fulham**

Heathrow terminal 5 | Heathrow terminal 4 | East Bedfont **148** **149** | Whitton | **Richmond** | Putney Roehampton | **Wandsworth 156** **157** | **158**

Stanwell | **Feltham 150** **151** | Twickenham **152** **153** | **154** **155** | Putney Vale | Southfields | Earlsfield

A30 | Strawberry Hill | Ham | *Richmond Park* A3 | A3

Ashford **170** **171** | Hanworth Hampton Hill **172** **173** | **Teddington 174** **175** | Kingston Vale **176** **177** | **Wimbledon 178** **179** | Tooting **180**

Staines | Charlton | A308 Hampton | *Bushey Park* Hampton Wick | Norbiton | **Merton**

Littleton Upper Halliford **192** **193** | Sunbury Molesey **194** **195** | **Kingston upon Thames 196** **197** | New Malden **198** **199** | Raynes Park **200** **201** | Mitcham **202**

M3 | Shepperton | **Walton-on-Thames** | Hampton Ct Thames Ditton | Surbiton | Motspur Park | **Morden** St Helier

Chertsey | | Hinchley Wood **212** **213** | Tolworth **214** **215** | **216** **217** | Carshalton **218**

Weybridge | Esher | Claygate | Chessington | Stoneleigh | Cheam | **Sutton**

A3 | A243 | Epsom | Ewell | A232 | A217

M25

A10

Herne
160
Tulse Hill

Scale
| 0 | 1 | 2 | 3 | 4 | 5 km |
| 0 | 1 | 2 | 3 miles |

Cockfosters 3

Clay Hill 4 Forty Hill 5 **Enfield** Enfield Town Enfield Wash 6 Enfield Lock 7 Brimsdown

Loug

Oakwood Bush Hill 16 17
Winchmore Hill 15 **Southgate**
Osidge

Ponders End 18 19
Lower Edmonton

Epping Forest
20 21 **Chingford**
Buckhurst Hill

Friern Barnet 31
Edmonton A406
32 33 34 35
Muswell Hill **Wood Green Tottenham** Higham Hill

Chingford Hatch **Woodford**
36 37
Woodford Green

Hornsey 49 50 51
Highgate Finsbury Park

Walthamstow
52 53
Upper Clapton

Snaresbrook
54 55
Wanstead

Barkingside
56 57
Newbury Park Goodmayes

Little Heath
58 59

A12

Romford

Tufnell Park 71
Stoke Newington Highbury
72 73
Camden Town Islington A10

Lower Clapton Lea Bridge
74 75
Hackney Hackney Wick

Leytonstone
76 77
Stratford Upton

A406
Ilford
78 79
Barking

Becontree
80 81
Dagenham

228 for central London

Park 93 A501
Finsbury
94 95
Marylebone **City of London**

Bethnal Green Bow
96 97
Stepney Tower Hamlets A11

West Ham
Newham 98 99
Canning Town

East Ham
100 101
Creekmouth
Beckton

Castle Green
102 103

A13

Mayfair 115
Southwark
116 117
Westminster Walworth Lambeth

Wapping
118 119
Bermondsey Isle of Dogs

Canary Wharf
Blackwall Silvertown
120 121
Greenwich

London City
122 123
Woolwich
Plumstead

Thamesmead
124 125
Abbey Wood Belvedere

Erith

Battersea
137
Clapham
Camberwell
138 139
Brixton

Deptford
140 141
Nunhead New Cross

Charlton
142 143
Blackheath **Lewisham**

Shooters Hill
144 145
Falconwood Welling

West Heath Lessness Heath
146 147
Bexleyheath

Crayford

A205
Herne Hill
159 160 161
Balham Tulse Hill Dulwich A205

Honor Oak Ladywell
162 163
Forest Hill **Catford**

Hither Green Lee
164 165
Grove Park

Eltham Avery Hill
166 167
New Eltham A20

A2
Blackfen Old Bexley
168 169

A2

Streatham
Furzedown 181 182 183
Norbury Upper Norwood

Crystal Palace
184 185
Penge Beckenham

Southend Downham
186 187
Plaistow **Bromley**
Bickley

Elmstead
188 189
Chislehurst

Sidcup
Foots Cray
190 191
St Paul's Cray

Swanley

A20

Thornton Heath
203 204 205
Beddington Corner A23 Selhurst

Elmers End Eden Park
206 207
Addiscombe

Shortlands
208 209
Hayes

Petts Wood
210 211
Southborough Broom Hill

A20

Beddington
Croydon
219 220 221
Wallington

Shirley A232
222 223
Addington Selsdon

West Wickham A232
224 225
New Addington Keston

Orpington
226 227
Farnborough

M25

A23

A21

A20

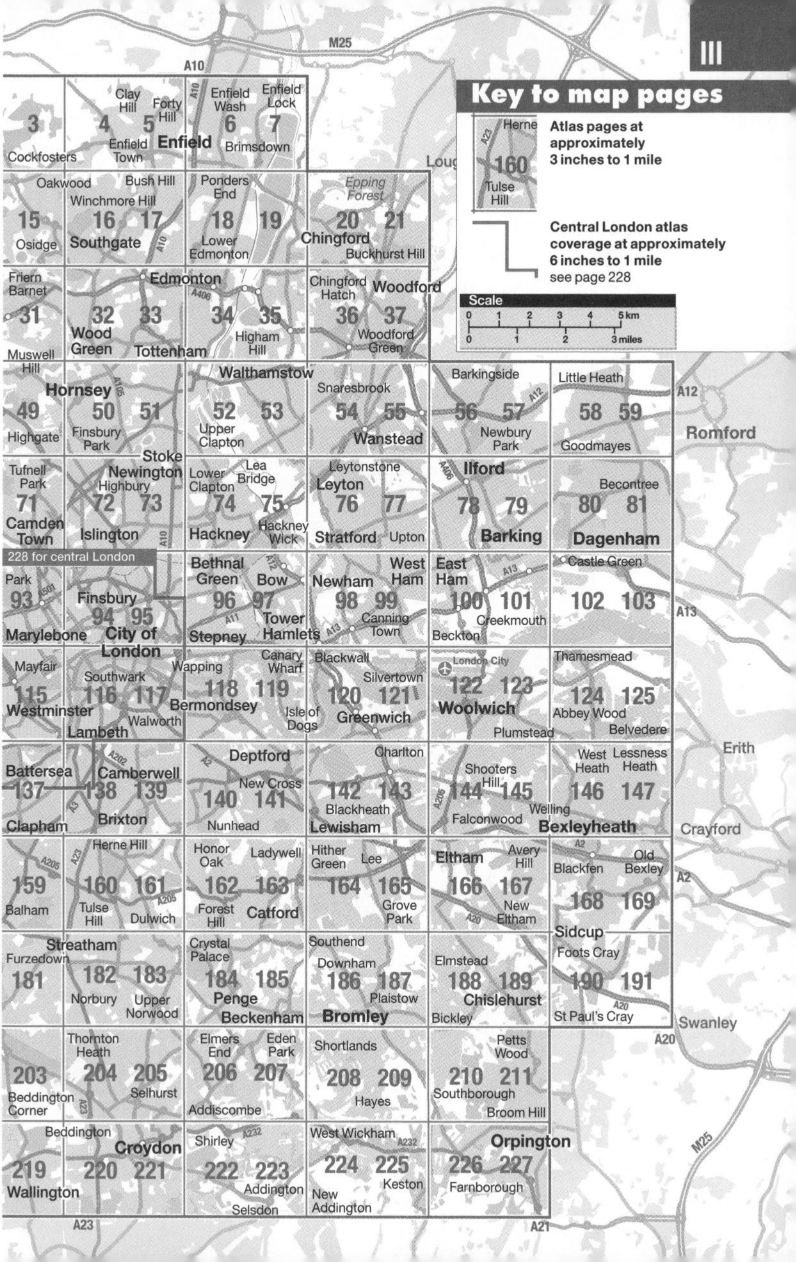

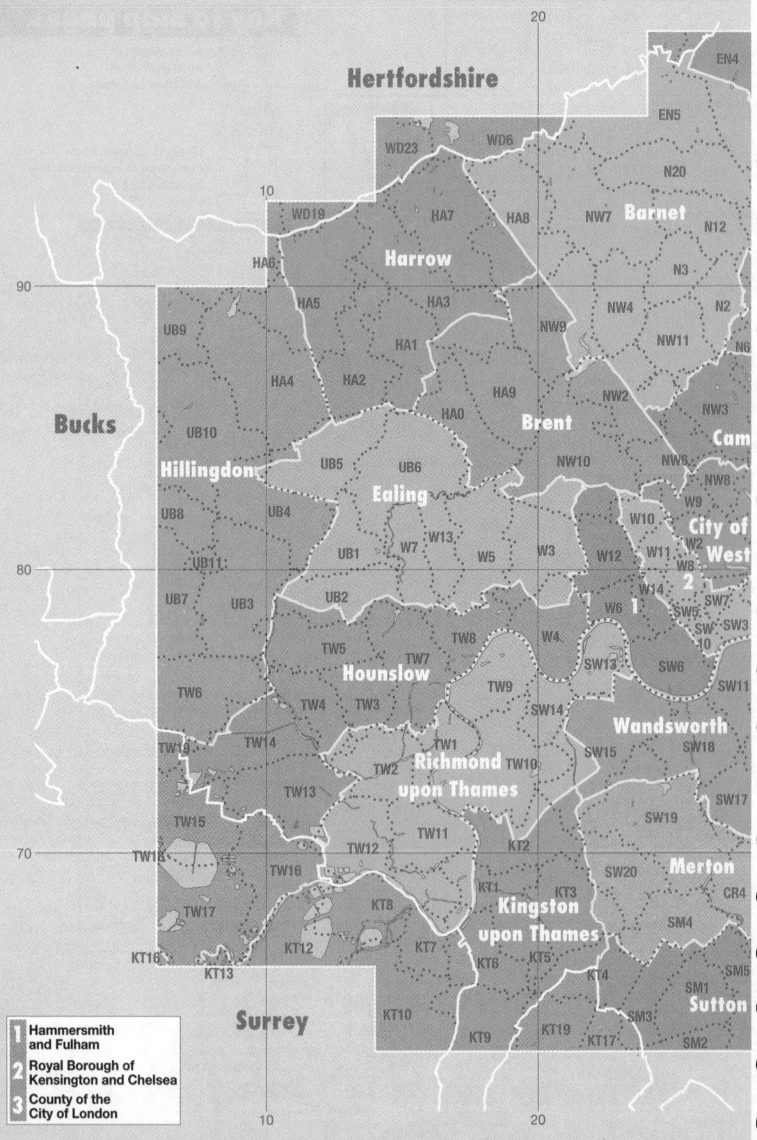

IV

Hertfordshire

Bucks

Surrey

1	Hammersmith and Fulham
2	Royal Borough of Kensington and Chelsea
3	County of the City of London

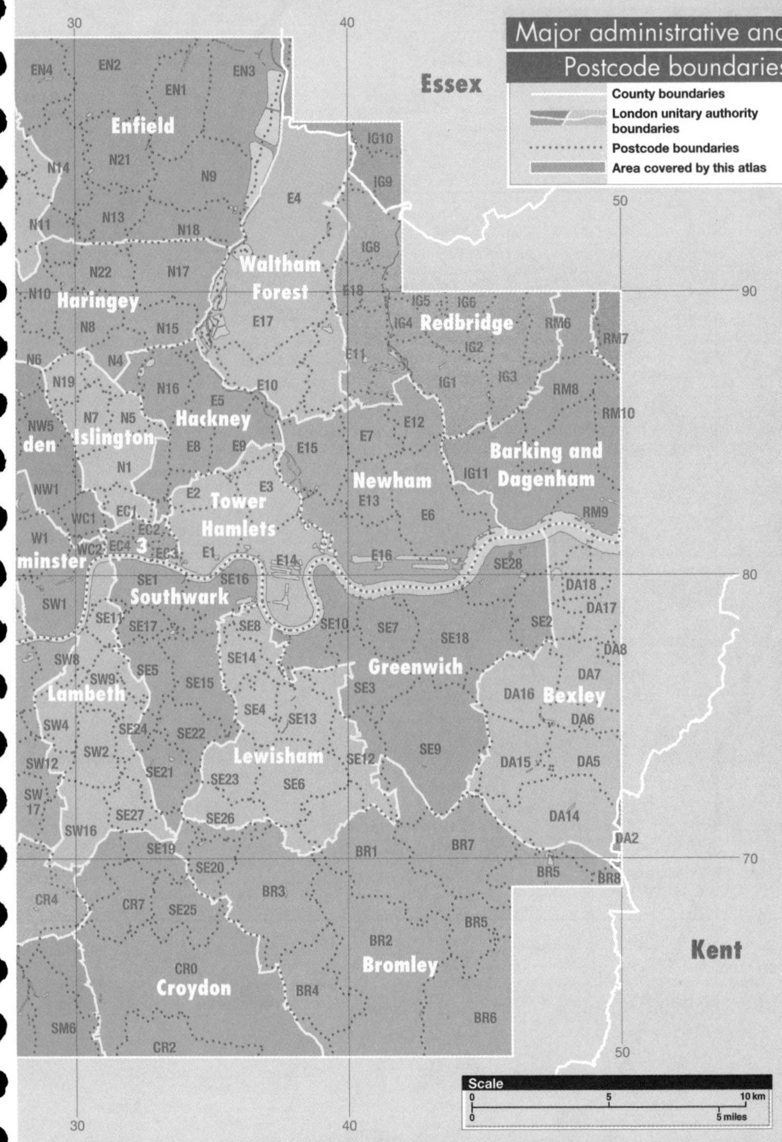

V

Major administrative and Postcode boundaries

- County boundaries
- London unitary authority boundaries
- Postcode boundaries
- Area covered by this atlas

Essex

Kent

EN4 EN2 EN1 EN3
Enfield
N14 N21 N9 IG10
IG9
N11 N13 N18 E4 IG8
N22 N17 E18
N10 Haringey N15 Waltham IG5 IG6
N8 Forest IG4 Redbridge RM6 RM7
N6 N19 N4 E17 E11 IG2 IG3 RM8
NW5 N16 E5 E10 IG1 RM10
N7 N5 Hackney E7 E12
den Islington E8 E9 E15 Newham IG11 Barking and
NW1 N1 E2 E3 Dagenham
WC1 EC1 Tower E13 E6 RM9
W1 WC2 EC2 Hamlets E14
minster EC4 EC3 E1 E16 SE28 DA18
SW1 SE1 SE16 DA17
Southwark SE10 SE7 SE2 DA8
SE11 SE8 SE18 DA7
SW8 SW9 SE5 SE17 SE14 Greenwich DA16 Bexley
Lambeth SE15 SE4 SE13 SE3 DA6
SW4 SW24 SW22 SE9 DA15 DA5
SW12 SW2 SE21 Lewisham SE12 DA14
SW SW27 SE23 SE6
17 SW16 SE26 DA2
SE19 BR1 BR7 70
CR4 SE20 BR5 BR8
CR7 SE25 BR3
SM6 CR0 BR2 BR5
CR2 Croydon BR4 Bromley BR6

Scale
0 — 5 — 10 km
0 — 5 miles

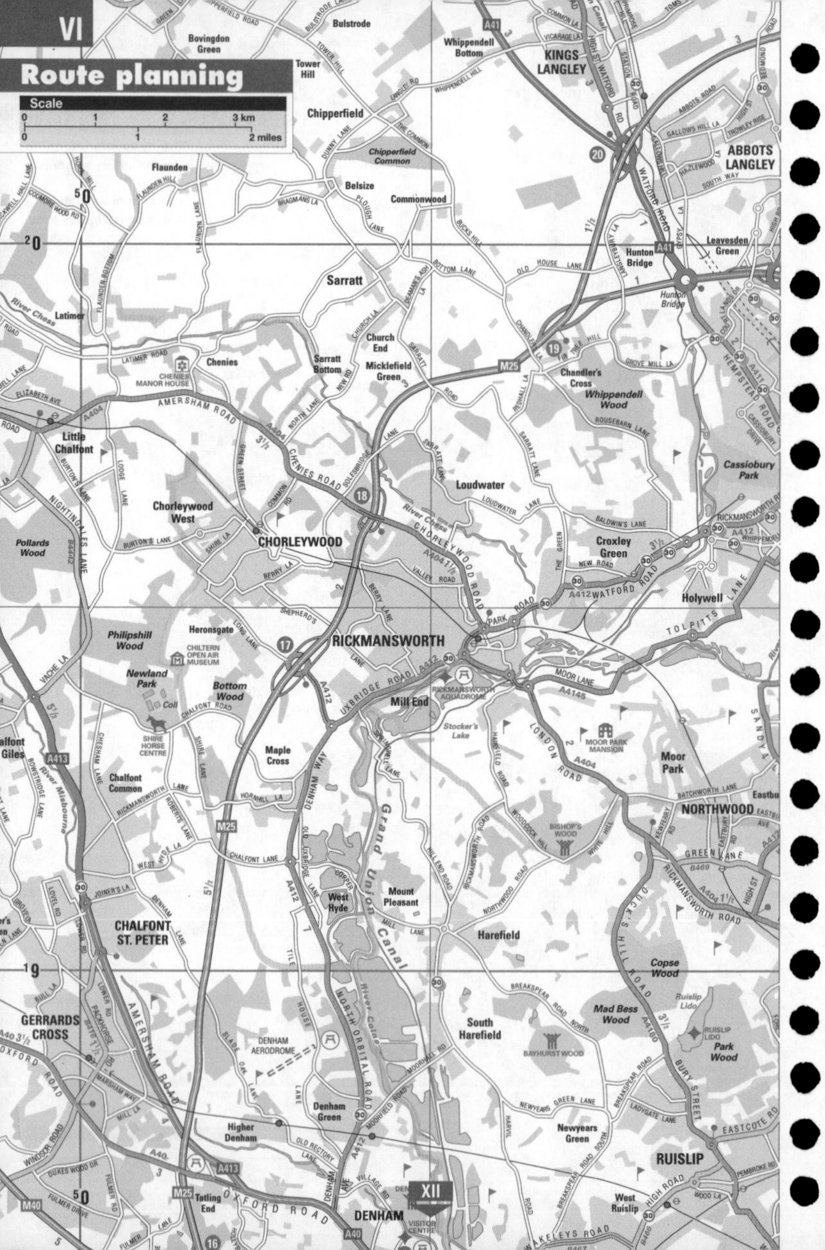
VI
Route planning
Scale
0
1
2
3 km
0
1
2 miles
Bulstrode
Bovingdon Green
Tower Hill
Chipperfield
Whippendell Bottom
KINGS LANGLEY
ABBOTS LANGLEY
Chipperfield Common
Flaunden
Belsize
Commonwood
Leavesden Green
Hunton Bridge
Sarratt
Latimer
River Chess
Church End
Chenies
CHENIES MANOR HOUSE
Sarratt Bottom
Micklefield Green
Chandler's Cross
Whippendell Wood
Little Chalfont
Loudwater
Cassiobury Park
Chorleywood West
CHORLEYWOOD
Pollards Wood
Croxley Green
Holywell
Philipshill Wood
Heronsgate
CHILTERN OPEN AIR MUSEUM
RICKMANSWORTH
Newland Park
Bottom Wood
Coll
RICKMANSWORTH AQUADROME
Mill End
Stocker's Lake
MOOR PARK MANSION
Moor Park
SHIRE HORSE CENTRE
Maple Cross
Chalfont St. Giles
River Misbourne
Chalfont Common
Grand Union Canal
NORTHWOOD
BISHOP'S WOOD
West Hyde
Mount Pleasant
CHALFONT ST. PETER
Harefield
Copse Wood
Ruislip Lido
GERRARDS CROSS
DENHAM AERODROME
South Harefield
Mad Bess Wood
BAYHURST WOOD
RUISLIP LIDO
Park Wood
River Colne
Denham Green
Higher Denham
Newyears Green
RUISLIP
Tatling End
DENHAM
VISITOR CENTRE
XII
West Ruislip
M25
M40
A40
A41
A404
A412
A413
A4145
A4180
M25
AMERSHAM ROAD
OXFORD ROAD
NORTH ORBITAL ROAD
WATFORD ROAD
LONDON ROAD
UXBRIDGE ROAD
RICKMANSWORTH ROAD
HIGH ROAD
BURY STREET
MOOR LANE
TOLPITTS LANE
CHORLEYWOOD ROAD
CHENIES ROAD
NIGHTINGALES LANE

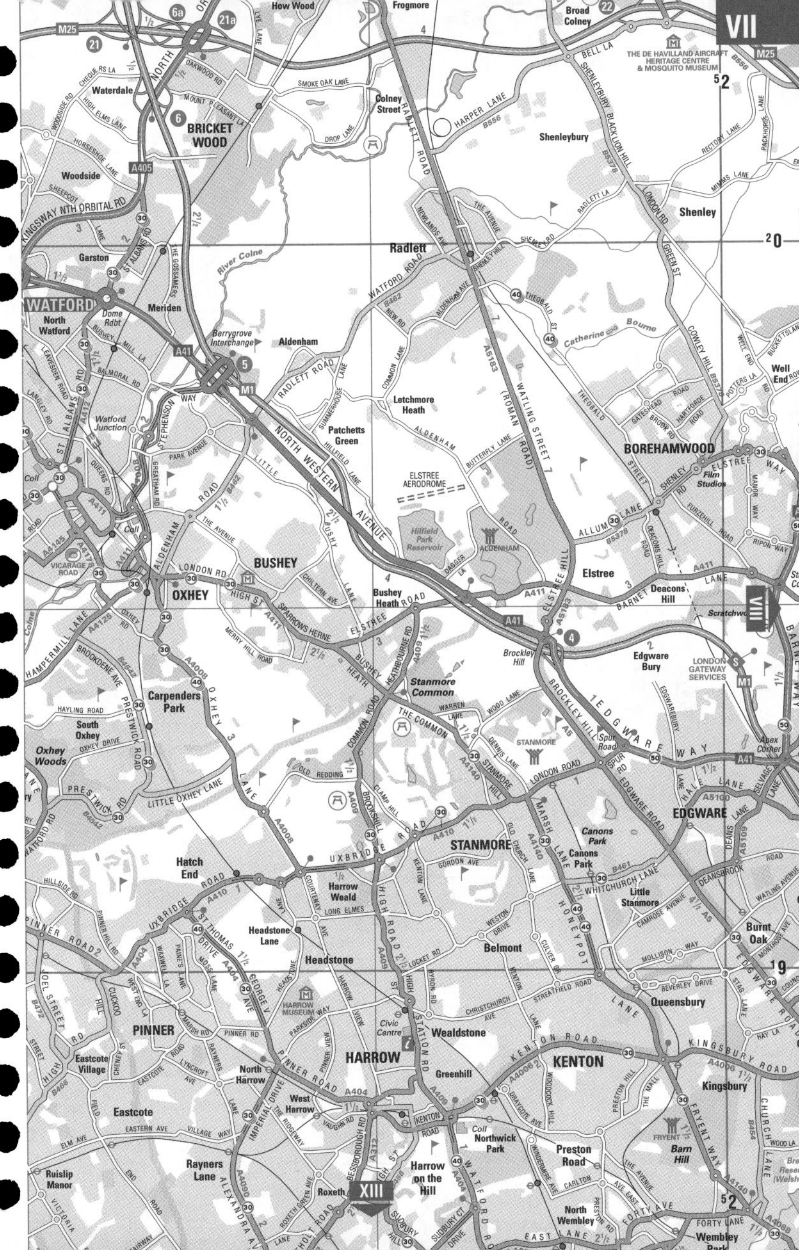

VII
Bricket Wood
Watford
Bushey
Oxhey
Radlett
Shenley
Borehamwood
Elstree
Stanmore
Edgware
Harrow
Pinner
Kenton
Wealdstone
Aldenham
Letchmore Heath
Patchetts Green
Carpenders Park
Hatch End
Harrow Weald
Headstone
Eastcote
Rayners Lane
North Harrow
West Harrow
Harrow on the Hill
Kingsbury
Queensbury
Burnt Oak
Belmont
Canons Park
Little Stanmore
Preston Road
North Wembley
Northwick Park
Wembley Park
Elstree Aerodrome
Hilfield Park Reservoir
The De Havilland Aircraft Heritage Centre & Mosquito Museum
London Gateway Services
Harrow Museum
VIII
XIII

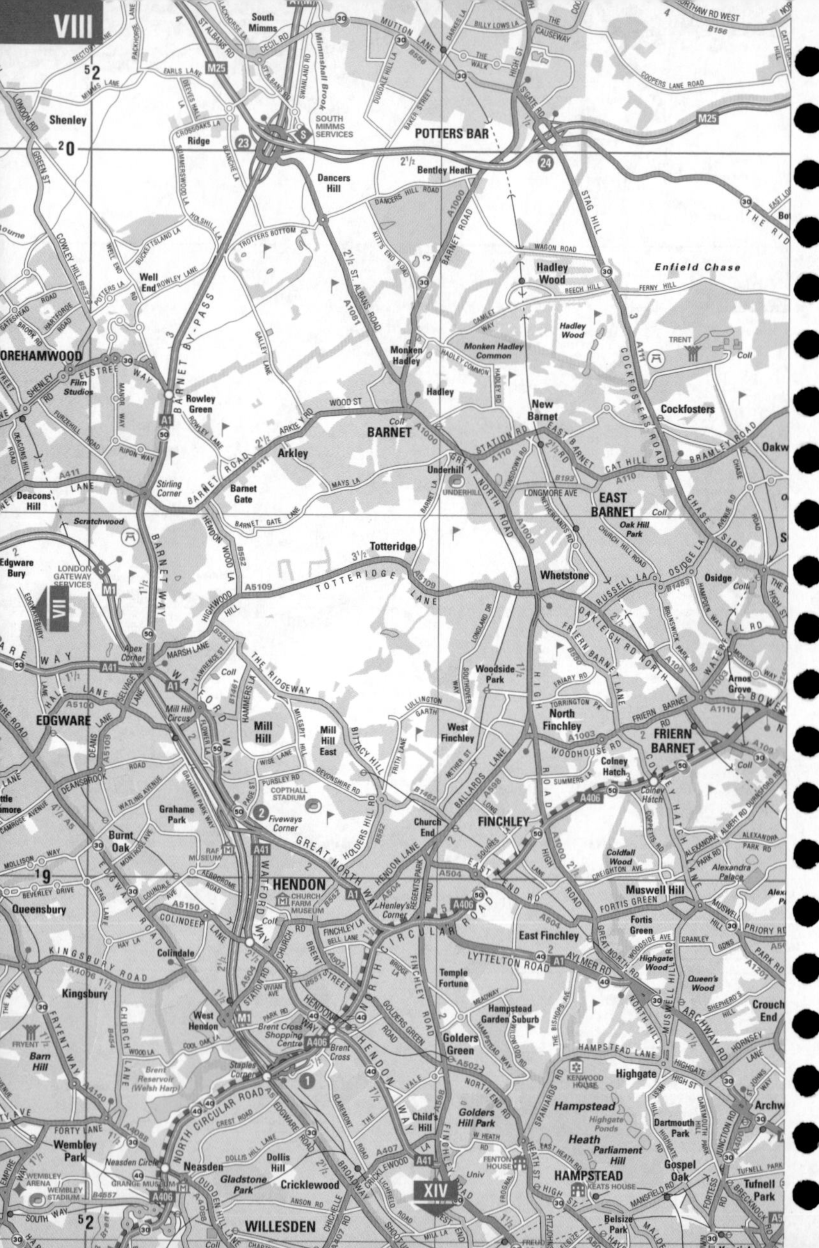
South Mimms
Shenley
Ridge
POTTERS BAR
SOUTH MIMMS SERVICES
Dancers Hill
Bentley Heath
Hadley Wood
Enfield Chase
Well End
OREHAMWOOD
Film Studios
Monken Hadley
Monken Hadley Common
Hadley
Rowley Green
Arkley
BARNET
New Barnet
Cockfosters
Underhill
EAST BARNET
Oak Hill Park
Deacons Hill
Stirling Corner
Barnet Gate
Scratchwood
Edgware Bury
LONDON GATEWAY SERVICES
Totteridge
Whetstone
Osidge
Apex Corner
EDGWARE
Mill Hill Circus
Mill Hill
Mill Hill East
West Finchley
Woodside Park
North Finchley
FRIERN BARNET
Arnos Grove
Colney Hatch
COPTHALL STADIUM
Fiveways Corner
Grahame Park
Burnt Oak
RAF MUSEUM
Church End
FINCHLEY
Coldfall Wood
Alexandra Palace
HENDON
CHURCH FARM MUSEUM
Henley's Corner
Muswell Hill
Fortis Green
Queensbury
Colindale
East Finchley
Highgate Wood
Queen's Wood
Kingsbury
Temple Fortune
Hampstead Garden Suburb
Crouch End
West Hendon
Brent Cross Shopping Centre
Brent Cross
Golders Green
Barn Hill
Staples Corner
Brent Reservoir (Welsh Harp)
KENWOOD HOUSE
Highgate
Hampstead
Highgate Ponds
Wembley Park
Child's Hill
Golders Hill Park
Heath
Parliament Hill
Dartmouth Park
Neasden Circle
Neasden
Dollis Hill
FENTON HOUSE
HAMPSTEAD
Gospel Oak
Tufnell Park
WEMBLEY ARENA
WEMBLEY STADIUM
GRANGE MUSEUM
Gladstone Park
Cricklewood
KEATS HOUSE
WILLESDEN
Belsize Park
Kentish
XIV
VII
M25
M1
A1
A41
A406
NORTH CIRCULAR ROAD
BARNET BY-PASS
GREAT NORTH ROAD
WATFORD WAY
TOTTERIDGE LANE
ARCHWAY RD

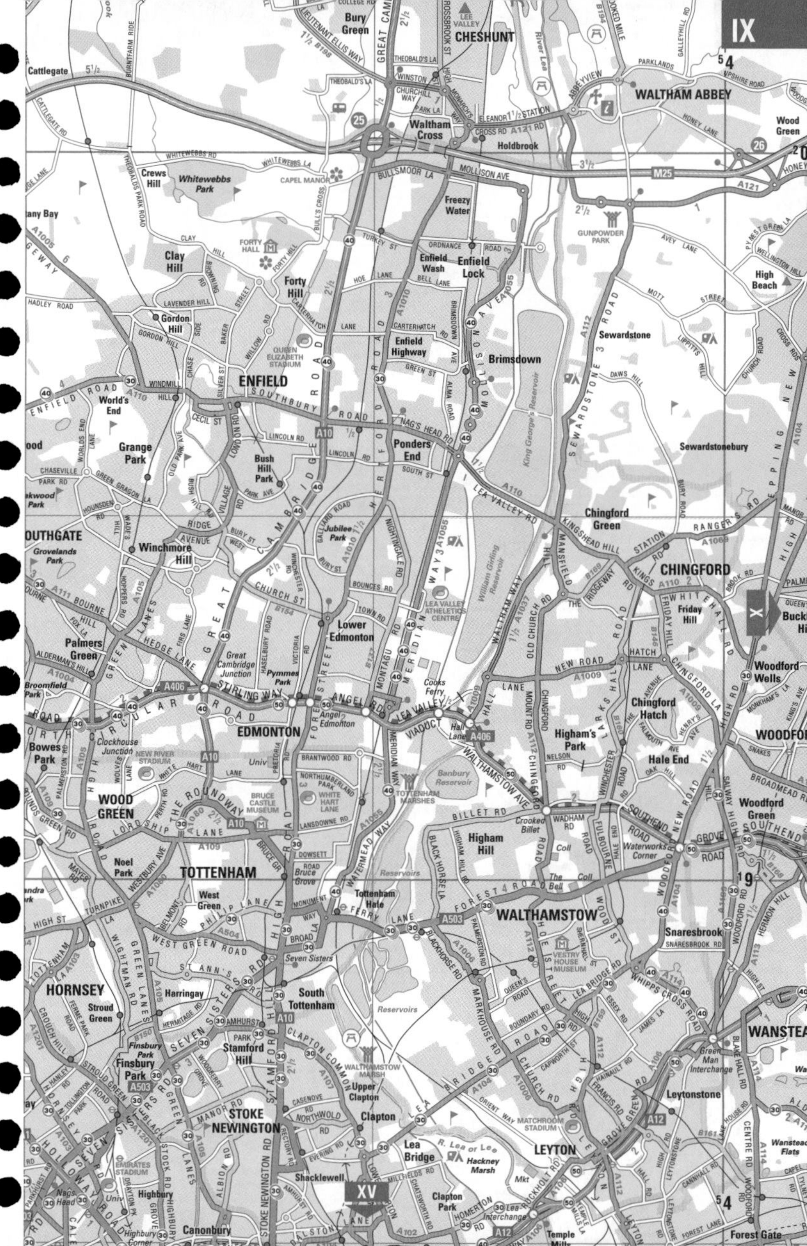
Bury Green
CHESHUNT
Cattlegate
WALTHAM ABBEY
Waltham Cross
Holdbrook
Wood Green
Crews Hill
Whitewebbs Park
CAPEL MANOR
Freezy Water
GUNPOWDER PARK
FORTY HALL
Clay Hill
Enfield Wash
Enfield Lock
High Beach
Forty Hill
Gordon Hill
Sewardstone
QUEEN ELIZABETH STADIUM
Enfield Highway
Brimsdown
ENFIELD
World's End
King George's Reservoir
Grange Park
Bush Hill Park
Ponders End
Sewardstonebury
Chingford Green
Jubilee Park
Winchmore Hill
Grovelands Park
CHINGFORD
William Girling Reservoir
LEA VALLEY ATHLETICS CENTRE
Friday Hill
Buckhurst Hill
Palmers Green
Lower Edmonton
Great Cambridge Junction
Pymmes Park
Woodford Wells
Broomfield Park
Cooks Ferry
Chingford Hatch
Angel Edmonton
EDMONTON
Higham's Park
WOODFORD
Bowes Park
Clockhouse Junction
NEW RIVER STADIUM
Hale End
Banbury Reservoir
WOOD GREEN
BRUCE CASTLE MUSEUM
WHITE HART LANE
TOTTENHAM MARSHES
Woodford Green
Crooked Billet
Higham Hill
Noel Park
Waterworks Corner
TOTTENHAM
Bruce Grove
Reservoirs
West Green
Tottenham Hale
WALTHAMSTOW
Snaresbrook
Seven Sisters
HORNSEY
VESTRY HOUSE MUSEUM
Harringay
South Tottenham
Stroud Green
Reservoirs
WANSTEAD
Finsbury Park
Stamford Hill
Green Man Interchange
WALTHAMSTOW MARSH
Upper Clapton
Leytonstone
STOKE NEWINGTON
Clapton
MATCHROOM STADIUM
EMIRATES STADIUM
Lea Bridge
Hackney Marsh
LEYTON
Wanstead Flats
Shacklewell
Highbury
Clapton Park
Lea Interchange
Highbury Corner
Canonbury
Temple Mills
Forest Gate
M25
A10
A406
A503
A12
XV
X

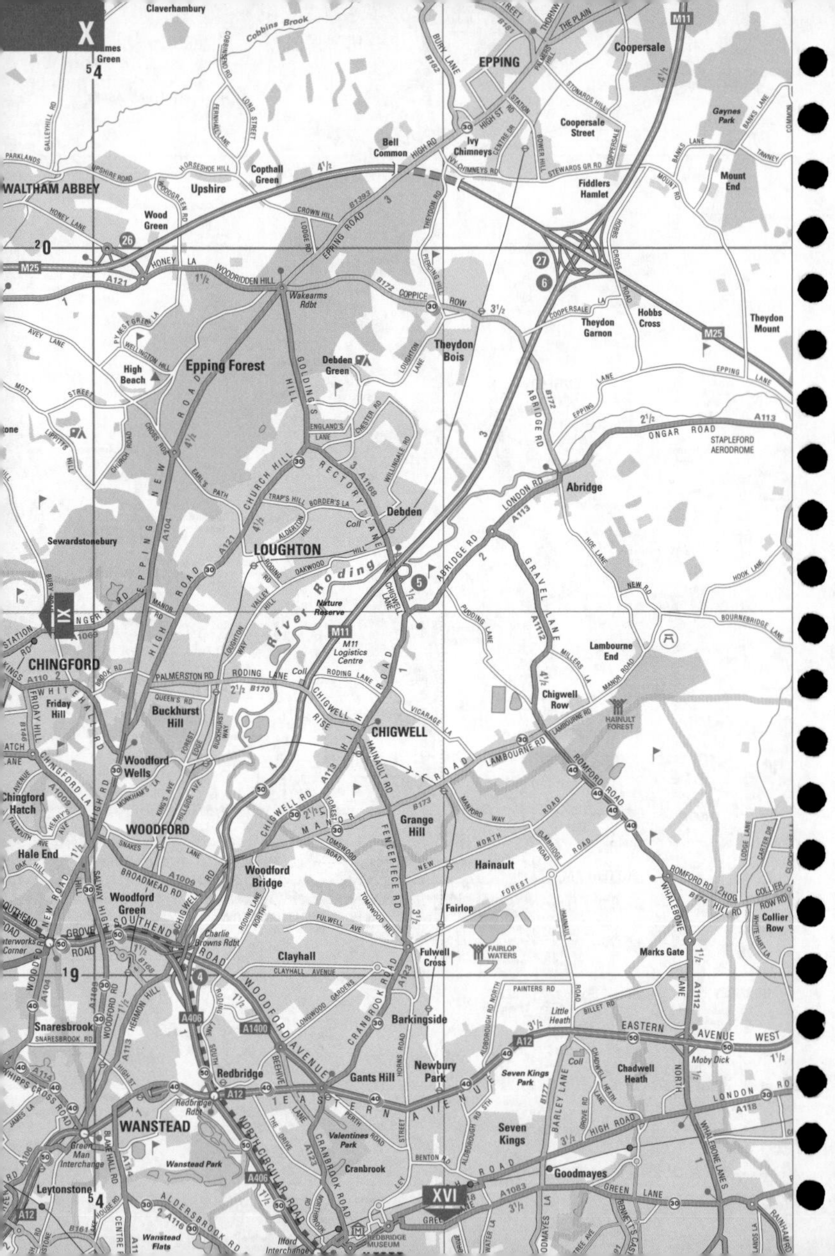

X
Claverhambury
Cobbins Brook
EPPING
Coopersale
Coopersale Street
Gaynes Park
Bell Common
Ivy Chimneys
Copthall Green
Fiddlers Hamlet
Mount End
WALTHAM ABBEY
Upshire
Wood Green
M25
M11
Wakearms Rdbt
Theydon Garnon
Hobbs Cross
Theydon Mount
Epping Forest
Debden Green
Theydon Bois
High Beach
STAPLEFORD AERODROME
Abridge
Debden
LOUGHTON
Sewardstonebury
River Roding
Nature Reserve
M11 Logistics Centre
Lambourne End
CHINGFORD
Friday Hill
Buckhurst Hill
Chigwell Row
CHIGWELL
HAINULT FOREST
Woodford Wells
Chingford Hatch
WOODFORD
Grange Hill
Hale End
Hainault
Woodford Bridge
Woodford Green
Fairlop
Charlie Browns Rdbt
FAIRLOP WATERS
Fulwell Cross
Collier Row
Marks Gate
Clayhall
Barkingside
Snaresbrook
Little Heath
Moby Dick
Redbridge
Gants Hill
Newbury Park
Seven Kings Park
Chadwell Heath
Redbridge Rdbt
WANSTEAD
Green Man Interchange
Valentines Park
Seven Kings
Wanstead Park
Cranbrook
Goodmayes
Leytonstone
XVI
IX
Wanstead Flats
Ilford Interchange
REDBRIDGE MUSEUM
EPPING ROAD
EPPING NEW ROAD
ONGAR ROAD
LONDON RD
ABRIDGE RD
GRAVEL LANE
ROMFORD ROAD
EASTERN AVENUE
EASTERN AVENUE WEST
WOODFORD AVENUE
NORTH CIRCULAR ROAD
HIGH ROAD
LAMBOURNE RD
MANOR ROAD
FENCEPIECE RD
CRANBROOK ROAD
WHALEBONE LANE
A12
A406
A1400
A113
A104
A121
A118

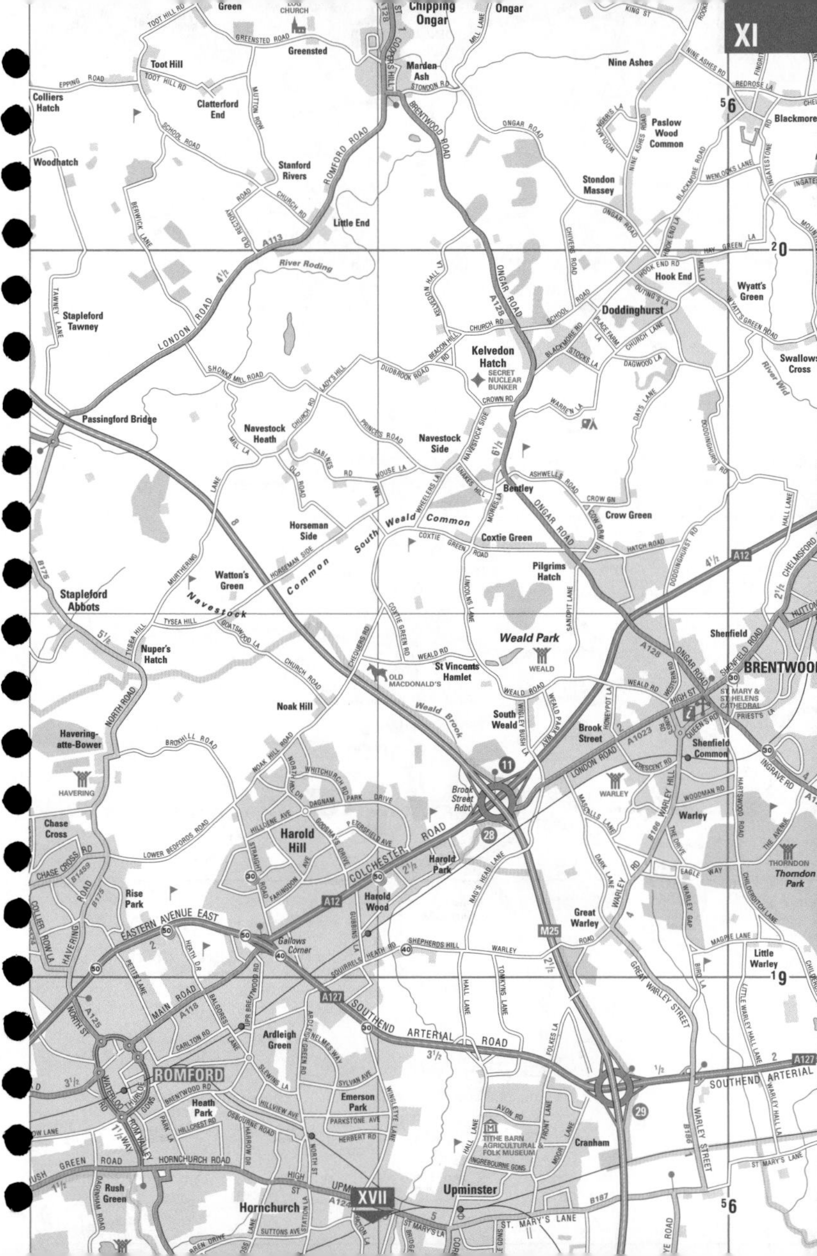
Chipping Ongar
Ongar
Green
Greensted
Toot Hill
Colliers Hatch
Clatterford End
Marden Ash
Nine Ashes
Paslow Wood Common
Blackmore
Woodhatch
Stanford Rivers
Stondon Massey
Little End
River Roding
Hook End
Wyatt's Green
Stapleford Tawney
Doddinghurst
Kelvedon Hatch
SECRET NUCLEAR BUNKER
Swallows Cross
Passingford Bridge
Navestock Heath
Navestock Side
Bentley
Crow Green
Horseman Side
South Weald Common
Coxtie Green
Pilgrims Hatch
Stapleford Abbots
Watton's Green
Navestock
Weald Park
Nuper's Hatch
St Vincents Hamlet
OLD MACDONALD'S
WEALD
Shenfield
BRENTWOOD
Noak Hill
South Weald
Brook Street
Shenfield Common
Havering-atte-Bower
HAVERING
Brook Street Rdbt
WARLEY
Warley
Chase Cross
Harold Hill
Harold Park
THORNDON
Thorndon Park
Rise Park
Harold Wood
Great Warley
Gallows Corner
Little Warley
Ardleigh Green
ROMFORD
Emerson Park
Heath Park
TITHE BARN AGRICULTURAL & FOLK MUSEUM
Cranham
Rush Green
Upminster
Hornchurch
XVII
A113
A128
A12
A1023
B186
M25
A127
SOUTHEND ARTERIAL ROAD
A118
A125
A124
B187
B175
B1459
EASTERN AVENUE EAST
COLCHESTER ROAD
LONDON ROAD
ONGAR ROAD
ROMFORD ROAD
BRENTWOOD ROAD
ST. MARY'S LANE
HORNCHURCH ROAD
56
20
19

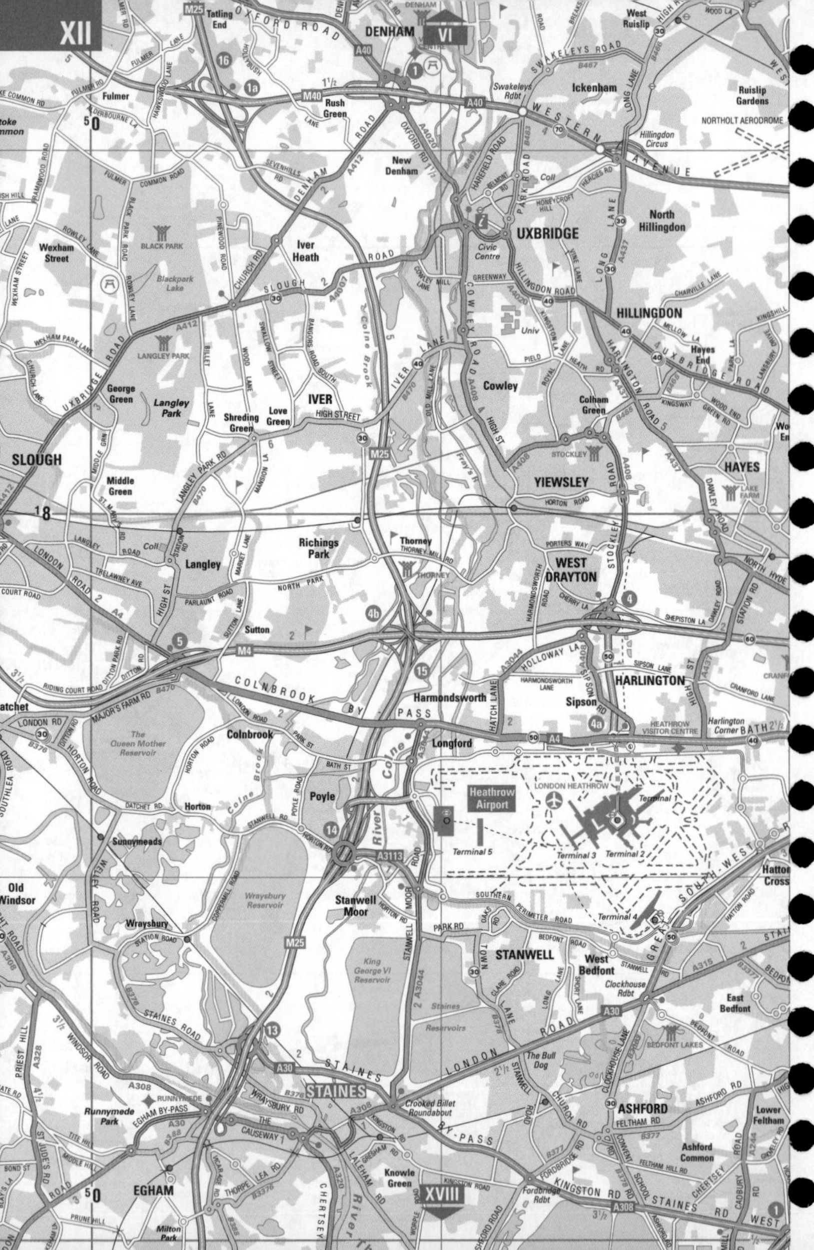

VI
DENHAM
Tatling End
OXFORD ROAD
M25
M40
A40
Fulmer
Stoke Common
Rush Green
Swakeleys Rdbt
SWAKELEYS ROAD
West Ruislip
Ickenham
Ruislip Gardens
NORTHOLT AERODROME
WESTERN AVENUE
Hillingdon Circus
New Denham
DENHAM ROAD
SEVENHILLS RD
FULMER COMMON ROAD
BLACK PARK
Blackpark Lake
Wexham Street
Iver Heath
SLOUGH ROAD
UXBRIDGE
Civic Centre
North Hillingdon
HILLINGDON ROAD
HILLINGDON
Univ
LANGLEY PARK
George Green
Langley Park
UXBRIDGE ROAD
IVER
Shreding Green
Love Green
HIGH STREET
Cowley
COWLEY ROAD
Colham Green
Hayes End
UXBRIDGE ROAD
HAYES
SLOUGH
Middle Green
LANGLEY PARK RD
STOCKLEY
YIEWSLEY
HORTON ROAD
LAKE FARM
Langley
Richings Park
Thorney
THORNEY
WEST DRAYTON
STOCKLEY ROAD
NORTH HYDE
LONDON ROAD
Sutton
M4
COLNBROOK BY-PASS
Harmondsworth
HOLLOWAY LA
Sipson
HARLINGTON
Datchet
Colnbrook
The Queen Mother Reservoir
Longford
HEATHROW VISITOR CENTRE
Harlington Corner
BATH RD
A4
Poyle
Horton
Heathrow Airport
LONDON HEATHROW
Terminal 1
Terminal 2
Terminal 3
Terminal 4
Terminal 5
River Colne
Sunnymeads
Old Windsor
Wraysbury Reservoir
Stanwell Moor
SOUTHERN PERIMETER ROAD
Hatton Cross
Wraysbury
King George VI Reservoir
STANWELL
West Bedfont
Clockhouse Rdbt
East Bedfont
Staines Reservoirs
BEDFONT LAKES
STAINES ROAD
WINDSOR ROAD
The Bull Dog
LONDON ROAD
STAINES
Crooked Billet Roundabout
RUNNYMEDE
Runnymede Park
EGHAM BY-PASS
ASHFORD
Lower Feltham
Ashford Common
EGHAM
Knowle Green
XVIII
Fordbridge Rdbt
KINGSTON RD
STAINES RD
Milton Park

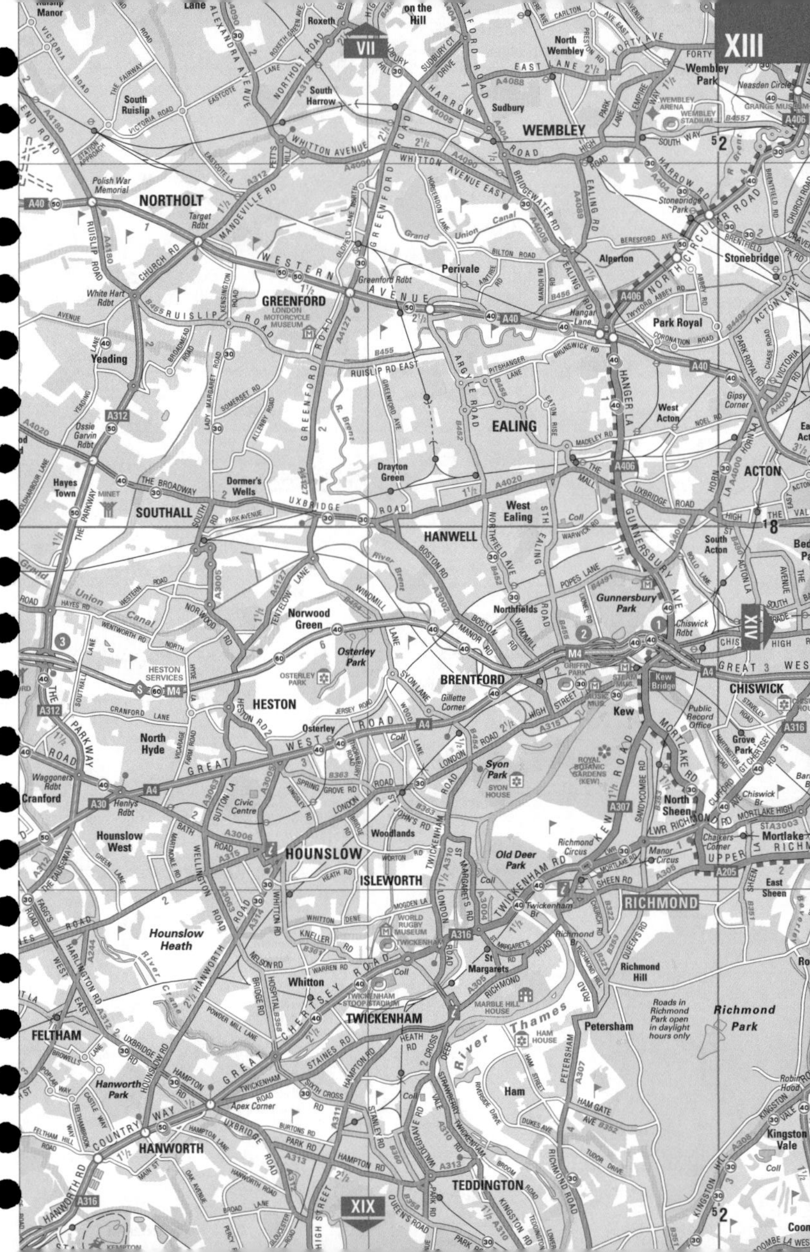

XIII
VII
XIX
XIV
Roxeth
on the Hill
North Wembley
Wembley Park
Neasden Circle
WEMBLEY ARENA
WEMBLEY STADIUM
South Ruislip
South Harrow
Sudbury
WEMBLEY
Polish War Memorial
NORTHOLT
Target Rdbt
Stonebridge Park
Stonebridge
Alperton
Perivale
White Hart Rdbt
GREENFORD
Greenford Rdbt
LONDON MOTORCYCLE MUSEUM
Hangar Lane
Park Royal
Yeading
WESTERN AVENUE
Grand Union Canal
NORTH CIRCULAR ROAD
West Acton
Gipsy Corner
EALING
Ossie Garvin Rdbt
Drayton Green
East Acton
ACTON
Hayes Town
Dormer's Wells
SOUTHALL
West Ealing
HANWELL
South Acton
UXBRIDGE ROAD
Gunnersbury Park
Norwood Green
Northfields
Chiswick Rdbt
HESTON SERVICES
Osterley Park
OSTERLEY PARK
BRENTFORD
GRIFFIN PARK
Kew Bridge
CHISWICK
HESTON
Gillette Corner
Kew
Public Record Office
North Hyde
Osterley
Grove Park
GREAT WEST ROAD
Syon Park
SYON HOUSE
ROYAL BOTANIC GARDENS (KEW)
Waggoners Rdbt
Cranford
Henlys Rdbt
Civic Centre
North Sheen
Chiswick Br
Hounslow West
HOUNSLOW
Woodlands
Richmond Circus
Old Deer Park
Chalkers Corner
Mortlake
ISLEWORTH
Manor Circus
East Sheen
Twickenham Br
RICHMOND
Hounslow Heath
WORLD RUGBY MUSEUM
TWICKENHAM
Richmond Br
St Margarets
Whitton
Richmond Hill
TWICKENHAM STOOP STADIUM
MARBLE HILL HOUSE
River Crane
River Thames
Roads in Richmond Park open in daylight hours only
Richmond Park
FELTHAM
Petersham
HAM HOUSE
Hanworth Park
Ham
Apex Corner
Robin Hood
Kingston Vale
HANWORTH
TEDDINGTON

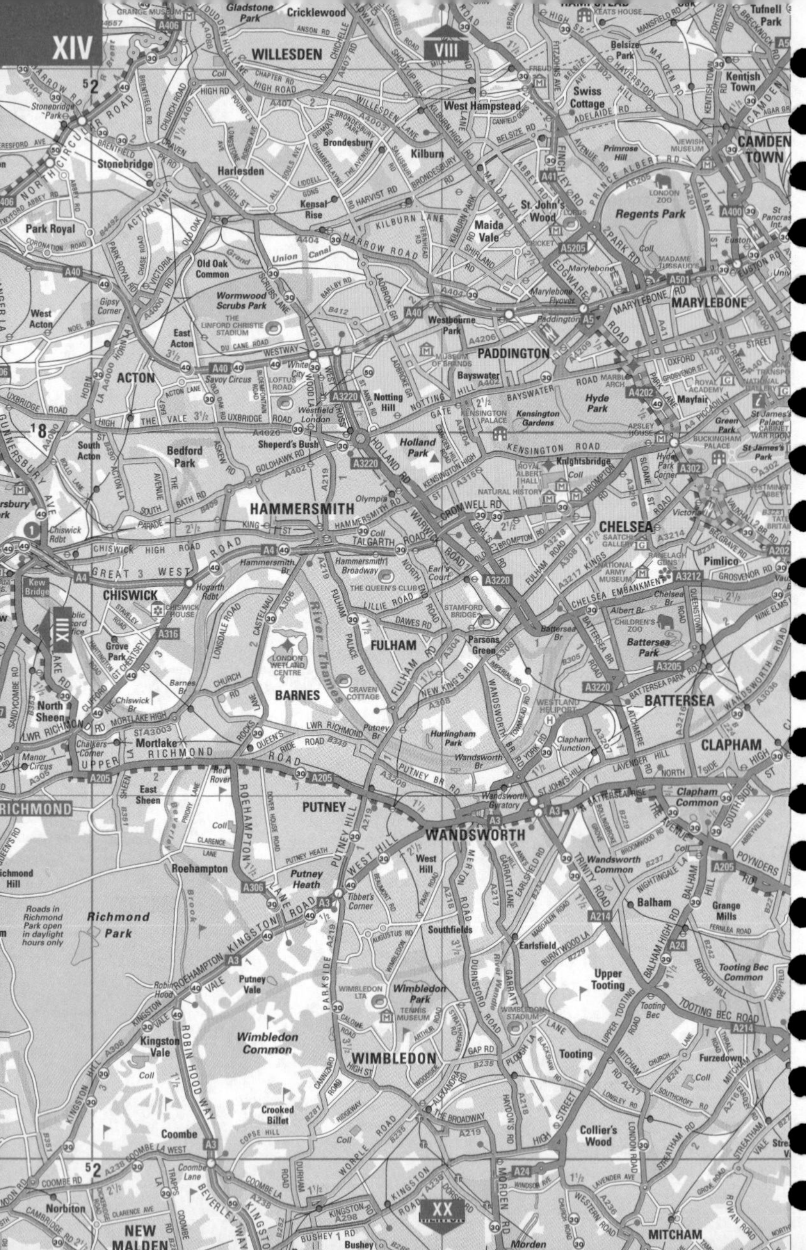

Gladstone Park
Cricklewood
WILLESDEN
VIII
West Hampstead
Belsize Park
Swiss Cottage
Kentish Town
Tufnell Park
CAMDEN TOWN
Primrose Hill
Stonebridge
Harlesden
Brondesbury
Kilburn
Kensal Rise
Park Royal
Regents Park
LONDON ZOO
St. John's Wood
Maida Vale
Old Oak Common
Grand Union Canal
MADAME TUSSAUD'S
Marylebone
MARYLEBONE
Wormwood Scrubs Park
Gipsy Corner
West Acton
East Acton
THE LINFORD CHRISTIE STADIUM
Westbourne Park
PADDINGTON
Paddington
ACTON
Savoy Circus
White City
Notting Hill
Westfield London
Bayswater
Hyde Park
Mayfair
Kensington Gardens
KENSINGTON PALACE
Green Park
BUCKINGHAM PALACE
St James's Park
South Acton
Bedford Park
Sheperd's Bush
Holland Park
Knightsbridge
Hyde Park Corner
NATURAL HISTORY
HAMMERSMITH
Olympia
CHELSEA
Victoria
Chiswick Rdbt
Earl's Court
Pimlico
Kew Bridge
CHISWICK
Hogarth Rdbt
CHISWICK HOUSE
Hammersmith Br
Hammersmith Broadway
THE QUEEN'S CLUB
STAMFORD BRIDGE
NATIONAL ARMY MUSEUM
Chelsea Br
Albert Br
CHILDREN'S ZOO
Battersea Park
XIII
Grove Park
FULHAM
Parsons Green
Battersea Br
LONDON WETLAND CENTRE
River Thames
North Sheen
Chiswick Br
Barnes Br
BARNES
CRAVEN COTTAGE
BATTERSEA
WESTLAND HELIPORT
Mortlake
Chalkers Corner
Manor Circus
Putney Br
Hurlingham Park
Clapham Junction
CLAPHAM
Wandsworth Br
RICHMOND
East Sheen
Red Rover
PUTNEY
Wandsworth Gyratory
WANDSWORTH
Clapham Common
Richmond Hill
Roehampton
Putney Heath
West Hill
Wandsworth Common
Tibbet's Corner
Balham
Grange Mills
Roads in Richmond Park open in daylight hours only
Richmond Park
Southfields
Earlsfield
Upper Tooting
Tooting Bec Common
Robin Hood
Putney Vale
WIMBLEDON LTA
Wimbledon Park
TENNIS MUSEUM
WIMBLEDON STADIUM
Tooting Bec
Kingston Vale
Wimbledon Common
WIMBLEDON
Tooting
Furzedown
Crooked Billet
Coombe
Collier's Wood
Norbiton
Coombe Lane
XX
NEW MALDEN
MITCHAM
Morden
Bushey

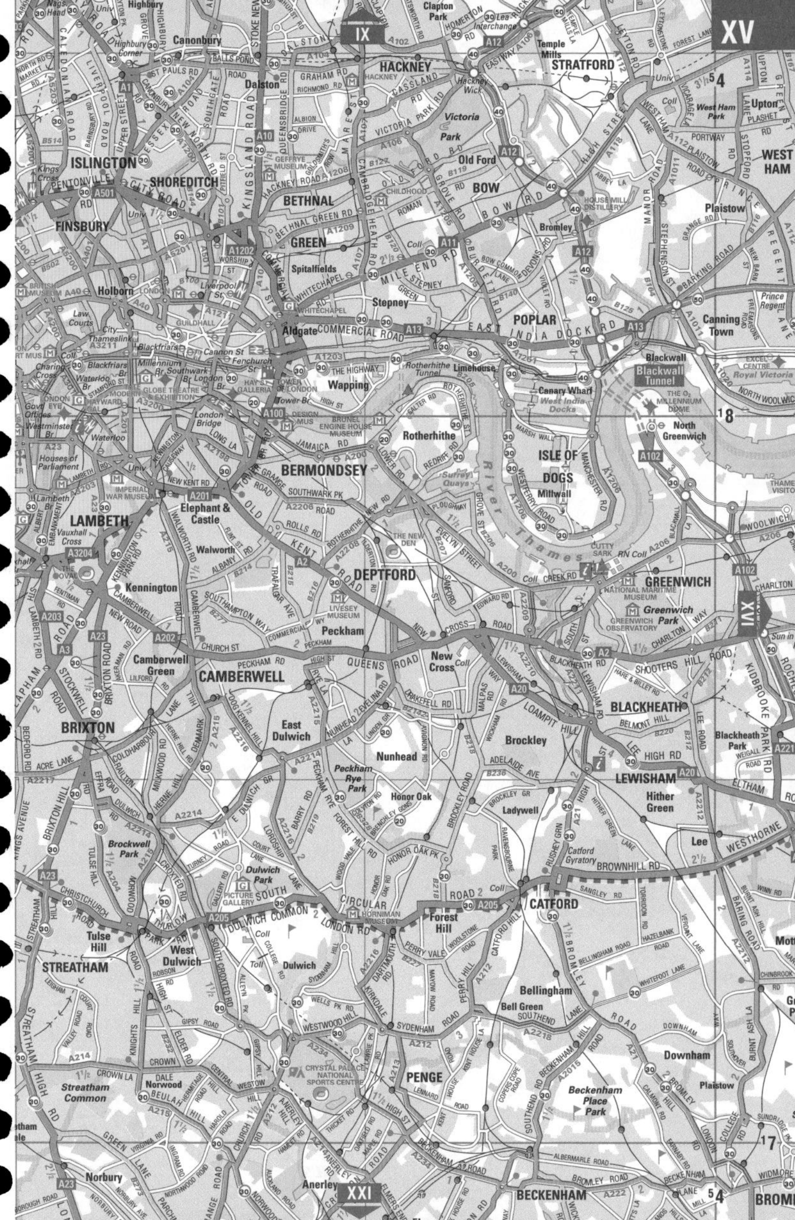
XV
IX
XVI
XXI
Highbury
Canonbury
Highbury Corner
Clapton Park
Homerton
Lea Interchange
Temple Mills
STRATFORD
HACKNEY
Hackney Wick
Dalston
ISLINGTON
SHOREDITCH
PENTONVILLE
Kings Cross
FINSBURY
Holborn
BETHNAL GREEN
Victoria Park
Old Ford
BOW
Bromley
West Ham Park
Upton
WEST HAM
Plaistow
Spitalfields
Stepney
POPLAR
Canning Town
Prince Regent
Aldgate
Liverpool St
Law Courts
City Thameslink
Blackfriars
Cannon St
Fenchurch St
Charing Cross
Waterloo Br
Millennium Br
Southwark Br
London Br
Tower Br
Wapping
Rotherhithe Tunnel
Limehouse
Canary Wharf
West India Docks
Blackwall
Blackwall Tunnel
EXCEL CENTRE
Royal Victoria Dock
THE O2 MILLENNIUM DOME
North Greenwich
Govt Offices
Westminster Br
Waterloo
London Bridge
Houses of Parliament
Rotherhithe
ISLE OF DOGS
Millwall
BERMONDSEY
Surrey Quays
Lambeth Br
LAMBETH
Elephant & Castle
Walworth
Vauxhall Cross
THE OVAL
Kennington
River Thames
CUTTY SARK
DEPTFORD
THE NEW DEN
GREENWICH
NATIONAL MARITIME MUSEUM
Greenwich Park
GREENWICH OBSERVATORY
LIVESEY MUSEUM
Peckham
New Cross
Camberwell Green
CAMBERWELL
BRIXTON
East Dulwich
Nunhead
Brockley
BLACKHEATH
Blackheath Park
LEWISHAM
Hither Green
Lee
Peckham Rye Park
Honor Oak
Ladywell
Brockwell Park
Catford Gyratory
Dulwich Park
PICTURE GALLERY
HORNIMAN MUSEUM
CATFORD
Forest Hill
Tulse Hill
West Dulwich
STREATHAM
Dulwich
Bellingham
Bell Green
Downham
CRYSTAL PALACE NATIONAL SPORTS CENTRE
PENGE
Streatham Common
Norwood
Beckenham Place Park
Plaistow
Norbury
Anerley
BECKENHAM
BROMLEY
Elmers End
South Norwood
Sun in the Sands
Motting
Grove Park

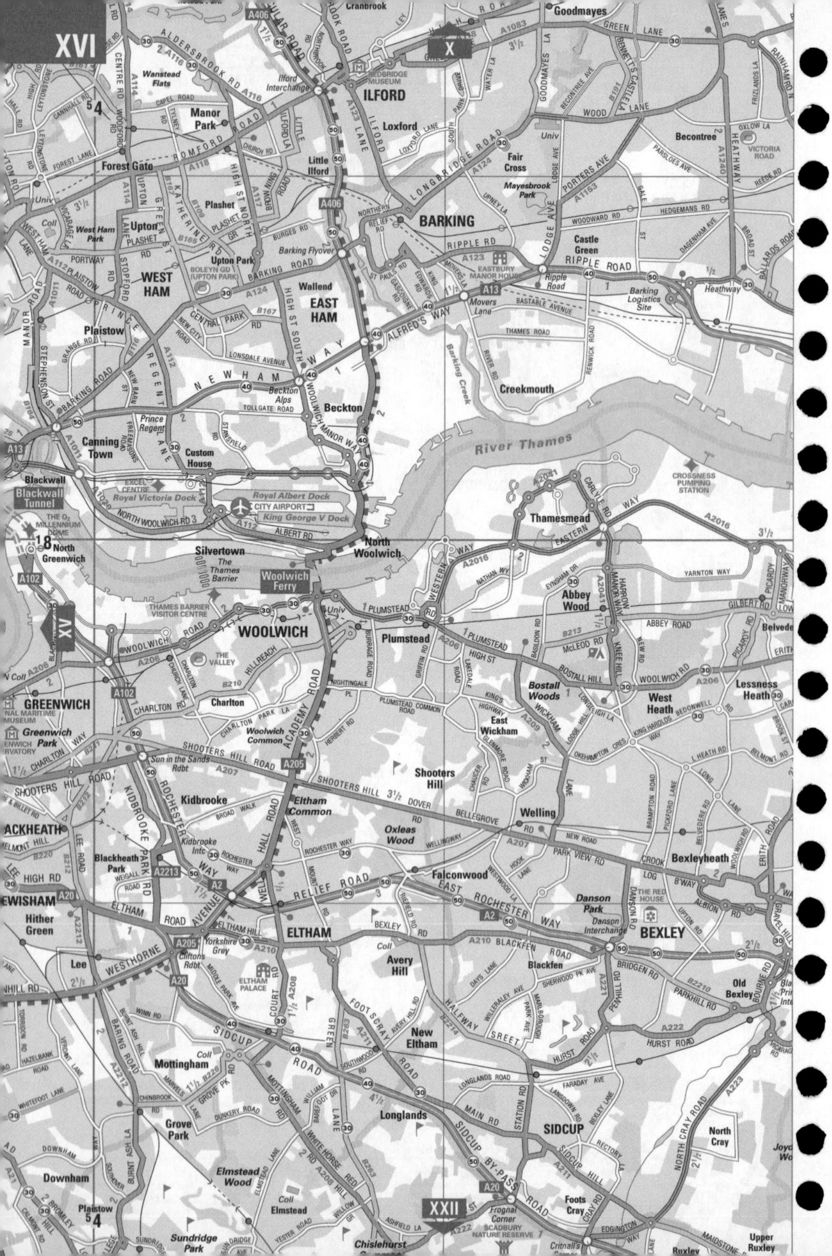

X
Goodmayes
Wanstead Flats
Manor Park
Ilford Interchange
REDBRIDGE MUSEUM
ILFORD
Loxford
Forest Gate
Little Ilford
Fair Cross
Mayesbrook Park
Becontree
VICTORIA ROAD
Plashet
West Ham Park
Upton
Upton Park
BOLEYN GD (UPTON PARK)
WEST HAM
Barking Flyover
BARKING
Castle Green
EASTBURY MANOR HOUSE
Ripple Road
Barking Logistics Site
Heathway
Wallend
EAST HAM
Movers Lane
Plaistow
Beckton Alps
Beckton
Barking Creek
Creekmouth
Canning Town
Prince Regent
Custom House
River Thames
CROSSNESS PUMPING STATION
Blackwall
Blackwall Tunnel
EXCEL CENTRE
Royal Victoria Dock
Royal Albert Dock
CITY AIRPORT
King George V Dock
THE O2 MILLENNIUM DOME
North Greenwich
Thamesmead
Silvertown
The Thames Barrier
North Woolwich
Woolwich Ferry
THAMES BARRIER VISITOR CENTRE
XV
Abbey Wood
WOOLWICH
Plumstead
THE VALLEY
GREENWICH
Charlton
Bostall Woods
West Heath
Lessness Heath
Greenwich Park
Woolwich Common
East Wickham
Sun in the Sands Rdbt
Shooters Hill
Kidbrooke
Eltham Common
Welling
Oxleas Wood
Kidbrooke Intc
Blackheath Park
Falconwood
Bexleyheath
THE RED HOUSE
Danson Park
Danson Interchange
Hither Green
Yorkshire Grey
ELTHAM
BEXLEY
Lee
Cliftons Rdbt
Avery Hill
Blackfen
ELTHAM PALACE
Old Bexley
New Eltham
Mottingham
Grove Park
Longlands
SIDCUP
North Cray
Downham
Elmstead Wood
Elmstead
Plaistow
XXII
Frognal Corner
SCADBURY NATURE RESERVE
Foots Cray
Sundridge Park
Chislehurst
Upper Ruxley

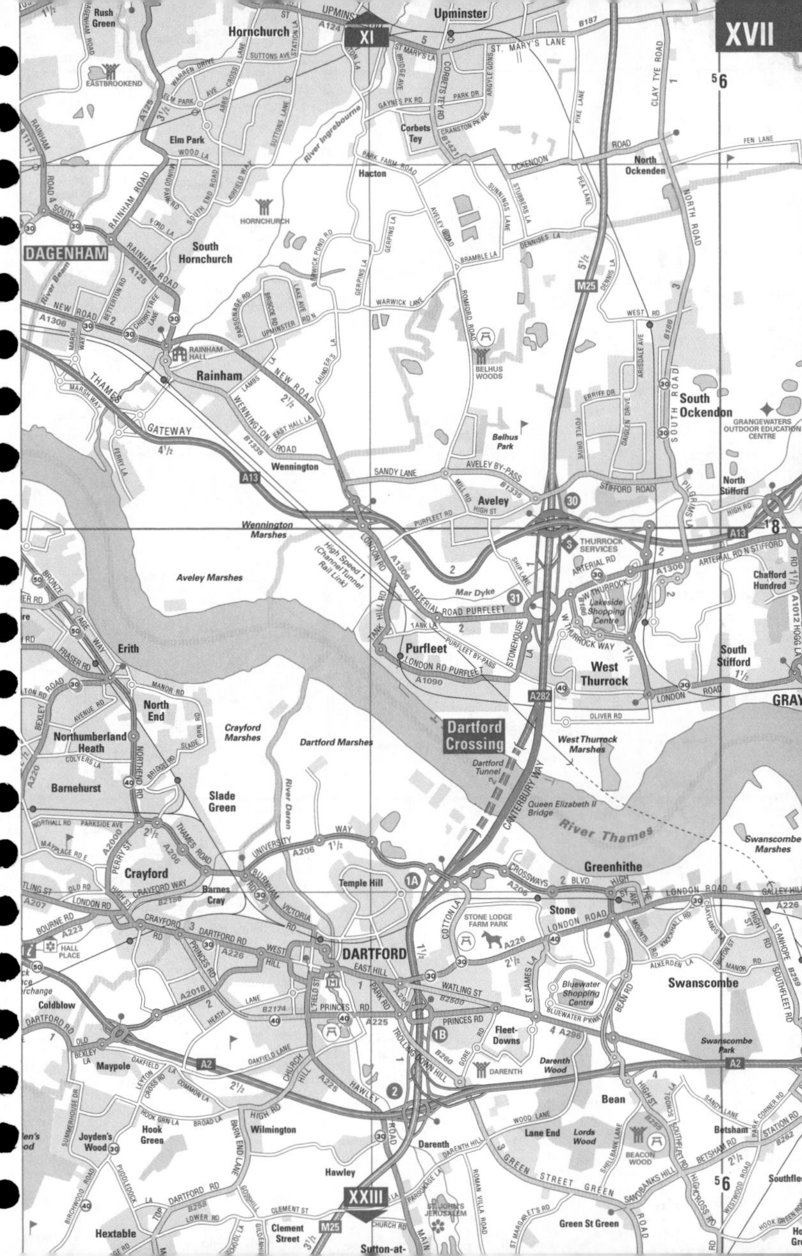
XVII
Rush Green
Hornchurch
Upminster
XI
EASTBROOKEND
Elm Park
Corbets Tey
Hacton
North Ockenden
HORNCHURCH
DAGENHAM
South Hornchurch
Rainham
RAINHAM HALL
BELHUS WOODS
South Ockendon
GRANGEWATERS OUTDOOR EDUCATION CENTRE
Belhus Park
Wennington
Aveley
North Stifford
Wennington Marshes
THURROCK SERVICES
High Speed 1 (Channel Tunnel Rail Link)
Aveley Marshes
Mar Dyke
Lakeside Shopping Centre
Chafford Hundred
Purfleet
West Thurrock
South Stifford
GRAYS
Erith
North End
Northumberland Heath
Crayford Marshes
Dartford Marshes
Dartford Crossing
Dartford Tunnel
West Thurrock Marshes
Barnehurst
Slade Green
River Darent
Queen Elizabeth II Bridge
River Thames
Swanscombe Marshes
Crayford
Barnes Cray
Temple Hill
Greenhithe
Stone
STONE LODGE FARM PARK
DARTFORD
HALL PLACE
Coldblow
Bluewater Shopping Centre
Swanscombe
Fleet-Downs
Maypole
DARENTH
Darenth Wood
Swanscombe Park
Bean
Joyden's Wood
Hook Green
Wilmington
Darenth
Lane End
Lords Wood
BEACON WOOD
Betsham
Hawley
Southfleet
XXIII
Hextable
Clement Street
ST JOHN'S JERUSALEM
Green St Green
Sutton-at-
River Ingrebourne
River Beam
M25
A13
A282
A2
A206
A226
A225
A296
A1306
A1090
A2018
A2000
A220
A223
A207
A125
A124
A1012
B187
B186
B1335
B1421
B2500
B2174
B2186
B260
B255
B258
B259
B262
UPMINSTER RD
ST. MARY'S LANE
CLAY TYE ROAD
OCKENDON ROAD
NORTH ROAD
SOUTH ROAD
RAINHAM ROAD
NEW ROAD
WARWICK LANE
ROMFORD ROAD
AVELEY BY-PASS
STIFFORD ROAD
SANDY LANE
LONDON RD
ARTERIAL ROAD PURFLEET
ARTERIAL RD N STIFFORD
LONDON RD PURFLEET
PURFLEET BY-PASS
OLIVER RD
CANTERBURY WAY
UNIVERSITY WAY
CROSSWAYS BLVD
LONDON ROAD
DARTFORD RD
CRAYFORD WAY
WATLING ST
PRINCES RD
EAST HILL
WEST HILL
HEATH LANE
OAKFIELD LANE
HAWLEY ROAD
GREEN STREET GREEN ROAD
DARTFORD RD

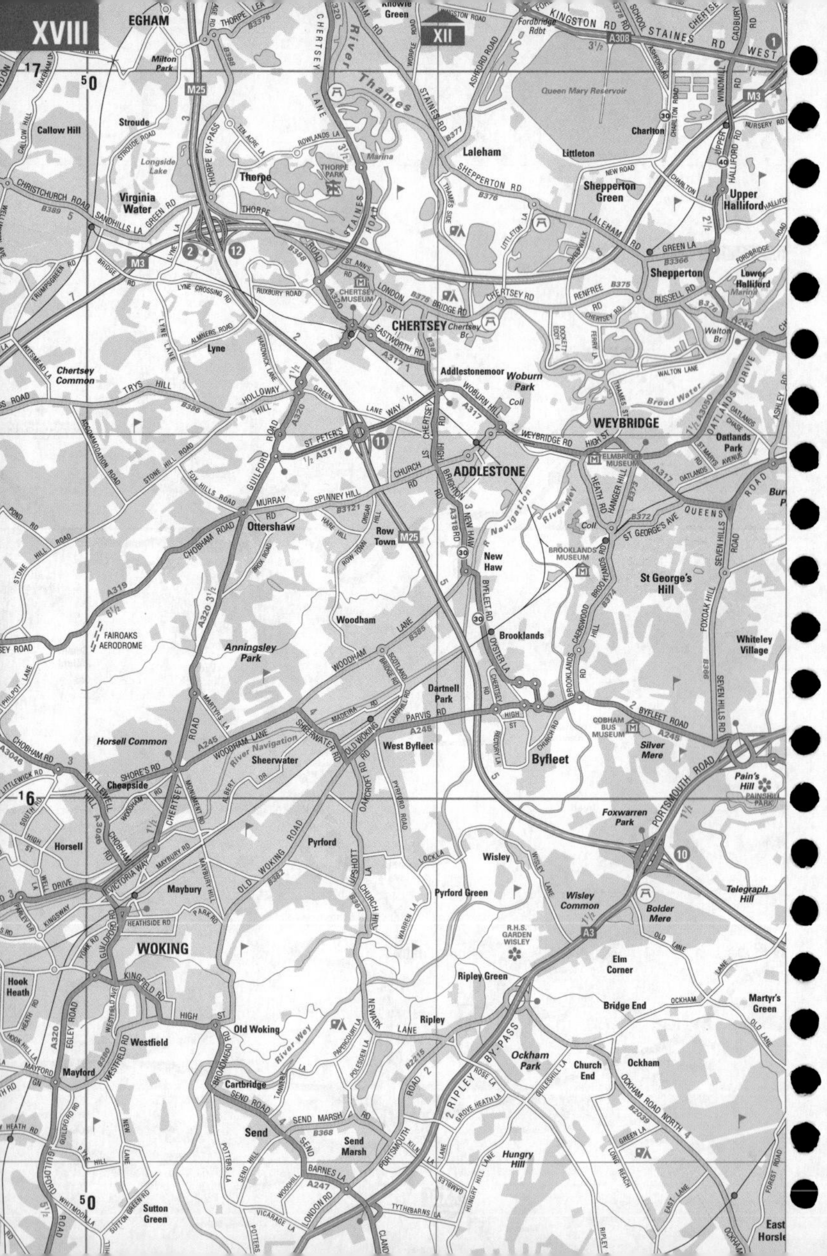

XII
EGHAM
Milton Park
Knowle Green
Queen Mary Reservoir
Callow Hill
Stroude
Longside Lake
Thorpe
THORPE PARK
Laleham
Littleton
Charlton
Shepperton Green
Upper Halliford
Virginia Water
Shepperton
Lower Halliford
CHERTSEY MUSEUM
CHERTSEY
Chertsey Br
Walton Br
Lyne
Chertsey Common
Addlestonemoor
Woburn Park
Broad Water
WEYBRIDGE
ELMBRIDGE MUSEUM
Oatlands Park
ADDLESTONE
Ottershaw
Row Town
New Haw
BROOKLANDS MUSEUM
St George's Hill
Woodham
Brooklands
FAIROAKS AERODROME
Anningsley Park
Whiteley Village
Dartnell Park
COBHAM BUS MUSEUM
Silver Mere
Horsell Common
West Byfleet
Sheerwater
Byfleet
Cheapside
Pain's Hill
PAINSHILL PARK
Foxwarren Park
Horsell
Pyrford
Wisley
Maybury
Pyrford Green
Wisley Common
Bolder Mere
Telegraph Hill
R.H.S. GARDEN WISLEY
WOKING
Elm Corner
Hook Heath
Ripley Green
Martyr's Green
Bridge End
Old Woking
Ripley
Westfield
Ockham Park
Church End
Ockham
Mayford
Cartbridge
Send
Send Marsh
Hungry Hill
Sutton Green
East Horsle
River Thames
River Wey
River Navigation

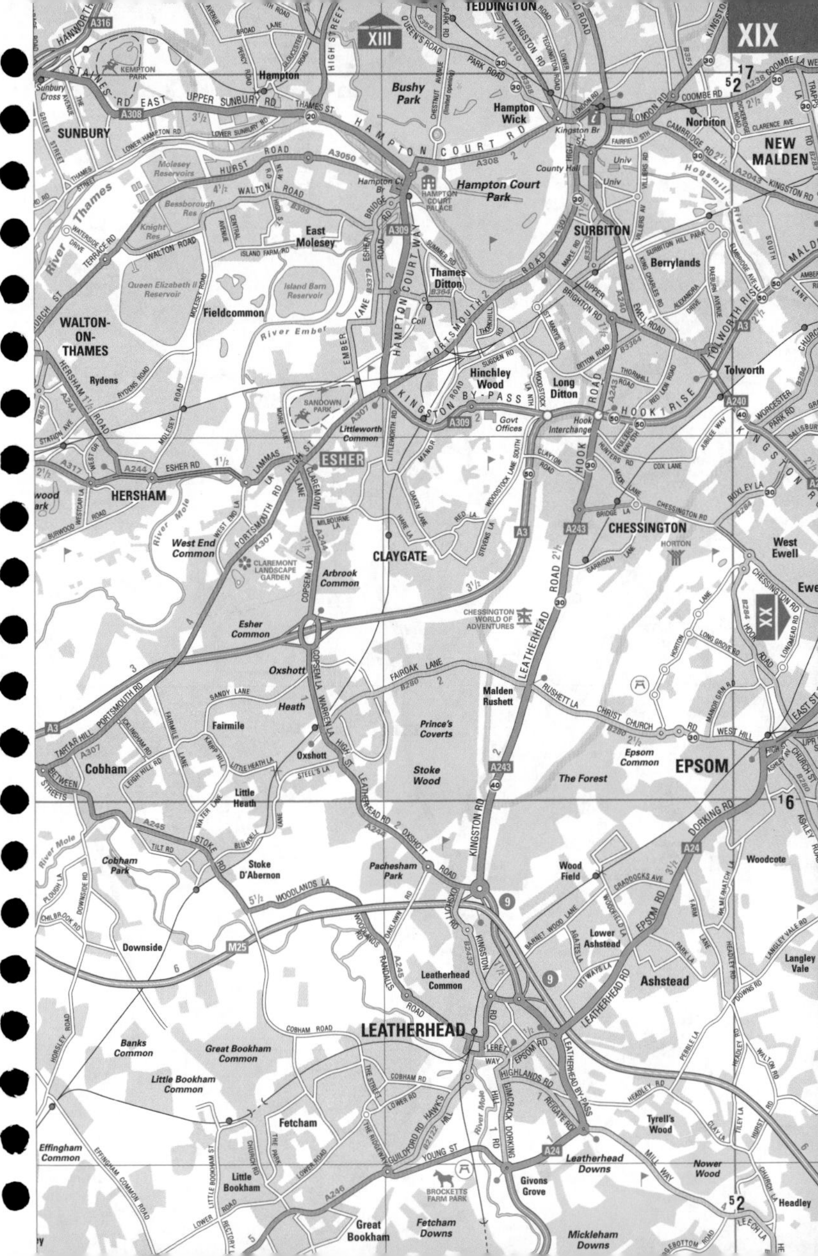
XIX
XIII
XX
TEDDINGTON
Hampton
Bushy Park
Hampton Wick
Kingston Br
Norbiton
NEW MALDEN
SUNBURY
Sunbury Cross
KEMPTON PARK
STAINES RD EAST
UPPER SUNBURY RD
HAMPTON COURT RD
Hampton Court Park
HAMPTON COURT PALACE
County Hall
Univ
SURBITON
Berrylands
Molesey Reservoirs
Bessborough Res
Knight Res
River Thames
East Molesey
Island Barn Reservoir
Queen Elizabeth II Reservoir
Fieldcommon
River Ember
Thames Ditton
WALTON-ON-THAMES
Rydens
SANDOWN PARK
Hinchley Wood
Long Ditton
Tolworth
TOLWORTH RISE
HOOK RISE
Hook Interchange
Govt Offices
KINGSTON BY-PASS
Littleworth Common
ESHER
HERSHAM
CHESSINGTON
HORTON
West Ewell
River Mole
West End Common
CLAREMONT LANDSCAPE GARDEN
Arbrook Common
CLAYGATE
CHESSINGTON WORLD OF ADVENTURES
Esher Common
Oxshott
Oxshott Heath
Fairmile
Malden Rushett
Prince's Coverts
Stoke Wood
Epsom Common
EPSOM
The Forest
Cobham
Little Heath
Cobham Park
Stoke D'Abernon
Pachesham Park
Wood Field
Woodcote
Downside
Leatherhead Common
Lower Ashstead
Ashstead
Langley Vale
LEATHERHEAD
Banks Common
Great Bookham Common
Little Bookham Common
Fetcham
Tyrell's Wood
Effingham Common
Leatherhead Downs
Nower Wood
Little Bookham
BROCKETTS FARM PARK
Givons Grove
Headley
Great Bookham
Fetcham Downs
Mickleham Downs
A3
A24
A240
A243
A244
A245
A246
A307
A308
A309
A316
A3050
M25
B280
B284
B364
B2122
B2430

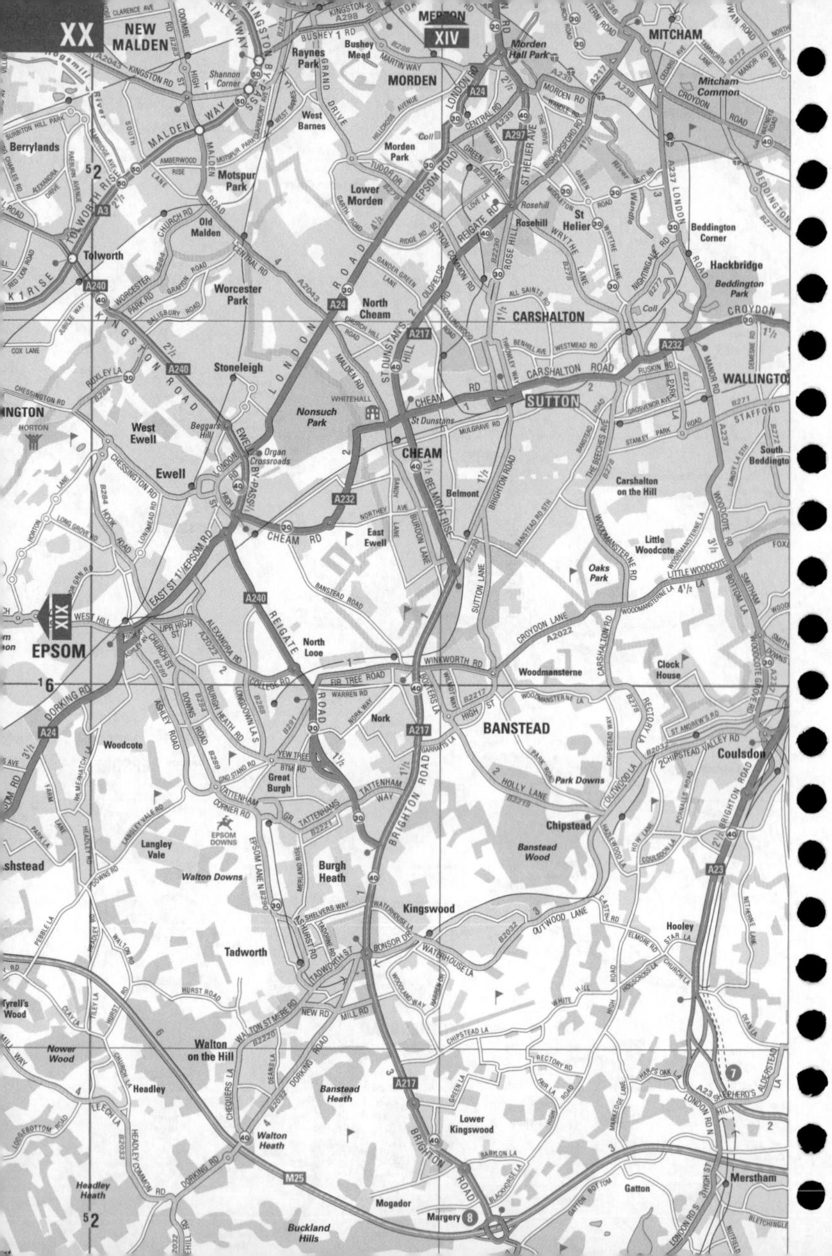
NEW MALDEN
MERTON
XIV
MITCHAM
Raynes Park
Bushey Mead
Morden Hall Park
Mitcham Common
MORDEN
Shannon Corner
West Barnes
Berrylands
Morden Park
Motspur Park
Lower Morden
Old Malden
Rosehill
St Helier
Beddington Corner
Tolworth
Hackbridge
Beddington Park
Worcester Park
North Cheam
CARSHALTON
Stoneleigh
WALLINGTON
SUTTON
Nonsuch Park
WHITEHALL
West Ewell
CHEAM
South Beddington
Ewell
Organ Crossroads
Belmont
Carshalton on the Hill
East Ewell
Little Woodcote
Oaks Park
XIX
EPSOM
North Looe
Woodmansterne
Clock House
Nork
BANSTEAD
Woodcote
Coulsdon
Great Burgh
Park Downs
Chipstead
EPSOM DOWNS
Langley Vale
Banstead Wood
Burgh Heath
Walton Downs
Kingswood
Hooley
Tadworth
Tyrell's Wood
Nower Wood
Walton on the Hill
Headley
Banstead Heath
Lower Kingswood
Walton Heath
Merstham
Headley Heath
Gatton
Mogador
Margery
Buckland Hills
M25
A24
A217
A240
A232
A23
A3
A2043
A297
A239
A237
A2022

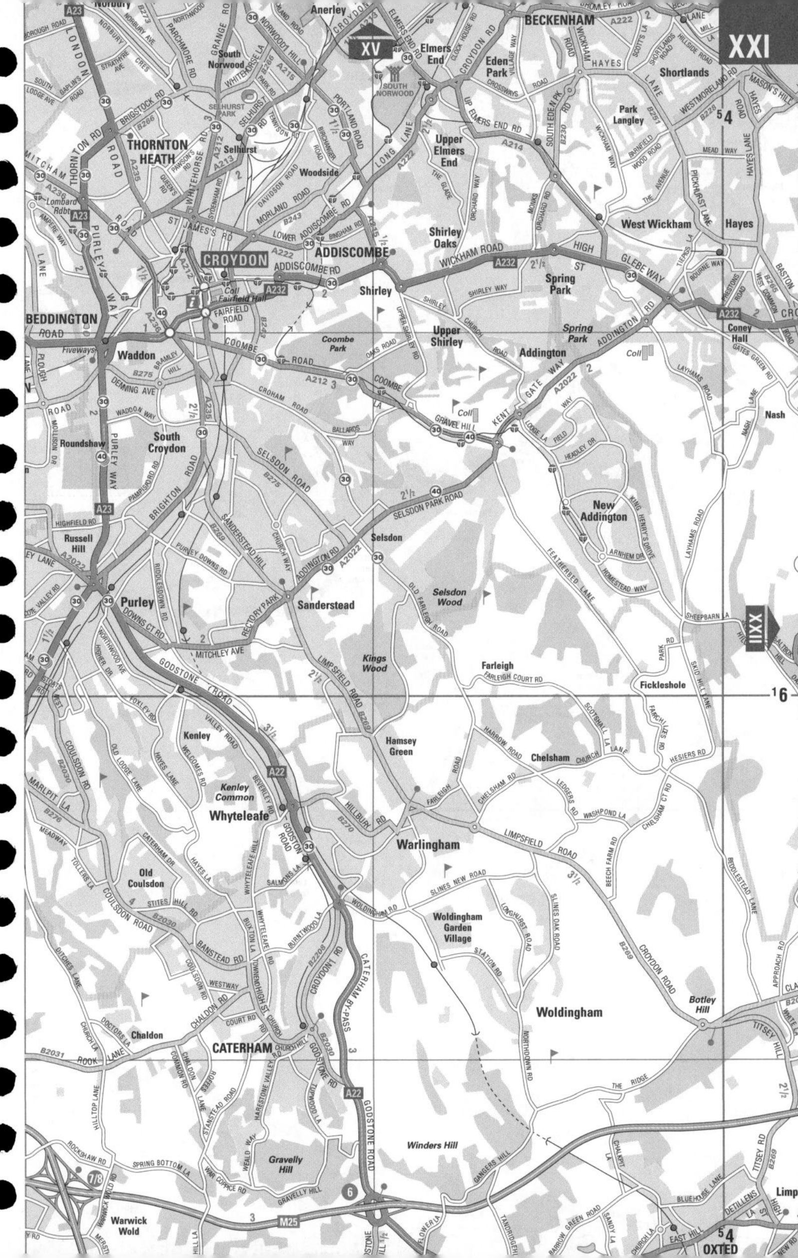
XV
XXII
Anerley
BECKENHAM
South Norwood
Elmers End
Eden Park
Shortlands
Park Langley
Selhurst
THORNTON HEATH
Upper Elmers End
Woodside
West Wickham
Hayes
Shirley Oaks
CROYDON
ADDISCOMBE
Shirley
Spring Park
BEDDINGTON
Upper Shirley
Addington
Coney Hall
Waddon
Coombe Park
Fiveways
Nash
Roundshaw
South Croydon
Selsdon
New Addington
Russell Hill
Purley
Sanderstead
Selsdon Wood
Kings Wood
Farleigh
Fickleshole
Kenley
Hamsey Green
Chelsham
Kenley Common
Whyteleafe
Warlingham
Old Coulsdon
Woldingham Garden Village
Woldingham
Botley Hill
Chaldon
CATERHAM
Winders Hill
Gravelly Hill
Warwick Wold
OXTED
Limpsfi
A23
A22
A232
A2022
A212
A222
A236
A235
A215
A214
M25
B269
B2030
B275
B270
B2031
LIMPSFIELD ROAD
CROYDON ROAD
GODSTONE ROAD
CATERHAM BY-PASS
BRIGHTON ROAD
PURLEY WAY
WICKHAM ROAD
ADDISCOMBE RD
SELSDON PARK ROAD
COULSDON ROAD
FEATHERBED LANE
LAYHAMS ROAD
16
54

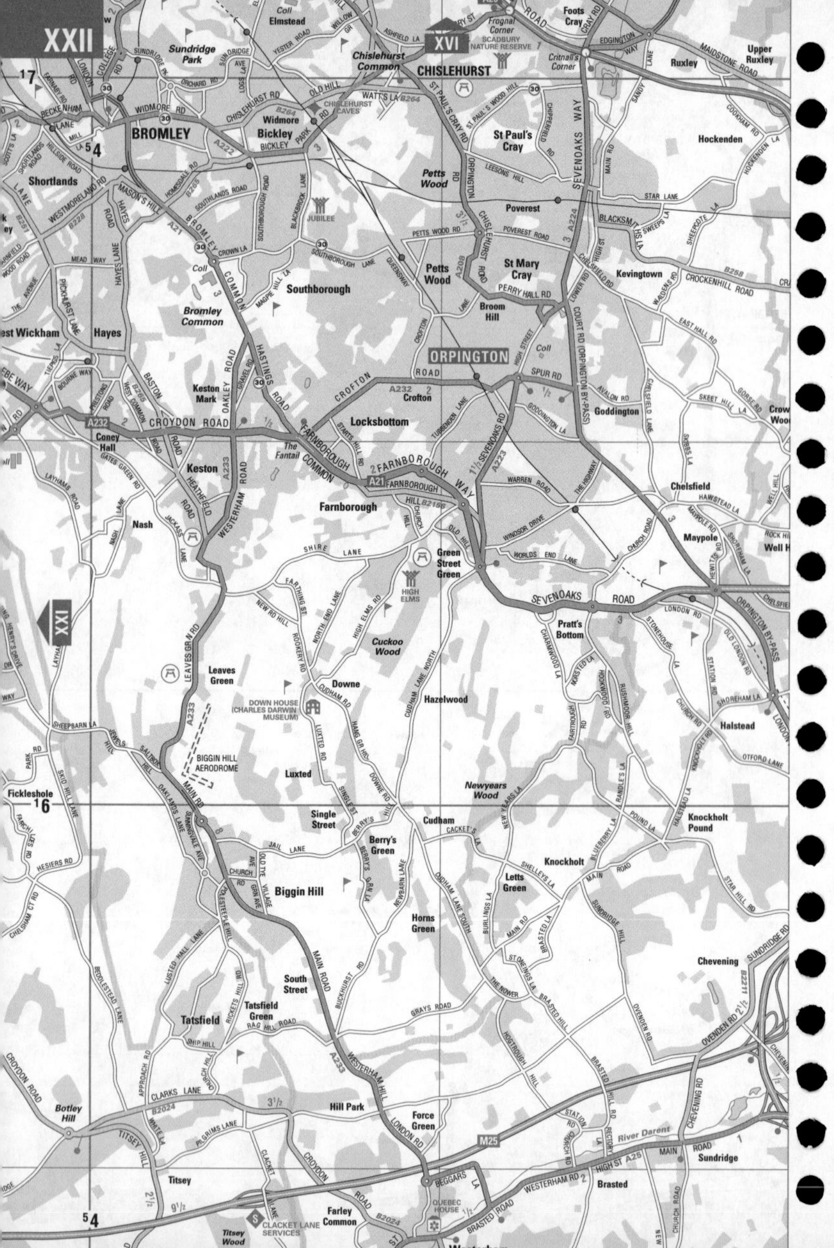

XVI
XXI
Elmstead
Sundridge Park
Chislehurst Common
CHISLEHURST
Frognal Corner
SCADBURY NATURE RESERVE
Foots Cray
Critnall's Corner
Ruxley
Upper Ruxley
BROMLEY
Widmore
Bickley
CHISLEHURST CAVES
St Paul's Cray
Hockenden
Shortlands
Petts Wood
Poverest
JUBILEE
St Mary Cray
Kevingtown
Southborough
Broom Hill
Bromley Common
Hayes
ORPINGTON
Keston Mark
Crofton
Locksbottom
Goddington
Coney Hall
The Fantail
Keston
Farnborough
Chelsfield
Nash
Green Street Green
HIGH ELMS
Maypole
Pratt's Bottom
Cuckoo Wood
Leaves Green
Downe
DOWN HOUSE (CHARLES DARWIN MUSEUM)
Hazelwood
Halstead
BIGGIN HILL AERODROME
Luxted
Newyears Wood
Fickleshole
Single Street
Cudham
Knockholt Pound
Berry's Green
Knockholt
Letts Green
Biggin Hill
Horns Green
Chevening
South Street
Tatsfield
Tatsfield Green
Botley Hill
Hill Park
Force Green
River Darent
Sundridge
Titsey
Brasted
QUEBEC HOUSE
Farley Common
CLACKET LANE SERVICES
Titsey Wood
Westerham
M25
A21
A232
A233
A223
A224
A208
A222
A25
B2024
B258
B2158
B2211
CROYDON ROAD
SEVENOAKS WAY
SEVENOAKS ROAD
FARNBOROUGH WAY
MAIN ROAD
WESTERHAM HILL
ORPINGTON BY-PASS

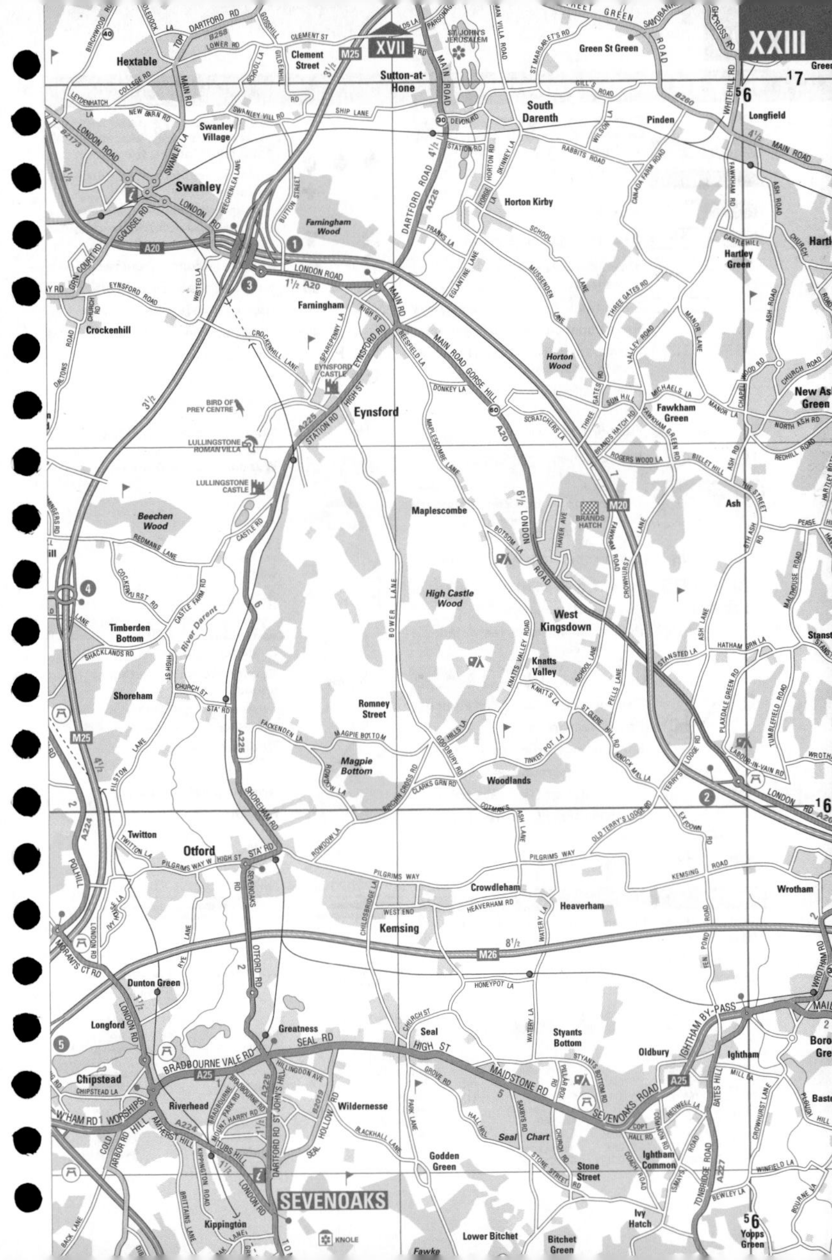

XVII
Hextable
Clement Street
Sutton-at-Hone
Green St Green
South Darenth
Pinden
Longfield
Swanley Village
Swanley
Horton Kirby
Farningham Wood
Farningham
Crockenhill
Hartley Green
Eynsford Castle
Bird of Prey Centre
Eynsford
Lullingstone Roman Villa
Lullingstone Castle
Horton Wood
Fawkham Green
New Ash Green
Beechen Wood
Maplescombe
Brands Hatch
Ash
High Castle Wood
Timberden Bottom
West Kingsdown
Knatts Valley
Shoreham
Romney Street
Magpie Bottom
Woodlands
Twitton
Otford
Crowdleham
Heaverham
Wrotham
Kemsing
Dunton Green
Longford
Greatness
Seal
Styants Bottom
Oldbury
Ightham
Chipstead
Riverhead
Wildernesse
Seal Chart
Godden Green
Stone Street
Ightham Common
SEVENOAKS
Kippington
Knole
Lower Bitchet
Bitchet Green
Ivy Hatch
Yopps Green
River Darent
M25
M20
M26
A20
A225
A25
A224
A227
B258
B260
B2173
B2019
London Road
Main Road
Dartford Road
Seal Rd
Maidstone Rd
Sevenoaks Road
Ightham By-Pass
Pilgrims Way
17
16
56

Key to map symbols

Roads

(22a)	Motorway with junction number
	Primary route – single, dual carriageway
	A road – single, dual carriageway
	B road – single, dual carriageway
	Through-route – single, dual carriageway
	Minor road – single, dual carriageway
	Road under construction
	Rural track, private road or narrow road in urban area
	Path, bridleway, byway open to all traffic, restricted byway
	Tunnel, covered road
(30) (30)	Speed camera – single, multiple
	Congestion Charge Zone boundary Roads within the zone are outlined in green
	Gate or obstruction, car pound
P P&R	Parking, park and ride
Crooked Billet	Road junction name
	Pedestrianised area, restricted access area

Public transport

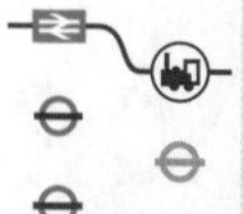

	Railway with National Rail station
	Private railway station
	London Underground station
	London Overground station
	Docklands Light Railway station
	Tramway or miniature railway
	Riverbus or ferry pier
	Bus or coach station, tram stop

Emergency services

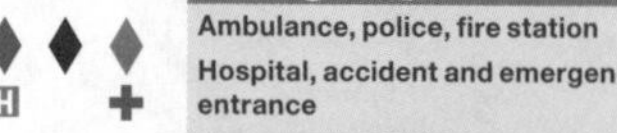

♦ ♦ ♦	Ambulance, police, fire station
H +	Hospital, accident and emergency entrance

General features

	Market, public amenity site
	Sports stadium, shopping centre
ℹ PO	Information centre, post office
VILLA House	Roman, non-Roman antiquity
100 .304	House number, spot height – metres
+	Christian place of worship
☪ ✡	Mosque, synagogue
◻	Other place of worship
	Houses, important buildings
	Woods, parkland/common
123	Adjoining page number

Leisure facilities

Δ ⌂	Camp site, caravan site
⚑ ✗ ※	Golf course, picnic site, view point

Boundaries

NW6	Postcode boundaries
Westminster	County and unitary authority boundaries

Water features

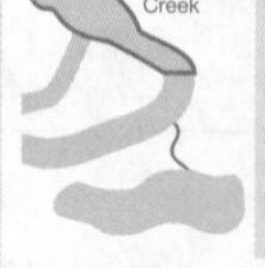

Barking Creek	Tidal water, water name
	River or canal – minor, major
	Stream
	Water

Scales

The map scale on the pages numbered in blue is 3.04 inches to 1 mile • 4.8cm to 1 km • 1:20833

| 0 | 220 yds | 440yds | 660yds | ½ mile |
| 0 | 250m | 500m | 750m | 1km |

The map scale on the pages numbered in red is 6.08 inches to 1 mile, see page 228

| 0 | 110 yds | 220yds | 330yds | ¼ mile |
| 0 | 125m | 250m | 375m | ½km |

Abbreviations

Acad	Academy	Drv Rng	Golf Driving Range	Meml	Memorial	Ret Pk	Retail Park
Allot Gdns	Allotments	Gn	Green	Mon	Monument	Sch	School
Bndstd	Bandstand	Gd	Ground	Mus	Museum	Sh Ctr	Shopping Centre
Btcl	Botanical	Hort	Horticultural	Nat Res	Nature Reserve	Sp	Sports
Bwg Gn	Bowling	Ind Est	Industrial Estate	Obsy	Observatory	Stad	Stadium
Cemy	Cemetery	Inst	Institute	Pav	Pavilion	Sw Pool	Swimming Pool
Ctr	Centre	Int	Interchange	Pk	Park	Tenn Cts	Tennis
C Ctr	Civic Centre	Ct	Law Court	Pl Fld	Playing Field	TH	Town Hall
CH	Club House	L Ctr	Leisure Centre	Pal	Royal Palace	Trad Est	Trading Estate
Ctry Pk	Country Park	LC	Level Crossing	PH	Public House	Univ	University
Coll	College	Liby	Library	Recn Gd	Recreation Ground	YH	Youth Hostel
Ct	Court	Mkt	Market	Resr	Reservoir		
Crem	Crematorium						
Crkt	Cricket						
Ent	Enterprise						
Ex H	Exhibition Hall						
Fball	Football						
Gdns	Gardens						
Glf C	Golf Course						
Glf Crs	Golf Course						

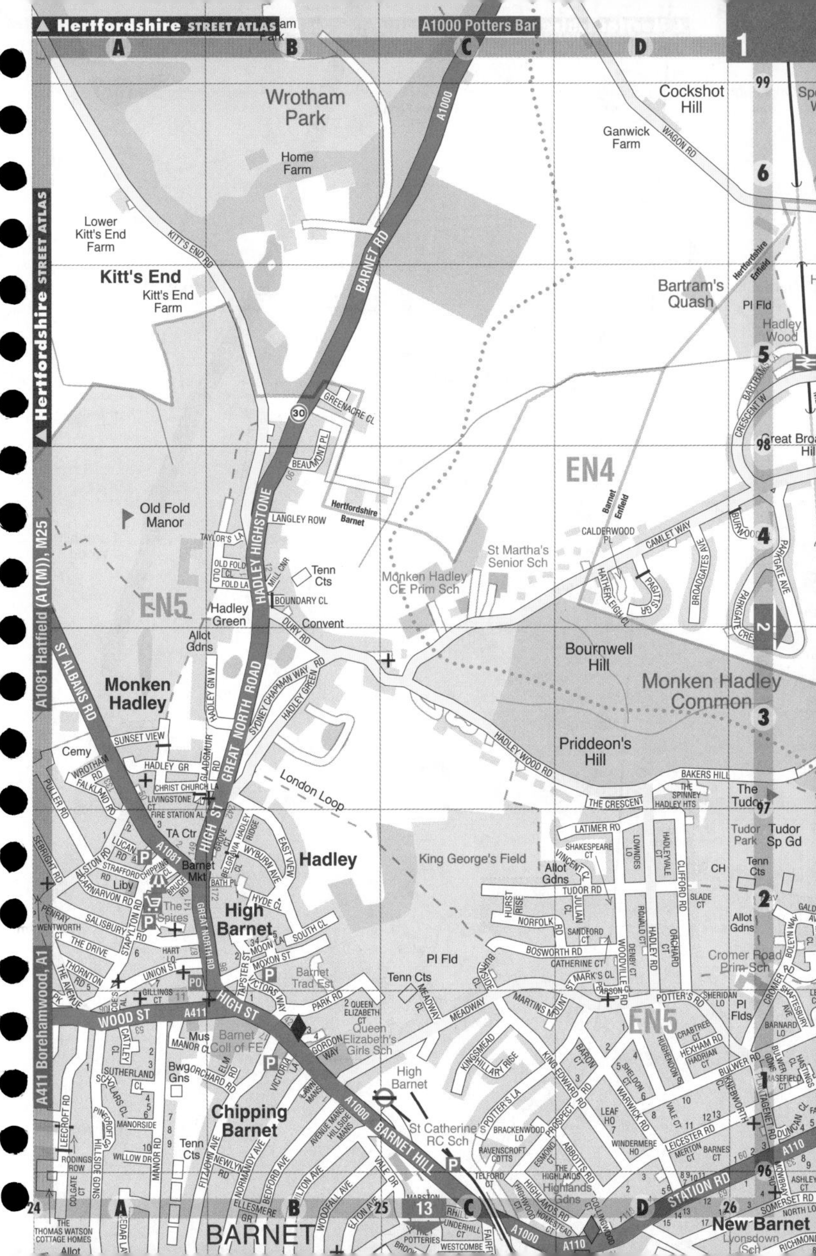
Wrotham Park
Home Farm
Cockshot Hill
Ganwick Farm
WAGON RD
Lower Kitt's End Farm
KITT'S END RD
Kitt's End
Kitt's End Farm
BARNET RD
A1000
Bartram's Quash
Pl Fld
Hadley Wood
GREENACRE CL
BEAUMONT PL
EN4
EN5
Old Fold Manor
LANGLEY ROW
HADLEY HIGHSTONE
TAYLOR'S LA
Hertfordshire Barnet
Barnet Enfield
CALDERWOOD PL
CAMLET WAY
St Martha's Senior Sch
Monken Hadley CE Prim Sch
Tenn Cts
BOUNDARY CL
Hadley Green
Convent
DURY RD
Allot Gdns
HATHERLEIGH CL
PAGITTS GR
BROADGATES AVE
PARKGATE AVE
PARKGATE CRES
Bournwell Hill
Monken Hadley Common
Priddeon's Hill
Monken Hadley
ST ALBANS RD
GREAT NORTH ROAD
SYDNEY CHAPMAN WAY
HADLEY GREEN RD
HADLEY GN W
SUNSET VIEW
Cemy
HADLEY GR
HADLEY WOOD RD
BAKERS HILL
The Tudor
London Loop
THE CRESCENT
THE SPINNEY
HADLEY HTS
CHRIST CHURCH LA
LIVINGSTONE CT
FIRE STATION AL
WROTHAM
FALKLAND RD
PULLER RD
TA Ctr
HIGH ST
LATIMER RD
SHAKESPEARE CT
VINCENT CL
LOWNDES CT
HADLEYVALE CT
CLIFFORD RD
Tudor Park
Tudor Sp Gd
Hadley
WYBURN AVE
EAST VIEW
King George's Field
Allot Gdns
Tenn Cts
CH
LUCAN RD
A1081
Barnet Mkt
ALSTON RD
STRAFFORD RD
CARNARVON RD
Liby
The Spires
SEBRIGHT RD
BATH PL
HYDE CL
TUDOR RD
HURST RISE
JULIAN CL
SLADE CT
High Barnet
NORFOLK RD
SANDFORD CT
RONALD CT
HADLEY RD
ORCHARD CT
Allot Gdns
GALDANA AVE
PENRAY
SALISBURY RD
WENTWORTH CT
THE DRIVE
STAPYLTON RD
HART LO
SOUTH CL
MOON LA
MOXON ST
BOSWORTH RD
CATHERINE CT
DENBY CT
WOODVILLE RD
Cromer Road Prim Sch
THORNTON RD
THE AVENUE
UNION ST
PO
GILLINGS CT
Barnet Trad Est
Pl Fld
Tenn Cts
BURNSIDE CL
ST MARK'S CL
CARSON CL
POTTER'S RD
SHERIDAN LO
Pl Flds
CROMER RD
WOOD ST
A411
VICTORS WAY
PARK RD
QUEEN ELIZABETH CT
MEADWAY CL
MEADWAY
MARTINS MOUNT
EN5
CRABTREE CT
HEXHAM RD
HADRIAN CT
BARNARD LO
SHAFTESBURY AVE
CATTLEY CL
Mus
MANOR CL
Barnet Coll of FE
GORDON WAY
Queen Elizabeth's Girls Sch
KINGSMEAD
HILLARY RISE
KING EDWARD RD
BARON CT
SHELDON CT
HUGHENDON
SUTHERLAND CL
Bwg Gns
ORCHARD RD
ELM
VICTORIA LA
LAWN MANS
High Barnet
BULWER RD
KNEBWORTH
BULWER GDNS
MASEFIELD CT
HASTINGS
SCHOLARS CL
PINECROFT
MANORSIDE
Chipping Barnet
AVENUE MANS
HILLSIDE MANS
A1000
BARNET HILL
St Catherine's RC Sch
BRACKENWOOD LO
PROSPECT RD
ABBOTTS RD
LEAF HO
WARWICK RD
VALE CT
LEICESTER RD
PLANTAGENET RD
DUNCAN CL
LEECROFT RD
RODINGS ROW
HILLSIDE GDNS
WILLOW DR
MANOR RD
Tenn Cts
FITZJOHN AVE
NEWLYN RD
NORMANDY AVE
BEDFORD AVE
MILTON AVE
WOODFALL AVE
VALE DR
RAVENSCROFT COTTS
ESMOND CT
THE HIGHLANDS
Highlands Gdns
WINDERMERE HO
MERTON CT
BARNES CT
STATION RD
A110
ASHLEY CT
MOWBRAY
COLGATE CT
ELLESMERE GR
ELTON AVE
TELFORD CT
MARSTON
HIGHWOOD CT
HIGHLANDS RD
HOMESTEAD
COLLINGWOOD
SOMERSET RD
NORTH LO
THE THOMAS WATSON COTTAGE HOMES
Allot
CEDAR LA
BARNET
RHILL
UNDERHILL CT
POTTERIES
WESTCOMBE
New Barnet
Lyonsdown Sch
RICHMOND
A411 Borehamwood, A1
A1081 Hatfield (A1(M)), M25
Hertfordshire STREET ATLAS

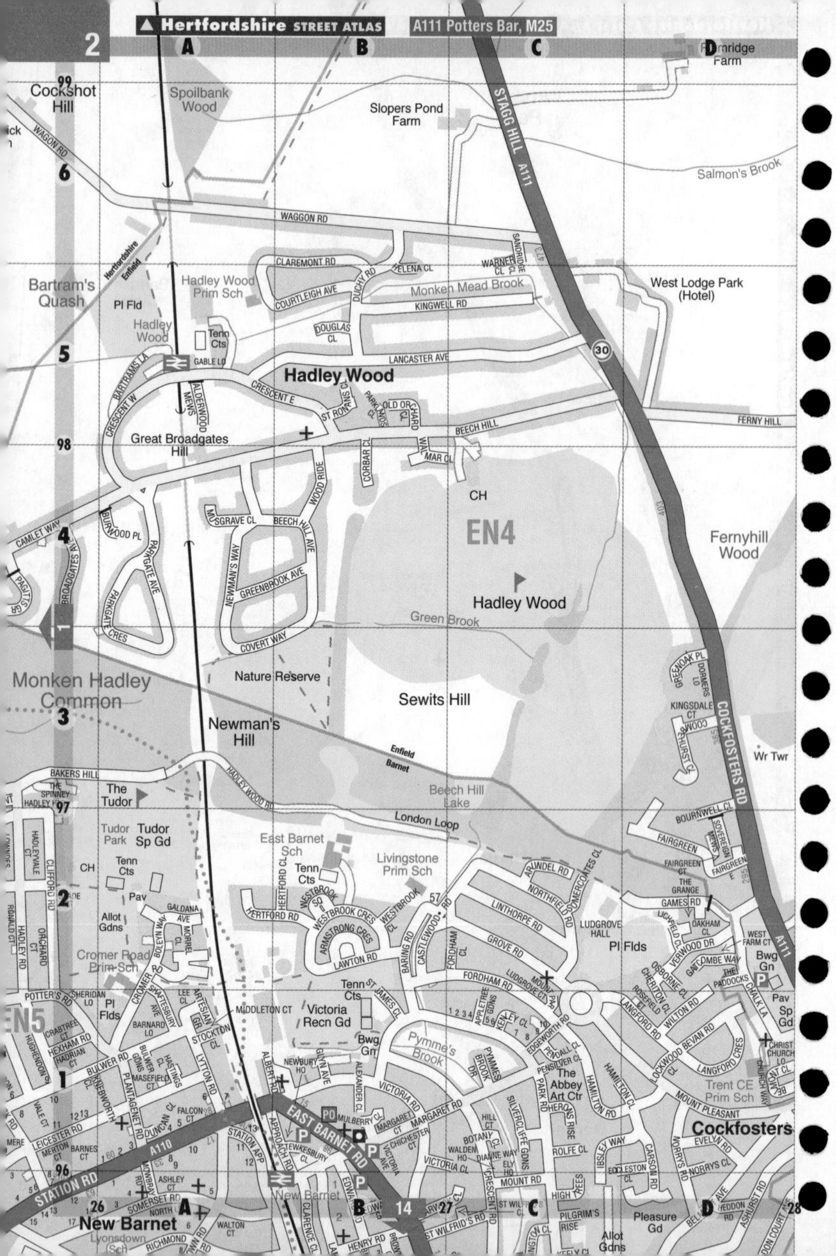
A
B
C
D
99
6
5
98
4
3
97
2
1
96
Cockshot Hill
Spoilbank Wood
Slopers Pond Farm
Ramridge Farm
STAGG HILL
A111
WAGON RD
Salmon's Brook
WAGGON RD
SANDRIDGE CL
Hertfordshire
Enfield
CLAREMONT RD
HELENA CL
WARNER CL
Bartram's Quash
Hadley Wood Prim Sch
Pl Fld
COURTLEIGH AVE
DUCHY RD
Monken Mead Brook
KINGWELL RD
West Lodge Park (Hotel)
Hadley Wood
Tenn Cts
DOUGLAS CL
30
GABLE LO
LANCASTER AVE
BARTRAMS LA
Hadley Wood
CRESCENT E
CRESCENT W
ALDERWOOD MEWS
ST RONANS CL
PARK RD
OLD ORCHARD CL
FERNY HILL
BEECH HILL
Great Broadgates Hill
CORBAR CL
MAR CL
WOOD RIDE
CH
EN4
MUSGRAVE CL
BEECH HILL AVE
BURWOOD PL
CAMLET WAY
PARKGATE AVE
Fernyhill Wood
NEWMAN'S WAY
GREENBROOK AVE
BROADGATES AV
PARKGATE CRES
Hadley Wood
Green Brook
COVERT WAY
Monken Hadley Common
Nature Reserve
Sewits Hill
GREENOAK PL
DORMERS
KINGSDALE CT
COCKFOSTERS RD
Newman's Hill
Enfield
Barnet
Wr Twr
BAKERS HILL
THE SPINNEY
The Tudor
HADLEY WOOD RD
Beech Hill Lake
BOURNWELL CL
SOVEREIGN MEWS
London Loop
Tudor Park
Tudor Sp Gd
East Barnet Sch
FAIRGREEN
HADLEYVALE CT
Livingstone Prim Sch
FAIRGREEN CT
CH
Tenn Cts
Tenn Cts
ARUNDEL RD
SOMERCOATES CL
THE GRANGE
CLIFFORD RD
HERTFORD CL
NORTHFIELD RD
GAMES RD
Pav
WESTBROOK SQ
WESTBROOK CL
57
LINTHORPE RD
GALDANA AVE
HERTFORD RD
WESTBROOK CRES
CASTLEWOOD RD
LUDGROVE HALL
LICHFIELD CL
OAKHAM CL
Allot Gdns
MORREL CL
BOLEYN WAY
ARMSTRONG CRES
BARING RD
FORDHAM CL
GROVE RD
Pl Flds
WEST FARM CT
RONALD CT
HADLEY RD
ORCHARD CT
VERWOOD DR
Bwg Gn
Cromer Road Prim Sch
LAWTON RD
MOUNT PDE
GATCOMBE WAY
THE PADDOCKS
CROMER RD
ST JAMES CL
FORDHAM RD
LUDGROVE CL
OSBORNE CL
CHERITON CL
ROSEFIELD CL
Pav Sp Gd
CHALK LA
POTTER'S RD
SHERIDAN LO
Pl Flds
LEE CL
ARTESIAN GR
Tenn Cts
APPLETREE GDNS
KENLEY CL
LANGFORD RD
WILTON RD
EN5
CRABTREE CT
SHAFTESBURY AVE
MIDDLETON CT
Victoria Recn Gd
EDGEWORTH RD
HEXHAM RD
BARNARD LO
STOCKTON CL
Pymme's Brook
PENDALL CL
LOCKWOOD BEVAN RD
CHRIST CHURCH LO
HUGHENDON CT
HADRIAN CT
Bwg Gn
PENSILVER CL
The Abbey Art Ctr
LANGFORD CRES
BULWER RD
BULWER GDNS
HASTINGS
NEWBURY HO
PYMMES BROOK DR
Trent CE Prim Sch
CHURCH WAY
KNEBWORTH
PLANTAGENET RD
MASEFIELD CT
LYTTON RD
ALBERT RD
GLYN AVE
ALEXANDER CL
VICTORIA RD
PARK RD
HAMILTON CL
HAMILTON RD
VALE CT
DUNCAN CL
FALCON CT
MULBERRY CL
MARGARET CT
MARGARET RD
HILL CT
SILVERCLIFFE GDNS
HERONS RISE
MOUNT PLEASANT
LEICESTER RD
EAST BARNET RD
Cockfosters
MERTON CT
BARNES CT
A110
STATION APP
APPROACH RD
TEWKESBURY CL
CHICHESTER CT
BOTANY CL
IBSLEY WAY
EVELYN RD
WALDEN HO
DIANNE WAY
ROLFE CL
STATION RD
MOWBRAY RD
ASHLEY CT
VICTORIA AVE
VICTORIA CL
ELY HO
NORRYS CL
NORRYS RD
EDWARD RD
MOUNT RD
CARSON RD
HIGH TREES
ECCLESTON CL
ASHURST RD
SOMERSET RD
NORTH LO
New Barnet
CRESCENT RD
ST WILFRIDS CL
New Barnet
WALTON CT
CLARENCE CL
ST WILFRID'S RD
PILGRIM'S RISE
Pleasure Gd
HEDDON RD
Lyonsdown Sch
RICHMOND
Allot Gdns
HENRY RD
HADDON COURT AVE
26
27
28
14
1

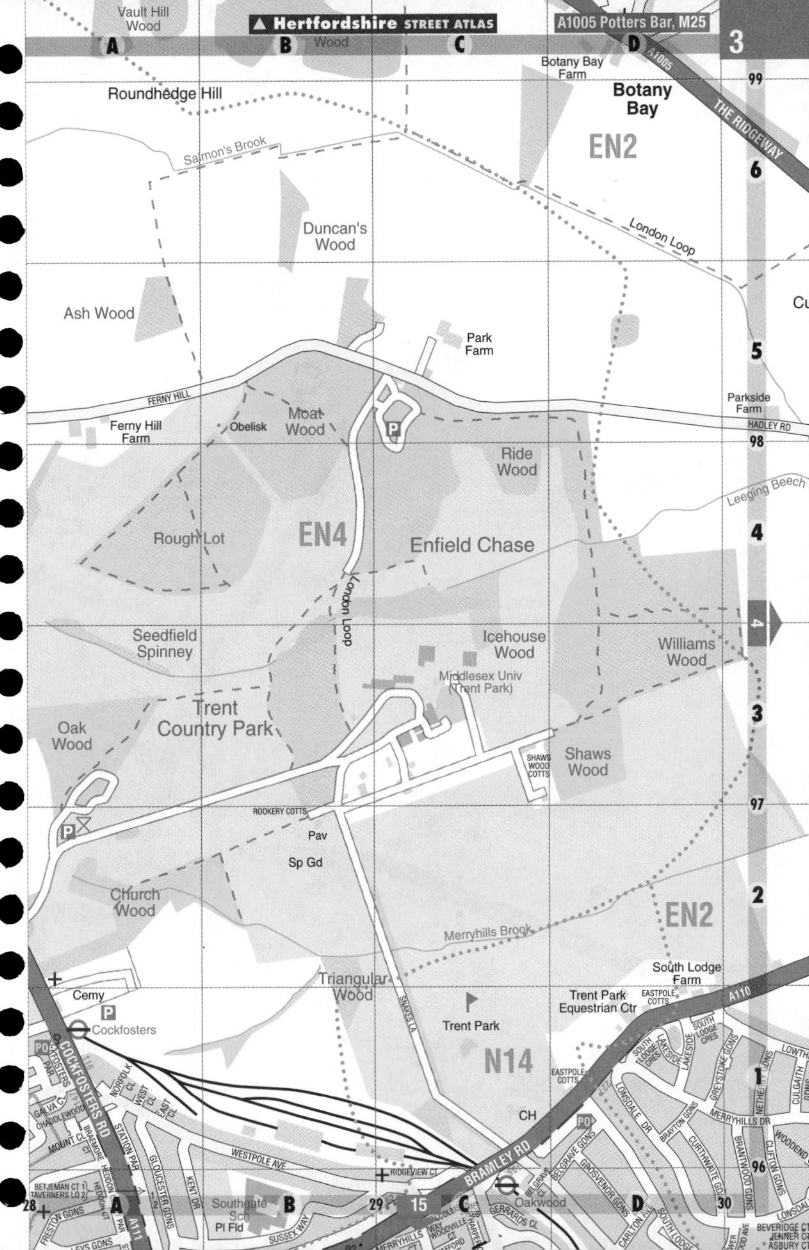

A **B** **C** **D** **3**

Vault Hill Wood

Wood

Botany Bay Farm

Botany Bay

99

THE RIDGEWAY

Roundhedge Hill

Salmon's Brook

EN2

6

Duncan's Wood

London Loop

Ash Wood

Cuc

5

Park Farm

Parkside Farm

FERNY HILL

HADLEY RD

98

Ferny Hill Farm

Moat Wood

Obelisk

P

Ride Wood

Leeging Beech G

EN4

Rough Lot

Enfield Chase

4

Seedfield Spinney

London Loop

Icehouse Wood

Williams Wood

4

3

Trent Country Park

Oak Wood

Middlesex Univ (Trent Park)

SHAWS WOOD COTTS

Shaws Wood

P

ROOKERY COTTS

97

Pav

Sp Gd

Church Wood

EN2

Merryhills Brook

South Lodge Farm

2

Triangular Wood

SUSSEX LO

Trent Park Equestrian Ctr

EASTPOLE COTTS

A110

Cemy

P

Cockfosters

Trent Park

N14

EASTPOLE COTTS

SOUTH LODGE

LOWTHER

1

CH

MERRYHILLS DR

WOODEND CL

96

COCKFOSTERS RD

WESTPOLE AVE

RIDGEVIEW CT

BRAMLEY RD

Oakwood

Southgate Pl Fld

28

A **B** 29 15 **C** 30 **D**

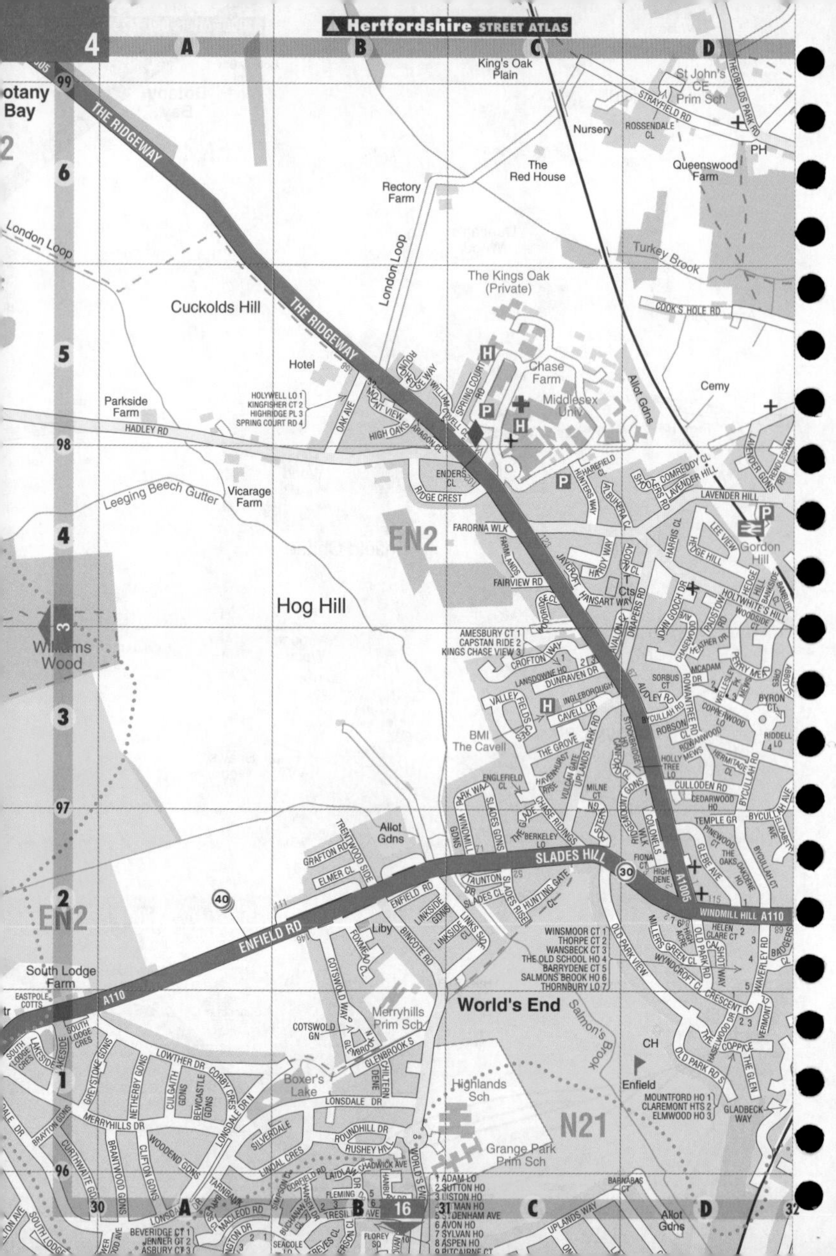

4

A B C D

99

Botany Bay

6

THE RIDGEWAY

King's Oak Plain

St John's CE Prim Sch

STRAYFIELD RD

ROSSENDALE CL

Nursery

Queenswood Farm

PH

The Red House

Rectory Farm

London Loop

London Loop

The Kings Oak (Private)

Turkey Brook

COOK'S HOLE RD

Cuckolds Hill

THE RIDGEWAY

Cerny

5

Hotel

HOLYWELL LO 1
KINGFISHER CL 2
HIGHRIDGE PL 3
SPRING COURT RD 4

Chase Farm

H

Middlesex Univ

P

H

Parkside Farm

HADLEY RD

OAK AVE

HIGH DANS

COMTESSE CL

LAVENDER HILL

98

ENDERS CL

RIDGE CREST

P

LAVENDER CL

P

Gordon Hill

Leeging Beech Gutter

Vicarage Farm

EN2

FARORNA WLK

FAIRVIEW RD

HANSART WAY

4

Hog Hill

AMESBURY CT 1
CAPSTAN RIDE 2
KINGS CHASE VIEW 3

CROFTON WAY

SORBUS RD

BYRON CT

RIDDELL LO

Williams Wood

3

LANSDOWNE RD

DUNRAVEN DR

INGLEBOROUGH

VALLEY RD

CAVELL DR

H

BMI The Cavell

COPPICEWOOD

97

THE GROVE

ENGLEFIELD RD

MILNE RD

CULLODEN RD

CEDARWOOD RD

TEMPLE GR

BYCULLA

Ailot Gdns

GRAFTON RD

ELMER CL

SLADES HILL

30

HIGH DENE

A1005

2

EN2

ENFIELD RD

TRENTWOOD SIDE

40

Liby

ENFIELD RD

LINSIDE

SLADES GDNS

RUNNING SATE

WINDMILL HILL A110

HELEN CL
CLARE CT 2

WAVERLEY RD

BINCOTE RD

COTSWOLD WAY

LINKS SIDE

WINSMOOR CT 1
THORPE CT 2
WANSBECK CT 3
THE OLD SCHOOL HO 4
BARRYDENE CT 5
SALMONS BROOK HO 6
THORNBURY LO 7

MILLERS GREEN

WYNDHOOT CL

CRESCENT RD

1

South Lodge Farm

EASTPOLE COTTS

A110

SOUTH LODGE CRES

LOWTHER DR

DORSET CRES

GLENBROOK N

Merryhills Prim Sch

COTSWOLD GN

World's End

Salmon's Brook

CH

Enfield

OLD PARK RD

MOUNTFORD HO 1
CLAREMONT HTS 2
ELMWOOD HO 3

GLADBECK WAY

96

MERRYHILLS DR

CLAYTON GDNS

Boxer's Lake

LONSDALE DR

Highlands Sch

RUSHEY

N21

Grange Park Prim Sch

30

A

BEVERIDGE CT 1
JENNER CT 2
ASBURY CT 3

SEAGULL

FLEMING

16

B

4 ADAM LO
2 SEFTON HO
3 LISTON HO
31 MAN HO
4 DENHAM AVE
6 AVON HO
7 SYLVAN AVE
8 ASPEN HO

C

UPLANDS WAY

BARNABAS

Ailot Gdns

D

32

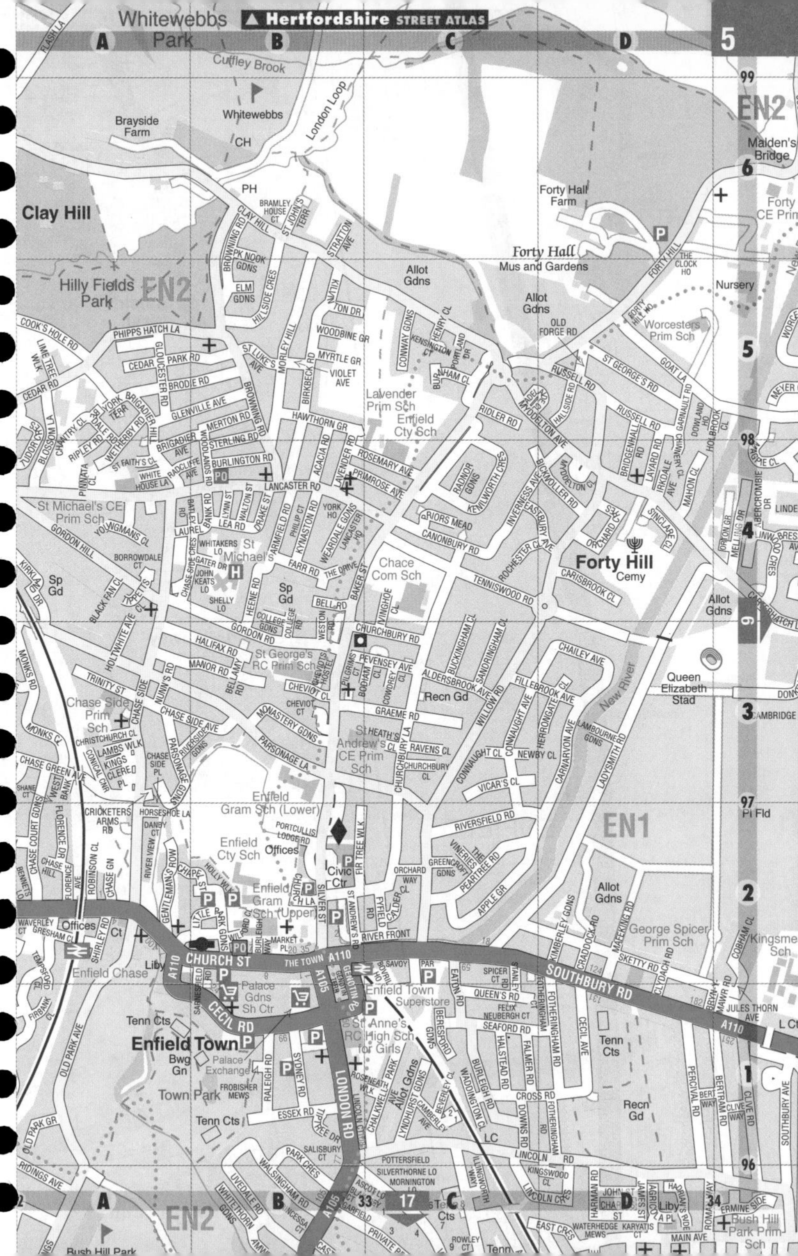
Whitewebbs Park
A
B
C
D
Cuffley Brook
Whitewebbs
Brayside Farm
CH
London Loop
99
EN2
Malden's Bridge
BULL'S CROSS
6
PH
Clay Hill
BRAMLEY HOUSE CT
ST JOHN'S TERR
CLAY HILL
BROWNING RD
PK NOOK GDNS
ELM GDNS
HILLSIDE CRES
STRATTON AVE
Forty Hall Farm
Forty Hall
Mus and Gardens
FORTY HILL
THE CLOCK HO
Forty Hill CE Prim Sch
Nursery
New River
Hilly Fields Park
EN2
Allot Gdns
KILVINTON DR
WOODBINE GR
MYRTLE GR
VIOLET AVE
MORLEY HILL
ST LUKE'S AVE
CONWAY GDNS
KENSINGTON CT
HENRY CL
PORTLAND DR
BURNHAM CL
Allot Gdns
OLD FORGE RD
FORTY HILL HO
Worcesters Prim Sch
WORCESTERS
5
COOK'S HOLE RD
PHIPPS HATCH LA
LIME TREE WLK
CEDAR PARK RD
GLOUCESTER RD
BRODIE RD
GLENVILLE AVE
MERTON RD
BIRKBECK RD
Lavender Prim Sch
Enfield Cty Sch
RUSSELL RD
ST GEORGE'S RD
GOAT LA
MEYER GN
CEDAR RD
YORK TERR
BRIGADIER HILL
DALE RD
WETHERBY RD
CHANTRY CL
RIPLEY RD
TUDOR CL
BLOSSOM LA
BRIGADIER AVE
STERLING RD
BROWNING RD
HAWTHORN GR
RIDLER RD
HALLSIDE RD
MYDDELTON AVE
RUSSELL RD
GARNAULT RD
DOWLAND HO
HOLBROOK CL
98
PINNATA CL
ST FAITH'S CL
WHITE HOUSE LA
RADCLIFFE AVE
WOODLANDS RD
BURLINGTON RD
PO
LANCASTER RD
ACACIA RD
LAVENDER RD
ROSEMARY AVE
PRIMROSE AVE
RADNOR GDNS
KEWLWORTH CRES
BICKWOLLER RD
MYDDELTON CL
BRIDGENHALL RD
LAYARD RD
IRKDALE AVE
CHINNERY CL
MAHON CL
ABERCROMBIE DR
LINDEN A
St Michael's CE Prim Sch
YOUNGMANS CL
LAUREL RD
BATLEY RD
BANK RD
LYNN ST
WALTON ST
DRAKE ST
LEA RD
ARMFIELD RD
PHILIP CT
KYNASTON RD
YORK HO
WEARDALE GDNS
LANCASTER HO
PRIORS MEAD
CANONBURY RD
INVERNESS AVE
EASTBURY AVE
ORCHARD CL
SINCLARE CL
MELLING DR
ORTON GR
LINWOOD CRES
BRESSEY AVE
4
GORDON HILL
BORROWDALE CT
WHITAKERS LO
GATER DR
CHASE SIDE CRES
JOHN KEATS LO
St Michael's
H
FARR RD
THE DRIVE
BAKER ST
Chace Com Sch
ROCHESTER CL
Forty Hill
Cemy
CARISBROOK CL
TENNISWOOD RD
Sp Gd
KIRKLAND DR
BLACK FAN CL
TIPPETTS CL
SHELLY LO
HEENE RD
Sp Gd
BELL RD
IVINGHOE CL
Allot Gdns
CARTERHATCH LA
COLLEGE GDNS
COLLEGE RD
WESTON RD
GORDON RD
HALIFAX RD
HOLTWHITE AVE
CHURCHBURY RD
CHAILEY AVE
BUCKINGHAM CL
SANDRINGHAM CL
MONKS RD
St George's RC Prim Sch
MANOR RD
BELLAMY RD
CHEVIOTS HOSTEL
PILGRIMS CT
PEVENSEY AVE
BODIAM CL
COWDREY CL
ALDERSBROOK AVE
WILLOW RD
FILLEBROOK AVE
HERRONGATE CL
Queen Elizabeth Stad
DONKEY LA
TRINITY ST
CHEVIOT CL
CHEVIOT CT
GRAEME RD
Recn Gd
3
CAMBRIDGE GD
Chase Side Prim Sch
CHASE SIDE
NUNN'S RD
CHASE SIDE AVE
MONASTERY GDNS
St Andrew's CE Prim Sch
HEATH'S CL
RAVENS CL
CHURCHBURY LA
CHURCHBURY CL
CONNAUGHT AVE
CONNAUGHT CL
NEWBY CL
CARNARVON AVE
LAMBOURNE GDNS
LADYSMITH RD
MONKS CL
CHRISTCHURCH CL
LAMBS WLK
KINGS CLERE PL
CONICAL CNR
PARK RD
RIVERSIDE GDNS
PARSONAGE GDNS
CHASE SIDE PL
PARSONAGE LA
CHASE GREEN AVE
SHANE CT
WEST BANK
VICAR'S CL
Enfield Gram Sch (Lower)
97
Pl Fld
CHASE COURT GDNS
FLORENCE DR
CRICKETERS ARMS RD
HORSESHOE LA
DANBY CT
RIVERSFIELD RD
EN1
PORTCULLIS LODGE RD
Enfield Cty Sch
Offices
FIR TREE WLK
Civic Ctr
VINERIES THE
PEARTREE RD
GREENCROFT GDNS
ORCHARD WAY
ROBINSON CL
CHASE GN
RIVER VIEW
GENTLEMAN'S ROW
CHAPEL ST
HOLLY WLK
CHASE HILL
BENNETS CL
Allot Gdns
Enfield Gram Sch (Upper)
CHURCH LA
SILVER ST
ST ANDREW'S RD
FYFIELD RD
CALDER CL
APPLE GR
2
KIMBERLEY GDNS
CRADDOCK RD
MAFEKING RD
George Spicer Prim Sch
COBHAM CL
Kingsmead Sch
WAVERLEY CT
GRESHAM CL
Offices
SHIRLEY RD
Ct
LITTLE PARK GDNS
WILFORD CL
BURLEIGH WAY
MARKET PL
PO
RIVER FRONT
TEMPSFORD CL
CHURCH ST
THE TOWN
A110
A105
SAVOY
PAR
SPICER CT
STANLEY RD
SOUTHBURY RD
SKETTY RD
CLYDACH RD
BRYN-Y-MAWR RD
Enfield Chase
Liby
SARNESFIELD RD
Palace Gdns Sh Ctr
GENOTIN TERR
GENOTIN RD
BOVRIL HO
Enfield Town
Superstore
EATON RD
QUEEN'S RD
FELIX NEUBERGH CT
FOTHERINGHAM RD
CECIL AVE
JULES THORN AVE
L Ctr
FIRBANK CL
Tenn Cts
CECIL RD
St Anne's RC High Sch for Girls
BERESFORD GDNS
SEAFORD RD
HALSTEAD RD
FALMER RD
Tenn Cts
Enfield Town
OLD PARK AVE
Bwg Gn
Palace Exchange
RALEIGH RD
SYDNEY RD
LONDON RD
ROSENEATH WLK
CHALKWELL PARK AVE
Allot Gdns
BEVERLEY CL
WADDINGTON CL
BURLEIGH RD
PERCIVAL RD
BERT WAY
BERTRAM RD
CLIVE WAY
CLIVE RD
SOUTHBURY AVE
1
Town Park
FROBISHER MEWS
ESSEX RD
TIPTREE DR
LINCOLN CT
LYNDHURST GDNS
CAMBERLEY AVE
CROSS RD
DOWNS RD
Recn Gd
OLD PARK GR
Tenn Cts
LC
LINCOLN RD
SALISBURY CT
PARK CRES
POTTERSFIELD
SILVERTHORNE LO
MORNINGTON LO
ILLINGWORTH WAY
KINGSWOOD CL
96
RIDINGS AVE
WALSINGHAM RD
UVEDALE RD
WHITETHORN GDNS
ASCOT LO
33
17
Tenn Cts
LINCOLN CRES
HARMAN RD
JOHN ST
CHARLES ST
JAMES ST
AGRICOLA PL
Liby
HADRIAN'S RIDE
ROMAN WAY
34
ERMINE SIDE
Bush Hill Park Prim Sch
EN2
GARFIELD
PRIVATE RD
ROWLEY CT
EAST CRES
WATERHEDGE MEWS
KARYATIS CT
MAIN AVE
Bush Hill Park

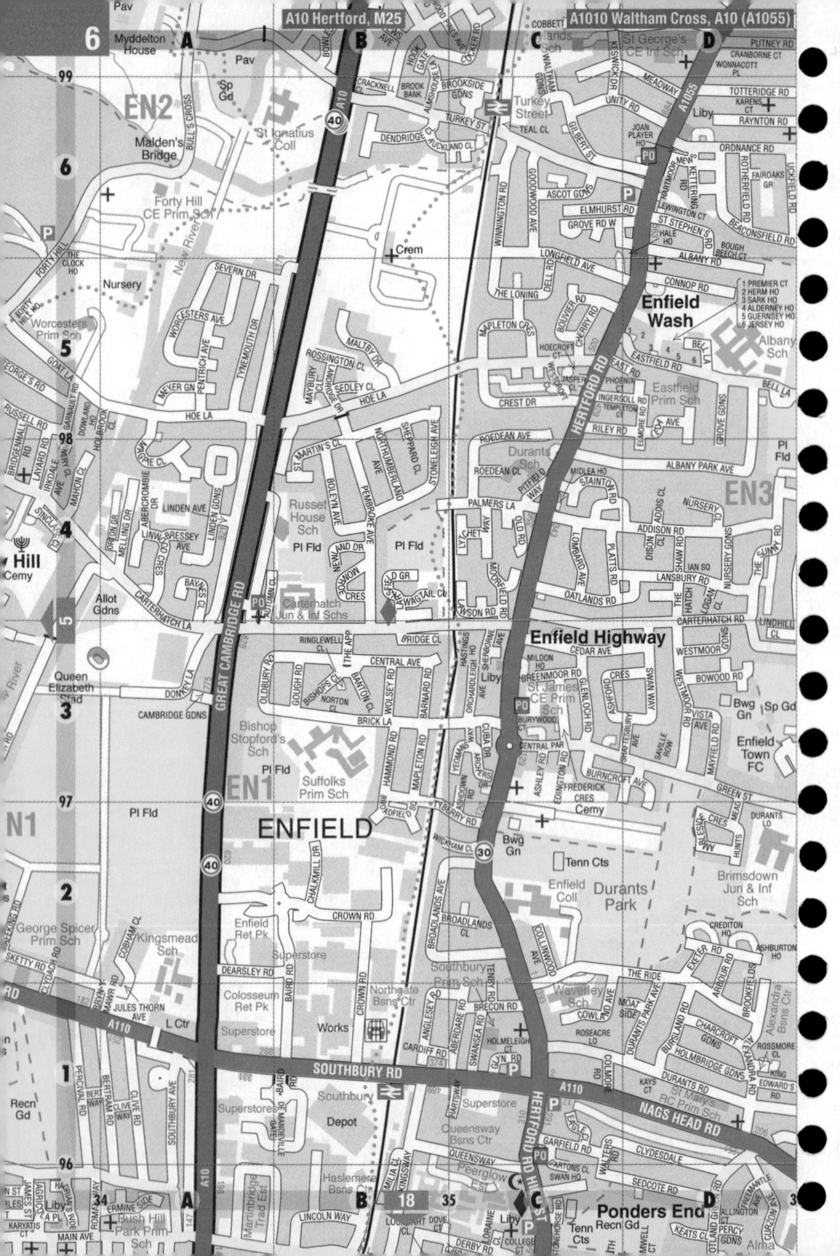
A10 Hertford, M25
A1010 Waltham Cross, A10 (A1055)
EN2
EN1
EN3
N1
Malden's Bridge
Forty Hill CE Prim Sch
St Ignatius Coll
Turkey Street
Crem
Nursery
Worcesters Prim Sch
Enfield Wash
Albany Sch
Eastfield Prim Sch
Durants Sch
Russet House Sch
Carterhatch Jun & Inf Schs
Allot Gdns
Enfield Highway
St James CE Prim Sch
Queen Elizabeth Stad
Bishop Stopford's Sch
Suffolks Prim Sch
ENFIELD
Enfield Town FC
Brimsdown Jun & Inf Sch
Enfield Coll
Durants Park
Tenn Cts
George Spicer Prim Sch
Kingsmead Sch
Enfield Ret Pk
Colosseum Ret Pk
Superstore
Southbury Prim Sch
Waverley Sch
Northgate Bsns Ctr
Works
Queensway Bsns Ctr
Haslemere Bsns Ctr
Martinbridge Trad Est
Peerglow Est
Ponders End
Recn Gd
Bush Hill Park Prim Sch
Southbury
Depot
Alexandra Bsns Ctr
St Mary's RC Prim Sch
GREAT CAMBRIDGE RD
HERTFORD RD
SOUTHBURY RD
NAGS HEAD RD
HOE LA
CARTERHATCH LA
CARTERHATCH RD
BRICK LA
CROWN RD
A110
A10
A1055
Pl Fld
Bwg Gn
Cemy

18

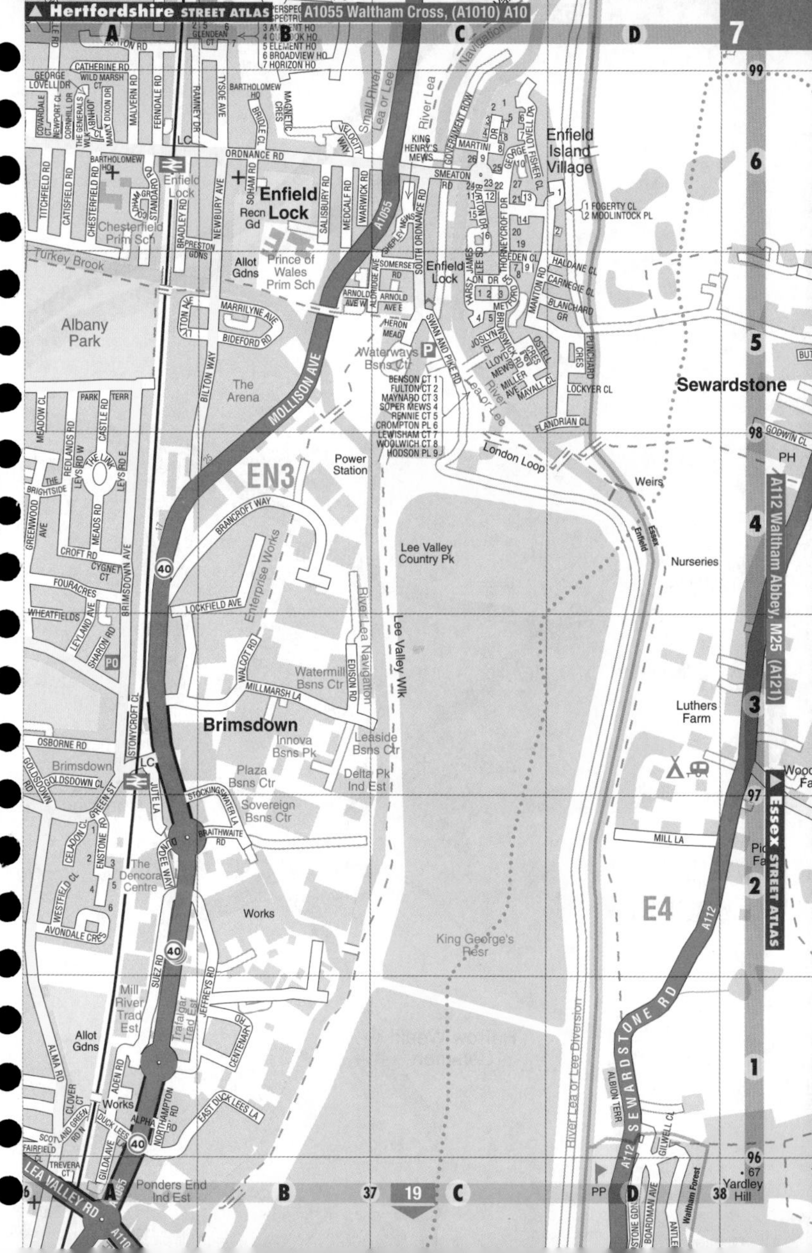

Enfield Lock

Enfield Island Village

Enfield Lock

Sewardstone

EN3

Albany Park

The Arena

Power Station

Lee Valley Country Pk

Brimsdown

Watermill Bsns Ctr

Innova Bsns Pk

Plaza Bsns Ctr

Sovereign Bsns Ctr

Leaside Bsns Ctr

Delta Pk Ind Est

Works

King George's Resr

E4

Luthers Farm

Nurseries

Weirs

Mill River Trad Est

Allot Gdns

Works

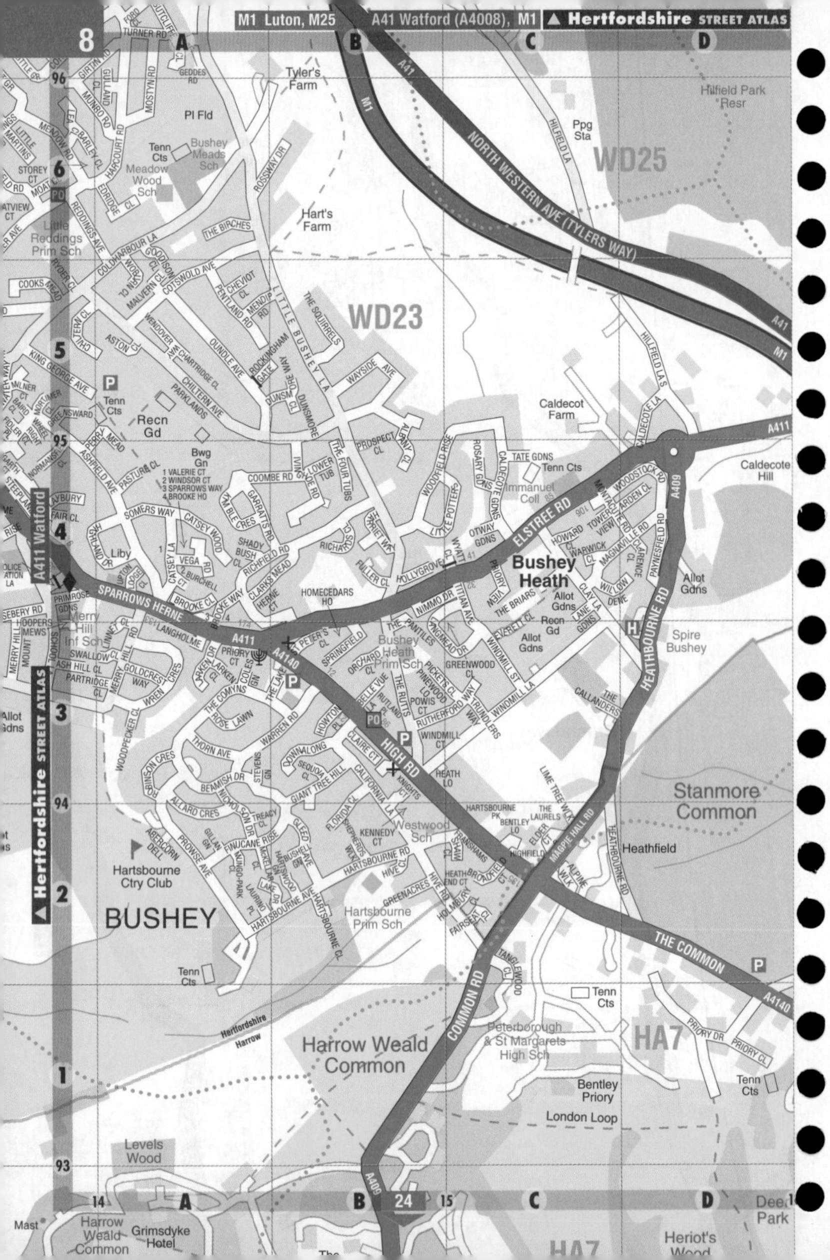
Tyler's Farm
Pl Fld
Hart's Farm
Hilfield Park Resr
Ppg Sta
WD25
NORTH WESTERN AVE (TYLERS WAY)
WD23
Caldecot Farm
Caldecote Hill
Immanuel Coll
Bushey Heath
Spire Bushey
Stanmore Common
Heathfield
Little Reddings Prim Sch
Bushey Meads Sch
Meadow Wood Sch
Recn Gd
Bwg Gn
Liby
Merry Hill Inf Sch
Bushey Heath Prim Sch
Westwood Sch
Hartsbourne Ctry Club
BUSHEY
Hartsbourne Prim Sch
Harrow Weald Common
Peterborough & St Margarets High Sch
HA7
Bentley Priory
London Loop
Levels Wood
Grimsdyke Hotel
Heriot's Wood
Deer Park
Hertfordshire
Harrow
SPARROWS HERNE
ELSTREE RD
HIGH RD
HEATHBOURNE RD
COMMON RD
THE COMMON
A411 Watford
A411
A4140
A409
A41
M1
1 VALERIE CT
2 WINDSOR CT
3 SPARROWS WAY
4 BROOKE HO
A411 Watford
▲ Hertfordshire STREET ATLAS

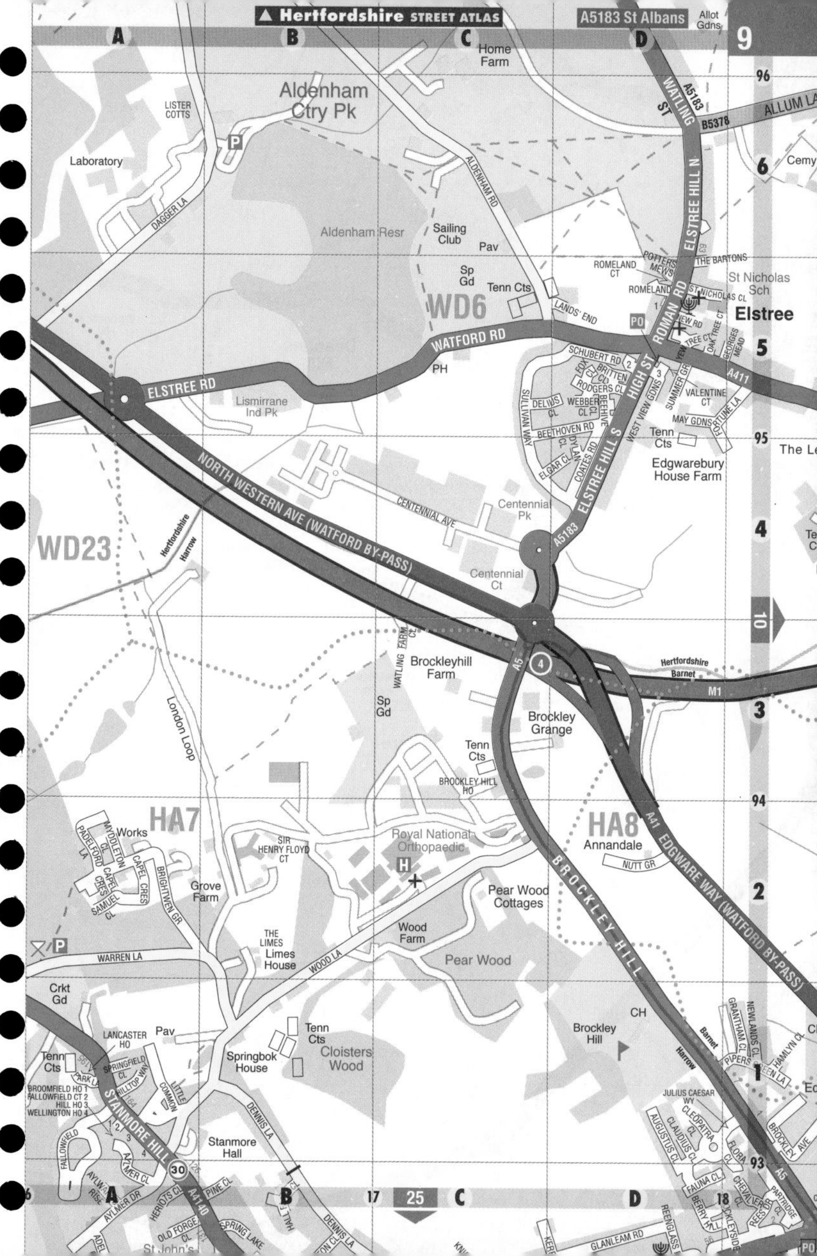
Home Farm
Aldenham Ctry Pk
LISTER COTTS
Laboratory
DAGGER LA
ALDENHAM RD
Aldenham Resr
Sailing Club
Pav
Sp Gd
Tenn Cts
WD6
WATLING ST
A5183
B5378
ALLUM LA
Cemy
ELSTREE HILL N
POTTERS MEWS
THE BARTONS
ROMELAND CT
ROMELAND
ST NICHOLAS CL
St Nicholas Sch
Elstree
LANDS' END
ROMAN RD
NEW RD
YEW TREE CT
OAK TREE CT
GEORGES MEAD
WATFORD RD
SCHUBERT RD
BRITTEN CL
RODGERS CL
HIGH ST
A411
ELSTREE RD
PH
Lismirrane Ind Pk
SULLIVAN WAY
DELIUS CL
WEBBER CL
BEEHIVE
WEST VIEW GDNS
SUMMER GR
VALENTINE CT
MAY GDNS
FORTUNE LA
BEETHOVEN RD
DYLAN CL
COATES RD
ELGAR CL
ELSTREE HILL S
Tenn Cts
Edgwarebury House Farm
The Le
NORTH WESTERN AVE (WATFORD BY-PASS)
CENTENNIAL AVE
Centennial Pk
A5183
WD23
Hertfordshire
Harrow
Centennial Ct
10
WATLING FARM CL
Brockleyhill Farm
A5
4
Hertfordshire
Barnet
M1
Sp Gd
London Loop
Brockley Grange
Tenn Cts
BROCKLEY HILL HO
HA7
HA8
Works
MYDDLETON CL
PADELFORD LA
CAPEL CRES
BRIGHTWEN GR
SAMUEL CL
SIR HENRY FLOYD CT
Royal National Orthopaedic
H
A41
EDGWARE WAY (WATFORD BY-PASS)
Annandale
NUTT GR
Grove Farm
Pear Wood Cottages
BROCKLEY HILL
WARREN LA
THE LIMES
Limes House
WOOD LA
Wood Farm
Pear Wood
Crkt Gd
CH
Brockley Hill
Barnet
Harrow
GRANTHAM CL
NEWLANDS CL
HAMLYN CL
PIPERS GREEN LA
LANCASTER HO
Pav
Tenn Cts
SPRINGFIELD CL
HILLTOP WAY
PARK LA
Springbok House
Tenn Cts
Cloisters Wood
BROOMFIELD HO 1
FALLOWFIELD CT 2
HILL HO 3
WELLINGTON HO 4
STANMORE HILL
COMMON
LITTLE COMMON
DENNIS LA
JULIUS CAESAR WY
CLEOPATRA CL
CLAUDIUS CL
AUGUSTUS CL
FLORA CL
BROCKLEY AVE
FALLOWFIELD
AYLMER CL
Stanmore Hall
30
AYLWARDS RISE
AYLMER DR
HERIOTS CL
PINE CL
A4140
FAUNA CL
BERRY HILL
CHEVALIER CL
PARTRIDGE
REES DR
OLD FORGE CL
SPRING LAKE
HALE LA
DENNIS LA
REENGLASS
GLANLEAM RD
PO
Allot Gdns

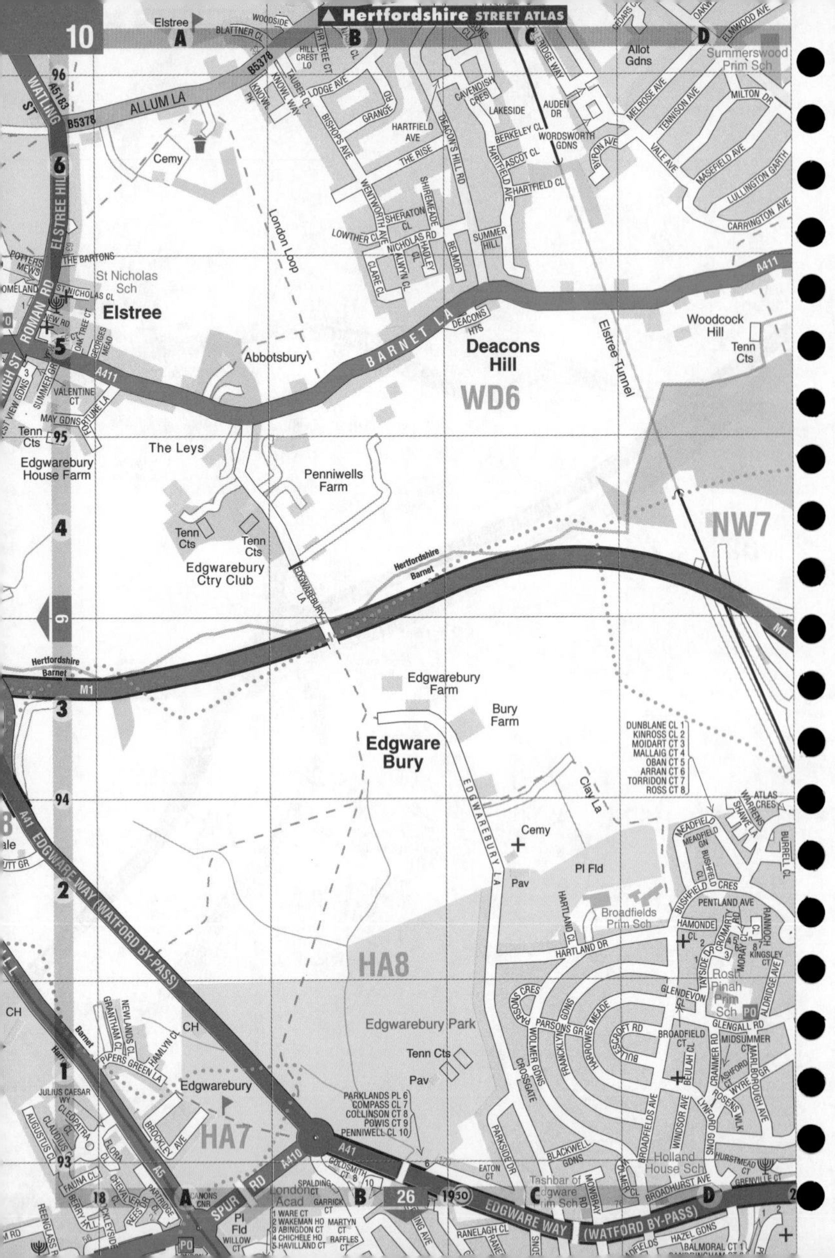
Elstree
Deacons Hill
Edgware Bury
WD6
NW7
HA8
HA7
Allot Gdns
Summerswood Prim Sch
Woodcock Hill
St Nicholas Sch
Abbotsbury
The Leys
Penniwells Farm
Edgwarebury House Farm
Edgwarebury Ctry Club
Edgwarebury Farm
Bury Farm
Broadfields Prim Sch
Edgwarebury Park
Holland House Sch
Rosh Pinah Prim Sch
London Loop
Elstree Tunnel
BARNET LA
ALLUM LA
EDGWARE WAY (WATFORD BY-PASS)
EDGWAREBURY LA
DUNBLANE CL 1
KINROSS CL 2
MOIDART CT 3
MALLAIG CT 4
OBAN CT 5
ARRAN CT 6
TORRIDON CT 7
ROSS CT 8
PARKLANDS PL 6
COMPASS CL 7
COLLINSON CT 8
POWIS CT 9
PENNIWELL CL 10
1 WARE CT
2 WAKEMAN HO
3 ABINGDON CT
4 CHICHELE HO
5 HAVILLAND CT

9
18
26
1950

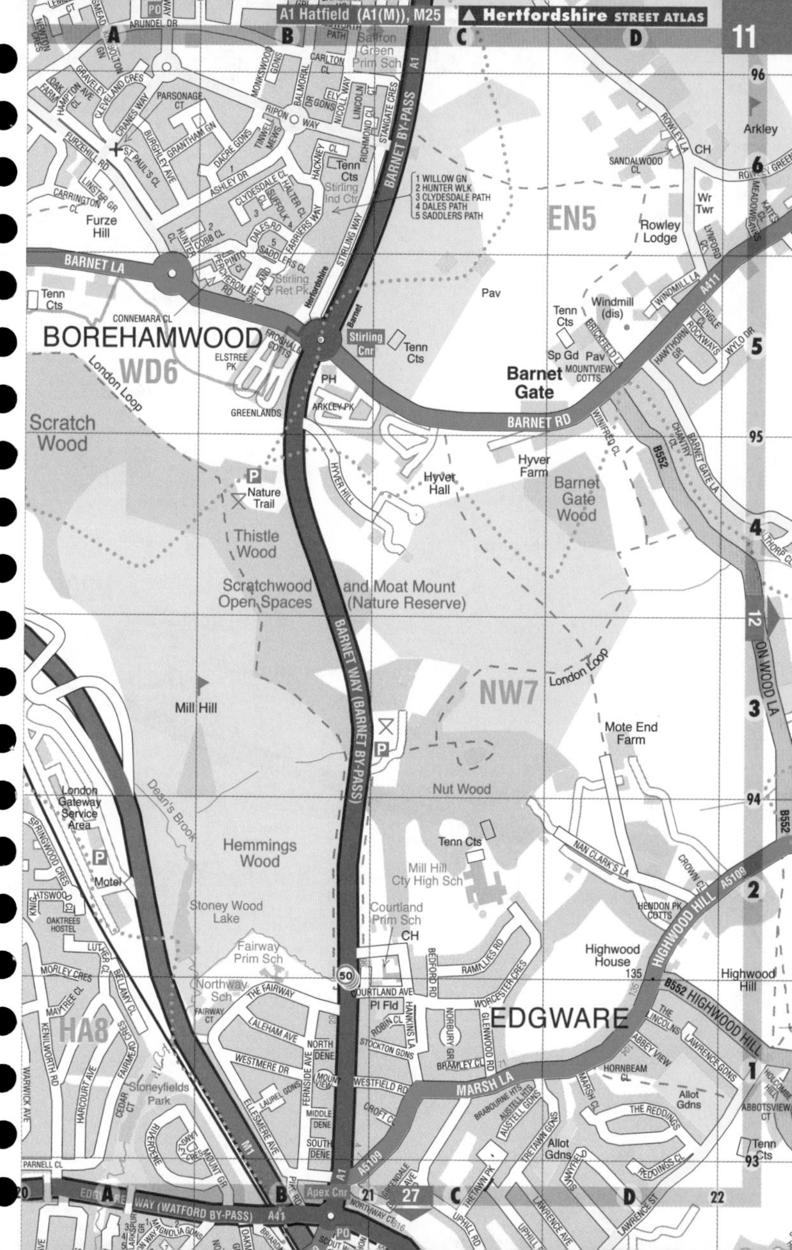
BOREHAMWOOD
EDGWARE
Barnet Gate
EN5
WD6
NW7
HA8
Furze Hill
Scratch Wood
Thistle Wood
Scratchwood and Moat Mount Open Spaces (Nature Reserve)
Mill Hill
London Gateway Service Area
Motel
Hemmings Wood
Stoney Wood Lake
Fairway Prim Sch
Northway Sch
Stoneyfields Park
Nut Wood
Mill Hill Cty High Sch
Courtland Prim Sch
Mote End Farm
Highwood House
Highwood Hill
Hyver Hall
Hyver Farm
Barnet Gate Wood
Rowley Lodge
Windmill (dis)
Arkley
Saffron Green Prim Sch
Stirling Ind Ctr
Stirling Ret Pk
Stirling Cnr
Nature Trail
London Loop
BARNET LA
BARNET RD
BARNET BY-PASS
BARNET WAY (BARNET BY-PASS)
MARSH LA
HIGHWOOD HILL
EDGWARE WAY (WATFORD BY-PASS)
1 WILLOW GN
2 HUNTER WLK
3 CLYDESDALE PATH
4 DALES PATH
5 SADDLERS PATH
Apex Cnr
A1
A41
A411
A5109
B552
M1
12
27
20
21
22
93
94
95
96
A B C D
1 2 3 4 5 6

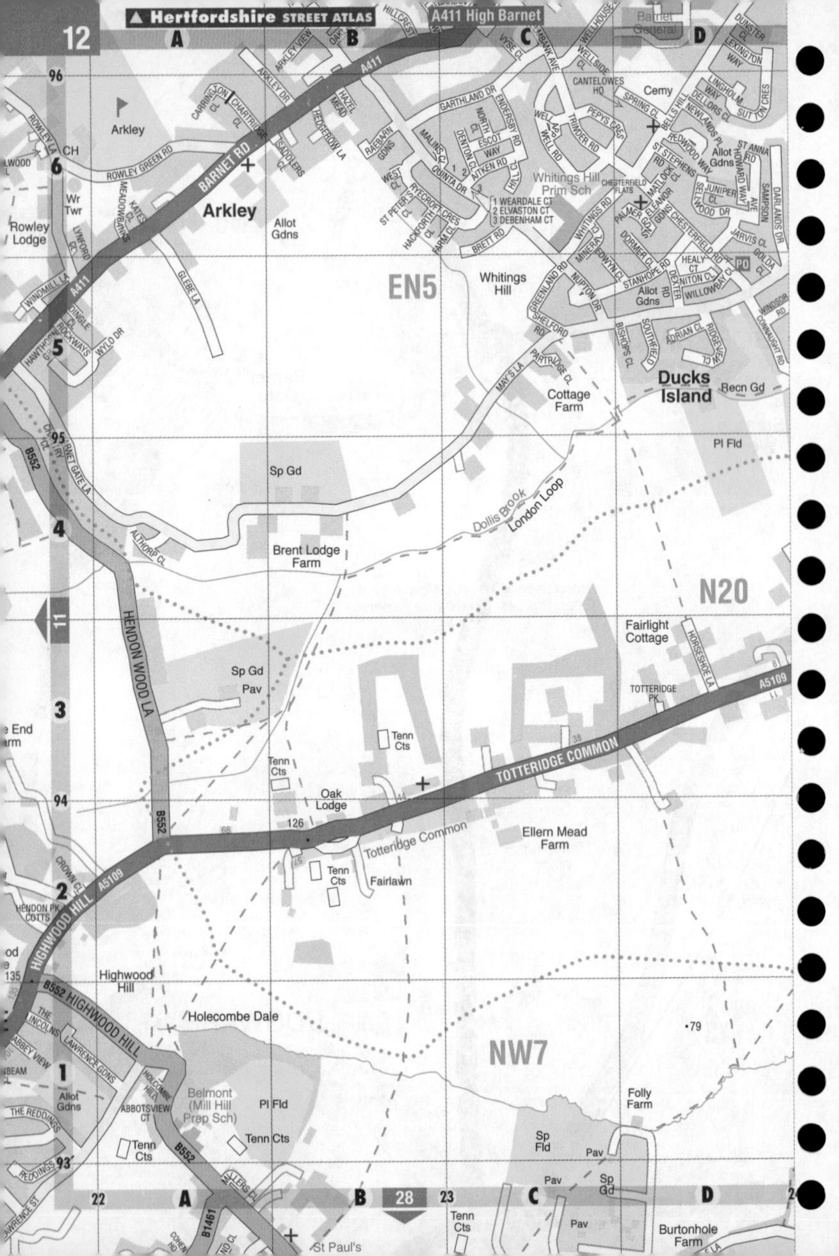
A411 High Barnet
A
B
C
D
Arkley
Arkley
BARNET RD
A411
ROWLEY GREEN RD
Rowley Lodge
Wr Twr
Allot Gdns
EN5
Whitings Hill
Whitings Hill Prim Sch
Cemy
Cottage Farm
Ducks Island
Becn Gd
Pl Fld
Sp Gd
Brent Lodge Farm
Dollis Brook
London Loop
N20
Fairlight Cottage
HORSESHOE LA
TOTTERIDGE PK
A5109
TOTTERIDGE COMMON
Sp Gd
Pav
Tenn Cts
Oak Lodge
Totteridge Common
Ellern Mead Farm
Fairlawn
HENDON WOOD LA
B552
HIGHWOOD HILL
A5109
Highwood Hill
Holecombe Dale
NW7
B552 HIGHWOOD HILL
Belmont (Mill Hill Prep Sch)
Pl Fld
Allot Gdns
Folly Farm
Sp Fld
Pav
Sp Gd
Burtonhole Farm
St Paul's
1 WEARDALE CT
2 ELVASTON CT
3 DEBENHAM CT
96
95
94
93
6
5
4
3
2
1
11
28
22
23

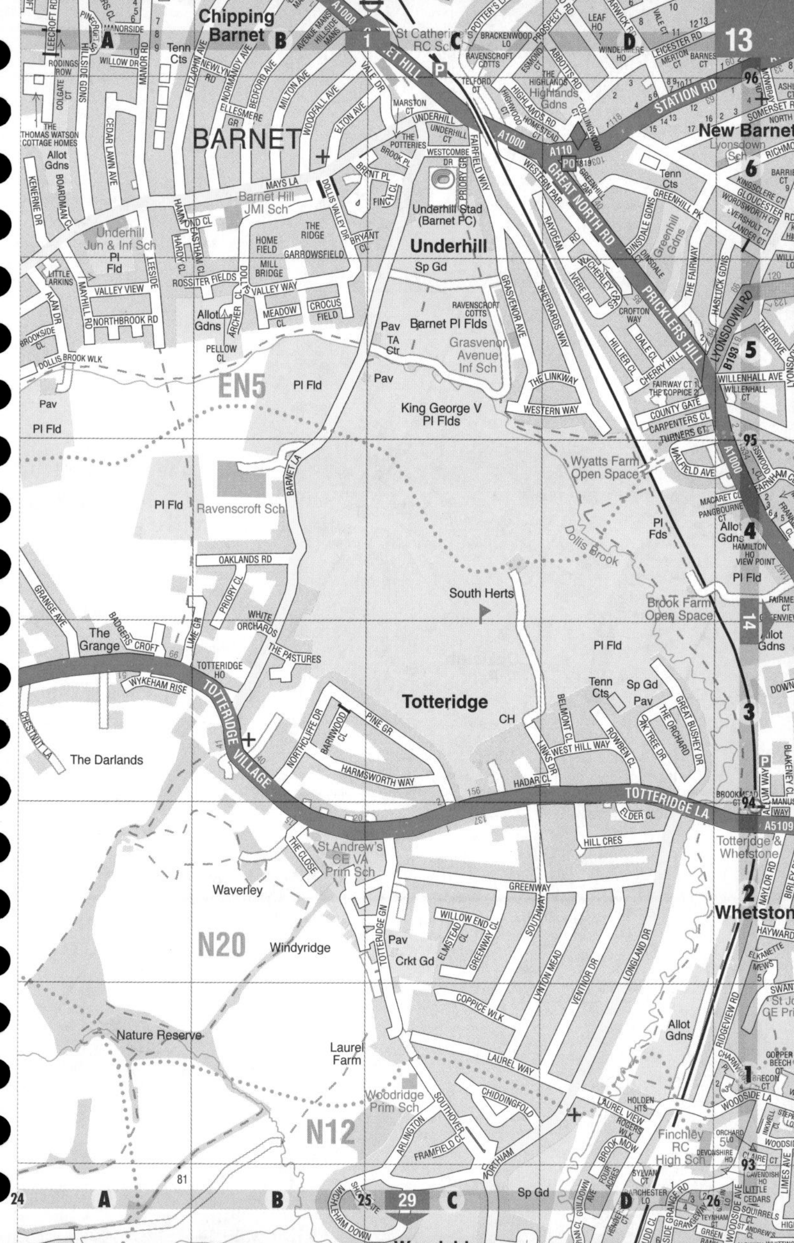
Chipping Barnet
BARNET
New Barnet
Underhill
Totteridge
Whetstone
EN5
N20
N12
A
B
C
D
1
2
3
4
5
6
24
25
26
29
14
93
94
95
96
A1000
A110
A5109
B193
STATION RD
GREAT NORTH RD
PRICKLERS HILL
TOTTERIDGE VILLAGE
TOTTERIDGE LA
LYONSDOWN RD
St Catherine's RC Sch
Barnet Hill JMI Sch
Underhill Jun & Inf Sch
Underhill Stad (Barnet FC)
Barnet Pl Flds
Grasvenor Avenue Inf Sch
King George V Pl Flds
Wyatts Farm Open Space
Dollis Brook
Ravenscroft Sch
South Herts
Brook Farm Open Space
The Grange
The Darlands
St Andrew's CE VA Prim Sch
Waverley
Windyridge
Nature Reserve
Laurel Farm
Woodridge Prim Sch
Finchley RC High Sch
Totteridge & Whetstone
Lyonsdown Sch
Highlands Gdns
Greenhill Gdns
Allot Gdns
Pl Fld
Pl Fds
Tenn Cts
Sp Gd
Pav
Crkt Gd
TA Ctr
CH
MAYS LA
OAKLANDS RD
GRANGE AVE
BARNET LA
WESTERN WAY
THE LINKWAY
GRASVENOR AVE
SHERRARDS WAY
FAIRFIELD WAY
HARMSWORTH WAY
NORTHCLIFFE DR
PINE GR
WEST HILL WAY
LINKS DR
BELMONT CL
ROWBEN CL
GREAT BUSHEY DR
THE ORCHARD
OAK TREE DR
HILL CRES
ELDER CL
GREENWAY
SOUTHWAY
LYNTON MEAD
VENTNOR DR
LONGLAND DR
COPPICE WLK
LAUREL WAY
LAUREL VIEW
TOTTERIDGE GN
WILLOW END
ELMSTEAD CL
GREENWAY CL
CHIDDINGFOLD
SOUTHOVER
ARLINGTON
FRAMFIELD CL
NORTHAM
BROOK MDW
FOUR ACRES
GUILDOWN AVE
WOODSIDE LA
WOODSIDE AVE
RIDGEVIEW RD
NAYLOR RD
BIRLEY RD
WYKEHAM RISE
BADGERS CROFT
LIME GR
PRIORY CL
WHITE ORCHARDS
THE PASTURES
THE CLOSE
CHESTNUT LA
DOLLIS BROOK WLK
NORTHBROOK RD
VALLEY VIEW
VALLEY WAY
ROSSITER FIELDS
MEADOW CL
CROCUS FIELD
GARROWSFIELD
HOME FIELD
MILL BRIDGE
THE RIDGE
BRYANT CL
DOLLIS VALLEY DR
MAYHILL RD
ALAN DR
BROOKSIDE CL
LEESIDE
HARDY CL
CEDAR LAWN AVE
HILLSIDE GDNS
MANOR RD
MANORSIDE
WILLOW DR
LEECROFT RD
KENERNE DR
BOARDMAN CL
ELLESMERE GR
NEWLYN RD
NORMANDY AVE
BEDFORD AVE
MILTON AVE
WOODFALL AVE
ELTON AVE
VALE DR
UNDERHILL
WESTCOMBE DR
PRIORY GR
BRENT PL
FINCH CL
WESTERN PAR
RAYDEAN RD
WYCHERLEY CR
IVERE DR
CROFTON WAY
DALE CL
HILLIER CL
CHERRY HILL
THE FAIRWAY
DINSDALE GDNS
GREENHILL PK
HASLUCK GDNS
WILLENHALL AVE
COUNTY GATE
CARPENTERS CL
TURNERS CT
WALFIELD AVE
FARNHAM CL
MACARET CL
PANGBOURNE CT
FRANKLIN CL
HAMILTON HO
VIEW POINT
THE DRIVE
RICHMOND
GLOUCESTER RD
KINGSCLERE CT
WORDSWORTH CT
LANDER CT
SOMERSET RD
ASHLEY CT
LEICESTER RD
BRACKENWOOD LO
RAVENSCROFT COTTS
HIGHLANDS GDNS
ABBOTTS RD
PROSPECT RD
COLLINGWOOD CT
HIGHWOOD CT
HOMESTEAD CT
TOTTERIDGE HO
HOLDEN HTS
ROGERS WLK
SYLVAN CT
BUDD CL
GREEN BANK
COPPER BEECH CT
CHARNWOOD PL
BRYANT CL
Sp Gd

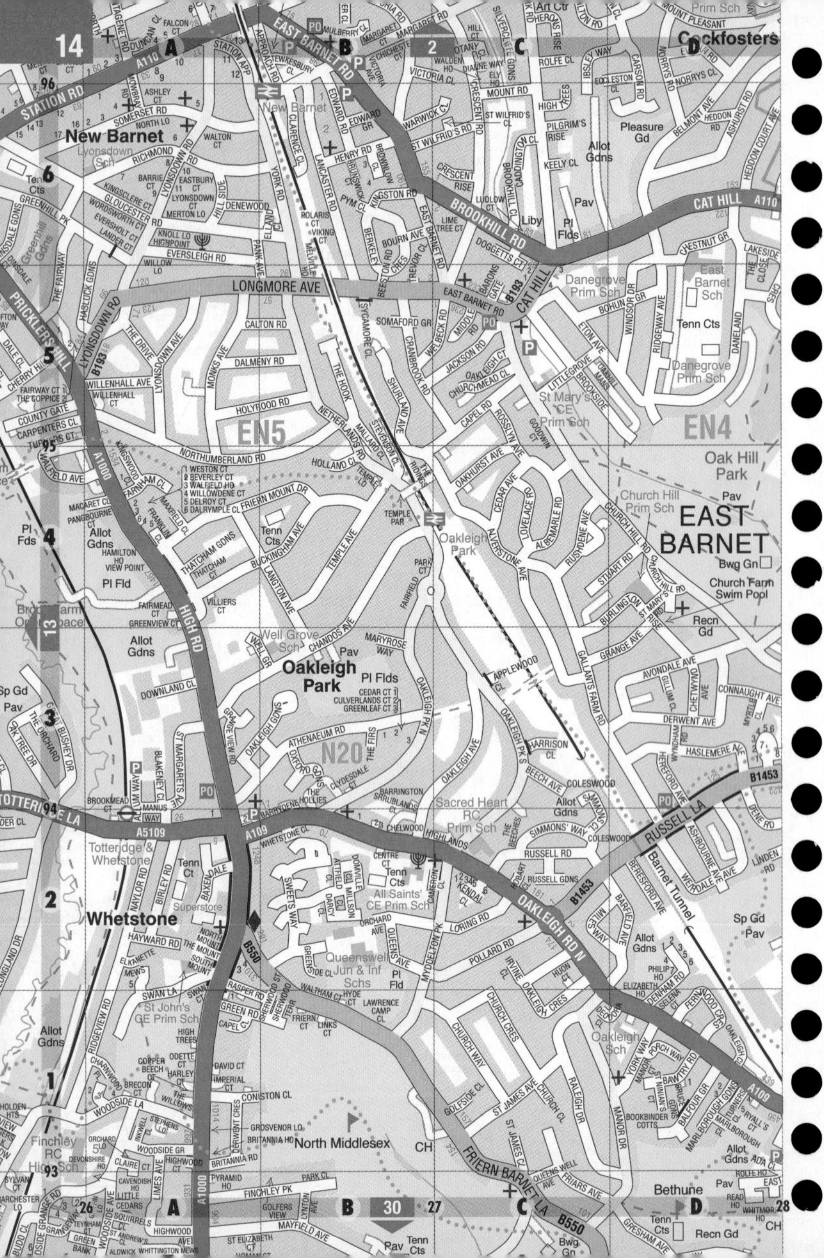

14
A
B
2
C
D
Cockfosters
Mount Pleasant
East Barnet Rd
Station Rd
A110
New Barnet
Lyonsdown Sch
Richmond Rd
Somerset Rd
Lyonsdown Rd
Approach Rd
Station App
Mulberry Cl
Margaret Rd
Victoria Cl
Tewkesbury Cl
Edward Rd
Clarence Cl
York Rd
Lancaster Rd
Henry Rd
Kingston Rd
Bourn Ave
Berkeley Cres
Beeston Rd
Trevor Cl
Brookhill Rd
Crescent Rise
Crescent Rd
Mount Rd
St Wilfrid's Rd
Warwick Cl
Silvercliffe Gdns
Rolfe Cl
Ibsley Way
Eccleston Cl
Carson Rd
Norrys Rd
Norrys Cl
Belmont Ave
Heddon Rd
Ashurst Rd
Heddon Court Ave
Pleasure Gd
Allot Gdns
Pav
Pl Flds
Liby
Cat Hill
A110
Chestnut Gr
Lakeside
The Close
Caddington Cl
Brookhill Cl
Pilgrim's Rise
High Trees
Keely Cl
Ludlow Ct
Doggetts Ct
Barons Gate
B193
Danegrove Prim Sch
East Barnet Sch
Tenn Cts
Daneland
Ridgeway Ave
Windsor Dr
Bohun Gr
Eton Ave
Littlegrove
Brookside
Greenhill Pk
Gloucester Rd
Kingsclere Ct
Wordsworth Ct
Eversholt Ct
Lander Ct
Greenhill Gdns
The Fairway
Hasluck Gdns
Eversleigh Rd
Willow Lo
Longmore Ave
Knoll Lo
Highpoint
Denewood
Hill Side
Park Ave
Melville Ho
Polaris Ct
Viking Ct
Elland Rd
Sycamore Cl
Somaford Gr
Welbeck Rd
Middle Rd
East Barnet Rd
Cranbrook Rd
Shurland Ave
The Hook
Netherlands Rd
Mallard Cl
Stevenson Cl
Calton Rd
Dalmeny Rd
Holyrood Rd
Monks Ave
The Drive
Lyonsdown Ave
Willenhall Ave
Pricklers Hill
B193
Jackson Rd
Oakleigh Ct
Churchmead Cl
Capel Rd
Rosslyn Ave
Goodwin Ct
St Mary's CE Prim Sch
EN5
EN4
Oak Hill Park
Northumberland Rd
Holland Cl
Temple Lo
The Ridings
County Gate
Carpenters Cl
Walfield Ave
Kingswood Ct
Farnham Cl
Franklin
Maxfield Cl
Friern Mount Dr
1 Weston Ct
2 Beverley Ct
3 Walfield Ho
4 Willowdene Ct
5 Delroy Ct
6 Dalrymple Cl
A1000
Macaret Cl
Pangbourne Ct
Allot Gdns
Hamilton Ho
View Point
Pl Fld
Pl Fds
Thatcham Gdns
Thatcham Ct
Buckingham Ave
Tenn Cts
Temple Ave
Temple Par
Oakleigh Park
Oakhurst Ave
Cedar Ave
Lovelace Rd
Albemarle Rd
Alverstone Ave
Rushdene Ave
Church Hill Rd
Church Hill Prim Sch
EAST BARNET
Bwg Gn
Church Farm Swim Pool
Stuart Rd
Burlington Rise
St Mary's Rise
Recn Gd
Langton Ave
Park Ct
Fairfield
Villiers Ct
Fairmead Ct
Greenview Ct
High Rd
Well Grove Sch
Chandos Ave
Well Gr
Maryrose Way
Oakleigh Park
Pl Flds
Cedar Ct
Culverlands Ct
Greenleaf Ct
Grange Ave
Gallants Farm Rd
Applewood Cl
Avondale Ave
Gillum Cl
Chetwynd Ave
Connaught Ave
Derwent Ave
Haslemere Ave
Downland Cl
Allot Gdns
Sp Gd
Pav
Great Bushey Dr
The Orchard
Oak Tree Dr
St Margarets Ave
Blakeney Cl
Oakleigh Gdns
Grange View Rd
Athenaeum Rd
The Firs
Oakleigh Pk N
Oakleigh Pk S
Oakleigh Ave
Harrison Cl
Beech Ave
Coleswood
Hereford Ave
B1453
N20
Clydesdale Ct
The Hollies
Barrington
Shrublands
Sacred Heart RC Prim Sch
Allot Gdns
Simmons Cl
Simmons' Way
The Beeches
Totteridge La
A5109
Brookmead Ct
Alum Way
Manus Way
Totteridge & Whetstone
A109
Whetstone Cl
Chelwood
Highlands
Russell Rd
Russell Gdns
Russell La
Barnet Tunnel
Ashbourne Ave
Weirdale Ave
Dene Rd
Linden Rd
Tenn Ct
Birley Rd
Naylor Rd
Baxendale
Superstore
Whetstone
Sweets Way
Centre Ct
Domville Cl
Attfield Cl
Millson Cl
Darcy Cl
Tenn Cts
All Saints' CE Prim Sch
Cameron Cl
Kendal Cl
Hobart Cl
Oakleigh Rd N
B1453
Beresford Ave
Barfield Ave
Miles Way
Sp Gd
Pav
Hayward Rd
North Mount
The Mount
South Mount
Elkanette Mews
Swan La
B550
Orchard Ave
Queens Ave
Greenside Cl
Queenswell Jun & Inf Schs
Pl Fld
Myddelton Pk
Loring Rd
Pollard Rd
Irvine Cl
Oakleigh Cres
Huon Ct
Allot Gdns
Philip Ho
Elizabeth Ho
Denham Rd
Selena Ct
Fernwood Cres
St John's CE Prim Sch
Ridgeview Rd
Rasper Rd
Green Rd
Capel Ct
Sherwood St
Sherwood Terr
Waltham Ct
Hyde Ct
Lawrence Camp Cl
Friern Ct
Links Ct
Church Way
Church Cres
Oakleigh Sch
York Way
Manor Ct
Porch Way
Bawtry Rd
St Ninian's Ct
Bruce Gdns
Allot Gdns
High Trees
Copper Beech Ct
Odette Ct
Harley Ct
David Ct
Imperial Ct
Charnwood Pl
Brecon Ct
The Willows
Woodside La
Coniston Cl
Golfside Cl
St James Ave
Church Cl
Raleigh Dr
Manor Dr
Balfour Gr
Marlborough Gdns
Turners Ct
Ryall's Ct
Marlborough Ct
A109
Bookbinder Cotts
Stephens Lo
Inkwell Cl
Woodside Gr
Derwent Cres
Grosvenor Lo
Britannia Ho
Britannia Rd
North Middlesex
CH
Friern Barnet La
St James Cl
Queens Well Ave
Friars Ave
Allot Gdns
Ada Cl
Rolfe Ho
Pav
Read Ho
Whitmore Ho
East
Finchley RC High Sch
Holden Hts
Orchard Lo
Devonshire Ho
Claire Ct
Highwood Ct
Cavendish Ho
Little Cedars
Limes Ave
Pyramid Ho
Park Cl
Finchley Pk
Golfers View
Lynton Ave
Mayfield Ave
Bethune
Sylvan Ct
Archester Lo
Grange Rd
Woodside Ave
Squirrels
Teynham Ct
St Andrew's Ct
Green Bank
Aldwick
Whittington Mews
Highwood
Avenue
St Elizabeth Ct
Budd Cl
Woodside Grange Rd
Longland Dr
Holden
Tenn Cts
Recn Gd
Gresham Ave
Bwg Gn
Tenn Cts
Rav
A
B
30
27
C
D
26
28
B550
1
2
3
4
5
6
13
93
94
95
96

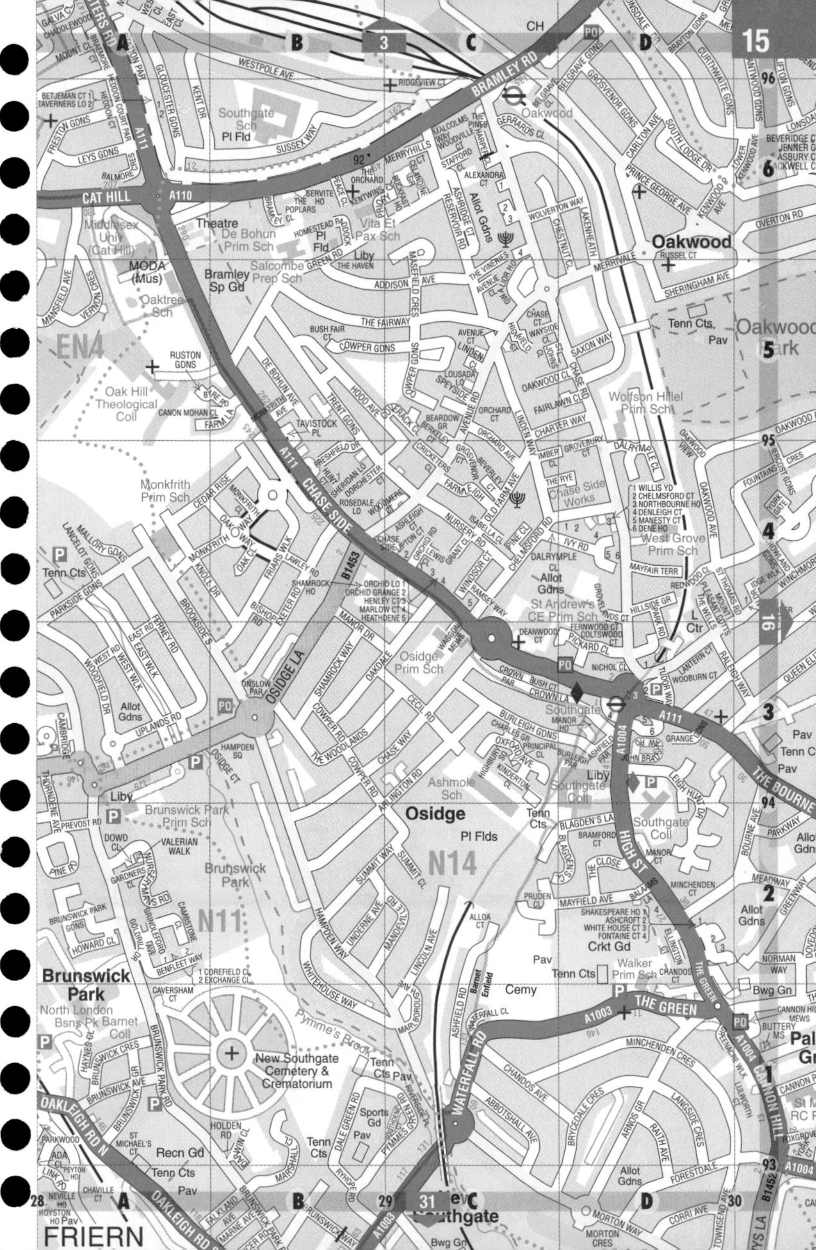
Southgate Sch
Pl Fld
Oakwood
Bramley Rd
Cat Hill
A111
A110
Theatre
De Bohun Prim Sch
Middlesex Univ (Cat Hill)
MODA (Mus)
Bramley Sp Gd
Salcombe Prep Sch
Vita Et Pax Sch
Oaktree Sch
EN4
Oak Hill Theological Coll
Allot Gdns
Wolfson Hillel Prim Sch
Oakwood Park
Tenn Cts
Pav
Monkfrith Prim Sch
Chase Side
Chase Side Works
West Grove Prim Sch
St Andrew's CE Prim Sch
L Ctr
Osidge Prim Sch
Osidge La
B1453
Southgate
Southgate Coll
Ashmole Sch
Liby
Osidge
Pl Flds
N14
N11
Brunswick Park Prim Sch
Brunswick Park
Crkt Gd
Walker Prim Sch
High St
A1004
The Bourne
The Green
A1003
Cemy
New Southgate Cemetery & Crematorium
Pymme's Brook
North London Bsns Pk Barnet Coll
Sports Gd
Recn Gd
Waterfall Rd
Oakleigh Rd N
Oakleigh Rd S
Cannon Hill
New Southgate
Bwg Gn
Friern
Palm Gr
Allot Gdns
Morton Way
Chandos Ave
Minchenden Cres
Waterfall Rd
A B C D
1 2 3 4 5 6
3
16
31
28
29
30

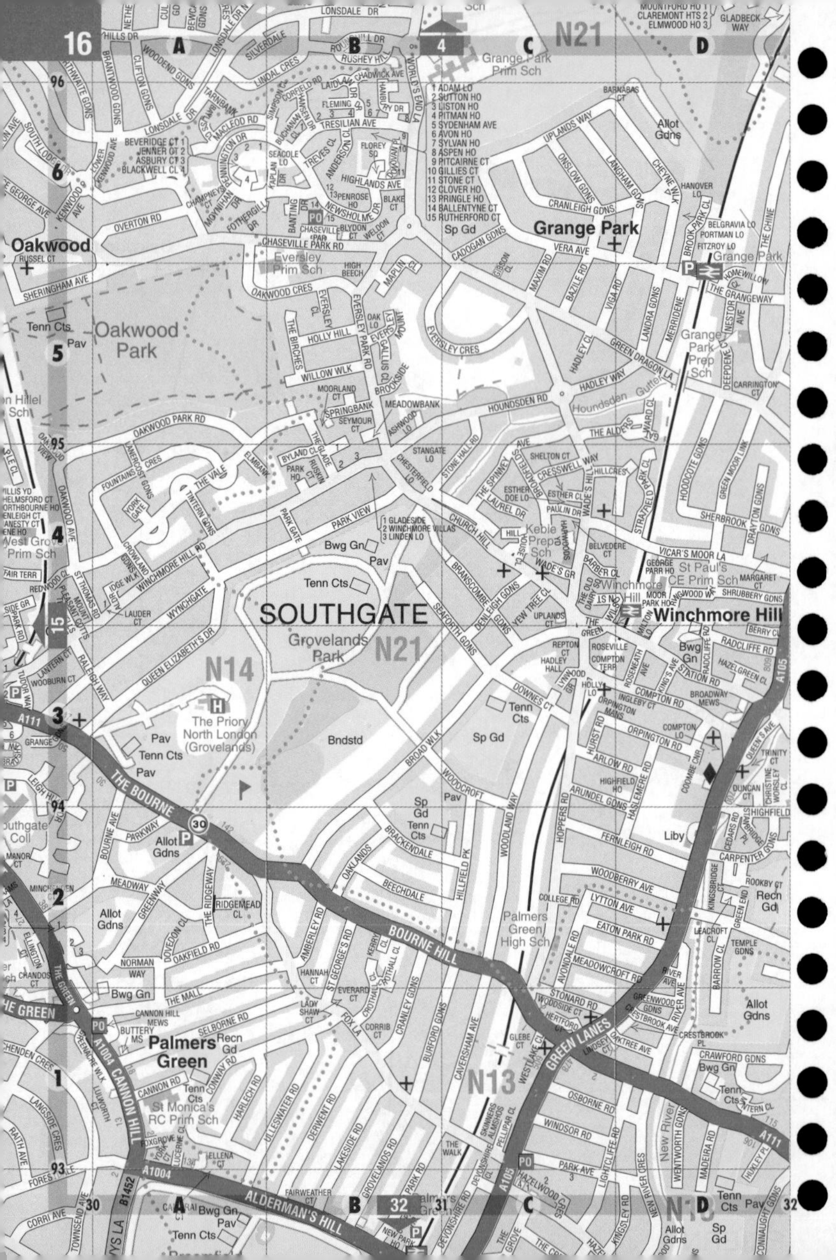

A
B
C
D
4
N21
96
95
94
93
6
5
4
3
2
1
30
31
32
Oakwood
Oakwood Park
Tenn Cts
Pav
Grange Park
Grange Park Prim Sch
Eversley Prim Sch
SOUTHGATE
Grovelands Park
N14
N21
N13
Winchmore Hill
Palmers Green
The Priory North London (Grovelands)
Bndstd
Sp Gd
Allot Gdns
Bwg Gn
Keble Prep Sch
St Paul's CE Prim Sch
Palmers Green High Sch
St Monica's RC Prim Sch
Grange Park Prep Sch
Houndsden Gutter
New River
Recn Gd
Liby
LONSDALE DR
RUSHEY HILL
CHADWICK AVE
WORLD'S END LA
LINDAL CRES
SILVERDALE
WOODEND GDNS
CLIFTON GDNS
BRANTWOOD GDNS
TARNBANK
MACLEOD RD
TRESILIAN AVE
HIGHLANDS AVE
NEWSHOLME DR
OVERTON RD
CHASEVILLE PARK RD
SHERINGHAM AVE
RUSSEL CT
OAKWOOD CRES
EVERSLEY CRES
EVERSLEY PARK RD
HOLLY HILL
WILLOW WLK
THE BIRCHES
BROOKSIDE
MEADOWBANK
SPRINGBANK
OAKWOOD PARK RD
OAKWOOD AVE
HOUNDSDEN RD
HADLEY WAY
GREEN DRAGON LA
UPLANDS WAY
CRANLEIGH GDNS
VERA AVE
CADOGAN GDNS
THE GRANGEWAY
CHURCH HILL
CHESTERFIELD LO
STONE HALL RD
CRESSWELL WAY
VICAR'S MOOR LA
STATION RD
COMPTON RD
ORPINGTON RD
ARLOW RD
FERNLEIGH RD
WOODBERRY AVE
LYTTON AVE
EATON PARK RD
MEADOWCROFT RD
STONARD RD
GREEN LANES
PARK VIEW
WINCHMORE HILL RD
WYNCHGATE
QUEEN ELIZABETH'S DR
RALEIGH WAY
THE BOURNE
BOURNE HILL
PARKWAY
MEADWAY
GREENWAY
THE RIDGEWAY
OAKFIELD RD
THE MALL
SELBORNE RD
CANNON RD
CANNON HILL
ALDERMAN'S HILL
BROAD WLK
WOODCROFT
BRACKENDALE
BEECHDALE
HILLFIELD PK
WOODLAND WAY
CAVERSHAM AVE
BURFORD GDNS
CRANLEY GDNS
FOX LA
DERWENT RD
LAKESIDE RD
GROVELANDS RD
ULLESWATER RD
HARLECH RD
OSBORNE RD
WINDSOR RD
PARK AVE
HAZELWOOD LA
NEW RIVER CRES
WENTWORTH GDNS
MADEIRA RD
CRAWFORD GDNS
A111
A105
A1004
B1452

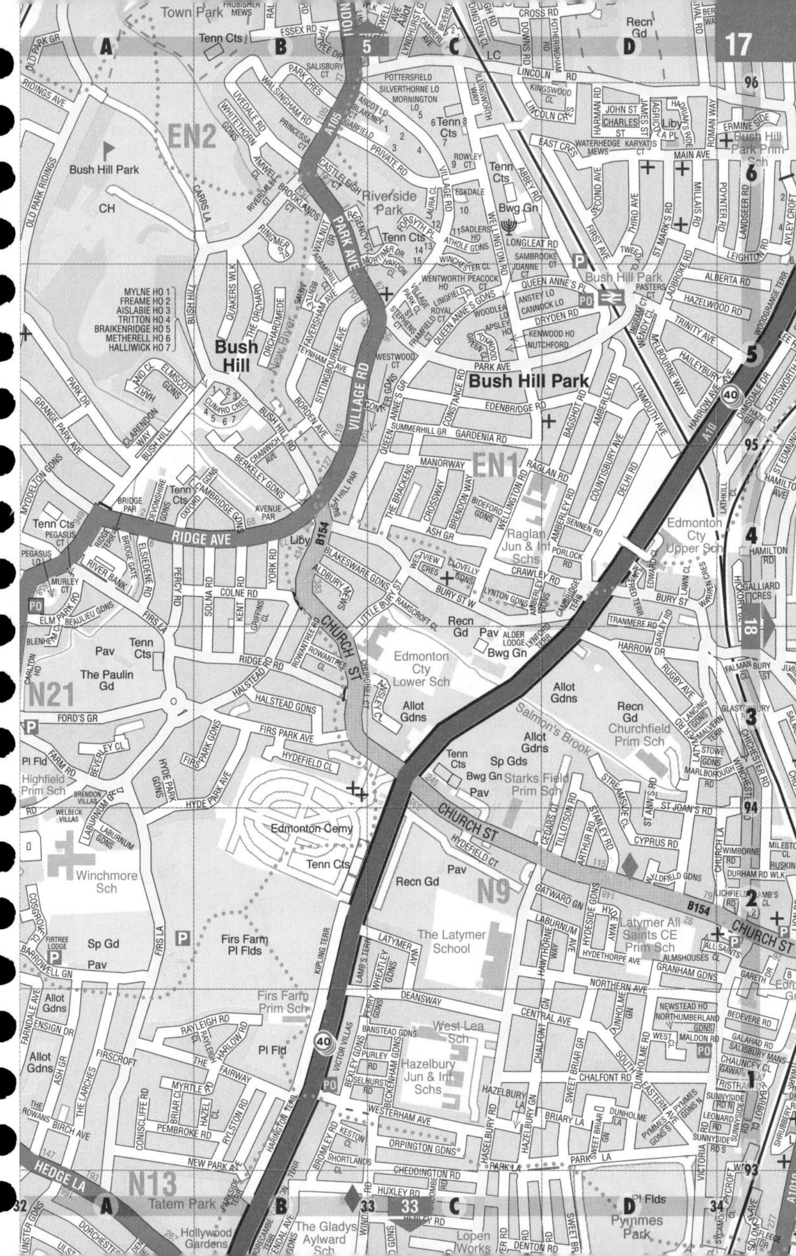
17
A
B
C
D
5
EN2
EN1
N21
N9
N13
Bush Hill Park
Bush Hill
Bush Hill Park
Town Park
Tenn Cts
Riverside Park
CH
MYLNE HO 1
FREAME HO 2
AISLABIE HO 3
TRITTON HO 4
BRAIKENRIDGE HO 5
METHERELL HO 6
HALLIWICK HO 7
RIDGE AVE
VILLAGE RD
PARK AVE
CHURCH ST
A105
A10
A1010
B154
HEDGE LA
Edmonton Cty Lower Sch
Edmonton Cty Upper Sch
Raglan Jun & Inf Schs
Churchfield Prim Sch
Starks Field Prim Sch
The Latymer School
Latymer All Saints CE Prim Sch
Hazelbury Jun & Inf Schs
West Lea Sch
Firs Farm Prim Sch
Firs Farm Pl Flds
Edmonton Cemy
Winchmore Sch
Highfield Prim Sch
The Paulin Gd
Salmon's Brook
Tatem Park
Pymmes Park
The Gladys Aylward Sch
Hollywood Gardens
Bush Hill Park Prim Sch
Recn Gd
Allot Gdns
Bwg Gn
Sp Gds
Pl Fld
Pav
Liby
PO
18
32
33
34
40
93
94
95
96
1
2
3
4
6

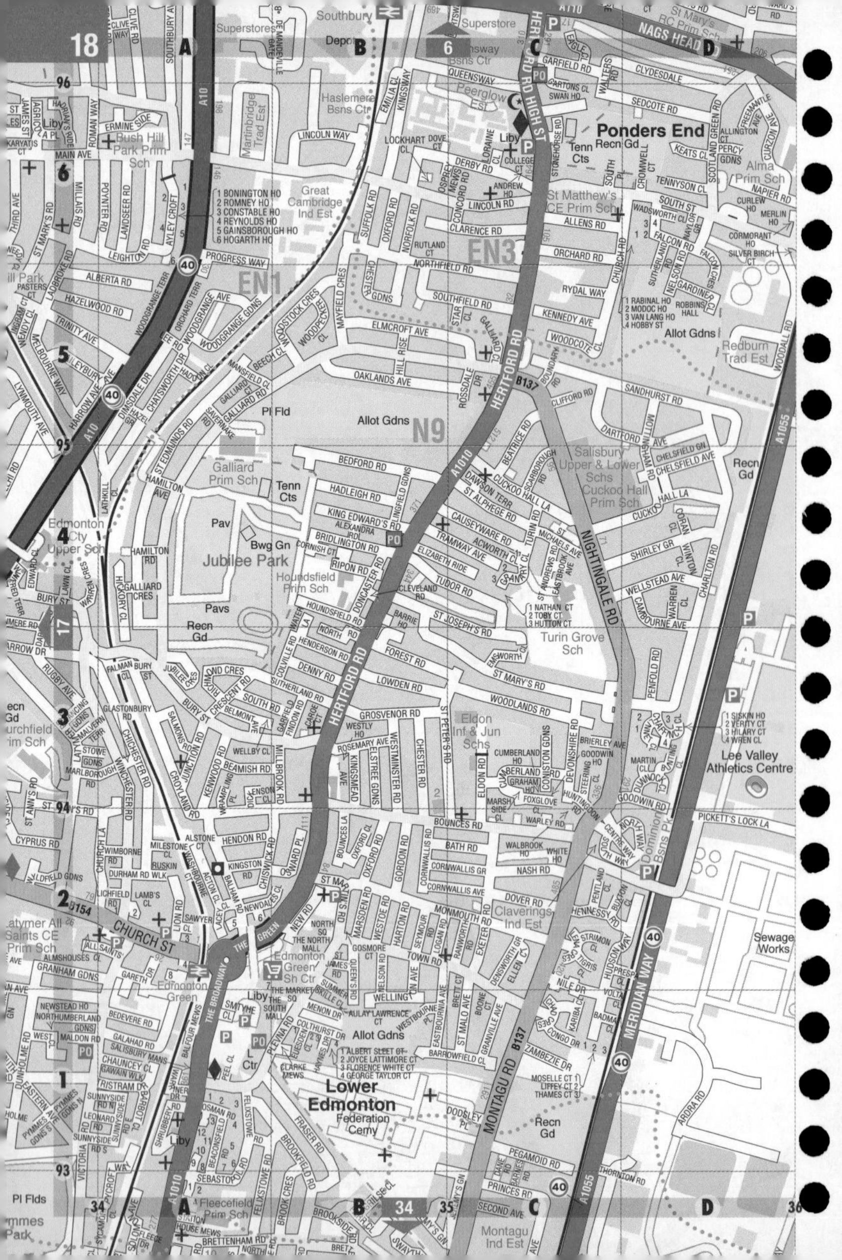

A
B
C
D
6
Southbury
Superstores
Depot
Superstore
NAGS HEAD RD
St Mary's RC Prim Sch
Haslemere Bsns Ctr
Martinbridge Trad Est
Peerglow Est
Ponders End
Recn Gd
Tenn Cts
Bush Hill Park Prim Sch
Great Cambridge Ind Est
1 BONINGTON HO
2 ROMNEY HO
3 CONSTABLE HO
4 REYNOLDS HO
5 GAINSBOROUGH HO
6 HOGARTH HO
St Matthew's CE Prim Sch
Alma Prim Sch
EN1
EN3
N9
PROGRESS WAY
LINCOLN WAY
QUEENSWAY
HERTFORD RD
HERTFORD RD HIGH ST
SOUTHBURY AVE
GARFIELD RD
CLYDESDALE
SEDCOTE RD
SOUTH ST
ALLENS RD
ORCHARD RD
RYDAL WAY
KENNEDY AVE
WOODCOTE CL
NORTHFIELD RD
SOUTHFIELD RD
ELMCROFT AVE
OAKLANDS AVE
SANDHURST RD
CLIFFORD RD
1 RABINAL HO
2 MODOC HO
3 VAN LANG HO
4 HOBBY ST
Allot Gdns
Redburn Trad Est
Pl Fld
Galliard Prim Sch
Salisbury Upper & Lower Schs
Cuckoo Hall Prim Sch
Recn Gd
Edmonton Cty Upper Sch
Jubilee Park
Pav
Bwg Gn
Pavs
Houndsfield Prim Sch
Turin Grove Sch
NIGHTINGALE RD
1 NATHAN CT
2 TOBY CT
3 HUTTON CT
BEDFORD RD
HADLEIGH RD
KING EDWARD'S RD
TRAMWAY AVE
ST JOSEPH'S RD
FOREST RD
LOWDEN RD
ST MARY'S RD
WOODLANDS RD
GROSVENOR RD
Eldon Inf & Jun Schs
1 SISKIN HO
2 VERITY CT
3 HILARY CT
4 WREN CL
Lee Valley Athletics Centre
PICKETT'S LOCK LA
Dominion Bsns Pk
BOUNCES RD
NASH RD
Claverings Ind Est
CHURCH ST
THE BROADWAY
THE GREEN
Edmonton Green
Edmonton Green Sh Ctr
Latymer All Saints CE Prim Sch
MERIDIAN WAY
Sewage Works
1 ALBERT SLEET CT
2 JOYCE LATTIMORE CT
3 FLORENCE WHITE CT
4 GEORGE TAYLOR CT
Lower Edmonton
Federation Cemy
MONTAGU RD
MOSELLE CT 1
LIFFEY CT 2
THAMES CT 3
ARDRA RD
PEGAMOID RD
THORNTON RD
Pl Flds
Fleecefield Prim Sch
BRETTENHAM RD
Montagu Ind Est
34
35
36
A10
A1010
A1055
B137
B154
40

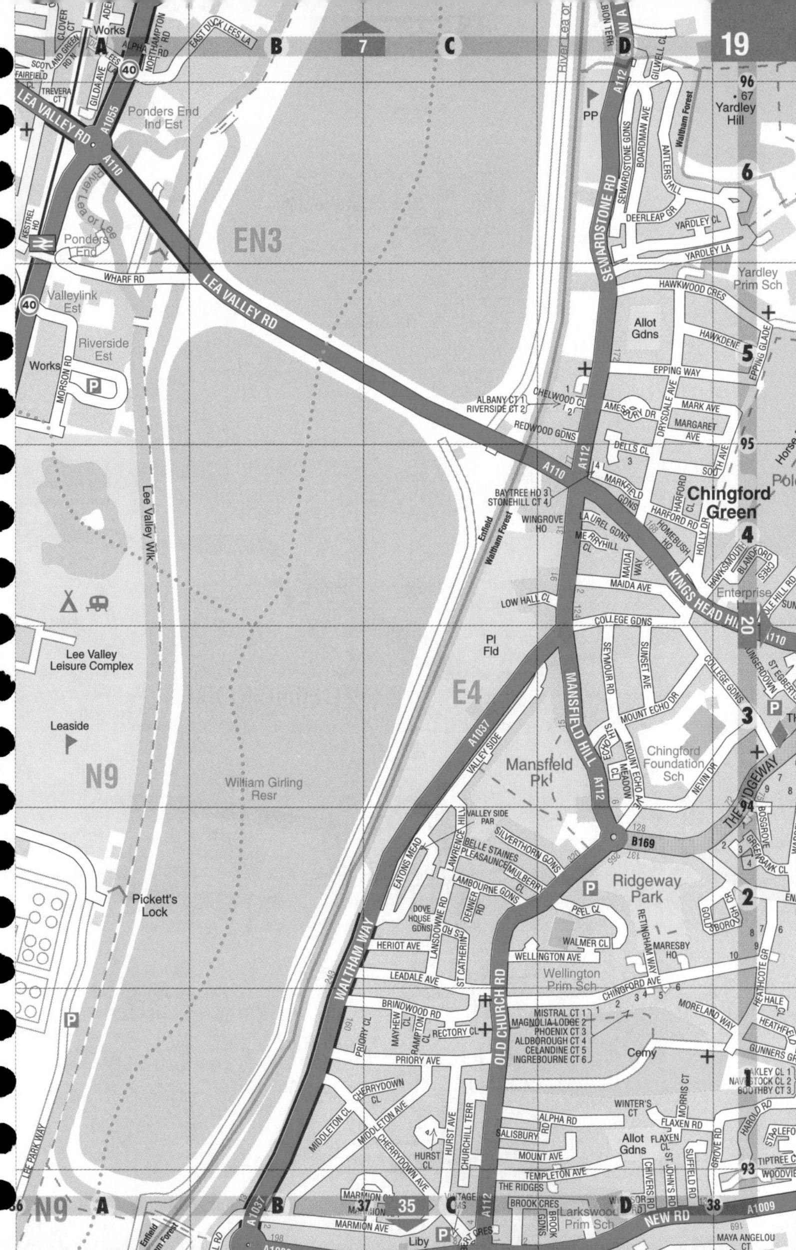
A
B
7
C
D
Works
CLOVER CT
GREEN RD N
SCOTLAND
FAIRFIELD CL
TREVERA CT
GILDA AVE
LEES
ALPHA RD
NORTHAMPTON RD
EAST DUCK LEES LA
40
A1055
LEA VALLEY RD
Ponders End Ind Est
A110
River Lea or Lee
KESTREL HO
Ponders End
WHARF RD
EN3
Valleylink Est
40
Riverside Est
Works
MORSON RD
P
LEA VALLEY RD
River Lea or Lee
SEWARDSTONE RD
A112
PP
GILWELL CL
SEWARDSTONE GDNS
BOARDMAN AVE
ANTLERS HILL
Waltham Forest
DEERLEAP GR
YARDLEY CL
YARDLEY LA
96
67
Yardley Hill
6
Yardley Prim Sch
HAWKWOOD CRES
Allot Gdns
HAWKDENE
EPPING GLADE
5
EPPING WAY
ALBANY CT 1
RIVERSIDE CT 2
CHELWOOD CL
AMESBURY DR
DRYSDALE AVE
MARK AVE
MARGARET AVE
REDWOOD GDNS
DELLS CL
SOUTH AVE
95
Horse Ride
A110
A112
MARKFIELD GDNS
HARFORD CL
Pole
Chingford Green
BAYTREE HO 3
STONEHILL CT 4
WINGROVE HO
LAUREL GDNS
MERRYHILL CL
HARFORD RD
HOMEBUSH HO
HOLLY DR
4
Enfield
Waltham Forest
MAIDA WAY
MAIDA AVE
HAWKSMOUTH
BLANDFORD CRES
KINGS HEAD HILL
Enterprise
LOW HALL CL
COLLEGE GDNS
SUNNY
20
A110
Lee Valley Wlk
Lee Valley Leisure Complex
Pl Fld
SEYMOUR RD
SUNSET AVE
COLLEGE GDNS
ST EGBERTS WAY
E4
MANSFIELD HILL
MOUNT ECHO DR
3
P
TH
Leaside
A1037
VALLEY SIDE
ECHO HTS
MOUNT ECHO AVE
Chingford Foundation Sch
THE RIDGEWAY
N9
William Girling Resr
Mansfield Pk
A112
MEADOW CL
NEVIN DR
94
VALLEY SIDE PAR
BOSGROVE
WARREN RD
B169
EATONS MEAD
LAWRENCE HILL
BELLE STAINES PLEASAUNCE
SILVERTHORN GDNS
MULBERRY CL
GREENBANK CL
LAMBOURNE GDNS
P
Ridgeway Park
2
ENDLE
Pickett's Lock
DOVE HOUSE GDNS
LANSDOWNE RD
DENNER RD
PEEL CL
RETINGHAM WAY
GOLDSBOROUGH
WALTHAM WAY
HERIOT AVE
ST CATHERINES RD
WALMER CL
WELLINGTON AVE
MARESBY HO
LEADALE AVE
OLD CHURCH RD
Wellington Prim Sch
HEATHCOTE GR
CHINGFORD AVE
HALE CL
P
BRINDWOOD RD
MISTRAL CT 1
MAGNOLIA LODGE 2
PHOENIX CT 3
ALDBOROUGH CT 4
CELANDINE CT 5
INGREBOURNE CT 6
MORELAND WAY
HEATHFIELD
PRIORY CL
MAYHEW CL
RAMPTON CL
RECTORY CL
PRIORY AVE
Cemy
GUNNERS GR
OAKLEY CL 1
NAVESTOCK CL 2
BOOTHBY CT 3
CHERRYDOWN CL
MIDDLETON AVE
WINTER'S CT
MORRIS CT
HAROLD RD
LEE PARK WAY
MIDDLETON CL
CHURCHILL TERR
HURST AVE
ALPHA RD
FLAXEN RD
SALISBURY RD
Allot Gdns
FLAXEN CL
STAPLEFORD
CHERRYDOWN AVE
HURST CL
MOUNT AVE
CHIVERS RD
ST JOHN'S RD
SUFFIELD RD
GROVE RD
TIPTREE CT
93
WOODVIEW
TEMPLETON AVE
THE RIDGES
MARMION CL
MARMION AVE
VINTAGE MS
BROOK CRES
BROOK GDNS
Larkswood Prim Sch
WINDSOR RD
D
NEW RD
38
A1009
N9
A
B
37
35
C
A1037
Enfield
Waltham Forest
A112
Liby
P
BERA CRES
MAYA ANGELOU CT

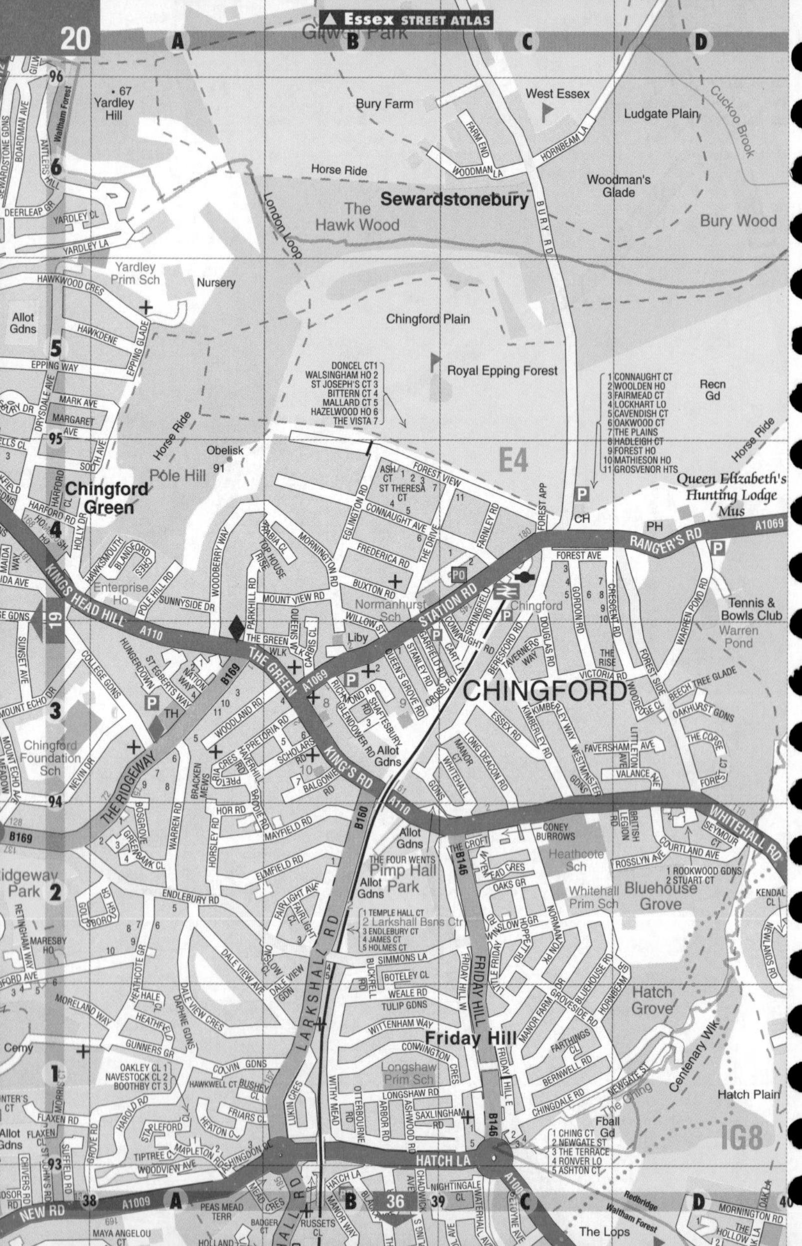

A
B
C
D
Bury Farm
West Essex
Ludgate Plain
Cuckoo Brook
Yardley Hill
Horse Ride
Woodman's Glade
Sewardstonebury
The Hawk Wood
Bury Wood
London Loop
Yardley Prim Sch
Nursery
Allot Gdns
Chingford Plain
Royal Epping Forest
DONCEL CT 1
WALSINGHAM HO 2
ST JOSEPH'S CT 3
BITTERN CT 4
MALLARD CT 5
HAZELWOOD HO 6
THE VISTA 7
1 CONNAUGHT CT
2 WOOLDEN HO
3 FAIRMEAD CT
4 LOCKHART LO
5 CAVENDISH CT
6 OAKWOOD CT
7 THE PLAINS
8 HADLEIGH CT
9 FOREST HO
10 MATHIESON HO
11 GROSVENOR HTS
Recn Gd
Obelisk
Pole Hill
Chingford Green
E4
Queen Elizabeth's Hunting Lodge Mus
Enterprise Ho
Normanhurst Sch
Chingford
Tennis & Bowls Club
Warren Pond
CHINGFORD
Chingford Foundation Sch
Heathcote Sch
Whitehall Prim Sch
Bluehouse Grove
Ridgeway Park
Pimp Hall Park
THE FOUR WENTS
1 TEMPLE HALL CT
2 Larkshall Bsns Ctr
3 ENDLEBURY CT
4 JAMES CT
5 HOLMES CT
1 ROOKWOOD GDNS
2 STUART CT
Hatch Grove
Friday Hill
Centenary Wlk
Longshaw Prim Sch
Hatch Plain
Cemy
OAKLEY CL 1
NAVESTOCK CL 2
BOOTHBY CT 3
Fball Gd
1 CHING CT
2 NEWGATE ST
3 THE TERRACE
4 RONVER LO
5 ASHTON CT
IG8
The Ching
Redbridge
Waltham Forest
The Lops
KINGS HEAD HILL
STATION RD
RANGER'S RD
THE GREEN
KING'S RD
THE RIDGEWAY
LARKSHALL RD
FRIDAY HILL
HATCH LA
WHITEHALL RD
NEW RD
BURY RD

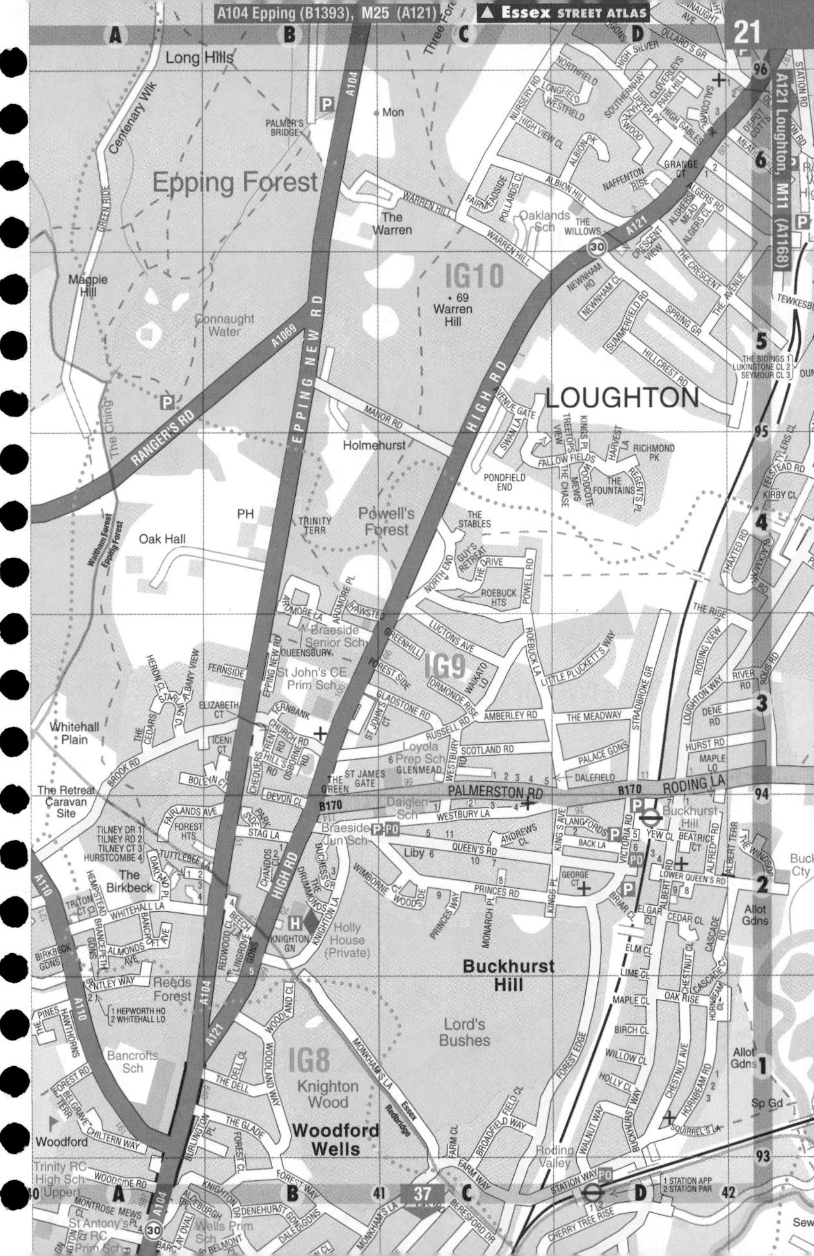
Long Hills
Epping Forest
Centenary Wlk
Green Ride
Palmer's Bridge
Mon
The Warren
Warren Hill
Magpie Hill
Connaught Water
IG10
69 Warren Hill
LOUGHTON
Oaklands Sch
The Willows
Epping New Rd
High Rd
Ranger's Rd
Manor Rd
Holmehurst
Powell's Forest
Trinity Terr
PH
Oak Hall
The Ching
Waltham Forest
Epping Forest
Pondfield End
Richmond Pk
The Fountains
The Stables
Roebuck Hts
IG9
Braeside Senior Sch
St John's CE Prim Sch
Whitehall Plain
Loyola Prep Sch
The Retreat Caravan Site
Palmerston Rd
Roding La
B170
Daiglen Sch
Braeside Jun Sch
Buckhurst Hill
The Birkbeck
Holly House (Private)
Reeds Forest
Buckhurst Hill
Lord's Bushes
IG8
Knighton Wood
Bancrofts Sch
Woodford
Woodford Wells
Roding Valley
Trinity RC High Sch (Upper)
St Antony's RC Prim Sch
Wells Prim Sch
Allot Gdns
Sp Gd
A121 Loughton, M11 (A1168)
A104
A121
A110
A1069
Monkham's La
Forest Edge
Station Way
1 Station App
2 Station Par
1 Hepworth Ho
2 Whitehall Lo
Tilney Dr 1
Tilney Rd 2
Tilney Ct 3
Hurstcombe 4
The Sidings 1
Lukinstone Cl 2
Seymour Cl 3
Essex
Redbridge
37

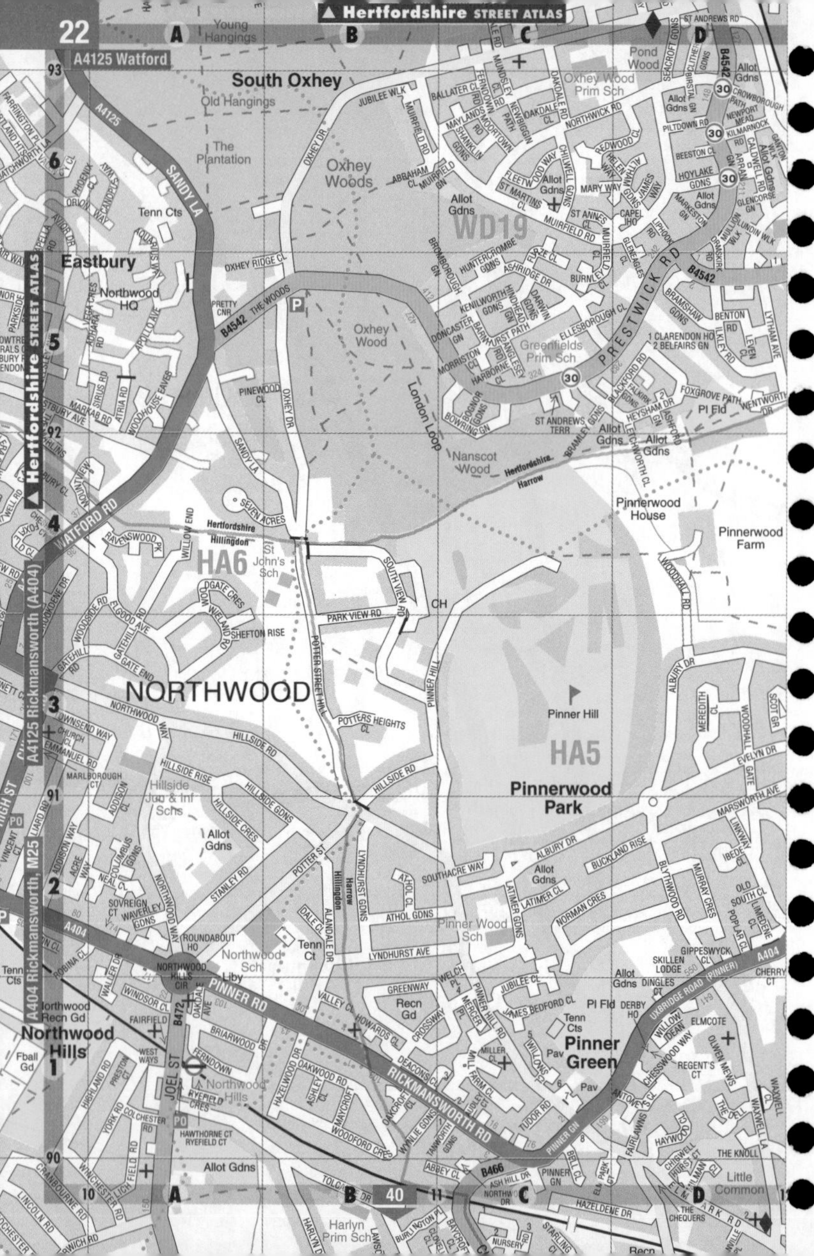
A4125 Watford
Young Hangings
South Oxhey
Old Hangings
The Plantation
Oxhey Woods
Oxhey Wood
Eastbury
Northwood HQ
Tenn Cts
Pond Wood
Oxhey Wood Prim Sch
Allot Gdns
WD19
Greenfields Prim Sch
London Loop
Nanscot Wood
Pinnerwood House
Pinnerwood Farm
Pl Fld
HA6
St John's Sch
CH
NORTHWOOD
Pinner Hill
HA5
Pinnerwood Park
Hillside Jun & Inf Schs
Pinner Wood Sch
Northwood Sch
Tenn Ct
Liby
Northwood Hills
Northwood Recn Gd
Fball Gd
Pinner Green
Pav
Little Common
Harlyn Prim Sch
SANDY LA
WATFORD RD
OXHEY DR
THE WOODS
B4542
PRESTWICK RD
MUIRFIELD RD
NORTHWICK RD
POTTER STREET HILL
PINNER HILL
HILLSIDE RD
NORTHWOOD WAY
PINNER RD
RICKMANSWORTH RD
UXBRIDGE ROAD (PINNER)
A404
B466
B472
JOEL ST
HIGH ST
A4125 Rickmansworth (A404)
A404 Rickmansworth, M25
▲ Hertfordshire STREET ATLAS
Hertfordshire
Hillingdon
Harrow
40

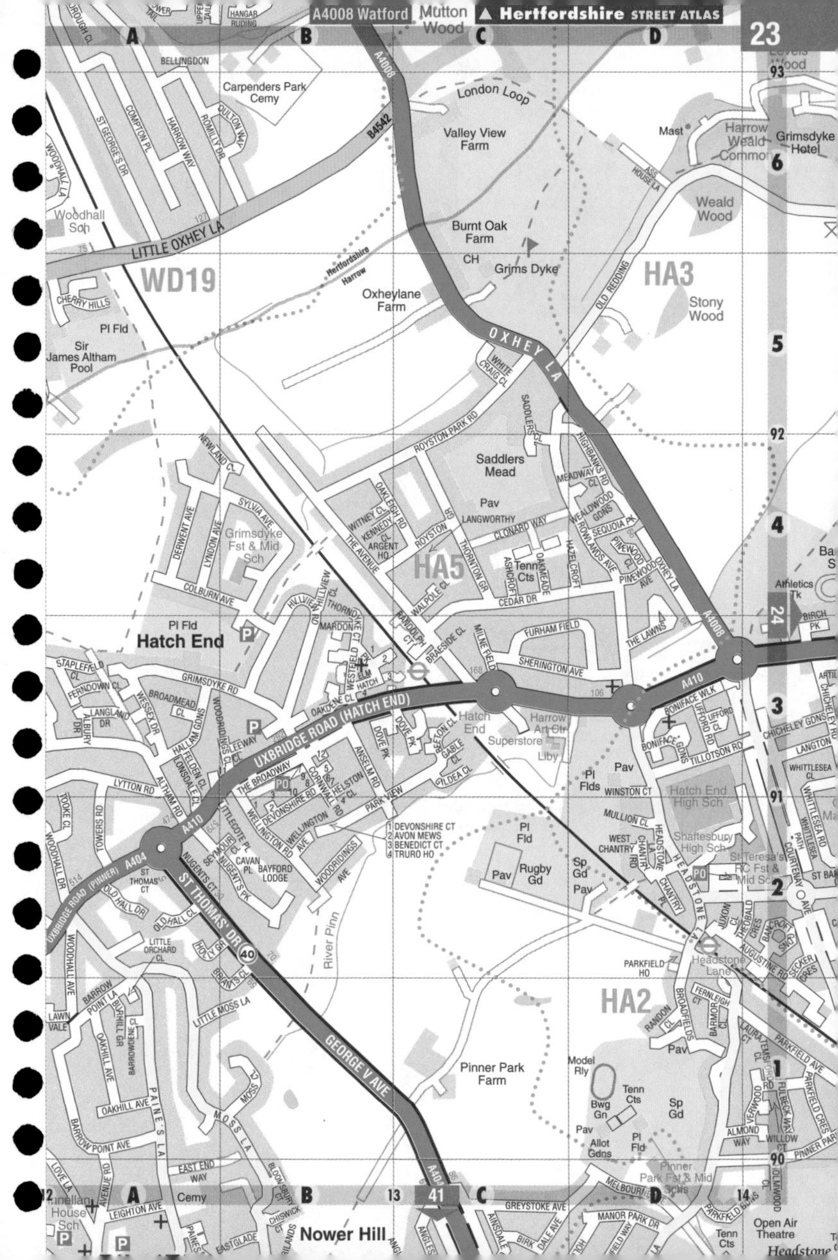
Mutton Wood
Carpenders Park Cemy
London Loop
Valley View Farm
Harrow Weald Common
Grimsdyke Hotel
Weald Wood
Burnt Oak Farm
Grims Dyke
WD19
HA3
HA5
HA2
Oxheylane Farm
Stony Wood
Woodhall Sch
Sir James Altham Pool
Saddlers Mead
Grimsdyke Fst & Mid Sch
Hatch End
UXBRIDGE ROAD (HATCH END)
OXHEY LA
LITTLE OXHEY LA
ST THOMAS' DR
GEORGE V AVE
Harrow Art Ctr
Hatch End High Sch
Shaftesbury High Sch
St Teresa's RC Fst & Mid Sch
Headstone Lane
Pinner Park Farm
Pinner Park Fst & Mid Schs
Athletics Tk
River Pinn
Nower Hill
Open Air Theatre
1 DEVONSHIRE CT
2 AVON MEWS
3 BENEDICT CT
4 TRURO HO

24
41

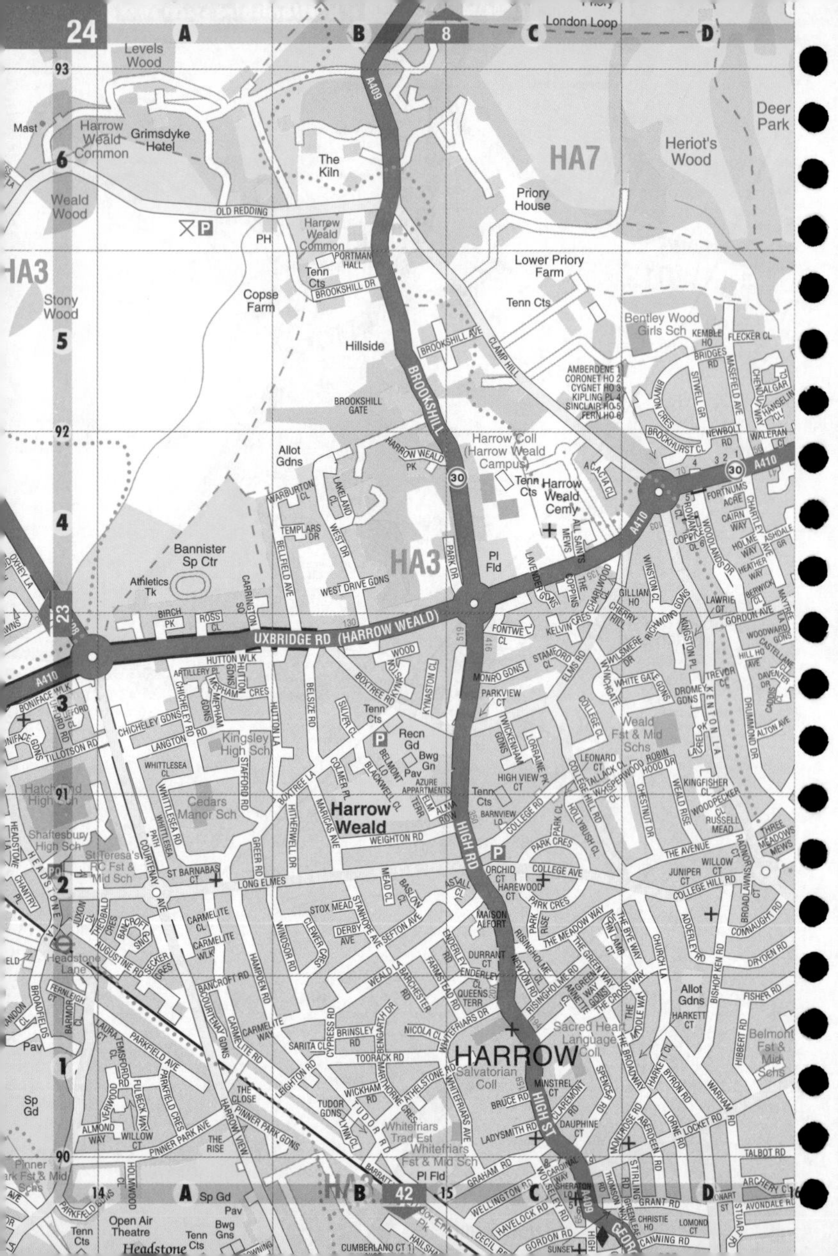
A
B
8
C
D
London Loop
Levels Wood
93
Mast
Harrow Weald Common
Grimsdyke Hotel
6
The Kiln
HA7
Heriot's Wood
Deer Park
Weald Wood
OLD REDDING
Priory House
PH
Harrow Weald Common
PORTMAN HALL
Lower Priory Farm
HA3
Stony Wood
Tenn Cts
BROOKSHILL DR
Copse Farm
Tenn Cts
5
Hillside
BROOKSHILL AVE
CLAMP HILL
Bentley Wood Girls Sch
BROOKSHILL
BROOKSHILL GATE
92
Allot Gdns
Harrow Coll (Harrow Weald Campus)
Harrow Weald Cemy
A410
4
Bannister Sp Ctr
Athletics Tk
HA3
Pl Fld
23
UXBRIDGE RD (HARROW WEALD)
3
Kingsley High Sch
Recn Gd
Bwg Gn
Pav
91
Hatch End High Sch
Cedars Manor Sch
Harrow Weald
HIGH RD
Weald Fst & Mid Schs
Shaftesbury High Sch
St Teresa's RC Fst & Mid Sch
2
LONG ELMES
COLLEGE AVE
Headstone Lane
Allot Gdns
1
HARROW
Sacred Heart Language Coll
Salvatorian Coll
Belmont Fst & Mid Schs
Sp Gd
Whitefriars Trad Est
Whitefriars Fst & Mid Sch
HIGH ST
90
Pinner Park Fst & Mid Schs
Pl Fld
14
A
Sp Gd
B
42
15
C
D
16
Open Air Theatre
Pav
Bwg Gns
Tenn Cts
Headstone

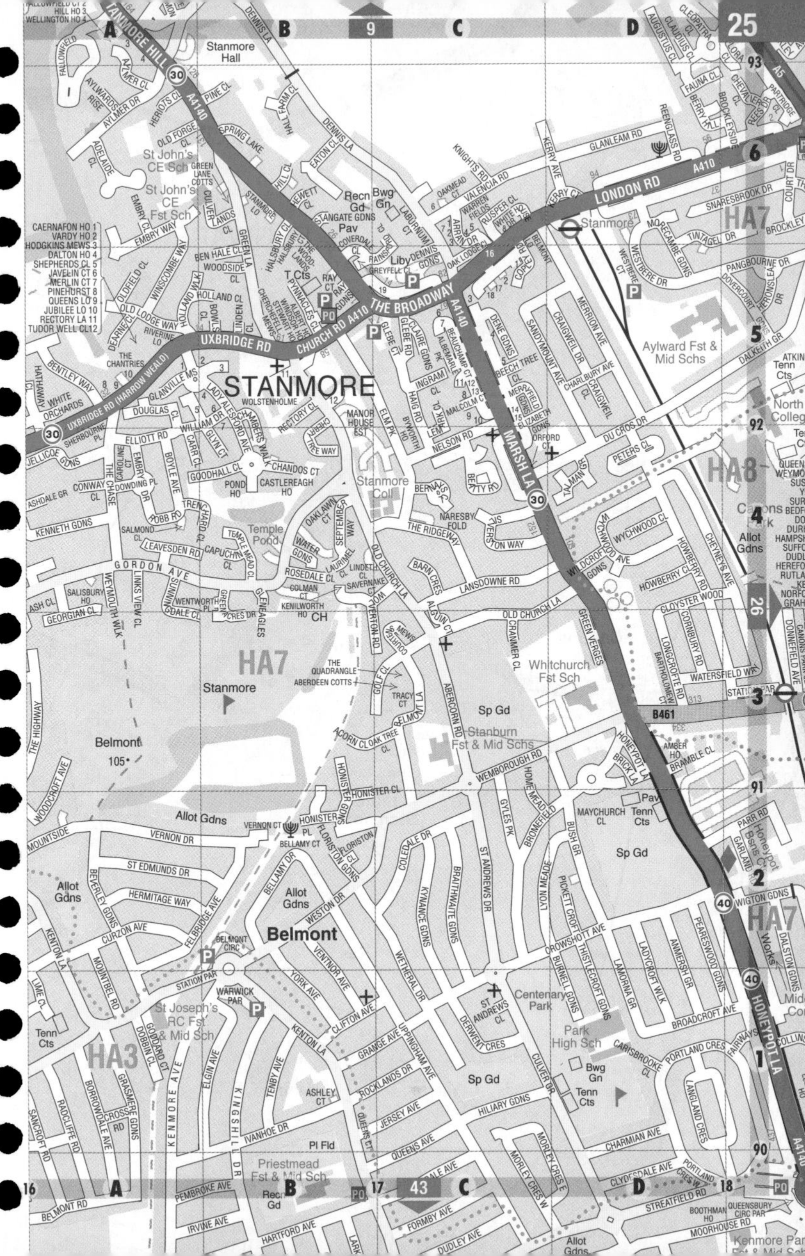
A
B
9
C
D
STANMORE HILL
Stanmore Hall
DENNIS LA
FALLOWFIELD
AYLMER CL
AYLWARDS RISE
AYLMER DR
HERIOTS CL
PINE CL
HALL FARM CL
A4140
OLD FORGE CL
SPRING LAKE
ADELAIDE CL
St John's CE Sch
GREEN LANE COTTS
St John's CE Fst Sch
EMBRY CL
EMBRY WAY
CULVER LANDS
HILL CL
EATON CL
HEWETT CL
Recn Gd
Bwg Gn
STANMORE LO
STANGATE GDNS
Pav
LABURNUM CT
Liby
DENNIS GDNS
GREYFELL CL
CAERNAFON HO 1
VARDY HO 2
HODGKINS MEWS 3
DALTON HO 4
SHEPHERDS CL 5
JAVELIN CT 6
MERLIN CT 7
PINEHURST 8
QUEENS LO 9
JUBILEE LO 10
RECTORY LA 11
TUDOR WELL CL12
BEN HALE CL
WOODSIDE CL
OLDFIELD CL
WINSCOMBE WAY
HOLLAND WLK
HOLLAND CL
OLD LODGE WAY
BOWLS CL
LINDEN CL
GREEN LA
HALSBURY CL
T Cts
PYNNACLES CL
RAY CT
RAY GDNS
CHURCH RD A410
THE BROADWAY
A4140
UXBRIDGE RD
UXBRIDGE RD (HARROW WEALD)
RIVERINE LO
THE CHANTRIES
DEARNE CT
HATHAWAY CL
BENTLEY WAY
WHITE ORCHARDS
STANMORE
WOLSTENHOLME
GLANVILLE MS
DOUGLAS CL
LADY ALESFORD AVE
WILLIAM DR
CHAMBERS WALK
RECTORY CL
MANOR HOUSE EST
ELM PK
GLEBE CT
GLEBE RD
CLAIRE GDNS
ALBEMARLE PK
BEAUCHAMP CT
HAIG RD
INGRAM CL
BYWORTH HO
LEMARK CL
MALCOLM CT
SHERBOURNE PL
JELLICOE GDNS
ELLIOTT RD
EMBRY DR
BOYLE AVE
CARR CL
GLYN CT
CHERRY TREE WAY
CHANDOS CT
GOODHALL CL
POND HO
CASTLEREAGH HO
Stanmore Coll
THE CHASE
CAROLINE CT
DOWDING PL
CONWAY CL
ASHDALE GR
ROBB RD
TRENCHARD CL
KENNETH GDNS
SALMOND CL
Temple Pond
OAKLAWN CT
SEPTEMBER WAY
LEAVESDEN RD
TEMPLE MEAD CL
CAPUCHIN CL
WATER GDNS
GORDON AVE
LINKS VIEW CL
LAURIMEL CL
ROSEDALE CL
LINDETH CL
SAVERNAKE CT
COLMAN CT
KENILWORTH HO
CH
SALISBURY HO
ASH CL
GEORGIAN CL
WENTWORTH PL
GLENEAGLES
WEYMOUTH WLK
OLD CHURCH LA
OVERTON RD
COURTENAY MEWS
ALGUIN CT
HA7
THE QUADRANGLE
ABERDEEN COTTS
GOLF CL
TRACY CT
BELMONT LA
Stanmore
Belmont
105
THE HIGHWAY
WOODCROFT AVE
ACORN CL
OAK TREE CL
HONISTER GDNS
HONISTER CL
HONISTER PL
VERNON CT
BELLAMY CT
Allot Gdns
MOUNTSIDE
VERNON DR
ST EDMUNDS DR
HERMITAGE WAY
BEVERLEY GDNS
FELBRIDGE AVE
CURZON AVE
KENTON LA
LIME CL
MOUNTBEL RD
BELMONT CIRC
STATION PAR
WARWICK PAR
St Joseph's RC Fst & Mid Sch
Tenn Cts
HA3
DOBBIN CL
GODDARD CT
ELGIN AVE
KENMORE AVE
KINGSHILL DR
BORROWDALE AVE
GRASMERE GDNS
CROSS RD
RADCLIFFE RD
SANCROFT RD
BELLAMY DR
FLORISTON GDNS
FLORISTON CL
Belmont
WESTON DR
VENTNOR AVE
YORK AVE
CLIFTON AVE
KENTON LA
GRANGE AVE
UPPINGHAM AVE
TENBY AVE
ROCKLANDS DR
ASHLEY CT
JERSEY AVE
QUEENS CT
IVANHOE DR
QUEENS AVE
Pl Fld
Priestmead Fst & Mid Sch
Recn Gd
PEMBROKE AVE
BELMONT RD
IRVINE AVE
HARTFORD AVE
FORMBY AVE
DUDLEY AVE
43
17
16
18
COLEDALE DR
KYNANCE GDNS
BRAITHWAITE GDNS
WETHERAL DR
ST ANDREWS DR
ST ANDREWS CL
DERWENT CRES
Centenary Park
CULVER DR
HILIARY GDNS
MORLEY CRES E
MORLEY CRES W
Sp Gd
GYLES PK
HOME MEAD
BROMEFIELD
WEMBOROUGH RD
ABERCORN RD
Stanburn Fst & Mid Schs
CRANMER CL
Whitchurch Fst Sch
GREEN VERGES
LANSDOWNE RD
BARN CRES
THE RIDGEWAY
NARESBY FOLD
VERSTON WAY
BERNAYS CL
BEATTY RD
NELSON RD
MARSH LA
ORFORD CT
ELIZABETH GDNS
MERRYFIELD GDNS
BEECH TREE CL
DENE GDNS
OAK LODGE CL
COPLEY RD
BELMONT
WHITE HOUSE DR
RUSPER CL
WARREN FIELDS
ARRAN DR
OAKMEAD CT
VALENCIA RD
KNIGHTS RD
KERRY AVE
KERRY CT
GLANLEAM RD
REENGLASS RD
LONDON RD
A410
Stanmore
MORECAMBE GDNS
WESTBERE CT
WESTBERE DR
TINTAGEL DR
SNARESBROOK DR
BROCKLEY CL
COURT DR
PANGBOURNE DR
DOVERCOURT GDNS
HERONSLEA DR
Aylward Fst & Mid Schs
DALKEITH GR
SANDYMOUNT AVE
CRAIGWEIL DR
MERRION AVE
CHARLBURY AVE
CRAIGWEIL CL
DU CROS DR
PETERS CL
TALMAN GR
WYCHWOOD AVE
WYCHWOOD CL
WILDCROFT GDNS
HOWBERRY CL
HOWBERRY RD
CHEYNEYS AVE
CLOYSTER WOOD
CORNBURY RD
LONGCROFTE RD
BARTHOLOMEW CT
WATERSFIELD WAY
STATION PAR
B461
HONEYPOT LA
BRICK LA
AMBER HO
BRAMBLE CL
MAYCHURCH CL
Pav
Tenn Cts
BUSH GR
LYON MEADE
PICKETT CROFT
THISTLECROFT GDNS
BURNELL GDNS
CROWSHOTT AVE
LAMORNA GR
LADYCROFT WLK
AMMERSH GR
PEARESWOOD GDNS
WIGTON GDNS
BROADCROFT AVE
Park High Sch
CARISBROOKE CL
PORTLAND CRES
FAIRWAYS
LANGLAND CRES
Bwg Gn
CHARMIAN AVE
CLYDESDALE AVE
PORTLAND CRES W
STREATFIELD RD
BOOTHMAN HO
QUEENSBURY CIRC PAR
MOORHOUSE RD
Allot Gdns
Kenmore Park
CLEOPATRA CL
AUGUSTUS CL
CLAUDIUS CL
FLORA CL
FAUNA CL
BERRY HILL
CHEVALIER CL
REES DR
PARTRIDGE
BROCKLEYSIDE
A5
HA7
HA8
Tenn Cts
North London Collegiate
Canons Park
Allot Gdns
BEDFORD
HAMPSHIRE
SUFFOLK
DUDLEY
HEREFORD
RUTLAND
NORFOLK
GRAHAM
DONNEFIELD AVE
CANONS PARK CL
26
Honeypot Bsns Cen
PARR RD
GARLAND RD
Works
DALSTON GDNS
COLLINS AVE
A4140
HONEYPOT LA
93
92
91
90
6
5
4
3
2
1

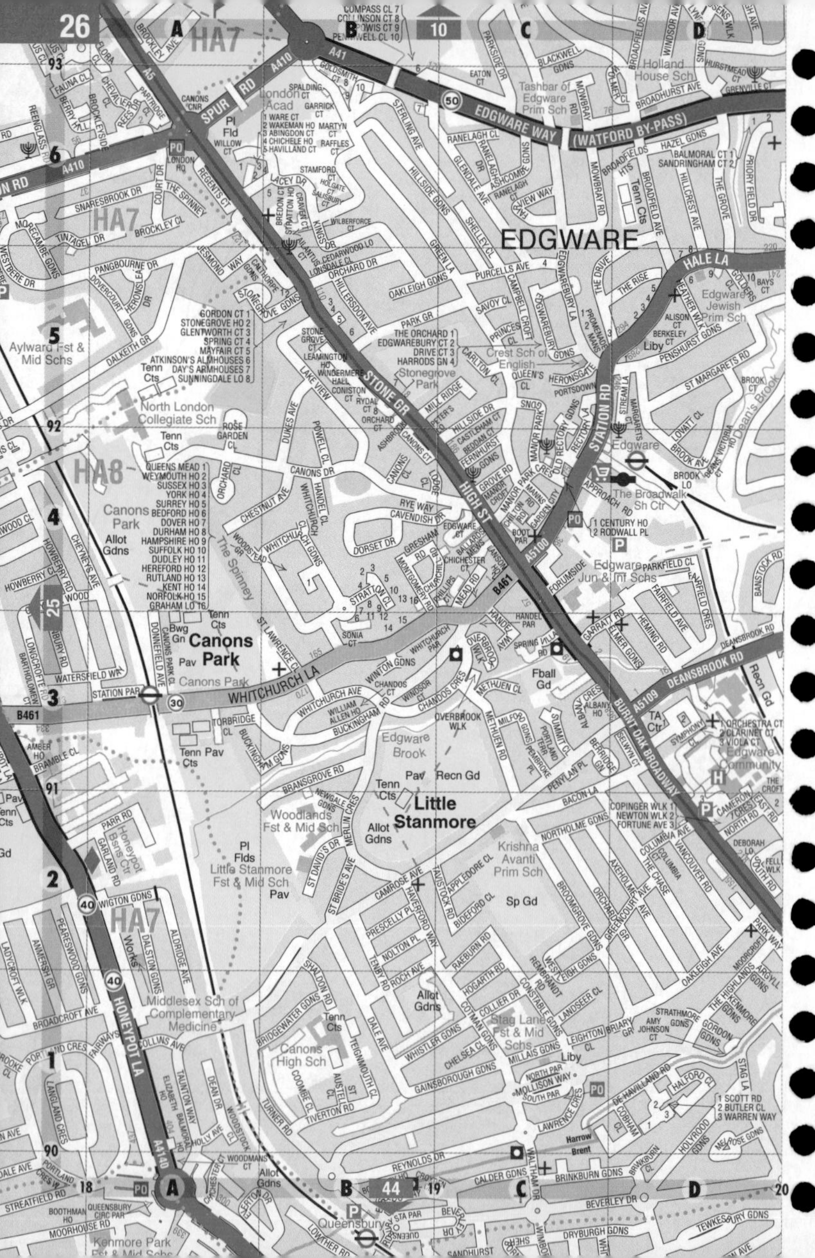

HA7
HA8
EDGWARE
Little Stanmore
Canons Park
EDGWARE WAY (WATFORD BY-PASS)
HIGH ST
STONE GR
STATION RD
BURNT OAK BROADWAY
WHITCHURCH LA
DEANSBROOK RD
HONEYPOT LA
SPUR RD
HALE LA
London Acad
North London Collegiate Sch
Aylward Fst & Mid Schs
Canons High Sch
Woodlands Fst & Mid Sch
Little Stanmore Fst & Mid Sch
Krishna Avanti Prim Sch
Stag Lane Fst & Mid Schs
Edgware Jun & Inf Schs
Edgware Jewish Prim Sch
Tashbar of Edgware Prim Sch
Holland House Sch
Crest Sch of English
Middlesex Sch of Complementary Medicine
The Broadwalk Sh Ctr
Edgware Community
Stonegrove Park
Edgware Brook
Queensbury
Kenmore Park Fst & Mid Schs
Honeypot Bsns Ctr

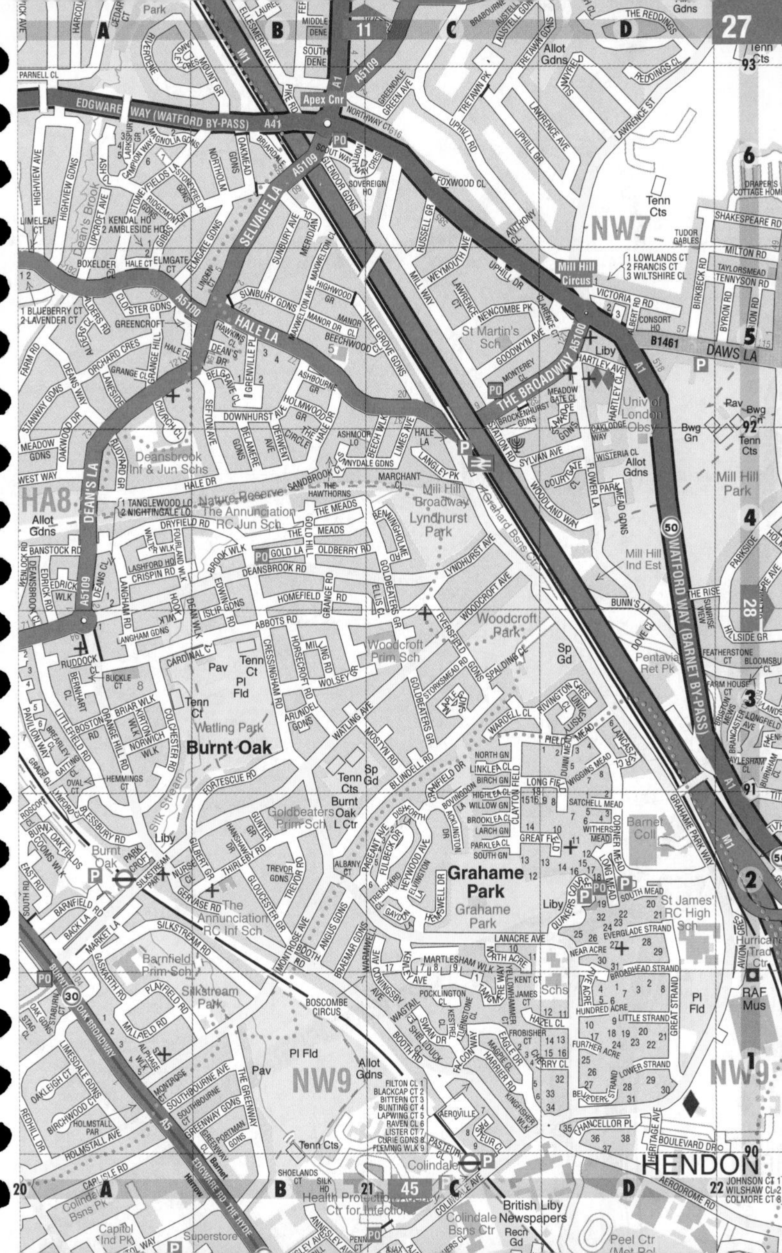
A
B
C
D
11
EDGWARE WAY (WATFORD BY-PASS)
A41
Apex Cnr
M1
A1
A5109
SELVAGE LA
HALE LA
A5100
DEAN'S LA
HALE DR
THE BROADWAY
Mill Hill Circus
DAWS LA
B1461
WATFORD WAY (BARNET BY-PASS)
NW7
HA8
NW9
Mill Hill Broadway
Lyndhurst Park
Woodcroft Park
Watling Park
Burnt Oak
Grahame Park
Barnet Coll
St James' RC High Sch
RAF Mus
Hurricane Trad Ctr
Colindale
HENDON
British Liby Newspapers
Colindale Bsns Ctr
Capitol Ind Pk
Peel Ctr
Mill Hill Park
Univ of London Obsy
Mill Hill Ind Est
Pentavia Ret Pk
Deansbrook Inf & Jun Schs
The Annunciation RC Jun Sch
The Annunciation RC Inf Sch
Woodcroft Prim Sch
Goldbeaters Prim Sch
Barnfield Prim Sch
Silkstream Park
Burnt Oak L Ctr
Health Protection Agency Ctr for Infections
BURNT OAK BROADWAY
EDGWARE RD THE HYDE
A5
28
45
20
21
22
1
2
3
4
5
6
93
92
91
90
JOHNSON CT 1
WILSHAW CL 2
COLMORE CT 3
FILTON CL 1
BLACKCAP CT 2
BITTERN CT 3
BUNTING CT 4
LAPWING CT 5
RAVEN CL 6
LISTER CT 7
CURIE GDNS 8
FLEMING WLK 9

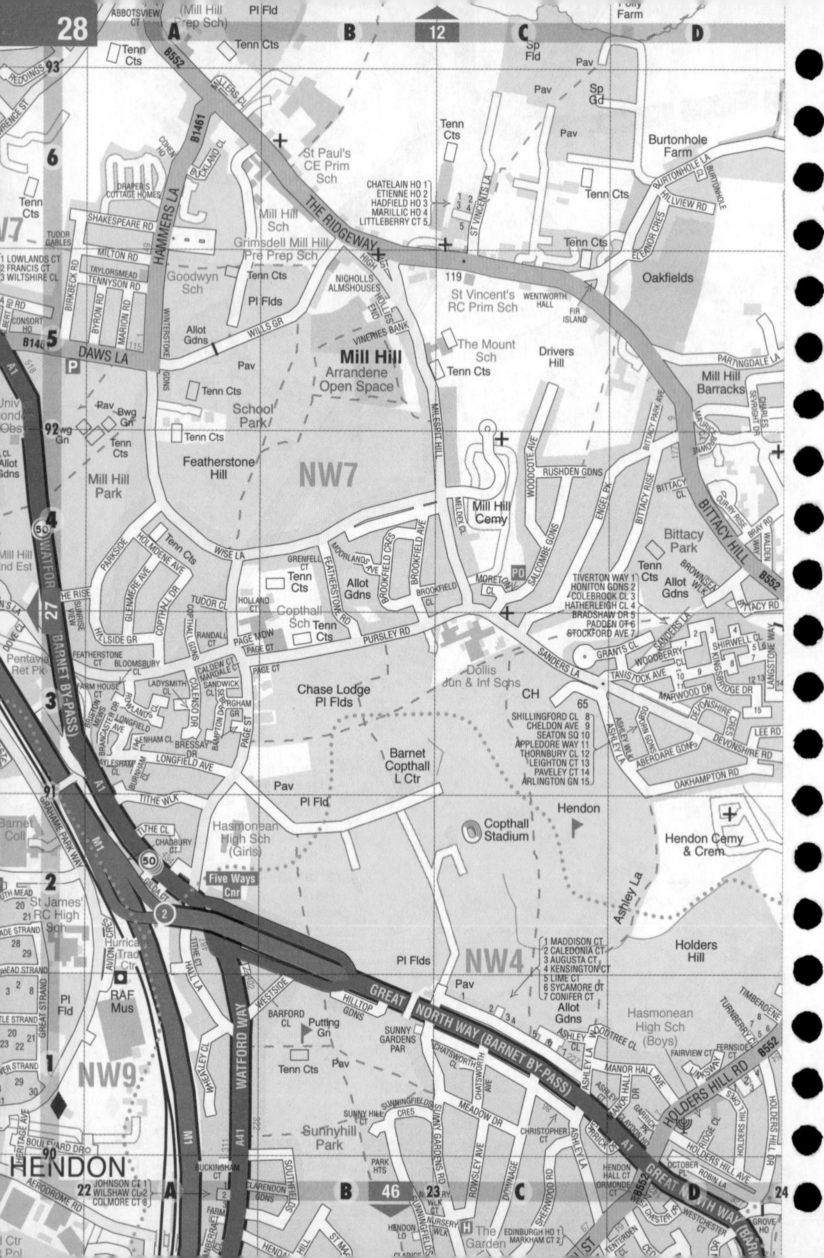

Mill Hill
NW7
NW4
NW9
HENDON
The Ridgeway
Mill Hill Arrandene Open Space
St Paul's CE Prim Sch
Mill Hill Sch
Grimsdell Mill Hill Pre Prep Sch
Goodwyn Sch
St Vincent's RC Prim Sch
The Mount Sch
Drivers Hill
Burtonhole Farm
Oakfields
Mill Hill Barracks
School Park
Featherstone Hill
Mill Hill Park
Mill Hill Cemy
Bittacy Park
Copthall Sch
Chase Lodge Pl Flds
Dollis Jun & Inf Schs
Barnet Copthall L Ctr
Copthall Stadium
Hendon
Hendon Cemy & Crem
Hasmonean High Sch (Girls)
Hasmonean High Sch (Boys)
Holders Hill
Five Ways Cnr
St James' RC High Sch
RAF Mus
Sunnyhill Park
Great North Way (Barnet By-Pass)
Watford Way
Hammers La
Daws La
Wise La
Pursley Rd
Sanders La
Bittacy Hill
Holders Hill Rd
Ashley La
Milespit Hill
Wills Gr
Partingdale La
Burtonhole La
Engel Pk
Bittacy Rise
Salcombe Gdns
Woodcote Ave
Rushden Gdns
Oakhampton Rd
Devonshire Rd
Longfield Ave
Tithe Wlk
Page St
Aerodrome Rd
CHATELAIN HO 1
ETIENNE HO 2
HADFIELD HO 3
MARILLIC HO 4
LITTLEBERRY CT 5
1 LOWLANDS CT
2 FRANCIS CT
3 WILTSHIRE CL
TIVERTON WAY 1
HONITON GDNS 2
COLEBROOK CL 3
HATHERLEIGH CL 4
BRADSHAW DR 5
PADDEN CT 6
STOCKFORD AVE 7
SHILLINGFORD CL 8
CHELDON AVE 9
SEATON SQ 10
APPLEDORE WAY 11
THORNBURY CL 12
LEIGHTON CT 13
PAVELEY CT 14
ARLINGTON GN 15
1 MADDISON CT
2 CALEDONIA CT
3 AUGUSTA CT
4 KENSINGTON CT
5 LIME CT
6 SYCAMORE CT
7 CONIFER CT
JOHNSON CT 1
WILSHAW CL 2
COLMORE CT 3
EDINBURGH HO 1
MARKHAM CT 2

12
27
46

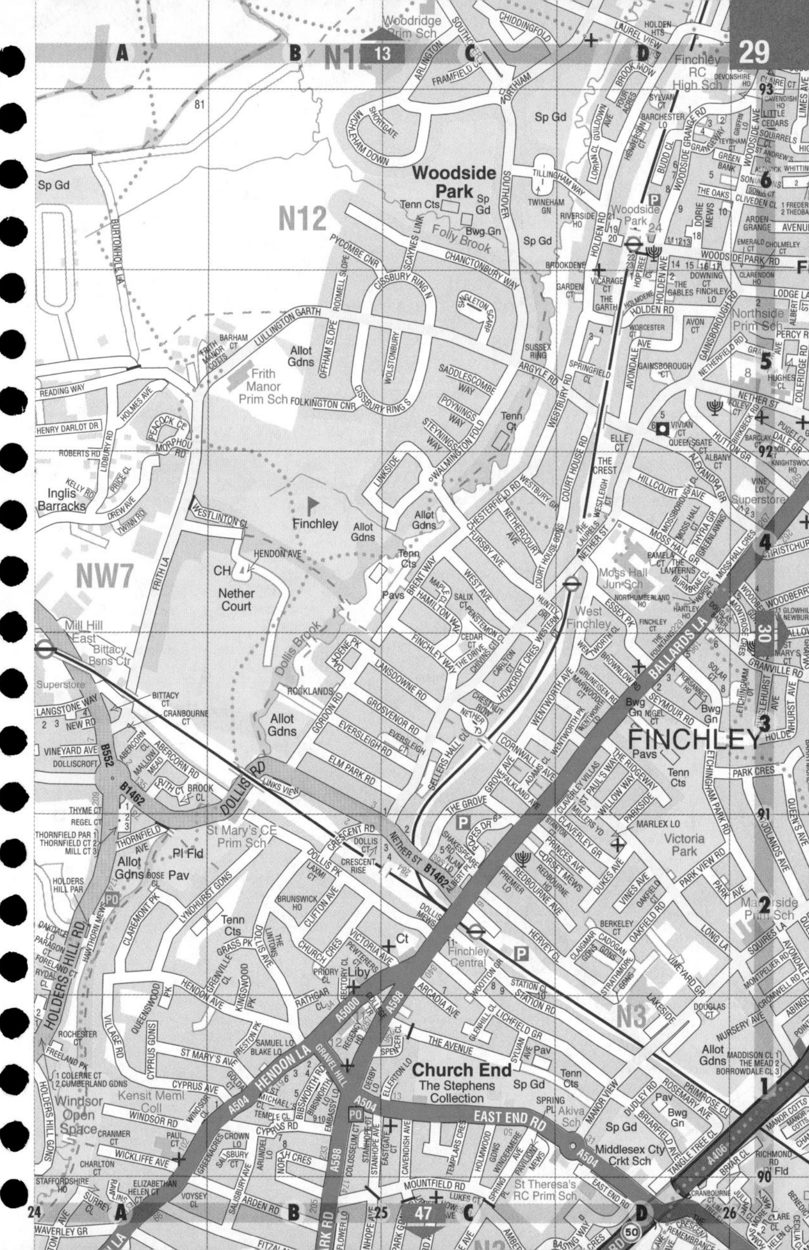
Woodside Park
N12
NW7
FINCHLEY
Church End
The Stephens Collection
Woodridge Prim Sch
Finchley RC High Sch
Frith Manor Prim Sch
Nether Court
Finchley
Mill Hill East
Inglis Barracks
West Finchley
Moss Hall Jun Sch
Northside Prim Sch
Victoria Park
Finchley Central
St Mary's CE Prim Sch
Windsor Open Space
Kensit Meml Coll
Middlesex Cty Crkt Sch
St Theresa's RC Prim Sch
Akiva Sch
N3
BALLARDS LA
HENDON LA
EAST END RD
DOLLIS RD
NETHER ST
HOLDERS HILL RD
FRITH LA
A B C D

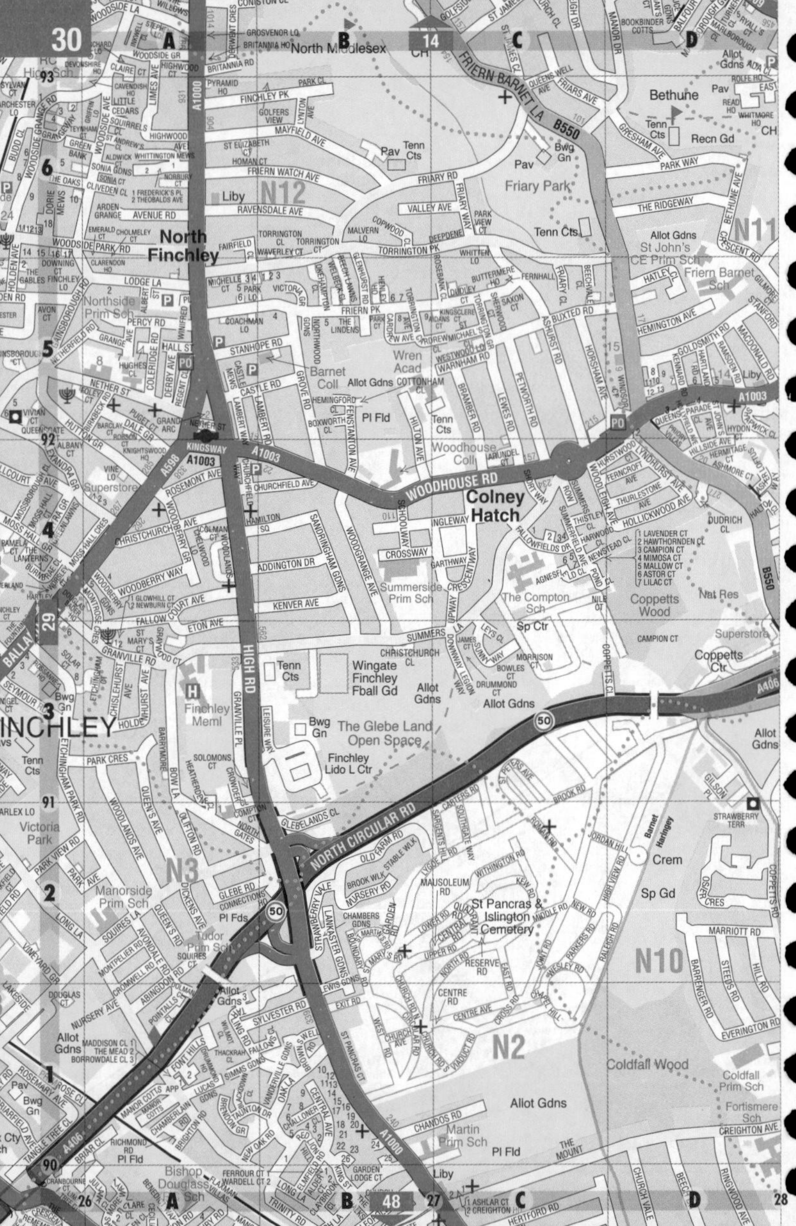

30
North Middlesex
North Finchley
N12
Friary Park
Bethune
Recn Gd
Friern Barnet Sch
St John's CE Prim Sch
N11
Northside Prim Sch
Barnet Coll
Wren Acad
Woodhouse Coll
Colney Hatch
Summerside Prim Sch
The Compton Sch
Coppetts Wood
Nat Res
Coppetts Ctr
Wingate Finchley Fball Gd
Finchley Meml
The Glebe Land Open Space
Finchley Lido L Ctr
FINCHLEY
Victoria Park
N3
Manorside Prim Sch
Tudor Prim Sch
St Pancras & Islington Cemetery
Crem
N10
N2
Coldfall Wood
Coldfall Prim Sch
Fortismere Sch
Martin Prim Sch
Bishop Douglass Sch
HIGH RD
NORTH CIRCULAR RD
WOODHOUSE RD
FRIERN BARNET LA
KINGSWAY
A1000
A1003
A406
A598
B550
14
48

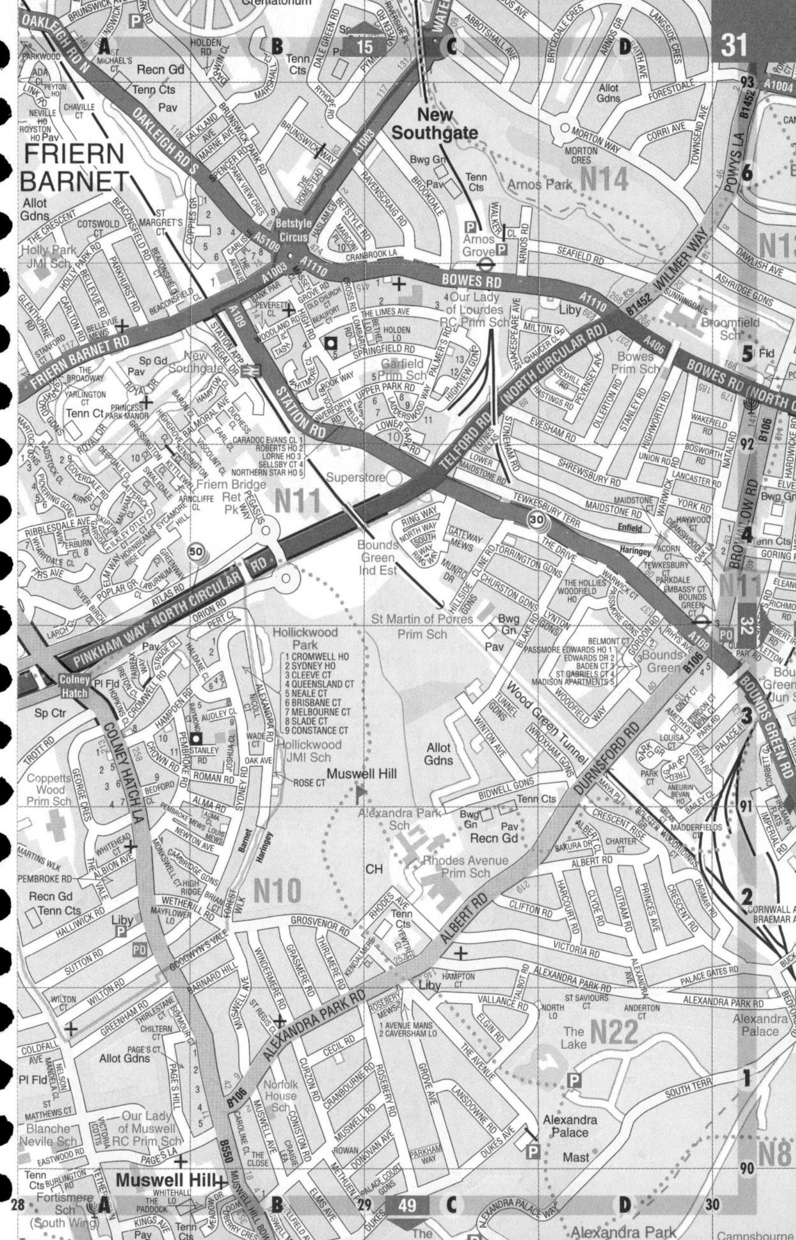
FRIERN BARNET
New Southgate
N14
N13
N11
N10
N22
N8
Muswell Hill
Alexandra Palace
Alexandra Park
Bounds Green
Arnos Grove
Colney Hatch
Friern Bridge Ret Pk
Bounds Green Ind Est
Hollickwood Park
Wood Green Tunnel
The Lake
Betstyle Circus
OAKLEIGH RD S
FRIERN BARNET RD
BOWES RD
PINKHAM WAY NORTH CIRCULAR RD
TELFORD RD (NORTH CIRCULAR RD)
STATION RD
COLNEY HATCH LA
DURNSFORD RD
ALBERT RD
ALEXANDRA PARK RD
BOUNDS GREEN RD
WILMER WAY
BROWNLOW RD
MUSWELL HILL BDWY

15
32
49

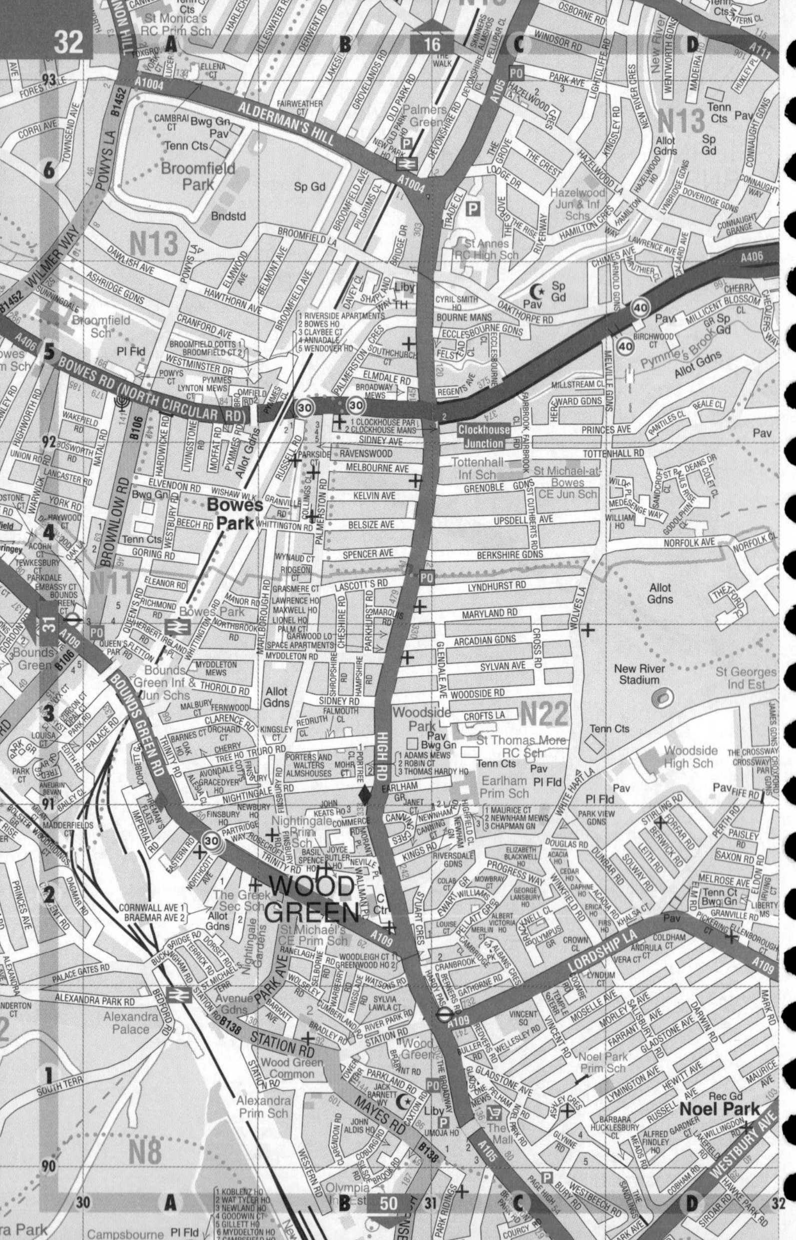
A
B
16
C
D
93
6
5
92
4
3
91
2
1
90
30
31
50
32
N13
N11
N22
N8
ALDERMAN'S HILL
A1004
B1452
POWYS LA
WILMER WAY
TOWNSEND AVE
CORRI AVE
FORESTDALE
Broomfield Park
Tenn Cts
Bwg Gn
Pav
Sp Gd
Bndstd
CAMBRAI CT
St Monica's RC Prim Sch
HARLECH
ULLESWATER RD
DERWENT RD
LAKESIDE
GROVELANDS RD
FAIRWEATHER
OLD PARK RD
Palmers Green
DEVONSHIRE RD
A105
OSBORNE RD
WINDSOR RD
PARK AVE
HAZELWOOD CRES
LIGHTCLIFFE RD
KINGSLEY RD
NEW RIVER CRES
WENTWORTH GDNS
MADEIRA RD
A111
CONNAUGHT GDNS
Hazelwood Jun & Inf Schs
HAZELWOOD LA
THE GROVE
THE CREST
LODGE DR
RIVERWAY
St Annes RC High Sch
TRADE CL
BRIDGE DR
BROOMFIELD LA
PILGRIMS CL
BROOMFIELD AVE
BELMONT AVE
ELMWOOD AVE
DAWLISH AVE
ASHRIDGE GDNS
HAWTHORN AVE
CRANFORD AVE
Broomfield Sch
Pl Fld
Bowes Prim Sch
A406
BOWES RD (NORTH CIRCULAR RD)
WESTMINSTER DR
Liby
TH
CYRIL SMITH HO
BOURNE MANS
ECCLESBOURNE GDNS
OAKTHORPE RD
Sp Gd
CHIMES AVE
LAWRENCE AVE
MILLICENT BLOSSOM CL
BIRCHWOOD CT
Pymme's Brook
Allot Gdns
MILLSTREAM CL
HEREWARD GDNS
PRINCES AVE
PANTILES CL
BEALE CL
Clockhouse Junction
SOUTHCHURCH CT
ELMDALE RD
BROADWAY MEWS
REGENTS AVE
PALMERSTON CRES
1 RIVERSIDE APARTMENTS
2 BOWES HO
3 CLAYBEE CT
4 ANNADALE
5 WENDOVER HO
1 CLOCKHOUSE PAR
2 CLOCKHOUSE MANS
SIDNEY AVE
RAVENSWOOD
MELBOURNE AVE
KELVIN AVE
BELSIZE AVE
SPENCER AVE
TOTTENHALL RD
Tottenhall Inf Sch
St Michael-at-Bowes CE Jun Sch
GRENOBLE GDNS
UPSDELL AVE
BERKSHIRE GDNS
NORFOLK AVE
LYNDHURST RD
MARYLAND RD
ARCADIAN GDNS
SYLVAN AVE
WOODSIDE RD
CROFTS LA
Allot Gdns
New River Stadium
St Georges Ind Est
Tenn Cts
Woodside High Sch
Bowes Park
STANLEY RD
HIGHWORTH RD
WAKEFIELD RD
BOSWORTH RD
UNION RD
LANCASTER RD
YORK RD
WARWICK RD
ELVENDON RD
WISHAW WLK
BROWNLOW RD
B106
GORING RD
ELEANOR RD
RICHMOND RD
NORTHBROOK RD
MARLBOROUGH RD
CHESHIRE RD
PARKHURST RD
LASCOTT'S RD
Bounds Green
A109
BOUNDS GREEN RD
Bounds Green Inf & Jun Schs
MYDDLETON MEWS
THOROLD RD
CLARENCE RD
FERNWOOD
Allot Gdns
SIDNEY RD
Woodside Park
St Thomas More RC Sch
Earlham Prim Sch
WHITE HART LA
HIGH RD
EARLHAM GR
NIGHTINGALE RD
TRURO RD
PALACE RD
Nightingale Prim Sch
WOOD GREEN
The Greek Sec Sch
CORNWALL AVE
BRAEMAR AVE
St Michael's CE Prim Sch
Nightingale Gardens
PARK AVE
Avenue Gdns
KINGS RD
PROGRESS WAY
DUNBAR RD
SOLWAY RD
LEITH RD
BERWICK RD
FORFAR RD
PERTH RD
PAISLEY RD
SAXON RD
MELROSE AVE
Tenn Ct
LORDSHIP LA
LYNDUM CT
MOSELLE AVE
MORLEY AVE
SALISBURY AVE
GLADSTONE AVE
DARWIN RD
MARK RD
Noel Park Prim Sch
Noel Park
Rec Gd
WESTBURY AVE
ALEXANDRA PARK RD
PALACE GATES RD
Alexandra Palace
BEDFORD RD
STATION RD
B138
Wood Green Common
Alexandra Prim Sch
MAYES RD
Wood Green
THE BROADWAY
The Mall
Liby
WESTERN RD
Olympia Ind Est
PARK RIDINGS
WESTBEECH RD
Campsbourne
Pl Fld
1 KOBLENZ HO
2 WAT TYLER HO
3 NEWLAND HO
4 GOODWIN CT
5 GILLETT HO
6 MYDDELTON HO
7 CAMPSFIELD HO

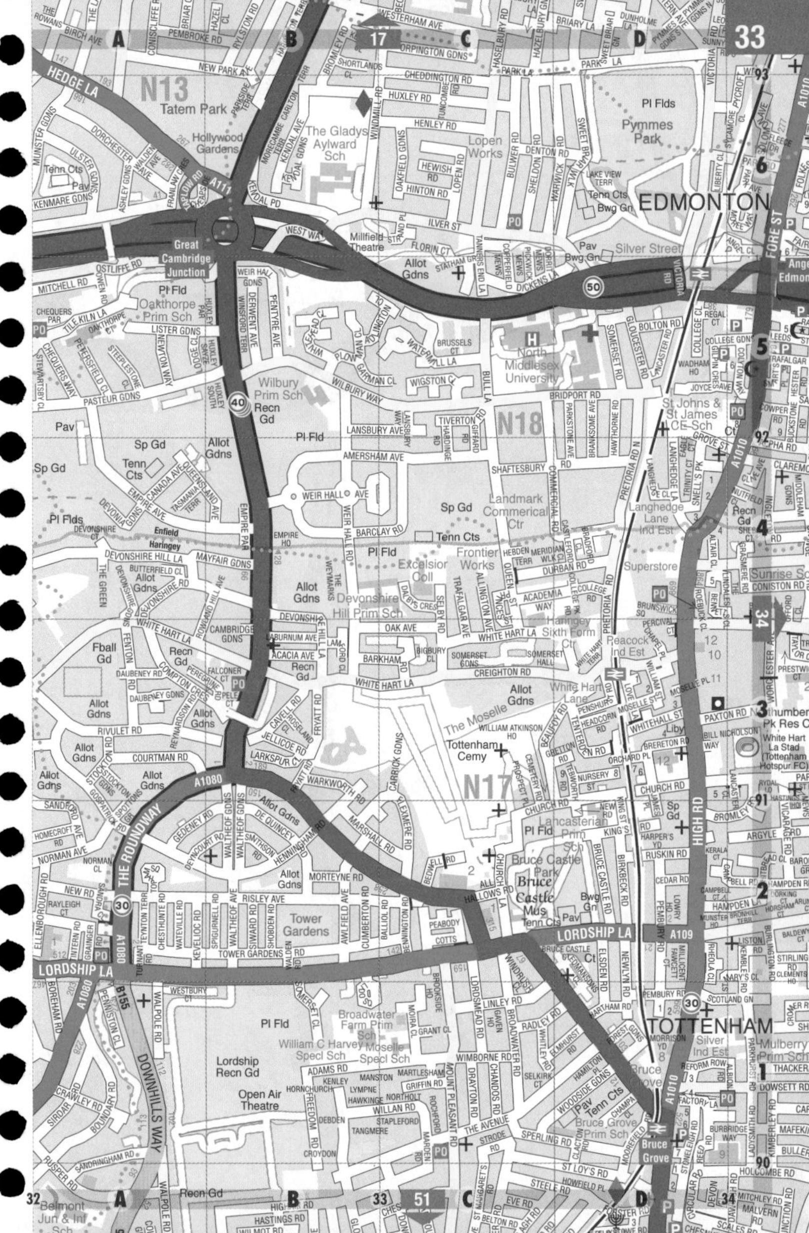

17
A
B
C
D
N13
Tatem Park
Hollywood Gardens
HEDGE LA
The Gladys Aylward Sch
Lopen Works
Pymmes Park
EDMONTON
Great Cambridge Junction
Millfield Theatre
Silver Street
Angel Edmonton
Oakthorpe Prim Sch
North Middlesex University
Wilbury Prim Sch
N18
St Johns & St James CE Sch
Landmark Commerical Ctr
Langhedge Lane Ind Est
Enfield
Haringey
Excelsior Coll
Frontier Works
Superstore
Sunrise Sch
Devonshire Hill Prim Sch
Haringey Sixth Form Ctr
Peacock Ind Est
34
The Moselle
Tottenham Cemy
N17
White Hart La Stad (Tottenham Hotspur FC)
Lancasterian Prim Sch
Bruce Castle Park
Bruce Castle Mus
THE ROUNDWAY
Tower Gardens
LORDSHIP LA
HIGH RD
Broadwater Farm Prim Sch
William C Harvey Specl Sch
Moselle Specl Sch
Lordship Recn Gd
Open Air Theatre
TOTTENHAM
Silver Ind Est
Mulberry Prim Sch
Bruce Grove
Bruce Grove Prim Sch
DOWNHILLS WAY
Belmont Jun & Inf Sch
51
32
33
34
A1010
A1080
A109
A111
B155
FORE ST
VICTORIA RD
PRETORIA RD
WHITE HART LA
DEVONSHIRE HILL LA
WEIR HALL AVE
BRUCE CASTLE RD

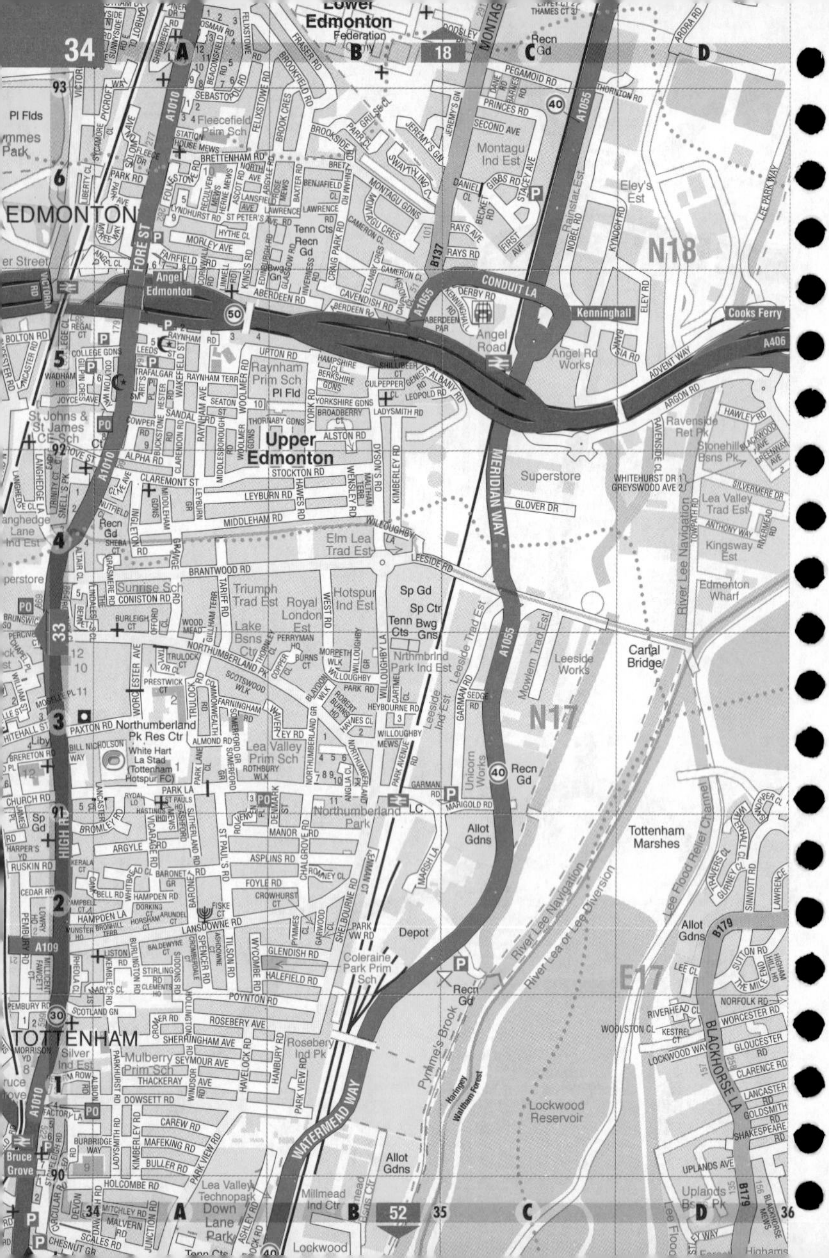

Lower Edmonton
Federation
18
Recn Gd
PEGAMOID RD
THORNTON RD
ARDRA RD
PRINCES RD
SECOND AVE
Montagu Ind Est
FELIXSTOWE RD
BROOKFIELD RD
FRASER RD
BROOK CRES
BAXTER RD
SEBASTOPOL RD
Fleecefield Prim Sch
STATION HOUSE MEWS
BRETTENHAM RD
PARK RD
EDMONTON
Pl Flds
CRAIG PARK RD
MONTAGU GDNS
MONTAGU CRES
Tenn Cts
Recn Gd
RAYS AVE
RAYS RD
FIRST AVE
STACEY AVE
Eley's Est
Rainstar Est
NOBEL RD
KYNOCH RD
N18
ELEY RD
LEE PARK WAY
MORLEY AVE
FAIRFIELD RD
KINGS RD
FORE ST
A1010
Angel Edmonton
ABERDEEN RD
CAVENDISH RD
CONDUIT LA
DERBY RD
Angel Road
Kenninghall
Cooks Ferry
A406
A1055
B137
ADVENT WAY
Angel Rd Works
BANKSIA RD
ARGON RD
UPTON RD
Raynham Prim Sch
Pl Fld
RAYNHAM TERR
RAYNHAM AVE
HAMPSHIRE CL
BERKSHIRE GDNS
YORKSHIRE GDNS
LADYSMITH RD
LEOPOLD RD
ALBANY RD
Ravenside Ret Pk
HAWLEY RD
Stonehill Bsns Pk
Upper Edmonton
ALSTON RD
STOCKTON RD
LEYBURN RD
MIDDLEHAM RD
WILLOUGHBY LA
MERIDIAN WAY
Superstore
GLOVER DR
WHITEHURST DR
GREYSWOOD AVE
SILVERMERE DR
Lea Valley Trad Est
ANTHONY WAY
Kingsway Est
River Lee Navigation
TOWPATH RD
Elm Lea Trad Est
LEESIDE RD
BRANTWOOD RD
Sunrise Sch
CONISTON RD
Triumph Trad Est
Royal London Est
Hotspur Ind Est
WEST RD
Sp Gd
Sp Ctr
Tenn Cts
Bwg Gns
Edmonton Wharf
Lake Bsns Ctr
NORTHUMBERLAND PK
Nrthmbrlnd Park Ind Est
Leeside Trad Est
Mowlem Trad Est
Leeside Works
Canal Bridge
SCOTSWOOD WLK
PRESTWICK CT
WORCESTER AVE
PAXTON RD
Northumberland Pk Res Ctr
White Hart La Stad (Tottenham Hotspur FC)
Lea Valley Prim Sch
Leeside Ind Est
GARMAN RD
N17
Unicorn Works
Recn Gd
PARK LA
Northumberland Park
MARIGOLD RD
Allot Gdns
Tottenham Marshes
Lee Flood Relief Channel
HIGH RD
CHURCH RD
BROMLEY RD
ARGYLE RD
ASPLINS RD
MANOR RD
FOYLE RD
LANSDOWNE RD
SHELBOURNE RD
Depot
River Lee Navigation
River Lea or Lee Diversion
A109
GLENDISH RD
HALEFIELD RD
Coleraine Park Prim Sch
POYNTON RD
Recn Gd
E17
Allot Gdns
B179
SUTTON RD
THE MILE END
NORFOLK RD
WORCESTER RD
GLOUCESTER RD
CLARENCE RD
LANCASTER RD
GOLDSMITH RD
SHAKESPEARE RD
BLACKHORSE LA
TOTTENHAM
ROSEBERY AVE
SHERRINGHAM AVE
SEYMOUR AVE
THACKERAY AVE
DOWSETT RD
CAREW RD
MAFEKING RD
BULLER RD
HOLCOMBE RD
Mulberry Prim Sch
Rosebery Ind Pk
Lockwood Reservoir
Pymme's Brook
Haringey
Waltham Forest
WATERMEAD WAY
Allot Gdns
Lea Valley Technopark
Down Lane Park
Millmead Ind Ctr
Lockwood
Bruce Grove
CHESNUT GR
SCALES RD
MALVERN RD
UPLANDS AVE
Uplands Bsns Pk
52
35
36
Highams

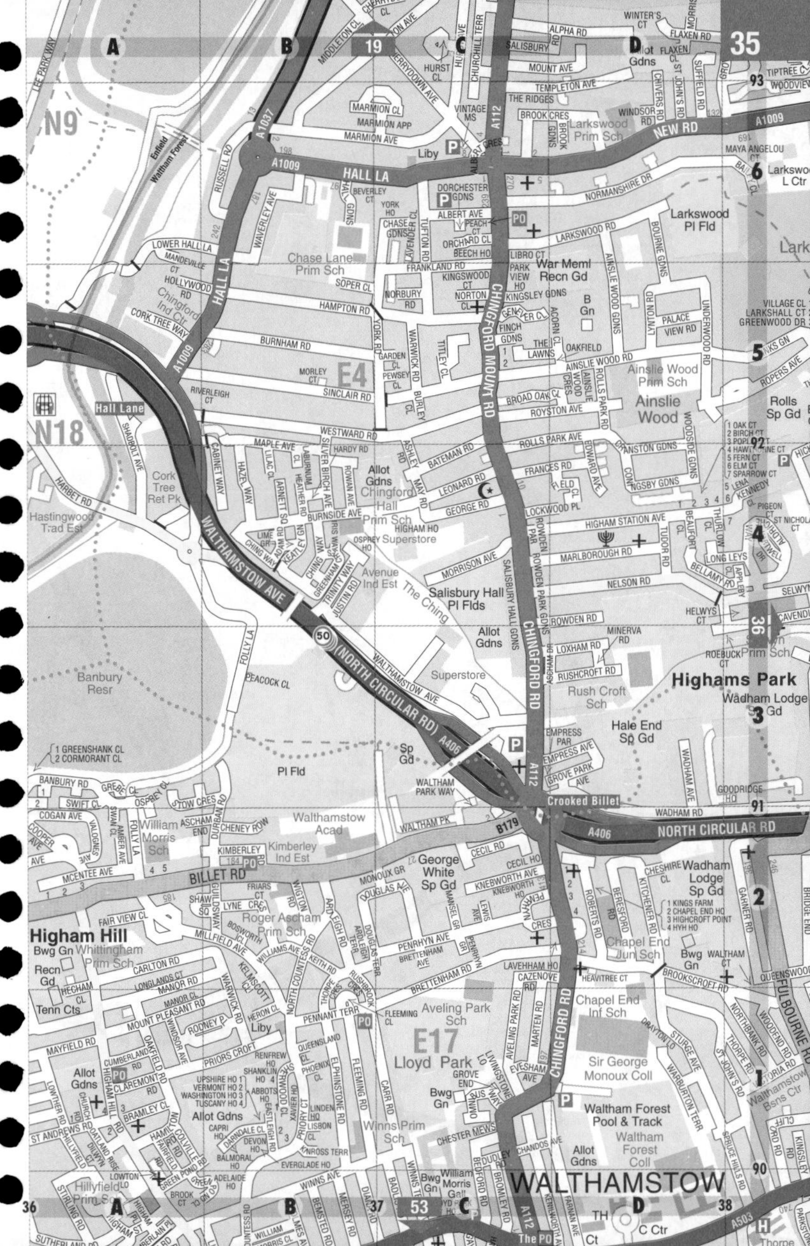
35
A
B
C
D
19
N9
E4
N18
E17
LEE PARK WAY
MIDDLETON CL
WINTER'S CT
MORRIS
ALPHA RD
FLAXEN RD
SALISBURY
MOUNT AVE
Allot Gdns
CHIVERS RD
ST JOHN'S RD
SUFFIELD RD
TIPTREE CT
WOODVIEW
93
HURST CL
CHURCHILL TERR
TEMPLETON AVE
THE RIDGES
VINTAGE MS
MARMION CL
MARMION APP
MARMION AVE
BROOK CRES
BROOK GDNS
WINDSOR RD
Larkswood Prim Sch
NEW RD
A1009
A1037
A112
Enfield
Waltham Forest
RUSSELL RD
HALL LA
Liby
ALBERT CRES
MAYA ANGELOU CT
BAILEY CL
6
Larkswood L Ctr
DORCHESTER GDNS
NORMANSHIRE DR
BEVERLEY CT
YORK HO
WAVERLEY AVE
ALBERT AVE
PEACH CT
PO
ORCHARD CL
BEECH HO
LARKSWOOD RD
Larkswood Pl Fld
CHASE GDNS
TUFTON RD
LAVENDER CL
LOWER HALL LA
MANDEVILLE CT
HOLLYWOOD RD
Chingford Ind Ctr
CORK TREE WAY
Chase Lane Prim Sch
FRANKLAND RD
LIBRO CT
PARK VIEW HO
War Meml Recn Gd
KINGSWOOD CT
KINGSLEY GDNS
NORTON CL
SOPER CL
NORBURY RD
HAMPTON RD
CHINGFORD MOUNT RD
AINSLIE WOOD GDNS
LYNTON RD
UNDERWOOD RD
PALACE VIEW RD
VILLAGE CL
LARKSHALL CT
GREENWOOD DR
FINCH GDNS
ACORN CL
B Gn
BURNHAM RD
YORK RD
WARWICK RD
TITLEY CL
THE LAWNS
OAKFIELD
AINSLIE WOOD RD
5
ROPERS AVE
GARDEN CL
PEWSEY CL
MORLEY CT
SINCLAIR RD
BURLEY CL
RIVERLEIGH CT
Hall Lane
BROAD OAK CL
AINSLIE WOOD CRES
ROLLS PARK RD
Ainslie Wood Prim Sch
Ainslie Wood
Rolls Sp Gd
ROYSTON AVE
WESTWARD RD
MAPLE AVE
HARDY RD
LAUREL AVE
ASHLEY RD
BATEMAN RD
ROLLS PARK AVE
EDWARD AVE
CRANSTON GDNS
WOODSIDE GDNS
1 OAK CT
2 BIRCH CT
3 POPLAR CT
4 HAWTHORNE CT
5 FERN CT
6 ELM CT
7 SPARROW CT
92
SHADBOLT AVE
CABINET WAY
HAZEL WAY
LILAC CL
SILVER BIRCH AVE
LABURNUM
HEATHER RD
ROWAN AVE
Allot Gdns
Chingford Hall Prim Sch
MAY RD
LEONARD RD
FRANCES RD
FIELD CL
CONINGSBY GDNS
LENA KENNEDY CL
Cork Tree Ret Pk
HARBET RD
Hastingwood Trad Est
ARNETT SQ
BURNSIDE AVE
GEORGE RD
LOCKWOOD PL
HIGHAM STATION AVE
BEAUFORT CL
THURLOW
PIGEON CT
ST NICHOLAS CT
ALDHOLME CT
4
LIME GR
ADAM RD
KEATLEY GN
CHING WAY
IRIS WAY
OSPREY HO
Superstore
HIGHAM HO
ROWDEN PAR
ROWDEN RD
MARLBOROUGH RD
TUDOR RD
LONG LEYS
CHING WAY
GREENHAM CL
TRINITY WAY
Avenue Ind Est
The Ching
MORRISON AVE
NELSON RD
BELLAMY RD
APPLEBY
SELWYN
JUSTIN RD
Salisbury Hall Pl Flds
ROWDEN PARK GDNS
SALISBURY HALL GDNS
HELWYS CT
CAVENDISH
WALTHAMSTOW AVE
50
(NORTH CIRCULAR RD)
FOLLY LA
Allot Gdns
CHINGFORD RD
ROWDEN RD
MINERVA RD
LOXHAM RD
ASCHAM DR
ROEBUCK CT
Selwyn Prim Sch
36
Banbury Resr
PEACOCK CL
WALTHAMSTOW AVE
Superstore
RUSHCROFT RD
Rush Croft Sch
Highams Park
Wadham Lodge Sp Gd
3
1 GREENSHANK CL
2 CORMORANT CL
Pl Fld
Sp Gd
A406
EMPRESS PAR
EMPRESS AVE
GROVE PARK AVE
Hale End Sp Gd
WADHAM AVE
WALTHAM PARK WAY
BANBURY RD
GREBE CL
OSPREY CL
SWIFT CL
STOW CRES
DURBAN RD
Crooked Billet
GOODRIDGE HO
91
COGAN AVE
VALOGNES AVE
SWAN CL
AMBER AVE
FOLLY LA
William Morris Sch
ASCHAM END
CHENEY ROW
Walthamstow Acad
WALTHAM PK
B179
WADHAM RD
NORTH CIRCULAR RD
COOPER AVE
KIMBERLEY RD
Kimberley Ind Est
George White Sp Gd
CECIL RD
CHESHIRE CL
Wadham Lodge Sp Gd
MCENTEE AVE
BILLET RD
FRIARS CT
MONOUX GR
DOUGLAS AVE
KNEBWORTH AVE
KNEBWORTH HO
PENRHYN AVE
ROBERTS RD
BERESFORD
KITCHENER RD
1 KINGS FARM
2 CHAPEL END HO
3 HIGHCROFT POINT
4 HYH HO
GAHNER RD
2
SHAW SQ
GUILDSWAY
LYNE CRES
WIGTON
Roger Ascham Prim Sch
ARDLEIGH RD
ARDLEIGH TERR
MANSEL GR
LEWIS AVE
Higham Hill
Bwg Gn
Whittingham Prim Sch
FAIR VIEW CL
MILLFIELD AVE
BOSWORTH
WILLIAMS AVE
KEITH RD
PENRHYN AVE
BRETTENHAM AVE
PENRHYN GR
Chapel End Jun Sch
Bwg Gn
WALTHAM CT
CARLTON RD
LONGLANDS CT
MANOR RD
KELMSCOTT CL
NORTH COUNTESS RD
RUSHBROOK CRES
BRETTENHAM RD
LAVEHHAM HO
CAZENOVE RD
HEAVITREE CT
BROOKSCROFT RD
QUEENSWOOD
FULBOURNE RD
Recn Gd
HECHAM CL
MANOR CL
MOUNT PLEASANT RD
WARWICK RD
HERON CL
THORPE CRES
FLEEMING CL
Aveling Park Sch
Chapel End Inf Sch
DRAYTON LO
NORTHBANK RD
WOODEND RD
Tenn Cts
RODNEY P
Liby
PENNANT TERR
PO
AVELING PARK RD
MARTEN RD
STURGE AVE
THORPE RD
ST JOHN'S RD
MAYFIELD RD
CUMBERLAND
OAKFIELD RD
WINDSOR RD
PRIORS CROFT
RENFREW HO
QUEENSLAND
ELPHINSTONE RD
FLEEMING RD
E17
Lloyd Park
LIVINGSTONE
EVESHAM AVE
Sir George Monoux Coll
WARBURTON TERR
VICTORIA RD
1
Walthamstow Bsns Ctr
Allot Gdns
HIGHAM HILL RD
CLAREMONT RD
SHANKLIN HO
PHOENIX CL
GROVE END
UPSHIRE HO 1
VERMONT HO 2
WASHINGTON HO 3
TUSCANY HO 4
ABBOTS HO
EASTLEIGH RD
XAVIER HO
LINDEN HO
CARR RD
Bwg Gn
Waltham Forest Pool & Track
CLIFF
LOWTHER RD
CHURCH HILL
BRAMLEY CL
Allot Gdns
PRIORY CT
ST ANDREWS RD
HILLYFIELD
OATLAND RISE
HAMILTON RD
COLVILLE RD
CAPRI HO
DARNDALE CL
DEVON HO
LISBON CL
KNROSS TERR
Winns Prim Sch
CHESTER MEWS
CHANDOS AVE
Waltham Forest Coll
Allot Gdns
SPRUCE HILLS RD
ORD RD
KINGSLEY
BALMORAL HO
EVERGLADE HO
LOWTON LO
GREEN POND RD
ADELAIDE RD
Hillyfield Prim Sch
BROOK CT
WINNS AVE
BWG Gn
William Morris Gall
BEDFORD RD
BROMLEY RD
DUDLEY RD
WALTHAMSTOW
90
36
A
B
37
53
C
D
38
STIRLING RD
HIGHAM ST
BEMSTED RD
MERSEY RD
DIANA RD
TH
C Ctr
A503
PARKSTONE
WILLIAM MORRIS CL
A112
KENILWORTH AVE
FARNAN AVE
SUTHERLAND RD
COUNTESS RD
The PO
Ct
Thorpe

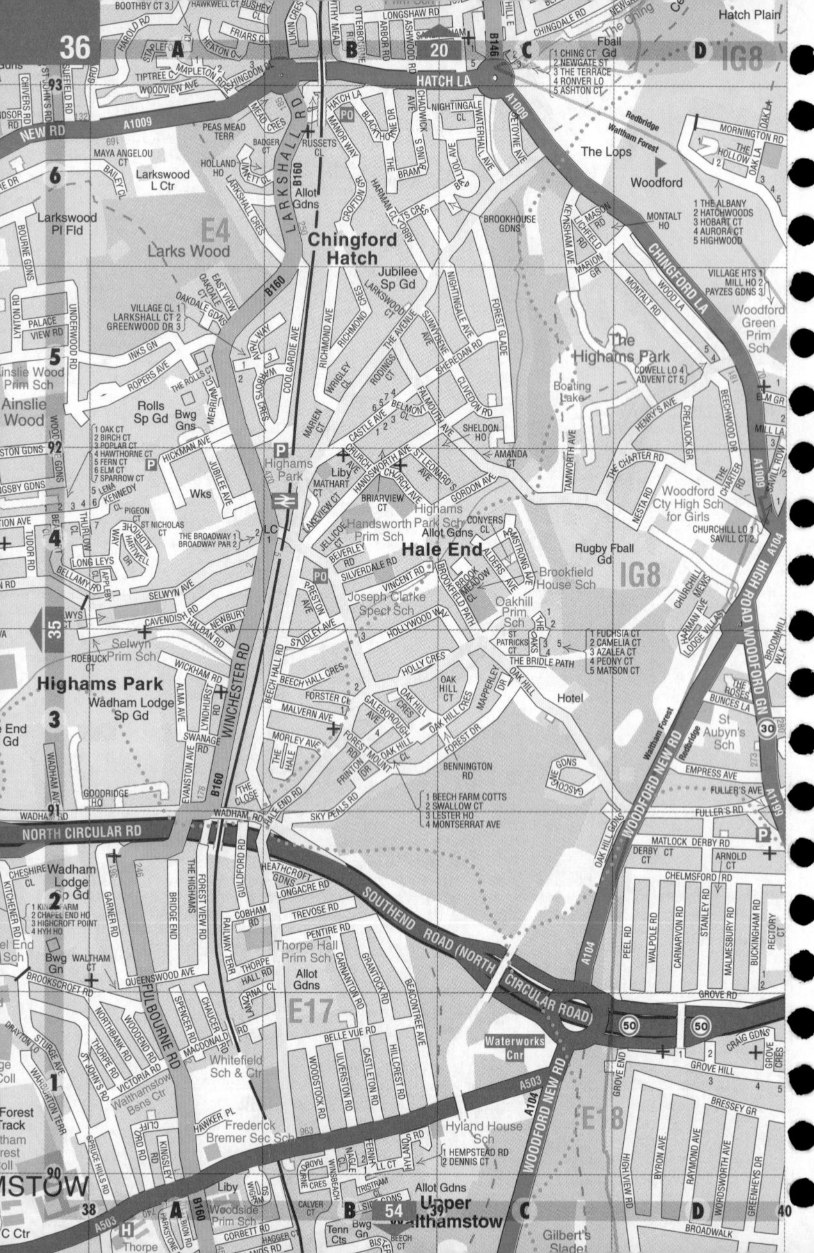

A
B
C
D
20
IG8
HATCH LA
NEW RD
A1009
Hatch Plain
Fball Gd
1 CHING CT
2 NEWGATE ST
3 THE TERRACE
4 RONVER LO
5 ASHTON CT
Larkswood L Ctr
Larkswood Pl Fld
E4
Larks Wood
Chingford Hatch
LARKSHALL RD
B160
Jubilee Sp Gd
The Lops
Woodford
CHINGFORD LA
1 THE ALBANY
2 HATCHWOODS
3 HOBART CT
4 AURORA CT
5 HIGHWOOD
Woodford Green Prim Sch
The Highams Park
Boating Lake
Ainslie Wood Prim Sch
Ainslie Wood
Rolls Sp Gd
Bwg Gns
Wks
Highams Park
Liby
Handsworth Prim Sch
Allot Gdns
Hale End
Rugby Fball Gd
Brookfield House Sch
Joseph Clarke Specl Sch
Oakhill Prim Sch
Woodford Cty High Sch for Girls
Selwyn Prim Sch
Highams Park
Wadham Lodge Sp Gd
WINCHESTER RD
1 FUCHSIA CT
2 CAMELIA CT
3 AZALEA CT
4 PEONY CT
5 MATSON CT
Hotel
St Aubyn's Sch
HIGH ROAD WOODFORD GN
WOODFORD NEW RD
1 BEECH FARM COTTS
2 SWALLOW CT
3 LESTER HO
4 MONTSERRAT AVE
NORTH CIRCULAR RD
SOUTHEND ROAD (NORTH CIRCULAR ROAD)
Wadham Lodge Sp Gd
Thorpe Hall Prim Sch
Allot Gdns
E17
Waterworks Cnr
E18
FULBOURNE RD
Whitefield Sch & Ctr
Walthamstow Bsns Ctr
Frederick Bremer Sec Sch
Hyland House Sch
1 HEMPSTEAD RD
2 DENNIS CT
Forest Track
Liby
Woodside Prim Sch
Allot Gdns
Upper Walthamstow
Tenn Cts
Bwg Gn
Gilbert's Slade
35
54
38
39
40

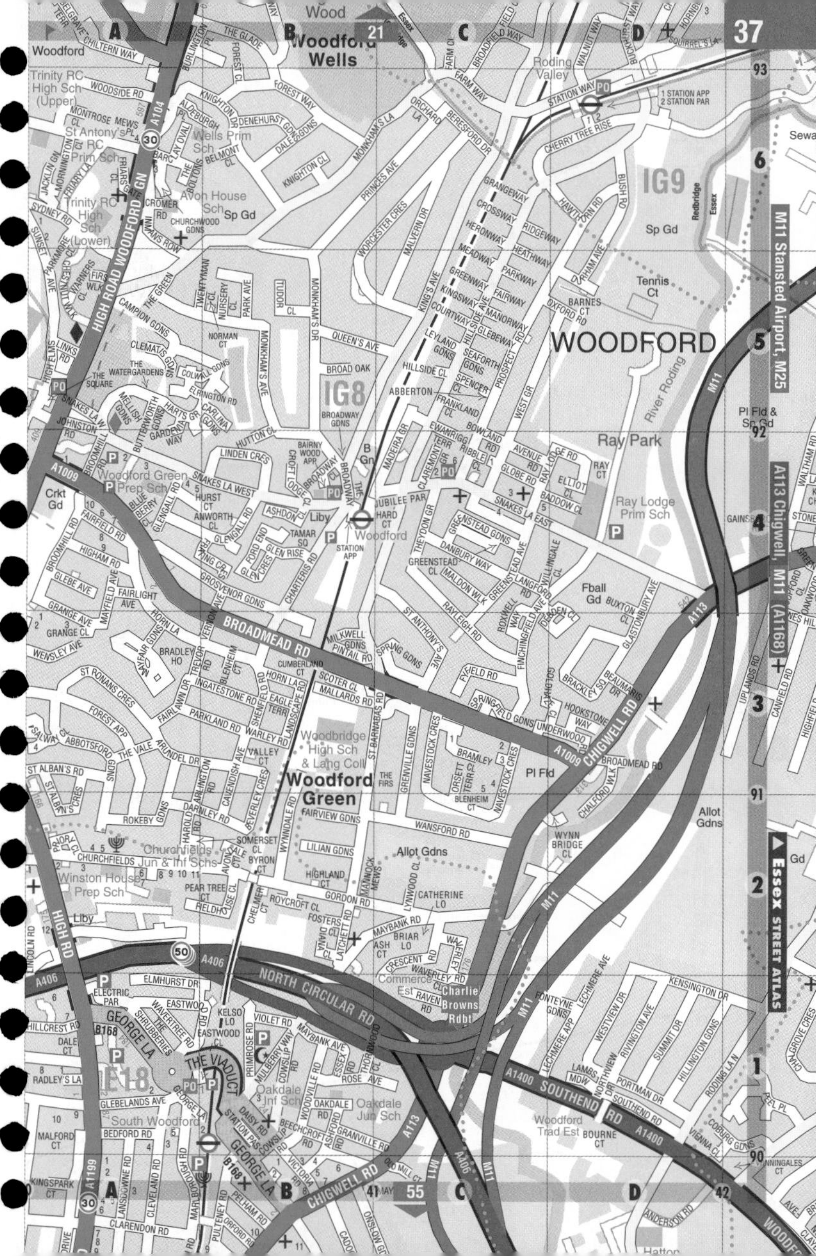
A
B
C
D
21
55
Woodford Wells
Woodford
WOODFORD
Woodford Green
South Woodford
Roding Valley
Ray Park
River Roding
IG8
IG9
E18
M11 Stansted Airport, M25
A113 Chigwell, M11 (A1168)
Essex STREET ATLAS
HIGH ROAD WOODFORD GN
HIGH RD
BROADMEAD RD
SNAKES LA WEST
SNAKES LA EAST
NORTH CIRCULAR RD
SOUTHEND RD
CHIGWELL RD
GEORGE LA
THE VIADUCT
THE BROADWAY
A104
A1009
A406
A113
A1400
A1199
B168
M11
Trinity RC High Sch (Upper)
Trinity RC High Sch (Lower)
St Antony's RC Prim Sch
Wells Prim Sch
Avon House Sch
Woodford Green Prep Sch
Woodbridge High Sch & Lang Coll
Churchfields Jun & Inf Schs
Winston House Prep Sch
Ray Lodge Prim Sch
Oakdale Inf Sch
Oakdale Jun Sch
Charlie Browns Rdbt
Commerce Est
Woodford Trad Est
Sp Gd
Tennis Ct
Fball Gd
Allot Gdns
Pl Fld
Crkt Gd
Liby
Sewage
Redbridge
Essex
93
92
91
90
6
5
4
3
2
1
42
41

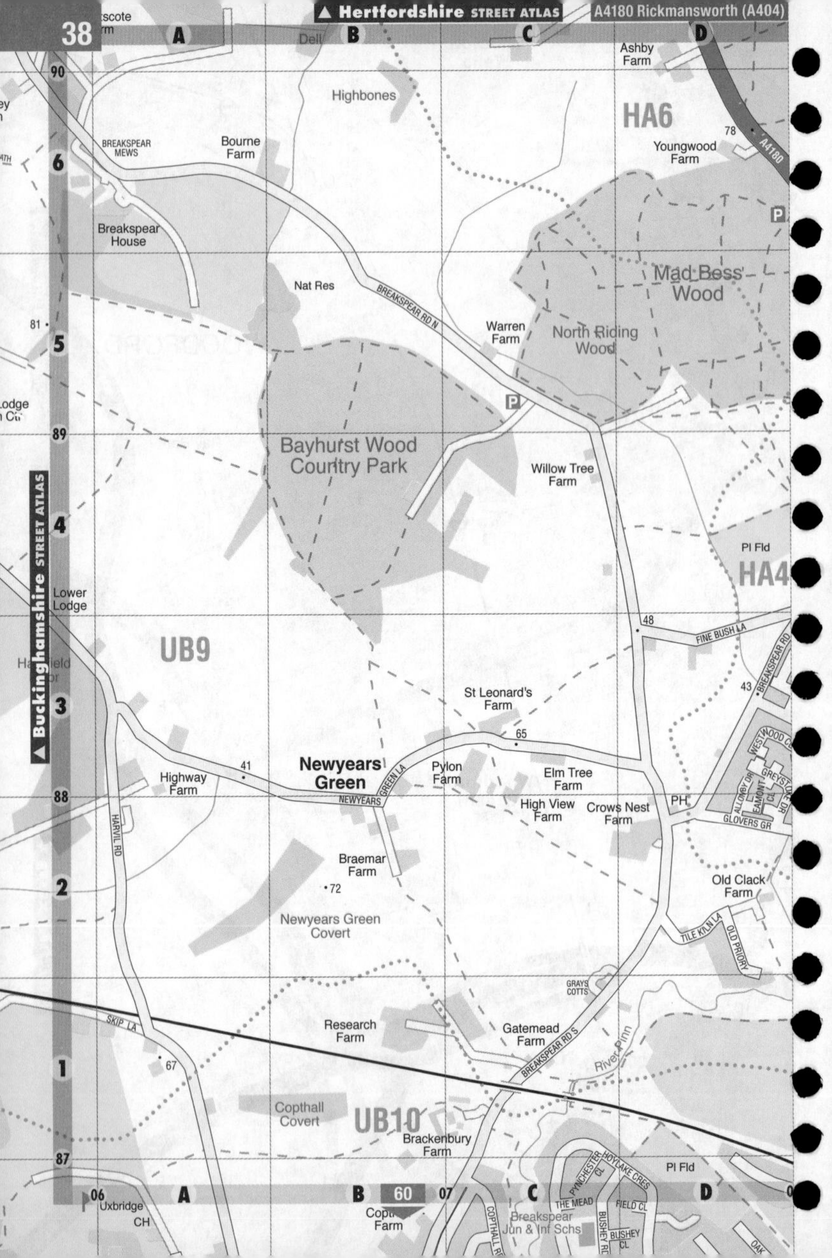

▲ Buckinghamshire STREET ATLAS

scote rm

Dell

Ashby Farm

Highbones

HA6

Breakspear Mews

Bourne Farm

Youngwood Farm

78

A4180

Breakspear House

Nat Res

BREAKSPEAR RD N

Mad Bess Wood

81

Warren Farm

North Riding Wood

Lodge n Ct

89

Bayhurst Wood Country Park

Willow Tree Farm

Pl Fld

HA4

Lower Lodge

48

FINE BUSH LA

BREAKSPEAR RD

UB9

43

St Leonard's Farm

65

WOOD CL

Highway Farm

41

GREEN LA

Newyears Green

Pylon Farm

Elm Tree Farm

GREEN

PH

88

NEWYEARS

High View Farm

Crows Nest Farm

GLOVERS GR

HARVIL RD

Braemar Farm

72

Old Clack Farm

Newyears Green Covert

TILE KILN LA

OLD PRIORY

GRAYS COTTS

SKIP LA

Research Farm

Gatemead Farm

BREAKSPEAR RD S

River Pinn

67

Copthall Covert

UB10

Brackenbury Farm

Pl Fld

87

06   A   Uxbridge CH

B   07

C

THE MEAD

BUSHEY RD

FIELD CL

D

Copt Farm

Breakspear Jun & Inf Schs

COPTHALL LA

PINCHESTER

HOTLAKE CRES

BUSHEY CL

OAK

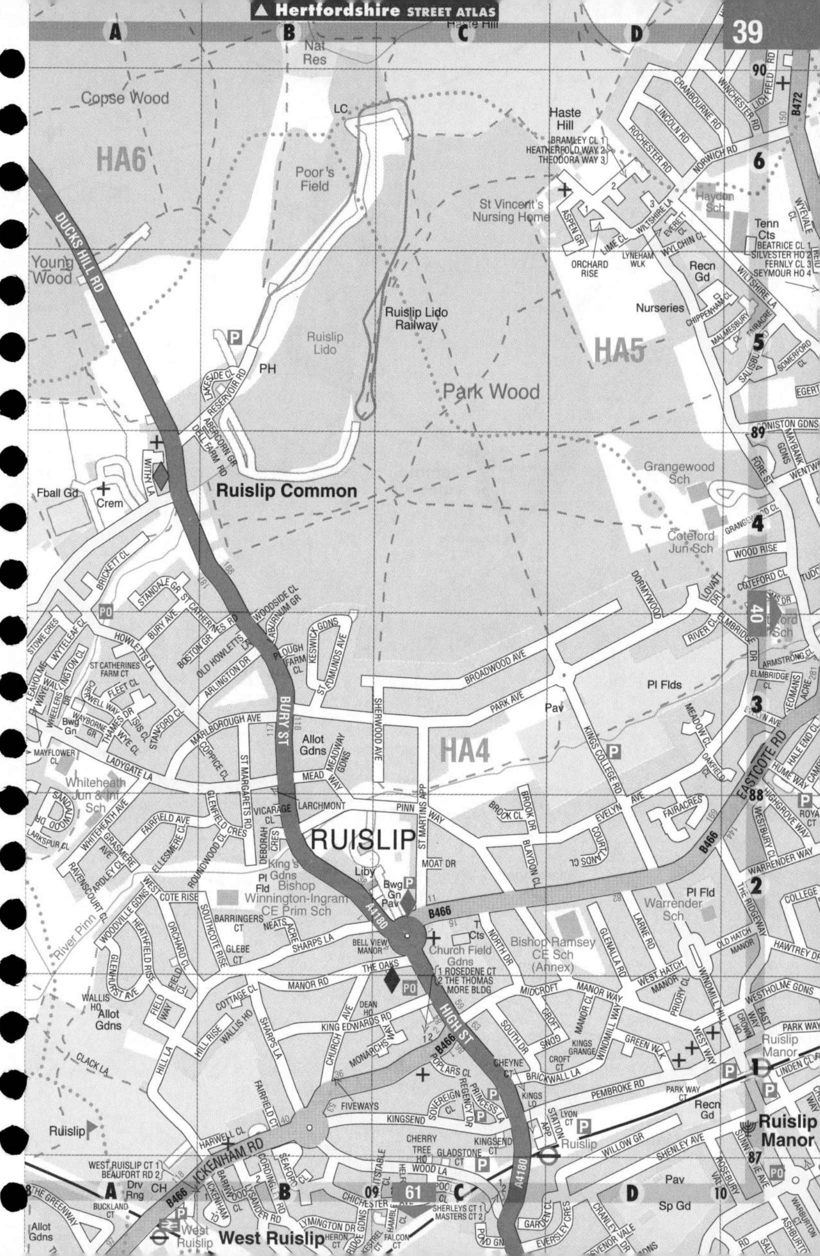

HA6

Copse Wood

Nat Res

Poor's Field

LC

Haste Hill

BRAMLEY CL 1
HEATHEROLD WAY 2
THEODORA WAY 3

St Vincent's Nursing Home

Hayden Sch

CHANBOURNE RD

INNES CT

KNIGHTLEY RD

LINCOLN RD

ROCHESTER RD

NORWICH RD

90

B472

6

Young Wood

Ducks Hill Rd

Ruislip Lido Railway

Ruislip Lido

Park Wood

HA5

Grangewood Sch

Cateford Jun Sch

WOOD RISE

CATEFORD CT

Recn Gd

Nurseries

Tenn Cts

BEATRICE CL 1
SILVESTER HO 2
FERNLY CL 3
SEYMOUR HO 4

ASPEN CT

LIME CL

WYCHIN CL

LYNEHAM WLK

ORCHARD RISE

WHITSHIRE

CHIPPENHAM

MALMESBURY

EGERT

WENTW

89

5

4

PH

Fball Gd

Crem

Ruislip Common

RESERVOIR RD

CHELTMAN RD

LAKESIDE CL

HERDON CL

WITHY LA

BRICKET CL

STANDALE

ST CATHERINES

BURY AVE

ST CATHERINES FARM CT

HOWLETTS LA

FLEET CL

STANFORD CL

BOSTON CR

OLD HOWLETTS LA

ARLINGTON CL

CHURCH LA

WOODSIDE CL

PARGRIM GR

KESWICK GDNS

ST CONANS RISE

ROUGH FARM CL

KESWICK AVE

DORMYWOOD

RIVER CAMBRIDGE

ARMSTRONG

ELMBRIDGE

LEEMANS

40

SAXON

ford Sch

3

STONE CRES

WYTELEAF CL

HOWELL CL

WELLS HO

WELLS WAY

MYE CL

LADYGATE LA

MAYFLOWER CL

BROADWOOD AVE

PARK AVE

KINGS COLLEGE RD

PAV

Pl Flds

MEADOW WAY

SHERWOOD AVE

Allot Gdns

MEAD

VICARAGE

LARCHMONT

ST MARTINS APP

PINN WAY

BROADWOOD AVE

EVELYN AVE

FAIRACRES

RIVER AVE

CANFIELD

HALCYON

ROYA

88

2

Whiteheath Jun & Inf Sch

MARLBOROUGH AVE

COPPICE CL

ST MARGARETS

GLENBROOK CL

ELLESMERE RD

WHITEHEATH AVE

FAIRFIELD AVE

LARKSPUR CL

VICARAGE

BRIDLE RD

RYDAL

CRES

COTE RISE

NEATSCOURT

SHARPS LA

BELL VIEW MANOR

THE OAKS

RUISLIP

King's Gdns

Bishop Winnington-Ingram CE Prim Sch

Liby

Pl Fld

Bwg Gn

MOAT DR

BLADDON CL

BROOK CL

ESOM CL

COURT

SOM CT

B466

Church Field Gdns

1 ROSEDENE CT
2 THE THOMAS MORE BLDG

Bishop Ramsey CE Sch (Annex)

WEST HATCH

OLD HATCH MANOR

WARRENDER WAY

Pl Fld

Warrender Sch

COLLEGE

HAWTREY DR

THE RIDGEWAY

WESTBURY RD

B466

River Pinn

BARRINGERS

CT

GLEBE

CT

ORCHARD CL

SOUTHCOTE RISE

WALLIS HO

Allot Gdns

CLACK LA

FREEMANS LA

STAINES AVE

GLENHURST AVE

HILL RISE

COTTAGE CL

WALLS RD

SHARPS LA

MANOR RD

CHERRY AVE

DEAN RD

MONARCHS

KING EDWARDS RD

POPLARS CL

CHEYNE

HIGH ST

B466

MIDCROFT

MANOR WAY

SOUTH DR

KINGS GRANGE

GREEN WAY

GREY CT

CROFT CT

BRICKWALL LA

PEMBROKE RD

MANOR CT

KINGS WAY

WEST HATCH

SHORT

LINNE RD

WEST HATCH

Ruislip Manor

PARK WAY

LINDEN CL

WESTHOLME GDNS

P

P

87

1

Ruislip ►

WEST RUISLIP CT 1
BEAUFORT RD 2

Drv Rng

CH

HILL LA

FAIRFIELD CT

HARWELL CL

FIVEWAYS

KINGSEND

CHERRY TREE CT

GLADSTONE CT

WOOD LA

SHENLEY AVE

WILLOW GR

LYON RD

STATION

Recn Gd

Ruislip

GARY

Pav

Sp Gd

Ruislip Manor

THE GREENWAY

Allot Gdns

BUCKLAND

WICKENHAM RD

B466

West Ruislip

SHERLEYS CT 1
MASTERS CT 2

West Ruislip

CHICHESTER

IDMINGTON DR

HERON CL

09

SOVEREIGN CT

SOVEREIGN

A4180

CHERRY CRES

CRANE VALE

10

B

61

C

D

A4180

A4180

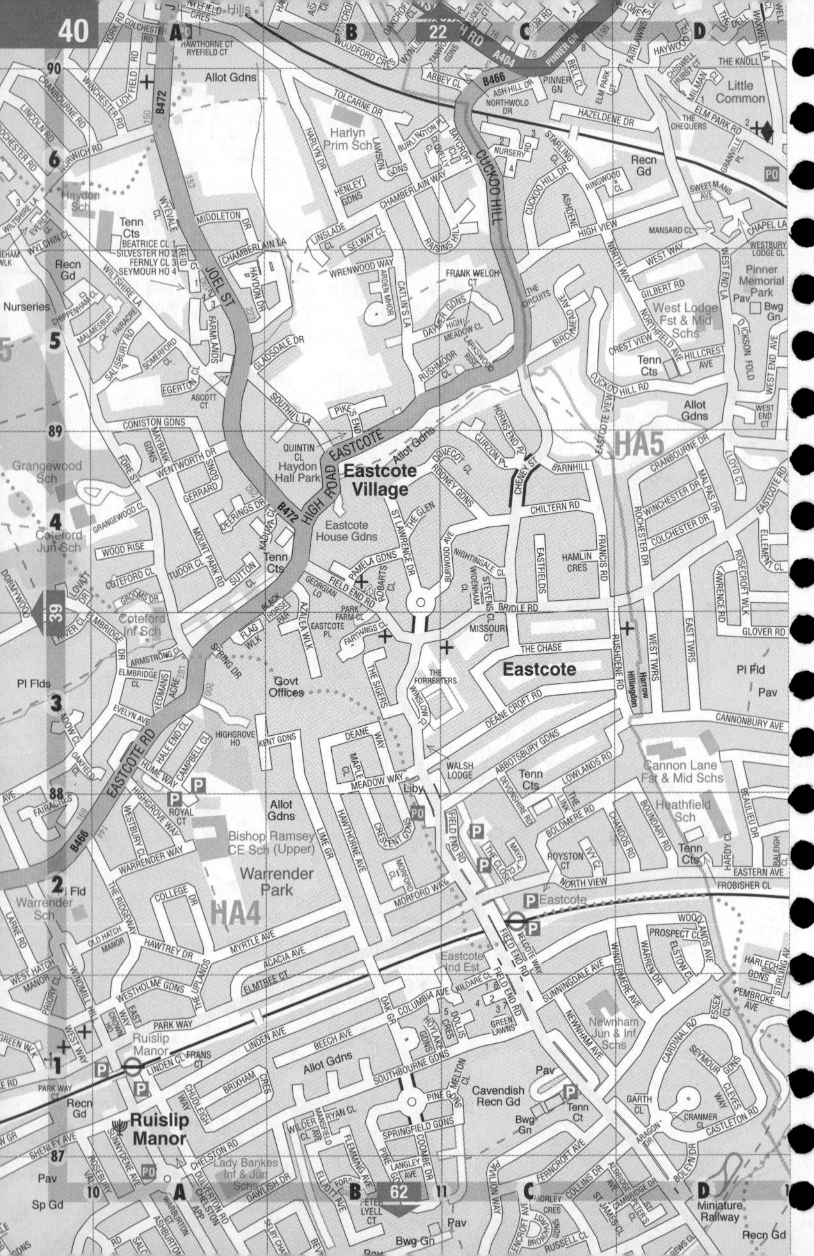

Eastcote Village
Eastcote
Ruislip Manor
HA5
HA4
Little Common
Harlyn Prim Sch
Haydon Sch
Grangewood Sch
Coteford Jun Sch
Coteford Inf Sch
Eastcote House Gdns
Haydon Hall Park
West Lodge Fst & Mid Schs
Pinner Memorial Park
Cannon Lane Fst & Mid Schs
Heathfield Sch
Bishop Ramsey CE Sch (Upper)
Warrender Park
Warrender Sch
Newnham Jun & Inf Schs
Cavendish Recn Gd
Lady Bankes Inf & Jun Schs
Govt Offices
Eastcote Ind Est
Miniature Railway
JOEL ST
HIGH ROAD EASTCOTE
CUCKOO HILL
EASTCOTE RD
FIELD END RD
PINNER RD
B472
B466
A404
22
39
62

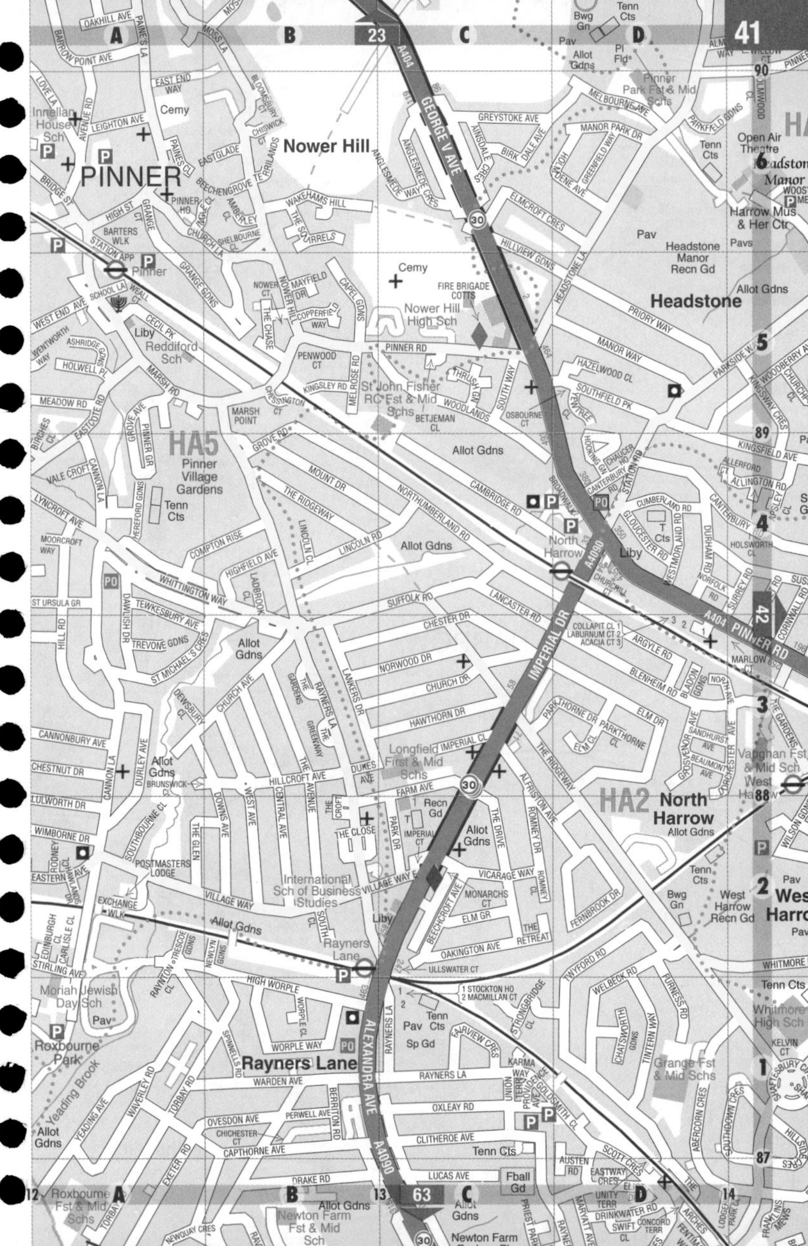
A
B
C
D
23
63
PINNER
Nower Hill
HA5
HA2
Headstone
North Harrow
West Harrow
Rayners Lane
Headstone Manor
Headstone Manor Recn Gd
Harrow Mus & Her Ctr
Open Air Theatre
Pinner Park Fst & Mid Schs
Nower Hill High Sch
St John Fisher RC Fst & Mid Schs
Reddiford Sch
Innellan House Sch
Pinner Village Gardens
Longfield First & Mid Schs
International Sch of Business Studies
Moriah Jewish Day Sch
Roxbourne Park
Roxbourne Fst & Mid Schs
Newton Farm Fst & Mid Sch
Newton Farm Ecology Pk
Grange Fst & Mid Schs
Vaughan Fst & Mid Sch
Whitmore High Sch
West Harrow Recn Gd
Yeading Brook
GEORGE V AVE
A404
A4090
IMPERIAL DR
ALEXANDRA AVE
PINNER RD
NORTHUMBERLAND RD
CAMBRIDGE RD
HEADSTONE LA
STATION RD
RAYNERS LA
HIGH WORPLE
WARDEN AVE
OXLEAY RD
CLITHEROE AVE
LUCAS AVE
DRAKE RD
MARSH RD
CANNON LA
WHITTINGTON WAY
VILLAGE WAY
CHURCH AVE
LANKERS DR
SUFFOLK RD
CHESTER DR
NORWOOD DR
CHURCH DR
HAWTHORN DR
HILLCROFT AVE
FARM AVE
THE RIDGEWAY
MOUNT DR
LINCOLN RD
GROVE RD
PRIORY WAY
MANOR WAY
HILLVIEW GDNS
ELMCROFT CRES
GREYSTOKE AVE
MELBOURNE AVE
MANOR PARK DR
KINGSFIELD AVE
CANTERBURY RD
ARGYLE RD
BLENHEIM RD
LANCASTER RD
TWYFORD RD
WELBECK RD
WHITMORE RD
SHAFTESBURY CIRC
WEST END AVE
HIGH ST
BRIDGE ST
CHURCH LA
ELM DR
VICARAGE WAY
OAKINGTON AVE
ULLSWATER CT
DEWSBURY CL
CANNONBURY AVE
CHESTNUT DR
LULWORTH DR
WIMBORNE DR
EASTERN AVE
STIRLING AVE
EXCHANGE WLK
POSTMASTERS LODGE
Allot Gdns
Cemy
Liby
Tenn Cts
Pav
Recn Gd
Fball Gd
Sp Gd
90
89
88
87
12
13
14
6
5
4
3
2
1
42

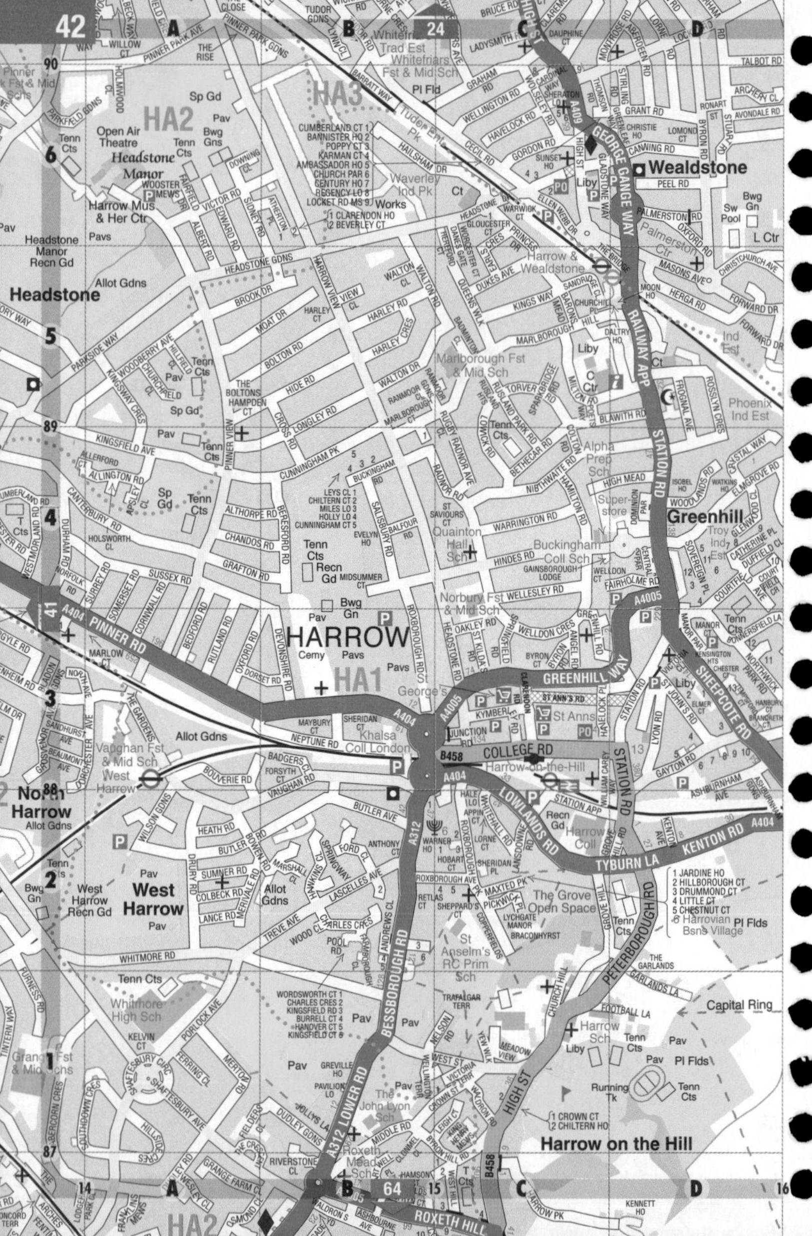
A
B
C
D
24
64
41
HA1
HA2
HA3
Headstone
Headstone Manor
Headstone Manor Recn Gd
Harrow Mus & Her Ctr
Open Air Theatre
Allot Gdns
Wealdstone
Harrow & Wealdstone
Greenhill
HARROW
West Harrow
North Harrow
Harrow on the Hill
Whitefriars Trad Est
Whitefriars Fst & Mid Sch
Tudor Ent Pk
Waverley Ind Pk
Palmerston Ctr
Phoenix Ind Est
Troy Ind Est
Marlborough Fst & Mid Sch
Alpha Prep Sch
Quainton Hall Sch
Buckingham Coll Sch
Norbury Fst & Mid Sch
Khalsa Coll London
Vaughan Fst & Mid Sch
Harrow-on-the-Hill
Harrow Coll
The Grove Open Space
St Anselm's RC Prim Sch
Whitmore High Sch
Grange Fst & Mid Schs
The John Lyon Sch
Roxeth Mead Sch
Harrow Sch
Capital Ring
Running Tk
Harrovian Bsns Village
Pinner Fst & Mid Schs
PINNER RD
A404
A4005
A409
A312
B458
GEORGE GANGE WAY
RAILWAY APP
STATION RD
SHEEPCOTE RD
GREENHILL WAY
COLLEGE RD
LOWLANDS RD
TYBURN LA
KENTON RD
BESSBOROUGH RD
LOWER RD
PETERBOROUGH RD
HIGH ST
ROXETH HILL
HEADSTONE GDNS
HEADSTONE RD
HARROW VIEW
PINNER VIEW
KINGSFIELD AVE
CUNNINGHAM PK
PARKSIDE WAY
WHITMORE RD
SHAFTESBURY AVE
SHAFTESBURY CIRC
CUMBERLAND CT 1
BANNISTER HO 2
POPPY CT 3
KARMAN CT 4
AMBASSADOR HO 5
CHURCH PAR 6
CENTURY HO 7
REGENCY LO 8
LOCKET RD MS 9
1 CLARENDON HO
2 BEVERLEY CT
LEYS CL 1
CHILTERN CT 2
MILES LO 3
HOLLY LO 4
CUNNINGHAM CT 5
WORDSWORTH CT 1
CHARLES CRES 2
KINGSFIELD RD 3
BURRELL CT 4
HANOVER CT 5
KINGSFIELD CT 6
1 JARDINE HO
2 HILLBOROUGH CT
3 DRUMMOND CT
4 LITTLE CT
5 CHESTNUT CT
6 Harrovian Bsns Village
1 CROWN CT
2 CHILTERN HO
14
15
16
87
88
89
90

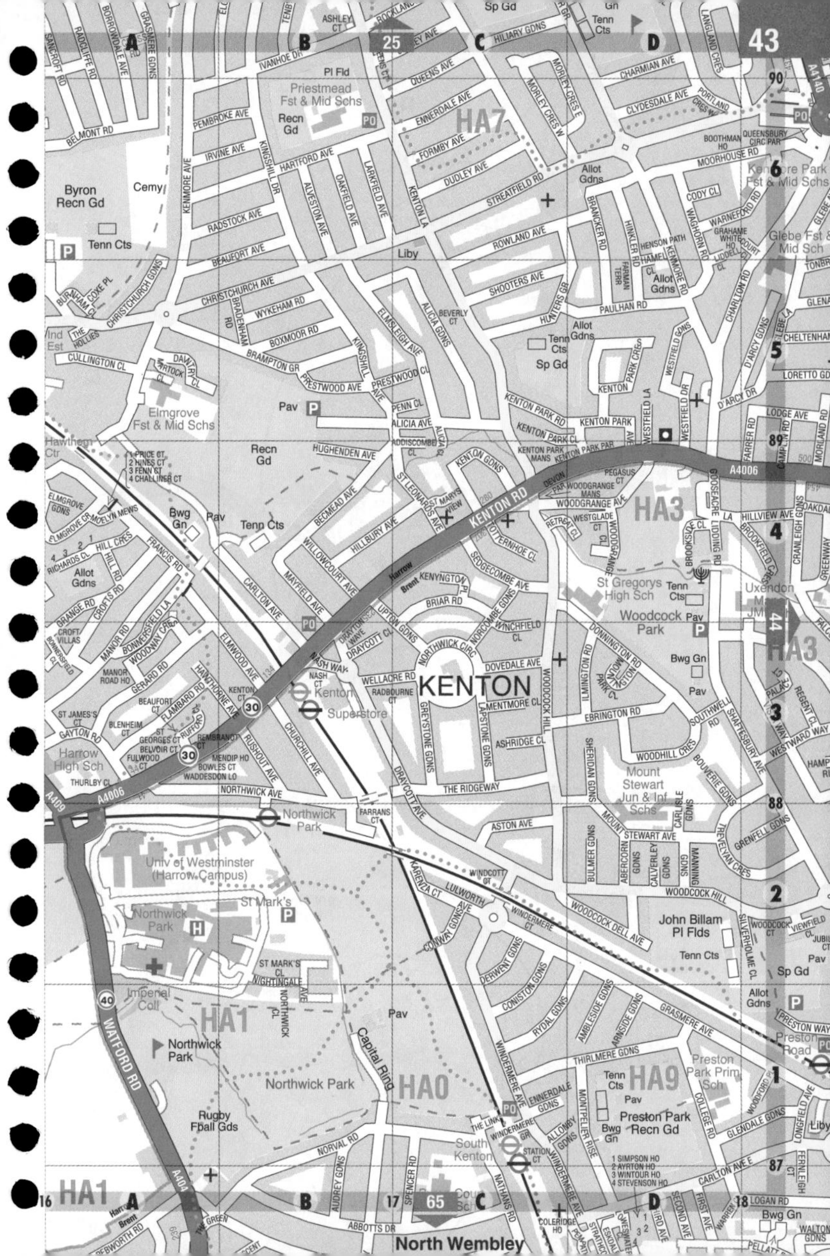
25
HA7
Priestmead Fst & Mid Schs
Recn Gd
Pl Fld
Byron Recn Gd
Cemy
Tenn Cts
KENMORE AVE
HARTFORD AVE
KENTON LA
STREATFIELD RD
Allot Gdns
MOORHOUSE RD
Kenmore Park Fst & Mid Schs
Glebe Fst & Mid Sch
Liby
SHOOTERS AVE
ROWLAND AVE
CHRISTCHURCH AVE
Elmgrove Fst & Mid Schs
Recn Gd
Pav
Sp Gd
KENTON PARK RD
KENTON RD
A4006
HA3
St Gregorys High Sch
Woodcock Park
Bwg Gn
KENTON
Kenton
Superstore
Harrow High Sch
NORTHWICK AVE
Northwick Park
THE RIDGEWAY
Mount Stewart Jun & Inf Schs
Univ of Westminster (Harrow Campus)
St Mark's
Northwick Park
Imperial Coll
HA1
Northwick Park
Rugby Fball Gds
Capital Ring
HA0
John Billam Pl Flds
Preston Road
HA9
Preston Park Prim Sch
Preston Park Recn Gd
South Kenton
WATFORD RD
A404
WINDERMERE AVE
WOODCOCK HILL
GRASMERE AVE
44
65
North Wembley

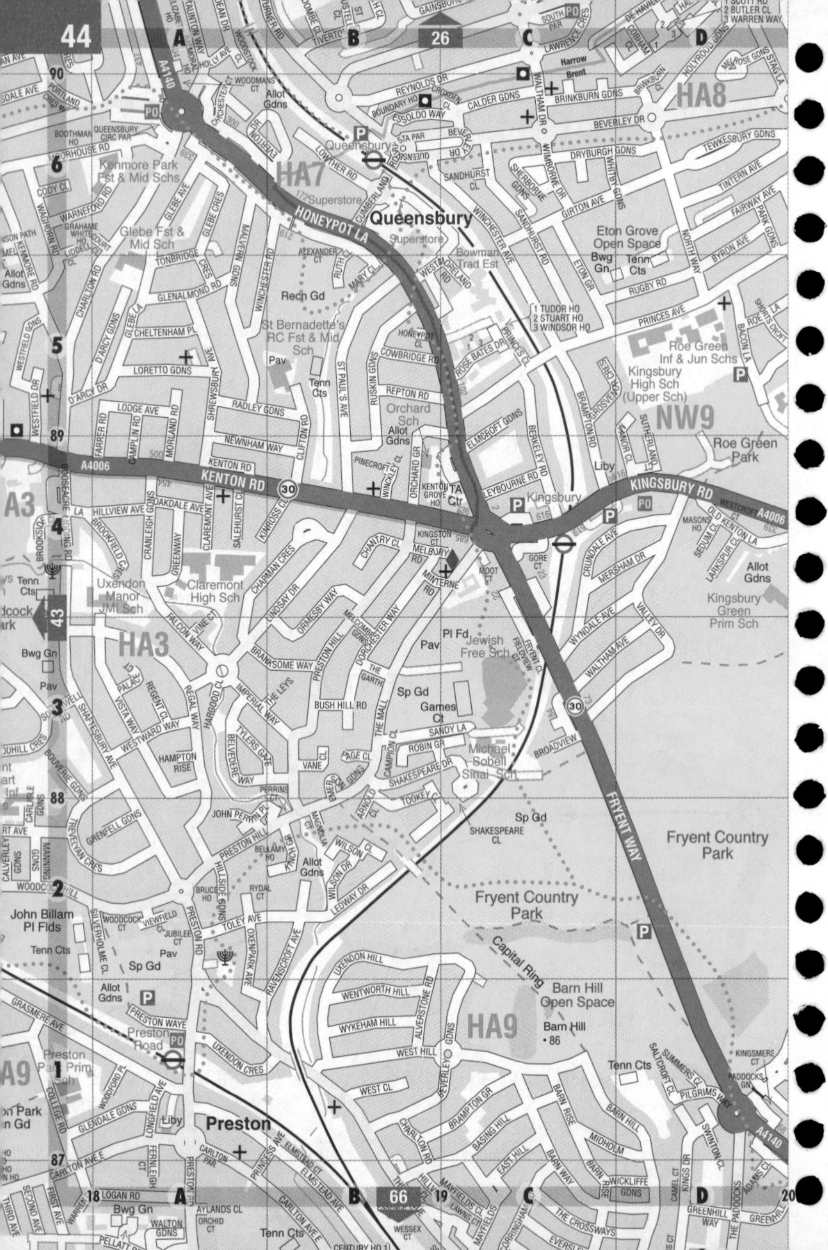
26
A
B
C
D
HA7
HA8
HA3
HA9
NW9
A3
A9
Queensbury
Kingsbury
Preston
HONEYPOT LA
KENTON RD
KINGSBURY RD
FRYENT WAY
A4140
A4006
Kenmore Park Fst & Mid Schs
Glebe Fst & Mid Sch
St Bernadette's RC Fst & Mid Sch
Orchard Sch
Claremont High Sch
Uxendon Manor JMI Sch
Jewish Free Sch
Michael Sobell Sinai Sch
Roe Green Inf & Jun Schs
Kingsbury High Sch (Upper Sch)
Kingsbury Green Prim Sch
Preston Park Prim Sch
Eton Grove Open Space
Roe Green Park
Fryent Country Park
Barn Hill Open Space
Barn Hill • 86
Capital Ring
John Billam Pl Flds
Bowman Trad Est
Superstore
Recn Gd
Allot Gdns
Tenn Cts
Bwg Gn
Pav
Sp Gd
Games Ct
Pl Fd
Liby
TA Ctr
Preston Road
1 TUDOR HO
2 STUART HO
3 WINDSOR HO
1 SCOTT RD
2 BUTLER CL
3 WARREN WAY
43
66
90
89
88
87
6
5
4
3
2
1
18
19
20

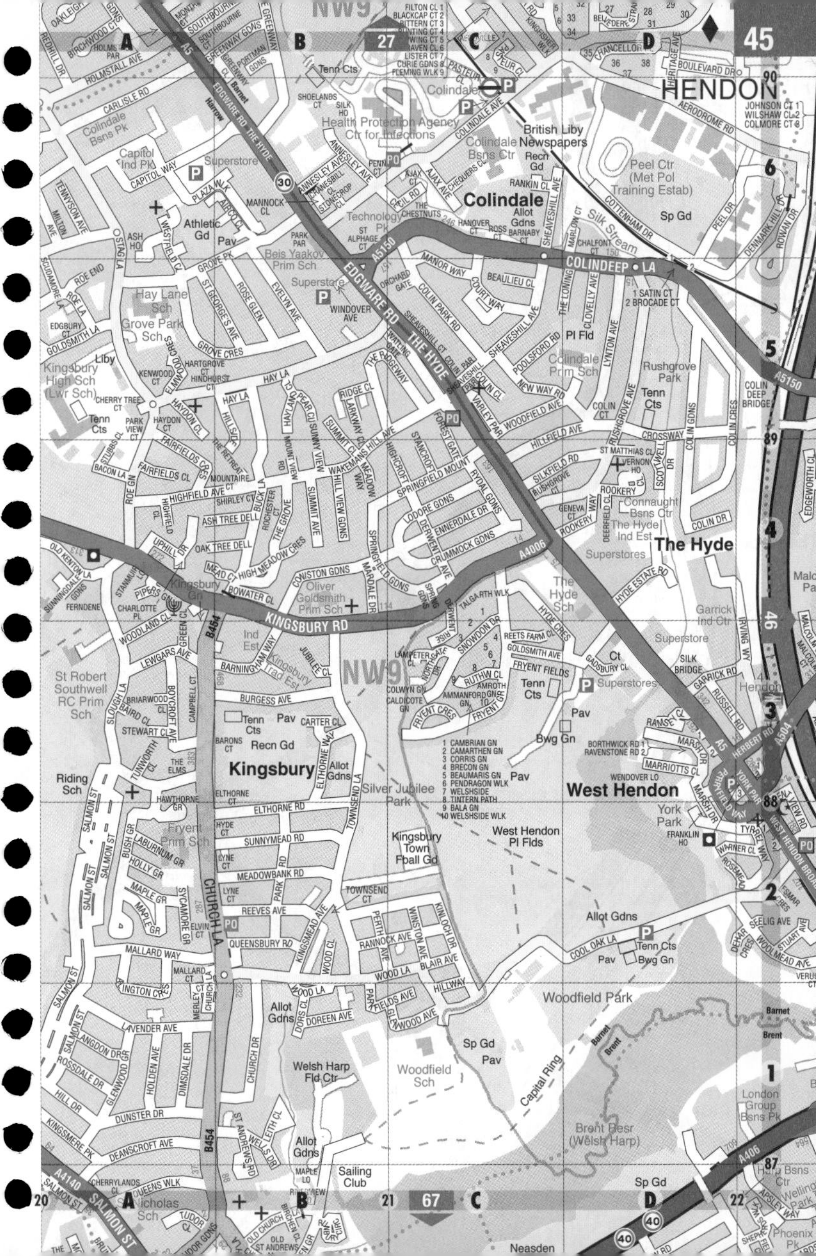
NW9
27
A
B
C
D
HENDON
Colindale
Tenn Cts
Health Protection Agency Ctr for Infections
British Liby Newspapers
Colindale Bsns Ctr
Recn Gd
Peel Ctr (Met Pol Training Estab)
Sp Gd
Colindale Bsns Pk
Capitol Ind Pk
Superstore
Athletic Gd
Pav
Technology Pk
Beis Yaakov Prim Sch
Allot Gdns
Silk Stream
COLINDEEP LA
Hay Lane Sch
Grove Park Sch
Liby
Kingsbury High Sch (Lwr Sch)
Pl Fld
Colindale Prim Sch
Rushgrove Park
Tenn Cts
Colin Deep Bridge
Connaught Bsns Ctr
The Hyde Ind Est
The Hyde
Superstores
The Hyde Sch
Kingsbury Gn
Oliver Goldsmith Prim Sch
KINGSBURY RD
Ind Est
Kingsbury Trad Est
Garrick Ind Ctr
Superstore
Silk Bridge
St Robert Southwell RC Prim Sch
Recn Gd
Kingsbury
Allot Gdns
Silver Jubilee Park
Bwg Gn
West Hendon
York Park
Riding Sch
Fryent Prim Sch
Kingsbury Town Fball Gd
West Hendon Pl Flds
CHURCH LA
Allot Gdns
Woodfield Park
Sp Gd
Pav
Welsh Harp Fld Ctr
Woodfield Sch
Capital Ring
Brent Resr (Welsh Harp)
Sailing Club
London Group Bsns Pk
St Nicholas Sch
Neasden
EDGWARE RD THE HYDE
A5
A5150
A4006
B454
A4140
A406
A504
SALMON ST
1
2
3
4
5
6
20
21
22
87
88
89
90
46
67

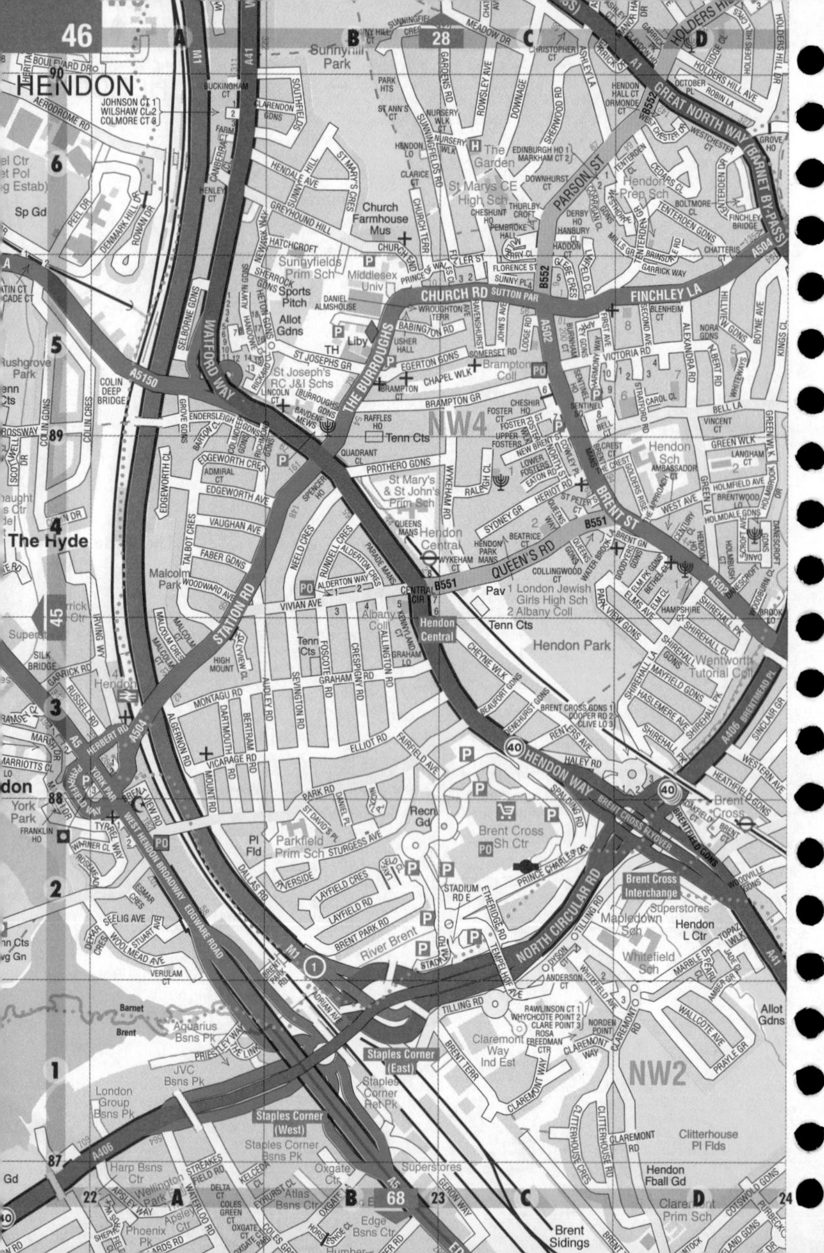
HENDON
28
Sunnyhill Park
AERODROME RD
BOULEVARD DR
WATFORD WAY
M1
A41
A5150
THE BURROUGHS
CHURCH RD
SUTTON PAR
FINCHLEY LA
GREAT NORTH WAY (BARNET BY-PASS)
PARSON ST
B552
A502
A504
A1
HOLDERS HILL
St Marys CE High Sch
The Garden
Church Farmhouse Mus
Sunnyfields Prim Sch
Middlesex Univ
Sports Pitch
Allot Gdns
Liby
TH
St Joseph's RC J&I Schs
Hendon Prep Sch
Brampton Coll
NW4
Tenn Cts
Hendon Central
QUEEN'S RD
B551
BRENT ST
Hendon Sch
St Mary's & St John's Prim Sch
Pav
1 London Jewish Girls High Sch
2 Albany Coll
Hendon Park
Wentworth Tutorial Coll
Malcolm Park
STATION RD
VIVIAN AVE
Albany Coll
Rushgrove Park
Colin Deep Bridge
The Hyde
Silk Bridge
Sp Gd
York Park
HENDON WAY
Brent Cross Sh Ctr
Brent Cross Interchange
BRENT CROSS FLYOVER
NORTH CIRCULAR RD
Recn Gd
Pl Fld
Parkfield Prim Sch
River Brent
WEST HENDON BROADWAY
EDGWARE ROAD
Barnet
Brent
Aquarius Bsns Pk
JVC Bsns Pk
London Group Bsns Pk
Staples Corner (East)
Staples Corner (West)
Staples Corner Ret Pk
Staples Corner Bsns Pk
Claremont Way Ind Est
NW2
Mapledown Sch
Whitefield Sch
Hendon L Ctr
Superstores
Allot Gdns
Clitterhouse Pl Flds
Hendon Fball Gd
Claremont Prim Sch
Harp Bsns Ctr
Wellington Park
Apsley Ctr
Phoenix Pk
Atlas Bsns Ctr
Oxgate Ctr
Edge Bsns Ctr
Brent Sidings
A406
A5
45
68
A
B
C
D
22
23
24
90
89
88
87
1
2
3
4
5
6

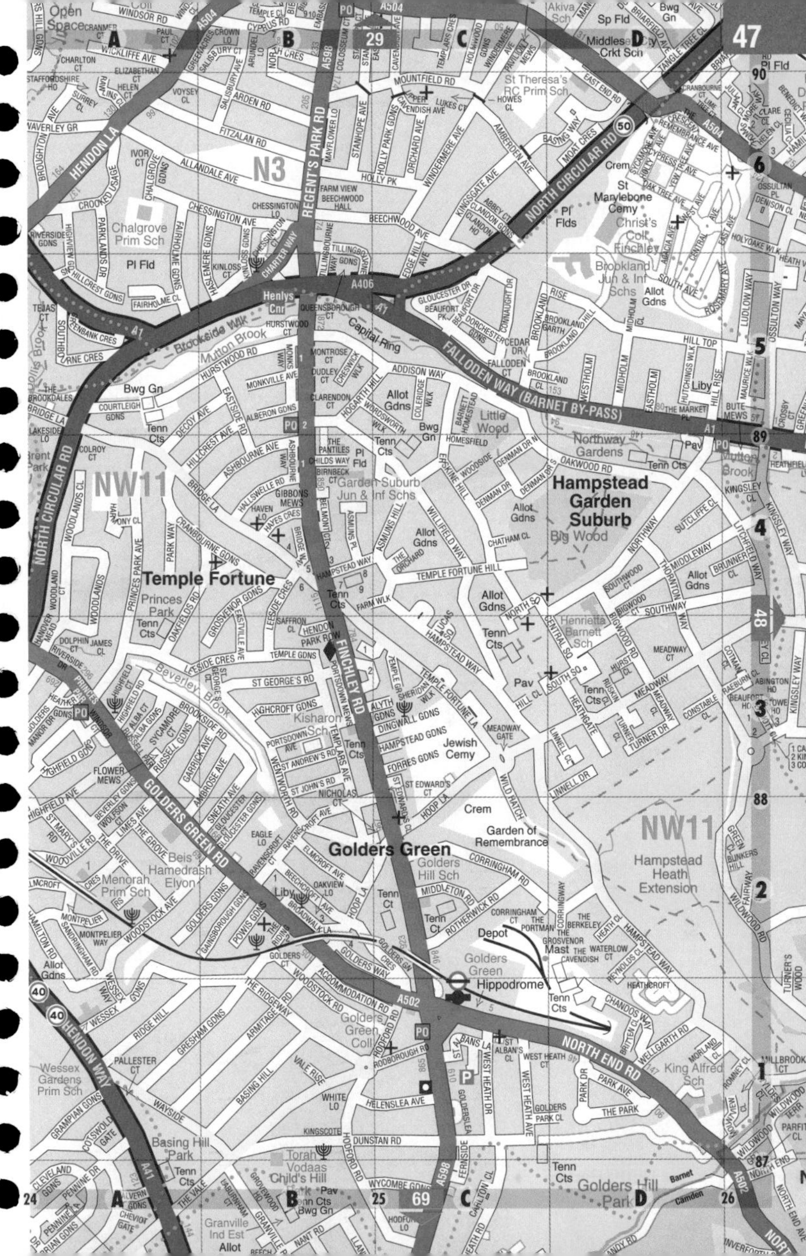
47
29
69
48
A
B
C
D
90
89
88
87
24
25
26
6
5
4
3
2
1
N3
NW11
NW11
Open Space
WINDSOR RD
CRANMER
WICKLIFFE AVE
CHARLTON CT
ELIZABETHAN CT
STAFFORDSHIRE HO
VOYSEY CL
ARDEN RD
FITZALAN RD
WAVERLEY GR
HENDON LA
ALLANDALE AVE
CROOKED USAGE
CHESSINGTON AVE
Chalgrove Prim Sch
Pl Fld
HILLCREST GDNS
FAIRHOLME CL
HASLEMERE GDNS
KINLOSS CT
CHARTER WAY
REGENT'S PARK RD
A598
A504
SALISBURY AVE
CYPRUS RD
MOUNTFIELD RD
LUKES CT
CAVENDISH AVE
STANHOPE AVE
HOLLY PARK GDNS
ORCHARD AVE
WINDERMERE AVE
HOLLY PK
FARM VIEW
BEECHWOOD HALL
BEECHWOOD AVE
CHESSINGTON LO
TILLINGBOURNE GDNS
EDGE HILL AVE
St Theresa's RC Prim Sch
EAST END RD
AMBERDEN AVE
KINGSGATE AVE
ABBEY CT
CLANDON GDNS
NORTH CIRCULAR RD
Crem
St Marylebone Cemy
Christ's Coll Finchley
Pl Flds
Brookland Jun & Inf Schs
Allot Gdns
SOUTH AVE
Sp Fld
Middlesex Cty Crkt Sch
Akiva Sch
Bwg Gn
Pl Fld
A406
A1
Henlys Cnr
QUEENSBOROUGH CT
HURSTWOOD CT
Capital Ring
Mutton Brook
Brookside Wlk
FALLODEN WAY (BARNET BY-PASS)
GLOUCESTER DR
BEAUFORT PK
DORCHESTER GDNS
CEDAR DR
FALLODEN CT
BROOKLAND RISE
BROOKLAND HILL
BROOKLAND CL
HILL TOP
MIDHOLM
WESTHOLM
EASTHOLM
HUTCHINGS WLK
HILL RISE
THE MARKET PL
Liby
BUTE MEWS
LUDLOW WAY
OSSULTON WAY
HURSTWOOD RD
MONTROSE CT
DUDLEY CT
CRESWICK WLK
MONKVILLE AVE
CLARENDON CT
ADDISON WAY
HOGARTH HILL
Allot Gdns
Bwg Gn
Little Wood
HOMESFIELD
Northway Gardens
Pav
Tenn Cts
OAKWOOD RD
Hampstead Garden Suburb
Big Wood
NORTH CIRCULAR RD
Bwg Gn
COURTLEIGH GDNS
THE BROOKDALES
BRIDGE LA
LAKESIDE
Brent Park
COLROY CT
Tenn Cts
DECOY AVE
HILLCREST AVE
EASTSIDE RD
ALBERON GDNS
ASHBOURNE AVE
THE PANTILES
CHILDS WAY
Pl Fld
Garden Suburb Jun & Inf Schs
HALLSWELLE RD
GIBBONS MEWS
HAVEN LO
HAYES CRES
BELMONT CT
ASMUNS HILL
ASMUNS PL
WILLIFIELD WAY
ERSKINE HILL
DENMAN DR
Allot Gdns
CHATHAM CL
NORTHWAY
SUTCLIFFE CL
KINGSLEY WAY
LITCHFIELD WAY
MIDDLEWAY
Allot Gdns
WOODLANDS CL
BRIDGE LA
CRANBOURNE GDNS
PARK WAY
PRINCES PARK AVE
Temple Fortune
Princes Park
OAKFIELDS RD
GROSVENOR GDNS
LEESIDE CRES
HAMPSTEAD WAY
TEMPLE FORTUNE HILL
THE ORCHARD
FARM WLK
Tenn Cts
SOUTHWOOD CT
THORNTON WAY
BRUNNER CL
BIGWOOD CT
SOUTHWAY
Allot Gdns
NORTH SQ
CENTRAL SQ
Henrietta Barnett Sch
HAMPSTEAD WAY
LUCAS SQ
SAFFRON CL
HENDON PARK ROW
FINCHLEY RD
TEMPLE GDNS
TEMPLE FORTUNE LA
SOUTH SQ
Pav
Tenn Cts
HILL CL
BIGWOOD RD
MEADWAY CT
MEADWAY
HURST CL
RUSKIN CL
HEATHGATE
TURNER DR
CONSTABLE CL
COTMAN CL
RAEBURN CL
ABINGTON HO
BEAUFORT HO
DOLPHIN CT
JAMES CL
HANOVER MEAD
RIVERSIDE DR
WOODLANDS
Tenn Cts
LEESIDE CRES
ST GEORGE'S RD
Beverley Brook
HIGHFIELD CT
HIGHFIELD RD
BROOKSIDE RD
ALBA CT
SYCAMORE CT
RUSSELL GDNS
HIGHCROFT GDNS
PORTSDOWN MEWS
ALYTH GDNS
DINGWALL GDNS
HAMPSTEAD GDNS
FORRES GDNS
Jewish Cemy
Kisharon Sch
MEADWAY GATE
PORTSDOWN AVE
ST ANDREW'S RD
ST JOHN'S RD
NICHOLAS CT
ST EDWARD'S CT
HOOP LA
WILD HATCH
LINNELL CL
LINNELL DR
Crem
Garden of Remembrance
GOLDERS MANOR DR
GARRICK AVE
AMBROSE AVE
SNEATH AVE
FLOWER MEWS
HIGHFIELD GDNS
HIGHFIELD AVE
ST MARY'S RD
WOODVILLE RD
THE DRIVE
LIMES AVE
THE GROVE
GOLDERS GREEN RD
GLOUCESTER GDNS
Beis Hamedrash Elyon
Menorah Prim Sch
EAGLE LO
RAVENSCROFT AVE
ELMCROFT AVE
Golders Green
Golders Hill Sch
CORRINGHAM RD
NW11
Hampstead Heath Extension
GREEN CL
BUNKERS HILL
FAIRWAY
WILDWOOD RD
BEECHCROFT AVE
OAKVIEW LO
Liby
BROADWALK LA
HOOP LA
Tenn Ct
MIDDLETON RD
ROTHERWICK RD
Tenn Ct
CORRINGHAM CT
THE PORTMAN
CORRINGWAY
THE BERKELEY
THE GROSVENOR
Mast
THE CAVENDISH
WATERLOW CT
Depot
Golders Green
Hippodrome
HEATH CL
HAMPSTEAD WAY
REYNOLDS CL
HEATHCROFT
CHANDOS WAY
Tenn Cts
WOODSTOCK AVE
MONTPELIER WAY
SANDRINGHAM RD
HAMILTON RD
Allot Gdns
GOLDERS GDNS
GAINSBOROUGH GDNS
POWIS GDNS
THE RIDINGS
GOLDERS CT
GOLDERS WAY
GOLDERS GN CRES
WOODSTOCK RD
ACCOMMODATION RD
A502
THE RIDGEWAY
WESSEX WAY
WESSEX GDNS
HENDON WAY
RIDGE HILL
GRESHAM GDNS
ARMITAGE RD
Golders Green Coll
HODFORD RD
RODBOROUGH RD
ST ALBANS LA
ST ALBAN'S CL
WEST HEATH CT
NORTH END RD
WELLGARTH RD
MORLAND CL
King Alfred Sch
MILLBROOK CT
TURNER'S WOOD
PALLESTER CT
Wessex Gardens Prim Sch
GRAMPIAN GDNS
WAYSIDE
BASING HILL
VALE RISE
WHITE LO
HELENSLEA AVE
GOLDERSLEA
WEST HEATH DR
WEST HEATH AVE
GOLDERS PARK CL
PARK DR
PARK AVE
THE PARK
WILDWOOD TERR
PARFITT CL
COTSWOLD GATE
Basing Hill Park
KINGSCOTE
DUNSTAN RD
Torah Vodaas
Child's Hill Park
Tenn Cts
Pav
Bwg Gn
WYCOMBE GDNS
FERNSIDE
CARLTON CL
Tenn Cts
Golders Hill Park
Barnet
Camden
NORTH END AVE
CLEVELAND GDNS
PENNINE DR
MALVERN GDNS
CHEVIOT GATE
THE VALE
LABURNHAM CT
GROVEWOOD HO
GRANVILLE RD
Granville Ind Est
Allot
NANT RD
A41
A598
A502
40
50

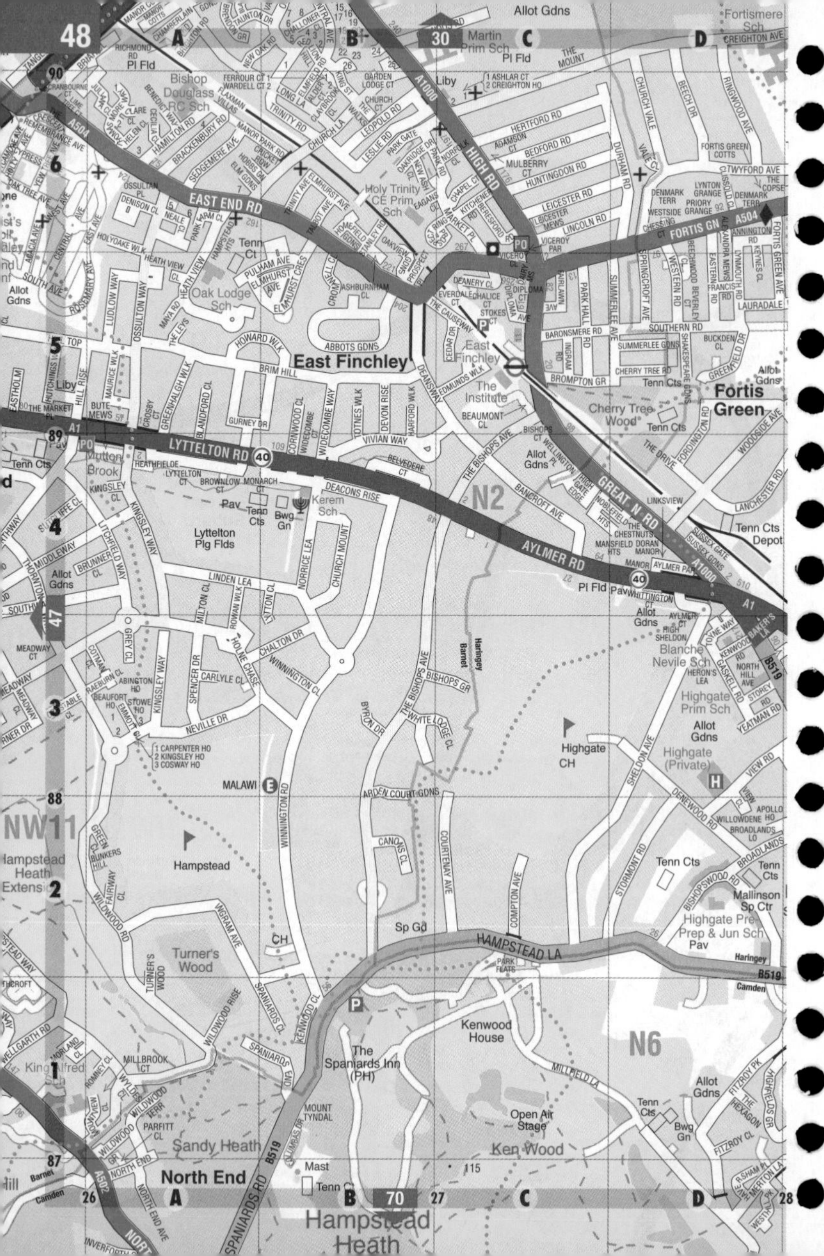

A
B
C
D
30
Martin Prim Sch
Allot Gdns
Fortismere Sch
CREIGHTON AVE
Pl Fld
THE MOUNT
Bishop Douglass RC Sch
Liby
A1000
HIGH RD
A504
EAST END RD
Holy Trinity CE Prim Sch
FORTIS GN
Tenn Ct
Oak Lodge Sch
East Finchley
East Finchley
The Institute
Cherry Tree Wood
Fortis Green
Tenn Cts
LYTTELTON RD
40
Mutton Brook
Lyttelton Plg Flds
Kerem Sch
Bwg Gn
N2
GREAT N RD
AYLMER RD
Tenn Cts Depot
A1
Blanche Nevile Sch
Highgate Prim Sch
Highgate CH
Highgate (Private)
Haringey
Barnet
MALAWI
NW11
Hampstead
Hampstead Heath Extension
Turner's Wood
CH
Sp Gd
HAMPSTEAD LA
B519
Camden
Mallinson Sp Ctr
Highgate Pre-Prep & Jun Sch
Kenwood House
The Spaniards Inn (PH)
N6
Open Air Stage
Ken Wood
Sandy Heath
King Alfred Sch
North End
SPANIARDS RD
A502
Mast
Hampstead Heath
26
27
28
70
47
90
89
88
87
6
5
4
3
2
1

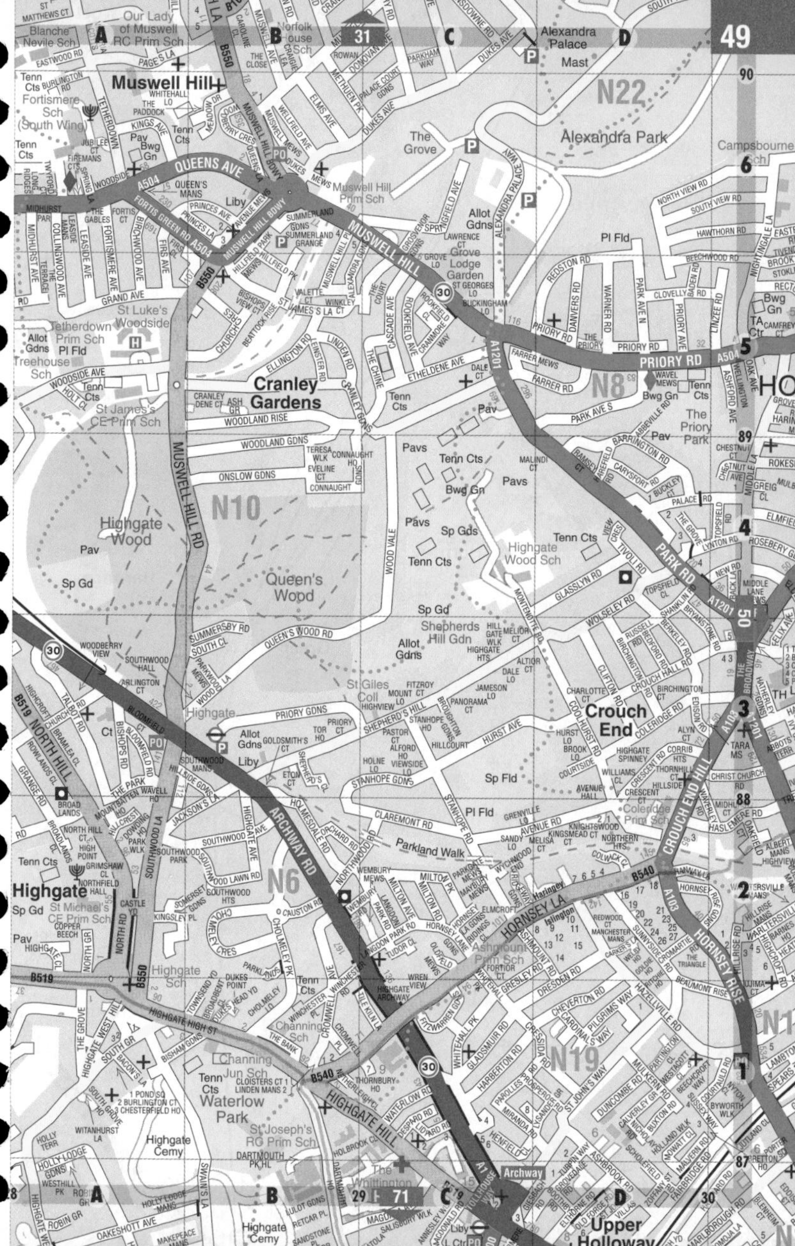
A
B
C
D
31
Muswell Hill
Alexandra Palace
Mast
N22
Alexandra Park
The Grove
Our Lady of Muswell RC Prim Sch
Blanche Nevile Sch
Norfolk House Sch
Fortismere Sch (South Wing)
Muswell Hill Prim Sch
Campsbourne Sch
QUEENS AVE
MUSWELL HILL BDWY
MUSWELL HILL
FORTIS GREEN RD
PRIORY RD
Grove Lodge Garden
Allot Gdns
Pl Fld
St Luke's Woodside
Tetherdown Prim Sch
Treehouse Sch
Cranley Gardens
St James's CE Prim Sch
N8
N10
The Priory Park
Highgate Wood
Queen's Wood
MUSWELL HILL RD
WOOD VALE
Highgate Wood Sch
PARK RD
Crouch End
Shepherds Hill Gdn
St Giles Coll
Highgate
ARCHWAY RD
HORNSEY LA
CROUCH END HILL
HORNSEY RISE
N6
N19
Coleridge Prim Sch
Parkland Walk
Highgate
St Michael's CE Prim Sch
Highgate Sch
Ashmount Prim Sch
Channing Sch
Channing Jun Sch
Waterlow Park
St Joseph's RC Prim Sch
Highgate Cemy
HIGHGATE HIGH ST
HIGHGATE HILL
NORTH HILL
Archway
Upper Holloway
The Whittington
29
71
30
50
1
2
3
4
5
6
87
88
89
90

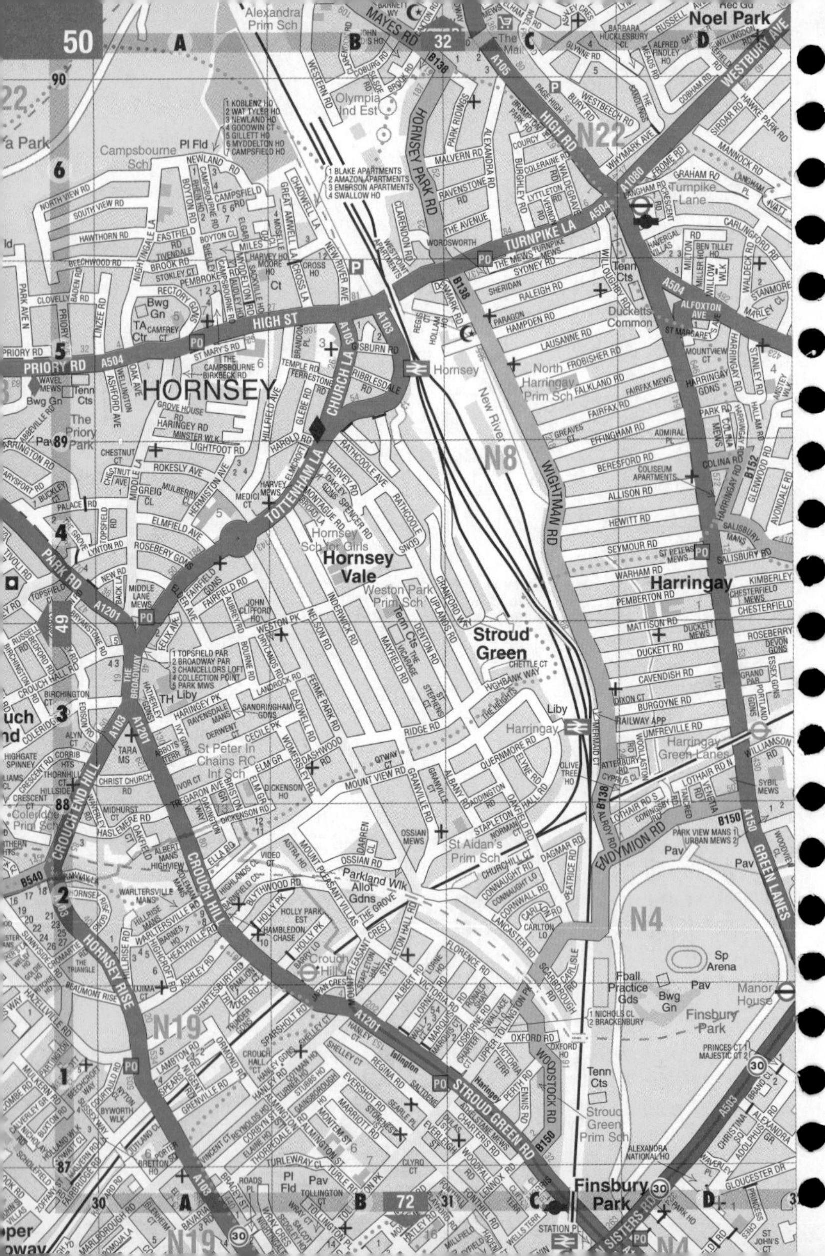

50
A
B
C
D
32
72
49
Noel Park
Alexandra Prim Sch
Olympia Ind Est
Campsbourne Sch
HORNSEY
Hornsey
The Priory Park
Hornsey Vale
Hornsey Sch for Girls
Weston Park Prim Sch
Stroud Green
Harringay
North Harringay Prim Sch
Turnpike Lane
Ducketts Common
Harringay Green Lanes
St Peter In Chains RC Inf Sch
Coleridge Prim Sch
St Aidan's Prim Sch
Parkland Wlk
Allot Gdns
Crouch Hill
Finsbury Park
Sp Arena
Fball Practice Gds
Manor House
Stroud Green Prim Sch
Finsbury Park
N22
N8
N4
N19
New River
HIGH RD
HIGH ST
PRIORY RD
TURNPIKE LA
HORNSEY PARK RD
CHURCH LA
TOTTENHAM LA
WIGHTMAN RD
GREEN LANES
CROUCH HILL
CROUCH END HILL
HORNSEY RISE
STROUD GREEN RD
PARK RD
THE BROADWAY
ENDYMION RD
WESTBURY AVE
MAYES RD
WOODSTOCK RD
SEVEN SISTERS RD
A504
A105
A103
A1201
A1080
B138
B150
B152
B540
A503

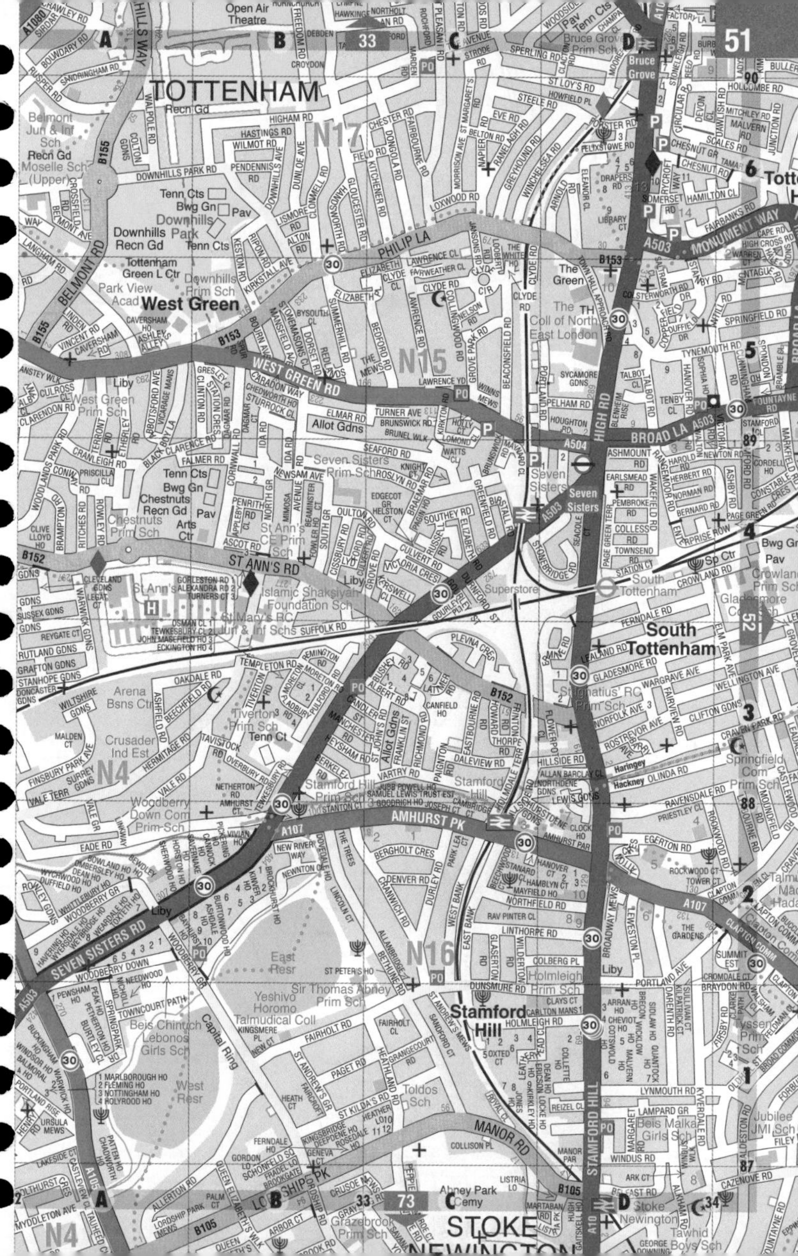
51
A
B
C
D
33
73
TOTTENHAM
N17
N15
N16
N4
West Green
South Tottenham
Stamford Hill
STOKE NEWINGTON
Tottenham Recn Gd
Downhills Park
Downhills Recn Gd
Tottenham Green L Ctr
Downhills Prim Sch
Park View Acad
Belmont Jun & Inf Sch
Moselle Sch (Upper)
West Green Prim Sch
Chestnuts Recn Gd
Chestnuts Prim Sch
Seven Sisters Prim Sch
St Ann's CE Prim Sch
Islamic Shakhsiyah Foundation Sch
St Mary's RC Jun & Inf Schs
Arena Bsns Ctr
Crusader Ind Est
Tiverton Prim Sch
Woodberry Down Com Prim Sch
Stamford Hill Prim Sch
East Resr
West Resr
Yeshivo Horomo Talmudical Coll
Sir Thomas Abney Prim Sch
Beis Chinuch Lebonos Girls Sch
Toldos Sch
Holmleigh Prim Sch
Beis Malka Girls Sch
Abney Park Cemy
Grazebrook Prim Sch
Tawhid Boys Sch
Jubilee JMI Sch
Tyssen Prim Sch
Springfield Com Prim Sch
Gladesmore Com Sch
Crowland Prim Sch
St Ignatius' RC Prim Sch
The Coll of North East London
Bruce Grove Prim Sch
Bruce Grove
Seven Sisters
South Tottenham
Stamford Hill
Superstore
Allot Gdns
Capital Ring
HIGH RD
STAMFORD HILL
WEST GREEN RD
ST ANN'S RD
SEVEN SISTERS RD
AMHURST PK
PHILIP LA
BROAD LA
MONUMENT WAY
MANOR RD
LORDSHIP PK
A10
A503
A504
A107
A105
B153
B152
B155
B105
Haringey
Hackney

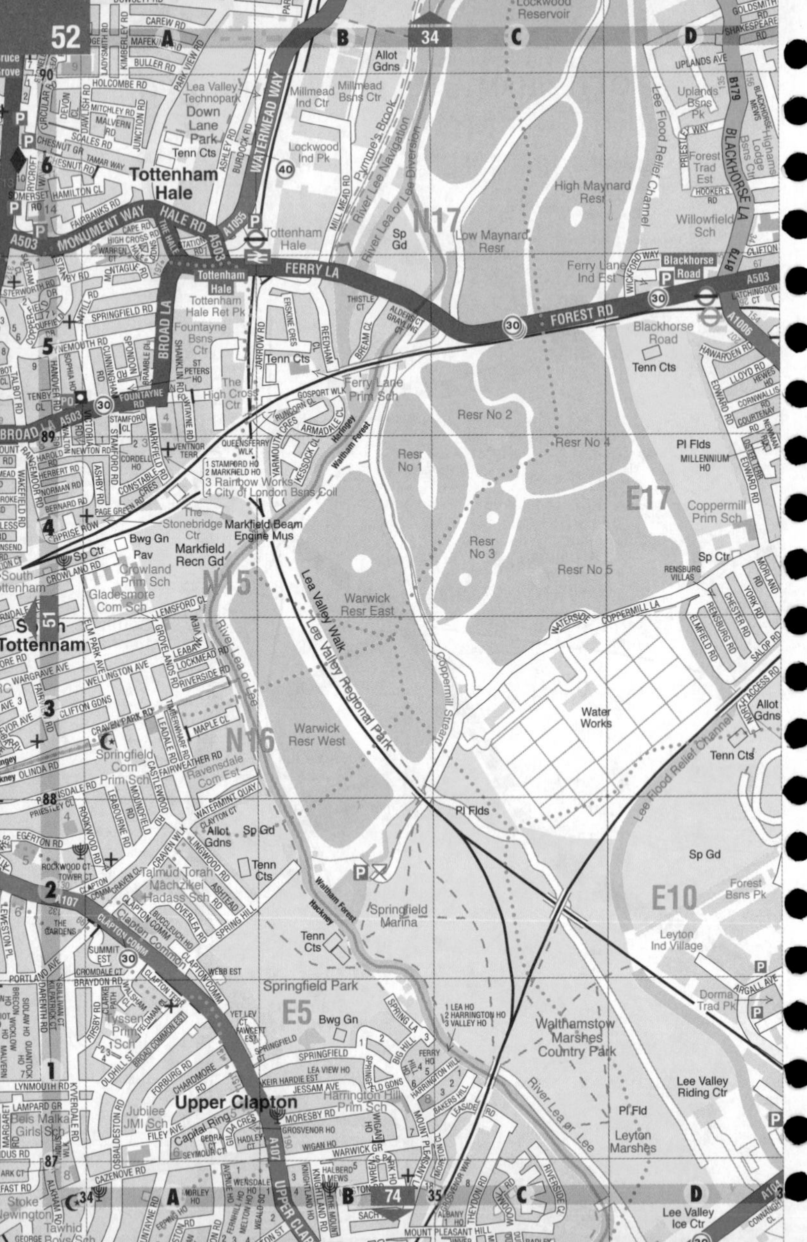

A
B
34
C
D
Lockwood Reservoir
Allot Gdns
Lea Valley Technopark
Down Lane Park
Millmead Ind Ctr
Millmead Bsns Ctr
Lockwood Ind Pk
Tenn Cts
Tottenham Hale
WATERMEAD WAY
Pymme's Brook
River Lee Navigation
River Lea or Lee Diversion
High Maynard Resr
Low Maynard Resr
Lee Flood Relief Channel
Uplands Bsns Pk
Forest Trad Est
Willowfield Sch
Blackhorse Lane Higham's Lodge Bsns Ctr
BLACKHORSE LA
N17
Sp Gd
MONUMENT WAY
HALE RD
FERRY LA
Ferry Lane Ind Est
Blackhorse Road
FOREST RD
A503
Tottenham Hale Ret Pk
Fountayne Bsns Ctr
BROAD LA
The High Cross Ctr
Ferry Lane Prim Sch
Blackhorse Road
Tenn Cts
Resr No 2
Resr No 4
Resr No 1
Pl Flds
Millennium HO
Bruce Grove
Tenby CL
BROAD LA
1 STAMFORD HO
2 MARKFIELD HO
3 Rainbow Works
4 City of London Bsns Coll
E17
Coppermill Prim Sch
The Stonebridge Ctr
Markfield Beam Engine Mus
Resr No 3
Resr No 5
Sp Ctr
Bwg Gn
Pav
Markfield Recn Gd
South Tottenham
Crowland Prim Sch
Gladesmore Com Sch
N15
Lea Valley Walk
Lee Valley Regional Park
Warwick Resr East
COPPERMILL LA
South Tottenham
51
Coppermill Stream
Water Works
River Lea or Lee
Warwick Resr West
N16
Allot Gdns
Springfield Com Prim Sch
Ravensdale Com Est
Lee Flood Relief Channel
Tenn Cts
Pl Flds
Allot Gdns
Sp Gd
Tenn Cts
Sp Gd
Talmud Torah Machzikei Hadass Sch
Springfield Marina
E10
Forest Bsns Pk
Leyton Ind Village
Clapton Common
Tenn Cts
Springfield Park
Dorma Trad Pk
E5
Bwg Gn
1 LEA HO
2 HARRINGTON HO
3 VALLEY HO
Walthamstow Marshes Country Park
Tyssen Prim Sch
Upper Clapton
Harrington Hill Prim Sch
Lee Valley Riding Ctr
Jubilee JMI Sch
Beis Malka Girls Sch
Capital Ring
Pl Fld
Leyton Marshes
River Lea or Lee
Stoke Newington
Tawhid Boys Sch
74
35
Lee Valley Ice Ctr

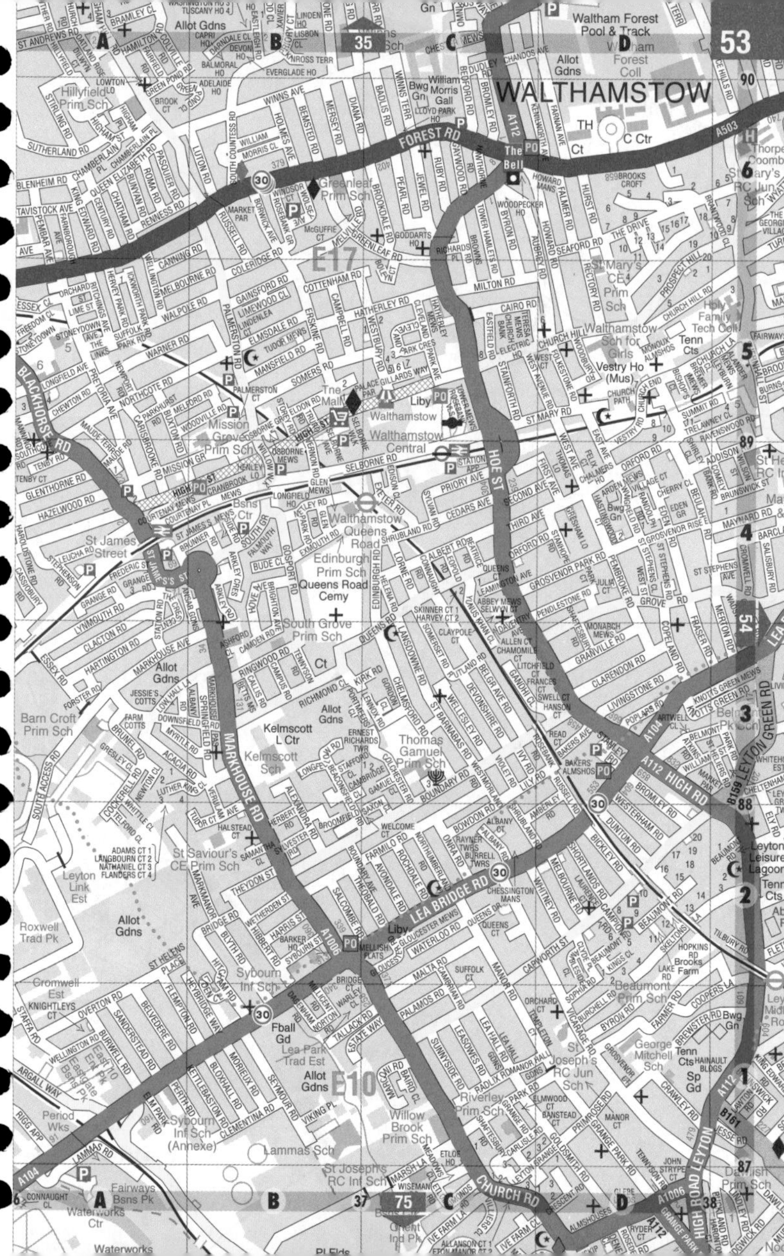

A
B
C
D
35
75
37
38
90
89
88
87
6
5
4
3
2
1
54
WALTHAMSTOW
Waltham Forest Pool & Track
Waltham Forest Coll
Allot Gdns
William Morris Gall
Bwg Gn
FOREST RD
A503
A112
The Bell
PO
TH
C Ctr
Ct
Thorpe Coombe
St Mary's RC Jun Sch
The Georgian Village
Hillyfield Prim Sch
Greenleaf Prim Sch
E17
E10
St Mary's CE Prim Sch
Holy Family Tech Coll
Walthamstow Sch for Girls
Vestry Ho (Mus)
Tenn Cts
CHURCH HILL
HOE ST
HIGH ST
The Mall
Liby
Walthamstow Central
Mission Grove Prim Sch
BLACKHORSE RD
St James Street
Walthamstow Queens Road
Edinburgh Prim Sch
Queens Road Cemy
South Grove Prim Sch
St Helen's RC Inf Sch
Maynard & Inf
Barn Croft Prim Sch
Kelmscott L Ctr
Kelmscott Sch
Thomas Gamuel Prim Sch
MARKHOUSE RD
Leyton Link Est
St Saviour's CE Prim Sch
Roxwell Trad Pk
Cromwell Est
LEA BRIDGE RD
A1006
A104
A112 HIGH RD
B159 LEYTON GREEN RD
Leyton Leisure Lagoon
Abbotts Park
Beaumont Prim Sch
Brooks Farm
Leyton Midland Road
George Mitchell Sch
Sp Gd
Sybourn Inf Sch
Fball Gd
Lea Park Trad Est
Eastgate Bsns Pk
Period Wks
Sybourn Inf Sch (Annexe)
Lammas Sch
Willow Brook Prim Sch
St Joseph's RC Jun Sch
Riverley Prim Sch
St Joseph's RC Inf Sch
Fairways Bsns Pk
Waterworks Ctr
CHURCH RD
HIGH ROAD LEYTON
B161
Dawlish Prim Sch
Waterworks

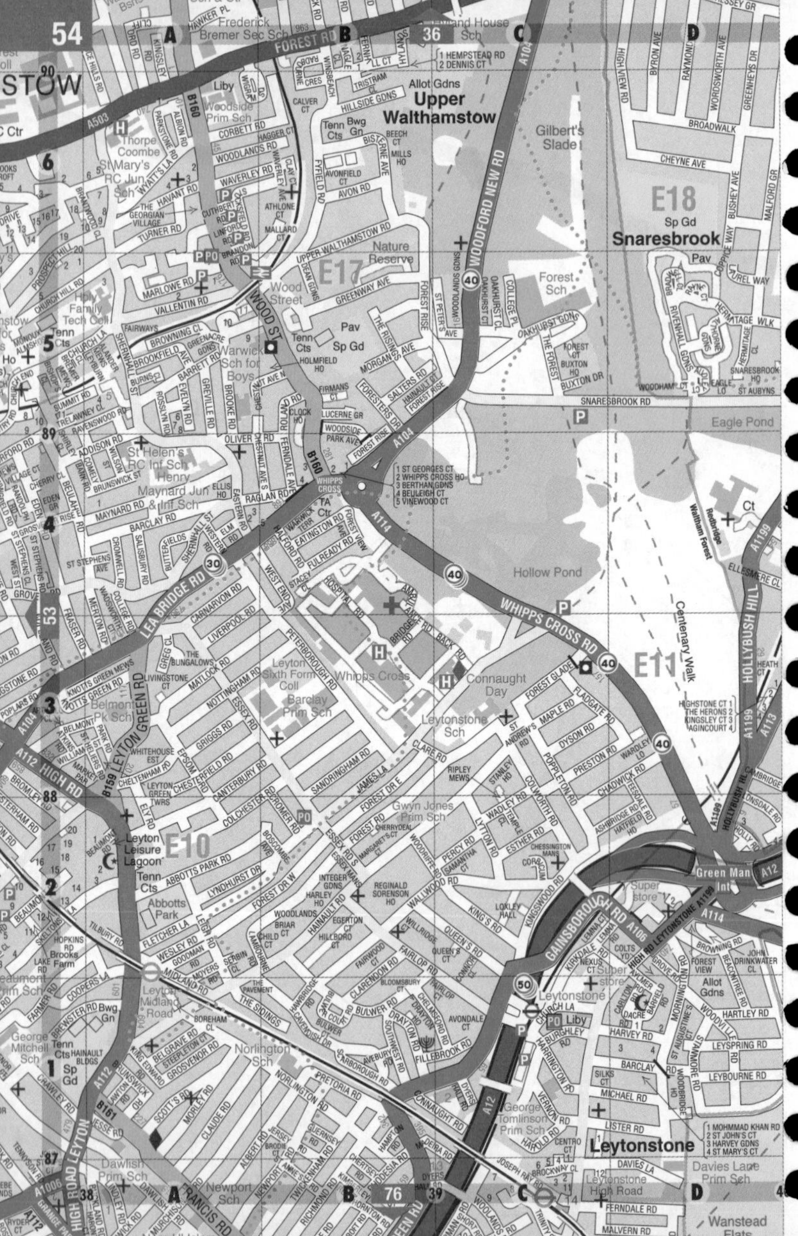

54
A
B
C
D
36
76
53
Upper Walthamstow
Snaresbrook
Leytonstone
E17
E18
E11
E10
FOREST RD
WOODFORD NEW RD
A104
A503
B160
A114
A112
A12
A106
A1199
B159
B161
WOOD ST
Wood Street
LEA BRIDGE RD
WHIPPS CROSS RD
Whipps Cross
HIGH RD
HIGH ROAD LEYTON
LEYTON GREEN RD
HOLLYBUSH HILL
SNARESBROOK RD
GAINSBOROUGH RD
HIGH RD LEYTONSTONE
Green Man Int
Eagle Pond
Hollow Pond
Centenary Walk
Gilbert's Slade
Nature Reserve
Allot Gdns
Forest Sch
Leytonstone Sch
Connaught Day
Leyton Sixth Form Coll
Barclay Prim Sch
Gwyn Jones Prim Sch
Norlington Sch
George Tomlinson Prim Sch
Davies Lane Prim Sch
Dawlish Prim Sch
Newport Sch
George Mitchell Sch
Beaumont Prim Sch
Leyton Leisure Lagoon
Abbotts Park
Brooks Farm
Leyton Midland Road
Leytonstone High Road
Wanstead Flats
Warwick Sch for Boys
St Helen's RC Inf Sch
Henry Maynard Jun & Inf Sch
Holy Family Tech Coll
Woodside Prim Sch
Thorpe Coombe
St Mary's RC Jun Sch
Frederick Bremer Sec Sch
Belmont Pk Sch
Noor Ul Islam

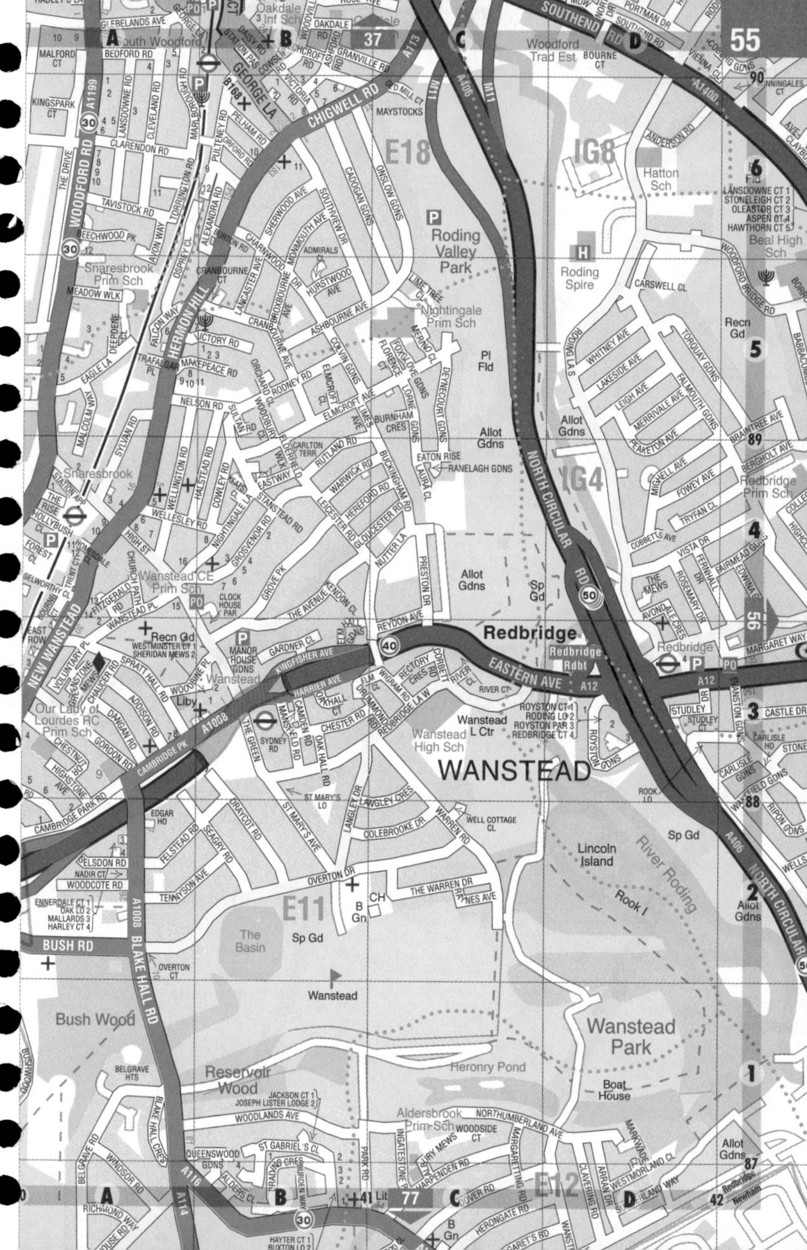

South Woodford
Woodford Trad Est
E18
IG8
Roding Valley Park
Nightingale Prim Sch
Hatton Sch
Beal High Sch
Roding Spire
Snaresbrook Prim Sch
Snaresbrook
Wanstead CE Prim Sch
Redbridge
Redbridge Prim Sch
IG4
NORTH CIRCULAR RD
EASTERN AVE
WANSTEAD
Wanstead L Ctr
Wanstead High Sch
Our Lady of Lourdes RC Prim Sch
E11
The Basin
Wanstead
Bush Wood
Reservoir Wood
Heronry Pond
Wanstead Park
Lincoln Island
River Roding
Boat House
Aldersbrook Prim Sch
E12
WOODFORD RD
HERMON HILL
CHIGWELL RD
NEW WANSTEAD
CAMBRIDGE PK
BLAKE HALL RD
BUSH RD
SOUTHEND RD
37
56
77

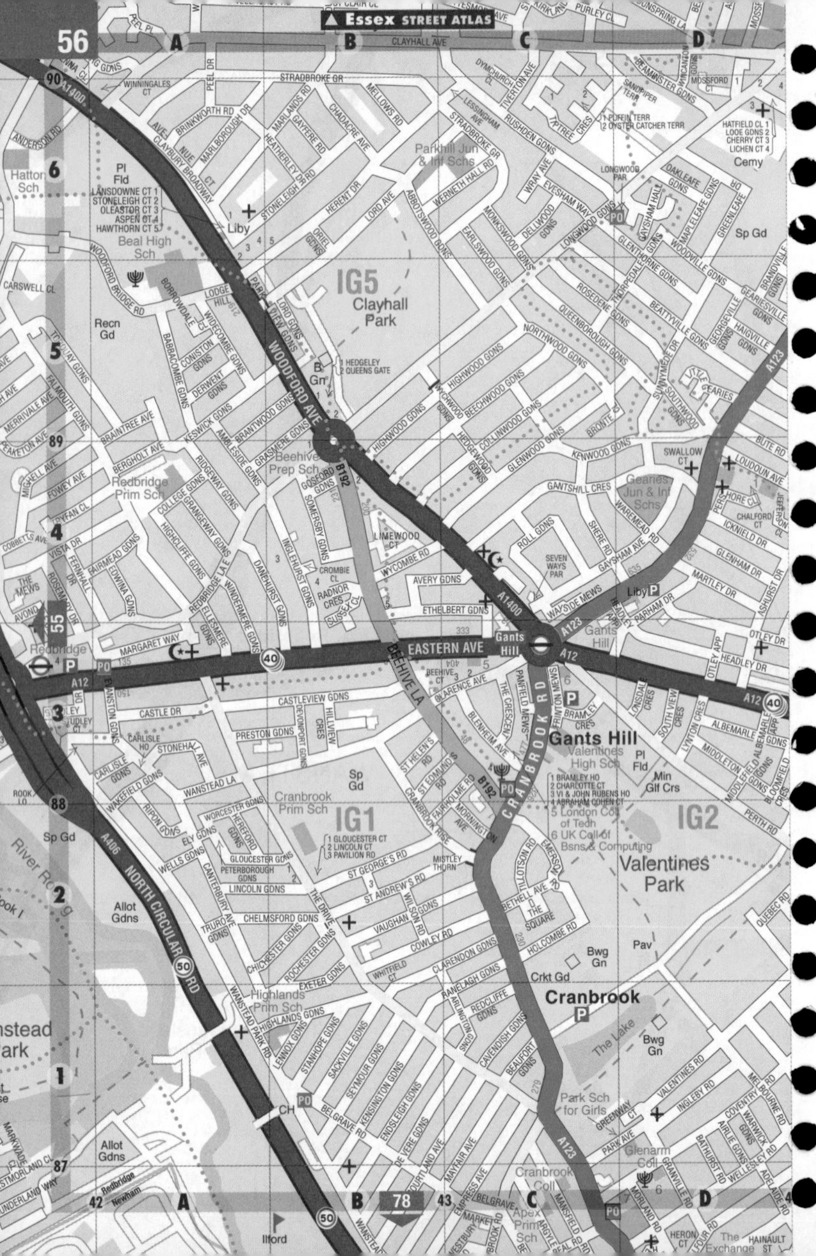
Clayhall Park
IG5
IG1
IG2
Gants Hill
Valentines Park
Cranbrook
WOODFORD AVE
EASTERN AVE
CRANBROOK RD
NORTH CIRCULAR RD
BEEHIVE LA
CLAYHALL AVE
Redbridge
Ilford
Beal High Sch
Valentines High Sch
Cranbrook Prim Sch
Highlands Prim Sch
Park Sch for Girls
The Lake

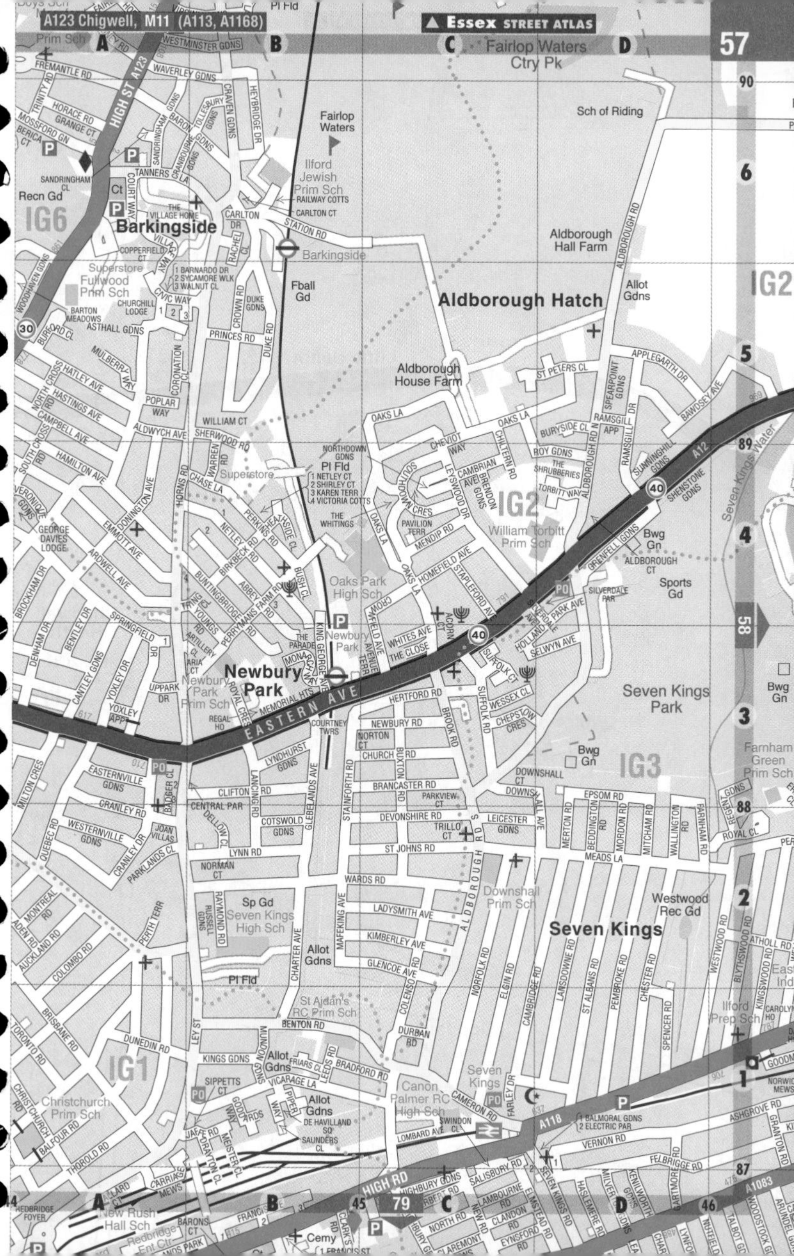
Fairlop Waters Ctry Pk
Fairlop Waters
Ilford Jewish Prim Sch
Sch of Riding
Barkingside
IG6
Aldborough Hall Farm
Aldborough Hatch
Aldborough House Farm
Fball Gd
Superstore
Fullwood Prim Sch
Recn Gd
IG2
William Torbitt Prim Sch
Oaks Park High Sch
Newbury Park
Newbury Park Prim Sch
EASTERN AVE
Seven Kings Park
IG3
Sports Gd
Bwg Gn
Farnham Green Prim Sch
Downshall Prim Sch
Seven Kings
Westwood Rec Gd
Sp Gd
Seven Kings High Sch
Allot Gdns
Pl Fld
St Aidan's RC Prim Sch
IG1
Christchurch Prim Sch
Canon Palmer RC High Sch
Ilford Prep Sch
New Rush Hall Sch
Redbridge Ent Ctr
Cemy
HIGH RD
A12
A118
A1083
58
79
HIGH ST A123
STATION RD
ALDBOROUGH RD N
ALDBOROUGH RD S
CAMERON RD
HERTFORD RD
BROOK RD
SUFFOLK RD
MEADS LA
ST JOHNS RD
WESTWOOD RD
SEVEN KINGS RD
Seven Kings Water

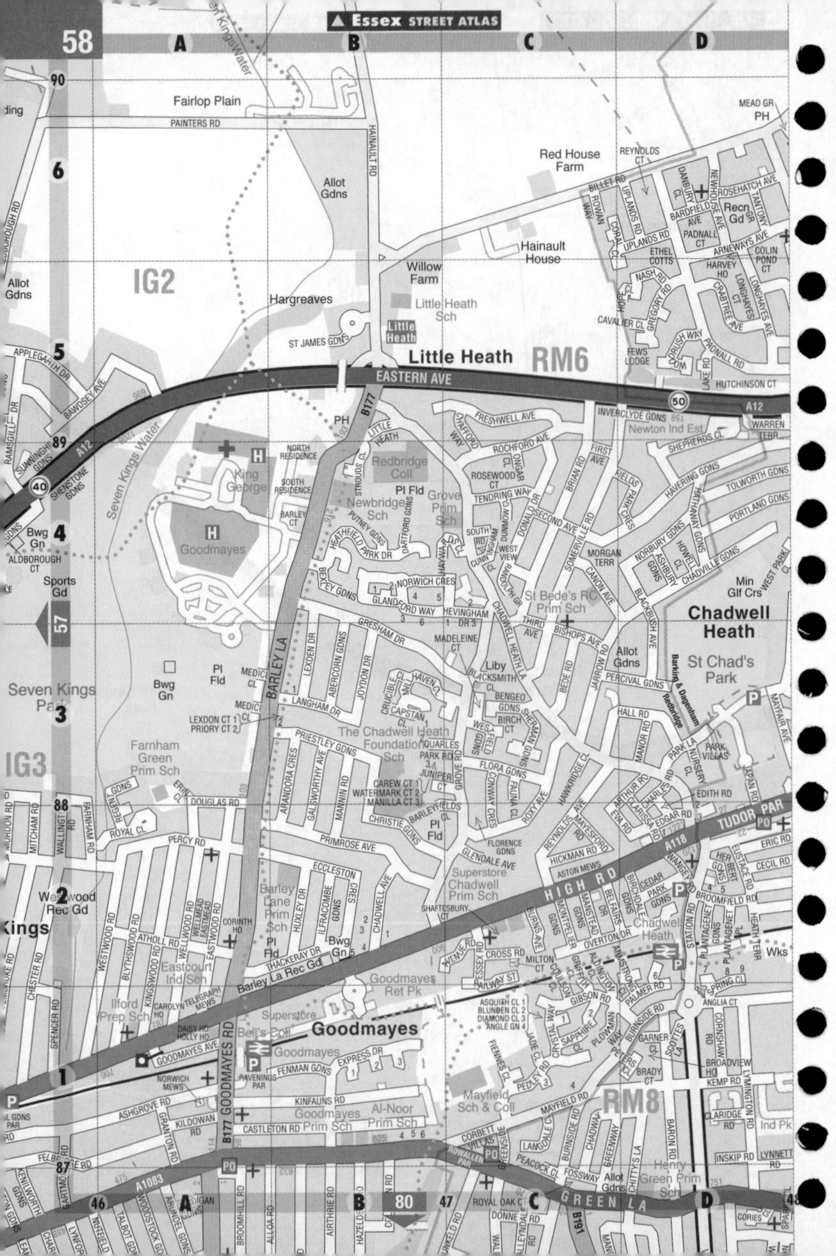
A
B
C
D
90
6
5
89
4
3
88
2
1
87
46
47
48
Fairlop Plain
PAINTERS RD
HAINAULT RD
Allot Gdns
Red House Farm
REYNOLDS CT
BILLET RD
ROWAN WAY
UPLANDS RD
CORAL CL
DANBURY CL
NEWHOUSE AVE
ROSEHATCH AVE
BARDFIELD AVE
TANTONY GR
Recn Gd
PADNALL CT
ARNEWAYS AVE
COLIN POND CT
ETHEL COTTS
HARVEY HO
NASH RD
GREGORY RD
CRABTREE AVE
LONGHAYES CT
LONGHAYES AVE
CAVALIER CL
MEAD GR
PH
Hainault House
Willow Farm
IG2
Hargreaves
Little Heath Sch
Little Heath
ST JAMES GDNS
Little Heath
RM6
FEWS LODGE
THRUSH WAY
PADNALL RD
LAKE RD
HUTCHINSON CT
EASTERN AVE
A12
50
40
APPLEGARTH DR
BAWDSEY AVE
RAMSGILL DR
SUNNINGHILL GDNS
SHENSTONE GDNS
Seven Kings Water
B177
PH
LITTLE HEATH
NORTH RESIDENCE
SOUTH RESIDENCE
King George
Goodmayes
Redbridge Coll
Pl Fld
STROUDS CL
Newbridge Sch
Grove Prim Sch
BARLEY CT
FRESHWELL AVE
CHAFFORD WAY
ROCHFORD AVE
ONGAR CL
ROSEWOOD CT
TENDRING WAY
DUNMOW CL
SECOND AVE
DONALD DR
BRIAN RD
FIRST AVE
INVERCLYDE GDNS
Newton Ind Est
SHEPHERDS CL
FIELDS PARK CRES
HAVERING GDNS
TOLWORTH GDNS
HATHAWAY GDNS
PORTLAND GDNS
NORBURY GDNS
HOWELL CL
ASHBURY GDNS
CHADVILLE GDNS
WEST PARK
Min Glf Crs
MORGAN TERR
CANON AVE
SOMERVILLE RD
WARREN TERR
Bwg Gn
ALDBOROUGH CT
Sports Gd
57
PUTNEY GDNS
DARTFORD GDNS
HEATHFIELD PARK DR
BEXLEY GDNS
NORWICH CRES
GLANDFORD WAY
HEVINGHAM DR
HAYWARDS CL
SOUTH RD
CUNNINGHAM CL
WEST VIEW
RANDOLPH GR
St Bede's RC Prim Sch
THIRD AVE
BISHOPS AVE
BLACKBUSH AVE
Chadwell Heath
St Chad's Park
Allot Gdns
JARROW RD
BEDE RD
GRESHAM DR
MADELEINE CT
CHADWELL HEATH LA
Liby
BLACKSMITH CL
BENGEO GDNS
BIRCH CT
SHERMAN GDNS
PERCIVAL GDNS
Barking & Dagenham
Redbridge
HALL RD
MANOR RD
PARK LA
PARK VILLAS
NURSERY
MAYFAIR AVE
JAPAN RD
Seven Kings Park
Pl Fld
Bwg Gn
MEDICI CL
LEXDON CT 1
PRIORY CT 2
BARLEY LA
LEXDEN DR
ABERCORN GDNS
JOYDON DR
LANGHAM DR
CRUCIBLE CL
HAVEN CL
CAPSTAN CL
WESTFIELD GDNS
The Chadwell Heath Foundation Sch
QUARLES PARK RD
JUNIPER CT
GROVE RD
FLORA GDNS
CONWAY CRES
FAUNA CL
ROXY AVE
HAWKRIDGE CL
ARTHUR RD
CHARLES RD
EDITH RD
CLARISSA RD
EVA RD
EDGAR RD
TUDOR PAR
IG3
Farnham Green Prim Sch
PRIESTLEY GDNS
ARANDORA CRES
GALSWORTHY AVE
MANNIN RD
CAREW CT 1
WATERMARK CT 2
MANILLA CT 3
BARLEYFIELDS CL
CHRISTIE GDNS
Pl Fld
FLORENCE GDNS
GLENDALE AVE
REYNOLDS AVE
MAYESFORD RD
HICKMAN RD
ASTON MEWS
A118
WANGEY RD
ERIC RD
CECIL RD
EUSTACE RD
HERBERT GDNS
BROOMFIELD RD
REGENT GDNS
ERIN CL
DOUGLAS RD
ROYAL CL
MITCHAM RD
WALLINGTON RD
FARNHAM RD
PERCY RD
PRIMROSE AVE
ECCLESTON CRES
CHADWELL AVE
Superstore
Chadwell Prim Sch
HIGH RD
BIRCHDALE GDNS
CEDAR PARK GDNS
STATION RD
PLANTAGENET GDNS
PLANTAGENET PL
HEATH TERR
Wks
Westwood Rec Gd
Kings
WESTWOOD RD
BLYTHSWOOD RD
ATHOLL RD
WELLWOOD RD
WELLMEAD
EASTMEAD
EASTWOOD RD
CORINTH HO
Barley Lane Prim Sch
HUXLEY DR
ILFRACOMBE GDNS
Pl Fld
Bwg Gn
THACKERAY DR
SHAFTESBURY CT
AVENUE RD
ESSEX RD
CROSS RD
MILTON CT
BURNS AVE
MONTPELIER GDNS
MANSTEAD GDNS
BELFAIRS DR
OVERTON DR
Chadwell Heath
ARMSTRONG CL
SPRING CL
CHESTER RD
KINGSWOOD RD
Eastcourt Ind Sch
Barley La Rec Gd
Goodmayes Ret Pk
RAILWAY ST
COULSON CL
GRIFFITH CL
ALDINGTON CL
PALMER RD
ANGLIA CT
Ilford Prep Sch
CAROLYN HO
TELEGRAPH MEWS
DAISY HO
HOLLY HO
Superstore
Bell's Coll
Goodmayes
ASQUITH CL 1
BLUNDEN CL 2
DIAMOND CL 3
ANGLE GN 4
CRYSTAL WAY
GIBSON RD
SAPPHIRE CL
PLOWMAN WAY
BURNSIDE RD
CORNSHAW RD
SPENCER RD
GOODMAYES AVE
GOODMAYES RD
Goodmayes
EXPRESS DR
FENMAN GDNS
RAVENINGS PAR
NORWICH MEWS
FIENNES CL
JADE CL
PEDLEY RD
PETERS CL
GARNER CL
SCOTTES LA
BRADY CT
BROADVIEW HO
KEMP RD
LYMINGTON RD
ASHGROVE RD
KINFAUNS RD
Mayfield Sch & Coll
MAYFIELD RD
RM8
KILDOWAN RD
GRANTON RD
Goodmayes Prim Sch
Al-Noor Prim Sch
CASTLETON RD
CLARIDGE RD
Ind Pk
CORBETT VILLAS
GREENSIDE
LANGDALE CL
BURNSIDE RD
CHADWAY
GREENWAY
CHITTY'S LA
BARON RD
INSKIP RD
LYNNETT RD
FELBRIDGE CL
ROWALLEN PAR
PEACOCK CL
FOSSWAY
Allot Gdns
Henry Green Prim Sch
A1083
PO
GREEN LA
B191
80
ROYAL OAK CT
DONNE RD
CARDIGAN GDNS
BROOMHILL RD
ALLOA RD
AIRTHRIE RD
ARUNDEL GDNS
WOODSTOCK GDNS
TALBOT GDNS
KENILWORTH GDNS
CORIES CL

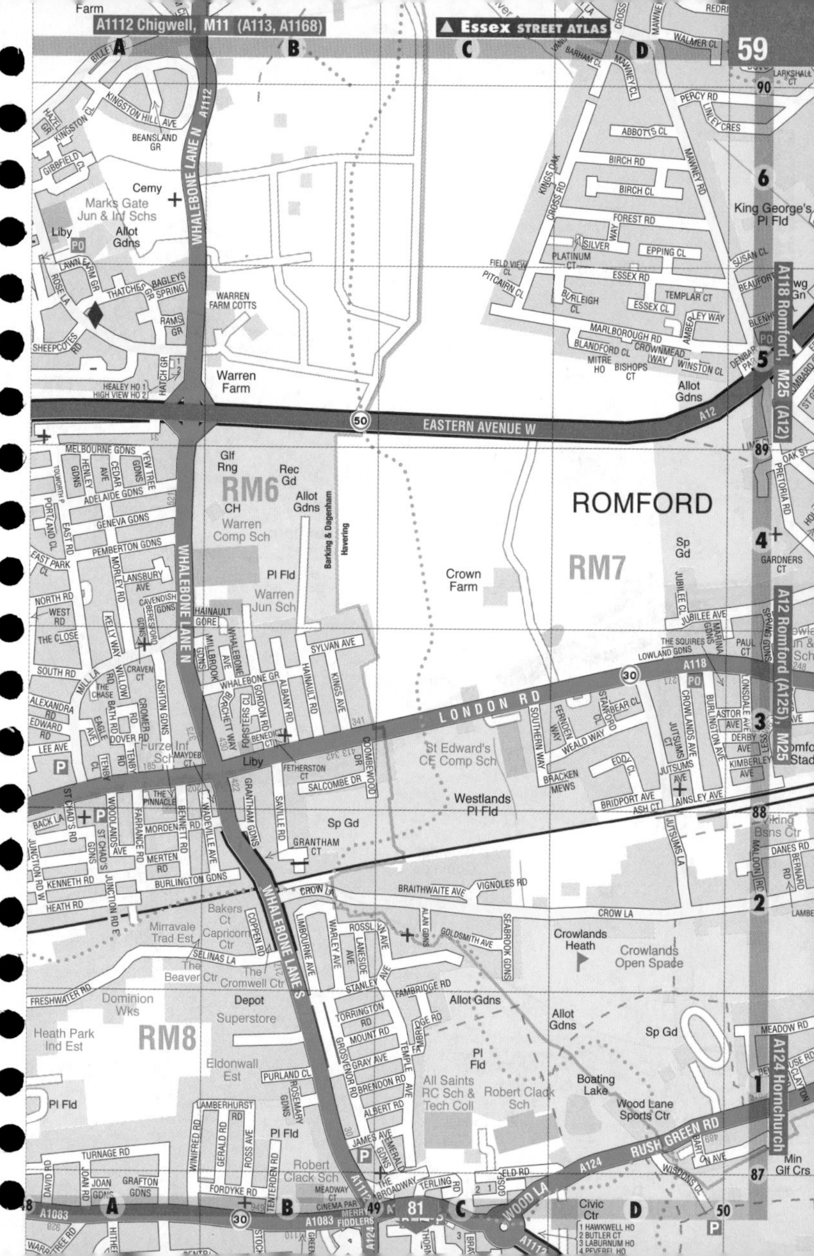

ROMFORD
RM6
RM7
RM8
WHALEBONE LANE N
WHALEBONE LANE S
EASTERN AVENUE W
LONDON RD
CROW LA
RUSH GREEN RD
WOOD LA
Marks Gate Jun & Inf Schs
Cemy
Allot Gdns
Warren Farm
Warren Comp Sch
Warren Jun Sch
Crown Farm
St Edward's CE Comp Sch
Westlands Pl Fld
Furze Inf Sch
Mirravale Trad Est
Capricorn Ctr
The Beaver Ctr
The Cromwell Ctr
Dominion Wks
Heath Park Ind Est
Superstore
Eldonwall Est
All Saints RC Sch & Tech Coll
Robert Clack Sch
Crowlands Heath
Crowlands Open Space
Boating Lake
Wood Lane Sports Ctr
King George's Pl Fld
Viking Bsns Ctr
Civic Ctr
A118 Romford, M25 (A12)
A12 Romford (A125), M25
A124 Hornchurch
1 HAWKWELL HO
2 BUTLER CT
3 LABURNUM HO
4 PEVEREL HO

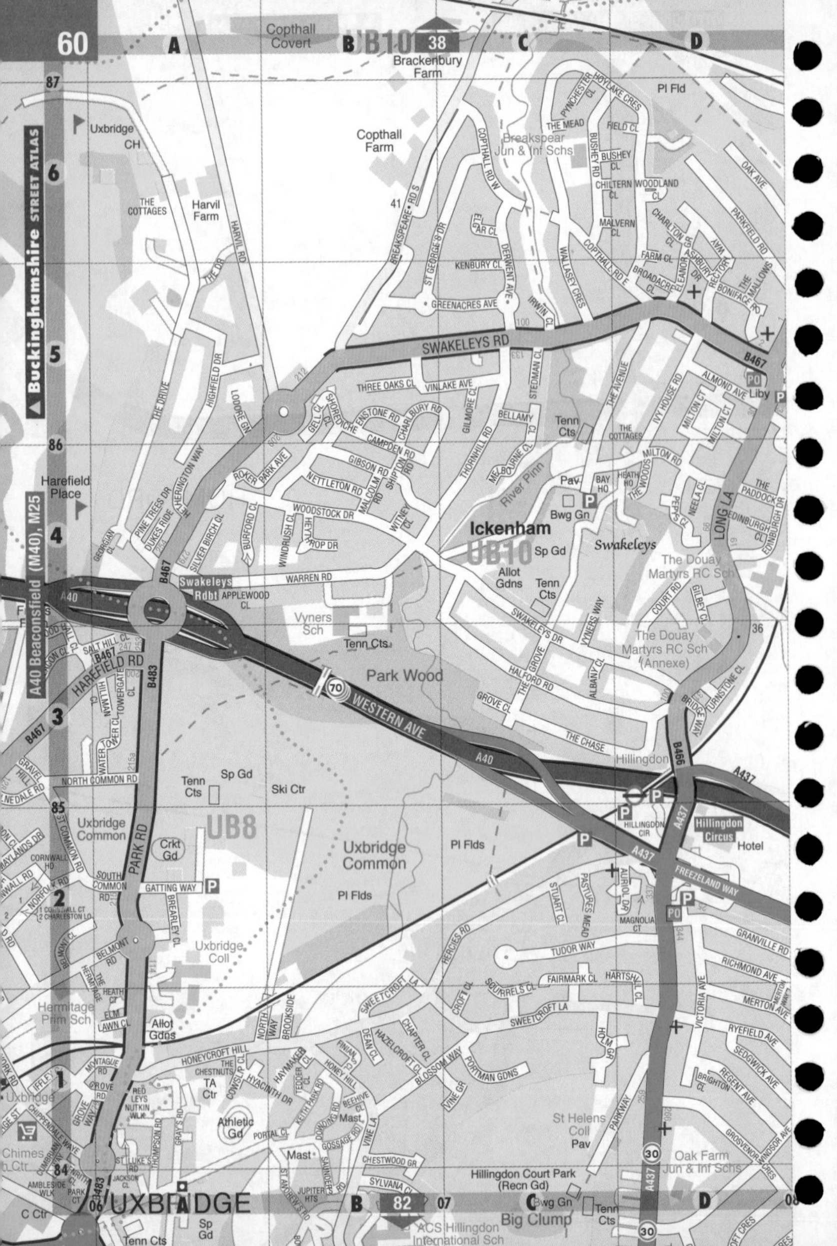

Buckinghamshire STREET ATLAS
A40 Beaconsfield (M40), M25
Copthall Covert
UB10
38
Brackenbury Farm
Copthall Farm
Uxbridge CH
Harvil Farm
THE COTTAGES
Breakspear Jun & Inf Schs
Pl Fld
SWAKELEYS RD
Harefield Place
Swakeleys Rdbt
Ickenham
UB10
Swakeleys
The Douay Martyrs RC Sch
The Douay Martyrs RC Sch (Annexe)
Vyners Sch
Tenn Cts
Park Wood
WESTERN AVE
A40
Hillingdon
Hillingdon Circus
Hotel
UB8
Ski Ctr
Uxbridge Common
Pl Flds
Uxbridge Coll
Hermitage Prim Sch
Allot Gdns
TA Ctr
Athletic Gd
St Helens Coll
Oak Farm Jun & Inf Schs
Hillingdon Court Park (Recn Gd)
UXBRIDGE
82
Big Clump
ACS Hillingdon International Sch
Chimes
C Ctr
LONG LA
FREEZELAND WAY
PARK RD
HAREFIELD RD

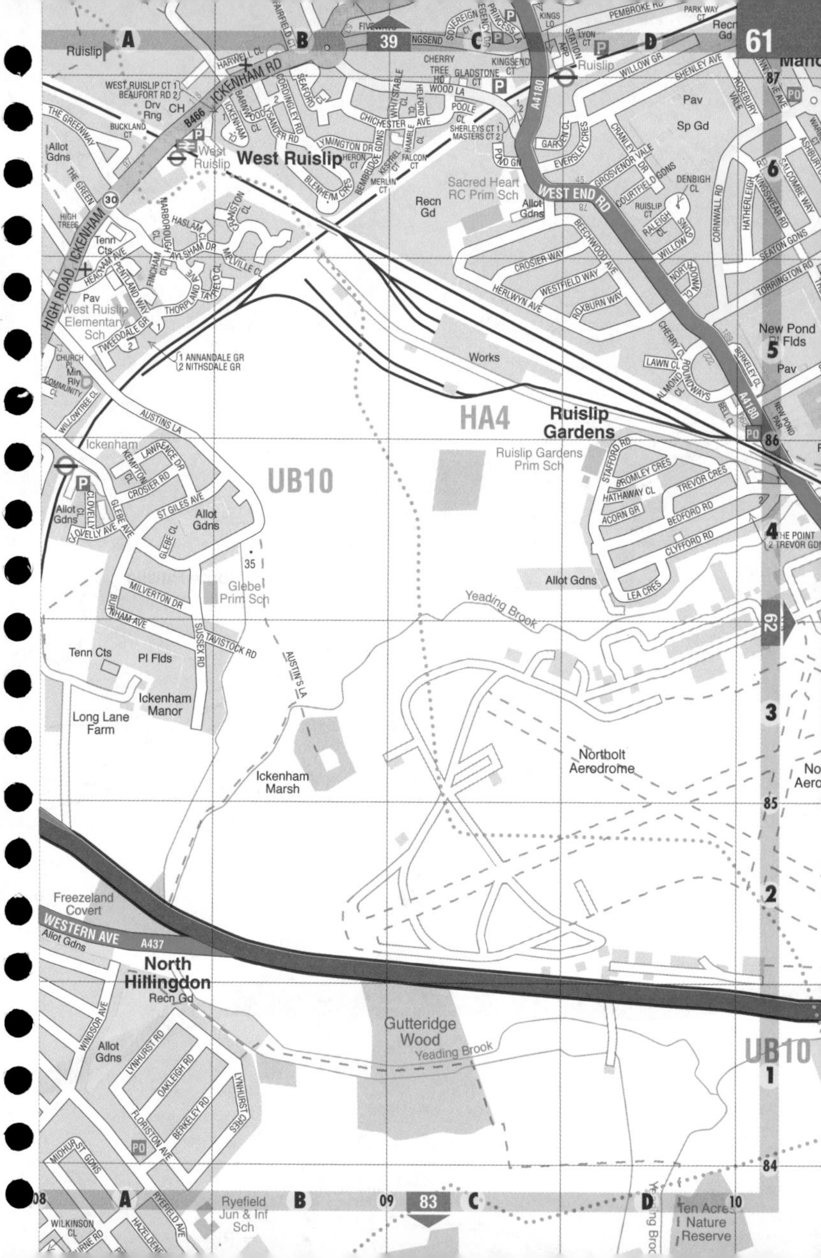

39
Ruislip
West Ruislip
ICKENHAM RD
B466
HIGH ROAD, ICKENHAM
30
WEST RUISLIP CT 1
BEAUFORT RD 2
Drv Rng
CH
BUCKLAND CT
THE GREENWAY
Allot Gdns
THE GREEN
HIGH TREES
Tenn Cts
Pav
West Ruislip Elementary Sch
HEACHAM AVE
PENTLAND WAY
TWEEDDALE GR
CHURCH PL
Min Rly
COMMUNITY CL
WILLOWTREE CL
1 ANNANDALE GR
2 NITHSDALE GR
HASLAM CL
NARBOROUGH CL
AYLSHAM DR
FINCHAM CL
THORPLAND AVE
TAYFIELD CL
MELVILLE CL
CRANSTON CL
HARWELL CL
CORDINGLEY RD
LYSANDER RD
SEAFORD
BARNWOOD CL
ICKENHAM CL
LYMINGTON DR
BLENHEIM CRES
HERON CT
BEMBRIDGE GDNS
KESTREL CT
MERLIN CT
FALCON CT
CHICHESTER AVE
WHITSTABLE CL
HAMBLE CL
HELFORD CL
WOOD LA
POOLE CL
SHERLEYS CT 1
MASTERS CT 2
CHERRY TREE HO
GLADSTONE CT
KINGSEND CT
SOVEREIGN
REGENCY DR
PRINCESS LA
KINGS LO
LYON CT
STATION APP
PEMBROKE RD
PARK WAY
Recn Gd
WILLOW GR
SHENLEY AVE
ROSEBURY VALE
A4180
GARDEN CL
POND GN
EVERSLEY CRES
CRANLEY DR
GROSVENOR VALE
COURTFIELD GDNS
DENBIGH CL
RUISLIP CT
RALEIGH CL
WILLOW GDNS
Pav
Sp Gd
CORNWALL RD
HATHERLEIGH RD
KINGSWEAR RD
SALCOMBE WAY
ASHBURTON
SEATON GDNS
TORRINGTON RD
6
Sacred Heart RC Prim Sch
Recn Gd
Allot Gdns
WEST END RD
CROSIER WAY
BEECHWOOD AVE
WESTFIELD WAY
HERLWYN AVE
ROXBURN WAY
NORTH VIEW CL
CHERRY CL
LAWN CL
ALMOND CL
ROUNDWAYS
BELL CL
BERKELEY CL
NEW POND PAR
New Pond Pl Flds
5
Pav
Works
HA4
Ruislip Gardens
Ruislip Gardens Prim Sch
STAFFORD RD
BROMLEY CRES
HATHAWAY CL
TREVOR CRES
ACORN GR
BEDFORD RD
CLYFFORD RD
LEA CRES
Allot Gdns
4
1 THE POINT
2 TREVOR GDNS
62
AUSTINS LA
Ickenham
KEMPTON CL
LAWRENCE DR
CROSIER RD
CLOVELLY CL
CLOVELLY AVE
GLEBE AVE
ST GILES AVE
GLEBE CL
Allot Gdns
UB10
35
Glebe Prim Sch
MILVERTON DR
BURNHAM AVE
SUSSEX RD
TAVISTOCK RD
AUSTIN'S LA
Yeading Brook
Tenn Cts
Pl Flds
Ickenham Manor
Long Lane Farm
Ickenham Marsh
Northolt Aerodrome
3
85
2
Freezeland Covert
WESTERN AVE
A437
Allot Gdns
North Hillingdon
Recn Gd
WINDSOR AVE
LYNHURST RD
OAKLEIGH RD
BERKELEY RD
LYNHURST CRES
FLORISTON AVE
MIDHURST GDNS
Gutteridge Wood
Yeading Brook
UB10
1
84
08
A
RYEFIELD AVE
WILKINSON CL
HAZELDENE
Ryefield Jun & Inf Sch
B
09
83
C
D
10
Ten Acres Nature Reserve

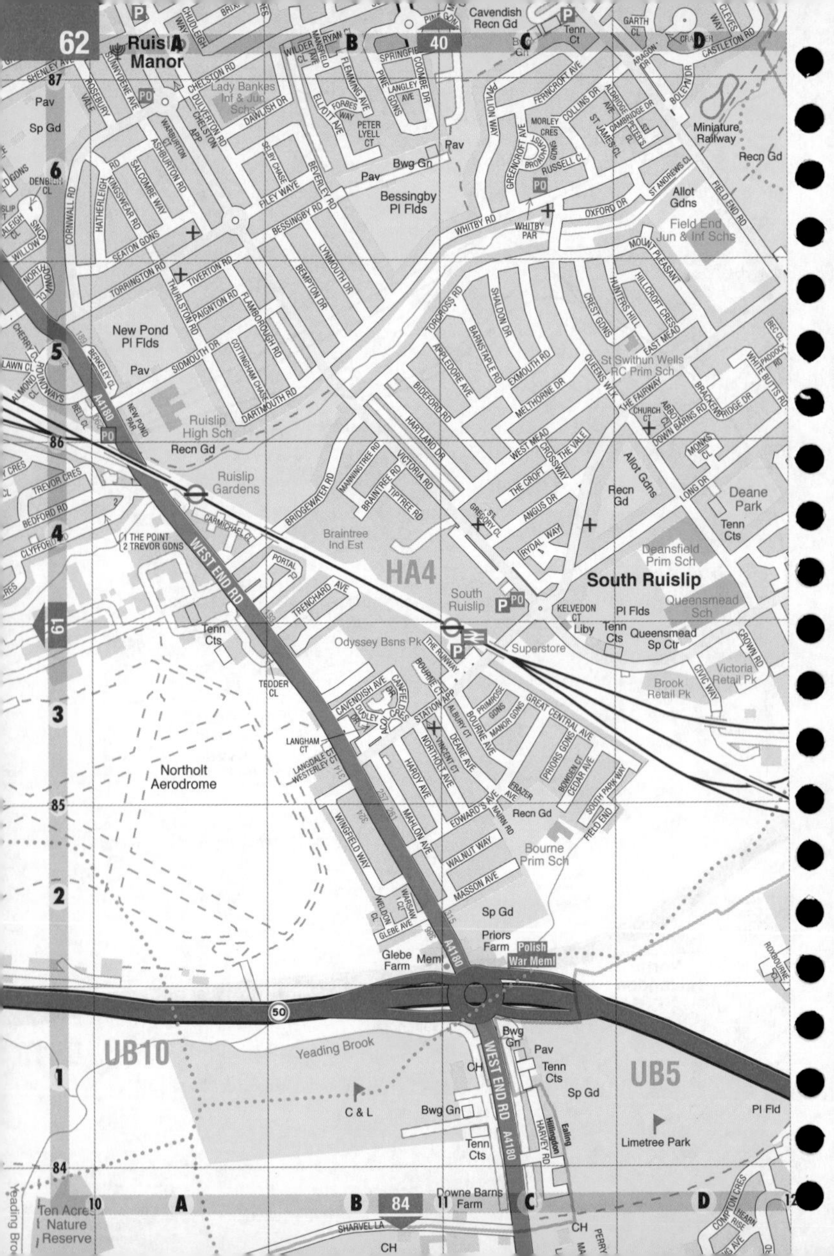
Ruislip Manor
Cavendish Recn Gd
Lady Bankes Inf & Jun Schs
Bessingby Pl Flds
Miniature Railway
Recn Gd
Allot Gdns
Field End Jun & Inf Schs
New Pond Pl Flds
Ruislip High Sch
Recn Gd
Ruislip Gardens
Braintree Ind Est
St Swithun Wells RC Prim Sch
Deane Park
Deansfield Prim Sch
HA4
South Ruislip
Queensmead Sch
Queensmead Sp Ctr
Odyssey Bsns Pk
Superstore
Victoria Retail Pk
Brook Retail Pk
Northolt Aerodrome
Bourne Prim Sch
Priors Farm
Polish War Meml
Glebe Farm
UB10
Yeading Brook
UB5
Limetree Park
Downe Barns Farm
Ten Acres Nature Reserve
WEST END RD
A4180
SHARVEL LA
40
61
84
50

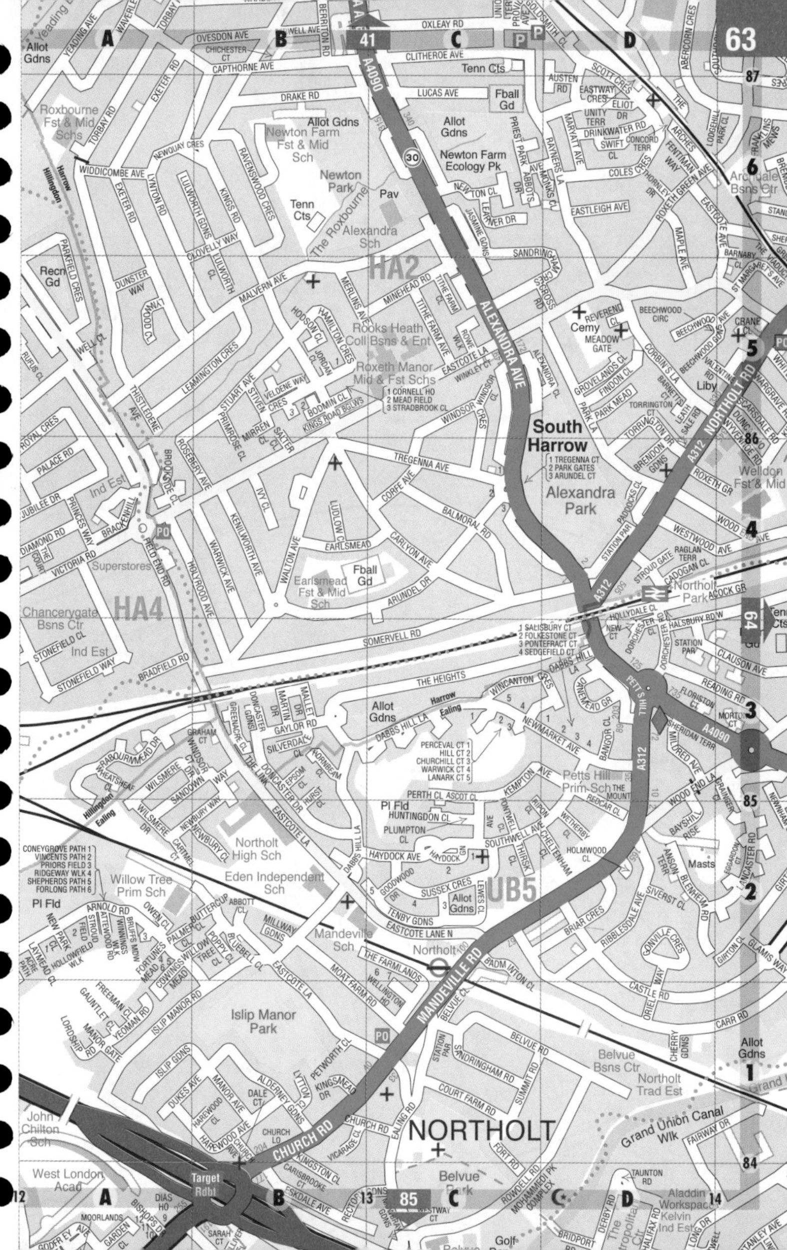
A
B
C
D
41
87
86
85
84
64
85
12
13
14
6
5
4
3
2
1
A4090
A312
HA2
HA4
UB5
South Harrow
NORTHOLT
Harrow
Hillingdon
Ealing
OXLEAY RD
OVESDON AVE
CHICHESTER CT
CAPTHORNE AVE
CLITHEROE AVE
Tenn Cts
DRAKE RD
LUCAS AVE
Fball Gd
Allot Gdns
Roxbourne Fst & Mid Schs
Newton Farm Fst & Mid Sch
Newton Farm Ecology Pk
Newton Park
The Roxbourne
Pav
Alexandra Sch
WIDDICOMBE AVE
NEWQUAY CRES
EXETER RD
LYNTON RD
LULLWORTH GDNS
KINGS RD
RAVENSWOOD CRES
TORBAY RD
CLOVELLY WAY
DUNSTER WAY
MALVERN AVE
MERLINS AVE
MINEHEAD RD
TITHE FARM AVE
TITHE FARM CL
ALEXANDRA AVE
SANDRINGHAM CRES
JASMINE GDNS
NEWTON CL
LEAMNER DR
PRIEST PARK AVE
ABBOTS DR
MONKS CL
RAYNERS LA
MARYATT AVE
AUSTEN RD
EASTWAY CRES
ELIOT DR
UNITY TERR
DRINKWATER RD
SWIFT CL
CONCORD TERR
COLES CRES
EASTLEIGH AVE
ROXETH GREEN AVE
FENTIMAN WAY
ARCHES
MAPLE AVE
EASTCOTE AVE
Archdale Bsns Ctr
BREMBER RD
STANLEY RD
Recn Gd
PARKFIELD CRES
Rooks Heath Coll Bsns & Ent
Roxeth Manor Mid & Fst Schs
1 CORNELL HO
2 MEAD FIELD
3 STRADBROOK CL
HODSON CL
HAMILTON CRES
JORDAN CL
STIVEN CRES
VELDENE WAY
BODMIN CL
KINGS ROAD BGLWS
EASTCOTE LA
WINKLEY CT
ROWE WLK
WINDSOR CRES
LEAMINGTON CRES
STUART AVE
PRIMROSE CL
MIRREN CL
SALTER CL
WELL CL
RUFUS CL
THISTLEDENE AVE
ROSEBERY AVE
ROYAL CRES
PALACE RD
JUBILEE DR
PRINCES WAY
BRACKENHILL
BROOKSIDE CL
DIAMOND RD
THE COURT
VICTORIA RD
Ind Est
Superstores
FIELD END RD
Chancerygate Bsns Ctr
STONEFIELD CL
STONEFIELD WAY
BRADFIELD RD
HOLYROOD AVE
WARWICK AVE
KENILWORTH AVE
IVY CL
WALTON AVE
LUDLOW CL
EARLSMEAD
CARLYON AVE
Earlsmead Fst & Mid Sch
ARUNDEL DR
TREGENNA AVE
CORFE AVE
BALMORAL RD
1 TREGENNA CT
2 PARK GATES
3 ARUNDEL CT
Alexandra Park
SOMERVELL RD
Cemy
REVEREND CL
MEADOW GATE
GROVELANDS CL
FINDON CL
PARK MEAD
PARK LA
CORBIN'S LA
BARNETTS CT
TORRINGTON CT
TORRINGTON DR
BRENDON GDNS
SALE PL
PADDOCKS CL
STATION PAR
BEECHWOOD CIRC
BEECHWOOD GDNS
CRANE CT
NORTHOLT RD
Liby
WHITBY RD
WARGRAVE RD
SCARSDALE RD
ROXETH GR
Welldon Park Fst & Mid Sch
WOOD END AVE
WESTWOOD AVE
RAGLAN TERR
STROUD GATE
CADOGAN CL
Northolt Park
ACOCK GR
HOLLYDALE CL
HALSBURY RD W
DORCHESTER RD
CLAUSON AVE
READING RD
FLORISTON CT
MORTON CT
SHERIDAN TERR
1 SALISBURY CT
2 FOLKESTONE CT
3 PONTEFRACT CT
4 SEDGEFIELD CT
DABBS HILL LA
THE HEIGHTS
WINCANTON CRES
NEWMARKET AVE
BANGOR CL
PETTS HILL
MILDRED AVE
WOOD END LA
BAYSHILL RISE
PERCEVAL CT 1
HILL CT 2
CHURCHILL CT 3
WARWICK CT 4
LANARK CT 5
Pl Fld
PERTH CL
ASCOT CL
HUNTINGDON CL
PLUMPTON CL
KEMPTON AVE
FONTWELL CL
RIPON CL
WETHERBY CL
Petts Hill Prim Sch
THE MOUNT
REDCAR CL
SOUTHWELL AVE
CHELTENHAM
THIRSK CL
HOLMWOOD CL
HAYDOCK AVE
GOODWOOD DR
SUSSEX CRES
LEWES CL
TENBY GDNS
Allot Gdns
EASTCOTE LANE N
Northolt
MANDEVILLE RD
BADMINTON CL
BRIAR CRES
RIBBLESDALE AVE
SIVERST CL
CONVILLE CRES
ANSON TERR
BLENHEIM RD
Masts
LANCASTER RD
GIRTON CL
GLAMIS WAY
CASTLE RD
ORIEL WAY
CARR RD
CHERRY GDNS
BELVUE RD
Belvue Bsns Ctr
Northolt Trad Est
Grand Union Canal Wlk
FAIRWAY DR
DONCASTER DR
GREENACRE CL
MARTIN DR
MALLET DR
GAYLOR RD
SILVERDALE
HORNBEAM
EPSOM CL
HURST CL
THE LINK
RABOURNMEAD DR
GRAHAM CT
WINDSOR CR
WHEATSHEAF
WILSMERE DR
SANDOWN WAY
NEWBURY WAY
NEWBURY CL
CARTMEL
Northolt High Sch
Eden Independent Sch
Willow Tree Prim Sch
CONEYGROVE PATH 1
VINCENTS PATH 2
PRIORS FIELD 3
RIDGEWAY WLK 4
SHEPHERDS PATH 5
FORLONG PATH 6
OWEN CL
BUTTERCUP
ABBOTT CL
MILLWAY GDNS
Mandeville Sch
ARNOLD RD
NEW PARK CL
HOLLOWFIELD WLK
STROUD FIELD
ATTEWOOD RD
BRUFFS MDW
WINNINGS WLK
FORTUNES MEAD
PALMER CL
COWINGS MEAD
WILLOW TREE CL
POPPY CL
BLUEBELL CL
EASTCOTE LA
THE FARMLANDS
MOAT FARM RD
WELLINGTON HO
LAYMEAD CL
ACRE PATH
FREEMAN CL
GAUNTLET CL
YEOMAN RD
LORDSHIP RD
MANOR GATE
ISLIP MANOR RD
Islip Manor Park
ISLIP GDNS
DUKES AVE
MANOR AVE
HAREWOOD CL
HAREWOOD AVE
DALE CT
ALDERNEY GDNS
LYTTON CL
PETWORTH CL
KINGSMEAD DR
CHURCH RD
CHURCH LO
VICARAGE CL
KINGSTON CL
CARISBROOKE
ESKDALE AVE
RECTORY
EALING RD
STATION PAR
SANDRINGHAM RD
COURT FARM RD
SUMMIT RD
FORT RD
ROWDELL RD
MOHAMMEDI PK COMPLEX
John Chilton Sch
West London Acad
Target Rdbt
DIAS HO
MOORLANDS
GARDEN CL
BISHOPS
SARAH CT
WESTWAY CT
Belvue Park
TAUNTON RD
DERBY RD
The Metropolitan Ctr
HALIFAX RD
Aladdin Workspace
Kelvin Ind Est
LONG DR
Golf
BRIDPORT
STANLEY AVE

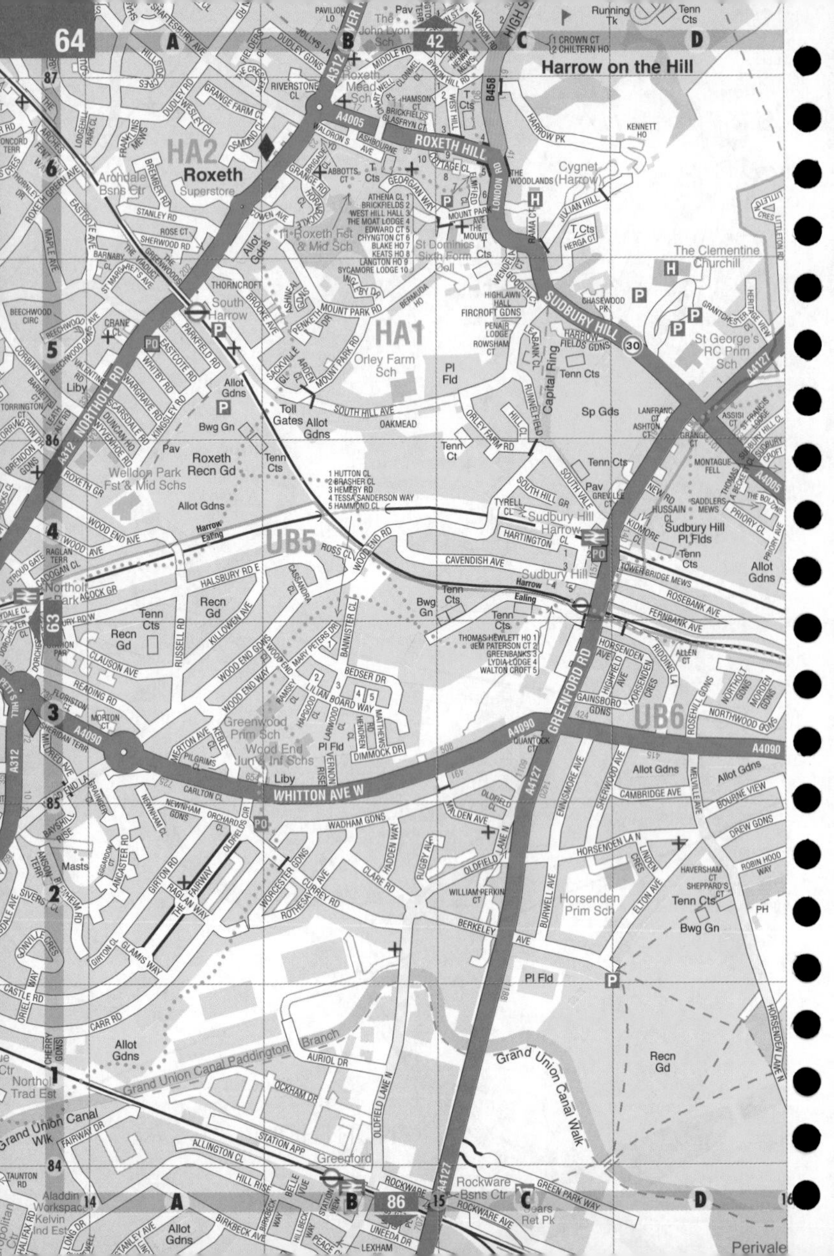

42
Harrow on the Hill
HA2
Roxeth
HA1
UB5
UB6
ROXETH HILL
SUDBURY HILL
NORTHOLT RD
GREENFORD RD
WHITTON AVE W
LONDON RD
A4090
A4127
A312
A4005
South Harrow
Sudbury Hill Harrow
Sudbury Hill
Northolt Park
Greenford
Orley Farm Sch
Roxeth Recn Gd
Welldon Park Fst & Mid Schs
Greenwood Prim Sch
Wood End Jun & Inf Schs
Horsenden Prim Sch
St George's RC Prim Sch
The Clementine Churchill
St Dominics Sixth Form Coll
Roxeth Fst & Mid Sch
Roxeth Mead Sch
The John Lyon Sch
Cygnet (Harrow)
Capital Ring
Grand Union Canal Paddington Branch
Grand Union Canal Walk
Northolt Trad Est
Rockware Bsns Ctr
Sears Ret Pk
Aladdin Workspace
Kelvin Ind Est
Perivale
A
B
C
D
86

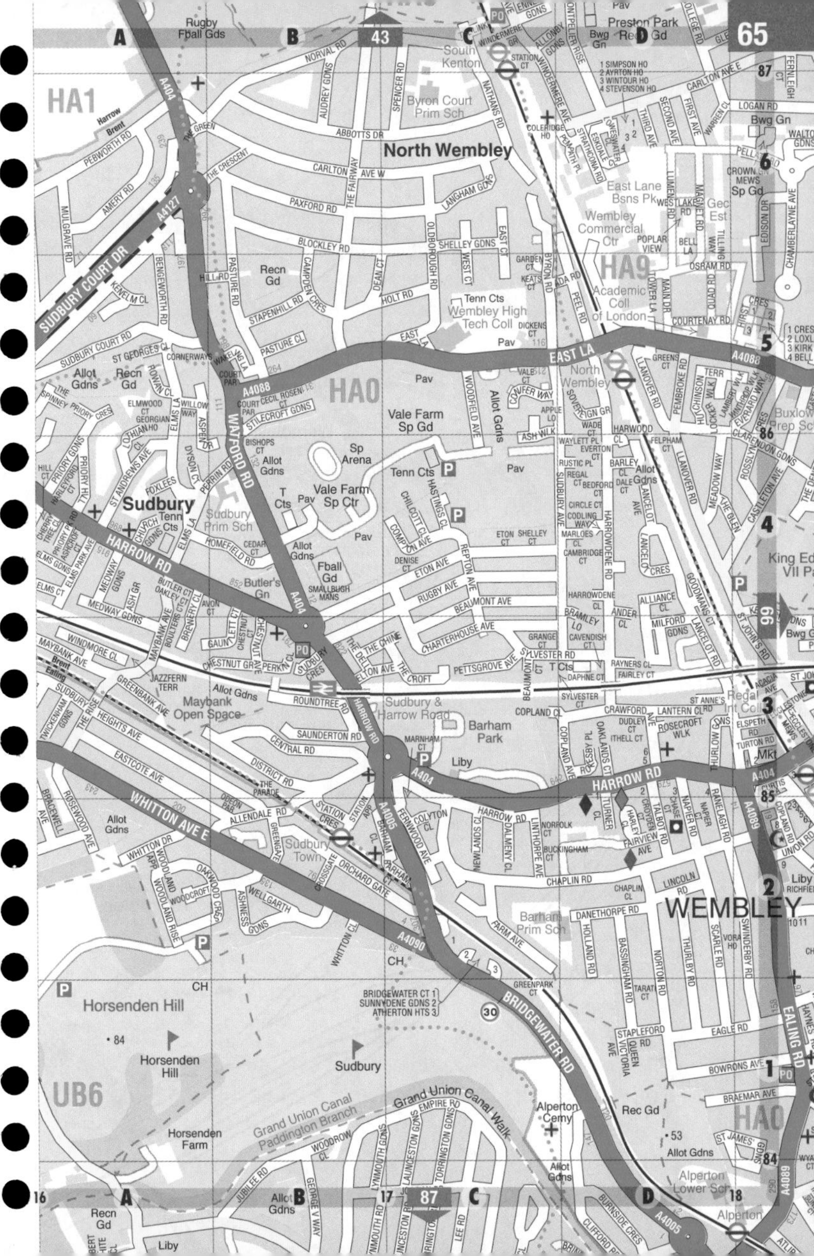
North Wembley
Sudbury
WEMBLEY
South Kenton
Preston Park
Byron Court Prim Sch
East Lane Bsns Pk
Wembley Commercial Ctr
Academic Coll of London
Wembley High Tech Coll
Vale Farm Sp Gd
Vale Farm Sp Ctr
Sp Arena
Sudbury Prim Sch
Butler's Gn
Maybank Open Space
Sudbury & Harrow Road
Barham Park
Sudbury Town
Barham Prim Sch
Horsenden Hill
Horsenden Farm
Grand Union Canal Paddington Branch
Grand Union Canal Walk
Alperton Cemy
Alperton Lower Sch
Alperton
Buxlow Prep Sch
King Edw VII Par
Regal Int Coll
HA1
HA0
HA9
UB6
WATFORD RD
HARROW RD
EAST LA
SUDBURY COURT DR
WHITTON AVE E
BRIDGEWATER RD
EALING RD
A404
A4088
A4127
A4005
A4090
A4089
BRIDGEWATER CT 1
SUNNYDENE GDNS 2
ATHERTON HTS 3
1 SIMPSON HO
2 AYRTON HO
3 WINTOUR HO
4 STEVENSON HO
1 CRESSW
2 LOXLEY
3 KIRK HO
4 BELL HO

43
87
66

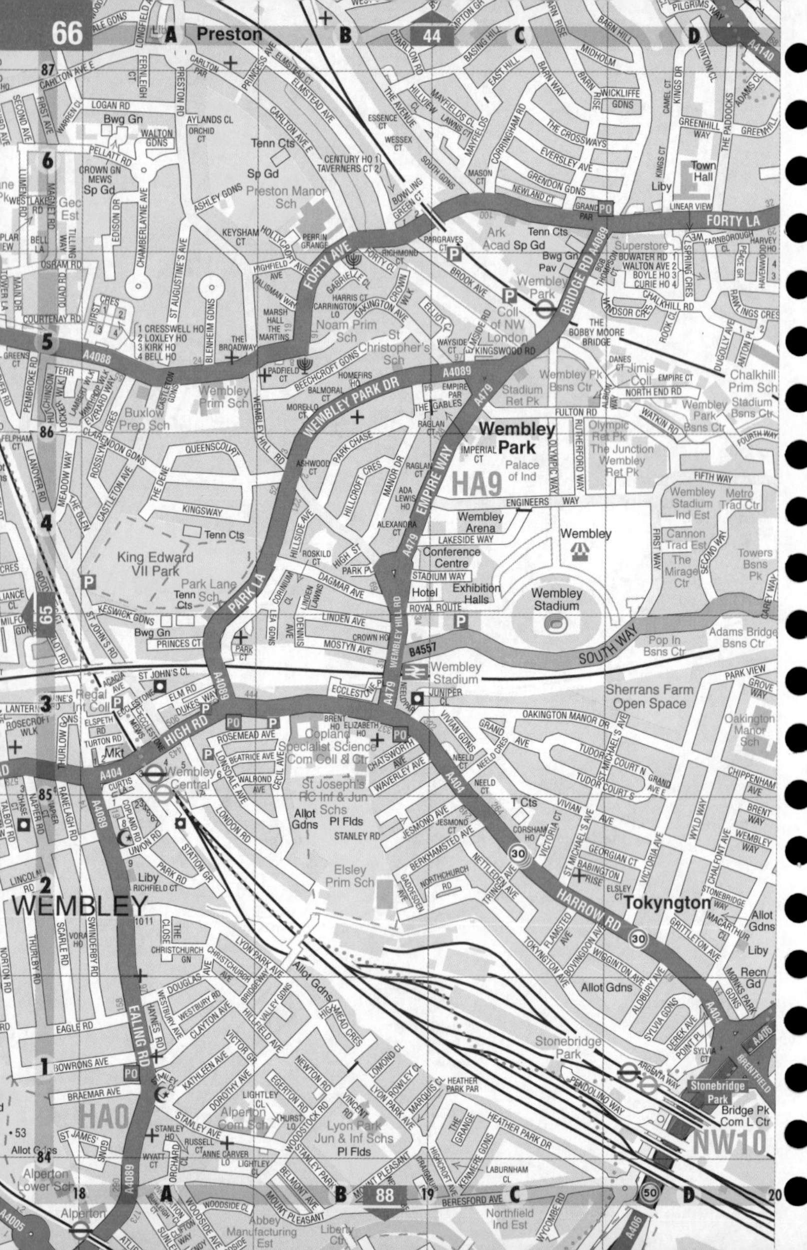
Preston
44
FORTY LA
FORTY AVE
WEMBLEY PARK DR
A4089
A4088
A479
EMPIRE WAY
BRIDGE RD
Wembley Park
HA9
Palace of Ind
Wembley Arena
Wembley
Conference Centre
Exhibition Halls
Wembley Stadium
SOUTH WAY
B4557
King Edward VII Park
PARK LA
HIGH RD
A404
Wembley Central
WEMBLEY
HAO
EALING RD
HARROW RD
Tokyngton
Stonebridge Park
NW10
Sherrans Farm Open Space
Preston Manor Sch
Noam Prim Sch
St Christopher's Sch
Wembley Prim Sch
Buxlow Prep Sch
Park Lane Sch
Copland Specialist Science Com Coll & Ctr
St Joseph's RC Inf & Jun Schs
Elsley Prim Sch
Alperton Com Sch
Lyon Park Jun & Inf Schs
Alperton Lower Sch
Abbey Manufacturing Est
Northfield Ind Est
Bridge Pk Com L Ctr
Chalkhill Prim Sch
Wembley Stadium Ind Est
Metro Trad Ctr
Cannon Trad Est
Towers Bsns Pk
Adams Bridge Bsns Ctr
Pop In Bsns Ctr
Oakington Manor Sch
Town Hall
Olympic Ret Pk
The Junction Wembley Ret Pk
Stadium Ret Pk
Wembley Pk Bsns Ctr
Ark Acad
Coll of NW London
65
88
A B C D
18 19 20

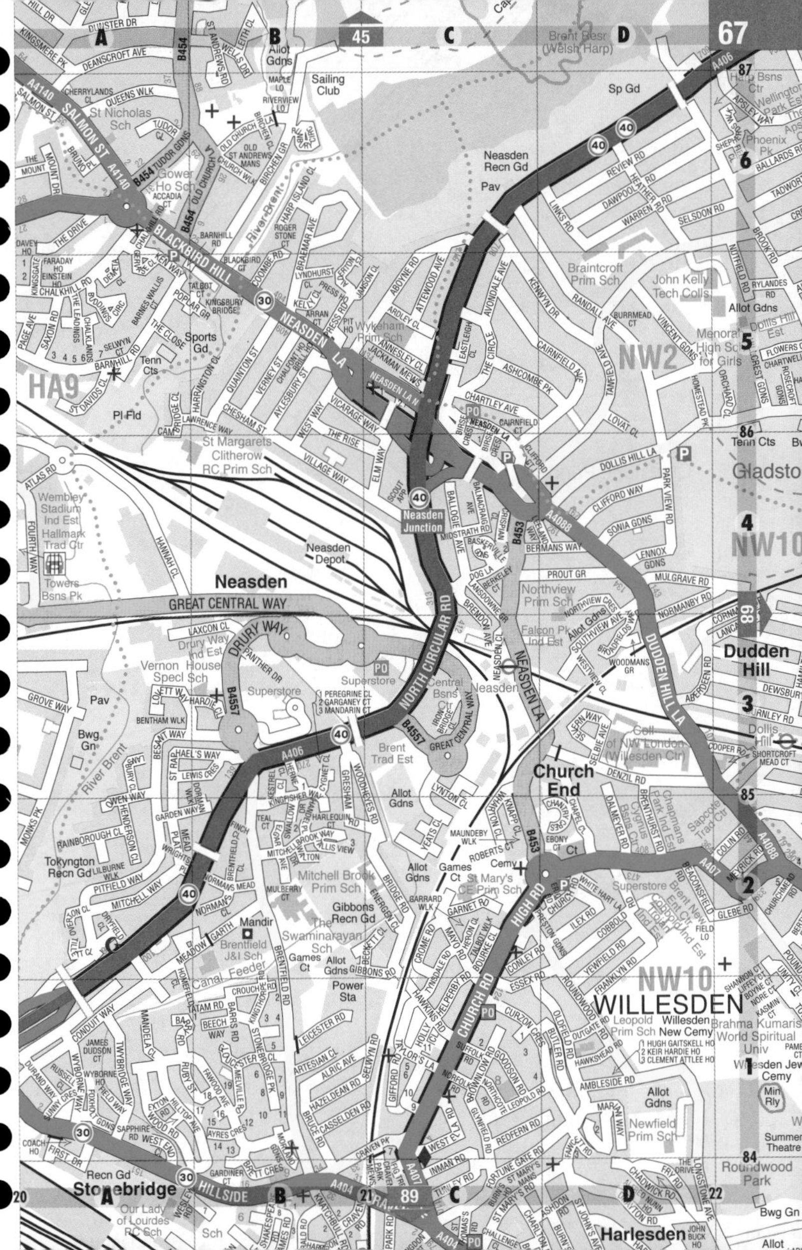
A
B
C
D
45
Brent Resr (Welsh Harp)
Sailing Club
Sp Gd
Allot Gdns
St Nicholas Sch
Gower Ho Sch
Neasden Recn Gd
Pav
SALMON ST
BLACKBIRD HILL
NEASDEN LA
Braintcroft Prim Sch
John Kelly Tech Colls
Allot Gdns
Menorah High Sch for Girls
Wykeham Prim Sch
Sports Gd
Tenn Cts
HA9
NW2
Pl Fld
St Margarets Clitherow RC Prim Sch
DOLLIS HILL LA
Gladstone
Tenn Cts
Wembley Stadium Ind Est
Hallmark Trad Ctr
Towers Bsns Pk
Neasden Junction
Neasden Depot
Neasden
NW10
GREAT CENTRAL WAY
NORTH CIRCULAR RD
DUDDEN HILL LA
Northview Prim Sch
Falcon Pk Ind Est
Dudden Hill
Drury Way Ind Est
Vernon House Specl Sch
Superstore
Central Bsns Ctr
Brent Trad Est
Pav
Bwg Gn
River Brent
Coll of NW London (Willesden Ctr)
Church End
Dollis Hill
Allot Gdns
Tokyngton Recn Gd
Mitchell Brook Prim Sch
Gibbons Recn Gd
Mandir
The Swaminarayan Sch
Brentfield J&I Sch
Games Ct
Allot Gdns
Power Sta
St Mary's CE Prim Sch
Cemy
Chapmans Park Ind Est
Cygnus Bsns Ctr
Sapcote Trad Ctr
Superstore
Brent New Ent Ctr
HIGH RD
CHURCH RD
NW10
WILLESDEN
Leopold Prim Sch
Willesden New Cemy
Brahma Kumaris World Spiritual Univ
Willesden Jewish Cemy
Allot Gdns
Newfield Prim Sch
Summer Theatre
Roundwood Park
Recn Gd
Stonebridge
HILLSIDE
Our Lady of Lourdes RC Sch
Sch
89
Harlesden
Bwg Gn
Allot
20
21
22
84
85
86
87
1
2
3
4
5
6

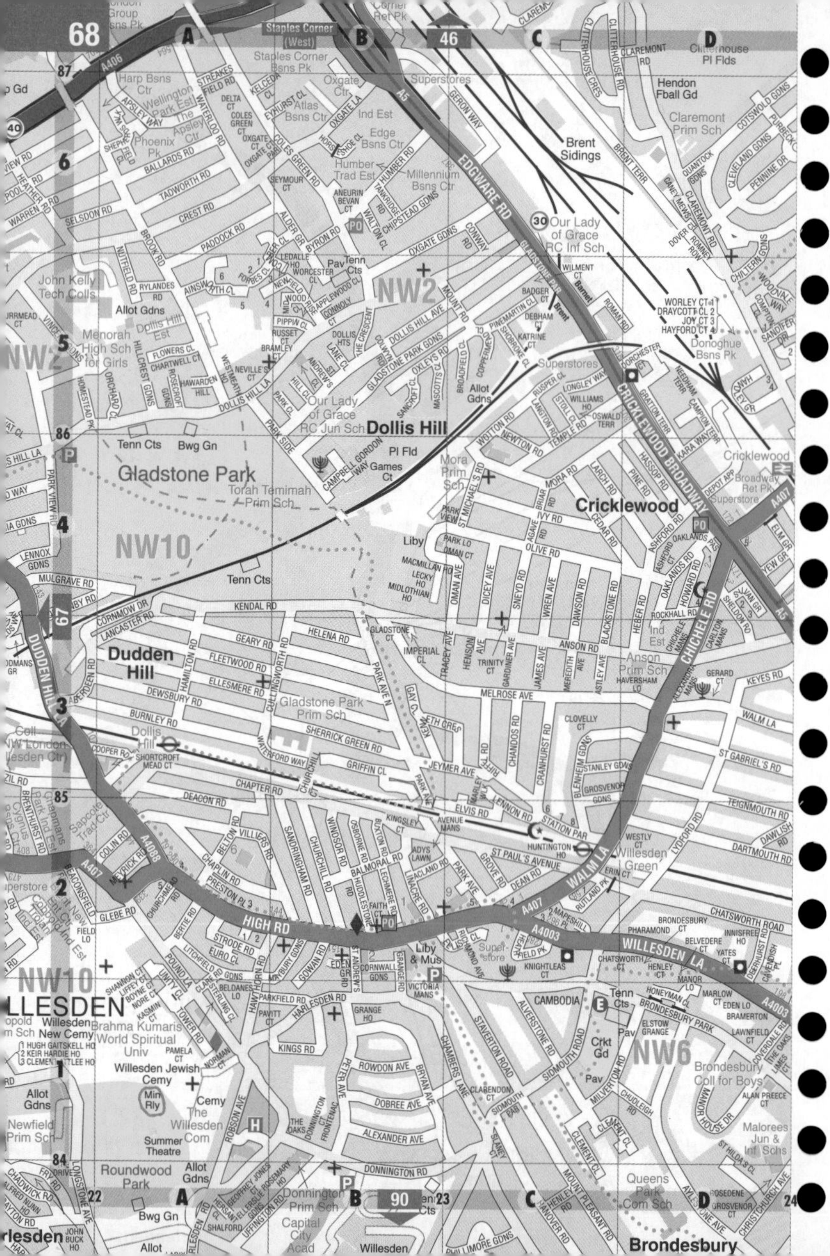
A
B
C
D
46
Staples Corner (West)
Staples Corner Bsns Pk
Clitterhouse Pl Flds
Hendon Fball Gd
Claremont Prim Sch
Brent Sidings
Superstores
Oxgate Ctr
Atlas Bsns Ctr
Ind Est
Edge Bsns Ctr
Humber Trad Est
Millennium Bsns Ctr
Harp Bsns Ctr
Wellington Park Est
The Apsley Ctr
Phoenix Pk
EDGWARE RD
A5
A406
CLITTERHOUSE CRES
CLITTERHOUSE RD
CLAREMONT RD
BRENT TERR
STREAKES FIELD RD
WATERLOO RD
APSLEY WAY
BALLARDS RD
TADWORTH RD
CREST RD
SELSDON RD
WARREN RD
PADDOCK RD
BROOK RD
NUTFIELD RD
RYLANDES RD
COLES GREEN RD
HUMBER RD
CHIPSTEAD GDNS
OXGATE GDNS
CONWAY RD
GERON WAY
Our Lady of Grace RC Inf Sch
Our Lady of Grace RC Jun Sch
John Kelly Tech Colls
Allot Gdns
Menorah High Sch for Girls
Dollis Hill Est
NW2
DOLLIS HILL AVE
DOLLIS HILL LA
GLADSTONE PARK GDNS
MOUNT RD
CRICKLEWOOD BROADWAY
Dollis Hill
Pl Fld
Games Ct
Tenn Cts
Bwg Gn
Gladstone Park
Torah Temimah Prim Sch
Mora Prim Sch
Cricklewood
Broadway Ret Pk
Superstore
Donoghue Bsns Pk
NW10
Liby
KENDAL RD
CORNMOW DR
LANCASTER RD
DUDDEN HILL LA
Dudden Hill
GEARY RD
HELENA RD
FLEETWOOD RD
ELLESMERE RD
DEWSBURY RD
BURNLEY RD
HAMILTON RD
CULLINGWORTH RD
Gladstone Park Prim Sch
SHERRICK GREEN RD
WATERFORD WAY
GRIFFIN CL
CHAPTER RD
DEACON RD
Dollis Hill
OLIVE RD
IVY RD
MORA RD
ANSON RD
MELROSE AVE
Anson Prim Sch
CHICHELE RD
WALM LA
ST GABRIEL'S RD
TEIGNMOUTH RD
DARTMOUTH RD
Willesden Green
STATION PAR
ST PAUL'S AVENUE
HIGH RD
A407
A4003
A4088
WILLESDEN LA
CHATSWORTH ROAD
Coll of NW London (Willesden Ctr)
Sapcote Trad Ctr
Liby & Mus
Super-store
CAMBODIA
Tenn Cts
Crkt Gd
Pav
NW6
Brondesbury Coll for Boys
BRONDESBURY PARK
WILLESDEN
Willesden New Cemy
Brahma Kumaris World Spiritual Univ
Willesden Jewish Cemy
Cemy
The Willesden Com
Summer Theatre
Allot Gdns
Newfield Prim Sch
Roundwood Park
Bwg Gn
Donnington Prim Sch
Capital City Acad
Queens Park Com Sch
Malorees Jun & Inf Schs
STAVERTON ROAD
CHAMBERS LANE
SIDMOUTH ROAD
ALEXANDER AVE
DONNINGTON RD
90
22
23
24
Brondesbury
Harlesden
67
1
2
3
4
5
6
84
85
86
87

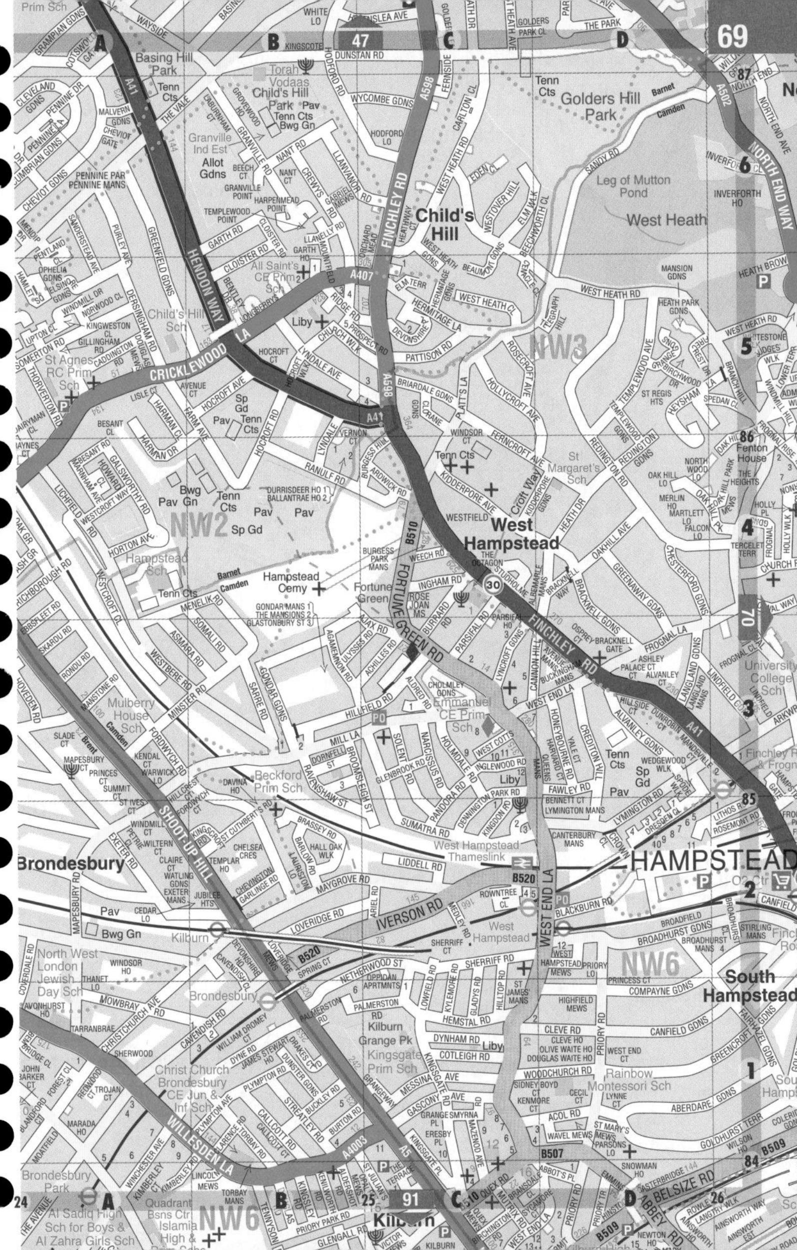

Child's Hill
West Hampstead
HAMPSTEAD
Brondesbury
South Hampstead
Kilburn
NW2
NW3
NW6
Golders Hill Park
West Heath
Leg of Mutton Pond
Hampstead Cemy
Fortune Green
Kilburn Grange Pk
Brondesbury Park
FINCHLEY RD
HENDON WAY
CRICKLEWOOD LA
FORTUNE GREEN RD
WEST END LA
SHOOT-UP HILL
WILLESDEN LA
IVERSON RD
WEST HEATH RD
NORTH END WAY
West Hampstead Thameslink
47
70
91

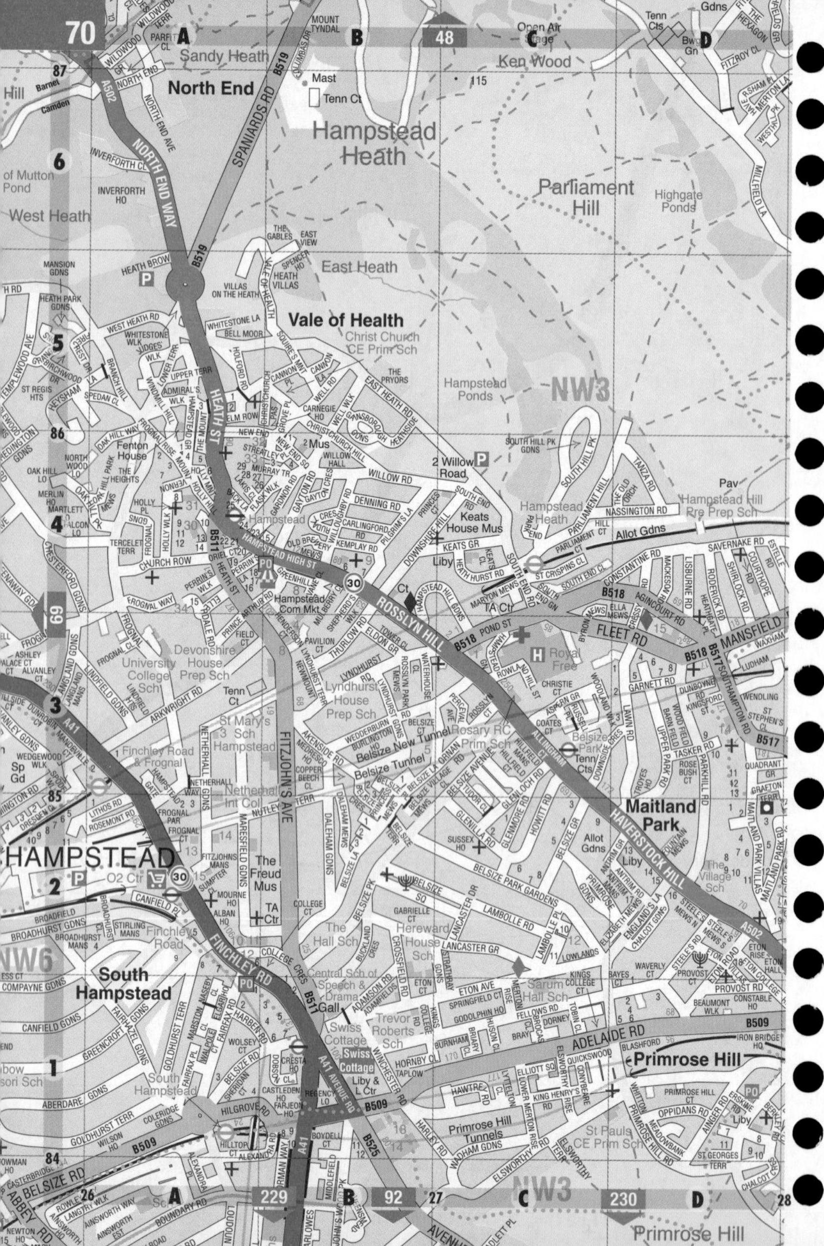

A
B
48
C
D
Sandy Heath
North End
Mast
Tenn Ct
Open Air Stage
Ken Wood
Hampstead Heath
Parliament Hill
Highgate Ponds
West Heath
of Mutton Pond
INVERFORTH HO
NORTH END WAY
SPANIARDS RD
NORTH END AVE
NORTH END
B519
A502
East Heath
Vale of Health
Christ Church CE Prim Sch
Hampstead Ponds
NW3
Fenton House
Hampstead
Keats House Mus
2 Willow Road
Hampstead Heath
Allot Gdns
Pav
Hampstead Hill Pre Prep Sch
HEATH ST
HAMPSTEAD HIGH ST
ROSSLYN HILL
B518
FLEET RD
MANSFIELD
Royal Free
Hampstead Com Mkt
Devonshire House Prep Sch
University College Sch
Tenn Ct
Lyndhurst House Prep Sch
St Mary's Sch Hampstead
Finchley Road & Frognal
Belsize New Tunnel
Belsize Tunnel
Rosary RC Prim Sch
Belsize Park
Netherhall Int Coll
FITZJOHN'S AVE
HAVERSTOCK HILL
Maitland Park
Allot Gdns
Liby
The Village Sch
HAMPSTEAD
O2 Ctr
The Freud Mus
TA Ctr
The Hall Sch
Hereward House Sch
Finchley Road
FINCHLEY RD
NW6
South Hampstead
Central Sch of Speech & Drama
Sarum Hall Sch
Swiss Cottage
Trevor Roberts Sch
Liby & L Ctr
ADELAIDE RD
Primrose Hill
Primrose Hill Tunnels
St Pauls CE Prim Sch
B509
A41
B525
B511
A41 AVENUE RD
229
92
230
NW3
Primrose Hill

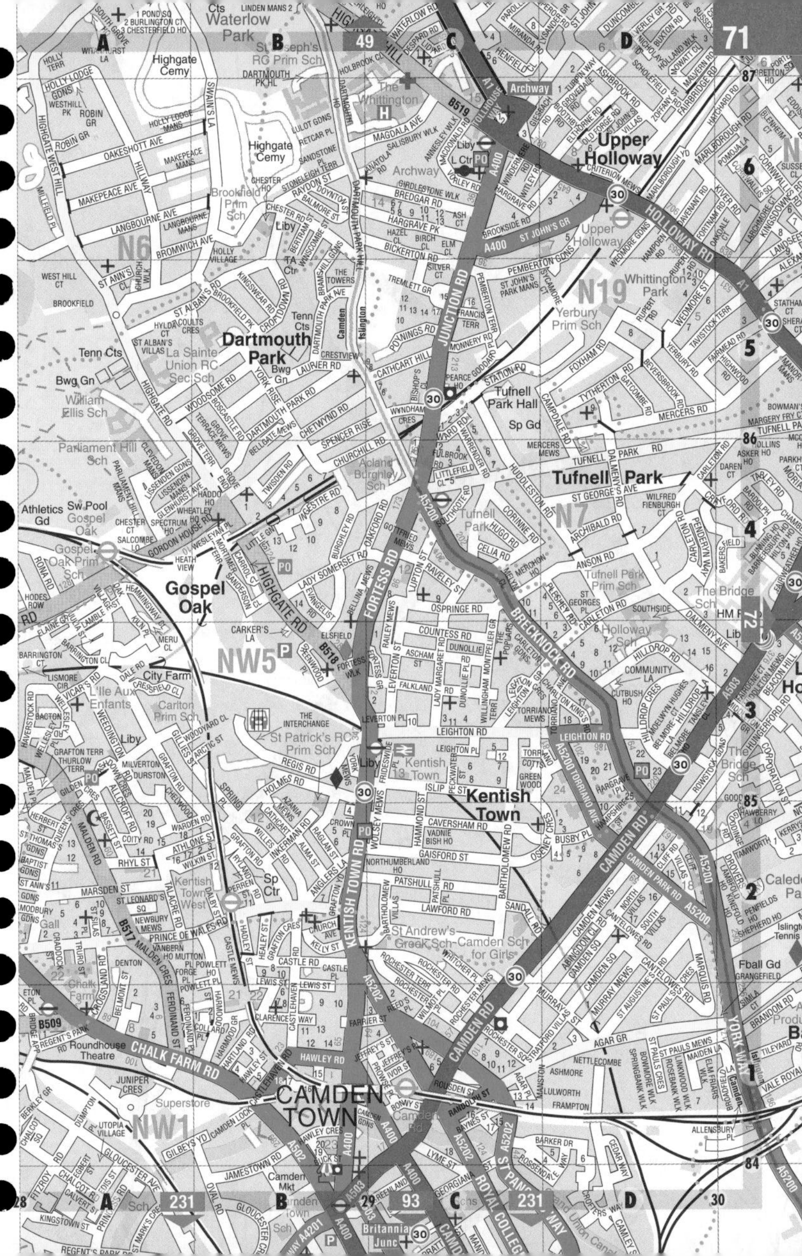

49
A
B
C
D
6
5
4
3
2
1
87
86
85
84
72
231
93
231
28
29
30
N6
N19
N7
NW5
NW1
Waterlow Park
Highgate Cemy
St Joseph's RC Prim Sch
The Whittington
Archway
Upper Holloway
Brookfield Prim Sch
Whittington Park
Yerbury Prim Sch
Dartmouth Park
La Sainte Union RC Sec Sch
William Ellis Sch
Parliament Hill Sch
Athletics Gd
Sw Pool
Gospel Oak
Gospel Oak Prim Sch
Tufnell Park Hall
Tufnell Park
Tufnell Park Prim Sch
Acland Burghley Sch
The Bridge Sch
Holloway Sch
City Farm
L'Ile Aux Enfants
Carlton Prim Sch
The Interchange
St Patrick's RC Prim Sch
Kentish Town
Kentish Town West
St Andrew's Greek Sch
Camden Sch for Girls
Chalk Farm
Roundhouse Theatre
Superstore
CAMDEN TOWN
Camden Mkt
Camden Rd
Britannia Junc
Caledonian Park
Islington Tennis C
Fball Gd
HIGHGATE WEST HILL
SWAIN'S LA
OAKESHOTT AVE
MAKEPEACE AVE
LANGBOURNE AVE
HIGHGATE RD
GORDON HOUSE RD
DARTMOUTH PARK HILL
DARTMOUTH PARK RD
JUNCTION RD
HOLLOWAY RD
FORTRESS RD
KENTISH TOWN RD
BRECKNOCK RD
CAMDEN RD
CHALK FARM RD
LEIGHTON RD
TUFNELL PARK RD
ST GEORGE'S AVE
YORK WAY
AGAR GR
HAWLEY RD
ROYAL COLLEGE ST
ST PANCRAS WAY
CAMDEN PARK RD
MALDEN RD
PRINCE OF WALES RD
GLOUCESTER AVE
A1
A400
A5200
A503
A5202
A502
B519
B518
B517
B509

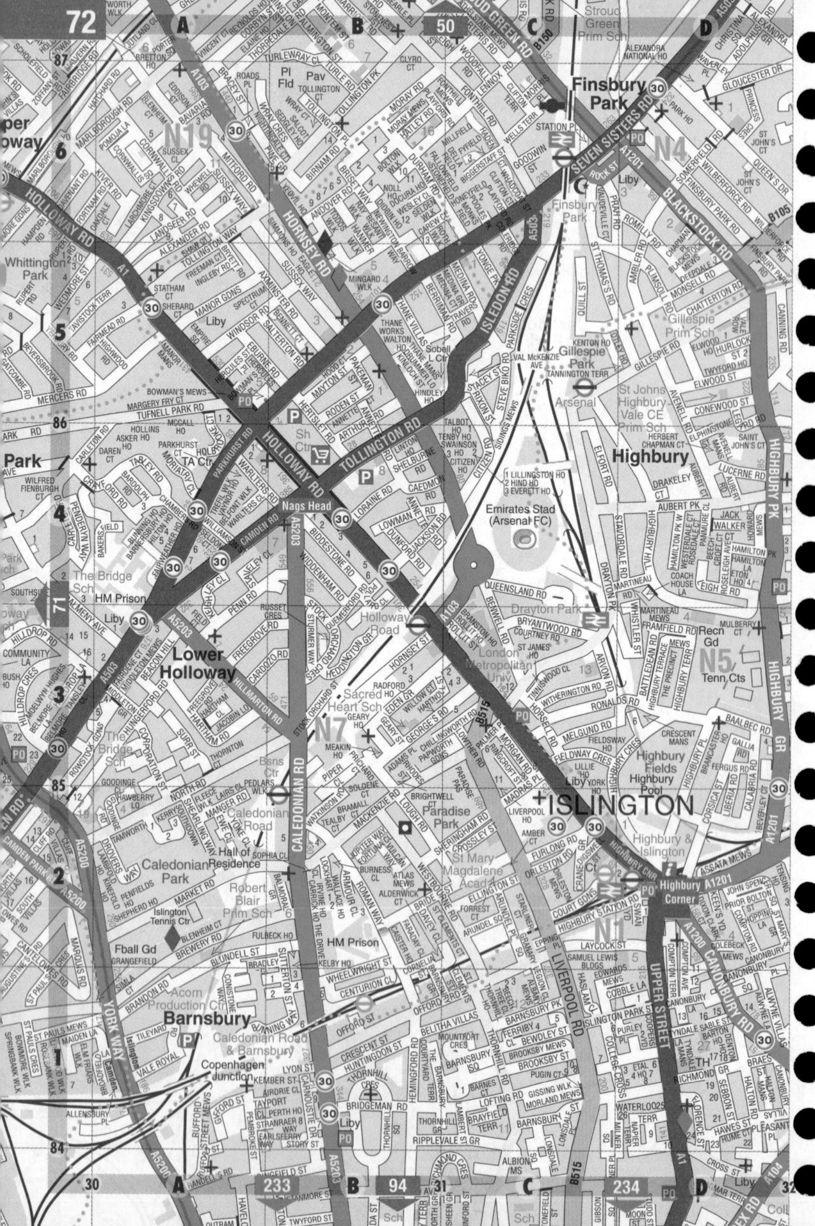

A
B
C
D
50
71
233
94
234
N19
N4
N5
N7
N1
Finsbury Park
Seven Sisters Rd
Blackstock Rd
Holloway Rd
Hornsey Rd
Tollington Rd
Isledon Rd
Camden Rd
Caledonian Rd
Highbury Pk
Highbury Gr
Liverpool Rd
Upper Street
Canonbury Rd
York Way
Nags Head
Highbury
Emirates Stad (Arsenal FC)
Arsenal
Holloway Road
Lower Holloway
HM Prison
Caledonian Road
Caledonian Park
Paradise Park
ISLINGTON
Highbury & Islington
Highbury Corner
Highbury Fields
Barnsbury
Caledonian Road & Barnsbury
Copenhagen Junction
Whittington Park
Drayton Park
Stroud Green Prim Sch
Gillespie Park
Tenn Cts
Sobell L Ctr

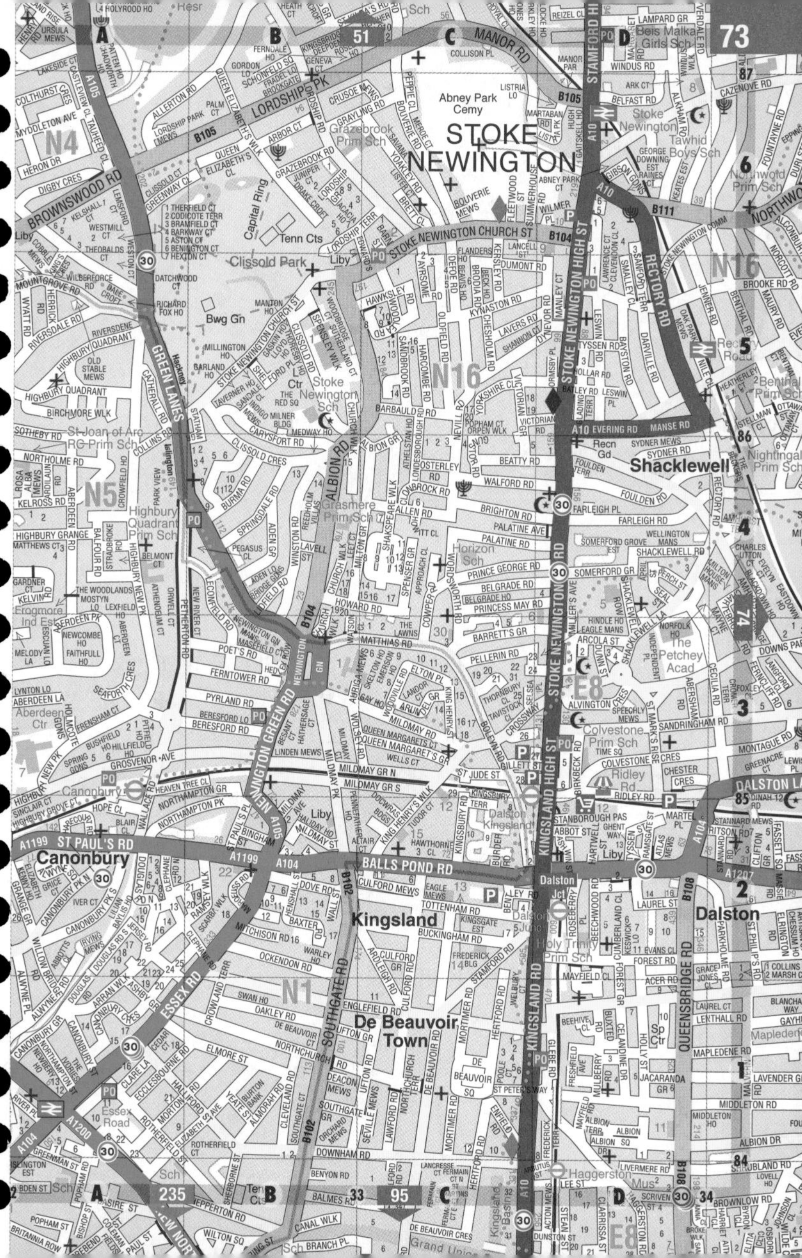

73
A
B
C
D
51
235
95
74
STOKE NEWINGTON
Abney Park Cemy
Shacklewell
Canonbury
Kingsland
Dalston
De Beauvoir Town
N4
N16
N5
N1
E8
Clissold Park
Capital Ring
Tenn Cts
Bwg Gn
Stoke Newington Sch
Grasmere Prim Sch
Horizon Sch
Highbury Quadrant Prim Sch
St Joan of Arc RC Prim Sch
Colvestone Prim Sch
Holy Trinity Prim Sch
The Petchey Acad
Nightingale Prim Sch
Grazebrook Prim Sch
Tawhid Boys Sch
Northwold Prim Sch
Beis Malka Girls Sch
Ridley Rd
Recn Gd
Dalston Kingsland
Dalston Junc
Haggerston
Rectory Road
Essex Road
Canonbury
Frogmore Ind Est
Aberdeen Ctr
Kingsland Basin
Grand Union
MANOR RD
LORDSHIP PK
BROWNSWOOD RD
GREEN LANES
STOKE NEWINGTON CHURCH ST
STOKE NEWINGTON HIGH ST
STAMFORD HILL
STOKE NEWINGTON RD
KINGSLAND HIGH ST
KINGSLAND RD
RECTORY RD
EVERING RD
MANSE RD
NORTHWOLD RD
ALBION RD
NEWINGTON GREEN RD
ST PAUL'S RD
BALLS POND RD
ESSEX RD
SOUTHGATE RD
QUEENSBRIDGE RD
DALSTON LA
A105
A10
A104
A1199
A1207
A1200
B105
B104
B111
B102
B108

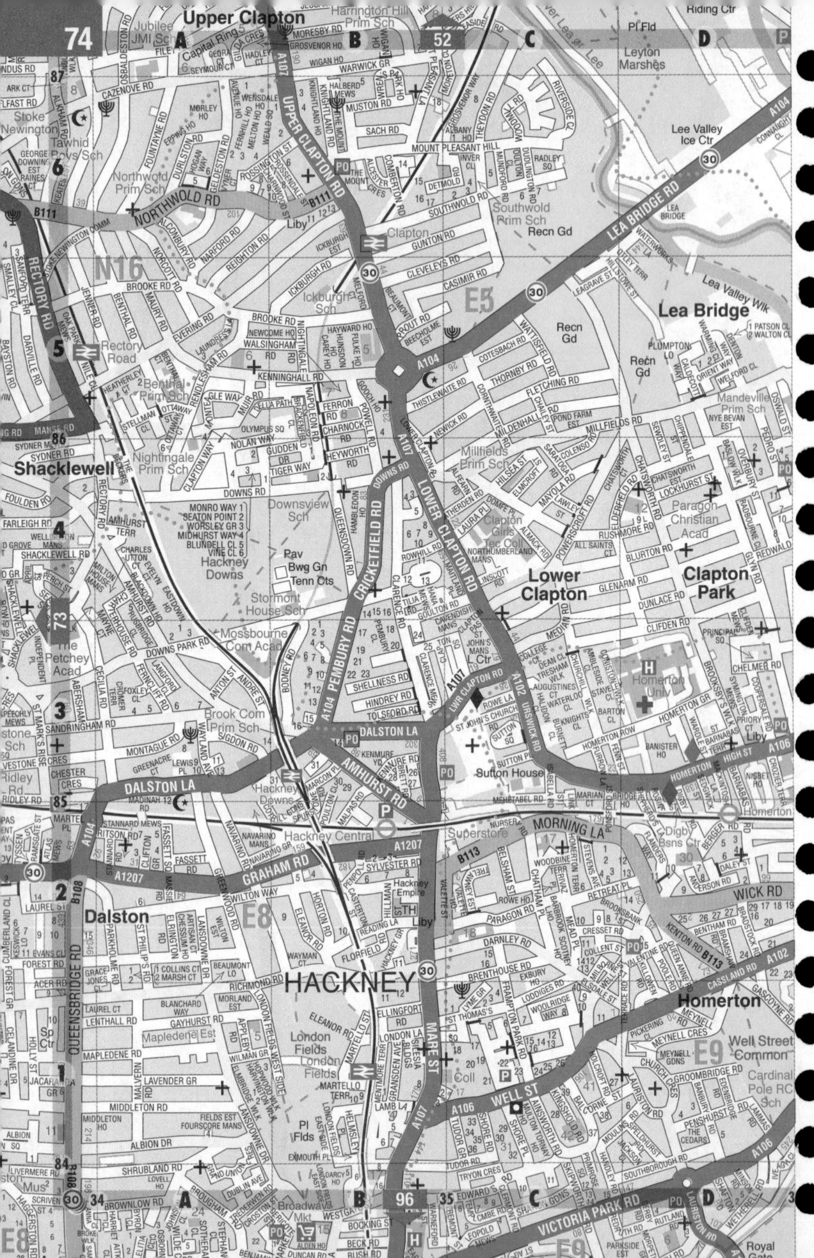

Upper Clapton
52
Riding Ctr
Pl Fld
Leyton Marshes
Lee Valley Ice Ctr
LEA BRIDGE RD
A104
Lea Bridge
Lea Valley Wlk
Stoke Newington
Tawhid Boys Sch
Northwold Prim Sch
NORTHWOLD RD
B111
UPPER CLAPTON RD
A107
CAZENOVE RD
MOUNT PLEASANT HILL
SOUTHWOLD RD
Southwold Prim Sch
Recn Gd
Clapton
N16
E5
RECTORY RD
Rectory Road
Benthal Prim Sch
Nightingale Prim Sch
KENNINGHALL RD
Shacklewell
Downsview Sch
Hackney Downs
Pav
Bwg Gn
Tenn Cts
Stormont House Sch
Mossbourne Com Acad
The Petchey Acad
CRICKETFIELD RD
PEMBURY RD
LOWER CLAPTON RD
Millfields Prim Sch
MILLFIELDS RD
Clapton Girls Tec Coll
Lower Clapton
Clapton Park
Paragon Christian Acad
Mandeville Prim Sch
Homerton Univ
HOMERTON HIGH ST
A106
Homerton
Sutton House
DALSTON LA
Brook Com Prim Sch
Hackney Downs
Hackney Central
AMHURST RD
MORNING LA
Superstore
Digby Bsns Ctr
WICK RD
GRAHAM RD
A1207
B113
Dalston
E8
QUEENSBRIDGE RD
B108
Hackney Empire
HACKNEY
MARE ST
London Fields
Mapledene Est
WELL ST
E9
Well Street Common
Cardinal Pole RC Sch
VICTORIA PARK RD
Broadway Mkt
96
73
Royal Gate

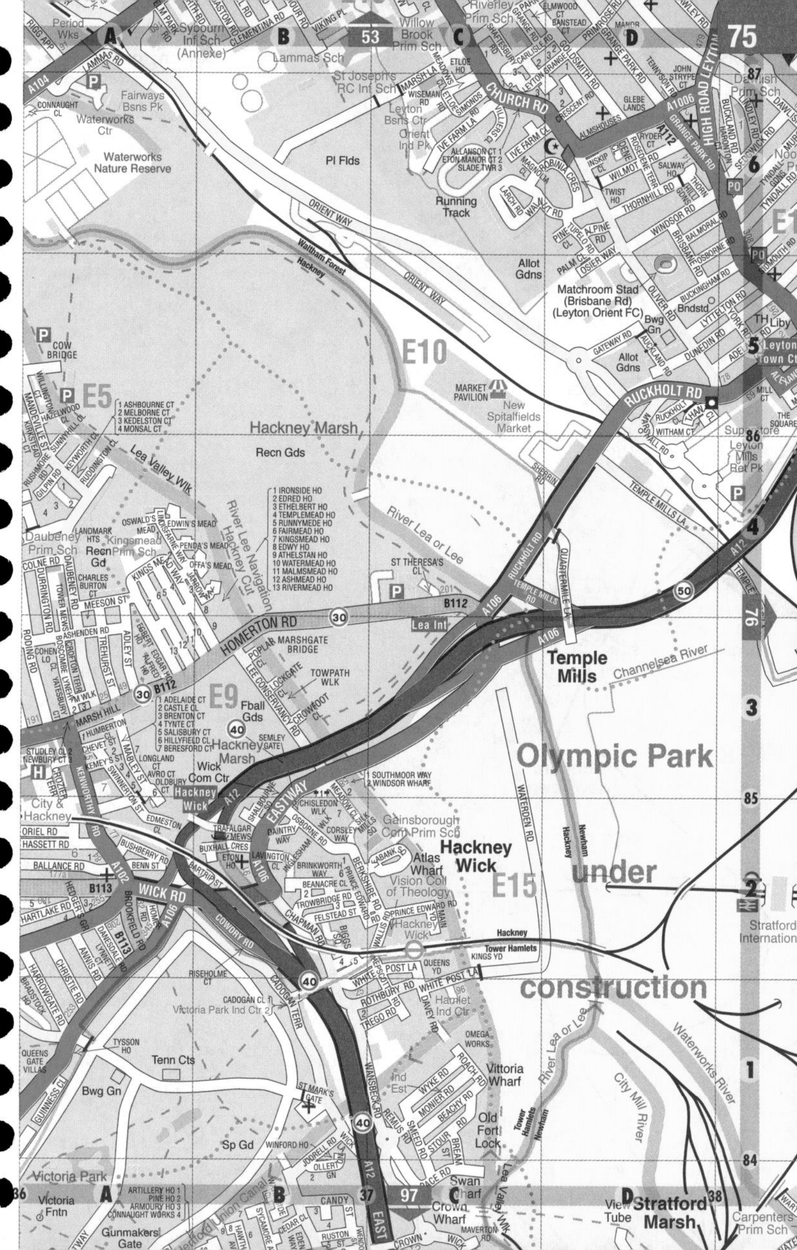

75

E10

E5

Hackney Marsh
Recn Gds

E9

Olympic Park

Hackney
Wick

E15

under

construction

Victoria Park

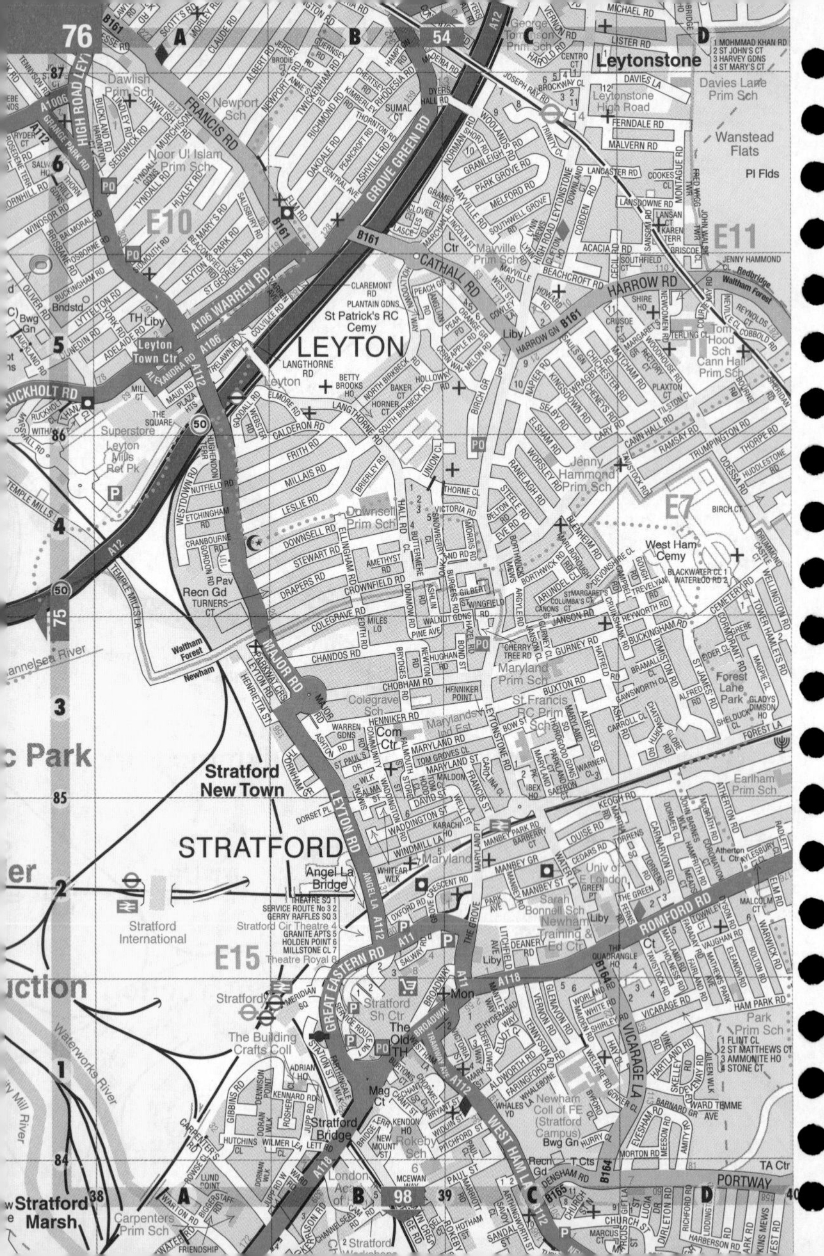

54
98
75
A
B
C
D
Leytonstone
LEYTON
STRATFORD
Stratford New Town
Stratford Marsh
E10
E11
E7
E15
Wanstead Flats
Pl Flds
HIGH ROAD LEYTON
FRANCIS RD
GROVE GREEN RD
HIGH ROAD LEYTONSTONE
CATHALL RD
HARROW RD
LEYTON RD
MAJOR RD
GREAT EASTERN RD
ROMFORD RD
VICARAGE LA
WEST HAM LA
BROADWAY
THE GROVE
PORTWAY
LEYTONSTONE RD
CANN HALL RD
BUCKINGHAM RD
CEMETERY RD
MARYLAND ST
ANGEL LA
A12
A11
A112
A118
A106
B161
B164
B165
Leyton Town Ctr
St Patrick's RC Cemy
West Ham Cemy
Forest Lane Park
Leyton Mills Ret Pk
Superstore
Stratford International
Stratford Sh Ctr
The Old TH
Newham Coll of FE (Stratford Campus)
Univ of E London
Sarah Bonnell Sch
Newham Training & Ed Ctr
Colegrave Sch
Downsell Prim Sch
Maryland Prim Sch
Jenny Hammond Prim Sch
Mayville Prim Sch
Dawlish Prim Sch
Newport Sch
Noor Ul Islam Prim Sch
Davies Lane Prim Sch
Leytonstone High Road
Tom Hood Sch
Cann Hall Prim Sch
St Francis RC Prim Sch
Earlham Prim Sch
Park Prim Sch
Rokeby Sch
Carpenters Prim Sch
The Building Crafts Coll
Stratford Cir Theatre
Theatre Royal
Angel La Bridge
Stratford Bridge
Waterworks River
Waltham Forest
Newham

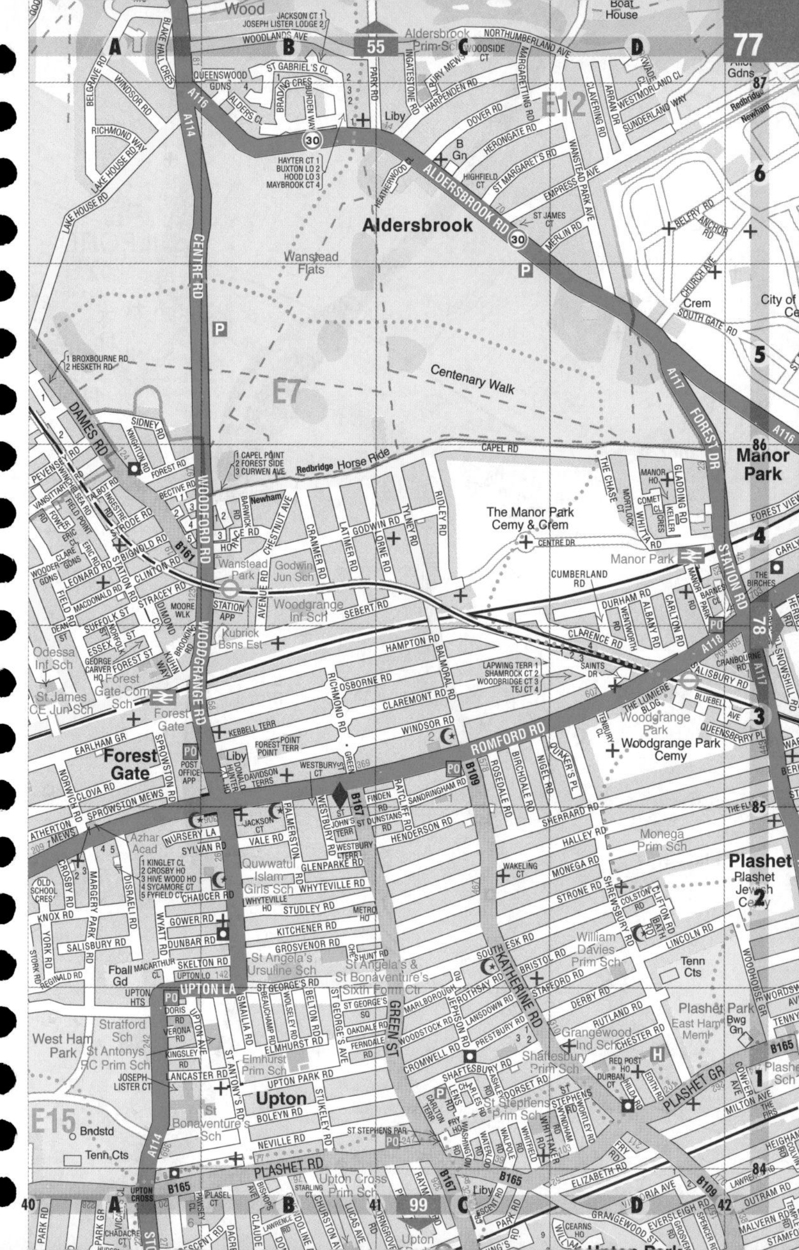

Aldersbrook
Wanstead Flats
Centenary Walk
Manor Park
Forest Gate
Plashet
Upton
The Manor Park Cemy & Crem
Woodgrange Park Cemy
West Ham Park
Plashet Park
E12
E7
E15
ALDERSBROOK RD
CENTRE RD
WOODFORD RD
WOODGRANGE RD
ROMFORD RD
FOREST DR
STATION RD
GREEN ST
KATHERINE RD
UPTON LA
PLASHET RD
PLASHET GR
CAPEL RD
DAMES RD
Redbridge Horse Ride
55
99

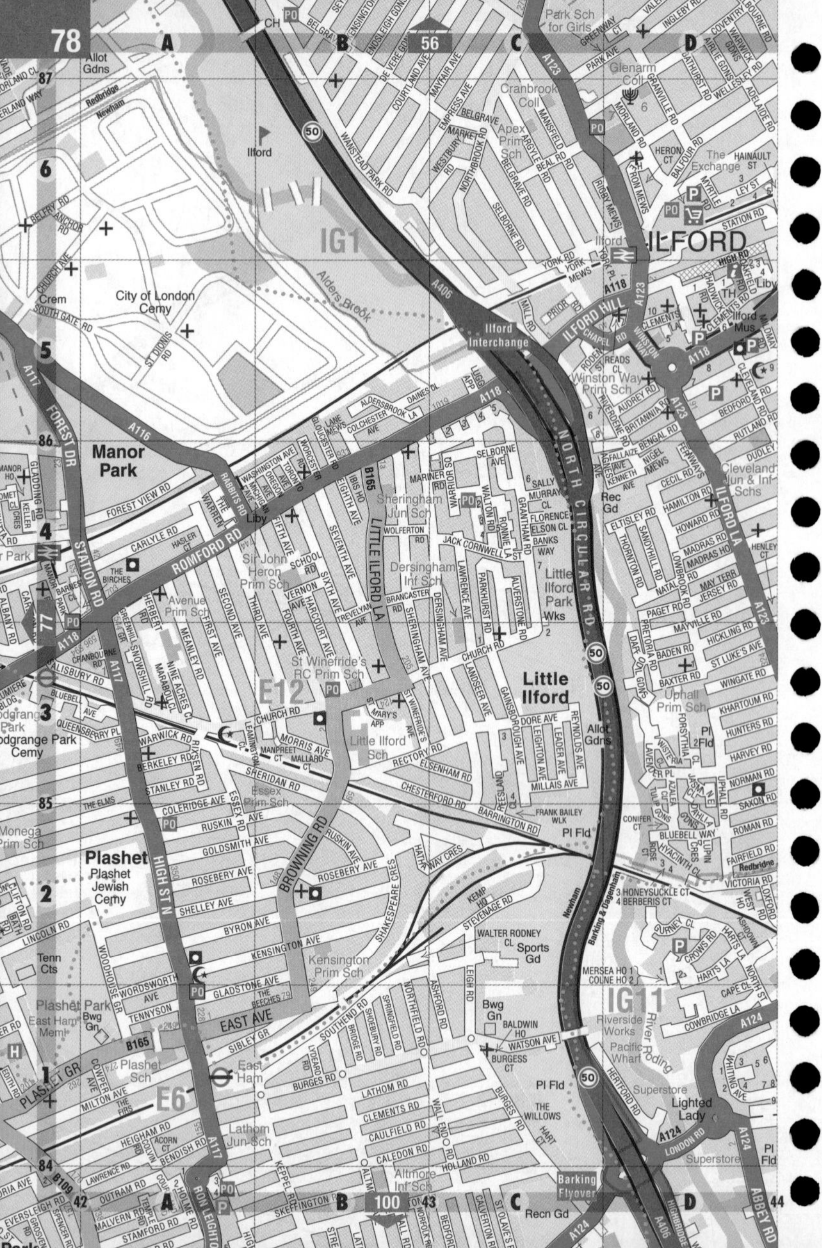
A
B
C
D
56
87
86
85
84
6
5
4
3
2
1
42
43
44
100
77
Allot Gdns
Redbridge
Newham
Ilford
IG1
Alders Brook
City of London Cemy
Crem
SOUTH GATE RD
ST DIONIS RD
CHURCH AVE
BELFRY RD
ANCHOR RD
Manor Park
A116
A117
FOREST DR
STATION RD
FOREST VIEW RD
CARLYLE RD
HASLER CT
ROMFORD RD
RABBITS RD
THE WARREN
Liby
THE BIRCHES
MANOR PARK
BARNES CL
GLADDING RD
KELLER CRES
MANOR HO
A118
CRANBOURNE RD
SALISBURY RD
BLUEBELL AVE
QUEENSBERRY PL
Wodgrange Park Cemy
WARWICK RD
BERKELEY RD
STANLEY RD
THE ELMS
COLERIDGE AVE
RUSKIN AVE
GOLDSMITH AVE
ROSEBERY AVE
SHELLEY AVE
BYRON AVE
KENSINGTON AVE
GLADSTONE AVE
WORDSWORTH AVE
TENNYSON
EAST AVE
SIBLEY GR
B165
Plashet
Plashet Jewish Cemy
Plashet Park
East Ham Meml
Bwg Gn
Plashet Sch
Tenn Cts
LINCOLN RD
WOODHOUSE GR
CLIFTON RD
BATH RD
Monega Prim Sch
PLASHET GR
COWPER AVE
MILTON AVE
THE FIRS
E6
HEIGHAM RD
ACORN CT
BENDISH RD
COLVIN RD
LAWRENCE RD
OUTRAM RD
MALVERN RD
STAMFORD RD
EVERSLEIGH RD
SPENCER RD
HOLME RD
RON LEIGHTON
B109
HIGH ST N
Avenue Prim Sch
Sir John Heron Prim Sch
SECOND AVE
FIRST AVE
THIRD AVE
FOURTH AVE
FIFTH AVE
SIXTH AVE
SEVENTH AVE
EIGHTH AVE
HARCOURT AVE
VERNON AVE
SCHOOL RD
TREVELYAN AVE
MEANLEY RD
NINE ACRES CL
HERBERT RD
GREENHILL GR
SNOWSHILL RD
MARABOU CL
RIXSEN RD
E12
CHURCH RD
MORRIS AVE
MANPREET CT
MALLARD
LEAMINGTON CL
SHERIDAN RD
Essex Prim Sch
BROWNING RD
RUSKIN AVE
St Winefride's RC Prim Sch
Little Ilford Sch
ST MARY'S APP
ST WINEFRIDE'S AVE
RECTORY RD
ELSENHAM RD
CHESTERFORD RD
BARRINGTON RD
HATHAWAY CRES
SHAKESPEARE CRES
Kensington Prim Sch
THE BEECHES
East Ham
SOUTHEND RD
LYDEARD RD
BRIDGE RD
SHOEBURY RD
SPRINGFIELD RD
NORTHFIELD RD
ASHFORD RD
BURGES RD
LATHOM RD
CLEMENTS RD
CAULFIELD RD
CALEDON RD
HOLLAND RD
WALL END RD
Lathom Jun Sch
Altmore Inf Sch
KEPPEL RD
SKEFFINGTON RD
CALVERTON RD
ST OLAVE'S RD
BEDFORD
Recn Gd
WASHINGTON AVE
MICHIGAN AVE
OREGON AVE
TORONTO AVE
WORCESTER RD
GLOUCESTER RD
LANE MEWS
COLCHESTER AVE
ALDERSBROOK LA
DAINES CL
IBIS HO
B165
LITTLE ILFORD LA
Sheringham Jun Sch
MARINER RD
WARRIOR SQ
WOLFERTON RD
WALTON RD
RONNIE LA
JACK CORNWELL ST
Dersingham Inf Sch
BRANCASTER RD
SHERINGHAM AVE
DERSINGHAM AVE
LAWRENCE AVE
PARKHURST RD
ALVERSTONE RD
SELBORNE AVE
SALLY MURRAY CL
FLORENCE ELSON CL
BANKS WAY
GRANTHAM RD
Little Ilford Park
Wks
Little Ilford
LANDSEER AVE
GAINSBOROUGH AVE
DORE AVE
LEIGHTON AVE
LEADER AVE
REYNOLDS AVE
MILLAIS AVE
REESLAND CL
FRANK BAILEY WLK
Pl Fld
Allot Gdns
KEMP HO
STEVENAGE RD
WALTER RODNEY CL
Sports Gd
LEIGH RD
Bwg Gn
BALDWIN HO
WATSON AVE
BURGESS CT
THE WILLOWS
HART CT
Barking Flyover
A124
A406
NORTH CIRCULAR RD
50
Barking & Dagenham
Ilford Interchange
A406
WANSTEAD PARK RD
COURTLAND AVE
MAYFAIR AVE
DE VERE GDNS
ENDSLEIGH GDNS
KENSINGTON
BELGRAVE
EMPRESS AVE
WESTBURY RD
MARKET
NORTHBROOK RD
Apex Prim Sch
Cranbrook Coll
MANSFIELD RD
ARGYLE RD
BEAL RD
BELGRAVE RD
SELBORNE RD
Park Sch for Girls
GREENWAY
PARK AVE
INGLEBY RD
VALE
Glenarm Coll
MORLAND RD
GRANVILLE RD
CATHURST RD
AIRLIE GDNS
WARWICK GDNS
WELLESLEY RD
COVENTRY RD
BOURNE RD
ADELAIDE RD
HERON CT
BALFOUR RD
MYRTLE
The Exchange
HAINAULT ST
LEY ST
STATION RD
RIGBY MEWS
FRON MEWS
A123
Ilford
ILFORD
YORK RD
YORK MEWS
YORK PL
A118
ILFORD HILL
MILL RD
PRIOR RD
CHAPEL RD
RODEN ST
READS CL
WINSTON WAY
Winston Way Prim Sch
CLEMENTS LA
CHADWICK RD
HIGH RD
TH
Liby
Ilford Mus
MILDMAY
AUDREY RD
RIVERDENE RD
BRITANNIA RD
BENGAL RD
FALLAIZE AVE
KENNETH AVE
AGNES AVE
NIGEL MEWS
FERNWAYS
CECIL RD
HAMILTON RD
HOWARD RD
MADRAS RD
MADRAS HO
ELTISLEY RD
THORNTON RD
SANDYHILL RD
LOWBROOK RD
NATAL RD
MAY TERR
JERSEY RD
PAGET RD
PRETORIA RD
MAYVILLE RD
BADEN RD
BAXTER RD
DAFFODIL GDNS
Rec Gd
CLEVELAND RD
BEDFORD RD
RUTLAND RD
DUDLEY
Cleveland Jun & Inf Schs
ILFORD LA
HENLEY CT
HICKLING RD
ST LUKE'S AVE
WINGATE RD
KHARTOUM RD
HUNTERS RD
HARVEY RD
NORMAN RD
SAXON RD
ROMAN RD
FAIRFIELD RD
VICTORIA RD
OXFORD RD
WEST HO
Uphall Prim Sch
FORSYTHIA CL
WISTERIA CL
LAVENDER PL
AZALEA CL
JASMINE CL
DAHLIA GDNS
TULIP GDNS
CONIFER CT
BLUEBELL WAY
LUPIN CRES
HYACINTH CL
ROSE LA
UPHALL RD
Pl Fld
3 HONEYSUCKLE CT
4 BERBERIS CT
Redbridge
GURNEY CL
CROWS RD
HARTS LA
ASHDOWN
NORTH ST
MERSEA HO
COLNE HO
CAPE CL
COWBRIDGE LA
IG11
Riverside Works
River Roding
Pacific Wharf
Superstore
HERTFORD RD
Lighted Lady
LONDON RD
WHITING AVE
A124
Superstore
ABBEY RD
HIGHBRIDGE RD
Pl Fld

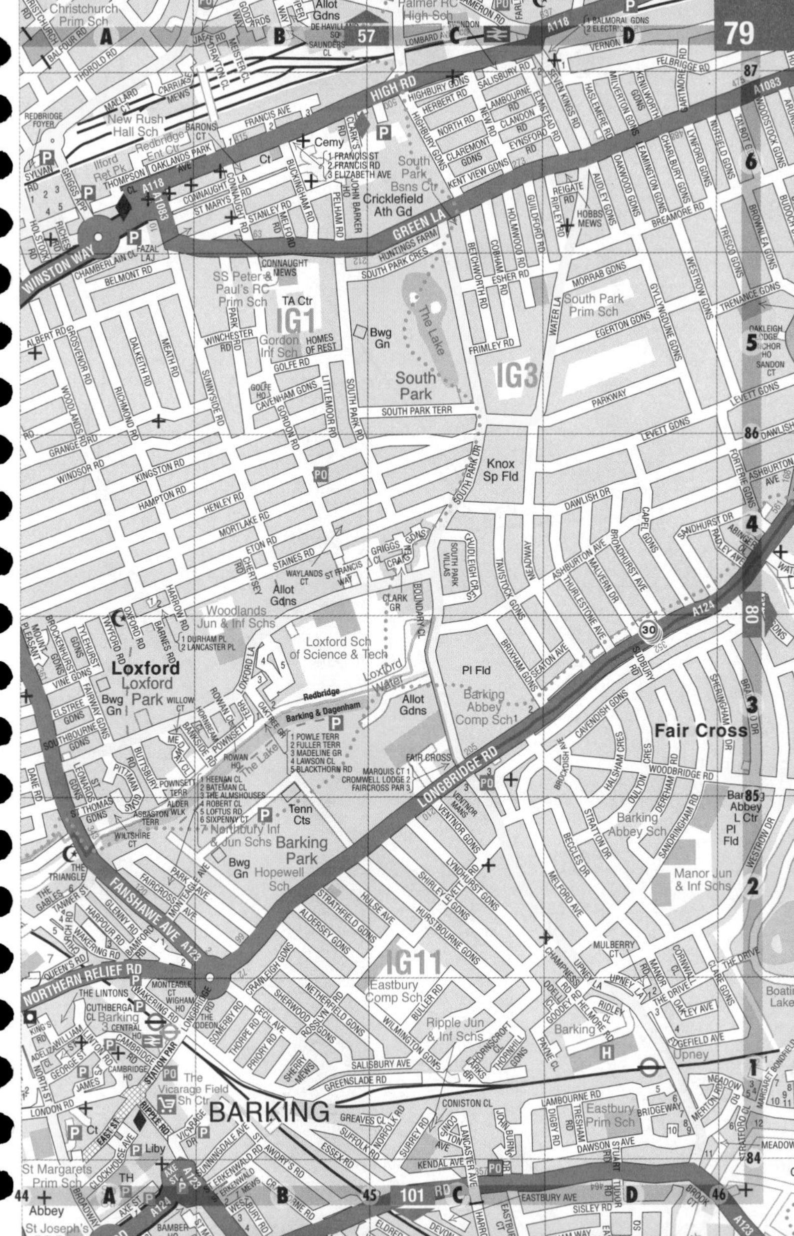
Loxford
Fair Cross
BARKING
IG1
IG3
IG11
South Park
Barking Park
Loxford Park
Cricklefield Ath Gd
Knox Sp Fld
HIGH RD
GREEN LA
LONGBRIDGE RD
FANSHAWE AVE
NORTHERN RELIEF RD
WINSTON WAY
A118
A1083
A124
A123
A177
57
80
101
87
86
85
84
44
45
46

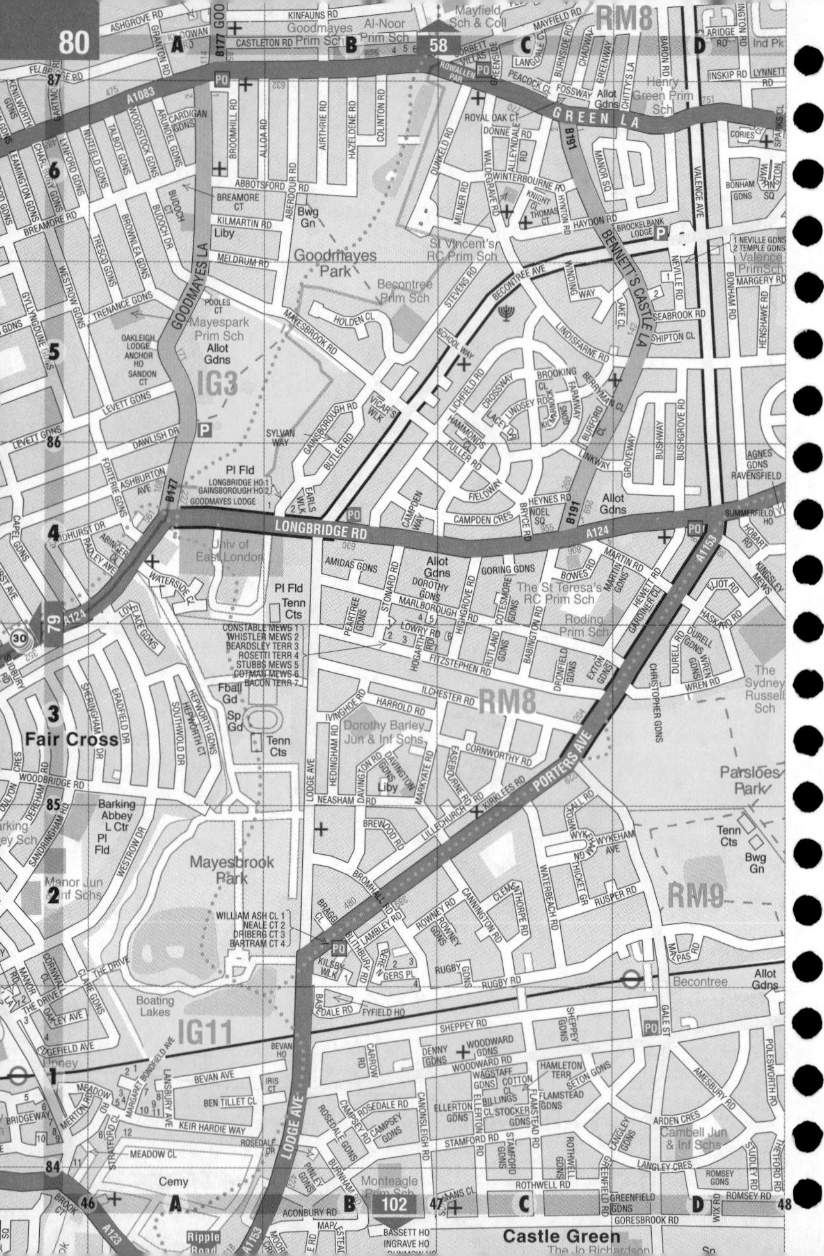

Goodmayes Park
Mayesbrook Park
Parsloes Park
Fair Cross
Castle Green
IG3
IG11
RM8
RM9
LONGBRIDGE RD
GREEN LA
GOODMAYES LA
BENNETT'S CASTLE LA
PORTERS AVE
LODGE AVE
BECONTREE AVE
Becontree
Univ of East London
Boating Lakes
Cemy

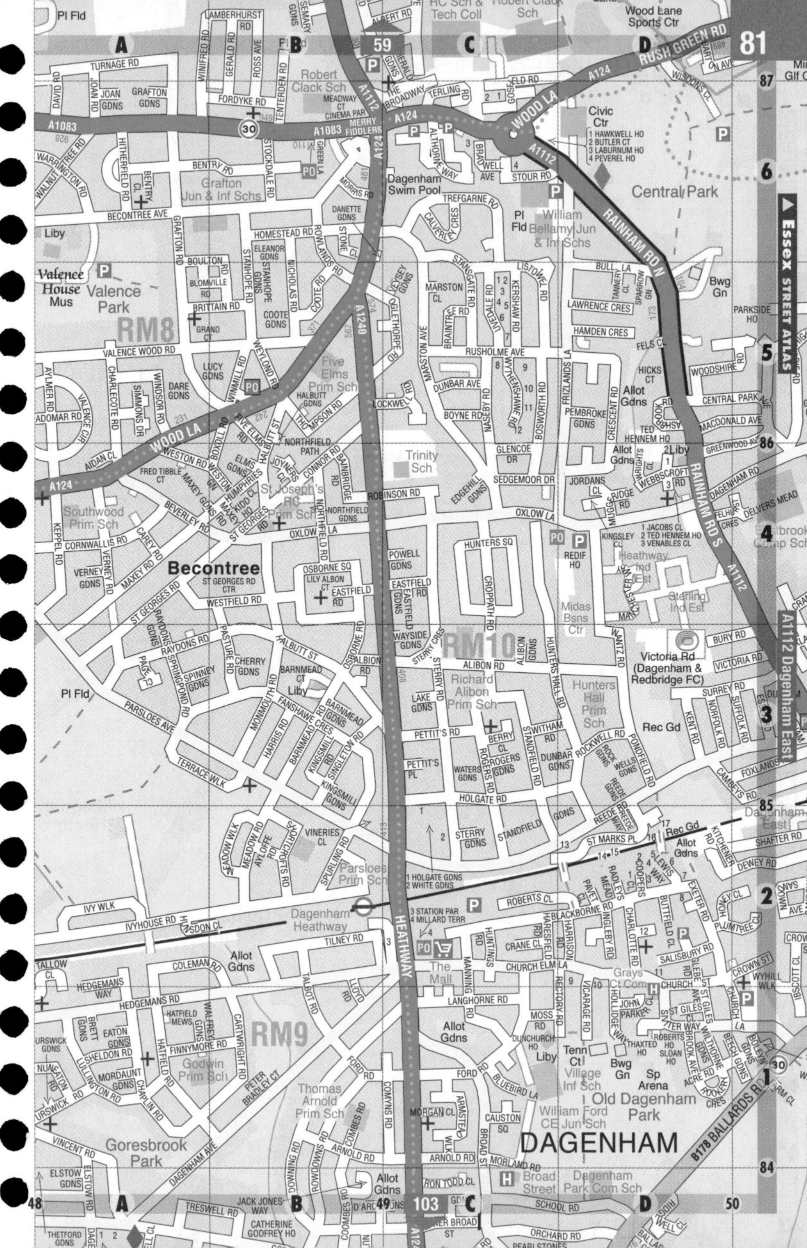
81
59
103
A
B
C
D
87
6
5
86
4
3
85
2
1
84
48
49
50
Essex STREET ATLAS
A1112 Dagenham East
RM8
RM10
RM9
Becontree
DAGENHAM
Pl Fld
RC Sch & Tech Coll
Robert Clack Sch
Wood Lane Sports Ctr
Min Glf Crs
RUSH GREEN RD
LAMBERHURST RD
ROSS AVE
GERALD RD
WINIFRED RD
TENTERDEN RD
TURNAGE RD
DAVID RD
JOAN RD
JOAN GDNS
GRAFTON GDNS
FORDYKE RD
Robert Clack Sch
MEADWAY CT
CINEMA PAR
MERRY FIDDLERS
THE BROADWAY
TERLING RD
A1083
A1112
A124
WOOD LA
Civic Ctr
1 HAWKWELL HO
2 BUTLER CT
3 LABURNUM HO
4 PEVEREL HO
WARRINGTON RD
WALNUT TREE RD
HITHERFIELD RD
BENTRY RD
BENTRY CL
STOCKDALE RD
GREEN LA
MORRIS RD
ALTHORNE WAY
BRADWELL AVE
STOUR RD
Dagenham Swim Pool
Grafton Jun & Inf Schs
BECONTREE AVE
Liby
TREFGARNE RD
CALVERLEY CRES
Pl Fld
William Bellamy Jun & Inf Schs
Central Park
RAINHAM RD N
Valence House Mus
Valence Park
GRAFTON RD
HOMESTEAD RD
DANETTE GDNS
STONE CL
ROWLANDS RD
BOULTON RD
BLOMVILLE RD
BRITTAIN RD
GRAND CT
ELEANOR GDNS
STANHOPE GDNS
STANHOPE RD
NICHOLAS RD
COOTE GDNS
COOTE RD
VEYSEY GDNS
OGLETHORPE RD
A1240
MARSTON CL
MARSTON AVE
STANSGATE RD
BRAINTREE RD
UVEDALE RD
KERSHAW RD
LISTOWEL RD
BULL LA
TANNERY CL
SPARROW GN
LAWRENCE CRES
HAMDEN CRES
FELS CL
Bwg Gn
PARKSIDE HO
VALENCE WOOD RD
LUCY GDNS
WINMILL RD
WEYLOND RD
DARE GDNS
WINDSOR RD
SIMMONS DR
CHARLECOTE RD
Five Elms Prim Sch
RUSHOLME AVE
DUNBAR AVE
LOCKWELL RD
WYTHENSHAWE RD
NASEBY RD
BOSWORTH RD
FRIZLANDS LA
HICKS CT
WOODSHIRE RD
Allot Gdns
CENTRAL PARK AVE
BOYNE RD
PEMBROKE GDNS
CRESCENT RD
TED HENNEM HO
MACDONALD AVE
AYLMER RD
VALENCE CIR
ADOMAR RD
FIVE ELMS RD
HALBUTT GDNS
THOMPSON RD
HALBUTT ST
BOXOLL RD
NORTHFIELD PATH
GLENCOE DR
GREENWOOD AVE
Allot Gdns
Liby
AIDAN CL
WESTON RD
FRED TIBBLE CT
ELMS GDNS
JOYNERS CL
CONNOR RD
BAINBRIDGE RD
Trinity Sch
SEDGEMOOR DR
WRIGHTS CL
WEBBSCROFT RD
RAINHAM RD S
DAGENHAM RD
EASTBROOK AVE
Southwood Prim Sch
St Joseph's RC Prim Sch
ROBINSON RD
EDGEHILL GDNS
JORDANS CL
MUGGERIDGE RD
DELVERS MEAD
FELHURST CRES
BEVERLEY RD
KEPPEL RD
CAREY RD
MAXEY GDNS
KIDD CL
ST GEORGES RD
NORTHFIELD GDNS
OXLOW LA
1 JACOBS CL
2 TED HENNEM HO
3 VENABLES CL
KINGSLEY CL
Eastbrook Comp Sch
CORNWALLIS RD
VERNEY RD
VERNEY GDNS
MAXEY RD
POWELL GDNS
HUNTERS SQ
REDIF HO
Heathway Ind Est
OSBORNE SQ
LILY ALBON CT
EASTFIELD RD
EASTFIELD GDNS
ST GEORGES RD CTR
WESTFIELD RD
CROPPATH RD
Midas Bsns Ctr
Sterling Ind Est
A1112
CRANMER
RAYDONS GDNS
RAYDONS RD
PASTURE RD
OSBORNE RD
WAYSIDE GDNS
STERRY CRES
ALBION GDNS
HUNTERS HALL RD
WANTZ RD
BURY RD
Victoria Rd (Dagenham & Redbridge FC)
VICTORIA RD
PAGE CL
SPRINGPOND RD
SPINNEY GDNS
CHERRY GDNS
BARNMEAD CT
ALBION RD
ALIBON RD
Richard Alibon Prim Sch
Hunters Hall Prim Sch
SURREY RD
Pl Fld
PARSLOES AVE
MONMOUTH RD
FANSHAWE CRES
BARNMEAD GDNS
LAKE GDNS
STERRY RD
KENT RD
NORFOLK RD
SUFFOLK RD
Rec Gd
HARRIS RD
BARNMEAD RD
KINGSMILL RD
SINGLETON RD
PETTIT'S RD
BERRY CL
WITHAM RD
STANDFIELD RD
ROCKWELL RD
PONDFIELD RD
TERRACE WLK
PETTIT'S PL
WATERS GDNS
ROGERS RD
ROGERS GDNS
DUNBAR GDNS
ROCK GDNS
WELLS GDNS
REEDE GDNS
CAMBEYS RD
FOXLANDS
KINGSMILL GDNS
HOLGATE RD
Dagenham East
MEADOW WLK
AYLOFFE RD
SHORTCROFTS RD
VINERIES CL
STERRY GDNS
STANDFIELD GDNS
REEDE RD
REEDE WAY
ST MARKS PL
Rec Gd
KITCHENER RD
SHAFTER RD
SPURLING RD
Parsloes Prim Sch
1 HOLGATE GDNS
2 WHITE GDNS
PAVET CL
RADLEYS MEAD
COOPERS LA
LEWIS WAY
EXETER RD
DEWEY RD
SANDOWN CT
IVY WLK
Dagenham Heathway
HEATHWAY
ROBERTS CL
BLACKBORNE RD
HARESFIELD RD
HARRISON RD
INGLEBY RD
CHARLOTTE RD
BUTTFIELD CL
HONEY CL
PLUMTREE CL
IVYHOUSE RD
HUNSDON CL
3 STATION PAR
4 MILLARD TERR
HUNTINGS RD
CRANE CL
SALISBURY RD
CROWN ST
TALLOW CL
COLEMAN RD
TILNEY RD
Allot Gdns
The Mall
MANNING RD
CHURCH ELM LA
RECTORY RD
VICARAGE RD
Grays Ct Com
CHURCH ST
GLEBE AVE
ST GILES RD
WYHILL WLK
SCOTT CL
HEDGEMANS WAY
HEDGEMANS RD
TALBOT RD
LLOYD RD
LANGHORNE RD
MOSS RD
HOLLIDGE WAY
JOHN PARKER CL
ST GILES CL
SITTER WAY
CHURCH LA
HATFIELD MEWS
WALFREY GDNS
BRETT GDNS
EATON GDNS
FINNYMORE RD
CARTWRIGHT RD
Allot Gdns
DUNCHURCH HO
ROBERTS HO
THAXTED HO
SLOAN HO
WILTHORNE GDNS
BEECH GDNS
BOLEYN GDNS
URSWICK GDNS
SHELDON RD
MORDAUNT GDNS
HATFIELD RD
Godwin Prim Sch
Liby
Tenn Ct
Bwg Gn
Sp Arena
BROOK AVE
ACRE RD
ROOKERY
NUNEATON RD
LULLINGTON RD
CHAPLIN RD
PETER BRADLEY CT
FORD RD
Village Inf Sch
Old Dagenham Park
BALLARDS RD
B178
URSWICK RD
Thomas Arnold Prim Sch
COMBES RD
COMYNS RD
MORGAN CL
ARMSTEAD WLK
BLUEBIRD LA
William Ford CE Jun Sch
CAUSTON SQ
VINCENT RD
Goresbrook Park
DAGENHAM AVE
ROWDOWNS RD
ARNOLD RD
BROAD ST
MORLAND RD
ELSTOW GDNS
ELSTOW RD
DOWNING RD
Allot Gdns
RON TODD CL
Broad Street
Dagenham Park Com Sch
JACK JONES WAY
TRESWELL RD
CATHERINE GODFREY HO
COOMBES RD
D'ARCY GDNS
BROAD ST
SCHOOL RD
ORCHARD RD
RIDGEWELL CL
THETFORD GDNS
PEARL STONES

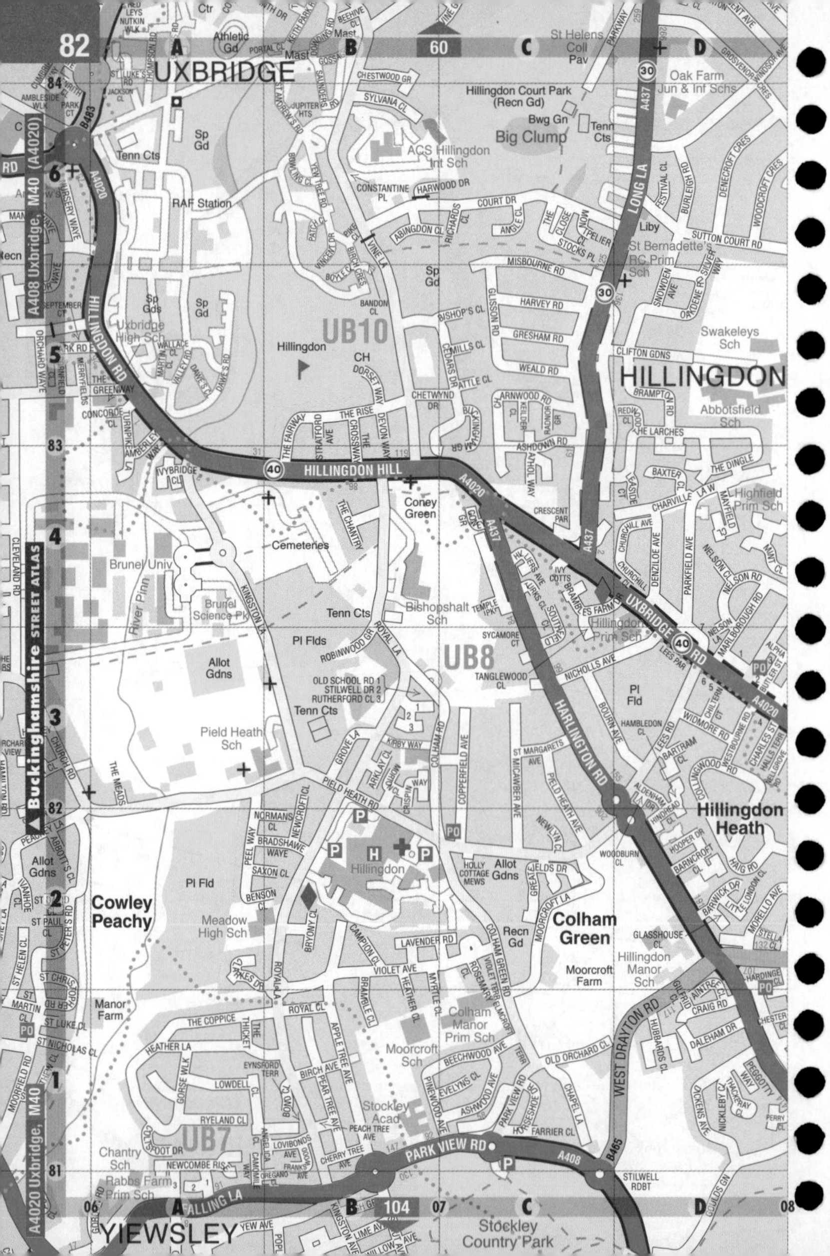

UXBRIDGE
HILLINGDON
Hillingdon Heath
Colham Green
Cowley Peachy
YIEWSLEY
UB10
UB8
UB7
HILLINGDON HILL
HILLINGDON RD
UXBRIDGE RD
HARLINGTON RD
LONG LA
PARK VIEW RD
FALLING LA
WEST DRAYTON RD
PIELD HEATH RD
Brunel Univ
Cemeteries
Hillingdon Court Park (Recn Gd)
Big Clump
ACS Hillingdon Int Sch
RAF Station
Uxbridge High Sch
Pield Heath Sch
Meadow High Sch
Bishopshalt Sch
Hillingdon Prim Sch
Hillingdon Manor Sch
Colham Manor Prim Sch
Moorcroft Sch
Stockley Acad
Chantry Sch
Rabbs Farm Prim Sch
Stockley Country Park
Swakeleys Sch
Abbotsfield Sch
Highfield Prim Sch
Oak Farm Jun & Inf Schs
St Helens Coll Pav
St Bernadette's RC Prim Sch
Manor Farm
Moorcroft Farm
Coney Green
Brunel Science Pk
A4020 Uxbridge, M40 (A4020)
A408 Uxbridge, M40
A4020 Uxbridge, M40
Buckinghamshire STREET ATLAS
60
104

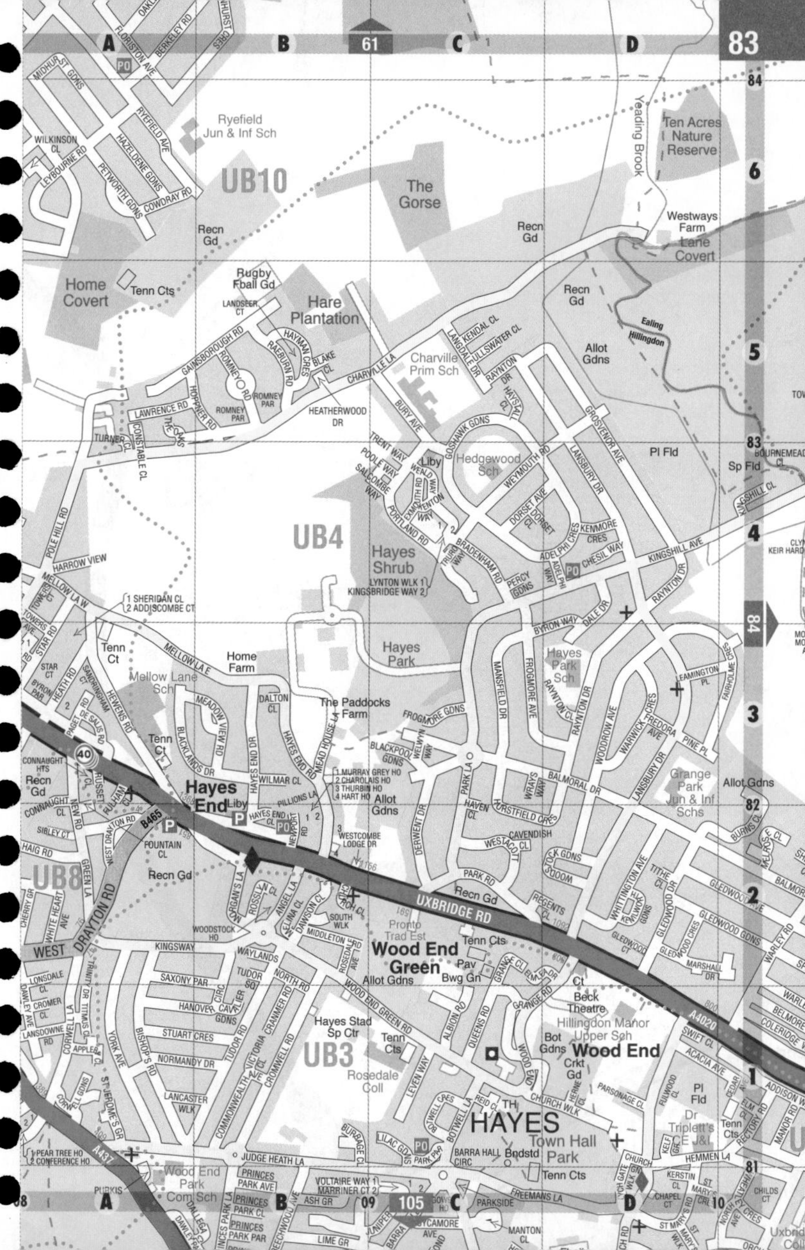

Ryefield Jun & Inf Sch
UB10
The Gorse
Ten Acres Nature Reserve
Yeading Brook
Westways Farm
Lane Covert
Recn Gd
Home Covert
Tenn Cts
Rugby Fball Gd
Hare Plantation
Charville Prim Sch
Allot Gdns
Ealing
Hillingdon
Hedgewood Sch
Pl Fld
Sp Fld
UB4
Hayes Shrub
Hayes Park
Hayes Park Sch
Home Farm
Mellow Lane Sch
The Paddocks Farm
Hayes End
Grange Park Jun & Inf Schs
UB8
UXBRIDGE RD
Pronto Trad Est
Wood End Green
Beck Theatre
Hillingdon Manor Upper Sch
Hayes Stad Sp Ctr
UB3
Rosedale Coll
Wood End
Crkt Gd
Bot Gdns
HAYES
Town Hall Park
Dr Triplett's CE J&I
Wood End Park Com Sch
UXBRIDGE RD

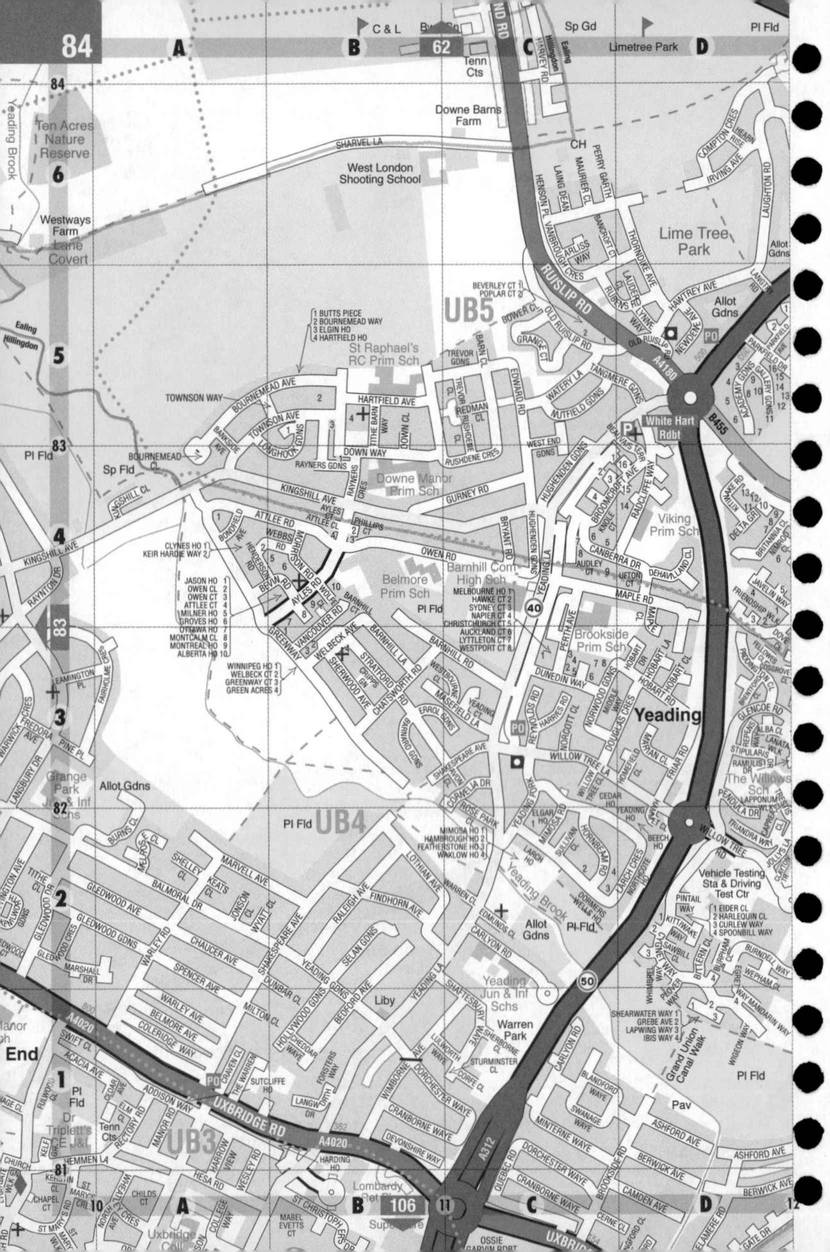
A
B
C
D
62
C & L
Tenn Cts
Sp Gd
Limetree Park
Pl Fld
Hillingdon
Ealing
Yeading Brook
Ten Acres Nature Reserve
6
Downe Barns Farm
SHARVEL LA
CH
West London Shooting School
Westways Farm
Lane Covert
HENSON PL
LAING DEAN
MAURIER CL
PERRY GARTH
VANBROUGH CRES
CARLISS WAY
BANCROFT CT
THORNDIKE AVE
Lime Tree Park
COMPTON CRES
HEARN RISE
IRVING AVE
LAUGHTON RD
Allot Gdns
RUISLIP RD
BEVERLEY CT 1
POPLAR CT 2
UB5
BOWER CL
OLD RUISLIP RD
LAUDER CL
RUBENS RD
LYNNE WAY
HAWTREY AVE
NEWDENE AVE
LANGTRY RD
PO
A4180
1 BUTTS PIECE
2 BOURNEMEAD WAY
3 ELGIN HO
4 HARTFIELD HO
St Raphael's RC Prim Sch
TREVOR GDNS
BARN CL
GRANGE CT
EDWARD RD
TANGMERE GDNS
Ealing
Hillingdon
5
TOWNSON WAY
BOURNEMEAD AVE
HARTFIELD AVE
TITHE BARN WAY
DOWN CL
TREVOR CL
REDMAN CL
RUSHDENE CL
WATERY LA
NUTFIELD GDNS
White Hart Rdbt
B455
PARKFIELD DR
ACADEMY GDNS
GALLERY GDNS
TOWNSON AVE
BANKSIDE AVE
LONGHOOK GDNS
DOWN WAY
WEST END GDNS
BEN JAMES TERR
83
Pl Fld
Sp Fld
BOURNEMEAD CL
RAYNERS GDNS
RAYNERS CRES
RUSHDENE CRES
HUGHENDEN GDNS
BROOMCROFT AVE
RADCLIFFE WAY
Downe Manor Prim Sch
KINGSHILL AVE
GURNEY RD
KINGSHILL CL
AYLES CT
ATTLEE CL
ATTLEE RD
BONDFIELD AVE
PHILLIPS CT
KNOLE CT
Viking Prim Sch
DELTA GR
BRITANNIA CL
NIMROD
4
CLYNES HO 1
KEIR HARDIE WAY 2
WEBBS
MORRISON RD
HENDERSON RD
OWEN RD
BRYANT RD
HUGHENDEN GDNS
YEADING LA
AUDLEY CT
CANBERRA DR
UFTON CT
DEHAVILLAND CL
KINGSHILL AVE
RAYNTON DR
JASON HO 1
OWEN CL 2
OWEN CT 3
ATTLEE CT 4
MILNER HO 5
GROVES HO 6
OTTAWA HO 7
MONTCALM CL 8
MONTREAL HO 9
ALBERTA HO 10
BEVIN RD
AYLES RD
WOLFE
BARNHILL CT
Belmore Prim Sch
Barnhill Com High Sch
MELBOURNE HO 1
HAWKE CT 2
SYDNEY CT 3
NAPIER CT 4
CHRISTCHURCH CT 5
AUCKLAND CT 6
LYTTLETON CT 7
WESTPORT CT 8
MAPLE RD
JAVELIN WAY
FRIENDSHIP WLK
83
VANCOUVER RD
GREENWAY
WELBECK AVE
BARNHILL LA
BARNHILL RD
Pl Fld
40
PERTH AVE
Brookside Prim Sch
HOBART DR
HOBART LA
HOBART CL
HOBART RD
WINNIPEG HO 1
WELBECK CT 2
GREENWAY CT 3
GREEN ACRES 4
LEAMINGTON PL
FAIRHOLME CRES
SHERWOOD AVE
CRIPPS GN
STRATFORD RD
CHATSWORTH RD
WESTBOURNE CL
MASEFIELD LA
YEADING CT
DUNEDIN WAY
NORWOOD GDNS
MIDDLE WAY
Yeading
GLENCOE RD
3
WARWICK CRES
FREDORA AVE
PINE PL
ERROL GDNS
BARNARD GDNS
PO
REYNOLDS RD
HARRES RD
NORCOTT CL
DOUGLAS CRES
MARAN CL
FRIAR RD
STIPULARIS DR
RAMULIS DR
LANSBURY DR
Grange Park Jun & Inf Schs
Allot Gdns
SHAKESPEARE AVE
AVON CT
CORNELIA DR
WILLOW TREE LA
HOMEFIELD CL
WILLOW TREE CL
CEDAR HO
YEADING HO
The Willows Sch
PENDULA DR
LAPPONUM WLK
82
Pl Fld
UB4
ROSE PARK
ELGAR HO
MIMOSA RD
SULLIVAN CL
HORNBEAM RD
BEECH HO
MIMOSA HO 1
HAMBROUGH HO 2
FEATHERSTONE HO 3
WAXLOW HO 4
WILLOW TREE
TRIANDRA WAY
BURNS CL
MELROSE CL
SHELLEY CL
MARVELL AVE
LOTHIAN AVE
LARCH HO
LARCH CRES
NORTHCOTE HO
Vehicle Testing Sta & Driving Test Ctr
2
TITHE CL
GLEDWOOD DR
GLEDWOOD AVE
BALMORAL DR
KEATS CL
JONSON CL
WYATT CL
RALEIGH AVE
FINDHORN AVE
WARREN CL
Yeading Brook
DORMERS WELLS HO
PINTAIL WAY
1 EIDER CL
2 HARLEQUIN CL
3 CURLEW WAY
4 SPOONBILL WAY
GLEDWOOD GDNS
GLEDWOOD CRES
WARLEY RD
CHAUCER AVE
SHAKESPEARE AVE
SELAN GDNS
EDMUNDS CL
Allot Gdns
Pl Fld
KITTIWAKE WAY
CYGNET WAY
SAWBILL CL
BITTERN CL
BURNHAM CL
BURNDELL WAY
WEPHAM CL
MARSHALL DR
SPENCER AVE
DUNBAR CL
YEADING GDNS
BEDFORD AVE
CARLYON RD
YEADING LA
SHAFTESBURY WAYE
Yeading Jun & Inf Schs
50
PLOVER WAY
WHIMBREL WAY
EGRET WAY
MANDARIN WAY
WARLEY AVE
BELMORE AVE
COLERIDGE WAY
MILTON CL
HOLLYWOOD GDNS
Liby
Warren Park
SHEARWATER WAY 1
GREBE AVE 2
LAPWING WAY 3
IBIS WAY 4
A4020
SWIFT CL
ACACIA AVE
CHEDDAR WAYE
FORSTERS WAY
LULWORTH WAYE
SHERBORNE CL
STURMINSTER CL
CORFE CL
CARLYON RD
Grand Union Canal Walk
WIGEON WAY
End
1
Pl Fld
FULWOOD CL
CEDAR AVE
ELM CL
PO
CRAVEN CL
THE WARREN
SUTCLIFFE HO
WIMBORNE AVE
DORCHESTER WAYE
BLANDFORD WAYE
Pl Fld
ADDISON WAY
UXBRIDGE RD
LANGWORTH DR
CRANBORNE WAYE
SWANAGE WAYE
Pav
Dr Triplett's CE J&I
Tenn Cts
RECTORY RD
MANOR RD
UB3
HARROW VIEW
WESLEY RD
A4020
DEVONSHIRE WAY
A312
MINTERNE WAYE
ASHFORD AVE
ASHFORD AVE
KELF GR
HEMMEN LA
81
HARDING HO
DORCHESTER WAYE
QUEBEC RD
BROOKSIDE RD
BERWICK AVE
CHURCH
KERSTIN CL
ST MARY'S CRES
CHAPEL CT
CHILDS CT
HESA RD
WHEATLEY CRES
NORTH AVE
COLLEGE WAY
Lombardy Ret Pk
CRANBORNE WAYE
CAMDEN AVE
BERWICK AVE
10
A
ST CHRISTOPHERS DR
B
106
11
C
D
12
ST MARY'S RD
Uxbridge Coll
MABEL EVETTS CT
Superstore
CERNE CL
UXBRIDGE
OSSIE GARVIN RDBT

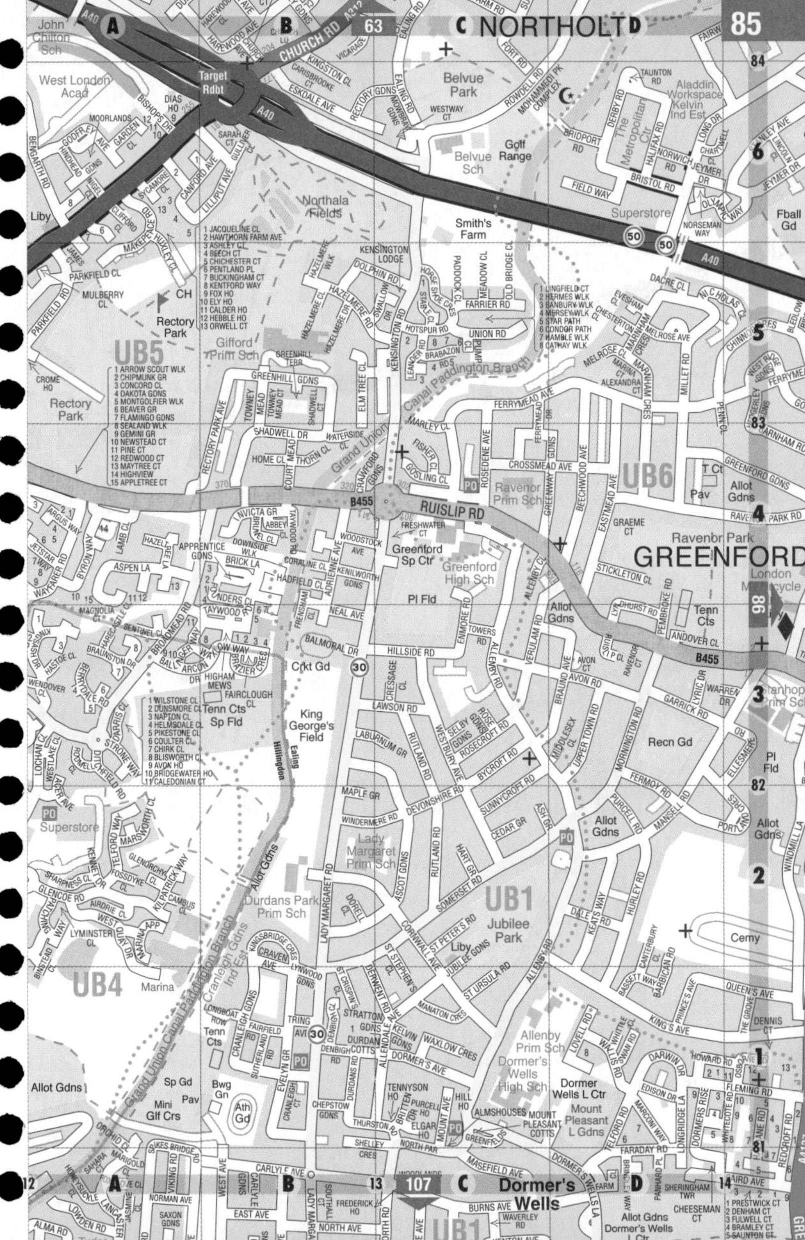
A
B
C
D
NORTHOLT
63
85
84
John Chilton Sch
West London Acad
Target Rdbt
CHURCH RD
A312
A40
Belvue Park
Belvue Sch
Golf Range
Aladdin Workspace
Kelvin Ind Est
The Metropolitan Ctr
Superstore
Fball Gd
Northala Fields
Smith's Farm
KENSINGTON LODGE
1 JACQUELINE CL
2 HAWTHORN FARM AVE
3 ASHLEY CL
4 BEECH CT
5 CHICHESTER CT
6 PENTLAND PL
7 BUCKINGHAM CT
8 KENTFORD WAY
9 FOX HO
10 ELY HO
11 CALDER HO
12 HEBBLE HO
13 ORWELL CT
1 LINGFIELD CT
2 HERMES WLK
3 BANBURY WLK
4 MERSEY WLK
5 STAR PATH
6 CONDOR PATH
7 HAMBLE WLK
8 CATHAY WLK
Rectory Park
Gifford Prim Sch
UB5
1 ARROW SCOUT WLK
2 CHIPMUNK GR
3 CONCORD CL
4 DAKOTA GDNS
5 MONTGOLFIER WLK
6 BEAVER GR
7 FLAMINGO GDNS
8 SEALAND WLK
9 GEMINI GR
10 NEWSTEAD CT
11 PINE CT
12 REDWOOD CT
13 MAYTREE CT
14 HIGHVIEW
15 APPLETREE CT
Grand Union Canal Paddington Branch
RUISLIP RD
B455
Ravenor Prim Sch
UB6
Ravenor Park
GREENFORD
London Motorcycle
Greenford Sp Ctr
Greenford High Sch
Pl Fld
Allot Gdns
Tenn Cts
Crkt Gd
King George's Field
1 WILSTONE CL
2 DUNSMORE CL
3 NAPTON CL
4 HELMSDALE CL
5 PIKESTONE CL
6 COULTER CL
7 CHIRK CL
8 BLISWORTH CL
9 AVON HO
10 BRIDGEWATER HO
11 CALEDONIAN CT
Tenn Cts Sp Fld
Stanhope Prim Sch
Recn Gd
Superstore
Lady Margaret Prim Sch
Durdans Park Prim Sch
UB1
Jubilee Park
Liby
Cemy
UB4
Marina
Cranleigh Gdns Ind Est
Allenby Prim Sch
Dormer's Wells High Sch
Dormer Wells L Ctr
Mount Pleasant L Gdns
Allot Gdns
Sp Gd
Pav
Mini Glf Crs
Bwg Gn
Ath Gd
1 PRESTWICK CT
2 DENHAM CT
3 FULWELL CT
4 BRAMLEY CT
5 SAUNTON CT
A4127
Allot Gdns Dormer's Wells L Ctr

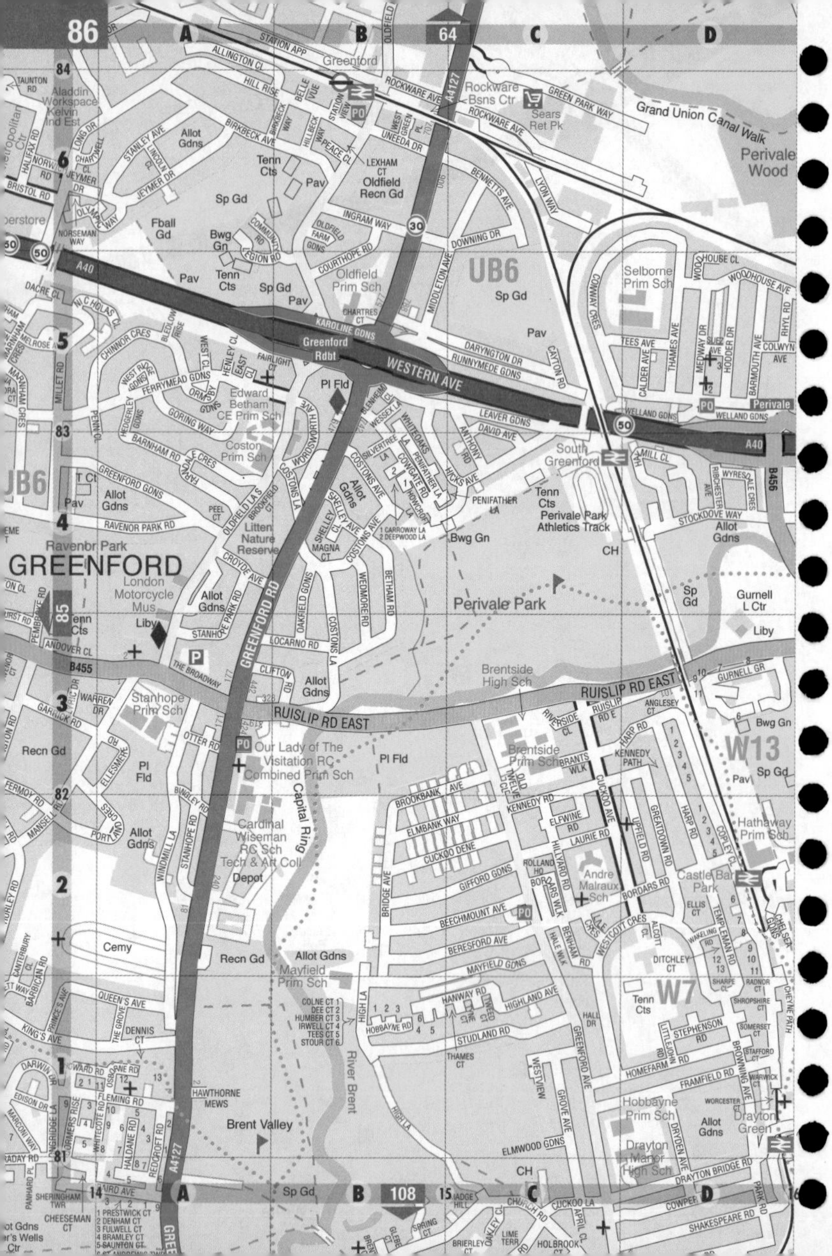

A
B
C
D
64
108
84
83
82
81
6
5
4
3
2
1
14
15
16
85
GREENFORD
UB6
W13
W7
Greenford
STATION APP
ALLINGTON CL
HILL RISE
BELLE VUE
STATION VIEW
ROCKWARE AVE
Rockware Bsns Ctr
Sears Ret Pk
GREEN PARK WAY
Grand Union Canal Walk
Perivale Wood
A4127
Aladdin Workspace
Kelvin Ind Est
TAUNTON RD
HALIFAX RD
NORWICH RD
BRISTOL RD
LONG DR
CHARTWELL
STANLEY AVE
LINCOLN RD
JEYMER DR
JEYMER AVE
BIRKBECK AVE
BIRKBECK WAY
HILLBECK WAY
WEST GREEN PL
UNEEDA DR
PEACE CL
LEXHAM CT
Oldfield Recn Gd
Allot Gdns
Tenn Cts
Pav
Sp Gd
Fball Gd
Bwg Gn
OLYMPIC WAY
NORSEMAN WAY
COMMUNITY RD
OLDFIELD FARM GDNS
INGRAM WAY
COURTHOPE RD
LEGION RD
DOWNING DR
BENNETTS AVE
LYON WAY
MIDDLETON AVE
Oldfield Prim Sch
A40
DACRE CL
NICHOLAS GDNS
BLEDLOW RISE
CHINNOR CRES
MELROSE AV
WEST CL
HENLEY CL
FAIRLIGHT CT
KAROLINE GDNS
Greenford Rdbt
CHARTRES CT
DARYNGTON DR
RUNNYMEDE GDNS
CAYTON RD
WESTERN AVE
CONWAY CRES
Selborne Prim Sch
WOODHOUSE CL
WOODHOUSE AVE
TEES AVE
THAMES AVE
CALDER AVE
MEDWAY DR
HODDER DR
BARMOUTH AVE
COLWYN AVE
RHYL RD
WELLAND GDNS
Perivale
MILLET RD
WEST RIDGE GDNS
FERRYMEAD GDNS
ORMSBY GDNS
HEDGERLEY GDNS
GORING WAY
Edward Betham CE Prim Sch
Pl Fld
WORDSWORTH AVE
BLENHEIM CL
WESSEX LA
WHITEOAKS LA
LEAVER GDNS
DAVID AVE
ANTHONY RD
BARNHAM RD
FARNDALE CRES
Coston Prim Sch
SILVERTREE LA
COWGATE RD
PENIFATHER LA
HICKS AVE
South Greenford
MILL CL
WYRESDALE CRES
RIBCHESTER AVE
B456
GREENFORD GDNS
T Ct
PEEL CT
OLDFIELD LA S
BROOKFIELD CT
COSTONS LA
COSTONS AVE
SHELLEY AVE
HOWCROFT LA
1 CARROWAY LA
2 DEEPWOOD LA
Perivale Park Athletics Track
STOCKDOVE WAY
RAVENOR PARK RD
Ravenor Park
Litten Nature Reserve
MAGNA CT
CH
London Motorcycle Mus
CROYDE AVE
STANHOPE PARK RD
GREENFORD RD
OAKFIELD GDNS
WEDMORE RD
BETHAM RD
Perivale Park
Gurnell L Ctr
Liby
PEMBROKE RD
ANDOVER CL
B455
THE BROADWAY
LOCARNO RD
CLIFTON RD
Brentside High Sch
RUISLIP RD EAST
GURNELL GR
ANGLESEY CT
Bwg Gn
GARRICK RD
WARREN DR
Stanhope Prim Sch
OTTER RD
RIVERSIDE CL
RUISLIP RD E
HARP RD
Recn Gd
ELLESMERE RD
Our Lady of The Visitation RC Combined Prim Sch
Brentside Prim Sch
BRANTS WLK
KENNEDY PATH
Capital Ring
FERMOY RD
MANSELL RD
PORTLAND CRES
BINGLEY RD
BROOKBANK AVE
OLD TWELVE CL
KENNEDY RD
ELFWINE RD
CUCKOO AVE
UPFIELD RD
GREATDOWN RD
Hathaway Prim Sch
COPLEY CL
ELMBANK WAY
LAURIE RD
CUCKOO DENE
Cardinal Wiseman RC Sch Tech & Art Coll
Depot
WINDMILL LA
STANHOPE RD
GIFFORD GDNS
ROLLAND HO
BORDARS WLK
HILLYARD RD
Andre Malraux Sch
BORDARS RD
Castle Bar Park
ELLIS CT
TEMPLEMAN RD
BRIDGE AVE
BEECHMOUNT AVE
CANTERBURY CL
BARBICAN RD
Cemy
BERESFORD AVE
HALE WLK
BENHAM RD
WESTCOTT CRES
ALCOTT CL
WAKELING CT
DITCHLEY CT
CHELSEA GDNS
Mayfield Prim Sch
MAYFIELD GDNS
HIGH LA
COLNE CT 1
DEE CT 2
HUMBER CT 3
IRWELL CT 4
TEES CT 5
STOUR CT 6
HANWAY RD
TYNE CT
TWEED CT
HIGHLAND AVE
HALL DR
RADNOR CT
SHARPE CL
SHROPSHIRE CT
QUEEN'S AVE
PRINCE'S AVE
KING'S AVE
THE GROVE
DENNIS CT
HOBBAYNE RD
STUDLAND RD
THAMES CT
Tenn Cts
STEPHENSON RD
SOMERSET CT
LITTLEJOHN RD
STAFFORD CT
CHEYNE PATH
DARWIN DR
EDISON DR
MARCONI WAY
FLEMING RD
HAWTHORNE MEWS
WESTVIEW
GREENFORD AVE
HOMEFARM RD
FRAMFIELD RD
BROWNING AVE
WARWICK CT
WORCESTER CT
River Brent
GROVE AVE
Hobbayne Prim Sch
Drayton Green
WHITECOTE RD
HALDANE RD
REDCROFT RD
Brent Valley
ELMWOOD GDNS
DRYDEN AVE
Drayton Manor High Sch
DRAYTON BRIDGE RD
PARK RD
PANHARD PL
SHERINGHAM TWR
CHEESEMAN CT
BAIRD AVE
1 PRESTWICK CT
2 DENHAM CT
3 FULWELL CT
4 BRAMLEY CT
5 SAUNTON CT
LADGE HILL
CHURCH RD
CUCKOO LA
APRIL CL
COWPER RD
SHAKESPEARE RD
SPRING CT
OAKLEY CL
LIME TERR
BRIERLEY CT
HOLBROOK CL
GLEBE CT

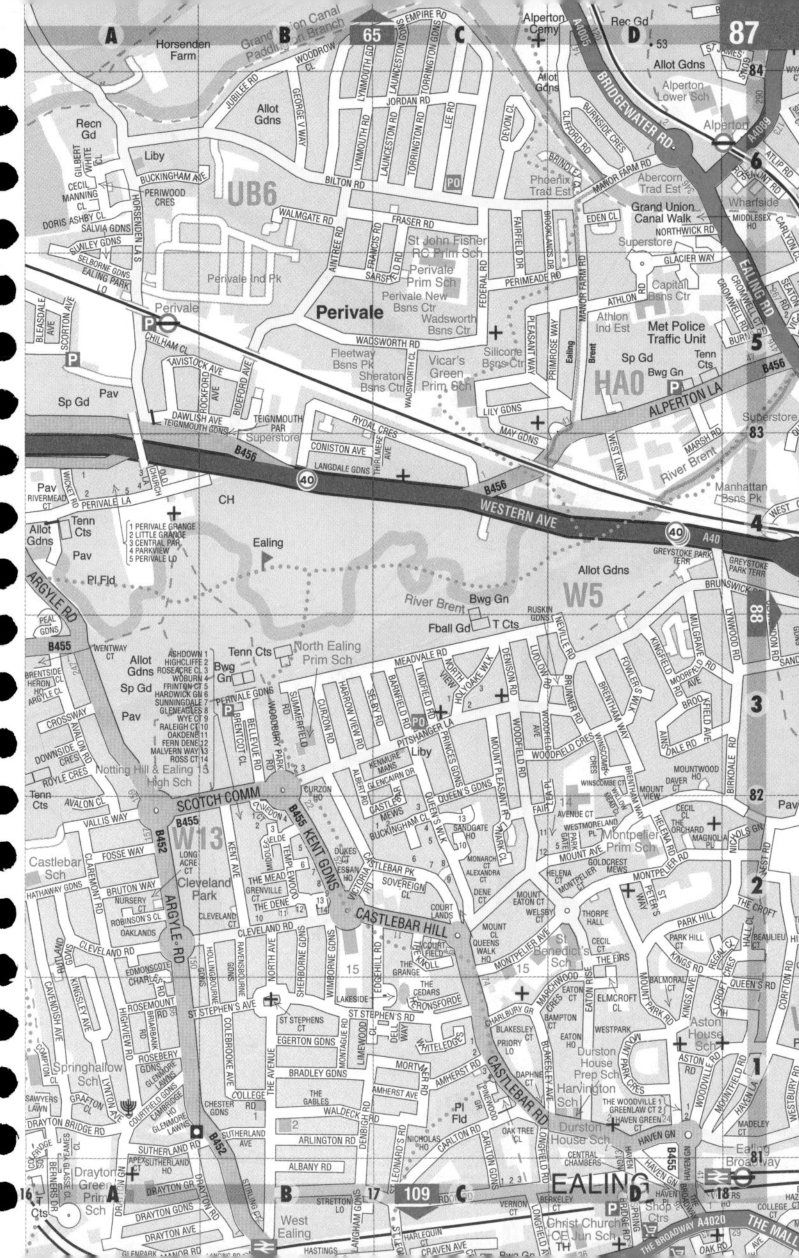

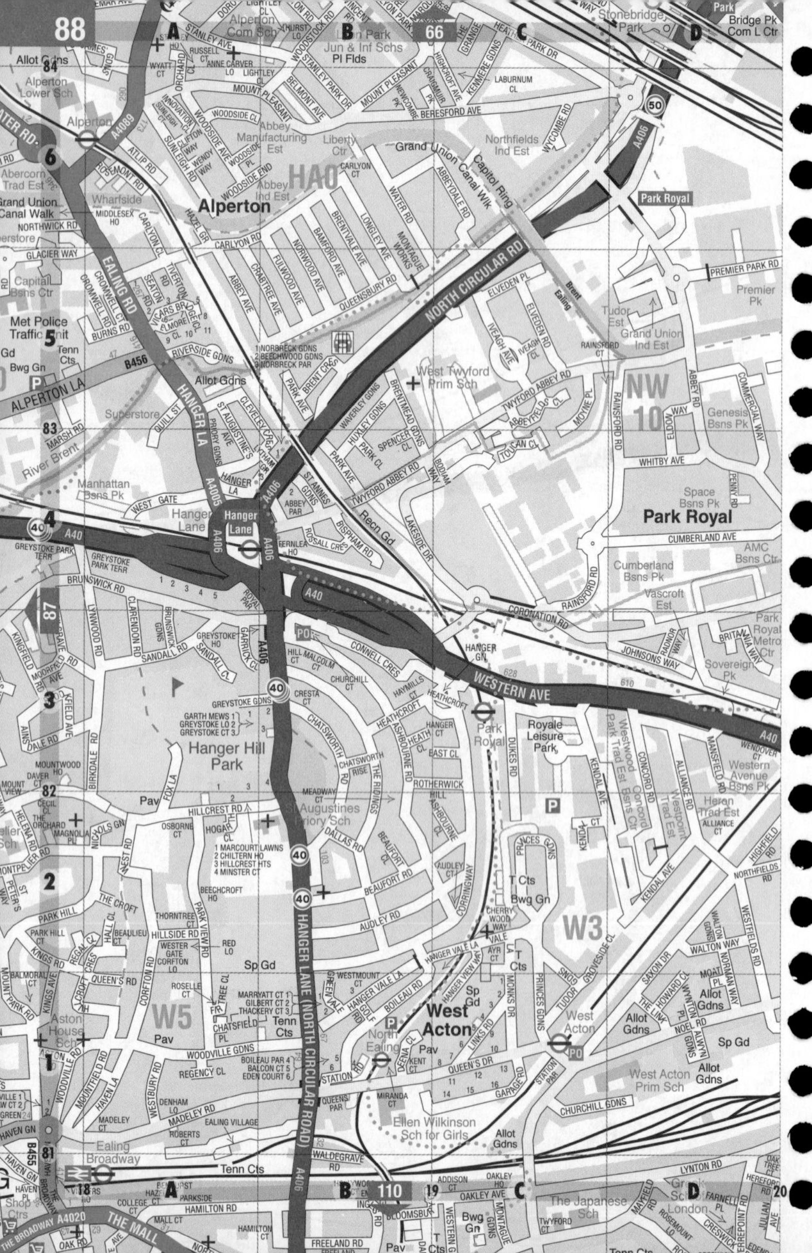

Alperton
Park Royal
West Acton
Hanger Hill Park
HA0
NW10
W3
W5
NORTH CIRCULAR RD
WESTERN AVE
HANGER LANE (NORTH CIRCULAR ROAD)
EALING RD
HANGER LA
ALPERTON LA
Grand Union Canal Walk
Ealing Broadway
North Ealing
Hanger Lane
Park Royal
West Acton
66
110
87

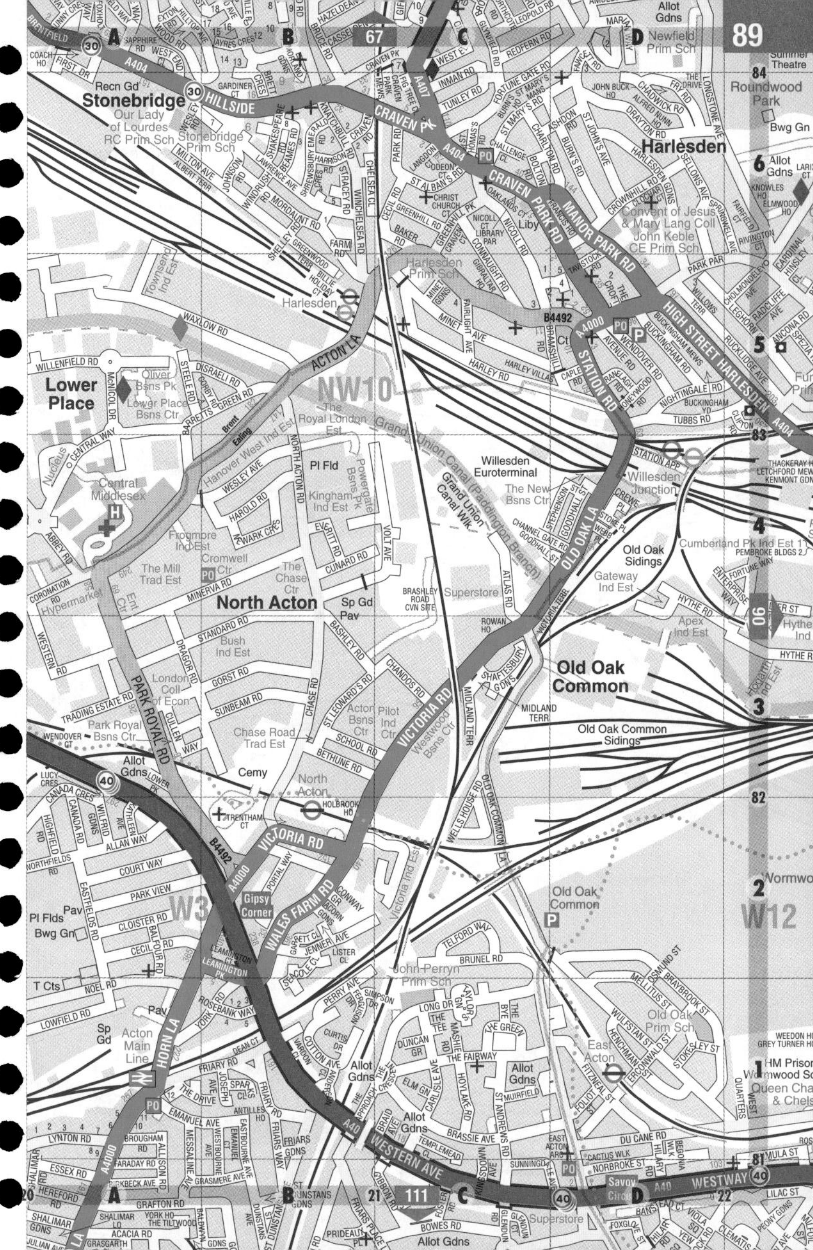
67
111
90
Stonebridge
Harlesden
Lower Place
North Acton
Old Oak Common
NW10
W3
W12
Recn Gd
Our Lady of Lourdes RC Prim Sch
Stonebridge Prim Sch
Newfield Prim Sch
Roundwood Park
Summer Theatre
Bwg Gn
Allot Gdns
Convent of Jesus & Mary Lang Coll
John Keble CE Prim Sch
Harlesden Prim Sch
Liby
Townsend Ind Est
Oliver Bsns Pk
Lower Place Bsns Ctr
The Royal London Est
Grand Union Canal (Paddington Branch)
Grand Union Canal Wlk
Willesden Euroterminal
The New Bsns Ctr
Willesden Junction
Old Oak Sidings
Cumberland Pk Ind Est
Gateway Ind Est
Apex Ind Est
Hythe Rd
Hogarth Ind Est
Hanover West Ind Est
Central Middlesex
Frogmore Ind Est
Cromwell Ctr
The Mill Trad Est
Hypermarket
Pl Fld
Powergate Bsns Pk
Kingham Ind Est
The Chase Ctr
Sp Gd Pav
Superstore
Brashley Road Cvn Site
Bush Ind Est
London Coll of Econ
Park Royal Bsns Ctr
Acton Bsns Ctr
Pilot Ind Ctr
Chase Road Trad Est
Westwood Bsns Ctr
Old Oak Common Sidings
Cemy
North Acton
Victoria Ind Est
Gipsy Corner
Old Oak Common
John Perryn Prim Sch
Old Oak Prim Sch
East Acton
Acton Main Line
HM Prison Wormwood Scrubs
Queen Charlotte's & Chelsea
Wormwood
Savoy Circus
Allot Gdns
Superstore
A404
A407
A4000
B4492
A40
HILLSIDE
CRAVEN PK
CRAVEN PARK RD
MANOR PARK RD
HIGH STREET HARLESDEN
STATION RD
ACTON LA
WAXLOW RD
OLD OAK LA
VICTORIA RD
PARK ROYAL RD
WALES FARM RD
HORN LA
WESTERN AVE
WESTWAY
OLD OAK COMMON LA
NORTH ACTON RD
CHASE RD
MINERVA RD
STANDARD RD
GORST RD
SUNBEAM RD
TELFORD WAY
BRUNEL RD
DU CANE RD
A
B
C
D
1
2
3
4
5
6
20
21
22
81
82
83
84

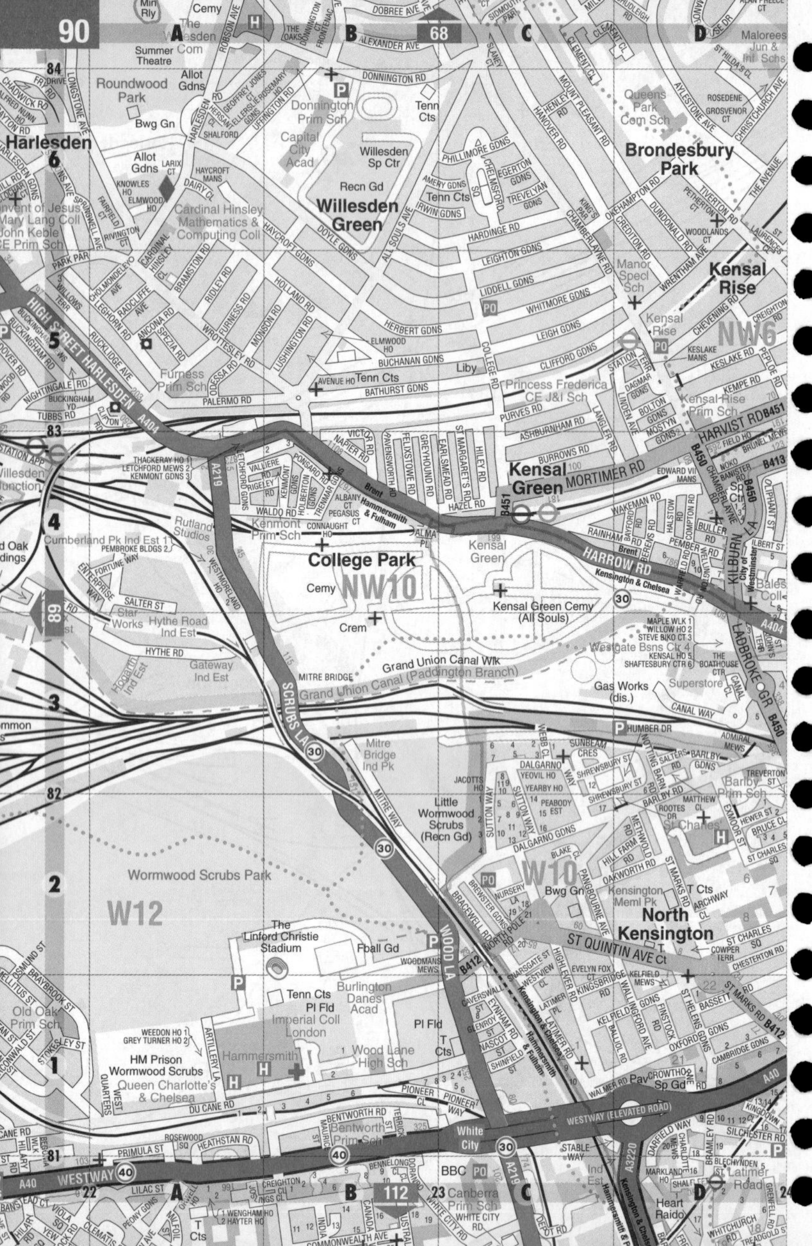

Harlesden
Willesden Green
Brondesbury Park
Kensal Rise
NW6
Kensal Green
College Park
NW10
Kensal Green Cemy (All Souls)
Grand Union Canal (Paddington Branch)
Grand Union Canal Wlk
Wormwood Scrubs Park
W12
Little Wormwood Scrubs (Recn Gd)
W10
North Kensington
The Linford Christie Stadium
HM Prison Wormwood Scrubs
Hammersmith
Queen Charlotte's & Chelsea
Imperial Coll London
Burlington Danes Acad
Wood Lane High Sch
White City
BBC
Westway
Westway (Elevated Road)
High Street Harlesden
Harrow Rd
Mortimer Rd
Scrubs La
Wood La
Ladbroke Gr
Kilburn La
St Quintin Ave
Willesden Sp Ctr
Donnington Prim Sch
Capital City Acad
Cardinal Hinsley Mathematics & Computing Coll
Furness Prim Sch
Kenmont Prim Sch
Princess Frederica CE J&I Sch
Kensal Rise Prim Sch
Queens Park Com Sch
Manor Specl Sch
Mitre Bridge Ind Pk
Gas Works (dis.)
Hythe Road Ind Est
Gateway Ind Est
Star Works
Cumberland Pk Ind Est
Westgate Bsns Ctr
Old Oak Prim Sch
Bentworth Prim Sch
Canberra Prim Sch
Latimer Road
Willesden Junction
Roundwood Park

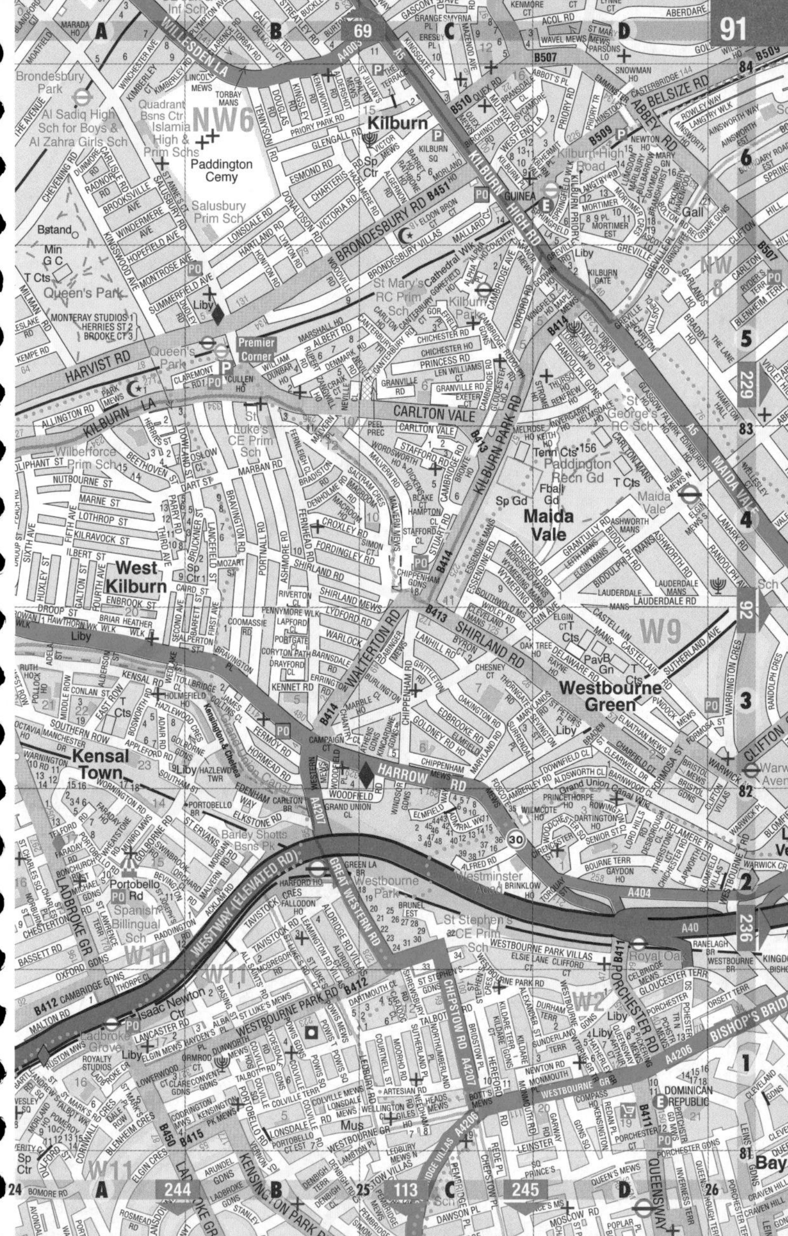
A
B
C
D
69
Brondesbury Park
Al Sadiq High Sch for Boys & Al Zahra Girls Sch
Quadrant Bsns Ctr
Islamia High & Prim Schs
NW6
Paddington Cemy
Kilburn
Salusbury Prim Sch
Bstand
Min G C
T Cts
Queen's Park
MONTERAY STUDIOS 1
HERRIES ST 2
BROOKE CT 3
Premier Corner
HARVIST RD
KILBURN LA
CARLTON VALE
St Luke's CE Prim Sch
Wilberforce Prim Sch
St Mary's RC Prim Sch
Kilburn Park
Kilburn High Road
KILBURN HIGH RD
BRONDESBURY RD
BRONDESBURY VILLAS
WILLESDEN LA
BELSIZE RD
ABBEY RD
MAIDA VALE
St George's RC Sch
Tenn Cts
Paddington Recn Gd
Fball Gd
Sp Gd
Maida Vale
Maida Vale
West Kilburn
SHIRLAND RD
W9
Westbourne Green
HARROW RD
Kensal Town
Grand Union Canal
Barley Shotts Bsns Pk
Portobello Rd
Spanish Billingual Sch
W10
W11
WESTWAY (ELEVATED RD)
GREAT WESTERN RD
Westbourne Park
St Stephen's CE Prim Sch
Westminster Acad
WESTBOURNE PARK VILLAS
Royal Oak
W2
Isaac Newton Ctr
Ladbroke Grove
LADBROKE GR
WESTBOURNE PARK RD
CHEPSTOW RD
PORCHESTER RD
WESTBOURNE GR
BISHOP'S BRIDGE
DOMINICAN REPUBLIC
QUEENSWAY
Mus
KENSINGTON PARK RD
Sp Ctr
229
92
236
244
113
245
84
83
82
81
24
25
26
6
5
4
3
2
1
A5
A404
A40
A4207
A4206
B507
B509
B510
B413
B414
B412
B411
B450
B415
B451
B4

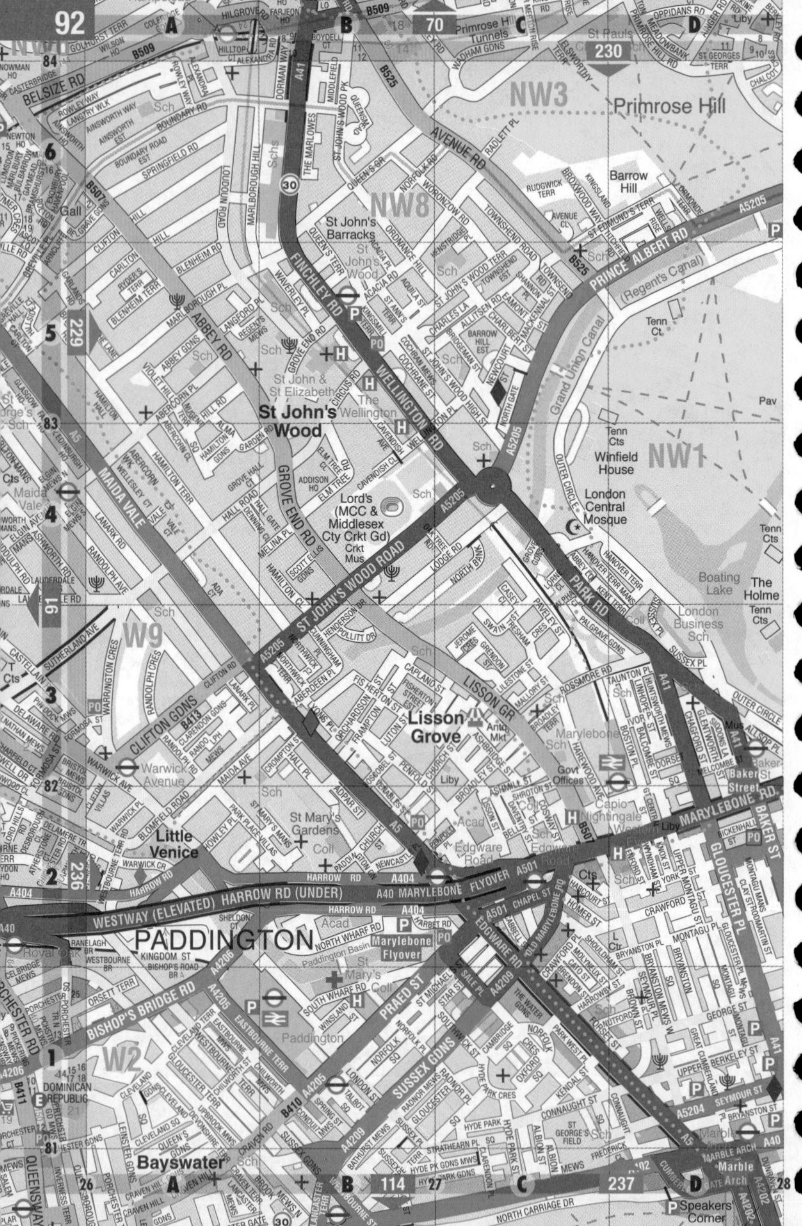

Hampstead
A
B
C
D
70
230
229
91
236
114
237
84
83
82
81
6
5
4
3
2
1
26
27
28
Primrose Hill Tunnels
St Pauls
NW3
Primrose Hill
NW8
NW1
W9
W2
BELSIZE RD
BOUNDARY RD
SPRINGFIELD RD
LOUDOUN ROAD
MARLBOROUGH HILL
ABBEY RD
FINCHLEY RD
WELLINGTON RD
AVENUE RD
ST JOHN'S WOOD PK
QUEEN'S GR
NORFOLK RD
WORONZOW RD
TOWNSHEND RD
ORDNANCE HILL
PRINCE ALBERT RD
(Regent's Canal)
Grand Union Canal
OUTER CIRCLE
Barrow Hill
St John's Barracks
St John's Wood
St John & St Elizabeth
The Wellington
Lord's (MCC & Middlesex Cty Crkt Gd)
Crkt Mus
Winfield House
London Central Mosque
Boating Lake
The Holme
London Business Sch
MAIDA VALE
Maida Vale
GROVE END RD
HAMILTON TERR
CLIFTON HILL
BLENHEIM RD
ST JOHN'S WOOD ROAD
ST JOHN'S WOOD HIGH ST
LODGE RD
PARK RD
LISSON GR
Lisson Grove
Marylebone
Govt Offices
Capio Nightingale
Baker Street
MARYLEBONE RD
BAKER ST
GLOUCESTER PL
CLIFTON GDNS
Warwick Avenue
WARWICK AVE
Little Venice
St Mary's Gardens
Edgware Road
HARROW RD
A40 MARYLEBONE FLYOVER
WESTWAY (ELEVATED) HARROW RD (UNDER)
PADDINGTON
Paddington Basin
Marylebone Flyover
St Mary's
Paddington
Royal Oak
BISHOP'S BRIDGE RD
EDGWARE RD
PRAED ST
SUSSEX GDNS
DOMINICAN REPUBLIC
Bayswater
QUEENSWAY
WESTBOURNE TERR
GLOUCESTER TERR
CONNAUGHT ST
SEYMOUR ST
GEORGE ST
CRAWFORD ST
Marble Arch
Speakers' Corner
NORTH CARRIAGE DR
NORTH RIDE
LANCASTER GATE

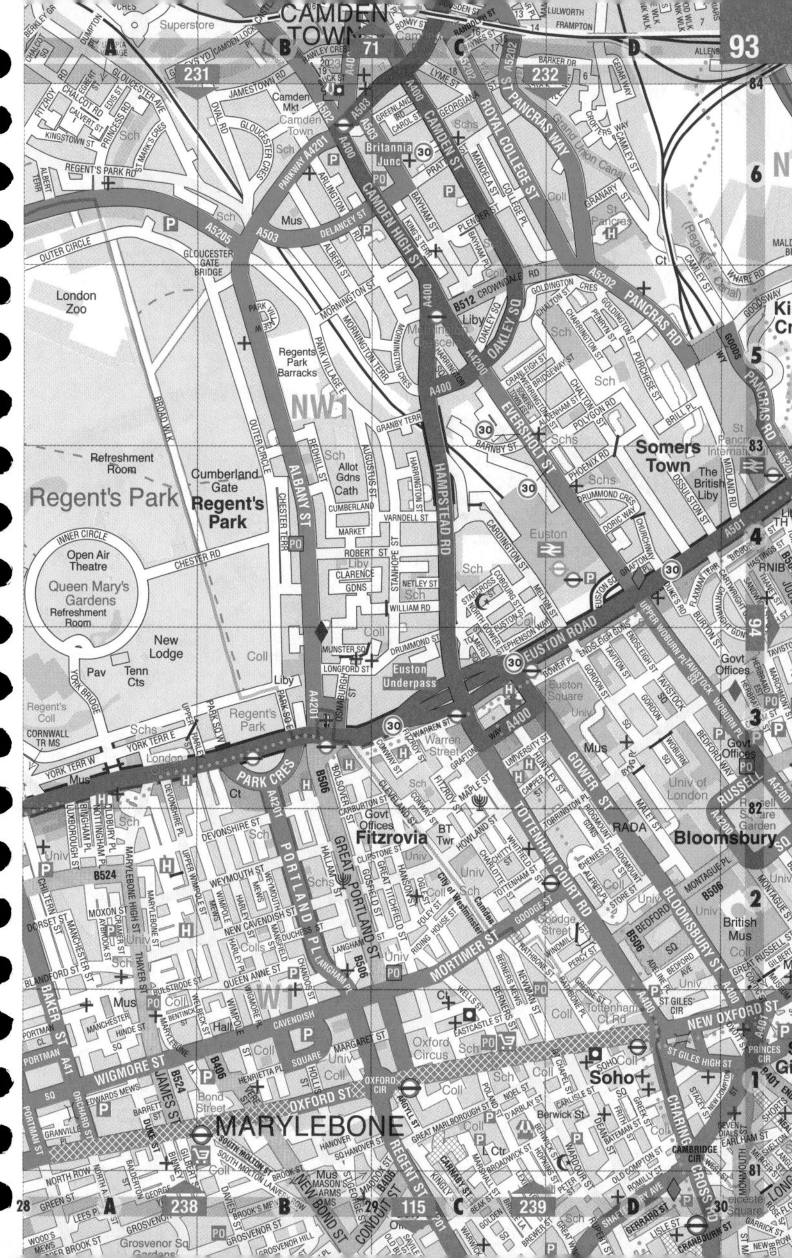

CAMDEN TOWN
Camden Mkt
Britannia Junc
Regent's Park
London Zoo
Regents Park Barracks
NW1
Refreshment Room
Cumberland Gate
Open Air Theatre
Queen Mary's Gardens
New Lodge
Somers Town
The British Liby
Euston
EUSTON ROAD
Euston Underpass
Warren Street
Euston Square
Univ of London
Bloomsbury
Fitzrovia
BT Twr
British Mus
Goodge Street
Tottenham Ct Rd
Oxford Circus
Bond Street
MARYLEBONE
Soho
W1
Grosvenor Sq Gardens
ALBANY ST
HAMPSTEAD RD
CAMDEN HIGH ST
PORTLAND PL
GREAT PORTLAND ST
TOTTENHAM COURT RD
GOWER ST
OXFORD ST
WIGMORE ST
REGENT ST
CHARING CROSS RD
NEW OXFORD ST
BAKER ST
MORTIMER ST
231
232
238
239
71
115
94

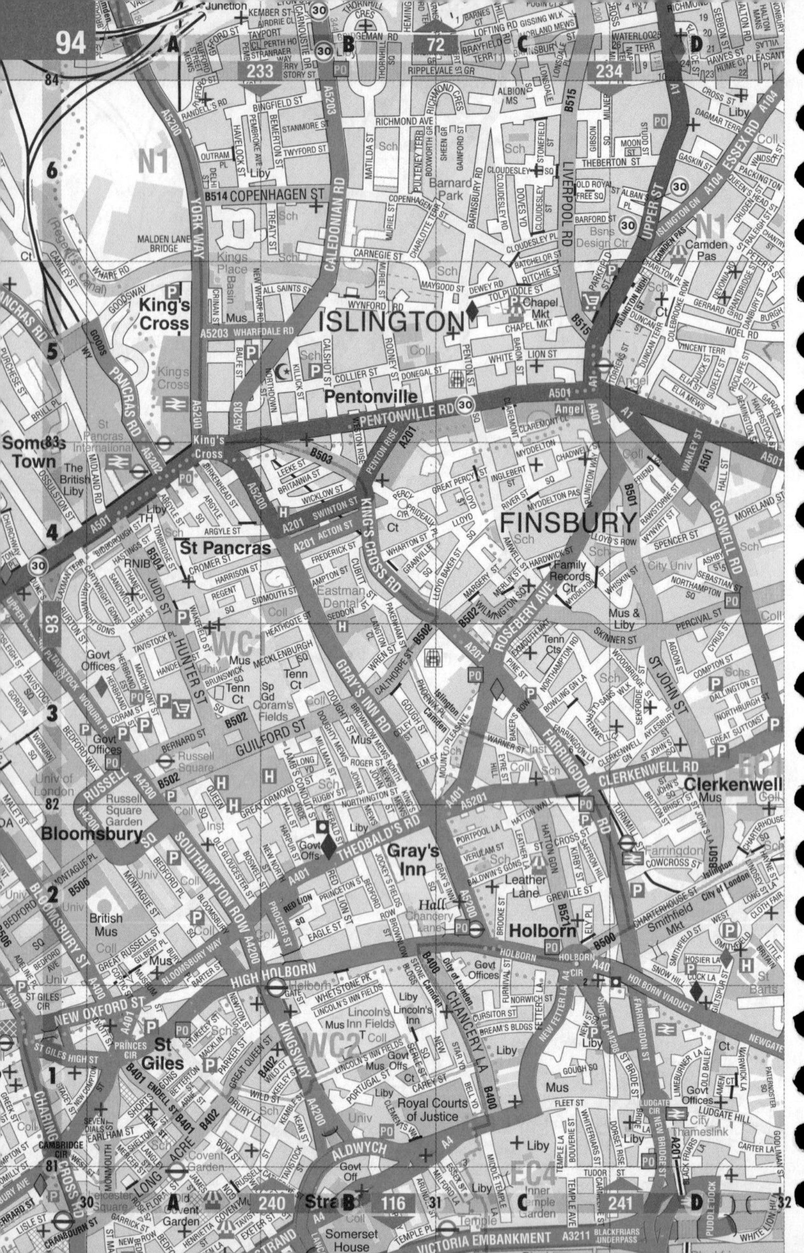

94
A
B
C
D
233
72
234
N1
King's Cross
ISLINGTON
Pentonville
PENTONVILLE RD
CALEDONIAN RD
YORK WAY
LIVERPOOL RD
UPPER ST
ESSEX RD
GOSWELL RD
COPENHAGEN ST
RICHMOND AVE
Barnard Park
Chapel Mkt
Angel
Camden Pas
FINSBURY
ROSEBERY AVE
KING'S CROSS RD
GRAY'S INN RD
FARRINGDON RD
ST JOHN ST
CLERKENWELL RD
Clerkenwell
Family Records Ctr
Somers Town
St Pancras
St Pancras International
The British Liby
EUSTON RD
JUDD ST
HUNTER ST
WC1
GUILFORD ST
Coram's Fields
Eastman Dental
Russell Square
Russell Square Garden
Univ of London
Bloomsbury
SOUTHAMPTON ROW
THEOBALD'S RD
Gray's Inn
Leather Lane
Holborn
HOLBORN
HOLBORN VIADUCT
Smithfield Mkt
British Mus
HIGH HOLBORN
NEW OXFORD ST
St Giles
KINGSWAY
WC2
Lincoln's Inn Fields
Lincoln's Inn
CHANCERY LA
Royal Courts of Justice
FLEET ST
EC4
Inner Temple Garden
ALDWYCH
STRAND
Somerset House
VICTORIA EMBANKMENT
BLACKFRIARS UNDERPASS
LONG ACRE
Covent Garden
CHARING CROSS RD
Leicester Square
Farringdon
City Thameslink
LUDGATE HILL
NEW BRIDGE ST
EC1
240
116
241
30
31
32

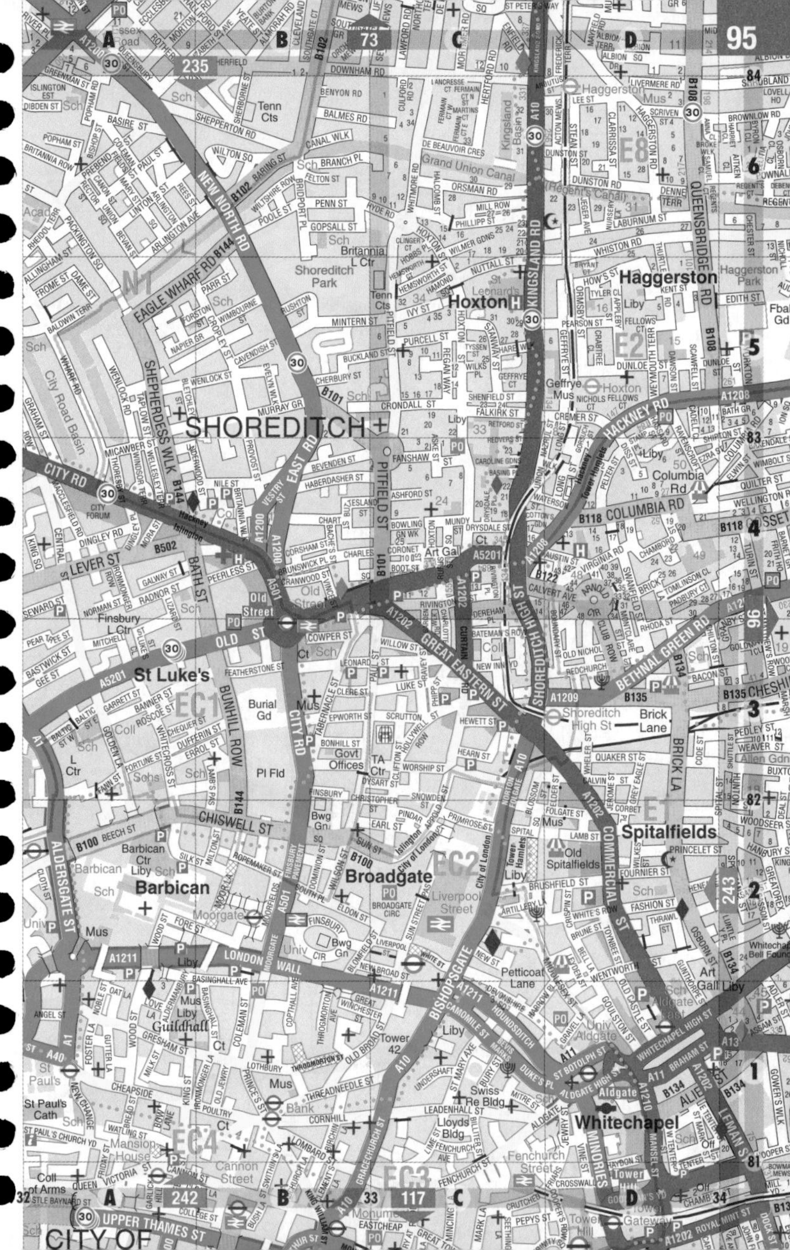
A
B
C
D
73
235
Essex Road
Haggerston
Hoxton
SHOREDITCH
St Luke's
Barbican
Broadgate
Spitalfields
Whitechapel
Shoreditch Park
Haggerston Park
Kingsland Basin
Grand Union Canal
(Regent's Canal)
City Road Basin
N1
E8
E2
E1
EC1
EC2
EC3
EC4
NEW NORTH RD
KINGSLAND RD
QUEENSBRIDGE RD
HACKNEY RD
CITY RD
OLD ST
EAST RD
PITFIELD ST
GREAT EASTERN ST
SHOREDITCH HIGH ST
COLUMBIA RD
BETHNAL GREEN RD
BRICK LA
COMMERCIAL ST
BISHOPSGATE
LONDON WALL
ALDERSGATE ST
BUNHILL ROW
CHISWELL ST
UPPER THAMES ST
MINORIES
WHITECHAPEL HIGH ST
LEMAN ST
EAGLE WHARF RD
SHEPHERDESS WLK
BATH ST
CURTAIN RD
Old Street
Moorgate
Liverpool Street
Aldgate
Aldgate East
Tower Hill
Tower Gateway
Shoreditch High St
Cannon Street
Mansion House
Monument
Bank
Fenchurch Street
St Paul's
Hoxton
Haggerston
Burial Gd
Pl Fld
Guildhall
Tower 42
Swiss Re Bldg
Lloyds Bldg
Petticoat Lane
Old Spitalfields
Geffrye Mus
Columbia Rd
Whitechapel Bell Foundry
St Paul's Cath
Coll of Arms
Barbican Ctr
Finsbury L Ctr
Britannia L Ctr
Govt Offices
Fball Gd
242
117
243
96
CITY OF

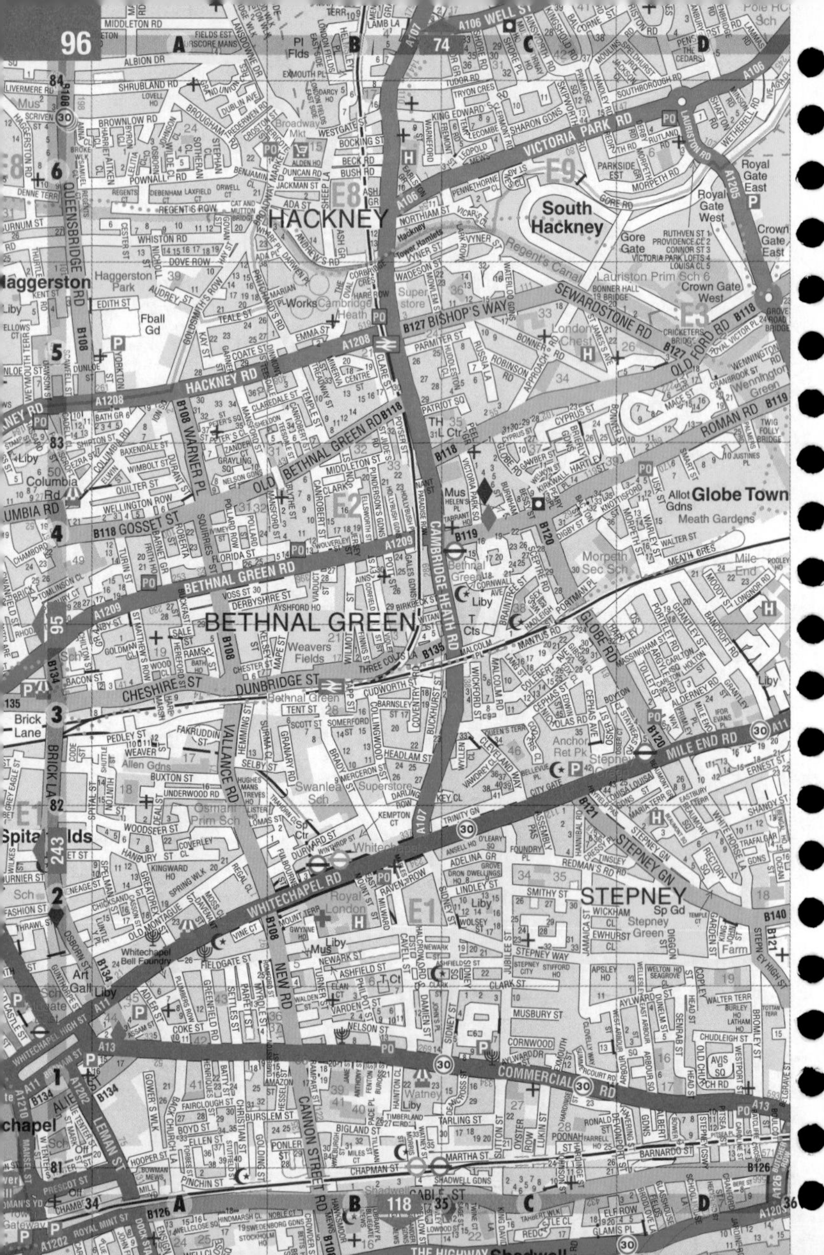

A
B
C
D
74
HACKNEY
E8
South Hackney
E9
Haggerston
Haggerston Park
Cambridge Heath
Regent's Canal
BETHNAL GREEN
E2
Globe Town
Meath Gardens
E3
Bethnal Green
Weavers Fields
Spitalfields
Whitechapel
E1
STEPNEY
Stepney Green
Royal London
Watney
Shadwell
118
95
243
HACKNEY RD
BETHNAL GREEN RD
CAMBRIDGE HEATH RD
VICTORIA PARK RD
ROMAN RD
OLD FORD RD
SEWARDSTONE RD
BISHOP'S WAY
MILE END RD
WHITECHAPEL RD
COMMERCIAL RD
CANNON STREET RD
NEW RD
VALLANCE RD
GLOBE RD
BRICK LA
QUEENSBRIDGE RD
WARNER PL
CHESHIRE ST
DUNBRIDGE ST
GOSSET ST
STEPNEY GN
STEPNEY WAY
CABLE ST
THE HIGHWAY
LEMAN ST
Brick Lane
Royal Gate East
Royal Gate West
Crown Gate East
Crown Gate West
Gore Gate
Allot Gdns
Mile End
Morpeth Sec Sch
Anchor Ret Pk
Swanlea Sch
Superstore
Osmani Prim Sch
Allen Gdns
Whitechapel Bell Foundry
Art Gall
Columbia Rd
Broadway Mkt
Lauriston Prim Sch
London Chest
Stepney Green Sp Gd
Farm
1
2
3
4
5
6
36

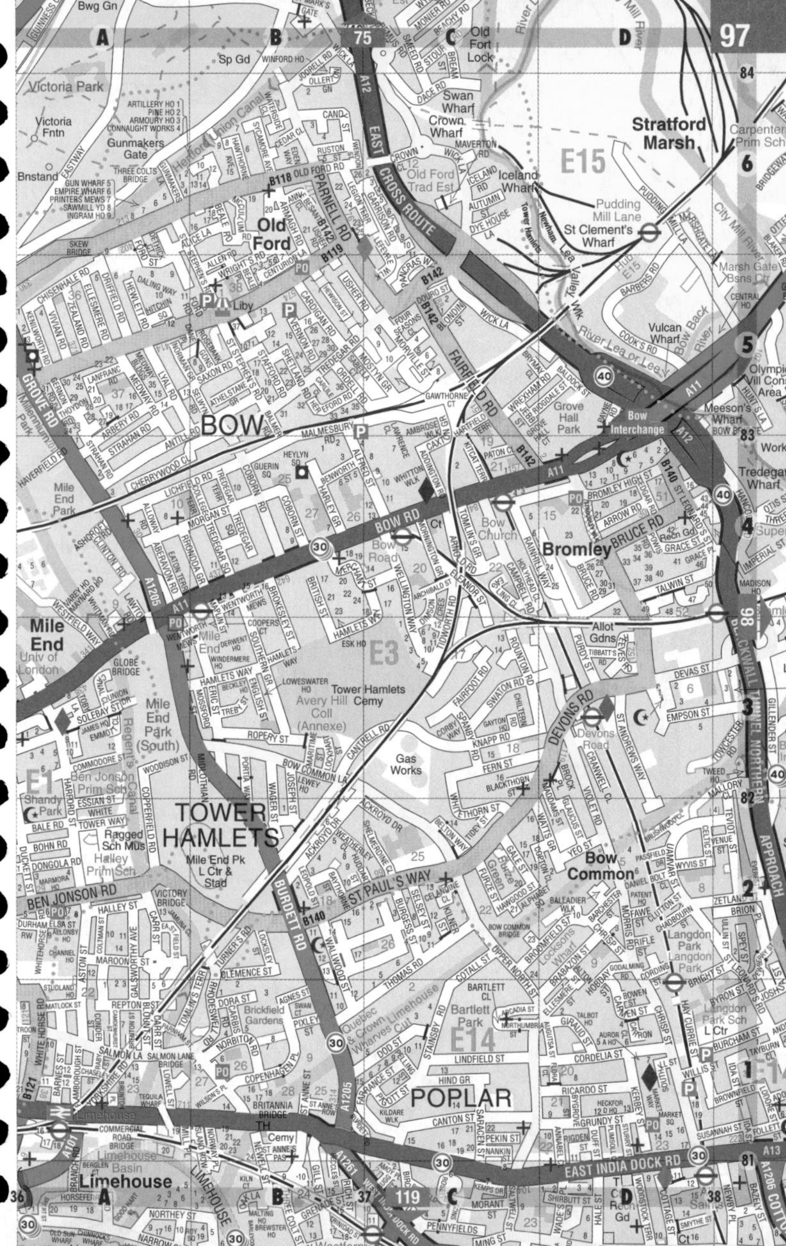

A
B
C
D
75
Victoria Park
Victoria Fntn
Gunmakers Gate
Old Ford
BOW
Bow Road
Bow Church
Bromley
Mile End
Mile End Park
Mile End Park (South)
TOWER HAMLETS
Tower Hamlets Cemy
E3
E15
E14
E1
Stratford Marsh
Old Fort Lock
Swan Wharf
Crown Wharf
Iceland Wharf
Pudding Mill Lane
St Clement's Wharf
Old Ford Trad Est
Grove Hall Park
Bow Interchange
Vulcan Wharf
Devons Road
Gas Works
Bow Common
Langdon Park
POPLAR
Bartlett Park
Limehouse
Limehouse Basin
EAST INDIA DOCK RD
BOW RD
CROSS ROUTE
GROVE RD
BURDETT RD
ST PAUL'S WAY
DEVONS RD
FAIRFIELD RD
BLACKWALL TUNNEL NORTHERN APPROACH
A12
A11
A13
A1205
B140
B142
119
98

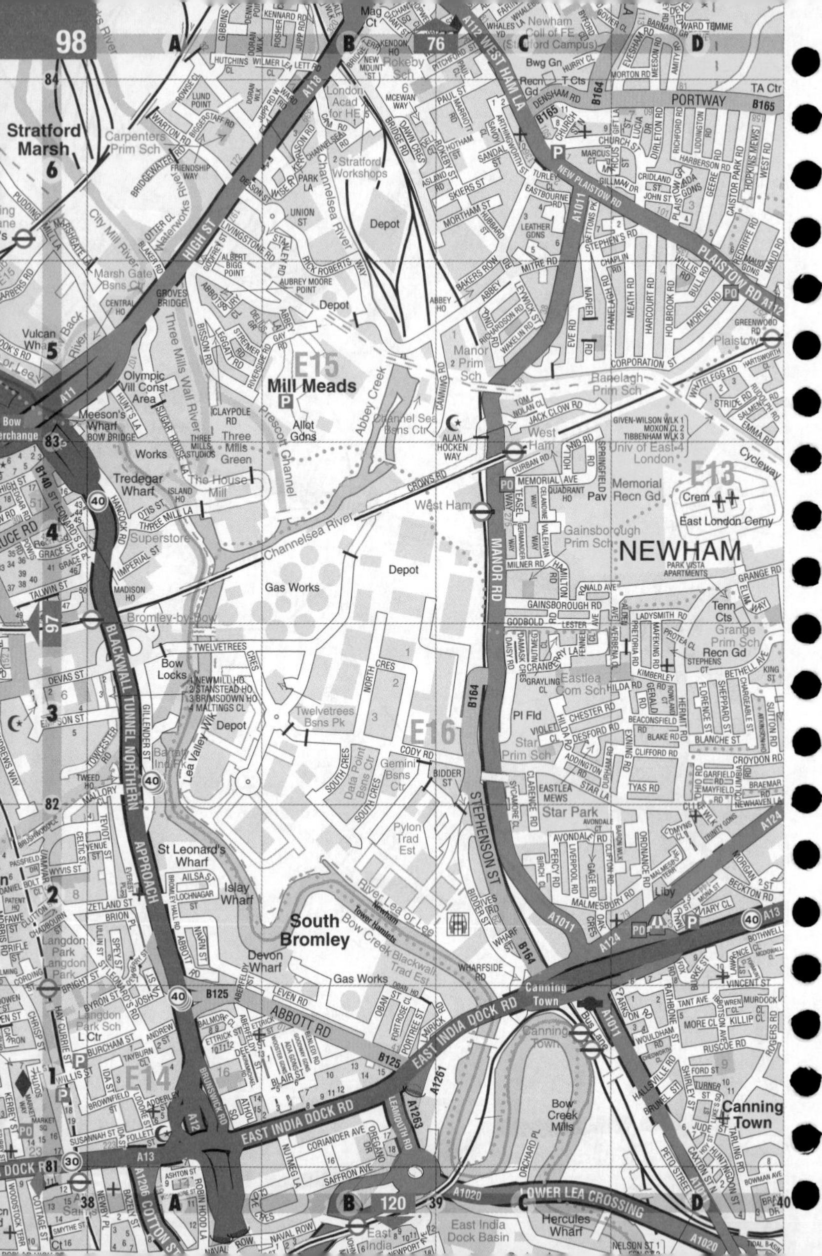
A
B
C
D
76
97
120
Stratford Marsh
6
5
4
3
2
1
84
83
82
81
Carpenters Prim Sch
City Mill River
Waterworks River
Marsh Gate Bsns Ctr
Vulcan Wharf
Bow Back River
Olympic Vill Const Area
Bow Interchange
Meeson's Wharf
BOW BRIDGE
Works
Tredegar Wharf
Superstore
Three Mills Wall River
Three Mills Green
The House Mill
Prescott Channel
E15
Mill Meads
Allot Gdns
Abbey Creek
Channel Sea Bsns Ctr
Channelsea River
Stratford Workshops
London Acad for HE
Rokeby Sch
Newham Coll of FE (Stratford Campus)
Depot
Gas Works
Bromley-by-Bow
Bow Locks
Twelvetrees Bsns Pk
Data Point Bsns Ctr
Gemini Bsns Ctr
Pylon Trad Est
E16
St Leonard's Wharf
Islay Wharf
Devon Wharf
South Bromley
Lea Valley Wlk
River Lea or Lee
Bow Creek
Blackwall Trad Est
Langdon Park
Langdon Park Sch
L Ctr
E14
BLACKWALL TUNNEL NORTHERN APPROACH
HIGH ST
A11
A12
A13
A118
A112
WEST HAM LA
A1011
MANOR RD
STEPHENSON ST
B164
B125
ABBOTT RD
EAST INDIA DOCK RD
LOWER LEA CROSSING
A1020
A1261
A1263
A1206
COTTON ST
Canning Town
Bow Creek Mills
East India Dock Basin
Hercules Wharf
East India
Manor Prim Sch
Ranelagh Prim Sch
West Ham
Univ of East London
Memorial Recn Gd
Pav
E13
Crem
East London Cemy
NEWHAM
Gainsborough Prim Sch
Eastlea Com Sch
Pl Fld
Star Prim Sch
Star Park
Tenn Cts
Grange Prim Sch
Recn Gd
Liby
Plaistow
PLAISTOW RD
PORTWAY
NEW PLAISTOW RD
Cycleway
Bwg Gn
Recn Gd
T Cts
TA Ctr

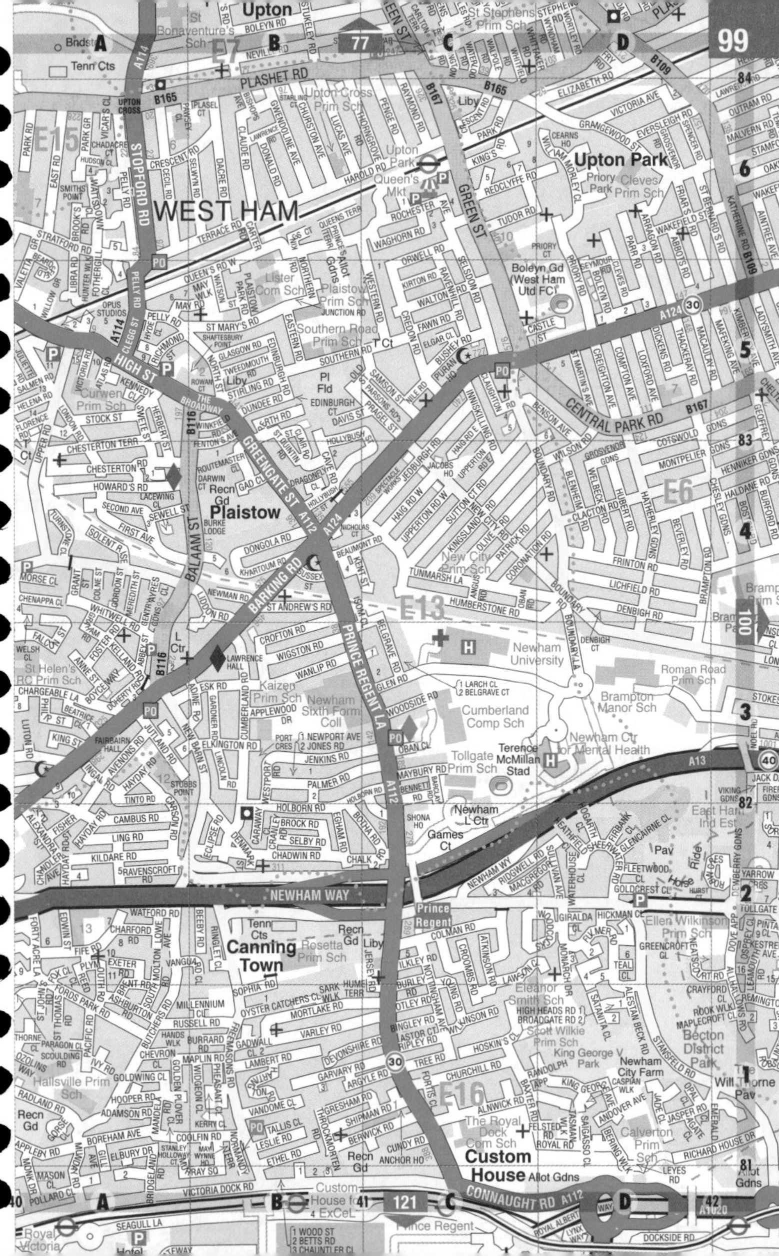
Upton
WEST HAM
Upton Park
Plaistow
Canning Town
Custom House
E15
E7
E13
E6
E16
HIGH ST
GREENGATE ST
BARKING RD
PRINCE REGENT LA
NEWHAM WAY
CENTRAL PARK RD
CONNAUGHT RD
STOPFORD RD
GREEN ST
PLASHET RD
BALAAM ST
Newham University
Boleyn Gd (West Ham Utd FC)
Newham L Ctr
A
B
C
D
77
100
121

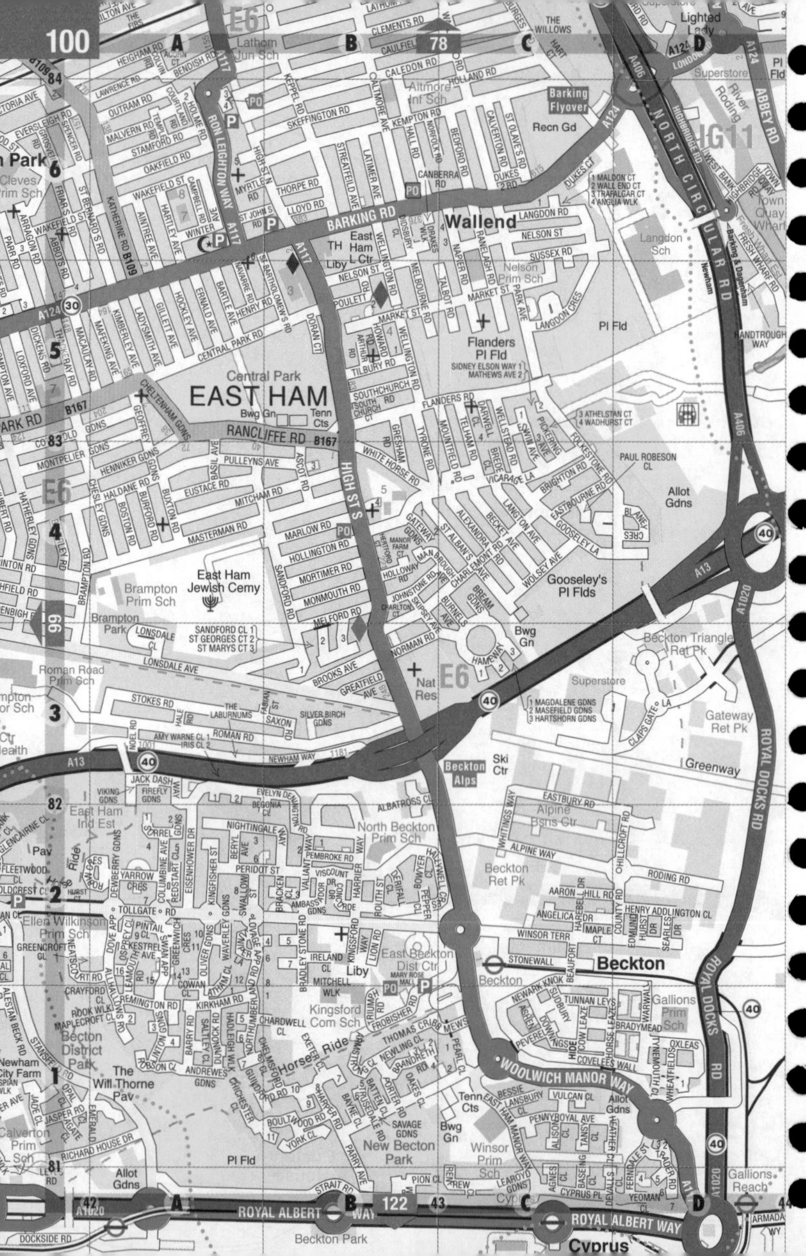

A
B
C
D
78
E6
Lathom Jun Sch
THE WILLOWS
Lighted Lady
HEIGHAM RD
BENDISH RD
CLEMENTS RD
CAULFIELD RD
CALEDON RD
HOLLAND RD
Altmore Inf Sch
Barking Flyover
VICTORIA AVE
LAWRENCE RD
OUTRAM RD
KEPPEL RD
CALTMORE AVE
SKEFFINGTON RD
KEMPTON RD
EVERSLEIGH RD
MALVERN RD
STAMFORD RD
RON LEIGHTON WAY
Recn Gd
NORTH CIRCULAR RD
IG11
ABBEY RD
River Roding
Superstore
OAKFIELD RD
STREATFEILD AVE
LATIMER AVE
HALL RD
NORFOLK RD
BEDFORD RD
CALVERTON RD
ST OLAVE'S RD
6
Cleves Prim Sch
WAKEFIELD ST
THORPE RD
LLOYD RD
CANBERRA RD
DUKES RD
DUKES CT
1 MALDON CT
2 WALL END CT
3 TRAFALGAR CT
4 ANGLIA WLK
KATHERINE RD
BARKING RD
Wallend
LANGDON RD
NELSON ST
SUSSEX RD
Langdon Sch
Town Quay Wharf
FRESH WHARF RD
Barking & Dagenham
Newham
East Ham L Ctr
TH
Liby
WELLINGTON RD
MELBOURNE RD
NAPIER RD
RANELAGH RD
Nelson Prim Sch
MARKET ST
PARK AVE
LANGDON CRES
A124
30
KIMBERLEY AVE
LADYSMITH AVE
GILLETT AVE
HOCKLEY AVE
ERNALD AVE
BARTLE AVE
HENRY RD
ST BARTHOLOMEW'S RD
POULETT RD
Pl Fld
HANDTROUGH WAY
5
CENTRAL PARK RD
Flanders Pl Fld
SIDNEY ELSON WAY 1
MATHEWS AVE 2
TILBURY RD
Central Park
EAST HAM
SOUTHCHURCH RD
FLANDERS RD
PARK RD
B167
CHELTENHAM GDNS
Bwg Gn
Tenn Cts
RANCLIFFE RD
3 ATHELSTAN CT
4 WADHURST CT
83
MONTPELIER GDNS
HENNIKER GDNS
PULLEYNS AVE
ASCOT RD
HIGH ST S
WHITE HORSE RD
GRESHAM RD
TYRONE RD
MOUNTFIELD RD
TELHAM RD
WELLSTEAD RD
PICKERING AVE
FOLKESTONE RD
PAUL ROBESON CL
E6
HALDANE RD
EUSTACE RD
MITCHAM RD
VICARAGE LA
BRIGHTON RD
EASTBOURNE RD
Allot Gdns
4
BOSTON RD
BURFORD RD
BUXTON RD
MASTERMAN RD
MARLOW RD
ALEXANDRA RD
BECKET AVE
LANGTON AVE
GOOSELEY LA
BLANEY CRES
40
HOLLINGTON RD
MORTIMER RD
MONMOUTH RD
HOLLOWAY RD
WOLSEY AVE
A13
Brampton Prim Sch
East Ham Jewish Cemy
SANDFORD RD
Gooseley's Pl Flds
A1020
99
Brampton Park
LONSDALE CL
SANDFORD CL 1
ST GEORGES CT 2
ST MARYS CT 3
MELFORD RD
NORMAN RD
Bwg Gn
HAMEWAY
Beckton Triangle Ret Pk
LONSDALE AVE
BROOKS AVE
GREATFIELD AVE
Nat Res
Roman Road Prim Sch
Superstore
3
STOKES RD
THE LABURNUMS
SAXON RD
SILVER BIRCH GDNS
1 MAGDALENE GDNS
2 MASEFIELD GDNS
3 HARTSHORN GDNS
CLAPS GATE LA
Gateway Ret Pk
ROYAL DOCKS RD
AMY WARNE CL 1
IRIS CL 2
ROMAN RD
NEWHAM WAY
Ski Ctr
Beckton Alps
Greenway
JACK DASH WAY
EVELYN DENNINGTON RD
ALBATROSS CL
EASTBURY RD
82
East Ham Ind Est
NIGHTINGALE WAY
North Beckton Prim Sch
Alpine Bsns Ctr
WHITINGS WAY
HILLCROFT RD
Pav
ALPINE WAY
PEMBROKE RD
PERIDOT ST
VISCOUNT DR
HARRIER WAY
Beckton Ret Pk
RODING RD
FLEETWOOD
YARROW CRES
2
TOLLGATE RD
AARON HILL RD
HENRY ADDLINGTON CL
ANGELICA DR
MAPLE CT
Ellen Wilkinson Prim Sch
WINSOR TERR
GREENCROFT CL
IRELAND CL
East Beckton Dist Ctr
Liby
STONEWALL
Beckton
MITCHELL WLK
MARY ROSE MALL
CRAYFORD CL
REMINGTON RD
KIRKHAM RD
Kingsford Com Sch
NEWARK KNOK
TUNNAN LEYS
Gallions Prim Sch
BRADYMEAD
ROOK WLK
MAPLECROFT CL
CHARDWELL CL
FROBISHER RD
THOMAS CRIBB MEWS
PEVEREL
COVELEES WALL
OXLEAS
Becton District Park
Horse Ride
NEWLING CL
WOOLWICH MANOR WAY
1
Newham City Farm
The Will Thorne Pav
ANDREWES GDNS
CHICHESTER CL
BRANDRETH RD
WHEATFIELDS
BESSIE LANSBURY CL
VULCAN CL
Allot Gdns
Tenn Cts
EAST HAM MANOR WAY
PENNYROYAL AVE
JASPER RD
BOULTWOOD RD
SAVAGE GDNS
Bwg Gn
Calverton Prim Sch
RICHARD HOUSE DR
YORK CL
New Becton Park
Winsor Prim Sch
ALISON CL
TANSY CL
HEATHER CL
FERNDALE ST
TRADER RD
81
Pl Fld
Allot Gdns
PARRY AVE
STRAIT RD
PION CL
LEAROYD GDNS
AGNES CL
BASING CL
DEVALLS CL
CYPRUS PL
YEOMAN CL
Gallions Reach
42
A
B
122
43
C
D
44
A1020
ROYAL ALBERT WAY
ROYAL ALBERT WAY
ARMADA WY
DOCKSIDE RD
Beckton Park
Cyprus

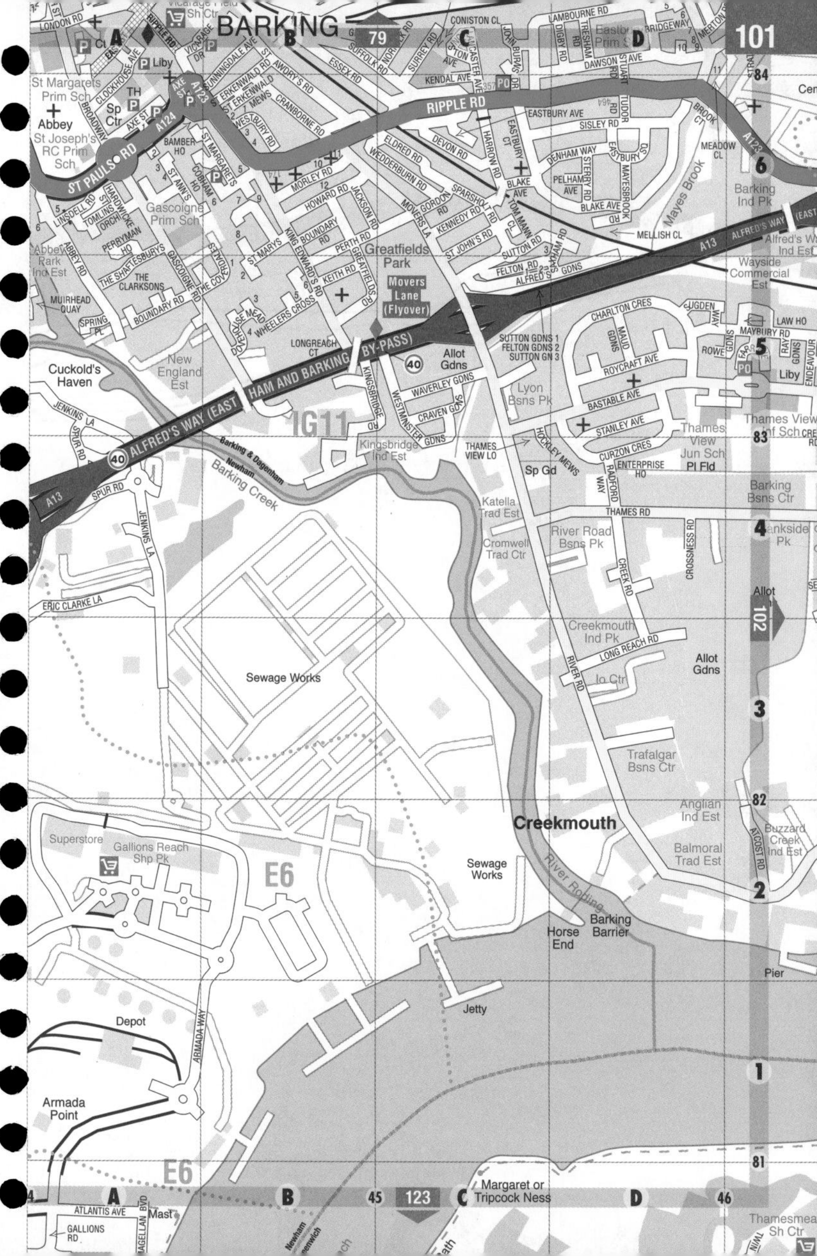
BARKING
79
A
B
C
D
Ripple Rd
St Pauls Rd
Alfred's Way (East Ham and Barking By-Pass)
A13
A123
A124
St Margarets Prim Sch
Abbey
St Joseph's RC Prim Sch
Gascoigne Prim Sch
Abbey Rark Ind Est
Muirhead Quay
Cuckold's Haven
New England Est
Greatfields Park
Movers Lane (Flyover)
Allot Gdns
Lyon Bsns Pk
IG11
Kingsbridge Ind Est
Barking Creek
Barking & Dagenham
Newham
Katella Trad Est
Cromwell Trad Ctr
River Road Bsns Pk
Creekmouth Ind Pk
Trafalgar Bsns Ctr
Anglian Ind Est
Balmoral Trad Est
Buzzard Creek Ind Est
Creekmouth
Sewage Works
River Roding
Barking Barrier
Horse End
Jetty
Pier
Superstore
Gallions Reach Shp Pk
E6
Depot
Armada Point
Armada Way
Margaret or Tripcock Ness
Thames View Inf Sch
Thames View Jun Sch
Barking Bsns Ctr
Barking Ind Pk
Alfred's Way Ind Est
Wayside Commercial Est
Mayes Brook
Thames Rd
River Rd
Creek Rd
Crossness Rd
Long Reach Rd
Eric Clarke La
Jenkins La
Spur Rd
Atlantis Ave
Gallions Rd
Magellan Blvd
Mast
Thamesmead Sh Ctr
Atcost Rd
6
5
4
3
2
1
84
83
82
81
102
45
46
123

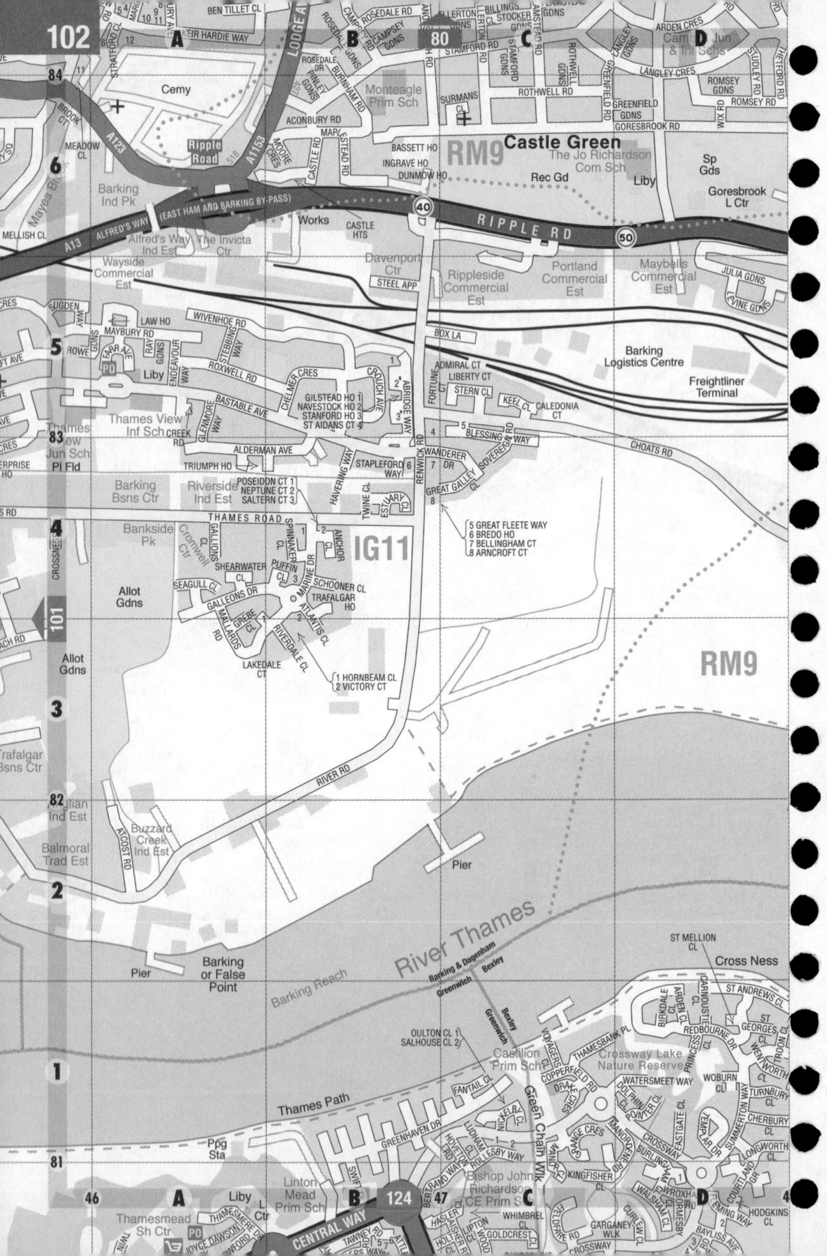
80
BEN TILLET CL
KEIR HARDIE WAY
LODGE AV
ROSEDALE RD
CAMPSEY GDNS
STAMFORD RD
ARDEN CRES
Cambell Jun & Inf Schs
LANGLEY CRES
ROMSEY GDNS
ROMSEY RD
Cemy
Monteagle Prim Sch
SURMANS CL
ROTHWELL RD
GREENFIELD GDNS
GORESBROOK RD
ACONBURY RD
MAPLESTEAD RD
BASSETT HO
INGRAVE HO
DUNMOW HO
RM9
Castle Green
The Jo Richardson Com Sch
Rec Gd
Liby
Sp Gds
Goresbrook L Ctr
Ripple Road
A123
A1153
MEADOW CL
Barking Ind Pk
A13 ALFRED'S WAY (EAST HAM AND BARKING BY-PASS)
Works
CASTLE HTS
RIPPLE RD
MELLISH CL
Alfred's Way Ind Est
The Invicta Ctr
Wayside Commercial Est
Davenport Ctr
STEEL APP
Rippleside Commercial Est
Portland Commercial Est
Maybells Commercial Est
JULIA GDNS
LEVINE GDNS
SUGDEN WAY
LAW HO
WIVENHOE RD
MAYBURY RD
BOX LA
ROWE GDNS
FARR AVE
RAY GDNS
STEBBING WAY
Barking Logistics Centre
Freightliner Terminal
PO
Liby
ENDEAVOUR WAY
ROXWELL RD
CHELMER CRES
CROUCH AVE
ABRIDGE WAY
ADMIRAL CT
LIBERTY CT
STERN CL
KEEL CL
CALEDONIA CT
FORTUNE CT
GILSTEAD HO 1
NAVESTOCK HO 2
STANFORD HO 3
ST AIDANS CT 4
BASTABLE AVE
Thames View Inf Sch
Thames View Jun Sch
Pl Fld
GLENMORE WAY
CREEK RD
BLESSING WAY
CHOATS RD
ALDERMAN AVE
TRIUMPH HO
HAVERING WAY
STAPLEFORD WAY
RENWICK RD
WANDERER DR
SOVEREIGN RD
GREAT GALLEY CL
Barking Bsns Ctr
Riverside Ind Est
POSEIDON CT 1
NEPTUNE CT 2
SALTERN CT 3
TWINE CL
ESTUARY CL
THAMES ROAD
Bankside Pk
Cromwell Ctr
CROSSNESS RD
GALLIONS CL
SPINNAKER CL
ANCHOR CL
IG11
5 GREAT FLEETE WAY
6 BREDO HO
7 BELLINGHAM CT
8 ARNCROFT CT
SHEARWATER CL
PUFFIN CL
MARINE DR
SCHOONER CL
TRAFALGAR HO
SEAGULL CL
GALLEONS DR
Allot Gdns
MALLARDS RD
GREBE CL
ATLANTIS CL
RIVERDALE CL
LAKEDALE CT
101
1 HORNBEAM CL
2 VICTORY CT
RM9
Allot Gdns
Trafalgar Bsns Ctr
RIVER RD
Anglian Ind Est
ATCOST RD
Buzzard Creek Ind Est
Balmoral Trad Est
Pier
River Thames
Pier
Barking or False Point
Barking Reach
Barking & Dagenham
Greenwich
Bexley
ST MELLION CL
Cross Ness
ST ANDREWS CL
BIRKDALE CL
ARDEN CL
CARNOUSTIE CL
REDBOURNE DR
ST GEORGES CL
OULTON CL 1
SALHOUSE CL 2
VOYAGERS
THAMESBANK PL
Castilion Prim Sch
Crossway Lake Nature Reserve
PRINCESS CL
WENTWORTH CL
COPPERFIELD RD
WATERSMEET WAY
WOBURN CL
TURNBURY CL
Thames Path
FANTAIL CL
DRAKE CRES
DOLPHIN CL
POINTER CL
EASTGATE CL
CHERBURY CL
NICKELBY CL
GRANGE CRES
MANORDENE RD
CROSSWAY
TEMPLAR DR
SUMMERTON WAY
LONGWORTH CL
Green Chain Wlk
GREENHAVEN DR
HOVETON RD
LUDHAM CL
ROLLESBY WAY
SURLINGHAM CL
Ppg Sta
KINGFISHER CL
WROXHAM
ORMESBY
COURTLAND GR
Linton Mead Prim Sch
BERTRAND WAY
Bishop John Richardson CE Prim Sch
WALSHAM CL
46
A
Liby
B
124
47
C
D
Thamesmead Sh Ctr
PO
THAMESMERE DR
CENTRAL WAY
JOYCE DAWSON
TAWNEY RD
HASLER CL
LIPTON CL
WHIMBREL CL
GOLDCREST
FIELDFARE RD
GARGANEY WLK
CURLEW CL
HODGKINS CL
FLEMING WAY
BAYLISS AVE
CROSSWAY

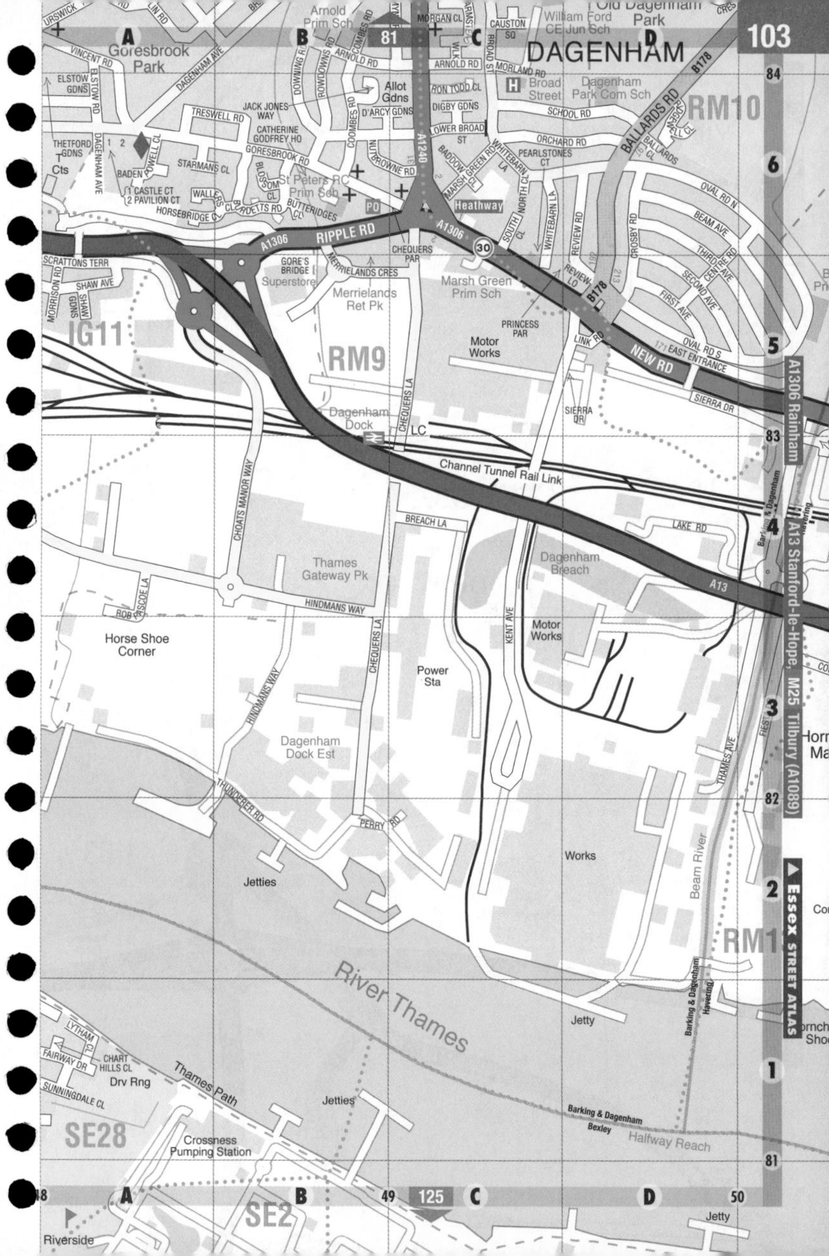
DAGENHAM
Goresbrook Park
Arnold Prim Sch
William Ford CE Jun Sch
Old Dagenham Park
81
A
B
C
D
84
83
82
81
6
5
4
3
2
1
RM10
RM9
IG11
SE28
SE2
RM1
URSWICK
VINCENT RD
ELSTOW GDNS
ELSTOW RD
DAGENHAM AVE
TRESWELL RD
JACK JONES WAY
CATHERINE GODFREY HO
GORESBROOK RD
THETFORD GDNS
Cts
BADEN
POWELL CL
STARMANS CL
1 CASTLE CT
2 PAVILION CT
WALLERS
BURDETTS RD
HORSEBRIDGE CL
BUTTERIDGES CL
St Peters RC Prim Sch
PO
DOWNING RD
ROWDOWNS RD
ARNOLD RD
COMBES RD
COOMBES RD
Allot Gdns
D'ARCY GDNS
NUTBROWNE RD
MORGAN CL
CAUSTON SQ
ARNOLD RD
MORLAND RD
BROAD ST
RON TODD CL
DIGBY GDNS
LOWER BROAD ST
BADDOW CL
MARSH GREEN RD
WHITEBARN LA
Broad Street
Dagenham Park Com Sch
SCHOOL RD
ORCHARD RD
PEARLSTONES CT
BALLARDS RD
BALLARDS CL
B178
Heathway
A1240
A1306
RIPPLE RD
CHEQUERS PAR
30
SOUTH CL
NORTH CL
WHITEBARN LA
REVIEW RD
REVIEW LO
CROSBY RD
OVAL RD N
BEAM AVE
THIRD AVE
CENTRE RD
SECOND AVE
FIRST AVE
OVAL RD S
EAST ENTRANCE
NEW RD
LINK RD
SIERRA DR
SCRATTONS TERR
MORRISON RD
SHAW AVE
SHAW GDNS
GORE'S BRIDGE
Superstore
MERRIELANDS CRES
Merrielands Ret Pk
Marsh Green Prim Sch
PRINCESS PAR
Motor Works
Dagenham Dock
CHEQUERS LA
LC
Channel Tunnel Rail Link
CHOATS MANOR WAY
BREACH LA
Thames Gateway Pk
HINDMANS WAY
ROBERT'S CL
PASCOE LA
Horse Shoe Corner
Dagenham Breach
LAKE RD
A13
KENT AVE
Motor Works
Power Sta
Dagenham Dock Est
THUNDERER RD
PERRY RD
THAMES AVE
Jetties
Works
Beam River
River Thames
Jetty
Barking & Dagenham
Havering
Bexley
Halfway Reach
LYTHAM CL
FAIRWAY DR
CHART HILLS CL
Drv Rng
SUNNINGDALE CL
Thames Path
Jetties
Crossness Pumping Station
Riverside
48
49
125
50
A1306 Rainham
A13 Stanford-le-Hope, M25 Tilbury (A1089)
Essex STREET ATLAS

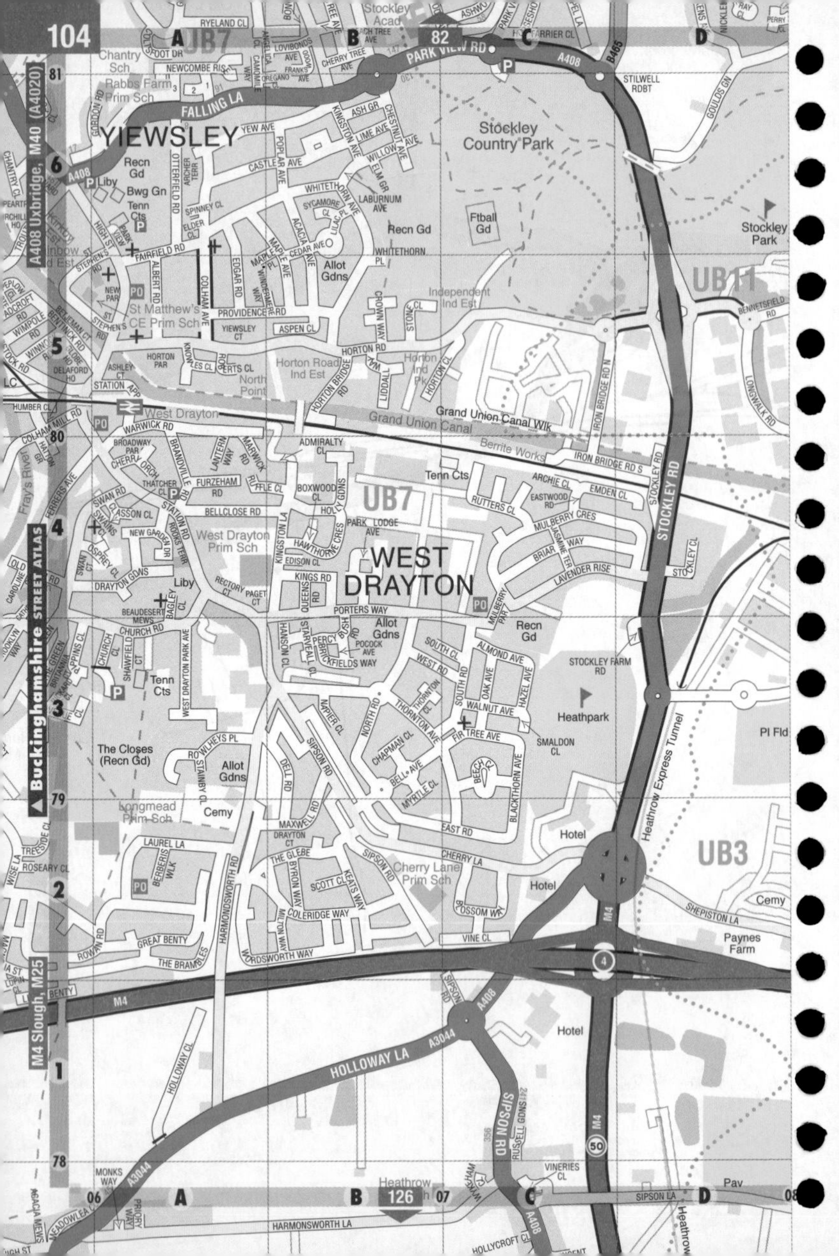

82
PARK VIEW RD
A408
FALLING LA
YIEWSLEY
Chantry Sch
Rabbs Farm Prim Sch
Stockley Country Park
Stockley Park
STILWELL RDBT
UB7
UB11
UB3
Recn Gd
Ftball Gd
Allot Gdns
Independent Ind Est
St Matthew's CE Prim Sch
Horton Road Ind Est
Horton Ind Pk
North Point
West Drayton
Grand Union Canal Wlk
Grand Union Canal
Berrite Works
IRON BRIDGE RD S
IRON BRIDGE RD N
STOCKLEY RD
West Drayton Prim Sch
WEST DRAYTON
Tenn Cts
Heathpark
STOCKLEY FARM RD
Heathrow Express Tunnel
Pl Fld
The Closes (Recn Gd)
Longmead Prim Sch
Cemy
Cherry Lane Prim Sch
Hotel
Paynes Farm
SHEPISTON LA
M4
HOLLOWAY LA
A3044
SIPSON RD
HARMONDSWORTH RD
HARMONDSWORTH LA
SIPSON LA
126
Pav
A408 Uxbridge, M40 (A4020)
Buckinghamshire STREET ATLAS
M4 Slough, M25

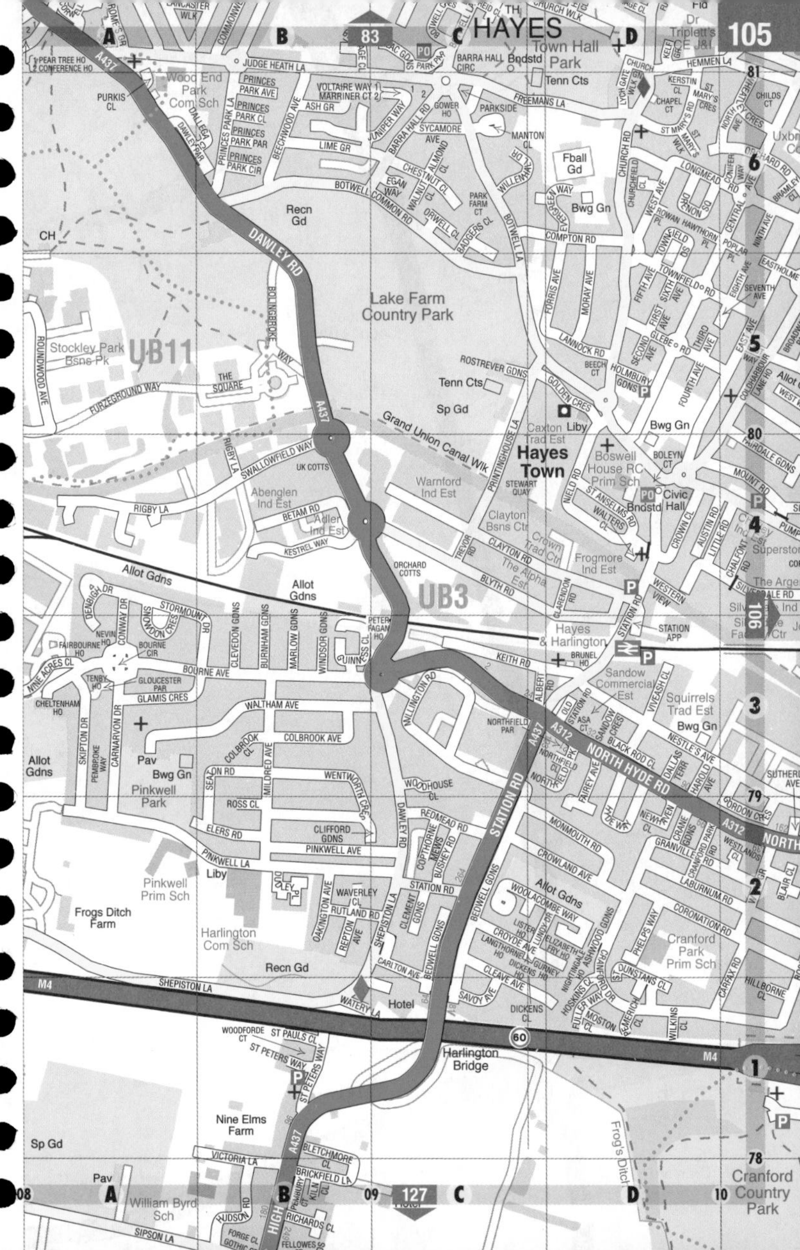

83
127
106
Town Hall Park
Hayes Town
Lake Farm Country Park
UB11
UB3
Stockley Park Bsns Pk
Grand Union Canal Wlk
Hayes & Harlington
Harlington Bridge
Cranford Country Park
Pinkwell Park
Frogs Ditch Farm
Nine Elms Farm
DAWLEY RD
STATION RD
NORTH HYDE RD
M4

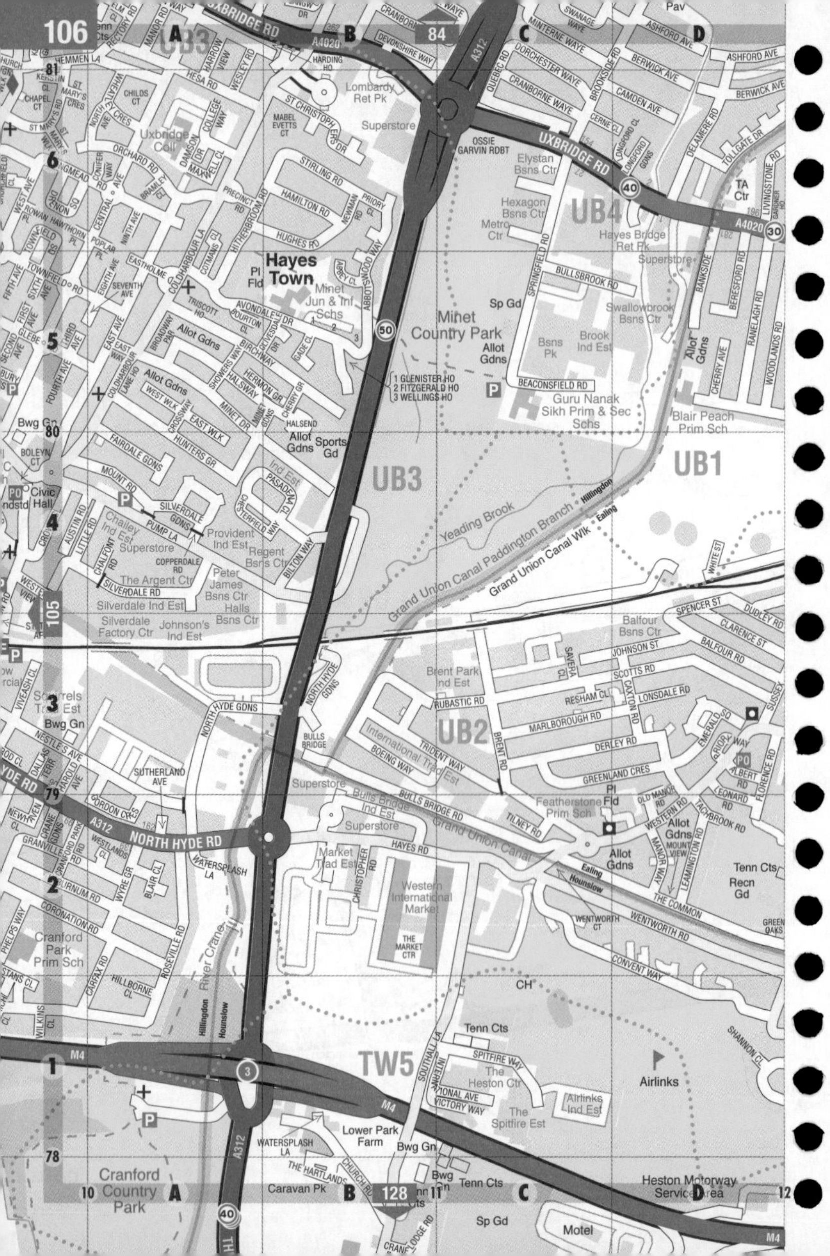
UXBRIDGE RD
A4020
84
A312
UB3
UB4
UB1
UB2
TW5
Lombardy Ret Pk
Superstore
OSSIE GARVIN RDBT
Elystan Bsns Ctr
Hexagon Bsns Ctr
Metro Ctr
Hayes Bridge Ret Pk
Uxbridge Coll
Hayes Town
Minet Jun & Inf Schs
Minet Country Park
Sp Gd
Swallowbrook Bsns Ctr
Bsns Pk
Brook Ind Est
Allot Gdns
Guru Nanak Sikh Prim & Sec Schs
Blair Peach Prim Sch
1 GLENISTER HO
2 FITZGERALD HO
3 WELLINGS HO
Sports Gd
Civic Hall
Yeading Brook
Grand Union Canal Paddington Branch
Grand Union Canal Wlk
Hillingdon
Ealing
Chailey Ind Est
Provident Ind Est
Regent Bsns Ctr
The Argent Ctr
Peter James Bsns Ctr
Halls Bsns Ctr
Silverdale Ind Est
Silverdale Factory Ctr
Johnson's Ind Est
Balfour Bsns Ctr
Brent Park Ind Est
International Trad Est
Squirrels Trad Est
Bwg Gn
NORTH HYDE RD
A312
Bulls Bridge Ind Est
Superstore
Market Trad Est
Western International Market
THE MARKET CTR
Featherstone Prim Sch
Grand Union Canal
Hounslow
Tenn Cts
Recn Gd
Cranford Park Prim Sch
River Crane
M4
The Heston Ctr
Airlinks Ind Est
The Spitfire Est
Airlinks
Lower Park Farm
Cranford Country Park
Caravan Pk
128
Heston Motorway Service Area
Motel
Sp Gd
105

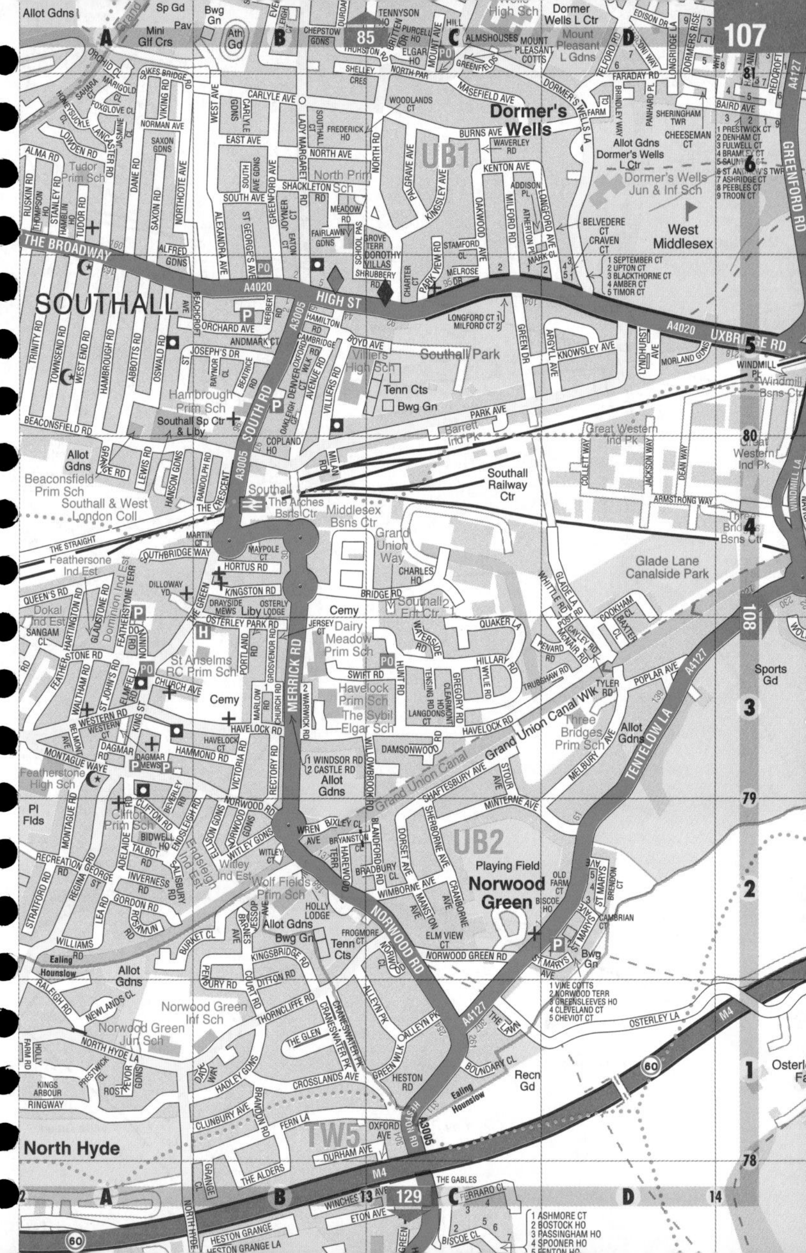
A
B
C
D
85
129
108
SOUTHALL
Dormer's Wells
Southall Park
UB1
UB2
TW5
Norwood Green
North Hyde
West Middlesex
THE BROADWAY
HIGH ST
A4020
UXBRIDGE RD
SOUTH RD
A3005
MERRICK RD
NORWOOD RD
HESTON RD
TENTELOW LA
A4127
GREENFORD RD
M4
Grand Union Canal
Grand Union Canal Wlk
Southall Railway Ctr
Glade Lane Canalside Park
Southall & West London Coll
Beaconsfield Prim Sch
Hambrough Prim Sch
Southall Sp Ctr & Liby
Dormer's Wells Jun & Inf Sch
Villiers High Sch
North Prim Sch
Tudor Prim Sch
Featherstone Ind Est
Dominion Ind Est
Dokal Ind Est
St Anselms RC Prim Sch
Havelock Prim Sch
The Sybil Elgar Sch
Dairy Meadow Prim Sch
Three Bridges Prim Sch
Featherstone High Sch
Clifton Prim Sch
Endsleigh Ind Est
Witley Ind Est
Wolf Fields Prim Sch
Norwood Green Inf Sch
Norwood Green Jun Sch
Middlesex Bsns Ctr
The Arches Bsns Ctr
Barrett Ind Pk
Great Western Ind Pk
Windmill Bsns Ctr
Three Bridges Bsns Ctr
Southall Ent Ctr
Playing Field
Sports Gd
Recn Gd
Allot Gdns
Cemy
Tenn Cts
Bwg Gn
Pl Flds
Ealing
Hounslow
1 PRESTWICK CT
2 DENHAM CT
3 FULWELL CT
4 BRAMLEY CT
5 SAUNTON CT
6 ST ANDREW'S TWR
7 ASHRIDGE CT
8 PEEBLES CT
9 TROON CT
1 SEPTEMBER CT
2 UPTON CT
3 BLACKTHORNE CT
4 AMBER CT
5 TIMOR CT
1 WINDSOR RD
2 CASTLE RD
1 VINE COTTS
2 NORWOOD TERR
3 GREENSLEEVES HO
4 CLEVELAND CT
5 CHEVIOT CT
1 ASHMORE CT
2 BOSTOCK HO
3 PASSINGHAM HO
4 SPOONER HO
5 FENTON HO
81
80
79
78
6
5
4
3
2
1
13
14

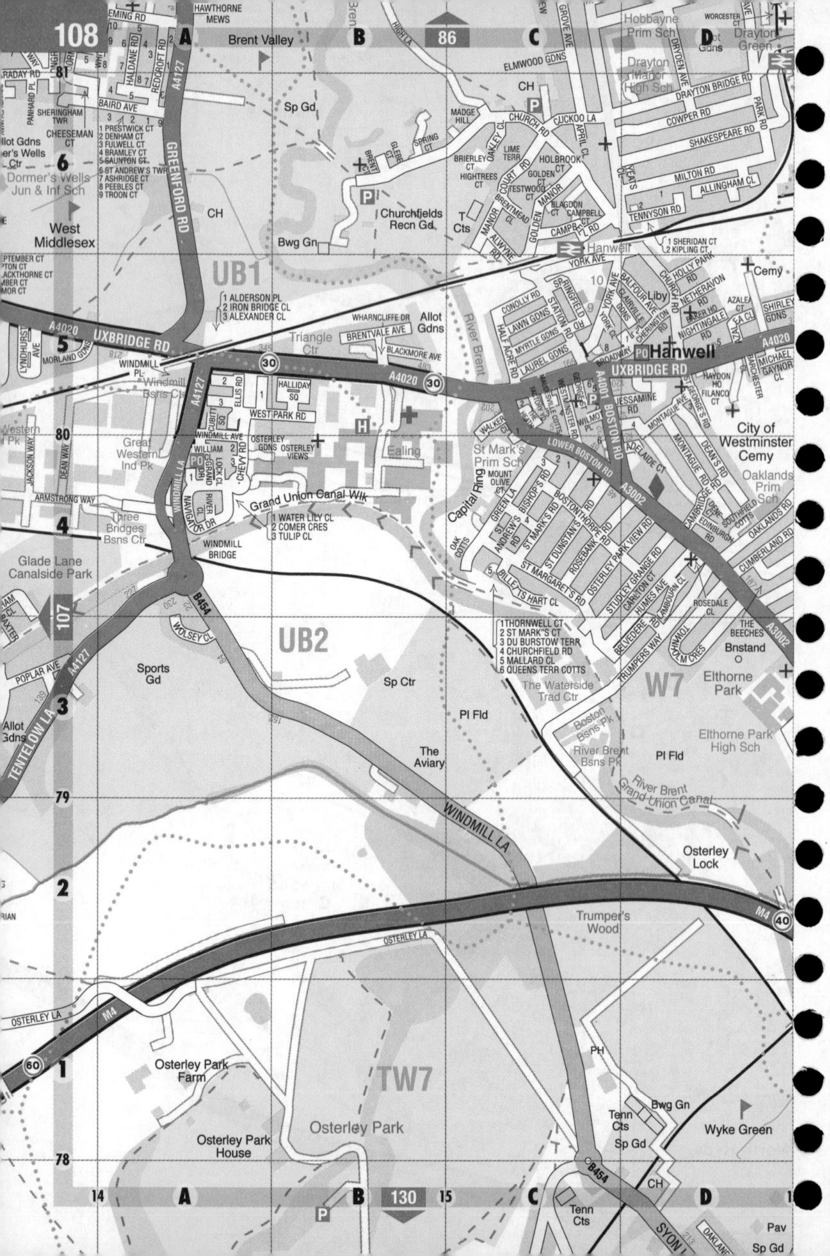

Brent Valley
86
Hobbayne Prim Sch
Drayton Green
Drayton Manor High Sch
ELMWOOD GDNS
DRAYTON BRIDGE RD
COWPER RD
SHAKESPEARE RD
MILTON RD
ALLINGHAM CL
TENNYSON RD
Sp Gd
GREENFORD RD
A4127
BAIRD AVE
HALDANE RD
REDCROFT RD
1 PRESTWICK CT
2 DENHAM CT
3 FULWELL CT
4 BRAMLEY CT
5 SAUNTON CT
6 ST ANDREW'S TWR
7 ASHRIDGE CT
8 PEEBLES CT
9 TROON CT
Dormer's Wells Jun & Inf Sch
West Middlesex
CH
Churchfields Recn Gd
Bwg Gn
CHURCH RD
CUCKOO LA
HOLBROOK CT
Hanwell
YORK AVE
1 SHERIDAN CT
2 KIPLING CT
UB1
1 ALDERSON PL
2 IRON BRIDGE CL
3 ALEXANDER CL
UXBRIDGE RD
A4020
Triangle Ctr
Allot Gdns
River Brent
Cemy
WINDMILL PL
Windmill Bsns Ctr
WEST PARK RD
Great Western Ind Pk
Ealing
St Mark's Prim Sch
LOWER BOSTON RD
A4001 BOSTON RD
A3002
City of Westminster Cemy
Oaklands Prim Sch
Grand Union Canal Wlk
1 WATER LILY CL
2 COMER CRES
3 TULIP CL
Three Bridges Bsns Ctr
WINDMILL BRIDGE
Glade Lane Canalside Park
Capital Ring
107
UB2
B454
WOLSEY CL
1 THORNWELL CT
2 ST MARK'S CT
3 DU BURSTOW TERR
4 CHURCHFIELD RD
5 MALLARD CL
6 QUEENS TERR COTTS
Sports Gd
Sp Ctr
The Waterside Trad Ctr
W7
Elthorne Park
Bnstand
Pl Fld
Boston Bsns Pk
River Brent Bsns Pk
Elthorne Park High Sch
The Aviary
River Brent
Grand Union Canal
WINDMILL LA
Osterley Lock
TENTELOW LA
POPLAR AVE
M4
Trumper's Wood
OSTERLEY LA
Osterley Park Farm
TW7
Osterley Park
Osterley Park House
PH
Bwg Gn
Tenn Cts
Sp Gd
Wyke Green
CH
SYON
130
14
15
A
B
C
D
1
2
3
4
5
6
78
79
80
81

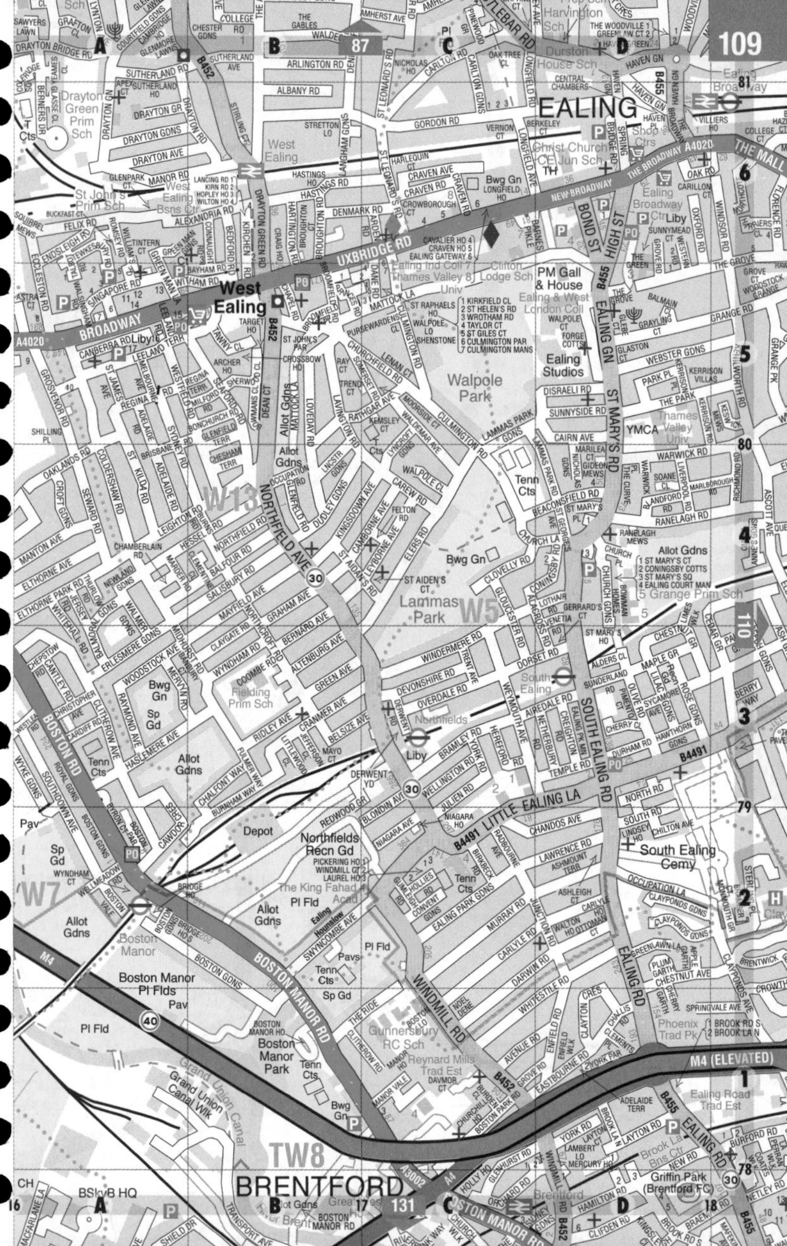
EALING
West Ealing
BRENTFORD
Walpole Park
Lammas Park
W13
W5
W7
TW8
Northfields
South Ealing
Boston Manor
Ealing Broadway
UXBRIDGE RD
BROADWAY
NEW BROADWAY
THE MALL
NORTHFIELD AVE
SOUTH EALING RD
BOSTON MANOR RD
BOSTON RD
WINDMILL RD
LITTLE EALING LA
M4 (ELEVATED)
Grand Union Canal
South Ealing Cemy
Griffin Park (Brentford FC)
87
110
131

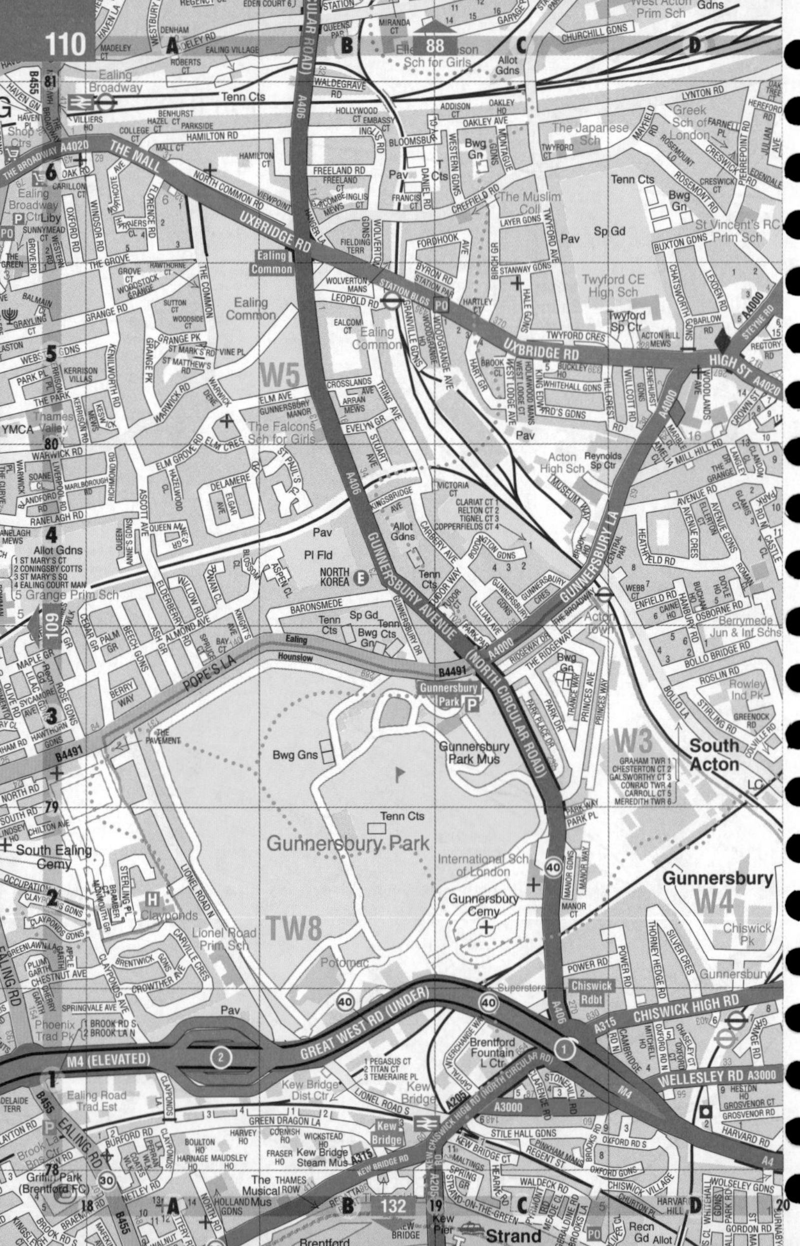
Ealing Common
W5
Gunnersbury Park
TW8
W3
South Acton
Gunnersbury
W4
UXBRIDGE RD
GUNNERSBURY AVENUE (NORTH CIRCULAR ROAD)
M4 (ELEVATED)
GREAT WEST RD (UNDER)
CHISWICK HIGH RD
POPE'S LA
Brentford
Strand
88
109
132

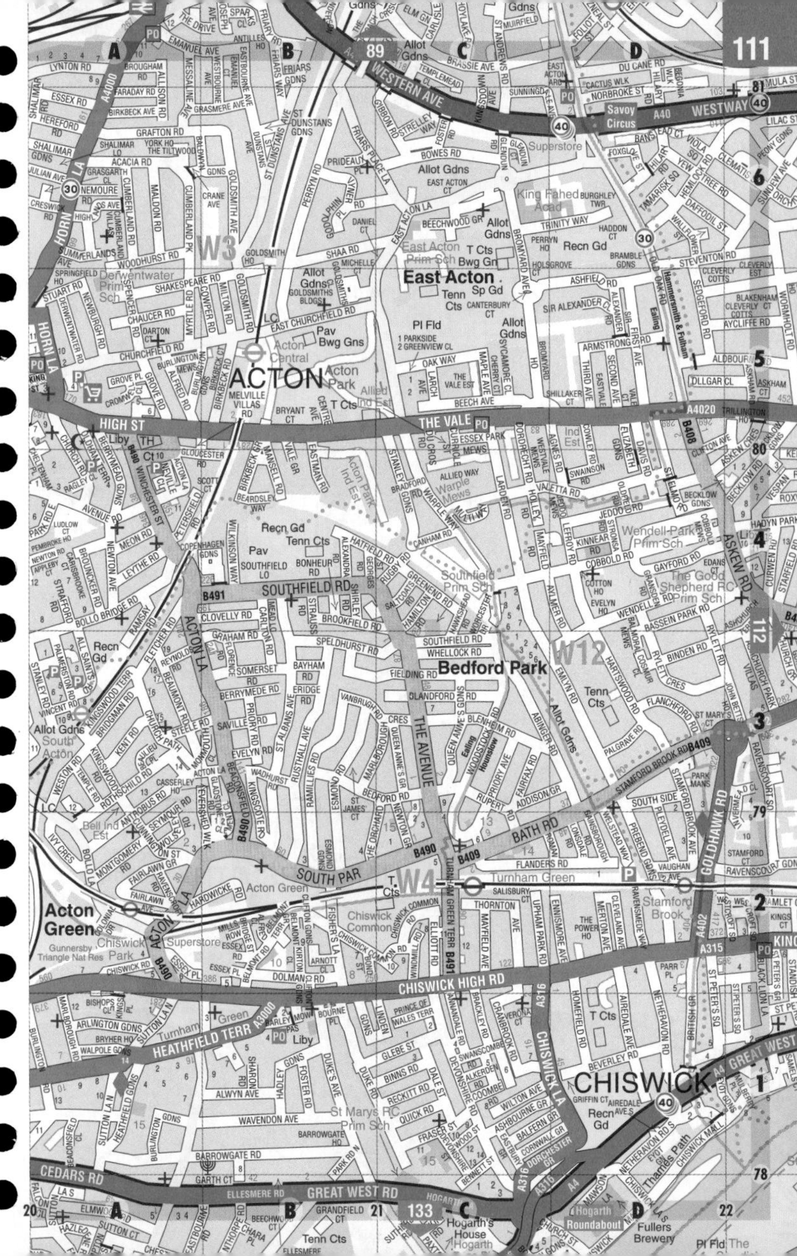
ACTON
East Acton
Bedford Park
CHISWICK
Acton Green
W3
W4
W12
WESTERN AVE
WESTWAY
Savoy Circus
HIGH ST
THE VALE
CHISWICK HIGH RD
GREAT WEST RD
CEDARS RD
SOUTH PAR
BATH RD
SOUTHFIELD RD
THE AVENUE
ACTON LA
HORN LA
ASKEW RD
GOLDHAWK RD
CHISWICK LA
HEATHFIELD TERR
TURNHAM GREEN TERR
Acton Central
Acton Park
Turnham Green
Stamford Brook
Chiswick Park
Hogarth Roundabout
Hogarth's House
Fullers Brewery
Gunnersby Triangle Nat Res
King Fahed Acad
Wendell Park Prim Sch
The Good Shepherd RC Prim Sch
Southfield Prim Sch
East Acton Prim Sch
Derwentwater Prim Sch
St Marys RC Prim Sch
Chiswick Common
Thames Path
89
133
112
80
79
81
78
20
21
22

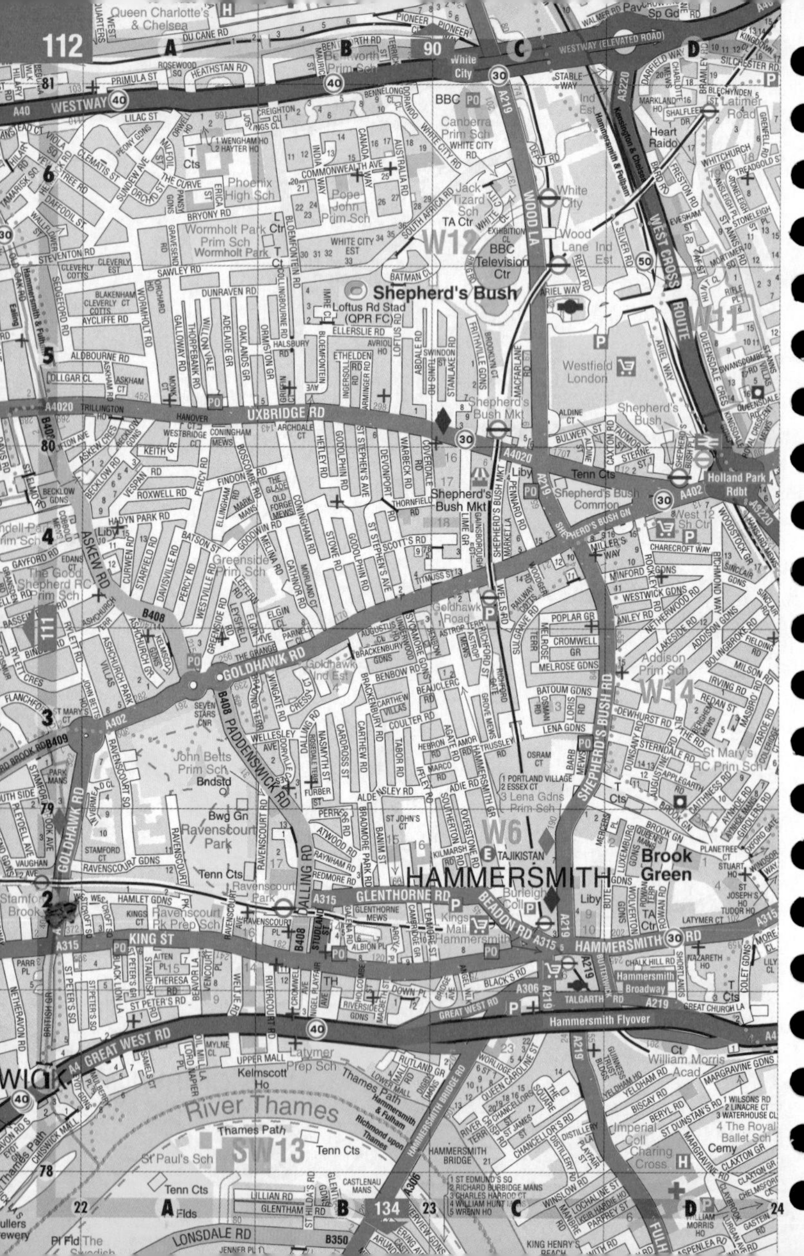

90
111
134
A
B
C
D
22
23
24
WESTWAY
WESTWAY (ELEVATED ROAD)
WEST CROSS ROUTE
DU CANE RD
UXBRIDGE RD
GOLDHAWK RD
KING ST
GREAT WEST RD
Hammersmith Flyover
HAMMERSMITH RD
GLENTHORNE RD
BEADON RD
SHEPHERD'S BUSH RD
SHEPHERD'S BUSH GN
WOOD LA
ASKEW RD
PADDENSWICK RD
DALLING RD
HAMMERSMITH BRIDGE RD
LONSDALE RD
W12
W11
W14
W6
SW13
Shepherd's Bush
HAMMERSMITH
Brook Green
White City
BBC Television Ctr
Loftus Rd Stad (QPR FC)
Westfield London
Shepherd's Bush Mkt
Shepherd's Bush Common
Ravenscourt Park
River Thames
Thames Path
Queen Charlotte's & Chelsea
Phoenix High Sch
Wormholt Park Prim Sch
Hammersmith Broadway
Kings Mall
Charing Cross
Imperial Coll
Hammersmith Bridge
Chiswick Mall

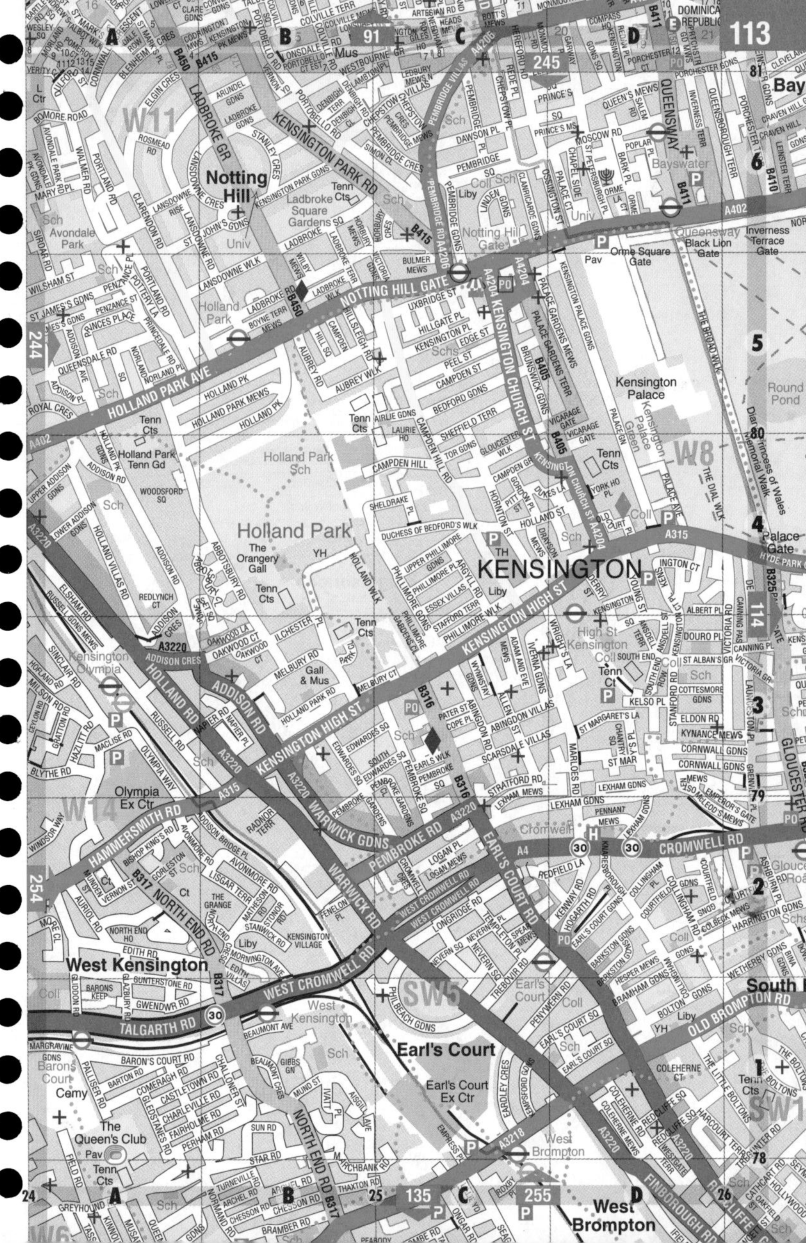

Notting Hill
KENSINGTON
Holland Park
Kensington Palace
West Kensington
Earl's Court
Earl's Court Ex Ctr
Olympia Ex Ctr
The Queen's Club
West Brompton
W11
W8
W14
SW5
NOTTING HILL GATE
HOLLAND PARK AVE
KENSINGTON HIGH ST
KENSINGTON CHURCH ST
CROMWELL RD
WEST CROMWELL RD
TALGARTH RD
HAMMERSMITH RD
NORTH END RD
EARL'S COURT RD
WARWICK RD
HOLLAND RD
ADDISON RD
LADBROKE GR
KENSINGTON PARK RD
PEMBROKE RD
OLD BROMPTON RD
GLOUCESTER RD
QUEENSWAY
FINBOROUGH RD
Round Pond
Bayswater
91
245
244
254
114
135
255

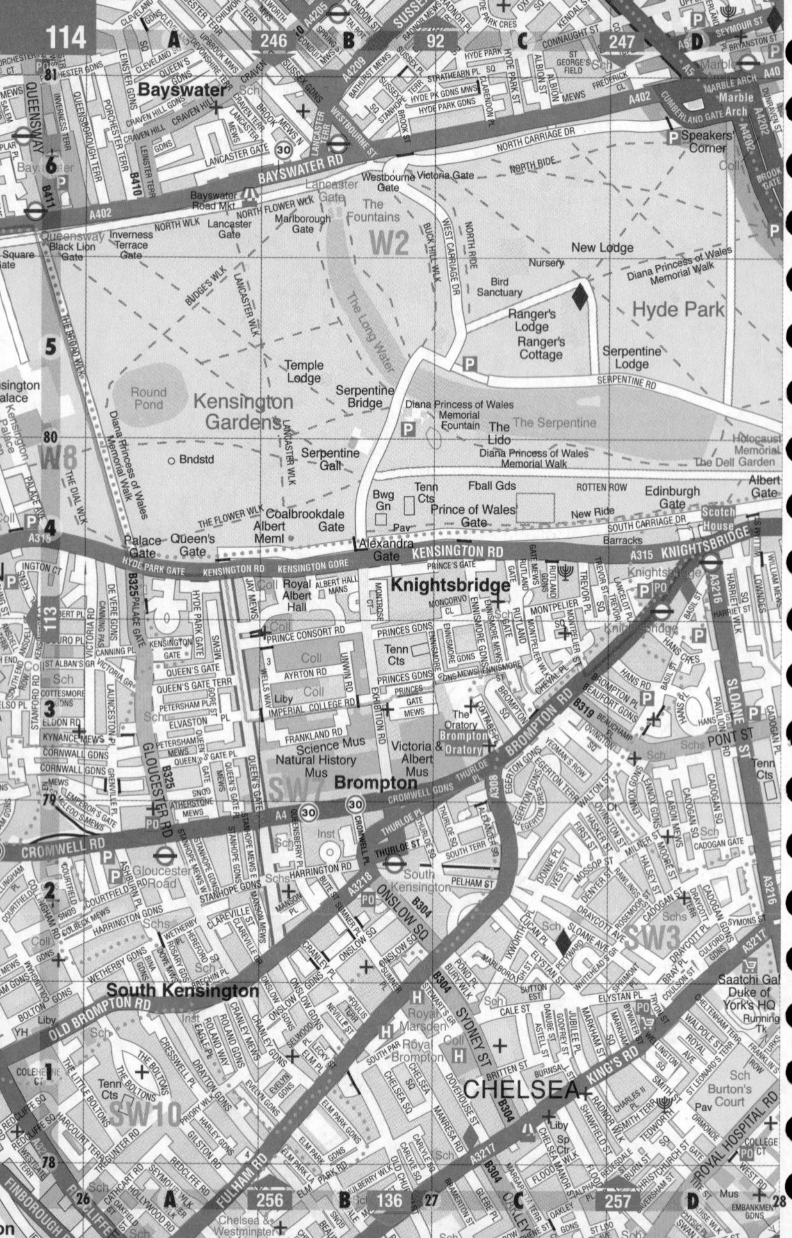

Bayswater
Hyde Park
Kensington Gardens
Knightsbridge
Brompton
South Kensington
CHELSEA
W2
W8
SW7
SW3
SW10
Marble Arch
Speakers' Corner
The Long Water
The Serpentine
Round Pond
Royal Albert Hall
Science Mus
Natural History Mus
Victoria & Albert Mus
Brompton Oratory
Royal Marsden
Royal Brompton
Saatchi Gal
Duke of York's HQ
Burton's Court
Holocaust Memorial
The Dell Garden
Kensington Palace
Albert Meml
Serpentine Gall
Bird Sanctuary
Ranger's Lodge
Ranger's Cottage
New Lodge
Temple Lodge
Serpentine Lodge
Serpentine Bridge
Diana Princess of Wales Memorial Fountain
Diana Princess of Wales Memorial Walk
The Lido
Scotch House
Barracks
Edinburgh Gate
Albert Gate
BAYSWATER RD
KENSINGTON RD
KNIGHTSBRIDGE
BROMPTON RD
CROMWELL RD
OLD BROMPTON RD
FULHAM RD
KING'S RD
SLOANE ST
SYDNEY ST
ROYAL HOSPITAL RD
GLOUCESTER RD
QUEENSWAY
246
92
247
256
136
257

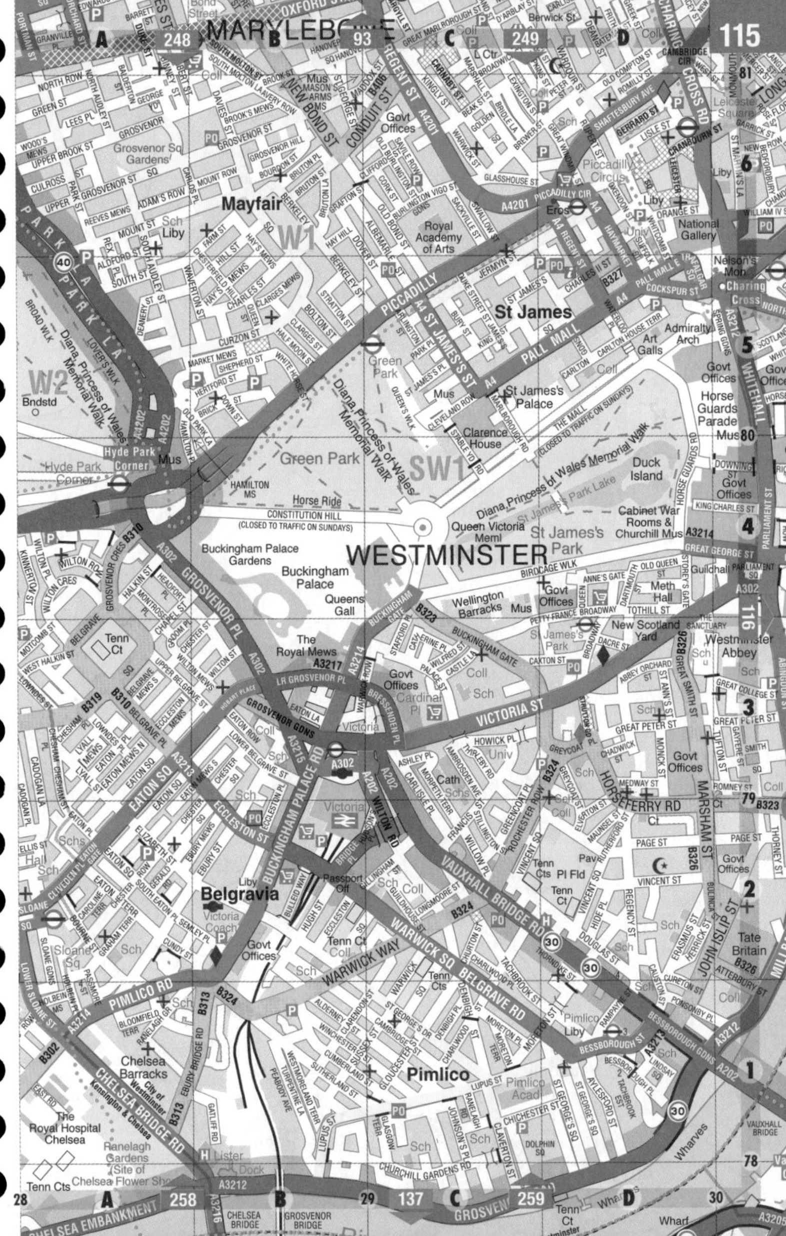
MARYLEBONE
248
93
249
A
B
C
D
OXFORD ST
Bond Street
Mayfair
W1
Grosvenor Sq Gardens
Royal Academy of Arts
Govt Offices
Piccadilly Circus
Eros
National Gallery
Leicester Square
CHARING CROSS RD
SHAFTESBURY AVE
REGENT ST
PICCADILLY
St James
PALL MALL
Admiralty Arch
Art Galls
Nelson's Mon
Charing Cross
WHITEHALL
Horse Guards Parade
Green Park
Diana, Princess of Wales Memorial Walk
SW1
St James's Palace
Clarence House
THE MALL
Duck Island
St James's Park Lake
W2
Bndstd
PARK LA
Hyde Park Corner
CONSTITUTION HILL
(CLOSED TO TRAFFIC ON SUNDAYS)
Horse Ride
Queen Victoria Meml
WESTMINSTER
St James's Park
Cabinet War Rooms & Churchill Mus
Buckingham Palace Gardens
Buckingham Palace
Queens Gall
The Royal Mews
Wellington Barracks
New Scotland Yard
Westminster Abbey
Guildhall
GREAT GEORGE ST
PARLIAMENT ST
VICTORIA ST
GROSVENOR PL
Victoria
HORSEFERRY RD
MARSHAM ST
Cath
Tate Britain
MILLBANK
Belgravia
EATON SQ
BUCKINGHAM PALACE RD
VAUXHALL BRIDGE RD
WARWICK WAY
BELGRAVE RD
Pimlico
Chelsea Barracks
The Royal Hospital Chelsea
Ranelagh Gardens (Site of Chelsea Flower Show)
CHELSEA BRIDGE RD
PIMLICO RD
CHELSEA EMBANKMENT
GROSVENOR RD
CHELSEA BRIDGE
GROSVENOR BRIDGE
VAUXHALL BRIDGE
Wharves
258
137
259
28
29
30
1
2
3
4
5
6
78
79
80
81
116

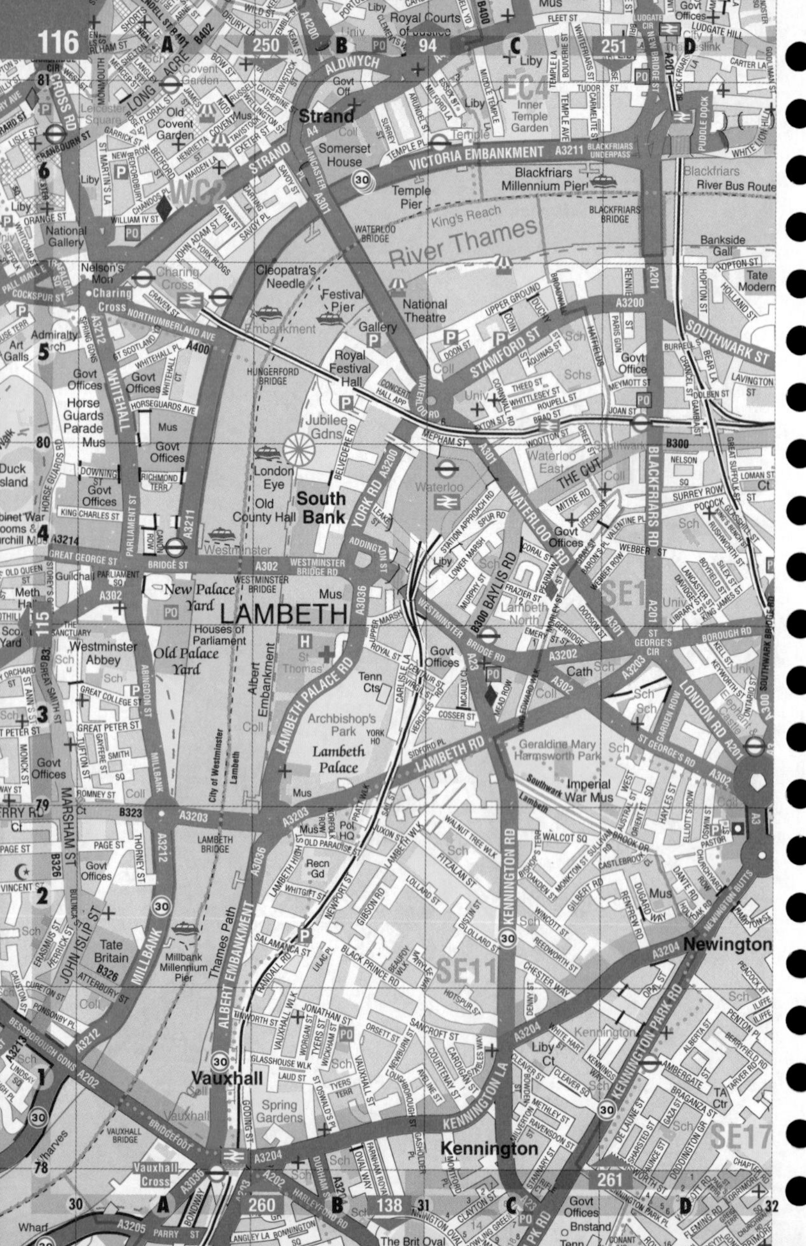
116
250
94
251
Royal Courts of Justice
Aldwych
Strand
Covent Garden
Long Acre
Old Covent Garden
Leicester Square
Cranbourn St
Charing Cross Rd
EC4
Inner Temple Garden
Somerset House
Temple Pier
Victoria Embankment
Blackfriars Millennium Pier
Blackfriars Underpass
Blackfriars Bridge
Blackfriars River Bus Route
Puddle Dock
King's Reach
River Thames
Waterloo Bridge
WC2
National Gallery
Nelson's Mon
Charing Cross
Cleopatra's Needle
Festival Pier
National Theatre
Bankside Gall
Tate Modern
Southwark St
Upper Ground
Stamford St
Embankment
Hungerford Bridge
Royal Festival Hall
Northumberland Ave
Whitehall
Admiralty Arch
Horse Guards Parade
Horseguards Ave
Jubilee Gdns
London Eye
Waterloo
Waterloo Rd
The Cut
Waterloo East
Blackfriars Rd
Duck Island
Horse Guards Rd
King Charles St
Cabinet War Rooms & Churchill Mus
Old County Hall
South Bank
York Rd
Westminster
Great George St
Bridge St
Westminster Bridge Rd
Parliament St
New Palace Yard
LAMBETH
Houses of Parliament
Old Palace Yard
Westminster Abbey
Lambeth North
Baylis Rd
SE1
St George's Cir
Borough Rd
London Rd
Elephant & Castle
St Thomas
Lambeth Palace Rd
Albert Embankment
Archbishop's Park
Lambeth Palace
Lambeth Rd
Geraldine Mary Harmsworth Park
Imperial War Mus
Millbank
Great Peter St
Marsham St
Lambeth Bridge
Horseferry Rd
Tate Britain
Millbank Millennium Pier
Thames Path
Kennington Rd
SE11
Newington
Newington Butts
Kennington Park Rd
Kennington
Kennington La
Vauxhall
Vauxhall Bridge
Vauxhall Cross
Spring Gardens
Bessborough Gdns
Bridgefoot
The Brit Oval
SE17
260
138
261
A
B
C
D
1
2
3
4
5
6
30
31
32
115

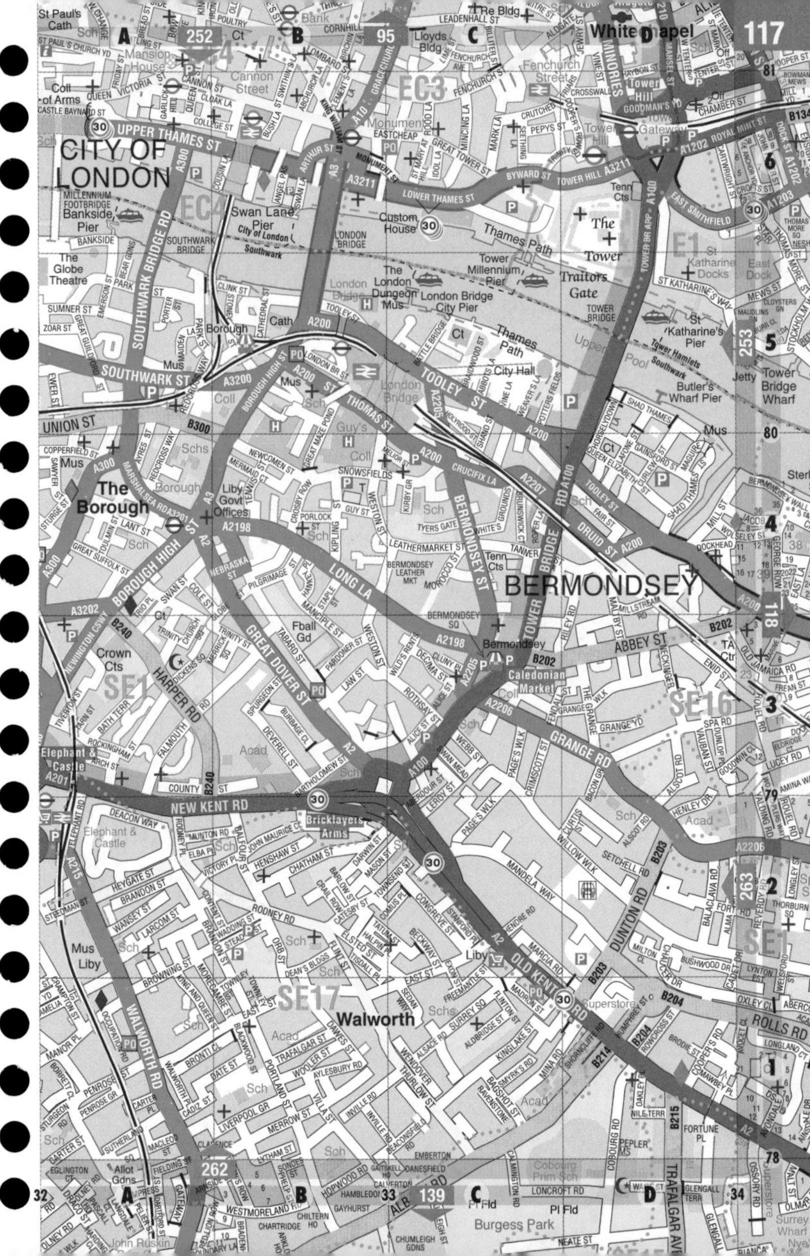

St Paul's Cath
A
252
Ct
B
95
Lloyds Bldg
C
Whitechapel
D
Mansion House
Cannon Street
EC3
Fenchurch Street
Coll of Arms
QUEEN VICTORIA ST
CANNON ST
LOMBARD ST
FENCHURCH ST
CRUTCHED FRIARS
PEPYS ST
Tower Hill
Tower Gateway
GOODMAN'S YD
CHAMBER ST
B134
ROYAL MINT ST
A1202
UPPER THAMES ST
CITY OF LONDON
Monument
EASTCHEAP
GREAT TOWER ST
BYWARD ST
TOWER HILL
A3211
MILLENNIUM FOOTBRIDGE
Bankside Pier
EC4
Swan Lane Pier
City of London
Southwark
Custom House
LOWER THAMES ST
Thames Path
The Tower
Tenn Cts
EAST SMITHFIELD
BANKSIDE
SOUTHWARK BRIDGE
LONDON BRIDGE
The Globe Theatre
The London Dungeon Mus
London Bridge City Pier
Tower Millennium Pier
Traitors Gate
E1
St Katharine Docks
East Dock
ST KATHARINE'S WAY
SUMNER ST
ZOAR ST
CLINK ST
Borough
Cath
TOOLEY ST
A200
TOWER BRIDGE
St Katharine's Pier
253
5
Tower Hamlets
Southwark
Upper Pool
Thames Path
City Hall
SOUTHWARK BRIDGE RD
SOUTHWARK ST
A3200
BOROUGH HIGH ST
London Bridge
Mus
Coll
Butler's Wharf Pier
Jetty
Tower Bridge Wharf
UNION ST
B300
Guy's
THOMAS ST
A2205
SHAD THAMES
80
Mus
COPPERFIELD ST
Schs
NEWCOMEN ST
SNOWSFIELDS
CRUCIFIX LA
A2207
TOOLEY ST
Sterling St
The Borough
A300
MARSHALSEA RD
A3201
Liby Govt Offices
Sch
BERMONDSEY ST
DRUID ST
A2198
LANT ST
GREAT SUFFOLK ST
TYERS GATE
LEATHERMARKET ST
Tenn Cts
TANNER
JACOB
4
DOCKHEAD
LONG LA
BERMONDSEY LEATHER MKT
BERMONDSEY
MALTBY ST
MILLSTREAM RD
A200
118
A3202
B240
Ct
TABARD ST
Fball Gd
BERMONDSEY SQ
Bermondsey
B202
ABBEY ST
B202
Crown Cts
SE1
HARPER RD
GREAT DOVER ST
PO
Caledonian Market
Coll
A2206
GRANGE RD
SE16
3
SPA RD
TIVERTON ST
ROCKINGHAM
Acad
Sch
LUCEY RD
Elephant & Castle
A201
COUNTY ST
B240
A2
A100
NEW KENT RD
30
Bricklayers Arms
79
Elephant & Castle
DEACON WAY
A215
HEYGATE ST
BRANDON ST
CHATHAM ST
MANDELA WAY
SETCHELL RD
B203
A2206
BALACLAVA RD
263
2
THORBURN SQ
SE1
RODNEY RD
DUNTON RD
Mus Liby
Liby
OLD KENT RD
MARCIA RD
BUSHWOOD DR
SE17
Walworth
Superstore
B204
ROLLS RD
WALWORTH RD
Schs
Acad
TRAFALGAR ST
AYLESBURY RD
Sch
1
LIVERPOOL GR
MERROW ST
INVILLE RD
BEACONSFIELD RD
Acad
B215
FORTUNE PL
A2
78
262
Allot Gdns
EMBERTON
Cobourg Prim Sch
COBOURG RD
PEPLER MS
32
A
B
33
139
C
Pl Fld
LONCROFT RD
D
TRAFALGAR AV
34
OLMAR ST
WESTMORELAND RD
CHARTRIDGE
Pl Fld
Burgess Park
Surrey Wharf
John Ruskin
NEATE ST

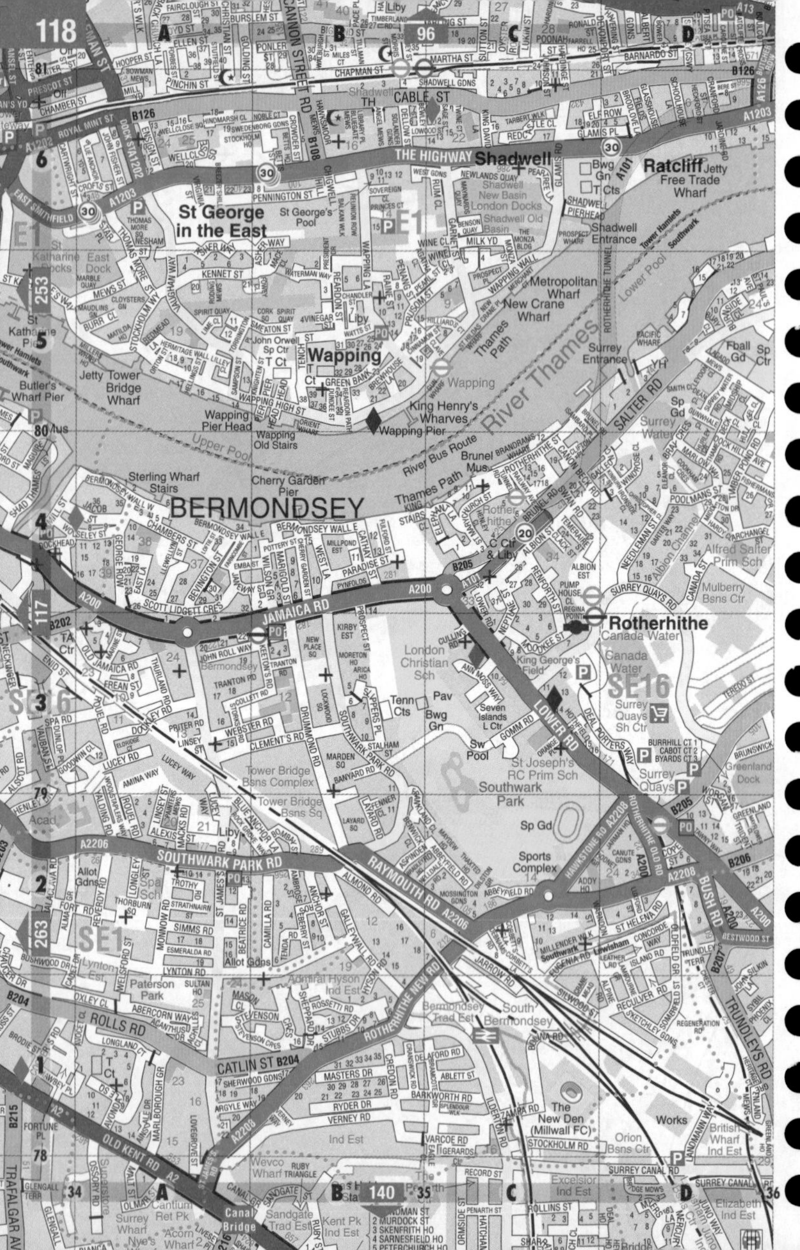
A
B
C
D
96
CANNON STREET RD
CABLE ST
Shadwell
THE HIGHWAY
Shadwell
Ratcliff
Jetty
Free Trade
Wharf
St George
in the East
St George's
Pool
E1
St
Katharine
Docks
East
Dock
Shadwell
New Basin
London Docks
Shadwell Old
Basin
Shadwell
Entrance
Metropolitan
Wharf
New Crane
Wharf
Thames
Path
Tower Hamlets
Southwark
Lower Pool
Wapping
Wapping
Wapping High St
John Orwell
Sp Ctr
Jetty Tower
Bridge
Wharf
Butler's
Wharf Pier
Wapping
Pier Head
Wapping
Old Stairs
King Henry's
Wharves
Wapping Pier
River Thames
River Bus Route
Upper Pool
Surrey
Entrance
Salter Rd
Brunel
Mus
Sterling Wharf
Stairs
Cherry Garden
Pier
Thames Path
BERMONDSEY
Bermondsey Wall E
Rotherhithe
Jamaica Rd
A200
Rotherhithe
Canada Water
Alfred Salter
Prim Sch
Mulberry
Bsns Ctr
Surrey Quays Rd
Albion Channel
Lower Rd
SE16
Surrey
Quays
Sh Ctr
London
Christian
Sch
Tenn
Cts
Pav
Bwg
Gn
Seven
Islands
L Ctr
King George's
Field
Canada
Water
Sw
Pool
St Joseph's
RC Prim Sch
Southwark
Park
Sp Gd
Sports
Complex
Tower Bridge
Bsns Complex
Tower Bridge
Bsns Sq
Southwark Park Rd
Raymouth Rd
SE1
Lynton
Est
Paterson
Park
Allot
Gdns
Admiral Hyson
Ind Est
Rotherhithe New Rd
Bermondsey
Trad Est
South
Bermondsey
Catlin St
Rolls Rd
Old Kent Rd
The
New Den
(Millwall FC)
Orion
Bsns Ctr
Works
British
Wharf
Ind Est
Surrey Canal Rd
Excelsior
Ind Est
Elizabeth
Ind Est
Trundleys Rd
Bush Rd
Evelyn St
Ind Est
Wevco
Wharf
Cantium
Ret Pk
Surrey
Wharf
Acorn
Wharf
Sandgate
Trad Est
Kent Pk
Ind Est
Canal
Bridge
140
34
35
36
117
253
263
Trafalgar Av
Fortune Pl
Glengall Terr

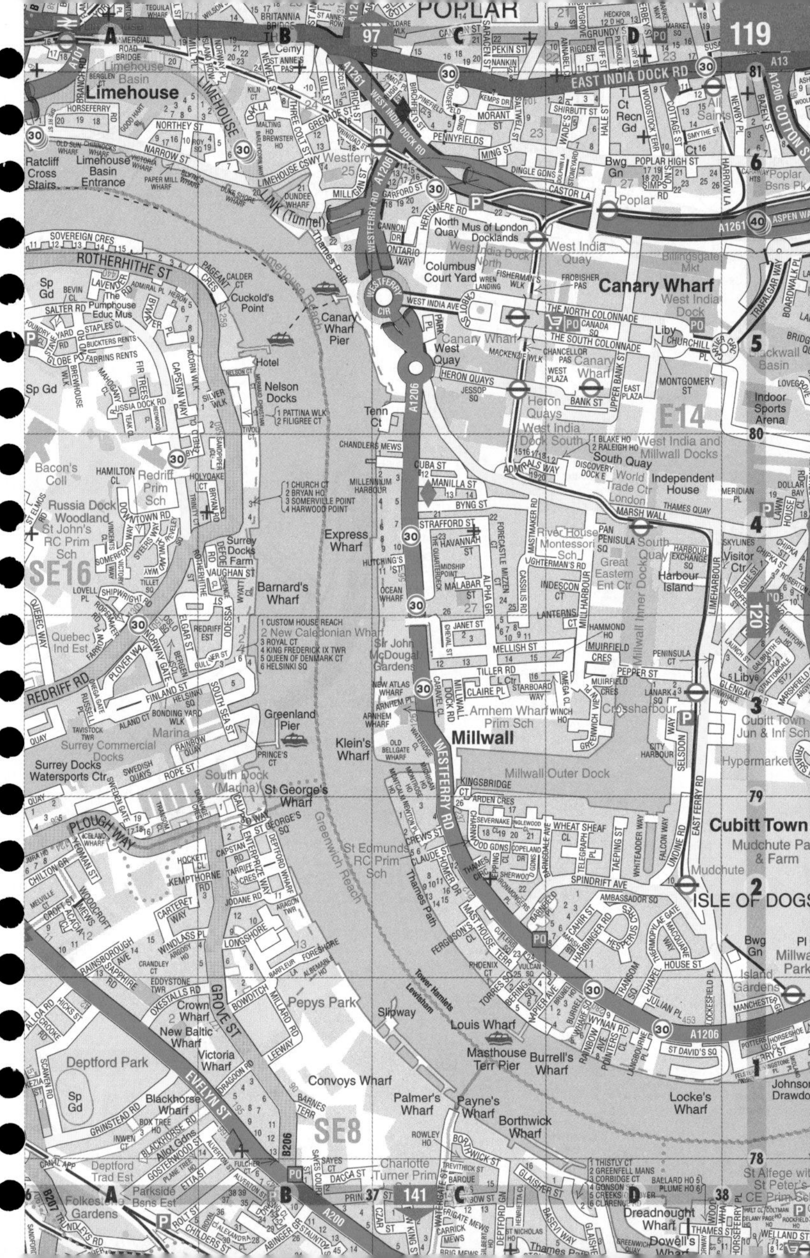
POPLAR
97
Limehouse
Limehouse Basin
Ratcliff Cross Stairs
Limehouse Basin Entrance
NARROW ST
LIMEHOUSE LINK (Tunnel)
Westferry
EAST INDIA DOCK RD
POPLAR HIGH ST
Poplar
All Saints
Poplar Bsns Pk
ASPEN WAY
Billingsgate Mkt
North Quay
Mus of London Docklands
West India Quay
Columbus Court Yard
Canary Wharf
West India Dock
Canary Wharf Pier
WESTFERRY CIR
West Quay
Heron Quays
West India Dock South
West India and Millwall Docks
South Quay
World Trade Ctr London
Independent House
MARSH WALL
Blackwall Basin
Indoor Sports Arena
E14
ROTHERHITHE ST
Cuckold's Point
Hotel
Nelson Docks
Sp Gd
Bacon's Coll
Redriff Prim Sch
Russia Dock Woodland
St John's RC Prim Sch
SE16
Surrey Docks Farm
Barnard's Wharf
Express Wharf
Quebec Ind Est
REDRIFF RD
Greenland Pier
Marina
Surrey Commercial Docks
Surrey Docks Watersports Ctr
South Dock (Marina)
St George's Wharf
Greenwich Reach
Sir John McDougal Gardens
Klein's Wharf
Millwall
Arnhem Wharf Prim Sch
Millwall Outer Dock
Millwall Inner Dock
Crossharbour
Great Eastern Ent Ctr
Harbour Island
Visitor Ctr
Cubitt Town Jun & Inf Sch
Hypermarket
Cubitt Town
Mudchute Park & Farm
Mudchute
ISLE OF DOGS
Island Gardens
Millwall Park
WESTFERRY RD
EAST FERRY RD
St Edmunds RC Prim Sch
Thames Path
PLOUGH WAY
GROVE ST
EVELYN ST
Deptford Park
Pepys Park
Slipway
Louis Wharf
Masthouse Terr Pier
Burrell's Wharf
Convoys Wharf
Palmer's Wharf
Payne's Wharf
Borthwick Wharf
Locke's Wharf
Johnson's Drawdock
SE8
Blackhorse Wharf
Crown Wharf
New Baltic Wharf
Victoria Wharf
Deptford Trad Est
Parkside Bsns Est
Folkestone Gardens
Charlotte Turner Prim
Dreadnought Wharf
Dowell's Wharf
St Alfege with St Peter's CE Prim Sch
120
141
A B C D
1 2 3 4 5 6
37 38
78 79 80 81

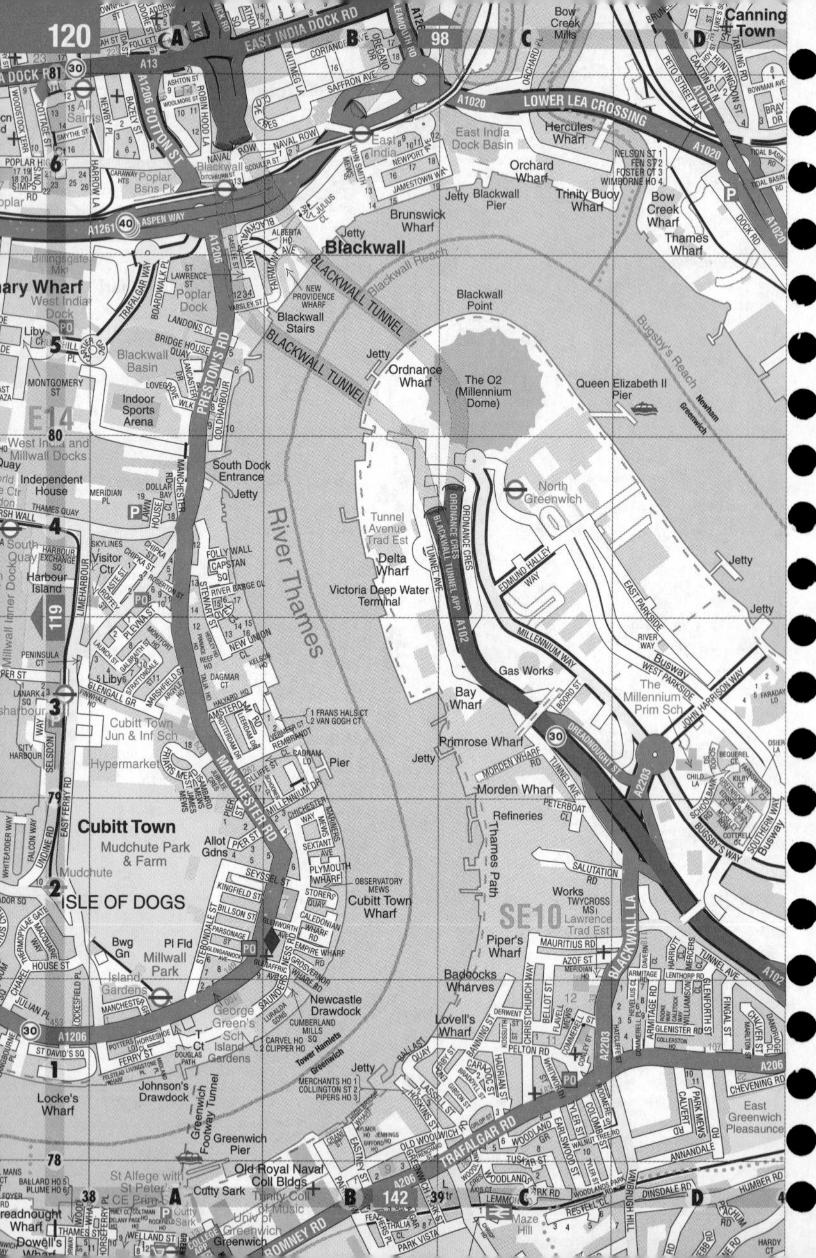
120
A
B
C
D
98
EAST INDIA DOCK RD
Bow Creek Mills
Canning Town
LOWER LEA CROSSING
A1020
A13
A1206
COTTON ST
ROBIN HOOD LA
NUTMEG LA
SAFFRON AVE
CORIANDER AVE
OREGANO DR
LEAMOUTH RD
ORCHARD PL
East India
NAVAL ROW
East India Dock Basin
Hercules Wharf
Orchard Wharf
Trinity Buoy Wharf
Bow Creek Wharf
Thames Wharf
NEWPORT AVE
JAMESTOWN WAY
JOHN SMITH MEWS
Blackwall
Jetty
Blackwall Pier
Brunswick Wharf
All Saints
POPLAR HIGH ST
Poplar
COTTAGE ST
WOODSTOCK TERR
NEWBY PL
BAZELY ST
HARROW LA
Poplar Bsns Pk
ASPEN WAY
A1261
Billingsgate Mkt
TRAFALGAR WAY
BOARDWALK PL
Poplar Dock
West India Dock
Blackwall Reach
BLACKWALL TUNNEL
NEW PROVIDENCE WHARF
Blackwall Stairs
Blackwall Point
Bugsby's Reach
Ordnance Wharf
The O2 (Millennium Dome)
Queen Elizabeth II Pier
Newham
Greenwich
Blackwall Basin
PRESTON'S RD
BRIDGE HOUSE QUAY
LANDONS CL
MONTGOMERY ST
Indoor Sports Arena
E14
West India and Millwall Docks
Independent House
MERIDIAN PL
THAMES QUAY
South Quay
South Dock Entrance
River Thames
North Greenwich
Tunnel Avenue Trad Est
Delta Wharf
Victoria Deep Water Terminal
ORDNANCE CRES
BLACKWALL TUNNEL APP
TUNNEL AVE
A102
EDMUND HALLEY WAY
EAST PARKSIDE
WEST PARKSIDE
MILLENNIUM WAY
RIVER WAY
Busway
JOHN HARRISON WAY
The Millennium Prim Sch
Gas Works
Bay Wharf
BOORD ST
DREADNOUGHT ST
Harbour Island
LIMEHARBOUR
Visitor Ctr
CHIPKA ST
FOLLY WALL
CAPSTAN SQ
RIVER BARGE CL
STEWART ST
NEW UNION CL
119
Millwall Inner Dock
PENINSULA CT
GLENGALL GR
MARSHFIELD ST
Cubitt Town Jun & Inf Sch
Hypermarket
FRIARS MEAD
MANCHESTER RD
Pier
MILLENNIUM DR
Primrose Wharf
MORDEN WHARF RD
Morden Wharf
Refineries
PETERBOAT CL
Thames Path
A2203
SCHOOLBANK RD
BUGSBY'S WAY
SOUTHERN WAY
Cubitt Town
Mudchute Park & Farm
EAST FERRY RD
UNDINE RD
FALCON WAY
WHITEADDER WAY
Allot Gdns
PIER ST
SEYSSEL ST
SEXTANT AVE
PLYMOUTH WHARF
OBSERVATORY MEWS
Cubitt Town Wharf
Mudchute
ISLE OF DOGS
KINGFIELD ST
BILLSON ST
STEBONDALE ST
CALEDONIAN WHARF
EMPIRE WHARF
SALUTATION RD
Works
SE10
Lawrence Trad Est
BLACKWALL LA
MAURITIUS RD
Piper's Wharf
Badcocks Wharves
Lovell's Wharf
TUNNEL AVE
Bwg Gn
Pl Fld
Millwall Park
Island Gardens
HOUSE ST
JULIAN PL
MANCHESTER GR
Newcastle Drawdock
George Green's Sch
A1206
FERRY ST
Island Gardens
Tower Hamlets
Greenwich
CHRISTCHURCH WAY
PELTON RD
HADRIAN ST
A206
CHEVENING RD
East Greenwich Pleasaunce
ST DAVID'S SQ
Locke's Wharf
Johnson's Drawdock
Greenwich Footway Tunnel
Jetty
Greenwich Pier
OLD WOOLWICH RD
TRAFALGAR RD
WOODLAND GR
EARLSWOOD ST
ANNANDALE
78
St Alfege with St Peter's CE Prim
Old Royal Naval Coll Bldgs
Cutty Sark
Trinity Coll of Music
Univ of Greenwich
142
39
Maze Hill
VANBRUGH HILL
DINSDALE RD
HUMBER RD
38
Dreadnought Wharf
Dowell's Wharf
ROMNEY RD
PARK VISTA
Greenwich

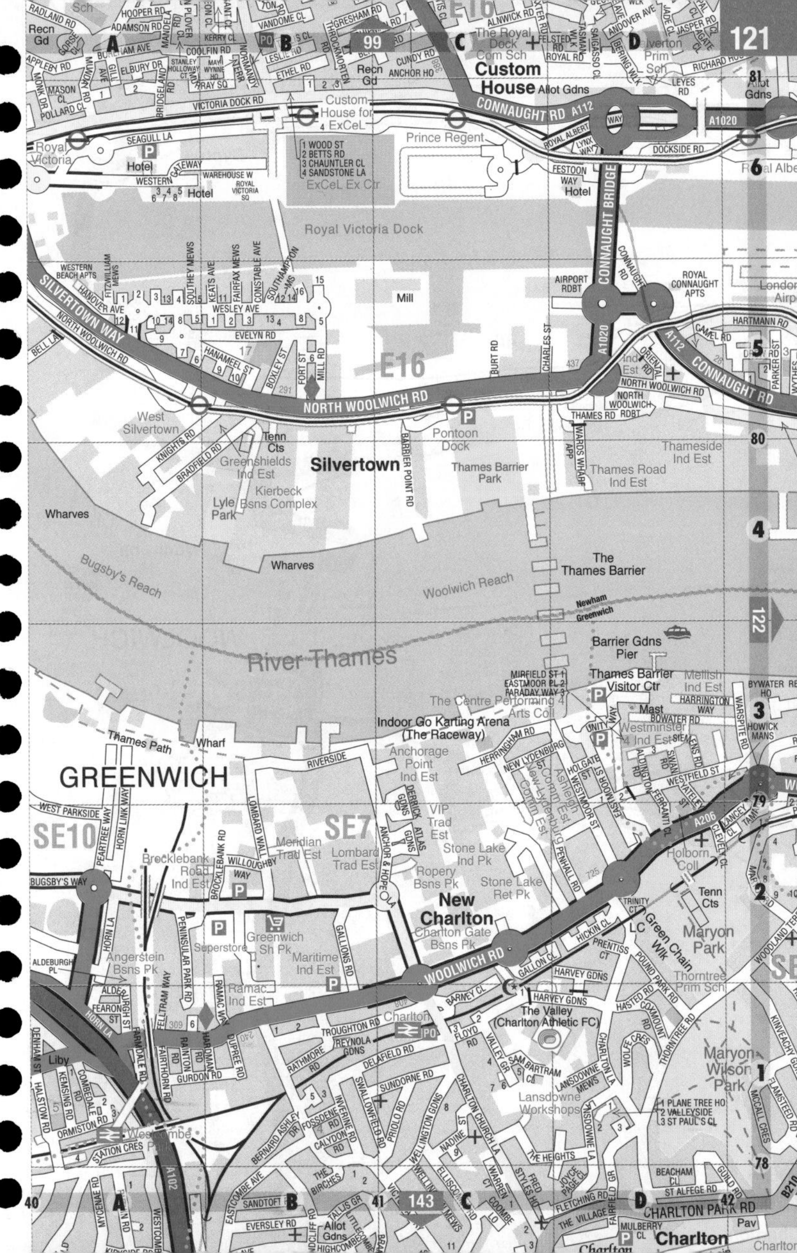
Custom House
Royal Victoria Dock
Silvertown
E16
River Thames
Woolwich Reach
Bugsby's Reach
The Thames Barrier
GREENWICH
SE10
SE7
New Charlton
Charlton
North Woolwich Rd
Woolwich Rd
Connaught Rd
Connaught Bridge
Silvertown Way
Prince Regent
ExCeL Ex Ctr
Thames Barrier Park
Pontoon Dock
West Silvertown
Maryon Park
Maryon Wilson Park
The Valley (Charlton Athletic FC)
Barrier Gdns Pier
Thames Barrier Visitor Ctr
Westcombe Park
99
122
143

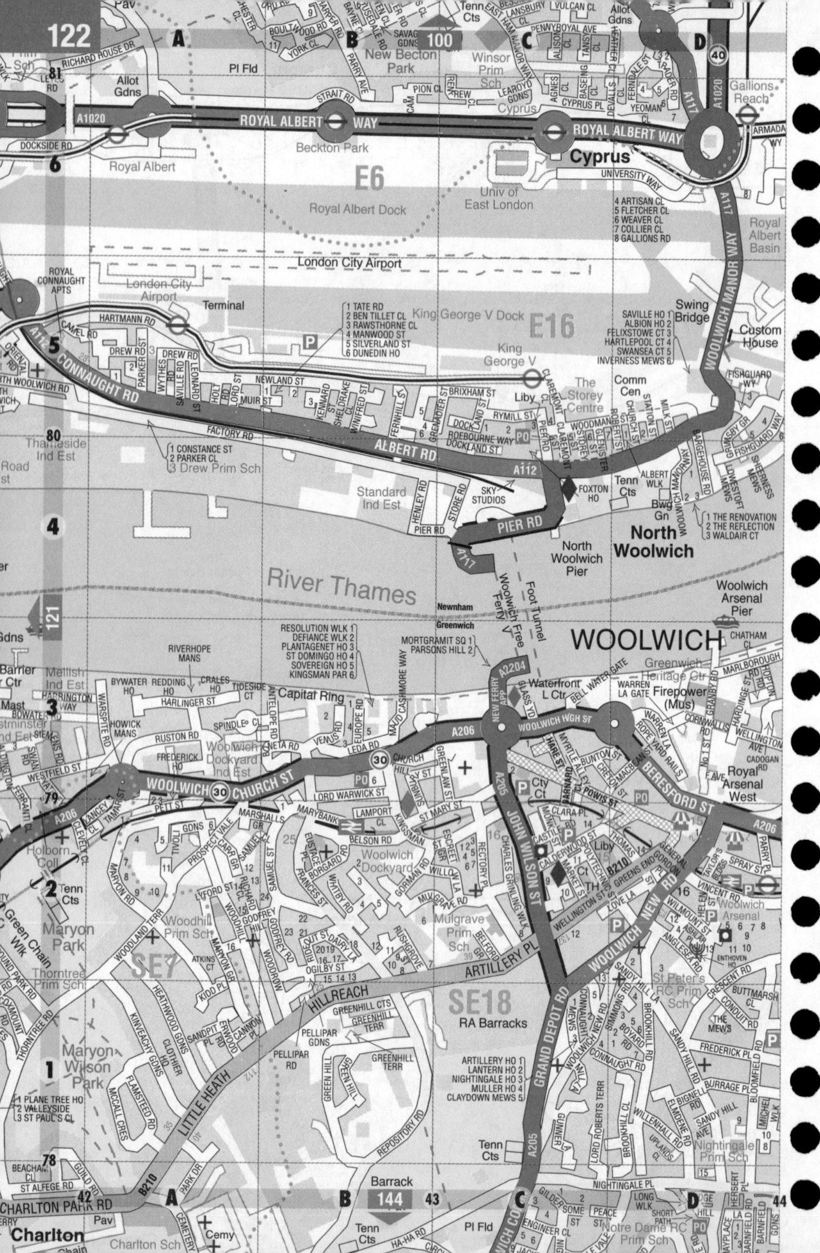

ROYAL ALBERT WAY
Beckton Park
Royal Albert
Cyprus
Gallions Reach
New Beckton Park
Winsor Prim Sch
E6
Royal Albert Dock
Univ of East London
London City Airport
Terminal
King George V Dock
E16
King George V
CONNAUGHT RD
ALBERT RD
PIER RD
North Woolwich Pier
North Woolwich
River Thames
Woolwich Free Ferry
Foot Tunnel
WOOLWICH MANOR WAY
Royal Albert Basin
Custom House
Swing Bridge
The Storey Centre
Standard Ind Est
Thameside Ind Est
WOOLWICH
Woolwich Arsenal Pier
Capital Ring
WOOLWICH CHURCH ST
WOOLWICH HIGH ST
BERESFORD ST
JOHN WILSON ST
Firepower (Mus)
Royal Arsenal West
Woolwich Dockyard
Woolwich Arsenal
SE7
SE18
RA Barracks
Maryon Park
Maryon Wilson Park
GRAND DEPOT RD
WOOLWICH NEW RD
ARTILLERY PL
HILLREACH
LITTLE HEATH
Charlton
CHARLTON PARK RD
Nightingale Prim Sch
St Peter's RC Prim Sch
Notre Dame RC Prim Sch
100
144
121

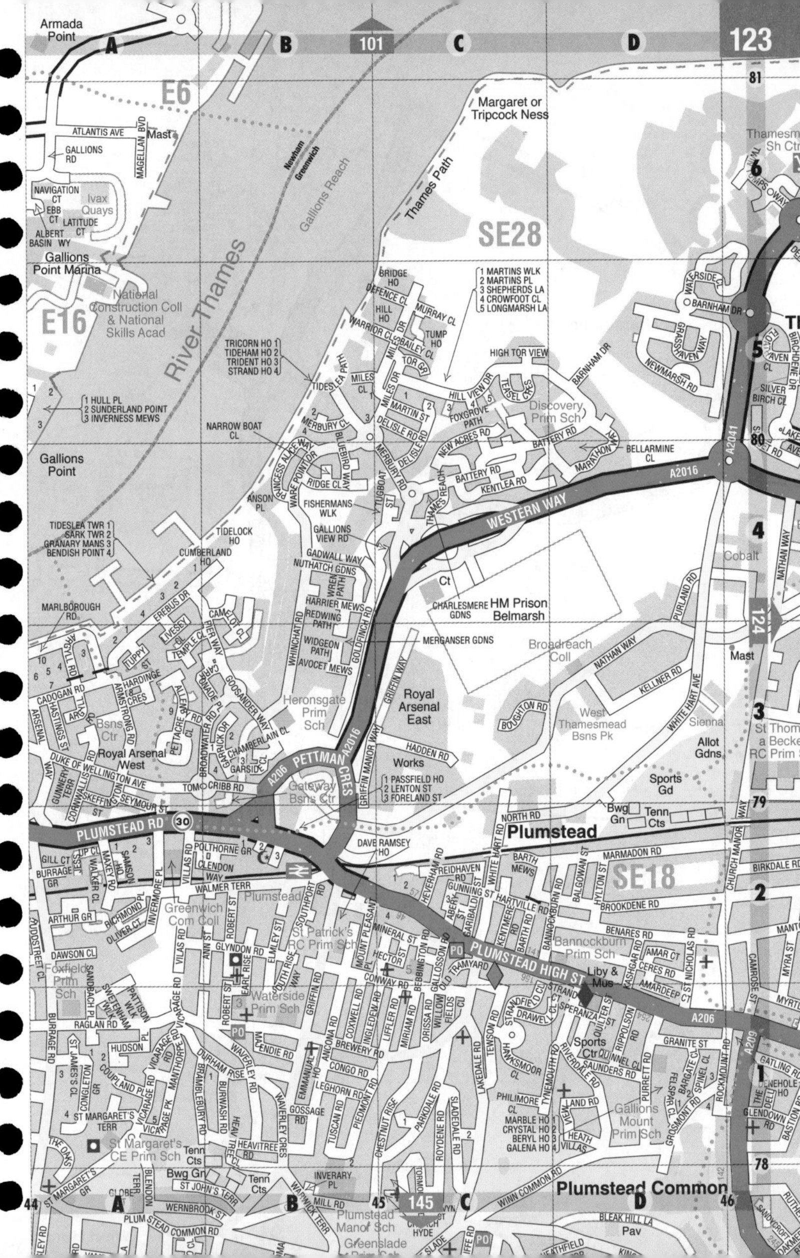

Armada Point
A
B
101
C
D
E6
Margaret or Tripcock Ness
Thamesmead Sh Ctr
ATLANTIS AVE
Mast
MAGELLAN BVD
GALLIONS RD
Newham
Greenwich
Gallions Reach
Thames Path
NAVIGATION CT
EBB CT
LATITUDE CT
ALBERT BASIN WY
Ivax Quays
SE28
Gallions Point Marina
River Thames
National Construction Coll & National Skills Acad
E16
1 MARTINS WLK
2 MARTINS PL
3 SHEPHERDS LA
4 CROWFOOT CL
5 LONGMARSH LA
WATERSIDE CL
BARNHAM DR
GRASSHAVEN WAY
NEWMARSH RD
TRICORN HO 1
TIDEHAM HO 2
TRIDENT HO 3
STRAND HO 4
HIGH TOR VIEW
1 HULL PL
2 SUNDERLAND POINT
3 INVERNESS MEWS
Discovery Prim Sch
NARROW BOAT CL
BELLARMINE CL
A2041
Gallions Point
A2016
WESTERN WAY
ANSON PL
FISHERMANS WLK
TIDESLEA TWR 1
SARK TWR 2
GRANARY MANS 3
BENDISH POINT 4
TIDELOCK HO
GALLIONS VIEW RD
CUMBERLAND HO
GADWALL WAY
NUTHATCH GDNS
Cobalt
NATHAN WAY
HARRIER MEWS
REDWING PATH
CHARLESMERE GDNS
HM Prison Belmarsh
MARLBOROUGH RD
124
WIDGEON PATH
MERGANSER GDNS
Broadreach Coll
AVOCET MEWS
Mast
Royal Arsenal East
Heronsgate Prim Sch
West Thamesmead Bsns Pk
Sienna
St Thomas a Beckett RC Prim Sch
Allot Gdns
Bsns Ctr
Royal Arsenal West
PETTMAN CRES
HADDEN RD
Works
Sports Gd
DUKE OF WELLINGTON AVE
1 PASSFIELD HO
2 LENTON ST
3 FORELAND ST
Gateway Bsns Ctr
79
PLUMSTEAD RD
NORTH RD
Bwg Gn
Tenn Cts
Plumstead
DAVE RAMSEY HO
MARMADON RD
BIRKDALE RD
SE18
Plumstead
BROOKDENE RD
Greenwich Com Coll
BENARES RD
St Patrick's RC Prim Sch
PLUMSTEAD HIGH ST
Bannockburn Prim Sch
Foxfield Prim Sch
Liby & Mus
Waterside Prim Sch
A206
Sports Ctr
Gallions Mount Prim Sch
PHILIMORE CL
MARBLE HO 1
CRYSTAL HO 2
BERYL HO 3
GALENA HO 4
78
St Margaret's CE Prim Sch
Tenn Cts
Bwg Gn
Tenn Cts
INVERARY PL
WINN COMMON RD
Plumstead Common
44
A
B
45
145
C
D
46
Plumstead Manor Sch
BLEAK HILL LA
Pav
Greenslade

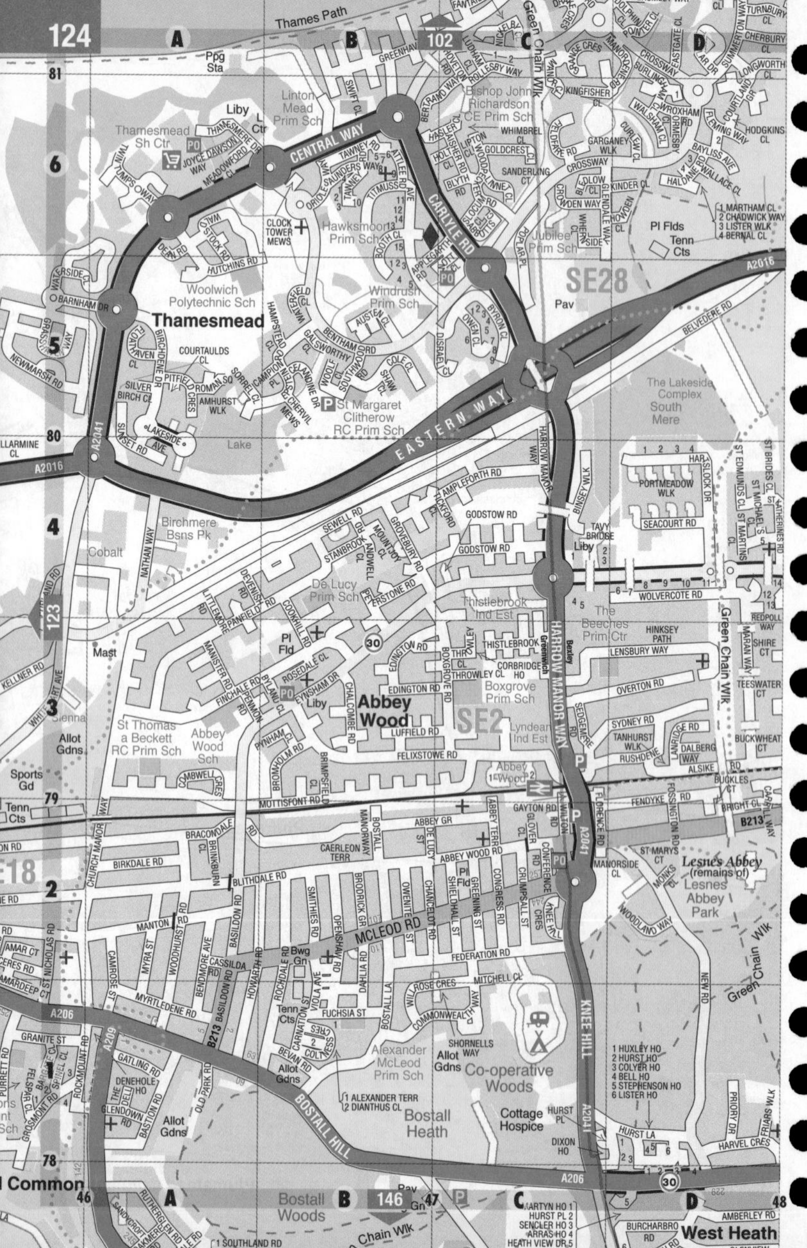

Thames Path
102
Ppg Sta
Linton Mead Prim Sch
Liby
L Ctr
Thamesmead Sh Ctr
PO
CENTRAL WAY
JOYCE DAWSON WAY
MEADOWFORD CL
THAMESMERE DR
NIMBUS RD
TUMPS WAY
Bishop John Richardson CE Prim Sch
WHIMBREL CL
KINGFISHER CL
GOLDCREST CL
SANDERLING CT
GARGANEY WLK
CROSSWAY
KINDER CL
CROWDEN WAY
BLEDLOW CL
GLENDALE WAY
WHERNSIDE
HOWDEN CL
Jubilee Prim Sch
Pl Flds
Tenn Cts
1 MARTHAM CL
2 CHADWICK WAY
3 LISTER WLK
4 BERNAL CL
HALDANE RD
WALLACE CL
BAYLISS AVE
FLEMING WAY
HODGKINS CL
COURTLAND GR
LONGWORTH CL
CHERBURY CL
TURNBURY CL
SUMMERTON WAY
WROXHAM RD
ORMESBY
WALSHAM CL
CURLEW CL
CROSSWAY
SURLINGHAM CL
EASTGATE CL
GRANGE CRES
MANORDENE RD
DOLPHIN CL
CLOCK TOWER MEWS
Hawksmoor Prim Sch
TAWNEY RD
SAUNDERS WAY
TITMUSS AVE
ATTLEE RD
CARLYLE RD
BOOTH CL
APPLEGARTH RD
Windrush Prim Sch
HUTCHINS RD
WATERSIDE CL
BARNHAM DR
Woolwich Polytechnic Sch
Thamesmead
GRASSMERE WAY
NEWMARSH RD
FLOATHAVEN CL
BIRCHDENE DR
COURTAULDS CL
PITFIELD CRES
ROMAN SQ
SILVER BIRCH CL
AMHURST WLK
SUNSET RD
LAKESIDE AVE
Lake
HAMPSTEAD CL
WATERFIELD CL
AUSTEN CL
BENTHAM RD
GALSWORTHY CL
SOUTHWOOD RD
COLE CL
SHAW CL
DISRAELI CL
BYRON CL
OWEN CL
CAMPION PL
CELANDINE DR
CHERVIL MEWS
St Margaret Clitherow RC Prim Sch
SE28
Pav
A2016
BELVEDERE RD
EASTERN WAY
The Lakeside Complex
South Mere
BELLARMINE CL
A2041
HARROW MANOR WAY
AMPLEFORTH RD
PORTMEADOW WLK
HARTSLOCK DR
SEACOURT RD
BINSEY WLK
TAVY BRIDGE
ST EDMUNDS CL
ST MARTINS
ST MICHAELS CL
ST BRIDES CL
ST KATHERINES RD
GODSTOW RD
TICKFORD CL
Birchmere Bsns Pk
Cobalt
NATHAN WAY
SEWELL RD
STANBROOK RD
MOUNTJOY CL
GROVEBURY RD
ANDWELL CL
PETERSTONE RD
De Lucy Prim Sch
DEVENISH RD
LITTLEMORE RD
PANFIELD RD
COOKHILL RD
WOLVERCOTE RD
Thistlebrook Ind Est
The Beeches Prim Ctr
HINKSEY PATH
Green Chain Wlk
REDPOLL WAY
Pl Fld
Mast
123
KELLNER RD
WHITEHART AVE
ROSEDALE CL
EYNSHAM DR
EDINGTON RD
THISTLEBROOK
THROWLEY CL
CORBRIDGE HO
LENSBURY WAY
MARAN WAY
SHIRE CT
TEESWATER CT
BOXGROVE RD
Boxgrove Prim Sch
MANISTER RD
FINCHALE RD
BYLAND CL
PENMON RD
Abbey Wood
Liby
CHALCOMBE RD
OVERTON RD
SEDGEMERE RD
SYDNEY RD
TANHURST WLK
LANRIDGE RD
DALBERG WAY
RUSHDENE
BUCKWHEAT CT
Sienna
Allot Gdns
St Thomas a Beckett RC Prim Sch
Abbey Wood Sch
PYNHAM CL
BROMHOLM RD
LUFFIELD RD
SE2
Lyndean Ind Est
FELIXSTOWE RD
Abbey Wood
ALSIKE RD
BUCKLES CT
Sports Gd
Tenn Cts
CAMBWELL CRES
BRIMPSFIELD CL
MOTTISFONT RD
GAYTON RD
WILTON RD
FLORENCE RD
FENDYKE RD
FOSSINGTON RD
BRIGHT CL
CARRILL WAY
B213
CHURCH MANOR WAY
BRACONDALE
BRINKBURN CL
ABBEY GR
BOSTALL MANORWAY
DE LUCY ST
ABBEY TERR
GLOVER RD
CONFERENCE CL
CAERLEON TERR
ABBEY WOOD RD
ST MARYS CT
MANORSIDE CL
Lesnes Abbey (remains of)
Lesnes Abbey Park
BIRKDALE RD
BLITHDALE RD
SMITHIES RD
BRODRICK GR
OWENITE ST
CHANCELOT RD
SHIELDHALL ST
GREENING ST
CONGRESS RD
CRUMPSALL ST
KNEE HILL CRES
WOODLAND WAY
MANTON RD
MCLEOD RD
OPENSHAW RD
WOODHURST RD
BENDMORE AVE
MYRA ST
CAMROSE ST
BASILDON RD
HOWARTH RD
ROCHDALE RD
Bwg Gn
DAHLIA RD
FEDERATION RD
ST NICHOLAS RD
CASSILDA RD
MYRTLEDENE RD
VIOLA AVE
BOSTALL LA
WILLROSE CRES
MITCHELL CL
COMMONWEALTH WAY
FUCHSIA ST
CARNATION ST
COLTNESS CRES
BEVAN RD
Tenn Cts
Alexander McLeod Prim Sch
Allot Gdns
SHORNELLS WAY
Co-operative Woods
KNEE HILL
NEW RD
A206
A209
GRANITE ST
GATLING RD
DENEHOLE HO
THE DELL
GLENDOWN RD
BASTION RD
OLD PARK RD
ROCKMOUNT RD
SPINEL CL
FELSPAR CL
GROSMONT RD
PURRETT RD
Allot Gdns
BOSTALL HILL
1 ALEXANDER TERR
2 DIANTHUS CL
Bostall Heath
Cottage Hospice
HURST PL
DIXON HO
1 HUXLEY HO
2 HURST HO
3 COLYER HO
4 BELL HO
5 STEPHENSON HO
6 LISTER HO
HURST LA
PRIORY DR
FRIARS WLK
HARVEL CRES
Common
146
Bostall Woods
MARTYN HO 1
HURST PL 2
SENCLER HO 3
ARRAS HO 4
HEATH VIEW DR 5
BURCHARBRO RD
AMBERLEY RD
West Heath
SANDYCROFT
RUTHERGLEN RD
1 SOUTHLAND RD

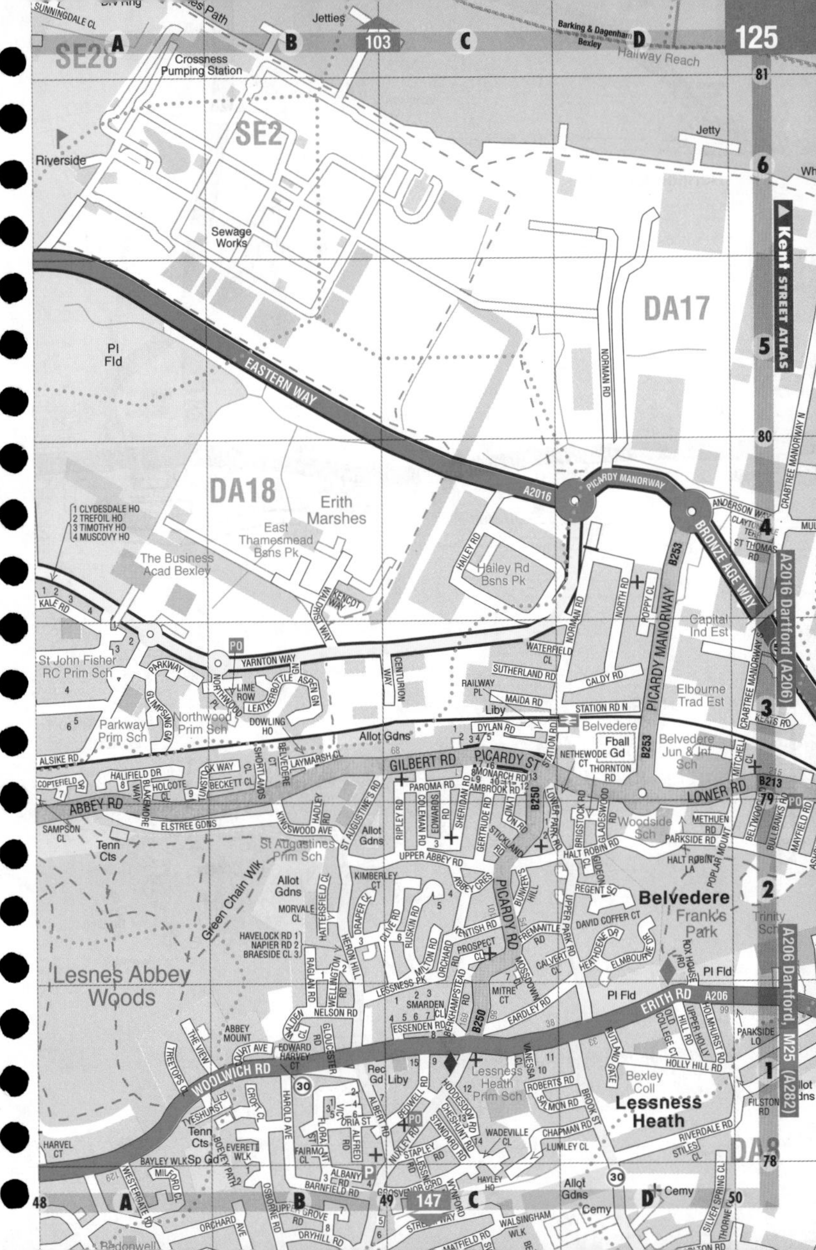

103
Barking & Dagenham
Bexley
Halfway Reach
Jetties
Crossness Pumping Station
SE28
SE2
Riverside
Sewage Works
Jetty
Kent STREET ATLAS
DA17
NORMAN RD
Pl Fld
EASTERN WAY
A2016
PICARDY MANORWAY
BRONZE AGE WAY
DA18
Erith Marshes
East Thamesmead Bsns Pk
The Business Acad Bexley
1 CLYDESDALE HO
2 TREFOIL HO
3 TIMOTHY HO
4 MUSCOVY HO
Hailey Rd Bsns Pk
HAILEY RD
KENCOT WAY
WALDRIST WAY
CRABTREE MANORWAY N
ANDERSON WAY
CLAYTON TERR
ST THOMAS RD
A2016 Dartford (A206)
Capital Ind Est
Elbourne Trad Est
CRABTREE MANORWAY S
KALE RD
St John Fisher RC Prim Sch
PARKWAY
YARNTON WAY
CENTURION WAY
WATERFIELD CL
SUTHERLAND RD
CALDY RD
NORTH RD
POPPY CL
B253
Parkway Prim Sch
GLIMPSING GN
Northwood Prim Sch
NORTHWOOD PL
LIME ROW
LEATHERBOTTLE GN
ASPEN GN
DOWLING HO
RAILWAY PL
MAIDA RD
STATION RD N
Liby
Belvedere
Fball Gd
Belvedere Jun & Inf Sch
KEATS RD
MITCHELL CL
Allot Gdns
DYLAN RD
ALSIKE RD
SHORTLANDS
BELVEDERE CT
LAYMARSH CL
GILBERT RD
PICARDY ST
STATION RD
NETHEWODE CT
THORNTON RD
COPTEFIELD DR
HALIFIELD DR
BLAKEMORE WAY
HOLCOTE CL
TUNSTOCK WAY
BECKETT CL
PAROMA RD
MONARCH RD
AMBROOK RD
B250
LOWER RD
B213
ABBEY RD
ELSTREE GDNS
KINGSWOOD AVE
HADLEY
ST AUGUSTINE'S RD
RIPLEY RD
COLEMAN RD
EDWARDS RD
SHERIDAN RD
GERTRUDE RD
LYNDON RD
LOWER PARK RD
BRIGSTOCK RD
GLADESWOOD
METHUEN RD
PARKSIDE RD
BELTWOOD
BULLBANKS RD
MAYFIELD RD
SAMPSON CL
Tenn Cts
St Augustines Prim Sch
STICKLAND RD
Woodside Sch
HALT ROBIN RD
HALT ROBIN LA
POPLAR MOUNT
UPPER ABBEY RD
Green Chain Wlk
KIMBERLEY CT
ABBEY CRES
PICARDY RD
BUNKERS HILL
GIDEON CL
REGENT SQ
Belvedere
Frank's Park
Trinity Sch
Allot Gdns
HATTERSFIELD CL
MORVALE CL
DRAPER CL
CLIVE RD
RUSKIN RD
KENTISH RD
FREMANTLE RD
UPPER PARK RD
DAVID COFFER CT
A206 Dartford, M25 (A282)
HAVELOCK RD 1
NAPIER RD 2
BRAESIDE CL 3
HERON HILL
PROSPECT CL
CALVERT CL
HEATHDENE DR
ELMBOURNE DR
FOX HOUSE RD
Pl Fld
Lesnes Abbey Woods
RAGLAN RD
WELLINGTON RD
LESSNESS PK
MILTON RD
ORCHARD RD
BERKHAMPSTEAD RD
MITRE CT
MOSSDOWN CL
Pl Fld
ERITH RD
A206
SMARDEN CL
EARDLEY RD
NELSON RD
ESSENDEN RD
WALDEN CL
ABBEY MOUNT
GLOUCESTER RD
OLD COLLEGE CT
HILL RD
UPPER HOLLY HILL RD
HOLMHURST RD
PARKSIDE LO
THE VIEW
COURT AVE
EDWARD HARVEY CT
VANESSA
RUTLAND GATE
HOLLY HILL RD
TREETOPS CL
WOOLWICH RD
Rec Gd
Liby
Lessness Heath Prim Sch
Bexley Coll
FILSTON RD
30
HAROLD AVE
CROFT CL
TYESHURST CL
BEDWELL RD
HODDESDON RD
CHESHUNT RD
ROBERTS RD
SALMON RD
BROOK ST
Lessness Heath
VICTORIA ST
FLORA ST
ALFRED RD
ALBERT RD
STANDARD RD
WADEVILLE CL
CHAPMAN RD
RIVERDALE RD
HARVEL CT
Tenn Cts
EVERETT WLK
BOEVEY PATH
FAIRMONT CL
NUXLEY RD
STAPLEY RD
LESSNESS AVE
LUMLEY CL
STILES CL
DA8
BAYLEY WLK
Sp Gd
MILFORD CL
WESTERGATE RD
ALBANY RD
BARNFIELD RD
WYNFORD
HAYLEY HO
Allot Gdns
Cemy
SILVER SPRING CL
GROSVENOR RD
147
OSBORNE RD
UPPER GROVE RD
ORCHARD AVE
STREAM WAY
WALSINGHAM WLK
THORNE CL
DRYHILL RD
MATFIELD RD
Bedonwell

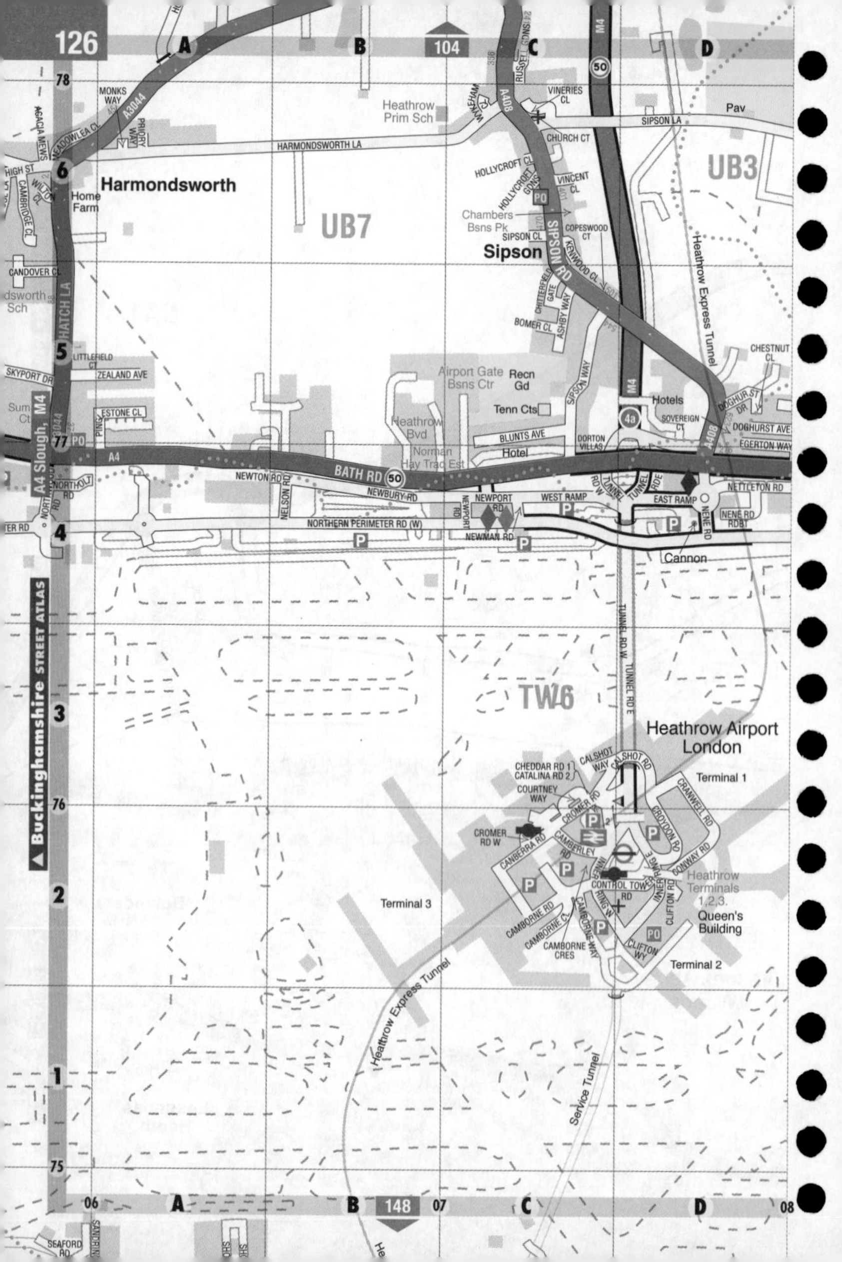

104
148
Harmondsworth
Sipson
Heathrow Airport London
UB7
UB3
TW6
HARMONDSWORTH LA
SIPSON LA
SIPSON RD
BATH RD
NORTHERN PERIMETER RD (W)
HATCH LA
A4 Slough, M4
Heathrow Express Tunnel
Service Tunnel
TUNNEL RD W
TUNNEL RD E
Terminal 1
Terminal 2
Terminal 3
Heathrow Terminals 1,2,3.
Queen's Building
Buckinghamshire STREET ATLAS

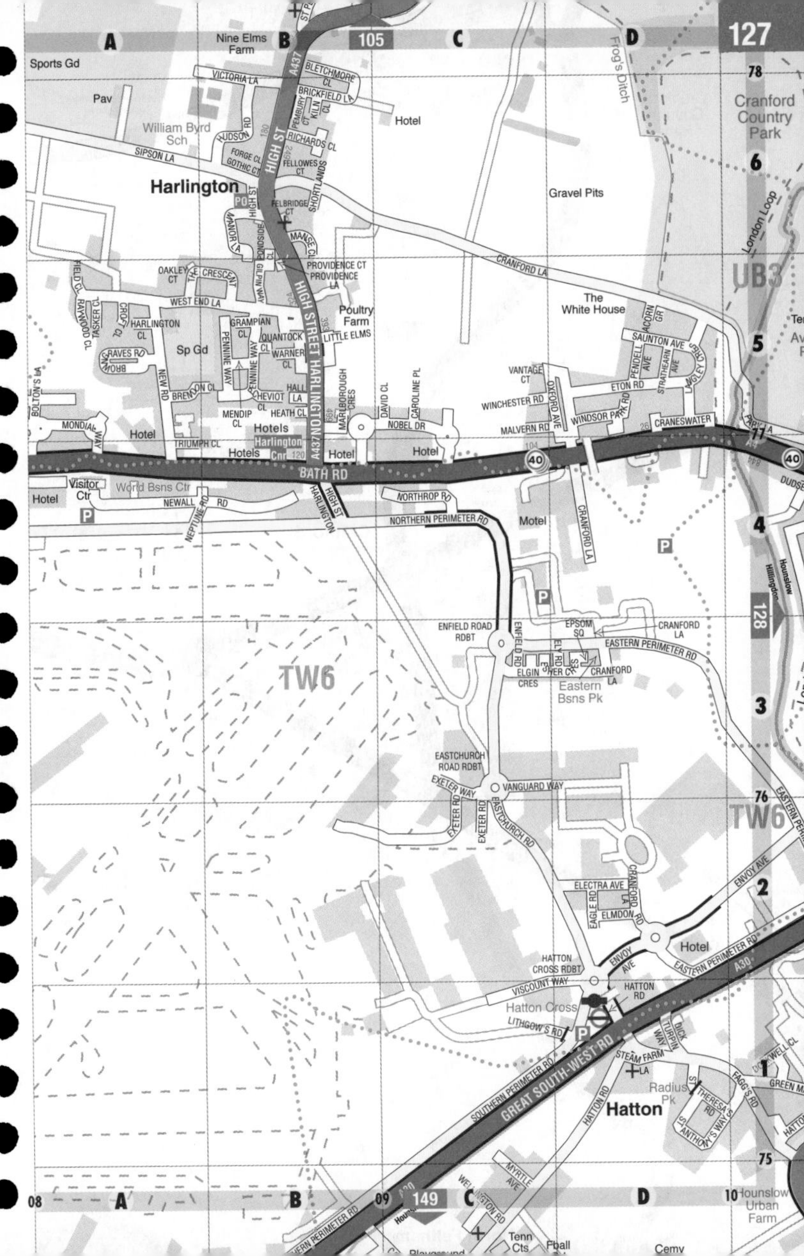

A
B
C
D
Nine Elms Farm
105
Sports Gd
Pav
William Byrd Sch
Harlington
Hotel
Gravel Pits
Frog's Ditch
Cranford Country Park
London Loop
UB3
The White House
Poultry Farm
Sp Gd
Hotels
Harlington Cnr
Hotel
Visitor Ctr
World Bsns Ctr
Motel
BATH RD
SIPSON LA
CRANFORD LA
HIGH ST
HIGH STREET HARLINGTON
NORTHERN PERIMETER RD
EASTERN PERIMETER RD
TW6
ENFIELD ROAD RDBT
EASTCHURCH ROAD RDBT
VANGUARD WAY
Eastern Bsns Pk
HATTON CROSS RDBT
Hatton Cross
GREAT SOUTH-WEST RD
SOUTHERN PERIMETER RD
Hatton
Radius Pk
Hounslow Urban Farm
128
149
08
09
10
78
76
75
Tenn Cts
Fball
Cemv

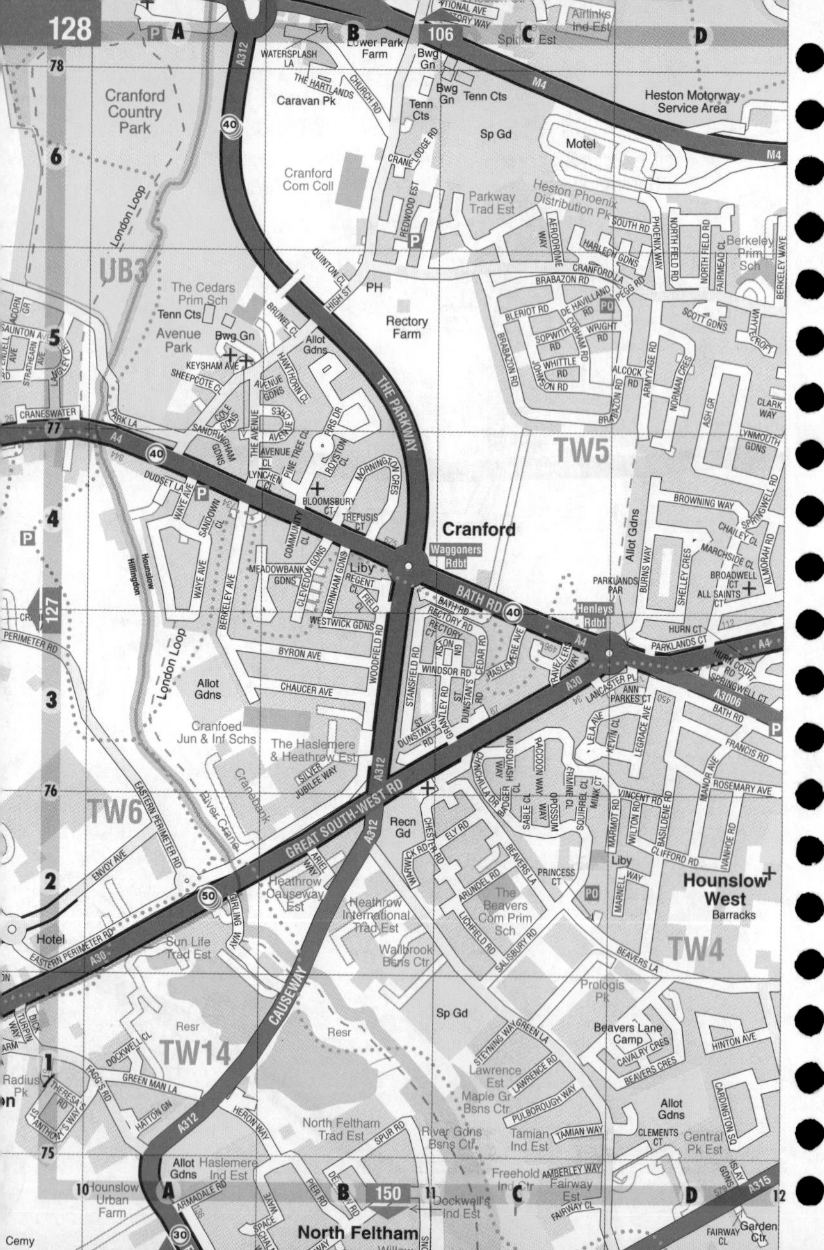

Cranford Country Park
Lower Park Farm
Caravan Pk
Heston Motorway Service Area
Motel
Cranford Com Coll
Parkway Trad Est
Heston Phoenix Distribution Pk
UB3
The Cedars Prim Sch
Avenue Park
Rectory Farm
TW5
Cranford
Waggoners Rdbt
Henleys Rdbt
BATH RD
THE PARKWAY
GREAT SOUTH-WEST RD
Cranfoed Jun & Inf Schs
The Haslemere & Heathrow Est
TW6
Heathrow Causeway Est
Heathrow International Trad Est
Sun Life Trad Est
Wallbrook Bsns Ctr
The Beavers Com Prim Sch
Hounslow West
Barracks
TW4
Prologis Pk
Beavers Lane Camp
TW14
Lawrence Est
Maple Gr Bsns Ctr
Tamian Ind Est
North Feltham Trad Est
River Gdns Bsns Ctr
Central Pk Est
Haslemere Ind Est
Hounslow Urban Farm
Freehold Ind Ctr
Fairway Est
Dockwell's Ind Est
North Feltham
Radius Pk
Hotel
Allot Gdns
Sp Gd
Recn Gd
Resr
London Loop
River Crane
Cranebank
Hounslow
Hillington
CAUSEWAY
EASTERN PERIMETER RD
M4
A4
A30
A312
A3006
A315
106
127
150

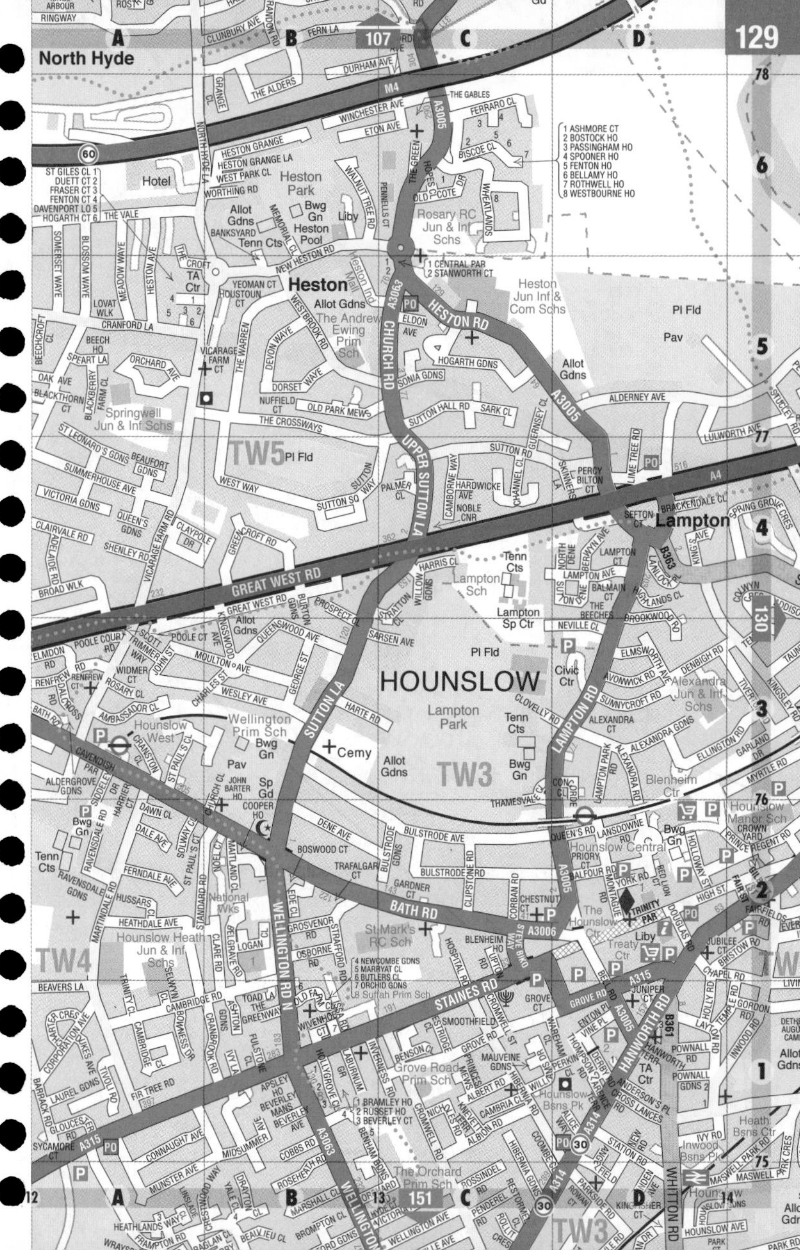
North Hyde
Heston
Lampton
HOUNSLOW
TW5
TW3
TW4
Hounslow West
Hounslow Central
Heston Park
Lampton Park
M4
GREAT WEST RD
A3005
A3063
A4
A315
A3006
A314
B363
B361
STAINES RD
BATH RD
HESTON RD
CHURCH RD
UPPER SUTTON LA
SUTTON LA
LAMPTON RD
WELLINGTON RD N
HANWORTH RD
WHITTON RD
1 ASHMORE CT
2 BOSTOCK HO
3 PASSINGHAM HO
4 SPOONER HO
5 FENTON HO
6 BELLAMY HO
7 ROTHWELL HO
8 WESTBOURNE HO
ST GILES CL 1
DUETT CT 2
FRASER CT 3
FENTON CT 4
DAVENPORT LO 5
HOGARTH CT 6
1 CENTRAL PAR
2 STANWORTH CT
4 NEWCOMBE GDNS
5 MARRYAT CL
6 BUTLERS CL
7 ORCHID GDNS
8 Suffah Prim Sch
1 BRAMLEY HO
2 RUSSET HO
3 BEVERLEY CT
Springwell Jun & Inf Schs
Rosary RC Jun & Inf Schs
Heston Jun Inf & Com Schs
The Andrew Ewing Prim Sch
Wellington Prim Sch
Lampton Sch
Alexandra Jun & Inf Schs
Hounslow Heath Jun & Inf Schs
St Mark's RC Sch
Grove Road Prim Sch
The Orchard Prim Sch
Hounslow Manor Sch
107
130
151
A
B
C
D
78
77
76
75
6
5
4
3
2
1
12
13
14

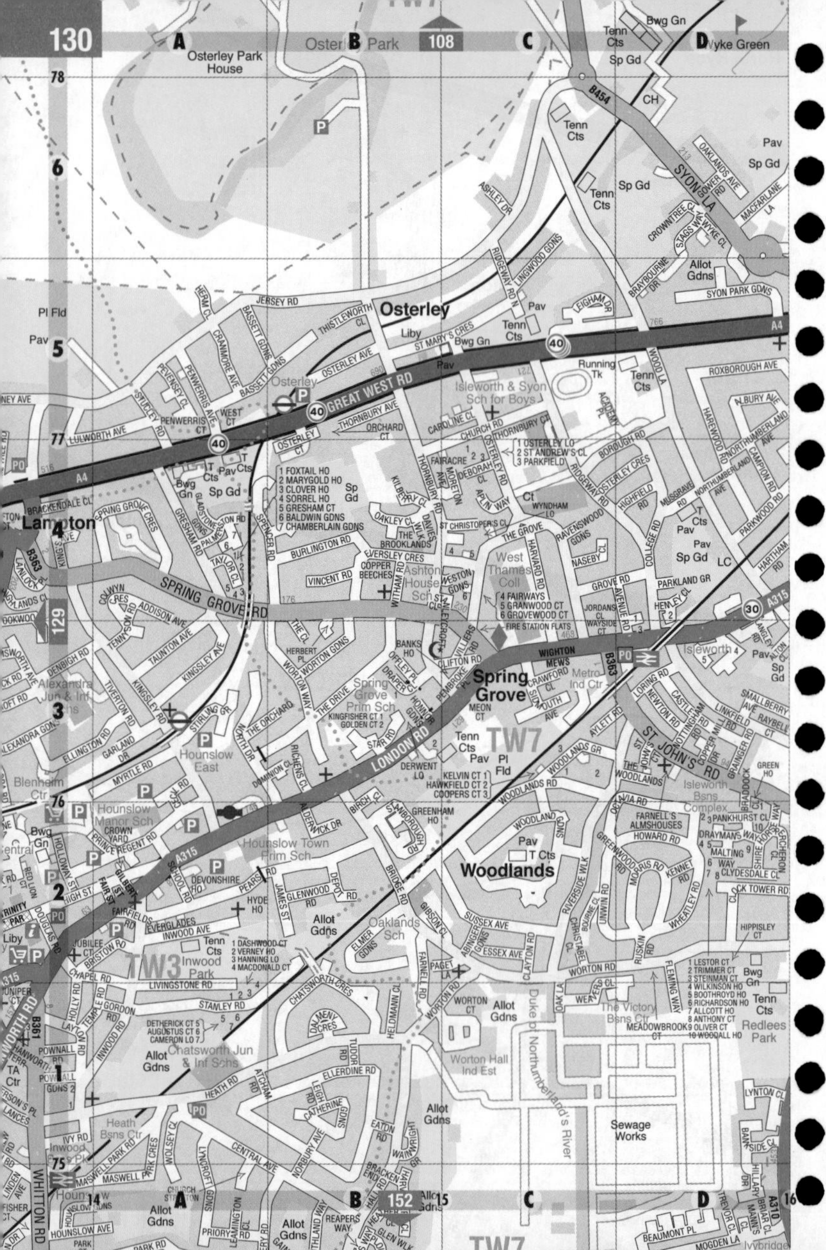

Osterley Park
108
Osterley Park House
Bwg Gn
Tenn Cts
Sp Gd
Wyke Green
B454
CH
Tenn Cts
Pav
Sp Gd
SYON LA
OAKLANDS AVE
GOWER RD
MACFARLANE LA
ASHLEY DR
Tenn Cts
Sp Gd
CROWNTREE CL
STAGS WAY
WYKE CL
RIDGEWAY RD N
LINGWOOD GDNS
BRAYBOURNE DR
Allot Gdns
SYON PARK GDNS
LEIGHAM DR
Pav
Pl Fld
JERSEY RD
HERM CL
BASSETT GDNS
THISTLEWORTH CL
Osterley
Liby
ST MARY'S CRES
Bwg Gn
Tenn Cts
A4
Pav
CRANMORE AVE
BASSETT GDNS
OSTERLEY AVE
Pav
Running Tk
Tenn Cts
WOOD LA
ROXBOROUGH AVE
PEVENSEY CL
PENWERRIS AVE
Osterley
GREAT WEST RD
Isleworth & Syon Sch for Boys
ACADEMY PL
ALBURY AVE
HAREWOOD RD
NORTHUMBERLAND AVE
LULWORTH AVE
STUCLEY RD
PENWERRIS CT
WEST CT
THORNBURY AVE
ORCHARD CT
CAROLINE CL
CHURCH RD
THORNBURY CT
1 OSTERLEY LO
2 ST ANDREW'S CL
3 PARKFIELD
BOROUGH RD
OSTERLEY CT
FAIRACRE
DEBORAH CL
OSTERLEY RD
RIDGEWAY RD
OSTERLEY CRES
CAMPION RD
PO
A4
T Cts
Pav
Bwg Gn
Sp Gd
1 FOXTAIL HO
2 MARYGOLD HO
3 CLOVER HO
4 SORREL HO
5 GRESHAM CT
6 BALDWIN GDNS
7 CHAMBERLAIN GDNS
Sp Gd
THORNBURY RD
MORETON AVE
KILBERRY CL
APLIN WAY
Ct
WYNDHAM LO
HIGHFIELD RD
MUSGRAVE RD
NORTHUMBERLAND AVE
PARKWOOD RD
BRACKENDALE CL
Lampton
SPRING GROVE CRES
GLADSTONE GDNS
GRESHAM RD
PALMERSTON RD
SPENCER RD
OAKLEY CL
DAVIES WLK
THE BROOKLANDS
ST CHRISTOPHER'S CL
THE GROVE
RAVENSWOOD GDNS
HARVARD RD
COLLEGE RD
T Cts
Pav
Pav
Sp Gd
LC
HARTHAM RD
KINGS AVE
B363
LANLOCK PL
TAYLOR CL
BURLINGTON RD
EVERSLEY CRES
COPPER BEECHES
Ashton House Sch
West Thames Coll
NASEBY CL
VINCENT RD
WESTON GDNS
GROVE RD
PARKLAND GR
129
COLWYN CRES
SPRING GROVE RD
ADDISON AVE
TENNYSON RD
WITHAM RD
STANLEYCROFT CL
4 FAIRWAYS
5 GRANWOOD CT
6 GROVEWOOD CT
FIRE STATION FLATS
JORDANS CL
WAYSIDE CT
AVENUE RD
HENLEY CL
A315
DENBIGH RD
TAUNTON AVE
KINGSLEY AVE
THE CL
HERBERT PL
WORTON GDNS
BANKS HO
OFFLEY PL
VILLIERS RD
CLIFTON RD
WIGHTON MEWS
B363
PO
Isleworth
Pav
Sp Gd
Alexandra Jun & Inf Schs
TIVERTON RD
KINGSLEY RD
STIRLING GR
WORTON WAY
THE DRIVE
DRAPER CL
HONNOR GDNS
PEMBROKE PL
Spring Grove
CRAWFORD CL
SIDMOUTH AVE
Metro Ind Ctr
LORING RD
NEWTON RD
CASTLE RD
NOTTINGHAM
SMALLBERRY AVE
LINKFIELD RD
RAYBELL CT
ALEXANDRA GDNS
ELLINGTON RD
GARLAND DR
Hounslow East
THE ORCHARD
NORTH DR
Spring Grove Prim Sch
KINGFISHER CT 1
GOLDEN CT 2
STAR RD
LONDON RD
MEON CT
Tenn Cts
TW7
Pav
Pl Fld
AYLETT RD
ST JOHN'S RD
COPPER MILL DR
GRAINGER RD
GREEN HO
Blenheim Ctr
MYRTLE RD
CECIL RD
DOMINION CL
RICHENS CL
DERWENT LO
KELVIN CT 1
HAWKFIELD CT 2
COOPERS CT 3
WOODLANDS GR
WOODLANDS RD
THE WOODLANDS
Isleworth Bsns Complex
BRADDOCK CL
Hounslow Manor Sch
CROWN YARD
PRINCE REGENT RD
ALDERWICK DR
BIRCH CL
SANBOROUGH
GREENHAM HO
WOODLAND GDNS
FARNELL'S ALMSHOUSES
HOWARD RD
PANKHURST CL
DRAYMANS WAY
SHIRE HORSE WAY
PERCHERON CL
MALTING WAY
CLYDESDALE CL
Bwg Gn
HOLLOWAY ST
Hounslow Town Prim Sch
Pav
T Cts
Woodlands
GREENWOOD RD
MORRIS RD
KENNET RD
A315
SCHOOL RD
DEVONSHIRE HO
PEARS RD
JAMES ST
GLENWOOD RD
DEPOT RD
BRIDGE RD
RIVERSIDE WLK
UNWIN RD
BOURNE CL
WHEATLEY RD
CLOCK TOWER RD
RED LION CT
HIGH ST
GILBERT ST
FAIR ST
TRINITY PAR
FAIRFIELDS
EVERGLADES
HYDE HO
Allot Gdns
Oaklands Sch
GIBSON CL
SUSSEX AVE
ABINGER GDNS
ESSEX AVE
CLAYTON RD
CHRISTABEL CL
RUSKIN RD
HIPPISLEY CT
Liby
DOUGLAS RD
JUBILEE CT
BRISTOW RD
INWOOD AVE
Tenn Cts
1 DASHWOOD CT
2 VERNEY HO
3 HANNING LO
4 MACDONALD CT
ELMER GDNS
PAGET LA
FARNELL RD
WORTON RD
FLEMING WAY
1 LESTOR CT
2 TRIMMER CT
3 STEINMAN CT
4 WILKINSON HO
5 BOOTHROYD HO
6 RICHARDSON HO
7 ALLCOTT HO
8 ANTHONY CT
9 OLIVER CT
10 WOODALL HO
Bwg Gn
Tenn Cts
TW3
Inwood Park
CHAPEL RD
LIVINGSTONE RD
CHATSWORTH CRES
HELDMANN CL
WEAVERS CL
OAK LA
The Victory Bsns Ctr
MEADOWBROOK CT
Redlees Park
HANWORTH RD
B361
HOLLY RD
TEMPLE RD
GORDON RD
STANLEY RD
DALMENY CRES
WORTON CT
Allot Gdns
Duke of Northumberland's River
LAYTON RD
DETHERICK CT 5
AUGUSTUS CT 6
CAMERON LO 7
INWOOD RD
Allot Gdns
Chatsworth Jun & Inf Schs
TUDOR RD
Worton Hall Ind Est
POWNALL RD
TA Ctr
ELLERDINE RD
ATCHAM RD
LEIGH RD
CATHERINE GDNS
HEATH RD
PO
EATON RD
Allot Gdns
LYNTON CL
Heath Bsns Ctr
WOLSEY CL
NORBURY AVE
WAINWRIGHT GR
Sewage Works
BANKSIDE CL
IVY RD
Inwood Ct
MASWELL PARK RD
MASWELL PARK CRES
LYNCROFT GDNS
CENTRAL AVE
BRACKEN END
HILLARY DR
Hounslow
WHITTON RD
MASWELL PK
CHURCH STREET
Allot Gdns
LEAMINGTON CL
PRIORY RD
Allot Gdns
REAPERS WAY
152
Allot Gdns
TREVOR CL
BRIAR CL
A310
HOUNSLOW GDNS
HOUNSLOW AVE
PARK RD
BEAUMONT PL
TW7
MOGDEN LA
Ivybridge

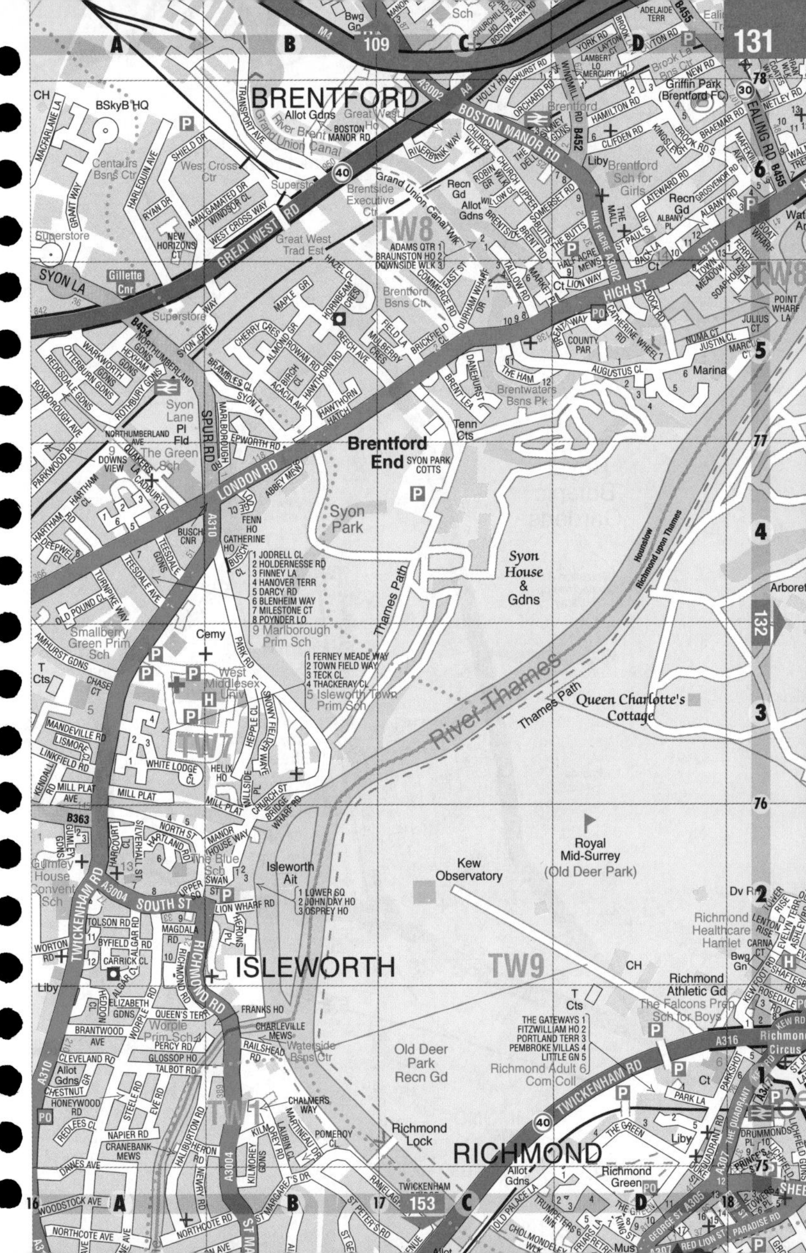
BRENTFORD
Brentford End
ISLEWORTH
RICHMOND
TW8
TW7
TW9
TW1
Syon Park
Syon House & Gdns
River Thames
Thames Path
Queen Charlotte's Cottage
Royal Mid-Surrey (Old Deer Park)
Kew Observatory
Old Deer Park Recn Gd
Isleworth Ait
Richmond Lock
Richmond Athletic Gd
Richmond Green
Richmond Healthcare Hamlet
Griffin Park (Brentford FC)
Brentford Sch for Girls
BSkyB HQ
Centaurs Bsns Ctr
West Cross Ctr
Great West Trad Est
Brentside Executive Ctr
Brentford Bsns Ctr
Brentwaters Bsns Pk
Grand Union Canal
GREAT WEST RD
BOSTON MANOR RD
HIGH ST
LONDON RD
SPUR RD
TWICKENHAM RD
SOUTH ST
RICHMOND RD
SYON LA
HALF ACRE
EALING RD
Marina
West Middlesex Univ
Smallberry Green Prim Sch
Gumley House Convent Sch
The Blue Sch
Worple Prim Sch
Waterside Bsns Ctr
The Falcons Prep Sch for Boys
Richmond Adult Com Coll
Hounslow
Richmond upon Thames
A
B
C
D
109
153
132
77
76
75
16
17
18

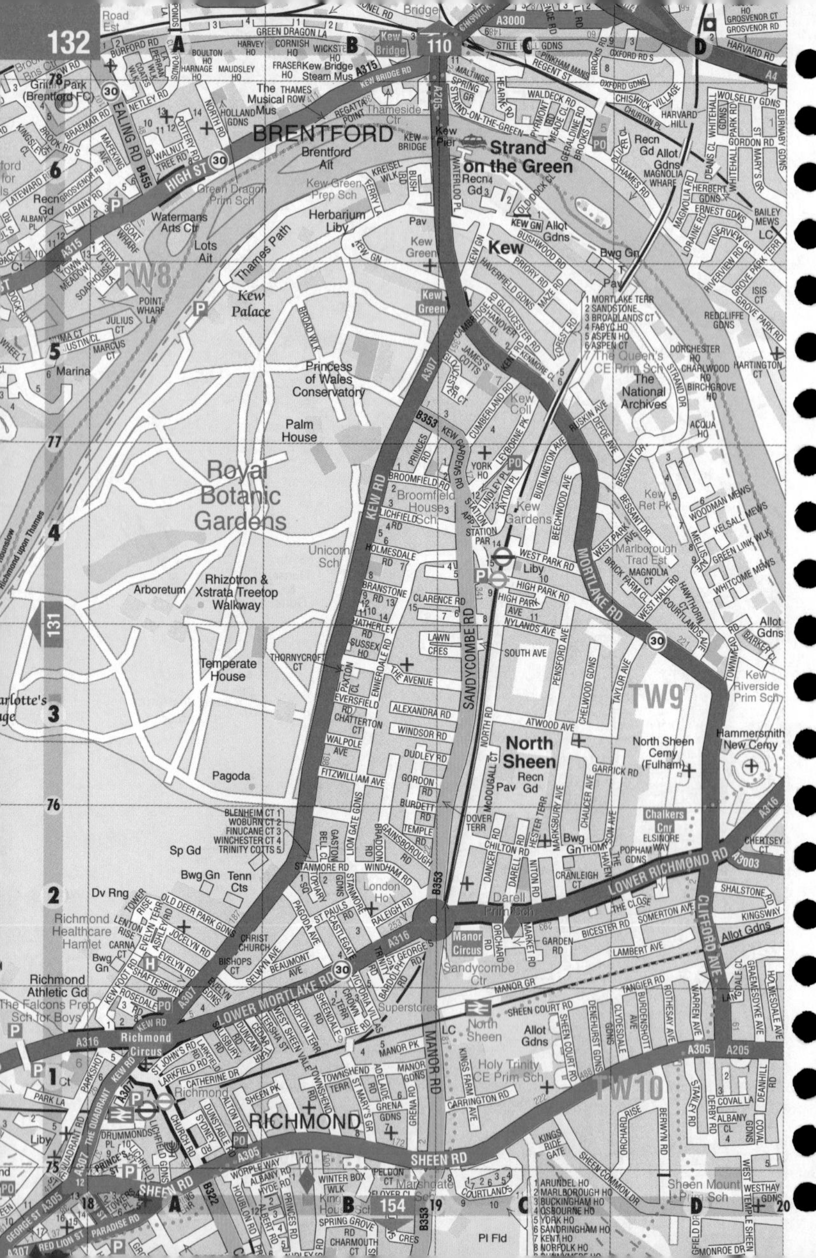
BRENTFORD
Strand on the Green
Kew
Kew Palace
Princess of Wales Conservatory
Palm House
Royal Botanic Gardens
Rhizotron & Xstrata Treetop Walkway
Arboretum
Temperate House
Pagoda
North Sheen
RICHMOND
Richmond Circus
Manor Circus
The National Archives
Hammersmith New Cemy
North Sheen Cemy (Fulham)
Kew Retail Pk
Marlborough Trad Est
Richmond Athletic Gd
Richmond Healthcare Hamlet
TW8
TW9
TW10
KEW RD
MORTLAKE RD
SANDYCOMBE RD
LOWER RICHMOND RD
LOWER MORTLAKE RD
SHEEN RD
MANOR RD
CLIFFORD AVE
KEW BRIDGE RD
HIGH ST
EALING RD
A316
A307
A205
A305
A315
B353
110
131
154

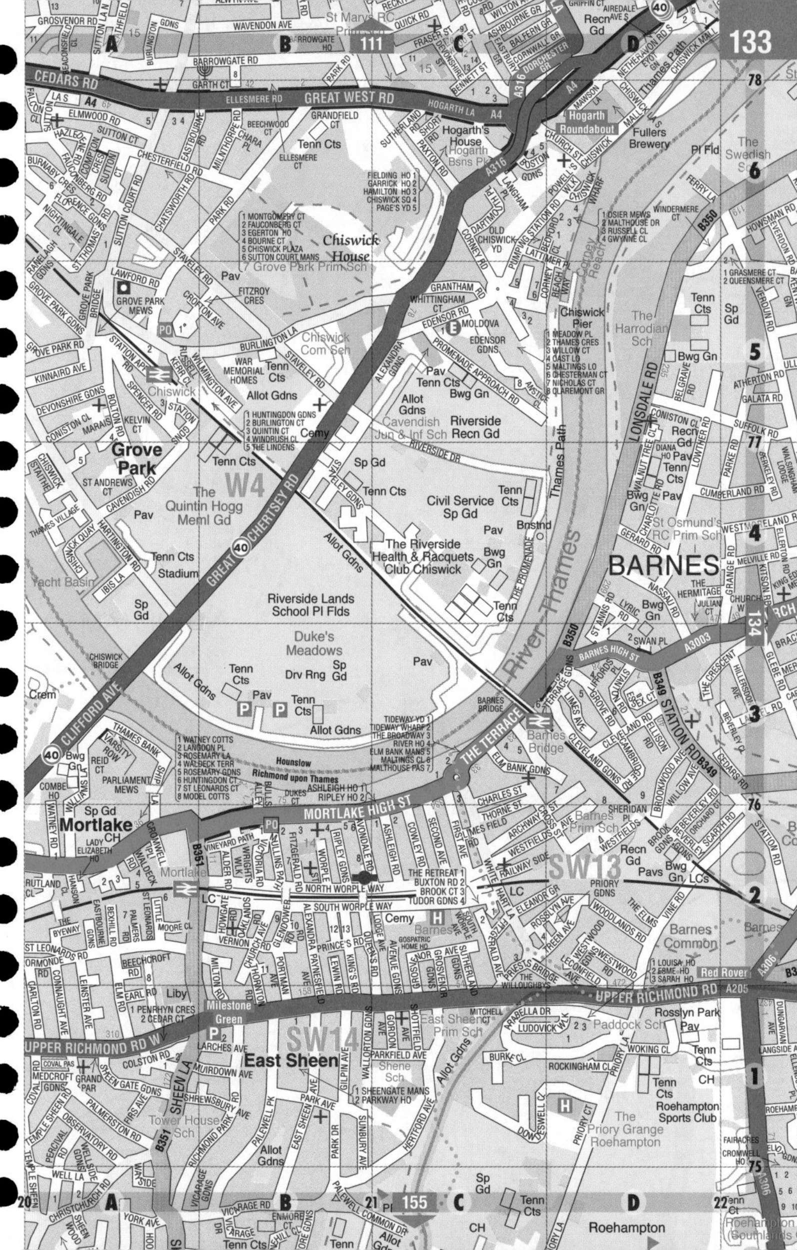
111
A
B
C
D
GROSVENOR RD
WAVENDON AVE
St Marys RC Prim Sch
BARROWGATE HO
BARROWGATE RD
GARTH CT
CEDARS RD
A4
GREAT WEST RD
ELLESMERE RD
HOGARTH LA
A316
DORCHESTER GR
Hogarth Roundabout
Fullers Brewery
Thames Path
CHISWICK MALL
Recn Gd
40
78
ELMWOOD RD
SUTTON CT
CHESTERFIELD RD
GRANDFIELD CT
BEECHWOOD CT
ELLESMERE CT
Tenn Cts
Hogarth's House
Hogarth Bsns Pk
FIELDING HO 1
GARRICK HO 2
HAMILTON HO 3
CHISWICK SQ 4
PAGE'S YD 5
1 MONTGOMERY CT
2 FAUCONBERG CT
3 EGERTON HO
4 BOURNE CT
5 CHISWICK PLAZA
6 SUTTON COURT MANS
7 Grove Park Prim Sch
Chiswick House
CHURCH ST
CHISWICK WHARF
POWELL'S WLK
BOSTON GDNS
PUMPING STATION RD
OLD CHISWICK YD
LATTIMER PL
CORNEY RD
CORNEY REACH WAY
Corney Reach
1 OSIER MEWS
2 MALTHOUSE DR
3 RUSSELL CL
4 GWYNNE CL
WINDERMERE CT
Pl Fld
The Swedish Sch
6
FERRY LA
B350
HOWSMAN RD
1 GRASMERE CT
2 QUEENSMERE CT
VERDUN RD
KENTWODE
RANELAGH GDNS
NIGHTINGALE CL
FLORENCE GDNS
BURNABY CRES
FAUCONBERG RD
ST THOMAS RD
SUTTON COURT RD
CHATSWORTH RD
PARK RD
STAVELEY RD
Pav
LAWFORD RD
GROVE PARK MEWS
GROVE PARK BRIDGE
GROVE PARK GDNS
CROFTON AVE
FITZROY CRES
GRANTHAM RD
WHITTINGHAM CT
EDENSOR RD
MOLDOVA
EDENSOR GDNS
Chiswick Pier
1 MEADOW PL
2 THAMES CRES
3 WILLOW CT
4 OAST LO
5 MALTINGS LO
6 CHESTERMAN CT
7 NICHOLAS CT
8 CLAREMONT GR
The Harrodian Sch
Tenn Cts
Sp Gd
Bwg Gn
5
BELGRAVE RD
ATHERTON RD
GALATA RD
PO
GROVE PARK RD
KINNAIRD AVE
STATION APP
KERR CL
RUSSELL
WILMINGTON AVE
Chiswick
BURLINGTON LA
Chiswick Com Sch
WAR MEMORIAL HOMES
Allot Gdns
ALEXANDRA GDNS
PROMENADE APPROACH RD
AMSTICE CL
Pav
Bwg Gn
Cavendish Jun & Inf Sch
Riverside Recn Gd
DEVONSHIRE GDNS
BOLTON RD
SPENCER RD
STATION GDNS
CONISTON CL
MARAIS
KELVIN CT
1 HUNTINGDON GDNS
2 BURLINGTON CT
3 QUINTIN CT
4 WINDRUSH CL
5 THE LINDENS
Cemy
RIVERSIDE DR
LONSDALE RD
CONISTON CL
Recn Gd
DIANA HO
LOWTHER RD
SUFFOLK RD
77
PARKE RD
BERKELEY RD
WALSINGHAM LODGE
FERRY RD
Grove Park
CHISWICK STAITHE
ST ANDREWS CT
CAVENDISH RD
W4
The Quintin Hogg Meml Gd
STAVELEY GDNS
Sp Gd
Civil Service Sp Gd
Thames Path
WALNUT TREE CL
CHARLOTTE RD
CUMBERLAND RD
St Osmund's RC Prim Sch
WESTMORELAND RD
THAMES VILLAGE
CHISWICK QUAY
HARTINGTON RD
Tenn Cts
Stadium
IBIS LA
Yacht Basin
GREAT CHERTSEY RD
Allot Gdns
The Riverside Health & Racquets Club Chiswick
Bnstnd
River Thames
THE PROMENADE
GERARD RD
BARNES
4
MELVILLE RD
ELLERTON RD
KITSON RD
KING EDWARD MEWS
NASSAU RD
THE HERMITAGE
JULIAN CT
CHURCH
134
Riverside Lands School Pl Flds
Duke's Meadows
Drv Rng
ST ANNS RD
LYRIC RD
SWAN PL
A3003
BARNES HIGH ST
B350
B349
STATION RD
CHISWICK BRIDGE
Crem
CLIFFORD AVE
P
Allot Gdns
BARNES BRIDGE
TIDEWAY YD 1
TIDEWAY WHARF 2
THE BROADWAY 3
RIVER HO 4
ELM BANK MANS 5
MALTINGS CL 6
MALTHOUSE PAS 7
TERRACE GDNS
LIMES AVE
GROVE RD
LILLFORD RD
STANTON RD
ESSEX CT
CLEVELAND RD
CAMBRIDGE RD
ELLISON RD
THE CRESCENT
HILLERSDON AVE
GLEBE RD
BEVERLEY CL
3
THAMES BANK
VARSITY ROW
REID CT
PARLIAMENT MEWS
1 WATNEY COTTS
2 LANGDON PL
3 ROSEMARY LA
4 WALDECK TERR
5 ROSEMARY GDNS
6 HUNTINGDON CT
7 ST LEONARDS CT
8 MODEL COTTS
Hounslow
Richmond upon Thames
ASHLEIGH HO 1
RIPLEY HO 2
DUKES CT
BULLS ALLEY
THE TERRACE
Barnes Bridge
CLEVELAND GDNS
ELM BANK GDNS
BROOKWOOD AVE
WILLOW AVE
CEDARS RD
COMBE HO
WATNEY RD
WILLIAMS LA
Sp Gd
Mortlake
LADY ELIZABETH HO
CROMWELL PL
WALDECK RD
PO
MORTLAKE HIGH ST
CHARLES ST
THORNE ST
ARCHWAY ST
LIMES FIELD
Barnes Prim Sch
SHERIDAN PL
WESTFIELDS AVE
BEVERLEY RD
ORCHARD CL
SCARTH RD
76
STATION RD
Barnes Com
B351
VINEYARD PATH
ALDER RD
WRIGHTS WLK
VICTORIA RD
MULLINS PATH
FITZGERALD RD
WORPLE ST
RIPLEY GDNS
AVONDALE RD
ASHLEIGH RD
COWLEY RD
SECOND AVE
FIRST AVE
WHITE HART LA
RAILWAY SIDE
SW13
Recn Gd
Pavs
Bwg Gn
LCs
RUTLAND CL
HANSON CL
Mortlake
LC
NORTH WORPLE WAY
SOUTH WORPLE WAY
THE RETREAT 1
BUXTON RD 2
BROOK CT 3
TUDOR GDNS 4
PRIORY GDNS
ELEANOR GR
2
EASTBOURNE GDNS
BEXHILL RD
PALMERS RD
ST LEONARDS RD
LITTLE
MOORE CL
THE BYEWAY
HOWGATE RD
OAKLANDS
GLENDOWER RD
ALEXANDRA RD
PRINCE'S RD
LODGE AVE
Cemy
H
Barnes Hosp
SOUTH WORPLE AVE
ROSSLYN AVE
TREEN AVE
WOODLANDS RD
THE ELMS
VINE RD
Barnes Common
Barnes
ST LEONARDS RD
ORMONDE RD
BEECHCROFT RD
VERNON RD
CHURCH AVE
PORTMAN AVE
PAYNESFIELD AVE
LEWIN RD
KING'S RD
QUEEN'S RD
AVENUE GDNS
GOSPATRIC HOME HO
GROSVENOR GDNS
SUTHERLAND GDNS
PRIESTS BRIDGE
THE WILLOUGHBYS
WESTWOOD GDNS
WESTWOOD RD
ECONFIELD AVE
1 LOUISA HO
2 EDME HO
3 SARAH HO
Red Rover
A306
B306
ELM RD
EARL RD
CARLTON RD
CONNAUGHT AVE
LEINSTER AVE
MILTON RD
THORNTON RD
Liby
1 PENRHYN CRES
2 CEDAR CT
Milestone Green
UPPER RICHMOND RD
A205
MITCHELL CT
ARABELLA DR
LUDOVICK WLK
Paddock Sch
Rosslyn Park
Pav
DUNGARVAN AVE
UPPER RICHMOND RD W
P
LARCHES AVE
SW14
East Sheen
WALLORTON GDNS
GORDON AVE
SHOTFIELD AVE
East Sheen Prim Sch
PARKFIELD AVE
Shene Sch
BURKE CL
ROCKINGHAM CL
WOKING CL
PRIORY LA
Tenn Cts
CH
LANGSIDE AVE
ELLENBOROUGH PL
COVAL PAS
MEDCROFT GDNS
GRAND PAR
COLSTON RD
MUIRDOWN AVE
SHEEN GATE GDNS
SHEEN LA
SHREWSBURY AVE
FIRS AVE
1 SHEENGATE MANS
2 PARKWAY HO
PARK AVE
EAST SHEEN AVE
GILPIN AVE
Allot Gdns
H
Roehampton Sports Club
1
ROEHAMPTON
TEMPLE SHEEN RD
PALMERSTON RD
OBSERVATORY RD
PERCIVAL RD
WELLSIDE GDNS
Tower House Sch
RICHMOND PARK RD
PALEWELL PK
PARK DR
SUNBURY AVE
HERTFORD AVE
DOWNESWELL CL
PRIORY CT
The Priory Grange Roehampton
FAIRACRES
CROMWELL HO
B351
WELL LA
WAY SIDE
VICARAGE GDNS
Allot Gdns
Sp Gd
75
A306
20
A
CHRISTCHURCH RD
VICARAGE RD
ENMORE CT
B
21
155
C
PALEWELL COMMON DR
Tenn Cts
D
22
Roehampton Univ (Southlands Coll)
YORK AVE
SHEEN WOOD
VICARAGE CL
Tenn Cts
CH
Roehampton
Allot Gdns

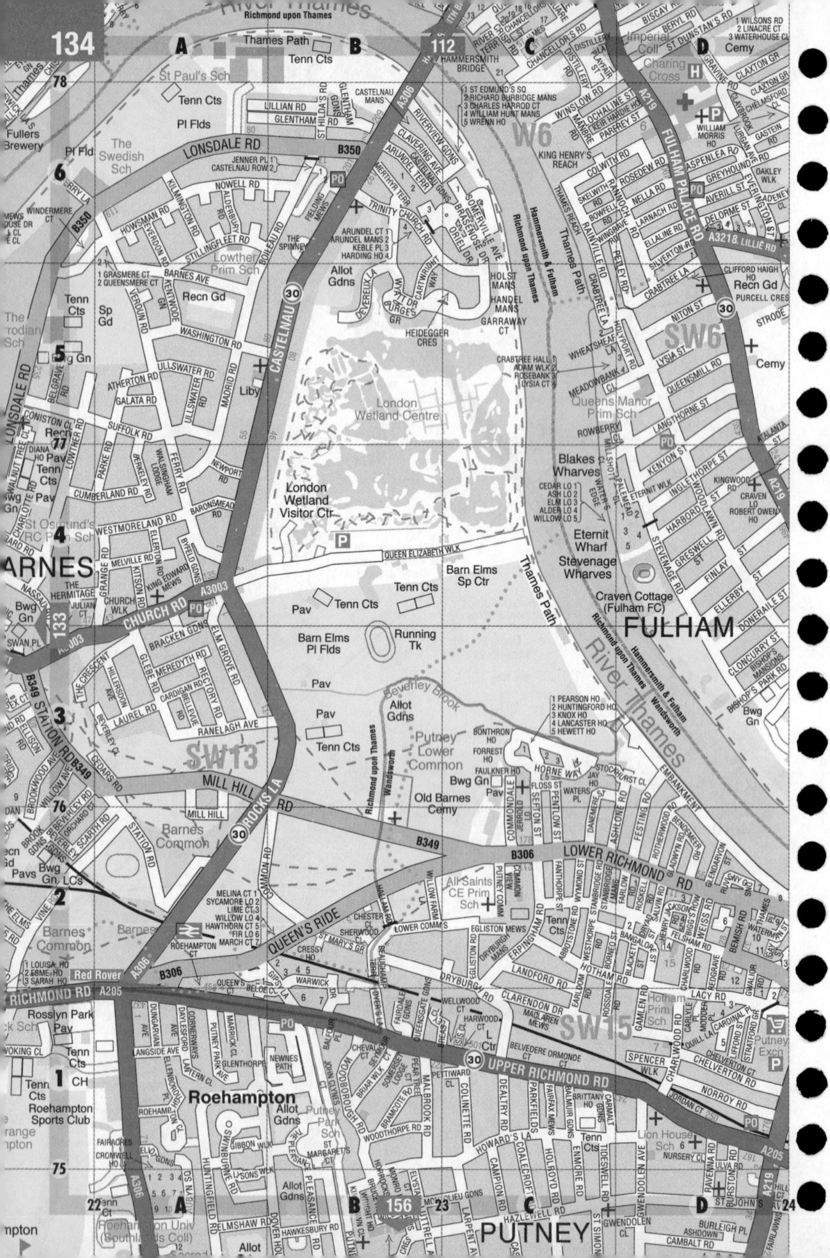

River Thames
Richmond upon Thames
Thames Path
Tenn Cts
St Paul's Sch
Pl Flds
Fullers Brewery
The Swedish Sch
LONSDALE RD
B350
CASTELNAU
A306
HAMMERSMITH BRIDGE
112
LILLIAN RD
GLENTHAM RD
CASTELNAU MANS
RIVERVIEW GDNS
CLAVERING AVE
ARUNDEL TERR
TRINITY CHURCH RD
NOWELL RD
KILMINGTON RD
HOWSMAN RD
STILLINGFLEET RD
BARNES AVE
Lowther Prim Sch
Recn Gd
Sp Gd
WASHINGTON RD
ULLSWATER RD
ATHERTON RD
GALATA RD
SUFFOLK RD
MADRID RD
Liby
Allot Gdns
DEVEREUX LA
WYATT DR
CARTWRIGHT WAY
HEIDEGGER CRES
HOLST MANS
HANDEL MANS
GARRAWAY CT
SOMERVILLE AVE
Hammersmith & Fulham
Richmond upon Thames
W6
WINSLOW RD
LOCHALINE ST
KEIR HARDIE HO
PARFREY ST
KING HENRY'S REACH
COLWITH RD
ROSEDEW RD
NELLA RD
LARNACH RD
ELLALINE RD
SILVERTON RD
CRABTREE LA
THAMES REACH
RAINVILLE RD
Imperial Coll
Charing Cross
ST DUNSTAN'S RD
BISCAY RD
BERYL RD
Cemy
WILLIAM MORRIS HO
FULHAM PALACE RD
A219
CLAXTON GR
GREYHOUND RD
ASPENLEA RD
AVERILL ST
DELORME ST
A3218 LILLIE RD
Recn Gd
PURCELL CRES
NITON ST
SW6
LYSIA ST
QUEENSMILL RD
LANGTHORNE ST
Queens Manor Prim Sch
KENYON ST
INGLETHORPE ST
HARBORD ST
WOODLAWN RD
GRESWELL ST
FINLAY ST
ELLERBY ST
DONERAILE ST
CLONCURRY ST
BISHOP'S PARK RD
Bwg Gn
FULHAM
Craven Cottage (Fulham FC)
Eternit Wharf
Stevenage Wharves
Blakes Wharves
STEVENAGE RD
London Wetland Centre
London Wetland Visitor Ctr
QUEEN ELIZABETH WLK
Barn Elms Sp Ctr
Barn Elms Pl Flds
Running Tk
Pav
Beverley Brook
Putney Lower Common
Old Barnes Cemy
Wandsworth
HORNE WAY
STOCKHURST CL
EMBANKMENT
ARNES
THE HERMITAGE
CHURCH RD
A3003
WESTMORELAND RD
CUMBERLAND RD
St Osmund's RC Prim Sch
Recn
Bwg Gn
133
SW13
RANELAGH AVE
LAUREL RD
MILL HILL RD
MILL HILL
ROCKS LA
Barnes Common
STATION RD
B349
B306
LOWER RICHMOND RD
COMMON RD
QUEEN'S RIDE
Barnes
ROEHAMPTON CT
Red Rover
RICHMOND RD
A205
Rosslyn Park
All Saints CE Prim Sch
EGLISTON MEWS
DRYBURGH RD
LANDFORD RD
CLARENDON DR
HOTHAM RD
Hotham Prim Sch
SW15
UPPER RICHMOND RD
30
Roehampton
Roehampton Sports Club
Allot Gdns
Putney Park Sch
ST MARGARET'S
Lion House Sch
PO
Putney Exch
NORROY RD
CHELVERTON RD
HOWARD'S LA
HAZLEWELL RD
156
PUTNEY
GWENDOLEN CL
Roehampton Univ (Southlands Coll)
A
B
C
D
1
2
3
4
5
6
22
23
24
75
76
77
78

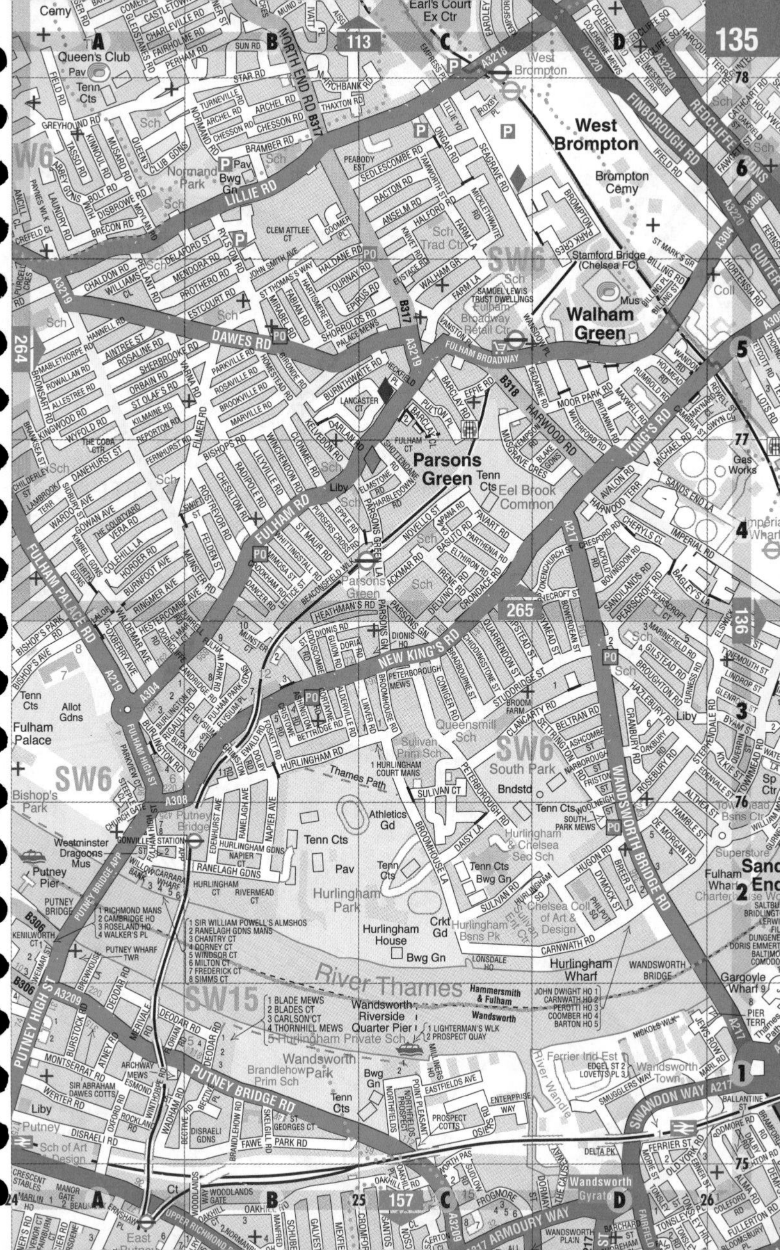

West Brompton
Brompton Cemy
Stamford Bridge (Chelsea FC)
Walham Green
Parsons Green
Eel Brook Common
Queen's Club
Normand Park
Fulham Palace
Bishop's Park
Putney Bridge
Putney Pier
Hurlingham Park
Hurlingham House
Hurlingham Wharf
South Park
Sands End
Fulham Wharf
Gas Works
Imperial Wharf
River Thames
Wandsworth Park
Wandsworth Riverside Quarter Pier
Wandsworth Town
Wandsworth Gyratory
Ferrier Ind Est
River Wandle
Putney
East Putney
W6
SW6
SW15
LILLIE RD
DAWES RD
FULHAM RD
FULHAM PALACE RD
FULHAM BROADWAY
NEW KING'S RD
KING'S RD
HURLINGHAM RD
PUTNEY BRIDGE RD
PUTNEY HIGH ST
WANDSWORTH BRIDGE RD
SWANDON WAY
ARMOURY WAY
NORTH END RD
FINBOROUGH RD
REDCLIFFE GDNS
HARWOOD RD
MUNSTER RD
UPPER RICHMOND RD
113
157
264
265
136

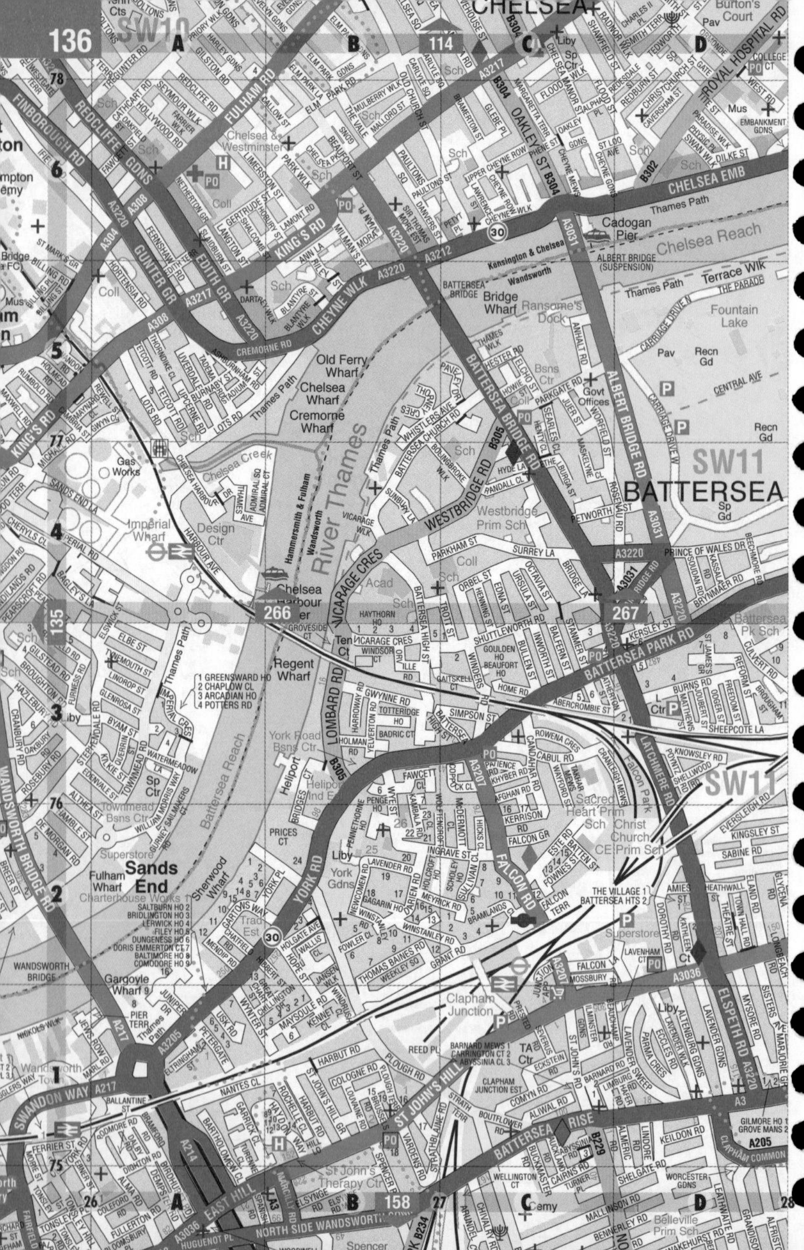
136
SW10
A
B
114
C
D
CHELSEA
Burton's Court
78
6
5
77
4
3
76
2
1
75
FINBOROUGH RD
REDCLIFFE GDNS
FULHAM RD
KING'S RD
OAKLEY ST
ROYAL HOSPITAL RD
CHELSEA EMB
Thames Path
Cadogan Pier
Chelsea Reach
ALBERT BRIDGE (SUSPENSION)
CHEYNE WLK
CREMORNE RD
GUNTER GR
EDITH GR
Chelsea & Westminster
BATTERSEA BRIDGE
Bridge Wharf
Ransome's Dock
Terrace Wlk
Fountain Lake
CARRIAGE DRIVE N
CENTRAL AVE
Recn Gd
Old Ferry Wharf
Chelsea Wharf
Cremorne Wharf
River Thames
BATTERSEA BRIDGE RD
ALBERT BRIDGE RD
Govt Offices
SW11
BATTERSEA
Gas Works
Chelsea Creek
Imperial Wharf
Design Ctr
WESTBRIDGE RD
Westbridge Prim Sch
VICARAGE CRES
PRINCE OF WALES DR
Chelsea Harbour Pier
266
267
135
BATTERSEA PARK RD
Regent Wharf
LOMBARD RD
BATTERSEA HIGH ST
York Road Bsns Ctr
Heliport
LATCHMERE RD
Falcon Park
SW11
Sacred Heart Prim Sch
Christ Church CE Prim Sch
Battersea Reach
Townmead Bsns Ctr
Superstore
Sands End
Fulham Wharf
Sherwood Wharf
YORK RD
FALCON RD
WANDSWORTH BRIDGE RD
WANDSWORTH BRIDGE
Gargoyle Wharf
Clapham Junction
ST JOHN'S HILL
BATTERSEA RISE
ELSPETH RD
LAVENDER SWEEP
SWANDON WAY
EAST HILL
NORTH SIDE WANDSWORTH COMMON
St John's Therapy Ctr
158
26
27
28
Belleville Prim Sch
CLAPHAM COMMON

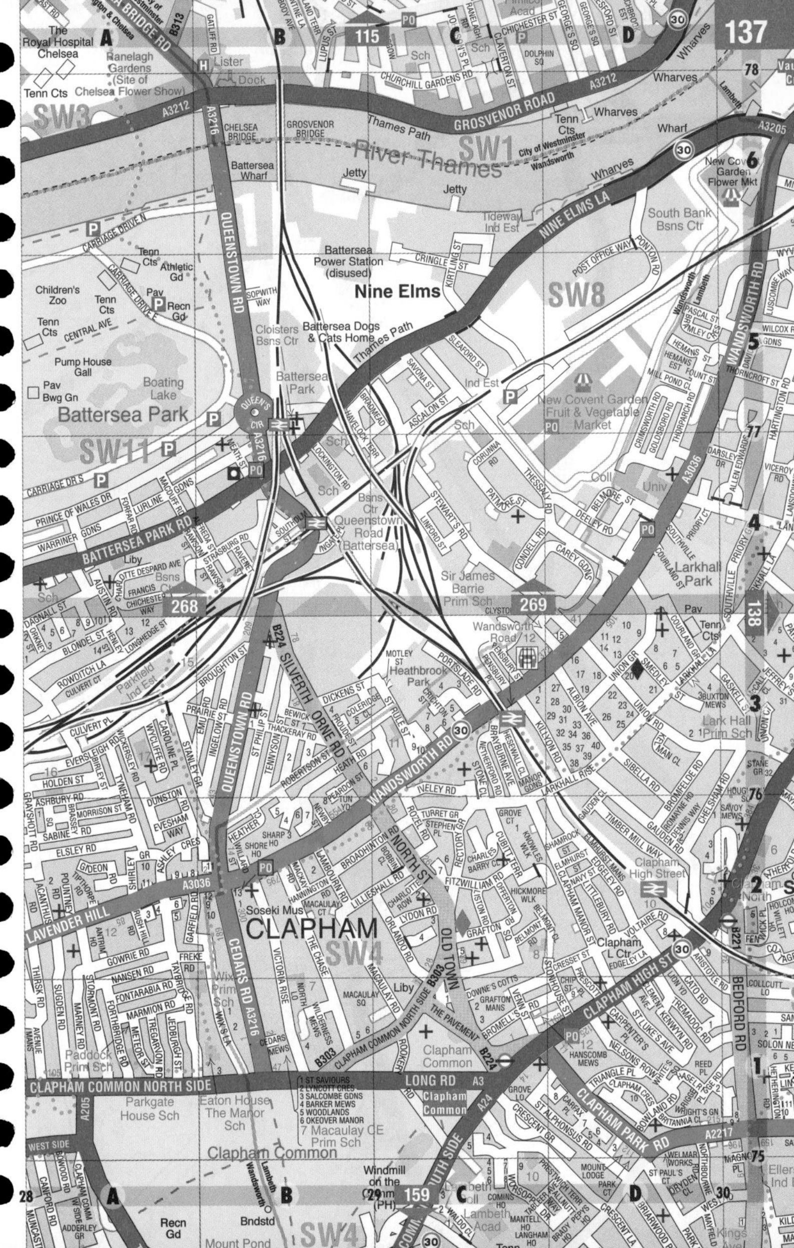

The Royal Hospital Chelsea
Ranelagh Gardens (Site of Chelsea Flower Show)
Tenn Cts
SW3
CHELSEA BRIDGE
GROSVENOR BRIDGE
GROSVENOR ROAD
Thames Path
River Thames
SW1
City of Westminster
Wandsworth
Battersea Wharf
Jetty
Wharves
Wharf
New Covent Garden Flower Mkt
NINE ELMS LA
Tideway Ind Est
South Bank Bsns Ctr
CARRIAGE DRIVE N
QUEENSTOWN RD
Battersea Power Station (disused)
Nine Elms
SW8
Children's Zoo
Athletic Gd
Recn Gd
CENTRAL AVE
Cloisters Bsns Ctr
Battersea Dogs & Cats Home
Pump House Gall
Boating Lake
Battersea Park
SW11
New Covent Garden Fruit & Vegetable Market
WANDSWORTH RD
CARRIAGE DR S
PRINCE OF WALES DR
BATTERSEA PARK RD
Queenstown Road (Battersea)
Larkhall Park
Sir James Barrie Prim Sch
268
269
138
Wandsworth Road
Heathbrook Park
Parkfield Ind Est
Lark Hall Prim Sch
SILVERTH ORNE RD
CEDARS RD
LAVENDER HILL
Soseki Mus
CLAPHAM
SW4
Clapham High Street
OLD TOWN
CLAPHAM HIGH ST
Clapham L Ctr
CLAPHAM COMMON NORTH SIDE
LONG RD
Clapham Common
1 ST SAVIOURS
2 LYNCOTT CRES
3 SALCOMBE GDNS
4 BARKER MEWS
5 WOODLANDS
6 OKEOVER MANOR
7 Macaulay CE Prim Sch
CLAPHAM PARK RD
Parkgate House Sch
Eaton House The Manor Sch
Windmill on the Common (PH)
WEST SIDE
Lambeth Acad
Mount Pond
159
Ellerslie Ind Est
BEDFORD RD

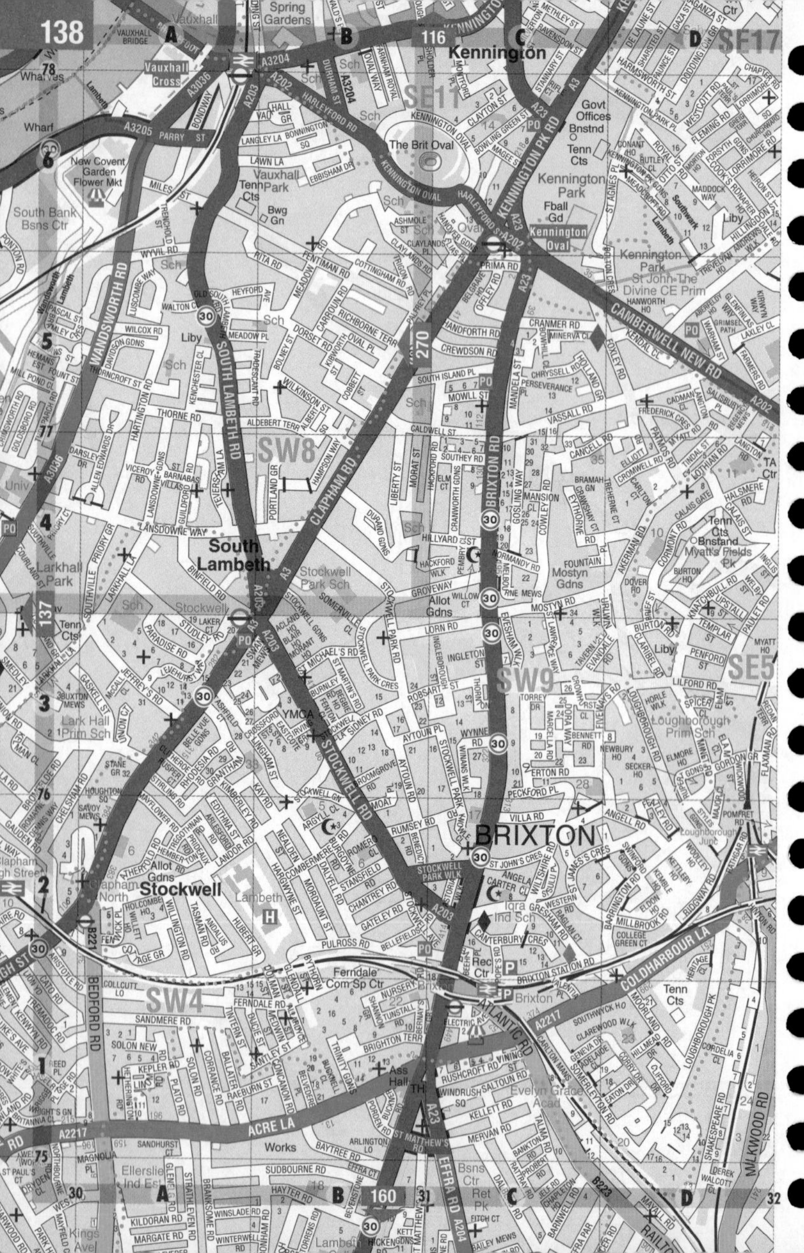

Vauxhall
Kennington
SE11
SE17
The Brit Oval
Kennington Park
SW8
South Lambeth
Stockwell
SW9
SE5
BRIXTON
SW4
Clapham North
Larkhall Park
Vauxhall Park
Myatt's Fields Pk
New Covent Garden Flower Mkt
SOUTH LAMBETH RD
WANDSWORTH RD
CLAPHAM RD
KENNINGTON PK RD
BRIXTON RD
STOCKWELL RD
CAMBERWELL NEW RD
COLDHARBOUR LA
ACRE LA
EFFRA RD
BEDFORD RD
116
270
137
160

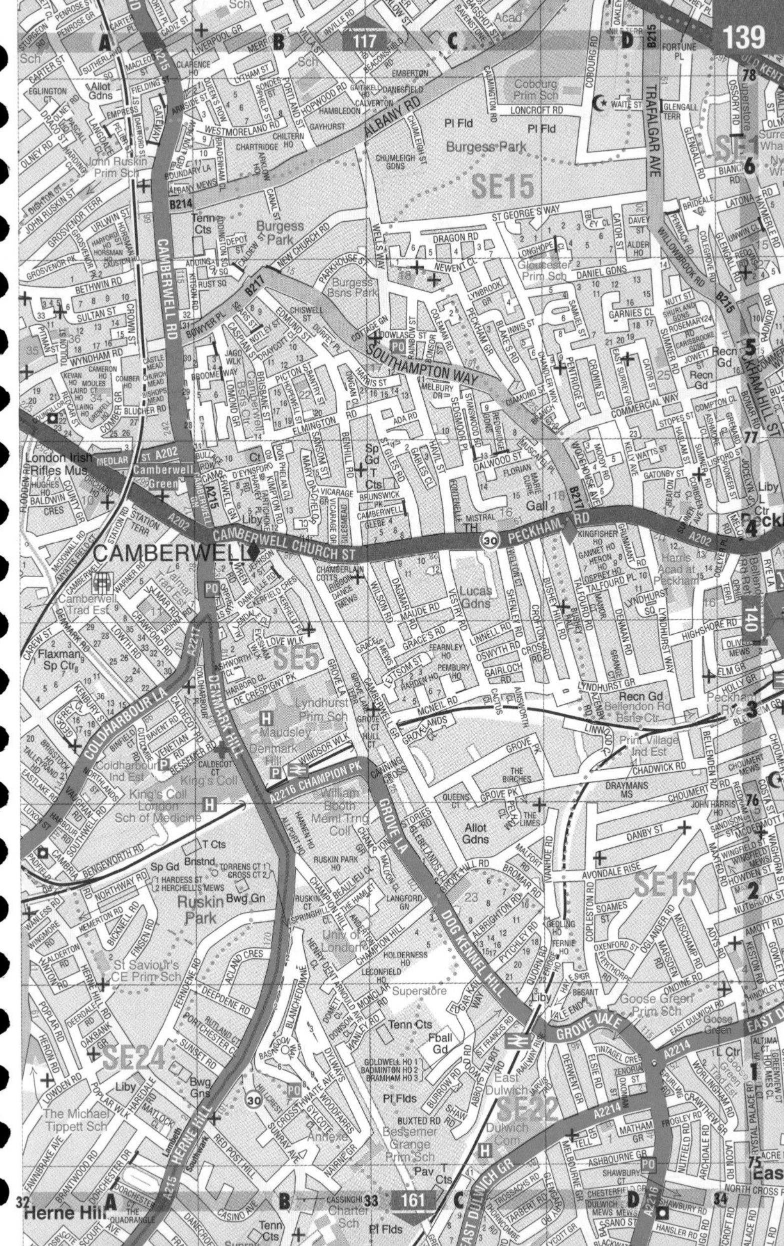
CAMBERWELL
SE15
SE5
SE24
SE22
Burgess Park
Camberwell Green
Peckham Rd
Camberwell Church St
Denmark Hill
Dog Kennel Hill
Grove Vale
East Dulwich
Herne Hill
Ruskin Park
Albany Rd
Southampton Way
Coldharbour La
Champion Pk
Trafalgar Ave
Peckham Hill St
Camberwell Rd
Lucas Gdns
King's Coll London Sch of Medicine
Maudsley
Denmark Hill
Peckham Rye
117
161
140

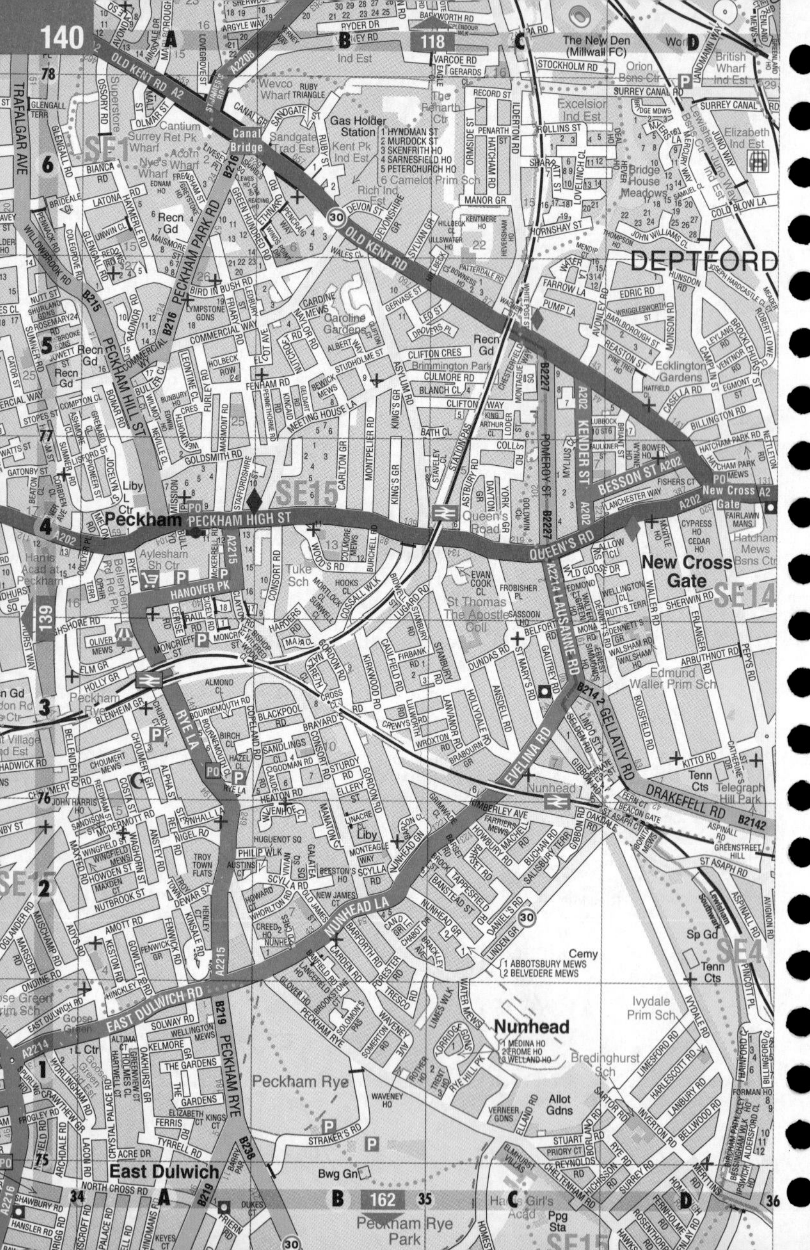

118
The New Den (Millwall FC)
OLD KENT RD A2
Canal Bridge
Gas Holder Station
1 HYNDMAN ST
2 MURDOCK ST
3 SKENFRITH HO
4 SARNESFIELD HO
5 PETERCHURCH HO
6 Camelot Prim Sch
DEPTFORD
SE1
SE15
SE14
SE4
Peckham
PECKHAM HIGH ST
PECKHAM HILL ST
PECKHAM PARK RD
Aylesham Sh Ctr
HANOVER PK
RYE LA
Queen's Road
QUEEN'S RD
KENDER ST
BESSON ST A202
New Cross Gate
LAUSANNE RD
GELLATLY RD
DRAKEFELL RD
EVELINA RD
Nunhead
NUNHEAD LA
EAST DULWICH RD
PECKHAM RYE
Peckham Rye
1 ABBOTSBURY MEWS
2 BELVEDERE MEWS
1 MEDINA HO
2 FROME HO
3 WELLAND HO
Bredinghurst Sch
Allot Gdns
Ivydale Prim Sch
Edmund Waller Prim Sch
St Thomas The Apostle Coll
Caroline Gardens
Ecklington Gardens
Telegraph Hill Park
East Dulwich
139
162
Peckham Rye Park
Harris Girl's Acad

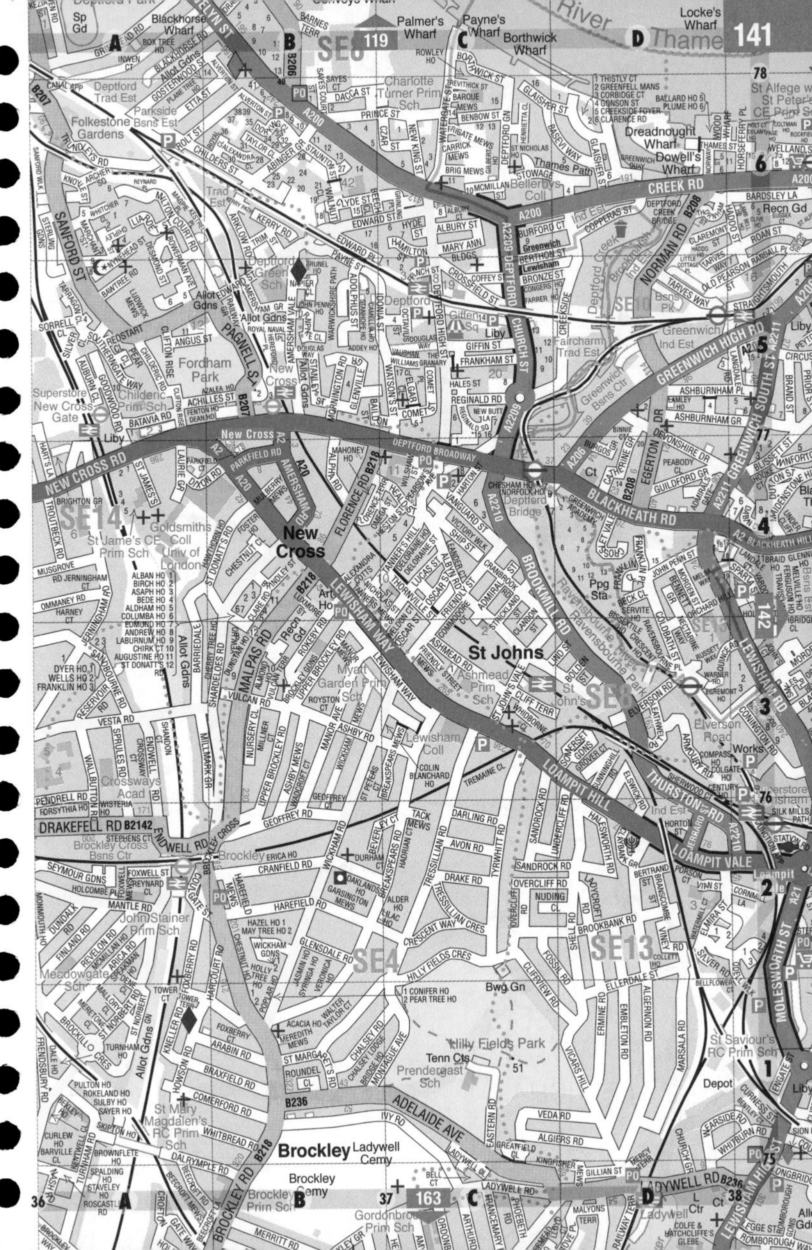

River Thames
Locke's Wharf
Palmer's Wharf
Payne's Wharf
Borthwick Wharf
Blackhorse Wharf
119
SE8
Deptford Trad Est
Folkestone Gardens
Parkside Bsns Est
Charlotte Turner Prim Sch
Dreadnought Wharf
Dowell's Wharf
St Alfege with St Peter's CE Prim Sch
Thames Path
Bellerbys Coll
CREEK RD
EVELYN ST
A200
PRINCE ST
GROVE ST
DEPTFORD CHURCH ST
DEPTFORD HIGH ST
CREEKSIDE
NORMAN RD
SANFORD ST
Trad Est
Deptford Green Sch
Deptford
Giffen Sq
Liby
Faircharm Trad Est
SE10
Bsns Pk
Greenwich Ind Est
GREENWICH HIGH RD
GREENWICH SOUTH ST
Fordham Park
Childeric Prim Sch
Superstore New Cross Gate
New Cross
NEW CROSS RD
DEPTFORD BROADWAY
BLACKHEATH RD
Deptford Bridge
Greenwich Bsns Ctr
SE14
Goldsmiths Coll Univ of London
St James's CE Prim Sch
New Cross
LEWISHAM WAY
AMERSHAM RD
FLORENCE RD
BROOKMILL RD
Ppg Sta
Ravensbourne Park
Ravensbourne River
St Johns
St John's
Ashmead Prim Sch
Myatt Garden Prim Sch
SE8
Recn Gd
Art Ho
MALPAS RD
LEWISHAM RD
142
Elverson Road
Works
Superstore Lewisham
Lewisham Coll
Crossways Acad
Allot Gdns
LOAMPIT HILL
LOAMPIT VALE
THURSTON RD
Ind Est
DRAKEFELL RD B2142
ENDWELL RD
Brockley Cross Bsns Ctr
Brockley
John Stainer Prim Sch
SE4
SE13
Meadowgate Sch
Hilly Fields Park
Bwg Gn
Tenn Cts
Prendergast Sch
HILLY FIELDS CRES
ADELAIDE AVE
MOLESWORTH ST
St Saviour's RC Prim Sch
Depot
Liby
St Mary Magdalen's RC Prim Sch
Brockley
Ladywell Cemy
Brockley Cemy
Brockley Prim Sch
Gordonbrock Prim Sch
163
LADYWELL RD
Ladywell
BROCKLEY RD
LEWISHAM HIGH ST
A B C D
36 37 38
75 76 77 78

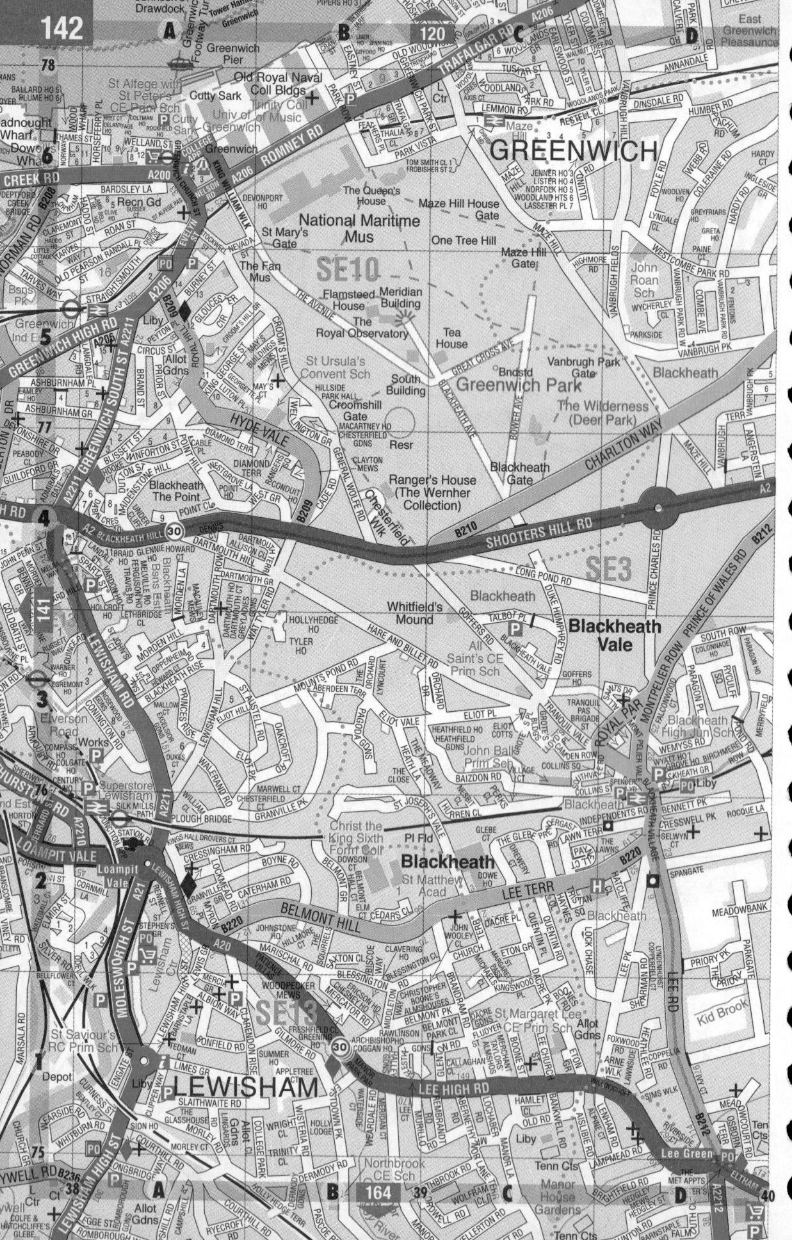

A
B
C
D
120
78
77
76
75
6
5
4
3
2
1
141
164
38
39
40
GREENWICH
SE10
SE3
SE13
LEWISHAM
Blackheath
Blackheath Vale
East Greenwich Pleasaunce
Greenwich Pier
Greenwich Footway Tun
Cutty Sark
Old Royal Naval Coll Bldgs
Trinity Coll
Univ of Music
St Alfege with St Peter's CE Prim Sch
National Maritime Mus
The Queen's House
Maze Hill House Gate
St Mary's Gate
The Fan Mus
One Tree Hill
Maze Hill Gate
Flamsteed House
Meridian Building
The Royal Observatory
Tea House
Greenwich Park
Bndstd
Vanbrugh Park Gate
St Ursula's Convent Sch
South Building
The Wilderness (Deer Park)
Croomshill Gate
Resr
Ranger's House (The Wernher Collection)
Blackheath Gate
John Roan Sch
CREEK RD
ROMNEY RD
TRAFALGAR RD
GREENWICH HIGH RD
GREENWICH SOUTH ST
HYDE VALE
CHARLTON WAY
SHOOTERS HILL RD
BLACKHEATH HILL
DARTMOUTH HILL
LEWISHAM RD
LEWISHAM HIGH ST
LOAMPIT VALE
BELMONT HILL
LEE TERR
LEE HIGH RD
LEE RD
MOLESWORTH ST
PRINCE OF WALES RD
MONTPELIER ROW
MAZE HILL
VANBRUGH HILL
WESTCOMBE PARK RD
LONG POND RD
GOFFERS RD
Whitfield's Mound
All Saint's CE Prim Sch
John Ball Prim Sch
Blackheath High Jun Sch
Christ the King Sixth Form Coll
St Matthew Acad
Pl Fld
St Margaret Lee CE Prim Sch
Northbrook CE Sch
St Saviour's RC Prim Sch
Manor House Gardens
Lee Green
Loampit Vale
Lewisham Ctr
Superstore
Elverson Road
Recn Gd
Allot Gdns
Liby
Depot
Tenn Cts
Kid Brook

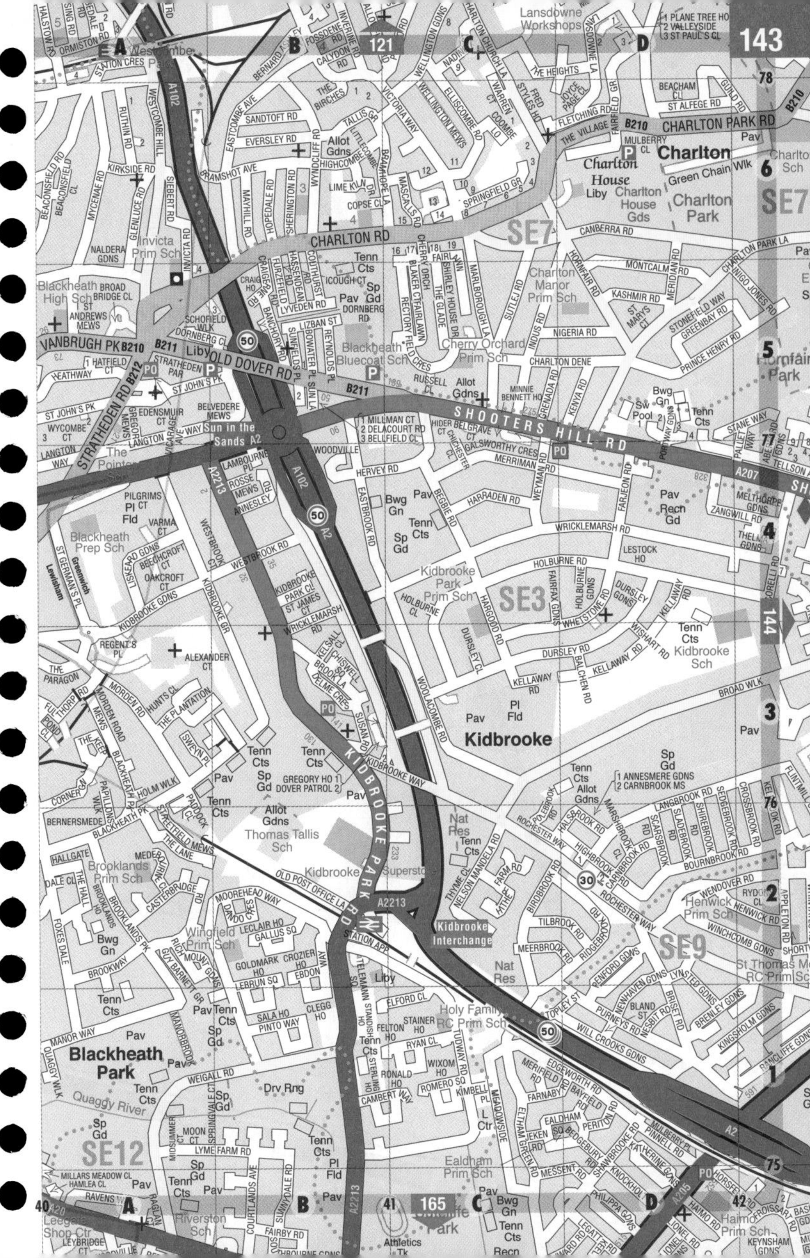
121
A
B
C
D
Lansdowne Workshops
1 PLANE TREE HO
2 VALLEYSIDE
3 ST PAUL'S CL
78
Westcombe Park
STATION CRES
ORMISTON RD
HALSTOW RD
A102
WESTCOMBE HILL
RUTHIN RD
BERNARD ASHLEY
FOSSDENE
INVERINE RD
CALYDON RD
WELLINGTON GDNS
CHARLTON CHURCH LA
LANSDOWNE LA
THE HEIGHTS
BEACHAM CL
ST ALFEGE RD
GUILD RD
B210
EASTCOMBE AVE
SANDTOFT RD
THE BIRCHES
VICTORIA WAY
WELLINGTON MEWS
ELLISCOMBE RD
WARREN CT
COOMBE LO
FRED STYLES HO
JOYCE PAGE CL
FLETCHING RD
FAIRFIELD GR
THE VILLAGE
CHARLTON PARK RD
Pav
EVERSLEY RD
TALLIS GR
Allot Gdns
MULBERRY CL
Charlton
Charlton Sch
Charlton House
Liby
Charlton House Gds
Green Chain Wlk
Charlton Park
6
SE7
BEACONSFIELD RD
BEACONSFIELD CL
MYCENAE RD
KIRKSIDE RD
GLENLUCE RD
SIEBERT RD
BRAMSHOT AVE
HIGHCOMBE
MAYHILL RD
HOPEDALE RD
SHERINGTON RD
WYNDCLIFF RD
LIME KILN DR
COPSE CL
MASCALLS RD
SPRINGFIELD GR
CHARLTON RD
CANBERRA RD
CHARLTON PARK LA
NALDERA GDNS
Invicta Prim Sch
INVICTA RD
Blackheath High Sch
BROAD BRIDGE CL
ST ANDREWS MEWS
CRAIGHOLM
CRAIGERNE RD
FURZEFIELD RD
HASSENDEAN RD
COUTHURST RD
ICOUGH CT
Tenn Cts
Sp Gd
Pav
DORNBERG RD
CHERRY ORCH
BLAKER CT
FAIRLAWN
SHIRLEY HOUSE DR
THE GLADE
RECTORY FIELD CRES
MARLBOROUGH LA
SUTLEJ RD
Charlton Manor Prim Sch
HORNFAIR RD
MONTCALM RD
MERIDIAN RD
KASHMIR RD
ST MARYS CT
STONEFIELD WAY
GREENBAY RD
INIGO JONES RD
SCHOFIELD WLK
DORNBERG CL
LYVEDEN RD
LIZBAN ST
BOWATER PL
REYNOLDS PL
SUNFIELDS PL
Blackheath Bluecoat Sch
Cherry Orchard Prim Sch
INDUS RD
NIGERIA RD
PRINCE HENRY RD
5
Hornfair Park
VANBRUGH PK
B211
Liby
OLD DOVER RD
50
HATFIELD CT
STRATHEDEN PAR
HEATHWAY
ST JOHN'S PK
STRATHEDEN RD
B212
RUSSELL CL
CHARLTON DENE
MINNIE BENNETT HO
GRENADA RD
KENYA RD
Bwg Gn
Sw Pool
Tenn Cts
STANE WAY
EDENSMUIR CT
BELVEDERE MEWS
WYCOMBE CT
GREGOR MEWS
LANGTON WAY
VICARAGE AVE
Sun in the Sands
A2
1 MILLMAN CT
2 DELACOURT RD
3 BELLFIELD CL
HIDER CT
BELGRAVE CT
CHICHESTER CL
SHOOTERS HILL RD
GALSWORTHY CRES
PO
WEYMAN RD
MERRIMAN RD
PORTWAY GDNS
PALLET WAY
ABE
77
TELLSON AVE
A207
The Pointer Sch
LAMBOURNE PL
ROSSE MEWS
ANNESLEY RD
WOODVILLE
HERVEY RD
A2213
A102
FARJEON RD
PILGRIMS PL
Pl Fld
VARMA CT
EASTBROOK RD
BEGBIE RD
HARRADEN RD
Pav
Recn Gd
MELTHORPE GDNS
ZANGWILL RD
Blackheath Prep Sch
WESTBROOK RD
WESTBROOK CT
Tenn Cts
Sp Gd
WRICKLEMARSH RD
4
THELMA GDNS
ST GERMAN'S PL
Lewisham
Greenwich
LISKEARD GDNS
BEECHCROFT CT
OAKCROFT CT
KIDBROOKE GDNS
KIDBROOKE GR
KIDBROOKE PARK CL
ST JAMES CT
WRICKLEMARSH RD
Kidbrooke Park Prim Sch
HOLBURNE CL
HOLBURNE RD
LESTOCK HO
SE3
HARGOOD RD
FAIRFAX GDNS
HOLBURNE GDNS
WHETSTONE RD
DURSLEY GDNS
KELLAWAY
CORELLI RD
144
REGENT'S PL
ALEXANDER CT
THE PARAGON
KELSALL CL
CHISWELL SQ
BROOK LA
DURSLEY CL
DURSLEY RD
BALCHEN RD
WISHART RD
KELLAWAY RD
Tenn Cts
Kidbrooke Sch
THORPE RD
MORDEN RD
HUNTS CL
THE PLANTATION
DELME CRES
WOOLACOMBE RD
KELLAWAY RD
BROAD WLK
3
SWEYN PL
PO
SUSAN RD
Pl Fld
Pav
Kidbrooke
Pav
THE KEEP
MORDEN ROAD MEWS
BLACKHEATH PK
PAPILLONS WLK
HOLM WLK
Tenn Cts
Sp Gd
GREGORY HO
DOVER PATROL
Pav
KIDBROOKE WAY
KIDBROOKE PARK RD
Tenn Cts
Allot Gdns
1 ANNESMERE GDNS
2 CARNBROOK MS
Sp Gd
FLINTMILL CRES
CORNER
BERNERSMEDE
PADDOCK CL
Allot Gdns
Thomas Tallis Sch
Nat Res
ROCHESTER WAY
POLEBROOK RD
HALSBROOK RD
MARSHBROOK CL
LANGBROOK RD
SEDGEBROOK RD
CROSSBROOK RD
KELL BROOK RD
76
SCARSBROOK RD
SLADEBROOK RD
SHIREBROOK RD
BOURNBROOK RD
HALLGATE
Brooklands Prim Sch
STREETFIELD MEWS
THE LANE
Kidbrooke
Superstore
NELSON MANDELA RD
THYME CL
FARM RD
HITHE
BIRDBROOK RD
HIGHBROOK RD
CARNBROOK RD
30
WENDOVER RD
RYDON CL
HENWICK RD
Henwick Prim Sch
2
WHINYATES RD
APPLETON RD
DALE CL
THE HALL
BROOKLANDS
CASTERBRIDGE RD
OLD POST OFFICE LA
MOOREHEAD WAY
DANDO CRES
A2213
Kidbrooke Interchange
TILBROOK RD
RIDGEBROOK RD
ROCHESTER WAY
WINCHCOMB GDNS
SHORTWAY
FOXES DALE
Bwg Gn
BROOKLANDS PK
Wingfield Prim Sch
LECLAIR HO
GALLUS SQ
STATION APP
MEERBROOK RD
SE9
St Thomas More RC Prim Sch
BROOKWAY
RICH
MOUNT GDNS
GUY BARNETT GR
GOLDMARK HO
CROZIER HO
EBDON WAY
TELEMANN SQ
Liby
Nat Res
RENFORD GDNS
LYNSTED GDNS
Tenn Cts
Pav
Tenn Cts
LEBRUN SQ
SALA HO
PINTO WAY
CLEGG HO
ELFORD CL
STANDISH HO
STAINER HO
FELTON HO
Holy Family RC Prim Sch
TOPLEY ST
NEWHAVEN GDNS
BLAND ST
PURNEYS RD
NESBIT RD
BRISET RD
BRENLEY GDNS
KINGSHOLM GDNS
MANOR WAY
Pav
Sp Gd
MANORBROOK
Tenn Cts
RYAN CL
TUDWAY RD
WILL CROOKS GDNS
50
Blackheath Park
Pav
WIXOM HO
RONALD HO
STERLING HO
MERIFIELD RD
EDGEWORTH RD
RANCLIFFE GDNS
1
OUAGGY WLK
Tenn Cts
WEIGALL RD
SPRINGVALE CT
Sp Gd
Drv Rng
CAMBERT WAY
ROMERO SQ
KIMBELL PL
MEADOWSIDE
FARNABY RD
BAYFIELD RD
Sp Gd
Quaggy River
L Ctr
ELTHAM GREEN RD
EALDHAM SQ
JEKEN RD
PERITON RD
BEDGEBURY RD
SHAWBROOKE RD
MULBERRY PL
PINNELL RD
KATHERINE GDNS
A2
Sp Gd
SE12
MIDSUMMER CT
MOON CT
LYME FARM RD
COURTLANDS AVE
SUNNYDALE RD
Tenn Cts
Pl Fld
A2213
Ealdham Prim Sch
MESSENT RD
KNOCKHOLT RD
75
MILLARS MEADOW CL
HAMLEA CL
RAVENS WAY
Pav
RAGLAN
Sp Gd
Tenn Cts
Pav
Pav
Pav
Bwg Gn
Tenn Cts
Recn
PO
HORSFELD
A205
FROISSART RD
BASKET GDNS
42
40
A20
Leegate Shop Ctr
LEYBRIDGE CT
Riverston Sch
FAIRBY RD
Athletics Tk
41
165
Park
PHILIPPA GDNS
LEGATT RD
HAIMO RD
Haimo Prim Sch
KEYNSHAM GDNS
MILN

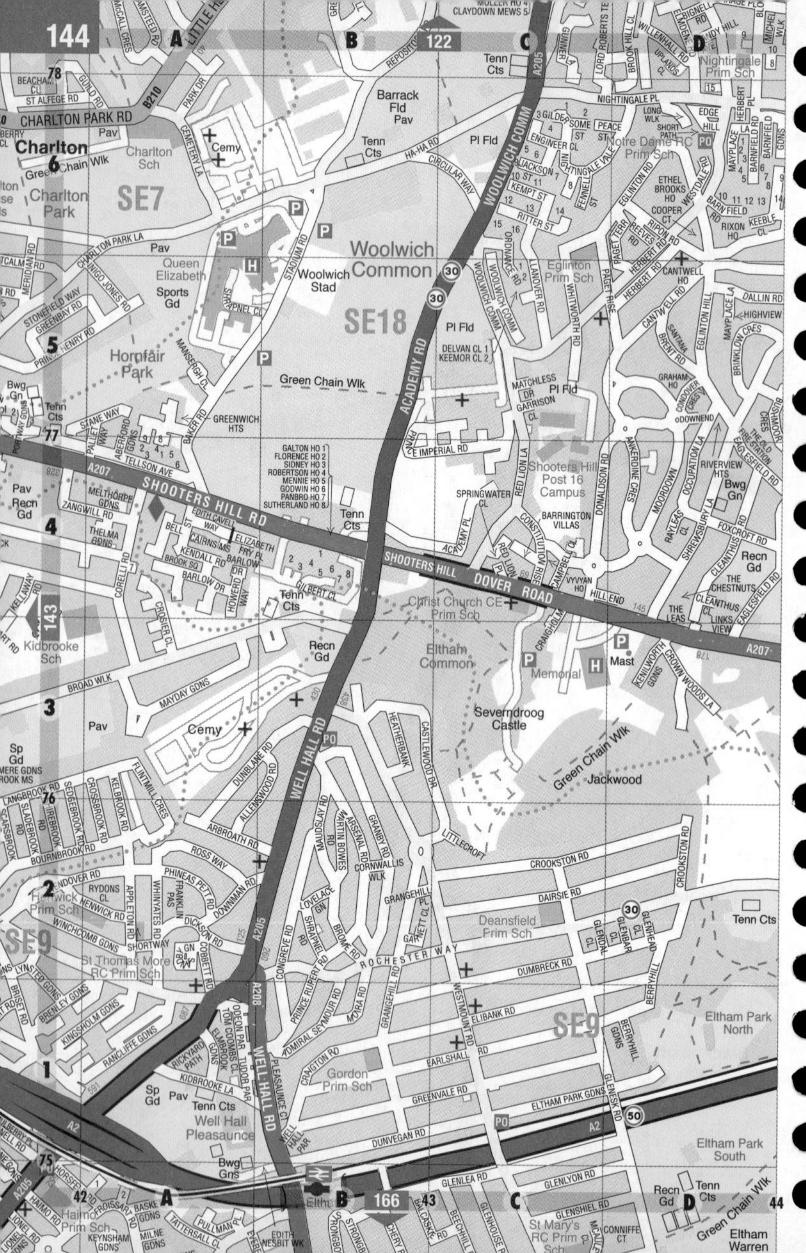
A
B
C
D
122
166
143
Charlton
Charlton Sch
Charlton Park
SE7
SE18
SE9
CHARLTON PARK RD
CHARLTON PARK LA
ST ALFEGE RD
BEACHAM CL
GUILD RD
PARK DR
CEMETERY LA
Cemy
Barrack Fld Pav
Tenn Cts
HA-HA RD
CIRCULAR WAY
Pl Fld
WOOLWICH COMM
A205
NIGHTINGALE PL
Nightingale Prim Sch
Notre Dame RC Prim Sch
ENGINEER CL
JACKSON ST
KEMPT ST
RITTER ST
GILDERSOME ST
PEACE ST
NIGHTINGALE VALE
FENNELL ST
EGLINTON RD
WESTDALE RD
MAYPLACE LA
BARNFIELD RD
RIXON HO
KEEBLE CL
COOPER CT
ETHEL BROOKS HO
HERBERT RD
PAGET TERR
PAGET RISE
CANTWELL HO
CANTWELL RD
EGLINTON HILL
DALLIN RD
HIGHVIEW
BRINKLOW CRES
Queen Elizabeth
Woolwich Stad
Woolwich Common
STADIUM RD
SHRAPNEL CL
Sports Gd
Eglinton Prim Sch
ORDNANCE RD
LANOVER RD
WHITWORTH RD
MEDIAN RD
INIGO JONES RD
STONEFIELD WAY
GREENBAY RD
PRINCE HENRY RD
Hornfair Park
MANSERGH CL
ACADEMY RD
DELVAN CL
KEEMOR CL
Green Chain Wlk
MATCHLESS DR
GARRISON CL
Pl Fld
GREENWICH HTS
BAKER RD
STANE WAY
PALLET WAY
ABERFORD GDNS
TELLSON AVE
PORTWAY GDNS
Bwg Gn
A207
SHOOTERS HILL RD
GALTON HO 1
FLORENCE HO 2
SIDNEY HO 3
ROBERTSON HO 4
MENNIE HO 5
GODWIN HO 6
PANBRO HO 7
SUTHERLAND HO 8
PRINCE IMPERIAL RD
RED LION LA
Shooters Hill Post 16 Campus
DONALDSON RD
ANKERDINE CRES
MOORDOWN
OCCUPATION LA
RIVERVIEW HTS
EAGLESFIELD RD
SPRINGWATER CL
BARRINGTON VILLAS
CONSTITUTION RISE
CAMPBELL CL
VYVYAN HO
HILL END
SHOOTERS HILL
DOVER ROAD
RAYLEAS CL
SHREWSBURY LA
FOXCROFT RD
CLEANTHUS RD
Recn Gd
THE CHESTNUTS
CLEANTHUS CL
THE LEAS
LINKS VIEW
MELTHORPE GDNS
ZANGWILL RD
THELMA GDNS
CORELLI RD
EDITH CAVELL WAY
ELIZABETH FRY PL
CAIRNS MS
KENDALL RD
BROOK SQ
BARLOW DR
HOWERD WAY
GILBERT CL
Pav
Recn Gd
KELLAWAY RD
Kidbrooke Sch
CROSIER CL
Christ Church CE Prim Sch
Eltham Common
Memorial
Mast
KENILWORTH GDNS
CROWN WOODS LA
BROAD WLK
MAYDAY GDNS
Cemy
Severndroog Castle
Jackwood
WELL HALL RD
HEATHERBANK
CASTLEWOOD DR
DUNBLANE RD
ALLENSWOOD RD
LANGBROOK RD
SEDGEBROOK RD
CROSSBROOK RD
KELBROOK RD
FLINTMILL CRES
SLADEBROOK RD
MIREBROOK RD
SCARSBROOK RD
BOURNBROOK RD
ARBROATH RD
ROSS WAY
MAUDSLAY RD
MARTIN BOWES RD
ARSENAL RD
GRANBY RD
CORNWALLIS WLK
LITTLECROFT
CROOKSTON RD
DAIRSIE RD
GRANGEHILL PL
PHINEAS PETT RD
FRANKLIN PAS
WHINYATES RD
APPLETON RD
RYDONS CL
HENWICK RD
DOWNMAN RD
DICKSON RD
WINCHCOMB GDNS
SHORTWAY
COBBETT RD
Deansfield Prim Sch
GLENDALE CL
GLENBARR CL
GLENHEAD CL
Tenn Cts
LOVELACE GN
SHRAPNEL RD
BROME RD
GARNETT CL
ROCHESTER WAY
DUMBRECK RD
BERRYHILL
CONGREVE RD
St Thomas More RC Prim Sch
BRISET RD
BRENLEY GDNS
KINGSHOLM GDNS
RANCLIFFE GDNS
PRINCE RUPERT RD
ADMIRAL SEYMOUR RD
MORA RD
GRANGEHILL RD
WESTMOUNT RD
ELIBANK RD
EARLSHALL RD
BERRYHILL GDNS
Eltham Park North
A208
ODEON PAR
TUDOR PAR
TOM COOMBS CL
ELMBROOK GDNS
RICKYARD PATH
KIDBROOKE LA
CRAIGTON RD
Gordon Prim Sch
GREENVALE RD
ELTHAM PARK GDNS
GLENESK RD
Sp Gd
Pav
Well Hall Pleasaunce
PLEASAUNCE CT
WELL HALL PAR
DUNVEGAN RD
A2
Eltham Park South
Bwg Gns
GLENLEA RD
GLENLYON RD
GLENSHIEL RD
Recn Gd
St Mary's RC Prim Sch
CONNIFFE CT
Eltham Warren
HORSFELD RD
HAIMO RD
Haimo Prim Sch
FROISSART RD
BASKERVILLE GDNS
TATTERSALL CL
PULLMAN PL
KEYNSHAM GDNS
MILNE GDNS
EDITH NESBIT WK
STRONGBOW RD
BALCASKIE RD
BEECHHILL RD
GLENHOUSE RD
CHERRY

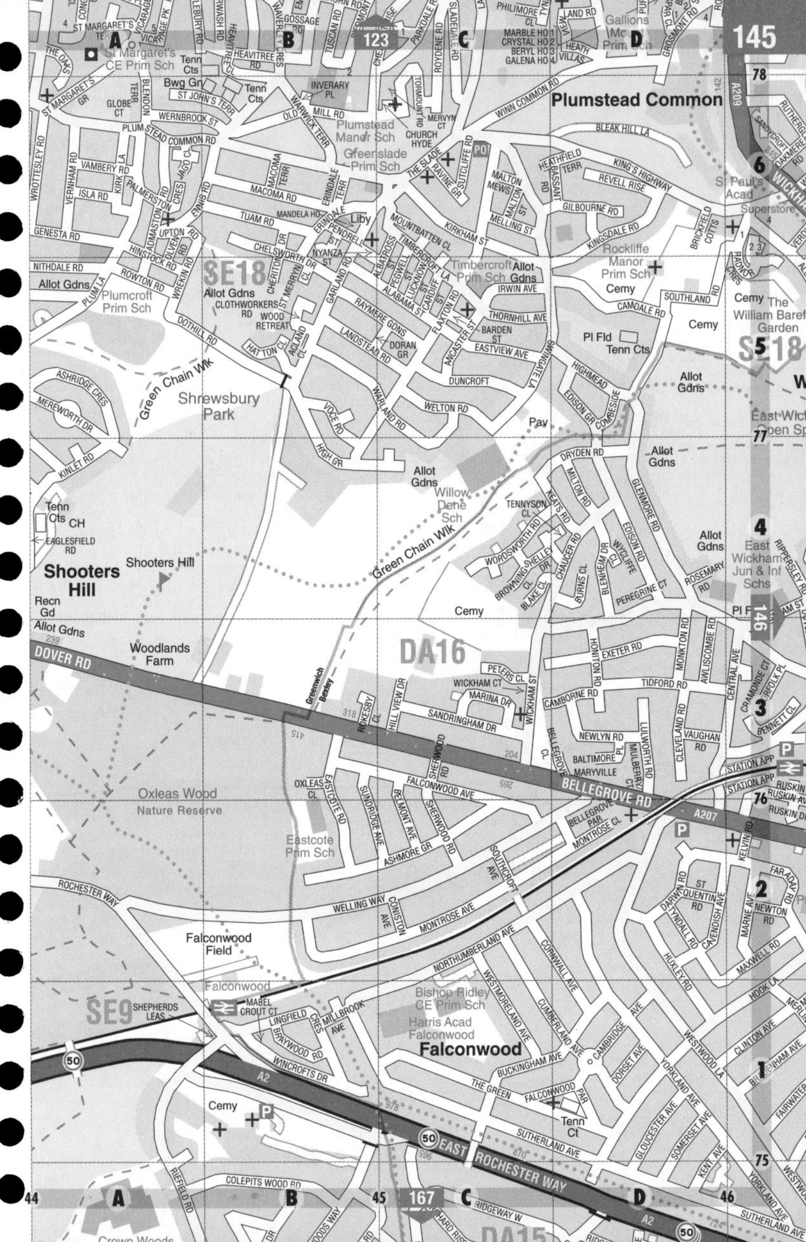

Plumstead Common
SE18
Shrewsbury Park
Shooters Hill
Woodlands Farm
DA16
Oxleas Wood
Nature Reserve
Falconwood Field
Falconwood
SE9
DOVER RD
BELLEGROVE RD
ROCHESTER WAY
EAST ROCHESTER WAY
Green Chain Wlk
123
146
167

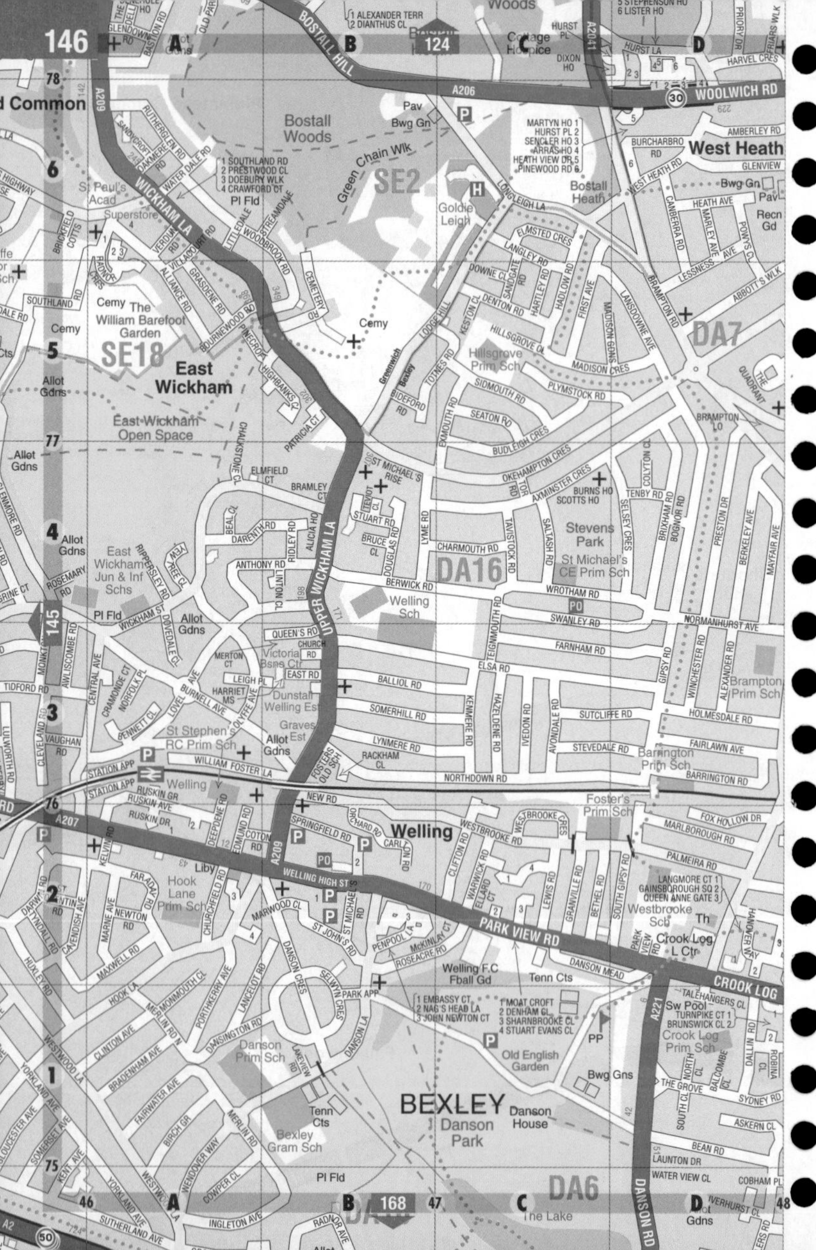

Bostall Woods
Bostall Heath
West Heath
East Wickham
East Wickham Open Space
Stevens Park
Welling
BEXLEY
Danson Park
Danson House
Old English Garden
SE2
SE18
DA16
DA7
DA6
WICKHAM LA
UPPER WICKHAM LA
BOSTALL HILL
WOOLWICH RD
WELLING HIGH ST
PARK VIEW RD
CROOK LOG
DANSON RD
Green Chain Wlk
124
168
145

125

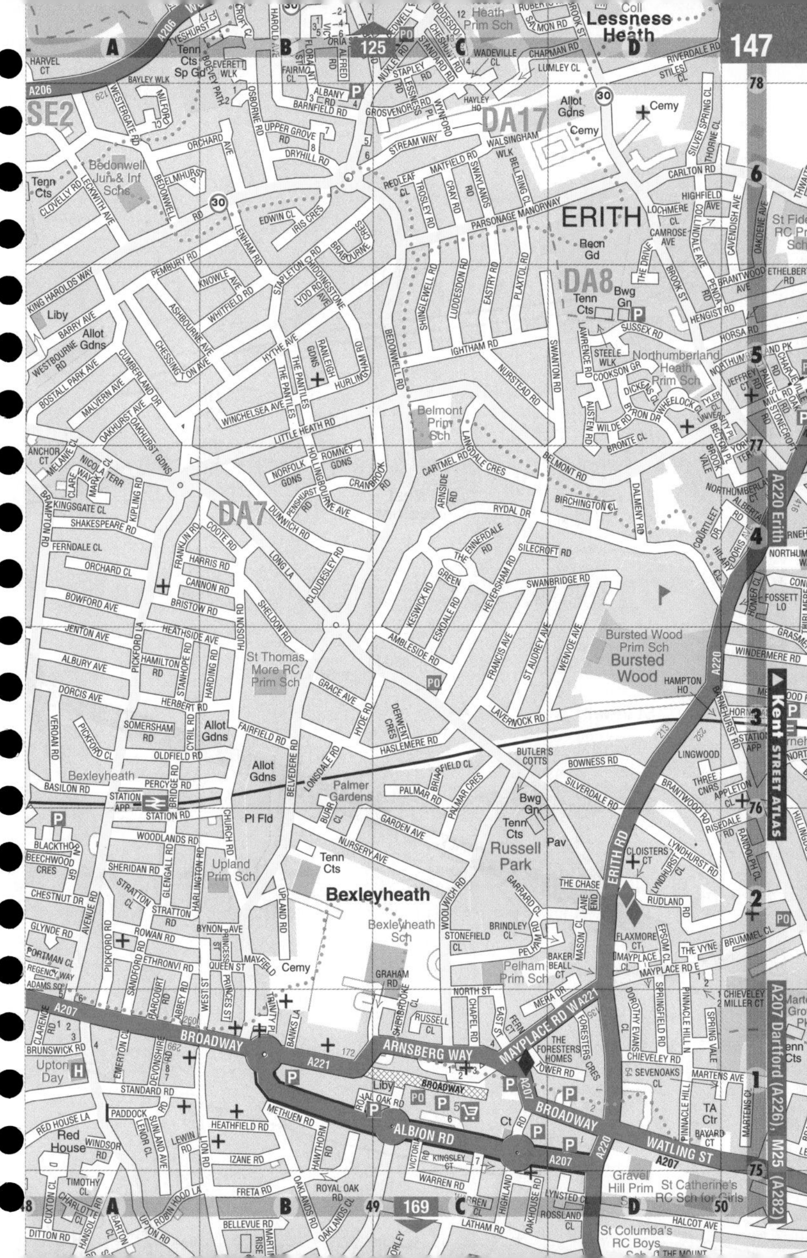

Lessness Heath
Heath Prim Sch
Coll
SE2
DA17
DA8
DA7
ERITH
Bexleyheath
Tenn Cts Sp Gd
Bedonwell Jun & Inf Schs
Tenn Cts
Liby
Allot Gdns
Cemy
Recn Gd
Tenn Cts
Bwg Gn
Northumberland Heath Prim Sch
St Fidelis RC Prim Sch
Belmont Prim Sch
St Thomas More RC Prim Sch
Bursted Wood Prim Sch
Bursted Wood
Palmer Gardens
Pl Fld
Russell Park
Pav
Upland Prim Sch
Bexleyheath Sch
Pelham Prim Sch
Upton Day
Red House
TA Ctr
Gravel Hill Prim Sch
St Catherine's RC Sch for Girls
St Columba's RC Boys Sch
Marten Grove Pk
Bexleyheath Station
A206
A207
A220
A221
BROADWAY
ARNSBERG WAY
MAYPLACE RD W
ERITH RD
WATLING ST
ALBION RD
PARSONAGE MANORWAY
BELMONT RD
LITTLE HEATH RD
IGHTHAM RD
BEDONWELL RD
LONG LA
HYDE RD
SHELDON RD
HUDSON RD
UPLAND RD
BELVEDERE RD
WOOLWICH RD
STATION RD
WOODLANDS RD
PICKFORD LA
DORCIS AVE
ALBURY AVE
JENTON AVE
BOWFORD AVE
ORCHARD CL
FERNDALE CL
SHAKESPEARE RD
KINGSGATE CL
BRAMPTON RD
CUMBERLAND DR
BOSTALL PARK AVE
WESTBOURNE RD
KING HAROLDS WAY
PEMBURY RD
LENHAM RD
WINCHELSEA AVE
HURLINGHAM RD
THE PANTILES
HYTHE AVE
STREAM WAY
WALSINGHAM WLK
BELLRING CL
SWAYLANDS RD
CRAY RD
TROSLEY RD
MATFIELD RD
REDLEAF CL
SHINGLEWELL RD
LUDDESDON RD
EASTRY RD
PLAXTOL RD
SWANTON RD
NURSTEAD RD
LANGDALE CRES
CARTMEL RD
RYDAL DR
ARNSIDE RD
ENNERDALE RD
KESWICK RD
ESKDALE RD
AMBLESIDE RD
HEVERSHAM RD
SWANBRIDGE RD
FRANCIS AVE
ST AUDREY AVE
WENVOE AVE
LAVERNOCK RD
HASLEMERE RD
DERWENT CRES
GRACE AVE
FAIRFIELD RD
LONSDALE RD
GARDEN AVE
NURSERY AVE
BRIARFIELD CL
PALMAR RD
PALMAR CRES
BOWNESS RD
SILVERDALE RD
BRANTWOOD RD
LYNDHURST RD
RUDLAND RD
MAYPLACE RD E
BRUMMEL CL
CHIEVELEY RD
MARTENS AVE
SEVENOAKS CL
SPRINGFIELD RD
PINNACLE HILL N
PINNACLE HILL
SPRING VALE
DOROTHY EVANS CL
FORESTERS CRES
THE FORESTERS HOMES
TOWER RD
MERA DR
NORTH ST
CHAPEL RD
EAST ST
RUSSELL CL
SHERBROOKE CL
GRAHAM RD
BANKS LA
TRINITY PL
MAYFIELD RD
QUEEN ST
PRINCESS ST
WEST ST
ABBEY RD
HARCOURT RD
SANDFORD RD
PICKFORD RD
AVENUE RD
CHESTNUT DR
GLYNDE RD
PORTMAN CL
REGENCY WAY
ADAMS SQ
BRUNSWICK RD
STANDARD RD
RED HOUSE LA
PADDOCK CL
HEATHFIELD RD
METHUEN RD
HAWTHORN RD
IZANE RD
FRETA RD
ROYAL OAK RD
OAKLANDS RD
BELLEVUE RD
LATHAM RD
VICTORIA RD
KINGSLEY CT
WARREN RD
HIGHLAND RD
OAKHOUSE RD
LYNSTED CL
ROSSLAND CL
HALCOT AVE
THE MOUNT
DITTON RD
UPTON RD
ROBIN HOOD LA
CARLTON RD
HIGHFIELD AVE
LOCHMERE CL
CAMROSE AVE
THE DRIVE
BROOK ST
PENDA RD
BRANTWOOD AVE
ETHELBERT RD
HENGIST RD
HORSA RD
SUSSEX RD
COOKSON GR
WILDE RD
BRONTE CL
BYRON DR
WHEELOCK CL
DICKENS CL
AUSTEN RD
LAWRENCE RD
STEELE WLK
BIRCHINGTON CL
DALMENY RD
SILECROFT RD
HILARY CL
DORIS AVE
COURTLEET DR
THE CHASE
GARRARD CL
BRINDLEY CL
PELHAM RD
STONEFIELD CL
MASON CL
FLAXMORE CT
MAYPLACE CL
EPSOM CL
THE VYNE
HAMPTON HO
BARNEHURST RD
LINGWOOD
THREE CNRS
APPLETON CL
RISEDALE RD
RANDOLPH CL
HILLINGDON RD
WINDERMERE RD
GRASMERE RD
THIRLMERE RD
FOSSETT LO
SILVER SPRING CL
THORNE CL
CAVENDISH AVE
OAKDENE AVE
RIVERDALE RD
STILES CL
LUMLEY CL
CHAPMAN RD
WADEVILLE CL
ALBANY RD
BARNFIELD RD
OSBORNE RD
UPPER GROVE RD
DRYHILL RD
ORCHARD AVE
WESTERGATE RD
MILFORD CL
BAYLEY WLK
HARVEL CT
TYESHURST CL
EDWIN CL
IRIS CRES
BRABOURNE CRES
STAPLETON RD
CHIDDINGSTONE AVE
LYDD RD
KNOWLE AVE
WHITFIELD RD
ASHBOURNE AVE
CHESSINGTON AVE
MALVERN AVE
OAKHURST AVE
OAKHURST GDNS
RANLEIGH GDNS
HOLLINGBOURNE AVE
NORFOLK GDNS
ROMNEY GDNS
CRANBROOK RD
PENSHURST RD
DUNWICH RD
CLOUDESLEY RD
COOTE RD
FRANKLIN RD
HARRIS RD
CANNON RD
BRISTOW RD
HEATHSIDE AVE
HAMILTON RD
STANHOPE RD
HARDING RD
HERBERT RD
SOMERSHAM RD
CYRIL RD
OLDFIELD RD
PERCY RD
BASILON RD
BRIDGE RD
CHURCH RD
VEROAN RD
BLACKTHORN
BEECHWOOD CRES
SHERIDAN RD
GLENGALL RD
HARLINGTON RD
STRATTON RD
BYNON AVE
ROWAN RD
ETHRONVI RD
EMERTON CL
DEVONSHIRE RD
LEWIN RD
LION RD
SUNLAND AVE
LENOR CL
WINDSOR RD
TIMOTHY CL
CHARLOTTE CL
CUXTON CL
BARTON CL
NICOLA TERR
ANCHOR CT
MELANIE CL
KIPLING RD
BARRY AVE
CLOVELLY RD
LECKWITH AVE
BELMHURST
A220 Erith
A207 Dartford (A226), M25 (A282)
Kent STREET ATLAS

169

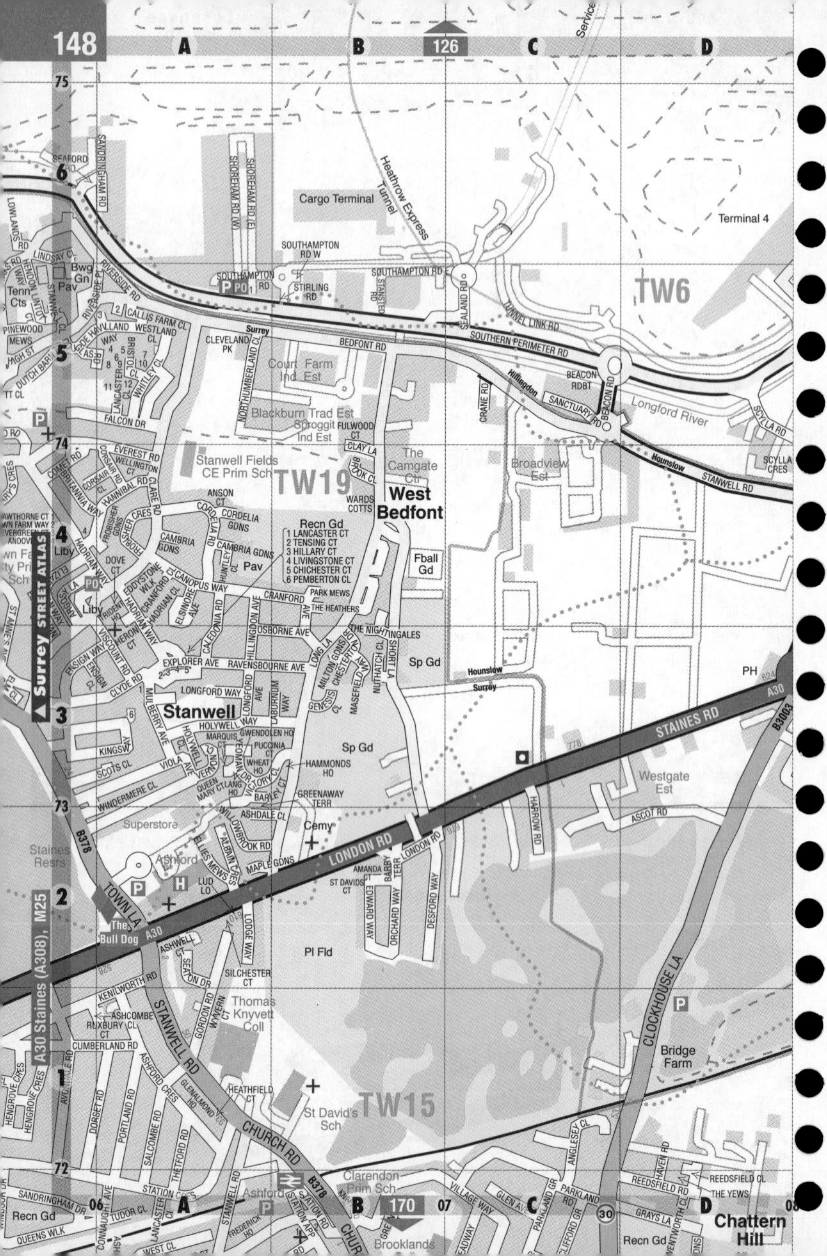
A
B
126
C
D
Cargo Terminal
Heathrow Express Tunnel
Terminal 4
TW6
Court Farm Ind Est
Blackburn Trad Est
Sproggit Ind Est
The Camgate Ctr
Broadview Est
Stanwell Fields CE Prim Sch
TW19
West Bedfont
Recn Gd
1 LANCASTER CT
2 TENSING CT
3 HILLARY CT
4 LIVINGSTONE CT
5 CHICHESTER CT
6 PEMBERTON CL
Fball Gd
Sp Gd
Stanwell
Westgate Est
Superstore
Staines Resrs
Ashford
Cemy
The Bull Dog
Pl Fld
Thomas Knyvett Coll
Bridge Farm
St David's Sch
TW15
Clarendon Prim Sch
Recn Gd
Chattern Hill
Brooklands
SOUTHERN PERIMETER RD
STANWELL RD
STAINES RD
LONDON RD
CLOCKHOUSE LA
STANWELL RD
CHURCH RD
TOWN LA
Surrey STREET ATLAS
A30 Staines (A308), M25
170

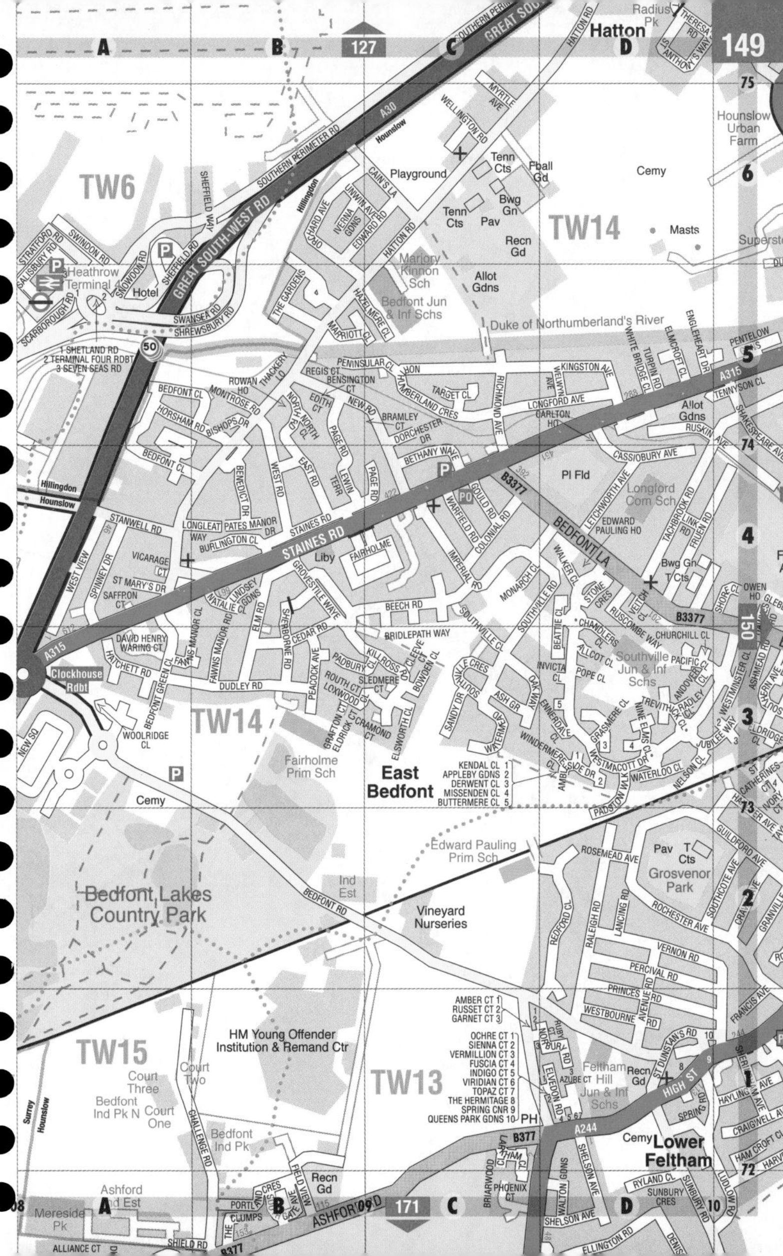
Hatton
TW6
TW14
East Bedfont
Bedfont Lakes Country Park
TW15
TW13
Lower Feltham
HM Young Offender Institution & Remand Ctr
Heathrow Terminal 4
Clockhouse Rdbt
Hounslow Urban Farm
Grosvenor Park
Vineyard Nurseries
Duke of Northumberland's River
STAINES RD
BEDFONT LA
GREAT SOUTH-WEST RD
1 SHETLAND RD
2 TERMINAL FOUR RDBT
3 SEVEN SEAS RD
KENDAL CL 1
APPLEBY GDNS 2
DERWENT CL 3
MISSENDEN CL 4
BUTTERMERE CL 5
AMBER CT 1
RUSSET CT 2
GARNET CT 3
OCHRE CT 1
SIENNA CT 2
VERMILLION CT 3
FUSCIA CT 4
INDIGO CT 5
VIRIDIAN CT 6
TOPAZ CT 7
THE HERMITAGE 8
SPRING CNR 9
QUEENS PARK GDNS 10
127
171
150

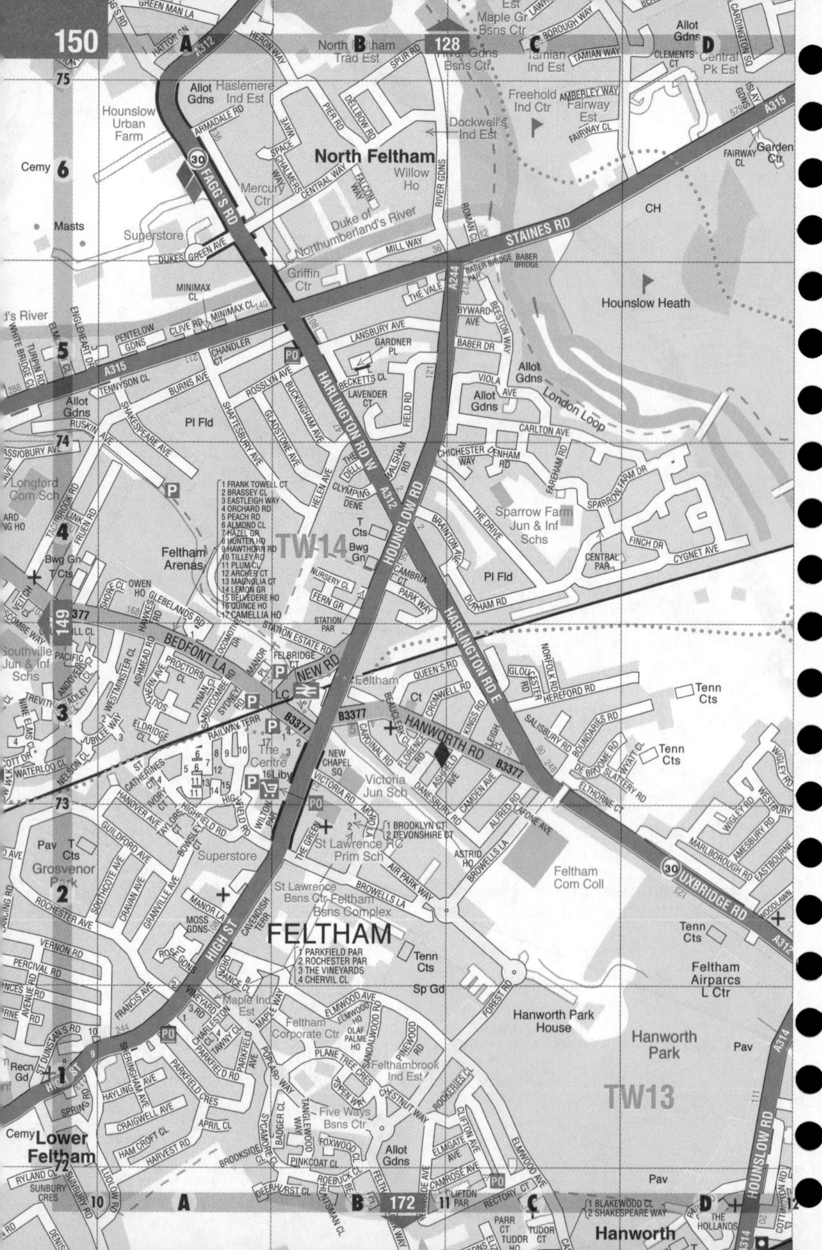
North Feltham
FELTHAM
Lower Feltham
Hanworth
TW14
TW13
Hounslow Heath
Hanworth Park
STAINES RD
HARLINGTON RD W
HARLINGTON RD E
HOUNSLOW RD
HIGH ST
HANWORTH RD
BEDFONT LA
UXBRIDGE RD
FAGG'S RD
NEW RD
1 FRANK TOWELL CT
2 BRASSEY CL
3 EASTLEIGH WAY
4 ORCHARD RD
5 PEACH RD
6 ALMOND CL
7 HAZEL GR
8 HUNTER HO
9 HAWTHORN RD
10 TILLEY RD
11 PLUM CL
12 ARCHER CT
13 MAGNOLIA CT
14 LEMON GR
15 BELVEDERE HO
16 QUINCE HO
17 CAMELLIA HO
1 BROOKLYN CT
2 DEVONSHIRE CT
1 PARKFIELD PAR
2 ROCHESTER PAR
3 THE VINEYARDS
4 CHERVIL CL
1 BLAKEWOOD CL
2 SHAKESPEARE WAY
128
149
172

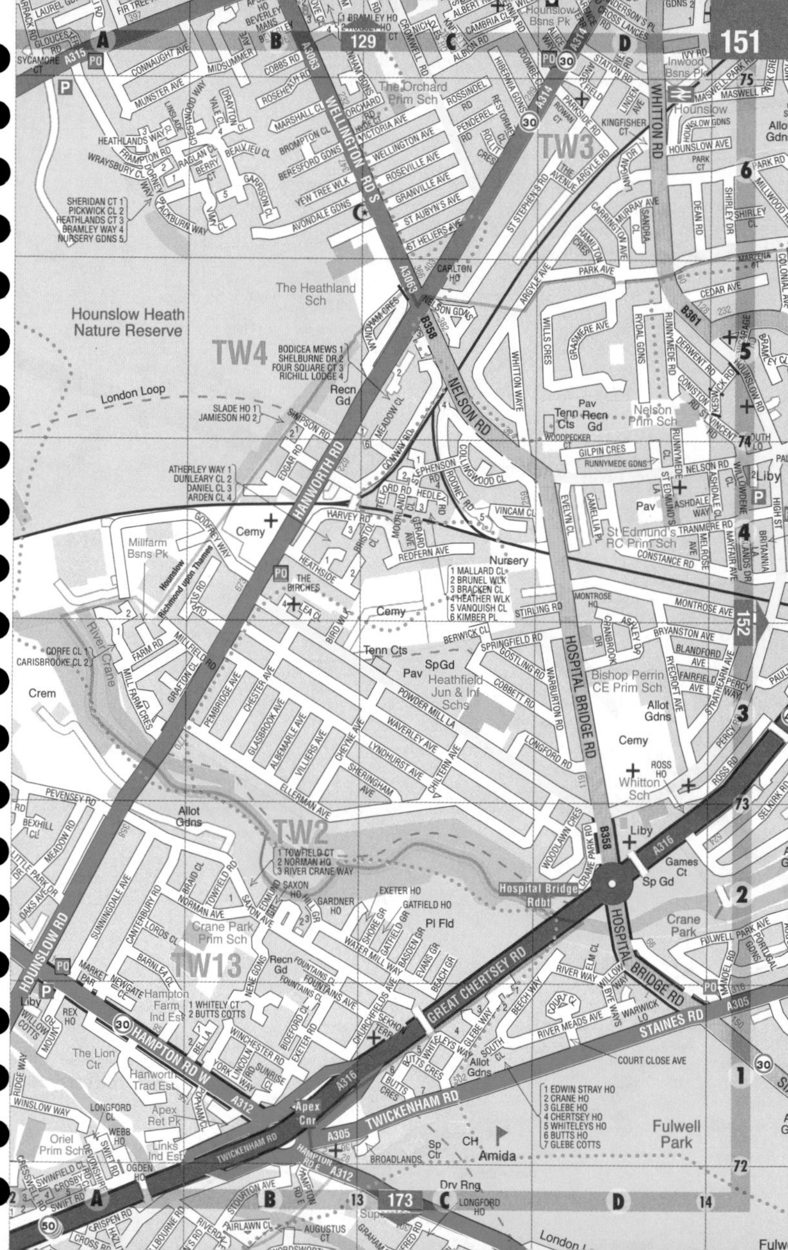

A
B
C
D
129
173
152
TW3
TW4
TW2
TW13
Hounslow Heath Nature Reserve
The Heathland Sch
The Orchard Prim Sch
London Loop
WELLINGTON RD S
HANWORTH RD
NELSON RD
HOSPITAL BRIDGE RD
WHITTON RD
HOUNSLOW RD
HAMPTON RD W
GREAT CHERTSEY RD
TWICKENHAM RD
STAINES RD
POWDER MILL LA
Hospital Bridge Rdbt
Apex Cnr
Crane Park
Fulwell Park
Crane Park Prim Sch
Heathfield Jun & Inf Schs
Bishop Perrin CE Prim Sch
St Edmund's RC Prim Sch
Nelson Prim Sch
Whitton Sch
Oriel Prim Sch
Hampton Farm Ind Est
Hanworth Trad Est
The Lion Ctr
Apex Ret Pk
Links Ind Est
Millfarm Bsns Pk
Hounslow Bsns Pk
Inwood Bsns Pk
River Crane
Amida
Hounslow
Richmond upon Thames
SHERIDAN CT 1
PICKWICK CL 2
HEATHLANDS CT 3
BRAMLEY WAY 4
NURSERY GDNS 5
BODICEA MEWS 1
SHELBURNE DR 2
FOUR SQUARE CT 3
RICHILL LODGE 4
SLADE HO 1
JAMIESON HO 2
ATHERLEY WAY 1
DUNLEARY CL 2
DANIEL CL 3
ARDEN CL 4
1 MALLARD CL
2 BRUNEL WLK
3 BRACKEN CL
4 HEATHER WLK
5 VANQUISH CL
6 KIMBER PL
CORFE CL 1
CARISBROOKE CL 2
1 TOWFIELD CT
2 NORMAN HO
3 RIVER CRANE WAY
1 WHITELY CT
2 BUTTS COTTS
1 EDWIN STRAY HO
2 CRANE HO
3 GLEBE HO
4 CHERTSEY HO
5 WHITELEYS HO
6 BUTTS HO
7 GLEBE COTTS

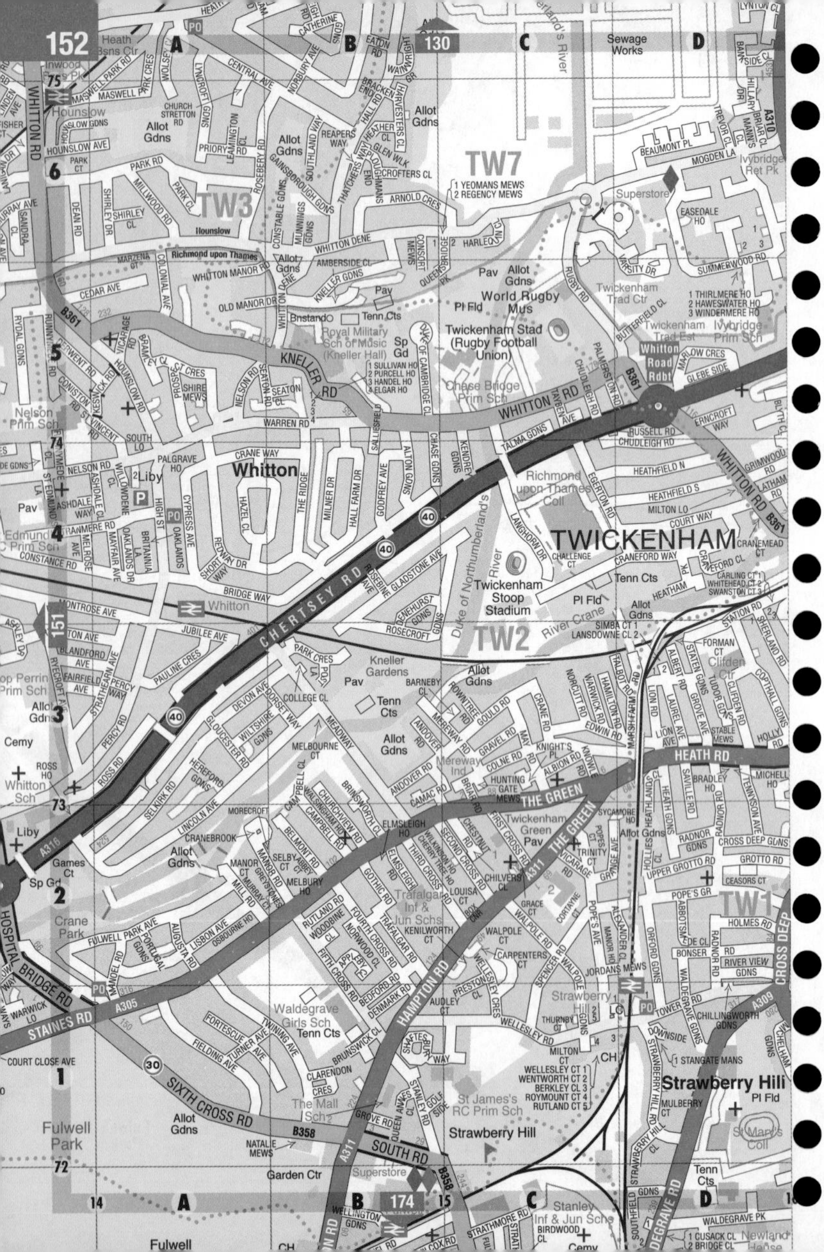

130
174
151
TW7
TW3
TW2
TW1
Whitton
TWICKENHAM
Strawberry Hill
Fulwell
Fulwell Park
Hounslow
Richmond upon Thames
Twickenham Stad (Rugby Football Union)
World Rugby Mus
Royal Military Sch of Music (Kneller Hall)
Twickenham Stoop Stadium
Richmond upon Thames Coll
Kneller Gardens
Crane Park
Sewage Works
Whitton Road Rdbt
WHITTON RD
CHERTSEY RD
KNELLER RD
HEATH RD
THE GREEN
HAMPTON RD
STAINES RD
SIXTH CROSS RD
SOUTH RD
HOSPITAL BRIDGE RD
CROSS DEEP
River Crane
Duke of Northumberland's River
Twickenham Trad Est
Ivybridge Ret Pk
Waldegrave Girls Sch
St James's RC Prim Sch
St Mary's Coll
Stanley Inf & Jun Schs
Trafalgar Inf & Jun Schs

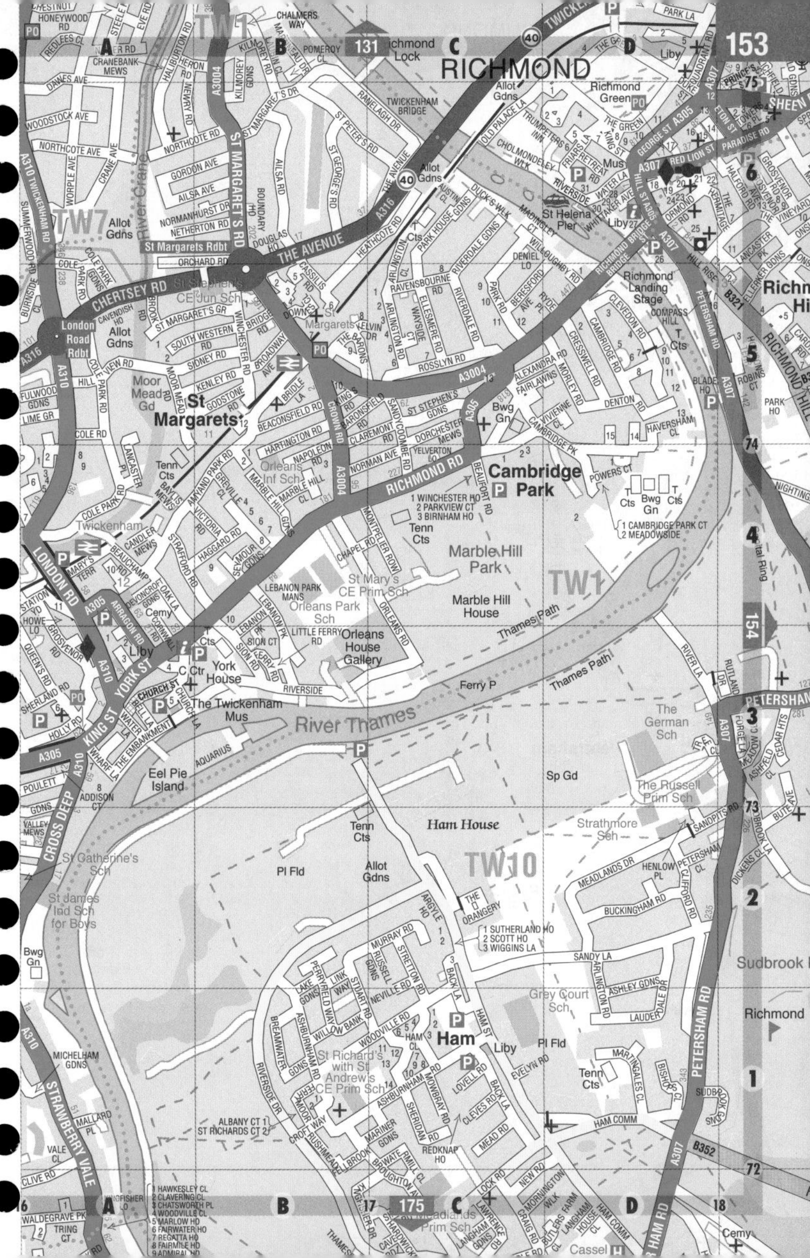
A
B
C
D
131
175
154
RICHMOND
Richmond Lock
Twickenham Bridge
Richmond Green
St Helena Pier
Richmond Landing Stage
Richmond Bridge
St Margarets
St Margarets Rdbt
London Road Rdbt
Cambridge Park
Marble Hill Park
Marble Hill House
Orleans House Gallery
Orleans Park Sch
St Mary's CE Prim Sch
Orleans Inf Sch
York House
The Twickenham Mus
Twickenham
River Thames
Thames Path
Eel Pie Island
Ferry P
Ham House
Ham
The German Sch
The Russell Prim Sch
Strathmore Sch
Grey Court Sch
St Richard's with St Andrew's CE Prim Sch
St Catherine's Sch
St James Ind Sch for Boys
St Stephen's CE Jun Sch
Moor Mead Gd
Sudbrook P
Richmond Hill
TW1
TW7
TW10
THE AVENUE
CHERTSEY RD
RICHMOND RD
ST MARGARET'S RD
PETERSHAM RD
RICHMOND HILL
HILL RISE
LONDON RD
KING ST
YORK ST
CROSS DEEP
STRAWBERRY VALE
TWICKENHAM RD
HAM ST
SANDY LA
MEADLANDS DR
BUCKINGHAM RD
HAM COMM
RIVERSIDE
CHURCH ST
THE EMBANKMENT
ORLEANS RD
MONTPELIER ROW
CROWN RD
ST PETER'S RD
RANELAGH DR
ROSSLYN RD
CAMBRIDGE PK
1 WINCHESTER HO
2 PARKVIEW CT
3 BIRNHAM HO
1 CAMBRIDGE PARK CT
2 MEADOWSIDE
1 SUTHERLAND HO
2 SCOTT HO
3 WIGGINS LA
ALBANY CT 1
ST RICHARDS CT 2
1 HAWKESLEY CL
2 CLAVERING CL
3 CHATSWORTH PL
4 WOODVILLE CL
5 MARLOW HO
6 FAIRWATER HO
7 REGATTA HO
8 FAIRMILE HO
9 ADMIRAL HO

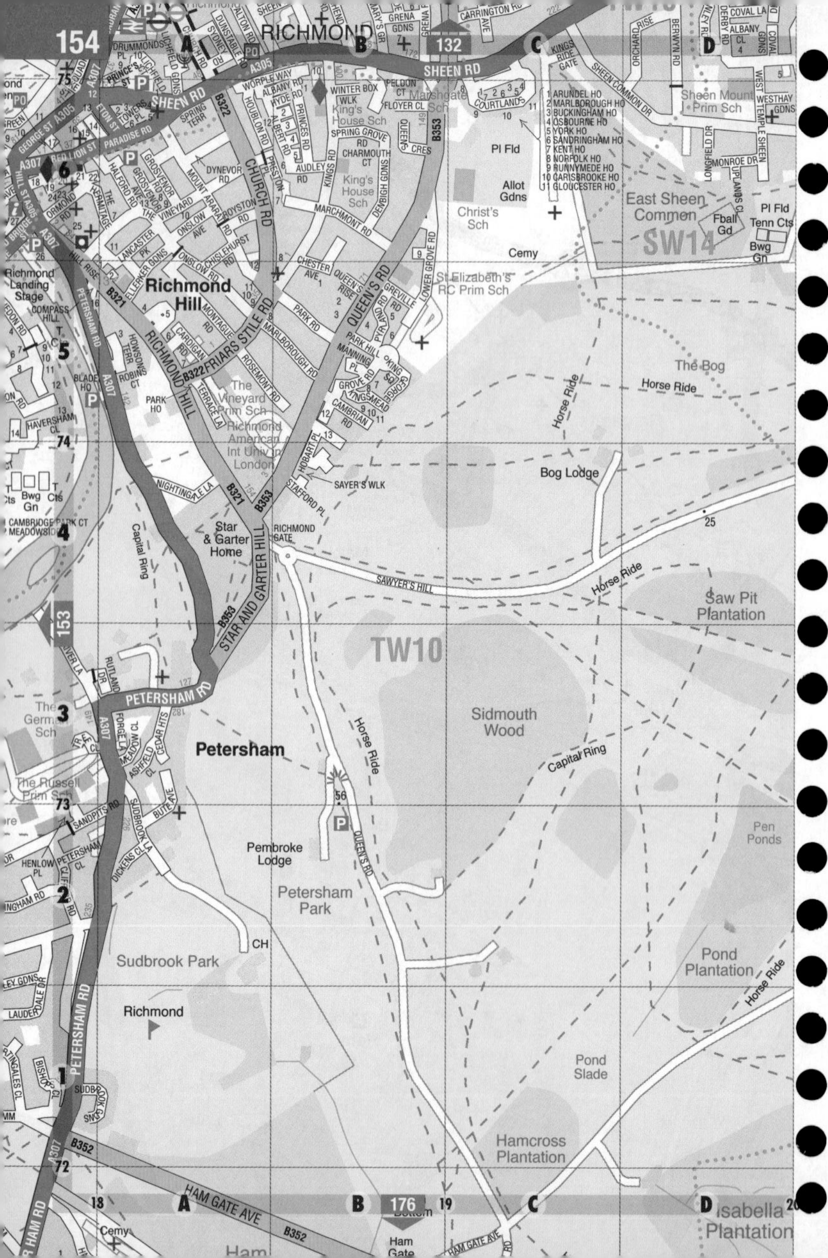
RICHMOND
132
SHEEN RD
Richmond Hill
Petersham
TW10
SW14
East Sheen Common
Sidmouth Wood
Saw Pit Plantation
Pen Ponds
Pond Plantation
Pond Slade
Hamcross Plantation
Isabella Plantation
Pembroke Lodge
Petersham Park
Sudbrook Park
Bog Lodge
The Bog
Horse Ride
Capital Ring
Star & Garter Home
STAR AND GARTER HILL
RICHMOND GATE
SAWYER'S HILL
QUEEN'S RD
PETERSHAM RD
HAM GATE AVE
153
176
Ham Gate
1 ARUNDEL HO
2 MARLBOROUGH HO
3 BUCKINGHAM HO
4 OSBOURNE HO
5 YORK HO
6 SANDRINGHAM HO
7 KENT HO
8 NORFOLK HO
9 RUNNYMEDE HO
10 CARISBROOKE HO
11 GLOUCESTER HO

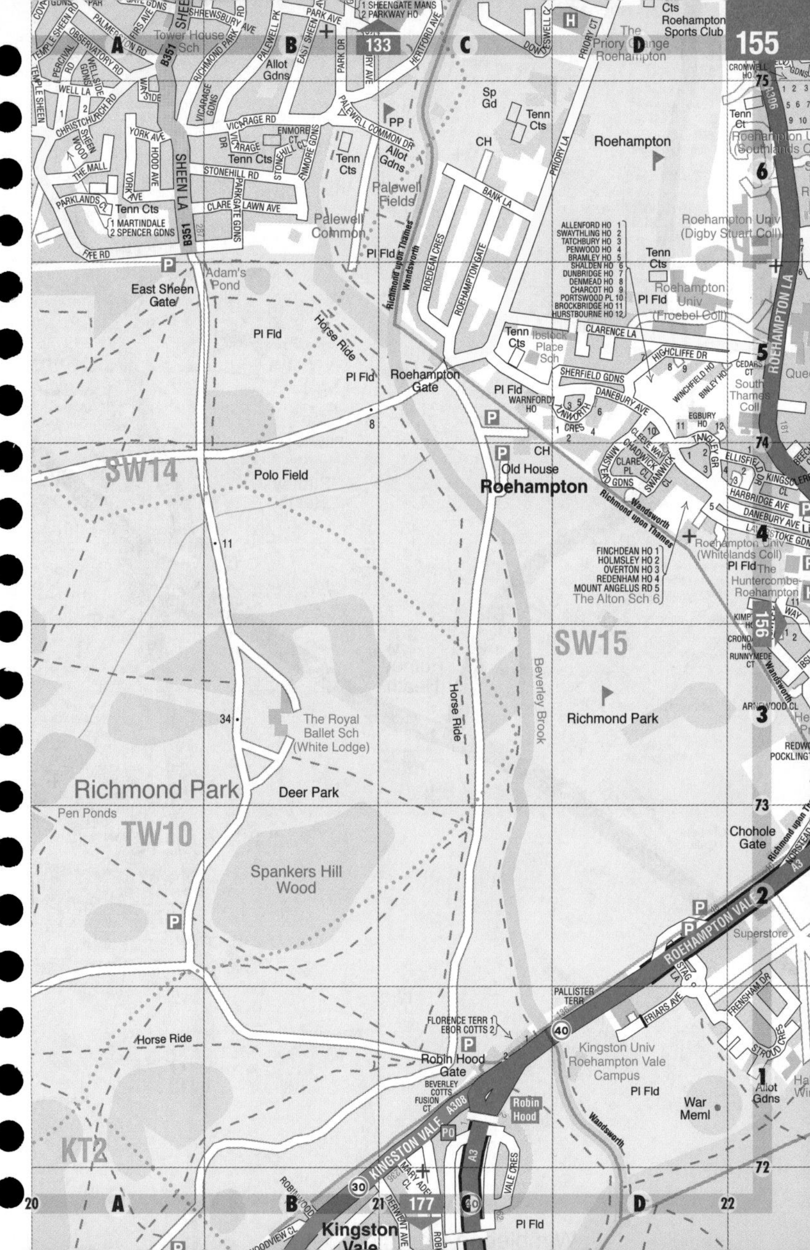

133
Tower House Sch
Allot Gdns
Sheen La
B351
Tenn Cts
1 Martindale
2 Spencer Gdns
Fife Rd
Palewell Fields
Palewell Common
Sp Gd
Tenn Cts
CH
Roehampton
The Priory Grange Roehampton
Roehampton Sports Club
Roehampton Univ (Southlands Coll)
Roehampton Univ (Digby Stuart Coll)
Roehampton Univ (Froebel Coll)
Allenford Ho 1
Swaythling Ho 2
Tatchbury Ho 3
Penwood Ho 4
Bramley Ho 5
Shalden Ho 6
Dunbridge Ho 7
Denmead Ho 8
Charcot Ho 9
Portswood Pl 10
Brockbridge Ho 11
Hurstbourne Ho 12
East Sheen Gate
Adam's Pond
Pl Fld
Horse Ride
Roehampton Gate
Ibstock Place Sch
Clarence La
Highcliffe Dr
Sherfield Gdns
Danebury Ave
South Thames Coll
Roehampton La
SW14
Polo Field
Old House
Roehampton
Richmond upon Thames
Wandsworth
Finchdean Ho 1
Holmsley Ho 2
Overton Ho 3
Redenham Ho 4
Mount Angelus Rd 5
The Alton Sch 6
Roehampton Univ (Whitelands Coll)
The Huntercombe-Roehampton
156
SW15
Beverley Brook
Richmond Park
The Royal Ballet Sch (White Lodge)
Deer Park
Pen Ponds
TW10
Spankers Hill Wood
Chohole Gate
Roehampton Vale
Superstore
A3
Pallister Terr
Friars Ave
Frensham Dr
Stroud Cres
Florence Terr 1
Ebor Cotts 2
Robin Hood Gate
Kingston Univ Roehampton Vale Campus
War Meml
Allot Gdns
Beverley Cotts
Fusion Ct
Kingston Vale
A308
Robin Hood
KT2
Vale Cres
177
Kingston Vale
Derwent Ave
20
21
22
A
B
C
D
75
74
73
72

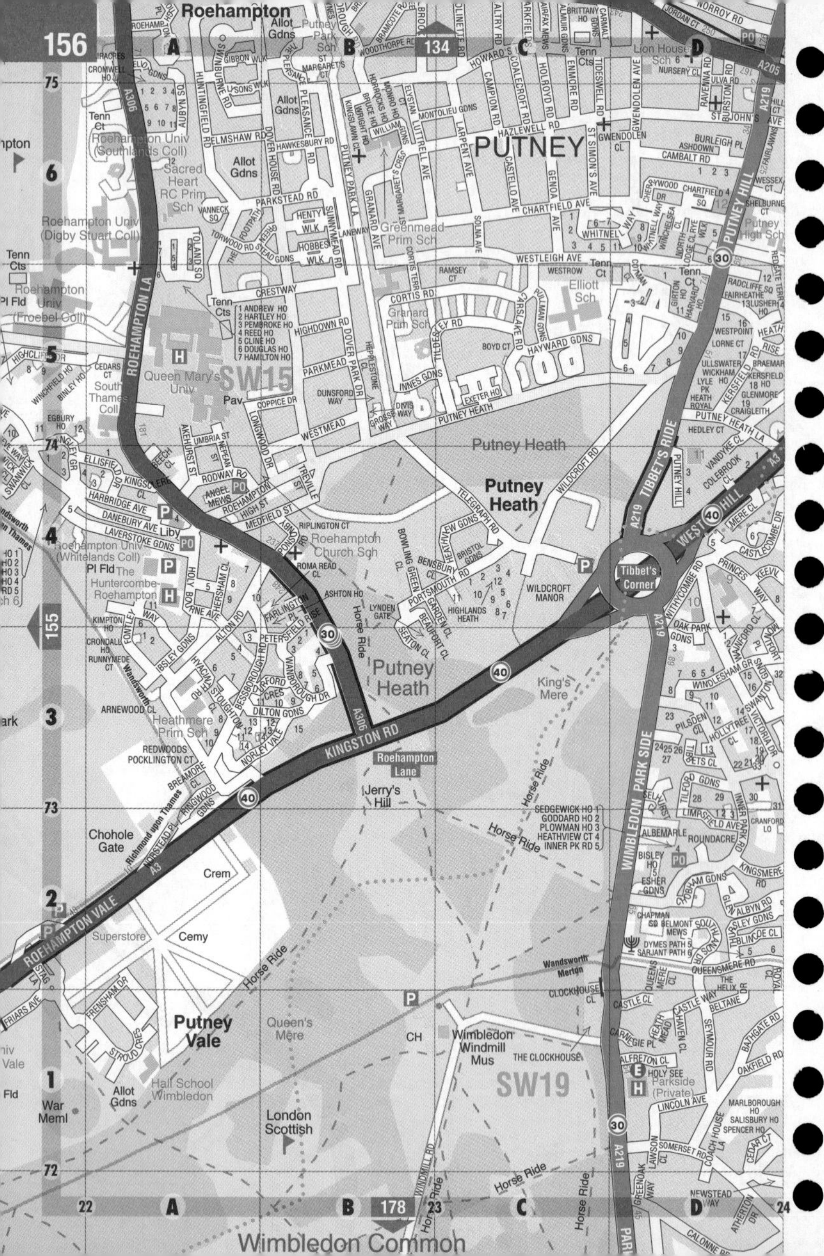

156
Roehampton
PUTNEY
Putney Heath
Putney Vale
Wimbledon Common
SW15
SW19
Tibbet's Corner
King's Mere
Queen's Mere
Jerry's Hill
Roehampton Lane
Wimbledon Windmill Mus
Wildcroft Manor
Highlands Heath
Queen Mary's Univ
Roehampton Univ (Southlands Coll)
Roehampton Univ (Digby Stuart Coll)
Roehampton Univ (Froebel Coll)
Roehampton Univ (Whitelands Coll)
Sacred Heart RC Prim Sch
Greenmead Prim Sch
Granard Prim Sch
Elliott Sch
Putney High Sch
Putney Park Sch
Roehampton Church Sch
Heathmere Prim Sch
Hall School Wimbledon
The Huntercombe-Roehampton
Parkside (Private)
London Scottish
Chohole Gate
Crem
Cemy
Superstore
War Meml
Allot Gdns
Horse Ride
ROEHAMPTON LA
KINGSTON RD
ROEHAMPTON VALE
TIBBET'S RIDE
PUTNEY HILL
WIMBLEDON PARK SIDE
WEST HILL
PUTNEY HEATH
PUTNEY PARK LA
DOVER PARK DR
DOVER HOUSE RD
WESTLEIGH AVE
CHARTFIELD AVE
HAZLEWELL RD
ST JOHN'S AVE
WINDMILL RD
A3
A306
A219
A205
134
155
178

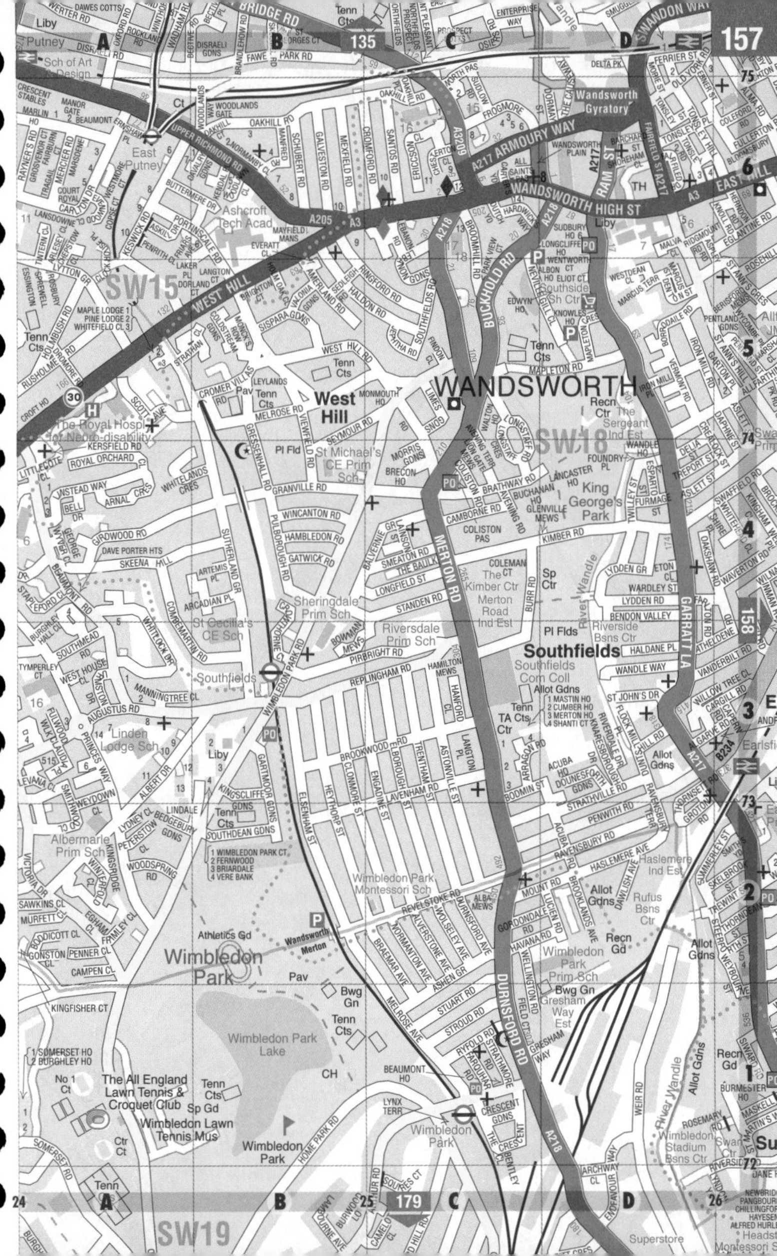

135
Putney
East Putney
SW15
WEST HILL
UPPER RICHMOND RD
Ashcroft Tech Acad
The Royal Hosp for Neuro-disability
West Hill
WANDSWORTH
Wandsworth Gyratory
ARMOURY WAY
WANDSWORTH HIGH ST
EAST HILL
BUCKHOLD RD
Southside Sh Ctr
MERTON RD
SW18
King George's Park
GARRATT LA
Southfields
Southfields Com Coll
Sheringdale Prim Sch
Riversdale Prim Sch
St Cecilia's CE Sch
St Michael's CE Prim Sch
The Kimber Ctr
Merton Road Ind Est
River Wandle
Linden Lodge Sch
Albermarle Prim Sch
Wimbledon Park Montessori Sch
WIMBLEDON PARK RD
DURNSFORD RD
REVELSTOKE RD
Haslemere Ind Est
Rufus Bsns Ctr
Wimbledon Park Prim Sch
Gresham Way Est
Wimbledon Park
Wimbledon Park Lake
Athletics Gd
The All England Lawn Tennis & Croquet Club
Wimbledon Lawn Tennis Mus
Wimbledon Stadium Bsns Ctr
Earlsfield
158
179
SW19
Superstore
Headstart Montessori Sch

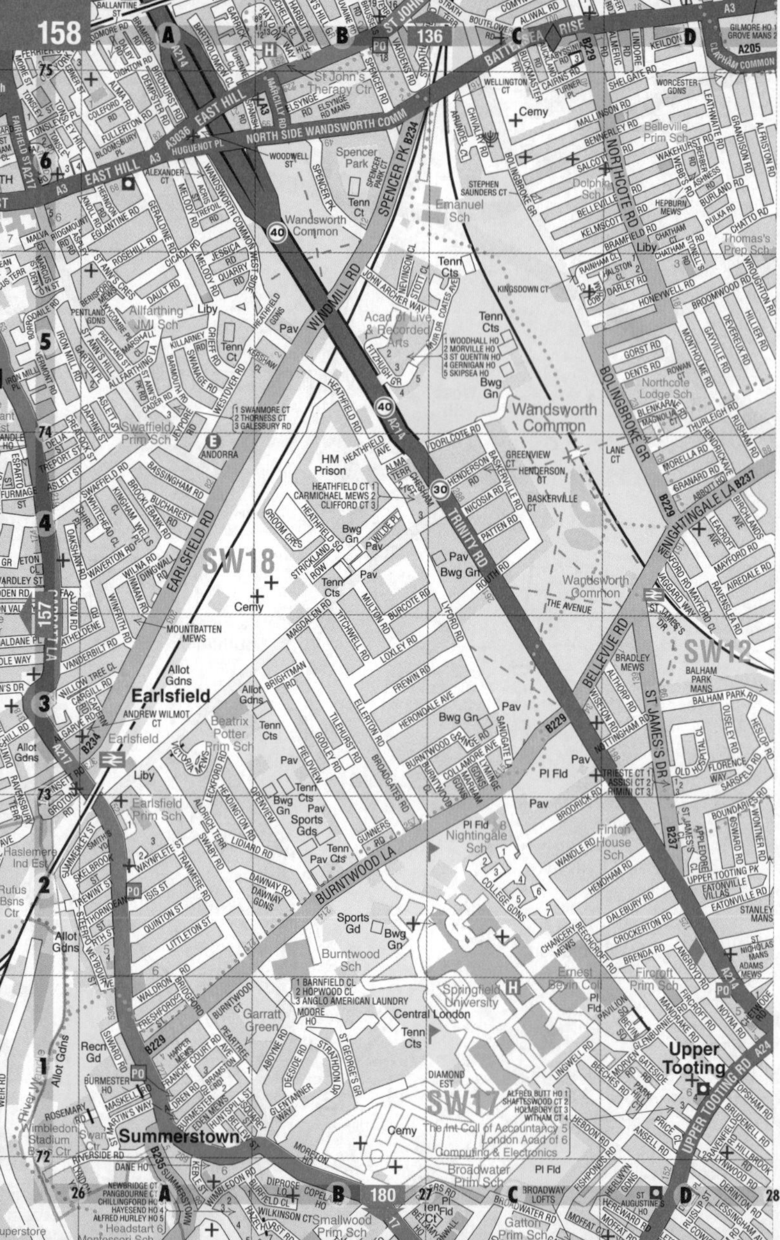
A
B
C
D
136
157
180
26
27
28
75
74
73
72
6
5
4
3
2
1
SW18
SW12
SW17
Earlsfield
Summerstown
Upper Tooting
Wandsworth Common
HM Prison
Spencer Park
Emanuel Sch
St John's Therapy Ctr
Allfarthing JMI Sch
Swaffield Prim Sch
Andorra
Acad of Live & Recorded Arts
Belleville Prim Sch
Dolphin Sch
Thomas's Prep Sch
Northcote Lodge Sch
Beatrix Potter Prim Sch
Earlsfield Prim Sch
Nightingale Sch
Finton House Sch
Burntwood Sch
Springfield University
Ernest Bevin Coll
Fircroft Prim Sch
Central London
Garratt Green
Diamond Est
The Int Coll of Accountancy
London Acad of Computing & Electronics
Broadwater Prim Sch
Gatton Prim Sch
Smallwood Prim Sch
Wimbledon Stadium Bsns Ctr
Haslemere Ind Est
Rufus Bsns Ctr
Headstart Montessori Sch
Superstore
EAST HILL
NORTH SIDE WANDSWORTH COMM
SPENCER PK
WINDMILL RD
TRINITY RD
EARLSFIELD RD
BURNTWOOD LA
NIGHTINGALE LA
BOLINGBROKE GR
NORTHCOTE RD
BELLEVUE RD
ST JAMES'S DR
UPPER TOOTING RD
CLAPHAM COMMON
BATTERSEA RISE
THE AVENUE
GARRATT LA
MAGDALEN RD
SUMMERSTOWN
A3
A205
A214
A217
A3036
A24
B229
B234
B235
B237

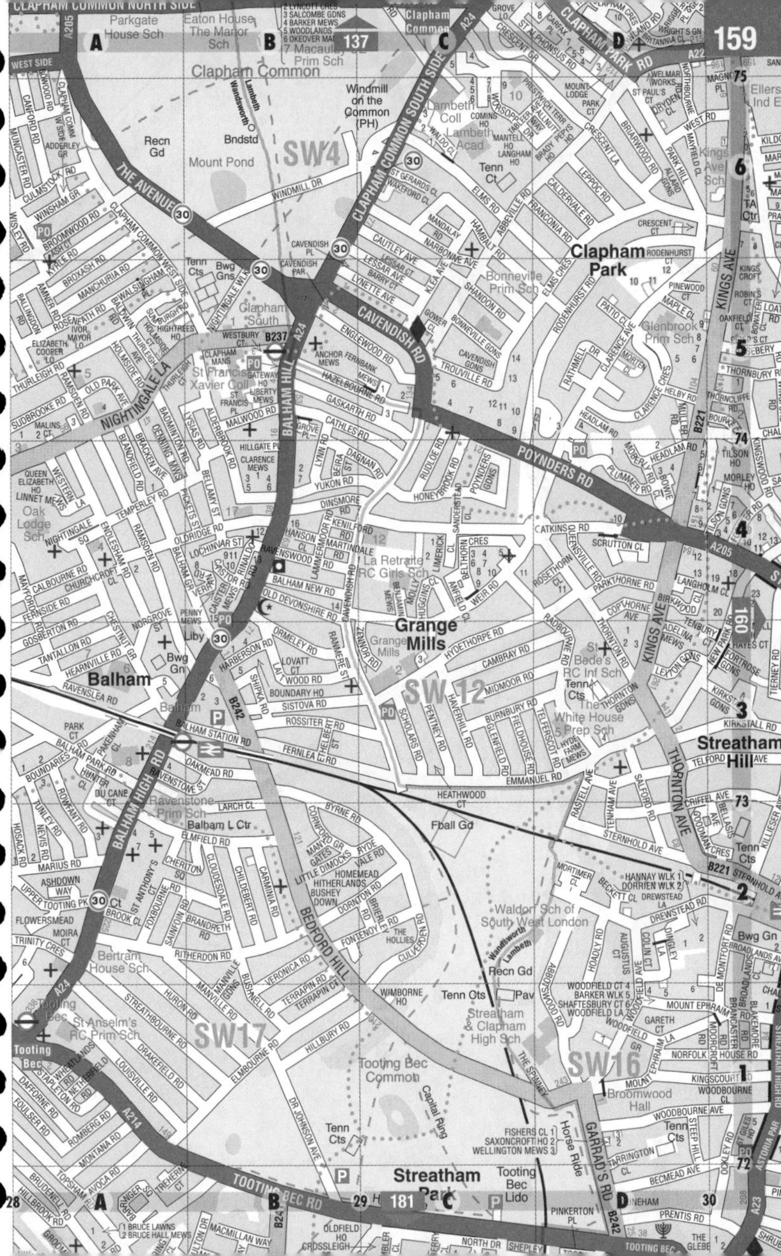

A
B
C
D
137
Clapham Common North Side
Parkgate House Sch
Eaton House The Manor Sch
Clapham Common
Clapham Common South Side
Clapham Park Rd
Windmill on the Common (PH)
Recn Gd
Bndstd
Mount Pond
SW4
The Avenue
Windmill Dr
Lambeth Coll
Lambeth Acad
Tenn Ct
Elms Rd
Abbeville Rd
Crescent La
Clapham Park
Ellerslie Ind Est
Kings Ave Sch
TA Ctr
Kings Ave
Bonneville Prim Sch
Cavendish Rd
Clapham South
Nightingale La
Balham Hill
St Francis Xavier Coll
Glenbrook Prim Sch
Poynders Rd
Tenn Cts
Bwg Gns
B237
A24
A205
A22
B221
B242
A214
A23
Oak Lodge Sch
La Retraite RC Girls Sch
Grange Mills
SW 12
St Bede's RC Inf Sch
White House Prep Sch
Thornton Ave
Streatham Hill
160
Balham
Liby
Bwg Gn
Balham Station Rd
Balham High Rd
Ravenstone Prim Sch
Balham L Ctr
Bedford Hill
Fball Gd
Emmanuel Rd
Heathwood Ct
Sternhold Ave
Waldorf Sch of South West London
Wandsworth
Lambeth
Recn Gd
Pav
Streatham & Clapham High Sch
Bertram House Sch
Tooting Bec
St Anselm's RC Prim Sch
SW17
Tooting Bec Common
Capital Ring
SW16
Broomwood Hall
Garrad's Rd
Horse Ride
Tenn Cts
Streatham Park
Tooting Bec Lido
Tooting Bec Rd
Streatham High Rd
28
29
181
30
75
6
5
74
4
3
73
2
1
72

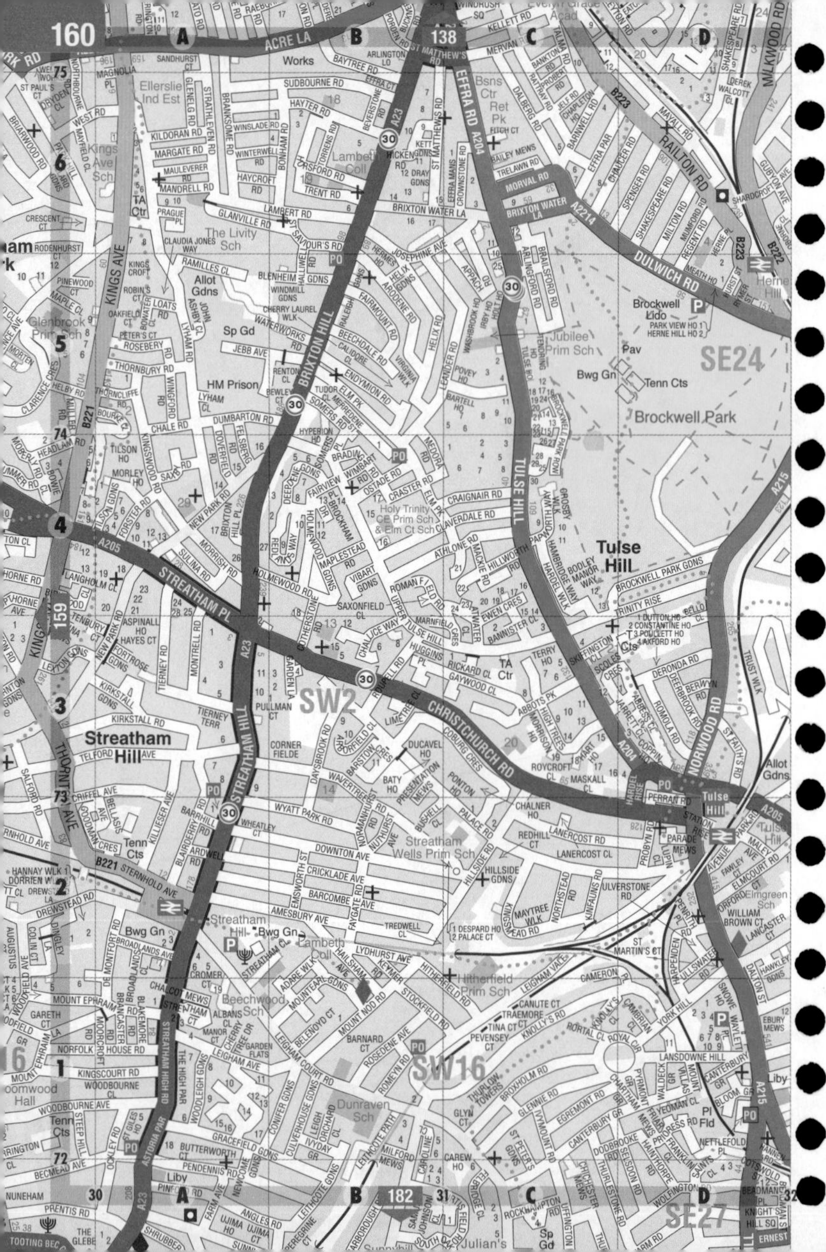

A
B
C
D
138
ACRE LA
Works
BAYTREE RD
ST MATTHEW'S RD
EFFRA RD
MERVAN RD
KELLETT RD
SUDBOURNE RD
Ellerslie Ind Est
Bsns Ctr
Ret Pk
HAYTER RD
KILDORAN RD
MARGATE RD
MAULEVERER RD
MANDRELL RD
WINSLADE RD
WINTERWELL RD
HAYCROFT RD
Kings Ave Sch
Lambeth Coll
TRENT RD
LAMBERT RD
GLANVILLE RD
BRIXTON WATER LA
MORVAL RD
TRELAWN RD
BAILEY MEWS
DALBERG RD
BARNWELL RD
EFFRA PAR
CHAUCER RD
SPENSER RD
SHAKESPEARE RD
MILTON RD
MUMFORD RD
REGENT RD
RAILTON RD
DULWICH RD
MILKWOOD RD
B223
A2214
A204
A23
The Livity Sch
RODENHURST CT
KINGS AVE
RAMILLES CL
JOSEPHINE AVE
BLENHEIM GDNS
Allot Gdns
Sp Gd
JEBB AVE
HM Prison
BRIXTON HILL
ENDYMION RD
TULSE HILL
BRAILSFORD RD
ARLINGFORD RD
Jubilee Prim Sch
Brockwell Lido
Pav
Bwg Gn
Tenn Cts
SE24
Brockwell Park
Herne Hill
Glenbrook Prim Sch
CLARENCE CRES
THORNBURY RD
LYHAM RD
DUMBARTON RD
CHALE RD
HEADLAM RD
NEW PARK RD
CRAIGNAIR RD
CLAVERDALE RD
Holy Trinity CE Prim Sch & Elm Ct Sch
ATHLONE RD
HILLWORTH RD
Tulse Hill
BROCKWELL PARK GDNS
TRINITY RISE
STREATHAM PL
A205
HOLMEWOOD RD
SAXONFIELD CL
CHRISTCHURCH RD
SW2
DERONDA RD
NORWOOD RD
Streatham Hill
TELFORD AVE
THORNTON AVE
STREATHAM HILL
KIRKSTALL RD
KIRKSTALL GDNS
TIERNEY TERR
CORNER FIELDE
PULLMAN CT
WAVERTREE RD
WYATT PARK RD
Streatham Wells Prim Sch
LANERCOST RD
LANERCOST CL
PERRAN RD
STATION RISE
Tulse Hill
B221
STERNHOLD AVE
DOWNTON AVE
CRICKLADE AVE
BARCOMBE AVE
AMESBURY AVE
HILLSIDE GDNS
ULVERSTONE RD
Streatham Hill
Bwg Gn
Lambeth Coll
Elmgreen Sch
WILLIAM BROWN CT
LANCASTER AVE
LEIGHAM VALE
Hitherfield Prim Sch
YORK HILL
Beechwood Sch
MOUNT EPHRAIM LA
NORFOLK HOUSE RD
KINGSCOURT RD
WOODBOURNE AVE
LEIGHAM AVE
LEIGHAM COURT RD
KNOLLY'S RD
SW16
LANSDOWNE HILL
Liby
Dunraven Sch
STREATHAM HIGH RD
ASTORIA PAR
A215
Tenn Cts
PENDENNIS RD
BUTTERWORTH CT
Liby
30
31
32
182
SE27

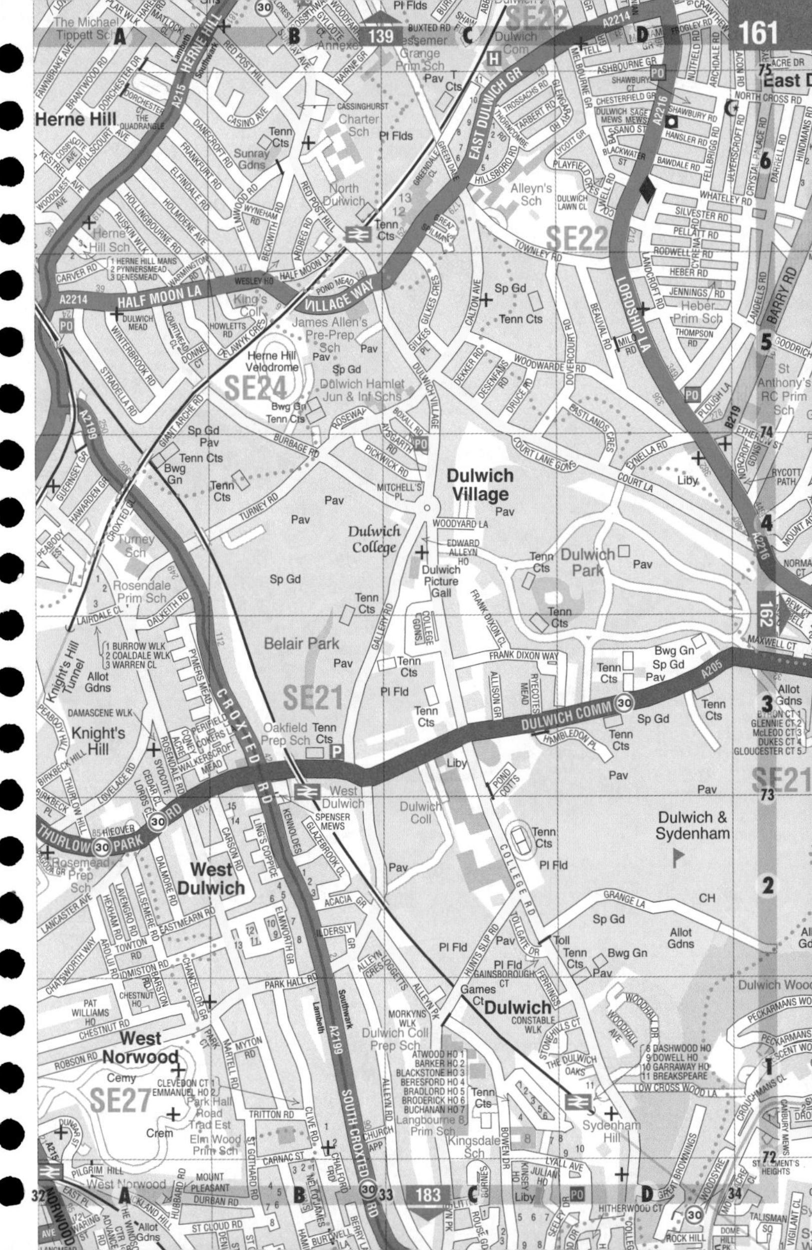
Herne Hill
SE22
SE24
SE21
SE27
Dulwich Village
Dulwich College
Dulwich Park
West Dulwich
Knight's Hill
West Norwood
Dulwich
Dulwich & Sydenham
East Dulwich
Herne Hill Velodrome
Belair Park
Sydenham Hill
HALF MOON LA
VILLAGE WAY
EAST DULWICH GR
LORDSHIP LA
DULWICH COMM
CROXTED RD
SOUTH CROXTED RD
COLLEGE RD
THURLOW PARK RD
BARRY RD
139
162
183

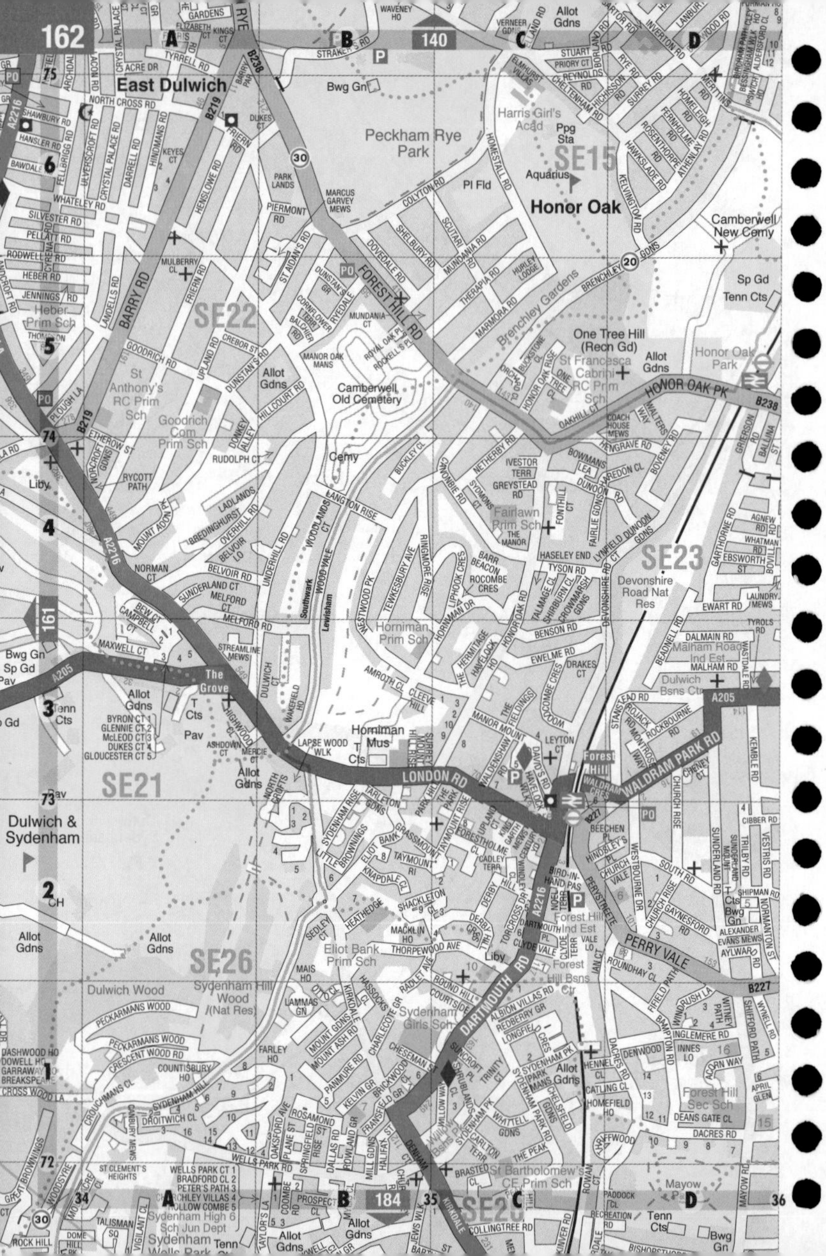
A
B
140
C
D
East Dulwich
Peckham Rye Park
Harris Girl's Acad
Ppg Sta
SE15
Aquarius
Honor Oak
Camberwell New Cemy
Sp Gd
Tenn Cts
SE22
Brenchley Gardens
One Tree Hill (Recn Gd)
St Francesca Cabrini RC Prim Sch
Allot Gdns
Honor Oak Park
HONOR OAK PK
B238
FOREST HILL RD
BARRY RD
B219
A2216
Heber Prim Sch
St Anthony's RC Prim Sch
Goodrich Com Prim Sch
Camberwell Old Cemetery
Cemy
Fairlawn Prim Sch
SE23
Devonshire Road Nat Res
Horniman Prim Sch
Malham Road Ind Est
Dulwich Bsns Ctr
A205
WALDRAM PARK RD
161
Bwg Gn
Sp Gd
The Grove
Horniman Mus
LONDON RD
Forest Hill
SE21
Dulwich & Sydenham
SE26
Eliot Bank Prim Sch
Forest Hill Ind Est
Forest Hill Bsns Ctr
PERRY VALE
B227
Dulwich Wood
Sydenham Hill Wood (Nat Res)
Sydenham Girls Sch
DARTMOUTH RD
Forest Hill Sec Sch
Willow Bsns Pk
St Bartholomew's CE Prim Sch
Mayow Pk
Sydenham High Sch Jun Dept
Sydenham Wells Park
184
34
35
36
SE26

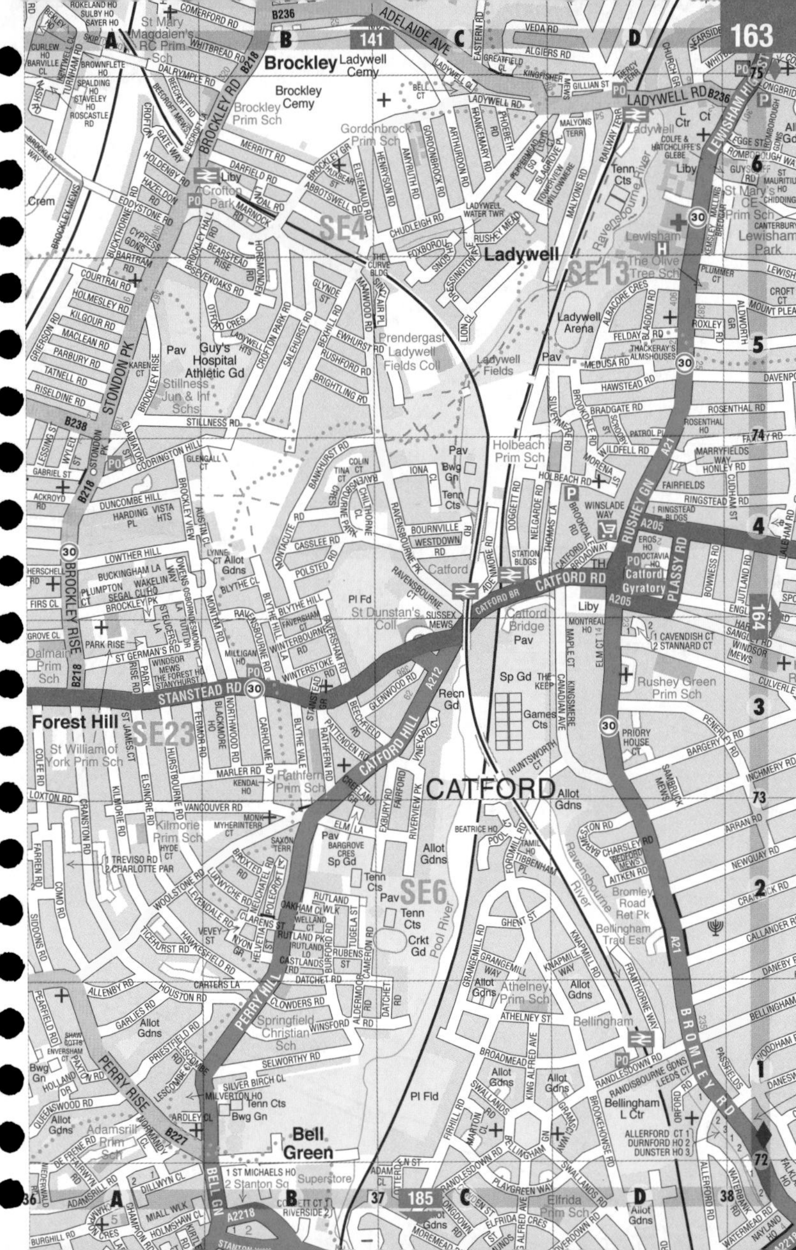
A
B
C
D
141
B236
ADELAIDE AVE
Brockley
Ladywell Cemy
Brockley Cemy
Brockley Prim Sch
St Mary Magdalen's RC Prim Sch
Gordonbrock Prim Sch
LADYWELL RD
Ladywell
BROCKLEY RD
B218
Crofton Park
Crem
SE4
Ladywell
SE13
Lewisham
The Olive Tree Sch
LEWISHAM HIGH ST
St Mary's CE Prim Sch
Lewisham Park
Ladywell Arena
Prendergast Ladywell Fields Coll
Ladywell Fields
Guy's Hospital Athletic Gd
Stillness Jun & Inf Schs
STONDON PK
B238
Holbeach Prim Sch
RUSHEY GN
A21
A205
Catford
CATFORD RD
Catford Gyratory
PLASSY RD
St Dunstan's Coll
Catford Bridge
BROCKLEY RISE
STANSTEAD RD
Forest Hill
SE23
St William of York Prim Sch
Rathfern Prim Sch
CATFORD HILL
A212
Rushey Green Prim Sch
CATFORD
Kilmorie Prim Sch
SE6
Pool River
Ravensbourne River
Bromley Road Ret Pk
Bellingham Trad Est
Athelney Prim Sch
Bellingham
Bellingham L Ctr
BROMLEY RD
PERRY HILL
PERRY RISE
B227
Springfield Christian Sch
Adamsrill Prim Sch
Bell Green
Superstore
BELL GN
A2218
Elfrida Prim Sch
185
36
37
38
72
73
74
75
164
1
2
3
4
5
6

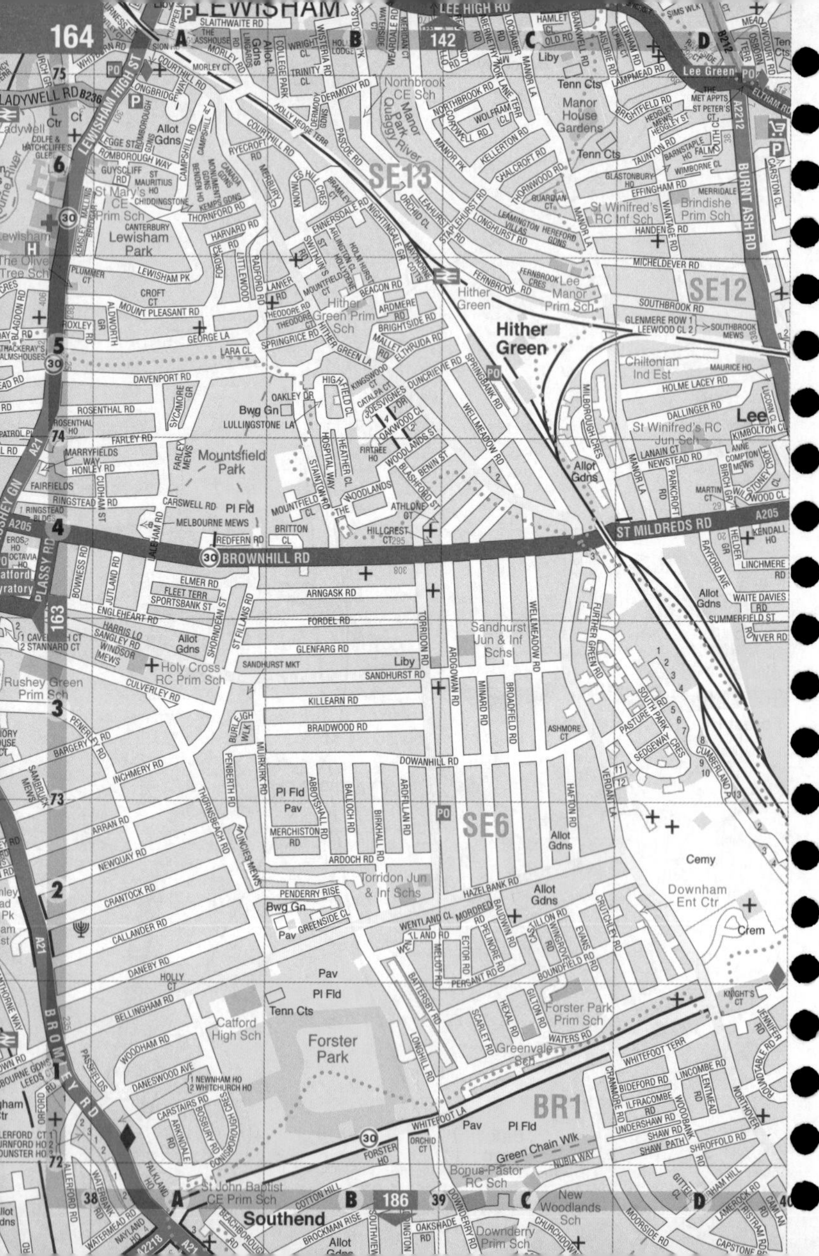

LEWISHAM
LEE HIGH RD
142
A
B
C
D
SLAITHWAITE RD
THE GLASSHOUSE
MORLEY RD
COURTHILL RD
MORLEY CT
WRIGHT CL
TRINITY CL
COLLEGE PARK
WISTERIA RD
HOLLY HEDGE TERR
DERMODY RD
Northbrook CE Sch
Manor Park
Quaggy River
HAMLET CL
OLD RD
MANOR LA
Liby
Tenn Cts
Manor House Gardens
NORTHBROOK RD
WOLFRAM CL
KELLERTON RD
CHALCROFT RD
THORNWOOD RD
LAMPMEAD RD
BRIGHTFIELD RD
Lee Green
THE MET APPTS
ST PETER'S CT
ELTHAM RD
A2212
BURNT ASH RD
B212
TAUNTON RD
BARNSTAPLE HO
WIMBORNE CL
GLASTONBURY HO
EFFINGHAM RD
MERRIDALE
Brindishe Prim Sch
St Winifred's RC Inf Sch
HANDEN RD
MICHELDEVER RD
SE12
SOUTHBROOK RD
GLENMERE ROW
LEEWOOD CL
SOUTHBROOK MEWS
LADYWELL RD
B236
LEWISHAM HIGH ST
Ladywell
L Ctr
COLFE & HATCHCLIFFE'S GLEBE
LONGBRIDGE WAY
LEGGE ST
ROMBOROUGH WAY
GUYSCLIFF RD
ST MAURITIUS HO
CHIDDINGSTONE
Allot Gdns
St Mary's CE Prim Sch
Lewisham
CANTERBURY
Lewisham Park
THORNFORD RD
HARVARD RD
RYECROFT RD
COURTHILL RD
SE13
ENNERSDALE RD
NIGHTINGALE GR
MAYTHORNE COTTS
STAPLEHURST RD
LONGHURST RD
LEAHURST RD
LEAMINGTON VILLAS
HEREFORD GDNS
FERNBROOK RD
FERNBROOK CRES
Lee Manor Prim Sch
Hither Green
The Olive Tree Sch
PLUMMER CT
LEWISHAM PK
CROFT CT
MOUNT PLEASANT RD
ALDWORTH GR
ROXLEY RD
GEORGE LA
THEODORE RD
LANIER RD
MOUNTFIELD RD
BEACON RD
Hither Green Prim Sch
ARDMERE RD
BRIGHTSIDE RD
SPRINGRICE RD
HITHER GREEN LA
MALLET RD
ELTHRUDA RD
LARA CL
DAVENPORT RD
ROSENTHAL RD
SYCAMORE GR
OAKLEY DR
HIGHFIELD CL
Bwg Gn
LULLINGSTONE LA
KINGSWOOD CT
CATALPA CT
DESVIGNES DR
DUNCRIEVIE RD
SPRINGBANK RD
WELLMEADOW RD
OAKWOOD CL
WOODLANDS ST
FIRTREE HO
BENIN ST
BLASHFORD ST
Chiltonian Ind Est
MAURICE HO
HOLME LACEY RD
DALLINGER RD
Lee
MILBOROUGH CRES
St Winifred's RC Jun Sch
KIMBOLTON CL
LANAIN CT
NEWSTEAD RD
ANNE COMPTON MEWS
PARKCROFT RD
MARTIN CT
BIRCH GR
WILDWOOD CL
STONEY CROFT
ST MILDREDS RD
A205
KENDALL HO
A21
RUSHEY GN
ROSENTHAL HO
PATROL PL
FARLEY RD
MARRYFIELDS WAY
HONLEY RD
Mountsfield Park
FARLEY MEWS
FAIRFIELDS
CUDHAM ST
RINGSTEAD RD
RINGSTEAD BLDGS
CARSWELL RD
Pl Fld
MELBOURNE MEWS
HOSPITAL WAY
HEATHER CL
STAINTON RD
THE WOODLANDS
MOUNTFIELD CL
ATHLONE CT
HILLCREST CT
BRITTON CL
REDFERN RD
BROWNHILL RD
PLASSY RD
Catford Gyratory
BOWNESS RD
JUTLAND RD
ELMER RD
FLEET TERR
SPORTSBANK ST
ENGLEHEART RD
HARRIS LO
SANGLEY RD
WINDSOR MEWS
Allot Gdns
SHORNDEAN ST
ST FILLANS RD
ARNGASK RD
FORDEL RD
GLENFARG RD
SANDHURST MKT
Liby
SANDHURST RD
TORRIDON RD
Sandhurst Jun & Inf Schs
WELLMEADOW RD
FURTHER GREEN RD
RAYFORD AVE
HELDER GR
LINCHMERE RD
Allot Gdns
WAITE DAVIES RD
SUMMERFIELD ST
RONVER RD
163
CAVELEIGH CT
STANNARD CT
Holy Cross RC Prim Sch
Rushey Green Prim Sch
CULVERLEY RD
BURLEIGH WLK
KILLEARN RD
BRAIDWOOD RD
ARDGOWAN RD
MINARD RD
BROADFIELD RD
ASHMORE CT
SOUTH PARK CRES
PASTURE RD
SEDGEWAY
CUMBERLAND PL
PENERLEY RD
BARGERY RD
INCHMERY RD
SAMBRUCK MEWS
PENBERTH RD
MUIRKIRK RD
THORNSBEACH RD
DOWANHILL RD
Pl Fld
Pav
ABBOTSHALL RD
BALLOCH RD
BIRKHALL RD
ARDFILLAN RD
SE6
HAFTON RD
VERDANT LA
Allot Gdns
Cemy
ARRAN RD
NEWQUAY RD
MERCHISTON RD
ARDOCH RD
MUNCIES MEWS
Torridon Jun & Inf Schs
CRANTOCK RD
PENDERRY RISE
Bwg Gn
GREENSIDE CL
HAZELBANK RD
Allot Gdns
Downham Ent Ctr
Crem
CALLANDER RD
WENTLAND CL
MORDRED RD
BAUDWIN RD
CASTILLON RD
WINGROVE RD
EVANS RD
CRUTCHLEY RD
DANEBY RD
HOLLY CT
Pav
Pl Fld
Tenn Cts
BELLINGHAM RD
MELLOT RD
ECTOR RD
PELLINORE RD
PERSANT RD
BOUNDFIELD RD
BATTERSBY RD
SCARLET RD
HEXAL RD
GILTON RD
Forster Park Prim Sch
WATERS RD
KNIGHT'S CT
JENNIFER RD
Catford High Sch
Forster Park
WOODHAM RD
DANESWOOD AVE
NEWNHAM HO
WHITCHURCH HO
LONGHILL RD
Greenvale Sch
WHITEFOOT TERR
BIDEFORD RD
LINCOMBE RD
LENTMEAD RD
NORTHOVER
ILFRACOMBE RD
UNDERSHAW RD
WOODBANK RD
SHAW RD
SHAW PATH
SHROFFOLD RD
BR1
CARSTAIRS RD
ARKINDALE RD
BOSBURY RD
CONISBOROUGH CRES
PASSFIELDS
BROMLEY RD
WHITEFOOT LA
FORSTER HO
ORCHID CT
Pav
Pl Fld
Green Chain Wlk
NUBIA WAY
Bonus Pastor RC Sch
ALLERFORD RD
WATERBANK RD
FALKLAND HO
St John Baptist CE Prim Sch
COTTON HILL
186
39
38
40
DOWNDERRY RD
New Woodlands Sch
GITTENS CL
MOORSIDE RD
LAMEROCK RD
TRISTRAM RD
CAPSTONE RD
Southend
BEACHBOROUGH
BROCKMAN RISE
SOUTHVIEW
OAKSHADE RD
Allot Gdns
Downderry Prim Sch
CHURCHDOWN
WATERMEAD RD
NAYLAND HO
A2218
LEEDS
ORFORD
TUNSTER HO
75
74
73
72
6
5
4
3
2
1

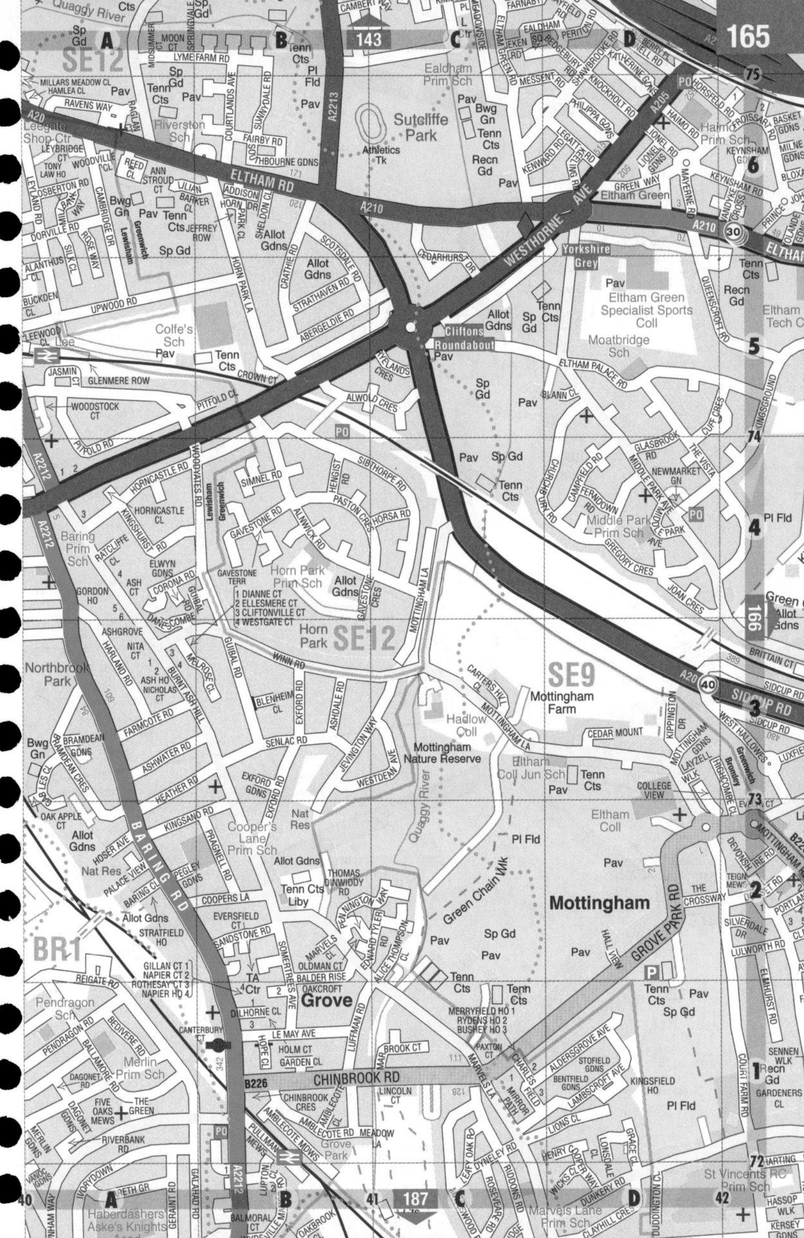

Quaggy River
143
SE12
LYME FARM RD
Ealdham Prim Sch
Sutcliffe Park
Athletics Tk
Riverston Sch
ELTHAM RD
A20
A2213
A210
A205
Leegate Shop Ctr
COURTLANDS AVE
SUNNYDALE RD
FAIRBY RD
WESTHORNE AVE
Eltham Green
Haimo Prim Sch
KEYNSHAM RD
Yorkshire Grey
Eltham Green Specialist Sports Coll
Moatbridge Sch
Eltham Hill Tech Coll
Colfe's Sch
Cliftons Roundabout
Lee
GLENMERE ROW
CROWN CT
PITFOLD RD
ELTHAM PALACE RD
HORN PARK LA
SCOTSDALE RD
STRATHAVEN RD
ABERGELDIE RD
Allot Gdns
Middle Park Prim Sch
MIDDLE PARK AVE
GREGORY CRES
JOAN CRES
Baring Prim Sch
Horn Park Prim Sch
Horn Park
SE12
SE9
A2212
MOTTINGHAM LA
SIDCUP RD
Mottingham Farm
Hadlow Coll
Mottingham Nature Reserve
Eltham Coll Jun Sch
Eltham Coll
Northbrook Park
BARING RD
Cooper's Lane Prim Sch
Quaggy River
Green Chain Wlk
Mottingham
GROVE PARK RD
BR1
Pendragon Sch
Merlin Prim Sch
Grove
CHINBROOK RD
B226
Grove Park
Haberdashers' Aske's Knights Acad
Marvels Lane Prim Sch
St Vincents RC Prim Sch
CASTLETON RD
166
187

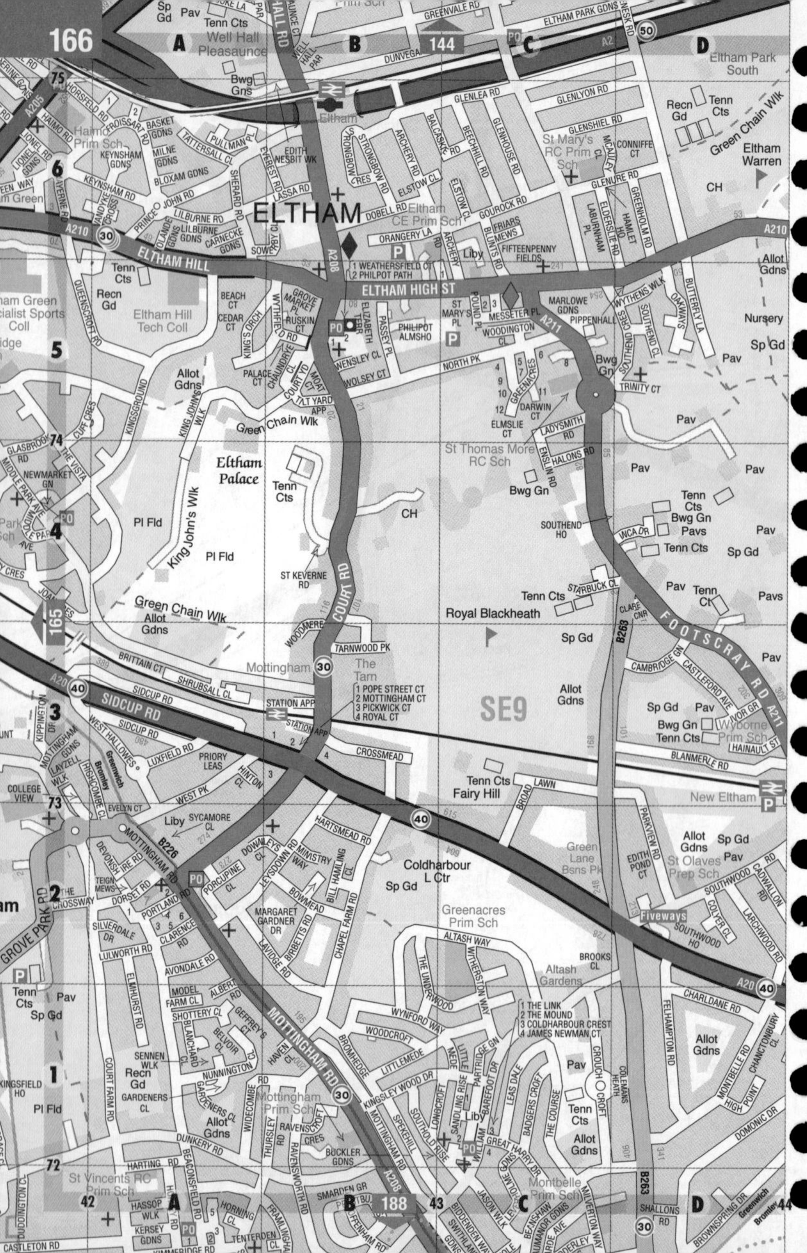

A
B
C
D
144
50
Well Hall Pleasaunce
Tenn Cts
Bwg Gns
Eltham
GREENVALE RD
ELTHAM PARK GDNS
DUNVEGAN
A2
Eltham Park South
Recn Gd
Tenn Cts
Green Chain Wlk
Eltham Warren
CH
GLENLEA RD
GLENLYON RD
GLENSHIEL RD
St Mary's RC Prim Sch
CONNIFFE CT
GLENURE RD
75
A205
HORSFIELD RD
FROISSART RD
BASKET GDNS
PULLMAN PL
TATTERSALL CL
Haimo Prim Sch
KEYNSHAM GDNS
MILNE GDNS
BLOXAM GDNS
EDITH NESBIT WK
EVEREST RD
STRONGBOW CRES
STRONGBOW RD
ARCHERY RD
BALCASKIE RD
BEECHHILL RD
GLENHOUSE RD
LASSA RD
ELSTOW CL
ELSTOW CL
6
KEYNSHAM RD
JOHN RD
SHERARD RD
ELTHAM
DOBELL RD
Eltham CE Prim Sch
GOUROCK RD
LABURNHAM PL
ELDERSLIE RD
HAMLET HO
GREENHOLM RD
LILBURNE RD
LILBURNE GDNS
CARNECKE GDNS
SOWE
ORANGERY LA
FRIARS MEWS
BLUNTS RD
FIFTEENPENNY FIELDS
Liby
A210
30
ELTHAM HILL
A208
1 WEATHERSFIELD CT
2 PHILPOT PATH
ELTHAM HIGH ST
Allot Gdns
Tenn Cts
Recn Gd
Eltham Hill Tech Coll
QUEENSCROFT RD
BEACH CT
CEDAR CT
KING'S ORCH
WYTHFIELD RD
GROVE MARKET PL
RUSKIN CT
ELIZABETH TERR
PASSEY PL
PHILIPOT ALMSHO
ST MARY'S PL
POUND PL
MESSETER PL
WOODINGTON CL
A211
MARLOWE GDNS
PIPPENHALL
WYTHENS WLK
SOUTHEND CRES
SOUTHEND CL
OAKWAYS
BUTTERFLY LA
Nursery
Sp Gd
Pav
5
KINGSGROUND
Allot Gdns
PALACE CT
CHAUNDRYE CL
COURT YD
MOAT CT
WENSLEY CL
WOLSEY CT
TILT YARD APP
NORTH PK
GREENACRES
DARWIN CT
ELMSLIE CT
Bwg Gn
TRINITY CT
KING JOHN'S WLK
Green Chain Wlk
CUFF CRES
74
GLASBROOK RD
THE VISTA
NEWMARKET GN
MIDDLE PARK AVE
Eltham Palace
Tenn Cts
LADYSMITH RD
HALONS RD
ENSLIN RD
St Thomas More RC Sch
Bwg Gn
Pav
4
Pl Fld
King John's Wlk
Pl Fld
CH
SOUTHEND HO
WICA DR
Tenn Cts
Bwg Gn
Pavs
Tenn Cts
Sp Gd
ST KEVERNE RD
COURT RD
STARBUCK CL
Tenn Cts
Royal Blackheath
Tenn Ct
Pavs
165
Green Chain Wlk
Allot Gdns
WOODMERE
CLARE CNR
B263
FOOTSCRAY RD
Sp Gd
TARNWOOD PK
BRITTAIN CT
SHRUBSALL CL
Mottingham
The Tarn
1 POPE STREET CT
2 MOTTINGHAM CT
3 PICKWICK CT
4 ROYAL CT
CAMBRIDGE GN
CASTLEFORD AVE
Allot Gdns
SE9
A20
40
SIDCUP RD
SIDCUP RD
STATION APP
3
KIPPINGTON DR
MOTTINGHAM GDNS
LAYZELL WLK
WEST HALLOWES
LUXFIELD RD
PRIORY LEAS
HINTON CL
CROSSMEAD
Sp Gd
Pav
Bwg Gn
Tenn Cts
IVOR GR
Wyborne Prim Sch
HAINAULT ST
BLANMERLE RD
COLLEGE VIEW
73
EVELYN CT
WEST PK
Liby
SYCAMORE CL
Tenn Cts
Fairy Hill
BROAD LAWN
New Eltham
B226
MOTTINGHAM RD
HARTSMEAD RD
DEVONSHIRE RD
PORCUPINE CL
DOWNLEYS
LEYSDOWN RD
MINISTRY WAY
BILL HAMLING CL
Coldharbour L Ctr
Sp Gd
Green Lane Bsns Pk
PARKVIEW RD
EDITH POND CT
Allot Gdns
Sp Gd
Pav
St Olaves Prep Sch
SOUTHWOOD CADWALLON
2
THE CROSSWAY
TEIGN MEWS
DORSET RD
PORTLAND RD
BOWMEAD
MARGARET GARDNER DR
CHAPEL FARM RD
Greenacres Prim Sch
Fiveways
SOUTHWOOD HO
COLYER CL
LARCHWOOD RD
GROVE PARK RD
SILVERDALE DR
CLARENCE RD
BIRBETTS RD
LAVIDGE RD
ALTASH WAY
THE UNDERWOOD
WITHERSTON WAY
BROOKS CL
Altash Gardens
LULWORTH RD
AVONDALE RD
Tenn Cts
Pav
Sp Gd
ELMHURST RD
MODEL FARM CL
ALBERT RD
SHOTTERY CL
BLANCHARD CL
BELVOIR CL
GEFFREY'S CT
WYNFORD WAY
1 THE LINK
2 THE MOUND
3 COLDHARBOUR CREST
4 JAMES NEWMAN CT
CHARLDANE RD
FELHAMPTON RD
Allot Gdns
CHANCTONBURY CL
1
KINGSFIELD HO
Pl Fld
COURT FARM RD
SENNEN WLK
Recn Gd
GARDENERS CL
NUNNINGTON
WIDECOMBE RD
HAVEN CL
WOODCROFT
BROMHEDGE
LITTLEMEDE
NEDE
LITTLE PARTRIDGE GN
KINGSLEY WOOD DR
Pav
CROUCH CROFT
COLEMANS HEATH
MONTBELLE RD
HIGH POINT
DOMONIC DR
Mottingham Prim Sch
Allot Gdns
THURSLEY RD
RAVENSCROFT CRES
RAVENSWORTH RD
MOTTINGHAM RD
SPEKEHILL
SOUTHOLD RISE
LONGCROFT
SANDLING RISE
BAREFOOT DR
Liby
LEAS DALE
BADGERS CROFT
THE COURSE
Tenn Cts
Allot Gdns
DUNKERY RD
BUCKLER GDNS
WILLIAM
GREAT HARRY DR
72
HARTING RD
BEACONSFIELD RD
St Vincents RC Prim Sch
A208
188
43
JASON WLK
Montbelle Prim Sch
B263
BROWNSPRING DR
42
A
B
C
D
44
SMARDEN GR
HASSOP WLK
KERSEY GDNS
HORNING CL
TENTERDEN CL
FRAMLINGHAM
DUDDINGTON CL
CASTLETON RD
KIMMERIDGE RD
BIDDENDEN WAY
BEANSHAW
MILVERTON WAY
SHALLONS RD
Greenwich
Bromley

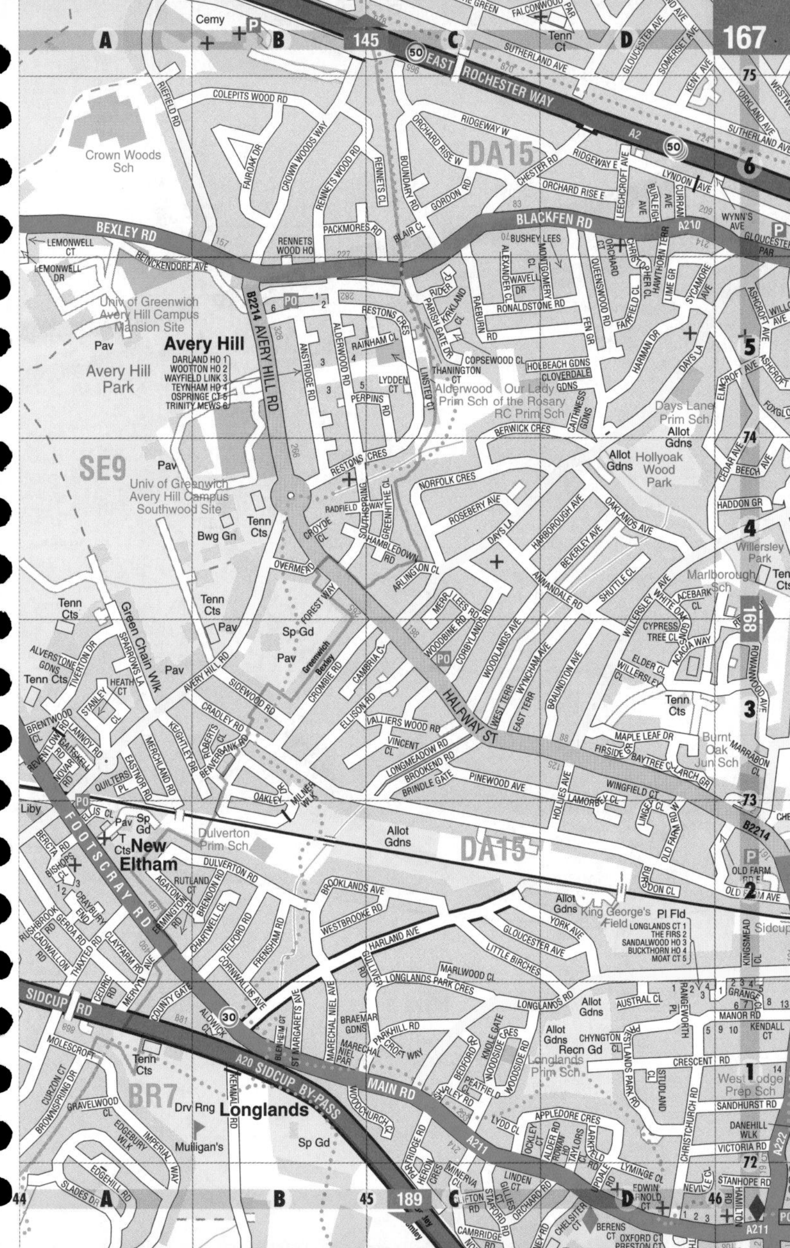

A
B
C
D
145
167
168
189
Cemy
Tenn Ct
FALCONWOOD PAR
SUTHERLAND AVE
GLOUCESTER AVE
SOMERSET AVE
KENT AVE
YORKLAND AVE
WESTWOOD LA
EAST ROCHESTER WAY
A2
COLEPITS WOOD RD
RIEFIELD RD
Crown Woods Sch
FAIROAK DR
CROWN WOODS WAY
RENNETS WOOD RD
RENNETS CL
BOUNDARY RD
ORCHARD RISE W
RIDGEWAY W
DA15
CHESTER RD
RIDGEWAY E
LEECHCROFT AVE
BURLEIGH AVE
CURRAN AVE
LYNDON AVE
ORCHARD RISE E
WYNN'S AVE
GORDON RD
BLAIR CL
PACKMORES RD
RENNETS WOOD HO
BEXLEY RD
BLACKFEN RD
A210
GLOUCESTER PAR
LEMONWELL CT
LEMONWELL DR
REINCKENDORF AVE
BUSHEY LEES
MONTGOMERY CL
ALEXANDER CL
WAVELL DR
ORCHARD CT
CHRISTOPHER CL
QUEENSWOOD RD
HAWTHORN TERR
LIME GR
SYCAMORE AVE
ASHCROFT AVE
WILLOW AVE
WELLINGTON
Univ of Greenwich Avery Hill Campus Mansion Site
B2214 AVERY HILL RD
PO
RESTONS CRES
RAINHAM CL
RIDER CL
PARISH GATE DR
KIRKLAND CL
RONALDSTONE RD
RAEBURN RD
FEN GR
FAIRFIELD CL
HARMAN DR
DAYS LA
Avery Hill
DARLAND HO 1
WOOTTON HO 2
WAYFIELD LINK 3
TEYNHAM HO 4
OSPRINGE CT 5
TRINITY MEWS 6
Pav
Avery Hill Park
ANSTRIDGE RD
ALDERWOOD RD
LYDDEN CT
PERPINS RD
LINSTED CT
THANINGTON CT
COPSEWOOD CL
HOLBEACH GDNS
CLOVERDALE GDNS
Alderwood Prim Sch
Our Lady of the Rosary RC Prim Sch
CAITHNESS GDNS
Days Lane Prim Sch
ELMCROFT AVE
ASHCROFT CRES
FOXGLOVE CL
BERWICK CRES
Allot Gdns
Hollyoak Wood Park
CEDAR AVE
BEECH AVE
SE9
Univ of Greenwich Avery Hill Campus Southwood Site
Tenn Cts
Bwg Gn
NORFOLK CRES
RADFIELD WAY
SOUTHSPRING
GREENHITHE CL
ROSEBERY AVE
HARBOROUGH AVE
BEVERLEY AVE
OAKLANDS AVE
HADDON GR
CROYDE CL
HAMBLEDOWN RD
ARLINGTON CL
Willersley Park
Marlborough Sch
OVERMEAD
FOREST WAY
ANNANDALE RD
SHUTTLE CL
WILLERSLEY AVE
WHITE OAK GDNS
ACEBARK CL
Sp Gd
Greenwich
Bexley
MERRILEES RD
CORBYLANDS RD
WOODBINE RD
WOODLANDS AVE
CYPRESS TREE CL
ACACIA WAY
ROWANWOOD AVE
ALVERSTONE GDNS
TIVERTON DR
SPARROWS LA
Green Chain Wlk
HEATH CT
STANLEY CL
CAMBRIA CL
CROMBIE RD
SIDEWOOD RD
ELLISON RD
WEST TERR
EAST TERR
WYNCHAM AVE
BRAUNDTON AVE
ELDER CL
WILLERSLEY CL
BRENTWOOD CL
LANNOY RD
CRADLEY RD
KEIGHTLEY DR
MERCHLAND RD
VALLIERS WOOD RD
HALFWAY ST
MAPLE LEAF DR
Burnt Oak Jun Sch
MARRABON CL
REVENTLOW RD
GAITSKELL RD
NOVAR RD
QUILTERS PL
EASTNOR RD
ROBERTS CL
BEAVERBANK RD
VINCENT CL
LONGMEADOW RD
BROOKEND RD
BRINDLE GATE
PINEWOOD AVE
HOLLIES AVE
FIRSIDE GR
BAYTREE CL
LARCH GR
WINGFIELD CT
LAMORBEY CL
LINGEY CL
OLD FARM RD W
Liby
OAKLEY PK
MILNER WLK
FOOTSCRAY RD
BERCTA RD
BISHOPS CL
New Eltham
Dulverton Prim Sch
DA15
B2214
OLD FARM RD E
OLD FARM AVE
BURSDON CL
CHESTNUT CL
RUTLAND CT
AGATON RD
DULVERTON RD
BRENDON RD
BROOKLANDS AVE
Allot Gdns
King George's Field
Pl Fld
LONGLANDS CT 1
THE FIRS 2
SANDALWOOD HO 3
BUCKTHORN HO 4
MOAT CT 5
Sidcup
KINGSMEAD
CRAYBURY END
RUSHBROOK RD
GERDA RD
CADWALLON RD
THAXTED RD
CLAYFARM RD
EMMINGTON RD
CHARTWELL CL
TELFORD RD
WESTBROOKE RD
FRENSHAM RD
YORK AVE
GLOUCESTER AVE
HARLAND AVE
LITTLE BIRCHES
MARLWOOD CL
LONGLANDS PARK CRES
GULLIVER RD
CEDRIC RD
MERVYN AVE
COUNTY GATE
CORNWALLIS AVE
LONGLANDS RD
Allot Gdns
AUSTRAL CL
RANGEWORTH PL
GRANGE CL
MANOR RD
KENDALL CT
SIDCUP RD
ALDWICK CL
BRAEMAR GDNS
MARECHAL NIEL AVE
MARECHAL NIEL PAR
BLENHEIM CT
ST MARGARETS AVE
PARKHILL RD
CROFT WAY
BEDFORD RD
KNOLE GATE
WOODSIDE CRES
WOODSIDE RD
Recn Gd
CHYNGTON CL
PRESTLANDS PARK RD
CRESCENT RD
STATION RD
MOLESCROFT
Tenn Cts
A20 SIDCUP BY-PASS
MAIN RD
VALLEY RD
PEATFIELD
Longlands Prim Sch
STUDLAND
CHRISTCHURCH RD
West Lodge Prep Sch
CURZON CT
BROWNSPRING DR
GRAVELWOOD CL
BR7
Drv Rng
Longlands
KEMNAL RD
WOODCHURCH CL
SANDHURST RD
DANEHILL WLK
A222
EDGEBURY WLK
IMPERIAL WAY
Mulligan's
Sp Gd
PARTRIDGE RD
HERON CRES
MINERVA CL
A211
LYDD CL
APPLEDORE CRES
ALDER RD
ROWAN RD
TAYLORS CL
LARKFIELD
LYMINGE CL
VICTORIA RD
EDGEHILL RD
SLADES DR
LINDEN CT
GILLIES CT
STAFFORD RD
ORCHARD RD
UPDALE RD
EDWIN ARNOLD CT
NEVILLE CL
STANHOPE RD
HAMILTON RD
CHAPLIN RD
CAMBRIDGE RD
CHELSITER CT
BERENS CT
OXFORD CT
PRESTON CT
44
45
46
1
2
3
4
5
6
72
73
74
75

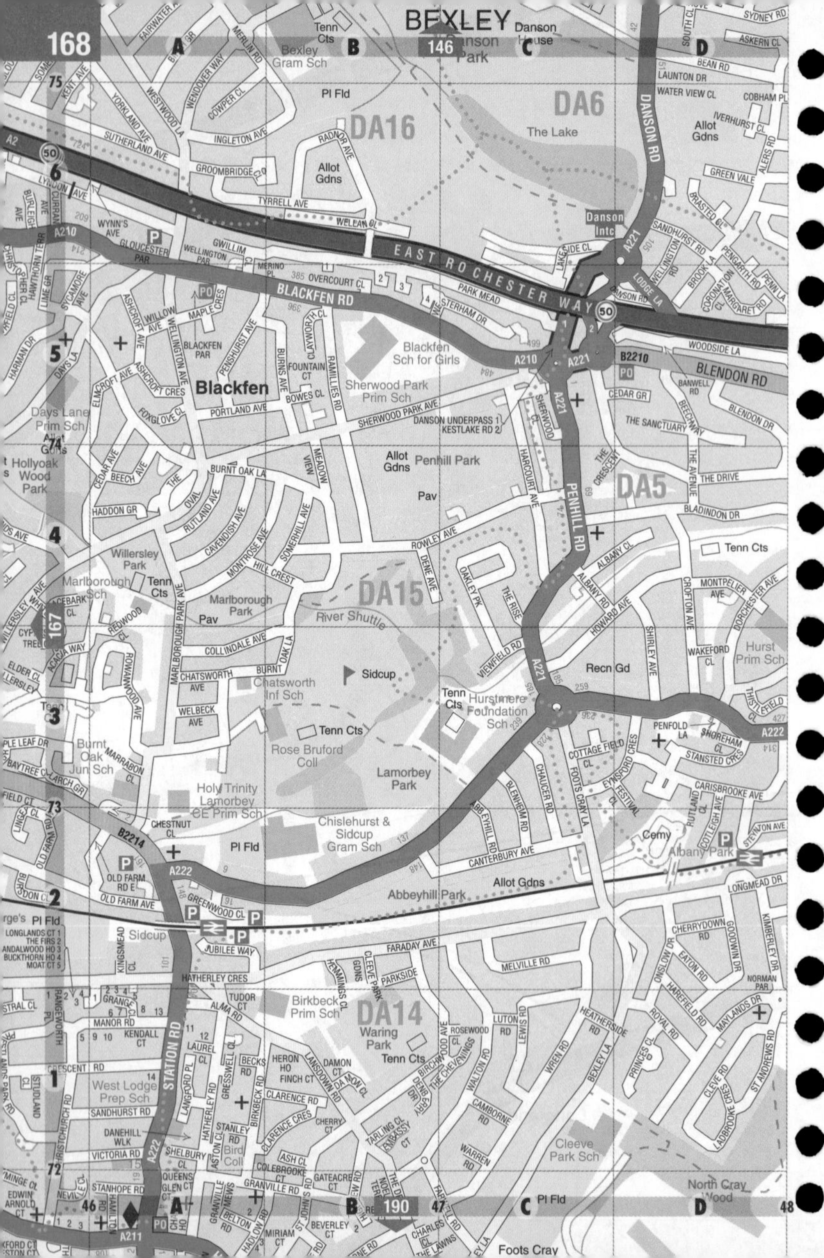
BEXLEY
146
Danson Park
Danson House
Bexley Gram Sch
Tenn Cts
Pl Fld
DA16
DA6
The Lake
Allot Gdns
DANSON RD
Danson Intc
EAST ROCHESTER WAY
BLACKFEN RD
A210
A221
B2210
BLENDON RD
Blackfen
Blackfen Sch for Girls
Sherwood Park Prim Sch
Days Lane Prim Sch
Hollyoak Wood Park
Allot Gdns
Penhill Park
Pav
DA5
PENHILL RD
DANSON UNDERPASS 1
KESTLAKE RD 2
Willersley Park
Marlborough Sch
Tenn Cts
Marlborough Park
Pav
DA15
River Shuttle
167
Sidcup
Chatsworth Inf Sch
Tenn Cts
Hurstmere Foundation Sch
Recn Gd
Hurst Prim Sch
Tenn Cts
Rose Bruford Coll
Lamorbey Park
Burnt Oak Jun Sch
Holy Trinity Lamorbey CE Prim Sch
Chislehurst & Sidcup Gram Sch
Pl Fld
B2214
A222
Cemy
Albany Park
Allot Gdns
Abbeyhill Park
Sidcup
Pl Fld
LONGLANDS CT 1
THE FIRS 2
ANDALWOOD HO 3
BUCKTHORN HO 4
MOAT CT 5
DA14
Birkbeck Prim Sch
Waring Park
Tenn Cts
STATION RD
West Lodge Prep Sch
Bird Coll
Cleeve Park Sch
North Cray Wood
190
Pl Fld
Foots Cray
A211
46
47
48
A
B
C
D
1
2
3
4
5
6
72
73
74
75

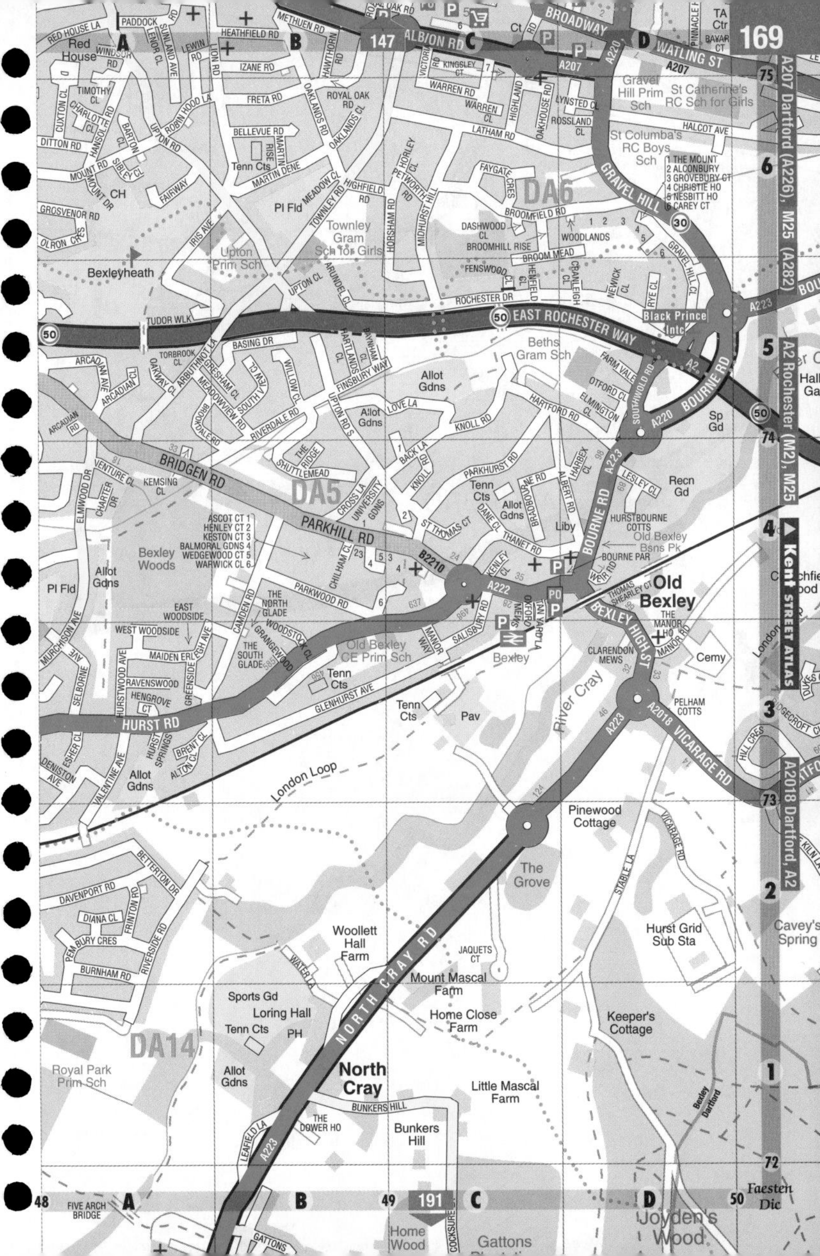

147
191
A
B
C
D
48
49
50
75
74
73
72
6
5
4
3
2
1
A207 Dartford (A226), M25 (A282)
A2 Rochester (M2), M25
A2018 Dartford, A2
Kent STREET ATLAS
DA6
DA5
DA14
BROADWAY
WATLING ST
ALBION RD
A207
A220
A223
A222
A2018
B2210
A2
EAST ROCHESTER WAY
GRAVEL HILL
BOURNE RD
BRIDGEN RD
PARKHILL RD
HURST RD
NORTH CRAY RD
VICARAGE RD
BEXLEY HIGH ST
RED HOUSE LA
Red House
PADDOCK
HEATHFIELD RD
METHUEN RD
HAWTHORN
IZANE RD
FRETA RD
ROYAL OAK RD
OAKLANDS RD
OAKLANDS CL
BELLEVUE RD
MARTIN RISE
MARTIN DENE
Tenn Cts
TIMOTHY CL
CHARLOTTE CL
CUXTON CL
HANSOL RD
DITTON RD
MOUNT RD
MOUNT DR
BARTON CL
SIBLEY CL
UPTON RD
ROBIN HOOD LA
FAIRWAY
CH
GROSVENOR RD
OLRON CRES
Bexleyheath
Upton Prim Sch
IRIS AVE
Pl Fld
MEADOW CL
TOWNLEY RD
HIGHFIELD RD
Townley Gram Sch for Girls
HORSHAM RD
HORLEY CL
PETWORTH RD
MIDHURST HILL
UPTON CL
ARUNDEL CL
VICTORIA
KINGSLEY CT
WARREN RD
WARREN CL
HIGHLAND
OAKHOUSE RD
LYNSTED CL
ROSSLAND CL
LATHAM RD
FAYGATE CRES
BROOMFIELD RD
DASHWOOD CL
BROOMHILL RISE
WOODLANDS
BROOM MEAD
FENSWOOD CL
HENFIELD CL
CRANLEIGH CL
NEWICK CL
RYE CL
GRAVEL HILL CL
ROCHESTER DR
Gravel Hill Prim Sch
St Catherine's RC Sch for Girls
HALCOT AVE
St Columba's RC Boys Sch
1 THE MOUNT
2 ALCONBURY
3 GROVEBURY CT
4 CHRISTIE HO
5 NESBITT HO
6 CAREY CT
Black Prince Intc
TUDOR WLK
TORBROOK CL
BASING DR
HARTLANDS CL
BAYNHAM CL
FINSBURY WAY
Beths Gram Sch
FARM VALE
OTFORD CL
ELMINGTON CL
SOUTHWOLD RD
HARTFORD RD
Hall
Sp Gd
ARCADIAN AVE
ARCADIAN CL
ARCADIAN RD
OAKWAY CL
ARBUTHNOT LA
GRESHAM CL
SOUTH VIEW CL
MEADOWVIEW RD
BROOKDALE RD
WILLOW CL
RIVERDALE RD
UPTON RD S
Allot Gdns
LOVE LA
KNOLL RD
BACK LA
THE RIDGE
SHUTTLEMEAD
PARKHURST RD
BRADBOURNE RD
ALBERT RD
HARBEX CL
LESLEY CL
Recn Gd
VENTURE CL
KEMSING CL
ELMWOOD DR
CHARTER DR
CROSS LA
UNIVERSITY GDNS
ST THOMAS CT
DANE CL
THANET RD
Liby
HURSTBOURNE COTTS
Old Bexley Bsns Pk
ASCOT CT 1
HENLEY CT 2
KESTON CT 3
BALMORAL GDNS 4
WEDGEWOOD CT 5
WARWICK CL 6
Bexley Woods
CHILHAM CL
KENLEY CL
BOURNE PAR
WEIR RD
THOMAS SHEARLEY CT
Old Bexley
THE MANOR HO
MANOR RD
PARKWOOD RD
THE NORTH GLADE
CAMDEN RD
EAST WOODSIDE
WEST WOODSIDE
MAIDEN ERLEGH AVE
WOODSTOCK CL
GRANGEWOOD
THE SOUTH GLADE
Old Bexley CE Prim Sch
MANOR WAY
SALISBURY RD
OXFORD MEWS
TAN YARD LA
Bexley
PO
CLARENDON MEWS
Cemy
MURCHISON AVE
SELBORNE AVE
HURSTWOOD AVE
RAVENSWOOD
HENGROVE CT
GREENSIDE
GLENHURST AVE
Pav
River Cray
PELHAM COTTS
RIDGECROFT CL
HILL CRES
ESHER CL
DENISTON AVE
VALENTINE AVE
HURST SPRINGS
BRENT CL
ALTON CL
London Loop
Pinewood Cottage
VICARAGE RD
BETTERTON DR
DAVENPORT RD
FRINTON RD
DIANA CL
RIVERSIDE RD
PEMBURY CRES
BURNHAM RD
The Grove
STABLE LA
Hurst Grid Sub Sta
Cavey's Spring
Woollett Hall Farm
JAQUETS CT
WATER LA
Mount Mascal Farm
Sports Gd
Loring Hall
PH
Home Close Farm
Keeper's Cottage
Royal Park Prim Sch
North Cray
Little Mascal Farm
Bexley
Dartford
BUNKERS HILL
THE DOWER HO
Bunkers Hill
LEAFIELD LA
FIVE ARCH BRIDGE
Home Wood
COCKSURE LA
GATTONS
Gattons
Joyden's Wood
Faesten Dic

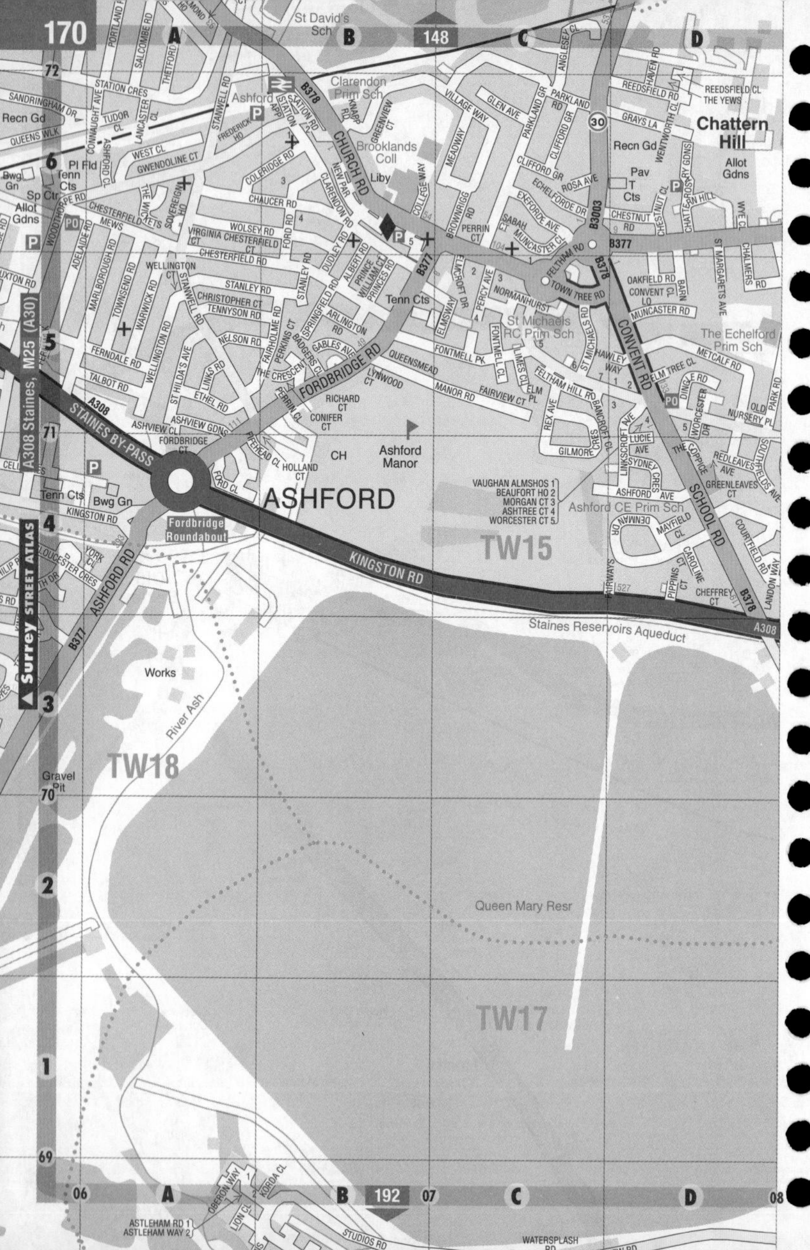

170
148
192
A
B
C
D
72
71
70
69
6
5
4
3
2
1
06
07
08
Surrey STREET ATLAS
A308 Staines, M25 (A30)
ASHFORD
TW15
TW18
TW17
Ashford
St David's Sch
Clarendon Prim Sch
Brooklands Coll
Liby
Chattern Hill
Recn Gd
Pav
T
Cts
Allot Gdns
Tenn Cts
Pl Fld
Bwg Gn
Sp Ctr
PO
St Michaels RC Prim Sch
The Echelford Prim Sch
Ashford Manor
CH
Ashford CE Prim Sch
Fordbridge Roundabout
Works
River Ash
Gravel Pit
Staines Reservoirs Aqueduct
Queen Mary Resr
STATION CRES
SANDRINGHAM DR
QUEENS WLK
CONNAUGHT AVE
TUDOR CL
ASHFORD CL
LANCASTER CL
THETFORD
SALCOMBE RD
PORTLAND RD
STANWELL RD
FREDERICK HO
WEST CL
GWENDOLINE CT
STATION APP
STATION RD
B378
CHURCH RD
KNAPP RD
GREENVIEW CT
COLERIDGE RD
NEW PAR
CLARENDON RD
CHAUCER RD
WOLSEY RD
VIRGINIA CT
CHESTERFIELD CT
CHESTERFIELD RD
CHESTERFIELD MEWS
WOODTHORPE RD
ADELAIDE RD
MARLBOROUGH RD
TOWNSEND RD
WARWICK RD
THE WICKETS
SOVEREIGN HO
FORD RD
DUDLEY RD
ALBERT RD
PRINCE WILLIAM CL
PRINCES RD
WELLINGTON CT
WELLINGTON RD
STANLEY RD
CHRISTOPHER CT
TENNYSON RD
NELSON RD
SPRINGFIELD RD
ARLINGTON RD
FAIRHOLME RD
PERKINS CT
BADGERS CL
GABLES AVE
THE CRESCENT
FORDBRIDGE RD
B377
COLLEGE WAY
MEADWAY
VILLAGE WAY
GLEN AVE
BROWNRIGG RD
PERRIN CT
ELMCROFT DR
ELMSWAY
PERCY AVE
NORMANHURST
FONTMELL PK
FONTMELL CL
LIMES CL
ELM PL
QUEENSMEAD
LYNWOOD CT
MANOR RD
FAIRVIEW CT
RICHARD CT
CONIFER CT
PERRIN CL
HOLLAND CT
FIREHEAD CL
FORD CL
ANGLESEY CL
PARKLAND GR
PARKLAND RD
CLIFFORD GR
CLIFFORD GR
ROSA AVE
ECHELFORDE DR
EXEFORDE AVE
SABAH CT
MUNCASTER CL
FELTHAM RD
TOWN TREE RD
B3003
B377
30
ST MICHAELS RD
HAWLEY WAY
FELTHAM HILL RD
REX AVE
GILMORE CRES
BANCROFT CL
LINKSCROFT AVE
LUCIE AVE
SYDNEY CRES
ASHFORD AVE
CONVENT RD
SCHOOL RD
OAKFIELD RD
CONVENT LO
BARN CL
MUNCASTER RD
REEDSFIELD RD
REEDSFIELD CL
THE YEWS
HAVEN RD
GRAYS LA
WENTWORTH CL
ROSARY GDNS
CHESTNUT RD
CHESTNUT CL
ST MARGARETS AVE
CHALMERS RD
WYE CL
METCALF RD
ELM TREE CL
DINGLE RD
WORCESTER DR
PARK RD
OLD NURSERY PL
THE COPPICE
REDLEAVES AVE
GREENLEAVES CT
SOUTHFIELDS AVE
DENMAN DR
MAYFIELD CL
CAROLINE CT
PIPPINS CT
CHEFFREY CT
COURTFIELD RD
LANDON WAY
FAIRWAYS
VAUGHAN ALMSHOS 1
BEAUFORT HO 2
MORGAN CT 3
ASHTREE CT 4
WORCESTER CT 5
A308
STAINES BY-PASS
ASHVIEW CL
ASHVIEW GDNS
FORDBRIDGE CT
ST HILDA'S AVE
LINKS RD
ETHEL RD
FERNDALE RD
TALBOT RD
KINGSTON RD
ASHFORD RD
B377
YORK CL
GLOUCESTER CRES
KINGSTON RD
OBERON WAY
KORDA CL
LION CL
STUDIOS RD
ASTLEHAM RD 1
ASTLEHAM WAY 2
WATERSPLASH RD

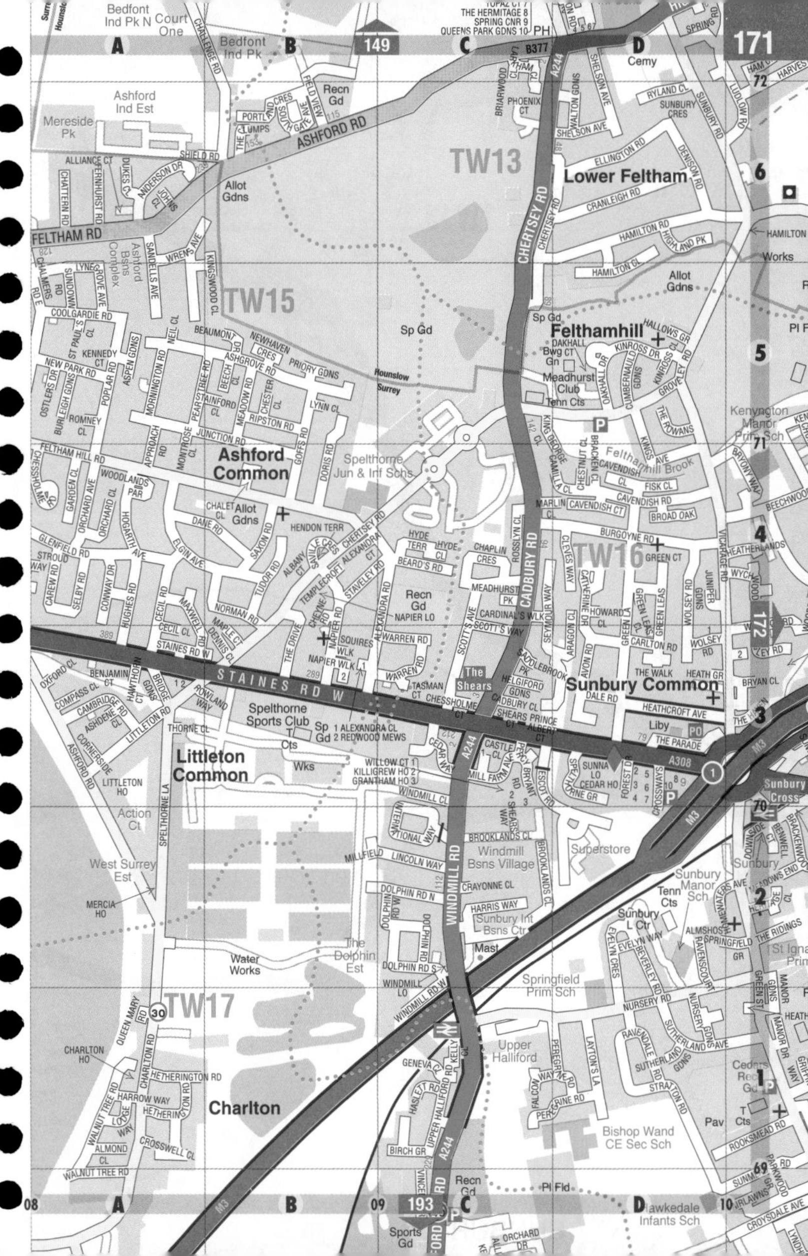

A
B
C
D
149
193
172
08
09
10
72
71
70
69
6
5
4
3
2
1
Bedfont Ind Pk N
Court One
Bedfont Ind Pk
CHALLENGE RD
TOPAZ CT 7
THE HERMITAGE 8
SPRING CNR 9
QUEENS PARK GDNS 10
PH
B377
A244
Cemy
SPRING RD
HAM CT
HARVEST
Recn Gd
FIELD VIEW
SOUTH GATE AVE
PORTLAND CRES
THE CLUMPS
Ashford Ind Est
Mereside Pk
ASHFORD RD
SHIELD RD
ALLIANCE CT
DUKES CL
FERNHURST RD
CHATTERN RD
ANDERSON DR
JOHNS CL
Allot Gdns
FELTHAM RD
LAKHAM CL
BRIARWOOD
PHOENIX CT
WALTON GDNS
SHELSON AVE
SUNBURY RD
RYLAND CL
SUNBURY CRES
LUDLOW RD
TW13
ELLINGTON RD
DENISON RD
Lower Feltham
CHERTSEY RD
CRANLEIGH RD
HAMILTON RD
HIGHLAND PK
HAMILTON CL
HAMILTON PA
Works
Allot Gdns
Sp Gd
Pl Fld
Felthamhill
HALLOWS GR
DAKHALL CT
Bwg Gn
KINROSS DR
KINROSS CL
CUMBERNAULD GDNS
OAKHALL DR
GROVELEY RD
Meadhurst Club
Tenn Cts
THE ROWANS
Kenyngton Manor Prim Sch
KING GEORGE CL
BRACKEN CL
CHESTNUT CL
CAMILLA CL
Felthamhill Brook
CAVENDISH CL
FISK CL
CAVENDISH RD
KINGS AVE
BRYONY WAY
MARLIN CL
CAVENDISH CT
BROAD OAK
BEECHWOOD
BURGOYNE RD
GREEN CT
VICARAGE RD
HEATHERLANDS
TW16
CLEVES WAY
CATHERINE DR
JUNIPER
WYCH WOOD
Ashford Bsns Complex
SANDELLS AVE
WRENS AVE
KINGSWOOD CL
TW15
LYNE GROVE AVE
SUNDOWN RD
CHALMERS RD E
COOLGARDIE RD
ST PAUL'S CL
KENNEDY CT
NEIL CL
BEAUMONT DR
NEWHAVEN CRES
PRIORY GDNS
Sp Gd
NEW PARK RD
ASPEN GDNS
MORNINGTON RD
ASHGROVE RD
BEECH CL
CHESTER CL
Hounslow
Surrey
OSTLERS DR
BURLEIGH GDNS
POPLAR RD
ROMNEY CL
PEARTREE RD
STAINFORD CL
MEADOW RD
RIPSTON RD
LYNN CL
JUNCTION RD
APPROACH RD
MONTROSE CL
FELTHAM HILL RD
GOFFS RD
DORIS RD
Ashford Common
Spelthorne Jun & Inf Schs
CHESSHOLME RD
GARDEN CL
ORCHARD AVE
WOODLANDS PAR
WOODLANDS CL
HOGARTH AVE
CHALET CL
Allot Gdns
HENDON TERR
DANE RD
SAXON RD
CHERTSEY RD
GLENFIELD RD
STROUD WAY
CAREW RD
SELBY RD
CONWAY DR
HUGHES RD
ELGIN AVE
TUDOR RD
ALBANY CT
SAVILE CRES
ALEXANDRA CT
TEMPLECROFT
HYDE TERR
HYDE CL
BEARD'S RD
CHAPLIN CRES
ROSSLYN CL
CADBURY RD
MEADHURST PK
Recn Gd
NAPIER LO
ALEXANDRA RD
STAVELEY RD
SCOTT'S AVE
SEYMOUR WAY
CARDINAL'S WLK
SCOTT'S WAY
ARAGON CL
HOWARD CL
GREEN LA CL
GREEN LEAS
WOLSEY RD
CECIL RD
MAXWELL RD
MAPLE CT
NORMAN RD
CHEYNE RD
NAPIER RD
THE DRIVE
SQUIRES WLK
WARREN RD
SADDLEBROOK PK
AVON RD
CARLTON RD
WOLSEY RD
CECIL CL
DENNIS CL
NAPIER WLK
WARREN CT
HELGIFORD GDNS
THE WALK
HEATH GR
BRYAN CL
STAINES RD W
The Shears
TASMAN CT
CHESSHOLME CT
Sunbury Common
DALE RD
HEATHCROFT AVE
OXFORD CL
BENJAMIN CT
HAWTHORN CT
BRIDGE GDNS
ROWLAND WAY
COMPASS CL
CAMBRIDGE RD
ASHDENE CL
LITTLETON RD
THORNE CL
Spelthorne Sports Club
Sp Gd
1 ALEXANDRA CL
2 REDWOOD MEWS
CADBURY CL
SHEARS CT
PRINCE ALBERT CT
Liby
PO
THE PARADE
A308
CORNERSIDE
ASHFORD RD
Littleton Common
T Cts
Wks
CEDAR WAY
CASTLE CL
PERCY AVE
BRYANT
MILL FARM AVE
ESCOT RD
SPELTHORNE GR
SUNNA LO
CEDAR HO
FOREST DR
CROSSWAYS
M3
Sunbury Cross
LITTLETON HO
WILLOW CT 1
KILLIGREW HO 2
GRANTHAM HO 3
Action Ct
WINDMILL CL
INTERNATIONAL WAY
SHEARS WAY
BROOKLANDS CL
Superstore
DOWNSIDE
BENWELL
BRACKENWOOD
West Surrey Est
SPELTHORNE LA
MILLFIELD
LINCOLN WAY
Windmill Bsns Village
BROOKLANDS RD
Sunbury
MEADOWS END
Sunbury Manor Sch
HOMEWATERS AVE
MERCIA HO
DOLPHIN RD N
CRAYONNE CL
Tenn Cts
HARRIS WAY
Sunbury Int Bsns Ctr
Sunbury L Ctr
EVELYN WAY
EVELYN CRES
BEVERLEY RD
ALMSHOUSES
SPRINGFIELD GR
THE RIDINGS
St Ignat Prim
WINDMILL RD
DOLPHIN RD W
DOLPHIN RD
The Dolphin Est
Mast
RAVENSCOURT
Water Works
DOLPHIN RD S
WINDMILL LO
WINDMILL RD W
Springfield Prim Sch
GREEN ST
MANOR GDNS
TW17
30
QUEEN MARY RD
NURSERY RD
NURSERY GDNS
SUTHERLAND AVE
HEATHL
MANOR RD
CHARLTON HO
CHARLTON RD
GENEVA CL
KELLY CL
Upper Halliford
PEREGRINE RD
FALCON WAY
LAYTON'S LA
RAVENDALE RD
SUTHERLAND GDNS
STRATTON RD
Cedars Recn Gd
GRIFFIN WAY
HETHERINGTON RD
HARROW WAY
HETHERINGTON RD
LOUISE WAY
Charlton
HASLETT RD
UPPER HALLIFORD RD
PEREGRINE RD
Bishop Wand CE Sec Sch
Pav
T Cts
ROOKSMEAD RD
WALNUT TREE RD
ALMOND CL
CROSSWELL CL
BIRCH GR
PARKWOOD
WALNUT TREE RD
VINCENT RD
Recn Gd
Pl Fld
Hawkedale Infants Sch
CROYSDALE AVE
Sports Gd
ORCHARD
P

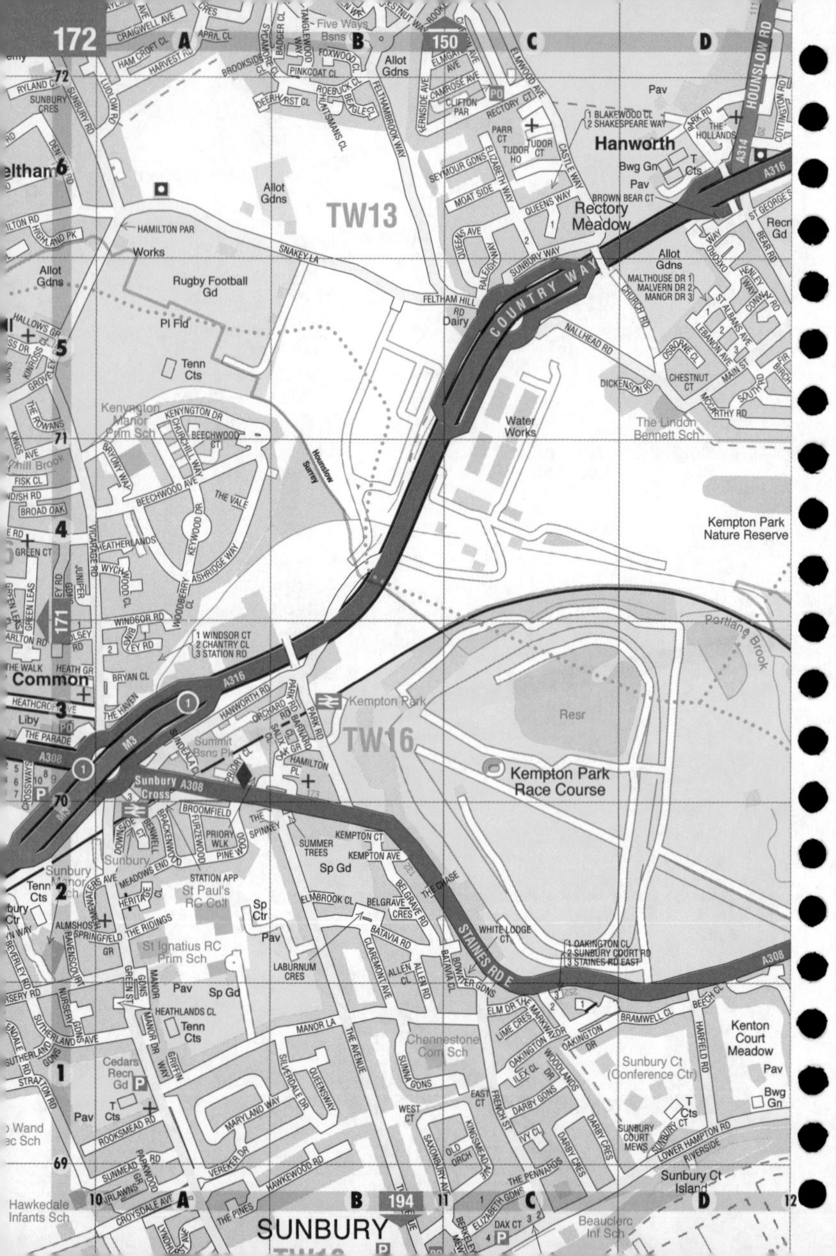

A
B
C
D
150
194
171
Hanworth
Rectory Meadow
TW13
TW16
Kempton Park
Kempton Park Race Course
Kempton Park Nature Reserve
Water Works
Resr
Portlane Brook
COUNTRY WAY
STAINES RD E
A316
A308
A314
M3
HOUNSLOW RD
Sunbury Cross
SUNBURY
Common
Feltham
Rugby Football Gd
Pl Fld
Allot Gdns
Tenn Cts
Works
Dairy
Kenyngton Manor Prim Sch
The Lindon Bennett Sch
Summit Bsns Pk
St Paul's RC Coll
St Ignatius RC Prim Sch
Chennestone Com Sch
Sunbury Ct (Conference Ctr)
Kenton Court Meadow
Sunbury Ct Island
Cedars Recn Gd
Hawkedale Infants Sch
Beauclerc Inf Sch
Five Ways Bsns Pk
SNAKEY LA
FELTHAM HILL RD
HAMILTON PAR
SUNBURY WAY
QUEENS WAY
NALLHEAD RD
DICKENSON RD
CHURCH RD
MANOR LA
THE AVENUE
LOWER HAMPTON RD
RIVERSIDE
HANWORTH RD
VICARAGE RD
BEECHWOOD AVE
KENYNGTON DR
ASHRIDGE WAY
THE VALE
KEYWOOD DR
1 BLAKEWOOD CL
2 SHAKESPEARE WAY
MALTHOUSE DR 1
MALVERN DR 2
MANOR DR 3
1 WINDSOR CT
2 CHANTRY CL
3 STATION RD
1 OAKINGTON CL
2 SUNBURY COURT RD
3 STAINES RD EAST

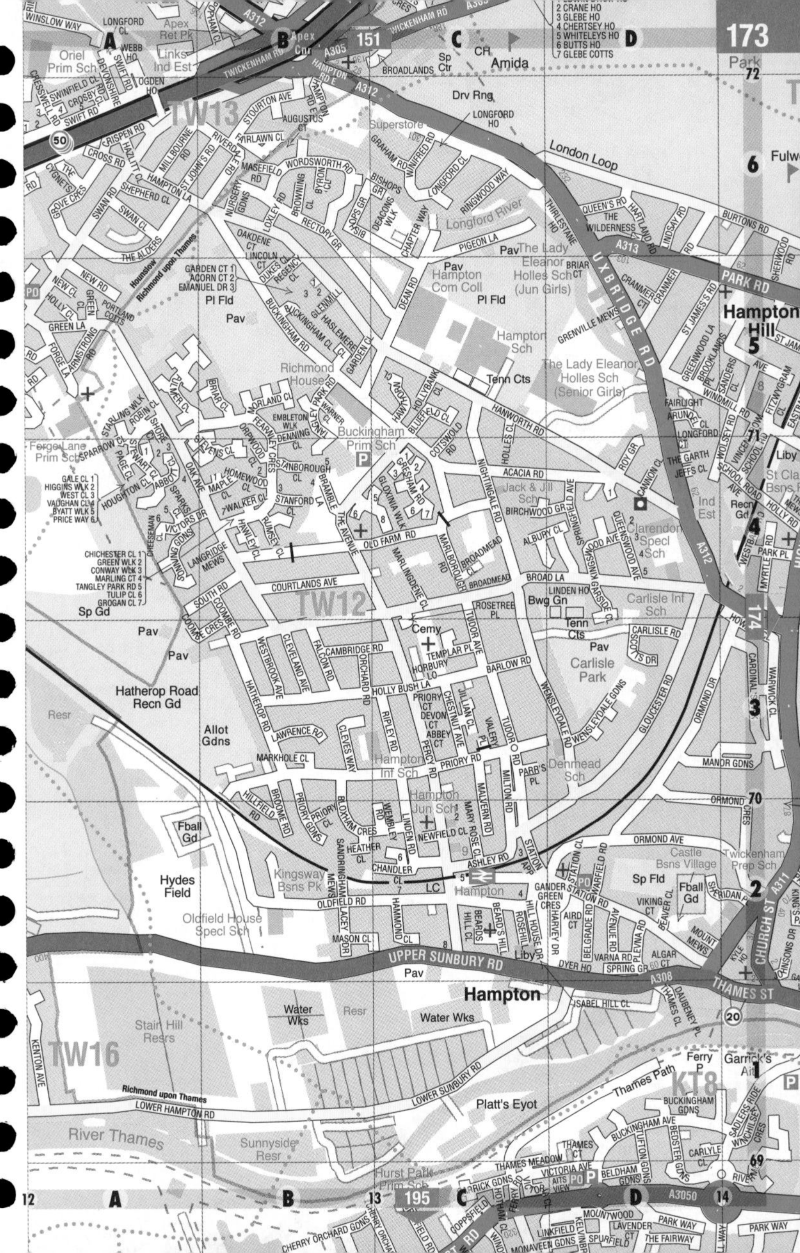

A
B
C
D
151
2 CRANE HO
3 GLEBE HO
4 CHERTSEY HO
5 WHITELEYS HO
6 BUTTS HO
7 GLEBE COTTS
WINSLOW WAY
LONGFORD CL
Apex Ret Pk
Apex Cnr
A312
TWICKENHAM RD
Sp Ctr
Amida
Oriel Prim Sch
WEBB HO
Links Ind Est
OGDEN HO
HAMPTON RD E
A305
BROADLANDS
Drv Rng
TW13
STOURTON AVE
AUGUSTUS CT
LONGFORD HO
Superstore
FAIRLAWN CL
CRISPEN RD
CROSS RD
MILLBOURNE RD
ST JOHN'S RD
HAMPTON LA
SHEPHERD CL
SWAN RD
SWAN CL
THE ALDERS
MASEFIELD RD
WORDSWORTH RD
BROWNING CL
BYRON CL
RECTORY GR
GRAHAM RD
WINIFRED RD
BISHOPS GR
DEACONS WLK
CHAPTER WAY
LONGFORD CL
RINGWOOD WAY
Longford River
PIGEON LA
London Loop
QUEEN'S RD
THE WILDERNESS
HARTLAND RD
LINDSAY RD
BURTONS RD
A313
THIRLESTANE HO
Fulwe
OAKDENE CT
LINCOLN CT
DUKES CT
REGENCY CT
GARDEN CT 1
ACORN CT 2
EMANUEL DR 3
Hounslow
Richmond upon Thames
Pl Fld
Pav
BUCKINGHAM RD
GLENMILL
HASLEMERE CL
BUCKINGHAM CL
GARDEN CL
DEAN RD
Pav
Hampton Com Coll
The Lady Eleanor Holles Sch (Jun Girls)
BRIAR CT
Pl Fld
UXBRIDGE RD
CRANMER CT
PARK RD
Hampton Hill
NEW RD
NEW CL
HOLLY CL
GREEN LA
PORTLAND COTTS
FORGE LA
ARMSTRONG RD
Richmond House
Hampton Sch
GRENVILLE MEWS
ST JAMES'S RD
GREENWOOD LA
BROOKLANDS PL
SANDERS CL
FITZWYGRAM CL
WINDMILL RD
Tenn Cts
The Lady Eleanor Holles Sch (Senior Girls)
FAIRLIGHT
ARUNDEL CL
LONGFORD CT
THE GARTH
JEFFS CL
WOLSEY RD
SCHOOL RD
HOLLY RD
Liby
St Clare Bsns Pk
Recn Gd
Ind Est
MORLAND CL
BRIAR CL
FILMER CL
EMBLETON WLK
DENNING CL
STARLING WLK
ROBIN CL
SPARROW CL
STEWART CL
PAGE CL
ABBOTT CL
SHORE CL
STEVENS CL
Forge Lane Prim Sch
Buckingham Prim Sch
HAWTHORN CL
HOLLYBANK CL
BLUEFIELD CL
COTSWOLD RD
HANWORTH RD
HOLLES CL
NIGHTINGALE RD
ROY GR
GALE CL 1
HIGGINS WLK 2
WEST CL 3
VAUGHAN CL 4
BYATT WLK 5
PRICE WAY 6
HOUGHTON CL
OAK AVE
MAPLE CL
HOMEWOOD CL
WALKER CL
STANFORD CL
STANBOROUGH CL
BRAMBLE LA
GRESHAM RD
GLOXINIA WLK
ACACIA RD
Jack & Jill Sch
BIRCHWOOD GR
CANNON CL
Clarendon Specl Sch
A312
CHEESEMAN CL
VICTORS DR
SPARKS CL
HAWLEY CL
RUMSEY CL
THE AVENUE
OLD FARM RD
MARLINGDENE CL
MARLBOROUGH RD
BROADMEAD
ALBURY CL
SPRINGFIELD AVE
KINGSWOOD AVE
QUEENSWOOD AVE
CHICHESTER CL 1
GREEN WLK 2
CONWAY WLK 3
MARLING CT 4
TANGLEY PARK RD 5
TULIP CL 6
GROGAN CL 7
LANGRIDGE MEWS
COURTLANDS AVE
TW12
BROAD LA
LINDEN HO
GARSIDE CL
Carlisle Inf Sch
174
Sp Gd
SOUTH RD
COOMBE RD
COOMBE CRES
ROSETREE PL
Bwg Gn
Tenn Cts
Pav
CARLISLE RD
SCOTTS DR
Pav
Cemy
TEMPLAR PL
TUDOR AVE
Carlisle Park
CARDINAL'S WK
WARWICK CL
Pav
WESTBROOK AVE
CLEVELAND AVE
FALCON RD
CAMBRIDGE RD
ORCHARD RD
HORBURY LO
BARLOW RD
WENSLEYDALE RD
WENSLEYDALE GDNS
GLOUCESTER RD
ORMOND DR
Hatherop Road Recn Gd
HATHEROP RD
HOLLY BUSH LA
PRIORY CT
DEVON CT
ABBEY CT
CHESTNUT AVE
JILLIAN CL
VALERY PL
TUDOR RD
Resr
Allot Gdns
LAWRENCE RD
CLEVES WAY
RIPLEY RD
PERCY RD
MANOR GDNS
MARKHOLE CL
Hampton Inf Sch
PRIORY RD
MILTON RD
PARR'S PL
Denmead Sch
HILLFIELD RD
BROOME RD
PRIORY GDNS
PRIORY CL
BLOXHAM CRES
WEMBLEY RD
LINDEN RD
Hampton Jun Sch
MARY ROSE CL
MALVERN RD
ORMOND CRES
Fball Gd
NEWFIELD CL
ORMOND AVE
HEATHER CL
SANDRINGHAM MEWS
ASHLEY RD
STATION APP
STATION CL
FAIRFIELD RD
Castle Bsns Village
Twickenham Prep Sch
Hydes Field
Kingsway Bsns Pk
CHANDLER CL
LC
Hampton
GANDER GREEN CRES
STATION RD
Sp Fld
Fball Gd
SHERIDAN PL
CHURCH ST
A311
OLDFIELD RD
HAMMOND CL
BEARDS HILL CL
BEARD'S HILL
ROSEHILL
HILL HOUSE DR
HARVEY DR
AIRD CT
BELGRADE RD
AVENUE RD
PLEVNA RD
VIKING CT
BEAVER CL
MOUNT MEWS
Oldfield House Specl Sch
LACEY DR
MASON CL
UPPER SUNBURY RD
Liby
DYER HO
VARNA RD
SPRING GR
ALGAR CT
A308
THAMES ST
Pav
Hampton
ISABEL HILL CL
THAMES CL
DAUBENEY PL
Water Wks
Resr
Water Wks
20
Stain Hill Resrs
TW16
KENTON AVE
LOWER SUNBURY RD
Ferry
Garrick's Ait
Thames Path
KT8
Richmond upon Thames
LOWER HAMPTON RD
Platt's Eyot
BUCKINGHAM GDNS
BUCKINGHAM AVE
River Thames
Sunnyside Resr
THAMES CT
UFFTON GDNS
BEDSTER GDNS
CARLYLE CL
SADLERS RIDE
WINCHILSEY CRES
THAMES MEADOW
VICTORIA AVE
Hurst Park Prim Sch
AITS VIEW
BELDHAM GDNS
195
A3050
14
12
13
MOUNTWOOD
PARK WAY
LAVENDER CT
LINKFIELD
SPURFIELD
THE FAIRWAY
MONAVEEN GDNS
CHERRY ORCHARD GDNS

Strawberry Hill
Fulwell Park
TW2
Fulwell
Hampton Hill
TW11
TW12
National Physical Laboratory
Canal Plantation
Round Plantation
Bushy Park
Willow Plantation
Woodland Gdn
Deer Park
Broom Clumps
Diana Fountain
Bushy House
Bartons Cottage
KT8
Hampton Court House
Hurst Park
Taggs Island
River Thames
SIXTH CROSS RD
SOUTH RD
WELLINGTON RD
FULWELL RD
STANLEY RD
PARK RD
HAMPTON RD
BROAD ST
HIGH ST
CHURCH ST
THAMES ST
HAMPTON COURT RD
WALDEGRAVE RD
CHURCH RD
QUEEN'S RD
1 Hampton Hill Bsns Pk
2 EDWARD CL
3 RADCLIFF MEWS
4 GORDON CT
5 DEERHURST CRES
6 PARK VIEW HO
7 PARK GATE CT
8 Hampton Hill Jun Sch
1 THE CEDARS
2 WHITE HERON MEWS
3 QUEEN'S HO
4 THE LINK
5 BRAGG RD
6 ADMIRALTY RD
7 Teddington Bsns Pk
1 FALSTAFF MS
2 PARKSIDE
1 CUSACK CL
2 BRIDGE CL
ROYAL MEWS 1
ROTARY CT 2
PALACE GATE 3
152
173
196

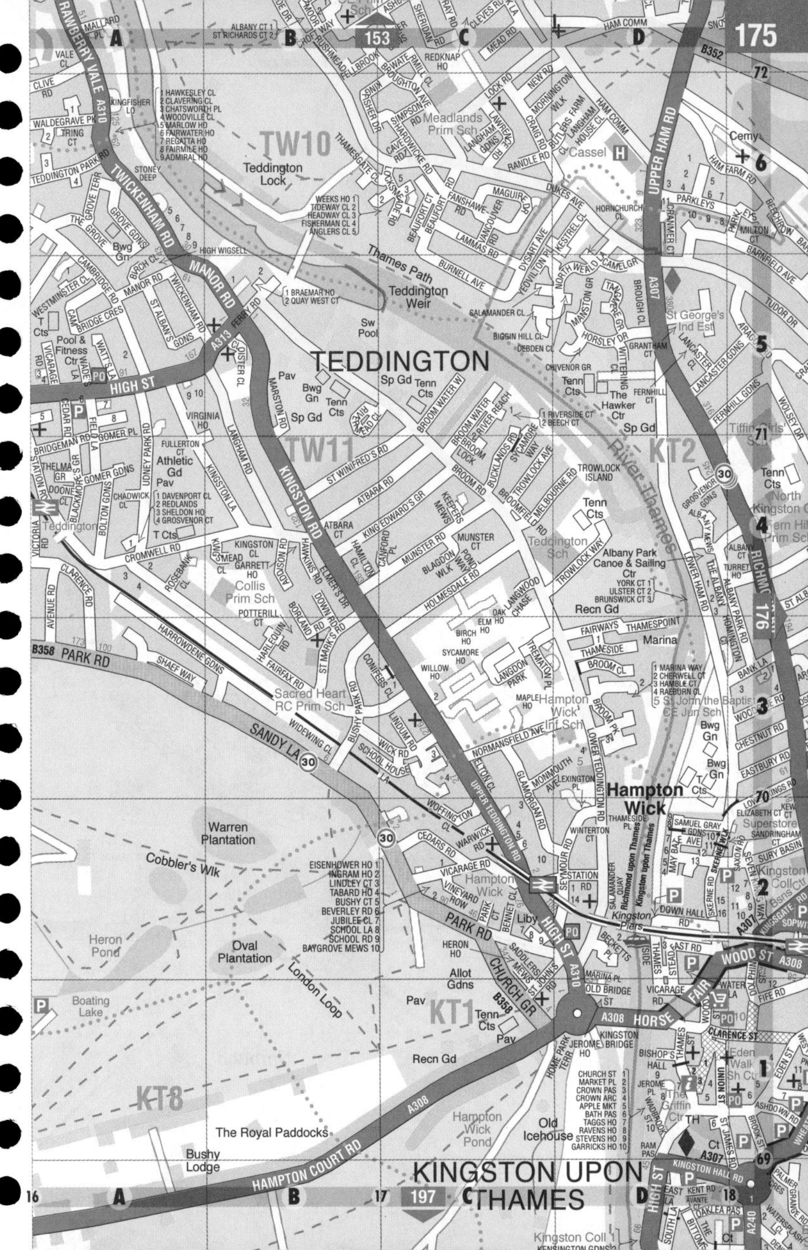
153
TEDDINGTON
TW10
TW11
KT2
KT1
KT8
Teddington Lock
Teddington Weir
Thames Path
River Thames
Meadlands Prim Sch
Cassel
UPPER HAM RD
TWICKENHAM RD
MANOR RD
HIGH ST
KINGSTON RD
FERRY RD
BROOM RD
BROOM WATER
BROOMFIELD RD
TROWLOCK AVE
TROWLOCK WAY
TROWLOCK ISLAND
MELBOURNE RD
St George's Ind Est
Tiffin Girls' Sch
North Kingston Ctr
Fern Hill Prim Sch
RICHMOND RD
Collis Prim Sch
Teddington Sch
Albany Park Canoe & Sailing Ctr
Recn Gd
Marina
St John the Baptist CE Jun Sch
Hampton Wick Inf Sch
Hampton Wick
Sacred Heart RC Prim Sch
PARK RD
SANDY LA
Warren Plantation
Cobbler's Wlk
Heron Pond
Oval Plantation
London Loop
Boating Lake
UPPER TEDDINGTON RD
LOWER TEDDINGTON RD
Kingston Piers
Kingston Bridge
HORSE FAIR
WOOD ST
CLARENCE ST
Eden Walk Sh Ctr
The Griffin Ctr
Kingston Coll Ctr
Superstore
The Royal Paddocks
Bushy Lodge
Hampton Wick Pond
Old Icehouse
HAMPTON COURT RD
KINGSTON UPON THAMES
197
176
Kingston Coll
Richmond upon Thames
Kingston upon Thames

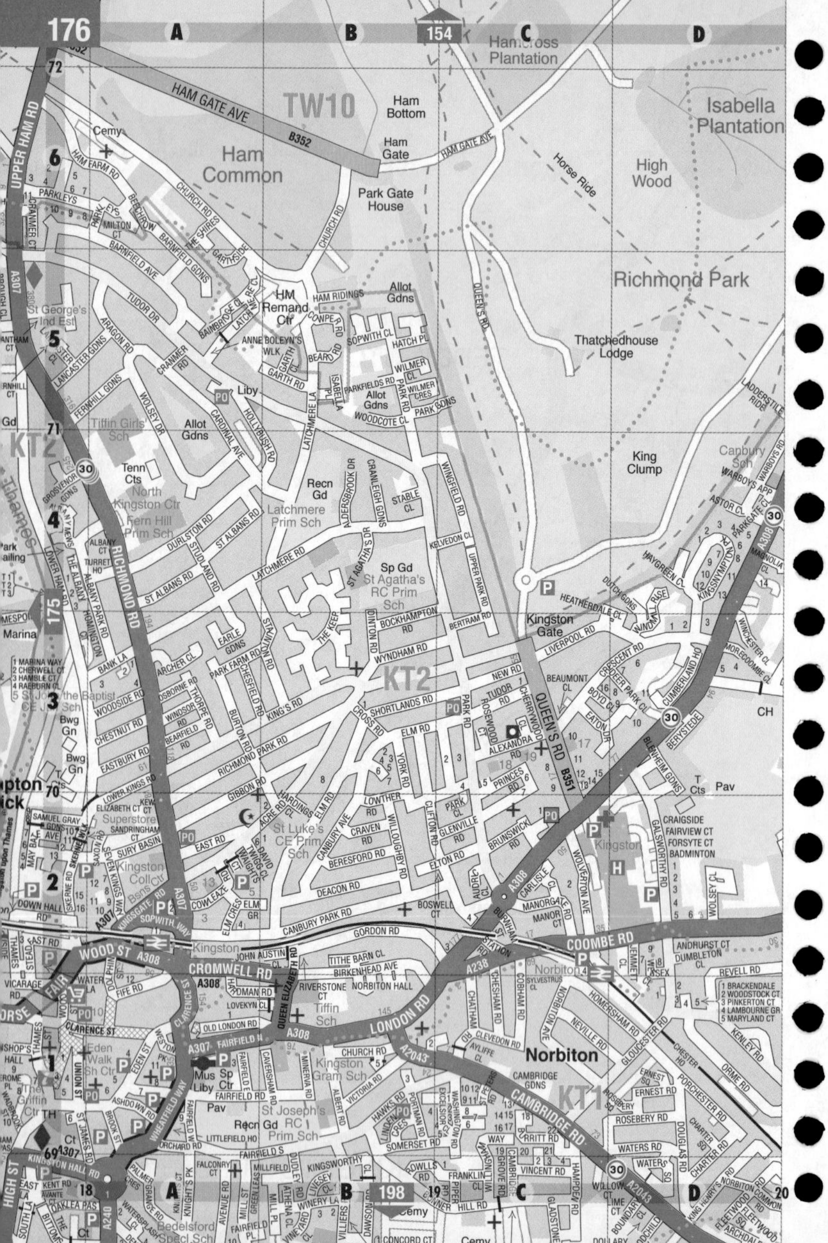
A
B
154
C
D
Hamcross Plantation
TW10
Ham Bottom
Isabella Plantation
HAM GATE AVE
B352
Ham Gate
Ham Common
High Wood
Horse Ride
Park Gate House
UPPER HAM RD
Richmond Park
HM Remand Ctr
Allot Gdns
St George's Ind Est
Thatchedhouse Lodge
QUEEN'S RD
Liby
Allot Gdns
Tiffin Girls' Sch
KT2
King Clump
Canbury Sch
Tenn Cts
North Kingston Ctr
Recn Gd
Latchmere Prim Sch
Fern Hill Prim Sch
RICHMOND RD
Sp Gd
St Agatha's RC Prim Sch
Kingston Gate
Marina
KT2
CH
Bwg Gn
St Luke's CE Prim Sch
Superstore
Kingston Coll
Kingston
COOMBE RD
CROMWELL RD
LONDON RD
Tiffin Sch
Norbiton
Eden Walk Sh Ctr
Kingston Gram Sch
Mus Liby
St Joseph's RC Prim Sch
Recn Gd
KT1
CAMBRIDGE RD
198
Cemy
Bedelsford Specl Sch
20

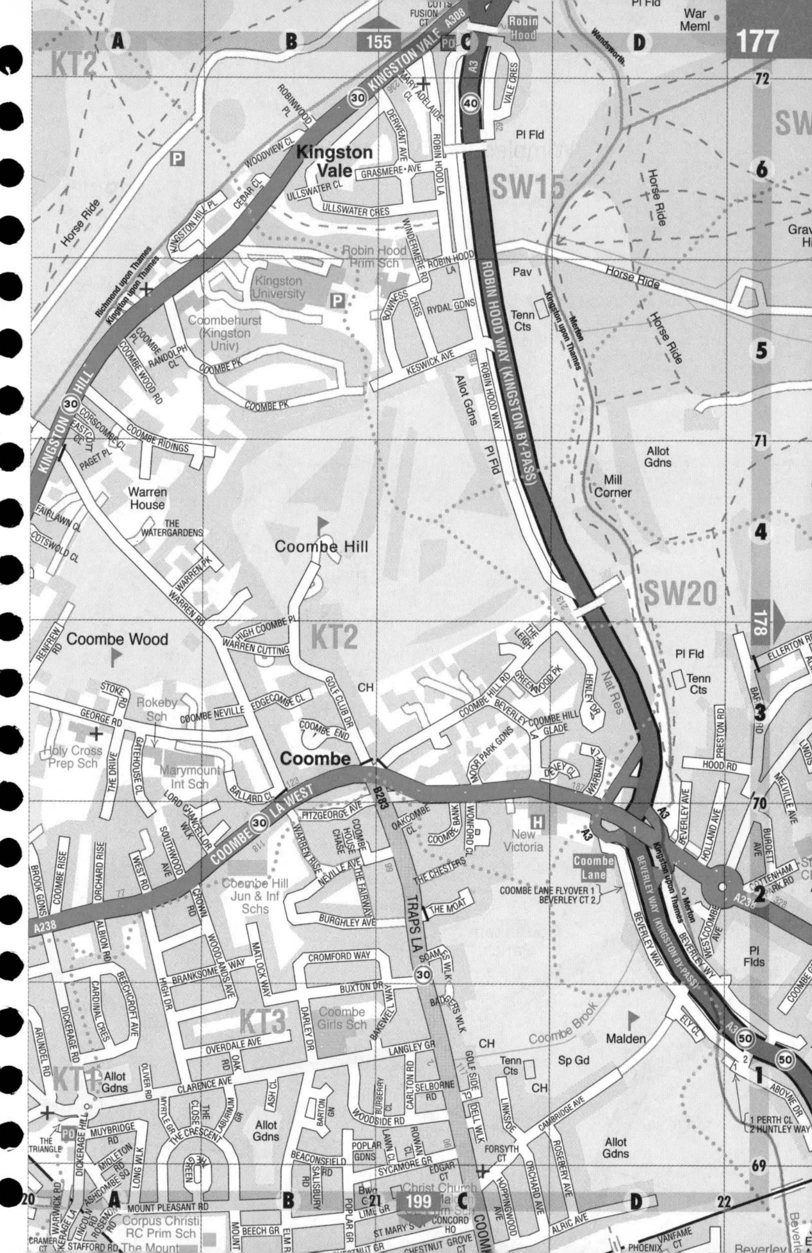
155
178
199
Kingston Vale
Coombe Hill
Coombe Wood
Coombe
Malden
Mill Corner
New Victoria
KT2
KT3
KT1
SW15
SW20
KINGSTON VALE
KINGSTON HILL
ROBIN HOOD WAY (KINGSTON BY-PASS)
COOMBE LA WEST
TRAPS LA
BEVERLEY WAY (KINGSTON BY-PASS)
Kingston University
Coombehurst (Kingston Univ)
Robin Hood Prim Sch
Rokeby Sch
Holy Cross Prep Sch
Marymount Int Sch
Coombe Hill Jun & Inf Schs
Coombe Girls Sch
Corpus Christi RC Prim Sch
Warren House
Horse Ride
Pl Fld
Allot Gdns
Tenn Cts
Pav
Coombe Lane
COOMBE LANE FLYOVER 1
BEVERLEY CT 2
1 PERTH CL
2 HUNTLEY WAY
Coombe Brook
Richmond upon Thames
Kingston upon Thames
Merton
Wandsworth

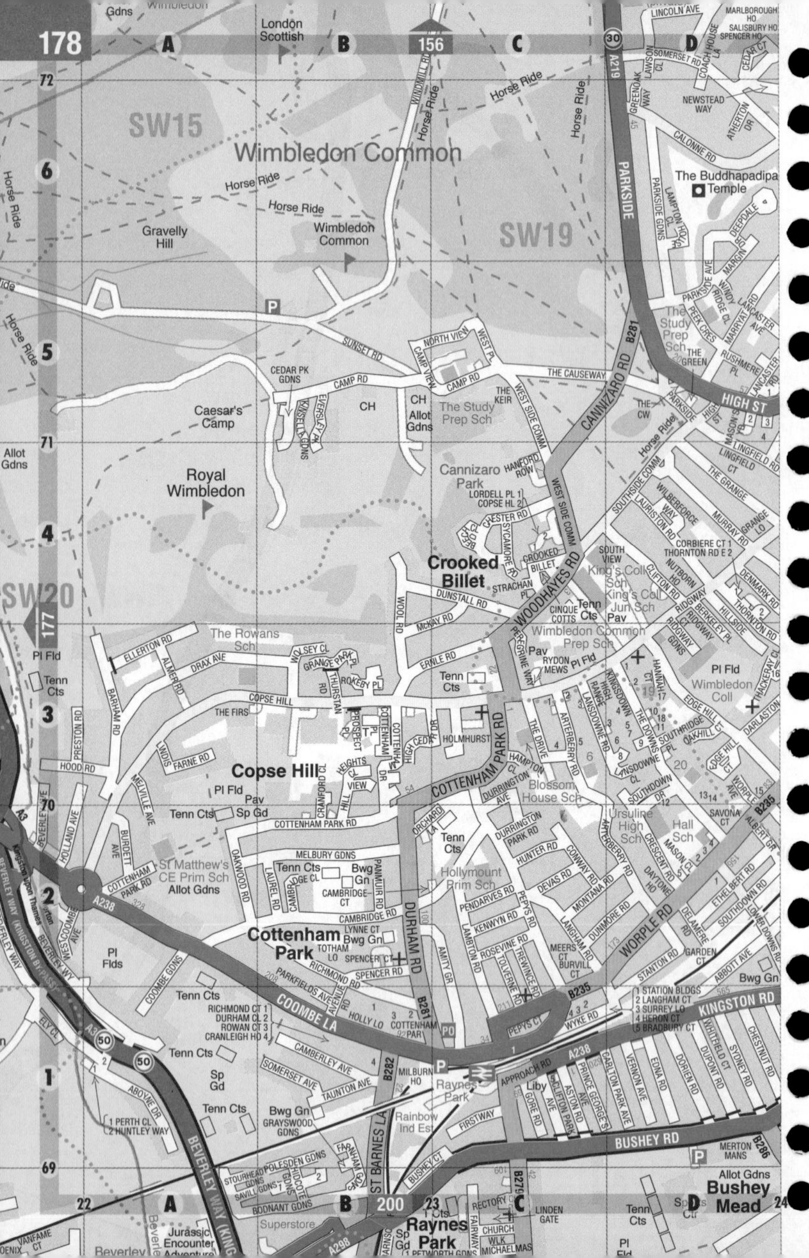
London Scottish
SW15
Wimbledon Common
Horse Ride
Gravelly Hill
Wimbledon Common
SW19
The Buddhapadipa Temple
PARKSIDE
LINCOLN AVE
SOMERSET RD
NEWSTEAD WAY
CALONNE RD
WINDMILL RD
SUNSET RD
CAMP RD
CEDAR PK GDNS
NORTH VIEW
CAMP VIEW
WEST PL
THE CAUSEWAY
CANNIZARO RD
HIGH ST
Caesar's Camp
CH
Allot Gdns
The Study Prep Sch
THE KEIR
WEST SIDE COMM
Royal Wimbledon
Cannizaro Park
HANFORD ROW
LORDELL PL
COPSE HL
CHESTER RD
SYCAMORE RD
Crooked Billet
WOODHAYES RD
SOUTHSIDE COMM
King's Coll Sch
King's Coll Jun Sch
Wimbledon Common Prep Sch
DUNSTALL RD
MCKAY RD
WOOL RD
ERNLE RD
SW20
The Rowans Sch
ELLERTON RD
DRAX AVE
WOLSEY CL
GRANGE PARK PL
ROKEBY PL
COPSE HILL
THE FIRS
PRESTON RD
BARHAM RD
HOOD RD
FARNE RD
Copse Hill
COTTENHAM PARK RD
HOLMHURST
THE DRIVE
ARTERBERRY RD
LANSDOWNE RD
THE DOWNS
SOUTHRIDGE PL
EDGE HILL
Pl Fld
Wimbledon Coll
Blossom House Sch
Ursuline High Sch
Hall Sch
DURRINGTON AVE
DURRINGTON PARK RD
HUNTER RD
CONWAY RD
Tenn Cts
Pl Fld
Pav
Sp Gd
St Matthew's CE Prim Sch
Allot Gdns
MELBURY GDNS
OAKWOOD RD
LAUREL RD
CAMBRIDGE CT
CAMBRIDGE RD
DURHAM RD
Hollymount Prim Sch
PENDARVES RD
KENWYN RD
ROSEVINE RD
DEVAS RD
MONTANA RD
DUNMORE RD
WORPLE RD
Cottenham Park
COOMBE LA
A238
A3
BEVERLEY WAY
Kingston upon Thames
RICHMOND RD
SPENCER RD
PARKFIELDS AVE
Pl Flds
COOMBE GDNS
PEPYS CT
WYKE RD
STATION BLDGS
KINGSTON RD
CAMBERLEY AVE
SOMERSET AVE
TAUNTON AVE
Raynes Park
Rainbow Ind Est
FIRSTWAY
APPROACH RD
GORE RD
ASTON RD
CARLTON PARK AVE
VERNON AVE
EDNA RD
DORIEN RD
DUPONT RD
SYDNEY RD
CHESTNUT RD
BUSHEY RD
MERTON MANS
ABOYNE DR
1 PERTH CL
2 HUNTLEY WAY
POLESDEN GDNS
STOURHEAD GDNS
SAVILL GDNS
BODNANT GDNS
ST BARNES LA
Superstore
Jurassic Encounter Adventure
Raynes Park
RECTORY
LINDEN GATE
Allot Gdns
Bushey Mead
Tenn Cts

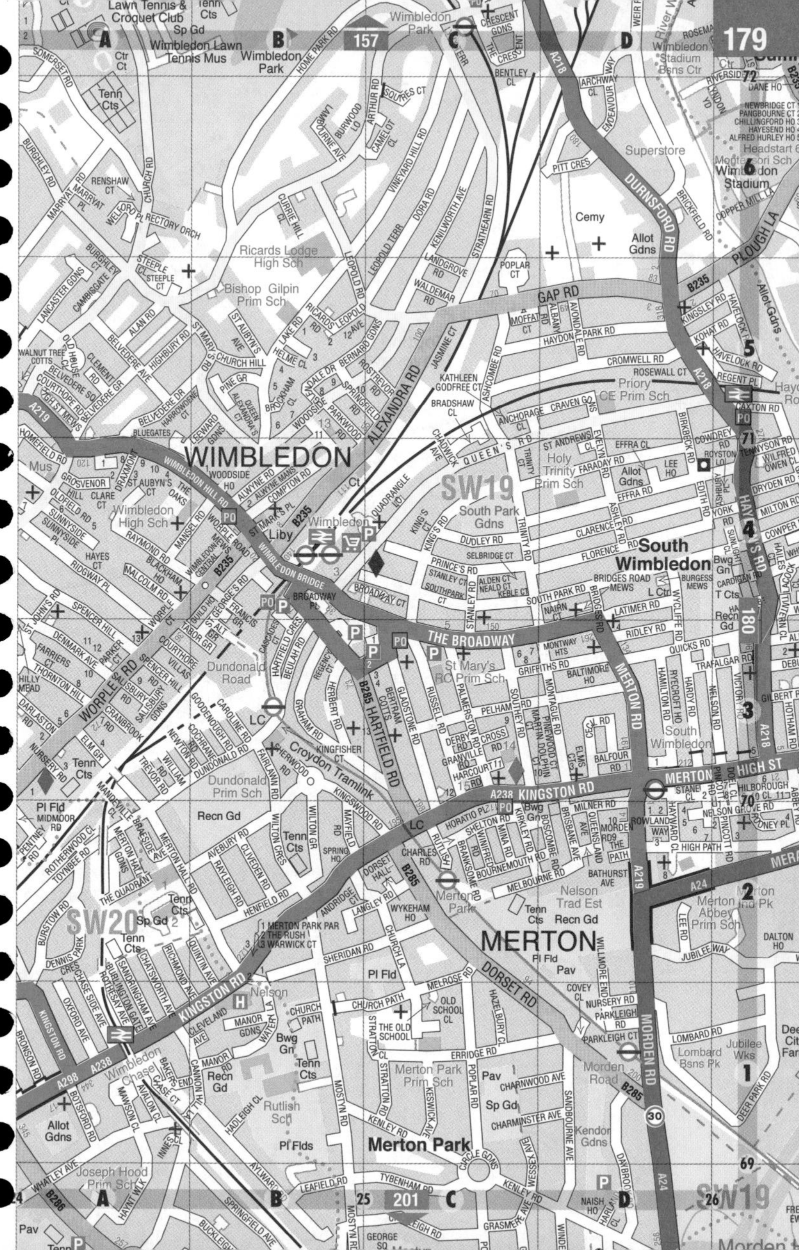
WIMBLEDON
SW19
South Wimbledon
MERTON
SW20
Merton Park
Wimbledon Park
Wimbledon Lawn Tennis Mus
Lawn Tennis & Croquet Club
Wimbledon Stadium
Ricards Lodge High Sch
Bishop Gilpin Prim Sch
Wimbledon High Sch
Dundonald Road
Dundonald Prim Sch
Croydon Tramlink
South Park Gdns
Holy Trinity Prim Sch
Priory CE Prim Sch
St Mary's RC Prim Sch
Merton Park Prim Sch
Rutlish Sch
Joseph Hood Prim Sch
Merton Abbey Prim Sch
Nelson Trad Est
Lombard Bsns Pk
Jubilee Wks
Deen City Farm
Kendor Gdns
Morden Road
Wimbledon Chase
THE BROADWAY
KINGSTON RD
MERTON HIGH ST
MERTON RD
MORDEN RD
DURNSFORD RD
HARTFIELD RD
ALEXANDRA RD
WORPLE RD
WIMBLEDON HILL RD
GAP RD
PLOUGH LA
DORSET RD
HAYDONS RD
A219
A218
A238
A24
A298
B235
B285
B286
157
201
180
A
B
C
D
1
2
3
4
5
6

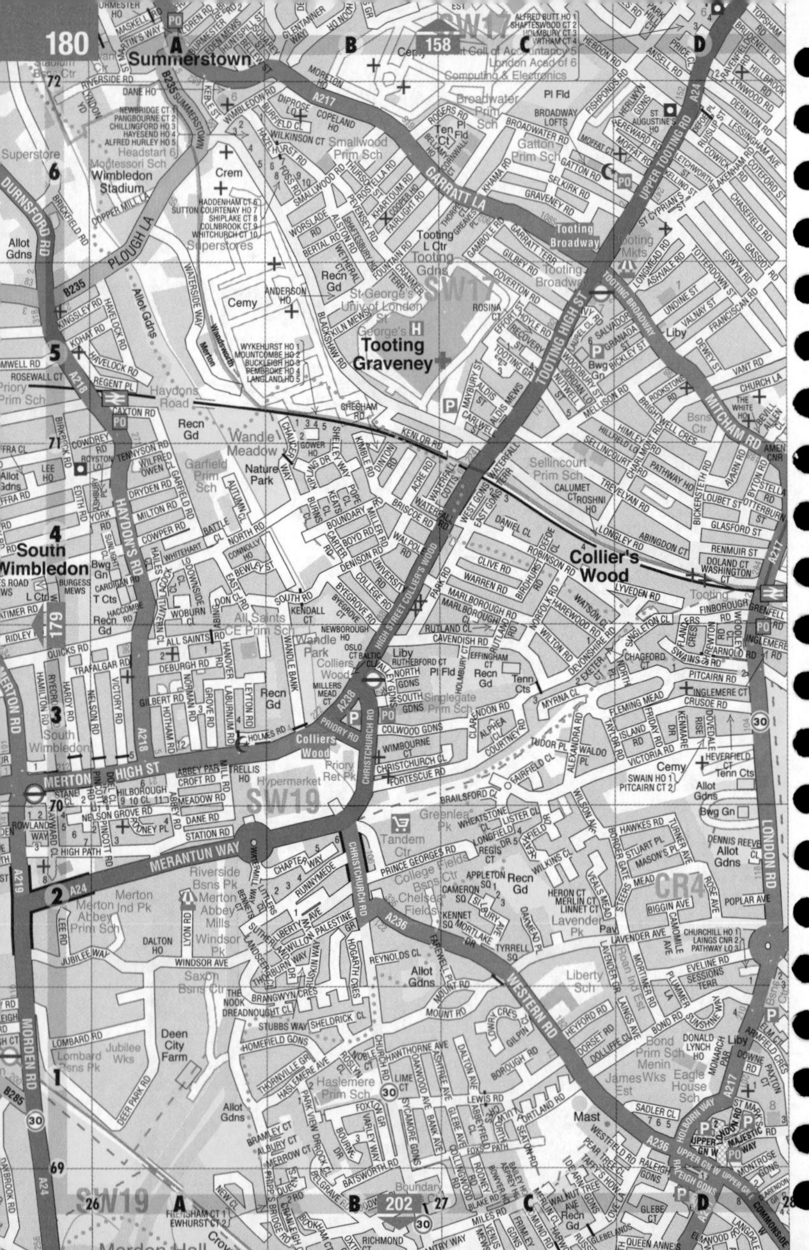
Summerstown
Wimbledon Stadium
Tooting Graveney
Collier's Wood
South Wimbledon
Tooting Broadway
Colliers Wood
Merton High St
Garratt La
Upper Tooting Rd
Tooting High St
High Street Colliers Wood
Mitcham Rd
London Rd
Western Rd
Merantun Way
Morden Rd
Haydon's Rd
Plough La
Durnsford Rd
SW17
SW19
CR4
158
179
202

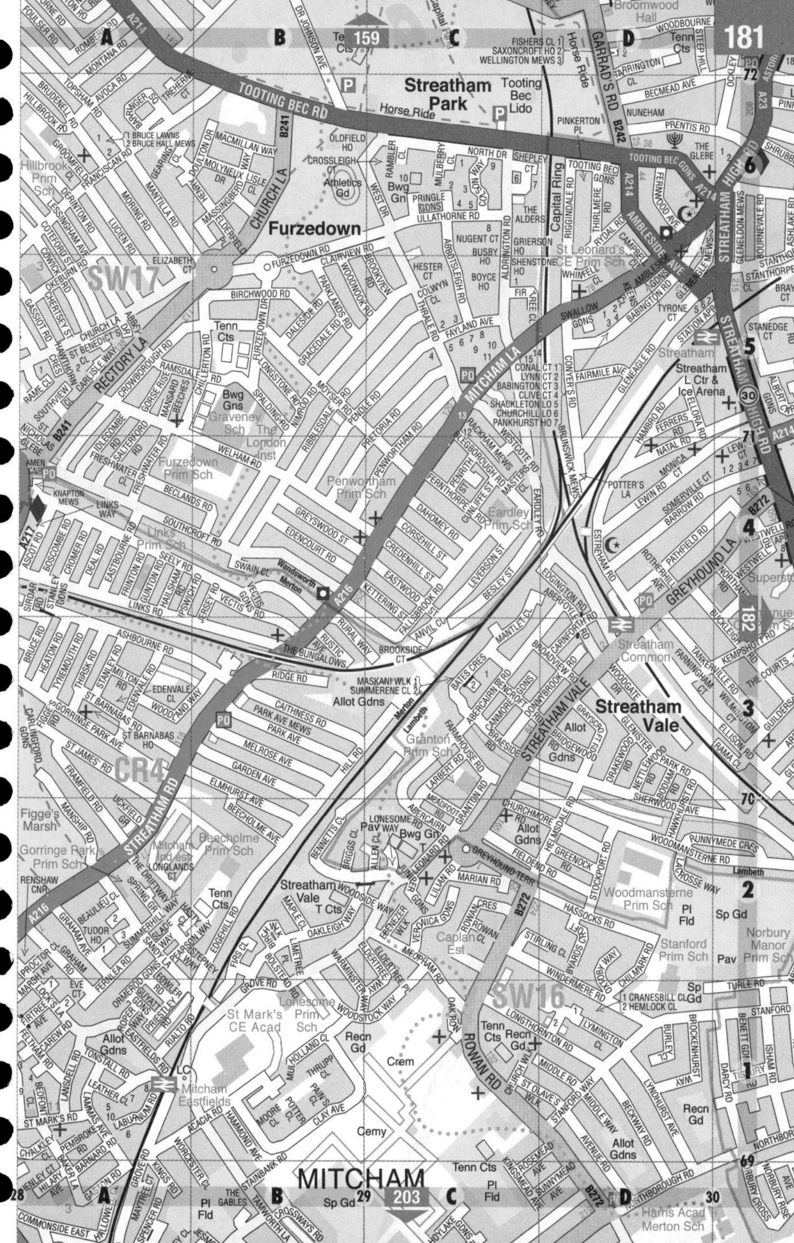
Streatham Park
Furzedown
SW17
Streatham Vale
CR4
SW16
MITCHAM
TOOTING BEC RD
MITCHAM LA
STREATHAM RD
STREATHAM VALE
STREATHAM HIGH RD
GREYHOUND LA
159
182
203

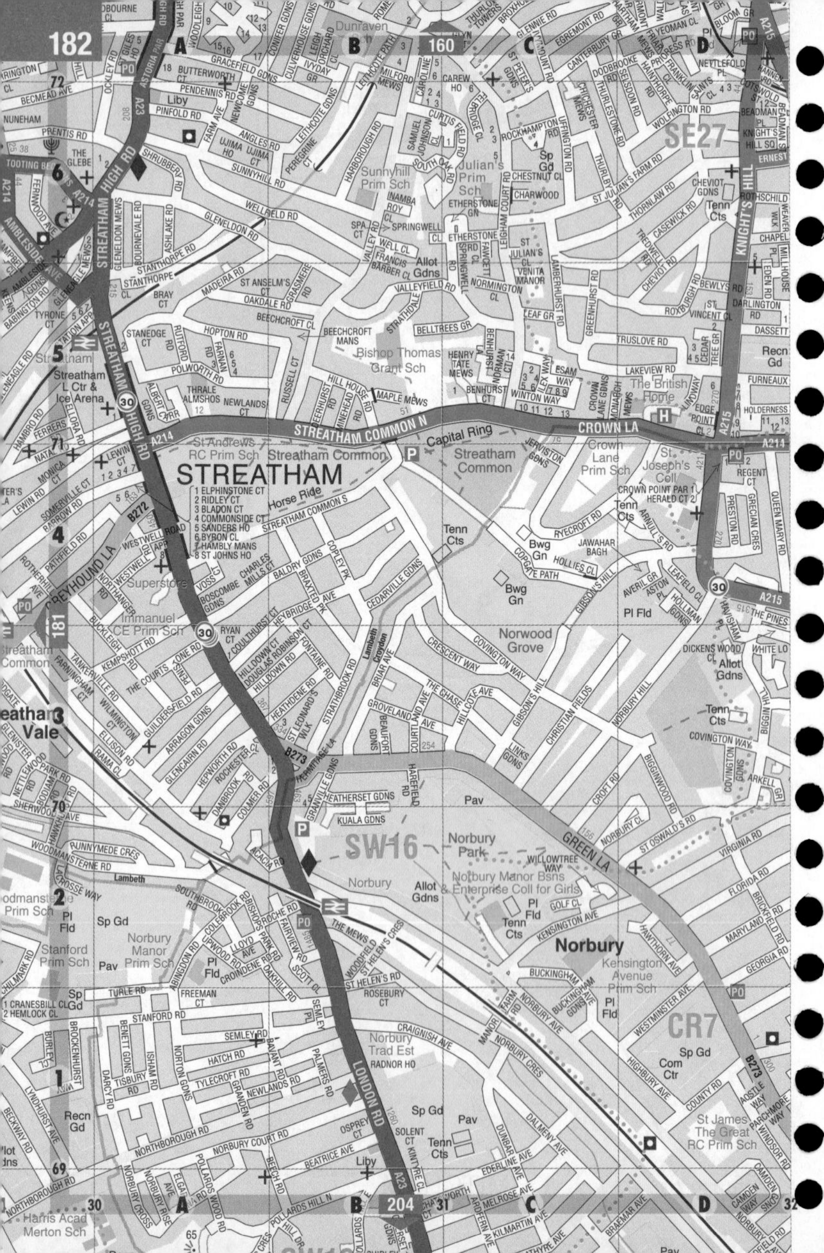
STREATHAM
Streatham Common
Norbury
SE27
SW16
CR7
STREATHAM HIGH RD
STREATHAM COMMON N
CROWN LA
LONDON RD
GREEN LA
KNIGHT'S HILL
Norwood Grove
Capital Ring
Horse Ride
Bishop Thomas Grant Sch
Sunnyhill Prim Sch
Julian's Prim Sch
The British Home
Crown Lane Prim Sch
St Joseph's Coll
St Andrews RC Prim Sch
Immanuel CE Prim Sch
Norbury Park
Norbury Manor Bsns & Enterprise Coll for Girls
Kensington Avenue Prim Sch
Norbury Trad Est
Norbury Manor Prim Sch
Stanford Prim Sch
St James The Great RC Prim Sch
Harris Acad Merton Sch
Streatham L Ctr & Ice Arena
Streatham Vale
1 ELPHINSTONE CT
2 RIDLEY CT
3 BLADON CT
4 COMMONSIDE CT
5 SANDERS HO
6 BYRON CL
7 HAMBLY MANS
8 ST JOHNS HO
160
181
204

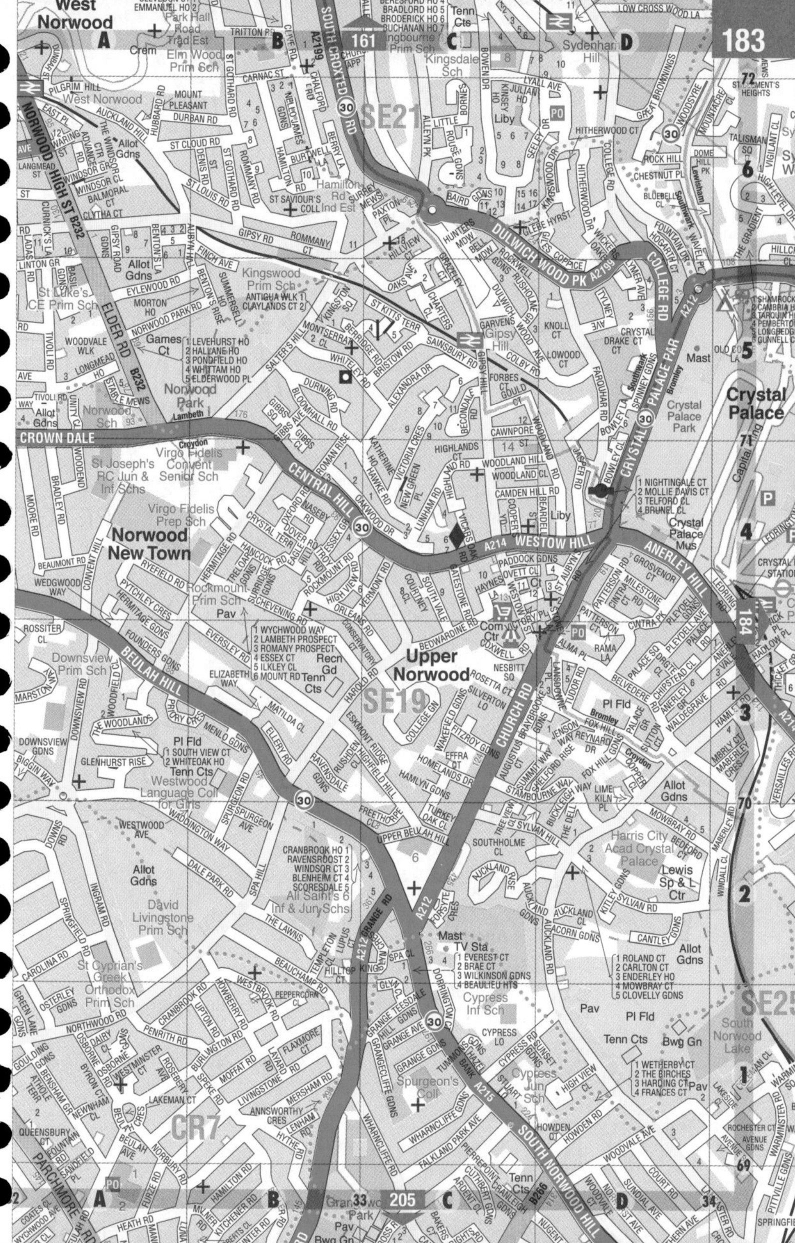
West Norwood
Crem
Park Hall Road Trad Est
Elm Wood Prim Sch
SOUTH CROXTED RD
161
Kingsdale Sch
Sydenham Hill
LOW CROSS WOOD LA
SE21
West Norwood
NORWOOD HIGH ST B232
AUCKLAND HILL
GIPSY RD
ROMMANY RD
Hamilton Rd Ind Est
DULWICH WOOD PK A2199
COLLEGE RD
HITHERWOOD DR
Kingswood Prim Sch
St Luke's CE Prim Sch
ELDER RD B232
Norwood Park
Norwood Sch
Gipsy Hill
CROWN DALE
Virgo Fidelis Convent Senior Sch
St Joseph's RC Jun & Inf Schs
Virgo Fidelis Prep Sch
CENTRAL HILL
Norwood New Town
Rockmount Prim Sch
WESTOW HILL A214
CRYSTAL PALACE PAR
Crystal Palace Park
Crystal Palace
Crystal Palace Mus
ANERLEY HILL
184
Upper Norwood
SE19
BEULAH HILL
Downsview Prim Sch
Westwood Language Coll for Girls
CHURCH RD
A212
Harris City Acad Crystal Palace
Lewis Sp & L Ctr
All Saint's Inf & Jun Schs
David Livingstone Prim Sch
St Cyprian's Greek Orthodox Prim Sch
Cypress Inf Sch
Cypress Jun Sch
Spurgeon's Coll
SE25
South Norwood Lake
CR7
PARCHMORE RD
SOUTH NORWOOD HILL
205
Grangewood Park

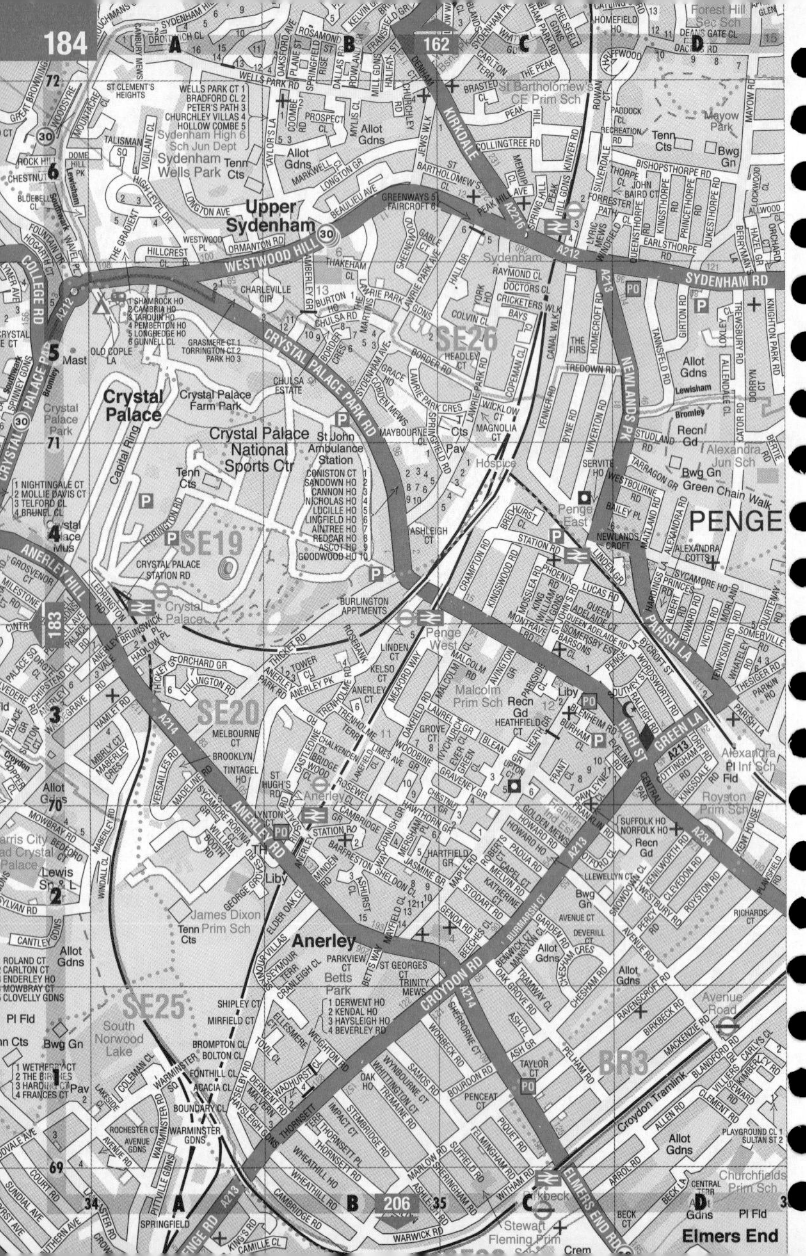
Upper Sydenham
Sydenham Wells Park
Crystal Palace
Crystal Palace National Sports Ctr
Crystal Palace Farm Park
SE26
SE19
SE20
SE25
BR3
PENGE
Anerley
Penge West
Penge East
Sydenham
Crystal Palace
Birkbeck
Elmers End
WESTWOOD HILL
CRYSTAL PALACE PARK RD
ANERLEY HILL
ANERLEY RD
CROYDON RD
SYDENHAM RD
KIRKDALE
NEWLANDS PK
PARISH LA
HIGH ST
COLLEGE RD
CRYSTAL PALACE PDE
ELMERS END RD
162
183
206

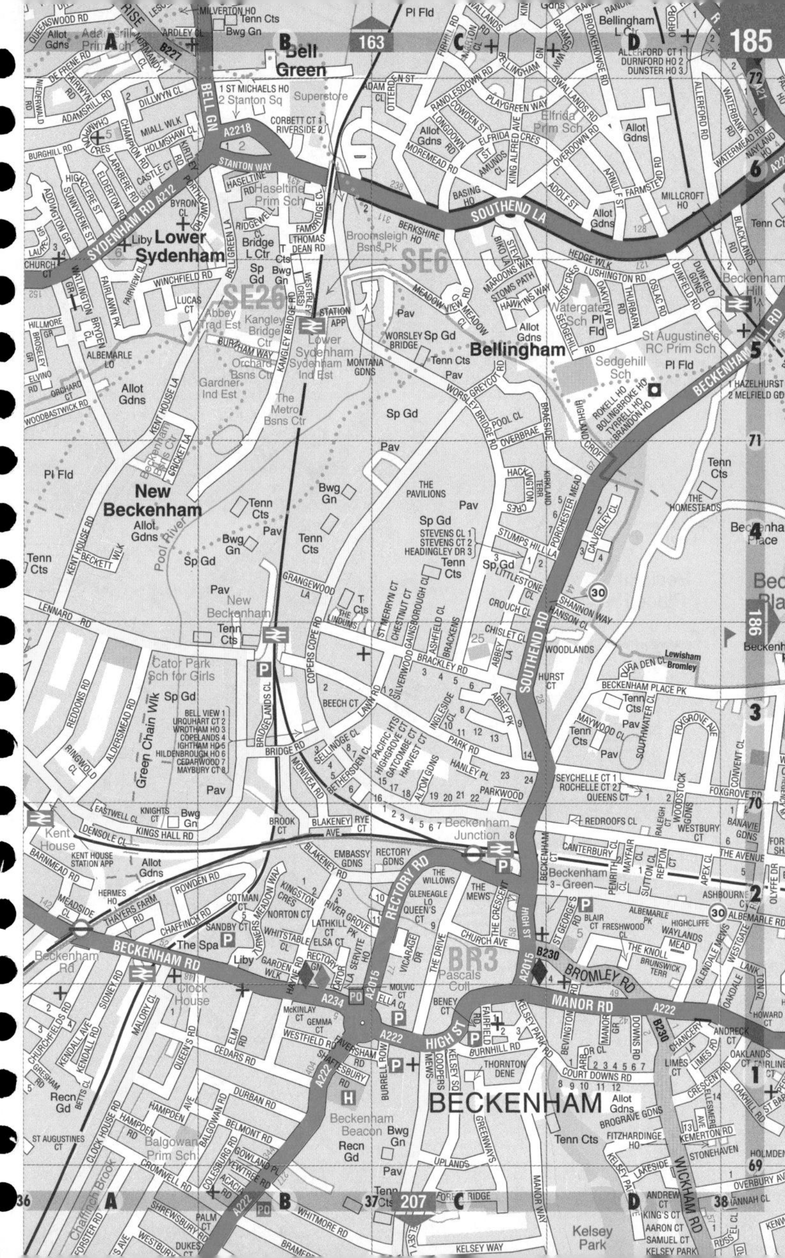

163
186
207
Bell Green
Lower Sydenham
New Beckenham
Bellingham
BECKENHAM
SE26
SE6
BR3
QUEENSWOOD RD
MILVERTON HO
Tenn Cts
Bwg Gn
Allot Gdns
Adamsrill Prim Sch
ARDLEY CL
NORMANDY CL
DE FRENE RD
FAIRWYN RD
NIEDERWALD RD
ADAMSRILL RD
DILLWYN CL
MIALL WLK
HOLMSHAW CL
CHAMPION CRES
BURGHILL RD
LARKBERE RD
CASTLE CT
ELDERTON RD
HIGHCLERE ST
SUNNYDENE ST
ADDINGTON GR
SYDENHAM RD A212
BELL GN
A2218
STANTON WAY
1 ST MICHAELS HO
2 Stanton Sq
Superstore
CORBETT CT 1
RIVERSIDE 2
HASELTINE RD
Haseltine Prim Sch
RIDGEWELL CL
FAMBRIDGE CL
THOMAS DEAN RD
Bridge L Ctr
Sp Gd
BYRON CL
Liby
WINCHFIELD RD
FAIRLAWN PK
WALLINGTON CL
FAIRVIEW CL
LUCAS CT
CHURCH CT
HILLMORE GR
BROSELEY GR
ELVINO RD
ALBEMARLE LO
ORCHARD CL
WOODBASTWICK RD
Abbey Trad Est
Kangley Bridge Ctr
BURGHAM WAY
Orchard Bsns Ctr
Gardner Ind Est
KANGLEY BRIDGE RD
WESTERLEY CRES
STATION APP
Lower Sydenham
Sydenham Ind Est
MONTANA GDNS
The Metro Bsns Ctr
KENT HOUSE LA
CRICKET LA
Beckenham Bsns Ctr
Pl Fld
Pool River
BECKETT WLK
KENT HOUSE RD
Pav
Broomsleigh Bsns Pk
BERKSHIRE HO
SOUTHEND LA
ADAM CL
OTTERDEN ST
FIRHILL RD
RANDLESDOWN RD
COWDEN ST
LONGDOWN
MOREMEAD RD
ELFRIDA CRES
ST AMUNDS CL
KING ALFRED AVE
BELLINGHAM GN
PLAYGREEN WAY
Elfrida Prim Sch
OVERDOWN RD
SWALLANDS RD
BROOKEHOWSE RD
Bellingham L Ctr
ALLERFORD CT 1
DURNFORD HO 2
DUNSTER HO 3
ALLERFORD RD
WATERBANK RD
WATERMEAD RD
NAYLAND HO
FALKLAND HO
BASING HO
ADOLF ST
ARNULF ST
FARMSTEAD RD
MILLCROFT HO
BLACKLANDS RD
HEDGE WLK
LUSHINGTON RD
OAKVIEW RD
THURBARN RD
OSLAC RD
DUNFIELD RD
DUNFIELD GDNS
Beckenham Hill
MAROONS WAY
STOMS PATH
HAWKINS WAY
BIKO
LEOF CRES
SEDGEHILL RD
Watergate Sch
St Augustine's RC Prim Sch
Sedgehill Sch
BECKENHAM HILL RD
1 HAZELHURST CT
2 MELFIELD GDNS
BENBURY CL
MEADOWVIEW RD
MEADOW
WORSLEY BRIDGE
WORSLEY BRIDGE RD
GREYCOT RD
POOL CL
OVERBRAE
BRAESIDE
HIGHLAND CROFT
ROKELL HO
BOLINGBROKE HO
TYRRELL HO
BRANDON HO
HACKINGTON CRES
KIRKLAND TERR
PORCHESTER MEAD
THE PAVILIONS
STEVENS CL 1
STEVENS CT 2
HEADINGLEY DR 3
STUMPS HILL LA
CALVERLEY CL
THE HOMESTEADS
Beckenham Place
Beckenham Place Pk
LITTLESTONE CL
CROUCH CL
SHANNON WAY
HANSON CL
CHISLET CL
WOODLANDS
HURST CT
Lewisham
Bromley
DURA DEN CL
BECKENHAM PLACE PK
SOUTHEND RD
GRANGEWOOD LA
THE LINDUMS
ST MERRYN CT
CHESTNUT CT
SILVERWOOD
GAINSBOROUGH CL
ASHFIELD CL
BRACKENS
ABBEY LA
BRACKLEY RD
New Beckenham
LENNARD RD
Cator Park Sch for Girls
REDDONS RD
ALDERSMEAD RD
RINGWOLD CL
Green Chain Wlk
BELL VIEW 1
URQUHART CT 2
WROTHAM HO 3
COPELANDS 4
IGHTHAM HO 5
HILDENBOROUGH HO 6
CEDARWOOD 7
MAYBURY CT 8
COPERS COPE RD
BRIDGELANDS CL
BEECH CT
LAWN RD
INGLESIDE CL
ABBEY PK
PARK RD
BRIDGE RD
SELLINDGE CL
PACIFIC HTS
HIGHGROVE CT
GATCOMBE CT
HARVEST CT
ALTON GDNS
HANLEY PL
PARKWOOD
MONIVEA RD
BETHERSDEN CL
MAYWOOD CL
SOUTHWATER CL
FOXGROVE AVE
CONVENT CL
FOXGROVE RD
SEYCHELLE CT 1
ROCHELLE CT 2
QUEENS CT
WOODSTOCK CT
RALEIGH CT
WESTBURY CT
REDROOFS CL
BANAVIE GDNS
FORSYTHE SHADES
THE AVENUE
EASTWELL CL
KNIGHTS CT
DENSOLE CL
KINGS HALL RD
Kent House
KENT HOUSE STATION APP
BARNMEAD RD
BROOK CT
BLAKENEY AVE
RYE CT
Beckenham Junction
CANTERBURY CL
PENRITH CL
MAYFAIR CL
SUTTON CL
REPTON CL
APEX CL
BRIARY LO
OLYFFE DR
ASHBOURNE
Beckenham Green
ALBEMARLE RD
ALBEMARLE PK
HIGHCLIFFE
WAYLANDS MEAD
THE KNOLL
BRUNSWICK TERR
GLENDALE MEWS
WESTGATE
LANKTON CL
HERMES HO
MEADSIDE CL
THAYERS FARM RD
ROWDEN RD
CHAFFINCH RD
COTMAN CL
EMBASSY GDNS
RECTORY GDNS
BLAKENEY RD
KINGSTON CRES
MEADOW WAY
NORTON CT
RIVER GROVE PK
LATHKILL CT
ELSA CT
WHITSTABLE CL
SANDBY CT
RECTORY RD
THE WILLOWS
GLENEAGLE LO
QUEEN'S CT
THE MEWS
THE CRESCENT
ST GEORGE'S RD
BLAIR CT
FRESHWOOD CL
CHURCH AVE
THE DRIVE
VICARAGE DR
Pascals Coll
BECKENHAM RD
The Spa
Liby
GARDEN WLK
RECTORY GN
CATOR RD
LA SERVITE HO
A2015
HIGH ST
B230
BROMLEY RD
MANOR RD
A222
Beckenham Rd
Clock House
SIDNEY RD
MALLORY CL
QUEEN'S RD
ELM RD
HAYNE RD
A234
MOLVIC CT
ELLA CL
McKINLAY CT
GEMMA CT
WESTFIELD RD
CEDARS RD
FAVERSHAM RD
SHAFTESBURY RD
BURRELL ROW
MEWS
COOPERS
KELSEY SQ
BENEY CT
FAIRFIELD RD
BURNHILL RD
KELSEY PARK RD
THORNTON DENE
BEVINGTON RD
MANOR GR
DOWNS RD
ARBOR CL
COURT DOWNS RD
CHANCERY LA
LIMES RD
LIMES CT
ANDRECK CT
HOWARD CT
HOLMOAK HO
HAVEN CT
THE MEWS
OAKDALE
CRESCENT RD
OAKLANDS CT
FAIRLINE CT
PERTH RD
OAKHILL RD
ST BARNABAS CL
CHURCHFIELDS RD
KENDALL AVE
KENDALL RD
BETTS CL
GRESHAM RD
Recn Gd
DURBAN RD
HAMPDEN AVE
HAMPDEN RD
BALGOWAN RD
BELMONT RD
CLOCK HOUSE RD
Balgowan Prim Sch
ST AUGUSTINES CT
CROMWELL RD
COLESBURG RD
GOWLAND PL
YEWTREE RD
ACACIA RD
Beckenham Beacon
Recn Gd
Bwg Gn
Allot Gdns
BROGRAVE GDNS
ELLESMERE AVE
KEMERTON RD
FITZHARDINGE HO
STONEHAVEN
HOLMDENE CT
LAKESIDE
WICKHAM RD
UPLANDS
GREENWAYS
MANOR WAY
FOREST RIDGE
OVERBURY AVE
ANDREW CT
KING'S CT
AARON CT
SAMUEL CT
KELSEY PARK
HANNAH CL
KENWOOD
RUSSELL CL
Kelsey Park
KELSEY WAY
Chaffinch Brook
FORSTER RD
SHREWSBURY RD
WESTBURY RD
PALM CT
DUKES CT
WHITMORE RD
BRAMERTON

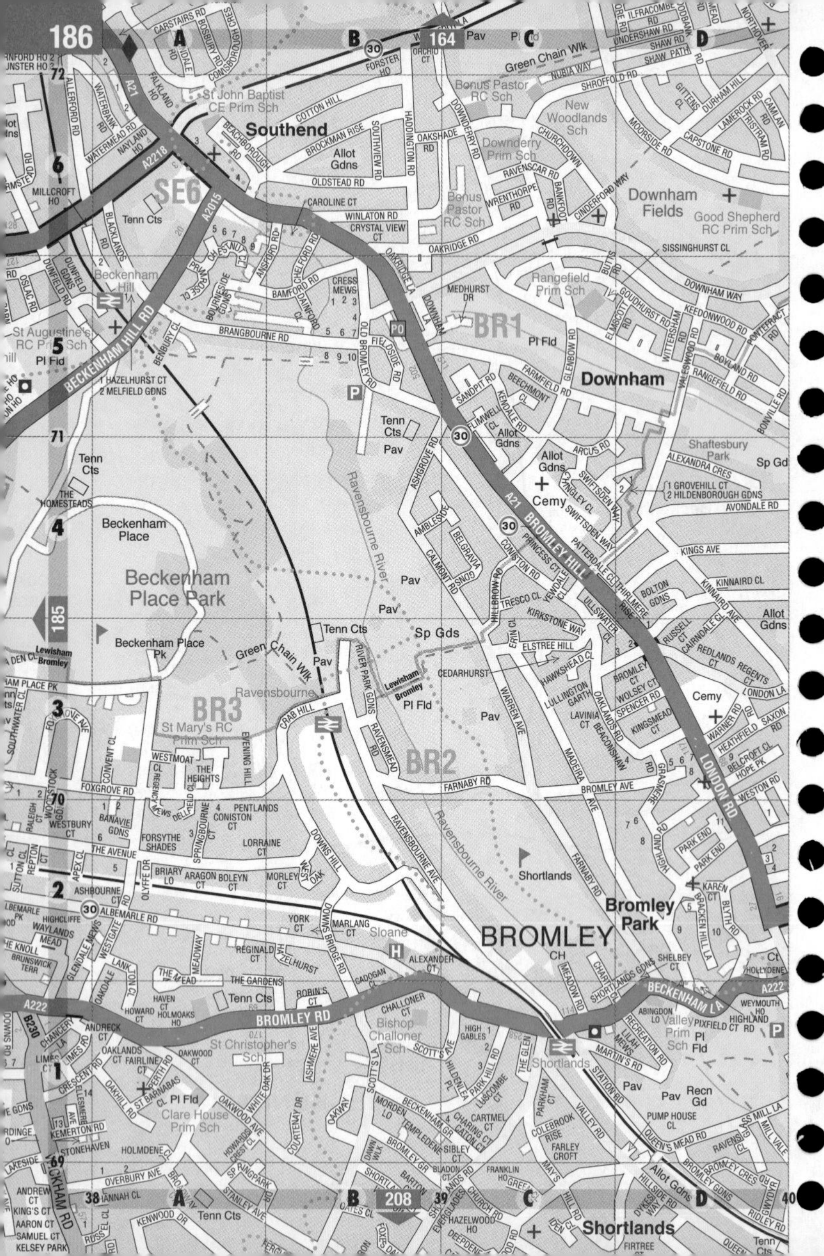

164
185
208
A
B
C
D
Southend
SE6
Downham
Downham Fields
BR1
BR2
BR3
BROMLEY
Bromley Park
Shortlands
Beckenham Place Park
Beckenham Place
Beckenham Place Pk
Beckenham Hill
Ravensbourne
Ravensbourne River
Green Chain Wlk
Lewisham
Bromley
St John Baptist CE Prim Sch
Bonus Pastor RC Sch
New Woodlands Sch
Downderry Prim Sch
Rangefield Prim Sch
Good Shepherd RC Prim Sch
Shaftesbury Park
St Augustine's RC Prim Sch
St Mary's RC Prim Sch
St Christopher's Sch
Bishop Challoner Sch
Clare House Prim Sch
Valley Prim Sch
Sloane
Allot Gdns
Tenn Cts
Pav
Pl Fld
Sp Gds
Cemy
Recn Gd
BECKENHAM HILL RD
BROMLEY HILL
LONDON RD
BROMLEY RD
BECKENHAM LA
A21
A2218
A2015
A222
B230
BRANGBOURNE RD
OLD BROMLEY RD
OAKRIDGE RD
DOWNHAM WAY
FARNABY RD
BROMLEY AVE
RAVENSBOURNE AVE
RIVER PARK GDNS
DOWNS HILL
ALBEMARLE RD
FOXGROVE RD
THE AVENUE
WARREN AVE
MADEIRA AVE
ASHGROVE RD
CONISTON RD
KINGS AVE
AVONDALE RD
HIGHLAND RD
SHORTLANDS GDNS
VALLEY RD
STATION RD
QUEEN'S MEAD RD
WICKHAM RD

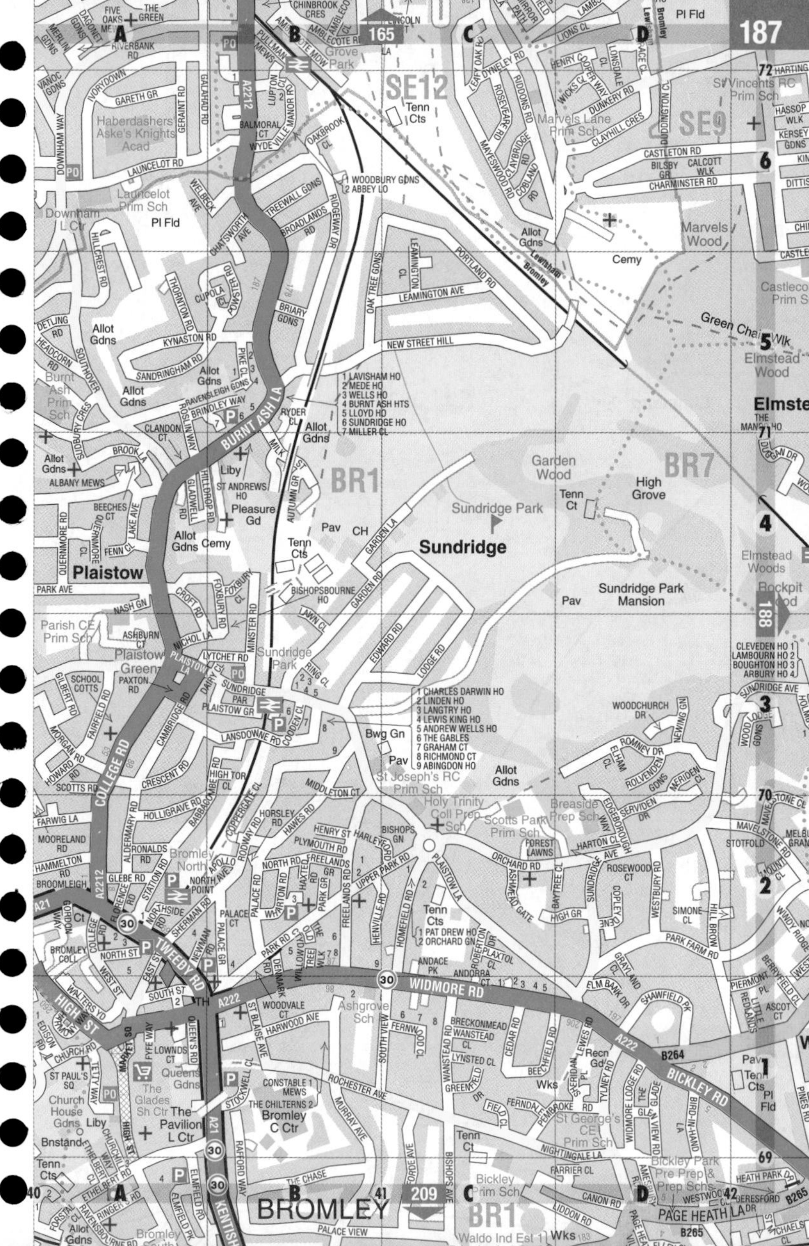
SE12
SE9
BR1
BR7
Grove Park
Plaistow
Sundridge
Sundridge Park
Sundridge Park Mansion
Elmstead
Elmstead Woods
Marvels Wood
Garden Wood
High Grove
Plaistow Green
Bromley North
BROMLEY
Haberdashers' Aske's Knights Acad
Launcelot Prim Sch
Downham L Ctr
Burnt Ash Prim Sch
Parish CE Prim Sch
St Joseph's RC Prim Sch
Holy Trinity Coll Prep Sch
Scotts Park Prim Sch
Breaside Prep Sch
Marvels Lane Prim Sch
St Vincents RC Prim Sch
Castlecombe Prim Sch
Ashgrove Sch
Bromley C Ctr
The Glades Sh Ctr
The Pavilion L Ctr
St George's CE Prim Sch
Bickley Prim Sch
Bickley Park Pre Prep & Prep Schs
Green Chain Wlk
BURNT ASH LA
COLLEGE RD
WIDMORE RD
BICKLEY RD
HIGH ST
TWEEDY RD
PLAISTOW LA
A2212
A222
A21
B264
B265
165
188
209

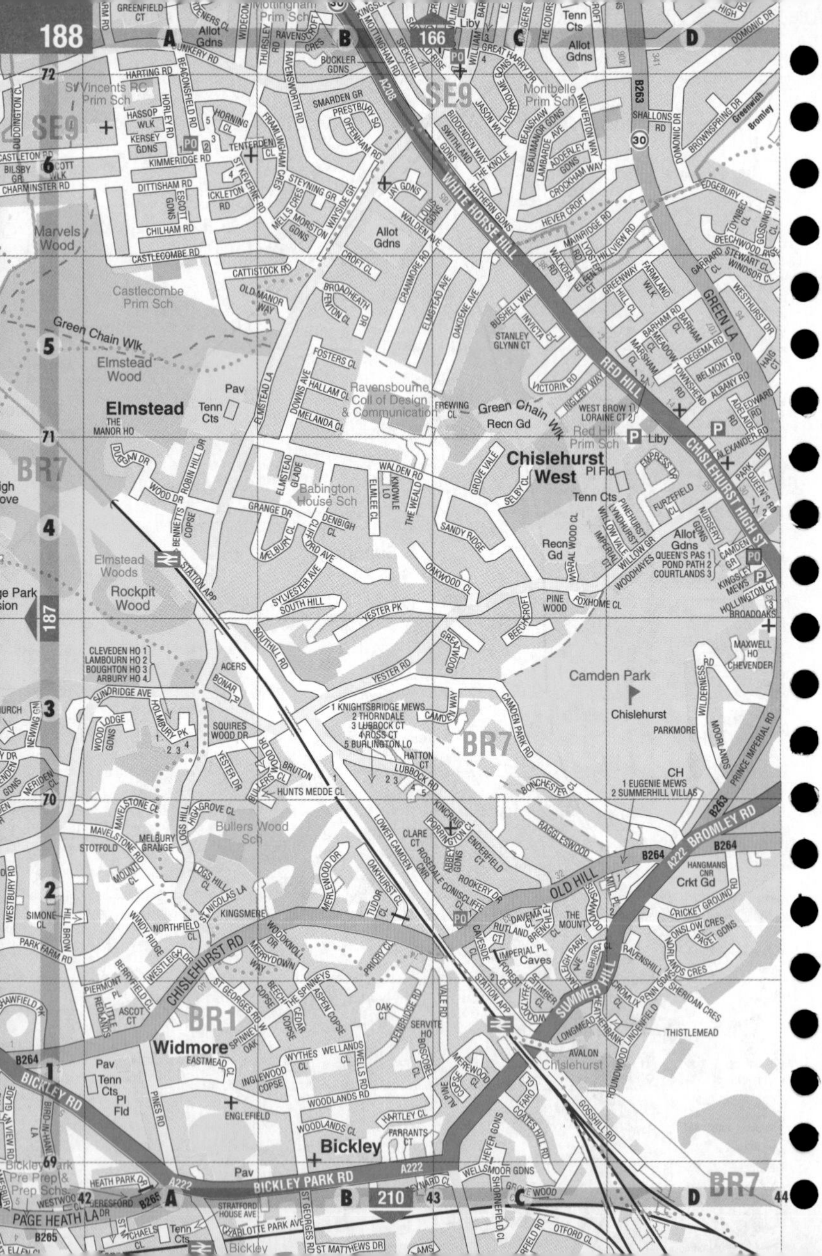

166
SE9
Allot Gdns
Tenn Cts
Liby
PO
Mottingham Prim Sch
St Vincents RC Prim Sch
Montbelle Prim Sch
Marvels Wood
Castlecombe Prim Sch
Green Chain Wlk
Elmstead Wood
Elmstead
THE MANOR HO
Pav
Ravensbourne Coll of Design & Communication
Recn Gd
Red Hill Prim Sch
Chislehurst West
Pl Fld
Babington House Sch
Elmstead Woods
Rockpit Wood
BR7
187
Camden Park
Chislehurst
PARKMORE
CH
1 EUGENIE MEWS
2 SUMMERHILL VILLAS
Bullers Wood Sch
BR1
Widmore
Caves
Chislehurst
Crkt Gd
Bickley
Bickley Park Pre Prep & Prep Schs
210
WHITE HORSE HILL
RED HILL
CHISLEHURST HIGH ST
GREEN LA
OLD HILL
SUMMER HILL
BROMLEY RD
CHISLEHURST RD
BICKLEY PARK RD
BICKLEY RD
PAGE HEATH LA
A208
A222
B263
B264
B265
ELMSTEAD LA
STATION APP
SOUTHILL RD
YESTER RD
YESTER PK
SOUTH HILL
SYLVESTER AVE
CAMDEN WAY
CAMDEN PARK RD
LUBBOCK RD
LOWER CAMDEN
WALDEN RD
WALDEN AVE
GRANGE DR
WOOD DR
SANDY RIDGE
OAKWOOD CL
WILLOW GR
FOXHOME CL
PRINCE IMPERIAL RD
1 KNIGHTSBRIDGE MEWS
2 THORNDALE
3 LUBBOCK CT
4 ROSS CT
5 BURLINGTON LO
CLEVEDEN HO 1
LAMBOURN HO 2
BOUGHTON HO 3
ARBURY HO 4
WEST BROW 1
LORAINE CT 2
QUEEN'S PAS 1
POND PATH 2
COURTLANDS 3
A B C D
1 2 3 4 5 6
69 70 71 72
42 43 44

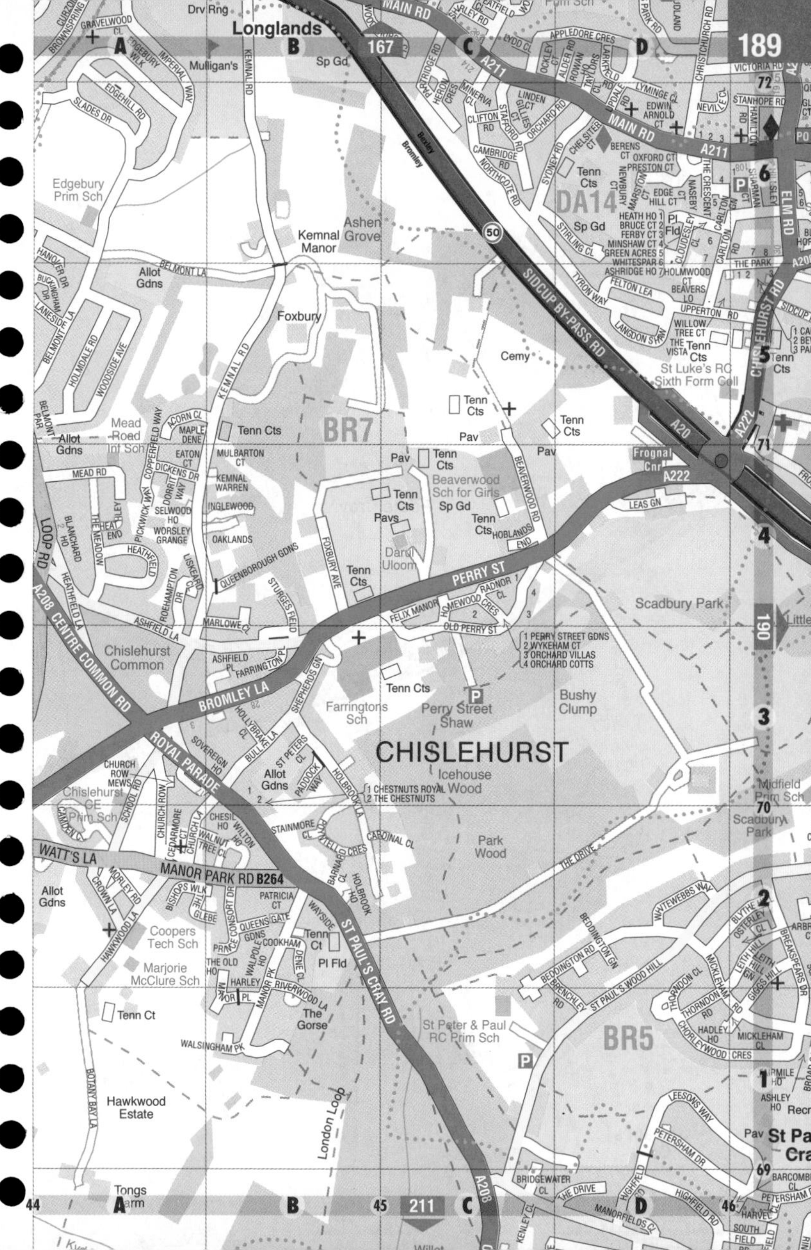
Longlands
Edgebury Prim Sch
Kemnal Manor
Ashen Grove
Foxbury
Allot Gdns
Mead Road Inf Sch
BR7
DA14
Cemy
Beaverwood Sch for Girls
Darul Uloom
Chislehurst Common
Farringtons Sch
Perry Street Shaw
Bushy Clump
Scadbury Park
CHISLEHURST
Icehouse Wood
Park Wood
Chislehurst CE Prim Sch
Coopers Tech Sch
Marjorie McClure Sch
St Peter & Paul RC Prim Sch
BR5
Hawkwood Estate
St Luke's RC Sixth Form Coll
Midfield Prim Sch
Frognal Cnr
SIDCUP BY-PASS RD
A20
A222
PERRY ST
BROMLEY LA
A208 CENTRE COMMON RD
ROYAL PARADE
ST PAUL'S CRAY RD
MANOR PARK RD B264
WATT'S LA
MAIN RD
A211
KEMNAL RD
CHISLEHURST RD
ELM RD
THE DRIVE
ST PAUL'S WOOD HILL
London Loop
Tongs Farm
167
211
190

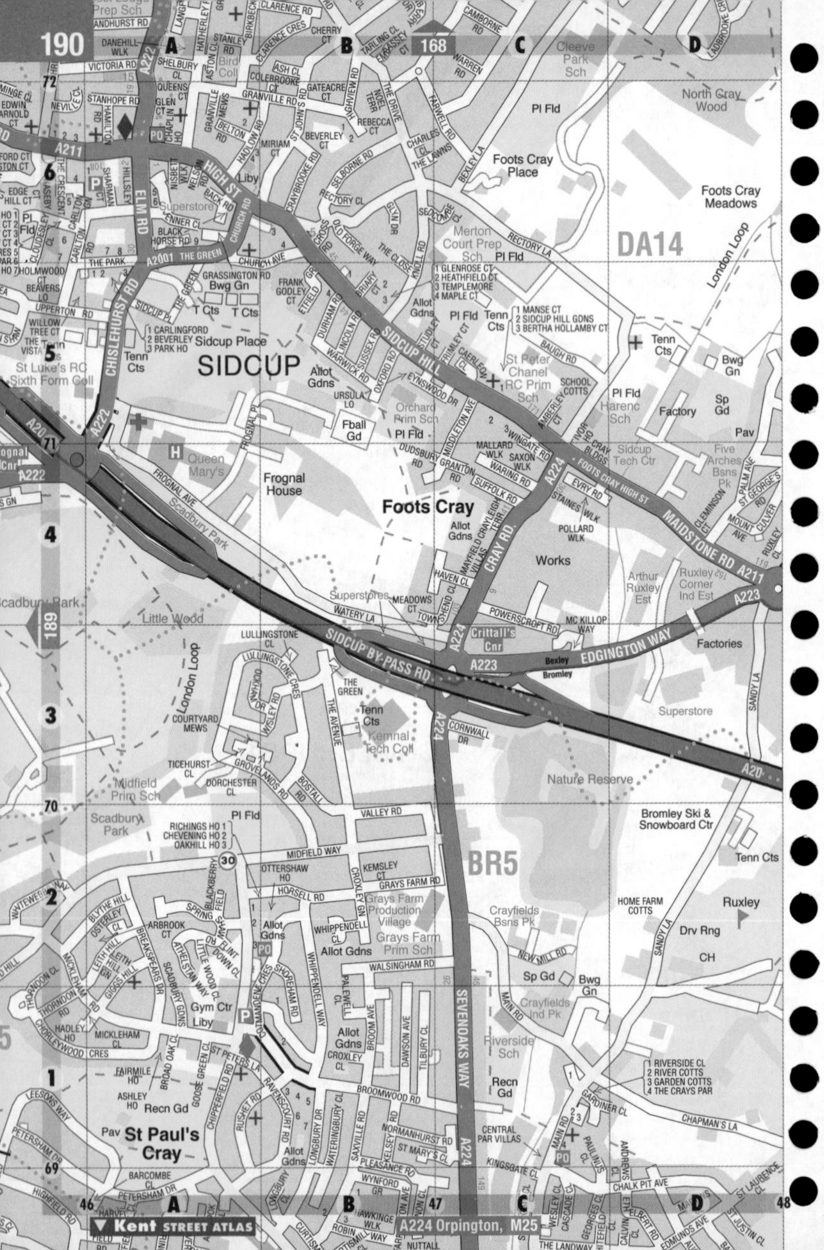

190
168
189
A
B
C
D
72
71
70
69
46
47
48
6
5
4
3
2
1
SIDCUP
Foots Cray
St Paul's Cray
Ruxley
DA14
BR5
Foots Cray Place
Foots Cray Meadows
North Cray Wood
Cleeve Park Sch
Merton Court Prep Sch
Sidcup Place
St Luke's RC Sixth Form Coll
Queen Mary's
Frognal House
Scadbury Park
Little Wood
London Loop
Nature Reserve
Bromley Ski & Snowboard Ctr
Kemnal Tech Coll
Grays Farm Production Village
Grays Farm Prim Sch
Midfield Prim Sch
Crayfields Bsns Pk
Crayfields Ind Pk
Riverside Sch
Arthur Ruxley Est
Ruxley Corner Ind Est
Five Arches Bsns Pk
Sidcup Tech Ctr
Harenc Sch
Orchard Prim Sch
St Peter Chanel RC Prim Sch
Crittall's Cnr
Frognal Cnr
HIGH ST
ELM RD
CHURCH RD
CHISLEHURST RD
SIDCUP HILL
FOOTS CRAY HIGH ST
MAIDSTONE RD
SIDCUP BY-PASS RD
EDGINGTON WAY
CRAY RD
SEVENOAKS WAY
FROGNAL AVE
WATERY LA
RECTORY LA
BEXLEY LA
SANDY LA
CHAPMAN'S LA
MIDFIELD WAY
VALLEY RD
BROOMWOOD RD
CHALK PIT AVE
A20
A211
A222
A223
A224
A2001
Bexley
Bromley
A224 Orpington, M25
Kent STREET ATLAS

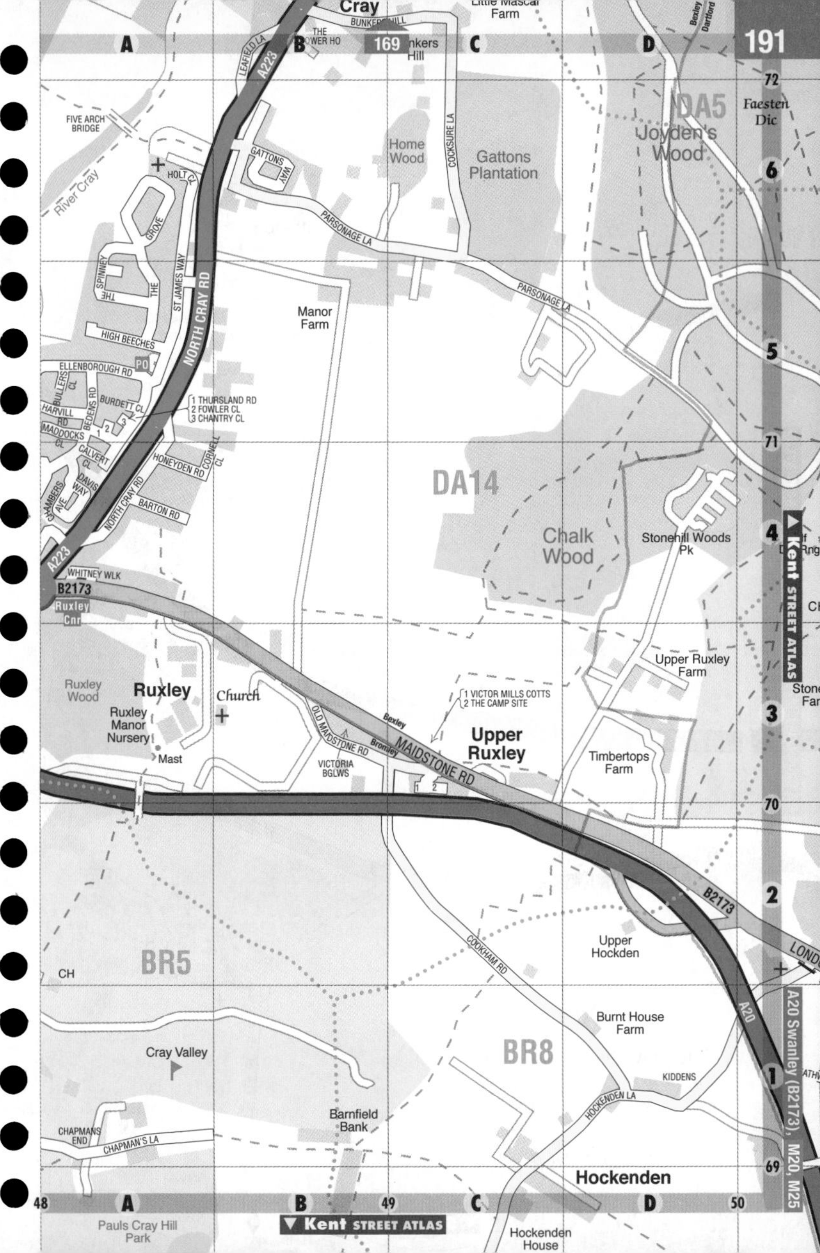

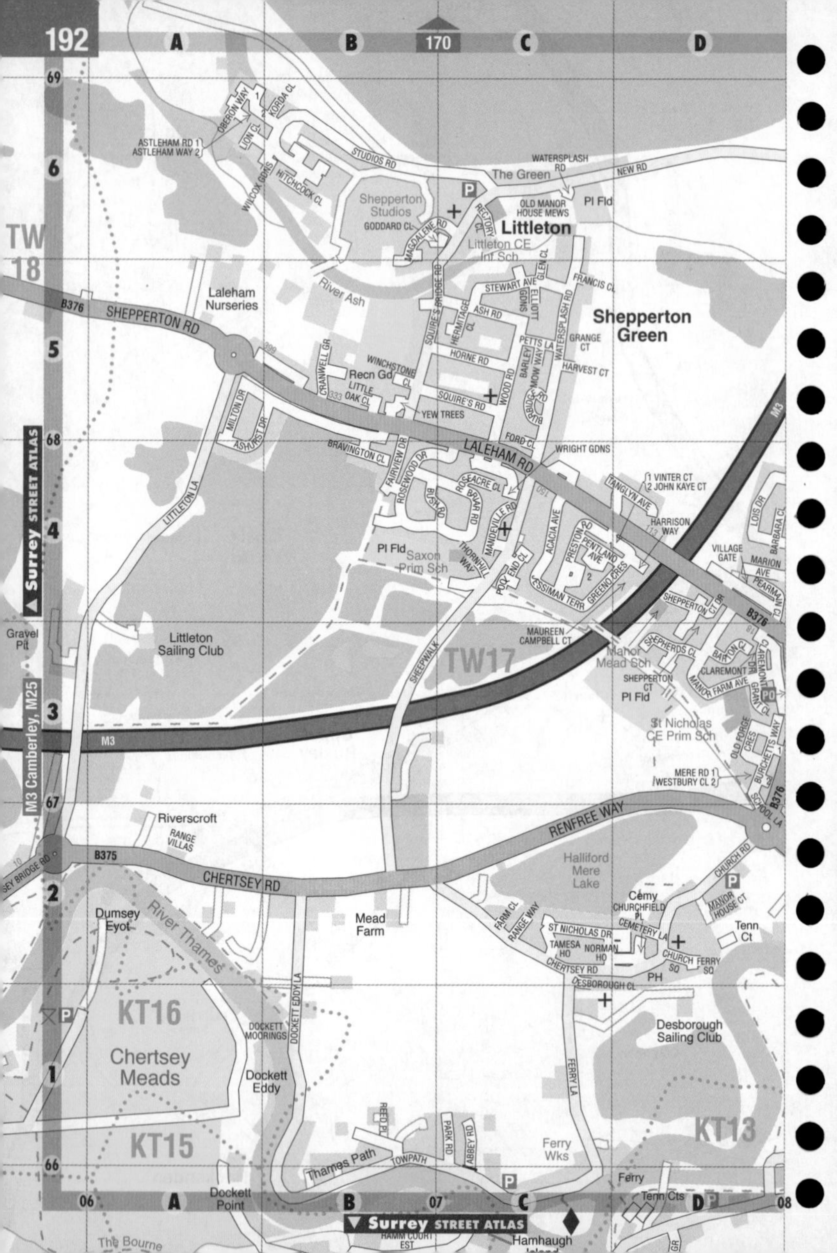
A
B
170
C
D
Littleton
Shepperton Green
Shepperton Studios
Laleham Nurseries
Littleton Sailing Club
TW17
TW 18
KT16
KT15
KT13
Chertsey Meads
Dumsey Eyot
Mead Farm
Dockett Eddy
Dockett Point
Halliford Mere Lake
Desborough Sailing Club
Riverscroft
River Ash
River Thames
SHEPPERTON RD
LALEHAM RD
CHERTSEY RD
RENFREE WAY
SHEEPWALK
LITTLETON LA
STUDIOS RD
The Green
NEW RD
WATERSPLASH RD
FERRY LA
DOCKETT EDDY LA
Thames Path
TOWPATH
M3
B376
B375
Saxon Prim Sch
Manor Mead Sch
St Nicholas CE Prim Sch
Littleton CE Inf Sch
Pl Fld
Recn Gd
Gravel Pit
Ferry Wks
Ferry
Tenn Cts
Cemy
PH
Surrey STREET ATLAS
M3 Camberley, M25
The Bourne
Hamhaugh Island
HAMM COURT EST
69
6
5
68
4
3
67
2
1
66
06
07
08

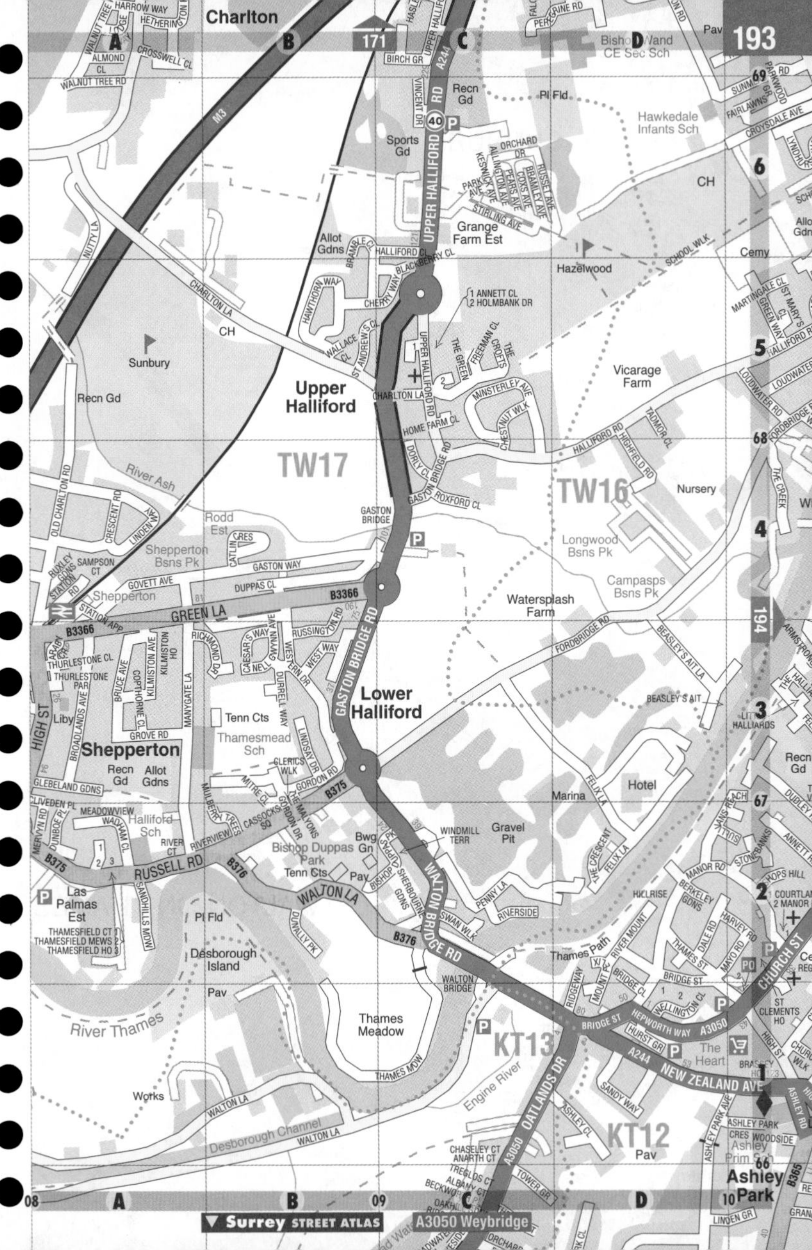
Charlton
171
A
B
C
D
HARROW WAY
HETHERINGTON RD
WALNUT TREE
ALMOND CL
CROSSWELL CL
WALNUT TREE RD
BIRCH GR
UPPER HALLIFORD RD
A244
Bishop Wand CE Sec Sch
PEREGRINE RD
Pav
M3
Recn Gd
Pl Fld
Hawkedale Infants Sch
FAIRLAWNS
CROYSDALE AVE
VINCENT DR
40
Sports Gd
ORCHARD DR
ALLINGTON AVE
KESWICK AVE
RUSSET AVE
BRAMLEY AVE
COXS AVE
PEARS AVE
PARK AVE
STIRLING AVE
CH
6
NUTTY LA
Grange Farm Est
Allot Gdns
BRAMBLE CL
HALLIFORD CL
BLACKBERRY CL
Hazelwood
SCHOOL WLK
Cemy
CHARLTON LA
HAWTHORN WAY
CHERRY WAY
1 ANNETT CL
2 HOLMBANK DR
MARTINGALE CL
ST MARY'S CL
GREEN WAY
WALLACE CL
ST ANDREW'S CL
THE GREEN
FREEMAN CL
THE CROFTS
5
HALLIFORD RD
Sunbury
Vicarage Farm
LOUDWATER RD
Recn Gd
Upper Halliford
MINSTERLEY AVE
CHESTNUT WLK
HOME FARM CL
TADMOR CL
FORDBRIDGE RD
68
TW17
DORLY CL
GASTON BRIDGE RD
HIGHFIELD RD
River Ash
OLD CHARLTON RD
CRESCENT RD
LINDEN WAY
TW16
ROXFORD CL
Nursery
THE CREEK
GASTON BRIDGE
Rodd Est
CATLIN CRES
Longwood Bsns Pk
4
Shepperton Bsns Pk
RUXLEY GDNS
SAMPSON CT
GASTON WAY
STATION RD
GOVETT AVE
DUPPAS CL
B3366
Shepperton
Campasps Bsns Pk
Watersplash Farm
194
STATION APP
GREEN LA
B3366
ARABY CL
THURLESTONE CL
THURLESTONE PAR
BRUCE AVE
COPTHORNE CL
KILMISTON AVE
KILMISTON HO
RICHMOND RD
CAESAR'S WAY
GWYNN AVE
NELL GWYNN AVE
RUSSINGTON RD
WESTERN DR
WEST WAY
DURRELL WAY
GASTON BRIDGE RD
BEASLEY'S AIT LA
ARMSTRONG
HIGH ST
Liby
BROADLANDS AVE
MANYGATE LA
Tenn Cts
Lower Halliford
BEASLEY'S AIT
3
LITTLE HALLIARDS
GROVE RD
Shepperton
Thamesmead Sch
LINDSAY DR
Recn Gd
Allot Gdns
CLERICS WLK
GORDON RD
GLEBELAND GDNS
B375
MITRE CL
THE MALYONS
Hotel
Marina
FELIX LA
CLIVEDEN PL
MEADOWVIEW
DUNBOE PL
MERVYN RD
WADHAM CL
Halliford Sch
RIVER CT
RIVERVIEW
MULBERRY TREES
CASSOCKS SQ
GORDON DR
Bwg Gn
WINDMILL TERR
Gravel Pit
67
DUDLEY RD
ANNETT RD
B375
RUSSELL RD
B376
Bishop Duppas Park
Tenn Cts
Pav
BISHOP DUPPAS PK
SHERBOURNE GDNS
WALTON BRIDGE RD
THE CRESCENT
FELIX LA
MANOR RD
STONEBANKS
HOPS HILL
HILLRISE
BERKELEY GDNS
Las Palmas Est
SANDHILLS MDW
WALTON LA
DUNALLY PK
PENNY LA
RIVERSIDE
2
1 COURTLANDS
2 MANOR PL
HARVEY RD
DALE RD
RIVER MOUNT
THAMES ST
MAYO RD
THAMESFIELD CT
THAMESFIELD MEWS
THAMESFIELD HO
Pl Fld
Desborough Island
SWAN WLK
B376
Thames Path
CHURCH ST
MOUNT PL
BRIDGE CL
BRIDGE ST
RIDGEWAY
Pav
WALTON BRIDGE
WELLINGTON CL
ST CLEMENTS HO
River Thames
Thames Meadow
BRIDGE ST
HEPWORTH WAY
A3050
HURST GR
KT13
The Heart
A244
NEW ZEALAND AVE
HIGH ST
CHURCH WLK
THAMES MDW
Works
WALTON LA
Engine River
OATLANDS DR
SANDY WAY
ASHLEY CL
ASHLEY PARK AVE
ASHLEY PARK CRES
WOODSIDE
ASHLEY RD
Desborough Channel
WALTON LA
CHASELEY CT
ANARTH CT
A3050
KT12
Pav
Ashley Prim Sch
66
Ashley Park
B365
TREGLOS CT
ALBANY CT
BECKWORTH
OAKHILL
TOWER GR
08
09
10
LINDEN GR
GRANGE

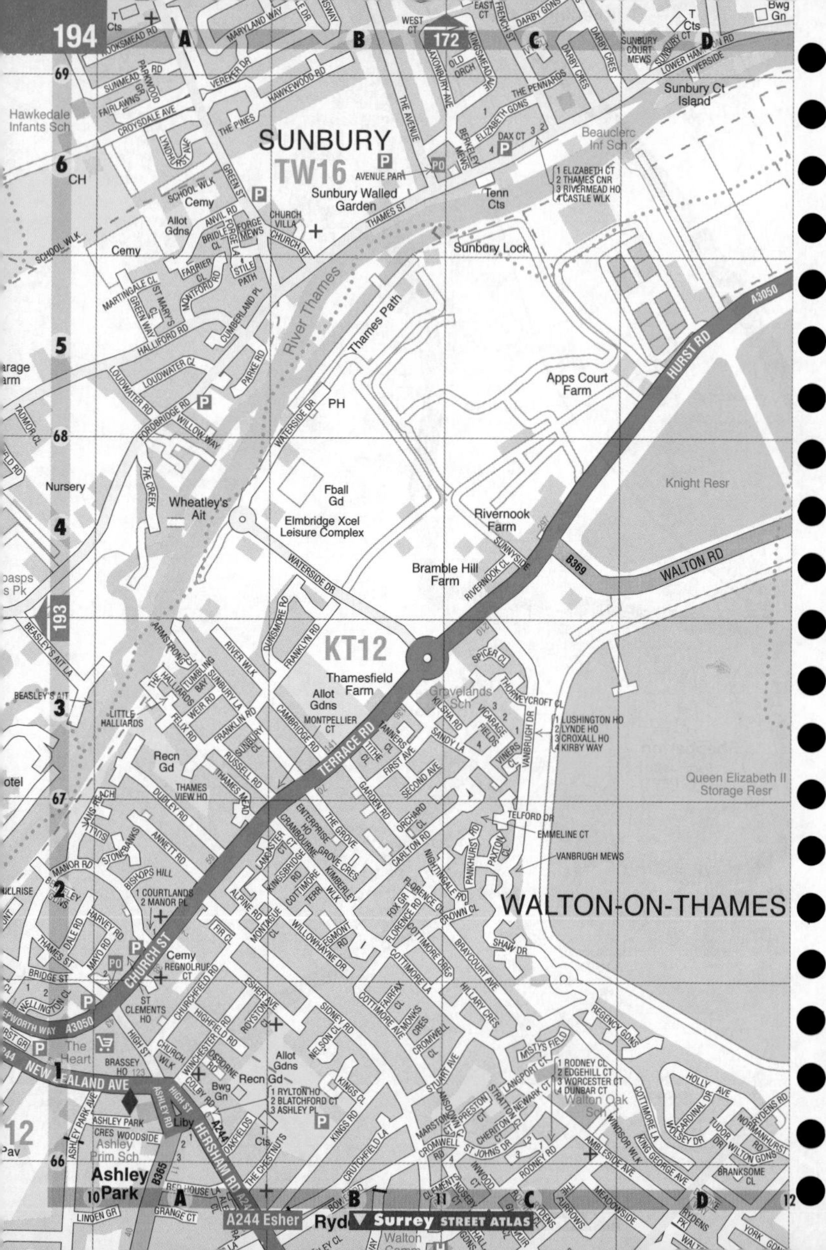

SUNBURY
TW16
Sunbury Walled Garden
Sunbury Lock
River Thames
Thames Path
Apps Court Farm
Knight Resr
Riverook Farm
Bramble Hill Farm
Elmbridge Xcel Leisure Complex
Fball Gd
Wheatley's Ait
KT12
Thamesfield Farm
Queen Elizabeth II Storage Resr
WALTON-ON-THAMES
Sunbury Ct Island
Ashley Park
HURST RD
WALTON RD
TERRACE RD
CHURCH ST
NEW ZEALAND AVE
HERSHAM RD
A3050
B369
A244
B365
1 ELIZABETH CT
2 THAMES CNR
3 RIVERMEAD HO
4 CASTLE WLK
1 LUSHINGTON HO
2 LYNDE HO
3 CROXALL HO
4 KIRBY WAY
1 RODNEY CL
2 EDGEHILL CT
3 WORCESTER CT
4 DUNBAR CT
1 RYLTON HO
2 BLATCHFORD CT
3 ASHLEY PL
1 COURTLANDS
2 MANOR PL

172
193
A244 Esher

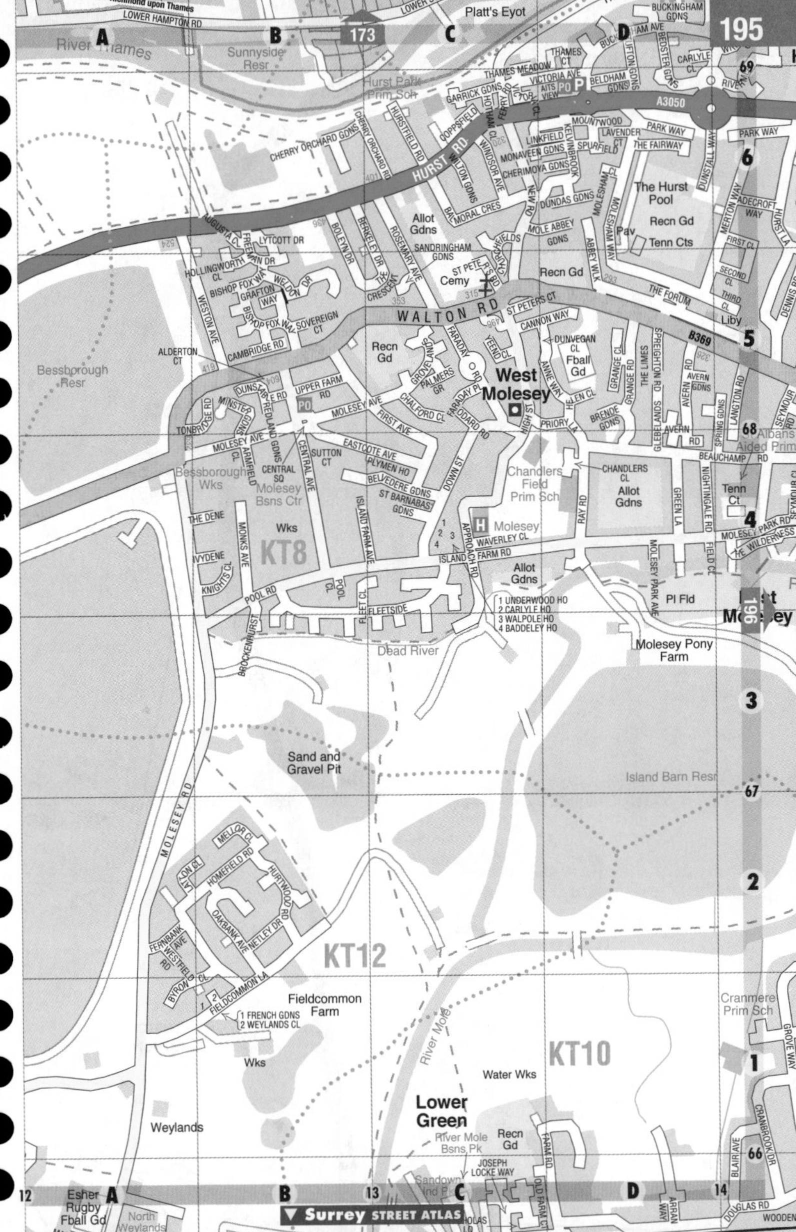
Richmond upon Thames
LOWER HAMPTON RD
River Thames
Sunnyside Resr
173
Platt's Eyot
Hurst Park Prim Sch
BUCKINGHAM GDNS
A3050
HURST RD
CHERRY ORCHARD GDNS
CHERRY ORCHARD RD
HURSTFIELD RD
WILTON GDNS
WINDSOR AVE
MOUNTWOOD
LAVENDER CT
PARK WAY
THE FAIRWAY
The Hurst Pool
Recn Gd
Pav
Tenn Cts
MOLESHAM WAY
MERTON WAY
ADECROFT WAY
HURST LA
FIRST CL
SECOND CL
THIRD CL
DENNIS RD
BALMORAL CRES
DUNDAS GDNS
MOLE ABBEY GDNS
ABBEY WLK
Allot Gdns
SANDRINGHAM GDNS
ST PETERS RD
Cemy
Recn Gd
THE FORUM
Liby
LYTCOTT DR
AUGUSTA CL
FREEMAN DR
HOLLINGWORTH CL
BISHOP FOX WAY
GRAFTON WAY
WELDON DR
SOVEREIGN CT
CAMBRIDGE RD
WESTON AVE
BOLEYN DR
BERKELEY DR
ROSEMARY AVE
THE CRESCENT
WALTON RD
ST PETERS CT
CANNON WAY
DUNVEGAN CL
Fball Gd
B369
GRANGE CL
THE LIMES
SPREIGHTON RD
AVERN RD
AVERN GDNS
Bessborough Resr
ALDERTON CT
Recn Gd
GROVELANDS
FARADAY RD
West Molesey
UPPER FARM RD
PO
MOLESEY AVE
FIRST AVE
CHALFORD CL
PALMERS GR
FARADAY PL
ODARD RD
HIGH ST
PRIORY LA
HELEN CL
BRENDE GDNS
GLEBELANDS
AVERN RD
SPRING GDNS
LANGTON RD
SEYMOUR RD
St Albans RC Aided Prim Sch
TONBRIDGE RD
MINSTER GDNS
DUNSTABLE RD
REDLAND GDNS
ARMFIELD CL
CENTRAL SQ
CENTRAL AVE
SUTTON CT
EASTCOTE AVE
PLYMEN HO
BELVEDERE GDNS
ST BARNABAS GDNS
DOWN ST
Chandlers Field Prim Sch
CHANDLERS CL
Allot Gdns
RAY RD
GREEN LA
NIGHTINGALE RD
BEAUCHAMP RD
Tenn Ct
Bessborough Wks
Molesey Bsns Ctr
Wks
KT8
THE DENE
MONKS AVE
IVYDENE
KNIGHTS CL
ISLAND FARM AVE
Molesey
WAVERLEY CL
APPROACH RD
ISLAND FARM RD
MOLESEY PARK AVE
FIELD CL
MOLESEY PARK RD
THE WILDERNESS
POOL RD
POOL CL
FLEET CL
FLEETSIDE
Allot Gdns
1 UNDERWOOD HO
2 CARLYLE HO
3 WALPOLE HO
4 BADDELEY HO
Pl Fld
196
East Molesey
BROCKENHURST
Dead River
Molesey Pony Farm
Sand and Gravel Pit
Island Barn Resr
MOLESEY RD
MELLOR CL
HOMEFIELD RD
HURTWOOD RD
LAYTON CL
OAKBANK AVE
NETLEY DR
FERNBANK AVE
WESTFIELD RD
BYRON CL
FIELDCOMMON LA
KT12
Fieldcommon Farm
1 FRENCH GDNS
2 WEYLANDS CL
Cranmere Prim Sch
GROVE WAY
River Mole
KT10
Wks
Water Wks
Lower Green
Weylands
River Mole Bsns Pk
Recn Gd
JOSEPH LOCKE WAY
FARM RD
OLD FARM CT
ARRAN WAY
BLAIR AVE
CRANBROOK DR
Sandown Ind Pk
Esher Rugby Fball Gd
North Weylands Ind Est
DOUGLAS RD
WOODEND
MILL RD
A B C D
12 13 14
1 2 3 4 5 6
66 67 68 69
Surrey STREET ATLAS

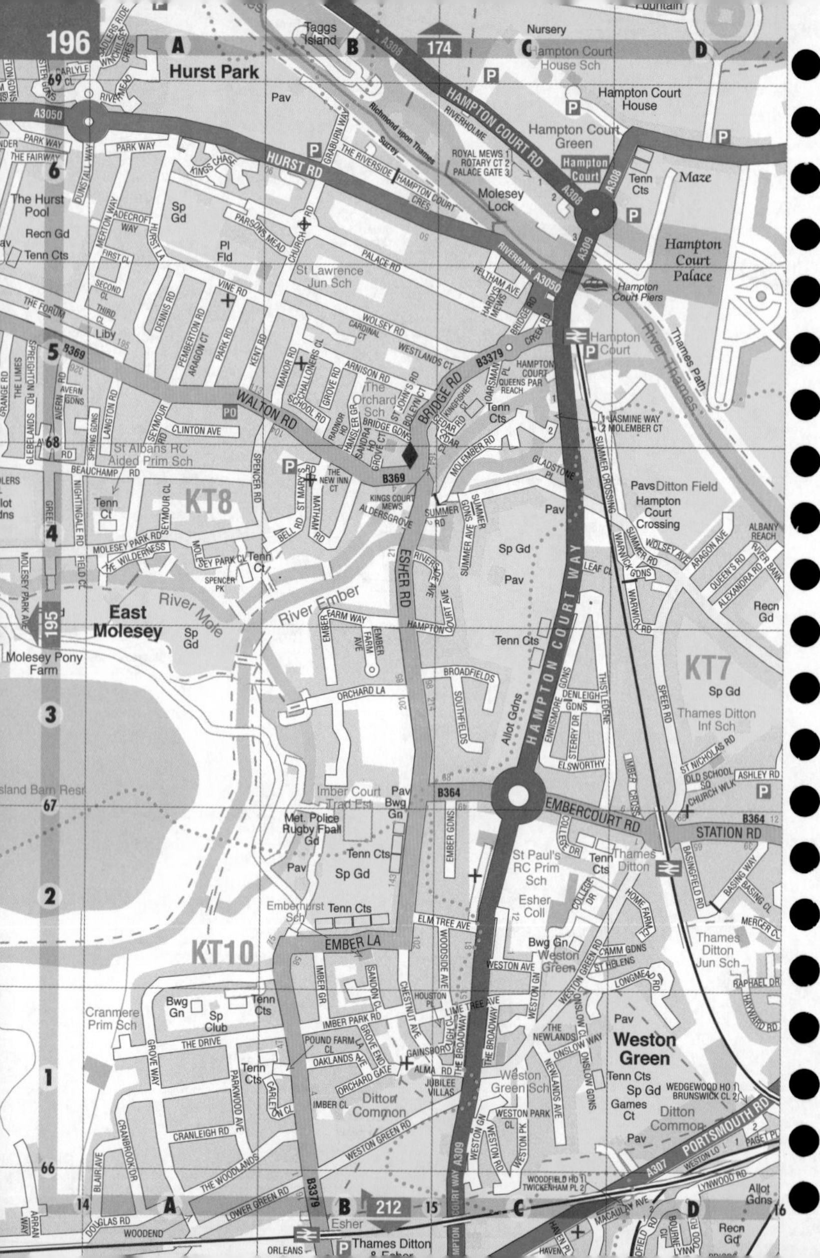
A
B
C
D
174
Taggs Island
Hurst Park
Nursery
Hampton Court House Sch
Hampton Court House
Hampton Court Green
Hampton Court
Hampton Court Palace
Hampton Court Piers
Maze
Molesey Lock
HAMPTON COURT RD
HURST RD
A3050
A308
A309
Richmond upon Thames
Surrey
RIVERBANK
PALACE RD
WOLSEY RD
WESTLANDS CT
BRIDGE RD
CREEK RD
B3379
B369
WALTON RD
The Hurst Pool
Recn Gd
Tenn Cts
Sp Gd
Pl Fld
St Lawrence Jun Sch
The Orchard Sch
St Albans RC Aided Prim Sch
KT8
KT7
KT10
East Molesey
River Mole
River Ember
River Thames
Thames Path
ESHER RD
HAMPTON COURT WAY
SUMMER RD
Ditton Field
Hampton Court Crossing
Thames Ditton Inf Sch
Allot Gdns
Imber Court Trad Est
Met. Police Rugby Fball Gd
Emberhurst Sch
EMBER LA
B364
EMBERCOURT RD
STATION RD
Thames Ditton
St Paul's RC Prim Sch
Esher Coll
Weston Green
Weston Green Sch
Thames Ditton Jun Sch
Ditton Common
Cranmere Prim Sch
Molesey Pony Farm
Island Barn Resr
PORTSMOUTH RD
A307
Esher
Thames Ditton & Esher
212
195
1
2
3
4
5
6
66
67
68
69
14
15
16

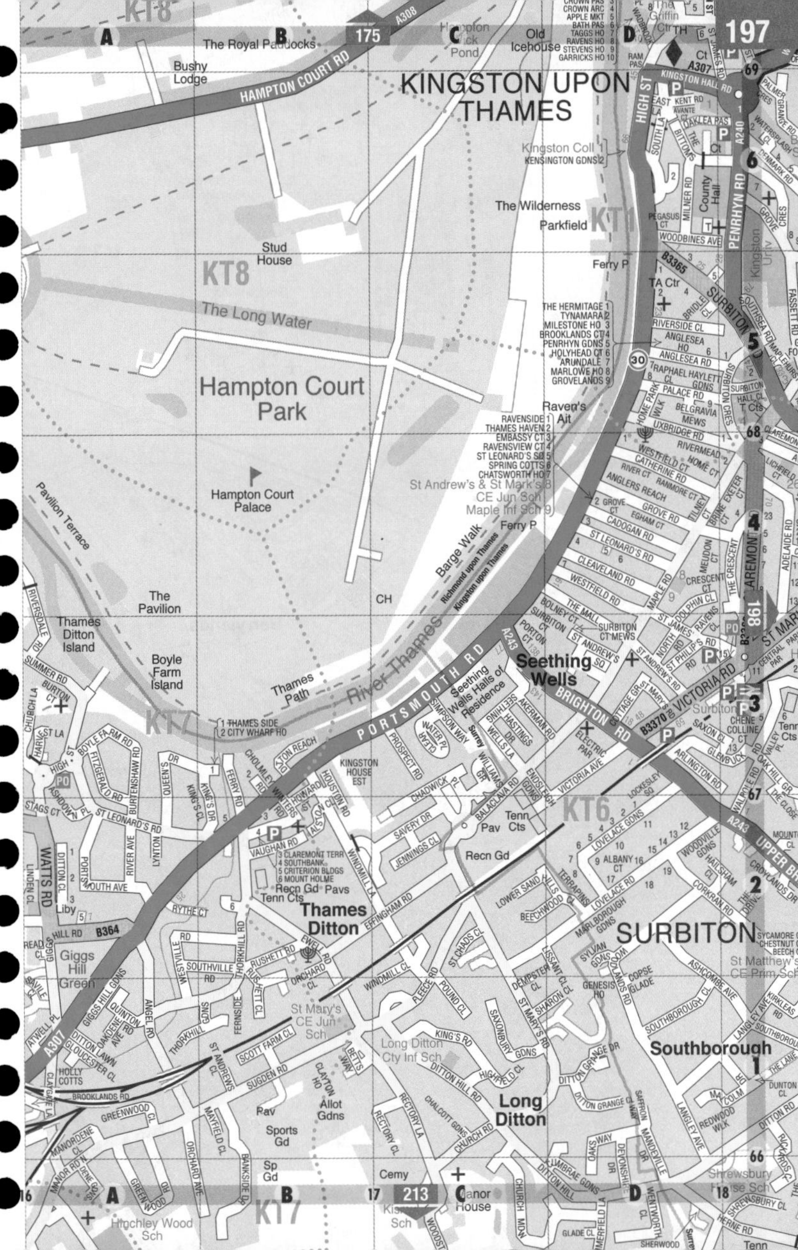
KINGSTON UPON THAMES
Hampton Court Park
Hampton Court Palace
The Long Water
The Royal Paddocks
Bushy Lodge
Stud House
Old Icehouse
The Wilderness
Parkfield
Raven's Ait
The Pavilion
Thames Ditton Island
Boyle Farm Island
River Thames
Barge Walk
Thames Path
Seething Wells
Thames Ditton
Giggs Hill Green
Long Ditton
SURBITON
Southborough
HAMPTON COURT RD
PORTSMOUTH RD
BRIGHTON RD
VICTORIA RD
UPPER BRIGHTON RD
PENRHYN RD
HIGH ST
KT1
KT6
KT7
KT8
175
198
213
66
67
68
69

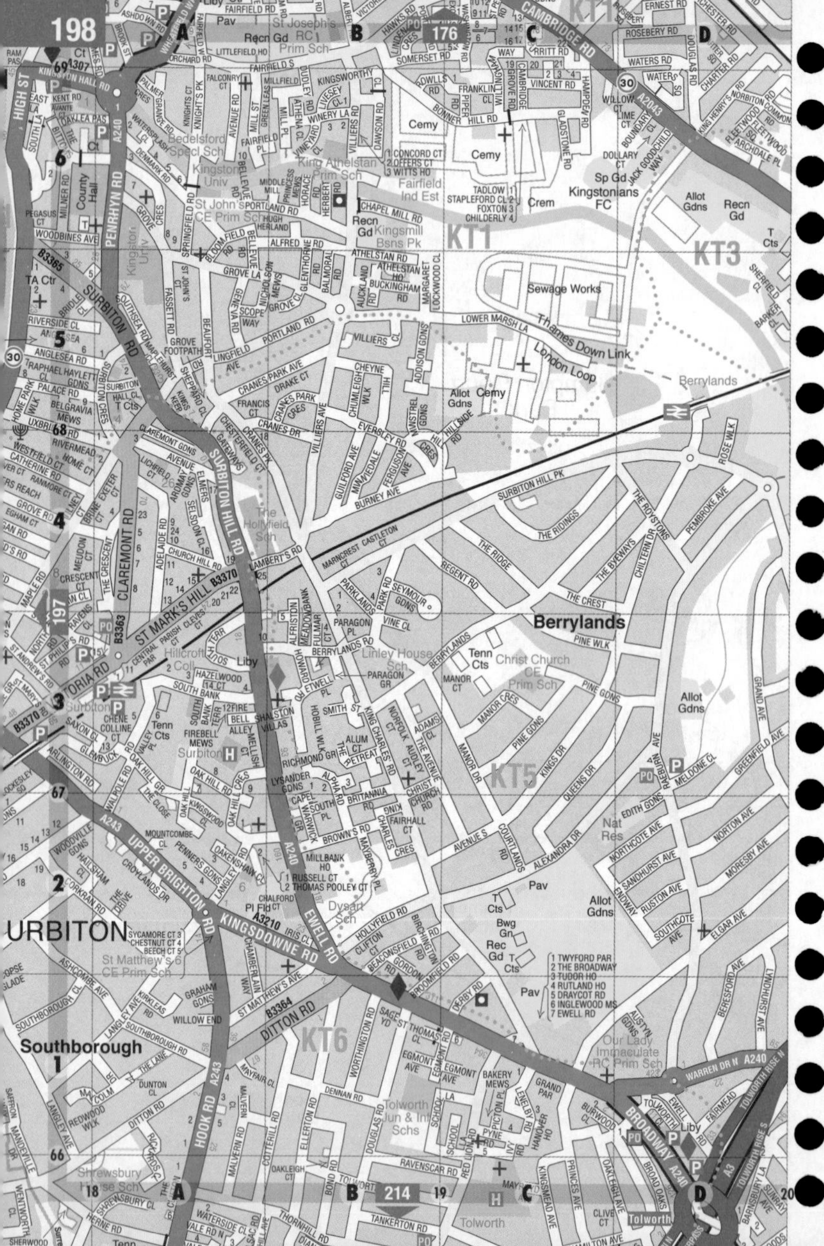
198
176
214
197
A
B
C
D
1
2
3
4
5
6
18
19
20
66
67
68
69
30
KT1
KT3
KT5
KT6
URBITON
Southborough
Berrylands
Tolworth
Surbiton
St Joseph's RC Prim Sch
Recn Gd
Pav
Liby
Fairfield Rd
Littlefield Ho
Orchard Rd
Kingston Hall Rd
High St
Fairfield S
Millfield
Kingsworthy Cl
Somerset Rd
Cambridge Rd
Ernest Rd
Rosebery Rd
Chester Rd
Waters Rd
Douglas Rd
Charter Rd
Waters Sq
Willow Ct
Lime Ct
Boundary Cl
A2043
King Henry's Rd
Norbiton Common Rd
Fleetwood Rd
Fleetwood Ct
Archdale Pl
Bonner Hill Rd
Franklin Cl
Vincent Rd
Hampden Rd
Gladstone Rd
Cambridge Grove Rd
Willingham Way
Piper Rd
Cemy
Crem
Kingstonians FC
Sp Gd
Dollary Ct
Jack Goodchild Way
Allot Gdns
Recn Gd
T Cts
1 Concord Ct
2 Offers Ct
3 Witts Ho
Fairfield Ind Est
Tadlow
Stapleford Cl
Foxton
Childerly
King Athelstan Prim Sch
Chapel Mill Rd
Kingsmill Bsns Pk
Bedelsford Specl Sch
Kingston Univ
County Hall
Penrhyn Rd
A240
Avenue Rd
Mill St
Dudley Rd
Athena Cl
Livesey Cl
Winery La
Vineyard Cl
Villiers Rd
Dawson Rd
Herbert Rd
Horace Rd
Princess Mews
Middle Mill
Portland Rd
Hugh Herland
St John's CE Prim Sch
Springfield Rd
Bloomfield Rd
Bellevue Rd
Grove Cres
Denmark Rd
Palmer Cres
Knight's Pk
Milner Rd
Pegasus Ct
Woodbines Ave
East La
Kent Rd
Avante Ct
South La
Oaklea Pas
Alfred Rd
Athelstan Rd
Athelstan Ho
Buckingham Rd
Glenthorne Rd
Balmoral Rd
Auckland Rd
Margaret Lockwood Cl
Grove La
Geneva Rd
Nicholson Mews
Scope Way
Grove Cl
Fassett Rd
St John's Ct
Beaufort Rd
Southsea Rd
Surbiton Rd
B3365
TA Ctr
Bridle Cl
Riverside Cl
Anglesea Rd
Raphael Haylett Gdns
Palace Rd
Home Park Wlk
Belgravia Mews
Uxbridge Rd
Rivermead
Westfield Ct
Catherine Rd
Home Ct
Ranmore Ct
Grove Rd
Egham Ct
Surbiton Cres
Surbiton Hall Cl
Lingfield Ave
Grove Footpath
Mapleburst
Sheppard Cl
Kings Keep
Villiers Cl
Cheyne Hill
Addison Gdns
Cranes Park Ave
Drake Ct
Cranes Park Cres
Chumleigh Wlk
Francis Ct
Cranes Dr
Eversley Rd
Villiers Ave
Minstrel Gdns
Hillside Rd
Hill Cres
Guilford Ave
Mimmedale
Ferguson Ave
Burney Ave
Allot Gdns
Cemy
Sewage Works
Lower Marsh La
Thames Down Link
London Loop
Berrylands
Rose Wlk
Surbiton Hill Pk
The Ridings
The Roystons
Pembroke Ave
The Ridge
Regent Rd
The Byeways
Chiltern Dr
The Crest
Seymour Gdns
Park Rd
Parklands
Marncrest Ct
Castleton Ct
Claremont Gdns
Avenue Elmers
Aromay Gdns
Lichfield Ct
Selsdon Cl
Adelaide Rd
Church Hill Rd
Claremont Rd
St Mark's Hill
B3370
B3363
Lambert's Rd
Surbiton Hill Rd
Chesterfield Ct
Gateways
Cranes Pk
The Hollyfield Sch
The Crescent
Crescent Ct
Meudon Ct
Brine Exeter Ct
Maple Rd
Ravens Ct
St Philips Rd
St Andrew's Rd
St Mary's Rd
Victoria Rd
Central Parade
Parish Ct
Cleves Ct
South Terr
Hillcroft Coll
Hazelwood
South Bank
South Bank Terr
Fire Bell Alley
Firebell Mews
Shalston Villas
Mellish Ct
Chene Colline Ct
Saxon Cl
Glenbuck Rd
Valley Pl
Tenn Cts
Surbiton
Alfriston
Meadowbank
Fulmar Ct
Paragon Pl
Vine Cl
Berrylands Rd
Howard Rd
Etwell Pl
Paragon Gr
Linley House Sch
Hobill Wlk
Smith St
King Charles' Rd
Norfolk Ct
Audley Ct
Adams Cl
The Avenue
Alum Ct
The Retreat
Richmond Gr
Lysander Gdns
Alpha Rd
Capel Gr
Warwick Gr
South Pl
Britannia Rd
King Charles Cres
Christ Church Rd
Fairhall Ct
Brown's Rd
Mayberry Pl
Millbank Ho
1 Russell Ct
2 Thomas Pooley Ct
Tenn Cts
Christ Church CE Prim Sch
Manor Ct
Manor Cres
Manor Dr
Pine Gdns
Kings Dr
Queens Dr
Pine Wlk
Avenue S
Courtlands Rd
Alexandra Dr
Raeburn Ave
Meldone Cl
Grand Ave
Greenfield Ave
Edith Gdns
Nat Res
Northcote Ave
Sandhurst Ave
Norton Ave
Moresby Ave
Endway
Ruston Ave
Southcote Ave
Elgar Ave
Pav
T Cts
Bwg Gn
Rec Gd
1 Twyford Par
2 The Broadway
3 Tudor Ho
4 Rutland Ho
5 Draycot Rd
6 Inglewood Ms
7 Ewell Rd
Oak Hill Rd
Oak Hill Cres
Oak Hill
Walpole Rd
The Close
Kingswood Ct
Mountcombe Cl
Penners Gdns
Oakenshaw Cl
Langley Rd
Arlington Rd
Lockesley Sq
Woodville Gdns
Hailsham
Corkran Rd
The Drive
Croylands Dr
A243
Upper Brighton Rd
Kingsdowne Rd
A3210
Iris Cl
Pl Fld
Chalford Ct
Dysart Sch
Ewell Rd
Hollyfield Rd
Clifton Rd
Beaconsfield Rd
Birchington Rd
Gordon Rd
Broomfield Rd
Sycamore Ct
Chestnut Ct
Beech Ct
St Matthew's CE Prim Sch
Chamberlain Way
St Matthew's Ave
Graham Gdns
Kirkleas Rd
Willow End
Copse Glade
Ashcombe Ave
Southborough Cl
Langley Ave
Southborough Rd
The Lane
Malcolm Dr
Redwood Wlk
Dunton Cl
Ditton Rd
B3364
Hook Rd
Mayfair Cl
Malvern Cl
Malvern Rd
Cotterill Rd
Ellerton Rd
Dennan Rd
Worthington Rd
Douglas Rd
Sage Yd
St Thomas Cl
Egmont Rd
Egmont Ave
Derby Rd
School La
Bakery Mews
Picton Pl
Lenelby Rd
Hanover Ho
Grand Par
Pyne Rd
Red Lion Rd
Ivy Rd
Kingsmead Ave
Princes Ave
Oakleigh Ave
Burwood Cl
Tolworth Cl
Ewell Ct
Fairmead
Warren Dr N
Tolworth Rise S
Broadway
Broad Oaks
Austyn Gdns
Beresford Ave
Lyndhurst Ave
Our Lady Immaculate RC Prim Sch
Tolworth Jun & Inf Schs
Ravenscar Rd
Oakleigh Ct
Bond Rd
Tolworth Rd
Tankerton Rd
Thornhill Rd
Clive Ct
Hamilton Ave
Barnsbury La
Sunray Ave
A3
Saffron Cl
Mandeville Dr
Wentworth Cl
Shrewsbury House Sch
Shrewsbury Cl
Herne Rd
Sherwood
Waterside Cl
Vale Rd N
Tenn

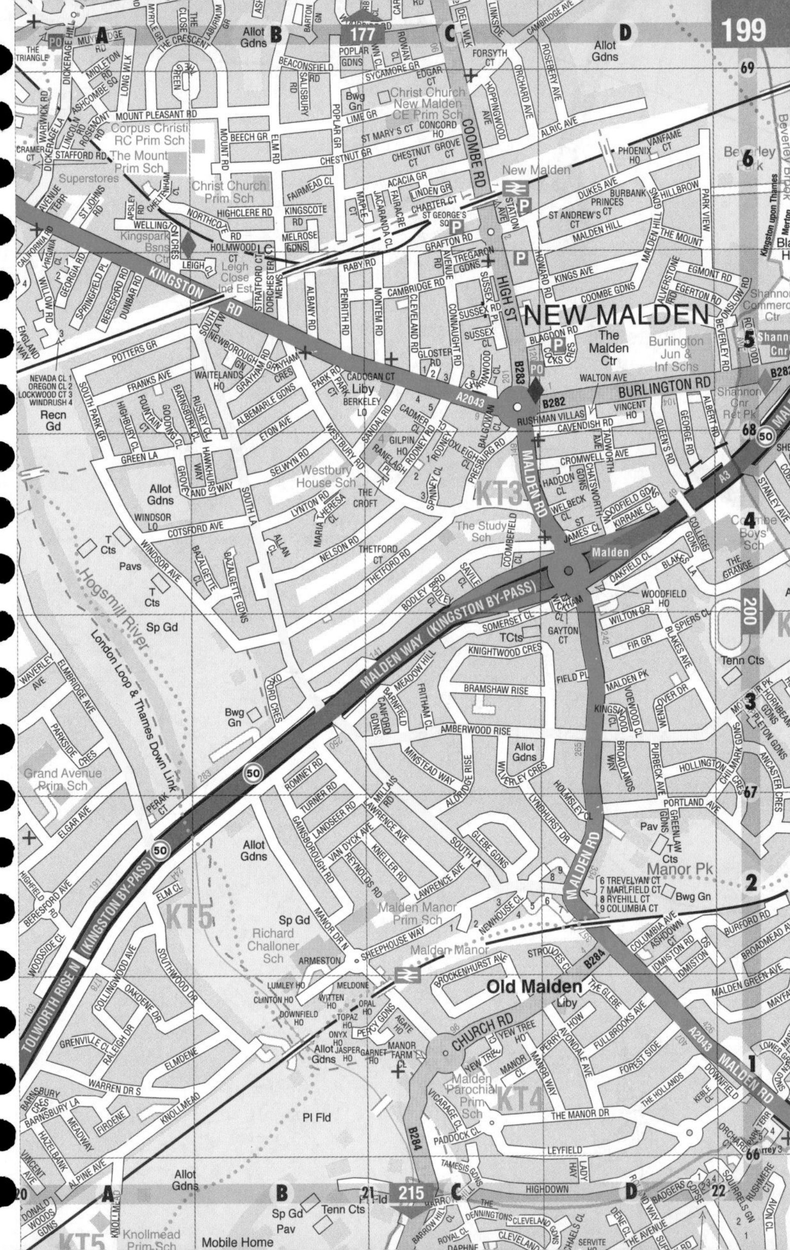

NEW MALDEN
Old Malden
New Malden
Malden
Malden Manor
KT3
KT4
KT5
A
B
C
D
177
200
215
1
2
3
4
5
6
66
67
68
69
Coombe Rd
High St
Kingston Rd
A2043
B283
B282
B284
A3
Malden Rd
Burlington Rd
Malden Way (Kingston By-Pass)
Tolworth Rise N (Kingston By-Pass)
Church Rd
Hogsmill River
London Loop & Thames Down Link
Allot Gdns
Corpus Christi RC Prim Sch
The Mount Prim Sch
Christ Church Prim Sch
Christ Church New Malden CE Prim Sch
Superstores
Kingspark Bsns Ctr
Leigh Close Ind Est
Westbury House Sch
The Study Sch
The Malden Ctr
Burlington Jun & Inf Schs
Shannon Commercial Ctr
Shannon Cnr Ret Pk
Coombe Boys' Sch
Grand Avenue Prim Sch
Malden Manor Prim Sch
Richard Challoner Sch
Malden Parochial Prim Sch
Knollmead Prim Sch
Manor Pk
Recn Gd
Sp Gd
Pavs
Pav
Bwg Gn
Tenn Cts
Liby
Pl Fld
Mobile Home
Beverley Brook
Kingston upon Thames
Merton
Mount Pleasant Rd
Beech Gr
Chestnut Gr
Kingsway
Alric Ave
Dukes Ave
Kings Ave
Coombe Gdns
Cavendish Rd
Cromwell Ave
Potters Gr
Franks Ave
Green La
Cotsford Ave
Nelson Rd
Thetford Rd
Amberwood Rise
Knightwood Cres
Bramshaw Rise
Malden Green Ave
Portland Ave
Sheephouse Way
Brockenhurst Ave
Fullbrooks Ave
Forest Side
The Manor Dr
Leyfield
Highdown
Warren Dr S
Knollmead
Elmdene
Southwood Dr
Barnsbury La
Alpine Ave
Nevada Cl 1
Oregon Cl 2
Lockwood Ct 3
Windrush 4
6 Trevelyan Ct
7 Marlfield Ct
8 Ryehill Ct
9 Columbia Ct

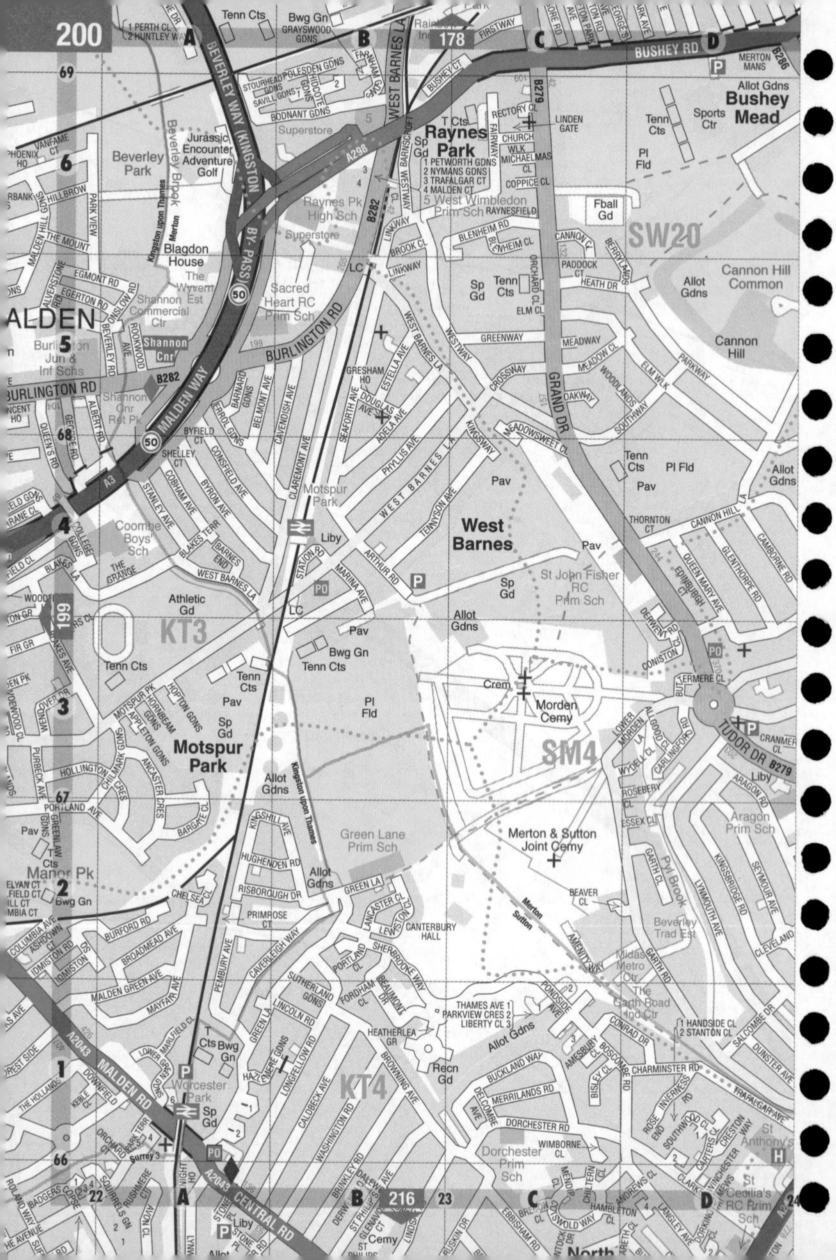
178
Raynes Park
Beverley Park
Blagdon House
ALDEN
Bushey Mead
SW20
Cannon Hill Common
Cannon Hill
West Barnes
KT3
Motspur Park
SM4
Morden Cemy
Merton & Sutton Joint Cemy
KT4
BUSHEY RD
BEVERLEY WAY (KINGSTON BY-PASS)
MALDEN WAY
BURLINGTON RD
WEST BARNES LA
GRAND DR
TUDOR DR
MALDEN RD
CENTRAL RD
Sacred Heart RC Prim Sch
Raynes Pk High Sch
Burlington Jun & Inf Schs
Coombe Boys' Sch
St John Fisher RC Prim Sch
Green Lane Prim Sch
Aragon Prim Sch
Dorchester Prim Sch
Worcester Park
Manor Pk
Beverley Trad Est
Midas Metro Ctr
The Garth Road Ind Ctr
Shannon Commercial Ctr
Jurassic Encounter Adventure Golf
1 PETWORTH GDNS
2 NYMANS GDNS
3 TRAFALGAR CT
4 MALDEN CT
5 West Wimbledon Prim Sch
1 PERTH CL
2 HUNTLEY WAY
THAMES AVE 1
PARKVIEW CRES 2
LIBERTY CL 3
1 HANDSIDE CL
2 STANTON CL

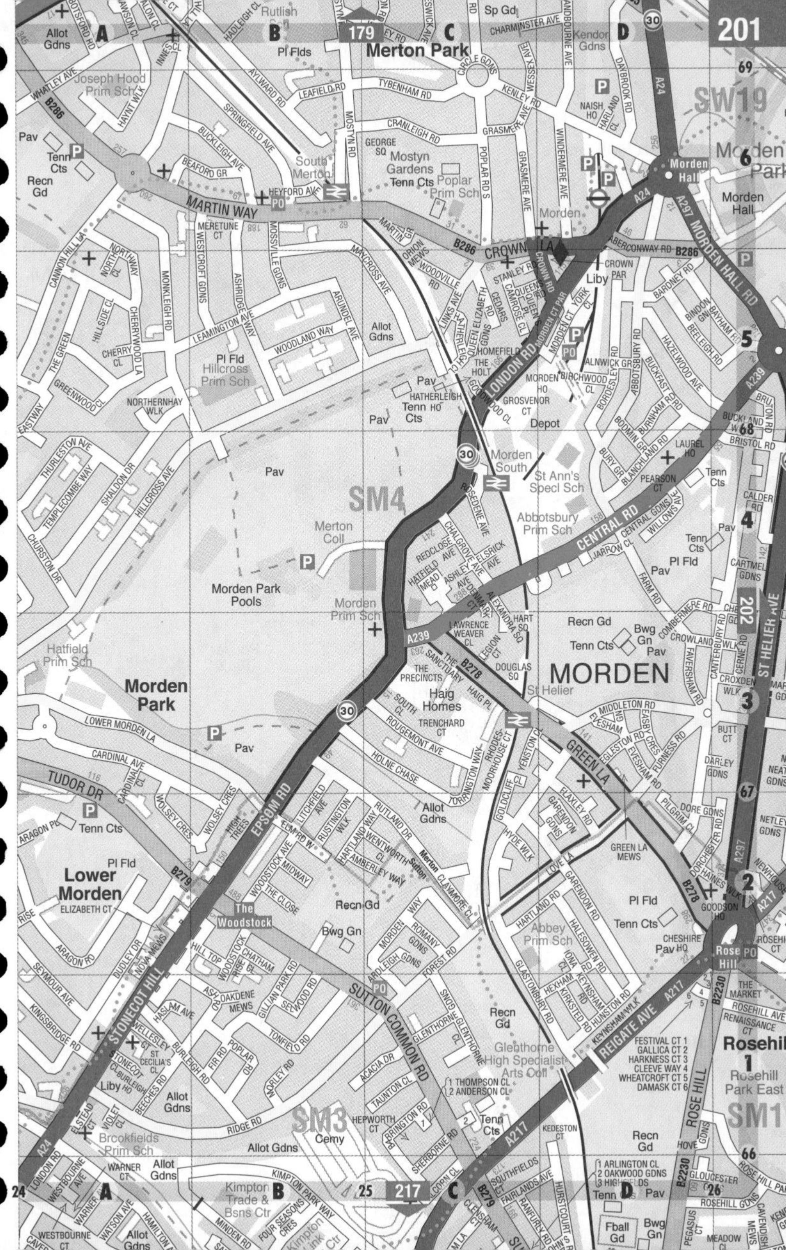

Merton Park
SW19
Morden Hall Park
Morden Hall
MARTIN WAY
South Merton
Mostyn Gardens
Poplar Prim Sch
Morden
CROWN LA
MORDEN HALL RD
LONDON RD
Joseph Hood Prim Sch
Hillcross Prim Sch
Morden South
St Ann's Specl Sch
Abbotsbury Prim Sch
CENTRAL RD
SM4
Merton Coll
Morden Park Pools
Morden Prim Sch
Hatfield Prim Sch
Morden Park
MORDEN
St Helier
Haig Homes
EPSOM RD
GREEN LA
ST HELIER AVE
Lower Morden
The Woodstock
STONECOT HILL
SUTTON COMMON RD
Abbey Prim Sch
Glebthorne High Specialist Arts Coll
REIGATE AVE
Rose Hill
Rosehill
Rosehill Park East
SM1
SM3
Brookfields Prim Sch
Kimpton Trade & Bsns Ctr
1 THOMPSON CL
2 ANDERSON CL
FESTIVAL CT 1
GALLICA CT 2
HARKNESS CT 3
CLEEVE WAY 4
WHEATCROFT CT 5
DAMASK CT 6
1 ARLINGTON CL
2 OAKWOOD GDNS
3 HIGHFIELDS

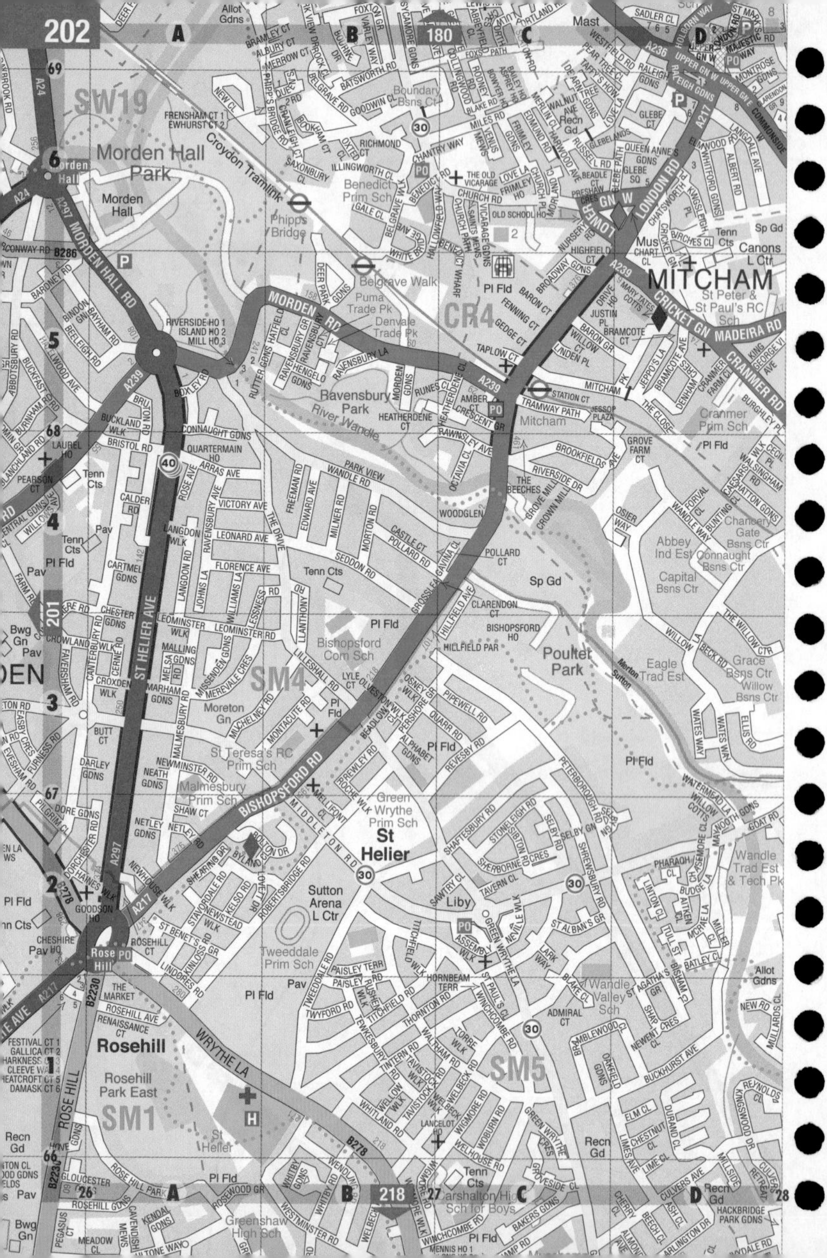
A
B
180
C
D
SW19
Morden Hall Park
Morden Hall
Croydon Tramlink
Phipps Bridge
Belgrave Walk
MORDEN HALL RD
MORDEN RD
Puma Trade Pk
Denvale Trade Pk
CR4
Ravensbury Park
River Wandle
Mitcham
MITCHAM
LONDON RD
CRICKET GN
MADEIRA RD
CRANMER RD
St Peter & St Paul's RC Sch
Cranmer Prim Sch
Canons L Ctr
Benedict Prim Sch
Boundary Bsns Ct
Abbey Ind Est
Capital Bsns Ctr
Connaught Bsns Ctr
Chancery Gate Bsns Ctr
Eagle Trad Est
Grace Bsns Ctr
Willow Bsns Ctr
Wandle Trad Est & Tech Pk
Poulter Park
Bishopsford Com Sch
BISHOPSFORD RD
ST HELIER AVE
SM4
St Teresa's RC Prim Sch
Malmesbury Prim Sch
Green Wrythe Prim Sch
St Helier
Sutton Arena L Ctr
Tweeddale Prim Sch
Wandle Valley Sch
SM5
WRYTHE LA
Rosehill
Rosehill Park East
SM1
ROSE HILL
St Helier
Carshalton High Sch for Boys
Greenshaw High Sch
Morton Sutton
Rose Hill
218
26
27
28

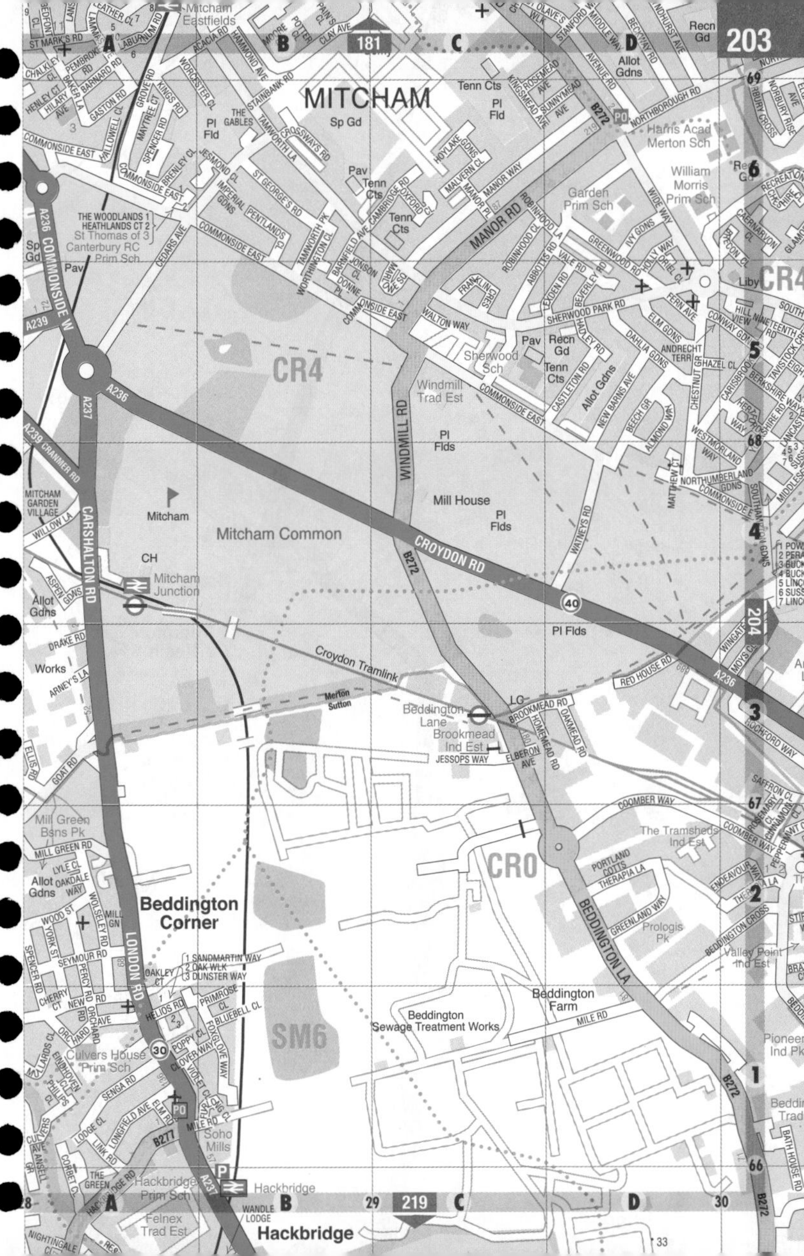

MITCHAM
Mitcham Eastfields
CR4
CR0
SM6
Mitcham Common
Mitcham Junction
Croydon Tramlink
Beddington Lane
Brookmead Ind Est
Windmill Trad Est
Mill House
Beddington Corner
Beddington Sewage Treatment Works
Beddington Farm
The Tramsheds Ind Est
Prologis Pk
Valley Point Ind Est
Pioneers Ind Pk
Mill Green Bsns Pk
Culvers House Prim Sch
Hackbridge Prim Sch
Hackbridge
Felnex Trad Est
Soho Mills
Harris Acad Merton Sch
William Morris Prim Sch
Garden Prim Sch
Sherwood Sch
St Thomas of Canterbury RC Prim Sch
MITCHAM GARDEN VILLAGE
COMMONSIDE EAST
COMMONSIDE W
CROYDON RD
CARSHALTON RD
LONDON RD
WINDMILL RD
MANOR RD
BEDDINGTON LA
NORTHBOROUGH RD
SHERWOOD PARK RD
MILE RD
COOMBER WAY
RED HOUSE RD
A236
A237
A239
B272
B277
181
204
219

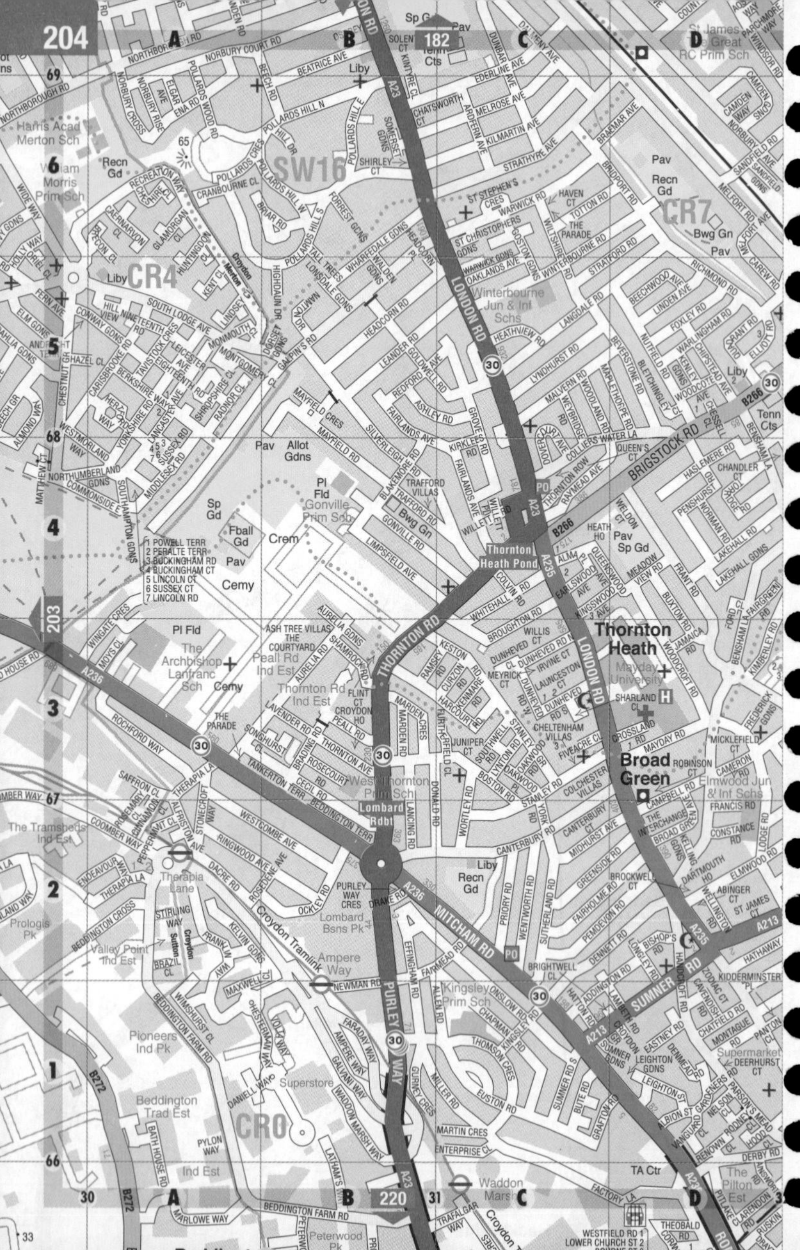

A
B
C
D
182
220
203
6
5
4
3
2
1
69
68
67
66
30
31
SW16
CR4
CR7
CR0
LONDON RD
THORNTON RD
PURLEY WAY
MITCHAM RD
BRIGSTOCK RD
SUMNER RD
A23
A235
A236
A213
B266
B272
Thornton Heath Pond
Thornton Heath
Broad Green
Lombard Rdbt
Mayday University
Winterbourne Jun & Inf Schs
Gonville Prim Sch
West Thornton Prim Sch
Kingsley Prim Sch
Elmwood Jun & Inf Schs
St James the Great RC Prim Sch
Harris Acad Merton Sch
William Morris Prim Sch
The Archbishop Lanfranc Sch
Peall Rd Ind Est
Thornton Rd Ind Est
The Tramsheds Ind Est
Valley Point Ind Est
Pioneers Ind Pk
Beddington Trad Est
Lombard Bsns Pk
Prologis Pk
Croydon Tramlink
Therapia Lane
Ampere Way
Waddon Marsh
Superstore
Supermarket
Crem
Cemy
Recn Gd
Liby
Pav
Bwg Gn
Allot Gdns
Fball Gd
Sp Gd
Pl Fld
TA Ctr
1 POWELL TERR
2 PERALTE TERR
3 BUCKINGHAM RD
4 BUCKINGHAM CT
5 LINCOLN CT
6 SUSSEX CT
7 LINCOLN RD
WESTFIELD RD 1
LOWER CHURCH ST 2

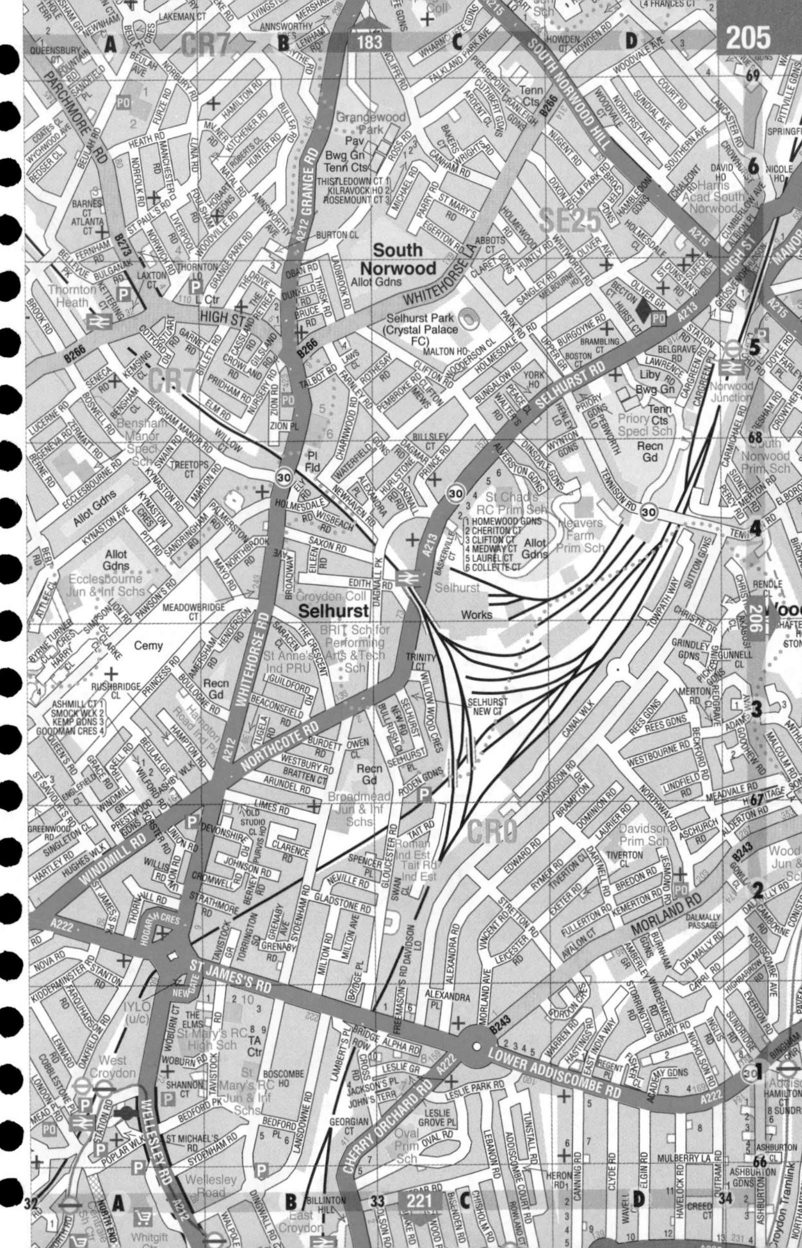
A
B
C
D
CR7
183
South Norwood
Allot Gdns
SE25
Grangewood Park
Selhurst Park (Crystal Palace FC)
Thornton Heath
HIGH ST
WHITEHORSE LA
SOUTH NORWOOD HILL
SELHURST RD
GRANGE RD
WHITEHORSE RD
Selhurst
Works
Croydon Coll
BRIT Sch for Performing Arts & Tech Sch
St Anne's Ind PRU
Recn Gd
Cemy
Ecclesbourne Jun & Inf Schs
Bensham Manor Specl Sch
Heavers Farm Prim Sch
St Chad's RC Prim Sch
Priory Specl Sch
Harris Acad South Norwood
Norwood Junction
South Norwood Prim Sch
Woodside Jun & Inf Sch
Davidson Prim Sch
Broadmead Jun & Inf Schs
Roman Ind Est
Tait Rd Ind Est
CR0
NORTHCOTE RD
WINDMILL RD
ST JAMES'S RD
LOWER ADDISCOMBE RD
MORLAND RD
CHERRY ORCHARD RD
WELLESLEY RD
West Croydon
St Mary's RC High Sch
St Mary's RC Jun & Inf Schs
Oval Prim Sch
Wellesley Road
East Croydon
Whitgift
Addiscombe
Croydon Tramlink
206
221
32
33
34
1
2
3
4
5
6

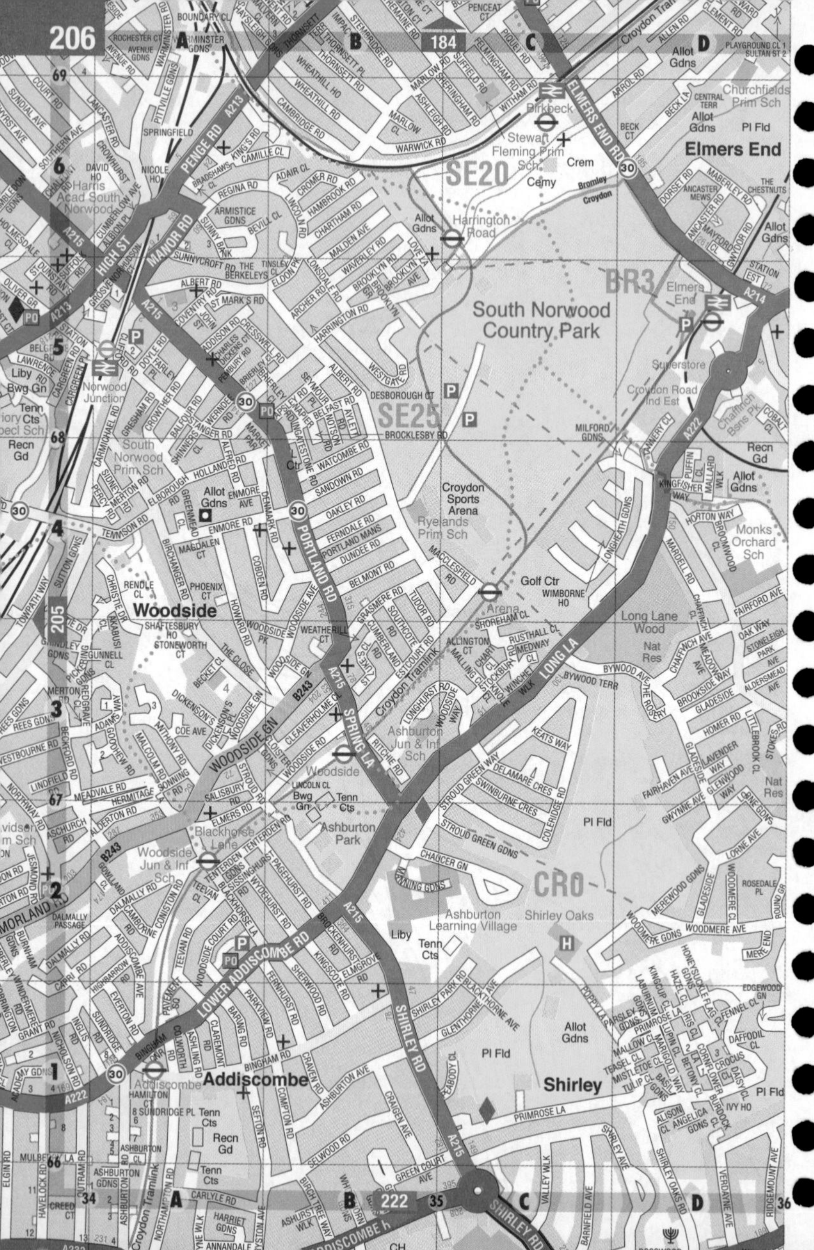

184
222
205
SE20
SE25
BR3
CR0
Elmers End
South Norwood Country Park
Woodside
Addiscombe
Shirley
Croydon Sports Arena
Ashburton Park
Ashburton Learning Village
Shirley Oaks
Long Lane Wood
Birkbeck
Harrington Road
Arena
Woodside
Blackhorse Lane
Addiscombe
Norwood Junction
Croydon Tramlink
PORTLAND RD
SPRING LA
SHIRLEY RD
LONG LA
LOWER ADDISCOMBE RD
WOODSIDE GN
PENGE RD
MANOR RD
HIGH ST
ELMERS END RD

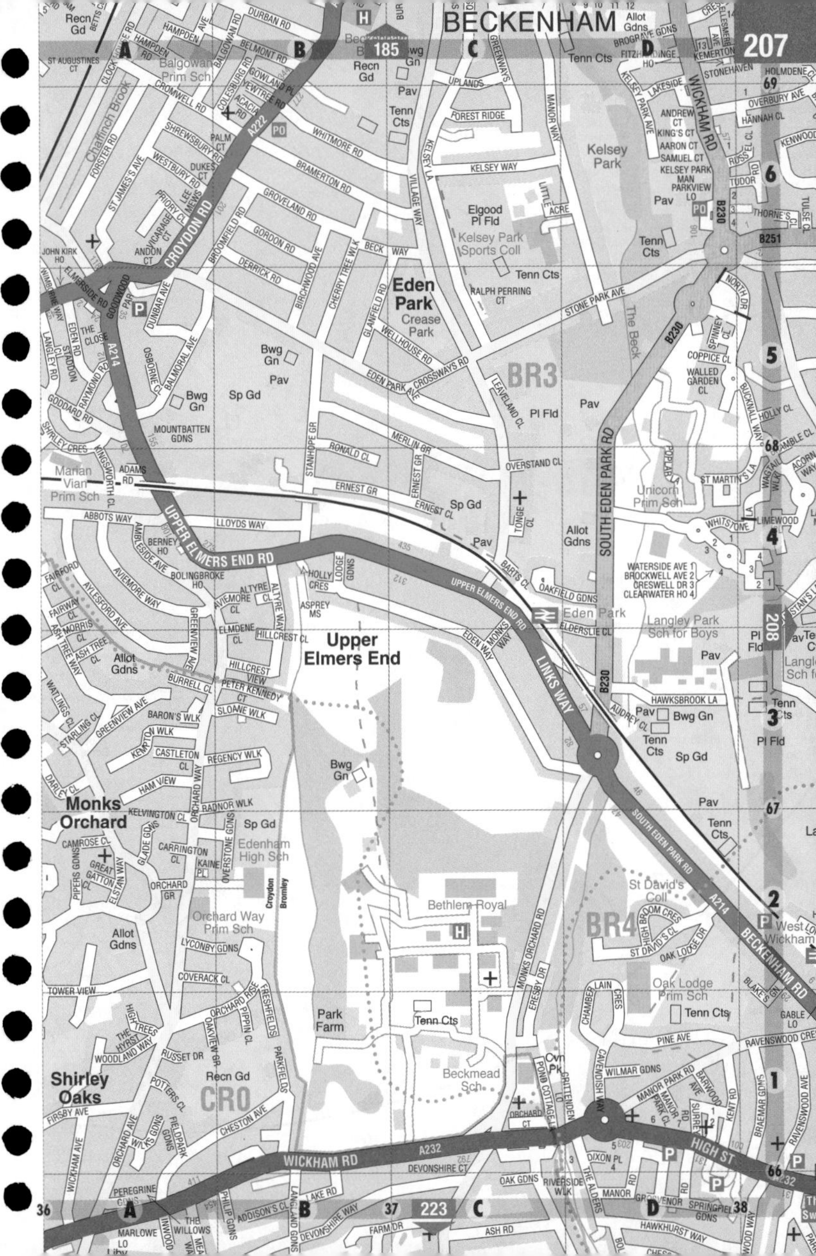

BECKENHAM
207
185
223
208
A
B
C
D
36
37
38
1
2
3
4
5
6
66
67
68
69
Recn Gd
BETTS CL
HAMPDEN AVE
HAMPDEN RD
BALGOWAN RD
DURBAN RD
BELMONT RD
ST AUGUSTINES CT
CLOCK HOUSE RD
Balgowan Prim Sch
COLESBURG RD
GOWLAND PL
YEWTREE RD
ACACIA RD
CROMWELL RD
Chaffinch Brook
FORSTER RD
SHREWSBURY RD
PALM CT
WHITMORE RD
WESTBURY RD
DUKES CT
ST JAMES'S AVE
LEE MEWS
PRIORY CL
VICARAGE CT
CROYDON RD
A222
BRAMERTON RD
GROVELAND RD
GORDON RD
DERRICK RD
BROOMFIELD RD
BIRCHWOOD AVE
CHERRY TREE WLK
BECK WAY
GLANFIELD RD
WELLHOUSE RD
JOHN KIRK HO
ELMERSIDE RD
ANDON CT
GOODWOOD PDE
DUNBAR AVE
NIMBORNE WAY
EDEN RD
THE CLOSE
LANGLEY RD
STADDON CL
RAYMOND RD
A214
OSBORNE CL
BALMORAL AVE
GODDARD RD
SHIRLEY CRES
MOUNTBATTEN GDNS
KINGSWORTH CL
ADAMS RD
Marian Vian Prim Sch
ABBOTS WAY
LLOYDS WAY
UPPER ELMERS END RD
BERNEY HO
AMBLESIDE AVE
AVIEMORE WAY
BOLINGBROKE HO
FAIRFORD CL
AYLESFORD AVE
FAIRWAY CL
MORRIS CL
ASH TREE WAY
ASH TREE CL
Allot Gdns
WATLINGS CL
STARLING CL
GREENVIEW AVE
GREENVIEW AVE
BURRELL CL
AVIEMORE CL
ALTYRE CL
ALTYRE WAY
ELMDENE CL
HILLCREST CL
HILLCREST VIEW
PETER KENNEDY CT
SLOANE WLK
BARON'S WLK
KEMPTON WLK
CASTLETON CL
REGENCY WLK
HAM VIEW
DARLEY CL
RADNOR WLK
KELVINGTON CL
ORCHARD WAY
Monks Orchard
CAMROSE CL
GREAT GATTON CL
PIPERS GDNS
ELSTAN WAY
GLADE GDNS
CARRINGTON CL
KAINE PL
OVERSTONE GDNS
ORCHARD GR
Edenham High Sch
Croydon
Bromley
Orchard Way Prim Sch
LYCONBY GDNS
COVERACK CL
TOWER VIEW
ORCHARD RISE
PIPPIN CL
FRESHFIELDS
OAKVIEW GR
HIGH TREES
THE HYRST
WOODLAND WAY
RUSSET DR
Recn Gd
POTTERS CL
Shirley Oaks
CR0
FIRSBY AVE
ORCHARD AVE
WILKS GDNS
FIELDPARK GDNS
CHESTON AVE
PARKFIELDS
WICKHAM AVE
WICKHAM RD
A232
DEVONSHIRE CT
PEREGRINE GDNS
PHILIP GDNS
INWOOD
THE WILLOWS
MARLOWE LO
ADDISON'S CL
LANGLAND GDNS
LAKE RD
DEVONSHIRE WAY
FARM DR
ASH RD
Upper Elmers End
HOLLY CRES
LODGE GDNS
ASPREY MS
Bwg Gn
Sp Gd
Pav
Park Farm
Bethlem Royal
Tenn Cts
Beckmead Sch
Recn Gd
Tenn Cts
UPLANDS
GREENWAYS
FOREST RIDGE
KELSEY LA
KELSEY WAY
VILLAGE WAY
MANOR WAY
LITTLE ACRE
Elgood Pl Fld
Kelsey Park Sports Coll
RALPH PERRING CT
STONE PARK AVE
Eden Park
Crease Park
CROSSWAYS RD
EDEN PARK AVE
STANHOPE GR
RONALD CL
MERLIN GR
ERNEST GR
ERNEST CL
BR3
LEAVELAND CL
Pl Fld
OVERSTAND CL
TONGE CL
BARTS CL
OAKFIELD GDNS
Eden Park
ELDERSLIE CL
MONKS WAY
EDEN WAY
LINKS WAY
SOUTH EDEN PARK RD
B230
AUDREY CL
Allot Gdns
Kelsey Park
The Beck
Allot Gdns
BROGRAVE GDNS
FITZHARDINGE HO
KEMERTON
ELLESMERE
STONEHAVEN
LAKESIDE
KELSEY PARK AVE
WICKHAM RD
ANDREW CT
KING'S CT
AARON CT
SAMUEL CT
KELSEY PARK MAN
PARKVIEW LO
HOLMDENE CL
OVERBURY AVE
HANNAH CL
KENWOOD
RUSSELL CL
TUDOR RD
THORNE'S CL
TULSE CL
B251
NORTH DR
SPINNEY CL
COPPICE CL
WALLED GARDEN CL
BUCKNALL WAY
HOLLY CL
GAMBLE CL
WAGTAIL WLK
ACORN WAY
POPLAR LA
ST MARTIN'S LA
Unicorn Prim Sch
WHITSTONE LA
LIMEWOOD
WATERSIDE AVE 1
BROCKWELL AVE 2
CRESWELL DR 3
CLEARWATER HO 4
STAN'S LA
Langley Park Sch for Boys
HAWKSBROOK LA
Langley Sch for
Sp Gd
Pl Fld
St David's Coll
BR4
HIGH BROOM CRES
ST DAVID'S CL
OAK LODGE DR
Oak Lodge Prim Sch
West Wickham
BECKENHAM RD
SOUTH EDEN PARK RD
BLAKE'S GN
GABLE LO
CHAMBERLAIN CRES
PINE AVE
RAVENSWOOD CRES
MONKS ORCHARD RD
ERESBY DR
Cvn Pk
POND COTTAGE LA
CRITTENDEN LO
ORCHARD CT
CAVENDISH WAY
WILMAR GDNS
MANOR PARK RD
MANOR PARK CL
MANOR RD
BARWOOD AVE
SURREY
KENT RD
BRAEMAR GDNS
RAVENSWOOD AVE
HIGH ST
DIXON PL
OAK GDNS
RIVERSIDE WLK
THE ALDERS
MANOR GROVE
SPRINGFIELD GDNS
HAWKHURST WAY
WOOD WAY
The Swan
Lan

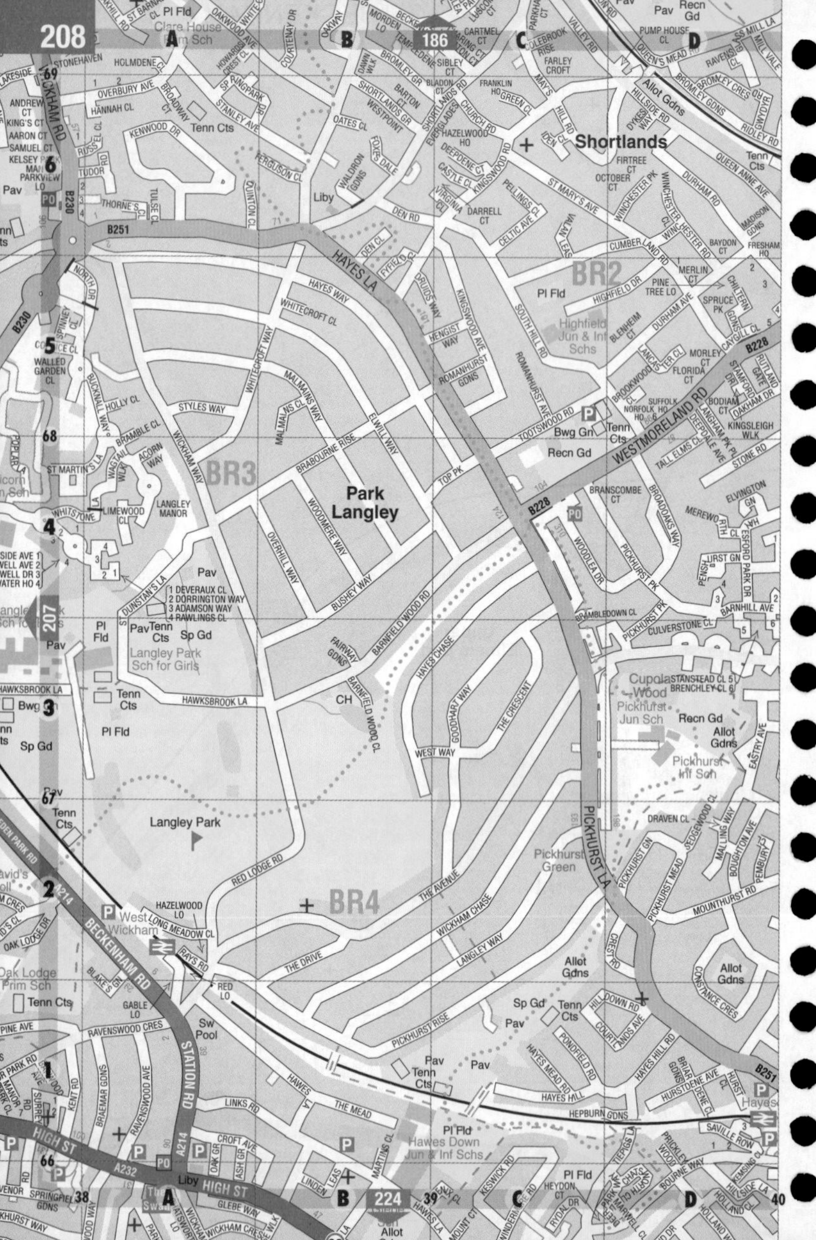
A
B
186
C
D
Clare House Prim Sch
Pl Fld
OAKWOOD AVE
COURTENAY DR
OAKWAY
MORDEN LO
BECKENHAM
CARTMEL CT
PARKHAM CT
COLEBROOK RISE
VALLEY RD
Pav
Recn Gd
PUMP HOUSE CL
QUEEN'S MEAD RD
SS MILL LA
MILL VALE
STONEHAVEN
HOLMDENE CL
LAKESIDE
WICKHAM RD
OVERBURY AVE
HANNAH CL
BROADWAY
STANLEY AVE
HOWARDS CREST CL
SPRINGPARK RD
Tenn Cts
KENWOOD DR
ANDREW CT
KING'S CT
AARON CT
SAMUEL CT
KELSEY PARK MANS
PARKVIEW LO
RUSSELL CL
TUDOR
THORNE'S CL
TULSE CL
FERGUSON CL
QUINTON CL
OATES CL
FOXES DALE
WALDRON GDNS
SHORTLANDS GR
WESTPOINT
BARTON CT
BROMLEY GR
TEMPLEDENE
SIBLEY CT
BLADON CT
SHORTLANDS RD
EVERGLADES
FRANKLIN HO
GREEN CL
CHURCH RD
HAZELWOOD HO
DEEPDENE CT
CASTLE CL
VIRGINIA CL
KINGSWOOD RD
DARRELL CT
PELLINGS CL
CELTIC AVE
HILL RD
IDEN CL
MAY'S
FARLEY CROFT
Shortlands
Allot Gdns
HILLSIDE RD
DYKES WAY
BROMLEY GDNS
BROMLEY CRES
RAVENSBOURNE
RIDLEY RD
Tenn Cts
QUEEN ANNE AVE
FIRTREE CT
OCTOBER CT
WINCHESTER PK
WINCHESTER CL
WINCHESTER RD
DURHAM RD
MADISON GDNS
BAYDON CT
FRESHAM HO
ST MARY'S AVE
VALAN LEAS
CUMBERLAND RD
Liby
DEN RD
DEN CL
FYFIELD CL
B251
HAYES LA
HAYES WAY
WHITECROFT CL
WHITECROFT WAY
NORTH DR
B230
SPINNEY CL
COPPICE CL
WALLED GARDEN CL
BUCKNALL WAY
HOLLY CL
BRAMBLE CL
WAGTAIL WLK
ACORN WAY
POPLAR LA
ST MARTIN'S LA
LIMEWOOD CL
WHITSTONE LA
LANGLEY MANOR
DRUIDS WAY
HENGIST WAY
KINGSWOOD AVE
ROMANHURST GDNS
ROMANHURST AVE
SOUTH HILL RD
Pl Fld
Highfield Jun & Inf Schs
HIGHFIELD DR
PINE TREE LO
MERLIN CT
CHILTERN GDNS
SPRUCE PK
BLENHEIM CT
DURHAM AVE
CAYGILL CL
MORLEY CT
LANCASTER CL
FLORIDA CT
B228
RUTLAND GATE
STAMFORD DR
OAKHAM DR
BODIAM CL
BROOKWOOD CL
SUFFOLK HO
NORFOLK HO
WESTMORELAND RD
LANGHAM PK PL
KINGSLEIGH WLK
TOOTSWOOD RD
Bwg Gn
Tenn Cts
Recn Gd
TALL ELMS CL
DEEPDALE AVE
STONE RD
STYLES WAY
MALMAINS CL
MALMAINS WAY
ELWILL WAY
BRABOURNE RISE
TOP PK
WICKHAM WAY
BR2
BR3
Park Langley
WOODMERE WAY
OVERHILL WAY
BUSHEY WAY
BARNFIELD WOOD RD
BRANSCOMBE CT
ELVINGTON GN
MEREWORTH CL
ESFORD PARK DR
WOODLEA DR
BROADOAKS WAY
PICKHURST PK
HURST GN
BARNHILL AVE
BRAMBLEDOWN CL
CULVERSTONE CL
Pav
1 DEVERAUX CL
2 DORRINGTON WAY
3 ADAMSON WAY
4 RAWLINGS CL
ST DUNSTAN'S LA
207
Pl Fld
Pav
Tenn Cts
Sp Gd
Langley Park Sch for Girls
FAIRWAY GDNS
HAYES CHASE
HAWKSBROOK LA
Bwg Gn
Tenn Cts
Pl Fld
Sp Gd
CH
BARNFIELD WOOD CL
GOODHART WAY
THE CRESCENT
WEST WAY
Cupola Wood
STANSTEAD CL
BRENCHLEY CL
Pickhurst Jun Sch
Recn Gd
Allot Gdns
EASTRY AVE
Pickhurst Inf Sch
Tenn Cts
Langley Park
EDEN PARK RD
RED LODGE RD
PICKHURST LA
DRAVEN CL
SEDGEWOOD CL
MALLING WAY
BOUGHTON AVE
PEMBURY CL
Pickhurst Green
PICKHURST GN
PICKHURST MEAD
MOUNTHURST RD
BR4
THE AVENUE
WICKHAM CHASE
LANGLEY WAY
THE DRIVE
HAZELWOOD LO
LONG MEADOW CL
West Wickham
A214
BECKENHAM RD
RAYS RD
OAK LODGE DR
Oak Lodge Prim Sch
BLAKE'S GN
Tenn Cts
RED LO
GABLE LO
PINE AVE
RAVENSWOOD CRES
Sw Pool
STATION RD
CREST RD
Allot Gdns
HILLDOWN RD
COURTLANDS AVE
Allot Gdns
CONSTANCE CRES
Sp Gd
Tenn Cts
Pav
PICKHURST RISE
HAYES MEAD RD
PONDFIELD RD
HAYES HILL RD
BRIAR GDNS
HURSTDENE AVE
HURST CL
DENE CL
B251
Hayes
SAVILLE ROW
BRAEMAR GDNS
RAVENSWOOD AVE
KENT RD
HAWES LA
THE MEAD
LINKS RD
Pav
Tenn Cts
Pav
HAYES HILL
HEPBURN GDNS
HIGH ST
A232
CROFT AVE
OAK GR
ASH GR
MARTINS CL
Pl Fld
Hawes Down Jun & Inf Schs
KESWICK RD
TIEPIGS LA
PRICKLEY WOOD
BOURNE WAY
HEMSING CL
HILLSIDE LA
HOLLAND CL
HOLLAND WAY
Liby
SPRINGPARK GDNS
38
A
LINDEN LEAS
B
224
39
HAWES LA
MOUNT CT
WINDERMERE RD
Pl Fld
HEYDON CT
RYDAL DR
C
D
40
GLEBE WAY
WICKHAM CRES
ROSE WLK
Allot Gdns

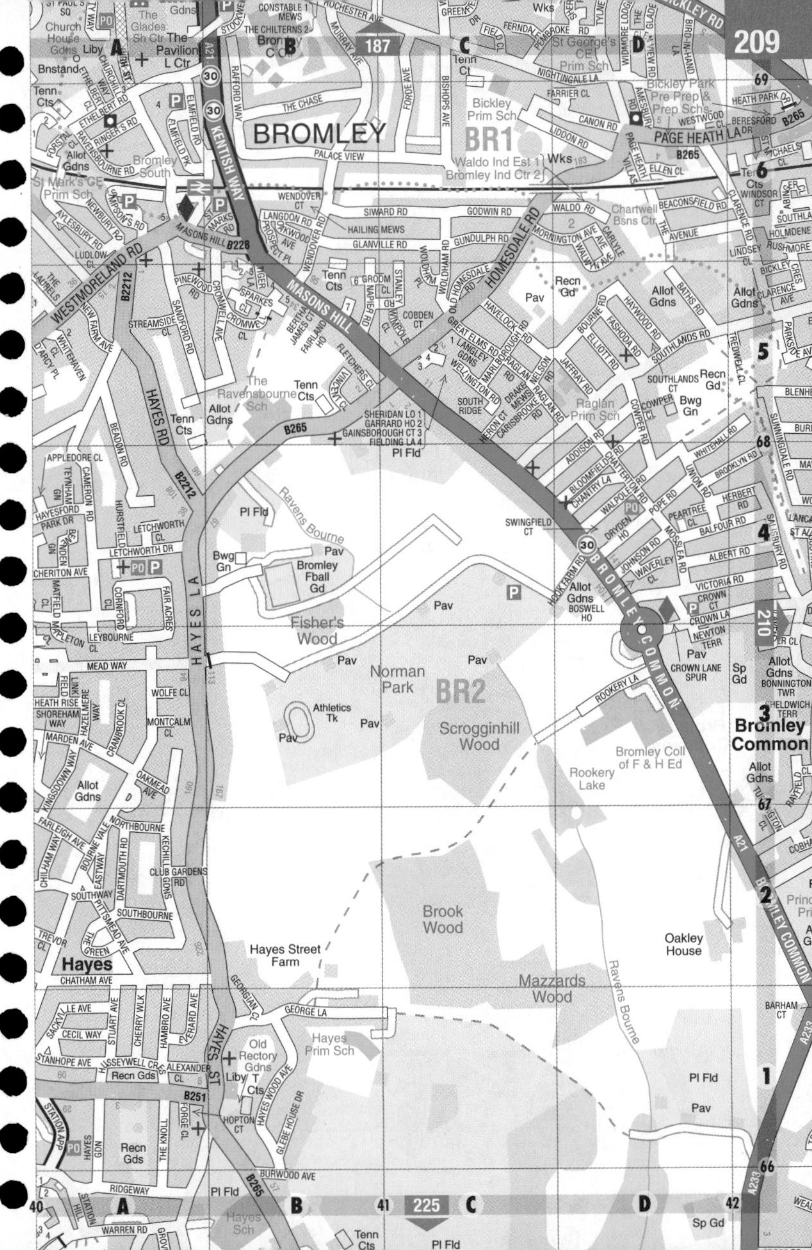

187
BROMLEY
BR1
BR2
KENTISH WAY
MASONS HILL
BROMLEY COMMON
HAYES LA
HAYES RD
HAYES ST
WESTMORELAND RD
HOMESDALE RD
PAGE HEATH LA
Bromley South
The Glades Sh Ctr
The Pavilion L Ctr
Bickley Prim Sch
Bickley Park Pre Prep & Prep Schs
Waldo Ind Est 1
Bromley Ind Ctr 2
Chartwell Bsns Ctr
St Mark's CE Prim Sch
St George's CE Prim Sch
The Ravensbourne Sch
Raglan Prim Sch
Bromley Fball Gd
Fisher's Wood
Norman Park
Athletics Tk
Scrogginhill Wood
Bromley Coll of F & H Ed
Rookery Lake
Brook Wood
Hayes Street Farm
Mazzards Wood
Oakley House
Ravens Bourne
Hayes Prim Sch
Old Rectory Gdns
Hayes
Bromley Common
Hayes Sch
SHERIDAN LO 1
GARRARD HO 2
GAINSBOROUGH CT 3
FIELDING LA 4
210
225
40
41
42
A
B
C
D
1
2
3
4
5
6

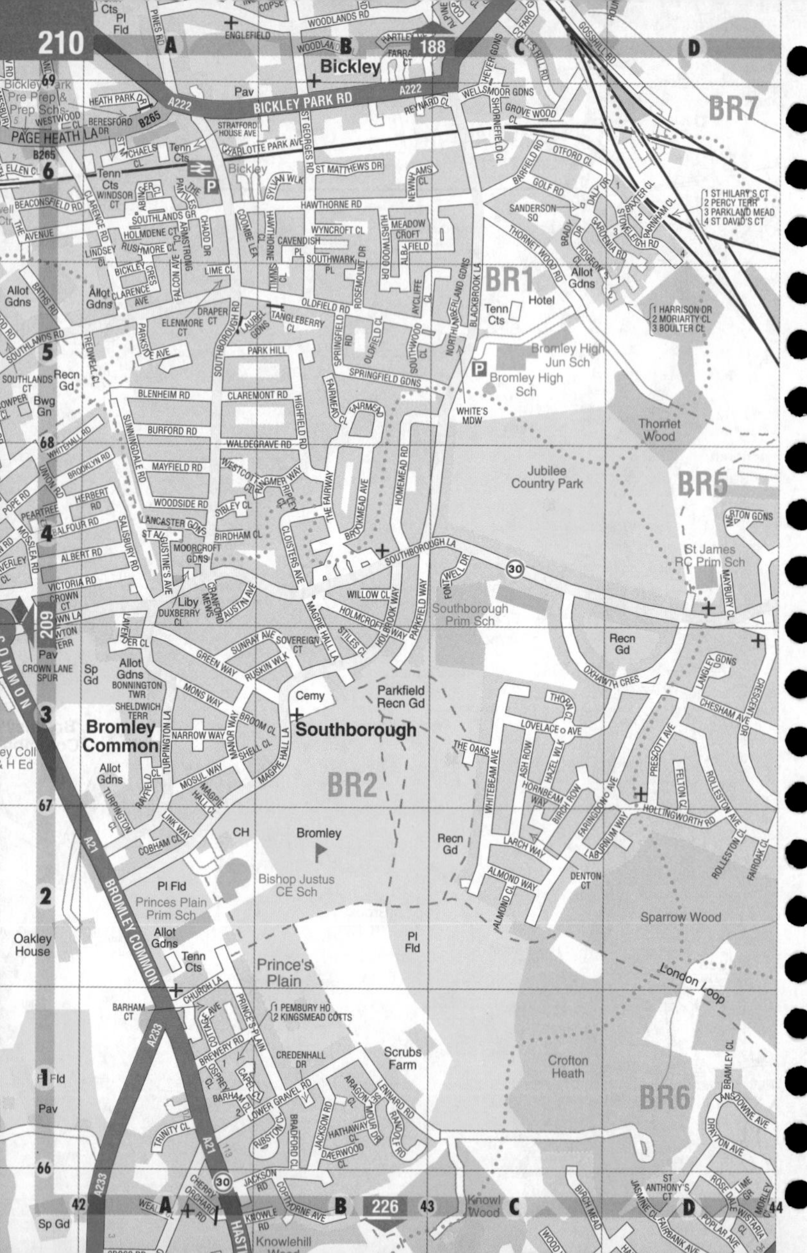
188
Bickley
BICKLEY PARK RD
A222
BR7
BR1
BR5
BR2
BR6
Bromley High Jun Sch
Bromley High Sch
Thornet Wood
Jubilee Country Park
St James RC Prim Sch
Southborough Prim Sch
SOUTHBOROUGH LA
Parkfield Recn Gd
Bromley Common
Southborough
Bishop Justus CE Sch
Princes Plain Prim Sch
Prince's Plain
Sparrow Wood
London Loop
Crofton Heath
Scrubs Farm
Oakley House
BROMLEY COMMON
A21
A233
209
226
Knowl Wood
Knowlehill Wood
1 ST HILARY'S CT
2 PERCY TERR
3 PARKLAND MEAD
4 ST DAVID'S CT
1 HARRISON DR
2 MORIARTY CL
3 BOULTER CL
1 PEMBURY HO
2 KINGSMEAD COTTS
42
43
44
69
68
67
66

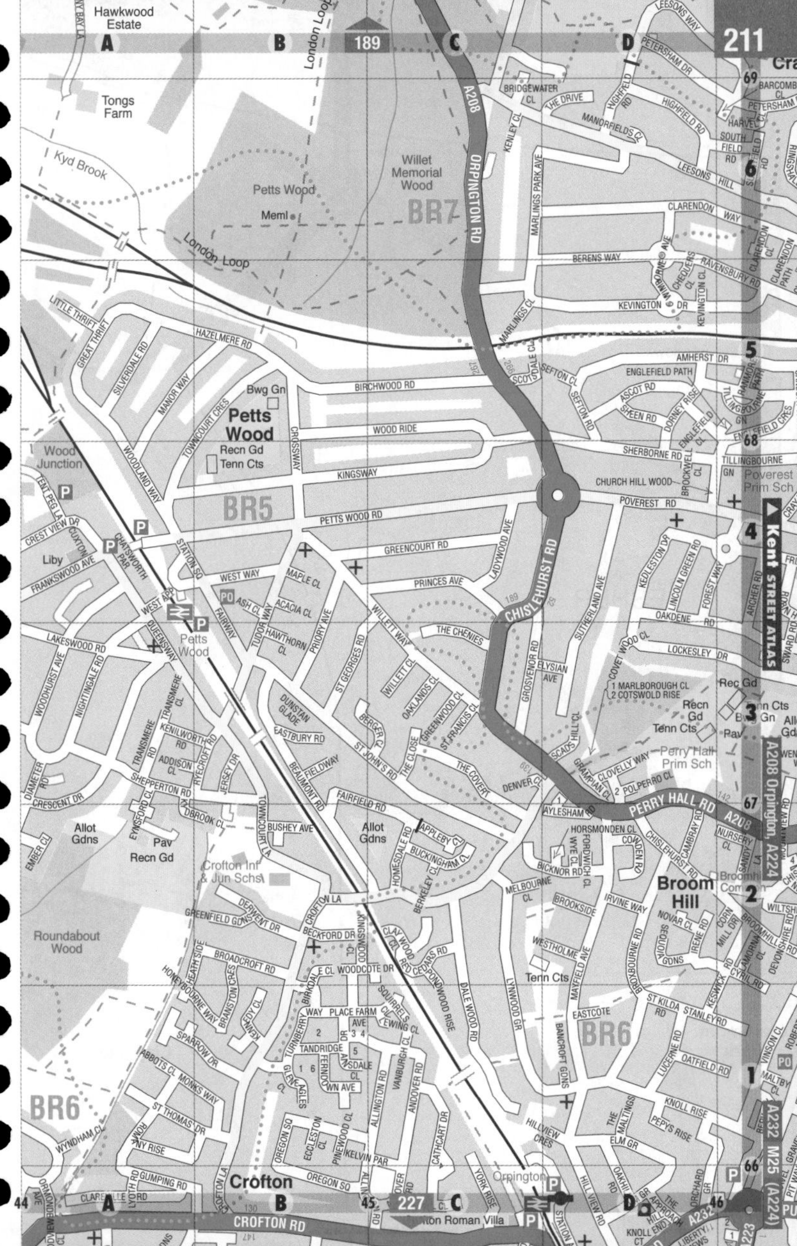
211
189
227
A
B
C
D
Hawkwood Estate
Tongs Farm
Kyd Brook
London Loop
Petts Wood
Meml
Willet Memorial Wood
BR7
A208
ORPINGTON RD
BRIDGEWATER CL
THE DRIVE
KENLEY CL
MANORFIELDS CL
HIGHFIELD RD
LEESONS WAY
PETERSHAM DR
LEESONS HILL
MARLINGS PARK AVE
CLARENDON WAY
BERENS WAY
KEVINGTON DR
KEVINGTON CL
MARLINGS CL
SCOTSDALE CL
SEFTON CL
SEFTON RD
AMHERST DR
ENGLEFIELD PATH
ASCOT RD
SHEEN RD
DORNEY RISE
SHERBORNE RD
TILLINGBOURNE GN
CHURCH HILL WOOD
Poverest Prim Sch
POVEREST RD
LITTLE THRIFT
GREAT THRIFT
SILVERDALE RD
HAZELMERE RD
MANOR WAY
TOWNCOURT CRES
Bwg Gn
Petts Wood
Recn Gd
Tenn Cts
BIRCHWOOD RD
WOOD RIDE
CROSSWAY
KINGSWAY
WOODLAND WAY
BR5
PETTS WOOD RD
Wood Junction
TENT PEG LA
CREST VIEW DR
CUXTON
Liby
FRANKSWOOD AVE
CHATSWORTH PAR
STATION SQ
GREENCOURT RD
WEST WAY
MAPLE CL
PRINCES AVE
LADYWOOD AVE
CHISLEHURST RD
SUTHERLAND AVE
KEDLESTON DR
LINCOLN GREEN RD
FOREST WAY
OAKDENE RD
LOCKESLEY DR
COVET WOOD CL
ASH CL
ACACIA CL
TUDOR WAY
FAIRWAY
PRIORY AVE
HAWTHORN CL
WILLETT WAY
THE CHENIES
GROSVENOR RD
ELYSIAN AVE
1 MARLBOROUGH CL
2 COTSWOLD RISE
Rec Gd
Recn Gd
Tenn Cts
Pav
Perry Hall Prim Sch
WEST APP
LAKESWOOD RD
QUEENSWAY
Petts Wood
WOODHURST AVE
NIGHTINGALE RD
TRANSMERE RD
TRANSMERE CL
ST GEORGES RD
WILLETT CL
OAKLANDS CL
GREENWOOD CL
ST FRANCIS CL
DUNSTAN GLADE
EASTBURY RD
BERGER CL
KENILWORTH RD
RYECROFT RD
ADDISON CL
JERSEY DR
DIAMETER RD
SHEPPERTON RD
CRESCENT DR
ST JOHN'S RD
THE CLOSE
THE COVERT
SCADS HILL CL
GRAMPIAN CL
CLOVELLY WAY
POLPERRO CL
DENVER CL
PERRY HALL RD
A208
FIELDWAY
BEAUMONT RD
FAIRFIELD RD
AYLESHAM RD
HORSMONDEN CL
WYE CL
FORDWICH CL
COWDEN RD
CAMBRAY RD
NURSERY CL
SANDY LA
Allot Gdns
Pav
Recn Gd
EYNSFORD CL
EMBER CL
TOWNCOURT LA
BUSHEY AVE
Allot Gdns
HOMESDALE RD
APPLEBY CL
BUCKINGHAM CL
BERKELEY CL
Crofton Inf & Jun Schs
MELBOURNE CL
BICKNOR RD
BROOKSIDE
IRVINE WAY
Broom Hill
Roundabout Wood
GREENFIELD GDNS
DERWENT DR
CROFTON LA
KINGSWOOD
BECKFORD DR
CLAYWOOD CL
RED CEDARS RD
WESTHOLME
NOVAR CL
SEQUOIA GDNS
IRENE RD
CORN MILL DR
LAMORNA CL
BROOMHILL RD
DEVONSHIRE RD
WILTSHIRE RD
CYRIL RD
BROADCROFT RD
HEATH SIDE
HONEYBOURNE WAY
BRANSTON CRES
BIRKDALE CL
WOODCOTE DR
SQUIRRELS
PONDWOOD RISE
DALE WOOD RD
LYNWOOD GR
MAYFIELD AVE
Tenn Cts
BROXBOURNE RD
KESWICK RD
ST KILDA RD
STANLEY RD
EDY CL
TURNBERRY WAY
PLACE FARM AVE
EWING CL
EASTCOTE
BR6
SPARROW DR
TANDRIDGE DR
FERNDOWN AVE
AINSDALE CL
GLENEAGLES CL
BANCROFT GDNS
LUCERNE RD
OATFIELD RD
ABBOTS CL
MONKS WAY
ALLINGTON RD
VANBURGH CL
ANDOVER RD
CATHCART DR
KNOLL RISE
BR6
WYNDHAM CL
ST THOMAS DR
ROWANY RISE
OREGON SQ
ECCLESTON CL
PINEWOOD CL
KELVIN PAR
HILLVIEW CRES
THE MALTINGS
PEPYS RISE
ELM GR
OREGON SQ
YORK RISE
HILL VIEW RD
OAKHILL RD
GUMPING RD
Crofton
Orpington
CRAY AVE
CROFTON RD
Crofton Roman Villa
STATION RD
ORCHARD GR
KNOLL CT
LIBERTY MEWS
A232
A223
M25 (A224)
A232
A208 Orpington, A224
Kent STREET ATLAS
44
45
46
1
2
3
4
5
6
66
67
68
69

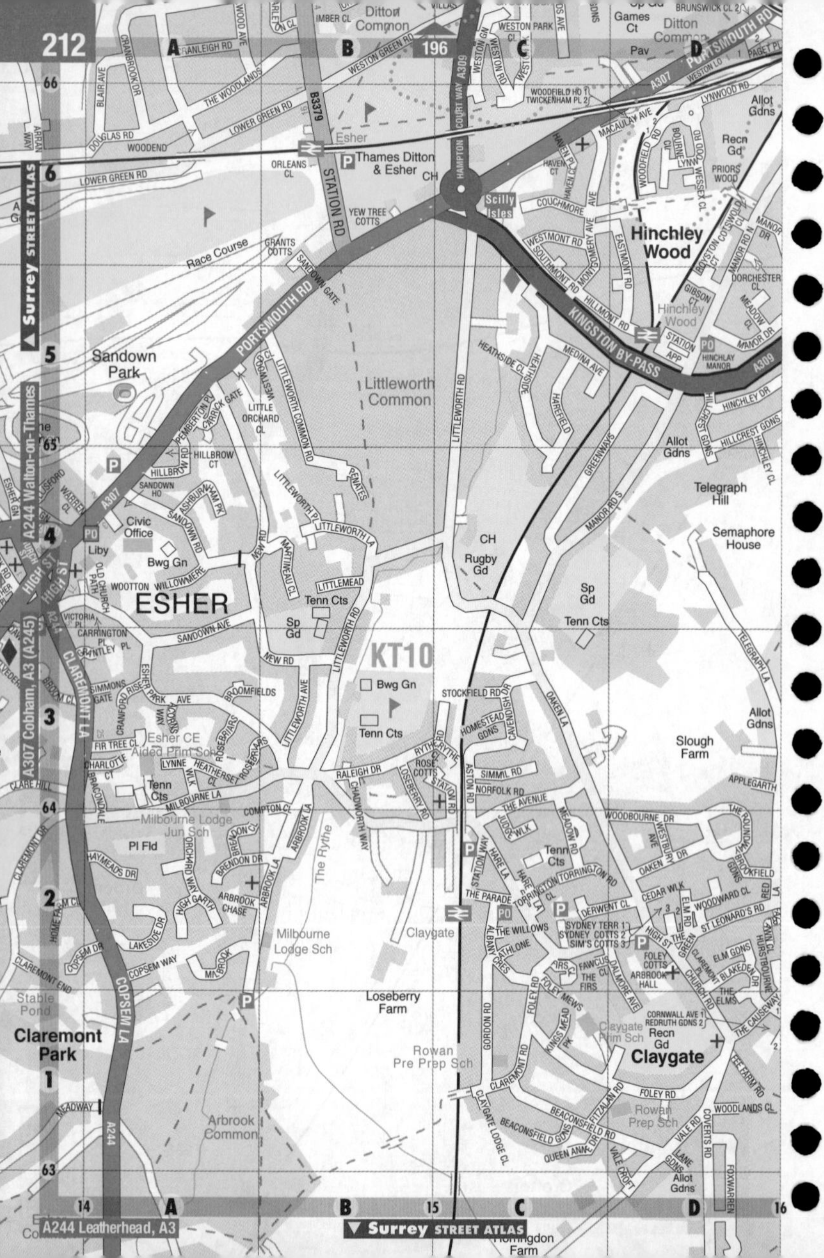
196
ESHER
Esher
Thames Ditton & Esher
Sandown Park
Race Course
Littleworth Common
KT10
Hinchley Wood
Claygate
Claremont Park
Arbrook Common
Telegraph Hill
Semaphore House
Slough Farm
Loseberry Farm
Rowan Pre Prep Sch
Milbourne Lodge Sch
Milbourne Lodge Jun Sch
Esher CE Aided Prim Sch
Claygate Prim Sch
Rowan Prep Sch
Civic Office
Scilly Isles
PORTSMOUTH RD
KINGSTON BY-PASS
LITTLEWORTH RD
COPSEM LA
CLAREMONT LA
HIGH ST
STATION RD
A307 Cobham, A3 (A245)
A244 Walton-on-Thames
A244 Leatherhead, A3
Surrey STREET ATLAS

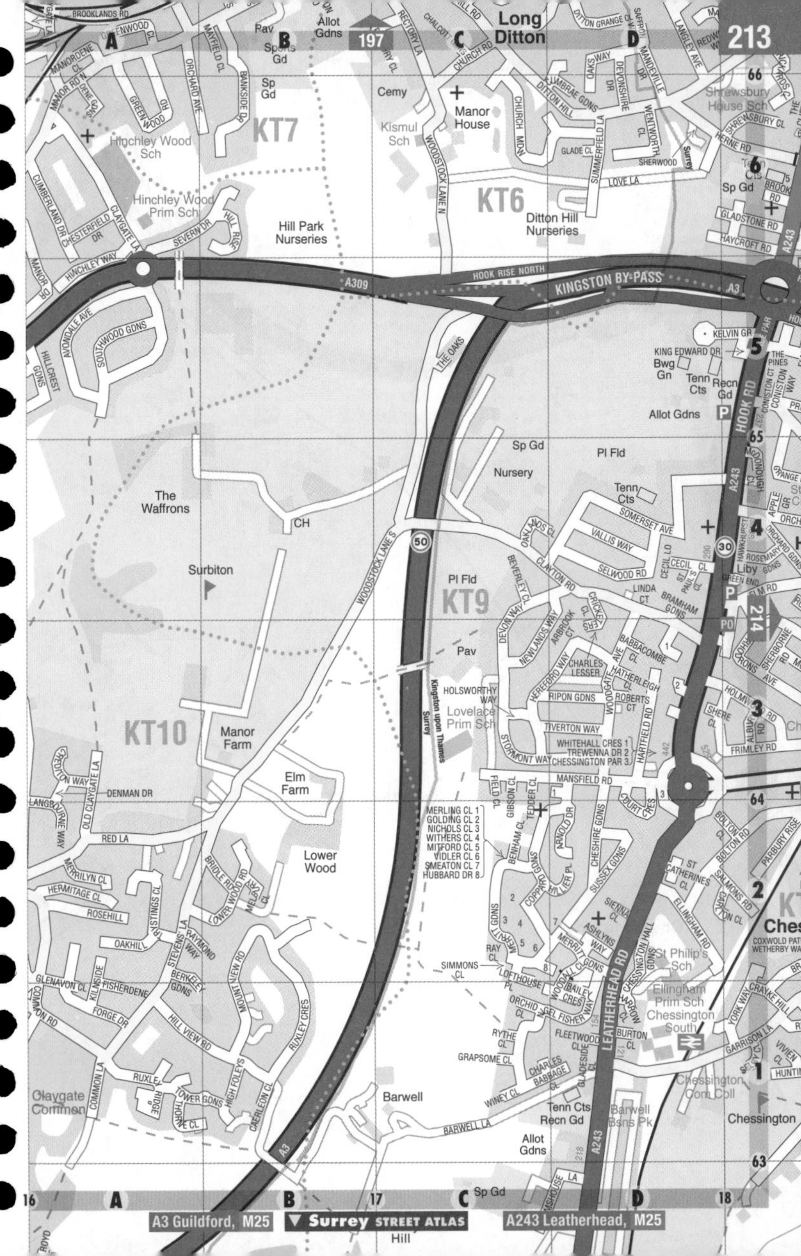
Long Ditton
197
KT7
KT6
KT9
KT10
Hinchley Wood Sch
Hinchley Wood Prim Sch
Hill Park Nurseries
Ditton Hill Nurseries
Manor House
Kismul Sch
Cemy
Shrewsbury House Sch
KINGSTON BY-PASS
HOOK RISE NORTH
A309
A3
A243
HOOK RD
LEATHERHEAD RD
The Waffrons
Surbiton
Manor Farm
Elm Farm
Lower Wood
Barwell
Barwell Bsns Pk
Lovelace Prim Sch
St Philip's Sch
Ellingham Prim Sch
Chessington South
Chessington Com Coll
Chessington
Claygate Common
Kingston upon Thames
Surrey
214
MERLING CL 1
GOLDING CL 2
NICHOLS CL 3
WITHERS CL 4
MITFORD CL 5
VIDLER CL 6
SMEATON CL 7
HUBBARD DR 8
WHITEHALL CRES 1
TREWENNA DR 2
CHESSINGTON PAR 3
COXWOLD PATH 1
WETHERBY WAY 2

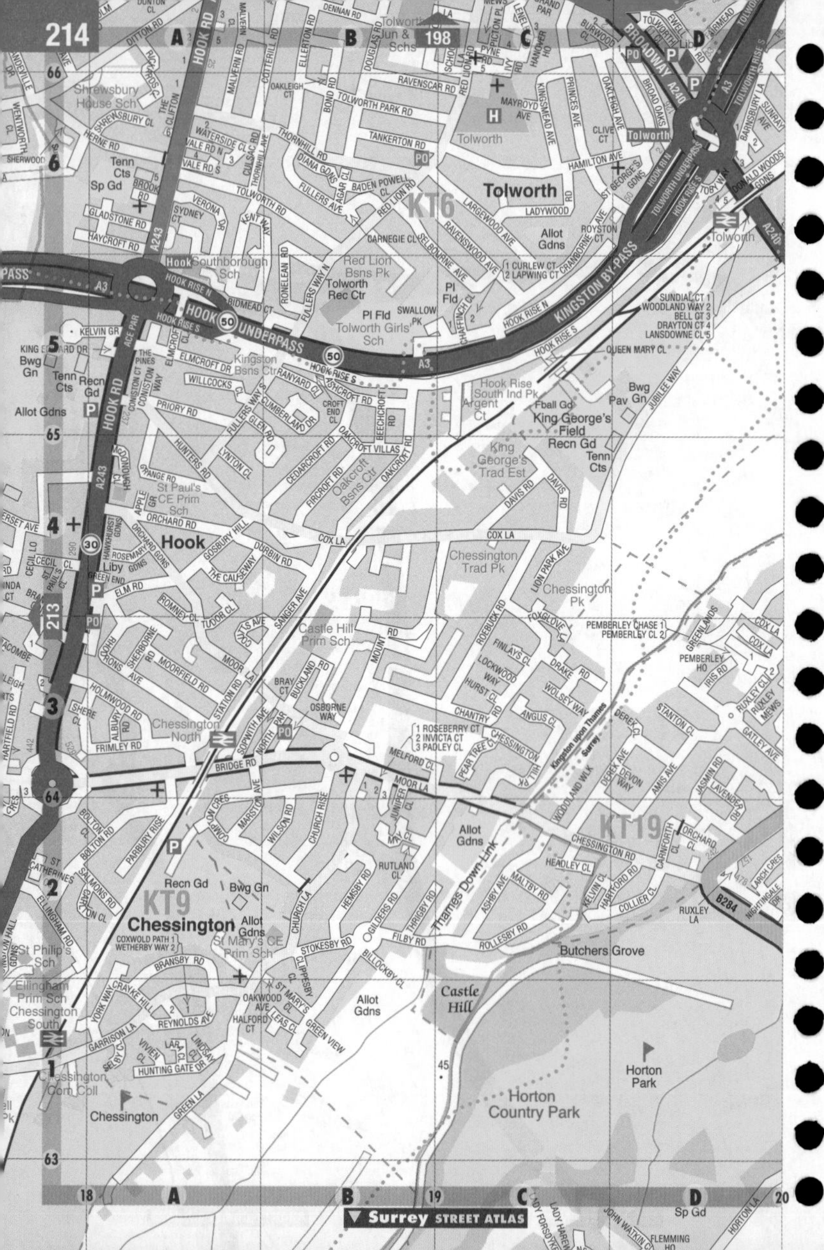

214
A
B
C
D
198
Tolworth Jun & Schs
HOOK RD
DITTON RD
MALVERN RD
COTTERILL RD
ELLERTON RD
DOUGLAS RD
DENNAN RD
PICTON PL
PYNE RD
RED LION RD
HANOVER HO
IVY RD
BROADWAY
A240
BURWOOD CL
TOLWORTH CL
FAIRMEAD
TOLWORTH RISE S
66
Shrewsbury House Sch
SHREWSBURY CL
THE CLIFTON
WENTWORTH CL
SHERWOOD
HERNE RD
WATERSIDE CL
VALE RD N
VALE RD S
CULSAC RD
THORNHILL AVE
OAKLEIGH CT
BOND RD
TOLWORTH PARK RD
RAVENSCAR RD
MAYROYD AVE
KINGSMEAD AVE
PRINCES AVE
OAKLEIGH AVE
BROAD OAKS
CLIVE CT
TANKERTON RD
THORNHILL RD
DIANA GDNS
AGAR CL
BADEN POWELL CL
Tolworth
HAMILTON AVE
ST GEORGE'S GDNS
HOOK RI N
TOLWORTH UNDERPASS
HOOK RISE S
TOBY WAY
BARNSBURY LA
SUNRAY AVE
DONALD WOODS GDNS
6
Tenn Cts
Sp Gd
BROOK RD
FULLERS AVE
TOLWORTH RD
VERONA DR
SYDNEY RD
KENT WAY
KT6
Tolworth
LARGEWOOD AVE
LADYWOOD RD
ROYSTON AVE
GLADSTONE RD
HAYCROFT RD
A243
CARNEGIE CL
SELBOURNE AVE
RAVENSWOOD AVE
Allot Gdns
CRANBORNE AVE
1 CURLEW CT
2 LAPWING CT
KINGSTON BY-PASS
Hook
Southborough Sch
RONELEAN RD
FULLERS WAY N
Red Lion Bsns Pk
Tolworth Rec Ctr
Pl Fld
CHAFFINCH CL
A3
HOOK RISE N
BIDMEAD CT
SWALLOW PK
Tolworth Girls' Sch
HOOK RISE S
HOOK UNDERPASS
50
KELVIN GR
5
KING EDWARD DR
ACE PAR
Bwg Gn
Tenn Cts
Recn Gd
THE PINES
ELMCROFT CL
ELMCROFT DR
Kingston Bsns Ctr
RANYARD CL
ASHCROFT RD
SUNDIAL CT 1
WOODLAND WAY 2
BELL CT 3
DRAYTON CT 4
LANSDOWNE CL 5
QUEEN MARY CL
JUBILEE WAY
Allot Gdns
CONISTON CT
CONISTON WAY
WILLCOCKS CL
FULLERS WAY S
CUMBERLAND DR
CROFT END CL
BEECHCROFT RD
Hook Rise South Ind Pk
Argent Ct
Fball Gd
King George's Field
Recn Gd
Bwg Gn
Pav
Tenn Cts
65
PRIORY RD
GLEN RD
OAKCROFT VILLAS
OAKCROFT RD
HUNTERS RD
LYNTON CL
CEDARCROFT RD
FIRCROFT RD
Oakcroft Bsns Ctr
King George's Trad Est
DAVIS RD
ORANGE RD
MONKSBOROUGH
St Paul's CE Prim Sch
APPLE GR
ORCHARD RD
4
Hook
COX LA
GOSBURY HILL
DURBIN RD
Chessington Trad Pk
LION PARK AVE
Chessington Pk
CECIL CL
HAWKHURST GDNS
ROSEMARY GDNS
ORCHARD GDNS
THE CAUSEWAY
Liby
GREEN END
ELM RD
ROMNEY CL
TUDOR CL
SANGER AVE
Castle Hill Prim Sch
MOUNT RD
ROEBUCK RD
FOXGLOVE LA
FINLAYS CL
LOCKWOOD WAY
DRAKE RD
WOLSEY WAY
PEMBERLEY CHASE 1
PEMBERLEY CL 2
GREENLANDS
PEMBERLEY HO
IRIS RD
COX LA
213
RHODRONS AVE
SHERBORNE RD
MOORFIELD RD
MOOR LA
COUTTS AVE
BRAY CT
BUCKLAND RD
HURST CL
CHANTRY RD
ANGUS CL
STANTON CL
RUXLEY CL
RUXLEY MEWS
GATLEY AVE
3
HOLMWOOD RD
SHERE CL
ALBURY RD
Chessington North
STATION RD
SOPWITH AVE
NORTH PAR
OSBORNE WAY
1 ROSEBERRY CT
2 INVICTA CT
3 PADLEY CL
CHESSINGTON HILL PK
PEAR TREE CL
Kingston upon Thames
Surrey
DEREK CL
DEREK AVE
DEVON WAY
AMIS AVE
JASMIN RD
LAVENDER RD
FRIMLEY RD
BRIDGE RD
MELFORD CL
MOOR LA
64
BOLTON CL
BOLTON RD
PARBURY RISE
COMPTON CRES
MARSTON AVE
WILSON RD
CHURCH RISE
JUNIPER CL
Allot Gdns
WOODLAND WALK
KT19
CHESSINGTON RD
HEADLEY CL
CARNFORTH CL
ORCHARD CL
ST CATHERINES
SALMONS RD
CARLTON CL
ELLINGHAM RD
2
Recn Gd
Bwg Gn
KT9
Chessington
Allot Gdns
CHURCH LA
HEMSBY RD
RUTLAND CL
GILDERS RD
THRIGBY RD
Thames Down Link
ASHBY AVE
MALTBY RD
KELVIN CL
HARTFORD RD
COLLIER CL
B284
RUXLEY LA
NIGHTINGALE DR
LARCH CRES
COXWOLD PATH 1
WETHERBY WAY 2
St Mary's CE Prim Sch
STOKESBY RD
FILBY RD
ROLLESBY RD
Butchers Grove
St Philip's Sch
BRANSBY RD
CLIPPESBY CL
BILLOCKBY CL
Castle Hill
Ellingham Prim Sch
Chessington South
YORK WAY
CRAYKE HILL
REYNOLDS AVE
OAKWOOD AVE
ST MARY'S CL
LEAS CL
HALFORD CT
GREEN VIEW
Allot Gdns
GARRISON LA
SELBY CL
VIVIEN CL
LARA CL
LINDSAY RD
HUNTING GATE DR
1
Chessington Com Coll
45
Horton Park
Horton Country Park
Chessington
GREEN LA
63
18
19
20
LADY FORSDYKE
LADY HAREWOOD
JOHN WATKIN CL
FLEMMING HO
HORTON LA
Sp Gd
Surrey STREET ATLAS

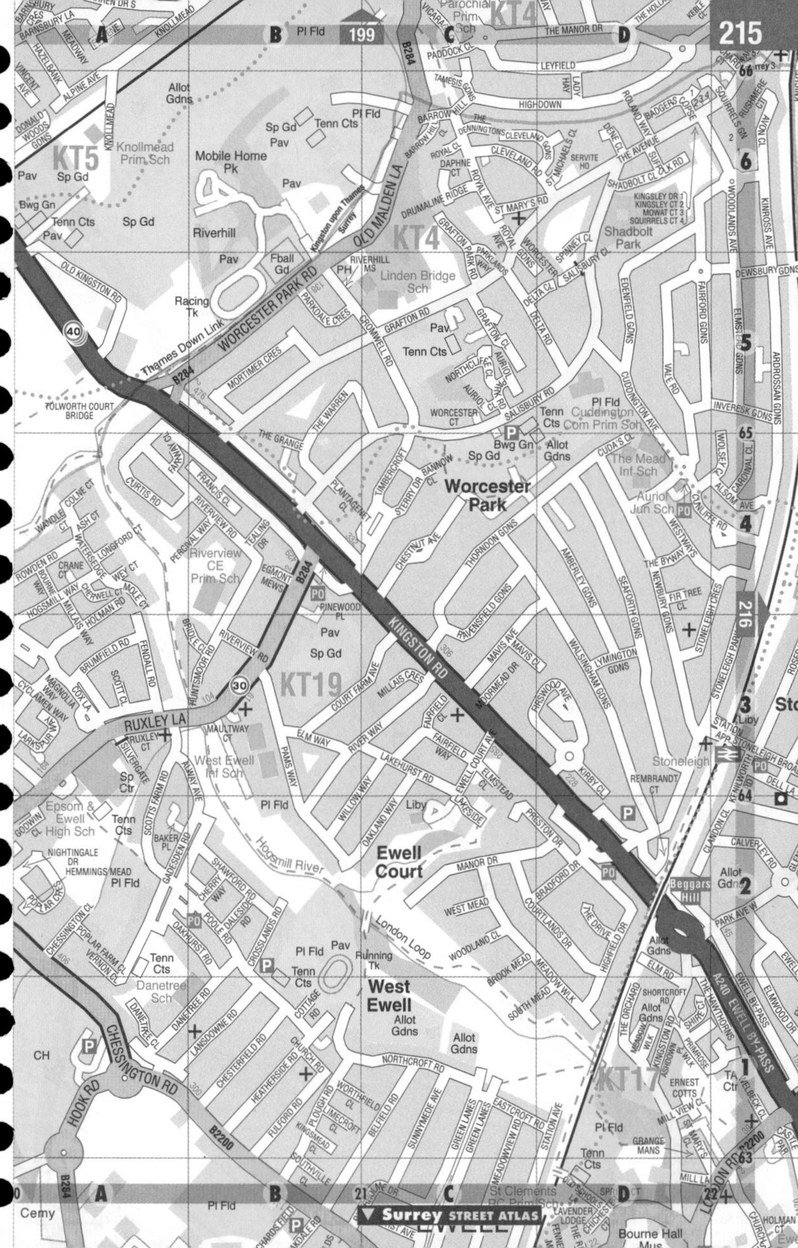
A
B
C
D
199
216
KT4
KT5
KT19
KT17
Worcester Park
Ewell Court
West Ewell
Stoneleigh
Beggars Hill
Knollmead Prim Sch
Linden Bridge Sch
Riverview CE Prim Sch
West Ewell Inf Sch
Epsom & Ewell High Sch
Danetree Sch
Cuddington Com Prim Sch
The Mead Inf Sch
Auriol Jun Sch
Shadbolt Park
Mobile Home Pk
Riverhill
Racing Tk
Thames Down Link
Hogsmill River
London Loop
KINGSTON RD
WORCESTER PARK RD
OLD MALDEN LA
RUXLEY LA
CHESSINGTON RD
HOOK RD
A240 EWELL BY-PASS
B284
B2200
Surrey STREET ATLAS

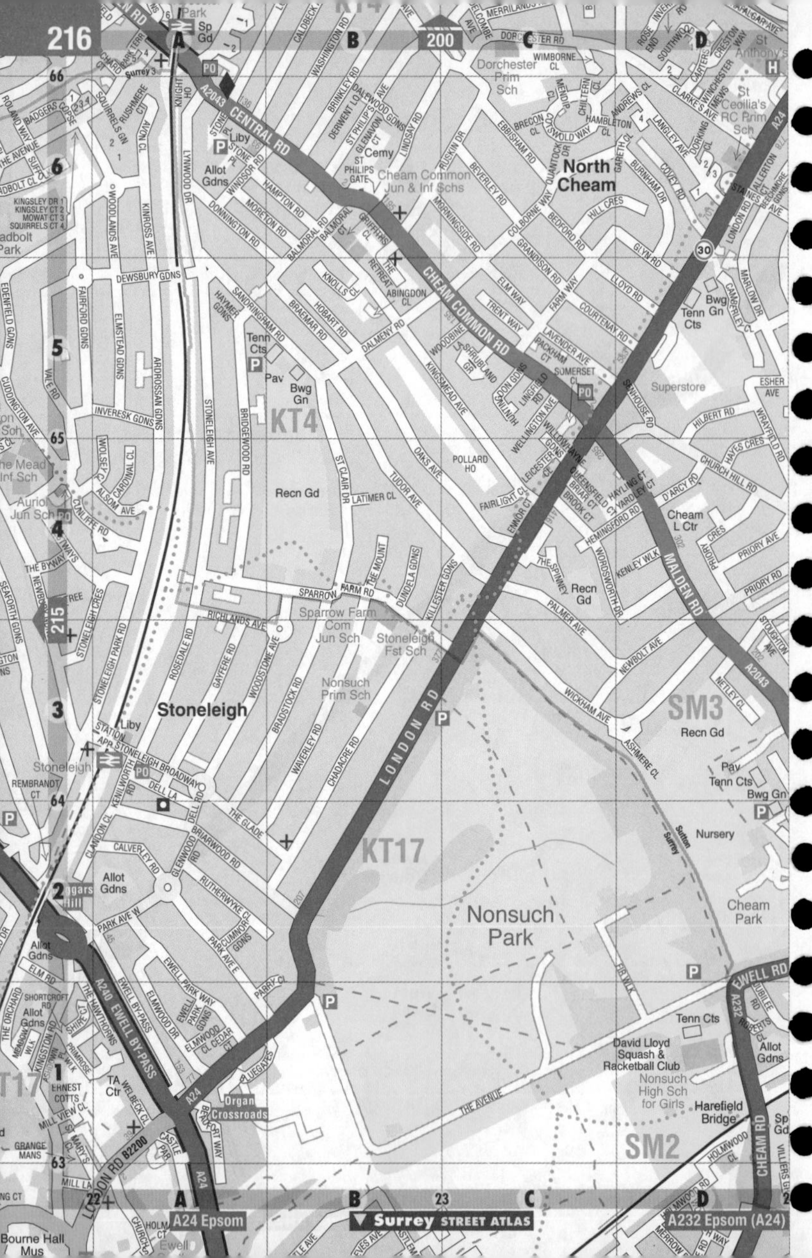
200
A
B
C
D
North Cheam
Stoneleigh
Nonsuch Park
KT4
KT17
SM3
SM2
CENTRAL RD
CHEAM COMMON RD
LONDON RD
MALDEN RD
EWELL BY-PASS
EWELL RD
CHEAM RD
THE AVENUE
STONELEIGH BROADWAY
SPARROW FARM RD
Dorchester Prim Sch
Cheam Common Jun & Inf Schs
Sparrow Farm Com Jun Sch
Stoneleigh Fst Sch
Nonsuch Prim Sch
Nonsuch High Sch for Girls
David Lloyd Squash & Racketball Club
Cheam Park
Harefield Bridge
Organ Crossroads
Superstore
Cheam L Ctr
Recn Gd
Allot Gdns
Tenn Cts
Bwg Gn
Pav
Nursery
215
6
5
4
3
2
1
66
65
64
63
22
23
A24 Epsom
A232 Epsom (A24)
Bourne Hall Mus

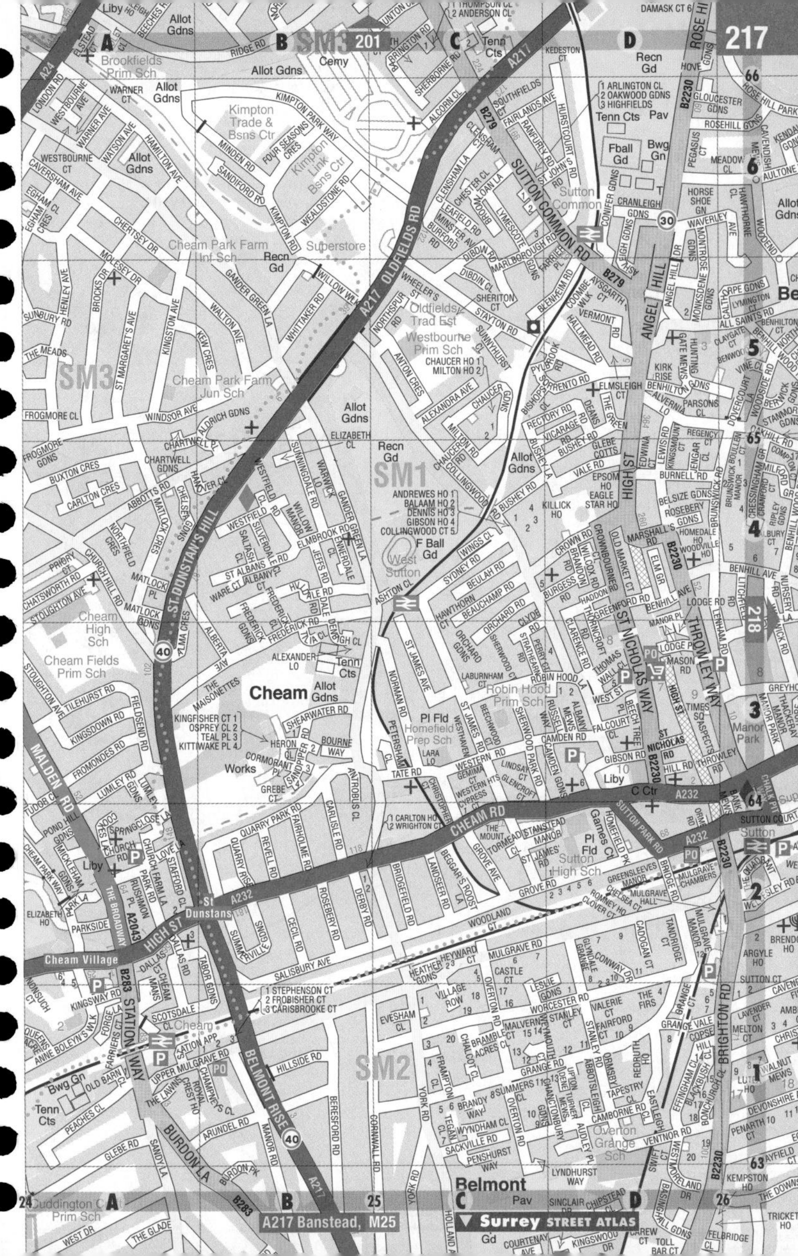

A
B
C
D
SM3
201
Brookfields Prim Sch
Allot Gdns
Cemy
RIDGE RD
Recn Gd
Tenn Cts
KIMPTON PARK WAY
Kimpton Trade & Bsns Ctr
Kimpton Link Bsns Ctr
MINDEN RD
FOUR SEASONS CRES
SANDIFORD RD
KIMPTON RD
WEALDSTONE RD
A217
OLDFIELDS RD
SUTTON COMMON RD
Sutton Common
B279
B2230
ROSE HILL
ROSEHILL GDNS
HOSE HILL PARK W
1 ARLINGTON CL
2 OAKWOOD GDNS
3 HIGHFIELDS
Fball Gd
Bwg Gn
Pav
CRANLEIGH GDNS
ANGEL HILL
30
66
6
Allot Gdns
LONDON RD
WESTBOURNE AVE
WARNER AVE
WATSON AVE
HAMILTON AVE
CAVERSHAM AVE
EGHAM CL
CHERTSEY DR
MOLESEY DR
Cheam Park Farm Inf Sch
Superstore
GANDER GREEN LA
WHITTAKER RD
WALTON AVE
KINGSTON AVE
HENLEY AVE
SUNBURY RD
THE MEADS
ST MARGARET'S AVE
KEW CRES
SM3
Cheam Park Farm Jun Sch
Oldfields Trad Est
Westbourne Prim Sch
CHAUCER HO 1
MILTON HO 2
ANTON CRES
ALEXANDRA AVE
VERMONT RD
ALL SAINTS RD
Ben
5
FROGMORE CL
WINDSOR AVE
ALDRICH GDNS
Allot Gdns
ELIZABETH CL
Recn Gd
SM1
Allot Gdns
ELMSLEIGH CT
HIGH ST
BENHILTON GDNS
PARSONS CL
65
FROGMORE GDNS
CHARTWELL GDNS
BUXTON CRES
CARLTON CRES
ABBOTTS RD
ST. DUNSTAN'S HILL
WESTFIELD CL
SUNNINGDALE RD
WARWICK LO
ANDREWES HO 1
BALAAM HO 2
DENNIS HO 3
GIBSON HO 4
COLLINGWOOD CT 5
F Ball Gd
West Sutton
BUSHEY RD
KILLICK HO
CROWN RD
MARSHALL'S GDNS
ROSEBERY GDNS
BELSIZE GDNS
4
CHATSWORTH RD
CHURCH HILL RD
STOUGHTON AVE
Cheam High Sch
Cheam Fields Prim Sch
MATLOCK PL
ASHTON CL
SYDNEY RD
BEULAH RD
BEAUCHAMP RD
ST NICHOLAS WAY
THROWLEY WAY
LODGE RD
218
40
ALMA CRES
ALBERTA AVE
FREDERICK GDNS
ALEXANDER LO
Tenn Cts
Cheam
Allot Gdns
SHEARWATER RD
KINGFISHER CT 1
OSPREY CL 2
TEAL PL 3
KITTIWAKE PL 4
HERON CL
BOURNE WAY
Works
ST JAMES AVE
NORMAN RD
Pl Fld
Homefield Prep Sch
Robin Hood Prim Sch
ROBIN HOOD LA
CAMDEN RD
Liby
C Ctr
A232
TIMES SQ
Manor Park
3
GREYHOUN
MALDEN RD
TILEHURST RD
KINGSDOWN RD
FROMONDES RD
LUMLEY RD
TUDOR CL
POND HILL GDNS
QUARRY PARK RD
REVELL RD
FAIRHOLME RD
CARLISLE RD
TATE RD
1 CARLTON HO
2 WRIGHTON CT
CHEAM RD
THE MOUNT
TORMEAD CL
STANSTEAD MANOR
Pl Fld
Games Ct
Sutton High Sch
SUTTON PARK RD
Sutton
64
SUTTON COURT RD
2
Liby
THE BROADWAY
A2043
HIGH ST
St Dunstans
BRIDGEFIELD RD
LANDSEER RD
BEGGAR'S ROOST LA
GROVE RD
MULGRAVE CHAMBERS
WOODLAND
Cheam Village
B283
STATION WAY
PARKSIDE
KINGSWAY RD
SALISBURY AVE
HEYWARD CT
MULGRAVE RD
CASTLE CT
WORCESTER RD
VALERIE CT
THE FIRS
GRANGE VALE
BRIGHTON RD
BRENDON HO
ARGYLE HO
SUTTON CT
1 STEPHENSON CT
2 FROBISHER CT
3 CARISBROOKE CT
Cheam
SCOTSDALE CL
STATION APP
HILLSIDE RD
EVESHAM CL
VILLAGE ROW
SM2
BRAMBLE ACRES CL
CHALCOT CL
GRANGE RD
MALVERN CT
FAIRFORD CT
TAPESTRY CL
Bwg Gn
OLD BARN CL
Tenn Cts
PEACHES CL
THE LAWNS
UPPER MULGRAVE RD
BELMONT RISE
BRANDY WAY
WYNDHAM CL
SACKVILLE RD
PENSHURST WAY
CAMBORNE RD
Overton Grange Sch
VENTNOR RD
1
DEVONSHIRE AVE
63
ARUNDEL RD
GLEBE RD
BURDON LA
MANOR RD
BERESFORD RD
CORNWALL RD
YORK RD
LYNDHURST WAY
Belmont
Pav
KEMPSTON HO
THE DOWNSW
24
Cuddington Prim Sch
B283
25
26
A217 Banstead, M25
Surrey STREET ATLAS
TRICKETT HO
WEST DR
THE GLADE
HOLLAND
COURTENAY AVE
KINGSWOOD DR
CAREW CT
TOLL BAR CT
FELBRIDGE CL
Gd

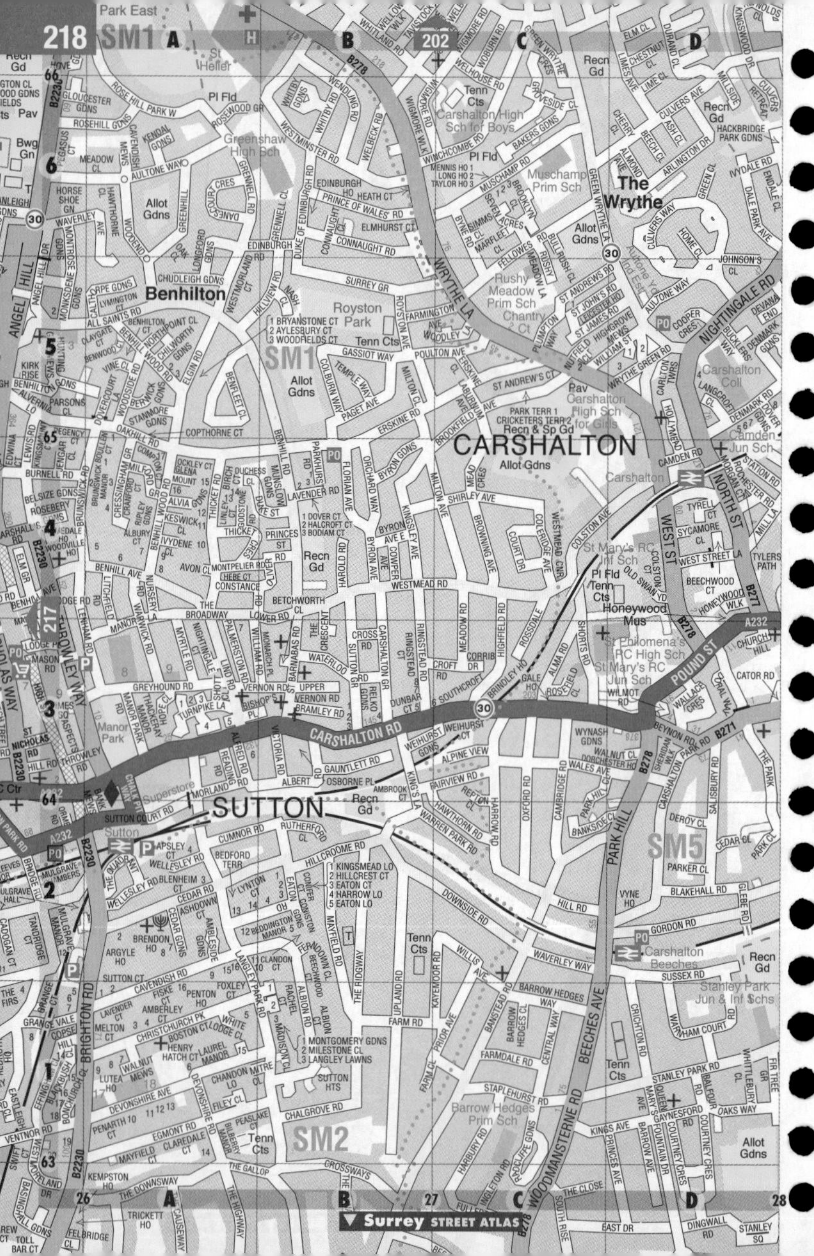
SM1
A
B
202
C
D
Park East
St Helier
B278
Recn Gd
Pl Fld
Greenshaw High Sch
Tenn Cts
Carshalton High Sch for Boys
Muschamp Prim Sch
The Wrythe
Allot Gdns
Benhilton
Royston Park
Rushy Meadow Prim Sch
Chantry Ct
Autone Yd Ind Est
Carshalton Coll
Pav
Carshalton High Sch for Girls
Recn & Sp Gd
CARSHALTON
Carshalton
Camden Jun Sch
St Mary's RC Inf Sch
Honeywood Mus
St Philomena's RC High Sch
St Mary's RC Jun Sch
Manor Park
Superstore
SUTTON
Sutton
SM5
Carshalton Beeches
Stanley Park Jun & Inf Schs
Barrow Hedges Prim Sch
Sutton Hts
SM2
WRYTHE LA
CARSHALTON RD
ANGEL HILL
THROWLEY WAY
BRIGHTON RD
PARK HILL
BEECHES AVE
WOODMANSTERNE RD
NORTH ST
WEST ST
POUND ST
NIGHTINGALE RD
DOWNSIDE RD
WAVERLEY WAY
GORDON RD
B2230
B277
B271
A232
A217
30
1
2
3
4
5
6
26
27
28
63
64
65
66
B
C
D
▼ Surrey STREET ATLAS

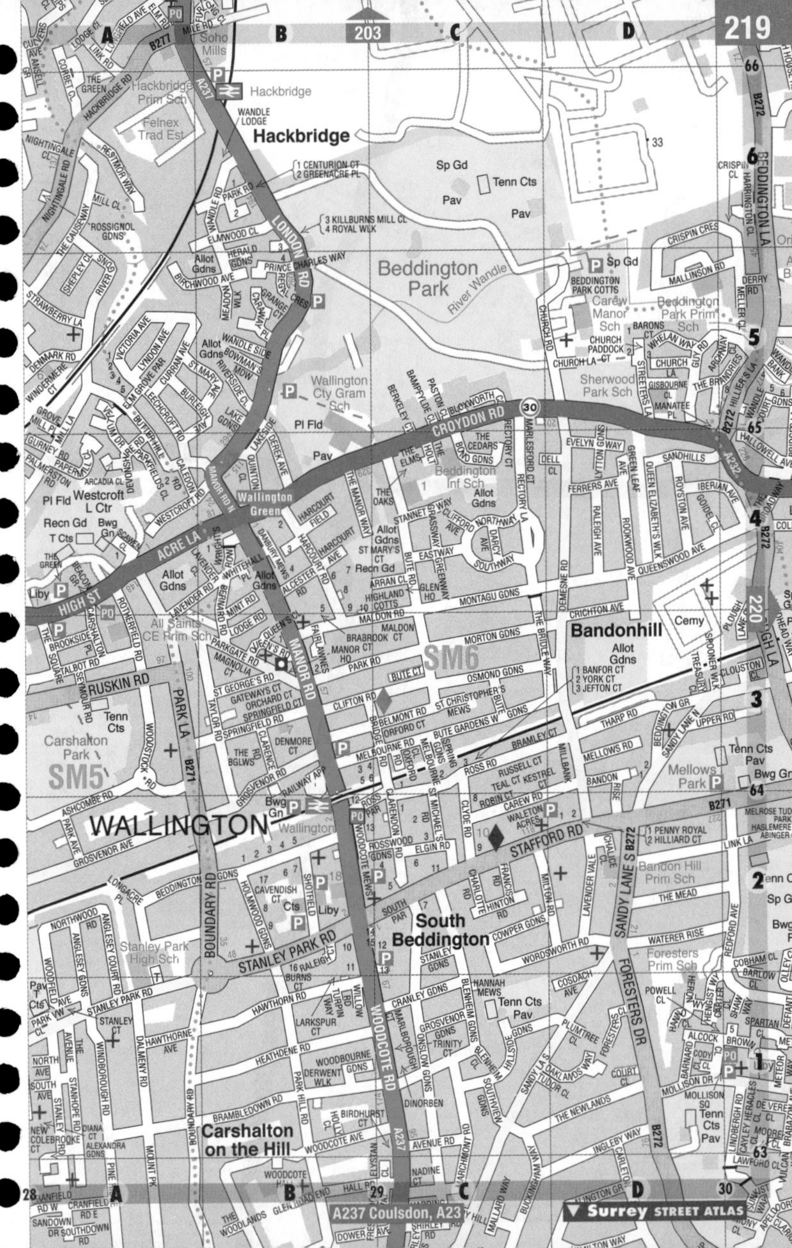
Hackbridge
Beddington Park
Wallington
WALLINGTON
Bandonhill
South Beddington
Carshalton on the Hill
SM5
SM6
London Rd
Croydon Rd
Manor Rd
Woodcote Rd
Stafford Rd
Stanley Park Rd
Park La
Boundary Rd
Sandy Lane S
Foresters Dr
Beddington La
Acre La
High St
Ruskin Rd
A237 Coulsdon, A23
Surrey STREET ATLAS

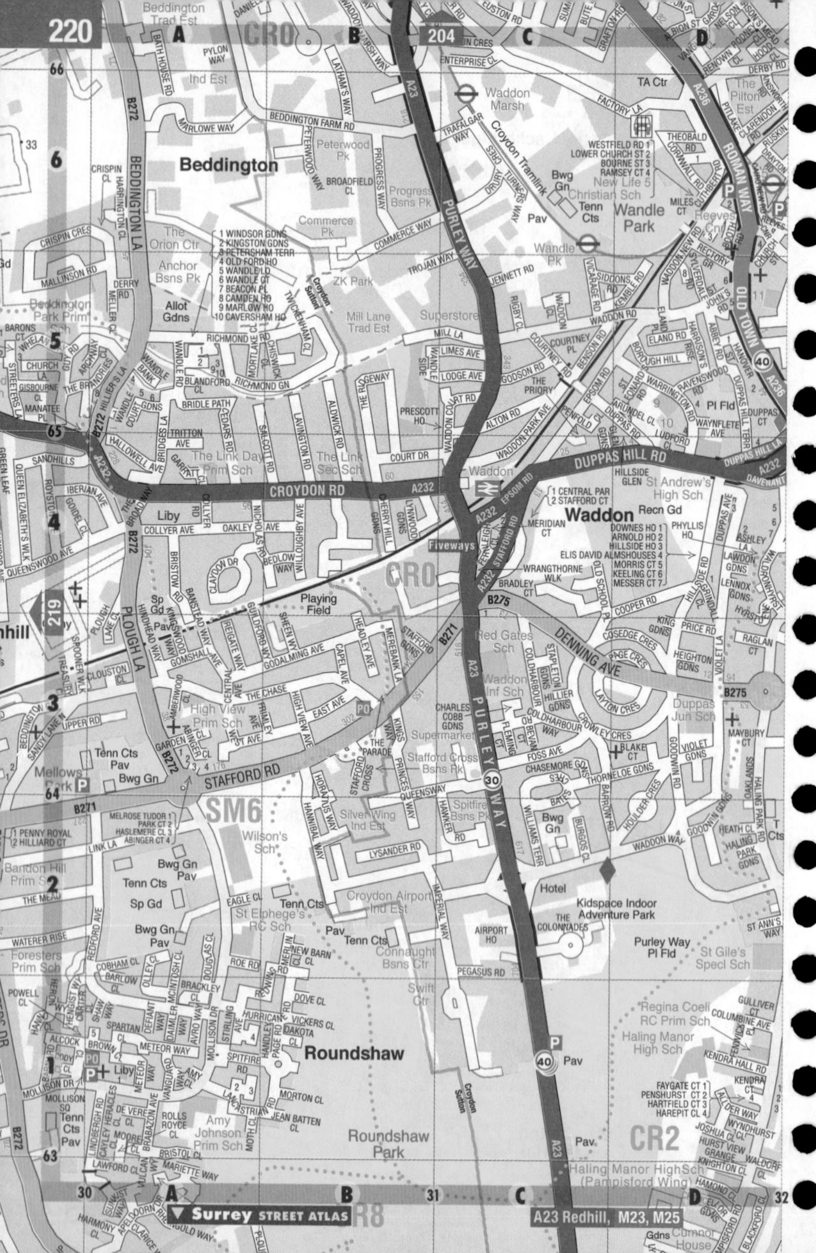
A
B
C
D
CR0
204
66
6
5
65
4
3
64
2
1
63
30
31
32
219
Beddington Trad Est
Beddington
Ind Est
Bath House Rd
Pylon Way
Marlowe Way
Beddington Farm Rd
Latham's Way
Peterwood Way
Peterwood Pk
Progress Way
Broadfield Cl
Progress Bsns Pk
Commerce Pk
Commerce Way
Trojan Way
ZK Park
Mill Lane Trad Est
Superstore
Enterprise Cl
Waddon Marsh
Trafalgar Way
Croydon Tramlink
Factory La
TA Ctr
Westfield Rd 1
Lower Church St 2
Bourne St 3
Ramsey Ct 4
New Life 5
Christian Sch
Bwg Gn
Tenn Cts
Pav
Wandle Park
Wandle Pk
Theobald Rd
Cornwall Rd
Miles Ct
Reeves Cnr
Roman Way
A236
Old Town
A23
Purley Way
B272
Beddington La
Crispin Cl
Harrington Cl
Crispin Cres
Mallinson Rd
Derry Rd
Meller Cl
The Orion Ctr
Anchor Bsns Pk
Allot Gdns
1 Windsor Gdns
2 Kingston Gdns
3 Petersham Terr
4 Old Ford Ho
5 Wandle Ld
6 Wandle Ct
7 Beacon Pl
8 Camden Ho
9 Marlow Ho
10 Caversham Ho
Twickenham Cl
Richmond Rd
Richmond Gn
Mortlake Cl
Chiswick Cl
Wandle Rd
Blandford
Bridle Path
Cedars Rd
Salcott Rd
Lavington Rd
Aldwick Rd
The Ridgeway
Mill La
Limes Ave
Lodge Ave
Wandle Side
Waddon Court Rd
Prescott Ho
Alton Rd
Waddon Park Ave
Godson Rd
The Priory
Courtney Rd
Courtney Pl
Benson Rd
Epsom Rd
Jennett Rd
Rigby Cl
Waddon Cl
Vicarage Rd
Siddons Rd
Kemble Rd
Waddon Rd
Waddon New Rd
Eland Rd
Eland Pl
Boroughh Hill
Harrison's Rise
Abbey Rd
St John's Rd
Hanover St
Warrington Rd
Ravenswood
Arundel Cl
Duppas Rd
Ludford Cl
Waynflete Ave
Duppas Hill Terr
Duppas Ct
Pl Fld
Duppas Hill Rd
Duppas Hill La
Davenant
Beddington Park Prim Sch
Barons Ct
Church La
Gisbourne Cl
Manatee Pl
Streeters La
Archway
The Brandries
Hillier's La
Wandle Bank
Wandle Ct
Gdns
Tritton Ave
Hallowell Ave
Bridges La
Garratt Cl
Sandhills
Queen Elizabeth's Wlk
Royston Ave
Iberian Ave
Goidel Cl
Queenswood Ave
Green Leaf
The Link Day Prim Sch
The Link Sec Sch
Croydon Rd
A232
Court Dr
Waddon
Liby
Collyer Ave
Collyer Rd
Oakley Ave
Nicholas Rd
Willoughby Ave
Cherry Hill Gdns
Lynwood Gdns
Claydon Dr
Bedlow Way
Bristow Rd
Banstead Way
Fiveways
1 Central Par
2 Stafford Ct
Meridian Ct
Stafford Rd
Fernleigh Cl
Wrangthorne Wlk
Bradley Ct
Old School Pl
St Andrew's High Sch
Hillside Glen
Recn Gd
Downes Ho 1
Arnold Ho 2
Hillside Ho 3
Elis David Almshouses 4
Morris Ct 5
Keeling Ct 6
Messer Ct 7
Phyllis Ho
Duppas Ave
Ashley La
Lawdon Gdns
Lennox Gdns
Waldronhyrst
Hillside Rd
Grindall Cl
Playing Field
Plough La
Plough Lane Cl
Spooner Wlk
Treasury Cl
Clouston Cl
Sp Gd
Pav
Hindhead Way
Kingswood Way
Gomshall Ave
Reigate Way
Guildford Way
Godalming Ave
Sheen Way
Capel Ave
Headley Ave
Merebank La
Stafford Gdns
B271
B275
Cooper Rd
Denning Ave
Cosedge Cres
Page Cres
Layton Cres
King Gdns
Price Rd
Heighton Gdns
Violet La
Raglan Ct
Red Gates Sch
Coldharbour Rd
Stapleton Gdns
Hillier Gdns
Waddon Inf Sch
Duppas Jun Sch
Maybury Ct
Beddington Gdns
Sandy Lane N
Upper Rd
Amberwood Cl
Central Ave
The Chase
High View Ave
Frimley Ave
East Ave
West Ave
High View Prim Sch
Abinger Cl
Garden Cl
Tenn Cts
Mellows Park
Bwg Gn
Stafford Rd
The Parade
Stafford Cross
Kings Way
Princes Way
Charles Cobb Gdns
Supermarket
Stafford Cross Bsns Pk
Fleming Ct
Bevan Ct
Coldharbour Way
Crowley Cres
Foss Ave
Chasemore Gdns
Blake Ct
Goodwin Rd
Violet Gdns
Thorneloe Gdns
Barrow Rd
Bates Cres
Williams Terr
Burgos Cl
Houlder Cres
Oaklands
Haling Park Rd
Goodwin Gdns
Heath Cl
Haling Park Gdns
SM6
Melrose Tudor 1
Park Ct 2
Haslemere Ct 3
Abinger Ct 4
1 Penny Royal
2 Hilliard Ct
Link La
Wilson's Sch
Queensway
Horatius Way
Hannibal Way
Silver Wing Ind Est
Hawker Rd
Spitfire Bsns Pk
Lysander Rd
Waddon Way
Bandon Hill Prim Sch
The Mead
Tenn Cts
Sp Gd
Bwg Gn
Pav
Eagle Cl
St Elphege's RC Sch
Croydon Airport Ind Est
Imperial Way
Hotel
Kidspace Indoor Adventure Park
The Colonnades
Airport Ho
St Ann's Way
Purley Way Pl Fld
St Gile's Specl Sch
Waterer Rise
Redford Ave
Foresters Prim Sch
Cobham Cl
Barlow Cl
Olley Cl
McIntosh Cl
Douglas Cl
Roe Rd
Merlin Cl
New Barn Cl
Connaught Bsns Ctr
Pegasus Rd
Swift Ctr
Brackley
Dove Cl
Powell Cl
Heron Cl
Hengist Way
Carter
Shaw
Defiant
Daimler
Avro Way
Hurricane Rd
Vickers Cl
Dakota Cl
Spartan Cl
Meteor Way
Mollison Dr
Stirling
Handley Rd
Page Rd
Roundshaw
Spitfire Rd
Alcock Cl
Brown Cl
Cody Cl
Liby
Mollison Sq
Meteor Way
Vanguard Way
Amy Cl
Morton Cl
Jean Batten Cl
Lancastrian Rd
De Vere Cl
Brabazon Ave
Rolls Royce Cl
Amy Johnson Prim Sch
Moth Cl
Lindbergh Rd
Cayley Cl
Heracles Cl
Moore Cl
Bristol Cl
Lawford Cl
Vulcan Cl
Mariette Way
Sunjet Way
Apeldoorn Dr
Harmony Cl
Clarice Way
Roundshaw Park
Pav
Croydon Sutton
Regina Coeli RC Prim Sch
Haling Manor High Sch
Gulliver Ct
Columbine Ave
Fenwick Pl
Kendra Hall Rd
Kendra Ct
Faygate Ct 1
Penshurst Ct 2
Hartfield Ct 3
Harepit Cl 4
Alder Way
Wyndhurst Cl
Joshua Cl
Hurst View Grange
Knighton Cl
Waldorf Cl
Hamond Cl
Haling Manor High Sch (Pampisford Wing)
CR2
Blackford Cl
Pampisford Rd
Cumnor House
Gdns
Surrey STREET ATLAS
R8
A23 Redhill, M23, M25

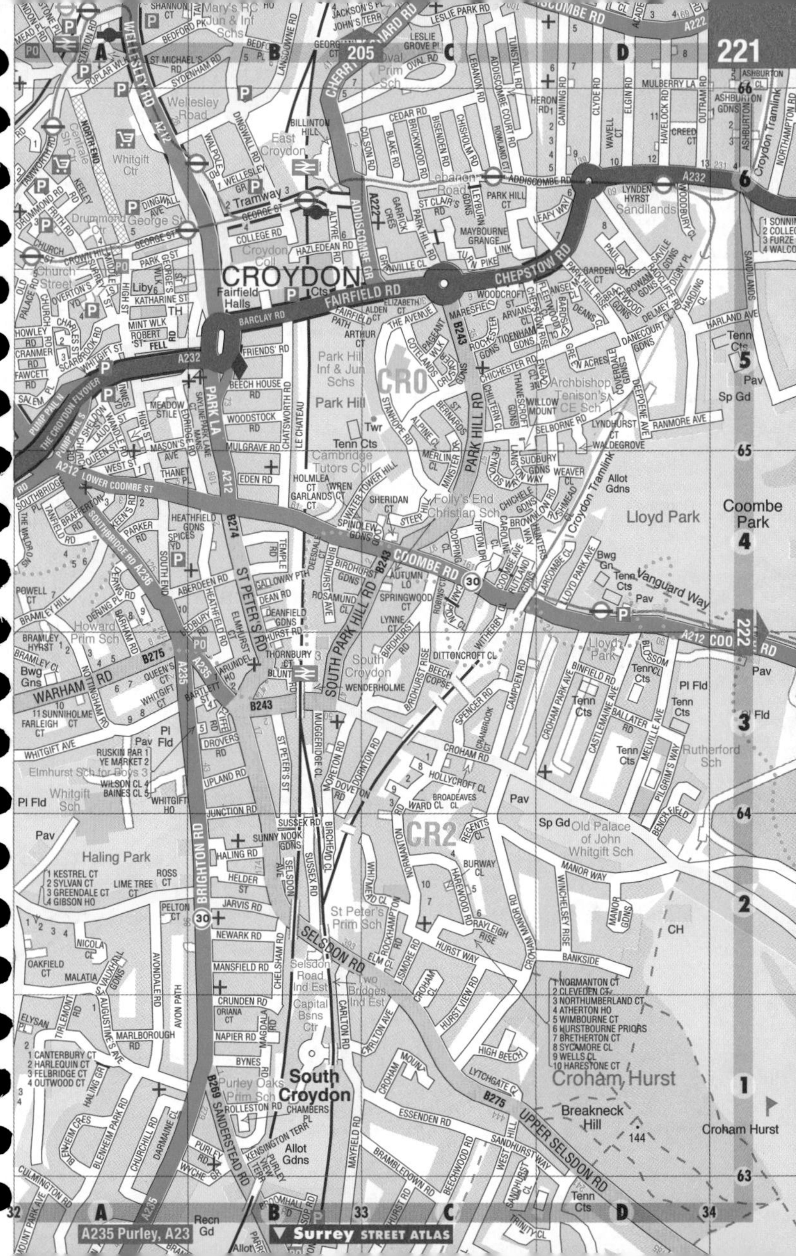
CROYDON
East Croydon
Whitgift Ctr
Wellesley Road
Park Hill
Lloyd Park
Coombe Park
South Croydon
Haling Park
Croham Hurst
Breakneck Hill
Lebanon Road
Sandilands
Addiscombe Rd
Fairfield Rd
Chepstow Rd
Coombe Rd
Park Hill Rd
South Park Hill Rd
Brighton Rd
Selsdon Rd
Upper Selsdon Rd
Wellesley Rd
Park La
St Peter's Rd
Croham Rd
Sanderstead Rd
Croydon Tramlink
Vanguard Way
Fairfield Halls
Old Palace of John Whitgift Sch
Whitgift Sch
Rutherford Sch
Archbishop Tenison's CE Sch
Park Hill Inf & Jun Schs
Folly's End Christian Sch
St Peter's Prim Sch
Purley Oaks Prim Sch
Elmhurst Sch for Boys
Howard Prim Sch
Croydon Coll
Cambridge Tutors Coll
Selsdon Road Ind Est
Two Bridges Ind Est
Capital Bsns Ctr
CR0
CR2
A232
A212
A222
A235
A236
B243
B274
B275
B269
205
222
A235 Purley, A23
Surrey STREET ATLAS

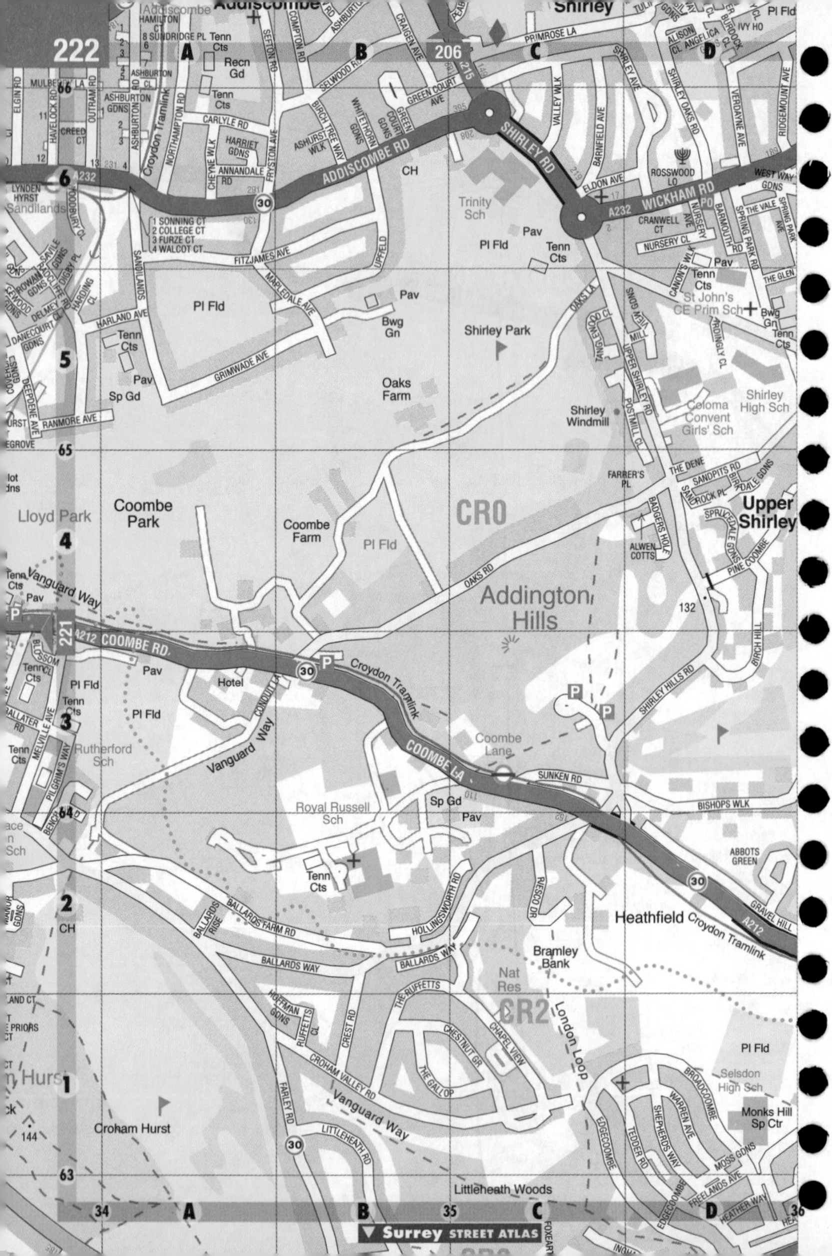
Addiscombe
Shirley
206
A232 ADDISCOMBE RD
SHIRLEY RD
A232 WICKHAM RD
Trinity Sch
Recn Gd
Pl Fld
Shirley Park
Oaks Farm
Shirley Windmill
St John's CE Prim Sch
Coloma Convent Girls' Sch
Shirley High Sch
Coombe Park
Lloyd Park
Coombe Farm
CR0
Upper Shirley
Addington Hills
OAKS RD
Vanguard Way
A212 COOMBE RD
Croydon Tramlink
Hotel
Rutherford Sch
Royal Russell Sch
COOMBE LA
Coombe Lane
SUNKEN RD
BISHOPS WLK
Heathfield
A212 GRAVEL HILL
BALLARDS FARM RD
BALLARDS WAY
HOLLINGSWORTH RD
Bramley Bank
Nat Res
CR2
London Loop
CROHAM VALLEY RD
Croham Hurst
Littleheath Woods
Selsdon High Sch
Monks Hill Sp Ctr
Pl Fld
34
35
36
A
B
C
D
66
65
64
63

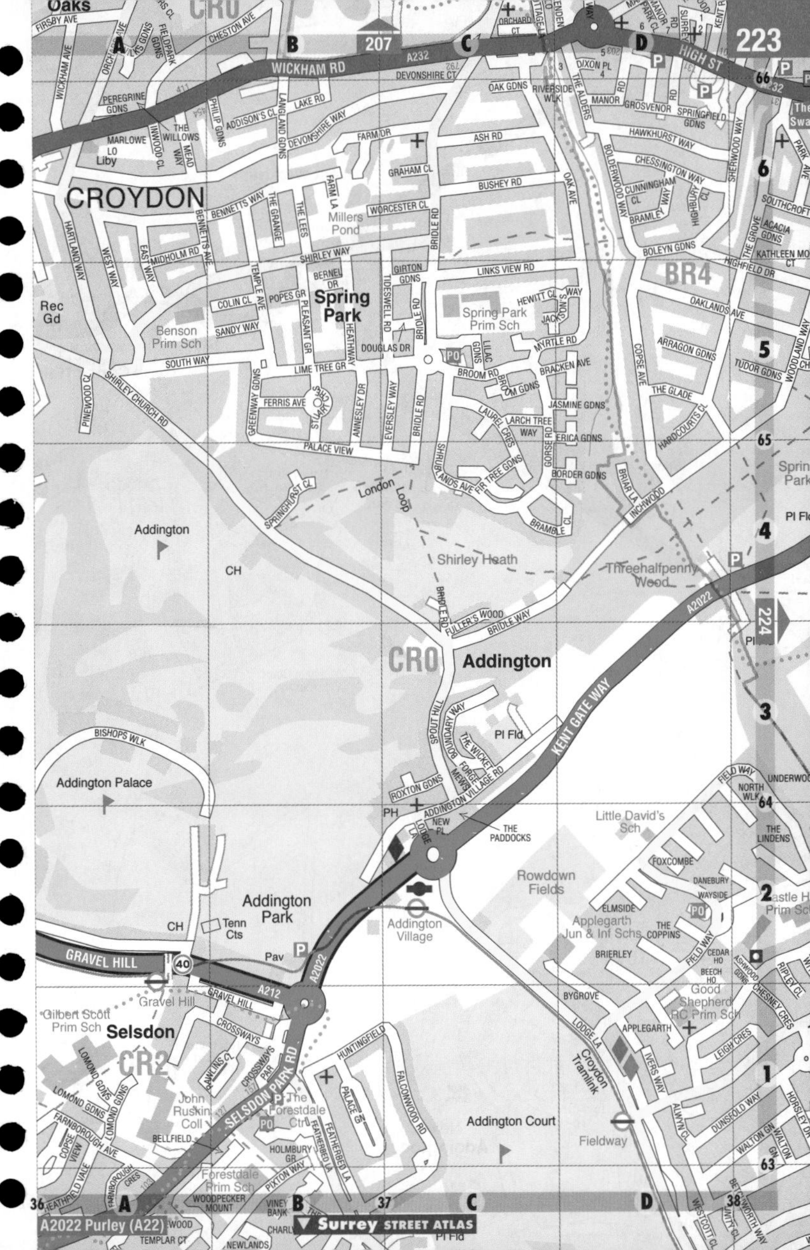

CROYDON
Spring Park
Addington
Selsdon
CR0
CR2
BR4
WICKHAM RD
A232
HIGH ST
SHIRLEY CHURCH RD
KENT GATE WAY
A2022
GRAVEL HILL
A212
SELSDON PARK RD
SPOUT HILL
ADDINGTON VILLAGE RD
LODGE LA
Millers Pond
Benson Prim Sch
Spring Park Prim Sch
Shirley Heath
Threehalfpenny Wood
London Loop
Addington Palace
Addington Park
Addington Village
Rowdown Fields
Little David's Sch
Applegarth Jun & Inf Schs
Good Shepherd RC Prim Sch
Croydon Tramlink
Addington Court
Fieldway
Gilbert Scott Prim Sch
Gravel Hill
John Ruskin Coll
The Forestdale Ctr
Forestdale Prim Sch
Rec Gd
Pl Fld
Tenn Cts
Pav
207
224
A2022 Purley (A22)

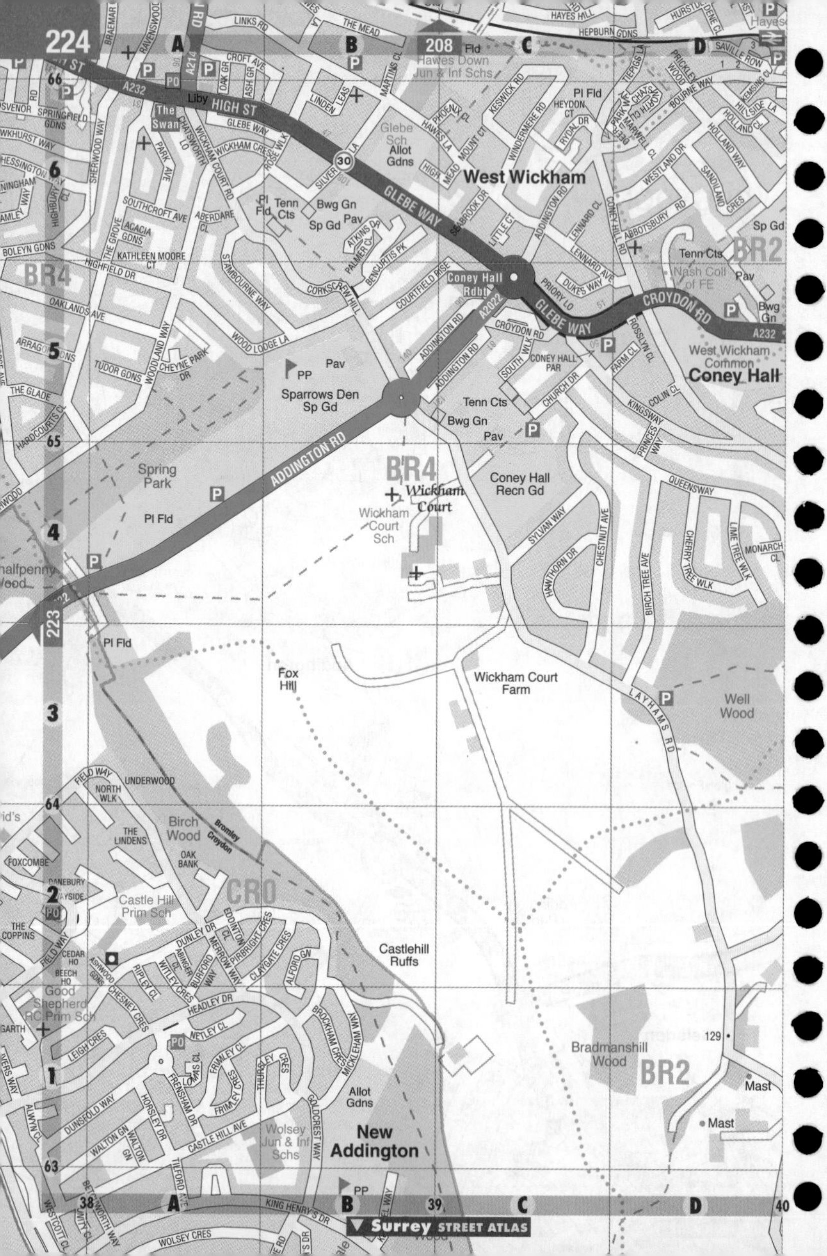

West Wickham
Coney Hall
New Addington
HIGH ST
GLEBE WAY
CROYDON RD
ADDINGTON RD
LAYHAMS RD
Coney Hall Rdbt
Spring Park
Sparrows Den Sp Gd
Wickham Court
Wickham Court Sch
Wickham Court Farm
Coney Hall Recn Gd
West Wickham Common
Nash Coll of FE
Hawes Down Jun & Inf Schs
Glebe Sch
Allot Gdns
Fox Hill
Birch Wood
Castle Hill Prim Sch
Castlehill Ruffs
Well Wood
Bradmanshill Wood
Good Shepherd RC Prim Sch
Wolsey Jun & Inf Schs
BR4
BR2
CR0
Bromley
Croydon
208
223

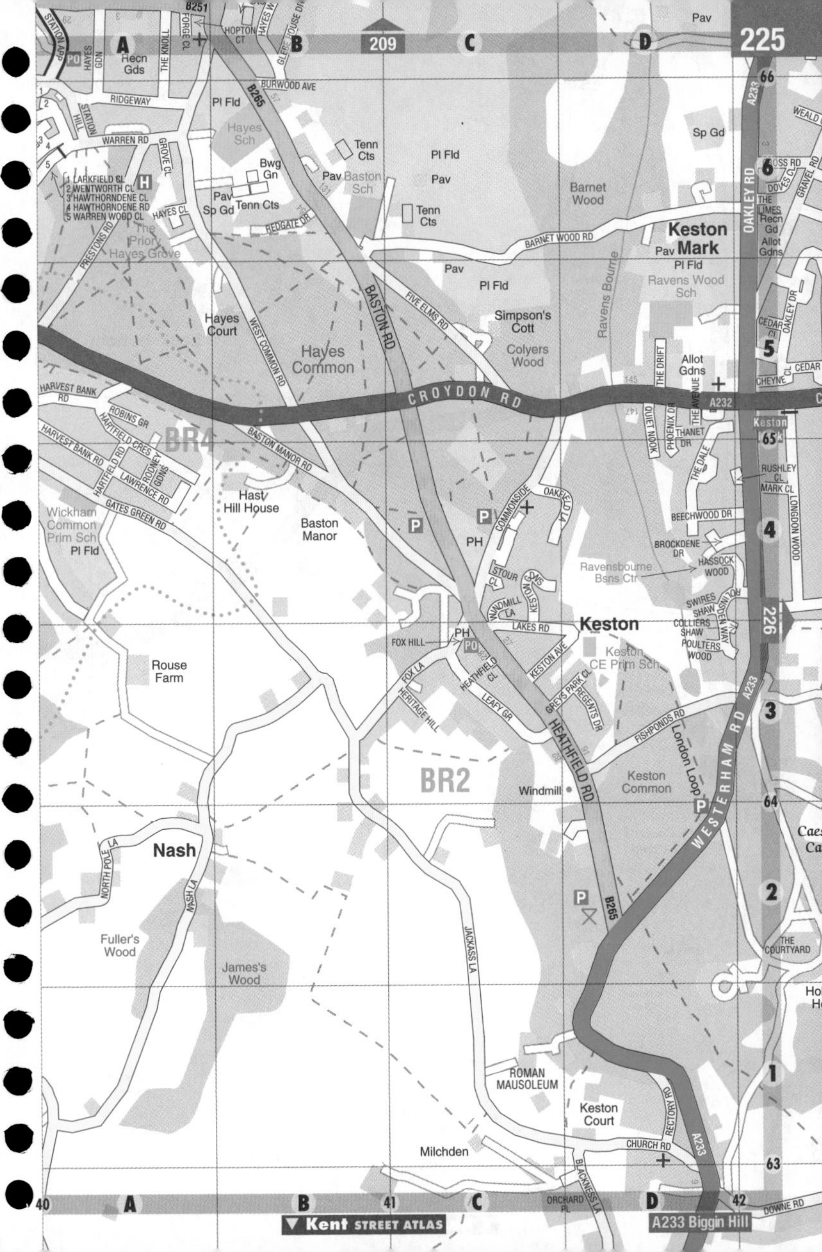
209
A
B
C
D
Recn Gds
Pl Fld
Hayes Sch
Tenn Cts
Bwg Gn
Pav
Baston Sch
Pl Fld
Pav
Tenn Cts
Pav Sp Gd
Tenn Cts
The Priory Hayes Grove
Barnet Wood
Keston Mark
Pav
Pl Fld
Ravens Wood Sch
Sp Gd
Pav
Pl Fld
Simpson's Cott
Colyers Wood
Hayes Court
Hayes Common
Allot Gdns
CROYDON RD
A232
BR4
BASTON RD
BASTON MANOR RD
Hast Hill House
Baston Manor
Wickham Common Prim Sch
Pl Fld
PH
Ravensbourne Bsns Ctr
Keston
Keston CE Prim Sch
Rouse Farm
BR2
Windmill
Keston Common
London Loop
WESTERHAM RD
A233
HEATHFIELD RD
B265
Nash
Fuller's Wood
James's Wood
ROMAN MAUSOLEUM
Keston Court
Milchden
CHURCH RD
RECTORY RD
BLACKNESS LA
ORCHARD PL
DOWNE RD
JACKASS LA
NASH LA
NORTH POLE LA
OAKLEY RD
THE COURTYARD
6
5
4
3
2
1
66
65
64
63
40
41
42
226

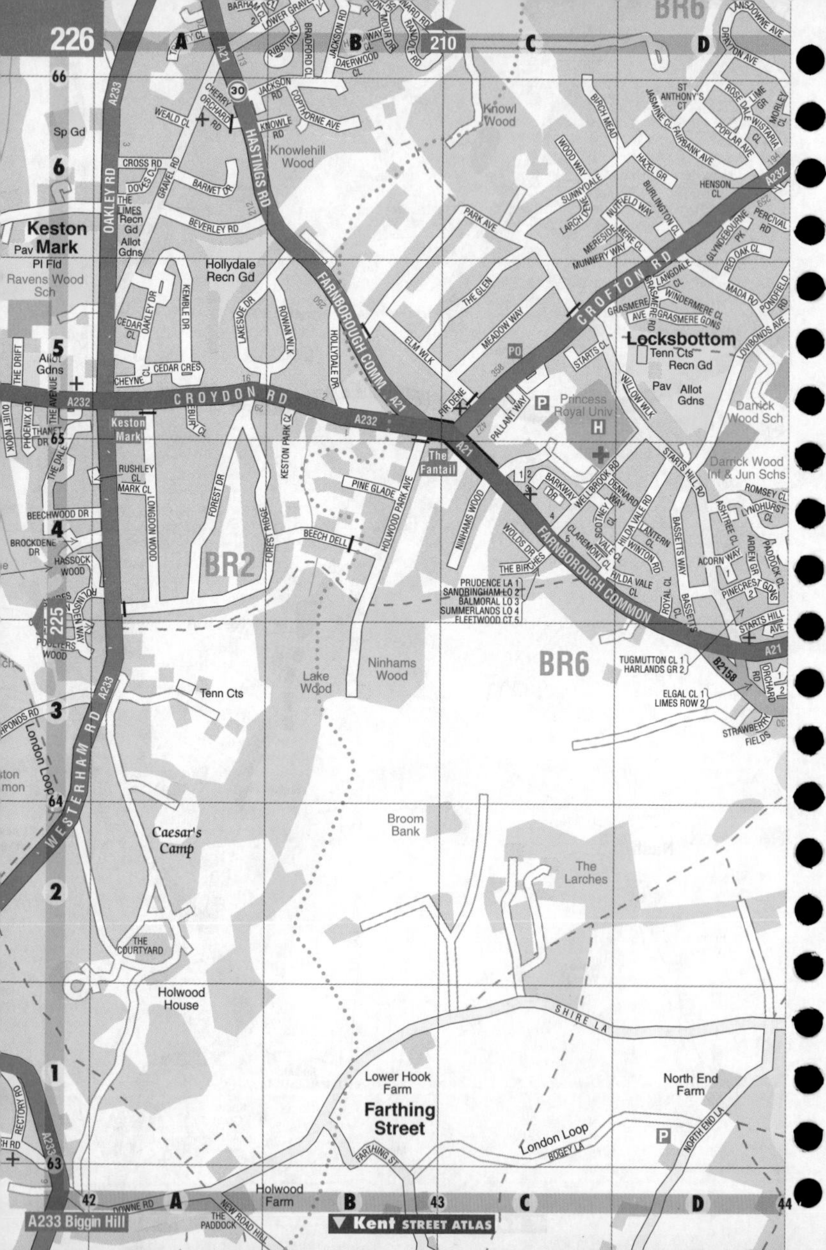

210
A
B
C
D
Keston Mark
Locksbottom
Croydon Rd
Crofton Rd
Farnborough Common
Farnborough Comm
Hastings Rd
Oakley Rd
Westerham Rd
A21
A232
A233
B2158
Knowl Wood
Knowlehill Wood
Hollydale Recn Gd
Ravens Wood Sch
Sp Gd
Pl Fld
Pav
Allot Gdns
The Limes Recn Gd
Princess Royal Univ
Tenn Cts Recn Gd
Darrick Wood Sch
Darrick Wood Inf & Jun Schs
The Fantail
BR2
BR6
Ninhams Wood
Lake Wood
Tenn Cts
Caesar's Camp
The Courtyard
Holwood House
Broom Bank
The Larches
Shire La
Lower Hook Farm
Farthing Street
North End Farm
London Loop
Bogey La
North End La
Holwood Farm
Downe Rd
New Road Hill
The Paddock
PRUDENCE LA 1
SANDRINGHAM LO 2
BALMORAL LO 3
SUMMERLANDS LO 4
FLEETWOOD CT 5
TUGMUTTON CL 1
HARLANDS GR 2
ELGAL CL 1
LIMES ROW 2
Strawberry Fields
225
66
6
5
65
4
3
64
2
1
63
42
43
44

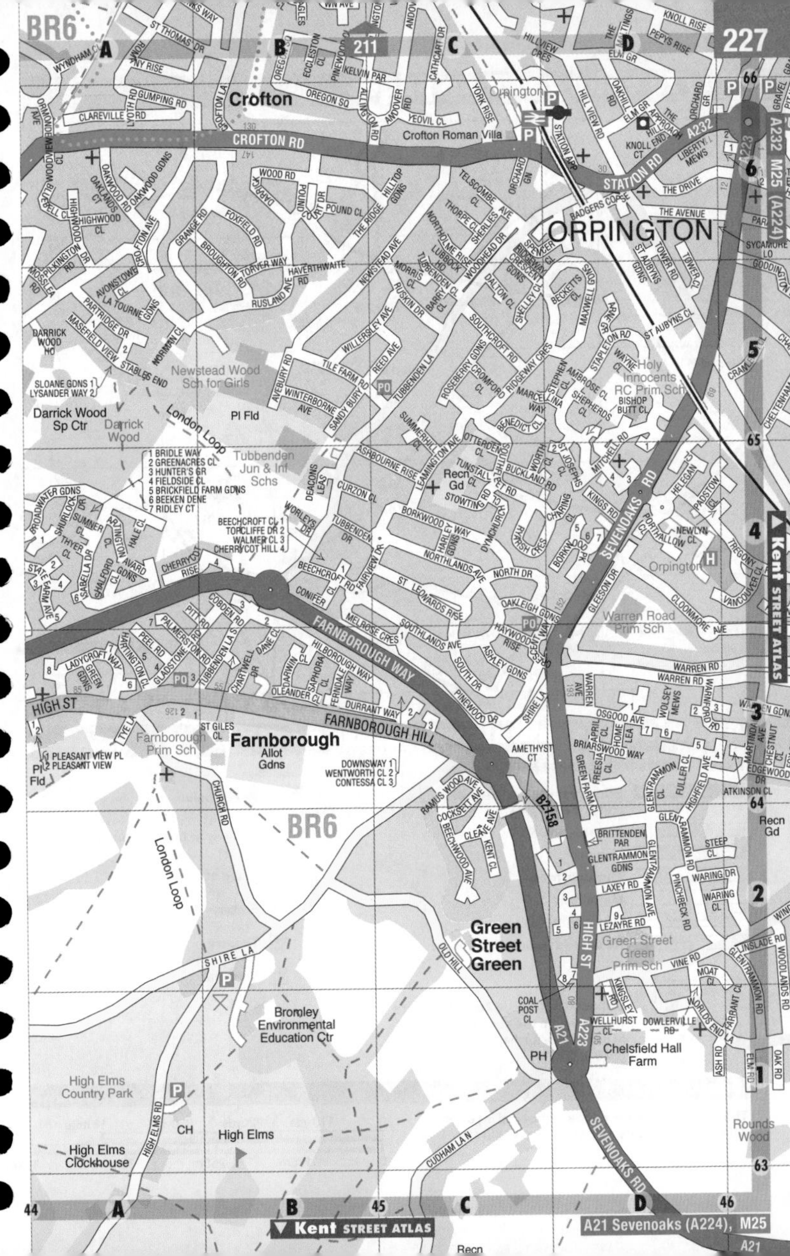
BR6
A
B
C
D
211
Crofton
CROFTON RD
Crofton Roman Villa
Orpington
ORPINGTON
STATION RD
STATION APP
A232
A223
M25
A232 M25 (A224)
ST THOMAS'S DR
WYNDHAM CL
CLAREVILLE RD
GUMPING RD
LYOTH RD
CROFTON LA
ECCLESTON CL
PINEWOOD CL
KELVIN PAR
OREGON SQ
ALLINGTON RD
ANDOVER RD
YEOVIL CL
CATHCART DR
YORK RISE
HILLVIEW CRES
KNOLL RISE
PEPYS RISE
ELM GR
OAKHILL RD
HILL VIEW RD
KNOLL CT
THE APPROACH
LIBERTY MEWS
ORCHARD GR
GRAVEL PIT WAY
THE DRIVE
THE AVENUE
BADGERS COPSE
ORCHARD GN
TELSCOMBE CL
THORPE CL
SHERLIES AVE
NORTHOLME RISE
LUBBOCK HO
TUBBENDEN CL
WOODHEAD DR
SPENCER CL
RIDGEWAY CRESCENT GDNS
WOOD RD
DARRICK CL
POUND CL
CROFT DR
THE RIDGE
HILLTOP GDNS
FOXFIELD RD
BROUGHTON RD
GRANGE RD
TORVER WAY
HAVERTHWAITE RD
RUSLAND AVE
NEWSTEAD AVE
MORRIS CL
RUSKIN DR
BARRY CL
OAKWOOD RD
OAKWOOD GDNS
OAKLANDS CT
CROFTON AVE
HIGHWOOD CL
HIGHWOOD DR
ORMONDE AVE
WOODVIEW CL
PILKINGTON RD
MOSSLEA RD
AVONSTOWE CL
LA TOURNE GDNS
PARTRIDGE DR
MASEFIELD VIEW
NORMAN CL
STABLES END
DARRICK WOOD HO
SLOANE GDNS 1
LYSANDER WAY 2
Newstead Wood Sch for Girls
Darrick Wood Sp Ctr
Darrick Wood
London Loop
Pl Fld
1 BRIDLE WAY
2 GREENACRES CL
3 HUNTER'S GR
4 FIELDSIDE CL
5 BRICKFIELD FARM GDNS
6 BEEKEN DENE
7 RIDLEY CT
Tubbenden Jun & Inf Schs
BEECHCROFT CL 1
TOPCLIFFE DR 2
WALMER CL 3
CHERRYCOT HILL 4
AVEBURY RD
TILE FARM RD
WILLERSLEY AVE
REED AVE
WINTERBORNE AVE
SANDY BURY
TUBBENDEN LA
PO
DALTON CL
SHELLEY CL
BECKETTS CL
MAXWELL GDNS
SOUTHCROFT RD
ROSEBERRY GDNS
CROMFORD CL
RIDGEWAY CRES
MARCELLINA WAY
STEPHEN CL
AMBROSE CL
STAPLETON RD
WAYNE CL
ARNE GR
ST AUBYNS CL
ST AUBYNS GDNS
TOWER RD
TOWER CL
Holy Innocents RC Prim Sch
BISHOP BUTT CL
SHEPHERDS CL
BENEDICT CL
SUMMERHILL CL
ASHBOURNE RISE
LEAMINGTON AVE
OTTERDEN CL
TUNSTALL CL
STOWTING RD
SOUTHFLEET RD
BUCKLAND RD
WORTH CL
ST JOSEPHS CL
MITCHELL RD
Recn Gd
DEACONS LEAS
CURZON CL
WORLEYS DR
TUBBENDEN DR
BORKWOOD WAY
HARLEY GDNS
DYMCHURCH CL
RYARSH CRES
CHARING CL
BORKWOOD PK
KINGS RD
SEVENOAKS RD
PORTHALLOW CL
HELEGAN CL
PADSTOW CL
NEWLYN CL
TREGONY RD
VANCOUVER CL
Orpington
H
BROADWATER GDNS
SHURLOCK DR
SUMMER CL
ARTINGTON CL
HALE CL
THYER CL
SABELLA DR
SHALFORD CL
AVARD GDNS
STATE FARM AVE
CHERRYCOT RISE
BEECHCROFT RD
FAIRVIEW DR
CONIFER CL
NORTHLANDS AVE
NORTH DR
ST LEONARDS RISE
OAKLEIGH GDNS
GLEESON DR
Warren Road Prim Sch
CLOONMORE AVE
COBDEN RD
PITT RD
PALMERSTON RD
PEEL RD
HARTINGTON CL
LADYCROFT WAY
GREEN GDNS
GLADSTONE RD
TUBBENDEN LA S
CHARTWELL DR
DANE CL
DARWIN CL
SAPHORA CL
HILBOROUGH WAY
FERNDALE WAY
OLEANDER CL
DURRANT WAY
FARNBOROUGH WAY
MELROSE CRES
SOUTHLANDS AVE
HAYWOOD RISE
CRESCENT WAY
ASHLEY GDNS
SOUTH DR
PINEWOOD DR
SHIRE LA
WARREN RD
WARREN AVE
OSGOOD AVE
WOLSEY MEWS
WARNFORD RD
WARREN GDNS
APRIL CL
HOME LEA
BRIARSWOOD WAY
FREESIA CL
GREEN FARM CL
GLENTRAMMON CL
FULLER CL
HIGHFIELD AVE
MARTINDALE AVE
CHESTNUT CL
FOX CL
EDGEWOOD DR
ATKINSON CL
HIGH ST
FARNBOROUGH HILL
Farnborough
Farnborough Prim Sch
ST GILES CL
TYE LA
Allot Gdns
1 PLEASANT VIEW PL
2 PLEASANT VIEW
Pl Fld
DOWNSWAY 1
WENTWORTH CL 2
CONTESSA CL 3
AMETHYST CT
B2158
RAMUS WOOD AVE
COCKSETT AVE
CLEAVE AVE
BEECHWOOD AVE
KENT CL
CHURCH RD
BR6
London Loop
BRITTENDEN PAR
GLENTRAMMON GDNS
GLENTRAMMON RD
GLENTRAMMON AVE
STEEP CL
WARING DR
WARING CL
LAXEY RD
PINCHBECK RD
LEZAYRE RD
Green Street Green
Green Street Green Prim Sch
VINE RD
MOAT CL
GLENTRAMMON RD
FARRANT CL
WOODLANDS RD
LINSLADE RD
WORLDS END LA
OLD HILL
SHIRE LA
COAL POST CL
KINGSLEY CT
WELLHURST CL
DOWLERVILLE RD
Chelsfield Hall Farm
A21
A223
PH
ASH RD
ELM RD
OAK RD
Bromley Environmental Education Ctr
High Elms Country Park
HIGH ELMS RD
CH
High Elms
High Elms Clockhouse
CUDHAM LA N
SEVENOAKS RD
Rounds Wood
Recn Gd
Kent STREET ATLAS
44
45
46
63
64
65
1
2
3
4
5
6
A21 Sevenoaks (A224), M25
Recn

Key to enlarged map pages

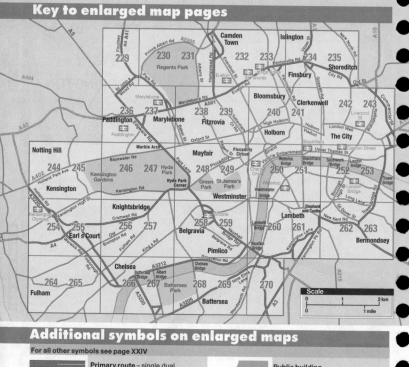

Additional symbols on enlarged maps

For all other symbols see page XXIV

Primary route – single,dual carriageway

A road – single, dual carriageway

B road

Through-route

Minor road

One way street

No access in direction shown

Congestion Charge Zone boundary
Roads within the zone are outlined in green – for further information call 0845 900 1234

Public building

Railway or bus station building

Place of interest

E Embassy

Theatre

Museum

Scale

The map scale on the pages numbered in red is 6.04 inches to 1 mile • 9.6cm to 1 km • 1: 10416

| 0 | 110 yds | 220yds | 330yds | ¼ mile |
| 0 | 125m | 250m | 375m | ½km |

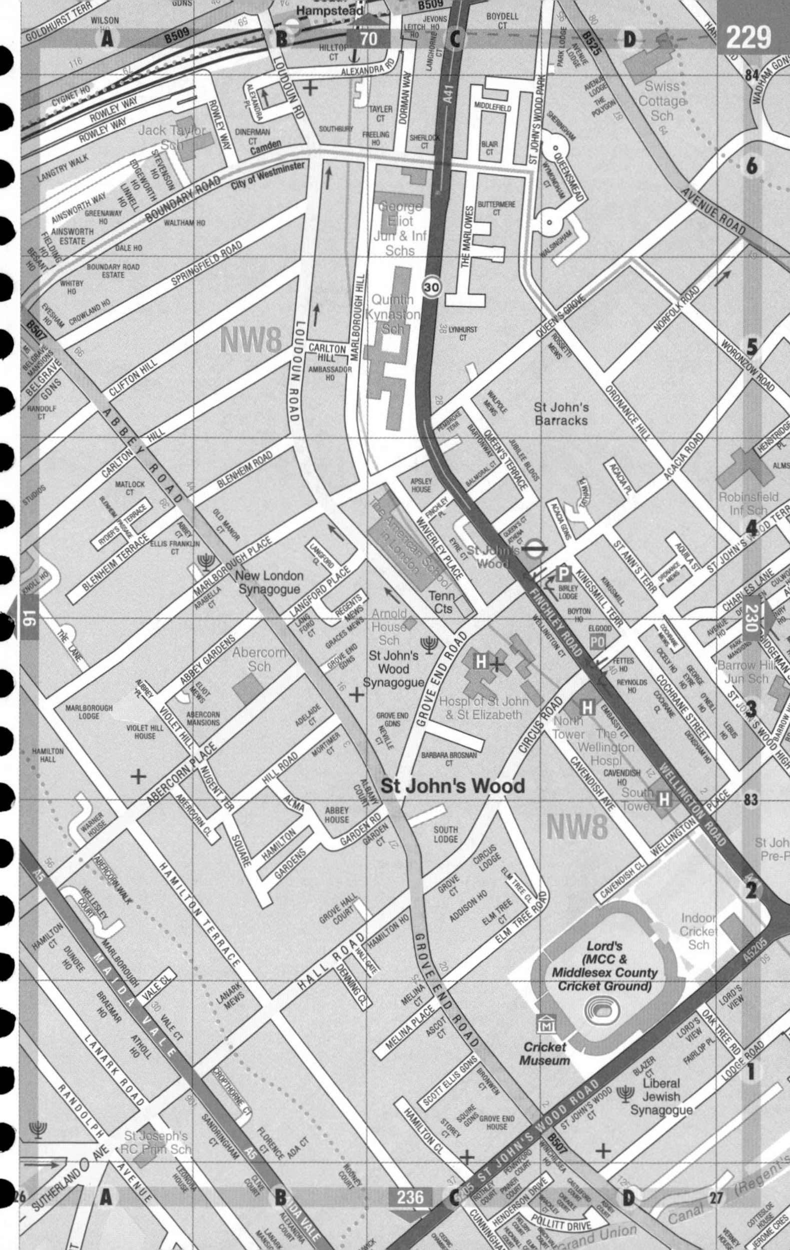

Hampstead
70
A
B
C
D
B509
GOLDHURST TERR
WILSON HO
HILLTOP CT
ALEXANDRA RD
LEITCH HO
JEVONS HO
LANGHORNE CT
BOYDELL CT
PARK LODGE
AVENUE LODGE
B525
Swiss Cottage Sch
84
WADHAM GDNS
CYGNET HO
ROWLEY WAY
LOUDOUN RD
ALEXANDRA PL
DORMAN WAY
TAYLER CT
SOUTHBURY
FREELING HO
SHERLOCK CT
A41
MIDDLEFIELD
BLAIR CT
ST JOHN'S WOOD PARK
SHERINGHAM
QUEENSMEAD
WYMONDHAM CT
AVENUE LODGE
THE POLYGON
Jack Taylor Sch
DINERMAN CT
Camden
City of Westminster
LANGTRY WALK
STEVENSON HO
EDGEWORTH HO
LINNELL HO
BOUNDARY ROAD
AINSWORTH WAY
GREENAWAY HO
AINSWORTH ESTATE
WALTHAM HO
DALE HO
BOUNDARY ROAD ESTATE
WHITBY HO
FIELDING HO
BESANT HO
EVESHAM HO
CROWLAND HO
SPRINGFIELD ROAD
George Eliot Jun & Inf Schs
THE MARLOWES
BUTTERMERE CT
WALSINGHAM
6
AVENUE ROAD
30
Quintin Kynaston Sch
LYNHURST CT
QUEEN'S GROVE
NORFOLK ROAD
NW8
B507
BELGRAVE MANSIONS
BELGRAVE GDNS
RANDOLF CT
CLIFTON HILL
CARLTON HILL
MARLBOROUGH HILL
LOUDOUN ROAD
AMBASSADOR HO
ROSSETTI MEWS
5
WORONZOW ROAD
ORDNANCE HILL
WALPOLE MEWS
St John's Barracks
ABBEY ROAD
PEMBROKE TERR
BARTON WAY
QUEEN'S TERRACE
JUBILEE BLDGS
BALMORAL CT
ACACIA ROAD
HENSTRIDGE PL
ALMSHOUSES
BLENHEIM ROAD
MATLOCK CT
STUDIOS
APSLEY HOUSE
ACACIA PL
Robinsfield Inf Sch
OLD MANOR CT
RYDER'S TERRACE
ABBEY CT
ELLIS FRANKLIN CT
BLENHEIM TERRACE
The American School in London
FINCHLEY PL
WAVERLEY PLACE
EYRE CT
St John's Wood
ACACIA GDNS
4
ST JOHN'S WOOD TERRACE
ST ANN'S TERR
AQUILA ST
MARLBOROUGH PLACE
LANGFORD CL
LANGFORD PLACE
New London Synagogue
KNOLL HO
ARABELLA CT
REGENTS MEWS
Tenn Cts
BIRLEY LODGE
KINGSMILL TERR
KINGSMILL
ORDNANCE MEWS
CHARLES LANE
CULWORTH HO
91
THE LANE
Arnold House Sch
GRACES MEWS
FINCHLEY ROAD
WELLINGTON CT
BOYTON HO
ELGOOD HO
PO
230
ABBEY GARDENS
Abercorn Sch
GROVE END GDNS
St John's Wood Synagogue
GROVE END ROAD
H
FETTES HO
REYNOLDS HO
CICELY HO
GEORGE EYRE HO
O'NEILL HO
Barrow Hill Jun Sch
AUBREY PL
ELIOT MEWS
ABERCORN MANSIONS
MARLBOROUGH LODGE
VIOLET HILL HOUSE
VIOLET HILL
16
ADELAIDE CT
Hospl of St John & St Elizabeth
CIRCUS ROAD
North Tower
The Wellington Hospl
EMBASSY CT
COCHRANE STREET
DENSHAM HO
3
ST JOHN'S WOOD HIGH STREET
HAMILTON HALL
ABERCORN PLACE
NUGENT TER
HILL ROAD
MORTIMER CT
GROVE END GDNS
NEVILLE CT
BARBARA BROSNAN CT
CAVENDISH AVE
CAVENDISH HO
South Tower
ALBANY COURT
St John's Wood
83
WARNER HOUSE
ABERCORN CL
ALMA
ABBEY HOUSE
GARDEN RD
GARDEN CT
SOUTH LODGE
NW8
WELLINGTON PLACE
WELLINGTON ROAD
St John's Pre-Prep
HAMILTON TERRACE
SQUARE
HAMILTON GARDENS
CIRCUS LODGE
CAVENDISH CL
ABERCORN WALK
WELLESLEY COURT
A5
GROVE CT
ELM TREE CL
2
GROVE HALL COURT
ADDISON HO
ELM TREE CT
ELM TREE ROAD
Indoor Cricket Sch
HAMILTON CT
DUNDEE HO
MAIDA VALE
HAMILTON HO
HALL ROAD
HALL GATE
GROVE END ROAD
Lord's (MCC & Middlesex County Cricket Ground)
A5205
MARLBOROUGH
VALE CL
LANARK MEWS
DENNING CL
MELINA CT
LORD'S VIEW
BRAEMAR HO
VALE CT
ATHOLL HO
MELINA PLACE
ASCOT CT
Cricket Museum
OAK TREE RD
LODGE ROAD
NORTH BANK
LANARK ROAD
CROPTHORNE CT
SCOTT ELLIS GDNS
BRONWEN CT
BLAZER CT
FAIRLOP PL
1
Liberal Jewish Synagogue
RANDOLPH
HAMILTON CL
SQUIRE GDNS
STOREY CT
GROVE END HOUSE
ST JOHN'S WOOD ROAD
ST JOHN'S WOOD CT
St Joseph's RC Prim Sch
SANDRINGHAM CT
FLORENCE CT
ADA CT
RODNEY COURT
WINCHILSEA HO
SUTHERLAND AVE
AVENUE
LEONORA HOUSE
CLIVE COURT
236
PINNER CT
HENDERSON DRIVE
POLLITT DRIVE
CUNNINGHAM
Canal (Regent's Ca
Grand Union
27
26
COTTESLOE HOUSE
JEROME CRES
MAIDA VALE
ALEXANDRA COURT
LANARK MANSIONS

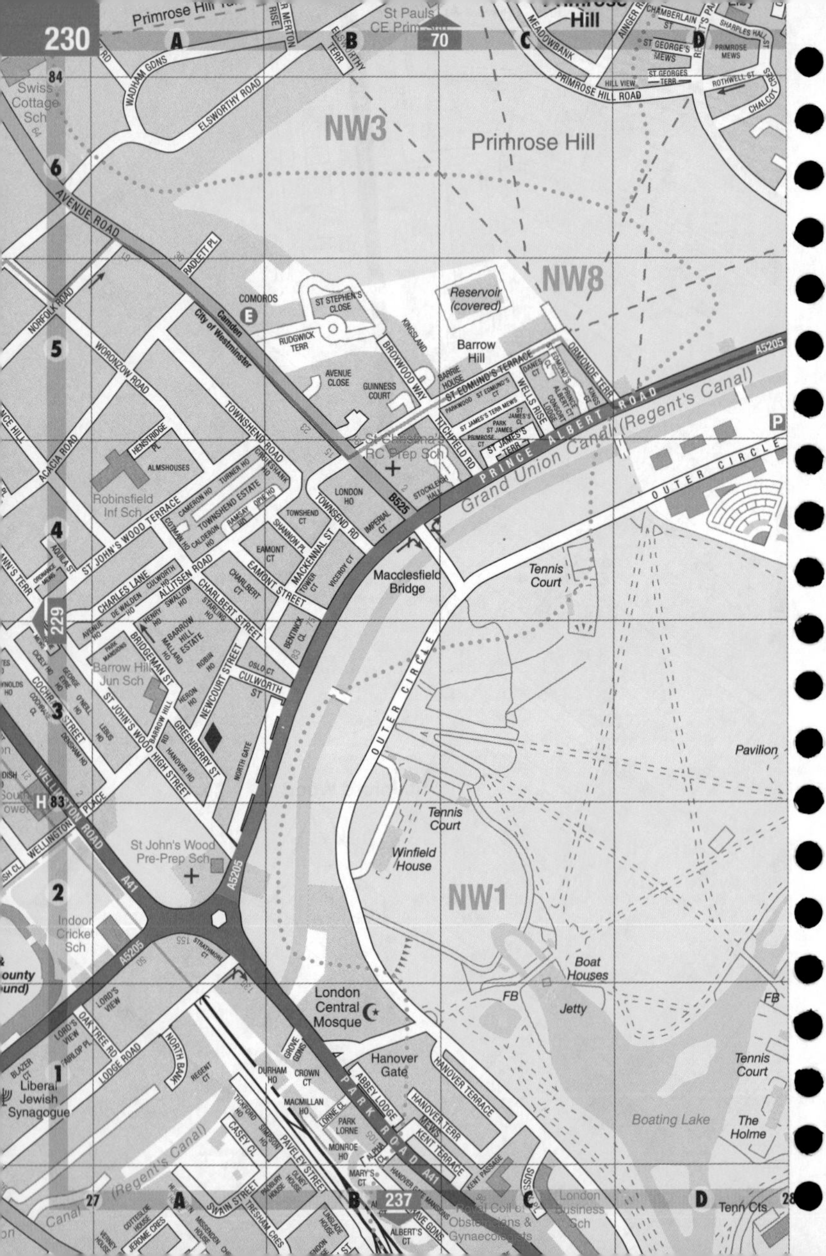

Primrose Hill
Hill
St Pauls
CE Prim
70
NW3
Primrose Hill
NW8
NW1
ELSWORTHY ROAD
WADHAM GDNS
AVENUE ROAD
Swiss Cottage Sch
CHAMBERLAIN ST
ST GEORGE'S MEWS
PRIMROSE MEWS
SHARPLES HALL ST
ROTHWELL ST
MEADOWBANK
AINGER RD
PRIMROSE HILL ROAD
CHALCOT CRES
Reservoir (covered)
Barrow Hill
COMOROS
ST STEPHEN'S CLOSE
RUDGWICK TERR
AVENUE CLOSE
GUINNESS COURT
BROXWOOD WAY
KINGSLAND
ST EDMUND'S TERRACE
ORMONDE TERR
WELLS RISE
A5205
PRINCE ALBERT ROAD
Grand Union Canal (Regent's Canal)
OUTER CIRCLE
Camden
City of Westminster
NORFOLK ROAD
WORONZOW ROAD
TOWNSHEND ROAD
ACACIA ROAD
HENSTRIDGE PL
ALMSHOUSES
Robinsfield Inf Sch
ST JOHN'S WOOD TERRACE
TOWNSHEND ESTATE
LONDON HO
TOWNSEND RD
B525
STOCKLEIGH HALL
IMPERIAL CT
Macclesfield Bridge
Tennis Court
CHARLES LANE
ALLITSEN ROAD
CHARLBERT STREET
EAMONT STREET
MACKENNAL ST
BENTINCK CL
229
OUTER CIRCLE
Barrow Hill Jun Sch
BARROW HILL ESTATE
NEWCOURT STREET
CULWORTH ST
OSLO CT
ST JOHN'S WOOD HIGH STREET
GREENBERRY ST
NORTH GATE
Pavilion
WELLINGTON ROAD
WELLINGTON PLACE
Tennis Court
Winfield House
St John's Wood Pre-Prep Sch
A41
A5205
Indoor Cricket Sch
STRATHMORE CT
Boat Houses
Jetty
FB
London Central Mosque
LORD'S VIEW
OAK TREE RD
LODGE ROAD
NORTH BANK
Liberal Jewish Synagogue
Hanover Gate
HANOVER TERRACE
PARK ROAD
ABBEY LODGE
Tennis Court
Boating Lake
The Holme
CASEY CL
PAVELEY STREET
KENT TERRACE
KENT PASSAGE
SWAIN STREET
TRESHAM CRES
237
London Business Sch
Tenn Cts

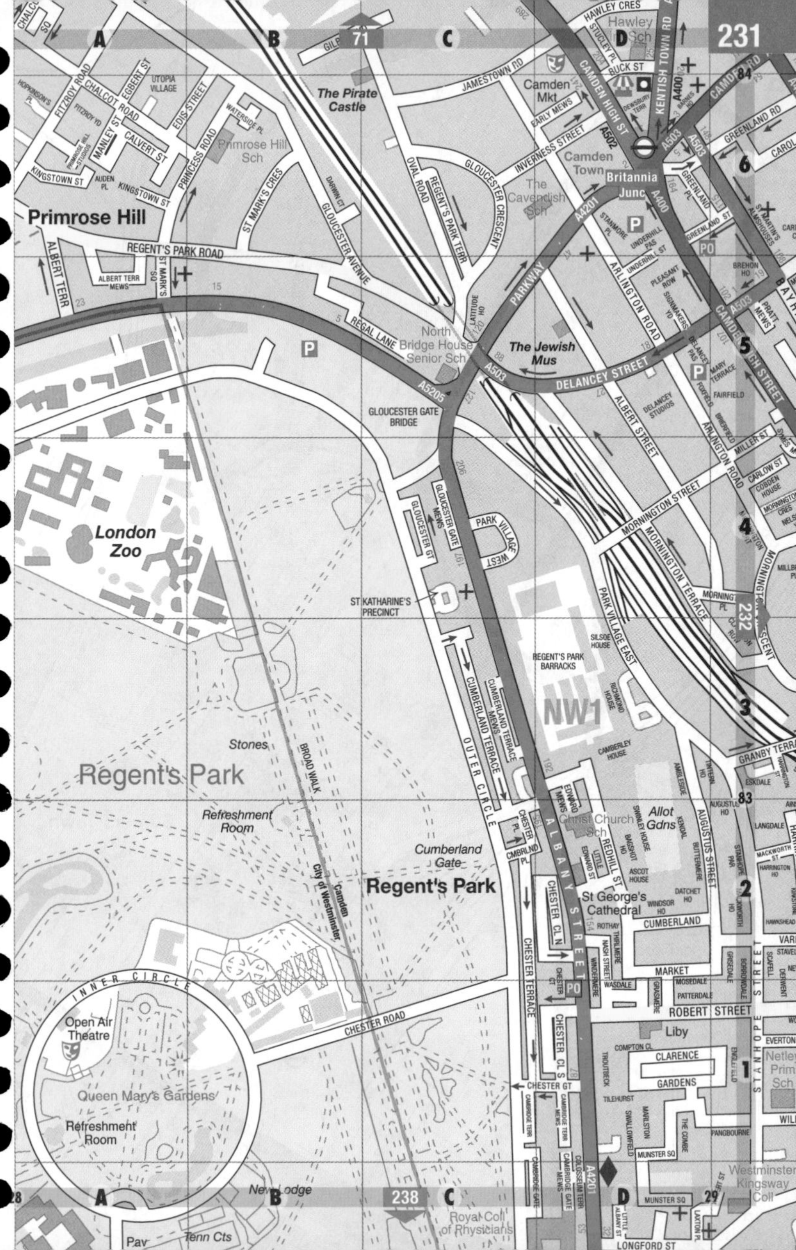
71
A
B
C
D
The Pirate Castle
Primrose Hill Sch
Utopia Village
Fitzroy Road
Chalcot Road
Egbert St
Edis Street
Manley St
Calvert St
Kingstown St
Princess Road
Waterside Pl
St Mark's Cres
Primrose Hill
Albert Terr
Regent's Park Road
Albert Terr Mews
St Mark's Sq
Gloucester Avenue
Oval Road
Regent's Park Terr
Gloucester Crescent
Jamestown Rd
Hawley Cres
Hawley Sch
Stucley Pl
Buck St
Camden High St
Kentish Town Rd
Camden Mkt
Early Mews
Inverness Street
Camden Town
Britannia Junc
The Cavendish Sch
Parkway
Arlington Road
Greenland Rd
Carol St
Delancey Street
The Jewish Mus
Regal Lane
North Bridge House Senior Sch
Gloucester Gate Bridge
Albert Street
Mornington Street
Mornington Terrace
Mornington Crescent
London Zoo
Gloucester Gate Mews
Gloucester Gt
Park Village West
Park Village East
St Katharine's Precinct
Regent's Park Barracks
NW1
Cumberland Terrace
Cumberland Terrace Mews
Outer Circle
Stones
Broad Walk
Regent's Park
Refreshment Room
Cumberland Gate
Camden
City of Westminster
Albany Street
Chester Pl
Redhill St
Augustus Street
Christ Church Sch
Allot Gdns
St George's Cathedral
Cumberland Market
Chester Terrace
Chester Cl N
Robert Street
Liby
Clarence Gardens
Stanhope Street
Netley Prim Sch
Inner Circle
Open Air Theatre
Queen Mary's Gardens
Refreshment Room
Chester Road
Chester Gt
Chester Cl S
Cambridge Terr
Colosseum Terr
Munster Sq
Westminster Kingsway Coll
New Lodge
238
Royal Coll of Physicians
Tenn Cts
Longford St
Granby Terrace
1
2
3
4
5
6

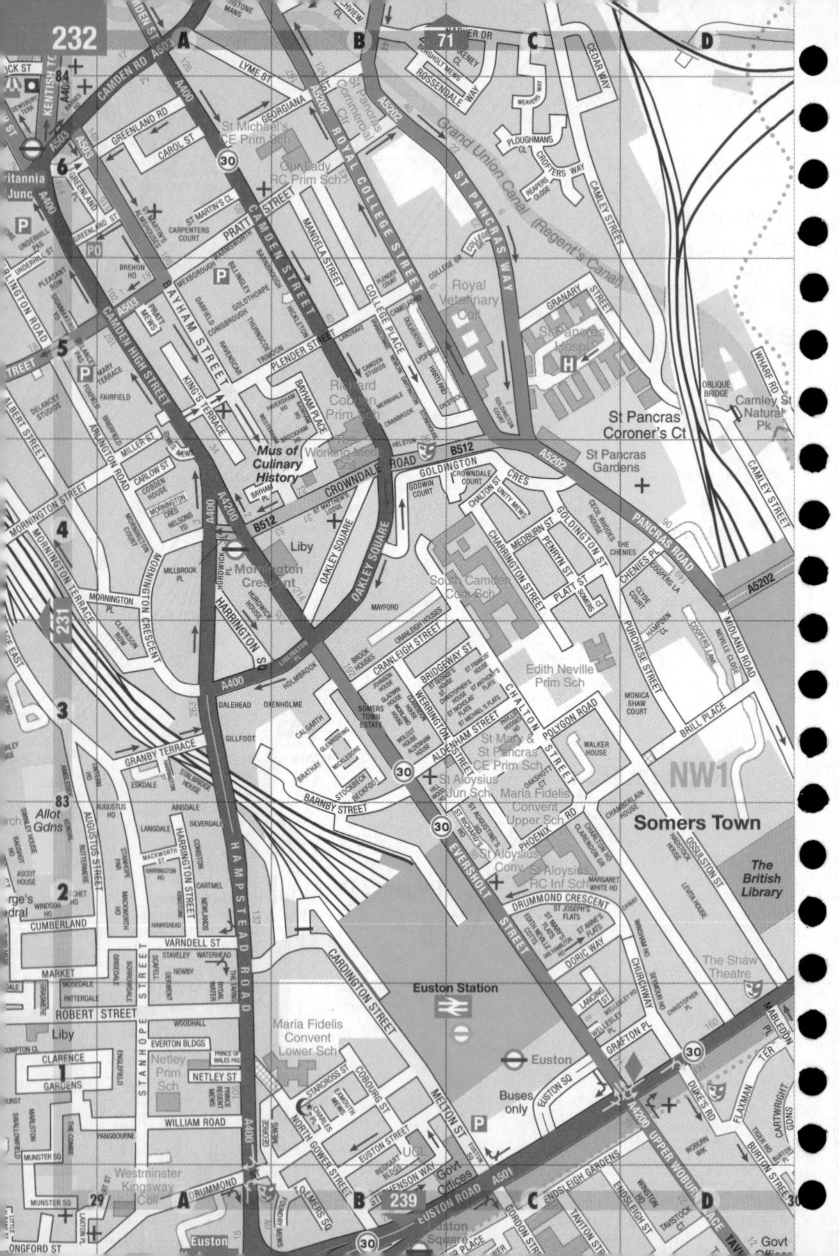

71
239
231
Camden Road
Royal College Street
St Pancras Way
Grand Union Canal (Regent's Canal)
Camden Street
Camden High Street
Bayham Street
Pratt Street
Plender Street
Crowndale Road
Oakley Square
Mornington Crescent
Mornington Terrace
Hampstead Road
Eversholt Street
Chalton Street
Polygon Road
Pancras Road
Midland Road
Brill Place
Ossulston Street
Churchway
Drummond Crescent
Cardington Street
Euston Road
Upper Woburn Place
Euston Station
Euston
Somers Town
NW1
The British Library
The Shaw Theatre
St Pancras Coroner's Ct
St Pancras Gardens
Royal Veterinary Coll
St Pancras Hospl
Camley St Natural Pk
Mus of Culinary History
Richard Cobden Prim Sch
The Working Mens Coll
Mornington Crescent
Liby
South Camden Com Sch
Edith Neville Prim Sch
St Mary & St Pancras CE Prim Sch
St Aloysius Jun Sch
Maria Fidelis Convent Upper Sch
St Aloysius Conv
St Aloysius RC Inf Sch
Maria Fidelis Convent Lower Sch
Netley Prim Sch
Westminster Kingsway Coll
UCL
Govt Offices
Buses only
Allot Gdns
Robert Street
Clarence Gardens
William Road
Varndell St
Granby Terrace
Barnby Street
Stanhope Street
Harrington Street
Augustus Street
Cumberland Market

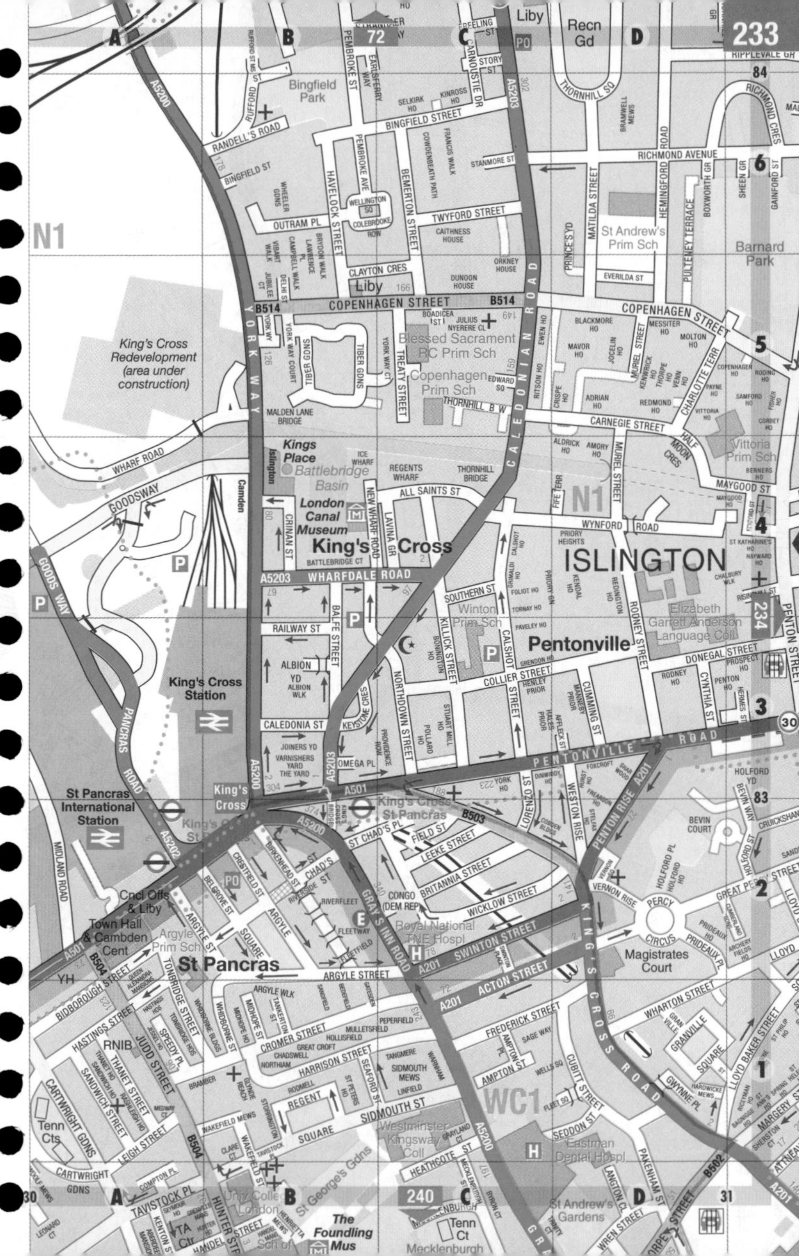

A
B
72
C
D
Liby
Recn Gd
PO
Bingfield Park
RANDELL'S ROAD
BINGFIELD ST
BINGFIELD STREET
RICHMOND AVENUE
RICHMOND CRES
THORNHILL SQ
CALEDONIAN ROAD
A5203
A5200
YORK WAY
N1
OUTRAM PL
TWYFORD STREET
HAVELOCK STREET
BEMERTON STREET
PEMBROKE ST
CLAYTON CRES
COPENHAGEN STREET
B514
St Andrew's Prim Sch
Barnard Park
BARNSBURY ROAD
King's Cross Redevelopment (area under construction)
Blessed Sacrament RC Prim Sch
Copenhagen Prim Sch
TREATY STREET
CARNEGIE STREET
CHARLOTTE TERR
Vittoria Prim Sch
MAYGOOD ST
WHARF ROAD
GOODSWAY
Kings Place
Battlebridge Basin
London Canal Museum
King's Cross
ALL SAINTS ST
WYNFORD ROAD
ISLINGTON
Pentonville
WHARFDALE ROAD
RAILWAY ST
BALFE STREET
CALEDONIA ST
Winton Prim Sch
Elizabeth Garrett Anderson Language Coll
DONEGAL STREET
COLLIER STREET
RODNEY STREET
CUMMING ST
PENTON STREET
234
King's Cross Station
GOODS WAY
PANCRAS ROAD
PENTONVILLE ROAD
A501
St Pancras International Station
King's Cross St Pancras
A5202
B503
PENTON RISE
A201
MIDLAND ROAD
GRAY'S INN ROAD
KING'S CROSS ROAD
Cncl Offs & Liby
Town Hall & Cambden Cent
Argyle Prim Sch
St Pancras
ARGYLE STREET
Royal National TNE Hospl
SWINTON STREET
ACTON STREET
WICKLOW STREET
BRITANNIA STREET
LEEKE STREET
FIELD ST
VERNON RISE
PERCY CIRCUS
GREAT PERCY STREET
Magistrates Court
LLOYD BAKER STREET
WHARTON STREET
GRANVILLE SQUARE
YH
B504
BIDBOROUGH STREET
HASTINGS STREET
RNIB
JUDD STREET
THANET STREET
CARTWRIGHT GDNS
LEIGH STREET
CROMER STREET
HARRISON STREET
SIDMOUTH ST
REGENT SQUARE
FREDERICK STREET
AMPTON ST
CUBITT STREET
WC1
Westminster Kingsway Coll
HEATHCOTE ST
Eastman Dental Hospl
TAVISTOCK PL
HUNTER ST
St George's Gdns
240
St Andrew's Gardens
The Foundling Mus
Mecklenburgh
Tenn Ct
MARGERY STREET
B502
30
31
1
2
3
4
5
6
83
84

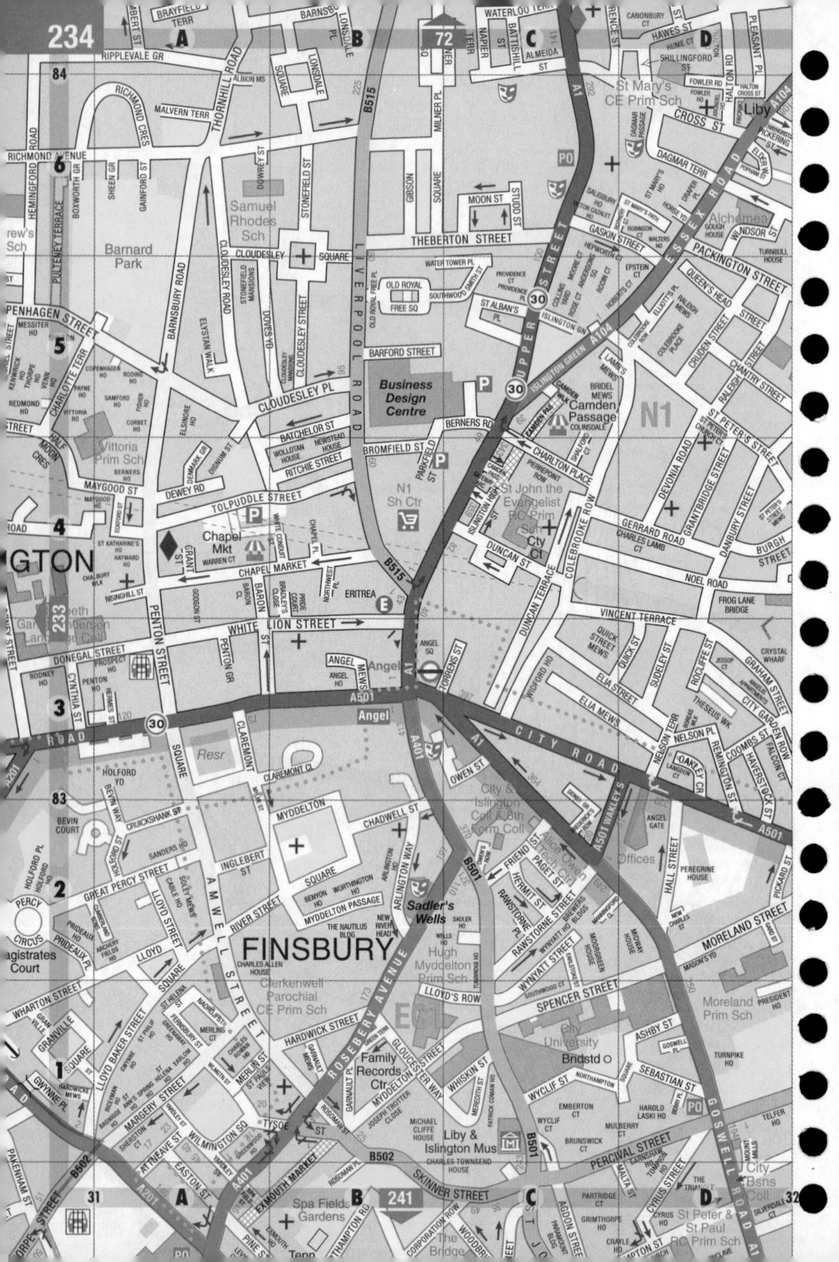
A
B
C
D
72
84
6
5
4
3
2
1
83
233
241
31
32
BRAYFIELD TERR
BARNSBURY
LONSDALE PL
WATERLOO TERR
NAPIER TERR
BATTISHILL ST
ALMEIDA ST
CANONBURY CT
HAWES ST
HUME CT
SHILLINGFORD ST
PLEASANT PL
RIPPLEVALE GR
ALBION MS
RICHMOND CRES
MALVERN TERR
THORNHILL ROAD
LONSDALE SQUARE
B515
MILNER PL
A1
St Mary's CE Prim Sch
FOWLER RD
HALTON RD
HALTON CROSS ST
CROSS ST
DAGMAR PASSAGE
DAGMAR TERR
Liby
A104
RICHMOND AVENUE
HEMINGFORD ROAD
BOXWORTH GR
SHEEN GR
GAINFORD ST
DOWREY ST
STONEFIELD ST
GIBSON SQUARE
PO
MOON ST
STUDD ST
ESSEX ROAD
Samuel Rhodes Sch
PULTENEY TERRACE
Barnard Park
CLOUDESLEY ROAD
CLOUDESLEY SQUARE
THEBERTON STREET
GASKIN STREET
Alchemea
GOUGH HOUSE
WINDSOR ST
PACKINGTON STREET
TURNBULL HOUSE
UPPER STREET
WATER TOWER PL
OLD ROYAL FREE SQ
OLD ROYAL FREE PL
LIVERPOOL ROAD
SOUTHWOOD SMITH ST
ST ALBAN'S PL
ISLINGTON GN
EPSTEIN CT
QUEEN'S HEAD STREET
COPENHAGEN STREET
BARNSBURY ROAD
STONEFIELD MANSIONS
DOVES YD
ELYSTAN WALK
CLOUDESLEY STREET
BARFORD STREET
ISLINGTON GREEN
LAMB'S MEWS
CRUDEN STREET
CHANTRY STREET
RALEIGH STREET
COPENHAGEN HO
RODING HO
SAMFORD HO
PAYNE HO
CHARLOTTE TERR
CLOUDESLEY PL
Business Design Centre
P
30
BRIDEL MEWS
Camden Passage
N1
REDMOND HO
VITTORIA HO
ELSINORE HO
BATCHELOR ST
BERNERS RD
CAMDEN PAS
CAMDEN WLK
COLINSDALE
ST PETER'S STREET
HALF MOON CRES
Vittoria Prim Sch
BERNERS HO
DENMARK GR
DIGNUM ST
WOLLOTAN HOUSE
NEWSTEAD HOUSE
RITCHIE STREET
BROMFIELD ST
PARKFIELD ST
CHARLTON PLACE
PIERREPONT ROW
DEVONIA ROAD
GRANTBRIDGE STREET
MAYGOOD ST
DEWEY RD
TOLPUDDLE STREET
N1 Sh Ctr
St John the Evangelist RC Prim Sch
COLEBROOKE ROW
DANBURY STREET
GERRARD ROAD
CHARLES LAMB CT
BURGH STREET
ROAD
GTON
ST KATHARINE'S HO
HAYWARD HO
Chapel Mkt
WARREN CT
GRANT ST
WHITE CONDUIT ST
CHAPEL PL
DUNCAN ST
Cty Ct
DUNCAN TERRACE
NOEL ROAD
CHAPEL MARKET
CHALBURY WLK
RISINGHILL ST
GODSON ST
BARON CL
BARON ST
BRADLEY'S CLOSE
PRIDE COURT
NORTHWEST PL
ERITREA
E
B515
FROG LANE BRIDGE
VINCENT TERRACE
WHITE LION STREET
QUICK STREET MEWS
QUICK ST
SUDELEY ST
ROCLIFFE ST
CRYSTAL WHARF
PENTON STREET
PENTON GR
DONEGAL STREET
PROSPECT HO
RODNEY HO
PENTON HO
HERMES ST
CYNTHIA ST
ANGEL MEWS
ANGEL HO
Angel
ANGEL SQ
TORRENS ST
WIDFORD HO
ELIA STREET
ELIA MEWS
GRAHAM STREET
CITY GARDEN ROW
THESEUS WK
A501
A1
CLAREMONT
Resr
CLAREMONT CL
A401
CITY ROAD
NELSON TERR
NELSON PL
REMINGTON ST
COOMBS ST
HAVERSTOCK ST
FALCON CT
OAKLEY CR
LANGDON CT
HOLFORD YD
BEVIN WAY
SQUARE
OWEN ST
City & Islington Coll & 6th Form Coll
A501 WAKLEY ST
ANGEL GATE
BEVIN COURT
CRUICKSHANK ST
MYDDELTON
CHADWELL ST
SANDERS HO
HOLFORD ST
INGLEBERT ST
ARLINGTON WAY
ARLINGTON HO
B501
OWEN'S ROW
FRIEND ST
Alice Owen Tech Ctr
PAGET ST
HERMIT ST
Offices
HALL STREET
PEREGRINE HOUSE
PICKARD ST
HOLFORD PL
GREAT PERCY STREET
CABLE HO
SOLEY MEWS
AMWELL STREET
SQUARE
BENYON HO
WORTHINGTON HO
MYDDELTON PASSAGE
Sadler's Wells
RAWSTORNE PL
RAWSTORNE STREET
BREWERS BLDGS
MIDWAY HOUSE
MORELAND STREET
PERCY CIRCUS
PRIDEAUX PL
Magistrates Court
ARCHERY FIELDS HO
LLOYD STREET
LLOYD SQUARE
RIVER STREET
THE NAUTILUS BLDG
NEW RIVER HEAD
SADLER HO
WELLS HO
Hugh Myddelton Prim Sch
TUNBRIDGE HO
WYNYATT HO
WYNYATT STREET
MOORGREEN HOUSE
FINSBURY
CHARLES ALLEN HOUSE
Clerkenwell Parochial CE Prim Sch
LLOYD'S ROW
SOUTHWOOD CT
SPENCER STREET
Moreland Prim Sch
PRESIDENT HO
WHARTON STREET
GRANVILLE SQUARE
LLOYD BAKER STREET
MERLINS CT
ROSEBERY AVENUE
HARDWICK STREET
GARNAULT MEWS
GREEN TERR
GLOUCESTER WAY
EC1
City University
ASHBY ST
GOSWELL PL
TURNPIKE HO
GWYNNE PL
HARDWICKE MEWS
MARGERY STREET
CHARLES ROWAN HO
MERLIN ST
ST PAUL'S VIEW
Family Records Ctr
GARNAULT PL
MYDDELTON ST
WHISKIN ST
MEREDITH ST
PATRICK COMAN HO
Bndstd
NORTHAMPTON SQUARE
SEBASTIAN ST
WYCLIF ST
EMBERTON CT
HAROLD LASKI HO
PO
TELFER HO
GOSWELL ROAD
SHERSTON CT
WILMINGTON SQ
TYSOE ST
JOSEPH TROTTER CLOSE
MICHAEL CLIFFE HOUSE
Liby & Islington Mus
WYCLIF CT
BRUNSWICK CT
MULBERRY CT
PERCIVAL STREET
EARNSHAW HO
TOMPION HO
MOUNT MILLS
PAKENHAM ST
B502
A201
ATTNEAVE ST
EASTON ST
EXMOUTH MARKET
ROSOMAN ST
ROSOMAN PL
B502
SKINNER STREET
CHARLES TOWNSEND HOUSE
MALTA ST
CYRUS STREET
THE TRIANGLE
City Bsns Coll
Spa Fields Gardens
NORTHAMPTON RD
CORPORATION ROW
PARTRIDGE CT
GRIMTHORPE HO
CYRUS HO
St Peter & St Paul RC Prim Sch
SILVERDALE CT
AGDON STREET
PARAMOUNT BLDG
PINE ST
EXMOUTH MEWS
The Bridge
WOODBRIDGE ST
CRAYLE HO
NORTHAMPTON ST
Tenn

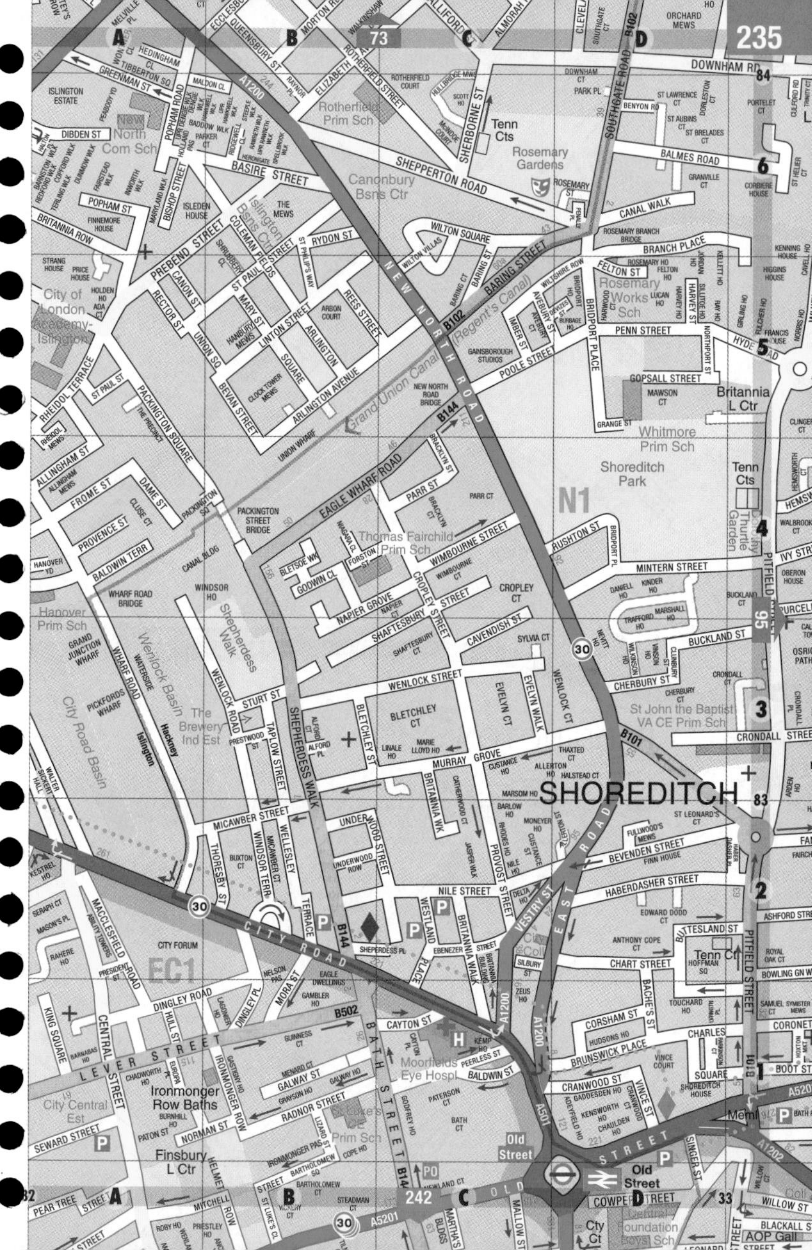

73
SHOREDITCH
N1
EC1
NEW NORTH ROAD
CITY ROAD
EAST ROAD
OLD STREET
LEVER STREET
SHEPPERTON ROAD
SOUTHGATE ROAD
DOWNHAM RD
PITFIELD STREET
SHEPHERDESS WALK
WENLOCK STREET
MURRAY GROVE
NILE STREET
HABERDASHER STREET
CHART STREET
CENTRAL STREET
BATH STREET
Grand Union Canal (Regent's Canal)
Wenlock Basin
City Road Basin
Shoreditch Park
Rosemary Gardens
Canonbury Bsns Ctr
Rotherfield Prim Sch
Thomas Fairchild Prim Sch
Whitmore Prim Sch
St John the Baptist VA CE Prim Sch
Hanover Prim Sch
City of London Academy-Islington
New North Com Sch
Britannia L Ctr
Ironmonger Row Baths
Finsbury L Ctr
Moorfields Eye Hospl
St Luke's CE Prim Sch
City Central Est
The Brewery Ind Est
Old Street
Central Foundation Boys Sch
242

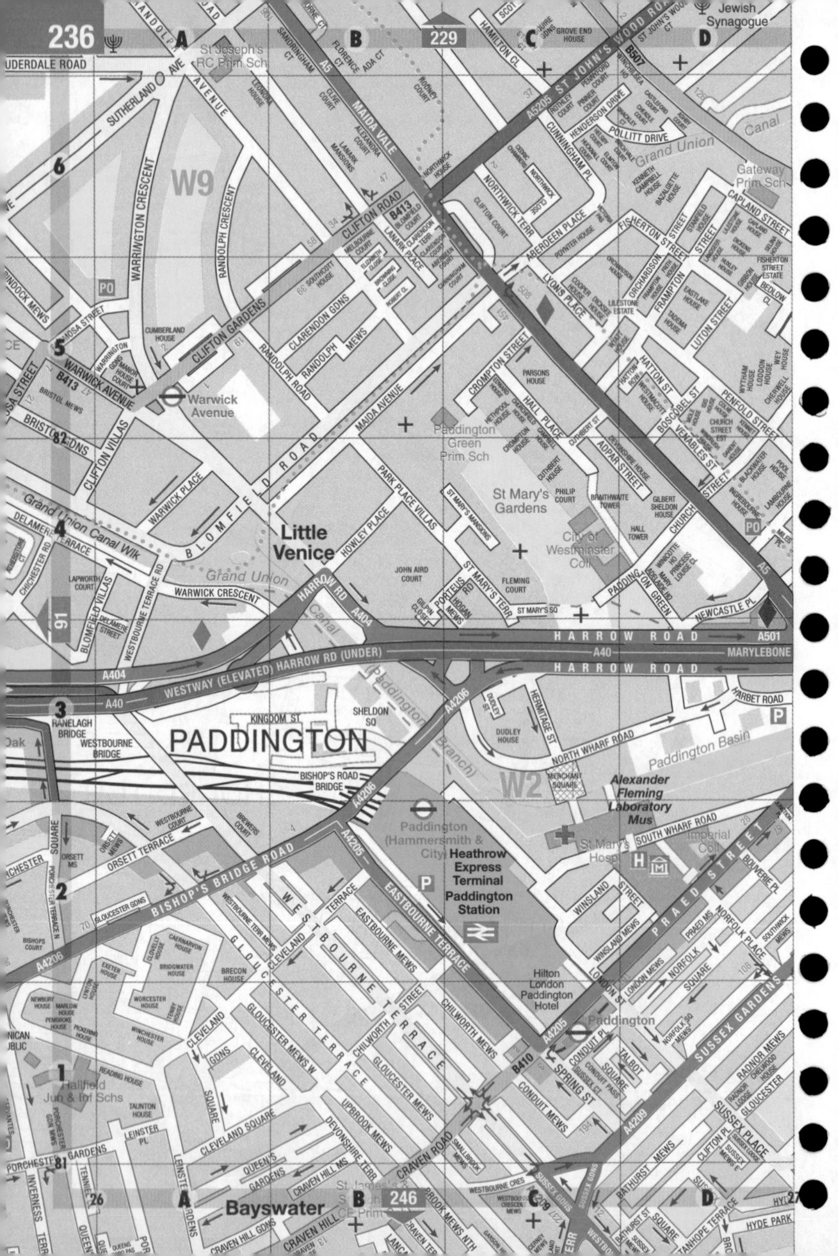
229
246
91
A
B
C
D
6
5
4
3
2
1
W9
W2
PADDINGTON
Little Venice
Bayswater
Warwick Avenue
Paddington Green Prim Sch
St Mary's Gardens
City of Westminster Coll
St Joseph's RC Prim Sch
Jewish Synagogue
Gateway Prim Sch
Alexander Fleming Laboratory Mus
St Mary's Hosp
Imperial Coll
Paddington (Hammersmith & City)
Heathrow Express Terminal Paddington Station
Hilton London Paddington Hotel
Paddington
Hallfield Jun & Inf Schs
Grand Union Canal
Grand Union Canal Wlk
Paddington Basin
Paddington Branch
MAIDA VALE
A5
ST JOHN'S WOOD ROAD
A5205
B507
CLIFTON ROAD
B413
CLIFTON GARDENS
WARWICK AVENUE
SUTHERLAND AVE
RANDOLPH AVENUE
WARRINGTON CRESCENT
RANDOLPH CRESCENT
RANDOLPH ROAD
CLARENDON GDNS
RANDOLPH MEWS
MAIDA AVENUE
BLOMFIELD ROAD
WARWICK PLACE
CLIFTON VILLAS
WARWICK CRESCENT
BLOMFIELD VILLAS
WESTBOURNE TERRACE RD
DELAMERE TERRACE
CHICHESTER RD
HARROW RD
A404
HARROW ROAD
A501
MARYLEBONE
A40
WESTWAY (ELEVATED)
HARROW RD (UNDER)
PARK PLACE VILLAS
HOWLEY PLACE
ST MARY'S TERR
CROMPTON STREET
HALL PLACE
ADPAR STREET
CHURCH STREET
LYONS PLACE
ABERDEEN PLACE
NORTHWICK TERR
CUNNINGHAM PL
HENDERSON DRIVE
POLLITT DRIVE
FISHERTON STREET
FRAMPTON STREET
LUTON STREET
CAPLAND STREET
PENFOLD STREET
BOSCOBEL ST
HATTON ST
VENABLES ST
NEWCASTLE PL
PADDINGTON GREEN
HARBET ROAD
NORTH WHARF ROAD
SOUTH WHARF ROAD
HERMITAGE ST
DUDLEY HOUSE
SHELDON SQ
KINGDOM ST
MERCHANT SQUARE
RANELAGH BRIDGE
WESTBOURNE BRIDGE
BISHOP'S ROAD BRIDGE
BISHOP'S BRIDGE ROAD
A4206
A4205
EASTBOURNE TERRACE
WESTBOURNE TERRACE
GLOUCESTER TERRACE
CHILWORTH STREET
CHILWORTH MEWS
CRAVEN ROAD
PRAED STREET
LONDON ST
WINSLAND STREET
NORFOLK PLACE
NORFOLK SQUARE
SUSSEX GARDENS
SUSSEX PLACE
SPRING ST
CONDUIT MEWS
TALBOT SQUARE
B410
A4209
ORSETT TERRACE
PORCHESTER SQUARE
PORCHESTER GARDENS
CLEVELAND SQUARE
CLEVELAND GDNS
LEINSTER PL
DEVONSHIRE TERR
UPBROOK MEWS
QUEEN'S GARDENS
GLOUCESTER MEWS
BATHURST MEWS
HYDE PARK
LAUDERDALE ROAD

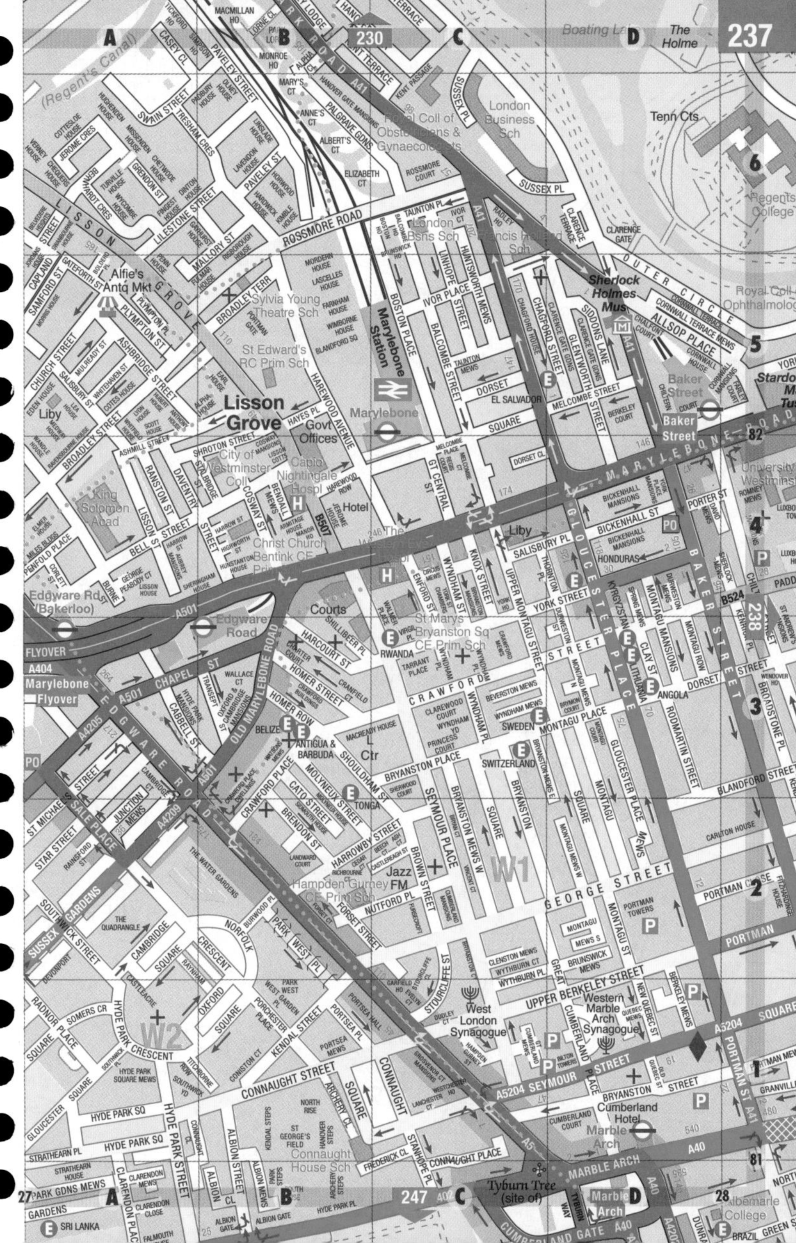
A
B
C
D
230
Boating Lake
The Holme
(Regent's Canal)
MACMILLAN HO
PARK ROAD
A41
CASEY CL
PAVELEY STREET
SWAIN STREET
TRESHAM CRES
HANOVER GATE MANSIONS
PALGRAVE GDNS
KENT PASSAGE
SUSSEX PL
Royal Coll of Obstetricians & Gynaecologists
London Business Sch
Tenn Cts
6
Regents College
ROSSMORE COURT
SUSSEX PL
ELIZABETH CT
JEROME CRES
LISSON GROVE
LILESTONE STREET
GRENDON ST
PAVELEY ST
ROSSMORE ROAD
TAUNTON PL
London Bsns Sch
Francis Holland Sch
CLARENCE TERRACE
CLARENCE GATE
OUTER CIRCLE
Sherlock Holmes Mus
MALLORY ST
CAPLAND ST
SAMFORD ST
Alfie's Antq Mkt
BROADLEY TERR
Sylvia Young Theatre Sch
MORDERN HOUSE
LASCELLES HOUSE
FARNHAM HOUSE
WIMBORNE HOUSE
BLANDFORD SQ
Marylebone Station
BOSTON PLACE
IVOR PLACE
LINHOPE STREET
HUNTSWORTH MEWS
CHAGFORD STREET
GLENTWORTH
SIDDONS LANE
CHALFONT COURT
ALLSOP PLACE
CORNWALL TERRACE
CORNWALL TERRACE MEWS
Royal Coll of Ophthalmologists
5
PLYMPTON ST
ASHBRIDGE STREET
CHURCH STREET
SALISBURY ST
St Edward's RC Prim Sch
HAREWOOD AVENUE
BALCOMBE STREET
TAUNTON MEWS
DORSET
EL SALVADOR
MELCOMBE STREET
BERKELEY COURT
Baker Street
YORK T
Stardome Madame Tussauds
Liby
Lisson Grove
HAYES PL
Govt Offices
Marylebone
SQUARE
MARYLEBONE ROAD
82
BROADLEY STREET
ASHMILL STREET
SHROTON STREET
City of Westminster Coll
Capio Nightingale Hospl
HAREWOOD ROW
GT CENTRAL ST
DORSET CL
BICKENHALL MANSIONS
PORTER ST
University of Westminster
King Solomon Acad
RANSTON ST
DAVENTRY ST
LISSON ST
COSWAY ST
BENDALL MEWS
B507
JEROME HOUSE
Hotel
174
BICKENHALL ST
LUXBOROUGH TOWER
4
BELL STREET
HARROW ST
Christ Church Bentinck CE Prim Sch
The Western Eye Hospl
Liby
SALISBURY PL
HONDURAS
P
PADDINGTON
PENFOLD PLACE
Edgware Rd (Bakerloo)
A501
Edgware Road
Courts
ENFORD ST
WYNDHAM ST
KNOX STREET
UPPER MONTAGU STREET
GLOUCESTER PLACE
KYRGYZSTAN
MONTAGU MANSIONS
BAKER STREET
B524
238
FLYOVER
A404
Marylebone Flyover
CHAPEL ST
OLD MARYLEBONE ROAD
HARCOURT ST
RWANDA
St Marys Bryanston Sq CE Prim Sch
CRAWFORD STREET
YORK STREET
CLAY ST
LITHUANIA
ANGOLA
MONTAGU ROW
DORSET
WENDOVER
BROADSTONE PL
3
HOMER STREET
CRANFIELD CT
BEVERSTON MEWS
WYNDHAM MEWS
SWEDEN
MONTAGU PLACE
EDGWARE ROAD
A4205
CABBELL ST
BELIZE
ANTIGUA & BARBUDA
HOMER ROW
MACREADY HOUSE
Ctr
CLAREWOOD COURT
WYNDHAM YD
PRINCESS COURT
SWITZERLAND
RODMARTIN STREET
PO
BRYANSTON PLACE
MOLYNEUX STREET
TONGA
SHOULDHAM ST
BRYANSTON SQUARE
MONTAGU SQUARE
BLANDFORD STREET
A4209
SALE PLACE
JUNCTION MEWS
ST MICHAELS ST
CRAWFORD PLACE
CATO STREET
BRENDON ST
SEYMOUR PLACE
BRYANSTON MEWS W
W1
CARLTON HOUSE
STAR STREET
HARROWBY STREET
Jazz FM
BROWN STREET
GEORGE STREET
PORTMAN TOWERS
PORTMAN CLOSE
2
THE WATER GARDENS
Hampden Gurney CE Prim Sch
NUTFORD PL
SUSSEX GARDENS
SOUTHWICK STREET
THE QUADRANGLE
CAMBRIDGE SQUARE
NORFOLK CRESCENT
PARK WEST PL
FORSET STREET
CLENSTON MEWS
MONTAGU MEWS S
BRUNSWICK MEWS
GREAT CUMBERLAND PLACE
PORTMAN
DEVONPORT
RADNOR PLACE
SOMERS CR
OXFORD SQUARE
PORCHESTER PLACE
KENDAL STREET
PORTSEA PL
STOURCLIFFE ST
West London Synagogue
UPPER BERKELEY STREET
Western Marble Arch Synagogue
BERKELEY MEWS
NEW QUEBEC ST
A5204
SQUARE
HYDE PARK CRESCENT
W2
HYDE PARK SQUARE MEWS
PORTSEA MEWS
CONNAUGHT
A5204 SEYMOUR STREET
PORTMAN ST
A41
1
PORTMAN MEWS S
GLOUCESTER SQUARE
CONNAUGHT STREET
ARCHERY CL
SQUARE
BRYANSTON STREET
GRANVILLE PL
HYDE PARK SQ
NORTH RISE
ST GEORGE'S FIELD
Cumberland Hotel
CUMBERLAND COURT
Marble Arch
A40
STRATHEARN PL
HYDE PARK SQ
Connaught House Sch
FREDERICK CL
CONNAUGHT PLACE
STANHOPE PL
A5
MARBLE ARCH
81
CLARENDON PLACE
HYDE PARK STREET
ALBION STREET
ALBION MEWS
Tyburn Tree (site of)
TYBURN WAY
Marble Arch
NORTH ROW
27
PARK GDNS MEWS
A
B
247
C
D
28
Albemarle College
GARDENS
SRI LANKA
ALBION GATE
HYDE PARK PL
CUMBERLAND GATE
A40
BRAZIL
GREEN STREET

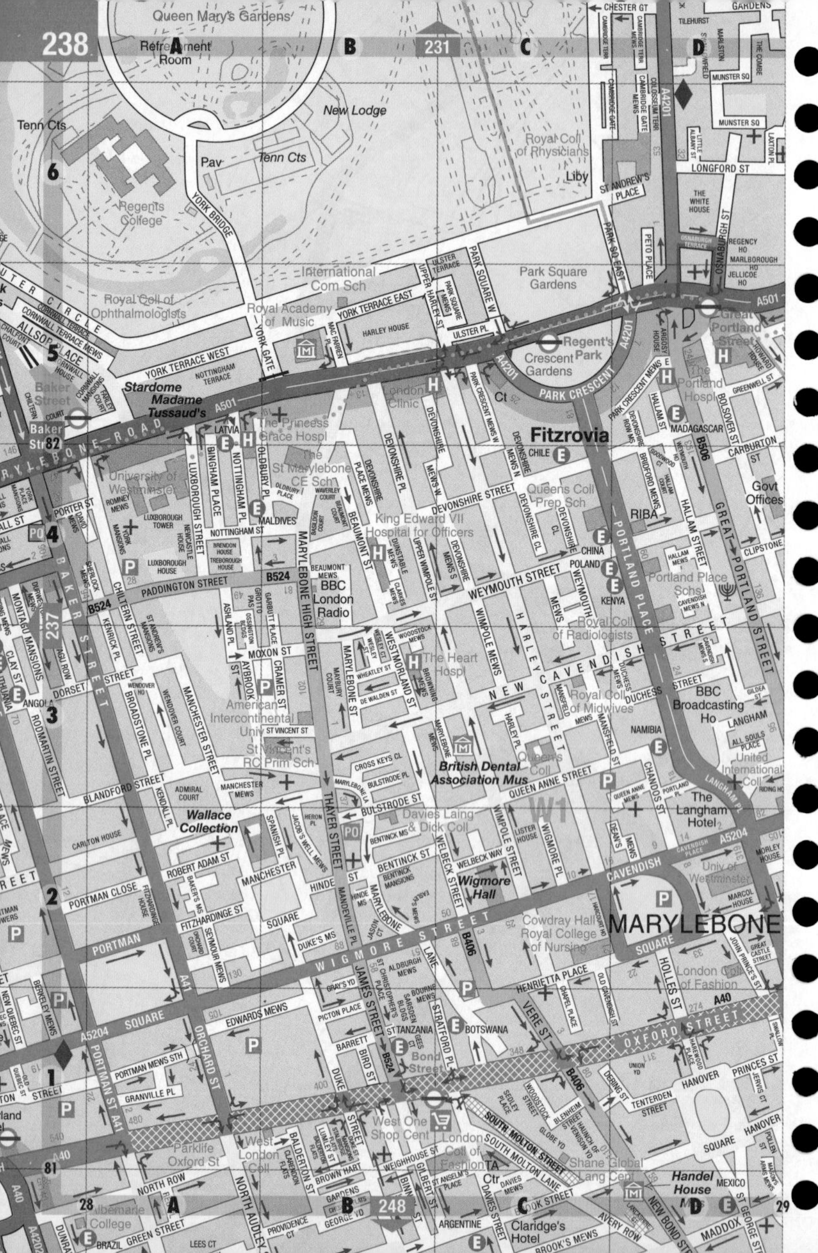
A
B
231
C
D
Queen Mary's Gardens
Refreshment Room
New Lodge
Tenn Cts
Pav
Regents College
YORK BRIDGE
Royal Coll of Physicians
Liby
CHESTER GT
CAMBRIDGE TERR
CAMBRIDGE TERR MEWS
CAMBRIDGE GATE
CAMBRIDGE GATE MEWS
COLOSSEUM TERR
TILEHURST
MARLSTON
THE COMBE
MUNSTER SQ
LONGFORD ST
ST ANDREW'S PLACE
THE WHITE HOUSE
OSNABURGH ST
OSNABURGH TERRACE
REGENCY HO
MARLBOROUGH HO
JELLICOE HO
PETO PLACE
PARK SQ EAST
Park Square Gardens
PARK SQUARE W
ULSTER TERRACE
PARK SQUARE MEWS
ULSTER PL
UPPER HARLEY ST
International Com Sch
Royal Coll of Ophthalmologists
OUTER CIRCLE
CORNWALL TERRACE
CORNWALL TERRACE MEWS
ALLSOP PLACE
CHALFONT HOUSE
CORNWALL HOUSE
CORNWALL MANSIONS
FARLEY COURT
Royal Academy of Music
YORK TERRACE EAST
YORK TERRACE WEST
YORK GATE
MAC FARREN PL
HARLEY HOUSE
NOTTINGHAM TERRACE
Stardome
Madame Tussaud's
A501
Regent's Park
Crescent Gardens
PARK CRESCENT
A4201
PARK CRESCENT MEWS W
PARK CRESCENT MEWS E
ARGOSY HOUSE
Great Portland Street
The Portland Hospl
HOWARD HOUSE
GREENWELL ST
BOLSOVER ST
Baker Street
CHILTERN COURT
MARYLEBONE ROAD
LATVIA
The Princess Grace Hospl
London Clinic
The St Marylebone CE Sch
DEVONSHIRE PLACE MEWS
DEVONSHIRE PL
DEVONSHIRE MEWS W
Fitzrovia
CHILE
DEVONSHIRE MEWS N
DEVONSHIRE ROW MS
HALLAM ST
MADAGASCAR
CARBURTON ST
B506
University of Westminster
ROMNEY MEWS
LUXBOROUGH TOWER
LUXBOROUGH STREET
BINGHAM PLACE
NOTTINGHAM PL
OLDBURY PL
WAVERLEY COURT
BEAUMONT COURT
DEVONSHIRE STREET
Queens Coll Prep Sch
DEVONSHIRE CL
RIBA
BRIDFORD MEWS
GREAT PORTLAND STREET
Govt Offices
PORTER ST
DAVID MEWS
YORK MANSIONS
NEWCASTLE HOUSE
MALDIVES
NOTTINGHAM ST
BRENDON HOUSE
TREBOROUGH HOUSE
LUXBOROUGH HOUSE
MARYLEBONE HIGH STREET
BEAUMONT ST
King Edward VII Hospital for Officers
DUNSTABLE MEWS
UPPER WIMPOLE ST
DEVONSHIRE MEWS S
CHINA
POLAND
KENYA
PORTLAND PLACE
HALLAM MEWS
CLIPSTONE
BAKER STREET
SHERLOCK MEWS
PADDINGTON STREET
B524
BEAUMONT MEWS
BBC London Radio
CLARKES MEWS
WEYMOUTH STREET
WEYMOUTH MEWS
Portland Place Schs
CAVENDISH MEWS N
MONTAGU MANSIONS
KENRICK PL
CHILTERN STREET
ST ANDREW'S MANSIONS
ASHLAND PL
GROTTO PAS
OSSINGTON BLDGS
GARBUTT PLACE
WESLEY ST
WOODSTOCK MEWS
WESTMORLAND ST
WIMPOLE MEWS
HARLEY STREET
Royal Coll of Radiologists
NEW CAVENDISH STREET
CAVENDISH MEWS S
237
CLAY ST
AGU ROW
DORSET STREET
WENDOVER HO
WENDOVER COURT
MANCHESTER STREET
MOXON ST
AYBROOK ST
CRAMER ST
MAYBURY COURT
MARYLEBONE ST
WHEATLEY ST
DE WALDEN ST
The Heart Hospl
BROWNING MEWS
DUCHESS MEWS
MANSFIELD MEWS
Royal Coll of Midwives
DUCHESS STREET
BBC Broadcasting Ho
GILDEA ST
LITHUANIA
ANGOLA
RODMARTIN STREET
BROADSTONE PL
American Intercontinental Univ
ST VINCENT ST
St Vincent's RC Prim Sch
CROSS KEYS CL
MARYLEBONE LA
BULSTRODE PL
MARYLEBONE MEWS
British Dental Association Mus
HARLEY PL
Queen's Coll
MANSFIELD ST
NAMIBIA
LANGHAM
ALL SOULS PLACE
United International Coll
BLANDFORD STREET
KENDALL PL
ADMIRAL COURT
MANCHESTER MEWS
BULSTRODE ST
THAYER STREET
QUEEN ANNE STREET
QUEEN ANNE MEWS
CHANDOS ST
PORTLAND PL
LANGHAM PL
The Langham Hotel
RIDING HO
Wallace Collection
CARLTON HOUSE
HERON PL
JACOB'S WELL MEWS
SPANISH PL
Davies Laing & Dick Coll
BENTINCK MS
WELBECK WAY
WIMPOLE STREET
LISTER HOUSE
WIGMORE PL
W1
DEAN'S MEWS
CAVENDISH PLACE
A5204
MORLEY HOUSE
Univ of Westminster
ROBERT ADAM ST
MANCHESTER SQUARE
BENTINCK ST
BENTINCK MANSIONS
WELBECK STREET
Wigmore Hall
CAVENDISH SQUARE
MARCOL HOUSE
PORTMAN CLOSE
FITZHARDINGE HOUSE
BAKER'S MS
FITZHARDINGE ST
HINDE ST
HINDE MS
MARYLEBONE LANE
EASLEY'S MEWS
Cowdray Hall Royal College of Nursing
HARCOURT HO
MARYLEBONE
PORTMAN
ORCHARD COURT
SEYMOUR MEWS
DUKE'S MS
MANDEVILLE PL
JASON CT
WIGMORE STREET
B406
HOLLES ST
London Coll of Fashion
JOHN PRINCE'S ST
GREAT CASTLE STREET
BERKELEY MEWS
NEW QUEBEC ST
A41
GRAY'S YD
ALDBURGH MEWS
BOURNE MEWS
HENRIETTA PLACE
OLD CAVENDISH ST
CHAPEL PLACE
A40
SWALLOW PL
PORTMAN SQUARE
A5204
EDWARDS MEWS
PICTON PLACE
ST CHRISTOPHER'S PLACE
SARSDEN BLDGS
STRATFORD PL
TANZANIA
BOTSWANA
VERE ST
OXFORD STREET
OLD QUEBEC ST
PORTMAN MEWS STH
GRANVILLE PL
ORCHARD ST
BARRETT
BIRD ST
JAMES STREET
DUKE STREET
Bond Street
DERING ST
UNION YD
HAREWOOD PLACE
TENTERDEN STREET
HANOVER
PRINCES ST
JERVIS CT
PORTMAN ST
West One Shop Cent
West London Coll
BALDERTON ST
CLARENDON FLATS
LUMLEY ST
LUMLEY FLATS
SEDLEY PLACE
WOODSTOCK STREET
BLENHEIM STREET
HAUNCH OF VENISON YD
GLOBE YD
SOUTH MOLTON STREET
SOUTH MOLTON LANE
Shane Global Lang Cent
HANOVER SQUARE
POLLEN ST
MADDOX ST
Parklife Oxford St
NORTH ROW
NORTH AUDLEY
BROWN HART GARDENS
WEIGHHOUSE ST
BINNEY ST
GILBERT ST
ST ANSELM'S PLACE
London Coll of Fashion
TA Ctr
DAVIES MEWS
BROOK STREET
Handel House Mus
MEXICO
ST GEORGE ST
Albemarle College
28
A
B
248
C
D
29
GEORGE YD
PROVIDENCE CT
ARGENTINE
DAVIES STREET
Claridge's Hotel
AVERY ROW
NEW BOND ST
BROOK'S MEWS
LEES CT
BRAZIL
GREEN STREET
A4202
1
2
3
4
5
6
82
81

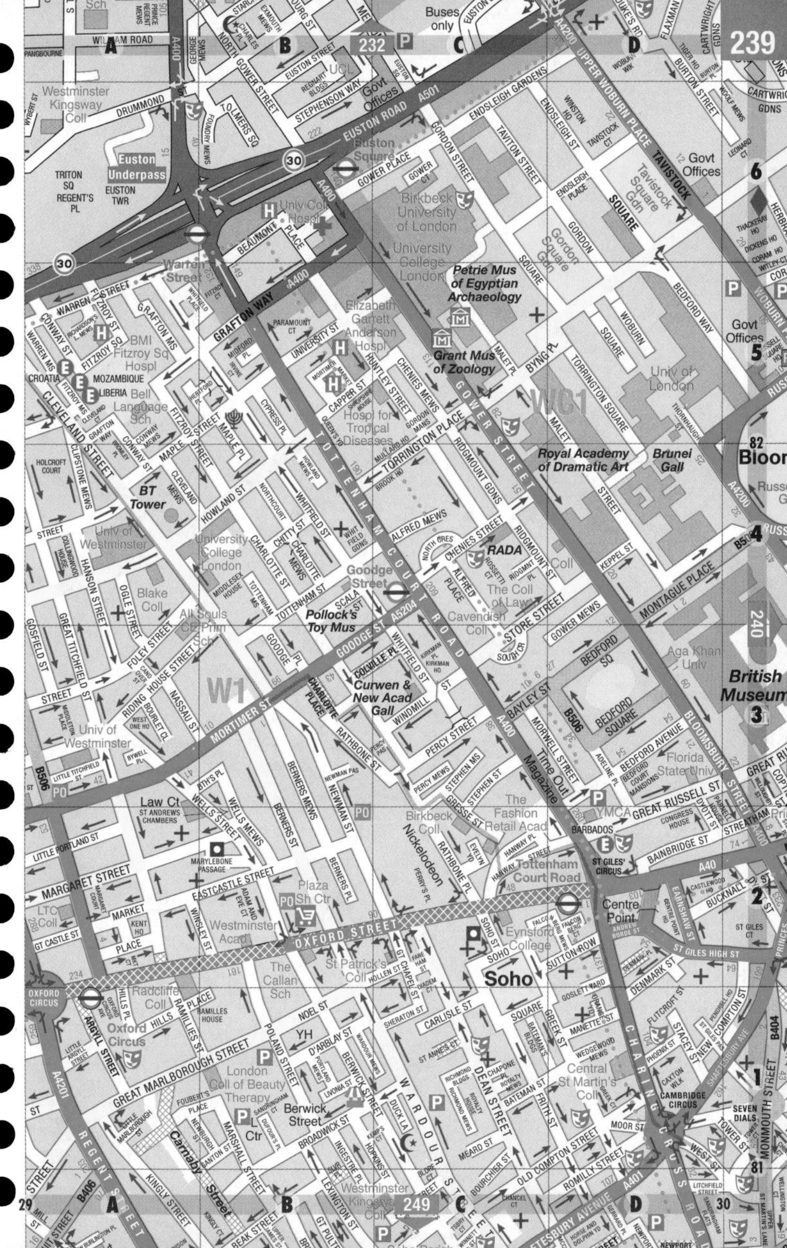
239
A
B
C
D
232
249
240
WILLIAM ROAD
Buses only
UPPER WOBURN PLACE
FLAXMAN
CARTWRIGHT GDNS
Westminster Kingsway Coll
DRUMMOND
GOWER STREET
EUSTON STREET
UCL
STEPHENSON WAY
Govt Offices
EUSTON ROAD
A501
ENDSLEIGH GARDENS
ENDSLEIGH ST
TAVISTOCK
TRITON SQ
REGENT'S PL
EUSTON TWR
Euston Underpass
Euston Square
GOWER PLACE
Univ Coll Hospl
BEAUMONT PLACE
Birkbeck University of London
University College London
GORDON STREET
TAVITON STREET
Tavistock Square Gdn
Gordon Square Gdn
SQUARE
Warren Street
WARREN STREET
GRAFTON WAY
A400
FITZROY SQ
CONWAY ST
BMI Fitzroy Sq Hospl
CROATIA
MOZAMBIQUE
LIBERIA
Bell Language Sch
Elizabeth Garrett Anderson Hospl
UNIVERSITY ST
Petrie Mus of Egyptian Archaeology
Grant Mus of Zoology
BEDFORD WAY
WOBURN SQUARE
TORRINGTON SQUARE
Univ of London
Govt Offices
WC1
CLEVELAND STREET
HUNTLEY STREET
CHENIES MEWS
CAPPER ST
Hospl for Tropical Diseases
TORRINGTON PLACE
RIDGMOUNT GDNS
Royal Academy of Dramatic Art
Brunei Gall
Blooms
Russell Sq Gardens
RUSSELL
BT Tower
HOWLAND ST
TOTTENHAM COURT ROAD
WHITFIELD ST
CHARLOTTE ST
ALFRED MEWS
CHENIES STREET
RADA
RIDGMOUNT ST
Coll
KEPPEL ST
MONTAGUE PLACE
Univ of Westminster
University College London
HANSON STREET
Blake Coll
Goodge Street
The Coll of Law
Cavendish Coll
STORE STREET
GOWER MEWS
All Souls CE Prim Sch
TOTTENHAM ST
Pollock's Toy Mus
GOODGE ST
A5204
GREAT TITCHFIELD ST
GOSFIELD ST
FOLEY STREET
RIDING HOUSE STREET
W1
Curwen & New Acad Gall
BEDFORD SQ
BEDFORD SQUARE
Aga Khan Univ
British Museum
MORTIMER ST
BAYLEY ST
B506
BEDFORD AVENUE
Florida State Univ
Univ of Westminster
NASSAU ST
RATHBONE ST
PERCY STREET
Time Out Magazine
BLOOMSBURY STREET
GREAT RUSSELL ST
Law Ct
WELLS STREET
BERNERS MEWS
NEWMAN ST
Birkbeck Coll
The Fashion Retail Acad
YMCA
BARBADOS
ST GILES' CIRCUS
LITTLE PORTLAND ST
MARGARET STREET
EASTCASTLE STREET
Plaza Sh Ctr
Nickelodeon
Tottenham Court Road
A40
Centre Point
EARNSHAW ST
BUCKNALL ST
LTC Coll
Westminster Acad
OXFORD STREET
Eynsford College
SUTTON ROW
ST GILES HIGH ST
OXFORD CIRCUS
The Callan Sch
St Patrick's Coll
Soho
DENMARK ST
Radcliffe Coll
Oxford Circus
ARGYLL STREET
RAMILLIES PLACE
NOEL ST
YH
CARLISLE ST
SOHO SQUARE
GREEK ST
MANETTE ST
NEW COMPTON ST
B404
GREAT MARLBOROUGH STREET
POLAND STREET
D'ARBLAY ST
London Coll of Beauty Therapy
BERWICK STREET
WARDOUR STREET
DEAN STREET
Central St Martin's Coll
CHARING CROSS ROAD
SHAFTESBURY AVE
CAMBRIDGE CIRCUS
SEVEN DIALS
MONMOUTH STREET
A4201
REGENT STREET
Carnaby Street
MARSHALL STREET
Berwick Street
BROADWICK ST
MEARD ST
OLD COMPTON STREET
ROMILLY STREET
MOOR ST
TOWER ST
WEST ST
KINGLY STREET
LEXINGTON ST
Westminster Kingsway Coll
A401
SHAFTESBURY AVENUE
B406
NEWPORT

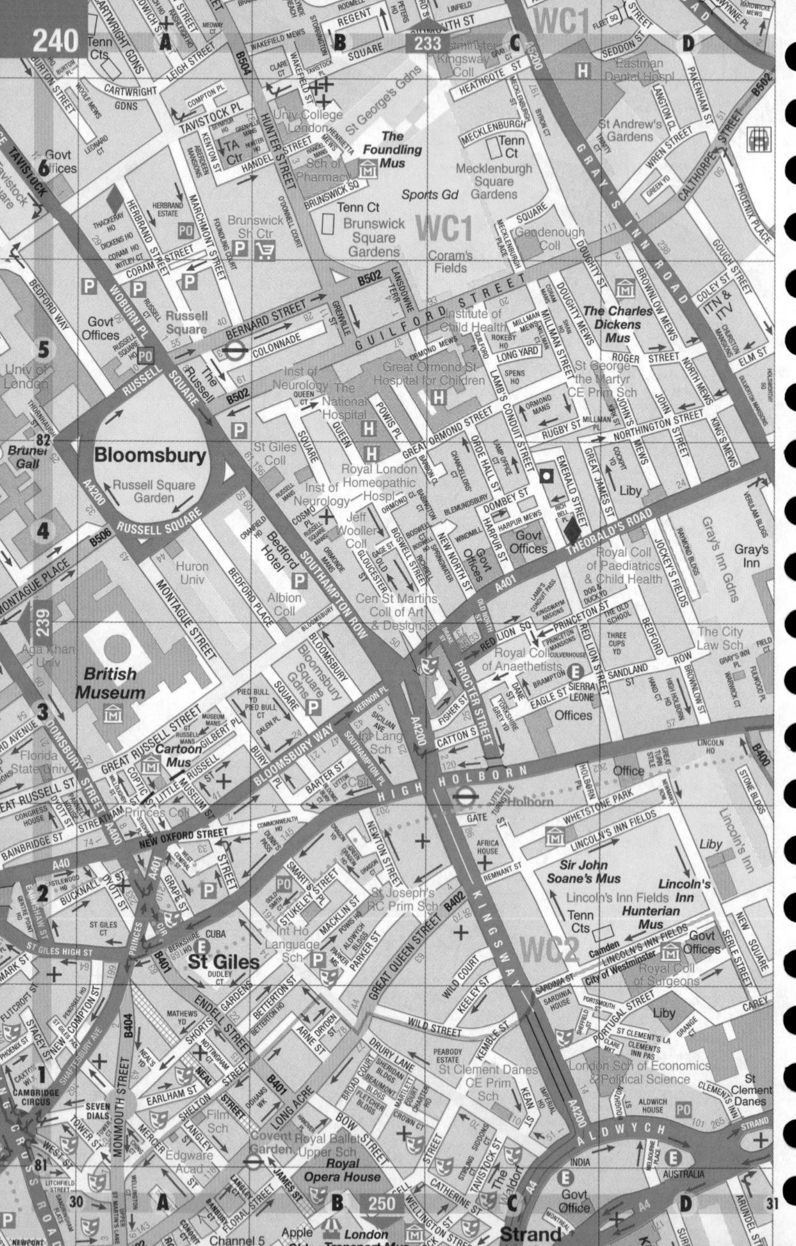
A
B
C
D
233
WC1
Tenn Cts
CARTWRIGHT GDNS
LEIGH STREET
REGENT SQUARE
WAKEFIELD MEWS
B504
BURTON STREET
CARTWRIGHT GDNS
COMPTON PL
TAVISTOCK PL
Univ College London
St George's Gdns
HEATHCOTE ST
MECKLENBURGH ST
Eastman Dental Hospl
PAKENHAM ST
B502
St Andrew's Gardens
WREN STREET
CALTHORPE STREET
PHOENIX PLACE
TAVISTOCK
Tavistock Square
Govt Offices
6
HUNTER STREET
HANDEL STREET
TA Ctr
The Foundling Mus
Sch of Pharmacy
BRUNSWICK SQ
MECKLENBURGH
Tenn Ct
Mecklenburgh Square Gardens
Sports Gd
GRAY'S INN ROAD
THACKERAY HO
HERBRAND ESTATE
HERBRAND STREET
MARCHMONT STREET
PO
Brunswick Sh Ctr
Tenn Ct
Brunswick Square Gardens
WC1
Coram's Fields
SQUARE
Goodenough Coll
DOUGHTY ST
BROWNLOW MEWS
GOUGH STREET
CORAM STREET
BEDFORD WAY
WOBURN PL
Govt Offices
Russell Square
BERNARD STREET
COLONNADE
B502
GUILFORD STREET
Institute of Child Health
DOUGHTY MEWS
MILLMAN STREET
The Charles Dickens Mus
COLEY STREET
ITN & ITV
ELM ST
5
Univ of London
RUSSELL SQUARE
The Russell
Inst of Neurology
The National Hospital
Great Ormond St Hospital for Children
LONG YARD
ROGER STREET
NORTH MEWS
St George the Martyr CE Prim Sch
LAMB'S CONDUIT STREET
RUGBY ST
NORTHINGTON STREET
JOHN STREET
KING'S MEWS
82
Brunei Gall
Bloomsbury
Russell Square Garden
St Giles Coll
POWIS PL
QUEEN SQUARE
GREAT ORMOND STREET
ORDE HALL ST
EMERALD STREET
GREAT JAMES ST
JOHN'S MEWS
Liby
A4200
Royal London Homeopathic Hospl
Inst of Neurology
4
RUSSELL SQUARE
B506
Jeff Wooller Coll
Bedford Hotel
NEW NORTH ST
DOMBEY ST
HARPUR MEWS
Govt Offices
THEOBALD'S ROAD
Gray's Inn Gdns
Gray's Inn
MONTAGUE PLACE
Huron Univ
BEDFORD PLACE
MONTAGUE STREET
SOUTHAMPTON ROW
Albion Coll
Cen St Martins Coll of Art & Design
A401
Royal Coll of Paediatrics & Child Health
JOCKEY'S FIELDS
239
Aga Khan Univ
British Museum
BLOOMSBURY SQUARE
Bloomsbury Square Gdns
RED LION SQ
PRINCETON ST
RED LION STREET
The City Law Sch
BEDFORD ROW
Royal Coll of Anaesthetists
PROCTER STREET
FISHER ST
EAGLE ST
SIERRA LEONE
Offices
SANDLAND ST
3
DOMSBURY STREET
Florida State Univ
GREAT RUSSELL STREET
Cartoon Mus
BLOOMSBURY WAY
VERNON PL
SOUTHAMPTON PL
A4200
CATTON S
BARTER ST
HIGH HOLBORN
Holborn
Office
LINCOLN HO
B400
GREAT RUSSELL ST
STREATHAM
Princes Coll
LITTLE RUSSELL
MUSEUM ST
WHETSTONE PARK
LINCOLN'S INN FIELDS
Lincoln's Inn
Liby
BAINBRIDGE ST
NEW OXFORD STREET
A40
NEWTON STREET
GATE
AFRICA HOUSE
REMNANT ST
Sir John Soane's Mus
Lincoln's Inn
2
BUCKNALL ST
DYOTT ST
A401
GRAPE ST
SHAFTESBURY
SMART'S PL
STUKELEY STREET
MACKLIN ST
St Joseph's RC Prim Sch
B402
KINGSWAY
Lincoln's Inn Fields
Tenn Cts
Hunterian Mus
NEW SQUARE
ST GILES HIGH ST
B401
CUBA
St Giles
Int Ho Language Sch
PARKER ST
GREAT QUEEN STREET
WC2
Camden
City of Westminster
LINCOLN'S INN FIELDS
Govt Offices
Royal Coll of Surgeons
SERLE STREET
NEW COMPTON ST
ENDELL STREET
BETTERTON ST
WILD COURT
KEELEY ST
PORTUGAL STREET
CAREY
SHAFTESBURY AVE
B404
MATHEWS YD
SHORTS GARDENS
ARNE ST
DRYDEN ST
WILD STREET
Liby
1
CAMBRIDGE CIRCUS
MONMOUTH STREET
SEVEN DIALS
EARLHAM ST
NEAL ST
B401
DRURY LANE
St Clement Danes CE Prim Sch
KEMBLE ST
London Sch of Economics & Political Science
St Clement Danes
CHARING CROSS ROAD
TOWER ST
SHELTON STREET
Film Sch
LONG ACRE
BOW STREET
KEAN ST
A4200
ALDWYCH
STRAND
81
WEST ST
MERCER
Edgware Acad
Covent Garden
Royal Ballet Upper Sch
Royal Opera House
CATHERINE ST
TAVISTOCK ST
The Waldorf
INDIA
AUSTRALIA
30
A
B
250
C
D
31
JAMES ST
FLORAL STREET
Govt Office
A4
Channel 5
Apple
London Transport Mus
WELLINGTON STREET
Strand

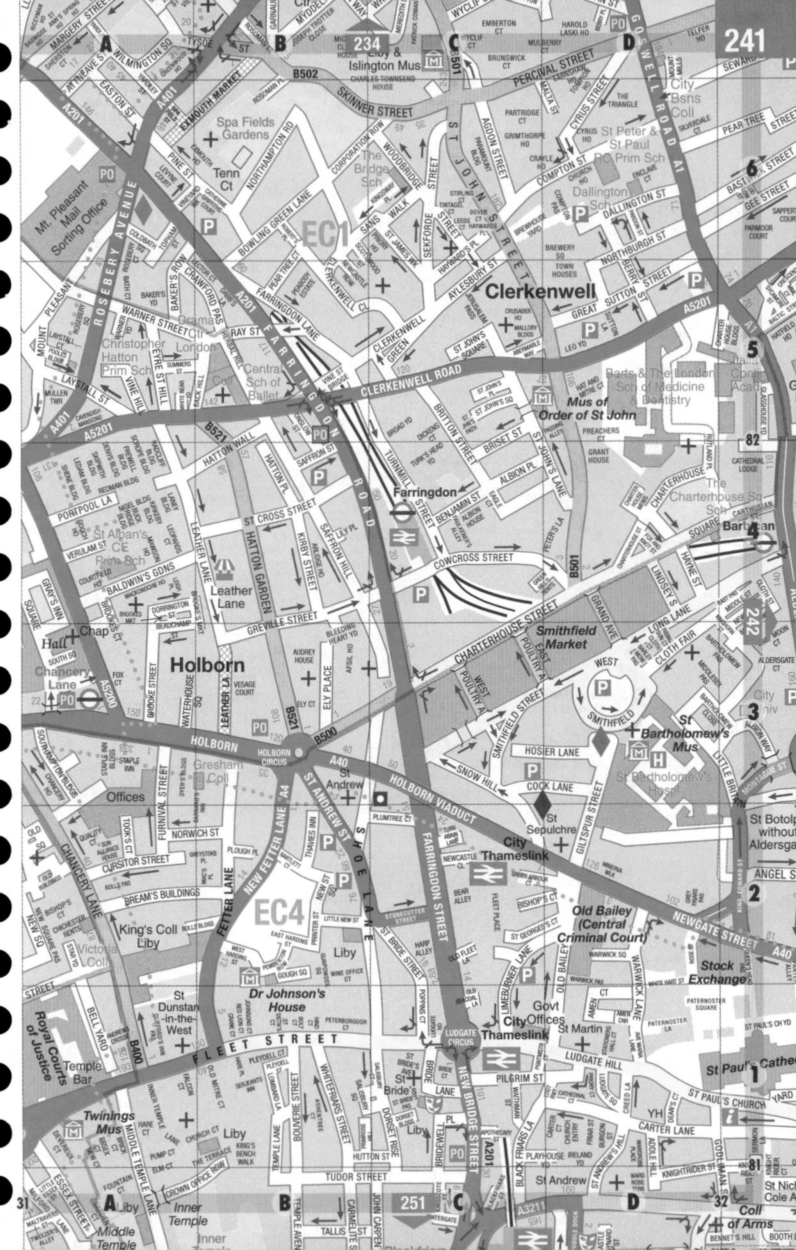

234
Liby & Islington Mus
PERCIVAL STREET
SKINNER STREET
GOSWELL ROAD A1
Spa Fields Gardens
EXMOUTH MARKET
WILMINGTON SQ
Mt. Pleasant Mail Sorting Office
ROSEBERY AVENUE
EC1
Clerkenwell
CLERKENWELL ROAD
FARRINGDON ROAD
Farringdon
Mus of Order of St John
Barts & The London Sch of Medicine & Dentistry
The Charterhouse Sq Sch
Barbican
CHARTERHOUSE STREET
Smithfield Market
Holborn
HATTON GARDEN
Leather Lane
HOLBORN
HOLBORN CIRCUS
HOLBORN VIADUCT
St Bartholomew's Mus
St Bartholomew's Hospl
St Sepulchre
City Thameslink
EC4
FARRINGDON STREET
Old Bailey (Central Criminal Court)
NEWGATE STREET
Stock Exchange
St Botolph without Aldersgate
CHANCERY LANE
King's Coll Liby
Dr Johnson's House
FLEET STREET
Royal Courts of Justice
Temple Bar
St Dunstan-in-the-West
LUDGATE CIRCUS
LUDGATE HILL
St Paul's Cathedral
NEW BRIDGE STREET
Twinings Mus
Inner Temple
Middle Temple
251
242

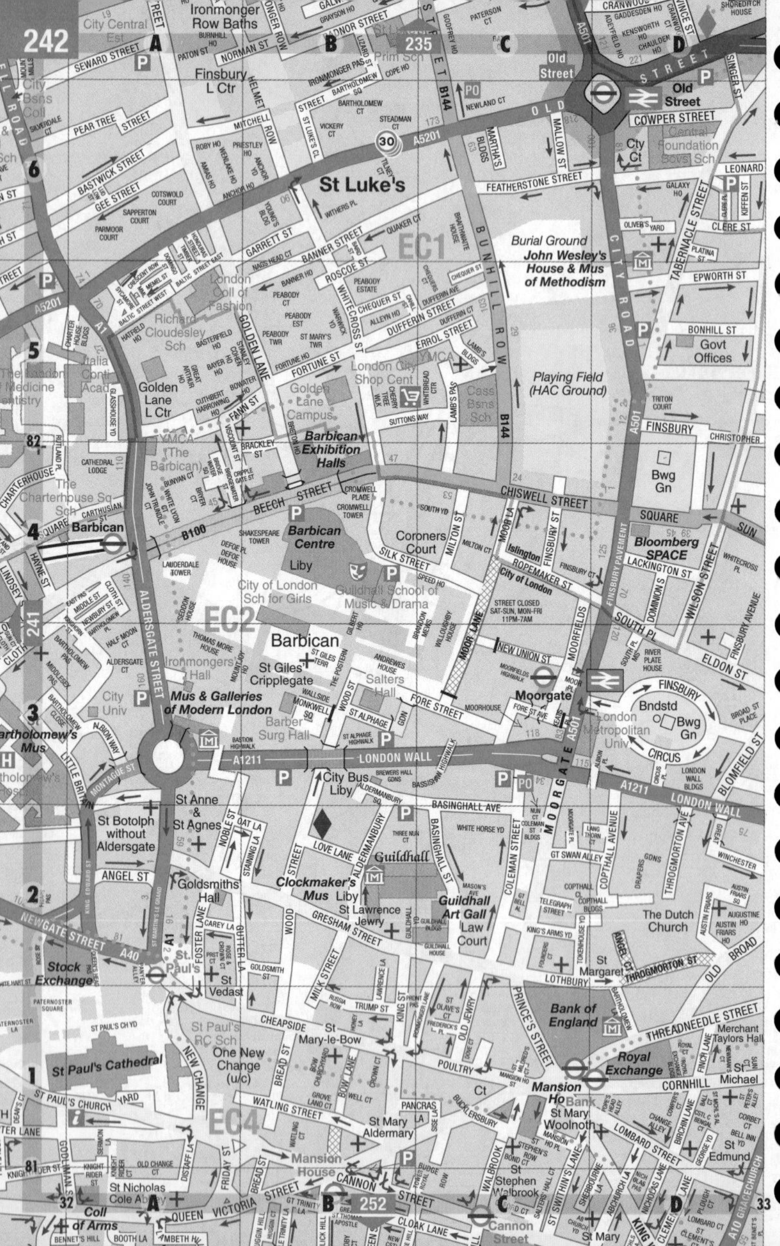

242
A
B
235
C
D
33
252
32
City Central Est
Ironmonger Row Baths
Seward Street
Norman St
Radnor Street
Finsbury L Ctr
Old Street
Old Street
St Luke's
EC1
Bunhill Row
City Road
Burial Ground
John Wesley's House & Mus of Methodism
Featherstone Street
Tabernacle Street
Epworth St
Bonhill St
Govt Offices
Playing Field (HAC Ground)
Chiswell Street
Finsbury Square
Bloomberg SPACE
Golden Lane
Golden Lane L Ctr
London Coll of Fashion
Richard Cloudesley Sch
Whitecross St
Fortune St
Banner Street
Bastwick Street
Gee Street
Pear Tree Street
Goswell Road
Beech Street
Barbican
Barbican Centre
Barbican Exhibition Halls
Coroners Court
Silk Street
Ropemaker St
Moor Lane
Milton St
Chiswell Street
City of London Sch for Girls
Guildhall School of Music & Drama
EC2
St Giles Cripplegate
Aldersgate Street
Mus & Galleries of Modern London
Ironmongers Hall
City Univ
Fore Street
Moorgate
London Wall
Finsbury Circus
London Metropolitan Univ
Moorfields
Eldon St
Wilson Street
St Bartholomew's Mus
Little Britain
St Botolph without Aldersgate
St Anne & St Agnes
Angel St
Goldsmiths' Hall
Newgate Street
Stock Exchange
St. Paul's
St Vedast
City Bus Liby
Basinghall Ave
Aldermanbury
Love Lane
Wood Street
Guildhall
Clockmaker's Mus
Liby
St Lawrence Jewry
Gresham Street
Guildhall Art Gall
Law Court
Coleman Street
Copthall Avenue
Throgmorton Ave
Lothbury
St Margaret
Throgmorton St
The Dutch Church
Old Broad
Bank of England
Threadneedle Street
Royal Exchange
Merchant Taylors Hall
Cornhill
St Michael
Mansion Ho
Bank
St Mary Woolnoth
Lombard Street
St Edmund
Prince's Street
Poultry
Cheapside
St Mary-le-Bow
St Paul's Cathedral
St Paul's Church Yard
St Paul's RC Sch
One New Change (u/c)
New Change
Bread St
Watling Street
St Mary Aldermary
Queen Victoria Street
Mansion House
Cannon Street
St Nicholas Cole Abbey
Coll of Arms
Carter Lane
St Stephen Walbrook
Walbrook
EC4
Cannon Street
Cloak Lane
King William

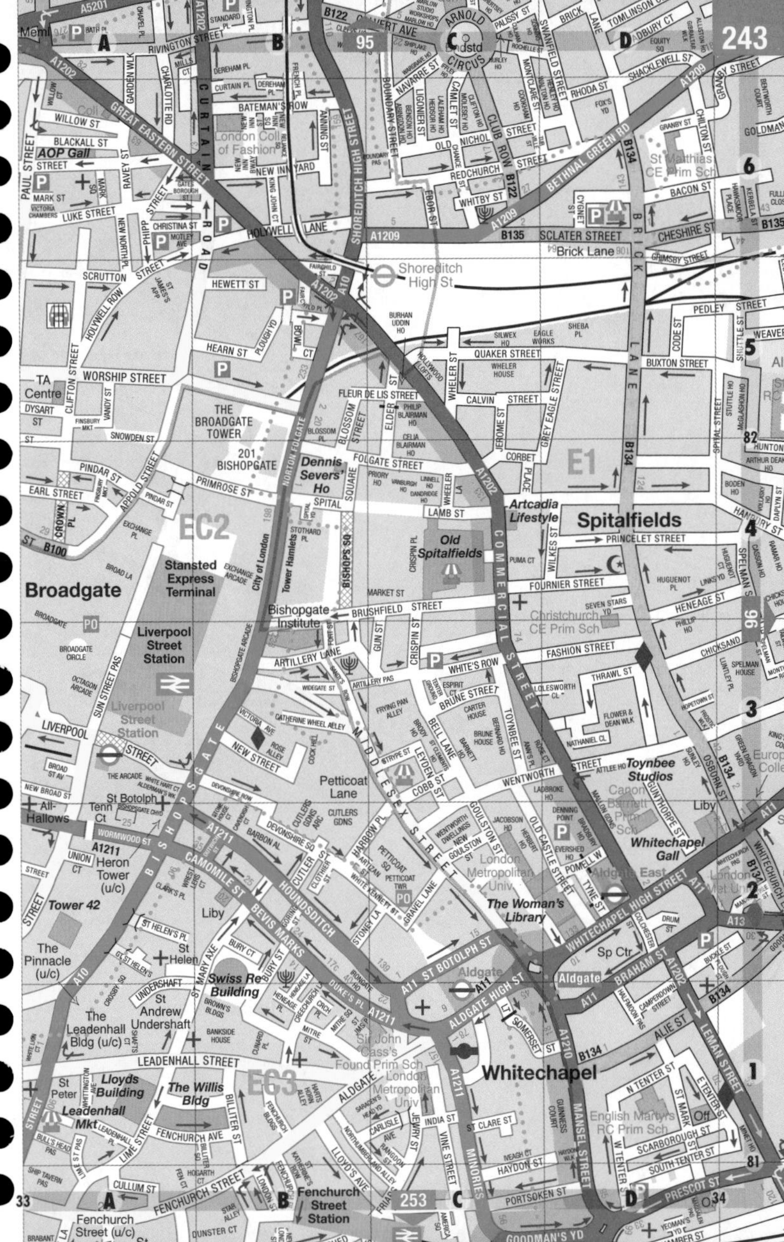

A B C D
95
Shoreditch High St
Brick Lane
Spitalfields
E1
EC2
Broadgate
Stansted Express Terminal
Liverpool Street Station
Old Spitalfields
Artcadia Lifestyle
Dennis Severs' Ho
The Broadgate Tower
201 Bishopgate
Bishopgate Institute
Petticoat Lane
Toynbee Studios
Whitechapel Gall
Aldgate East
Aldgate
The Woman's Library
Swiss Re Building
Tower 42
The Pinnacle (u/c)
Heron Tower (u/c)
The Leadenhall Bldg (u/c)
Lloyds Building
The Willis Bldg
Leadenhall Mkt
EC3
Whitechapel
Fenchurch Street Station
253
Great Eastern Street
Curtain Road
Shoreditch High Street
Bethnal Green Rd
Commercial Street
Bishopsgate
Houndsditch
Middlesex Street
Leadenhall Street
Fenchurch Street
Aldgate High St
Whitechapel High Street
Mansell Street
Leman Street
Minories
Brick Lane
Christchurch CE Prim Sch
London Metropolitan Univ
English Martyrs RC Prim Sch
Sir John Cass's Found Prim Sch
European College
1 2 3 4 5 6
33 34 81 82

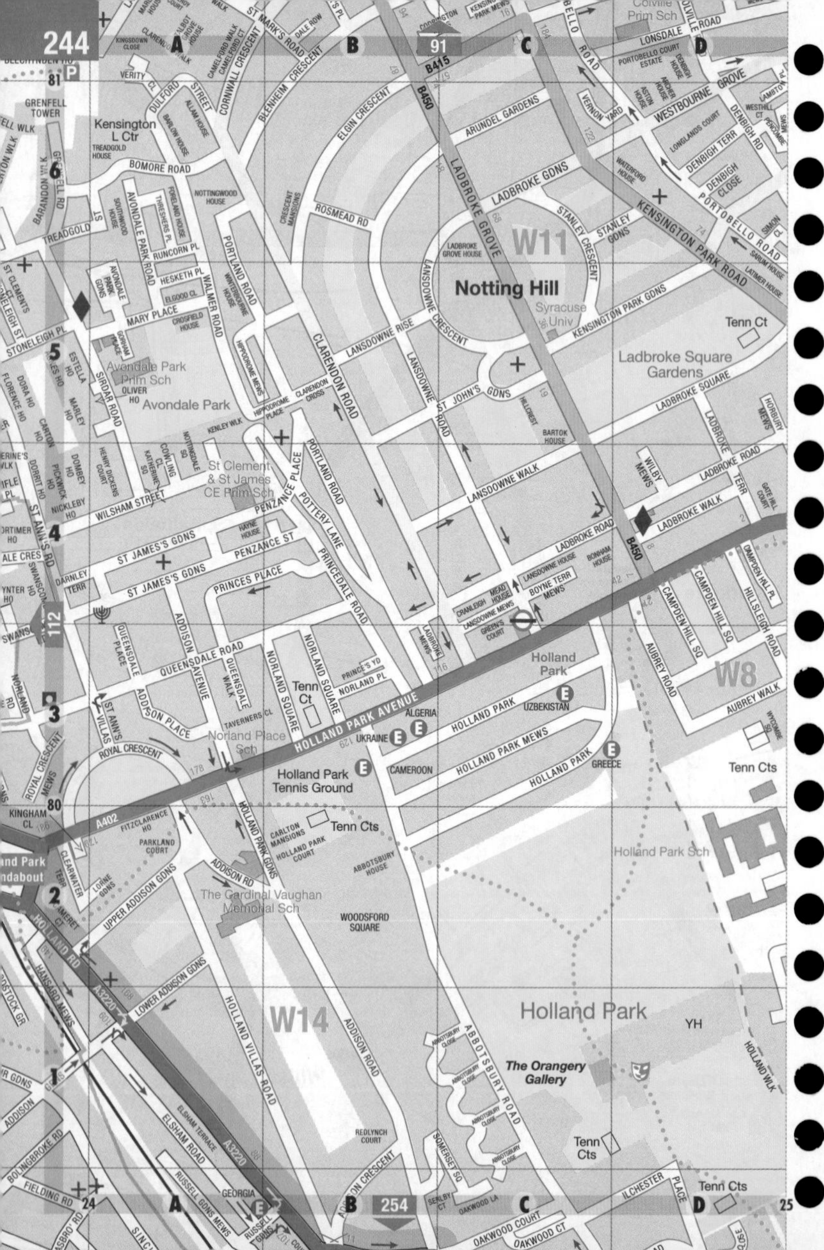
A
B
C
D
91
B415
B450
Colville Prim Sch
LONSDALE ROAD
PORTOBELLO COURT ESTATE
KENSINGTON PARK MEWS
CORNWALL CRESCENT
CAMELFORD WALK
CAMELFORD CT
ST MARK'S ROAD
DALE ROW
BLENHEIM CRESCENT
KINGSDOWN CLOSE
VERITY CL
DULFORD STREET
GRENFELL TOWER
Kensington L Ctr
TREADGOLD HOUSE
BOMORE ROAD
BARANDON WLK
GRENFELL RD
TREADGOLD ST
ALLAM HOUSE
BARLOW HOUSE
ELGIN CRESCENT
ARUNDEL GARDENS
VERNON YARD
WESTBOURNE GROVE
DENBIGH RD
DENBIGH TERR
DENBIGH CLOSE
LONGLANDS COURT
ASTON HOUSE
ARCHER HOUSE
DENBIGH HOUSE
WATERFORD HOUSE
LADBROKE GDNS
KENSINGTON PARK ROAD
PORTOBELLO ROAD
SIMON CL
SARUM HOUSE
LATIMER HOUSE
CRESCENT MANSIONS
ROSMEAD RD
LADBROKE GROVE
LADBROKE GROVE HOUSE
W11
STANLEY CRESCENT
STANLEY GDNS
Notting Hill
Syracuse Univ
KENSINGTON PARK GDNS
Tenn Ct
Ladbroke Square Gardens
LADBROKE SQUARE
HORBURY MEWS
NOTTINGWOOD HOUSE
AVONDALE PARK ROAD
SOUTHWOOD HOUSE
THRESHERS PL
FORELAND HOUSE
RUNCORN PL
HESKETH PL
ELGOOD CL
MARY PLACE
CROSFIELD HOUSE
WALMER ROAD
PORTLAND ROAD
WINTERBOURNE HOUSE
HIPPODROME MEWS
HIPPODROME PLACE
CLARENDON CROSS
CLARENDON ROAD
LANSDOWNE RISE
LANSDOWNE CRESCENT
LANSDOWNE ROAD
ST JOHN'S GDNS
HILLCREST
BARTOK HOUSE
ST CLEMENTS CT
STONELEIGH ST
STONELEIGH PL
AVONDALE PARK GDNS
GORHAM PLACE
Avondale Park Prim Sch
OLIVER HO
Avondale Park
ESTELLA
DORA HO
FLORENCE HO
MARLEY
CARTON HO
SIRDAR ROAD
KENLEY WLK
HENRY DICKENS COURT
KATHERINE SQ
COWLING CL
NOTTINGDALE SQ
St Clement & St James CE Prim Sch
DOMBEY HO
PICKWICK HO
DORRIT HO
NICKLEBY HO
WILSHAM STREET
PENZANCE PLACE
PORTLAND ROAD
POTTERY LANE
LANSDOWNE WALK
WILBY MEWS
LADBROKE TERR
LADBROKE ROAD
GATE HILL COURT
LADBROKE WALK
ST ANN'S RD
HAYNE HOUSE
PENZANCE ST
ST JAMES'S GDNS
PRINCEDALE ROAD
LADBROKE ROAD
BONHAM HOUSE
LANSDOWNE HOUSE
BOYNE TERR MEWS
MEAD HOUSE
CRANLEIGH
LANSDOWNE MEWS
GREEN'S COURT
DARNLEY TERR
SWANSCOMBE
PRINCES PLACE
112
CAMPDEN HILL PL
CAMPDEN HILL SQ
HILLSLEIGH ROAD
AUBREY ROAD
QUEENSDALE PLACE
ADDISON AVENUE
QUEENSDALE ROAD
QUEENSDALE WALK
NORLAND SQUARE
PRINCE'S YD
NORLAND PL
LADBROKE MEWS
Holland Park
W8
AUBREY WALK
NORLAND RD
ST ANN'S VILLAS
ADDISON PLACE
TAVERNERS CL
Tenn Ct
HOLLAND PARK AVENUE
ALGERIA
HOLLAND PARK
UZBEKISTAN
WYCOMBE SQ
ROYAL CRESCENT MEWS
ROYAL CRESCENT
Norland Place Sch
UKRAINE
HOLLAND PARK MEWS
GREECE
CAMEROON
Tenn Cts
Holland Park Tennis Ground
KINGHAM CL
A402
FITZCLARENCE HO
PARKLAND COURT
CARLTON MANSIONS
HOLLAND PARK COURT
Tenn Cts
HOLLAND PARK GDNS
ABBOTSBURY HOUSE
Holland Park Sch
CLEARWATER TERR
LORNE GDNS
UPPER ADDISON GDNS
ADDISON RD
The Cardinal Vaughan Memorial Sch
WOODSFORD SQUARE
HOLLAND RD
HANSARD MEWS
A3220
LOWER ADDISON GDNS
HOLLAND VILLAS ROAD
W14
ADDISON ROAD
ABBOTSBURY ROAD
ABBOTSBURY CLOSE
Holland Park
YH
The Orangery Gallery
HOLLAND WLK
ELSHAM TERRACE
ELSHAM ROAD
REDLYNCH COURT
Tenn Cts
ADDISON CRESCENT
SOMERSET SQ
ILCHESTER PLACE
BOLINGBROKE RD
FIELDING RD
RUSSELL GDNS MEWS
GEORGIA
RUSSELL GDNS
254
SERLBY CT
OAKWOOD LA
OAKWOOD COURT
OAKWOOD CT
Tenn Cts
1
2
3
4
5
6
24
25
80
81

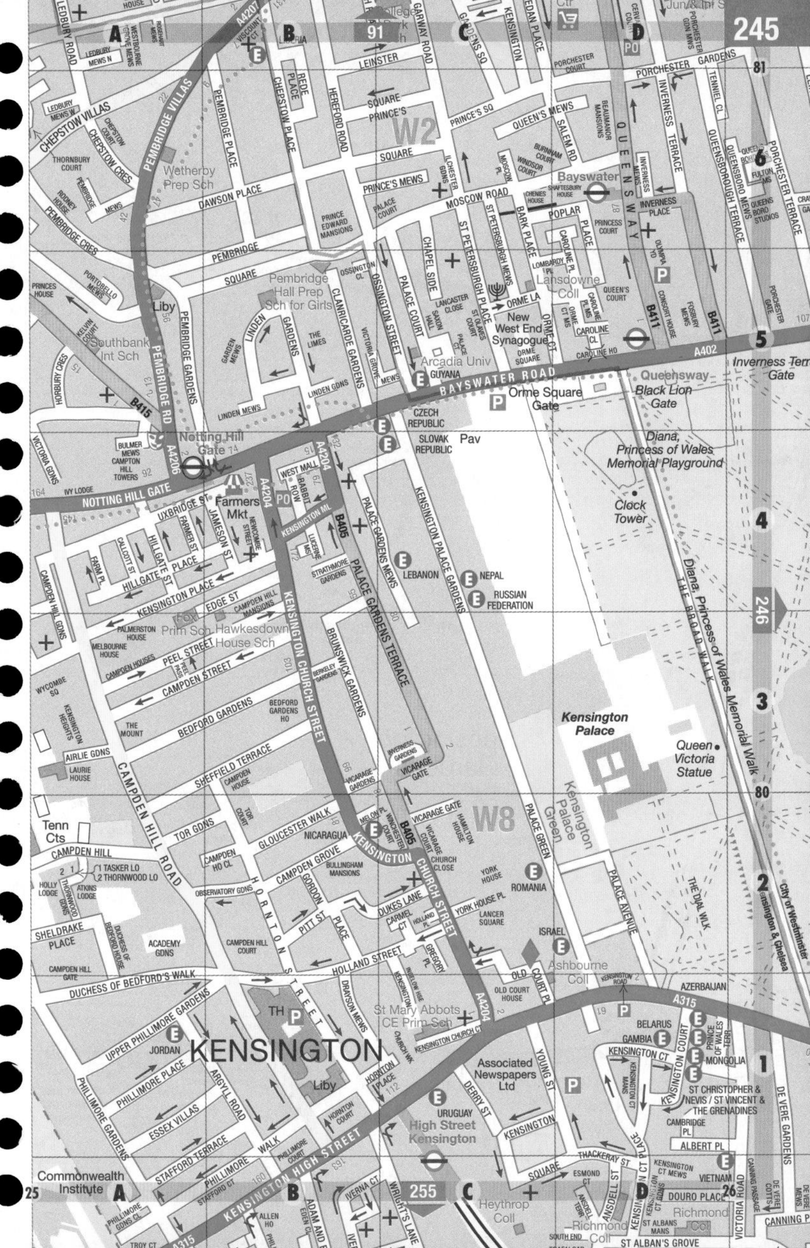

W2
W8
KENSINGTON
Bayswater
Queensway
Notting Hill Gate
High Street Kensington
Kensington Palace
Kensington Palace Gardens
Diana, Princess of Wales Memorial Playground
Diana, Princess of Wales Memorial Walk
Clock Tower
Queen Victoria Statue
Inverness Terrace Gate
Black Lion Gate
Orme Square Gate
New West End Synagogue
Pembridge Hall Prep Sch for Girls
Wetherby Prep Sch
Southbank Int Sch
Arcadia Univ
Lansdowne Coll
Fox Prim Sch
Hawkesdown House Sch
Farmers Mkt
Associated Newspapers Ltd
St Mary Abbots CE Prim Sch
Ashbourne Coll
Heythrop Coll
Richmond Coll
Commonwealth Institute
Tenn Cts
BAYSWATER ROAD
NOTTING HILL GATE
KENSINGTON HIGH STREET
KENSINGTON CHURCH STREET
CAMPDEN HILL ROAD
PEMBRIDGE VILLAS
PEMBRIDGE RD
QUEENSWAY
THE BROAD WALK

91
246
255

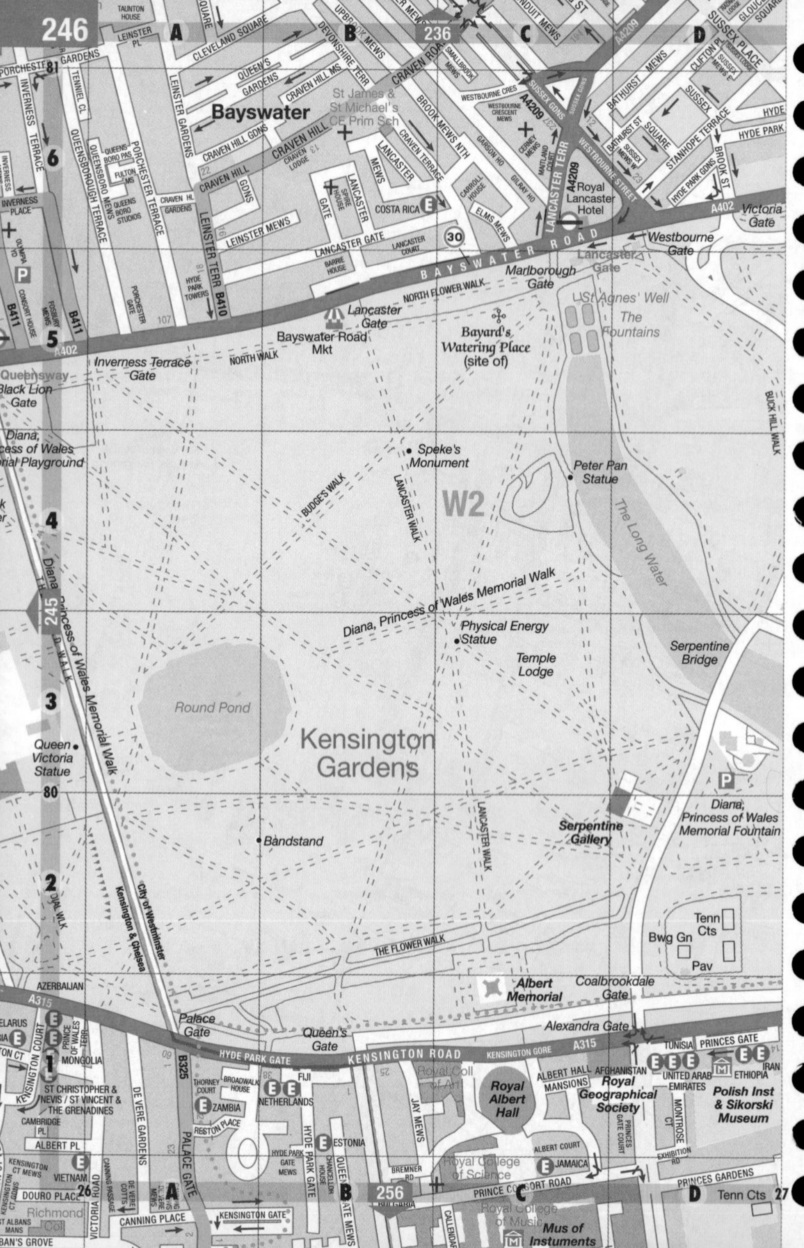

Bayswater
Kensington Gardens
W2
Round Pond
The Long Water
Bayswater Road
Kensington Road
Hyde Park Gate
Lancaster Gate
Leinster Terr
Lancaster Terr
Royal Lancaster Hotel
Lancaster Walk
Budge's Walk
North Walk
North Flower Walk
The Flower Walk
Diana, Princess of Wales Memorial Walk
Speke's Monument
Peter Pan Statue
Physical Energy Statue
Temple Lodge
Serpentine Bridge
Serpentine Gallery
Bandstand
Queen Victoria Statue
Albert Memorial
Coalbrookdale Gate
Alexandra Gate
Queen's Gate
Palace Gate
Royal Albert Hall
Royal Geographical Society
Royal Coll of Art
Royal College of Science
Royal College of Music
Mus of Instuments
Polish Inst & Sikorski Museum
Bayard's Watering Place (site of)
Bayswater Road Mkt
Inverness Terrace Gate
Marlborough Gate
Westbourne Gate
Victoria Gate
St Agnes' Well
The Fountains
Diana, Princess of Wales Memorial Fountain
Buck Hill Walk
Tenn Cts
Bwg Gn
Pav

236
245
256

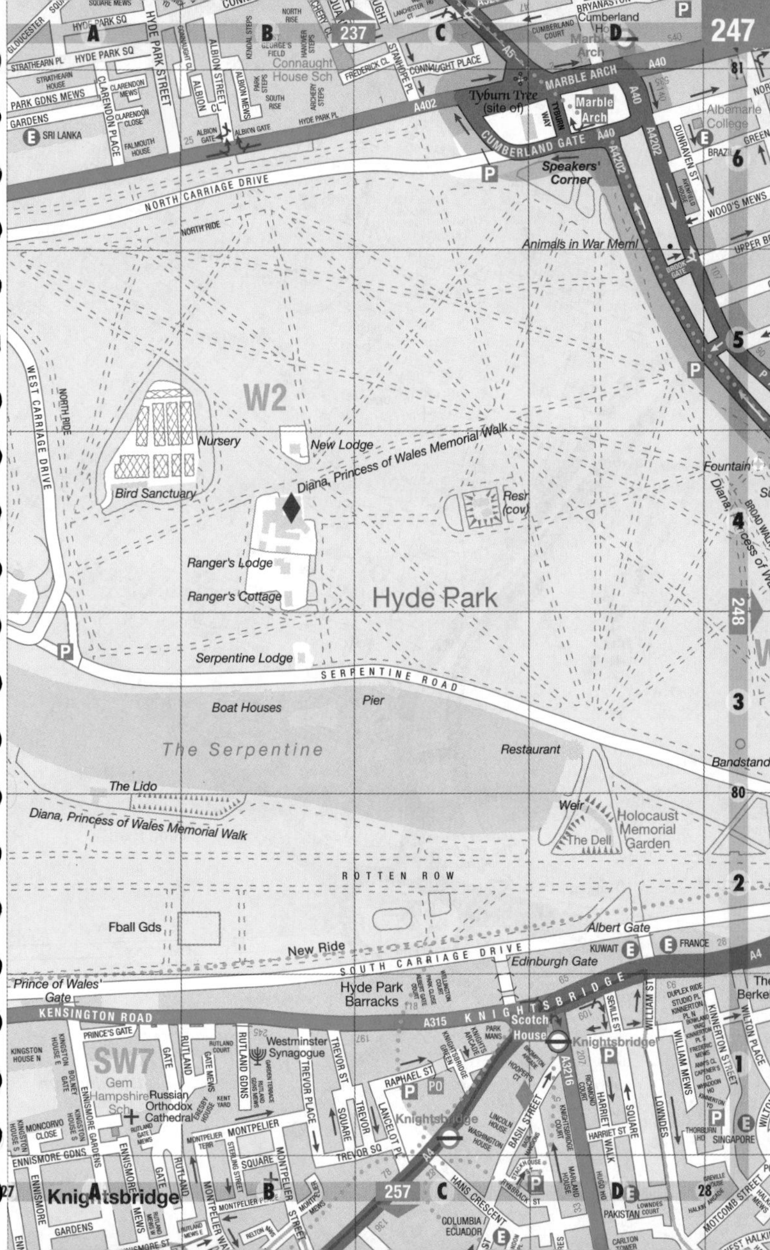

Hyde Park

W2

Nursery
New Lodge
Diana, Princess of Wales Memorial Walk
Bird Sanctuary
Resr (cov)
Ranger's Lodge
Ranger's Cottage
Serpentine Lodge
SERPENTINE ROAD
Boat Houses
Pier
The Serpentine
Restaurant
Bandstand
The Lido
Diana, Princess of Wales Memorial Walk
Weir
Holocaust Memorial Garden
The Dell
ROTTEN ROW
Fball Gds
New Ride
Albert Gate
SOUTH CARRIAGE DRIVE
Edinburgh Gate
Kuwait
France
Prince of Wales' Gate
Hyde Park Barracks
The Berkeley
KENSINGTON ROAD
KNIGHTSBRIDGE
Scotch House
Knightsbridge
Kingston House N
PRINCE'S GATE
SW7
Westminster Synagogue
Raphael St
Gem Hampshire Sch
Russian Orthodox Cathedral
Knightsbridge
Singapore

NORTH CARRIAGE DRIVE
NORTH RIDE
WEST CARRIAGE DRIVE
Tyburn Tree (site of)
MARBLE ARCH
Marble Arch
Connaught House Sch
CUMBERLAND GATE
Speakers' Corner
Animals in War Meml
Albemarle College
Brazil
Sri Lanka
HYDE PARK SQ
HYDE PARK STREET
Connaught Place
Fountain
Subw
Montpelier
Knightsbridge

Columbia
Ecuador

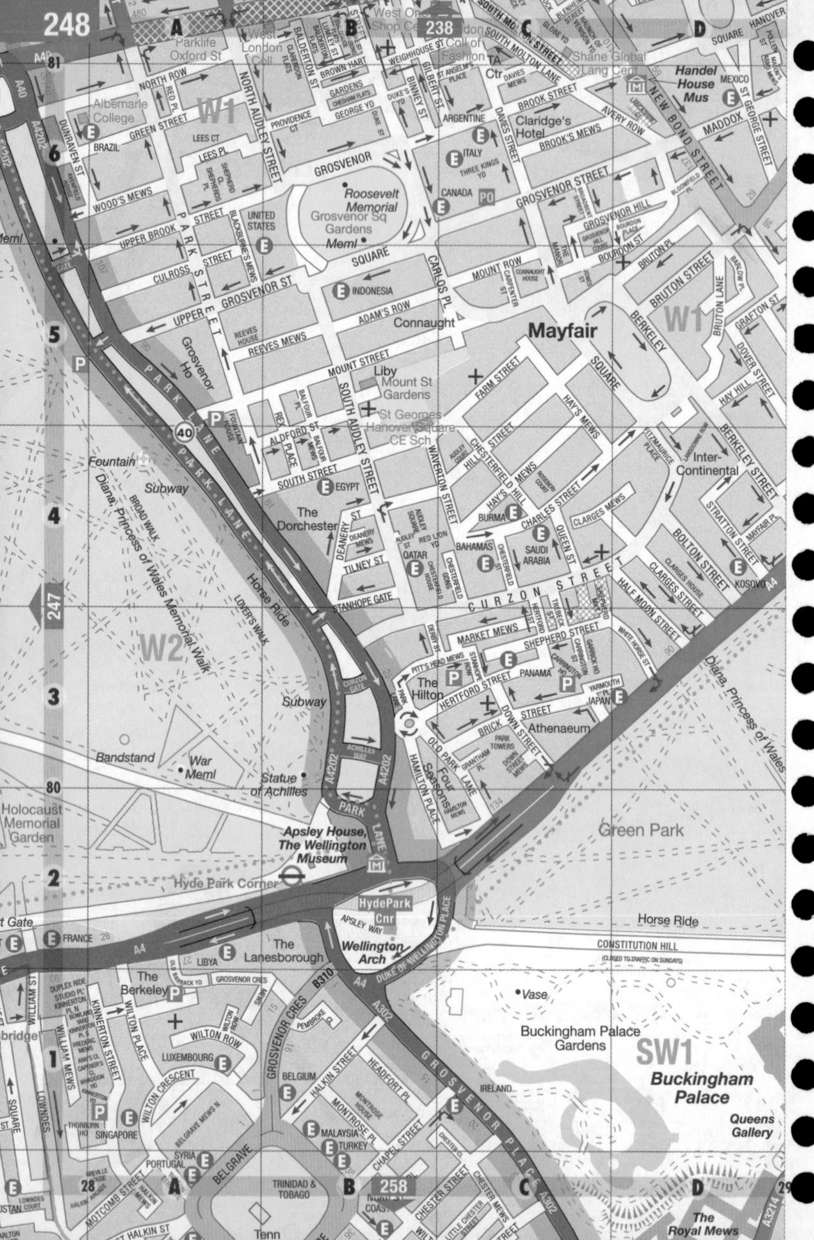

248
A
B
C
D
238
247
258
W1
W2
SW1
Mayfair
Parklife Oxford St
West London Coll
West One Shop Ctr
London Coll of Fashion
TA Ctr
Shane Global Lang Cent
Handel House Mus
Albemarle College
Claridge's Hotel
Roosevelt Memorial
Grosvenor Sq Gardens
Meml
Connaught
Grosvenor Ho
Liby
Mount St Gardens
St Georges Hanover Square CE Sch
The Dorchester
Inter-Continental
The Hilton
Four Seasons
Athenaeum
Fountain
Subway
Diana, Princess of Wales Memorial Walk
Broad Walk
Horse Ride
Lover's Walk
Bandstand
War Meml
Statue of Achilles
Holocaust Memorial Garden
Apsley House, The Wellington Museum
Hyde Park Corner
HydePark Cnr
Apsley Way
Wellington Arch
The Lanesborough
The Berkeley
Green Park
Constitution Hill
(CLOSED TO TRAFFIC ON SUNDAYS)
Vase
Buckingham Palace Gardens
Buckingham Palace
Queens Gallery
The Royal Mews
North Row
Green Street
Upper Brook Street
Upper Grosvenor St
Park Street
Park Lane
North Audley Street
South Audley Street
Grosvenor Square
Grosvenor Street
Brook Street
Brook's Mews
South Molton Street
South Molton Lane
New Bond Street
Avery Row
Maddox
St George Street
Davies Street
Mount Row
Mount Street
Adam's Row
Reeves Mews
Carlos Pl
Bruton Street
Bruton Pl
Bruton Lane
Berkeley Square
Berkeley Street
Hay Hill
Dover Street
Farm Street
Hay's Mews
Chesterfield Hill
Charles Street
Queen St
Curzon Street
Clarges Street
Clarges Mews
Bolton Street
Half Moon Street
Stratton Street
Shepherd Street
Hertford Street
Down Street
Brick Street
Old Park Lane
Hamilton Place
Waverton Street
Tilney St
Stanhope Gate
Deanery St
South Street
Aldford St
Rex Place
Market Mews
Achilles Way
Curzon Gate
Duke of Wellington Place
Grosvenor Place
Grosvenor Cres
Wilton Place
Wilton Row
Wilton Crescent
Kinnerton Street
William Mews
Lowndes Square
Halkin Street
Headfort Pl
Montrose Pl
Chapel Street
Chester Street
Belgrave
Motcomb Street
Indonesia
Egypt
United States
Canada
Italy
Argentine
Mexico
Burma
Bahamas
Qatar
Saudi Arabia
Panama
Japan
Kosovo
France
Libya
Luxembourg
Belgium
Singapore
Syria
Portugal
Malaysia
Turkey
Trinidad & Tobago
Ireland
A4
A4202
A302
B310
A40

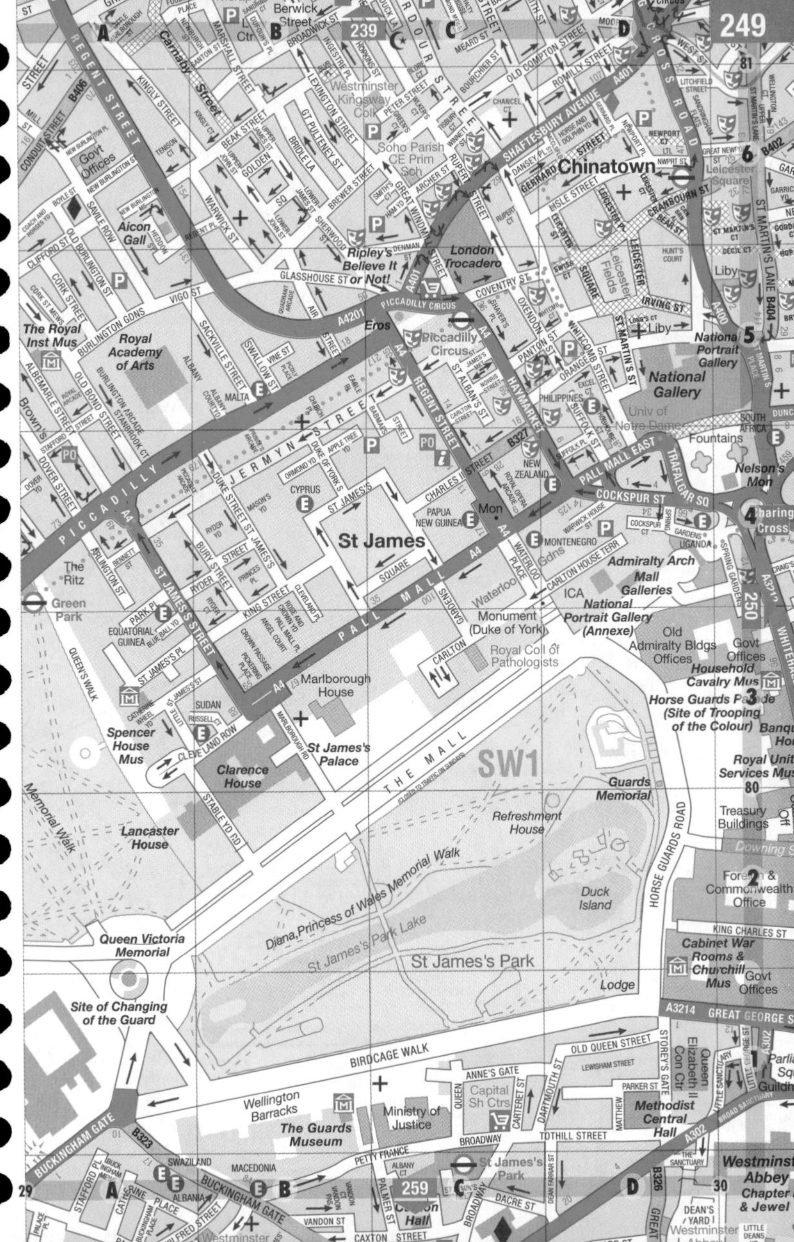

Regent Street
Carnaby Street
Berwick Street
Broadwick St
Old Compton Street
Shaftesbury Avenue
Chinatown
Gerrard Street
Lisle Street
Leicester Square
Cranbourn St
Charing Cross Road
St Martin's Lane
Govt Offices
Aicon Gall
Warwick St
Golden Sq
Brewer Street
Ripley's Believe It or Not!
London Trocadero
Glasshouse St
Vigo St
Piccadilly Circus
Eros
Coventry St
Leicester Fields
Irving St
National Portrait Gallery
National Gallery
Univ of Notre Dame
Fountains
Nelson's Mon
Trafalgar Sq
Charing Cross
The Royal Inst Mus
Royal Academy of Arts
Burlington Arcade
Sackville Street
Jermyn Street
Haymarket
Pall Mall East
Cockspur St
Piccadilly
St James
St James's Square
Pall Mall
The Ritz
Green Park
St James's Street
King Street
Waterloo Place
Admiralty Arch
Mall Galleries
ICA
National Portrait Gallery (Annexe)
Monument (Duke of York)
Royal Coll of Pathologists
Old Admiralty Bldgs Offices
Govt Offices
Household Cavalry Mus
Horse Guards Parade (Site of Trooping of the Colour)
Whitehall
Marlborough House
St James's Palace
Clarence House
Spencer House Mus
Lancaster House
The Mall
SW1
Guards Memorial
Refreshment House
Horse Guards Road
Royal United Services Muse
Treasury Buildings
Downing St
Foreign & Commonwealth Office
King Charles St
Duck Island
Diana, Princess of Wales Memorial Walk
St James's Park Lake
St James's Park
Queen Victoria Memorial
Site of Changing of the Guard
Cabinet War Rooms & Churchill Mus
Govt Offices
Lodge
Great George St
Birdcage Walk
Old Queen Street
Wellington Barracks
The Guards Museum
Ministry of Justice
Capital Sh Ctrs
Queen Elizabeth II Con Ctr
Methodist Central Hall
Broadway
Tothill Street
Petty France
St James's Park
Buckingham Gate
Westminster Abbey
Caxton Street
Memorial Walk
Queen's Walk

239
250
259

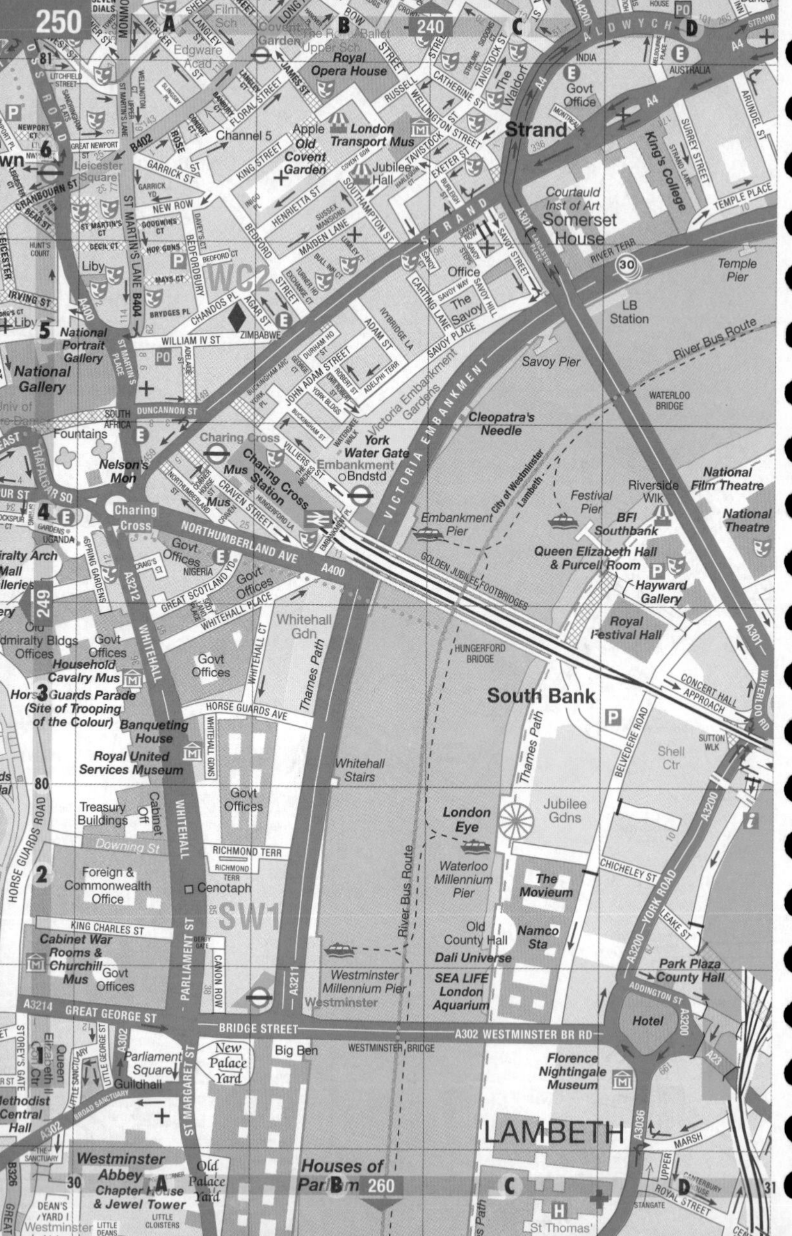

Royal Opera House
London Transport Mus
Old Covent Garden
Jubilee Hall
Strand
Courtauld Inst of Art
Somerset House
King's College
National Portrait Gallery
National Gallery
Charing Cross
Nelson's Mon
Fountains
WC2
The Savoy
Savoy Pier
Cleopatra's Needle
York Water Gate
Embankment
Victoria Embankment Gardens
Festival Pier
BFI Southbank
National Film Theatre
National Theatre
Queen Elizabeth Hall & Purcell Room
Hayward Gallery
Royal Festival Hall
Golden Jubilee Footbridges
Hungerford Bridge
South Bank
Waterloo Bridge
Household Cavalry Mus
Horse Guards Parade (Site of Trooping of the Colour)
Banqueting House
Royal United Services Museum
Whitehall
Treasury Buildings
Downing St
Foreign & Commonwealth Office
Cenotaph
SW1
Cabinet War Rooms & Churchill Mus
London Eye
Jubilee Gdns
Waterloo Millennium Pier
The Movieum
Old County Hall
Dali Universe
SEA LIFE London Aquarium
Westminster Millennium Pier
Westminster
Big Ben
Westminster Bridge
Park Plaza County Hall
Florence Nightingale Museum
LAMBETH
Houses of Parliament
Westminster Abbey
Chapter House & Jewel Tower
Parliament Square
Methodist Central Hall
St Thomas' Hospl
River Bus Route
Thames Path

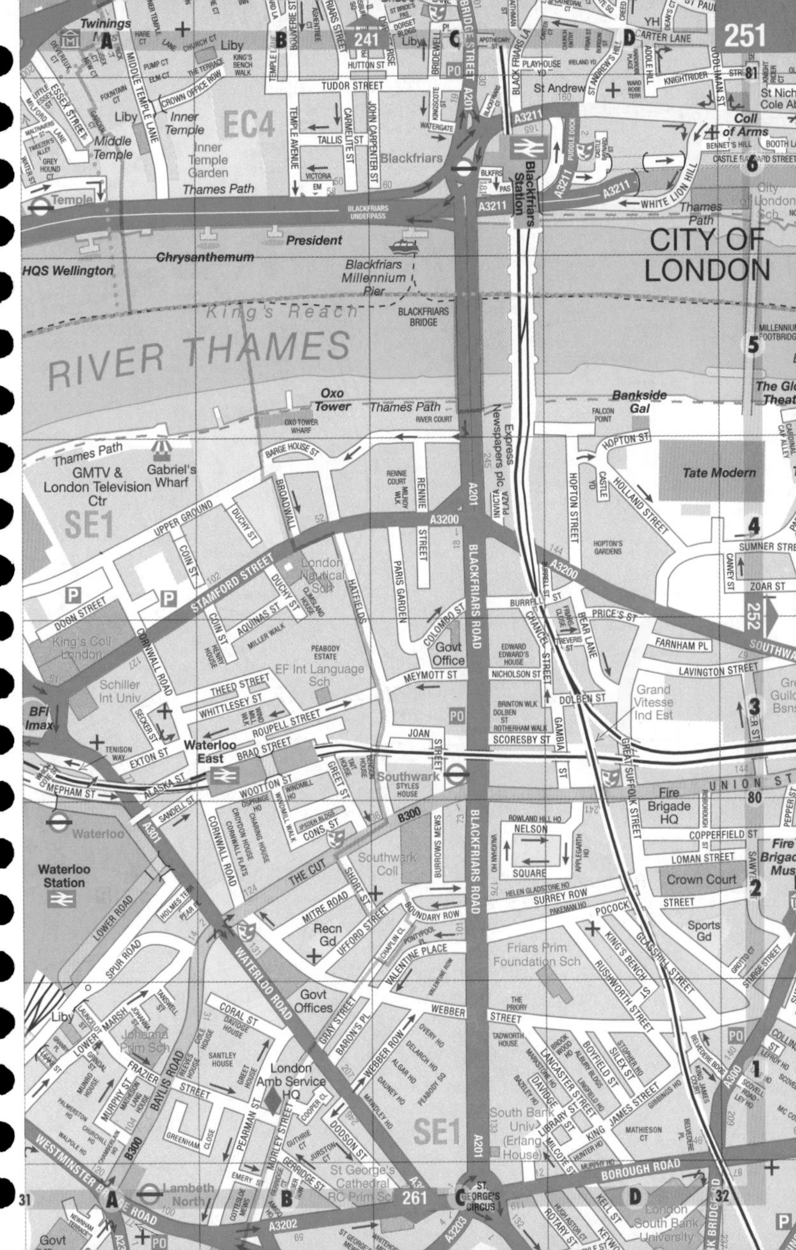

RIVER THAMES
King's Reach
CITY OF LONDON
EC4
SE1
Blackfriars Station
Blackfriars Millennium Pier
BLACKFRIARS BRIDGE
MILLENNIUM FOOTBRIDGE
Oxo Tower
Bankside Gal
Tate Modern
The Globe Theatre
Thames Path
GMTV & London Television Ctr
Gabriel's Wharf
Inner Temple
Middle Temple
Inner Temple Garden
Temple
HQS Wellington
Chrysanthemum
President
BLACKFRIARS UNDERPASS
Waterloo East
Waterloo Station
Waterloo
Southwark
Southwark Coll
King's Coll London
Schiller Int Univ
BFI Imax
London Nautical Sch
EF Int Language Sch
PEABODY ESTATE
Govt Office
Express Newspapers plc
Grand Vitesse Ind Est
Fire Brigade HQ
Fire Brigade Mus
Crown Court
Sports Gd
Recn Gd
Friars Prim Foundation Sch
Govt Offices
London Amb Service HQ
Johanna Prim Sch
South Bank Univ (Erlang House)
St George's Cathedral RC Prim Sch
London South Bank University
Lambeth North
ST. GEORGE'S CIRCUS
STAMFORD STREET
BLACKFRIARS ROAD
WATERLOO ROAD
SOUTHWARK STREET
UNION STREET
BOROUGH ROAD
WESTMINSTER BRIDGE ROAD
THE CUT
UPPER GROUND
TUDOR STREET
QUEEN VICTORIA ST
BRIDGE STREET
CARTER LANE
WHITE LION HILL
A201
A3200
A3211
A301
A300
A3202
A3203
B300
241
252
261
31
32

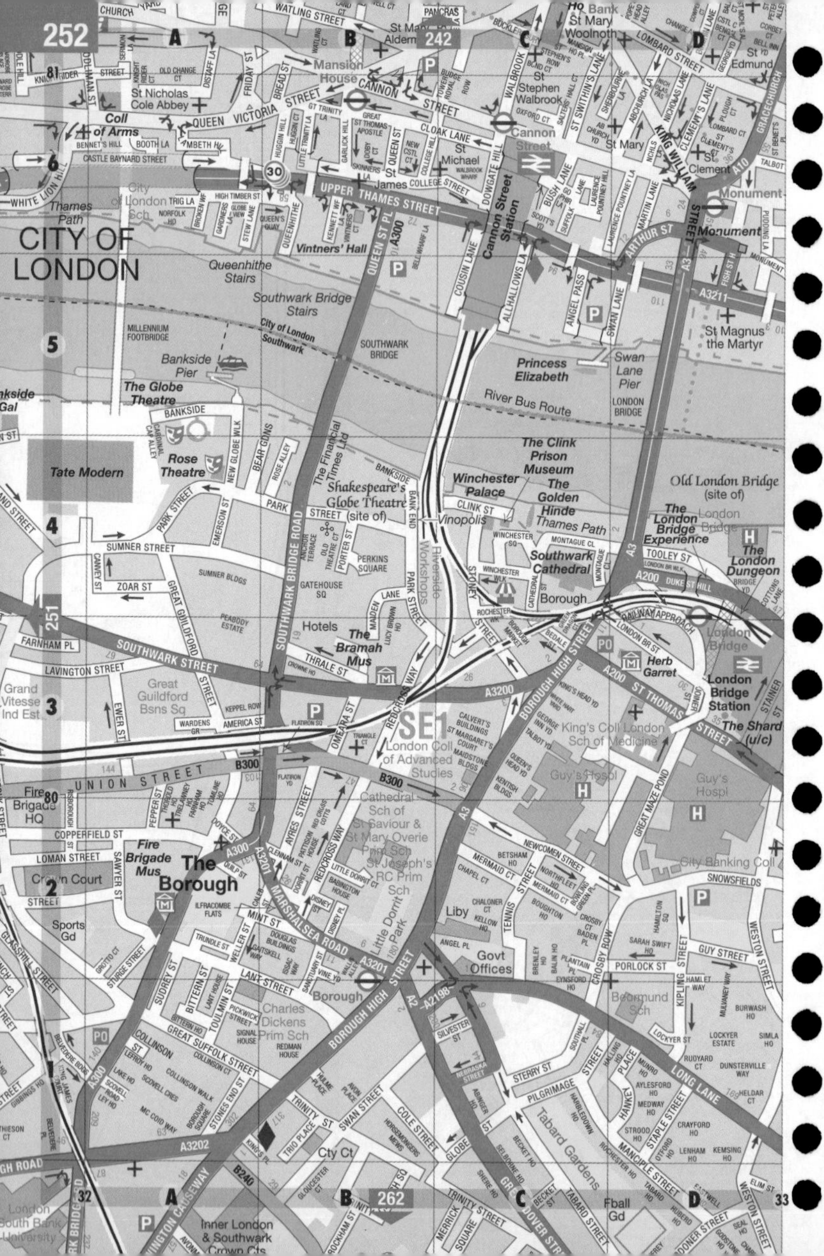
252
A
B
C
D
242
262
CITY OF LONDON
St Mary Aldermary
Mansion House
St Nicholas Cole Abbey
Coll of Arms
QUEEN VICTORIA STREET
CANNON STREET
WATLING STREET
FRIDAY ST
BREAD ST
CASTLE BAYNARD STREET
WHITE LION HILL
Thames Path
City of London Sch
UPPER THAMES STREET
St James
St Michael
Vintners' Hall
Queenhithe Stairs
Southwark Bridge Stairs
MILLENNIUM FOOTBRIDGE
City of London
Southwark
SOUTHWARK BRIDGE
Bankside Pier
The Globe Theatre
Bankside Gal
BANKSIDE
Tate Modern
Rose Theatre
St Mary Woolnoth
St Stephen Walbrook
Cannon Street
Cannon Street Station
St Mary
St Clement
KING WILLIAM STREET
Monument
ARTHUR ST
LOMBARD STREET
St Edmund
GRACECHURCH
A10
A3211
St Magnus the Martyr
Princess Elizabeth
Swan Lane Pier
River Bus Route
LONDON BRIDGE
The Clink Prison Museum
The Golden Hinde
Winchester Palace
Old London Bridge (site of)
Shakespeare's Globe Theatre (site of)
The Financial Times Ltd
Vinopolis
Thames Path
The London Bridge Experience
The London Dungeon
Southwark Cathedral
TOOLEY ST
DUKE ST HILL
Borough
Riverside Workshops
London Bridge
London Bridge Station
The Shard (u/c)
Herb Garret
RAILWAY APPROACH
ST THOMAS STREET
SUMNER STREET
PARK STREET
SOUTHWARK BRIDGE ROAD
SOUTHWARK STREET
A3200
Hotels
The Bramah Mus
SE1
London Coll of Advanced Studies
King's Coll London Sch of Medicine
Guy's Hospl
Great Guildford Bsns Sq
Grand Vitesse Ind Est
UNION STREET
B300
Fire Brigade HQ
Fire Brigade Mus
The Borough
Crown Court
Sports Gd
Cathedral Sch of St Saviour & St Mary Overie Prim Sch
St Joseph's RC Prim Sch
Little Dorrit Park
MARSHALSEA ROAD
BOROUGH HIGH STREET
A3
A2
Liby
Govt Offices
NEWCOMEN STREET
City Banking Coll
SNOWSFIELDS
GREAT MAZE POND
WESTON STREET
GUY STREET
LONG LANE
Bermondsey Sch
Charles Dickens Prim Sch
Borough
LANT STREET
GREAT SUFFOLK STREET
A3202
Cty Ct
Tabard Gardens
GREAT DOVER STREET
Fball Gd
Inner London & Southwark Crown Cts
London South Bank University
32
33

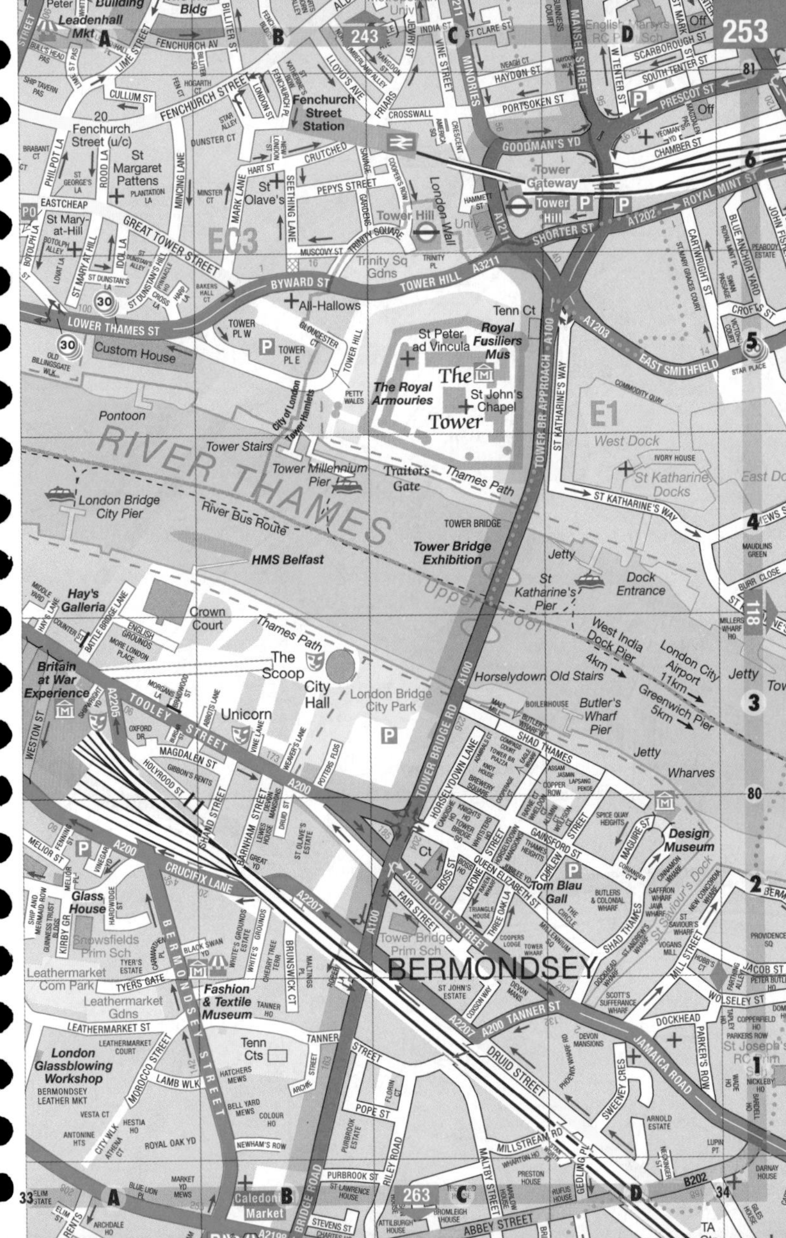
Fenchurch Street Station
Tower Gateway
Tower Hill
EC3
E1
The Tower
The Royal Armouries
Royal Fusiliers Mus
St Peter ad Vincula
St John's Chapel
Traitors Gate
RIVER THAMES
Upper Pool
Tower Millennium Pier
London Bridge City Pier
HMS Belfast
Tower Bridge Exhibition
St Katharine Docks
West Dock
East Dock
St Katharine's Pier
Dock Entrance
Hay's Galleria
Crown Court
The Scoop
City Hall
London Bridge City Park
Britain at War Experience
Unicorn
Design Museum
Tom Blau Gall
Glass House
Fashion & Textile Museum
London Glassblowing Workshop
Leathermarket Gdns
Leathermarket Com Park
BERMONDSEY
Custom House
All-Hallows
Pontoon
St Margaret Pattens
St Olave's
St Mary-at-Hill
Fenchurch Street (u/c)
Leadenhall Mkt
LOWER THAMES ST
BYWARD ST
TOWER HILL
EAST SMITHFIELD
TOOLEY STREET
BERMONDSEY STREET
JAMAICA ROAD
DRUID STREET
TOWER BRIDGE RD
TOWER BR APPROACH
ABBEY STREET
TANNER ST
CRUCIFIX LANE
West India Dock Pier 4km
London City Airport 11km
Greenwich Pier 5km
Horselydown Old Stairs
Butler's Wharf Pier
Thames Path
River Bus Route
243
263
118

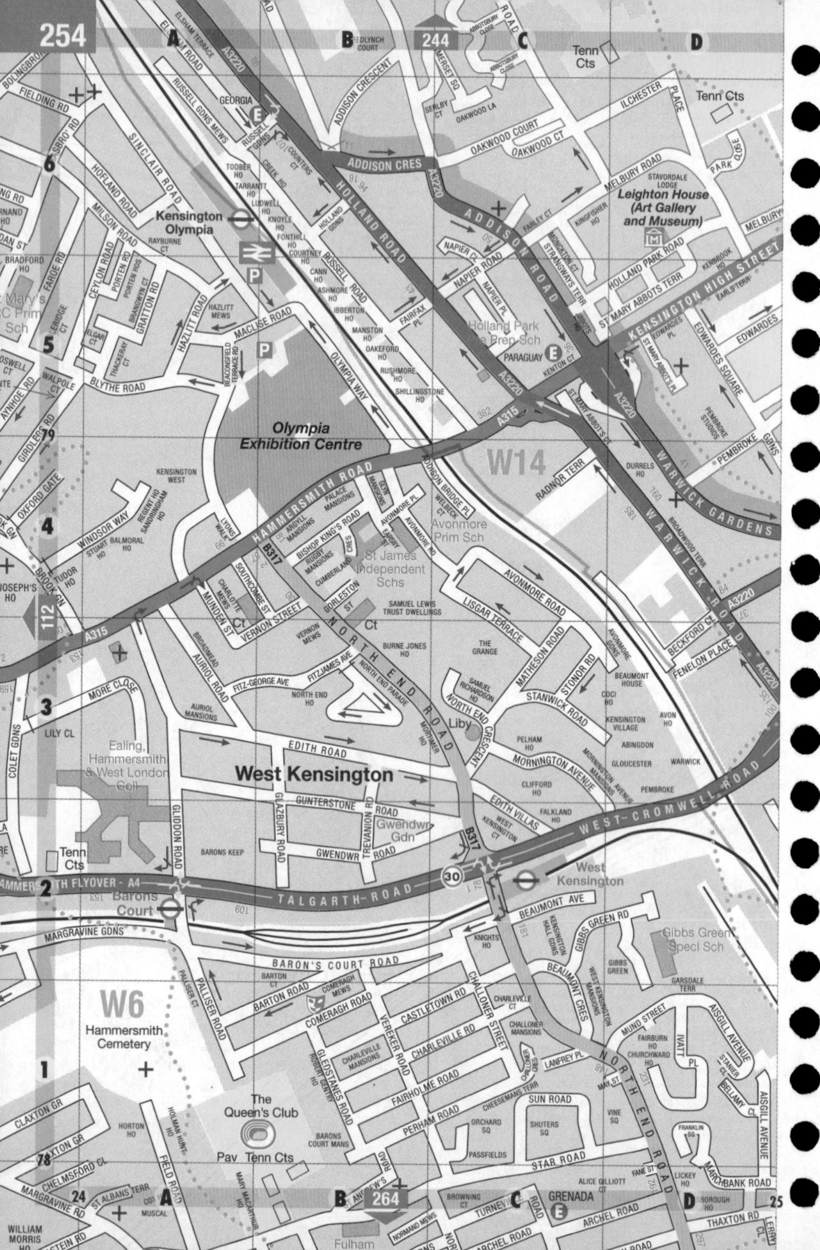
A
B
C
D
244
264
112
ELSHAM TERRACE
ELSHAM ROAD
RUSSELL GDNS MEWS
RUSSELL GDNS
GEORGIA
REDLYNCH COURT
ADDISON CRESCENT
SOMERSET SQ
ABBOTSBURY CLOSE
ABBOTSBURY ROAD
Tenn Cts
SERLBY CT
OAKWOOD LA
OAKWOOD COURT
OAKWOOD CT
ILCHESTER PLACE
PARK CLOSE
MELBURY ROAD
STAVORDALE LODGE
Leighton House (Art Gallery and Museum)
MELBURY
ADDISON CRES
A3220
HOLLAND ROAD
ADDISON ROAD
COUNTERS CT
CREEK HO
TODBER HO
TARRANTT HO
LUDWELL HO
KNOYLE HO
FONTHILL HO
COURTNEY HO
CANN HO
ASHMORE HO
IBBERTON HO
MANSTON HO
OAKEFORD HO
RUSHMORE HO
SHILLINGSTONE HO
HOLLAND GDNS
RUSSELL ROAD
FAIRFAX PL
NAPIER CL
NAPIER ROAD
NAPIER PL
FARLEY CT
MONCKTON CT
STRANGWAYS TERR
KINGFISHER HO
HOLLAND PARK ROAD
KENBROOK HO
EARLS TERR
ST MARY ABBOTS TERR
KENSINGTON HIGH STREET
ABBOTS HO
Holland Park Pre Prep Sch
PARAGUAY
KENTON CT
EDWARDES PL
ST MARY ABBOTS PL
EDWARDES SQUARE
EDWARDES
PEMBROKE STUDIOS
PEMBROKE GDNS
ST MARY ABBOT'S CT
A315
W14
RADNOR TERR
DURRELS HO
WARWICK GARDENS
WARWICK ROAD
BROADWOOD TERR
FIELDING RD
BOLINGBROKE
SINCLAIR ROAD
HOFLAND ROAD
MILSON ROAD
Kensington Olympia
RAYBURNE CT
BRADFORD HO
FAROE RD
CEYLON ROAD
PORTEN RD
PORTEN HOS
BRANGWYN CT
GRATTON RD
St Mary's RC Prim Sch
HAZLITT ROAD
HAZLITT MEWS
MACLISE ROAD
BEACONSFIELD TERRACE RD
OLYMPIA WAY
ELGAR CT
THACKERAY CT
BOSWELL CT
WALPOLE CT
AYNHOE RD
BLYTHE ROAD
GIRDLERS RD
Olympia Exhibition Centre
KENSINGTON WEST
OXFORD GATE
REGENT HO
SANDRINGHAM HO
WINDSOR WAY
STUART HO
BALMORAL HO
TUDOR HO
BROOK GN
ST JOSEPH'S HO
LYONS WALK
HAMMERSMITH ROAD
ARGYLL MANSIONS
PALACE MANSIONS
GLYN MANSIONS
AVONMORE PL
ADDISON BRIDGE PL
WELBECK CT
Avonmore Prim Sch
BISHOP KING'S ROAD
RUGBY MANSIONS
CUMBERLAND CRES
EARSBY ST
AVONMORE RD
St James Independent Schs
B317
SOUTHCOMBE ST
CHARLOTTE MEWS
MUNDEN ST
VERNON STREET
GORLESTON ST
SAMUEL LEWIS TRUST DWELLINGS
AVONMORE ROAD
LISGAR TERRACE
BECKFORD CL
FENELON PLACE
VERNON MEWS
BURNE JONES HO
NORTH END ROAD
THE GRANGE
MATHESON ROAD
STONOR RD
AVONMORE GDNS
BEAUMONT HOUSE
COCI HO
BROADMEAD
AURIOL ROAD
FITZ-GEORGE AVE
FITZJAMES AVE
NORTH END PARADE
NORTH END HO
SAMUEL RICHARDSON HO
STANWICK ROAD
KENSINGTON VILLAGE
AVON HO
MORE CLOSE
LILY CL
COLET GDNS
AURIOL MANSIONS
MORTIMER HO
Liby
NORTH END CRESCENT
PELHAM HO
ABINGDON
GLOUCESTER
WARWICK
PEMBROKE
EDITH ROAD
MORNINGTON AVENUE
MORNINGTON AVENUE MANSIONS
Ealing, Hammersmith & West London Coll
West Kensington
CLIFFORD HO
WEST CROMWELL ROAD
GUNTERSTONE ROAD
TREVANION RD
GLAZBURY ROAD
EDITH VILLAS
FALKLAND HO
WEST KENSINGTON CT
Gwendwr Gdn
GLIDDON ROAD
BARONS KEEP
GWENDWR ROAD
HAMMERSMITH FLYOVER - A4
TALGARTH ROAD
Barons Court
West Kensington
BEAUMONT AVE
KENSINGTON HALL GDNS
GIBBS GREEN RD
Gibbs Green Specl Sch
MARGRAVINE GDNS
KNIGHTS HO
BARON'S COURT ROAD
BARTON CT
BARTON ROAD
COMERAGH MEWS
COMERAGH ROAD
CHALLONER STREET
CHARLEVILLE CT
BEAUMONT CRES
WEST KENSINGTON MANSIONS
GIBBS GREEN
GARSDALE TERR
W6
Hammersmith Cemetery
PALLISER ROAD
PALLISER CT
CASTLETOWN RD
CHALLONER MANSIONS
MUND STREET
AISGILL AVENUE
FAIRBURN HO
CHURCHWARD HO
IVATT PL
STANIER CL
BELLAMY CL
CHARLEVILLE MANSIONS
VEREKER ROAD
CHARLEVILLE RD
LANFREY PL
GLEDSTANES ROAD
ROBERT GENTRY HO
FAIRHOLME ROAD
CHEESEMANS TERR
SUN ROAD
MAY ST
VINE SQ
CLAXTON GR
The Queen's Club
PERHAM ROAD
ORCHARD SQ
SHUTERS SQ
FRANKLIN SQ
HORTON HO
HOLMAN HUNT HO
FIELD ROAD
Pav Tenn Cts
BARONS COURT MANS
PASSFIELDS
STAR ROAD
MARCHBANK ROAD
CHELMSFORD CL
ST ALBANS TERR
MARGRAVINE RD
MARY MACARTHUR HO
ST ANDREW'S ROAD
ALICE GILLIOTT CT
FANE ST
LICKEY HO
BROWNING CT
TURNEVILLE ROAD
GRENADA
ARCHEL ROAD
THAXTON RD
LEBRY CL
COX HO
MUSCAL
WILLIAM MORRIS HO
NORMAND MEWS
Fulham
24
25
78
79
1
2
3
4
5
6
30

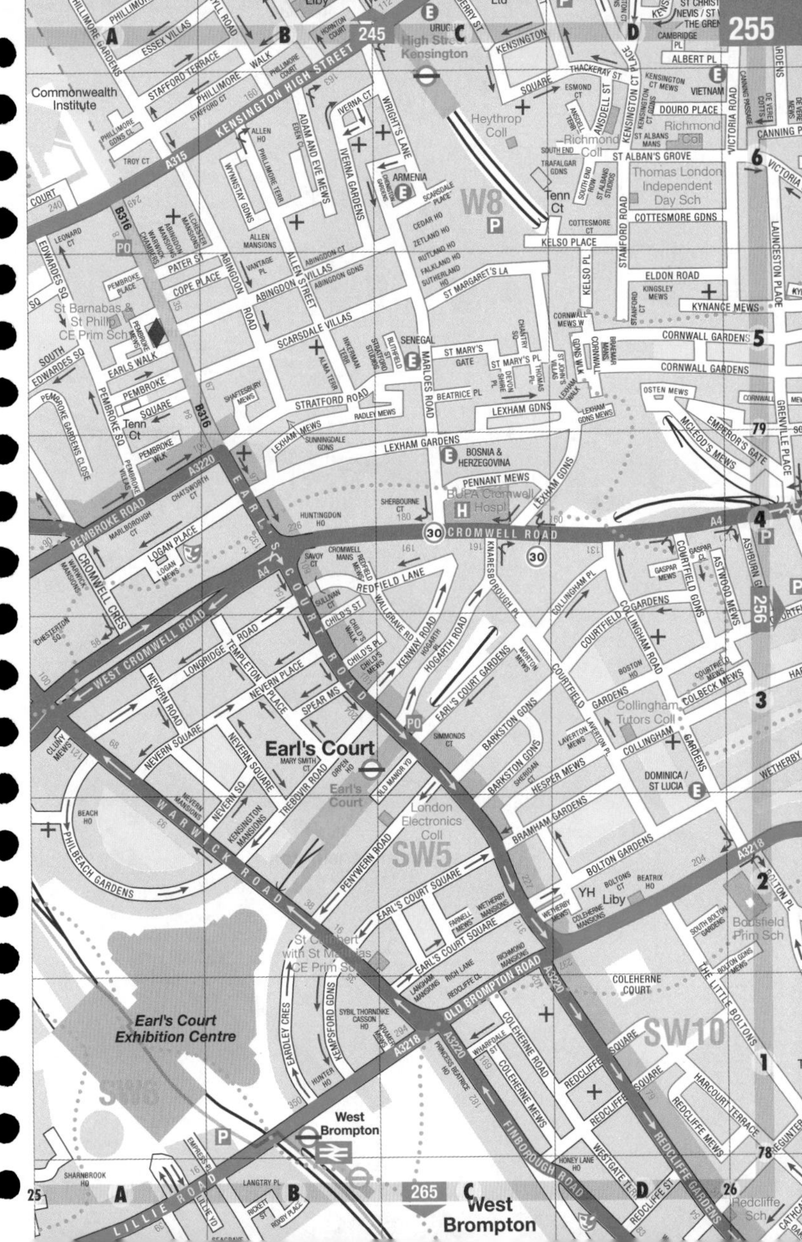

Kensington High Street
High Street Kensington
Commonwealth Institute
Heythrop Coll
Richmond Coll
Thomas London Independent Day Sch
W8
Cromwell Road
BUPA Cromwell Hospl
Earl's Court
Earl's Court Road
West Cromwell Road
Warwick Road
London Electronics Coll
SW5
Collingham Tutors Coll
Old Brompton Road
Earl's Court Exhibition Centre
St Cuthbert with St Matthias CE Prim Sch
St Barnabas & St Philip CE Prim Sch
Bousfield Prim Sch
SW10
Redcliffe Gardens
Finborough Road
Lillie Road
West Brompton
Redcliffe Sch
245
256
265

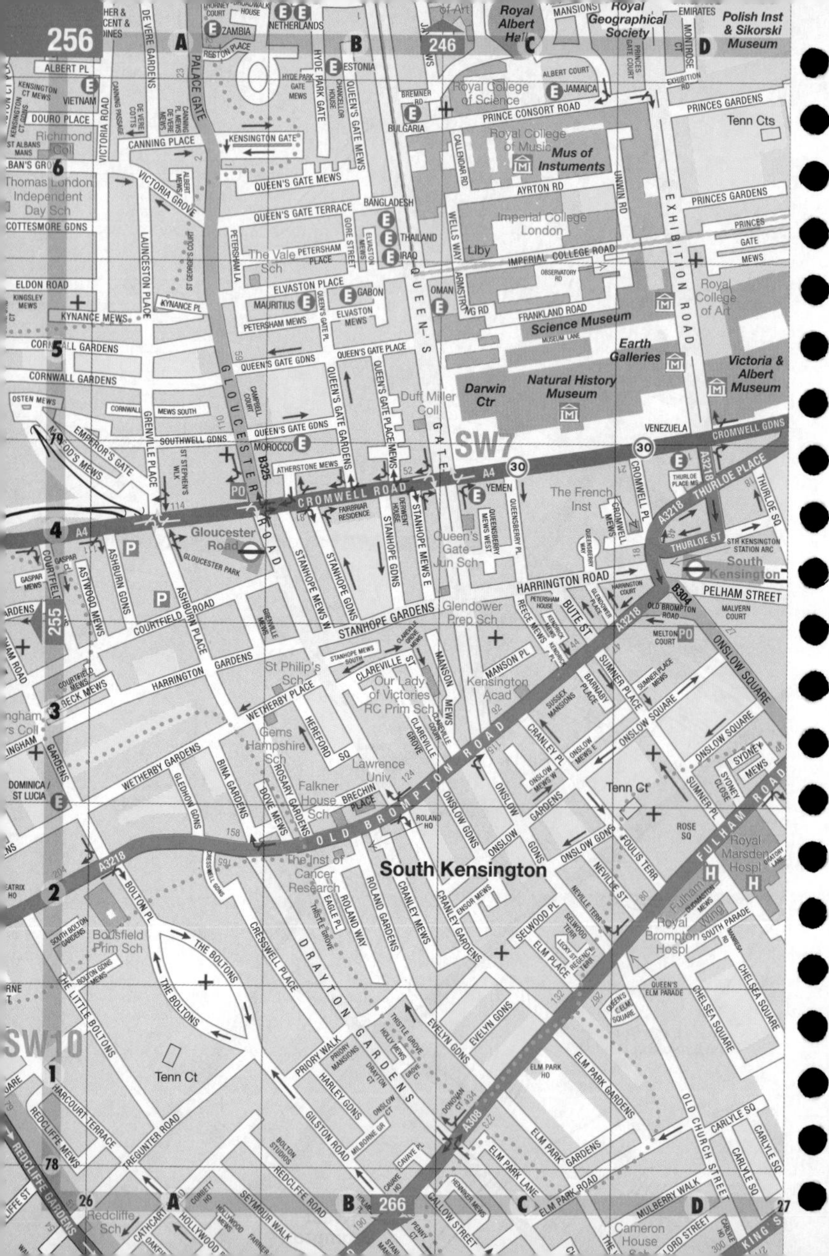

Royal Albert Hall
Royal Geographical Society
Polish Inst & Sikorski Museum
246
Royal College of Science
Royal College of Music
Mus of Instuments
Imperial College London
Science Museum
Earth Galleries
Natural History Museum
Darwin Ctr
Victoria & Albert Museum
Royal College of Art
SW7
CROMWELL ROAD
CROMWELL GDNS
GLOUCESTER ROAD
Gloucester Road
South Kensington
The French Inst
Queen's Gate Jun Sch
Duff Miller Coll
Glendower Prep Sch
St Philip's Sch
Our Lady of Victories RC Prim Sch
Kensington Acad
Gems Hampshire Sch
Lawrence Univ
Falkner House Sch
The Inst of Cancer Research
OLD BROMPTON ROAD
FULHAM ROAD
South Kensington
Royal Marsden Hospl
Royal Brompton Hospl
Bousfield Prim Sch
THE BOLTONS
Tenn Ct
Tenn Cts
Richmond Coll
Thomas London Independent Day Sch
Cameron House Sch
Redcliffe Sch
SW10
255
266
DRAYTON GARDENS
ONSLOW SQUARE
HARRINGTON ROAD
PALACE GATE
EXHIBITION ROAD
QUEEN'S GATE
PRINCE CONSORT ROAD
IMPERIAL COLLEGE ROAD
CORNWALL GARDENS
ELM PARK GARDENS
OLD CHURCH STREET
CHELSEA SQUARE
A B C D
1 2 3 4 5 6

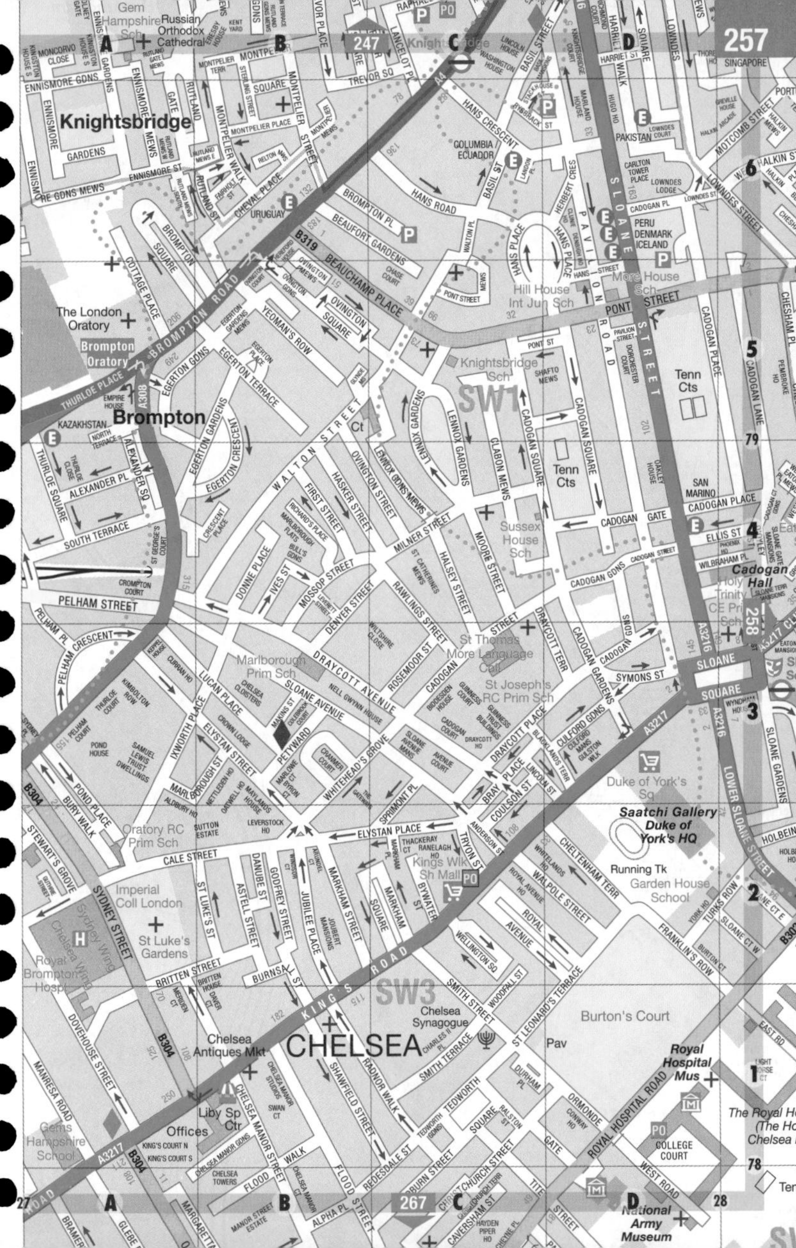
Knightsbridge
Brompton
CHELSEA
SW1
SW3
The London Oratory
Brompton Oratory
Russian Orthodox Cathedral
Saatchi Gallery Duke of York's HQ
Royal Hospital Mus
National Army Museum
Cadogan Hall
Chelsea Antiques Mkt
Chelsea Synagogue
Burton's Court
Imperial Coll London
St Luke's Gardens
Royal Brompton Hosp
The Royal Hos (The Hom Chelsea Pe
KING'S ROAD
SLOANE STREET
BROMPTON ROAD
SYDNEY STREET
247
258
267

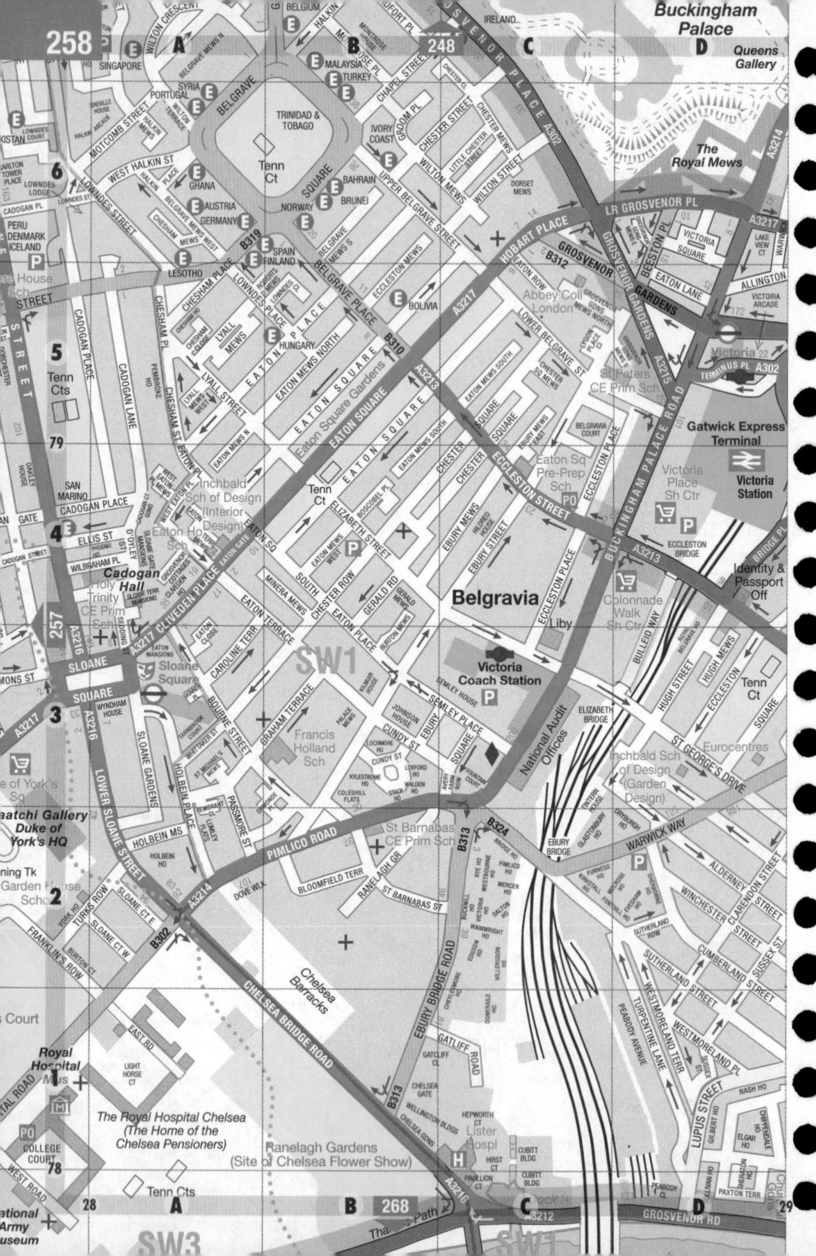

258
248
257
268
A
B
C
D
28
29
6
5
4
3
2
1
79
78
Buckingham Palace
Queens Gallery
The Royal Mews
Belgravia
SW1
SW3
Victoria
Victoria Station
Gatwick Express Terminal
Victoria Place Sh Ctr
Victoria Coach Station
Identity & Passport Off
Colonnade Walk Sh Ctr
National Audit Offices
Eurocentres
Inchbald Sch of Design (Garden Design)
Inchbald Sch of Design (Interior Design)
Eaton Ho Sch
Cadogan Hall
Holy Trinity CE Prim Sch
Sloane Square
Francis Holland Sch
St Barnabas CE Prim Sch
Abbey Coll London
St Peters CE Prim Sch
Eaton Sq Pre-Prep Sch
Liby
Chelsea Barracks
Ranelagh Gardens (Site of Chelsea Flower Show)
The Royal Hospital Chelsea (The Home of the Chelsea Pensioners)
Royal Hospital Mus
National Army Museum
Saatchi Gallery Duke of York's HQ
Lister Hospl
Tenn Ct
Tenn Cts
Eaton Square Gardens
BELGRAVE SQUARE
EATON SQUARE
EATON PLACE
BELGRAVE PLACE
GROSVENOR PLACE
GROSVENOR GARDENS
LR GROSVENOR PL
HOBART PLACE
UPPER BELGRAVE STREET
LOWER BELGRAVE ST
CHESTER SQUARE
CHESTER STREET
WILTON CRESCENT
WILTON STREET
WILTON MEWS
MOTCOMB STREET
WEST HALKIN ST
LOWNDES STREET
LOWNDES PLACE
CHESHAM PLACE
CHESHAM ST
CADOGAN PLACE
CADOGAN LANE
LYALL STREET
ELIZABETH STREET
ECCLESTON STREET
ECCLESTON PLACE
EBURY STREET
EBURY MEWS
BUCKINGHAM PALACE ROAD
BEESTON PL
VICTORIA SQUARE
ALLINGTON ST
EATON LANE
TERMINUS PL
ECCLESTON BRIDGE
BULLEID WAY
HUGH STREET
HUGH MEWS
ECCLESTON SQUARE
ST GEORGE'S DRIVE
WARWICK WAY
ALDERNEY STREET
CLARENDON STREET
WINCHESTER STREET
CUMBERLAND STREET
SUSSEX ST
SUTHERLAND STREET
WESTMORELAND TERR
WESTMORELAND PL
TURPENTINE LANE
PEABODY AVENUE
LUPUS STREET
GROSVENOR RD
EBURY BRIDGE
EBURY BRIDGE ROAD
ELIZABETH BRIDGE
SEMLEY PLACE
EBURY SQUARE
CUNDY ST
PIMLICO ROAD
BOURNE STREET
PASSMORE ST
HOLBEIN PLACE
HOLBEIN MS
SLOANE GARDENS
LOWER SLOANE STREET
CHELSEA BRIDGE ROAD
CLIVEDEN PLACE
EATON TERRACE
CAROLINE TERR
GRAHAM TERRACE
CHESTER ROW
GERALD RD
MINERA MEWS
ELLIS ST
WILBRAHAM PL
CADOGAN STREET
SEDDING ST
SLOANE SQUARE
TURKS ROW
FRANKLIN'S ROW
BLOOMFIELD TERR
RANELAGH GR
ST BARNABAS ST
DOVE WLK
GATLIFF ROAD
EAST RD
WEST ROAD
Thames Path
A3217
A3216
A3214
A3213
A3215
A302
A3212
B310
B312
B313
B319
B324
B302

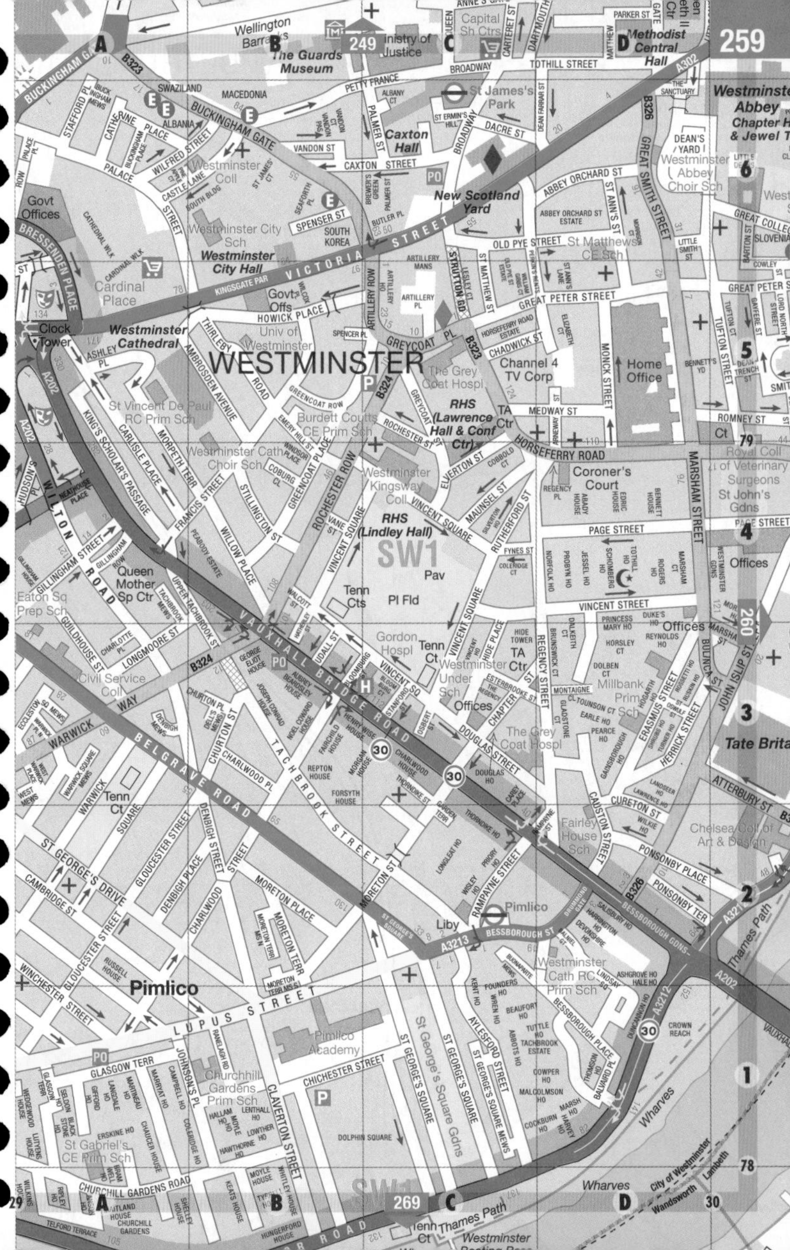

Wellington Barracks
The Guards Museum
249
Ministry of Justice
Capital Sh Ctrs
Methodist Central Hall
TOTHILL STREET
BROADWAY
PETTY FRANCE
BUCKINGHAM GATE
St James's Park
Westminster Abbey
Chapter House & Jewel Tower
DEAN'S YARD
Westminster Abbey Choir Sch
Caxton Hall
CAXTON STREET
New Scotland Yard
ABBEY ORCHARD ST
GREAT SMITH STREET
VICTORIA STREET
Westminster City Sch
Westminster City Hall
Govt Offices
BRESSENDEN PLACE
Cardinal Place
Westminster Cathedral
Clock Tower
WESTMINSTER
Univ of Westminster
OLD PYE STREET
St Matthews CE Sch
GREAT PETER STREET
GREAT COLLEGE ST
HORSEFERRY ROAD
Channel 4 TV Corp
Home Office
The Grey Coat Hospl
RHS (Lawrence Hall & Conf Ctr)
St Vincent De Paul RC Prim Sch
Burdett Coutts CE Prim Sch
Westminster Cath Choir Sch
ROCHESTER ROW
Westminster Kingsway Coll
Coroner's Court
Royal Coll of Veterinary Surgeons
St John's Gdns
MARSHAM STREET
PAGE STREET
RHS (Lindley Hall)
SW1
VINCENT SQUARE
Tenn Cts
Pl Fld
Pav
Queen Mother Sp Ctr
Eaton Sq Prep Sch
Civil Service Coll
WILTON ROAD
VAUXHALL BRIDGE ROAD
Gordon Hospl
Westminster Under Sch
Millbank Prim Sch
Offices
260
Tate Britain
ATTERBURY ST
Chelsea Coll of Art & Design
The Grey Coat Hospl
Fairley House Sch
BELGRAVE ROAD
WARWICK WAY
TACHBROOK STREET
PONSONBY PLACE
ST GEORGE'S DRIVE
Pimlico
BESSBOROUGH ST
Westminster Cath RC Prim Sch
Thames Path
LUPUS STREET
Pimlico Academy
St George's Square Gdns
Churchhill Gardens Prim Sch
CLAVERTON STREET
CHICHESTER STREET
DOLPHIN SQUARE
St Gabriel's CE Prim Sch
CHURCHILL GARDENS ROAD
GROSVENOR ROAD
Wharves
City of Westminster
Lambeth
Wandsworth
269
Thames Path
Westminster Boating Base
A B C D
1 2 3 4 5 6
78 79
29 30

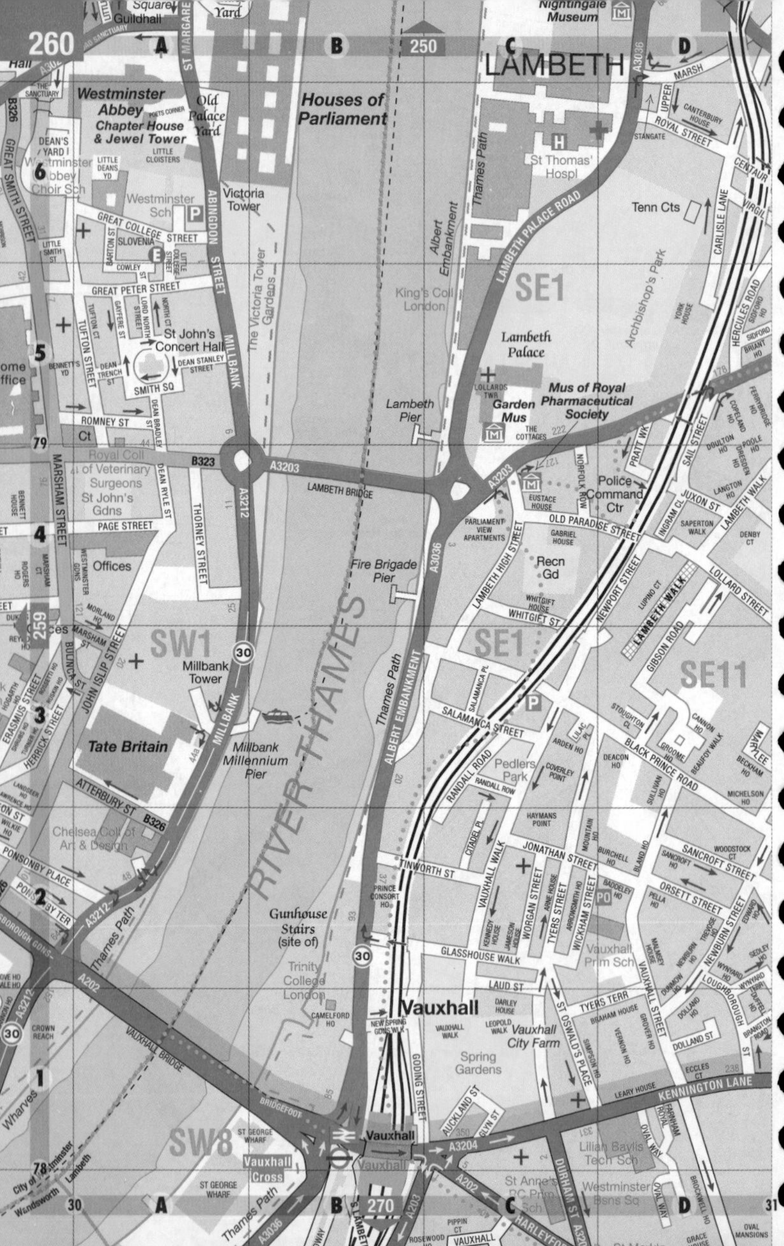
A
B
250
C
D
LAMBETH
Westminster Abbey
Chapter House & Jewel Tower
Old Palace Yard
Houses of Parliament
Victoria Tower
Nightingale Museum
Guildhall
THE SANCTUARY
GREAT SMITH STREET
DEAN'S YARD
Westminster Abbey Choir Sch
LITTLE DEANS YD
LITTLE CLOISTERS
Westminster Sch
ST MARGARET
ABINGDON STREET
GREAT COLLEGE STREET
BARTON ST
SLOVENIA
COWLEY ST
GREAT PETER STREET
TUFTON ST
GAYFERE ST
LORD NORTH STREET
NORTH CT
St John's Concert Hall
DEAN STANLEY STREET
DEAN TRENCH ST
SMITH SQ
Home Office
ROMNEY ST
DEAN BRADLEY ST
MILLBANK
The Victoria Tower Gardens
King's Coll London
Albert Embankment
Thames Path
St Thomas' Hospl
UPPER MARSH
CANTERBURY HOUSE
ROYAL STREET
STANGATE
CENTAUR
VIRGIL
Tenn Cts
CARLISLE LANE
Archbishop's Park
YORK HOUSE
HERCULES ROAD
LAMBETH PALACE ROAD
SE1
Lambeth Palace
LOLLARDS TWR
Garden Mus
Mus of Royal Pharmaceutical Society
Lambeth Pier
THE COTTAGES
Royal Coll of Veterinary Surgeons
St John's Gdns
MARSHAM STREET
B323
A3203
LAMBETH BRIDGE
A3212
DEAN RYLE ST
THORNEY STREET
PAGE STREET
Offices
EUSTACE HOUSE
NORFOLK ROW
Police Command Ctr
PRATT WK
SAIL STREET
JUXON ST
LAMBETH WALK
OLD PARADISE STREET
PARLIAMENT VIEW APARTMENTS
LAMBETH HIGH STREET
GABRIEL HOUSE
Recn Gd
Fire Brigade Pier
A3036
WHITGIFT HOUSE
WHITGIFT ST
NEWPORT STREET
LOLLARD STREET
GIBSON ROAD
SE11
SW1
MORLAND HO
MARSHAM ST
BULINCA ST
JOHN ISLIP STREET
Millbank Tower
Tate Britain
ERASMUS STREET
HERRICK STREET
Millbank Millennium Pier
RIVER THAMES
ALBERT EMBANKMENT
SALAMANCA PL
SALAMANCA STREET
ARDEN HO
LILAC PL
STOUGHTON CL
CANNON HO
BLACK PRINCE ROAD
DEACON HO
RANDALL ROAD
RANDALL ROW
Pedlers Park
COVERLEY POINT
HAYMANS POINT
ATTERBURY ST
B326
Chelsea Coll of Art & Design
PONSONBY PLACE
PONSONBY TER
CITADEL PL
VAUXHALL WALK
JONATHAN STREET
BURCHELL HO
SANCROFT STREET
ORSETT STREET
TINWORTH ST
PRINCE CONSORT HO
WORGAN STREET
TYERS STREET
WICKHAM STREET
Gunhouse Stairs (site of)
Trinity College London
GLASSHOUSE WALK
Vauxhall Prim Sch
VAUXHALL STREET
NEWBURN STREET
LOUGHBOROUGH
BESSBOROUGH GDNS
A202
A3212
Thames Path
VAUXHALL BRIDGE
LAUD ST
Vauxhall
TYERS TERR
BRAHAM HOUSE
NEW SPRING GDNS WLK
VAUXHALL WALK
LEOPOLD WALK
Vauxhall City Farm
Spring Gardens
ST OSWALD'S PLACE
DOLLAND ST
CROWN REACH
Wharves
BRIDGEFOOT
GODING STREET
AUCKLAND ST
GLYN ST
KENNINGTON LANE
LEARY HOUSE
SW8
ST GEORGE WHARF
Vauxhall Cross
A3204
A202
Lilian Baylis Tech Sch
OVAL WAY
St Anne's RC Prim Sch
Westminster Bsns Sq
DURHAM ST
HARLEYFORD
BROCKWELL HO
OVAL MANSIONS
City of Westminster
Wandsworth
Lambeth
30
A
B
270
C
D
31
30
1
2
3
4
5
6
78
79
259

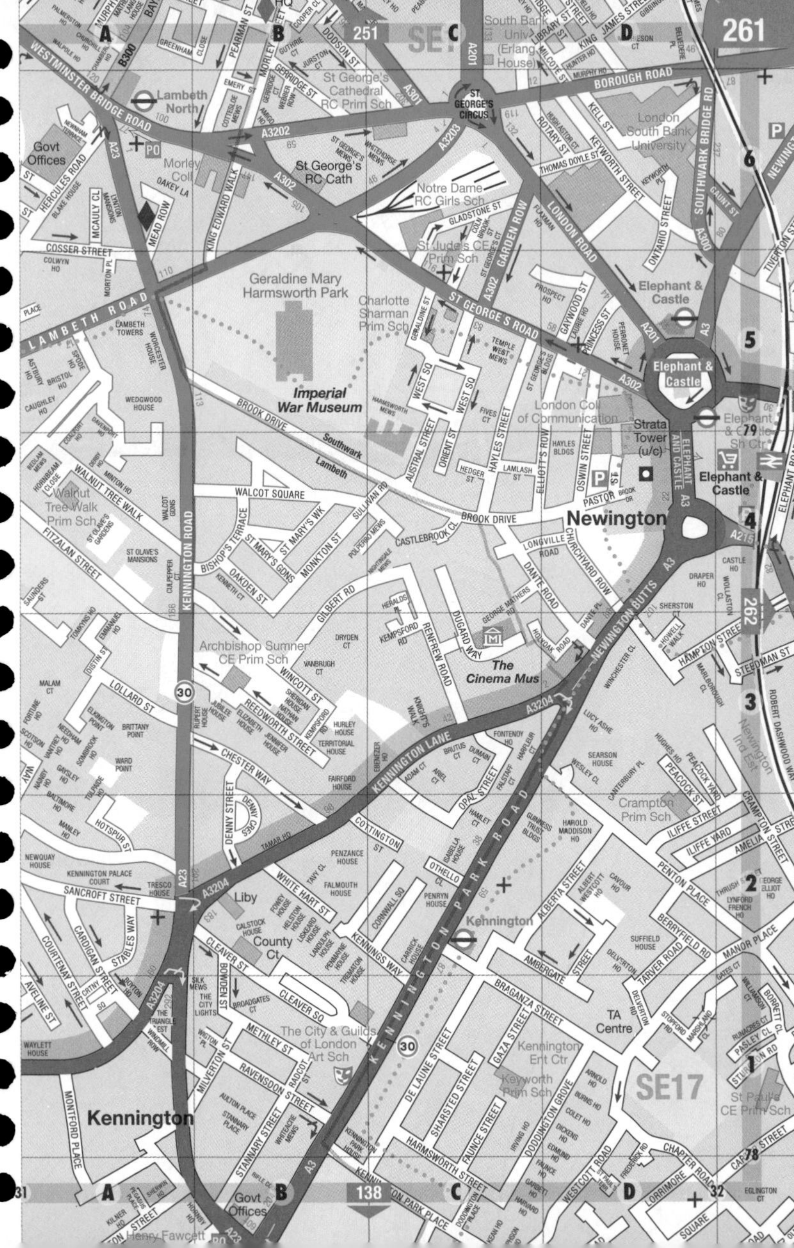

251
261
262
138
A
B
C
D
SE1
SE17
6
5
4
3
2
1
79
78
31
32
HQ
Westminster Bridge Road
Lambeth North
Govt Offices
Hercules Road
Blake House
Morley Coll
Oakey La
Mead Row
King Edward Walk
A3202
A302
A23
B300
St George's Cathedral RC Prim Sch
St George's RC Cath
St George's Circus
A201
A301
A3203
Borough Road
South Bank Univ (Erlang House)
London South Bank University
Southwark Bridge Rd
Newington
Gaunt St
Library St
King James Street
Rotary St
Keyworth Street
Thomas Doyle St
London Road
Ontario Street
A300
Notre Dame RC Girls Sch
Gladstone St
St Jude's CE Prim Sch
Garden Row
Gaywood St
Princess St
Perronet Ho
Prospect Ho
Elephant & Castle
A3
A302
St George's Road
Temple West Mews
Charlotte Sharman Prim Sch
Geraldine St
Geraldine Mary Harmsworth Park
Imperial War Museum
West Sq
Cosser Street
Colwyn Ho
Morton Pl
Lambeth Road
Lambeth Towers
Worcester House
Brook Drive
Southwark
Lambeth
Austral Street
Orient St
Fives Ct
Hayles Street
London Coll of Communication
Strata Tower (u/c)
Elephant and Castle
Elephant & Castle Sh Ctr
Elephant Road
Hayles Bldgs
Oswin Street
Elliott's Row
Hedger St
Lamlash St
Pastor St
Brook Dr
Newington
A215
Tiverton Street
Wedgwood House
Walnut Tree Walk
Walnut Tree Walk Prim Sch
Fitzalan Street
St Olave's Mansions
Walcot Gdns
Kennington Road
Walcot Square
Bishop's Terrace
St Mary's Wk
St Mary's Gdns
Monkton St
Oakden St
Sullivan Rd
Castlebrook Cl
Longville Road
Churchyard Row
Dante Road
Castle Ho
Wollaston Cl
Draper Ho
Sherston Ct
Hampton Street
Steedman St
Robert Dashwood Way
Newington Butts
Gilbert Rd
Dryden Ct
Vanbrugh Ct
Kempsford Rd
Renfrew Road
Dugard Way
The Cinema Mus
Holyoak Road
Archbishop Sumner CE Prim Sch
Wincott St
Reedworth Street
Lollard St
Chester Way
Hurley House
Territorial House
Fairford House
Kennington Lane
A3204
Winchester Cl
Lucy Ashe Ho
Searson House
Wesley Cl
Canterbury Pl
Peacock St
Peacock Yard
Crampton Prim Sch
Crampton Street
Iliffe Street
Iliffe Yard
Amelia Street
Newington Ind Est
Penton Place
Denny Street
Denny Cres
Tamar Ho
Cottington St
Penzance House
Falmouth House
White Hart St
Opal Street
Hamlet Ct
Othello Cl
Harold Maddison Ho
Guinness Trust Bldgs
Alberta Street
Manor Place
Berryfield Rd
Tarver Road
Suffield House
Hotspur St
Newquay House
Kennington Palace Court
Sancroft Street
Tresco House
Liby
Stables Way
Courtenay Street
Cardigan Street
Aveline Street
County Ct
Cleaver St
Cleaver Sq
Bowden St
The City Lights
Kennings Way
Cornwall Sq
Carrick House
Kennington
Kennington Park Road
Ambergate Street
Braganza Street
TA Centre
Delverton Rd
The Triangle Est
Waylett House
Methley St
Milverton St
Ravensdon Street
Radcot St
The City & Guilds of London Art Sch
Kennington Ent Ctr
Keyworth Prim Sch
De Laune Street
Gaza Street
Sharsted Street
Faunce Street
Doddington Grove
Harmsworth Street
Westcott Road
Chapter Road
Lorrimore Square
St Paul's CE Prim Sch
Carter Street
Eglinton Ct
Pasley Cl
Sturgeon Rd
Borrett Cl
Montford Place
Kennington
Stannary Street
Kennington Park Place
Govt Offices
Kennington Park House
Henry Fawcett
Kilner Ho

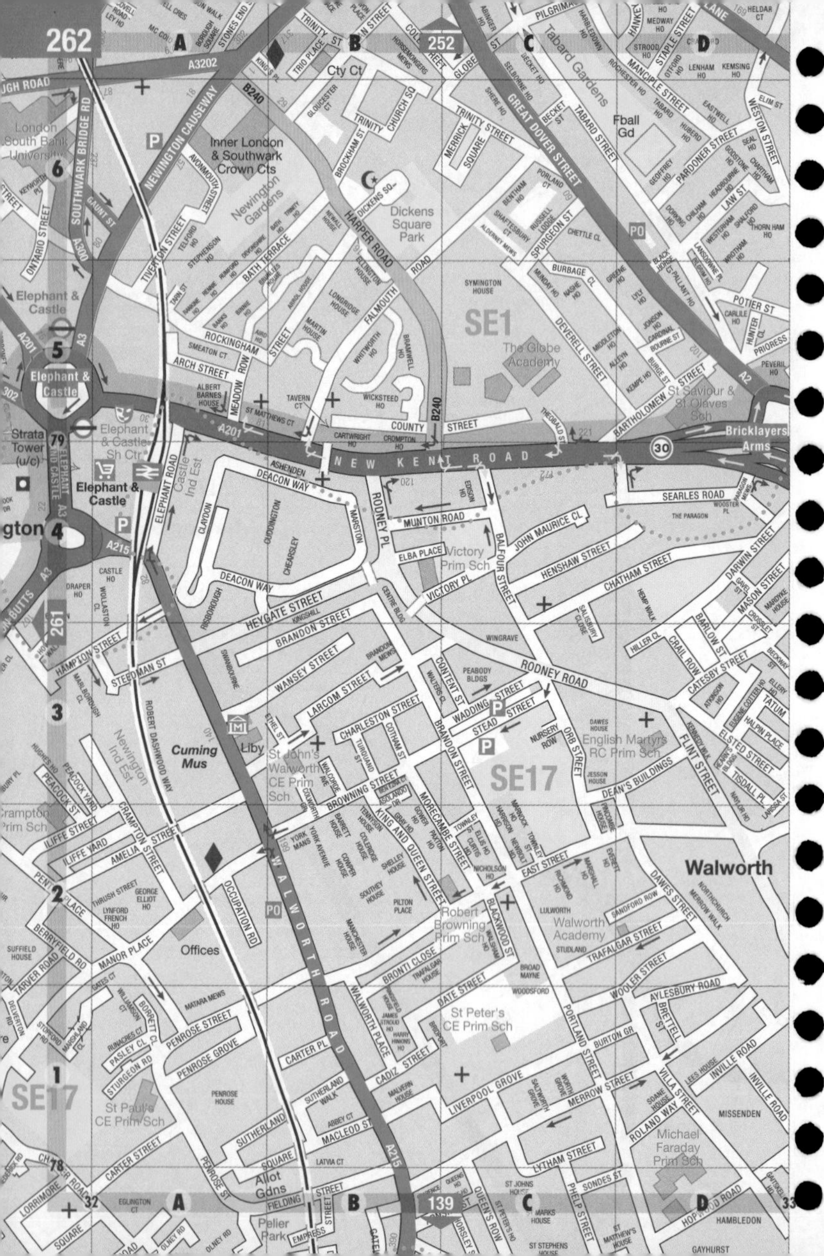

262
A
B
C
D
252
139
261
A3202
B240
A201
A3
A215
A2
B240
A300
Newington Causeway
Southwark Bridge Rd
Southwark Bridge Road
London South Bank University
Inner London & Southwark Crown Cts
Newington Gardens
Cty Ct
Trinity St
Trinity Church Sq
Trinity Street
Merrick Square
Tabard Gardens
Tabard Street
Great Dover Street
Fball Gd
Harper Road
Dickens Square Park
Pilgrimage Street
Manciple Street
Staple Street
Pardoner Street
Weston Street
Law St
Potier St
Prioress
Bartholomew Street
St Saviour & St Olaves Sch
Bricklayers Arms
SE1
The Globe Academy
Deverell Street
Burbage Cl
Spurgeon St
Symington House
Elephant & Castle
Strata Tower (u/c)
Elephant & Castle Sh Ctr
Rockingham Street
Arch Street
Meadow Row
Smeaton Ct
Falmouth Road
County Street
New Kent Road
Ashenden
Deacon Way
Rodney Pl
Munton Road
Elba Place
Victory Prim Sch
Victory Pl
Balfour Street
John Maurice Cl
Henshaw Street
Chatham Street
Searles Road
The Paragon
Darwin Street
Mason Street
Elephant Road
Castle Ind Est
Heygate Street
Brandon Street
Wansey Street
Larcom Street
Hampton Street
Steedman St
Robert Dashwood Way
Cuming Mus
Liby
St John's Walworth CE Prim Sch
Charleston Street
Browning Street
Wadding Street
Stead Street
Rodney Road
Wingrave
Peabody Bldgs
Catesby Street
Barlow St
Crail Row
Flint Street
Dean's Buildings
Orb Street
English Martyrs RC Prim Sch
SE17
Morecambe Street
King and Queen Street
York Avenue
East Street
Walworth
Dawes Street
Newington Ind Est
Crampton Prim Sch
Crampton Street
Iliffe Street
Iliffe Yard
Amelia Street
Penton Place
Berryfield Rd
Manor Place
Offices
Occupation Rd
Walworth Road
Robert Browning Prim Sch
Blackwood St
Walworth Academy
Trafalgar Street
Sandford Row
Wooler Street
Aylesbury Road
Brettell St
Bronti Close
Bate Street
St Peter's CE Prim Sch
Portland Street
Burton Gr
Liverpool Grove
Merrow Street
Villa Street
Inville Road
Missenden
Roland Way
Michael Faraday Prim Sch
Penrose Street
Penrose Grove
Penrose House
Carter Pl
Cadiz Street
Walworth Place
Sutherland Walk
Sutherland Square
Macleod St
Carter Street
St Paul's CE Prim Sch
Lytham Street
Sondes St
Phelp Street
Queen's Row
Allot Gdns
Fielding Street
Pelier Park
Empress Street
Hopwood Road
Hambledon
Gayhurst
Lorrimore Square
Tarver Road
Marshland Cl
Sturgeon Rd
Pasley Cl
Borrett Cl
Matara Mews
Olney Rd

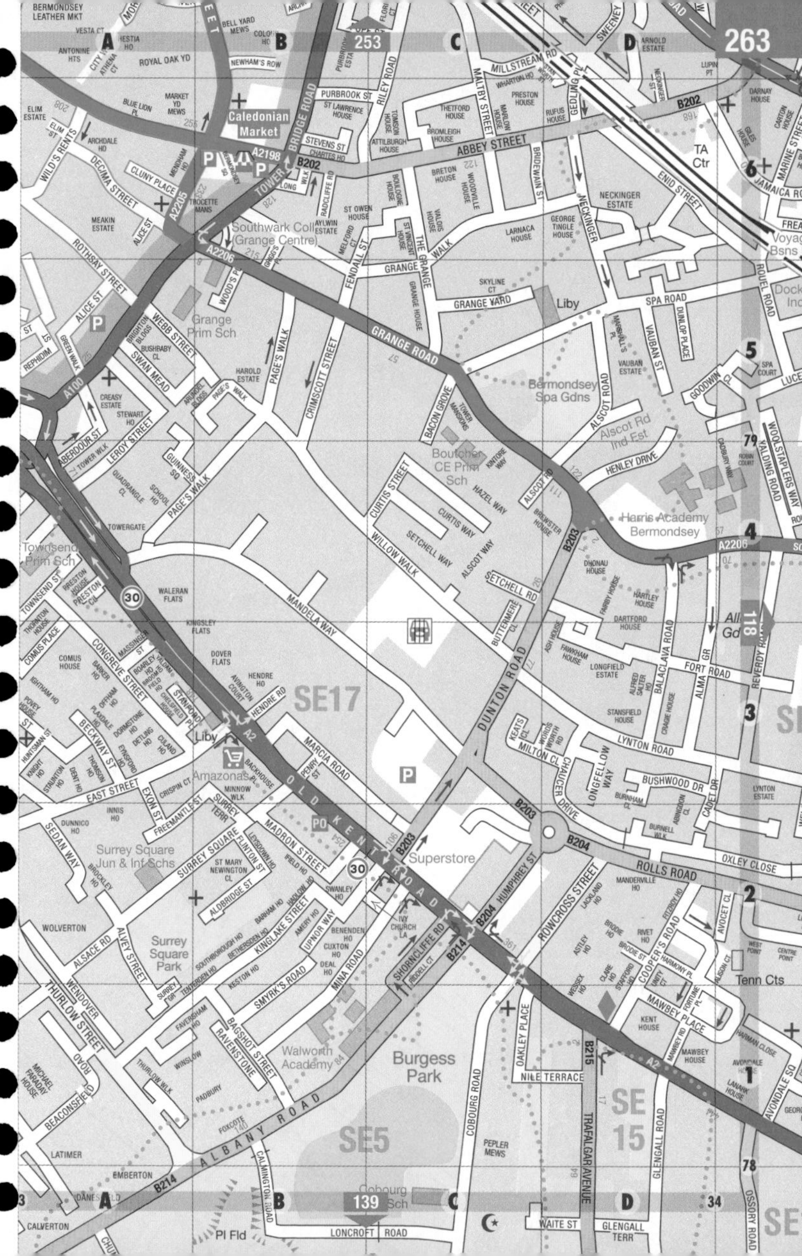
253
A
B
C
D
BERMONDSEY LEATHER MKT
VESTA CT
ANTONINE HTS
ROYAL OAK YD
BELL YARD MEWS
NEWHAM'S ROW
Caledonian Market
PURBROOK ST
RILEY ROAD
MILLSTREAM RD
ARNOLD ESTATE
MALTBY STREET
ST LAWRENCE HOUSE
STEVENS ST
ELIM ESTATE
BLUE LION PL
MARKET YD MEWS
WILD'S RENTS
DECIMA STREET
ARCHDALE HO
CLUNY PLACE
TOWER BRIDGE ROAD
A2198
B202
ABBEY STREET
BRETON HOUSE
BRIDEWAIN ST
NECKINGER
NECKINGER ESTATE
ENID STREET
TA Ctr
JAMAICA ROAD
MARINE STREET
DARNAY HOUSE
MEAKIN ESTATE
ALICE ST
A2205
TROCETTE MANS
Southwark Coll (Grange Centre)
A2206
ROTHSAY STREET
ST OWEN HOUSE
RADCLIFFE RD
AYLWIN ESTATE
MELFORD CT
FENDALL ST
GRANGE WALK
THE GRANGE
LARNACA HOUSE
GEORGE TINGLE HOUSE
Voyager Bsns Est
SKYLINE CT
GRANGE YARD
Liby
SPA ROAD
DUNLOP PLACE
VAUBAN ST
VAUBAN ESTATE
ROUEL ROAD
Dockley Ind
ALICE ST
P
Grange Prim Sch
WEBB STREET
BRIGHTON BLDGS
BUSHBABY CL
SWAN MEAD
GRANGE ROAD
PAGE'S WALK
CRIMSCOTT STREET
HAROLD ESTATE
GREEN WALK
REPHIDIM ST
A100
CREASY ESTATE
STEWART HO
LEROY STREET
ABERDOUR ST
TOWER WLK
BACON GROVE
TOWER MANSIONS
Bermondsey Spa Gdns
ALSCOT ROAD
Alscot Rd Ind Est
GOODWIN CL
SPA COURT
LUCEY
Boutcher CE Prim Sch
KINTORE WAY
HENLEY DRIVE
ALSCOT RD
CURTIS STREET
CURTIS WAY
HAZEL WAY
GUINNESS SQ
QUADRANGLE CL
SCHOOL HO
TOWERGATE
Harris Academy Bermondsey
BREWSTER HOUSE
WOOLSTAPLERS WAY
YALDING ROAD
CADBURY WAY
Townsend Prim Sch
SETCHELL WAY
ALSCOT WAY
WILLOW WALK
B203
A2206
4
5
6
79
TOWNSEND ST
PRESTON HOUSE
PRESTON CL
30
WALERAN FLATS
MANDELA WAY
SETCHELL RD
DHONAU HOUSE
HARTLEY HOUSE
DARTFORD HOUSE
BUTTERMERE CL
ASH HOUSE
FAWKHAM HOUSE
LONGFIELD ESTATE
BALACLAVA ROAD
ALMA GR
FORT ROAD
118
REVERDY ROAD
THORNTON HOUSE
COMUS PLACE
COMUS HOUSE
CONGREVE STREET
KINGSLEY FLATS
DOVER FLATS
AVINGTON COURT
HENDRE HO
HENDRE RD
DUNTON ROAD
SE17
ALFRED SALTER HO
STANSFIELD HOUSE
CRAGIE HOUSE
3
SE
ROARLEY HO
STANFORD PL
Liby
A2
MARCIA ROAD
KEATS CL
WORDSWORTH RD
MILTON CL
CHAUCER DRIVE
LONGFELLOW WAY
LYNTON ROAD
BUSHWOOD DR
CADET DR
LYNTON ESTATE
WELSFORD ST
BECKWAY ST
HUNTSMAN ST
EAST STREET
EXON ST
CRISPIN CT
Amazonas
BACKHOUSE PL
MINNOW WLK
OLD KENT ROAD
P
B203
BURNHAM CL
ABINGDON CL
BURNELL WLK
B204
OXLEY CLOSE
ROLLS ROAD
INNIS HO
DUNNICO HO
SEDAN WAY
FREEMANTLE ST
SURREY TERR
PO
MADRON STREET
106
Superstore
Surrey Square Jun & Inf Schs
SURREY SQUARE
ST MARY NEWINGTON CL
FLINTON ST
ALDBRIDGE ST
SWANLEY HO
HUMPHREY ST
ROWCROSS STREET
MANDERVILLE HO
2
WOLVERTON
ALSACE RD
ALVEY STREET
Surrey Square Park
KINGLAKE STREET
UPNOR WAY
IVY CHURCH LA
SHORNCLIFFE RD
B214
COOPER'S ROAD
AVOCET CL
HARMONY PL
Tenn Cts
THURLOW STREET
WENDOVER
SMYRK'S ROAD
MINA ROAD
KESTON HO
BENENDEN HO
CUXTON HO
DEAL HO
RIDDELL CT
OAKLEY PLACE
MAWBEY PLACE
KENT HOUSE
MAWBEY HOUSE
HARMAN CLOSE
AVONDALE SQ
1
MICHAEL FARADAY HOUSE
BEACONSFIELD ROAD
THURLOW WLK
WINSLOW
FAVERSHAM HO
BAGSHOT STREET
RAVENSTONE
PADBURY
Walworth Academy
Burgess Park
COBOURG ROAD
NILE TERRACE
B215
SE 15
GLENGALL ROAD
LATIMER
FOXCOTE
ALBANY ROAD
SE5
PEPLER MEWS
TRAFALGAR AVENUE
78
EMBERTON
B214
CALMINGTON ROAD
139
Cobourg Sch
34
OSSORY ROAD
CALVERTON
Pl Fld
LONCROFT ROAD
WAITE ST
GLENGALL TERR

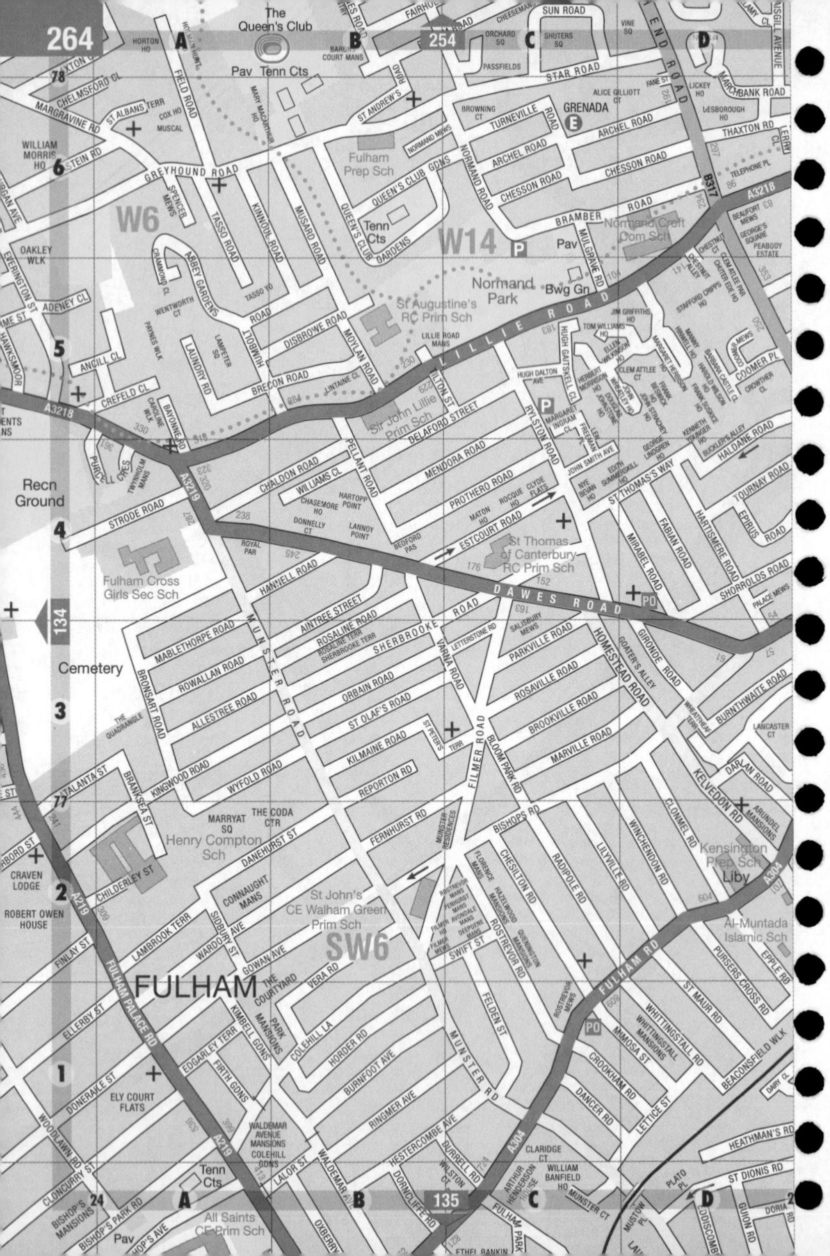

The Queen's Club
Pav Tenn Cts
W6
W14
SW6
FULHAM
GRENADA
Fulham Prep Sch
Normand Park
St Augustine's RC Prim Sch
Sir John Lillie Prim Sch
St Thomas of Canterbury RC Prim Sch
Fulham Cross Girls Sec Sch
Henry Compton Sch
St John's CE Walham Green Prim Sch
All Saints CE Prim Sch
Kensington Prep Sch
Al-Muntada Islamic Sch
Normand Croft Com Sch
Recn Ground
Cemetery
LILLIE ROAD
DAWES ROAD
FULHAM PALACE RD
FULHAM RD
MUNSTER ROAD
GREYHOUND ROAD
MARGRAVINE RD
STAR ROAD
ARCHEL ROAD
CHESSON ROAD
BRAMBER ROAD
FILMER ROAD
HOMESTEAD ROAD
KELVEDON RD
BURNTHWAITE ROAD
SHORROLDS ROAD
TOURNAY ROAD
HALDANE ROAD
STRODE ROAD
CHALDON ROAD
MENDORA ROAD
PROTHERO ROAD
ESTCOURT ROAD
DELAFORD STREET
BRECON ROAD
DISBROWE ROAD
MOYLAN ROAD
MUSARD ROAD
KINNOUL ROAD
TASSO ROAD
ABBEY GARDENS
FIELD ROAD
NORMAND ROAD
TURNEVILLE ROAD
SUN ROAD
A3218
A3219
A219
A304
B317
254
134
135

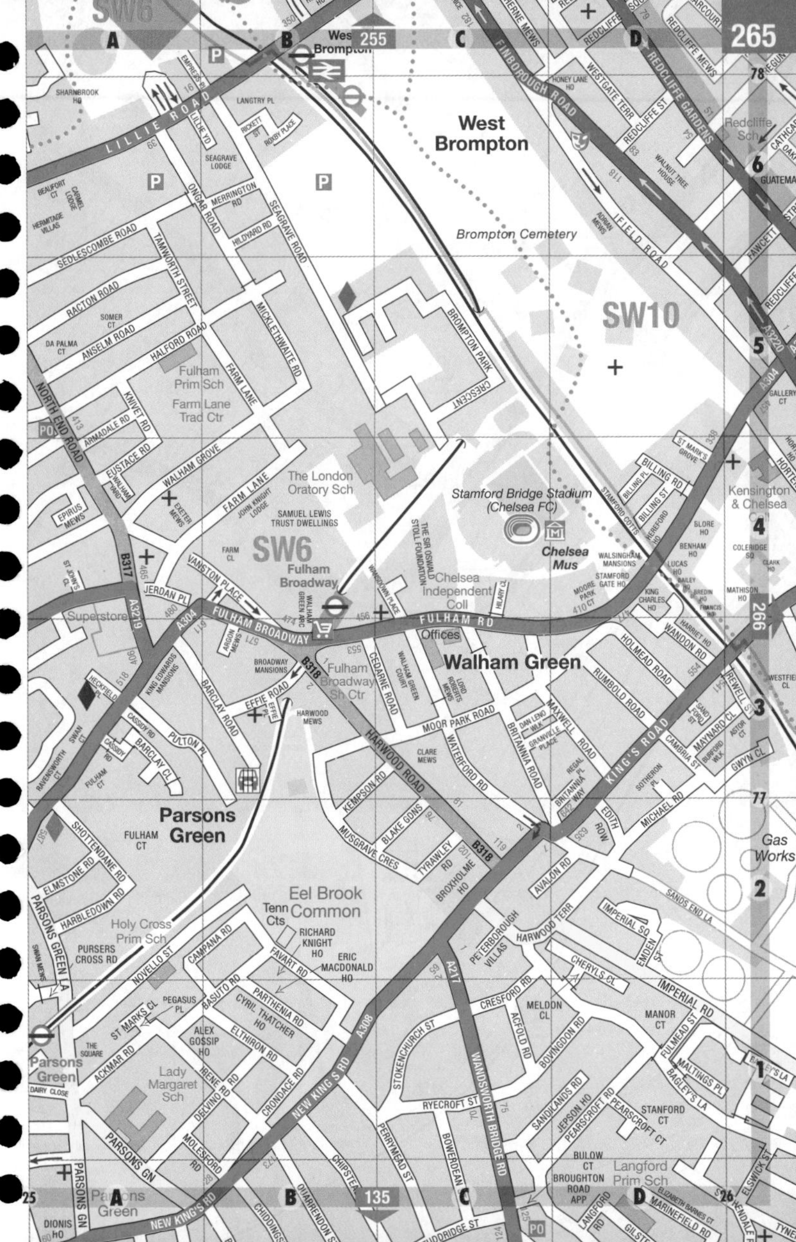

A
B
C
D
255
West Brompton
Brompton Cemetery
SW10
SW6
Stamford Bridge Stadium (Chelsea FC)
Chelsea Mus
Fulham Broadway
Walham Green
Parsons Green
Eel Brook Common
Gas Works
LILLIE ROAD
FINBOROUGH ROAD
REDCLIFFE GARDENS
IFIELD ROAD
NORTH END ROAD
FULHAM BROADWAY
FULHAM RD
KING'S ROAD
HARWOOD ROAD
NEW KING'S RD
WANDSWORTH BRIDGE RD
IMPERIAL RD
SEAGRAVE ROAD
BROMPTON PARK CRESCENT
The London Oratory Sch
Fulham Prim Sch
Farm Lane Trad Ctr
Kensington & Chelsea Coll
Chelsea Independent Coll
Fulham Broadway Sh Ctr
Holy Cross Prim Sch
Lady Margaret Sch
Langford Prim Sch
Redcliffe Sch
Superstore
Offices
135
266

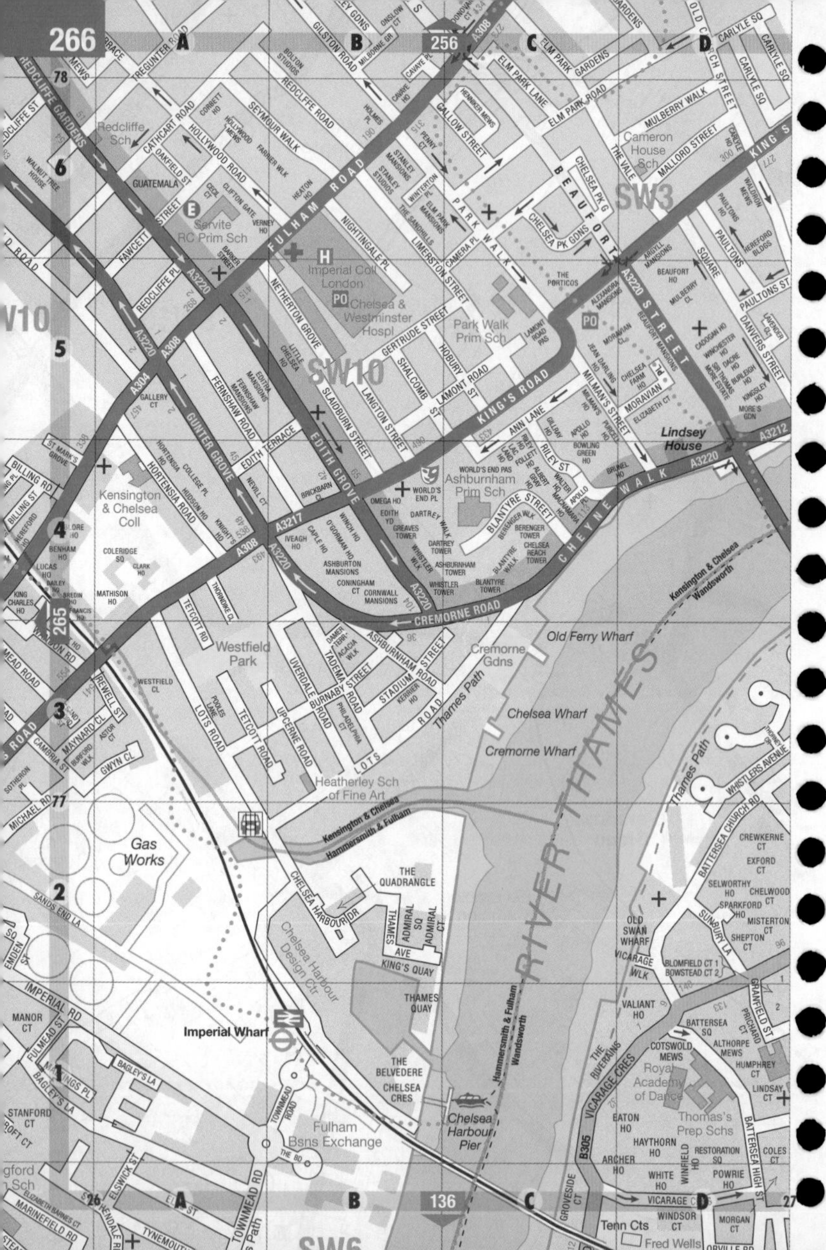
A
B
C
D
256
78
6
5
4
3
77
2
1
26
27
136
265
SW10
SW3
SW6
W10
FULHAM ROAD
A308
A3220
A304
A3217
A3212
B305
KING'S ROAD
CHEYNE WALK
CREMORNE ROAD
LOTS ROAD
GUNTER GROVE
EDITH GROVE
BEAUFORT STREET
REDCLIFFE GARDENS
REDCLIFFE ROAD
ELM PARK GARDENS
ELM PARK LANE
ELM PARK ROAD
OLD CHURCH STREET
CARLYLE SQ
MULBERRY WALK
MALLORD STREET
THE VALE
PARK WALK
LIMERSTON STREET
CALLOW STREET
GILSTON ROAD
SEYMOUR WALK
HOLLYWOOD ROAD
CATHCART ROAD
TREGUNTER ROAD
FAWCETT STREET
REDCLIFFE PL
NETHERTON GROVE
NIGHTINGALE PL
GERTRUDE STREET
SHALCOMB ST
LANGTON STREET
HOBURY ST
LAMONT ROAD
SLAIDBURN STREET
FERNSHAW ROAD
EDITH TERRACE
HORTENSIA ROAD
MILMAN'S STREET
RILEY ST
BLANTYRE STREET
DARTREY WALK
PAULTONS SQUARE
PAULTONS ST
DANVERS STREET
ASHBURNHAM ROAD
BURNABY STREET
TADEMA ROAD
UVERDALE ROAD
UPCERNE ROAD
TETCOTT ROAD
STADIUM STREET
CHELSEA HARBOUR DR
KING'S QUAY
THAMES QUAY
VICARAGE CRES
BATTERSEA CHURCH RD
BATTERSEA HIGH ST
SUNBURY LA
GRANFIELD ST
WHISTLERS AVENUE
IMPERIAL RD
SANDS END LA
TOWNMEAD RD
BAGLEY'S LA
MARINEFIELD RD
ELSWICK ST
TYNEMOUTH
Redcliffe Sch
Servite RC Prim Sch
Imperial Coll London
Chelsea & Westminster Hospl
Park Walk Prim Sch
Cameron House Sch
Ashburnham Prim Sch
Kensington & Chelsea Coll
Lindsey House
Westfield Park
Cremorne Gdns
Old Ferry Wharf
Chelsea Wharf
Cremorne Wharf
Heatherley Sch of Fine Art
Gas Works
Chelsea Harbour Design Ctr
Imperial Wharf
Chelsea Harbour Pier
Fulham Bsns Exchange
Royal Academy of Dance
Thomas's Prep Schs
Tenn Cts
Fred Wells
Thames Path
RIVER THAMES
Kensington & Chelsea
Hammersmith & Fulham
Wandsworth

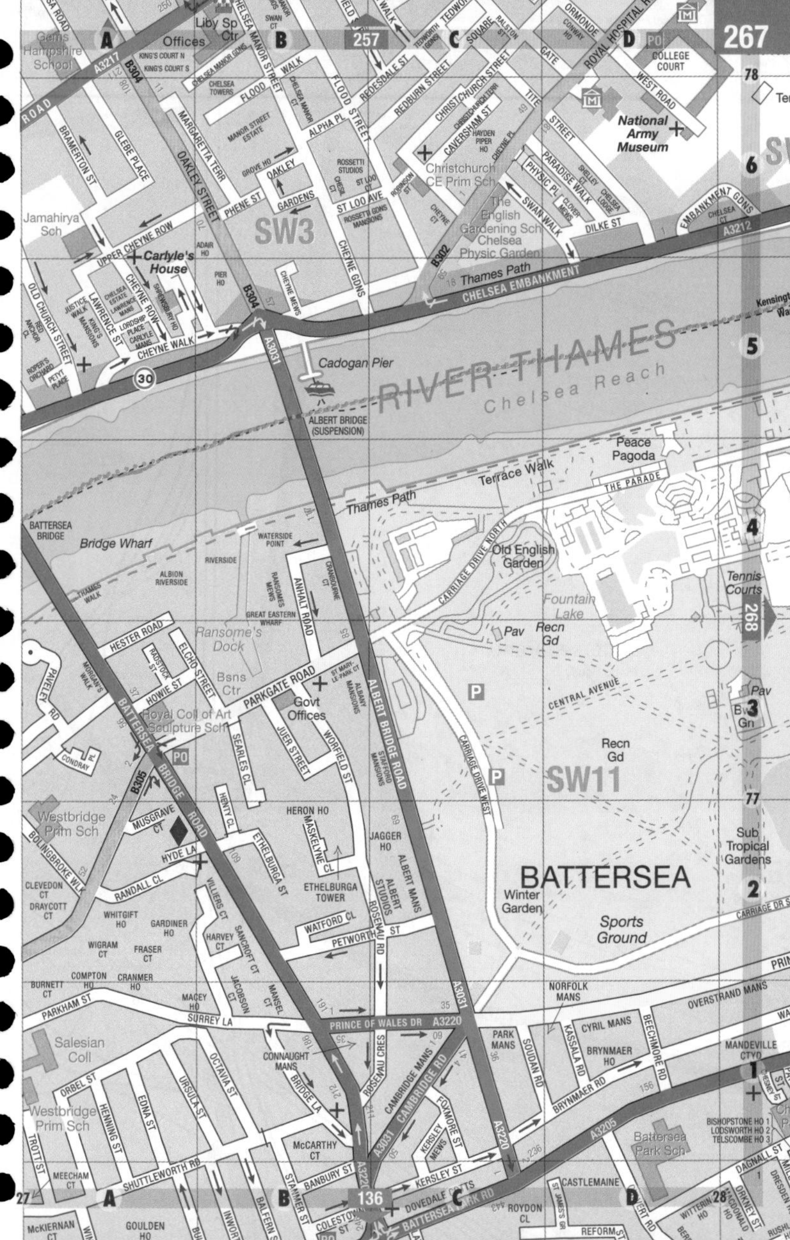

RIVER THAMES
Chelsea Reach
SW3
SW11
BATTERSEA
National Army Museum
Carlyle's House
Chelsea Physic Garden
The English Gardening Sch
Christchurch CE Prim Sch
Cadogan Pier
ALBERT BRIDGE (SUSPENSION)
BATTERSEA BRIDGE
Bridge Wharf
Peace Pagoda
Terrace Walk
Thames Path
Old English Garden
Fountain Lake
Recn Gd
Winter Garden
Sports Ground
Sub Tropical Gardens
Tennis Courts
Ransome's Dock
Bsns Ctr
Govt Offices
Royal Coll of Art Sculpture Sch
Westbridge Prim Sch
Salesian Coll
Battersea Park Sch
Jamahirya Sch
Gems Hampshire School
Liby Sp Ctr
Offices
COLLEGE COURT
CHELSEA EMBANKMENT
CHEYNE WALK
OAKLEY STREET
ALBERT BRIDGE ROAD
BATTERSEA BRIDGE ROAD
PARKGATE ROAD
PRINCE OF WALES DR
CARRIAGE DRIVE NORTH
CARRIAGE DRIVE WEST
CENTRAL AVENUE
THE PARADE
CAMBRIDGE RD
BATTERSEA PARK RD
ROYAL HOSPITAL ROAD
FLOOD STREET
CHEYNE ROW
OLD CHURCH STREET
SURREY LA
PARKHAM ST
A3031
A3220
A3212
A3205
B304
B302
B305
A3217
257
268
136

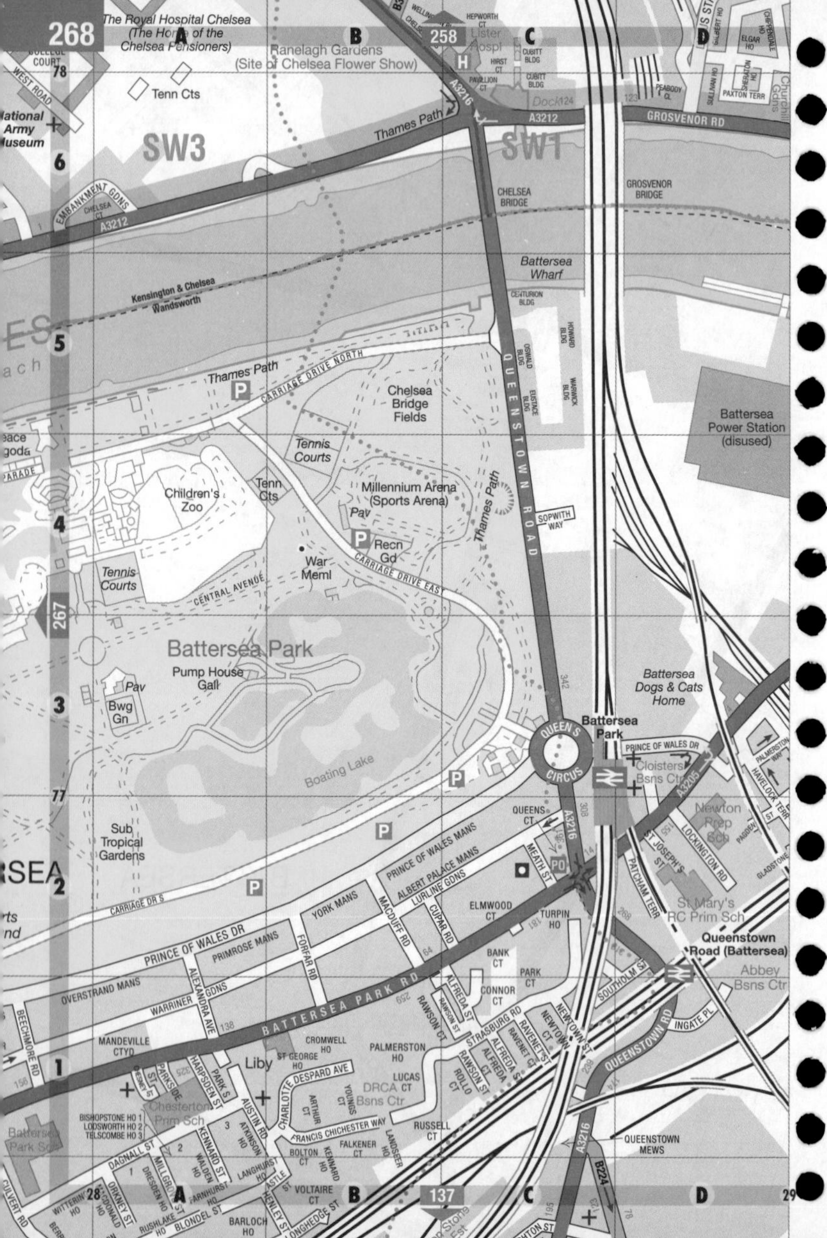

The Royal Hospital Chelsea
(The Home of the Chelsea Pensioners)
Ranelagh Gardens
(Site of Chelsea Flower Show)
258
Lister Hospl
Tenn Cts
SW3
SW1
Thames Path
A3216
A3212
GROSVENOR RD
CHELSEA BRIDGE
GROSVENOR BRIDGE
EMBANKMENT GDNS
Kensington & Chelsea
Wandsworth
Battersea Wharf
CARRIAGE DRIVE NORTH
Chelsea Bridge Fields
Tennis Courts
Children's Zoo
Millennium Arena
(Sports Arena)
QUEENSTOWN ROAD
SOPWITH WAY
Battersea Power Station
(disused)
War Meml
Recn Gd
CARRIAGE DRIVE EAST
CENTRAL AVENUE
Battersea Park
Pump House Gall
Boating Lake
Bwg Gn
Sub Tropical Gardens
Battersea Dogs & Cats Home
Battersea Park
QUEEN'S CIRCUS
PRINCE OF WALES DR
Cloisters Bsns Ctr
Newton Prep Sch
St Mary's RC Prim Sch
Queenstown Road (Battersea)
Abbey Bsns Ctr
PRINCE OF WALES MANS
ALBERT PALACE MANS
YORK MANS
PRIMROSE MANS
OVERSTRAND MANS
BATTERSEA PARK RD
ELMWOOD CT
TURPIN HO
BANK CT
PARK CT
CONNOR CT
NEWTOWN ST
QUEENSTOWN RD
INGATE PL
MANDEVILLE CTYD
Liby
DRCA Bsns Ctr
CHARLOTTE DESPARD AVE
FRANCIS CHICHESTER WAY
PALMERSTON HO
RUSSELL CT
QUEENSTOWN MEWS
Chesterton Prim Sch
Battersea Park Sch
267
137

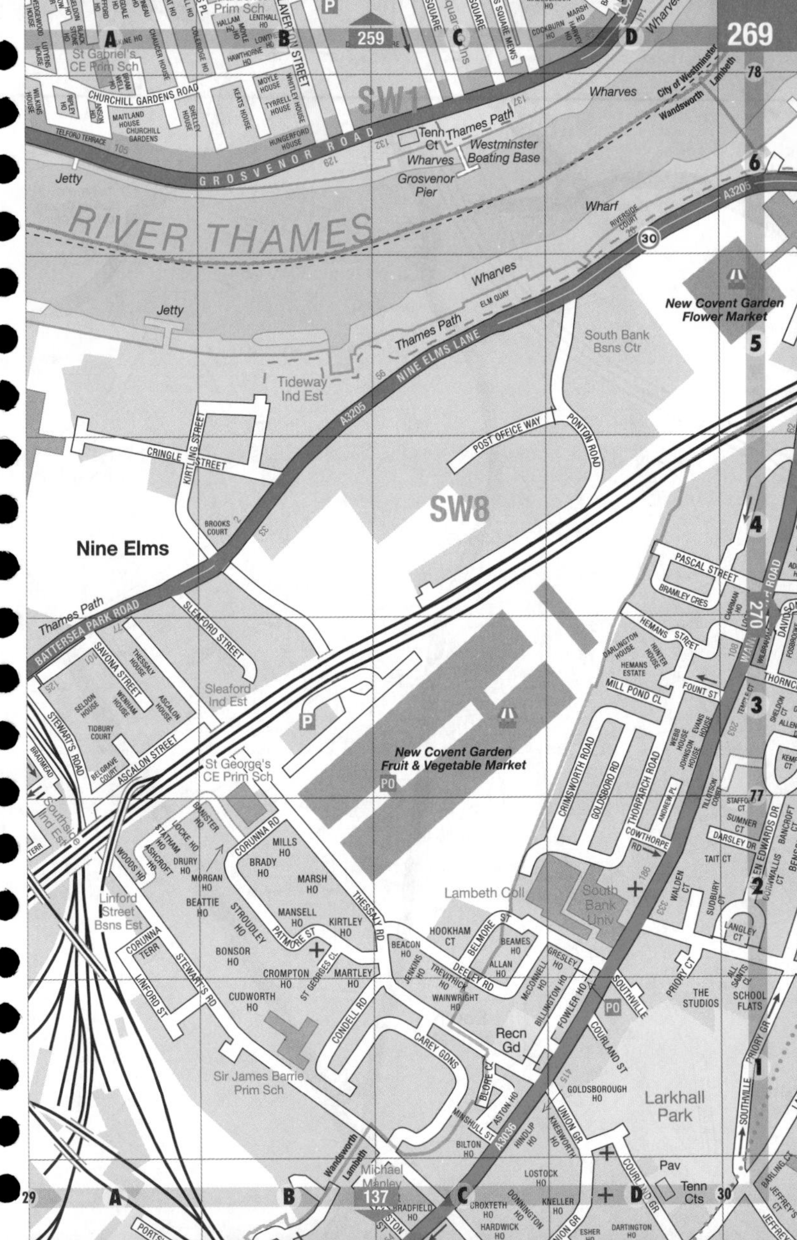
259
SW1
St Gabriel's CE Prim Sch
CHURCHILL GARDENS ROAD
CLAVERTON STREET
GROSVENOR ROAD
Thames Path
Westminster Boating Base
Grosvenor Pier
Wharves
Jetty
RIVER THAMES
Wharf
City of Westminster
Wandsworth
Lambeth
A3205
New Covent Garden Flower Market
South Bank Bsns Ctr
NINE ELMS LANE
Tideway Ind Est
POST OFFICE WAY
PONTON ROAD
CRINGLE STREET
KIRTLING STREET
SW8
Nine Elms
BATTERSEA PARK ROAD
SLEAFORD STREET
SAVONA STREET
ASCALON STREET
Sleaford Ind Est
STEWART'S ROAD
St George's CE Prim Sch
New Covent Garden Fruit & Vegetable Market
PASCAL STREET
BRAMLEY CRES
HEMANS STREET
MILL POND CL
CRIMSWORTH ROAD
GOLDSBORO RD
THORPARCH ROAD
COWTHORPE RD
Lambeth Coll
South Bank Univ
CORUNNA RD
THESSALY RD
PATMORE ST
Linford Street Bsns Est
LINFORD ST
DEELEY RD
BELMORE ST
CONDELL RD
CAREY GDNS
Recn Gd
COURLAND ST
Sir James Barrie Prim Sch
A3036
Larkhall Park
PRIORY GR
SOUTHVILLE
THE STUDIOS
SCHOOL FLATS
Michael Manley
137
Tenn Cts
Pav
29
30
A
B
C
D
1
2
3
4
5
6
77
78

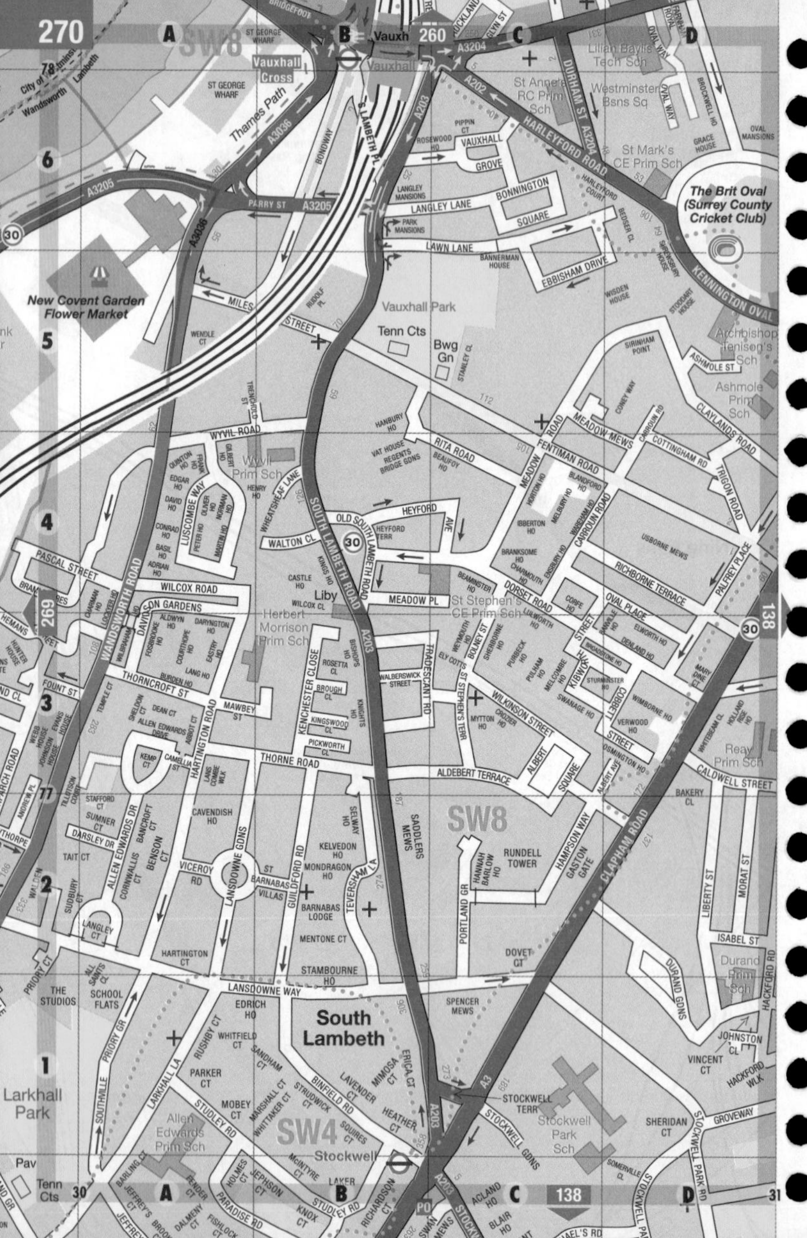
Vauxhall
Vauxhall Cross
St George Wharf
Thames Path
New Covent Garden Flower Market
Vauxhall Park
Tenn Cts
Bwg Gn
The Brit Oval (Surrey County Cricket Club)
Kennington Oval
Harleyford Road
Durham St
Lilian Baylis Tech Sch
St Anne's RC Prim Sch
Westminster Bsns Sq
St Mark's CE Prim Sch
Vauxhall Grove
Bonnington Square
Langley Lane
Lawn Lane
Ebbisham Drive
Miles Street
Parry St
Bondway
S Lambeth Pl
Archbishop Tenison's Sch
Ashmole St
Ashmole Prim Sch
Claylands Road
Meadow Mews
Fentiman Road
Meadow Road
Rita Road
Carroun Road
Cottingham Rd
Trigon Road
Usborne Mews
Richborne Terrace
Palfrey Place
Wyvil Road
Wyvil Prim Sch
Wheatsheaf Lane
South Lambeth Road
Old South Lambeth Road
Heyford Ave
Walton Cl
Luscombe Way
Pascal Street
Wilcox Road
Davidson Gardens
Wandsworth Road
Thorncroft St
Mawbey St
Hartington Road
Meadow Pl
St Stephen's CE Prim Sch
Dorset Road
Oval Place
Kibworth Street
Cobbett Street
Wilkinson Street
Albert Square
Aldebert Terrace
Tradescant Rd
Walberswick Street
Kenchester Close
Herbert Morrison Prim Sch
Liby
Thorne Road
SW8
Saddlers Mews
Rundell Tower
Hampson Way
Gaston Gate
Clapham Road
Caldwell Street
Reay Prim Sch
Bakery Cl
Liberty St
Morat St
Isabel St
Durand Prim Sch
Durand Gdns
Hackford Rd
Lansdowne Gdns
Viceroy Rd
St Barnabas Villas
Guildford Rd
Teversham La
Portland Gr
Dovet Ct
Lansdowne Way
Spencer Mews
South Lambeth
Priory Gr
Larkhall La
Larkhall Park
Southville
Studley Rd
Allen Edwards Prim Sch
SW4
Stockwell
Stockwell Park Sch
Stockwell Gdns
Stockwell Terr
Stockwell Park Rd
Groveway
Sheridan Ct
Vincent Ct
Johnston Cl
Hackford Wlk
Binfield Rd
Paradise Rd
Richardson Ct
Stockwell Rd
A3
A203
A202
A3204
A3205
A3036
SW8

260
269
138
138

Index

Place name May be abbreviated on the map

Location number Present when a number indicates the place's position in a crowded area of mapping

Locality, town or village Shown when more than one place has the same name

Postcode district District for the indexed place

Map page number and grid square References to the large-scale maps on pages 229–270 are underlined in red

Example: **Church Rd** 6 Beckenham BR2....**53** C6 **228** C6

Cities, towns and villages are listed in CAPITAL LETTERS. **Public and commercial buildings** are highlighted in magenta. **Places of interest** are highlighted in blue with a star★

Abbreviations used in the index

Acad	**Academy**	Ct	**Court**	Hts	**Heights**	Pl	**Place**
App	**Approach**	Ctr	**Centre**	Ind	**Industrial**	Prec	**Precinct**
Arc	**Arcade**	Ctry	**Country**	Inst	**Institute**	Prom	**Promenade**
Ave	**Avenue**	Cty	**County**	Int	**International**	Rd	**Road**
Bglw	**Bungalow**	Dr	**Drive**	Intc	**Interchange**	Recn	**Recreation**
Bldg	**Building**	Dro	**Drove**	Junc	**Junction**	Ret	**Retail**
Bsns, Bus	**Business**	Ed	**Education**	L	**Leisure**	Sh	**Shopping**
Bvd	**Boulevard**	Emb	**Embankment**	La	**Lane**	Sq	**Square**
Cath	**Cathedral**	Est	**Estate**	Liby	**Library**	St	**Street**
Cir	**Circus**	Ex	**Exhibition**	Mdw	**Meadow**	Sta	**Station**
Cl	**Close**	Gd	**Ground**	Meml	**Memorial**	Terr	**Terrace**
Cnr	**Corner**	Gdn	**Garden**	Mkt	**Market**	TH	**Town Hall**
Coll	**College**	Gn	**Green**	Mus	**Museum**	Univ	**University**
Com	**Community**	Gr	**Grove**	Orch	**Orchard**	Wk, Wlk	**Walk**
Comm	**Common**	H	**Hall**	Pal	**Palace**	Wr	**Water**
Cott	**Cottage**	Ho	**House**	Par	**Parade**	Yd	**Yard**
Cres	**Crescent**	Hospl	**Hospital**	Pas	**Passage**		
Cswy	**Causeway**	HQ	**Headquarters**	Pk	**Park**		

Index of towns, villages, streets, hospitals, industrial estates, railway stations, schools, shopping centres, universities and places of interest

176 Gall★ NW5.......**71** A2
201 Bishopgate EC2 **243** B4

A

Aaron Ct BR3....... **207** D6
Aaron Hill Rd E6.....**100** C2
Abady Ho SW1...... **259** D4
Abberley Mews 9 SW8..............**137** B2
Abberton IG8.........**37** C5
Abbess Cl
11 Newham E6 ..... **100** A2
Streatham SW2..... **160** D3
Abbeville Mews 3 SW4............. **137** D1
Abbeville Rd
Clapham Pk SW4.... **159** C6
Hornsey N8 ....**49** D5
Abbey Ave HA0 ....**88** A5
Abbey Bsns Ctr SW8....... **137** B4 **268** D2
Abbey Cl Hayes UB3 ..**106** B5
Northolt UB5 ....**85** B4
Pinner HA5...........**40** C6
Abbey Coll London SW1........**115** B3 **258** C5
Abbey Cres DA17 ....**125** C2
Abbey Ct
6 Bedford Pk W12 .. **111** C3
Camberwell SE17.... **262** B1
Church End N3........**47** C6
Abbey Ct *continued*
5 Edgware HA8 ......**26** D5
Hampton TW12 ..... **173** C3
St John's Wood NW8 . **229** A4
Twickenham TW2.....**152** B2
Abbeydale Rd HA0 ....**88** C6
Abbey Dr SW17 ......**181** A5
Abbeyfield Cl CR4....**180** C1
Abbeyfield Rd SE16 ..**118** C2
Abbeyfields Cl NW10..**88** C5
Abbey Gdns
10 Bermondsey SE16 .... **118** A2
Chislehurst BR7..... **188** C2
St John's Wood NW8 ....**92** A5 **229** B3
West Kensington W6 ...... **135** A6 **264** A5
Abbey Gr SE2........**124** B2
Abbeyhill Rd DA15 ...**168** C2
Abbey Ho
Newham E15 ....**98** C5
St John's Wood NW8 . **229** B2
Abbey Ind Est
Ealing HA0...........**88** B6
Mitcham CR4 .... **202** D4
Abbey La
Beckenham BR3..... **185** C3
Mill Meads E15 ....**98** B5
Abbey Lane Commercial Est 1 E15 ....**98** C5
Abbey Lo
Bromley SE12........**187** B6
Abbey Lo *continued*
1 Ealing W5 .... **109** C6
Lisson Gr NW8...... **230** B1
Abbey Manufacturing Est HA0 ....**88** B6
Abbey Mews
Brentford TW7........**131** B4
Walthamstow E17 .....**53** C4
Abbey Mount DA17 ..**125** B1
Abbey Orchard St SW1 ...... **115** D3 **259** D6
Abbey Orchard Street Est SW1 .... **259** D6
Abbey Par
Ealing NW10 ....**88** B4
Merton SW19....... **180** A3
Abbey Park Ind Est IG11............. **101** A6
Abbey Pk BR3 ....**185** C3
Abbey Prim Sch SM4.............. **201** C2
Abbey Rd
Barking IG11....... **100** D6
Bexley DA7......... **147** A1
Croydon CR0 .... **220** D5
Enfield EN1 ....**17** C6
Erith DA17 .... **125** A3
Ilford IG2...........**57** B4
Lower Halliford TW17 **192** C1
Merton SW19....... **180** A2
Newham E15 ....**98** C5
St John's Wood NW8 ....**92** A5 **229** A4
Abbey Rd *continued*
Wembley NW10.......**88** D5
Abbey Sports Ctr IG11.............. **101** A6
Abbey St
Bermondsey SE1 ...... **117** D3 **263** C6
Newham E13 ....**99** A3
Abbey Terr SE2 ......**124** C2
Abbey Trad Est SE26. .**185** B5
Abbey View NW7......**11** D1
Abbey Wlk KT8 ..... **195** D5
ABBEY WOOD **124** B3
Abbey Wood Rd SE2 .**124** C2
Abbey Wood Sch SE2............... **124** A3
Abbey Wood Sta SE2............... **124** C3
Abbot Cl HA4 ....**62** D5
Abbot Ct SW8 ...... **270** A3
Abbot Ho 14 E14.... **119** D6
Abbotsbury Cl
Kensington W14 ......**113** B4 **244** C1
Mill Meads E15 ....**98** A5
Abbotsbury Gdns HA5................**40** C3
Abbotsbury Ho W14. **244** B2
Abbotsbury Mews SE15..............**140** C2
Abbotsbury Prim Sch SM4.............. **201** D4
Abbotsbury Rd
Coney Hall BR2, BR4............. **224** D6
Kensington W14 ......**113** B4 **244** C1
Morden SM4 .... **201** D5
Abbots Cl BR5 ....**211** A1
Abbots Ct SE25 ......**205** C6
Abbots Dr HA2........**63** C6
Abbotsfield Sch UB10 **82** D5
Abbotsford Ave N15...**51** A5
Abbotsford Gdns IG8 .**37** A3
Abbotsford Rd IG3....**80** B6
Abbots Gdns N2 ......**48** B5
Abbots Gn CR0, CR2 . **222** D2
Abbots Green CR2 .. **222** D2
Abbotshade Rd 15 SE16............. **118** D5
Abbotshall Ave N14...**15** C1
Abbotshall Rd SE6 ...**164** B2
Abbots Ho
Kensington W14..... **254** C5
Pimlico SW1........ **259** C1
Walthamstow E17 .....**35** B1
Abbots La SE1........**117** C5 **253** B3
Abbotsleigh Cl SM2. **217** D1
Abbotsleigh Rd SW16 ....**181** C5

Abbotsmede Cl
TW1 152 D2
Abbots Pk SW2 160 C3
Abbot's Pl NW6 91 D6
Abbots Rd
Burnt Oak HA8 27 B3
Newham E6 99 D6
Abbot St E8 73 D2
Abbots Terr N8 50 A3
Abbotstone Ho 4 E5 74 A6
Abbotstone Rd
SW15 134 C2
Abbotsview Ct NW7 12 A1
Abbots Way BR3 207 A4
Abbotswell Rd SE4 163 B6
Abbotswood Cl 7
DA17 125 A3
Abbotswood Gdns
IG5 56 B6
Abbotswood Rd
London SE22 139 C1
Streatham SW16 159 D1
Abbotswood Way
UB3 106 B5
Abbott Ave SW20 178 D2
Abbott Cl
Hampton TW12 173 A4
Northolt UB5 63 B2
Abbott Ho SW12 158 D4
Abbott Rd E14 98 B1
Abbotts Cl
Canonbury N1 73 A2
Romford RM7 59 D6
Woolwich SE28 124 C6
Abbotts Cres
Chingford E4 36 B6
Enfield EN2 4 D3
Abbotts Ct HA2 64 B6
Abbotts Dr HA0 65 B6
Abbotts Park Rd E10 54 A2
Abbotts Rd Barnet EN5 1 D1
Cheam SM3 217 A4
Mitcham CR4 203 C5
Southall UB1 107 A5
Abbotts Wharf 4
E14 97 C1
Abbott's Wlk DA7 146 D5
Abchurch La EC2,
EC4 117 B6 252 D6
Abchurch Yd EC4 252 C6
Abdale Rd W12 112 B5
Abel Ho
7 Kennington
SE11 138 C6
1 Woolwich SE18 123 A2
Abenglen Ind Est
UB3 105 B4
Aberavon Rd E3 97 A4
Abercairn Rd SW16 181 C3
Aberconway Rd
SM4 201 D5
Abercorn Cl
Finchley NW7 29 A3
St John's Wood
NW8 92 A4 229 A2
Abercorn Cres HA2 41 D1
Abercorn Dell WD23 8 A2
Abercorn Gdns
Harrow HA3 43 D2
Ilford RM6 58 B3
Abercorn Gr HA4 39 B5
Abercorn Mans NW8 229 B3
Abercorn Mews 10
TW10 132 B1
Abercorn Pl
NW8 92 A5 229 A3
Abercorn Rd
Finchley NW7 29 A3
Stanmore HA7 25 C3
Abercorn Sch
NW8 92 A5 229 B3
Abercorn Trad Est
HA0 87 D6
Abercorn Way SE1 118 A1
Abercorn Wlk
NW8 92 A4 229 A2
Abercrombie Dr EN1 6 A4
Abercrombie Ho 1
W12 112 B6
Abercrombie St
SW11 136 C3
Aberdale Ct 22 SE16 118 D4
Aberdare Cl BR4 224 A6
Aberdare Gdns
Finchley NW7 28 D3
South Hampstead NW6 69 D1
Aberdare Rd EN3 6 C1
Aberdeen Cotts HA7 25 C3
Aberdeen Ct
Canonbury N5 73 A3
Paddington W2 236 C5
Aberdeen Ctr N5 73 A3
Aberdeen La N5 73 A3
Aberdeen Mans WC1 240 A6
Aberdeen Par N18 34 B5
Aberdeen Pk N5 73 A3
Aberdeen Pl
NW8 92 B3 236 C6
Aberdeen Rd
Canonbury N5 73 A4
Croydon CR0 221 B4
Dudden Hill NW10 67 D3
Edmonton N18 34 B5
Harrow HA3 24 D1
Aberdeen Terr SE3 142 B3
Aberdour Rd IG3 80 B6
Aberdour St
SE1 117 C2 263 A4
Aberfeldy Ho SE5 138 D5
Aberfeldy St E14 98 A1
Aberford Gdns SE18 144 A4
Aberfoyle Rd SW16 181 D4
Abergeldie Rd SE12 165 B5
Abernethy Rd SE13 142 C1
Abersham Rd E8 73 D3
Abery St SE18 123 C2
Ability Plaza 8 E8 73 D1
Ability Twrs EC1 235 A2
Abingdon W14 254 D3
Abingdon Cl
Fulham SE1 263 D2
Hillingdon UB10 82 B6
Kentish Town NW1 71 D2
North Cheam KT4 216 B5
Wimbledon SW19 180 A4
Abingdon Ct
Earl's Ct W8 255 B5
Edgware HA8 26 A6
Upper Tooting SW17 180 D4
Abingdon Gdns W8 255 B5
Abingdon Ho
Bromley BR1 187 B3
Spitalfields E2 243 C6
Abingdon Lo
2 Barnet EN5 1 A1
Bromley BR2 186 D1
Abingdon Mans W8 255 A6
Abingdon Rd
Finchley N3 30 A1
Kensington
W8 113 C3 255 B5
Thornton Heath
SW16 182 A2
Abingdon St
SW1 116 A3 260 A6
Abingdon Villas
W8 113 C3 255 B5
Abinger Cl
Barking IG11 80 A4
Bickley BR1 210 A6
New Addington CR0 224 A2
Wallington SM6 220 A3
Abinger Ct
3 Ealing W5 109 C6
Thornton Heath CR0 204 D2
Wallington SM6 220 A3
Abinger Gdns TW7 130 C2
Abinger Gr SE8 141 B6
Abinger Ho
Borough The SE1 252 C1
2 Kingston u T KT2 176 D3
Abinger Mews W9 91 C3
Abinger Rd W4 111 C3
Abington Ho NW11 48 A3
Ablett St SE16 118 C1
Abney Gdns 5 N16 73 D6
Abney Park Cemetery★
N16 73 C6
Abney Park Ct N16 73 D6
Aborfield 6 NW5 71 C3
Aboyne Dr SW20 178 A1
Aboyne Rd
Neasden NW10 67 C5
Wandsworth SW17 158 B1
Abraham Cl WD19 22 B6
Abraham Cohen Ct
IG1 56 C3
Abraham Fisher Ho 2
E12 78 C3
Abridge Way IG11 102 B5
Abyssinia Cl SW11 136 C1
Abyssinia Rd SW11 136 C1
Acacia Ave
Brentford TW8 131 B5
East Finchley N2 47 D6
Hayes UB3 83 D1
Littleton TW17 192 C4
Ruislip HA4 40 B2
Tottenham N17 33 B3
Wembley HA9 66 A3
Yiewsley UB7 104 B6
Acacia Bsns Ctr 1
E11 76 C5
Acacia Cl
Penge SE20 184 A1
Petts Wood BR5 211 B4
Rotherhithe SE8 119 A2
Stanmore HA7 24 C4
Acacia Ct Harrow HA1 41 D3
5 West Norwood
SW16 182 C5
Acacia Dr SM3 201 C1
Acacia Gdns
St John's Wood
NW8 229 D4
West Wickham BR4 224 A6
Acacia Gr
Dulwich SE21 161 B2
Kingston u T KT3 199 C6
Acacia Ho
Brockley SE4 141 B1
1 New Malden KT3 199 C5
Stoke Newington N16 73 B6
Wood Green N22 32 C2
Acacia Lo 6 N3 29 B1
Acacia Pl NW8 92 B5 229 D4
Acacia Rd Acton W3 111 A6
Beckenham BR3 207 B6
Enfield EN2 5 B4
Hampton TW12 173 C4
Leyton E11 76 C6
Mitcham CR4 181 B1
St John's Wood
NW8 92 B5 229 D4
Thornton Heath
SW16 182 A2
Walthamstow E17 53 A3
Wood Green N22 32 C2
Acacias Lo EN4 14 B6
Acacias The EN4 14 B6
Acacia Way DA15 167 D3
Acacia Wlk SW10 266 B3
Academia Way N17 33 C4
Academic Coll of London
HA0 65 D5
Academy Ct 13 E2 96 C4
Academy Gdns
Croydon CR0 205 D1
Kensington W8 245 A2
Northolt UB5 84 D5
Academy Pl
Hounslow TW7 130 C5
Woolwich SE18 144 C4
Academy Rd SE18 144 B5
Academy Sch The 9
NW3 70 B4
Academy The 2 N19 49 C1
Acad of Live & Recorded
Arts SW18 158 B5
Acanthus Dr SE1 118 A1
Acanthus Rd SW11 137 A2
Accadia Ct NW9 67 A6
Accommodation Rd
NW11 47 B1
Ace Par KT9 214 A5
Acer Ave UB4 85 A2
Acer Ct
2 Cricklewood NW2 68 D4
3 Enfield EN3 7 A2
Acer Rd E8 73 D1
Acers BR7 188 A3
Acfold Rd SW6 265 C1
Achilles Cl SE1 118 A1
Achilles Ho 16 E2 96 B5
Achilles Rd NW6 69 C3
Achilles St SE14 141 A5
Achilles Way W1 248 B3
Acklam Rd W10 91 B2
Acklington Dr NW9 27 C2
Ackmar Rd
SW6 135 C4 265 A1
Ackroyd Dr E3 97 C2
Ackroyd Rd SE23 163 A4
Acland Burghley Sch
NW5 71 B4
Acland Cl SE18 145 B5
Acland Cres SE5 139 B2
Acland Ho SW9 138 B3
Acland Rd NW2 68 B2
Acock Gr UB5 64 A4
Acol Cres HA4 62 B3
Acol Ct 3 NW6 69 C1
Acol Rd NW6 69 D1
Aconbury Rd RM9 102 B6
Acorn Cl Chingford E4 35 D5
Chislehurst BR7 189 A5
Enfield EN2 4 D4
1 Hampton TW12 173 D4
Stanmore HA7 25 B3
Acorn Ct 5 Bow E3 97 C5
Hampton TW12 173 B5
Ilford IG2 57 C4
Upton Pk E6 78 A1
Wood Green N11 31 D4
Acorn Gdns
North Acton W3 89 B2
South Norwood SE19 183 D2
Acorn Gr
Harlington UB3 127 D5
Ruislip HA4 61 D4
Acorn Par 7 SE15 140 B5
Acorn Production Ctr
N7 72 A1
Acorns The 21
SW19 156 D3
Acorns Way KT10 212 A3
Acorn Way
Beckenham BR3 208 A4
Forest Hill SE23 162 D1
Orpington BR6 226 D4
Acorn Wharf SE15 140 A6
Acorn Wlk SE16 119 A5
Acqua Ho TW9 132 D5
Acre Dr SE22 140 A1
Acrefield Ho 4 NW4 46 D5
Acre La Brixton SW2 138 B1
Wallington SM5 219 A4
Acre Path UB5 63 A2
Acre Rd
Dagenham RM10 81 D1
Kingston u T KT2 176 B2
Mitcham SW19 180 B4
Acre Way HA6 22 A2
Acris St SW18 158 A6
ACS Hillingdon
International Sch
UB10 82 B6
Action Ct TW15 171 A2
ACTON 111 B5
Acton Bsns Ctr NW10 89 B3
Acton Central Ind Est 4
W3 110 D5
Acton Central Sta
W3 111 B5
Acton Cl N9 18 A2
ACTON GREEN 111 A2
Acton High Sch W3 110 C4
Acton Hill Mews
W3 110 D5
Acton Ho 5 Acton W3 89 A1
16 Haggerston E8 95 D6
Acton La
Acton Green W4 111 A2
Acton W3 111 A4
Harlesden NW10 89 B5
Acton Main Line Sta
W3 89 A1
Acton Mews E8 95 D6
Acton Park Ind Est
W3 111 B4
Acton St WC1 94 B4 233 C1
Acton Town Sta W3 110 C4
Acton Vale Ind Pk
W3 111 D5
Acton & West London
Coll 16 W3 110 D5
Acuba Ho SW18 157 D3
Acuba Rd SW18 157 D2
Acworth Cl N9 18 C4
Acworth Ho 1 SE18 144 D6
Ada Ct Islington N1 235 A5
St John's Wood
W9 92 A4 229 B1
Ada Gdns
Plaistow E15 98 D6
South Bromley E14 98 B1
Ada Ho 23 E2 96 A6
Adair Cl SE25 206 B6
Adair Ho SW3 267 B6
Adair Rd W10 91 A3
Adair Twr 7 W10 91 A3
Ada Kennedy Ct 6
SE10 142 A5
Ada Lewis Ho HA9 66 B4
Adam Cl SE6 185 C6
Adam Ct
Newington SE11 261 C3
15 Sutton SM1 218 A4
Adam & Eve Ct W1 239 B2
Adam & Eve Mews
W8 113 C3 255 B6
Adamfields NW3 70 B1
Adam Lo N21 16 B6
Adam Rd E4 35 B4
Adams Bridge Bsns Ctr
HA9 66 D3
Adams Cl Finchley N3 29 C3
Surbiton KT5 198 B3
Wembley Pk NW9 66 D6
Adams Ct E17 53 A3
Adams Gardens Est 5
SE16 118 C4
Adams Ho
3 South Bromley
E14 98 B1
3 Streatham SW16 181 C5
Adams Mews
Upper Tooting
SW17 158 D2
Wood Green N22 32 B3
Adamson Ct N2 48 C6
Adamson Rd
Hampstead NW3 70 B1
Newham E16 99 A1
Adamson Way BR3 208 A4
Adams Pl N7 72 B3
Adams Qtr TW8 131 C6
Adams Rd
Beckenham BR3 207 A4
Tottenham N17 33 B1
Adamsrill Cl EN1 17 B5
Adamsrill Prim Sch
SE26 163 A1
Adamsrill Rd SE26 185 A6
Adam's Row
W1 115 A6 248 B5
Adams Sq DA6 147 A2
Adam St
WC2 116 A6 250 B5
Adams Way CR0 206 A3
Adams Wlk 11 KT1 176 A1
Adam Wlk SW6 134 C5
Ada Pl E2 96 A6
Ada Rd
Camberwell SE5 139 C5
Wembley HA0, HA9 65 D5
Adare Wlk SW16,
SW2 160 B2
Ada St E8 96 B6
Adcot Wlk 6 BR6 227 D4
Adderley Gdns SE9 188 C6
Adderley Gr SW11 159 A6
Adderley Rd HA3 24 D2
Adderley St E14 98 A1
Addey Ho SE8 141 B5
Addey & Stanhope Sch
11 SE14 141 C4
ADDINGTON 223 C3
Addington Ct 7
SW14 133 B2
Addington Dr N12 30 B4
Addington Gr SE26 185 A6
Addington Ho 13
SW9 138 B3
Addington Rd Bow E3 97 C4
Newham E16 98 C3
Stroud Green N4 50 C3
Thornton Heath CR0 204 C1
West Wickham BR4 224 C6
West Wickham BR4,
CR0 224 B4
Addington Sq SE5 139 B5
Addington St
SE1 116 B4 250 D1
Addington Village Rd
CR0 223 C3
Addington Village Sta
CR0 223 C2
Addis Cl EN3 6 D4
ADDISCOMBE 206 A1
Addiscombe Ave
CR0 206 A2
Addiscombe Cl HA3 43 C4
Addiscombe Court Rd
CR0 221 C6
Addiscombe Ct UB10 83 A3
Addiscombe Rd CR0 222 B6

Addiscombe Sta
CR0 206 A1
Addis Ho 15 E1 96 C2
Addison Ave
Hounslow TW3 130 A4
Notting Hill
W11 113 A5 244 A3
Southgate N14 15 C5
Addison Bridge Pl
W14 113 B2 254 C4
Addison Cl
Northwood HA6 22 A2
Orpington BR5 211 A3
Addison Cres
W14 113 A3 254 B6
Addison Ct
3 Belmont SM2 217 D1
Ealing W5 110 C6
Twickenham TW1 153 A3
Addison Dr SE12 165 B6
Addison Gdns
Hammersmith W14 112 D3
Kingston u T KT5 198 B5
Addison Gr W4 111 C3
Addison Ho
NW8 92 B4 229 C2
Addison Park Mans 12
W14 112 D4
Addison Pl
Notting Hill
W11 113 A5 244 A3
Southall UB1 107 C6
Addison Prim Sch
W14 112 D3
Addison Rd
Bromley BR2 209 D4
Croydon SE25 206 A5
Enfield EN3 6 D4
Kensington
W14 113 B3 254 C6
Teddington TW11 175 B4
Walthamstow E17 54 A4
Wanstead E11 55 A3
Addison's Cl CR0 223 B6
Addison Way
Hampstead Garden Suburb
NW11 47 C5
Hayes UB3 84 A1
Northwood HA6 22 A2
Addle Hill EC4 241 D1
Addlestone Ho 4
W10 90 C2
Addy Ho SE16 118 C2
Adecroft Way KT8 196 A6
Adela Ave KT3 200 B5
Adela Ho 9 W6 112 C1
Adelaide Ave SE4 141 C1
Adelaide Cl
Brixton SW9 138 C1
Enfield EN1 5 C5
Stanmore HA7 25 A6
Adelaide Ct
15 Beckenham BR3 185 C3
Hackney E5 75 A3
Hanwell W7 108 D4
St John's Wood NW8 229 B3
Adelaide Gdns RM6 59 A4
Adelaide Gr W12 112 A5
Adelaide Ho E17 53 B6
Adelaide Rd
Ashford TW15 170 A6
Chislehurst BR7 188 D5
Ealing W13 109 A4
Heston TW5 129 A4
Ilford IG1 78 D6
Kingston u T KT6 198 A4
Leyton E10 76 A5
Primrose Hill NW3 70 C1
Richmond TW9 132 B1
Southall UB2 107 A2
Teddington TW11 174 D4
2 Wandsworth
SW18 157 C6
Adelaide St WC2 250 A5
Adelaide Terr TW8 109 D1
Adela St W10 91 A3
Adelina Gr E1 96 C2
Adelina Mews SW12 159 D3
Adeline Pl
WC1 93 D2 239 D3
Adelphi Cres UB4 83 D4
Adelphi Ct
19 Finchley N2 30 B1
20 Rotherhithe SE16 118 D4
Adelphi Terr WC2 250 B5
Adelphi Way UB4 83 D4
Adeney Cl W6 134 D6
Aden Gr N16 73 B4
Aden Ho 15 E1 96 D2
Aden Lo N16 73 B4
Adenmore Rd SE6 163 C4
Aden Rd Enfield EN3 7 A1
Ilford IG1 57 A2
Adeyfield Ho EC1 235 D1
Adhara Rd HA6 22 A5
Adie Rd W6 112 C3
Adine Rd E13 99 B3
Adisham Ho 4 E5 74 B3
Adler Ind Est UB3 105 B4
Adler St E1 96 A1
Adley St E5 75 A3
Adlington Cl N18 33 C5
Admaston Rd SE18 145 A6
Admiral Ct
Barking IG11 102 C5
Carshalton SM5 202 C1
Chelsea
SW10 136 A4 266 B2
Hendon NW4 46 A4
Marylebone W1 238 A3
Admiral Ho TW11 175 A6
Admiral Hyson Ind Est
SE16 118 B1
Admiral Mews W10 90 D3
Admiral Pl
Harringay N8 50 D5
Rotherhithe SE16 119 A5
Admirals Cl E18 55 B5
Admirals Ct
Bermondsey SE1 253 C3
3 Newham E6 100 D1
32 Putney SW19 156 D3
Admiral Seymour Rd
SE9 144 B1
Admirals Gate SE10 141 D4
Admiral Sq
SW10 136 A4 266 B2
Admiral St SE8 141 C4
Admirals Way E14 119 C4
Admiral's Wlk NW3 70 A5
Admiralty Arch★
SW1 249 D4
Admiralty Cl
1 London SE8 141 C4
West Drayton UB7 104 B4
Admiralty Rd TW11 174 D4
Admiralty Way
TW11 174 D4
Admiral Wlk W9 91 C2
Adolf St SE6 185 D6
Adolphus Rd N4 50 D1
Adolphus St SE8 141 B5
Adomar Rd RM8 81 A5
Adpar St W2 92 B2 236 C4
Adrian Ave NW2 46 B1
Adrian Bolt Ho 2 E2 96 B4
Adrian Cl EN5 12 D5
Adrian Ho
Islington N1 233 D5
South Lambeth SW8 270 A4
Stratford E15 76 B1
Adrian Mews SW10 265 D6
Adriatic Bldg 18 E14 119 A6
Adriatic Ho 18 E1 96 D3
Adrienne Ave UB1 85 B4
Adron Ho 13 SE16 118 C2
Adstock Ho 5 N1 72 D1
Advance Rd SE27 183 A6
Advent Ct IG8 36 D5
Adventurers Ct 17
E14 120 B6
Advent Way N18 34 D5
Adyar Ct 7 SW19 179 A3
Adys Lawn NW2 68 B2
Adys Rd SE15 139 D2
Aegean Apts 7 E16 121 A6
Aegon Ho 3 E14 119 D3
Aerodrome Rd NW4,
NW9 45 D6
Aerodrome Way
TW5 128 C6
Aeroville NW9 27 C1
Affleck St N1 233 D3
Afghan Rd SW11 136 C3
Africa Ho WC2 240 C2
Afsil Ho EC1 241 B3
Aga Khan Univ WC1 239 D3
Agamemnon Rd NW6 69 B3
Agar Cl KT6 214 B6
Agar Gr NW1 71 D1
Agar Ho 6 KT1 198 A6
Agar Pl NW1 71 C1
Agar St WC2 250 B5
Agate Cl E16 99 D1
Agate Ho
New Malden KT4 199 C1
12 Penge SE26 184 B5
Agate Rd W6 112 C3
Agatha Cl E1 118 C5
Agaton Rd SE9 167 A2
Agave Rd NW2 68 C4
Agdon St EC1 94 D3 241 C6
Agincourt E11 54 D3
Agincourt Rd NW3 70 D4
Agnes Ave IG1 78 D4
Agnes Cl E6 122 C6
Agnes Ct 11 SW18 136 B1
Agnesfield Cl N12 30 C4
Agnes Gdns RM8 80 D4
Agnes Ho 13 W11 112 D6
Agnes Rd W3 111 D4
Agnes St E14 97 B1
Agnew Rd SE23 162 D4
Agricola Pl EN1 17 D6
Aicon Gall★ SW1 249 A6
Aidan Cl RM8 81 A4
Aidans Ct N12 30 C5
Aigburth Mans 5
SW9 138 C5
Ailantus Ct HA8 26 B5
Aileen Wlk E15 76 D1
Ailsa Ave TW1 153 B6
Ailsa Rd TW1 153 B6
Ailsa St E14 98 A2
Ainger Rd NW3 70 D1
Ainsdale NW1 232 A2
Ainsdale Cl BR6 211 B1
Ainsdale Cres HA5 41 C6
Ainsdale Dr SE1 118 A1
Ainsdale Rd W5 87 D3
Ainsley Ave RM7 59 D3
Ainsley Cl N9 17 C3
Ainsley St E2 96 B4
Ainslie Ct 2 HA0 88 A5
Ainslie Ho 1 E4 35 C5
Ainslie Wlk 8 SW12 159 B4
Ainslie Wood Cres
E4 35 D5
Ainslie Wood Gdns
E4 35 D5
Ainslie Wood Prim Sch
E4 35 D5
Ainslie Wood Rd E4 35 D5
Ainsty St 20 SE16 118 C4
Ainsworth Cl
Camberwell SE5 139 C3
Dollis Hill NW2 68 A5
Ainsworth Est
NW8 92 A6 229 A6
Ainsworth Ho NW8 91 D6
Ainsworth Rd
Croydon CR0 220 D6
Hackney E9 74 C1
Ainsworth Way
NW8 92 A6 229 A6
Aintree Ave E6 100 A6
Aintree Cl UB8 82 D2
Aintree Ho SE26 184 B4
Aintree Rd UB6 87 B5
Aintree St
SW6 135 A5 264 B4
Airborne Ho 10 SM6 219 B4
Airco Cl NW9 45 B6
Aird Ct TW12 173 D2
Aird Ho SE1 262 A5
Airdrie Cl
Barnsbury N1 72 B1
Hayes UB4 85 A2
Airedale Ave W4 111 D1
Airedale Ave S W4 111 D1
Airedale Rd
Balham SW12 158 D4
Ealing W5 109 D3
Airlie Gdns Ilford IG1 56 D1
Kensington
W8 113 C5 245 A3
Airlinks Ind Est TW5 106 C1
Air Park Way TW13 150 B2
Airport Gate Bsns Ctr
UB7 126 C5
Airport Ho CR0 220 C2
Airport Rdbt E16 121 D5
Air St W1 249 B5
Airthrie Rd IG3 80 B6
Aisgill Ave
SW5 113 B1 254 D1
Aisher Rd SE28 124 C6
Aislabie Ho N21 17 B5
Aislibie Rd SE12 142 C1
Aiten Pl W6 112 A2
Aithan Ho 15 E14 97 B1
Aitken Cl
Carshalton CR4 202 D2
Hackney E8 96 A6
Aitken Rd Barnet EN5 12 C6
Catford SE6 163 D2
Aits View KT8 195 D6
Ajax Ave NW9 45 C6
Ajax Ct NW9 45 C6
Ajax Ho 15 E2 96 B5
Ajax Rd NW6 69 C3
Akabusi Cl SE25 206 A3
Akbar Ho 7 E14 119 D2
Akehurst St SW15 156 A4
Akenside Ct 3 NW3 70 B3
Akenside Rd NW3 70 B3
Akerman Rd
Brixton SW9 138 D4
Kingston u T KT6 197 C3
Akintaro Ho 7 SE8 141 B6
Akiva Sch N3 29 D1
Alabama St SE18 145 C5
Alacross Rd W5 109 D4
Aladdin Workspace
UB6 85 D6
Alamaro Lo 5 SE10 120 D3
Alandale Dr HA5 22 B2
Aland Ct SE16 119 A3
Alander Mews E17 54 A5
Alan Dr EN5 13 A5
Alan Gdns RM7 59 C2
Alan Hocken Way
E15 98 C5
Alan Lo N3 29 C2
Alan Preece Ct NW6 68 D1
Alan Rd SW19 179 A5
Alanthus Cl SE12 165 A5
Alaska Bldg 12 SE13 141 D4
Alaska St SE1 251 A3
Alastor Ho 10 E14 120 A3
Alba Cl UB4 84 D3
Albacore Cres SE13 163 D5
Alba Gdns NW11 47 A3
Albain Cres TW15 148 A2
Alba Mews SW18,
SW19 157 C2
Alban Ho
Hampstead NW3 70 A2
New Cross SE14 141 B4
Albans Cl SW16 160 A1
Albany W1 249 A5
Albany Cl Bushey WD23 8 B5
Ickenham UB10 60 C3
Mortlake SW14 132 D1
Sidcup DA5 168 D4
West Green N15 51 A5
Albany Coll NW4 46 C4
Albany Coll Hendry Ho
NW4 46 B4
Albany Cres
Claygate KT10 212 C2
Edgware HA8 26 C3
Albany Ct
Ashford TW15 171 B4
Cheam SM1 217 B4
Chingford E4 19 D5
College Pk NW10 90 B4
Finchley N12 29 D4
Grahame Pk HA8 27 B2
Kingston u T KT2 176 A4
NW8 229 C3
Richmond TW10 153 B1
Surbiton KT6 197 D2
Walthamstow E10 53 C2
Westminster SW1 259 C6
8 Whitechapel E1 96 A1
Albany Ctyd W1 249 B5
Albany Ho
6 Brentford TW8 132 A6
Edgware HA8 26 C3
Upper Clapton E5 74 C6
Albany Mans SW11 267 B3
Albany Mews
Camberwell SE5 139 A6
Islington N1 72 C1
Kingston u T KT2 175 D4
Plaistow BR1 187 A4
Sutton SM1 217 D3
Albany Par 4 TW8 132 A6
Albany Park Ave EN3 6 D4
Albany Park Rd KT2 176 A4
Albany Park Sta
DA14 168 D2
Albany Pas 12 TW10 154 A6
Albany Pk Canoe &
Sailing Ctr KT2 175 D4
Albany Pl TW8 131 D6
Albany Rd
Brentford TW8 131 D6
Camberwell SE5 139 C6
Chislehurst BR7 188 D5
Dagenham RM6 59 B3
Ealing W13 109 B6
Enfield EN3 6 D5
Erith DA17 147 B6
Leyton E10 53 C2
Manor Pk E12 77 D4
New Malden KT3 199 B5
Richmond TW10 154 A6
Sidcup DA5 168 C4
Stroud Green N4 50 C3
Upper Edmonton N18 34 C5
Walthamstow E17 53 A3
Wimbledon SW19 179 D5
Albany Reach KT7 196 D4
Albany Sch EN3 6 D5
Albany St
NW1 93 B4 231 D2
Albany Terr 6
TW10 154 B6
Albany The
Kingston u T KT2 175 D4
Woodford IG8 36 D6
Albany View IG9 21 A3
Albany Wlk N15 50 D5
Alba Pl W11 91 B1
Albatross 31 NW9 27 D1
Albatross Cl E6 100 B3
Albatross St SE18 145 C5
Albemarle SW19 156 D2
Albemarle App IG2 56 D3
Albemarle Ave TW2 151 B3
Albemarle Coll W1 247 D6
Albemarle Gdns
Ilford IG2 56 D3
New Malden KT3 199 B5
Albemarle Ho
2 Brixton SW9 138 C2
Rotherhithe SE8 119 B2
Albemarle Lo SE26 185 A5
Albemarle Mans
NW3 69 D4
Albemarle Pk
Beckenham BR3 185 D2
Stanmore HA7 25 C5
Albemarle Prim Sch
SW19 157 A2
Albemarle Rd
Beckenham BR2,
BR3 186 A2
East Barnet EN4 14 C4
Albemarle St
W1 115 C6 249 A5
Albemarle Way EC1 241 C5
Alberon Gdns NW11 47 B5
Alberta Ave SM1 217 B3
Alberta Ct 1 TW10 154 B6
Alberta Ho
Blackwall E14 120 A5
Hayes UB4 84 B4
Alberta Rd EN1 18 A5
Alberta St
SE17 116 D1 261 D2
Albert Ave
Chingford E4 35 C6
South Lambeth SW8 270 C3
Albert Barnes Ho
SE1 262 A5
Albert Basin Way
E16 123 A6
Albert Bigg Point
E15 98 A6
Albert Bridge Rd
SW11 136 D5 267 C3
Albert Carr Gdns
SW16 182 A5
Albert Cl
11 Hackney E9 96 B6
Wood Green N22 31 D2
Albert Cotts 2 E1 96 A2
Albert Cres E4 35 C6
Albert Ct
Knightsbridge SW7 246 C1
9 Putney SW19 157 A3
Albert Dr SW19 157 A3
Albert Emb
SE1 116 A2 260 B3

Albert Gate Ct SW1 247 C1
Albert Gdns E1 96 D1
Albert Gr SW20 178 D2
Albert Gray Ho SW10 266 C4
Albert Hall Mans
SW7 114 B4 246 C1
Albert Ho
Stanmore HA7 25 B5
5 Wanstead E18 55 B6
2 Woolwich SE28 123 A3
Albert Mans
Battersea SW11 267 C2
Hornsey N8 50 A2
Albert Meml★
SW7 114 B4 246 C1
Albert Mews W8 256 A6
Albert Palace Mans
SW11 268 B2
Albert Pl Finchley N3 29 C2
Kensington
W8 113 D4 245 D1
Albert Rd
Ashford TW15 170 B5
Bromley Comm BR2 209 D4
Buckhurst Hill IG9 21 D2
Chislehurst SE9 166 A1
Croydon SE25 206 B5
Dagenham RM8 59 C1
Ealing W5 87 B3
East Barnet EN4 2 A1
Erith DA17 125 B1
Finsbury Pk N4 50 B2
Hampton TW12 174 A5
Harrow HA2 42 A6
Hayes UB3 105 C3
Hendon NW4 46 D5
Hounslow TW3 129 C1
Ilford IG1 79 A5
Kilburn NW6 91 B5
Kingston u T KT1 176 B1
Leyton E10 54 A1
Mill Hill NW7 27 D5
Mitcham CR4 202 D6
Newham E16 122 B4
New Malden KT3 199 D5
Penge SE20 184 D4
Richmond TW10 154 B6
Sidcup DA5 169 D4
Southall UB2 106 D3
South Tottenham N15 51 C3
Sutton SM1 218 B3
Teddington TW11 174 D4
Twickenham TW1 152 D3
Walthamstow E17 53 C4
4 Wanstead E18 55 B6
Wood Green N22 31 C2
Yiewsley UB7 104 A5
Albert's Ct NW1 237 B6
Albert Sleet Ct N9 18 B1
Albert Sq Leyton E15 76 C3
South Lambeth
SW8 138 B5 270 C3
Albert St
Camden Town
NW1 93 B6 231 D5
North Finchley N12 30 A5
Albert Starr Ho 7
SE8 118 D2
Albert Studios SW11 267 C2
Albert Terr
Buckhurst Hill IG9 21 D2
Camden Town
NW1 93 A6 231 A5
Stonebridge NW10 89 A6
Albert Terr Mews
NW1 231 A5
Albert Victoria Ho
N22 32 C2
Albert Way SE15 140 B5
Albert Westcott Ho
SE17 261 D2
Albert Whicher Ho 3
E17 54 A5
Albert Wlk E16 122 D4
Albion Ave
Clapham SW8 137 D3
Muswell Hill N10 31 A2
Albion Cl W2 247 B6
Albion Coll
WC1 94 A2 240 B3
Albion Ct
7 Hammersmith
W6 112 B2
Albion Ct *continued*
Sutton SM2 218 B1
2 Woolwich SE18 122 A2
Albion Dr E8 74 A1
Albion Est SE16 118 C4
Albion Gate W2 247 B6
Albion Gdns 1 W6 112 B2
Albion Gr N16 73 C4
Albion Hill IG10 21 D6
Albion Ho
17 Deptford SE8 141 C5
EC1 241 C4
Newham E16 122 D5
Albion Mews
Bayswater
W2 114 C6 247 B6
6 Hammersmith W6 112 B2
Islington N1 234 A6
Albion Pk IG10 21 D6
Albion Pl
Broadgate EC2 242 D3
Clerkenwell EC1 241 C4
Hammersmith W6 112 B2
South Norwood SE25 206 A6
Albion Prim Sch 34
SE16 118 C4
Albion Rd
Bexley DA6 147 C1
Dagenham RM10 81 B3
Hayes UB3 83 C1
Hounslow TW3 129 C1
Kingston u T KT2 177 A2
Stoke Newington N16 73 B4
Sutton SM2 218 B1
Tottenham N17 34 A1
Twickenham TW2 152 C3
Walthamstow E17 54 A6
Albion Riverside
SW11 267 A4
Albion Sq E8 73 D1
Albion St
Bayswater
W2 114 C6 247 B6
Rotherhithe SE16 118 C4
Thornton Heath CR0 204 D1
Albion Terr
Hackney E8 73 D1
Sewardstone E4 7 D1
Albion Villas Rd SE23,
SE26 162 C1
Albion Way
Barbican EC1 242 A3
Lewisham SE13 142 A1
Wembley HA9 66 C5
Albion Wlk N1 233 B3
Albion Works Studios 14
E8 74 A3
Albion Yd N1 233 B3
Albon Ho SW18 157 D5
Albrighton Rd SE5,
SE22 139 C2
Albuhera Cl EN2 4 C4
Albury Ave
Bexleyheath DA7 147 A3
Hounslow TW7 130 D5
Albury Bldgs SE1 251 D1
Albury Cl TW12 173 D4
Albury Ct
4 Croydon CR0 221 A4
Deptford SE8 141 C6
Mitcham CR4 180 B1
6 Northolt UB5 84 C4
Ruislip HA4 62 C3
Sutton SM1 218 A4
Albury Dr HA5 22 D3
Albury Lo 7 SW2 160 B4
Albury Mews E12 77 C6
Albury Rd KT9 214 A3
Albury St SE8 141 C6
Albyfield BR1 210 B6
Albyn Rd SE8 141 C4
Alcester Cres E5 74 B6
Alcester Ct 4 SM6 219 B4
Alcester Rd SM6 219 B4
Alchemea Coll of Audio
Engineering
N1 94 D6 234 D6
Alcock Cl SM6 219 D1
Alcock Rd TW5 128 D5
Alconbury DA6 169 D6
Alconbury Rd E5 74 A6
Alcorn Cl SM3 217 C6
Alcott Cl W7 86 D2
Aldborough Ct
Chingford E4 19 D1
Ilford IG2 57 D4
ALDBOROUGH
HATCH 57 C5
Aldborough Rd IG2 57 D6
Aldborough Rd N
IG2 57 D4
Aldborough Rd S IG3 57 C2
Aldbourne Rd W12 112 A5
Aldbridge St
SE17 117 C1 263 B2
Aldburgh Mews W1 238 B2
Aldbury Ave HA9 66 D1
Aldbury Ho SW3 257 A3
Aldbury Mews N9 17 B4
Aldebert Terr
SW8 138 B5 270 C3
Aldeburgh Cl 16 E5 74 B6
Aldeburgh Pl
Greenwich SE10 121 A2
Woodford IG8 37 A6
Aldeburgh St SE10 121 A1
Alden Ave E15 98 D4
Alden Ct
South Croydon CR0 221 C5
Wimbledon SW19 179 C4
Aldenham Ctry Pk
WD6 9 B6
Aldenham Dr UB8 82 D3
Aldenham Ho NW1 232 B3
Aldenham Rd WD6 9 C6
Aldenham St
NW1 93 D5 232 C3
Alden Ho E8 96 B6
Aldensley Rd W6 112 B3
Alderbrook Prim Sch 17
SW12 159 B4
Alderbrook Rd
SW12 159 B5
Alderbury Rd SW13 134 A6
Alder Ct
East Finchley N2 48 B6
3 West Norwood
SW16 182 C5
Alder Gr NW2 68 B6
Aldergrove Gdns
TW4 129 A3
Aldergrove Ho 3 E5 74 A6
Alder Ho
Camberwell SE15 139 D6
1 Maitland Pk NW3 70 D2
St Johns SE4 141 C2
Alderley Ho 36 SW8 137 D3
Alder Lo SW6 134 D4
Alder Lodge N9 17 C3
Alderman Ave IG11 102 A4
Aldermanbury
EC2 95 A1 242 B2
Aldermanbury Sq
EC2 242 B3
Alderman Ct 13 N11 30 D5
Alderman Judge Mall 6
KT1 176 A1
Alderman's Hill N13 32 B6
Alderman's Wlk EC2 243 A3
Aldermary Rd BR1 187 A2
Aldermead 2 TW3 129 D1
Alder Mews 12 N19 71 C6
Aldermoor Rd SE6 163 B1
Alderney Ave TW5 129 D5
Alderney Gdns UB5 63 B1
Alderney Ho
20 Canonbury N1 73 A2
Enfield EN3 6 D5
Alderney Mews SE1 262 C6
Alderney Rd E1 96 D3
Alderney St
SW1 115 B1 258 D2
Alder Rd
Mortlake SW14 133 B2
Sidcup DA14 167 D1
Alders Ave IG8 36 C4
ALDERSBROOK 77 C6
Aldersbrook Ave EN1 5 C3
Aldersbrook Dr KT2 176 B4
Aldersbrook La E12 78 B5
Aldersbrook Prim Sch
E12 77 C6
Aldersbrook Rd E11,
E12 77 C6
Alders Cl Ealing W5 109 D3
Edgware HA8 27 A5
Wanstead E11 77 B6
Alders Ct N17 52 B5
Aldersey Gdns IG11 79 B2
Aldersford Cl SE4 140 D1
Aldersgate Ct EC1 242 A3
Aldersgate St
EC1 95 A2 242 A3
Aldersgrove KT8 196 B4
Aldersgrove Ave SE9,
SE12 165 D1
Aldershot Rd NW6 91 B6
Aldersmead Ave
CR0 206 D3
Aldersmead Rd BR3 185 A3
Alderson Pl UB2 108 A5
Alderson St W10 91 A3
Alders Rd HA8 27 A5
Alders The
Feltham TW13 173 A6
Heston TW5 129 B6
Southgate N21 16 C5
Streatham SW16 181 C6
West Wickham BR4 223 D6
Alderton 9 KT2 176 D2
Alderton Cl NW10 67 B5
Alderton Cres NW4 46 B4
Alderton Ct KT8 195 B5
Alderton Rd
Croydon CR0 206 A2
Herne Hill SE24 139 A2
Alderton Way NW4 46 B4
Alderville Rd SW6 135 B3
Alderwick Ct N7 72 B2
Alderwick Dr TW3 130 B2
Alder Wlk IG11 79 A2
Alderwood Mews EN4 2 A5
Alderwood Prim Sch
SE9 167 C5
Alderwood Rd SE9 167 B5
Aldford St
W1 115 A5 248 B4
Aldgate EC3 95 C1 243 B1
Aldgate East Sta
E1 95 D1 243 D2
Aldgate High St
EC3 95 D1 243 C1
Aldgate Sta
EC3 95 D1 243 C1
Aldham Hall 1 E11 55 A3
Aldham Ho SE4 141 B4
Aldine Ct W12 112 C5
Aldine St W12 112 C4
Aldington Cl RM8 58 C1
Aldington Ct 1 E8 74 A1
Aldington Rd SE18 121 D3
Aldis Mews
3 Holdbrook EN3 7 C6
Upper Tooting SW17 180 C5
Aldis St SW17 180 C5
Aldred Rd NW6 69 C3
Aldren Rd SW17 158 A1
Aldriche Way E4 36 A4
Aldrich Gdns SM3 217 B5
Aldrich Terr SW18 158 A2
Aldrick Ho N1 233 D4
Aldridge Ave
Edgware HA8 10 D1
Holdbrook EN3 7 C5
Ruislip HA4 62 D6
Stanmore HA7 26 A2
Aldridge Ct W11 91 B2
Aldridge Rd Villas
W11 91 B2
Aldridge Rise KT3 199 C3
Aldridge Wlk N14 16 A4
Aldrington Rd SW16 181 C6
Aldsworth Cl W9 91 D3
Aldwich Ho WC2 240 D1
Aldwick Cl SE9 167 B1
Aldwick Ct N12 30 A6
Aldwick Rd CR0 220 B4
Aldworth Gr SE13 164 A5
Aldworth Rd E15 76 C1
Aldwych WC2 94 B1 240 D1
Aldwych Ave IG6 57 A5
Aldwych Bldgs WC2 240 B2
Aldwyn Ho SW8 270 A3
Alers Rd DA6 168 D6
Alesia Cl N22 32 A3
Alestan Beck Rd E16 99 D1
Alexa Ct 4 SM2 217 C2
Alexander Ave NW10 68 B1
Alexander Cl
Barnet EN4 2 B1
Hayes BR2 209 A1
Sidcup DA15 167 C5
Southall UB2 108 A5
Twickenham TW2 152 D2
Alexander Ct
Beckenham BR3 186 B2
Greenwich SE3 143 B3
Alexander Ct *continued*
Stanmore HA7 44 B6
14 Surbiton KT6 197 D2
Wandsworth SW18 158 A6
Alexander Evans Mews
SE23 162 D2
Alexander Fleming
Laboratory Mus★
W2 236 D2
Alexander Ho
8 Kingston u T
KT2 176 A2
15 Millwall E14 119 C3
16 Sutton SM2 218 A2
Alexander Lo SM1 217 B3
Alexander McLeod Prim
Sch SE2 124 B1
Alexander Mews 2
W2 91 D1
Alexander Pl SW7 257 A4
Alexander Rd
Bexley DA7 146 D3
Chislehurst BR7 188 D5
Upper Holloway N19 72 A6
Alexander Sq
SW3 114 C2 257 A4
Alexander St W2 91 C1
Alexander Terr SE2 124 B1
Alexandra Ave
Battersea SW11 268 A1
Harrow HA2 63 C5
Southall UB1 107 B6
Sutton SM1 217 C5
Wood Green N22 31 D2
Alexandra Bsns Ctr
EN3 6 D1
Alexandra Cl
Ashford TW15 171 B3
Deptford SE8 141 B6
Harrow HA2 63 D5
Alexandra Cotts
New Cross SE14 141 B4
Penge SE20 184 D4
Alexandra Cres BR1 186 D4
Alexandra Ct
Ashford TW15 171 B4
Ealing W5 87 C2
Greenford UB6 85 D5
Hounslow TW3 129 D3
Paddington W9 236 B6
4 Shacklewell N16 73 D4
5 Shepherd's Bush
W12 112 A4
Southgate N14 15 C6
Wembley HA9 66 B4
Alexandra Dr
Surbiton KT5 198 C2
West Norwood SE19 183 C5
Alexandra Gdns
Chiswick W4 133 C5
Cranley Gdns N10 49 B5
Hounslow TW3 129 D3
Wallington SM5 219 A1
Alexandra Gr
Finchley N12 29 D4
Finsbury Pk N4 50 D1
Alexandra Ho 13
W6 112 C1
Alexandra Inf Sch
19 Kingston u T
KT2 176 C3
Penge BR3 184 D3
Alexandra Jun & Inf Schs
TW3 129 D3
Alexandra Jun Sch
SE26 184 D4
Alexandra Mans
Chelsea SW3 266 C5
Cricklewood NW2 68 D3
6 Hampstead NW6 69 C3
9 Shepherd's Bush
W12 112 C5
Alexandra Mews N2 48 D6
Alexandra National Ho
N4 72 D6
Alexandra Pal★ N22 31 D1
Alexandra Palace Sta
N22 32 A1
Alexandra Palace Way
N10 49 C6
Alexandra Park Rd N10,
N22 31 D2
Alexandra Park Sch
N11 31 C2
Alexandra Pl
Croydon CR0 205 C1

Alexandra Pl *continued*
South Norwood SE25 . . 205 B4
St John's Wood
NW8 . . . . 92 A6 229 B6
Alexandra Prim Sch
N22 . . . . 32 B1
Alexandra Rd
Acton W4 . . . . 111 B4
Ashford TW15 . . . . . . 171 C4
10 Brentford TW8 . . . 131 D6
Croydon CR0 . . . . 205 C2
Dagenham RM6 . . . . 59 A3
Edmonton N9 . . . . 18 B4
Enfield EN3 . . . . 6 D1
Hampstead NW8 . . . . . . 70 B1
Hendon NW4 . . . . 46 D5
Hornsey N8, N22 . . . . . . 50 C6
Hounslow TW3 . . . . . . 129 D3
Kingston u T KT2 . . . . 176 C3
Leyton E10 . . . . 76 A5
Mitcham SW19 . . . . . 180 C3
Mortlake SW14 . . . . . . 133 B2
Muswell Hill N10 . . . . . . 31 B3
Penge SE26 . . . . 184 D4
Richmond TW9 . . . . 132 B3
Thames Ditton KT7 . . . 196 D4
Tottenham N15 . . . . 51 B4
Twickenham TW1 . . . . 153 C5
Wallend E6 . . . . 100 C4
Walthamstow E17 . . . . . 53 B2
Wanstead E18 . . . . 55 B6
Wimbledon SW19 . . . 179 C5
Alexandra Sch HA2 . . 63 C6
Alexandra Sq SM4 . . . 201 C4
Alexandra St
5 Deptford SE14 . . . . 141 A5
Newham E16 . . . . 99 A2
Alexandra Wlk 8
SE19 . . . . 183 C5
Alexandria Rd W13 . . 109 B6
Alex Gossip Ho SW6 265 A1
Alexis St SE16 . . . . . 118 A2
Al Falah Sch 7 E5 . . . . 74 B5
Alfearn Rd E5 . . . . 74 C4
Alfie's Antique Mkt★
NW8 . . . . 92 C3 237 A5
Alford Ct
18 Belmont SM2 . . . . 217 D1
Shoreditch N1 . . . . . . 235 B3
Alford Gn CR0 . . . . 224 B2
Alford Ho
Crouch End N6 . . . . 49 C3
6 Woolwich SE18 . . . 144 D6
Alford Pl N1 . . . . 235 B3
Alfoxton Ave N8, N15 . . 50 D5
Alfreda Ct SW11 . . . . 268 C1
Alfreda St
SW11 . . . . . . 137 B4 268 C1
Alfred Butt Ho
SW17 . . . . 158 D1
Alfred Cl W4 . . . . 111 B2
Alfred Findley Ho
N22 . . . . 32 D1
Alfred Gdns UB1 . . . . . 107 A6
Alfred Ho E9 . . . . 75 A3
Alfred Hurley Ho
SW17 . . . . 180 A6
Alfred Mews W1,
WC1 . . . . 239 C4
Alfred Nunn Ho
NW10 . . . . 89 D6
Alfred Pl WC1 . . 93 D2 239 C4
Alfred Prior Ho 7
E12 . . . . 78 C4
Alfred Rd Acton W3 . . . 111 A5
Buckhurst Hill IG9 . . . . . 21 D2
Croydon SE25 . . . . 206 A4
Erith DA17 . . . . 125 B1
Feltham TW13 . . . . . . 150 C2
Kingston u T KT1 . . . . . 198 B6
Leyton E15 . . . . 76 D3
Paddington W2 . . . . 91 C2
Sutton SM1 . . . . 218 A3
Alfred Salter Ho SE1 263 D3
Alfred Salter Prim Sch
SE16 . . . . 118 D4
Alfred's Gdns IG11 . . . 101 C5
Alfred St E3 . . . . 97 B4
Alfred's Way (East Ham & Barking By-Pass)
IG11 . . . . 101 B5
Alfred's Way Ind Est
IG11 . . . . 102 A6
Alfred Villas 9 E17 . . . 54 A5
Alfreton Cl SW19 . . . 156 D1
Alfriston KT5 . . . . 198 B3
Alfriston Ave
Harrow HA2 . . . . 41 C2
Thornton Heath CR0 . 204 A2
Alfriston Cl 5 KT5 . . . 198 B3
Alfriston Rd SW11 . . . 158 D6
Algar Cl
Isleworth TW7 . . . . 131 A2
Stanmore HA7 . . . . 24 D5
Algar Ct TW12 . . . . . . 173 D2
Algar Ho SE1 . . . . 251 C1
Algar Rd TW7 . . . . 131 A2
Algarve Rd SW18 . . . 157 D3
Algernon Rd
Hendon NW4 . . . . 46 A3
Kilburn NW6 . . . . 91 C6
Lewisham SE13 . . . . . 141 D1
Algers Cl IG10 . . . . 21 D6
Algers Rd IG10 . . . . 21 D6
Alghers Mead IG10 . . . 21 D6
Algiers Rd SE13 . . . . . 141 C1
Alguin Ct HA7 . . . . 25 C3
Alibon Gdns RM10 . . . . 81 C3
Alibon Rd RM10 . . . . . . 81 C3
Alice Cl 13 EN5 . . . . 2 A1
Alice Ct 10 N3 . . . . 29 C2
Alice Gilliott Ct W14 264 D6
Alice La E3 . . . . 97 B6
Alice Mews 3
TW11 . . . . 174 D5
Alice Owen Tech Ctr
EC1 . . . . 234 C2
Alice Shepherd Ho 12
E14 . . . . 120 A4
Alice St SE1 . . 117 C3 263 A5
Alice Thompson Cl
SE12 . . . . 165 C2
Alice Walker Cl 8
SE24 . . . . 138 D1
Alice Way TW3 . . . . . . 129 D1
Alicia Ave HA3 . . . . 43 C5
Alicia Cl HA3 . . . . 43 C5
Alicia Gdns HA3 . . . . . . 43 C5
Alicia Ho DA16 . . . . . . 146 B4
Alie St E1 . . . . . 95 D1 243 D1
Alington Cres NW9 . . . 45 A1
Alison Cl
Croydon CR0 . . . . 206 D1
Newham E6 . . . . 100 C1
Alison Ct HA8 . . . . 26 D5
Aliwal Rd SW11 . . . . . . 136 C1
Alkerden Rd W4 . . . . . 111 C1
Al Khair Prim & Sec Sch
7 CR0 . . . . 205 C1
Alkham Rd N16 . . . . 73 D6
Allam Ho W11 . . . . 244 A6
Allan Barclay Cl N15 . . 51 D3
Allanbridge N16 . . . . . . 51 C2
Allan Cl KT3 . . . . 199 B4
Allandale Ave N3 . . . . . 47 B6
Allan Ho SW8 . . . . 269 C2
Allanson Ct E10 . . . . . . 75 C6
Allan Way W3 . . . . 89 A2
Allard Cres WD23 . . . . . . 8 A2
Allard Gdns SW4 . . . . 159 D6
Allardyce St SW4,
SW9 . . . . 138 B1
Allbrook Cl TW11 . . . . 174 C5
Allbrook Ho 4
SW15 . . . . 156 A4
Allcot Cl TW14 . . . . . . 149 D3
Allcott Ho TW7 . . . . . . 130 D2
Allcroft Rd NW5 . . . . . . 71 A2
Allder Way CR2 . . . . . 220 D1
Allenby Cl UB6 . . . . 85 C4
Allenby Prim Sch
UB1 . . . . 85 C1
Allenby Rd
Forest Hill SE23 . . . . . 163 A1
Southall UB1 . . . . 85 C3
Woolwich SE28 . . . . . 123 A3
Allen Cl
Streatham CR4 . . . . . . 181 C2
Sunbury TW16 . . . . 172 B2
Allen Ct
Greenford UB6 . . . . 64 D3
Walthamstow E17 . . . . . 53 C3
Allendale Ave UB1 . . . . 85 C1
Allendale Cl
Camberwell SE5 . . . . . . 139 B4
Forest Hill SE26 . . . . . 184 D5
Allendale Rd UB6 . . . . . 65 B2
Allen Edwards Dr
SW8 . . . . 138 A4 270 A2
Allen Edwards Prim Sch
SW4 . . . . 138 A4 270 A1
Allenford Ho SW15 . . 155 D5
All England Lawn Tennis & Croquet Club The
SW19 . . . . 157 A1
Allen Ho W8 . . . . 255 B6
Allen Mans W8 . . . . . . 255 B6
Allen Rd Old Ford E3 . . . 97 B5
Penge BR3 . . . . 184 D1
Stoke Newington N16 . . 73 C4
Sunbury TW16 . . . . 172 B1
Thornton Heath CR0 . 204 C1
Allensbury Pl
7 Camden Town
NW1 . . . . 71 D1
Camden Town NW1 . . . . 72 A1
Allens Rd EN3 . . . . 18 C6
Allen St W8 . . . 113 C3 255 B5
Allenswood 12
SW19 . . . . 157 A3
Allenswood Rd SE9 . . . 144 B3
Allerdale Ho 7 N4 . . . . . 51 B2
Allerford Ct
Catford SE6 . . . . 163 D1
Harrow HA2 . . . . 42 A4
Allerford Rd SE6 . . . . 185 D6
Allerton Ct
5 Hendon NW4 . . . . . . 28 D1
North Cheam SM3 . . . 216 D6
Allerton Ho
4 Merton SW19 . . . . . 180 A3
Shoreditch N1 . . . . 235 D3
Allerton Rd N16 . . . . . . 73 A6
Allerton St N1 . . . . 235 D2
Allerton Wlk 11 N7 . . . . 72 B6
Allestree Rd
SW6 . . . . 135 A5 264 A3
Alleyn Cres SE21 . . . . . 161 B2
Alleyndale Rd RM8 . . . . 80 C6
Alleyn Ho
Bermondsey SE1 . . . . . 262 C5
St Luke's EC1 . . . . 242 B5
Alleyn Pk
Dulwich SE21 . . . . 161 C1
Southall UB2 . . . . 107 C1
Alleyn Rd SE21 . . . . . . 161 C1
Alleyn's Sch SE22 . . . . 161 C6
Allfarthing JMI Sch
SW18 . . . . 158 A5
Allfarthing La SW18 . . 158 A5
Allgood Cl SM4 . . . . . . 200 D3
Allgood St 10 E2 . . . . . . 95 D5
Allhallows La EC4 . . . 252 C5
Allhallows Rd E6 . . . . 100 A1
All Hallows Rd N17 . . . . 33 C2
Alliance Cl HA0 . . . . 65 D4
Alliance Ct Acton W3 . . 88 D2
Ashford TW15 . . . . 171 A6
Alliance Rd Acton W3 . . 88 D3
East Wickham SE18 . . 146 A5
1 Newham E16 . . . . 99 C2
Allied Ind Est W3 . . . . 111 C5
Allied Way W3 . . . . . . 111 C4
Allingham Cl W7 . . . . 108 D6
Allingham Ct NW3 . . . . 70 C3
Allingham Mews N1 235 A4
Allingham St
N1 . . . . 95 A5 235 A4
Allington Ave
Tottenham N17 . . . . 33 C4
Upper Halliford TW17 193 C6
Allington Cl
Greenford UB6 . . . . 64 A1
3 Wimbledon SW19 . . 178 D5
Allington Ct
6 Clapham SW8 . . . . . 137 C3
Croydon CR0 . . . . 206 C3
Enfield EN3 . . . . 18 D6
Allington Rd
Harrow HA2 . . . . 42 A4
Hendon NW4 . . . . 46 B3
Kensal Rise W10 . . . . . . 91 A5
Orpington BR6 . . . . . . 211 C1
Allington St SW1 . . . . 258 D5
Allison Cl SE10 . . . . . . 142 A4
Allison Gr SE21 . . . . . . 161 C3
Allison Rd Acton W3 . . 111 A6
Harringay N8 . . . . 50 D4
Alliston Ho 27 E2 . . . . . 95 D4
Allitsen Rd
NW8 . . . . 92 C5 230 A4
All Nations Ho 10 E8 . . 74 B1
Allnutt Way SW4 . . . . . 159 D6
Alloa Ct N14 . . . . 15 C2
Alloa Rd IG3 . . . . 80 A6
Allom Ct 11 SW4 . . . . . 138 A3
Allonby Dr HA4 . . . . 38 D2
Allonby Gdns HA9 . . . . 43 C1
Allonby Ho E14 . . . . 97 A2
Alloway Rd E3 . . . . 97 A4
Allport Ho SE5 . . . . 139 B2
Allport Mews 44 E1 . . . . 96 C3
All Saints' Benhilton CE Prim Sch 3 SM1 . . 217 D5
All Saints CE Prim Sch
8 Fulham SW6 . . . . . . 135 A3
Merton SW19 . . . . 180 A3
Putney SW15 . . . . 134 C2
All Saints' CE Prim Sch
Blackheath Vale
SE3 . . . . 142 C3
Child's Hill NW2 . . . . 69 B5
East Barnet N20 . . . . 14 B2
Wallington SM5 . . . . . . 219 A3
All Saints Church 9
N19 . . . . 71 D5
All Saints' Cl N9 . . . . . . 18 A2
All Saints Ct
Heston TW5 . . . . 128 D4
Lower Clapton E5 . . . . . . 74 C4
10 Shadwell E1 . . . . . . 118 C6
All Saints Dr SE3 . . . . 142 D3
All Saints Ho 2 W11 . . . 91 B2
All Saint's Inf & Jun Schs
SE19 . . . . 183 C2
All Saints Mews HA3 . . . 24 C4
All Saints Pas SW18 . . 157 C6
All Saints RC Sch & Tech Coll RM8 . . . . 59 C1
All Saints Rd
Merton SW19 . . . . 180 A3
Notting Hill W11 . . . . 91 B1
Sutton SM1 . . . . 218 A5
All Saints' Rd W3 . . . . 111 A3
All Saints St
N1 . . . . 94 B5 233 C4
All Saints Sta E14 . . . 119 D6
All Saints Twr 19 E10 . . 53 D2
Allsop Pl NW1 . 92 D3 237 D5
All Souls Ave NW10 . . . 90 B6
All Souls CE Prim Sch
W1 . . . . 93 C2 239 A4
All Souls Pl W1 . . . . . 238 D3
Allum La WD6 . . . . 10 A6
Allum Way N20 . . . . 14 A3
Allwood Cl SE26 . . . . 184 D6
Alma Ave E4 . . . . 36 A3
Alma Birk Ho 1 NW6 . . 69 B1
Almack Rd E5 . . . . 74 C4
Alma Cl N10 . . . . 31 B2
Alma Cres SM1 . . . . . . 217 A3
Alma Gr SE1 . 117 D2 263 D3
Alma Ho
7 Brentford TW8 . . . 132 A6
2 Edmonton N9 . . . . . . 34 A6
Alma Pl
College Pk NW10 . . . . . . 90 B4
Penge SE19 . . . . 183 D3
Thornton Heath CR7 . 204 C4
Alma Prim Sch
21 Bermondsey
SE16 . . . . 118 A2
Enfield EN3 . . . . 18 D6
Alma Rd
Carshalton SM5 . . . . . 218 C3
Enfield EN3 . . . . 7 A1
Muswell Hill N10 . . . . . . 31 B3
Sidcup DA14 . . . . 168 A1
Southall UB1 . . . . 107 A6
Thames Ditton KT10,
KT7 . . . . 196 C1
Wandsworth SW18 . . 158 A6
Alma Row HA3 . . . . 24 B2
Alma Sq NW8 . . 92 A4 229 B2
Alma St
Camden Town NW5 . . . . 71 B2
Stratford New Town
E15 . . . . 76 B2
Alma Terr
Earl's Ct W8 . . . . 255 B5
Wandsworth SW18 . . . 158 B4
Almeida St 10 N1 . . . . . 72 D1
Almeric Rd SW11 . . . . 136 D1
Almer Rd SW20 . . . . . . 178 A3
Almington St N4 . . . . . . 50 B1
Almond Ave
Carshalton SM5 . . . . . 218 D6
Ealing W5 . . . . 110 A3
Uxbridge UB10 . . . . 60 D5
West Drayton UB7 . . . 104 C3
Almond Cl
Bromley BR2 . . . . 210 C2
Charlton TW17 . . . . . . 171 A1
Feltham TW14 . . . . . . 150 A3
Almond Cl *continued*
Hayes UB3 . . . . 105 C6
Peckham SE15 . . . . . . 140 A3
Ruislip HA4 . . . . 61 D5
Almond Gr TW8 . . . . . . 131 B5
Almond Ho SE4 . . . . . . 141 B3
Almond Rd
Bermondsey SE16 . . . . 118 B2
Tottenham N17 . . . . 34 A3
Almonds Ave IG9 . . . . . 21 A2
Almond Way
Bromley BR2 . . . . 210 C2
Harrow HA2 . . . . 24 A1
Mitcham CR4 . . . . 203 D5
Almorah Rd
De Beauvoir Town N1 . . . 73 B1
Heston TW5 . . . . 128 D4
Almshouse La EN1 . . . . . 6 B6
Almshouses
Edmonton N9 . . . . 17 D2
Leyton E10 . . . . 75 D6
Southall UB1 . . . . 85 C1
Sunbury TW16 . . . . 171 D2
Almshouses The
IG11 . . . . 79 A2
Al-Muntada Islamic Sch
SW6 . . . . 135 B4 264 D2
Alnmouth Ct 10 UB1 . . 86 A1
Al-Noor Prim Sch
IG3 . . . . 58 B1
Alnwick 8 N17 . . . . 34 B3
Alnwick Gr SM4 . . . . . 201 D5
Alnwick Rd
Eltham SE12 . . . . 165 B4
Newham E16 . . . . 99 C1
Alonso Ho 4 DA17 . . . 125 C1
ALPERTON 88 A6
Alperton Com Sch
HA0 . . . . 66 B1
Alperton La UB6 . . . . . . 87 D5
Alperton Lower Sch
HA0 . . . . 87 D6
Alperton St W10 . . . . . . 91 B3
Alperton Sta HA0 . . . . . 88 A6
Alphabet Gdns SM5 . . 202 B3
Alphabet Sq E3 . . . . 97 C2
Alpha Bsns Ctr E17 . . . 53 B4
Alpha Cl NW8 . . 92 C4 230 B1
Alpha Ct 6 NW5 . . . . . . 71 B2
Alpha Est The UB3 . . 105 C4
Alpha Gr E14 . . . . 119 C4
Alpha Ho
19 Brixton SW4 . . . . . . 138 B1
Kilburn NW6 . . . . 91 C5
Lisson Gr NW8 . . . . . . 237 B5
Alpha Pl
Chelsea
SW3 . . . . 136 C6 267 B6
Kilburn NW6 . . . . 91 C5
Alpha Prep Sch HA1 . . 42 C4
Alpha Rd Chingford E4 . . 19 D1
Croydon CR0 . . . . 205 C1
Edmonton N18 . . . . 34 A4
Enfield EN3 . . . . 7 A1
Hillingdon UB10 . . . . 82 D3
New Cross SE14 . . . . . 141 B4
Surbiton KT5 . . . . 198 B3
Teddington TW12 . . . . 174 B5
Alpha St SE15 . . . . 140 A3
Alphea Cl SW19 . . . . . 180 C3
Alpine Ave KT5 . . . . . . 215 A6
Alpine Bsns Ctr E6 . . . 100 C2
Alpine Cl CR0 . . . . 221 C5
Alpine Copse BR1 . . . . 188 C1
Alpine Ct SE12 . . . . . . 142 D1
Alpine Gr 37 E9 . . . . 74 C1
Alpine Rd
Deptford SE16 . . . . 118 D1
Leyton E10 . . . . 75 D6
Walton-on-T KT12 . . . 194 A2
Alpine View SM5 . . . . 218 C3
Alpine Way E6 . . . . . . 100 C2
Alpine Wlk HA7 . . . . 8 C2
Alric Ave
Kingston u T KT3 . . . . 199 D6
Willesden NW10 . . . . . . 67 B1
Al-risaala Sec Sch 1
SW17 . . . . 180 D6
Alroy Rd N4 . . . . 50 C2
Alsace Rd
SE17 . . . . 117 C1 263 A2

Al Sadiq High Sch for Boys & Al Zahra Girls Sch NW6 ... 91 A6
Alscot Rd
SE1 ... 117 D3 263 D5
Alscot Road Ind Est
SE1 ... 263 D5
Alscot Way SE1 ... 263 C4
Alsike Rd DA18 ... 125 A3
Alsom Ave KT19, KT4 ... 216 A4
Alston Cl KT7 ... 197 B2
Alston Ct 2 EN5 ... 1 A2
Alstone Ct N9 ... 18 A2
Alston Rd
Edmonton N18 ... 34 B5
High Barnet EN5 ... 1 A2
Upper Tooting SW17 ... 180 B6
Altair Cl N17 ... 33 D4
Altair Ct N1 ... 73 B2
Altash Way SE9 ... 166 C2
Altenburg Ave W13 ... 109 B3
Altenburg Gdns
SW11 ... 136 D1
Alt Gr SW19 ... 179 B3
Altham Gdns WD19 ... 22 D6
Altham Rd HA5 ... 23 A3
Althea St SW6 ... 135 D2
Althorne Gdns E18 ... 54 D5
Althorne Way RM10 ... 81 C6
Althorp Cl EN5 ... 12 A4
Althorpe Mews
SW11 ... 266 D1
Althorpe Rd HA1 ... 42 A4
Althorp Rd SW17 ... 158 D3
Altima Ct SE22 ... 140 A1
Altior Ct N6 ... 49 C3
Altmore Ave E6 ... 100 B6
Altmore Inf Sch E6 ... 100 B6
Alton Ave HA7 ... 24 D3
Alton Cl
Isleworth TW7 ... 130 D3
Sidcup DA5 ... 169 A3
Alton Ct 18 BR3 ... 185 C3
Alton Gdns
Beckenham BR3 ... 185 C3
Twickenham TW2 ... 152 B4
Alton Ho 3 E3 ... 97 D4
Alton Rd
Croydon CR0 ... 220 C5
Richmond TW10, TW9 ... 132 A1
Roehampton SW15 ... 156 A3
Tottenham N17 ... 51 B6
Alton Sch The SW15 ... 155 D4
Alton St E14 ... 97 D2
Altyre Cl BR3 ... 207 B4
Altyre Rd CR0 ... 221 B6
Altyre Way BR3 ... 207 B4
Alum Ct KT5 ... 198 B3
Alumni Ct SE1 ... 253 D2
Alvanley Ct NW3 ... 69 D3
Alvanley Gdns NW6 ... 69 D3
Alvanley Ho 14 SW9 ... 138 C4
Alvernia Lo SM1 ... 217 D5
Alverstone Ave
East Barnet EN4 ... 14 C4
Wimbledon SW18, SW19 ... 157 C2
Alverstone Gdns
SE9 ... 167 A3
Alverstone Ho 11
SE11 ... 138 C6
Alverstone Rd
Little Ilford E12 ... 78 C4
New Malden KT3 ... 199 D5
Wembley HA9 ... 44 B1
Willesden NW2 ... 68 C1
Alverston Gdns
SE25 ... 205 C4
Alverton St SE8 ... 141 B6
Alveston Ave HA3 ... 43 B6
Alveston Sq 5 E18 ... 37 A1
Alvey St SE17 ... 263 A2
Alvia Gdns SM1 ... 218 A4
Alvington Cres E8 ... 73 D3
Alway Ave KT19 ... 215 B3
Alwen Cotts CR0 ... 222 D4
Alwold Cres SE12 ... 165 C5
Alwyn Ave W4 ... 111 B1
Alwyn Cl
Borehamwood WD6 ... 10 B5
New Addington CR0 ... 223 D1
Alwyne La N1 ... 72 D1
Alwyne Mans SW19 ... 179 B4
Alwyne Pl N1 ... 73 A1
Alwyne Rd
Canonbury N1 ... 73 A1
Ealing W7 ... 108 C6
Wimbledon SW19 ... 179 B4
Alwyne Sq N1 ... 73 A2
Alwyne Villas N1 ... 72 D1
Alwyn Gdns Acton W3 ... 88 D1
Hendon NW9 ... 46 A5
Alyn Ct N8 ... 49 D3
Alyth Gdns NW11 ... 47 C3
Alzette Ho 11 E2 ... 96 D5
Amalgamated Dr
TW8 ... 131 B6
Amanda Ct
Ashford TW15 ... 148 B2
Chingford E4 ... 36 C4
Aman Dalvi Ho 2
SW18 ... 157 A4
Amar Ct SE18 ... 123 D2
Amardeep Ct SE18 ... 123 D1
Amazon Apartments
N8 ... 50 B6
Amazonas
SE1 ... 117 C2 263 B3
Amazon St E1 ... 96 B1
Ambassador Cl TW3 ... 129 A3
Ambassador Ct
9 Hampstead NW6 ... 69 C3
Hendon NW4 ... 46 D4
Ambassador Gdns
E6 ... 100 B2
Ambassador Ho
Harrow HA3 ... 42 C6
St John's Wood NW8 ... 229 B5
Ambassador Sq E14 ... 119 D2
Amber Ave E17 ... 35 A2
Amber Ct
Feltham TW13 ... 149 C1
Islington N7 ... 72 C2
Mitcham CR4 ... 202 C5
Southall UB1 ... 107 D5
Amberden Ave N3 ... 47 C6
Amberdene HA7 ... 24 D4
Ambergate St
SE17 ... 116 D1 261 D2
Amber Gr NW2 ... 46 D1
Amber Ho HA7 ... 25 D3
Amberley Cl
2 Orpington BR6 ... 227 D3
Pinner HA5 ... 41 B6
Amberley Ct
2 Brixton SW9 ... 138 D2
Sidcup DA14 ... 190 C5
Sutton SM2 ... 218 A1
Amberley Gdns
Enfield EN1 ... 17 C4
Worcester Pk KT19 ... 215 D4
Amberley Gr
Croydon CR0 ... 205 D2
Penge SE26 ... 184 B5
Amberley Ho
8 Barnet EN5 ... 1 D1
7 Ealing W7 ... 108 C5
Amberley Rd
Buckhurst Hill IG9 ... 21 C3
Enfield EN1 ... 17 D5
Palmers Green N13 ... 16 B2
Walthamstow E10 ... 53 D2
Westbourne Green W9 ... 91 C2
West Heath SE2 ... 146 D6
Amberley Way
Heston TW4 ... 150 C6
Morden SM4 ... 201 B2
Romford RM7 ... 59 D5
Uxbridge UB10 ... 82 A5
Amberside Cl TW2 ... 152 B5
Amber Wharf 29 E2 ... 95 D6
Amberwood Cl SM6 ... 220 A3
Amberwood Rise
KT3 ... 199 C3
Amblecote Cl SE12 ... 165 B1
Amblecote Mdws
SE12 ... 165 B1
Amblecote Rd SE12 ... 165 B1
Ambler Prim Sch 2
N4 ... 72 D6
Ambler Rd N4 ... 72 D5
Ambleside
Catford BR1 ... 186 B4
13 Putney SW19 ... 157 A3
Regent's Pk NW1 ... 231 D3
Ambleside Ave
Beckenham BR3 ... 207 A4
Streatham SW16 ... 181 D6
Ambleside Ave *continued*
Walton-on-T KT12 ... 194 C1
Ambleside Cl
Lower Clapton E9 ... 74 C3
5 Tottenham N17 ... 51 D6
Walthamstow E10 ... 53 D2
Ambleside Cres EN3 ... 6 D2
Ambleside Dr TW14 ... 149 D3
Ambleside Gdns
Redbridge IG4 ... 56 A4
Streatham SW16 ... 181 D5
Sutton SM2 ... 218 A2
Wembley HA9 ... 43 D1
Ambleside Ho HA8 ... 27 A5
Ambleside Point 1
SE15 ... 140 C5
Ambleside Rd
Bexleyheath DA7 ... 147 C3
Willesden NW10 ... 67 D1
Ambrook Ct SM1 ... 218 B3
Ambrook Rd DA17 ... 125 C3
Ambrosden Ave
SW1 ... 115 C3 259 B5
Ambrose Ave NW11 ... 47 B3
Ambrose Cl
6 Newham E6 ... 100 B2
Orpington BR6 ... 227 D5
Ambrose Ho 9 E14 ... 97 C2
Ambrose Mews 2
SW11 ... 136 D3
Ambrose St SE16 ... 118 B2
Ambrose Wlk E3 ... 97 C5
Ambulance Rd E11 ... 54 B4
AMC Bsns Ctr NW10 ... 88 D4
Amelia Cl W3 ... 110 D4
Amelia Ho 5 W6 ... 112 C1
Amelia St
SE17 ... 117 A1 262 A2
Amen Cnr
Holborn EC4 ... 241 D1
Streatham SW17 ... 181 A4
Amen Ct EC4 ... 94 D1 241 D1
Amenity Way SM4 ... 200 C2
American Intercontinental Univ
W1 ... 93 A2 238 B3
American Sch in London The NW8 ... 92 B5 229 C4
American Univ in London The 3 N7 ... 72 B5
America Sq EC3 ... 253 C6
America St SE1 ... 252 A3
Amerland Rd SW18 ... 157 B5
Amersham Ave N18 ... 33 B4
Amersham Gr SE14 ... 141 B5
Amersham Rd
New Cross SE14 ... 141 B4
Thornton Heath CR0 ... 205 B3
Amersham Vale SE14, SE8 ... 141 B5
Amery Gdns NW10 ... 90 B6
Amery Ho SE17 ... 263 B2
Amery Rd HA1 ... 65 A6
Amesbury Ave SW2 ... 160 B2
Amesbury Cl KT4 ... 200 C1
Amesbury Ct EN2 ... 4 C3
Amesbury Dr E4 ... 19 D5
Amesbury Rd
Bromley BR1 ... 209 D6
Dagenham RM9 ... 80 D1
Feltham TW13 ... 150 D2
Amesbury Twr 4
SW8 ... 137 C3
Ames Cotts 12 E3 ... 97 A2
Ames Ho 10 E2 ... 96 D5
Amethyest Ct 1 EN3 ... 7 A2
Amethyst Cl N11 ... 31 D3
Amethyst Ct BR6 ... 227 C3
Amethyst Rd E15 ... 76 B4
Amherst Ave W13 ... 87 C1
Amherst Dr BR5 ... 211 D5
Amherst Gdns 2
W13 ... 87 C1
Amherst Rd W13 ... 87 C1
Amhurst Ct N4 ... 51 B2
Amhurst Gdns TW7 ... 131 A3
Amhurst Par N16 ... 51 D2
Amhurst Pk N4, N16 ... 51 C2
Amhurst Rd E8, N16 ... 74 A4
Amhurst Terr E8 ... 74 A4
Amhurst Wlk SE28 ... 124 A5
Amias Ho EC1 ... 242 A6
Amidas Gdns RM8 ... 80 B4
Amiel St 15 E1 ... 96 C3
Amies St SW11 ... 136 D2
Amigo Ho SE1 ... 261 B6
Amina Way SE16 ... 118 A3
Amis Ave KT19 ... 214 D3
Amity Gr SW20 ... 178 C2
Amity Rd E15 ... 76 D1
Ammanford Gn NW9 ... 45 C3
Ammonite Ho 3 E15 ... 76 D1
Amner Rd SW11 ... 159 A5
Amora 8 HA7 ... 25 C6
Amor Rd W6 ... 112 C3
Amory Ho N1 ... 233 D4
Amott Rd SE15 ... 140 A2
Amoy Pl E14 ... 119 C6
Ampere Way Sta
CR0 ... 204 B1
Ampleforth Rd SE2 ... 124 C4
Ampton Pl WC1 ... 233 C1
Ampton St
WC1 ... 94 B4 233 C1
Amroth Cl SE23 ... 162 B3
Amroth Gn NW9 ... 45 C3
Amstel Ct 12 SE15 ... 139 D5
Amsterdam Rd E14 ... 120 A3
Amundsen Ct 7
E14 ... 119 C1
Amundsen Ho 6
NW10 ... 67 B1
Amwell Cl EN2 ... 17 B6
Amwell St EC1 94 C4 234 A2
Amyand Cotts 12
TW1 ... 153 B5
Amyand Park Gdns 2
TW1 ... 153 B4
Amyand Park Rd
TW1 ... 153 B4
Amy Cl SM6 ... 220 A1
Amy Johnson Ct HA8 ... 26 D1
Amy Johnson Prim Sch
SM6 ... 220 A1
Amyruth Rd SE4 ... 163 C6
Amy Warne Cl E6 ... 100 A3
Anarth Ct KT13 ... 193 C1
Anatola Rd N19 ... 71 C6
Ancaster Cres KT3 ... 200 A3
Ancaster Mews CR0 ... 206 D6
Ancaster Rd BR3 ... 206 D6
Ancaster St SE18 ... 145 C5
Anchorage Cl SW19 ... 179 C5
Anchorage Point 1
E14 ... 119 C4
Anchorage Point Ind Est
SE7 ... 121 C3
Anchor Bsns Pk CR0, SM6 ... 220 A5
Anchor Cl IG11 ... 102 B4
Anchor Ct
Bexley DA7 ... 147 A4
5 Enfield EN1 ... 17 C6
Anchor Ho Ilford IG3 ... 80 A5
Newham E16 ... 99 C1
St Luke's EC1 ... 242 A6
Anchor & Hope La
SE7 ... 121 C2
Anchor Mews SW12 ... 159 B5
Anchor Rd E12 ... 77 D6
Anchor Ret Pk E1 ... 96 C3
Anchor St SE16 ... 118 B2
Anchor Terr SE1 ... 252 B4
Anchor Yd EC1 ... 242 B6
Ancill Cl W6 ... 135 A6 264 A5
Ancona Rd
Plumstead SE18 ... 123 B1
Willesden Green NW10 90 A5
Andace Pk BR1 ... 187 C2
Andalus Rd SW9 ... 138 A2
Andaman Ho 3 E1 ... 97 A2
Ander Cl HA0 ... 65 D4
Andersens Wharf 9
E14 ... 97 B1
Anderson Cl
Morden SM3 ... 201 C1
North Acton W3 ... 89 B1
Southgate N21 ... 16 B6
Anderson Ct NW2 ... 46 C2
Anderson Dr TW15 ... 171 A6
Anderson Ho
1 Barking IG11 ... 101 B5
10 Blackwall E14 ... 120 A6
Upper Tooting SW17 ... 180 B5
Anderson Rd
Homerton E9 ... 74 D2
Redbridge IG8 ... 55 D6
Anderson's Pl TW3 ... 129 D1
Andersons Sq N1 ... 234 C5
Anderson St SW3 ... 257 C2
Anderson Way
Erith DA17 ... 125 D4
Anderson Way *continued*
Erith DA17 ... 125 D4
Anderton Cl SE5 ... 139 B2
Anderton Ct N22 ... 31 D1
Andhurst Ct KT2 ... 176 D2
Andmark Ct UB1 ... 107 B5
Andon Ct BR3 ... 207 A6
Andorra Ct BR1 ... 187 C2
Andover Ave E16 ... 99 D1
Andover Cl
East Bedfont TW14 ... 149 D3
Greenford UB6 ... 85 D3
Andover Ho 5 N7 ... 72 B6
Andover Pl NW6 ... 91 D5
Andover Rd
Finsbury Pk N7 ... 72 B6
Orpington BR6 ... 211 C1
Twickenham TW2 ... 152 B3
Andoversford Ct 2
SE15 ... 139 C6
Andrecht Terr CR4 ... 203 D5
Andreck Ct BR3 ... 186 A1
Andre Malraux Sch
W7 ... 86 C2
Andre St E8 ... 74 A3
Andrew Borde St
WC2 ... 239 D2
Andrew Ct
Beckenham BR3 ... 207 D6
2 Forest Hill SE23 ... 162 D2
Andrewes Ct 2 W7 ... 108 C5
Andrewes Gdns E6 ... 100 A1
Andrewes Ho
Barbican EC2 ... 242 B3
Sutton SM1 ... 217 C4
Andrew Ewing Prim Sch
The TW5 ... 129 B5
Andrew Ho
Enfield EN3 ... 18 C6
New Cross SE4 ... 141 B3
Putney SW15 ... 156 A6
Andrew Logan's Glasshouse* SE1 ... 253 A2
Andrew Marvell Ho 12
N16 ... 73 C4
Andrew Pl SW8 ... 269 D2
Andrew Reed Ho 3
SW18 ... 157 A4
Andrews Cl
Buckhurst Hill IG9 ... 21 C2
Harrow HA1 ... 42 B2
North Cheam KT4 ... 216 D6
Sidcup BR5 ... 190 D1
Andrews Crosse
WC2 ... 241 A1
Andrew's Rd E8 ... 96 B6
Andrew St E14 ... 98 A1
Andrews Wharf 14 E8 96 B6
Andrews Wlk SE17 ... 138 D6
Andrew Wells Ho
BR1 ... 187 B3
Andrew Wilmot Ct
SW18 ... 158 A3
Andridge Ct SW19 ... 179 B2
Andringham Lo 4
BR1 ... 187 B2
Andrula Ct N22 ... 32 D2
Andwell Cl SE2 ... 124 B4
ANERLEY ... 184 B2
Anerley Ct SE20 ... 184 B3
Anerley Gr SE19 ... 183 D3
Anerley Hill SE19 ... 183 D4
Anerley Park Rd
SE20 ... 184 B3
Anerley Pk SE20 ... 184 B3
Anerley Rd SE20 ... 184 B2
Anerley Sta SE20 ... 184 B2
Anerley Station Rd
SE20 ... 184 B2
Anerley Vale SE19 ... 184 A3
Aneurin Bevan Ct
NW2 ... 68 B6
Aneurin Bevan Ho
N11 ... 31 D3
Anfield Cl SW12 ... 159 C4
Angel EC1 ... 94 D5 234 D3
Angela Carter Cl
SW9 ... 138 C2
Angela Ct 2 SE23 ... 162 C3
Angela Davis Ind Est 20
SW9 ... 138 D1
Angel Cl
Edmonton N18 ... 34 A6
Hampton TW12 ... 174 A5
Angel Corner Par 6
N18 ... 34 A6

Angel Ct
Broadgate EC2 ... 242 D2
St James SW1 ... 249 B3
5 Willesden NW2 ... 68 A2
Angel Edmonton N18 ... 34 A5
Angelfield TW3 ... 151 D6
Angel Gate EC1 ... 234 D2
Angel Hill SM1 ... 217 D5
Angel Hill Dr SM1 ... 217 D5
Angel Ho N1 ... 234 B3
Angelica Cl UB7 ... 82 B1
Angelica Dr E6 ... 100 C2
Angelica Gdns CR0 ... 206 D1
Angelina Ho 2
SE15 ... 140 A4
Angelis Appartments
N1 ... 234 D3
Angel La Hayes UB3 ... 83 B2
Stratford E15 ... 76 B2
Angell Park Gdns 4
SW9 ... 138 C2
Angell Rd SW9 ... 138 D2
Angel Mews
Finsbury N1 ... 234 B3
Putney SW15 ... 156 A4
Stepney E1 ... 118 B6
Angel Pas
EC4 ... 117 B6 252 C5
Angel Pl
Borough The SE1 ... 252 C2
1 Edmonton N18 ... 34 A5
Angel Rd Harrow HA1 ... 42 C3
Thames Ditton KT7 ... 197 A1
Angel Rd (North Circular Rd) N18 ... 34 B5
Angel Rd Works N18 ... 34 C5
Angel Road Sta N18 ... 34 C5
Angel Sq N1 ... 234 B3
Angel St EC1 ... 95 A1 242 A2
Angel Sta EC1 ... 94 C5 234 B3
Angel Wlk W6 ... 112 C2
Angerstein Bsns Pk
SE10 ... 121 A2
Angerstein La SE3 ... 142 D4
Anglebury 5 W2 ... 91 C1
Angle Cl UB10 ... 82 C6
Angle Gn RM8 ... 58 C1
Anglers Cl TW10 ... 175 C6
Anglers La NW5 ... 71 B2
Anglers Reach KT6 ... 197 D4
Anglesea Ave 4
SE18 ... 122 D2
Anglesea Ho KT1 ... 197 D5
Anglesea Mews 12
SE18 ... 122 D2
Anglesea Rd
Kingston u T KT1 ... 197 D5
Woolwich SE18 ... 122 D2
Anglesey Cl TW15 ... 148 C1
Anglesey Court Rd
SM5 ... 219 A2
Anglesey Ct W7 ... 86 D3
Anglesey Gdns SM5 ... 219 A2
Anglesey Ho 13 E14 ... 97 C1
Anglesey Rd
Enfield EN3 ... 6 B1
South Oxhey WD19 ... 22 C5
Anglesmede Cres
HA5 ... 41 C6
Anglesmede Way
HA5 ... 41 C6
Angles Rd SW16 ... 182 A6
Anglia Cl N17 ... 34 B3
Anglia Ct RM8 ... 58 D1
Anglia Ho 13 E14 ... 97 A1
Anglian Ind Est
IG11 ... 101 D2
Anglian Rd E11 ... 76 B5
Anglia Wlk E6 ... 100 C6
Anglo American Laundry
SW17 ... 158 A1
Anglo Rd 16 E3 ... 97 B5
Angrave Ct 4 E8 ... 95 D6
Angrave Pas 5 E8 ... 95 D6
Angus Cl KT9 ... 214 C3
Angus Dr HA4 ... 62 C4
Angus Gdns NW9 ... 27 B2
Angus Ho 12 SW12 ... 159 D4
Angus Rd E13 ... 99 C4
Angus St SE14 ... 141 A5
Anhalt Rd
SW11 ... 136 C5 267 B4
Animals in War Meml★
W1 ... 247 D6
Ankerdine Cres
SE18 ... 144 D4

Anlaby Rd TW11 ... 174 C5
Anley Rd W14 ... 112 D4
Anmersh Gr HA7 ... 25 D2
Annabel Cl E14 ... 97 D1
Anna Cl E8 ... 95 D6
Annadale N22 ... 32 B5
Annandale Gr UB10 ... 61 A5
Annandale Rd
Chiswick W4 ... 111 C1
Croydon CR0 ... 222 A6
Greenwich SE10 ... 120 D1
Sidcup DA15 ... 167 D4
Anna Neagle Cl 2
E7 ... 77 A4
Anne Boleyn's Wlk
Belmont SM3 ... 217 A1
Kingston u T KT2 ... 176 A5
Anne Compton Mews
SE12 ... 164 D4
Anne Goodman Ho 3
E1 ... 96 C1
Anne Kerr Ct 18
SW15 ... 156 D5
Anne's Ct NW8 ... 237 B6
Annesley Ave NW9 ... 45 B6
Annesley Cl NW10 ... 67 C5
Annesley Dr CR0 ... 223 B5
Annesley Ho
31 Brixton SW9 ... 138 C4
15 Kennington SW9 ... 138 C5
Annesley Rd SE3 ... 143 B4
Annesley Wlk N19 ... 71 C6
Annesmere Gdns
SE3 ... 143 D2
Anne St E13 ... 99 A3
Annett Cl TW17 ... 193 C5
Annette Cl HA3 ... 24 C1
Annette Cres 16 N1 ... 73 A1
Annette Ct N7 ... 72 B5
Annette Rd N7 ... 72 B4
Annette White Lo 20
N2 ... 30 B1
Annett Rd KT12 ... 194 A2
Anne Way KT8 ... 195 D5
Annie Besant Cl E3 ... 97 B6
Annie Taylor Ho 2
E12 ... 78 C4
Anning St EC2 ... 243 B6
Annington Rd N2 ... 48 D6
Annis Rd E9 ... 75 A2
Ann La SW10 ... 136 B6 266 C5
Ann Moss Way SE16 ... 118 C3
Ann Parkes Ct TW5 ... 128 D3
Ann's Cl SW1 ... 248 A1
Ann's Pl E1 ... 243 C3
Ann St SE18 ... 123 B2
Ann Stroud Ct SE12 ... 165 A6
Annsworthy Ave
CR7 ... 205 B6
Annsworthy Cres
CR7 ... 183 B1
Annunciation RC Inf Sch
The HA8 ... 27 B2
Annunciation RC Jun Sch
The HA8 ... 27 B4
Ansar Gdns E17 ... 53 B4
Ansdell Rd SE15 ... 140 C3
Ansdell St
W8 ... 113 D3 255 D6
Ansdell Terr
W8 ... 113 D3 255 D6
Ansell Gr SM5 ... 203 A1
Ansell Ho E1 ... 96 C2
Ansell Rd SW17 ... 158 D1
Anselm Cl CR0 ... 221 D5
Anselm Rd
Hatch End HA5 ... 23 B3
West Brompton
SW6 ... 135 C6 265 A5
Ansford Rd BR1, SE6 ... 186 B6
Ansleigh Pl W11 ... 112 D6
Anson 30 NW9 ... 27 D1
Anson Ct TW19 ... 148 A4
Anson Ho
Pimlico SW1 ... 269 A6
6 Tower Hamlets E1 ... 97 A3
Anson Pl SE28 ... 123 B4
Anson Prim Sch NW2 ... 68 D3
Anson Rd
Cricklewood NW2 ... 68 C3
Tufnell Pk N7 ... 71 D4
Anson Terr UB5 ... 63 D2
Anstey Ct 6 W3 ... 110 D4
Anstey Ho 7 E9 ... 96 C6
Anstey Lo EN1 ... 17 C5
Anstey Rd SE15 ... 140 A2

Anstey Wlk N15 ... 51 A5
Anstice Cl W4 ... 133 C5
Anstridge Rd SE9 ... 167 B5
Antelope Rd SE18 ... 122 B3
Antenor Ho 11 E2 ... 96 B5
Anthony Cl NW7 ... 27 C6
Anthony Cope Ct N1 ... 235 D2
Anthony Ct
Harrow HA1 ... 42 B2
Isleworth TW7 ... 130 D2
Anthony Ho NW8 ... 237 A5
Anthony Kendal Ho 4
E5 ... 74 B5
Anthony Rd
Croydon SE25 ... 206 A3
East Wickham DA16 ... 146 A4
Greenford UB6 ... 86 C4
Anthony St E1 ... 96 B1
Antigua Wlk SE19 ... 183 B5
Antilles Bay 19 E14 ... 120 A4
Antilles Ho W3 ... 89 B1
Antill Rd Mile End E3 ... 97 A4
Tottenham Hale N15 ... 52 A5
Antill Terr 5 E1 ... 96 D1
Antlers Hill E4 ... 19 D6
Anton Cres SM1 ... 217 C5
Antoneys Cl HA5 ... 22 D1
Antonine Hts SE1 ... 253 A1
Anton Pl HA9 ... 66 D5
Anton St E8 ... 74 A3
Antony Ho
4 Deptford SE14 ... 140 D5
2 Rotherhithe SE16 ... 118 C2
Antrim Gr NW3 ... 70 D2
Antrim Ho SW11 ... 137 A2
Antrim Mans NW3 ... 70 D2
Antrim Rd NW3 ... 70 D2
Antrobus Cl SM1 ... 217 B3
Antrobus Rd W4 ... 111 A3
Anvil Cl SW16 ... 181 C3
Anvil Ho 10 N9 ... 18 A1
Anvil Rd TW16 ... 194 A6
Anworth Cl IG8 ... 37 B4
AOP Gall★ EC2 ... 243 A6
Apex Cl BR3 ... 185 D2
Apex Cnr
Edgware NW7 ... 27 B6
Twickenham TW13 ... 151 B1
Apex Ct W13 ... 87 A1
Apex Ind Est NW10 ... 89 D3
Apex Lo 10 EN5 ... 14 A6
Apex Prim Sch
3 Barking IG11 ... 79 A1
Ilford IG1 ... 78 C6
Apex Ret Pk TW13 ... 151 B1
Aphrodite Ct 11 E14 ... 119 C2
Aplin Ct 4 SM1 ... 217 D2
Aplin Way TW7 ... 130 C4
Apollo Ave
Bromley BR1 ... 187 B2
Loughton HA6 ... 22 A5
Apollo Bldg 2 E14 ... 119 C2
Apollo Ho
Chelsea SW10 ... 266 C5
32 Hackney E2 ... 96 B5
Highgate N6 ... 48 D2
Apollo Ind Bsns Ctr 29
SE8 ... 140 D6
Apollo Pl
Chelsea SW10 ... 266 C4
6 Leyton E11 ... 76 C5
Apollo Studios 18
NW5 ... 71 D3
Apollo Way 1 SE18 ... 123 B3
Apostle Way CR7 ... 182 D1
Apothecary St EC4 ... 241 C1
Appach Rd SW2 ... 160 C5
Appin Ct HA1 ... 42 C2
Appleby Cl
Chingford E4 ... 36 A4
Hayes UB3, UB8 ... 83 A1
Orpington BR5 ... 211 C2
Twickenham TW2 ... 152 B2
West Green N15 ... 51 B4
Appleby Ct W3 ... 111 A4
Appleby Gdns TW14 ... 149 D3
Appleby Rd
Hackney E8 ... 74 A1
Newham E16 ... 99 A1
Appleby St E2 ... 95 D5
Appledore Ave HA4 ... 62 C5
Appledore Cl
Bromley BR2 ... 209 A4
Edgware HA8 ... 26 C2
Upper Tooting SW12, SW17 ... 158 D2

Appledore Cres
DA14 ... 167 D1
Appledore Way NW7 ... 28 D3
Appleford 8 NW5 ... 71 C3
Appleford Ho 6 W10 ... 91 A3
Appleford Rd W10 ... 91 A3
Applegarth
Claygate KT10 ... 212 D3
New Addington CR0 ... 223 D1
Apple Garth TW8 ... 109 D2
Applegarth Dr IG2 ... 57 D5
Applegarth Ho
Borough The SE1 ... 251 D2
9 Camberwell SE15 ... 140 A5
Applegarth Inf Sch
CR0 ... 223 D2
Applegarth Jun Sch
CR0 ... 223 D2
Applegarth Rd
Hammersmith W14 ... 112 D3
Woolwich SE28 ... 124 C6
Apple Gr
Chessington KT9 ... 214 A4
Enfield EN1 ... 5 C2
Apple Lo HA0 ... 65 C5
Apple Mkt KT1 ... 175 D1
Apple Mkt★ WC2 ... 250 B6
Apple Rd E11 ... 76 C5
Appleshaw Ho 4
SE5 ... 139 C2
Appleton Ct 30 E8 ... 74 B3
Appleton Gdns KT3 ... 200 A3
Appleton Rd SE9 ... 144 A2
Appleton Sq CR4 ... 180 C2
Apple Tree Ave UB7 ... 82 B1
Appletree Cl 5
SE20 ... 184 B2
Appletree Ct
Lewisham SE13 ... 142 B1
Northolt UB5 ... 85 A4
Appletree Gdns EN4 ... 2 C1
Apple Tree Yd SW1 ... 249 B4
Applewood Cl
Dollis Hill NW2 ... 68 B5
Ickenham UB10 ... 60 A4
Oakleigh Pk N20 ... 14 C3
Applewood Dr E13 ... 99 B3
Appold St EC2 ... 95 C2 243 A4
Apollo Ct 7 SW9 ... 138 C4
Apprentice Gdns UB5 ... 85 B4
Apprentice Way 5
E5 ... 74 B4
Approach Cl N16 ... 73 C4
Approach Rd
Ashford TW15 ... 171 A4
Bethnal Green E2 ... 96 C5
East Molesey KT8 ... 195 C4
Edgware HA8 ... 26 C4
Merton SW20 ... 178 C1
New Barnet EN4, EN5 ... 2 B1
Approach The
Acton W3 ... 89 B1
Enfield EN1 ... 6 B3
Hendon NW4 ... 46 D4
Orpington BR6 ... 227 D6
Aprey Gdns NW4 ... 46 C5
April Cl Ealing W7 ... 108 C6
Feltham TW13 ... 150 A1
Orpington BR6 ... 227 D3
April Ct 20 E2 ... 96 A5
April Glen SE23 ... 162 D1
April St E8 ... 73 D4
Apsley Cl HA2 ... 42 A4
Apsley Ct SM2 ... 218 A2
Apsley Ctr The NW2 ... 68 A6
Apsley Ho Enfield EN1 ... 17 C5
Hounslow TW4 ... 129 B1
Stepney E1 ... 96 C2
St John's Wood NW8 ... 229 C4
Apsley Ho, The Wellington Mus★
SW1 ... 115 A4 248 B2
Apsley Rd
Croydon SE25 ... 206 B5
Kingston u T KT3 ... 199 A6
Apsley Way
Dollis Hill NW2 ... 68 A6
Mayfair W1 ... 248 B2
Aquarius TW1 ... 153 B3
Aquarius Bsns Pk
NW2 ... 46 A1
Aquarius Way HA6 ... 22 A6
Aquila St NW8 ... 92 B5 229 D4
Aquinas St
SE1 ... 116 C5 251 B3
Arabella Ct NW8 ... 229 B4

Arabella Dr SW15 ... 133 C1
Arabia Cl E4 ... 20 B4
Arabian Ho 3 E1 ... 97 A3
Arabin Rd SE4 ... 141 B1
Aragon Ave KT7 ... 196 D4
Aragon Cl
Ashford TW16 ... 171 D3
Bromley BR2 ... 210 B1
Enfield EN2 ... 4 B5
Aragon Ct
Beckenham BR3 ... 186 A2
East Molesey KT8 ... 196 A5
Aragon Dr HA4 ... 40 D1
Aragon Pl SM4 ... 201 A2
Aragon Prim Sch
SM4 ... 200 D2
Aragon Rd
Kingston u T KT2 ... 176 A5
West Barnes SM4 ... 201 A2
Aragon Twr SE8 ... 119 B2
Arakan Ho 4 N16 ... 73 B4
Aral Ho 14 E1 ... 96 D3
Arandora Cres RM6 ... 58 B2
Aranya Ct 3 E17 ... 35 A1
Arapiles Ho 6 E14 ... 98 B1
Arbery Rd E3 ... 97 A5
Arbon Ct N1 ... 235 B5
Arbor Cl BR3 ... 185 D1
Arbor Ct N16 ... 73 B6
Arborfield Cl SW2 ... 160 B3
Arborfield Ho 7
E14 ... 119 C6
Arbor Rd E4 ... 20 B1
Arbour Ho 3 E1 ... 96 D1
Arbour Rd EN3 ... 6 D2
Arbour Sq E1 ... 96 D1
Arbroath Rd SE9 ... 144 A2
Arbrook Chase KT10 ... 212 A2
Arbrook Ct
Chessington KT9 ... 213 D3
St Paul's Cray BR5 ... 190 A2
Arbrook Hall KT10 ... 212 D2
Arbrook La KT10 ... 212 B2
Arbury Ho BR1 ... 188 A3
Arbury Terr 3 SE26 ... 162 B1
Arbuthnot La DA5 ... 169 A5
Arbuthnot Rd SE14 ... 140 D3
Arbutus St E8 ... 95 D6
Arcade Ho 7 NW11 ... 47 B4
Arcade The
Broadgate EC2 ... 243 A3
2 Eltham SE9 ... 166 C5
1 Tufnell Pk N7 ... 72 A4
Walthamstow E17 ... 53 C5
Arcadia Ave N3 ... 29 C2
Arcadia Centre The
W5 ... 109 D6
Arcadia Cl SM5 ... 219 A4
Arcadian Ave DA5 ... 169 A5
Arcadian Cl DA5 ... 169 A5
Arcadian Gdns N22 ... 32 C3
Arcadian Ho SW6 ... 136 A3
Arcadian Pl SW18 ... 157 B4
Arcadian Rd DA5 ... 169 A5
Arcadia St E14 ... 97 C1
Arcadia Univ
W2 ... 113 D6 245 C5
Archangel St SE16 ... 118 D4
Archbishop Coggan Ho
SE13 ... 142 B1
Archbishop Lanfranc Sch
The CR0 ... 204 A3
Archbishop's Pl 1
SW2 ... 160 B4
Archbishop Sumner CE Prim Sch
SE11 ... 116 C2 261 B3
Archbishop Tenison's CE Sch CR0 ... 221 D5
Archbishop Tenison's Sch SE11 ... 138 B6 270 D5
Archdale Bsns Ctr
HA2 ... 64 A6
Archdale Ct W12 ... 112 B5
Archdale Ho SE1 ... 263 A6
Archdale Pl KT3 ... 198 D6
Archdale Rd SE22 ... 139 D1
Archdeacon Cambridge's CE Prim Sch 2
TW2 ... 152 C2
Archel Rd
W14 ... 135 B6 264 C6
Archer Cl Barnet EN5 ... 13 B5

Archer Cl *continued*
Kingston u T KT2 .... 176 A3
Archer Ct TW13 ...... 150 A3
Archer Ho
1 Battersea SW11 ... 136 B3
Ealing W13 ... 109 B5
24 Hoxton N1 ... 95 C6
1 New Cross SE14 .. 141 A4
Notting Hill W11 ... 244 D6
Archer Mews TW12 .. 174 A4
Archer Rd SE25 ... 206 B5
Archers Ct 3 CR2 ... 221 A3
Archers Dr EN3 ... 6 C3
Archers Lo 22 SE16 .. 118 A1
Archer Sq SE14 ... 141 A6
Archer St W1 ... 249 C6
Archer Terr UB7 ... 104 A6
Archery Cl
Harrow HA3 ... 42 D6
Paddington W2 ... 237 B1
Archery Fields Ho
WC1 ... 234 A2
Archery Rd SE9 ... 166 B6
Archery Stps W2 ... 247 B6
Arches Bsns Ctr The
UB2 ... 107 B4
Arches The
Harrow HA2 ... 63 D6
Strand WC2 ... 250 B4
Archgate Bsns Ctr 1
N12 ... 30 A5
Archibald Mews W1 248 C5
Archibald Rd N7 ... 71 D4
Archibald St E3 ... 97 C4
Archie Cl UB7 ... 104 C4
Archie St SE1 ... 253 B1
Arch St SE1 ... 117 A3 262 A5
Archway N19 ... 71 C6
Archway Bsns Ctr 5
N19 ... 71 D5
Archway Cl
North Kensington
W10 ... 90 D2
2 Upper Holloway
N19 ... 71 C6
Wallington SM6 ... 220 A5
Wimbledon SW19 ... 179 D6
Archway Hts 5 N19 ... 49 C1
Archway L Ctr N19 ... 71 C6
Archway Mews
SW15 ... 135 A1
Archway Rd N6 ... 49 B2
Archway St SW13,
SW14 ... 133 C2
Archway Sta N19 ... 71 C6
Arcola St E8 ... 73 D3
Arcon Dr UB5 ... 85 A3
Arctic St NW5 ... 71 B3
Arcus Rd BR1 ... 186 C4
Ardbeg Rd SE24 ... 161 B6
Arden 17 SW19 ... 156 D3
Arden Cl
Bushey Heath WD23 ... 8 D4
Erith SE28 ... 102 D1
Harrow HA1 ... 64 B5
Twickenham TW2 ... 151 B4
Arden Court Gdns N2 . 48 B3
Arden Cres
Dagenham RM9 ... 80 D1
Millwall E14 ... 119 C2
Arden Gr BR6 ... 226 D4
Arden Grange N12 ... 30 A6
Arden Ho
21 Hoxton N1 ... 95 C5
29 Stockwell SW9 ... 138 A3
Vauxhall SE11 ... 260 C3
Arden Mews E17 ... 53 D4
Arden Mhor HA5 ... 40 B5
Arden Rd Ealing W13 .. 109 C6
Finchley N3 ... 47 B6
Ardent Cl SE25 ... 205 C6
Ardent Ho 30 E3 ... 97 A5
Ardfern Ave SW16 ... 204 C6
Ardfillan Rd SE6 ... 164 B2
Ardgowan Rd SE6 ... 164 C3
Ardilaun Rd N5 ... 73 A4
Ardingly Cl CR0 ... 222 D5
Ardleigh Gdns SM3 .. 201 C2
Ardleigh Ho 4 IG11 .. 101 A6
Ardleigh Rd
Kingsland N1 ... 73 C2
Walthamstow E17 ... 35 B2
Ardleigh Terr E17 ... 35 B2
Ardley Cl
Forest Hill SE6 ... 163 A1
Neasden NW10 ... 67 C5
Ruislip HA4 ... 39 A2
Ardlui Rd SE27 ... 161 A2
Ardmay Gdns KT6 ... 198 A4
Ardmere Rd SE13 ... 164 B5
Ardmore La IG9 ... 21 B4
Ardmore Pl IG9 ... 21 B4
Ardoch Rd SE6 ... 164 B2
Ardra Rd N9 ... 18 D1
Ardrossan Gdns KT4 . 216 A5
Ardshiel Cl 6 SW15 . 134 D2
Ardwell Ave IG6 ... 57 A4
Ardwell Rd SW2 ... 160 A2
Ardwick Rd NW2 ... 69 C4
Arena Bsns Ctr N4 ... 51 A3
Arena Est N4 ... 50 D3
Arena Sta SE25 ... 206 C4
Arena The EN3 ... 7 B5
Ares Ct 16 E14 ... 119 C2
Arethusa Ho 8 E14 . 119 D2
Argali Ho 3 DA18 ... 125 A3
Argall Ave E10 ... 52 D1
Argall Way E10 ... 53 A1
Argenta Way NW10 ... 66 D1
Argent Ct KT6 ... 214 C5
Argent Ctr The UB3 . 106 A4
Argent Ho HA5 ... 23 B4
Argo Bsns Ctr 7
NW6 ... 91 C4
Argon Mews SW6 ... 265 B3
Argon Rd N18 ... 34 D5
Argos Ct 5 SW9 ... 138 C4
Argos Ho 8 E2 ... 96 B5
Argosy Ho
Fitzrovia W1 ... 238 D5
Rotherhithe SE8 ... 119 A2
Argus Way UB5 ... 85 A4
Argyle Cl W13 ... 87 A3
Argyle Ho
Cubitt Town E14 ... 120 A3
Richmond TW10 ... 153 C2
Sutton SM2 ... 218 A2
Teddington TW11 ... 174 C5
Argyle Mans 4 NW2 .. 68 D4
Argyle Pl W6 ... 112 B2
Argyle Prim Sch
WC1 ... 94 A4 233 A2
Argyle Rd Ealing W13 .. 87 A2
Edmonton N18 ... 34 A6
Harrow HA2 ... 41 D3
Hounslow TW3 ... 151 D6
Ilford IG1 ... 78 C6
Leyton E15 ... 76 C4
Newham E16 ... 99 B1
Stepney E1 ... 96 D3
Tottenham N17 ... 34 A2
Woodside Pk N12 ... 29 C5
Argyle Sq
WC1 ... 94 A4 233 B2
Argyle St WC1 . 94 A4 233 B2
Argyle Way SE16 ... 118 A1
Argyle Wlk WC1 ... 233 B1
Argyll Ave UB1 ... 107 D5
Argyll Cl SW9 ... 138 B2
Argyll Ct 15 SW2 ... 160 A4
Argyll Gdns HA8 ... 26 D2
Argyll Mans
Chelsea SW3 ... 266 D6
West Kensington W14 254 B4
Argyll Rd
Kensington
W8 ... 113 C4 245 B1
Woolwich SE18 ... 123 A3
Argyll St W1 ... 93 C1 239 A1
Aria Ct IG2 ... 57 A3
Arica Ho SE16 ... 118 B3
Arica Rd SE4 ... 141 A2
Ariel Ct
5 Belvedere DA17 .. 125 C1
5 Hammersmith
W12 ... 112 A3
Newington SE11 ... 261 C3
Ariel Rd NW6 ... 69 C2
Ariel Way
Hounslow TW4 ... 128 B2
Shepherd's Bush W11,
W12 ... 112 D5
Aristotle Rd SW4 ... 137 D2
Arizona Bldg 10
SE13 ... 141 D4
Ark Acad HA9 ... 65 C6
Arkansas Ho 21 N19 ... 49 D2
Ark Ct N16 ... 73 D6
Arkell Gr SW16 ... 182 D3
Arkindale Rd SE6 ... 164 A1
Arklay Cl UB8 ... 82 B3
ARKLEY ... 12 A6
Arkley Cres E17 ... 53 B4
Arkley Dr EN5 ... 12 B6
Arkley Pk EN5 ... 11 B5
Arkley Rd E17 ... 53 B4
Arklow Ho SE17 ... 139 B6
Arklow Mews 4
KT6 ... 214 A6
Arklow Rd SE14 ... 141 B6
Arklow Road Trad Est
SE14 ... 141 B6
Arkwright Ho 23
SW2 ... 160 A4
Arkwright Mans 1
NW3 ... 70 A3
Arkwright Rd NW3 ... 70 A3
Arlesey Cl SW15 ... 157 A6
Arlesford Rd SW9 ... 138 A2
Arless Ho 8 HA1 ... 42 D4
Arlidge Ho EC1 ... 241 B4
Arlingford Rd SW2 ... 160 C5
Arlington N12 ... 13 C1
Arlington Ave
N1 ... 95 A6 235 B5
Arlington Cl
Lewisham SE13 ... 164 B6
Sidcup DA15 ... 167 C4
Sutton SM1 ... 217 C6
Twickenham TW1 ... 153 C5
Arlington Ct
13 Acton W3 ... 110 D5
Highgate N6 ... 49 A3
4 Twickenham TW1 . 153 C5
Arlington Dr
Carshalton SM5 ... 218 D6
Ruislip HA4 ... 39 B3
Arlington Gdns
Acton Green W4 ... 111 A1
Ilford IG1 ... 56 C1
Arlington Gn NW7 ... 28 D3
Arlington Ho
3 Deptford SE8 ... 141 B6
Finsbury EC1 ... 234 B2
1 Shepherd's Bush
W12 ... 112 B5
Arlington Lo SW2 ... 138 B1
Arlington Park Mans 1
W4 ... 111 A1
Arlington Pl 7 SE10 . 142 A5
Arlington Rd
Ashford TW15 ... 170 B5
Camden Town
NW1 ... 93 B6 231 D5
Ealing W13 ... 87 B1
Osidge N14 ... 15 C3
Richmond TW10 ... 153 D2
Surbiton KT6 ... 197 D3
Teddington TW11 ... 174 D6
Twickenham TW1 ... 153 C5
Woodford IG8 ... 37 B3
Arlington Sq
N1 ... 95 A6 235 B5
Arlington St
SW1 ... 115 C5 249 A4
Arlington Way
EC1 ... 94 C4 234 B2
Arliss Way UB5 ... 84 C6
Arlow Rd N21 ... 16 C3
Armada Ct 11 SE8 ... 141 C6
Armadale Cl N17 ... 52 B5
Armadale Rd
Feltham TW14 ... 150 A6
West Brompton SW6 . 265 A5
Armada St 10 SE8 ... 141 C6
Armada Way
Newham E6 ... 101 B1
Newham E16 ... 122 D6
Armagh Rd E3 ... 97 B6
Armeston KT3 ... 199 B2
Armfield Cl KT8 ... 195 B4
Armfield Cotts 3
SW19 ... 180 D1
Armfield Cres CR4 ... 180 D1
Armfield Rd EN2 ... 5 B4
Arminger Rd W12 ... 112 B5
Armistice Gdns
SE25 ... 206 A6
Armitage Ho
NW1 ... 92 C2 237 B4
Armitage Rd
Golders Green NW11 ... 47 B1
Greenwich SE10 ... 120 D1
Armour Cl N7 ... 72 B2
Armoury Ho E3 ... 97 A6
Armoury Rd SE8 ... 141 D3
Armoury Way SW18 .. 157 C6
Armsby Ho 17 E1 ... 96 C2
Armstead Wlk RM10 .. 81 C1
Armstrong Ave IG8 ... 36 C4
Armstrong Cl
Bickley BR1 ... 210 A6
Dagenham RM8 ... 58 D2
Newham E6 ... 100 B1
Pinner HA5 ... 40 A3
Walton-on-T KT12 ... 194 A3
Armstrong Cres EN4 ... 2 B2
Armstrong Ho 8
SW15 ... 156 D5
Armstrong Rd
East Acton W3 ... 111 D5
Feltham TW13 ... 173 A5
Knightsbridge SW7 ... 256 C5
10 Willesden NW10 ... 67 C1
Woolwich SE18 ... 123 A3
Armstrong Way UB2 107 D4
Armytage Rd TW5 ... 128 D5
Arnal Cres SW18 ... 157 A4
Arncliffe NW6 ... 91 D6
Arncliffe Cl N11 ... 31 A4
Arncroft Ct IG11 ... 102 B4
Arndale Wlk 6
SW18 ... 157 D6
Arndell Ho 16 SM1 ... 218 A4
Arne Gr BR6 ... 227 D5
Arne Ho SE11 ... 260 C2
Arne St WC2 ... 94 A1 240 B1
Arnett Sq E4 ... 35 B4
Arneways Ave RM6 ... 58 D6
Arneway St SW1 ... 259 D5
Arne Wlk SE3 ... 142 D1
Arnewood Cl SW15 ... 156 A3
Arney's La CR4 ... 203 A3
Arngask Rd SE6 ... 164 B4
Arnhem Pl E14 ... 119 C3
Arnhem Way 3
SE22 ... 161 C6
Arnhem Wharf E14 . 119 C3
Arnhem Wharf Prim Sch
E14 ... 119 C3
Arnison Rd KT8 ... 196 B5
Arnold Ave E EN3 ... 7 C5
Arnold Ave W EN3 ... 7 B5
Arnold Cir E2 ... 95 D4
Arnold Cl HA3 ... 44 B2
Arnold Cres TW7 ... 152 B6
Arnold Ct E18 ... 36 D2
Arnold Dr KT9 ... 213 D2
Arnold Est SE1 ... 253 D1
Arnold Gdns N13 ... 32 D5
Arnold Ho
Croydon CR0 ... 220 D4
Newington SE17 ... 261 D1
9 Stoke Newington
N16 ... 73 C5
Arnold House Sch
NW8 ... 92 B5 229 C3
Arnold Rd Bow E3 ... 97 C4
Dagenham RM10 ... 81 C1
Mitcham SW17 ... 180 D3
Northolt UB5 ... 63 A2
Tottenham N15 ... 51 D6
Arnos Gr N14 ... 15 D1
Arnos Grove Ct 4
N11 ... 31 C5
Arnos Grove Sta N11 .. 31 C6
Arnos Rd N11 ... 31 C6
Arnot Ho 27 SE5 ... 139 A5
Arnott Cl
Acton Green W4 ... 111 B2
Thamesmead SE28 ... 124 C5
Arnould Ave SE5 ... 139 B1
Arnsberg Way DA6,
DA7 ... 147 C1
Arnside Gdns HA9 ... 43 D1
Arnside Ho 2 SE17 .. 139 B6
Arnside Rd DA7 ... 147 C4
Arnside St SE17 ... 139 A6
Arnulf St SE6 ... 185 D6
Arnull's Rd SW16 ... 182 D4
Arodene Rd SW2 ... 160 B5
Arosa Rd 8 TW1 ... 153 D5
Arragon Gdns
Streatham SW16 ... 182 A3
West Wickham BR4 .. 223 D5
Arragon Rd
Newham E6 ... 99 D6
4 Twickenham TW1 . 153 A3
Wandsworth SW18 .. 157 C3
Arran Cl SM6 ... 219 C4
Arran Ct Edgware HA8 .. 10 D2
Arran Ct *continued*
32 Hendon NW9 ... 27 D1
Neasden NW10 ... 67 B5
Arrandene Ho 3
BR5 ... 190 B1
Arran Dr
Stanmore HA7 ... 25 C6
Wanstead E12 ... 77 D6
Arran Ho
5 Canary Wharf
E14 ... 120 A5
Stoke Newington N16 .. 51 D1
Arran Mews W5 ... 110 B5
Arran Rd SE6 ... 164 A2
Arran Wlk N1 ... 73 A1
Arras Ave SM4 ... 202 A4
Arras Ho SE2 ... 146 D6
Arrol Ho SE1 ... 262 B5
Arrol Rd BR3 ... 206 D6
Arrowe Ct 6 E5 ... 74 B4
Arrow Ho 23 N1 ... 95 C6
Arrow Rd E3 ... 97 D4
Arrow Scout Wlk
UB5 ... 85 A4
Arrowsmith Ho SE11 260 C2
Arsenal Rd SE9 ... 144 B2
Arsenal Sta N5 ... 72 C5
Arsenal Way SE18 ... 123 A3
Arta Ho 26 E1 ... 96 C1
Artcadia Lifestyle★
EC2 ... 243 C4
Artemis Ct 14 E14 ... 119 C2
Artemis Pl SW18 ... 157 B4
Arterberry Rd SW20,
SW19 ... 178 D2
Artesian Cl NW10 ... 67 B1
Artesian Gr EN5 ... 2 A1
Artesian Rd W2 ... 91 C1
Artesian Wlk 4 E11 ... 76 C5
Arthingworth St E15 .. 98 C6
Arthur Ct
Battersea SW11 ... 268 B1
10 North Kensington
W10 ... 90 D1
Paddington W2 ... 91 D1
South Croydon CR0 ... 221 B5
Arthur Deakin Ho 1
E1 ... 96 A2
Arthurdon Rd SE4 ... 163 C6
Arthur Gr SE18 ... 123 A2
Arthur Henderson Ho
9 Crouch End N19 ... 49 D2
9 Fulham SW6 ... 135 B3
Arthur Newton Ho 19
SW11 ... 136 B2
Arthur Rd
Dagenham RM6 ... 58 D3
Edmonton N9 ... 17 D2
6 Kingston u T KT2 . 176 C3
Lower Holloway N7 ... 72 B4
Newham E6 ... 100 B5
West Barnes KT3 ... 200 B4
Wimbledon SW19 ... 179 C6
Arthur Ruxley Est
DA14 ... 190 D4
Arthur St
EC4 ... 117 B6 252 D6
Arthur Wade Ho 7
E2 ... 95 D4
Arthur Walls Ho 3
E12 ... 78 C5
Artichoke Hill 8 E1 .. 118 B6
Artichoke Mews 5
SE5 ... 139 B4
Artichoke Pl SE5 ... 139 B4
Artillery Cl IG2 ... 57 A3
Artillery Ho Bow E3 ... 97 A6
Westminster SW1 ... 259 C5
Woolwich SE18 ... 122 C1
Artillery La
Broadgate
E1 ... 95 C2 243 B3
North Kensington W12 .. 90 A1
Artillery Pas E1 ... 243 B3
Artillery Pl
Harrow Weald HA3 ... 24 A3
Westminster SW1 ... 259 C5
Woolwich SE18 ... 122 C2
Artillery Row SW1 .. 259 C5
Artington Cl BR6 ... 227 A4
Artisan Cl E16 ... 122 D6
Artisan Ct E8 ... 74 A2
Artisan Mews 9
NW10 ... 90 D4
Artisan Quarter 10
NW10 ... 90 D4

Artizan St E1 . . . . **243** B2
Arton Wilson Ho **12**
  SW15 . . . .**156** A6
Art Pilgrim★ NW3 . . . .**70** B1
Artsdepot★ N12 . . . . . .**30** A5
Arts Educational Sch The
  10 W4 . . . .**111** C2
Arwell Cl E10 . . . .**53** D3
Arundale KT1 . . . .**197** D5
Arundel Ave SM4 . . . . .**201** B5
Arundel Bldgs SE1 . . . .**263** B5
Arundel Cl
  Croydon CR0 . . . .**220** D5
  Hampton TW12 . . . . . .**173** D5
  Leyton E15 . . . .**76** C4
  Sidcup DA5 . . . .**169** B5
  Wandsworth SW11 . . . .**158** C6
Arundel Ct
  Barnes SW13 . . . .**134** B6
  Beckenham BR2 . . . . .**186** C1
  2 Bexley DA6 . . . .**147** A1
  Chelsea SW3 . . . .**257** B2
  Colney Hatch N12 . . . . .**30** C4
  3 Croydon CR0 . . . . . .**220** D5
  Harrow HA2 . . . .**63** C4
  Putney SW15 . . . .**156** D6
  Tottenham N17 . . . .**34** A2
Arundel Dr
  Borehamwood WD6 . . .**11** A6
  Harrow HA2 . . . .**63** C4
  Woodford IG8 . . . .**37** A3
Arundel Gdns
  Burnt Oak HA8 . . . .**27** B3
  Ilford IG3 . . . .**80** A6
  Notting Hill
  W11 . . . . . . **113 B6 244** C6
  Southgate N21 . . . .**16** C3
Arundel Gr N16 . . . .**73** C3
Arundel Ho
  Croydon CR0 . . . .**221** B3
  Islington N1 . . . . .**94** D6 **234** D6
  Richmond TW10 . . . . . .**154** C6
  3 South Acton W3 . . . . .**110** D4
Arundel Lo
  Church End N3 . . . .**29** B1
  9 Upper Holloway
  N19 . . . .**72** A6
Arundel Mans
  Barnes SW13 . . . .**134** B6
  Fulham SW6 . . . .**264** D2
Arundel Pl N1, N7 . . . . .**72** C2
Arundel Rd
  Belmont SM2 . . . .**217** B1
  Cockfosters EN4 . . . . . .**2** C2
  Hounslow TW4 . . . . . .**128** C2
  Kingston u T KT1 . . . . .**177** A1
  Thornton Heath CR0 . . .**205** B3
Arundel Sq N7 . . . .**72** C2
Arundel St
  WC2 . . . .**116 B6 250** D6
Arundel Terr SW13 . . . .**134** B6
Arungford Mews **12**
  SW2 . . . .**160** C6
Arun Ho **3** KT2 . . . . .**175** D2
Arvon Rd N5 . . . .**72** C3
Asa Ct UB3 . . . .**105** D3
Asaph Ho SE14 . . . . . .**141** B4
Asbaston Terr IG11 . . . .**79** A2
Asbury Ct N21 . . . .**16** A6
Ascalon Ct **16** SW2 . . .**160** B4
Ascalon Ho SW8 . . . . .**269** A3
Ascalon St
  SW8 . . . . . . **137** C5 **269** A3
Ascham Dr E4 . . . .**35** C3
Ascham End E17 . . . . . .**35** A2
Ascham St NW5 . . . . . .**71** C3
Aschurch Rd CR0 . . . . .**205** D2
Ascot Cl
  Borehamwood WD6 . . .**10** C6
  Northolt UB5 . . . .**63** C3
Ascot Ct
  8 Brixton SW4 . . . . .**138** A1
  Bromley BR1 . . . .**188** A1
  Old Bexley DA5 . . . . . .**169** B4
  St John's Wood NW8 . . .**229** C1
Ascot Gdns Enfield EN3 . . .**6** C6
  Southall UB1 . . . .**85** C2
Ascot Ho
  6 Acton Green W4 . . .**111** A1
  1 Paddington W9 . . . . .**91** C2
  Penge SE26 . . . .**184** B4
  Regent's Pk NW1 . . . . .**231** D2
Ascot Lo Enfield EN1 . . .**17** B4
  Paddington NW6 . . . . . .**91** D5
Ascot Par **9** SW4 . . . .**138** A1
Ascot Rd **12** HA7 . . . . .**25** C1

Ascot Rd
  East Bedfont TW14 . . .**148** D2
  Edmonton N18 . . . .**34** A6
  Newham E6 . . . .**100** B4
  Orpington BR5 . . . . . .**211** D5
  Streatham SW17 . . . . .**181** A4
  Tottenham N15 . . . .**51** B4
Ascott Ave W5 . . . .**110** A4
Ascott Ct UB5 . . . .**40** A5
Ashbourne Ave
  East Barnet N20 . . . . . .**14** D2
  Erith DA7 . . . .**147** A5
  Harrow HA2 . . . .**64** B1
  Temple Fortune NW11 . . .**47** B4
  Willesden E18 . . . .**55** B5
Ashbourne Ct
  Ealing W5 . . . .**88** C2
  18 Woodside Pk N12 . . .**29** C6
Ashbourne Coll
  W8 . . . .**113** D4 **245** C1
Ashbourne Gr
  Chiswick W4 . . . .**111** C1
  East Dulwich SE22 . . . .**139** D1
  Edgware NW7 . . . .**28** B4
Ashbourne Lo **2** N13 . . .**32** C6
Ashbourne Par **8**
  NW11 . . . .**47** B5
Ashbourne Rd
  Ealing W5 . . . .**88** C3
  Mitcham CR4 . . . .**181** A3
Ashbourne Rise BR6 . .**227** C4
Ashbourne Terr **1**
  SW19 . . . .**179** C3
Ashbourne Way
  NW11 . . . .**47** B5
Ashbridge Ct **3** W6 . . .**112** B3
Ashbridge Rd E11 . . . . .**54** D2
Ashbridge St
  NW8 . . . .**92** C3 **237** A5
Ashbrook HA8 . . . .**26** B4
Ashbrook Rd
  Dagenham RM10 . . . . .**81** D5
  Upper Holloway N19 . . . .**71** D6
Ashburn Gdns SW7 . . .**256** A4
Ashburnham Cl N2 . . . . .**48** B5
Ashburnham Gdns
  HA1 . . . .**42** D3
Ashburnham Gr
  SE10 . . . .**141** D5
Ashburnham Pk
  KT10 . . . .**212** A4
Ashburnham Pl
  SE10 . . . .**141** D5
Ashburnham Prim Sch
  SW10 . . . .**266** C4
Ashburnham Rd
  Chelsea
  SW10 . . . . **136** A5 **266** C4
  Kensal Rise NW10 . . . . .**90** C5
  Richmond TW10 . . . . .**153** B1
Ashburnham Retreat **3**
  SE10 . . . .**141** D5
Ashburnham Twr
  SW10 . . . .**266** C4
Ashburn Pl
  SW7 . . . . . . **114** A2 **256** A3
Ashburton Ave
  Croydon CR0 . . . .**206** B1
  Ilford IG3 . . . .**79** D4
Ashburton Cl CR0 . . . .**206** A1
Ashburton Ct **11** HA5 . .**40** D6
Ashburton Gdns
  CR0 . . . .**222** A6
Ashburton Ho
  2 Wallington SM6 . . .**219** D3
Ashburton Jun & Inf Sch
  CR0 . . . .**206** B1
Ashburton Learning
  Village CR9 . . . .**206** B2
Ashburton Mans
  SW10 . . . .**266** B4
Ashburton Rd
  Croydon CR0 . . . .**222** A6
  Newham E16 . . . .**99** A1
  Ruislip HA4 . . . .**62** A6
Ashburton Terr **2**
  E13 . . . .**99** A5
Ashbury Dr UB10 . . . . . .**60** D5

Ashbury Gdns RM6 . . . . .**58** D4
Ashbury Pl SW19 . . . . .**180** A4
Ashbury Rd SW11 . . . .**137** A2
Ashby Ave KT19, KT9 . .**214** C2
Ashby Ct NW8 . . . .**236** D6
Ashby Gr N1 . . . .**73** A1
Ashby Grange **7**
  SM6 . . . .**219** C2
Ashby Ho
  6 Brixton SW9 . . . . .**138** D3
  17 Islington N1 . . . . . .**73** A1
  3 Northolt UB5 . . . . . .**85** B3
  14 Surbiton KT6 . . . . .**198** A3
Ashby Mews
  10 Clapham Pk
  SW2 . . . .**160** B3
  New Cross SE4 . . . . . .**141** B3
Ashby Rd
  New Cross SE4 . . . . . .**141** B3
  South Tottenham N15 . . . .**52** A4
Ashby St EC1 . . . .**94** D4 **234** D4
Ashby Way UB7 . . . . . .**126** C5
Ashby Wlk CR0 . . . . . .**205** A3
Ashchurch Ct **2**
  W12 . . . .**112** A3
Ashchurch Gr W12 . . . .**112** A3
Ashchurch Park Villas
  W12 . . . .**112** A3
Ashchurch Terr
  W12 . . . .**112** A3
Ash Cl
  Carshalton SM5 . . . . .**218** D6
  Edgware HA8 . . . .**27** A6
  Kingston u T KT3 . . . . .**177** A6
  Penge SE20 . . . .**184** C1
  Petts Wood BR5 . . . . .**211** B4
  Sidcup DA14 . . . .**168** B1
  Stanmore HA7 . . . .**25** A4
Ashcombe Ave KT6 . . .**197** D2
Ashcombe Ct **1**
  SW15 . . . .**156** D6
Ashcombe Gdns HA8 . . .**26** C6
Ashcombe Ho **10** E3 . . .**97** D4
Ashcombe Pk NW2 . . . . .**67** C5
Ashcombe Rd
  Wallington SM5 . . . . . .**219** A2
  Wimbledon SW19 . . . . .**179** C5
Ashcombe Sq KT3 . . . .**199** A6
Ashcombe St SW6 . . . .**135** D3
Ashcroft
  Hatch End HA5 . . . .**23** C4
  Osidge N14 . . . .**15** D2
Ashcroft Ave DA15 . . . .**168** A5
Ashcroft Cres DA15 . . .**168** A5
Ashcroft Ct
  8 Eltham SE9 . . . . .**166** C5
  Wembley HA0 . . . .**65** A4
  3 Whetstone N20 . . . . .**14** B2
Ashcroft Ho SW8 . . . . .**269** A2
Ashcroft Rd Bow E3 . . . .**97** A4
  Chessington KT9 . . . . .**214** B5
Ashcroft Sq **3** W6 . . . .**112** C2
Ashcroft Tech Acad
  SW15 . . . .**157** B6
Ash Ct Chingford E4 . . . .**20** B4
  Clapham SW11 . . . . . .**159** A6
  Lee SE12 . . . .**165** A4
  Marylebone W1 . . . . . .**237** C2
  Romford RM7 . . . .**59** D3
  2 Rotherhithe SE16 . .**119** A5
  Upper Holloway N19 . . . .**71** C6
  West Ewell KT19 . . . . .**215** A4
  2 West Norwood
  SW27 . . . .**182** C5
  9 Wimbledon SW19 . .**179** A3
  Woodford E18 . . . .**37** C2
Ashdale Cl
  Stanwell TW19 . . . . . .**148** A4
  Twickenham TW2 . . . . .**152** A4
Ashdale Gr HA7 . . . .**24** D4
Ashdale Ho N4 . . . .**51** B2
Ashdale Rd SE12 . . . . .**165** B3
Ashdale Way TW2 . . . . .**152** A4
Ashdene
  6 Deptford SE15 . . . .**140** B5
  Pinner HA5 . . . .**40** C6
Ashdene Ct TW15 . . . . .**171** A3
Ashdon Cl IG8 . . . .**37** B4
Ashdon Rd NW10 . . . . . .**89** D6
Ashdown Ealing W13 . . . .**87** B2
  Putney SW15 . . . .**156** D6
Ashdown Cl **13** BR3 . . .**185** D1
Ashdown Cres NW5 . . . .**71** A3
Ashdown Ct
  Dulwich SE22 . . . .**162** A3

Ashdown Ct continued
  Ilford IG1 . . . .**78** D2
  New Malden KT4 . . . . .**199** D2
  Sutton SM2 . . . .**218** A2
Ashdowne Ct N17 . . . . . .**34** A2
Ashdown Ho **7** E5 . . . . .**74** A6
Ashdown Pl
  Ewell KT17 . . . .**215** D1
  Thames Ditton KT7 . . .**197** A2
Ashdown Rd
  Enfield EN3 . . . .**6** C3
  Hillingdon UB10 . . . . . .**82** C5
  Kingston u T KT1 . . . . .**176** A1
Ashdown Way SW17 . . .**159** A2
Ashdown Wlk **2**
  E14 . . . .**119** C2
Ashe Ho **2** TW1 . . . . . .**153** D5
Ashen E6 . . . .**100** C1
Ashenden SE17 . . . . . .**262** B4
Ashenden Rd E5 . . . .**75** A3
Ashen Gr SW19 . . . . . .**157** C2
Ashentree Ct EC4 . . . . .**241** B1
Asher Loftus Way
  N11 . . . .**30** C4
Asher Way E1 . . . .**118** A6
Ashfield Ave
  Bushey WD23 . . . .**8** A4
  Feltham TW13 . . . .**150** B3
Ashfield Cl
  Beckenham BR3 . . . . .**185** C3
  Richmond TW10 . . . . .**154** A3
Ashfield Gr SW9 . . . . . .**138** A3
Ashfield Ho **5** N5 . . . . .**73** A3
Ashfield La BR7 . . . . . .**189** A3
Ashfield Par N14 . . . . . .**15** D3
Ashfield Pl BR7 . . . . . .**189** A3
Ashfield Rd
  East Acton W3 . . . . . .**111** D5
  New Southgate N14 . . . .**15** C1
  Tottenham N4 . . . .**51** A3
Ashfield St E1 . . . .**96** C2
  4 Whitechapel E1 . . . .**96** C2
Ashfield Yd **11** E1 . . . . .**96** C2
ASHFORD **170** A4
Ashford Ave
  Ashford TW15 . . . . . .**170** D4
  Hayes UB4 . . . .**84** D1
  Hornsey N8 . . . .**50** A5
Ashford Bsns Complex
  TW15 . . . .**171** A6
Ashford CE Prim Sch
  TW15 . . . .**170** D4
Ashford Cl
  Ashford TW15 . . . . . .**170** A6
  Walthamstow E17 . . . . .**53** B3
Ashford
COMMON **171** B4
Ashford Cres EN3 . . . . . .**6** C3
Ashford Ct
  Cricklewood NW2 . . . . .**68** D4
  Edgware HA8 . . . .**10** D1
Ashford Ho
  8 Brixton SW9 . . . . .**138** D1
  11 Deptford SE8 . . . .**141** B6
Ashford Hospl TW15 . . .**148** A2
Ashford Ind Est
  TW15 . . . .**171** A6
Ashford Mews N17 . . . . .**34** A2
Ashford Rd
  Cricklewood NW2 . . . . .**68** D4
  Feltham TW13, TW15 . .**171** B3
  Littleton TW15, TW17 . .**171** A3
  Staines TW18 . . . .**170** A4
  Wallend E6 . . . .**78** C1
  Woodford E18 . . . .**37** B1
Ashford St N1 . . . .**95** C4
Ashford Sta TW15 . . . . .**170** B6
Ash Gr
  Cranley Gardens N10 . . .**49** B5
  Cricklewood NW2 . . . . .**69** A4
  Hampton TW12 . . . . . .**173** C2
  Hornsey N19 . . . .**50** A2
  Richmond TW9 . . . . . .**132** C1
  Thames Ditton KT7 . . .**196** D3
  Thornton Heath CR7 . . .**204** B5
  Tottenham Hale N17 . . .**52** A6
  Upton E7 . . . .**77** C1
  Walton-on-T KT12 . . . .**194** A1
  Westminster
  SW1 . . . . . .**115** C3 **259** A5
Ashley Prim Sch
  KT12 . . . .**194** A1
Ashley Rd
  Ashford TW15 . . . . . .**171** B5
  Catford BR1 . . . .**186** B4
  Mitcham Sch BR1 . . . .**187** B1
  Ash Hill Dr HA5 . . . .**40** C6

Ash Ho
  3 Canary Wharf
  E14 . . . .**120** A4
  Fulham SE1 . . . .**263** D3
  Kenton NW9 . . . .**45** A6
  Lewisham SE12 . . . . . .**165** A4
  2 Teddington TW11 . .**175** C3
Ashingdon Cl E4 . . . . . .**20** A1
Ashington **1** NW5 . . . . .**71** B2
Ashington Ho **10** E1 . . . .**96** B3
Ashington Rd SW6 . . . . .**135** B3
Ashlake Rd SW16 . . . . .**182** A6
Ashland Pl W1 . . . .**238** A4
Ashlar Ct N2 . . . .**48** C6
Ashlar Pl SE18 . . . .**122** D2
Ashleigh Commercial Est
  SE7 . . . .**121** D3
Ashleigh Ct
  Ealing W5 . . . .**109** D2
  Osidge N14 . . . .**15** C4
  Penge SE26 . . . .**184** B4
Ashleigh Gdns SM1 . . .**217** D6
Ashleigh Ho
  Mortlake SW14 . . . . . .**133** C2
  1 Streatham SW16 . .**182** B6
Ashleigh Point **8**
  SE26 . . . .**162** D1
Ashleigh Rd
  Mortlake SW14 . . . . . .**133** C2
  Penge SE20 . . . .**206** B6
Ashley Ave SM4 . . . . . .**201** C4
Ashley Cl Hendon NW4 . . .**28** C1
  Oatlands Pk KT12,
  KT13 . . . .**193** D1
  Pinner Green HA5 . . . . .**22** B4
Ashley Cres
  Clapham SW11 . . . . . .**137** A2
  Wood Green N22 . . . . . .**32** C1
Ashley Ct
  Hampstead NW3 . . . . . .**69** D3
  Hendon NW4 . . . .**28** C1
  10 Kingsland N16 . . . .**73** C3
  New Barnet EN5 . . . . . .**14** A6
  Northolt UB5 . . . .**85** A6
  Stanmore HA7 . . . .**25** B1
  Yiewsley UB7 . . . .**104** A5
Ashley Dr
  Borehamwood WD6 . . .**11** B6
  Hounslow TW7 . . . . . .**130** C6
  Twickenham TW2 . . . . .**151** D3
Ashley Gdns
  Edmonton N13 . . . .**33** A6
  Orpington BR6 . . . . . .**227** C3
  Richmond TW10 . . . . .**153** D2
  Wembley HA9 . . . .**66** A6
Ashley Ho BR5 . . . .**190** A1
Ashley La
  Croydon CR0 . . . .**220** D4
  Edgware NW7 . . . .**28** D3
  Hendon NW4 . . . .**28** C1
Ashley Park Ave
  KT12 . . . .**193** D1
Ashley Park Cres
  KT12 . . . .**194** A1
Ashley Pl
  Walton-on-T KT12 . . . .**194** A1
  Westminster
  SW1 . . . . . .**115** C3 **259** A5
Ashley Prim Sch
  KT12 . . . .**194** A1
Ashley Rd
  Chingford E4 . . . .**35** C4
  Enfield EN3 . . . .**6** C3
  Hampton TW12 . . . . . .**173** C2
  Hornsey N19 . . . .**50** A2
  Richmond TW9 . . . . . .**132** C1
  Thames Ditton KT7 . . .**196** D3
  Thornton Heath CR7 . . .**204** B5
  Tottenham Hale N17 . . .**52** A6
  Upton E7 . . . .**77** C1
  Walton-on-T KT12 . . . .**194** A1
  Westminster
  SW1 . . . . . .**115** C3 **259** A5
Ashleys Alley N15 . . . . .**51** A5
Ashley Wlk NW7 . . . . . .**28** D3
Ashling Ho **2** N17 . . . . .**33** D1
Ashling Rd CR0 . . . . . .**206** A1
Ashlin Rd E15 . . . .**76** B4

Ash Lo
2 Ashford TW16 171 D3
Fulham SW6 134 D4
Ashlone Rd SW15 134 D2
Ashlyns Way KT9 213 D2
Ashmead 4 N14 15 C6
Ashmead Bsns Ctr 2
E16 98 B3
Ashmead Gate BR1 187 C2
Ashmead Ho E9 75 A3
Ashmead Mews 1
SE8 141 C3
Ashmead Prim Sch
SE8 141 C3
Ashmead Rd
East Bedfont TW14 150 A3
St Johns SE8 141 C3
Ashmere Ave BR3 186 B1
Ashmere Cl SM3 216 D3
Ashmere Gr 11 SW2,
SW4 138 A1
Ashmere Ho 10 SW2 138 A1
Ashmill Ct CR0 205 A3
Ashmill St
NW8 92 C2 237 A4
Ashmole Prim Sch
SW8 138 B6 270 D5
Ashmole Sch N14 15 C3
Ashmole St
SW8 138 B6 270 D5
Ashmoor Lo NW7 27 B4
Ashmore NW1 71 D1
Ashmore Cl SE15 139 D5
Ashmore Ct
Catford SE6 164 C3
Colney Hatch N11 30 D4
Heston TW5 129 C6
Ashmore Gr DA16 145 C2
Ashmore Ho W14 254 B5
Ashmore Rd W9 91 B4
Ashmount Prim Sch
N19 49 C2
Ashmount Rd
Crouch End N19 49 D2
South Tottenham N15 51 D4
Ashmount Terr W5 109 D2
Ashneal Gdns HA1 64 B5
Ashness Gdns UB6 65 B2
Ashness Rd SW11 158 D6
Ashpark Ho 4 E14 97 B1
Ash Rd Cheam SM3 201 B1
Croydon CR0 223 C6
Littleton TW17 192 C5
Orpington BR6 227 D1
Plashet E15 76 D3
Ashridge Cl HA3 43 C3
Ashridge Cres SE18 145 A5
Ashridge Ct
Southall UB1 108 A6
Southgate N14 15 C6
Ashridge Dr WD19 22 C5
Ashridge Gdns
Bowes Pk N13 32 A5
Pinner HA5 41 A5
Ashridge Ho DA14 189 D6
Ashridge Way
Ashford TW16 172 A4
Merton SM4 201 B5
Ash Row BR2 210 C3
Ashtead Ct 15 SW19 156 D3
Ashtead Rd E5 52 A2
Ashton Cl SM1 217 C4
Ashton Ct
1 Beckenham BR3 185 B2
Chingford E4 20 C1
Harrow HA1 64 D5
Ashton Gdns
Dagenham RM6 59 A3
Hounslow TW4 129 B1
Ashton Ho
13 Kennington SW9 138 C5
Roehampton SW15 156 B4
Ashton House Sch
TW7 130 B4
Ashton Rd E15 76 B3
Ashton St E14 120 A6
Ashtree Ave CR4 180 B1
Ashtree Cl BR6 226 D4
Ash Tree Cl
Croydon CR0 207 A3
1 Surbiton KT6 198 A1
Ashtree Ct TW15 170 D5
Ash Tree Dell NW9 45 B4
Ash Tree Villas CR0 204 B3
Ash Tree Way CR0 207 A3
Ashurst Cl SE20 184 B2
Ashurst Dr
Ilford IG2, IG6 57 A4
Littleton TW17 192 A4
Ashurst Lo 4 N5 72 D3
Ashurst Rd
Cockfosters EN4 14 D6
Colney Hatch N12 30 C5
Ashurst Wlk CR0 222 B6
Ashvale Rd SW17 180 D5
Ashview Cl TW15 170 A5
Ashview Gdns TW15 170 A5
Ashville Rd E11 76 B6
Ashwater Rd SE12 165 A3
Ashway Ctr 5 KT2 176 A2
Ashwell Cl 8 E6 100 A1
Ashwell Ct TW15 148 A2
Ashwin St E8 73 D2
Ash Wlk HA0 65 C4
Ashwood Ave UB8 82 C1
Ashwood Ct HA9 66 B4
Ashwood Gdns
Hayes UB3 105 D2
New Addington CR0 224 A2
Ashwood Ho 10 NW4 46 C5
Ashwood Lo
9 New Barnet EN5 13 D6
Southgate N21 16 B5
Ashwood Pk 6 SM2 217 C1
Ashwood Rd E4 20 B1
Ashworth Cl SE5 139 B3
Ashworth Mans W9 91 D4
Ashworth Rd W9 91 D4
Aske Ho 2 N1 95 C4
Asker Ho N7 72 A4
Askern Cl DA6 146 D1
Aske St N1 95 C4
Askew Cres W12 112 A4
Askew Mans 14
W12 112 A4
Askew Rd W12 112 A4
Askham Ct W12 112 A5
Askham Lo 5 SE12 165 A4
Askham Rd W12 112 A5
Askill Dr SW15 157 A6
Asland Rd E15 98 B6
Aslett St SW18 158 A4
Asmara Rd NW2 69 A3
Asmuns Hill NW11 47 C4
Asmuns Pl NW11 47 B4
Asolando Dr SE17 262 B3
Aspect Ho 7 E14 120 A4
Aspects SM1 217 D3
Aspen Cl Ealing W5 110 B4
13 Upper Holloway
N19 71 C6
Yiewsley UB7 104 B5
Aspen Copse BR1 188 B1
Aspen Ct 10 Acton W3 89 A1
12 Hackney E8 74 A3
Redbridge IG5 56 A6
Richmond TW9 132 C5
Aspen Dr HA0 65 A5
Aspen Gdns
Ashford TW15 171 A5
2 Hammersmith W6 112 B1
Mitcham CR4 203 A4
Aspen Gn DA18 125 B3
Aspen Gr HA5 39 D6
Aspen Ho
8 Deptford SE15 140 C6
4 Maitland Pk NW3 70 D2
Richmond TW9 132 C5
2 Sidcup DA15 168 A1
Southgate N21 16 B6
Aspen La UB5 85 A4
Aspenlea Rd W6 134 D6
Aspen Lo 1 SW19 179 B4
Aspen Way
Canary Wharf E14 120 A6
Feltham TW13 150 B1
Aspern Gr NW3 70 C3
Aspinall Ho SW12 160 A3
Aspinall Rd SE4 140 D2
Aspinden Rd SE16 118 B2
Aspire Bld 10 SW15 157 B6
Aspley Rd SW18 157 D6
Asplins Rd N17 34 B2
Asprey Ho CR4 202 C6
Asprey Mews BR3 207 B4
Asquith Cl RM8 58 C1
Assam SE1 253 D3
Assam St E1 96 A1
Assata Mews N1 72 D2
Assembly Pas E1 96 C2
Assembly Wlk SM5 202 C2
Assheton-Bennett Ho 15
KT6 198 A4
Ass House La HA3 23 D6
Assisi Ct
Upper Tooting
SW12 158 D3
Wembley HA0 64 D5
Assunah Sch 8 N17 33 D1
Astall Cl HA3 24 C2
Astbury Bsns Pk 5
SE15 140 C4
Astbury Ho SE11 261 A5
Astbury Rd SE15 140 C4
Astell St SW3 114 C1 257 B2
Aster Ct 3 HA8 27 A6
Aster Ho 8 SE13 142 A3
Aste St E14 120 A4
Astey's Row 1 N1 73 A1
Asthall Gdns IG6 57 A5
Astins Ho 4 E17 53 D5
Astleham Rd TW17 192 A6
Astleham Way TW17 192 A6
Astle St SW11 137 A3
Astley Ave NW2 68 C3
Astley Ho Fulham SE1 263 D2
39 Paddington W2 91 C2
8 West Norwood
SE27 183 A6
Aston Ave HA3 43 C2
Aston Cl Bushey WD23 8 A5
Sidcup DA14 168 A1
Aston Ct
Stoke Newington N4 73 A6
3 Wimbledon SW19 178 C3
10 Woodford IG8 37 A4
Aston Gn TW5 128 C3
Aston Ho
Notting Hill W11 244 D6
South Lambeth SW8 269 C1
Aston House Sch W5 87 D1
Aston Mews RM6 58 C2
Aston Pl SW16 182 D4
Aston Rd
Claygate KT10 212 C3
Ealing W5 87 D1
Merton SW20 178 C1
Aston St E14 97 A2
Astonville St SW18 157 C3
Astor Ave RM7 59 D3
Astor Cl KT2 176 D4
Astor Ct
Colney Hatch N12 30 C4
Newham E16 99 C1
Walham Green SW6 266 A3
Astoria Mans 18
SW16 160 A1
Astoria Par SW16 160 A1
Astoria Wlk SW9 138 C2
Astra Ct W13 109 A5
Astra Ho 4 Bow E3 97 B4
Hornsey N4 50 B2
Astrid Ho TW13 150 C2
Astrop Mews W6 112 C3
Astrop Terr W6 112 C4
Astwood Mews SW7 256 A4
Asylum Rd SE15 140 B5
Atalanta St
SW6 134 D5 264 A3
Atbara Ct TW11 175 B4
Atbara Rd TW11 175 B4
Atcham Rd TW3 130 A1
Atcost Rd IG11 102 A2
Atheldene Rd SW18 158 A3
Athelney Prim Sch
SE6 163 C1
Athelney St SE6 163 C1
Athelstan Ct E6 100 C5
Athelstane Gr E3 97 B5
Athelstane Mews N4 50 C1
Athelstan Gdns 8
NW6 69 A1
Athelstan Ho
Hackney Wick E9 75 B3
Kingston u T KT1 198 B5
Stoke Newington N16 73 C4
Athelstan House Sch 9
TW12 173 C2
Athelstan Rd KT1 198 B5
Athelstan Way BR5 190 A2
Athelstone Rd HA3 24 B1
Athena Cl Harrow HA2 64 C6
Kingston u T KT1 198 B6
Athena Ct
Bermondsey SE1 253 A1
Athena Ct *continued*
St John's Wood NW8 229 C4
Athenaeum Pl 3 N10 49 B6
Athenaeum Rd N20 14 B3
Athenia Ho 7 E14 98 B1
Athenlay Rd SE15 162 D6
Athenoeum Ct N5 73 A4
Athens Gdns W9 91 C3
Atherden Rd E5 74 C4
Atherfield Ct SW18 157 D5
Atherfold Rd SW9 138 A2
Atherley Way TW4 151 B4
Atherstone Ct W2 91 D2
Atherstone Mews
SW7 114 A2 256 B4
Atherton Dr SW19 178 D6
Atherton Ho CR2 221 C2
Atherton Hts HA0 65 C2
Atherton L Ctr E15 76 D2
Atherton Mews E7 77 A2
Atherton Pl
Harrow HA2 42 B6
Southall UB1 107 C6
Atherton Rd
Barnes SW13 134 A5
Stratford E7 76 D2
Atherton St SW11 136 C3
Athlone KT10 212 C2
Athlone Cl 24 E5 74 B3
Athlone Ct
Lewisham SE6 164 B4
Upper Walthamstow
E17 54 B6
Athlone Ho
16 Camden Town
NW5 71 A2
9 Stepney E1 96 C1
Athlone Rd SW2 160 C4
Athlone St NW5 71 A2
Athlon Ind Est HA0 87 D5
Athlon Rd HA0 87 D5
Athol Cl HA5 22 B2
Athol Ct 15 N4 72 B6
Athole Gdns EN1 17 C6
Athole Terr CR7 183 A1
Athol Gdns HA5 22 B2
Atholl Ho W9 229 A1
Atholl Rd IG3 58 A2
Athol Sq E14 98 A1
Athol Way UB10 82 C4
Atkins Ct
13 Old Ford E3 97 B6
Woolwich SE7 122 A2
Atkins Dr BR4 224 B6
Atkins Lo W8 245 A2
Atkinson Ct 3 E10 53 D2
Atkinson Ho
11 Battersea SW11 137 A3
Battersea SW11 268 A1
15 Hackney E2 96 A5
Newham E13 98 D3
Walworth SE17 262 D3
Atkinson Rd E16 99 C2
Atkinson's Almhouses
HA8 26 B5
Atkins Rd
Streatham SW4,
SW12 159 D4
Walthamstow E10 53 D3
Atlanta Bldg 8
SE13 141 D4
Atlanta Ct CR7 205 A6
Atlantic Ct 10 E14 120 B6
Atlantic Ho
5 Putney SW15 157 B6
4 Tower Hamlets E1 97 A2
Atlantic Rd SW2, SW9,
SE24 138 C1
Atlantis Ave E16 123 A6
Atlantis Cl IG11 102 B4
Atlas Bsns Ctr NW2 68 B6
Atlas Cres HA8 10 D2
Atlas Gdns SE7 121 C2
Atlas Mews
Dalston E8 73 D2
Islington N7 72 B2
Atlas Rd
Friern Barnet N11 31 A4
Newham E13 99 A5
North Acton NW10 89 C4
Wembley HA9 67 A4
Atlip Rd HA0 88 A6
Atney Rd SW15 135 A1
Atria Rd HA6 22 A5
Atrium 9 IG9 21 D2
Atterbury Rd N4 50 D3
Atterbury St
SW1 116 A2 260 A3
Attewood Ave NW10 67 C5
Attewood Rd UB5 63 A2
Attfield Cl N20 14 B2
Attilburgh Ho SE1 263 C6
Attleborough Ct 4
SE21 162 B2
Attle Cl UB10 82 C5
Attlee Cl Hayes UB4 84 B4
Thornton Heath CR7 205 A4
Attlee Ct UB4 84 B4
Attlee Ho E1 243 D3
Attlee Rd Hayes UB4 84 B4
Thamesmead SE28 124 B6
Attlee Terr 3 E17 53 D5
Attneave St WC1 234 A1
Atwater Cl SW2 160 C3
Atwell Pl KT7 197 A1
Atwell Rd 6 SE15 140 A3
Atwood Ave TW9 132 C3
Atwood Ho SE21 161 C1
Atwood Rd W6 112 B2
Aubert Ct N5 72 D4
Aubert Pk N5 72 D4
Aubert Rd N5 72 D4
Aubrey Beardsley Ho
SW1 259 B3
Aubrey Mans NW1 237 A4
Aubrey Moore Point
E15 98 A5
Aubrey Pl NW8 229 A3
Aubrey Rd Hornsey N8 50 A4
Kensington
W14 113 B5 244 D3
Walthamstow E17 53 D6
Aubrey Wlk
W14 113 B5 244 D3
Auburn Cl SE14 141 A5
Aubyn Hill SE27 183 B6
Aubyn Sq SW15 156 A6
Auckland Cl Enfield EN1 6 B6
South Norwood SE19 183 D2
Auckland Ct UB4 84 C3
Auckland Gdns
SE19 183 D2
Auckland Hill SE27 183 A6
Auckland Ho 11
W12 112 B6
Auckland Rd
Clapham SW11 136 C1
Ilford IG1 57 A2
Kingston u T KT1 198 B5
Leyton E10 75 D5
South Norwood SE19 183 D2
Auckland Rise SE19 183 C2
Auckland St SE11 260 C1
Audax 23 NW9 27 D1
Auden Dr WD6 10 C6
Auden Pl NW1 231 A6
Audley Cl
8 Clapham SW11 137 A2
Muswell Hill N10 31 B3
Audley Ct Ealing W5 88 C2
Mayfair W1 248 C4
Northolt UB5 84 C4
Pinner Green HA5 22 C1
Snaresbrook E11, E18 54 D5
Surbiton KT5 198 B3
Twickenham TW2 152 B1
Audley Dr 3 E16 121 B5
Audley Gdns IG3 79 D6
Audley Ho N8 50 A5
Audley Pl SM2 217 D1
Audley Rd Ealing W5 88 B2
Enfield EN2 4 D3
Hendon NW4 46 B3
Richmond TW10 154 B6
Audley Sq W1 248 B4
Audley St W1 248 B4
Audrey Cl BR3 207 D3
Audrey Gdns HA0 65 B6
Audrey Ho EC1 241 B3
Audrey Rd IG1 78 D5
Audrey St E2 96 A5
Audric Cl KT2 176 C2
Augurs La 3 E13 99 B4
Augusta Cl KT8 195 B6
Augusta Ct NW4 28 C1
Augusta Rd TW2 152 A2
Augusta St E14 97 D1
Augustine Ho
Broadgate EC2 242 D2
New Cross SE4 141 B4
Augustine Rd
Hammersmith W14 112 D3

Augustine Rd *continued*
Harrow Weald HA3 . . . . 24 A2
Augustines Ct E9 . . . . 74 C3
Augustus Cl
Brentford TW8 . . . . 131 D5
Hammersmith W12 . . . 112 B3
Stanmore HA7 . . . . 9 D1
Augustus Ct
Feltham TW13 . . . . 173 B6
Isleworth TW3 . . . . 130 A1
8 Putney SW19 . . . . 157 A3
South Norwood SE19 . 183 C3
Streatham SW16 . . . 159 D2
Augustus Ho NW1 . . 232 A2
Augustus Rd
33 Putney SW19 . . . . 156 D3
Putney SW19 . . . . 157 A3
Augustus St
NW1 . . . . 93 B4 231 D2
Aulay Lawrence Ct
N9 . . . . 18 B1
Aultone Way
Carshalton SM5 . . . . 218 D5
Sutton SM1 . . . . 218 A6
Aultone Yd Ind Est
SM5 . . . . 218 D5
Aulton Pl SE11 . . . . 261 B1
Aura Ho 3 TW9 . . . . 132 D4
Aurelia Gdns CR0 . . . . 204 B3
Aurelia Rd CR0 . . . . 204 B3
Auriga Mews N1 . . . . 73 B3
Auriol Cl KT4 . . . . 215 C5
Auriol Dr
Greenford UB6 . . . . 64 B1
Hillingdon UB10 . . . . 60 D2
Auriol Jun Sch KT19 215 D4
Auriol Mans W14 . . . . 254 A3
Auriol Park Rd KT4 . . 215 C5
Auriol Rd
W14 . . . . 113 A2 254 A3
Aurora Bldg 4 E14 . . 120 A5
Aurora Ct IG8 . . . . 36 D6
Aurora Ho E14 . . . . 97 D1
Austell Gdns NW7 . . . . 11 C1
Austell Hts NW7 . . . . 11 C1
Austen Cl SE28 . . . . 124 B5
Austen Ho 5 NW6 . . . . 91 C4
Austen Rd Erith DA8 . 147 D5
Harrow HA2 . . . . 63 D6
Austin Ave BR1, BR2 . . 210 A4
Austin Cl
Forest Hill SE23 . . . . 163 B4
Twickenham TW1 . . . . 153 C6
Austin Ct
9 Enfield EN1 . . . . 17 C6
9 Newham E6 . . . . 99 C6
Austin Friars EC2 . . . . 242 D2
Austin Friars Ho EC2 242 D2
Austin Friars Sq EC2 242 D2
Austin Ho
6 Brixton SW2 . . . . 160 B6
19 Kingston u T KT6 . . 198 A4
1 New Cross SE14 . . . 141 B5
Austin Rd
Battersea
SW11 . . . . 137 A4 268 A1
Hayes UB3 . . . . 105 D4
Austins Ct SE15 . . . . 140 A2
Austins La UB10 . . . . 61 A5
Austin St E2 . . . . 95 D4
Austral Cl DA15 . . . . 167 D1
Australia Rd W12 . . . . 112 B6
Austral St
SE11 . . . . 116 D2 261 C4
Austyn Gdns KT5 . . . . 198 D1
Autumn Cl Enfield EN1 . . 6 A4
Wimbledon SW19 . . . 180 A4
Autumn Gr BR1 . . . . 187 B4
Autumn Lo CR2 . . . . 221 C4
Autumn Rise 9 W4 . . 111 B1
Autumn St E3 . . . . 97 C6
Avalon BR7 . . . . 188 C1
Avalon Cl Ealing W13 . . 87 A2
Enfield EN2 . . . . 4 C3
Merton SW20 . . . . 179 A1
Avalon Ct CR0 . . . . 205 D2
Avalon Rd Ealing W13 . . 87 A3
Parsons Green
SW6 . . . . 135 D4 265 C2
Avante Ct KT1 . . . . 197 D6
Avard Gdns BR6 . . . . 227 A4
Avarn Rd SW17 . . . . 180 D4
Avebury Ct N1 . . . . 235 C5
Avebury Rd
Leytonstone E11 . . . . 54 B1
Merton SW19 . . . . 179 B2
Avebury Rd *continued*
Orpington BR6 . . . . 227 B5
Avebury St N1 . . . . 235 C5
Aveley Ct 15 E5 . . . . 74 B6
Aveley Mans 1 IG11 . . 78 D1
Aveline St
SE11 . . . . 116 C1 261 A1
Aveling Ho 12 N19 . . . . 71 C5
Aveling Park Rd E17 . . 35 C1
Aveling Park Sch E17 . 35 C1
Ave Maria La EC4 . . . 241 D1
Avenell Mans N5 . . . . 72 D4
Avenell Rd N5 . . . . 72 D5
Avenfield Ho W1 . . . . 247 D6
Avening Rd SW18 . . . . 157 C4
Avening Terr SW18 . . . 157 C4
Avenons Rd E13 . . . . 99 A3
Avenue Cl
Cranford TW5 . . . . 128 B4
Primrose Hill
NW8 . . . . 92 C6 230 B5
Southgate N14 . . . . 15 C5
Avenue Cres
Cranford TW5 . . . . 128 B5
South Acton W3 . . . . 110 D4
Avenue Ct
Chelsea SW3 . . . . 257 C3
Cricklewood NW2 . . . . 69 A5
Ealing W5 . . . . 87 D2
Penge SE20 . . . . 184 C2
Redbridge IG5 . . . . 56 A6
Southgate N14 . . . . 15 C5
Avenue Elmers KT6 . . 198 A4
Avenue Gate IG10 . . . . 21 C5
Avenue Gdns
Cranford TW5 . . . . 128 B5
Mortlake SW14 . . . . 133 C2
South Acton W3 . . . . 110 D4
South Norwood SE25 . 184 A1
Teddington TW11 . . . . 174 D4
Avenue Hall N6 . . . . 49 D3
Avenue Ho
St John's Wood
NW8 . . . . 230 A3
Upper Clapton N16 . . . . 74 A6
Willesden Green NW10 90 B5
Avenue House Sch 2
W13 . . . . 87 B1
Avenue Ind Est E4 . . . . 35 B4
Avenue Lo 12 NW8 . . . . 70 B1
Avenue Mans
Barnet EN5 . . . . 1 B1
Clapham SW11 . . . . 137 A1
Hampstead NW3 . . . . 69 D3
Muswell Hill N10 . . . . 31 C1
Willesden NW2 . . . . 68 B2
Avenue Mews N10 . . . . 49 B6
Avenue Par
Southgate N21 . . . . 17 B4
Sunbury TW16 . . . . 194 B6
Avenue Park Rd SE21,
SE27 . . . . 160 D2
Avenue Prim Sch E12 . 78 A3
Avenue Rd
Bexley DA6, DA7 . . . . 147 A2
Brentford TW8 . . . . 109 C1
Crouch End N6 . . . . 49 D2
Feltham TW13 . . . . 149 D1
Forest Gate E7 . . . . 77 B4
Hampton TW12 . . . . 173 D2
Harlesden NW10 . . . . 89 D5
Hounslow TW7 . . . . 130 D4
Ilford RM6 . . . . 58 C2
Kingston u T KT1 . . . . 198 A6
Mitcham SW16 . . . . 181 D1
New Malden KT3 . . . . 199 C5
North Finchley N12 . . . . 30 A6
Penge BR3, SE20 . . . . 184 D2
Pinner HA5 . . . . 41 A6
Primrose Hill
NW8 . . . . 92 C6 230 A6
South Acton W3 . . . . 110 D4
Southall UB1 . . . . 107 B5
Southgate N14 . . . . 15 C5
South Norwood SE25 . 184 A1
Teddington TW11 . . . . 175 A4
Tottenham N15 . . . . 51 B4
Wallington SM6 . . . . 219 C1
Wimbledon SW20 . . . . 178 B1
Woodford IG8 . . . . 37 C4
Avenue Road Sta
BR3 . . . . 184 D1
Avenue S KT5 . . . . 198 C2
Avenue Terr
Ilford IG2 . . . . 57 C3
Kingston u T KT3 . . . . 199 A6
Avenue The Barnet EN5 . 1 A2
Beckenham BR3 . . . . 186 A2
Bedford Pk W4 . . . . 111 C3
Bromley BR1 . . . . 209 D6
Brondesbury Pk NW6 . . 91 A6
8 Buckhurst Hill IG9 . . 21 C2
Chingford E4 . . . . 36 B5
Clapham SW4 . . . . 159 A6
Claygate KT10 . . . . 212 C3
Cranford TW5 . . . . 128 A4
Ealing W13 . . . . 87 B1
Finchley N3 . . . . 29 C1
Friern Barnet N11 . . . . 31 B5
Greenwich SE10 . . . . 142 B5
Hampton TW12 . . . . 173 B4
Harrow HA3 . . . . 24 D2
Hatch End HA5 . . . . 23 B4
Hornsey N8 . . . . 50 C6
Hounslow TW3 . . . . 151 D6
Isleworth TW1 . . . . 153 B6
Keston Mark BR2 . . . . 225 D5
Loughton IG10 . . . . 21 D5
Muswell Hill N10 . . . . 31 C1
4 New Malden KT4 . . 200 A1
Orpington BR6 . . . . 227 D6
Pinner HA5 . . . . 41 B3
Richmond TW9 . . . . 132 B3
Sidcup DA5 . . . . 168 D4
South Croydon CR0 . . 221 C5
Stoneleigh KT17, SM3 216 C1
St Paul's Cray BR5 . . . . 190 B3
Sunbury TW16 . . . . 172 B1
Surbiton KT5 . . . . 198 B3
Tottenham N17 . . . . 33 C1
Uxbridge UB10 . . . . 60 D5
Wallington SM5 . . . . 219 A1
Wandsworth SW18,
SW12 . . . . 158 C4
Wanstead E11 . . . . 55 B4
Wembley HA9 . . . . 44 B1
West Wickham BR4 . . 208 C2
Worcester Pk KT4 . . . . 215 D6
Averil Gr SW16 . . . . 182 D4
Averill St W6 . . . . 134 D6
Avern Gdns KT8 . . . . 195 D5
Avern Rd KT8 . . . . 195 D5
Avery Ct 1 SE20 . . . . 184 B3
Avery Farm Row
SW1 . . . . 258 C3
Avery Gdns IG2 . . . . 56 B4
AVERY HILL 167 B5
Avery Hill Coll (Mile End
Annexe) E3 . . . . 97 B3
Avery Hill Rd SE9 . . . . 167 B3
Avery Row
W1 . . . . 115 B6 248 D6
Aviary Cl E16 . . . . 98 D2
Aviemore Cl BR3 . . . . 207 B4
Aviemore Way BR3 . . . 207 A4
Avignon Rd SE4 . . . . 140 D2
Avingdor Ct 10 W3 . . . 111 A5
Avington Ct SE1 . . . . 263 B3
Avington Gr SE20 . . . . 184 C3
Avion Cres NW7, NW9 . . 28 A2
Avis Sq E1 . . . . 96 D1
Avoca Rd SW17 . . . . 181 A6
Avocet Cl SE1 . . . . 118 A1
Avocet Mews SE28 . . . 123 B3
Avon Cl Hayes UB4 . . . . 84 C3
Sutton SM1 . . . . 218 A4
Worcester Pk KT4 . . . . 216 A6
Avon Ct 1 Acton W3 . . . 89 A1
11 Chingford E4 . . . . 20 A3
Greenford UB6 . . . . 85 D3
North Finchley N12 . . . . 29 D5
10 Putney SW15 . . . . 157 A6
Wembley HA0 . . . . 65 A4
Avondale N22 . . . . 32 A3
Avondale Ave
Barnet EN4 . . . . 14 D3
Finchley N12 . . . . 29 D5
Hinchley Wood KT10 . 213 A5
Neasden NW2 . . . . 67 C5
New Malden KT4 . . . . 199 D1
Avondale Cres
Enfield EN3 . . . . 7 A2
Redbridge IG4 . . . . 55 D4
Avondale Ct
Canning Town E16 . . . . 98 C2
Leytonstone E11 . . . . 54 C1
9 Sutton SM2 . . . . 218 A1
Woodford E18 . . . . 37 B2
Avondale Dr UB3 . . . . 106 B5
Avondale Gdns TW4 . . 151 B6
Avondale Ho
11 Bermondsey
SE1 . . . . 118 A1
6 Mortlake SW14 . . . . 133 B2
Avondale Mans SW6 . 264 C2
Avondale Park Gdns
W11 . . . . 113 A6 244 A5
Avondale Park Prim Sch
W11 . . . . 113 A6 244 A5
Avondale Park Rd
W11 . . . . 113 A6 244 A6
Avondale Pavement 7
SE1 . . . . 118 A1
Avondale Rd
Bexley DA16 . . . . 146 C3
Bromley BR1 . . . . 186 D4
Chislehurst SE9 . . . . 166 A2
Finchley N3 . . . . 30 A2
Harringay N15 . . . . 50 D4
Harrow HA3 . . . . 42 D6
Mortlake SW14 . . . . 133 B2
Newham E16 . . . . 98 C2
South Croydon CR2 . . 221 A2
Southgate N13 . . . . 16 C2
Walthamstow E17 . . . . 53 C2
Wimbledon SW19 . . . . 179 D5
Avondale Rise SE15 . 139 D2
Avondale Sq SE1 . . . . 118 A1
Avonfield Ct E17 . . . . 54 B6
Avon Ho
2 Islington N1 . . . . 72 C1
7 Kingston u T KT2 . . 175 D2
Northolt UB5 . . . . 85 A3
Southgate N21 . . . . 16 B6
14 Stoke Newington
N16 . . . . 73 B4
West Kensington W14 254 D3
Avon House Sch IG8 . . 37 A6
Avonhurst Ho NW6 . . . . 69 A1
Avonley Rd SE14 . . . . 140 C5
Avon Mews HA5 . . . . 23 B2
Avonmore Gdns
W14 . . . . 254 D3
Avonmore Pl W14 . . . . 254 B4
Avonmore Prim Sch
W14 . . . . 113 A2 254 B4
Avonmore Rd
W14 . . . . 113 B2 254 C4
Avonmouth St SE1 . . 262 A6
Avon Path CR0 . . . . 221 A1
Avon Pl SE1 . . . . 252 B1
Avon Rd
Ashford TW16 . . . . 171 D3
Greenford UB6 . . . . 85 D3
St Johns SE4 . . . . 141 C2
Upper Walthamstow
E17 . . . . 54 B6
Avonstowe Cl BR6 . . . 227 A5
Avon Way E18 . . . . 55 A6
Avonwick Rd TW3 . . . . 129 D3
Avril Way E4 . . . . 36 A5
Avriol Ho W12 . . . . 112 B5
Avro Ct E9 . . . . 75 A3
Avro Way SM6 . . . . 220 A1
Awlfield Ave N17 . . . . 33 B2
Awliscombe Rd
DA16 . . . . 145 D3
Axeholm Ave HA8 . . . . 26 D2
Axe St IG11 . . . . 101 A6
Axford Ho SW2 . . . . 160 D3
Axiom Apartments 5
BR2 . . . . 209 B5
Axis Ct
7 Bermondsey
SE16 . . . . 118 A4
Greenwich SE10 . . . . 142 C6
Axminster Cres
DA16 . . . . 146 C4
Axminster Rd N7 . . . . 72 B5
Axon Pl 5 IG1 . . . . 79 A6
Aybrook St
W1 . . . . 93 A2 238 A3
Aycliffe Cl BR1 . . . . 210 B5
Aycliffe Rd W12 . . . . 112 A5
Ayerst Ct 1 E10 . . . . 54 A2
Aylands Cl HA9 . . . . 66 A6
Aylesbury Cl E7 . . . . 76 D2
Aylesbury Ct SM1 . . . . 218 A5
Aylesbury Ho 13
SE15 . . . . 140 A6
Aylesbury Rd
Bromley BR2 . . . . 209 A6
Walworth
SE17 . . . . 117 B1 262 D1
Aylesbury St
Clerkenwell
EC1 . . . . 94 D3 241 C5
Neasden NW10 . . . . 67 B5
Ayles Ct UB4 . . . . 84 B4
Aylesford Ave BR3 . . . 207 A4
Aylesford Ho SE1 . . . . 252 D1
Aylesford St
SW1 . . . . 115 D1 259 C1
Aylesham Cl NW7 . . . . 28 A3
Aylesham Rd BR6 . . . . 211 D2
Aylesham Sh Ctr
SE15 . . . . 140 A4
Ayles Rd UB4 . . . . 84 B4
Aylestone Ave NW6 . . . 90 D6
Aylestone Ct 10 HA0 . . 66 A2
Aylett Rd
Croydon SE25 . . . . 206 B5
Isleworth TW7 . . . . 130 C3
Ayley Croft EN1 . . . . 18 A6
Ayliffe Cl KT1 . . . . 176 C1
Aylmer Cl HA7 . . . . 25 A6
Aylmer Ct N2 . . . . 48 D4
Aylmer Dr HA7 . . . . 25 A6
Aylmer Ho SE10 . . . . 120 B1
Aylmer Par N2 . . . . 48 D4
Aylmer Rd
Acton W12 . . . . 111 D4
Dagenham RM8 . . . . 81 A5
East Finchley N2 . . . . 48 C4
Leytonstone E11 . . . . 54 D1
Ayloffe Rd RM9 . . . . 81 B2
Aylsham Dr UB10 . . . . 61 A6
Aylton Est 28 SE16 . . 118 C4
Aylward Fst & Mid Schs
HA7 . . . . 25 D5
Aylward Rd
Forest Hill SE23 . . . . 162 D2
Merton SW20 . . . . 201 B6
Aylwards Rise HA7 . . . . 25 A6
Aylward St E1 . . . . 96 D1
Aylwin Est SE1 . . . . 263 B6
Aynhoe Mans W14 . . 112 D2
Aynhoe Rd W14 . . . . 112 D3
Ayr Ct W3 . . . . 88 C2
Ayres Cl E13 . . . . 99 A4
Ayres Cres NW10 . . . . 67 B1
Ayres St SE1 . . 117 A4 252 B2
Ayrsome Rd N16 . . . . 73 C5
Ayrton Gould Ho 9
E2 . . . . 96 D4
Ayrton Ho HA9 . . . . 65 D6
Ayrton Rd
SW7 . . . . 114 B3 256 C6
Aysgarth Ct SM1 . . . . 217 D5
Aysgarth Rd SE21 . . . . 161 C4
Ayshford Ho E1 . . . . 96 B4
Ayston Ho 19 SE8 . . . . 118 D2
Aytoun Ct 17 SW9 . . . . 138 B3
Aytoun Pl SW9 . . . . 138 B3
Aytoun Rd SW9 . . . . 138 B3
Azalea Cl Ealing W7 . . 108 D5
Ilford IG1 . . . . 78 D3
Azalea Ct
Chingford IG8 . . . . 36 C3
Ealing W7 . . . . 108 D5
Azalea Ho
2 Feltham TW13 . . . . 150 B3
New Cross SE14 . . . . 141 B5
Azalea Wlk HA5 . . . . 40 B3
Azania Mews NW5 . . . . 71 B2
Azenby Rd SE15 . . . . 139 D3
Azhar Acad E7 . . . . 77 A2
Azof St SE10 . . . . 120 C2
Azov Ho 10 E1 . . . . 97 A3
Aztec Ct 8 N16 . . . . 73 C2
Azure Appartments
HA3 . . . . 24 B3
Azure Ct TW13 . . . . 149 D1
Azure Ho 28 E2 . . . . 96 A4

B

Baalbec Rd N5 . . . . 72 D3
Babbacombe Cl KT9 213 D3
Babbacombe Gdns
IG4 . . . . 56 A5
Babbacombe Rd
BR1 . . . . 187 A2
Baber Bridge Par
TW14 . . . . 150 C5
Baber Dr TW14 . . . . 150 C5

Babington Ct
Bloomsbury WC1 240 B4
Streatham SW16 181 D5
Babington Ho SE1 252 B2
Babington House Sch
BR7 188 B4
Babington Rd
Dagenham RM8 80 C4
Hendon NW4 46 B5
Streatham SW16 181 D5
Babington Rise HA9 66 C2
Babmaes St SW1 249 C5
Bacchus Wlk 12 N1 95 C5
Bache's St N1 95 B4 235 D1
Back Church La E1 96 A1
Back Hill EC1 241 B5
Backhouse Pl SE1 263 B3
Back La
Brentford TW8 131 D6
Buckhurst Hill IG9 21 D2
Burnt Oak HA8 27 A2
Dagenham RM6 59 A2
Hampstead NW3 70 A4
Hornsey N8 50 A4
Richmond TW10 153 C2
Sidcup DA5 169 C4
Backley Gdns SE25 206 A3
Back Rd
Leytonstone E11 54 C3
Sidcup DA14 190 A6
Teddington TW11 174 C3
Bacon Gr
SE1 117 D3 263 C5
Bacon La
Edgware HA8 26 C2
Queensbury NW9 44 D5
Bacon's Coll SE16 119 A4
Bacon's La N6 49 A1
Bacon St E2 95 D3 243 D6
Bacon Terr RM8 80 B3
Bacton NW5 71 A3
Bacton St E2 96 C4
Baddeley Cl 11 EN3 7 C6
Baddeley Ho
East Molesey KT8 195 C4
Vauxhall SE11 260 D2
Baddow Cl
Dagenham RM10 103 C6
Woodford IG8 37 D4
Baddow Wlk N1 235 A6
Baden Ct N11 31 D3
Baden Pl SE1 252 C2
Baden Powell Cl
Dagenham RM9 103 A6
Surbiton KT6 214 B6
Baden Powell Ho 11
DA17 125 C3
Baden Powell Sch 8
E5 74 B5
Baden Rd Hornsey N8 49 D5
Ilford IG1 78 D3
Badger Cl
Feltham TW13 150 B1
Hounslow TW4 128 C2
Ilford IG2 57 A2
Badger Ct
Chingford E4 36 B6
Dollis Hill NW2 68 C5
Badgers Cl
Ashford TW15 170 B5
Enfield EN2 4 D2
Harrow HA1 42 B3
Hayes UB3 105 C6
Badgers Copse
Orpington BR6 227 D6
Worcester Pk KT4 215 D6
Badgers Croft
Barnet N20 13 A3
Chislehurst SE9 166 C1
Badgers Hole CR0 222 D4
Badgers Wlk KT3 177 C1
Badlis Rd E17 53 C6
Badma Cl N9 18 C1
Badminton KT2 176 D2
Badminton Cl
Harrow HA1 42 C5
Northolt UB5 63 C2
Badminton Ct 9 N4 51 A2
Badminton Ho SE22 139 C1
Badminton Mews 9
E16 121 A5
Badminton Rd
SW12 159 A5
Badric Ct SW11 136 B3
Badsworth Rd 3
SE5 139 A4
Bagley Cl UB7 104 A4
Bagley's La
SW6 135 D4 265 D1
Bagleys Spring RM6 59 A5
Bagnigge Ho WC1 234 A1
Bagshot Ho NW1 231 D2
Bagshot Rd EN1 17 D5
Bagshot St
SE17 117 C1 263 B1
Baildon 27 E2 96 C5
Baildon St SE8 141 B5
Bailey Cl Chingford E4 36 A6
Wood Green N11 31 D3
Woolwich SE28 123 C5
Bailey Cres KT9 213 D1
Bailey Ct
4 Chingford E4 36 B5
9 Shepherd's Bush
W12 112 A4
Bailey Ho
Mitcham CR4 202 C6
11 Penge SE26 184 B5
Walham Green SW10 265 D4
Bailey Mews
Brixton SW2 160 C6
Chiswick W4 132 D6
Bailey Pl SE26 184 D4
Bainbridge cl KT2 176 A5
Bainbridge Rd RM9 81 B4
Bainbridge St WC1 239 D2
Baines Cl CR2 221 B3
Bain Ho 23 SW9 138 A3
Baird Ave UB1 108 A6
Baird Cl
Kingsbury NW9 45 A3
Walthamstow E10 53 C1
Baird Gdns SE19 183 C6
Baird Ho
12 Belvedere DA17 125 C3
29 Shepherd's Bush
W12 112 B6
Baird Rd EN1 6 B1
Baird St EC1 242 B6
Bairny Wood App IG8 37 B4
Baizdon Rd SE3 142 C3
Baker Beall Ct DA7 147 D2
Baker Ct E11 76 B5
Baker Ho
12 Bromley E3 97 D4
Ealing W7 108 D5
Baker La CR4 203 A6
Baker Pl KT19 215 A2
Baker Rd
Harlesden NW10 89 C6
Kidbrooke SE18 144 A4
Bakers' Almshouses
E10 53 D3
Bakers Ave E17 53 D3
Bakers Ct RM8 59 B2
Bakers Ct SE25 205 C6
Bakers End SW20 179 A1
Bakers Field N7 72 A4
Bakers Gdns SM5 218 C6
Bakers Hall Ct EC3 253 B5
Bakers Hill Barnet EN5 1 D3
Upper Clapton E5 52 C1
Bakers Ho W5 109 D5
Baker's La N6 48 D3
Bakers Mews 9
BR6 227 D2
Baker's Mews W1 238 A2
Bakers Pas 22 NW3 70 A4
Bakers Rents 13 E2 95 D4
Bakers Row E15 98 C5
Baker's Row
EC1 94 C3 241 A5
Baker St Enfield EN1 5 B4
Marylebone
W1 92 D2 237 D4
Baker Street
W1 92 D2 237 D4
Baker Street Sta
NW1 92 D3 237 D5
Baker's Yd EC1 241 A5
Bakery Cl SW9 270 D3
Bakery Mews KT6 198 C1
Bakewell Way KT3 177 C1
Balaam Ho SM1 217 C4
Balaam L Ctr E13 99 A3
Balaams La N14 15 D2
Balaam St E13 99 B4
Balaclava Rd
Bermondsey
SE1 117 D2 263 D3
Kingston u T KT6 197 C2
Bala Gn NW9 45 C3
Balcaskie Rd SE9 166 B6
Balchen Rd SE3 143 D3
Balchier Rd SE22 162 B5
Balcombe Cl DA6 146 D1
Balcombe Ho
Lisson Gr NW1 237 C6
3 Streatham SW2 160 B3
Balcombe St
NW1 92 D3 237 C5
Balcon Ct W5 88 B1
Balcorne St E9 74 C1
Balder Rise SE12 165 B2
Balderton Flats W1 238 B1
Balderton St
W1 93 A1 238 B1
Baldewyne Ct N17 34 A2
Baldock Ho 31 SE5 139 A3
Baldock St E3 97 D5
Baldrey Ho 1 SE10 120 D1
Baldry Gdns SW16 182 B4
Baldwin Cres SE5 139 A4
Baldwin Gdns TW3 130 A4
Baldwin Ho
15 Streatham SW2 160 C3
Wallend E12 78 C1
Baldwin Rd SW12 159 A5
Baldwin's Gdns
EC1 94 C2 241 A4
Baldwin St EC1 235 C1
Baldwin Terr
N1 95 A5 235 A4
Baldwyn Gdns W3 111 B6
Balearic Apts 3
E16 121 A6
Bale Rd E1 97 A2
Bales Coll W10 90 D4
Balfern Gr W4 111 C1
Balfern St SW11 136 C3
Balfe St N1 94 A5 233 B3
Balfour Ave W7 108 D5
Balfour Bsns Ctr
UB2 106 D3
Balfour Gr N20 14 D1
Balfour Ho 4 W10 90 D2
Balfour Mews
Edmonton N9 18 A1
Mayfair W1 248 B4
Balfour Pl
Mayfair W1 248 B5
Putney SW15 134 B1
Balfour Rd
Bromley Comm BR2 209 D4
Croydon SE25 206 A5
Ealing W13 109 B4
Harrow HA1 42 B4
Highbury N5 73 A4
Hounslow TW3 129 D2
Ilford IG1 57 A1
Merton SW19 179 D3
North Acton W3 89 A2
Southall UB2 106 D3
Wallington SM5 218 D1
Balfour St
SE17 117 B2 262 C4
Balfron Twr 4 E14 98 A1
Balgonie Rd E4 20 B3
Balgowan Cl KT3 199 C5
Balgowan Prim Sch
BR3 185 A1
Balgowan Rd BR3 185 B1
Balgowan St SE18 123 D2
BALHAM 159 A3
Balham Gr SW12 159 A4
Balham High Rd SW12,
SW17 159 A3
Balham Hill SW12 159 B5
Balham L Ctr SW12 159 B2
Balham New Rd
SW12 159 B4
Balham Park Mans
SW12 158 D3
Balham Park Rd SW12,
SW17 159 A3
Balham Rd N9 18 A2
Balham Sta SW12 159 B3
Balham Station Rd
SW12 159 B3
Balin Ho SE1 252 C2
Balkan Wlk E1 118 B6
Balladier Wlk E14 97 D2
Ballamore Rd BR1 165 A1
Ballance Rd E9 75 A2
Ballantine St SW18 136 A1
Ballantrae Ho NW2 69 B4
Ballantyne Cl 5
SE9 188 A6
Ballard Cl KT2 177 B3
Ballard Ho SE10 141 D6
Ballards Cl RM10 103 D6
Ballards Farm Rd CR0,
CR2 222 A2
Ballards La N3 29 D3
Ballards Mews HA8 26 C4
Ballards Rd
Dagenham RM10 103 D6
Dollis Hill NW2 68 A6
Ballards Rise CR2 222 A2
Ballards Way CR0,
CR2 222 B2
Ballast Quay SE10 120 B1
Ballater Cl WD19 22 C6
Ballater Rd
Brixton SW2, SW4 138 A1
South Croydon CR2 221 D3
Ball Ct EC3 242 D1
Ballentyne Ct N21 16 B6
Ballina St SE23 162 D4
Ballin Ct 14 E14 120 A4
Ballingdon Rd SW11 159 A5
Ballinger Point 18 E3 97 D4
Ballinger Way UB5 85 A3
Balliol Ave E4 36 C6
Balliol Ho 11 SW15 156 D5
Balliol Rd
Bexley DA16 146 B3
North Kensington W10 90 D1
Tottenham N17 33 C2
Balloch Rd SE6 164 B2
Ballogie Ave NW10 67 C4
Ballow Cl 15 SE5 139 C5
Ball's Pond Pl 3 N1 73 B2
Ball's Pond Rd N1 73 C2
Balmain Cl W5 109 D5
Balmain Ct TW3 129 D4
Balman Ho 3 SE16 118 D2
Balmer Rd E3 97 B5
Balmes Rd N1 95 B6 235 D6
Balmoral Ave
Beckenham BR3 207 A5
Friern Barnet N11 31 B5
Balmoral Cl 1
SW15 156 D5
Balmoral Cres KT8 195 C6
Balmoral Ct
18 Belmont SM2 217 C1
Ealing W5 87 D1
Edgware HA8 26 D6
Grove Pk SE12 187 B6
North Cheam KT4 216 B6
21 Rotherhithe SE16 118 D5
St John's Wood NW8 229 C4
Wembley HA9 66 B5
West Norwood SE27 183 A6
Balmoral Dr
Borehamwood WD6 11 B6
Hayes UB4 83 D3
Southall UB1 85 B3
Balmoral Gdns
Ealing W13 109 A3
Ilford IG3 57 D1
Old Bexley DA5 169 B4
Balmoral Gr N7 72 B2
Balmoral Ho
2 Isle Of Dogs
E14 119 D3
Stanmore HA7 26 A1
Stoke Newington N4 51 A1
Walthamstow E17 35 B1
West Kensington W14 254 A4
Balmoral Lo BR6 226 C4
Balmoral Mews
W12 111 D3
Balmoral Rd
Forest Gate E7 77 C3
Harrow HA2 63 C4
Kingston u T KT1 198 B5
Leyton E10 75 D6
North Cheam KT4 216 B6
Willesden NW2 68 B2
Balmoral Trad Est
IG11 101 D2
Balmore Cl E14 98 A1
Balmore Cres EN4 15 A6
Balmore St N19 71 B6
Balmuir Gdns SW15 134 C1
Balnacraig Ave NW10 67 C4
Balniel Gate SW1 259 D2
Balsam Ho 9 E14 119 D6
Baltic Apts 5 E16 121 A6
Baltic Cl SW19 180 B3
Baltic Ho 7 SE5 139 A3
Baltic St E
EC1 95 A3 242 A5
Baltic St W
EC1 95 A3 242 A5
Baltimore Ho
Clapham SW18 136 A1
Kennington SE11 261 A2
Merton SW19 179 D3
Baltimore Pl DA16 145 D3
Balvaird Pl SW1 259 D1
Balvernie Gr SW18 157 C4
Bamber Ho IG11 101 A6
Bamber Rd 5 SE15 139 D4
Bamborough Gdns 12
W12 112 C4
Bamburgh 9 N17 34 B3
Bamford Ave HA0 88 B5
Bamford Rd
Barking IG11 79 A2
Catford BR1 186 B5
Bampfylde Cl SM6 219 C5
Bampton Ct W5 87 D1
Bampton Dr NW7 28 A3
Bampton Rd SE23 162 D1
Banavie Gdns BR3 186 A2
Banbury Cl EN2 4 D4
Banbury Ct
11 Belmont SM2 217 C1
Ealing W13 109 A3
Strand WC2 250 A6
Banbury Ho 5 E9 74 D1
Banbury Rd
Higham Hill E17 35 A3
Homerton E9 74 D1
Banbury St 3 SW11 136 C3
Banbury Wlk UB5 85 C5
Banchory Rd SE3 143 B5
Bancroft Ave
East Finchley N2 48 C4
Woodford IG9 21 A2
Bancroft Cl TW15 170 C5
Bancroft Ct
Northolt UB5 84 C6
South Lambeth SW8 270 A2
Bancroft Gdns
Harrow Weald HA3 24 A2
Orpington BR6 211 D1
Bancroft Ho 11 E1 96 C3
Bancroft Rd
Bethnal Green E1 96 D3
Harrow Weald HA3 24 A1
Bancrofts Sch IG8 21 A1
Bandon Cl UB10 82 B5
BANDONHILL 219 D3
Bandon Hill Prim Sch
SM6 219 D2
Bandon Rise SM6 219 D3
Banff Ho 1 NW3 70 C2
Banfield Rd SE15 140 B2
Banfor Ct SM6 219 C3
Bangabandhu Prim Sch
88 E2 96 C4
Bangalore St SW15 134 D2
Bangor Cl UB5 63 D3
Banim St W6 112 B2
Banister Ho
Hackney E9 74 D3
Nine Elms SW8 269 B2
9 West Kilburn W10 91 A4
Banister Rd W10 90 D4
Bank Ave CR4 180 B1
Bank Bldgs 13 SW16 181 C5
Bank Ct SW11 268 C2
Bank End SE1 252 B4
Bankfoot Rd BR1 186 C6
Bankhurst Rd SE6 163 B4
Bank La
Kingston u T KT2 176 A3
Roehampton SW15 155 C6
Bank Mews SM1 218 A2
Bank of England*
EC2 242 C1
Bank of England Mus*
EC2 95 B1 242 C1
Bank Par N11 31 B5
Banks Ho
Isleworth TW7 130 C3
Newington SE1 262 A5
Banksia Rd N18 34 D5
Bankside
Borough The
SE1 117 A6 252 A5

Bankside continued
Borough The SE1 ... 252 B4
Enfield EN2 ... 4 D4
Southall UB1 ... 106 D5
South Croydon CR2 ... 221 D2
Bankside Ave
1 Lewisham SE13 ... 142 A2
Northolt UB5 ... 84 A5
Bankside Cl
Carshalton SM5 ... 218 C2
Isleworth TW7 ... 130 D1
Bankside Dr KT7 ... 213 B6
Bankside Gall★
SE1 ... 116 D6 251 D5
Bankside Ho EC3 ... 243 B1
Bankside Pier
SE1 ... 117 A6 252 A5
Bankside Pk IG11 ... 102 A4
Bankside Rd IG1 ... 79 B3
Bankside Way 6
SE19 ... 183 C4
Banks La DA6 ... 147 B1
Bank St E14 ... 119 D5
Bank Sta EC3 ... 95 B1 242 D1
Banks Way E12 ... 78 C4
Banksyard TW5 ... 129 B6
Bank The N6 ... 49 B1
Bankton Rd SW2 ... 138 C1
Bankwell Rd SE13 ... 142 C1
Banner Ct 5 SE16 ... 118 C2
Banner Ho EC1 ... 242 B5
Bannerman Ho SW8 270 C5
Banner St EC1 95 A3 242 B6
Banning Ho 4
SW19 ... 156 D3
Banning St SE10 ... 120 C1
Bannister Cl
Greenford UB6 ... 64 B3
Streatham SW2 ... 160 C3
Bannister Ho
28 Deptford SE14 ... 140 D6
Harrow HA3 ... 42 C6
Bannister Sports Ctr
HA3 ... 24 A4
Bannockburn Prim Sch
SE18 ... 123 D2
Bannockburn Rd
SE18 ... 123 D2
Bannow Cl KT19 ... 215 C4
Banqueting Ho★
SW1 ... 250 A3
Banstead Ct
East Acton W12 ... 111 D6
Stoke Newington N4 ... 51 A1
Walthamstow E10 ... 53 D1
Banstead Gdns N9 ... 17 C1
Banstead Rd SM5 ... 218 C1
Banstead St SE15 ... 140 C2
Banstead Way SM6 ... 220 A3
Banstock Rd HA8 ... 26 D4
Banting Dr N21 ... 16 B6
Banting Ho 6 NW2 ... 68 A5
Bantock Ct 1 N20 ... 14 D2
Bantock Ho 8 W10 ... 91 A4
Banton Cl EN1 ... 6 B3
Bantry Ho 18 E1 ... 96 D3
Bantry St SE5 ... 139 B5
Banville Ho SW8 ... 270 D3
Banwell Rd DA5 ... 168 D5
Banyan Ho 8 NW3 ... 69 D2
Banyard Rd SE16 ... 118 B3
Baptist Gdns NW5 ... 71 A2
Barandon Wlk 6
W11 ... 112 D6
Barbanel Ho 26 E1 ... 96 C3
Barbara Brosnan Ct
NW8 ... 229 C3
Barbara Castle Cl
SW6 ... 264 D5
Barbara Cl TW17 ... 192 D4
Barbara Hucklesbury Cl
N22 ... 32 D1
Barbara Martin Ho 1
N11 ... 31 C5
Barbara Rudolph Ct 5
N19 ... 50 A2
Barbara Ward Ct 3
E11 ... 76 C6
Barbauld Rd N16 ... 73 C5
Barber Beaumont Ho 21
E1 ... 96 D4
Barber Cl N21 ... 16 C4
Barberry Ct E15 ... 76 C2
Barbers Alley 1 E13 ... 99 B4
Barbers Rd E15 ... 97 D5
BARBICAN ... 95 A2
Barbican★
EC2 ... 95 A2 242 B3
Barbican Ctr★
EC2 ... 95 A2 242 B4
Barbican Rd UB1 ... 85 D1
Barb Mews W6 ... 112 C3
Barbon Alley EC3 ... 243 B2
Barbon Cl WC1 ... 240 C4
Barbot Cl N9 ... 18 A1
Barbrook Ho E9 ... 74 C2
Barchard St SW18 ... 157 D6
Barchester Cl W7 ... 108 D5
Barchester Lo N12 ... 29 D6
Barchester Rd HA3 ... 24 B1
Barchester St E14 ... 97 D2
Barclay Cl
SW6 ... 135 C5 265 A3
Barclay Ct N12 ... 30 A5
Barclay Ho 21 E9 ... 74 C1
Barclay Oval IG8 ... 37 A6
Barclay Prim Sch E10 54 B3
Barclay Rd
Edmonton N18 ... 33 B4
Leyton E11 ... 54 D1
Newham E13 ... 99 C3
Parsons Green
SW6 ... 135 C5 265 B3
South Croydon CR0 ... 221 B5
Walthamstow E17 ... 54 A4
Barcombe Ave SW2 ... 160 B2
Barcom Trad Est 1
CR0 ... 204 A2
Bardell Ho 17 SE1 ... 118 A4
Barden St SE18 ... 145 C5
Bardfield Ave RM6 ... 58 D6
Bardney Rd SM4 ... 201 D5
Bardolph Rd
Richmond TW9 ... 132 B2
Tufnell Pk N7 ... 72 A4
Bard Rd W10 ... 112 D6
Bardsey Pl 41 E1 ... 96 C3
Bardsey Wlk 5 N1 ... 73 A2
Bardsley Cl CR0 ... 221 D5
Bardsley Ho 6 SE10 ... 142 A6
Bardsley La SE10 ... 142 A6
Barents Ho 10 E1 ... 96 D3
Barfett St W10 ... 91 B3
Barfield Ave N20 ... 14 D2
Barfield Rd
Bromley BR1, BR7 ... 210 C6
Leytonstone E11 ... 54 D1
Barfleur La SE8 ... 119 B2
Barford Cl NW4 ... 28 A2
Barford Ho 23 E3 ... 97 B5
Barford St N1 ... 94 C6 234 B5
Barforth Rd SE15 ... 140 B2
Barfreston Way
SE20 ... 184 B2
Bargate Cl
New Malden KT3 ... 200 A2
Plumstead Comm
SE18 ... 123 D1
Bargehouse Rd E16 ... 122 D4
Barge House St SE1 ... 251 B4
Barge La 10 E3 ... 97 B6
Bargery Rd SE6 ... 163 D3
Bargrove Cl 8 SE20 ... 184 A3
Bargrove Cres SE6 ... 163 B2
Barham Cl
Chislehurst BR7 ... 188 D5
Keston Mark BR2 ... 210 A1
Wembley HA0 ... 65 C2
Barham Ct
8 Croydon CR2 ... 221 A4
Keston Mark BR2 ... 210 A1
Wembley HA0 ... 65 C2
Woodside Pk N12 ... 29 B5
Barham Ho SE17 ... 263 B2
Barham Prim Sch
HA0 ... 65 C2
Barham Rd
Chislehurst BR7 ... 188 D5
Croydon CR2 ... 221 A3
Wimbledon SW20 ... 178 A3
Baring Cl SE12 ... 165 A2
Baring Ct N1 ... 235 C5
Baring Ho 15 E14 ... 97 C1
Baring Prim Sch
SE12 ... 165 A4
Baring Rd Barnet EN4 ... 2 B2
Croydon CR0 ... 206 A1
Grove Pk SE12 ... 165 A2
Baring St N1 ... 95 B6 235 C5
Barker Cl
Kingston u T KT3 ... 198 D5
Richmond TW9 ... 132 D3
Barker Dr NW1 ... 71 D1
Barker Ho
Dulwich SE21 ... 161 C1
3 Harringay N15 ... 50 D5
Walthamstow E17 ... 53 B2
Walworth SE17 ... 263 A3
Barker Mews SW4 ... 137 B1
Barker St SW10 ... 266 A6
Barker Wlk SW16 ... 159 D1
Barkham Rd N17 ... 33 C3
BARKING ... 79 B1
Barking Abbey Comp Sch (Sports & Humanities Coll)) IG11 ... 79 C3
Barking Abbey L Ctr
IG11 ... 80 A2
Barking Abbey (ruins of)★ IG11 ... 101 A6
Barking Abbey Sch (Sports & Humanities Coll) IG11 ... 79 D2
Barking Bsns Ctr
IG11 ... 102 A4
Barking Flyover IG11 ... 78 D1
Barking Hospl IG11 ... 79 D1
Barking Ind Pk IG11 102 A6
Barking Rd
East Ham E6 ... 100 B6
Plaistow E13 ... 99 B4
BARKINGSIDE ... 57 A6
Barkingside Sta IG6 ... 57 B6
Barking Sta IG11 ... 79 A1
Bark Pl W2 ... 113 D6 245 C6
Barkston Gdns
SW5 ... 113 D2 255 C3
Barkway Cl BR6 ... 226 C4
Barkway Ct N4 ... 73 A6
Barkwith Ho 27
SE14 ... 140 D6
Barkworth Rd SE16 ... 118 C1
Barlborough St
SE14 ... 140 D5
Barlby Gdns W10 ... 90 D3
Barlby Prim Sch W10 ... 90 D3
Barlby Rd W10 ... 90 D2
Barley Cl Bus WD23 ... 8 A6
Wembley HA9 ... 65 D4
Barleycorn Way E14 ... 119 B6
Barley Ct Ilford IG3 ... 58 B4
Stanwell TW19 ... 148 A3
Barleyfields Cl RM6 ... 58 C2
Barley La IG3 ... 58 B3
Barley Lane Prim Sch
RM6 ... 58 B2
Barley Mow Pas
Chiswick W4 ... 111 B1
Clerkenwell EC1 ... 241 D3
Barley Mow Way
TW17 ... 192 C5
Barley Shotts Bsns Pk
W10 ... 91 B2
Barling 6 NW1 ... 71 B1
Barling Ct 1 SW4 ... 138 A3
Barlings Ho 2 SE4 ... 140 D1
Barloch Ho 14 SW11 ... 137 A3
Barlow Cl SM6 ... 220 A1
Barlow Dr SE18 ... 144 A4
Barlow Ho
14 Bermondsey
SE16 ... 118 B2
Notting Hill W11 ... 244 A6
Shoreditch N1 ... 235 C2
Barlow Pl W1 ... 248 D5
Barlow Rd Acton W3 ... 110 D5
Brondesbury NW6 ... 69 B2
Hampton TW12 ... 173 C3
Barlow St
SE17 ... 117 B2 262 D3
Barmeston Rd SE6 ... 163 D2
Barmor Cl HA2 ... 23 D1
Barmouth Ave UB6 ... 86 D5
Barmouth Ho 6 N7 ... 72 B6
Barmouth Rd
Croydon CR0 ... 222 D6
Wandsworth SW18 ... 158 A5
Barnabas Ct N21 ... 16 D6
Barnabas Ho EC1 ... 235 A1
Barnabas Lo SW8 ... 270 B2
Barnabas Rd E9 ... 74 D3
Barnaby Cl HA2 ... 64 A6
Barnaby Ct NW9 ... 45 C6
Barnaby Pl SW7 ... 256 C3
Barnard Cl
Chislehurst BR7 ... 189 B2
Sunbury TW16 ... 172 B3
Wallington SM6 ... 219 D1
Barnard Cl continued
Woolwich SE18 ... 122 C3
Barnard Ct SW16 ... 160 B1
Barnard Gdns
Hayes UB4 ... 84 B3
West Barnes KT3 ... 200 A5
Barnard Gr E15 ... 76 D1
Barnard Hill N10 ... 31 B2
Barnard Ho 17 E2 ... 96 B4
Barnard Lo
New Barnet EN5 ... 2 A1
10 Paddington W9 ... 91 C2
Barnard Mews
SW11 ... 136 C1
Barnardo Dr IG6 ... 57 A5
Barnardo Gdns 1
E1 ... 118 D6
Barnardo St E1 ... 96 D1
Barnard Rd
Clapham SW11 ... 136 C1
Enfield EN1 ... 6 B3
Mitcham CR4 ... 181 A1
Barnard's Inn EC4 ... 241 B2
Barnbrough NW1 ... 232 A5
Barnby Sq 1 E15 ... 98 C6
Barnby St
Somers Town
NW1 ... 93 C4 232 B2
2 West Ham E15 ... 98 C6
Barn Cl
Ashford TW15 ... 170 D5
19 Kentish Town NW5 ... 71 D3
Northolt UB5 ... 84 C5
Barn Cres HA7 ... 25 C4
Barncroft Cl UB8 ... 82 D2
Barn Croft Prim Sch
E17 ... 53 A3
Barneby Cl TW2 ... 152 C3
Barnehurst Rd DA7 ... 147 D3
Barn Elms Sp Ctr
SW15 ... 134 C4
Barnersbury Ho N7 ... 72 A4
BARNES ... 133 D4
Barnes Ave
Barnes SW13 ... 134 A5
Southall UB2 ... 107 B2
Barnes Bridge Sta
SW13 ... 133 C3
Barnes Cl E12 ... 77 D4
Barnes Common★
SW13 ... 134 A2
Barnes Ct Barnet EN5 ... 1 D1
Islington N1 ... 72 C1
3 Newham E16 ... 99 C2
South Norwood CR7 ... 205 A6
Woodford IG8 ... 37 D5
Wood Green N22 ... 32 A3
Barnes End KT3 ... 200 A4
Barnes High St
SW13 ... 133 D3
Barnes Ho
8 Barking IG11 ... 101 B6
14 Bethnal Green E2 ... 96 C5
Camden Town NW1 ... 231 D6
26 Deptford SE14 ... 140 D6
Hornsey N19 ... 50 A2
Barnes Hospl SW14 ... 133 C2
Barnes Prim Sch
SW13 ... 133 D2
Barnes Qtr 6 TW8 ... 131 C5
Barnes Rd
Edmonton N18 ... 34 C6
Ilford IG1 ... 79 A3
Barnes St E14 ... 97 A1
Barnes Sta SW13 ... 134 A2
Barnes Terr SE8 ... 119 B1
Barnes Wallis Ct HA9 ... 67 A5
BARNET ... 13 B6
Barnet By-Pass WD6 ... 11 C6
Barnet Coll (Grahame Park) NW9 ... 27 D2
Barnet Coll (North London Bsns Pk)
N11 ... 15 A1
Barnet Coll (Stanhope Rd) N12 ... 30 B5
Barnet Coll (Wood St)
EN5 ... 1 B1
Barnet Dr BR2 ... 226 A6
BARNET GATE ... 11 C5
Barnet Gate La EN5 ... 11 D4
Barnet Gr E2 ... 96 A4
Barnet Hill EN5 ... 1 C1
Barnet Hill JMI Sch
EN5 ... 13 B6
Barnet Ho 35 SE5 ... 139 A3
Barnet La
Barnet EN5, N20 ... 13 B4
Borehamwood WD6 ... 10 B5
Barnet Mus★ EN5 ... 1 A1
Barnet Rd Barnet EN5 ... 1 B5
Edgware EN5 ... 11 C5
Barnett Ho E1 ... 243 C3
Barnett Homestead
NW11 ... 47 C5
Barnet Trad Est EN5 ... 1 B2
Barnetts Ct HA2 ... 63 D5
Barnett St 18 E1 ... 96 B1
Barnet Way (Barnet By-Pass) EN5, NW7, WD6 11 B3
Barnet Wood Rd
BR2 ... 225 C6
Barney Cl SE7 ... 121 C1
Barnfield KT3 ... 199 C3
Barn Field NW3 ... 70 D3
Barnfield Ave
Croydon CR0 ... 222 C6
Kingston u T KT2 ... 176 A5
Mitcham CR4 ... 203 B6
Barnfield Cl
London N4 ... 50 A2
Wandsworth SW17 ... 158 A1
Barnfield Gdns
Kingston u T KT2 ... 176 A5
Shooters Hill SE18 ... 144 D6
Barnfield Pl E14 ... 119 C2
Barnfield Prim Sch
HA8 ... 27 A2
Barnfield Rd
Burnt Oak HA8 ... 27 A2
Ealing W5 ... 87 C3
Erith DA17 ... 147 B6
Shooters Hill SE18 ... 144 D6
Barnfield Wood Cl
BR3 ... 208 B3
Barnfield Wood Rd
BR3 ... 208 B3
Barnham Dr SE28 ... 123 D5
Barnham Rd UB6 ... 86 A4
Barnham St SE1 ... 253 B2
Barnhill HA5 ... 40 C4
Barn Hill HA9 ... 44 D1
Barnhill Ave BR2 ... 208 D4
Barnhill Com High Sch
UB4 ... 84 C4
Barnhill Ct UB4 ... 84 B4
Barnhill La UB4 ... 84 B3
Barnhill Rd Hayes UB4 ... 84 C3
Wembley HA9 ... 67 A5
Barnhurst Path WD19 ... 22 C5
Barningham Way
NW9 ... 45 B3
Barnlea Cl TW13 ... 151 A2
Barnmead Ct RM9 ... 81 B3
Barnmead Gdns RM9 ... 81 B3
Barnmead Rd
Dagenham RM9 ... 81 B3
Penge BR3 ... 185 A2
Barn Rise HA9 ... 66 C6
BARNSBURY ... 72 A1
Barnsbury Cl KT3 ... 199 A5
Barnsbury Cres KT5 ... 199 A1
Barnsbury Gr N7 ... 72 B1
Barnsbury Ho 12
SW4 ... 159 D5
Barnsbury La KT5 ... 199 A1
Barnsbury Pk N1 ... 72 C1
Barnsbury Rd
N1 ... 94 C6 234 A5
Barnsbury Sq N1 ... 72 C1
Barnsbury St N1 ... 72 C1
Barnsbury Terr N1 ... 72 B1
Barnscroft SW20 ... 200 B6
Barnsdale Ave E14 ... 119 C2
Barnsdale Rd W9 ... 91 B3
Barnsley St E1 ... 96 B3
Barn St N16 ... 73 C6
Barnstaple Ho SE12 ... 164 D6
Barnstaple La SE13 ... 142 A1
Barnstaple Rd HA4 ... 62 C5
Barnston Wlk N1 ... 235 A6
Barnview Lo HA3 ... 24 C2
Barn Way HA9 ... 66 C6
Barnwell Ho 1 SE5 ... 139 C4
Barnwell Rd SW2 ... 160 C6
Barnwood Cl
Barnet N20 ... 13 B3
Ruislip HA4 ... 61 B6
Westbourne Green W9 ... 91 D3

Baron Cl
Friern Barnet N11 31 B5
Islington N1 234 A4
Baron Ct Barnet EN5 1 D1
Mitcham CR4 202 C5
Baroness Rd 5 E2 95 D4
Baronet Gr N17 34 A2
Baronet Rd N17 34 A2
Baron Gdns IG6 57 A6
Baron Gr CR4 202 C5
Baron Ho 6 SW19 180 B2
Baron Rd RM8 58 D1
Barons 14 BR3 185 D1
Barons Court Mans
W14 254 B1
Baron's Court Rd
W14 113 A1 254 B2
Barons Court Sta
W14 113 A1 254 A2
Barons Ct Ilford IG1 79 B6
Kingsbury NW9 45 B3
Wallington SM6 219 D5
Baronsfield Rd TW1 153 B5
Barons Gate
East Barnet EN4 14 C5
13 South Acton W4 111 A3
Barons Keep
W14 113 A1 254 A2
Barons Lo 9 E14 120 A2
Barons Mead HA1 42 C5
Baronsmead Rd
SW13 134 A4
Baronsmede W5 110 B4
Baronsmere Ct 9 EN5 1 A1
Baronsmere Rd N2 48 C5
Baron's Pl
SE1 116 C4 251 B1
Baron St N1 94 C5 234 A4
Barons The TW1 153 B5
Baron's Wlk CR0 207 A3
Baron Wlk E16 98 D2
Barque Mews SE8 141 C6
Barrack Rd TW4 129 A1
Barradell Ho 15
W14 112 D3
Barra Hall Cir UB3 83 C1
Barra Hall Rd UB3 105 C6
Barrass Cl 7 EN3 7 C6
Barratt Ave N22 32 B1
Barratt Ho 15 N1 72 D1
Barratt Ind Pk
Poplar E3 98 A3
Southall UB1 107 C5
Barratt Way HA3 42 B6
Barr Beacon SE23 162 C4
Barrenger Rd N10 30 D1
Barret Ho NW6 91 C6
Barrett Ct 2 NW10 89 C5
Barrett Rd E17 54 A5
Barrett's Gr N16 73 C3
Barretts Green Rd
NW10 89 B5
Barrett St W1 93 A1 238 B1
Barrhill Rd SW2 160 A2
Barrie Ct EN5 14 A6
Barriedale SE14 141 A3
Barrie Ho Acton W3 111 A4
Bayswater W2 246 B5
Edmonton N9 18 B4
Primrose Hill NW8 230 B5
8 Stoke Newington
N16 73 C5
Barrier Gdns Pier
SE18 121 D3
Barrier Point Rd
E16 121 C4
Barringers Ct HA4 39 B2
Barringer Sq SW17 181 A6
Barrington N20 14 B3
Barrington Cl NW5 71 A3
Barrington Ct
9 Acton W3 110 D4
Kentish Town NW5 71 A3
4 Muswell Hill N10 31 B1
31 South Lambeth
SW9 138 A3
Barrington Prim Sch
DA7 146 D3
Barrington Rd
Bexley DA7 146 D3
Brixton SW9 138 D2
Cheam SM3 201 C1
Hornsey N8 49 D4

Barrington Rd *continued*
Little Ilford E12 78 C2
Barrington Villas
SE18 144 C4
Barrington Wlk 9
SE19 183 C4
Barrow Ave SM5 218 D1
Barrow Cl N21 16 D2
Barrow Ct 6 SE6 164 D3
Barrowdene Cl HA5 23 A1
Barrowell Gn N21 17 A2
Barrowfield Cl N9 18 C1
Barrowgate Ho W4 111 B1
Barrowgate Rd W4 111 B1
Barrow Hedges Cl
SM5 218 C1
Barrow Hedges Prim Sch
SM5 218 C1
Barrow Hedges Way
SM5 218 C1
Barrow Hill KT4 215 C6
Barrow Hill Cl KT4 215 C6
Barrow Hill Est
NW8 92 C5 230 A3
Barrow Hill Jun Sch
NW8 92 C5 230 A3
Barrow Hill Rd NW8 230 A3
Barrow Point Ave
HA5 23 A1
Barrow Point La HA5 23 A1
Barrow Rd
Croydon CR0 220 C3
Streatham SW16 181 D4
Barrow Wlk 1 TW8 109 C1
Barrs Rd NW10 67 B1
Barry Ave Erith DA7 147 A5
South Tottenham N15 51 D3
Barry Cl BR6 227 C5
Barry Ct SW4 159 C5
Barrydene N20 14 B2
Barrydene Ct EN2 4 D2
Barry Ho 4 SE16 118 B1
Barry Lo N4 50 B2
Barrymore N12 30 A3
Barry Par SE22 140 A1
Barry Rd
London SE22 162 A6
Newham E6 100 A1
Willesden NW10 67 A1
Barry Terr TW15 148 B2
Barset Rd SE15 140 C2
Barsons Cl SE20 184 C3
Barston Rd SE27 161 A1
Barstow Cres SW2 160 B3
Bartell Ho SW2 160 C5
Barter St WC1 94 A2 240 B3
Barters Wlk HA5 41 A6
Barth Mews SE18 123 C2
Bartholomew Cl
Barbican EC1 242 A3
Wandsworth SW18 136 A1
Bartholomew Ct
16 Blackwall E14 120 B6
Edgware HA8 25 D3
St Luke's EC1 242 B6
Bartholomew Ho
22 Camberwell SE5 139 A3
Enfield EN3 7 A6
Bartholomew La EC2 242 D1
Bartholomew Pas
EC1 241 D3
Bartholomew Pl EC1 242 A3
Bartholomew Rd
NW5 71 C2
Bartholomew Sq
18 Bethnal Green E1 96 B3
St Luke's EC1 242 B6
Bartholomew St
SE1 117 B3 262 D5
Bartholomew Villas
NW5 71 C2
Barth Rd SE18 123 C2
Bartle Ave E6 100 A5
Bartle Rd W11 91 A1
Bartlett Cl E14 97 C1
Bartlett Ct EC4 241 B2
Bartletts Cotts 4 EN5 1 A2
Bartletts Ho 10 RM10 81 D2
Bartlett St CR2 221 B3
Bartok Ho W11 244 C5
Barton Ave RM7 59 D1
Barton Cl Bexley DA6 169 A6
Hackney E9 74 C3
Hendon NW4 46 A5
2 Newham E6 100 B1
Peckham SE15 140 B2

Barton Cl *continued*
Shepperton TW17 192 D3
Barton Ct
Beckenham BR2 208 B6
10 South Lambeth
SW4 138 A3
3 Sutton SM1 217 D2
West Kensington W14 254 B2
Barton Gn KT3 177 B1
Barton Ho
8 Bromley E3 97 D4
Islington N1 72 D1
Sands End SW6 135 D2
Barton Mdws IG6 57 A5
Barton Rd
Sidcup DA14 191 A4
West Kensington
W14 113 A1 254 B1
Barton St SW1 260 A6
Bartons The WD6 9 D5
Bartonway NW8 229 C4
Bartram Cl UB8 82 D3
Bartram Ct RM9 80 B2
Bartram Rd SE4 163 A5
Bartrams La EN4 2 A5
Bartrip St E9 75 B2
Barts Cl BR3 207 C4
Barts & The London Sch
of Medicine & Dentistry
EC1 94 D3 241 D5
Barville Cl SE4 141 A1
Barwell Bsns Pk
KT9 213 D1
Barwell Ho 7 E2 96 A3
Barwell La KT9 213 C1
Barwick Dr UB8 82 D2
Barwick Ho 7 W3 111 A4
Barwick Rd E7 77 B4
Barwood Ave BR4 207 D1
Bascome St 13 SW2 160 C5
Basden Gr TW13 151 C2
Base Apartments 8
N1 73 A1
Basedale Rd RM9 80 B1
Baseing Cl E6 122 C6
Baseline Business
Studios 18 W11 112 D6
Basevi Way SE8 141 D6
Bashley Rd NW10 89 B3
Basil Ave E6 100 A4
Basil Ct 11 EN5 2 A1
Basildene Rd TW4,
TW5 128 D2
Basildon Ct W1 238 B4
Basildon Rd SE2 124 A1
Basil Gdns
Croydon CR0 206 D1
West Norwood SE27 183 A5
Basil Ho
South Lambeth SW8 270 A4
22 Whitechapel E1 96 A1
Basil Mans SW1 247 C1
Basilon Rd DA7 147 A3
Basil Spence Ho N22 32 B2
Basil St
Knightsbridge
SW1 114 D4 247 C1
Knightsbridge SW1,
SW3 114 D3 257 C6
Basin App 20 E14 97 A1
Basing Cl KT7 196 D2
Basing Ct 13 SE15 139 D4
Basingdon Way SE5 139 B1
Basing Dr DA5 169 B5
Basingfield Rd KT7 196 D2
Basinghall Ave
EC2 95 B1 242 C2
Basinghall St
EC2 95 B1 242 C2
Basing Hill
London NW11 47 B1
Wembley HA9 44 C1
Basing Ho
7 Barking IG11 101 B6
Catford SE6 185 C6
Basing House Yd 22
E2 95 C4
Basing Pl E2 95 C4
Basing St W11 91 B1
Basing Way
London N3 47 D6
Thames Ditton KT7 196 D2
Basire St N1 95 A6 235 B6
Baskerville Ct
South Norwood
SE25 205 C4

Baskerville Ct *continued*
Wandsworth SW18 158 C4
Baskerville Gdns
NW10 67 C4
Baskerville Rd
SW18 158 C4
Basket Gdns SE9 166 A6
Basle Ho 3 E15 76 C3
Baslow Cl HA3 24 B2
Baslow Wlk E5 74 D4
Basnett Rd 9 SW11 137 A2
Basque Ct 21 SE16 118 D4
Bassano St SE22 161 D6
Bassant Rd SE18 145 D6
Bassein Park Rd
W12 111 D4
Bassett Gdns TW7 130 A5
Bassett Ho RM9 102 B6
Bassett House Sch 22
W10 90 D1
Bassett Rd W10 90 D1
Bassetts Cl BR6 226 D4
Bassett St NW5 71 A2
Bassetts Way BR6 226 D4
Bassett Way UB1 85 D1
Bassingbourn Ho 3
N1 72 D1
Bassingham Rd
Wandsworth SW18 158 A4
Wembley HA0 65 D2
Bassishaw Highwalk
EC2 242 C3
Basswood Cl 5
SE15 140 B2
Bastable Ave IG11 102 A5
Basterfield Ho EC1 242 A5
Bastion Highwalk
EC2 242 A3
Bastion Rd SE18, SE2 124 A1
Baston Manor Rd BR2,
BR4 225 B4
Baston Rd BR2 225 B5
Baston Sch BR2 225 B6
Bastwick St
EC1 95 A3 242 A6
Basuto Rd
SW6 135 C4 265 B1
Batavia Cl TW16 172 C2
Batavia Ho 1 SE14 141 A5
Batavia Mews 3
SE14 141 A5
Batavia Rd
Deptford SE14 141 A5
Sunbury TW16 172 B2
Batchelor St
N1 94 C6 234 B5
Bateman Cl IG11 79 A2
Bateman Ho 8
SE17 138 D6
Bateman Rd E4 35 C4
Bateman's Bldgs W1 239 C1
Bateman's Row
EC2 95 C3 243 B6
Bateman St
W1 93 D1 239 C1
Bates Cres
Croydon CR0 220 C3
Streatham SW16 181 C3
Bateson St 3 SE18 123 C2
Bate St 10 E14 119 B6
Bath Cl SE15 140 B5
Bath Ct Finsbury EC1 235 C1
3 Forest Hill SE26 162 A1
Holborn EC1 241 A5
Bathgate Ho 8
SW9 138 D4
Bathgate Rd SW19 156 D1
Bath Gr E2 96 A5
Bath Ho
Bethnal Green E2 96 A3
Borough The SE1 262 B6
Bath House Rd CR0 204 A1
Bath Pas KT1 175 D1
Bath Pl Barnet EN5 1 B2
14 Hammersmith W6 112 C1
11 Shoreditch EC2 95 C4
Bath Rd Acton W4 111 C2
Cranford TW3, TW4,
TW5 128 C4
Dagenham RM6 59 A3
Harlington TW6, UB7,
TW5 127 B4
Harmondsworth TW6,
UB7 126 B4
Lower Edmonton N9 18 C2
Upton E7 77 D2

Baths Rd BR1, BR2 209 D5
Bath St EC1 95 B4 235 C1
Bath Terr
SE1 117 A3 262 A6
Bathurst Ave SW19 179 D2
Bathurst Gdns NW10 90 B5
Bathurst Ho 2 W12 112 B6
Bathurst Mews
W2 114 B6 246 D6
Bathurst Rd IG1 56 D1
Bathurst St W2 246 D6
Bathway 11 SE18 122 C2
Batley Cl CR4 202 D2
Batley Pl 3 N16 73 D5
Batley Rd Enfield EN2 5 B4
Shacklewell N16 73 D5
Batman Cl W12 112 B5
Batoum Gdns W6 112 C3
Batson Ho 20 E1 96 A1
Batson St W12 112 A4
Batsworth Rd CR4 202 B6
Battenburg Wlk 10
SE19 183 C5
Batten Cl E6 100 B1
Batten Ho
7 London SW4 159 C6
8 Walthamstow E17 53 D6
10 West Kilburn W10 91 A4
Batten St SW11 136 C2
Battersby Rd SE6 164 B1
BATTERSEA 136 D4
Battersea Bridge Rd
SW11 136 C5 267 A3
Battersea Bsns Ctr
SW11 137 A2
Battersea Church Rd
SW11 136 B4 266 D2
Battersea Dogs & Cats
Home SW8 137 B5 268 D3
Battersea High St
SW11 136 B3
Battersea Hts SW11 136 D2
Battersea Park*
SW11 137 A5 268 A3
Battersea Park Rd SW11,
SW8 267 D1
Battersea Park Sch
SW11 136 D4 267 D1
Battersea Park Sta
SW8 137 B5 268 C3
Battersea Power
Station(dis)
SW8 137 B6 268 D6
Battersea Rise
SW11 136 C1
Battersea Sq SW11 266 D1
Battery Rd SE28 123 C4
Battishill St 9 N1 72 D1
Battlebridge Ct NW1 233 B4
Battle Bridge La
SE1 117 C5 253 A3
Battle Cl SW19 180 A4
Battledean Rd N5 72 D3
Battle Ho 8 SE15 140 A6
Battle House Mews 7
EN5 2 A1
Batty St E1 96 A1
Baty Ho SW2 160 B3
Baudwin Rd SE6 164 C2
Baugh Rd DA14 190 C5
Baulk The SW18 157 C4
Bavant Rd SW16 182 B1
Bavaria Rd N19 72 A6
Bavdene Mews NW4 46 B5
Bavent Rd SE5 139 A3
Bawdale Rd SE22 161 D6
Bawdsey Ave IG2 57 D5
Bawtree Rd SE14 141 A5
Bawtry Rd N20 14 D1
Baxendale N20 14 A2
Baxendale St E2 96 A4
Baxter Cl
Bromley BR1 210 D6
Hillingdon UB10 82 D4
Southall UB2 107 D3
Baxter Ho 11 E3 97 D4
Baxter Rd
Edmonton N18 34 B6
Ilford IG1 78 D3
Islington N1 73 B2
Newham E16 99 C1
Bayard Ct DA7 147 D1
Baycliffe Ho 8 E9 74 D2
Baycroft Cl HA5 40 C6
Bay Ct Ealing W5 110 A3
7 Stepney E1 96 D3

Baydon Ct BR2 208 D6
Bayer Ho EC1 242 A5
Bayes Ct NW3 70 D1
Bayeux Ho 10 SE7 143 C6
Bayfield Ho 3 SE4 140 D1
Bayfield Rd SE9 143 D1
Bayford Lodge HA5 23 B2
Bayford Rd NW10 90 D4
Bayford St Ind Ctr 4 E8 74 B1
Bayford St 5 E8 74 B1
Baygrove Mews KT1 175 C2
Bayham Pl NW1 93 C6 232 B5
Bayham Rd
Acton W4 111 B3
Ealing W13 109 B5
Morden SM4 202 A5
Bayham St NW1 93 C6 232 A5
Bay Ho UB10 60 C4
Bayhurst Ho N4 51 A2
Bayhurst Wood Country Park UB9 38 B4
Bayleaf Cl TW12 174 B5
Bayley St WC1 239 C3
Bayley Wlk SE2 125 A1
Baylis Mews TW1 153 A4
Baylis Rd SE1 116 C4 251 A1
Bayliss Ave SE28 124 D6
Bayliss Cl
4 Southall UB1 85 D1
Southgate N21 16 A6
Bayne Cl E6 100 B1
Baynes Cl EN1 6 A4
Baynes Mews 2 NW3 70 B2
Baynes St NW1 71 C1
Baynham Cl DA5 169 B5
Bayon Ho 27 N19 49 D2
Bayonne Rd W6 264 A5
Bays Cl SE26 184 C5
Bays Ct HA8 26 D5
Bayshill Rise UB5 63 D2
Bayston Rd N16 73 D5
BAYSWATER 114 A6
Bayswater Rd W2 114 B6 246 C5
Bayswater Rd Mkt* W2 114 A6 246 B5
Bayswater Sta W2 113 D6 245 D6
Bayton Ct 2 E8 74 A1
Baytree Cl
Bromley BR1 187 D2
Sidcup DA15 167 D3
Baytree Ho E4 19 D4
Baytree Rd SW2 138 B1
Bazalgette Cl KT3 199 B4
Bazalgette Gdns KT3 199 B4
Bazalgette Ho NW8 236 D6
Bazeley Ho SE1 251 C1
Bazely St E14 120 A6
Bazile Rd N21 16 C5
BBC Television Ctr W12 112 C5
Beacham Cl SE7 143 D6
Beachborough Rd BR1 186 A6
Beachcroft Ave UB1 107 B5
Beachcroft Rd E11 76 C5
Beach Ct SE9 166 A5
Beach Gr TW13 151 C2
Beach Ho SW5 255 A2
Beachy Rd E3 75 C1
Beaconfield Terrace Rd W14 254 A5
Beacon Gate SE14 140 D2
Beacon Gr SM5 219 A4
Beacon Hill N7 72 A3
Beacon Ho
11 Camberwell SE5 139 C5
7 Isle Of Dogs E14 119 D1
10 Penge SE26 184 B5
South Lambeth SW8 269 C2
Beacon Pl CR0 220 A5
Beacon Rd
Harlington TW19, TW6 148 C5
Hither Green SE13 164 B5
Beacon Rdbt TW6 148 C5
Beacons Cl 10 E6 100 A2
Beaconsfield Cl
Acton Green W4 111 A1
Beaconsfield Cl *continued*
Friern Barnet N11 31 A5
Greenwich SE3 143 A6
Beaconsfield Ct N11 31 A5
Beaconsfield Gdns KT10 212 C1
Beaconsfield Par 1 SE9 188 A6
Beaconsfield Prim Sch UB2 107 A5
Beaconsfield Rd
Acton W4 111 B3
Bromley BR1 209 D6
Claygate KT10 212 C1
Ealing W5 109 D4
Edmonton N9 18 A1
Elmstead SE9 188 A6
Enfield EN3 6 D6
Friern Barnet N11 31 A6
Greenwich SE3 143 A5
Hayes UB4 106 C5
Kingston u T KT3 177 B1
Leyton E10 76 A5
Newham E16 98 D3
Southall UB1 107 A5
South Tottenham N15 51 C5
Surbiton KT5 198 B2
Thornton Heath CR0 205 B3
Twickenham TW1 153 B5
Walthamstow E17 53 B3
Walworth SE17 117 C1 263 A1
Willesden NW10 67 D2
Beaconsfield Wlk SW6 135 B4 264 D1
Beaconshaw BR1 186 C3
Beacontree Ave E17 36 B1
Beacontree Rd E11 54 D2
Beadle Ct CR4 202 C6
Beadlow Cl SM4 202 B3
Beadman Pl SE27 182 D6
Beadman St SE27 182 D6
Beadnell Rd SE23 162 D3
Beadon Rd
Bromley BR2 209 A4
Hammersmith W6 112 C2
Beaford Gr SW20 201 B6
Beagle Cl TW13 172 B6
Beak St W1 115 C6 249 B6
Beal Cl DA16 146 A4
Beale Cl N13 32 D5
Beale Ho 7 SW9 138 B3
Beale Pl E3 97 B5
Beale Rd E3 97 B6
Beal High Sch IG5 56 A5
Beal Rd IG1 78 C6
Beam Ave RM10 103 D6
Beames Ho SW8 269 C2
Beames Rd NW10 89 B6
Beaminster Ct N15 51 B4
Beaminster Gdns IG6 56 D6
Beaminster Ho SW8 270 C4
Beamish Dr WD23 8 A3
Beamish Ho 7 SE16 118 C2
Beamish Rd N9 18 A3
Beanacre Cl E9 75 B2
Bean Rd DA6 146 D1
Beanshaw SE9 188 C6
Beansland Gr RM6 59 A6
Bear Alley EC4 241 C2
Bear Cl RM7 59 D3
Bear Croft Ho 6 SW6 135 B3
Beardell St SE19 183 D4
Beardow Gr N14 15 C5
Beard Rd KT2 176 B5
Beardsfield E13 99 A5
Beard's Hill TW12 173 C2
Beards Hill Cl TW12 173 C2
Beardsley Terr RM8 80 B3
Beardsley Way W3 111 B4
Beard's Rd TW15, TW16 171 C4
Bearfield Rd KT2 176 A3
Bear Gdns SE1 117 A5 252 A4
Bear La SE1 116 D5 251 D3
Bear Rd TW13 172 D6
Bear St WC2 249 D6
Bearstead Rise SE4 163 B6
Bearsted Terr 7 BR3 185 C2
Beasley's Ait TW17 193 D3
Beasley's Ait La TW16, TW17 193 D3
Beaton Cl SE15 139 D4
Beatrice Ave
Thornton Heath SW16 182 B1
Wembley HA9 66 A3
Beatrice Cl
Newham E13 99 A3
Pinner HA5 40 A5
Beatrice Ct
Buckhurst Hill IG9 21 D2
Hendon NW4 46 C4
Beatrice Ho
1 Brixton SW2 160 B6
Forest Hill SE6 163 C2
4 Hammersmith W6 112 C1
2 Stepney E1 96 D2
Beatrice Lo 3 N12 30 A4
Beatrice Pl W8 255 C5
Beatrice Rd
Bermondsey SE1 118 A2
Edmonton N9 18 C4
Finsbury Pk N4 50 C2
2 Richmond TW10 154 B6
Southall UB1 107 B5
Walthamstow E17 53 C4
Beatrice Tate Sch 33 E2 96 B4
Beatrice Webb Ho 4 E3 97 A5
Beatrix Ho SW5 255 D2
Beatrix Potter Prim Sch SW18 158 A3
Beatson Wlk 23 SE16 118 D5
Beattie Cl TW14 149 D3
Beattie Ho SW8 269 B2
Beattock Rise N10 49 B5
Beatty Ho 16 E14 119 C4
Beatty Rd
Stanmore HA7 25 C4
Stoke Newington N16 73 C4
Beattyville Gdns IG6 56 D5
Beauchamp Cl 17 W4 111 A3
Beauchamp Ct HA7 25 C5
Beauchamp Pl SW3 114 C3 257 B5
Beauchamp Rd
Clapham SW11 136 D1
East Molesey KT8 196 A4
South Norwood SE19 183 B2
Sutton SM1 217 C4
Twickenham TW1 153 A4
Upton E7 77 B1
Beauchamp St EC1 241 A3
Beauchamp Terr SW15 134 B2
Beauclerc Inf Sch TW16 194 C6
Beauclerc Rd W6 112 B3
Beauclere Ho 1 SM2 218 A1
Beauclerk Cl TW13 150 B3
Beauclerk Ho 10 SW16 160 A1
Beaudesert Mews UB7 104 A4
Beaufort E6 100 C2
Beaufort Ave HA3 43 B6
Beaufort Cl
Chingford E4 35 D4
Ealing W5 88 B2
Putney SW19 156 B4
Beaufort Ct
Friern Barnet N11 31 B5
Harrow HA3 43 A3
3 New Barnet EN5 14 A6
Richmond TW10 175 C6
West Brompton SW6 265 A6
Beaufort Dr NW11 47 C5
Beaufort Gdns
Hendon NW4 46 C3
Heston TW5 129 A4
Ilford IG1 56 C1
Knightsbridge SW3 114 C3 257 B6
South Norwood SW16 182 B3
Beaufort Ho
Ashford TW15 170 D5
Battersea SW11 136 C3
Chelsea SW3 266 D5
Hampstead Garden Suburb NW11 48 A3
20 Millwall E14 119 C4
Pimlico SW1 259 C1
8 South Tottenham N15 51 D5
Beaufort Ho *continued*
1 Wimbledon SW20 178 D2
Beaufort Mans SW3 266 D5
Beaufort Mews SW6 264 D6
Beaufort Pk NW11 47 C5
Beaufort Rd Ealing W5 88 B2
Kingston u T KT1, KT5, KT6 198 A5
Richmond TW10 175 C6
Ruislip HA4 61 B6
Twickenham TW1 153 C4
Beaufort St SW3 136 B6 266 C6
Beaufort Way KT17 216 A1
Beaufoy Ho
South Lambeth SW8 270 C4
3 West Norwood SE27 160 D1
Beaufoy Rd
11 London SW8 137 B2
Tottenham N17 33 C3
Beaufoy Wlk SE11 116 B2 260 D3
Beaulieu Ave
Forest Hill SE26 184 B6
1 Newham E16 121 B5
Beaulieu Cl
Camberwell SE5 139 B2
Colindale NW9 45 C5
Hounslow TW4 151 B6
Mitcham CR4 181 A2
14 Twickenham TW1 153 D5
Beaulieu Ct W5 88 A2
Beaulieu Dr HA5 40 D2
Beaulieu Gdns N21 17 A4
Beaulieu Ho 6 NW4 28 D1
Beaulieu Hts CR7 183 C2
Beaulieu Pl W4 111 A3
Beaumanor Gdns SE9 188 C6
Beaumanor Mans W2 245 D6
Beaumaris 5 N11 32 A4
Beaumaris Dr IG8 37 D3
Beaumaris Gn NW9 45 C3
Beaumaris Twr 2 W3 110 D4
Beaumont SW15 157 A6
Beaumont Ave
Harrow HA2 41 D3
Richmond TW9 132 B2
Wembley HA0 65 C4
West Kensington W14 113 B1 254 C2
Beaumont Bldgs WC2 240 B1
Beaumont Cl
East Finchley N2 48 C5
Kingston u T KT2 176 C3
Beaumont Cres W14 113 B1 254 C1
Beaumont Ct
10 Acton Green W4 111 A1
16 Hendon NW9 27 D1
Lower Clapton E5 74 B5
Marylebone W1 238 B4
7 Mile End E1 97 A4
6 Mitcham CR4 181 A1
Wembley HA0 65 C3
17 Wimbledon SW19 178 D3
Beaumont Dr
Ashford TW15 171 B5
New Malden KT4 200 B2
Beaumont Gdns NW3 69 C5
Beaumont Gr E1 96 D3
Beaumont Ho
12 Leyton E10 53 D2
1 Streatham SW2 160 A3
West Kensington W14 254 D3
Wimbledon SW19 157 C1
Beaumont Lo E8 74 A2
Beaumont Pl
Barnet EN5 1 B4
Fitzrovia NW1, WC1, W1 93 C3 239 B6
Isleworth TW7 152 D6
Beaumont Prim Sch E10 53 D1
Beaumont Rd
Leyton E10 53 D2
Newham E13 99 B4
Orpington BR5 211 B3
Putney SW15, SW19 157 A4
South Acton W4 111 A3
South Norwood SE19 183 A4
Beaumont Rise N19 49 D1
Beaumont Sq E1 96 D2
Beaumont St W1 238 B4
Beaumont Terr 1 SE13 164 C4
Beaumont Wlk NW3 70 D1
Beauvais Terr UB5 84 D4
Beauvale 6 NW1 71 A1
Beauval Rd SE22 161 D5
Beaverbank Rd SE9 167 B3
Beaver Cl
Hampton TW12 173 D2
9 Penge SE20 184 A3
West Barnes SM4 200 C2
Beaver Ctr The RM8 59 A2
Beaver Gr UB5 85 A4
Beavers Com Prim Sch The TW4 128 C2
Beavers Cres TW4 128 D1
Beavers La TW4 128 C2
Beavers Lo DA14 189 D5
Beaverwood Rd BR7 189 C4
Beaverwood Sch for Girls BR7 189 C4
Beavis Ho N16 73 C5
Beavor La W6 112 A1
Bebbington Rd SE18 123 C2
Beblets Cl 4 BR6 227 D3
Bec Cl HA4 62 D5
Beccles Dr IG11 79 D2
Beccles St E14 119 B6
Bechervaise Ct 2 E10 53 D1
Beck Cl SE13 141 D4
Beck Ct BR3 206 D6
BECKENHAM 185 C1
Beckenham Beacon Hospl BR3 185 B1
Beckenham Bsns Ctr BR3 185 A4
Beckenham Ct BR3 185 C2
Beckenham Gdns N9 17 C1
Beckenham Gr BR2 186 B1
Beckenham Hill Rd BR3, SE6 186 A5
Beckenham Hill Sta SE6 186 A5
Beckenham Junction Sta BR3 185 C2
Beckenham La BR1, BR2 186 D1
Beckenham Place Pk BR3 185 D3
Beckenham Rd
Penge BR3 185 A2
West Wickham BR3, BR4 208 A2
Beckenham Rd Sta BR3 185 A2
Beckers The N16 74 A4
Becket Ave E6 100 C4
Becket Cl
Croydon SE25 206 A3
2 Merton SW19 179 D2
Becket Fold 10 HA1 42 D4
Becket Ho SE1 252 C1
Becket Rd N18 34 C6
Becket St SE1 262 C6
Beckett Cl
Abbey Wood DA17 125 B3
Streatham SW16 159 D2
Willesden NW10 67 C2
Beckett Ho
28 London SW9 138 A3
15 Stepney E1 96 C2
Becketts Cl
Feltham TW14 150 B5
Orpington BR6 227 D5
Becketts Pl KT1 175 D2
Beckett Wlk BR3 185 A4
Beckfoot NW1 232 B3
Beckford Cl W14 254 D3
Beckford Dr BR5 211 B2
Beckford Ho 18 N16 73 C3
Beckford Prim Sch NW6 69 B3
Beckford Rd CR0 205 D3
Beckham Ho SE11 260 D3
Beck Ho
4 Edmonton N18 34 A5
Stoke Newington N16 73 C5
Beckington 18 NW5 71 A2
Beck La BR3 206 D6
Beckley Ho E3 97 B3

Becklow Gdns
Chiswick W12 111 D4
1 Shepherd's Bush W12 112 A4
Becklow Mews 7 W12 112 A4
Becklow Rd W12 112 A4
Beckmead Sch BR3 207 C1
Beck Rd E8 96 B6
Mitcham CR4 202 D3
Beck River Pk 10 BR3 185 C2
Becks Rd DA14 168 A1
BECKTON 100 D2
Beckton Alps E6 100 C3
Beckton Alps Ski Ctr E6 100 C3
Beckton Park Sta E6 122 B6
Beckton Rd E16 98 D2
Beckton Ret Pk E6 100 C2
Beckton Sta E6 100 C2
Beckton Triangle Ret Pk E6 100 D3
Beck Way BR3 207 B6
Beckway Rd SW16 181 D1
Beckway St SE17 117 C2 263 A3
Beckwith Ho 22 E2 96 B5
Beckwith Rd SE24 161 B6
Beclands Rd SW17 181 A4
Becmead Ave
Harrow HA3 43 B4
Streatham SW16 181 D6
Becondale Rd SE19 183 C5
BECONTREE 81 A4
Becontree Ave RM8 80 C5
Becontree Prim Sch RM8 80 B5
Becontree Sta RM9 80 D2
Bective Pl SW15 135 B1
Bective Rd
Forest Gate E7 77 A4
Putney SW15 135 B1
Becton Pl DA8 147 D5
Bedale Rd EN2 5 A5
Bedale St SE1 252 C3
Beddan Ct HA8 26 C4
BEDDINGTON 220 A6
BEDDINGTON CORNER 203 A2
Beddington Cross CR0 204 A2
Beddington Farm Rd CR0 204 A1
Beddington Gdns SM5, SM6 219 A2
Beddington Gn BR5 189 D2
Beddington Gr SM6 219 D3
Beddington Inf Sch SM6 219 C4
Beddington La
Wallington CR0 203 D2
Wallington CR0 220 A6
Beddington Lane Sta CR0 203 C3
Beddington Manor SM2 218 B2
Beddington Park Cotts SM6 219 D5
Beddington Park Prim Sch CR0 219 D5
Beddington Rd
Ilford IG3 57 D2
St Paul's Cray BR5 189 D2
Beddington Terr CR0 204 B2
Beddington Trad Est CR0 204 A1
Bede Cl HA5 22 D2
Bedefield WC1 233 B1
Bede Ho London SE14 141 B4
5 Putney SW15 156 D5
Bedelsford Specl Sch KT1 198 A6
Bedens Rd DA14 191 A5
Bede Rd RM6 58 C3
Bedevere Rd N9 18 A1
Bedfont Cl
East Bedfont TW14 149 A5
Mitcham CR4 181 A1
Bedfont Green Cl TW14 149 A3
Bedfont Ind Pk TW15 149 B1
Bedfont Ind Pk N TW15 149 A1
Bedfont Jun & Inf Schs TW14 149 C5
Bedfont La TW14, TW13 149 D4
Bedfont Lakes Ctry Pk TW14 149 A2
Bedfont Rd
East Bedfont TW13, TW14 149 B2
Stanwell TW19 148 B5
Bedford Ave
Barnet EN5 13 B6
Bloomsbury WC1 93 D2 239 D3
Hayes UB4 84 B1
Bedfordbury WC2 116 A6 250 A5
Bedford Cl
Chiswick W4 133 D6
Muswell Hill N10 31 A3
Bedford Cnr 3 W4 111 C2
Bedford Court Mans WC1 239 D3
Bedford Ct
6 Richmond TW9 132 B1
South Norwood SE19 183 D2
St James WC2 250 A5
Wembley HA0 65 D4
Bedford Gardens Ho W8 245 B3
Bedford Gdns W8 113 C5 245 B3
Bedford Hill SW12 159 B2
Bedford Ho
2 Acton W4 111 C2
Edgware HA8 26 B3
7 Stockwell SW4 138 A1
Bedford Mews SE6 163 D2
BEDFORD PARK 111 C3
Bedford Park Cnr 5 W4 111 C2
Bedford Park Mans 4 W4 111 B2
Bedford Pas SW6 264 B4
Bedford Pk CR0 205 A1
Bedford Pl
Bloomsbury WC1 94 A2 240 A4
Croydon CR0 205 B1
Bedford Rd
Acton W4 111 C3
Barking E6 100 C6
Crouch End N8 49 D3
Ealing W13 109 B6
East Finchley N2 48 C6
Edgware NW7 11 C1
Edmonton N9 18 B4
Harrow HA1 42 A3
Ilford IG1 78 D5
North Cheam KT4 216 C6
Ruislip HA4 61 D4
Sidcup DA15 167 C1
South Tottenham N15 51 C5
Stockwell SW2, SW4 138 A1
Twickenham TW2 152 B1
Walthamstow E17 53 C6
Woodford E18 37 A1
Wood Green N22 32 A1
Bedford Row WC1 94 B2 240 D3
Bedford Sq WC1 93 D2 239 D3
Bedford St WC2 116 A6 250 B5
Bedford Terr SM2 218 A2
Bedford Villas 3 SM5 218 D5
Bedford Way WC1 93 D3 239 D5
Bedgebury Gdns SW19 157 A2
Bedgebury Rd SE9 143 D1
Bedivere Rd BR1 165 A1
Bedlam Mews SE11 261 A4
Bedlow Cl NW8 236 D5
Bedlow Way CR0 220 B4
Bedonwell Inf Sch DA17 147 A6
Bedonwell Jun Sch DA17 147 A6
Bedonwell Rd
Bexley DA17 147 A6
Bedonwell Rd *continued*
Erith DA7 147 C5
Bedser Cl
Kennington SE11 270 D6
South Norwood CR7 205 A6
Bedser Ct 7 SW4 138 A3
Bedser Dr UB6 64 B3
Bedster Gdns KT8 195 D6
Bedwardine Rd SE19 183 C3
Bedwell Ct 4 RM6 58 D2
Bedwell Gdns UB3 105 C2
Bedwell Ho 18 SW9 138 C3
Bedwell Rd
Belvedere DA17 125 C1
Tottenham N17 33 C2
Beeby Rd E16 99 B2
Beech Ave Acton W3 111 C5
Brentford TW8 131 B5
4 Chigwell IG9 21 B2
East Barnet N20 14 C3
Ruislip HA4 40 B1
Sidcup DA15 168 A4
Beech Cl
Ashford TW15 171 B5
Carshalton SM5 218 D6
Deptford SE8 141 B6
Enfield N9 18 B5
Putney SW15 156 A4
Sunbury TW16 172 D1
West Drayton UB7 104 C3
Wimbledon SW19 178 C4
Beech Copse
Bickley BR1 188 B1
South Croydon CR2 221 C3
Beechcroft
Chislehurst West BR7 188 C3
3 Kingston u T KT2 176 D2
Beechcroft Ave
Golders Green NW11 47 B2
Harrow HA2 41 C2
Kingston u T KT1, KT3 177 A1
Beechcroft Cl
Heston TW5 129 A5
Orpington BR6 227 B4
Streatham SW16 182 B5
Beechcroft Ct
3 Golders Green NW11 47 B2
Greenwich SE3 143 A4
8 Woodside Pk N12 29 D6
Beech Croft Ct N5 72 D4
Beechcroft Gdns HA9 66 B5
Beechcroft Ho W5 88 A2
Beechcroft Lo 6 SM2 218 A1
Beechcroft Mans SW16 182 B5
Beechcroft Rd
Chessington KT9 214 B5
Mortlake SW14 133 A2
Orpington BR6 227 B4
Upper Tooting SW17 158 C2
Woodford E18 37 B1
Beechcroft Way N19 49 D1
Beech Ct
Beckenham BR3 185 B3
3 Buckhurst Hill IG9 21 D2
Child's Hill NW2 69 B6
Hayes UB3 105 D5
6 Ilford E12 78 C5
Marylebone W1 237 C2
Northolt UB5 85 A6
43 Notting Hill W2 91 C2
7 Rotherhithe SE16 119 A5
Surbiton KT6 198 A2
Teddington TW11 175 C4
Walthamstow E17 54 B6
4 West Norwood SW16 182 C5
Beechdale N21 16 B2
Beechdale Rd SW2 160 B5
Beech Dell BR2, BR6 226 B4
Beechdene 4 SE15 140 B4
Beech Dr N2 48 D6
Beechen Cliff Way 2 TW7 130 D3
Beechengrove HA5 41 B6
Beechen Pl SE23 162 C2
Beeches Ave SM5 218 C1
Beeches Cl SE20 184 C2
Beeches Ct BR1 187 A4
Beeches Prim Ctr The SE2 124 C3
Beeches Rd
Cheam SM3 201 A1
Upper Tooting SW17 158 D1
Beeches The
Ealing W7 108 D4
East Barnet N20 14 C2
East Ham E12 78 B1
Hounslow TW3 129 D4
Mitcham CR4 202 C4
1 Upper Holloway N19 50 A1
Beechey Ho 30 E1 118 B5
Beech Farm Cotts IG8 36 B3
Beechfield Cotts 5 BR1 187 C1
Beechfield Ct 7 CR2 221 A4
Beechfield Rd
Bromley BR1 187 C1
Forest Hill SE6 163 B3
Harringay N4 51 A3
Beech Gdns
Dagenham RM10 81 D1
Ealing W5 110 A3
Beech Gr
Kingston u T KT3 199 B6
Mitcham CR4 203 D5
Beech Hall Cres E4 36 B3
Beech Hall Rd E4 36 B3
Beech Hill EN4 2 C5
Beech Hill Ave EN4 2 B4
Beechhill Rd SE9 166 C6
Beech Ho Chingford E4 35 C6
Hayes UB4 84 D2
Heston TW5 129 A5
6 Maitland Pk NW3 70 D2
New Addington CR0 223 D2
22 Rotherhithe SE16 118 C4
7 Sidcup DA15 168 A1
5 Stoke Newington N16 73 B6
12 Wallington SM6 219 C2
Beech House Rd CR0 221 B5
Beech La IG9 21 B2
Beech Lawns N12 30 B5
Beechmont Cl BR1 186 C5
Beechmore Gdns SM3 216 D6
Beechmore Rd SW11 136 D4 267 D1
Beechmount Ave W7 86 C2
Beecholme 15 N12 29 D6
Beecholme Ave CR4 181 B2
Beecholme Est E5 74 B5
Beecholme Prim Sch CR4 181 B2
Beech Rd
Bowes Pk N11 32 A4
East Bedfont TW14 149 C4
Thornton Heath SW16 204 B6
Beechrow KT2 176 A6
Beech St EC2 95 A2 242 B4
Beech Tree Cl
Islington N1 72 C1
Stanmore HA7 25 C5
Beech Tree Glade E4 20 D3
Beech Tree Pl SM1 217 D3
Beechvale Cl N12 30 C5
Beechway DA5 168 D5
Beech Way
Twickenham TW2 151 C1
Willesden NW10 67 B1
Beech Wlk NW7 27 C4
Beechwood Ave
Ashford TW16 172 A4
East Finchley N3 47 C6
Greenford UB6 85 D4
Harrow HA2 63 D5
Hayes UB3 105 B6
Hillingdon UB8 82 C1
Orpington BR6 227 C2
Richmond TW9 132 C4
Ruislip HA4 61 D6
Thornton Heath CR7 204 D5
Beechwood Circ HA2 63 D5
Beechwood Cl
Edgware NW7 27 C5
Fortis Green N2 48 D5
Surbiton KT6 197 D2
Beechwood Cres DA7 147 A2
Beechwood Ct
Ashford TW16 172 A5
Beechwood Ct *continued*
Carshalton SM5 218 D4
Cheam SM1 217 C3
Chiswick W4 133 B6
Stamford Hill N16 51 C2
Sutton SM2 218 B2
Beechwood Dr
Keston BR2 225 D4
Woodford IG8 36 D5
Beechwood Gdns
Ealing NW10 88 B4
Harrow HA2 63 D5
Ilford IG5 56 C5
Beechwood Gr W3 111 C6
Beechwood Hall N3 47 B6
Beechwood Ho 23 E2 96 A5
Beechwood Mews 2 N9 18 A2
Beechwood Pk E18 55 A6
Beechwood Rd
Dalston E8 73 D2
London N8 50 A5
South Croydon CR2 221 C1
Beechwood Rise BR7 188 D6
Beechwood Sch SW16 160 A1
Beechwoods Ct 5 SE19 183 D5
Beechworth Cl NW3 69 C6
Beecroft La SE4 163 A6
Beecroft Mews SE4 163 A6
Beecroft Rd SE4 163 A6
Beehive Cl Dalston E8 73 D1
Elstree WD6 9 D5
Hillingdon UB10 60 B1
Beehive Ct IG1 56 B3
Beehive La IG1 56 B3
Beehive Pl SW9 138 C2
Beehive Prep Sch IG4 56 B4
Beeken Dene BR6 227 A4
Beeleigh Rd SM4 201 D5
Beeston Cl
5 Dalston E8 74 A3
South Oxhey WD19 22 D6
Beeston Pl SW1 258 D6
Beeston Rd EN4 14 B5
Beeston's Ho SE15 140 B2
Beeston Way TW14 150 C5
Beethoven Rd WD6 9 D5
Beethoven St W10 91 A4
Beeton Cl HA5 23 C3
Begbie Ho SW9 138 B3
Begbie Rd SE3 143 C4
Beggars Hill KT17 215 D2
Beggar's Roost La SM1 217 C2
Begonia Cl E6 100 B3
Begonia Pl 1 TW12 173 C4
Begonia Wlk W12 89 D1
Beira St SW12 159 B4
Beis Chinuch Lebonos Girls Sch N4 51 A2
Beis Hamedrash Elyon NW11 47 A2
Beis Malka Girls Sch N16 51 D1
Beis Rochel d'Satmar Girls Sch 1 N16 51 C2
Beis Soroh Schneirer (Sch) 4 NW4 46 A3
Beis Yaakov Prim Sch NW9 45 B6
Bekesbourne St 17 E14 97 A1
Belcroft Cl BR1 186 D3
Beldanes Lo NW10 68 A1
Beldham Gdns KT8 195 D6
Belenoyd Ct SW16 160 B1
Belfairs Dr RM6 58 C2
Belfairs Gn WD19 22 D5
Belfast Rd
Croydon SE25 206 B5
Stoke Newington N16 73 D6
Belfield Rd KT19 215 C1
Belfont Wlk N7 72 A4
Belford Gr SE18 122 C2
Belford Ho 7 E8 95 D6
Belfort Rd SE15 140 C3
Belfry Cl 33 SE16 118 B1
Belfry Rd E12 77 D6
Belgrade Ho N16 73 C4
Belgrade Rd
Hampton TW12 173 D2
Stoke Newington N16 73 C4

Belgrave Cl
1 Acton W3 .... 111 A4
Burnt Oak NW7 .... 27 B5
Southgate N14 .... 15 C6
Belgrave Cres TW16 .. 172 B2
Belgrave Ct
8 Acton Green W4 .. 111 A1
Charlton SE3 .... 143 C5
22 Limehouse E14 .... 119 B6
Newham E13 .... 99 C3
Nine Elms SW8 ..... 269 A3
Belgrave Gdns
Kilburn NW8 .... 91 D6
Southgate N14 .... 3 D1
1 Stanmore HA7 ..... 25 C5
St John's Wood NW8 . 229 A5
Belgrave Ho SW9 .... 138 C5
Belgrave Hts E11 ...... 55 A1
Belgrave Mans NW8 229 A5
Belgrave Market IG1 .. 78 C6
Belgrave Mews N
SW1 .... 248 A1
Belgrave Mews S
SW1 .... 115 A3 258 B6
Belgrave Mews W
SW1 .... 258 A6
Belgrave Pl
SW1 .... 115 A3 258 B5
Belgrave Rd
Barnes SW13 .... 133 D5
Hounslow TW4 .... 129 B2
Leyton E10 .... 54 A1
Mitcham CR4 .... 202 B6
Newham E13 .... 99 C3
Redbridge IG1 .... 56 B1
South Norwood SE25. 205 D5
Sunbury TW16 .... 172 B2
Walthamstow E17 ..... 53 C3
Wanstead E11 .... 55 A1
Westminster
SW1 ..... 115 C2 259 A3
Belgrave Sq
SW1 .... 115 A3 258 A6
Belgrave St E1 .... 96 D1
Belgrave Terr IG8 ..... 21 A1
Belgrave Wlk CR4 .... 202 B6
Belgrave Wlk Sta
CR4 .... 202 B5
Belgrave Yd SW1 ... 258 C5
BELGRAVIA 115 B2
Belgravia Cl EN5 .... 1 B2
Belgravia Ct SW1 ... 258 C5
Belgravia Gdns BR1 .. 186 C4
Belgravia Ho
11 London SW4 ..... 159 D5
1 Teddington TW11 . 175 C3
Belgravia Lo N21 ..... 16 D6
Belgravia Mews
KT1 .... 197 D5
Belgrove St WC1 .... 233 B2
Belham Wlk 13 SE5 .. 139 B4
Belinda Rd 8 SW9 .. 138 D2
Belitha Villas N1 ..... 72 C1
Bel La TW13 .... 151 B1
Bellamy Cl
Edgware HA8 .... 11 A1
13 Millwall E14 ..... 119 C4
Uxbridge UB10 .... 60 C5
West Kensington SW5 254 D1
Bellamy Ct HA7 .... 25 B2
Bellamy Dr HA7 .... 25 B2
Bellamy Ho
Harrow HA3 .... 44 A2
Heston TW5 .... 129 C6
Upper Tooting SW17 .. 180 B6
Bellamy Rd
Chingford E4 .... 35 D4
Enfield EN2 .... 5 B3
Bellamy's Ct 16
SE16 .... 118 D5
Bellamy St SW12 ..... 159 B4
Bellarmine Cl SE28 .. 123 D4
Bellasis Ave SW2 .... 160 A2
Bell Ave UB7 .... 104 B3
Bell Cl Pinner HA5 ..... 40 C6
Ruislip HA4 .... 61 D5
Bellclose Rd UB7 .... 104 A4
Bell Ct Hendon NW4 .... 46 C5
Ladywell SE13 .... 163 C6
Tolworth KT5 .... 214 D6
Bell Dr SW18 .... 157 A4
Bellefields Rd SW9 .. 138 B2
Bellegrove Cl DA16 . 145 D3
Bellegrove Par
DA16 .... 145 D2
Bellegrove Rd DA16. 145 D3
Bellenden Prim Sch 5
SE15 .... 140 A2
Bellenden Rd SE15 .. 139 D3
Bellenden Rd Ret Pk
SE15 .... 140 A4
Bellendon Road Bsns Ctr
SE15 .... 139 D3
Bellerbys Coll SE8 .. 141 C6
Belle Staines Pleasaunce
E4 .... 19 C2
Belleville Prim Sch
SW11 .... 158 D6
Belleville Rd SW11 .. 158 D6
Belle Vue UB6 .... 86 B6
Belle Vue Gdns SW9 .. 138 A3
Belle Vue La WD23 ..... 8 B3
Bellevue Mews N11 .... 31 A5
Bellevue Pk CR7 ..... 205 A5
Bellevue Pl E1 .... 96 C3
Bellevue Rd
Barnes SW13 .... 134 A3
Bexley DA6 .... 169 B6
Ealing W13 .... 87 B3
Friern Barnet N11 ..... 31 A5
Kingston u T KT1 .... 198 A6
Upper Tooting SW17 . 158 D3
Belle Vue Rd
Chingford E17 .... 36 B1
8 Hendon NW4 .... 46 C5
Bellew St SW17 .... 158 A1
Bellfield CR0 .... 223 B1
Bellfield Ave HA3 ..... 24 B4
Bellfield Cl SE3 ...... 143 B5
Bell Flats 4 NW2 ..... 68 A2
Bellflower Cl 2 E6 .. 100 A2
Bellflower Ct SE13 .. 141 D1
Bellgate Mews NW5 .. 71 B5
Bell Gn SE26 .... 185 B6
Bellgrave Lo 9 W4 . 110 D1
BELL GREEN 163 B1
Bell Green La SE26 ... 185 B6
Bell Ho
6 Dagenham RM10 ... 81 D2
Greenwich SE10 .... 142 A6
15 Streatham SW2 .. 160 C4
Wembley HA9 .... 66 A5
West Heath SE2 .... 124 D1
Bellina Mews NW5 .... 71 C4
Bell Ind Est 2 W4 .. 111 A2
BELLINGHAM 185 C5
Bellingham 10 N17 ..... 34 B3
Bellingham Ct IG11 .. 102 B4
Bellingham Gn SE6 . 163 C1
Bellingham L Ctr
SE6 .... 163 D1
Bellingham Rd SE6 . 164 A1
Bellingham Sta SE6. 163 D1
Bellingham Trad Est
SE6 .... 163 D2
Bell Inn Yd EC3 ..... 242 D1
Bell La Enfield EN3 ...... 6 D5
Hendon NW4 .... 46 D5
Newham E16 .... 121 A5
Spitalfields E1 . 95 D2 243 C3
Twickenham TW1 .... 153 A3
Wembley HA9 .... 65 D6
Bell Lane Prim Sch 7
NW4 .... 46 D5
Bell Language Sch
W1 .... 93 C3 239 A5
Bellmaker Ct 13 E3 ... 97 C2
Bell Mdw SE19 .... 183 C6
Bell Moor NW3 .... 70 A5
Bellmore Ct 5 CR0 . 205 D1
Bello Cl SE24, SW2 ... 160 D3
Bellot Gdns 1 SE10 . 120 C1
Bellot St SE10 .... 120 C1
Bell Rd
East Molesey KT8 .... 196 B4
Enfield EN1 .... 5 B4
Hounslow TW3 .... 129 D1
Bellring Cl DA17 ..... 147 C6
Bell's Coll IG3 .... 58 A1
Bells Hill EN5 .... 12 D6
Bell St
Kidbrooke SE18 ..... 144 A4
Paddington
NW1 .... 92 C2 237 A4
Bell The E17 .... 53 C6
Bell View BR3 .... 185 B3
Bellview Ct 1 TW3 .. 129 D1
Bell View Manor HA4 .. 39 C2
Bell Water Gate
SE18 .... 122 C3
Bell Wharf La EC4 ... 252 B6
Bellwood Rd SE15 .. 140 D1
Bell Yard Mews SE1 . 253 B1
Bell Yd WC2 ... 94 C1 241 A1
BELMONT 25 B2
Belmont Ave
Bowes Pk N13 .... 32 B5
Cockfosters EN4 .... 14 D6
Edmonton N9 .... 18 A3
Falconwood DA16 .... 145 C2
Southall UB2 .... 107 A3
Tottenham N17 .... 51 A6
Wembley HA0 .... 88 B6
West Barnes KT3 .... 200 A5
Belmont Circ HA3 ..... 25 B2
Belmont Cl
Chingford E4 .... 36 B5
Clapham SW4 .... 137 C2
Cockfosters EN4 .... 2 D1
Totteridge N20 .... 13 D3
Uxbridge UB8 .... 60 A2
Woodford IG8 .... 37 B6
Belmont Ct
Highbury N5 .... 73 A4
6 Stamford Hill N16 ... 51 C1
Temple Fortune NW11 .. 47 B4
1 Whetstone N20 ..... 14 A1
Wood Green N11 .... 31 D3
Belmont Fst & Mid Schs
HA3 .... 24 D1
Belmont Gr
Chiswick W4 .... 111 B2
Lewisham SE13 .... 142 B2
Belmont Hall Ct
SE13 .... 142 B2
Belmont Hill SE13 .... 142 B2
Belmont Jun & Inf Sch
N22 .... 51 A6
Belmont La
Chislehurst BR7 ..... 189 A5
Stanmore HA7 .... 25 C3
Belmont Lo
Harrow HA3 .... 24 B3
Stanmore HA7 .... 25 C6
Belmont Mews
SW19 .... 156 D2
Belmont (Mill Hill Prep
Sch) NW7 .... 12 A1
Belmont Par
Chislehurst BR7 ..... 189 A5
2 Temple Fortune
NW11 .... 47 B4
Belmont Park Cl
SE13 .... 142 C1
Belmont Park Rd E10 . 53 D3
Belmont Pk SE13 .... 142 C1
Belmont Pk Sch E10 .. 54 A3
Belmont Prim Sch
10 Chiswick W4 ..... 111 B2
Erith DA8 .... 147 C5
Belmont Rd
Beckenham BR3 ..... 185 B1
Chislehurst BR7 ..... 188 D5
Clapham SW4 .... 137 C2
Croydon SE25 .... 206 B4
Erith DA8 .... 147 D4
Harrow HA3 .... 43 A6
Ilford IG1 .... 79 A5
London W4 .... 111 B2
Twickenham TW2 ..... 152 B2
Uxbridge UB8 .... 60 A2
Wallington SM6 ..... 219 C3
West Green N15, N17 .. 51 A5
Belmont Rise SM1,
SM2 .... 217 B1
Belmont St NW1 .... 71 A1
Belmont Terr W4 ..... 111 B2
Belmor WD6 .... 10 C5
Belmore Ave UB4 ..... 84 A1
Belmore Ho N7 .... 71 D3
Belmore La N7 .... 71 D3
Belmore Prim Sch
UB4 .... 84 B4
Belmore St
SW8 .... 137 D4 269 C2
Beloe Cl SW15 .... 134 A1
Belper Ct 11 E5 .... 74 D4
Belsham St E9 .... 74 C2
Belsize Ave
Bowes Pk N13 .... 32 B4
Ealing W13 .... 109 B3
Maitland Pk NW3 ..... 70 C3
Belsize Court Garages 1
NW3 .... 70 B3
Belsize Cres NW3 ..... 70 B2
Belsize Ct NW3 .... 70 B3
Belsize Gdns SM1 ... 217 D4
Belsize Gr NW3 .... 70 C2
Belsize La NW3 .... 70 B3
Belsize Mews NW3 .... 70 B2
Belsize Park Gdns
NW3 .... 70 C2
Belsize Park Mews 1
NW3 .... 70 B2
Belsize Park Sta NW3 70 C3
Belsize Pk NW3 .... 70 B2
Belsize Pl NW3 .... 70 B3
Belsize Rd
Harrow HA3 .... 24 B3
Kilburn NW6 .... 91 D6
Belsize Sq NW3 .... 70 B2
Belsize Terr NW3 ..... 70 B2
Belson Rd SE18 ...... 122 B2
Beltane Dr SW19 .... 156 D1
Belthorn Cres SW12 .. 159 C4
Belton Rd Leyton E11 .. 76 C4
Sidcup DA14 .... 190 A6
Tottenham N17 .... 51 C6
Upton E7 .... 77 B1
Willesden NW2 .... 68 A2
Belton Way E3 .... 97 C2
Beltran Rd SW6 .... 135 D3
BELVEDERE 125 D2
Belvedere Ave
SW19 .... 179 A5
Belvedere Bldgs SE1 251 D1
Belvedere Cl TW11 ... 174 C5
Belvedere Ct
Abbey Wood DA17 .... 125 B3
Brondesbury NW2 ..... 68 D2
7 Clapham Pk SW4 . 159 D5
East Finchley N2 ..... 48 B4
8 Kingston u T KT2 .. 176 C3
Putney SW15 .... 134 C1
33 Shoreditch N1 ..... 95 C6
Southall UB1 .... 107 D6
Southgate N21 .... 16 C4
Belvedere Dr SW19 .. 179 A5
Belvedere Gdns KT8 . 195 C4
Belvedere Gr SW19 .. 179 A5
Belvedere Ho TW14 .. 150 A3
Belvedere Htss NW8 237 A6
Belvedere Jun & Inf Sch
DA17 .... 125 D3
Belvedere Mews
Greenwich SE3 ..... 143 B5
Nunhead SE15 ..... 140 C2
Belvedere Pl
Brixton SW2 .... 138 B1
Lambeth SE1 .... 251 D1
Belvedere Rd
Bexleyheath DA7 .... 147 B3
Erith SE2, SE28 ..... 124 D5
Hanwell W7 .... 108 D3
Lambeth SE1 116 B5 250 D3
Penge SE19 .... 183 D3
Walthamstow E10 ..... 53 A1
Belvedere Sq SW19 .. 179 A5
Belvedere Sta DA17. 125 D3
Belvedere Strand
NW9 .... 27 D1
Belvedere The SW10 266 B1
Belvedere Way HA3 ... 44 A3
Belvoir Cl SE9 .... 166 A1
Belvoir Ct HA3 .... 43 A3
Belvoir Lo SE22 ...... 162 A4
Belvoir Rd SE22 ...... 162 A4
Belvue Bsns Ctr UB5 .. 63 D1
Belvue Cl UB5 .... 63 C1
Belvue Rd UB5 .... 63 C1
Belvue Sch UB5 .... 85 C6
Bembridge Cl NW6 .... 69 A1
Bembridge Gdns HA4 61 B6
Bembridge Ho
9 Deptford SE8 ..... 119 B2
Wandsworth SW18 .. 157 D5
Bemersyde Point 6
E13 .... 99 B4
Bemerton St
N1 .... 94 B6 233 C6
Bemish Rd SW15 .... 134 D2
Bempton Dr HA4 .... 62 B5
Bemsted Rd E17 .... 53 B6
Benabo Ct 6 E8 .... 74 A3
Benares Rd SE18,
SE2 .... 123 D2
Benbow Ct W6 .... 112 B3
Benbow Ho 12 SE8 .. 141 C6
Benbow Rd W6 .... 112 B3
Benbow St SE8 .... 141 C6
Benbury Cl BR1 .... 186 A5
Bence Ho 13 SE8 ..... 119 A2
Bench Field CR2 .... 221 D3
Bencroft Rd SW16 ... 181 C3
Bencurtis Pk BR4 .... 224 B6
Bendall Mews NW1 . 237 B4
Bendemeer Rd
SW15 .... 134 D2
Benden Ho SE13 ..... 164 A6
Bendish Point SE28 .. 123 A4
Bendish Rd E6 .... 78 A1
Bendmore Ave SE2 .. 124 A2
Bendon Valley
SW18 .... 157 D4
Benedict Cl
9 Erith DA17 .... 125 A3
Orpington BR6 .... 227 C5
Benedict Ct
Dagenham RM9 .... 59 B3
Pinner HA5 .... 23 B2
Benedict Dr TW14 .... 149 B4
Benedict House Sch 15
DA15 .... 168 A1
Benedict Prim Sch
CR4 .... 202 B6
Benedict Rd
London SW9 .... 138 B2
Mitcham CR4 .... 202 B6
Benedict Way N2 ..... 48 A6
Benedict Wharf CR4 . 202 C6
Benenden Gn BR2 ... 209 A4
Benenden Ho SE17 .. 263 B2
Benett Gdns SW16 ... 182 A1
Beney Ct BR3 .... 185 C1
Ben Ezra Ct SE17 .... 262 B3
Benfleet Cl SM1 ..... 218 A5
Benfleet Ct 6 E8 ..... 95 D6
Benfleet Way N11 ..... 15 A2
Bengal Ct EC3 .... 242 D1
Bengal Ho E1 .... 96 D2
Bengal Rd IG1 .... 78 D5
Bengarth Dr HA3 ..... 24 B1
Bengarth Rd UB5 ..... 85 A6
Bengeo Gdns RM6 .... 58 C3
Bengeworth Rd
Camberwell SE5 ..... 139 A2
Harrow HA1 .... 65 A5
Ben Hale Cl HA7 .... 25 B5
Benham Cl KT9 .... 213 C2
Benham Gdns TW3,
TW4 .... 151 B6
Benham Ho SW10 .... 265 D4
Benham Rd W7 .... 86 C2
Benham's Pl 11 NW3 .. 70 A4
Benhill Ave SM1 ..... 218 A4
Benhill Rd
London SE5 .... 139 B4
Sutton SM1 .... 218 B4
Benhill Wood Rd
SM1 .... 218 A4
BENHILTON 218 A5
Benhilton Ct SM1 .... 218 A5
Benhilton Gdns
SM1 .... 217 D5
Benhurst Ct
Ealing W5 .... 110 A6
12 Penge SE20 .... 184 B2
West Norwood SW16 182 C5
Benhurst La SW16 ... 182 C5
Benington Ct N4 ..... 73 A6
Benin St SE13 .... 164 B4
Benjafield Cl N18 ..... 34 B6
Benjamin Cl E8 .... 96 A6
Benjamin Ct
4 Ealing W7 .... 108 C5
4 Erith DA17 .... 147 B6
Littleton TW15 .... 171 A3
Benjamin Franklin
House* SW1 .... 250 A4
Benjamin Ho 12 W3. 110 D5
Benjamin Mews
SW12 .... 159 C4
Benjamin St EC1 .... 241 C4
Ben Jonson Ct 30 N1 .. 95 C5
Ben Jonson Prim Sch
E1 .... 97 A3
Ben Jonson Rd E1 ..... 97 A2
Benledi Rd E14 .... 98 B1
Bennelong Cl W12 .... 90 B1
Bennerley Rd SW11 . 158 D6
Bennet Cl KT1 .... 175 C2
Bennets Ct SW19 .... 180 A2
Bennetsfield Rd
UB11 .... 104 D5
Bennet's Hill EC4 ... 251 D6
Bennets Lo EN2 .... 5 A2

Bennett Cl
Twickenham TW4 151 A6
Welling DA16 146 A3
Bennett Ct
Hampstead NW6 69 D2
Lower Holloway N7 72 B5
7 South Acton W3 110 D4
Bennett Gr SE13 141 D4
Bennett Ho
2 Streatham SW4 159 D4
Westminster SW1 259 D4
Bennett Pk SE3 142 D2
Bennett Rd
Brixton SW9 138 C3
Dagenham RM6 59 A2
Newham E13 99 C3
Bennetts Ave
Croydon CR0 223 A6
Greenford UB6 86 C6
Bennett's Castle La
RM8 80 D5
Bennetts Cl
Mitcham CR4, SW16 181 B2
Tottenham N17 33 D4
Bennetts Copse BR7 188 A4
Bennett St
Chiswick W4 111 C1
St James SW1 249 A4
Bennetts Way CR0 223 B6
Bennett's Yd SW1 259 D5
Benn Ho
Bethnal Green E2 96 A4
7 Greenwich SE7 121 C1
Benningholme Rd
HA8 27 C4
Bennington Rd
Chingford IG8 36 C3
Tottenham N17 33 C2
Benn St E9 75 A2
Benns Wlk 8 TW9 132 A1
Bensbury Cl SW15 156 C4
Bensham Cl CR7 205 A5
Bensham Gr CR7 183 A1
Bensham La CR0,
CR7 204 D3
Bensham Manor Rd
CR7 205 A5
Bensham Manor Specl
Sch CR7 205 A4
Bensington Ct TW14 149 B5
Bensley Cl 7 N11 30 D5
Ben Smith Way 21
SE16 118 A3
Benson Ave E13, E6 99 D5
Benson Cl
Hillingdon UB8 82 A2
Hounslow TW3 129 C1
Benson Ct
Holdbrook EN3 7 C5
South Lambeth SW8 270 A2
1 Tufnell Pk N19 71 C4
Benson Ho
Lambeth SE1 251 B3
1 Richmond TW10 153 C1
Shoreditch E2 243 C6
Benson Prim sch
CR0 223 A5
Benson Quay E1 118 C6
Benson Rd
Croydon CR0 220 C5
Forest Hill SE23 162 C3
Bentall Sh Ctr The 10
KT1 176 A1
Bentfield Gdns SE9 165 D1
Benthal Ct N16 74 A5
Benthal Prim Sch
N16 74 A5
Benthal Rd N16 74 A5
Bentham Ct 11 N1 73 A1
Bentham Ho SE1 262 C6
Bentham Rd
Homerton E9 74 D2
Woolwich SE28 124 B5
Bentham Wlk NW10 67 A3
Ben Tillet Cl E16 122 B5
Ben Tillet Ho E17 50 D6
Bentinck Cl NW8 230 B3
Bentinck Ho
4 Richmond TW10 153 C1
4 Shepherd's Bush
W12 112 B6
Bentinck Mans W1 238 B2
Bentinck Mews W1 238 B2
Bentinck Rd UB7 104 A5
Bentinck St
W1 93 A1 238 B2
Bentley Cl SW19 157 C1
Bentley Ct SE13 142 A1
Bentley Dr
Child's Hill NW2 69 B5
Ilford IG2 57 A3
Bentley Ho 6 Bow E3 97 C3
4 Camberwell SE5 139 C4
Bentley Lo WD23 8 C2
Bentley Mews EN1 17 B5
Bentley Rd N1 73 C2
Bentley Way
Stanmore HA7 25 A5
Woodford IG8 21 A1
Bentley Wood Girls Sch
HA7 24 D5
Benton Rd
Ilford IG1, IG2 57 B1
South Oxhey WD19 22 D5
Benton's La SE27 183 A6
Benton's Rise SE27 183 B5
Bentry Cl RM8 81 A6
Bentry Rd RM8 81 B6
Bentworth Ct 1 E2 96 A3
Bentworth Prim Sch
W12 90 B1
Bentworth Rd W12 90 B1
Ben Uri Gall★ NW8 91 D6
Benwell Ct TW16 172 A2
Benwell Rd N7 72 C3
Benwick Cl SE16 118 B2
Benwick Ct SE20 184 C2
Benwood Ct SM1 218 A5
Benworth St E3 97 B4
Benyon Ho EC1 234 B2
Benyon Rd N1 95 B6 235 D6
Benyon Wharf 31 E8 95 C6
Beormund Sch
SE1 117 B4 252 D1
Bequerel Ct SE10 120 D3
Berberis Ct IG1 78 D2
Berberis Ho 17 E3 97 C2
Berberis Wlk UB7 104 A2
Berber Par 8 SE18 144 A4
Berber Pl 2 E14 119 C6
Berber Rd SW11 158 D6
Berberry Cl 5 HA8 27 A6
Bercta Rd SE9 167 A2
Berebinder Ho 21 E3 97 B5
Berengers Pl RM9 80 B2
Berenger Twr SW10 266 C4
Berenger Wlk SW10 266 C4
Berens Ct DA14 189 D6
Berens Rd NW10 90 D4
Berens Way BR5,
BR7 211 D6
Beresford Ave
Ealing W7 86 C2
Friern Barnet N20 14 D2
Tolworth KT5 199 A2
Twickenham TW1 153 C5
Wembley HA0 88 C6
Beresford Ct
Homerton E9 75 A3
11 Twickenham TW1 153 C5
Beresford Dr
Bickley BR1 210 A6
Woodford IG8 37 C6
Beresford Gdns
Dagenham RM6 59 A4
Enfield EN1 5 C1
Hounslow TW4 151 B6
Beresford Ho
Dulwich SE21 161 C1
15 Stockwell SW4 138 A1
Beresford Lo N4 73 B3
Beresford Rd
Belmont SM2 217 B1
Canonbury N5 73 B3
Chingford E4 20 C3
East Finchley N2 48 C6
Harringay N8 50 D4
Harrow HA1 42 B4
Kingston u T KT2 176 B2
New Malden KT3 199 A5
Southall UB1 106 D5
Walthamstow E17 35 D2
Beresford Sq 1
SE18 122 D2
Beresford Square Mkt
SE18 122 D2
Beresford Terr 3 N5 73 A3
Bere St E1 118 D6
Berestede Rd 4
W6 111 D1
Bergen Ho 1 SE5 139 A3
Bergenia Ho 1
TW13 150 B3
Bergen Sq SE16 119 A3
Berger Cl BR5 211 C3
Berger Prim Sch 30
E9 74 D2
Berger Rd E9 74 D2
Berghem Mews
W14 112 D3
Bergholt Ave IG4 56 A4
Bergholt Cres N16 51 C2
Bergholt Mews 4
NW1 71 D1
Berglen Ct E14 119 A6
Berica Ct IG6 57 A6
Bering Sq E14 119 C1
Bering Wlk E16 99 D1
Berisford Mews
SW18 158 A5
Berkeley Ave
Cranford TW4 128 A3
Erith DA16 146 D4
Northolt UB6 64 C2
Berkeley Cl
Borehamwood WD6 10 C6
Broom Hill BR5 211 C2
2 Kingston u T KT2 176 A3
Ruislip HA4 62 A5
Berkeley Cres EN4 14 B6
Berkeley Ct
Ealing W5 109 C6
Edgware HA8 26 D5
Finchley N3 29 D2
1 Golders Green
NW11 47 B2
Marylebone NW1 237 D5
Southgate N14 15 C5
Wallington SM6 219 C4
Willesden NW10 67 C4
Berkeley Dr KT8 195 C6
Berkeley Gdns
Claygate KT10 213 A2
Kensington W8 245 B3
Southgate N21 17 B4
Walton-on-T KT12 193 D2
Berkeley Ho
17 Bow E3 97 C4
11 Brentford TW8 131 D6
8 Deptford SE8 119 B1
Berkeley Lo Enfield EN2 4 C2
New Malden KT3 199 C5
Berkeley Mews
Marylebone W1 237 D1
Sunbury TW16 194 C6
Berkeley Pl SW19 178 D4
Berkeley Prim Sch
TW5 128 D5
Berkeley Rd
Barnes SW13 134 A4
Crouch End N8 49 D3
Hillingdon UB10 61 A1
Manor Pk E12 78 A3
Queensbury NW9 44 C4
Stamford Hill N15 51 B3
Berkeley Sq
W1 115 B6 248 D5
Berkeley St
W1 115 B5 248 D4
Berkeleys The SE25 206 A5
Berkeley The NW11 47 D2
Berkeley Waye TW5 128 D5
Berkeley Wlk 1 N7 72 B6
Berkhampstead Rd
DA17 125 C1
Berkhamsted Ave
HA9 66 C2
Berkley Cl TW2 152 C1
Berkley Ct 8 TW1 153 A4
Berkley Gr NW1 71 A1
Berkley Rd NW1 70 D1
Berkshire Ct 1 W7 86 D3
Berkshire Gdns
Bowes Pk N13 32 C4
Upper Edmonton N18 34 B5
Berkshire Ho
Catford SE6 185 C6
St Giles WC2 240 A2
Berkshire Rd E9 75 B2
Berkshire Way CR4 204 A5
Bermans Way NW10 67 D4
BERMONDSEY 118 A4
Bermondsey Leather Mkt
SE1 253 A1
Bermondsey Sq SE1 263 B6
Bermondsey St
SE1 117 C4 253 A1
Bermondsey Sta
SE16 118 B3
Bermondsey Trad Est
SE16 118 C1
Bermondsey Wall E
SE16 118 B4
Bermondsey Wall W SE1,
SE16 118 A4
Bermuda Ho HA1 64 B5
Bernal Cl SE28 124 D6
Bernard Angell Ho 4
SE10 142 B6
Bernard Ashley Dr
SE7 121 B1
Bernard Ave W13 109 B3
Bernard Cassidy St 2
E16 98 D2
Bernard Gdns SW19 179 B5
Bernard Ho E1 243 C3
Bernard Rd
South Tottenham
N15 51 D4
Wallington SM5, SM6 219 B4
Bernard Shaw Ct 5
NW1 71 C1
Bernard Shaw Ho 2
NW10 89 B6
Bernard St
WC1 94 A3 240 B5
Bernays Cl HA7 25 C4
Bernay's Gr SW9 138 B1
Bernel Dr CR0 223 B5
Berne Rd CR7 205 A4
Berners Dr W13 109 A6
Berners Ho N1 234 A4
Bernersmede SE3 143 A2
Berners Mews
W1 93 C2 239 B3
Berners Pl W1 239 B2
Berners Rd
Islington N1 234 C5
Wood Green N22 32 C1
Berners St W1 93 C1 239 B2
Berner Terr 27 E1 96 A1
Berney Ho BR3 207 A4
Berney Rd CR0 205 B2
Bernhard Baron Ho 23
E1 96 A1
Bernhardt Cres NW8 237 A6
Bernhart Cl HA8 27 A3
Bernie Grant Ho 40
E9 74 C1
Bernwell Rd E4 20 C1
Bernwood Ho 6 N4 51 B2
Berridge Gn HA8 26 C3
Berridge Mews NW6 69 C3
Berridge Rd SE19 183 C5
Berriman Rd N7 72 B5
Berrite Works UB7 104 C4
Berriton Rd HA2 41 B1
Berrybank Cl 4 E4 20 A2
Berry Cl
Dagenham RM10 81 C3
Southgate N21 16 D3
Berry Cotts 2 E14 97 A1
Berry Ct TW4 151 B6
Berrydale Rd UB4 85 A3
Berryfield Cl BR1 188 A1
Berry Field Cl 8 E17 53 D5
Berryfield Rd
SE17 116 D1 261 D2
Berryhill SE9 144 D1
Berry Hill HA7 25 D6
Berryhill Gdns SE9 144 D1
Berry Ho
10 Battersea SW11 136 D3
25 Bethnal Green E1 96 B3
Berry La SE21 183 B6
BERRYLANDS 198 C3
Berrylands
Surbiton KT5 198 C3
West Barnes SW20 200 C5
Berrylands Ct 16
SM2 217 D1
Berrylands Rd KT5 198 B3
Berrylands Sta KT5 198 D5
Berryman Cl RM8 80 C5
Berryman's La SE26 184 D6
Berrymead Gdns
W3 111 A4
Berrymede Inf Sch
W3 110 D4
Berrymede Jun Sch
W3 110 D4
Berrymede Rd W4 111 B3
Berry Pl EC1 234 D1
Berry St EC1 241 D5
Berry Way W5 110 A3
Bertal Rd SW17 180 B6
Bertha Hollamby Ct
DA14 190 C5
Bertha James Ct
BR2 209 B5
Bertha Neubergh Ho 1
SE5 139 A4
Berthan Gdns E17 54 B4
Berthon St SE8 141 C6
Bertie Rd
Penge SE26 184 D4
Willesden NW10 68 A2
Bertram Cotts SW19 179 C3
Bertram Rd Enfield EN1 6 A1
Hendon NW4 46 A3
Kingston u T KT2 176 C3
Bertram St N19 71 B6
Bertrand Ho 11
SW16 160 A1
Bertrand St SE13 141 D2
Bertrand Way SE28 124 C6
Bert Rd CR7 205 A4
Bert Reilly Ho 1
SE18 123 B1
Bertrum House Sch
SW17 159 A2
Bert Way EN1 5 D1
Berwick Ave UB4 106 D6
Berwick Cl
Harrow HA7 24 D4
Twickenham TW2 151 C3
Berwick Cres DA15 167 C5
Berwick Ct 8 BR3 185 C2
Berwick Gdns SM1 218 A5
Berwick Ho 10 N2 30 B1
Berwick Rd
Newham E16 99 C1
Tottenham N22 32 D2
Welling DA16 146 B4
Berwick St
W1 93 C1 239 B1
Berwick Street Mkt★
W1 93 C1 239 B1
Berwyn Ave TW3 129 D4
Berwyn Ho 3 N16 51 D1
Berwyn Rd
Mortlake SW14,
TW10 132 D1
Streatham SE24 160 D3
Beryl Ave E6 100 A2
Beryl Harding Ho 3
SW19 178 D3
Beryl Ho SE18 123 D1
Beryl Rd W6 112 D1
Berystede KT2 176 D3
Besant Cl NW2 69 A5
Besant Ct
Canonbury N1 73 B3
15 Thamesmead
SE28 124 B6
Besant Ho NW8 229 A5
Besant Pl SE22 139 D1
Besant Rd NW2 69 A4
Besant Way NW10 67 A3
Besant Wlk N7 72 B6
Besford Ho 26 E2 96 A5
Besley St SW16 181 C4
Bessant Dr TW9 132 D4
Bessborough Gdns
SW1 115 D1 259 D2
Bessborough Pl
SW1 115 D1 259 D2
Bessborough Rd
Harrow HA1 42 B1
Roehampton SW15 156 A3
Bessborough St
SW1 115 D1 259 C2
Bessborough Wks
KT8 195 B4
Bessemer Ct 7 NW1 71 C1
Bessemer Grange Prim
Sch SE5 139 C1
Bessemer Park Ind Est
3 SE24 138 D1
Bessemer Rd SE5 139 A3
Bessie Lansbury Cl
E6 100 C1
Bessingby Rd HA4 62 B6
Bessingham Wlk
SE4 162 D6

Besson St SE14 ..... 140 D4
Bessy St E2 ..... 96 C4
Bestwood St SE8 ... 118 D2
Beswick Mews 1 NW6 ..... 69 D2
Betam Rd UB3 ..... 105 B4
Beta Pl 20 SW4 ..... 138 B1
Betchworth Cl SM1 .. 218 B3
Betchworth Ho 8 N7 ..... 71 D3
Betchworth Rd IG3 ... 79 C5
Betham Rd UB6 ..... 86 B4
Bethany Ct 8 DA6 ... 147 A1
Bethany Waye TW14 . 149 C4
Bethecar Rd HA1 ..... 42 C4
Bethel Cl NW4 ..... 46 D4
Bethell Ave Ilford IG1 .. 56 C2
 Newham E13, E16 ..... 98 D3
Bethel Lo N11 ..... 31 C5
Bethel Rd DA16 ..... 146 C2
Bethersden Cl BR3 .. 185 B3
Bethersden Ho SE17 263 B2
Bethesda Ct 5 SE20 ..... 184 C3
Beth Jacob Gram Sch 6 NW4 ..... 46 D5
Bethlehem Ho 13 E14 ..... 119 B6
Bethlem Royal Hospl BR3 ..... 207 C2
BETHNAL GREEN 96 B4
Bethnal Green Rd
 Bethnal Green E2 ..... 96 A4
 Shoreditch E1, E2 ..... 95 D3 243 D6
Bethnal Green Sta
 Bethnal Green E1 ..... 96 B3
 Bethnal Green E2 ..... 96 C4
Bethnal Green Tech Coll 49 E2 ..... 95 D4
Beths Gram Sch DA5 ..... 169 D5
Bethune Ave N11 ..... 30 D6
Bethune Rd
 North Acton NW10 ..... 89 B3
 Stamford Hill N16 ..... 51 C2
Bethwin Rd SE5 ..... 139 A5
Betjeman Cl HA5 ..... 41 C5
Betjeman Ct EN4 ..... 15 A6
Betony Cl CR0 ..... 206 D1
Betoyne Ave E4 ..... 36 C6
Betsham Ho SE1 ..... 252 C2
Betspath Ho 6 N11 ... 31 C5
Betstyle Circus N11 ... 31 B6
Betstyle Ho 2 N10 ... 31 A3
Betstyle Rd N11 ..... 31 B6
Betterton Dr DA14 ... 169 A2
Betterton Ho WC2 .. 240 B1
Betterton St WC2 ..... 94 A1 240 B1
Bettons Pk E15 ..... 98 C6
Bettridge Rd SW6 ..... 135 B3
Betts Cl BR3 ..... 185 A1
Betts Ho E1 ..... 118 B6
Betts Mews E17 ..... 53 B3
Betts Rd E16 ..... 121 B6
Betts St E1 ..... 118 B6
Betts Way
 Long Ditton KT6 ..... 197 B1
 Penge SE20 ..... 184 B2
Bettswood Ct 15 SE20 ..... 184 B2
Betty Brooks Ho E11 .. 76 B5
Betty Layward Prim Sch 1 N16 ..... 73 B5
Betty May Gray Ho 2 E14 ..... 120 A2
Beulah Ave CR7 ..... 183 A1
Beulah Cl HA8 ..... 10 D1
Beulah Cres CR7 ..... 183 A1
Beulah Gr CR0 ..... 205 A3
Beulah Hill SE19 ..... 183 A3
Beulah Inf Sch 2 CR7 ..... 205 A6
Beulah Jun Sch 1 CR7 ..... 205 A6
Beulah Rd
 Merton SW19 ..... 179 B3
 South Norwood CR7 .. 205 A6
 Sutton SM1 ..... 217 C4
 Walthamstow E17 ..... 53 D4
Beuleigh Ct E17 ..... 54 B4
Bevan Ave IG11 ..... 80 A1
Bevan Ct
 Croydon CR0 ..... 220 C3
 10 Twickenham TW1 . 153 D5
Bevan Ho IG11 ..... 80 B1
Bevan Rd
 Cockfosters EN4 ..... 2 D1
 Plumstead Comm SE2 . 124 B1
Bevan St N1 ... 95 A6 235 B5
Bev Callender Cl 4 SW8 ..... 137 B2
Bevenden St N1 ..... 95 B4 235 D2
Bevercote Wlk 1 DA17 ..... 147 B6
Beveridge Ct
 Southgate N21 ..... 16 A6
 1 Thamesmead SE28 ..... 124 B6
Beveridge Rd 1 NW10 ..... 67 C1
Beverley DA14 ..... 190 A5
Beverley Ave
 Hounslow TW4 ..... 129 B1
 Sidcup DA15 ..... 167 D4
 Wimbledon SW20 ... 177 D2
Beverley Cl
 Barnes SW13 ..... 134 A3
 Chessington KT9 ..... 213 C4
 Edmonton N21 ..... 17 A3
 Enfield EN1 ..... 5 C1
 6 Wandsworth SW11 ..... 136 B1
Beverley Cotts SW15 ..... 155 C1
Beverley Cres IG8 ..... 37 B2
Beverley Ct
 9 Acton Green W4 .. 111 A1
 5 Acton W12 ..... 111 C4
 Brockley SE4 ..... 141 B2
 6 Cheam SM2 ..... 217 C2
 Chingford Hatch E4 ..... 35 B6
 Fortis Green N2 ..... 48 D5
 Harrow HA2 ..... 42 B6
 Hounslow TW4 ..... 129 B1
 Islington N5 ..... 72 D2
 Northolt UB5 ..... 84 C5
 Oakleigh Pk N20 ..... 14 A4
 Oakwood N14 ..... 15 C4
 Sidcup DA14 ..... 190 B6
 Wimbledon SW20 ... 177 D2
Beverley Dr HA8 ..... 44 C6
Beverley Gdns
 Barnes SW13 ..... 133 D2
 Hendon NW11 ..... 47 A2
 2 New Malden KT4 . 200 A1
 Stanmore HA7 ..... 25 A2
 Wembley HA9 ..... 44 C1
Beverley Ho 5 BR1 .. 186 B5
Beverley Hyrst 10 CR0 ..... 221 D6
Beverley La KT2 ..... 177 C3
Beverley Lo 6 TW10 ..... 154 A6
Beverley Mans TW4 .. 129 B1
Beverley Path 9 SW13 ..... 133 D3
Beverley Rd
 Barnes SW13 ..... 133 D2
 Chingford E4 ..... 36 B4
 Chiswick W4 ..... 111 D1
 Dagenham RM9 ..... 81 A4
 Keston Mark BR2 ..... 226 A6
 Mitcham CR4 ..... 203 D5
 Newham E6 ..... 99 D4
 North Cheam KT4 ..... 216 C6
 Penge SE20 ..... 184 B1
 Ruislip HA4 ..... 62 B6
 Southall UB2 ..... 107 A3
 Sunbury TW16 ..... 171 D2
 Teddington KT1 ..... 175 C2
 West Barnes KT3 ..... 200 A5
Beverley Trad Est SM4 ..... 200 D2
Beverley Way KT3, SW20, KT2 ..... 177 D2
Beverley Way (Kingston By-Pass) KT3, SW20 ..... 200 A6
Beverly Ct HA3 ..... 43 C5
Beversbrook Rd N19 .. 71 D5
Beverstone Rd
 London SW2 ..... 160 B6
 Thornton Heath CR7 . 204 D5
Beverston Mews NW1 ..... 237 C3
Bevill Allen Cl SW17 180 D5
Bevill Cl SE25 ..... 206 A6
Bevin Cl SE16 ..... 119 A5
Bevin Ct WC1 ..... 233 D2
Bevington Prim Sch 15 W10 ..... 91 A2
Bevington Rd
 Beckenham BR3 ..... 185 D1
 Kensal Town W10 ..... 91 A2
Bevington St SE16 ... 118 A4
Bevin Ho
 35 Bethnal Green E2 ... 96 C4
 8 Bow E3 ..... 97 C4
Bevin Rd UB4 ..... 84 B4
Bevin Sq SW17 ..... 158 D1
Bevin Way WC1 ..... 234 A2
Bevis Marks EC3 ..... 95 C1 243 B2
Bewcastle Gdns EN2 ... 4 A1
Bew Ct SE21 ..... 162 A4
Bewdley Ho N4 ..... 51 A2
Bewdley St N1 ..... 72 C1
Bewick Mews SE15 .. 140 B5
Bewick St SW8 ..... 137 B3
Bewley Ct SW2 ..... 160 B5
Bewley Ho 7 E1 ..... 118 B6
Bewley St Stepney E1 . 118 B6
 Wimbledon SW19 ..... 180 A4
Bewlys Rd SE27 ..... 182 D5
Bexhill Cl TW13 ..... 151 A2
Bexhill Rd
 Catford SE4 ..... 163 B5
 Mortlake SW14 ..... 133 A2
 Wood Green N11 ..... 31 D5
Bexhill Wlk 6 E15 ..... 98 C6
BEXLEY 146 B1
Bexley Coll (Erith Rd Campus) DA17 ..... 125 D1
Bexley Gdns
 Edmonton N9 ..... 17 B1
 Ilford RM6 ..... 58 B4
Bexley Gram Sch DA16 ..... 146 B1
BEXLEYHEATH 147 B2
Bexleyheath Sch DA8 ..... 147 C2
Bexleyheath Sta DA7 ..... 147 A3
Bexley High St DA5 . 169 D3
Bexley Ho SE4 ..... 141 A1
Bexley La DA14 ..... 168 C1
Bexley Rd SE9 ..... 167 A6
Bexley Sta DA5 ..... 169 C3
Beynon Rd SM5 ..... 218 D3
BFI Imax (Cinema) SE1 ..... 116 C5 251 A3
BFI Southbank★ SE1 250 D4
Bglws The SM6 ..... 219 B3
Bianca Rd SE1, SE15 .. 140 A6
Bibsworth Lo N3 ..... 29 B1
Bibsworth Rd N3 ..... 29 B1
Bicester Rd TW9 ..... 132 D2
Bickenhall Mans W1 237 D4
Bickenhall St W1 ..... 92 D2 237 D4
Bickersteth Rd SW17 ..... 180 D4
Bickerton Rd N19 ..... 71 C6
BICKLEY 188 B1
Bickley Cres BR1 ..... 210 A5
Bickley Ct
 10 Merton SW19 ..... 179 C3
 1 Stanmore HA7 ..... 25 C6
Bickley Park Rd BR1, BR7 ..... 210 B6
Bickley Pk Pre Prep Sch BR1 ..... 209 D6
Bickley Pk Prep Sch BR1 ..... 209 D6
Bickley Prim Sch BR1 ..... 209 C6
Bickley Rd
 Bromley BR1 ..... 187 D1
 Leyton E10 ..... 53 D2
Bickley St SW17 ..... 180 D5
Bickley Sta BR1 ..... 210 A6
Bicknell Ho 34 E1 ..... 96 A1
Bicknell Rd SE5 ..... 139 A2
Bicknoller Rd EN1 ..... 5 D4
Bicknor Ho 2 E5 ..... 74 B3
Bicknor Rd BR6 ..... 211 D2
Bidborough Cl 3 BR2 ..... 208 D4
Bidborough St N1, WC1 ..... 94 A4 233 A1
Biddenden Way SE9 . 188 C6
Biddenham Ho 18 SE16 ..... 118 D2
Bidder St E16 ..... 98 C2
Biddesden Ho SW3 . 257 C3
Biddestone Rd N7 ..... 72 B4
Biddulph Ho 22 SE18 ..... 122 B2
Biddulph Mans W9 ..... 91 D4
Biddulph Rd W9 ..... 91 D4
Bideford Ave UB6 ..... 87 B5
Bideford Cl
 Edgware HA8 ..... 26 C2
 Twickenham TW13 ..... 151 B1
Bideford Gdns EN1 ..... 17 C4
Bideford Rd
 Catford BR1 ..... 164 D1
 East Wickham DA16 .. 146 B5
 Enfield EN3 ..... 7 B5
 Ruislip HA4 ..... 62 B5
Bidmead Ct KT6 ..... 214 A5
Bidwell Gdns N11 ..... 31 C3
Bidwell Ho
 Southall UB2 ..... 107 A2
 3 Willesden NW2 ..... 68 A5
Bidwell St SE15 ..... 140 B4
Big Ben★ SW1 ..... 250 B1
Bigbury Cl N17 ..... 33 C3
Biggerstaff Rd E15 ..... 98 A6
Biggerstaff St N4 ..... 72 C6
Biggin Ave CR4 ..... 180 D2
Biggin Hill SE19 ..... 182 D3
Biggin Hill Cl KT2 ..... 175 C5
Biggin Way SE19 ..... 183 A3
Bigginwood Rd SW16 ..... 182 D2
Bigg's Row SW15 ..... 134 D2
Biggs Sq E9 ..... 75 B2
Big Hill E5 ..... 52 B1
Bigland Green Prim Sch 41 E1 ..... 96 B1
Bigland St E1 ..... 96 B1
Bignell Rd SE18 ..... 122 D1
Bignold Rd E7 ..... 77 A4
Bigwood Ct NW11 ..... 47 D4
Bigwood Rd NW11 ..... 47 D3
Biko Ho 1 NW10 ..... 67 B1
Bilberry Ho 18 E3 ..... 97 C2
Bilberry Manor SM2 . 218 A1
Billet Rd Ilford RM6 ..... 58 C6
 Walthamstow E17 ..... 35 B2
Billetts Hart Cl W7 .. 108 C4
Bill Hamling Cl SE9 .. 166 B2
Billie Holiday Ct NW10 ..... 89 B5
Billingford Cl SE4 ..... 140 D1
Billing Ho 7 E1 ..... 96 D1
Billingley NW1 ..... 232 A5
Billing Pl SW10 ..... 135 D5 265 D4
Billing Rd SW10 ..... 135 D5 265 D4
Billings Cl RM9 ..... 80 C1
Billingsgate Mkt E14 ..... 119 D5
Billing St SW10 ..... 135 D5 265 D4
Billington Ho SW8 .. 269 D1
Billington Rd SE14 .. 140 D5
Billinton Hill CR0 ..... 221 B6
Billiter Sq EC3 ..... 243 B1
Billiter St EC3 . 95 C1 243 B1
Bill Nicholson Way N17 ..... 33 D3
Billockby Cl KT9 ..... 214 B2
Billsley Ct SE25 ..... 205 C5
Billson St E14 ..... 120 A2
Bilsby Gr SE9 ..... 187 D6
Bilton Ho SW8 ..... 269 C1
Bilton Rd UB6 ..... 87 B6
Bilton Twrs W1 ..... 237 D1
Bilton Way Enfield EN3 ... 7 B5
 Hayes UB3 ..... 106 B4
Bina Gdns SW5 ..... 114 A2 256 A3
Binbrook Ho 13 W10 .. 90 C2
Bincote Rd EN2 ..... 4 B2
Binden Rd W12 ..... 111 D3
Bindon Gn SM4 ..... 201 D5
Binfield Ct SE5 ..... 139 A3
Binfield Rd
 London SW4 ..... 138 A4 270 B1
 South Croydon CR2 .. 221 D3
Bingfield St N1 ..... 94 B6 233 C6
Bingham Cnr CR0 ..... 206 A1
Bingham Pl W1 ..... 93 A2 238 A4
Bingham Point 11 SE18 ..... 122 D2
Bingham Rd CR0 ..... 206 B1
Bingham St N1 ..... 73 B2
Bingley Rd
 Ashford TW16 ..... 172 A3
 Newham E16 ..... 99 C1
 Southall UB6 ..... 86 A2
Binley Ho SW15 ..... 155 D5
Binney St W1 .. 93 A1 238 B1
Binnie Ct SE10 ..... 141 D5
Binnie Ho SE1 ..... 262 A5
Binns Rd W4 ..... 111 C1
Binns Terr 3 W4 ..... 111 C1
Binsey Wlk 1 SE2 ... 124 C4
Binstead Cl UB4 ..... 85 A2
Binstead Ho SW18 .. 157 D5
Binyon Cres HA7 ..... 24 D5
Binyon Ho 8 N16 ..... 73 C4
Birbeck Ho 4 N19 ..... 49 D1
Birbetts Rd SE9 ..... 166 B2
Bircham Path SE4 .. 140 D1
Birchanger Rd SE25 .. 206 A4
Birch Ave
 Edmonton N13 ..... 17 A1
 Hillingdon UB7 ..... 82 B1
Birch Cl
 Brentford TW8 ..... 131 B5
 Buckhurst Hill IG9 ..... 21 D1
 Hounslow TW3 ..... 130 B3
 Newham E16 ..... 98 C2
 Peckham SE15 ..... 140 A3
 Romford RM7 ..... 59 D6
 Teddington TW11 ..... 175 A5
 Upper Holloway N19 ... 71 C6
Birch Cres UB10 ..... 82 B6
Birch Ct Chingford E4 ... 35 D4
 Forest Gate E7 ..... 76 D4
 Ilford RM6 ..... 58 C3
 Sutton SM1 ..... 218 A4
 9 Wallington SM6 ... 219 B4
 7 Woodside Pk N12 ... 29 D6
Birchdale Gdns RM6 .. 58 D2
Birchdale Rd E7 ..... 77 C3
Birchdene Dr SE28 ... 124 A5
Birchdown Ho 32 E3 .. 97 D4
Birchen Cl NW9 ..... 67 B6
Birchend Cl CR2 ..... 221 B2
Birchen Gr NW9 ..... 67 B6
Birches Cl
 Mitcham CR4 ..... 202 D6
 Pinner HA5 ..... 41 A4
Birches The
 2 Beckenham BR2 .. 208 D5
 Bushey WD23 ..... 8 A6
 Camberwell SE5 ..... 139 C3
 Greenwich SE7 ..... 143 B6
 Manor Pk E12 ..... 78 A4
 Orpington BR6 ..... 226 C4
 Southgate N21 ..... 16 B5
 South Norwood SE25 . 183 D1
 Twickenham TW4 ..... 151 B4
Birchfield Ho 3 E14 ..... 119 C6
Birchfield St E14 ..... 119 C6
Birch Gn NW9 ..... 27 C3
Birch Gr Acton W3 ..... 110 C6
 Bexley DA16 ..... 146 A1
 Lewisham SE12 ..... 164 D4
 Leyton E11 ..... 76 C5
 Upper Halliford TW17 171 C1
Birchgrove Ho TW9 . 132 D5
Birch Hill CR0 ..... 222 D3
Birch Ho
 New Cross Gate SE14 ..... 141 B4
 Teddington TW11 ..... 175 C3
 8 Tulse Hill SW2 ..... 160 C5
Birchington Cl DA7 . 147 D4
Birchington Ct
 Crouch End N8 ..... 49 D3
 2 Kilburn NW6 ..... 91 D6
Birchington Ho 1 E5 . 74 B3
Birchington Rd
 Crouch End N8 ..... 49 D3
 Kilburn NW6 ..... 91 C6
 Surbiton KT5 ..... 198 B2
Birchin La EC3 ..... 242 D1
Birchlands Ave SW12 ..... 158 D4
Birch Mead BR2, BR6 ..... 226 C6
Birchmead Ave HA5 ... 40 C5
Birchmere Bsns Pk SE2 ..... 124 A4

Birchmere Lo 18 SE16 118 B1
Birchmere Row SE3 142 D3
Birchmore Wlk N5 73 A5
Birch Pk HA3 24 A3
Birch Rd
Feltham TW13 172 D5
Romford RM7 59 D6
Birch Row BR2 210 C3
Birch Tree Ave BR4 224 D4
Birch Tree Ho 16 SE7 143 C6
Birch Tree Way CR0 222 B6
Birch Vale Ct NW8 236 D6
Birchway UB3 106 A5
Birch Wlk CR4 181 B2
Birchwood Ave
Beckenham BR3 207 B5
Hackbridge SM5, SM6 219 B5
Muswell Hill N10 49 A6
Sidcup DA14 168 C1
Birchwood Cl SM4 201 D5
Birchwood Ct
Burnt Oak HA8 27 A1
Edmonton N13 32 D5
Birchwood Dr NW3 69 D5
Birchwood Gr TW12 173 C4
Birchwood Rd
Orpington BR5 211 C5
Streatham SW17 181 B5
Birdbrook Rd SE3 143 C2
Birdcage Wlk SW1 115 D4 249 C1
Bird Coll DA14 168 A1
Birdham Cl BR1 210 A4
Birdhurst Ave CR2 221 B4
Birdhurst Ct SM6 219 C1
Birdhurst Gdns CR2 221 B4
Birdhurst Rd
London SW18 158 A6
Mitcham SW19 180 C4
South Croydon CR2 221 C3
Birdhurst Rise CR2 221 C3
Bird In Bush Rd SE15 140 A5
Bird-in-Hand La BR1 187 D1
Bird-In-Hand Pas SE23 162 C2
Bird In Hand Yd 24 NW3 70 A4
Birdsall Ho 5 SE5 139 C2
Birdsfield La 12 E3 97 B6
Bird St W1 238 B1
Bird Wlk TW2 151 B3
Birdwood Ave 4 SE13 164 B5
Birdwood Cl TW11 174 C6
Birkbeck Ave
Acton W3 111 A6
Greenford UB6 86 A6
Birkbeck Coll W1 93 D1 239 C2
Birkbeck Ct W3 111 B5
Birkbeck Gdns IG8 21 A2
Birkbeck Gr W3 111 B4
Birkbeck Hill SE21 160 D3
Birkbeck Mews 5 E8 73 D3
Birkbeck Pl SE21 161 A2
Birkbeck Prim Sch DA14 168 B1
Birkbeck Rd
Acton W3 111 B5
Dalston E8 73 D3
Ealing W5 109 C2
Edgware NW7 27 D5
Enfield EN2 5 B5
Hornsey N8 50 A5
Ilford IG2 57 B4
North Finchley N12 30 A5
Penge BR3 184 D1
Sidcup DA14 168 A1
Tottenham N17 33 D2
Wimbledon SW19 179 D4
Birkbeck St E2 96 B4
Birkbeck Sta SE20 206 C6
Birkbeck Univ of London WC1 93 D3 239 C6
Birkbeck Way UB6 86 B6
Birkdale Ave HA5 41 C6
Birkdale Cl
30 Bermondsey SE16 118 B1
Crofton BR6 211 B2
Erith SE28 102 D1
Birkdale Ct 3 UB1 86 A1
Birkdale Gdns CR0 222 D4
Birkdale Rd
Abbey Wood SE2 124 A2
Ealing W5 88 A3
Birkenhead Ave KT2 176 B2
Birkenhead Ho 11 N7 72 C3
Birkenhead St WC1 94 A4 233 B2
Birkhall Rd SE6 164 B2
Birkwood Cl SW12 159 D4
Birley Lo NW8 229 D4
Birley Rd N20 14 A2
Birley St SW11 137 A3
Birnam Rd N4 72 B6
Birnbeck Ct NW11 47 B4
Birnham Ho TW1 153 C4
Birrell Ho 9 SW9 138 B3
Birse Cres NW10 67 C4
Birstal Gn WD19 22 D6
Birstall Rd N15 51 C4
Birtwhistle Ho 5 E3 97 B6
Biscay Ho 11 E1 96 D3
Biscay Rd W6 112 D1
Biscoe Cl TW5 129 C6
Biscoe Ho UB2 107 D2
Biscoe Way SE13 142 B2
Biscott Ho 3 E3 97 D3
Bisenden Rd CR0 221 C6
Bisham Cl CR4 202 D1
Bisham Gdns N6 49 A1
Bishop Butt Cl BR6 227 D5
Bishop Challoner Collegiate Sch 28 E1 96 C1
Bishop Challoner Sch BR2 186 B1
Bishop Ct 20 SW2 160 C5
Bishop Douglass RC Sch N2 48 A6
Bishop Duppa's Almshouses 7 TW10 154 A6
Bishop Duppas Pk TW17 193 C2
Bishop Fox Way KT8 195 B5
Bishop Gilpins Prim Sch SW19 179 B5
Bishop John Robinson CE Prim Sch SE28 124 C6
Bishop Justus CE Sch BR2 210 A2
Bishop Ken Rd HA3 24 D2
Bishop King's Rd W14 113 A2 254 B4
Bishop Perrin CE Prim Sch TW2 151 D3
Bishop Ramsey CE Sch (Annexe) HA4 39 D2
Bishop Ramsey CE Sch (Upper) HA4 40 A2
Bishop Rd N14 15 B4
Bishop Ridley CE Prim Sch DA16 145 C1
Bishops Ave
Borehamwood WD6 10 B6
Bromley BR1 209 C6
Ilford RM6 58 C3
Newham E13 99 B6
Bishop's Ave SW6 135 A3
Bishops Ave The N2 48 B3
Bishopsbourne Ho BR1 187 B3
Bishop's Bridge Rd W2 92 A1 236 A2
Bishops Cl
Acton Green W4 111 A1
Barnet EN5 12 D5
Enfield EN1 6 B3
New Eltham SE9 167 A2
Richmond TW10 153 D1
Sutton SM1 217 C5
Bishop's Cl
Dartmouth Pk N19 71 C5
Hillingdon UB10 82 C5
Walthamstow E17 53 D5
Bishopscourt 8 CR0 221 D6
Bishops Ct
1 Ashford TW16 171 D3
13 Bayswater W2 91 D1
Bishops Ct *continued*
East Finchley N2 48 C5
Richmond TW9 132 A2
Romford RM7 59 D5
Wembley HA0 65 B4
Bishop's Ct
Holborn EC4 241 C2
Holborn WC2 241 A2
Bishopsdale Ho 8 NW6 91 C6
Bishops Dr
East Bedfont TW14 149 B5
Northolt UB5 85 A6
Bishopsford Com Sch SM4 202 B3
Bishopsford Ho SM4 202 C3
Bishopsford Rd SM4 202 B3
Bishopsgate EC2 95 C1 243 A2
Bishopsgate Arc E1 243 B3
Bishopsgate Churchyard EC2 243 A2
Bishopsgate Inst EC2 95 C2 243 B3
Bishops Gn BR1 187 C2
Bishops Gr
East Finchley N2 48 C3
Feltham TW12 173 B6
Bishop's Hall KT1 175 D1
Bishopshalt Sch UB8 82 B4
Bishops Hill KT12 194 A2
Bishops Ho SW8 270 B3
Bishop's Mans SW6 134 D3
Bishops Mead SE5 139 A5
Bishops Park Rd SW16 182 A2
Bishop's Park Rd SW6 134 D3
Bishop's Pl SM1 218 A3
Bishops Rd
Fulham SW6 135 B4 264 C2
Highgate N6 49 A3
Bishop's Rd
Hanwell W7 108 C4
Hayes UB3 83 A1
Thornton Heath CR0 204 D2
Bishops Sq E1 243 B4
Bishop St N1 95 A6 235 A6
Bishop's Terr SE11 116 C2 261 B4
Bishopsthorpe Rd SE26 184 D6
Bishopstone Ho 4 SW11 137 A3
Bishop Stopford's Sch EN1 6 B3
Bishops View Ct N10 49 B5
Bishop's Way E2 96 C5
Bishops Wlk
Chislehurst BR7 189 A2
South Croydon CR0, CR9 223 A3
Bishopswood Rd N6 48 D2
Bishop Thomas Grant Sch SW16 182 B5
Bishop Wand CE Sec Sch TW16 171 D1
Bishop Wilfred Wood Cl SE15 140 A3
Bishop Wilfred Wood Ct 3 E13 99 C5
Bishop Winnington-Ingram CE Prim Sch HA4 39 B2
Bisley Cl KT4 200 C1
Bisley Ho SW19 156 D2
Bispham Rd NW10 88 B4
Bissextile Ho SE13 141 D3
Bisson Rd E15 98 A5
Bisterne Ave E17 54 B6
Bittacy Bsns Ctr NW7 29 A3
Bittacy Cl NW7 28 D4
Bittacy Ct NW7 29 A3
Bittacy Hill NW7 28 D4
Bittacy Park Ave NW7 28 D5
Bittacy Rd NW7 28 D4
Bittacy Rise NW7 28 D4
Bittern Cl UB4 84 D2
Bittern Ct Chingford E4 20 B4
7 Deptford SE8 141 C6
Hendon NW9 27 C1
Bittern Ho SE1 252 A1
Bittern St SE1 252 A1
Bittoms The KT1 197 D6
Bixley Cl UB2 107 B2
Blackall St EC2 243 A6
Blackberry Cl TW17 193 C5
Blackberry Farm Cl TW5 129 A5
Blackberry Field BR5 190 A2
Blackbird Ct NW9 67 B5
Blackbird Hill NW9 67 B5
Blackborne Rd RM10 81 D2
Black Boy La N15 51 A4
Blackbrook La BR1, BR2 210 C5
Blackburn 28 NW9 27 D1
Blackburn Ct 21 SW2 160 C5
Blackburne's Mews W1 248 A5
Blackburn Rd NW6 69 D2
Blackburn Trad Est TW19 148 B5
Blackburn Way TW4 151 A6
Blackbush Ave RM6 58 D4
Blackbush Cl SM2 217 D1
Blackcap Ct NW9 27 C1
Blackdown Cl N2 30 A1
Blackdown Ho E8 74 A4
Blackett St SW15 134 D2
Black Fan Cl EN2 5 A4
BLACKFEN 168 A5
Blackfen Par DA15 168 A5
Blackfen Rd DA15 168 B5
Blackfen Sch for Girls DA15 168 B5
Blackford Rd WD19 22 D5
Blackfriars Bridge EC4 251 C5
Blackfriars Ct EC4 251 C6
Black Friars La EC4 94 D1 241 C1
Blackfriars Pas EC4 251 C6
Blackfriars Pier EC4 251 C6
Blackfriars Rd SE1 116 D5 251 C3
Blackfriars Underpass EC4 116 C6 251 B6
Blackham Ho SW19 179 A4
BLACKHEATH 142 C2
Blackheath★ SE3 142 C4
Blackheath Ave SE3 142 C5
Blackheath Bluecoat Sch SE3 143 B5
Blackheath Bsns Est SE10 142 A4
Blackheath Gr SE3 142 D3
Blackheath High Jun Sch SE3 142 D3
Blackheath High Sch SE3 143 A5
Blackheath Hill SE10 142 A4
Blackheath Hospl SE3 142 C2
BLACKHEATH PARK 143 A1
Blackheath Pk SE3 143 A2
Blackheath Prep Sch SE3 143 A4
Blackheath Rd SE10 141 D4
Blackheath Rise SE13 142 A3
Blackheath Sta SE3 142 D2
BLACKHEATH VALE 142 D3
Blackheath Vale SE3 142 C3
Blackheath Village SE3 142 D3
Black Horse Ct SE1 262 D6
Blackhorse La
Croydon CR0 206 A2
Higham Hill E17 34 D1
Blackhorse La Sta CR0 206 A2
Blackhorse Mews E17 52 D6
Black Horse Par HA5 40 B4
Blackhorse Rd
Deptford SE8 141 A6
Walthamstow E17 53 A5
Black Horse Rd DA14 190 A6
Blackhorse Road E17 52 D5
Blackhorse Road Sta E17 52 D5
Blacklands Dr UB4 83 A3
Blacklands Rd SE6 186 A6
Blacklands Terr SW3 257 D3
Black Lion La W6 112 A2
Black Lion Mews 4 W6 112 A2
Blackmore Ave UB1 108 B5
Blackmore Dr NW10 66 D1
Blackmore Ho
Forest Hill SE23 163 B3
Islington N1 233 D5
2 Wandsworth SW18 157 D6
Blackmore's Gr TW11 175 A4
Blackmore Twr 1 W3 111 A3
Blackness La BR2 225 D1
Blackpool Gdns UB4 83 C3
Blackpool Rd SE15 140 B3
Black Prince Intc DA6 169 D5
Black Prince Rd SE1, SE11 116 B2 260 D3
Black Rod Cl UB3 105 D3
Black Roof Ho 9 SE5 138 D4
Blackshaw Rd SW17 180 B5
Blacksmith Cl RM6 58 C3
Blacksmiths Ho 7 E17 53 C5
Black's Rd W6 112 C2
Blackstock Ho 2 N5 72 D5
Blackstock Mews N4 72 D5
Blackstock Rd N4, N5 72 D6
Blackstone Ho
Dulwich SE21 161 C1
Pimlico SW1 259 A1
Blackstone Rd NW2 68 C4
Black Swan Yd SE1 253 A2
Blackthorn Ave UB7 104 C3
Blackthorn Ct
20 Camberwell SE15 139 D5
Heston TW5 129 A5
4 Leyton E15 76 B4
6 West Norwood SW16 182 C5
Blackthorne Ave CR0 206 C1
Blackthorne Ct
2 Littleton TW15 171 A3
Southall UB1 107 D5
Blackthorne Dr E4 36 B6
Blackthorn Gr DA7 147 A2
Blackthorn Rd IG1 79 B3
Blackthorn St E3 97 C3
Blacktree Mews 11 SW9 138 C2
BLACKWALL 120 B6
Blackwall Sta E14 120 A6
Blackwall Trad Est E14 98 B2
Blackwall Tunnel E14, SE10 120 B5
Blackwall Tunnel App SE10 120 C4
Blackwall Tunnel Northern Approach E14, E3 98 A3
Blackwall Way E14 120 A6
Blackwater Cl E7 76 D4
Blackwater Ho NW8 236 D4
Blackwater St SE22 161 D6
Blackwell Cl
10 Clapton Pk E5 74 D4
Harrow HA3 24 B3
Southgate N21 16 A6
Blackwell Gdns HA8 10 C1
Blackwell Ho 3 SW4 159 D5
Blackwood Ho 11 E1 96 B3
Blackwood St SE17 117 B1 262 C2
Blade Ho TW1 153 D5
Blade Mews SW15 135 B1
Bladen Ho 4 E1 96 D1
Blades Ct
4 Hammersmith W6 112 B1
Putney SW15 135 B1
Blades Ho 12 SE11 138 C6
Blades Lo 16 SW2 160 C5
Bladindon Dr DA5 168 D4
Bladon Ct
Beckenham BR2 208 C6

Bladon Ct *continued*
Streatham SW16 182 A4
Bladon Gdns HA2 41 D3
Blagden's Cl N14 15 D2
Blagden's La N14 15 D2
Blagdon Ct W7 108 C6
Blagdon Rd
London SE13 163 D5
New Malden KT3 199 D5
Blagdon Wlk TW11 175 C4
Blagrove Rd 1 W10 91 B2
Blair Ave London NW9 45 C2
Thames Ditton KT10 212 A6
Blair Cl
Avery Hill DA15 167 C6
Canonbury N1 73 A2
Hayes UB3 106 A2
Blair Ct
Beckenham BR3 185 D2
8 Carshalton SM5 218 D5
7 Catford SE6 164 D3
St John's Wood NW8 229 C6
Blairderry Rd SW2 160 A2
Blairgowrie Ct 13 E14 98 B1
Blair Ho SW9 138 B3
Blair Peach Prim Sch
UB1 106 D5
Blair St E14 98 B1
Blake Apartments N8 50 B6
Blake Ave IG11 101 D6
Blake Cl Bexley DA16 145 C4
Carshalton SM5 202 C1
Hayes UB4 83 B5
Blake Coll W1 93 C2 239 A4
Blake Ct
8 Bermondsey
SE16 118 B1
9 Clapham SW8 137 C3
Croydon CR2 220 D3
Kilburn NW6 91 C4
Southgate N21 16 B6
Blakeden Dr KT10 212 D2
Blake Gdns
SW6 135 D4 265 C2
Blake Hall Cres E11 55 A1
Blakehall Rd SM5 218 D2
Blake Hall Rd E11 55 A2
Blake Ho
6 Beckenham BR3 185 D4
2 Deptford SE8 141 C6
Harrow HA1 64 C6
Isle Of Dogs E14 119 D4
1 Kentish Town N19 71 D3
Lambeth SE1 261 A6
14 Stoke Newington
N16 73 C4
Blake Lo N3 29 B1
Blake Mews 15 TW9 132 C4
Blakemore Rd
Streatham SW16 160 A1
Thornton Heath CR7 204 B4
Blakemore Way
DA17 125 A3
Blakeney Ave BR3 185 B2
Blakeney Cl
5 Camden Town
NW1 71 D1
4 Dalston E8 74 A3
Whetstone N20 14 A3
Blakeney Ct EN2 17 B6
Blakeney Rd BR3 185 B2
Blakenham Ct W12 112 A5
Blakenham Rd
SW17 180 D6
Blaker Ct SE7 143 C5
Blake Rd
Croydon CR0 221 C6
Mitcham CR4 202 C6
Newham E16 98 D3
Wood Green N11 31 C3
Blaker Rd E15 98 A6
Blakes Ave KT3 199 D3
Blakes Cl W10 90 C2
Blake's Gn BR4 208 A1
Blakes La KT3 199 D4
Blakesley Ave W5 87 C1
Blakesley Ct W5 87 C1
Blakesley Ho 4 E12 78 C5
Blake's Rd SE15 139 C5
Blakes Terr KT3 200 A4
Blakesware Gdns N9 17 B4
Blakewood Cl TW13 172 C6
Blakewood Ct 5
SE20 184 B3
Blanca Ho 16 N1 95 C5
Blanchard Cl SE9 166 A1
Blanchard Gr EN3 7 D5
Blanchard Ho
Chislehurst BR7 189 A4
7 Twickenham TW1 153 D5
Blanchard Way E8 74 A2
Blanch Cl SE15 140 C5
Blanchedowne SE5 139 B1
Blanche Nevile Sch
Highgate N6 48 D3
Muswell Hill N10 31 A1
Blanche St E16 98 D3
Blanchland Rd SM4 201 D4
Blandfield Rd SW12 159 A4
Blandford Ave
2 Beckenham BR3 185 A1
Twickenham TW2 151 D3
Blandford Cl
London N2 48 A5
Romford RM7 59 D5
Wallington CR0 220 A5
Blandford Cres E4 20 A4
Blandford Ct
Brondesbury Pk NW6 69 A1
6 De Beauvoir Town
N1 73 C1
Blandford Ho SW8 270 C4
Blandford Rd
Acton W4 111 C3
Ealing W5 109 D4
Penge BR3 184 D1
Southall UB2 107 C2
Teddington TW11 174 C5
Blandford Sq NW1 237 B5
Blandford St
W1 93 A2 238 A3
Blandford Waye UB4 84 C1
Bland Ho SE11 260 D2
Bland St SE9 143 D1
Blaney Cres E6 100 D4
Blanmerle Rd SE9 166 D3
Blann Cl SE9 165 D5
Blantyre St
SW10 136 B5 266 C4
Blantyre Twr SW10 266 C4
Blantyre Wlk
SW10 136 B5 266 C4
Blashford NW3 70 D1
Blashford St SE13 164 B4
Blasker Wlk 8 E14 119 D1
Blatchford Ct KT12 194 A1
Blatchford Ho 8
RM10 81 C5
Blawith Rd HA1 42 D5
Blaxland Ho 12 W12 112 B6
Blaydon Cl HA4 39 C2
Blaydon Ct 4 UB5 63 C2
Blaydon Wlk N17 34 B3
Blazer Ct NW8 229 D1
Bleak Hill La SE18 145 D6
Blean Gr SE20 184 C3
Bleasdale Ave UB6 87 A5
Blechynden Ho 17
W10 90 D1
Blechynden St W10 112 D6
Bledlow Cl SE28 124 C6
Bledlow Rise UB6 86 A5
Bleeding Heart Yd
EC1 241 B3
Blegborough Rd
SW16 181 C4
Blemundsbury WC1 240 C4
Blendon Dr DA5 168 D5
Blendon Path 9
BR1 186 D3
Blendon Rd DA5 168 D5
Blendon Terr SE18 145 A6
Blendworth Point 4
SW15 156 B3
Blenheim 26 SW19 156 D3
Blenheim Ave IG2 56 C3
Blenheim Bsns Ctr
CR4 180 D1
Blenheim Centre 7
SE20 184 D3
Blenheim Cl
Edmonton N21 17 A3
Eltham SE12 165 B3
Greenford UB6 86 B5
Wallington SM6 219 C1
West Barnes SW20 200 C6
Blenheim Cres
Notting Hill W11 91 A1
Notting Hill W11 244 B6
Ruislip HA4 61 B6
South Croydon CR2 221 A1
Blenheim Ct
Barnsbury N7 72 A2
Beckenham BR2 208 D5
5 Hampton TW12 173 C2
Harrow HA3 43 A3
Hendon NW4 46 D5
Longlands DA14 167 B1
Richmond TW9 132 B2
17 Rotherhithe SE16 118 D5
South Norwood SE19 183 C2
Sutton SM2 218 A2
Upper Holloway N19 72 A6
Woodford IG8 37 B3
Blenheim Ctr TW3 129 D2
Blenheim Dr DA16 145 D4
Blenheim Gdns
Clapham Pk SW2 160 B5
Dollis Hill NW2 68 C3
Kingston u T KT2 176 D3
Wallington SM6 219 C1
Wembley HA9 66 A5
Blenheim Gr SE15 140 A3
Blenheim Ho
6 Edmonton N9 18 A1
Hounslow TW3 129 C2
8 Woolwich SE18 123 A3
Blenheim Par 2
UB10 82 D3
Blenheim Park Rd
CR2 221 A1
Blenheim Pas NW8 229 A4
Blenheim Pl TW11 174 D5
Blenheim Rd
Acton W4 111 C3
Bromley BR1, BR2 210 A5
Harrow HA2 41 D3
Leyton E15 76 C4
Newham E6 99 D4
Northolt UB5 63 D2
Penge SE20 184 C3
Sidcup DA15 168 C3
St John's Wood
NW8 92 A5 229 B4
Sutton SM1 217 D5
Walthamstow E17 53 A6
West Barnes SW20 200 C6
Blenheim Rise N15 51 D5
Blenheim St W1 238 C1
Blenheim Terr
NW8 92 A5 229 A4
Blenheim Way TW7 131 A4
Blenkarne Rd SW11 158 D5
Bleriot 27 NW9 27 D1
Bleriot Rd TW5 128 C5
Blessbury Rd HA8 27 A2
Blessed Dominic RC Sch
NW9 27 D1
Blessed Sacrament RC
Prim Sch N1 94 B6 233 C5
Blessington Cl SE13 142 B2
Blessington Rd SE13 142 B1
Blessing Way IG11 102 C5
Bletchingley Cl CR7 204 D5
Bletchington Ct 2
DA17 125 C2
Bletchley Ct N1 235 C3
Bletchley St
N1 95 A5 235 B3
Bletchmore Cl UB3 105 B1
Bletsoe Wlk N1 235 B4
Blewbury Ho 3 SE2 124 C4
Blick Ho 1 SE16 118 C3
Bligh Ho 4 SE27 183 A6
Blincoe Cl SW19 156 D2
Blissett St SE10 142 A4
Blissland Ct 5 N12 30 A4
Bliss Mews 14 W10 91 A4
Blisworth Cl UB4 85 A3
Blisworth Ho 12 E2 96 A6
Blithbury Rd RM9 80 B2
Blithdale Rd SE2 124 A2
Blithfield St W8 255 C5
Blockley Rd HA0 65 B6
Bloemfontein Ave
W12 112 B5
Bloemfontein Rd
W12 112 B6
Blomfield Ct
Battersea SW11 266 D2
Paddington W9 236 B6
Blomfield Ho 4
E14 119 D6
Blomfield Mans 3
W12 112 C5
Blomfield Rd
W9 92 A2 236 A4
Blomfield St
EC2 95 B2 242 D3
Blomfield Villas W9 236 A4
Blomville Rd RM8 81 A5
Blondel St SW11 137 A3
Blondin Ave W5 109 C3
Blondin St E3 97 C5
Bloomburg St SW1 259 B3
Bloomfield Cres IG2 56 D3
Bloomfield Ct N6 49 A3
Bloomfield Ho 19 E1 96 A2
Bloomfield Pl W1 248 D6
Bloomfield Rd
Bromley Comm BR2 209 D4
Highgate N6 49 A3
Kingston u T KT1 198 A6
Woolwich SE18 122 D1
Bloomfield Terr
SW1 115 A1 258 B2
Bloom Gr SE27 160 D1
Bloomhall Rd SE19 183 B5
Bloom Park Rd SW6 264 C3
Bloomsberg Space*
EC1 242 D4
BLOOMSBURY 93 D2
Bloomsbury Cl
Ealing W5 110 B6
Edgware NW7 28 A3
Bloomsbury Ct
Cranford TW5 128 B4
Leytonstone E11 54 B1
Pinner HA5 41 B6
St Giles WC1 240 B3
Bloomsbury Ho 10
SW4 159 D5
Bloomsbury
International Language
Sch WC1 94 A2 240 B3
Bloomsbury Pl
London SW18 158 A6
St Giles WC1 240 B3
Bloomsbury Sq
WC1 94 A2 240 B3
Bloomsbury St
WC1 93 D2 239 D3
Bloomsbury Way
WC1 94 A2 240 B3
Blore Cl SW8 269 C1
Blore Ct W1 249 C6
Blore Ho SW10 265 D4
Blossom Cl
Dagenham RM9 103 B6
Ealing W5 110 A4
South Croydon CR2 221 D3
Blossom House Sch
SW20 178 C3
Blossom La EN2 5 A4
Blossom Pl E1 243 B5
Blossom St E1 95 C3 243 B5
Blossom Way
Hillingdon UB10 60 B1
West Drayton UB7 104 C2
Blossom Waye TW5 129 A5
Blount St E14 97 A1
Bloxam Gdns SE9 166 A6
Bloxhall Rd E10 53 B1
Bloxham Cres TW12 173 B2
Bloxworth Cl SM6 219 C5
Blucher Rd SE5 139 A5
Blue Anchor Alley 4
TW9 132 A1
Blue Anchor La
SE16 118 B2
Blue Anchor Yd E1 118 A6
Blue Ball Yd SW1 249 A3
Bluebell Ave E12 78 A3
Bluebell Cl
Forest Hill SE26 183 D6
Hackbridge SM6 203 B1
10 Hackney E9 96 C6
Northolt UB5 63 B2
Orpington BR6 227 A6
Bluebell Ct 4 N12 14 A1
Bluebell Way IG1 78 D2
Blueberry Cl IG8 37 A4
Blueberry Ct
Edgware HA8 27 A5
3 Enfield EN2 4 D3
Bluebird La RM10 81 C1
Bluebird Way SE28 123 B4
Bluefield Cl TW12 173 C5
Blue Gate Fields Jun &
Inf Schs 22 E1 118 C6
Bluegate Mews E1 118 B6
Bluegates
Stoneleigh KT17 216 A1
Bluegates *continued*
Wimbledon SW19 179 A5
Bluehouse Rd E4 20 C1
Blue Lion Pl SE1 263 A6
Blue Point Ct 2 HA1 42 D4
Blueprint Apartments 15
SW12 159 B4
Blue Sch The TW7 131 A2
Blundell Cl E8 74 A4
Blundell Rd HA8 27 C3
Blundell St N7 72 A2
Blunden Cl RM8 58 C1
Blunt Rd CR0 221 B3
Blunts Ave UB7 126 C5
Blunts Rd SE9 166 C6
Blurton Rd E5 74 D4
Blydon Ct N21 16 B6
Blyth Cl
4 Cubitt Town E14 120 B2
Twickenham TW1 152 D5
Blythe Cl SE23 163 B4
Blythe Hill
Forest Hill SE6 163 B4
St Paul's Cray BR5 190 A2
Blythe Hill La SE6 163 B3
Blythe Ho 8 SE11 138 C6
Blythe Mews 2
W14 112 D3
Blythendale Ho 34 E2 96 A5
Blythe Rd
W14 113 A3 254 A5
Blythe St E2 96 B4
Blytheswood Pl 4
SW16 182 B6
Blythe Vale SE6 163 B3
Blythewood 5 SM1 218 B3
Blyth Rd
Bromley BR1 186 D2
Hayes UB3 105 C4
Walthamstow E17 53 B2
Woolwich SE28 124 C6
Blyth's Wharf E14 119 A6
Blythswood Rd IG3 58 A2
Blythwood Pk 10
BR1 186 D2
Blythwood Rd
London N4 50 A2
Pinner HA5 22 D2
BMI Fitzroy Square
Hospl W1 93 C3 239 A5
BMI The Cavell Hospl
EN2 4 C3
Bnois Jerusalem Girls
Sch 2 N16 51 B2
Boades Mews 3
NW3 70 B4
Boadicea St N1 233 C5
Boardman Ave E4 19 D6
Boardman Cl EN5 13 A6
Boardwalk Pl E14 120 A5
Boarhound 25 NW9 27 D1
Boarley Ho SE17 263 A3
Boatemah Wlk 21
SW9 138 C3
Boathouse Ctr The
W10 90 D3
Boathouse Wlk 24
SE15 139 D5
Boat Lifter Way 19
SE16 119 A2
Bob Anker Cl 1 E13 99 A4
Bobbin Cl SW4 137 C2
Bobby Moore Bridge The
HA9 66 C5
Bob Marley Way 11
SE24 138 C1
Bobov Foundation Sch
4 N16 51 D2
Bob Thompson Ct
HA9 66 D5
Bockhampton Rd
KT2 176 B3
Bocking St E8 96 B6
Boddicott Cl SW19 157 A2
Boddington Gdns
W3 110 C4
Boddington Ho 2
SE14 140 C4
Bodeney Ho 10 SE5 139 C4
Boden Ho 4 E1 96 A2
Bodiam Cl EN1 5 C3
Bodiam Ct
Beckenham BR2 208 D5

Bodiam Ct *continued*
Sutton SM1 . . . . **218** A4
Bodiam Rd SW16 . . . **181** D3
Bodiam Way NW10 . . . . **88** B4
Bodicea Mews W4 . . **151** C5
W12 . . . . **112** D4
Bodley Cl KT3 . . . . . . **199** C4
Bodley Manor Way
SE24 . . . . **160** C4
Bodley Rd KT3 . . . . . **199** C4
Bodmin N9 NW9 . . . . . . **27** D1
Bodmin Cl SM4 . . . . . **201** D4
Bodmin Gr SM4 . . . . . **201** D4
Bodmin St SW18 . . . . **157** C3
Bodnant Gdns SW20 . **200** B6
Bodney Rd E5, E8 . . . . **74** B3
Boeing Way UB2 . . . . **106** B3
Boevey Path DA17 . . . **125** B1
Bogart Ct 13 E14 . . . **119** C6
Bognor Gdns WD19 . . . **22** C5
Bognor Rd DA16 . . . . **146** D4
Bohemia Pl 1 E8 . . . . **74** B2
Bohn Rd E1 . . . . **97** A2
Bohun Gr EN4 . . . . . . **14** D5
Boileau Par W5 . . . . . **88** B1
Boileau Rd
Barnes SW13 . . . . . . **134** B6
Ealing W5 . . . . **88** B1
Boilerhouse SE1 . . . . **253** C3
Boisseau Ho 3 E1 . . . . **96** C2
Bolden St SE8 . . . . . **141** D3
Boldero Pl NW8 . . . . . **237** A5
Bolderwood Way
BR4 . . . . **223** D6
Boldmere Rd HA5 . . . . **40** C4
Boleyn Ave E6 . . . . . . **99** C6
Boleyn Ct
Beckenham BR3 . . . . . **207** A4
Buckhurst Hill IG9 . . . . **21** B3
East Molesey KT8 . . . **196** B5
Hayes UB3 . . . . **105** D4
Walthamstow E17 . . . **53** C1
Boleyn Dr
East Molesey KT8 . . . **195** B6
Ruislip HA4 . . . . **62** D6
Boleyn Gdns BR4 . . . **223** D6
Boleyn Ground (Upton
Park) (West Ham Utd
FC) E13, E6 . . . . **99** C5
Boleyn Rd Newham E6 . **99** D5
Stoke Newington N16 . **73** C3
Upton E7 . . . . **77** B1
Boleyn Way EN5 . . . . . . **2** A2
Bolina Rd SE16 . . . . . **118** C1
Bolingbroke Gr
SW11 . . . . **158** D5
Bolingbroke Ho
Beckenham BR3 . . . . . **207** A4
Catford BR3 . . . . **185** D5
Bolingbroke Rd
W14 . . . . **112** D3
Bolingbroke Way UB3,
UB11 . . . . **105** B6
Bolingbroke Wlk
SW11 . . . . . **136** C4 **267** A2
Bollo Bridge Rd W3 . **111** A4
Bollo Ct 2 W3 . . . . . **111** A3
Bollo La W3 . . . . **110** D3
Bolney Ct KT6 . . . . . **197** D4
Bolney Gate SW7 . . . **247** A1
Bolney St
SW8 . . . . . . **138** B5 **269** C3
Bolsover St
W1 . . . . **93** B3 **238** D5
Bolstead Rd CR4 . . . . **181** B2
Bolster Gr N22 . . . . . . **31** D2
Bolt Ct EC4 . . . . **241** B1
Boltmore Cl NW4 . . . . **46** D6
Bolton Cl
Chessington KT9 . . . . **214** A2
Penge SE20 . . . . **184** A1
Bolton Cres SE5 . . . . **138** D5
Bolton Dr SM4 . . . . . . **202** B2
Bolton Gdns
Bromley BR1 . . . . **186** D4
Kensal Rise NW10 . . . . **90** D5
South Kensington
SW5 . . . . . **113** D1 **255** D2
Teddington TW11 . . . . **175** A4
Bolton Gdns Mews
SW10 . . . . **256** A2

Bolton Ho 4 SE10 . . . **120** C1
Bolton Pl SW5 . . . . . **256** A2
Bolton Rd
Chessington KT9 . . . . **214** A1
Chiswick W4 . . . . **133** A5
Edmonton N18 . . . . . . **33** D5
Harlesden NW10 . . . . . **89** C6
Harrow HA1 . . . . **42** B5
Kilburn NW8 . . . . **91** D6
Stratford E15 . . . . . . **76** D2
Boltons Cl SW5 . . . . **255** D2
Bolton's La TW6,
UB7 . . . . **127** A5
Bolton Stw11 11 5 **85 248** D4
Boltons The
Harrow HA1 . . . . **42** A5
South Kensington
SW10 . . . . . **114** A1 **256** A2
6 Stratford E15 . . . . . **76** D2
Wembley HA0 . . . . **64** D2
Woodford **37** A6
Bolton Studios SW10 **256** B1
Bolton Wlk N7 . . . . . . **72** B6
Bombay St SE16 . . . **118** C4
Bombay St SE16 . . . **118** B2
Bomer Cl UB7 . . . . . **126** C5
Bomore Rd
W11 . . . . . . **113** A6 **244** A6
Bonar Pl BR7 . . . . . . **188** A3
Bonar Rd SE15 . . . . . **140** A5
Bonchester Cl BR7 . . **188** C3
Bonchurch Cl SM2 . . **217** D1
Bonchurch Rd
Ealing W13 . . . . **109** B5
Kensal Town W10 . . . . **91** A2
Bond Cl UB7 . . . . **82** B1
Bond Ct EC4 . . . . . . **242** C1
Bondfield Ave UB4 . . . **84** A4
Bondfield Rd 4 E6 . . . **100** B2
Bond Gdns SM6 . . . . **219** C4
Bond Ho 4 NW6 . . . . . **91** B5
Bonding Yard Wlk
SE16 . . . . **119** A3
Bond Prim Sch CR4 . **180** D1
Bond Rd
Mitcham CR4 . . . . **180** D1
Surbiton KT6 . . . . . . **214** B6
Bond St Chiswick W4 . **133** B1
Ealing W5 . . . . **109** D6
Stratford E15 . . . . . . **76** D3
Bond Street Sta
W1 . . . . **93** A1 **238** B1
Bondway
SW8 . . . . . . **138** A4 **270** B6
Bonfield Rd SE13 . . . **142** A1
Bonham Gdns RM8 . . . **80** C6
Bonham Ho W11 . . . . **244** C4
Bonham Rd
Brixton SW2 . . . . **160** B6
Dagenham RM8 . . . . . **80** D5
Bonheur Rd W4 . . . . . **111** B4
Bonhill St EC2 **95** B3 **242** D5
Boniface Gdns HA3 . . . **23** D3
Boniface Rd UB10 . . . . **60** D5
Boniface Wlk HA3 . . . . **23** D3
Bonington Ho
Enfield EN1 . . . . **18** A6
Pentonville N1 . . . . . **233** C1
Bonita Mews SE13 . . **140** D2
Bonne Marche Terr
Mews 18 SE27 . . . . **183** C6
Bonner Hill Rd KT1 . **198** C6
Bonner Ho 3 SW15 . . **156** A6
Bonner Prim Sch
E2 . . . . **96** C5
Bonner Rd E2 . . . . . . **96** C5
Bonnersfield Cl HA1 . . **43** A3
Bonnersfield La
Greenhill HA1 . . . . **42** D3
Kenton HA1, HA3 . . . . **43** A3
Bonner St E2 . . . . **96** C5
Bonneville Gdns
SW4 . . . . **159** C5
Bonneville Prim Sch
SW4 . . . . **84** D5
Bonnington Ct 14
UB5 . . . . **84** D5
Bonnington Ho 9
N1 . . . . **233** A2
Bonnington Sq
SW8 . . . . . . **138** B6 **270** C6
Bonnington Twr
BR2 . . . . **210** A3
Bonny St NW1 . . . . . . **71** C1
Bonser Rd TW1 . . . . . **152** D2

Bonsor Ho SW8 . . . . . **269** B2
Bonsor St SE5 . . . . . **139** C5
Bonthron Ho SW15 . . **134** C3
Bonus Pastor RC Sch
BR1 . . . . **186** C6
Bonville Gdns 1
NW4 . . . . **46** A5
Bonville Rd BR1 . . . . **186** D5
Bookbinder Cotts
N20 . . . . **14** D1
Booker Cl 1 E3 . . . . . . **97** B2
Booker Rd 5 N18 . . . . . **34** A5
Bookham Ct CR4 . . . . **202** B6
Boone Ct N9 . . . . **18** C1
Boones Rd SE13 . . . . **142** C1
Boone St SE13 . . . . . **142** C1
Boord St SE10 . . . . . **120** C3
Boothby Ct E4 . . . . **20** A1
Boothby Ho 2
SW16 . . . . **181** C5
Boothby Rd N19 . . . . . . **71** D6
Booth Cl
10 Hackney E9 . . . . . . **96** B6
Thamesmead SE28 . . **124** B6
Booth Ho
2 Streatham SW2 . . . **160** C4
Streatham SW8 . . . . . . **181** C5
Booth La EC4 . . . . . . **252** A6
Boothman Ho HA3 . . . . **43** D6
Booth Rd
Croydon CR0 . . . . **220** D6
Hendon NW9 . . . . **27** C1
Boothroyd Ho TW7 . . **130** D2
Booth's Pl W1 . . . . . . **239** B3
Boot Par HA8 . . . . **26** D4
Boot St N1 . . . . **95** C4
Bordars Rd W7 . . . . . . **86** D2
Bordars Wlk W7 . . . . . **86** C2
Bordeaux Ho 1 E15 . . **76** C3
Borden Ave EN1 . . . . . . **17** B5
Border Cres SE26 . . . **184** B5
Border Gate CR4 . . . . **180** D2
Border Gdns CR0 . . . . **223** D4
Border Rd SE26 . . . . . **184** B5
Bordesley Rd SM4 . . . **201** D5
Bordeston Ct 11
TW8 . . . . **131** C5
Bordley Ct 8 N20 . . . . **14** D2
Bordon Wlk 5
SW15 . . . . **156** A4
Boreas Wlk N1 . . . . . **234** D3
Boreham Ave E16 . . . . **99** A1
Boreham Cl E11 . . . . . **54** A1
Boreham Rd N22 . . . . . **33** A1
BOREHAMWOOD . . . **11** A5
Boreman Ho 1
SE10 . . . . **142** A6
Borgard Rd SE18 . . . . **122** B2
Borkwood Pk BR6 . . . **227** D4
Borkwood Way BR6 . . **227** C4
Borland Rd
London SE15 . . . . **140** C1
Teddington TW11 . . . **175** B3
Borneo St SW15 . . . . **134** C2
Borough High St
SE1 . . . . **117** B5 **252** C4
Borough Hill CR0 . . . **220** D5
Borough Mkt★
SE1 . . . . . . **117** B5 **252** C5
Borough Rd
Hounslow TW7 . . . . . **130** D4
7 Kingston u T KT2 . . **176** C3
Lambeth SE1 **116** D3 **261** D6
Mitcham CR4 . . . . **180** C1
Borough Sq SE1 . . . . **252** A1
Borough Sta
SE1 . . . . **117** A4 **252** B1
BOROUGH THE **117** A4
Borrett Cl
SE17 . . . . . . **117** A1 **262** A1
Borrodaile Rd SW18 **157** D5
Borrowdale NW1 . . . . **232** A1
Borrowdale Ave HA3 . . **25** A1
Borrowdale Cl
Finchley N2 . . . . **30** A1
Redbridge IG4 . . . . . . **56** A5
Borrowdale Ct EN2 . . . . **5** A4
Borthwick Mews E15 **76** C4
Borthwick Rd
Leyton E15 . . . . **76** C4
London NW9 . . . . **45** D3
Borthwick St SE8 . . . **119** C1
Borwick Ave E17 . . . . . **53** B6
Bosbury Rd SE6 . . . . **164** A1
Boscastle Rd NW5 . . . . **71** B5
Boscobel Cl BR1 . . . . **188** B1

Boscobel Ho 4 E8 . . . . **74** B2
Boscobel Pl SW1 . . . . **258** B4
Boscobel St
NW8 . . . . . . **92** B3 **236** D4
Boscombe Ave E10 . . . **54** B2
Boscombe Circus
NW4 . . . . **27** B1
Boscombe Cl E5 . . . . . **75** A3
Boscombe Gdns
SW16 . . . . **182** A4
Boscombe Ho CR0 . . **205** A1
Boscombe Rd
Merton SW19 . . . . . . **179** D2
North Cheam KT4 . . . **200** D1
Shepherd's Bush W12 **112** A4
Streatham SW17 . . . . **181** A4
Bosco Cl N3 . . . . **29** A2
Bosgrove E4 . . . . **20** A2
Boss Ho SE1 . . . . . . **253** C2
Boss St SE1 . . . . **253** C2
Bostall Hill SE2 . . . . **124** B1
Bostall La SE2 . . . . . **124** B1
Bostall Manorway
SE2 . . . . **124** B2
Bostall Park Ave
DA7 . . . . **147** A5
Bostall Rd BR5 . . . . . **190** B3
Bostock Ho NW5 . . . . **129** C6
Boston Bsns Pk W7 . . **108** C3
Boston Ct
South Norwood
SE25 . . . . **205** D5
Sutton SM2 . . . . **218** A1
Boston Gdns
Brentford TW8 . . . . . **109** B2
Chiswick W4 . . . . **133** C6
Boston Gr HA4 . . . . . . **39** A3
Boston Ho
24 Camberwell SE5 . . **139** A3
Earl's Ct SW5 . . . . . **255** D3
Lisson Gr NW1 . . . . . **237** C6
Boston Lo W13 . . . . . **109** C1
Boston Manor Ho
TW8 . . . . **109** B1
Boston Manor Rd
TW8 . . . . **131** B6
Boston Manor Sta
TW8 . . . . **109** A2
Boston Par W7 . . . . . **109** A2
Boston Park Rd
TW8 . . . . **109** C1
Boston Pl
NW1 . . . . . . **92** D3 **237** C5
Boston Rd
Burnt Oak HA8 . . . . . . **27** A3
Ealing W7 . . . . **109** A2
Newham E6 . . . . **100** A4
Thornton Heath CR0 . **204** C3
3 Walthamstow E17 . . **53** C3
Bostonthorpe Rd
W7 . . . . **108** C4
Boston Vale W7 . . . . **109** A2
Boston U 22 E14 . . . . **119** C4
Boswell Ct
Bloomsbury WC1 . . . **240** B4
Bromley BR2 . . . . **209** D4
5 Streatham SW16 . . **181** C5
Boswell Rd CR7 . . . . **205** A5
Boswell St
WC1 . . . . . . **94** A2 **240** B4
Boswood Ct TW4 . . . . **129** B2
Bosworth Cl E17 . . . . **35** B2
Bosworth Ho 4 W10 . . **91** A3
Bosworth Rd
Barnet EN5 . . . . **1** C2
Dagenham RM10 . . . . **81** C5
Kensal Town W10 . . . . **91** A3
Wood Green N11 . . . . . **31** D4
Botany Bay La BR7 . **189** A1
Botany Cl EN4 . . . . . . **2** C1
Boteley Cl E4 . . . . **20** C2
Botham Cl 6 HA8 . . . . **27** A3
Botha Rd E13 . . . . **99** C2
Bothwell Cl E16 . . . . . **98** D2
Bothwell St 8 W6 . . . **133** A4
Botolph Alley EC3 . . **253** A6
Botolph La EC3 . . . . **253** A6
Botsford Rd SW20 . . **179** A1
Bott's Mews W2 . . . . . **91** C1
Botwell Common Rd
UB3 . . . . **105** C6

Botwell Cres UB3 . . . . **83** C1
Botwell House RC Prim
Sch UB3 . . . . **105** D4
Botwell La UB3 . . . . . **105** C6
Boucher Cl TW11 . . . . **174** D5
Bouchier Ho N2 . . . . **30** B1
Bough Beech Ct EN3 . . **6** D6
Boughton Ave BR2 . . **208** D2
Boughton Ho
Borough The SE1 . . . **252** C2
Bromley BR1 . . . . . . **188** A3
Boughton Rd SE28 . . **123** C3
Boulcott St E1 . . . . . . **96** C1
Boulevard Dr NW9 . . . **27** D1
Boulevard The
Chelsea SW6 . . . . **266** C3
4 Upper Tooting
SW17 . . . . **159** A2
Boullen St SM1 . . . . . **218** A4
Boulogne Ho SE1 . . . **263** C6
Boulogne Rd CR0 . . . **205** A3
Boulter Cl BR1 . . . . . **210** C5
Boulter Ho 4 SE14 . . **140** C4
Boulters Ct HA0 . . . . . **65** A4
Boulton Ho TW8 . . . . **110** A1
Boulton Rd RM8 . . . . . **81** B6
Boultwood Rd E6 . . . **100** B1
Bounces La N9 . . . . . . **18** B2
Bounces Rd N9 . . . . . **18** C2
Boundaries Mans 3
SW12 . . . . **159** A3
Boundaries Rd
Feltham TW13 . . . . . . **150** C3
Upper Tooting SW12 . **159** A3
Boundary Ave E17 . . . . **53** B2
Boundary Bsns Ct
CR4 . . . . **202** B6
Boundary Cl
Barnet EN5 . . . . **1** B4
Ilford IG3 . . . . **79** C4
Kingston u T KT1 . . . **198** D6
Penge SE20 . . . . **184** A1
Southall UB2 . . . . . . **107** C1
Boundary Ct
3 Edmonton N18 . . . . **33** C3
9 New Southgate N11 **31** B6
Boundary Ho
Balham SW12 . . . . . . **159** B3
1 Camberwell SE5 . . **139** A5
3 Edgware HA8 . . . . . **44** B6
Isleworth TW1 . . . . . **153** B6
16 Notting Hill W11 . . **112** D5
Boundary La
Camberwell SE17 . . . **139** A6
Newham E13, E6 . . . . **99** D3
Boundary Pas E2 . . . **243** C6
Boundary Rd
Avery Hill DA15 . . . . **167** C6
Barking IG11 . . . . **101** A5
London N2 . . . . **30** B2
Newham E13 . . . . **99** D4
Pinner HA5 . . . . **40** D2
Ponders End N9 . . . . . **18** C5
Walthamstow E17 . . . . **53** C3
Boundary Road Est
NW8 . . . . . . **92** A6 **229** B6
Boundary Row SE1 . . **251** C2
Boundary St
E2 . . . . **95** D3 **243** C6
Boundary Way CR0 . **223** C6
Boundfield Rd SE6 . . **164** C2
Bounds Green Ct
N11 . . . . **31** D4
Bounds Green End
N11 . . . . **31** C4
Bounds Green Jun & Inf
Schs N11 . . . . **32** A3
Bounds Green Rd
London N11 . . . . **31** D4
Wood Green N22 . . . . . **32** A3
Bounds Green Sta
N11 . . . . **31** D3
Bourbon Ho 9 SE6 . . **186** B6
Bourchier St W1 . . . **249** C6
Bourdillon Ct 2
Stevenage **166** A2
Bourdon Pl W1 . . . . . **248** D6
Bourdon Rd SE20 . . . **184** C1
Bourdon St
W1 . . . . **115** B6 **248** D5

Bourke Cl
London SW4 . . . . 160 A5
Willesden NW10 . . . . . . 67 C2
Bourlet Cl W1 . . . . . . 239 A3
Bourn Ave
Hillingdon UB8 . . . . 82 C3
New Barnet EN4 . . . . . . 14 B6
West Green N15 . . . . . . 51 B5
Bournbrook Rd SE3, SE9 . . . . 143 D2
Bourne Ave
Hayes UB3 . . . . 105 B3
Palmers Green N14 . . . . 16 A2
Ruislip HA4 . . . . 62 C3
Bourne Cir UB3 . . . . . . 105 A3
Bourne Cl
Hinchley Wood KT7 . . 212 D6
Isleworth TW7 . . . . . . 130 C2
Bourne Ct
Chiswick W4 . . . . 133 A6
Ruislip HA4 . . . . 62 B3
Wanstead E11 . . . . 55 A4
Woodford IG8 . . . . 37 D1
Bourne Dr CR4 . . . . . . 180 B1
Bourne Gdns E4 . . . . . . 35 D6
Bourne Hill N13 . . . . . . 16 B2
Bourne Ho
4 Ashford TW15 . . . . 170 C5
3 Buckhurst Hill IG9 . . 21 D1
5 Clapham SW4 . . . . . 137 C1
1 Dollis Hill NW2 . . . . . 68 A5
Bourne Mans N13 . . . . . 32 C5
Bournemead Ave UB5 . . . . 84 A5
Bournemead Cl UB5 . . 84 A4
Bournemead Way UB5 . . . . 84 B5
Bourne Mews W1 . . . 238 B1
Bournemouth Cl SE15 . . . . 140 A3
Bournemouth Ct 6 SM1 . . . . 218 A3
Bournemouth Rd
London SE15 . . . . 140 A3
Merton SW19 . . . . 179 C2
Bourne Par DA5 . . . . 169 D4
Bourne Pl W4 . . . . 111 B1
Bourne Prim Sch HA4 . . . . 62 C2
Bourne Rd
Bexley DA5 . . . . 169 D5
Bromley BR2 . . . . 209 D5
Hornsey N8 . . . . 50 A3
Leyton E7, E11 . . . . 76 D5
Bournes Ho 4 N15 . . . 51 C3
Bourneside 5 N14 . . . . 15 D3
Bourneside Cres 6 N14 . . . . 15 D3
Bourneside Gdns SE6 . . . . 186 A5
Bourne St
Belgravia SW1 . . . . . 115 A2 258 A3
Croydon CR0 . . . . 220 D6
Bourne Terr W2 . . . . 91 D2
Bourne The N14 . . . . . . 16 A3
Bourne Vale BR2 . . . . 209 A2
Bournevale Rd SW16 . . . . 182 A6
Bourne View UB6 . . . . . 64 D3
Bourne Way
Cheam SM1 . . . . 217 B3
Coney Hall BR2, BR4 . 224 D6
West Ewell KT19 . . . . 215 A4
Bournewood Rd SE18 . . . . 146 A5
Bournville Rd SE6 . . . 163 C4
Bournwell Cl EN4 . . . . . . 2 D3
Bourton Cl UB3 . . . . . . 106 A5
Bousfield Prim Sch SW10 . . . . . . 114 A1 256 A2
Bousfield Rd SE14 . . 140 D3
Boutcher CE Prim Sch SE1 . . . . 117 D2 263 C4
Boutflower Rd SW11 . . . . 136 C1
Bouverie Ct 4 SW16 . . . . 182 A5
Bouverie Gdns HA3 . . . 43 D3
Bouverie Mews N16 . . 73 C6
Bouverie Pl W2 . . . . . 236 D2
Bouverie Rd
Harrow HA1 . . . . 42 A3
Stoke Newington N16 . . 73 C6
Bouverie St EC4 . . . . 94 C1 241 B1
Bouvier Rd EN3 . . . . 6 C5
Boveney Rd SE23 . . . 162 D4
Bovill Rd SE23 . . . . . . 162 D4
Bovingdon Ave HA9 . . . 66 C2
Bovingdon Cl 4 N19 . . 71 C6
Bovingdon La NW9 . . . 27 C2
Bovingdon Rd SW6 . . . . . . 135 D4 265 D1
Bovril Ho EN1 . . . . 5 C2
BOW 97 B5
Bowater Cl
Clapham Pk SW2 . . . . 160 A5
Kingsbury NW9 . . . . 45 B4
Bowater Gdns TW16 . 172 C2
Bowater Ho EC1 . . . . 242 B5
Bowater Pl SE3 . . . . . . 143 B5
Bowater Rd
Greenwich SE18 . . . . 121 D3
Wembley HA9 . . . . 66 D5
Bow Brook The 20 E2 . . . . 96 D5
Bow Church Sta E3 . . . 97 C4
BOW COMMON 97 D2
Bow Common La E3 . . 97 B3
Bowden Cl TW14 . . . . . 149 C3
Bowden Ct HA4 . . . . 62 C3
Bowden Ho 29 E3 . . . . . 97 D4
Bowden St SE11 . . . . 116 C1 261 B1
Bowditch SE8 . . . . 119 B1
Bowdon Rd E17 . . . . 53 C2
Bowen Ct 2 N5 . . . . . . 72 D4
Bowen Dr SE21 . . . . . . 161 C1
Bowen Rd HA1 . . . . 42 A2
Bowen St E14 . . . . 97 D1
Bower Ave SE3 . . . . . . 142 C5
Bower Cl UB5 . . . . 84 C5
Bowerdean St SW6 . 135 D3
Bower Ho SE14 . . . . . 140 D4
Bowerman Ave SE14 . . . . 141 A6
Bowerman Ct 1 N19 . . 71 D6
Bowers Ho 5 IG11 . . . 78 D1
Bower St E1 . . . . 96 D1
Bowers Wlk 1 E6 . . . . 100 B1
Bowery Ct 16 RM10 . . . 81 D2
Bowes Cl DA15 . . . . . . 168 B5
Bowes Ho N13 . . . . 32 B5
Bowes-Lyon Hall 13 E16 . . . . 121 A5
Bowes Lyon Ho 2 TW10 . . . . 153 C1
BOWES PARK 32 A4
Bowes Park Sta N22 . . 32 A3
Bowes Prim Sch N11 . . 31 D5
Bowes Rd Acton W3 . . 111 C6
Dagenham RM8 . . . . 80 C4
New Southgate N11 . . . . 31 C5
Walton-on-T KT12 . . . . 194 B1
Bowes Rd (North Circular Rd) N13 . . . . 32 A5
Bowfell Rd W6 . . . . 134 C6
Bowford Ave DA7 . . . . 147 A4
Bowhill Cl SW9 . . . . . . 138 C5
Bow Ho 1 E3 . . . . 97 C4
Bowie Cl SW4 . . . . . . 159 D4
Bow La
Barbican EC2, EC4 . . . . 95 A1 242 B1
Finchley N12 . . . . 30 A3
Bowland Ho N4 . . . . 51 A2
Bowland Rd
London SW4 . . . . 137 D1
Woodford IG8 . . . . 37 C4
Bowland Yd SW1 . . . . 247 D1
Bowl Ct EC2 . . . . 243 B5
Bowles Ct
Finchley N12 . . . . 30 C3
Harrow HA3 . . . . 43 A3
Bowles Rd 1 SE1 . . . . 140 A6
Bowley Cl SE19 . . . . . 183 D4
Bowley Ho 6 SE16 . . . 118 A3
Bowley La SE19 . . . . . 183 D5
Bowling Cl UB10 . . . . . . 82 B6
Bowling Green Cl SW19 . . . . 156 B4
Bowling Green Ct HA9 . . . . 66 B6
Bowling Green Ho SW10 . . . . 266 C4
Bowling Green La EC1 . . . . 94 C3 241 B6
Bowling Green Pl SE1 . . . . 252 C2
Bowling Green Row 1 SE18 . . . . 122 B2
Bowling Green St SE11 . . . . 138 C6
Bowling Green Wlk N1 . . . . 95 C4
Bowls Cl HA7 . . . . 25 B5
Bowman Ave E16 . . . 120 D6
Bowman Homes W5 . . . . 109 D4
Bowman Mews
St George in t East E1 . . . . 118 A6
Wandsworth SW18 . . . 157 B3
Bowmans Cl W13 . . . . 109 B5
Bowmans Lea SE23 . 162 C4
Bowman's Meadow SM6 . . . . 219 B5
Bowman's Mews N7 . . 72 A5
Bowman's Pl N7 . . . . . . 72 A5
Bowman Trad Est NW9 . . . . 44 C5
Bowmar Lo 13 EN5 . . . . . 1 D1
Bowmead SE9 . . . . 166 B2
Bowmore Wlk NW1 . . . 71 D1
Bowness Cl 5 E8 . . . . . 73 D2
Bowness Cres KT2, SW15 . . . . 177 C5
Bowness Dr TW4 . . . . 129 A1
Bowness Ho SE15 . . . . 140 C5
Bowness Rd
Catford SE6 . . . . 163 D4
Erith DA7 . . . . 147 D3
Bowood Rd
Clapham SW11 . . . . . 159 A6
Enfield EN3 . . . . 6 D3
Bow Rd E3 . . . . 97 C4
Bowring Gn WD19 . . . . 22 C5
Bow Road Sta E3 . . . . . 97 C4
Bowrons Ave HA0 . . . . . 65 D1
Bowry Ho 14 E14 . . . . . 97 B2
Bow Sec Sch 19 E3 . . . 97 C4
Bowsley Ct TW13 . . . . 150 A2
Bowsprit Point 1 E14 . . . . 119 C3
Bow St
St Giles WC2 . . 94 A1 240 B1
Stratford E15 . . . . 76 C3
Bowstead Ct SW11 . . 266 D1
Bow Triangle Bsns Ctr 17 E3 . . . . 97 C3
Bowyer Cl E6 . . . . 100 B2
Bowyer Ho
Mitcham CR4 . . . . 202 C6
27 Shoreditch N1 . . . . . 95 C6
Wandsworth SW18 . . 157 D5
Bowyer Pl SE5 . . . . . . 139 A5
Bowyer St 15 SE5 . . . 139 A5
Boxall Rd SE21 . . . . . 161 C5
Box Cnr TW2 . . . . 152 C2
Boxelder Cl HA8 . . . . . . 27 A5
Boxgrove Prim Sch SE2 . . . . 124 C3
Boxgrove Rd SE2 . . . 124 C3
Box La IG11 . . . . 102 C5
Boxley Ho 3 E5 . . . . . . 74 B3
Boxley Rd SM4 . . . . . . 202 A5
Boxley St E16 . . . . 121 B5
Boxmoor Ho
16 Hackney E2 . . . . 96 A6
9 Shepherd's Bush W11 . . . . 112 D5
Boxmoor Rd HA3 . . . . . 43 B5
Boxoll Rd RM9 . . . . 81 B5
Boxshall Ho 7 SE18 . 144 D6
Box Tree Ho SE8 . . . . 119 A1
Boxtree La HA3 . . . . 24 B3
Boxtree Rd HA3 . . . . . . 24 B3
Boxwood Cl UB7 . . . . . 104 B4
Boxworth Cl N12 . . . . . . 30 B5
Boxworth Gr N1 . . . . 94 B6 233 D6
Boyard Rd SE18 . . . . . 122 D1
Boyce Ho
Streatham SW16 . . . . 181 C5
1 West Kilburn W10 . . . 91 B4
Boyce Way E13 . . . . 99 A3
Boycroft Ave NW9 . . . . 45 A3
Boyd Ave UB1 . . . . 107 B5
Boyd Cl KT2 . . . . 176 C3
Boyd Ct SW15 . . . . 156 C5
Boydell Ct NW8 . . . . . . 70 B1
Boyden Ho 8 E17 . . . . . 54 A6
Boyd Rd SW19 . . . . 180 B4
Boyd St E1 . . . . 96 A1
Boyfield St SE1 . . . . 116 D4 251 D1
Boyland Rd BR1 . . . . 186 D5
Boyle Ave HA7 . . . . 25 A4
Boyle Cl UB10 . . . . 82 B5
Boyle Farm Rd KT7 . . 197 A3
Boyle Ho
13 Belvedere DA17 . . 125 C3
Wembley HA9 . . . . 66 D5
Boyle St W1 . . . . 249 A6
Boyne Ave NW4 . . . . 46 D5
Boyne Ct NW10 . . . . 68 A1
Boyne Ho 10 E5 . . . . 74 B6
Boyne Rd
Dagenham RM10 . . . . . . 81 C5
Lewisham SE13 . . . . . . 142 B2
Boyne Terr Mews W11 . . . . 113 B5 244 C4
Boyson Rd 10 SE17 . . . 139 B6
Boyton Cl London N8 . . . 50 A6
Stepney E1 . . . . 96 D3
Boyton Ho
Kennington SE11 . . . . 261 A1
St John's Wood NW8 . 229 D4
Boyton Rd N8 . . . . 50 A6
Brabant Ct EC3 . . . . . 253 A6
Brabant Rd N22 . . . . 32 B1
Brabazon Ave SM6 . . . 220 A1
Brabazon Rd
Heston TW5 . . . . 128 D5
Northolt UB5 . . . . 85 C5
Brabazon St E14 . . . . . . 97 D2
Brabner Ho 3 E2 . . . . . 96 A4
Brabourne Cl 7 SE19 . . . . 183 C5
Brabourne Cres DA7 147 B6
Brabourne Hts NW7 . . . 11 C1
Brabourne Rise BR3 . 208 B4
Brabourn Gr SE15 . . . 140 C3
Brabrook Ct SM6 . . . . 219 B3
Brabstone Ho 2 UB6 . 86 D5
Bracer Ho 1 N1 . . . . . . 95 C5
Bracewell Ave UB6 . . . . 65 A2
Bracewell Rd W10 . . . . 90 C2
Bracewood Gdns CR0 . . . . 221 D5
Bracey Mews 1 N4 . . . . 72 A6
Bracey St N4 . . . . 72 A6
Bracken Ave
Balham SW12 . . . . 159 A4
Croydon CR0 . . . . 223 C5
Brackenbridge Dr HA4 . . . . 62 D5
Brackenbury N4 . . . . . . 50 B1
Brackenbury Gdns W6 . . . . 112 B3
Brackenbury Prim Sch 4 W6 . . . . 112 B3
Brackenbury Rd
East Finchley N2 . . . . . . 48 A6
Hammersmith W6 . . . . 112 B3
Bracken Cl
Ashford TW16 . . . . . . 171 D4
Newham E6 . . . . 100 B2
Twickenham TW4 . . . . 151 C4
Brackendale
Kingston u T KT1 . . . . 176 D1
Southgate N21 . . . . 16 B2
Brackendale Cl TW5 . . . . 129 D4
Brackendale Ct 2 BR3 . . . . 185 C3
Bracken End TW7 . . . . 152 B6
Brackenfield Cl E5 . . . . 74 B5
Bracken Gdns SW13 . 134 A3
Brackenhill HA4 . . . . . . 63 A4
Bracken Hill Cl 5 BR1 . . . . 186 D2
Bracken Hill La BR1 . 186 D2
Bracken Ho 15 E3 . . . . . 97 C2
Bracken Mews
Chingford E4 . . . . 20 A3
Romford RM7 . . . . 59 D3
Brackens BR3 . . . . 185 C3
Brackens The EN1 . . . . 17 C4
Bracken The E4 . . . . 20 A2
Brackenwood TW16 . 172 A2
Brackenwood Lo EN5 . . 1 C1
Brackley Ave SE15 . . . 140 C2
Brackley Cl SM6 . . . . . 220 A1
Brackley Ct NW8 . . . . 236 D6
Brackley Rd
Beckenham BR3 . . . . . 185 C3
Chiswick W4 . . . . 111 C1
Brackley Sq IG8 . . . . 37 D3
Brackley St EC1 . . . . . 242 B4
Brackley Terr 6 W4 . . . . 111 C1
Bracklyn Ct N1 . . . . . 235 C4
Bracklyn St N1 . . . . . 235 C4
Bracknell Cl N22 . . . . . . 32 C2
Bracknell Gate NW3 . . 69 D3
Bracknell Gdns NW3 . . 69 D4
Bracknell Way NW3 . . . 69 D4
Bracondale KT10 . . . . 212 A3
Bracondale Rd SE2 . . 124 A2
Braconhyrst HA1 . . . . . 42 C2
Bradbeer Ho 24 E2 . . . . 96 C4
Bradbourne Ct 11 SM2 . . . . 217 D2
Bradbourne Rd DA5 . . 169 C4
Bradbourne St SW6 . . 135 C3
Bradbury Cl UB2 . . . . . 107 B2
Bradbury Ct
4 Barnet EN5 . . . . 1 D1
2 Greenwich SE3 . . . . 143 A5
Merton SW20 . . . . 178 C1
Bradbury Ho E1 . . . . . 243 D2
Bradbury St 28 N16 . . . 73 C3
Bradby Ho NW8 . . . . 91 D5
Braddock Cl TW7 . . . . 130 D3
Braddon Rd TW9 . . . . . 132 B2
Braddyll St SE10 . . . . 120 C1
Bradenham 11 SE17 . . 139 B6
Bradenham Ave DA16 . . . . 146 A1
Bradenham Cl SE17 . . 139 B6
Bradenham Rd
Harrow HA3 . . . . 43 B5
Hayes UB4 . . . . 83 C4
Braden St W9 . . . . 91 D3
Bradfield Ct 14 NW1 . . 71 B1
Bradfield Dr IG11 . . . . . 80 A3
Bradfield Ho 15 SW8 . . . . 137 D3
Bradfield Rd
Newham E16 . . . . 121 B4
Ruislip HA4 . . . . 63 A3
Bradford Cl
Bromley BR2 . . . . 210 B1
Forest Hill SE26 . . . . . 184 B6
Tottenham N17 . . . . 33 D4
Bradford Dr KT19 . . . . 215 D2
Bradford Ho 4 W14 . . . . 112 D3
Bradford Rd
Acton W3 . . . . 111 C4
Ilford IG1 . . . . 57 C1
Bradgate Rd SE6 . . . . 163 D5
Brading Cres E11 . . . . . 77 B6
Brading Rd
Streatham SW2 . . . . . . 160 B4
Thornton Heath CR0 . . 204 B3
Brading Terr W12 . . . . 112 A3
Bradiston Rd W9 . . . . . . 91 B4
Bradley Cl N7 . . . . 72 B2
Bradley Ct CR0 . . . . . . 220 C4
Bradley Gdns W13 . . . . 87 B1
Bradley Ho
Bermondsey SE16 . . . . 118 B2
1 Bromley E3 . . . . 97 D4
Twickenham TW1 . . . . 152 D3
Woodford IG8 . . . . 37 A3
Bradley Mews SW12 . 158 D3
Bradley Rd Enfield EN3 . . 7 A6
Upper Norwood SE19 . 183 A4
Wood Green N22 . . . . . . 32 B1
Bradley's Cl N1 . . . . . 234 B4
Bradley Stone Rd E6 . . . . 100 B2
Bradlord Ho SE21 . . . . 161 C1
Bradman Row 7 HA8 . . . . 27 A3
Bradmead SW8 . . . . 137 C5 269 A3
Bradmore Ct 2 EN3 . . . 7 A2
Bradmore Park Rd W6 . . . . 112 B2
Bradon 24 NW9 . . . . 27 D1
Bradshaw Cl SW19 . . . 179 C4
Bradshaw Dr NW7 . . . . 28 D3
Bradshawe Waye UB8 . . . . 82 B2
Bradshaws Cl SE25 . . 206 A6
Bradsole Ho 13 BR3 . . 185 C3
Brad St SE1 . . . 116 C5 251 B3
Bradstock Ho E9 . . . . . . 75 A1
Bradstock Rd
Homerton E9 . . . . 74 D2
Stoneleigh KT17 . . . . . 216 B3
Bradwell Ave RM10 . . . 81 C6
Bradwell Cl E18 . . . . . . 54 D5

Bradwell Ho
8 Kilburn NW6 . . . . 91 D6
9 Walthamstow E17 . . . 53 D6
Bradwell Mews 5
N18 . . . . 34 A6
Bradwell St 24 E1 . . . . . 96 D4
Brady Ct RM8 . . . . 58 D1
Brady Dr BR1 . . . . 210 C6
Brady Ho
London SW4 . . . . 159 D6
South Lambeth SW8 . 269 B2
Bradymead E6 . . . . 100 D1
Brady St E1 . . . . 96 B3
Braeburn Ct 1 EN4 . . . . 2 C1
Brae Ct
2 Kingston u T
KT2 . . . . 176 C2
South Norwood SE25 . 183 C2
Braefoot Ct SW15 . . . 156 D6
Braemar SW15 . . . . . 156 D5
Braemar Ave
Thornton Heath
CR7 . . . . 204 D6
Welsh Harp NW10 . . . . . 67 B6
Wembley HA0 . . . . 66 A1
Wimbledon SW18,
SW19 . . . . 157 C2
Wood Green N22 . . . . . . 32 A2
Braemar Ct
4 Brentford TW8 . . . 131 D6
5 Catford SE6 . . . . . 164 D3
Braemar Gdns
Hendon NW9 . . . . 27 B2
Longlands DA15 . . . . . . 167 B1
West Wickham BR4 . . 208 A1
Braemar Ho
Richmond TW11 . . . . . . 175 B5
St John's Wood W9 . . 229 A1
Braemar Mans W8 . . 255 D5
Braemar Rd
Brentford TW8 . . . . . . 131 D6
Newham E13 . . . . 98 D3
North Cheam KT4 . . . . . . 216 B5
South Tottenham N15 . . . 51 C4
Braemore Ct EN4 . . . . 3 A1
Braeside BR3 . . . . 185 D5
Braeside Ave SW19 . . 179 A2
Braeside Cl HA5 . . . . . . 23 C3
Braeside Jun Sch
IG9 . . . . 21 C2
Braeside Rd SW16 . . . 181 C3
Braeside Senior Sch
IG9 . . . . 21 B3
Braes St N1 . . . . 72 D1
Braesyde Cl DA17 . . . . 125 B2
Brafferton Rd CR0 . . . 221 A4
Braganza St
SE17 . . . . 116 D1 261 C1
Bragg Cl RM8 . . . . 80 B2
Bragg Rd TW11 . . . . . 174 D4
Braham Ho SE11 . . . . . 260 D1
Braham St E1 . . . . 243 D2
Brahma Kumaris World
Spiritual Univ NW10 68 A1
Braid Ave W3 . . . . 89 C1
Braid Cl TW13 . . . . 151 B2
Braid Ho SE10 . . . . 142 A4
Braidwood Ho 2
CR7 . . . . 204 D5
Braidwood Rd SE6 . . . 164 B3
Braidwood St
SE1 . . . . 117 C5 253 A3
Braikenridge Ho N21 . . 17 B5
Brailsford Cl SW19 . . . 180 C3
Brailsford Rd SW2 . . . 160 C5
Braintcroft Prim Sch
NW2 . . . . 67 D5
Brainton Ave TW14 . . . 150 C4
Braintree Ave IG4 . . . . . 56 A5
Braintree Ho 6 E1 . . . . 96 C3
Braintree Ind Est HA4 62 B4
Braintree Rd
Dagenham RM10 . . . . . . 81 C5
Ruislip HA4 . . . . 62 B4
Braintree St E2 . . . . 96 C4
Braithwaite Ave RM7 . . 59 C2
Braithwaite Gdns
HA7 . . . . 25 C2
Braithwaite Ho EC1 . 242 C6
Braithwaite Rd EN3 . . . . 7 B2
Braithwaite Twr W2 . 236 C4
Brake Shear Ho 1
EN5 . . . . 1 B2
Bramah Gn SW9 . . . . . 138 C4
Bramah Mus of Tea &
Coffee The★ SE1 . . 252 B3
Bramalea Cl N6 . . . . 49 A3
Bramall Cl E15 . . . . 76 D3
Bramall Ct N7 . . . . 72 B2
Bramber WC1 . . . . . . 233 A1
Bramber Ct TW8 . . . . . 110 A2
Bramber Ho 9 KT2 . . 176 A2
Bramber Rd
Colney Hatch N12 . . . . . 30 C5
Fulham W14 . . 135 B6 264 C6
Bramble Acres Cl
SM2 . . . . 217 C1
Bramblebury Rd
SE18 . . . . 123 A1
Bramble Cl
Beckenham BR3 . . . . . 208 A4
Croydon CR0 . . . . 223 D4
Hillingdon UB8 . . . . 82 B1
South Tottenham N15 . . . 52 A5
Stanmore HA7 . . . . 25 D3
Upper Halliford TW17 . 193 B6
Brambledown 8 N4 . . 50 A2
Brambledown Cl BR2,
BR4 . . . . 208 C4
Brambledown Rd
South Croydon CR2 . . 221 C1
Wallington SM5, SM6 . . 219 B1
Bramble Gdns W12 . 111 D6
Bramble Ho 16 E3 . . . . 97 C2
Bramble La TW12 . . . . 173 B4
Brambles Cl TW7,
TW8 . . . . 131 B5
Brambles Farm Dr
UB10 . . . . 82 C4
Brambles The
West Drayton UB7 . . . 104 A2
8 Wimbledon SW19 . . 179 B5
Bramblewood Cl
SM5 . . . . 202 C1
Brambling Ct
25 Deptford SE8 . . . . . 141 B6
South Norwood SE25 . 205 D5
Bramblings The E4 . . . . 36 B6
Bramcote Ave CR4 . . . 202 D5
Bramcote Ct CR4 . . . 202 D5
Bramcote Gr SE16 . . . 118 C1
Bramcote Rd SW15 . . 134 B1
Bramdean Cres
SE12 . . . . 165 A3
Bramdean Gdns
SE12 . . . . 165 A3
Bramerton NW6 . . . . . . 68 D1
Bramerton Rd BR3 . . . 207 B6
Bramerton St
SW3 . . . . 136 C6 267 A6
Bramfield Ct N4 . . . . . . 73 A6
Bramfield Rd SW11 . 158 D6
Bramford Ct N14 . . . . . . 15 D2
Bramford Rd SW18 . . . 136 A1
Bramham Gdns
Chessington KT9 . . . . 213 D4
South Kensington
SW5 . . . . . . 113 D1 255 D2
Bramham Ho SE22 . . . 139 C1
Bramhope La SE7 . . . . 143 B6
Bramlands Cl SW11 . . 136 C2
Bramley Ave TW17 . . . 193 C6
Bramley Cl
Croydon CR2 . . . . 221 A3
East Barnet N14 . . . . 15 B6
Edgware NW7 . . . . 11 C1
Hayes UB3 . . . . 106 A6
Higham Hill E17 . . . . 35 A1
Orpington BR6 . . . . 210 D1
Pinner HA5 . . . . 39 D6
Twickenham TW2 . . . . 152 A5
Woodford IG8 . . . . 37 C3
Bramley Cres
Ilford IG2 . . . . 56 C3
Nine Elms
SW8 . . . . . 137 D5 269 D4
Bramley Ct
2 Barnet EN4 . . . . 2 C1
7 Chingford E4 . . . . 20 A3
Dollis Hill NW2 . . . . 68 B5
Feltham TW14 . . . . . . 149 C5
Hither Green SE13 . . . . 164 B6
Mitcham CR4 . . . . 180 B1
Southall UB1 . . . . 108 A6
Wallington SM6 . . . . . 219 C3
Welling DA16 . . . . 146 B4
Bramley Gdns WD19 . . 22 C5
Bramley Hill CR2 . . . . . 221 A4
Bramley Ho
Hounslow TW3 . . . . 129 B1
Ilford IG2 . . . . 56 C3
1 Kingston u T KT2 . . 176 D3
19 North Kensington
W10 . . . . 90 D1
Roehampton SW15 . . 155 D5
Bramley House Ct EN2 . 5 B6
Bramleyhyrst CR2 . . . 221 A3
Bramley Lo HA0 . . . . . . 65 D4
Bramley Rd
Ealing W5 . . . . 109 C3
North Kensington W10 . 90 D1
Southgate N14 . . . . 15 C6
Sutton SM1 . . . . 218 B3
Bramley Way
Hounslow TW4 . . . . . . 151 B6
West Wickham BR4 . . 223 D6
Brampton WC1 . . . . . . 240 C3
Brampton Cl 14 E5 . . . . 74 B6
Brampton Coll NW4 . . . 46 C5
Brampton Ct NW4 . . . . 46 B5
Brampton Gr
Harrow HA3 . . . . 43 B5
Hendon NW4 . . . . 46 C5
Wembley HA9 . . . . 44 C1
Brampton La 6 NW4 . 46 C5
Brampton Lo DA7 . . . 146 D5
Brampton Manor Sch
E6 . . . . 99 D3
Brampton Park Rd
N22 . . . . 50 C6
Brampton Prim Sch
Bexley DA7 . . . . 146 D3
Newham E6 . . . . 100 A4
Brampton Rd
Bexleyheath DA7 . . . . 147 A4
Croydon CR0 . . . . 205 D3
Harringay N15 . . . . 51 A4
Hillingdon UB10 . . . . 82 D5
Newham E6 . . . . 99 D4
Queensbury NW9 . . . . . 44 C5
Bramshaw Gdns
WD19 . . . . 22 D5
Bramshaw Rd E9 . . . . . 74 D2
Bramshaw Rise KT3 . . 199 C3
Bramshill Gdns NW5 . . 71 B5
Bramshill Rd NW10 . . . 89 D5
Bramshot Ave SE7 . . . 143 B6
Bramshott Ct 3
KT6 . . . . 198 A3
Bramshurst NW8 . . . . . 91 D6
Bramston Rd
Harlesden NW10 . . . . . . 90 A5
Wandsworth SW17 . . 158 A1
Bramwell Cl TW16 . . . 172 D1
Bramwell Ho
Borough The SE1 . . . . 262 B5
Chelsea SW1 . . . . 269 A6
Bramwell Mews N1 . 233 D6
Brancaster Dr NW7 . . . 28 A3
Brancaster Ho
22 Globe Town E1 . . . . . 96 D4
Islington N5 . . . . 72 D3
Brancaster Rd
Ilford E12 . . . . 78 B4
Newbury Pk IG2 . . . . 57 C3
Streatham SW16 . . . . 160 A1
Brancepeth Gdns IG9 21 A2
Branch Hill NW3 . . . . . . 70 A5
Branch Ho 13 SM1 . . . 218 A4
Branch Pl N1 . . 95 B6 235 D6
Branch Rd E14 . . . . 119 A6
Branch St SE15 . . . . . 139 C5
Brancker Rd HA3 . . . . . 43 D6
Brancroft Way EN3 . . . . 7 B4
Brandan Ho 11 HA1 . . . 42 D4
Brand Cl N4 . . . . 50 D1
Branden Lo 13 W4 . . . 111 A1
Brandlehow Prim Sch
SW15 . . . . 135 B1
Brandlehow Rd
SW15 . . . . 135 B1
Brandon Ho BR3 . . . . 185 D5
Brandon Mews
Barbican EC2 . . . . 242 C4
Walworth SE17 . . . . . 262 B3
Brandon Pl N8 . . . . 50 B5
Brandon Rd
Barnsbury N7 . . . . 72 A1
Southall UB2 . . . . 107 B1
Sutton SM1 . . . . 217 D4
Walthamstow E17 . . . . . 54 A6
Brandon St
SE17 . . . . 117 A2 262 B3
Brandram Rd SE13 . . . 142 C1
Brandrams Wharf
SE16 . . . . 118 C4
Brandreth Ct HA1 . . . . . 42 D3
Brandreth Rd
Newham E6 . . . . 100 B1
Upper Tooting SW17 . . 159 B2
Brandries The SM6 . . 219 D5
Brand St SE10 . . . . 142 A5
Brandville Gdns IG6 . . 56 D5
Brandville Rd UB7 . . . 104 A4
Brandy Way SM2 . . . . . 217 C1
Brangbourne Rd
BR1 . . . . 186 A5
Brangton Rd SE11 . . 260 D1
Brangwyn Cres
SW19 . . . . 180 B1
Brangwyn Ct W14 . . . 254 A5
Branham Ho 1
SE18 . . . . 122 D1
Branksea St
SW6 . . . . 135 A5 264 A3
Branksome Ave N18 . . 33 D5
Branksome Cl
Teddington TW11 . . . . . 174 B6
Walton-on-T KT12 . . . . 194 D1
Branksome Ct 6 N2 . . 48 A6
Branksome Ho SW8 . 270 C4
Branksome Rd
London SW2 . . . . 160 A6
Merton SW19 . . . . 179 C2
Branksome Way
Harrow HA3 . . . . 44 B3
Kingston u T KT3 . . . . . 177 B2
Bransby Ct 4 N16 . . . . 73 C4
Bransby Rd KT9 . . . . . 214 A2
Branscombe NW1 . . 232 B5
Branscombe Ct BR2 . 208 C4
Branscombe Gdns
N21 . . . . 16 C4
Branscombe St
SE13 . . . . 141 D2
Bransdale Cl NW6 . . . . 91 C6
Bransgrove Rd HA8 . . . 26 B3
Branston Cres BR5 . . . 211 B1
Branstone Ct 9
TW9 . . . . 132 B4
Branstone Rd TW9 . . . 132 B4
Branston Ho N7 . . . . . . 72 C3
Brants Wlk W7 . . . . 86 C3
Brantwood Ave
Erith DA8 . . . . 147 D5
Isleworth TW7 . . . . . . 131 A1
Brantwood Cl E17 . . . . 53 D6
Brantwood Gdns
Enfield EN2 . . . . 16 A6
Redbridge IG4 . . . . 56 A5
Brantwood Ho 9
SE5 . . . . 139 A5
Brantwood Rd
Erith DA7 . . . . 147 D3
Herne Hill SE24 . . . . . 161 A6
Tottenham N17 . . . . 34 A4
Brasenose Dr SW13 . 134 C6
Brasher Cl UB6 . . . . 64 B3
Brashley Road Cvn Site
NW10 . . . . 89 C4
Brassett Point 3 E15 . 98 C6
Brassey Cl TW14 . . . . . 150 A3
Brassey Ho
1 Millwall E14 . . . . . . 119 D2
Walton-on-T KT12 . . . . 194 A1
Brassey Rd NW6 . . . . . 69 B2
Brassey Sq SW11 . . . . 137 A2
Brassie Ave W3 . . . . 89 C1
Brass Talley Alley 31
SE16 . . . . 118 D4
Brasted Cl
Bexley DA6 . . . . 168 D6
Forest Hill SE26 . . . . . 184 C6
Brasted Lo 11 BR3 . . . 185 C3
Brathay NW1 . . . . 232 B3
Brathway Rd SW18 . . . 157 C4
Bratley St 11 E1 . . . . . . 96 A3
Bratten Ct CR0 . . . . . . 205 B3
Braund Ave UB6 . . . . . . 85 D3
Braundton Ave
DA15 . . . . 167 D3
Braunston Dr UB4 . . . . 85 A3
Braunston Ho TW8 . . . 131 C6
Bravington Cl TW17 . . 192 B4
Bravington Pl W9 . . . . . 91 B3
Bravington Rd W9 . . . . 91 B4
Brawne Ho 12 SE17 . . 138 D6
Braxfield Rd SE4 . . . . 141 B1
Braxted Pk SW16 . . . . 182 B4
Bray NW3 . . . . 70 C1
Brayard's Rd SE15 . . . 140 B3
Braybourne Dr TW7 . 130 D5
Braybrooke Gdns
SE19 . . . . 183 C3
Braybrook St W12 . . . . 89 D1
Brayburne Ave SW4 . 137 C3
Braycourt Ave KT12 . . 194 C2
Bray Cres SE16 . . . . . 118 D4
Bray Ct
Chessington KT9 . . . . 214 B3
Streatham SW16 . . . . 182 A5
Braydon Rd N16 . . . . . . 52 A1
Bray Dr E16 . . . . 120 D6
Brayfield Terr N1 . . . . . 72 C1
Brayford Sq 12 E1 . . . . 96 C1
Bray Pl SW3 . 114 D2 257 C3
Bray Rd NW7 . . . . 28 D4
Brayton Gdns EN2 . . . . . 3 D1
Braywick Ct 9 KT2 . . 176 C3
Braywood Rd SE9 . . . . 145 B1
Brazier Cres UB5 . . . . . 85 B3
Brazil Cl CR0 . . . . 204 A2
Breach La RM9 . . . . . . 103 C4
Bread St EC2, EC4 . . . 242 B1
Breakspeare SE21 . . . 161 D1
Breakspear Jun & Inf
Schs UB10 . . . . 60 C6
Breakspear Rd HA4,
UB9 . . . . 38 D3
Breakspear Road N
UB9 . . . . 38 B5
Breakspear Road S UB9,
UB10 . . . . 38 C1
Breakspears Dr BR5 . 190 A2
Breakspears Mews
SE4 . . . . 141 C3
Breakspears Rd SE4 . 141 C2
Breakwell Ct 16 W10 . . 91 A3
Bream Cl N17 . . . . 52 B5
Bream Gdns E6 . . . . . 100 C4
Breamore Cl SW15 . . . 156 A3
Breamore Ct IG3 . . . . . 80 A6
Breamore Ho 21
SE15 . . . . 140 A5
Breamore Rd IG3 . . . . . 79 D6
Bream's Bldgs
EC4 . . . . 94 C1 241 A2
Bream St E3 . . . . 75 C1
Breamwater Gdns
TW10 . . . . 153 B1
Brearley Cl
Burnt Oak HA8 . . . . 27 A3
Uxbridge UB8 . . . . 60 A2
Breaside Prep Sch
BR1 . . . . 187 D2
Breasley Cl SW15 . . . 134 B1
Brechin Pl
SW7 . . . . 114 A2 256 B3
Brecknock Prim Sch 18
N7 . . . . 71 D2
Brecknock Rd N19 . . . . 71 D3
Breckonmead BR1 . . . 187 C1
Brecon Cl
Mitcham CR4 . . . . 204 A6
North Cheam KT4 . . . . 216 C6
Brecon Ct
7 Eltham SE9 . . . . . . 166 C5
Whetstone N12 . . . . 14 A1
Brecon Gn NW9 . . . . 45 C3
Brecon Ho
Stamford Hill N16 . . . . . 51 D1
Wandsworth SW18 . . . 157 C4
Brecon Rd Enfield EN3 . . 6 C1
Fulham W6 . . . 135 A6 264 B5
Brede Cl E6 . . . . 100 C4
Bredel Ho 1 E14 . . . . . 97 C2
Bredgar SE13 . . . . 163 D6
Bredgar Rd N19 . . . . . . 71 C6
Bredhurst Cl SE20 . . . 184 C4
Bredinghurst SE22 . . . 162 A4
Bredinghurst Sch
SE15 . . . . 140 D1
Bredin Ho SW10 . . . . 265 D4
Bredo Ho IG11 . . . . . . 102 B4
Bredon Ct HA8 . . . . 26 B6
Bredon Rd CR0 . . . . . 205 D2
Breer St SW6 . . . . 135 D2
Breezer's Ct 22 E1 . . . 118 A6
Breezer's Hill E1 . . . . . 118 A6
Brehon Ho NW1 . . . . 232 A5
Bremans Row 1
SW18 . . . . 158 A2
Brember Rd HA2 . . . . . . 64 A6
Bremer Mews E17 . . . . . 53 D5
Bremner Rd SW7 . . . 256 B6

Brenchley Cl
Chislehurst BR7 ..... 188 C2
Hayes BR2 .... 208 D3
Brenchley Gdns SE15, SE22, SE23 .... 162 D5
Brenchley Rd BR5 ... 189 D1
Bren Ct 27 EN3 .... 7 C6
Brenda Rd SW17 .... 158 D2
Brende Gdns KT8 ... 195 D5
Brendon Ave NW10 ... 67 C4
Brendon Cl
Esher KT10 .... 212 A2
Harlington UB7 ..... 127 A5
Brendon Ct
3 London N20 .... 14 C2
Southall UB2 .... 107 D2
Brendon Dr KT10 ... 212 A2
Brendon Gdns
Harrow HA2 .... 63 D4
Ilford IG2 .... 57 C4
Brendon Gr N2 .... 30 A1
Brendon Ho
Marylebone W1 ..... 238 A4
Sutton SM2 .... 218 A2
Brendon Rd
Dagenham RM8 .... 59 C1
New Eltham SE9 ...... 167 B2
Brendon St
W1 .... 92 C1 237 B2
Brendon Villas N21 .... 17 A3
Brendon Way EN1 ...... 17 C4
Brenley Cl CR4 .... 203 A6
Brenley Gdns SE9 ... 143 D1
Brenley Ho SE1 ..... 252 C2
Brennands Ct 14 N19 .. 71 C5
Brent Adult Comm Education Service Coll 9 NW10 .... 89 B6
Brent Cl DA5 .... 169 A3
Brentcot Cl W13 ...... 87 B3
Brent Cres NW10 ..... 88 B5
Brent Cross Flyover NW2, NW4 .... 46 D2
Brent Cross Gdns
NW4 .... 46 D3
Brent Cross Interchange
NW2, NW4 .... 46 D2
Brent Cross Sh Ctr
NW4 .... 46 C2
Brent Cross Sta
NW11 .... 46 D2
Brent Ct
5 Acton W12 ...... 111 C3
Ealing W7 .... 108 B6
Hendon NW11 .... 46 D2
Brentfield NW10 ...... 66 D1
Brentfield Cl NW10 ... 67 B2
Brentfield Gdns NW2 . 46 D2
Brentfield Ho 7
NW10 .... 67 B1
Brentfield Jun & Inf Sch
NW10 .... 67 B2
Brentfield Rd NW10 ... 67 B2
BRENTFORD 131 B6
Brentford Bsns Ctr
TW8 .... 131 C5
Brentford Cl UB4 ..... 84 D3
BRENTFORD END ... 131 C4
Brentford Fountain L Ctr
W4 .... 110 C1
Brentford Ho 6
TW1 .... 153 B4
Brentford Sch for Girls
TW8 .... 131 D6
Brentford Sta TW8 .. 131 C6
Brent Gn NW4 .... 46 D4
Brentham Way W5 .... 87 D3
Brent Ho
3 Catford BR1 ...... 186 B5
16 Hackney E9 .... 74 C2
Wembley HA9 .... 66 B3
Brenthouse Rd E9 .... 74 C2
Brenthurst Rd NW10 .. 67 D2
Brent Knoll Sch 15
SE26 .... 162 D1
Brent Lea TW8 .... 131 C5
Brent Mans NW4 ...... 46 C4
Brentmead Cl W7 .... 108 C6
Brentmead Gdns
NW10 .... 88 B5
Brentmead Pl NW11 .. 46 D3
Brent Mus★ NW10 .... 68 B2
Brent New Ent Ctr
NW10 .... 67 D2
Brenton Ct E9 .... 75 A3
Brenton St E14 .... 97 A1
Brent Park Ind Est
UB2 .... 106 C3
Brent Park Rd NW4 ... 46 B2
Brent Pl EN5 .... 13 B6
Brent Rd
Brentford TW8 ...... 131 C6
Newham E16 .... 99 A2
Southall UB2 .... 106 C3
Woolwich SE18 ..... 144 D5
Brentside TW8 .... 131 C6
Brentside Cl W13 ..... 87 A3
Brentside Executive Ctr
TW8 .... 131 B6
Brentside High Sch
W7 .... 86 C3
Brentside Prim Sch
W7 .... 86 C3
Brent St NW4 .... 46 C4
Brent Trad Est NW10 .. 67 C3
Brentvale Ave
Southall UB1 .... 108 B5
Wembley HA0 .... 88 B6
Brent View Rd NW9 ... 46 A2
Brentwaters Bsns Pk
TW8 .... 131 C5
Brent Way
Brentford TW8 ...... 131 D5
Finchley N3 .... 29 C4
Wembley HA9 .... 66 D2
Brentwick Gdns
TW8 .... 110 A2
Brentwood Cl SE9 ... 167 A3
Brentwood Ho 2
SE18 .... 143 D5
Brentwood Lo NW4 ... 46 D4
Brereton Ho 4 SW2 . 160 C4
Brereton Rd N17 ...... 33 D3
Bressay Dr NW7 ...... 28 A3
Bressenden Pl
SW1 .... 115 C3 259 A6
Bressey Ave EN1 .... 6 A4
Bressey Gr E18 .... 36 D1
Bretherton Ct CR2 ... 221 C2
Breton Ho
Bermondsey SE1 .... 263 C6
St Luke's EC2 .... 242 B5
Brett Cl
15 Northolt UB5 ...... 84 D4
Stoke Newington N16 .. 73 C6
Brett Cres NW10 ...... 89 B6
Brett Ct N9 .... 18 C2
Brettell St SE17 ..... 262 D1
Brettenham Ave E17 .. 35 C2
Brettenham Prim Sch 10
N18 .... 34 A6
Brettenham Rd
Edmonton N18 .... 34 A6
Walthamstow E17 ..... 35 C2
Brett Ho 1 SW15 .... 156 D4
Brett House Cl 2
SW15 .... 156 D4
Brettinghurst 8
SE1 .... 118 A1
Bretton Ho N19 .... 50 A1
Brett Pas 28 E8 .... 74 B3
Brett Rd Barnet EN5 .... 12 C6
Hackney E8 .... 74 B3
Brewers Bldgs EC1 .. 234 C2
Brewers Ct W2 ...... 236 A2
Brewer's Gn SW1 ... 259 C6
Brewers Hall Gdns
EC2 .... 242 B3
Brewers La 11 TW9 .. 153 D6
Brewer St
W1 .... 115 C6 249 B6
Brewery Cl HA0 .... 65 A4
Brewery Ind Est The
N1 .... 235 B3
Brewery Mews Bsns Ctr
1 TW7 .... 131 A2
Brewery Rd
Islington N7 .... 72 A2
Keston Mark BR2 .... 210 A1
Plumstead SE18 ..... 123 B1
Brewery Sq
Bermondsey SE1 .... 253 C3
Clerkenwell EC1 ..... 241 D6
Brewhouse La
Putney SW15 .... 135 A2
Wapping E1 .... 118 B5
Brewhouse Rd 3
SE18 .... 122 B2
Brewhouse Wlk
SE16 .... 119 A5
Brewhouse Yd EC1 .. 241 C6
Brewood Rd RM8 ..... 80 B2
Brewster Gdns W10 ... 90 C2
Brewster Ho
Bermondsey SE1 .... 263 D4
Poplar E14 .... 119 B6
Brewster Rd E10 ...... 53 D1
Brian Ct N10 .... 31 B2
Brian Rd RM6 .... 58 C4
Briant Ho SE1 ...... 260 D5
Briants Cl HA5 .... 23 B1
Briant St SE14 ...... 140 D5
Briar Ave SW16 ...... 182 B3
Briarbank Rd W13 .... 87 A1
Briar Cl
Buckhurst Hill IG9 ..... 21 D2
Edmonton N13 .... 17 A1
Finchley N2 .... 30 A1
Hampton TW12 ...... 173 B5
Isleworth TW7 ...... 152 D6
Briar Cres UB5 .... 63 D2
Briar Ct 7 Bow E3 .... 97 C5
Cheam SM3 .... 216 C4
9 Dalston E8 .... 73 D1
Hampton TW12 ...... 173 D5
Leytonstone E11 ...... 54 B2
Briardale
Edgware HA8 .... 27 B6
Wandsworth SW19 ... 157 B3
Briardale Gdns NW3 .. 69 C5
Briardale Ho 12 N16 .. 51 C1
Briarfield Ave N3 ..... 29 D1
Briarfield Cl DA7 .... 147 C3
Briar Gdns BR2 ..... 208 D1
Briaris Cl 11 N17 ...... 34 B3
Briar La CR0 .... 223 D4
Briar Lo E18 .... 37 C2
Briar Rd
Cricklewood NW2 ..... 68 C4
Harrow HA3 .... 43 C4
Littleton TW17 ...... 192 C4
Thornton Heath
SW16 .... 204 B6
Twickenham TW2 .... 152 C3
Briars The WD23 .... 8 C4
Briarswood Way
BR6 .... 227 D3
Briar The 11 SM1 .... 218 A4
Briarview Ct E4 .... 36 B4
Briar Way UB7 .... 104 C4
Briar Wlk
Burnt Oak HA8 .... 27 A3
Putney SW15 .... 134 B1
West Kilburn W10 ..... 91 A3
Briarwood Cl
Feltham TW13 ...... 149 C1
Kingsbury NW9 .... 45 A3
Briarwood Ct 5
KT4 .... 200 A1
Briarwood Dr HA6 .... 22 A1
Briarwood Rd
London SW4 .... 159 D6
Stoneleigh KT17 ..... 216 A2
Briary Cl NW3 .... 70 C1
Briary Ct
10 Canning Town
E16 .... 98 D1
Sidcup DA14 .... 190 B5
Briary Gdns BR1 ..... 187 B5
Briary Gr HA8 .... 26 D1
Briary La N9 .... 17 D1
Briary Lo BR3 .... 186 A2
Brickbarn Cl SW10 .. 266 B4
Brick Ct EC4 .... 241 A1
Brickett Cl HA4 .... 39 A4
Brick Farm Cl TW9 .. 132 D4
Brickfield Cl TW8 .... 131 C5
Brickfield Cotts
SE18 .... 145 D6
Brickfield Farm Gdns
BR6 .... 227 A4
Brickfield La
Edgware EN5 .... 11 D5
Harlington UB3 ..... 127 B6
Brickfield Rd
South Norwood CR7,
SW16 .... 182 D2
Wimbledon SW19 ... 179 D6
Brickfields HA2 .... 64 B6
Brickfields Way UB7 . 104 B3
Brick La Enfield EN1 ..... 6 B3
Northolt UB5 .... 85 B4
Shoreditch E2 .... 95 D4
Spitalfields E1 . 95 D3 243 D5
Stanmore HA7 .... 25 D3
Brick Lane Mkt★
E2 .... 95 D3 243 D6
Bricklayers Arms
SE1 .... 262 D5
Brick St W1 .. 115 B5 248 C3
Brickwall La HA4 ..... 39 D1
Brickwood Cl SE26 ... 162 B1
Brickwood Rd CR0 .. 221 C6
Brickworth Ho 26
SW9 .... 138 C4
Brideale Cl SE15 .... 139 D6
Bride Ct EC4 .... 241 C1
Bride La EC4 ... 94 D1 241 C1
Bridel Mews N1 ..... 234 C5
Bride St N7 .... 72 B2
Bridewain St SE1 ... 263 C6
Bridewell Pl
Holborn EC4 .... 241 C1
20 Wapping E1 .... 118 B5
Bridford Mews W1 .. 238 D4
Bridge Acad The E2 ... 95 D6
Bridge App NW3 ...... 71 A1
Bridge Ave Ealing W7 .. 86 B2
Hammersmith W6 ... 112 C1
Bridge Avenue Mans 1
W6 .... 112 C1
Bridge Bsns Ctr The 2
UB2 .... 107 C4
Bridge Cl Enfield EN1 ... 6 B3
13 North Kensington
W10 .... 90 D1
Teddington TW11 .... 174 D6
Walton-on-T KT12 ... 193 D1
Bridge Ct
9 Blackwall E14 ..... 120 B6
Leyton E10 .... 53 B2
2 Walton-on-T KT12 . 193 D1
7 Willesden NW10 .... 67 C1
Bridge Dr N13 .... 32 B6
Bridge End E17 .... 36 A2
Bridge End Cl 4
KT2 .... 176 C2
Bridge Field Ho 7
W2 .... 91 D1
Bridgefield Rd SM1 .. 217 C2
Bridgefoot
SE1 .... 116 A1 260 B1
Bridge Gate N21 ...... 17 A4
Bridge Gdns
Canonbury N16 .... 73 B4
East Molesey KT8 .... 196 B5
Littleton TW15 ...... 171 A3
Bridge Ho
Brockley SE4 .... 141 B1
1 Camden Town NW1 .. 71 A1
Ealing TW8 .... 109 A2
Homerton E9 .... 74 D3
Woolwich SE28 ...... 123 C5
Bridge Ho S TW8 .... 109 A2
Bridge House Quay
E14 .... 120 A5
Bridge La
Battersea
SW11 ..... 136 C4 267 B1
Temple Fortune NW11 .. 47 B4
Bridgeland Rd E16 ... 121 A6
Bridgelands Cl BR3 .. 185 B3
Bridge L Ctr SE26 ... 185 B6
Bridgeman Ho 19 E9 .. 74 C1
Bridgeman Rd
Islington N1 .... 72 B1
Teddington TW11 .... 175 A4
Bridgeman St
NW8 .... 92 C5 230 A3
Bridge Meadows
SE14 .... 140 D6
Bridgend Rd SW18 ... 136 A1
Bridgenhall Rd EN1 .... 5 D4
Bridgen Ho 9 E1 ...... 96 B1
Bridgen Rd DA5 ..... 169 A4
Bridge Par
7 Croydon CR0 ..... 220 D5
Edmonton N21 .... 17 A4
Bridge Pk
7 London SW18 .... 157 C6
Wembley NW10 .... 66 D1
Bridge Pk Com L Ctr
NW10 .... 66 D1
Bridge Pl
Belgravia
SW1 ..... 115 B2 258 D4
Croydon CR0 .... 205 B1
Bridgepoint Lofts 2
E7 .... 77 C1
Bridgeport Pl 4 E1 .. 118 A5
Bridge Rd
Beckenham BR3 ..... 185 B3
Bexleyheath DA7 .... 147 A3
Bridge Rd *continued*
Chessington KT9 .... 214 A3
East Ham E6 .... 78 B1
East Molesey KT8 ... 196 C5
Isleworth TW3, TW7 .. 130 B2
Southall UB2 .... 107 C4
Stratford Marsh E15 ... 98 B6
Sutton SM2 .... 217 D2
Twickenham TW1 .... 153 B5
Wallington SM6 ..... 219 C3
Walthamstow E17 ..... 53 B2
Wembley HA9 .... 66 C5
Willesden NW10 ...... 67 C2
Wood Green N22 ...... 32 A2
Bridge Row CR0 ..... 205 B1
Bridge Sch The
Clerkenwell
EC1 .... 94 D3 241 C6
Lower Holloway N7 .... 72 A3
Bridges Ct SW11 .... 136 B3
Bridges Ho 15 SE5 ... 139 B5
Bridges La CR0 ...... 220 A4
Bridges Rd
Stanmore HA7 .... 24 D5
Wimbledon SW19 ... 179 D4
Bridges Road Mews
SW19 .... 179 D4
Bridge St
Chiswick W4 .... 111 B2
Pinner HA5 .... 41 A6
Richmond TW10 ..... 153 D6
Walton-on-T KT12 ... 193 D2
Westminster
SW1 ...... 116 A4 250 B1
Bridge Terr E15 .... 76 B1
Bridge The HA3 .... 42 D5
Bridgetown Cl 5
SE19 .... 183 C5
Bridgeview 2 W6 ... 112 C1
Bridgewater Cl BR7 . 211 C6
Bridgewater Ct HA0 ... 65 C2
Bridgewater Gdns
HA8 .... 26 B1
Bridgewater Ho UB5 .. 85 A3
Bridgewater Rd
Ruislip HA4 .... 62 B4
Stratford Marsh E15 ... 98 A6
Wembley HA0 .... 65 C1
Bridgewater Sq EC2 242 A4
Bridgewater St EC2 . 242 A4
Bridgeway
Barking IG11 .... 79 D1
Wembley HA0 .... 66 B1
Bridge Way
London NW11 .... 47 B4
Twickenham TW2 .... 152 A4
Uxbridge UB10 .... 60 D3
Bridgeway St
NW1 .... 93 C5 232 B3
Bridge Wharf 18 E2 ... 96 D5
Bridge Wharf Rd
TW7 .... 131 B2
Bridgewood Cl SE20 . 184 B3
Bridgewood Rd
North Cheam KT17,
KT4 .... 216 A4
Streatham SW16 .... 181 D3
Bridge Yd SE1 ...... 252 D4
Bridgford St SW17,
SW18 .... 158 A1
Bridgman Rd W4 .... 111 A3
Bridgnorth Ho 10
SE15 .... 140 A6
Bridgwater Ho W2 .. 236 A2
Bridle Cl Enfield EN3 .... 7 B6
Kingston u T KT1 .... 197 D5
Sunbury TW16 ...... 194 A6
West Ewell KT19 .... 215 B3
Bridle La
Marylebone
W1 .... 115 C6 249 B6
Twickenham TW1 .... 153 B5
Bridle Path CR0 ..... 220 A5
Bridle Path The IG8 ... 36 C3
Bridlepath Way
TW14 .... 149 C3
Bridle Rd
Addington CR0 ...... 223 C4
Claygate KT10 ...... 213 B2
Croydon CR0 .... 223 C6
Pinner HA5 .... 40 C4

Bridle Way
Addington CR0 223 C3
Orpington BR6 227 A4
Bridle Way The SM6 219 C3
Bridlington Ho SW18 136 A1
Bridlington Rd N9 18 B4
Bridport SE17 262 B1
Bridport Ave RM7 59 D3
Bridport Ho
6 Edmonton N18 34 A5
Shoreditch N1 235 D5
Bridport Pl N1 95 B6 235 D5
Bridport Rd
Edmonton N18 33 D5
Greenford UB6 85 D6
Thornton Heath CR7 204 D6
Bridstow Pl W2 91 C1
Brief St SE5 138 D4
Brierfield NW1 232 A5
Brierley CR0 223 D2
Brierley Ave N9 18 C3
Brierley Cl SE25 206 A5
Brierley Ct W7 108 C6
Brierley Rd Leyton E11 76 B4
Upper Tooting SW12 159 C2
Brierly Gdns E2 96 C5
Brigade Cl HA2 64 B6
Brigade St SE3 142 D3
Brigadier Ave EN2 5 A4
Brigadier Hill EN2 5 A5
Briggeford Cl 5 E5 74 A6
Briggs Cl CR4 181 B2
Briggs Ho 20 E2 95 D4
Bright Cl DA17 124 D2
Bright Ct 8 SE28 124 C5
Brightfield Rd SE12 164 D6
Brightling Rd SE4 163 B5
Brightlingsea Pl 5 E14 119 B6
Brightman Rd SW18 158 B3
Brighton Ave E17 53 B4
Brighton Bldgs SE1 263 A5
Brighton Cl UB10 60 D1
Brighton Ct SW15 157 B5
Brighton Dr 3 UB5 63 C2
Brighton Gr SE14 141 A4
Brighton Ho 7 SE5 139 B4
Brighton Rd
Belmont SM2 217 D1
Finchley N2 30 A1
South Croydon CR2 221 B2
Stoke Newington N16 73 C4
Surbiton KT6 197 D3
Sutton SM2 218 A1
Wallend E6 100 C4
Brighton Terr SW9 138 B1
Brightside Rd SE13 164 B5
Brightside The EN3 7 A4
Bright St E14 97 D2
Brightwell Cl CR0 204 C1
Brightwell Cres SW17 180 D5
Brightwell Ct N7 72 B3
Brightwells 1 SW6 135 D3
Brightwen Gr HA7 9 A2
Brig Mews SE8 141 C6
Brigstock Ho SE5 139 A3
Brigstock Par 1 CR7 204 C4
Brigstock Rd
Belvedere DA17 125 D2
Thornton Heath CR7 204 D4
Brill Ho NW10 67 B5
Brill Pl NW1 93 D5 232 D3
Brim Hill N2 48 B5
Brimpsfield Cl SE2 124 B3
BRIMSDOWN 7 B3
Brimsdown Ave EN3 7 A4
Brimsdown Ho E3 98 A3
Brimsdown Jun & Inf Sch EN3 6 D2
Brimsdown Sta EN3 7 A3
Brimstone Ho 4 E15 76 C1
Brindishe Prim Sch SE12 164 D6
Brindle Gate DA15 167 C3
Brindley Cl
Bexleyheath DA7 147 D2
Wembley HA0 87 D6
Brindley Ho
Carshalton SM1 218 C3
37 Notting Hill W2 91 C2
Brindley Ho *continued*
22 Streatham SW12 160 A4
Brindley St SE14 141 B4
Brindley Way
Bromley BR1 187 B5
Southall UB1 107 D6
Brindwood Rd E4 19 C1
Brine Ct KT6 197 D4
Brine Ho 11 E3 97 A5
Brinkburn Cl
Abbey Wood SE2 124 A2
Edgware HA8 44 D6
Brinkburn Gdns HA8 44 C6
Brinkley 18 KT1 176 C1
Brinkley Rd KT4 216 B6
Brinklow Cres SE18 144 D5
Brinklow Ho W2 91 D2
Brinkworth Rd IG5 56 A6
Brinkworth Way E9 75 B2
Brinsdale Rd NW4 46 D6
Brinsley Ho 17 E1 96 C1
Brinsley Rd HA3 24 B1
Brinsley St 35 E1 96 B1
Brinsworth Cl TW2 152 B2
Brinton Wlk SE1 251 C3
Brion Pl E14 98 A2
Brisbane Ave SW19 179 D2
Brisbane Ct N10 31 B3
Brisbane Ho 3 W12 112 B6
Brisbane Rd
Ealing W13 109 A4
Ilford IG1 57 A1
Leyton E10 75 D6
Brisbane St SE5 139 B5
Briscoe Cl E11 76 D6
Briscoe Rd SW19 180 B4
Briset Rd SE9 143 D1
Briset St EC1 94 D3 241 C5
Briset Way N7 72 B6
Bristol Cl
Stanwell TW19 148 A5
Twickenham TW4 151 C4
Wallington SM6 220 A1
Bristol Ct 11 TW19 148 A5
Bristol Gdns
Putney SW15 156 C4
Westbourne Green W9 91 D3
Bristol Ho
1 Barking IG11 80 A1
SE11 261 A5
Bristol Mews W9 91 D3
Bristol Park Rd 1 E17 53 A5
Bristol Rd
Greenford UB6 85 D6
Morden SM4 202 A4
Upton E7 77 D2
Briston Gr N8 50 A3
Briston Mews NW7 28 A3
Bristowe Cl 24 SW2 160 C5
Bristow Rd
Bexleyheath DA7 147 A4
Hounslow TW3 130 A2
Wallington CR0 220 A4
West Norwood SE19 183 C5
Britannia Building N1 235 C2
Britannia Cl
London SW4 137 D1
Northolt UB5 84 D4
Britannia Gate 11 E16 121 A5
Britannia Ho N20 14 A1
Britannia Junc NW1 231 D6
Britannia La TW2 152 A4
Britannia L Ctr N1 95 C6
Britannia Rd
Ilford IG1 78 D5
23 Millwall E14 119 C2
Surbiton KT5 198 B2
Walham Green SW6 135 D5 265 C3
Whetstone N12 14 A1
Britannia Row N1 95 A6 235 A6
Britannia St WC1 94 B4 233 C2
Britannia Village Prim Sch 17 E16 121 B5
Britannia Way NW10 88 D3
Britannia Wlk N1 235 C2
British Coll of Osteopathic Medicine NW3 70 A2
British Dental Association Mus★ W1 238 C3
British Gr W4 111 D1
British Grove Pas 2 W4 111 D1
British Grove S 3 W4 111 D1
British Home The (Hospl) SE27 182 D5
British Legion Rd E4 20 D2
British Library Newspapers NW9 45 C6
British Library The★ WC1 93 D4 232 D2
British Mus★ WC1 94 A2 240 A3
British Optical Association Mus★ SW1 250 A4
British St E3 97 B4
British Wharf Ind Est SE14 140 D6
Britley Ho 16 E14 97 B1
Brit Oval The (Surrey Cnty Crkt Club) SE11 138 C6 270 D6
BRIT Performing Arts & Tech Sch SE25 205 B3
Brittage Rd 11 NW10 67 C1
Brittain Ct SE9 166 A3
Brittain Rd RM8 81 B5
Brittany Ho SW15 134 C1
Brittany Point SE11 261 A3
Britten Cl Elstree WD6 9 D5
Golders Green NW11 47 D1
Brittenden Cl 1 BR6 227 D2
Brittenden Par BR6 227 D2
Britten Dr UB1 85 C1
Britten Ho SW3 257 B2
Britten St SW3 114 C1 257 A2
Britton Cl SE6 164 B4
Britton St EC1 94 D3 241 C5
Brixham Cres HA4 40 A1
Brixham Gdns IG3 79 C3
Brixham Rd DA16 146 D4
Brixham St E16 122 C5
BRIXTON 138 C2
Brixton Day Coll 6 SW9 138 A2
Brixton Hill SW2 160 B5
Brixton Hill Ct 5 SW2 160 B6
Brixton Hill Pl SW2 160 A4
Brixton Mkt★ SW9 138 C1
Brixton Oval 7 SW2 138 C1
Brixton Rd SW9 138 C4
Brixton Rec Ctr SW9 138 C2
Brixton Sta SW9 138 C1
Brixton Station Rd SW9 138 C2
Brixton Water La SW2 160 B6
Broadacre Cl UB10 60 D5
Broadbent Cl N6 49 B1
Broadbent St W1 248 C6
Broadberry Ct N18 34 B5
Broadbridge Cl SE3 143 A5
Broad Common Est N16 52 A1
Broadcoombe CR2 222 D1
Broadcroft Ave HA7 25 D1
Broadcroft Rd BR5 211 B2
Broad Ct WC2 240 B1
Broadeaves Cl CR2 221 C3
Broadfield NW6 69 D2
Broadfield Cl
Croydon CR0 220 B6
Dollis Hill NW2 68 C5
Broadfield Ct
Bushey WD23 8 C2
Edgware HA8 10 D1
Broadfield La NW1 72 A1
Broadfield Rd SE6 164 C3
Broadfields
Harrow HA2 23 D1
Thames Ditton KT8 196 C3
Broadfields Ave
Edgware HA8 10 D1
Southgate N21 16 C4
Broadfields Hts HA8 26 D6
Broadfields Prim Sch HA8 10 C2
Broadfield Sq EN1 6 B3
Broadfields Way NW10 67 D3
Broadfield Way IG9 21 C1
Broadford Ho 12 E1 97 A3
BROADGATE 95 C2
Broadgate EC2 95 C2 243 A4
Broadgate Circ EC2 95 C2 243 A3
Broadgate Rd E16 99 D1
Broadgates Ave EN4 1 D4
Broadgates Ct SE11 261 B1
Broadgates Rd SW18 158 B3
Broadgate Twr The EC2 243 B5
BROAD GREEN 204 D3
Broad Green Ave CR0 204 D2
Broadhead Strand NW9 27 D2
Broadheath Dr BR7 188 B5
Broadhinton Rd SW4 137 C2
Broadhurst Ave
Edgware HA8 26 D6
Ilford IG3 79 D4
Broadhurst Cl
Hampstead NW6 70 A2
9 Richmond TW10 154 B6
Broadhurst Gdns
Hampstead NW6 69 D2
Ruislip HA4 62 C6
Broadhurst Mans NW6 69 D2
Broad La
Broadgate EC2 243 A4
Hampton TW12 173 C4
Hornsey Vale N8 50 B4
South Tottenham N15 51 D5
South Tottenham N15 52 A5
Broadlands
Feltham TW13 151 C1
Highgate N6 49 A2
Broadlands Ave
Enfield EN3 6 B2
Shepperton TW17 193 A3
Streatham SW16 160 A2
Broadlands Cl
Enfield EN3 6 C2
Highgate N6 49 A2
Streatham SW16 160 A2
Broadlands Ct TW9 132 C5
Broadlands Lo N6 48 D2
Broadlands Mans 2 SW16 160 A2
Broadlands Rd
Grove Pk BR1 187 B6
Highgate N6 48 D2
Broadlands Way KT3 199 D3
Broad Lawn SE9 166 C3
Broadlawns Ct HA3 24 D2
Broadley St NW8 92 C2 237 A4
Broadley Terr NW1 92 C3 237 B5
Broadmayne SE17 262 C2
Broadmead
Catford SE6 163 C1
Hampton TW12 173 C4
West Kensington W14 254 A3
Broadmead Ave KT4 200 A2
Broadmead Cl
Hampton TW12 173 C4
Pinner HA5 23 A3
Broadmead Ct 6 IG8 37 A4
Broadmead Inf Sch CR0 205 B2
Broadmead Jun Sch CR0 205 B3
Broadmead Rd
Northolt UB5 85 A3
Woodford IG8 37 B3
Broad Oak
Ashford TW16 171 D4
Woodford IG8 37 B5
Broad Oak Cl
Chingford E4 35 C5
St Paul's Cray BR5 190 A1
Broadoak Ct 8 SW9 138 C2
Broadoak Ho 11 NW6 91 D6
Broadoaks BR7 188 D4
Broad Oaks KT6 214 D6
Broadoaks Way BR2 208 D4
Broadreach Coll SE28 123 D3
Broad St Ave EC2 243 A3
Broad Sanctuary SW1 250 A1
Broad St
Dagenham RM10 81 C1
Teddington TW11 174 D4
Broadstone Ho SW8 270 C3
Broadstone Pl W1 238 A3
Broad Street NHS Walk-in Ctr RM10 103 C6
Broad Street Pl EC2 242 D3
Broadview NW9 44 C3
Broadview Est TW19 148 C4
Broadview Ho RM8 58 D1
Broadview Rd SW16 181 D3
Broadwalk
Harrow HA2 41 D4
Snaresbrook E18 54 D6
Broadwalk Ho SW7 246 A1
Broadwalk La NW11 47 B2
Broadwalk Sh Ctr The HA8 26 D4
Broadwall SE1 116 C5 251 B4
Broadwater Farm Prim Sch N17 33 B1
Broadwater Gdns BR6 227 A4
Broadwater Prim Sch SW17 180 C6
Broadwater Rd
Plumstead SE18 123 B3
Tottenham N17 33 C1
Upper Tooting SW17 180 C6
Broadway
Barking IG11 101 A6
Bexley DA6 147 C1
Bexleyheath DA6 147 B1
Hanwell W7 108 C5
Stratford E15 76 B1
Tolworth KT6 198 D1
West Ealing W13 109 A5
Westminster SW1 115 D3 259 C6
Broadway Arc 3 W6 112 C2
Broadway Ave
Thornton Heath CR0 205 B4
Twickenham TW1 153 B5
Broadway Bldgs 5 W7 108 C5
Broadway Cl IG8 37 B4
Broadway Ct
Beckenham BR3 208 A6
Wimbledon SW19 179 C4
Broadway Ctr The 6 W6 112 C2
Broadway Gdns
Mitcham CR4 202 C5
Woodford IG8 37 B4
Broadway Ho 2 E8 96 B6
Broadway Ho 5 SW19 179 C3
Broadway Lofts SW17 180 C6
Broadway Mans SW6 265 B3
Broadway Market E8 96 B6
Broadway Market Mews 21 E8 96 A6
Broadway Mews
Bowes Pk N13 32 B5
Southgate N21 16 D3
Stamford Hill E5 51 D2
Broadway Mkt E8 96 B6
Broadway Par
Chingford E4 36 A4
Hayes UB3 106 A5
Hornsey N8 50 A3
West Drayton UB7 104 A4
Broadway Pl SW19 179 B4
Broadway Ret Pk NW2 68 D4
Broadway Sh Ctr 5 DA6 147 C1
Broadway The
Barnes SW13 133 C3
Bedington CR0 220 A4
Cheam SM3 217 A2
Chingford E4 36 B4
Dagenham RM8 81 C6
Ealing W5 109 D6
Edgware NW7 27 D5
Edmonton N9 18 A1

Broadway The *continued*
Friern Barnet N11 31 A5
Greenford UB6 86 A3
Harrow HA3 24 D1
Hornsey N8 50 A3
Merton SW19 179 C3
Newham E13 99 B5
Pinner HA5 23 B3
South Acton W3 110 C4
Southall UB1 107 A6
2 Southgate N14 15 D3
Stanmore HA7 25 C5
Sutton SM1 218 A4
Thames Ditton KT10 196 C1
Tolworth KT6 198 C1
Wembley HA9 66 A5
Woodford IG8 37 B4
Wood Green N22 32 C1
Broadway Wlk 4 E14 119 C3
Broadwell Ct TW5 128 D4
Broadwick St W1 93 C1 239 B1
Broad Wlk
Eltham SE3, SE18 144 A3
Heston TW5 129 A4
Mayfair W1 115 A5 248 A4
Regent's Pk NW1 93 A5 231 B3
Richmond TW9 132 B5
Southgate N21 16 B3
Broad Wlk The W8 113 D5 245 D3
Broadwood Ave HA4 39 C3
Broadwood Terr W14 254 D4
Broad Yd EC1 241 C5
Brocade Ct NW9 45 D5
Brocas Cl NW3 70 C1
Brockbridge Ho SW15 155 D5
Brockdene Dr BR2 225 D4
Brockdish Ave IG11 79 D3
Brockelbank Lo RM8 80 D6
Brockenhurst KT8 195 B3
Brockenhurst Ave KT4 199 C1
Brockenhurst Gdns
Edgware NW7 27 C5
Ilford IG1 79 A3
Brockenhurst Mews 9 N18 34 A6
Brockenhurst Rd CR0 206 B2
Brockenhurst Way SW16 181 D1
Brocket Ho 16 SW8 137 D3
Brockham Cl SW19 179 B5
Brockham Cres CR0 224 B1
Brockham Ct
17 Belmont SM2 217 D1
8 South Croydon CR2 221 A3
Brockham Dr
Ilford IG2 57 A4
Streatham SW2 160 B4
Brockham Ho
Camden Town NW1 232 B5
11 Streatham SW2 160 B4
Brockham St SE1 262 B6
Brockhurst Cl HA7 24 D4
Brockhurst Ho N4 51 B2
Brockill Cres SE4 141 A1
Brocklebank Ho 7 E16 122 C5
Brocklebank Rd
Greenwich SE7 121 B2
Wandsworth SW18 158 A4
Brocklebank Road Ind Est SE7 121 A2
Brocklehurst St SE14 140 D5
Brocklesby Rd SE25 206 B5
BROCKLEY 141 B1
Brockley Ave HA7 10 A1
Brockley Cl HA7 26 A6
Brockley Cross SE4 141 B2
Brockley Cross Bsns Ctr SE4 141 A2
Brockley Gdns SE4 141 B3
Brockley Gr SE4 163 B6
Brockley Hall Rd SE4 163 A6
Brockley Hill HA7, HA8 9 D2
Brockley Hill Ho HA7 9 C3
Brockley Ho SE17 263 A2
Brockley Mews SE4 163 A6
Brockley Pk SE23 163 A4
Brockley Prim Sch SE4 163 B6
Brockley Rd SE4 163 B6
Brockley Rise SE23 163 A4
Brockleyside HA7 26 A6
Brockley Sta SE4 141 A2
Brockley View SE23 163 A4
Brockley Way SE4 163 A6
Brockman Rise BR1 186 B6
Brockmer Ho 5 E1 118 B6
Brock Pl E3 97 D3
Brock Rd E13 99 B2
Brocks Dr SM3 217 A5
Brockshot Cl 1 TW8 131 D6
Brock St SE15 140 C2
Brockway Cl E11 76 C6
Brockweir 28 E2 96 C5
Brockwell Ave BR3 207 D4
Brockwell Cl BR5 211 D4
Brockwell Ct
2 London SW2 160 C6
Thornton Heath CR0 204 D2
Brockwell Ho SE11 270 D6
Brockwell Lido SE24 160 D5
Brockwell Park* SE24 160 D5
Brockwell Park Gdns SE24 160 D4
Brockwell Park Row SW2 160 C5
Brockworth 8 KT2 176 D2
Broderick Ho SE21 161 C1
Brodia Rd N16 73 C5
Brodick Ho 12 E3 97 B5
Brodie Ct E10 54 B1
Brodie Ho
Bermondsey SE1 263 D2
7 Wallington SM6 219 B4
Brodie Rd
Chingford E4 20 A2
Enfield EN2 5 A5
Brodie St SE1 117 D1 263 D2
Brodlove La E1 118 D6
Brodrick Gr SE2 124 B2
Brodrick Rd SW17 158 C2
Brody Ho E1 243 C3
Brograve Gdns BR3 185 D1
Broken Wharf EC4 252 A6
Brokesley St E3 97 B4
Broke Wlk Hackney E8 95 D6
1 Hackney E8 96 A6
Bromar Rd SE5 139 C2
Bromborough Gn WD19 22 C5
Bromefield HA7 25 C2
Bromehead St 8 E1 96 C1
Bromell's Rd SW4 137 C1
Brome Rd SE9 144 B2
Bromfelde Rd SW4 137 D3
Bromfield Ct 20 SE16 118 A3
Bromfield St N1 234 B4
Bromhall Rd RM8 80 B2
Bromhedge SE9 166 B1
Bromholm Rd SE2 124 B3
Bromleigh Ct 1 SE21, SE22 162 B2
Bromleigh Ho SE1 263 C6
BROMLEY BR1 186 C2
E3 97 D4
Bromley Ave BR1 186 C3
Bromley-by-Bow Sta E3 98 A4
Bromley Coll BR1 187 A2
Bromley Coll of F & H Ed (Rookery Lane Campus) BR2 209 D3
Bromley Comm BR2 209 D4
BROMLEY COMMON 210 A3
Bromley Cres
Beckenham BR2 208 D6
Ruislip HA4 61 D4
Bromley Ct BR1 186 D3
Bromley Gdns BR2 208 D6
Bromley Gr BR2 186 B1
Bromley Hall Rd E14 98 A2
Bromley High Jun Sch BR1 210 C5
Bromley High Sch BR1 210 C5
Bromley High St E3 97 D4
Bromley Hill BR1 186 C4
Bromley Ho 5 BR1 187 A2
Bromley Ind Ctr BR1 209 D6
Bromley La BR7 189 B3
Bromley Lo 2 W3 89 A1
Bromley Manor Mans 3 BR1 209 A6
Bromley North Sta BR1 187 A2
BROMLEY PARK 186 D2
Bromley Pk 11 BR1 186 D2
Bromley Pl W1 239 A4
Bromley Rd
Beckenham BR3 185 D2
Bromley BR2, BR3 186 B1
Catford SE6 163 D1
Chislehurst BR7 188 D2
Edmonton N18 17 B1
Leyton E10 53 D3
Tottenham N17 34 A2
Walthamstow E17 53 C6
Bromley Road Inf Sch 5 BR3 185 D2
Bromley Road Ret Pk SE6 163 D2
Bromley Ski & Snowboard Ctr BR5 190 D1
Bromley South Sta BR2 209 A6
Bromley St E1 96 D1
BROMPTON 114 B3
Brompton Arc SW1 247 D1
Brompton Cl
Hounslow TW4 151 B6
Penge SE20 184 A1
Brompton Ct 4 HA7 25 C6
Brompton Gr N2 48 C5
Brompton Ho 3 N9 34 A6
Brompton Oratory SW3 114 C3 257 A5
Brompton Park Cres SW6 135 D6 265 C5
Brompton Pl SW3 114 C3 257 B6
Brompton Rd SW3 114 C3 257 A5
Brompton Sq SW3 114 C3 257 A6
Bromstone Ho 19 SW9 138 C4
Bromwich Ave N6 71 A6
Bromwich Ho 3 TW10 154 A5
Bromyard Ave W3 111 C6
Bromyard Ho
Acton W3 111 C5
3 Peckham SE15 140 B5
Bron Ct NW6 91 C6
BRONDESBURY 69 A2
Brondesbury Coll for Boys 10 NW6 69 A1
Brondesbury Ct NW2 68 D2
Brondesbury Mews 11 NW6 69 C1
BRONDESBURY PARK 90 D6
Brondesbury Park Sta NW6 91 A6
Brondesbury Pk NW6 68 D1
Brondesbury Rd NW6 91 C5
Brondesbury Sta NW6 69 B1
Brondesbury Villas NW6 91 C5
Bronhill Terr N17 34 A2
Bronsart Rd SW6 135 A5 264 A3
Bronson Rd SW20 179 A1
Bronte Cl Erith DA8 147 D5
1 Forest Gate E7 77 A4
Ilford IG2 56 C5
Bronte Ct 8 W14 112 D3
Bronte Ho
Kilburn NW6 91 C4
6 Stoke Newington N16 73 C3
Bronti Cl SE17 117 A1 262 B2
Bronwen Ct NW8 229 C1
Bronze Age Way DA17 125 D4
Bronze St SE8 141 C5
Brook Ave
Dagenham RM10 81 D1
Edgware HA8 26 D4
Wembley HA9 66 C5
Brook Bank EN1 6 B6
Brookbank Ave W7 86 B2
Brookbank Rd SE13 141 D2
Brook Cl Acton W3 110 C5
Finchley N12 29 A3
Ruislip HA4 39 C2
Stanwell TW19 148 B4
Upper Tooting SW17 159 A2
West Barnes SW20 200 B6
Brook Com Prim Sch E8 74 A3
Brook Cres
Chingford E4 35 D6
Edmonton N9 34 B6
Brook Ct
Barking IG11 101 D6
Beckenham BR3 185 B2
5 Brentford TW8 131 D6
Cheam SM3 216 C4
Edgware HA8 26 D5
2 Leyton E11 76 C5
Mortlake SW14 133 C2
Walthamstow E17 53 A6
Brookdale N11 31 C6
Brookdale Rd
Catford SE6 163 D4
Lewisham SE6 163 D5
Sidcup DA5 169 A5
Walthamstow E17 53 C6
Brookdales The NW4 47 A5
Brookdene N12 29 D6
Brookdene Rd SE18, SE2 123 D2
Brook Dr Harrow HA1 42 A5
Newington SE11 116 D2 261 C4
Ruislip HA4 39 C2
Brooke Ave HA2 64 A5
Brooke Cl WD23 8 A4
Brooke Ct Kilburn W10 91 A5
7 Kingston u T KT2 175 D6
Brooke Ho
Bushey WD23 8 A4
4 New Cross Gate SE14 141 A4
Brookehowse Rd SE6 163 D1
Brookend Rd DA15 167 C3
Brooke Rd
Shacklewell E5, N16 74 A5
Walthamstow E17 54 A5
Brookes Ct EC1 241 A4
Brooke's Mkt EC1 241 B4
Brooke St EC1 94 C2 241 A3
Brooke Way WD23 8 A4
Brookfield
Dartmouth Pk N6 71 A5
1 Finsbury Pk N4 72 C6
Brookfield Ave
Carshalton SM1, SM5 218 C5
Ealing W5 87 D3
Mill Hill NW7 28 B4
Walthamstow E17 54 A5
Brookfield Cl NW7 28 B4
Brookfield Cres
Harrow HA3 44 A4
Mill Hill NW7 28 B4
Brookfield Ct
Greenford UB6 86 A4
1 London N12 29 D6
Brookfield Gdns KT10 212 D2
Brookfield Ho 23 E2 96 B5
Brookfield House Sch IG8 36 C4
Brookfield Path IG8 36 C4
Brookfield Pk NW5 71 B5
Brookfield Prim Sch
Cheam SM3 201 A1
Dartmouth Pk N19 71 B6
Brookfield Rd
Acton W4 111 B4
Edmonton N9 18 B1
Homerton E9 75 A2
Brookfields EN3 6 D1
Brookfields Ave CR4 202 C4
Brookgate N16 73 B6
Brook Gate W1 114 D6 247 D5
Brook Gdns
Barnes SW13 133 D2
Brook Gdns *continued*
Chingford E4 35 D6
Kingston u T KT2 177 A2
Brook Gn W6 112 D2
BROOK GREEN 112 D2
Brook Green Flats 11 W14 112 D3
Brookhill Cl
East Barnet EN4 14 C6
Woolwich SE18 122 D1
Brookhill Ct 2 EN4 14 C5
Brookhill Rd
East Barnet EN4 14 C6
Woolwich SE18 122 D1
Brook Ho
3 Clapham Pk SW4 159 C6
Ealing W3 110 C4
3 Edmonton N9 18 A1
4 Hammersmith W6 112 C2
Marylebone WC1 239 C4
4 Twickenham TW1 153 A4
Brook Hos NW1 232 B3
Brookhouse Gdns E4 36 C6
Brook House Sixth Form Coll 5 E5 74 B5
Brook Ind Est UB4 106 C5
Brooking Cl RM8 80 C5
Brooking Rd E7 77 A3
Brook La Bexley DA5 168 D5
Greenwich SE3 143 B3
Plaistow BR1 187 A4
Brook La N 3 TW8 131 D6
Brookland Cl NW11 47 C5
Brookland Garth NW11 47 D5
Brookland Hill NW11 47 D5
Brookland Jun & Inf Schs NW11 47 D5
Brookland Rise NW11 47 C5
Brooklands Ave
New Eltham DA15 167 B2
Wandsworth SW18 157 D2
Brooklands Cl TW16 171 C2
Brooklands Coll TW15 170 B6
Brooklands Court Apartments 3 NW6 69 B1
Brooklands Ct
10 Clapham SW8 137 C3
Enfield N21 17 B6
Kingston u T KT1 197 D5
2 London NW6 69 B1
2 Mitcham CR4 180 B1
Brooklands Dr UB6 87 D6
Brooklands Ho SE3 143 A2
Brooklands Pk SE3 143 A2
Brooklands Pl TW12 173 D5
Brooklands Prim Sch SE3 143 A2
Brooklands Rd KT7 197 A1
Brooklands The TW7 130 B4
Brook Lane Bns Ctr TW8 109 D1
Brooklea Cl NW9 27 C2
Brook Lo
Crouch End N8 49 D3
Edgware HA8 26 D4
Hendon NW4 46 D4
Brooklyn SE20 184 A3
Brooklyn Ave SE25 206 B5
Brooklyn Cl SM5 218 C6
Brooklyn Ct
Feltham TW13 150 B2
Shepherd's Bush W12 112 C5
Brooklyn Gr SE25 206 B5
Brooklyn Rd
Bromley BR2 210 A4
Croydon SE25 206 B5
Brookmarsh Ind Est SE10 141 D5
Brook Mdw N12 13 D1
Brook Mead KT19 215 C2
Brookmead Ave BR1, BR2 210 B4
Brookmead Ct N20 14 A2
Brookmead Ind Est CR4 203 C3
Brook Meadow Cl IG8 36 C4
Brookmead Rd CR0 203 C3

Brook Mews N
W2 ... 114 A6 246 B6
Brookmill Rd SE8 ... 141 C4
Brook Park Cl N21 ... 16 D6
Brook Pl EN5 ... 13 C6
Brook Rd
Buckhurst Hill IG9 ... 21 A3
Dollis Hill NW2 ... 68 A6
Finchley N12 ... 30 C3
Hornsey N8 ... 50 A5
Ilford IG2 ... 57 C3
South Norwood CR7 ... 205 A5
Surbiton KT6 ... 214 A6
Twickenham TW1 ... 153 A5
Wood Green N22 ... 50 B6
Brook Ret Pk HA4 ... 62 D3
Brook Road S
Brentford TW8 ... 109 D1
Brentford TW8 ... 131 D6
Brooks Ave E6 ... 100 B3
Brooksbank Ho 7 E9 ... 74 C2
Brooksbank St 9 E9 ... 74 C2
Brooksby Ho 9 N1 ... 72 C1
Brooksby Mews N1 ... 72 C1
Brooksby St N1 ... 72 C1
Brooksby's Wlk E9 ... 74 D3
Brooks Cl SE9 ... 166 C2
Brookscroft E17 ... 53 D6
Brookscroft Rd E17 ... 35 D2
Brooks Ct
3 London SW4 ... 138 A3
Nine Elms SW8 ... 269 B4
Brooks Farm★ E10 ... 53 D2
Brookshill HA3 ... 24 B5
Brookshill Ave HA3 ... 24 C5
Brookshill Dr HA3 ... 24 B5
Brookshill Gate HA3 ... 24 B5
Brooks Ho 6 SW2 ... 160 C3
Brookside
Broom Hill BR6 ... 211 D2
East Barnet EN4 ... 14 C5
Hillingdon UB10 ... 60 B1
Southgate N21 ... 16 B5
Wallington SM5 ... 219 A3
Brookside Cl
Barnet EN5 ... 13 A5
Feltham TW13 ... 150 A1
Harrow HA3 ... 43 D4
South Harrow HA2,
HA4 ... 63 A4
Brookside Cres 1
KT4 ... 200 A1
Brookside Ct SW16 ... 181 C3
Brookside Gdns EN1 ... 6 C6
Brookside Ho N17 ... 33 C1
Brookside Prim Sch
UB4 ... 84 C4
Brookside Rd
Edmonton N9 ... 34 B6
Hayes UB4 ... 106 C6
Temple Fortune NW11 ... 47 B3
Upper Holloway N19 ... 71 C6
Brookside S EN4 ... 15 A4
Brookside Way CR0 ... 206 D3
Brooks La W4 ... 132 C6
Brook's Mans 5 IG3 ... 58 B1
Brook's Mews
W1 ... 115 B6 248 C6
Brook's Par 6 IG3 ... 58 B1
Brook Sq SE18 ... 144 A4
Brooks Rd W4 ... 110 C1
Brook's Rd E13 ... 99 A6
Brook St
Bayswater
W2 ... 114 B6 246 D6
Erith DA8 ... 147 D5
Kingston u T KT1 ... 176 A1
Mayfair W1 ... 115 B6 248 C6
7 Tottenham N17 ... 33 D1
Brookstone Ct SE15 ... 140 B1
Brooksville Ave NW6 ... 91 A6
Brook Vale DA8 ... 147 D4
Brookview Ct 11 EN1 ... 17 C6
Brookview Rd SW16 ... 181 C5
Brookville Rd
SW6 ... 135 B5 264 C3
Brookway SE3 ... 143 A2
Brook Wlk
Burnt Oak HA8 ... 27 B4
Finchley N2 ... 30 B2
Brookwood Ave
SW13 ... 133 D3
Brookwood Cl BR2 ... 208 D5
Brookwood Ho SE1 ... 251 D1
Brookwood Rd
Hounslow TW3 ... 129 D4
Wandsworth SW18 ... 157 C3
Broom Ave BR5 ... 190 B1
Broom Cl
Bromley Comm BR2 ... 210 A3
Teddington KT1,
TW11 ... 175 D3
Broomcroft Ave UB5 ... 84 C4
Broome Ct 3 TW9 ... 132 C4
Broome Ho 7 E5 ... 74 B3
Broome Rd TW12 ... 173 B2
Broome Way SE5 ... 139 B5
Broom Farm SW6 ... 135 C3
Broomfield
7 Camden Town
NW1 ... 71 A1
Sunbury TW16 ... 172 A2
Walthamstow E17 ... 53 B2
Broomfield Ave N13 ... 32 B5
Broomfield Cotts
N13 ... 32 A5
Broomfield Ct N13 ... 32 A5
Broomfield Ho
Stanmore HA7 ... 9 A1
4 St Paul's Cray BR5 ... 190 B1
Walworth SE17 ... 263 A3
Broomfield House Sch
TW9 ... 132 B4
Broomfield La N13 ... 32 B6
Broomfield Pl W13 ... 109 B5
Broomfield Rd
Beckenham BR3 ... 207 B6
Bexley DA6 ... 169 C6
Bowes Pk N13 ... 32 A5
Dagenham RM6 ... 58 D2
Ealing W13 ... 109 B5
Richmond TW9 ... 132 B4
Surbiton KT5 ... 198 B1
Teddington TW11 ... 175 C4
Broomfields KT10 ... 212 A3
Broomfield Sch N14 ... 31 D5
Broomfield St E14 ... 97 D2
Broom Gdns CR0 ... 223 C5
Broomgrove Gdns
HA8 ... 26 C2
Broomgrove Rd
SW9 ... 138 B3
BROOM HILL ... 211 D2
Broomhill Ct 2 IG8 ... 37 A4
Broomhill Rd
Broom Hill BR6 ... 211 D2
Ilford IG3 ... 80 A6
Wandsworth SW18 ... 157 C6
Woodford IG8 ... 37 A4
Broomhill Rise DA6 ... 169 C6
Broomhill Wlk IG8 ... 36 D3
Broomhouse La
SW6 ... 135 C2
Broomhouse Rd
SW6 ... 135 C3
Broomleigh BR1 ... 187 A2
Broomloan La SM1 ... 217 C6
Broom Lock TW11 ... 175 C4
Broom Mead DA6 ... 169 C6
Broom Pk KT1 ... 175 D3
Broom Rd
Croydon CR0 ... 223 C5
Teddington TW11 ... 175 C4
Broomsleigh Bsns Pk
SE26 ... 185 B5
Broomsleigh St NW6 ... 69 B3
Broom Water TW11 ... 175 C5
Broom Water W
TW11 ... 175 C5
Broomwood Cl CR0 ... 206 D4
Broomwood Hall (Lower
Sch) 5 SW12 ... 159 A5
Broomwood Hall Sch
(Lower Sch) SW16 159 D1
Broomwood Hall Sch
(Upper Sch) 3
SW12 ... 159 A4
Broomwood Rd
London SW11 ... 159 A6
St Paul's Cray BR5 ... 190 B1
Broseley Gr SE26 ... 185 A5
Broster Gdns SE25 ... 205 D6
Brougham Rd
Acton W3 ... 89 A1
Hackney E8 ... 96 A6
Brougham St SW11 ... 136 D3
Brough Cl
Kingston u T KT2 ... 175 D5
South Lambeth SW8 ... 270 B3
Broughton Ave
London N3 ... 47 A6
Richmond TW10 ... 175 C6
Broughton Ct W13 ... 109 B6
Broughton Dr 19
SW9 ... 138 D1
Broughton Gdns N6 ... 49 C3
Broughton Ho 10
SW19 ... 179 A3
Broughton Rd
Ealing W13 ... 109 B6
Orpington BR6 ... 227 B6
Sands End SW6 ... 135 D3
Thornton Heath CR7 ... 204 C3
Broughton Road App 2
SW6 ... 135 D3
Broughton St SW8 ... 137 B3
Brouncker Rd W3 ... 111 A4
Browells La TW13 ... 150 B2
Brown Bear Ct
TW13 ... 172 D6
Brown Cl SM6 ... 220 A1
Browne Ho
13 Deptford SE8 ... 141 C5
9 Penge SE26 ... 184 B5
Brownfield St E14 ... 98 A1
Brownflete Ho SE4 ... 141 A1
Browngraves Rd
UB7 ... 127 A5
Brown Hart Gdns
W1 ... 248 B6
Brownhill Rd SE6 ... 164 A4
Browning Ave
Carshalton SM1 ... 218 C4
Ealing W7 ... 86 D1
North Cheam KT4 ... 200 B1
Browning Cl
Bexley DA16 ... 145 C4
Feltham TW12 ... 173 B6
Paddington W9 ... 236 B5
Walthamstow E17 ... 54 A5
Browning Ct W14 ... 264 C6
Browning Ho
2 London SE14 ... 141 A4
7 Shepherd's Bush
W12 ... 90 C1
10 Stoke Newington
N16 ... 73 C4
Browning Mews W1 ... 238 B3
Browning Rd
Enfield EN2 ... 5 B5
Leytonstone E11 ... 54 D2
Plashet E12 ... 78 B2
Browning St
SE17 ... 117 A2 262 B3
Browning Way TW5 ... 128 D4
Brownlea Gdns IG3 ... 80 A6
Brownlow Cl EN4 ... 14 B6
Brownlow Ct
2 Bowes Pk N11 ... 32 A4
Hampstead Garden Suburb
N2 ... 48 A4
Brownlow Ho 10
SE16 ... 118 A4
Brownlow Lo 1 N11 ... 32 A4
Brownlow Mews
WC1 ... 94 B3 240 D5
Brownlow Rd
Bowes Pk N11 ... 32 A4
6 Ealing W13 ... 109 A5
Finchley N3 ... 29 D3
3 Forest Gate E7 ... 77 A4
Hackney E8 ... 96 A6
South Croydon CR0 ... 221 D4
Willesden NW10 ... 67 C1
Brownlow St
WC1 ... 94 B2 240 D3
Brownrigg Rd TW15 ... 170 C6
Brown's Bldgs EC3 ... 243 B1
Brownsea Wlk NW7 ... 28 D4
Brownspring Dr SE9 ... 166 D1
Browns Rd E17 ... 53 C6
Brown's Rd KT5, KT6 ... 198 B2
Brown St W1 ... 92 D1 237 C2
Brownswell Rd N2 ... 30 B1
Brownswood Rd N4 ... 73 A6
Broxash Rd SW11 ... 159 A5
Broxbourne Ave E18 ... 55 B5
Broxbourne Ho 1 E3 ... 97 D3
Broxbourne Rd
Broom Hill BR6 ... 211 D2
Wanstead E7 ... 77 A5
Broxholme Cl 4
SE25 ... 205 B5
Broxholme Ho SW6 ... 265 C2
Broxholm Rd SE27,
SW16 ... 160 C1
Broxted Rd SE6 ... 163 B2
Broxwood Way
NW8 ... 92 C6 230 B5
Bruce Ave TW17 ... 193 A3
Bruce Castle Ct N17 ... 33 C2
Bruce Castle Mus★
N17 ... 33 C2
Bruce Castle Rd N17 ... 33 D2
Bruce Cl
North Kensington
W10 ... 90 D2
Welling DA16 ... 146 B4
Bruce Ct DA15 ... 189 D6
Bruce Gdns N20 ... 14 D1
Bruce Glasier Ho 13
N19 ... 49 D2
Bruce Gr N17 ... 33 D1
Bruce Grove N17 ... 33 D1
Bruce Grove Prim Sch
N17 ... 33 D1
Bruce Grove Sta N17 ... 33 D1
Bruce Hall Mews
SW17 ... 181 A6
Bruce Ho
4 Clapham Pk
SW4 ... 159 D5
5 Greenhill HA1 ... 42 D4
3 North Kensington
W10 ... 90 D2
Preston HA3 ... 44 A2
Putney SW15 ... 156 B6
Bruce Lawns SW17 ... 181 A6
Bruce Rd Barnet EN5 ... 1 A2
Bromley E3 ... 97 D4
Harrow HA3 ... 24 C1
Mitcham CR4 ... 181 A3
South Norwood SE25 ... 205 B5
Willesden NW10 ... 67 B1
Bruckner St W10 ... 91 B4
Brudenell Rd SW17 ... 181 A6
Bruffs Meadow UB5 ... 63 A2
Bruges Pl 16 NW1 ... 71 C1
Brumfield Rd KT19 ... 215 A3
Brune Ho E1 ... 243 C3
Brunei Gall★ WC1 ... 239 D4
Brunel Cl
Cranford TW5 ... 128 B5
Northolt UB5 ... 85 B4
Penge SE19 ... 183 D4
Brunel Ct 8 SW13 ... 133 D3
Brunel Est W2 ... 91 C2
Brunel Ho
Chelsea SW10 ... 266 D4
4 Gospel Oak NW5 ... 71 B4
Hayes UB3 ... 105 D3
Millwall E14 ... 119 D1
New Cross SE8 ... 141 B5
25 Streatham SW2 ... 160 A4
Brunel Mews NW10 ... 90 D4
Brunel Mus★ SE16 ... 118 C4
Brunel Pl 7 UB1 ... 85 D1
Brunel Rd Acton W3 ... 89 C2
Walthamstow E17 ... 53 A3
Wapping SE16 ... 118 C5
Brunel Science Pk
UB8 ... 82 A4
Brunel St E16 ... 98 D1
Brunel Univ UB8 ... 82 A4
Brunel Wlk
South Tottenham N15 ... 51 C5
Twickenham TW4 ... 151 C4
Brune St E1 ... 95 D2 243 C3
Brunlees Ho SE1 ... 262 B5
Brunner Cl NW11 ... 48 A4
Brunner Ho 6 SE6 ... 186 A6
Brunner Rd Ealing W5 ... 87 D3
Walthamstow E17 ... 53 B4
Bruno Ct 5 E8 ... 74 A2
Bruno Pl NW9 ... 67 A6
Brunswick Ave N11 ... 15 A1
Brunswick Cl
Bexley DA6 ... 146 D1
Pinner HA5 ... 41 A3
Thames Ditton KT7 ... 196 D1
Twickenham TW2 ... 152 B1
Brunswick Cres N11 ... 15 A1
Brunswick Ct
Bermondsey
SE1 ... 117 C4 253 B2
Finsbury EC1 ... 234 C1
Kingston u T KT2 ... 175 D4
New Barnet EN4 ... 14 B6
2 Penge SE19 ... 184 A3
Westminster SW1 ... 259 D3
Brunswick Ct *continued*
2 Wimbledon SW19 ... 179 A3
Brunswick Gdns
Ealing W5 ... 88 A3
Kensington
W8 ... 113 C5 245 B3
Brunswick Gr N11 ... 15 A1
Brunswick Ho
Church End N3 ... 29 B2
4 Haggerston E2 ... 95 D5
Lisson Gr NW1 ... 237 C6
Brunswick Lo 6 E4 ... 20 A2
Brunswick Manor
SM1 ... 218 A4
Brunswick Mews
Marylebone W1 ... 237 D2
Streatham SW16 ... 181 D4
BRUNSWICK PARK ... 15 A1
Brunswick Park Gdns
N11 ... 15 A2
Brunswick Park Prim
Sch
Brunswick Pk N14 ... 15 A2
22 Camberwell SE5 ... 139 B5
Brunswick Park Rd
N11 ... 15 A1
Brunswick Pk SE5 ... 139 C4
Brunswick Pl
Penge SE19 ... 184 A3
Shoreditch N1 ... 95 B4 235 D1
Brunswick Quay
SE16 ... 118 D3
Brunswick Rd
Bexley DA6 ... 147 A1
Ealing W5 ... 88 A4
Holdbrook EN3 ... 7 C5
Kingston u T KT2 ... 176 C2
Leyton E10 ... 54 A1
Poplar E14 ... 98 A1
South Tottenham N15 ... 51 C4
South Tottenham N15 ... 51 C5
Sutton SM1 ... 217 D4
Brunswick Sh Ctr
WC1 ... 94 A3 240 B6
Brunswick Sq
St Pancras
WC1 ... 94 A3 240 B6
Tottenham N17 ... 33 D4
Brunswick St E17 ... 54 A4
Brunswick Terr BR3 ... 185 D2
Brunswick Villas 2
SE5 ... 139 C4
Brunswick Way N11 ... 31 B6
Brunton Pl E14 ... 97 A1
Brushfield St
E1 ... 95 D2 243 C4
Brushwood Lo 1
DA17 ... 125 C2
Brussels Ct N18 ... 33 C5
Brussels Rd SW11 ... 136 B1
Bruton Cl BR7 ... 188 B3
Bruton La
W1 ... 115 B6 248 D5
Bruton Pl
W1 ... 115 B6 248 D5
Bruton Rd SM4 ... 202 A5
Bruton St
W1 ... 115 B6 248 D5
Bruton Way W13 ... 87 A2
Brutus Ct SE11 ... 261 C3
Bryan Ave NW10 ... 68 B1
Bryan Cl TW16 ... 172 A3
Bryan Ct W1 ... 237 C2
Bryan Ho SE16 ... 119 B4
Bryan Rd SE16 ... 119 B4
Bryanston Ave TW2 ... 151 D3
Bryanston Cl UB2 ... 107 B2
Bryanston Ct W1 ... 237 C2
Bryanstone Ct SM1 ... 218 A5
Bryanstone Rd N8 ... 49 D4
Bryanston Ho 12
SE15 ... 139 D4
Bryanston Mans W1 ... 237 C4
Bryanston Mews E
W1 ... 237 C3
Bryanston Mews W
W1 ... 92 D1 237 C2
Bryanston Pl
W1 ... 92 D2 237 C3
Bryanston Sq
W1 ... 92 D1 237 C2
Bryanston St
W1 ... 92 D1 237 D1
Bryant Cl EN5 ... 13 B6
Bryant Ct Acton W3 ... 111 B5
Haggerston E2 ... 95 D5

Bryant Rd UB5.......84 C4
Bryant St E15.......76 C1
Bryantwood Rd N5,
  N7.................72 C2
Brycedale Cres N14...15 D1
Bryce Ho 25 SE14...140 D6
Bryce Rd RM8........80 A4
Brydale Ho 2 SE16..118 D2
Bryden Cl SE26.....185 A5
Bryden St SE15......76 B3
Brydon Wlk N1......233 B6
Bryer Ct EC2.......242 A4
Bryett Rd N7........97 C5
Brymay Cl E3........97 C5
Brymon Ct W1.......237 D3
Brynmaer Ho SW11..140 B1
Brynmaer Rd
  SW11.......136 C4 267 D1
Bryn-y-Mawr Rd EN1..5 D1
Bryony Cl UB8.......82 B2
Bryony Rd W12.....112 A6
Bryony Way TW16...172 A4
B Sky B Hq TW7....131 A6
BT Twr * W1...93 C2 239 A4
Buccleuch Ho E5.....54 A2
Buchanan Cl N21....16 B6
Buchanan Ct
  SE16..............118 D2
Buchan Gdns
  NW10..............90 B5
Buchanan Ho
  Dulwich SE21......161 C1
  Wandsworth SW18...157 C4
Buchan Ho W3......110 D4
Buchan Rd SE15....140 C2
Bucharest Rd SW18..158 A4
Buckden Cl
  Fortis Green N2....48 D5
  Lee SE12..........165 A5
Buckfast Ct W13....109 A6
Buckfast Ho N14.....15 C4
Buckfast SM4......201 D5
Buckfast St E2......96 A4
Buck Hill Wlk
  W2..........114 B6 246 D5
Buckhold Rd SW18..157 C5
Buckhurst Ave CR4,
  SM5..............202 C5
Buckhurst Ct 7 IG9..21 D2
BUCKHURST HILL....21 C5
Buckhurst Hill Ho 3
  IG9...............21 B2
Buckhurst Hill Sta
  IG9...............21 B2
Buckhurst Ho 19 N7..71 D3
Buckhurst St E1.....96 B3
Buckhurst Way IG9...21 C1
Buckingham Ave
  East Molesey KT8...173 B4
  Falconwood DA16...145 C1
  Feltham TW14......151 A6
  Oakleigh Pk N20....14 B4
  South Norwood CR7..182 C2
  St James SW1......250 B5
  Wembley UB6.......87 A4
Buckingham Cl
  Broom Hill BR5....211 C2
  Ealing W5..........87 C2
  Enfield EN1.........5 C3
  Hampton TW12.....173 B4
Buckingham College
  Prep Sch 10 HA2....41 C2
Buckingham College Sch
  HA1...............42 C4
Buckingham Ct
  Ealing W7.........86 D3
  Hendon NW4........46 A6
  Mitcham CR4......204 A4
  Northolt UB5.......85 A6
  Welling HA0.......65 C2
Buckingham Gdns
  East Molesey KT8...173 B4
  Edgware HA8.......26 B3
  South Norwood CR7..182 C1
Buckingham Gate
  SW1.......115 C3 259 B6
Buckingham Ho
  2 Acton W3........88 C1
  Finsbury Pk N4....111 A1
  Richmond TW10....154 C6
Buckingham La
  SE23..............163 A4

Buckingham Lo N10...49 C5
Buckingham Mans
  NW6...............69 D3
Buckingham Mews
  Harlesden NW10....89 D5
  7 Kingsland N1.....73 C2
  Westminster SW1...259 A6
Buckingham Pal *
  SW1.......115 C4 259 A5
Buckingham Palace Rd
  SW1.......115 B2 258 D4
Buckingham Par 11
  HA7...............25 C5
Buckingham Pl SW1..259 A6
Buckingham Prim Sch
  TW12.............173 B5
Buckingham Rd
  Edgware HA8.......26 A5
  Hampton TW12,
  TW13.............173 B5
  Harlesden NW10....89 D5
  Harrow HA1........42 B4
  Ilford IG1.........79 B6
  Kingsland N1......73 C2
  Kingston u T KT1...198 B5
  Leyton E10........75 D5
  Mitcham CR4......204 A4
  Richmond TW10....153 D2
  Stratford E15......76 B1
  Wanstead E11......54 B1
  Woodford E18......36 D2
  Wood Green N22....32 A2
Buckingham Way
  SM6..............219 C1
Buckingham Yd
  NW10.............89 D5
Buck La NW9........28 A6
Buckland Cl NW7....28 A6
Buckland Ct
  6 Shoreditch N1....95 C5
  Uxbridge UB10.....61 A6
Buckland Rd
  Chessington KT9...214 B3
  Leyton E10........76 A6
  Orpington BR6.....227 C4
Buckland Rise HA5..22 D2
Bucklands Rd TW11..175 C4
Buckland St
  N1.......95 B5 235 D3
Buckland Way KT4...200 C1
Buckleigh Ave
  SW20.............201 B6
  Morden SM4.......202 A5
Buckle Ct HA8......27 A3
Buckleigh Ave SW16..201 B6
Buckleigh Ho SW16..180 B5
Buckleigh Way SE19..183 D3
Buckler Gdns SE9...166 B1
Buckler's Alley SW6..264 C3
Bucklers' Alley EC2,
  EC4..............242 C1
Buckler's' Way SM5..218 D5
Buckles Ct DA17....124 D2
Buckle St
  5 Whitechapel E1...96 A1
  Whitechapel E1....243 D2
Buckley Cl SE23....162 B4
Buckley Ct
  5 Brondesbury NW6..69 B1
  London N8.........110 C5
Buckley Ho N3......110 C5
Buckley Rd NW6.....69 B1
Buckmaster Cl 11
  SW9..............138 C2
Buckmaster Ho 11
  N7................72 B4
Buckmaster Rd
  SW11.............136 C1
Bucknall St WC1....240 A2
Bucknall Way BR3...208 A5
Bucknell Cl SW2....138 B1
Buckner Rd SW2....138 B1
Buckrell Rd E4......20 B2
Buckridge Bldg EC1..241 A4
Buckshead Ho 10 W2..91 C2
Buck St NW1.........71 B1
Buckstone Cl SE23..162 C5
Buckstone Rd N18...34 A5
Buckters Rents
  SE16..............119 A5
Buckthorne Rd SE4..163 A6
Buckthorn Ho DA15..167 D1

Buckwheat Ct DA18.124 D3
Budd Cl N12........29 D6
Buddings Circ HA9...67 A5
Bude Cl E17........53 B4
Budge La CR4......202 D2
Budge Row EC4.....242 C1
Budge's Wlk
  W2..........114 A6 246 B4
Budleigh Cres DA16.146 C4
Budleigh Ho 19
  SE15..............140 A6
Budoch Ct IG3......80 A6
Budoch Dr IG3......80 A6
Buer Rd SW6.......135 A3
Bugsby's Way SE10..120 D2
Buick Ho 4 E3......97 C3
Building 36 7 E16..123 A3
Building 47 6 E16..123 A3
Building 48 E16....123 A3
Building 49 5 E16..123 A3
Building 50 3 E16..123 A3
Building Crafts Coll The
  E15...............76 B1
Bulbarrow NW8.....91 D6
Bulganak Rd CR7...205 A5
Bulinca St
  SW1.......115 D2 259 D3
Bullace Row SE5...139 B4
Bullard Rd TW11...174 D4
Bullards Pl 13 E2...96 D4
Bull Dog The (Juct)
  SW15.............148 A2
Bulleid Way
  SW1.......115 B2 258 D3
Bullen Ho 13 E1....96 B3
Bullen St SW11.....136 C3
Buller Cl SE15.....140 A5
Buller Rd Barking IG11 79 C1
  Kensal Green NW10..90 D4
  South Norwood CR7..205 B6
  Tottenham N17......34 A1
  Wood Green N22....32 C1
Bullers Wood Dr
  BR7..............188 B3
Bullers Wood Sch
  BR7..............188 B3
Bullescroft Rd HA8..10 D1
Bullfinch Cl 4 SE21..161 B2
Bullingham Mans
  W8...............245 B2
Bull Inn Ct WC2....250 B5
Bullivant St 9 E14..120 A6
Bull La
  Chislehurst BR7....189 B3
  Dagenham RM10....81 D5
  Edmonton N18......33 C5
Bull Rd E15........98 D5
Bullrush Cl
  Carshalton SM5...218 C6
  Thornton Heath CR0..205 C3
Bull's Alley SW14...133 B3
Bull's Bridge Ind Est
  UB2..............106 B2
Bullsbrook Rd UB4..106 C5
Bull's Cross EN1, EN2..6 A6
Bull's Gdns SW3....257 B4
Bull's Head Pas EC3..243 A1
Bull Yd SE15.......140 A4
Bulmer Gdns HA3....43 D2
Bulmer Mews
  W11.......113 C5 245 A4
Bulow Ct 11 SW6...135 D3
Bulstrode Ave TW3..129 C2
Bulstrode Gdns
  TW3..............129 C2
Bulstrode Pl W1....238 B3
Bulstrode Rd TW3..129 C2
Bulstrode St
  W1.......93 A1 238 B2
Bulwer Court Rd E11..54 B1
Bulwer Gdns EN5....2 A1
Bulwer Rd
  Edmonton N18......33 C6
  Leytonstone E11....54 B1
  New Barnet EN5....2 A1
Bulwer St W12......112 C5
Bunbury Ho SE15...140 A5
Bunces La IG8......36 D3
Bungalow Rd SE25..205 C5
Bungalows The
  Leyton E10........54 A3
  Mitcham SW16.....181 B3

Bunhill Row
  EC1.......95 B3 242 C5
Bunhouse Pl SW1...258 B2
Bunkers Hill
  London NW11......48 A2
  North Cray DA14...169 B1
Bunker's Hill DA17..125 C2
Bunning Ho N7......72 A4
Bunning Way N7.....72 B1
Bunsen Ho 2 E3.....97 A5
Bunsen St 8 E3......97 A5
Buntingbridge Rd
  IG2...............57 B5
Bunting Cl London N9..18 D3
  Mitcham CR4......202 D4
Bunting Ct NW9.....27 D2
Bunton St SE18.....122 C3
Bunyan Ct EC2.....242 A4
Bunyan Rd E17......53 A6
Buonaparte Mews
  SW1..............259 C2
Burbage Cl
  Bermondsey
  SE1.......117 B3 262 C6
  Hayes UB3.........83 B1
Burbage Ho
  18 Deptford SE14...140 D6
  Shoreditch N1.....235 D5
Burbage Rd SE21,
  SE24.............161 B4
Burbage Sch 30 N1..235 C5
Burbank KT3.......199 D6
Burberry Cl KT3....177 C1
Burberry Ct 8 N3...29 D3
Burbridge Rd W7...192 C5
Burbridge Way N17..34 A1
Burcham St E14.....98 A1
Burcharbro Rd SE2..146 D6
Burchell Ct WD23...8 A4
Burchell Ho SE11...260 D2
Burchell Rd
  Leyton E10........53 D1
  London SE15......140 B4
Burcher Gale Gr 5
  SE15.............139 C5
Burchets Way
  TW17.............192 D3
Burcote Rd SW18...158 B4
Burden Cl TW8......109 C1
Burden Ho SW8.....270 A3
Burdenshott Ave
  TW10.............122 D3
Burden Way E11.....77 B6
Burder Cl N1.......73 C2
Burder Rd N1.......73 C2
Burdett Ave SW20...178 B2
Burdett Cl
  2 Ealing W7......108 D5
  Sidcup DA14......191 A5
Burdett Coutts &
  Townshend CE Prim
  Sch SW1...115 D2 259 D3
Burdett Mews W2...91 D2
Burdett Rd
  Richmond TW9....132 B2
  Thornton Heath CR0..205 B3
  Tower Hamlets E3...97 B2
Burdetts Rd RM9...103 A6
Burdock Cl CR0....206 D1
Burdock Rd N17....52 A6
Burdon La SM2.....217 A2
Burdon Pk SM2.....217 A1
Burfield Cl SW17...180 B6
Burford Cl
  Dagenham RM8.....80 C5
  Ickenham UB10.....60 A4
  Ilford IG6.........57 A5
Burford Ct SE8.....141 C6
Burford Gdns N13...16 B1
Burford Ho
  1 Brentford TW8...110 A1
  5 South Lambeth
  SW9..............270 C4
Burford Rd
  Brentford TW8....110 A1
  Bromley BR1......210 A5
  Forest Hill SE6....163 B2
  Newham E6.........99 A4
  New Malden KT4...200 A2
  5 Stratford Marsh
  E15...............98 B3
  Sutton SM1.......217 C6
Burford Way CR0...224 A2

Burford Wlk SW6...265 D3
Burgate Ct 9 SW9..138 C2
Burges Gr SW13....134 B5
Burges Rd E6.......78 B1
Burgess Ave NW9...45 B3
Burgess Bsns Pk
  SE5...............139 B5
Burgess Cl 4 TW13.173 A6
Burgess Ct
  2 London N20......14 D2
  5 Southall UB1.....85 D1
  Wallend E12.......78 C1
Burgess Hill NW2...69 C4
Burgess Ho 5 SE5..139 B5
Burgess Mews
  SW19.............179 D4
Burgess Park Mans
  NW6...............69 C4
Burgess Rd
  Leyton E15.........76 C4
  Sutton SM1.......217 D4
Burgess St E14......97 C2
Burge St SE1.......262 D5
Burgh House &
  Hampstead Mus *
  NW3...............70 D4
Burghill Rd SE26...185 A6
Burghley Ave
  Borehamwood WD6...11 A6
  Kingston u T KT3...177 B2
Burghley Cl SW19...179 A5
Burghley Hall Cl
  SW19.............157 A3
Burghley Ho SW19..157 A1
Burghley Pl CR4....202 D5
Burghley Rd
  Camden Town NW5...71 B4
  Leytonstone E11....54 C1
  London N8.........50 C6
  Wimbledon SW19...179 A6
Burghley Twr W3...111 D6
Burgh St N1...94 C6 234 D4
Burgon St EC4.....241 D1
Burgos Cl CR0.....220 C2
Burgos Gr SE10....141 C4
Burgoyne Rd
  Ashford TW16......171 D4
  Brixton SW9.......138 B2
  Harringay N4.......50 D3
  South Norwood SE25..205 D5
Burham Cl SE20....184 C3
Burhan Uddin Ho 21 E1 243 C5
Burhill Gr HA5......23 A1
Buriton Ho 9 SW15..156 B3
Burke Cl SW15.....133 C1
Burke Ho SW11.....136 B1
Burke Lodge E13....99 B4
Burke St E16.......98 D2
Burket Cl UB2.....107 B2
Burland Rd SW11...158 D6
Burleigh Ave
  Bexley DA15.......167 D6
  Hackbridge SM6....219 B5
Burleigh Cl RM7.....59 D5
Burleigh Coll W6...112 C2
Burleigh Ct N17.....34 A4
Burleigh Gdns
  Ashford TW15......171 A5
  Osidge N14.........15 C3
Burleigh Ho
  Cheam SM3........201 A1
  Chelsea SW3.......266 D5
  5 North Kensington
  W10..............91 D2
Burleigh Lo 3
  SW19.............179 D2
Burleigh Par N14....15 D3
Burleigh Pl SW15...156 D6
Burleigh Rd
  Cheam SM3........201 A1
  Enfield EN1.........5 C1
  Hillingdon UB10....82 D6
Burleigh St WC2....250 C5
Burleigh Way EN2....5 B2
Burleigh Wlk SE6..164 A3
Burley Cl Chingford E4..35 C5
  Mitcham SW16.....181 D1
Burley Ho E1.......96 D1
Burley Rd E16......99 C2
Burlington Apartments
  SE20..............184 B3
Burlington Arc W1..249 A5

Burlington Ave
Richmond TW9 132 C4
Romford RM7 59 D3
Burlington Cl
East Bedfont TW14 149 B4
[5] Newham E6 100 A1
Orpington BR6 226 D6
Paddington W9 91 C3
Pinner HA5 40 B6
Burlington Ct
Chiswick W4 133 A5
Highgate N6 49 A1
Burlington Danes Acad W12 90 B1
Burlington Gate SW20 179 A1
Burlington Gdns
Acton Green W4 111 A1
Acton W3 111 A5
Dagenham RM6 59 A2
[4] Fulham SW6 135 A3
Marylebone W1 115 C6 249 A5
Burlington Ho NW3 70 B3
Burlington Inf Sch KT3 199 D5
Burlington Jun Sch KT3 199 D5
Burlington La W4 133 B5
Burlington Lo BR7 188 B3
Burlington Lodge SW6 135 A3
Burlington Mews
Acton W3 111 A5
[2] Putney SW15 157 B6
Burlington Park Ho [6] HA7 25 C6
Burlington Pl
Fulham SW6 135 A3
Woodford IG8 21 A1
Burlington Rd
Acton Green W4 111 A1
Enfield EN2 5 B4
Fulham SW6 135 A3
Hounslow TW7 130 B4
Muswell Hill N10 49 A6
New Malden KT3 199 D5
South Norwood CR7 183 B1
Tottenham N17 34 A2
Burlington Rise EN4 14 D4
Burma Rd N16 73 B4
Burmarsh [6] NW5 71 A2
Burmarsh Ct SE20 184 C2
Burma Terr [11] SE19 183 C5
Burmester Ho SW17 158 A1
Burmester Rd SW17 158 A1
Burnaby Cres W4 133 A6
Burnaby Ct [31] SE16 118 A4
Burnaby Gdns W4 132 D6
Burnaby St SW10 136 A5 266 B3
Burnand Ho [3] W14 112 D3
Burnbrae Cl N12 29 D4
Burnbury Rd SW12 159 C3
Burncroft Ave EN3 6 C3
Burndell Way UB4 84 D2
Burne Jones Ho W14 254 B3
Burnell Ave
Richmond TW10 175 C5
Welling DA16 146 A3
Burnell Gdns HA7 25 D1
Burnell Ho [18] SW2 160 C3
Burnell Rd SM1 217 D4
Burnell Wlk SE1 263 D2
Burnels Ave E6 100 C4
Burness Cl N7 72 B2
Burne St NW1 237 A4
Burnett Cl E9 74 C3
Burnett Ct SW11 267 A1
Burnett Ho [6] SE13 142 A3
Burney Ave KT5 198 B4
Burney Ho [4] SW16 181 C5
Burney St SE10 142 A5
Burnfoot Ave SW6 135 A4 264 B1
Burnham NW3 70 C1
Burnham Ave UB10 61 A4
Burnham Cl
Bermondsey SE1 263 D3
Enfield EN1 5 C5
Harrow HA3 43 A5
Hendon NW7 28 A3
Burnham Cres E11 55 C5
Burnham Ct
Bayswater W2 245 D6
Hendon NW4 46 C5
[15] Stanmore HA7 25 C5
Burnham Dr KT4 216 D6
Burnham Est [8] E2 96 C4
Burnham Gdns
Cranford TW4 128 B4
Croydon CR0 205 D2
Hayes UB3 105 B3
Burnham Rd
Chingford Hatch E4 35 B5
Dagenham RM9 102 B6
Morden SM4 201 D5
Sidcup DA14 169 A2
Burnham St
Bethnal Green E2 96 C4
Kingston u T KT2 176 C2
Burnham Way
Ealing W13 109 B3
Penge SE26 185 B5
Burnhill Ho EC1 235 A1
Burnhill Rd BR3 185 C1
Burnley Cl WD19 22 C5
Burnley Rd
London SW9 138 B3
Willesden NW10 68 A3
Burnsall St SW3 114 C1 257 B2
Burns Ave
Blackfen DA15 168 B5
Feltham TW14 150 A5
Ilford RM6 58 C2
Southall UB1 107 C6
Burns Cl Bexley DA16 145 D4
Hayes UB4 84 A2
Mitcham SW17 180 B4
Walthamstow E17 54 A5
Burns Ct
Tottenham N17 34 B3
Wallington SM6 219 B1
Burns Ho
[18] Bethnal Green E2 96 C4
Bexley DA16 146 C4
[1] Islington N7 72 B2
Kennington SE17 261 D1
[11] Stoke Newington N16 73 C4
Burn's Ho NW10 89 C6
Burnside Ave E4 35 B4
Burnside Cl Barnet EN5 1 C2
Rotherhithe SE16 118 D5
Twickenham TW1 153 A5
Burnside Cres HA0 87 D6
Burnside Ct [1] SM6 219 A5
Burnside Rd RM8 58 D1
Burns Rd
Battersea SW11 136 D3
Ealing W13 109 B4
Wembley HA0 88 A5
Burn's Rd NW10 89 D6
Burns Way TW5 128 D4
Burnt Ash Hill
Lee SE12 164 D5
Lewisham SE12 165 A3
Burnt Ash Hts BR1 187 B5
Burnt Ash La BR1, SE12 187 B5
Burnt Ash Prim Sch BR1 187 A5
Burnt Ash Rd SE12 164 D6
Burnthwaite Rd SW6 135 B5 264 D3
BURNT OAK 27 B3
Burnt Oak Broadway HA8 26 D3
Burnt Oak Fields HA8 27 A2
Burnt Oak Jun Sch DA15 168 A3
Burnt Oak La DA15 168 B3
Burnt Oak L Ctr HA8 27 B2
Burnt Oak Sta HA8 27 A2
Burntwood Cl SW18 158 C3
Burntwood Ct SW17 158 A1
Burntwood Grange Rd SW18 158 C3
Burntwood La SW17 158 B2
Burntwood Sch SW17 158 B2
Burntwood View [6] SE19 183 D5
Buross St E1 96 B1
Burpham Cl UB4 84 D2
Burrage Ct [17] SE16 118 D2
Burrage Gr SE18 123 A2
Burrage Pl SE18 122 D1
Burrage Rd SE18 123 A1
Burrard Ho [11] E2 96 C5
Burrard Rd
Newham E16 99 B1
West Hampstead NW6 69 C4
Burr Cl
Bexleyheath DA7 147 B2
St George in t East E1 118 A5
Burrell Cl
Croydon CR0 207 A3
Edgware HA8 10 D2
Burrell Ct HA1 42 B2
Burrell Ho [4] TW1 153 B4
Burrell Row BR3 185 C1
Burrells [9] BR3 185 D1
Burrell St SE1 116 D5 251 C4
Burrell's Wharf Sq E14 119 D1
Burrell Twrs E10 53 C2
Burrhill Ct SE16 118 D3
Burritt Rd KT1 176 C1
Burrmead Ct NW2 67 D5
Burroughs Gdns NW4 46 B5
Burroughs The NW4 46 B5
Burrow Ho [19] SW9 138 B3
Burrow Rd SE22 139 C1
Burrows Mews SE1 251 C2
Burrows Rd NW10 90 C4
Burrow Wlk SE21 161 A4
Burr Rd SW18 157 C4
Bursar St SE1 253 A3
Bursdon Cl DA15 167 D2
Bursland Rd EN3 6 D1
Burslem St E1 96 A1
Bursted Wood Prim Sch DA7 147 D3
Burstock Rd SW15 135 A1
Burston Rd SW15 156 D6
Burstow Rd SW20 179 A2
Burtenshaw Rd KT7 197 A3
Burtley Cl N4 51 A1
Burton Bank N1 73 B1
Burton Cl
Chessington KT9 213 D1
South Norwood CR7 205 B6
Burton Ct
Chelsea SW3 257 D2
[10] Friern Barnet N11 30 D5
Thames Ditton KT7 197 A3
Burton Dr EN3 7 C6
Burton Gdns TW5 129 B4
Burton Gr SE17 262 C1
Burton Ho
[8] Bermondsey SE16 118 B4
Brixton SE5 138 D4
Penge SE26 184 B5
Burtonhole Cl NW7 28 D6
Burtonhole La
Finchley NW7, NW12 29 A6
Mill Hill NW7 28 D6
Burton La [3] SW9 138 C3
Burton Lo [6] SW15 157 B6
Burton Mews SW1 258 B3
Burton Pl WC1 232 D1
Burton Rd
[7] Brixton SW9 138 C3
Brixton SW9 138 D3
Brondesbury NW6 69 B1
Kingston u T KT2 176 A3
Wanstead E18 55 B6
Burtons Ct E15 76 B1
Burtons Rd TW12 174 A6
Burton St WC1 93 D3 239 D6
Burtonwood Ho N4 51 B2
Burt Rd E16 121 C5
Burtt Ho [6] N1 95 C4
Burtwell La SE21, SE27 183 B6
Burvill Ct SW20 178 C2
Burwash Ho SE1 252 D1
Burwash Rd SE18 123 B1
Burway Cl CR2 221 C2
Burwell [2] KT1 176 C1
Burwell Ave UB6 64 C2
Burwell Cl [27] E1 96 B1
Burwell Rd E10 53 A1
Burwell Wlk [14] E3 97 C3
Burwood Ave
Hayes BR2 225 B6
Pinner HA5 40 C4
Burwood Cl KT6 198 C1
Burwood Ho [11] SW9 138 D1
Burwood Lo SW19 179 B6
Burwood Pl Barnet EN4 2 A4
Paddington W2 237 B2
Bury Ave Hayes UB4 83 C5
Ruislip HA4 39 A3
Bury Cl SE16 118 D5
Bury Ct EC3 243 B2
Buryfield Ct [23] SE8 118 D2
Bury Gr SM4 201 D4
Bury Hall Villas N9 17 D4
Bury Pl WC1 94 A2 240 B3
Bury Rd Chingford E4 20 C6
Dagenham RM10 81 D3
Hornsey N22 50 C6
Bury St W N9 17 C4
Buryside Cl IG2 57 D5
Bury St Edmonton N9 18 A3
Ruislip HA4 39 B3
St James SW1 115 C5 249 B4
Whitechapel EC3 95 C1 243 B2
Bury Wlk SW3 114 C1 257 A2
Burywood Ct EN3 6 C3
Busbridge Ho [24] E14 97 C2
Busby Ho SW16 181 C6
Busby Mews [5] NW1 71 D2
Busby Pl NW5 71 D2
Busch Cl TW7 131 B4
Busch Cnr TW7 131 B4
Bushbaby Cl SE1 263 A5
Bushberry Rd E9 75 A2
Bush Cl IG2 57 B4
Bush Cotts [12] SW18 157 C6
Bush Ct London N14 15 C3
[7] Shepherd's Bush W12 112 D4
Bushell Cl SW2 160 B2
Bushell Gn WD23 8 B2
Bushell Ho [3] SE27 183 A6
Bushell St [18] E1 118 A5
Bushell Way BR7 188 C5
BUSHEY 8 A2
Bushey Ave
Crofton BR5 211 B2
Snaresbrook E18 54 D6
Bushey Cl
Chingford E4 20 A1
Ickenham UB10 60 C6
Bushey Ct SW20 178 B1
Bushey Down SW12 159 B2
Bushey Hall SE5 139 D4
BUSHEY HEATH 8 C4
Bushey Heath Prim Sch WD23 8 B3
Bushey Hill Rd SE5 139 D4
Bushey Ho SE12 165 C1
Bushey La SM1 217 C4
Bushey Lees DA15 167 D5
BUSHEY MEAD 200 D6
Bushey Meads Sch WD23 8 A6
Bushey Rd
Croydon CR0 223 C6
Hayes UB3 105 C2
Ickenham UB10 60 C6
Newham E13 99 C5
South Tottenham N15 51 C3
Sutton SM1 217 C4
West Barnes SW20 178 D1
Bushey Way BR3 208 B4
Bush Fair Ct N14 15 B5
Bushfield Cl HA8 10 D2
Bushfield Cres HA8 10 D2
Bushfield Ho N5 73 A3
Bush Gr London NW9 45 A2
Stanmore HA7 25 D2
Bushgrove Rd RM8 80 D5
BUSH HILL 17 B5
Bush Hill N21 17 A5
Bush Hill Par EN1 17 B4
BUSH HILL PARK 17 C5
Bush Hill Park Prim Sch EN1 18 A6
Bush Hill Park Sta EN1 17 D5
Bush Hill Rd
Enfield N21 17 B5
Harrow HA3 44 B3
Bush Ind Est NW10 89 B3
Bush La EC4 117 B6 252 C6
Bushmead Cl [7] N15 51 D5
Bushmoor Cres SE18 144 D5
Bushnell Rd SW17 159 B1
Bush Rd
Bermondsey SE8 118 D2
Hackney E8 96 B6
Littleton TW17 192 B4
Richmond TW9 132 B6
Wanstead E11 55 A2
Woodford IG9 37 D6
Bushway RM8 80 D5
Bushwood E11 55 A1
Bushwood Dr SE1 117 D2 263 D3
Bushwood Rd TW9 132 C6
Bushy Ct KT1 175 C2
Bushy Park Gdns TW12 174 B5
Bushy Park Rd TW11 175 B3
Bushy Rd TW11 174 D3
Business Acad Bexley The DA18 125 A4
Business Design Ctr★ N1 94 C6 234 B5
Buspace Studios [3] W10 91 A3
Butcher Row E1 96 D1
Butchers Rd E16 99 A1
Bute Ave TW10 154 A2
Bute Ct SM6 219 C3
Bute Gardens W SM6 219 C3
Bute Gdns
Hammersmith W6 112 D2
Wallington SM6 219 C3
Bute House Prep Sch [2] W6 112 D2
Bute Mews NW11 48 A4
Bute Rd Ilford IG6 56 D4
Thornton Heath CR0 204 C1
Wallington SM6 219 C4
Bute St SW7 114 B2 256 C4
Bute Wlk [18] N1 73 B2
Butfield Ho [6] E9 74 C2
Butler Ave HA1 42 B2
Butler Cl HA8 26 D1
Butler Ct
Dagenham RM8 81 C6
Wembley HA0 65 A4
Butler Ho
[32] Bethnal Green E2 96 C4
[5] Brixton SW9 138 D4
[11] Poplar E14 97 B1
Butler Pl SW1 259 C6
Butler Rd
Dagenham RM8 80 B4
Harrow HA1 42 A2
Willesden NW10 67 D1
Butlers Cl TW3 129 B1
Butlers & Colonial Wharf SE1 253 D2
Butler's Cotts DA7 147 C3
Butlers Farm Cl TW10 175 D6
Butler St
[33] Bethnal Green E2 96 C4
Hillingdon UB10 82 D3
Butler's Wharf W SE1 253 C3
Butley Ct [8] E3 97 A5
Butt Ct SM4 202 A3
Buttercup Cl UB5 63 B2
Butterfield Cl
[1] Bermondsey SE16 118 B4
Tottenham N17 33 A4
Twickenham TW1 152 D5
Butterfield Ho [4] EN2 4 D3
Butterfield Mews [15] SE18 144 D6
Butterfields E17 54 A4
Butterfield Sq [10] E6 100 B1
Butterfly Ct [1] E6 100 B4
Butterfly La SE9 166 D5
Butterfly Wlk [2] SE5 139 B4
Butter Hill SM5, SM6 219 A4
Butteridges Cl RM9 103 B6
Buttermere NW1 231 D2
Buttermere Cl
Bermondsey SE1 263 C3
East Bedfont TW14 149 D3
Leyton E11 76 B4
West Barnes SM4 200 D3
Buttermere Ct NW8 229 C6

Buttermere Dr SW15 ... 157 A6
Buttermere Ho
London N12 ... 30 C5
13 Tower Hamlets E3 ... 97 B4
Buttermere Wlk 9 E8 ... 73 D2
Butterwick W6 ... 112 C2
Butterworth Ct SW16 ... 160 A1
Butterworth Gdns IG8 ... 37 A5
Buttery Mews N4 ... 16 A1
Buttesland St N1 ... 95 B4 235 D2
Buttfield Cl RM10 ... 81 D2
Buttmarsh Cl SE18 ... 122 D1
Buttsbury Rd IG1 ... 79 A3
Butts Cotts TW13 ... 151 B1
Butts Cres TW13 ... 151 C1
Butts Ho TW13 ... 151 C1
Butts Piece UB5 ... 84 B5
Butts Rd BR1 ... 186 C5
Butts The TW8 ... 131 D6
Buxhall Cres E9 ... 75 B2
Buxlow Prep Sch HA9 ... 66 A5
Buxted Rd
Camberwell SE22 ... 139 C1
Colney Hatch N12 ... 30 C5
Dalston E8 ... 73 D1
Buxton Cl London N9 ... 18 C2
Woodford IG8 ... 37 D4
Buxton Cres SM3 ... 217 A4
Buxton Ct
1 Leyton E11 ... 54 D2
Shoreditch N1 ... 235 B2
Buxton Dr
Kingston u T KT3 ... 177 B1
Leytonstone E11 ... 54 C5
Buxton Gdns W3 ... 110 D6
Buxton Ho
Leytonstone E11 ... 54 C5
3 London SW11 ... 136 B1
Buxton Lo E11 ... 77 B6
Buxton Mews SW4 ... 137 D3
Buxton Rd
Chingford E4 ... 20 B4
Ilford IG2 ... 57 C3
Mortlake SW14 ... 133 C2
Newham E6 ... 100 A4
Stratford E15 ... 76 C3
Thornton Heath CR7 ... 204 D4
Upper Holloway N19 ... 49 D1
Walthamstow E17 ... 53 A5
Willesden NW2 ... 68 B2
Buxton St E1 ... 95 D3 243 D5
Buzzard Creek Ind Est IG11 ... 102 A2
Byam Shaw Sch of Art 8 N19 ... 71 D6
Byam St SW6 ... 136 A3
Byards Croft SW16 ... 181 D2
Byards Ct SE16 ... 118 D3
Byas Ho 6 E3 ... 97 B4
Byatt Wlk TW12 ... 173 A4
Bychurch End 11 TW11 ... 174 D5
Bycroft Rd UB1 ... 85 C3
Bycroft St SE20 ... 184 D3
Bycullah Ave EN2 ... 4 D3
Bycullah Ct EN2 ... 4 D2
Bycullah Rd EN2 ... 4 D3
Byefield Cl SE16 ... 119 A4
Byegrove Ct SW19 ... 180 B4
Byegrove Rd SW19 ... 180 B4
Byelands Cl 12 SE16 ... 118 D5
Bye The W3 ... 89 C1
Bye Ways TW2 ... 151 D1
Byeways The KT5 ... 198 D4
Byeway The SW14 ... 133 A2
Bye Way The HA3 ... 24 D2
Byfeld Gdns SW13 ... 134 A4
Byfield Ct KT3 ... 200 A5
Byfield Rd TW7 ... 131 A2
Byford Cl E15 ... 76 C1
Bygrove CR0 ... 223 D1
Bygrove Prim Sch 21 E14 ... 97 D1
Bygrove St E14 ... 97 D1
Byland Cl
Abbey Wood SE2 ... 124 B3
Carshalton SM4 ... 202 B2
Southgate N21 ... 16 B4
Byne Rd
Carshalton SM5 ... 218 C6
Byne Rd *continued*
Forest Hill SE26 ... 184 C5
Bynes Rd CR2 ... 221 B1
Byng Pl WC1 ... 93 D3 239 C5
Byng St E14 ... 119 C4
Bynon Ave DA7 ... 147 B2
Byre Rd N14 ... 15 B5
Byrne Cl 2 CR0 ... 204 D3
Byrne Ho 11 SW2 ... 160 B6
Byrne Rd SW12 ... 159 B2
Byron Ave
Borehamwood WD6 ... 10 C6
Cranford TW4 ... 128 B3
Plashet E12 ... 78 A2
Queensbury NW9 ... 44 D6
Sutton SM1 ... 218 B4
West Barnes KT3 ... 200 A4
Woodford E18 ... 36 D1
Byron Ave E SM1 ... 218 B4
Byron Cl
Feltham TW12 ... 173 B6
Forest Hill SE26 ... 185 A6
Hackney E8 ... 96 A6
Streatham SW16 ... 182 A4
Thamesmead SE28 ... 124 C5
Walton-on-T KT12 ... 195 A1
Byron Court Prim Sch HA0 ... 65 C6
Byron Ct Chelsea SW3 257 B3
Dulwich SE21 ... 162 A3
Ealing W7 ... 109 A2
Enfield EN2 ... 4 D3
3 Hampstead NW6 ... 70 A1
Harrow HA1 ... 42 C3
4 New Barnet EN5 ... 2 A1
Paddington W9 ... 91 C3
1 Richmond TW10 ... 175 D6
South Norwood CR7 ... 183 A1
St Pancras WC1 ... 240 C6
11 Wanstead E11 ... 55 A5
Woodford E18 ... 37 B2
Byron Dr
East Finchley N2 ... 48 B3
Erith DA8 ... 147 D5
Byron Gdns SM1 ... 218 B4
Byron Hill Rd HA1, HA2 ... 64 C6
Byron Ho 5 BR3 ... 185 D4
Byron Mews
Hampstead NW3 ... 70 C4
2 Maida Vale W9 ... 91 C3
Byron Par UB10 ... 83 A3
Byron Rd
Dollis Hill NW2 ... 68 B6
Ealing W5 ... 110 B5
Edgware NW7 ... 28 A5
Harrow HA1 ... 42 C3
Leyton E10 ... 53 D1
Walthamstow E17 ... 53 C6
Wealdstone HA3 ... 24 D1
Wembley HA0 ... 65 C5
Byron St E14 ... 98 A1
Byron Way Hayes UB4 ... 83 D3
Northolt UB5 ... 85 A4
West Drayton UB7 ... 104 B2
Bysouth Cl N15 ... 51 B5
Bythorn St SW9 ... 138 B1
Byton Rd SW17 ... 180 D4
Byward Ave TW14 ... 150 C5
Byward St EC3 ... 117 C6 253 B5
Bywater Ho SE18 ... 122 A3
Bywater Pl SE16 ... 119 A5
Bywater St SW3 ... 114 D1 257 C2
Byway The KT19 ... 215 D4
Bywell Pl W1 ... 239 A3
Bywood Ave CR0 ... 206 D3
Bywood Terr CR0 ... 206 C3
Byworth Ho HA7 ... 25 C4
Byworth Wlk N19 ... 50 A1

C

Cabbell St NW1 ... 92 C2 237 A3
Cabinet Off SW1 ... 250 A2
Cabinet War Rooms & Churchill Mus★ SW1 ... 115 D4 249 D2
Cabinet Way E4 ... 35 B4
Cable Ho WC1 ... 234 A2
Cable Pl SE10 ... 142 A4
Cable St E1 ... 118 B6
Cabot Ct SE16 ... 118 D3
Cabot Sq E14 ... 119 C5
Cabot Way 3 E6 ... 99 D6
Cabul Rd SW11 ... 136 C3
Cactus Cl SE5 ... 139 C3
Cactus Wlk W12 ... 89 D1
Cadbury Cl
Ashford TW16 ... 171 C3
Isleworth TW7 ... 131 A4
Cadbury Rd TW16 ... 171 C4
Cadbury Way 1 SE16 ... 118 A2
Caddington Cl EN4 ... 14 C6
Caddington Rd NW2 ... 69 A5
Caddis Cl HA7 ... 24 D3
Cadell Cl E2 ... 95 D5
Cadell Ho 12 E2 ... 95 D5
Cade Rd SE10 ... 142 B4
Cader Rd SW18 ... 158 A5
Cadet Dr SE1 ... 117 D1 263 D2
Cade Tyler Ho 10 SE10 ... 142 A4
Cadiz St SE17 ... 117 A1 262 B1
Cadley Terr SE23 ... 162 C2
Cadman Cl SW9 ... 138 D5
Cadmer Cl KT3 ... 199 C5
Cadmore Ho 4 N1 ... 72 D1
Cadmus Cl 9 SW4 ... 137 D2
Cadmus Ct 6 SW9 ... 138 C4
Cadnam Lo E14 ... 120 B3
Cadnam Point 15 SW15 ... 156 B3
Cadogan Cl
Beckenham BR3 ... 186 B1
Hackney Wick E9 ... 75 B1
Harrow HA2 ... 63 D4
Teddington TW11 ... 174 C5
Cadogan Ct
Chelsea SW3 ... 257 C3
New Malden KT3 ... 199 C5
Sutton SM2 ... 217 D2
Cadogan Ct Gdns SW1 ... 258 A4
Cadogan Gate SW1 ... 114 D2 257 D4
Cadogan Gdns
Chelsea SW3 ... 114 D2 257 D3
Finchley N3 ... 29 D2
Southgate N21 ... 16 C6
Wanstead E18 ... 55 B6
Cadogan Hall★ SW1 258 A4
Cadogan Ho SW3 ... 266 D5
Cadogan La SW1 ... 115 A3 258 A5
Cadogan Pl SW1 ... 114 D3 257 D5
Cadogan Rd
Kingston u T KT6 ... 197 D4
Woolwich SE18 ... 122 D3
Woolwich SE18 ... 123 A3
Cadogan Sq SW1 ... 114 D3 257 D5
Cadogan St SW3 ... 114 D2 257 C3
Cadogan Terr E9 ... 75 B1
Cadoxton Ave 3 N15 ... 51 D3
Cadwallon Rd SE9 ... 167 A2
Caedmon Rd N7 ... 72 B4
Caerleon Cl
Claygate KT10 ... 213 B1
Sidcup DA14 ... 190 C5
Caerleon Terr SE2 ... 124 B2
Caernafon Ho HA7 ... 25 A5
Caernarvon Cl CR4 ... 204 A6
Caernarvon Ct 3 KT5 ... 198 B4
Caernarvon Ho W2 ... 236 A2
Caesar Ct 25 E2 ... 96 D5
Caesar's Way TW17 ... 193 B3
Caesars Wlk CR4 ... 202 D4
Cahill St EC1 ... 242 B5
Cahir St E14 ... 119 D2
Cain Ct 2 W5 ... 87 C2
Caine Ho W3 ... 110 D4
Cain's La TW14 ... 149 C6
Caird St W10 ... 91 B4
Cairn Ave W5 ... 109 D5
Cairndale Cl BR1 ... 186 D3
Cairnfield Ave NW2 ... 67 D5
Cairnfield Ct NW2 ... 67 C5
Cairngorm Cl 3 TW11 ... 175 A5
Cairn Ho 3 SW19 ... 180 C3
Cairns Ho 3 N7 ... 72 B4
Cairns Mews SE18 ... 144 A4
Cairns Rd SW11 ... 158 C6
Cairn Way HA7 ... 24 D4
Cairo New Rd CR0 ... 220 D6
Cairo Rd E17 ... 53 C5
Caister Ho N7 ... 72 B2
Caistor Ho
10 Balham SW12 ... 159 B4
5 West Ham E15 ... 98 D6
Caistor Mews SW12 ... 159 B4
Caistor Park Rd E15 ... 98 D6
Caistor Rd SW12 ... 159 B4
Caithness Gdns DA15 ... 167 D5
Caithness Ho N1 ... 233 C6
Caithness Rd
Hammersmith W14 ... 112 D3
Mitcham CR4 ... 181 B3
Calabria Rd N5 ... 72 D3
Calais Gate SE5 ... 138 D4
Calais St SE5 ... 138 D4
Calbourne Rd SW12 ... 159 A4
Calcott Wlk SE9 ... 187 D6
Calcraft Ho 10 E2 ... 96 C5
Caldbeck Ave KT4 ... 200 B1
Caldecot Ct SE5 ... 139 A3
Caldecote 3 KT1 ... 176 C1
Caldecote Gdns WD23 ... 8 C4
Caldecote La WD23 ... 8 D5
Caldecot Rd SE5 ... 139 A3
Caldecott Way E5 ... 74 D5
Calder Ave UB6 ... 86 D5
Calder Cl EN1 ... 5 C2
Calder Ct SE16 ... 119 B5
Calder Gdns HA8 ... 44 C6
Calder Ho UB5 ... 85 A6
Calderon Ho NW8 ... 230 A4
Calderon Pl 20 W10 ... 90 C2
Calderon Rd E11 ... 76 B5
Calder Rd SM4 ... 202 A4
Caldervale Rd SW4 ... 159 D6
Calderwood Pl EN4 ... 1 D4
Calderwood St SE18 ... 122 C2
Caldew Ct NW7 ... 28 A3
Caldew St SE5 ... 139 B5
Caldicote Gn NW9 ... 45 C3
Caldon Ho 2 UB5 ... 85 B3
Caldwell Rd WD19 ... 22 D6
Caldwell St SW9 ... 138 B5 270 D3
Caldy Rd DA17 ... 125 D3
Caldy Wlk 19 N1 ... 73 A2
Caleb St SE1 ... 252 B2
Caledonia Ct
Barking IG11 ... 102 C5
Hendon NW4 ... 28 C1
Caledonia Ho 15 E14 ... 97 A1
Caledonian Cl 1 IG3 ... 58 B1
Caledonian Ct UB5 ... 85 A3
Caledonian Market SE1 ... 117 C3 263 B6
Caledonian Rd
Islington N1 ... 94 B6 233 C5
Lower Holloway N7 ... 72 B2
Caledonian Road & Barnsbury Sta N7 ... 72 B1
Caledonian Road Sta N7 ... 72 B2
Caledonian Sq 6 NW1 ... 71 D2
Caledonian Wharf Rd E14 ... 120 B2
Caledonia Rd TW19 ... 148 A3
Caledonia St N1 ... 233 B3
Caledon Rd
East Ham E6 ... 78 B1
Hackbridge SM5, SM6 219 A4
Cale St SW3 ... 114 C1 257 A2
Caletock Way SE10 ... 120 D1
Calgarth NW1 ... 232 B3
Calgary Ct 30 SE16 ... 118 C4
Caliban Twr 9 N1 ... 95 C5
Calico Ho 4 SW11 ... 136 A2
Calico Row 5 SW11 ... 136 A2
Calidore Cl SW2 ... 160 B5
California Bldg 2 SE13 ... 141 D4
California La WD23 ... 8 B3
California Rd KT3 ... 199 A6
Callaby Terr 11 N1 ... 73 B2
Callaghan Cl SE13 ... 142 C1
Callahan Cotts 8 E1 ... 96 C2
Callander Rd SE6 ... 164 A2
Callanders The WD23 ... 8 C3
Callan Sch The W1 ... 93 C1 239 B2
Callard Ave N13 ... 32 D6
Callcott Ct NW6 ... 69 B1
Callcott Rd NW6 ... 69 B1
Callcott St W8 ... 245 A4
Callendar Rd SW7 ... 256 C6
Callingham Cl 13 E14 ... 97 B2
Callingham Ho 1 SW4 ... 138 A2
Callis Farm Cl TW19 ... 148 A5
Callis Rd E17 ... 53 B3
Callonfield 3 E17 ... 53 A5
Callow St SW3 ... 136 B6 266 C6
Calmington Rd SE5 ... 139 C6
Calmont Rd BR1 ... 186 C4
Calonne Rd SW19 ... 178 D6
Calshot Ho N1 ... 233 C4
Calshot Rd TW6 ... 126 D3
Calshot St N1 ... 94 B5 233 C3
Calshot Way
Enfield EN2 ... 4 D2
Harlington TW6 ... 126 C3
Calstock NW1 ... 232 C5
Calstock Ho SE11 ... 261 B2
Calthorpe Gdns
Edgware HA8 ... 26 B5
Sutton SM1 ... 218 A5
Calthorpe St WC1 ... 94 B3 240 D6
Calton Ave SE21 ... 161 C5
Calton Rd EN5 ... 14 B5
Calumet Ct SW17 ... 180 C4
Calver 13 NW5 ... 71 B4
Calver Ct E17 ... 54 B6
Calverley Cl BR3 ... 185 D4
Calverley Cres RM10 ... 81 C6
Calverley Gdns HA3 ... 43 D2
Calverley Gr N19 ... 49 D1
Calverley Rd KT17 ... 216 A2
Calvert Ave E2 ... 95 D4
Calvert Cl
Belvedere DA17 ... 125 D2
Sidcup DA14 ... 191 A4
Calvert Ct
1 London N19 ... 49 C1
5 Richmond TW9 ... 132 B1
Calvert Ho 9 W12 ... 112 B6
Calverton SE5 ... 139 C6
Calverton Prim Sch E16 ... 99 D1
Calverton Rd E6 ... 100 C6
Calvert Rd SE10 ... 120 D1
Calvert's Bldgs SE1 ... 252 C3
Calvert St NW1 ... 93 A6 231 A6
Calvin St E1 ... 95 D3 243 C5
Calydon Rd SE7 ... 121 B1
Calypso Cres 6 SE15 ... 139 D5
Calypso Way SE8, SE16 ... 119 B2
Camac Rd TW2 ... 152 B3
Camarthen Gn NW9 ... 45 C3
Cambalt Ho 3 SW15 ... 156 D6
Cambalt Rd SW15 ... 156 D6
Cambay Ho 7 E1 ... 97 A3
Cambell Jun & Inf Schs RM9 ... 80 D1
Camber Ho 4 SE15 ... 140 C6
Camberley Ave
Enfield EN1 ... 5 C1
Wimbledon SW20 ... 178 B1
Camberley Cl SM3 ... 216 D5
Camberley Ct 15 SM2 ... 217 D1
Camberley Ho NW1 ... 231 D3
Camberley Rd TW6 ... 126 C2
Cambert Way SE9 ... 143 B1
CAMBERWELL ... 139 A4
Camberwell Bsns Ctr SE5 ... 139 B5
Camberwell Church St SE5 ... 139 B4
Camberwell Coll of Arts
16 Camberwell SE5 ... 139 C4
25 Camberwell SE15 ... 139 D5
Camberwell Glebe SE5 ... 139 C4
Camberwell Gn SE5 ... 139 B4
Camberwell Gr SE5 ... 139 C3
Camberwell Green SE5 ... 139 A4

Camberwell New Rd SW9 138 D5
Camberwell Rd SE5 139 A5
Camberwell Station Rd SE5 139 A4
Camberwell Trad Est SE5 139 A4
Cambeys Rd RM10 81 D3
Cambisgate SW19 179 A5
Camborne Ave W13 109 C4
Camborne Cl TW6 126 C2
Camborne Cres TW6 126 C2
Camborne Rd
Belmont SM2 217 D1
Bexley DA16 145 D3
Croydon CR0 206 A2
Harmondsworth TW6 126 C2
Sidcup DA14 168 C1
Wandsworth SW18 157 C4
West Barnes SM4 200 D4
Camborne Way
Harlington TW6 126 C2
Heston TW5 129 C4
Cambourne Ave N9 18 D4
Cambourne Mews 6 W11 91 A1
Cambrai Ct N13 32 A6
Cambray Rd
Broom Hill BR6 211 D2
Streatham SW12 159 C3
Cambria 6 BR3 185 D1
Cambria Cl
Hounslow TW3 129 C1
Sidcup DA15 167 C3
Cambria Ct TW14 150 B4
Cambria Gdns TW19 148 A4
Cambria Ho
Forest Hill SE26 184 A6
14 Limehouse E14 97 A1
Cambria Lo 3 SW15 157 B6
Cambrian Ave IG2 57 C4
Cambrian Cl SE27 160 D1
Cambrian Ct UB2 107 D2
Cambrian Gn NW9 45 C4
Cambrian Rd
Leyton E10 53 C1
Richmond TW10 154 B5
Cambria Rd SE5 139 A2
Cambria St SW6 135 D5 265 D3
Cambridge Ave
Falconwood DA16 145 D1
Greenford UB6 64 D3
Kilburn NW6 91 C5
Kingston u T KT3, SW20 177 D1
Cambridge Barracks Rd 11 SE18 122 B2
Cambridge Cir WC2 93 D1 239 D1
Cambridge Cl
East Barnet EN4 15 A3
Hounslow TW4 129 A1
Walthamstow E17 53 B3
Willesden NW10 67 A5
Wimbledon SW20 178 B2
Wood Green N22 32 C2
Cambridge Cotts TW9 132 C6
Cambridge Cres
20 Bethnal Green E2 96 B5
Teddington TW11 175 A5
Cambridge Ct
4 Barnet EN5 1 B2
26 Bethnal Green E2 96 B5
7 Hammersmith W6 112 C2
2 Kilburn NW6 91 C5
Marylebone W2 237 A3
Stamford Hill N16 51 C2
Wembley HA0 65 D4
Wimbledon SW20 178 B2
Cambridge Dr
Lee SE12 165 A6
Ruislip HA4 62 D6
Cambridge Gate NW1 238 C6
Cambridge Gate Mews NW1 238 D6
Cambridge Gdns
Enfield EN1 6 A3
Kilburn NW6 91 C5
Cambridge Gdns *continued*
Kingston u T KT1 176 C1
Muswell Hill N10 31 B2
North Kensington W10 91 A1
Southgate N21 17 B4
Tottenham N17 33 B3
Cambridge Gn SE9 166 D3
Cambridge Gr
Hammersmith W6 112 B2
Penge SE20 184 B2
Cambridge Grove Rd
13 Kingston u T KT1 176 C1
Kingston u T KT1 198 C6
Cambridge Heath Rd E1, E2 96 B4
Cambridge Heath Sta E2 96 B5
Cambridge Ho
Barking IG11 79 A1
Ealing W13 87 A1
Fulham SW6 135 A2
2 Teddington TW11 175 A5
8 Woolwich SE18 122 B2
Cambridge Mans SW11 267 C1
Cambridge Par EN1 6 A4
CAMBRIDGE PARK 153 C4
Cambridge Park Ct TW1 153 D4
Cambridge Park Rd E11 55 A2
Cambridge Pas 9 E9 74 C1
Cambridge Pk
Twickenham TW1 153 D5
Wanstead E11 55 A3
Cambridge Pl W8 245 D1
Cambridge Rd
Barking IG11 79 A1
Barnes SW13 133 D3
Battersea SW11 136 D4 267 C1
Carshalton SM5 218 C3
3 Chingford E4 20 B3
East Molesey KT8 195 B5
Hampton TW12 173 B3
Hanwell W7 108 D4
Harrow HA2 41 C4
Hounslow TW4 129 A1
Ilford IG3 57 C1
Kilburn NW6 91 C4
Kilburn NW6 91 C5
Kingston u T KT1 176 C1
Leytonstone E11 54 D3
Littleton TW15 171 A3
Mitcham CR4 203 C6
New Malden KT3 199 C5
Penge SE20 206 B6
Plaistow BR1 187 A3
Richmond TW9 132 C5
Sidcup DA14 189 C6
Southall UB1 107 B5
Teddington TW11 175 A5
Twickenham TW1 153 D5
Walton-on-T KT12 194 B3
Wimbledon SW20 178 B2
Cambridge Rd N W4 110 D1
Cambridge Rd S 3 W4 110 D1
Cambridge Row SE18 122 D1
Cambridge Sch 15 W6 112 B2
Cambridge Sq W2 92 C1 237 A2
Cambridge St SW1 115 C1 259 A2
Cambridge Terr
Edmonton N9 17 D4
Regent's Pk NW1 231 C1
Cambridge Terr Mews NW1 231 D1
Cambridge Tutors Coll CR0 221 C4
Cambstone Cl N11 15 A2
Cambus Cl UB4 85 A2
Cambus Rd E16 99 A2
Cam Ct 2 SE15 139 D6
Camdale Rd SE18 145 D5
Camden Ave
Feltham TW13 150 C3
Hayes UB4 106 D6
Camden Cl BR7 189 A2
Camden Coll of English 8 NW1 71 A1
Camden Ct 9 DA17 125 C1
Camden Gdns
Camden Town NW1 71 B1
Sutton SM1 217 D3
Thornton Heath CR7 204 D6
Camden Gr BR7 188 D4
Camden High St NW1 93 C6 232 A5
Camden Hill Rd SE19 183 C4
Camden Ho
6 Deptford SE8 119 B1
Wallington CR6 220 A5
Camdenhurst St E14 97 A1
Camden Jun Sch SM5 218 D4
Camden Lock Pl NW1 71 B1
Camden Mews NW1 71 D2
Camden Mkt* NW1 93 B6 231 D6
Camden Park Rd
Camden Town NW1 71 D2
Chislehurst West BR7 188 C3
Camden Pas* N1 94 D6 234 C5
Camden Rd
Camden Town NW1 93 B6 231 D6
Carshalton SM5 218 D4
Old Bexley DA5 169 B4
Sutton SM1 217 D3
Walthamstow E17 53 B3
Wanstead E11 55 B3
Camden Road Sta NW1 71 C1
Camden Row SE3 142 C3
Camden Sch for Girls The NW5 71 C2
Camden Sq NW1 71 D2
Camden St NW1 93 C6 232 B5
Camden Studios NW1 232 B5
Camden Terr 17 NW1 71 D2
CAMDEN TOWN 71 B1
Camden Town Sta NW1 93 B6 231 D6
Camden Way
Chislehurst West BR7 188 C3
Thornton Heath CR7 204 D6
Camden Wlk N1 234 C5
Cameford Ct 20 SW12 160 A4
Camelford NW1 232 B5
Camelford Ct 15 W11 91 A1
Camelford Ho SE1 260 B1
Camelford Wlk 13 W11 91 A1
Camel Gr KT2 175 D5
Camelia Ct IG8 36 C4
Camellia Ct 20 BR3 185 C3
Camellia Ho
Feltham TW13 150 A3
New Cross SE8 141 B5
Camellia Pl TW2 151 D4
Camellia St SW8 270 A3
Camelot Cl
Plumstead SE18 123 B4
Wimbledon SW19 179 C6
Camelot Ho 15 NW1 71 D2
Camelot Prim Sch SE15 140 B6
Camel Rd E16 121 D5
Camera Pl SW10 266 C6
Camera Press Gall The* SE1 253 C2
Cameret Ct 6 W11 112 D4
Cameron Cl
East Barnet N20 14 C2
Edmonton N18 34 B5
Cameron Cres HA8 26 D2
Cameron Ct 3 SW19 157 A3
Cameron Ho
8 Bromley BR1 186 D2
Camberwell SE5 139 A5
St John's Wood NW8 230 A4
Cameron House Sch SW10 266 D6
Cameron Lo TW3 130 A1
Cameron Pl SW16 160 C2
Cameron Rd
Bromley BR2 209 A4
Forest Hill SE6 163 B2
Ilford IG3 57 C1
Cameron Rd *continued*
Thornton Heath CR0 204 D3
Cameron Sq CR4 180 C2
Camerton Cl 8 E8 73 D2
Camfrey Ct N8 50 A5
Camgate Ctr The TW19 148 B4
Camilla Cl TW16 171 D4
Camilla Ct 12 SM2 217 C1
Camilla Rd SE16 118 B2
Camille Cl SE25 206 A6
Camlan Rd BR1 186 D6
Camlet St E2 243 C6
Camlet Way EN4 1 D4
Camley St Natural Pk* NW1 232 D5
Camley St NW1 93 D5 232 D4
Camm 23 NW9 27 D1
Camm Gdns
5 Kingston u T KT1 176 B1
Thames Ditton KT7 196 D2
Camomile Ave CR4 180 D2
Camomile St EC3 95 C1 243 B2
Camomile Way UB7 82 A1
Campaign Ct W9 91 B3
Campana Rd SW6 135 C4 265 B2
Campasps Bsns Pk TW16 193 D4
Campbell Ave IG6 57 A5
Campbell Cl
Ruislip HA4 40 A3
Shooters Hill SE18 144 C4
Streatham SW16 181 D6
Twickenham TW2 152 B3
Campbell Croft HA8 26 C5
Campbell Ct
Dulwich SE21 162 A3
Ealing W7 108 C6
Kingsbury NW9 45 A3
South Kensington SW7 256 A5
Tottenham N17 33 D2
Campbell Gordon Way NW2 68 B4
Campbell Ho
Paddington W2 236 C5
Pimlico SW1 259 A1
30 Shepherd's Bush W12 112 B6
6 Wallington SM6 219 B4
Campbell Rd Bow E3 97 C4
Ealing W7 108 C6
Newham E6 100 A6
Stratford E15 76 D4
Thornton Heath CR0 204 D3
Tottenham N17 34 A2
Twickenham TW2 152 B2
Walthamstow E17 53 B5
Campbell Wlk N1 233 B6
Campdale Rd N7 71 D5
Campden Cres
Dagenham RM8 80 C4
Wembley HA0 65 B5
Campden Gr W8 113 C4 245 B2
Campden Hill W8 113 C4 245 A2
Campden Hill Ct W8 245 B2
Campden Hill Gate W8 245 A2
Campden Hill Gdns W8 245 A4
Campden Hill Mans W8 245 B4
Campden Hill Pl W14 244 D4
Campden Hill Rd W8 113 C4 245 A2
Campden Hill Sq W14 113 B5 244 D4
Campden Ho 4 NW6 70 B1
Campden Hos W8 245 A3
Campden House Cl W8 245 B2
Campden Rd
Ickenham UB10 60 B4
South Croydon CR2 221 C3
Campden St W8 113 C5 245 A3
Campden Way RM8 80 B4
Campe Ho 1 N10 31 A3
Campen Cl SW19 157 A2
Camperdown St E1 243 D1
Campfield Rd SE9 165 D4
Campion Cl
Harrow HA3 44 B3
Hillingdon UB8 82 B2
Newham E6 122 B6
South Croydon CR2 221 C4
Campion Ct
London N12 30 C4
10 Wembley HA0 88 A5
Campion Gdns IG8 37 A5
Campion Ho 15 N16 73 C3
Campion Pl SE28 124 B5
Campion Rd
Hounslow TW7 130 D4
Leyton E10 53 D2
Putney SW15 156 C6
Campion Terr NW2 68 D5
Campion Way HA8 27 A6
Camplin Rd HA3 44 A4
Camplin St SE14 140 D5
Camp Rd SW19 178 C5
Campsbourne Ho 3 N8 50 A5
Campsbourne Rd
Hornsey N8 50 A5
Hornsey N8 50 A6
Campsbourne Sch N8 50 A6
Campsbourne The N8 50 A5
Campsey Gdns RM9 80 B1
Campsey Rd RM9 80 B1
Campsfield Ho N8 50 A6
Campsfield Rd N8 50 A6
Campshill Pl SE13 164 A6
Campshill Rd SE13 164 A6
Camp Site The BR8 191 C3
Campton Hill Twrs W8 245 A4
Campus Rd E17 53 B3
Camp View SW19 178 B5
Cam Rd E15 98 B6
Camrose Ave
Edgware HA8 26 B2
Erith DA8 147 D6
Feltham TW13 172 C6
Camrose Cl
Croydon CR0 207 A2
Morden SM4 201 C5
Camrose St SE2 124 A2
Camsey Ho 8 SW2 160 B6
Canada Ave N18 33 A4
Canada Cres W3 89 A3
Canada Gdns SE13 164 A6
Canada Rd W3 89 A2
Canada Sq E14 119 D5
Canada St SE16 118 D4
Canada Water Sta SE16 118 D3
Canada Way W12 112 B6
Canadian Ave SE6 163 D3
Canal App SE8 141 A6
Canal Bldg N1 235 A4
Canal Bridge SE15 140 A6
Canal Bvd 7 NW1 71 D2
Canal Cl Mile End E1 97 A3
North Kensington W10 90 D3
Canal Gr SE15 140 B6
Canal Head Public Sq 1 SE15 140 A4
Canal Path 22 E2 95 D6
Canalside Studios 29 N1 95 C6
Canal St SE5 139 B6
Canal Way W10 90 D3
Canal Wlk
Croydon CR0 205 D3
Forest Hill SE26 184 C5
Shoreditch N1 95 B6 235 D6
CANARY WHARF 119 D5
Canary Wharf* E14 119 D5
Canary Wharf Pier (River Bus) E14 119 B5
Canary Wharf Sta E14 119 D5
Canary Wharf Sta (DLR) E14 119 C5
Canberra Cl NW4 46 A6
Canberra Dr UB4 84 C4
Canberra Ho 7 HA4 40 C1
Canberra Prim Sch W12 112 B6
Canberra Rd
Charlton SE7 143 D6
Ealing W13 109 A5
Erith DA7 146 D6

Canberra Rd *continued*
Harlington TW6 126 C2
Newham E6 100 B6
Canbury 2000 Bsns Pk 3 KT2 176 A2
Canbury Ave KT2 176 B2
Canbury Ct 3 KT2 176 A3
Canbury Mews SE26 162 A1
Canbury Park Rd KT2 176 B2
Canbury Sch KT2 176 D4
Cancell Rd SW9 138 C4
Candahar Rd SW11 136 C3
Candida Ct 9 NW1 71 B1
Candishe Ho SE1 253 C2
Candle Gr SE15 140 B2
Candlelight Ct 5 E15 76 D2
Candlemakers 24 SW11 136 B2
Candler Mews TW1 153 A4
Candler St N15 51 B3
Candover St W1 239 A3
Candy St E3 97 B6
Caney Mews NW2 68 D6
Canfield Dr HA4 62 B3
Canfield Gdns NW6 69 D1
Canfield Ho N15 51 C3
Canfield Pl NW6 70 A2
Canford Ave UB5 85 A6
Canford Cl EN2 4 C3
Canford Gdns KT3 199 C3
Canford Pl TW11 175 C4
Canford Rd SW11 159 A6
Canham Rd
Acton W3 111 C4
South Norwood SE25 205 C6
Canmore Gdns SW16 181 C3
Cann Hall Prim Sch E11 76 D5
Cann Hall Rd E11 76 D4
Cann Ho W14 254 B5
Canning Cres N22 32 B2
Canning Cross SE5 139 C3
Canning Ct N22 32 B2
Canning Ho 23 W12 112 B6
Canning Pas W8 114 A3 256 A6
Canning Pl W8 114 A3 256 A6
Canning Pl Mews W8 256 A6
Canning Rd
Croydon CR0 221 D6
Harrow HA3 42 D6
Highbury N5 72 D5
Walthamstow E17 53 A6
West Ham E15 98 C5
Cannington 14 NW5 71 A2
Cannington Rd RM9 80 C2
CANNING TOWN 99 B2
Canning Town E16 98 C1
Canning Town Sta E16 98 C1
Cannizaro Rd SW19 178 D5
Cannock Ho N4 51 B2
Cannock Lo EN1 17 C5
Cannonbury Ave HA5 40 D3
Cannon Cl
Hampton TW12 173 D4
West Barnes SW20 200 C6
Cannon Dr 21 E14 119 C6
Cannon Hill
Palmers Green N14 16 A1
West Hampstead NW6 69 C3
Cannon Hill La SM4, SW20 201 A5
Cannon Hill Mews N14 16 A1
Cannon Ho
Lambeth SE11 260 D3
Penge SE26 184 B4
Cannon La
Hampstead NW3 70 B5
Pinner HA5 41 A3
Cannon Lane Fst & Mid Schs HA5 40 D3
Cannon Pl
Hampstead NW3 70 B5
Woolwich SE7 122 A1
Cannon Rd Erith DA7 147 B4
Palmers Green N14 16 A1
Cannon St EC4 117 A6 252 B6
Cannon Street Rd E1 96 B1
Cannon Street Sta EC4 117 B6 252 C6
Cannon Trad Est HA9 66 D4
Cannon Way KT8 195 D5
Cannon (W End of General Roy's Base Line)* TW6 126 D4
Cannon Wharf Bsns Ctr 12 SE8 119 A2
Canon Ave RM6 58 C4
Canon Barnett Prim Sch E1 95 D1 243 D2
Canon Beck Rd SE16 118 C4
Canonbie Rd SE23 162 C4
CANONBURY 73 A2
Canonbury Bsns Ctr N1 235 B6
Canonbury Cres N1 73 A1
Canonbury Ct 21 N1 72 D1
Canonbury Gr N1 73 A1
Canonbury Hts 6 N1 73 B2
Canonbury La N1 72 D1
Canonbury Pk N N1 73 A2
Canonbury Pk S N1 73 A2
Canonbury Pl N1 72 D2
Canonbury Prim Sch 4 N1 72 D2
Canonbury Rd
Enfield EN1 5 C4
Islington N1 72 D1
Canonbury Sq N1 72 D1
Canonbury St N1 73 A1
Canonbury Sta N1, N5 73 A3
Canonbury Villas N1 72 D1
Canonbury Yd E 26 N1 73 A2
Canon Mohan Cl N14 15 B5
Canon Murnane Rd SE1 263 C5
Canon Palmer RC High Sch IG3 57 C1
Canon Rd BR1 209 D6
Canon Row SW1 116 A4 250 A1
Canons Cl
East Finchley N2 48 B2
Edgware HA8 26 B4
Canons Cnr HA8 26 A6
Canons Ct
Edgware HA8 26 B4
Leyton E15 76 C4
Canons Dr HA8 26 B4
Canons High Sch HA8 26 B1
Canons L Ctr CR4 202 D5
Canonsleigh Rd RM9 80 B1
CANONS PARK 26 A3
Canons Park Cl HA8 26 A3
Canons Park Sta HA8 26 A3
Canon St N1 95 A6 235 A5
Canon's Wlk CR0 222 D5
Canopus Way
Northwood HA6 22 A6
Stanwell TW19 148 A4
Canrobert St E2 96 B4
Cantelowes Ho EN5 12 D6
Cantelowes Rd NW1 71 D2
Canterbury SE13 164 A6
Canterbury Ave
Redbridge IG1 56 A2
Sidcup DA15 168 C2
Canterbury Cl
Beckenham BR3 185 D2
16 Camberwell SE5 139 A3
7 Newham E6 100 B1
North Cheam KT4 216 D6
Southall UB6 85 D2
Canterbury Cres SW9 138 C2
Canterbury Ct
Acton W3 111 C5
4 Ashford TW15 170 B6
Eltham SE12 165 B1
15 Hendon NW9 27 D1
Kilburn NW6 91 C5
South Croydon CR2 221 A1
Thornton Heath CR0 204 C2
Canterbury Gr SE27, SW16 160 C1
Canterbury Hall KT4 200 B2
Canterbury Ho
2 Barking IG11 80 A1
6 Bromley E3 97 D4
Lambeth SE1 260 D6
Canterbury Ind Pk 15 SE15 140 C6
Canterbury Mans NW6 69 D2
Canterbury Pl SE17 261 D3
Canterbury Rd
Feltham TW13 151 A2
Harrow HA1, HA2 42 A4
Kilburn NW6 91 C5
Leyton E10 54 A3
Morden SM4 202 A3
Thornton Heath CR0 204 C2
Canterbury Terr NW6 91 C5
Cantium Ret Pk SE1 140 A6
Cantley Gdns
Ilford IG2 57 A3
South Norwood SE19 183 D2
Cantley Rd W7 109 A3
Canton St E14 97 C1
Cantrell Rd E3 97 C3
Cantwell Ho SE18 144 D5
Cantwell Rd SE18 144 D5
Canute Ct SW16 160 C1
Canute Gdns SE16 118 D2
Canute Ho 1 TW8 131 C5
Canvey St SE1 252 A4
Cape Cl IG11 78 D1
Cape Henry Ct 15 E14 120 B6
Capel KT5 198 B2
Capel Ave SM6 220 B3
Capel Cl
Keston Mark BR2 210 A1
Whetstone N20 14 A1
Capel Cres HA7 9 A2
Capel Ct SE20 184 C2
Capel Gdns Ilford IG3 79 D4
Pinner HA5 41 B5
Capel Ho
17 Hackney E9 74 C1
South Oxhey WD19 22 D6
Capella Ho 1 SE7 143 B6
Capel Lo
5 Richmond TW9 132 B4
12 Streatham SW2 160 B4
Capel Point E7 77 B4
Capel Rd
East Barnet EN4 14 C5
Forest Gate E7, E12 77 C4
Capener's Cl SW1 248 A1
Cape Rd N17 52 A6
Capern Rd SW18 158 A3
Cape Yd 6 E1 118 A5
Capio Nightingale Hospl NW1 92 C2 237 B4
Capital Bsns Ctr
South Croydon CR0 221 B1
Wembley HA0 87 D5
Capital City Acad NW10 90 B6
Capital East Apts 8 E16 121 A6
Capital Ind Est
Belvedere DA17 125 D3
Mitcham CR4 202 D4
Capital Interchange Way TW8 110 C1
Capital Sh Ctrs SW1 249 C1
Capital Wharf 14 E1 118 A5
Capitol Ind Pk NW9 45 A6
Capitol Way NW9 45 A6
Capland Ho NW8 236 D6
Capland St NW8 92 B3 236 D6
Caplan Est CR4 181 C2
Caple Ho SW10 266 B4
Caple Rd NW10 89 D5
Capper St WC1 93 C3 239 B5
Caprea Cl UB4 84 D2
Capricorn Ctr RM8 59 B2
Capri Ho E17 35 B1
Capri Rd CR0 205 D2
Capstan Cl RM6 58 B3
Capstan Ho 6 E14 120 A2
Capstan Rd SE8 119 B2
Capstan Ride EN2 4 C3
Capstan Sq E14 120 A4
Capstan Way SE16 119 A5
Capstone Rd BR1 186 D6
Capthorne Ave HA2 41 B1
Capuchin Cl HA7 25 B4
Capulet Mews 1 E16 121 A5
Capworth St E10 53 D2
Caradoc Cl W2 91 C1
Caradoc Evans Cl N11 31 B5
Caradoc St SE10 120 C1
Caradon Cl 4 E11 76 C6
Caradon Ct 7 TW1 153 C5
Caradon Way N15 51 B5
Cara Ho 10 N1 72 C1
Caranday Villas 5 W11 112 D5
Caravel Cl E14 119 C3
Caravelle Gdns 1 UB5 84 D4
Caravel Mews 14 SE8 141 C6
Caraway Cl E13 99 B2
Caraway Hts E14 120 A6
Caraway Pl SM6 219 B5
Carberry Rd 12 SE19 183 C4
Carbery Ave W3 110 B4
Carbis Cl E4 20 B3
Carbis Rd E14 97 B1
Carbroke Ho 9 E9 96 C6
Carburton St W1 93 B3 238 D5
Cardale St 1 E14 120 A3
Cardamom Ct 1 E12 78 C4
Carden Rd SE15 140 B2
Cardiff Ho 9 SE15 140 A6
Cardiff Rd Ealing W7 109 A3
Enfield EN3 6 B1
Cardiff St SE18 145 C5
Cardigan Ct 3 W7 86 D3
Cardigan Gdns IG3 80 A6
Cardigan Rd
Barnes SW13 134 A3
Bow E3 97 B5
Richmond TW10 154 A5
Wimbledon SW19 180 A4
Cardigan St SE11 116 C1 261 A2
Cardigan Wlk 19 N1 73 A1
Cardinal Ave
Kingston u T KT2 176 A4
West Barnes SM4 201 A3
Cardinal Bourne St SE1 262 D5
Cardinal Cap Alley SE1 252 A5
Cardinal Cl
Burnt Oak HA8 27 B3
Chislehurst BR7 189 B2
West Barnes SM4 201 A3
Worcester Pk KT19, KT4 216 A4
Cardinal Cres KT3 177 A1
Cardinal Ct KT8 196 B5
Cardinal Dr KT12 194 D1
Cardinal Hinsley Cl NW10 90 A5
Cardinal Hinsley Mathematics & Computing Coll NW10 90 A6
Cardinal Pl SW15 134 D1
Cardinal Pl SW1 115 C3 259 A5
Cardinal Pole RC Sch
London E9 74 D1
London E9 75 A3
Cardinal Rd
Feltham TW13 150 B3
Ruislip HA4 40 D1
Cardinal Road Inf Sch 5 TW13 150 B3
Cardinals Way N19 49 D1
Cardinal's Wlk
Ashford TW16 171 C4
Hampton TW12 174 A3
Cardinal Vaughan Meml Sch The W14 244 A2
Cardinal Way HA3 42 C6
Cardinal Wiseman RC Sch UB6 86 A2
Cardinal Wlk SW1 259 A5
Cardine Mews SE15 140 B5
Cardington Sq TW4 128 D1
Cardington St NW1 93 C4 232 B1
Cardozo Rd N7 72 A3
Cardrew Ave N12 30 B5
Cardrew Cl N12 30 B5
Cardrew Ct 8 N12 30 B5
Cardross St W6 112 B3
Cardwell Prim Sch 25 SE18 122 B2
Cardwell Rd 3 N7 72 A4
Career Ct 11 SE16 118 D4
Carew Cl N7 72 B6
Carew Ct
15 Deptford SE14 140 D6
Ilford RM6 58 B3
Carew Ho
West Norwood SW16 160 C1
23 Woolwich SE18 122 B2
Carew Manor Sch SM6 219 D5
Carew Rd
Ashford TW15 171 A4
Ealing W13 109 C4
Mitcham CR4 181 A1
Thornton Heath CR7 204 D5
Tottenham N17 34 A1
Wallington SM6 219 C2
Carew St SE5 139 A3
Carey Ct Bexley DA6 169 D6
20 Camberwell SE5 139 A5
Carey Gdns SW8 137 D4 269 C1
Carey Ho E5 74 B5
Carey La EC2 242 A2
Carey Pl SW1 259 C3
Carey Rd RM9 81 A4
Carey St WC2 94 B1 240 D1
Carey Way HA9 66 D4
Carfax Pl SW4 137 D1
Carfax Rd UB3 106 A2
Carfree Cl 5 N1 72 C1
Cargill Rd SW18 158 A3
Cargreen Pl SE25 205 D5
Cargreen Rd SE25 205 D5
Cargrey Ho 9 HA7 25 C5
Carholme Rd SE23 163 B3
Carillon Ct W5 109 D6
Carinthia Ct 5 SE8 119 A2
Carisbrook 2 N10 31 B1
Carisbrook Cl EN1 5 D4
Carisbrooke Ave DA5 168 D3
Carisbrooke Cl
Stanmore HA7 25 D1
Twickenham TW4 151 A4
Carisbrooke Ct
Acton W3 111 A4
Belmont SM2 217 B1
Northolt UB5 85 B6
1 Streatham SW16 160 B1
Carisbrooke Gdns SE15 139 D5
Carisbrooke Ho
10 Kingston u T KT2 176 A2
Richmond TW10 154 C6
Carisbrooke Rd
Bromley BR2 209 C5
Mitcham CR4 204 A5
Walthamstow E17 53 A4
Carker's La
Crouch End N19 49 B2
Gospel Oak NW5 71 B3
Carleton Ave SM6 219 D1
Carleton Cl KT10 196 B1
Carleton Gdns N19 71 C3
Carleton Ho 4 N8 50 A4
Carleton Rd N7 71 D4
Carley Ct 6 N12 30 B5
Carlile Cl E3 97 B5
Carlile Ho SE1 262 D5
Carlina Gdns IG8 37 B5
Carling Ct TW1 152 D4
Carlingford DA14 190 A5
Carlingford Gdns CR4 181 A3
Carlingford Rd
Hampstead NW3 70 B4
London N15 50 D6
West Barnes SM4 200 D3
Carlisle Ave Acton W3 89 C1
Whitechapel EC3 243 C1
Carlisle Cl
Kingston u T KT2 176 C2
Pinner HA5 41 A2
Carlisle Gdns
Harrow HA3 43 D2
Redbridge IG1 56 A3
Carlisle Ho
6 Dartmouth Pk NW5 71 C5
Redbridge IG1 56 A3

Carlisle Inf Sch TW12 173 D4
Carlisle La SE1 116 B3 260 D6
Carlisle Lo 1 N3 29 B1
Carlisle Pl London N11 31 B6
Westminster SW1 115 C3 259 A5
Carlisle Rd
Cheam SM1 217 B2
Finsbury Pk N4 50 C2
Hampton TW12 173 D3
Hendon NW9 45 A6
Kilburn NW6 91 A6
Leyton E10 53 C1
Carlisle St W1 93 D1 239 C1
Carlisle Way SW17 181 A5
Carlisle Wlk 6 E8 73 D2
Carlos Pl W1 115 B6 248 C5
Carlow St NW1 232 A4
Carlson Ct SW15 135 B1
Carlton Ave
Feltham TW14 150 C5
Harrow HA3 43 B4
Hayes UB3 105 C2
South Croydon CR2 221 C1
Southgate N14 15 D6
Carlton Ave E HA9 65 D6
Carlton Ave W HA0 65 B6
Carlton Cl
Chessington KT9 213 D2
Child's Hill NW3 69 C6
Edgware HA8 26 C5
Northolt UB5 64 A3
Carlton Cres SM3 217 A4
Carlton Ct
Brixton SW9 138 D4
Ealing W7 108 D4
Finchley N3 29 C3
Ilford IG6 57 B6
Kilburn NW6 91 D5
11 Penge SE20 184 B2
South Norwood SE19 183 D2
8 Willesden NW2 68 C2
Carlton Dr Ilford IG6 57 B6
Putney SW15 157 A6
Carlton Gdns
Ealing W5 109 C6
St James SW1 115 D5 249 C3
Carlton Gn DA14 189 D6
Carlton Gr SE15 140 B4
Carlton Hill NW8 92 A5 229 A4
Carlton Ho
Cheam SM1 217 B2
Edmonton N21 17 A3
Feltham TW14 149 D5
Hounslow TW4 151 C5
8 Kilburn NW6 91 B5
Kilburn NW6 91 C5
Marylebone W1 237 D2
Carlton House Terr SW1 115 D5 249 D4
Carlton Lo N4 50 C2
Carlton Mans
Brixton SW9 138 C1
Cricklewood NW2 68 D3
Kensington W14 244 B2
Maida Vale W9 91 D4
7 South Hampstead NW6 69 C1
Stamford Hill N16 51 D1
Carlton Par HA9 44 A1
Carlton Park Ave SW20 178 D1
Carlton Prim Sch NW5 71 A3
Carlton Rd Acton W4 111 B4
Ashford TW16 171 D3
Ealing W5 87 C1
Erith DA8 147 D6
Finsbury Pk N4 50 C2
Friern Barnet N11 31 A5
Higham Hill E17 35 A2
Kingston u T KT3 177 C1
Leytonstone E11 54 D1
Manor Pk E12 77 D4
Mortlake SW14 133 A1
Sidcup DA14 189 D6
South Croydon CR2 221 B1
Walton-on-T KT12 194 B2
Welling DA16 146 B2
Carlton Sq E1 96 D3
Carlton St SW1 249 C5
Carltons The 5 SW15 157 A6
Carlton Terr
Edmonton N18 33 B6
Forest Hill SE26 162 C1
Upton E7 77 C1
Wanstead E11 55 B4
Carlton Tower Pl SW1 257 D6
Carlton Twrs SM5 218 D5
Carlton Vale NW6 91 C5
Carlton Vale Inf Sch 12 NW6 91 B4
Carlwell St SW17 180 C5
Carlyle Ave
Bromley BR1 209 D6
Southall UB1 107 B6
Carlyle Cl
East Molesey KT8 173 D1
Hampstead Garden Suburb N2 48 A3
Carlyle Gdns UB1 107 B6
Carlyle Ho
4 Camberwell SE5 139 A5
Chelsea SW3 266 D6
Ealing W5 109 D2
East Molesey KT8 195 C4
12 Stoke Newington N16 73 C5
Carlyle Lo 6 EN5 14 A6
Carlyle Mans SW3 267 A5
Carlyle Mews 24 E1 96 D3
Carlyle Pl SW15 134 D1
Carlyle Rd
Croydon CR0 222 A6
Ealing W5 109 C2
Manor Pk E12 78 A4
1 Stonebridge NW10 89 B6
Woolwich SE28 124 C6
Carlyle's Ho★ SW3 267 A5
Carlyle Sq SW3 114 B1 256 D1
Carlyon Ave HA2 63 C4
Carlyon Cl HA0 88 A6
Carlyon Ct HA0 88 B6
Carlyon Mans 1 HA0 88 A5
Carlyon Rd Hayes UB4 84 C2
Wembley HA0 88 A6
Carlys Cl BR3 184 D1
Carmalt Gdns SW15 134 C1
Carmarthen Ct 4 W7 86 D3
Carmarthen Ho 8 SW15 156 C4
Carmarthen Pl SE1 253 A2
Carmel Ct
Kensington W8 245 C2
Wembley Pk HA9 66 D6
Carmelite Cl HA3 24 A2
Carmelite Rd HA3 24 A1
Carmelite St EC4 116 C6 251 B6
Carmelite Way HA3 24 A1
Carmelite Wlk HA3 24 A2
Carmel Lo SW6 265 A6
Carmen St E14 97 D1
Carmichael Cl
8 London SW11 136 B2
Ruislip HA4 62 A4
Carmichael Ct 5 SW13 133 D3
Carmichael Ho
17 Dulwich SE21 183 C6
6 Poplar E14 120 A6
Carmichael Mews SW18 158 B4
Carmichael Rd SE25 206 A5
Carminia Rd SW17 159 B2
Carnaby St★ W1 93 C1 239 A1
Carnac St SE21, SE27 161 B1
Carna Ct TW9 132 A2
Carnanton Rd E17 36 B2
Carnarvon Ave EN1 5 D3
Carnarvon Dr UB3 105 A3
Carnarvon Rd
Barnet EN5 1 A2
Leyton E10 54 A4
Stratford E15 76 D2
Woodford E18 36 D2
Carnation St SE2 124 B1
Carnbrook Mews SE3 143 D2
Carnbrook Rd SE3 143 D2
Carnecke Gdns SE9 166 A6
Carnegie Cl
Holdbrook EN3 7 D5
Surbiton KT6 214 B6
Carnegie Ho NW3 70 B5
Carnegie Pl SW19 156 D1
Carnegie St N1 94 B6 233 D5
Carnforth Cl KT19 214 D2
Carnforth Rd SW16 181 D3
Carnicot Ho 9 SE15 140 B4
Carnoustie Cl SE28 102 D1
Carnoustie Dr N1 72 B1
Carnwath Ho SW6 135 D2
Carnwath Rd SW6 135 D2
Caroe Ct N9 18 B3
Carol Cl NW4 46 D5
Carole Ho 13 SE20 184 B2
Carolina Cl E15 76 C3
Carolina Rd CR7 183 A2
Caroline Cl
Bayswater W2 245 D5
Hounslow TW7 130 C5
Muswell Hill N10 31 B1
South Croydon CR0 221 C4
Streatham SW16 160 B1
Caroline Ct
Ashford TW15 170 D4
Catford SE6 186 B6
Stanmore HA7 25 A4
17 Surbiton KT6 197 D2
23 Woodside Pk N12 29 D6
Caroline Gdns E2 95 C4
Caroline Ho
Bayswater W2 245 D5
20 Hammersmith W6 112 C1
Caroline Martyn Ho 8 N19 49 D2
Caroline Pl
Bayswater W2 245 D5
Clapham SW11 137 A3
Harlington UB3 127 C5
Caroline Pl Mews W2 245 D5
Caroline Rd SW19 179 B3
Caroline St E1 96 D1
Caroline Terr SW1 115 A2 258 A3
Caroline Wlk W6 264 A5
Carol St NW1 93 C6 232 A6
Carolyn Ho IG3 58 A1
Caronia Ct 4 SE16 119 A2
Carpenter Gdns N21 16 D2
Carpenter Ho
London NW11 48 A3
11 Tower Hamlets E14 97 C2
5 Tufnell Pk N19 71 D4
Carpenters Cl EN5 13 D5
Carpenters Ct
Camden Town NW1 232 A6
5 Dagenham RM10 81 D2
Twickenham TW2 152 C2
Carpenter's Pl SW4 137 D1
Carpenters Prim Sch E15 98 A6
Carpenter St W1 248 C5
Carradale Ho 2 E14 98 A1
Carrara Cl 18 SW9 138 D1
Carrara Wharf SW6 135 A2
Carr Cl HA7 25 A4
Carr Gr SE18 122 A2
Carriage Dr E SW11 137 A5 268 B4
Carriage Drive E SW11 137 A5 268 B4
Carriage Drive N SW11, SW8 137 A6 268 B5
Carriage Dr N
Battersea SW8, SW11 136 D5 267 C4
Battersea SW8, SW11 137 A6 268 B5
Carriage Dr S SW11 137 A4 268 A2
Carriage Dr W SW11 136 D5 267 C3
Carriage Mews IG1 79 A6
Carriage Pl 14 SW16 181 C5
Carrick Cl TW7 131 A2
Carrick Gate KT10 212 A5
Carrick Gdns N17 33 C3
Carrick Ho
Islington N7 72 B2
Kennington SE11 261 C2
Carrick Mews SE8 141 C6
Carrill Way DA17 124 D3
Carrington Ave
Borehamwood WD6 10 D6
Hounslow TW3 151 D6
Carrington Cl
Barnet EN5 12 A6
Borehamwood WD6 11 A6
Croydon CR0 207 A2
Carrington Ct
London SW11 136 C1
3 New Malden KT3 199 C5
Southgate N21 16 D5
Carrington Gdns 4 E7 77 A4
Carrington Ho
Mayfair W1 248 C3
7 Merton SW19 179 C3
Carrington Lo
3 Richmond TW10 154 A6
Wembley HA9 66 B5
Carrington Pl KT10 212 A4
Carrington Rd TW10 132 C1
Carrington Sq HA3 24 A3
Carrington St W1 248 C3
Carrol Cl NW5 71 B4
Carroll Cl E15 76 D3
Carroll Ct Acton W3 110 D3
4 Shacklewell E5 74 A5
Carroll Ho W2 246 C6
Carronade Pl SE18 123 B3
Carron Cl E14 97 D1
Carroun Rd SW8 138 B5 270 C4
Carroway La UB6 86 B4
Carrow Rd RM9 80 B1
Carr Rd Northolt UB5 64 A1
Walthamstow E17 35 C1
Carrs La N21 17 B6
Carr St 5 E14 97 A1
CARSHALTON 218 C4
Carshalton Beeches Sta SM5 218 D2
Carshalton Coll SM5 218 D5
Carshalton Gr SM1 218 B3
Carshalton High Sch for Boys SM5 218 C6
Carshalton High Sch for Girls SM5 218 C5
CARSHALTON ON THE HILL 219 B1
Carshalton Park Rd SM5 218 D3
Carshalton Pl SM5 219 A3
Carshalton Rd
Mitcham CR4 203 A4
Sutton SM1, SM5 218 B3
Carshalton Sta SM5 218 D4
Carslake Rd SW15 156 C5
Carson Rd
Cockfosters EN4 2 D1
Dulwich SE21 161 B2
Newham E16 99 A2
Carstairs Rd SE6 164 A1
Carston Cl SE12 164 D6
Carswell Cl IG4 55 D5
Carswell Rd SE6 164 A4
Carter Cl NW9 45 B3
Carter Ct EC4 241 D1
Carteret Ho 8 W12 112 B6
Carteret St SW1 249 C1
Carteret Way SE8 119 A2
Carterhatch Jun & Inf Schs EN1 6 B4
Carterhatch La EN1 6 A4
Carterhatch Rd EN3 6 D4
Carter Ho
11 London SW2 160 C6
Spitalfields E1 243 C3
Carter La EC4 94 D1 241 D1
Carter Pl SE17 117 A1 262 B1
Carter Rd
Mitcham SW19 180 B4
Newham E13 99 B6
Carters Cl
10 Kentish Town NW5 71 D2
North Cheam KT4 200 D1
Carters Hill Cl SE9 165 C3
Carters La SE23 163 B1
Carters Rd N2 30 C3
Carter St SE17 117 A1 262 A1
Carter's Yd SW18 157 C6
Carthew Rd W6 112 B3
Carthew Villas W6 112 B3
Carthusian St EC1 242 A4
Cartier Circ E14 120 A5
Carting La WC2 116 A6 250 B5
Cart La E4 20 C3
Cartmel NW1 232 A2
Cartmel Cl N17 34 B3
Cartmel Ct
Beckenham BR2 186 C1
Northolt UB5 63 A2
Cartmel Gdns SM4 202 A4
Cartmel Rd DA7 147 C4
Carton Ho
4 Bermondsey SE16 118 A3
2 Dollis Hill NW2 68 A5
12 Shepherd's Bush W11 112 D6
Cartoon Mus The★ WC1 94 A2 240 A3
Cartwright Gdns WC1 94 A4 233 A1
Cartwright Ho SE1 262 B5
Cartwright Rd RM9 81 B1
Cartwright St E1 117 D6 253 D5
Cartwright Way SW13 134 B5
Carvel Ho E14 120 A1
Carver Cl 15 W4 111 A3
Carver Rd SE24 161 A5
Carville Cres TW8 110 A2
Caryl Ho 6 SW19 156 D3
Cary Rd E11 76 C5
Carysfort Rd
Canonbury N16 73 B4
London N8 49 D4
Casby Ho 7 SE16 118 A3
Cascade Ave N10 49 C5
Cascade Cl IG9 21 D2
Cascade Rd IG9 21 D2
Cascadia Ho 22 KT1 176 C1
Casella Rd SE14 140 D5
Casewick Rd SE27 182 D6
Casey Cl NW8 92 C4 230 B1
Casimir Rd E5 74 C5
Casino Ave SE24 161 B6
Caspian Ho 10 E1 96 D2
Caspian St SE5 139 B5
Caspian Wlk E16 99 D1
Cassandra Cl UB5 64 B4
Cassandra Ct 7 NW2 68 C2
Cass Bsns Sch EC1 95 B3 242 C5
Casselden Rd NW10 67 B1
Cassel Hospl TW10 175 D6
Cassell Ho 21 SW9 138 A3
Casserley Ho W4 111 B3
Cass Ho 23 E9 74 D2
Cassidy Rd SW6 265 A3
Cassilda Rd SE2 124 A2
Cassilis Rd
Millwall E14 119 C4
Twickenham TW1 153 B5
Cassinghurst SE24 161 B6
Cassiobury Ave TW14 149 D4
Cassiobury Rd E17 53 A4
Cassland Rd
Homerton E9 74 D2
South Norwood CR7 205 B5
Casslee Rd SE6 163 B4
Cassocks Sq TW17 193 B2
Casson Ho 11 E1 96 A2
Casson St E1 96 A2
Castalia Sq 6 E14 120 A4
Castellain Mans W9 91 D3
Castellain Rd W9 91 D3
Castellane Cl HA7 24 D3
Castell Ho 11 SE8 141 C5
Castello Ave SW15 156 C6
Castelnau SW13 134 B5
Castelnau Gdns SW13 134 B6
Castelnau Mans SW13 134 B6
Castelnau Row SW13 134 B6
Casterbridge
Kilburn NW6 91 D6
3 Notting Hill W11 91 C1
Casterbridge Rd SE3 143 A2
Casterton St E8 74 B2
Castile Rd SE18 122 C2

Castilion Prim Sch
SE28 102 C1
Castillon Rd SE6 164 C2
Castlands Rd SE6 163 B2
Castleacre W2 237 A1
Castle Ave
Chingford E4 36 B5
Yiewsley UB7 104 B6
Castlebar Ct 5 W5 87 C2
Castlebar Hill W5 87 C2
Castlebar Mews W5 87 C2
Castle Bar Park Sta
W7 86 D2
Castlebar Pk W5 87 B2
Castlebar Rd W5 87 C1
Castlebar Sch W13 87 A2
Castle Baynard St
EC4 117 A6 252 A6
Castlebrook Cl
SE11 116 D2 261 C4
Castle Bsns Village
TW12 173 D2
Castle Cl
12 Acton W3 111 A4
Ashford TW16 171 C3
Beckenham BR2 208 C6
Homerton E9 75 A3
South Acton W3 110 D4
Wimbledon SW19 156 D1
Castlecombe Dr
SW19 156 D4
Castlecombe Prim Sch
SE9 188 A5
Castlecombe Rd
SE9 188 A6
Castle Ct
Belmont SM2 217 C2
City of London EC3 242 D1
Dagenham RM9 103 A6
Forest Hill SE26 185 A6
Morden SM4 202 B4
Castleden Ho NW6 70 B1
Castledine Rd SE20 184 B3
Castle Dr IG4 56 A3
Castleford Ave SE9 166 D3
Castleford Cl N17 33 D4
Castleford Ct NW8 236 D6
Castlefrank Ho 20 N1 95 C4
Castlegate TW9 132 B2
CASTLE GREEN 102 C6
Castleham Ct HA8 26 C4
Castlehaven Rd NW1 71 B1
Castle Hill Ave CR0 224 A1
Castle Hill Prim Sch
Chessington KT9 214 B3
New Addington CR0 224 A2
Castle Ho
17 Belmont SM2 217 C1
3 Chingford E4 36 B5
Newington SE1 262 A4
South Lambeth SW8 270 B4
Castle Hts RM9 102 B6
Castle Ind Est SE17 262 A4
Castle La
SW1 115 C3 259 A6
Castleleigh Ct EN2 17 B6
Castlemaine 8
SW11 136 D3
Castlemaine Ave
CR2 221 D3
Castlemaine St 2 E1 96 B2
Castle Mead SE5 139 A5
Castle Mews
Camden Town NW1 71 B2
North Finchley N12 30 A5
Castle Par KT17 216 A1
Castle Pl
8 Acton W4 111 C2
Camden Town NW1 71 B2
Castle Point 4 E13 99 C5
Castle Rd
Camden Town NW1 71 B2
Dagenham RM9 102 B6
Enfield EN3 7 A5
Isleworth TW7 130 D3
North Finchley N12 30 B5
Northolt UB5 63 D1
Southall UB2 107 B3
Castlereagh Ho HA7 25 B4
Castlereagh St W1 237 C2
Castle St E6 99 C5
Castleton Ave HA9 66 A4
Castleton Cl CR0 207 A3
Castleton Ct KT5 198 B4
Castleton Gdns HA9 66 A5
Castleton Ho 3 E14 120 A2
Castleton Rd
Chingford E17 36 B1
Ilford IG3 58 B1
Mitcham CR4 203 D5
Mottingham SE12,
SE9 187 D6
Ruislip HA4 40 D1
Castletown Rd
W14 113 A1 254 B1
Castleview Cl N4 73 A6
Castleview Gdns IG1 56 B3
Castle Way
Feltham TW13 172 C6
Wimbledon SW19 156 D1
Castle Wlk TW16 194 C6
Castlewood Dr SE9 144 B3
Castlewood Ho WC1 239 D2
Castlewood Rd
Barnet EN4 2 B2
Stamford Hill N16 52 A3
Castle Yd Highgate N6 49 A2
Lambeth SE1 251 D4
18 Richmond TW10 153 D6
Castor La E14 119 D6
Catalina Rd TW6 126 C2
Catalpa Ct SE13 164 B5
Caterham Rd SE13 142 B2
Catesby Ho 25 E9 74 C1
Catesby St
SE17 117 B2 262 D3
CATFORD 163 C3
Catford Br SE6 163 C4
Catford Bridge Sta
SE6 163 C4
Catford Broadway
SE6 163 D4
Catford Gyratory
SE6 163 D4
Catford High Sch
SE6 164 A1
Catford Hill SE6 163 C3
Catford Rd SE6 163 C4
Catford Sh Ctr SE6 163 D4
Catford Sta SE6 163 C4
Cathall L Ctr E11 76 C6
Cathall Rd E11 76 B5
Cathay Ho SE16 118 B4
Cathay St 12 SE16 118 B4
Cathay Wlk UB5 85 C5
Cathcart Dr BR6 211 C1
Cathcart Hill N19 71 C5
Cathcart Rd
SW10 136 A6 266 A6
Cathcart St NW5 71 B2
Cathedral Ct EC4 241 D1
Cathedral Lo EC1 242 A4
Cathedral Sch of St
Saviour & St Mary
Overie Prim Sch
SE1 117 A4 252 B2
Cathedral St
SE1 117 B5 252 C4
Cathedral Wlk SW1 259 A6
Catherall Rd N5, N16 73 A5
Catherine Baird Ct 12
SW12 159 B4
Catherine Ct
Barnet EN5 1 D2
1 Ilford IG2 57 A3
2 Southgate N14 15 C6
3 Wimbledon SW19 179 B5
Catherine Dr
Ashford TW16 171 D4
Richmond TW9 132 A1
Catherine Gdns
TW3 130 B1
Catherine Godfrey Ho
RM9 103 B6
Catherine Gr SE10 141 D4
Catherine Griffiths Ct
EC1 241 B6
Catherine Ho
Isleworth TW7 131 B4
16 Shoreditch N1 95 C6
Catherine Lo E18 37 C2
Catherine Pl
Harrow HA1 42 D4
Westminster
SW1 115 C3 259 A6
Catherine Rd
Enfield EN3 7 A6
Kingston u T KT6 197 D4
Catherine St
WC2 116 B6 250 C6
Catherine Wheel Alley
E1 243 B3
Catherine Wheel Rd
TW8 131 D5
Catherine Wheel Yd
SW1 249 A3
Catherwood Ct N1 235 C3
Cat Hill EN4 14 D6
Cathles Rd SW12 159 B5
Cathnor Rd W12 112 B4
Catisfield Rd EN3 7 A6
Catlin Cres TW17 193 B4
Catling Cl SE23 162 D1
Catlin's La HA5 40 B5
Catlin St SE16 118 B1
Catman Ho N4 50 B1
Caton Ct BR2 186 C1
Cato Rd SW4 137 D1
Cator La BR3 185 B2
Cator Park Sch for Girls
BR3 185 A3
Cator Rd
Penge SE20, SE26 184 D5
Wallington SM5 218 D3
Cator St
Camberwell SE15 139 D5
Camberwell SE15 139 D6
Cato St W1 92 C1 237 B2
Catsey La WD23 8 A4
Catsey Wood WD23 8 A4
Catterick Cl N11 31 A4
Cattistock Rd SE9 188 B5
Cattley Cl EN5 1 A1
Catton St WC1 240 C3
Caughley Ho SE11 261 A5
Caulfield Ct 15 NW1 71 C1
Caulfield Rd
East Ham E6 78 B1
London SE15 140 B3
Causeway TW14,
TW4 128 B1
Causeway The
Carshalton SM5 219 A6
Chessington KT9 214 A4
Claygate KT10 212 D1
East Finchley N2 48 C5
Teddington TW11 174 D4
Wandsworth SW18 157 D6
Wimbledon SW19 178 C5
Causeyware Rd N9 18 C4
Causton Cotts 3 E14 97 A1
Causton Ho SE5 139 A5
Causton Rd N6 49 B2
Causton Sq RM10 81 C1
Causton St
SW1 115 D1 259 D2
Cautley Ave SW4 159 C6
Cavalier Cl RM6 58 D5
Cavalier Gdns UB3 83 B1
Cavalier Ho W5 109 C6
Cavalry Cres TW4 128 D1
Cavalry Gdns SW15 157 B6
Cavan Pl HA5 23 B2
Cavaye Ho SW10 266 B6
Cavaye Pl SW10 256 B1
Cavell Ct 5 N19 71 C6
Cavell Dr EN2 4 C3
Cavell Ho 8 N1 95 C6
Cavell Rd N17 33 B3
Cavell St E1 96 B2
Cavendish Ave
Ealing W13 87 A1
Falconwood DA16 145 D2
Finchley N3 29 C1
Harrow HA1 64 C4
Ruislip HA4 62 B3
Sidcup DA15 168 A4
St John's Wood
NW8 92 B5 229 D3
West Barnes KT3 200 B5
Woodford IG8 37 B3
Cavendish Cl
Ashford TW16 171 D4
Brondesbury NW6 69 B2
Edmonton N18 34 B5
Hayes UB4 83 C2
3 Putney SW15 157 A6
St John's Wood
NW8 92 B4 229 D2
Cavendish Coll
WC1 93 D2 239 C4
Cavendish Cres WD6 10 C6
Cavendish Ct
Ashford TW16 171 D4
Catford SE6 163 D3
5 Chingford E4 20 C4
Wallington SM6 219 B2
Wembley HA0 65 D3
Cavendish Ct *continued*
Whitechapel EC2 243 B2
Cavendish Dr
Claygate KT10 212 C3
Edgware HA8 26 B4
Leytonstone E11 54 B1
Cavendish Gdns
Barking IG11 79 D3
Clapham Pk SW4 159 C5
Dagenham RM6 59 A4
Ilford IG1 56 C1
Cavendish Ho
London N12 30 A6
5 Muswell Hill N10 31 A3
3 Richmond TW10 153 C1
South Lambeth SW8 270 A2
St John's Wood NW8 229 D3
Twickenham TW1 153 A5
Cavendish Jun & Inf Sch
W4 133 C5
Cavendish Mans
2 Clapham Pk
SW12 159 C5
Hackney E5 74 C3
Holborn EC1 241 A5
8 West Hampstead
NW6 69 C3
Cavendish Mews
SM1 218 A6
Cavendish Mews N
W1 238 D4
Cavendish Mews S
W1 238 D3
Cavendish Par
Balham SW12 159 B5
Hounslow TW4 129 A3
Cavendish Pl
Balham SW4 159 B5
Bromley BR1 210 B6
Brondesbury NW2 68 D2
Marylebone W1 238 D2
Cavendish Rd
Ashford TW16 171 D4
Brondesbury NW6 69 B1
Chingford E4 36 A4
Chiswick W4 133 A4
Clapham Pk SW12 159 C5
Edmonton N18 34 B5
Harringay N4 50 D3
Mitcham SW19 180 C3
New Malden KT3 199 D5
Sutton SM2 218 A1
Thornton Heath CR0 204 D1
Cavendish Sch 14
SE16 118 C2
Cavendish Sch The
NW1 93 B6 231 D6
Cavendish Sq
W1 93 B1 238 D2
Cavendish St
N1 95 B5 235 C3
Cavendish Terr
Feltham TW13 150 A2
11 Tower Hamlets E3 97 B4
Cavendish The NW11 47 D2
Cavendish Way BR4 207 D1
Cavenham Gdns IG1 79 B5
Cave Rd Newham E13 99 B4
Richmond TW10 175 C6
Caverleigh Way KT4 200 B2
Caversham Ave
Cheam SM3 217 A6
Palmers Green N13 16 C1
Caversham Ct N11 15 A1
Caversham Ho
8 Kingston u T
KT1 176 A1
7 Peckham SE15 140 A6
Wallington CR0 220 A5
West Green N15 51 A5
Caversham Lo N10 31 C1
Caversham Rd
Kentish Town NW5 71 C2
Kingston u T KT1 176 B1
West Green N15 51 A5
Caversham St
SW3 136 D6 267 C6
Caverswall St W12 90 C1
Caveside Cl BR7 188 C2
Cavour Ho SE17 261 D2
Cawdor Cres W7 109 A2
Cawnpore St SE19 183 C5
Cawston Ct 8 BR1 186 D3
Caxton Gr E3 97 C4
Caxton Hall★ SW1 259 C6
Caxton Mews 9
TW8 131 D5
Caxton Rd
Shepherd's Bush
W12 112 D4
Southall UB2 106 D3
Wimbledon SW19 180 A5
Wood Green N22 32 B1
Caxton St N E16 98 D1
Caxton St
SW1 115 D3 259 C6
Caxton Trad Est
UB3 105 C5
Caxton Wlk WC2 239 D1
Cayford Ho 1 NW3 70 D3
Caygill Cl BR2 208 D5
Cayley Cl SM6 220 A1
Cayley Prim Sch 22
E14 97 A1
Cayley Rd UB2 107 D3
Cayton Pl EC1 235 C1
Cayton Rd UB6 86 C5
Cayton St EC1 235 C1
Cazenove Mans 1
N16 74 A6
Cazenove Rd
Stoke Newington N16 74 A6
Walthamstow E17 35 C2
Cearns Ho E6 99 D6
Ceasors Ct TW1 152 D2
Cecil Ave Barking IG11 79 B1
Enfield EN1 5 D1
Wembley HA9 66 B3
Cecil Cl
Chessington KT9 213 D4
Ealing W5 87 D2
Littleton TW15 171 A3
Cecil Ct
Chelsea SW10 266 A6
12 Croydon CR0 221 D6
Ealing W5 87 D2
South Hampstead NW6 69 D1
St James WC2 250 A5
Cecile Pk N8 50 A3
Cecil Ho E17 35 C2
Cecilia Cl N2 48 A6
Cecilia Rd E8 74 A3
Cecil Lo KT9 213 D4
Cecil Manning Cl
UB6 87 A6
Cecil Mans 2 SW17 159 A2
Cecil Pk HA5 41 A5
Cecil Pl CR4 202 D4
Cecil Rd Acton W3 89 A2
Ashford TW15 171 A4
Cheam SM1, SM2 217 B2
Colindale NW9 45 C6
Dagenham RM6 58 D2
Enfield EN2 5 B1
Harlesden NW10 89 C6
Harrow HA3 42 C6
Hounslow TW3 130 A3
Ilford IG1 78 D4
Leyton E11 76 C5
Merton SW19 179 D3
Muswell Hill N10 31 B1
Newham E13 99 A6
Osidge N14 15 C3
Thornton Heath CR0 204 B3
Walthamstow E17 35 C2
Cecil Rhodes Ho
NW1 232 C4
Cecil Rosen Ct HA0 65 B5
Cecil Way BR2 209 A1
Cedar Ave
Dagenham RM6 59 A4
East Barnet EN4 14 C4
Enfield EN3 6 C3
Hayes UB3 84 A1
Ruislip HA4 62 C3
Sidcup DA15 168 A4
Twickenham TW2 152 A5
Yiewsley UB7 104 B6
Cedar Cl
Buckhurst Hill IG9 21 D2
East Molesey KT8 196 C5
Keston Mark BR2 226 A5
Kingston u T KT2 177 B6
Old Ford E3 97 B6
Wallington SM5 218 D2
West Norwood SE21 161 A2
Cedar Copse BR1 188 B1
Cedar Cres BR2 226 A5

Cedarcroft Rd KT9 ... 214 B4
Cedar Ct
7 Brentford TW8 ... 131 D6
19 Charlton SE7 ... 143 C6
Edgware HA8 ... 11 A1
Eltham SE9 ... 166 A5
Finchley N3 ... 29 C3
Islington N1 ... 73 A1
Marylebone W1 ... 237 B2
Mortlake SW14 ... 133 A1
1 Muswell Hill N10 ... 31 B1
5 New Southgate N11 31 C5
Oakleigh Pk N20 ... 14 B3
Stoneleigh KT17 ... 216 A1
3 Sutton SM2 ... 218 A2
6 Wanstead E11 ... 55 B4
Wembley HA0 ... 65 B4
Wimbledon SW19 ... 156 D1
5 Woodford E18 ... 37 A2
Cedar Dr
Hampstead Garden Sub
NW11 ... 47 C5
London N2 ... 48 C5
Pinner HA5 ... 23 C4
Cedar Gdns SM2 ... 218 A2
Cedar Gr Ealing W5 ... 110 A3
Sidcup DA5 ... 168 D5
Southall UB1 ... 85 C2
Cedar Grange 10 EN1 ... 17 C6
Cedar Ho
Ashford TW16 ... 171 D3
5 Cubitt Town E14 ... 120 A4
Hayes UB4 ... 84 C3
Kensington W8 ... 255 C6
New Addington CR0 ... 223 D2
New Cross Gate SE14 140 D4
5 Richmond TW9 ... 132 D4
16 Rotherhithe SE16 ... 118 D4
Wood Green N22 ... 32 C2
Cedar Hts TW10 ... 154 A3
Cedarhurst BR1 ... 186 C3
Cedarhurst Dr SE9 ... 165 C6
Cedar Lawn Ave EN5 ... 13 A6
Cedar Lo
Brondesbury NW2 ... 69 B2
Fulham SW6 ... 134 D4
Cedarmore Ct BR7 ... 189 A2
Cedar Mount SE9 ... 165 D3
Cedarne Rd
SW6 ... 135 D5 265 C3
Cedar Park Gdns
RM6 ... 58 D2
Cedar Park Rd EN2 ... 5 A5
Cedar Pk Gdns
SW19 ... 178 B5
Cedar Pl 3 SE7 ... 121 C1
Cedar Rd
Bromley BR1 ... 187 C1
Cranford TW5 ... 128 C3
Cricklewood NW2 ... 68 C4
Croydon CR0 ... 221 C6
East Bedfont TW14 ... 149 B3
East Molesey KT8 ... 196 C5
Enfield EN2 ... 5 A5
Sutton SM2 ... 218 A2
Teddington TW11 ... 175 A5
Tottenham N17 ... 33 D2
Cedar Rise N14 ... 15 A4
Cedars Ave
Mitcham CR4 ... 203 A6
Walthamstow E17 ... 53 C4
Cedars Cl
Hendon NW4 ... 46 D6
Lewisham SE13 ... 142 B2
Cedars Ct
Edmonton N9 ... 17 D2
Putney SW15 ... 156 A5
Cedars Dr UB10 ... 82 C5
Cedars Ho
21 London SW2 ... 138 B1
15 Walthamstow E17 ... 53 D6
5 West Norwood
SW27 ... 182 D5
Cedars Manor Sch
HA3 ... 24 A2
Cedars Mews SW4 ... 137 B1
Cedars Prim Sch The
TW5 ... 128 A5
Cedars Rd
Barnes SW13 ... 134 A3
Beckenham BR3 ... 185 B1
Clapham SW4 ... 137 B1
Cedars Rd *continued*
4 Lower Edmonton
N9 ... 18 A2
Morden SM4 ... 201 C5
Stratford E15 ... 76 C2
Teddington KT8 ... 175 C2
Wallington CR0 ... 220 A4
Winchmore Hill N21 ... 16 D2
Cedars The
Buckhurst Hill IG9 ... 21 A3
Ealing W13 ... 87 C1
Hackney E9 ... 74 D1
4 Kingston u T KT2 ... 176 D2
Teddington TW11 ... 174 D4
Wallington SM6 ... 219 C4
Cedar Terr
9 Dagenham RM8 ... 58 D2
Richmond TW9 ... 132 A1
Cedar Tree Gr SE27 ... 182 D5
Cedarville Gdns
SW16 ... 182 B4
Cedar Way
Ashford TW16 ... 171 C3
Camden Town
NW1 ... 93 D6 232 C6
Cedar Wlk KT10 ... 212 D2
Cedarwood BR3 ... 185 B3
Cedarwood Ho EN2 ... 4 D3
Cedarwood Lo HA8 ... 26 B5
Cedra Ct N16 ... 52 A1
Cedric Chambers
NW8 ... 236 C6
Cedric Rd SE9 ... 167 A1
Celadon Cl EN3 ... 7 A2
Celandine Cl E3, E14 ... 97 C2
Celandine Ct E4 ... 19 D1
Celandine Dr
Dalston E8 ... 73 D1
Woolwich SE28 ... 124 B5
Celandine Gr N14 ... 15 C6
Celandine Way E15 ... 98 C4
Celbridge Mews W2 ... 91 D1
Celestial Gdns SE13 ... 142 B1
Celia Blairman Ho
E1 ... 243 C4
Celia Ct 7 TW9 ... 132 B4
Celia Ho 10 N1 ... 95 C5
Celia Rd N19 ... 71 C4
Celtic Ave BR2 ... 208 C6
Celtic St E14 ... 97 D2
Cemetery La
Lower Halliford
TW17 ... 192 D2
Woolwich SE7 ... 144 A6
Cemetery Rd
East Wickham SE2 ... 146 B5
Forest Gate E7 ... 76 D4
Tottenham N17 ... 33 C3
Cenacle Cl NW3 ... 69 C5
Cenotaph* SW1 ... 250 A2
Centaur Ct 3 TW8 ... 110 A1
Centaurs Bsns Pk
TW7 ... 131 A6
Centaur St
SE1 ... 116 B3 260 D6
Centenary Rd EN3 ... 7 B1
Centennial Ave WD6 ... 9 C4
Centennial Ct WD6 ... 9 C4
Centennial Pk HA7,
WD6 ... 9 C4
Central Ave
Battersea
SW11 ... 136 D5 267 D3
East Finchley N2 ... 47 D6
East Molesey KT8 ... 195 B4
Edmonton N9 ... 17 D1
Enfield EN1 ... 6 B3
Finchley N2 ... 30 B1
Hayes UB3 ... 106 A6
Isleworth TW3, TW7 ... 130 A1
Leyton E11 ... 76 B6
Pinner HA5 ... 41 B2
Wallington SM6 ... 220 A3
Welling DA16 ... 146 A3
Central Bsns Ctr
NW10 ... 67 C3
Central Chambers
W5 ... 109 D6
Central Cir NW4 ... 46 B4
Central Ct 2 SE18 ... 122 D2
Centrale Ctr CR0 ... 221 A6
Centrale Sta CR0 ... 221 A6
Central Foundation Boys'
Sch EC2 ... 95 B3 242 D6
Central Foundation
Lower Girls Sch The 10
E3 ... 97 A4
Central Foundation
Upper Girls Sch The 27
E3 ... 97 B4
Central Gdns SM4 ... 201 D4
Central Hill SE19 ... 183 B4
Central Ho
Barking IG11 ... 79 A1
Mill Meads E15 ... 98 A5
Central Mans
8 London NW4 ... 46 B4
1 Streatham SW16 ... 182 A6
Central Middlesex Hospl
NW10 ... 89 A4
Central Par
Croydon CR0 ... 220 C4
Ealing UB6 ... 87 A4
Enfield EN3 ... 6 C3
Feltham TW14 ... 150 C4
Harrow HA1 ... 42 D4
Heston TW5 ... 129 C5
Ilford IG2 ... 57 B3
Penge SE20 ... 184 D3
South Acton W3 ... 110 D4
2 Streatham SW16 ... 182 A6
Surbiton KT6 ... 198 A3
8 Walthamstow E17 ... 53 C5
Central Park Ave
RM10 ... 81 D5
Central Park Prim Sch 7
E6 ... 99 D5
Central Park Rd E6 ... 99 D5
Central Par Villas
BR5 ... 190 C1
Central Pk Est TW4 ... 128 D1
Central Public Health
Laboratories NW9 ... 45 C6
Central Rd Finchley N2 ... 30 C2
Morden SM4 ... 201 D4
Wembley HA0 ... 65 B3
Worcester Pk KT4 ... 216 A6
Central St Martins Coll
EC1 ... 94 C3 241 B5
Central St Martin's Coll
of Art & Design
W1 ... 93 D1 239 D1
Central St Martins Coll
of Art & Design (The
London Inst)
WC1 ... 94 B2 240 C3
Central Sch of Ballet
EC1 ... 94 C3 241 B5
Central Sch of Speech &
Drama NW3 ... 70 B1
Central Sq
East Molesey KT8 ... 195 B5
Hampstead Garden Suburb
NW11 ... 47 D3
4 Wembley HA9 ... 66 A3
Central St EC1 95 A4 235 A1
Central Terr BR3 ... 206 D6
Central Way
Feltham TW14 ... 150 B6
Lower Place NW10 ... 89 A4
Sutton SM5 ... 218 C1
Thamesmead SE28 ... 124 B6
Centre Acad 2
SW11 ... 136 B1
Centre Ave Acton W3 ... 111 B5
Finchley N2 ... 30 C1
Centre Bldg SE17 ... 262 B4
Centre Common Rd
BR7 ... 189 A3
Centre Court Sh Ctr 3
SW19 ... 179 B4
Centre Ct N20 ... 14 B2
Centre Dr E7 ... 77 C4
Centre Hts 5 NW3 ... 70 B1
Centre Point 3 SE1 ... 118 A1
Centre Point Ho
WC2 ... 239 D2
Centre Rd
Dagenham RM10 ... 103 D5
Finchley N2 ... 30 C1
Wanstead E7, E11 ... 77 A6
Centre St E2 ... 96 B5
Centre The TW13 ... 150 B3
Centre The Performing
Arts Coll SE18 ... 121 D3
Centreway 4 IG1 ... 79 A6
Centre Way N9 ... 18 D2
Centro Ct E11 ... 54 C1
Centurian Sq 9
SE18 ... 144 A4
Centurian Way
DA18 ... 125 C3
Centurion Bldg SW8 268 C5
Centurion Cl N7 ... 72 B1
Centurion Ct
Hackbridge SM6 ... 219 B6
7 Woolwich SE18 ... 122 B2
Centurion La E3 ... 97 B5
Centurion Lodge 2
RM10 ... 81 D2
Centurion Way
DA18 ... 125 C3
Century Cl NW4 ... 46 D4
Century Ho
Edgware HA8 ... 26 C3
Harrow HA3 ... 42 C6
Lewisham SE13 ... 141 D3
Wembley HA9 ... 66 B6
Century Rd E17 ... 53 A6
Century Yd SE23 ... 162 C2
Cephas Ave E1 ... 96 C3
Cephas Ho 9 E1 ... 96 C3
Cephas St E1 ... 96 C3
Ceres Ct 12 KT1 ... 176 A1
Ceres Rd SE18 ... 123 D2
Cerise Rd SE15 ... 140 A4
Cerne Cl UB4 ... 106 C6
Cerne Rd SM4 ... 202 A3
Cerney Mews W2 ... 246 C6
Cervantes Ct 12 W2 ... 91 D1
Cester St E2 ... 96 A6
Ceylon Rd
6 Hammersmith
W14 ... 112 D3
Kensington W14 ... 254 A5
Chabot Dr SE15 ... 140 B2
Chace Com Sch EN1 ... 5 C4
Chadacre Ave IG5 ... 56 B6
Chadacre Ct E15 ... 99 A6
Chadacre Ho 10
SW9 ... 138 D1
Chadacre Rd KT17 ... 216 B3
Chadbourn St E14 ... 97 D2
Chadbury Ct NW7 ... 28 A2
Chad Cres N9 ... 18 C1
Chadd Dr BR1 ... 210 A6
Chadd Gn 2 E13 ... 99 A6
Chaddlewood EN4 ... 3 A1
Chadston Ho 17 N1 ... 72 D1
Chadswell WC1 ... 233 B1
Chadview Ct 2 RM6 ... 58 D2
Chadville Gdns RM6 ... 58 D4
Chadway RM8 ... 58 C1
Chadwell Ave RM6 ... 58 B2
CHADWELL HEATH ... 58 D4
Chadwell Heath
Foundation Sch The
RM6 ... 58 B3
Chadwell Heath Ind Pk
RM8 ... 58 D1
Chadwell Heath La
RM6 ... 58 C3
Chadwell Heath Sta
RM6 ... 58 D2
Chadwell La N8 ... 50 B6
Chadwell Prim Sch
RM6 ... 58 C2
Chadwell St
EC1 ... 94 C4 234 B2
Chadwick Ave
Chingford E4 ... 36 B6
Enfield N21 ... 4 B1
Wimbledon SW19 ... 179 C4
Chadwick Cl
12 Ealing W7 ... 86 D2
Roehampton SW15 ... 155 D4
Teddington TW11 ... 175 A4
Chadwick Ct 4
SE28 ... 124 B5
Chadwick Pl KT6 ... 197 C3
Chadwick Rd
Harlesden NW10 ... 89 D6
Ilford IG1 ... 78 D5
Leytonstone E11 ... 54 D3
Peckham SE15 ... 139 D3
Chadwick St
SW1 ... 115 D3 259 C5
Chadwick Way SE28 ... 124 D6
Chadwin Rd E13 ... 99 B2
Chadworth Ho
Finsbury EC1 ... 235 A1
Finsbury Pk N4 ... 51 A1
Chadworth Way
KT10 ... 212 B3
Chaffey Ho 6 SE7 ... 121 C1
Chaffinch Ave CR0 ... 206 D3
Chaffinch Bsns Pk
CR0 ... 206 D5
Chaffinch Cl
Croydon CR0 ... 206 D3
Edmonton N9 ... 18 D3
Tolworth KT6 ... 214 C5
Chaffinch Rd BR3 ... 185 A2
Chafford Way RM6 ... 58 C5
Chagford Ct SW19 ... 180 C3
Chagford Ho
38 Bromley E3 ... 97 D4
Marylebone NW1 ... 237 C5
Chagford St
NW1 ... 92 D3 237 D5
Chailey Ave EN1 ... 5 D3
Chailey Cl TW5 ... 128 D4
Chailey Ind Est UB3 ... 106 A4
Chailey St E5 ... 74 C5
Chalbury Ho 8 SW9 ... 138 B1
Chalbury Wlk N1 ... 234 A4
Chalcombe Rd SE2 ... 124 B3
Chalcot Cl SM2 ... 217 C1
Chalcot Cres
NW1 ... 92 D6 230 D6
Chalcot Gdns NW3 ... 70 D2
Chalcot Mews SW16 ... 160 A1
Chalcot Rd
NW1 ... 93 A6 231 A6
Chalcot Sch 21 NW1 ... 71 B1
Chalcot Sq NW1 ... 71 A1
Chalcott Gdns KT6 ... 197 C1
Chalcroft Rd SE13 ... 164 C6
Chaldon Rd
SW6 ... 135 A5 264 B4
Chale Rd SW2 ... 160 A5
Chalet Cl TW15 ... 171 B4
Chalfont Ave HA9 ... 66 D2
Chalfont Ct
3 Belvedere DA17 ... 125 C1
12 Harrow HA1 ... 42 D3
Hendon NW9 ... 45 D6
Marylebone NW1 ... 237 D5
Chalfont Gn N9 ... 17 C1
Chalfont Ho
2 Bermondsey
SE16 ... 118 B3
Willesden NW10 ... 67 B5
Chalfont Rd
Edmonton N9 ... 17 D1
Hayes UB3 ... 106 A4
South Norwood SE25 ... 205 D6
Chalfont Way W13 ... 109 B3
Chalfont Wlk 5 HA5 ... 22 C1
Chalford 7 NW3 ... 70 A2
Chalford Cl KT8 ... 195 C5
Chalford Ct Ilford IG2 ... 56 D4
15 Putney SW15 ... 156 D5
Surbiton KT6 ... 198 B2
Chalford Rd SE21 ... 183 B6
Chalford Wlk IG8 ... 37 D3
Chalgrove Ave SM4 ... 201 C4
Chalgrove Gdns N3 ... 47 A6
Chalgrove Prim Sch
N3 ... 47 A6
Chalgrove Rd
Sutton SM2 ... 218 B1
Tottenham N17 ... 34 B2
Chalice Cl SM6 ... 219 D2
Chalice Ct N2 ... 48 C5
Chalkenden Cl SE20 ... 184 B3
Chalkers Cnr TW9 ... 132 D2
Chalk Farm Rd NW1 ... 71 A1
Chalk Farm Sta NW3 ... 71 A1
Chalkhill Prim Sch
HA9 ... 66 D5
Chalkhill Rd HA9 ... 67 A5
Chalk Hill Rd W6 ... 112 D2
Chalk La EN4 ... 2 D1
Chalklands HA9 ... 67 A5
Chalkley Cl CR4 ... 181 A1
Chalkmill Dr EN1 ... 6 B2
Chalk Pit Ave BR5 ... 190 C1
Chalk Pit Way SM1 ... 218 A3
Chalk Rd E13 ... 99 C2
Chalkstone Cl DA16 ... 146 A4
Chalkwell Ho 10 E1 ... 96 D1
Chalkwell Park Ave
EN1 ... 5 C1
Challenge Cl NW10 ... 89 C6
Challenge Ct TW2 ... 152 C4
Challenge Rd TW15 ... 149 B1
Challenger Ho 7
E14 ... 119 A6
Challice Way SW2 ... 160 B3
Challiner Ct HA1 ... 43 A4
Challin St 1 SE20 ... 184 C2

Challis Rd TW8 . . . . . 109 D1
Challoner Cl N2 . . . . . 30 B1
Challoner Cres W14 . . 254 C1
Challoner Ct BR2 . . . . 186 B1
Challoner St
W14 . . . . 113 B1 254 C1
Challoners Cl KT8 . . 196 B5
Challoner St
W14 . . . . 113 B1 254 C1
Chalmers Ho
13 London SW11 . . . . 136 A2
Walthamstow E17 . . . . 53 D4
Chalmers Rd TW15 . . 170 D5
Chalmers Rd E
TW15 . . . . 171 A5
Chalmers Way
Feltham TW14 . . . . . . 150 B6
Isleworth TW1 . . . . . . 131 B1
Chalmer's Wlk 16
SE17 . . . . 138 D6
Chalner Ho SW2 . . . . 160 C3
Chalsey Lodge SE4 . . 141 B1
Chalsey Rd SE4 . . . . . 141 B1
Chalton Dr N2 . . . . 48 B3
Chalton St
NW1 . . . . 93 D4 232 C3
Chamberlain Cl
Ilford IG1 . . . . 79 A5
Plumstead SE18 . . . . . 123 B3
Chamberlain Cotts
SE5 . . . . 139 B4
Chamberlain Cres
BR4 . . . . 207 D1
Chamberlain Gdns
TW3 . . . . 130 A4
Chamberlain Ho
E1 . . . . 118 C6
Chamberlain La HA5 . . 40 A5
Chamberlain Pl E17 . . 53 A6
Chamberlain Rd
Ealing W13 . . . . 109 A4
Finchley N2 . . . . 30 A1
Chamberlain St 7
NW1 . . . . 70 D1
Chamberlain Way
Pinner HA5 . . . . 40 B6
Surbiton KT6 . . . . 198 A2
Chamberlain Wlk 5
TW13 . . . . 173 A6
Chamberlayne Ave
HA9 . . . . 66 A6
Chamberlayne Mans 3
NW10 . . . . 90 D4
Chamberlayne Rd
NW10 . . . . 90 C6
Chambers Ave DA14 .191 A4
Chambers Bsns Pk
UB7 . . . . 126 C6
Chambers Gdns N2 . . . 30 B2
Chambers Ho 2
SW16 . . . . 181 C6
Chambers La NW10 . . . 68 C1
Chambers PI CR2 . . . 221 B1
Chambers Rd N7 . . . . . 72 A4
Chambers St SE16 . .118 A4
Chamber St
E1 . . . . 117 D6 253 D6
Chambers Walk HA7 . . 25 B5
Chambon PI 7 W6 . . 112 A2
Chambord St 2 . . . . . . 95 D4
Chambord St E2 . . . . . 95 D4
Chamomile Ct E17 . . . 53 C3
Champa 2 N17 . . . . 33 D1
Champion Cres
SE26 . . . . 185 A6
Champion Gr SE5 . . . 139 B2
Champion Hill SE5 . . 139 B2
Champion Pk SE5 . . . 139 B2
Champion Rd SE26 . . 185 A6
Champlain Ho 20
W12 . . . . 112 B6
Champness Cl 9
SE27 . . . . 183 B6
Champness Rd IG11 . . 79 D1
Champneys SE17 . . . 217 B1
Champneys Cl SM2 . . 16 A6
Chancel Ct W1 . . . . . 249 C6
Chancellor Gr SE21 . . 161 A1
Chancellor Ho
South Kensington
SW7 . . . . 256 B6
13 Wapping E1 . . . . . 125 C6
Chancellor Pl NW9 . . . 27 D1
Chancellors Ct WC1 . 240 D4
Chancellors Loft N8 . . 50 A3

Chancellor's Rd W6 . . 112 C1
Chancellors St W6 . . 112 C1
Chancellors Wharf 2
W6 . . . . 112 C1
Chancelot Rd SE2 . . . 124 B2
Chancel St
SE1 . . . . 116 B5 251 C3
Chancery Bldgs 14
E1 . . . . 118 C6
Chancerygate Bsns Ctr
HA4 . . . . 63 A3
Chancery Gate Bsns Ctr
CR4 . . . . 202 D4
Chancery Ho WC2 . . . 241 A3
Chancery La
Beckenham BR3 . . . . . 185 C1
Holborn EC4 . . 94 C1 241 A2
Chancery Lane Sta
WC1 . . . . 94 C2 241 A3
Chancery Mews
SW17 . . . . 158 C2
Chance St E2 . . . . 95 D4
Chanctonbury Cl
SE9 . . . . 166 D1
Chanctonbury Gdns
SM2 . . . . 217 D1
Chanctonbury Way
N12 . . . . 29 C6
Chanderia Ct 5
CR0 . . . . 4 A5
Chandler Ho 7 N12 . . . 30 A5
Chandler Ave E16 . . . . 99 A2
Chandler Cl TW12 . . . 173 C2
Chandler Ct
Feltham TW14 . . . . . . 150 A5
Thornton Heath CR7 . . 204 D4
2 Tolworth KT5 . . . . . 198 D1
8 Wallington SM6 . . . 219 B2
Chandlers Cl
East Bedfont TW14 . . 149 D4
East Molesey KT8 . . . 195 D4
Chandlers Field Prim
SchKT8 . . . . 195 C4
Chandlers Mews
E14 . . . . 119 C4
Chandler St 1
E1 . . . . 118 B5
Chandlers Way 11
SE24 . . . . 138 C2
Chandler Way SE15 . . 139 D5
Chandlery Ho 2 E1 . . . 96 A1
Chandon Lo SW2 . . . 218 A1
Chandos Ave
Ealing W5 . . . . 109 D2
New Southgate N14 . . 15 C1
Oakleigh Pk N20 . . . . . 14 A3
Walthamstow E17 . . . . 35 C1
Chandos Bsns Ctr 13
SW9 . . . . 73 A1
Chandos Cl IG9 . . . . . . 21 B2
Chandos Ct HA8 . . . . . 26 C3
Chandos Ct
Edgware HA8 . . . . 26 B3
Palmers Green N14 . . 15 C4
Stanmore HA7 . . . . . . 25 B4
Chandos Pl
WC2 . . . . 116 A6 250 A5
Chandos Rd
Cricklewood NW2 . . . . 68 C3
Finchley N2 . . . . 30 C1
Harrow HA1 . . . . 42 A4
Old Oak Comm NW10 . . 89 C3
Walthamstow E17 . . . . 35 C1
Stratford New Town
E15 . . . . 76 B3
Tottenham N17 . . . . . . 33 C1
Chandos St
W1 . . . . 93 B2 238 D2
Chandos Way NW11 . . 47 D1
Change Alley EC3 . . . 242 D1
Channel Cl TW5 . . . . . 129 D2
Channel Gate Rd
NW10 . . . . 89 C4
Channel Ho E14 . . . . . 97 A2
Channel Sea Bsns Ctr
E15 . . . . 98 A5
Channelsea Rd E15 . . 98 B6
Channing Jun Sch
N6 . . . . 49 B1
Channing Sch N6 . . . . 49 B1
Channon St 3 KT6 . . . 198 A6
Chantrey Rd SW9 . . . 138 B2
Chantries The HA7 . . . 25 A5
Chantry Cl
2 Abbey Wood
SE2 . . . . 124 C3
Edgware NW7 . . . . 11 D4

Chantry Cl continued
Enfield EN2 . . . . 5 A5
Harrow HA3 . . . . 44 B4
Sidcup DA14 . . . . 191 A5
Sunbury TW16 . . . . . . 172 A3
West Kilburn W9 . . . . . 91 B3
Chantry Cres NW10 . . 67 D2
Chantry Ct SM5 . . . . 218 C5
Chantry Cl SW6 . . . . 135 A2
Chantry La BR2 . . . . . 209 D4
Chantry Pl HA3 . . . . . . 23 D2
Chantry Rd
Chessington KT9 . . . . 214 C3
Harrow HA3 . . . . 23 D2
Chantry Sch AB7 . . . 104 B6
Chantry Sq
W8 . . . . 113 D3 255 C5
Chantry St N1 . . . . . . 234 D5
Chantry The UB8 . . . 104 B2
Chantry The CR4 . . . 202 B6
Chant Sq E15 . . . . 76 B1
Chant St E15 . . . . 76 B1
Chapel Cl
Borough The SE1 . . . 252 C2
East Finchley N2 . . . . 48 C6
Hayes UB3 . . . . 105 D6
Chapel End Inf Sch
E17 . . . . 35 D2
Chapel End Jun Sch
E17 . . . . 35 D2
Chapel Farm Rd SE9 . 166 B2
Chapel Hill N2 . . . . 30 C1
Chapel House St
E14 . . . . 119 D2
Chapel La
6 Dagenham RM6 . . . 58 D2
Hillingdon UB8 . . . . . . 82 C1
Pinner HA5 . . . . 40 D6
Chapel Mill Rd KT1 . . 198 B6
Chapel Mkt *
N1 . . . . 94 C5 234 A3
Chapel Pl
Islington N1 . . . . 234 B4
Marylebone W1 . . . . . 238 C2
12 Shoreditch EC2 . . . 95 C4
Tottenham N17 . . . . . . 33 C1
Chapel Rd
Bexleyheath DA7 . . . . 147 C1
Ealing W13 . . . . 109 B5
Hounslow TW3 . . . . . 129 D2
Ilford IG1 . . . . 78 D1
Twickenham TW1 . . . 153 B4
West Norwood SE27 . . 182 D6
Chapel Side
W2 . . . . 113 D6 245 C5
Chapel St Enfield EN2 . . 5 B2
Paddington
NW1 . . . . . . 92 C2 237 A3
Westminster
SW1 . . . . . . .115 A4 248 B1
Chapel View CR2 . . . 222 C1
Chapel Wlk NW4 . . . . 46 C5
Chaplin 2 NW2 . . . . . 160 C6
Chaplin Cl
Lambeth SE1 . . . . . . 251 C2
Wembley HA0 . . . . . . 65 D2
Chaplin Cres TW16 . . 151 D6
Chaplin Ho
6 London SW9 . . . . . 138 C1
Sidcup DA14 . . . . 190 A6
Chaplin Rd
Dagenham RM9 . . . . . 81 A1
3 Tottenham N17 . . . 51 D6
Wembley HA0 . . . . . . 65 D2
West Ham E15 . . . . . . 98 B5
Willesden NW2 . . . . . . 68 A3
Chaplow Cl SW6 . . . 136 A3
Chapman Cl UB7 . . . 104 B3
Chapman Cres HA3 . . 44 A4
Chapman Gn N22 . . . . 32 C2
Chapman Ho
20 Stepney E1 . . . . . 96 B1
2 West Norwood
SE27 . . . . 160 D1
Chapman Rd
Belvedere DA17 . . . . 125 D1
Hackney Wick E9 . . . . 75 B1
Thornton Heath CR0 . 204 C1
Chapmans End BR5 . . 191 A1
Chapmans La BR5 . . 191 A1
Chapmans Park Ind Est
NW10 . . . . 67 D2
Chapman Sq SW19 . . 156 D2
Chapman St E1 . . . . . 118 B6

Chapone Pl W1 . . . . . 239 C1
Chapter Cl
Hillingdon UB10 . . . . . 60 B1
South Acton W4 . . . . 111 A3
Chapter House & Jewel
Twr * SW1 . . . . 260 A6
Chapter Rd
Kennington
SE17 . . . . . . 116 D1 261 D1
Willesden NW2 . . . . . . 68 A3
Chapter St SW1 . . . . 259 C3
Chapter Way
Hampton TW12 . . . . . 173 C6
Mitcham SW19 . . . . . 180 B2
Chara PI W4 . . . . 133 B6
Charcot Ho SW5 . . . 155 D5
Charcroft Ct 11
W14 . . . . 112 C4
Charcroft Gdns EN3 . . 6 D1
Chard Ho 7 N7 . . . . . . 72 B6
Chardin Ho 10 SW9 . . 138 C4
Chardin Rd 11 W4 . . . 111 C1
Chardmore Rd N16 . . 52 A1
Cardwell Cl E6 . . . . . 100 B1
Charecroft Way
W12 . . . . 112 C4
Charfield Ct 9
SW9 . . . . 91 D3
Charford Rd E16 . . . . 99 A2
Chargeable La E13 . . 99 A3
Chargeable St E16 . . 98 D3
Chargrove Cl 24
SE16 . . . . 118 D4
Charing Cl BR6 . . . . . 227 D4
Charing Cross
SW1 . . . . . . .116 A5 250 A4
Charing Cross Hospl
W6 . . . . 112 D1
Charing Cross Rd
WC2 . . . . 93 D1 239 D1
Charing Cross Sta
WC2 . . . . 116 A5 250 A6
Charing Ho SE1 . . . . 251 B2
Chariot Cl 3 E3 . . . . . 97 C6
Charlbert Ct NW8 . . . 230 A4
Charlbert St
NW8 . . . . 92 C5 230 A4
Charlbury Ave HA7 . . 25 D5
Charlbury Gdns IG3 . . 79 D6
Charlbury Gr W5 . . . . 87 C2
Charlbury Ho 11 E12 . 78 C5
Charlbury Rd UB10 . . 60 B5
Charldane Rd SE9 . . 166 D1
Charlecote Gr SE26 . 162 B1
Charlecote Rd RM8 . . 81 A5
Charlemont Rd E6 . . 100 C4
Charles Allen Ho
EC1 . . . . 234 A2
Charles Auffray Ho 3
E1 . . . . 96 C2
Charles Babbage Cl
KT9 . . . . 213 C1
Charles Barry Cl
SW4 . . . . 137 C2
Charles Bradlaugh Ho 2
N17 . . . . 34 B3
Charles Burton Ct E5 . 75 A4
Charles Cl DA14 . . . . 190 B6
Charles Cobb Gdns
CR0 . . . . 220 C3
Charles Coveney Rd 6
SE15 . . . . 139 D4
Charles Cres HA1 . . . 42 B2
Charles Ct 5 TW11 . . 174 C5
Charles Darwin Ho
6 Bethnal Green E2 . . 96 B4
Bromley BR1 . . . . 187 B3
Charles Dickens Ct
SE25 . . . . 206 A5
Charles Dickens Ho 1
E2 . . . . 96 B4
Charles Dickens Mus
The * WC1 . . . 94 B3 240 D5
Charles Dickens Prim
SchSE1 . . . . 117 A4 252 A1
Charles Edward Brooke
Sch 11 SW9 . . . . . . 138 D4
Charles Edward Brooke
Sch (Dennen Site) 10
SE5 . . . . 138 D4
Charlesfield SE12 . . . 165 C1
Charles Flemwell Mews
7 E16 . . . . 121 A5
Charles Goddard Ho 3
HA0 . . . . 65 D3
Charles Gr N14 . . . . . 15 C3

Charles Grinling Wlk
SE18 . . . . 122 C2
Charles Haller St 2
SW2 . . . . 160 C4
Charles Harrod Ct
SW13 . . . . 134 C6
Charles Ho
Southall UB2 . . . . 107 C4
1 Tottenham N17 . . . 33 D3
Charles Hobson Ho 4
NW10 . . . . 67 C1
Charles Rocking Ho 9
W3 . . . . 111 A4
Charles II Pl
SW3 . . . . 114 D1 257 C1
Charles II St
SW1 . . . . 115 D5 249 C4
Charles La
NW8 . . . . 92 C5 230 A4
Charles Lamb Ct N1 . 234 D4
Charles Lesser KT9 . 213 D3
Charles Mackenzie Ho
SE16 . . . . 118 A3
Charlesmere Gdns
SE28 . . . . 123 C4
Charles Mills Ct
SW16 . . . . 182 A4
Charles PI NW1 . . . . 232 B1
Charles Rd
Dagenham RM6 . . . . . 58 D3
Ealing W13 . . . . 87 A1
Merton SW19 . . . . . . 179 C2
Romford IG1 . . . . 77 C1
Charles Rowan Ho
WC1 . . . . 234 A1
Charles Sevright Dr
NW7 . . . . 28 D5
Charles Sq N1 . 95 B4 235 D1
Charles St
Barnes SW13 . . . . . . 133 C3
Croydon CR0 . . . . . . 221 A5
Enfield EN1 . . . . 17 C6
Hillingdon UB10 . . . . . 82 D3
Hounslow TW3 . . . . . 129 B3
Mayfair W1 . . . 115 B5 248 A4
Newham E16 . . . . 121 C5
Charles Staunton Ho 8
SE27 . . . . 183 B6
Charleston Cl TW13 . 150 A1
Charleston St SE17 . 262 B3
Charles Townsend Ho
EC1 . . . . 241 C6
Charles Utton Ct E8 . . 74 A4
Charles Whincup Rd
E16 . . . . 121 B5
Charlesworth Ho 6
E14 . . . . 97 C1
Charleville Cir SE26 . 184 A5
Charleville Ct SW5 . . 254 C1
Charleville Mans
W14 . . . . 254 B1
Charleville Mews
TW7 . . . . 131 B1
Charleville Rd
W14 . . . . 113 B1 254 C1
Charlie Browns Rdbt
E18 . . . . 37 C1
Charlmont Rd SW17 . 180 D4
Charlotte Cl DA6 . . . . 169 A6
Charlotte Ct
Crouch End N8 . . . . . . 49 D3
Esher KT10 . . . . 212 A3
10 Hammersmith W6 . 112 A2
Ilford IG2 . . . . 56 C3
11 Wembley HA0 . . . 66 A1
Charlotte Despard Ave
SW11 . . . . . . 137 A4 268 B1
Charlotte Ho 12 W6 . 112 C1
Charlotte Mews
Marylebone W1 . . . . 239 B4
North Kensington W10 . 90 D1
West Kensington W14 . 254 A1
Charlotte Par 3
BR1 . . . . 210 A6
Charlotte Pl
Kenton NW9 . . . . 45 A4
Marylebone W1 . . . . 239 B3
Westminster SW1 . . . 259 A3
Charlotte Rd
Barnes SW13 . . . . . . 133 D4
Dagenham RM10 . . . . 81 D2

Charlotte Rd *continued*
Shoreditch
EC2 ....95 C3 243 A6
Wallington SM6 ..... 219 C2
Charlotte Row SW4 . .137 C2
Charlotte Sharman Prim
Sch SE11 . 116 D3 261 C5
Charlotte Sq 5
TW10 ....154 B5
Charlotte St
W1 ....93 C2 239 B4
Charlotte Terr
N1 ....94 B6 233 D5
Charlotte Turner Prim
Sch SE8 .... 141 C6
CHARLTON 143 D6
171 B1
Charlton Church La
SE7 ....121 C1
Charlton Cl UB10 .....60 D6
Charlton Cres IG11 . 101 D5
Charlton Ct
Finchley N3 ....29 A1
25 Hackney E2........95 D6
17 Kentish Town N7.....71 D3
Newham E6 ....100 B4
Charlton Dene SE7 . . 143 D5
Charlton Gate Bsns Pk
SE7 .... 121 C2
Charlton Ho
5 Brentford TW8 ... 132 A6
Charlton TW17........ 171 A1
Somers Town NW1... 232 C2
Charlton King's Rd
NW5 ....71 D3
Charlton La
Greenwich SE7 ..... 121 D1
Upper Halliford TW17 .193 B5
Upper Halliford TW17 193 C5
Charlton Lo 1 NW11. . 47 B3
Charlton Manor Prim
Sch SE7 .... 143 D5
Charlton Park La
SE7 ....144 A6
Charlton Park Rd
SE7 .... 143 D6
Charlton Pl
N1.........94 D5 234 C4
Charlton Rd
Charlton TW17...... 171 A1
Edmonton N9 ....18 D4
Greenwich SE3, SE7....143 B6
Harlesden NW10 ......89 C6
Harrow HA3..........43 D5
Wembley HA9 ....44 B1
Charlton Sch SE7 .... 144 A6
Charlton Sta SE7 ... 121 C1
Charlton Way SE10,
SE3 ....142 C4
Charlwood Cl HA3 ....24 C4
Charlwood Ho
Richmond TW9...... 132 D5
1 Streatham SW2 .... 160 B3
Westminster SW1 ... 259 C3
Charlwood Pl
SW1 ....115 C2 259 B3
Charlwood Rd
SW15 .... 134 D1
Charlwood St
SW1 ....115 C1 259 B2
Charlwood Terr 5
SW15 .... 134 D1
Charman Ho
18 London SW2...... 160 C5
South Lambeth SW8 . 270 A4
Charmian Ave HA7....25 D1
Charmian Ho 19 N1....95 C5
Charminster Ave
SW19 .... 179 D1
Charminster Ct 3
KT6 .... 197 D2
Charminster Rd
Mottingham SE12,
SE9 .... 187 D6
North Cheam KT4.... 200 D1
Charmouth Ct TW10. .154 B6
Charmouth Ho SW8. 270 C4
Charmouth Rd DA16 .146 C4
Charnock Ho 22
W12 ....112 B6
Charnock Rd E5 ......74 B5
Charnwood Ave
SW19 .... 179 D1
Charnwood Cl KT3 . . .199 C5
Charnwood Dr E18. . . .55 B5
Charnwood Gdns
E14 ....119 C2
Charnwood Ho 9 E5. 74 B6
Charnwood Pl N20....14 A1
Charnwood Rd
Hillingdon UB10........82 C5
South Norwood SE25. .205 B5
Charnwood St E5 .....74 B6
Charolais Ho UB4.....83 B2
Charrington Ho 42
E1.................96 C3
Charrington Rd 2
CR0...............221 A6
Charrington St
NW1 ....93 D5 232 C4
Charsley Rd SE6 .... 163 D2
Chart Cl Bromley BR2 .186 C2
Croydon CR0 .... 206 C3
Mitcham CR4 .... 202 D5
Charter Ave IG2 ......57 B2
Charter Bldgs 14
SE10 .... 141 D4
Charter Cres TW4....129 A1
Charter Ct
Finsbury Pk N4.........50 C1
Kingston u T KT3 .... 199 C6
Marylebone W1 ..... 237 B3
Southall UB1 .... 107 C5
Wood Green N22 ....31 D2
Charter Dr DA5 ......169 A4
Charter Ho WC2 .... 240 B1
Charterhouse Ave
HA0 ....65 C3
Charterhouse Bldgs
EC1 .... 242 A5
Charterhouse Mews
EC1 .... 241 D4
Charterhouse Rd E8 . .74 A3
Charterhouse Sq
EC1 ....94 D2 241 D4
Charterhouse Square
Sch The EC1. .94 D2 241 D4
Charterhouse St EC1 241 C3
Charterhouse Works
SW18 .... 136 A1
Charteris Rd
Finsbury Pk N4.........50 C1
Kilburn NW6 ....91 B6
Woodford IG8 ....37 B4
Charteris Sp Ctr NW6 .91 C6
Charter Rd KT1 ..... 198 D6
Charter Rd The IG8 ...36 D4
Charter Sch SE24 ....161 B6
Charters Cl SE19.....183 C5
Charter Sq KT1 ..... 176 D1
Charter Way
London NW3 ....47 B5
Southgate N14.........15 D5
Chartes Ho SE1..... 263 B6
Chartfield Ave
SW15 ....156 C6
Chartfield Sq SW15 . 156 D6
Chartham Ct 12
SW9 ....138 C2
Chartham Gr SE27 .. 160 D1
Chartham Ho SE1... 262 D6
Chartham Rd SE25...206 B6
Chart Hills Cl SE28 ...103 A1
Chart Ho 7 SW19... 180 D1
Chart House The 5
E14 .... 119 D1
Chartley Ave
Harrow HA7..........24 D4
Neasden NW2 ....67 C5
Charton Cl 5 DA17 ..147 B6
Chartres Ct UB6 ......86 B5
Chartridge SE17 .....139 B6
Chartridge Cl
Barnet EN5 ....12 A6
Bushey WD23...........8 A5
Chartridge Ct 6 HA7 .25 C5
Chart St N1....95 B4 235 D2
Chartwell 25 SW19.. 156 D3
Chartwell Bsns Ctr
BR1 .... 209 D6
Chartwell Cl
2 Croydon CR0.......205 B1
Greenford UB6..........85 D6
Sidcup SE9 ....167 B2
Chartwell Ct
10 Barnet EN5...........1 A1
Dollis Hill NW2........68 A5
Chartwell Ct *continued*
2 Woodford IG8........37 A3
Chartwell Dr BR6 ....227 B3
Chartwell Gdns SM3 .217 A4
Chartwell Lo 5 BR3 .185 C3
Chartwell Pl
Cheam SM3 ....217 B4
Harrow HA2..........64 B6
Chartwell Way 3
SE20 ....184 B2
Charville Ct 8 HA1 ...42 D3
Charville La UB4 .....83 C5
Charville La W UB10 ..82 D4
Charville Prim Sch
UB4 ....83 C5
Charwood SW16 .....182 C6
Chase Bridge Prim Sch
TW2 .... 152 C5
Chase Court Gdns EN2 . 5 A2
Chase Ct
Chelsea SW3 .... 257 C5
Isleworth TW7....... 131 A3
Merton SW20....... 179 A1
Southgate N14.........15 C5
Wembley HA0 ....65 D2
Chase Ctr The NW10 . .89 B4
Chase Farm Hospl EN2 4 C5
Chasefield Rd SW17 180 D6
Chase Gdns
Chingford E4 ....35 C6
Twickenham TW2......152 B4
Chase Gn EN2 ....5 A2
Chase Green Ave EN2 . . 5 A3
Chase Hill EN2..........5 A2
Chase La IG6 ....57 B4
Chase Lane Prim Sch
E4.................35 B6
Chaseley Ct
Gunnersbury W4 .... 110 D1
Oatlands Pk KT13.... 193 C1
Chaseley St E14 ......97 A1
Chasemore Cl CR4 .. 202 D2
Chasemore Gdns
CR0...............220 C3
Chasemore Ho SW6. 264 B4
Chase Rd
North Acton NW10.....89 B3
Southgate N14.........15 D5
Chase Ridings EN2.....4 C3
Chase Road Trad Est
NW10 ....89 B3
Chase Side
East Barnet N14 ....15 B4
Enfield EN2 ....5 A3
Chase Side Ave
Enfield EN2 ....5 A3
Merton SW20....... 179 A1
Chase Side Cres EN2....5 A4
Chase Side Pl EN2 .....5 A3
Chase Side Prim Sch
EN2 ....5 A3
Chase Side Works
N14 ....15 D4
Chase The
Bromley BR1 ....209 B6
Clapham SW4 ....137 B2
Dagenham RM6 ....59 A3
Eastcote HA5..........40 C3
Edgware HA8..........26 D2
Erith DA7 .... 147 D2
Ickenham UB10........60 C3
Loughton IG10.........21 D4
Manor Pk E12..........77 D4
Pinner HA5............41 B5
South Norwood SW16 182 C3
Stanmore HA7 ....25 A4
Sunbury TW16 ....172 B2
Wallington CR0, SM6. .220 B3
Chaseville Par N21....16 B6
Chaseville Park Rd
N21................16 B6
Chase Way N14........15 C3
Chasewood Ave EN2 ...4 D3
Chasewood Ct 4
NW7 ....27 B5
Chasewood Pk HA1 ...64 C5
Chateau The 4
SM5 .... 218 D5
Chatelain Ho NW7 ....28 C6
Chater Ho 6 E2 ......96 D4
Chatfield Rd
London SW11........ 136 A2
Thornton Heath CR0 . 204 D1
Chatham Ave BR2....209 A2
Chatham Cl
Cheam SM3 ....201 B2
Chatham Cl *continued*
Hampstead Garden Suburb
NW11 ....47 C4
Woolwich SE18 ......122 B3
Chatham Ct SW11... 158 D6
Chatham Ho
7 London SE5....... 139 C3
6 Wallington SM6 ...219 B3
21 Woolwich SE18....122 B2
Chatham Pl E9 ....74 C2
Chatham Rd
Clapham SW11 ...... 158 D6
Kingston u T KT1, KT2. 176 C1
Walthamstow E17 .....53 A6
1 Woodford E18........36 D1
Chatham St
SE17 ....117 B2 262 D4
Chatsfield Pl W5......88 A1
Chatsworth Ave
Grove Pk BR1........187 B6
Hendon NW4 ....28 C1
Merton SW20........ 179 A1
Sidcup DA15........ 168 A3
Wembley HA9 ....66 B3
Chatsworth Cl
Coney Hall BR2,
BR4 .... 224 D6
Hendon NW4 ....28 C1
Chatsworth Cres TW3,
TW7 ....130 B2
Chatsworth Ct
Brondesbury NW2.....68 D2
Clapton Pk E5.........74 D4
Earl's Ct W8......... 255 A4
5 Stanmore HA7 .....25 C5
Thornton Heath
SW16 ....204 B6
Chatsworth Dr EN1 ...18 A5
Chatsworth Est E5....74 D4
Chatsworth Gdns
Acton W3 .... 110 D5
Harrow HA2...........41 D1
New Malden KT3 .... 199 D4
Chatsworth Ho
2 Bromley BR2...... 209 A5
Kingston u T KT6 .... 197 D4
Chatsworth Inf Sch
Isleworth TW3....... 130 A1
Sidcup DA15........ 168 A3
Chatsworth Jun Sch
TW3 .... 130 A1
Chatsworth Lo
1 Chiswick W4........111 B1
West Wickham BR4 .. 224 A6
Chatsworth Par BR5 .211 A4
Chatsworth Pl
Mitcham CR4 .... 202 D6
Teddington TW11.... 175 A6
Chatsworth Rd
Brondesbury NW2.....68 D2
Cheam SM3 .... 217 A4
Chiswick W4 .... 133 A6
Clapton Pk E5.........74 D4
Ealing W5............88 B3
Hayes UB4............84 B3
South Croydon CR0 ...221 B5
Stratford E15..........76 D3
Chatsworth Rise W5 . . 88 B3
Chatsworth Way
SE27 ....161 A1
Chattenden Ho 8 N4 . 51 B2
Chatteris Ct NW4 .....46 D6
CHATTERN HILL.... 170 D6
Chattern Hill TW15.. 170 D6
Chattern Rd TW15 ...171 A6
Chatterton Ct TW9...132 B3
Chatterton Rd
Bromley Comm BR2.. 209 D4
Highbury N4..........72 D5
Chatton Ct 5 NW9....46 A5
Chatto Rd SW11 .... 158 D6
Chaucer Ave
Cranford TW4 ....128 B3
Hayes UB4............84 A2
Richmond TW9...... 132 C3
Chaucer Cl N11........31 D5
Chaucer Ct
14 New Barnet EN5....13 D6
17 Stoke Newington
N16 ....73 C4
Chaucer Dr
SE1........ 117 D2 263 D3
Chaucer Gdns SM1 . .217 C5
Chaucer Gn CR0 .....206 C2
Chaucer Ho
Harrow HA2...........41 D4
Chaucer Ho *continued*
Pimlico SW1......... 259 A1
Sutton SM1 .... 217 C5
2 West Norwood
SE27 .... 183 A6
Chaucer Rd
Acton W3 ....111 A5
Ashford TW15 ....170 B6
Bexley DA16......... 145 D4
Chingford E17 ....36 A1
Herne Hill SE24 ..... 160 D6
Sidcup DA15........ 168 C3
Sutton SM1 .... 217 C4
Upton E7 ....77 A2
Wanstead E11 ....55 A3
Chaucer Way SW17 . .180 B5
Chaulden Ho EC1 ... 235 D1
Chauncey Cl N9 ......18 A1
Chaundrye Cl SE9....166 B5
Chauntler Cl E16.....121 B6
Chaville Ct N11........31 A6
Cheadle Ct NW8 .... 236 D6
Cheadle Ho 17 E14....97 B1
CHEAM..............217 B3
Cheam Common Inf Sch
KT4 ....216 B6
Cheam Common Jun Sch
KT4 ....216 B6
Cheam Common Rd
KT4................216 C5
Cheam Court Flats 1
SM3 ....217 A2
Cheam Fields Prim Sch
SM3 .... 217 A3
Cheam High Sch
SM3 .... 217 A4
Cheam L Ctr SM3 ... 216 D4
Cheam Mans SM3....217 A1
Cheam Park Farm Inf
Sch SM3 .... 217 A5
Cheam Park Farm Jun
Sch SM3.......... 217 A5
Cheam Park Way
SM3 ....217 A2
Cheam Rd
Belmont SM2, SM3. . . 216 D1
Cheam SM1 .... 217 C2
Cheam St 6 SE15.....140 B2
Cheam Sta SM2..... 217 A1
Cheam Village SM3 . .217 A2
Cheapside
Barbican EC2 ..95 A1 242 B1
Edmonton N13..........33 A6
Chearsley SE17...... 262 B4
Cheddar Cl 1 N11.....31 A4
Cheddar Rd TW6.....126 C3
Cheddar Waye UB4 ...84 B1
Cheddington Ho 9
E2.................96 A6
Cheddington Rd N18. 33 C6
Chedworth Cl E16 ....98 D1
Chedworth Ho
London N15 ....51 B5
2 Stoke Newington E5 74 A6
Cheeseman Cl
TW12 ....173 A4
Cheeseman Ct UB1 . 107 D6
Cheesemans Terr
W14 .... 254 C1
Cheffrey Ct TW15 ... 170 D4
Cheldon Ave NW7.....28 D3
Chelford Rd BR1 .....186 B5
Chelmer Cres IG11....102 B5
Chelmer Ct E18........37 B2
Chelmer Rd E9 ....74 D3
Chelmsford Cl
Fulham W6............134 D6
Newham E6 ....100 B1
Chelmsford Ct N14.....15 D4
Chelmsford Gdns IG1 56 B2
Chelmsford Ho 5 N7 .72 B4
Chelmsford Rd
Leytonstone E11 ......54 B1
London N14 ....15 C4
Walthamstow E17 .....53 C3
Woodford E18 ....36 D2
Chelmsford Sq NW10 .90 C6
CHELSEA.......... 114 C1
Chelsea Antiques Mkt★
SW3........114 C1 257 B1
Chelsea Barracks★
SW1.......115 A1 258 B1
Chelsea Bridge
SW1 ....137 B6 268 C6
Chelsea Bridge Rd
SW1 ....115 A1 258 B1

Chelsea Cl
Edgware HA8 26 C1
Hampton TW12 174 A5
New Malden KT4 200 A2
Stonebridge NW10 89 B6
Chelsea Cloisters SW3 257 B3
Chelsea Coll of Art & Design SW1 116 A1 260 A2
Chelsea Cres
Brondesbury NW2 69 B2
Chelsea SW10 266 B1
Chelsea Ct
Chelsea SW3 268 A6
6 Chingford E4 20 A3
Sutton SM2 217 D2
Chelsea Emb SW3 136 D6 267 C5
Chelsea Est SW3 267 A5
Chelsea Farm Ho SW10 266 D5
Chelsea Fields SW19 180 B2
Chelsea Gate SW1 258 B1
Chelsea Gdns
Cheam SM3 217 A4
Chelsea SW1 258 B1
Ealing W13 86 D2
Chelsea Harbour Design Ctr SW10 266 B2
Chelsea Harbour Dr SW10 136 A4 266 B2
Chelsea Harbour Pier SW10 266 C1
Chelsea Ind Coll SW6 256 C3
Chelsea Lo SW3 267 D6
Chelsea Manor Ct SW3 267 B6
Chelsea Manor Gdns SW3 257 B1
Chelsea Manor St SW3 114 C1 257 B1
Chelsea Manor Studios SW3 257 B1
Chelsea Mus* SW6 265 D4
Chelsea Park Gdns SW3 136 B6 266 C6
Chelsea Physic Gdn* SW1 267 C6
Chelsea Reach Twr SW10 266 C4
Chelsea Sp Ctr SW3 114 C1 257 B1
Chelsea Sq SW3 114 B1 256 D1
Chelsea Twrs SW3 267 B6
Chelsea & Westminster Hospl SW10 136 A6 266 B5
Chelsfield Ave N9 18 D4
Chelsfield Gdns SE26 162 C1
Chelsfield Gn N9 18 D4
Chelsfield Ho SE17 263 A3
Chelsfield Point 3 E9 74 D1
Chelsham Ho 1 SW4 137 D2
Chelsham Rd
London SW4 137 D2
South Croydon CR2 221 B2
Chelsiter Ct DA14 189 D6
Chelston App HA4 62 A6
Chelston Ct 2 E11 55 B4
Chelston Rd HA4 40 A1
Chelsworth Dr SE18 145 B6
Cheltenham Ave 10 TW1 153 A4
Cheltenham Cl
Kingston u T KT3 199 A6
Northolt UB5 63 D2
Cheltenham Ct 8 HA7 25 C5
Cheltenham Gdns E6 100 A5
Cheltenham Ho UB3 105 A3
Cheltenham Pl
10 Acton W3 110 D5
Acton W3 111 A4
Harrow HA3 44 A5
1 South Acton W3 110 D4
Cheltenham Rd
Leyton E10 54 A3
London SE15 162 C6
Cheltenham Terr SW3 114 D1 257 D2
Cheltenham Villas CR7 204 C3
Chelverton Ct SW15 134 D1
Chelverton Rd SW15 134 D1
Chelwood
Gospel Oak NW5 71 A3
London N20 14 B2
Chelwood Cl E4 19 D5
Chelwood Ct
Battersea SW11 266 D2
9 South Croydon CR2 221 A3
Chelwood Gdns TW9 132 C3
Chelwood Ho W2 236 D1
Chelwood Lo N12 30 A4
Chenappa Cl E13 99 A4
Chenduit Way HA7 24 D5
Chene Colline Ct KT6 198 A3
Cheney Ct SE23 162 D3
Cheney Row E17 35 B2
Cheneys Rd E11 76 C5
Cheney St HA5 40 C4
Chenies Ho W2 245 C6
Chenies Mews WC1 239 C5
Chenies Pl NW1 232 D4
Chenies St WC1 93 D2 239 C4
Chenies The
Orpington BR6 211 C3
Somers Town NW1 232 D4
Cheniston Gdns W8 255 C6
Chennestone Prim Sch TW16 172 B1
Chepstow Cl SW15 157 A6
Chepstow Cres
Ilford IG3 57 C3
Notting Hill W11 113 C6 245 A6
Chepstow Ct W11 245 A6
Chepstow Gdns UB1 85 B1
Chepstow Pl W2 113 C6 245 B6
Chepstow Rd
Croydon CR0 221 D6
Ealing W7 109 A3
Paddington W2 91 C1
Chepstow Rise CR0 221 C5
Chepstow Villas W11 113 C6 245 A6
Chequers IG9 21 B3
Chequers Cl
London NW9 45 C6
Orpington BR5 211 D5
Chequers Ct
7 Croydon CR0 205 D1
St Luke's EC1 242 C5
Chequers Ho NW8 237 A6
Chequers La RM9 103 C5
Chequers Par
Dagenham RM9 103 C6
Edmonton N13 33 A5
Chequer St EC1 95 A3 242 B5
Chequers The HA5 40 D6
Chequers Way N13 32 D5
Cherbury Cl SE28 102 D1
Cherbury Ct N1 235 D3
Cherbury St N1 95 B5 235 D3
Cherchefells Mews HA7 25 B5
Cherimoya Gdns KT8 195 D6
Cherington Rd W7 108 D5
Cheriton Ave BR2 209 A4
Cheriton Cl
Cockfosters EN4 2 D1
10 Ealing W5 87 C2
Cheriton Ct
4 Lee SE12 165 A4
South Norwood SE25 205 C4
Walton-on-T KT12 194 C1
Cheriton Dr SE18 145 B6
Cheriton Ho 9 E5 74 B3
Cheriton Sq SW17 159 A2
Cherry Ave UB1 106 D5
Cherry Blossom Cl N13 32 D5
Cherry Cl
Carshalton SM5 218 D6
Ealing W5 109 D3
Cherry Cl *continued*
Merton SM4 201 A5
Ruislip HA4 61 D5
7 Streatham SW2 160 C4
Walthamstow E17 53 D4
Cherrycot Hill BR6 227 B4
Cherrycot Rise BR6 227 A4
Cherry Cres TW8 131 B5
Cherry Croft Gdns 3 HA5 23 B3
Cherry Ct Acton W3 111 C5
Hackbridge CR4 203 A1
Ilford IG6 56 D6
Pinner HA5 22 D2
5 Rotherhithe SE16 119 A5
Sidcup DA14 168 B1
Cherrydeal Ct E11 54 B2
Cherrydown Ave E4 19 C1
Cherrydown Cl E4 19 C1
Cherrydown Rd DA14 168 D2
Cherry Garden Ho 7 SE16 118 B4
Cherry Garden Sch 20 SE16 118 A2
Cherry Garden St SE16 118 B4
Cherry Garth TW8 109 D1
Cherry Gdns
Dagenham RM9 81 B3
Northolt UB5 63 D1
Cherry Gr Hayes UB3 106 B5
Hillingdon UB8 83 A2
Cherry Hill
New Barnet EN5 13 D5
Stanmore HA3 24 C4
Cherry Hill Gdns CR0 220 B4
Cherry Hills WD19 23 A5
Cherry La UB7 104 C2
Cherrylands Cl NW9 67 A6
Cherry Lane Prim Sch UB7 104 B2
Cherry Laurel Wlk SW2 160 B5
Cherry Orch
Charlton SE7 143 C6
West Drayton UB7 104 A4
Cherry Orchard Gdns
7 Croydon CR0 205 B1
East Molesey KT8 195 B6
5 South Croydon CR0 221 B6
Cherry Orchard Prim Sch SE7 143 C5
Cherry Orchard Rd
Croydon CR0 205 C1
East Molesey KT8 195 C6
Keston Mark BR2 226 A6
Cherry Rd EN3 6 C5
Cherry Tree Ave UB7 82 B1
Cherry Tree Cl
11 Hackney E9 96 C6
Wembley HA0 65 A4
Cherry Tree Ct
1 Camden Town NW1 71 C1
17 Charlton SE7 143 C6
Kingsbury NW9 45 A5
11 Peckham SE15 140 B4
3 Woodford E18 36 D1
Cherry Tree Dr SW16 160 A1
Cherry Tree Hill N6 48 D4
Cherrytree Ho 8 W10 90 D4
Cherry Tree Ho
London SE14 141 B3
Ruislip HA4 39 C1
Twickenham TW2 152 B2
Wood Green N22 32 A3
Cherry Tree Rd
London N2 48 D5
Stratford E15 76 C3
Cherry Tree Rise IG9 37 D6
Cherry Trees Sch The 22 E3 97 C4
Cherry Tree Terr SE1 253 B2
Cherry Tree Way HA7 25 B4
Cherry Tree Wlk
Beckenham BR3 207 B5
Coney Hall BR4 224 D4
St Luke's EC1 242 B5
Cherry Way
Upper Halliford TW17 193 C5
West Ewell KT19 215 B2
Cherry Wlk BR2 209 A1
Cherrywood Cl
Bow E3 97 A4
Kingston u T KT2 176 C3
Cherrywood Ct 1 TW11 175 A5
Cherrywood Dr SW15 156 D6
Cherrywood La SM4, SW20 201 A5
Cherry Wood Way W5 88 C2
Chertsey Ct SW14 132 D2
Chertsey Dr SM3 217 A6
Chertsey Ho
Feltham TW13 151 C1
37 Shoreditch E2 95 D4
Chertsey Rd
Ashford TW15, TW16 171 B4
Feltham TW13, TW16 171 C6
Ilford IG1 79 B4
Leyton E11 76 B6
Lower Halliford TW17 192 C2
Shepperton TW17 192 A2
Twickenham TW2 152 B4
Chertsey St SW17 181 A5
Chervil Cl TW13 150 A1
Chervil Mews SE28 124 B5
Cherwell Ct
Teddington KT1 175 D3
West Ewell KT19 215 A4
Cherwell Ho NW8 236 D5
Cherwell Way HA4 39 A3
Cheryls Cl SW6 135 D4 265 D2
Cheseman St SE26 162 B1
Chesfield Rd KT2 176 A3
Chesham Ave BR2, BR5 210 D3
Chesham Cl SW1 258 A5
Chesham Cres SE20 184 C2
Chesham Ct SW18 158 B4
Chesham Flats W1 248 B6
Chesham Ho SW1 258 A5
Chesham Mews SW1 258 A6
Chesham Pl SW1 115 A3 258 A5
Chesham Rd
Kingston u T KT1, KT2 176 C1
Mitcham SW19 180 B4
Penge SE20 184 C2
Chesham St
Westminster SW1 115 A3 258 A5
Willesden NW10 67 B5
Chesham Terr W13 109 B4
Cheshire Cl
Chingford E17 35 D2
Mitcham CR4, SW16 204 A6
Cheshire Gdns KT9 213 D2
Cheshire Ho SM4 201 D2
Cheshire Rd N22 32 B4
Cheshire St E2 95 D3 243 D6
Cheshir Ho NW4 46 C5
Chesholm Rd N16 73 C5
Cheshunt Ho
Hendon NW4 46 C6
9 Kilburn NW6 91 D6
Cheshunt Rd
Belvedere DA17 125 C1
Upton E7 77 B2
Chesil Ct
17 Bethnal Green E2 96 C5
Chelsea SW3 267 B6
Chesil Ho BR7 189 B2
Chesilton Rd SW6 135 B4 264 C2
Chesil Way UB4 83 D4
Chesley Gdns E6 100 A4
Chesney Cres CR0 224 A1
Chesney Ct W9 91 C3
Chesney Ho SE13 142 B1
Chesney St SW11 268 A1
Chesnut Gr N17 51 D6
Chesnut Rd N17 51 D6
Chessell Cl CR7 204 D5
Chessholme Ct TW16 171 C3
Chessholme Rd TW15 171 A4
Chessing Ct N2 48 D6
CHESSINGTON 214 A2
Chessington Ave
Church End N3 47 B6
Erith DA7 147 A5
Chessington Cl KT19 215 A2
Chessington Com Coll KT9 213 D1
Chessington Ct
London N3 47 B6
Pinner HA5 41 B5
Chessington Hall Gdns KT9 213 D1
Chessington Hill Pk KT9 214 C3
Chessington Ho 19 SW8 137 D3
Chessington Lo N3 47 B6
Chessington Mans
Leyton E10 53 C2
Leytonstone E11 54 C2
Chessington North Sta KT9 214 A3
Chessington Par KT9 213 D3
Chessington Pk KT9 214 C4
Chessington Rd KT19 215 B1
Chessington South Sta KT9 213 D1
Chessington Trade Pk KT9 214 C4
Chessington Way BR4 223 D6
Chesson Rd W14 135 B6 264 D6
Chessum Ho E8 74 A2
Chesswood Way HA5 22 D1
Chestbrook Ct 12 EN1 17 C6
Chester Ave
Richmond TW10 154 B5
Twickenham TW2 151 B3
Chester Cl
Ashford TW15 171 B5
Barnes SW13 134 B2
Hayes UB8 82 D1
Knightsbridge SW1 248 C1
1 Richmond TW10 154 B5
Sutton SM1 217 C6
Chester Close N NW1 231 D2
Chester Close S NW1 231 D1
Chester Cres E8 73 D3
Chester Ct
2 Acton W3 88 C1
Bermondsey SE8 118 D1
4 Camberwell SE5 139 B5
Gospel Oak NW5 71 A4
Harrow HA1 42 D3
Regent's Pk NW1 231 D1
Chester Dr HA2 41 C3
Chesterfield Ct
Ashford TW15 170 A6
Kingston u T KT6 198 A4
Lewisham SE13 142 A2
Chesterfield Dr KT10 213 A6
Chesterfield Flats EN5 12 D6
Chesterfield Gdns
Greenwich SE10 142 B5
Harringay N4 50 D4
Mayfair W1 248 C4
Chesterfield Gr SE22 161 D6
Chesterfield Hill W1 115 B5 248 C4
Chesterfield Ho
Highgate N6 49 A1
Mayfair W1 248 B4
6 Streatham SW16 181 C5
Chesterfield Lo N21 16 B4
Chesterfield Mews
Ashford TW15 170 A6
Harringay N4 50 D4
Chesterfield Prim Sch EN3 7 A6

Chesterfield Rd
Ashford TW15 170 A5
Barnet EN5 12 D6
Chiswick W4 133 A6
Enfield EN3 7 A6
Finchley N3 29 C4
Leyton E10 54 A3
West Ewell KT19 215 B1
Chesterfield St W1 248 C4
Chesterfield Way
Hayes UB3 106 A4
Peckham SE15 140 C5
Chesterford Gdns
NW3 69 D4
Chesterford Ho 4
SE18 143 D5
Chesterford Rd E12 78 B3
Chester Gate NW1 231 D1
Chester Gdns
Ealing W13 87 B1
Enfield EN3 18 B5
Morden SM4 202 A3
Chester Ho
5 Barnet EN5 1 D1
Dartmouth Pk N19 71 B6
1 Deptford SE8 141 B6
Kingston u T KT1 176 D1
Chesterman Ct W4 133 C5
Chester Mews
Belgravia SW1 258 C6
Walthamstow E17 35 C1
Chester Pl NW1 231 C2
Chester Rd
Avery Hill DA15 167 C6
Dartmouth Pk N19 71 B6
Edmonton N9 18 B3
Hounslow TW4 128 B2
Ilford IG3 57 D2
Newham E16 98 C3
Regent's Pk
NW1 93 B4 231 C2
Tottenham N17 51 C6
Upton E7 77 D1
Walthamstow E17 52 D4
Wanstead E11 55 B3
Wimbledon SW19,
SW20 178 C4
Chester Row
SW1 115 A2 258 B4
Chester Sq
SW1 115 B2 258 C4
Chester Sq Mews
SW1 258 C5
Chester St
Bethnal Green E2 96 A3
Westminster
SW1 115 A3 258 B6
Chesters The KT3 177 C2
Chester Terr
NW1 93 B4 231 C2
Chesterton Cl
Greenford UB6 85 D5
Wandsworth SW18 157 C6
Chesterton Ct W3 110 D3
Chesterton Dr TW19 148 B3
Chesterton Ho
20 Battersea SW11 136 B2
3 Kensal Town W10 91 A2
3 Sutton SM1 218 A4
Chesterton Prim Sch
SW11 137 A4 268 A1
Chesterton Rd
Kensal Town W10 91 A2
Newham E13 99 A4
Chesterton Sq W8 255 A3
Chesterton Terr
6 Kingston u T
KT1 176 C1
Newham E13 99 A4
Chester Way
SE11 116 C2 261 B3
Chesthunte Rd N17 33 A2
Chestnut Alley SW6 264 D5
Chestnut Ave
Brentford TW8 109 D2
Buckhurst Hill IG9 21 D1
Coney Hall BR4 224 C4
Edgware HA8 26 B4
Forest Gate E7 77 B4
Hampton TW12 173 C3
Hornsey N8 50 A4
Kingston u T KT8,
KT11 174 D2
Chestnut Ave *continued*
11 Mortlake SW14 133 B2
Thames Ditton KT10 196 B1
Wembley HA0 65 B3
Worcester Pk KT19 215 C4
Yiewsley UB7 104 B6
Chestnut Ave N E17 54 B5
Chestnut Ave S E17 54 B4
Chestnut Cl
Buckhurst Hill IG9 21 D2
Carshalton SM5 202 D1
Catford SE6 186 A6
Chattern Hill TW15 170 D6
Harlington UB7 126 D5
Hayes UB3 105 C6
New Cross Gate SE14 141 B4
Sidcup DA15 168 A2
Southgate N14 15 D6
1 Stoke Newington
N16 73 B6
Sunbury Comm TW16 171 D4
West Norwood SW16 182 C6
Chestnut Ct
Beckenham BR3 185 C3
7 Cheam SM2 217 C2
5 Croydon CR0 221 A4
Feltham TW13 172 D5
Harrow HA1 42 C2
Hornsey N8 50 A4
Hounslow TW3 129 C2
Kingston u T KT3 199 C6
Surbiton KT6 198 A2
Wembley HA0 65 B3
West Brompton SW6 264 D6
Chestnut Dr
Bexley DA7 147 A2
Harrow HA3 24 D2
Pinner HA5 41 A3
Wanstead E11 55 A3
Chestnut Gr
Cockfosters EN4 14 D6
Ealing W5 109 D3
Isleworth TW7 131 A1
Kingston u T KT3 199 B6
Mitcham CR4 203 D5
Penge SE20 184 C3
South Croydon CR2 222 B1
Upper Tooting SW12 159 A3
Wembley HA0 65 B3
Chestnut Grove Sch 6
SW12 159 A3
Chestnut Ho
1 Acton W4 111 C2
Brockley SE4 141 B2
7 Maitland Pk NW3 70 D2
West Norwood SE27 161 A1
Chestnut La N20 13 A3
Chestnut Pl SE19 183 D6
Chestnut Rd
Ashford TW15 170 D6
Kingston u T KT2 176 A3
Twickenham TW2 152 C2
West Barnes SW20 178 D1
West Norwood SE21,
SE27 161 A1
Chestnut Rise SE18 123 C1
Chestnut Row N3 29 C3
Chestnuts Ct 3 E17 54 A6
Chestnuts Prim Sch
N15 51 A4
Chestnuts Royal
BR7 189 B3
Chestnuts The
Chislehurst BR7 189 B3
Colindale NW9 45 C6
East Finchley N2 48 D4
7 Erith DA17 125 B1
1 Highbury N5 72 D4
Penge BR3 206 D6
8 Pinner HA5 23 B3
Shooters Hill SE18 144 D4
Uxbridge UB10 60 A1
Walton-on-T KT12 194 B1
Chestnut Way TW13 150 B1
Chestnut Wlk
Upper Halliford
TW17 193 C5
Woodford IG8 37 A5
Cheston Ave CR0 207 B1
Chestwood Gr UB10 60 B1
Chettle Cl SE1 262 C6
Chettle Ct N8 50 C3
Chetwode Ho NW8 237 A6
Chetwode Rd SW17 158 D1
Chetwood Wlk 13
E6 100 A2
Chetwynd Ave EN4 14 D3
Chetwynd Dr UB10 82 B5
Chetwynd Rd NW5 71 B5
Cheval Ct SW15 134 B1
Chevalier Cl HA7 26 A6
Cheval Pl
SW7 114 C3 257 B6
Cheval St E14 119 C3
Chevender BR7 188 D3
Cheveney Wlk 2
BR2 209 A6
Chevening Ho BR5 190 A2
Chevening Rd
Cubitt Town SE10 120 D1
Kilburn NW6 91 A6
South Norwood SE19 183 B4
Chevenings The
DA14 168 C1
Cheverell Ho 25 E2 96 A5
Cheverton Rd N19 49 D1
Chevet St E9 75 A3
Chevington NW2 69 B2
Cheviot 4 N17 34 B3
Cheviot Cl
Bushey WD23 8 A5
Enfield EN1 5 B3
Harlington UB3 127 B5
Cheviot Ct
16 Deptford SE14 140 C5
Enfield EN2 5 B3
Southall UB2 107 D2
Cheviot Gate NW2 69 A6
Cheviot Gdns
Cricklewood NW2 69 A6
West Norwood SE27 182 D6
Cheviot Ho N16 51 D1
Cheviot Rd SE27 182 D5
Cheviots Hostel EN1 5 B3
Cheviot Way IG2 57 C5
Chevron Cl E16 99 A1
Chevy Rd UB2 108 A4
Chewton Rd E17 53 A5
Cheylesmore Ho
SW1 258 C2
Cheyne Ave
Snaresbrook E18 54 D6
Twickenham TW2 151 B3
Cheyne Cl
6 Hendon NW4 46 B4
Keston Mark BR2 226 A5
Cheyne Ct
Chelsea SW3 267 C6
1 Croydon CR0 221 D6
Ruislip HA4 39 C1
4 Wallington SM6 219 B2
Cheyne Gdns
SW3 136 C6 267 B5
Cheyne Hill KT5 198 B5
Cheyne Mews
SW3 136 C6 267 B5
Cheyne Park Dr BR4 224 A5
Cheyne Path W7 86 D1
Cheyne Pl SW3 267 C6
Cheyne Rd TW15 171 B4
Cheyne Row
SW3 136 C6 267 A5
Cheyne Wlk
Chelsea
SW10 136 B5 266 C4
Croydon CR0 222 A6
Hendon NW4 46 C3
Southgate N21 16 D6
Cheyney Ho 2 E9 74 D2
Cheyneys Ave HA8 25 D4
Chichele Gdns CR0 221 C4
Chichele Ho HA8 26 B6
Chichele Mans NW2 68 D3
Chichele Rd NW2 68 D3
Chicheley Gdns HA3 24 A3
Chicheley Rd HA3 24 A3
Chicheley St SE1 250 D2
Chichester Ave HA4 61 B6
Chichester Cl
Hampton TW12 173 B4
Kidbrooke SE3 143 C4
Newham E6 100 A1
Chichester Ct
Barnet EN4 2 B1
2 Camden Town NW1 71 C1
Edgware HA8 26 C4
Harrow HA2 41 B1
Northolt UB5 85 A6
3 Sidcup DA5 169 C4
Stanmore HA7 44 A6
Stanwell TW19 148 A3
Chichester Gdns IG1 56 B2
Chichester Ho
Kilburn NW6 91 C5
2 Kingston u T KT2 176 D2
Chichester Mews
SE27 182 C6
Chichester Rd
Bayswater W2 91 D2
Edmonton N9 18 A3
Kilburn NW6 91 C5
Leyton E11 76 C5
South Croydon CR0 221 C5
Chichester Rents
WC2 241 A2
Chichester St
SW1 115 C1 259 B1
Chichester Way
Cubitt Town E14 120 B2
Feltham TW14 150 C4
Chicksand Ho 14 E1 96 A2
Chicksand St
E1 95 D2 243 D3
Chicksand Street E1 96 A2
Chiddingfold N12 13 C1
Chiddingstone SE13 164 A6
Chiddingstone Ave
DA7 147 B5
Chiddingstone St
SW6 135 C3
Chieveley Par DA7 147 D2
Chieveley Rd DA7 147 D1
Chignell Pl 7 W13 109 A5
Chigwell Ct 1 E9 75 A2
Chigwell Hill E1 118 B6
Chigwell Hurst Ct
HA5 40 D6
Chigwell Rd
Wanstead E18 55 B6
Woodford IG8 37 D3
Chiham Ho 5 SE15 140 C6
Chilchester Ct 3
BR3 207 D6
Chilcombe Ho 6
SW15 156 A4
Chilcot Cl 13 E14 97 D1
Chilcott Cl HA0 65 C4
Child Ct E11 54 B2
Childebert Rd SW17 159 B2
Childeric Prim Sch
SE14 141 A5
Childeric Rd SE14 141 A5
Childerley St
SW6 135 A4 264 A2
Childerly KT1 198 C6
Childers St SE8 141 B6
Child La SE10 120 D3
Childrens House Upper
Sch 15 N1 73 C2
Childs Ct UB3 106 A6
CHILD'S HILL 69 C6
Child's Hill Sch NW2 69 A5
Childs La 11 SE19 183 C4
Child's Mews SW5 255 B3
Child's Pl SW5 255 B3
Child's St SW5 255 B3
Childs Way NW11 47 B4
Child's Wlk SW5 255 B3
Chilham Cl
Old Bexley DA5 169 B4
Wembley UB6 87 A5
Chilham Ct 13 SW9 138 C2
Chilham Ho SE1 262 D6
Chilham Rd SE9 188 A6
Chilham Way BR2 209 A2
Chillerton Rd SW17 181 B5
Chillingford Ho
SW17 180 A6
Chillington Dr SW11 136 B1
Chillingworth Gdns
TW1 152 D1
Chillingworth Rd N7 72 C3
Chilmark Gdns KT3 200 A3
Chilmark Rd SW16 181 D2
Chiltern Ave
Bushey WD23 8 A5
Twickenham TW2 151 C3
Chiltern Cl Bus WD23 8 A5
Ickenham UB10 60 C6
North Cheam KT4 216 C6
South Croydon CR0 221 C5
Chiltern Ct
15 Deptford SE14 140 C5
6 East Barnet N20 14 C2
11 Eltham SE9 166 C5
Harrow HA1 42 B4
Hillingdon UB8 82 D3
Marylebone NW1 237 D5
Chiltern Ct *continued*
Muswell Hill N10 31 A1
1 New Barnet EN5 14 A6
Chiltern Dene EN2 4 B1
Chiltern Dr KT5 198 D4
Chiltern Gdns •
Beckenham BR2 208 D5
Cricklewood NW2 68 D5
Chiltern Ho
Camberwell SE17 139 B6
Ealing W5 88 A2
5 Edmonton N9 18 A1
Harrow HA1 42 C1
4 Kensal Town W10 91 A2
5 Stamford Hill N16 51 D1
Chiltern Pl 18 E5 74 B6
Chiltern Rd Bow E3 97 C3
Ilford IG2 57 C4
Pinner HA5 40 C4
Chiltern St
W1 93 A2 238 A4
Chilterns The BR1 187 B1
Chiltern Way IG8 21 A1
Chilthorne Cl SE6 163 B4
Chilton Ave W5 109 D2
Chilton Gr SE8 119 A2
Chiltonian Ind Est
SE12 164 D5
Chilton Rd
Edgware HA8 26 C4
Richmond TW9 132 C2
Chilton St E2 95 D3 243 D6
Chiltons The 1 E18 37 A1
Chilvers Cl TW2 152 C2
Chilver St SE10 120 D1
Chilwell Gdns WD19 22 C6
Chilworth Ct 8
SW19 156 D3
Chilworth Gdns
SM1 218 A5
Chilworth Mews
W2 92 B1 236 C1
Chilworth St
W2 92 A1 236 B1
Chimes Ave N13 32 D6
Chimes Sh Ctr The
UB8 60 A1
Chimney Ct 23 E1 118 B5
Chimneys Ct 2
SW19 178 C3
China Ct 1 E1 118 B5
China Hall Mews 16
SE16 118 C3
China Mews 17 SW2 160 B4
Chinbrook Cres
SE12 165 B1
Chinbrook Rd SE12 165 B1
Chinchilla Dr TW4 128 C3
Chindit Ho 11 N16 73 B4
Chine The London N10 49 C5
Southgate N21 16 D6
Wembley HA0 65 B3
Ching Ct Chingford E4 20 C1
St Giles WC2 240 A1
Chingdale Rd E4 20 C1
CHINGFORD 20 C3
Chingford Ave E4 19 D2
Chingford CE Inf Sch 10
E4 20 B3
Chingford CE Jun Sch 9
E4 20 B3
Chingford Foundation
Sch E4 19 D3
CHINGFORD GREEN 20 A4
Chingford Hall Com Prim
Sch E4 35 B4
CHINGFORD HATCH 36 B6
Chingford Ind Ctr E4 35 A5
Chingford La IG8 36 D5
Chingford Mount Rd
E4 35 C5
Chingford Rd
Highams Pk E4 35 C3
Walthamstow E17 35 D1
Chingford Sta E4 20 C4
Chingley Cl BR1 186 C4
Ching Way E4 35 B4
Chinnery Cl EN1 5 D4
Chinnocks Wharf
E14 119 A6
Chinnor Cres UB6 86 A5
Chipka St E14 120 A4
Chipley St SE14 141 A6
Chipmunk Gr UB5 85 A4
Chippendale Ho
SW1 258 D1

Chippendale St E5 ... 74 D5
Chippenham [4] KT1 ... 176 B1
Chippenham Ave HA9 ... 66 D3
Chippenham Cl HA5 ... 39 D5
Chippenham Gdns NW6 ... 91 C4
Chippenham Mews W9 ... 91 C3
Chippenham Rd W9 ... 91 C3
Chipperfield Rd BR5 ... 190 A1
CHIPPING BARNET ... 1 B1
Chipping Cl EN5 ... 1 A2
Chip St SW4 ... 137 D1
Chipstead Ave CR7 ... 204 D5
Chipstead Cl SE19 ... 183 D3
Chipstead Gdns NW2 ... 68 B6
Chipstead Ho [4] SW2 ... 160 A3
Chipstead St SW6 ... 135 C3
Chirk Cl UB4 ... 85 A3
Chirk Ct SE4 ... 141 B3
Chisenhale Prim Sch [36] E3 ... 97 A5
Chisenhale Rd E3 ... 97 A5
Chisholm Ct [1] W6 ... 112 A1
Chisholm Rd
  Croydon CR0 ... 221 C6
  [13] Richmond TW10 ... 154 B5
Chisledon Wlk E9 ... 75 B2
CHISLEHURST ... 189 C3
Chislehurst Ave N12 ... 30 A3
Chislehurst CE Prim Sch BR7 ... 189 A3
Chislehurst High St BR7 ... 188 D4
Chislehurst Rd
  Bromley BR1, BR7 ... 188 A2
  Broom Hill BR6 ... 211 D2
  Orpington BR5, BR6, BR7 ... 211 C4
  Richmond TW10 ... 154 A6
  Sidcup DA14 ... 190 A5
Chislehurst & Sidcup Gram Sch DA15 ... 168 B2
Chislehurst Sta BR7 ... 188 C1
CHISLEHURST WEST ... 188 C4
Chislet [5] NW5 ... 71 A2
Chislet Cl BR3 ... 185 C3
Chisley Rd [5] N15 ... 51 C3
Chiswell Sq SE3 ... 143 B3
Chiswell St
  Barbican EC1 ... 95 B2 242 C4
  Camberwell SE5 ... 139 B5
CHISWICK ... 111 D1
Chiswick & Bedford Park Prep Sch [13] W4 ... 111 C2
Chiswick Cl CR0 ... 220 B5
Chiswick Common Rd W4 ... 111 B2
Chiswick Com Sch W4 ... 133 B5
Chiswick Ct HA5 ... 41 B6
Chiswick Green Studios [1] W4 ... 111 A2
Chiswick High Rd W4 ... 111 C2
Chiswick High Road (North Circular Rd) W4 ... 110 C1
Chiswick Ho★ W4 ... 133 B6
Chiswick La W4 ... 111 C1
Chiswick La S W4 ... 133 D6
Chiswick Mall W4 ... 111 D1
Chiswick Park Sta W4 ... 111 A2
Chiswick Pier W4 ... 133 D5
Chiswick Pk W4 ... 110 D2
Chiswick Plaza W4 ... 133 A6
Chiswick Quay W4 ... 133 A4
Chiswick Rd
  Acton W4 ... 111 A2
  Edmonton N9 ... 18 A2
Chiswick Rdbt W4 ... 110 C1
Chiswick Sq W4 ... 133 C6
Chiswick Sta W4 ... 133 A5
Chiswick Staithe W4 ... 133 A4
Chiswick Terr [6] W4 ... 111 A2
Chiswick Village W4 ... 132 D6
Chiswick Wharf W4 ... 133 D6
Chitterfield Gate UB7 ... 126 C5
Chitty's La RM8 ... 80 D6
Chitty St W1 ... 93 C2 239 B4
Chivalry Rd SW11 ... 158 C6
Chivelston [27] SW19 ... 156 D3
Chivenor Gr KT2 ... 175 D5
Chivers Rd E4 ... 35 D6
Chivins Ct N3 ... 29 C3
Choats Manor Way RM9 ... 103 B4
Choats Rd IG11 ... 102 D4
Chobham Gdns SW19 ... 156 D2
Chobham Rd E15 ... 76 B3
Cholmeley Cres N6 ... 49 B2
Cholmeley Ct N12 ... 30 A6
Cholmeley Lo N6 ... 49 B1
Cholmeley Pk N6 ... 49 B2
Cholmley Gdns NW6 ... 69 C3
Cholmley Rd KT7 ... 197 B3
Cholmondeley Ave NW10 ... 90 A5
Cholmondeley Wlk TW9 ... 153 C6
Chopin's Ct [13] E1 ... 118 B5
Chopwell Cl E15 ... 76 B1
Chorleywood Cres BR5 ... 190 A1
Choumert Gr SE15 ... 140 A3
Choumert Mews SE15 ... 140 A3
Choumert Rd SE15 ... 139 D3
Choumert Sq [4] SE15 ... 140 A3
Chow Sq [2] E8 ... 73 D3
Chrisp Ho SE10 ... 142 C6
Chrisp St E14 ... 97 D1
Christabel Cl TW7 ... 130 C2
Christ Church TW9 ... 132 A2
Christchurch Ave
  Brondesbury Pk NW6 ... 69 A1
  Finchley N12 ... 30 A4
  Harrow HA3 ... 42 D5
  Harrow HA3 ... 43 A5
  [5] Teddington TW11 ... 175 A5
  Wembley HA0 ... 66 A2
Christ Church Bentinck CE Prim Sch NW1 ... 92 C2 237 B4
Christ Church Brondesbury CE Jun & Inf Sch NW6 ... 69 B1
Christ Church CE Jun Sch W5 ... 109 D6
Christchurch CE Prim Sch SW3 ... 136 D6 267 C6
Christ Church CE Prim Sch
  Battersea SW11 ... 136 C2
  [35] Camberwell SW9 ... 138 C4
  Cubitt Town SE10 ... 120 C1
  [6] Forest Hill SE23 ... 162 D2
  Shooters Hill SE18 ... 144 C4
  Surbiton KT5 ... 198 C3
Christ Church CE Prim Sch, Hampstead NW3 ... 70 B5
Christchurch CE Sch E1 ... 95 D2 243 D3
Christchurch Cl
  Enfield EN2 ... 5 A3
  Finchley N12 ... 30 B3
  Mitcham SW19 ... 180 B3
Christchurch Ct UB4 ... 84 C3
Christ Church Ct
  [1] Brondesbury Pk NW6 ... 69 A1
  Harlesden NW10 ... 89 C6
Christchurch Gdns HA3 ... 43 A5
Christchurch Gn HA0 ... 66 A2
Christchurch Hill NW3 ... 70 B4
Christchurch Ho [2] SW2 ... 160 A3
Christ Church La EN5 ... 1 A3
Christchurch Lo EN4 ... 2 D1
Christ Church New Malden CE Prim Sch KT3 ... 199 C6
Christchurch Pas NW3 ... 70 A5
Christchurch Pk SM2 ... 218 A1
Christchurch Prim Sch IG1 ... 57 A1
Christ Church Prim Sch KT3 ... 199 B6
Christchurch Rd
  Ilford IG1 ... 57 A1
  Mitcham SW19 ... 180 B3
  Mortlake SW14 ... 155 A6
  Sidcup DA15 ... 167 D1
  Streatham SW2 ... 160 C3
Christ Church Rd
  [1] Beckenham BR3 ... 185 C1
  Hornsey N8 ... 50 A3
  Surbiton KT5 ... 198 B3
Christ Church Sch NW1 ... 93 B4 231 D2
Christchurch Sq [2] E9 ... 96 C6
Christchurch St SW3 ... 136 D6 267 C6
Christ Church Streatham CE Prim Sch [13] SW2 ... 160 B3
Christchurch Terr SW3 ... 267 C6
Christchurch Way SE10 ... 120 C1
Christian Ct SE16 ... 119 B5
Christian Fields SW16 ... 182 C3
Christian St E1 ... 96 A1
Christie Ct
  Maitland Pk NW3 ... 70 C3
  [2] Upper Holloway N19 ... 72 A6
Christie Dr SE25 ... 206 A4
Christie Gdns RM6 ... 58 B2
Christie Ho
  Bexley DA6 ... 169 D6
  [2] Cubitt Town SE10 ... 120 D1
  Harrow HA3 ... 42 D6
  [4] West Wickham BR4 ... 207 D1
Christie Rd E9 ... 75 A2
Christina Sq N4 ... 50 D1
Christina St EC2 ... 243 A6
Christine Worsley Cl N21 ... 16 D3
Christopher Ave W7 ... 109 A3
Christopher Boone's Almshouses SE13 ... 142 B1
Christopher Cl
  Bexley DA15 ... 167 D6
  Rotherhithe SE16 ... 118 D4
Christopher Ct
  Ashford TW15 ... 170 A5
  [12] Barnet EN5 ... 1 D1
  [6] Croydon CR0 ... 206 A1
  Hendon NW4 ... 28 C1
  [23] Surbiton KT6 ... 198 A4
  Sutton SM1 ... 217 C3
Christopher France Ho [6] E1 ... 97 A4
Christopher Gdns RM9 ... 80 D3
Christopher Hatton Prim Sch EC1 ... 94 C3 241 A5
Christopher Lo [2] N6 ... 49 D2
Christopher Pl NW1 ... 232 D1
Christopher Rd UB2 ... 106 B2
Christopher St EC2 ... 95 B3 242 D5
Christ's Coll Finchley NW11 ... 47 D6
Christ's Sch TW10 ... 154 C6
Christ the King RC Prim Sch [7] N4 ... 72 B6
Christ the King Sixth Form Coll SE13 ... 142 B2
Christ the Redeemer Bible Coll [1] E15 ... 76 C2
Chryssell Rd SW9 ... 138 C5
Chubworthy St [5] SE14 ... 141 A6
Chudleigh [1] DA14 ... 190 B6
Chudleigh Cres IG3 ... 79 C4
Chudleigh Gdns SM1 ... 218 A5
Chudleigh Rd
  Hampstead NW6 ... 68 D1
  London SE4 ... 163 C6
  Twickenham TW1, TW2 ... 152 D4
Chudleigh St E1 ... 96 D1
Chudleigh Way HA4 ... 40 A1
Chulsa Rd SE26 ... 184 B5
Chumleigh Gdns SE5 ... 139 C6
Chumleigh St SE5 ... 139 C6
Chumleigh Wlk KT5 ... 198 B5
Church App SE21 ... 161 B1
Church Ave
  Beckenham BR3 ... 185 C2
  Camden Town NW1 ... 71 B2
  Chingford E4 ... 36 B4
  Finchley N2 ... 30 B2
  Mortlake SW14 ... 133 B2
  Northolt UB5 ... 63 B1
  Pinner HA5 ... 41 B3
  Ruislip HA4 ... 39 B1
  Sidcup DA14 ... 190 B5
  Southall UB2 ... 107 A3
  Wanstead E12 ... 77 D5
Churchbank E17 ... 53 C5
Churchbury Cl EN1 ... 5 C3
Churchbury La EN1 ... 5 C3
Churchbury Rd
  Eltham SE9 ... 165 D4
  Enfield EN1 ... 5 C3
Church Cl
  Edgware HA8 ... 27 A5
  Friern Barnet N20 ... 14 C1
  Hayes UB4 ... 83 B2
  Hounslow TW4 ... 129 B3
  Kensington W8 ... 245 C2
  West Drayton UB7 ... 104 A3
Church Cres
  Church End N3 ... 29 B2
  Cranley Gdns N10 ... 49 B5
  Friern Barnet N20 ... 14 C1
  Hackney E9 ... 74 D1
Churchcroft Cl SW12 ... 159 A4
Church Ct
  East Finchley N2 ... 48 B6
  Forest Hill SE26 ... 185 A5
  Harmondsworth UB7 ... 126 C6
  Holborn EC4 ... 241 B1
  [16] Richmond TW10 ... 153 D6
  Rotherhithe SE16 ... 119 B4
  Ruislip HA4 ... 62 D5
  [5] West Norwood SE27 ... 182 D6
Churchdale Ct [1] W4 ... 110 D1
Churchdown BR1 ... 186 C6
Church Dr
  Coney Hall BR4 ... 224 C5
  Harrow HA2 ... 41 C3
  Welsh Harp NW9 ... 45 B1
Church Elm La RM10 ... 81 C2
Church End NW4 ... 46 B6
CHURCH END N3 ... 29 C1
  NW10 ... 67 D3
Church End E17 ... 53 D5
Church Entry EC4 ... 241 D1
Church Estate Almshouses [8] TW9 ... 132 B1
Church Farmhouse Mus★ NW4 ... 46 B6
Church Farm La SM3 ... 217 A2
Church Farm Swimming Pool EN4 ... 14 D4
Churchfield Ave N12 ... 30 B4
Churchfield Cl
  Harrow HA2 ... 42 A5
  Hayes UB3 ... 105 D6
Churchfield Ho W2 ... 236 C5
Churchfield Mans [5] SW6 ... 135 B3
Churchfield Pl TW17 ... 192 D2
Churchfield Prim Sch N9 ... 17 D3
Churchfield Rd
  Acton W3 ... 111 A5
  Ealing W13 ... 109 C5
  Hanwell W7 ... 108 C4
  Walton-on-T KT12 ... 194 A1
  Welling DA16 ... 146 A2
Churchfields
  East Molesey KT8 ... 195 C6
  Greenwich SE10 ... 142 A6
  Woodford E18 ... 37 A2
Churchfields Ave TW13 ... 151 C1
Churchfields Jun & Inf Sch E18 ... 37 A2
Churchfields Prim Sch BR3 ... 206 D6
Churchfields Rd BR3 ... 185 A1
Churchfield Way N12 ... 30 A4
Church Garth [4] N19 ... 71 D6
Church Gate SW6 ... 135 A2
Church Gdns
  Ealing W5 ... 109 D4
  Wembley HA0 ... 65 A4
Church Gn
  [4] Brixton SW9 ... 138 C3
  Hayes UB3 ... 83 D1
Church Gr
  London SE13 ... 163 D6
  Teddington KT1 ... 175 C1
Church Hill
  Harrow HA1 ... 42 C1
  Southgate N21 ... 16 C4
  Wallington SM5 ... 218 D3
  Walthamstow E17 ... 53 D5
  Wimbledon SW19 ... 179 B5
  Woolwich SE18 ... 122 B3
Churchhill Gardens Prim Sch SW1 ... 115 C1 259 B1
Church Hill Prim Sch EN4 ... 14 D4
Church Hill Rd
  Cheam SM1, SM3 ... 217 A4
  East Barnet EN4 ... 14 D4
  Kingston u T KT6 ... 198 A4
  Walthamstow E17 ... 53 D5
Church Hill Wood BR5 ... 211 D4
Church Ho EC1 ... 241 D6
Church Hyde SE18 ... 145 C6
Churchill Ave
  Harrow HA3 ... 43 B3
  Hillingdon UB10 ... 82 D4
Churchill Cl
  East Bedfont TW14 ... 149 D3
  Hillingdon UB10 ... 82 D4
Churchill Ct Ealing W5 ... 88 B3
  Edmonton N9 ... 17 B3
  [4] Farnborough BR6 ... 227 A3
  Finsbury Pk N4 ... 50 C2
  Harrow HA2 ... 41 D4
  [7] Ilford IG1 ... 78 D5
  Northolt UB5 ... 63 C3
  Peckham SE15 ... 140 A3
  Willesden NW2 ... 68 B3
  [9] Woolwich SE18 ... 122 B2
Churchill Gdns
  Acton W3 ... 88 C1
  Pimlico SW1 ... 137 C6 269 A6
Churchill Gdns Rd SW1 ... 137 C6 269 A6
Churchill Ho
  Brentford TW8 ... 109 C1
  Mitcham CR4 ... 180 D2
Churchill Lo
  Streatham SW16 ... 181 D5
  Woodford IG8 ... 36 D4
Churchill Lodge IG6 ... 57 A5
Churchill Mews IG8 ... 36 D4
Churchill Pl
  Canary Wharf E14 ... 119 D5
  Harrow HA1 ... 42 C5
Churchill Rd
  Edgware HA8 ... 26 C4
  Gospel Oak NW5 ... 71 B4
  Newham E16 ... 99 C1
  South Croydon CR2 ... 221 A1
  Willesden NW2 ... 68 B2
Churchill Terr E4 ... 19 C1
Churchill Way
  Ashford TW16 ... 172 A4
  Bromley BR1 ... 187 A1
Churchill Wlk E9 ... 74 C3
Church La
  Chessington KT9 ... 214 B2
  Chislehurst BR7 ... 189 A2
  Dagenham RM10 ... 81 D1
  Ealing W5 ... 109 D4
  East Finchley N2 ... 48 B6
  Edmonton N9 ... 18 A2
  Enfield EN1 ... 5 B2
  Harrow HA3 ... 24 D2
  Hornsey N8 ... 50 B5
  Keston Mark BR2 ... 210 A1
  Kingsbury NW9 ... 45 B2
  Leytonstone E11 ... 54 C1
  Merton SW19 ... 179 C2
  Pinner HA5 ... 41 B6
  Teddington TW11 ... 174 D5
  Thames Ditton KT7 ... 197 A3
  Tottenham N17 ... 33 C2

Church La *continued*
Twickenham TW1 153 A3
Upper Tooting SW17 181 A5
Wallington SM6 219 D5
Walthamstow E17 53 D5
Churchlands Way 3 KT4 216 D6
Churchley Rd SE26 184 B6
Churchley Villas SE26 184 B6
Church Lo UB5 63 B1
Church Manor Way SE18, SE2 124 A2
Church Mdw KT6 213 C6
Church Mead SE5 139 A5
Churchmead Cl EN4 14 C5
Churchmead Rd NW10 68 A2
Churchmore Rd SW16 181 D2
Church Mount N2 48 B4
Church Paddock Ct SM6 219 D5
Church Par
5 Ashford TW15 170 B6
Harrow HA3 42 C6
Church Path
Merton SW19 179 C1
Mitcham CR4 202 C6
South Acton W4 111 A3
Walthamstow E17 53 D5
Wanstead E11 55 A4
Church Pl Ealing W5 109 D4
Mitcham CR4 202 C6
St James SW1 249 B5
Uxbridge UB10 61 A5
Church Rd Acton W3 111 A4
Ashford TW15 170 B6
Barking IG11 79 A2
Barnes SW13 134 A4
Beckenham BR2 208 C6
Bexleyheath DA7 147 B2
Bromley BR1, BR2 187 A1
Buckhurst Hill IG9 21 B3
24 Canonbury N1 73 A2
Cheam SM3 217 A2
Claygate KT10 212 D1
Cranford TW5 128 B6
Croydon CR0 221 A5
Ealing W7 108 C6
East Molesey KT8 196 B6
Enfield EN3 18 C6
Farnborough BR6 227 B3
Feltham TW13 172 D5
Hayes UB3 105 D6
Hendon NW4 46 C5
Heston TW5 129 C5
Higham Hill E17 35 A1
Highgate N6 49 A3
Hillingdon UB8 82 A3
Hounslow TW7 130 C5
Ilford IG2 57 C3
Keston BR2 225 D1
Kingston u T KT1 176 B1
Leyton E10 75 C6
Long Ditton KT6 197 C1
Lower Halliford TW17 192 D2
Manor Pk E12 78 A3
Mitcham CR4 202 C6
Mitcham CR4, SW19 180 B1
New Malden KT4 199 C1
Northolt UB5 85 A6
Richmond TW10 176 A6
Richmond TW10, TW9 154 A6
Sidcup DA14 190 A6
Southall UB2 107 B3
South Norwood SE19 183 C3
Stanmore HA7 25 B5
Teddington TW11 174 D5
Tottenham N17 33 D3
Wallington SM6 219 D5
Welling DA16 146 B3
West Drayton UB7 104 A3
West Ewell KT19 215 B1
Willesden NW10 67 C1
Wimbledon SW19 179 A6
Church Rd N N2 30 B2
Church Rd S N2 30 B2
Church Rise
Chessington KT9 214 B2
Forest Hill SE23 162 D2
Church Row
Chislehurst BR7 189 A2
Hampstead NW3 70 A4
Church Row Mews BR7 189 A3
Church St N E15 98 C6
Church St Sta CR0 221 A6
Church Sq TW17 192 D2
Church St
Chiswick W4 133 D6
Croydon CR0 220 D6
Croydon CR0 221 A6
Dagenham RM10 81 D2
Edmonton N9 17 C2
Enfield EN2 5 B2
Hampton TW12 174 A2
Isleworth TW7 131 B3
Kingston u T KT1 175 D1
Lisson Gr NW8 92 C3 237 A5
Newham E16 122 D5
Sunbury TW16 194 B6
Twickenham TW1 153 A3
Walton-on-T KT12 194 A2
West Ham E15 98 D6
Church Street Est NW8 236 D5
Church Stretton Rd TW3 152 A6
Church Studios 16 NW1 71 D2
Church Terr
Hendon NW4 46 B6
Lewisham SE13 142 C2
21 Richmond TW10 153 D6
Church Vale
Forest Hill SE23 162 D2
Muswell Hill N2 48 D6
Churchview Rd TW2 152 B2
Church Villa TW16 194 B6
Churchward Ho
Camberwell SE17 138 D6
West Kensington SW5 254 D1
Churchway NW1 232 D2
Church Way
Cockfosters EN4 2 D1
Friern Barnet N20 14 C1
Church Wlk
Barnes SW13 134 A4
Brentford TW8 131 C6
Canonbury N16 73 B4
Child's Hill NW2 69 B5
Dartmouth Pk N6 71 A5
Hayes UB3 83 D1
Mitcham SW16 181 C1
15 Richmond TW10 153 D6
Thames Ditton KT7 196 D3
Walton-on-T KT12 194 A1
Welsh Harp NW9 67 B6
West Barnes SW20 200 C6
Churchwood Gdns IG8 37 A6
Churchyard Row SE11 116 D2 261 D4
Churnfield 2 N4 72 C6
Churston Ave E13 99 B6
Churston Cl 16 SW2 160 C3
Churston Dr SM4 201 A4
Churston Gdns N11 31 C4
Churston Mans WC1 240 D5
Churton Pl
Brentford W4 132 D6
Pimlico SW1 259 B3
Churton St SW1 115 C2 259 B3
Chute Ho 17 SW9 138 C3
Chuter Ede Ho SW6 264 D5
Chyngton Cl DA15 167 D1
Chyngton Ct HA1 64 C6
Cibber Rd SE23 162 D2
Cicada Rd SW18 158 A6
Cicely Ho NW8 229 D3
Cicely Rd SE15 140 A4
Cinderford Way BR1 186 C6
Cinema Mus The★ SE11 261 C3
Cinema Par RM8 81 B6
Cinnabar Wharf Central 16 E1 118 A5
Cinnabar Wharf East 15 E1 118 A5
Cinnabar Wharf West 17 E1 118 A5
Cinnamon Cl
8 Camberwell SE15 139 D5
Thornton Heath CR0 204 A2
Cinnamon Row 3 SW11 136 A2
Cinnamon St E1 118 B5
Cinnamon Wharf SE1 253 D2
Cinque Cotts SW19 178 C4
Cintra Ct SE19 183 D4
Cintra Pk SE19 183 D3
Circle Ct HA0 65 D4
Circle Gdns SW19 179 C1
Circle Ho 14 E14 98 B1
Circle The
Bermondsey SE1 253 D2
Burnt Oak NW7 27 B4
Neasden NW2 67 C5
Circuits The HA5 40 C5
Circular Rd London N2 30 B2
Tottenham N17 51 D6
Circular Way SE18 144 C6
Circus Lo NW8 229 C2
Circus Mews W1 237 C4
Circus Pl EC2 242 D3
Circus Rd NW8 92 B5 229 C3
Circus St SE10 142 A5
Cirencester St W2 91 D2
Cirrus 17 NW9 27 D1
Cirrus Cl 4 SM6 220 A1
Cissbury Ho 6 SE26 162 A1
Cissbury Rd N15 51 B4
Cissbury Ring N N12 29 C5
Cissbury Ring S N12 29 B5
Citadel Pl SE11 260 C2
Citizen Ho N7 72 C4
Citizen Rd N7 72 C4
Citron Terr 4 SE15 140 B2
Citrus Ho 14 SE8 119 B1
City Banking Coll SE1 117 B4 252 D2
City Bsns Coll EC1 94 D4 234 D1
City Bsns Ctr 33 SE16 118 C4
City Central Est EC1 235 A1
City Coll N1 235 C2
City Coll of London The WC1 240 D3
City Forum EC1 95 A4 235 A2
City Garden Row N1 94 D5 234 D3
City Gate E1 96 C3
City & Guilds of London Art Sch The SE11 116 C1 261 B1
City & Hackney Ctr for Mental Health (Hospl) E9 75 A3
City Hall★ SE1 117 C5 253 B3
City Harbour E14 119 D3
City & Islington 6th Form Coll EC1 94 D4 234 C2
City & Islington Coll (Ctr for Applied Sciences) EC1 94 D4 234 C2
City & Islington Coll (Ctr for Bsns, Arts & Technology) 8 N7 72 A4
City & Islington Coll (Ctr for Health, Social & Child Care) 7 N7 72 B4
City & Islington Coll (Ctr for Lifelong Learning) 3 N4 72 D6
City Law Sch The EC1 240 D3
City Lights The SE11 261 B1
CITY OF LONDON 117 A6
City of London Acad-Islington N1 95 A6 235 A5
City of London Acad The SE1 118 A1
City of London Bsns Coll N15 52 A5
City of London Information Ctr★ EC4 241 D1
City of London Sch EC4 117 A6 252 A6
City of London Sch for Girls EC2 95 A2 242 B4
City of Westminster Coll W2 92 B2 236 C4
City of Westminster Coll, Cosway Street Ctr NW1 92 C2 237 B4
City of Westminster Coll, Maida Vale Ctr 1 W9 91 D4
City of Westminster Coll, Queens Park Ctr 10 W9 91 C4
City Prospect 5 SE19 183 C4
City Rd EC1 95 A4 235 B2
City Thameslink Sta EC4 94 D1 241 C1
City University EC1 94 D4 234 C1
City View 3 IG1 79 A6
City Wharf Ho KT7 197 B3
City Wlk SE1 253 A1
Civic Way Ilford IG6 57 A5
Ruislip HA4 62 D3
Civil Service Coll SW1 115 C2 259 A3
Clabon Mews SW1 114 D2 257 C4
Clack St SE16 118 C4
Clacton Rd
Newham E6 99 D4
Tottenham N17 33 D1
Walthamstow E17 53 A3
Claigmar Gdns N3 29 D2
Claire Ct
Brondesbury NW2 69 A2
Bushey WD23 8 B3
4 Pinner HA5 23 B3
Whetstone N12 14 A1
Claire Gdns HA7 25 C5
Claire Pl E14 119 C3
Clairvale Rd TW5 129 A4
Clairview Rd SW16 181 B5
Clairville Gdns W7 108 C5
Clairville Point 12 SE23 162 D1
Clamp Hill HA7 24 C5
Clancarty Rd SW6 135 C3
Clandon Cl
South Acton W3 110 D4
Stoneleigh KT17 216 A2
Clandon Ct
Plaistow BR1 187 A4
Sutton SM2 218 B2
Clandon Gdns N3 47 C6
Clandon Ho
East Finchley N3 47 C6
12 Kingston u T KT2 176 D4
Clandon Rd IG3 79 C6
Clandon St SE8 141 C3
Clanfield Ho 12 SW15 156 A3
Clanricarde Gdns W2 113 C6 245 B5
CLAPHAM 137 B2
Clapham Common★ SW4 137 B1
Clapham Common North Side SW4 137 A1
Clapham Common South Side SW4 159 C6
Clapham Common Sta SW4 137 C1
Clapham Common West Side
Clapham SW4, SW11 136 D1
Clapham SW11 159 A6
Clapham Computer & Secretarial Coll 1 SW11 158 D6
Clapham Court Terr 2 SW4 160 A6
Clapham Cres SW4 137 D1
Clapham Ct 3 SW4 160 A6
Clapham High St SW4 137 D1
Clapham High Street Sta SW4 137 D2
Clapham Junction Est SW11 136 C1
Clapham Junction Sta SW11 136 C1
Clapham L Ctr SW4 137 D2
Clapham Manor Ct 1 SW4 137 C2
Clapham Manor Prim Sch 8 SW4 137 C2
Clapham Manor St SW4 137 D2
Clapham Mans SW4 159 B5
Clapham North Bsns Ctr 10 SW4 137 D2
Clapham North Sta SW4 138 A2
CLAPHAM PARK 159 D6
Clapham Park Rd SW4 137 D1
Clapham Park Terr 4 SW2 160 A6
Clapham Rd SW9 138 B5 270 D4
Clapham South Sta SW4 159 B5
Claps Gate La E6 100 D3
Clapton Comm E5 52 A2
Clapton Girls Tec Coll E5 74 C4
CLAPTON PARK 74 D4
Clapton Pas E5 74 C3
Clapton Sq E5 74 C3
Clapton Sta E5 74 B6
Clapton Terr E5 52 A1
Clapton Way E5 74 A4
Clara Grant Ho 10 E14 119 C3
Clara Grant Prim Sch The 18 E3 97 C3
Clara Pl SE18 122 C2
Clare Cl
Borehamwood WD6 10 B5
East Finchley N2 48 A6
Clare Cnr SE9 166 D4
Clare Ct
Chislehurst BR7 188 B2
St Pancras WC1 233 B1
Wimbledon SW19 179 A4
Claredale Ct SM2 218 A1
Claredale Ho 3 E2 96 B5
Claredale St E2 96 A5
Clare Gdns
Barking IG11 80 A1
Forest Gate E7 77 A4
Notting Hill W11 91 A1
Clare Ho
Bermondsey SE1 263 D2
4 Burnt Oak HA8 27 A1
5 Ealing W7 108 D5
6 Old Ford E3 97 B6
Clare House Prim Sch BR3 186 A1
Clare La N1 73 A1
Clare Lawn Ave SW14 155 B6
Clare Mews SW6 265 C3
Clare Mkt WC2 240 D1
Claremont
1 Putney SW15 157 A6
Shepperton TW17 192 D3
Claremont Ave
Harrow HA3 44 A4
Sunbury TW16 172 B2
West Barnes KT3 200 B4
Claremont Cl
Finsbury N1 94 C5 234 B3
Newham E16 122 C5
Orpington BR6 226 C4
4 Streatham SW2 160 B3
Claremont Ct 1 W9 91 B5
Claremont Dr TW17 192 D3
Claremont Gdns
Ilford IG3 79 C6
Kingston u T KT6 198 A4
Claremont Gr
Chiswick W4 133 C5
Woodford IG8 37 C4
Claremont High Sch HA3 44 A4
Claremont Ho 15 SM2 217 C1
Claremont Hts EN2 4 D1
Claremont La KT10 212 A3
Claremont Lo 12 SW19 178 D3
Claremont Pk N3 29 A2
Claremont Pl KT10 212 D2
Claremont Prim Sch NW2 68 D6
Claremont Rd
Bromley BR1 210 B5
Claygate KT10 212 C1
Croydon CR0 206 A1
Ealing W13 87 A2
Forest Gate E7 77 C3

Claremont Rd *continued*
Hadley Wood EN4 . . . 2 B6
Harrow HA3 . . . 24 C1
Hendon NW2 . . . 68 D6
Higham Hill E17 . . . 35 A1
Highgate N6 . . . 49 C2
Kingston u T KT6 . . . 198 A4
Leyton E7 . . . 76 B5
Teddington TW11 . . . 174 D6
Twickenham TW1 . . . 153 C5
West Kilburn W9 . . . 91 B5
Claremont Sq N1 . . . 94 C5 234 A3
Claremont St
Edmonton N18 . . . 34 A4
Greenwich SE10 . . . 141 D6
Newham E16 . . . 122 C4
Claremont Terr KT7 . . . 197 B2
Claremont Way NW2 . . . 46 C1
Claremont Way Ind Est NW2 . . . 46 C1
Clarence Ave
Bromley BR1, BR2 . . . 210 A5
Clapham Pk SW4 . . . 159 D5
Ilford IG2 . . . 56 C3
Kingston u T KT3 . . . 177 B1
Clarence Cl
Bushey WD23 . . . 8 D4
New Barnet EN4 . . . 14 B6
Clarence Cres
Clapham Pk SW4 . . . 159 D5
Sidcup DA14 . . . 168 B1
Clarence Ct
Edgware NW7 . . . 27 D5
[10] Hammersmith W6 . . . 112 B2
[5] North Finchley N12 . . . 30 B5
Clarence Gate NW1 . . . 237 D6
Clarence Gate Gdns NW1 . . . 237 D5
Clarence Gdns NW1 . . . 93 B4 231 D1
Clarence Ho SE17 . . . 139 A6
Clarence Ho★ SW1 . . . 115 C5 249 B3
Clarence La SW15 . . . 155 D5
Clarence Mews
Balham SW12 . . . 159 B4
Hackney E5 . . . 74 B3
[1] Rotherhithe SE16 . . . 118 D5
Clarence Pl [25] E5 . . . 74 B3
Clarence Rd
Bexley DA6 . . . 147 A1
Brentford W4 . . . 110 C1
Bromley BR1, BR2 . . . 210 A6
Brondesbury NW6 . . . 69 B1
Chislehurst SE9 . . . 166 A2
Enfield EN3 . . . 18 C6
Greenwich SE8 . . . 141 D6
Harringay N15 . . . 51 A4
Higham Hill E17 . . . 34 D1
Lower Clapton E5 . . . 74 B4
Manor Pk E12 . . . 77 D3
Newham E16 . . . 98 C3
Richmond TW9 . . . 132 C4
Sidcup DA14 . . . 168 B1
Sutton SM1 . . . 217 D3
Teddington TW11 . . . 175 A4
Thornton Heath CR0 . . . 205 B2
Wallington SM6 . . . 219 B3
Wimbledon SW19 . . . 179 D4
Wood Green N22 . . . 32 A3
Clarence St
Kingston u T KT1, KT2 . . . 176 A1
[5] Richmond TW9 . . . 132 A1
Southall UB2 . . . 106 D3
Clarence Terr
Hounslow TW3 . . . 129 D1
Lisson Gr NW1 . . . 237 D6
Clarence Way NW1 . . . 71 B1
Clarence Wlk [9] SW4 . . . 138 A3
Clarendon Cl
Bayswater W2 . . . 247 A6
[38] Hackney E9 . . . 74 C1
Clarendon Cres TW2 . . . 152 B1
Clarendon Cross W11 . . . 244 B5
Clarendon Ct
London NW11 . . . 47 B5
Mitcham SM4 . . . 202 C4
Paddington W9 . . . 236 B6
[1] Richmond TW9 . . . 132 C4
Willesden NW2 . . . 68 C1
Clarendon Dr SW15 . . . 134 C1
Clarendon Flats W1 . . . 238 B1
Clarendon Gdns
Hendon NW4 . . . 46 B6
Paddington W9 . . . 92 A3 236 B5
Redbridge IG1 . . . 56 B2
Wembley HA9 . . . 66 A4
Clarendon Gr
Mitcham CR4 . . . 202 D6
Somers Town NW1 . . . 232 C2
Clarendon Ho
Harrow HA2 . . . 42 B6
North Finchley N12 . . . 30 A5
Somers Town NW1 . . . 232 B3
South Oxhey WD19 . . . 22 D5
Clarendon Mews
Bayswater W2 . . . 247 A6
Old Bexley DA5 . . . 169 D3
Clarendon Pl W2 . . . 114 C6 247 A6
Clarendon Prim Sch TW15 . . . 170 B6
Clarendon Rd
Ashford TW15 . . . 170 B6
Croydon CR0 . . . 220 D6
Ealing W5 . . . 88 A3
Edmonton N18 . . . 34 A5
Harrow HA1 . . . 42 C3
Hayes UB3 . . . 105 D4
Hornsey N8 . . . 50 B6
Leytonstone E11 . . . 54 B1
Mitcham SW19 . . . 180 C3
Notting Hill W11 . . . 113 A6 244 B5
Wallington SM6 . . . 219 C2
Walthamstow E17 . . . 53 D3
Wanstead E18 . . . 55 A6
West Green N15 . . . 51 A5
Wood Green N22 . . . 32 B1
Clarendon Rise SE13 . . . 142 A1
Clarendon Specl Sch TW12 . . . 173 D4
Clarendon St SW1 . . . 115 B1 258 D2
Clarendon Terr W9 . . . 236 B6
Clarendon Way
Enfield N21 . . . 17 A5
Orpington BR5, BR7 . . . 211 D6
Clarendon Wlk [11] W11 . . . 91 A1
Clarens St SE6 . . . 163 B2
Clare Pl SW15 . . . 155 D4
Clare Point NW2 . . . 46 D1
Clare Rd
Hounslow TW4 . . . 129 B2
Leytonstone E11 . . . 54 B3
New Cross Gate SE14 . . . 141 B4
Northolt UB6 . . . 64 B2
Stanwell TW19 . . . 148 A4
Willesden NW10 . . . 68 A1
Clare St E2 . . . 96 B5
Claret Gdns SE25 . . . 205 C5
Clareville Ct SW7 . . . 256 B3
Clareville Gr SW7 . . . 114 A2 256 B3
Clareville Grove Mews SW7 . . . 256 B3
Clareville Rd BR5 . . . 227 A6
Clareville St SW7 . . . 114 A2 256 B3
Clare Way DA7 . . . 147 A4
Clarewood Ct W1 . . . 237 C3
Clarewood Wlk SW9 . . . 138 C1
Clarges Ho W1 . . . 248 D4
Clarges Mews W1 . . . 115 B5 248 C4
Clarges St W1 . . . 115 B5 248 D4
Clariat Ct W3 . . . 110 C4
Claribel Rd SW9 . . . 138 D3
Clarice Ct NW4 . . . 46 B6
Claridge Ct SW6 . . . 264 C1
Claridge Rd RM8 . . . 58 D1
Clarinet Ct HA8 . . . 26 D3
Clarissa Ho [7] E14 . . . 97 D1
Clarissa Rd RM6 . . . 58 D2
Clarissa St E8 . . . 95 D6
Clark Ct [17] NW10 . . . 67 B1
Clarke Cl CR0 . . . 205 A3
Clarke Ho
[2] London SW4 . . . 137 C2
[5] Richmond TW10 . . . 153 C1
Clarke Mans [9] IG11 . . . 79 D1
Clarke Mews N9 . . . 18 B1
Clarke Path N16 . . . 52 A1
Clarke's Ave KT4, SM3 . . . 216 D6
Clarkes Dr UB8 . . . 82 A2
Clarkes Mews W1 . . . 238 B4
Clark Gr IG3 . . . 79 C4
Clark Ho SW10 . . . 266 A4
Clark Lawrence Ct [10] SW11 . . . 136 B2
Clarks Mead WD23 . . . 8 B4
Clarkson Rd E16 . . . 98 D1
Clarkson Row NW1 . . . 232 A3
Clarkson St E2 . . . 96 B4
Clarksons The IG11 . . . 101 A5
Clark's Pl EC2 . . . 243 A2
Clark's Rd IG1 . . . 79 B6
Clark St E1 . . . 96 C2
Clark Way TW5 . . . 128 D5
Classic Mans [33] E9 . . . 74 C1
Classinghall Ho [14] SW15 . . . 156 D5
Classon Cl UB7 . . . 104 A4
Claude Rd Leyton E10 . . . 54 A1
London SE15 . . . 140 B3
Newham E13 . . . 99 B6
Claude St E14 . . . 119 C2
Claudia Jones Way SW2 . . . 160 A5
Claudia Pl SW19 . . . 157 A3
Claudius Cl HA7 . . . 9 D1
Claughton Rd E13 . . . 99 C5
Clauson Ave UB5 . . . 64 A3
Clavell St [8] SE10 . . . 142 A6
Claverdale Rd SW2 . . . 160 C4
Clavering Ave SW13 . . . 134 B6
Clavering Cl TW1 . . . 175 A6
Clavering Ho SE13 . . . 142 B1
Clavering Rd E12 . . . 77 D6
Claverings Ind Est N9 . . . 18 C2
Claverley Gr N3 . . . 29 D2
Claverley Villas N3 . . . 29 D3
Claverton St SW1 . . . 115 C1 259 B1
Clave St E1 . . . 118 C5
Claxton Gr W6 . . . 112 D1 254 A1
Clay Ave CR4 . . . 181 B1
Claybank Gr SE13 . . . 141 D2
Claybee Ct N22 . . . 32 B5
Claybourne Mews [2] SE19 . . . 183 D3
Claybridge Rd SE12 . . . 187 C6
Claybrook Cl N2 . . . 48 B6
Claybrook Rd W6 . . . 134 D6
Claybury Broadway IG5 . . . 56 A6
Clay Ct E17 . . . 54 B6
Claydon SE17 . . . 262 A4
Claydon Dr CR0 . . . 220 A4
Claydon Ho NW4 . . . 28 D1
Claydown Mews SE18 . . . 122 C1
Clayfarm Rd SE9 . . . 167 A2
CLAYGATE . . . 212 D1
Claygate Cres CR0 . . . 224 B2
Claygate Ct SM1 . . . 218 A5
Claygate La
Hinchley Wood KT10 . . . 213 A6
Thames Ditton KT7 . . . 197 A1
Claygate Lodge Cl KT10 . . . 212 C1
Claygate Prim Sch KT10 . . . 212 C1
Claygate Rd W13 . . . 109 B3
Claygate Sta KT10 . . . 212 C2
CLAYHALL . . . 56 B6
Clayhall Ct [20] E3 . . . 97 B5
CLAY HILL . . . 5 A6
Clay Hill EN2 . . . 5 B6
Clayhill Cres SE12, SE9 . . . 187 D6
Clay La Bushey WD23 . . . 8 C4
Stanwell TW19 . . . 148 B4
Claylands Ct SE19 . . . 183 B5
Claylands Pl SW8 . . . 138 C5
Claylands Rd SW8 . . . 138 B6 270 D5
Claymill Ho [2] SE18 . . . 123 A1
Claymore Cl SM3, SM4 . . . 201 C2
Claymore Ct [4] E17 . . . 35 A2
Claypole Ct E17 . . . 53 C4
Claypole Dr TW5 . . . 129 A4
Claypole Rd E15 . . . 98 A5
Clayponds Ave TW8 . . . 110 A2
Clayponds Gdns W5 . . . 109 D2
Clayponds Hospl W5 . . . 110 A2
Clayponds La TW8 . . . 110 A1
Clays Ct N16 . . . 51 D1
Clay St W1 . . . 92 D2 237 D3
Clayton [22] NW9 . . . 27 D1
Clayton Ave HA0 . . . 66 A1
Clayton Bsns Ctr UB3 . . . 105 C4
Clayton Cl [3] E6 . . . 100 B1
Clayton Cres
Brentford TW8 . . . 109 D1
Islington N1 . . . 233 C5
Clayton Ct
[1] Higham Hill E17 . . . 35 A1
Stamford Hill N16 . . . 52 A2
Clayton Field NW9 . . . 27 C2
Clayton Ho
[22] Hackney E9 . . . 74 C1
Long Ditton KT7 . . . 197 B1
Clayton Mews SE10 . . . 142 B4
Clayton Rd
Chessington KT10, KT9 . . . 213 D4
Hayes UB3 . . . 105 C4
Isleworth TW7 . . . 130 C2
Peckham SE15 . . . 140 A4
Clayton St SE11 . . . 138 C6
Clayton Terr UB4 . . . 84 D2
Claytonville Terr DA17 . . . 125 D4
Clay Wood Cl BR6 . . . 211 C2
Clayworth Cl DA15 . . . 168 B5
Cleanthus Cl SE18 . . . 144 D4
Cleanthus Rd SE18 . . . 144 D4
Clearbrook Way [13] E1 . . . 96 C1
Clearmont Ho UB2 . . . 107 C3
Clearwater Ho BR3 . . . 207 D4
Clear Water Ho [9] TW10 . . . 154 A6
Clearwater Pl KT6 . . . 197 C3
Clearwater Terr [4] W11 . . . 112 D4
Clearwell Dr W9 . . . 91 D3
Cleave Ave
Hayes UB3 . . . 105 C2
Orpington BR6 . . . 227 C2
Cleaveland Rd KT6 . . . 197 D4
Cleaver Ho [6] NW3 . . . 70 D1
Cleaverholme Cl SE25 . . . 206 B3
Cleaver Sq SE11 . . . 116 C1 261 B1
Cleaver St SE11 . . . 116 C1 261 B2
Cleave's Almshos [1] KT2 . . . 176 A1
Cleeve Ct
East Bedfont TW14 . . . 149 C3
Muswell Hill N10 . . . 31 B3
Cleeve Hill SE23 . . . 162 B3
Cleeve Ho [15] E2 . . . 95 C4
Cleeve Park Gdns DA14 . . . 168 B2
Cleeve Park Sch DA14 . . . 168 C1
Cleeve Way
Cheam SM1 . . . 201 D1
Roehampton SW15 . . . 155 D4
Cleeve Workshops [14] E2 . . . 95 C4
Clegg Ho SE3 . . . 143 B1
Clegg St Newham E13 . . . 99 A5
[16] Wapping E1 . . . 118 B5
Cleland Ho [19] E2 . . . 96 C5
Clematis Gdns IG8 . . . 37 A5
Clematis St W12 . . . 112 A6
Clem Atlee Par SW6 . . . 264 D5
Clem Attlee Ct SW6 . . . 135 B6 264 D5
Clemence St E14 . . . 97 B2
Clement Attlee Ho NW10 . . . 67 D1
Clement Ave SW4 . . . 137 D1
Clement Cl Acton W4 . . . 111 B2
Hampstead NW6 . . . 68 C1
Clement Danes Ho [2] W12 . . . 90 B1
Clement Gdns UB3 . . . 105 C2
Clement Ho
[14] Deptford SE8 . . . 119 A2
[17] North Kensington W10 . . . 90 C2
Clementhorpe Rd RM9 . . . 80 C2
Clementina Rd E10 . . . 53 B1
Clementine Churchill Hospl The HA1 . . . 64 D5
Clementine Cl W13 . . . 109 B4
Clementine Wlk [4] IG8 . . . 37 A3
Clement Rd
Penge BR3 . . . 184 D1
Wimbledon SW19 . . . 179 A5
Clements Ave [1] E16 . . . 121 A6
Clements Cl [19] N12 . . . 29 D6
Clements Ct
Hounslow TW4 . . . 128 D1
[5] Ilford IG1 . . . 78 D5
Clements Ho N17 . . . 34 A2
Clements Inn WC2 . . . 94 B1 240 D1
Clements Inn Pas WC2 . . . 240 D1
Clements La IG1 . . . 78 D5
Clement's La EC2, EC4 . . . 117 B6 252 D6
Clements Pl TW8 . . . 109 D1
Clements Rd
East Ham E6 . . . 78 B1
Ilford IG1 . . . 78 D5
Clement's Rd SE16 . . . 118 B3
Cleminson Ct DA14 . . . 190 D4
Clemson Ho [9] E8 . . . 95 D6
Clendon Way SE18 . . . 123 B2
Clennam St SE1 . . . 252 B2
Clensham Ct SM3 . . . 217 C6
Clensham La SM1 . . . 217 C6
Clenston Mews W1 . . . 237 C2
Clent Ho [4] N16 . . . 51 D1
Cleopatra Cl HA7 . . . 9 D1
Cleopatra's Needle★ WC2 . . . 116 B6 250 C5
Clephane Rd [13] N1 . . . 73 A2
Clephane Rd N N1 . . . 73 A2
Clephane Rd S N1 . . . 73 B2
Clere Pl EC2 . . . 242 D6
Clere St EC2 . . . 95 B3 242 D6
Clerics Wlk TW17 . . . 193 B3
CLERKENWELL . . . 94 D3
Clerkenwell Cl EC1 . . . 94 C3 241 B5
Clerkenwell Gn EC1 . . . 94 D3 241 C5
Clerkenwell Parochial CE Prim Sch EC1 . . . 94 C4 234 A1
Clerkenwell Rd EC1 . . . 94 D3 241 C5
Clermont Rd E9 . . . 96 C6
Cleveden Ct CR2 . . . 221 C3
Cleveden Ho BR1 . . . 188 A3
Clevedon Ct
Battersea SW11 . . . 267 A2
Dulwich SE21 . . . 161 B1
Clevedon Gdns
Cranford TW5 . . . 128 B4
Hayes UB3 . . . 105 B3
Clevedon Ho [4] SM1 . . . 218 A4
Clevedon Mans NW5 . . . 71 A4
Clevedon Rd
Kingston u T KT1 . . . 176 C1
Penge SE20 . . . 184 D2
Twickenham TW1 . . . 153 D5
Cleve Ho NW6 . . . 69 D1
Cleveland Ave
Chiswick W4 . . . 111 D2
Hampton TW12 . . . 173 B3
Merton SW20 . . . 179 B1
Cleveland Cres WD6 . . . 11 A6
Cleveland Ct
Ealing W13 . . . 87 B2
Marylebone W1 . . . 239 B5
Southall UB2 . . . 107 D2
Cleveland Gdns
Barnes SW13 . . . 133 D3
Harringay N4, N15 . . . 51 A4
Hendon NW2 . . . 68 D6
Paddington W2 . . . 92 A1 236 A1
Worcester Pk KT4 . . . 215 D6
Cleveland Gr [39] E1 . . . 96 C3
Cleveland Ho [7] N2 . . . 30 B1

Cleveland Inf Sch
IG1 .78 D5
Cleveland Jun Sch
IG1 .78 D5
Cleveland Mans
8 Brixton SW9 138 C5
4 Brondesbury NW6 69 B1
Paddington W9 91 C3
Cleveland Mews W1 239 A4
Cleveland Park Ave
E17 53 C5
Cleveland Park Cres
E17 53 C5
Cleveland Pk TW19 148 A5
Cleveland Pl SW1 249 B4
Cleveland Rd
Barnes SW13 133 D3
Bexley DA16 145 D3
Ealing W13 87 B2
Edmonton N9 18 B4
Ilford IG1 78 D5
Isleworth TW7 131 A1
Islington N1 73 B1
New Malden KT3 199 C5
14 South Acton W4 111 A3
Wanstead E18 55 A6
Worcester Pk KT4 215 C6
Cleveland Rise SM4 200 D2
Cleveland Row
SW1 115 C5 249 B3
Cleveland Sq
W2 92 A1 236 A1
Cleveland St
W1 93 C3 239 A5
Cleveland Terr
W2 92 A1 236 B2
Cleveland Way E1 96 C3
Cleveley Cres W5 88 B5
Cleveleys Rd E5 74 B5
Clevely Cl SE7 121 D2
Clevendon Cl N16 73 D5
Cleve Rd
Sidcup DA14 168 D1
South Hampstead NW6 69 D1
Cleverly Cotts W12 111 D5
Cleverly Est W12 112 A6
Cleves Ct KT6 198 A3
Cleves Prim Sch E6 99 D6
Cleves Rd Newham E6 99 D5
Richmond TW10 153 C1
Cleves Way
Ashford TW16 171 D4
Hampton TW12 173 B3
Ruislip HA4 40 D1
Clewer Cres HA3 24 B2
Clewer Ct 2 E10 53 C1
Clewer Ho 6 SE2 124 D4
Cley Ho SE4 140 D1
Clichy Ho 32 E1 96 C2
Clifden Centre (Richmond Adult & Com Coll) TW1 152 D3
Clifden Ho 6 TW8 131 D6
Clifden Mews E5 74 D3
Clifden Rd
Brentford TW8 131 D6
Homerton E5 74 D3
Twickenham TW1 152 D3
Cliff Ct 14 NW1 71 D2
Cliffe Ho 4 SE10 120 D1
Cliffe Rd CR2 221 B3
Cliffe Wlk 2 SM1 218 A3
Clifford Ave
Elmstead BR7 188 B4
Mortlake SW14 133 A3
Mortlake SW14, TW9 132 D2
Wallington SM6 219 C4
Clifford Cl UB5 85 A6
Clifford Ct
Bayswater W2 91 D2
Wandsworth SW18 158 B4
Willesden NW10 67 C4
Clifford Dr SW9 138 D1
Clifford Gdns
Hayes UB3 105 B2
Kensal Green NW10 90 C5
Clifford Gr TW15 170 C6
Clifford Haigh Ho
SW6 134 D5
Clifford Ho
2 Beckenham BR3 185 D4
West Kensington W14 254 C3
Clifford Lo 5 N3 29 B1
Clifford Rd Barnet EN5 1 D2
Chingford E17 36 A1
Croydon SE25 206 A5
Hounslow TW4 128 D2
Newham E16 98 D3
Ponders End N9 18 C5
Richmond TW10 153 D2
Wembley HA0 87 D6
Clifford's Inn Pas
EC4 241 A1
Clifford St
W1 115 C6 249 A5
Clifford Way NW10 67 D4
Cliff Rd NW1 71 D2
Cliff Road Studios 13
NW1 71 D2
Cliffsend Ho 23
SW9 138 C4
Cliff Terr SE8 141 C3
Cliffview Rd SE13 141 C2
Cliff Villas NW1 71 D2
Cliff Wlk E16 98 D2
Clifton Ave
Church End N3 29 B2
Feltham TW13 150 C1
Shepherd's Bush
W12 111 D5
Stanmore HA7 25 B1
Walthamstow E17 52 D6
Wembley HA9 66 B2
Clifton Cl 8 BR6 227 A3
Clifton Cres SE15 140 B5
Clifton Ct
1 Beckenham BR3 185 D2
Finsbury Pk N4 72 C6
Paddington NW8 236 C6
Peckham SE15 140 B5
Putney SW15 156 D6
South Norwood SE25 205 C4
9 Stanwell TW19 148 A5
Surbiton KT5 198 B2
3 Woodford IG8 37 A4
Clifton Gate SW10 266 A6
Clifton Gdns
Chiswick W4 111 B2
Enfield EN2 16 A6
Hillingdon UB10 82 D5
Paddington
W9 92 A3 236 A5
South Tottenham N15 51 D3
2 Temple Fortune
NW11 47 B3
Clifton Gr E8 74 A2
Clifton Hill
NW8 92 A6 229 A5
Clifton Ho Leyton E11 76 C6
Shoreditch E2 243 C6
Clifton Lodge Sch
W5 109 C6
Clifton Mans 4
SW9 138 C1
Clifton Mews SE25 205 C5
Clifton Par TW13 172 C6
Clifton Park Ave
SW20 178 C1
Clifton Pl
Paddington W2 236 D1
Rotherhithe SE16 118 C4
Clifton Prim Sch
UB2 107 A2
Clifton Rd
Bexley DA16 146 C2
Crouch End N8 49 D3
Finchley N3 30 A2
Greenford UB6 86 B3
Harlesden NW10 90 A5
Harlington TW6 126 D2
Harrow HA3 44 B4
Ilford IG2 57 B3
Isleworth TW7 130 C3
Kingston u T KT2 176 B2
Newham E16 98 C2
Paddington
W9 92 A3 236 B6
Sidcup DA14 189 C6
Southall UB2 107 A2
South Norwood SE25 205 C5
Teddington TW11 174 C6
Upton E7 77 D2
Wallington SM6 219 B3
Wimbledon SW19 178 D4
Wood Green N22 31 C2
Clifton Rise SE14 141 A5
Cliftons Roundabout SE9,
SE12 165 C5
Clifton St EC2 95 C3 243 A5
Clifton Terr N4 72 C6
Clifton The KT6 214 A6
Clifton Villas
W9 92 A2 236 A4
Cliftonville Ct SE12 165 A3
Clifton Way
Harlington TW6 126 D2
Peckham SE15 140 C5
Wembley HA0 88 A6
Climsland Ho SE1 251 B4
Clinch Ct 11 E16 99 A2
Cline Ho SW15 156 A6
Cline Rd N11 31 C4
Clinger Ct N1 95 C6
Clink Prison Mus The★
SE1 252 C4
Clink St SE1 117 B5 252 C4
Clinton Ave
Bexley DA16 146 A1
East Molesey KT8 196 A5
Clinton Ho
New Malden KT3 199 B1
6 Surbiton KT6 197 D2
Clinton Rd Bow E3 97 A4
Forest Gate E7 77 A4
West Green N15 51 B5
Clipper Appts 12
SE10 142 A6
Clipper Cl 3 SE16 118 D4
Clipper Ho E14 120 A1
Clipper Way SE13 142 A1
Clippesby Cl KT9 214 B2
Clipstone Ho 10
SW15 156 A6
Clipstone Mews W1 239 A4
Clipstone Rd TW3 129 C2
Clipstone St
W1 93 C2 239 A4
Clissold Cl N2 48 D6
Clissold Cres N16 73 B4
Clissold Ct N4 73 A6
Clissold Ho 4 N16 73 B6
Clissold Rd N16 73 B5
Clitheroe Ave HA2 41 C1
Clitheroe Rd SW9 138 A3
Clitherow Ave W7 109 A3
Clitherow Rd TW8 109 C1
Clitterhouse Cres
NW2 46 C1
Clitterhouse Rd NW2 46 C1
Clive Ave N18 34 A4
Clive Ct
Paddington W9 236 B6
Streatham SW16 181 D5
Tolworth KT6 214 C6
Cliveden Cl N12 30 A6
Cliveden Ho SW1 258 A4
Cliveden Pl
Belgravia
SW1 115 A2 258 A4
Shepperton TW17 193 A3
Cliveden Rd SW19 179 B2
Clivedon Ct
Ealing W13 87 B2
6 New Barnet EN5 2 A1
Clivedon Rd E4 36 C5
Clive Ho
18 Clapham SW8 137 D3
3 Croydon CR0 205 D1
Greenwich SE10 142 A6
Clive Lloyd Ho N15 51 A4
Clive Lo NW4 46 D3
Clive Rd
Belvedere DA17 125 C2
Enfield EN1 6 A1
Feltham TW14 150 A5
Mitcham SW19 180 C4
Teddington TW1 175 A6
West Norwood SE21,
SE27 161 B1
Clivesdale Dr UB3 106 B5
Clive Way EN1 6 A1
Cloak La EC4 117 B6 252 C6
Clochar Ct NW10 89 D6
Clock Ct 2 E11 55 B5
Clock Ho
Stamford Hill N16 51 D2
Walthamstow E17 54 B5
Clock Ho The EN2 5 D6
Clockhouse Ave
IG11 101 A6
Clockhouse Cl
SW19 156 C2
Clock House Ct 1
BR3 185 A1
Clockhouse Junc
N13 32 C5
Clockhouse La TW14,
TW15 148 D2
Clockhouse Mans
N13 32 C5
Clockhouse Par N13 32 C5
Clock House Par E11 55 B3
Clockhouse Pl
SW15 157 A5
Clock House Rd
BR3 185 A1
Clockhouse Rdbt
TW14 149 A3
Clock House Sta
BR3 185 A2
Clockhouse The
SW19 156 C1
Clockmakers' Mus★
EC2 95 A1 242 B2
Clocktower Mews 6
W7 108 C5
Clock Tower Mews
Islington N1 235 B5
Thamesmead SE28 124 B6
Clock Tower Pl 1
N7 72 A2
Clock Tower Rd
TW7 130 D2
Clock View Cres 2
N7 72 A2
Cloister Cl TW11 175 B5
Cloister Gdns
Croydon SE25 206 B3
Edgware HA8 27 A5
Cloister Rd Acton W3 89 A2
Child's Hill NW2 69 B6
Cloisters Ave BR1,
BR2 210 B4
Cloisters Ct
Erith DA7 147 D2
Highgate N6 49 B1
Cloisters Ho 8
SW19 179 C3
Cloisters The 22
SW9 138 C4
Clonard Way HA5 23 C4
Clonbrock Rd N16 73 C4
Cloncurry St SW6 134 D3
Clone Ct 4 W12 111 C3
Clone The 5 KT2 176 D3
Clonmel Cl HA2 42 B1
Clonmell Rd N17 51 B6
Clonmel Rd
Fulham
SW6 135 B4 264 D2
Teddington TW11 174 B6
Clonmore St SW18 157 B3
Cloonmore Ave BR6 227 D4
Clorane Gdns NW3 69 C5
Close The
Beckenham BR3 207 A5
Cheam SM3 201 B2
Chingford E4 36 A3
Cockfosters EN4 14 D6
Croydon SE25 206 A3
Dagenham RM6 59 A3
Eastcote HA5 40 C2
Harrow HA2 24 A1
Hillingdon UB10 82 C6
Hounslow TW7 130 B3
Ilford IG2 57 C3
Kingston u T KT3 177 A1
Lewisham SE3 142 B3
Mitcham CR4 202 D5
Mortlake TW9 132 D2
Muswell Hill N10 31 B1
1 Old Bexley DA5 169 C4
Palmers Green N14 15 D2
Petts Wood BR5 211 C3
Rayners La HA5 41 B2
Sidcup DA14 190 B5
Surbiton KT6 198 A3
Totteridge N20 13 B2
Wembley HA0 66 A2
Wembley Pk HA9 67 A5
Cloth Ct EC1 241 D3
Cloth Fair EC1 94 D2 241 D3
Clothier Ho SE7 122 A1
Clothier St EC3 243 B2
Cloth St EC1 95 A2 242 A4
Clothworkers Rd
SE18 145 B5
Cloudesdale Rd
SW17 159 B2
Cloudesley Cl DA14 189 D6
Cloudesley Mans N1 234 B5
Cloudesley Pl
N1 94 C6 234 B5
Cloudesley Rd
Erith DA7 147 B4
Islington N1 94 C6 234 A5
Cloudesley Sq
N1 94 C6 234 B6
Cloudesley St
N1 94 C6 234 B5
Clouston Cl SM6 220 A3
Clova Rd E7 77 A3
Clove Cres E14 120 B6
Clovelly Ave
London NW9 45 D5
Uxbridge UB10 61 A4
Clovelly Cl Pinner HA5 40 C6
Uxbridge UB10 61 A4
Clovelly Ct NW2 68 C3
Clovelly Gdns
Enfield EN1 17 C4
South Norwood SE19 183 D2
Clovelly Ho W2 236 A2
Clovelly Rd
Acton W4 111 B4
Ealing W5 109 C4
Erith DA7 147 A6
Hornsey N8 49 D5
Hounslow TW3 129 C3
Clovelly Way
Harrow HA2 63 B6
Orpington BR6 211 D3
Stepney E1 96 C1
Clover Cl E11 76 B6
Clover Ct Enfield EN3 7 A1
Sutton SM2 217 D2
Cloverdale Gdns
DA15 167 D5
Clover Ho
Hounslow TW3 130 A4
Southgate N21 16 B6
Cloverleys IG10 21 D6
Clover Mews SW3 267 D6
Clover Way SM6 203 A1
Clove St 9 E13 99 A3
Clowders Rd SE6 163 B1
Clowes Ho 3 SW4 138 A1
Clowns Mus★ E8 95 D6
Clowser Cl 4 SM1 218 A3
Cloysters Gn E1 118 A5
Cloyster Wood HA8 25 D4
Club Gardens Rd
BR2 209 A2
Club Row E2 95 D3 243 C6
Clumps The TW15 171 B6
Clunbury Ave UB2 107 B1
Clunbury St N1 235 D3
Clunie Ho SW1 257 D6
Cluny Mews SW5 255 A3
Cluny Pl SE1 117 C3 263 A6
Cluse Ct N1 235 A4
Clutton St E14 97 D2
Clydach Rd EN1 5 D1
Clyde Cir N15 51 C5
Clyde Ct NW1 232 D4
Clyde Flats SW6 264 C4
Clyde Ho 9 KT2 175 D2
Clyde Pl E10 53 D2
Clyde Rd
Croydon CR0 221 D6
South Tottenham N15 51 C5
Stanwell TW19 148 A3
Sutton SM1 217 C3
Wallington SM6 219 C2
Wood Green N22 31 D2
Clydesdale EN3 6 D1
Clydesdale Ave HA7 43 D6
Clydesdale Cl
Borehamwood WD6 11 B6
Isleworth TW7 130 D2
Clydesdale Ct N20 14 B3
Clydesdale Gdns
TW10 132 D1
Clydesdale Ho
Abbey Wood DA18 125 A4
4 Notting Hill W11 91 B1
Clydesdale Path WD6 11 B6
Clydesdale Rd W11 91 B1
Clyde St SE8 141 B6
Clyde Terr SE23 162 C2
Clyde Vale SE23 162 C2
Clyde Works 10
SM6 219 C2
Clyfford Rd HA4 61 D4
Clymping Dene
TW14 150 B4

Clynes Ho
6 Dagenham RM10 ... 81 C5
3 Globe Town E2 ... 96 D4
Hayes UB4 ... 84 A4
Clyro Ct N4 ... 50 B1
Clyston St SW8 ... 137 C3
Clytha Ct SE27 ... 183 A6
Coach Ho NW10 ... 67 A1
Coach & Horses Yd W1 ... 249 A6
Coach House La
Highbury N5 ... 72 D4
Wimbledon SW19 ... 156 D1
Coach House Mews SE23 ... 162 D5
Coach House Yd 5 NW3 ... 70 B4
Coachmaker Mews 5 SW9 ... 138 A2
Coachman Lo N12 ... 30 A5
Coalbrook Mans 3 SW12 ... 159 B3
Coaldale Wlk SE21 ... 161 A4
Coalecroft Rd SW15 ... 156 C6
Coalport Ho SE11 ... 261 A4
Coal Post Cl BR6 ... 227 D2
Coatbridge Ho 8 N1 ... 72 B1
Coates Ave SW18 ... 158 C5
Coates Cl CR7 ... 205 A6
Coates Ct NW3 ... 70 C3
Coates Hill Rd BR1 ... 188 C1
Coates Rd WD6 ... 9 D4
Coate St E2 ... 96 A5
Coates Wlk TW8 ... 110 A1
Cobalt SE2 ... 124 A4
Cobalt Cl CR0 ... 206 D5
Cobb Cl WD6 ... 11 A6
Cobbett Rd
Kidbrooke SE9 ... 144 A2
Twickenham TW2 ... 151 C3
Cobbetts Ave IG4 ... 55 D4
Cobbett St SW8 ... 138 B5 270 D3
Cobble La N1 ... 72 D1
Cobble Mews N4, N5 ... 73 A5
Cobbler's Wlk TW11 174 D3
Cobblestone Pl CR0 ... 205 A1
Cobbold Ct SW1 ... 259 C4
Cobbold Ind Est NW10 ... 67 D2
Cobbold Mews W12 ... 111 D4
Cobbold Rd
Bedford Pk W12 ... 111 D4
Leyton E11 ... 76 D5
Willesden NW10 ... 67 D2
Cobb's Hall 1 SW6 ... 134 D6
Cobbs Rd TW4 ... 129 B1
Cobb St E1 ... 243 C3
Cobden Bldgs WC1 ... 233 C2
Cobden Ct
Bromley BR2 ... 209 C5
9 Thamesmead SE28 ... 124 C5
Cobden Ho
11 Bethnal Green E2 ... 96 A4
Regent's Pk NW1 ... 232 A4
Cobden Mews SE26 ... 184 B5
Cobden Rd
Croydon SE25 ... 206 A4
Leyton E11 ... 76 C6
Orpington BR6 ... 227 B4
Cobham 21 NW9 ... 27 D1
Cobham Ave KT3 ... 200 A4
Cobham Cl
2 Blackfen DA15 ... 168 B5
Bromley BR2 ... 210 A2
Clapham SW11 ... 158 C5
Edgware HA8 ... 26 D1
Enfield EN1 ... 6 A2
Wallington SM6 ... 220 A2
Cobham Ct CR4 ... 180 B1
Cobham Ho IG11 ... 101 A6
Cobham Mews 3 NW1 ... 71 D1
Cobham Pl DA6 ... 168 D6
Cobham Rd
Chingford E17 ... 36 A2
Harringay N22 ... 50 D6
Heston TW5 ... 128 C5
Ilford IG3 ... 79 C5
Kingston u T KT1, KT2 ... 176 C1
Cobland Rd SE12 ... 187 C6
Coborn Mews 9 E3 ... 97 B4
Coborn Rd E3 ... 97 B4
Coborn St E3 ... 97 B4
Cobourg Prim Sch SE5 ... 139 D6
Cobourg Rd SE5 ... 139 D6
Cobourg St NW1 ... 93 C4 232 B1
Coburg Cl SW1 ... 259 B4
Coburg Cres SW2 ... 160 C3
Coburg Dwellings 11 E1 ... 118 C6
Coburg Gdns IG5 ... 37 D1
Coburg Rd N22 ... 32 B1
Cochrane Cl NW8 ... 229 D3
Cochrane Ct 3 E10 ... 53 C1
Cochrane Ho 15 E14 ... 119 C4
Cochrane Mews NW8 ... 92 B5 229 D3
Cochrane Rd SW19 ... 179 B3
Cochrane St NW8 ... 92 B5 229 D3
Coci Ho W14 ... 254 D3
Cockburn Ho SW1 ... 259 D1
Cockerell Rd E17 ... 53 A3
COCKFOSTERS ... 2 D1
Cockfosters Par EN4 ... 3 A1
Cockfosters Rd EN4 ... 2 D3
Cockfosters Sta EN4 ... 3 A1
Cock Hill E1 ... 243 B3
Cock La EC1 ... 94 D2 241 D3
Cockpit Yd WC1 ... 240 D4
Cocks Cres KT3 ... 199 D5
Cocksett Ave BR6 ... 227 C2
Cockspur Ct SW1 ... 249 D4
Cockspur St SW1 ... 115 D5 249 D4
Cocksure La DA14 ... 191 C6
Coda Ctr The SW6 ... 135 A4 264 B2
Code St E1 ... 95 D3 243 D5
Codicote Ho 22 SE8 ... 118 D2
Codicote Terr N4 ... 73 A6
Codling Cl 12 E1 ... 118 A5
Codling Way HA0 ... 65 D4
Codrington Ct 3 SE16 ... 119 A5
Codrington Hill SE23 ... 163 A4
Codrington Ho 7 E1 ... 96 B3
Codrington Mews W11 ... 91 A1
Cody Cl Harrow HA3 ... 43 D6
Wallington SM6 ... 219 D1
Cody Rd E16 ... 98 B3
Coe Ave SE25 ... 206 A3
Coe's Alley EN5 ... 1 A1
Coffey St SE8 ... 141 C5
Cogan Ave E17 ... 35 A2
Cohen Ho NW7 ... 28 A6
Cohen Lo E5 ... 75 A3
Coin St SE1 ... 116 C5 251 A4
Coity Rd NW5 ... 71 A2
Cokers La SE21 ... 161 B3
Coke St E1 ... 96 A1
Colab Ct N22 ... 32 C2
Colas Mews 7 NW6 ... 91 C6
Colbeck Mews SW5 ... 113 D2 255 D3
Colbeck Rd HA1 ... 42 A2
Colberg Pl N16 ... 51 D2
Colbert 1 SE5 ... 139 D4
Colborne Ct 8 SW19 ... 179 D2
Colborne Ho 8 E14 ... 119 C6
Colborne Way KT4 ... 216 C6
Colbrook Ave UB3 ... 105 B3
Colbrook Cl UB3 ... 105 B3
Colburn Ave HA5 ... 23 A4
Colburn Way SM1 ... 218 B5
Colby Rd
Walton-on-T KT12 ... 194 A1
West Norwood SE19 ... 183 C5
Colchester Ave E12 ... 78 B5
Colchester Dr HA5 ... 40 D4
Colchester Ho 17 SW8 ... 137 D3
Colchester Rd
Burnt Oak HA8 ... 27 A3
Leyton E10 ... 54 A2
Pinner HA6 ... 22 A1
Walthamstow E17 ... 53 C3
Colchester St E1 ... 243 D2
Colchester Villas CR7 ... 204 C3
Coldbath Sq EC1 ... 241 A6
Coldbath St SE13 ... 141 D3
Cold Blow La SE14 ... 140 D6
Coldershaw Rd W13 ... 109 A4
Coldfall Ave N10 ... 31 A1
Coldfall Prim Sch N10 ... 30 D1
Coldham Ct N22 ... 32 D2
Coldham Gr EN3 ... 7 A6
Coldharbour E14 ... 120 A5
Coldharbour Crest SE9 ... 166 C1
Coldharbour Ind Est SE5 ... 139 A3
Coldharbour La
Brixton SW9 ... 138 D2
Bushey WD23 ... 8 A6
Hayes UB3 ... 106 A5
Coldharbour Lane Ho UB3 ... 106 A5
Coldharbour Pl SE5 ... 139 B3
Coldharbour Rd CR0 ... 220 C3
Coldharbour Sports Ctr SE9 ... 166 B2
Coldharbour Way CR0 ... 220 C3
Coldstream Gdns SW18 ... 157 B5
Colebeck Mews N1 ... 72 D2
Colebert Ave E1 ... 96 C3
Colebert Ho 21 E1 ... 96 C3
Colebrook Cl
Edgware NW7 ... 28 D3
Putney SW19 ... 156 D4
Colebrook Ct SW3 ... 257 B3
Colebrooke Ave W13 ... 87 B1
Colebrooke Ct DA14 ... 190 B6
Colebrooke Dr E11 ... 55 C2
Colebrooke Pl N1 ... 234 D5
Colebrooke Row
Islington N1 ... 233 B6
Islington N1 ... 94 D5 234 C4
Islington N1 ... 234 D5
Colebrook Ho 1 E14 ... 97 D1
Colebrook Rd SW16 ... 182 A2
Colebrook Rise BR2 ... 186 C1
Colebrook Way N11 ... 31 B5
Coleby Path 21 SE5 ... 139 B5
Colechurch Ho 9 SE1 ... 118 A1
Cole Cl SE28 ... 124 B5
Cole Court Lo 9 TW1 ... 153 A4
Coledale Dr HA7 ... 25 C2
Colefax Bldg 12 E1 ... 96 A1
Coleford Rd SW18 ... 158 A6
Cole Gdns TW5 ... 128 A5
Colegrave Rd E15 ... 76 B3
Colegrave Sch E15 ... 76 B3
Colegrove Rd SE15 ... 139 D6
Coleherne Ct SW10 ... 113 D1 255 D1
Coleherne Mans SW5 ... 255 D2
Coleherne Mews SW10 ... 113 D1 255 C1
Coleherne Rd SW10 ... 113 D1 255 C1
Colehill Gdns SW6 ... 264 A1
Colehill La SW6 ... 135 A4 264 B1
Cole Ho SE1 ... 251 B1
Coleman Cl SE25 ... 184 A1
Coleman Ct SW18 ... 157 C4
Coleman Fields N1 ... 95 A6 235 B6
Coleman Mans N19 ... 50 A2
Coleman Rd
Belvedere DA17 ... 125 C2
Camberwell SE5 ... 139 C5
Dagenham RM9 ... 81 A2
Colemans Heath SE9 ... 166 D1
Coleman St EC2 ... 95 B1 242 C2
Coleman Street Bldgs EC2 ... 242 C2
Colenso Dr NW7 ... 28 A3
Colenso Rd Ilford IG2 ... 57 C2
Lower Clapton E5 ... 74 C4
Cole Park Gdns TW1 ... 153 A5
Cole Park Rd TW1 ... 153 A5
Cole Park View 2 TW1 ... 153 A5
Colepits Wood Rd SE9 ... 167 B6
Coleraine Park Prim Sch N17 ... 34 B2
Coleraine Rd
Greenwich SE3 ... 142 D6
Hornsey N8, N22 ... 50 C6
Cole Rd TW1 ... 153 A5
Coleridge Ave
Carshalton SM1 ... 218 C4
Plashet E12 ... 78 A2
Coleridge Cl SW8 ... 137 B3
Coleridge Ct
Hammersmith W14 ... 112 D3
15 New Barnet EN5 ... 13 D6
2 Richmond TW10 ... 175 D6
Coleridge Gdns NW6 ... 70 A1
Coleridge Ho
Pimlico SW1 ... 259 B1
Walworth SE17 ... 262 B2
Wembley HA9 ... 65 D6
Coleridge Prim Sch N8 ... 49 D2
Coleridge Rd
Ashford TW15 ... 170 B6
Crouch End N8 ... 49 D3
Croydon CR0 ... 206 C2
Finsbury Pk N4, N7 ... 72 C6
North Finchley N12 ... 30 A5
Walthamstow E17 ... 53 B5
Coleridge Sq
Chelsea SW10 ... 266 A4
Ealing W13 ... 87 A1
Coleridge Way
Borehamwood WD6 ... 10 C6
Hayes UB4 ... 84 A1
West Drayton UB7 ... 104 B2
Coleridge Wlk NW11 ... 47 C5
Colerne Ct NW4 ... 29 A1
Colesburg Rd BR3 ... 185 B1
Coles Cres HA2 ... 63 D6
Coles Ct SW11 ... 266 D1
Coles Gn WD23 ... 8 A3
Coles Green Ct NW2 ... 68 A6
Coles Green Rd NW2 ... 68 B6
Coleshill Flats SW1 ... 258 B3
Coleshill Rd TW11 ... 174 C4
Cole St SE1 ... 117 A4 252 B1
Colestown St 4 SW11 ... 136 C3
Coleswood N20 ... 14 C3
Colesworth Ho 1 HA8 ... 27 A1
Colet Cl N13 ... 32 D4
Colet Gdns W14 ... 112 D2
Colet Ho SE17 ... 261 D1
Colette Ct 5 SE16 ... 118 D4
Coley St WC1 ... 94 B3 240 D5
Colfe & Hatchcliffe's Glebe SE13 ... 163 D6
Colfe Rd SE23 ... 163 A3
Colfe's Sch SE12 ... 165 A5
Colgate Ct EN5 ... 13 A6
Colgate Ho SE13 ... 141 D3
Colgate Pl 10 EN3 ... 7 C6
Colham Ave UB7 ... 104 A5
COLHAM GREEN ... 82 C2
Colham Green Rd UB8 ... 82 C2
Colham Manor Prim Sch UB8 ... 82 C1
Colham Rd UB8 ... 82 B3
Colina Mews N8, N15 ... 50 D5
Colina Rd N8, N15 ... 50 D4
Colin Blanchard Ho SE4 ... 141 C3
Colin Cl Colindale NW9 ... 45 C5
Coney Hall BR4 ... 224 D5
Croydon CR0 ... 223 B5
Colin Cres NW9 ... 45 D5
Colin Ct
Forest Hill SE6 ... 163 B4
Hendon NW9 ... 45 D5
Streatham SW16 ... 159 D2
COLINDALE ... 45 C6
Colindale Ave NW9 ... 45 C6
Colindale Bsns Ctr NW9 ... 45 C6
Colindale Bsns Pk NW9 ... 45 A6
Colindale Prim Sch NW9 ... 45 D5
Colindale Sta NW9 ... 45 C6
Colindeep Gdns NW4 ... 46 A5
Colindeep La NW9, NW4 ... 45 D5
Colin Dr NW9 ... 45 D4
Colinette Rd SW15 ... 134 C1
Colin Gdns NW9 ... 45 D5
Colin Par NW9 ... 45 C5
Colin Park Rd NW9 ... 45 C5
Colin Pond Ct RM6 ... 58 D6
Colin Rd NW10 ... 68 A2
Colinsdale N1 ... 234 C5
Colinton Rd IG3 ... 80 B6
Colin Winter Ho 45 E1 ... 96 C3
Coliseum Apartments N8 ... 50 D4
Coliston Pas SW18 ... 157 C4
Coliston Rd SW18 ... 157 C4
Collamore Ave SW18 ... 158 C3
Collapit Cl HA1 ... 41 D3
Collard Pl NW1 ... 71 B1
Collard's Almshouses 1 E17 ... 54 A4
Collcutt Lo SW4 ... 138 A1
Collection Point N8 ... 50 A3
College App SE10 ... 142 A6
College Ave HA3 ... 24 C2
College Cl
Edmonton N18 ... 33 D5
Hackney E5 ... 74 C3
Harrow HA3 ... 24 C3
Twickenham TW2 ... 152 B3
College Cres NW3 ... 70 B2
College Cross N1 ... 72 C1
College Ct
Chelsea SW3 ... 114 D1 257 D1
Croydon CR0 ... 222 A6
Ealing W5 ... 110 A6
Enfield EN3 ... 18 C6
3 Hammersmith W6 ... 112 C1
Hampstead NW3 ... 70 B2
College Dr Ruislip HA4 ... 40 A2
Thames Ditton KT7 ... 196 C2
College Fields Bsns Ctr SW19 ... 180 B2
College Gdns
Chingford E4 ... 20 A3
Dulwich SE21 ... 161 C3
Edmonton N18 ... 34 A5
Enfield EN2 ... 5 B4
New Malden KT3 ... 199 D4
Redbridge IG4 ... 56 A4
Upper Tooting SW17 ... 158 C2
College Gn SE19 ... 183 C3
College Gr NW1 ... 232 C6
College Green Ct SW9 ... 138 D2
College Hill EC4 ... 252 B6
College Hill Rd HA3 ... 24 C3
College La NW5 ... 71 B4
College Mews 5 SW18 ... 157 D6
College of North West London HA9 ... 65 C5
COLLEGE PARK ... 90 B4
College Park Cl SE13 ... 142 B1
College Park Rd N17 ... 33 D4
College Park Sch 20 W2 ... 91 D1
College Pl
Camden Town NW1 ... 93 C6 232 B5
Chelsea SW10 ... 266 A4
Walthamstow E17 ... 54 C5
College Pt 3 E15 ... 76 D2
College Rd
Dulwich SE19, SE21 ... 161 C2
Ealing W13 ... 87 B1
Enfield EN2 ... 5 B3
Harrow HA1 ... 42 C3
Harrow Weald HA3 ... 24 C2
Hounslow TW7 ... 130 D4
Kensal Green NW10 ... 90 C5
Mitcham SW19 ... 180 B4
Plaistow BR1 ... 187 A3
South Croydon CR0 ... 221 B6
Southgate N21 ... 16 C2
Tottenham N17 ... 33 D4
Walthamstow E17 ... 54 A4
Wembley HA9 ... 43 D1
College Rdbt 1 KT1 ... 198 A6
College St EC4 ... 117 A6 252 B6
College Terr Bow E3 ... 97 B4
Church End N3 ... 29 B1
College View SE9 ... 165 D3

College Way
Ashford TW15 .... 170 B6
Hayes UB3 .... 106 A6
College Wlk 10 KT1 .. 198 A6
Collent Ho 12 E9 ...... 74 C2
Collent St E9 .... 74 C2
Collerston Ho SE10 . 120 D1
Colless Rd N15 .... 51 D4
Collette Ct SE25 ..... 205 C4
Collette Ho N16 .... 51 D1
Collett Ho SE13 ..... 141 D2
Collett Rd SE16 ...... 118 A3
Collett Way UB2 .... 107 D4
Colley Ho 12 N7 .... 71 D3
Collier Cl
Newham E16 .... 122 D6
West Ewell KT19 ..... 214 D2
Collier Dr HA8 .... 26 C1
Colliers Shaw BR2 . 225 D3
Collier St N1 .. 94 B5 233 C3
Colliers Water La
CR7 .... 204 C4
Colliers Wood SW19 . 180 B3
COLLIER'S WOOD ... 180 C4
Collier's Wood Sta
SW19 .... 180 B3
Collindale Ave
Erith DA8 .... 147 D6
Sidcup DA15 .... 168 A3
Collingbourne Rd
W12 .... 112 B5
Collingham Gdns
SW5 ...... 113 D2 255 D3
Collingham Pl
SW5 ...... 113 D2 255 D4
Collingham Rd
SW5 ...... 113 D2 255 D3
Collingham Tutors Coll
SW5 .... 113 D2 255 D3
Collings Cl N22 .... 32 B4
Collington Ho 2
SE7 .... 143 B6
Collington St SE10 ... 120 B1
Collingtree Rd SE26 .. 184 C6
Collingwood Ave
London N10 .... 49 A5
Tolworth KT5 .... 199 A1
Collingwood Cl
2 Penge SE20 .... 184 B2
Twickenham TW2,
TW4 .... 151 C4
Collingwood Ct
London NW4 .... 46 C4
New Barnet EN5 .... 13 D6
Sutton SM1 .... 217 C4
Collingwood Ho
27 Bethnal Green E1 ... 96 B3
Marylebone W1 .... 239 A4
Collingwood Rd
Hillingdon UB8 .... 82 D3
Mitcham CR4 .... 202 C6
South Tottenham N15 ... 51 C5
Sutton SM1 .... 217 C4
Collingwood Sch 7
SM6 .... 219 B3
Collingwood St E1 ..... 96 B3
Collins Ave HA7 .... 26 A1
Collins Ct Dalston E8 ... 74 A2
1 Loughton IG10 ...... 21 D6
Collins Dr HA4 .... 62 C6
Collins Ho
8 Barking IG11 .... 78 D1
6 Cubitt Town SE10 . 120 D1
4 Poplar E14 ...... 120 A6
Collinson Ct
Borough The SE1 .... 252 A1
Edgware HA8 .... 26 B6
Collinson Ho 14
SE15 .... 140 A5
Collinson St SE1 .... 252 A1
Collinson Wlk SE1 .. 252 A1
Collins Rd N5, N16 ..... 73 A4
Collins Sq SE3 ...... 142 D3
Collins St SE3 .... 142 C3
Collins Yd N1 .... 234 C5
Collinwood Ave EN3 .... 6 C2
Collinwood Gdns IG5 .. 56 C5
Collison Pl N16 .... 51 C1
Collis Prim Sch
TW11 .... 175 B4
Coll of Arms★
EC4 .... 117 A6 252 A6
Coll of Central London
The EC2 .... 243 A6
Coll of Law The
(Bloomsbury)
EC1 .... 93 D2 239 C4
Coll of Law The
(Moorgate)
EC1 .... 95 B3 242 C5
Coll of North East
London The N15 ..... 51 D5
Coll of NW London 15
NW6 .... 91 C6
Coll of NW London
(Willesden Centre)
NW10 .... 67 D3
Coll of Optometrists The
SW1 .... 250 A4
Coll Sharp Ct 42 E2 ... 95 D4
Coll's Rd SE15 .... 140 C4
Collyer Ave CR0 .... 220 A4
Collyer Pl SE15 .... 140 A4
Collyer Rd CR0 .... 220 A4
Colman Ct London N12 30 A4
Stanmore HA7 .... 25 B4
Colman Rd E16 .... 99 C2
Colmans Wharf 5
E14 .... 97 D2
Colmar Cl 3 E1 .... 96 D3
Colmer Pl HA3 .... 24 B3
Colmer Rd SW16 ..... 182 A3
Colmore Ct NW4 .... 46 A6
Colmore Mews SE15 . 140 B4
Colmore Rd EN3 .... 6 C1
Colnbrook Ct SW17 .. 180 B6
Colnbrook St SE1 .... 261 C6
Colne Ct Ealing W7 ..... 86 B1
West Ewell KT19 ..... 215 A4
Colne Ho Barking IG11 . 78 D2
Paddington NW8 .... 236 D5
Colne Rd
Clapton Pk E5 .... 75 A4
Southgate N21 .... 17 B4
Twickenham TW1,
TW2 .... 152 C3
Colne St E13 .... 99 A4
COLNEY HATCH 30 C4
Colney Hatch N10 ...... 31 A3
Colney Hatch La N10 ... 31 A3
Cologne Rd SW11 ..... 136 B1
Coloma Convent Girl's
Sch CR0 .... 222 D5
Colombo Rd IG1 .... 57 A2
Colombo St SE1 .... 251 C3
Colomb St SE10 .... 120 C1
Colonades The 4
SE5 .... 139 B4
Colonels Wlk EN2 .... 4 D2
Colonial Ave TW2 .... 152 A5
Colonial Dr W4 .... 111 A2
Colonial Rd TW14 ..... 149 C4
Colonnade WC1 ..... 240 B5
Colonnade Ho SE3 .. 142 D3
Colonnades The
Croydon CR0 .... 220 C2
6 Hackney E8 .... 74 B2
Colonnade The 12
SE8 .... 119 B2
Colonnade Wlk Sh Ctr
SW1 .... 258 D4
Colorado Bldg 9
SE13 .... 141 D4
Colosseum Ct N3 ...... 29 B1
Colosseum Ret Pk EN1 6 A1
Colosseum Terr
NW1 .... 238 D6
Colour Ho SE1 ...... 253 B1
Colroy Ct NW4 .... 47 A4
Colson Rd CR0 .... 221 C6
Colson Way SW16 ..... 181 C6
Colstead Ho 22 E1 ..... 96 B1
Colsterworth Rd N15 .. 51 D5
Colston Ave SM1,
SM5 .... 218 C4
Colston Ct SM5 ...... 218 D4
Colston Rd
Mortlake SW14 ..... 133 A1
Upton E7 .... 77 D2
Colthurst Cres N4 ..... 73 A6
Colthurst Dr N9 .... 18 B1
Coltman Ho SE10 ..... 142 A6
Coltman St E14 .... 97 A2
Colt Mews 5 EN3 .... 7 C6
Coltness Cres SE2 .... 124 B1
Colton Gdns N17 .... 51 A6
Colton Rd HA1 .... 42 C4
Coltsfoot Dr UB7 .... 82 A1
Coltswood Ct N14 .... 15 D3
Colts Yd E11 .... 54 D2
Columba Ho SE14 ..... 141 B4
Columbas Dr NW3 .... 48 B1
Columbia Ave
Edgware HA8 .... 26 D2
New Malden KT4 ..... 199 D2
Ruislip HA4 .... 40 B1
Columbia Ct
Edgware HA8 .... 26 D2
New Malden KT3 .... 199 D2
Columbia Ho 18 E3 ... 97 C4
Columbia Point 7
SE16 .... 118 C3
Columbia Prim Sch 50
E2 .... 95 D4
Columbia Rd
9 Hackney E2 .... 96 A5
Newham E13 .... 98 D3
Shoreditch E2 .... 95 D4
Columbia Road Flower
Mkt★ E2 .... 95 D4
Columbine Ave
Croydon CR2 .... 220 D1
Newham E6 .... 100 A2
Columbus Gdns HA6 ... 22 A2
Colveiw Ct SE9 ..... 165 D3
Colverson Ho 14 E1 .... 96 C2
Colvestone Cres E8 ... 73 D3
Colvestone Prim Sch
E8 .... 73 D3
Colville Gdns W11 .... 91 B1
Colville Ho
32 Bethnal Green E2 ... 96 C5
Notting Hill W11 .... 91 B1
Colville Mews W11 ..... 91 B1
Colville Pl W1 ...... 239 B3
Colville Prim Sch 5
W11 .... 91 B1
Colville Rd
Edmonton N9 .... 18 B3
Higham Hill E17 .... 35 A1
Leyton E11 .... 76 A5
Notting Hill W11 .... 91 B1
South Acton W3 ...... 110 D3
Colville Sq W11 .... 91 B1
Colville Terr W11 ...... 91 B1
Colvin Cl SE26 .... 184 C5
Colvin Gdns
Chingford E4 .... 20 A1
Wanstead E11 .... 55 B5
Colvin Rd
Thornton Heath
CR7 .... 204 C4
Upton Pk E6 .... 78 A1
Colwall Gdns IG8 .... 37 A5
Colwall Ho 18 SW9 .... 138 B3
Colwell Rd SE22 .... 161 D6
Colwick Cl N6 .... 49 D2
Colwith Rd W6 .... 134 C6
Colwood Gdns
SW19 .... 180 B3
Colworth Gr SE17 ... 262 B3
Colworth Rd
Croydon CR0 .... 206 A1
Leytonstone E11 ...... 54 C2
Colwyn Ave UB6 .... 86 D5
Colwyn Cl SW16 ..... 181 C5
Colwyn Cres TW3 .... 130 A4
Colwyn Gn NW9 ...... 45 C3
Colwyn Ho SE1 ..... 261 A5
Colwyn Rd NW2 .... 68 B5
Colyer Cl SE9 .... 166 D2
Colyer Ho SE2 ...... 124 D1
Colyton Cl
Erith DA16 .... 146 D4
Wembley HA0 .... 65 C2
Colyton La 14 SW16 .. 182 C5
Colyton Rd SE22 .... 162 B6
Colyton Way N18 ..... 34 A5
Combe Ave SE3 ...... 142 D5
Combedale Rd SE10 . 121 A1
Combe Ho
Mortlake SW14 ..... 133 A3
20 Paddington W2 ..... 91 C2
Combe Lane Sta
CR0 .... 222 C3
Combemartin Rd
SW18 .... 157 A3
Combe Mews 4
SE3 .... 142 D5
Comber Cl NW2 ...... 68 B6
Comber Gr SE5 .... 139 A5
Comber Grove Prim Sch
34 SE5 .... 139 A5
Comber Ho SE5 ...... 139 A5
Combermere Rd
London SW9 .... 138 B2
Morden SM4 .... 201 D4
Comberton 10 KT1 ... 176 C1
Comberton Rd E5 ..... 74 B6
Combeside SE18 .... 145 D5
Combes Rd RM9 .... 81 B1
Combe The NW1 ..... 231 D1
Combwell Cres SE2 .. 124 A3
Com Coll Hackney The
17 E8 .... 96 B6
Comely Bank Rd E17 .. 54 A4
Comeragh Mews
W14 .... 254 B1
Comeragh Rd
W14 .... 113 A1 254 B1
Comer Cres UB2 ...... 108 A4
Comerford Rd SE4 ... 141 B1
Comer Ho 10 EN5 ...... 2 A1
Comet Cl E12 .... 77 D4
Comet Pl SE8 .... 141 C5
Comet St SE8 .... 141 C5
Comfort St 6 SE15 .. 139 C6
Comins Ho SW4 ..... 159 C6
Commerce Est E18 ... 37 C1
Commerce Pk CR0 ... 220 B6
Commerce Rd
Brentford TW8 .... 131 C5
Wood Green N22 ...... 32 B2
Commerce Way CR0 . 220 B6
Commercial Rd
Edmonton N18 .... 33 C4
Stepney E1 .... 96 C1
Whitechapel E1 .... 96 A1
Commercial St
E1 .... 95 D2 243 C4
Commercial Way
Peckham SE15 .... 140 A5
Wembley NW10 .... 88 D5
Commerell Pl SE10 . 120 D1
Commerell St SE10 .. 120 C1
Commodity Quay E1 253 D5
Commodore Ct SE8 . 141 C4
Commodore Ho 7
E14 .... 120 A6
Commodore St E1 .... 97 A3
Commondale SW15 .. 134 C2
Common La KT10 ... 213 A1
Common Rd
Barnes SW13 .... 134 A2
Claygate KT10 ...... 213 A1
Stanmore HA7 .... 8 C1
Commonside BR2 ... 225 C4
Commonside Ct
SW16 .... 182 A4
Commonside E CR4 .. 203 B6
Commonside W CR4 . 203 A6
Common The
Ealing W5 .... 110 A5
Southall UB2 ...... 106 D2
Stanmore HA7 .... 8 D2
1 Stratford E15 .... 76 D2
Common View
SW15 .... 134 C2
Commonwealth Ave
Hayes UB3 .... 83 B1
25 Shepherd's Bush
W12 .... 112 B6
21 Shepherd's Bush
W12 .... 112 B6
Commonwealth Ho
WC1 .... 240 B2
Commonwealth Rd
N17 .... 34 A3
Commonwealth Way
SE2 .... 124 C1
Community Cl
Cranford TW5 .... 128 B4
Uxbridge UB10 .... 61 A5
Community La N7 .... 71 D3
Community Rd
Greenford UB6 .... 86 A6
Stratford New Town
E15 .... 76 B3
Comodore Ho SW18 . 136 A1
Como Rd SE23 .... 163 A2
Compania Bldg 12
E1 .... 118 D6
Compass Cl
Edgware HA8 .... 26 B6
Littleton TW15 .... 171 A3
Compass Ct SE1 .... 253 C3
Compass Hill TW10 . 153 D5
Compass Ho
Bayswater W2 .... 91 D1
London SE8 .... 141 D3
Compass Point 10
E14 .... 119 C6
Compayne Gdns
NW6 .... 69 D1
Compton Ave
Islington N1 .... 72 D2
London N6 .... 48 C2
Newham E6 .... 99 D5
Wembley HA0 .... 65 C4
Compton Cl
5 Burnt Oak HA8 ..... 27 A3
Camberwell SE15 .... 139 D5
Cricklewood NW11 .... 68 D5
Ealing W13 .... 87 A1
Esher KT10 .... 212 B3
Regent's Pk NW1 .... 231 D1
Compton Cres
Chessington KT9 .... 214 A2
Chiswick W4 .... 133 A6
Northolt UB5 .... 84 D6
Tottenham N17 .... 33 A3
Compton Ct
London N12 .... 30 A2
Sutton SM1 .... 218 A4
9 West Norwood
SE19 .... 183 C5
Compton Ho SW11 ... 267 A2
Compton Lo N21 .... 16 D3
Compton Pas EC1 ... 241 D6
Compton Pl
Bloomsbury WC1 ..... 240 A6
South Oxhey WD19 .... 23 A6
Compton Rd
Croydon CR0 .... 206 B1
Hayes UB3 .... 105 D6
Islington N1 .... 72 D2
Kensal Green NW10 ... 90 D4
Southgate N21 .... 16 D3
Wimbledon SW19 ..... 179 B4
Compton Rise HA5 .... 41 B4
Compton Sch The
N12 .... 30 C4
Compton St
EC1 .... 94 D3 241 D6
Compton Terr
Islington N1 .... 72 D2
Southgate N21 .... 16 C3
Comreddy Cl EN2 ..... 4 D4
Comus Ho SE17 ..... 263 A3
Comus Pl
SE17 .... 117 C2 263 A3
Comyn Rd SW11 ..... 136 C1
Comyns Cl E16 .... 98 D2
Comyns Rd RM9 .... 81 C1
Comyns The WD23 ..... 8 A3
Conal Ct SW16 ...... 181 D5
Conant Ho SE11 ..... 138 D6
Conant Mews 1 E1 .. 118 A6
Concanon Rd SW2,
SW4 .... 138 B1
Concert Hall App
SE1 .... 116 B5 250 D3
Concord Bsns Ctr
W3 .... 88 D2
Concord Cl UB5 .... 85 A4
Concord Ct KT1 ...... 198 B6
Concorde Cl
Hounslow TW3 ...... 129 D3
Uxbridge UB10 .... 82 A5
Concorde Dr E6 ...... 100 B2
Concorde Way SE16 . 118 D2
Concord Ho
Kingston u T KT3 .... 199 C6
5 Tottenham N17 ..... 33 D3
Concordia Wharf 10
E14 .... 120 A5
Concord Rd Acton W3 .. 88 D3
Enfield EN3 .... 18 C6
Concord Terr HA2 ..... 63 D6
Concourse The
32 Edgware NW9 ..... 27 D2
7 Edmonton N9 ...... 18 A2
Condell Rd
SW8 .... 137 C4 269 B1
Conder St E14 .... 97 A1
Condor Path UB5 ..... 85 C5
Condover Cres SE18 144 D5
Condray Pl SW11 ... 267 A3
Conduit Ct WC2 .... 250 A6
Conduit Ho SE10 ..... 142 B4
Conduit La
London N18 .... 34 C5
South Croydon CR0 .. 222 A3
Conduit Mews
W2 .... 92 B1 236 C1
Conduit Pas W2 .... 236 C1

Conduit Pl W2 236 C1
Conduit Rd SE18 122 D1
Conduit St
W1 115 C6 249 A6
Conduit Way NW10 67 A1
Conewood St N5 72 D5
Coney Acre SE21 161 A3
Coney Burrows E4 20 C2
Coney Gr UB8 82 C4
Coneygrove Path
UB5 63 A2
CONEY HALL 224 D5
Coney Hall Par BR4 224 C5
Coney Hall Rdbt
BR4 224 C5
Coney Hill Rd BR4 224 D6
Coney Way SW8 270 D5
Conference Cl 3 E4 20 A2
Conference Ho UB8 83 A1
Conference Rd SE2 124 C2
Congers Ho SE8 141 C5
Congleton Gr SE18 123 A1
Congo Dr N9 18 C1
Congo Rd SE18 123 B1
Congress Ho WC1 239 D2
Congress Rd SE2 124 C2
Congreve Ho 10 N16 73 C3
Congreve Rd SE9 144 B2
Congreve St
SE17 117 C2 263 A3
Congreve Wlk 6 E16 99 D2
Conical Cnr EN2 5 A3
Conifer Cl BR6 227 B4
Conifer Ct
Ashford TW15 170 B5
Hendon NW4 28 C1
Ilford IG1 78 D2
23 Putney SW19 156 D3
Sutton SM2 218 B2
Conifer Gdns
Enfield EN1 17 C5
Streatham SW16 160 B1
Sutton SM1 217 D6
Conifer Ho SE4 141 B1
Conifers Cl TW11 175 C3
Conifer Way
Hayes UB3 106 A6
Wembley HA0 65 C5
Coniger Rd SW6 135 C3
Coningham Ct SW10 266 B4
Coningham Mews
W12 112 A5
Coningham Rd W12 112 B4
Coningsby Ave NW9 27 C1
Coningsby Cotts
W5 109 D4
Coningsby Ct 4
CR4 181 A1
Coningsby Gdns E4 35 D4
Coningsby Rd
Ealing W5 109 D4
Harringay N4 50 D2
Conington Rd SE13 142 A3
Conisbee Ct 3 N14 15 C6
Conisborough Cres
SE6 164 A1
Conisbrough NW1 232 A5
Coniscliffe Cl BR7 188 C2
Coniscliffe Rd N13 17 A1
Coniston NW1 232 A2
Coniston Ave
Barking IG11 79 C1
Ealing UB6 87 B4
Falconwood DA16 145 C2
Coniston Cl
Barking IG11 79 C1
Barnes SW13 133 D5
Chiswick W4 133 A5
West Barnes SM4 200 D3
Whetstone N20 14 A1
Coniston Ct
Beckenham BR3 186 A2
Chessington KT9 214 A5
Edgware HA8 26 B5
4 Finchley NW7 29 A3
Marylebone W2 237 B1
Penge SE26 184 B4
6 Rotherhithe SE16 118 D4
3 Wallington SM6 219 B4
Conistone Way N7 72 A1
Coniston Gdns
Edmonton N9 18 C3
Kingsbury NW9 45 B4
Pinner HA5 40 A5
Redbridge IG4 56 A5
Sutton SM2 218 B2

Coniston Gdns *continued*
Wembley HA9 43 C1
Coniston Ho
14 Bow E3 97 B4
18 Camberwell SE5 139 A5
Coniston Rd
Catford BR1 186 C4
Croydon CR0 206 A2
Muswell Hill N10 31 B1
Tottenham N17 34 A4
Twickenham TW2 151 D5
Coniston Way KT9 214 A5
Coniston Wlk E9 74 C3
Conlan St W10 91 A3
Conley Rd NW10 67 C2
Conley St SE10 120 C1
Connaught Ave
Ashford TW15 170 A6
Barnet EN4 14 D3
Chingford E4 20 B4
Enfield EN1 5 C3
Hounslow TW4 129 A1
Mortlake SW14 133 A1
Connaught Bridge
E16 121 D6
Connaught Bsns Ctr
London NW9 45 D4
Mitcham CR4 202 D4
Wallington CR0 220 B2
Connaught Cl
Carshalton SM1 218 B6
Enfield EN1 5 C3
Hillingdon UB8 83 A3
Lea Bridge E10 75 A6
Marylebone W2 237 B1
Connaught Ct
1 Chingford E4 20 C4
9 Walthamstow E17 53 D5
Connaught Day Hospl
E11 54 C3
Connaught Dr NW11 47 C5
Connaught Gdns
Cranley Gdns N10 49 B4
Edmonton N13 32 D6
Morden SM4 202 A5
Connaught Grange
N13 32 D6
Connaught Ho
College Pk NW10 90 B4
London N10 49 B4
Mayfair W1 248 C5
Connaught House Sch
W2 92 C1 237 B1
Connaught Hts UB10 83 A3
Connaught La IG1 79 B6
Connaught Lo N4 50 C2
Connaught Mans
Battersea SW11 267 B1
3 Brixton SW9 138 C1
15 Canonbury N16 73 B4
Fulham SW6 264 A2
Connaught Mews
Ilford IG1 79 B6
Woolwich SE18 122 C1
Connaught Pl W2 237 C1
Connaught Rd
Barnet EN5 12 D5
Carshalton SM1 218 B6
Chingford E4 20 C3
Ealing W13 109 B6
Finsbury Pk N4 50 C2
Harlesden NW10 89 C5
Harrow HA3 24 D2
Ilford IG1 79 B6
Leytonstone E11 54 B1
Newham E16 121 D5
New Malden KT3 199 C5
5 Richmond TW10 154 B6
Teddington TW11,
TW12 174 B5
Walthamstow E17 53 C4
Woolwich SE18 122 D1
Connaught Sch for Girls
2 E11 54 C1
Connaught Sch for Girls
(Annexe) 13 E11 76 C6
Connaught Sq
W2 92 D1 237 C1
Connaught St
W2 92 C1 237 B1
Connaught Way N13 32 D6
Connaught Works E3 97 A6
Connections Ho N2 30 B2
Connell Cres W5 88 B3
Connell Ct 6 SE14 140 D6
Connell Ho 6 SM6 219 C2

Connemara Cl WD6 11 B5
Conniffe Ct SE9 166 D6
Connington 5 KT1 176 C1
Connington Cres E4 20 B1
Connolly Ho SW19 180 A4
Connoly Ct NW2 68 B5
Connop Rd EN3 6 D5
Connor Cl E11 54 C2
Connor Ct SW11 268 C1
Connor Rd RM9 81 B4
Connor St E9 96 D6
Conolly Rd W7 108 C5
Conrad Dr KT4 200 D1
Conrad Ho
8 Limehouse SE16 119 A6
South Lambeth SW8 270 A4
12 Stoke Newington
N16 73 C3
Conrad Twr W3 110 D3
Conroy Ct 6 DA14 190 A6
Conservatory Ct
SE19 183 C3
Consfield Ave KT3 200 A4
Consort Ho
Bayswater W2 245 D5
Edgware NW7 27 D5
Consort Lo NW8 230 C5
Consort Mews TW7 152 B6
Consort Rd SE15 140 B3
Cons St SE1 251 B2
Constable Ave E16 121 B5
Constable Cl
12 Friern Barnet N11 30 D5
Hampstead Garden Suburb
NW11 47 D3
Hayes UB4 83 A5
Constable Cres N15 52 A4
Constable Ct 11
SE16 118 B1
Constable Gdns
Edgware HA8 26 C1
Isleworth TW7 152 B6
Constable Ho
Enfield EN1 18 A6
25 Millwall E14 119 C4
13 Northolt UB5 84 D5
Primrose Hill NW3 70 D1
Constable Mews
Bromley BR1 187 B1
Dagenham RM8 80 B4
Constable Wlk SE21 161 C1
Constance Cres BR2 208 D1
Constance Ct N10 31 B3
Constance Rd
Enfield EN1 17 C5
Sutton SM1 218 A4
Thornton Heath CR0 204 D2
Twickenham TW2 151 D4
Constance St E16 122 A5
Constant Ho 20 E14 119 D6
Constantine Ho
SW2 160 D3
Constantine Pl UB10 82 B6
Constantine Rd NW3 70 C4
Constitution Hill
W1 115 B4 248 D2
Constitution Rise
SE18 144 C4
Consul Ho 5 E3 97 C3
Content St
SE17 117 B2 262 C3
Contessa Cl BR6 227 C3
Control Tower Rd
TW6 126 D2
Convair Wlk 11 UB5 84 D4
Convent Cl BR3 186 A3
Convent Gdns
Ealing W5 109 C2
Notting Hill W11 91 B1
Convent Hill SE19 183 A4
Convent Lo TW15 170 D5
Convent of Jesus & Mary
Language Coll
NW10 89 D6
Convent of Jesus & Mary
RC Inf Sch 5 NW2 68 C2
Convent Rd TW15 170 D5
Convent Way UB2 106 D2
Conway Cl HA7 25 A4
Conway Cres
Dagenham RM6 58 C3
Greenford UB6 86 C5
Conway Dr
Ashford TW15 171 A4
Hayes UB3 105 A3
Sutton SM2 217 D2

Conway Gdns
Enfield EN2 5 C5
Mitcham CR4 204 A5
Wembley HA9 43 C2
Conway Gr W3 89 B2
Conway Ho
Chelsea SW3 257 D1
5 Millwall E14 119 D2
6 Streatham SW2 160 A3
Conway Mews W1 239 A5
Conway Prim Sch 5
SE18 123 C2
Conway Rd
Dollis Hill NW2 68 C6
Feltham TW13 172 D5
Harlington TW6 126 D2
Harringay N15 51 A4
Palmers Green N14 16 A1
Plumstead SE18 123 C2
Twickenham TW4 151 C4
Wimbledon SW20 178 C2
Conway St W1 93 C3 239 A5
Conway Wlk TW12 173 B4
Conybeare NW3 70 C1
Conyers Cl IG8 36 C4
Conyer's Rd SW16 181 D5
Conyer St 21 E3 97 A5
Cooden Cl BR1 187 B3
Cookes Cl E11 76 D6
Cookes La SM3 217 A2
Cooke St 2 IG11 101 A6
Cookham Cl UB2 107 D4
Cookham Cres SE16 118 D4
Cookham Dene Cl
BR7 189 B2
Cookham Ho E2 243 C6
Cookham Rd BR8,
DA14 191 C2
Cookhill Rd SE2 124 B3
Cooks Ferry N18 34 D5
Cook's Hole Rd EN2 5 A5
Cookson Gr DA8 147 D5
Cook's Rd
Camberwell SE17 138 D6
Stratford Marsh E15 97 D5
Coolfin Rd E16 99 B1
Coolgardie Ave E4 36 B5
Coolgardie Rd
TW15 171 A5
Coolhurst Rd N8 49 D3
Cool Oak La NW9 45 D2
Coomassie Rd W9 91 B3
COOMBE 177 B3
Coombe Ave CR0 221 C4
Coombe Bank KT2,
KT3 177 C2
Coombe Boys' Sch
KT3 200 A4
Coombe Cl
Edgware HA8 26 B1
Hounslow TW3 129 C1
Coombe Cnr N21 16 D3
Coombe Cres TW12 173 A3
Coombe Ct 2 BR3 185 B2
Coombe Dr HA4 40 B1
Coombe End KT2 177 B3
Coombefield Cl KT3 199 C4
Coombe Gdns
New Malden KT3 199 D5
Wimbledon SW20 178 A2
Coombe Girls Sch
KT3 177 B1
Coombe Hill Glade
KT2 177 C3
Coombe Hill Inf Sch
KT2 177 B2
Coombe Hill Jun Sch
KT2 177 B2
Coombe Hill Rd KT2 177 C3
Coombe Ho 13 N7 71 D3
Coombe House Chase
KT3 177 B2
Coombehurst Cl EN4 2 D3
Coombehurst (Kingston
University) KT2 177 A5
Coombe La CR0 222 B3
Coombe Lane Flyover
SW20 177 D2
Coombe La W KT2 177 B2
Coombe Lea BR1 210 A6
Coombe Lo SE7 143 C6
Coombe Neville KT2 177 B3
Coombe Pk KT2 177 B5
Coombe Pl KT2 177 A5
Coombe Rd
Bushey WD23 8 B4

Coombe Rd *continued*
Chiswick W4 111 C1
Ealing W13 109 B3
Forest Hill SE26 184 B6
Hampton TW12 173 B4
New Malden KT3 199 C6
Norbiton KT2 176 C2
South Croydon CR0,
CR2 221 C4
Willesden NW10 67 B5
Wood Green N22 32 C2
Coomber Ho SW6 135 D2
Coombe Ridings
KT2 177 A5
Coombe Rise KT2 177 A2
Coomber Way CR0 203 D3
Coombes Rd RM9 103 B6
Coombe Wlk SM1 217 D5
Coombewood Dr
RM6 59 B3
Coombe Wood Rd
KT2 177 A5
Coombs St N1 234 D3
Coomer Mews SW6 264 D5
Coomer Pl
SW6 135 B6 264 D5
Cooms Wlk HA8 27 A2
Cooperage Cl 5 N17 33 D4
Cooperage The SE1 253 C3
Cooper Ave E17 35 A2
Cooper Cl SE1 251 B1
Cooper Cres SM5 218 D5
Cooper Ct SE18 144 D6
Cooper Ho
Hounslow TW4 129 B2
Paddington NW8 236 C5
Upper Tooting SW17 180 B6
7 West Norwood
SW27 182 D5
Cooper Rd
Croydon CR0, CR9 220 D4
Hendon NW4 46 D3
Willesden NW10 68 A3
Coopersale Cl 3 IG8 37 C3
Coopersale Rd E9 74 D3
Coopers Cl
Bethnal Green E1 96 C3
Dagenham RM10 81 D2
Coopers Ct
9 Acton W3 111 A5
4 Friern Barnet N20 14 D1
Isleworth TW7 130 D3
Tower Hamlets E3 97 B3
Coopers La
Grove Pk SE12 165 B2
London E10 54 A1
Somers Town NW1 232 D3
Cooper's Lane Prim Sch
SE12 165 B2
Coopers Lo SE1 253 C2
Coopers Mews BR3 185 C1
Cooper's Rd
SE1 117 D1 263 D2
Cooper's Row
EC3 117 D6 253 C6
Cooper St 10 E16 98 D2
Coopers Tech Sch
BR7 189 A2
Coopers Yd N1 72 D1
Cooper's Yd SE19 183 C4
Coote Gdns RM8 81 B5
Coote Rd
Dagenham RM8 81 B5
Erith DA7 147 B4
Cope Ho EC1 235 B1
Copeland Dr E14 119 C2
Copeland Ho
Lambeth SE11 260 D5
Upper Tooting SW17 180 B6
Copeland Rd
London SE15 140 B3
Walthamstow E17 53 D3
Copelands BR3 185 B3
Copeman Cl SE26 184 C5
Copenhagen Gdns
W4 111 B4
Copenhagen Ho N1 234 A5
Copenhagen Pl E14 97 B1
Copenhagen Prim Sch
N1 94 B6 233 C5
Copenhagen St
N1 94 B6 233 C5
Cope Pl W8 113 C3 255 A5

Copers Cope Rd BR3 185 B3
Cope St SE16 118 D2
Copeswood Ct UB7 126 C5
Copford Wlk N1 235 A6
Copgate Path SW16 182 C4
Copinger Wlk HA8 26 D2
Copland Ave HA0 65 D3
Copland Cl HA0 65 C3
Copland Ho UB1 107 B4
Copland Mews [8] HA0 66 A2
Copland Rd HA0 66 A2
Copland Specialist Science Com Coll HA9 66 B3
Copleston Rd SE15 139 D2
Copley Cl
[15] Camberwell SE17 138 D6
Ealing W7 86 D2
Copley Dene BR1 187 D2
Copley Pk SW16 182 B4
Copley Rd HA7 25 C5
Copley St E1 96 D2
Coppard Gdns KT9 213 C2
Coppedhall [2] SE21 161 B2
Coppelia Rd SE3 142 D1
Coppen Rd RM8 59 B2
Copperas St SE8 141 D6
Copper Beech N6 49 A2
Copperbeech Cl NW3 70 B3
Copper Beech Ct N20 14 A1
Copper Beeches TW7 130 B4
Copper Cl
Penge SE19 183 D3
Tottenham N17 34 B3
Copperdale Rd UB3 106 A4
Copperfield Ave UB8 82 C3
Copperfield Ct
Blackheath SE3 142 D2
Ilford IG6 57 A6
Copperfield Dr N15 51 D5
Copperfield Ho [12] SE1 118 A4
Copperfield Mews N18 33 C5
Copperfield Rd
Stepney E3 97 A2
Thamesmead SE28 102 C1
Copperfields
[5] Beckenham BR3 186 A2
Harrow HA1 42 C2
Copperfields Ct W3 110 C4
Copperfield St SE1 117 A4 252 A2
Copperfield Way
Chislehurst BR7 189 A4
Pinner HA5 41 B5
Coppergate Cl BR1 187 B2
Coppermead Cl NW2 68 C5
Copper Mews [19] W4 111 A3
Copper Mill Dr TW7 130 D3
Coppermill La E17 52 D4
Copper Mill La SW17 180 A6
Coppermill Prim Sch E17 52 D4
Copper Row SE1 253 C3
Copperwood Lo EN2 4 D3
Coppetts Cl N12 30 D3
Coppetts Ctr N12 30 D3
Coppetts Rd N10 30 D2
Coppetts Wood Prim Sch N10 31 A2
Coppice Cl
Beckenham BR3 207 D5
Harrow HA7 24 D4
Ruislip HA4 39 B3
West Barnes SW20 200 C6
Coppice Dr SW15 156 B5
Coppice The
Ashford TW15 170 D4
Enfield EN2 4 D1
Hillingdon UB7 82 A1
New Barnet EN5 13 D5
Coppice Way E18 54 D6
Coppice Wlk N20 13 C1
Coppies Gr N11 31 B6
Copping Cl CR0 221 C4
Coppin Ho SW2 160 D3
Coppins The
[2] Ilford RM6 58 B2
New Addington CR0 223 D2
Stanmore HA3 24 C4
Coppock Cl SW11 136 C3
Coppsfield KT8 195 C6
Copse Ave BR4 223 D5
Copse Cl SE7 143 B6
Copse Ct SW15 157 A6
Copse Glade KT6 197 D1
COPSE HILL 178 B3
Copse Hill
Belmont SM2 217 D1
Wimbledon SW19 178 C4
Wimbledon SW20 178 B3
Copsem Dr KT10 212 A2
Copsem La KT10 212 A1
Copsem Way KT10 212 A2
Copse The
Chingford E4 20 D3
Muswell Hill N2 48 D6
Copse View CR2 223 A1
Copsewood Cl DA15 167 C5
Coptefield Dr DA17 125 A3
Copthall Ave EC2 95 B1 242 D2
Copthall Bldgs EC2 242 D2
Copthall Cl EC2 242 C2
Copthall Dr NW7 28 A4
Copthall Gdns
Hendon NW7 28 A3
Twickenham TW1 152 D3
Copthall L Ctr NW4 28 B2
Copthall Rd E UB10 60 C5
Copthall Rd W UB10 60 C6
Copthall Sch NW7 28 B3
Copthall Stadium NW4 28 C2
Copthorne Ave
Bromley BR2 226 B6
Streatham SW12 159 D4
Copthorne Chase [3] TW15 170 B6
Copthorne Cl TW17 193 A3
Copthorne Ct SM1 218 A5
Copthorne Mews UB3 105 C2
Coptic St WC1 94 A2 240 A3
Copton Cl E3 97 C2
Copwood Cl N12 30 B6
Coral Apts [6] E16 121 A6
Coral Cl RM6 58 C6
Coral Ho [5] E1 97 A3
Coraline Cl UB1 85 B4
Coralline Wlk [4] SE2 124 C4
Coral Row [14] SW11 136 A2
Coral St SE1 116 C4 251 B1
Coram Ho
Bloomsbury WC1 240 A6
[9] Chiswick W4 111 C1
Coram Mans WC1 240 C5
Coram St WC1 94 A3 240 A5
Coran Cl N9 18 D4
Corban Rd TW3 129 C2
Corbar Cl EN4 2 B4
Corbden Cl SE15 139 D4
Corbet Cl CR4, SM6 219 A6
Corbet Ct EC3 242 D1
Corbet Ho N1 234 A5
Corbet Pl E1 95 D2 243 C4
Corbett Ct SE26 185 B6
Corbett Gr N22 32 A3
Corbett Ho SW10 266 A6
Corbett Rd
Walthamstow E17 54 A6
Wanstead E11 55 C3
Corbett's La SE16 118 C2
Corbetts Pas [8] SE16 118 C2
Corbett Villas RM8 58 C1
Corbicum E11 54 C2
Corbidge Ct SE8 141 D6
Corbiere Ct SW19 178 D4
Corbiere Ho [5] N1 95 C6
Corbin Ho [7] E3 97 D4
Corbin's La HA2 63 D5
Corbridge [5] N17 34 B3
Corbridge Cres E2 96 B5
Corbridge Ho SE2 124 C3
Corby Cres EN2 4 A1
Corbylands Rd DA15 167 C3
Corbyn St N4, N19 50 A1
Corby Rd NW10 89 B5
Corby Way E3 97 C3
Cordelia Cl SE24 138 D1
Cordelia Gdns TW19 148 A4
Cordelia Ho [26] N1 95 C5
Cordelia Rd TW19 148 A4
Cordelia St E14 97 D1
Cordell Ho N15 51 D4
Cordingley Rd HA4 61 B6
Cording St E14 97 D2
Cordwainers Ct [18] E9 74 C1
Cordwainers Wlk [9] E13 99 A5
Cordwain Ho [7] N18 34 A5
Cordwell Rd SE13 164 C6
Corefield Cl N11 15 A2
Corelli Rd SE3 144 A4
Corfe Ave HA2 63 C4
Corfe Cl Hayes UB4 84 C1
Twickenham TW4 151 A3
Corfe Ho SW8 270 C4
Corfe Lodge [15] SE21 161 B2
Corfe Twr [6] W3 111 A4
Corfield Rd N21 16 B6
Corfield St E2 96 B4
Corfton Lo W5 88 A2
Corfton Rd W5 88 A2
Coriander Ave E14 98 B1
Coriander Ct SE1 253 D2
Cories Cl RM8 80 D6
Corigan Ct [6] E11 76 C6
Corinium Cl HA9 66 B4
Corinne Rd N19 71 C4
Corinth Ho IG3 58 A2
Cork St Mews W1 249 A5
Corkscrew Hill BR4 224 B5
Cork Sq E1 118 B5
Cork St W1 115 C6 249 A5
Cork Tree Ho [3] SW27 182 D5
Cork Tree Ret Pk N18 35 A4
Cork Tree Way E4 35 A5
Corlett St NW1 237 A4
Cormont Rd SE5 138 D4
Cormorant Cl E17 35 A3
Cormorant Ct
[36] Deptford SE8 141 B6
[13] Dulwich SE21 161 B2
Cormorant Ho EN3 18 D6
Cormorant Pl SM1 217 B3
Cormorant Rd E7 76 D3
Cornbury Ho [5] SE8 141 B6
Cornbury Rd HA8 25 D3
Cornel Ho [4] DA15 168 A1
Cornelia Dr UB4 84 C3
Cornelia St N7 72 B2
Cornelion Cotts [1] SM6 219 B3
Cornelius Ct [4] N12 30 A5
Cornell Bldg [9] E1 96 A1
Cornell Cl DA14 191 A4
Cornell Ct [4] EN3 7 A2
Cornell Ho HA2 63 B5
Corner Fielde SW2 160 B3
Corner Gn SE3 143 A3
Corner House St WC2 250 A4
Corner Mead NW9 27 D2
Cornerside TW15 171 A3
Cornerstone Ct [13] E1 96 A3
Cornerways
Harrow HA1 65 A5
Putney SW15 134 A1
Corney Rd W4 133 C6
Corney Reach Way W4 133 C5
Cornflower La CR0 206 D1
Cornflower Terr SE22 162 B5
Cornford Cl BR2 209 A4
Cornford Gr SW12 159 B2
Cornhill EC3 95 B1 242 D1
Cornhill Dr EN3 7 A6
Cornick Ho [7] SE16 118 B3
Cornish Ct N9 18 B4
Cornish Gr SE20 184 B2
Cornish Ho
Brentford TW8 110 B1
[7] Camberwell SE17 138 D6
Cornmill La SE13 142 A2
Cornmow Dr NW10 68 A3
Cornshaw Rd RM8 58 D1
Cornthwaite Rd E5 74 C5
Cornwall Ave
Bethnal Green E2 96 C4
Claygate KT10 212 D1
Cornwall Ave *continued*
Falconwood DA16 145 D2
Finchley N3 29 C3
Southall UB1 85 C2
Wood Green N22 32 A2
Cornwall Cl IG11 79 D2
Cornwall Cres W11 91 A1
Cornwall Ct
[5] Ealing W7 86 D3
[5] Pinner HA5 23 B3
Upper Tooting SW17 180 C6
Cornwall Dr BR5 190 C3
Cornwall Flats SE1 251 B2
Cornwall Gdns
Kensington SW7 113 D3 255 D5
Willesden NW10 68 B2
Cornwall Gdns Wlk SW7 255 D5
Cornwall Gr W4 111 C1
Cornwall Ho
Marylebone NW1 237 D5
[3] Putney SW15 156 C4
Cornwallis Ave
London N9 18 C2
New Eltham SE9 167 B2
Cornwallis Ct SW8 270 A2
Cornwallis Gr N9 18 C2
Cornwallis Ho [24] W12 112 B6
Cornwallis Rd
Dagenham RM9 81 A4
Edmonton N9 18 B2
Upper Holloway N19 72 A6
Walthamstow E17 52 D5
Woolwich SE18 122 D3
Woolwich SE18 123 A3
Cornwallis Sq
[3] Finsbury Park N4 72 C6
London N19 72 A6
Cornwallis Wlk SE9 144 B2
Cornwall Mans
Chelsea SW10 266 B4
Marylebone NW1 237 D5
Cornwall Mews S SW7 256 A5
Cornwall Mews W SW7 255 D5
Cornwall Rd
Belmont SM2 217 B1
Croydon CR0 220 D6
Edmonton N18 34 A5
Finsbury Pk N4 50 C2
Harrow HA1 42 A3
Lambeth SE1 116 C4 251 B2
Pinner HA5 23 B3
Ruislip HA4 61 D6
Twickenham TW1 153 A3
West Green N15 51 B4
Cornwall Sq SE11 261 C2
Cornwall St [4] E1 118 B6
Cornwall Terr NW1 237 D5
Cornwall Terrace Mews NW1 237 D5
Corn Way E11 76 C5
Cornwood Cl N2 48 B5
Cornwood Dr E1 96 C1
Cornworthy Rd RM8 80 C3
Corona Rd SE12 165 A4
Coronation Ave [1] N16 73 D4
Coronation Cl
Bexley DA5 168 D5
Ilford IG6 57 A5
Coronation Ct
[19] North Kensington W10 90 C2
Stratford E15 76 D2
Coronation Rd
Acton NW10 88 C3
Hayes UB3 105 D2
Newham E13 99 C4
Coronet Ho HA7 24 D4
Coronet Par [9] HA0 66 A2
Coronet St N1 95 C4
Corporation Ave TW4 129 A1
Corporation Row EC1 241 B6
Corporation St
Lower Holloway N7 72 A3
West Ham E15 98 D5
Corpus Christi RC Prim Sch
[19] Brixton SW2 160 B6
Kingston u T KT3 199 A6
Corrance Rd SW2, SW4 138 A1
Corri Ave N14 31 D6
Corrib Ct N13 16 B1
Corrib Dr SM1 218 C3
Corrib Hts N8 49 D3
Corrigan Cl NW4 46 C6
Corringham Ct NW11 47 C2
Corringham Ho [11] E1 96 D1
Corringham Rd
London NW11 47 C2
Wembley HA9 66 C6
Corringway Ealing W5 88 C2
Golders Green NW11 47 D2
Corris Gn NW9 45 C3
Corry Dr SW9 138 D1
Corry Ho [2] E14 119 D6
Corsair Cl TW19 148 A4
Corsair Rd TW19 148 A4
Corscombe Cl KT2 177 A5
Corsehill St SW16 181 C4
Corsell Ho [5] TW8 131 C5
Corsham Ho HA9 66 C2
Corsham St N1 95 B4 235 D1
Corsica St N5 72 D2
Corsley Way E9 75 B2
Cortayne Ct TW2 152 C2
Cortayne Rd SW6 135 B3
Cortis Rd SW15 156 B5
Cortis Terr SW15 156 B5
Corunna Rd SW8 137 C4 269 B2
Corunna Terr SW8 269 A2
Corvette Sq [5] SE10 142 B6
Corwell Gdns UB8 83 A1
Corwell La UB8 83 A1
Coryton Path W9 91 B3
Cosbycote Ave SE24 161 A6
Cosdach Ave SM6 219 D1
Cosedge Cres CR0, CR9 220 D3
Cosgrove Cl
Edmonton N21 17 A2
Hayes UB4 84 D3
Cosgrove Ho [11] E2 96 A6
Cosmo Pl WC1 240 B4
Cosmur Cl W12 111 D3
Cossall Wlk SE15 140 B4
Cossar Mews [10] SW2 160 C6
Cosser St SE1 116 C3 261 A6
Costa St SE15 140 A3
Coston Prim Sch UB6 86 A4
Costons Ave UB6 86 B4
Costons La UB6 86 B4
Coston Wlk [4] SE4 140 D1
Cosway Ho NW11 48 A3
Cosway Mans NW1 237 B4
Cosway St NW1 92 C2 237 B4
Cotall St E14 97 C2
Coteford Cl HA5 40 A4
Coteford Inf Sch HA5 40 A3
Coteford Jun Sch HA5 39 D4
Coteford St SW17 181 A6
Cotelands CR0 221 C5
Cotesbach Rd E5 74 C5
Cotes Ho NW8 237 A5
Cotesmore Gdns RM8 80 C4
Cotford Rd CR7 205 A5
Cotham St SE17 262 B3
Cotherstone Cl SW2 160 B3
Cotleigh Ave DA5 168 D2
Cotleigh Rd NW6 69 C1
Cotman Cl
London NW11 48 A3
Putney SW15 156 D6
Cotman Ct BR3 185 B2
Cotmandene Cres BR5 190 A1
Cotman Gdns HA8 26 C1
Cotman Ho
[5] Northolt UB5 84 D5
St John's Wood NW8 230 A4
Cotman Mews RM8 80 C3
Cotmans Cl UB3 106 A5
Coton Rd DA16 146 A2
Cotrill Gdns E8 74 B2
Cotsford Ave KT3 199 B4
Cotswold Ave WD23 8 A5

Cotswold Cl
Hinchley Wood KT10 212 D6
Kingston u T KT2 177 A4
Cotswold Ct
London N11 31 A6
St Luke's EC1 242 A6
3 Wembley UB6 86 D5
Cotswold Gate NW2 47 A1
Cotswold Gdns
Hendon NW2 68 D6
Ilford IG2 57 B2
Newham E6 99 D5
Cotswold Gn EN2 4 B1
Cotswold Ho N16 51 D1
Cotswold Mews SW11 266 D1
Cotswold Rd TW12 173 C4
Cotswold Rise BR6 211 D3
Cotswold St SE27 182 D6
Cotswold Way
Enfield EN2 4 B2
North Cheam KT4 216 C6
Cottage Ave BR2 210 A1
Cottage Cl
Harrow HA2 64 C6
Ruislip HA4 39 B1
Cottage Field Cl DA14 168 C3
Cottage Gn SE5 139 B5
Cottage Gr
London SW9 138 A2
Surbiton KT6 197 D3
Cottage Pl SW3 114 C3 257 A5
Cottage Rd KT19 215 B1
Cottage St E14 119 D6
Cottages The
Ickenham UB10 60 A6
Lambeth SE1 260 C5
Uxbridge UB10 60 D5
Cottage Wlk 2 N16 73 D5
Cottenham Dr
London NW9 45 D6
Wimbledon SW20 178 B3
Cottenham Ho 5 N19 72 A6
Cottenham Par SW20 178 B1
COTTENHAM PARK 178 B2
Cottenham Park Rd SW20 178 C3
Cottenham Pl SW20 178 B3
Cottenham Rd E17 53 B5
Cotterill Rd KT6 198 B1
Cottesbrook St 9 SE14 141 A5
Cottesloe Ho NW8 237 A6
Cottesloe Mews SE1 261 B6
Cottesmore Ct W8 255 D6
Cottesmore Gdns W8 113 D3 255 D6
Cottimore Ave KT12 194 B1
Cottimore Cres KT12 194 B2
Cottimore La KT12 194 B2
Cottimore Terr KT12 194 B2
Cottingham Chase HA4 62 A5
Cottingham Rd
Penge SE20 184 D3
South Lambeth SW8 138 B5 270 D4
Cottington Rd TW13 172 D6
Cottington St SE11 261 C2
Cotton Ave W3 89 B1
Cotton Cl
Dagenham RM9 80 C1
12 Leyton E11 76 C6
Cottongrass Cl 1 CR0 206 D1
Cottonham Cl N12 30 B5
Cotton Hill BR1 186 B6
Cotton Ho
Bedford Pk W12 111 D4
18 Streatham SW12 160 A4
Cotton Row SW11 136 B2
Cotton's Gdns E2 95 C4
Cottons La SE1 252 D4
Cotton St E14 120 A6
Cottrell Ct SE10 120 D2
Cotts Cl 13 W7 86 D2
Couchman Ho 8 SW4 159 C5
Couchmore Ave KT10 212 C6
Coulgate St SE4 141 A2
Coulsdon Ct 4 N8 49 D4
Coulsdon Ho 5 SW2 160 A3
Coulson Cl RM8 58 C1
Coulson St SW3 114 D1 257 C2
Coulter Cl UB4 85 A3
Coulter Rd W6 112 B3
Coulthurst Ct SW16 182 A3
Coults Cres NW5 71 A5
Councillor St SE5 139 A5
Counters Ct W14 254 B6
Counter St SE1 253 A3
Countess Rd NW5 71 C3
Countisbury Ave EN1 17 D4
Countisbury Ho SE26 162 A1
Country Way TW13, TW16 172 C5
County Gate
Longlands SE9 167 A1
New Barnet EN5 13 D5
County Gr SE5 139 A4
County Ho
22 Herne Hill SE24 138 D1
9 South Lambeth SW9 138 C4
County Par TW8 131 D5
County Rd
Newham E6 100 D2
South Norwood CR7 182 D1
County St SE1 117 A3 262 B5
Coupland Pl SE18 123 A1
Courcy Rd N8, N22 50 C6
Courier Ho 17 SW2 160 C4
Courland Gr SW8 137 D3
Courland St SW8 137 D4 269 D1
Course The SE9 166 C1
Courtauld Ho 12 E2 96 A5
Courtauld Inst of Art★ WC2 250 C6
Courtauld Rd N19 50 A1
Courtaulds Cl SE28 124 A5
Court Ave DA17 125 B1
Court Cl Harrow HA3 44 A6
Twickenham TW13, TW2 151 D1
Wallington SM6 219 D1
Court Close Ave TW13, TW2 151 D1
Court Cres KT9 213 D2
Court Downs Rd BR3 185 D1
Court Dr
Carshalton SM1 218 C4
Edgware HA7 26 A6
Hillingdon UB10 82 C6
Wallington CR0 220 B4
Courtenay Ave
Harrow HA3 24 A2
Highgate N6 48 C2
Courtenay Dr BR3 186 B1
Courtenay Gdns HA3 24 A1
Courtenay Mews E17 53 A4
Courtenay Pl E17 53 A4
Courtenay Rd
Leyton E11 76 D5
North Cheam KT4, SM3 216 C5
Penge BR3, SE20 184 D4
Walthamstow E17 52 D5
Courtenay Rd HA9 65 D5
Courtenay Sq SE11 261 A1
Courtenay St SE11 116 C1 261 A2
Courtens Mews HA7 25 C3
Court Farm Ave KT19 215 B3
Court Farm Ind Est TW19 148 B5
Court Farm Rd
Chislehurst SE9 166 A1
Northolt UB5 63 C1
Courtfield W13 87 C2
Courtfield Ave HA1 42 D4
Courtfield Cres HA1 42 D4
Courtfield Gdns
Ealing W13 87 A1
Ruislip HA4 61 D6
South Kensington SW5 113 D2 255 D3
Courtfield Ho EC1 241 A4
Courtfield Mews SW7 255 D3
Courtfield Rd
Ashford TW15 170 D4
South Kensington SW7 114 A2 256 A3
Courtfield Rise BR4 224 B5
Courtgate Cl NW7 27 D4
Court Gdns N7 72 C2
Courthill Rd SE13 142 A1
Courthope Ho
14 Rotherhithe SE16 118 C3
South Lambeth SW8 270 A3
Courthope Rd
Gospel Oak NW3 70 D4
Greenford UB6 86 B5
Wimbledon SW19 179 A5
Courthope Villas SW19 179 A3
Court House Gdns N3 29 C4
Court House Rd N12 29 D4
Court La SE21 161 D4
Courtland Ave
Chingford E4 20 D2
Edgware NW7 11 C1
Redbridge IG1 78 B6
South Norwood SW16 182 B3
Courtland Gr SE28 124 D6
Courtland Prim Sch NW7 11 C2
Courtland Rd E6 100 A6
Courtlands
11 Beckenham BR3 185 D1
8 Belmont SM2 217 D1
Chislehurst BR7 188 D4
Ealing W5 87 C2
Richmond TW10 154 C6
5 Upper Clapton E5 52 B1
Walton-on-T KT12 194 A2
Courtlands Ave
Hampton TW12 173 B4
Hayes BR2 208 D1
Lee SE12 165 B6
Richmond TW9 132 D3
Courtlands Cl HA4 39 D2
Courtlands Dr KT19 215 D2
Courtlands Rd KT5 198 C2
Court Lane Gdns SE21 161 C4
Courtleet Dr DA8 147 D4
Courtleigh 6 NW11 47 B4
Courtleigh Ave EN4 2 B5
Courtleigh Gdns NW11 47 A5
Court Lo 11 DA17 125 C1
Courtman Rd N17 33 A3
Court Mans 8 W6 112 A2
Court Mead UB5 85 B4
Courtmead Cl SE24 161 A5
Courtnell St W2 91 C1
Courtney Cl SE19 183 C4
Courtney Cres SM5 218 D1
Courtney Ct N7 72 C3
Courtney Ho
1 Hendon NW4 46 C5
Kensington W14 254 B6
Courtney Pl CR0 220 C5
Courtney Rd
Croydon CR0 220 C5
Islington N7 72 C3
Mitcham SW19 180 C3
Courtney Twrs IG2 57 B3
Courtney Way TW6 126 C2
Court One TW15 149 A1
Court Par HA0 65 B5
Courtrai Rd SE23 163 A5
Court Rd Eltham SE9 166 B4
Southall UB2 107 B1
South Norwood SE25 205 D6
Uxbridge UB10 60 D4
Court Royal SW15 157 A6
Courtside
Crouch End N8 49 D3
Forest Hill SE23 162 C1
Court St
2 Bromley BR1 187 A1
3 Stepney E1 96 B2
Courts The SW16 182 A3
Court The London N10 49 C5
Ruislip HA4 63 A4
Court Three TW15 149 A1
Court Two TW15 149 A1
Courtville Ho 12 W10 91 A4
Courtway IG8 37 C5
Court Way Acton W3 89 A2
Colindale NW9 45 C5
Ilford IG6 57 A6
Twickenham TW1, TW2 152 D4
Courtyard Apartments TW11 174 B5
Courtyard Mews BR5 190 A3
Courtyard The
Fulham SW6 135 A4 264 A1
Islington N1 72 B1
Keston BR2 226 A2
Thornton Heath CR0 204 B3
13 Wandsworth SW18 136 B1
Court Yd SE9 166 B5
Cousin La EC4 117 B6 252 C5
Cousins Cl 2 UB7 104 A6
Cousins Ct 2 NW9 46 A5
Couthurst Rd SE3 143 B5
Coutts Ave KT9 214 A3
Couzens Ho 8 E3 97 B2
Coval Gdns SW14 132 D1
Coval La SW14 132 D1
Coval Pas SW14 133 A1
Coval Rd SW14 133 A1
Covardale Ct EN3 7 A6
Covelees Wall E6 100 C1
Covell Ct 16 SE8 141 C5
Covent Garden Sta WC2 94 A1 240 B1
Coventry Cl
Kilburn NW6 91 C6
9 Newham E6 100 B1
Coventry Rd
Bethnal Green E1 96 B3
Croydon SE25 206 A5
Ilford IG1 56 D1
Coventry St W1 249 C5
Coverack Cl
Croydon CR0 207 A2
Southgate N14 15 C5
Coverdale Cl HA7 25 B5
Coverdale Gdns CR0 221 D5
Coverdale Rd
Brondesbury NW2 69 A2
Friern Barnet N11 31 A4
Hammersmith W12 112 B4
Hampstead NW6 68 D1
Coverdales The IG11 101 B5
Coverham Ho 5 SE4 140 D1
Coverley Cl E1 96 A2
Coverley Point SE11 260 C3
Coverton Rd SW17 180 C5
Coverts Rd KT10 212 D1
Covert The BR6 211 C3
Covert Way EN4 2 A3
Covet Wood Cl BR5 211 D3
Covey Cl SW19 179 D1
Covey Rd KT4, SM3 216 D6
Covington Gdns SW16 182 D3
Covington Way
South Norwood SW16 182 C3
South Norwood SW16 182 D3
Cowan Cl E6 100 A2
Cowan Ct 14 NW10 67 B1
Cowan Lo 6 IG8 37 C4
Cowbridge La IG11 78 D1
Cowbridge Rd HA3 44 B5
Cowcross St EC1 94 D2 241 C4
Cowdenbeath Path N1 233 C6
Cowden Rd BR6 211 D2
Cowden St SE6 185 C6
Cowdray Hall Royal Coll of Nursing W1 93 B1 238 C2
Cowdray Ho 22 SE22 139 C2
Cowdray Rd UB10 83 A6
Cowdrey Cl EN1 5 C3
Cowdrey Rd SW19 180 A5
Cowdry Rd E9 75 B2
Cowell Lo E4 36 D5
Cowen Ave HA2 64 B6
Cowen Ho 4 SE18 144 D6
Cowgate Rd UB6 86 B4
Cowick Rd SW17 180 D6
Cowings Mead UB5 63 A2
Cowland Ave EN3 6 C1
Cow Leaze E6 100 C1
Cowleaze Rd KT2 176 A2
Cowley Ct 8 E18 37 A1
Cowley La E11 76 C5
COWLEY PEACHY 82 A2
Cowley Pl NW4 46 C4
Cowley Rd
Brixton SW9 138 C4
East Acton W3 111 D5
16 Kennington SW9 138 C5
Mortlake SW14 133 C2
Redbridge IG1 56 B2
Wanstead E11 55 B4
Cowley St SW1 260 A5
Cowling Cl W11 244 A4
Cowper Ave
Sutton SM1 218 B4
Upton Pk E6 78 A1
Cowper Cl
Bexley DA16 168 A6
Bromley BR2 209 D5
Cowper Gdns
Southgate N14 15 C5
Wallington SM6 219 C2
Cowper Ho
Pimlico SW1 259 D1
Walworth SE17 262 B2
Cowper Rd Acton W3 111 B5
6 Belvedere DA17 125 C2
Bromley BR2 209 D5
Ealing W7 108 D6
East Barnet N14 15 B3
Edmonton N18 34 A5
Kingston u T KT2 176 B5
Stoke Newington N16 73 C4
Wimbledon SW19 180 A4
Cowper's Ct EC3 242 D1
Cowper St EC1, EC2 95 B3 242 D6
Cowper Terr W10 90 D2
Cowslip Cl UB10 60 A1
Cowslip Rd E18 37 B1
Cowthorpe Rd SW8 269 D2
Cox Ct 3 EN4 2 C1
Coxe Pl HA3 43 A5
Cox Ho W6 264 A6
Cox La
Chessington KT9 214 B4
West Ewell KT19 215 A3
Coxmount Rd SE7 121 D1
Coxs Ave TW17 193 C6
Coxson Way SE1 253 C1
Coxwell Rd
Plumstead SE18 123 B1
South Norwood SE19 183 C3
Coxwold Path KT9 214 A1
Coysh Ct 8 SW15 157 A6
Crabbs Croft Cl 7 BR6 227 A3
Crab Hill BR3 186 B3
Crabtree Ave
Dagenham RM6 58 D5
Wembley HA0 88 B5
Crabtree Cl E2 95 D5
Crabtree Ct EN5 1 D1
Crabtree Hall SW6 134 C5
Crabtree La SW6 134 D5
Cracknell Cl EN1 6 B6
Craddock Rd EN1 5 D2
Craddock St NW5 71 A2
Cradley Rd SE9 167 B3
Cragie Ho SE1 263 D3
Craig Dr UB8 82 D1
Craigen Ave CR0 206 B1
Craigen Gdns IG1, IG3 79 C4
Craigerne Rd SE3 143 B5
Craig Gdns E18 36 D1
Craig Ho Ealing W13 109 B6
Greenwich SE3 143 B5
Craigholm SE18 144 C4
Craigie Lea N10 31 B1
Craigleith SW15 156 D5
Craigmuir Pk HA0 88 B6
Craignair Rd SW2 160 C4
Craignish Ave SW16 182 B1
Craig Park Rd N18 34 B6
Craig Rd TW10 175 C6
Craig's Ct SW1 250 A4

Craigside KT2 176 D2
Craigton Rd SE9 144 B1
Craigweil Cl HA7 25 D5
Craigweil Dr HA7 25 D5
Craigwell Ave TW13 150 A1
Craik Ct NW6 91 B5
Crail Row SE17 117 B2 262 D3
Crales Ho SE18 122 A3
Cramer Ct KT3 199 A6
Cramer St W1 93 A2 238 B3
Cramhurst Ho 3 SM1 218 B3
Crammond Cl W6 264 A5
Cramond Ct TW14 149 C3
Cramonde Ct DA16 146 A3
Crampton Prim Sch SE17 116 D1 261 D2
Crampton Rd SE20 184 C4
Crampton St SE17 117 A1 262 A2
Cranberry Cl 2 UB5 84 D5
Cranberry La E16 98 C3
Cranborne Ave
Southall UB2 107 C2
Tolworth KT6, KT9 214 C5
Cranborne Rd IG11 101 B6
Cranborne Waye
Hayes UB4 84 B1
Hayes UB4 106 C6
Cranbourn Alley WC2 249 D6
Cranbourne Cl SW16 204 A6
Cranbourne Ct
East Finchley N2 47 D6
2 Edgware HA8 26 D5
Finchley NW7 29 A3
SW11 267 B4
Walton-on-T KT12 194 B2
Wanstead E18 55 B5
Cranbourne Dr HA5 40 D4
Cranbourne Gdns
Ilford IG6 57 A6
Temple Fortune NW11 47 B4
Cranbourne Rd
Leyton E15 76 A4
London N10 31 B1
Manor Pk E12 78 A3
Northwood HA6 39 D6
Cranbourn Ho 6 SE16 118 B4
Cranbourn Pas 5 SE16 118 B4
Cranbourn St WC2 115 D6 249 D6
CRANBROOK 56 C1
Cranbrook NW1 232 B5
Cranbrook Cl BR2 209 A3
Cranbrook Coll (Boys) IG1 78 C6
Cranbrook Ct
8 Brentford TW8 131 D6
South Croydon CR2 221 C3
Cranbrook Dr
Thames Ditton KT10 196 A1
Twickenham TW2 151 D3
Cranbrook Ho
5 Hackney E5 74 B3
South Norwood SE19 183 B2
Cranbrook La N11 31 B6
Cranbrook Mews E17 53 B4
Cranbrook Pk N22 32 C2
Cranbrook Prim Sch IG1 56 B2
Cranbrook Rd
Chiswick W4 111 C1
Erith DA7 147 B4
Hounslow TW4 129 B1
Ilford IG1, IG2 56 C3
New Barnet EN4 14 B5
South Norwood CR7 183 A1
St Johns SE8 141 C4
Wimbledon SW19 179 A3
Cranbrook Rise IG1 56 B2
Cranbrook St E2 96 D5
Cranbury Rd SW6 135 D3
Crandale Ho 8 E5 74 B3
Crandley Ct SE8 119 A2
Crane Ave Acton W3 111 A6
Isleworth TW7 153 A6
Cranebank TW4 128 B2
Cranebank Mews TW1 131 A1
Cranebrook TW2 152 A2
Crane Cl
Dagenham RM10 81 C2
Harrow HA2 64 A5
Crane Ct
7 Acton W12 111 C4
Holborn EC4 241 B1
West Ewell KT19 215 A4
Craneford Cl TW2 152 D4
Craneford Way TW2 152 D4
Crane Gdns UB3 105 D2
Crane Gr N7 72 C2
Crane Ho 24 Bow E3 97 A5
9 Catford BR1 186 B5
Feltham TW13 151 C1
10 Peckham SE15 139 D4
Crane Lodge Rd TW5 128 B6
Crane Mead SE16 118 D2
Crane Mead Ct TW1 152 D4
Crane Park Prim Sch TW13 151 B2
Crane Park Rd TW2 151 D2
Crane Rd
Stanwell TW19 148 C5
Twickenham TW2 152 C3
Cranesbill Cl
Kenton NW9 45 B6
Mitcham SW16 181 D1
Cranes Dr KT5 198 B5
Cranes Park Ave KT5, KT6 198 B5
Cranes Park Cres KT5 198 B5
Cranes Pk KT5, KT6 198 A4
Crane St
Greenwich SE10 120 B1
6 Peckham SE15 139 D4
Craneswater TW6 127 D5
Craneswater Pk UB2 107 B1
Cranes Way WD6 11 A6
Crane Way TW2 152 A4
Cranfield Ct
Marylebone NW1 237 B3
2 Woodford IG8 37 A6
Cranfield Dr NW9 27 C3
Cranfield Ho WC1 240 B4
Cranfield Rd SE4 141 B2
CRANFORD 128 C4
Cranford Ave
Bowes Pk N13 32 A5
Stanwell TW19 148 B4
Cranford Cl
Stanwell TW19 148 A4
Wimbledon SW20 178 B3
Cranford Com Coll TW5 128 B6
Cranford Cotts 8 E1 118 D6
Cranford Ct SM1 218 A4
Cranford Ctry Pk TW5 128 A6
Cranford Dr UB3 105 D2
Cranford Jun & Inf Schs TW4 128 B3
Cranford La
Harlington TW6 127 D4
Harlington UB3 127 C5
Heston TW5 128 C5
Cranford Lo SW19 156 D2
Cranford Mews BR2 210 A4
Cranford Park Prim Sch UB3 105 D2
Cranford Park Rd UB3 105 D2
Cranford Rd TW6 127 D2
Cranford Rise KT10 212 A3
Cranford St E1 118 D6
Cranford Way N8 50 C4
Cranhurst Rd NW2 68 C3
Cranleigh W11 244 C4
Cranleigh Cl
Bexley DA5 169 D5
Penge SE20 184 B1
Cranleigh Ct
1 Barnet EN5 1 D1
Mitcham CR4 202 B6
Richmond TW9 132 C2
Southall UB1 85 B1
4 Stamford Hill N16 51 C1
Cranleigh Gardens Ind Est UB1 85 B2
Cranleigh Gdns
Barking IG11 79 B2
Harrow HA3 44 A4
Kingston u T KT2 176 B4
Southall UB1 85 B1
Southgate N21 16 C6
South Norwood SE25 205 C6
Sutton SM1 217 D6
Cranleigh Ho SW20 178 B1
Cranleigh Hos NW1 232 B3
Cranleigh Mews SW11 136 D3
Cranleigh Rd
Feltham TW13 171 D6
Harringay N15 51 A4
Merton SW19 201 C6
Thames Ditton KT10 196 A1
Cranleigh St NW1 93 C5 232 B3
Cranley Dene Ct N10 49 B5
Cranley Dr Ilford IG2 57 A2
Ruislip HA4 61 D6
CRANLEY GARDENS 49 B5
Cranley Gdns
London N10 49 B5
Palmers Green N13 16 B1
South Kensington SW7 114 B1 256 C2
Wallington SM6 219 C1
Cranley Mews SW7 114 A1 256 B2
Cranley Par 2 SE9 188 A6
Cranley Pl SW7 114 B2 256 C3
Cranley Rd Ilford IG2 57 A2
Newham E13 99 B2
Cranmer Ave W13 109 B3
Cranmer Cl
Ruislip HA4 40 D1
Stanmore HA7 25 C3
West Barnes SM4 200 D3
Cranmer Ct
Chelsea SW3 257 B3
Church End N3 29 A1
Hampton TW12 173 D5
Kingston u T KT2 175 D6
Cranmere Prim Sch KT10 196 A1
Cranmer Farm Cl CR4 202 D5
Cranmer Ho SW11 267 A2
Cranmer Prim Sch CR4 202 D5
Cranmer Rd
Brixton SW9 138 C5
Croydon CR0 221 A5
Edgware HA8 10 D1
Forest Gate E7 77 B4
Hampton TW12 173 D5
Hayes UB3 83 B1
Kingston u T KT2 176 A5
Mitcham CR4 202 D5
Cranmer Terr SW17 180 B5
Cranmore Ave TW7 130 A5
Cranmore Rd
Catford BR1 164 D1
Elmstead BR7 188 B5
Cranmore Way N10 49 C5
Cranston Cl
Hounslow TW3, TW4 129 A3
Uxbridge UB10 61 B6
Cranston Ct 6 N20 14 D2
Cranston Gdns E4 35 D4
Cranston Rd SE23 163 A2
Cranswick Rd SE16 118 B1
Crantock Rd SE6 164 A2
Cranwell Cl E3 97 D3
Cranwell Ct
Croydon CR0 222 D6
6 Hendon NW9 27 D3
Cranwell Gr TW17 192 B5
Cranwell Rd TW6 126 D3
Cranwich Ave N21 17 B4
Cranwich Rd N16 51 C2
Cranwood Ct EC1 235 D1
Cranwood St EC1 95 B4 235 D1
Cranworth Cres 7 E4 20 B3
Cranworth Gdns SW9 138 C4
Cranworth Ho 6 N7 72 B4
Craster Rd SW2 160 B4
Craston Ho 2 SE5 139 C3
Crathie Rd SE12 165 B5
Crathorne Ho N2 30 B1
Cravan Ave TW13 150 A2
Craven Ave
Ealing W5 109 C6
Southall UB1 85 B2
Craven Cl Hayes UB4 84 A1
Stamford Hill N16 52 A2
Craven Cottage (Fulham FC) SW6 134 D4
Craven Ct
Dagenham RM6 59 A3
Edgware HA8 26 B6
Harlesden NW10 89 C6
Southall UB1 107 D5
Craven Gdns
Barking IG11 101 C5
Ilford IG6 57 B6
Wimbledon SW19 179 D5
Craven Hill W2 114 A6 246 B6
Craven Hill Gdns W2 114 A6 246 A6
Craven Hill Mews W2 246 B6
Craven Ho Ealing W5 109 C6
16 Finchley N2 30 B1
2 Mortlake SW14 133 B2
Craven Lo
Bayswater W2 246 B6
Fulham SW6 134 D4
Craven Mews 6 SW11 137 A2
Craven Park Mews NW10 89 C6
Craven Park Rd
Harlesden NW10 89 C6
South Tottenham N15 52 A3
Craven Pas WC2 250 A4
Craven Pk NW10 89 C6
Craven Rd
Croydon CR0 206 B1
Ealing W5 109 C6
Kingston u T KT2 176 B2
Paddington W2 92 A1 236 B1
Stonebridge NW10 89 B6
Craven St WC2 116 A5 250 A4
Craven Terr W2 114 A6 246 B6
Craven Wlk E5, N16 52 A2
Crawford Ave HA0 65 D3
Crawford Bldgs NW1 237 B3
Crawford Cl TW7 130 C3
Crawford Ct SE18 146 A6
Crawford Gdns
Edmonton N13 16 D1
Northolt UB5 85 B4
Crawford Mews W1 237 C3
Crawford Pas EC1 241 B5
Crawford Pl W1 92 C2 237 B3
Crawford Place Dwellings NW1 237 B3
Crawford Point 4 E16 98 D1
Crawford Prim Sch SE5 139 A4
Crawford Rd SE5 139 A3
Crawford St
Marylebone W1 92 D2 237 C3
16 Willesden NW10 67 B1
Crawley Rd
Enfield EN1 17 D4
Leyton E10 53 D1
Tottenham N22 33 A1
Crawshay Ct SW9 138 C4
Crawshay Ho 13 N16 73 B4
Crawthew Gr SE22 139 D1
Cray Bldgs DA14 190 C4
Craybrooke Rd DA14 190 B6
Craybury End SE9 167 A2
Crayfields Bsns Pk BR5 190 C2
Crayfields Ind Pk BR5 190 C1
Crayford Cl E6 100 A1
Crayford Ho
Bermondsey SE1 252 D1
5 Lower Holloway N7 72 A4
Crayford Rd N7 72 A4
Crayke Hill KT9 214 A1
Crayle Ho EC1 241 D6
Crayleigh Terr DA14 190 C4
Crayonne Cl TW16 171 C2
Cray Rd Erith DA17 147 C6
Sidcup DA14 190 C4
Crays Par The BR5 190 C1
Crealock Gr IG8 36 D5
Crealock St SW18 157 D5
Creasy Est SE1 263 A5
Crebor St SE22 162 A5
Credenhall Dr BR2 210 B1
Credenhill Ho 2 SE15 140 B5
Credenhill St SW16 181 C4
Crediton Hill NW6 69 D3
Crediton Ho EN3 6 D2
Crediton Rd NW10 90 D6
Crediton Way KT10 213 A3
Credon Rd
Bermondsey SE16 118 B1
Newham E13 99 C5
Creechurch La EC3 243 B1
Creechurch Pl EC3 243 B1
Creed Ct 5 E1 97 A4
Creed Ho SE15 140 B2
Creed La EC4 241 D1
Creek Ho W14 254 B6
CREEKMOUTH 101 D2
Creekmouth Ind Pk IG11 101 D3
Creek Rd
Barking IG11 101 D4
East Molesey KT8 196 C5
Greenwich SE10, SE8 141 D6
Creek Road Ind Est SE8 141 D6
Creekside SE8 141 D5
Creekside Foyer SE8 141 D6
Creek The TW16 194 A4
Creeland Gr SE6 163 B3
Crefeld Cl W6 135 A6 264 A5
Creffield Rd W3, W5 110 C6
Creighton Ave
London N2, N10 30 D1
Newham E6 99 D5
Creighton Cl W12 112 B6
Creighton Ho N2 48 C6
Creighton Rd
Ealing W5 109 D3
Kensal Rise NW6 90 D5
Tottenham N17 33 C3
Cremer Bsns Ctr 8 E2 95 D5
Cremer Ho 9 SE8 141 C5
Cremer St E2 95 D5
Cremorne Rd SW10 136 B5 266 C4
Creon Ct 3 SW9 138 C4
Crescent EC3 253 C6
Crescent Arc 1 SE10 142 A6
Crescent Court Bsns Ctr 1 E16 98 B3
Crescent Ct
Clapham Pk SW4 159 D6
Crouch End N8 49 D3
Kingston u T KT6 197 D4
14 Sidcup DA15 168 A1
Crescent Dr BR5 211 A3
Crescent E EN4 2 A5
Crescent Gdns
Ruislip HA4 40 B2
Wimbledon SW19 157 C1
Crescent Gr
London SW4 137 C1
Mitcham CR4 202 C5
Crescent Ho
London SE13 141 D3
5 Wimbledon SW20 178 D2
Crescent La SW4 159 D6
Crescent Mans
Islington N5 72 D3
Notting Hill W11 244 B6
Crescent Par UB10 82 C4
Crescent Pl SW3 257 B4
Crescent Rd
Beckenham BR3 185 D1
Chingford E4 20 C4
Church End N3 29 B2
Crouch End N8 49 D3
Dagenham RM10 81 D5
East Barnet EN4 14 C6
Edmonton N9 18 A3
Enfield EN2 4 D1
Friern Barnet N11 30 D6
Harringay N15 50 D6

Crescent Rd *continued*
Kingston u T KT2 176 D3
Leyton E10 75 D6
Plaistow BR1 187 A3
Shepperton TW17 193 A4
Sidcup DA15 167 D1
Upton Pk E6 99 C6
West Ham E13 99 A6
Wimbledon SW20 178 D2
Woodford E18 37 C2
Wood Green N22 31 D2
Woolwich SE18 122 D2
Crescent Rise
East Barnet EN4 14 C6
3 Finchley N3 29 C2
Wood Green N22 31 D2
Crescent Row EC1 242 A5
Crescent St N1 72 B1
Crescent Stables SW15 157 A6
Crescent The
Acton W3 89 C1
Ashford TW15 170 B5
Barnes SW13 134 A3
Barnet EN5 1 D3
Beckenham BR3 185 C2
Bexley DA5 168 C4
Coombe KT3 177 A1
Dollis Hill NW2 68 B5
East Finchley N2 47 D6
East Molesey KT8 195 C5
Friern Barnet N11 31 A6
Harlington UB7 127 B5
Harrow HA2 42 A1
Ilford IG2 56 C3
Loughton IG10 21 D5
Lower Halliford TW17 193 D2
Sidcup DA14 189 D6
Southall UB1 107 A4
Surbiton KT6 198 A4
Sutton SM1 218 B3
Thornton Heath CR0 205 B3
Walthamstow E17 53 A4
Wembley HA0 65 B6
West Wickham BR4 208 C3
Wimbledon SW19 157 C1
Crescent View IG10 21 D6
Crescent W EN4 2 A5
Crescentway N12 30 C4
Crescent Way
London SE4 141 C2
Orpington BR6 227 C3
South Norwood SW16 182 C3
Crescent Wood Rd SE21, SE26 162 A1
Cresford Rd SW6 135 D4 265 C1
Crespigny Rd NW4 46 B3
Cressage Cl UB1 85 C3
Cressage Ho 9 TW8 132 A6
Cressall Ho 14 E14 119 C3
Cresset Ho 8 E9 74 C2
Cresset Rd E9 74 C2
Cresset St SW4 137 D2
Cressfield Cl NW5 71 A3
Cressida Rd N19 49 D1
Cressingham Ct 1 DA17 125 C3
Cressingham Gr SM1 218 A4
Cressingham Rd
Burnt Oak HA8 27 B3
Lewisham SE13 142 A2
Cressington Cl 4 N16 73 C3
Cress Mews BR1 186 B5
Cresswell Gdns SW5 256 A2
Cresswell Ho HA9 66 A5
Cresswell Pk SE3 142 D2
Cresswell Pl SW10 114 A1 256 B2
Cresswell Rd
Croydon SE25 206 A5
Feltham TW13 173 A6
Twickenham TW1 153 D5
Cresswell Way N21 16 C4
Cressy Ct
Hammersmith W6 112 B3
6 Stepney E1 96 C2
36 Stepney E1 96 C2
Cressy Ho SW13 134 B2
Cressy Hos 7 E1 96 C2
Cressy Pl E1 96 C2
Cressy Rd NW3 70 D4
Cresta Ct W5 88 B3
Cresta Ho 7 Bow E3 97 C3
Hampstead NW6 70 B1
Crestbrook Ave N13 16 D1
Crestbrook Pl N13 16 D1
Crest Ct NW4 46 C4
Crest Dr EN3 6 C5
Crestfield St N1, WC1 233 B2
Crest Gdns HA4 62 C5
Crest Ho 3 TW15 170 C5
Creston Way KT4 200 D1
Crest Rd
Dollis Hill NW2 68 A6
Hayes BR2 208 D2
South Croydon CR2 222 B1
Crest Sch of English HA8 26 C5
Crest The
Edmonton N13 32 C6
Finchley N12 29 D4
Hendon NW4 46 C4
Surbiton KT5 198 C4
10 West Norwood SW27 182 D5
Crestview NW5 71 B5
Crest View HA5 40 D5
Crest View Dr BR5 211 A4
Crestway SW15 156 B5
Crestwood Way TW4 151 A6
Creswell Dr BR3 207 D4
Creswick Ct W3 110 D6
Creswick Rd W3 110 D6
Creswick Wlk
7 Bow E3 97 C4
Temple Fortune NW11 47 B5
Creton St SE18 122 C3
Crewdson Rd SW9 138 C5
Crewe Pl NW10 89 D4
Crewkerne Ct SW11 266 D2
Crews St E14 119 C2
Crewys Rd
Child's Hill NW2 69 B6
London SE15 140 B3
Crichton Ave SM6 219 D4
Crichton Rd SM5 218 D1
Crichton St SW8 137 C3
Cricket Ct 2 E6 100 B4
Cricketers Arms Rd EN2 5 A3
Cricketers Cl
Chessington KT9 213 D4
Oakwood N14 15 C4
Cricketers Mews 4 SW18 157 D6
Cricketers Terr SM5 218 C5
Cricketers Wlk SE26 184 C5
Cricketfield Rd E5 74 B4
Cricket Gn CR4 202 D5
Cricket Green Specl Sch 1 CR4 202 C6
Cricket Ground Rd BR7 188 D2
Cricket La BR3 185 A4
Cricket Row N2 48 B6
Cricklade Ave SW2 160 B2
CRICKLEWOOD 68 D4
Cricklewood Broadway NW2 68 D4
Cricklewood La NW2 69 B5
Cricklewood Sta NW2 68 D4
Cridland St E15 98 D6
Crieff Ct 3 TW11 175 C3
Crieff Rd SW18 158 A5
Criffel Ave SW2 159 D3
Crimscott St SE1 117 C3 263 B5
Crimsworth Rd SW8 137 D5 269 D3
Crinan St N1 94 A5 233 B4
Cringle St SW8 137 C5 269 A4
Cripplegate St EC1 242 B4
Cripps Gn UB4 84 B3
Crispe Ho
4 Barking IG11 101 B5
Islington N1 233 D5
Crispen Rd TW13 173 A6
Crispian Cl NW10 67 C4
Crispin Cl SM6 220 A6
Crispin Cres SM6 219 D6
Crispin Ct SE17 263 A3
Crispin Mews 10 NW11 47 B4
Crispin Pl E1 243 C4
Crispin Rd HA8 27 A4
Crispin St E1 95 D2 243 C3
Crispin Way UB8 82 B3
Crisp Rd W6 112 C1
Cristowe Rd SW6 135 B3
Criterion Bldgs KT7 197 B2
Criterion Mews N19 71 D6
Crittall's Cnr DA14 190 C3
Crittenden Lo BR4 207 C1
Crockerton Rd SW17 158 D2
Crockham Way SE9 188 C6
Crocus Cl CR0 206 D1
Crocus Field EN5 13 B5
Croft Ave BR4 208 A1
Croft Cl Edgware NW7 11 C1
Elmstead BR7 188 B5
Erith DA17 125 B1
Harlington UB7 127 A5
Hillingdon UB10 60 C1
Croft Ct London SE13 164 A5
Ruislip HA4 39 D1
Croftdown Rd NW5 71 B5
Croft End Cl KT9 214 B5
Crofters Cl TW7 152 B6
Crofters Ct 9 SE8 119 A2
Crofters Way NW1 93 D6 232 C6
Croft Gdns
Ealing W7 109 A4
Ruislip HA4 39 D1
Croft Ho
Putney SW15 157 A5
11 West Kilburn W10 91 A4
Croft Lodge Cl IG8 37 B4
Croft Mews 3 N12 14 A1
CROFTON 227 B6
Crofton Ave
Chiswick W4 133 B5
Orpington BR6 227 A6
Sidcup DA5 168 D4
Crofton Gate Way SE4 163 A6
Crofton Gr E4 36 B6
Crofton Inf Sch BR5 211 B2
Crofton Jun Sch BR5 211 B2
Crofton La BR5, BR6 211 B2
Crofton Park Rd SE4 163 B5
Crofton Park Sta SE4 163 A6
Crofton Rd
Camberwell SE5 139 C3
Locksbottom BR6 226 C5
Newham E13 99 B3
Crofton Roman Villa* BR6 227 C6
Crofton Terr
Homerton E5 75 A3
Richmond TW9 132 B1
Crofton Way
Enfield EN2 4 C3
New Barnet EN5 13 D5
Croft Rd
Carshalton SM1 218 C3
Enfield EN3 7 A4
Merton SW19 180 A3
Plaistow BR1 187 A4
South Norwood SW16 182 C3
Crofts Ho 21 E2 96 A5
Croftside The 3 SE25 206 A6
Crofts La N22 32 C3
Crofts Rd HA1 43 A4
Crofts St E1 118 A6
Croft St SE8 119 A2
Crofts The TW17 193 C5
Croft The Barnet EN5 1 A1
Chingford E4 20 C2
Ealing W5 88 A2
Edgware HA8 26 D3
Harlesden NW10 89 D5
Heston TW5 129 A5
New Malden KT3 199 C4
Pinner HA5 41 B2
Ruislip HA4 62 C4
Wembley HA0 65 C3
Croft Villas HA1 43 A3
Croft Way
Richmond TW10 153 B1
Sidcup DA15 167 C1
Crogsland Rd NW1 71 A1
Croham Cl CR2 221 C1
Croham Manor Rd CR2 221 C2
Croham Mount CR2 221 C1
Croham Park Ave CR2 221 D3
Croham Rd CR2 221 C3
Croham Valley Rd CR2 222 B1
Croindene Rd SW16 182 A2
Crokesley Ho 2 HA8 27 A1
Cromartie Rd N19 49 D2
Cromarty Ct 7 BR1 187 C1
Cromarty Ho 8 E1 97 A2
Cromarty Rd HA8 10 D2
Cromberdale Ct N17 34 A2
Crombie Cl IG4 56 B4
Crombie Mews 5 SW11 136 C3
Crombie Rd DA15 167 B3
Cromdale Ct N16 51 D2
Crome Ho UB5 85 A5
Cromer Cl UB8 83 A1
Cromer Ct
Streatham SW16 160 A1
Wandsworth SW18 157 B5
Crome Rd NW10 67 C2
Cromer Mans 6 SM1 217 D3
Cromer Pl 5 BR6 211 B1
Cromer Rd Barnet EN5 2 A2
Croydon SE25 206 B6
Dagenham RM6 59 A3
Harlington TW6 126 C3
Leyton E10 54 B2
Streatham SW17 181 A4
Tottenham N17 34 A1
Woodford IG8 37 A6
Cromer Rd W TW6 126 C2
Cromer Road Prim Sch EN5 2 A2
Cromer St WC1 94 A4 233 B1
Cromer Terr
Dalston E8 74 A3
3 Ilford RM6 58 B4
Cromer Villas Rd SW18 157 B5
Cromford Cl BR6 227 C5
Cromford Path 1 E5 74 D4
Cromford Rd SW18 157 C6
Cromford Way KT3 177 B2
Cromlix Cl BR7 188 D1
Crompton Ct SW3 257 A4
Crompton Ho
Borough The SE1 262 B5
Paddington W2 236 C5
South Lambeth SW8 269 B1
Crompton Pl EN3 7 C5
Crompton St W2 92 B3 236 C5
Cromwell Ave
Bromley BR2 209 B5
Hammersmith W6 112 B2
Highgate N6 49 B1
New Malden KT3 199 D4
Cromwell Cl
Acton W3 111 A5
Bromley BR2 209 B5
East Finchley N2 48 B5
2 Gunnersbury W4 110 D1
Walton-on-T KT12 194 B1
Cromwell Cres SW5 113 C2 255 A4
Cromwell Ct
Enfield EN3 18 D6
15 Kingston u T KT2 176 C3
Wembley HA0 88 A5
Cromwell Ctr
Barking IG11 102 A4
North Acton NW10 89 B4
Cromwell Ctr The RM8 59 B2
Cromwell Est E10 53 A1
Cromwell Gdns SW7 114 B3 256 D5
Cromwell Gr W6 112 C3
Cromwell Ho
Battersea SW11 268 B1
2 Croydon CR0 220 D5
Muswell Hill N10 31 B3
Putney SW15 134 A1
Cromwell Hospl (BUPA) SW5 113 D2 255 C4
Cromwell Lo
Barking IG11 79 C3
40 Bethnal Green E1 96 C3
Cromwell Mans SW5 255 B4
Cromwell Mews SW7 256 D4
Cromwell Pl
5 Acton W3 111 A5
Barbican EC1 242 B4
Highgate N6 49 B1
Mortlake SW14 133 A2
South Kensington SW7 114 B2 256 D4
Cromwell Rd
Beckenham BR3 207 A6
Brixton SW9 138 D4
Feltham TW13 150 B3
Finchley N3 30 A2
Hayes UB3 83 B1
Hounslow TW3 129 C1
Kingston u T KT2 176 A2
Muswell Hill N10 31 A3
South Kensington SW7 256 B4
Teddington TW11 175 A4
Thornton Heath CR0 205 B2
Upton E7 77 C1
Walthamstow E17 54 A4
Walton-on-T KT12 194 B1
Wembley HA0 88 A5
Wimbledon SW19 179 D5
Worcester Pk KT4 215 C5
Cromwell St TW3 129 C1
Cromwell Trad Ctr IG11 101 C4
Cromwell Twr EC2 242 B4
Crondace Rd SW6 135 C4 265 B1
Crondall Ct 7 N1 95 C5
Crondall Ho SW15 156 A3
Crondall Pl 15 N1 95 C5
Crondall St N1 95 C5
Crone Ct 5 NW6 91 B5
Cronin St SE15 139 D5
CROOKED BILLET 178 C4
Crooked Billet
Chingford E4 35 C3
Wimbledon SW19 178 C4
Crooked Billet Yd 18 E2 95 C4
Crooked Usage N3 47 A6
Crooke Rd SE8 119 A1
Crookham Rd SW6 135 B4 264 C1
Crook Log DA6 146 D1
Crook Log L Ctr DA7 146 D2
Crook Log Prim Sch DA6 146 D1
Crookston Rd SE9 144 C2
Croombs Rd E16 99 C2
Croom's Hill SE10 142 B5
Croom's Hill Gr SE10 142 A5
Cropley Ct N1 235 C4
Cropley St N1 95 B5 235 C4
Croppath Rd RM10 81 C4
Cropthorne Ct W9 229 B1
Crosbie 10 NW9 27 D1
Crosbie Ho 20 E17 53 D6
Crosby Cl TW13 173 A6
Crosby Ct
Borough The SE1 252 C2
East Finchley N2 48 A5
7 New Southgate N11 31 B6
Crosby Ho
18 Cubitt Town E14 120 A3
Forest Gate E7 77 A2
Crosby Rd
Dagenham RM10 103 D6
Upton E7 77 A2
Crosby Row SE1 117 B4 252 C2
Crosby Sq EC3 243 A2
Crosby Wlk
3 Dalston E8 73 D2
Streatham SE24 160 C4
Crosfield Ct 3 W10 90 D1
Crosfield Ho W11 244 A5
Crosier Cl SE3 144 A3
Crosier Rd UB10 61 A4
Crosier Way HA4 61 C5
Crosland Pl 5 SW11 137 A2
Crossbow Ho
Ealing W13 109 B5
15 Shoreditch N1 95 C6
Crossbrook Rd SE3 144 A2
Cross Cl SE15 140 B3

Cross Ct London SE5 . . 139 B2
[11] Thamesmead
SE28 . . . . 124 B6
Cross Deep TW1 . . . . . 153 A2
Cross Deep Gdns
TW1 . . . . 152 D2
Crossfield Rd
Hampstead NW3 . . . . . . 70 B2
London N17 . . . . 51 A6
Crossfield St SE8 . . . 141 C5
Crossford St SW9 . . . . 138 B3
Crossgate
Edgware HA8 . . . . 10 C1
Wembley UB6 . . . . 65 B2
Crossharbour Sta
E14 . . . . 119 D3
Cross Ho N8 . . . . 50 B5
Cross Keys Cl
[5] Edmonton N9 . . . . . . 18 A2
Marylebone W1 . . . . . 238 B3
Cross La
City of London EC3 . . . 253 A5
Hornsey N8 . . . . 50 B5
Old Bexley DA5 . . . . . 169 B4
Cross Lances Rd
TW3 . . . . 129 D1
Crossland Rd CR7 . . . 204 D3
Crosslands Ave
Ealing W5 . . . . 110 B5
Southall UB2 . . . . 107 B1
Crosslands Rd KT19 . . 215 B2
Crossleigh Ct
[3] New Cross SE14 . . . 141 B5
Streatham SW16 . . . . . 181 B6
Crosslet St SE17 . . . . 262 D4
Crosslet Vale SE10 . . 141 D4
Crossley St N7 . . . . 72 C2
Crossman Hos [19]
SW12 . . . . 160 A4
Crossmead SE9 . . . . . . 166 B3
Crossmead Ave UB6 . . 85 C4
Crossmount Ho [13]
SE5 . . . . 139 A5
Crossness Rd IG11 . . 101 D4
Cross Rd Belmont HA3 . . 25 A1
Camberwell SE5 . . . . . 139 C3
Chingford E4 . . . . 20 C3
Croydon CR0 . . . . 205 B1
Enfield EN1 . . . . 5 C1
Feltham TW13 . . . . . . 173 A6
Finchley N2 . . . . 30 C1
Friern Barnet N11 . . . . . 31 B5
Harrow HA1 . . . . 42 B4
Ilford RM6 . . . . 58 C2
Keston Mark BR2 . . . . 226 A6
Kingston u T KT2 . . . . . 176 B3
Merton SW19 . . . . 179 C3
Romford RM7 . . . . 59 C6
Sidcup DA14 . . . . 190 B6
South Harrow HA2 . . . . . 63 D5
Sutton SM1 . . . . 218 B3
Wood Green N22 . . . . . . 32 C3
Cross St
[2] Edmonton N18 . . . . . 34 A5
Hampton TW12 . . . . . . 174 A5
Islington N1 . . . 94 D6 234 D6
Mortlake SW13 . . . . . . 133 C2
Crossthwaite Ave SE5,
SE24 . . . . 139 B1
Crosstrees Ho [7]
E14 . . . . 119 C3
Crosswall
EC3 . . . . 117 D6 253 C6
Crossway
Dagenham RM8 . . . . 80 C5
Ealing W13 . . . . 87 A3
Enfield EN1 . . . . 17 C4
Finchley N12 . . . . 30 B4
Hayes UB3 . . . . 106 A5
Hendon NW9 . . . . 45 D5
Kingsland E8, N16 . . . . . 73 C3
Petts Wood BR5 . . . . . . 211 B4
Pinner HA5 . . . . 22 B1
Ruislip HA4 . . . . 62 C4
Thamesmead SE28 . . . 102 D1
West Barnes KT3,
SW20 . . . . 200 C5
Woodford IG8 . . . . 37 C6
Crossway Ct SE4 . . . . 141 A3
Crossway Par N22 . . . . 32 D3
Crossways
Ashford TW16 . . . . . . 171 D3
South Croydon CR2 . . . 223 B1
Crossways *continued*
Sutton SM2 . . . . 218 B1
Crossways Acad
SE4 . . . . 141 A3
Crossways Par CR2 . . 223 B1
Crossways Rd
Beckenham BR3 . . . . . 207 C5
Mitcham CR4 . . . . 203 B6
Crossways The
Heston TW5 . . . . 129 B5
Wembley HA9 . . . . 66 C6
Crossway The
Chislehurst SE9 . . . . . 165 D2
Hillingdon UB10 . . . . . . 82 B5
Tottenham N22 . . . . 32 D3
Cross Way The HA3 . . . 24 C1
Crosswell Cl TW17 . . . 171 A1
Croston St E8 . . . . 96 A6
Crothall Cl N13 . . . . . . 16 B1
Crouch Ave IG11 . . . . . 102 B5
Crouch Cl BR3 . . . . 185 C4
Crouch Croft SE9 . . . . 166 C1
CROUCH END 49 D3
Crouch End Hill N8 . . . 49 D2
Crouch Hall Ct N19 . . . 50 A1
Crouch Hall Rd N8 . . . . 49 D3
Crouch Hill N4, N8,
N19 . . . . 50 A2
Crouch Hill Sta N4 . . . . 50 B2
Crouchmans Cl SE21,
SE26 . . . . 162 A1
Crouch Rd NW10 . . . . . 67 B1
Crowborough Ct
W13 . . . . 109 C6
Crowborough Path
WD19 . . . . 22 D6
Crowborough Rd
SW17 . . . . 181 A5
Crowden Way SE28 . . 124 C6
Crowder Cl N12 . . . . . . 30 A3
Crowder St E1 . . . . 118 B6
Crowfield Ho N5 . . . . . . 73 A4
Crowfoot Cl
Hackney Wick E9 . . . . . . 75 B3
Woolwich SE28 . . . . . 123 C5
Crowhurst SE25 . . . . . 206 A6
Crowhurst Cl SW9 . . . 138 C3
Crowhurst Ct N17 . . . . 34 B2
Crowhurst Ho [21]
SW9 . . . . 138 B3
Crow La RM7, RM8 . . . . . 59 D2
Crowland Ave UB3 . . . 105 D2
Crowland Gdns N14 . . . 16 A4
Crowland Ho NW8 . . . 229 A5
Crowland Prim Sch
N15 . . . . 52 A4
Crowland Rd
South Norwood CR7 . . . 205 B5
South Tottenham N15 . . 51 D4
Crowlands Ave RM7 . . . 59 D3
Crowland Terr N1 . . . . . 73 B1
Crowland Wlk SM4 . . . 202 A3
Crowley Cres CR0 . . . . 220 C3
Crowline Wlk [1] N1 . . . 73 A2
Crowmarsh Gdns
SE23 . . . . 162 C4
Crown Arc KT1 . . . . . . 175 D1
Crown Bldgs [4] E4 . . . . 20 B3
Crownbourne Ct
SM1 . . . . 217 D4
Crown Cl Bow E3 . . . . . . 97 C6
Edgware NW7 . . . . 11 D2
Hampstead NW6 . . . . . . 69 D2
Hayes UB3 . . . . 105 D4
Walton-on-T KT12 . . . . 194 C2
Wood Green N22 . . . . . . 32 C2
Crown Close Bsns Ctr [12]
E3 . . . . 97 C6
Crown Ct
Bromley BR1 . . . . 209 D4
City of London EC4 . . . 242 B1
Harrow HA2 . . . . 42 C1
Lee SE12 . . . . 165 B5
[11] Muswell Hill N10 . . . . 31 A3
[4] Putney SW15 . . . . . 134 D1
St Giles WC2 . . . . 240 B1
St John's Wood NW8 . . 230 B1
[3] Twickenham TW1 . . . 153 B4
Crown Dale SE19 . . . . 183 A5
Crowndale Ct NW1 . . 232 C4
Crowndale Rd
NW1 . . . . 93 C5 232 B4
Crowne Ho SE1 . . . . . . 252 B3
Crownfield Ave IG2 . . . 57 C4
Crownfield Rd E15 . . . . 76 B4
Crowngate Ho [33] E3 . . 97 B5
Crown Hill CR0 . . . . . . 221 A5
Crownhill Rd NW10 . . . 89 D6
Crown Ho Ruislip HA4 . . 40 A1
Wembley HA9 . . . . 66 B3
[3] Woolwich SE18 . . . 123 A2
Crown La
Bromley Comm BR2 . . 209 D4
Chislehurst BR7 . . . . . 189 A2
Merton SM4 . . . . 201 C6
Osidge N14 . . . . 15 C3
South Norwood SE19,
SW16 . . . . 182 C5
Crown Lane Gdns
SE27 . . . . 182 C5
Crown Lane Prim Sch
SE27 . . . . 182 D5
Crown Lane Spur
BR2 . . . . 209 D3
Crownleigh Ct SW2 . . 160 C6
Crown Lo
Chelsea SW3 . . . . 257 B3
Finchley N3 . . . . 29 B1
Crownmead Way
RM7 . . . . 59 D5
Crown Mews
[2] Newham E13 . . . . . . 99 C6
[9] Stepney E1 . . . . 96 D2
Crown Mill CR4 . . . . . . 202 C4
Crown Office Row
EC4 . . . . 251 A6
Crown Par
London N14 . . . . 15 C3
Morden SM4 . . . . 201 D5
Crown Pas
Kingston u T KT1 . . . . 175 D1
St James SW1 . . . . 249 B3
Crown Pl
Broadgate EC2 . . . . . . 243 A4
Kentish Town NW5 . . . . . 71 B2
Crown Point Par
SE19 . . . . 182 D4
Crown Rd Enfield EN1 . . . 6 B2
Ilford IG6 . . . . 57 B5
Kingston u T KT3 . . . . 177 A2
Morden SM4 . . . . 201 D5
Muswell Hill N10 . . . . . . 31 A3
Ruislip HA4 . . . . 62 D3
Sutton SM1 . . . . 217 D4
Twickenham TW1 . . . . . 153 B5
Crown Reach SW1 . . . 259 D1
Crown St Acton W3 . . . 110 D5
Camberwell SE5 . . . . . 139 A5
Dagenham RM10 . . . . . . 81 D2
Harrow HA2 . . . . 42 C1
Crownstone Ct [1]
SW2 . . . . 160 C6
Crownstone Rd
SW2 . . . . 160 C6
Crown Terr TW9 . . . . . 132 B1
Crown Trad Ctr UB3 . 105 C4
Crowntree Cl TW7 . . 130 D6
Crown Way UB7 . . . . . 104 B5
Crown Wlk HA9 . . . . 66 B5
Crown Woods La
SE18 . . . . 144 D3
Crown Woods Sch
SE9 . . . . 167 A6
Crown Woods Way
SE9 . . . . 167 B6
Crown Yard TW3 . . . . 130 A2
Crowshott Ave HA7 . . . 25 D2
Crows Rd
Barking IG11 . . . . 78 D2
Mill Meads E3, E15 . . . . 98 B4
Crowther Ave TW8 . . . 110 A2
Crowther Cl
SW6 . . . . 135 B6 264 D5
Crowther Rd SE25 . . . 206 A5
Crowthorne Cl
SW18 . . . . 157 B3
Crowthorne Rd W10 . . 90 D1
Croxall Ho KT12 . . . . . 194 C3
Croxden Cl HA8 . . . . . . 44 C6
Croxden Wlk SM4 . . . 202 A3
Croxford Gdns N22 . . . 32 D3
Croxley Cl BR5 . . . . . . 190 B1
Croxley Gn BR5 . . . . . . 190 B2
Croxley Rd W9 . . . . 91 B4
Croxted Cl SE21 . . . . . 161 A4
Croxted Rd SE21,
SE24 . . . . 161 B3
Croxteth Ho [11] SW8 . 137 D3
Croxton [17] KT1 . . . . . 176 C1
Croyde Ave
Greenford UB6 . . . . 86 A4
Hayes UB3 . . . . 105 C2
Croyde Cl DA15 . . . . . 167 B4
Croyden Ct HA0 . . . . . . 65 D2
CROYDON 221 B5
Croydon N17 . . . . 33 B1
Croydon Airport Ind Est
CR0 . . . . 220 B2
Croydon Coll CR0 . . . . 221 B6
Croydon Coll Annexe [10]
CR0 . . . . 205 B1
Croydon Coll (Selhurst
Tertiary Ctr) SE25 . . 205 B4
Croydon Flyover The
CR0 . . . . 221 A5
Croydon Gr CR0 . . . . 204 D1
Croydon Ho
Lambeth SE1 . . . . 251 B2
Thornton Heath CR0 . . 204 B3
Croydon Prim
Independant Sch [8]
CR0 . . . . 205 C1
Croydon Rd
Bandonhill CR0, SM5,
SM6 . . . . 219 C5
Beckenham BR3 . . . . . 207 A6
Coney Hall BR2, BR4 . 224 D5
Harlington TW6 . . . . . 126 D2
Keston Mark BR2, BR4,
BR6 . . . . 225 C5
Mitcham CR0, CR4 . . . 203 C4
Newham E13 . . . . 98 D3
Penge SE20 . . . . 184 C2
Waddon CR0 . . . . 220 B4
Croydon Rd Ind Est
BR3 . . . . 206 D5
Croydon's Sports Arena
SE25 . . . . 206 C4
Croydon Valley Trade Pk
[2] CR0 . . . . 204 A2
Croyland Rd N9 . . . . . . 18 A3
Croylands Dr KT6 . . . . 198 A2
Croysdale Ave TW16 . 194 A6
Crozier Ho
Blackheath Pk SE3 . . . 143 B2
South Lambeth SW8 . . 270 C3
Crozier Terr E9 . . . . 74 D3
Crucible Ct RM6 . . . . . . 58 B3
Crucifix La
SE1 . . . . 117 C4 253 A2
Cruden Ho [15] Bow E3 . . 97 B5
[11] Camberwell SE17 . 138 D6
Cruden St N1 . . 94 D6 234 D5
Cruickshank St WC1 234 A2
Cruikshank Ho NW8 230 B4
Cruikshank Rd E15 . . . . 76 C3
Crummock Gdns
NW9 . . . . 45 C4
Crumpsall St SE2 . . . . 124 C2
Crundale Ave NW9 . . . . 44 C4
Crunden Rd CR2 . . . . . 221 B1
Crusader Gdns CR0 . . 221 C5
Crusader Ho EC1 . . . . 241 C5
Crusader Ind Est N4 . . 51 A3
Crusoe Ct E11 . . . . 76 D5
Crusoe Mews N16 . . . . 73 B6
Crusoe Rd CR4 . . . . . . 180 D3
Crutched Friars
EC3 . . . . 117 C6 253 B6
Crutchfield La KT12 . . 194 B1
Crutchley Rd SE6 . . . . 164 C2
Crystal Ct SE19 . . . . . 183 D5
Crystal Ctr The [1]
HA1 . . . . 42 D4
Crystal Ho SE18 . . . . . 123 D1
CRYSTAL PALACE . . . 184 A5
Crystal Palace Farm Pk★
SE20 . . . . 184 A5
Crystal Palace Mus★
SE19 . . . . 183 D4
Crystal Palace National
Sports Ctr SE19 . . . 184 A4
Crystal Palace Par
SE19 . . . . 183 D5
Crystal Palace Park Rd
SE26 . . . . 184 B5
Crystal Palace Rd
SE22 . . . . 162 A6
Crystal Palace Sta
SE19 . . . . 184 A4
Crystal Palace Station Rd
SE19 . . . . 184 A4
Crystal Terr SE19 . . . . 183 B4
Crystal View Ct BR1 . . 186 B6
Crystal Way
Dagenham RM8 . . . . 58 C1
Harrow HA1 . . . . 42 D4
Crystal Wharf N1 . . . 234 D3
Cuba Dr EN3 . . . . 6 C3
Cuba St E14 . . . . 119 C4
Cubitt Bldg SW1 . . . . 258 C1
Cubitt Ho [4] SW4 . . . . 159 C5
Cubitt Sq UB2 . . . . 108 A5
Cubitt St WC1 . . 94 B4 233 D1
Cubitt Terr SW4 . . . . . 137 C2
CUBITT TOWN 120 A2
Cubitt Town Jun & Inf
Sch E14 . . . . 120 A3
Cuckoo Ave W7 . . . . 86 C3
Cuckoo Dene W7 . . . . . 86 B2
Cuckoo Hall La N9 . . . . 18 D4
Cuckoo Hall Prim Sch
N9 . . . . 18 C4
Cuckoo Hill HA5 . . . . . . 40 C6
Cuckoo Hill Dr HA5 . . . 40 C6
Cuckoo Hill Rd HA5 . . . 40 D5
Cuckoo La W7 . . . . 108 C6
Cuda's Cl KT19 . . . . . . 215 D4
Cuddington SE17 . . . . 262 B4
Cuddington Ave KT19,
KT4 . . . . 215 D5
Cuddington Com Prim
Sch KT4 . . . . 215 D5
Cudham La N BR6 . . . . 227 C1
Cudham St SE6 . . . . . . 164 A4
Cudworth Ho SW8 . . . 269 B1
Cudworth St E1 . . . . 96 B3
Cuff Cres SE9 . . . . 165 D5
Cuffley Ho [3] W10 . . . . 90 C2
Cuff Point [12] E2 . . . . . 95 D4
Culand Ho SE17 . . . . . 263 A3
Culford Gdns
SW3 . . . . 114 D2 257 D3
Culford Gr N1 . . . . 73 C2
Culford Mans SW3 . . . 257 D3
Culford Mews N1 . . . . . 73 C2
Culford Rd
Kingsland N1 . . . . 73 C2
Shoreditch N1 . . . . 95 C6
Culgaith Gdns EN2 . . . . . 4 A1
Culham Ho
[21] Paddington W2 . . . . 91 C2
[33] Shoreditch E2 . . . . . 95 D4
Cullen Ho W9 . . . . 91 B5
Cullen Way NW10 . . . . . 89 A3
Culling Rd SE16 . . . . . 118 C3
Cullington Cl HA3 . . . . . 43 A5
Cullingworth Rd
NW10 . . . . 68 B3
Culloden Cl [21] SE16 . . 118 A1
Culloden Prim Sch [16]
E14 . . . . 98 A1
Culloden Rd EN2 . . . . . . 4 D3
Cullum St EC3 . . . . . . 253 A6
Culmington Mans
W13 . . . . 109 C6
Culmington Par
W13 . . . . 109 C6
Culmington Rd
Ealing W13, W5 . . . . . 109 C5
South Croydon CR2 . . . 221 A1
Culmore Rd SE15 . . . . 140 C5
Culmstock Rd SW11 . . 159 A6
Culpepper Cl N18 . . . . . 34 B5
Culpepper Ct SE11 . . . 261 A4
Culross Bldgs NW1 . . 233 A4
Culross Cl N15 . . . . 51 A5
Culross St
W1 . . . . 115 A6 248 A5
Culsac Rd KT6 . . . . . . 214 A6
Culver Ct SW18 . . . . . 157 D5
Culverden Rd SW12 . . 159 C2
Culver Gr HA7 . . . . 25 C1
Culverhouse WC1 . . . . 240 C3
Culverhouse Gdns
SW16 . . . . 160 B1
Culverin Ct [1] N7 . . . . . 72 B3
Culverlands Cl HA7 . . . 25 B6
Culverlands Ct N20 . . . 14 B3
Culverley Rd SE6 . . . . 164 A3
Culvers Ave SM5 . . . . 218 D6
Culvers House Prim Sch
CR4 . . . . 203 A1
Culvers Retreat
SM5 . . . . 218 D6
Culverstone Cl BR2 . 208 D4
Culvers Way SM5 . . . 218 D6
Culvert Ct SW11 . . . . 137 A3
Culverton Ct [8]
DA14 . . . . 190 A6
Culvert Pl SW11 . . . . . 137 A3
Culvert Rd
London SW11 . . . . 136 D3
South Tottenham N15 . . 51 C4

Culworth Ho NW8 230 A4
Culworth St NW8 230 A3
Cumber Ho SW18 157 C3
Cumberland Ave
- Falconwood DA16 145 D1
- Wembley NW10 88 D4
Cumberland Bsns Pk NW10 88 D4
Cumberland Cl
- Dalston E8 73 D2
- 2 Twickenham TW1 153 B5
- 8 Wimbledon SW20 178 D3
Cumberland Comp Sch E13 99 C3
Cumberland Cres W14 254 B4
Cumberland Ct
- 4 Croydon CR0 205 B1
- 7 Finchley N3 29 B1
- Harrow HA1 42 C6
- Marylebone W1 237 D1
- Woodford IG8 37 B3
Cumberland Dr
- Chessington KT9 214 B5
- Erith DA7 147 A5
- Hinchley Wood KT10 213 A6
Cumberland Gate W1 114 D6 247 D6
Cumberland Gdns
- Church End NW4 29 A1
- Finsbury WC1 234 A2
Cumberland Ho
- Edmonton N9 18 C3
- Kingston u T KT2 176 D3
- Paddington W9 236 A5
- 1 Putney SW15 156 C4
- Woolwich SE28 123 B4
Cumberland Mans
- Marylebone W1 237 C2
- 7 West Hampstead NW6 69 C3
Cumberland Market NW1 93 B4 231 D2
Cumberland Mills Sq E14 120 B1
Cumberland Park Ind Est NW10 90 A4
Cumberland Pk W3 111 A6
Cumberland Pl
- Catford SE6 164 D3
- Regent's Pk NW1 231 C2
- Sunbury TW16 194 A5
Cumberland Rd
- Acton W3 111 A6
- Ashford TW15 148 A1
- Barnes SW13 134 A4
- Beckenham BR2 208 D6
- Croydon SE25 206 B3
- Edmonton N9 18 C3
- Hanwell W7 108 D4
- Harrow HA1 41 D4
- Higham Hill E17 35 A1
- Manor Pk E12 77 D4
- Newham E13 99 B3
- Richmond TW9 132 C5
- Stanmore HA7, HA8 44 B6
- Wood Green N22 32 B1
Cumberland St SW1 115 B1 258 D2
Cumberland Terr NW1 231 C3
Cumberland Terrace Mews NW1 231 C3
Cumberland Villas W3 111 A6
Cumberland Wharf 12 SE16 118 C4
Cumberlow Ave SE25 206 A6
Cumbernauld Gdns TW16 171 D5
Cumberton Rd N17 33 B2
Cumbrae Gdns KT6 213 D6
Cumbrian Gdns NW2 69 A6
Cuming Mus* SE17 262 A3
Cumming St N1 233 D3
Cumnor Cl 23 SW9 138 B3
Cumnor Gdns KT17 216 A2
Cumnor Rd SM2 218 A2
Cunard Cres N21 17 B5
Cunard Pl EC3 243 B1
Cunard Rd NW10 89 B4
Cunard Wlk 3 SE16 119 A2
Cundy Rd E16 99 C1
Cundy St SW1 115 A2 258 B3
Cunliffe Rd KT19 215 D4
Cunliffe St SW16 181 C4
Cunningham Cl
- Dagenham RM6 58 C4
- West Wickham BR4 223 D6
Cunningham Ct
- Harrow HA1 42 B4
- Paddington W2 236 C5
Cunningham Ho 16 SE5 139 B5
Cunningham Pk HA1 42 B4
Cunningham Pl NW8 92 B3 236 C6
Cunningham Rd N15 52 A5
Cunnington St W4 111 A2
Cupar Rd SW11 268 B2
Cupola Cl BR1 187 B5
Cureton St SW1 115 D2 259 D3
Curie Gdns NW9 27 C1
Curie Ho 1 HA9 67 A5
Curlew Cl SE28 124 D6
Curlew Ct KT6 214 C5
Curlew Ho
- Brockley SE4 141 A1
- Enfield EN3 18 D6
- 7 Peckham SE15 139 D4
Curlew St SE1 117 D4 253 D2
Curlew Way UB4 84 D2
Curness St SE13 142 A1
Curnick's La SE27 183 A6
Curran Ave
- Bexley DA15 167 D6
- Hackbridge SM6 219 A5
Curran Ho SW3 257 A3
Currey Rd UB6 64 B2
Curricle St W3 111 C5
Currie Hill Cl SW19 179 B6
Currie Ho 13 SW12 159 D4
Curry Rise NW7 28 D4
Cursitor St EC4 94 C1 241 A2
Curtain Pl EC2 243 B6
Curtain Rd EC2 95 C3 243 B6
Curthwaite Gdns EN2 15 D6
Curtis Dr W3 89 B1
Curtis Field Rd SW16 182 C6
Curtis Ho
- 7 London N11 31 C5
- Walworth SE17 262 C2
Curtis La HA0 66 A3
Curtis Rd
- Twickenham TW4 151 B4
- West Ewell KT19 215 A4
Curtis St SE1 117 D2 263 C4
Curtis Way
- Bermondsey SE1 263 C4
- 7 Thamesmead SE28 124 B6
Curtlington Ho 3 HA8 27 A1
Curve Bldg The SE4 163 B6
Curve The Ealing W5 109 D4
- Shepherd's Bush W12 112 A6
Curwen Ave E7 77 B4
Curwen & New Acad Gall* W1 239 C3
Curwen Prim Sch E13 99 A5
Curwen Rd W12 112 A4
Curzon Ave
- Enfield EN3 18 D6
- Stanmore HA7 25 A2
Curzon Cl BR6 227 B4
Curzon Cres
- Barking IG11 101 D4
- Willesden NW10 67 C1
Curzon Ct SE9 167 A1
Curzon Gate W1 248 B3
Curzon Ho W5 87 B3
Curzon Pl HA5 40 C4
Curzon Rd Ealing W5 87 B3
- Muswell Hill N10 31 B1
- Thornton Heath CR7 204 C3
Curzon Sq W1 248 B3
Curzon St W1 115 B5 248 C4
Cusack Cl TW1 174 D6
Custance Ho N1 235 C3
Custance St N1 235 C2
CUSTOM HOUSE 121 C6
Custom House EC3 117 C6 253 A5
Custom House for ExCeL Sta E16 121 B6
Custom House Reach SE16 119 B3
Cutbush Ho N7 71 D3
Cutcombe Rd SE5 139 A3
Cuthberga Cl IG11 79 A1
Cuthbert Gdns SE25 205 C6
Cuthbert Harrowing Ho EC1 242 A5
Cuthbert Ho W2 236 C4
Cuthbert Rd
- Croydon CR0 220 D6
- 8 Edmonton N18 34 A6
- Walthamstow E17 54 A6
Cuthbert St W2 236 C5
Cuthill Wlk 3 SE5 139 B4
Cutlers Gdns EC2 243 B2
Cutlers Gdns Arc EC2 243 B2
Cutlers Sq E14 119 C2
Cutler St EC2 243 B2
Cut The SE1 116 C4 251 B2
Cutty Sark* SE10 142 A6
Cutty Sark Ho 10 E14 119 D2
Cutty Sark Ret Development SE10 142 A6
Cutty Sark Sta SE10 142 A6
Cuxton BR5 211 A4
Cuxton Cl DA6 169 A6
Cuxton Ho SE17 263 B2
Cyclamen Cl 4 TW12 173 C4
Cyclamen Way KT19 215 A3
Cyclops Mews 12 E14 119 C2
Cygnet Ave TW14 150 D4
Cygnet Cl NW10 67 B3
Cygnet Ct EN3 7 A4
Cygnet Ho
- Harrow HA7 24 D4
- St John's Wood NW8 229 A6
Cygnet Hospl Harrow HA1 64 C6
Cygnet House N 18 E14 97 D1
Cygnet House S 19 E14 97 D1
Cygnet St E1 243 D6
Cygnets The TW13 173 A6
Cygnet Way UB4 84 D2
Cygnus Bsns Ctr NW10 67 D2
Cymbeline Ct 6 HA1 42 D3
Cyna Ct 5 E11 55 A3
Cynthia St N1 233 D3
Cyntra Pl 8 E8 74 B1
Cypress Ave
- London N2 47 D6
- Twickenham TW2 152 A4
Cypress Cl 9 E5 74 A6
Cypress Ct
- Cheam SM1 217 C2
- 5 Leyton E11 76 B4
- 7 West Norwood SW16 182 C5
Cypress Gdns SE4 163 A6
Cypress Ho SE14 140 D4
Cypress Inf Sch SE25 183 C1
Cypress Jun Sch SE25 183 C1
Cypress Lo SE25 183 C1
Cypress Pl W1 239 B5
Cypress Rd
- Harrow HA3 24 B1
- South Norwood SE25 183 C1
Cypress Tree Cl DA15 167 D3
CYPRUS 122 C6
Cyprus Ave N3 29 A1
Cyprus Cl N4 50 C3
Cyprus Ct 9 N3 29 B1
Cyprus Gdns N3 29 A1
Cyprus Ho 10 N3 29 B1
Cyprus Pl
- 23 Bethnal Green E2 96 C5
- Newham E6 122 C6
Cyprus Rd
- Church End N3 29 B1
- Edmonton N9 17 D2
Cyprus St E2 96 C5
Cyprus Sta E6 122 C6
Cyrena Rd SE22 161 D6
Cyril Jackson Prim Sch (North Bldg) 24 E14 119 B6
Cyril Jackson Prim Sch (South Bldg) 25 E14 119 B6
Cyril Lo 2 DA14 190 A6
Cyril Mans SW11 267 D1
Cyril Rd DA7 147 A3
Cyril Smith Ho N13 32 B5
Cyril Thatcher Ho SW6 265 B1
Cyrus Ho EC1 241 D6
Cyrus St EC1 94 D3 241 D6
Czar St SE8 141 C6

D

Daairy Mews N2 48 C5
Dabbs Hill La UB5 63 C3
Dabb's La EC1 241 B5
Dabin Cres SE10 142 A4
Dacca St SE8 141 B6
Dace Rd E3 97 C6
Dacre Cl UB6 85 D5
Dacre Gdns
- Borehamwood WD6 11 B6
- Lewisham SE13 142 C1
Dacre Ho SW3 266 D5
Dacre Pk SE13 142 C1
Dacre Pl SE13 142 C2
Dacre Rd
- Leytonstone E11 54 D1
- Newham E13 99 B6
- Thornton Heath CR0 204 A2
Dacres Rd SE23 162 D1
Dacre St SW1 115 D3 259 C6
Dade Way UB2 107 B1
Daerwood Cl BR2 210 B1
Daffodil Cl CR0 206 D1
Daffodil Gdns IG1 78 D3
Daffodil Pl 7 TW12 173 C4
Daffodil St W12 111 D6
Dafforne Rd SW17 159 A1
DAGENHAM 81 D1
Dagenham Ave
- Dagenham RM9 81 B1
- Dagenham RM9 103 A6
Dagenham Dock Estate RM9 103 B3
Dagenham Dock Sta RM9 103 B5
Dagenham East Sta RM10 81 D3
Dagenham Heathway Sta RM9 81 B2
Dagenham Park Com Sch RM10 103 D6
Dagenham Rd
- Dagenham RM10 81 D4
- London E10 53 B1
Dagenham & Redbridge Football Grd RM10 81 D3
Dagenham Swimming Pool RM10 81 C6
Dagger La WD23 9 A6
Dagmar Ave HA9 66 B4
Dagmar Ct
- Cubitt Town E14 120 A3
- South Tottenham N15 51 B5
Dagmar Gdns NW10 90 D5
Dagmar Mews UB2 107 A3
Dagmar Pas N1 234 D6
Dagmar Rd
- Camberwell SE5 139 C4
- Finsbury Pk N4 50 C2
- 4 Kingston u T KT2 176 C3
- Southall UB2 107 A3
- South Norwood SE25 205 C4
- West Green N15 51 B5
- Wood Green N22 31 D2
Dagmar Terr N1 94 D6 234 D6
Dagnall Pk SE25 205 C4
Dagnall Rd SE25 205 C4
Dagnall St SW11 137 A4 268 A1
Dagnan Rd SW12 159 C4
Dagobert Ho 27 E1 96 C2
Dagonet Gdns BR1 165 A1
Dagonet Rd BR1 165 A1
Dahlia Gdns
- Ilford IG1 78 D2
- Mitcham CR4 203 D5
Dahlia Rd SE2 124 B2
Dahomey Rd SW16 181 C4
Daiglen Sch IG9 21 C2
Daimler Ho 8 E3 97 C3
Daimler Way SM6 220 A1
Daines Cl E12 78 B5
Dainford Cl BR1 186 B5
Dainton Cl 1 BR1 187 B2
Dainton Ho 22 W2 91 C2
Daintry Cl HA3 43 A5
Daintry Way E9 75 B2
Dairsie Ct 3 BR1 187 C1
Dairsie Rd SE9 144 C2
Dairy Cl Bromley BR1 187 B3
- South Norwood CR7 183 A1
- Willesden NW10 90 A6
Dairy La SE18 122 B2
Dairyman Cl NW2 69 A5
Dairy Meadow Prim Sch UB2 107 B3
Daisy Cl CR0 206 D1
Daisy Dormer Ct 11 SW9 138 B1
Daisy Ho IG3 58 A1
Daisy La SW6 135 C2
Daisy Rd Newham E16 98 C3
- Woodford E18 37 B1
Dakin Pl 9 E1 97 A2
Dakota bldg 6 SE13 141 D4
Dakota Cl SM6 220 B1
Dakota Gdns UB5 85 A4
Dalberg Rd SW2 160 C6
Dalberg Way SE2 124 D3
Dalbury Ho 6 SW9 138 B1
Dalby Rd SW18 136 A1
Dalbys Cres N17 33 C4
Dalby St NW5 71 B2
Dalcross Rd TW4, TW5 129 A3
Dale Ave Edgware HA8 26 B1
- Hounslow TW4 129 A2
Dalebury Rd SW17 158 D2
Dale Cl
- Blackheath Pk SE3 143 A2
- New Barnet EN5 13 D5
- Pinner HA5 22 B2
Dale Croft N4 73 A5
Dale Ct
- Cranley Gdns N8 49 C5
- 3 Kingston u T KT2 176 B3
- Northolt UB5 63 B1
- Wembley HA0 65 D4
- Woodford E18 37 A1
Dale Dr UB4 83 D4
Dalefield IG9 21 D3
Dale Gdns IG8 37 B6
Dale Gr N12 30 A5
Dale Green Rd N11 15 B1
Dalehaed NW1 232 A3
Daleham Dr UB8 82 D1
Daleham Gdns NW3 70 B2
Daleham Mews NW3 70 B2
Dale Ho London SE4 141 A1
- St John's Wood NW8 229 A6
Dale Lo N6 49 C3
Dalemain Ho 5 SW8 137 D3
Dalemain Mews 12 E16 121 A5
Dale Park Ave SM5 218 D6
Dale Park Rd SE19 183 B2
Dale Rd
- Ashford TW16 171 D3
- Camberwell SE17 138 D6
- Cheam SM1 217 B4
- Gospel Oak NW5 71 A3
- Southall UB6 85 D2
- Walton-on-T KT12 193 D2
Dale Row W11 91 A1
Daleside Rd
- Streatham SW17 181 B5
- West Ewell KT19 215 B2
Dales Path WD6 11 B6
Dales Rd WD6 11 B6
Dale St W4 111 C1
Dale The BR2 225 D4
Dale View Ave E4 20 A2
Dale View Cres E4 20 A1
Dale View Gdns E4 20 B1
Daleview Rd N15 51 C3
Dalewood Gdns KT4 216 B6
Dale Wood Rd BR6 211 C1

Daley Ho [6] W12 90 B1
Daley St E9 74 D2
Daley Thompson Way [7] SW8 137 B2
Dalgarno Gdns W10 90 C2
Dalgarno Way W10 90 C3
Daling Way E3 97 A5
Dali Universe★ SE1 250 C2
Dalkeith Ct SW1 259 D3
Dalkeith Gr HA7 26 A5
Dalkeith Ho [6] SW9 138 D4
Dalkeith Rd Ilford IG1 79 A5
West Norwood SE21 161 A4
Dallas Ct SM3 217 A2
Dallas Rd
Cheam SM3 217 A2
Ealing W5 88 B2
Forest Hill SE26 162 B1
Hendon NW4 46 A2
Dallas Terr UB3 105 D3
Dallega Cl UB3 105 B6
Dallinger Rd SE12 164 D5
Dalling Rd W6 112 B2
Dallington Sch EC1 94 D3 241 D6
Dallington St EC1 94 D3 241 D6
Dallin Rd Bexley DA6 146 D1
Woolwich SE18 144 D5
Dalmain Prim Sch SE23 163 A3
Dalmain Rd SE23 162 D3
Dalmally Pas CR0 205 D2
Dalmally Passage CR0 205 D3
Dalmally Rd CR0 206 A2
Dalmeny Ave
Thornton Heath SW16 182 C1
Tufnell Pk N7 71 D4
Dalmeny Avenue Est [3] N7 71 D4
Dalmeny Cl HA0 65 C2
Dalmeny Cres TW3 130 B1
Dalmeny Ct [4] SW4 138 A3
Dalmeny Rd
Erith DA8 147 D4
New Barnet EN5 14 A5
North Cheam KT4 216 B5
Tufnell Pk N7 71 D4
Wallington SM5 219 A1
Dalmeyer Rd NW10 67 D2
Dalmore Ave KT10 212 D2
Dalmore Rd SE21 161 A2
Dalrymple Cl
Barnet N20 14 A4
London N14 15 D4
Dalrymple Rd SE4 141 A1
DALSTON 74 A2
Dalston Gdns HA7 26 A1
Dalston Jct E8 73 D2
Dalston Junction Sta E8 73 C2
Dalston Kingsland Sta E8 73 D3
Dalston La E8 74 A3
Dalton Ave CR4 180 C1
Dalton Cl Hayes UB4 83 B3
Orpington BR6 227 C5
Dalton Ho
[7] Balham SW12 159 B4
[10] Bow E3 97 A5
[19] Deptford SE14 140 D6
Merton SW19 180 A2
Stanmore HA7 25 B5
Dalton St SE27 160 D1
Daltry Ho HA1 42 D5
Dalwood St SE5 139 C4
Daly Dr BR1 210 C6
Dalyell Rd SW9 138 B2
Damascene Wlk SE21 161 A3
Damask Cres E16 98 C3
Damask Ct SM1 201 D1
Damer Ho [9] TW10 154 B5
Damer Terr SW10 266 B3
Dames Rd E7 77 A5
Dame St N1 95 A5 235 A4
Damien Ct [12] E1 96 B1
Damien St E1 96 B1
Damon Cl DA14 168 B1
Damon Ct DA14 168 B1
Damon Ho [2] N12 30 B5
Damory Ho [1] SE16 118 C2
Damson Dr UB3 106 A6
Damsonwood Rd UB2 107 C3
Danbrook Rd SW16 182 A3
Dan Bryant Ho [5] SW12 159 C4
Danbury Cl RM6 58 D6
Danbury Mans [3] IG11 78 D1
Danbury Mews SM5, SM6 219 B4
Danbury St N1 94 D5 234 D4
Danbury Way IG8 37 C4
Danby Ct EN2 5 A2
Danby Ho
[23] Hackney E9 74 C1
[3] West Kilburn W10 91 B4
Danby St SE15 139 D2
Dancastle Ct [7] N3 29 C2
Dancer Rd
Fulham SW6 135 B4 264 C1
Richmond TW9 132 C2
Dando Cres SE3 143 B2
Dandridge Cl SE10 120 D1
Dandridge Ho E1 243 C4
Danebury
New Addington CR0 223 D2
[18] North Kensington W10 90 C2
Danebury Ave SW15 155 D5
Daneby Rd SE6 164 A2
Dane Cl
Farnborough BR6 227 B3
Sidcup DA5 169 C4
Danecourt Gdns CR0 221 D5
Danecroft Rd SE24 161 B6
Daneglen Ct [18] HA7 25 C5
Danegrove Prim Sch (Ridgeway Ave) EN4 14 D5
Danegrove Prim Sch (Windsor Dr) EN4 14 C5
Danehill Wlk DA14 168 A1
Dane Ho
[15] London SE5 139 A3
Upper Tooting SW17 180 A6
Danehurst TW8 131 C5
Danehurst Gdns IG4 56 B4
Danehurst St SW6 135 A4 264 A2
Daneland EN4 14 D5
Danemead Gr UB5 63 D3
Danemere St SW15 134 C2
Dane Pl E3 97 B5
Dane Rd
Ashford TW15 171 B4
Ealing W13 109 C5
Ilford IG1 79 A3
Lower Edmonton N18 18 C1
Merton SW19 180 A2
Southall UB1 107 A6
Danesbury Rd TW13 150 B3
Danescombe SE12 165 A3
Danescourt Cres SM1 218 A6
Danescroft
Hendon NW4 46 D4
[3] North Finchley N12 30 A5
Danescroft Ave NW4 46 D4
Danescroft Gdns NW4 46 D4
Danes Ct
Primrose Hill NW8 230 C5
Wembley HA9 66 D5
Danesdale Rd E9 75 A2
Danesfield SE5 139 C6
Danes Gate HA1 42 C6
Danes Ho [10] W10 90 C2
Dane St WC1 240 C3
Daneswood Ave SE6 164 A1
Danethorpe Rd HA0 65 D2
Danetree Cl KT19 215 A1
Danetree Rd KT19 215 A1
Danetree Sch KT19 215 A1
Danette Gdns RM8 81 B6
Daneville Rd SE5 139 B4
Danford Ho [9] N11 31 C5
Dangan Rd E11 55 A3
Daniel Almshouse NW4 46 B5
Daniel Bolt Cl E14 97 D2
Daniel Cl London N18 34 C6
Daniel Cl *continued*
Twickenham TW4 151 B4
Upper Tooting SW17 180 C4
Daniel Ct Acton W3 111 C6
[3] Beckenham BR3 185 C3
[7] Edgware HA8 26 D5
[10] Hendon NW9 27 C2
Daniel Gdns SE15 139 D5
Daniel Ho [1] HA5 22 C1
Daniell Ho N1 235 D4
Daniell Way CR0 204 B1
Daniel Pl NW4 46 B2
Daniel Rd W5 110 B6
Daniel's Rd SE15 140 C2
Dan Leno Wlk SW6 265 C3
Dansey Pl W1 249 C6
Dansington Rd DA16 146 A1
Danson Cres DA16 146 B2
Danson House★ DA6 146 C1
Danson Intc DA5 168 C5
Danson La DA16 146 B1
Danson Mead DA16 146 C2
Danson Prim Sch DA16 146 A1
Danson Rd DA5 168 D6
Danson Underpass DA5 168 C5
Dante Pl SE11 261 D3
Dante Rd SE11 116 D2 261 C4
Danube Ct [13] SE15 139 D5
Danube St SW3 114 C1 257 B2
Danvers Ho [35] E1 96 A1
Danvers Rd N8 49 D5
Danvers St SW3 136 B6 266 D5
Da Palma Ct SW6 265 A5
Daphne Ct Ealing W5 87 C1
Wembley HA0 65 D3
Worcester Pk KT4 215 C6
Daphne Gdns E4 20 A1
Daphne Ho N22 32 C2
Daphne St SW18 158 A5
Daplyn St [6] E1 96 A2
D'arblay St W1 93 C1 239 B1
Darby Cres TW16 172 C1
Darby Gdns TW16 172 C1
Darcy Ave SM6 219 C4
Darcy Cl N20 14 B2
D'arcy Dr HA3 43 D5
D'arcy Gdns
Dagenham RM9 103 B6
Harrow HA3 44 A5
Darcy Ho E8 96 B6
D'arcy Pl BR2 209 A5
Darcy Rd
Isleworth TW7 131 A4
Thornton Heath SW16 182 A1
D'arcy Rd SM3 216 D4
Dare Ct [2] E10 54 A2
Dare Gdns RM8 81 A5
Darell Prim Sch TW9 132 C2
Darell Rd TW9 132 C2
Daren Ct N7 72 A4
Darent Ho
[4] Catford BR1 186 B5
Lisson Gr NW8 236 D4
Darenth Rd
Stamford Hill N16 51 D1
Welling DA16 146 A4
Darfield NW1 232 A5
Darfield Rd SE4 163 B6
Darfield Way W10 90 D1
Darfur St [2] SW15 134 D2
Dargate Cl SE19 183 D3
Darien Ho
[16] London SW11 136 B2
[11] Stepney E1 96 D2
Darien Rd SW11 136 B2
Daring Ho [23] E3 97 A5
Darland Ho SE9 167 B5
Darlands Dr EN5 12 D6
Darlan Rd SW6 135 B5 264 D3
Darlaston Rd SW19 179 A3
Darley Cl CR0 207 A3
Darley Dr KT3 177 B1
Darley Gdns SM4 201 D3
Darley Ho SE11 260 C1
Darley Rd
Clapham SW11 158 D5
Edmonton N9 17 D3
Darling Ho [12] TW1 153 D5
Darling Rd SE4 141 C2
Darling Row E1 96 B3
Darlington Ct [8] SE6 164 D3
Darlington Ho
South Lambeth SW8 269 D3
[2] Surbiton KT6 197 D2
Darlington Rd SE27 182 D5
Darmaine Cl CR2 221 A1
Darnall Ho [4] SE10 142 A4
Darnay Ho [3] SE16 118 A3
Darndale Cl E17 35 B1
Darnell Ho [9] SE10 142 A5
Darnley Ho [7] E14 97 A1
Darnley Rd
Hackney E9 74 C2
Woodford IG8 37 B2
Darnley Terr [12] W11 112 D5
Darrell Ct BR2 208 C6
Darrell Rd SE22 162 A6
Darren Cl N4 50 B2
Darrick Wood Ho BR6 227 A5
Darrick Wood Inf Sch BR6 226 D5
Darrick Wood Jun Sch BR6 226 D4
Darrick Wood Rd BR6 227 B6
Darrick Wood Sch BR6 226 D5
Darrick Wood Sports Ctr BR6 227 A5
Darris Cl UB4 85 A3
Darsley Dr SW8 138 A4 270 A2
Dartford Ave N9 18 D5
Dartford Gdns RM6 58 B4
Dartford Ho SE1 263 D4
Dartford St SE17 139 A6
Dartington NW1 232 B5
Dartington Ho
Bayswater W2 91 D2
[7] London SW8 137 D3
Dartle Ct [29] SE16 118 A4
Dartmoor Wlk [18] E14 119 C2
Dartmouth Cl W11 91 C1
Dartmouth Ct SE10 142 A4
Dartmouth Gr SE10 142 A4
Dartmouth Hill SE10 142 A4
Dartmouth Ho
Dartmouth Pk N19 71 B6
[11] Kingston u T KT2 176 A2
Lewisham SE10 142 A3
Thornton Heath CR0 204 D2
DARTMOUTH PARK 71 B5
Dartmouth Park Ave NW5 71 B5
Dartmouth Park Hill N19 71 B6
Dartmouth Park Rd NW5 71 B5
Dartmouth Pl
Chiswick W4 133 C6
Forest Hill SE23 162 C2
Dartmouth Rd
Brondesbury NW2 68 D2
Forest Hill SE23, SE26 162 C1
Hayes BR2 209 A2
Hendon NW4 46 A3
Ruislip HA4 62 A5
Dartmouth Row SE10 142 A4
Dartmouth St SW1 115 D4 249 D1
Dartmouth Terr SE10 142 B4
Dartnell Rd CR0 205 D2
Darton Ct W3 111 A5
Dartrey Twr SW10 266 C4
Dartrey Wlk SW10 136 A5 266 B4
Dart St W10 91 B4
Darul Uloom BR7 189 C4
Darville Rd N16 73 D5
Darwell Cl E6 100 C5
Darwen Pl E2 96 B6
Darwin Cl
Farnborough BR6 227 B3
Darwin Cl *continued*
New Southgate N11 15 B1
Darwin Ct
Eltham SE9 166 C5
Newham E13 99 B4
Primrose Hill NW1 231 B6
Darwin Ctr★ SW7 256 C5
Darwin Dr UB1 85 D1
Darwin Gdns WD19 22 C5
Darwin Ho
[8] London SE13 142 A3
[2] Wembley HA9 67 A5
Darwin Rd
Ealing W5 109 C2
Falconwood DA16 145 D2
Tottenham N22 32 D1
Darwin St SE17 117 B2 262 D4
Daryngton Dr UB6 86 C5
Daryngton Ho SW8 270 A3
Dashwood Cl DA6 169 C6
Dashwood Ct TW3 130 A1
Dashwood Ho SE21 161 D1
Dashwood Rd N8 50 B3
Dassett Rd SE27 182 D5
Data Point Bsns Ctr E16 98 B3
Datchelor Pl [14] SE5 139 B4
Datchet Ho NW1 231 D2
Datchet Rd SE6 163 B2
Datchett Ho [40] E2 95 D4
Datchwood Ct N4 73 A5
Datchworth Ct [7] EN1 17 C6
Datchworth Ho [8] N1 72 D1
Date St SE17 117 B1 262 C1
Daubeney Gdns N17 33 A3
Daubeney Pl TW12 173 D1
Daubeney Prim Sch E5 75 A4
Daubeney Rd
Clapton Pk E5 75 A4
Tottenham N17 33 A3
Daubeney Twr [2] SE8 119 B1
Dault Rd SW18 158 A5
Dauney Ho SE1 251 C1
Dauphine Ct HA3 24 C1
Dave Adams Ho [8] E3 97 B5
Davenant Ho [20] E1 96 A2
Davenant Rd
Croydon CR0, CR9 220 D4
Upper Holloway N19 71 D6
Davenant St E1 96 A2
Davenport Cl TW11 175 A4
Davenport Ctr IG11 102 B5
Davenport Ho SE11 261 A5
Davenport Lo TW3 129 A5
Davenport Mews [6] W12 112 B5
Davenport Rd
London SE6 164 A5
Sidcup DA14 169 A2
Daventer Dr HA7 24 D3
Daventry Ave E17 53 C3
Daventry St NW1 92 C2 237 A4
Dave Porter Hts SW19 157 A4
Dave Ramsey Ho SE18 123 B2
Daver Ct
Chelsea SW3 257 B1
Ealing W5 87 D3
Davern Cl SE10 120 D2
Davey Cl
Bowes Pk N13 32 B5
Islington N7 72 B2
Davey Ho HA9 67 A6
Davey Rd E9 75 C1
Davey's Ct WC2 250 A6
Davey St SE15 139 D6
David Ave UB6 86 C5
David Cl UB3 127 C5
David Coffer Ct DA17 125 D2
David Ct N20 14 A1
David Devine Ho [7] E8 74 A3
David Game Coll SW7 256 C3
Davidge Ho SE1 251 B1
Davidge St SE1 116 D4 251 D1

David Henry Waring Ct TW14 ... 149 A3
David Hewitt Ho 2 E3 ... 97 D2
David Ho
8 Putney SW15 ... 156 A6
South Lambeth SW8 ... 270 A4
South Norwood SE25 ... 206 A6
David Lee Point 4 E15 ... 98 C6
David Livingstone Prim Sch CR7 ... 183 A2
David Mews W1 ... 237 D4
David Rd RM8 ... 81 A6
Davidson Gdns SW8 ... 138 A5 270 A4
Davidson Ho 7 N19 ... 71 C4
Davidson Lo CR0 ... 205 C2
Davidson Prim Sch CR0 ... 205 D2
Davidson Rd CR0 ... 205 D3
Davidson Terrs E7 ... 77 B3
David's Rd SE23 ... 162 C3
David St E15 ... 76 B3
David Twigg Cl KT2 ... 176 A2
Davies Cl CR0 ... 206 A3
Davies La E11 ... 76 D6
Davies Laing & Dick Coll W1 ... 93 A1 238 B2
Davies Lane Prim Sch E11 ... 76 D6
Davies Mews W1 ... 248 C6
Davies St W1 ... 115 B6 248 C6
Davies Walk TW7 ... 130 B4
Davina Ho
Brondesbury NW2 ... 69 B2
14 Hackney E5 ... 74 B3
Da Vinci Ct 12 SE16 ... 118 B1
Davington Ct 19 SM2 ... 217 C1
Davington Gdns RM8 ... 80 B3
Davington Rd RM8 ... 80 B3
Davis Ct 1 N20 ... 14 B2
Davis Ho 35 W12 ... 112 B6
Davis Rd
Bedford Pk W3 ... 111 D4
Chessington KT9 ... 214 C4
Davis St E13 ... 99 B5
Davisville Rd W12 ... 112 A4
Davis Way DA14 ... 191 A4
Davmor Ct TW8 ... 109 C1
Dawes Ave TW7 ... 131 A1
Dawe's Cl UB10 ... 82 A5
Dawes Ho SE17 ... 262 C3
Dawes Rd SW6 ... 135 B5 264 C4
Dawe's Rd UB10 ... 82 A5
Dawes St SE17 ... 117 B1 262 D2
Dawley Ave UB8 ... 83 A1
Dawley Par UB3 ... 105 A6
Dawley Rd
Harlington UB3 ... 105 C2
Hayes UB3 ... 105 B6
Dawlish Ave
Bowes Pk N13 ... 32 A5
Wandsworth SW18 ... 157 D2
Wembley UB6 ... 87 A5
Dawlish Dr Ilford IG3 ... 79 D4
Pinner HA5 ... 41 A3
Ruislip HA4 ... 62 B6
Dawlish Prim Sch E10 ... 54 A1
Dawlish Rd
Brondesbury NW2 ... 68 D2
Leyton E10 ... 76 A6
Tottenham Hale N17 ... 52 A6
Dawnay Gdns SW18 ... 158 B2
Dawnay Rd SW17, SW18 ... 158 B2
Dawn Cl TW4 ... 129 A2
Dawn Cres E15 ... 98 B6
Dawn Wlk BR2 ... 186 B1
Dawpool Rd NW2 ... 67 D6
Daws La NW7 ... 28 A5
Dawson Ave
Barking IG11 ... 79 D1
St Paul's Cray BR5 ... 190 B1
Dawson Cl Hayes UB3 ... 83 B2
Woolwich SE18 ... 123 A2
Dawson Gdns 10 IG11 ... 79 D1
Dawson Ho
23 Bethnal Green E2 ... 96 C4
5 Camberwell SE5 ... 139 C4
Dawson Pl W2 ... 113 C6 245 B6
Dawson Rd
Cricklewood NW2 ... 68 C4
Kingston u T KT1 ... 198 B6
Dawson St E2 ... 95 D5
Dawson Terr N9 ... 18 C4
Dax Ct TW16 ... 194 C6
Daybrook Rd SW19 ... 201 D6
Day Ho 2 SE5 ... 139 A5
Daylesford Ave SW15 ... 134 A1
Daymer Gdns HA5 ... 40 C5
Daynor Ho 4 NW6 ... 91 C6
Day's Armhouses HA8 26 B5
Daysbrook Rd SW2 ... 160 B3
Days La DA15 ... 167 C4
Days Lane Prim Sch DA15 ... 167 D5
Daytone Ho SW20 ... 178 D2
Dayton Gr SE15 ... 140 C4
Deaconess Ct 5 N15 ... 51 D5
Deacon Ho SE11 ... 260 D3
Deacon Mews N1 ... 73 B1
Deacon Rd
Kingston u T KT2 ... 176 B2
Willesden NW2 ... 68 A2
Deacons Cl HA5 ... 22 B1
DEACONS HILL ... 10 C5
Deacon's Hill Rd WD6 ... 10 C6
Deacons Hts WD6 ... 10 C5
Deacons Leas BR6 ... 227 B4
Deacons Rise N2 ... 48 B4
Deacons Wlk TW12 ... 173 C6
Deacon Way SE17 ... 117 A2 262 B4
Deal Ct
13 Hendon NW9 ... 27 D1
7 Southall UB1 ... 86 A1
Deal Ho
Deptford SE15 ... 140 D6
Walworth SE17 ... 263 B2
Deal Porters Way SE16 ... 118 D3
Deal Rd SW17 ... 181 A4
Deal St E1 ... 96 A2
Dealtry Rd SW15 ... 134 C1
Deal Wlk 3 SW9 ... 138 C5
Dean Bradley St SW1 ... 260 A5
Dean Cl Hackney E9 ... 74 C3
Hillingdon UB10 ... 60 B1
Rotherhithe SE16 ... 118 D5
Dean Coll of London 4 N7 ... 72 B5
Deancross St E1 ... 96 C1
Dean Ct Acton W3 ... 89 B1
Ealing W13 ... 109 B5
10 Kingston u T KT2 ... 176 C3
South Lambeth SW8 ... 270 A3
Wembley HA0 ... 65 B5
Dean Dr HA7 ... 26 A1
Deane Ave HA4 ... 62 C3
Deane Croft Rd HA5 ... 40 C3
Deanery Cl N2 ... 48 C5
Deanery Mews W1 ... 248 B4
Deanery Rd E15 ... 76 C2
Deanery St W1 ... 115 A5 248 B4
Deane Way HA4 ... 40 B3
Dean Farrar St SW1 ... 259 D6
Deanfield Gdns CR0 ... 221 B4
Dean Gdns E17 ... 54 B5
Deanhill Ct 2 SW14 132 D1
Deanhill Rd SW14 ... 132 D1
Dean Ho London N4 ... 51 A2
New Cross SE14 ... 141 B5
Ruislip HA4 ... 39 B1
Stamford Hill N16 ... 51 D1
18 Stepney E1 ... 96 C1
Dean Rd Croydon CR0 ... 221 B4
Hampton TW12 ... 173 C5
Hounslow TW3 ... 151 D6
Thamesmead SE28 ... 124 A6
Willesden NW2 ... 68 C2
Dean Ryle St SW1 ... 260 A4
Dean's Bldgs SE17 ... 117 B2 262 D3
Deansbrook Cl HA8 ... 27 A3
Deansbrook Jun & Inf Schs NW7 ... 27 A4
Deansbrook Rd
Burnt Oak HA8 ... 27 B4
Edgware HA8 ... 26 D3
Deans Cl
Burnt Oak HA8 ... 27 A4
Chiswick W4 ... 132 D6
South Croydon CR0 ... 221 D5
Deanscroft Ave NW9 ... 45 A1
Deans Ct HA8 ... 26 D4
Dean's Ct EC4 ... 241 D1
Deans Dr N13 ... 32 D4
Dean's Dr HA8 ... 27 B5
Deansfield Prim Sch
Eltham SE9 ... 144 C2
Ruislip HA4 ... 62 D4
Deans Gate Cl SE23 ... 162 D1
Dean's Gateway 9 SE10 ... 141 C4
Deanshanger Ho 21 SE8 ... 118 D2
Dean's La HA8 ... 27 A4
Dean's Mews W1 ... 238 D2
Deans Rd SM1 ... 217 D5
Dean's Rd W7 ... 108 D4
Dean St Forest Gate E7 ... 77 A3
Soho W1 ... 93 D1 239 C1
Dean Stanley St SW1 260 A5
Deansway
East Finchley N2 ... 48 B5
Edmonton N9 ... 17 C1
Deans Way HA8 ... 27 A5
Deanswood N11 ... 31 D4
Dean's Yd SW1 ... 259 D6
Dean Trench St SW1 260 A5
Dean Way UB2 ... 107 D4
Dean Wlk HA8 ... 27 B3
Deanwood Ct N14 ... 15 C3
Dearmer Ho 6 SW2 ... 160 C4
Dearne Cl HA7 ... 25 A5
De'arn Gdns CR4 ... 202 C6
Dearsley Rd EN1 ... 6 A2
Deason St E15 ... 98 A6
Deauville Ct
14 London SW4 ... 159 C5
4 Rotherhithe SE16 ... 118 D4
Deauville Mans 13 SW4 ... 159 C5
De Barowe Mews
4 Highbury N5 ... 72 D4
1 London N5 ... 72 D3
Debdale Ho 20 E2 ... 96 A6
Debden N17 ... 33 B1
Debden Cl
7 Edgware NW9 ... 27 C2
Kingston u T KT2 ... 175 D5
Woodford IG8 ... 37 D3
De Beauvoir Cres N1 ... 95 C6
De Beauvoir Ct N1 ... 73 B1
De Beauvoir Pl 5 N1 ... 73 C2
De Beauvoir Prim Sch 13 N1 ... 73 C2
De Beauvoir Rd N1 ... 73 C1
De Beauvoir Sq N1 ... 73 C1
DE BEAUVOIR TOWN ... 73 C1
Debenham Ct
Barnet EN5 ... 12 C6
Hackney E8 ... 96 A6
Debham Ct NW2 ... 68 C5
Debnams Rd SE16 ... 118 C2
De Bohun Ave N14 ... 15 B5
De Bohun Prim Sch N14 ... 15 B6
Deborah Cl TW7 ... 130 C4
Deborah Cres HA4 ... 39 B2
Deborah Ct 7 E18 ... 55 B6
Deborah Lo HA8 ... 26 D2
De Broome Rd TW13 ... 150 C3
De Burgh Ho 10 SW19 ... 180 A3
Deburgh Rd SW19 ... 180 A3
Debussy 9 NW9 ... 27 D1
Decimal Ctr 1 UB2 ... 107 C4
Decima St SE1 ... 117 C3 263 A6
Decimus Cl 1 CR7 ... 205 B5
Deck Cl SE16 ... 118 D5
Decoy Ave NW11 ... 47 A5
De Crespigny Pk SE5 ... 139 B3
Dedham Ho 1 SE6 ... 186 A6
Dee Ct W7 ... 86 B1
Deeley Rd SW8 ... 137 D4 269 C2
Deena Cl W3 ... 88 B1
Deen City Farm* SW19 ... 180 A1
Deepdale Highbury N4 ... 72 D5
Deepdale *continued*
Wimbledon SW19 ... 178 D6
Deepdale Ave BR2 ... 208 D5
Deepdale Cl N11 ... 31 A4
Deepdene N12 ... 30 C6
Deepdene Ave CR0 ... 221 D5
Deepdene Cl E11 ... 55 A5
Deepdene Ct
Beckenham BR2 ... 208 C6
Southgate N21 ... 16 D5
Deepdene Gdns SW2 ... 160 B4
Deepdene Ho N16 ... 51 B1
Deepdene Lo 5 SW2 ... 160 B4
Deepdene Mans SW6 ... 264 C2
Deepdene Point 9 SE26 ... 162 D1
Deepdene Rd
London SE5, SE24 ... 139 B1
Welling DA16 ... 146 A2
Deepwell Cl TW7 ... 131 A4
Deepwood La UB6 ... 86 B4
Deerbrook Rd SE24, SW2 ... 160 D3
Dee Rd TW9 ... 132 B1
Deerdale Rd SE24 ... 139 A1
Deerfield Cl NW9 ... 45 D4
Deerhurst
7 Kingston u T KT2 ... 176 D2
5 Streatham SW16 ... 182 A5
Deerhurst Cl TW13 ... 172 B6
Deerhurst Cres TW12 ... 174 A5
Deerhurst Ct CR0 ... 204 D1
Deerhurst Ho 6 SE15 ... 140 A6
Deerhurst Rd
Brondesbury NW2 ... 68 D2
Streatham SW16 ... 182 B5
Deerings Ct 2 N20 ... 14 B2
Deerings Dr HA5 ... 40 A4
Deerleap Gr E4 ... 19 D6
Deer Lo SW6 ... 135 A2
Deer Park Cl KT2 ... 176 D3
Deer Park Gdns CR4 ... 202 B5
Deer Park Rd SW19 ... 180 A1
Deer Park Way BR4 ... 224 D6
Deesdale Ct CR2 ... 221 B4
Deeside Rd SW17 ... 158 B1
Dee St E14 ... 98 A1
Defence Cl SE28 ... 123 C5
Defiance Wlk SE18 ... 122 B3
Defiant 18 NW9 ... 27 D1
Defiant Way SM6 ... 220 A1
Defoe Ave TW9 ... 132 C5
Defoe Cl SW17 ... 180 C4
Defoe Ho
Barbican EC2 ... 242 A4
5 Stoke Newington N16 ... 73 C5
Defoe Pl Barbican EC2 242 A4
Upper Tooting SW17 ... 180 D6
Defoe Rd
Rotherhithe SE16 ... 119 B4
Stoke Newington N16 ... 73 C5
De Frene Rd SE26 ... 163 A1
De Gama Pl 8 E14 ... 119 C1
Degema Rd BR7 ... 188 D5
Dehar Cres NW9 ... 46 A2
De Haviland Dr 8 SE18 ... 122 D1
Dehavilland Cl UB5 ... 84 D4
De Havilland Rd
Edgware HA8 ... 26 D1
Heston TW5 ... 128 C5
De Havilland Sq IG1 ... 57 B1
Dehavilland Studios E5 ... 74 C6
De Havilland Way TW19 ... 148 A5
Dekker Ho 19 SE5 ... 139 B5
Dekker Rd SE21 ... 161 C5
Delacourt Rd SE3 ... 143 B5
Delafield Ho 25 E1 ... 96 A1
Delafield Rd SE7 ... 121 C1
Delaford Rd SE16 ... 118 B1
Delaford St SW6 ... 135 A6 264 B5
Delamare Cres CR0 ... 206 C3
Delamere Gdns NW7 ... 27 B4
Delamere Ho 4 N4 ... 51 B2
Delamere Rd
Ealing W5 ... 110 A4
Delamere Rd *continued*
Hayes UB4 ... 106 D6
Wimbledon SW20 ... 178 D2
Delamere St W2 ... 236 A3
Delamere Terr W2 ... 91 D2
Delancey Pas NW1 ... 231 D5
Delancey St NW1 ... 93 B6 231 D5
Delancey Studios NW1 ... 231 D5
Delany Ho SE10 ... 142 A6
Delarch Ho SE1 ... 251 C1
De Laune St SE17 ... 116 D1 261 C1
Delaware Rd W9 ... 91 D3
Delawyk Cres SE24 ... 161 B5
Delcombe Ave KT4 ... 200 C1
Delft Ho 8 KT2 ... 176 B3
Delft Way 2 SE22 ... 161 C6
Delhi Rd EN1 ... 17 D4
Delhi St N1 ... 94 A6 233 B5
Delia St SW18 ... 157 D4
Delisle Rd SE28 ... 123 C5
Delius Cl WD6 ... 9 C5
Delius Gr E15 ... 98 A5
Dellafield N4 ... 72 C6
Della Path E5 ... 74 B5
Dellbow Rd TW14 ... 150 B6
Dell Cl
Stratford Marsh E15 ... 98 B6
Wallington SM6 ... 219 D4
Woodford IG8 ... 21 B1
Dellfield Cl BR3 ... 186 A2
Dell La KT17 ... 216 A3
Dellors Cl EN5 ... 12 D6
Dellow Cl IG2 ... 57 B2
Dellow Ho 6 E1 ... 118 B6
Dellow St E1 ... 118 B6
Dell Rd Enfield EN3 ... 6 C5
Stoneleigh KT17 ... 216 A2
West Drayton UB7 ... 104 B3
Dells Cl Chingford E4 ... 19 D4
Teddington TW11 ... 174 D4
Dell's Mews SW1 ... 259 B3
Dell The
Brentford TW8 ... 131 C6
Feltham TW14 ... 150 B4
Pinner HA5 ... 22 D1
Plumstead Comm SE2 124 A1
South Norwood SE19 ... 183 D2
Wembley HA0 ... 65 B3
Woodford IG8 ... 21 B1
Dell Way W13 ... 87 C1
Dell Wlk KT3 ... 177 C1
Dellwood Gdns IG5 ... 56 C6
Delme Cres SE3 ... 143 B3
Delmey Cl CR0 ... 221 D5
Deloraine Ho SE8 ... 141 C4
Deloraine St SE8 ... 141 C4
Delorme St W6 ... 134 D6
Delphian Ct 5 SW16 ... 182 C6
Delroy Ct N20 ... 14 A4
Delta Bldg 7 E14 ... 98 A1
Delta Cl KT4 ... 215 D5
Delta Ct NW2 ... 68 A6
Delta Gr UB5 ... 84 D4
Delta Ho N1 ... 235 C2
Delta Pk SW18 ... 135 D1
Delta Pk Ind Est EN3 ... 7 B3
Delta Point 5 E2 ... 96 A4
Delta Rd KT4 ... 215 C5
Delta St 4 E2 ... 96 A4
De Lucy Prim Sch SE2 ... 124 B4
De Lucy St SE2 ... 124 B2
Delvan Cl SE18 ... 144 C5
Delverton Ho SE17 ... 261 D2
Delverton Rd SE17 ... 261 D1
Delvino Rd SW6 ... 135 C4 265 B1
De Mandeville Gate EN1 ... 6 B1
Demesne Rd SM6 ... 219 D4
Demeta Cl HA9 ... 67 A5
De Montfort Ct 1 SW16 ... 160 A1
De Montfort Rd SW16 ... 160 A2
De Morgan Rd SW6 ... 135 D2
Dempster Cl KT6 ... 197 C1
Dempster Rd SW18 ... 158 A6
Denberry Dr DA14 ... 168 B1

Denbigh Cl
Cheam SM1 217 B3
Elmstead BR7 188 B4
Notting Hill
W11 113 B6 244 D6
Ruislip HA4 61 D6
Southall UB1 85 B1
Denbigh Ct
1 Ealing W7 86 D2
Newham E6 99 D4
Denbigh Dr UB3 105 A4
Denbigh Gdns TW10 154 B6
Denbigh Ho
Knightsbridge SW1 257 D6
7 Notting Hill W11 91 B1
Notting Hill W11 244 D6
Denbigh Mews SW1 259 A3
Denbigh Pl
SW1 115 C1 259 A2
Denbigh Rd
Ealing W13 87 B1
Hounslow TW3 129 D3
Newham E6 99 D4
Notting Hill
W11 113 B6 244 D6
Southall UB1 85 B1
Denbigh St
SW1 115 C1 259 B2
Denbigh Terr
W11 113 B6 244 D6
Denbridge Rd BR1,
BR7 188 B1
Denbury Ho 48 E3 97 D4
Denby Ct Barnet EN5 1 D2
Lambeth SE11 260 D4
Dence Ho 15 E2 96 A4
Denchworth Ho 14
SW9 138 C3
Den Cl BR2, BR3 208 B6
Dencliffe 2 TW15 170 C5
Dencora Centre The
EN3 7 A2
Dendridge Cl EN1 6 B6
Dene Ave
Blackfen DA15 168 B4
Hounslow TW3 129 B2
Dene Cl Brockley SE4 141 A1
Hayes BR2 208 D1
Leyton E10 75 D6
Worcester Pk KT4 215 D6
Denecroft Cres UB10 82 D6
Dene Ct Ealing W5 87 C2
Hanwell W7 108 D4
Dene Gdns
Hinchley Wood KT7 213 A6
Stanmore HA7 25 C5
Dene Ho N14 15 D4
Denehole Ho SE18 124 A1
Denehurst Gdns
Acton W3 110 D5
Hendon NW4 46 C3
Richmond TW10 132 C1
Twickenham TW2 152 B4
Woodford IG8 37 B6
Dene Mans 1 NW6 69 C2
Dene Rd
Buckhurst Hill IG9 21 D3
Friern Barnet N11 14 D2
Denesmead SE24 161 A6
Dene The Ealing W13 87 B2
East Molesey KT12,
KT8 195 B4
South Croydon CR0 222 D4
Wembley HA9 66 A4
Denewood EN5 14 A6
Denewood Ho 6
SM1 218 A4
Denewood Rd N6 48 D2
Dengie Wlk N1 235 A6
Denham Cl DA16 146 C2
Denham Cres CR4 202 D5
Denham Ct
Forest Hill SE26 162 B1
Southall UB1 108 A6
Denham Dr IG2 57 A3
Denham Ho 32 W12 112 B6
Denham Lo W5 88 A1
Denham Rd
Feltham TW14 150 C4
Friern Barnet N20 14 D1
Denham St SE10 121 A1
Denham Way IG11 101 D6
Denholme Rd W9 91 B4
Deniel Lo TW9 153 C6
Denise Ct HA0 65 C4
Denison Cl N2 48 A6
Denison Rd Ealing W5 87 C3
Feltham TW13 171 D6
Mitcham SW19 180 B4
Deniston Ave DA5 169 A3
Denland Ho SW8 270 D3
Denleigh Ct N14 15 D4
Denleigh Gdns
Southgate N21 16 C4
Thames Ditton KT7 196 C3
Denman Dr
Ashford TW15 170 D4
Claygate KT10 213 A3
Hampstead Garden Suburb
NW11 47 C4
Denman Dr N NW11 47 C4
Denman Dr S NW11 47 C4
Denman Ho 1 N16 73 C6
Denman Rd SE15 139 D3
Denman St W1 249 C5
Denmark Ave SW19 179 A3
Denmark Ct SM4 201 C4
Denmark Gdns SM5 218 D5
Denmark Gr N1 234 A4
Denmark Hill SE5 139 B3
Denmark Hill Dr NW9 46 A6
Denmark Hill Sta
SE5 139 B3
Denmark Ho 9 SE7 122 A2
Denmark Mans 14
SE5 139 A3
Denmark Pl
2 Bromley E3 97 C4
Soho WC2 239 D2
Denmark Rd
Bromley BR1 187 B2
Camberwell SE5 139 A3
Carshalton SM5 218 D5
Croydon SE25 206 B4
Ealing W13 109 B6
Hornsey N8 50 C5
Kilburn NW6 91 B5
Kingston u T KT1 198 A6
Twickenham TW2 152 B1
Wimbledon SW19 178 D4
Denmark St
8 Leyton E11 76 C5
Newham E13 99 B2
Soho WC2 239 D2
Tottenham N17 34 B3
Denmark Terr NW2 48 D6
Denmead Ho SW15 155 D5
Denmead Rd CR0 204 D1
Denmead Sch TW12 173 D3
Denmore Ct SM6 219 B3
Dennan Rd KT6 198 B1
Dennard Way BR6 226 C4
Denner Rd E4 19 C2
Denne Terr E8 95 D6
Dennett Rd CR0 204 C2
Dennett's Gr SE14 140 D3
Dennett's Rd SE14 140 C4
Denning Ave CR0 220 C3
Denning Cl
Hampton TW12 173 B5
St John's Wood
NW8 92 A4 229 B1
Denning Mews
SW12 159 A4
Denning Point E1 243 D2
Denning Rd NW3 70 B4
Dennington Cl 17 E5 74 B6
**Dennington Park
Mansions** 12 NW6 69 C3
Dennington Park Rd
NW6 69 C2
Denningtons The
KT4 215 C6
Dennis Ave HA9 66 B3
Dennis Cl TW15 171 B3
Dennis Ct
Chingford E17 36 B1
Greenford UB6 86 A1
Lewisham SE10 142 A4
Dennis Gdns HA7 25 C5
Dennis Ho 4 Bow E3 97 B5
Sutton SM1 217 C4
Dennis La HA7 25 B6
Dennison Point E15 76 A1
Dennis Par 1 N14 15 D3
Dennis Park Cres
SW20 179 A2
Dennis Rd KT8 196 A5
Dennis Reeve Cl
CR4 180 D2
Dennis Severs' House★
E1 243 B4
Dennis Way SW4 137 D2
Denny Cl 15 E6 100 A2
Denny Cres SE11 261 B2
Denny Gdns RM9 80 B1
Denny Rd N9 18 B3
Denny St
SE11 116 C1 261 B2
Den Rd BR2 208 B6
Densham Ho NW8 229 D3
Densham Rd E15 98 C6
Densole Cl BR3 185 A2
Denstone Ho 5
SE15 140 A6
Densworth Gr N9 18 C2
Dent Ho SE17 263 A3
Denton NW1 71 A2
Denton Cl EN5 12 C6
Denton Ct BR2 210 C2
Denton Ho N1 72 D1
Denton Rd
Bexley DA16 146 C5
Edmonton N18 33 C6
Hornsey N8 50 B3
Twickenham TW1 153 D5
Denton St SW18 157 D5
Denton Way E5 74 D5
Dents Rd SW11 158 D5
Denvale Trade Pk
CR4 202 B5
Denver Cl BR6 211 C3
Denver Ct UB1 107 B5
Denver Rd N16 51 C2
Denwood SE23 162 D1
Denyer Ho 1 NW5 71 B4
Denyer St
SW3 114 C2 257 B4
Denys Bldg EC1 241 A4
Denziloe Ave UB10 82 D4
Denzil Rd NW10 67 D3
Deodar Rd SW15 135 A1
Deodora Cl N20 14 D1
Depot App NW2 68 D4
Depot Rd
Isleworth TW3,
TW7 130 B2
Shepherd's Bush W12 112 C6
Depot St SE5 139 B6
DEPTFORD 140 D6
Deptford Bridge
SE8 141 C4
Deptford Bridge Sta
SE8 141 C4
Deptford Broadway SE8,
SE14 141 C4
Deptford Church St
SE8 141 C5
Deptford Ferry Rd 24
E14 119 C2
Deptford Gn SE8 141 C6
Deptford Green Sch
SE14 141 B5
Deptford Green Sch
(Annex) 12 SE14 141 A5
Deptford High St
SE8 141 C5
Deptford Park Prim Sch
2 SE8 119 A1
Deptford Sta SE8 141 C5
Deptford Trad Est
SE8 141 A6
Deptford Wharf SE8 119 B2
De Quincey Mews 3
E16 121 A5
De Quincey Rd N17 33 B2
Derby Ave
Harrow HA3 24 B2
North Finchley N12 30 A5
Romford RM7 59 D3
Derby Ct
8 Clapton Pk E5 74 D4
Woodford E18 36 D2
Derby Gate SW1 250 A2
Derby Hill SE23 162 C2
Derby Hill Cres
SE23 162 C2
Derby Ho
Hendon NW4 46 C6
Lambeth SE11 261 A4
Pinner HA5 22 D1
4 Wallington SM6 219 B3
Derby Lo N3 29 B1
Derby Rd
Cheam SM1, SM2 217 B2
Edmonton N18 34 C5
Enfield EN3 18 C6
Greenford UB6 85 D6
Hounslow TW3 129 D1
Merton SW19 179 C3
Mortlake SW14 132 D1
South Hackney E9 96 D6
Surbiton KT5, KT6 198 C1
Thornton Heath CR0 204 D1
Upton E7 77 D1
Woodford E18 36 D2
Derby Rd Ind Est
TW3 129 D1
Derbyshire St E2 96 A4
Derby St W1 248 B3
Dereham Ho 7 SE4 140 D1
Dereham Pl EC2 243 B6
Dereham Rd IG11 79 D3
Derek Ave
Chessington KT19 214 D3
Wallington SM6 219 B4
Wembley HA9 66 D1
Derek Cl KT19 214 D3
Derek Walcott Cl
SE24 160 D6
Dericote St E8 96 B6
Deri Dene Cl 2
TW19 148 A5
Derifall Cl E6 100 B2
Dering Pl CR0 221 A4
Dering Rd CR0 221 A4
Dering St W1 238 D1
Derinton Rd SW17 181 A6
Derley Rd UB2 106 D3
Dermody Gdns SE13 164 B6
Dermody Rd SE13 164 B6
Deronda Rd SE24,
SW2 160 D3
Deroy Cl SM5 218 D2
Derrick Gdns SE7 121 C2
Derrick Ho 13 SW2 160 C3
Derrick Rd BR3 207 B5
Derrycombe Ho 18
W2 91 C2
Derry Rd CR0, SM6 220 A5
Derry St W8 113 D4 245 C1
Dersingham Ave E12 78 C4
Dersingham Inf Sch
E12 78 C3
Dersingham Rd NW2 69 A5
Derwent NW1 232 A1
Derwent Ave
Barnet EN4 14 D3
Burnt Oak NW7 27 B4
Edmonton N18 33 B5
Hyde The NW9 45 C4
Kingston u T SW15 177 C6
Pinner HA5 23 A4
Uxbridge UB10 60 C5
Derwent Cl
Claygate KT10 212 D2
East Bedfont TW14 149 D3
Derwent Cres
Bexleyheath DA7 147 C3
Stanmore HA7 25 C1
Whetstone N20 14 A1
Derwent Ct
2 Hammersmith
W6 112 A2
Hornsey N8 50 A3
8 Rotherhithe SE16 118 D4
Derwent Dr
Crofton BR5 211 B2
Hayes UB4 83 C2
Derwent Gdns
Redbridge IG4 56 A5
Wembley HA9 43 C2
Derwent Gr SE22 139 D1
Derwent Ho
Penge SE20 184 B1
South Kensington
SW7 256 B4
Tower Hamlets E3 97 B3
Derwent Lo
Hounslow TW7 130 B3
North Cheam KT4 216 B6
Derwent Rd
Ealing W5 109 C3
Palmers Green N13 16 B1
Penge SE20 184 B1
Southall UB1 85 B1
Twickenham TW2 151 D5
West Barnes SM4 200 D3
Derwent Rise NW9 45 C3
Derwent St SE10 120 C1
Derwentwater Mans 2
W3 111 A5
Derwentwater Prim Sch
W3 111 A5
Derwentwater Rd
W3 111 A5
Derwent Wlk SM6 219 B1
Derwent Yd W5 109 C3
De Salis Rd UB10 83 A3
Desborough Cl
Bayswater W2 91 D2
Lower Halliford TW17 192 C2
Desborough Ct SE25 206 B5
Desborough Ho W14 264 D6
Desenfans Rd SE21 161 C5
Deseret Ho 6 CR4 202 D6
Desford Rd E16 98 C3
Desford Way TW15 148 B2
Design Mus★ SE1 253 D2
Desmond Ho 4 EN4 14 C5
Desmond St SE14 141 A6
Desmond Tutu Dr
SE23 163 A3
Despard Ho SW2 160 C2
Despard Rd N19 49 C1
Dessouter 19 NW9 27 D1
Desvignes Dr SE13 164 B5
Detherick Ct TW3 130 A1
Dethick Ct E3 97 A6
Detling Ho SE17 263 A3
Detling Rd BR1 187 A5
Detmold Rd E5 74 C6
Devalls Cl E6 122 C6
Devana End SM5 218 D5
Devas Rd SW20 178 C2
Devas St E3 97 D3
Devema Cl BR7 188 C2
Devenay Rd E15 76 D1
Devenish Rd SE2 124 A4
Deventer Cres 8
SE22 161 C6
Deveraux Cl BR3 208 A4
De Vere Cl SM6 220 A1
De Vere Cotts W8 256 A6
De Vere Ct 1 E5 74 B5
De Vere Gdns
Kensington
W8 114 A4 246 A1
Redbridge IG1 56 B1
Deverell St
SE1 117 B3 262 C5
De Vere Mews W8 256 A6
Devereux Ct WC2 241 A1
Devereux Ho 7
SW15 156 A6
Devereux La SW13 134 B5
Devereux Rd SW11 158 D5
Deverill Ct SE20 184 C2
Devey Cl KT2 177 B5
Devitt Ho 5 E14 119 D6
Devizes St N1 235 D5
Devon Ave TW2 152 A3
Devon Cl Chigwell IG9 21 B2
Tottenham N17 51 D6
Wembley UB6 87 C6
Devoncroft Gdns
TW1 153 A4
Devon Ct 3 Acton W3 88 C1
2 Ealing W7 86 D2
Hampton TW12 173 C3
Devon Gdns N4 50 D3
Devon Ho
9 Penge SE20 184 B3
Walthamstow E17 35 B1
6 Wanstead E11 55 A4
Devonhurst Pl 4
W4 111 B1
Devonia Gdns N18 33 A4
Devonia Rd
N1 94 D5 234 D4
Devon Mans SE1 253 B2
Devon Par HA3 43 C4
Devonport W2 237 A2
Devonport Gdns IG1 56 B3
Devonport Ho
Greenwich SE10 142 A6
23 Paddington W2 91 C2
Devonport Rd W12 112 B4
Devonport St E1 96 D1
Devon Rd IG11 101 C6
Devon Rise N2 48 B5
Devonshire Ave
SM2 218 A1
Devonshire Cl
Edmonton N13 32 C6

Devonshire Cl *continued*
Leyton E15 76 C4
Marylebone W1 238 C4
Devonshire Cres
NW7 28 D3
Devonshire Ct
14 Balham SW12 159 B4
Croydon CR0 207 C1
Feltham TW13 150 B2
Pinner HA5 23 B2
6 Richmond TW9 132 B4
Tottenham N17 33 A4
Devonshire Dr
London SE10 141 D4
Long Ditton KT6 213 D6
Devonshire Gdns
Chiswick W4 133 A5
Edmonton N21 17 A4
Tottenham N17 33 A4
Devonshire Gr SE15 140 B6
Devonshire Hall 15
E9 74 C2
Devonshire Hill La
N17 33 A4
Devonshire Hill Prim Sch
N17 33 B4
Devonshire Ho
Brondesbury NW6 69 B2
Hounslow TW3 130 A2
Newington SE1 262 A6
Paddington W2 236 D4
2 Putney SW15 156 C4
10 Sutton SM2 218 A1
Westminster SW1 259 D2
Whetstone N12 14 A1
Devonshire House Prep Sch NW3 70 A3
Devonshire Mews 2
W4 111 C1
Devonshire Mews N
W1 238 C4
Devonshire Mews S
W1 238 C4
Devonshire Mews W
W1 238 B4
Devonshire Pl
Child's Hill NW2 69 C5
Kensington W8 255 C5
Marylebone
W1 93 A2 238 B4
Devonshire Place Mews
W1 238 B4
Devonshire Prim Sch 18
SM2 218 A1
Devonshire Rd
Bexley DA6 147 A1
Chislehurst SE9 166 A2
Chiswick W4 111 C1
Ealing W5 109 C3
Eastcote HA5 40 C2
Edmonton N9 18 C3
Feltham TW13 173 A6
Forest Hill SE23 162 C4
Hackbridge SM5, SM6 219 A4
Harrow HA1 42 B3
Hatch End HA5 23 B2
Ilford IG2 57 C2
Mill Hill NW7 28 D3
Mitcham SW19 180 C3
Newham E16 99 B1
Palmers Green N13 32 C6
Southall UB1 85 C2
Sutton SM2 218 A1
Thornton Heath CR0 205 B2
Tottenham N17 33 A4
Walthamstow E17 53 C3
Devonshire Rd Nat Res★
SE23 162 D4
Devonshire Row EC2 243 B3
Devonshire Row Mews
W1 238 D5
Devonshire Sq
Bromley BR2 209 B5
Whitechapel
EC2 95 C1 243 B2
Devonshire St
Chiswick W4 111 C1
Marylebone
W1 93 B2 238 C4
Devonshire Terr
W2 92 A1 236 B1
Devonshire Way
Croydon CR0, CR9 223 B6
Hayes UB4 84 B1
Devons Rd E3 97 D3
Devons Road Sta E3 97 D3
Devon St SE15 140 B6
Devon Way
Chessington KT9 213 C3
Ewell KT19 214 D3
Hillingdon UB10 82 B5
Devon Waye TW5 129 B5
De Walden Ho NW8 230 A4
De Walden St W1 238 B3
Dewar Ho 2 SW17 180 C5
Dewar St SE15 140 A2
Dewberry Gdns E6 100 A2
Dewberry St E14 98 A2
Dewey Rd
Dagenham RM10 81 D2
Islington N1 94 C5 234 A4
Dewey St SW17 180 D5
Dewhurst Rd W14 112 D3
Dewlands Ct 7 NW4 28 D1
Dewsbury Cl HA5 41 A3
Dewsbury Ct 5 W4 111 A2
Dewsbury Gdns KT4 216 A5
Dewsbury Rd NW10 68 A3
Dewsbury Terr NW1 231 D6
Dexter Ho 2 DA18 125 A3
Dexter Rd EN5 12 D5
Deyncourt Rd N17 33 A2
Deynecourt Gdns E11 55 C5
D'eynsford Rd SE5 139 B4
Dhonau Ho SE16 263 D4
Diadem Ct W1 239 C2
Dial Wlk The
W8 113 D4 245 D2
Diameter Rd BR5 211 A3
Diamond Cl RM8 58 C1
Diamond Ct 8 W7 108 C5
Diamond Est SW17 158 C1
Diamond Ho 22 E3 97 A5
Diamond Rd HA4 63 A4
Diamond St
18 London NW10 67 B1
SE15 139 C5
Diamond Terr SE10 142 A4
Diana Cl
27 Deptford SE8 141 B6
Sidcup DA14 169 A2
Woodford E18 37 B2
Diana Ct SM5 219 A1
Diana Gdns KT6 214 B6
Diana Ho
Barnes SW13 133 D4
4 Brixton SW2 160 B6
Diana, Princess of Wales Mml Fountain★
W2 114 C5 246 D2
Diana, Princess of Wales Mml Wlk
W2 114 A5 246 A3
Diana Rd E17 53 B6
Dianne Ct SE12 165 A3
Dianne Way EN4 2 C1
Dianthus Cl SE2 124 B1
Dias Ho UB5 85 A6
Dibden Ho 8 SE5 139 C5
Dibden St N1 95 A6 235 A6
Dibdin Cl SM1 217 C5
Dibdin Ho W9 91 D5
Dibdin Rd SM1 217 C6
Dicey Ave NW2 68 C4
Dickens Ave
Finchley N3 30 A2
Hayes UB8 82 D1
Dickens Cl Erith DA8 147 D5
Hayes UB3 105 C2
Richmond TW10 154 A2
Dickens Ct
Clerkenwell EC1 241 C5
10 Wanstead E11 55 A5
Wembley HA0 65 C5
Dickens Dr BR7 189 A4
Dickens Ho
Bloomsbury WC1 240 A6
8 Erith DA17 125 B1
Hayes UB3 105 C2
Kennington SE17 261 D1
Kilburn NW6 91 C4
Paddington NW8 236 D6
Dickens La N18 33 C5
Dickenson Cl N9 18 A3
Dickenson Ho N8 50 B3
Dickenson Rd
Feltham TW13 172 D5
Hornsey N8 50 A2
Dickenson's La SE25 206 A3
Dickenson's Pl SE25 206 A3
Dickens Rd E6 99 D5
Dickens Sq
SE1 117 A3 262 B6
Dickens St SW8 137 B3
Dickens Wood Cl
SE19 182 D3
Dickerage Hill
Kingston u T KT3 177 A1
Kingston u T KT3 199 A6
Dickerage La KT3 199 A6
Dickerage Rd KT1, KT2, KT3 177 A1
Dickinson Ho 18 E2 96 A4
Dicksee Ho NW8 236 C5
Dick Shepherd Ct 17
SW2 160 C5
Dickson Fold HA5 40 D5
Dickson Ho
3 Charlton SE18 144 A4
4 Stepney E1 96 B1
Dickson Rd SE9 144 A2
Dick Turpin Way
TW14 127 D1
Didbin Ho N7 72 B6
Didsbury Cl E6 100 B6
Digby Bsns Ctr E9 74 D2
Digby Cres N4 73 A6
Digby Gdns RM10 103 C6
Digby Mans W6 112 C1
Digby Pl CR0 221 D5
Digby Rd Barking IG11 79 D1
Homerton E9 74 D2
Digby St E2 96 C4
Diggon St E1 96 D2
Dighton Ct SE17 139 A6
Dighton Rd SW18 136 A1
Dignum St N1 234 A4
Digswell St N7 72 C2
Dilhorne Cl SE12 165 B1
Dilke St SW3 136 D6 267 D6
Dilloway Yd UB2 107 A4
Dillwyn Cl SE26 185 A6
Dilston Cl 1 UB5 84 C4
Dilston Gr SE16 118 C2
Dilton Gdns SW15 156 B3
Dilwyn Ct E17 35 A1
Dimes Pl 9 W6 112 B2
Dimmock Dr UB6 64 B3
Dimond Cl E7 77 A4
Dimsdale Dr
Enfield EN1 18 A5
Welsh Harp NW9 45 A1
Dimsdale Wlk 4 E13 99 A5
Dimson Cres E3 97 C4
Dinerman Ct NW8 229 B6
Dingle Cl EN5 11 D5
Dingle Ct 16 HA7 25 C5
Dingle Gdns E14 119 C6
Dingle Rd TW15 170 D5
Dingles Ct HA5 22 D1
Dingle The UB10 82 D4
Dingley La SW16 159 D2
Dingley Pl EC1 95 A4 235 B1
Dingley Rd
EC1 95 A4 235 A1
Dingwall Ave CR0 221 A6
Dingwall Gdns NW11 47 C3
Dingwall Rd
South Croydon CR0 221 B6
Wandsworth SW18 158 A4
Dinmont Ho 27 E2 96 A5
Dinmont St 1 E2 96 B5
Dinmore Ho 6 E9 96 C6
Dinnington Ho 17 E1 96 B3
Dinorben SM6 219 C1
Dinsdale Ct EN5 13 D6
Dinsdale Gdns
New Barnet EN5 13 D6
South Norwood SE25 205 C4
Dinsdale Rd SE3 142 D6
Dinsmore Rd SW12 159 B4
Dinton Ho NW8 237 A6
Dinton Rd
Kingston u T KT2 176 B3
Mitcham SW19 180 B4
Dinwiddy Ho N1 233 C3
Dionis Ho SW6 135 C3
Diploma Ave N2 48 C5
Diploma Ct N2 48 C5
Diprose Lo SW17 180 B6
Dirleton Rd E15 98 D6
Disbrowe Rd
W6 135 A6 264 B5
Discovery Bsns Pk 13
SE16 118 A3
Discovery Dock E
E14 119 D4
Discovery Ho 1
E14 120 A6
Discovery Prim Sch
SE28 123 C5
Dishforth La NW9 27 C2
Disley Ct 2 UB1 85 D1
Disney Pl SE1 252 B2
Disney St SE1 252 B2
Dison Cl EN3 6 D4
Disraeli Cl
1 Acton W4 111 B2
Thamesmead SE28 124 C5
Disraeli Gdns SW15 135 B1
Disraeli Rd
Acton NW10 89 B5
Ealing W5 109 D5
Putney SW15 135 A1
Upton E7 77 A2
Diss St E2 95 D4
Distaff La EC4 252 A6
Distillery La W6 112 C1
Distillery Rd W6 112 C1
Distillery Wlk 14
TW8 132 A6
Distin Ct 3 SM1 217 D3
Distin St
SE11 116 C2 261 A3
District Rd HA0 65 B3
Ditchburn St E14 120 A6
Ditchfield Rd UB4 85 A3
Ditchley Ct W7 86 D2
Dittisham Rd SE9 188 A6
Ditton Cl KT7 197 A2
Dittoncroft Cl CR0 221 C4
Ditton Grange Cl
KT6 197 D1
Ditton Grange Dr
KT6 197 D1
Ditton Hill KT6 213 D6
Ditton Hill Rd KT6 197 C1
Ditton Ho 10 E5 74 B3
Ditton Lawn KT7 197 A1
Ditton Pl 6 SE20 184 B2
Ditton Rd Bexley DA6 169 A6
Southall UB2 107 B1
Surbiton KT6 198 B1
Ditton Reach KT7 197 B3
Divis Way SW15 156 B5
Dixon Cl 4 E6 100 B1
Dixon Clark Ct N1 72 D2
Dixon Ct N4 50 C3
Dixon Ho
20 North Kensington NW10 90 D1
West Heath SE2 124 C1
Dixon Pl BR4 207 D1
Dixon Rd
London SE14 141 A4
South Norwood SE25 205 D6
Dixon's Alley 10
SE16 118 B4
Dixon Way 9 NW10 67 C1
Dobbin Cl HA3 25 A1
Dobell Rd SE9 166 B6
Dobree Ave NW10 68 B1
Dobson Cl NW6 70 B1
Dobson Ho 18 SE14 140 D6
Doby Ct EC4 252 B6
Dockers Tanner Rd 26
E14 119 C2
Dockett Eddy La KT16,
TW17 192 B1
Dockett Moorings
KT16 192 B1
Dockhead
SE1 117 D4 253 D1
Dockhead Wharf
SE1 253 D2
Dock Hill Ave SE16 118 D4
Docklands Ct 20 E14 97 B1
Dockland St E16 122 C5
Docklands Visitor Ctr★
E14 120 A4
Dockley Rd SE16 118 A3
Dockley Road Ind Est 11
SE16 118 A3
Dock Offices 12
SE16 118 C3
Dock Rd
Brentford TW8 131 D5
Canning Town E16 120 D6
Dockside Rd E16 121 D6
Dock St E1 118 A6
Dockwell Cl TW14 128 A1
Dockwell's Ind Est
TW14 150 B6
Doctor Johnson Ho 2
SW16 181 D6
Doctors Cl SE26 184 C5
Doctor Spurstowe Almshouses 9 E8 74 B2
Docura Ho N7 72 B6
Docwras Bldgs N1 73 C2
Dodbrooke Rd SE27 160 D1
Dodd Ho 18 SE16 118 B2
Doddington Gr
SE17 116 D1 261 D1
Doddington Pl 4
SE17 138 D6
Dodsley Pl N9 18 C1
Dodson St
SE1 116 C4 251 B1
Dod St E14 97 C1
Doebury Wlk SE18 146 A6
Doel Cl SW19 180 A3
Dog & Duck Yd WC1 240 C4
Doggett Rd SE6 163 C4
Doggetts Ct EN4 14 C6
Doghurst Ave UB3 126 D5
Doghurst Dr UB7 126 D5
Dog Kennel Hill
SE22 139 C2
Dog Kennel Hill Sch 23
SE22 139 C2
Dog La NW10 67 C4
Dogrose Ct 14 NW9 46 A5
Doherty Rd E13 99 A3
Dokal Ind Est UB2 107 A4
Doland Ct SW17 180 D4
Dolben Ct SW1 259 D3
Dolben St
SE1 116 D5 251 D3
Dolby Rd SW6 135 B3
Doleman Ho 19
SE10 141 D4
Dolland Ho SE11 260 D1
Dolland St SE11 260 D1
Dollar Bay E14 120 A4
Dollary Ct KT3 198 D6
Dolliffe Cl CR4 180 D1
Dollis Ave N3 29 B2
Dollis Brook Wlk EN5 13 A5
Dollis Cres HA4 40 C1
Dolliscroft NW7 29 A3
Dollis Ct N3 29 B2
DOLLIS HILL 68 B5
Dollis Hill Ave NW2 68 B5
Dollis Hill Est NW2 68 A5
Dollis Hill La NW2 68 A5
Dollis Hill Sta NW2 68 A3
Dollis Hts NW2 68 B5
Dollis Jun & Inf Schs
NW7 28 C3
Dollis Mews N3 29 C2
Dollis Pk N3 29 B2
Dollis Rd N3, NW7 29 B3
Dollis Valley Dr EN5 13 B6
Dollis Valley Way
EN5 13 B5
Dolman Cl N3 30 A1
Dolman Rd W4 111 B2
Dolman St SW4 138 B1
Dolphin Cl
Kingston u T KT6 197 D4
2 Rotherhithe SE16 118 D4
Thamesmead SE28 102 D1
Dolphin Ct
London NW11 47 A3
Merton SW19 179 C3
Tufnell Pk N7 71 D4
2 Wallington SM6 219 B2
Dolphin Est The
TW16 171 B2
Dolphin La E14 119 D6
Dolphin Rd
Charlton TW16 171 C2
Northolt UB5 85 B5
Dolphin Rd N TW16 171 C2
Dolphin Rd S TW16 171 C2
Dolphin Rd W TW16 171 C2
Dolphin Sch SW11 158 D6
Dolphin Sq
SW1 115 C1 259 B1
Dolphin St KT2 176 A2
Dolphin Twr 21 SE8 141 B6
Dombey Ho
13 Bermondsey
SE1 118 A4

Dombey Ho *continued*
4 Shepherd's Bush W11 112 D5
Dombey St WC1 240 C4
Dome Hill Pk SE26 183 D6
Domelton Ho SW18 157 D5
Domett Cl SE5 139 B1
Domfe Pl E5 74 C4
Domingo St EC1 242 A5
Dominica Cl 6 E6 99 D5
Dominion Bsns Pk N9 18 D2
Dominion Cl TW3 130 B3
Dominion Ind Est UB2 107 A4
Dominion Par HA1 42 D4
Dominion Rd
Croydon CR0 205 D2
Southall UB2 107 A3
Dominion St EC2 95 B2 242 D4
Dominion Wks RM8 59 A1
Domonic Dr SE9 166 D1
Domville Cl N20 14 B2
Donaghue Cotts 11 E14 97 A2
Donald Dr RM6 58 C4
Donald Lynch Ho CR4 180 D1
Donald Rd
Newham E13 99 B6
Thornton Heath CR0 204 B2
Donaldson Rd
Kilburn NW6 91 B6
Shooters Hill SE18 144 C4
Donald Woods Gdns KT5 215 A6
Doncaster Dr UB5 63 B3
Doncaster Gdns
London N4 51 A3
Northolt UB5 63 B3
Doncaster Gn WD19 22 C5
Doncaster Rd N9 18 B4
Doncel Ct E4 20 B4
Donegal Ho 2 E1 96 C3
Donegal St N1 94 B5 233 D3
Doneraile Ho SW1 258 C1
Doneraile St SW6 134 D4
Dongola Rd
Newham E13 99 B4
Tottenham N17 51 C6
Tower Hamlets E1 97 A2
Dongola Rd W 5 E13 99 B4
Don Gratton Ho 23 E1 96 A2
Donhead Sch 19 SW19 178 D3
Donington Ave IG6 57 A4
Donkey Alley SE22 162 A5
Donkey La EN1 6 A3
Donkin Ho 15 SE16 118 B2
Donne Ct SE24 161 A5
Donnefield Ave HA8 26 A3
Donne Ho
18 Canonbury N16 73 B4
14 Deptford SE14 140 D6
11 Poplar E14 97 C1
Donnelly Ct SW6 264 B4
Donne Pl
Chelsea SW3 114 C2 257 B4
Mitcham CR4 203 B5
Donne Rd RM8 80 C6
Donnington Ct
11 Camden Town NW1 71 B1
Willesden NW10 68 B1
Donnington Ho 12 SW8 137 D3
Donnington Prim Sch NW10 90 B6
Donnington Rd
Harrow HA3 43 D3
Willesden Green NW10 90 B6
Worcester Pk KT4 216 A6
Donnybrook Rd SW16 181 D3
Donoghue Bsns Pk NW2 68 D5
Donovan Ave N10 31 C1
Donovan Ct SW7 256 C1
Donovan Ho 4 E1 118 C6
Donovan Pl N21 16 B6
Don Phelan Cl SE5 139 B4
Doone Cl TW11 175 A4
Doon St SE1 116 C5 251 A4
Doradus Ct 20 SW19 156 D3
Dora Ho
11 Shepherd's Bush W11 112 D6
1 Tower Hamlets E14 97 B1
Doral Way SM5 218 D3
Doran Ct E6 100 B5
Dorando Cl W12 112 B6
Doran Gr SE18 145 C5
Doran Manor N2 48 D4
Doran Wlk
Stratford E15 76 A1
Stratford Marsh E15 98 A6
Dora Rd SW19 179 C6
Dora St E14 97 B1
Dora Way SW9 138 C3
Dorcas Ct 9 SW18 136 B1
Dorchester Ave
Edmonton N13 33 A6
Harrow HA2 42 A3
Sidcup DA5 168 D4
Dorchester Cl
Hinchley Wood KT10 212 D6
Northolt UB5 63 D3
St Paul's Cray BR5 190 B3
Dorchester Ct
Cricklewood NW2 68 D5
1 De Beauvoir Town N1 73 C1
East Barnet N14 15 B4
Herne Hill SE24 161 A6
Knightsbridge SW1 257 D5
1 Muswell Hill N10 49 B6
5 Streatham SW16 160 A2
2 Woodford E18 36 D2
Dorchester Dr
Feltham TW14 149 C5
Herne Hill SE24 161 A6
Dorchester Gdns
Chingford E4 35 C6
East Finchley NW11 47 C5
Dorchester Gr W4 111 D1
Dorchester Ho
Richmond TW9 132 D5
Wallington SM5 218 D3
Dorchester Mews
New Malden KT3 199 B5
Twickenham TW1 153 C5
Dorchester Prim Sch KT4 200 C1
Dorchester Rd
Cheam SM4 202 A2
North Cheam KT4 200 C1
Northolt UB5 63 D3
Dorchester Way HA3 44 B3
Dorchester Waye
Hayes UB4 84 B1
Hayes UB4 84 C1
Dorcis Ave DA7 147 A3
Dordrecht Rd W3 111 C5
Dore Ave E12 78 C3
Doreen Ave NW9 45 B1
Doreen Capstan Ho 5 E11 76 C5
Dore Gdns SM4 201 D2
Dorell Cl UB1 85 B2
Dorey Ho 7 TW8 131 C5
Doria Rd SW6 135 B3
Doric Ho 7 E2 96 D5
Doric Way NW1 93 D4 232 C2
Dorie Mews N12 29 D6
Dorien Rd SW20 178 D1
Doris Ashby Cl UB6 87 A6
Doris Emmerton Ct SW18 136 A1
Doris Rd
Ashford TW15 171 B4
Upton E7 77 A1
Dorking Cl
Deptford SE8 141 B6
North Cheam KT4 216 D6
Dorking Ct N17 34 A2
Dorking Ho SE1 262 D6
Dorland Ct SW15 157 B5
Dorlcote Rd SW18 158 C4
Dorleston Ct N1 235 D6
Dorly Cl TW17 193 C4
Dorman Pl 6 N9 18 A2
Dorman Way NW8 92 B6 229 C6
Dorman Wlk NW10 67 B2
Dorma Trad Pk E10 52 D1
Dormay St SW18 157 D6
Dormer Cl Barnet EN5 12 D6
Stratford E15 76 D2
Dormer's Ave UB1 85 C1
Dormers Lo EN4 2 D3
Dormers Rise UB1 85 D1
DORMER'S WELLS 107 C6
Dormer's Wells High Sch UB1 85 C1
Dormers Wells Ho UB4 84 C2
Dormer's Wells Inf Sch UB1 107 D6
Dormer's Wells Jun Sch UB1 107 D6
Dormer's Wells La UB1 107 C5
Dormer's Wells L Ctr UB1 107 D6
Dormer Wells L Ctr UB1 85 D1
Dormstone Ho SE17 263 A3
Dormywood HA4 39 D4
Dornberg Cl SE3 143 A5
Dornberg Rd SE3 143 B5
Dorncliffe Rd SW6 135 A3
Dorney NW3 70 C1
Dorney Ct SW6 135 A2
Dorney Rise BR5 211 D5
Dorney Way TW4 151 A6
Dornfell St NW6 69 B3
Dornoch Ho 26 E3 97 B5
Dornton Rd
South Croydon CR2 221 C3
Upper Tooting SW12, SW17 159 C2
Dorothy Ave HA0 66 A1
Dorothy Barley Jun & Inf Schs RM8 80 B3
Dorothy Charrington Ho 1 SE22 162 A6
Dorothy Evans Cl DA7 147 D1
Dorothy Gdns RM8 80 B4
Dorothy Pettingel Ho 1 SM1 217 D5
Dorothy Rd SW11 136 D2
Dorothy Villas UB1 107 C5
Dorrell Pl 18 SW9 138 C2
Dorrien Wlk SW16 159 D2
Dorrington Ct SE25 183 C1
Dorrington Point 20 E3 97 D4
Dorrington St EC1 241 A4
Dorrington Way BR3 208 A4
Dorrit Ho 2 W11 112 D5
Dorrit Mews N18 33 C5
Dorrit St SE1 252 B2
Dorrit Way BR7 189 A4
Dorryn Ct SE26 184 D5
Dors Cl NW9 45 B1
Dorset Ave
Falconwood DA16 145 D1
Hayes UB4 83 C4
Southall UB2 107 C2
Dorset Bldgs EC4 241 C1
Dorset Cl Hayes UB4 83 C4
Marylebone NW1 237 C4
Dorset Ct
3 Ealing W7 86 D2
3 London N1 73 C1
4 Northolt UB5 85 B4
Dorset Dr HA8 26 B4
Dorset Gdns SW16 204 B5
Dorset Hall SW19 179 C2
Dorset Ho 1 SE20 184 B2
Dorset Mans 2 W6 134 D6
Dorset Mews
Belgravia SW1 258 C6
Finchley N3 29 C2
Dorset Pl E15 76 B2
Dorset Rd
Ashford TW15 148 A1
Chislehurst SE9 166 A2
Ealing W5 109 D3
Harrow HA1 42 A3
Merton SW19 179 C1
Mitcham CR4 180 C1
Penge BR3 206 D6
South Lambeth SW8 138 B5 270 C4
Upton E7 77 C1
West Green N15 51 B5
Wood Green N22 32 A2
Dorset Rise EC4 94 D1 241 C1
Dorset Road Inf Sch 7 SE9 166 A2
Dorset Sq NW1 92 D3 237 C5
Dorset St W1 92 D2 237 D3
Dorset Way
Hillingdon UB10 82 B5
Twickenham TW2 152 B3
Dorset Waye TW5 129 B5
Dorton Cl 6 SE15 139 C5
Dorton Villas UB7 126 C4
Dorville Cres W6 112 B3
Dorville Rd SE12 165 A6
Dothill Rd SE18 145 A5
Douai Gr TW12 174 A2
Douay Martyrs RC Sch (Annexe) The UB10 60 D3
Douay Martyrs RC Sch The UB10 60 D4
Doughty Ct 11 E1 118 B5
Doughty Mews WC1 94 B3 240 C5
Doughty St WC1 94 B3 240 C5
Douglas 20 NW9 27 D1
Douglas Ave
Walthamstow E17 35 C2
Wembley HA0 66 A1
West Barnes KT3 200 B5
Douglas Bader Ho N3 29 D4
Douglas Bldgs SE1 252 B2
Douglas Cl
Hadley Wood EN4 2 B5
Stanmore HA7 25 A5
Wallington SM6 220 A2
Douglas Cres UB4 84 D3
Douglas Ct London N3 29 D1
5 South Hampstead NW6 69 C1
1 Upper Tooting SW17 180 C4
Douglas Dr CR0 223 C5
Douglas Gracey Ho 1 SW18 157 A4
Douglas Ho
Isleworth TW1 153 B6
Putney SW15 156 A5
Westminster SW1 259 C3
Douglas Johnstone Ho SW6 264 C5
Douglas Mews NW2 69 A5
Douglas Path E14 120 A1
Douglas Rd
Chingford E4 20 C3
Hounslow TW3 129 D2
Ilford IG3 58 A3
Islington N1 73 A1
Kilburn NW6 91 B6
Kingston u T KT1 176 D1
5 Newham E16 99 A2
Stanwell TW19 148 A5
Surbiton KT6 198 B1
Thames Ditton KT10 212 A6
Welling DA16 146 B4
Wood Green N22 32 C2
Douglas Rd N N1 73 A2
Douglas Rd S N1 73 A2
Douglas Robinson Ct SW16 182 A3
Douglas Sq SM4 201 C3
Douglas St SW1 115 D2 259 C3
Douglas Terr E17 35 B2
Douglas Waite Ho NW6 69 D1
Douglas Way SE8 141 B5
Doulton Ho SE11 260 D4
Doulton Mews 4 NW6 69 D2
Dounesforth Gdns SW18 157 D3
Douro Pl W8 113 D3 255 D6
Douro St E3 97 C5
Douthwaite Sq 11 E1 118 A5
Dove App E6 100 A2
Dove Cl Hendon NW7 27 D3
Northolt UB5 84 D3
Wallington SM6 220 B1
Dovecot Cl HA5 40 C4
Dovecote Gdns 8 SW14 133 B2
Dove Ct
City of London EC2 242 C1
Enfield EN3 18 B6
Stanwell TW19 148 A4
Dovedale Ave HA3 43 C3
Dovedale Cl DA16 146 A3
Dovedale Cotts 6 SW11 136 D3
Dovedale Ho N16 51 B2
Dovedale Rd SE22 162 B5
Dovedale Rise CR4 180 D3
Dovedon Cl N14 16 A2
Dove House Gdns E4 19 C2
Dovehouse Mead IG11 101 B5
Dovehouse St SW3 114 C1 257 A1
Dove Mews SW7 114 A1 256 B2
Dove Pk HA5 23 C3
Dover Cl NW2 68 D6
Dovercourt Ave CR7 204 C5
Dovercourt Gdns HA7 26 A5
Dovercourt La SM1 218 A5
Dovercourt Rd SE22 161 D5
Dover Ct
Clerkenwell EC1 241 C6
17 Greenwich SE10 141 D4
Sutton SM1 218 B4
Dove Rd N1 73 B2
Doverfield Rd SW2 160 A4
Dover Flats SE1 263 B3
Dover Gdns SM5 218 D5
Dover Ho
7 Beckenham BR3 185 C3
Brixton SE5 138 D4
11 Deptford SE15 140 C6
Edgware HA8 26 B3
14 Penge SE20 184 B2
Dover House Rd SW15 156 B6
Doveridge Gdns N13 32 D6
Dover Mans 16 SW9 138 C2
Dove Row E2 96 A6
Dover Park Dr SW15 156 B5
Dover Patrol SE3 143 C3
Dover Rd
Dagenham RM6 59 A3
Lower Edmonton N9 18 C2
South Norwood SE19 183 B4
Wanstead E12 77 C6
Woolwich SE18 145 A3
Dover St W1 115 C5 249 A4
Dover Terr TW9 132 C3
Dover Yd W1 249 A4
Doves Cl BR2 226 A6
Doves Yd N1 94 C6 234 A5
Dovet Ct SW8 270 C2
Doveton Ho 7 E1 96 C3
Doveton Rd CR2 221 B3
Doveton St 8 E1 96 C3
Dove Wlk SW1 258 A2
Dovey Lo 4 N1 72 C1
Dowanhill Rd SE6 164 B3
Dowd Cl N11 15 A2
Dowdeny Cl 12 NW5 71 C3
Dowdeswell Cl SW15 133 C1
Dowding Ho N6 49 A2
Dowding Pl HA7 25 A4
Dowding Rd UB10 60 B1
Dowe Ho SE3 142 C2
Dowell Ho SE21 161 D1
Dower Ho The DA14 169 B1
Dowes Ho 13 SW16 160 A1
Dowgate Hill EC4 252 C6
Dowland Ho EN1 5 D5
Dowland St W10 91 A4
Dowlas St SE5 139 C5
Dowlen Ct 14 E14 119 C4
Dowler Ct 2 KT2 176 B2
Dowler Ho 32 E1 96 A1
Dowlerville Rd BR6 227 D2
Dowling Ho DA17 125 B3
Dowman Cl 2 SW19 179 D3
Downage NW4 46 C6
Downalong WD23 8 B3
Down Barns Rd HA4 62 D5
Downbarton Ho 11 SW9 138 C4
Downbury Mews 13 SW18 157 C6
Down Cl UB5 84 B5

Downderry Prim Sch BR1 186 C6
Downderry Rd BR1 186 C6
Downe Cl DA16 146 C5
Downe Ho 9 SE7 143 C6
Downe Manor Prim Sch UB5 84 B4
Downend SE18 144 D5
Downend Ct 1 SE15 139 C6
Downe Rd CR4 180 D1
Downer's Cotts SW4 137 C1
Downes Cl TW1 153 B5
Downes Ct N21 16 C3
Downes Ho CR0 220 D4
Downey Ho 6 E1 96 D3
Downfield KT4 200 A1
Downfield Cl W9 91 D3
Downfield Ho KT3 199 B1
Down Hall Rd KT2 175 D2
DOWNHAM 186 C5
Downham Ct 1 N1 73 B1
Downham Ent Ctr SE6 164 D2
Downham La BR1 186 B5
Downham L Ctr BR1 187 A6
Downham Rd N1 73 B1
Downham Way BR1 186 C6
Downhills Ave N17 51 B6
Downhills Park Rd N17 51 A6
Downhills Prim Sch N15 51 B5
Downhills Way N17 33 A1
Downhurst Ave NW7 27 B5
Downhurst Ct NW4 46 C6
Downing Cl HA2 42 A6
Downing Ct N12 29 D5
Downing Dr UB6 86 C6
Downing Ho
9 Merton SW19 179 C3
2 North Kensington W10 90 D1
4 Putney SW15 156 A6
Downing Rd RM9 81 B1
Downings E6 100 C1
Downing St★ SW1 116 A4 250 A2
Downland Cl N20 14 A3
Downland Ct E11 76 C6
Downleys Cl SE9 166 B2
Downman Rd SE9 144 A2
Down Pl W6 112 B1
Down Rd TW11 175 B4
Down St Mews W1 248 C3
Downs Ave
Elmstead BR7 188 B5
Pinner HA5 41 B2
Downs Bridge Rd BR3 186 B2
Downs Ct
16 Hackney E8 74 B3
13 Wimbledon SW19 178 D3
Downsell Prim Sch E15 76 B4
Downsell Rd E15 76 B4
Downsfield Rd E17 53 A3
Downshall Ave IG3 57 C3
Downshall Ct IG3 57 C3
Downshall Prim Sch IG3 57 C2
Downs Hill BR2, BR3 186 B2
Downshire Hill NW3 70 B4
Downside
2 Putney SW15 157 A6
Sunbury TW16 172 A2
Twickenham TW1 152 D1
Downside Cl SW19 180 A4
Downside Cres
Ealing W13 87 A3
Maitland Pk NW3 70 C3
Downside Rd SM2 218 C2
Downside Wlk UB5 85 B4
Downs La 2 E5 74 B4
Downs Park Rd E5, E8 74 A3
Downs Rd
Beckenham BR3 185 D1
Enfield EN1 5 C1
Shacklewell E5, N16 74 A4
South Norwood CR7 183 A2
Down St
East Molesey KT8 195 C4
Mayfair W1 115 B5 248 C3
Downs The SW19, SW20 178 D3
Downs View TW7 131 A4
Downsview Gdns SE19 183 A3
Downs View Lo 9 KT6 198 A3
Downsview Prim Sch SE19 183 A3
Downsview Rd SE19 183 A3
Downsview Sch E5 74 B4
Downsway BR6 227 C3
Downton Ave SW2 160 B2
Downtown Rd SE16 119 A4
Downway N12 30 C3
Down Way UB5 84 B4
Dowrey St N1 234 A6
Dowsett Rd N17 34 A1
Dowson Cl SE5 139 B1
Dowson Ct SE13 142 B2
Dowson Ho 8 E1 96 D1
Doyce St SE1 252 A2
Doyle Gdns NW10 90 B6
Doyle Ho W3 110 D4
Doyle Rd SE25 206 A5
D'Oyley St SW1 258 A4
Doynton St N19 71 B6
Draco St SE17 139 A6
Dragon Ct WC2 240 B2
Dragonfly Cl E13 99 B4
Dragon Rd SE15 139 C6
Dragon Yd WC1 240 B2
Dragoon Rd SE8 119 B1
Dragor Rd NW10 89 A3
Drake Cl 30 SE16 118 D4
Drake Cres SE28 102 C1
Drake Croft N16 73 B6
Drake Ct
Dulwich SE19 183 D5
5 Hammersmith W12 112 B4
Kingston u T KT5 198 B5
Drakefell Rd SE4, SE14 140 D2
Drakefield Rd SW17 159 A1
Drake Hall 13 E16 121 B5
Drake Ho
2 Limehouse E14 119 A6
20 Stepney E1 96 C2
Drakeley Ct N5 72 D4
Drake Mews BR2 209 C5
Drake Rd
Brockley SE4 141 C2
Chessington KT9 214 C3
Harrow HA2 63 B6
Mitcham CR4 203 A3
Thornton Heath CR0 204 B2
Drakes Ct SE23 162 C3
Drakes Ctyd NW6 69 B1
Drake St Enfield EN2 5 B4
Holborn WC1 240 C3
Drakes Wlk E6 100 B6
Drakewood Rd SW16 181 D3
Drama Ctr London EC1 94 C3 241 B5
Draper Cl
Belvedere DA17 125 B2
Hounslow TW7 130 B3
Draper Ct BR1 210 A5
Draper Ho SE1 261 D4
Draper Pl N1 234 D6
Drapers Almhouses 5 E3 97 C4
Draper's Cottage Homes NW7 28 A6
Drapers Gdns EC2 242 D2
Drapers Rd Enfield EN2 4 D4
Leyton E15 76 B4
Tottenham N17 51 D6
Drappers Way 8 SE16 118 A2
Draven Cl BR2 208 D2
Drawell Cl SE18 123 C1
Drax Ave SW20 178 A3
Draxmont SW19 179 A4
Draycot Rd
Tolworth KT6 198 C1
Wanstead E11 55 B2
Draycott Ave
Chelsea SW3 114 C2 257 B3
Harrow HA3 43 C3
Draycott Cl
Camberwell SE5 139 B5
Cricklewood NW2 68 D5
Harrow HA3 43 B3
Draycott Ct SW11 267 A2
Draycott Ho SW3 257 C3
Draycott Pl SW3 114 D2 257 C3
Draycott Terr SW3 114 D2 257 D3
Drayford Cl W9 91 B3
Dray Gdns SW2 160 B6
Draymans Ct 4 SW9 138 B2
Draymans Mews SE15 139 D3
Draymans Way TW7 130 D2
Drayside Mews UB2 107 B4
Drayson Mews W8 113 C4 245 B1
Drayton Ave
Ealing W13 109 A6
Orpington BR6 210 D1
Drayton Bridge Rd
Ealing W7, W13 108 D6
Ealing W13 87 A1
Drayton Cl
Hounslow TW4 151 B6
Ilford IG1 57 B1
Drayton Ct
South Kensington SW10 256 B1
Tolworth KT5 214 D6
West Drayton UB7 104 B2
Drayton Gdns
Ealing W13 109 A6
Southgate N21 16 D4
South Kensington SW10 114 A1 256 B1
West Drayton UB7 104 A4
Drayton Gn W13 109 A6
Drayton Gr W13 109 A6
Drayton Green Prim Sch W13 109 A6
Drayton Green Rd W13 109 B6
Drayton Green Sta W7 86 D1
Drayton Ho
14 Camberwell SE5 139 B5
Leytonstone E11 54 B1
Drayton Lo E17 35 D1
Drayton Manor High Sch W7 86 D1
Drayton Park Mews 12 N5 72 C3
Drayton Park Prim Sch 13 N5 72 C3
Drayton Park Sta N5 72 C3
Drayton Pk N5, N7 72 C4
Drayton Rd
Croydon CR0 220 D6
Ealing W13 109 B6
Harlesden NW10 89 D6
Leytonstone E11 54 B1
Tottenham N17 33 C1
Drayton Waye HA3 43 B3
DRCA Business Pk SW11 137 A4 268 B1
Dreadnought Cl SW19 180 B1
Dreadnought St SE10 120 C3
Drenon Sq UB3 105 D6
Dresden Cl NW6 69 D2
Dresden Ho
5 Clapham SW11 137 A3
Lambeth SE11 260 D4
Dresden Rd N19 49 D1
Dressington Ave SE4 163 C5
Drew Ave NW7 29 A4
Drewery Ct SE3 142 C2
Drewett Ho 31 E1 96 A1
Drew Gdns UB6 64 D2
Drew Ho 12 SW16 160 A1
Drew Prim Sch E16 122 A5
Drew Rd E16 122 A5
Drewstead La SW16 159 D2
Drewstead Rd SW16 159 D2
Driberg Ct RM9 80 B2
Driffield Ct 4 NW9 27 C2
Driffield Rd E3 97 A5
Drift The BR2 225 D5
Driftway Ho 19 E3 97 B5
Driftway The CR4 181 A2
Drinkwater Ho 11 SE5 139 B5
Drinkwater Rd HA2 63 D6
Drive Ct HA8 26 C5
Drive Ho CR4 202 C5
Drive Mans 1 SW6 135 A3
Drive The Acton W3 89 A1
Ashford TW15 171 B3
Barking IG11 79 D1
Barking IG11 80 A2
Barnet EN5 1 A2
Beckenham BR3 185 C2
Bexley DA5 168 D4
Buckhurst Hill IG9 21 C4
Chingford E4 20 B4
Chislehurst BR7 189 D2
Edgware HA8 26 C5
Enfield EN2 5 B4
Erith DA8 147 D6
Feltham TW14 150 C4
Finchley N3 29 C3
Fortis Green N6 48 D4
Harlesden NW10 89 D6
Harrow HA2 41 C2
Hendon NW11 47 A2
Hounslow TW3, TW7 130 B3
Ickenham UB10 60 A5
Islington N7 72 B2
Kingston u T KT2 177 A3
Morden SM4 202 B4
New Barnet EN5 14 A5
Orpington BR6 227 D6
Redbridge IG1 56 B2
Sidcup DA14 190 B6
South Norwood CR7 205 B5
St Paul's Cray BR7 211 D6
Surbiton KT6 198 A2
Thames Ditton KT10 196 A1
Walthamstow E17 53 D6
Wanstead E18 55 A6
Wembley Pk HA9 67 A6
West Ewell KT19 215 D2
West Wickham BR4 208 B2
Wimbledon SW19, SW20 178 C3
Wood Green N11 31 D4
Dr Johnson Ave SW17 159 B1
Dr Johnson's House★ EC4 241 B1
Droitwich Cl SE26 162 A1
Dromey Gdns HA3 24 D3
Dromore Rd SW15 157 A5
Dronfield Gdns RM8 80 C3
Dron Ho E1 96 C2
Droop St W10 91 A3
Drovers Ct
3 Kingston u T KT1 176 A1
Lewisham SE13 142 A2
Drovers Pl SE15 140 B5
Drovers Rd CR2 221 B3
Drovers Way N7 72 A2
Dr Triplett's CE Jun & Inf Sch UB3 83 D1
Druce Rd SE21 161 C5
Druid St SE1 117 D4 253 C1
Druids Way BR2 208 B5
Drumaline Ridge KT4 215 C6
Drummer Lo N7 72 B5
Drummond Castle Ct E7 76 D4
Drummond Cres NW1 93 D4 232 C2
Drummond Ct
Finchley N12 30 C3
Harrow HA1 42 C2
Drummond Ctr CR0 221 A6
Drummond Dr HA7 24 D3
Drummond Gate SW1 259 D2
Drummond Ho
13 Bethnal Green E2 96 A5
Finchley N2 30 A1
Drummond Rd
Bermondsey SE16 118 B3
Croydon CR0 221 A6
Wanstead E11 55 C3
Drummonds Pl TW9 132 A1
Drummond St NW1 93 C3 239 A6
Drummonds The IG9 21 B2
Drum St E1 243 D2
Drury Cres CR0 220 C6
Drury Ho SW8 269 A2
Drury La WC2 94 A1 240 B1
Drury Rd HA1 42 A2
Drury Way NW10 67 B3
Drury Way Ind Est NW10 67 B3
Dryad St SW15 134 D2
Dryburgh Gdns NW9 44 C6
Dryburgh Ho SW1 258 D2
Dryburgh Mans SW15 134 C2
Dryburgh Rd SW15 134 C2
Dryden Ave W7 86 D1
Dryden Bldg 10 E1 96 A1
Dryden Cl SW4 159 D6
Dryden Ct
Lambeth SE11 261 B3
11 Richmond TW10 175 D6
Dryden Ho
Bromley Comm BR2 209 D4
6 Camberwell SE5 139 C4
16 Stoke Newington N16 73 C5
Dryden Rd
Bexley DA16 145 D4
Enfield EN1 17 D5
Harrow HA3 24 D2
Wimbledon SW19 180 A4
Dryden St WC2 240 B1
Dryer Ct 21 EN3 7 C6
Dryfield Cl NW10 67 A2
Dryfield Rd HA8 27 A4
Dryfield Wlk 1 SE8 141 C6
Dryhill Rd DA17 147 B6
Dryland Ave 5 BR6 227 D4
Drylands Rd N8 50 A3
Drysdale Ave E4 19 D5
Drysdale Flats 3 E8 73 D3
Drysdale Ho 19 E2 95 C4
Drysdale Pl N1 95 C4
Drysdale St N1 95 C4
Dublin Ave E8 96 A6
Du Burstow Terr W7 108 C4
Ducal St 25 E2 95 D4
Ducane Cl 6 W12 90 C1
Du Cane Ct SW12 159 A3
Du Cane Rd W12 90 A1
Ducavel Ho SW2 160 B3
Duchess Cl
London N11 31 B5
Sutton SM1 218 A4
Duchess Gr IG9 21 B2
Duchess Mews W1 238 D3
Duchess of Bedford Ho W8 245 A2
Duchess of Bedford's Wlk W8 113 C4 245 A1
Duchess St W1 93 B2 238 D3
Duchy Rd EN4 2 B5
Duchy St SE1 116 C5 251 B4
Ducie Ho
8 Charlton SE7 143 C6
2 Putney SW15 156 C6
Ducie St SW4 138 B1
Duckett Mews N4 50 D3
Duckett Rd N4 50 D3
Duckett St E1 97 A2
Duck La W1 239 C1
Duck Lees La EN3 7 A1
Ducks Hill Rd HA4, HA6 39 A5
DUCKS ISLAND 12 D5
Duck's Wlk TW1 153 C6
Du Cros Dr HA7 25 D4
Du Cros Rd W3 111 C5
DUDDEN HILL 68 A3
Dudden Hill La NW10 67 D3
Duddington Cl SE9 187 D6
Dudley Ave HA3 43 C6
Dudley Ct
Colney Hatch N12 30 C5
Marylebone W1 237 C1
St Giles WC2 240 A2
Temple Fortune NW11 47 B5
14 Wanstead E11 55 A4
Wembley HA0 65 D3
Dudley Dr Ruislip HA4 62 B3
West Barnes SM4 201 A2
Dudley Gdns
Ealing W13 109 B4
Harrow HA2 42 B1
Dudley Ho
13 Brixton SW9 138 C3
Edgware HA8 26 B3
Paddington W2 236 C3
Dudley Mews 14 SW2 160 C5

Dudley Pl UB3 ... 105 B2
Dudley Rd
Ashford TW15 ... 170 B6
East Bedfont TW14 ... 149 B3
Finchley N3 ... 29 D1
Harrow HA2 ... 64 A6
Ilford IG1 ... 78 D4
Kilburn NW6 ... 91 B5
Kingston u T KT1 ... 198 B6
Richmond TW9 ... 132 B3
Southall UB2 ... 106 D3
Walthamstow E17 ... 35 C1
Walton-on-T KT12 ... 194 A2
Wimbledon SW19 ... 179 C4
Dudley St W2 ... 236 C3
Dudlington Rd E5 ... 74 C6
Dudmaston Mews SW3 ... 256 D2
Dudrich Cl N11, N12 ... 30 D4
Dudsbury Rd DA14 ... 190 B4
Dudset La TW5 ... 128 A4
Duett Ct TW3 ... 129 A5
Duffell Ho SE11 ... 260 D1
Dufferin Ave EC1 ... 242 C5
Dufferin Ct EC1 ... 242 C5
Dufferin St EC1 ... 95 A3 242 B5
Duffield Cl HA1 ... 42 D4
Duffield Dr N15 ... 51 D5
Duffield Ho N4 ... 51 A2
Duff Miller Coll SW7 ... 114 A3 246 B5
Duff St E14 ... 97 D1
Dufour's Pl W1 ... 239 B1
Dugard Way SE11 ... 116 D2 261 C3
Dugdale Ho 10 N7 ... 71 D3
Duggan Dr BR7 ... 188 A4
Dugolly Ave HA9 ... 66 D5
Duke Gdns IG6 ... 57 B5
Duke Humphrey Rd SE3 ... 142 C3
Duke Of Cambridge Cl TW2 ... 152 B5
Duke Of Edinburgh Rd SM1 ... 218 B6
Duke Of Wellington Ave SE18 ... 123 A3
Duke of Wellington Pl SW1, W1 ... 248 B2
Duke of York's Sq SW3 ... 114 D2 257 D3
Duke of York St SW1 ... 249 B4
Duke Rd Chiswick W4 ... 111 B1
Ilford IG6 ... 57 B5
Duke St Hill SE1 ... 252 D4
Duke St St James's SW1 ... 115 C5 249 B4
Dukes Ave
Edgware HA8 ... 26 B5
Finchley N3 ... 29 D2
Hornsey N10 ... 49 C6
Hounslow TW4 ... 129 A1
Kingston u T KT3 ... 199 D6
Northolt UB5 ... 63 A1
Rayners La HA2, HA5 ... 41 B3
Richmond KT2, TW10 ... 175 D6
Wealdstone HA1 ... 42 C5
Duke's Ave W4 ... 111 B1
Dukes Cl
Ashford TW15 ... 171 A6
Hampton TW12 ... 173 B5
Dukes Ct Barking E6 ... 100 C6
Beckenham BR3 ... 207 A6
Dulwich SE22 ... 162 A3
Ealing W13 ... 87 B2
East Dulwich SE22 ... 162 B6
Lewisham SE13 ... 142 A3
Mortlake SW14 ... 133 B3
Dukes Gate 4 W4 ... 111 A2
Dukes Green Ave TW14 ... 150 A6
Dukes Head Yd N6 ... 49 B1
Duke's Ho SW1 ... 259 D4
Duke Shore Wharf E14 ... 119 B6
Dukes La W8 ... 113 D4 245 C2
Dukes Mews N10 ... 49 B6
Duke's Mews W1 ... 238 B2
Duke's Pl EC3 ... 95 C1 243 B1
Dukes Point N6 ... 49 B1
Dukes Rd Acton W3 ... 88 C3
Barking E6 ... 100 C6
Duke's Rd WC1 ... 93 D4 232 D1
Dukes Ride UB10 ... 60 A4
Duke St
Marylebone W1 ... 93 A1 238 B1
Richmond TW10, TW9 ... 153 D6
Sutton SM1 ... 218 B4
Dukesthorpe Rd SE26 ... 184 D6
Duke Street Mans W1 ... 238 B1
Dukes Way
Coney Hall BR4 ... 224 C5
Wembley HA9 ... 66 A3
Duke's Yd W1 ... 248 B6
Dulas St N4 ... 50 B1
Dulford St W11 ... 113 A6 244 A6
Dulka Rd SW11 ... 158 D6
Dulverton NW1 ... 232 B5
Dulverton Ct 12 KT6 ... 198 A4
Dulverton Mans WC1 ... 240 D5
Dulverton Prim Sch SE9 ... 167 B2
Dulverton Rd
New Eltham SE9 ... 167 B2
Ruislip HA4 ... 62 A6
DULWICH ... 161 C1
Dulwich Bsns Ctr SE23 ... 162 D3
Dulwich Coll SE21 ... 161 C2
Dulwich Coll Prep Sch SE21 ... 161 C1
Dulwich Com Hospl SE22 ... 139 C1
Dulwich Comm SE21 ... 161 C3
Dulwich Ct SE22 ... 162 B3
Dulwich Hamlet Jun Sch SE21 ... 161 B5
Dulwich Lawn Cl SE22 ... 161 D6
Dulwich L Ctr SE22 ... 140 A1
Dulwich Mead SE24 ... 161 A5
Dulwich Mews
1 East Dulwich SE22 ... 139 D1
East Dulwich SE22 ... 161 D6
Dulwich Oaks The SE21 ... 161 D1
Dulwich Picture Gall★ SE21 ... 161 C4
Dulwich Rd SE24 ... 160 D5
DULWICH VILLAGE ... 161 C4
Dulwich Village SE21 ... 161 C5
Dulwich Village CE Inf Sch SE21 ... 161 C5
Dulwich Wood Ave SE19 ... 183 C5
Dulwich Wood Pk SE19 ... 183 C6
Dumain Ct SE11 ... 261 C3
Du Maurier Ho 2 NW3 ... 70 D3
Dumbarton Ct 16 SW2 ... 160 A4
Dumbarton Rd SW2 ... 160 A5
Dumbleton Cl KT2 ... 176 D2
Dumbreck Rd SE9 ... 144 C2
Dumont Rd N16 ... 73 C5
Dumphreys Ho 5 SW4 ... 159 D4
Dumpton Pl NW1 ... 71 A1
Dunally Pk TW17 ... 193 B2
Dunbar Ave
Beckenham BR3 ... 207 A5
Dagenham RM10 ... 81 C5
Thornton Heath SW16 ... 182 C1
Dunbar Cl UB4 ... 84 A2
Dunbar Ct
3 London N12 ... 29 D6
Sutton SM1 ... 218 B3
Walton-on-T KT12 ... 194 C1
Dunbar Gdns RM10 ... 81 D3
Dunbar Rd
New Malden KT3 ... 199 A5
Tottenham N22 ... 32 D2
Upton E7 ... 77 A2
Dunbar St SE27 ... 161 A1
Dunbar Wharf 20 E14 ... 119 B6
Dunblane Cl HA8 ... 10 D2
Dunblane Rd SE9 ... 144 A3
Dunboe Pl TW17 ... 193 A2
Dunboyne Rd NW3 ... 70 D3
Dunbridge Ho SW15 ... 155 D5
Dunbridge St
Bethnal Green E2 ...
Bethnal Green E2 ... 96 B3
Duncan Cl EN5 ... 2 A1
Duncan Ct
5 London N12 ... 29 D5
3 Poplar E14 ... 98 A2
Southgate N21 ... 16 D3
Duncan Gr W3 ... 89 C1
Duncan Ho
Harrow HA2 ... 64 A5
3 Primrose Hill NW3 ... 70 D1
Duncannon Ho SW1 ... 259 D1
Duncannon St WC2 ... 250 A5
Duncan Rd
Hackney E8 ... 96 B6
Richmond TW9 ... 132 A1
Duncan St N1 ... 94 D5 234 C4
Duncan Terr N1 ... 94 D5 234 C4
Dunch St 33 E1 ... 96 B1
Dunchurch Ho RM10 ... 81 C1
Duncombe Hill SE23 ... 163 A4
Duncombe Ho 7 SW19 ... 156 D3
Duncombe Prim Sch N19 ... 50 A1
Duncombe Rd N19 ... 49 D1
Duncrievie Rd SE13 ... 164 B5
Duncroft SE18 ... 145 C5
Dundalk Ho 2 E1 ... 96 C1
Dundalk Rd SE4 ... 141 A2
Dundas Gdns KT8 ... 195 D6
Dundas Ho 12 E2 ... 96 C5
Dundas Mews 4 EN3 ... 7 C6
Dundas Rd SE15 ... 140 C3
Dundee Ct 36 E1 ... 118 B5
Dundee Ho W9 ... 229 A2
Dundee Rd
Croydon SE25 ... 206 B4
Newham E13 ... 99 B5
Dundee St E1 ... 118 B5
Dundee Way EN3 ... 7 A2
Dundee Wharf E14 ... 119 B6
Dundela Gdns KT17, KT4 ... 216 B4
Dundonald Cl 6 E6 ... 100 A1
Dundonald Prim Sch SW19 ... 179 B3
Dundonald Rd
Brondesbury Pk NW10 ... 90 D6
Merton SW19 ... 179 B3
Dundonald Road Sta SW19 ... 179 B3
Dundry Ho 8 SE26 ... 162 A1
Duneaves HA1 ... 64 C5
Dunedin Ho E16 ... 122 B5
Dunedin Rd Ilford IG1 ... 57 A1
Leyton E10 ... 75 D5
Dunedin Way UB4 ... 84 C3
Dunelm Gr SE27 ... 161 A1
Dunelm St E1 ... 96 D1
Dunfield Gdns SE6 ... 185 D5
Dunfield Rd SE6 ... 185 D5
Dunford Ct 9 HA5 ... 23 B3
Dunford Rd N7 ... 72 B4
Dungarvan Ave SW15 ... 134 A1
Dungeness Ho SW18 ... 136 A1
Dunheved Cl CR7 ... 204 C3
Dunheved Ct 2 CR7 ... 204 C3
Dunheved Rd N CR7 ... 204 C3
Dunheved Rd S CR7 ... 204 C3
Dunheved Rd W CR7 ... 204 C3
Dunhill Point 12 SW15 ... 156 B3
Dunholme Gn N9 ... 17 D1
Dunholme La N9 ... 17 D1
Dunholme Rd N9 ... 17 D1
Dunkeld Ho 15 E14 ... 98 B1
Dunkeld Rd
Dagenham RM8 ... 80 C6
South Norwood SE25 ... 205 B5
Dunkery Rd SE9 ... 166 A1
Dunkirk St 12 SE27 ... 183 A6
Dunlace Rd E5 ... 74 D4
Dunleary Cl TW4 ... 151 B4
Dunley Dr CR0 ... 224 A2
Dunlin Ct 12 SE21 ... 161 B2
Dunlin Ho 18 SE16 ... 118 D2
Dunloe Ave N17 ... 51 B6
Dunloe Ct 7 E2 ... 95 D5
Dunloe St E2 ... 95 D5
Dunlop Pl SE16 ... 117 D3 263 D5
Dunmore Point 15 E2 ... 95 D4
Dunmore Rd
Kilburn NW6 ... 91 A6
Wimbledon SW20 ... 178 D2
Dunmow Cl
Dagenham RM6 ... 58 C4
3 Feltham TW13 ... 173 A6
Dunmow Ho
Dagenham RM9 ... 102 B6
Vauxhall SE11 ... 260 D2
Dunmow Rd E15 ... 76 B4
Dunmow Wlk N1 ... 235 A6
Dunnage Cres SE16 ... 119 A2
Dunne Mews 11 NW5 ... 71 C3
Dunnet Ho 27 E3 ... 97 B5
Dunnico Ho SE17 ... 263 A2
Dunn Mead NW9 ... 27 D3
Dunnock Cl N9 ... 18 D3
Dunnock Ct 11 SE21 ... 161 B2
Dunnock Rd E6 ... 100 A1
Dunn's Pas WC1 ... 240 B2
Dunn St E8 ... 73 D3
Dunollie Pl NW5 ... 71 C3
Dunollie Rd NW5 ... 71 C3
Dunoon Gdns SE23 ... 162 D4
Dunoon Ho N1 ... 233 C5
Dunoon Rd SE23 ... 162 C4
Dunraven Dr EN2 ... 4 C3
Dunraven Ho 12 TW9 ... 132 B4
Dunraven Rd W12 ... 112 A5
Dunraven Sch SW16 ... 160 B1
Dunraven St W1 ... 114 D6 247 D6
Dunrobin Ct NW3 ... 69 D3
Dunsany Rd W14 ... 112 D3
Dunsfold Ct 14 SM2 ... 217 D1
Dunsfold Ho
10 Kingston u T KT2 ... 176 D4
4 Streatham SW2 ... 160 B4
Dunsfold Way CR0 ... 223 D1
Dunsford Way SW15 ... 156 B5
Dunsmore Cl
Bushey WD23 ... 8 B5
Hayes UB4 ... 85 A3
Dunsmore Rd KT12 ... 194 B3
Dunsmore Way WD23 ... 8 B5
Dunsmure Rd N16 ... 51 C1
Dunstable Ct 3 SE3 ... 143 A5
Dunstable Mews W1 ... 238 B4
Dunstable Rd
East Molesey KT8 ... 195 B5
Richmond TW10, TW9 ... 132 A1
Dunstall Ho 9 SE15 ... 140 A4
Dunstall Rd SW19, SW20 ... 178 C4
Dunstall Way KT8 ... 195 D6
Dunstall Welling Est DA16 ... 146 B3
Dunstan Cl 2 N2 ... 48 A6
Dunstan Glade BR5 ... 211 B3
Dunstan Ho SE4 ... 141 B3
Dunstan Hos 5 E1 ... 96 C2
Dunstan Rd NW11 ... 47 C1
Dunstan's Gr SE22 ... 162 B5
Dunstan's Rd SE22 ... 162 A5
Dunster Ave SM4 ... 200 D1
Dunster Ct EC3 ... 253 B6
Dunster Dr NW9 ... 45 A1
Dunster Gdns NW6 ... 69 B1
Dunster Ho SE6 ... 163 D1
Dunsterville Way SE1 ... 252 D1
Dunster Way
Carshalton CR4 ... 203 A1
Harrow HA2 ... 63 A5
Dunston Rd
Clapham SW11 ... 137 A3
Hackney E8 ... 95 D6
Dunston St E8 ... 95 D6
Dunton Cl KT6 ... 198 A1
Dunton Ct 5 SE26 ... 162 B2
Dunton Ho 14 SW16 ... 160 A1
Dunton Rd
Bermondsey SE1 ... 117 D2 263 C3
Leyton E10 ... 53 D2
Duntshill Rd SW18 ... 157 D3
Dunvegan Cl KT8 ... 195 D5
Dunvegan Rd SE9 ... 144 B1
Dunwich Ct 2 RM6 ... 58 B4
Dunwich Rd DA7 ... 147 B4
Dunworth Mews W11 ... 91 B1
Duplex Ride SW1 ... 247 D1
Dupont Rd SW20 ... 178 D1
Duppas Ave CR0 ... 220 D4
Duppas Cl TW17 ... 193 B4
Duppas Ct CR0 ... 220 D5
Duppas Hill La CR0 ... 220 D4
Duppas Hill Rd CR0 ... 220 D4
Duppas Hill Terr CR0 ... 220 D5
Duppas Jun Sch CR0 ... 220 D3
Duppas Rd CR0 ... 220 D5
Dupree Rd SE7 ... 121 B1
Dura Den Cl BR3 ... 185 D3
Durand Cl SM5 ... 202 D1
Durand Gdns SW9 ... 138 B4 270 D1
Durand Prim Sch SW9 ... 138 B4 270 D2
Durand Way NW10 ... 67 A1
Durants Lo EN3 ... 6 D2
Durants Park Ave EN3 ... 6 D1
Durants Rd EN3 ... 6 D1
Durants Sch EN3 ... 6 C4
Durant St E2 ... 96 A4
Durban Ct E7 ... 77 D1
Durban Ho 28 W12 ... 112 B6
Durban Rd
Beckenham BR3 ... 185 B1
Ilford IG2 ... 57 C1
Newham E15 ... 98 C4
Tottenham N17 ... 33 D4
Walthamstow E17 ... 35 B2
West Norwood SE27 ... 183 B6
Durbin Ho 18 N9 ... 18 A1
Durbin Rd KT9 ... 214 B4
Durdan Cotts UB5 ... 85 B1
Durdans Ho 3 NW1 ... 71 C1
Durdans Park Prim Sch UB1 ... 85 B2
Durdans Rd UB1 ... 85 B1
Durell Gdns RM9 ... 80 D3
Durell Rd RM9 ... 80 D3
Durfey Pl SE5 ... 139 B5
Durford Cres SW15 ... 156 B3
Durham Ave
Beckenham BR2 ... 208 D5
Hounslow TW5 ... 107 B1
Woodford IG8 ... 37 D5
Durham Cl SW20 ... 178 B1
Durham Ct
2 Barnet EN5 ... 1 B2
Brockley SE4 ... 141 C2
4 Kilburn NW6 ... 91 C5
Teddington TW11 ... 174 C6
Durham Hill BR1 ... 186 D6
Durham Ho
3 Barking IG11 ... 80 A1
7 Dartmouth Pk NW5 ... 71 C5
Edgware HA8 ... 26 B3
Lisson Gr NW8 ... 230 B1
Durham House St WC2 ... 250 B5
Durham Pl
Chelsea SW3 ... 257 C1
Ilford IG1 ... 79 A4
Durham Rd
Beckenham BR2 ... 208 D6
Ealing W5 ... 109 D3
Edmonton N9 ... 18 A2
Feltham TW14 ... 150 C4
Harrow HA1 ... 41 D4
Lower Holloway N4, N7 ... 72 B6
Manor Pk E12 ... 77 D4
Muswell Hill N2 ... 48 D6
Newham E16 ... 98 C3
Sidcup DA14 ... 190 B5
Wimbledon SW20 ... 178 B2
Durham Rise SE18 ... 123 B1
Durham Row E1 ... 97 A2
Durham St SE11 ... 138 B6 270 C6
Durham Terr W2 ... 91 D1
Durham Wharf Dr TW8 ... 131 C5
Durley Ave HA5 ... 41 A3
Durley Rd N16 ... 51 C2
Durlock Ho 16 SW9 ... 138 C4
Durlston Rd
Kingston u T KT2 ... 176 A4

Durlston Rd *continued*
Stoke Newington E5 ... 74 A6
Durnford Ho SE6 ... 163 D1
Durnford St
4 Greenwich SE10 ... 142 A6
South Tottenham N15 ... 51 C4
Durning Rd SE19 ... 183 B5
Durnsford Ave SW18, SW19 ... 157 C2
Durnsford Ct 5 EN3 ... 7 A2
Durnsford Rd
London N11 ... 31 D3
Wimbledon SW18, SW19 ... 157 C1
Durnston Ct 2 SM1 ... 217 D2
Durrant Ct HA3 ... 24 C2
Durrant Way BR6 ... 227 B3
Durrell Rd SW6 ... 264 C1
Durrell Way TW17 ... 193 B3
Durrels Ho W14 ... 254 D4
Durrington Ave SW20 ... 178 C3
Durrington Park Rd SW20 ... 178 C2
Durrington Rd E5 ... 75 A4
Durrington Twr 3 SW8 ... 137 C3
Durrisdeer Ho NW2 ... 69 B4
Dursley Cl SE3 ... 143 C3
Dursley Gdns SE3 ... 143 D4
Dursley Rd SE3 ... 143 C3
Durston NW5 ... 71 A3
Durston House Prep Sch W5 ... 87 D1
Durston House Sch W5 ... 87 D1
Durward St E1 ... 96 B2
Durweston Mews W1 ... 237 D4
Durweston St W1 ... 237 D3
Dury Rd EN5 ... 1 B3
Dutch Gdns KT2 ... 176 D4
Dutch Yd SW18 ... 157 C6
Dutton Ho SW2 ... 160 D3
Dutton St SE10 ... 142 A4
Duxberry Cl BR2 ... 210 A4
Duxford 21 KT1 ... 176 C1
Duxford Ho 10 SE2 ... 124 D4
Dwight Ct 3 SW6 ... 135 A3
Dycer Ho 10 E9 ... 74 D2
Dye House La E3 ... 97 C6
Dyer Ho
Hampton TW12 ... 173 D2
New Cross SE4 ... 141 A3
Dyer's Bldgs EC1 ... 241 A3
Dyers Hall Rd
Leyton E11 ... 76 B6
Leytonstone E11 ... 54 C1
Dyer's La SW15 ... 134 B1
Dykes Ct 11 SW2 ... 160 B3
Dykes Way BR2 ... 208 D6
Dylan Cl WD6 ... 9 D4
Dylan Rd
Belvedere DA17 ... 125 C3
2 Brixton SE24 ... 138 D1
Dylways SE5 ... 139 B1
Dymchurch Cl
Ilford IG5 ... 56 C6
Orpington BR6 ... 227 C4
Dymchurch Ho 12 E5 ... 74 B3
Dymes Path SW19 ... 156 D2
Dymock St SW6 ... 135 D2
Dyneley Rd SE12 ... 165 C1
Dyne Rd NW6 ... 69 B1
Dynevor Rd
Richmond TW10 ... 154 A6
Shacklewell N16 ... 73 D5
Dynham Rd NW6 ... 69 C1
Dyott St Soho WC1 ... 239 D2
St Giles WC1, WC2 ... 94 A1 240 A2
Dysart Ave KT2, TW10 ... 175 C6
Dysart Sch KT6 ... 198 B2
Dysart St EC2 ... 95 C3 243 A5
Dyson Ct London NW2 ... 46 C2
Wembley HA0 ... 65 A4
Dyson Ho 3 SE10 ... 120 D1
Dyson Rd
Leytonstone E11 ... 54 C3
Stratford E15 ... 76 D2
Dyson's Rd N18 ... 34 B4

E

Eade Rd N4 ... 51 A2
Eagans Cl N2 ... 48 B6
Eagle Ave RM6 ... 59 A3
Eagle Cl
Bermondsey SE16 ... 118 C1
Enfield EN3 ... 6 C1
Wallington SM6 ... 220 A2
Eagle Ct
10 Dulwich SE21 ... 161 B2
Edmonton N18 ... 33 D4
Holborn EC1 ... 241 C4
6 Wanstead E11 ... 55 A5
Eagle Dr NW9 ... 27 C1
Eagle Dwellings EC1 ... 235 B2
Eagle Hill SE19 ... 183 B4
Eagle Ho
22 Bethnal Green E1 ... 96 B3
Finsbury Pk N7 ... 72 B5
Eagle House Sch CR4 ... 180 D1
Eagle Hts 10 SW11 ... 136 C2
Eagle La E11 ... 55 A5
Eagle Lo
Leytonstone E11 ... 54 D5
London NW11 ... 47 B2
Eagle Mans N16 ... 73 D3
Eagle Mews N1 ... 73 C2
Eagle Pl
South Kensington SW7 ... 114 A1 256 B2
St James SW1 ... 249 B5
Eagle Rd Hatton TW6 ... 127 D2
Wembley HA0 ... 65 D1
Eaglesfield Rd SE18 ... 144 D4
Eagle St WC1 ... 94 B2 240 C3
Eagle Star Ho SM1 ... 217 D4
Eagle Terr IG8 ... 37 B3
Eagle Trad Est CR4 ... 202 D3
Eagle Wharf SE1 ... 253 C3
Eagle Wharf Rd N1 ... 95 A5 235 B4
Eagle Works E1 ... 243 D5
Eagling Cl E3 ... 97 C4
Ealcom Ct W5 ... 110 B5
Ealdham Prim Sch SE9 ... 143 C1
Ealdham Sq SE9 ... 143 C1
EALING ... 109 D6
Ealing Broadway Ctr W5 ... 109 D6
Ealing Broadway Sta W5 ... 109 D6
Ealing Coll 1 W13 ... 87 B1
Ealing Coll of Higher Ed W5 ... 109 D5
Ealing Common W5 ... 110 B6
Ealing Common Sta W5 ... 110 B5
Ealing Court Man W5 ... 109 D4
Ealing Gateway W5 ... 109 C6
Ealing Gn W5 ... 109 D5
Ealing, Hammersmith & West London Coll W14 ... 113 A1 254 A2
Ealing Hospl UB1 ... 108 B4
Ealing Ind Coll W5 ... 109 C6
Ealing Park Gdns W5 ... 109 C2
Ealing Park Lo UB6 ... 87 A5
Ealing Park Mans W5 ... 109 D3
Ealing Rd
Brentford TW8 ... 109 D2
Northolt UB5 ... 63 C1
Wembley HA0 ... 66 A1
Ealing Road Trad Est TW8 ... 109 D1
Ealing Studios★ W5 ... 109 D5
Ealing Village W5 ... 88 A1
Ealing & West London Coll W5 ... 109 D5
Eamann Casey Ho 33 SW9 ... 138 C4
Eamont Cl HA4 ... 38 D2
Eamont Ct NW8 ... 230 B4
Eamont St NW8 ... 92 C5 230 B4
Eardley Cres SW5 ... 113 C1 255 B1
Eardley Point 9 SE18 ... 122 D2
Eardley Rd
Belvedere DA17 ... 125 C1
Streatham SW16 ... 181 C4
Eardley Sch SW16 ... 181 C4
Earl Cl N11 ... 31 B5
Earldom Rd SW15 ... 134 C1
Earle Gdns KT2 ... 176 A3
Earle Ho SW1 ... 259 D3
Earlham Gr
Forest Gate E7 ... 77 A3
Wood Green N22 ... 32 B3
Earlham Prim Sch
Stratford E7 ... 76 D3
Wood Green N22 ... 32 C3
Earlham St WC2 ... 94 A1 240 A1
Earl Ho NW1 ... 237 B5
Earlom Ho WC1 ... 234 A1
Earl Rd SW14 ... 133 A1
Earl Rise SE18 ... 123 B2
EARL'S COURT ... 113 C1
Earl's Court Ex Ctr★ SW5 ... 113 C1 255 A1
Earl's Court Gdns SW5 ... 113 D2 255 C3
Earl's Court Rd SW5, W8 ... 113 C2 255 B4
Earl's Court Sq SW5 ... 113 D1 255 C2
Earl's Court Sta SW5 ... 113 C2 255 B3
Earls Cres HA1 ... 42 C5
Earlsdown Ho 6 IG11 ... 101 B5
Earlsferry Way N1 ... 72 A1
EARLSFIELD ... 158 A3
Earlsfield Ho 16 KT2 ... 175 D2
Earlsfield Prim Sch SW18 ... 158 A2
Earlsfield Rd SW18 ... 158 A4
Earlsfield Sta SW18 ... 158 A3
Earlshall Rd SE9 ... 144 C1
Earlsmead HA2 ... 63 B4
Earlsmead Fst & Mid Sch HA2 ... 63 B4
Earlsmead Prim Sch 3 N15 ... 51 D5
Earlsmead Rd
Kensal Green NW10 ... 90 C4
South Tottenham N15 ... 51 D4
Earl St EC2 ... 95 C2 243 A4
Earls Terr W8 ... 254 D5
Earlsthorpe Mews 3 SW12 ... 159 A5
Earlsthorpe Rd SE26 ... 184 D6
Earlstoke St EC1 ... 234 C2
Earlston Gr E9 ... 96 B6
Earls Wlk
Dagenham RM8 ... 80 B4
Kensington W8 ... 113 C3 255 A5
Earlswood Ave CR7 ... 204 C4
Earlswood Cl 10 SE10 ... 120 C1
Earlswood Gdns IG5 ... 56 C6
Earlswood Ho 2 SW2 ... 160 B3
Earlswood St SE10 ... 120 C1
Early Mews NW1 ... 231 D6
Earnshaw Ho EC1 ... 234 D1
Earnshaw St WC1, WC2 ... 239 D2
Earsby St W14 ... 254 B4
Earth Galleries★ SW7 ... 114 B3 256 D5
Easby Cres SM4 ... 201 D3
Easebourne Rd RM8 ... 80 C3
Easedale Ho TW7 ... 152 D6
Eashing Point 5 SW15 ... 156 B3
Easleys Mews W1 ... 238 B2
East 10 Ent Pk E10 ... 53 A1
EAST ACTON ... 111 C5
East Acton Arc W3 ... 89 D1
East Acton Ct W3 ... 111 C6
East Acton La W3 ... 111 C6
East Acton Prim Sch W3 ... 111 C6
East Acton Sta W12 ... 89 D1
East Arbour St E1 ... 96 D1
East Ave Croydon CR0 ... 220 B3
East Finchley NW2 ... 48 A6
Hayes UB3 ... 106 A5
Plashet E12 ... 78 A1
Southall UB1 ... 107 B6
East Ave *continued*
Walthamstow E17 ... 53 D5
East Bank N16 ... 51 C2
Eastbank Cl 2 E17 ... 53 D4
Eastbank Rd TW12 ... 174 A5
EAST BARNET ... 14 D4
East Barnet Rd EN4 ... 2 B1
East Barnet Sch
Barnet EN4 ... 2 B2
East Barnet EN4 ... 14 D5
East Beckton District Ctr E6 ... 100 B2
EAST BEDFONT ... 149 C3
East Block 5 E1 ... 118 D6
Eastbourne Ave W3 ... 89 B1
Eastbourne Gdns SW14 ... 133 A2
Eastbourne Mews W2 ... 92 A1 236 B2
Eastbourne Rd
Brentford TW8 ... 109 D1
Chiswick W4 ... 133 A6
Feltham TW13 ... 150 D2
South Tottenham N15 ... 51 C3
Streatham SW17 ... 181 A4
Wallend E6 ... 100 C4
West Ham E15 ... 98 C6
Eastbourne Terr W2 ... 92 A1 236 B2
Eastbournia Ave N9 ... 18 B1
Eastbrook Ave N9 ... 18 C4
Eastbrook Rd SE3 ... 143 B4
EASTBURY ... 22 A5
Eastbury Ave
Barking IG11 ... 101 C6
Enfield EN1 ... 5 D4
Mo Pk HA6 ... 22 A5
Eastbury Comp Sch IG11 ... 79 C2
Eastbury Ct
Barking IG11 ... 101 C6
New Barnet EN5 ... 14 A6
Eastbury Gr W4 ... 111 C1
Eastbury Inf Sch IG11 ... 79 D1
Eastbury Rd
Kingston u T KT2 ... 176 A3
Newham E6 ... 100 C3
Orpington BR5 ... 211 B3
Eastbury Sq IG11 ... 101 D6
Eastbury Terr E1 ... 96 D3
Eastcastle St W1 ... 93 C1 239 B2
Eastcheap EC3 ... 117 C6 253 A6
East Churchfield Rd W3 ... 111 B5
Eastchurch Rd TW6 ... 127 C2
Eastchurch Road Rdbt TW6 ... 127 C3
East Cl Cockfosters EN4 ... 3 A1
Ealing W5 ... 88 C3
Greenford UB6 ... 86 A5
Eastcombe Ave SE7 ... 143 B6
EASTCOTE ... 40 C3
Eastcote BR6 ... 211 D1
Eastcote Ave
East Molesey KT8 ... 195 C4
Harrow HA2 ... 64 A6
Wembley UB6 ... 65 A3
Eastcote Ind Est HA4 ... 40 C2
Eastcote La
Harrow HA2 ... 63 C5
Northolt UB5 ... 63 B2
Eastcote La N UB5 ... 63 C2
Eastcote Pl HA5 ... 40 B3
Eastcote Prim Sch DA16 ... 145 B2
Eastcote Rd
Bexley DA16 ... 145 B3
Harrow HA2 ... 64 A5
Pinner HA5 ... 40 D4
Ruislip HA4 ... 40 A3
Eastcote St SW9 ... 138 B3
Eastcote Sta HA5 ... 40 C2
Eastcote View HA5 ... 40 C5
EASTCOTE VILLAGE ... 40 B4
Eastcott Cl KT2 ... 177 A5
Eastcourt Ind Sch IG3 ... 58 A1
East Cres Enfield EN1 ... 17 D6
Friern Barnet N11 ... 30 D6
Eastcroft Rd KT19 ... 215 C1
East Cross Route
Bow E3 ... 97 C6
Hackney Wick E9 ... 75 B3
East Croydon Sta CR0 ... 221 B6
East Ct
Sunbury TW16 ... 172 C1
Wembley HA0 ... 65 C6
Eastdown Ho E8 ... 74 A4
Eastdown Pk SE13 ... 142 B1
East Duck Lees La EN3 ... 7 B1
EAST DULWICH ... 162 A6
East Dulwich Gr SE22 ... 161 C6
East Dulwich Rd SE15, SE22 ... 140 A1
East Dulwich Sta SE22 ... 139 C1
East End Computing & Bsns Coll 37 E1 ... 96 B1
East End Rd
East Finchley N2, N3 ... 48 A6
Finchley N3 ... 29 C1
East End Way HA5 ... 41 A6
East Entrance RM10 ... 103 D5
Eastern Ave
Gants Hill IG1, IG2, IG4 ... 56 C3
Newbury Pk IG2 ... 57 B3
Pinner HA5 ... 40 D2
Wanstead E11 ... 55 C3
Eastern Avenue W RM7 ... 59 C5
Eastern Bsns Pk TW16 ... 127 D3
Eastern Perimeter Rd TW14 ... 127 D3
Eastern Quay 15 E16 ... 121 B5
Eastern Rd
Brockley SE4 ... 141 C1
Fortis Green N2 ... 48 D5
Newham E13 ... 99 B5
Walthamstow E17 ... 54 A4
Wood Green N22 ... 32 A2
Easternville Gdns IG2 ... 57 A3
Eastern Way SE28 ... 124 B4
East Ferry Rd E14 ... 119 D2
Eastfield Gdns RM10 ... 81 C4
Eastfield Prim Sch EN3 ... 6 D5
Eastfield Rd
Dagenham RM9 ... 81 B4
Dagenham RM10 ... 81 C4
Enfield EN3 ... 6 D5
Hornsey N8 ... 50 A6
Walthamstow E17 ... 53 C5
Eastfields HA5 ... 40 C4
Eastfields Ave SW18 ... 135 C1
Eastfields Rd
Acton W3 ... 89 A2
Mitcham CR4 ... 181 A1
Eastfield St E14 ... 97 A2
EAST FINCHLEY ... 48 B5
East Finchley Sta N2 ... 48 C5
Eastgate Bsns Pk E10 ... 53 A1
Eastgate Cl SE28 ... 102 D1
Eastgate Ct N3 ... 29 C1
East Gdns SW17 ... 180 C4
Eastglade HA5 ... 41 B6
EAST HAM ... 100 A5
Eastham Cl EN5 ... 13 B6
East Ham Ind Est E6 ... 100 A2
East Ham L Ctr E6 ... 100 B6
East Ham Manor Way E6 ... 100 C1
East Ham Meml Hospl E7 ... 77 D1
East Ham Sta E6 ... 78 A1
East Harding St EC4 ... 241 B2
East Heath Rd NW3 ... 70 B5
East Hill
London SW18 ... 158 A6
Wembley HA9 ... 44 C1
Eastholm NW11 ... 47 D5
Eastholme UB3 ... 106 A5
East India Bldgs 9 E14 ... 119 C6
East India Ct 7 SE16 ... 118 C4
East India Dock Basin★ E14 ... 120 C6
East India Dock Rd E14 ... 119 D6
East India Dock Road Tunnel 18 E14 ... 98 B1

East India Sta E14 ... 120 B6
East India Way CR0 . 205 D1
East La
5 Bermondsey SE16 ... 118 A4
Bermondsey SE16 ... 118 A4
Kingston u T KT1 ... 197 D6
Wembley HA0, HA9 ... 65 D5
Eastlake Ho NW8 ... 236 D5
Eastlake Rd SE5 ... 139 A3
Eastland Ct 2 BR1 ... 187 C1
Eastlands Cres SE21 161 D5
East Lane Bsns Pk HA9 ... 65 D6
Eastlea Com Sch E16 . 98 C3
Eastlea Mews E16 ... 98 C3
Eastleigh Ave HA2 ... 63 D6
Eastleigh Cl
Belmont SM2 ... 217 D1
Neasden NW2 ... 67 C5
Eastleigh Rd E17 ... 35 B1
Eastleigh Way TW14 . 150 A3
Eastleigh Wlk 9 SW15 ... 156 A4
East London Coll 14 E11 ... 76 C6
Eastman Dental Hospl WC1 ... 94 B3 240 C6
Eastman Ho 7 SW4 . 159 C5
Eastman Rd W3 ... 111 B4
East Mascalls 15 SE7 ... 143 C6
Eastmead IG3 ... 58 A2
East Mead HA4 ... 62 D5
Eastmead Ave UB6 ... 85 D4
Eastmead Cl BR1 ... 188 A1
Eastmearn Rd SE21, SE27 ... 161 A2
EAST MOLESEY ... 196 A4
Eastmont Rd KT10 .. 212 D6
Eastmoor Pl SE7 ... 121 D3
Eastmoor St SE7 ... 121 D3
East Mount St E1 ... 96 B2
Eastney Rd CR0 ... 204 D1
Eastney St SE10 ... 120 B1
Eastnor Rd SE9 ... 167 A3
Easton Ho 4 SE27 .. 160 D1
Easton St WC1 ... 241 A6
East Park Cl RM6 ... 59 A4
East Parkside SE10 . 120 D4
East Pas EC1 ... 242 A4
East Pl SE27 ... 183 A6
East Plaza E14 ... 119 D5
East Point 4 SE1 ... 118 A1
Eastpole Cotts N14 ... 3 D1
East Poultry Ave EC1 241 C3
East Putney Sta SW15 ... 157 A6
East Ramp TW6 ... 126 D4
East Rd Burnt Oak HA8 .. 27 A2
Chelsea SW1 115 A1 258 A1
Dagenham RM6 ... 59 A4
East Barnet EN4 ... 15 A3
East Bedfont TW14 ... 149 B4
Enfield EN3 ... 6 C5
Finchley N2 ... 30 C2
Kingston u T KT2 ... 176 A2
Newham E15 ... 99 A6
Shoreditch N1 . 95 B4 235 D2
Welling DA16 ... 146 B3
West Drayton UB7 ... 104 C2
Wimbledon SW19 ... 180 A4
East Rochester Way DA5, DA15, SE9 ... 168 C5
East Row
Kensal Town W10 ... 91 A3
Wanstead E11 ... 55 A3
Eastry Ave BR2 ... 208 D3
Eastry Ho SW8 ... 270 A3
Eastry Rd DA8 ... 147 C5
EAST SHEEN ... 133 B1
East Sheen Ave SW14 ... 133 B1
East Sheen Prim Sch SW14 ... 133 C1
Eastside Rd NW11 ... 47 B5
East Smithfield E1 ... 117 D6 253 D5
East St Barking IG11 ... 79 A1
Bexleyheath DA7 ... 147 C1
Brentford TW8 ... 131 C5
Bromley BR1 ... 187 A1
East St *continued*
Walworth SE17 ... 117 B1 262 C2
East Surrey Gr SE15 . 139 D5
East Tenter St E1 ... 95 D1 243 D1
East Terr DA15 ... 167 C3
East Thamesmead Bsns Pk DA18 ... 125 B4
East Towers HA5 ... 40 D3
Eastvale W3 ... 111 D5
East View Barnet EN5 ... 1 B2
Chingford E4 ... 36 A5
Hampstead NW3 ... 70 B6
Eastview Ave SE18 ... 145 C5
East View Ho 13 N2 ... 30 B1
Eastville Ave NW11 ... 47 B3
Eastway Hayes BR2 ... 209 A2
Merton SM4, SW20 .. 201 A5
South Hackney E3, E9 .. 97 A6
Wallington SM6 ... 219 C4
Wanstead E11 ... 55 B4
East Way
Croydon CR0 ... 223 A5
Hayes UB3 ... 106 A5
Ruislip HA4 ... 40 A1
Eastway Cres HA2 ... 63 D6
Eastwell Cl BR3 ... 185 A2
Eastwell Ho SE1 ... 262 D6
Eastwick Ct 2 SW19 ... 156 D3
EAST WICKHAM ... 146 A5
East Wickham Inf Sch DA16 ... 145 D4
East Wickham Jun Sch DA16 ... 146 A4
East Wlk
East Barnet EN4 ... 15 A3
Hayes UB3 ... 106 A5
Eastwood Cl
2 Islington N7 ... 72 C3
7 Tottenham N17 ... 34 B3
Woodford E18 ... 37 A1
Eastwood Rd
Ilford IG3 ... 58 A2
Muswell Hill N10 ... 31 A1
West Drayton UB7 ... 104 C4
Woodford E18 ... 37 A1
East Woodside DA5 .. 169 A3
Eastwood St SW16 .. 181 C4
Eatington Rd E10 ... 54 B4
Eaton Cl
Belgravia SW1 ... 258 A3
Stanmore HA7 ... 25 B6
Eaton Ct
Chislehurst BR7 ... 189 A4
Ealing W5 ... 87 D1
Edgware HA8 ... 26 C6
Southall UB1 ... 107 B6
Sutton SM2 ... 218 B2
6 Woodford E18 ... 37 A1
Eaton Dr
Brixton SW9 ... 138 D1
Kingston u T KT2 ... 176 C3
Eaton Gate SW1 ... 115 A2 258 A4
Eaton Gdns RM9 ... 81 A1
Eaton Ho
Battersea SW11 ... 266 D1
Ealing W5 ... 87 D1
23 Limehouse E14 ... 119 B6
Eaton House Sch SW1 ... 115 A2 258 A4
Eaton House The Manor Sch SW4 ... 137 B1
Eaton La SW1 ... 115 B3 258 D5
Eaton Lo SM2 ... 218 B2
Eaton Mans SW1 ... 258 A3
Eaton Mews N SW1 ... 115 A3 258 B5
Eaton Mews S SW1 ... 115 B3 258 C5
Eaton Mews W SW1 . 258 B4
Eaton Park Rd N13 ... 16 D2
Eaton Pl SW1 ... 115 A3 258 B5
Eaton Rd Enfield EN1 ... 5 C1
Hendon NW4 ... 46 C4
Isleworth TW3, TW7 .. 130 B1
Sidcup DA14 ... 168 D2
Sutton SM2 ... 218 B2
Eaton Rise Ealing W5 .. 87 D1
Wanstead E11 ... 55 C4
Eaton Row SW1 ... 115 B3 258 C5
Eatons Mead E4 ... 19 C2
Eaton Sq SW1 ... 115 A3 258 B5
Eaton Sq Pre-Prep Sch SW1 ... 115 B2 258 C4
Eaton Sq Prep Sch SW1 ... 115 C2 259 A4
Eaton Terr
Belgravia SW1 ... 115 A2 258 B4
Bow E3 ... 97 A4
Eaton Terr Mews SW1 ... 258 A4
Eatonville Rd SW17 . 158 D2
Eatonville Villas SW17 ... 158 D2
Ebb Ct E16 ... 123 A6
Ebbisham Dr SW8 ... 138 B6 270 C5
Ebbisham Rd KT4 ... 216 C6
Ebbsfleet Rd NW2 ... 69 A4
Ebdon Way SE3 ... 143 B2
Ebenezer Ho SE11 .. 261 C3
Ebenezer Mussel Ho 5 E2 ... 96 C5
Ebenezer St N1 ... 235 C2
Ebenezer Wlk CR4 ... 181 C2
Ebley Cl SE15 ... 139 D6
Ebner St SW18 ... 157 D6
Ebony Ct NW10 ... 67 D2
Ebony Ho
27 Bethnal Green E2 ... 96 A4
10 West Hampstead NW3 ... 69 D2
Ebor Cotts SW15 ... 155 C1
Ebor St E1, E2 ... 243 C6
Ebrington Rd HA3 ... 43 D3
Ebsworth St SE23 ... 162 D4
Eburne Rd N7 ... 72 A5
Ebury Bridge Rd SW1 ... 115 A1 258 B1
Ebury Cl BR2 ... 226 A5
Ebury Mews
Belgravia SW1 ... 115 B2 258 C4
West Norwood SE27 . 160 D1
Ebury Mews E SW1 . 258 C5
Ebury Sq SW1 ... 258 B3
Ebury St SW1 ... 115 B2 258 C4
Ecclesbourne Cl N13 .. 32 C5
Ecclesbourne Gdns N13 ... 32 C5
Ecclesbourne Inf Sch CR7 ... 205 A4
Ecclesbourne Jun Sch CR7 ... 205 A4
Ecclesbourne Rd
Islington N1 ... 73 A1
Thornton Heath CR7 . 205 A4
Eccles Ct SE11 ... 260 D1
Eccleshill 3 BR2 ... 208 D5
Eccles Rd SW11 ... 136 D1
Eccleston Cl
Cockfosters EN4 ... 2 D1
Crofton BR6 ... 211 B1
Eccleston Cres RM6 ... 58 B2
Ecclestone Ct HA9 ... 66 A3
Ecclestone Mews HA9 ... 66 A3
Ecclestone Pl HA9 ... 66 B3
Eccleston Ho 1 SW2 ... 160 C5
Eccleston Mews SW1 ... 115 A3 258 B5
Eccleston Pl SW1 ... 115 B2 258 C4
Eccleston Rd W13 ... 109 A5
Eccleston Sq SW1 ... 115 B2 258 D3
Eccleston Sq Mews SW1 ... 259 A3
Eccleston St SW1 ... 115 B2 258 C4
Echelforde Dr TW15 .. 170 C6
Echelford Prim Sch The TW15 ... 170 D5
Echo Hts E4 ... 19 D3
Eckford St N1 ... 234 A4
Eckington Ho N15 ... 51 B3
Eckstein Rd SW11 ... 136 C1
Eclipse Rd E13 ... 99 B2
Ector Rd SE6 ... 164 C2
Edam Ct 11 DA14 ... 168 A1
Edans Ct W12 ... 111 D4
Edbrooke Rd W9 ... 91 C3
Eddinton Cl CR0 ... 224 A2
Eddisbury Ho 7 SE26 ... 162 A1
Eddiscombe Rd SW6 ... 135 B3
Eddison Ct N19 ... 72 A6
Eddy Cl RM7 ... 59 D3
Eddystone Rd SE4 ... 163 A6
Eddystone Twr SE8 ... 119 A1
Eddystone Wlk TW19 ... 148 A4
Ede Cl TW4 ... 129 B2
Edenbridge Cl 29 SE16 ... 118 B1
Edenbridge Rd
Enfield EN1 ... 17 C5
Hackney E9 ... 74 D1
Eden Cl
Child's Hill NW3 ... 69 C6
Enfield EN3 ... 7 C5
Kensington W8 ... 255 B6
Wembley HA0 ... 87 D6
Edencourt W5 ... 88 B1
Edencourt Rd SW16 .. 181 B4
Eden Ct 3 N3 ... 29 B1
Edendale W3 ... 110 D6
Edenfield Gdns KT4 . 215 D5
Eden Gr Islington N7 ... 72 B3
Walthamstow E17 ... 53 D4
Willesden NW10 ... 68 B2
Edenham High Sch CR0 ... 207 B2
Edenham Way W10 ... 91 B2
Eden High Sch 9 W6 ... 112 A1
Eden Ho
15 Battersea SW11 .. 136 C2
Lisson Gr NW8 ... 237 A5
Edenhurst Ave SW6 .. 135 B2
Eden Ind Sch UB5 ... 63 B2
Eden Lodge NW6 ... 68 D1
Eden Mews SW17 ... 158 A1
EDEN PARK ... 207 C5
Eden Park Ave BR3 ... 207 C4
Eden Park Sta BR3 ... 207 C4
Eden Rd Croydon CR0 221 B4
Penge BR3 ... 185 A2
Walthamstow E17 ... 53 D4
West Norwood SE27 . 182 D5
Edensmuir Ct SE3 ... 143 A5
Edensor Gdns W4 ... 133 C5
Edensor Rd W4 ... 133 C5
Eden St KT1, KT2 ... 176 A1
Edenvale Cl CR4 ... 181 A3
Edenvale Rd CR4 ... 181 A3
Edenvale St SW6 ... 136 A3
Eden Way
Beckenham BR3 ... 207 C3
Bow E3 ... 97 B6
Eden Wlk 5 KT1 ... 176 A1
Eden Wlk Sh Ctr KT2 ... 176 A1
Ederline Ave SW16 .. 182 C1
Edgar Ct KT3 ... 199 C6
Edgar Ho Homerton E9 . 75 A3
South Lambeth SW8 . 270 A4
Wanstead E11 ... 55 A2
Edgar Kail Way SE22 ... 139 C1
Edgarley Terr SW6 .. 264 A1
Edgar Rd Bromley E3 ... 97 D4
Dagenham RM6 ... 58 D2
Twickenham TW4 ... 151 B4
Yiewsley UB7 ... 104 A5
Edgar Wallace Cl 4 SE15 ... 139 C5
Edgbury Ct NW9 ... 45 A5
Edgcott Ho 2 W10 ... 90 C2
Edgeborough Way BR1 ... 187 D2
Edge Bsns Ctr NW2 ... 68 B6
Edgebury BR7, SE9 .. 188 D6
Edgebury Prim Sch BR7 ... 189 A6
Edgebury Wlk BR7 ... 167 A1
Edgecombe Cl KT2 ... 177 B3
Edgecombe Ho
4 London SE5 ... 139 C3
Putney SW19 ... 157 A4
Edgecoombe CR2 ... 222 C1
Edgecote Cl 7 W3 ... 111 A5
Edgecot Gr N15 ... 51 C4
Edgecumbe Ct 2 CR0 ... 206 A1
Edgefield Ave IG11 ... 79 D1
Edgefield Ct 3 IG11 ... 79 D1
Edge Hill
Shooters Hill SE18 ... 144 D6
Wimbledon SW19 ... 178 D3
Edge Hill Ave N3 ... 47 C5
Edgehill Ct KT12 ... 194 C1
Edge Hill Ct
Sidcup DA14 ... 189 D6
Wimbledon SW19 ... 178 D3
Edgehill Gdns RM10 ... 81 C4
Edgehill Ho 4 SW9 . 138 D3
Edgehill Rd
Ealing W13 ... 87 C2
Longlands BR7 ... 189 A6
Mitcham CR4 ... 181 B2
Edgeley La SW4 ... 137 D2
Edgeley Rd SW4 ... 137 D2
Edgel St SW18 ... 135 D1
Edge Point Cl SE27 .. 182 D5
Edge St W8 ... 113 C5 245 B4
Edgewood Dr BR6 .. 227 D3
Edgewood Gn CR0 .. 206 D1
Edgeworth Ave NW4 . 46 A4
Edgeworth Cl NW4 ... 46 A4
Edgeworth Cres NW4 . 46 A4
Edgeworth Ct 10 EN4 .. 2 C1
Edgeworth Ho NW8 . 229 A6
Edgeworth Rd
Barnet EN4 ... 2 C1
Eltham SE9 ... 143 D1
Edgington Rd SW16 . 181 D4
Edgington Way DA14 ... 190 D3
Edgson Ho SW1 ... 258 C2
EDGWARE ... 26 C6
Edgware Acad WC2 . 240 B1
EDGWARE BURY ... 10 B3
Edgwarebury Ct HA8 .. 26 C5
Edgwarebury Gdns HA8 ... 26 C5
Edgwarebury La
Edgware Bury HA8 ... 10 C2
Edgware HA8 ... 26 C5
Edgware Community Hospl HA8 ... 26 D3
Edgware Ct HA8 ... 26 C4
Edgware Jewish Prim Sch HA8 ... 26 D5
Edgware Jun & Inf Schs HA8 ... 26 C4
Edgware Rd
Dollis Hill NW2 ... 68 C6
Paddington W1, W2, NW1, NW8 ... 92 C2 237 A3
Edgware Road Sta (Bakerloo) NW1 ... 92 C2 237 A3
Edgware Road Sta (Met, Distr, Circle) NW1 . 237 B3
Edgware Road The Hyde NW9 ... 45 C5
Edgware Road West Hendon Broadway NW9 ... 46 A2
Edgware Sta HA8 ... 26 D4
Edgware Way (Watford By-Pass) HA8 ... 27 A6
Edinburgh Cl
7 Bethnal Green E2 ... 96 C5
Pinner HA5 ... 41 A2
Uxbridge UB10 ... 60 D4
Edinburgh Ct
1 Catford SE6 ... 164 D3
2 Kingston u T KT1 .. 198 A6
Newham E13 ... 99 B5
10 Rotherhithe SE16 . 118 D5
West Barnes SM4 ... 200 D4
Edinburgh Dr UB10 ... 60 D4
Edinburgh Ho
3 Acton W3 ... 89 B1
Carshalton SM1 ... 218 B6
Hendon NW4 ... 46 C6
Maida Vale W9 ... 91 D4
Edinburgh Prim Sch E17 ... 53 B4
Edinburgh Rd
Carshalton SM1 ... 218 B6
Edmonton N18 ... 34 A5
Hanwell W7 ... 108 D4
Newham E13 ... 99 B5
Walthamstow E17 ... 53 C4
Edington 20 NW5 ... 71 A2
Edington Rd
Abbey Wood SE2 ... 124 B3
Enfield EN3 ... 6 C3
Edison Bldg 7 E14 .. 119 C4

Edison Cl
Walthamstow E17 ... 53 C4
West Drayton UB7 ... 104 B4
Edison Ct SE10 ... 120 D3
Edison Dr
Southall UB1 ... 85 D1
Wembley HA9 ... 66 A6
Edison Gr SE18 ... 145 D5
Edison Ho
Walworth SE1 ... 262 C4
7 Wembley HA9 ... 67 A5
Edison Rd
Bexley DA16 ... 145 D4
Brimsdown EN3 ... 7 B3
Bromley BR2 ... 187 A1
Crouch End N8 ... 49 D3
Edis St NW1 ... 93 A6 231 B6
Editha Mans SW10 ... 266 A5
Edith Cavell Cl 2
N19 ... 50 A2
Edith Cavell Way
SE18 ... 144 A4
Edith Ct TW14 ... 149 B5
Edith Gdns KT5 ... 198 D2
Edith Gr
SW10 ... 136 A5 266 B4
Edith Ho 6 W6 ... 112 C1
Edithna St SW9 ... 138 A2
Edith Nesbit Wlk
SE9 ... 166 B6
Edith Neville Cotts
NW1 ... 232 C2
Edith Neville Prim Sch
NW1 ... 93 D5 232 C3
Edith Pond Ct SE9 ... 166 D2
Edith Ramsay Ho 2
E1 ... 97 A2
Edith Rd
Dagenham RM6 ... 58 D2
South Norwood SE25 ... 205 B4
Stratford New Town
E15 ... 76 B3
Upton Pk E6 ... 77 D1
West Kensington
W14 ... 113 A2 254 B3
Wimbledon SW19 ... 179 D4
Wood Green N11 ... 31 D3
Edith Row SW6 ... 265 D2
Edith St E2 ... 96 A5
Edith Summerskill Ho
SW6 ... 264 C4
Edith Terr
SW10 ... 136 A5 266 A4
Edith Villas
W14 ... 113 B1 254 C2
Edith Yd SW10 ... 266 B4
Edmansons' Cl N17 ... 33 D2
Edmeston Cl E9 ... 75 A2
Edmond Ct SE14 ... 140 C4
Edmonscote W13 ... 87 A2
EDMONTON ... 33 D6
Edmonton Ct 5
SE16 ... 118 C3
Edmonton Cty Lower Sch
N9 ... 17 C3
Edmonton Cty Upper Sch
EN1 ... 17 D4
Edmonton Green Sh Ctr
N9 ... 18 B2
Edmonton Green Sta
N9 ... 18 A2
Edmonton Wharf
N18 ... 34 D4
Edmund Gr TW13 ... 151 B2
Edmund Halley Way
SE10 ... 120 C4
Edmund Ho
Kennington SE17 ... 261 D1
New Cross Gate SE14 ... 141 B4
Edmund Hurst Dr
E6 ... 100 D2
Edmund Rd
Mitcham CR4 ... 202 C6
Welling DA16 ... 146 A2
Edmundsbury Ct Est 16
SW9 ... 138 B1
Edmunds Cl UB4 ... 84 C2
Edmund St SE5 ... 139 B5
Edmunds Wlk N2 ... 48 C5
Edmund Waller Prim Sch
SE14 ... 140 D3
Ednam Ho SE15 ... 140 A6
Edna Rd SW20 ... 178 D1
Edna St
SW11 ... 136 C4 267 A1
Edred Ho E9 ... 75 A4
Edrich Ho SW4 ... 270 A1
Edric Ho SW1 ... 259 D4
Edrick Rd HA8 ... 27 A4
Edrick Wlk HA8 ... 27 A4
Edric Rd SE14 ... 140 D5
Edridge Cl WD23 ... 8 A6
Edridge Ho 9 SE27 ... 160 D1
Edridge Rd CR0 ... 221 B5
Edward Alderton Theatre★
DA7 ... 146 D2
Edward Alleyn Ho
SE21 ... 161 C4
Edward Ave
Chingford E4 ... 35 D4
Morden SM4 ... 202 B4
Edward Betham CE Prim Sch UB6 ... 86 A5
Edward Cl
Edmonton N9 ... 17 D4
Hampton TW12 ... 174 A5
Edward Ct
2 Ealing W5 ... 87 B3
Harrow HA1 ... 64 C6
2 Newham E16 ... 99 A2
Edward Dodd Ct N1 ... 235 D2
Edward Edward's Ho
SE1 ... 251 C3
Edwardes Pl W8 ... 254 D5
Edwardes Sq
W8 ... 113 B3 254 D5
Edward Friend Ho 6
N16 ... 73 C5
Edward Gr EN4 ... 14 B6
Edward Harvey Ct
DA17 ... 125 B1
Edward Ho
Paddington W2 ... 236 C5
Vauxhall SE11 ... 260 D2
Edward Kennedy Ho 18
W10 ... 91 A3
Edward Mann Cl 13
E1 ... 96 D1
Edward Mans 8
IG11 ... 79 D1
Edward Mews NW1 ... 231 D3
Edward Pauling Ho
TW14 ... 149 D4
Edward Pauling Prim Sch TW13 ... 149 C2
Edward Pinner Ct 5
KT6 ... 214 A6
Edward Pl SE8 ... 141 B6
Edward Rd
Bromley BR1 ... 187 C3
Chislehurst BR7 ... 188 D5
Croydon CR0 ... 205 C2
Dagenham RM6 ... 59 A3
Hampton TW12 ... 174 A5
Harrow HA2 ... 42 A6
Hatton TW14 ... 149 C6
New Barnet EN4 ... 14 B6
Northolt UB5 ... 84 C5
Penge SE20 ... 184 D4
Walthamstow E17 ... 52 D4
Edward Robinson Ho 3
SE14 ... 140 D5
Edward's Ave HA4 ... 62 C2
Edwards Cl 1 KT4 ... 216 D6
Edward's Cotts 11 N1 ... 72 D1
Edwards Dr N11 ... 31 D3
Edwards Ho 7
TW10 ... 153 C1
Edward's La N16 ... 73 C6
Edwards Language Sch
6 W5 ... 110 A6
Edwards Mews
Islington N1 ... 72 C1
Marylebone
W1 ... 93 A1 238 A1
Edward Sq
Islington N1 ... 233 C5
1 Rotherhithe SE16 ... 119 A5
Edwards Rd DA17 ... 125 C2
Edward St
New Cross SE14 ... 141 B5
10 Newham E16 ... 99 A3
Edward Temme Ave
E15 ... 76 D1
Edward Tyler Rd
SE12 ... 165 C2
Edward VII Mans
NW10 ... 90 D4
Edward Way TW15 ... 148 B2
Edward Wilson Prim Sch
2 W2 ... 91 D2
Edwina Ct SM1 ... 217 D4
Edwina Gdns IG4 ... 56 A4
Edwin Arnold Ct
DA15 ... 189 D6
Edwin Ave E6 ... 100 C5
Edwin Cl DA7 ... 147 B6
Edwin Ho SE15 ... 140 A5
Edwin Pl 10 CR0 ... 205 B1
Edwin Rd
Burnt Oak HA8 ... 27 B4
Twickenham TW1,
TW2 ... 152 C3
Edwin's Mead E9 ... 75 A4
Edwin St
Bethnal Green E1 ... 96 C3
Newham E16 ... 99 A2
Edwin Stray Ho
TW13 ... 151 C1
Edwin Ware Ct 4
HA5 ... 22 C1
Edwy Ho E9 ... 75 B4
Edwyn Cl EN5 ... 12 D5
Edwyn Ho SW18 ... 157 D5
Eel Pie Island★
TW1 ... 153 A3
Effie Pl SW6 ... 265 B3
Effie Rd SW6 ... 135 C5 265 B3
Effingham Cl SM2 ... 217 D1
Effingham Ct SW19 ... 180 C3
Effingham Ho
37 Clapham SW8 ... 137 D3
9 Kingston u T KT2 ... 176 D4
Effingham Lo 1
KT6 ... 198 A4
Effingham Rd
Hornsey N8 ... 50 C5
Lewisham SE12 ... 164 D6
Thames Ditton KT6,
KT7 ... 197 C2
Thornton Heath CR0 ... 204 B2
Effort St SW17 ... 180 C5
Effra Cl SW19 ... 179 D4
Effra Ct London SW2 ... 160 B6
South Norwood SE19 ... 183 C3
Effra Mans SW2 ... 160 C6
Effra Par SW2 ... 160 C6
Effra Rd London SW2 ... 160 C6
Wimbledon SW19 ... 179 D4
Effra Road Ret Pk
SW2 ... 160 C6
EF International Language Sch SE1 ... 251 B3
Egan Way UB3 ... 105 C6
Egbert Ho E9 ... 75 A3
Egbert St
NW1 ... 93 A6 231 A6
Egbury Ho SW15 ... 155 D5
Egerton Cl HA5 ... 40 A5
Egerton Cres
SW3 ... 114 C2 257 B4
Egerton Ct
Leytonstone E11 ... 54 B2
5 Richmond TW10 ... 154 A6
Egerton Dr SE10 ... 141 D4
Egerton Gdns
Ealing W13 ... 87 B1
Hendon NW4 ... 46 B5
Ilford IG3 ... 79 D5
Knightsbridge
SW3 ... 114 C3 257 A5
Willesden NW10 ... 90 C6
Egerton Gdns Mews
SW3 ... 257 B5
Egerton Ho W4 ... 133 A6
Egerton Pl SW3 ... 257 B5
Egerton Rd
New Malden KT3 ... 199 D5
South Norwood SE25 ... 205 C6
Stamford Hill N16 ... 51 D2
Twickenham TW2 ... 152 C4
Wembley HA0 ... 66 B1
Egerton Terr
SW3 ... 114 C3 257 B5
Egerton Way UB3 ... 126 D5
Eggardon Ct UB5 ... 64 A2
Egham Cl
Cheam SM3 ... 217 A6
Putney SW19 ... 157 A2
Egham Cres SM3 ... 217 A6
Egham Ct KT6 ... 197 D4
Egham Rd E13 ... 99 B2
Eglantine Rd SW18 ... 158 A6
Egleston Rd SM4 ... 201 D3
Eglington Ct SE17 ... 139 A6
Eglington Rd E4 ... 20 B4
Eglinton Hill SE18 ... 144 D5
Eglinton Prim Sch
SE18 ... 144 C6
Eglinton Rd SE18 ... 144 D6
Egliston Mews
SW15 ... 134 C2
Egliston Rd SW15 ... 134 C2
Egmont Ave KT6 ... 198 B1
Egmont Mews KT19 ... 215 B4
Egmont Rd
New Malden KT3 ... 199 D5
Sutton SM2 ... 218 A1
Tolworth KT6 ... 198 C1
Walton-on-T KT12 ... 194 B2
Egmont St SE14 ... 140 D5
Egremont Ho SE13 ... 141 D3
Egremont Rd SE27 ... 160 C1
Egret Ho 11 SE16 ... 118 D2
Egret Way UB4 ... 84 D2
Eider Cl Hayes UB4 ... 84 D2
Stratford E7 ... 76 D3
Eider Ct 38 SE8 ... 141 B6
Eighteenth Rd CR4 ... 204 A5
Eighth Ave
Hayes UB3 ... 106 A5
Ilford E12 ... 78 B4
Eileen Ct BR7 ... 188 C5
Eileen Rd SE25 ... 205 B4
Eindhoven Cl SM5 ... 203 A1
Einstein Ho HA9 ... 67 A5
Eisenhower Dr E6 ... 100 A2
Eisenhower Ho KT8 ... 175 C2
Elaine Ct 13 NW3 ... 70 D2
Elaine Gr NW5 ... 71 A3
Elaine Ho N4 ... 50 A1
Elam Cl SE5 ... 138 D3
Elam St SE5 ... 138 D3
Elan Ct E1 ... 96 B2
Eland Pl CR0 ... 220 D5
Eland Rd
Clapham SW11 ... 136 D2
Croydon CR0 ... 220 D5
Elba Pl SE17 ... 117 A2 262 B4
Elberon Ave CR0 ... 203 C3
Elbe St SW6 ... 136 A3
Elborough Rd SE25 ... 206 A4
Elborough St SW18 ... 157 C3
Elbourne Trad Est
DA17 ... 125 D3
Elbury Dr E16 ... 99 A1
Elcho St
SW11 ... 136 C5 267 B3
Elcot Ave SE15 ... 140 B5
Elder Ave N8 ... 50 A4
Elderberry Ct 2 EN2 ... 4 D3
Elderberry Gr 10
SE27 ... 183 A6
Elderberry Rd W5 ... 110 A4
Elder Cl Barnet N20 ... 13 D3
Sidcup DA15 ... 167 D3
Yiewsley UB7 ... 104 A6
Elder Ct WD23 ... 8 C2
Elderfield Ho 4
E14 ... 119 C6
Elderfield Pl SW17 ... 181 B6
Elderfield Rd E5 ... 74 C4
Elderfield Wlk E11 ... 55 B4
Elderflower Way E15 ... 76 C1
Elder Gdns 9 SE27 ... 183 A6
Elder Oak Cl SE20 ... 184 B2
Elder Rd SE27 ... 183 A5
Elderslie Cl BR3 ... 207 D3
Elderslie Rd SE9 ... 166 C6
Elder St E1 ... 95 D3 243 C5
Elderton Rd SE26 ... 185 A6
Eldertree Pl CR4 ... 181 C2
Eldertree Way CR4 ... 181 C2
Elder Wlk
Islington N1 ... 234 D6
2 Lewisham SE13 ... 142 A2
Elderwood Pl SE27 ... 183 A5
Eldon Ave
Croydon CR0 ... 222 C6
Heston TW5 ... 129 C5
Eldon Ct NW6 ... 91 C6
Eldon Gr NW3 ... 70 B3
Eldon Ho SW9 ... 138 D2
Eldon Jun & Inf Schs
N9 ... 18 C3
Eldon Pk SE25 ... 206 B5
Eldon Rd Edmonton N9 ... 18 C3
Kensington
W8 ... 113 D3 255 D5
Tottenham N22 ... 32 D2
Walthamstow E17 ... 53 B5
Eldon St EC2 ... 95 B2 242 D3
Eldonwall Est RM8 ... 59 B1
Eldon Way NW10 ... 88 D5
Eldred Rd IG11 ... 101 C6
Eldrick Ct TW14 ... 149 B3
Eldridge Cl TW14 ... 150 A3
Eldridge Ct
Bermondsey SE16 ... 118 A3
14 Dagenham RM10 ... 81 D2
Eleanor Cl
Rotherhithe SE16 ... 118 D4
South Tottenham N15 ... 51 D6
Eleanor Cres NW7 ... 28 D6
Eleanor Ct 13 E2 ... 96 A6
Eleanor Gdns
Barnet EN5 ... 12 D6
Dagenham RM8 ... 81 B6
Eleanor Gr
Mortlake SW13 ... 133 C2
Uxbridge UB10 ... 60 D5
Eleanor Ho
18 Hammersmith
W6 ... 112 C1
1 Kentish Town NW5 ... 71 C3
6 Merton SW19 ... 179 D2
Eleanor Palmer Prim Sch
12 NW5 ... 71 C4
Eleanor Rathbone Ho 1
N6 ... 49 D2
Eleanor Rd
Bowes Pk N11 ... 32 A4
Hackney E8 ... 74 B1
Stratford E15 ... 76 D2
Eleanor Smith Sch 2
E13 ... 99 B5
Eleanor Smith Sch (West Beckton Site) E16 ... 99 C2
Eleanor St E3 ... 97 C4
Eleanor Wlk 24 SE18 ... 122 B2
Electra Ave TW6 ... 127 D2
Electra Ct 6 NW2 ... 68 C2
Electric Ave SW9 ... 138 C1
Electric Ho 13 Bow E3 ... 97 C4
Walthamstow E17 ... 53 C5
Electric La 2 SW9 ... 138 C1
Electric Mans 1
SW9 ... 138 C1
Electric Par Ilford IG3 ... 57 D1
Surbiton KT6 ... 197 D3
Woodford E18 ... 37 A1
Elenmore Ct BR1 ... 210 A5
Elephant & Castle
Newington
SE1 ... 116 D3 261 D5
Newington SE1 ... 261 D4
Elephant & Castle Sh Ctr
SE1 ... 117 A2 262 A4
Elephant & Castle Sta
Lambeth
SE1 ... 116 D3 261 D5
Newington
SE17 ... 117 A2 262 A4
Elephant La SE16 ... 118 C4
Elephant Rd
SE17 ... 117 A2 262 A4
Elers Rd Ealing W13 ... 109 C4
Hayes UB3 ... 105 B2
Eley Rd N18 ... 34 D5
Eley's Est N18 ... 34 D6
Elfindale Rd SE24 ... 161 A6
Elfin Gr TW11 ... 174 D5
Elford Cl SE9 ... 143 C1
Elfort Rd N5 ... 72 C4
Elfrida Cres SE6 ... 185 C6
Elfrida Prim Sch
SE6 ... 185 C6
Elf Row E1 ... 118 C6
Elfwine Rd W7 ... 86 C2
Elgal Cl BR6 ... 226 D3
Elgar N8 ... 50 A6
Elgar Ave Ealing W5 ... 110 A4
Thornton Heath
SW16 ... 204 A6
Tolworth KT5, KT6 ... 198 D2
Willesden NW10 ... 67 B2
Elgar Cl
Buckhurst Hill IG9 ... 21 D2
Deptford SE8 ... 141 C5
Elstree WD6 ... 9 D4
Ickenham UB10 ... 60 C6
Newham E13 ... 99 C5
Elgar Ct W14 ... 254 A5
Elgar Ho Hayes UB4 ... 84 C2
Isleworth TW2 ... 152 B5

Elgar Ho *continued*
Pimlico SW1 258 D1
Southall UB1 85 C1
South Hampstead NW6 70 A1
Elgar St SE16 119 A3
Elgin Ave
Ashford TW15 171 A4
Hammersmith W12 112 B3
Harrow HA3 25 B1
Westbourne Green W9 91 D3
Elgin Cl W12 112 B4
Elgin Cres
Hatton TW6 127 C3
Notting Hill W11 113 A6 244 B6
Elgin Ct
6 Croydon CR0 221 A4
Westbourne Green W9 91 D3
Elgin Ho Northolt UB5 84 B5
8 Poplar E14 97 D1
Elgin Mans W9 91 D4
Elgin Mews W11 91 A1
Elgin Mews N W9 91 D4
Elgin Mews S W9 91 D4
Elgin Rd
Croydon CR0 221 D6
Ilford IG3 57 C2
Sutton SM1 218 A5
Wallington SM6 219 C2
Wood Green N22 31 C1
Elgood Ave HA6 22 A3
Elgood Cl W11 244 A3
Elgood Ho NW8 229 D3
Elham Cl BR1 187 D3
Elham Ho 13 E5 74 B3
Elia Mews N1 94 D5 234 C3
Elias Pl SW8 138 C6
Elia St N1 94 D5 234 C3
Elibank Rd SE9 144 C1
Elim Est SE1 263 A6
Elim St SE1 263 A6
Elim Way E13 98 D4
Eliot Bank SE23, SE26 162 B2
Eliot Bank Prim Sch SE26 162 B2
Eliot Cotts SE3 142 C3
Eliot Ct SW18 157 D5
Eliot Dr HA2 63 D6
Eliot Gdns SW15 134 A1
Eliot Hill SE13 142 A3
Eliot Ho 10 TW10 154 B5
Eliot Mews NW8 229 A3
Eliot Pk SE13 142 A3
Eliot Pl SE3 142 C3
Eliot Rd RM9 80 D4
Eliot Vale SE3 142 B3
Elis David Almshouses CR0 220 D4
Elizabethan Ct N3 47 A6
Elizabeth Ave
Enfield EN2 4 D2
Ilford IG1 79 B6
Islington N1 73 B1
Shoreditch N1 95 A6 235 B6
Elizabeth Barnes Ct 5 SW6 135 D3
Elizabeth Blackwell Ho N22 32 C2
Elizabeth Blount Ct 4 E14 97 A1
Elizabeth Cl
Cheam SM1 217 B4
Paddington W9 236 B5
12 Poplar E14 97 D1
Elizabeth Clyde Cl N15 51 C5
Elizabeth Cooper Lo SW12 159 A5
Elizabeth Cotts 5 TW9 132 C4
Elizabeth Ct
Buckhurst Hill IG9 21 B3
Chelsea SW10 266 D5
East Dulwich SE22 140 A1
Kingston u T KT2 176 A2
Marylebone NW8 237 B6
South Croydon CR0 221 C5
Sunbury TW16 194 C6
3 Teddington TW11 174 C5
Upper Tooting SW17 181 A5
West Barnes SM4 201 A2
Westminster SW1 259 D5
Elizabeth Ct *continued*
6 Woodford Green E18 37 A2
2 Woodford Green IG8 37 C3
10 Woolwich SE18 122 B2
Elizabeth Finn Ho 1 W12 112 A3
Elizabeth Fry Ho UB3 105 D2
Elizabeth Fry Pl SE18 144 A4
Elizabeth Garrett Anderson Ho 9 DA17 125 C3
Elizabeth Garrett Anderson Hospl NW1 93 C3 239 B5
Elizabeth Garrett Anderson Language Coll N1 94 B5 233 D3
Elizabeth Gdns
East Acton W3 111 D5
Isleworth TW7 131 A1
Stanmore HA7 25 C5
Sunbury TW16 194 C6
Elizabeth Ho
Cheam SM3 217 A2
Friern Barnet N20 14 D1
15 Hammersmith W6 112 C1
Lambeth SE11 261 B3
Stanmore HA7 26 A1
Wembley HA9 66 B3
Elizabeth Ind Est SE14 140 D6
Elizabeth Kenny Ho N1 73 A2
Elizabeth Mews
28 Hackney E2 96 A5
Maitland Pk NW3 70 D2
Elizabeth Pl N15 51 B5
Elizabeth Rd
Newham E6 99 D6
South Tottenham N15 51 C4
Elizabeth Ride N9 18 B4
Elizabeth Selby Inf Sch 31 E2 96 A4
Elizabeth Sq 13 SE16 119 A6
Elizabeth St SW1 115 A2 258 B4
Elizabeth Terr SE9 166 B5
Elizabeth Way
Feltham TW13 172 C6
South Norwood SE19 183 B3
Elkanette Mews N20 14 A2
Elkington Point SE11 261 A3
Elkington Rd E13 99 B3
Elkstone Rd W10 91 B2
Ella Cl BR3 185 C1
Ellacombe Ho 1 SW2 160 C4
Ellaline Rd W6 134 D6
Ella Mews NW3 70 D4
Ellanby Cres N18 34 B5
Elland Cl EN5 14 B6
Elland Ho 18 E14 97 B1
Elland Rd SE15 140 C1
Ella Rd N4, N8 50 A2
Ellard Ct DA16 146 C2
Elle Ct N12 29 D5
Ellement Cl HA5 40 D4
Ellena Ct N14 16 A1
Ellenborough Ct N22 32 D2
Ellenborough Ho 5 W12 112 B6
Ellenborough Pl SW15 134 A1
Ellenborough Rd
Sidcup DA14 191 A5
Tottenham N22 33 A2
Ellen Cl BR1 209 D6
Ellen Ct
4 Chingford E4 20 A3
Lower Edmonton N9 18 C2
Ellen Miller Ho 2 E17 54 A4
Ellen St E1 96 A1
Ellen Webb Dr HA3 42 C6
Ellen Wilkinson Ho
12 Dagenham RM10 81 C5
7 Globe Town E2 96 D4
West Brompton SW6 264 D5
Ellen Wilkinson Prim Sch E6 100 A2
Ellen Wilkinson Sch for Girls W3 88 B1
Elleray Rd TW11 174 D4
Ellerby St SW6 134 D4
Ellerdale Cl 15 NW3 70 A4
Ellerdale Rd NW3 70 A3
Ellerdale St SE13 141 D2
Ellerdine Rd TW3 130 B1
Ellerker Gdns TW10 154 A5
Ellerman Ave TW2, TW4 151 B3
Ellerslie Ct 6 SM6 219 B2
Ellerslie Gdns NW10 90 A6
Ellerslie Ind Est SW2 160 A6
Ellerslie Rd W12 112 B5
Ellerton Ct W3 110 D4
Ellerton Gdns RM9 80 C1
Ellerton Lo N3 29 C1
Ellerton Rd
Barnes SW13 134 A4
Dagenham RM9 80 C1
Surbiton KT6 198 B1
Wandsworth SW17, SW18 158 B3
Wimbledon SW20 178 A3
Ellery Cl 5 NW10 89 D5
Ellery Ho SE17 262 D3
Ellery Rd SE19 183 B3
Ellery St SE15 140 B3
Ellesborough Cl WD19 22 C5
Ellesmere Ave
Beckenham BR3 185 D1
Edgware NW7 11 B1
Ellesmere Cl
Leytonstone E11 54 D4
Ruislip HA4 39 A2
Ellesmere Ct
Chiswick W4 133 B6
Lewisham SE12 165 A3
Penge SE20 184 B1
Ellesmere Gdns IG4 56 A3
Ellesmere Gr EN5 13 B6
Ellesmere Rd Bow E3 97 A5
Chiswick W4 133 B6
Greenford UB6 86 A3
Twickenham TW1 153 C5
Willesden NW10 68 A3
Ellesmere St E14 97 D1
Ellies Mews TW15 148 A2
Ellingfort Rd E8 74 B1
Ellingham Prim Sch KT9 213 D1
Ellingham Rd
Chessington KT9 213 D2
Leyton E15 76 B4
Shepherd's Bush W12 112 A4
Ellington Ct N14 15 D2
Ellington Ho SE1 262 B5
Ellington Rd
Cranley Gdns N10 49 B5
Feltham TW13 171 D6
Hounslow TW3 129 D3
Ellington St N7 72 C2
Elliot Cl Stratford E15 76 C1
Wembley HA9 66 C5
Woodford IG8 37 D4
Elliot Ct 6 N15 51 D5
Elliot Rd NW4 46 B3
Elliott Ave HA4 62 B6
Elliott Gdns TW17 192 C5
Elliott Ho 3 CR7 204 D5
Elliott Rd Acton W4 111 C2
Brixton SW9 138 D4
Bromley BR2 209 D5
Camberwell SW9 138 D4
Stanmore HA7 25 A4
Thornton Heath CR7 204 D5
Elliott Sch SW15 156 C5
Elliott's Pl N1 234 D5
Elliott Sq NW3 70 C1
Elliott's Row SE11 116 D2 261 D4
Ellis Cl Burnt Oak HA8 27 C4
New Eltham SE9 167 A2
Willesden NW10 68 C2
Elliscombe Mount 11 SE7 143 C6
Elliscombe Rd SE7 143 C6
Ellis Ct W7 86 D2
Ellisfield Dr SW15 156 A4
Ellis Franklin Ct NW8 229 A4
Ellis Ho
Walthamstow E17 54 A4
Ellis Ho *continued*
Walworth SE17 262 C2
Ellison Gdns UB2 107 B2
Ellison Ho 1 SE13 142 A3
Ellison Rd
Barnes SW13 133 D3
New Eltham DA15 167 B3
Streatham SW16 182 A3
Ellis Rd Mitcham CR4 202 D3
Southall UB2 108 A5
Ellis St SW1 115 A2 258 A4
Elliston Ho 8 SE18 122 C2
Ellora Rd SW16 181 D5
Ellswood Ct 18 KT6 197 D2
Ellsworth St E2 96 B4
Ellwood Ct 1 W9 91 D3
Elmar Ct SW6 135 A3
Elmar Rd N15 51 B5
Elm Ave Ealing W5 110 B5
Ruislip HA4 40 B2
Elmbank N14 16 A4
Elm Bank Dr BR1 187 D1
Elm Bank Gdns SW13 133 C3
Elm Bank Mans SW13 133 C3
Elmbank Way W7 86 B2
Elmbourne Dr DA17 125 D2
Elmbourne Rd SW17 159 B1
Elmbridge Ave KT5 199 A3
Elmbridge Cl HA4 40 A3
Elmbridge Dr HA4 40 A3
Elmbridge Wlk E8 74 A1
Elmbridge Xcel Leisure Complex KT12 194 B4
Elmbrook 3 E18 55 A6
Elmbrook Cl TW16 172 B2
Elmbrook Gdns SE9 144 A1
Elmbrook Rd SM1 217 B4
Elm Cl
Buckhurst Hill IG9 21 D2
Carshalton SM5 202 D1
Harrow HA2 41 D3
Hayes UB3 84 A1
Hendon NW4 46 D4
South Croydon CR2 221 C2
Tolworth KT5 199 A2
Twickenham TW13, TW2 151 D2
Upper Holloway N19 71 C6
Wanstead E11 55 B3
West Barnes SW20 200 C5
Elmcote HA5 22 D1
Elmcourt Rd SE21, SE27 160 D2
Elm Court Sch SE27 161 A2
Elm Cres Ealing W5 110 A4
Kingston u T KT2 176 A2
Elmcroft Highgate N6 49 C2
Hornsey Vale N8 50 B4
Elmcroft Ave
Blackfen DA15 168 A5
Enfield N9 18 B5
Golders Green NW11 47 B2
Wanstead E11 55 B5
Elmcroft Cl
Chessington KT9 214 A5
Ealing W5 87 D1
Feltham TW14 149 D5
Wanstead E11 55 B5
Elmcroft Cres
Harrow HA2 41 C6
Hendon NW11 47 A2
Elmcroft Dr
Ashford TW15 170 C5
Chessington KT9 214 A5
Elmcroft Gdns NW9 44 C4
Elmcroft St E5 74 C4
Elmcroft Terr UB8 82 C1
Elm Ct
5 Ashford TW16 171 D3
Brixton SW9 138 C4
Catford SE6 163 D3
Chingford E4 36 A4
4 Finchley N3 29 C2
Lewisham SE13 142 B2
Mitcham CR4 180 D1
42 Notting Hill W2 91 C2
Strand EC4 251 A6
Elm Ct Sch SE27 160 B4
Elmdale Rd N13 32 B5
Elmdene KT5 199 A1
Elmdene Cl BR3 207 B4
Elmdene Rd SE18 122 D1
Elmdon Rd
Hatton TW6 127 D2
Elmdon Rd *continued*
Hounslow TW5 129 A3
Elm Dr Harrow HA2 41 D3
Sunbury TW16 172 C1
Elmer Cl EN2 4 B2
Elmer Ct HA1 42 D3
Elmer Gdns
Edgware HA8 26 D3
Isleworth TW7 130 B2
Elmer Ho NW1 237 A4
Elmer Rd SE6 164 A4
Elmer's Dr TW11 175 B4
ELMERS END 206 D6
Elmers End Rd BR3, SE20 206 C6
Elmers End Sta BR3 206 D5
Elmerside Rd BR3 207 A5
Elmers Rd SE25 206 A2
Elmfield Ave
London N8 50 A4
1 Mitcham CR4 181 A2
Teddington TW11 174 D5
Elmfield Cl HA1 64 C6
Elmfield Ct DA16 146 B4
Elmfield Ho
6 Canonbury N5 73 A3
22 London N2 30 B1
Paddington W9 91 C3
Elmfield Mans 5 SW17 159 A2
Elmfield Pk BR1 209 A6
Elmfield Rd
Bromley BR1 209 A6
Chingford E4 20 B2
East Finchley N2 48 B6
Southall UB2 107 A3
Upper Tooting SW17 159 B2
Walthamstow E17 52 D3
Elmfield Way
Paddington W9 91 C2
South Croydon CR2 221 D1
Elm Friars Wlk NW1 71 D1
Elmgate Ave TW13 150 C1
Elmgate Ct HA8 27 A5
Elmgate Gdns HA8 27 B6
Elm Gdns
Claygate KT10 212 D2
East Finchley N2 48 A6
Enfield EN2 5 B5
Mitcham CR4 203 D5
Elm Gn W3 89 C1
Elm Gr
Cricklewood NW2 68 D4
Harrow HA2 41 C2
Hornsey N8 50 A3
Kingston u T KT2 176 A2
Orpington BR6 211 D1
Peckham SE15 140 A3
Sutton SM1 217 D4
Wimbledon SW19 179 A3
Woodford IG8 36 D5
Yiewsley UB7 104 B6
Elmgreen Cl 8 E15 98 C6
Elmgreen Sch The SE27 160 B2
Elmgrove Cres HA1 43 A4
Elmgrove Fst & Mid Schs HA3 43 A5
Elmgrove Gdns HA1 43 A4
Elm Grove Par SM6 219 A5
Elmgrove Rd
Croydon CR0 206 B2
Harrow HA1 42 D4
Elm Grove Rd
Barnes SW13 134 A3
Ealing W5 110 A4
Elm Hall Gdns E11 55 B3
Elm Hatch HA5 23 B3
Elm Ho
4 Cubitt Town E14 120 A4
2 Kingston u T KT2 176 B3
Teddington TW11 175 C3
Elmhurst DA17 147 A6
Elmhurst Ave
London N2 48 B6
Mitcham CR4 181 B3
Elmhurst Cres N2 48 B5
Elmhurst Ct
Carshalton SM5 218 B6
Croydon CR0 221 B3
Elmhurst Dr E18 37 A1
Elmhurst Lo 3 SM2 218 A1
Elmhurst Mans SW4 137 D2
Elmhurst Prim Sch E7 77 B1

Elmhurst Rd
Chislehurst SE9 .... 166 A1
Enfield EN3 .... 6 C6
Tottenham N17 .... 33 D1
Upton E7 .... 77 B1
Elmhurst Sch for Boys CR2 .... 221 B3
Elmhurst St SW4 .... 137 D2
Elmhurst Villas SE15 .... 140 C1
Elmington Cl DA5 .... 169 D5
Elmington Rd SE5 .... 139 B5
Elmira St SE13 .... 141 D2
Elm La SE6 .... 163 B2
Elm Lawn Cl UB8 .... 60 A1
Elmlea Dr UB3 .... 83 D2
Elm Lea Trad Est N17 .... 34 B4
Elmlee Cl BR7 .... 188 B4
Elmley Cl 12 E6 .... 100 A2
Elmley St SE18 .... 123 B2
Elm Lo SW6 .... 134 D4
Elmore Cl HA0 .... 88 A5
Elmore Ho SW9 .... 138 D3
Elmore Rd Enfield EN3 .... 6 D5
Leyton E11 .... 76 B5
Elmore St N1 .... 73 B1
Elm Park Ave N15 .... 52 A3
Elm Park Ct HA5 .... 40 C6
Elm Park Gdns
Chelsea SW10 .... 114 B1 256 C1
Hendon NW4 .... 46 D4
Elm Park Ho SW10 .... 256 C1
Elm Park La SW3 .... 114 B1 256 C1
Elm Park Mans SW10 .... 266 B6
Elm Park Rd
Chelsea SW3 .... 136 B6 266 C6
Edmonton N21 .... 17 A4
Finchley N3 .... 29 B3
Pinner HA5 .... 40 D6
South Norwood SE25 .... 205 D6
Walthamstow E10 .... 53 A1
Elm Pk Stanmore HA7 .... 25 C5
Streatham SW2 .... 160 B4
Elm Pl Ashford TW15 .... 170 C5
SW7 .... 114 B1 256 C2
Elm Quay SW8 .... 269 C5
Elm Rd Barnet EN5 .... 1 B1
Beckenham BR3 .... 185 B1
Chessington KT9 .... 214 A4
Claygate KT10 .... 212 D2
East Bedfont TW14 .... 149 B4
Hackbridge SM6 .... 203 A1
Kingston u T KT2 .... 176 B2
Leyton E11 .... 76 B6
Mortlake SW14 .... 133 A1
New Malden KT3 .... 199 B6
Sidcup DA14 .... 190 A6
South Norwood CR7 .... 205 B5
Stoneleigh KT17 .... 215 D2
Stratford E7 .... 76 D2
Tottenham N22 .... 32 D2
Walthamstow E17 .... 54 A4
Wembley HA9 .... 66 A3
Elm Rd W SM4 .... 201 B2
Elm Row NW3 .... 70 A5
Elms Ave Hendon NW4 .... 46 D4
Muswell Hill N10 .... 49 B6
Elmscott Gdns N21 .... 17 A5
Elmscott Rd BR1 .... 186 D5
Elms Cotts 1 CR4 .... 180 D1
Elms Cres SW4 .... 159 D5
Elms Ct
Merton SW19 .... 179 D3
Wembley HA0 .... 65 A4
Elmsdale Rd E17 .... 53 B5
Elms Gdns
Dagenham RM9 .... 81 B4
Wembley HA0 .... 65 A4
Elmshaw Rd SW15 .... 156 A6
Elmside CR0 .... 223 D2
Elmside Rd HA9 .... 66 C5
Elms La HA0 .... 65 B4
Elmsleigh Ave HA3 .... 43 C5
Elmsleigh Ct SM1 .... 217 D5
Elmsleigh Ho TW2 .... 152 B2
Elmsleigh Rd TW2 .... 152 B2
Elmslie Ct SE9 .... 166 C5
Elmslie Point 2 E3 .... 97 B2
Elms Mews W2 .... 246 C6
Elms Park Ave HA0 .... 65 A4
Elms Rd
Clapham Pk SW4 .... 159 C6

Elms Rd *continued*
Harrow HA3 .... 24 C3
Elm St WC1 .... 94 B3 240 D5
ELMSTEAD 188 A5
Elmstead Ave
Elmstead BR7 .... 188 B5
Wembley HA9 .... 66 B6
Elmstead Cl
Totteridge N20 .... 13 C2
West Ewell KT19 .... 215 C3
Elmstead Ct HA9 .... 44 B1
Elmstead Gdns KT4 .... 216 A5
Elmstead Glade BR7 .... 188 B4
Elmstead La BR7 .... 188 B5
Elmstead Rd IG3 .... 79 D6
Elmstead Woods Sta BR7 .... 188 A4
Elmsted Cres DA16 .... 146 C6
Elms The
5 Ashford TW15 .... 170 C5
Barnes SW13 .... 133 D2
Claygate KT10 .... 212 D1
Croydon CR0 .... 205 A1
3 Harlesden NW10 .... 89 C5
Kingsbury NW9 .... 45 A3
Plashet E12 .... 78 A2
Wallington SM6 .... 219 C4
Elmstone Rd SW6 .... 265 A2
Elmsway TW15 .... 170 C5
Elmsworth Ave TW3 .... 129 D3
Elm Terr
Child's Hill NW2 .... 69 C5
3 Eltham SE9 .... 166 C5
Harrow HA3 .... 24 B2
Elmton Ct NW8 .... 236 C6
Elm Tree Ave KT10 .... 196 C2
Elm Tree Cl
Ashford TW15 .... 170 D5
Northolt UB5 .... 85 B5
St John's Wood NW8 .... 92 B4 229 C2
Elmtree Ct HA4 .... 40 A1
Elm Tree Ct
5 Camberwell SE5 .... 139 A4
18 Charlton SE7 .... 143 C6
St John's Wood NW8 .... 229 C2
Elmtree Rd TW11 .... 174 C5
Elm Tree Rd NW8 .... 92 B4 229 C2
Elm View Ct UB2 .... 107 C2
Elm Way London N11 .... 31 A4
North Cheam KT4 .... 216 C5
West Ewell KT19 .... 215 B3
Willesden NW10 .... 67 C4
Elm Wlk
Child's Hill NW3 .... 69 C6
Orpington BR6 .... 226 B5
West Barnes SW20 .... 200 D5
Elmwood Ave
Bowes Pk N13 .... 32 A5
Feltham TW13 .... 150 B1
Harrow HA3 .... 43 B3
Elmwood Cl
Hackbridge SM6 .... 219 B6
Stoneleigh KT17 .... 216 A1
Elmwood Cres NW9 .... 45 A5
Elmwood Ct
Battersea SW11 .... 268 C2
Walthamstow E10 .... 53 C1
Wembley HA0 .... 65 A5
Elmwood Dr
Sidcup DA5 .... 169 A4
Stoneleigh KT17 .... 216 A1
Elmwood Gdns W7 .... 86 C1
Elmwood Ho
Enfield EN2 .... 4 D1
Feltham TW13 .... 150 B1
Elmwood Inf Sch CR0 .... 204 D3
Elmwood Jun Sch CR0 .... 204 D2
Elm Wood Prim Sch SE27 .... 161 B1
Elmwood Rd
Chiswick W4 .... 133 A6
Herne Hill SE24 .... 161 B6
Mitcham CR4 .... 202 D6
Thornton Heath CR0 .... 204 D2
Elmworth Gr SE21 .... 161 B2
Elnathan Mews W9 .... 91 D3
Elphinstone Ct SW16 .... 182 A4
Elphinstone Rd E17 .... 35 B1
Elphinstone St N5 .... 72 D4
Elrington Rd
Dalston E8 .... 74 A2

Elrington Rd *continued*
Woodford IG8 .... 37 A5
Elsa Ct BR3 .... 185 B2
Elsa Rd DA16 .... 146 C3
Elsa St E1 .... 97 A2
Elsdale Ho 14 E9 .... 74 C2
Elsdale St E9 .... 74 C1
Elsden Mews E2 .... 96 C5
Elsden Rd N17 .... 33 D2
Elsenham Rd E12 .... 78 C3
Elsenham St SW18, SW19 .... 157 B2
Elsfield NW5 .... 71 B3
Elsham Rd
Kensington W14 .... 113 A4 244 A1
Leyton E11 .... 76 C4
Elsham Terr W14 .... 244 A1
Elsiedene Rd N21 .... 17 A4
Elsie Lane Ct W2 .... 91 D2
Elsiemaud Rd SE4 .... 163 B6
Elsie Rd SE22 .... 139 D1
Elsinge Rd EN1 .... 6 B6
Elsinore Ave TW19 .... 148 A4
Elsinore Gdns NW2 .... 69 A5
Elsinore Ho
12 Camberwell SE5 .... 139 A3
Islington N1 .... 234 A5
7 Woolwich SE7 .... 122 A2
Elsinore Rd SE23 .... 163 A3
Elsinore Way TW9 .... 132 D2
Elsley Ct HA9 .... 66 D2
Elsley Prim Sch HA9 .... 66 B2
Elsley Rd SW11 .... 137 A2
Elsley Sch 8 SW17 .... 158 C2
Elspeth Rd
London SW11 .... 136 D1
Wembley HA0 .... 66 A3
Elsrick Ave SM4 .... 201 C4
Elstan Way CR0 .... 207 A2
Elstead Ct SM3 .... 201 A1
Elstead Ho 9 SW2 .... 160 B4
Elsted St SE17 .... 117 B2 262 D3
Elstow Cl Eltham SE9 .... 166 B6
Ruislip HA4 .... 40 D2
Elstow Gdns RM9 .... 103 A6
Elstow Grange NW6 .... 68 D1
Elstow Rd RM9 .... 103 A6
ELSTREE 10 A5
Elstree Gdns
Abbey Wood DA17 .... 125 A2
Edmonton N9 .... 18 B3
Ilford IG1 .... 79 A3
Elstree Hill BR1 .... 186 C3
Elstree Hill N WD6 .... 9 D6
Elstree Hill S WD6 .... 9 D4
Elstree Ho 3 HA7 .... 25 C6
Elstree Pk WD6 .... 11 B5
Elstree Rd
Bushey WD23 .... 8 C4
Elstree WD6 .... 9 A5
Elswick Rd SE13 .... 141 D3
Elswick St SW6 .... 136 A3
Elsworth Cl TW14 .... 149 C3
Elsworthy KT7 .... 196 C3
Elsworthy Rd NW3 .... 92 C6 230 A6
Elsworthy Rise NW3 .... 70 C1
Elsworthy Terr NW3 .... 70 C1
Elsynge Rd SW18 .... 158 B6
Elsynge Road Mans SW18 .... 158 B6
ELTHAM 166 B6
Eltham CE Prim Sch SE9 .... 166 B6
Eltham Coll SE9 .... 165 D2
Eltham Coll Jun Sch SE9 .... 165 D3
Eltham Green Rd SE9 .... 165 C6
Eltham Green Specialist Sports Coll SE9 .... 165 D5
Eltham High St SE9 .... 166 B5
Eltham Hill SE9 .... 166 A6
Eltham Hill Tech Coll SE9 .... 166 A5
Eltham Pal★ SE9 .... 166 A4
Eltham Palace Rd SE9 .... 165 D5
Eltham Park Gdns SE9 .... 144 C1
Eltham Rd SE9, SE12 .... 165 B6
Eltham Sta SE9 .... 166 B6
Elthiron Rd SW6 .... 135 C4 265 B1

Elthorne Ave W7 .... 109 A4
Elthorne Ct
Feltham TW13 .... 150 C3
Kingsbury NW9 .... 45 B3
Elthorne Park High Sch W7 .... 108 D3
Elthorne Park Rd W7 .... 109 A4
Elthorne Rd
London NW9 .... 45 B2
Upper Holloway N19 .... 71 D6
Elthorne Sp Ctr W7 .... 108 D3
Elthorne Way NW9 .... 45 B3
Elthruda Rd SE13 .... 164 B5
Eltisley Rd IG1 .... 78 D4
Elton Ave Barnet EN5 .... 13 B6
Wembley HA0 .... 65 B3
Wembley UB6 .... 64 D2
Elton Cl KT1 .... 175 C3
Elton Ho 3 E3 .... 97 B6
Elton Lo 4 W5 .... 110 A6
Elton Pl N16 .... 73 C3
Elton Rd KT2 .... 176 C2
Elton St 11 N16 .... 73 C3
Eltringham St SW18 .... 136 A1
Elvaston Ct EN5 .... 12 C6
Elvaston Mews SW7 .... 256 B6
Elvaston Pl SW7 .... 114 A3 256 B5
Elveden Ho 17 SW9 .... 138 D1
Elveden Pl NW10 .... 88 C5
Elveden Rd NW10 .... 88 C5
Elvedon Rd TW13 .... 149 D1
Elvendon Rd N13 .... 32 A4
Elver Gdns 10 E2 .... 96 A4
Elverson Rd SE8 .... 141 D3
Elverson Rd Sta SE8 .... 141 D3
Elverton St SW1 .... 115 D2 259 C4
Elvin Ct NW9 .... 45 A2
Elvington Gn BR2 .... 208 D4
Elvington La NW9 .... 27 C2
Elvin Ho 2 E9 .... 74 C2
Elvino Rd SE26 .... 185 A5
Elvis Rd NW2 .... 68 C2
Elwill Way BR3 .... 208 B5
Elwin St E2 .... 96 A4
Elwood Ho N5 .... 72 D5
Elwood St N4, N5 .... 72 D5
Elworth Ho SW8 .... 270 D3
Elwyn Gdns SE12 .... 165 A4
Ely Cl SW20 .... 177 D1
Ely Cotts SW8 .... 270 C3
Ely Court Flats SW6 .... 264 A1
Ely Ct Holborn EC1 .... 241 B3
3 Maida Vale NW6 .... 91 C5
Ely Gdns
Borehamwood WD6 .... 11 B6
Redbridge IG1 .... 56 A2
Ely Ho Barnet EN4 .... 2 C1
Northolt UB5 .... 85 A6
22 Peckham SE15 .... 140 A5
Elyne Rd N4 .... 50 C3
Ely Pl EC1 .... 94 C2 241 B3
Ely Rd Hatton TW6 .... 127 D3
Hounslow TW4 .... 128 C2
Leyton E10 .... 54 A2
Thornton Heath CR0 .... 205 B4
Elysan Pl CR2 .... 221 A1
Elysian Ave BR5 .... 211 D3
Elysium Gate 7 SW6 .... 135 B3
Elysium Pl SW6 .... 135 B3
Elysium St SW6 .... 135 B3
Elystan Bsns Ctr UB4 .... 106 C6
Elystan Ct SW15 .... 156 B6
Elystan Pl SW3 .... 114 D1 257 C2
Elystan St SW3 .... 114 C2 257 B3
Elystan Wlk N1 .... 234 A5
Emanuel Ave W3 .... 89 A1
Emanuel Ct Acton W3 .... 89 B1
10 Leyton E10 .... 53 D2
Emanuel Dr TW12 .... 173 B5
Emanuel Sch SW11 .... 158 C6
Embankment SW15 .... 134 D3
Embankment Gdns SW3 .... 136 D6 267 D6
Embankment Pier WC2 .... 116 A5 250 B4
Embankment Pl WC2 .... 250 B4
Embankment Sta WC2 .... 116 A5 250 B4

Embankment The TW1 .... 153 A3
Embassy Ct
Ealing W5 .... 110 B6
Kingston u T KT6 .... 197 D4
Sidcup DA14 .... 168 B1
St John's Wood NW8 .... 229 D3
7 Wallington SM6 .... 219 B2
8 Wanstead E18 .... 55 A6
Welling DA16 .... 146 B2
Wood Green N11 .... 31 D4
Embassy Gdns BR3 .... 185 B2
Embassy Ho 2 NW6 .... 69 C1
Embassy Lo N3 .... 29 B1
Emba St SE16 .... 118 A4
Ember Cl BR5 .... 211 A2
Embercourt Rd KT10, KT7, KT8 .... 196 C3
Ember Ct
2 Acton W12 .... 111 C3
14 Hendon NW9 .... 27 D1
Ember Farm Ave KT8 .... 196 B3
Ember Farm Way KT8 .... 196 B4
Ember Gdns KT10, KT8 .... 196 C2
Ember Ho 8 BR1 .... 186 B5
Emberhurst Sch KT10 .... 196 B2
Ember La KT10, KT8 .... 196 B2
Emberson Ho 7 E17 .... 54 A5
Emberton SE5 .... 139 C6
Emberton Ct EC1 .... 234 C1
Embleton Rd SE13 .... 141 D1
Embleton Wlk TW12 .... 173 B5
Embry Cl HA7 .... 25 A6
Embry Dr HA7 .... 25 A4
Embry Way HA7 .... 25 A6
Emden Cl UB7 .... 104 C4
Emden St SW6 .... 265 D2
Emerald Cl E16 .... 100 A1
Emerald Ct N12 .... 30 A6
Emerald Gdns RM8 .... 59 C1
Emerald Rd NW10 .... 89 B6
Emerald Sq UB2 .... 106 D3
Emerald St WC1 .... 94 B2 240 C4
Emerson Apartments N8 .... 50 B6
Emerson Ct 8 SW19 .... 179 A4
Emerson Gdns HA3 .... 44 B3
Emerson Ho N16 .... 73 C3
Emerson Rd IG1 .... 56 C2
Emerson St SE1 .... 117 A5 252 A4
Emerton Cl DA6 .... 147 A1
Emery Hill St SW1 .... 259 B5
Emery St SE1 .... 116 C3 261 B6
Emilia Cl EN3 .... 18 B6
Emily St 7 E16 .... 98 D1
Emirates Stad (Arsenal FC) N7 .... 72 C4
Emlyn Gdns 3 W12 .... 111 C3
Emlyn Rd W12 .... 111 D3
Emmanual Ho SE18 .... 123 B1
Emmanuel CE Prim Sch NW6 .... 69 C3
Emmanuel Ct 3 EN4 .... 14 D3
Emmanuel Ho
Dulwich SE21 .... 161 B1
Lambeth SE11 .... 261 A3
Emmanuel Rd
Northwood HA6 .... 22 A3
Streatham SW12 .... 159 D3
Emma Rd E13 .... 98 D5
Emma St E2 .... 96 B5
Emmeline Ct KT12 .... 194 C2
Emminster NW6 .... 91 D6
Emmott Ave IG6 .... 57 A4
Emmott Cl
London NW11 .... 48 A3
Mile End E1 .... 97 A3
Emperor's Gate SW7 .... 114 A2 256 A4
Empingham Ho 20 SE8 .... 118 D2
Empire Ave N18 .... 33 A4
Empire Ct HA9 .... 66 D5
Empire Ho
Brompton SW3 .... 257 A5
Edmonton N18 .... 33 B4

Empire Par
Edmonton N18 33 B4
Wembley HA9 66 C5
Empire Rd UB6 65 C1
Empire Sq N19 72 A5
Empire Way HA9 66 C4
Empire Wharf E3 97 A6
Empire Wharf Rd E14 120 B2
Empress Ave
Chingford E4 35 D3
Ilford IG1 78 C6
Wanstead E12 77 D6
Woodford IG8 36 D3
Empress Dr BR7 188 D4
Empress Mews 36 SE5 139 A3
Empress Par E4 35 C3
Empress Pl SW5 113 C1 255 A1
Empress St SE17 139 A6
Empson St E3 97 D3
Emsworth Cl N9 18 C3
Emsworth St SW2 160 B2
Emu Rd SW8 137 B3
Ena Rd SW16 204 A6
Enard Ho 28 E3 97 B5
Enbrook St W10 91 A4
Enclave Ct EC1 241 D6
Endale Cl SM5 218 D6
Endeavour Way
Barking IG11 102 A5
Thornton Heath CR0 204 A2
Wimbledon SW19 179 D6
Endell St WC2 94 A1 240 A1
Enderby St SE10 120 C1
Enderfield Ct BR7 188 C2
Enderley Cl HA3 24 C2
Enderley Ho SE19 183 D2
Enderley Rd HA3 24 C2
Endersby Rd EN5 12 C6
Enders Cl EN2 4 C4
Endersleigh Gdns NW4 46 A5
Endlebury Ct E4 20 B2
Endlebury Rd E4 20 A2
Endlesham Ct 2 SW12 159 A4
Endlesham Rd SW12 159 A4
Endsleigh Gdns
Bloomsbury WC1 93 D3 239 C6
Ilford IG1 56 D1
Kingston u T KT6 197 C3
Endsleigh Ind Est UB2 107 B2
Endsleigh Mans 4 SW16 160 A1
Endsleigh Pl WC1 239 D6
Endsleigh Rd
Ealing W13 109 A6
Southall UB2 107 A2
Endsleigh St WC1 93 D3 239 D6
Endway KT5 198 D2
Endwell Rd SE4 141 A3
Endymion Rd
Harringay N4 50 D2
Tulse Hill SW2 160 B5
Energen Cl NW10 67 C2
ENFIELD 6 B2
Enfield Chase Sta EN2 5 A2
Enfield Cloisters 7 N1 95 C4
Enfield Coll EN3 6 C2
Enfield Cty Sch (Lower Sch) EN2 5 C5
Enfield Cty Sch (Upper Sch) EN2 5 B2
Enfield Gram Sch (Lower) EN1 5 B3
Enfield Gram Sch (Upper) EN2 5 B2
ENFIELD HIGHWAY 6 C3
Enfield Ho 24 SW9 138 A3
ENFIELD LOCK 7 B6
Enfield Lock Sta EN3 7 A6
Enfield Rd
Brentford TW8 109 D1
De Beauvoir Town E8, N1 73 C1
Enfield Rd *continued*
Enfield EN2 4 A2
Hatton TW6 127 C3
South Acton W3 110 D4
Enfield Ret Pk EN1 6 A2
Enfield Road Rdbt TW6 127 C3
ENFIELD TOWN 5 B1
Enfield Town Sta EN1 5 B2
ENFIELD WASH 6 D5
Enfield Wlk TW8 109 D1
Enford St W1 92 D2 237 C4
Engadine Cl CR0 221 D5
Engadine St SW18 157 C3
Engate St SE13 142 A1
Engel Pk NW7 28 C4
Engineer Cl SE18 144 C6
Engineers Way HA9 66 C4
England's La NW3 70 D2
England Way KT3 199 A5
Englefield
Bromley BR1 188 A1
Regent's Pk NW1 232 A1
Englefield Cl
Enfield EN2 4 C3
Orpington BR5 211 D5
Thornton Heath CR0 205 A3
Englefield Path BR5 211 D5
Englefield Rd N1 73 C1
Engleheart Dr TW14 149 D5
Engleheart Rd SE6 164 A4
Englewood Rd SW12 159 C5
English Gardening Sch The SW3 136 D6 267 C6
English Grounds SE1 253 A3
English Martyrs RC Prim Sch
Walworth SE17 117 B2 262 D3
Whitechapel E1 95 D1 243 D1
English St E3 97 B3
Enid St SE16 117 D3 263 D6
Enid Stacy Ho 11 N19 49 D2
Enmore Ave SE25 206 A4
Enmore Ct SW14 155 B6
Enmore Gdns SW14 155 B6
Enmore Rd
Croydon SE25 206 A4
Putney SW15 156 C6
Southall UB1 85 C3
Ennerdale Ave HA3, HA7 43 C6
Ennerdale Cl
Cheam SM1 217 B4
East Bedfont TW14 149 D3
Ennerdale Ct E11 55 A2
Ennerdale Dr NW9 45 C4
Ennerdale Gdns HA9 43 C1
Ennerdale Ho 3 N4 51 B2
Ennerdale Rd
Erith DA7 147 C4
Richmond TW9 132 B3
Ennersdale Rd SE13 164 B6
Ennis Ho 16 E14 97 D1
Ennismore Ave
Chiswick W4 111 D2
Greenford UB6 64 C3
Ennismore Gdns
Knightsbridge SW7 114 C3 257 A6
Thames Ditton KT7 196 C3
Ennismore Gdns Mews SW7 114 C3 257 A6
Ennismore Mews SW7 114 C3 257 A6
Ennismore St SW7 114 C3 257 A6
Ennis Rd London N4 50 C1
Shooters Hill SE18 145 A6
Ennor Ct KT4 216 C4
Ensbury Ho SW8 270 C4
Ensign Cl TW19 148 A3
Ensign Ct 12 E1 118 A6
Ensign Dr N13 17 A1
Ensign Ho 19 E14 119 C4
Ensign St E1 118 A6
Ensign Way
Stanwell TW19 148 A3
2 Wallington SM6 220 A1
Enslin Rd SE9 166 C4
Ensor Mews SW7 256 C2
Enstone Rd Enfield EN3 7 A2
Enstone Rd *continued*
Ickenham UB10 60 B5
Enterprise Cl CR0 204 C1
Enterprise Ho IG11 101 D4
Enterprise Ho E4 20 A4
Enterprise Ho
36 Hackney E9 74 C1
Walton-on-T KT12 194 B2
Enterprise Row N15 51 D4
Enterprise Way
College Pk NW10 90 A4
Teddington TW11 174 D4
Wandsworth SW18 135 C1
Enterprise Works EN3 7 B4
Enterprize Way SE8 119 B2
Enthoven Ho SE18 122 D2
Enton Pl TW3 129 D1
Enversham Ct SE23 163 A1
Envoy Ave TW6 127 D2
Epirus Mews SW6 265 A4
Epirus Rd SW6 135 B5 264 D4
Epping Cl
Millwall E14 119 C2
Romford RM7 59 D6
Epping Forest★ IG10 21 B6
Epping Glade E4 20 A5
Epping Ho 8 E5 74 A6
Epping New Rd IG9 21 B5
Epping Pl N1 72 C2
Epping Way E4 19 D5
Epple Rd SW6 135 B4 264 D2
Epsom Cl Erith DA7 147 D2
Northolt UB5 63 B3
Epsom & Ewell High Sch KT19 215 A3
Epsom Ho SM1 217 D4
Epsom Rd
Croydon CR0 220 C4
Ilford IG3 57 D3
Leyton E10 54 A3
Morden SM3, SM4 201 B2
Epsom Sq TW6 127 D3
Epstein Ct N1 234 D5
Epstein Rd SE28 124 B5
Epworth Rd TW7, TW8 131 B5
Epworth St EC2 95 B3 242 D5
Equity Sq 29 E2 95 D4
Erasmus St SW1 115 D2 259 D3
Erconwald St W12 89 D1
Erebus Dr SE28 123 B4
Eresby Dr BR3 207 C1
Eresby Ho SW7 247 B1
Eresby Pl NW6 69 C1
Erica Ct SW4 270 B1
Erica Gdns CR0 223 D5
Erica Ho London SE4 141 B2
6 Wimbledon SW19 179 A3
Wood Green N22 32 C2
Erica St W12 112 A6
Eric Cl E7 77 A4
Eric Clarke La IG11 101 A4
Ericcson Cl SW18 157 C6
Eric Fletcher Ct 15 N1 73 A1
Eric Macdonald Ho SW6 265 B1
Eric Rd
Dagenham RM6 58 D2
Forest Gate E7 77 A4
Willesden NW10 67 D2
Eric Shipman Terr 2 E13 99 A3
Ericson Ho
London SE13 142 B1
Stamford Hill N16 51 D1
Eric St E3 97 B3
Eric Wilkins Ho 14 SE1 118 A1
Eridge Ho SE22 139 D2
Eridge House Sch 13 SW6 135 B3
Eridge Rd W4 111 B3
Erin Cl Bromley BR1 186 C3
Ilford IG3 58 A3
Erin Ct NW2 68 C2
Erindale SE18 145 B6
Erindale Ct 1 BR3 185 C2
Erindale Terr SE18 145 B6
ERITH 147 D6
Erith Rd
Belvedere DA17 125 D1
Erith Rd *continued*
Erith DA7 147 D2
Erlanger Rd SE14 140 D3
Erlesmere Gdns W13 109 A3
Ermine Cl TW4 128 C3
Ermine Ho 3 N17 33 D3
Ermine Rd
London SE13 141 D1
South Tottenham N15 51 D3
Ermine Side EN1 18 A6
Ermington Rd SE9 167 A2
Ernald Ave E6 100 A5
Erncroft Way TW1 152 D5
Ernest Ave SE27 182 D6
Ernest Bevin Coll SW17 158 C2
Ernest Cl BR3 207 C4
Ernest Cotts KT17 215 D1
Ernest Gdns W4 132 D6
Ernest Gr BR3 207 B4
Ernest Rd KT1 176 D1
Ernest Richards Twr E17 53 B3
Ernest Simmonds Ho SE14 140 C3
Ernest Sq KT1 176 D1
Ernest St E1 96 D3
Ernle Rd SW20 178 C3
Ernshaw Pl SW15 157 A6
Eros Ho SE6 163 D4
Eros (Shaftesbury Meml)★ W1 115 D6 249 C5
Erpingham Rd SW15 134 C2
Erridge Rd SW19 179 C1
Errington Manor 6 SM5 218 D5
Errington Rd W9 91 B3
Errol Gdns Hayes UB4 84 B3
West Barnes KT3 200 A5
Errol St EC1 95 A3 242 B5
Erskine Cl SM1 218 C5
Erskine Cres N17 52 B5
Erskine Hill NW11 47 C4
Erskine Ho
7 Charlton SE7 143 C6
Pimlico SW1 259 A1
Erskine Rd
Carshalton SM1 218 B5
Primrose Hill NW3 70 D1
Walthamstow E17 53 B5
Erwood Rd SE7 122 A1
Esam Way SW16 182 C5
Escot Rd TW16 171 C3
Escott Gdns SE9 188 A6
Escot Way EN5 12 C6
Escreet Gr SE18 122 C2
Escuan Lo N5 73 A3
ESHER 212 A4
Esher Ave
Cheam SM3 216 D5
Walton-on-T KT12 194 A1
Esher CE Prim Sch KT10 212 A3
Esher Cl DA5 169 A3
Esher Coll KT7 196 C2
Esher Cres TW6 127 D3
Esher Gdns SW19 156 D2
Esher Ho 8 SW8 137 D3
Esher Mews 4 CR4 202 D6
Esher Park Ave KT10 212 A3
Esher Rd
East Molesey KT8 196 B4
Ilford IG3 79 C5
Esher Sta KT10 212 B6
Eskdale Enfield EN1 17 C6
Regent's Pk NW1 232 A3
Eskdale Ave UB5 85 B6
Eskdale Cl HA9 65 D6
Eskdale Rd DA7 147 C4
Esk Ho E3 97 B3
Eskmont Ridge SE19 183 C3
Esk Rd E13 99 B3
Esmar Cres NW9 46 A2
Esme Ho SW15 133 D1
Esmeralda Rd SE1 118 A2
Esmond Ct Barnet EN5 1 C1
Kensington W8 255 D6
Esmond Gdns W4 111 B2
Esmond Rd
Acton W4 111 B3
Kilburn NW6 91 B6
Esmond St SW15 135 A1
Esparto St SW18 157 D4
Espirit Ct E1 243 C3
Espirit Ho 6 SW15 157 A6
Essan Ho W13 87 B2
Essence Ct HA9 66 B6
Essenden Rd
Belvedere DA17 125 C1
South Croydon CR2 221 C1
Essendine Mans W9 91 C4
Essendine Prim Sch 11 W9 91 C4
Essendine Rd W9 91 C4
Essex Ave TW7 130 C2
Essex Cl Romford RM7 59 D5
Ruislip HA4 40 D1
Walthamstow E17 53 A5
West Barnes SM4 200 D2
Essex Ct
Barnes SW13 133 D3
Hammersmith W6 112 C3
Holborn EC4 241 A1
South Norwood SE19 183 B4
Essex Gdns N4 50 D3
Essex Gr SE19 183 B4
Essex Ho 4 Acton W3 88 C1
2 Poplar E14 97 D1
Essex Lo 5 N10 31 B1
Essex Mans E11 54 B2
Essex Park Mews W3 111 C5
Essex Pk N3 29 D4
Essex Pl W4 111 A2
Essex Place Sq 5 W4 111 B2
Essex Prim Sch E12 78 A3
Essex Rd Acton W3 111 A6
Barking IG11 79 B1
Chingford E4 20 C3
Chiswick W4 111 B2
Enfield EN2 5 B1
Ilford RM6 58 C2
Islington N1 94 D6 234 D6
Leyton E10 54 A3
Plashet E12 78 A2
Romford RM7 59 D5
Walthamstow E17 53 A3
Willesden NW10 67 C1
Woodford E18 37 B1
Essex Rd S E11 54 B2
Essex Road Sta N1 73 A1
Essex St
Forest Gate E7 77 A3
Strand WC2 116 C6 251 A6
Essex Twr 4 SE20 184 B2
Essex Villas W8 113 C4 245 A1
Essian St E1 97 A2
Essington SW15 157 A5
Essoldo Way HA8 44 B6
Estate Way E10 53 B1
Estcourt Rd
Croydon SE25 206 B3
Fulham SW6 135 B5 264 C4
Estella Ave KT3 200 B5
Estella Ho 15 W11 112 D6
Estelle Rd NW3 70 D4
Esterbrooke St SW1 259 C3
Este Rd SW11 136 C2
Esther Cl N21 16 C4
Esther Doe Lo N21 16 C4
Esther Rd E11 54 C2
Estoria Cl 22 SW2 160 C4
Estreham Rd SW16 181 D4
Estridge Cl TW3 129 C1
Estuary Cl IG11 102 B4
Eswyn Rd SW17 180 D5
Etal Ho N1 72 D1
Etchingham Ct N12 30 A3
Etchingham Park Rd N3 29 D3
Etchingham Rd E15 76 A4
Eternit Wlk SW6 134 D4
Etfield Gr DA14 190 B5
Ethelbert Cl BR1 209 A6
Ethelbert Gdns IG2 56 C4
Ethelbert Ho E9 75 A4
Ethelbert Rd
Bromley BR1, BR2 209 A6
Wimbledon SW20 178 D2
Ethelbert St SW12 159 B3
Ethel Brooks Ho SE18 144 D6
Ethelburga St SW11 136 C4 267 B2

Ethelburga Twr
SW11 267 B2
Ethel Cotts RM6 58 D6
Etheldene Ave N10 49 C5
Ethelden Rd W12 112 B5
Ethel Rankin Ct [8]
SW6 135 B3
Ethel Rd
Ashford TW15 170 A5
Newham E16 99 B1
Ethel St SE17 262 B3
Ethelworth Ct [4]
SW2 160 C3
Etheridge Rd NW2 46 C2
Etherley Rd N15 51 A4
Etherow St SE22 162 A4
Etherstone Gn
SW16 182 C6
Etherstone Rd SW16 182 C6
Ethnard Rd SE15 140 B6
Ethronvi Rd DA7 147 A2
Etienne Ho NW7 28 C6
Etloe Ho E10 53 C1
Etloe Rd E10 75 C6
Eton Ave
East Barnet EN4 14 C5
Finchley N12 30 A3
Heston TW5 129 C6
New Malden KT3 199 B5
Primrose Hill NW3 70 C1
Wembley HA0 65 C4
Eton Cl SW18 157 D4
Eton College Rd NW3 70 D2
Eton Ct
Hampstead NW3 70 B1
Highgate N6 49 B3
Wembley HA0 65 C4
Eton Garages [11]
NW3 70 C2
Eton Gr
Lewisham SE13 142 C2
Queensbury NW9 44 C5
Eton Hall NW3 70 D2
Eton Ho Hackney E9 75 B2
Highbury N5 72 D4
Eton Manor Ct E10 75 C6
Eton Pl NW1 71 A1
Eton Rd
Harlington UB3 127 D5
Ilford IG1 79 B4
Maitland Pk NW3 70 D2
Eton Rise NW3 70 D2
Eton St TW10 154 A6
Eton Villas NW3 70 D2
Etta St SE8 141 A6
Ettrick Ho [8] E5 74 B6
Ettrick St E14 98 A1
Etwell Pl KT5 198 B3
Euesden Cl N9 18 B1
Eugene Cotter Ho
SE17 262 D3
Eugenia Rd SE16 118 C2
Eugenie Mews BR7 188 D2
Eureka Rd [8] KT1 176 C1
Euro Bsns Ctr [3] E15 98 D6
Eurocentres
SW1 115 B2 258 D3
Euro Cl NW10 68 A2
Eurolink Bsns Ctr
SW2 160 C6
Europa Pl EC1 235 A1
European Coll [45] E1 96 A1
Europe Rd SE18 122 B3
Eustace Bldg SW8 268 C5
Eustace Ho SE11 260 C4
Eustace Pl SE18 122 B2
Eustace Rd
Dagenham RM6 58 D2
Newham E6 100 A4
Walham Green
SW6 135 C5 265 A4
Euston Ct [5] HA0 66 A2
Euston Rd
Fitzrovia
NW1 93 C3 239 B6
Thornton Heath CR0 204 C1
Euston Sq NW1 232 C1
Euston Square Sta
WC1 93 C3 239 B6
Euston St
NW1 93 C4 232 B1
Euston Sta
NW1 93 D4 232 C1
Euston Underpass
NW1 239 A6
Evan Cook Cl SE15 140 C4
Evandale Rd SW9 138 C3
Evangelist Rd NW5 71 B4
Evans Cl E8 73 D2
Evans Gr TW13 151 C2
Evans Ho
[34] Shepherd's Bush
W12 112 B6
South Lambeth SW8 269 D3
Evans Rd SE6 164 C2
Evanston Ave E4 36 A3
Evanston Gdns IG4 56 A3
Eva Rd RM6 58 D2
Eve Ct CR4 181 A1
Evelina Mans [9]
SE5 139 B5
Evelina Rd
London SE15 140 C3
Penge SE20 184 D3
Eveline Ct N10 49 B4
Eveline Lowe Prim Sch
[28] SE1 118 A1
Eveline Rd CR4 180 D2
Evelyn Ave
London NW9 45 B5
Ruislip HA4 39 D2
Evelyn Cl TW2 151 D4
Evelyn Cres TW16 171 D2
Evelyn Ct
Chislehurst SE9 166 A2
Marylebone W1 237 C1
Shacklewell E8 74 A4
Shoreditch N1 235 C3
Evelyn Denington Ct [2]
N1 72 D1
Evelyn Denington Rd
E6 100 A3
Evelyn Dr HA5 22 D3
Evelyn Fox Ct W10 90 C2
Evelyn Gdns
Richmond TW9 132 A1
South Kensington
SW7 114 B1 256 C1
Evelyn Gr Ealing W5 110 B5
Southall UB1 85 B1
Evelyn Grace Acad
SW9 138 C1
Evelyn Ho
Bedford Pk W12 111 D4
[3] Brixton SW2 160 B6
Harrow HA1 42 B4
[18] Spitalfields E1 96 A2
Evelyn Rd Acton W4 111 B3
Cockfosters EN4 2 D1
Ham TW10 153 C1
Newham E16 121 B5
Richmond TW9 132 A2
Walthamstow E17 54 A5
Wimbledon SW19 179 D4
Evelyns Cl UB8 82 C1
Evelyn St
Greenwich SE10 142 A6
SE8 119 A1
Evelyn Terr TW9 132 A2
Evelyn Way
Sunbury TW16 171 D2
Wallington SM6 219 D4
Evelyn Wlk N1 95 B5 235 C3
Evelyn Yd W1 239 C2
Evening Hill BR3 186 A3
Evenlode Ho [5] SE2 124 C4
Evenwood Cl SW15 157 A6
Everard Ave BR2 209 A1
Everard Ct N13 16 B1
Everard Ho [33] E1 96 A1
Everard Way HA9 66 A5
Everatt Cl SW18 157 B6
Eve Rd
Isleworth TW7 131 A1
Leyton E11 76 C4
Tottenham N17 51 C6
West Ham E15 98 C5
Everdale Ct N2 48 C5
Everdon Rd SW13 134 A6
Everest Ct
[6] Chislehurst SE9 166 A2
South Norwood SE19 183 C2
Everest Pl E14 98 A2
Everest Rd
Eltham SE9 166 B6
Stanwell TW19 148 A4
Everett Cl Bushey WD23 8 C3
Pinner HA5 39 D6
Everett Ho
Islington N7 72 C4
Walworth SE17 262 C2
Everett Wlk DA17 125 B1
Everglade Ho E17 35 B1
Everglades
Beckenham BR2 208 C6
Hounslow TW3 130 A2
Everglade Strand
NW9 27 D2
Evergreen Cl SE20 184 C3
Evergreen Ct [6]
SM2 218 A2
Evergreen Sq [3] E8 73 D1
Evergreen Way UB3 105 D6
Everilda St N1 233 D5
Evering Rd E5, N16 74 A5
Everington Rd N10 30 D1
Everington St W6 134 D6
Everitt Rd NW10 89 B4
Everleigh St N4 50 B1
Eversfield Ct SE12 165 B2
Eversfield Gdns HA8,
NW7 27 C3
Eversfield Rd TW9 132 B3
Evershed Ho E1 243 D2
Evershed Wlk W4 111 B2
Eversholt Ct EN5 14 A6
Eversholt St
NW1 93 D4 232 C2
Evershot Rd N4 50 B1
Eversleigh Ct N3 29 C3
Eversleigh Rd
Clapham SW11 137 A3
Finchley N3 29 B3
New Barnet EN5 14 A6
Newham E6 99 D6
Eversley Ave HA9 66 C6
Eversley Cl N21 16 B5
Eversley Cres
Hounslow TW7 130 B4
Ruislip HA4 61 D6
Southgate N21 16 C5
Eversley Ho [12] E2 96 A4
Eversley Mount N21 16 B5
Eversley Park Rd N21 16 B5
Eversley Pk SW19 178 B5
Eversley Prim Sch
N21 16 B5
Eversley Rd
Greenwich SE7 143 B6
Kingston u T KT5 198 B4
South Norwood SE19 183 B3
Eversley Way CR0 223 C5
Everthorpe Rd SE15 139 D2
Everton Bldgs NW1 232 A1
Everton Ct HA0 65 D4
Everton Dr HA7 44 A6
Everton Rd CR0 206 A1
Evesham Ave E17 35 C1
Evesham Cl
Belmont SM2 217 C1
Greenford UB6 85 D5
Evesham Ct
[2] Ealing W13 109 A5
[2] Richmond TW10 154 B5
Evesham Gn SM4 201 D3
Evesham Ho
[1] Bethnal Green E2 96 C5
Pimlico SW1 258 D2
St John's Wood NW8 229 A5
Evesham Rd
London N11 31 D5
Morden SM4 201 D3
Stratford E15 76 D1
Evesham St W11 112 D6
Evesham Way
Clapham SW11 137 A2
Ilford IG5 56 C6
Evesham Wlk
Brixton SW9 138 C3
Camberwell SE5 139 B3
Evry Rd DA14 190 C4
Ewald Rd SW6 135 B3
Ewanrigg Terr IG8 37 C5
Ewart Gr N22 32 C2
Ewart Pl [13] E3 97 B5
Ewart Rd SE23 162 D4
Ewe Cl N7 72 A2
EWELL 215 C1
Ewell By-Pass KT17 216 A1
EWELL COURT 215 C2
Ewell Court Ave
KT19 215 C3
Ewell Park Gdns
KT17 216 A1
Ewell Park Way
KT17 216 A1
Ewell Rd
Cheam SM2, SM3 216 D2
Ewell Rd *continued*
Surbiton KT6 198 B2
Thames Ditton KT6,
KT7 197 B2
Tolworth KT6 198 D1
Ewelme Rd SE23 162 C3
Ewen Cres SW2 160 C4
Ewen Henderson Ct [10]
SE14 141 A5
Ewen Ho N1 233 C5
Ewer St SE1 117 A5 252 A3
Ewhurst [19] SW15 156 D5
Ewhurst Cl E1 96 C2
Ewhurst Ct CR4 202 B6
Ewhurst Rd SE4 163 B5
Exbury Ho Hackney E9 74 C2
[4] London SW9 138 B1
Exbury Rd SE6 163 C2
Excel Ct WC2 249 D5
Excel Ex Ctr E16 121 B6
Excelsior Cl KT1 176 C1
Excelsior Coll N17 33 C3
Excelsior Gdns SE13 142 A3
Excelsior Ind Est
SE16 140 C6
Exchange Apartments [4]
BR2 209 B5
Exchange Arc EC2 243 B4
Exchange Cl N11 15 A2
Exchange Ct WC2 250 B5
Exchange Mans [2]
NW11 47 B2
Exchange Pl EC2 243 A4
Exchange The IG1 78 D6
Exchange Wlk HA5 41 A2
Exeforde Ave TW15 170 C6
Exeter Cl E6 100 B1
Exeter Ct Kilburn NW6 91 C5
Kingston u T KT6 198 A4
Mitcham SW19 180 C3
Exeter Gdns IG1 56 B1
Exeter Ho
[7] Barking IG11 80 A1
Feltham TW13 151 C2
Paddington W2 236 A2
[11] Peckham SE15 140 A6
Putney SW15 156 C5
Exeter Mans NW2 69 A2
Exeter Mews
Fulham SW6 265 A4
[12] Hampstead NW6 69 D2
Exeter Rd
Bexley DA16 145 D3
Brondesbury NW2 69 A2
Croydon CR0 205 D2
Dagenham RM10 81 D2
East Barnet N14 15 B4
Enfield EN3 6 D2
Harrow HA2 63 A6
Hatton TW6 127 C2
Lower Edmonton N9 18 C2
Newham E16 99 A2
Twickenham TW13 151 B1
Walthamstow E17 53 C4
Exeter St
WC2 116 B6 250 C6
Exeter Way
Hatton TW6 127 C3
[2] New Cross SE14 141 B5
Exford Ct SW11 266 D2
Exford Gdns SE12 165 B3
Exford Rd SE12 165 B3
Exhibition Cl W12 112 C6
Exhibition Rd
SW7 114 B3 256 D6
Exit Rd N2 30 B1
Exmoor Ho [25] E3 97 A5
Exmoor St W10 90 D2
Exmouth Ho
Clerkenwell EC1 241 B6
[6] Millwall E14 119 D2
Exmouth Market
EC1 94 C3 241 B6
Exmouth Mews NW1 232 B1
Exmouth Pl E8 74 B1
Exmouth Rd
Bexley DA16 146 C5
Hayes UB4 83 C4
Ruislip HA4 62 C5
Walthamstow E17 53 B4
Exmouth St E1 96 C1
Exning Rd E16 98 D3
Exonbury NW8 91 D6
Exon St SE17 117 C2 263 A3
Explorer Ave TW19 148 A3
Explorers Ct [6] E14 120 B6
Express Dr IG3 58 B1
Express Wharf [10]
E14 119 C4
Exton Cres NW10 67 A1
Exton Gdns RM8 80 C3
Exton Rd NW10 67 A1
Exton St SE1 116 C5 251 A3
Eyebright Cl [3] CR0 206 D1
Eyhurst Cl NW2 68 A6
Eylewood Rd SE27 183 A5
Eynella Rd SE21 161 D4
Eynham Rd W12 90 C1
Eynsford Cl BR5 211 A3
Eynsford Coll
W1 93 D1 239 C2
Eynsford Cres DA5 168 D3
Eynsford Ho
Borough The SE1 252 C2
[12] Deptford SE15 140 C6
Walworth SE17 263 A3
Eynsford Rd IG3 79 C6
Eynsford Terr UB7 82 B1
Eynsham Dr SE2 124 B3
Eynswood Dr DA14 190 C5
Eyot Gdns W6 111 D1
Eyot Gn W4 111 D1
Eyre Ct NW8 229 C4
Eyre St Hill
EC1 94 C3 241 A5
Eysham Ct [12] EN5 13 D6
Eythorne Rd SW9 138 C4
Ezra St E2 95 D4

F

Faber Gdns NW4 46 A4
Fabian Rd
SW6 135 B5 264 D4
Fabian St E6 100 B3
Fabyc Ho TW9 132 C5
Factory La
Croydon CR0 220 D6
Tottenham N17 33 D1
Factory Rd E16 122 A5
Factory Yd W7 108 C5
Fagg's Rd TW14 150 A6
Fairacre
Hounslow TW7 130 B4
Kingston u T KT3 199 C6
Pinner HA5 40 A5
Fairacres
Putney SW15 134 A1
Ruislip HA4 39 D2
Fair Acres BR2 209 A4
Fairbairn Gn [1]
SW9 138 D4
Fairbairn Hall E13 99 A3
Fairbank Ave BR6 226 D6
Fairbanks Rd N17 52 A6
Fairbourne Ho UB3 105 A3
Fairbourne Rd N17 51 C6
Fairbriar Residence
SW7 256 B4
Fairbridge Rd N19 71 D6
Fairbrook Cl N13 32 C5
Fairbrook Rd N13 32 C4
Fairburn Ct SW15 157 A6
Fairburn Ho
[9] Stamford Hill N16 51 C1
West Kensington SW5 254 D1
Fairby Ho SE1 263 D4
Fairby Rd SE12 165 B6
Faircharm Trad Est
SE8 141 D5
Fairchild Cl [6]
SW11 136 B3
Fairchild Ho
[13] Hackney E9 74 C1
Pimlico SW1 259 B3
[5] Shoreditch N1 95 C4
Fairchild Pl EC2 243 B5
Fairchild St EC2 243 B5
Fairclough Cl UB5 85 B3
Fairclough St E1 96 A1
Faircourt [14] NW3 70 D2
Faircroft
[6] Forest Hill SE26 184 C6
Stoke Newington N16 51 B1
FAIR CROSS 79 D3
Fair Cross IG11 79 C3
Faircross Ave IG11 79 A2
Faircross Par IG11 79 C3

Fairdale Gdns
Hayes UB3 106 A4
Putney SW15 134 B1
Fairdene Ct N7 72 A3
Fairey Ave UB3 105 D3
Fairfax Cl KT12 194 B1
Fairfax Gdns SE3 143 C4
Fairfax Ho
11 Brixton SW9 138 C3
5 Ealing W5 88 A4
6 Putney SW15 156 A6
Fairfax Mews
London N8 50 D5
Newham E16 121 B5
Putney SW15 134 C1
Fairfax Pl
Kensington W14 254 B5
South Hampstead NW6 70 A1
Fairfax Rd Acton W4 111 C3
Hornsey N8 50 C5
South Hampstead NW6 70 A1
Teddington TW11 175 B3
Fairfax Way N10 31 A3
Fairfield
Camden Town NW1 232 A5
Oakleigh Pk N20 14 B4
Pinner HA6 22 A1
4 Stepney E1 96 C2
Fairfield Ave
Edgware HA8 26 D3
Hendon NW4 46 B3
Ruislip HA4 39 A2
Twickenham TW2 151 D3
Fairfield Cl
Blackfen DA15 167 D5
Enfield EN3 7 A1
Mitcham SW19 180 C3
North Finchley N12 30 A6
West Ewell KT19 215 C3
Fairfield Cres HA8 26 D4
Fairfield Ct
Harlesden NW10 90 A6
1 London SW18 157 D6
Ruislip HA4 39 B1
8 Woodford IG8 37 A4
Fairfield Dr
Harrow HA2 42 A6
Wandsworth SW18 157 D6
Wembley UB6 87 C6
Fairfield E KT1 176 A1
Fairfield Gdns N8 50 A4
Fairfield Gr SE7 143 D6
Fairfield Ind Est KT1 198 B6
Fairfield N KT1, KT2 176 A1
Fairfield Path CR0 221 B5
Fairfield Pl KT1 198 A6
Fairfield Rd
Beckenham BR3 185 C1
Bexleyheath DA7 147 B3
Bow E3 97 C5
Edmonton N18 34 A6
Higham Hill E17 35 A1
Hornsey N8 50 A4
Ilford IG1 78 D2
Kingston u T KT1 176 A1
Petts Wood BR5 211 B3
Plaistow BR1 187 A3
Southall UB1 85 B1
South Croydon CR0 221 C5
Woodford IG8 37 A4
Yiewsley UB7 104 A6
Fairfields SE6 163 D4
Fairfield S KT1 176 B1
Fairfields Cl NW9 45 A4
Fairfields Cres NW9 45 A4
Fairfields Rd TW3 130 A2
Fairfield St SW18 157 D6
Fairfield W KT1 176 A1
Fairfield Way
Barnet EN5 13 C6
West Ewell KT19 215 C3
Fairfoot Rd E3 97 C3
Fairford SE6 163 C3
Fairford Ave CR0 206 D4
Fairford Cl CR0 207 A4
Fairford Ct SM2 217 D1
Fairford Gdns KT4 215 D5
Fairford Ho SE11 261 B3
Fairgreen EN4 2 D2
Fairgreen Ct EN4 2 D2
Fair Green Ct 1
CR4 202 D6
Fairgreen E EN4 2 D2
Fairgreen Rd CR7 204 D4
Fairhall Ct KT6 198 B2
Fairhaven Ave CR0 206 D3
Fairhaven Ct 7 CR2 221 A3
Fairhazel Gdns NW6 70 A1
Fairheathe SW15 156 D5
Fairholme TW14 149 C4
Fairholme Cl N3 47 A5
Fairholme Cres UB4 84 A3
Fairholme Gdns N3 47 A5
Fairholme Ho 4
KT3 199 C5
Fairholme Prim Sch
TW14 149 B3
Fairholme Rd
Ashford TW15 170 B5
Cheam SM1 217 B2
Harrow HA1 42 D4
Ilford IG1 56 C2
Thornton Heath CR0 204 C2
West Kensington
W14 113 A1 254 B1
Fairholt Cl N16 51 C1
Fairholt Rd N16 51 B1
Fairholt St SW7 257 B6
Fairhurst 4 NW6 70 A2
Fairland Ho BR2 209 B5
Fairland Rd E15 76 D1
Fairlands Ave
Sutton SM1 217 C6
Thornton Heath CR7 204 C4
Woodford IG9 21 A2
Fairlands Ct 6 SE9 166 C5
Fairlawn SE7 143 C6
Fairlawn Ave
Acton W4 111 A2
Bexley DA7 146 D3
East Finchley N2 48 C5
Fairlawn Cl
Claygate KT10 212 D2
Feltham TW13 173 B6
Kingston u T KT2 177 A4
Southgate N14 15 D5
Fairlawn Ct 3 W4 111 A2
Fairlawn Dr IG8 37 A3
Fairlawnes SM6 219 B3
Fairlawn Gdns UB1 107 B6
Fairlawn Gr W4 111 A2
Fairlawn Mans SE14 140 D4
Fairlawn Pk SE26 185 A5
Fairlawn Prim Sch
SE23 162 C4
Fairlawn Rd SW19 179 B3
Fairlawns
4 Bowes Pk N11 32 A4
10 Chingford E4 20 A2
Pinner HA5 22 D1
Putney SW15 156 D6
Sunbury TW16 194 A6
Twickenham TW1 153 C5
Fairlead Ho 6 E14 119 C3
Fairlea Pl W5 87 D3
Fair Lea Pl W5 87 C2
Fairleas 12 BR3 185 D1
Fairley Ct HA0 65 D3
Fairley House Sch
SW1 259 D2
Fairlie Ct
22 Bromley E3 97 D4
1 Tufnell Pk N7 71 D4
Fairlie Gdns SE23 162 C4
Fairlight TW12 173 D5
Fairlight Ave
Chingford E4 20 B2
Harlesden NW10 89 C5
Woodford IG8 37 A4
Fairlight Cl
Cheam KT4 216 C4
Chingford E4 20 B2
Fairlight Ct
Greenford UB6 86 B5
4 Harlesden NW10 89 C5
Fairlight Rd SW17 180 B6
Fairline Ct BR3 186 A1
Fairlop Ct E11 54 C1
Fairlop Pl NW8 229 D1
Fairlop Rd E11 54 B2
Fairmark Cl UB10 60 C2
Fairmead
Bromley BR1 210 B5
Tolworth KT5, KT6 198 D1
Fairmead Cl
Bromley BR1 210 B5
Heston TW5 128 D5
Kingston u T KT3 199 B6
Fairmead Cres HA8 11 A1
Fairmead Ct
3 Chingford E4 20 C4
Oakleigh Pk N20 14 A4
Fairmead Gdns IG4 56 A4
Fairmead Ho E9 75 A4
Fairmead Rd
Lower Holloway N7,
N19 72 A5
Thornton Heath CR0 204 C2
Fairmeadside IG10 21 C6
Fairmile Ave SW16 181 D5
Fairmile Ho
St Paul's Cray BR5 190 A1
Teddington TW11 175 A6
Fairmont Ave E14 120 B5
Fairmont Cl DA17 125 B1
Fairmont Ho 1 E3 97 C3
Fairmount Rd SW2 160 B5
Fairoak Cl BR5 210 D2
Fairoak Dr SE9 167 B6
Fairoaks Gr EN3 6 D6
Fairseat Cl WD23 8 C2
Fair St
Bermondsey
SE1 117 D4 253 C2
Hounslow TW3 130 A2
Fairstead Lo 4 IG8 37 A4
Fairstead Wlk N1 235 A6
Fairthorn Rd SE7,
SE10 121 A1
Fairview Ave HA0 65 D2
Fairview Cl SE26 185 A5
Fair View Cl E17 35 A2
Fairview Cres HA2 41 C1
Fairview Ct
Ashford TW15 170 C5
Hendon NW4 28 D1
Kingston u T KT2 176 D2
Fairview Dr
Littleton TW17 192 B4
Orpington BR6 227 B4
Fairview Gdns IG8 37 B2
Fairview Ho 14 SW2 160 B4
Fairview Pl SW2 160 B4
Fairview Rd
Carshalton SM1,
SM5 218 C3
Enfield EN2 4 C4
South Tottenham N15 51 D3
Thornton Heath
SW16 182 B2
Fairview Way HA8 26 C6
Fairwall Ho 9 SE5 139 C4
Fairwater Ave DA16 146 A1
Fairwater Ho TW11 175 A6
Fairway Bexley DA6 169 A6
Petts Wood BR5 211 B4
West Barnes SW20 200 C6
Woodford IG8 37 C5
Fairway Ave NW9 44 D6
Fairway Cl
Croydon CR0 207 A4
Heston TW4 150 C6
Hounslow TW4 150 D6
North End NW11 48 A2
West Ewell KT19 215 A4
Fairway Ct
Edgware NW7 11 B1
12 Eltham SE9 166 C5
New Barnet EN5 13 D5
13 Rotherhithe SE16 118 D4
Fairway Dr
Erith SE28 103 A1
Greenford UB6 63 D1
Fairway Est TW4 150 C6
Fairway Gdns
Ilford IG1 79 A3
West Wickham BR3 208 B3
Fairway Prim Sch
NW7 11 B2
Fairways
Ashford TW15 170 D4
10 Chingford E4 20 A3
4 Hounslow TW7 130 C4
Stanmore HA7 26 A1
Teddington TW11 175 D3
Walthamstow E17 54 A5
Fairways Bsns Pk
E10 75 A6
Fairway The Acton W3 89 C1
Bromley BR1, BR2 210 B4
East Molesey KT8 195 D6
Edgware NW7 11 B1
Edmonton N13 17 B1
Hillingdon UB10 82 B5
Kingston u T KT3 177 B2
Fairway The *continued*
New Barnet EN5 13 D5
Northolt UB5 64 A2
Ruislip HA4 62 D5
Southgate N14 15 C5
Wembley HA0 65 B6
Fairweather Cl N15 51 C5
Fairweather Ct N13 32 B6
Fairweather Ho N7 72 A4
Fairweather Rd N16 52 A3
Fairwood Ct E11 54 B2
Fairwyn Rd SE26 185 A6
Faith Ct NW2 68 B2
Faithfull Ho N5 73 A3
Fakenham Cl
Hendon NW7 28 A3
5 Northolt UB5 63 C2
Fakruddin St E1 96 A3
Falcon Ave BR1 210 A5
Falconberg Ct W1 239 D2
Falconberg Mews
W1 239 D2
Falconbrook Prim Sch 26
SW11 136 B2
Falcon Cl
Chiswick W4 133 A6
Lambeth SE1 251 D4
Falcon Cres EN3 18 D6
Falcon Ct
9 Dulwich SE21 161 B2
Holborn EC4 241 A1
Islington N1 234 D3
New Barnet EN5 2 A1
Ruislip HA4 61 C6
6 Wanstead E18 55 B6
Falcon Dr TW19 148 A5
Falconer Ct N17 33 A3
Falconer Wlk 12 N7 72 B6
Falcon Gr SW11 136 C2
Falcon Ho
11 London SE15 139 D4
9 Merton SW19 179 D2
Falconhurst 4 KT6 198 A4
Falcon La SW11 136 C2
Falcon Lo
11 Paddington W9 91 C2
West Hampstead NW3 69 D4
Falcon Pk Ind Est
NW10 67 C3
Falcon Point SE1 251 D5
Falcon Rd
Battersea SW11 136 C2
Enfield EN3 18 D6
Hampton TW12 173 B3
Falconry Ct KT1 198 A6
Falcon Sch for Girls The
W5 110 B5
Falcons Pre Prep Sch
The 1 W4 132 D6
Falcons Prep Sch for
Boys The TW9 132 A1
Falcons Sch for Girls The
W5 110 B5
Falcon St E13 99 A3
Falcon Terr SW11 136 C2
Falcon Way
Feltham TW14 150 B6
Harrow HA3 44 A3
Hendon NW9 27 C1
Millwall E14 119 D2
Sunbury TW16 171 C1
Wanstead E11 55 A5
FALCONWOOD 145 C1
Falconwood Ave
DA16 145 C3
Falconwood Ct SE3 142 D3
Falconwood Par
DA16 145 D1
Falconwood Rd CR0 223 C1
Falconwood Sta SE9 145 B1
Falcourt Cl SM1 217 D3
Falkener Ct SW11 268 B1
Falkirk Ct 11 SE16 118 D5
Falkirk Gdns WD19 22 D5
Falkirk Ho W9 91 D4
Falkirk St N1 95 C5
Falkland Ave
Finchley N3 29 C3
Friern Barnet N11 31 B6
Falkland Ho
Catford SE6 186 A6
Kensington W8 255 C5
West Kensington W14 254 C2
Falkland Park Ave
SE25 183 C1
Falkland Pl 2 NW5 71 C3
Falkland Rd Barnet EN5 1 A3
Hornsey N8 50 C5
Kentish Town NW5 71 C3
Falkner House Sch
SW7 256 B2
Fallaize Ave IG1 78 D4
Falling La UB7 104 A6
Falloden Ct NW11 47 C5
Falloden Way (Barnet By-Pass) NW11 47 C5
Fallodon Ho
6 London SW8 137 D3
Paddington W11 91 B2
Fallow Court Ave
N12 30 A4
Fallow Ct 20 SE16 118 A1
Fallowfield
Lower Holloway N4 72 B6
Stanmore HA7 9 A1
Fallowfield Ct HA7 9 A1
Fallow Fields IG10 21 C4
Fallowfields Dr N12 30 C4
Fallows Cl N2 30 B1
Fallsbrook Rd SW16 181 C4
Falman Cl N9 18 A3
Falmer Rd Enfield EN1 5 C1
Walthamstow E17 53 D6
West Green N15 51 B4
Falmouth Ave E4 36 C5
Falmouth Cl
London SE12 164 D6
Wood Green N22 32 B3
Falmouth Gdns IG4 55 D5
Falmouth Ho
Bayswater W2 247 A6
Kennington SE11 261 B2
15 Kingston u T KT2 175 D2
6 Pinner HA5 23 B3
Falmouth Rd
SE1 117 A3 262 B5
Falmouth St E15 76 B3
Falmouth Way E17 53 B4
Falstaff Ct SE11 261 C3
Falstaff Ho 18 N1 95 C5
Falstaff Mews TW12 174 B5
Fambridge Cl SE26 185 B6
Fambridge Rd RM8 59 C1
Fane St W14 264 D6
Fan Mus The ★ SE10 142 A5
Fann St EC1 95 A3 242 B5
Fanshawe Ave IG11 79 A2
Fanshawe Cres RM9 81 B3
Fanshawe Rd TW10 175 C6
Fanshaw Ho 6 E17 53 D6
Fanshaw St N1 95 C4
Fantail Cl SE28 102 C1
Fantail The BR6 226 B5
Fanthorpe St SW15 134 C2
Faraday Ave DA14 168 B2
Faraday Cl N7 72 B2
Faraday Ho
2 Balham SW12 159 B4
4 Belvedere DA17 125 C3
6 Gospel Oak NW5 71 B4
5 Hampton TW12 173 D4
Kensal Town W10 91 A2
6 Poplar E14 119 B6
Wembley HA9 67 A5
Faraday Lo SE10 120 D3
Faraday Pl KT8 195 C5
Faraday Rd
Acton W3 111 A6
East Molesey KT8 195 C5
Kensal Town W10 91 A2
Southall UB1 107 D6
Stratford E15 76 D2
Welling DA16 146 A2
Wimbledon SW19 179 D4
Faraday Way
Greenwich SE18 121 D3
Thornton Heath CR0 204 B1
Fareham Ho 13
SW15 156 A3
Fareham Rd TW14 150 C4
Fareham St W1 239 C2
Farendon Ho 15
SM2 218 A2
Farewell Pl CR4 180 C2
Faringdon Ave BR2 210 C3
Faringford Rd E15 76 C1
Farjeon Ho NW6 70 B1
Farjeon Rd SE3 143 D4
Farleigh Ave BR2 209 A2
Farleigh Ct CR2 221 A3
Farleigh Ho 7 KT2 176 D4
Farleigh Pl N16 73 D4

Farleigh Rd N16 73 D4
Farleycroft [1] CR0 206 A1
Farley Croft BR2 186 C1
Farley Ct
Kensington W14 254 C6
Marylebone NW1 238 A5
Farley Dr IG3 57 C1
Farley Ho SE26 162 B1
Farley Mews SE6 164 A4
Farley Pl SE25 206 A5
Farley Rd
Catford SE6 164 A4
South Croydon CR2 222 B1
Farlington Pl SW15 156 B4
Farlow Rd SW15 134 D2
Farlton Rd SW18 157 D4
Farman Gr [2] UB5 84 D4
Farman Terr HA3 43 D5
Farm Ave
Child's Hill NW2 69 B5
Harrow HA2, HA5 41 C3
Streatham SW16 182 A6
Wembley HA0 65 C2
Farmborough Cl HA1 42 B2
Farm Cl Barnet EN5 12 C6
Buckhurst Hill IG9 21 C1
Coney Hall BR4 224 D5
Lower Halliford TW17 192 C2
Southall UB1 107 D6
Sutton SM2 218 B1
Uxbridge UB10 60 D6
Walham Green SW6 265 B4
Farmcote Rd SE12 165 A3
Farm Cotts E17 53 A3
Farm Ct NW4 46 A6
Farmdale Rd
Greenwich SE10 121 A1
Sutton SM5 218 C1
Farm Dr CR0 223 B6
Farm End E4 20 C6
Farmer Ho [4] SE16 118 B3
Farmer Rd E10 53 D1
Farmers Mkt*
W8 113 C5 245 B4
Farmers Rd SE5 138 D5
Farmer St W8 245 A4
Farmfield Rd BR1 186 C5
Farm House Ct NW7 28 A3
Farmhouse Rd
SW16 181 C3
Farmilo Rd E17 53 C2
Farmington Ave
SM1 218 B5
Farm La Croydon CR0 223 B6
East Barnet N14 15 B5
Walham Green
SW6 135 C5 265 B4
Farmlands Enfield EN2 4 C4
Pinner HA5 40 A5
Farmlands The UB5 63 C2
Farmland Wlk BR7 188 D5
Farm Lane Trad Ctr
SW6 135 C6 265 B5
Farmleigh N14 15 C4
Farmleigh Ho SW9 160 D6
Farm Pl W8 245 A4
Farm Rd Edgware HA8 27 A5
Edmonton N21 17 A3
Morden SM4 201 D4
Stonebridge NW10 89 B6
Sutton SM2 218 B1
Thames Ditton KT10 195 C1
Twickenham TW4 151 A3
Farm St W1 115 B6 248 C5
Farmstead Ct [3]
SM6 219 B3
Farmstead Rd
Catford SE6 185 D6
Harrow HA3 24 B1
Farm Vale DA5 169 D5
Farm View N3 47 B6
Farmway RM8 80 C5
Farm Way
Buckhurst Hill IG9 37 C6
North Cheam KT4 216 C5
Farm Wlk NW11 47 C4
Farnaby Ho [2] W10 91 B4
Farnaby Rd
Bromley BR1, BR2 186 C2
Kidbrooke SE9 143 C1
Farnan Ave E17 53 D6
Farnan Hall [6]
SW16 182 A5
Farnan Rd SW16 182 A5
FARNBOROUGH 227 B3
Farnborough Ave
South Croydon CR2 223 A1
Walthamstow E17 53 A6
Farnborough Cl HA9 66 D6
Farnborough Comm
Keston Mark BR2,
BR6 226 B5
Orpington BR6 226 C4
Farnborough Cres
[3] Hayes BR2 208 D1
South Croydon CR2 223 A1
Farnborough Ct [2]
BR6 227 A3
Farnborough Hill
BR6 227 C3
Farnborough Ho [1]
SW15 156 A3
Farnborough Prim Sch
BR6 227 A3
Farnborough Way
BR6 227 B3
Farncombe St SE16 118 A4
Farndale Ave N13 17 A1
Farndale Cres UB6 86 A4
Farndale Ho [3] NW6 91 D6
Farnell Mews SW5 255 C2
Farnell Pl W3 110 D6
Farnell Rd TW7 130 B2
Farnell's Almshouses
TW7 130 D3
Farnfield Ho [12]
SW2 160 B6
Farnham Cl N20 14 A4
Farnham Ct
[2] Cheam SM3 217 A2
[1] Southall UB1 86 A1
[2] Stamford Hill N16 51 C1
Farnham Gdns
SW20 178 B1
Farnham Green Prim Sch
IG3 58 A3
Farnham Ho
Borough The SE1 252 A3
Marylebone NW1 237 B5
Farnham Pl SE1 251 D3
Farnham Rd
Bexley DA16 146 C3
Ilford IG3 57 D2
Farnham Royal
SE11 116 B1 260 D1
Farnhurst Ho [7]
SW11 137 A3
Farningham Ct
SW16 181 D3
Farningham Ho [9]
N4 51 B2
Farningham Rd N17 34 A3
Farnley Ho [13] SW8 137 D3
Farnley Rd
Chingford E4 20 C4
South Norwood SE25 205 B5
Farnsworth Ct SE10 120 D3
Farnsworth Ho [8]
SW27 182 D5
Farnworth Ho [5]
E14 120 B2
Faro Cl BR1 188 C1
Faroe Rd W14 112 D3
Farorna Wlk EN2 4 C4
Farquhar Rd
Dulwich SE19 183 D5
Wimbledon SW19 157 C1
Farquharson Rd
CR0 205 A1
Farrance Rd RM6 59 A2
Farrance St E14 97 C1
Farrans Ct HA3 43 B2
Farrant Ave N22 32 D1
Farrant Cl BR6 227 D1
Farrant Ho [14] SW11 136 B2
Farrants Ct BR1 188 B1
Farr Ave IG11 102 A5
Farrell Ho E1 96 C1
Farren Rd SE23 163 A2
Farrer Ho SE8 141 C5
Farrer Mews N8 49 C5
Farrer Rd Harrow HA3 44 A5
Hornsey N8 49 D5
Farrer's Pl CR0 222 D4
Farrier Cl
Bromley BR1 209 D6
Hillingdon UB8 82 C1
Sunbury TW16 194 A5
Farrier Pl SM1 217 D6
Farrier Rd UB5 85 C5
Farriers Ct
Belmont SM2 217 A1
Wimbledon SW19 179 A3
Farriers Mews SE15 140 C2
Farrier St NW1 71 C1
Farriers Way WD6 11 B6
Farrier Wlk
SW10 136 A6 266 A6
Farringdon La
EC1 94 C3 241 B5
Farringdon Rd
EC1 94 C3 241 B5
Farringdon St
EC4 94 D1 241 C2
Farringdon Sta
EC1 94 D2 241 C4
Farrington Pl BR7 189 B3
Farringtons Sch
BR7 189 B3
Farrins Rents SE16 119 A5
Farrow La SE14 140 C5
Farrow Pl SE16 119 A3
Farr Rd EN2 5 B4
Farthingale Wlk E15 76 B1
Farthing Alley [8]
SE1 118 A4
Farthing Ct [3] NW7 29 A3
Farthing Fields [8]
E1 118 B5
Farthings Cl
Chingford E4 20 C1
Pinner HA5 40 B3
Farthing St BR6 226 B1
Farthings The [1]
KT2 176 C2
FARTHING STREET 226 B1
Farwell Rd DA14 190 C6
Farwig La BR1 187 A2
Fashion Retail Acad The
W1 239 C2
Fashion St E1 95 D2 243 D3
Fashion & Textile Mus*
SE1 253 A2
Fashoda Rd BR2 209 D5
Fassett Rd Dalston E8 74 A2
Kingston u T KT1 198 A5
Fassett Sq E8 74 A2
Fauconberg Ct W4 133 A6
Fauconberg Rd W4 133 A6
Faulkner Cl [6] RM8 58 D2
Faulkner Ho SW15 134 C3
Faulkner's Alley EC1 241 C4
Faulkner St SE14 140 C4
Fauna Cl
Dagenham RM6 58 C3
Stanmore HA7 25 D6
Faunce Ho [1] SE17 138 D6
Faunce St
SE17 116 D1 261 C1
Favart Rd
SW6 135 C4 265 B2
F Ave SE18 122 D3
Faversham Ave
Chingford E4 20 D3
Enfield EN1 17 B5
Faversham Ct SE6 163 B3
Faversham Ho
Camden Town NW1 232 B5
Walworth SE17 263 A1
Faversham Rd
Beckenham BR3 185 B1
Forest Hill SE6 163 B3
Morden SM4 201 D3
Fawcett Cl
London SW11 136 B3
West Norwood SW16 182 C6
Fawcett Est E5 52 A1
Fawcett Ho [25] SW9 138 A3
Fawcett Rd
Croydon CR0 221 A5
Willesden NW10 67 D1
Fawcett St
SW10 136 A6 266 A6
Fawcus Cl KT10 212 C2
Fawe Park Rd SW15 135 B1
Fawe St E14 97 D2
Fawkham Ho SE1 263 D3
Fawley Ct SE27 160 D2
Fawley Lo [2] E14 120 B2
Fawley Rd NW6 69 D3
Fawnbrake Ave
SE24 161 A6
Fawn Rd E13 99 C5
Fawns Manor Cl
TW14 149 A3
Fawns Manor Rd
TW14 149 B3
Fawood Ave NW10 67 B1
Fayetville Ho [26] N19 49 D2
Faygate Cres DA6 169 C6
Faygate Ct CR2 220 D1
Faygate Rd SW2 160 B2
Fayland Ave SW16 181 C5
Fazal Laj IG1 79 A6
Fazerley Ct [49] W2 91 C2
Fearnley Cres TW12 173 B4
Fearnley Ho SE5 139 C3
Fearon St SE10 121 A1
Featherbed La CR0 223 B1
Feathers Pl SE10 142 B6
Featherstone Ave [4]
SE23 162 C2
Featherstone Ct NW7 28 A3
Featherstone High Sch
UB2 107 A3
Featherstone Ho UB4 84 C2
Featherstone Ind Est
UB2 107 A3
Featherstone Prim Sch
UB2 106 C2
Featherstone Rd
Mill Hill NW7 28 B4
Southall UB2 107 A3
Featherstone St
EC1 95 B3 242 C6
Featherstone Terr
UB2 107 A3
Featley Rd SW9 138 D2
Federal Rd UB6 87 C5
Federation Rd SE2 124 C2
Fee Farm Rd KT10 212 D1
Felbridge Ave HA7 25 B2
Felbridge Cl SW16 182 C6
Felbridge Ct
Croydon CR2 221 A1
Feltham TW13 150 B3
Harlington UB3 127 B6
Felbridge Ho [21]
SE22 139 C2
Felbrigge Rd IG3 57 D1
Felday Rd SE13 163 D5
Felden Cl HA5 23 A3
Felden St
SW6 135 B4 264 C1
Feldman Cl N16 52 A1
Feldspar Ct [6] EN3 7 A2
Felgate Mews [4]
W6 112 B2
Felhampton Rd SE9 166 D1
Felhurst Cres RM10 81 D4
Feline Ct [1] EN4 14 C5
Felix Ave N8 50 A3
Felix Ct E17 53 D4
Felix La TW17 193 D3
Felix Manor BR7 189 C4
Felix Neubergh Ct EN1 5 C1
Felix Rd Ealing W13 109 A6
Walton-on-T KT12 194 A3
Felix St [19] E2 96 B5
Felixstowe Ct E16 122 D5
Felixstowe Rd
Abbey Wood SE2 124 B3
College Pk NW10 90 B4
Edmonton N9 34 A6
Tottenham N17 51 D6
Fellbrigg Rd SE22 161 D6
Fellbrigg St [21] E1 96 B3
Fellbrook TW10 153 B1
Fell Ho [11] N19 71 C5
Fellmongers Yd [1]
CR0 221 A5
Fellowes Cl UB4 84 D3
Fellowes Ct UB3 127 B6
Fellowes Rd SM5 218 C6
Fellows Ct E2 95 D5
Fellows Rd NW3 70 C1
Fell Rd CR0 221 A5
Fells Haugh [6] W3 89 A1
Felltram Way SE7 121 A1
Fell Wlk HA8 26 D2
Felmersham Cl [2]
SW4 137 D1
Felmingham Rd
SE20 184 C1
Felnex Trad Est
SM6 219 A6
Felpham Ct HA9 65 D4
Felsberg Rd SW2 160 A4
Fels Cl RM10 81 D5
Felsham Ho [5]
SW15 134 D2
Felsham Mews [14]
SW15 134 D2
Felsham Rd SW15 134 D2
Felspar Cl SE18 123 D1
Felstead Cl N13 32 C5
Felstead Rd E11 55 A2
Felstead St E9 75 B2
Felstead Wharf E14 120 A1
Felsted Rd E16 99 D1
FELTHAM 150 B2
Feltham Airparcs L Ctr
TW13 150 D2
Feltham Arenas
TW14 150 A4
Feltham Ave KT8 196 C5
Felthambrook Ind Est
TW13 150 B1
Felthambrook Way
TW13 172 B6
Feltham Bsns Complex
TW13 150 B2
Feltham Com Sch
TW13 150 C2
Feltham Corporate Ctr
TW13 150 B1
FELTHAMHILL 171 D5
Feltham Hill Jun & Inf
Schs TW13 149 D1
Feltham Hill Rd
Ashford TW15 171 A4
Feltham TW13 172 C5
Feltham Rd
Ashford TW15 171 A6
Mitcham CR4 181 A1
Feltham Sta TW13 150 B3
Felton Cl BR5 210 D3
Felton Gdns IG11 101 C5
Felton Ho
Kidbrooke SE9 143 C1
Shoreditch N1 235 D5
Felton Lea DA14 189 D5
Felton Rd
Barking IG11 101 C5
Ealing W13 109 C4
Felton St N1 95 B6 235 D5
Fenchurch Ave
EC3 95 C1 243 A1
Fenchurch Bldgs
EC3 243 B1
Fenchurch Pl EC3 253 B6
Fenchurch St
EC3 117 C6 253 B6
Fenchurch Street Sta
EC3 117 C6 253 B6
Fen Ct EC3 253 A6
Fendall Rd KT19 215 A3
Fendall St
SE1 117 C3 263 B5
Fender Ct [5] SW4 138 A3
Fendt Cl [8] E16 98 D1
Fendyke Rd SE2,
DA17 124 D3
Fenelon Pl
W14 113 B2 254 D3
Fen Gr DA15 167 D5
Fenham Rd SE15 140 B5
Fenman Ct N17 34 B2
Fenman Gdns IG3 58 B1
Fenn Cl BR1 187 A4
Fenn Ct HA1 43 A4
Fennel Cl
Croydon CR0 206 D1
Newham E16 98 C3
Fennell St SE18 144 C6
Fenner Cl SE16 118 B2
Fenner Ho [25] E1 118 B5
Fenner Sq [9] SW11 136 B2
Fenn Ho TW7 131 B4
Fenning Ct CR4 202 C5
Fenning St SE1 253 A2
Fenn St E9 74 C3
Fen St E16 120 D6
Fenstanton [3] N4 50 B1
Fenstanton Ave N12 30 B5
Fenstanton Prim Sch [20]
SW2 160 C3
Fenswood Cl DA5 169 C5
Fentiman Rd
SW8 138 B5 270 C4
Fentiman Way HA2 63 D6
Fenton Cl
[16] Dalston E8 73 D2
Elmstead BR7 188 B5

Fenton Cl *continued*
South Lambeth SW9 138 B3
Fenton Ct TW3 129 A5
Fenton Ho
Deptford SE14 141 A5
Heston TW5 129 C6
Fenton House★ NW3 70 A5
Fenton Rd N17 33 A3
Fentons SE3 142 D5
Fenton's Ave E13 99 B5
Fenton St E1 96 B1
Fenwick Cl 16 SE18 144 C6
Fenwick Gr SE15 140 A2
Fenwick Pl
Croydon CR2 220 D1
Stockwell SW9 138 A2
Fenwick Rd SE15 140 A2
Ferby Ct DA15 189 D6
Ferdinand Ho 1
NW1 71 B1
Ferdinand Pl NW1 71 A1
Ferdinand St NW1 71 A1
Ferguson Ave KT5 198 B4
Ferguson Cl BR2, BR3 208 B6
Ferguson Dr W3 89 B1
Ferguson Ho SE10 142 A4
Ferguson's Cl E14 119 C2
Fergus Rd N5 72 D3
Fermain Ct E N1 95 C6
Fermain Ct N N1 95 C6
Fermain Ct W N1 95 C6
Ferme Park Rd N4, N8 50 B3
Fermor Rd SE23 163 A3
Fermoy Rd
Greenford UB6 85 D3
West Kilburn W9 91 B3
Fern Ave CR4 203 D5
Fernbank IG9 21 B3
Fernbank Ave
Walton-on-T KT12 195 A2
Wembley HA0 64 D3
Fernbank Mews SW12 159 C5
Fernbrook Cres SE13 164 C5
Fernbrook Dr HA2 41 D2
Fernbrook Rd SE13 164 C5
Fern Cl 3 N1 95 C5
Ferncliff Rd E8 74 A3
Ferncroft Ave
London N12 30 D4
Ruislip HA4 62 C6
West Hampstead NW3 69 C4
Fern Ct
Bexleyheath DA7 147 C1
Chingford E4 36 A4
New Cross Gate SE14 140 D3
Ferndale BR1 187 C1
Ferndale Ave
Hounslow TW4 129 A2
Walthamstow E17 54 B4
Ferndale Cl DA7 147 A4
Ferndale Com Sp Ctr SW9 138 B1
Ferndale Ct 3 SE3 142 D5
Ferndale Ho N16 51 B1
Ferndale Rd
Ashford TW15 170 A5
Brixton SW4, SW9 138 B1
Croydon SE25 206 B4
Enfield EN3 7 A6
Leyton E11 76 D6
South Tottenham N15 51 D4
Upton E7 77 B1
Ferndale St E6 100 D1
Ferndale Way BR6 227 B3
Ferndene NW9 45 A4
Fern Dene W13 87 B2
Ferndene Rd SE24 139 A1
Fernden Way RM7 59 D3
Ferndown
5 Kingston u T KT6 198 A4
Pinner HA6 22 A1
7 Wanstead E18 55 A6
Ferndown Ave BR6 211 B1
Ferndown Cl
Pinner HA5 23 A3
Sutton SM2 218 B2
Ferndown Ct 6 UB1 86 A1
Ferndown Lo 17 E14 120 A3
Ferndown Rd
Eltham SE9 165 D4
South Oxhey WD19 22 C6
Ferney Meade Way TW7 131 A3
Ferney Rd EN4 15 A3
Fern Gr TW14 150 B4
Fernhall N12 30 C5
Fernhall Dr IG4 55 D4
Fernham Rd CR7 205 A6
Fernhead 12 SM1 218 A4
Fernhead Rd W9 91 B4
Fernhill Ct
Chingford E17 36 B1
Kingston u T KT2 175 D5
Fernhill Gdns KT2 176 A5
Fernhill Ho E5 74 A6
Fern Hill Pl 3 BR6 227 A3
Fern Hill Prim Sch KT2 176 A4
Fernhill St E16 122 B5
Fern Ho HA7 24 D4
Fernholme Rd SE15 162 D6
Fernhurst Gdns HA8 26 C4
Fernhurst Rd
Ashford TW15 171 A6
Croydon CR0 206 B1
Fulham SW6 135 A4 264 B2
Fernie Ho SE22 139 D2
Fern La TW5 107 B1
Fernlea Ho NW10 88 B4
Fernlea Rd
Balham SW12 159 B3
Mitcham CR4 181 A2
Fernleigh Cl
Croydon CR0 220 C4
West Kilburn W9 91 B4
Fernleigh Ct
Harrow HA2 23 D1
Wembley HA9 44 A1
Fernleigh Rd N21 16 D2
Fern Lo 13 SW16 182 C5
Fernly Cl HA5 40 A5
Fernsbury St WC1 234 A1
Fernshaw Mans SW10 266 A5
Fernshaw Rd SW10 136 A6 266 A5
Fernside
Buckhurst Hill IG9 21 B3
Golders Green NW11 47 C1
Thames Ditton KT7 197 B1
Fernside Ave
Edgware NW7 11 B1
Feltham TW13 172 B6
Fernside Ct NW4 28 D1
Fernside Rd SW12 159 A4
Ferns Rd E15 76 D2
Fern St E3 97 C3
Fernthorpe Rd SW16 181 C4
Ferntower Rd N5 73 B3
Fernways IG1 78 D4
Fern Wlk 18 SE16 118 A1
Fernwood
Wandsworth SW19 157 B3
Wood Green N22 32 A3
Fernwood Ave
Streatham SW16 181 D6
Wembley HA0 65 C2
Fernwood Cl BR1 187 C1
Fernwood Cres N20 14 D1
Fernwood Ct N14 15 D3
Ferny Hill EN4 3 A5
Ferranti Cl SE18 121 D3
Ferraro Cl TW5 129 C6
Ferrers Ave
Wallington SM6 219 D4
West Drayton UB7 104 A4
Ferrers Rd SW16 181 D5
Ferrestone Rd N8 50 B5
Ferrey Mews 19 SW9 138 C3
Ferriby Cl N1 72 C1
Ferrier Ind Est SW18 135 D1
Ferrier Point 6 E16 99 A2
Ferrier St SW18 135 D1
Ferring Cl HA2 42 A1
Ferrings SE21 161 C1
Ferris Ave CR0 223 B5
Ferris Rd SE22 140 A1
Ferron Rd E5 74 B5
Ferrour Ct N2 48 B6
Ferrybridge Ho SE11 260 D5
Ferrydale Lo 4 NW4 46 C5
Ferry Ho E5 52 B1
Ferry Island Ret Pk N17 52 A6
Ferry La
Barnes SW13 133 D6
Brentford TW8 132 A6
Lower Halliford TW17 192 C1
Richmond TW9 132 B6
Tottenham Hale N17 52 B5
Ferry Lane Ind Est E17 52 D5
Ferry Lane Prim Sch N17 52 B5
Ferrymead Ave UB6 85 C5
Ferrymead Dr UB6 85 C5
Ferrymead Gdns UB6 86 A5
Ferrymoor TW10 153 B1
Ferry Quays Ctyd 13 TW8 131 D6
Ferry Rd
Barnes SW13 134 A4
East Molesey KT8 195 C6
Richmond TW11 175 B5
Thames Ditton KT7 197 B3
Twickenham TW1 153 B3
Ferry Sq
1 Brentford TW8 132 A6
Lower Halliford TW17 192 D2
Ferry St E14 120 A1
Ferry Wks TW17 192 C1
Festing Rd SW15 134 D2
Festival Cl
Hillingdon UB10 82 D6
Sidcup DA5 168 D3
Festival Ct
Cheam SM1 201 D1
5 Dalston E8 73 D1
Festival Pier SE1 116 B5 250 C4
Festoon Way E16 121 D6
Fetherston Ct RM6 59 B3
Fetter La EC4 94 C1 241 B2
Fettes Ho NW8 229 D3
Fews Lodge RM6 58 D5
Ffinch St SE8 141 C5
Fidgeon Cl BR1 210 C6
Field Cl Bromley BR1 187 C1
Buckhurst Hill IG9 21 C1
Chessington KT9 213 C3
Chingford E4 35 D4
Cranford TW4 128 B4
East Molesey KT8 195 D4
Harlington UB7 127 A5
Ruislip HA4 39 A1
Uxbridge UB10 60 D6
Willesden NW2 68 A6
Fieldcommon La KT12 195 B1
Field Ct
Hampstead NW3 70 A3
Holborn WC1 240 D3
Lower Holloway N7 72 A3
Wimbledon SW19 157 C1
Fieldend TW11 174 D6
Field End HA4 62 C2
Field End Jun & Inf Schs HA4 62 D6
Fieldend Rd SW16 181 C2
Field End Rd HA5, HA4 40 C1
Fielders Cl
2 Enfield EN1 5 C1
Harrow HA2 42 A1
Fieldfare Rd SE28 124 C6
Fieldgate Mans 25 E1 96 A2
Fieldgate St E1 96 A2
Field Ho
4 Edmonton N9 34 A6
Kensal Green NW10 90 D4
8 Richmond TW10 153 C1
Fieldhouse Cl E18 37 B2
Fieldhouse Rd SW12 159 C3
Fielding Ave TW2 152 A1
Fielding Ho
Chiswick W4 133 C6
6 Kilburn NW6 91 C4
St John's Wood NW8 229 A6
Fielding La BR2 209 C5
Fielding Mews SW13 134 B6
Fielding Prim Sch W13 109 B3
Fielding Rd
Acton W4 111 C3
Hammersmith W14 112 D3
Fielding St SE17 139 A6
Fieldings The SE23 162 C3
Fielding Terr W5 110 B6
Field La
Brentford TW8 131 C5
Teddington TW11 175 A5
Field Lo NW10 67 D2
Field Mead NW9, NW7 27 D3
Fieldpark Gdns CR0 207 A1
Field Pl KT3 199 D3
Field Point E7 77 A4
Field Rd
Feltham TW14 150 B5
Forest Gate E7 77 A4
Fulham W6 135 A6 264 A6
Tottenham N17 51 C6
Fieldsend Rd SM3 217 A3
Fields Est E8 74 A1
Fieldside Cl BR6 227 A4
Fieldside Rd BR1 186 B5
Fields Park Cres RM6 58 D4
Field St WC1 233 C2
Fieldsway Ho N5 72 C3
Fieldview SW17, SW18 158 B3
Field View TW13 171 B6
Field View Cl RM7 59 C6
Fieldview Ct
2 Islington N5 72 D3
London NW9 44 C3
Fieldway
Dagenham RM8 80 C4
Petts Wood BR5 211 B3
Field Way
Greenford UB6 85 D6
New Addington CR0 223 D2
Ruislip HA4 39 A1
Willesden NW10 67 A1
Fieldway Cres N5, N7 72 C3
Fieldway Sta CR0 223 D1
Fieldwick Ho 14 E9 74 D2
Fiennes Cl RM8 58 C1
Fife Ct 5 W3 88 C1
Fifehead Cl TW15 170 A4
Fife Rd
Kingston u T KT2 176 A1
Mortlake SW14 155 A6
Newham E16 99 A2
Tottenham N22 32 D3
Fife Terr N1 233 D4
Fifield Path SE23 162 D1
Fifteenpenny Fields SE9 166 C6
Fifth Ave Hayes UB3 105 D5
Ilford E12 78 B4
West Kilburn W10 91 A4
Fifth Cross Rd TW2 152 B2
Fifth Way HA9 66 D4
Figge's Rd CR4 181 A3
Fig Tree Cl NW10 89 C6
Filanco Ct W7 108 D5
Filby Rd KT9 214 B2
Filey Ave N16 52 A1
Filey Cl SM2 218 A1
Filey Ho SW18 136 A1
Filey Waye HA4 62 B6
Filigree Ct SE16 119 B5
Fillebrook Ave EN1 5 D3
Fillebrook Rd E11 54 C1
Filmer Ho SW6 264 B2
Filmer Mews SW6 264 B2
Filmer Rd SW6 135 B5 264 C3
Filston Rd DA8 125 D1
Filton Cl NW9 27 C1
Filton Ct 14 SE14 140 C5
Finborough Rd
Upper Tooting SW17 180 D4
West Brompton SW10 135 D6 265 D6
Finchale Rd SE2 124 A3
Fincham Cl UB10 61 A5
Finch Ave SE27 183 B6
Finch Cl Barnet EN5 13 C6
Willesden NW10 67 B2
Finch Ct DA14 168 B1
Finchdean Ho SW15 155 D4
Finch Dr TW14 150 D4
Finch Gdns E4 35 C5
Finch Ho 1 SE8 141 D5
Finchingfield Ave IG8 37 C3
Finch La EC2, EC3 242 D1
FINCHLEY 29 D3
Finchley Central Sta N3 29 C2
Finchley Ct N3 29 D4
Finchley La NW4 46 D5
Finchley Lido L Ctr N12 30 B3
Finchley Lo N12 29 D5
Finchley Meml Hospl N12 30 A3
Finchley Pk N12 30 B6
Finchley Pl NW8 229 C4
Finchley RC High Sch N12 13 D1
Finchley Rd
Hampstead NW3 70 A2
London NW11 47 B3
St John's Wood NW8 229 C4
Finchley Road & Frognal Sta NW3 70 A3
Finchley Road Sta NW3 70 A2
Finchley Way N3 29 C3
Finch Lo 15 W9 91 C2
Finch Mews 3 SE15 139 D4
Finch's Ct 10 E14 119 D6
Finden Rd E7 77 C3
Findhorn Ave UB4 84 B2
Findhorn St 8 E14 98 A1
Findon Cl Harrow HA2 63 D5
Wandsworth SW18 157 C5
Findon Rd
Edmonton N9 18 B3
Shepherd's Bush W12 112 A4
Fine Bush La HA4 38 D3
Fineran Ct 16 SW11 136 B1
Fingal St SE10 120 D1
Fingest Ho NW8 237 A6
Finians Cl UB10 60 B1
Finland Rd SE4 141 A2
Finland St SE16 119 A3
Finlays Cl KT9 214 C3
Finlay St SW6 134 D4
Finley Ct 21 SE5 139 A5
Finmere Ho 1 N4 51 A2
Finnemore Ho N1 235 A6
Finney La TW7 131 A4
Finn Ho N1 235 D2
Finnis St E2 96 B3
Finnymore Rd RM9 81 A1
FINSBURY 94 C4
Finsbury Ave EC2 242 D3
Finsbury Cir EC2 95 B2 242 D3
Finsbury Cotts N22 32 A3
Finsbury Ct EC2 242 C4
Finsbury Ho N22 32 A2
Finsbury L Ctr EC1 95 A3 235 A1
Finsbury Market EC2 243 A4
Finsbury Mkt EC2 243 A5
FINSBURY PARK 72 C6
Finsbury Park Ave N4 51 A3
Finsbury Park Rd N4, N5 72 D6
Finsbury Park Sta N4 72 C6
Finsbury Pavement EC2 95 B2 242 D4
Finsbury Rd N22 32 B2
Finsbury Sq EC2 95 B2 242 D4
Finsbury St EC2 242 C4
Finsbury Way DA5 169 B5
Finsen Rd SE5 139 A2
Finstock Rd W10 90 D1
Finton House Sch SW17 158 D2
Finucane Ct TW9 132 B2
Finucane Rise WD23 8 A2
Finwhale Ho E14 119 D3
Fiona Ct Enfield EN2 4 D2
9 Kilburn NW6 91 B5
Firbank Cl Enfield EN2 5 A1
Newham E16 99 D2
Firbank Rd SE15 140 B3
Fir Cl KT12 194 A2
Fircroft N1 94 D6 234 D6
Fircroft Gdns HA1 64 C5
Fircroft Prim Sch SW17 158 D1

Fircroft Rd
Chessington KT9 214 B4
Upper Tooting SW17 158 D1
Firdene KT5 199 A1
Fir Dene BR6 226 C5
Fire Bell Alley KT6 198 A3
Firebell Mews KT6 198 A3
Fire Brigade Cotts HA5 41 C5
Fire Brigade Pier SE1 260 B4
Firecrest Dr NW3 69 D5
Firefly 7 NW9 27 D1
Firefly Gdns E6 100 A3
Firemans Cotts N10 49 A6
Fireman's Flats N22 32 A2
Firepower (The Royal Artillery Mus)★ SE18 122 D3
Fire Station Alley EN5 1 A3
Fire Station Flats TW7 130 C3
Fire Station Mews 4 BR3 185 D2
Firethorn Cl 4 HA8 27 A6
Fir Gr KT3 199 D3
Fir Grove Rd 25 SW9 138 C3
Firhill Rd SE6 163 C1
Fir Island NW7 28 C5
Firle Ho 7 W10 90 C2
Fir Lo SW15 134 B1
Firmans Ct E17 54 B5
Firmston Ho 9 SW14 133 B2
Fir Rd Cheam SM3 201 B1
Feltham TW13 172 D5
Firs Ave
Fortis Green N10 49 A5
Friern Barnet N11 31 A4
Mortlake SW14 133 A1
Firsby Ave CR0 207 A1
Firsby Rd N16 52 A1
Firs Cl Claygate KT10 212 C2
Forest Hill SE23 163 A4
Mitcham CR4 181 B2
Muswell Hill N10 49 A6
Firscroft N13 17 A1
Firs Dr TW5 128 B5
Firs Farm Prim Sch N13 17 B1
Firs Ho N22 32 C2
Firside Gr DA15 167 D3
Firs La N21, N13 17 A2
Firs Park Ave N21 17 B3
Firs Park Gdns N21 17 B3
First Ave Bexley DA7 146 C5
Chadwell Heath RM6 58 C4
Dagenham RM10 103 D5
East Acton W3 111 D5
East Molesey KT8 195 C5
Edmonton N18 34 C6
Enfield EN1 17 D6
Hayes UB3 105 D5
Hendon NW4 46 C5
Manor Pk E12 78 A3
Mortlake SW14 133 C2
Newham E13 99 A4
Walthamstow E17 53 D4
Walton-on-T KT12 194 B3
Wembley HA9 65 D6
West Kilburn W10 91 B3
First Cl KT8 196 A6
First Cross Rd TW2 152 C2
First Dr NW10 67 A1
Firs The
Belmont SM2 217 D1
Claygate KT10 212 C2
Ealing W5 87 D2
Forest Hill SE26 184 C5
Oakleigh Pk N20 14 B3
2 Penge SE26 184 B5
Sidcup DA15 167 D1
Upton Pk E6 78 A1
Wimbledon SW20 178 A3
Woodford IG8 37 C3
First St SW3 114 C2 257 B4
Firstway SW20 178 C1
First Way HA9 66 D4
Firs Wlk IG8 37 A5
Firswood Ave KT19 215 D3
Firth Gdns SW6 135 A4 264 A1
Firtree Ave CR4 181 A1
Fir Tree Ave UB7 104 C3
Fir Tree Cl Ealing W5 88 A1
Fir Tree Cl *continued*
Esher KT10 212 A3
5 Orpington BR6 227 D3
Streatham SW16 181 C5
Worcester Pk KT19 215 D4
Firtree Ct BR2 208 D6
Fir Tree Gdns CR0 223 C4
Fir Tree Gr SM5 218 D1
Firtree Ho SE13 164 B4
Fir Tree Ho 11 SE14 140 C5
Firtree Lodge N21 17 A2
Fir Tree Rd TW4 129 A1
Fir Trees Cl SE16 119 A5
Fir Tree Wlk EN1 5 B2
Fir Wlk KT17, SM3 216 D2
Fisher Cl
Croydon CR0 205 D1
Holdbrook EN3 7 C6
Southall UB6 85 C4
Fisherdene KT10 213 A1
Fisher Ho
Islington N1 234 A5
9 Shadwell E1 118 C6
2 Tufnell Pk N19 71 C5
Fisherman Cl TW10 175 C6
Fishermans Dr SE16 118 D4
Fishermans Wlk SE28 123 C4
Fisherman's Wlk E14 119 C5
Fisher Rd HA3 24 D1
Fishers Cl SW16 159 D1
Fishers Ct
London SE14 140 D4
6 Teddington TW11 174 D5
Fisher's La W4 111 B2
Fisher St
Holborn WC1 240 C3
Newham E16 99 A2
Fisherton St NW8 92 B3 236 D6
Fisherton Street Est NW8 92 B3 236 D5
Fishguard Way E16 122 D5
Fishlock Ct 6 SW4 138 A3
Fishponds Rd
Keston BR2 225 D3
Upper Tooting SW17 180 C6
Fish St Hill EC3 252 D5
Fisk Cl TW16 171 D4
Fiske Ct Barking IG11 101 B5
1 Merton SW19 180 A3
Sutton SM2 218 A1
Tottenham N17 34 A2
Fitch Ct London SW2 160 C6
8 Mitcham CR4 181 A1
Fitzalan Rd
Church End N3 47 B6
Claygate KT10 212 C1
Fitzalan St SE11 116 C2 261 A4
Fitzclarence Ho W11 244 A2
Fitzgeorge Ave KT2, KT3 177 B2
Fitz-George Ave W14 254 A3
Fitzgerald Ave SW14 133 C2
Fitzgerald Ct 1 E10 53 D1
Fitzgerald Ho
15 Brixton SW9 138 C3
Hayes UB3 106 B5
14 Poplar E14 97 D1
Fitzgerald Rd
Mortlake SW14 133 B2
Thames Ditton KT7 197 A3
Wanstead E11 55 A4
Fitzhardinge Ho
Beckenham BR3 185 D1
Marylebone W1 238 A2
Fitzhardinge St W1 238 A2
Fitzherbert Ho 11 TW10 154 B5
Fitzhugh Gr SW18 158 B5
Fitzjames Ave
Croydon CR0 222 A6
West Kensington W14 254 B3
Fitzjohn Ave EN5 1 B1
Fitzjohn's Ave NW3 70 B3
Fitzjohns Mans NW3 70 A2
Fitzjohns Prim Sch 4 NW3 70 B3
Fitzmaurice Ho 17 SE16 118 B2
Fitzmaurice Pl W1 248 D4
Fitzneal St W12 89 D1
FITZROVIA 93 C2
Fitzroy Cl N6 48 D1
Fitzroy Cres W4 133 B5
Fitzroy Ct London N6 49 C3
Marylebone W1 239 B5
Fitzroy Gdns SE19 183 C3
Fitzroy Ho
Bermondsey SE1 263 D2
12 Tower Hamlets E14 97 B1
Fitzroy Lo N21 16 D6
Fitzroy Mews W1 239 A5
Fitzroy Pk N6 48 D1
Fitzroy Rd NW1 93 A6 231 A6
Fitzroy Sq W1 239 A5
Fitzroy St W1 93 C3 239 A5
Fitzroy Yd NW1 231 A6
Fitzstephen Rd RM8 80 C3
Fitzwarren Gdns N19 49 C1
Fitzwilliam Ave TW9 132 B3
Fitzwilliam Cl 8 EN4 14 D3
Fitzwilliam Ho
4 Higham Hill E17 35 A1
Richmond TW9 131 D1
Fitzwilliam Hts 1 SE23 162 C2
Fitzwilliam Mews E16 121 A5
Fitzwilliam Rd SW4 137 C2
Fitzwygram Cl TW12 174 A5
Five Acre NW9 27 D1
Fiveacre Cl CR7 204 C3
Five Arch Bridge DA14 191 A6
Five Arches Bsns Pk DA14 190 D4
Five Elms Prim Sch RM8 81 B5
Five Elms Rd
Dagenham RM9 81 B5
Keston Mark BR2 225 C5
Five Oaks Mews BR1 165 A1
Fives Ct SE11 261 C5
Fiveways
Chislehurst SE9 166 D2
Croydon CR0 220 C4
Ruislip HA4 39 B1
Five Ways Bsns Ctr TW13 150 B1
Five Ways Cnr NW4 28 A2
Fiveways Rd SW9 138 C3
Flack Ct 15 E10 53 D2
Fladbury Rd N15 51 B3
Fladgate Rd E11 54 C3
Flag Cl CR0 206 D1
Flag Wlk HA5 40 A3
Flambard Rd HA1, HA3 43 A3
Flamborough Ho 12 SE15 140 A4
Flamborough Rd HA4 62 A5
Flamborough St E14 97 A1
Flamingo Ct 2 SE8 141 C5
Flamingo Gdns UB5 85 A4
Flamstead Gdns RM9 80 C1
Flamstead Rd RM9 80 C1
Flamsted Ave HA9 66 C2
Flamsteed Ct 15 SE13 141 D4
Flamsteed Ho★ SE10 142 B5
Flamsteed Rd SE7 122 A1
Flanchford Rd W12 111 D3
Flanders Cres SW17 180 D4
Flanders Ct E17 53 A3
Flanders Ho N16 73 C5
Flanders Mans 1 W4 111 D2
Flanders Rd
Acton W4 111 C2
Wallend E6 100 C5
Flanders Way E9 74 D2
Flandrian Cl EN3 7 D5
Flank St 9 E1 118 A6
Flansham Ho 2 E14 97 B1
Flash La EN2 5 A6
Flask Cotts 4 NW3 70 B4
Flask Wlk NW3 70 B4
Flatford Ho 2 SE6 186 A6
Flather Cl 12 SW16 181 C5
Flatiron Sq SE1 252 B3
Flatiron Yd SE1 252 B3
Flavell Mews SE10 120 C1
Flaxen Cl E4 19 D1
Flaxen Rd E4 19 D1
Flaxley Rd SM4 201 D2
Flaxman Ct
12 Belvedere DA17 125 C1
Soho W1 239 C1
Flaxman Ho
10 Chiswick W4 111 C1
Newington SE1 261 D6
Flaxman Rd SE5 138 D3
Flaxman Sp Ctr SE5 139 A3
Flaxman Terr WC1 93 D4 232 D1
Flaxman Villas N2 48 A6
Flaxmore Ct
Erith DA7 147 D2
South Norwood CR7 183 B1
Flaxton Rd SE18 145 C5
Flecker Cl HA7 24 D5
Flecker Ho 6 SE5 139 B5
Fleece Dr N9 34 A6
Fleecefield Prim Sch N18 34 A6
Fleece Rd KT6 197 C1
Fleece Wlk N7 72 A2
Fleeming Cl E17 35 B1
Fleeming Rd E17 35 B1
Fleet Cl
East Molesey KT8 195 B4
Ruislip HA4 39 A3
Fleet Ct 1 W12 111 C3
Fleetfield WC1 233 B2
Fleet Ho
6 Brixton SW2 160 C6
4 Limehouse E14 119 A6
Fleet Pl EC4 241 C2
Fleet Prim Sch 15 NW3 70 D3
Fleet Rd NW3 70 D3
Fleetside KT8 195 C4
Fleet Sq WC1 233 D1
Fleet St EC4 94 C1 241 B1
Fleet Street Hill 10 E1 96 A3
Fleet Terr SE6 164 A4
Fleetway WC1 233 B2
Fleetway West Bsns Pk UB6 87 B5
Fleet Wood 6 N16 73 D6
Fleetwood Cl
Chessington KT9 213 D1
Newham E16 99 D2
South Croydon CR0 221 D5
Fleetwood Ct
1 Newham E6 100 B2
Orpington BR6 226 C4
8 Stanwell TW19 148 A5
Fleetwood Rd
Kingston u T KT3 198 D6
Willesden NW10 68 A3
Fleetwood Sq KT3 198 D6
Fleetwood St N16 73 C6
Fleetwood Way WD19 22 C6
Fleming Cl 4 W9 91 C3
Fleming Ct
Croydon CR0 220 C3
Paddington W2 236 C4
Fleming Dr N21 16 B6
Fleming Ho
14 Bermondsey SE16 118 A4
Finsbury Pk N4 51 A1
5 Wembley HA9 67 A5
Fleming Mead CR4 180 D3
Fleming Rd
Camberwell SE17 138 D6
Southall UB1 86 A1
Fleming Way
Isleworth TW7 130 D1
Thamesmead SE28 124 D6
Fleming Wlk NW9 27 C1
Flemming Ave HA4 62 B6
Flempton Rd E10 53 A1
Fletcher Bldgs WC2 240 B1
Fletcher Cl E16 122 D6
Fletcher Ct 9 NW5 71 B4
Fletcher Ho 16 N16 73 C4
Fletcher La E10 54 A2
Fletcher Path 7 SE8 141 C5
Fletcher Rd W4 111 A3
Fletchers Cl BR2 209 B5
Fletcher St 16 E1 118 A6
Fletching Rd
Charlton SE7 143 D6
Lower Clapton E5 74 C5
Fletton Rd N11 32 A3
Fleur De Lis St E1 243 C5
Fleur Gates 7 SW19 156 D4
Flexmere Rd N17 33 C2
Flimwell Cl BR1 186 C5
Flinders Ho 28 E1 118 B5
Flint Cl
8 Green Street Green BR6 227 D2
1 Stratford E15 76 D1
Flint Ct CR0 204 B3
Flint Down Cl BR5 190 A2
Flintmill Cres SE3, SE9 144 A3
Flinton St SE17 117 C1 263 B2
Flint St SE17 117 B2 262 D3
Flitcroft St WC2 239 D1
Flitton Ho 7 N1 72 D1
Floathaven Cl SE28 124 A5
Flock Mill Pl SW18 157 D3
Flockton St
20 Bermondsey SE16 118 A4
3 Bermondsey SE16 118 A4
Flodden Rd SE5 139 A4
Flood La 5 TW1 153 A3
Flood St SW3 136 C6 267 B6
Flood Wlk SW3 136 C6 267 B6
Flora Cl Edgware HA7 10 A1
Poplar E14 97 D1
Flora Gardens Prim Sch 17 W6 112 B2
Flora Gdns
Dagenham RM6 58 C3
2 Hammersmith W6 112 B2
Floral St WC2 116 A6 250 A6
Flora St DA17 125 B1
Florence Ave
Enfield EN2 5 A2
Morden SM4 202 A4
Florence Cl KT12 194 B2
Florence Ct
18 New Barnet EN5 13 D6
St John's Wood W9 229 B1
Wanstead E11 55 C5
5 Wimbledon SW19 179 A4
Florence Dr EN2 5 A2
Florence Elson Cl E12 78 C4
Florence Gdns
Chiswick W4 133 A6
Ilford RM6 58 C2
Florence Ho
20 Bermondsey SE16 118 B1
2 Brixton SW2 160 B6
Kidbrooke SE18 144 B4
5 Kingston u T KT2 176 B3
10 Shepherd's Bush W11 112 D6
7 Wandsworth SW18 136 B1
Florence Mans
Fulham SW6 264 C2
4 Hendon NW4 46 B4
Florence Nightingale Ho 14 N1 73 A2
Florence Nightingale Mus★ SE1 250 D1
Florence Rd
Abbey Wood SE2 124 C2
Acton W4 111 B3
5 Beckenham BR3 185 A1
Bromley BR1 187 A2
Ealing W5 110 A6
Feltham TW13 150 B3
Finsbury Pk N4 50 C2
6 Kingston u T KT2 176 B3
New Cross Gate SE14 141 B4
Southall UB2 106 D3
7 Upton Pk E6 99 C6
Walton-on-T KT12 194 B2
West Ham E13 99 A5
Wimbledon SW19 179 D4
Florence Root Ho 3 IG4 56 B4
Florence St
Islington N1 72 D1
London NW4 46 C5

Florence St *continued*
Newham E16 ... 98 D3
Florence Terr
Kingston u T SW15 ... 155 C1
New Cross Gate SE14 ... 141 B4
Florence Way SW12 ... 158 D3
Florence White Ct N9 ... 18 B1
Florentine Ho 3 IG1 ... 78 D6
Flores Ho 13 E1 ... 96 D2
Florey Sq N21 ... 16 B6
Florfield Rd E8 ... 74 B2
Florian SE5 ... 139 C4
Florian Ave SM1 ... 218 B4
Florian Rd SW15 ... 135 A1
Florida Cl WD23 ... 8 B2
Florida Ct BR2 ... 208 D5
Florida Rd CR7 ... 182 D2
Florida St E2 ... 96 A4
Florida State Univ
WC1 ... 93 D2 239 D3
Florin Ct
Bermondsey SE1 ... 253 C1
Edmonton N18 ... 33 C6
8 St George in t East
SE1 ... 118 A6
Floris Pl 7 SW4 ... 137 C2
Floriston Ave UB10 ... 61 A1
Floriston Cl HA7 ... 25 B2
Floriston Ct UB5 ... 63 D3
Floriston Gdns HA7 ... 25 B2
Florys Ct 7 SW19 ... 157 A3
Floss St SW15 ... 134 C3
Flower & Dean Wlk
E1 ... 243 D3
Flower La NW7 ... 27 D4
Flower Mews NW11 ... 47 A3
Flowerpot Cl N15 ... 51 D3
Flower Pot Cl N15 ... 51 D3
Flowers Cl NW2 ... 68 A5
Flowersmead SW17 ... 159 A2
Flowers Mews 1
N19 ... 71 C6
Flower Wlk The
SW7 ... 114 A4 246 B2
Floyd Rd SE7 ... 121 C1
Floyer Cl TW10 ... 154 B6
Fludyer St SE13 ... 142 C1
Flynn Ct 19 E14 ... 119 C6
Fogerty Cl EN3 ... 7 D6
Foley Cotts KT10 ... 212 D2
Foley Ct N12 ... 30 A5
Foley Ho 19 E1 ... 96 C1
Foley Mews KT10 ... 212 C2
Foley Rd KT10 ... 212 C1
Foley St W1 ... 93 C2 239 A3
Folgate St E1 ... 95 D2 243 C4
Foliot Ho N1 ... 233 C4
Foliot St W12 ... 89 D1
Folkestone Ct UB5 ... 63 D3
Folkestone Rd
Edmonton N18 ... 34 A6
Wallend E6 ... 100 C4
Walthamstow E17 ... 53 D5
Folkingham La 6
NW9 ... 27 C2
Folkington Cnr N12 ... 29 B5
Folland 6 NW9 ... 27 D1
Follett Ho SW10 ... 266 C4
Follett St E14 ... 98 A1
Folly La
Higham Hill E17 ... 35 A2
Walthamstow E4 ... 35 B3
Folly's End Christian Sch
CR2 ... 221 C4
Folly Wall E14 ... 120 A4
Fonda Ct 14 E14 ... 119 C6
Fontaine Ct
3 Beckenham BR3 ... 185 B2
Southgate N14 ... 15 D2
Fontaine Rd SW16 ... 182 B3
Fontarabia Rd SW11 ... 137 A1
Fontenelle SE5 ... 139 C4
Fontenoy Ho SE11 ... 261 C3
Fontenoy Rd SW12,
SW17 ... 159 C2
Fonteyne Gdns IG8 ... 37 D1
Fonthill Cl SE20 ... 184 A1
Fonthill Ct SE23 ... 162 C4
Fonthill Ho
Kensington W14 ... 254 B6
Pimlico SW1 ... 258 D2
Fonthill Mews N4 ... 72 B6
Fonthill Rd N4 ... 72 C6
Font Hills N2 ... 30 A1
Fontley Way SW15 ... 156 A4
Fontmell Cl TW15 ... 170 C5
Fontmell Pk TW15 ... 170 C5
Fontwell Cl
Harrow HA3 ... 24 C3
Northolt UB5 ... 63 C2
Fontwell Dr BR2 ... 210 C4
Football La HA1 ... 42 C1
Footpath The SW15 ... 156 A6
FOOTS CRAY ... 190 B4
Foots Cray High St
DA14 ... 190 D4
Foots Cray La DA14 ... 168 C3
Footscray Rd SE9 ... 166 D3
Forber Ho 25 E2 ... 96 C4
Forbes Cl NW2 ... 68 A5
Forbes Ct SE19 ... 183 C5
Forbes Ho 2 W4 ... 110 C1
Forbes St E1 ... 96 A1
Forbes Way HA4 ... 62 B6
Forburg Rd N16 ... 52 A1
Fordbridge Ct TW15 ... 170 A4
Fordbridge Rd
Ashford TW15 ... 170 B5
Lower Halliford TW16,
TW17 ... 193 D3
Sunbury TW16 ... 194 A5
Fordbridge Rdbt
TW15 ... 170 A4
Ford Cl
Ashford TW15 ... 170 A4
12 Bow E3 ... 97 A5
Harrow HA1 ... 42 B2
Littleton TW17 ... 192 C4
Thornton Heath CR7 ... 204 D4
Fordcombe 18 NW5 ... 71 A2
Forde Ave BR1 ... 209 C6
Fordel Rd SE6 ... 164 B3
Ford End IG8 ... 37 B4
Fordham 4 KT1 ... 176 C1
Fordham Cl
Cockfosters EN4 ... 2 C2
North Cheam KT4 ... 200 B1
Fordham Ho 11
SE14 ... 141 A5
Fordham Rd EN4 ... 2 C2
Fordham St 13 E1 ... 96 A1
Ford Ho
2 New Barnet EN5 ... 13 D6
2 Woolwich SE18 ... 122 D1
Fordhook Ave W5 ... 110 C6
Fordingley Rd W9 ... 91 B4
Fordington Ho 2
SE26 ... 162 B1
Fordington Rd N6 ... 48 D5
Fordmill Rd SE6 ... 163 C2
Ford Rd
Ashford TW15 ... 170 B6
Bow E3 ... 97 B5
Dagenham RM10 ... 81 C1
Ford's Gr N21 ... 17 A3
Fords Park Rd E16 ... 99 A1
Ford Sq E1 ... 96 B2
Ford St Bow E3 ... 97 A5
Canning Town E16 ... 98 D1
Fordwich Cl BR6 ... 211 D2
Fordwych Ct NW2 ... 69 A2
Fordwych Rd NW2 ... 69 A3
Fordyce Ho 3
SW16 ... 181 C6
Fordyce Rd SE13 ... 164 A6
Fordyke Rd RM8 ... 81 B6
Forecastle Ct E14 ... 119 C4
Foreign &
Commonwealth Office
SW1 ... 250 A2
Foreland Ct NW4 ... 29 A2
Foreland Ho W11 ... 244 A6
Foreland St SE18 ... 123 B2
Foreshore SE8 ... 119 B2
Fore St
Barbican EC2 ... 95 A2 242 B3
Edmonton N18 ... 34 A6
Pinner HA5 ... 40 A4
Forest App
Chingford E4 ... 20 C4
Woodford IG8 ... 37 A3
Forest Ave E4 ... 20 C4
Forest Bsns Pk E17 ... 52 D2
Forest Cl
Brondesbury NW6 ... 69 A1
Chislehurst BR7 ... 188 C2
Wanstead E11 ... 55 A4
Woodford IG8 ... 37 B6
Forest Ct Chingford E4 ... 20 D3
Forest Ct *continued*
Leytonstone E11 ... 54 C5
14 Woodside Pk N12 ... 29 D6
Forestdale N14 ... 31 D6
Forestdale Ctr The
CR0 ... 223 B1
Forestdale Prim Sch
CR0 ... 223 B1
Forest Dene Ct 2
SM2 ... 218 A2
Forest Dr
Ashford TW16 ... 171 D3
Chingford IG8 ... 36 C3
Keston Mark BR2 ... 226 A4
Wanstead E12 ... 77 D5
Forest Dr E E11 ... 54 B3
Forest Dr W E11 ... 54 B2
Forest Edge IG9 ... 21 D1
Forester Rd SE15 ... 140 B2
Foresters Cl SM6 ... 219 D1
Foresters Cres DA7 ... 147 D1
Foresters Dr
Wallington SM6 ... 219 D1
Walthamstow E17 ... 54 B5
Foresters Homes The
DA7 ... 147 D1
Foresters Prim Sch
SM6 ... 219 D1
FOREST GATE ... 77 A3
Forest Gate NW9 ... 45 C4
Forest Gate Com Sch
E7 ... 77 A3
Forest Gate Sta E7 ... 77 A3
Forest Gdns N17 ... 33 D1
Forest Glade
Chingford E4 ... 36 C5
Leytonstone E11 ... 54 C3
Forest Gr E8 ... 73 D2
FOREST HILL ... 163 A3
Forest Hill SE23 ... 162 C3
Forest Hill Bsns Ctr
SE23 ... 162 C2
Forest Hill Ct 6
SE26 ... 162 B1
Forest Hill Ind Est
SE23 ... 162 C2
Forest Hill Rd SE22 ... 162 B5
Forest Hill Sec Sch
SE23 ... 162 D1
Forest Hill Sta SE23 ... 162 C2
Forest Ho 9 E4 ... 20 C4
Forestholme Cl
SE23 ... 162 C2
Forest Ho The SE23 ... 163 A3
Forest Hts IG9 ... 21 A2
Forest La E7, E15 ... 76 D3
Forest Lawns BR1 ... 187 C2
Forest Lea 3 E11 ... 54 D2
Forest Lo 1 SE23 ... 162 C1
Forest Mount Rd IG8 ... 36 B3
Forest Point E7 ... 77 B3
Forest Rd Dalston E8 ... 73 D2
Edmonton N9 ... 18 B3
Feltham TW13 ... 150 C1
Forest Gate E7 ... 77 A4
Leytonstone E11 ... 54 B2
Morden SM3, SM4 ... 201 C2
Richmond TW9 ... 132 C5
Romford RM7 ... 59 D6
Walthamstow E17 ... 53 C6
Woodford IG8 ... 21 A1
Fore Street Ave EC2 ... 242 C3
Forest Ridge
Beckenham BR3 ... 207 C6
Bromley BR2 ... 226 B4
Forest Rise E17 ... 54 B5
Forest Sch E17 ... 54 C5
Forest Side
Buckhurst Hill IG9 ... 21 C3
Chingford E4 ... 20 D3
Forest Gate E7 ... 77 B4
New Malden KT4 ... 199 D1
Forest St E7 ... 77 A3
Forest The E11 ... 54 C5
Forest Trad Est E17 ... 52 D6
Forest View
Chingford E4 ... 20 B4
Leytonstone E11 ... 54 D2
Forest View Ave E10 ... 54 B4
Forest View Rd
Chingford E17 ... 36 A2
Manor Pk E12 ... 78 A4
Forest Way
Orpington BR5 ... 211 D4
Sidcup DA15 ... 167 B4
Forest Way *continued*
9 Upper Holloway
N19 ... 71 C6
Woodford IG8 ... 37 B6
Forest Wlk N10 ... 31 B2
Forfar Rd
London
SW11 ... 137 A4 268 B2
Tottenham N22 ... 32 D2
Forge Cl
Harlington UB3 ... 127 B6
Hayes BR2 ... 209 A1
Forge Cotts W5 ... 109 D5
Forge Dr KT10 ... 213 A1
Forge La
Belmont SM3 ... 217 A1
Feltham TW13 ... 173 A5
Richmond TW10 ... 154 A3
Sunbury TW16 ... 194 A6
Forge Lane Prim Sch
TW13 ... 173 A5
Forge Lo 2 TW7 ... 131 A2
Forge Mews
Addington CR0 ... 223 C3
Sunbury TW16 ... 194 A6
Forge Pl NW1 ... 71 A2
Forlong Path UB5 ... 63 A2
Forman Ct TW1 ... 152 D3
Forman Ho SE4 ... 140 D1
Formby Ave HA3, HA7 ... 43 C6
Formby Ct 9 N7 ... 72 C3
Formosa Ho 1 E1 ... 97 A3
Formosa St W9 ... 91 D3
Formunt Cl E16 ... 98 D2
Forres Gdns NW11 ... 47 C3
Forrest Ct N7 ... 72 C2
Forrester Path SE26 ... 184 C6
Forresters The HA5 ... 40 B3
Forrest Gdns SW16 ... 204 B6
Forrest Ho SW15 ... 134 C3
Forris Ave UB3 ... 105 D5
Forset Ct W1 ... 237 B2
Forset St W1 ... 92 C1 237 B2
Forstal Cl BR2 ... 209 A6
Forster Cl IG8 ... 36 B3
Forster Ho SE6 ... 164 B1
Forster Park Prim Sch
SE6 ... 164 C1
Forster Rd
Beckenham BR3 ... 207 A6
Streatham SW2 ... 160 A4
Thornton Heath CR0 ... 205 A2
Tottenham N17 ... 51 D6
Walthamstow E17 ... 53 A3
Forsters Cl RM6 ... 59 B3
Forsters Way UB4 ... 84 B1
Forston St N1 ... 95 A5 235 B4
Forsyte Cres SE19 ... 183 C2
Forsyte Ct KT2 ... 176 D2
Forsyth Ct
13 Dagenham RM10 ... 81 D2
Harrow HA1 ... 42 B3
Kingston u T KT3 ... 177 C1
Forsythe Shades
BR3 ... 186 A2
Forsyth Gdns SE17 ... 138 D6
Forsyth Ho
14 Hackney E9 ... 74 C1
Pimlico SW1 ... 259 B3
Forsythia Cl IG1 ... 78 D3
Forsythia Ho SE4 ... 141 A2
Forsyth Pl EN1 ... 17 C6
Forterie Gdns IG3 ... 80 A4
Fortescue Ave
1 Hackney E8 ... 74 B1
Twickenham TW2 ... 152 A1
Fortescue Rd
Burnt Oak HA8 ... 27 B3
Mitcham SW19 ... 180 B3
Fortess Gr NW5 ... 71 C3
Fortess Rd NW5 ... 71 C4
Fortess Wlk NW5 ... 71 B3
Forthbridge Rd
SW11 ... 137 A1
Forth Ho 30 E3 ... 97 B5
Forties The 9 NW5 ... 71 C3
Fortior Ct N6 ... 49 C2
Fortis Cl E16 ... 99 C1
Fortis Ct N10 ... 49 A6
Fortis Gn N2, N10 ... 48 D6
FORTIS GREEN ... 48 D5
Fortis Green Ave N2 ... 48 D5
Fortis Green Cotts
N2 ... 48 D6
Fortismere Ave N10 ... 49 A6
Fortismere Sch N10 ... 30 D1
Fortismere Sch (South
Wing) N10 ... 49 A6
Fortnam Rd N19 ... 71 D6
Fortnums Acre HA7 ... 24 D4
Fort Rd
Bermondsey
SE1 ... 117 D2 263 D3
Northolt UB5 ... 63 C1
Fortrose Cl E14 ... 98 B1
Fortrose Gdns SW12,
SW2 ... 160 A3
Fort St Broadgate E1 ... 243 B3
Newham E16 ... 121 B5
Fortuna Cl N7 ... 72 B2
Fortune Ave HA8 ... 26 D2
Fortune Ct
Barking IG11 ... 102 B5
6 Dalston E8 ... 73 D1
Fortune Gate Rd
NW10 ... 89 C6
Fortune Green Rd
NW6 ... 69 C4
Fortune Ho
Lambeth SE11 ... 261 A3
St Luke's EC1 ... 242 B5
Fortune La WD6 ... 9 D5
Fortunes Mead UB5 ... 63 A2
Fortune St
EC1 ... 95 A3 242 B5
Fortune Way NW10 ... 90 A4
Fortune Wlk 4
SE28 ... 123 B3
Forty Acre La E16 ... 99 A2
Forty Ave HA9 ... 66 B6
Forty Cl HA9 ... 66 B5
Forty Hall Mus & Gdns*
EN2 ... 5 D6
FORTY HILL ... 5 D4
Forty Hill EN2 ... 5 D5
Forty Hill CE Prim Sch
EN2 ... 6 A6
Forty Hill Ho EN1 ... 5 D5
Forty La HA9 ... 66 D6
Forum Cl 7 E3 ... 97 C6
Forumside HA8 ... 26 C4
Forum The KT8 ... 195 D5
Forval Cl CR4 ... 202 D4
Forward Bsns Ctr The 3
E16 ... 98 B3
Forward Dr HA3 ... 42 D5
Fosbrooke Ho SW8 ... 270 A3
Fosbury Ho 7 SW9 ... 138 B1
Fosbury Mews W2 ... 245 D5
Foscote Mews W9 ... 91 C2
Foscote Rd NW4 ... 46 B3
Foskett Ho 21 N2 ... 30 B1
Foskett Rd SW6 ... 135 B3
Foss Ave CR0, CR9 ... 220 C3
Fossdene Prim Sch 4
SE7 ... 121 B1
Fossdene Rd SE7 ... 121 B1
Fossdyke Cl UB4 ... 85 A2
Fosse Way W13 ... 87 A2
Fossil Rd SE13 ... 141 C2
Fossington Rd DA17 ... 124 D2
Foss Rd SW17 ... 180 B6
Fossway RM8 ... 80 C6
Foster Ct
6 Camden Town
NW1 ... 71 C1
Canning Town E16 ... 120 D6
Hendon NW4 ... 46 C5
Foster Ho SE14 ... 141 B4
Foster La EC2 ... 95 A1 242 A2
Foster Rd Acton W3 ... 111 C6
Chiswick W4 ... 111 B1
Newham E13 ... 99 A3
Fosters Cl
Elmstead BR7 ... 188 B5
Woodford E18 ... 37 B2
Fosters Old Sch
DA16 ... 146 B3
Foster's Prim Sch
DA16 ... 146 C2
Foster St NW4 ... 46 C5
Foster Wlk NW4 ... 46 C5
Fothergill Cl E13 ... 99 A5
Fothergill Dr N21 ... 16 A6
Fotheringham Ct EN1 ... 5 D1
Fotheringham Rd EN1 ... 5 D1
Foubert's Pl W1 ... 239 A1
Foulden Rd N16 ... 73 D4
Foulden Terr N16 ... 73 D4
Foulis Terr
SW7 ... 114 B1 256 D2
Foulser Rd SW17 ... 159 A1

Foulsham Rd CR7 205 B6
Foundary Ho 6 E14 97 D2
Founder Cl 2 E6 100 D1
Founders Cl UB5 85 B4
Founders Ct EC2 242 C2
Founders Gdns
SE19 183 A3
Founders Ho SW1 259 C2
Foundling Ct WC1 240 A6
Foundling Mus The*
WC1 94 A3 240 B6
Foundry Cl SE16 119 A5
Foundry Mews NW1 239 B6
Foundry Pl Stepney E1 96 C2
Wandsworth SW18 157 D4
Fountain Cl UB8 83 A2
Fountain Ct
Belgravia SW1 258 C3
Blackfen DA15 168 B5
New Malden KT3 199 A5
5 Penge SE26 184 C4
14 Shepherd's Bush
W11 112 D4
Strand EC4 251 A6
Fountain Dr
Dulwich SE19 183 D6
Wallington SM5 218 D1
Fountain Green Sq 34
SE16 118 A4
Fountain Ho
33 Bermondsey
SE16 118 A4
3 Brondesbury Pk
NW6 69 A1
Mayfair W1 248 A4
5 Mitcham SW19 180 D1
Fountain Mews
1 Highbury N5 73 A4
Maitland Pk NW3 70 D2
Fountain Pl SW9 138 C4
Fountain Rd
South Norwood CR7 183 A1
Upper Tooting SW17 180 B6
Fountains Ave TW13 151 B1
Fountains Cl TW13 151 B1
Fountains Cres N14 16 A4
Fountains The
London N3 29 D3
Loughton IG10 21 D4
Fountayne Bsns Ctr
N15 52 A5
Fountayne Rd
South Tottenham N15 52 A5
Stoke Newington N16 74 A6
Fount St
SW8 137 D5 269 D3
Fouracres EN3 7 A4
Four Acres N12 29 D6
Fourland Wlk HA8 27 A4
Fournier St
E1 95 D2 243 D4
Fourscore Mans E8 74 A1
Four Seasons Cl E3 97 C5
Four Seasons Cres
SM3 217 B6
Four Square Ct TW4 151 C5
Fourth Ave
Hayes UB3 105 D5
Ilford E12 78 B4
West Kilburn W10 91 A4
Fourth Cross Rd
TW2 152 B2
Fourth Way
Wembley HA9 66 D4
Wembley HA9 67 A4
Four Tubs The WD23 8 B4
Fourways 2 CR0 221 D6
Four Wents The E4 20 B2
Fovant Ct 5 SW8 137 C3
Fowey Ave IG4 55 D4
Fowey Cl E1 118 B5
Fowey Ho SE11 261 B2
Fowler Cl
London SW11 136 B2
Sidcup DA14 191 A5
Fowler Ho
5 Camberwell SE5 139 C3
Islington N1 94 D6 234 D6
South Lambeth SW8 269 D1
West Green N15 51 B4
Fowler Rd
Forest Gate E7 77 A4
Islington N1 94 D6 234 D6
Mitcham CR4 181 A1
Fowler's Wlk W5 87 D3
Fownes St SW11 136 C2

Fox and Knot St EC1 241 D4
Foxberry Ct SE4 141 B1
Foxberry Rd SE4 141 A2
Foxborough Gdns
SE4 163 C6
Foxbourne Rd SW17 159 A2
Foxbury Ave BR7 189 B4
Foxbury Cl BR1 187 B4
Foxbury Rd BR1 187 B4
Fox Cl
Bethnal Green E1 96 C3
Elstree WD6 9 D5
Newham E16 99 A2
Foxcombe CR0 223 D2
Foxcombe Cl 1 E6 99 D5
Foxcombe Rd 6
SW15 156 A3
Foxcote SE5 263 B1
Foxcroft WC1 233 D3
Foxcroft Rd SE18 144 D4
Fox Ct EC1 241 A3
Foxdene Cl 12 E18 55 B6
Foxes Dale
Beckenham BR2 208 B6
Blackheath Pk SE3 143 A2
Foxfield NW1 231 D5
Foxfield Prim Sch
SE18 123 A1
Foxfield Rd BR6 227 B6
Foxglove Cl
Bexley DA15 168 A5
Edmonton N9 18 C3
Southall UB1 107 A6
Foxglove Ct 11 HA0 88 A5
Foxglove Gdns E11 55 C5
Foxglove La KT9 214 C4
Foxglove Path SE28 123 C5
Foxglove St W12 111 D6
Foxglove Way SM6 203 B1
Fox Gr KT12 194 B2
Foxgrove N14 16 A1
Foxgrove Ave BR3 185 D3
Foxgrove Path WD19 22 D5
Foxgrove Rd BR3 186 A3
Foxham Rd N19 71 D5
Fox Hill Keston BR2 225 C3
Penge SE19 183 D3
Fox Hill Gdns SE19 183 D3
Fox Ho
2 London SW11 136 B1
Northolt UB5 85 A6
Foxhole Rd 2 SE9 166 A6
Fox Hollow Cl 1
SE18 123 C1
Fox Hollow Dr DA7 146 D2
Foxholt Gdns NW10 67 A1
Foxhome Cl BR7 188 C4
Fox House Rd DA17 125 D1
Fox La Ealing W5 88 A3
Keston BR2 225 C3
Palmers Green N13 16 B1
Foxlees HA0 65 A4
Foxley Cl E8 74 A3
Foxley Ct SM2 218 A1
Foxley Ho 4 E3 97 D4
Foxley Rd
Camberwell SW9 138 D5
Thornton Heath CR7 204 D5
Foxley Sq 3 SW9 138 D4
Foxmead Cl EN2 4 B2
Foxmore St SW11 267 C1
Fox Prim Sch
W8 113 C5 245 A3
Fox Rd E16 98 D2
Foxs Path CR4 180 C1
Fox's Yd E2 243 D6
Foxtail Ho TW3 130 A4
Foxton KT1 198 C6
Foxton Gr CR4 180 B1
Foxton Ho E16 122 C4
Foxwarren KT10 212 D1
Foxwell Mews SE4 141 A2
Foxwell St SE4 141 A2
Foxwood Cl
Edgware NW7 27 C6
Feltham TW13 150 B1
Foxwood Green Cl
EN1 17 C5
Foxwood Rd SE3 142 D1
Foyle Rd
Greenwich SE3 142 D6
Tottenham N17 34 A2
Fradel Lo N16 51 B1
Framfield Cl N12 13 C1
Framfield Ct EN1 17 C5

Framfield Rd
Ealing W7 86 D1
Islington N5 72 D3
Mitcham CR4 181 A3
Framlingham Cl 2
E5 74 C6
Framlingham Cres
SE9 188 B6
Framlingham Ct 5
RM6 58 B4
Frampton NW1 71 D1
Frampton Cl SM2 217 C1
Frampton Ct 3 W3 111 A4
Frampton Ho NW8 236 D5
Frampton Park Rd
E9 74 C1
Frampton Rd TW4 151 A6
Frampton St
NW8 92 B3 236 D5
Francemary Rd SE4 163 C6
Frances Ct
South Norwood
SE25 183 D1
Walthamstow E17 53 C3
Frances & Dick James Ct
2 NW7 29 A3
Frances Rd E4 35 C4
Frances St SE18 122 B2
Franche Court Rd
SW17 158 A1
Francis Ave
Bexleyheath DA7 147 C3
Feltham TW13 150 A1
Ilford IG1 79 B6
Francis Barber Cl
SW16 182 B6
Franciscan Prim Sch 3
SW17 181 A5
Franciscan Rd
SW17 181 A6
Francis Chichester Way
SW11 137 A4 268 B1
Francis Cl
6 Cubitt Town E14 120 B2
Littleton TW17 192 C5
West Ewell KT19 215 B4
Francis Ct
12 Deptford SE14 140 D6
Ealing W5 110 B6
Edgware NW7 27 D5
Kingston u T KT5 198 A5
Francis Gr SW19 179 B4
Francis Ho
Harlesden NW10 89 D6
11 Shoreditch N1 95 C6
Walham Green SW10 265 D4
Francis Holland Sch
Belgravia
SW1 115 A2 258 B3
Marylebone
NW1 92 D3 237 C6
Francis Rd
Fortis Green N2 48 D5
Harrow HA1 43 A4
Hounslow TW4 128 D3
Ilford IG1 79 B6
Leyton E10 76 A6
Pinner HA5 40 C4
Thornton Heath CR0 204 D2
Wallington SM6 219 C2
Wembley UB6 87 C6
Francis Snary Lo 11
SW18 157 C6
Francis St Ilford IG1 79 B6
Stratford E15 76 C3
Westminster
SW1 115 C2 259 B4
Francis Terr N19 71 C5
Francis Terrace Mews 16
N19 71 C5
Francis Wlk N1 233 C6
Francklyn Gdns HA8 10 C1
Franconia Rd SW4 159 D6
Frank Bailey Wlk E12 78 C2
Frank Barnes Sch 13
NW3 70 B1
Frank Beswick Ho
SW6 264 D5
Frank Burton Cl 5
SE7 121 B1
Frank Dixon Cl SE21 161 C3
Frank Dixon Way
SE21 161 C3
Frankfurt Rd SE24 161 A6

Frank Godley Ct
DA14 190 B5
Frankham Ho 8
SE8 141 C5
Frankham St SE8 141 C5
Frank Ho SW8 270 A4
Frankland Cl
Bermondsey SE16 118 B2
Woodford IG8 37 C5
Frankland Ho 4
SW12 159 B4
Frankland Rd
Brompton
SW7 114 B3 256 C5
Chingford E4 35 C5
Franklin Bldg 5
E14 119 C4
Franklin Cl
Greenwich SE13 141 D4
Kingston u T KT1 198 C6
Oakleigh Pk N20 14 A4
West Norwood SE27 160 D1
Franklin Cres CR4 203 C5
Franklin Ho
Beckenham BR2 208 C6
New Cross SE4 141 A3
26 Wapping E1 118 B5
West Hendon NW9 45 D2
Franklin Ind Est
SE20 184 C2
Franklin Pas SE9 144 A2
Franklin Pl SE13 141 D4
Franklin Rd
Bexleyheath DA7 147 A4
Penge SE20 184 C3
Walton-on-T KT12 194 A3
Franklins Mews HA2 64 A6
Franklin Sq SW5 254 D1
Franklin's Row
SW3 114 D1 257 D2
Franklin St
43 Bromley E3 97 D4
South Tottenham N15 51 C3
Franklin Way CR0 204 A2
Franklyn Rd
Walton-on-T KT12 194 B3
Willesden NW10 67 D2
Franks Ave KT3 199 A5
Franks Ho TW7 131 B1
Frank Slater Ho 4
IG3 58 B1
Frank Soskice Ho
SW6 264 D5
Frank St 5 E13 99 A3
Frankswood Ave
Hillingdon UB7 82 B1
Petts Wood BR2, BR5 211 A4
Frank Towell Ct
TW14 150 A3
Frank Welch Ct HA5 40 C5
Frank Whymark Ho 4
SE16 118 C4
Franlaw Cres N13 33 A6
Frans Ct HA4 40 A1
Fransfield Gr SE26 162 B1
Frans Hals Ct E14 120 B3
Franshams WD23 8 C2
Frant Cl SE20 184 C3
Franthorne Way
SE6 163 D1
Frant Rd CR7 204 D4
Fraserburgh Ho 29
E3 97 B5
Fraser Cl 3 E6 100 A1
Fraser Ct
Battersea SW11 267 A2
Heston TW3 129 A5
Fraser Ho
Brentford TW8 110 B1
40 Clapham SW8 137 D3
3 Woolwich SE18 122 C2
Fraser Rd
Edmonton N9 18 B1
Walthamstow E17 53 D3
Wembley UB6 87 C6
Fraser Regnart Ct 12
NW5 70 D3
Fraser St W4 111 C1
Frating Cres IG8 37 B4
Frazer Ave HA4 62 C3
Frazier St
SE1 116 C4 251 A1
Freame Ho N21 17 B5
Frean St SE16 118 A3
Frearson Ho WC1 233 D2

Freda Corbett Cl 10
SE15 140 A5
Frederica Rd E4 20 B4
Frederica St 4 N7 72 B1
Frederick Blg N1 73 C2
Frederick Bremer Sec
Sch E17 36 A1
Frederick Charrington
Ho 4 E1 96 C3
Frederick Cl
Cheam SM1 217 B3
Marylebone
W2 114 D6 247 C6
Frederick Cres
Camberwell SW9 138 D5
Enfield EN3 6 C3
Frederick Ct SW6 135 A2
Frederick Gdns
Cheam SM1 217 B3
Thornton Heath CR0 204 D3
Frederick Ho
Ashford TW15 170 A6
Southall UB1 107 B6
Woolwich SE7 122 A3
Frederick Pl SE18 122 D1
Frederick Rd SM1 217 B3
Frederick's Pl
City of London EC2 242 C1
North Finchley N12 30 A6
Frederick Sq 11
SE16 119 A6
Frederick's Row EC1 234 C2
Frederick St
WC1 94 B4 233 C1
Frederick Terr E8 73 D1
Frederic Mews SW1 248 A1
Frederic St E17 53 A4
Fredora Ave UB4 83 D3
Fred Styles Ho SE7 143 C6
Fred Tibble Ct RM9 81 A4
Fred Wigg Twr E11 76 D6
Freedom Cl E17 53 A5
Freedom Rd N17 33 B1
Freedom St SW11 136 D3
Freegrove Rd N7 72 A3
Freehold Ind Ctr
TW4 150 C6
Freeland Ct W5 110 B6
Freeland Pk N3 29 A1
Freeland Rd W5 110 B6
Freelands Ave CR2 222 D1
Freelands Gr BR1 187 B2
Freelands Rd BR1 187 B2
Freeling Ho NW8 229 C6
Freeling St 7 N1 72 B1
Freeman Cl
Northolt UB5 63 A1
Upper Halliford TW17 193 C5
Freeman Ct SW16 182 A1
Freeman Dr KT8 195 B5
Freeman Ho 13 SW2 160 A4
Freeman Rd SM4 202 B4
Freemans La UB3 105 C6
Freemantle Ave EN3 18 D6
Freemantle St
SE17 117 C1 263 A2
Freemasons Pl 6
CR0 205 C1
Freemasons Rd E16 99 B1
Freemason's Rd
CR0 205 C1
Freemens Hos 1
SW9 138 B1
Freesia Cl BR6 227 D3
Freethorpe Cl SE19 183 C2
Freezeland Way
UB10 60 D2
Freke Rd SW11 137 A2
Fremantle Ho 14 E1 96 B3
Fremantle Rd
Belvedere DA17 125 C2
Ilford IG6 57 A6
Fremont St E9 96 C6
French Gdns KT12 195 B1
French Inst The
SW7 114 B2 256 C4
French Pl E1 243 B6
French St TW16 172 C1
Frendsbury Rd SE4 141 A1
Frensham Cl UB1 85 B4
Frensham Ct
Canonbury N5 73 A3
4 London NW9 46 A5

Frensham Ct *continued*
Mitcham CR4 202 B6
Frensham Dr
New Addington CR0 224 A1
Roehampton SW15 156 A2
Frensham Ho 7 KT6 198 A4
Frensham Rd SE9 167 B2
Frensham St SE15 140 A6
Frere St 6 SW11 136 C3
Fresham Ho BR2 208 D6
Freshfield Ave E8 73 D1
Freshfield Cl SE13 142 B1
Freshfield Dr N14 15 B4
Freshfields CR0 207 B1
Freshford St SW17, SW18 158 A1
Freshwater Cl SW17 181 A4
Freshwater Ct UB1 85 C4
Freshwater Rd
Dagenham RM8 59 A1
Streatham SW17 181 A4
Freshwell Ave RM6 58 C5
Fresh Wharf Est IG11 100 D6
Fresh Wharf Rd IG11 100 D5
Freshwood Cl BR3 185 D2
Freston Gdns EN4 15 A6
Freston Pk N3 29 B1
Freston Rd W10, W11 112 D6
Freswick Ho 6 SE8 119 A2
Freta Rd DA6 169 B6
Freud Mus The* NW3 70 A2
Frewell Bldg EC1 241 A4
Frewing Cl BR7 188 C5
Frewin Rd SW18 158 B3
Friar Mews SE27 160 D1
Friar Rd UB4 84 D3
Friars Ave London N20 30 C6
Putney SW15 157 A6
Roehampton SW15 155 D1
Friars Cl Chingford E4 20 A1
Ilford IG1 57 B1
Lambeth SE1 251 D3
16 Northolt UB5 84 D4
Friars Ct
5 Wallington SM6 219 B4
Walthamstow E17 35 B2
Friars Gate Cl IG8 37 A6
Friars Gdns W3 89 B1
Friars La TW9 153 D6
Friars Mead E14 120 A3
Friars Mews SE9 166 C6
Friars Place La W3 111 B6
Friars Prim Foundation Sch SE1 116 D4 251 D1
Friar's Rd E6 99 D6
Friars Stile Pl 9 TW10 154 A5
Friars Stile Rd TW10 154 A5
Friar St EC4 241 D1
Friars Way W3 89 B1
Friars Wlk London N14 15 B4
West Heath SE2 124 D1
Friary Cl N12 30 C5
Friary La IG8 37 A6
Friary Park Ct 12 W3 89 A1
Friary Rd Acton W3 89 B1
London N12 30 C6
Peckham SE15 140 A5
Friary Way N12 30 C6
Friday Grove Mews 11 SW12 159 C4
FRIDAY HILL 20 C1
Friday Hill E4 20 C1
Friday Hill E E4 20 C1
Friday Hill W E4 20 C2
Friday Rd CR4 180 D3
Friday St EC4 117 A6 252 A6
Frideswide Pl NW5 71 C3
Friendly Pl 16 SE13 141 D4
Friendly St SE8 141 C4
Friendly Street Mews SE8 141 C3
Friendship Way E15 98 A6
Friendship Wlk UB5 84 D4
Friends' Rd CR0 221 B5
Friend St EC1 94 D4 234 C2
FRIERN BARNET 31 A6
Friern Barnet La N20 30 C6
Friern Barnet Rd N11 31 A5
Friern Barnet Sch N11 30 D5
Friern Bridge Ret Pk N11 31 B4
Friern Ct N20 14 B1
Friern Mount Dr N20 14 A4
Friern Pk N12 30 B5
Friern Rd SE22 162 A5
Friern Watch Ave N12 30 B6
Frigate Ho 7 E14 120 A2
Frigate Mews SE8 141 C6
Frimley Ave SM6 220 B3
Frimley Cl
New Addington CR0 224 A1
Putney SW19 157 A2
Frimley Cres CR0 224 A1
Frimley Ct DA14 190 C5
Frimley Gdns CR4 202 C6
Frimley Ho CR4 202 C6
Frimley Rd
Chessington KT9 214 A3
Ilford IG3 79 C5
Frimley Way E1 96 D3
Frinstead Ho 1 W10 112 D6
Frinton Ct W13 87 B2
Frinton Dr IG8 36 B3
Frinton Mews IG2 56 C3
Frinton Rd
Newham E6 99 D4
Sidcup DA14 169 A2
South Tottenham N15 51 C3
Streatham SW17 181 A4
Friston St SW6 135 D3
Friswell Pl 1 DA6 147 C1
Fritham Cl KT3 199 C3
Frith Ct NW7 29 A3
Frith Ho
Bethnal Green E2 96 A4
Paddington NW8 236 D5
Frith La NW7 29 A4
Frith Manor Cotts N12 29 B5
Frith Manor Prim Sch N12 29 B5
Frith Rd Croydon CR0 221 A6
Leyton E11 76 B4
Frith St W1 93 D1 239 C1
Frithville Ct 2 W12 112 C5
Frithville Gdns W12 112 C5
Frizlands La RM10 81 D5
Frobisher Cl HA5 40 D2
Frobisher Cres TW19 148 A4
Frobisher Ct
Belmont SM2 217 B1
6 Forest Hill SE23 162 B2
1 Greenwich SE10 142 B6
Hendon NW9 27 C1
3 Shepherd's Bush W12 112 C4
Frobisher Gdns TW19 148 A4
Frobisher Ho
3 Ealing W5 88 A4
27 Wapping E1 118 B5
Frobisher Mews EN2 5 B1
Frobisher Pas E14 119 C5
Frobisher Pl SE14 140 C4
Frobisher Rd
London N8 50 C5
Newham E6 100 B1
Frobisher St SE10 142 C6
Froghall Cotts EN5 11 B5
Frogley Rd SE22 139 D1
Frogmore SW18 157 C6
Frogmore Ave UB4 83 C3
Frogmore Cl SM3 217 A5
Frogmore Ct UB2 107 B2
Frogmore Est NW10 89 A4
Frogmore Gdns
Cheam SM3 217 A4
Hayes UB4 83 C3
Frogmore Ind Est
Hayes UB3 105 D4
Highbury N5 73 A4
Frognal NW3 70 A3
Frognal Ave
Harrow HA1 42 D5
Sidcup DA14 190 A4
Frognal Cl NW3 70 A3
Frognal Cnr BR7 189 D4
Frognal Ct NW3 70 A2
Frognal Gdns NW3 70 A4
Frognal La NW3 69 D3
Frognal Par NW3 70 A2
Frognal Pl DA14 190 A5
Frognal Rise NW3 70 A4
Frognal Way NW3 70 A4
Froissart Rd SE9 166 A6
Frome Ho SE15 140 C1
Frome Rd N22 50 D6
Frome St N1 95 A5 235 A4
Fromondes Rd SM3 217 A3
Fromow's Cnr 14 W4 111 A1
Frontenac NW10 68 B1
Frontier Works N17 33 C4
Frosbery Ct 23 EN3 7 C6
Frostic Wlk E1 243 D3
Froude St SW8 137 B3
Fruen Rd TW14 149 D4
Fryatt Rd N17 33 B3
Frye Ct 5 E3 97 B4
Fryent Cl NW9 44 C3
Fryent Cres NW9 45 C3
Fryent Ctry Park HA3, HA9, NW9 44 C2
Fryent Fields NW9 45 C3
Fryent Gr NW9 45 C3
Fryent Prim Sch NW9 45 A2
Fryent Way HA9, NW9 44 D2
Fry Ho E6 77 C1
Frying Pan Alley E1 243 C3
Fry Rd
Harlesden NW10 89 D6
Upton Pk E6 77 D1
Fryston Ave CR0 222 A6
Fuchsia St SE2 124 B1
Fulbeck Dr NW9 27 C2
Fulbeck Ho N7 72 B2
Fulbeck Way HA2 24 A1
Fulbourn 9 KT1 176 C1
Fulbourne Rd E17 36 A1
Fulbourne St E1 96 B2
Fulbrook Rd N19 71 C4
Fulcher Ct 40 SE8 141 B6
Fulcher Ho
13 Deptford SE8 119 B1
10 Shoreditch N1 95 C6
Fulford Mans 3 N19 72 A5
Fulford Rd KT19 215 B1
Fulford St SE16 118 B4
FULHAM 134 D3
Fulham Broadway SW6 135 C5 265 B3
Fulham Broadway Sh Ctr SW6 265 B3
Fulham Broadway Sta SW6 135 C5 265 B4
Fulham Bsns Exchange SW6 266 B1
Fulham Cl UB10 83 A3
Fulham Cross Girls Sec Sch SW6 135 A5 264 A3
Fulham Ct SW6 135 C4 265 A2
Fulham High St SW6 135 A3
Fulham Pal* SW6 135 A3
Fulham Palace Rd SW6, W6 134 D6
Fulham Park Gdns SW6 135 B3
Fulham Park Rd SW6 135 B3
Fulham Prep Sch
6 Fulham SW6 135 A3
Fulham W14 135 A6 264 B6
Fulham Prim Sch SW6 135 C6 265 A5
Fulham Rd
Chelsea SW10 136 A6 266 B6
Fulham SW6 135 B4 264 D2
Fulke Ho E5 74 B5
Fullbrooks Ave KT4 199 D1
Fuller Cl
4 Bethnal Green E2 96 A3
Bushey WD23 8 B4
Orpington BR6 227 D3
Fuller Rd RM8 80 C4
Fullers Ave KT6 214 B6
Fuller's Ave IG8 36 D3
Fullers Ho 6 SW18 157 C6
Fuller's Rd E18 36 D3
Fuller St NW4 46 C5
Fullers Way N KT6 214 B5
Fullers Way S KT9 214 A5
Fuller's Wood CR0 223 C3
Fuller Terr IG1 79 B3
Fullerton Ct TW11 175 A4
Fullerton Rd
Croydon CR0 205 D2
Wandsworth SW18 158 A6
Fuller Way UB3 105 D1
Fullwood Prim Sch IG6 57 A5
Fullwood's Mews N1 235 D2
Fulmar Ct
6 Dulwich SE21 161 B2
10 Ealing W13 86 D3
Surbiton KT5 198 B3
Fulmar Ho
12 Bermondsey SE16 118 D2
Marylebone NW8 237 B5
Fulmead St SW6 265 D1
Fulmer Cl TW12 173 A5
Fulmer Rd E16 99 D2
Fulmer Way W13 109 B3
Fulneck 1 E1 96 C2
Fulready Rd E10 54 B4
Fulstone Cl TW4 129 B1
Fulthorp Rd SE3 143 A3
Fulton Ct EN3 7 C5
Fulton Mews W2 246 A6
Fulton Rd HA9 66 C5
Fulwell Ct
Southall UB1 108 A6
Teddington TW11 174 C6
Fulwell Park Ave TW2 152 A2
Fulwell Rd TW11, TW12 174 B6
Fulwell Sta TW11 174 B6
Fulwood Ave HA0 88 B5
Fulwood Cl UB3 83 D1
Fulwood Ct
Harrow HA3 43 A3
Stanwell TW19 148 B5
Fulwood Gdns TW1 153 A5
Fulwood Pl WC1 240 D3
Fulwood Wlk SW19 157 A3
Furber St W6 112 B3
Furham Field HA5 23 C3
Furley Ho 7 SE15 140 A5
Furley Rd SE15 140 A5
Furlong Cl SM6 203 B1
Furlong Rd N7 72 C2
Furmage St SW18 157 D4
Furneaux Ave SE27 182 D5
Furness Ho SW1 258 C2
Furness Lo 4 SW14 132 D1
Furness Prim Sch NW10 90 A5
Furness Rd
Harlesden NW10 90 A5
Harrow HA2 41 D1
Morden SM4 201 D3
Sands End SW6 135 D3
Furnival St EC4 94 C1 241 A2
Furrow La E9 74 C3
Furrows The KT12 194 C1
Fursby Ave N3 29 C4
Fursecroft W1 237 C2
Further Acre NW9 27 D1
Furtherfield Cl CR0 204 C3
Further Green Rd SE6 164 C3
Furze Cl WD19 22 C5
Furze Ct CR0 222 A6
FURZEDOWN 181 B6
Furzedown Dr SW17 181 B5
Furzedown Prim Sch SW17 181 A4
Furzedown Rd SW17 181 B5
Furzefield Cl BR7 188 D4
Furzefield Rd SE3 143 B5
Furzeground Way UB11 105 A5
Furzeham Rd UB7 104 A4
Furzehill Rd WD6 11 A6
Furze Inf Sch RM6 59 A3
Furzeland Ho 2 KT3 199 C2
Furze Rd CR7 205 A6
Furze St E3 97 C2
Furzewood TW16 172 A2
Fuschia Ct IG8 36 C4
Fuscia Ct TW13 149 D1
Fusion Ct SW15 155 C1
Futters Ct 1 NW10 89 C5
Fyfe Way BR1 187 A1
Fyfield N4 72 C6
Fyfield Cl BR2, BR3 208 B5
Fyfield Ct E7 77 A2
Fyfield Ho RM9 80 B1
Fyfield Rd
5 Brixton SW9 138 C2
Enfield EN1 5 C2
Walthamstow E17 54 B6
Woodford IG8 37 C3
Fynes St SW1 259 C4

G

Gable Cl HA5 23 C3
Gable Ct SE26 184 B6
Gable Ho 12 W4 111 C2
Gable Lo
Hadley Wood EN4 2 A5
5 North Finchley N12 30 A5
West Wickham BR4 208 A1
Gables Ave TW15 170 B5
Gables Cl
Camberwell SE5 139 C4
Lewisham SE12 165 A3
Gables The
Barking IG11 79 A2
Bromley BR1 187 B3
3 Clapham SW4 137 C2
Ealing W13 87 B1
Hampstead NW3 70 B6
Heston TW5 129 C6
Mitcham CR4 203 B6
Muswell Hill N10 49 A6
North Finchley N12 29 D5
Wembley HA9 66 B5
Gabriel Cl 1 TW13 173 A6
Gabriel Ho SE11 260 C4
Gabrielle Cl HA9 66 B5
Gabrielle Ct NW3 70 B2
Gabriel Mews NW2 69 B6
Gabriel St SE23 163 A4
Gabriel's Wharf* SE1 251 A4
Gad Cl E13 99 B4
Gaddesden Ave HA9 66 B2
Gaddesden Ho EC1 235 D1
Gade Cl UB3 106 B5
Gadesden Rd KT19 215 A2
Gadsbury Cl NW9 45 D3
Gadsden Ho
6 Homerton E9 74 D2
8 Kensal Town W10 91 A3
Gadwall Cl E16 99 B1
Gadwall Way SE28 123 B4
Gagarin Ho SW11 136 B2
Gage Rd E16 98 C2
Gage St WC1 240 B4
Gainford Ho 18 E2 96 B4
Gainford St N1 94 C6 234 A6
Gainsboro Gdns UB6 64 C3
Gainsborough Ave E12 78 C3
Gainsborough Cl
Beckenham BR3 185 C3
Thames Ditton KT10 196 C1
Gainsborough Ct
11 Barnet EN5 1 D1
6 Bermondsey SE16 118 B1
Bromley BR2 209 C5
Dulwich SE21 161 C2
North Finchley N12 29 D5
Shepherd's Bush W12 112 C4
Gainsborough Gdns
Edgware HA8 26 C1
Golders Green NW11 47 B2
Hampstead NW3 70 B5
Isleworth TW7 152 B6
Gainsborough Ho
Dagenham RM8 80 B4
Enfield EN1 18 A6
Finsbury Pk N4 50 B1
3 Hampstead NW3 70 A4
5 Limehouse E14 119 A6
Westminster SW1 259 D3
Gainsborough Lodge HA1 42 C4
Gainsborough Mews 5 SE26 162 B1
Gainsborough Prim Sch
Hackney Wick E9 75 C2
Newham E15 98 C4
Gainsborough Rd
Bedford Pk W4 111 D2

Gainsborough Rd *continued*
Dagenham RM8 . . . . 80 B5
Hayes UB4 . . . . 83 B5
Leytonstone E11 . . . . . . 54 C2
Newham E15 . . . . 98 C4
New Malden KT3 . . . . . 199 B2
North Finchley N12 . . . . 29 D5
Richmond TW9 . . . . 132 B2
Gainsborough Sq DA6 . . . . 146 D2
Gainsborough St 3 E9 . . . . 75 B2
Gainsborough Studios N1 . . . . 235 C5
Gainsborough Twr 7 UB5 . . . . 84 D5
Gainsfield Ct 3 E11 . . 76 C5
Gainsford Rd E17 . . . . . 53 B5
Gainsford St SE1 . . . . 117 D4 253 D2
Gairloch Ho 2 NW1 . . 71 D1
Gairloch Rd SE5 . . . . . 139 C3
Gaisford St NW5 . . . . . 71 C2
Gaitskell Ct SW11 . . . 136 C3
Gaitskell Ho
Camberwell SE17 . . . . . 139 B6
2 Newham E6 . . . . 99 D6
3 Walthamstow E17 . . . 53 D6
Gaitskell Rd SE9 . . . . . 167 A3
Gaitskell Way SE1 . . . 252 A2
Galahad Rd
Edmonton N9 . . . . 18 A1
Grove Pk BR1 . . . . 187 A6
Galata Rd SW13 . . . . . . 134 A5
Galatea Sq SE15 . . . . . 140 B2
Galaxy Bldg 6 E14 . . . 119 C2
Galaxy Ho EC2 . . . . . . 242 D6
Galba Ct 1 TW8 . . . . . 131 D5
Galbraith St E14 . . . . . 120 A3
Galdana Ave EN5 . . . . . . 2 A2
Galeborough Ave IG8 36 B3
Gale Cl
Hampton TW12 . . . . . 173 A4
Mitcham CR4 . . . . 202 B6
Gale Ho
10 Brixton SW2 . . . . . . 160 B6
Carshalton SM5 . . . . . 218 C3
Galena Ho
5 Hammersmith W6 . . . . 112 B2
Plumstead Comm SE18 . . . . 123 D1
Galena Rd W6 . . . . 112 B2
Galen Pl WC1 . . . . 240 B3
Galesbury Rd SW18 . . 158 A5
Gales Gdns E2 . . . . 96 B4
Gale St
Dagenham RM9 . . . . 80 D1
Tower Hamlets E3 . . . . . 97 C2
Galgate Cl 4 SW19 . . 157 A3
Gallants Farm Rd EN4 . . . . 14 C3
Galleon Cl SE16 . . . . . 118 D4
Galleon Ho 8 E14 . . . 120 A2
Galleons Dr IG11 . . . . 102 A4
Galleries of Modern London★ EC1 . . . . . 242 A3
Gallery Ct SW10 . . . . 266 A5
Gallery Gdns UB5 . . . . . 84 D5
Gallery Rd SE21 . . . . . . 161 B3
Galleywall Rd SE16 . . 118 B2
Galleywall Road Trad Est 12 SE16 . . . . 118 B2
Galleywood Ho 1 W10 . . . . 90 C2
Gallia Rd N5 . . . . 72 D3
Galliard Cl N9 . . . . 18 C5
Galliard Cres N9 . . . . . . 18 A4
Galliard Ct N9 . . . . 18 A5
Galliard Prim Sch N9 . 18 A4
Galliard Rd N9 . . . . 18 A5
Gallica Ct SM1 . . . . . . 201 D1
Gallions Cl IG11 . . . . . 102 A4
Gallions Mount Prim Sch SE18 . . . . 123 D1
Gallions Prim Sch E6 . . . . 100 D1
Gallions Rd E16 . . . . . . 123 A6
Gallions Reach Shp Pk IG11 . . . . 101 A2
Gallions Reach Sta E16 . . . . 122 D6
Gallions View Rd SE28 . . . . 123 C4
Gallon Cl SE7 . . . . 121 C2
Gallop The
South Croydon CR2 . . . 222 B1
Sutton SM2 . . . . 218 A1
Gallosson Rd SE18 . . . 123 C2
Galloway Path CR0 . . . 221 B4
Galloway Rd W12 . . . . 112 A5
Gallus Cl N21 . . . . 16 B5
Gallus Sq SE3 . . . . 143 B2
Galpin's Rd CR4, CR7 . 204 B5
Galsworthy Ave
Ilford RM6 . . . . 58 B2
Tower Hamlets E14 . . . . 97 A2
Galsworthy Cl SE28 . . 124 B5
Galsworthy Cres SE3 . . . . 143 C4
Galsworthy Ct W3 . . 110 D3
Galsworthy Ho 4 W11 . . . . 91 A1
Galsworthy Rd
Cricklewood NW2 . . . . . 69 A4
Kingston u T KT2 . . . . 176 D2
Galton Ho SE18 . . . . . . 144 B4
Galton St W10 . . . . 91 A4
Galva Cl EN4 . . . . 3 A1
Galvani Way CR0 . . . . . 204 B1
Galveston Ho 2 E1 . . . 97 A3
Galveston Rd SW15 . . 157 B6
Galway Cl 28 SE16 . . . 118 B1
Galway Ho
Finsbury EC1 . . . . 235 B1
7 Stepney E1 . . . . 96 D2
Galway St EC1 95 A4 235 B1
Galy 5 NW9 . . . . 27 D1
Gambetta St 3 SW8 . 137 B3
Gambia St SE1 . . . . 116 D5 251 D3
Gambler Ho EC1 . . . . 235 B1
Gambole Rd SW17 . . . 180 C6
Games Ho 6 SE7 . . . . . 143 C6
Games Rd EN4 . . . . 2 D2
Gamlen Rd SW15 . . . 134 D1
Gamma Ct 9 CR0 . . . . 205 B1
Gamuel Cl E17 . . . . 53 C3
Gander Green Cres TW12 . . . . 173 C2
Gander Green La KT4, SM1, SM3 . . . . 217 B5
Gandhi Cl E17 . . . . 53 C3
Gandolfi St 5 SE15 . . 139 C6
Ganley Ct 18 SW11 . . . 136 B2
Gannet Ct 5 SE21 . . . 161 B2
Gannet Ho SE15 . . . . 139 D4
Ganton St W1 . . . . . . 239 B1
Ganton Wlk WD19 . . . . . 22 D6
GANTS HILL 56 C3
Gants Hill IG2 . . . . 56 C3
Gantshill Cres IG2 . . . . 56 C4
Gants Hill Sta IG2 . . . . 56 C3
Gap Rd SW19 . . . . 179 D5
Garage Rd W3 . . . . 88 C1
Garand Ct 2 N7 . . . . . . 72 B3
Garbett Ho 2 SE17 . 138 D6
Garbutt Pl W1 . . . . . . 238 B3
Garden Ave
Bexleyheath DA7 . . . . 147 C2
Mitcham CR4 . . . . 181 B3
Garden City HA8 . . . . . 26 C4
Garden Cl
Ashford TW15 . . . . . . 171 A4
Chingford E4 . . . . 35 C5
Grove Pk SE12 . . . . 165 B1
Hampton TW12 . . . . . . 173 B5
Northolt UB5 . . . . 85 A6
Roehampton SW15 . . . 156 B4
Ruislip HA4 . . . . 61 D6
Wallington SM6 . . . . . . 220 A3
Garden Cotts BR5 . . . . 190 C1
Garden Ct
5 Belmont SM2 . . . . 217 C1
10 Eltham SE9 . . . . . . 166 C5
Hampton TW12 . . . . . . 173 B5
North Finchley N12 . . . . 29 D5
4 Richmond TW9 . . . . 132 B4
12 South Acton W4 . . 111 A3
South Croydon CR0 . . 221 D5
4 Stanmore HA7 . . . . . 25 C5
St John's Wood NW8 . 229 C2
Strand EC4 . . . . 251 A6
Wembley HA0 . . . . 65 C5
Wimbledon SW20 . . . . 178 D2
Gardeners Cl SE9 . . . . 166 A1
Gardeners Rd CR0 . . 204 D1
Garden Flats SW16 . . . 160 A1
Garden Ho
2 Finchley N2 . . . . 30 B1
Garden Ho *continued*
12 South Lambeth SW9 . . . . 138 A3
Garden Hospl The NW4 . . . . 46 C6
Garden House Sch SW3 . . . . 114 D1 257 D2
Gardenia Ct 1 BR3 . . 185 C3
Gardenia Rd
Bromley BR1 . . . . 210 C6
Enfield EN1 . . . . 17 C5
Gardenia Way IG8 . . . . 37 A5
Garden La
Bromley BR1 . . . . 187 B4
Streatham SW2 . . . . . . 160 B3
Garden Lodge Ct N2 . . 48 B6
Garden Mews W2 . . . . 245 B5
Garden Mus★ SE1 . . 260 C5
Garden Pl 28 E2 . . . . . . 95 D6
Garden Prim Sch CR4 . . . . 203 D6
Garden Rd
Bromley BR1 . . . . 187 B4
Finchley N2 . . . . 30 B2
Penge SE20 . . . . 184 C2
Richmond TW9 . . . . . . 132 C2
St John's Wood NW8 . . . . 92 A4 229 B2
Walton-on-T KT12 . . . . 194 B2
Garden Row SE1 . . . . 116 D3 261 C6
Garden Royal 16 SW15 . . . . 156 D5
Garden St E1 . . . . 96 D2
Gardens The
Beckenham BR3 . . . . . 186 A2
East Bedfont TW14 . . . 149 B5
East Dulwich SE22 . . . 140 A1
Harrow HA1, HA2 . . . . . 42 A3
Pinner HA5 . . . . 41 B3
Stamford Hill N16 . . . . . 51 D2
Garden Suburb Jun & Inf Schs NW11 . . . . 47 B4
Garden Terr
Knightsbridge SW7 . . 247 B1
Pimlico SW1 . . . . 259 C2
Garden Way NW10 . . . . 67 A2
Garden Wlk
Beckenham BR3 . . . . . . 185 B2
Shoreditch EC2 . . . . 95 C3 243 A6
Gardiner Ave NW2 . . . . 68 C3
Gardiner Cl
Chislehurst BR5 . . . . . 190 C1
Dagenham RM8 . . . . 80 D4
Enfield EN3 . . . . 18 D5
Gardiner Ct NW10 . . . . 89 B6
Gardiner Ho SW11 . . 267 A2
Gardner Cl E11 . . . . 55 B3
Gardner Ct
Highbury N5 . . . . 73 A4
Hounslow TW3 . . . . 129 C2
Tottenham N22 . . . . 32 D1
Gardner Ho
Feltham TW13 . . . . 151 B2
Southall UB1 . . . . 106 D6
Gardner Ind Est SE26 . . . . 185 B5
Gardner Pl TW14 . . . . . 150 B5
Gardner Rd E13 . . . . 99 B3
Gardners Cl N11 . . . . . . 15 A2
Gardners La EC4 . . . . 252 A6
Gardnor Mans 14 NW3 . . . . 70 A4
Gardnor Rd NW3 . . . . . . 70 B4
Gard St EC1 . . . . 234 D2
Garendon Gdns SM4 . . . . 201 D2
Garendon Rd SM4 . . 201 D2
Garenne Ct 8 E4 . . . . . 20 A3
Gareth Cl KT4 . . . . 216 D6
Gareth Ct SW16 . . . . . 159 D1
Gareth Gr BR1 . . . . 187 A6
Garfield Edmonton N9 . . 18 B3
Enfield EN2 . . . . 17 B6
Garfield Ho W2 . . . . . . 237 C1
Garfield Mews 7 SW11 . . . . 137 A2
Garfield Prim Sch London N11 . . . . 31 C5
Wimbledon SW19 . . . 180 A4
Garfield Rd
Chingford E4 . . . . 20 B3
Clapham SW11 . . . . . 137 A2
Enfield EN3 . . . . 6 C1
Newham E13 . . . . 98 D3
Garfield Rd *continued*
3 Twickenham TW1 . 153 A3
Wimbledon SW19 . . . 180 A4
Garford St E14 . . . . 119 C6
Garganey Ct NW10 . . . . 67 B2
Garganey Wlk SE28 . . 124 C6
Garibaldi St SE18 . . . . 123 C2
Garland Ct 12 E14 . . . . 119 C6
Garland Dr TW3 . . . . . . 130 A3
Garland Ho
12 Kingston u T KT2 . . . . 176 A2
Stoke Newington N16 . . 73 B5
Garland Rd
Plumstead Comm SE18 . . . . 145 B5
Stanmore HA7 . . . . 26 A2
Garlands Ct CR0 . . . . . 221 B4
Garlands Ho NW8 . . . . . 91 D5
Garlands La HA1 . . . . . . 42 D1
Garlands The HA1 . . . . . 42 D2
Garlick Hill EC4 . . . . 117 A6 252 B6
Garlies Rd SE23 . . . . . . 163 A1
Garlinge Ho 12 SW9 . . 138 C4
Garlinge Rd NW2 . . . . . 69 B2
Garman Cl N18 . . . . 33 B5
Garman Rd N17 . . . . 34 C3
Garnault Mews EC1 . 234 B1
Garnault Pl EC1 . . . . . 234 B1
Garnault Rd EN1 . . . . 5 D5
Garner Cl RM8 . . . . 58 D1
Garner Rd E17 . . . . 36 A2
Garner St E2 . . . . 96 A5
Garnet Ct TW13 . . . . . . 149 C1
Garnet Ho KT4 . . . . 199 B1
Garnet Rd
South Norwood CR7 . . . 205 B5
Willesden NW10 . . . . . . 67 C2
Garnet St E1 . . . . 118 C6
Garnett Cl SE9 . . . . 144 B2
Garnett Ho 5 NW3 . . . 70 D3
Garnett Rd NW3 . . . . . . 70 D3
Garnett Way 3 E17 . . . 35 A2
Garnet Wlk 8 E6 . . . . 100 A2
Garnham Cl 2 N16 . . . 73 D6
Garnham St 1 N16 . . . 73 D6
Garnies Cl SE15 . . . . . 139 D5
Garrad's Rd SW16 . . 159 D1
Garrard Cl
Bexleyheath DA7 . . . . 147 C2
Chislehurst BR7 . . . . . 188 D5
Garrard Ho BR2 . . . . . . 209 C5
Garrard Wlk NW10 . . . . 67 C2
Garratt Cl CR0 . . . . 220 A4
Garratt Ho 8 N16 . . . . . 51 C1
Garratt La
Upper Tooting SW17, SW18 . . . . 180 C6
Wandsworth SW18 . . 157 D3
Garratt Park Sec Specl Sch 6 SW18 . . . . . . 158 A2
Garratt Rd HA8 . . . . 26 C3
Garratts Rd WD23 . . . . . . 8 A4
Garratt Terr SW17 . . . . 180 C6
Garraway Ct SW13 . . . 134 C5
Garraway Ho SE21 . . 161 D1
Garrett Cl W3 . . . . 89 B2
Garrett Ho
8 Shepherd's Bush W12 . . . . 90 B1
Teddington TW11 . . . . . 175 B4
Garrett St EC1 . 95 A3 242 B6
Garrick Ave NW11 . . . . 47 A3
Garrick Cl Ealing W5 . . . 88 A3
1 Richmond TW9 . . . 153 D6
Wandsworth SW18 . . 136 A1
Garrick Cres CR0 . . . . 221 C6
Garrick Ct HA8 . . . . 26 B6
Garrick Dr
Hendon NW4 . . . . 28 C1
Plumstead SE18 . . . . . . 123 B3
Garrick Gdns KT8 . . . . 195 C6
Garrick Ho
Chiswick W4 . . . . 133 C6
2 Kingston u T KT1 . . 198 A5
Mayfair W1 . . . . 248 C3
7 Streatham SW16 . . 181 C5
Garrick Ind Ctr NW9 . . 45 D4
Garrick Pk NW4 . . . . . . 28 D1
Garrick Rd
Greenford UB6 . . . . 85 D3
Richmond TW9 . . . . . . 132 C3
West Hendon NW9 . . . . 45 D3
Garrick's Ait KT8 . . . . 174 A1
Garricks Ho KT1 . . . . 175 D1
Garrick St WC2 . . . . 116 A6 250 A6
Garrick's Villa TW12 . . 174 A1
Garrick Way NW4 . . . . . 46 D5
Garrick Yd WC2 . . . . . 250 A6
Garrison Cl
Hounslow TW4 . . . . 151 B6
Shooters Hill SE18 . . . 144 C5
Garrison La KT9 . . . . . 214 A1
Garrowsfield EN5 . . . . . 13 B6
Garsdale Cl N11 . . . . . . 31 A4
Garsdale Terr SW5 . . 254 D2
Garside Cl
Hampton TW12 . . . . . 173 D4
Plumstead SE28 . . . . . . 123 B3
Garside Ct 5 N20 . . . . . 14 D2
Garsington Mews SE4 . . . . 141 B2
Garson Ho W2 . . . . . . 246 C6
Garston Ho 6 N1 . . . . . 72 D1
Garter Way SE16 . . . . 118 D4
Garth Cl
Kingston u T KT2 . . . . . 176 B5
Ruislip HA4 . . . . 40 D1
West Barnes SM4 . . . 200 D2
Garth Ct Chiswick W4 . 133 B6
11 Harrow HA1 . . . . 42 D3
Garth Dr N9 . . . . 18 A2
Garth Ho NW2 . . . . 69 B6
Garthland Dr EN5 . . . . . 12 C6
Garth Mews W5 . . . . . . 88 A3
Garthorne Rd SE23 . . 162 D4
Garth Rd
Child's Hill NW2 . . . . 69 B6
8 Chiswick W4 . . . . . . 111 B1
Kingston u T KT2 . . . . . 176 B5
West Barnes SM4 . . . 200 D2
Garth Road Ind Ctr The SM4 . . . . 200 D1
Garthside TW10 . . . . . . 176 A5
Garth The
Hampton TW12 . . . . . 173 D4
Harrow HA3 . . . . 44 B3
North Finchley N12 . . . . 29 D5
Garthway N12 . . . . 30 C4
Gartmoor Gdns SW19 . . . . 157 B3
Gartmore Rd IG3 . . . . . 79 D6
Garton Ho 6 N6 . . . . . . 49 D2
Garton Pl SW18 . . . . . . 158 A5
Gartons Cl EN3 . . . . 6 C1
Gartons Way SW11 . . . 136 A2
Garvary Rd E16 . . . . 99 B1
Garvens SE19 . . . . 183 C5
Garway Rd W2 . . . . 91 D1
Garwood Cl N17 . . . . . . 34 B2
Garwood Lo N22 . . . . . . 32 B3
Gascoigne Gdns IG8 . . 36 C3
Gascoigne Pl 17 E2 . . . 95 D4
Gascoigne Prim Sch IG11 . . . . 101 A6
Gascoigne Rd IG11 . . 101 A5
Gascony Ave NW6 . . . . 69 C1
Gascoyne Ho 2 E9 . . . 74 D1
Gascoyne Rd E9 . . . . . . 74 D1
Gaselee St E14 . . . . . . 120 A6
Gasholder Pl SE11 . . . . . . 116 B1 260 D1
Gaskarth Rd
Balham SW12 . . . . 159 B5
Burnt Oak HA8 . . . . 27 A1
Gaskell Rd N6 . . . . 48 D3
Gaskell St SW4 . . . . . . 138 A3
Gaskin Ho N16 . . . . 73 B5
Gaskin St N1 . . 94 D6 234 C6
Gaspar Cl SW7 . . . . . . 255 D4
Gaspar Mews SW5 . . 255 D4
Gassiot Rd SW17 . . . . 180 D6
Gassiot Way SM1 . . . . 218 B5
Gasson Ho 24 SE14 . . 140 D6
Gastein Rd W6 . . . . . 134 D6
Gastigny Ho EC1 . . . . 235 B1
Gaston Bell Cl TW9 . . . 132 B2
Gaston Bridge Rd TW17 . . . . 193 B3
Gaston Gate SW8 . . . 270 C2
Gaston Rd CR4 . . . . . . 203 A6
Gaston Way TW17 . . . . 193 B4
Gataker Ho 5 SE16 . . 118 B3
Gataker St 6 SE16 . . . 118 B3
Gatcliff Cl SW1 . . . . . 258 B1
Gatcombe Ct BR3 . . . . 185 C3

Gatcombe Ho [20] SE22 139 C2
Gatcombe Mews W5 110 B6
Gatcombe Rd
[8] Newham E16 121 A5
Tufnell Pk N19 71 D5
Gatcombe Way EN4 2 D2
Gateacre Ct DA14 190 B6
Gate End HA6 22 A3
Gatefield Ct SE15 140 A2
Gateforth St NW8 237 A5
Gate Hill Ct W11 244 D4
Gatehill Rd HA6 22 A3
Gate Ho [4] KT6 198 A1
Gatehouse Cl KT2 177 A3
Gatehouse Sch [26] E2 96 D5
Gatehouse Sq SE1 252 B4
Gateley Ho [6] SE4 140 D1
Gateley Rd SW9 138 B2
Gate Mews SW7 114 C4 247 B1
Gater Dr EN2 5 B4
Gates [4] NW9 27 D1
Gatesborough St EC2 243 A6
Gates Ct SE17 262 A2
Gatesden WC1 233 B1
Gates Green Rd BR2, BR4 225 A4
Gateside Rd SW17 158 D1
Gate St WC2 94 B1 240 C2
Gatestone Ct [10] SE19 183 C4
Gatestone Rd SE19 183 C4
Gateway SE17 139 A6
Gateway Arc N1 234 C4
Gateway Bsns Ctr SE28 123 B3
Gateway Gdns E6 100 B4
Gateway Ho
Balham SW12 159 B5
[3] Barking IG11 101 A6
[3] Upper Tooting SW17 180 C4
Gateway Ind Est NW10 90 A3
Gateway Mews
Friern Barnet N11 31 C4
[4] London E8 73 D3
Gateway Prim Sch NW8 92 B3 236 D6
Gateway Rd E15 75 D5
Gateway Ret Pk E6 100 D3
Gateways KT6 198 A4
Gateways Ct SM6 219 B3
Gateways The
Chelsea SW3 257 B3
Richmond TW9 131 D1
Gateway Trad Est NW10 89 D4
Gatfield Gr TW13 151 C2
Gatfield Ho TW13 151 C2
Gathorne Rd N22 32 C2
Gathorne St [19] E2 96 D5
Gatley Ave KT19 214 D3
Gatliff Rd SW1 115 B1 258 C1
Gatling Rd SE18, SE2 124 A1
Gatonby St SE15 139 D4
Gatting Cl HA8 27 A3
Gatting Way UB8 60 A2
Gatton Prim Sch SW17 180 C6
Gatton Rd SW17 180 C6
Gattons Way DA14 191 B6
Gatward Cl N21 16 D5
Gatward Gn N9 17 D2
Gatwick Ho [3] E14 97 B1
Gatwick Rd SW18 157 B4
Gauden Cl SW4 137 D2
Gauden Rd SW4 137 D2
Gaugin Ct [13] SE16 118 B1
Gauntlet [1] NW9 27 D1
Gauntlet Cl UB5 63 A1
Gauntlett Ct HA0 65 B3
Gauntlett Rd SM1 218 B3
Gaunt St SE1 262 A6
Gautrey Rd SE15 140 C3
Gautrey Sq [5] E6 100 B1
Gavel St SE17 262 D4
Gaven Ho N17 33 C1
Gaverick Mews [3] E14 119 C2
Gavestone Cres SE12 165 B4
Gavestone Rd SE12 165 B4
Gavestone Terr SE12 165 B4
Gaviller Pl [3] E5 74 B4
Gavina Cl SM4 202 C4
Gavin Ho [1] SE18 123 C2
Gawain Wlk N9 18 A1
Gawber St E2 96 C4
Gawsworth Cl E15 76 D3
Gawthorne Ct E3 97 C5
Gay Cl NW2 68 B3
Gaydon Ho W2 91 D2
Gaydon La NW9 27 C2
Gayfere Rd
Redbridge IG5 56 B6
Stoneleigh KT17 216 A3
Gayfere St SW1 116 A3 260 A5
Gayford Rd W12 111 D4
Gay Ho N16 73 C3
Gayhurst SE17 139 B6
Gayhurst Ct [9] UB5 84 C4
Gayhurst Ho NW8 237 B6
Gayhurst Prim Sch [5] E8 74 A1
Gayhurst Rd E8 74 A1
Gaylor Rd UB5 63 B3
Gaymead NW8 91 D6
Gaynesford Rd
Forest Hill SE23 162 D2
Wallington SM5 218 D1
Gay Rd E15 98 B5
Gaysham Ave IG2 56 D4
Gaysham Hall IG5 56 D6
Gaysley Ho SE11 261 A3
Gay St SW15 134 D2
Gayton Cres NW3 70 B4
Gayton Ct
[3] Harrow HA1 42 D3
New Malden KT3 199 D4
Gayton Ho E3 97 C3
Gayton Rd
Abbey Wood SE2 124 C3
Hampstead NW3 70 B4
Harrow HA1 43 A3
Gayville Rd SW11 158 D5
Gaywood Cl SW2 160 C3
Gaywood Rd E17 53 C6
Gaywood St SE1 261 D5
Gaza St SE17 116 D1 261 C1
Gaze Ho [11] E14 98 B1
Gean Ct [3] E11 76 B4
Gearies Inf Sch IG2 56 D4
Gearies Jun Sch IG2 56 D4
Geariesville Gdns IG6 56 D5
Gearing Cl SW17 181 A6
Geary Ho N7 72 B3
Geary Rd NW10 68 A3
Geary St N7 72 B3
GEC Est HA9 65 D6
Geddes Pl [3] DA6 147 C1
Gedeney Rd N17 33 A2
Gedge Ct CR4 202 C5
Gedling Ho SE22 139 D2
Gedling Pl SE1 263 D6
Geere Rd E15 98 D6
Gees Ct W1 238 B1
Gee St EC1 95 A3 242 A6
Geffrey's Ct SE9 166 A1
Geffrye Ct N1 95 C5
Geffrye Mus★ E2 95 D5
Geffrye St E2 95 D5
Geldart Rd SE15 140 B5
Geldeston Rd E5 74 A6
Gellatly Rd SE14 140 D3
Gell Cl UB10 60 B5
Gemima Ct SM1 217 C3
Gemini Bsns Ctr E16 98 B3
Gemini Gr UB5 85 A4
Gemini Ho [11] E3 97 C6
Gemma Ct BR3 185 B1
Gems Hampshire Sch (Main Sch) SW7 257 A1
Gems Hampshire Sch (The Early Years) SW7 256 B3
General Gordon Pl SE18 122 D2
Generals Wlk The EN3 7 A6
General Wolfe Rd SE10 142 B4
Genesis Bsns Pk NW10 88 D5
Genesis Cl TW19 148 B3
Genesis Ho KT6 197 D1
Genesta Rd SE18 145 A6
Geneva Cl TW17 171 C1
Geneva Ct
Hendon NW9 45 D4
[1] Putney SW15 156 D6
Stoke Newington N16 51 B1
Geneva Dr SW9 138 C1
Geneva Gdns RM6 59 A4
Geneva Rd
Kingston u T KT1 198 A5
Thornton Heath CR7 205 A4
Genever Cl E4 35 C5
Genista Rd N18 34 B5
Genoa Ave SW15 156 C6
Genoa Ho [19] E1 96 D3
Genoa Rd SE20 184 C2
Genotin Rd EN1 5 B2
Genotin Terr EN1 5 B2
Gentleman's Row EN2 5 A2
Gentry Gdns E13 99 A4
Geoffrey Cl SE5 139 A3
Geoffrey Ct SE4 141 B2
Geoffrey Gdns E6 100 A5
Geoffrey Ho SE1 262 D6
Geoffrey Jones Ct NW10 90 A6
Geoffrey Rd SE4 141 B2
George Akass Ho [5] SE18 123 A1
George Beard Rd [11] SE8 119 B2
George Beare Lo [9] SW4 159 C6
George Belt Ho [8] E2 96 D4
George Carver Ho E7 77 A3
George Comberton Wlk [4] E12 78 C3
George Cres N10 31 A3
George Ct
Buckhurst Hill IG9 21 D2
St James WC2 250 B5
George Davies Lodge IG6 57 A4
George Downing Est N16 73 D6
George Eliot Ho SW1 259 B3
George Eliot Jun & Inf Schs NW8 92 B6 229 C6
George Elliot Ho SE17 262 A2
George Elliston Ho [13] SE1 118 A1
George Eyre Ho NW8 229 D3
George Gange Way HA3 42 D6
George Green's Sch E14 120 A1
George Groves Rd SE20 184 A2
George Ho [8] SE26 184 B5
George Inn Yd SE1 252 C3
George La
Hayes BR2 209 B1
Lewisham SE13 164 A5
Wanstead E18 55 B6
Woodford E18 37 A1
George Lansbury Ho
[7] Bow E3 97 B4
[3] Willesden NW10 67 C1
Wood Green N22 32 C2
George Lashwood Ct [12] SW9 138 B1
George Leybourne Ho [15] E1 118 A6
George Lindgren Ho SW6 264 D4
George Loveless Ho [4] E2 95 D4
George Lovell Dr
Enfield EN3 7 A6
Holdbrook EN3 7 C6
George Mathers Rd SE11 261 C4
George Mews
[27] Brixton SW9 138 C3
NW1 232 A1
George Mitchell Sch E10 53 D1
George Parr Ho N21 16 D4
George Peabody Ct NW1 237 A4
George Rd
Chingford E4 35 C4
Kingston u T KT2 177 A3
New Malden KT3 199 D4
George Row SE16 118 A4
Georges Mead WD6 10 A5
George Spicer Prim Sch EN1 5 D2
George Sq SW19 201 C6
George's Rd N7 72 B3
George's Sq SW6 264 D6
George St
Barking IG11 79 A1
[6] Canning Town E16 98 D1
Ealing W7 108 C5
Hounslow TW3, TW5 129 B3
Marylebone W1 92 D1 237 D2
Richmond TW10 153 D6
Southall UB2 107 A2
South Croydon CR0 221 B6
George Street Sta CR0 221 A6
George Taylor CT N9 18 B1
George Tingle Ho SE1 263 D6
George Tomlinson Prim Sch E11 54 C1
Georgetown Cl [4] SE19 183 C5
Georgette Pl SE10 142 A5
George Vale Ho [35] E2 96 A5
George V Ave HA2, HA5 41 C6
Georgeville Gdns IG6 56 D5
George V Way UB6 87 B6
George Walter Ho [11] SE16 118 C2
George Wyver Cl SW18 157 A4
George Yd
City of London EC3 242 D1
Mayfair W1 115 A6 248 B6
Georgiana St NW1 93 C6 232 B6
Georgian Cl
Hayes BR2 209 B1
Ickenham UB10 60 A4
Stanmore HA7 25 A3
Georgian Ct
Croydon CR0 205 B1
[12] Hackney E9 96 C6
[3] Hendon NW4 46 B4
Wembley HA9 66 D2
Georgian Ho HA0 65 A5
Georgian Lo HA5 40 B4
Georgian Village The E17 54 A6
Georgian Way HA1 64 B6
Georgia Rd
New Malden KT3 199 A5
South Norwood CR7 182 D2
Georgina Ct [5] TW1 153 C5
Georgina Gdns [10] E2 95 D4
Geraint Rd BR1 187 A6
Geraldine Ct [6] NW9 46 A5
Geraldine Rd
Brentford W4 132 C6
Wandsworth SW18 158 A6
Geraldine St SE11 261 C5
Gerald Mews SW1 258 B4
Gerald Rd
Belgravia SW1 115 A2 258 B4
Dagenham RM8 59 B1
Newham E16 98 D3
Gerard Ave TW4 151 C4
Gerard Ct NW2 68 D3
Gerard Rd
Barnes SW13 133 D4
Harrow HA1 43 A3
Gerards Cl SE16 118 C1
Gerboa Ct [6] E4 36 B5
Gerda Rd SE9 167 A2
Germander Way E15 98 C4
German Sch The TW10 153 D3
Gernigan Ho SW18 158 B5
Gernon Rd E3 97 A5
Geron Way NW2 68 C6
Gerrard Gdns HA5 40 A4
Gerrard Ho [5] SE14 140 D5
Gerrard Pl W1 249 D6
Gerrard Rd N1 94 D5 234 D4
Gerrards Cl N14 15 C6
Gerrard's Ct W5 109 D3
Gerrard St W1 115 D6 249 D6
Gerridge Ct SE1 261 B6
Gerridge St SE1 116 C3 261 B6
Gerry Raffles Sq E15 76 B2
Gertrude Rd DA17 125 C2
Gertrude St SW10 136 A6 266 B5
Gervase Cl HA9 67 A5
Gervase Rd HA8 27 B2
Gervase St SE15 140 B5
Getters Talmud Torah [3] N16 51 B2
Ghent St SE6 163 C2
Ghent Way E8 73 D2
Giant Arches Rd SE24 161 A5
Giant Tree Hill WD23 8 B3
Gibbards Cott [1] IG11 79 D1
Gibbfield Cl RM6 59 A6
Gibbings Ho SE1 251 D1
Gibbins Rd E15 76 A1
Gibbon Ho NW8 236 D5
Gibbon Rd Acton W3 111 C6
Kingston u T KT2 176 A3
Nunhead SE15 140 C3
Gibbons Mews NW11 47 B4
Gibbons Rd NW10 67 C2
Gibbon's Rents SE1 253 A3
Gibbon Wlk SW15 134 A1
Gibbs Ave SE19 183 B5
Gibbs Cl SE19 183 B5
Gibbs Gn
Edgware HA8 27 A6
West Kensington W14 113 B1 254 D2
Gibbs Green Rd W14 113 B1 254 C2
Gibbs Green Specl Sch W14 113 B1 254 D2
Gibbs Ho
[6] Balham SW12 159 B4
[2] Bromley BR1 186 D2
Gibbs Rd N18 34 C6
Gibbs Sq SE19 183 B5
Gibraltar Ho NW10 89 C5
Gibraltar Wlk [28] E2 95 D4
Gibson Bsns Ctr [10] N17 33 D3
Gibson Cl
Bethnal Green E1 96 C3
Chessington KT9 213 C3
Isleworth TW7 130 B2
Southgate N21 16 C5
Gibson Ct
[9] Friern Barnet N11 30 D5
Hinchley Wood KT10 212 D5
Gibson Gdns N16 73 D6
Gibson Ho
South Croydon CR2 221 A2
Sutton SM1 217 C4
Gibson Rd
Dagenham RM8 58 C1
Ickenham UB10 60 B4
Lambeth SE11 260 D3
Sutton SM1 217 D3
Gibson's Hill SW16 182 C3
Gibson Sq N1 94 C6 234 B6
Gibson St SE10 120 C1
Gideon Cl DA17 125 D2
Gideon Mews W5 109 D4
Gideon Rd SW11 137 A2
Giesbach Rd N19 71 D6
Giffard Rd N18 33 C4
Giffen Square Mkt★ SE8 141 C5
Giffin St SE8 141 C5
Gifford Gdns W7 86 C2
Gifford Ho
[5] Clapham SW4 137 D1
Greenwich SE10 120 B1
Pimlico SW1 259 A1
Gifford Prim Sch UB5 85 B5
Gifford Rd NW10 67 C1
Gifford St N1 72 A1
Gift La E15 98 D6
Giggs Hill BR5 190 A2
Giggs Hill Gdns KT7 197 A1
Giggs Hill Rd KT7 197 A2

Gilbert Cl
Kidbrooke SE18 144 B4
1 Merton SW19 179 D2
Gilbert Ct W5 88 B1
Gilbert Gr HA8 27 B2
Gilbert Ho
Barbican EC2 242 B3
Deptford SE8 141 C6
5 Globe Town E2 96 D4
Pimlico SW1 258 D1
South Lambeth SW8 270 A4
5 Walthamstow E17 54 A6
Gilbert Pl
WC1 94 A2 240 A3
Gilbert Rd
Belvedere DA17 125 C3
Lambeth
SE11 116 C2 261 B4
Merton SW19 180 A3
Pinner HA5 40 D5
Plaistow BR1 187 A3
Gilbert Scott Prim Sch
CR2 223 A1
Gilbert Sheldon Ho
W2 236 D4
Gilbertson Ho 11
E14 119 C3
Gilbert St Enfield EN3 6 C6
Hounslow TW3 130 A2
Leyton E15 76 C4
Marylebone
W1 93 A1 238 B1
Gilbert White Cl UB6 87 A6
Gilbey Cl UB10 60 D4
Gilbey Rd SW17 180 C5
Gilbeys Yd NW1 71 A1
Gilbourne Rd SE18 145 D6
Gilby Ho 5 E9 74 D2
Gilda Ave EN3 19 A6
Gilda Cres N16 52 A1
Gilda Ct NW7 28 A2
Gildea Cl HA5 23 C3
Gildea St W1 238 D3
Gilden Cres NW5 71 A3
Gildersome St SE18 144 C6
Gilders Rd KT9 214 B2
Giles Coppice SE19 183 D6
Giles Ho
5 Bermondsey
SE16 118 A3
Notting Hill W11 91 C1
Gilesmead SE5 139 B4
Gilfrid Cl UB8 82 D1
Gilkes Cres SE21 161 C5
Gilkes Pl SE21 161 C5
Gillam Ho 9 SE16 118 C2
Gillan Ct SE12 165 B1
Gillan Gn WD23 8 A2
Gillards Mews 6 E17 53 C5
Gillards Way E17 53 C5
Gill Ave E16 99 A1
Gill Ct SE18 123 A2
Gillender St E3 98 A3
Gillespie Prim Sch
N5 72 D5
Gillespie Rd N4, N5 72 D5
Gillett Ave E6 100 A5
Gillette Cnr TW7 131 A5
Gillett Ho N8 50 A6
Gillett Pl 27 E8 73 C3
Gillett Rd CR7 205 B5
Gillett St E8, N16 73 C3
Gillfoot NW1 232 A3
Gillham Terr N17 34 A3
Gillian Ho HA3 24 C4
Gillian Park Rd SM3 201 B1
Gillian St SE13 163 D6
Gillies Ct
Sidcup DA14 189 C6
Southgate N21 16 B6
Gillies St NW5 71 A3
Gilling Ct 5 NW3 70 C2
Gillingham Ho SW1 259 A4
Gillingham Mews
SW1 259 A4
Gillingham Rd NW2 69 A5
Gillingham Row
SW1 259 A4
Gillingham St
SW1 115 C2 259 A4
Gillings Ct EN5 1 A1
Gillison Wlk 19 SE16 118 A3
Gillman Dr E15 98 D6
Gillman Ho 24 E2 96 A5
Gillray Ho
Chelsea SW10 266 C5

Gillray Ho *continued*
2 Sutton SM1 218 B3
Gills Ct 2 EN5 14 A6
Gill St E14 119 B6
Gillum Cl EN4 14 D3
Gilmore Cl UB10 60 C5
Gilmore Cres TW15 170 C4
Gilmore Ct N11 30 D5
Gilmore Ho SW4 136 D1
Gilmore Rd SE13 142 B1
Gilpin Ave SW14 133 B1
Gilpin Cl
Mitcham CR4 180 C1
Paddington W2 236 B4
Gilpin Cres
Edmonton N18 33 D5
Twickenham TW2 151 D4
Gilpin Ho
9 Edmonton N9 18 A1
New Malden KT3 199 C4
Gilpin Rd E5 75 A4
Gilpin Way UB3 127 B5
Gilray Ho W2 246 C6
Gilsland Rd CR7 205 B5
Gilson Pl N10 30 D3
Gilstead Ho IG11 102 B5
Gilstead Rd SW6 135 D3
Gilston Rd
SW10 114 A1 256 B1
Gilton Rd SE6 164 C1
Giltspur St
EC1 94 D1 241 D2
Gilwell Cl E4 7 D1
Gilwell Ct 7 E5 74 B4
Gippeswyck Cl HA5 22 D2
Gipsy Cnr W3 89 B2
Gipsy Hill SE19 183 C5
Gipsy Hill Sta SE19 183 C5
Gipsy La SW15 134 B2
Gipsy Rd
Bexley DA16 146 D3
West Norwood SE27 183 B6
Gipsy Road Gdns
SE27 183 A6
Giralda Cl E16 99 D2
Giraud St E14 97 D1
Girdlers Rd W14 112 D2
Girdlestone Wlk N19 71 C6
Girdwood Rd SW18,
SW19 157 A4
Girling Ho 9 N1 95 C6
Girling Way TW14 128 A2
Gironde Rd
SW6 135 B5 264 D3
Girtin Ho
6 Belmont SM2 217 D1
4 Northolt UB5 84 D5
Girton Ave NW9 44 C6
Girton Cl UB5 64 A2
Girton Gdns CR0 223 C5
Girton Ho SW15 156 D5
Girton Rd
Forest Hill SE26 184 D5
Northolt UB5 64 A2
Girton Villas 6 W10 90 D1
Gisbourne Cl SM6 219 D5
Gisburn Ho 23 SE15 140 A5
Gisburn Mans N8 50 B5
Gisburn Rd N8 50 B5
Gissing Wlk N1 72 C1
Gittens Cl BR1 186 D6
Given-Wilson Wlk
E13 98 D5
Glacier Way HA0 87 D5
Gladbeck Way EN2 4 D1
Gladding Rd E12 77 D4
Gladebury Ct 2
SW19 179 B4
Glade Cl KT6 213 D6
Glade Gdns CR0 207 A2
Glade La UB2 107 D4
Gladeside
Croydon CR0 206 D3
Southgate N21 16 B4
Gladeside Cl KT9 213 D1
Gladesmore Com Sch
N15 52 A4
Gladesmore Rd N15 51 D3
Glades Sh Ctr The
BR1 187 A1
Gladeswood Rd
DA17 125 D2
Glade The
Bromley BR1 187 D1
Charlton SE7 143 C5
Croydon CR0 206 D3

Glade The *continued*
Enfield EN2 4 C3
Hammersmith W12 112 B4
Southgate N21 16 B4
Stoneleigh KT17 216 A2
West Wickham BR4 223 D5
Woodford IG8 21 B1
Gladiator St SE23 163 A4
Glading Terr N16 73 D5
Gladioli Cl 6 TW12 173 C4
Gladsdale Dr HA5 40 B5
Gladsmuir Rd
Barnet EN5 1 A3
Upper Holloway N19 49 C1
Gladstone Ave
Feltham TW14 150 B5
Plashet E12 78 A1
Tottenham N22 32 D1
Twickenham TW2 152 B4
Gladstone Ct
12 Merton SW19 179 C3
Ruislip HA4 61 C6
Westminster SW1 259 D3
Willesden NW2 68 B3
Gladstone Gdns
TW3 130 A4
Gladstone Ho
6 Mitcham SW19 180 D1
16 Poplar E14 97 C1
Gladstone Mews
3 Penge SE20 184 C3
Wood Green N22 32 C1
Gladstone Par NW2 68 C5
Gladstone Park Gdns
NW2 68 B5
Gladstone Park Sch
NW10 68 B3
Gladstone Pl KT8 196 C4
Gladstone Rd
Acton W4 111 B3
Buckhurst Hill IG9 21 C3
Farnborough BR6 227 A3
Kingston u T KT1 198 C6
Merton SW19 179 C3
Southall UB2 107 A4
Surbiton KT6 214 A6
Thornton Heath CR0 205 B2
Gladstone St SE1 261 C6
Gladstone Terr SW8 268 D2
Gladstone Way HA3 42 C6
Gladwell Rd
London N8 50 B3
Plaistow BR1 187 A4
Gladwin Ho NW1 232 B3
Gladwyn Rd SW15 134 D2
Gladys Aylward Sch The
N18 33 B6
Gladys Dimson Ho
E7 76 D3
Gladys Rd NW6 69 C1
Glaisher St SE8 141 D6
Glamis Cres UB3 105 A3
Glamis Ct W3 110 D4
Glamis Est 3 E1 118 D6
Glamis Pl E1 118 C6
Glamis Rd E1 118 C6
Glamis Way UB5 64 A2
Glamorgan Cl CR4,
SW16 204 A6
Glamorgan Ct 4 W7 86 D2
Glamorgan Rd KT1 175 C3
Glandford Way RM6 58 B4
Glanfield Rd BR3 207 B5
Glanleam Rd HA7 25 D6
Glanville Ho 4
SW12 159 C4
Glanville Mews HA7 25 A5
Glanville Rd
Bromley BR2 209 B6
Clapham Pk SW2 160 A6
Glasbrook Ave TW2 151 B3
Glasbrook Rd SE9 165 D4
Glasbury Ho 5 SW9 138 B1
Glaserton Rd N16 51 C2
Glasford St SW17 180 D4
Glasfryn Ct HA2 64 B6
Glasgow Ho W9 91 D5
Glasgow Rd
Edmonton N18 34 B5
Newham E13 99 B5
Glasgow Terr
SW1 115 C1 259 A1
Glasier Ct 6 E15 76 C1
Glasse Cl W13 109 A6
Glasshill St
SE1 116 D4 251 D2

Glasshouse Cl UB8 82 D2
Glasshouse Fields
E1 118 D6
Glasshouse St
W1 115 C6 249 B5
Glasshouse The
SE13 142 A1
Glasshouse Wlk
SE11 116 B1 260 C2
Glasshouse Yd EC1 242 A5
Glasslyn Rd N8 49 D4
Glassmill La BR2 186 D1
Glass St 4 E2 96 B3
Glass Yd SE18 122 C3
Glastonbury Ave IG8 37 D4
Glastonbury Ct
12 Deptford SE14 140 C5
1 Ealing W13 109 A5
Glastonbury Ho
London SE12 164 D6
Pimlico SW1 258 C2
Glastonbury Pl 22 E1 96 C1
Glastonbury Rd
Edmonton N9 18 A3
Morden SM4 201 C2
Glastonbury St NW6 69 B3
Glaston Ct W5 109 D5
Glaucus St E3 97 D2
Glazbury Rd
W14 113 A1 254 B2
Glazebrook Cl SE21 161 B2
Glazebrook Rd
TW11 174 D3
Gleave Ct 7 N20 14 D2
Glebe Ave Enfield EN2 4 D2
Harrow HA3 44 A6
Mitcham CR4 180 C1
Ruislip HA4 62 B2
Uxbridge UB10 61 A4
Woodford IG8 37 A4
Glebe Cl
1 Chiswick W4 111 C1
Uxbridge UB10 61 A4
Glebe Cotts
Feltham TW13 151 C1
Sutton SM1 217 D4
Glebe Cres
Harrow HA3 44 A6
Hendon NW4 46 C5
Glebe Ct Ealing W5 109 D5
Hanwell W7 108 B6
Lewisham SE3 142 C2
Mitcham CR4 202 D6
Palmers Green N13 16 C1
Ruislip HA4 39 B2
Stanmore HA7 25 C5
Glebe Fst & Mid Sch
HA3 44 A5
Glebe Gdns KT3 199 C2
Glebe Ho
8 Bermondsey
SE16 118 B3
Feltham TW13 151 C1
7 Woolwich SE18 122 C2
Glebe House Dr BR2 209 B1
Glebehyrst SE19 183 C6
Glebe La Barnet EN5 12 A5
Harrow HA3 44 A5
Glebeland Gdns
TW17 193 A3
Glebelands
East Molesey KT8 195 D5
Leyton E10 75 D6
Mitcham CR4 202 C6
Glebelands Ave
Ilford IG2 57 B2
Woodford E18 37 A1
Glebelands Cl
Camberwell SE5 139 C2
Finchley N2 30 B2
Glebelands Rd
TW14 150 A4
Glebe Path CR4 202 D6
Glebe Pl
SW3 136 C6 267 A6
Glebe Prim Sch UB10 61 B4
Glebe Rd
Barnes SW13 134 A3
Belmont SM2 217 A1
Bromley BR1 187 A2
Dagenham RM10 81 D2
Dalston E8 73 D1
Finchley N3 30 A2
Hayes UB3 105 D5
Hornsey N8 50 B5
Stanmore HA7 25 C5

Glebe Rd *continued*
Wallington SM5 218 D2
Willesden NW10 68 A2
Glebe Sch BR4 224 B6
Glebe Side TW1 152 D5
Glebe Sq CR4 202 D6
Glebe St W4 111 C1
Glebe The
Chislehurst BR7 189 A2
Lewisham SE3 142 C2
New Malden KT4 199 D1
Streatham SW16 181 D6
West Drayton UB7 104 B2
Glebeway IG8 37 C5
Glebe Way
Feltham TW13 151 C1
West Wickham BR4 224 B6
Gledhow Gdns SW5 256 A3
Gledstanes Rd
W14 113 A1 254 B1
Gledwood Ave UB4 84 A2
Gledwood Cres UB4 83 D2
Gledwood Ct UB4 83 D2
Gledwood Dr UB4 83 D2
Gledwood Gdns UB4 84 A2
Gleed Ave WD23 8 B2
Gleeson Dr BR6 227 D4
Glegg Pl 3 SW15 134 D1
Glenaffric Ave E14 120 B2
Glen Albyn Rd
SW19 156 D2
Glenalla Rd HA4 39 D2
Glenalmond Ho
Ashford TW15 148 A1
2 Putney SW15 156 D5
Glenalmond Rd HA3 44 A5
Glenalvon Way 5
SE18 122 A2
Glena Mount SM1 218 A4
Glenarm Coll IG1 78 D6
Glenarm Rd E5 74 D4
Glen Ave TW15 170 C6
Glenavon Cl KT10 213 A1
Glenavon Ct KT4 216 B6
Glenavon Lo 5 E18 55 A6
Glenavon Rd E15 76 C1
Glenbarr Cl SE9 144 D2
Glenbow Rd BR1 186 C5
Glenbrook N EN2 4 B1
Glenbrook Prim Sch
SW4 159 D5
Glenbrook Rd NW6 69 C3
Glenbrook S EN2 4 B1
Glenbuck Ct 6 KT6 198 A3
Glenbuck Rd KT6 198 A3
Glenburnie Rd
SW17 158 D1
Glencairn Dr W5 87 C3
Glencairne Cl E16 99 D2
Glencairn Rd SW16 182 A3
Glen Cl TW17 192 C5
Glencoe Ave IG2 57 C2
Glencoe Dr RM10 81 C4
Glencoe Mans 6
SW9 138 C5
Glencoe Rd UB4 84 D3
Glencorse Gn WD19 22 D6
Glen Cres IG8 37 B4
Glencroft Ct SM1 217 C3
Glen Ct
6 Bromley BR1 186 D3
9 Penge SE20 184 B2
Sidcup DA14 190 A6
Glendale Ave
Edgware HA8 26 C6
Ilford RM6 58 C2
Wood Green N22 32 C3
Glendale Cl SE9 144 C2
Glendale Dr SW19 179 B5
Glendale Gdns HA9 44 A1
Glendale Mews BR3 185 D2
Glendale Way SE28 124 C6
Glendall St SW9 138 B1
Glendarvon St
SW15 134 D2
Glendevon Cl HA8 10 D1
Glendish Rd N17 34 B2
Glendor Gdns NW7 27 B6
Glendower Gdns 10
SW14 133 B2
Glendower Pl SW7 256 C4
Glendower Prep Sch
SW7 114 B2 256 C4

Glendower Rd
Chingford E4 20 B3
Mortlake SW14 133 B2
Glendown Ho 2 E8 74 A3
Glendown Rd SE2 124 A1
Glendun Ct W3 111 C6
Glendun Rd W3 111 C6
Gleneagle Lo BR3 185 C2
Gleneagle Mews SW16 181 D5
Gleneagle Rd SW16 181 D5
Gleneagles
Ealing W13 87 B2
Stanmore HA7 25 B4
Gleneagles Cl
21 Bermondsey SE16 118 B1
Crofton BR6 211 B1
South Oxhey WD19 22 D6
Gleneagles Ct 4 TW11 175 A5
Gleneagles Gn 1 BR6 211 B1
Gleneagles Twr 2 UB1 86 A1
Gleneldon Mews SW16 182 A6
Gleneldon Rd SW16 182 A6
Glenelg Rd SW2 160 A6
Glenesk Rd SE9 144 D1
Glenfarg Rd SE6 164 B3
Glenfield Cres HA4 39 B2
Glenfield Rd
Ashford TW15 171 A4
Ealing W13 109 B4
Streatham SW12 159 C3
Glenfield Terr W13 109 B5
Glenfinlas Way SE5 138 D5
Glenforth St SE10 120 D1
Glengall Ct SE23 163 A4
Glengall Gr E14 120 A3
Glengall Pass 2 NW6 91 C6
Glengall Rd
Bexley DA7 147 A2
Camberwell SE15 139 D6
Edgware HA8 10 D1
Kilburn NW6 91 B6
Woodford IG8 37 B4
Glengall Terr SE15 139 D6
Glengarnock Ave E14 120 A2
Glengarry Rd SE22 161 D6
Glen Gdns CR0 220 C4
Glenham Dr IG2 56 D4
Glenhead Cl SE9 144 D2
Glenhill Cl N3 29 C1
Glen Ho
6 Newham E16 122 C5
Wallington SM6 219 C4
Glenhouse Rd SE9 166 C6
Glenhurst 4 BR3 186 A2
Glenhurst Ave
Gospel Oak NW5 71 A4
Ruislip HA4 39 A1
Sidcup DA5 169 B3
Glenhurst Ct 1 SE19 183 D5
Glenhurst Rd
Brentford TW8 109 C1
North Finchley N12 30 B5
Glenhurst Rise SE19 183 A3
Glenilla Rd NW3 70 C2
Glenister Ho UB3 106 B5
Glenister Park Rd SW16 181 D3
Glenister Rd SE10 120 D1
Glenister St E16 122 C5
Glenkerry Ho 1 E14 98 A1
Glenlea Rd SE9 166 C6
Glenloch Ct 2 NW3 70 C2
Glenloch Rd
Enfield EN3 6 C3
Maitland Pk NW3 70 C3
Glenluce Rd SE3 143 A6
Glenlyon Rd SE9 166 C6
Glenmead IG9 21 C3
Glenmere Ave NW7 28 A4
Glenmere Row
Lee SE12 165 A5
Lewisham SE12 164 D5
Glen Mews E17 53 B4
Glenmill TW12 173 B5
Glenmore SW15 156 D5
Glenmore Ho 6 TW10 154 A5
Glenmore Lawns W13 87 A1
Glenmore Rd
Bexley DA16 145 D4
Maitland Pk NW3 70 C2
Glenmore Way IG11 102 A5
Glenmount Path 1 SE18 123 A1
Glennie Ct SE21 162 A3
Glennie Ho SE10 142 A4
Glennie Rd SE27, SW16 160 C1
Glenny Rd IG11 79 A2
Glenorchy Cl UB4 85 A2
Glenpark Ct W13 109 A6
Glenparke Rd E7 77 B2
Glen Rd
Chessington KT9 214 A5
Newham E13 99 C3
Walthamstow E17 53 B4
Glenridding NW1 232 B3
Glen Rise IG8 37 B4
Glenrosa St SW6 136 A3
Glenrose Ct DA14 190 B5
Glenrose Ho 9 SM1 218 A4
Glenroy St W12 90 C1
Glensdale Rd SE4 141 B2
Glenshaw Mans 7 SW9 138 C5
Glenshiel Rd SE9 166 C6
Glentanner Way SW17 158 B1
Glentham Gdns SW13 134 B6
Glentham Rd SW13 134 B6
Glen The
Beckenham BR2 186 C1
Eastcote Village HA5 40 B4
Enfield EN2 4 D1
Locksbottom BR6 226 C5
Rayners La HA5 41 A2
Southall UB2 107 B1
South Croydon CR0 222 D5
Wembley HA9 65 D4
Glenthorne Ave CR0 206 C1
Glenthorne Cl SM3 201 C1
Glenthorne Gdns
Cheam SM3 201 C1
Ilford IG6 56 D5
Glenthorne High Specialist Arts Coll SM3 201 C1
Glenthorne Mews W6 112 B2
Glenthorne Rd
Friern Barnet N11 31 A5
Hammersmith W6 112 B2
Kingston u T KT1 198 B5
Walthamstow E17 53 A4
Glenthorpe SW15 134 A1
Glenthorpe Rd SM4 200 D4
Glenton Rd SE13 142 C1
Glentrammon Ave BR6 227 D2
Glentrammon Cl BR6 227 D3
Glentrammon Gdns BR6 227 D2
Glentrammon Rd BR6 227 D2
Glentworth Ct HA8 26 B5
Glentworth St NW1 92 D3 237 D5
Glenure Rd SE9 166 C6
Glenview SE2 146 D6
Glen View Rd BR1 187 D1
Glenville Ave EN2 5 A5
Glenville Gr SE8 141 B5
Glenville Mews SW18 157 C4
Glenville Rd KT2 176 C2
Glen Wlk TW7 152 B6
Glenwood Ave NW9 45 C1
Glenwood Cl HA1 42 D4
Glenwood Ct
7 Sidcup DA14 190 A6
6 Wanstead E18 55 A6
Glenwood Gdns IG2 56 C4
Glenwood Gr NW9 45 A1
Glenwood Ho 3 EN5 13 D6
Glenwood Rd
Edgware NW7 11 C1
Forest Hill SE6 163 C3
Glenwood Rd *continued*
Harringay N15 50 D4
Hounslow TW3 130 B2
Stoneleigh KT17 216 A2
Glenwood Way CR0 206 D3
Glenworth Ave E14 120 B2
Gliddon Rd W14 113 A1 254 A2
Glimpsing Gn DA18 125 A3
Glisson Rd UB10 82 C5
Globe Acad The SE1 117 B3 262 C5
Globe Ct SE18 145 A6
Globe Pond Rd SE16 119 A5
Globe Prim Sch 37 E2 96 C4
Globe Rd
Bethnal Green E1, E2 96 C3
Stratford E15 76 D3
Woodford IG8 37 C4
Globe St SE1 117 B4 252 C1
Globe Terr 9 E2 96 C4
Globe Theatre The* SE1 117 A5 252 A5
GLOBE TOWN 96 D4
Globe View EC4 252 A6
Globe Yd W1 238 C1
Glossop Ho TW7 131 A1
Gloster Rd KT3 199 C5
Gloucester W14 254 D3
Gloucester Ave
Camden Town NW1 93 A6 231 B6
Falconwood DA16 145 D1
Sidcup DA15 167 C2
Gloucester Cir SE10 142 A5
Gloucester Cl
Thames Ditton KT7 197 A1
Willesden NW10 67 B1
Gloucester Cres
Camden Town NW1 93 B6 231 C6
Staines TW18 170 A4
Gloucester Ct
6 Acton W3 88 C1
10 Belmont SM2 217 C1
Borough The SE1 262 B6
City of London EC3 253 B5
Dulwich SE22 162 A3
5 Ealing W7 86 D2
Golders Green NW11 47 B2
Harrow HA1 42 C6
Redbridge IG1 56 B2
Richmond TW9 132 C5
8 Surbiton KT6 197 D2
Gloucester Dr
Finsbury Pk N4 72 D6
London NW11 47 C5
Gloucester Gate NW1 231 C4
Gloucester Gate Mews NW1 231 C4
Gloucester Gdns
Cockfosters EN4 15 A6
Golders Green NW11 47 B2
Paddington W2 236 A2
Redbridge IG1 56 A2
Sutton SM1 217 D6
Gloucester Gr HA8 27 B2
Gloucester Ho
Kilburn NW6 91 C5
Richmond TW10 154 C6
Gloucester Lo 9 CR0 221 D6
Gloucester Mews
Paddington W2 236 B1
Walthamstow E17 53 C2
Gloucester Mews W W2 236 B1
Gloucester Par
Bexley DA15 168 A6
Hayes UB3 105 A3
Gloucester Pk SW7 256 A4
Gloucester Pl W1 92 D2 237 D4
Gloucester Pl Mews W1 92 D2 237 D3
Gloucester Prim Sch SE15 139 C5
Gloucester Rd
Acton W3 111 A4
Croydon CR0 205 C2
Ealing W5 109 C4
Edmonton N18 33 D5
Enfield EN2 5 A5
Gloucester Rd *continued*
Erith DA17 125 B1
Feltham TW13 150 C3
Hampton TW12 173 D3
Harrow HA1 41 D4
Higham Hill E17 34 D1
Hounslow TW4 129 A1
Ilford E12 78 B4
Kingston u T KT1, KT2 176 D1
Leyton E10 53 C2
New Barnet EN5 14 A6
Richmond TW9 132 C5
South Kensington SW7 114 A2 256 A4
Teddington TW11 174 C5
Tottenham N17 51 B6
Twickenham TW2 152 A3
Wanstead E11 55 C4
Gloucester Road Sta SW7 114 A2 256 A4
Gloucester Sq
6 Hackney E2 96 A6
Paddington W2 92 C1 237 A1
Gloucester St SW1 115 C1 259 A2
Gloucester Terr W2 92 A1 236 B1
Gloucester Way EC1 234 B1
Gloucester Wlk W8 113 C4 245 B2
Glover Cl SE2 124 C2
Glover Dr N18 34 C4
Glover Ho
London SE15 140 B1
2 South Hampstead NW6 70 A1
Glover Rd HA5 40 D3
Glovers Gr HA4 38 D2
Glovers Lo 24 TW10 153 D6
Glowhill Ct N12 30 A3
Gloxinia Wlk TW12 173 C4
Glycena Rd SW11 136 D2
Glyn Ave EN4 2 B1
Glyn Cl SE25 183 C2
Glyn Ct Stanmore HA7 25 B4
West Norwood SE27 160 C1
Glyndale Grange SM2 217 D2
Glyndebourne Ct 5 UB5 84 C4
Glyndebourne Pk BR6 226 D6
Glynde Mews SW3 257 B5
Glynde Rd DA7 147 A2
Glynde Reach WC1 233 B1
Glynde St SE4 163 B5
Glyndon Rd SE18 123 B2
Glyn Dr DA14 190 B6
Glynfield Rd NW10 67 C1
Glyn Mans W14 254 B4
Glynne Rd N22 32 C1
Glyn Rd Clapton Pk E5 74 D4
Enfield EN3 6 C1
North Cheam KT4, SM3 216 D6
Glyn St SE11 260 C1
Glynwood Ct 7 SE23 162 C2
Goater's Alley SW6 264 D3
Goat La EN1 5 D5
Goat Rd CR4 202 D2
Goat Wharf TW8 132 A6
Godalming Ave SM6 220 B3
Godalming Rd E14 97 D2
Godbold Rd E15 98 C4
Goddard Cl TW17 192 B6
Goddard Ct HA3 25 A1
Goddard Ho SW19 156 D2
Goddard Pl N19 71 C5
Goddard Rd BR3 207 A5
Goddards Way IG1 57 B1
Goddarts Ho E17 53 C6
Godfrey Ave
Northolt UB5 85 A6
Twickenham TW2 152 B4
Godfrey Hill SE18 122 A2
Godfrey Ho EC1 235 C1
Godfrey Rd SE18 122 B2
Godfrey St
Chelsea SW3 114 C1 257 B2
Mill Meads E15 98 A5
Godfrey Way TW4 151 B4
Goding St SE11 116 A1 260 B1
Godley Rd SW18 158 B3
Godliman St EC4 252 A6
Godman Rd SE15 140 B3
Godolphin Cl N13 32 D4
Godolphin Ho
Primrose Hill NW3 70 C1
7 Streatham SW2 160 C3
Godolphin & Latymer Sch 16 W6 112 B2
Godolphin Pl W3 111 B6
Godolphin Rd W12 112 B4
Godson Rd CR0 220 C5
Godson St N1 234 A4
Godstone Ct 1 N16 51 C1
Godstone Ho
Borough The SE1 262 D6
1 Kingston u T KT2 176 D4
Godstone Rd
Sutton SM1 218 A4
Twickenham TW1 153 B5
Godstow Rd SE2 124 C4
Godwin Cl
Shoreditch N1 235 B4
West Ewell KT19 215 A2
Godwin Ct NW1 232 B4
Godwin Ho
2 Haggerston E2 95 D5
Kidbrooke SE18 144 B4
Kilburn NW6 91 D5
Godwin Jun Sch E7 77 B4
Godwin Prim Sch RM9 81 A1
Godwin Rd
Bromley BR1, BR2 209 C6
Forest Gate E7 77 B4
Godwyn Ho 13 KT6 198 A3
Goffers Ho SE3 142 C3
Goffers Rd SE3, SE13 142 C3
Goffs Rd TW15 171 B4
Goffton Ho 14 SW9 138 B3
Goidel Cl SM6 219 D4
Golborne Gdns
5 Kensal Town W10 91 A3
West Kilburn W10 91 B3
Golborne Mews 9 W10 91 A2
Golborne Rd W10 91 A2
Golda Cl EN5 12 D5
Golda Ct N3 29 B1
Goldbeaters Gr HA8 27 C3
Goldbeaters Prim Sch HA8 27 B2
Goldcliff Cl SM4 201 C2
Goldcrest Cl
Newham E16 99 D2
Woolwich SE28 124 C6
Goldcrest Mews W5 87 D2
Goldcrest Way
Bushey WD23 8 A3
New Addington CR0 224 B1
Golden Cres UB3 105 D5
Golden Cross Mews 2 W11 91 B1
Golden Ct
4 Barnet EN4 2 C1
Ealing W7 108 C6
Hounslow TW3 130 B3
10 Richmond TW9 153 D6
Golden Hinde The* SE1 252 C4
Golden Hind Pl 5 SE8 119 B2
Golden La EC1 95 A3 242 B5
Golden Lane Campus EC1 95 A3 242 B5
Golden Lane L Ctr EC1 95 A3 242 A5
Golden Manor W7 108 C6
Golden Mews SE20 184 C2
Golden Par 2 E17 54 A6
Golden Plover Cl E16 99 A1
Golden Sq W1 115 C6 249 B6
Golders Cl HA8 26 D5
Golders Ct NW11 47 B2
Golders Gdns NW11 47 B2
GOLDERS GREEN 47 B2
Golders Green Coll NW11 47 C1
Golders Green Cres NW11 47 C2
Golders Green Rd NW11 47 A2
Golders Green Sta NW11 47 C1

Golders Hill Sch NW11 47 C2
Golderslea NW11 47 C1
Golders Manor Dr NW11 47 A3
Golders Park Cl NW11 47 C1
Golders Rise NW4 46 D4
Golders Way NW11 47 B2
Golderton 2 NW4 46 C5
Goldfinch Rd SE28 123 B3
Goldhawk Ind Est W6 112 B3
Goldhawk Mews 2 W12 112 B4
Goldhawk Rd W12 112 A3
Goldhawk Road Sta W12 112 C4
Goldhaze Cl IG8 37 D3
Gold Hill HA8 27 B4
Goldhurst Terr NW6 70 A1
Goldie Ho N19 49 D2
Goldie Leigh Hospl SE2 146 C6
Golding Cl KT9 213 C2
Golding Ct 7 IG1 78 C5
Golding St E1 96 A1
Goldington Cres NW1 232 C4
Goldington Ct NW1 232 C5
Goldington St NW1 93 D5 232 C4
Gold La HA8 27 B4
Goldman Cl E2 96 A3
Goldmark Ho SE3 143 B2
Goldney Rd W9 91 C3
Goldrill Dr N11 15 A2
Goldsboro Rd SW8 137 D5 269 D3
Goldsborough Cres E4 20 A2
Goldsborough Ho SW8 269 D1
Goldsdown Cl EN3 7 A3
Goldsdown Rd EN3 7 A3
Goldsmid St 2 SE18 123 C1
Goldsmith Ave
Acton W3 111 B6
Dagenham RM7 59 C2
Hyde The NW9 45 C3
Plashet E12 78 A2
Goldsmith Cl HA2 41 D1
Goldsmith Ct
Edgware HA8 26 B6
St Giles WC1 240 B2
Goldsmith Ho W3 111 B6
Goldsmith La NW9 45 A5
Goldsmith Rd
Acton W3 111 B5
Friern Barnet N11 30 D5
Higham Hill E17 34 D1
Leyton E10 53 D1
Peckham SE15 140 A4
Goldsmiths Bldgs W3 111 B5
Goldsmiths Cl W3 111 B5
Goldsmiths Coll, Univ of London SE14 141 A4
Goldsmith's Ct N6 49 B3
Goldsmith's Pl 6 NW6 91 D6
Goldsmith's Row E2 96 A5
Goldsmith's Sq 17 E2 96 A5
Goldsmith St EC2 242 B2
Goldthorpe NW1 232 A5
Goldwell Ho SE22 139 C1
Goldwell Rd CR7 204 B5
Goldwin Cl SE14 140 C4
Goldwing Cl E16 99 A1
Golf Cl
South Norwood SW16 182 C2
Stanmore HA7 25 C3
Golf Club Dr KT2 177 B3
Golfe Ho IG1 79 B5
Golfe Rd IG1 79 B5
Golfers View N12 30 B6
Golf Rd Bromley BR1 210 C6
Ealing W5 88 B1
Golf Side TW2 152 B1
Golfside Cl N20 14 C1
Golf Side Cl KT3 177 C1
Gollogly Terr 9 SE7 121 C1
Gomer Gdns TW11 175 A4
Gomer Pl TW11 175 A4
Gomm Rd SE16 118 C3
Gomshall Ave SM6 220 A3
Gondar Gdns NW6 69 B3
Gondar Mans NW6 69 B3
Gonson St SE8 141 D6
Gonston Cl SW19 157 A2
Gonville Cres UB5 63 D2
Gonville Ct 6 EN4 14 D3
Gonville Ho 6 SW15 156 D5
Gonville Prim Sch CR7 204 B4
Gonville Rd CR7 204 B4
Gonville St SW6 135 A2
Gooch Ho
Holborn EC1 241 A4
Lower Clapton E5 74 B5
Goodall Ho 10 SE4 140 D1
Goodall Rd E11 76 A5
Goodbehere Ho 7 SE27 183 A6
Gooden Ct HA1 64 C5
Goodenough Coll WC1 94 B3 240 C6
Goodenough Rd SW19 179 B3
Goodey Rd IG11 79 D1
Goodfaith Ho 18 E14 119 D6
Goodge Pl W1 239 B3
Goodge St W1 93 C2 239 B3
Goodge Street Sta W1 93 D2 239 C4
Goodhall Cl HA7 25 B4
Goodhall St NW10 89 D4
Good Hart Pl E14 119 A6
Goodhart Way BR4 208 C3
Goodhew Rd CR0 206 A3
Goodhope Ho 17 E14 119 D6
Gooding Cl KT3 199 A4
Goodinge Cl N7 72 A2
Goodinge Rd N7 72 A2
Gooding Ho 4 SE7 121 C1
Goodison Cl WD23 8 A6
Goodland Ho 1 KT3 199 C2
Goodman Cres
Streatham SW2 159 D2
Thornton Heath CR0 205 A3
Goodman Rd E10 54 A2
Goodmans Ct HA0 65 D4
Goodman's Stile 17 E1 96 A1
Goodman's Yd E1, EC3 117 D6 253 C6
GOODMAYES 58 B1
Goodmayes Ave IG3 58 A1
Goodmayes Hospl IG3 58 A4
Goodmayes La IG3 80 A5
Goodmayes Lodge RM8 80 A4
Goodmayes Prim Sch IG3 58 B1
Goodmayes Rd IG3 58 A1
Goodmayes Ret Pk RM6 58 B2
Goodmayes Sta IG3 58 A1
Goodrich Com Prim Sch SE22 162 A5
Goodrich Ct 9 W10 90 D1
Goodrich Ho
20 Bethnal Green E2 96 C5
Stamford Hill N16 51 C2
Goodrich Rd SE22 162 A5
Goodridge Ho E17 36 A3
Good Shepherd RC Prim Sch
Catford BR1 186 D6
New Addington CR0 223 D1
Good Shepherd RC Prim Sch The W12 111 D4
Goodson Ho SM4 202 A2
Goodson Rd NW10 67 C1
Goodspeed Ho 20 E14 119 D6
Goodsway NW1 94 A5 233 A4
Goodway Gdns E14 98 B1
Goodwill Ho 22 E14 119 D6
Goodwin Cl
Bermondsey SE16 117 D3 263 D5
Mitcham CR4 202 B6
Goodwin Ct
East Barnet EN4 14 C5
Hornsey N8 50 A6
2 Mitcham SW19 180 C3
Goodwin Dr DA14 168 D2
Goodwin Gdns CR0, CR2 220 D2
Goodwin Ho
Edmonton N9 18 C3
2 Peckham SE15 140 B2
Goodwin Rd
Croydon CR0 220 D3
Edmonton N9 18 D3
Shepherd's Bush W12 112 A4
Goodwins Ct WC2 250 A6
Goodwin St N4 72 C6
Goodwood Ave EN3 6 C6
Goodwood Cl
Morden SM4 201 C5
11 Stanmore HA7 25 C5
Goodwood Ct W1 238 D4
Goodwood Dr UB5 63 C2
Goodwood Ho
3 Acton Green W4 111 A1
Penge SE26 184 B4
Goodwood Lo 1 SM6 219 D5
Goodwood Mans 3 SW9 138 C2
Goodwood Par BR3 207 A5
Goodwood Rd SE14 141 A5
Goodwyn Ave NW7 27 C5
Goodwyn Sch NW7 28 A5
Goodwyn's Vale N10 31 B2
Goodyear Ho 8 N2 30 B1
Goodyers Gdns NW4 46 D4
Goosander Ct 34 NW9 27 D1
Goosander Way SE18, SE28 123 B3
Gooseacre La HA3 43 D4
Goose Green Cl BR5 190 A1
Goose Green Prim Sch SE22 139 D1
Goose Green Trad Est SE22 140 A1
Gooseley La E6 100 C4
Goose Sq 8 E6 100 B1
Goossens Cl 1 SM1 218 A3
Gophir La EC4 252 C6
Gopsall St N1 95 B6 235 D5
Gordon Ave
Chingford E4 36 C4
Isleworth TW1 153 B6
Mortlake SW14 133 C1
Stanmore HA7 25 A4
Gordonbrock Prim Sch SE4 163 C6
Gordonbrock Rd SE4 163 C6
Gordon Cl E17 53 C3
Gordon Cres
Croydon CR0 205 D1
Hayes UB3 106 A2
Gordon Ct
Edgware HA8 26 B5
Hampton TW12 174 A5
5 Shepherd's Bush W12 90 C1
18 Wimbledon SW20 178 D3
Gordondale Rd SW18, SW19 157 C2
Gordon Dr TW17 193 B2
Gordon Gdns HA8 26 D1
Gordon Gr SE5 138 D3
Gordon Hill EN2 5 A4
Gordon Hill Sta EN2 4 D4
Gordon Ho
2 Ealing W5 88 A4
Lee SE12 165 A4
17 Shadwell E1 118 C6
Gordon Hospl SW1 115 D2 259 C3
Gordon House Rd NW5 71 A4
Gordon Inf Sch IG1 79 B5
Gordon Lo N16 51 B1
Gordon Mans
3 Barnet EN5 1 B1
Marylebone WC1 239 C5
Gordon Pl W8 113 C4 245 B2
Gordon Prim Sch SE9 144 B1
Gordon Rd
Ashford TW15 148 A1
Gordon Rd *continued*
Avery Hill DA15 167 C6
Barking IG11 101 C6
Beckenham BR3 207 B6
Chingford E4 20 C4
Chiswick W4 132 D6
Claygate KT10 212 C1
Dagenham RM6 59 B3
Ealing W13 109 C6
Edmonton N9 18 B2
Enfield EN2 5 B3
Finchley N3 29 B3
Harrow HA3 42 C6
Ilford IG1 79 B5
Isleworth TW3 130 A1
Kingston u T KT2 176 B2
Leyton E15 76 A4
Peckham SE15 140 B3
Richmond TW9 132 B3
Shepperton TW17 193 B3
Southall UB2 107 A2
Surbiton KT5 198 B2
Wallington SM5 218 D2
Wanstead E11 55 A3
Woodford E18 37 B2
Wood Green N11 31 D3
Yiewsley UB7 104 A6
Gordon Sq WC1 93 D3 239 D6
Gordon St
Bloomsbury WC1 93 D3 239 C6
Newham E13 99 A4
Gordon Way
Barnet EN5 1 B1
Bromley BR1 187 A2
Gore Ct NW9 44 C4
Gorefield Ho NW6 91 C5
Gorefield Pl NW6 91 C5
Gore Rd Hackney E9 96 C6
Merton SW20 178 C1
Goresbrook L Ctr RM9 102 D6
Goresbrook Rd RM9 102 D6
Gore St SW7 114 A3 256 B6
Gorham Ho 12 SW4 159 C5
Gorham Pl W11 244 A5
Goring Gdns RM8 80 C4
Goring Rd N11 32 A4
Goring St EC3 243 B2
Goring Way UB6 86 A5
Gorleston Rd N15 51 B4
Gorleston St W14 113 A2 254 B4
Gorman Rd SE18 122 B2
Gorringe Park Ave CR4 181 A3
Gorringe Park Prim Sch CR4 181 A2
Gorse Cl E16 99 A1
Gorsefield Ho 6 E14 119 C6
Gorse Rd CR0 223 C5
Gorse Rise SW17 181 A5
Gorse Wlk UB7 82 A1
Gorst Rd
London SW11 158 D5
North Acton NW10 89 B3
Gorsuch Pl 1 E2 95 D4
Gorsuch St E2 95 D4
Gosberton Rd SW12 159 A3
Gosbury Hill KT9 214 A4
Gosfield Rd RM8 59 C1
Gosfield St W1 93 C2 239 A3
Gosford Gdns IG4 56 B4
Gosford Ho 25 E3 97 B5
Goshawk Gdns UB4 83 C5
Goslett Yd WC2 239 D2
Gosling Cl UB6 85 C4
Gosling Ho 2 E1 118 C6
Gosling Way SW9 138 C4
Gosmore Ct N9 18 B2
Gospatric Home Ho SW14 133 C2
Gospatrick Rd N17 33 A2
GOSPEL OAK 71 A4
Gospel Oak Prim Sch NW5 71 A4
Gospel Oak Sta NW5 71 A4
Gosport Ho 9 SW15 156 A3
Gosport Rd E17 53 B4
Gosport Wlk N17 52 B5
Gossage Rd
Hillingdon UB10 60 B1
Gossage Rd *continued*
Plumstead SE18 123 B1
Gosset St E2 96 A4
Gosshill Rd BR7 188 C1
Gossington Cl BR7 188 D6
Gosterwood St SE8 141 A6
Gostling Rd TW2 151 C3
Goston Gdns CR7 204 C6
Goswell Pl EC1 234 D1
Goswell Rd EC1 94 D4 234 D2
Gothic Ct
17 Camberwell SE5 139 A5
Harlington UB3 127 B6
Gothic Rd TW2 152 B2
Gottfried Mews NW5 71 C4
Goudhurst Ho 7 SE20 184 C3
Goudhurst Rd BR1 186 D5
Gough Ho
Islington N1 234 D6
4 Kingston u T KT1 176 A1
Gough Rd Enfield EN1 6 B3
Stratford E15 76 D4
Gough Sq EC4 94 C1 241 B2
Gough St WC1 94 B3 240 D5
Gough Wlk 14 E14 97 C1
Gould Ct SE19 183 C5
Goulden Ho SW11 136 C3
Goulding Gdns CR7 183 A1
Gouldman Ho 33 E1 96 C3
Gould Rd
East Bedfont TW14 149 C4
Twickenham TW2 152 C3
Gould's Gn UB8 104 D6
Gould Terr 26 E8 74 B3
Goulston St E1 95 D1 243 C2
Goulton Rd E5 74 B4
Gourley Pl N15 51 C4
Gourley St N15 51 C4
Gourock Rd SE9 166 C6
Govan St E2 96 A6
Gover Ct 8 SW4 138 A3
Government Row EN3 7 C6
Govett Ave TW17 193 A4
Govier Cl E15 76 C1
Gowan Ave SW6 135 A4 264 A2
Gowan Ho 22 E2 95 D4
Gowan Lea 4 E18 55 A5
Gowan Rd NW10 68 B2
Gower Cl SW4 159 C5
Gower Ct WC1 239 C6
Gower Ho
2 Barking IG11 79 A1
Hayes UB3 105 C6
Upper Tooting SW17 180 B4
12 Walthamstow E17 53 D6
Walworth SE17 262 B2
Gower House Sch NW9 67 A6
Gower Mews WC1 239 D4
Gower Pl NW1, WC1 93 D3 239 C6
Gower Rd
Hounslow TW7 130 D6
Upton E7 77 A2
Gower Sch The 4 N7 72 A2
Gower St WC1 93 D3 239 C5
Gower's Wlk E1 96 A1
Gowland Pl BR3 185 B1
Gowlett Rd SE15 140 A2
Gowlland Cl CR0 206 A2
Gowrie Rd SW11 137 A2
Graburn Way KT8 196 B6
Grace Ave DA7 147 B3
Grace Bsns Ctr CR4 202 D3
Gracechurch St EC2, EC4 252 D6
Grace Cl
Burnt Oak HA8 27 A3
Mottingham SE9 165 D1
Grace Ct
5 Croydon CR0 220 D5
Twickenham TW2 152 C2
Gracedale Rd SW16 181 B5
Gracedyer Ho N22 32 A3
Gracefield Gdns SW16 160 A1
Gracehill 2 E1 96 C2

Grace Ho
Kennington SE11 .... 270 D6
Penge SE26 .... 184 B5
Grace Jones Cl E8 .... 74 A2
Grace Path 2 SE26 .. 184 C6
Grace Pl E3 .... 97 D4
Grace Rd CR0 .... 205 A3
Graces Alley 14 SE1 .. 118 A6
Graces Mews NW8 .. 229 B3
Grace's Mews SE5 .. 139 C3
Grace's Rd SE5 .... 139 C3
Grace St E3 .... 97 D4
Gradient The SE26 .. 184 A6
Graeme Ct UB6 .... 85 D4
Graeme Rd EN1 .... 5 C3
Graemesdyke Ave
SW14 .... 132 D1
Grafton Cl Ealing W13 .. 87 A1
Twickenham TW4 .... 151 B3
Worcester Pk KT4 ... 215 C5
Grafton Cres NW1 .... 71 B2
Grafton Ct
10 Dalston E8 .... 74 A3
East Bedfont TW14 ... 149 B3
Grafton Gdns
Dagenham RM8 .... 81 A6
Harringay N4 .... 51 A3
Grafton Ho 16 Bow E3 . 97 C4
12 Deptford SE8 .... 119 B1
Grafton Jun & Inf Schs
RM8 .... 81 B6
Grafton Mans SW4 .. 137 C1
Grafton Mews W1 .. 239 A5
Grafton Park Rd
KT4 .... 215 C6
Grafton Pl
NW1 .... 93 D4 232 D1
Grafton Prim Sch 5
N7 .... 72 A5
Grafton Rd Acton W3 . 111 A6
Dagenham RM8 .... 81 A6
Enfield EN2 .... 4 B2
Gospel Oak NW5 .... 71 A3
Harrow HA1 .... 42 A4
Kingston u T KT3 .... 199 C6
Thornton Heath CR0 . 204 C1
Worcester Pk KT4 ... 215 C5
Grafton Sq SW4 .... 137 C2
Grafton St
W1 .... 115 B6 248 D5
Grafton Terr NW5 .... 71 A3
Grafton Way
East Molesey KT8 .... 195 B5
Marylebone W1 .... 239 B5
Grafton Yd NW5 .... 71 B2
Graham Ave
Ealing W13 .... 109 B4
Mitcham CR4 .... 181 A2
Graham Cl CR0 .... 223 C6
Graham Ct
Bromley BR1 .... 187 B3
5 Deptford SE14 ... 140 D6
Northolt UB5 .... 63 B3
GRAHAME PARK 27 C2
Grahame Park Way NW7,
NW9 .... 27 D2
Grahame White Ho
HA3 .... 43 D6
Graham Gdns KT6 ... 198 A1
Graham Ho
5 Balham SW12 .... 159 B4
6 Barnet EN5 .... 1 D1
Edmonton N9 .... 18 C3
6 Tufnell Pk N19 .... 71 D4
Woolwich SE18 .... 144 D5
Graham Lo
Edgware HA8 .... 26 B4
Hendon NW4 .... 46 B3
Graham Mans
11 Barking IG11 .... 80 A1
2 Hackney E8 .... 74 B2
Graham Rd
Acton W4 .... 111 B3
Bexleyheath DA6 .... 147 C1
Dalston E8 .... 74 A2
Hampton TW12 .... 173 C6
Harringay N15 .... 50 D6
Harrow HA3 .... 42 C6
Hendon NW4 .... 46 B3
Merton SW19 .... 179 B3
Mitcham CR4 .... 181 A2
Newham E13 .... 99 A3
Graham St N1 . 94 D5 234 D3
Graham Terr
SW1 .... 115 A2 258 B3
Graham Twr W3 .... 110 D3
Grainger Cl UB5 .... 64 A3
Grainger Ct 22 SE5 ... 139 A5
Grainger Rd
Isleworth TW7 .... 130 D3
Tottenham N22 .... 33 A2
Gramer Cl E11 .... 76 B6
Grampian Cl
Harlington UB3 .... 127 B5
Orpington BR6 .... 211 D3
15 Sutton SM2 .... 218 A1
Grampian Gdns NW2 .. 47 A1
Grampians The 10
W14 .... 112 D4
Gramsci Way SE6 ... 163 D1
Granada St SW17 ... 180 D5
Granard Ave SW15 ... 156 B6
Granard Bsns Ctr
NW7 .... 27 C4
Granard Ho 20 E9 .... 74 D2
Granard Prim Sch
SW15 .... 156 B5
Granard Rd SW11,
SW12 .... 158 D4
Granary Cl N9 .... 18 C4
Granary Ct 3 RM6 .... 58 D2
Granary Mans SE28 .. 123 A4
Granary Rd E1 .... 96 B3
Granary Sq N1 .... 72 C2
Granary St
NW1 .... 93 D6 232 C5
Granary The SE8 .... 141 C5
Granby Ho 13 SE18 ... 122 B2
Granby Pl SE1 .... 251 A1
Granby Rd
Eltham SE9 .... 144 B2
Woolwich SE18 .... 122 D3
Granby St
Bethnal Green E2 .... 96 A3
Shoreditch E2 .... 243 D6
Granby Terr
NW1 .... 93 C5 232 A3
Grand Arc N12 .... 30 A5
Grand Ave
Clerkenwell EC1 .... 241 D4
Fortis Green N10 .... 49 A5
Tolworth KT5 .... 198 D3
Wembley HA9 .... 66 C3
Grand Ave E HA9 .... 66 D3
Grand Avenue Prim Sch
KT5 .... 199 A3
Grand Ct RM8 .... 81 A5
Grand Depot Rd
SE18 .... 122 C1
Grand Dr
Southall UB2 .... 108 A4
West Barnes SM4,
SW20 .... 200 C5
Granden Rd SW16 ... 182 A1
Grandfield Ct W4 .... 133 B6
Grandison Rd
London SW11 .... 158 D6
North Cheam KT4 .... 216 C5
Grand Junction Wharf
N1 .... 235 A3
Grand Par London N4 .. 50 D3
Mortlake SW14 .... 133 A1
Tolworth KT6 .... 198 C1
Wembley HA9 .... 66 C6
Grand Union Cl W9 ... 91 B2
Grand Union Cres E8 .. 96 A6
Grand Union Ind Est
NW10 .... 88 D5
Grand Union Way
UB2 .... 107 C4
Grand Vitesse Ind Est
SE1 .... 251 D3
Granfield St SW11 .. 266 D1
Grange Ave
East Barnet EN4 .... 14 D3
North Finchley N12 .... 30 A5
South Norwood SE25 . 183 C1
Stanmore HA7 .... 25 C1
Totteridge N20 .... 13 A4
Twickenham TW2 .... 152 C2
Woodford IG8 .... 37 A3
Grange Cl
East Molesey KT8 ... 195 D5
Edgware HA8 .... 27 A5
Hayes UB3 .... 83 C2
Heston TW5 .... 129 B6
Sidcup DA15 .... 168 A1
Woodford IG8 .... 37 A3
Grangecliffe Gdns
SE25 .... 183 C1
Grangecourt Rd N16 .. 51 C1
Grange Cres SE28 .... 102 C1
Grange Ct
Belmont SM2 .... 217 D1
4 Finchley N12 .... 30 A4
Hackbridge SM6 .... 219 B5
Harrow HA1 .... 64 D5
Ilford IG6 .... 57 A6
Littleton TW17 .... 192 C5
Loughton IG10 .... 21 D6
Northolt UB5 .... 84 C5
Peckham SE15 .... 139 D3
Pinner HA5 .... 41 A6
Strand WC2 .... 240 D1
Wembley HA0 .... 65 C3
1 Willesden NW10 .... 67 C4
Grange Dr BR7 .... 188 B4
Grange Farm Cl HA2 .. 64 A6
Grange Farm Est
TW17 .... 193 C6
Grangefield NW1 .... 72 A1
Grange Fst & Mid Schs
HA2 .... 41 D1
Grange Gdns
London N14 .... 15 D3
Pinner HA5 .... 41 A5
South Norwood SE25 . 183 C1
West Hampstead NW3 . 69 D5
Grange Gr N1 .... 73 A2
Grange Hill
Edgware HA8 .... 27 A5
South Norwood SE25 . 183 C1
Grangehill Pl SE9 .... 144 B2
Grangehill Rd SE9 .... 144 B1
Grange Ho
6 Barking IG11 .... 101 B6
Bermondsey SE1 .... 263 C5
Willesden NW10 .... 68 B1
Grange La SE21 .... 161 D2
Grange Lo SW19 .... 178 D4
Grange Mans KT17 .. 215 D1
Grangemill 11 NW5 ... 71 B4
Grangemill Rd SE6 .. 163 C2
GRANGE MILLS 113 C3
Grange Mills SW12 .. 159 C3
Grangemill Way SE6 . 163 C2
GRANGE PARK 16 C6
Grange Park Ave N21 . 17 A5
Grange Park Jun & Inf
Schs UB4 .... 83 D3
Grange Park Pl
SW20 .... 178 B3
Grange Park Prep Sch
N21 .... 16 D5
Grange Park Prim Sch
N21 .... 4 C1
Grange Park Rd
Leyton E10 .... 53 D1
South Norwood CR7 ... 205 B6
Grange Park Sta N21 .. 16 D5
Grange Pk W5 .... 110 A5
Grange Pl NW6 .... 69 C1
Grange Prim Sch
Bermondsey
SE1 .... 117 C3 263 A5
Ealing W5 .... 109 D4
Newham E13 .... 98 D4
Grange Rd
Barnes SW13 .... 134 A4
Belmont SM2 .... 217 C1
Bermondsey
SE1 .... 117 D3 263 C5
Borehamwood WD6 .... 10 B6
Burnt Oak HA8 .... 27 B4
Chessington KT9 .... 214 A4
Ealing W5 .... 110 A5
East Molesey KT8 ... 195 D5
Greenhill HA1 .... 43 A4
Gunnersbury W4 .... 110 D1
Hayes UB3 .... 83 C1
Highgate N6 .... 49 A3
Ilford IG1 .... 79 A4
Kingston u T KT1 .... 198 A6
Leyton E10 .... 53 C1
Newham E13 .... 98 D4
Orpington BR6 .... 227 A6
Roxeth HA2 .... 64 B6
Southall UB1 .... 107 A4
South Norwood SE19,
SE25 .... 183 B1
Tottenham N17 .... 34 A4
Walthamstow E17 .... 53 A4
Willesden NW10 .... 68 B2
Grange St N1 .... 235 D5
Grange The
Bermondsey
SE1 .... 117 D3 263 C5
Cockfosters EN4 .... 2 D2
Croydon CR0 .... 223 B6
Ealing W13 .... 87 C2
7 Gunnersbury W4 .. 110 D1
Hammersmith W12 .... 112 B3
19 Maitland Pk NW3 ... 70 D2
South Acton W3 .... 110 D4
3 Walthamstow E17 .... 53 A4
4 Wanstead E18 .... 55 A6
Wembley HA0 .... 66 C1
West Barnes KT3 .... 200 A4
West Ewell KT19 .... 215 B4
West Kensington
W14 .... 113 B2 254 C3
Wimbledon SW19 ... 178 D4
Grange Vale SM2 .... 217 D1
Grange View Rd N20 .. 14 A3
Grangeway
London N12 .... 29 D6
South Hampstead NW6 69 C1
Woodford IG8 .... 37 C6
Grangeway Gdns IG4 . 56 A4
Grangeway The N21 ... 16 D5
Grange Wlk
SE1 .... 117 D3 263 C5
Grangewood DA5 .... 169 B3
Grangewood Cl HA5 .. 40 A4
Grangewood Ind Sch
E7 .... 77 D1
Grangewood La BR3 . 185 B4
Grangewood Sch
HA5 .... 39 D4
Grangewood St E6 .... 99 D6
Grange Yd
SE1 .... 117 D3 263 C5
Granham Gdns N9 .... 17 D2
Granite Apts E15 .... 76 B2
Granite St SE18 .... 123 D1
Granleigh Rd E11 .... 76 C6
Grannary The 10
SE16 .... 118 C4
Gransden Ave E8 .... 74 B1
Gransden Ho 1 SE8 .. 119 B1
Gransden Rd W12 ... 111 D4
Grantbridge St
N1 .... 94 D5 234 D4
Grantchester 12
KT1 .... 176 C1
Grantchester Cl HA1 .. 64 D5
Grant Cl London N14 .... 15 C4
Shepperton TW17 ... 192 D3
Tottenham N17 .... 33 C1
Grant Ct
2 Chingford E4 .... 20 A3
11 Hendon NW9 .... 27 D1
Grantham Cl HA8 .... 10 A1
Grantham Ct
Dagenham RM6 .... 59 B2
Kingston u T KT2 .... 175 D5
9 Rotherhithe SE16 . 118 D4
Grantham Gdns RM6 .. 59 B2
Grantham Gn WD6 .... 11 A6
Grantham Ho
Ashford TW16 .... 171 C3
12 Peckham SE15 ... 140 A6
Grantham Pl W1 .... 248 C3
Grantham Rd
Chiswick W4 .... 133 C5
Little Ilford E12 .... 78 C4
South Lambeth SW9 . 138 A3
Grant Ho
38 Clapham SW8 .... 137 D3
Clerkenwell EC1 .... 241 D4
Grantley Ho
2 Deptford SE14 ... 140 D6
5 Putney SW19 .... 156 D3
Grantley Pl KT10 .... 212 A3
Grantley Rd TW4,
TW5 .... 128 C3
Grantley St E1 .... 96 D3
Grant Mus of Zoology★
WC1 .... 93 D3 239 C5
Grantock Rd E17 .... 36 B2
Granton Prim Sch
SW16 .... 181 C3
Granton Rd Ilford IG3 .. 58 A1
Sidcup DA14 .... 190 C4
Streatham SW16 .... 181 C2
Grant Pl 2 CR0 .... 205 D1
Grant Rd
Battersea SW11 .... 136 C2
Croydon CR0 .... 205 D1
Grant Rd *continued*
Harrow HA3 .... 42 D6
Grants Cl NW7 .... 28 D3
Grants Cotts KT10 .... 212 B6
Grant St Islington N1 . 234 A4
Newham E13 .... 99 A4
Grantully Rd W9 .... 91 D4
Grant Way TW7 .... 131 A6
Granville Ave
Feltham TW13 .... 150 A2
Hounslow TW3, TW4 . 151 C6
Lower Edmonton N9 ... 18 C1
Granville Cl CR0 .... 221 C6
Granville Ct
8 Deptford SE14 ... 141 A5
Hornsey N4 .... 50 B3
Shoreditch N1 .... 235 D6
Granville Gdns
Ealing W5 .... 110 B5
South Norwood SW16 182 B3
Granville Gr SE13 .... 142 A2
Granville Ho 18 E14 ... 97 C1
Granville Ind Est
NW2 .... 69 B6
Granville Mans 8
W12 .... 112 C4
Granville Mews
DA14 .... 190 A6
Granville Pk SE13 .... 142 B2
Granville Pl
London N12 .... 30 A3
Marylebone
W1 .... 93 A1 238 A1
Pinner HA5 .... 40 D6
Walham Green SW6 .. 265 C3
Granville Point NW2 .. 69 B6
Granville Rd
Bexley DA16 .... 146 C2
Bowes Pk N13 .... 32 B4
Child's Hill NW2 .... 69 B6
Finchley N12 .... 30 A3
Hayes UB3 .... 105 D2
Hillingdon UB10 .... 60 D2
Hornsey N4, N8 .... 50 B3
Ilford IG1 .... 78 D6
Kilburn NW6 .... 91 C5
Merton SW19 .... 179 C3
Sidcup DA14 .... 190 B6
Tottenham N22 .... 32 D2
Walthamstow E17 .... 53 D3
Wandsworth SW18 ... 157 B4
Woodford E18 .... 37 B1
Granville Sq
3 Camberwell
SE15 .... 139 C5
Finsbury WC1 .. 94 B4 233 D1
Granville St WC1 .... 233 D1
Granwood Ct 5
TW7 .... 130 C4
Grape St WC2 .... 240 A2
Grapsome Cl KT9 .... 213 C1
Grasdene Rd SE18 ... 146 A5
Grasgarth Cl W3 .... 111 A6
Grasmere NW1 .... 231 D1
Grasmere Ave
Acton W3 .... 111 B6
Kingston u T SW15 ... 177 C6
Locksbottom BR6 .... 226 D5
Merton SW19 .... 201 C6
Ruislip HA4 .... 39 A2
Twickenham TW3 .... 151 D5
Wembley HA9 .... 43 D1
Grasmere Cl TW14 .. 149 D3
Grasmere Ct
Barnes SW13 .... 134 A6
Bowes Pk N22 .... 32 B4
Forest Hill SE26 .... 184 A5
7 Sutton SM2 .... 218 A2
Grasmere Gdns
Harrow HA3 .... 25 A1
Locksbottom BR6 .... 226 D5
Redbridge IG4 .... 56 B4
Grasmere Ho 20 N16 .. 73 B4
Grasmere Point 2
SE15 .... 140 C5
Grasmere Prim Sch
N16 .... 73 B4
Grasmere Rd
Bromley BR1 .... 186 D3
Croydon SE25 .... 206 B4
Locksbottom BR6 .... 226 D5
Muswell Hill N10 .... 31 B2
3 Newham E13 .... 99 A5
Streatham SW16 .... 182 B5
Tottenham N17 .... 34 A4

Grasshaven Way SE28 . . . . . 123 D5
Grassington Cl N11 . . . 31 A4
Grassington Rd DA14 . . . . . 190 A6
Grassmere Ct [6] EN1 . . 17 C6
Grassmount SE23 . . . . 162 B2
Grass Pk N3 . . . . 29 B2
Grassway SM6 . . . . . . 219 C4
Grasvenor Ave EN5 . . . 13 C5
Grasvenor Avenue Inf Sch EN5 . . . . . 13 C5
Grateley Ho [10] SW15 . . . . . 156 B3
Gratton Rd W14 . . . . . 113 A3 254 A5
Gratton Terr NW2 . . . . 68 D5
Graveley [16] KT1 . . . . 176 C1
Graveley Ave WD6 . . . . 11 A6
Graveley Ho [7] SE8 . . 119 A2
Gravel Hill
Bexley DA6 . . . . 169 D6
Church End N3 . . . . . . 29 B1
South Croydon CR0, CR2 . . . . . . 223 B1
Gravel Hill Cl DA6 . . . 169 D5
Gravel Hill Prim Sch DA6 . . . . . . 169 D6
Gravel Hill Sta CR0 . . 223 A2
Gravel La E1 . . . 95 D1 243 C2
Gravel Rd
Keston Mark BR2 . . . . 226 A6
Twickenham TW2 . . . . 152 C3
Gravelwood Cl BR7 . . 167 A1
Gravenel Gdns [5] SW17 . . . . . . 180 C5
Graveney Gr SE20 . . . 184 C3
Graveney Rd SW17 . . . 180 C6
Graveney Sch SW17 . . 181 B5
Gravesend Rd W12 . . . 112 A6
Graves Est DA16 . . . . 146 B3
Gray Ave RM8 . . . . 59 B1
Gray Ct [8] KT2 . . . . . 175 D6
Grayfriars Pas EC1 . . 241 D2
Grayham Cres KT3 . . . 199 B5
Grayham Rd KT3 . . . . . 199 B5
Gray Ho SE17 . . . . . . 262 B2
Grayland Cl BR1 . . . . 187 D2
Grayland Ct WC1 . . . . 233 C1
Grayling Cl E16 . . . . . . 98 C3
Grayling Ct
Ealing W5 . . . . 109 D5
Tottenham Hale N17 . . . 52 B5
Grayling Rd N16 . . . . . 73 B6
Grayling Sq E2 . . . . . . 96 A4
Grays Cotts UB9 . . . . . 38 C1
Grays Court Com Hospl RM10 . . . . 81 D1
Grayscroft Rd SW16 . 181 D3
Grays Farm Prim Sch BR5 . . . . 190 B2
Grays Farm Production Village BR5 . . . . . 190 B2
Grays Farm Rd BR5 . . 190 B2
Grayshott Ct [10] SM2 . . . . 217 D1
Grayshott Rd SW11 . . 137 A2
Gray's Inn★ WC1 . . . . . . 94 B2 240 D4
Gray's Inn Pl WC1 . . . 240 D3
Gray's Inn Rd WC1 . . . . . . 94 B3 240 D6
Gray's Inn Sq WC1 . . . . . . 94 C2 241 A4
Grays La TW15 . . . . . . 170 D6
Grayson Ho EC1 . . . . 235 B1
Gray's Rd UB10 . . . . . . 60 A1
Gray St SE1 . . . 116 C4 251 B1
Grayswood Gdns SW20 . . . . 178 B1
Grayswood Point [14] SW15 . . . . 156 A3
Gray's Yd W1 . . . . 238 B2
Graywood Ct N12 . . . . . 30 A3
Grazebrook Rd N16 . . . 73 B6
Grazeley Ct SE19 . . . . 183 C5
Great Amwell La N8 . . . 50 B6
Great Arthur Ho EC1 242 A5
Great Bell Alley EC2 . 242 C2
Great Benty UB7 . . . . 104 A2
Great Brownings SE21 . . . . 183 D6
Great Bushey Dr N20 . . 13 D3
Great Cambridge Ind Est EN1 . . . . 18 B6
Great Cambridge Junction N13, N18 . . . 33 B6
Great Cambridge Rd
Edmonton N9, N18 . . . . 17 C3
Enfield EN1 . . . . 6 A3
Great Castle St W1 . . 239 A2
Great Central Ave HA4 . . . . 62 C3
Great Central St NW1 . . . . . . 92 D2 237 C4
Great Central Way NW10 . . . . 67 B4
Great Chapel St W1 . . . . 93 D1 239 C2
Great Chart St SW11 . . . . 136 A1
Great Chertsey Rd
Chiswick SW14, W4 . . 133 B4
Feltham TW13, TW2 . . 151 C1
Great Church La W6 . . . . 112 D1
Great College St SW1 . . . . . . 116 A3 260 A6
Great Croft WC1 . . . . 233 B1
Great Cross Ave SE3 . . . . 142 C5
Great Cumberland Mews W1 . . . . 237 C1
Great Cumberland Pl W1 . . . . 92 D1 237 D1
Great Dover St SE1 . . . . . . 117 B3 262 C6
Greatdown Rd W7 . . . . 86 D2
Great Eastern Bldgs [10] E8 . . . . 74 B2
Great Eastern Ent Ctr E14 . . . . 119 D4
Great Eastern Pier E14 . . . . 119 C1
Great Eastern Rd E15 . 76 B2
Great Eastern St EC2 . . . . . . 95 C3 243 A6
Great Eastern Wharf SW11 . . . . 267 B3
Great Elms Rd BR2 . . 209 C5
Great Field
Hendon NW9 . . . . 27 D2
[7] Kentish Town NW5 . . 71 C3
Greatfield Ave E6 . . . . 100 B3
Greatfield Cl
London SE4 . . . . 141 C1
[4] Tufnell Pk N19 . . . . . 71 C4
Greatfields Dr UB8 . . . . 82 C2
Greatfields Rd IG11 . . 101 B5
Great Fleete Way IG11 . . . . 102 C5
Great Galley Cl IG11 . 102 C4
Great Gatton Cl CR0 . 207 A2
Great George St SW1 . . . . . . 116 A4 250 A1
Great Guildford Bsns Sq SE1 . . . . 252 A3
Great Guildford St SE1 . . . . . . 117 A5 252 A3
Great Hall The [1] E11 . 55 B5
Greatham Wlk [8] SW15 . . . . 156 A3
Great Harry Dr SE9 . . 166 C1
Great James St WC1 240 C4
Great Marlborough St W1 . . . . 93 C1 239 A1
Great Maze Pond SE1 . . . . . . 117 B4 252 D2
Great Newport St WC2 . . . . 250 A6
Great North Rd
Barnet EN5 . . . . 1 A2
East Finchley N2 . . . . . 48 C5
New Barnet EN5 . . . . . 13 D6
Great North Way (Barnet By-Pass) NW4 . . . . . . 46 D6
Greatorex Ho [13] E1 . . . 96 A2
Greatorex St E1 . . . . . . 96 A2
Great Ormond St Hospl for Children WC1 . . . . . . 94 B3 240 C5
Great Ormond St WC1 . . . . . . 94 B3 240 C5
Great Percy St WC1 . . . . . . 94 C4 234 A2
Great Peter St SW1 . . . . . 115 D3 259 D5
Great Portland St W1 . . . . . . 93 B2 238 D4
Great Portland Street Sta W1 . . . . 93 B3 238 D5
Great Pulteney St W1 . . . . 249 B6
Great Queen St WC2 . . . . . . 94 A1 240 B2
Great Russell Mans WC1 . . . . 240 A3
Great Russell St WC1 . . . . . . 94 A2 240 A3
Great St Helen's EC3 243 A2
Great St Thomas Apostle EC4 . . . . 252 B6
Great Scotland Yd SW1, WC2 . . . . 116 A5 250 A4
Great Smith St SW1 . . . . . 115 D3 259 D6
Great South West Rd TW6, TW14, TW4 . . . . 148 B6
Great South-West Rd TW5 . . . . 128 B2
Great Spilmans SE22 . . . . 161 C6
Greatstone Ho [10] SE20 . . . . 184 C3
Great Strand NW9 . . . . 27 D1
Great Suffolk St SE1 . . . . . . 116 D5 251 D3
Great Sutton St EC1 . . . . 94 D3 241 D5
Great Swan Alley EC2 . . . . 242 C2
Great Thrift BR5 . . . . . 211 A5
Great Titchfield St W1 . . . . 93 C2 239 A3
Great Tower St EC3 . . . . 117 C6 253 A6
Great Trinity La EC4 . 252 B6
Great Turnstile WC2 . 240 D3
Great Western Ind Pk UB1, UB2 . . . . 108 A4
Great Western Rd W2, W9 . . . . 91 B2
Great West Ho TW8 . 131 C6
Great West Rd
Brentford TW7, TW8 . . . . 131 B6
Chiswick W4, W6 . . . . 133 B6
Heston TW5, TW7 . . . 129 B4
Hounslow TW5, TW7 . . 130 B5
Great West Road Cedars Rd W4 . . . . 133 A6
Great West Road Hogarth La W4 . . . . 133 C6
Great West Trad Est TW8 . . . . 131 B6
Great Winchester St EC2 . . . . 95 B1 242 D2
Great Windmill St W1 . . . . . . 115 D6 249 C6
Greatwood BR7 . . . . . 188 C3
Great Yd SE1 . . . . 253 B2
Greaves Cl IG11 . . . . . . 79 C1
Greaves Cotts [10] E14 . . 97 A2
Greaves Ct N8 . . . . 50 C5
Greaves Pl SW17 . . . . . 180 C6
Greaves Twr SW10 . . 266 B4
Grebe [3] NW9 . . . . 27 D1
Grebe Ave UB4 . . . . 84 D1
Grebe Cl
Barking IG11 . . . . 102 A3
Higham Hill E17 . . . . . . 35 A3
Stratford E7 . . . . 76 D3
Grebe Ct Cheam SM1 . . 217 B3
[16] Cubitt Town E14 . . 120 A4
Grebe Terr [4] KT1 . . . . 198 A6
Grecian Cres SE19 . . 182 D4
Greek Ct W1 . . . . 239 D1
Greek Sch of London W3 . . . . 110 D6
Greek Sec Sch of London N22 . . . . 32 B2
Greek St W1 . . . 93 D1 239 D1
Greenacre Cl
Barnet EN5 . . . . 1 B5
Northolt UB5 . . . . 63 B3
Greenacre Ct E8 . . . . . . 74 A3
Greenacre Gdns E17 . . 54 A5
Greenacre Pl SM6 . . . 219 B6
Greenacres
Bushey WD23 . . . . 8 B2
Church End N3 . . . . 29 A1
Eltham SE9 . . . . 166 C5
Green Acres
Hayes UB4 . . . . 84 B3
Sidcup DA14 . . . . 189 D6
South Croydon CR0 . . 221 D5
Greenacres Ave UB10 . 60 C5
Greenacres Cl BR6 . . . 227 A4
Greenacres Dr HA7 . . . 25 B3
Greenacres Prim Sch SE9 . . . . 166 C2
Greenacre Sq [26] SE16 . . . . 118 D4
Greenacre Wlk N14 . . . 15 D1
Green Arbour Ct EC1 241 C2
Green Ave
Ealing W13 . . . . 109 B3
Edgware NW7 . . . . 27 C6
Greenaway Gdns NW3 . . . . 69 D4
Greenaway Ho
Finsbury WC1 . . . . . . 234 A1
St John's Wood NW8 . 229 A6
Greenaway Terr TW19 . . . . 148 A3
Green Bank
London N12 . . . . 29 D6
Wapping E1 . . . . 118 B5
Greenbank Ave HA0 . . . 65 A3
Greenbank Cl E4 . . . . . . 20 A2
Greenbank Cres NW4 . 47 A5
Greenbank Lo [2] BR7 . . . . 188 C2
Greenbanks HA1 . . . . . . 64 C4
Greenbay Rd SE7 . . . 143 D5
Greenberry St NW8 . 230 A3
Greenbrook Ave EN4 . . . 2 A4
Green CE Prim Sch The [14] N17 . . . . 51 D6
Green CE Sch Holy Trinity (Inf Annexe) The [10] N15 . . . . 51 D5
Green Cl
Beckenham BR2 . . . . 208 C6
Carshalton SM5 . . . . . 218 D6
Feltham TW13 . . . . . . 173 A5
Kingsbury NW9 . . . . . . 45 A3
North End NW11 . . . . . 48 A2
Greencoat Pl SW1 . . . . . . 115 C2 259 B4
Greencoat Row SW1 259 B5
Greencourt Ave HA8 . . 26 D2
Green Court Ave CR0 . . . . 222 B6
Green Court Gdns CR0 . . . . 222 B6
Greencourt Ho [25] E1 . . 96 D3
Greencourt Rd BR5 . . 211 C4
Greencroft HA8 . . . . . . 27 A5
Greencroft Ave HA4 . . . 62 C6
Greencroft Cl E16 . . . . . 99 D2
Greencroft Gdns
Enfield EN1 . . . . 5 C2
South Hampstead NW6 70 A1
Greencroft Rd TW5 . . 129 B4
Green Ct
Ashford TW16 . . . . . . 171 D4
[2] Willesden NW10 . . . . 67 C4
Greendale NW7 . . . . 27 C6
Green Dale SE22 . . . . . 161 C6
Greendale Cl SE22 . . . 161 C6
Greendale Ct CR2 . . . . 221 A2
Green Dr UB1 . . . . 107 C5
Green Dragon Ct SE1 . . . . 252 C3
Green Dragon Ho WC1 . . . . 240 B2
Green Dragon La
Brentford TW8 . . . . . . 110 B1
Southgate N21 . . . . 16 D5
Green Dragon Prim Sch TW8 . . . . 132 A6
Green Dragon Yd [24] E1 . . . . 96 A2
Greene Ct [20] SE14 . . . 140 D6
Greene Ho SE1 . . . . . 262 C5
Green Elms IG6 . . . . 57 A6
Green End
Chessington KT9 . . . . 214 A4
Edmonton N21 . . . . 16 D2
Greenend Rd W4 . . . . 111 C4
Greener Ct [26] EN3 . . . . . 7 C6
Greener Ho [3] SW4 . . 137 D2
Green Farm Cl BR6 . . 227 D3
Greenfell Mans SE8 . 141 D6
Greenfield Ave KT5 . 198 D3
Greenfield Ct SE9 . . . 166 A1
Greenfield Dr
Bromley BR1 . . . . 187 C1
Fortis Green N2 . . . . . . 48 D5
Greenfield Gdns
Cricklewood NW2 . . . . . 69 A5
Crofton BR5 . . . . 211 B2
Greenfield Gdns *continued*
Dagenham RM9 . . . . . 102 D6
Greenfield Ho [28] SW19 . . . . 156 D3
Greenfield Rd
Dagenham RM9 . . . . . 102 C6
South Tottenham N15 . . . 51 C4
Whitechapel E1 . . . . . . 96 A1
Greenfields UB1 . . . . . . 85 C1
Greenfields Prim Sch WD19 . . . . 22 C5
Greenfield Way HA2 . . 41 D6
GREENFORD 86 A4
Greenford Ave
Ealing W7 . . . . 86 C1
Southall UB1 . . . . 107 B6
Greenford Gdns UB6 . . 86 A4
Greenford High Sch UB6 . . . . 85 C4
Greenford Rd
Greenford UB6 . . . . 86 A3
Sudbury HA1, UB6 . . . . . 64 C3
Sutton SM1 . . . . 217 D4
Greenford Rdbt UB6 . . 86 B5
Greenford Sp Ctr UB1 . . . . 85 C4
Greenford Sta UB6 . . . . 86 B6
Greengate UB6 . . . . 65 B2
Greengate St E13 . . . . . 99 B4
Green Gdns BR6 . . . . . 227 A3
Greenhalgh Wlk N2 . . . 48 A5
Greenham Cl SE1 . . . . 251 A1
Greenham Cres E4 . . . . 35 B4
Greenham Ho
[5] Hackney E9 . . . . 96 C6
Isleworth TW7 . . . . . . 130 B2
Greenham Rd N10 . . . . . 31 A1
Greenhaven Dr SE28 102 B1
Greenheath Bsns Ctr [3] E2 . . . . 96 B3
Green Hedges [8] TW1 . . . . 153 C5
Greenheys Dr E18 . . . . . 54 D6
GREENHILL 42 D4
Greenhill
Buckhurst Hill IG9 . . . . . 21 C3
Hampstead NW3 . . . . . . 70 B4
Sutton SM1 . . . . 218 A6
Wembley Pk HA9 . . . . . . 66 D6
Green Hill SE18 . . . . . . 122 B1
Greenhill Cts SE7 . . . . 122 B1
Greenhill Gdns UB5 . . . 85 B5
Greenhill Gr E12 . . . . . . 78 A4
Greenhill Par EN5 . . . . . 13 D6
Greenhill Pk
Harlesden NW10 . . . . . . 89 C6
New Barnet EN5 . . . . . . 13 D6
Greenhill Rd
Harlesden NW10 . . . . . . 89 C6
Harrow HA1 . . . . 42 C3
Greenhill's Rents EC1 . . . . 241 C4
Greenhills Terr [16] N1 . . 73 B2
Greenhill Terr
Northolt UB5 . . . . 85 B5
Woolwich SE18 . . . . . 122 B1
Greenhill Way
Harrow HA1 . . . . 42 C3
Wembley Pk HA9 . . . . . . 66 D6
Greenhithe Cl DA15 . . 167 C4
Green Ho TW7 . . . . 130 D3
Greenholm Rd SE9 . . 166 D6
Green Ho The [5] SW19 . . . . 157 A3
Green Hundred Rd SE15 . . . . 140 A6
Greenhurst Rd SE27 . . 182 C5
Greening Ho SE13 . . . 142 B1
Greening St SE2 . . . . . 124 C2
Green La
Ashford TW16 . . . . . . 171 D4
Chessington KT9 . . . . 214 A1
Chislehurst SE9 . . . . . 166 D1
Dagenham RM8 . . . . 81 B6
East Molesey KT8 . . . 195 D4
Edgware HA8 . . . . 26 C5
Feltham TW13 . . . . . . 173 A5
Hanwell W7 . . . . 108 C4
Hendon NW4 . . . . 46 D4
Hillingdon UB8 . . . . 83 A2
Hounslow TW4 . . . . . . 128 C1
Ilford IG1, IG3 . . . . 79 C6
Morden SM4 . . . . 201 D3

Green La *continued*
New Malden KT3 .... 199 A4
New Malden KT4 .... 200 A1
Penge SE20 .... 184 D3
Shepperton TW17 ... 193 A4
South Norwood CR7,
SW16 .... 182 C2
Stanmore HA7 .... 25 B5
Greenland Cres UB2 106 D3
Greenland Ho
Bermondsey SE8 .... 118 D1
4 Mile End E1........97 A3
Greenland Mews
SE8............... 118 D1
Greenland Pl NW1 .. 231 D6
Greenland Quay
SE16............... 118 D2
Greenland Rd
Barnet EN5 ....12 C5
Camden Town
NW1 ....93 C6 232 A6
Greenlands
Borehamwood WD6.... 11 B5
Chessington KT19 ... 214 D3
Greenland St NW1 .. 231 D6
Greenland Way CR0. 203 D2
Green Lane Bsns Pk
SE9............... 166 C2
Green Lane Cotts
HA7...................25 B6
Green Lane Gdns
CR7..................183 A1
Green Lane Mews
SM4 .... 201 D3
Green Lane Prim Sch
KT4 ....200 B2
Green Lanes
London N4, N8, N15....50 D2
Palmers Green N13....16 C1
West Ewell KT19 .... 215 C1
Greenlaw Ct W5 ....87 D1
Greenlaw Gdns KT3. 199 D2
Greenlawn La TW8.. 109 D2
Greenlawns N12......29 D4
Green Lawns
Ruislip HA4 ....40 C1
8 Woolwich SE18... 122 D2
Greenlaw St SE18....122 C3
Green Leaf Ave SM6. 219 D4
Greenleaf Cl 8
SW2 ....160 C4
Greenleaf Ct N20 .....14 B3
Greenleafe Dr IG6 ....56 D6
Greenleaf Prim Sch
E17.....................53 B6
Greenleaf Rd
5 Newham E6 ....99 C6
Walthamstow E17 .....53 B6
Greenleaf Way HA3 ...42 D6
Greenlea Pk SW19.. 180 C2
Green Leas
Ashford TW16 ...... 171 D4
Kingston u T KT1 .... 198 A6
Green Leas Cl TW16. 171 D4
Greenleaves Ct
TW15 .... 170 D4
Green Link Wlk
TW9 .... 132 D4
Green Man Gdns
W13 ....109 A6
Green Man Intc E11...54 D2
Green Man La
Ealing W13......... 109 A5
Hatton TW14 .... 128 A1
Greenman St
N1...........95 A6 235 A6
Greenmead Cl SE25..206 A4
Greenmead Prim Sch
SW15.................156 B6
Green Moor Link N21 .16 D4
Greenmoor Rd EN3 .... 6 C3
Greenoak Pl EN4........2 D3
Green Oaks UB2 .... 106 D2
Greenoak Way
SW19 .... 178 D6
Greenock Rd
Mitcham SW16 ..... 181 D2
11 South Acton W3 ... 111 A3
Greeno Cres TW17 ...192 C4
Green Park★ SW1,
W1.........115 B4 248 D2
Greenpark Ct HA0 ....65 C1
Green Park Sta
W1.......... 115 C5 249 A4
Green Park Way UB6..86 C6
Green Pond Cl E17....53 B6
Green Pond Rd E17 ...53 A6
Green Pt E15 ....76 C2
Green Rd
East Barnet N14.........15 B5
Whetstone N20 ....14 A1
Green Ride IG10, E4 ...21 A6
Greenroof Way
SE10................ 120 D3
Green Sch (Girls) The
TW7.................. 131 A4
Greens Ct Soho W1 .. 249 C6
Wembley HA9 ....65 D5
Green's Ct W11...... 244 C3
Greens End SE18..... 122 D2
Greenshank Cl E17....35 A3
Greenshaw High Sch
SM1................... 218 A6
Greenshields Ind Est
E16....................121 B5
Greenside
Dagenham RM8........58 C1
Sidcup DA5......... 169 A3
Greenside Cl
Catford SE6 ....164 B2
Whetstone N20 ....14 B2
Greenside Prim Sch
W12.............. 112 A4
Greenside Rd
Shepherd's Bush
W12 .... 112 A4
Thornton Heath CR0 . 204 C2
Greenslade Prim Sch
SE18....................145 B6
Greenslade Rd IG11...79 B1
Greensleeves Ho
UB2.............. 107 D2
Greensleeves Manor
SM2 .... 217 D2
Green St Enfield EN3 .... 6 D3
Mayfair W1 . 115 A6 248 A6
Newham E13 ....99 C6
Sunbury TW16 ...... 172 A1
Upton E7 ....77 C1
Greenstead Ave IG8...37 C4
Greenstead Cl IG8 ....37 C4
Greenstead Gdns
Putney SW15..........156 B6
Woodford IG8 ....37 C4
Greenstone Mews
E11......................55 A3
GREEN STREET
GREEN 227 C2
Green Street Green Prim
Sch BR6 .... 227 D2
Greenstreet Hill
SE4.............. 140 D2
Greensward Ho
SW6...................136 A3
Green Terr EC1 .... 234 B1
Green The Acton W3 ...89 C1
Buckhurst Hill IG9.....21 B3
Chingford E4 ....20 B3
Claygate KT10 ...... 212 D2
Ealing W5........... 109 D6
Edmonton N9...........18 A2
Erith DA7 .... 147 C4
Falconwood DA16 ... 145 C1
Feltham TW13 ....150 B2
Grove Pk BR1........ 165 A1
Hackbridge SM6 .... 219 A6
Hayes BR2.......... 209 A2
Heston TW5.......... 129 C6
Kingston u T KT3 .... 177 A1
Merton SM4.......... 201 A5
Palmers Green N14.....15 D1
Richmond TW9...... 131 D1
7 Richmond TW9 ... 153 D6
Sidcup DA14......... 190 A5
Southall UB2 ....107 B4
Southgate N21.........16 C4
St Paul's Cray BR5 ....190 B3
Stratford E15...........76 D2
Sutton SM1 .... 217 D5
Tottenham N17 ....33 A4
Twickenham TW2..... 152 C2
Upper Halliford TW17 193 C5
Uxbridge UB10.........61 A6
Wallington SM5 ..... 219 A4
Wanstead E11 ....55 B3
Wembley HA0 ....65 A6
Wimbledon SW19 ... 178 D5
Woodford IG8 ....37 A5
Green Vale
Bexley DA6......... 168 D6
Ealing W5..............88 B1
Greenvale Rd SE9....144 C1
Greenvale Sch SE23. 164 C1
Green Verges HA7.....25 D3
Green View KT9.......214 B1
Greenview Ave CR0 . 207 A3
Greenview Cl W3 ....111 C5
Greenview Ct
Ashford TW15 .... 170 B6
East Dulwich SE22.... 140 A1
Oakleigh Pk N20........14 A4
Wandsworth SW18 ... 158 C4
Greenway
Chislehurst BR7..... 188 D5
Dagenham RM8........58 C1
Harrow HA3............44 A4
Hayes UB4.............84 B3
Palmers Green N14....16 A2
Pinner HA5............22 B1
Totteridge N20.........13 C2
Wallington SM6 ..... 219 C4
West Barnes SW20 .. 200 C5
Woodford IG8 ....37 C5
Green Way
Bromley Comm BR2.. 210 A3
Eltham SE9........... 165 D6
Sunbury TW16 ...... 194 A5
Greenway Ave E17 ....54 B5
Greenway Cl
Finsbury Pk N4.........73 A6
Friern Barnet N11 .....31 A4
Hendon NW9 ....27 B1
2 South Tottenham
N15...................51 D5
Totteridge N20.........13 C2
Greenway Ct
Hayes UB4.............84 B3
Ilford IG1...............56 D1
2 Newham E15 ......98 C5
Greenway Gdns
Croydon CR0 ....223 B5
Greenford UB6.........85 D4
Hendon NW9 ....27 B1
Green Way Gdns HA3 .24 C1
Greenways
Beckenham BR3..... 185 C1
5 Forest Hill SE26 .. 184 C6
Hinchley Wood KT10 . 212 C4
Greenways The 1
TW1...................153 A5
Greenway The
Harrow HA3...........24 C2
Hendon NW9 ....27 B1
Hounslow TW4.........129 B1
Pinner HA5............41 B3
Uxbridge UB8...........82 A5
West Ruislip UB10.....61 A6
Greenwell St W1.... 238 D5
GREENWICH.........142 C6
Greenwich Acad
SE10.............. 141 D4
Greenwich Borough
Mus★ SE18 .... 123 D1
Greenwich Bsns Ctr
SE10.............. 141 D5
Greenwich Bsns Pk
SE10.............. 141 D5
Greenwich Church St
SE10..................142 A6
Greenwich Coll 17
SE10............... 142 A5
Greenwich Com Coll
Plumstead Ctr
SE18.............. 123 A2
Greenwich Cres E6 ..100 A2
Greenwich Ct 11 E1....96 B1
Greenwich Heritage
Ctr★ SE18 .... 122 D3
Greenwich High Rd
SE10.............. 141 D5
Greenwich Ho SE13..164 B5
Greenwich Hts SE18 .144 A5
Greenwich Ind Est
SE10.............. 141 D5
Greenwich London Coll
15 SE18............. 122 C2
Greenwich Mkt 2
SE10.................142 A6
Greenwich Mkt★
SE10..................142 A6
Greenwich Park★
SE10..................142 C5
Greenwich Park St
SE10..................142 B6
Greenwich Quay
SE8................ 141 D6
Greenwich Sh Pk
SE7.................121 B2
Greenwich South St
SE10.................142 A4
Greenwich Sta SE10 141 D5
Greenwich View Pl
E14.................119 D3
Green Wlk
Bermondsey SE1 .... 263 A5
Hampton TW12 ......173 B4
Hendon NW4 ....46 D4
Ruislip HA4 ....39 D1
Southall UB2 .... 107 C1
Green Wlk The E4.....20 B3
Greenwood
8 Putney SW19 .... 156 D4
3 Woodford IG8......37 A3
Green Wood NW5.....71 C3
Greenwood Ave
Dagenham RM10......81 D4
Enfield EN3 ....7 A4
Greenwood Cl
Bushey WD23...........8 C3
Merton SM4......... 201 A5
Orpington BR5 ...... 211 C3
Sidcup DA15......... 168 A2
Thames Ditton KT7... 197 A1
Greenwood Dr E4.....36 B5
Greenwood Gdns
N13...................16 D1
Greenwood Ho
Finsbury WC1....... 234 A1
8 Nunhead SE4 .... 140 D1
Wood Green N22 ......32 C2
Greenwood La
TW12............. 173 D5
Greenwood Mans 9
IG11..................80 A1
Greenwood Pk KT2 ..177 C3
Greenwood Pl NW5 ...71 B3
Greenwood Prim Sch
UB5 ....64 A3
Greenwood Rd
Dalston E8............74 A2
Hinchley Wood KT7 .. 213 A6
Isleworth TW7...... 130 D2
Mitcham CR4 .... 203 D6
Thornton Heath CR0 . 205 A2
West Ham E13.........98 D5
Greenwoods The
HA2..................64 A5
Greenwood Terr
NW10................89 B5
Green Wrythe Cres
SM5 ....202 C1
Green Wrythe La
SM5 ....202 C2
Green Wrythe Prim Sch
SM5..................202 B3
Green Yd WC1 ...... 240 D6
Greer Rd HA3..........24 A2
Greet Ho SE1 .... 251 B1
Greet St SE1 ..116 C5 251 B3
Greg Cl E10............54 A3
Gregor Mews SE3....143 A5
Gregory Cres SE9 ... 165 D4
Gregory Ho SE3.......143 B3
Gregory Pl W8...... 245 C2
Gregory Rd
Dagenham RM6........58 D5
Southall UB2 .... 107 C3
Greig City Acad 6
N8 ....50 A5
Greig Cl N8.............50 A4
Greig Ho 9 TW10....153 C1
Greig Terr SE17 ...... 138 D6
Grenaby Ave CR0 ....205 B2
Grenaby Rd CR0 .....205 B2
Grenada Ho 18 E14...119 B6
Grenada Rd SE7 .....143 C5
Grenade St E14.......119 B6
Grenadier St E16 ....122 C5
Grena Gdns TW9.....132 B1
Grena Rd TW10, TW9..132 B1
Grenard Cl SE15 .....140 A5
Grendon Gdns HA9 ...66 C6
Grendon Ho
29 Hackney E9........74 C1
Pentonville N1 ...... 233 C3
Grendon St
NW8.........92 C3 237 A6
Grenfell Ct NW7 ......28 B4
Grenfell Gdns
Harrow HA3..........44 A2
Grenfell Gdns *continued*
Ilford IG2...............57 D4
Grenfell Ho SE5......139 A5
Grenfell Rd
Mitcham CR4,
SW17 .... 180 D4
Shepherd's Bush
W11 .... 112 D6
Grenfell Twr 5
W11 .... 112 D6
Grenfell Wlk 4
W11 .... 112 D6
Grengate Lodge 2
E13....................99 B4
Grenier Apartments 11
SE15..................140 B5
Grennell Cl SM1 .....218 B6
Grennell Rd SM1.....218 A6
Grenoble Gdns N13 ...32 C4
Grenville Cl
Church End N3.........29 B2
Tolworth KT5 .... 199 A1
Grenville Ct
3 Dulwich SE19 .... 183 D5
Ealing W13............87 B2
Edgware HA8...........26 D6
Grenville Gdns IG8 ...37 C3
Grenville Ho
26 Bow E3............97 A5
4 Deptford SE8 .... 141 C6
Grenville Lo N6.......49 C2
Grenville Mans WC1 240 A6
Grenville Mews
Hampton TW12 ..... 173 D5
South Kensington
SW7 .... 256 A3
Grenville Pl
Burnt Oak NW7 ....27 B5
South Kensington
SW7 ..... 114 A2 256 A4
Grenville Rd N19......50 A1
Grenville St WC1..... 240 B5
Gresham Almshouses 3
SW9...................138 B1
Gresham Ave N20.....30 D6
Gresham Cl Enfield EN2 . 5 A2
Sidcup DA5..........169 B5
Gresham Coll
EC1 ....94 C2 241 B3
Gresham Ct TW3.....130 A4
Gresham Dr RM6 .....58 B3
Gresham Gdns NW11. .47 A1
Gresham Ho
4 Teddington
TW11 .... 174 D5
3 Thames Ditton
KT7.................. 197 A2
West Barnes KT3.....200 B5
Gresham Lo E17 ......53 D4
Gresham Pl 2 N19....71 D6
Gresham Rd
Beckenham BR3..... 185 A1
Brixton SW9........ 138 C2
Canning Town E16 .....99 B1
Croydon SE25....... 206 A5
East Ham E6.........100 B5
Edgware HA8..........26 B4
Hampton TW12 ..... 173 C4
Hillingdon UB10........82 C5
Hounslow TW3, TW5 . 130 A4
Willesden NW10 ......67 B3
Gresham St
EC2.........95 A1 242 B2
Gresham Way SW19..157 C1
Gresham Way Est
SW19.............. 157 D1
Gresley Cl London N15 .51 B5
Walthamstow E17 .....53 A3
Gresley Ho SW8 ..... 269 D2
Gresley Rd N19 ....49 C2
Gressenhall Rd
SW18.................157 B4
Gressenham Ct 7
HA7...................25 C6
Gresse St W1 ..93 D1 239 C2
Gresswell Cl DA14 ...168 A1
Greswell St SW6.... 134 D4
Greta Ho SE3 .... 142 D6
Gretton Ho 2 E2 .....96 C4
Gretton Rd N17 ....33 D3
Greville Cl TW1 ......153 B4
Greville Ct
Harrow HA1...........64 C4
3 Lower Clapton E5 ...74 B5
Greville Hall NW6.....91 D5

Greville Ho
Harrow HA2 42 B1
Knightsbridge SW1 258 A6
Putney SW15 134 D2
Greville Lo
5 Bayswater W2 91 D1
16 London N12 29 D6
Greville Mews 5
NW6 91 D6
Greville Pl W9 91 D5
Greville Rd
Kilburn NW6 91 D5
Richmond TW10 154 B5
Walthamstow E17 54 A5
Greville St
EC1 94 C2 241 B4
Grey Cl NW11 48 A3
Grey Coat Hospital The
SW1 115 D2 259 C3
SW1 115 D3 259 C5
Greycoat Pl
SW1 115 D3 259 C5
Greycoat St
SW1 115 D3 259 C5
Greycot Rd BR3 185 C5
Grey Court Sch
TW10 153 C1
Grey Eagle St
E1 95 D3 243 D5
Greyfell Cl HA7 25 B5
Greyfriars 16 SE26 162 A1
Greyfriars Ho SE3 142 D6
Grey Ho 27 W12 112 B6
Greyhound Ct WC2 251 A6
Greyhound Hill NW4 46 B6
Greyhound La SW16 181 D4
Greyhound Rd
College Pk NW10 90 B4
Fulham W6 135 A6 264 A6
Sutton SM1 218 A3
Tottenham N17 51 C6
Greyhound Terr
SW16 181 C2
Greyladies Gdns
SE10 142 A3
Greys Park Cl BR2 225 D3
Greystead Rd SE23 162 C4
Greystoke Ave HA5 41 C6
Greystoke Ct W5 88 B3
Greystoke Dr HA4 38 D3
Greystoke Gdns
Ealing W5 88 B3
Enfield EN2 3 D1
Greystoke Ho
Ealing W5 88 A3
Peckham SE15 140 A6
Greystoke Lo W5 88 B3
Greystoke Park Terr
W5 88 A4
Greystoke Pl EC4 241 B2
Greystone Gdns HA3 43 C3
Greystones TW2 152 A2
Greyswood St SW16 181 B4
Greytiles TW11 174 D4
Grey Turner Ho W12 90 A1
Grice Ct N1 73 A2
Grierson Ho SW16 181 C6
Grierson Rd
Forest Hill SE23 162 D4
Forest Hill SE23 163 A5
Griffin Cl NW10 68 B3
Griffin Ct
8 Brentford TW8 132 A6
Chiswick W4 111 D1
Shepherd's Bush W12 112 B5
Griffin Ctr TW14 150 B5
Griffin Ctr The KT1 175 D1
Griffin Gate 1
SW15 134 D2
Griffin Lo N12 30 A6
Griffin Manor Way
SE28 123 B3
Griffin Park (Brentford
FC) TW8 131 D6
Griffin Rd
Plumstead SE18 123 B1
Tottenham N17 33 C1
Griffins Cl N21 17 B4
Griffin Way
Sunbury TW16 172 A1
Woolwich SE28 123 C3
Griffith Cl RM8 58 C1
Griffiths Cl KT4 216 B6
Griffiths Ho 2 SE18 144 D6
Griffiths Rd SW19 179 D3
Griffon Ho 3 SW11 136 C2
Griggs App IG1 79 A6
Griggs Cl IG1 79 C4
Grigg's Pl SE1 263 B5
Griggs Rd E10 54 A3
Grilse Cl N9 34 B6
Grimaldi Ho N1 233 C4
Grimsby Gr E16 122 D5
Grimsby St
8 Bethnal Green E2 96 A3
Shoreditch E2 243 D6
Grimsdell Mill Hill Pre
Prep Sch NW7 28 B5
Grimsdyke Fst & Mid Sch
HA5 23 B4
Grimsdyke Rd HA5 23 A3
Grimsel Path SE5 138 D5
Grimshaw Cl N6 49 A2
Grimston Rd SW6 135 B3
Grimthorpe Ho EC1 241 C6
Grimwade Ave CR0 222 A5
Grimwade Cl SE15 140 C2
Grimwood Rd TW1 152 D4
Grindall Cl CR0 220 D4
Grindall Ho 25 E1 96 B3
Grindal St SE1 251 A1
Grindleford Ave N11 15 A2
Grindley Gdns CR0 205 D3
Grindley Ho 3 E3 97 B2
Grinling Gibbons Prim
Sch 42 SE8 141 B6
Grinling Ho 6 SE18 122 C2
Grinling Pl SE8 141 C6
Grinstead Rd SE8 119 A1
Grisedale NW1 232 A2
Grittleton Ave HA9 66 D2
Grittleton Rd W9 91 C3
Grizedale Terr 8
SE23 162 B2
Grogan Cl TW12 173 B4
Groombridge Cl
DA16 168 A6
Groombridge Ho 1
SE20 184 D3
Groombridge Rd E9 74 D1
Groom Cl BR2 209 B5
Groom Cres SW18 158 B4
Groome Ho SE11 260 D3
Groomfield Cl SW17 181 A6
Groom Pl
SW1 115 A3 258 B6
Grooms Dr HA5 40 A4
Grosmont Rd SE18 123 D1
Grosse Way SW15 156 B5
Grosslea SM4 202 B4
Grosvenor Ave
Canonbury N5 73 A3
Harrow HA2 41 D3
Hayes UB4 83 D5
Mortlake SW14 133 C2
Richmond TW10 154 A6
Wallington SM5, SM6 219 A2
Grosvenor Bridge
SW1 137 B6 268 D6
Grosvenor Cotts
SW1 258 A4
Grosvenor Court Mans
W2 237 C1
Grosvenor Cres
Hillingdon UB10 82 D6
Queensbury NW9 44 C5
Westminster
SW1 115 A4 248 B1
Grosvenor Cres Mews
SW1 248 A1
Grosvenor Ct
4 Acton W3 110 C5
Brondesbury Pk NW6 90 D6
3 Ealing W5 110 A6
3 Edgware NW7 27 B5
Gunnersbury W4 110 D1
Leyton E10 53 D1
Morden SM4 201 C5
Oakwood N14 15 C4
Penge SE19 183 D4
22 Poplar E14 97 B1
Putney SW15 157 A6
1 Sutton SM2 218 A2
Teddington TW11 175 A4
3 Wanstead E11 55 B4
2 Wimbledon SW19 179 A4
Grosvenor Gdns
Cricklewood NW2 68 C3
Hornsey N10 49 C6
Kingston u T KT2 175 D4
Mortlake SW14 133 C2
Newham E6 99 D4
Grosvenor Gdns *continued*
Southgate N14 15 D6
Temple Fortune NW11 47 B4
Wallington SM6 219 C1
Westminster
SW1 115 B3 258 D5
Woodford IG8 37 B4
Grosvenor Gdns Mews E
SW1 258 D6
Grosvenor Gdns Mews N
SW1 258 C5
Grosvenor Gdns Mews S
SW1 258 D5
Grosvenor Hill
Mayfair W1 115 B6 248 C6
Wimbledon SW19 179 A4
Grosvenor Hill Ct
W1 248 C6
Grosvenor Ho
5 Sutton SM1 217 D3
Upper Clapton E5 52 A1
Grosvenor Hts E4 20 C4
Grosvenor Lo
London N20 14 A1
4 Woodford E18 36 D1
Grosvenor Par 1
W5 110 C5
Grosvenor Park SE5 139 A5
Grosvenor Park Rd
E17 53 D4
Grosvenor Pier SW1 269 C6
Grosvenor Pk SE5 139 A6
Grosvenor Pl
SW1 115 B4 248 C1
Grosvenor Rd
Acton Green W4 111 A1
Bexley DA6 169 A6
Brentford TW8 131 D6
Croydon SE25 206 A5
Dagenham RM8 59 B1
Ealing W7 109 A5
Edmonton N9 18 B3
Erith DA17 147 C6
Finchley N3 29 C3
Hounslow TW3, TW4 129 B2
Ilford IG1 79 A5
Leyton E10 54 A1
Muswell Hill N10 31 B2
Newham E6 99 D6
Orpington BR6 211 C3
Pimlico SW1 137 C6 269 B6
Richmond TW10 154 A6
Southall UB2 107 B3
Twickenham TW1 153 A3
Upton E7 77 B2
Wallington SM6 219 B3
Wanstead E11 55 B4
West Wickham BR4 223 D6
Grosvenor Residences 1
W14 112 D3
Grosvenor Rise E E17 53 D4
Grosvenor Sq
W1 115 A6 248 B6
Grosvenor St
W1 115 B6 248 C6
Grosvenor Terr SE5 139 A6
Grosvenor The NW11 47 D2
Grosvenor Vale HA4 61 D6
Grosvenor Way E5 74 C6
Grosvernor Wharf Rd
E14 120 B2
Grote's Bldgs SE3 142 C3
Grote's Pl SE3 142 C3
Groton Rd SW18 157 D2
Grotto Ct SE1 252 A2
Grotto Pas W1 238 A4
Grotto Rd TW1 152 D2
Grove Ave
Cheam SM1 217 C2
Ealing W7 86 C1
Finchley N3 29 C3
Pinner HA5 41 A5
Twickenham TW1 152 D3
Wood Green N10 31 C1
Grovebury Ct
Bexley DA6 169 D6
Southgate N14 15 D4
Grovebury Rd SE2 124 B4
Grove Cl
Forest Hill SE23 163 A3
Hayes BR2 225 A6
Ickenham UB10 60 C3
Kingston u T KT1 198 B5
Grove Cres
Feltham TW13 173 A6
Kingsbury NW9 45 B5
Grove Cres *continued*
Kingston u T KT1 198 A6
Walton-on-T KT12 194 B2
Woodford E18 36 D1
Grove Crescent Rd
E15 76 B2
Grove Ct Barnet EN5 1 B2
Camberwell SE5 139 C3
Clapham SW4 137 C2
Ealing W5 110 A5
East Molesey KT8 196 B4
3 Forest Hill SE26 185 A6
Hounslow TW3 129 C1
8 Kingston u T KT1 198 A6
New Malden KT3 199 C6
Penge SE20 184 B3
Seething Wells KT6 197 D4
South Kensington
SW10 256 B1
St John's Wood NW8 229 C2
Grovedale Rd N19 71 D6
Grove Dwellings E1 96 C2
Grove End
Gospel Oak NW5 71 B4
Woodford E18 36 D1
Grove End Gdns
NW8 229 B3
Grove End Ho NW8 229 C1
Grove End La KT10 196 B1
Grove End Rd
NW8 92 B4 229 C1
Grove Farm Ct CR4 202 D4
Grovefield 1 N11 31 B6
Grove Footpath KT5 198 A5
Grove Gdns Enfield EN3 6 D5
Hendon NW4 46 A5
Lisson Gr NW8 92 C4 230 B1
Teddington TW11 175 A6
Grove Glade Shop Hall
W13 109 A5
Grove Green Rd E11 76 B6
Grove Hall Ct Bow E3 97 C5
St John's Wood
NW8 92 A4 229 B2
Grove Hill Harrow HA1 42 C2
Woodford E18 36 D1
Grovehill Ct BR1 186 D4
Grove Hill Rd
Camberwell SE5 139 C2
Harrow HA1 42 D2
Grove Ho
Blackheath SE3 142 D3
Chelsea SW3 267 B6
Hendon N3 46 D6
Grove House Rd N8 50 A5
Grove La
Camberwell SE5 139 C2
Hillingdon UB8 82 B3
Kingston u T KT1 198 A5
Groveland Ave
SW16 182 B3
Groveland Ct EC4 242 B1
Groveland Rd BR3 207 B6
Grovelands
East Molesey KT8 195 C5
Kingston u T KT1 197 D5
Grovelands Cl
Camberwell SE5 139 C3
Harrow HA2 63 D5
Grovelands Ct N14 15 D4
Grovelands Rd
Palmers Green N13 16 B1
South Tottenham N15 52 A3
St Paul's Cray BR5 190 A3
Grovelands Sch
KT12 194 B3
Groveland Way KT3 199 B4
Grove Lane Terr
SE5 139 B3
Groveley Ho 7 N4 51 A2
Groveley Rd TW13,
TW16 171 D5
Grove Lo
Clapham SW4 137 C1
Cranley Gdns N10 49 C5
Grove Mans
London SW4 136 D1
2 Shepherd's Bush
W6 112 C4
3 Stamford Hill N16 52 A1
Grove Market Pl
SE9 166 B5
Grove Mews W6 112 C3
Grove Mill CR4 202 C4
Grove Mill Pl SM5 219 A5
GROVE PARK SE9 165 B1
GROVE PARK *continued*
W4 133 A4
Grove Park Ave E4 35 D3
Grove Park Bridge
W4 133 A5
Grove Park Gdns
W4 133 A5
Grove Park Mews
W4 133 A5
Grove Park Prim Sch
W4 133 A6
Grove Park Rd
Chiswick W4 132 D5
Mottingham SE9,
SE12 165 D2
South Tottenham N15 51 C5
Grove Park Sch NW9 45 A5
Grove Park Sta SE12 165 B1
Grove Park Terr W4 132 D6
Grove Pk
Camberwell SE5 139 C3
Kingsbury NW9 45 B5
Wanstead E11 55 B4
Grove Pl Acton W3 111 A5
Balham SW12 159 B5
Hampstead NW3 70 B5
Grove Prim Sch RM6 58 C4
Grover Ct SE13 141 D3
Grove Rd Acton W3 111 A5
Barnes SW13 133 D3
Belmont SM2 217 C2
Bow E3 97 A5
Brentford TW8 109 C1
Chingford E4 20 A1
Cockfosters EN4 2 C2
Dagenham RM6 58 C3
Ealing W5 109 D6
East Molesey KT8 196 B5
Edgware HA8 26 C4
8 Erith DA17 147 B6
Friern Barnet N11 31 B5
Hounslow TW3 129 C1
Kingston u T KT6 197 D4
Leytonstone E11 54 D2
Merton SW19 180 A3
Mitcham CR4 181 B1
North Finchley N12 30 B5
Pinner HA5 41 B4
Richmond TW10 154 B5
Shepperton TW17 193 A3
South Tottenham N15 51 C4
Spring Gr TW7 130 C4
Thornton Heath CR7 204 C5
Twickenham TW2 152 B1
Uxbridge UB8 60 A1
Walthamstow E17 53 D4
Willesden NW2 68 C2
Woodford E18 36 D1
Grove Rd Prim Sch
TW3 129 C1
Grove Rd W EN3 6 C6
Grover Ho
4 London SW4 159 C6
Vauxhall SE11 260 D1
Groves Ho UB4 84 B4
Groveside Cl
Acton W3 88 C1
Carshalton SM5 218 C6
Groveside Ct SW11 136 B3
Groveside Rd E4 20 C1
Grove St
Deptford SE8 119 B1
Edmonton N18 33 D4
Grovestile Waye
TW14 149 B4
Grove Terr
Gospel Oak NW5 71 B4
Southall UB1 107 C6
Teddington TW11 175 A6
Grove Terrace Mews
NW5 71 B5
Grove The
Bexley DA6 146 D1
Dulwich SE21 162 A3
Ealing W5 110 A5
Edgware HA8 26 D6
Edmonton N13 32 C6
Enfield EN2 4 C3
Finchley N3 29 C3
Hendon NW11 47 A2
Highgate N6 49 A1
Hornsey N8 49 D4
Hounslow TW7 130 C4

Grove The *continued*
Ickenham UB10 ....60 C3
Kingsbury NW9 ....45 B4
Sidcup DA14........191 A6
Southall UB6 ....86 A1
Stratford E15.........76 C2
Stroud Green N4 ......50 B2
Teddington TW11.... 175 A6
1 Twickenham TW1 ..153 B5
Walton-on-T KT12 ....194 B2
West Wickham BR4 .. 224 A6
Grove Vale
Chislehurst West
BR7.............. 188 C4
East Dulwich SE22... 139 D1
Groveway
Dagenham RM8.......80 D4
South Lambeth
SW9 ..... 138 B4 270 D1
Grove Way
Thames Ditton KT10.. 196 A1
Wembley HA9 ....67 A3
Grovewood 9 TW9 ..132 C4
Grove Wood Cl BR1 ..210 C6
Grovewood Ct 6
TW7..............130 C4
Grovewood Ho NW2 ..69 B6
Grummant Rd SE15. 139 D4
Grundy St E14........97 D1
Gruneisen Rd N3 ......29 D3
Guardian Angels RC Prim
Sch 9 E3...........97 A4
Guardian Ct SE12......164 C6
Guards Mus The★
SW1........115 C4 249 B1
Gubyon Ave SE24 ... 160 D6
Gudden Dr E5 ....74 B4
Guerin Sq E3...........97 B4
Guernsey Cl TW5 ....129 C5
Guernsey Gr SE24....161 A4
Guernsey Ho
10 Canonbury N1......73 A2
Enfield EN3 ....6 D5
Guernsey Rd
11 Canonbury N1......73 A2
Leytonstone E11 ......54 B1
Guibal Rd SE12 ....165 B3
Guildersfield Rd
SW16..............182 A3
Guildford Ave TW13 ..150 A2
Guildford Gr SE10... 141 D4
Guildford Ho 23 SE5. .139 A3
Guildford Rd
Chingford E17 ....36 A2
Ilford IG3............79 C6
Newham E6 ....100 B1
South Lambeth
SW8 ....138 A4 270 B2
Thornton Heath CR0 ..205 B3
Guildford Way SM6 ..220 A3
Guildhall Art Gall★
EC2 ....95 A1 242 B2
Guildhall Ho EC2.... 242 C2
Guildhall Sch Music &
Drama EC2 ..95 A2 242 B4
Guildhall Yd EC2..... 242 B2
Guild Ho SW19 ......179 B4
Guildhouse St
SW1 ....115 C2 259 A3
Guildown Ave N12 ....29 D6
Guild Rd SE7 .... 143 D6
Guildsway E17.........35 B2
Guilford Ave KT5.....198 B4
Guilford Pl WC1..... 240 C5
Guilford St
WC1.........94 A3 240 B5
Guilfoyle 2 NW9 .....27 D1
Guillemot Ct 28 SE8. .141 B6
Guinness Cl
Hayes UB3...........105 B3
Homerton E9 ....75 A1
Guinness Ct
Chelsea SW3 .... 257 C3
6 Croydon CR0...... 221 D6
Finsbury EC1 .... 235 B1
Primrose Hill NW8.... 230 B5
Whitechapel E1 ...... 243 D1
Guinness Sq SE1.... 263 A4
Guinness Trust Bldgs
Bermondsey SE1 .... 253 A2
7 Bethnal Green E2 ...96 A5
Chelsea SW3 .... 257 C3
Hammersmith W6 .... 112 C1
Guinness Trust Bldgs
continued
Kennington SE11.... 261 C2
Guion Rd SW6 ....135 B3
Gujarat Ho 1 N16 ....73 C5
Gulland Cl WD23........8 A6
Gulland Wlk 21 N1....73 A2
Gullane Ho 24 E3 .....97 B5
Gull Cl SM6..........220 A1
Gulliver Cl UB5 ....85 B6
Gulliver Ct CR2 ..... 220 D1
Gulliver Rd DA15.....167 C2
Gulliver St SE16......119 B3
Gulston Wlk SW3.... 257 D3
Gumleigh Rd W5 ....109 C2
Gumley Gdns TW7 ...131 A2
Gumley House Convent
Sch (Girls) TW7 ... 131 A2
Gumping Rd BR5 ....227 A6
Gundulph Rd BR2....209 C6
Gunmakers La E3.....97 A6
Gunnel Cl SE20 ......184 A6
Gunnell Cl SE25......206 A3
Gunnell Ct 3 CR4....180 C2
Gunnels Ct &
Hastingwood Ct 6
IG9.................21 C2
Gunner Dr 9 EN3.......7 C6
Gunner La SE18.......122 C1
GUNNERSBURY.... 110 D2
Gunnersbury Avenue
(North Circular Rd)
W3 ....110 C3
Gunnersbury Cl 8
W4 .... 110 D1
Gunnersbury Cres
W3 ....110 C4
Gunnersbury Ct 8
W3 .... 110 D4
Gunnersbury Dr W5. .110 B4
Gunnersbury Gdns
W3 ....110 C4
Gunnersbury La W3. .110 C4
Gunnersbury Manor
W5 ....110 B5
Gunnersbury Mews 6
W4 .... 110 D1
Gunnersbury Park
W3 ....110 C3
Gunnersbury Park Mus★
W3................110 C3
Gunnersbury RC Sch
TW8............. 109 C1
Gunnersbury Sta
W4................110 D1
Gunnersbury Triangle
Nat Res★ W12 .....111 A2
Gunners Gr E4.......20 A1
Gunners Rd SW18....158 B2
Gunnery Terr SE18 ....123 A3
Gunning St SE18.....123 C2
Gunpowder Sq EC4 . 241 B2
Gun St E1 .... 243 C3
Gunstor Rd N16.......73 C4
Gunter Gr
Chelsea
SW6 ..... 136 A5 266 A4
Hendon HA8...........27 B2
Gunterstone Rd
W14 ....113 A1 254 B2
Gunthorpe St
E1..........95 D1 243 D2
Gunton Rd
Streatham SW17.... 181 A4
Upper Clapton E5......74 B6
Gunwhale Cl SE16 .. 118 D5
Gun Wharf
Old Ford E3 ....97 A6
Wapping E1 .... 118 C5
Gurdon Ho 7 E14.....97 C1
Gurdon Rd SE7 ....121 A1
Gurnell Gr W13 ....86 D3
Gurnell L Ctr W13.....86 D4
Gurney Cl
Barking IG11 ....78 D2
Higham Hill E17 ....34 D2
Stratford E15.........76 C3
Gurney Cres CR0.....204 B1
Gurney Dr N2.........48 A5
Gurney Ho
3 Bayswater W2 .....91 D1
14 Bethnal Green E2 ...96 A5
Hayes UB3.......... 105 C2
Gurney Rd
London SW6......... 136 A2
Northolt UB5 ....84 C4
Gurney Rd *continued*
Stratford E15.........76 C3
Wallington SM5..... 219 A4
Guru Nanak Sikh Prim &
Sec Schs UB4 .... 106 C5
Guthrie Ct SE1...... 251 B1
Guthrie St SW3 .... 257 A2
Gutter La EC2. .95 A1 242 A2
Guyatt Gdns CR4.....181 A1
Guy Barnett Gr SE3 ...143 A2
Guy Rd SM6 .... 219 D5
Guyscliff Rd SE13....164 A6
Guy's Hospl
SE1......... 117 B4 252 D2
Guy's Retreat IG9.....21 C4
Guy St SE1 ...117 B4 252 D2
Gwalior Ho N14........15 C5
Gwalior Rd SW15 ... 134 D2
Gwendolen Ave
SW15 .... 156 D6
Gwendolen Cl SW15 156 D6
Gwendolen Ho
TW19 ....148 A3
Gwendoline Ave E13 .. 99 B6
Gwendoline Ct
TW15 ....170 A6
Gwendwr Rd
W14 ....113 A1 254 B2
Gwent Ct 13 SE16 ... 118 D5
Gwillim Cl DA15 .....168 A6
Gwilym Maries Ho 11
E2..................96 B4
Gwydor Rd BR3..... 206 D6
Gwydyr Rd BR2..... 208 D6
Gwyn Cl SW6 .136 A5 266 A3
Gwyn Jones Prim Sch
E11.................54 B2
Gwynne Ave CR0.... 206 D2
Gwynne Cl W4...... 133 D6
Gwynne Ho
Finsbury WC1........ 234 A1
6 Streatham SW2 ...160 B3
3 Wanstead E11......55 A4
Whitechapel E1 ....96 B2
Gwynne Pl WC1..... 233 D1
Gwynne Rd SW11 ....136 B3
Gye Ho 2 SW4 ......138 A1
Gylcote Cl SE5.......139 B1
Gyles Pk HA7 ....25 C2
Gyllyngdune Gdns
IG3................79 D5

H

Haarlem Rd 12 W14 . 112 D3
Haberdasher Pl 4
N1..................95 C4
Haberdashers' Aske's
Hatcham Coll SE4. 141 A3
Haberdashers' Aske's
Knights Acad BR1. 187 A6
Haberdasher St
N1..........95 B4 235 D2
Haccombe Rd SW19 .180 A4
HACKBRIDGE.......219 B6
Hackbridge Park Gdns
SM5 .... 218 D6
Hackbridge Prim Sch
SM5............... 203 A1
Hackbridge Rd SM5,
SM6 ....219 A6
Hackbridge Sta SM6 .219 B6
Hackford Rd
SW9 ....138 B4 270 D2
Hackford Wlk SW9...138 C4
Hackforth Cl EN5 .....12 B6
Hackington Cres
BR3...............185 C4
HACKNEY 74 B2
Hackney Central Sta
E8..................74 B2
Hackney Cl WD6 ......11 B6
Hackney Com Coll 33
N1 ....95 C4
Hackney Downs Sta
E8..................74 B3
Hackney Empire E8...74 B2
Hackney Free &
Parochial CE Sec Sch
18 E9................74 C2
Hackney Gr E8........74 B2
Hackney Rd E2 ....96 A5
HACKNEY WICK......75 C2
Hackney Wick E9......75 B2
Hackney Wick Sta E9 .75 C2
Hackworth Point 24
E3..................97 D4
Hacon Sq 12 E8........74 B1
Hadar Cl N20.........13 D3
Haddenham Ct
SW17 ....180 B6
Hadden Rd SE28 .....123 C3
Hadden Way UB6 .....64 B2
Haddington Rd BR1 ..186 B6
Haddo Ho
Gospel Oak NW5 ......71 B4
Greenwich SE10 .... 141 D6
Haddon Cl Enfield EN1 .18 A5
New Malden KT3 .... 199 D4
Haddon Ct
East Acton W3 ...... 111 D6
Hendon NW4 ....46 C6
Haddon Gr DA15 ......168 A4
Haddon Rd SM1 ..... 217 D4
Haddo St SE10.......142 A6
Haden Ct N4..........72 C6
Hadfield Cl UB1.......85 B4
Hadfield Ho
Edgware NW7 ....28 C6
37 Whitechapel E1.....96 A1
Hadleigh Cl
17 Bethnal Green E1...96 C3
Merton SW20.........179 B1
Hadleigh Ct 8 E4.....20 C4
Hadleigh Ho 16 E1....96 C3
Hadleigh Lo 5 IG8 ...37 A4
Hadleigh Rd N9........18 B4
Hadleigh St E2 ....96 C4
Hadleigh Wlk 1 E6. .100 A1
HADLEY 1 B2
Hadley Cl
Borehamwood WD6....10 B5
Southgate N21.........16 C5
Hadley Ct
1 London N3 ....29 D3
Stamford Hill N16 .....52 A1
Hadley Gdns
Chiswick W4 ....111 B1
Southall UB2 ....107 B1
Hadley Gn W EN5 ......1 B3
Hadley Gr EN5 ....1 A3
Hadley Green Rd EN5 .. 1 B3
Hadley Hall N21 ....16 C3
Hadley Highstone EN5 . 1 B4
Hadley Ho BR5...... 189 D1
Hadley Hts EN5 ....1 D3
Hadley Rd Barnet EN5....1 D2
Belvedere DA17.......125 B2
Enfield EN2 ....4 A5
Mitcham CR4 .... 203 D5
Hadley Ridge EN5.......1 B2
Hadley St NW1.........71 B2
Hadleyvale Ct EN5 .....1 D2
Hadley View 9 EN5 ....1 D1
Hadley Way N21 ....16 C5
HADLEY WOOD........2 B5
Hadley Wood Prim Sch
EN4 ....2 A5
Hadley Wood Rd
Barnet EN4 ....2 A3
Barnet EN5 ....1 C3
Hadley Wood Sta EN4 .. 2 A5
Hadlow Coll
(Mottingham Ctr)
SE12............... 165 C3
Hadlow Ho SE17 .... 263 B2
Hadlow Pl SE19.......184 A3
Hadlow Rd
Bexley DA16........ 146 C5
Sidcup DA14........ 190 A6
Hadrian Cl
5 Old Ford E3........97 C6
Stanwell TW19...... 148 A4
Hadrian Ct Barnet EN5 ..1 D1
11 Belmont SM2 .... 217 D1
Brockley SE4 .... 141 C2
Hadrian Est 33 E2.....96 A5
Hadrian's Ride EN1 ...17 D6
Hadrian St SE10 ......120 C1
Hadrian Way TW19...148 A4
Hadstock Ho NW1 ... 232 D2
Hadyn Park Ct 13
W12 ....112 A4
Hadyn Park Rd W12..112 A4
Hafer Rd SW11 ..... 136 D1
Hafton Rd SE6.......164 C2
Haggard Rd TW1.....153 B4
Hagger Ct E17........54 B6
HAGGERSTON 95 D5
Haggerston Rd E8 ....95 D6
Haggerston Sch 15
E2..................95 D5
Haggerston Sta E2....95 D6
Haggerston Studios 30
E8..................95 D6
Hague Prim Sch 21
E2..................96 B3
Hague St 30 E2 ....96 A4
Ha-Ha Rd SE7, SE18 ..144 B6
Haig Ct BR7 .... 188 D5
Haig Ho 4 E2 ....96 A5
Haig Pl SM4 ....201 C3
Haig Rd Hillingdon UB8 .83 A2
Stanmore HA7 ....25 C5
Haig Rd E E13 ....99 C5
Haig Rd W E13........99 C4
Haigville Gdns IG6....56 D5
Hailes Cl SW19 ......180 A4
Haileybury Ave EN1 ...17 D5
Hailey Rd DA18 ......125 C4
Hailey Rd Bsns Pk
DA18 .... 125 C4
Hailing Mews BR2 ...209 B6
Hailsham Ave SW2....160 B2
Hailsham Cl KT6.... 197 D2
Hailsham Dr HA1 .....42 B6
Hailsham Rd SW17...181 A4
Hailsham Terr N18 ....33 B5
Haimo Prim Sch
SE9............... 165 D6
Haimo Rd SE9 ...... 165 D6
Hainault Bldgs E10 ....54 A1
Hainault Bridge Par 5
IG1.................78 D6
Hainault Ct E17.......54 B5
Hainault Gore RM6....59 A4
Hainault Rd
Dagenham RM6 ....59 B3
Ilford RM6............58 B6
Leytonstone E11 ......54 B2
Hainault St Ilford IG1 ..78 D6
New Eltham SE9..... 166 D3
Haines Wlk SM4 .... 201 D2
Hainford Cl SE4..... 140 D1
Haining Cl 3 W4 ....110 C1
Hainthorpe Rd SE27 182 D6
Hainton Cl E1 ....96 B1
Halberd Mews E5......74 B6
Halbutt Gdns RM9 ....81 B5
Halbutt St RM9 ....81 B4
Halcomb St N1 ....95 C6
Halcot Ave DA6..... 169 D6
Halcroft Ct SM1......218 B4
Halcrow St E1 ....96 B2
Halcyon Ho 3 EN1....17 C6
Haldane Cl
Holdbrook EN3..........7 D5
Muswell Hill N10 ....31 B3
Haldane Pl SW18 ... 157 D3
Haldane Rd
Fulham
SW6 ..... 135 B6 264 D5
Newham E6 .... 100 A4
Southall UB1 ....86 A1
Thamesmead SE28 ... 124 D6
Haldan Rd E4..........36 A4
Haldon Rd SW18......157 B5
Hale Cl Chingford E4 ...20 A1
Edgware HA8..........27 A5
Orpington BR6....... 227 A4
Hale Ct HA8 ....27 A5
Hale Dr NW7 ....27 B4
HALE END 36 C4
Hale End Cl HA4 ......40 A3
Hale End Rd E17 ......36 B2
Halefield Rd N17......34 B2
Hale Gdns Acton W3 ..110 C5
Tottenham Hale N17 ...52 A6
Hale Grove Gdns
NW7................27 C5
Hale Ho Enfield EN3.....6 D6
Westminster SW1.... 259 D2
Hale La NW7, HA8 .....27 B5
Hale Lo HA1 ....42 C2
Hale Rd Newham E6...100 A3
Tottenham Hale N17 ...52 A6
Hales Ct 6 TW11 ....175 A5
Hales Ho 3 SW12....159 B4
Halesowen Rd SM4 . 201 D2
Hales Prior N1....... 233 C3
Hales St SE8.......... 141 C5
Hale St E14......... 119 D6
Halesworth Cl 3 E5 ..74 C6
Halesworth Rd SE13 141 D2
Hale The Chingford E4 . 36 B3
Tottenham Hale N17 ...52 A6

Hale Wlk W7 . . . . .86 C2
Haley Rd NW4 . . . . .46 C3
Halfacre 14 HA7 . . . . . .25 C5
Half Acre
Brentford TW8. . . . . . 131 D6
2 Wanstead E18. . . . . .55 A6
Half Acre Mews
TW8 . . . . 131 D6
Half Acre Rd W7 . . . . .108 C5
Half Moon Cres N1. . 233 D4
Half Moon Ct EC1 . . . 242 A3
Half Moon La SE24. . .161 A5
Halfmoon Pas E1 . . . 243 D1
Half Moon St
W1 . . . . .115 B5 248 D3
Halford Cl HA8. . . . . . . .26 D1
Halford Ct KT9. . . . . . .214 A1
Halford Ho 9 SW15. 156 D6
Halford Rd
Ickenham UB10. . . . . . .60 C3
Leyton E10. . . . . .54 B4
Richmond TW10. . . . . 154 A6
West Brompton
SW6 . . . . . 135 C6 265 A5
Halfway St DA15 . . . . .167 C3
Haliburton Rd TW1,
TW7 . . . . .131 A1
Haliday Ho N1. . . . . . . .73 B2
Haliday Wlk 4 N1 . . . .73 B2
Halidon Cl E9. . . . . .74 C3
Halifax 8 NW9 . . . . . . .27 D1
Halifax Cl TW11. . . . . .174 C4
Halifax Rd Enfield EN2. . . 5 B3
Greenford UB6. . . . . . . .85 D6
Halifax St SE26 . . . . . .162 B1
Halifield Dr DA17 . . . . .125 A3
Haling Gr CR2 . . . . . . .221 A1
Haling Manor High Sch
CR2 . . . . 220 D1
Haling Park Gdns
CR2. . . . . 220 D2
Haling Park Rd
Croydon CR2 . . . . 220 D3
South Croydon CR2 . . 221 A2
Haling Rd CR2. . . . . . .221 B2
Haliwell Ho 10 NW6. . . .91 D6
Halkett Ho 1 E2. . . . . .96 C6
Halkin Arc
SW1 . . . . . . 114 D3 257 D6
Halkin Mews SW1 . . 258 A6
Halkin Pl SW1 . . . . . . 258 A6
Halkin St
SW1 . . . . . . .115 A4 248 B1
Hallam Cl BR7 . . . . . . .188 B5
Hallam Ct W1. . . . . . . 238 D4
Hallam Gdns HA5 . . . . .23 A3
Hallam Ho
17 London SW9. . . . . . 138 C4
Pimlico SW1. . . . . 259 B1
Hallam Mews W1 . . . 238 D4
Hallam Rd
Barnes SW13. . . . . . . .134 B2
Harringay N15. . . . . . . .50 D5
Hallam St W1. . 93 B2 238 D4
Hallane Ho SE27 . . . . .183 A5
Hall Cl W5. . . . . .88 A2
Hall Ct TW11. . . . . 174 D5
Hall Dr Ealing W7 . . . . . .86 C1
Forest Hill SE26 . . . . . 184 C5
Halley Gdns SE13 . . . .142 B1
Halley Ho
16 Bethnal Green E2 . . .96 A5
8 Cubitt Town SE10 . 120 D1
Halley Prim Sch E14 . .97 A2
Halley Rd E7, E12. . . . . .77 D2
Halley St E14 . . . . .97 A2
Hall Farm Cl HA7 . . . . . .25 B6
Hall Farm Dr TW2. . . .152 B4
Hallfield Jun & Inf Schs
21 W2 . . . . .91 D1
Hallgate SE3 . . . . .143 A2
Hall Gate NW8 92 A4 229 B2
Hall Gdns E4 . . . . .35 B6
Halliards The KT12. . .194 A3
Halliday Ho 10 E1. . . . . .96 A1
Halliday Sq UB2 . . . . .108 B5
Halliford Cl TW17 . . . .193 C6
Halliford Rd
Sunbury TW16 . . . . . . 194 A5
Upper Halliford TW16,
TW17 . . . . 193 D5
Halliford Sch TW17 . 193 A2
Halliford St N1 . . . . . . .73 B1
Hallingbury Ct 1
E17. . . . . .53 D6
Halling Ho SE1 . . . . . 252 D1
Hallings Wharf Studios
2 E15 . . . . .98 B6
Halliwell Ct 4 SE22. .162 A6
Halliwell Rd SW2 . . . .160 B5
Halliwick Court Par 2
N12. . . . . .30 D5
Halliwick Ct 1 N12 . . .30 D5
Halliwick Ho N21 . . . . .17 B5
Halliwick Rd N10 . . . . .31 A2
Hall La
Chingford Hatch E4 . . . .35 B5
Harlington UB3 . . . . . .127 B5
Hendon NW4 . . . . .28 A1
Hall Lane E4. . . . . .35 A5
Hallmark Trad Ctr
HA9 . . . . .67 A4
Hallmead Rd SM1. . . 217 D5
Hall Oak Wlk NW6 . . . . .69 B2
Hallowell Ave CR0 . . .220 A4
Hallowell Cl CR4. . . . .203 A6
Hallowfield Way
CR4. . . . . .202 C6
Hallows Gr TW16. . . . 171 D5
Hall Pl W2. . . . . 92 B3 236 C5
Hall Rd
Dagenham RM6 . . . . . . .58 D3
Isleworth TW7. . . . . . .152 B6
Leyton E15 . . . . .76 B4
Newham E6 . . . . .100 B6
St John's Wood
NW8 . . . . 92 A4 229 B2
Halls Bsns Ctr UB3. . 106 A3
Hall Sch SW20. . . . . . 178 D2
Hall Sch The NW3. . . . .70 B2
Hall Sch Wimbledon
SW15. . . . . 156 A1
Hallside Rd EN1 . . . . 5 D5
Hall St
Finsbury EC1 . . 94 D4 234 D2
North Finchley N12 . . . .30 A5
Halls Terr UB10 . . . . . . .82 D3
Hallsville Prim Sch
E16. . . . . .99 A1
Hallsville Rd E16. . . . . .98 D1
Hallswelle Par 1
NW11. . . . . .47 B4
Hallswelle Rd NW11 . .47 B4
Hall The SE3 . . . . .143 A2
Hall Twr W2 . . . . 236 D4
Hall View SE9. . . . . . . 165 D2
Hallywell Cres E6. . . .100 B2
Halons Rd SE9. . . . . . .166 C4
Halpin Pl
SE17. . . . . . . .117 B2 262 D3
Halsbrook Rd SE3. . . 143 D2
Halsbury Cl HA7 . . . . . .25 B6
Halsbury Ct HA7 . . . . . .25 B6
Halsbury Ho 4 N7. . . .72 B4
Halsbury Rd W12 . . . .112 B5
Halsbury Rd E UB5 . . . .64 A4
Halsbury Rd W UB5 . . .63 D3
Halsend UB3 . . . . .106 B5
Halsey St
SW3 . . . . . . 114 D2 257 C4
Halsham Cres IG11 . . . .79 D3
Halsmere Rd SE5 . . . 138 D4
Halstead Cl 2 CR0. . .221 A5
Halstead Ct
Shoreditch N1 . . . . . . 235 D3
Walthamstow E17 . . . . .53 B2
Halstead Gdns N21 . . .17 B3
Halstead Rd
Edmonton N21. . . . . . . .17 B3
Enfield EN1 . . . . 5 C1
Wanstead E11 . . . . .55 B4
Halston Cl SW11. . . . 158 D5
Halstow 12 NW5 . . . . . .71 A2
Halstow Prim Sch 5
SE10. . . . . 121 A1
Halstow Rd
Greenwich SE3,
SE10 . . . . 121 A1
Kensal Green NW10 . . .90 D4
Halsway UB3 . . . . .106 A5
Halter Cl WD6 . . . . .11 B6
Halton Cl N11 . . . . .30 D4
Halton Cross St
N1. . . . . .94 D6 234 D6
Haltone Ho 1 SW4 . . 137 D3
Halton Ho 22 N1. . . . . .72 D1
Halton Mans N1 . . . . . .72 D1
Halton Pl N1 . . . . 235 A6
Halton Rd N1. . 94 D6 234 D6
Halt Robin La DA17 . . 125 D2
Halt Robin Rd DA17 . 125 D2
Halyard Ho E14. . . . . .120 A3
HAM 153 C1
Hamara Ghar 4 E13 . . 99 C6
Hambalt Rd SW4. . . . .159 C6
Hamble Cl HA4 . . . . . . .61 C6
Hamble Ct KT1 . . . . . . 175 D3
Hambledon SE17 . . . .139 B6
Hambledon Chase
N4. . . . . .50 A2
Hambledon Cl UB8. . . .82 D3
Hambledon Ct
5 Ealing W5 . . . . 110 A6
9 Wallington SM6 . . .219 B2
Hambledon Gdns
SE25. . . . . 205 D6
Hambledon Ho
2 Kingston u T
KT2 . . . . 176 D4
Lower Clapton E5. . . . . .74 B4
Hambledon Pl SE21 . 161 D3
Hambledon Rd
SW18 . . . . .157 B4
Hambledown Rd
DA15. . . . . .167 C4
Hamble St SW6. . . . . . 135 D2
Hambleton Cl KT4 . . .216 C6
Hamble Wlk UB5. . . . . .85 C5
Hambley Ho 5 SE16 . .118 B2
Hamblin Ho UB1 . . . . .107 A6
Hambly Mans SW16. .182 A4
Hamblyn Ct N16 . . . . . .51 D2
Hambridge Way
SW2 . . . . .160 C4
Hambro Ave BR2. . . . .209 A1
Hambrook Ct 12 NW5 . 71 B4
Hambrook Rd SE25 . .206 B6
Hambro Rd SW16 . . . 181 D5
Hambrough Ho UB4. . .84 C2
Hambrough Prim Sch
UB1 . . . . .107 B5
Hambrough Rd UB1. .107 A5
Ham Cl TW10 . . . . .153 C1
Ham Comm TW10. . . 153 D1
Ham Croft Cl TW13. . .150 A1
Ham Ct 12 NW9. . . . . . .27 D1
Hamden Cres RM10. . .81 D5
Hamel Cl HA3. . . . . .43 D5
Hamers Ho 19 SW2 . .160 C4
Hameway E6 . . . . .100 C3
Ham Farm Rd KT2,
TW10 . . . . .176 A6
Hamfrith Rd E15. . . . . .76 D2
Ham Gate Ave TW10. .176 A6
Ham Ho★ TW10. . . . . .153 C2
Hamilton Ave
Cheam SM3 . . . . 217 A6
Edmonton N9. . . . . .18 A4
Ilford IG6. . . . . .57 A4
Tolworth KT6, SM3. . . 214 C6
Hamilton Cl
Ashford TW13 . . . . . . 171 D5
Cockfosters EN4 . . . . 2 D1
Rotherhithe SE16. . . . 119 A4
St John's Wood
NW8 . . . . 92 B4 229 C1
Teddington TW11. . . . .175 B4
Tottenham N17 . . . . . . .51 D6
Hamilton Cres
Edmonton N13. . . . . . . .32 C6
Harrow HA2. . . . . .63 B5
Hounslow TW3. . . . . . 151 D6
Hamilton Ct
9 Catford SE6 . . . . . 164 D3
Croydon CR0 . . . . 206 A1
Ealing W5. . . . . .110 B6
St John's Wood W9 . . 229 A2
Hamilton Gdns
NW8. . . . . 92 A4 229 B2
Hamilton Hall
NW8. . . . . 92 A5 229 A3
Hamilton Ho
23 Bow E3 . . . . .97 B4
Chiswick W4 . . . . 133 C6
Kensington W8. . . . . . 245 C2
Oakleigh Pk N20. . . . . . .14 A4
1 Poplar E14 . . . . . . .119 B6
Putney SW15. . . . . 156 A6
10 Richmond TW9 . . . 132 C4
St John's Wood NW8 . 229 C2
Hamilton La N5. . . . . . .72 D4
Hamilton Lo 37 E1 . . . .96 C3
Hamilton Mews W1. . 248 C2
Hamilton Par TW13 . .172 A6
Hamilton Pk N5 . . . . . .72 D4
Hamilton Pk W N5 . . . .72 D4
Hamilton Pl
Mayfair W1 . .115 A5 248 B3
Hamilton Pl *continued*
Sunbury TW16 . . . . . . .172 B3
Tottenham N17 . . . . . . .33 D1
Hamilton Rd
Acton W4 . . . . 111 C4
Barnet EN4 . . . . 2 C1
Bexleyheath DA7 . . . . 147 A3
Brentford TW8. . . . . . 131 D6
Ealing W5. . . . . 110 A6
East Finchley N2 . . . . . .48 A6
Edmonton N9. . . . . .18 A4
Feltham TW13 . . . . . . 171 D6
Harrow HA1. . . . . .42 C4
Hayes UB3 . . . . .106 B6
Hendon NW11 . . . . .47 A2
Higham Hill E17 . . . . . . .35 A1
Ilford IG1. . . . . .78 D4
Merton SW19. . . . . . . 179 D3
Newham E15 . . . . .98 C4
Sidcup DA15. . . . . 190 A6
Southall UB1 . . . . .107 B5
South Norwood CR7. . .205 B6
Twickenham TW2. . . . . 152 C3
West Norwood SE27 . .183 B6
Willesden NW10 . . . . . .68 A3
Hamilton Road Ind Est
SE27. . . . . .183 B6
Hamilton Road Mews 1
SW19 . . . . 179 D3
Hamilton Sq
Bermondsey SE1 . . . . 252 D2
Finchley N12 . . . . .30 A4
Hamilton St SE8 . . . . .141 C6
Hamilton Terr
NW8. . . . . 92 A4 229 B2
Hamilton Way
Edmonton N13. . . . . . . .32 D6
Finchley N3 . . . . .29 C4
Hamlea Cl SE12. . . . . .165 A6
Hamlet Cl SE13 . . . . . .142 C1
Hamlet Ct
14 Enfield EN1. . . . . . . .17 C6
1 Hammersmith W6 112 A2
Kennington SE11 . . . . 261 C2
Hamlet Gdns W6. . . . .112 A2
Hamlet Ho SE9 . . . . . .166 C6
Hamlet Ind Ctr E9. . . . .75 C1
Hamleton Terr RM9 . . .80 C1
Hamlet Rd SE19. . . . . .184 A3
Hamlet Sq NW2. . . . . . .69 A5
Hamlets Way E3 . . . . . .97 B3
Hamlet The SE5. . . . . .139 B2
Hamlet Way SE1 . . . . 252 D2
Hamlin Cres HA5 . . . . .40 C4
Hamlyn Cl HA8 . . . . . . .10 A1
Hamlyn Gdns SE19. . .183 C3
Hamlyn Ho 3 TW13. .150 B3
Hammelton Ct 4
BR1. . . . . 186 D2
Hammelton Gn 2
SW9 . . . . 138 D4
Hammelton Rd BR1 . .187 A2
Hammers La NW7 . . . .28 A6
Hammersley Ho 8
SE14. . . . . .140 C5
HAMMERSMITH 112 C2
Hammersmith Bridge Rd
W6, SW13. . . . . .112 C1
Hammersmith Broadway
Hammersmith W6 . . . 112 C1
5 Hammersmith W6 112 C2
Hammersmith Flyover
W6 . . . . .112 C1
Hammersmith Gr
W6 . . . . .112 C3
Hammersmith Hospl
W12. . . . . .90 B1
Hammersmith Rd
Hammersmith W6 . . . 112 D2
Kensington W14. . . . . 254 B4
Hammersmith Sta
W6. . . . . 112 C2
Hammersmith Terr 6
W6 . . . . .112 A1
Hammet Cl UB4. . . . . . .84 D2
Hammett St EC3 . . . . 253 C6
Hammond Ave CR4 . .181 B1
Hammond Cl
Barnet EN5 . . . . .13 B6
Greenford UB6. . . . . . . .64 B3
Hampton TW12 . . . . . 173 C2
Hammond Ct
1 Leyton E10 . . . . .75 D6
1 Walthamstow E17. . .53 A4
Hammond Ho
10 Deptford SE14 . . . 140 C5
Millwall E14. . . . . 119 D3
Hammond Lo 6 W9 . . .91 C2
Hammond Rd
Enfield EN1 . . . . 6 B3
Southall UB2 . . . . 107 A3
Hammonds Cl RM8 . . .80 C5
Hammonds Ho
TW19 . . . . .148 B3
Hammond St NW5 . . . .71 C2
Hammond Way 2
SE28. . . . . .124 B6
Hamonde Cl HA8 . . . . .10 D2
Hamond Sq N1 . . . . . . .95 C5
Ham Park Rd E15 . . . . .76 D1
Hampden Ave BR3 . . .185 A1
Hampden Cl NW1. . . 232 D4
Hampden Ct
Harrow HA1. . . . . .42 A5
10 Muswell Hill N10. . . .31 A3
Hampden Gurney CE
Prim Sch W1 92 C1 237 B2
Hampden Gurney St
W1 . . . . 237 C1
Hampden La N17 . . . . .34 A2
Hampden Rd
Beckenham BR3. . . . . 185 A1
Harrow HA3. . . . . .24 A1
Hornsey N8 . . . . .50 C5
Kingston u T KT1 . . . . 198 C6
Muswell Hill N10 . . . . . .31 A3
Tottenham N17 . . . . . . .34 A2
Upper Holloway N19 . . .71 D6
Hampden Sq N14 . . . . .15 B3
Hampden Way N14 . . . 15 B2
Hampshire Cl N18 . . . .34 B5
Hampshire Ct
6 Barnes SW13. . . . 133 D3
Hendon NW4 . . . . .46 D4
Hampshire Ho HA8 . . .26 B3
Hampshire Hog La
3 Hammersmith
W6 . . . . .112 B1
11 Hammersmith W6 . .112 B2
Hampshire Rd N22. . . .32 B3
Hampshire St NW5. . . .71 D2
Hampson Way
SW8 . . . . .138 B4 270 C2
HAMPSTEAD 70 A3
Hampstead Cl SE28 . .124 B5
Hampstead Coll of Fine
Arts & Humanities 12
NW3. . . . . .70 C2
Hampstead Com Mkt★
NW3. . . . . .70 B4
HAMPSTEAD GARDEN SUBURB. 47 D4
Hampstead Gate
NW3 . . . . .70 A3
Hampstead Gdns
NW11. . . . . .47 C3
Hampstead Gn NW3 . .70 C3
Hampstead Gr NW3. . .70 A5
Hampstead Heath★
NW3. . . . . .70 B6
Hampstead Heath Pre
Prep Sch NW3 . . . . . .70 D4
Hampstead Heath Sta
NW3. . . . . .70 C4
Hampstead High Sch 3
NW3. . . . . .70 A3
Hampstead High St
NW3 . . . . .70 B4
Hampstead Hill Gdns
NW3 . . . . .70 C4
Hampstead Hill Sch 1
NW3. . . . . .70 C3
Hampstead Hts N2. . . .48 A6
Hampstead La N6. . . . .48 C2
Hampstead Parochial CE
Prim Sch 30 NW3. . . .70 A4
Hampstead Rd
NW1 . . . . 93 C4 232 A2
Hampstead Sch NW2 . 69 A4
Hampstead Sq 1
NW3 . . . . .70 A5
Hampstead Sta NW3. .70 A4
Hampstead Way
NW11 . . . . .47 A3
Hampstead West 4
NW6 . . . . .69 C2

Hampstead Wlk 1 E3 97 B6
HAMPTON 173 C1
Hampton Cl
Borehamwood WD6 11 A6
Friern Barnet N11 31 B5
Kilburn NW6 91 C4
Wimbledon SW20 178 C3
Hampton Com Coll TW12 173 C5
Hampton Court Ave KT8 196 C3
Hampton Court Cres KT8 196 B6
Hampton Court Landing Stage KT8 196 C6
Hampton Court Pal★ KT8 196 D6
Hampton Court Par KT8 196 C5
Hampton Court Rd KT1, KT8 197 B6
Hampton Court Sta KT8 196 C5
Hampton Court Way KT10, KT7, KT8 196 C3
Hampton Ct
Hampton KT8 196 C6
1 Islington N1 72 D2
19 Rotherhithe SE16 118 D5
Wood Green N22 31 C2
Hampton Ct House Sch KT8 174 C1
Hampton Farm Ind Est TW13 151 A1
HAMPTON HILL 174 A5
Hampton Hill Bsns Pk TW12 174 A5
Hampton Hill Jun Sch TW12 174 A5
Hampton Ho DA7 147 D3
Hampton Inf Sch TW12 173 C3
Hampton Jun Sch TW12 173 C2
Hampton La TW13 173 A6
Hampton Pool (Open Air) TW12 174 A3
Hampton Rd
Chingford Hatch E4 35 B5
Forest Gate E7 77 C3
Ilford IG1 79 A4
Leytonstone E11 54 B1
North Cheam KT4 216 B6
Teddington TW11, TW12 174 C5
Thornton Heath CR0 205 A3
Twickenham TW2 152 B1
Hampton Rd E TW13 151 B1
Hampton Rd W TW13 151 A1
Hampton Rise HA3 44 A3
Hampton Road Ind Pk CR0 205 A3
Hampton Sch TW12 173 C5
Hampton St SE1 116 D2 261 D3
Hampton Sta TW12 173 C2
HAMPTON WICK 175 D3
Hampton Wick Inf Sch TW11 175 D3
Hampton Wick Sta KT1 175 C2
Ham Ridings TW10 176 B5
Ham Shades Cl 1 DA15 168 A1
Hamson Ct HA2 64 B6
Ham St TW10 153 C1
Hamstead Gates 11 NW5 71 B2
Ham The TW8 131 C5
Ham View CR0 207 A3
Ham Yd W1 249 C6
Hanameel St E16 121 B5
Hana Mews E5 74 B4
Hanbury Cl NW4 46 C6
Hanbury Ct HA1 42 D3
Hanbury Dr
2 Leyton E11 54 D2
Southgate N21 16 B6
Hanbury Ho
8 Bethnal Green E1 96 A2
South Lambeth SW8 270 B5
Hanbury Mews N1 235 B5
Hanbury Rd
South Acton W3 110 D4
Tottenham N17 34 B1
Hanbury St E1 95 D2 243 D4
Hancocke Ho 4 E17 53 D6
Hancock Nunn Ho 1 NW3 70 D1
Hancock Rd
Bromley E3 98 A4
South Norwood SE19 183 B4
Handa Wlk 3 N1 73 A2
Handcroft Rd CR0 204 D1
Hand Ct WC1 240 D3
Handel Cl HA8 26 B4
Handel Ho TW2 152 B5
Handel House Museum★ W1 115 B6 248 D6
Handel Mans
Barnes SW13 134 C5
Bloomsbury WC1 240 B6
Handel Par HA8 26 C3
Handel Pl NW10 67 B2
Handel St WC1 94 A3 240 B6
Handel Way HA8 26 C3
Handen Rd SE12 164 D6
Handforth Rd
Brixton SW9 138 C5
6 Ilford IG1 78 D5
Handley Gr NW2 68 D5
Handley Page Rd SM6 220 B1
Handley Rd E9 96 C6
Handowe Cl NW4 46 A5
Handside Cl KT4 200 D1
Hands Wlk E16 99 A1
Handsworth Ave E4 36 B4
Handsworth Prim Sch E4 36 B4
Handsworth Rd N17 51 B6
Handtrough Way IG11 100 D5
Hanford Cl SW18 157 C3
Hanford Row SW19 178 C4
Hanger Ct W5 88 C3
Hanger Gn W5 88 C3
Hanger Lane Sta W5 88 A4
Hanger La (North Circular Rd) W5 88 B2
Hanger Vale La W5 88 B1
Hanger View Way W3 88 C2
Hangmans Cnr BR7 188 D2
Hankey Pl SE1 117 B4 252 D1
Hankins La NW7 11 C1
Hanley Ct N4 50 B1
Hanley Gdns N4 50 B1
Hanley Pl BR3 185 C3
Hanley Rd N4, N19 50 A1
Hanmer Wlk N7 72 B6
Hannah Cl
Beckenham BR3 208 A6
Wembley NW10 67 A4
Hannah Ct
Palmers Green N13 16 B2
5 Sutton SM1 217 D2
Wimbledon SW19 178 D3
Hannah Mary Way 17 SE1 118 A2
Hannah Mews SM6 219 C1
Hannay La N8 49 D2
Hannay Wlk SW16 159 D2
Hannell Rd SW6 135 A5 264 B4
Hannen Ho SE5 139 B2
Hannen Rd SE27 160 D1
Hannibal Rd
Stanwell TW19 148 A4
Stepney E1 96 C2
Hannibal Way CR0 220 B2
Hanning Lo TW3 130 A1
Hannington Rd SW4 137 B2
Hanno Cl SM6 219 D1
Hanover Ave
Feltham TW13 150 A2
Newham E16 121 A5
Hanover Circ UB3 83 B1
Hanover Cl
Cheam SM3 217 B4
Richmond TW9 132 C5
Hanover Ct
Colindale NW9 45 C6
Harrow HA1 42 B2
1 Penge SE19 184 A3
Hanover Ct *continued*
11 Pinner HA5 23 B3
Shepherd's Bush W12 112 A5
Stamford Hill N16 51 D2
Hanover Dr BR7 189 A6
Hanover Gate Mans NW1 237 B6
Hanover Gdns SE11 138 C6
Hanover Ho
1 New Barnet EN5 2 A1
St John's Wood NW8 230 A3
Tolworth KT6 198 C1
Hanover Lo N21 16 D6
Hanover Mans 5 SW2 160 C6
Hanover Mead NW11 47 A3
Hanover Pk SE15 140 A4
Hanover Pl 16 Bow E3 97 B4
St Giles WC2 240 B1
Hanover Prim Sch N1 95 A5 235 A4
Hanover Rd
Merton SW19 180 A3
South Tottenham N15 51 D5
Willesden NW10 90 C6
Hanover Sq W1 93 B1 238 D1
Hanover St
Croydon CR0 220 D5
Marylebone W1 93 B1 238 D1
Hanover Stps W2 237 B1
Hanover Terr
Isleworth TW7 131 A4
Lisson Gr NW1 92 D4 230 C1
Hanover Terrace Mews NW1 92 C4 230 B1
Hanover Way DA6 146 D2
Hanover West Ind Est NW10 89 B4
Hanover Yd N1 235 A4
Hansard Mews W14 112 D4
Hansart Way EN2 4 C4
Hanscomb Mews SW4 137 C1
Hans Cres SW1 114 D3 257 C6
Hanselin Cl HA7 24 D5
Hansen Dr N21 16 B6
Hanshaw Dr HA8 27 B2
Hansler Ct 14 SW19 157 A3
Hansler Gr KT8 196 B5
Hansler Rd SE22 161 D6
Hansol Rd DA6 169 A6
Hanson Cl
Balham SW12 159 B4
Beckenham BR3 185 D4
Mortlake SW14 133 A2
West Drayton UB7 104 B3
Hanson Ct E17 53 D3
Hanson Gdns UB1 107 A4
Hanson Ho 2 E1 118 A6
Hanson St W1 93 C2 239 A4
Hans Pl SW1 114 D3 257 C6
Hans Rd SW3 114 D3 257 C6
Hans St SW1 114 D3 257 D5
Hanway Ho 25 SW9 138 C4
Hanway Pl W1 239 C2
Hanway Rd W7 86 C1
Hanway St W1 239 C2
HANWELL 108 D5
Hanwell Sta W7 108 C6
HANWORTH 172 D6
Hanworth Ho SE5 138 D5
Hanworth Rd
Ashford TW16 172 A3
Feltham TW13 150 B3
Hampton TW12 173 C5
Hounslow TW3, TW4 129 D1
Twickenham TW4 151 B4
Hanworth Terr TW3 129 D1
Hanworth Trad Est TW13 151 A1
Hapgood Cl UB6 64 B3
Harben Rd NW6 70 A1
Harberson Rd
Balham SW12 159 B3
West Ham E15 98 D6
Harberton Rd N19 49 C1
Harbet Rd
Highams Pk N18 35 A4
Paddington W2 92 B2 236 D3
Harbex Cl DA5 169 D4
Harbinger Prim Sch 11 E14 119 D2
Harbinger Rd E14 119 D2
Harbin Ho 5 SW2 160 C3
Harbledown Ho SE1 252 C1
Harbledown Rd SW6 265 A2
Harbord Cl
Camberwell SE15 139 C5
London SE5 139 B3
Harbord Ho 5 SE16 118 D2
Harbord St SW6 134 D4
Harborne Cl WD19 22 C5
Harborough Ave DA15 167 D4
Harborough Rd SW16 182 B6
Harbour Ave SW10 136 A4 266 B1
Harbour Cl 2 CR4 181 A2
Harbour Exchange Sq E14 119 D4
Harbour Rd SE5 139 A2
Harbridge Ave SW15 156 A4
Harbury Rd SM5 218 C1
Harbut Rd SW11 136 B1
Harcombe Rd N16 73 C5
Harcourt Ave
Edgware HA8 11 A1
Little Ilford E12 78 B3
Sidcup DA15 168 C4
Wallington SM6 219 B4
Harcourt Cl TW7 131 A2
Harcourt Field SM6 219 B4
Harcourt Ho
5 Chingford E4 36 B5
27 Clapham SW8 137 D3
Marylebone W1 238 C2
4 Willesden NW10 68 C2
Harcourt Lo 2 SM6 219 B4
Harcourt Rd
Bexley DA6 147 A1
Brockley SE4 141 B2
Bushey WD23 8 A6
Merton SW19 179 C3
Thornton Heath CR7 204 C3
Wallington SM6 219 B4
West Ham E15 98 D5
Wood Green N22 31 D2
Harcourt St W1 92 C2 237 B3
Harcourt Terr SW10 113 D1 255 D1
Hardcastle Cl SE25 206 A3
Hardcastle Ho
3 New Cross Gate SE14 141 A4
8 Peckham SE15 140 A4
Hardcourts Cl BR4 223 D5
Hard Ct IG8 37 C4
Hardel Rise SW2 160 D3
Hardel Wlk SE24, SW2 160 C4
Harden Ct 1 SE7 122 A2
Harden Ho SE5 139 C3
Harders Rd SE15 140 B3
Hardess St SE24 139 A2
Hardham Ho 5 SW2 160 C5
Hardie Cl NW10 67 B3
Harding Cl
Camberwell SE17 139 A6
South Croydon CR0 221 D5
Harding Ct SE25 183 D1
Hardinge Cl UB8 82 D1
Hardinge Cres SE18 123 A3
Hardinge Rd
Edmonton N18 33 C4
Willesden NW10 90 C6
Hardinge St
Stepney E1 96 C1
Woolwich SE18 122 D3
Harding Ho
Barnes SW13 134 B6
Hayes UB3 84 B1
14 Woolwich SE18 122 B2
Harding Pl SE23 163 A4
Harding Rd DA7 147 B3
Hardings Cl KT2 176 B2
Hardings La SE20 184 D4
Hardington 2 NW1 71 A1
Hardman Rd
Greenwich SE7 121 B1
Kingston u T KT2 176 A1
Hardwick Cl 7 HA7 25 C5
Hardwick Ct 8 E11 55 A3
Hardwicke Ave TW5 129 C4
Hardwicke Ho 10 E3 97 D4
Hardwicke Mews WC1 233 D1
Hardwicke Rd
Acton W4 111 B2
Bowes Pk N13 32 A4
Richmond TW10 175 C6
Hardwicke St IG11 101 A6
Hardwick Gn W13 87 B2
Hardwick Ho
10 London SW8 137 D3
Marylebone NW8 237 B6
Hardwick St EC1 94 C4 234 B1
Hardwick's Way SW18 157 C6
Hardwidge St SE1 253 A2
Hardy Ave
4 Newham E16 121 A5
Ruislip HA4 62 B3
Hardy Cl Barnet EN5 13 A6
Pinner HA5 40 D2
Rotherhithe SE16 118 D4
Hardy Cotts 2 SE10 142 B6
Hardy Ct
Greenwich SE3 142 D6
9 Wanstead E11 55 A5
Hardyng Ho 4 E17 53 A5
Hardy Pas N22 32 C1
Hardy Rd
Greenwich SE3 142 D6
Merton SW19 179 D3
Walthamstow E4 35 B4
Hardys Mews KT8 196 C5
Hardy Way EN2 4 C4
Hare and Billet Rd SE3 142 B3
Harebell Dr E6 100 C2
Harecastle Cl UB4 85 A3
Harecourt Rd N1 73 A2
Hare Ct EC4 241 A1
Haredale Ho 24 SE16 118 A4
Haredale Rd SE24 139 A1
Haredon Cl SE23 162 D4
Harefield KT10 212 C5
Harefield Cl EN2 4 C4
Harefield Ct 4 SW19 179 C3
Harefield Mews SE4 141 B2
Harefield Rd
Brockley SE4 141 B2
Hornsey N8 49 D4
Sidcup DA14 168 D1
South Norwood SW16 182 B3
Uxbridge UB8 60 A3
Hare La KT10 212 C2
Hare Marsh E2 96 A3
Harenc Sch DA14 190 C5
Harepit Cl CR2 220 D1
Hare Pl EC4 241 B1
Hare Row E2 96 B5
Haresfield Rd RM10 81 C2
Hare St SE18 122 C3
Harestone Ct CR2 221 C2
Hare Wlk N1 95 C5
Harewood Ave
Lisson Gr NW1 92 C3 237 B5
Northolt UB5 63 B1
Harewood Cl UB5 63 B1
Harewood Ct HA3 24 C2
Harewood Pl W1 238 D1
Harewood Rd
Hounslow TW7 130 D4
Mitcham SW19 180 C4
South Croydon CR2 221 C2
Harewood Row NW1 237 B4
Harewood Terr UB2 107 B2
Harfield Gdns 1 SE5 139 C2
Harfield Rd TW16 172 D1
Harfleur Ct SE11 261 C3
Harford Cl E4 19 D4
Harford Ho
Camberwell SE5 139 A6
Notting Hill W11 91 B2
Harford Mews 6 N19 71 D5
Harford Rd E4 19 D4
Harford St E1 97 A3
Harford Wlk N2 48 B5
Hargood Cl HA3 44 A3
Hargood Rd SE3 143 C4

Hargrave Mans 3 N19 71 D6
Hargrave Park Prim Sch 14 N19 71 C6
Hargrave Pk N19 71 C6
Hargrave Pl N7 71 D3
Hargrave Rd N19 71 C6
Hargraves Ho 14 W12 112 B6
Hargwyne St SW9 138 B2
Haringey Pk N8 50 A3
Haringey Rd N8 50 A5
Haringey Sixth Form Ctr N17 33 D4
Harington Terr N18 17 B1
Harkett Cl HA3 24 D1
Harkett Ct HA3 24 D1
Harkness Ct SM1 201 D1
Harkness Ho 30 E1 96 A1
Harland Ave
Sidcup DA15 167 C2
South Croydon CR0 222 A5
Harland Cl SW19 201 D6
Harland Rd SE12 165 A3
Harlands Gr BR6 226 D4
Harlech Ct 1 SE23 162 C3
Harlech Gdns TW5 128 C5
Harlech Rd N14 16 A1
Harlech Twr 5 W3 111 A4
Harlequin Ave TW8 131 A6
Harlequin Cl
Hayes UB4 84 D2
Isleworth TW7 152 C6
Harlequin Ct
Croydon CR2 221 A1
Ealing W5 109 C6
Willesden NW10 67 B2
Harlequin Ho 1 DA18 125 A3
Harlequin Rd TW11 175 B3
Harlescott Rd SE15 140 D1
HARLESDEN 89 D6
Harlesden Gdns NW10 89 D6
Harlesden Plaza 2 NW10 89 D5
Harlesden Prim Sch NW10 89 C5
Harlesden Rd NW10 90 A6
Harlesden Sta NW10 89 B5
Harleston Cl 4 E5 74 C6
Harley BR7 189 B2
Harley Cl HA0 65 D2
Harley Cres HA1 42 B5
Harley Ct Harrow HA1 42 B5
Wanstead E11 55 A2
Whetstone N20 14 A1
Harleyford BR1 187 C2
Harleyford Ct
Kennington SW8 270 C6
Wembley HA0 65 A4
Harleyford Manor 8 W3 111 A5
Harleyford Rd SE11 138 B6 270 C6
Harleyford St SE11 138 C6
Harley Gdns
Orpington BR6 227 C4
South Kensington SW10 114 A1 256 B1
Harley Gr E3 97 B4
Harley Ho
Leytonstone E11 54 B2
Marylebone NW1 238 B5
Harley Pl W1 93 B2 238 C3
Harley Rd
Hampstead NW3 70 B1
Harlesden NW10 89 C5
Harrow HA1 42 B5
Harley St W1 93 B2 238 C3
Harley Villas NW10 89 C5
Harling Ct 3 SW11 136 D3
Harlinger St SE18 122 A3
HARLINGTON 127 A6
Harlington Cl UB7 127 A5
Harlington Cnr UB3 127 B4
Harlington Com Sch UB3 105 B2
Harlington Rd
Bexley DA7 147 A2
Hillingdon UB8 82 C3
Harlington Rd E TW13, TW14 150 C3
Harlington Rd W TW14 150 B5
Harlowe Ho 13 E8 95 D6
Harlow Mans 2 IG11 78 D1
Harlow Rd N13 17 B1
Harlyn Dr HA5 40 B6
Harlyn Prim Sch HA5 40 B6
Harlynwood 19 SE5 139 A5
Harman Ave IG8 36 D4
Harman Cl
10 Bermondsey SE1 118 A1
Chingford E4 36 B6
Cricklewood NW2 69 A5
Harman Dr
Blackfen DA15 167 D5
Cricklewood NW2 69 A4
Harman Rd EN1 17 D6
HARMONDSWORTH 126 A6
Harmondsworth La UB7 126 B6
Harmondsworth Rd UB7 104 A2
Harmon Ho 7 SE8 119 B2
Harmony Cl NW11 47 A4
Harmony Way
Bromley BR1 187 A1
Hendon NW4 46 C5
Harmood Gr NW1 71 B1
Harmood Ho 2 NW1 71 B1
Harmood St NW1 71 B1
Harmsworth St SE17 116 D1 261 C1
Harmsworth Way N20 13 C3
Harnage Ho TW8 110 A1
Harney Ct SE14 141 A4
Harold Ave
Erith DA17 125 B1
Hayes UB3 105 D3
Harold Ct
14 Rotherhithe SE16 118 D4
6 Teddington TW11 174 C5
Harold Est SE1 263 B5
Harold Gibbons Ct 12 SE7 143 C6
Harold Ho 16 E2 96 D5
Harold Laski Ho EC1 234 D1
Harold Maddison Ho SE17 261 D2
Harold Rd
Chingford E4 20 A1
Hornsey N8 50 B5
Leytonstone E11 54 C1
Newham E13 99 B6
North Acton NW10 89 B4
South Norwood SE19 183 B3
South Tottenham N15 51 D4
Sutton SM1 218 B4
Woodford IG8 37 A2
Haroldstone Rd E17 53 A4
Harold Wilson Ho SW6 264 D5
Haronton Ct E10 76 A6
Harp Alley EC4 241 C2
Harp Bsns Ctr The NW2 68 A6
Harpenden Rd
Wanstead E12 77 C6
West Norwood SE27, SW16 160 D2
Harpenmead Point NW2 69 B6
Harper Cl N14 15 C6
Harper Ho 3 SW9 138 D2
Harper Mews SW17 158 A1
Harper Rd
Bermondsey SE1 117 A3 262 B6
Newham E6 100 B1
Harper's Yd N17 33 D2
Harp Island Cl NW10 67 B6
Harp La EC3 253 A5
Harpley Sq E1 96 D3
Harpour Rd IG11 79 A2
Harp Rd W7 86 D3
Harpsden St SW11 268 A1
Harpur Mews WC1 240 C4
Harpur St WC1 94 B2 240 C4
Harraden Rd SE3 143 C4
Harrier Ave E11 55 B3
Harrier Ct TW4 129 A3
Harrier Ho 9 SW11 136 C2
Harrier Mews SE28 123 B4
Harrier Rd NW9 27 C1
Harriers Cl W5 110 A6
Harrier Way E6 100 B2
Harries Rd UB4 84 C3
Harriet Cl E8 96 A6
Harriet Gdns CR0 222 A6
Harriet Ho
Walham Green SW6 265 D3
1 Walthamstow E17 53 D4
Harriet Mews DA16 146 B3
Harriet St SW1 114 D4 247 D1
Harriet Tubman Cl 21 SW2 160 C4
Harriet Way WD23 8 B4
Harriet Wlk SW1 114 D4 247 D1
HARRINGAY 50 D4
Harringay Gdns N8 50 D5
Harringay Green Lanes Sta N4 50 D3
Harringay Rd N15 50 D5
Harringay Sta N4 50 C3
Harrington Cl
Wallington CR0 220 A6
Willesden NW10 67 B5
Harrington Ct
6 South Croydon CR0 221 B6
South Kensington SW7 256 D4
9 West Kilburn W9 91 B4
Harrington Gdns SW7 114 A2 256 A3
Harrington Hill E5 52 B1
Harrington Hill Prim Sch E5 52 B1
Harrington Ho
2 Bromley BR1 187 A2
Regent's Pk NW1 232 A2
Upper Clapton E5 52 C1
Westminster SW1 259 D2
Harrington Rd
Croydon SE25 206 B5
Leytonstone E11 54 C1
South Kensington SW7 114 B2 256 C4
Harrington Road Sta SE25 206 C6
Harrington Sq NW1 93 C5 232 A3
Harrington St NW1 93 C4 232 A2
Harrington Way SE18 121 D3
Harriott Cl SE10 120 D2
Harriott Ho 11 E1 96 C1
Harris Acad at Peckham SE15 139 D4
Harris Acad Bermondsey SE1 117 D2 263 D4
Harris Acad Falconwood DA16 145 C1
Harris Acad Merton Sch CR4 203 D6
Harris Acad South Norwood SE25 205 D6
Harris City Acad Crystal Palace SE19 183 D2
Harris Cl Enfield EN2 4 D4
Heston TW5 129 C4
Harris Cotts 1 E15 98 D6
Harris Ct HA9 66 B5
Harris Girl's Acad SE15 162 C6
Harris Ho 11 Bow E3 97 C4
7 Brixton SW9 138 C2
Harris Lo SE6 164 A3
Harrison Cl N20 14 C3
Harrison Dr BR1 210 D5
Harrison Ho SE17 262 C2
Harrison Rd
Dagenham RM10 81 D2
Stonebridge NW10 89 B6
Harrisons Ct 1 SE14 140 D6
Harrison's Rise CR0 220 D5
Harrison St WC1 94 A4 233 B1
Harrison Way TW17 192 D4
Harris Rd
Dagenham RM9 81 B3
Erith DA7 147 B4
Harris St
Camberwell SE5 139 B5
Walthamstow E17 53 B2
Harris Way TW16 171 C2
Harrodian Sch The SW13 133 D5
Harrods Gn HA8 26 C5
Harrogate Ct
2 Forest Hill SE26 162 A1
9 New Southgate N11 31 A4
Harrold Ho 1 NW3 70 A1
Harrold Rd RM8 80 B3
Harrovian Bsns Village 6 HA1 42 C2
HARROW 42 B3
Harrow Arts Ctr* HA5 23 C3
Harrow Ave EN1 17 D5
Harroway Rd SW11 136 B3
Harrowby St W1 92 C1 237 B2
Harrow Cl KT9 213 D1
Harrow Coll HA1 42 C2
Harrow Coll (Harrow Weald Campus) HA3 24 C4
Harrowdene Cl HA0 65 D4
Harrowdene Ct SW19 179 A5
Harrowdene Gdns TW11 175 A3
Harrowdene Rd HA0 65 D4
Harrow Dr N9 17 D3
Harrowes Meade HA8 10 C1
Harrow Fields Gdns HA1 64 C5
Harrowgate Ho 22 E9 74 D2
Harrowgate Rd E9 75 A1
Harrow Gn E11 76 C5
Harrow High Sch HA1 43 A3
Harrow La E14 120 A6
Harrow Lo SM2 218 B2
Harrow Manor Way SE2 124 C3
Harrow Mus & Her Ctr* HA2 42 A6
HARROW ON THE HILL 42 C1
Harrow-on-the-Hill Sta HA1 42 C3
Harrow Pk HA1 64 C6
Harrow Pl E1 95 C1 243 B2
Harrow Rd
Ashford TW15 148 C2
Barking IG11 101 C6
Carshalton SM5 218 C2
Ilford IG1 79 A4
Leyton E11 76 D5
Little Venice W2 92 A2 236 B3
2 Newham E6 100 A6
Sudbury HA0 65 A4
Tokyngton HA9 66 C2
Wembley HA0 65 D3
Westbourne Green W2, W9 91 C3
Harrow Sch HA1 42 C1
Harrow St NW1 237 A4
Harrow View
Harrow HA1, HA2 42 B5
Hayes UB3 84 A1
Hillingdon UB10 83 A4
Harrow View Rd W5 87 B3
Harrow Way
Charlton TW17 171 A1
South Oxhey WD19 23 A6
HARROW WEALD 24 B2
Harrow Weald Pk HA3 24 B4
Harrow & Wealdstone Sta HA1 42 C5
Harry Cl CR7 205 A3
Harry Ct 15 NW9 46 A5
Harry Gosling Prim Sch 41 E1 96 A1
Harry Hinkins Ho SE17 262 B1
Harry Lambourn Ho 10 SE15 140 B5
Harston 15 KT1 176 C1
Harston Dr EN3 7 C5
Hart Ct E12 78 C1
Harte Rd TW3 129 B3
Hartfield Ave
Borehamwood WD6 10 C6
Northolt UB5 84 B5
Hartfield Cl WD6 10 C6
Hartfield Cres
Coney Hall BR4 225 A5
Merton SW19 179 B3
Hartfield Ct CR2 220 D1
Hartfield Gr SE20 184 C2
Hartfield Ho UB5 84 B5
Hartfield Rd
Chessington KT9 213 D3
Hayes BR4 225 A4
Merton SW19 179 C3
Hartfield Terr E3 97 C5
Hartford Ave HA3 43 B6
Hartford Rd
Old Bexley DA5 169 C5
West Ewell KT19 214 D2
Hart Gr Ealing W5 110 C5
Southall UB1 85 C2
Hartgrove Ct NW9 45 A5
Hart Grove Ct 3 W5 110 C5
Hartham Cl
Isleworth TW7 131 A4
Lower Holloway N7 72 A3
Hartham Rd
Isleworth TW7 131 A4
Lower Holloway N7 72 A3
Tottenham N17 33 D1
Hart Ho Hayes UB4 83 B2
Streatham SW2 160 C3
Harting Rd SE9 166 A1
Hartington Cl
Farnborough BR6 227 A3
Harrow HA1 64 C4
Hartington Ct
Chiswick W4 132 D5
South Lambeth SW8 270 A2
Hartington Rd
Chiswick W4 133 A4
Ealing W13 109 B6
Newham E16 99 B1
Southall UB2 107 A3
South Lambeth SW8 138 A5 270 A3
Twickenham TW1 153 B5
Walthamstow E17 53 A3
Hartismere Rd SW6 135 B5 264 D4
Hartlake Rd E9 75 A2
Hartland NW1 232 B5
Hartland Cl
Edgware HA8 10 C2
Enfield N21 17 A5
Hartland Ct 5 N11 30 D5
Hartland Dr
Edgware HA8 10 C2
Ruislip HA4 62 B4
Hartland Rd
Camden Town NW1 71 B1
Cheam SM4 201 D2
Friern Barnet N11 30 D5
Hampton TW12 173 D6
Isleworth TW7 131 A2
Kilburn NW6 91 B6
Stratford E15 76 D1
Hartlands Cl DA5 169 B5
Hartlands The TW5 128 B6
Hartland Way
Croydon CR0 223 A6
Morden SM4 201 B2
Hartlepool Ct E16 122 D5
Hartley Ave
Edgware NW7 27 D5
Newham E6 100 A6
Hartley Cl
Bickley BR1 188 B1
Edgware NW7 27 D5
Hartley Ct Ealing W5 110 C5
5 Mitcham CR4 180 C2
Hartley Ho
Bermondsey SE1 263 D4
Finchley N3 29 D4
Putney SW15 156 A6
Hartley Prim Sch 7 E6 100 A6
Hartley Rd
Bexley DA16 146 C5
Leytonstone E11 54 D1
Thornton Heath CR0 205 A2
Hartley St E2 96 C4
Hart Lo EN5 1 A2
Hartmann Rd E16 122 A5
Hartmoor Mews EN3 6 D6
Hartnoll Ho 4 N7 72 C3

Hartnoll St N7 . . . . 72 B3
Harton Cl BR1 . . . . . . 187 D2
Harton Lodge 2
SE8 . . . . 141 C4
Harton Rd N9 . . . . 18 B2
Harton St SE8 . . . . 141 C4
Hartopp Ct 20 N16 . . . . 73 C5
Hartopp Point SW6 . 264 B4
Hartsbourne Ave
WD23 . . . . 8 B2
Hartsbourne Cl WD23 . . 8 B2
Hartsbourne Ct 5
UB1 . . . . 86 A1
Hartsbourne Pk WD23 . . 8 C2
Hartsbourne Prim Sch
WD23 . . . . 8 B2
Hartsbourne Rd WD23 . 8 B2
Harts Gr IG8 . . . . 37 A5
Hartshill Cl UB10 . . . . . 60 D2
Hartshorn Alley EC3 243 B1
Hartshorn Gdns E6 . . 100 C3
Harts La IG11 . . . . 78 D2
Hart's La SE14 . . . . 141 A4
Hartslock Dr SE2 . . . 124 D4
Hartsmead Rd SE9 . . . 166 B2
Hart Sq SM4 . . . . 201 C3
Hart St EC3 . . . . 253 B6
Hartsway EN3 . . . . 6 C1
Hartswood Gn WD23 . . . 8 B2
Hartswood Ho 10
SW2 . . . . 160 A3
Hartswood Rd W12 . 111 D3
Hartsworth Cl E13 . . . . 98 D5
Hartville Rd SE18 . . . . 123 C2
Hartwell Cl 12 SW2 . . 160 B3
Hartwell Ct SE22 . . . . 140 A1
Hartwell Dr E4 . . . . 36 A4
Hartwell Ho 2 SE7 . . 121 B1
Hartwell St E8 . . . . 73 D2
Harvard Ct
9 Eltham SE9 . . . . . . 166 C5
West Hampstead NW6 . 69 D3
Harvard Hill W4 . . . . 132 D6
Harvard Ho
3 Camberwell
SE17 . . . . 138 D6
Putney SW15 . . . . 156 D5
Harvard Mans 18
SW11 . . . . 136 B1
Harvard Rd
11 Acton Green W4 . . 111 A1
Gunnersbury W4 . . . . 110 D1
Hounslow TW7 . . . . 130 C4
Lewisham SE13 . . . . . 164 A6
Harvel Cres SE2 . . . . 124 D1
Harvel Ct SE2 . . . . 125 A1
Harvest Bank Rd
BR4 . . . . 225 A5
Harvest Ct
Beckenham BR3 . . . . . 185 C3
Littleton TW17 . . . . . . 192 C5
Harvesters Cl TW7 . . . 152 B6
Harvest La
Loughton IG10 . . . . 21 D4
Thames Ditton KT7 . . . 197 A3
Harvest Rd TW13 . . . . . 150 A1
Harvey Ct
Battersea SW11 . . . . 267 B2
Walthamstow E17 . . . . . 53 C4
Harvey Dr TW12 . . . . . . 173 C2
Harvey Gdns
Greenwich SE7 . . . . . 121 C1
Leytonstone E11 . . . . . . 54 D1
Harvey Ho
1 Barking IG11 . . . . . . 79 A1
10 Bethnal Green E1 . . . 96 B3
Brentford TW8 . . . . . . 110 A1
Dagenham RM6 . . . . 58 D5
Hornsey N8 . . . . 50 A6
Pimlico SW1 . . . . 259 D1
Shoreditch N1 . . . . . . 235 D5
Wembley Pk HA9 . . . . . 66 D6
Harvey Lo 8 W9 . . . . . . 91 C2
Harvey Mews N8 . . . . . . 50 B4
Harvey Point 7 E16 . . . 99 A2
Harvey Rd
15 Camberwell SE5 . . . 139 B4
Hillingdon UB10 . . . . 82 C5
Hornsey Vale N8 . . . . . . 50 B4
Ilford IG1 . . . . 78 D3
Leytonstone E11 . . . . . . 54 D1
Ruislip UB5 . . . . 62 C1
Twickenham TW4 . . . . . 151 B4
Harvey Rd *continued*
Walton-on-T KT12 . . . 194 A2
Harvey St N1 . . . . 235 D5
Harvill Rd
Newyears Green UB9 . . 38 A2
Sidcup DA14 . . . . 191 A5
Harvil Rd UB9, UB10 . . . 38 A2
Harvington Sch W5 . . . 87 D1
Harvington Wlk E8 . . . 74 A1
Harvist Rd NW6 . . . . 91 A5
Harwell Cl HA4 . . . . 39 B1
Harwood Ave
Bromley BR1 . . . . 187 B1
Mitcham CR4 . . . . 202 C6
Harwood Cl
London N12 . . . . 30 C4
Wembley HA0 . . . . 65 D4
Harwood Ct
Putney SW15 . . . . 134 C1
Shoreditch N1 . . . . . . 235 D5
Harwood Dr UB10 . . . . . 82 B6
Harwood Point SE16 119 B4
Harwood Rd
SW6 . . . . 135 D5 265 C3
Harwoods Yd N21 . . . . . 16 C4
Harwood Terr
SW6 . . . . . . 135 D4 265 C2
Hascombe Ho 11
SW15 . . . . 156 B3
Hascombe Terr 2
SE5 . . . . 139 B3
Haselbury Rd N9 . . . . . 17 C1
Haseley End SE23 . . . 162 C4
Haselrigge Rd SW4 . 137 D1
Haseltine Prim Sch
SE26 . . . . 185 B6
Haseltine Rd SE26 . . . 185 B6
Haselwood Dr EN2 . . . . . 4 D1
Haskard Rd RM9 . . . . . . 80 D4
Hasker St
SW3 . . . . 114 C2 257 B4
Haslam Ave SM3 . . . . . 201 A1
Haslam Cl Islington N1 72 C1
Uxbridge UB10 . . . . 61 A6
Haslam Ct N11 . . . . 31 B6
Haslam Ho 12 N1 . . . . . 73 A1
Haslam St SE15 . . . . . 139 D4
Haslemere Ave
Barnet EN4 . . . . 14 D3
Cranford TW5 . . . . . . 128 C3
Ealing W13 . . . . 109 A3
Hendon NW4 . . . . 46 D3
Mitcham CR4, SW19 . . 180 B1
Wandsworth SW18 . . 157 D2
Haslemere Bsns Ctr
EN1 . . . . 18 B6
Haslemere Cl
Hampton TW12 . . . . . . 173 B5
Wallington SM6 . . . . . 220 A3
Haslemere Ct 5 N16 . . 51 C1
Haslemere Gdns N3 . . 47 B5
Haslemere & Heathrow
Est The TW4 . . . . 128 B3
Haslemere Ind Est
Feltham TW14 . . . . . . 150 A6
Wandsworth SW18 . . 157 D2
Haslemere Prim Sch
CR4 . . . . 180 B1
Haslemere Rd
Bexleyheath DA7 . . . . 147 C3
Hornsey N8 . . . . 50 A2
Ilford IG3 . . . . 79 D6
Southgate N21 . . . . 16 D3
Thornton Heath CR7 . 204 D4
Hasler Cl SE28 . . . . . . 124 C6
Hasler Ct E12 . . . . 78 A4
Haslett Rd TW17 . . . . . 171 C1
Hasluck Gdns EN5 . . . . 14 A5
Hasmonean High Sch
(Boys) NW4 . . . . 28 D1
Hasmonean High Sch
(Girls) NW7 . . . . 28 A2
Hasmonean Prim Sch 1
NW4 . . . . 46 D4
Hassard St E2 . . . . 95 D5
Hassendean Rd SE3 . . 143 B5
Hassett Rd E9 . . . . 75 A2
Hassocks Cl SE23,
SE26 . . . . 162 B1
Hassocks Rd SW16 . . 181 D2
Hassock Wood BR2 . . 225 D4
Hassop Rd NW2 . . . . 68 D4
Hassop Wlk SE9 . . . . . 188 A6
Hasted Rd SE7 . . . . . . 121 D1
Hasting Ct TW11 . . . . . 174 B5
Hastings Ave IG6 . . . . . 57 A5
Hastings Cl
New Barnet EN5 . . . . 2 A1
17 Peckham SE15 . . . 140 A5
Wembley HA0 . . . . 65 C4
Hastings Dr KT6 . . . . . 197 C3
Hastings Ho
Ealing W13 . . . . 109 B6
Enfield EN3 . . . . 6 C3
18 Shepherd's Bush
W12 . . . . 112 B6
Tottenham N17 . . . . 34 A2
6 Woolwich SE18 . . . . 122 B2
Hastings Hos WC1 . . . 233 A1
Hastings Pl 1 CR0 . . 205 D1
Hastings Rd
Croydon CR0 . . . . 205 D1
Ealing W13 . . . . 109 B6
Keston Mark BR2 . . . . 226 A6
Tottenham N17 . . . . 51 B6
Wood Green N11 . . . . . . 31 D5
Hastings St
St Pancras
WC1 . . . . 94 A4 233 A1
Woolwich SE18 . . . . . 123 A3
Hastingwood Ct
1 Newham E6 . . . . . . 100 B5
Walthamstow E17 . . . . . 53 D4
Hastingwood Trad Est
N18 . . . . 35 A4
Hastoe Cl UB4 . . . . 85 A3
Hasty Cl CR4 . . . . 181 A2
Hatcham Mews Bsns Ctr
SE14 . . . . 140 D4
Hatcham Park Mews
SE14 . . . . 140 D4
Hatcham Park Rd
SE14 . . . . 140 D4
Hatcham Rd SE15 . . . . 140 C6
Hatchard Rd N19 . . . . . 72 A6
Hatchcroft NW4 . . . . . . 46 B6
HATCH END 23 A3
Hatch End High Sch
HA3 . . . . 23 D2
Hatch End Sta HA5 . . . . 23 C3
Hatchers Mews SE1 . 253 B1
Hatchett Rd TW14 . . . . 149 A3
Hatchfield Ho 8 N15 . 51 C3
Hatch Gr RM6 . . . . 59 A5
Hatch Ho
9 Muswell Hill N10 . . . . 31 A3
14 Richmond TW10 . . . 153 C1
Hatch La E4 . . . . 20 C1
Hatch Pl KT2 . . . . 176 B5
Hatch Rd SW16 . . . . . . 182 A1
Hatch The EN3 . . . . 6 D4
Hatchwoods IG8 . . . . . . 36 D6
Hatcliffe Almshouses 8
SE10 . . . . 120 C1
Hatcliffe Cl SE3 . . . . . 142 D2
Hatcliffe St SE10 . . . . 120 D1
Hatfield Cl
Deptford SE14 . . . . . . 140 D5
Ilford IG6 . . . . 56 D6
Mitcham CR4 . . . . 202 B5
Hatfield Ct
Greenwich SE3 . . . . . 143 A5
8 Northolt UB5 . . . . 84 C4
Hatfield Ho
16 Kingston u T
KT6 . . . . 198 A4
Leytonstone E11 . . . . . . 54 D2
St Luke's EC1 . . . . 242 A5
Hatfield Mead SM4 . . 201 C4
Hatfield Mews RM9 . . . 81 A1
Hatfield Prim Sch
SM4 . . . . 201 A3
Hatfield Rd
Acton W4 . . . . 111 B4
Dagenham RM9 . . . . 81 A1
10 Ealing W13, W7 . . . 109 A5
Stratford E15 . . . . 76 C3
Hatfields SE1 116 C5 251 B4
Hathaway Cl
Bromley BR2 . . . . 210 B1
Ruislip HA4 . . . . 61 D4
Stanmore HA7 . . . . 25 A5
Hathaway Cres E12 . . . 78 C2
Hathaway Gdns
Ealing W13 . . . . 87 A2
Ilford RM6 . . . . 58 D4
Hathaway Ho 3 N1 . . . 95 C4
Hathaway Prim Sch
W13 . . . . 86 D2
Hathaway Rd CR0 . . . 204 D2
Hatherleigh Cl
Barnet EN4 . . . . 1 D4
Hatherleigh Cl *continued*
Chessington KT9 . . . . 213 D3
Edgware NW7 . . . . 28 D3
Morden SM4 . . . . 201 C5
Hatherleigh Ho SM4 . 201 C5
Hatherleigh Rd HA4 . . 62 A6
Hatherley Cres
DA14 . . . . 168 A2
Hatherley Ct 6 W2 . . . 91 D1
Hatherley Gdns
London N8 . . . . 50 A3
Newham E6 . . . . 99 D4
Hatherley Gr W2 . . . . . 91 D1
Hatherley Ho 2 E17 . . 53 C5
Hatherley Mews E17 . . 53 C5
Hatherley Rd
Richmond TW9 . . . . . . 132 B4
Sidcup DA14 . . . . 168 A1
Walthamstow E17 . . . . . 53 C5
Hatherley St SW1 . . . . 259 B3
Hathern Gdns SE9 . . . 188 C6
Hatherop Rd TW12 . . . 173 B3
Hathersage Ct N1 . . . . . 73 B3
Hathersley Ho 3
SW2 . . . . 160 C4
Hathorne Cl 3 SE15 . 140 B3
Hathway Ho 3 SE15 . 140 C3
Hathway St 4 SE15 . . 140 C3
Hatley Ave IG6 . . . . 57 A5
Hatley Cl N11 . . . . 30 D5
Hatley Rd N4, N7 . . . . . . 72 B6
Hat & Mitre Ct EC1 . . . 241 D5
Hatstone Ct 2 NW3 . . . 70 A3
Hatteraick St 6
SE16 . . . . 118 C4
Hattersfield Cl DA17 . 125 B2
HATTON 127 D1
Hatton Cl SE18 . . . . . . 145 B5
Hatton Cross Rdbt
TW6 . . . . 127 D2
Hatton Cross Sta
TW6 . . . . 127 D1
Hatton Ct BR7 . . . . 188 B3
Hatton Gdn
EC1 . . . . 94 C2 241 B4
Hatton Gdns CR4 . . . . 202 D4
Hatton Gn TW14 . . . . . 128 A1
Hatton Ho 17 E1 . . . . . 118 A6
Hatton Pl EC1 . . . . 241 B4
Hatton Rd
Hatton TW14, TW6 . . . 149 C6
Thornton Heath CR0 . 204 C1
Hatton Row NW8 . . . . 236 D5
Hatton Sch IG8 . . . . 55 D6
Hatton St NW8 . . . . . . 236 D5
Hatton Wall
EC1 . . . . 94 C2 241 B4
Haughmond 4 N12 . . . 29 D6
Haunch of Venison Yd
W1 . . . . 238 C1
Hauteville Court Gdns 2
W6 . . . . 111 D3
Havana Rd SW18,
SW19 . . . . 157 C2
Havannah St E14 . . . . 119 C4
Havant Rd E17 . . . . 54 A6
Havelock Cl 13 W12 . 112 B6
Havelock Ct
8 Peckham SE15 . . . . 140 B5
Southall UB2 . . . . 107 B3
Havelock Hall 8
CR0 . . . . 205 D1
Havelock Ho
4 Croydon CR0 . . . . . 205 D1
Forest Hill SE23 . . . . . 162 C3
Havelock Pl HA1 . . . . . . 42 C3
Havelock Prim Sch
UB2 . . . . 107 B3
Havelock Rd
Belvedere DA17 . . . . . 125 B2
Bromley BR2 . . . . 209 C5
Croydon CR0 . . . . 221 D6
Harrow HA3 . . . . 42 C6
Southall UB2 . . . . 107 C3
Tottenham N17 . . . . 34 A1
Wimbledon SW19 . . . . 180 A5
Havelock St Ilford IG1 . 78 D6
Islington N1 . . . 94 A6 233 B6
Havelock Terr
SW8 . . . . 137 B5 268 D3
Havelock Wlk SE23 . . 162 C2
Haven Cl
Chislehurst SE9 . . . . . 166 B1
Hayes UB4 . . . . 83 C3
Hinchley Wood KT10 . 212 C6
Sidcup DA14 . . . . 190 C4
Haven Cl *continued*
Wimbledon SW19 . . . 156 D1
Haven Ct
Beckenham BR3 . . . . . 186 A1
Hinchley Wood KT10 . 212 C6
Thornton Heath CR7 . 204 C6
Haven Gn W5 . . . . 87 D1
Haven Green Ct W5 . . . 87 D1
Havenhurst Rise EN2 . . . 4 C3
Haven La W5 . . . . 88 A1
Haven Lo
15 Enfield EN1 . . . . 17 C6
Temple Fortune NW11 . . 47 B4
7 Woolwich SE18 . . . . 122 D2
Haven Pl Ealing W5 . . . 109 D6
Hinchley Wood KT10 . 212 C6
Havenpool NW8 . . . . 91 D6
Haven Rd TW15 . . . . . . 148 D1
Haven St 18 NW1 . . . . . 71 B1
Havenswood Ct 14
KT2 . . . . 176 D4
Haven The
Ashford TW16 . . . . . . 172 A3
East Barnet N14 . . . . . . 15 B5
Richmond TW9 . . . . . . 132 C2
Havenwood HA9 . . . . . . 66 D5
Havercourt 3 NW3 . . . 70 C2
Haverfield Gdns
TW9 . . . . 132 C5
Haverfield Rd E3 . . . . . 97 A4
Haverford Way HA8 . . . 26 B2
Havergal Villas N15 . . . 50 D6
Haverhill Rd
Chingford E4 . . . . 20 A3
Streatham SW12 . . . . 159 C3
Havering 8 NW1 . . . . . . 71 B1
Havering Gdns RM6 . . . 58 D4
Havering Ho N4 . . . . . . 51 A2
Havering St E1 . . . . 96 D1
Havering Way IG11 . . 102 B4
Haverley 15 SW20 . . . 178 D3
Haversham Cl TW1 . . 153 D5
Haversham Ct UB6 . . . . 64 D2
Haversham Lo NW2 . . . 68 D3
Haversham Pl N6 . . . . . 70 D6
Haverstock Ct 2
BR5 . . . . 190 B1
Haverstock Hill NW3 . . 70 D2
Haverstock Rd NW5 . . . 71 A3
Haverstock Sch 22
NW1 . . . . 71 A2
Haverstock St
N1 . . . . 94 D5 234 D3
Haverthwaite Rd
BR6 . . . . 227 B5
Havilland Ct HA8 . . . . . 26 B6
Havil St SE5 . . . . 139 C4
Havisham Ho 25
SE16 . . . . 118 A4
Havisham Pl SW16 . . 182 D3
Hawarden Gr SE24 . . . 161 A4
Hawarden Hill NW2 . . . 68 A5
Hawarden Rd E17 . . . . . 52 D5
Hawberry Lo N7 . . . . . . 72 A2
Hawbridge Rd E11 . . . . 54 B1
Hawes Down Inf Sch
BR4 . . . . 208 B1
Hawes Down Jun Sch
BR4 . . . . 208 B1
Hawes La BR4 . . . . 224 C6
Hawes Rd
Bromley BR1 . . . . 187 B2
Edmonton N18 . . . . 34 B4
Hawes St N1 . . . . 72 D1
Haweswater Ho
TW1 . . . . 152 D6
Hawfinch 29 NW9 . . . . . 27 D2
Hawgood St E3 . . . . 97 C2
Hawkdene E4 . . . . 20 A5
Hawke Ct UB4 . . . . 84 C3
Hawkedale Inf Sch
TW16 . . . . 193 D6
Hawke Ho 20 E1 . . . . . . 96 D3
Hawke Park Rd N22 . . . 50 D6
Hawke Pl 29 SE16 . . . 118 D4
Hawker 28 NW9 . . . . . . 27 D2
Hawker Ct 14 KT2 . . . 176 C3
Hawker Ctr The KT2 . 175 D5
Hawke Rd SE19 . . . . . 183 C4
Hawker Pl E4 . . . . 36 A1
Hawker Rd CR0 . . . . . 220 C2
Hawkesbury Rd
SW15 . . . . 156 B6
Hawkesdown House Sch
W2 . . . . 113 C5 245 B3

Hawkesfield Rd SE23 163 B2
Hawkesley Cl TW1 175 A6
Hawkes Rd
Feltham TW14 150 A4
Mitcham CR4 180 D2
Hawkesworth Ho 5 SW4 159 C5
Hawke Twr 4 SE14 141 A6
Hawkewood Rd TW16 194 A6
Hawkfield Ct TW7 130 C3
Hawk Ho 7 SW11 136 C2
Hawkhurst Gdns KT9 214 A4
Hawkhurst Rd SW16 181 D2
Hawkhurst Way
New Malden KT3 199 B4
West Wickham BR4 223 D6
Hawkinge N17 33 B1
Hawkins Cl
Burnt Oak NW7 27 B5
Harrow HA1 42 B2
Hawkins Ho
3 Deptford SE8 141 C6
10 Richmond TW10 153 C1
Hawkins Rd
Teddington TW11 175 B4
Willesden NW10 67 C1
Hawkins Way SE6 185 C5
Hawkley Gdns SE27 160 D2
Hawkridge 19 NW5 71 A2
Hawkridge Cl RM6 58 C3
Hawksbrook La BR3 208 A3
Hawkshaw Cl 28 SW2 160 A4
Hawkshead NW1 232 A2
Hawkshead Cl BR1 186 C3
Hawkshead Rd
Acton W4 111 C4
Willesden NW10 67 D1
Hawkslade Rd SE15 162 D6
Hawksley Rd N16 73 C5
Hawks Mews 10 SE10 142 A5
Hawksmoor Cl
2 Newham E6 100 A1
Plumstead Comm SE18 123 C1
Hawksmoor Mews E1 118 B6
Hawksmoor Pl 2 E2 96 A3
Hawksmoor Prim Sch SE28 124 B6
Hawksmoor St 5 W6 134 D6
Hawksmouth E4 20 A4
Hawks Rd KT1 176 B1
Hawkstone Rd SE16 118 C2
Hawkwell Ct E4 20 A1
Hawkwell Ho RM8 81 C6
Hawkwell Wlk N1 235 B6
Hawkwood Cres E4 19 D5
Hawkwood La BR7 189 A2
Hawkwood Mount 1 E5 52 B1
Hawlands Dr HA5 41 A2
Hawley Cl TW12 173 B4
Hawley Cres NW1 71 B1
Hawley Inf Sch 23 NW1 71 B1
Hawley Mews 4 NW1 71 B1
Hawley Rd
3 Camden Town NW1 71 B1
London N18 34 D5
Hawley St NW1 71 B1
Hawley Way TW15 170 D5
Haworth Ho 7 SW2 160 C5
Hawstead Rd SE6 163 D5
Hawsted IG9 21 B4
Hawthorn Ave
Bowes Pk N13 32 A5
South Norwood CR7 182 D2
Hawthorn Cl
Cranford TW5 128 B5
Hampton TW12 173 C5
Petts Wood BR5 211 B3
Hawthorn Cres SW17 181 A5
Hawthorn Ct
Littleton TW15 171 A3
2 Pinner HA5 22 C1
Putney SW15 134 B2
Redbridge IG5 56 B6
Hawthorn Ct *continued*
Richmond TW9 132 D4
Sutton SM1 217 C4
8 West Norwood SW16 182 C5
Hawthorn Ctr HA1 43 A4
Hawthornden Cl N12 30 C4
Hawthorndene Cl BR2 225 A6
Hawthorndene Rd BR2 225 A6
Hawthorn Dr
Coney Hall BR4 224 C4
Harrow HA2 41 C3
Hawthorne Ave
Harrow HA3 43 A3
Mitcham CR4 180 B1
Old Ford E3 97 B6
Ruislip HA4 40 B2
Wallington SM5 219 A1
Hawthorne Cl
Bickley BR1 210 B6
Kingsland N1 73 C2
Sutton SM1 218 A6
Hawthorne Cres UB7 104 B4
Hawthorne Ct
Chingford E4 35 D4
Ealing W5 110 A5
Pinner HA6 22 A1
Hawthorne Gr NW9 45 A2
Hawthorne Ho SW1 259 B1
Hawthorne Mews UB6 86 A1
Hawthorne Rd
Bickley BR1 210 B6
Edmonton N18 33 D5
Walthamstow E17 53 C6
Hawthorne Way N9 17 D2
Hawthorn Farm Ave UB5 85 A6
Hawthorn Gdns W5 109 D3
Hawthorn Gr
Edgware EN5 11 D5
Enfield EN2 5 B5
Penge SE20 184 B2
Hawthorn Hatch TW8 131 B5
Hawthorn Ho SE14 141 B4
Hawthorn Mews NW7 29 A2
Hawthorn Pl UB3 105 D6
Hawthorn Rd
Bexleyheath DA6 147 B1
Brentford TW8 131 B5
Carshalton SM1 218 C2
Feltham TW14 150 A3
Hornsey N8 50 A6
Wallington SM5, SM6 219 B1
Willesden NW10 68 A1
Woodford IG9 37 D6
Hawthorns IG8 21 A1
Hawthorns The
2 Cheam SM2 217 C2
Edgware NW7 27 B4
Stoneleigh KT17 216 A1
Hawthorn Terr DA15 167 D6
Hawthorn Way TW17 193 B5
Hawthorn Wlk W10 91 A3
Hawtrey Ave UB5 84 D5
Hawtrey Dr HA4 40 A2
Hawtrey Rd NW3 70 C1
Haxted Rd BR1 187 B2
Haybridge Ho 1 E5 74 C6
Hay Cl E15 76 D1
Haycroft Gdns NW10 90 B6
Haycroft Mans NW10 90 A6
Haycroft Rd
London SW2 160 A6
Surbiton KT6 214 A6
Hay Currie St E14 97 D1
Hayday Rd E16 99 A2
Hayden Piper Ho SW3 267 C6
Hayden's Pl W11 91 B1
Haydock Ave UB5 63 C2
Haydock Gn UB5 63 C2
Haydock Green Flats 2 UB5 63 C2
Haydock Lo 2 SM6 219 D5
Haydon Cl Enfield EN1 17 C6
Kingsbury NW9 45 A5
Haydon Ct NW9 45 A5
Haydon Dr HA5 40 A5
Haydon Ho W7 108 D5
Haydon Park Rd SW19 179 D5
Haydon Rd RM8 80 C6
Haydon Sch HA5 39 D6
Haydon's Rd SW19 180 A4
Haydons Road Sta SW19 180 A5
Haydon St E1, EC3 117 D6 253 C6
Haydon Way SW11 136 B1
Haydon Wlk E1 243 D1
HAYES BR2 209 A2
UB3 83 C1
Hayes Bridge Ret Pk UB4 106 D6
Hayes Chase BR4 208 C3
Hayes Cl BR2 225 A6
Hayes Cres
Cheam SM3 216 D4
Temple Fortune NW11 47 B4
Hayes Ct
23 Camberwell SE5 139 A5
Streatham SW12 160 A3
Wimbledon SW19 179 A4
HAYES END 83 B3
Hayes End Cl UB4 83 B2
Hayes End Dr UB4 83 B3
Hayesend Ho SW17 180 A6
Hayes End Rd UB4 83 B3
Hayesford Park Dr BR2 208 D4
Hayes Gdn BR2 209 A1
Hayes Gr SE15, SE22 139 D1
Hayes & Harlington Sta UB3 105 D3
Hayes Hill BR2 208 C1
Hayes Hill Rd BR2 208 D1
Hayes La
Beckenham BR2, BR3 208 B5
Hayes BR2 209 A4
Hayes Mead Rd BR2 208 C1
Hayes Park Sch UB4 83 D3
Hayes Pl NW1 237 B5
Hayes Prim Sch BR2 209 B1
Hayes Rd
Bromley BR2 209 A5
Southall UB2 106 B2
Hayes Sch BR2 225 B6
Hayes St BR2 209 B1
Hayes Sta BR2 208 D1
Hayes Stadium Sp Ctr UB3 83 B1
HAYES TOWN 106 B5
Hayes Way BR3 208 B5
Hayes Wood Ave BR2 209 B1
Hayfield Pas E1 96 C3
Hayfield Yd 43 E1 96 C3
Hayford Ct NW2 68 D5
Haygarth Pl 2 SW19 178 D5
Haygreen Cl KT2 176 D4
Hay Hill W1 115 B6 248 D5
Hayhurst N1 234 D6
Hay La NW9 45 B5
Hayland Cl NW9 45 B5
Hay Lane Sch NW9 45 A5
Hayles Bldgs SE11 261 D4
Hayles St SE11 116 D2 261 C4
Haylett Gdns KT1 197 D5
Hayley Ho DA17 147 C6
Hayling Ave TW13 150 A1
Hayling Cl 20 N16 73 C3
Hayling Ct SM3 216 C4
Haymaker Cl UB10 60 B1
Hayman Cres UB4 83 B5
Haymans Point SE11 260 C2
Haymarket SW1 115 D6 249 C5
Haymeads Dr KT10 212 A2
Haymer Gdns KT4 216 A5
Haymerle Ho 6 SE15 140 A5
Haymerle Rd SE15 140 A6
Haymerle Sch 15 SE15 140 A6
Haymill Cl UB6 86 D4
Haymills Ct W5 88 B3
Hayne Ho W11 244 A4
Hayne Rd BR3 185 B2
Haynes Cl
Friern Barnet N11 15 A1
Lewisham SE3 142 C2
Tottenham N17 34 B3
Haynes Dr N9 18 B1
Haynes Ho 3 E9 74 D2
Haynes La SE19 183 C4
Haynes Rd HA0 66 A1
Hayne St EC1 94 D2 241 D4
Haynt Wlk SW20 201 A6
Hay's Galleria★ SE1 253 A4
Hay's La SE1 253 A4
Haysleigh Gdns SE20 184 A1
Haysleigh Ho SE20 184 B1
Hay's Mews W1 115 B5 248 C4
Hay St E2 96 A6
Haystall Cl UB4 83 C5
Hayter Ct E11 77 B6
Hayter Ho W12 112 A6
Hayter Rd SW2 160 B6
Haythorn Ho SW11 136 B4 266 D1
Hayton Cl 11 E8 73 D2
Hayward Cl SW19 179 D2
Hayward Ct
14 London SW4 138 A3
Mitcham CR4 180 B1
Hayward Gallery★ SE1 116 B5 250 D4
Hayward Gdns SW15 156 C5
Hayward Ho
Islington N1 234 A4
Lower Clapton E5 74 B5
Hayward Rd
London N20 14 A2
Thames Ditton KT7 196 D1
Haywards Cl RM6 58 C4
Haywards Pl EC1 241 C6
Hayward's Pl EC1 241 C6
Haywood Cl HA5 22 D1
Haywood Ct N11 31 D4
Haywood Lo 23 N7 71 D3
Haywood Rd BR2 209 D5
Haywood Rise BR6 227 C3
Hazel Ave UB7 104 C3
Hazelbank KT5 199 A1
Hazel Bank SE25 183 C1
Hazelbank Rd SE6 164 C2
Hazelbourne Rd SW12 159 B5
Hazelbury Cl SW19 179 C1
Hazelbury Gn N9 17 C1
Hazelbury Inf Sch N9 17 C1
Hazelbury Jun Sch N9 17 C1
Hazelbury La N9 17 C1
Hazel Cl
Brentford TW8 131 B5
Croydon CR0 206 D1
Edmonton N13 17 B1
Hendon NW9 27 D1
Mitcham CR4 203 D5
Peckham SE15 140 A3
Twickenham TW2 152 A4
Upper Holloway N19 71 C6
Hazelcroft HA5 23 D4
Hazelcroft Cl UB10 60 B1
Hazel Ct Ealing W5 110 A6
8 Rotherhithe SE16 119 A5
9 West Norwood SW16 182 C5
Hazeldean Rd NW10 67 B1
Hazeldene Dr HA5 40 C6
Hazeldene Gdns UB10 83 A6
Hazeldene Rd
Bexley DA16 146 C3
Ilford IG3 80 B6
Hazeldon Rd SE4 163 A6
Hazel Gdns HA8 26 D6
Hazel Gr
Dagenham RM6 59 A6
Enfield EN1 18 A5
Feltham TW14 150 A3
Forest Hill SE26 184 D6
Orpington BR6 226 D6
Wembley HA0 88 A6
Hazelgreen Cl N21 16 D3
Hazel Ho London SE4 141 B2
12 Maitland Pk NW3 70 D2
Hazelhurst BR3 186 B2
Hazelhurst Ct SE6 186 A5
Hazelhurst Rd SW17 180 B6
Hazellville Rd N19 49 D1
Hazel Mead EN5 12 B6
Hazelmere Cl
Feltham TW14 149 C5
Hazelmere Cl *continued*
Northolt UB5 85 B5
Hazelmere Ct 10 SW2 160 B3
Hazelmere Dr UB5 85 B5
Hazelmere Rd
Kilburn NW6 91 B6
Northolt UB5 85 B5
Petts Wood BR5 211 B5
Hazelmere Way BR2 209 A3
Hazelmere Wlk UB5 85 B5
Hazel Rd
Kensal Green NW10 90 C4
Stratford E15 76 C3
Hazeltree La UB5 85 A4
Hazel Way
Bermondsey SE1 263 C4
Walthamstow E4 35 B4
Hazel Wlk BR2 210 C3
Hazelwood IG10 21 D6
Hazelwood Ave SM4 201 D5
Hazelwood Cl
Clapton Pk E5 75 A5
Ealing W5 110 A4
Harrow HA2 41 D5
Hazelwood Cres N13 32 C6
Hazelwood Ct
1 Edmonton N13 32 C6
Surbiton KT6 198 A3
1 Willesden NW10 67 C5
Hazelwood Dr HA5 22 B1
Hazelwood Ho
Beckenham BR2 208 C6
Chingford E4 20 B4
11 Deptford SE8 119 A2
Edmonton N13 32 D6
2 Sutton SM1 218 A4
Hazelwood Jun & Inf Schs N13 32 C6
Hazelwood La N13 32 C6
Hazelwood Lo BR4 208 A2
Hazelwood Mans SW6 264 C2
Hazelwood Rd
Enfield EN1 17 D5
Walthamstow E17 53 A4
Hazlebury Rd SW6 135 D3
Hazledean Rd CR0 221 B6
Hazledene Rd W4 133 A6
Hazlemere 3 DA14 190 A6
Hazlemere Gdns KT4 200 A1
Hazlewell Rd SW15 156 C6
Hazlewood Cres W10 91 A3
Hazlewood Twr W10 91 B3
Hazlitt Cl TW13 173 A6
Hazlitt Ct 4 SE28 124 C5
Hazlitt Mews W14 254 A5
Hazlitt Rd W14 113 A3 254 A5
Heacham Ave UB10 61 A5
Headbourne Ho SE1 262 D6
Headcorn 10 NW5 71 A2
Headcorn Pl CR7 204 B5
Headcorn Rd
Plaistow BR1 187 A5
Thornton Heath CR7 204 B5
Tottenham N17 33 D3
Headfort Pl SW1 115 A4 248 B1
Headingley Dr BR3 185 C4
Headington Rd SW18 158 A2
Headlam Rd SW4 159 D4
Headlam St E1 96 B3
Headley App IG2 56 D4
Headley Ave CR0, SM6 220 B3
Headley Cl KT19 214 C2
Headley Ct SE26 184 C5
Headley Dr Ilford IG2 56 D3
New Addington CR0 224 A1
Headley Ho 5 BR5 190 B1
Heads Mews W11 91 C1
Head St E1 96 D1
Headstart Montessori Sch SW17 180 A6
HEADSTONE 41 D5
Headstone Dr HA1, HA3 42 C6
Headstone Gdns HA2 42 A5
Headstone La
Harrow HA2, HA3 23 D2

Headstone La *continued*
Headstone HA2 41 D5
Headstone Lane Sta HA3 23 D2
Headstone Manor★ HA2 42 A6
Headstone Rd HA1 42 C3
Headway Cl TW10 175 C6
Heald St SE8, SE14 141 C4
Healey Ho RM6 59 A5
Healey St NW1 71 B2
Healy Ct EN5 12 D5
Healy Dr 1 BR6 227 D4
Healy Ho
12 Kennington SW9 138 C5
2 Tower Hamlets E3 97 C3
Heanor Ct 4 E5 74 D4
Hearne Rd W4 132 C6
Hearn Rise UB5 84 D6
Hearn's Bldgs SE17 262 D3
Hearnshaw St 1 E14 97 A1
Hearn St EC2 95 C3 243 B5
Hearnville Rd SW12 159 A3
Heart Hospl The W1 93 A2 238 B3
Heart Raido W11 112 D6
Heart The KT12 193 D1
Heatham Pk TW2 152 D4
Heath Ave DA7 146 D6
Heathbourne Rd WD23 8 D3
Heathbrook Prim Sch 11 SW4 137 C3
Heath Brow NW3 70 A5
Heath Bsns Ctr The TW3 130 A1
Heath Cl
Croydon CR2 220 D2
Ealing W5 88 B3
Golders Green NW11 47 D2
Harlington UB3 127 B5
Heathcote Gr E4 20 A2
Heathcote Point 25 E9 74 D2
Heathcote Rd TW1 153 B6
Heathcote Sch E4 20 C2
Heathcote St WC1 94 B4 233 C1
Heathcroft Ealing W5 88 B3
Golders Green NW11 47 D1
Heathcroft Ave TW16 171 D3
Heathcroft Gdns E4 36 B2
Heath Ct
Carshalton SM5 218 B6
Eltham SE9 167 A3
2 Hampstead NW3 70 A2
Leytonstone E11 54 D3
Stoke Newington N16 51 B1
Uxbridge UB8 60 A1
Heathdale Ave TW4 129 A2
Heathdene N14 15 C4
Heathdene Dr DA17 125 D2
Heathdene Rd
South Norwood SW16 182 B3
Wallington SM5, SM6 219 B1
Heath Dr
West Barnes SW20 200 C5
West Hampstead NW3 69 D4
Heathedge SE23, SE26 162 B2
Heath End Ct WD23 8 C2
Heatherbank
Chislehurst BR7 188 C1
Eltham SE9 144 B3
Heather Cl
Clapham SW8 137 B2
Hampton TW12 173 B2
Hillingdon UB8 82 B2
Hither Green SE13 164 B4
Isleworth TW7 152 B6
Newham E6 100 C1
Heather Ct
South Lambeth SW4 270 B1
6 West Norwood SW16 182 C6
Heatherdale Cl KT2 176 D3
Heatherdene Cl
London N12 30 A2
Mitcham CR4 202 C5
Heatherdene Ct CR4 202 B5
Heatherdene Mans 2 TW1 153 D5
Heather Dr EN2 4 D3
Heatherfold Way HA5, HA6 39 D6
Heather Gdns
Belmont SM2 217 C2
Hendon NW11 47 A3
Heather Ho 11 E14 98 A1
Heather La UB7 82 A1
Heatherlands TW16 172 A4
Heatherlea Gr KT4 200 B1
Heatherley Ct N16 74 A5
Heatherley Dr IG5 56 B6
Heatherley Sch of Fine Art SW10 266 B3
Heather Lo N16 51 C1
Heather Park Dr HA0 66 C1
Heather Park Par HA0 66 B1
Heather Rd
Dollis Hill NW2 67 D6
Lewisham SE12 165 A3
Walthamstow E4 35 B4
Heatherset Cl KT10 212 A3
Heatherset Gdns SW16 182 B3
Heatherside Rd
Sidcup DA14 168 C1
West Ewell KT19 215 B1
Heathers The TW19 148 B4
Heather Way HA7 24 D4
Heather Wlk
Edgware HA8 26 D5
Twickenham TW4 151 C4
West Kilburn W10 91 A3
Heatherwood Cl E12 77 C6
Heatherwood Dr UB4 83 B5
Heathfield
Chingford E4 20 A1
Chislehurst BR7 189 A4
Heathfield Ave SW18 158 B4
Heathfield Cl
Keston BR2 225 C3
Newham E16 99 D2
Heathfield Ct
Ashford TW15 148 A1
3 Bow E3 97 C5
5 Chiswick W4 111 B1
Penge SE20 184 C3
Sidcup DA14 190 B5
8 Sutton SM2 218 A2
Wandsworth SW18 158 B4
Heathfield Dr CR4 180 C2
Heathfielde N2 48 A4
Heathfield Gdns
Acton Green W4 111 A1
Blackheath SE3 142 C3
Croydon CR0 221 B4
Hendon NW11 46 D3
Wandsworth SW18 158 B5
Heathfield Ho SE3 142 C3
Heathfield House Sch 15 W4 111 A1
Heathfield Inf Sch TW2 151 C3
Heathfield Jun Sch TW2 151 C3
Heathfield La BR7 189 A4
Heathfield N TW1, TW2 152 D4
Heathfield Park Dr RM6 58 B4
Heathfield Pk NW2 68 C2
Heathfield Rd
Bexleyheath DA6 147 B1
Bromley BR1 186 D3
Croydon CR0 221 B4
Keston BR2 225 D3
South Acton W3 110 D4
Wandsworth SW18 158 B5
Heathfield Rise HA4 39 A2
Heathfield S TW1, TW2 152 D4
Heathfield Sch HA5 40 D2
Heathfield Sq SW18 158 B4
Heathfield Terr
Chiswick W4 111 B1
Plumstead Comm SE18 145 D6
Heathfield Vale CR2 223 A1
Heathgate NW11 47 D3
Heathgate Pl NW3 70 D4
Heath Gdns TW1 152 D2
Heath Gr
Ashford TW16 171 D3
Penge SE20 184 C3
Heath Ho
Thornton Heath CR7 204 C4
Uxbridge UB10 60 D4
Heath House Prep Sch 1 SE8 142 D3
Heath Hurst Rd NW3 70 C4
Heath La SE3 142 B3
Heathland Rd N16 51 C1
Heathland Sch The TW4 151 B5
Heathlands Cl
Sunbury TW16 172 A1
Twickenham TW1 152 D3
Heathlands Ct
Hounslow TW4 151 A6
Mitcham CR4 203 A6
Heathlands Way TW4 151 A6
Heathlee Rd SE3 142 D1
Heathley End BR7 189 A4
Heath Lo WD23 8 B3
Heath Mans
5 Hampstead NW3 70 A4
Putney SW15 156 D5
Heathman's Rd SW6 135 B4 264 D1
Heath Mead SW19 156 D1
Heathmere Prim Sch SW15 156 A3
Heath Park Dr BR1 210 A6
Heath Park Gdns NW3 69 D5
Heath Park Ind Est RM8 59 A1
Heathpool Ct 8 E1 96 B3
Heath Rd
Clapham SW8 137 B3
Dagenham RM6 59 A2
Harrow HA1 42 A2
Hillingdon UB10 83 A3
Isleworth TW3, TW7 130 A1
South Norwood CR7 205 A6
Twickenham TW1 152 D3
Heath Rise
Hayes BR2 209 A3
Putney SW15 156 D5
Heathrow Airport London TW6 126 D3
Heathrow Bvd UB7 126 B5
Heathrow Causeway Est TW4 128 B2
Heathrow International Trad Est TW4 128 B2
Heathrow Prim Sch UB7 126 B6
Heathrow Terminal 4 Sta TW6 149 A5
Heathrow Terminals 1, 2, 3 Sta TW6 126 D2
Heath Royal SW15 156 D5
Heath's Cl EN1 5 C3
Heathshott 8 TW10 154 A5
Heathside
Hampstead NW3 70 B4
Hinchley Wood KT10 212 C5
Twickenham TW4 151 B4
Heath Side BR5 211 A2
Heathside Ave DA7 147 A3
Heathside Cl
Hinchley Wood KT10 212 C5
Ilford IG2 57 B4
Heathside Prep Sch 32 NW3 70 A4
Heath St NW3 70 A5
Heathstan Rd W12 90 A1
Heath Terr RM6 58 D2
Heath The W7 108 C5
Heath View
Gospel Oak NW5 71 A4
London N2 48 A5
Heath View Cl N2 48 A5
Heathview Ct SW19 156 D2
Heath View Dr SE2 146 D6
Heathview Gdns SW15 156 C4
Heathview Rd CR7 204 C5
Heath Villas
Hampstead NW3 70 B5
Plumstead Comm SE18 123 D1
Heathville Rd N4, N19 50 A2
Heathwall St SW11 136 D2
Heathway
Croydon CR0 223 B5
Heathway *continued*
Dagenham RM10 81 C2
Dagenham RM10 103 C6
Greenwich SE3 143 A5
Woodford IG8 37 C5
Heathway Ct NW3 69 C6
Heathway Ind Est RM10 81 D4
Heathwood Ct
1 Hounslow TW3 129 D1
Streatham SW12 159 C3
Heathwood Gdns SE7 122 A1
Heathwood Point 7 SE26 162 D1
Heaton Cl E4 20 A1
Heaton Ct 3 N20 14 D2
Heaton Ho
Chelsea SW10 266 B6
6 Peckham SE15 140 B3
Heaton Rd
London SE15 140 B3
Mitcham CR4 181 A3
Heaven Tree Cl N1 73 A3
Heaver Rd 23 SW11 136 B2
Heavers Farm Prim Sch SE25 205 D4
Heavitree Cl SE18 123 B1
Heavitree Ct E17 35 D2
Heavitree Rd 2 SE18 123 B1
Hebble Ho UB5 85 A6
Hebden Ct 24 E2 95 D6
Hebden Terr N17 33 C4
Hebdon Rd SW17 158 C1
Hebe Ct SM1 218 A4
Heber Prim Sch SE22 161 D5
Heber Rd
Cricklewood NW2 68 D4
East Dulwich SE22 161 D5
Hebron Rd W6 112 B3
Hecham Cl E17 35 A2
Heckfield Pl SW6 135 C5 265 A3
Heckford Ho E14 97 D1
Heckford St E1 118 D6
Hector 31 NW9 27 D2
Hector Cl 8 N9 18 A2
Hector Ct
1 London SW9 138 C4
Putney SW15 156 D6
Hector Ho 14 E2 96 B5
Hector St SE18 123 C2
Heddington Gr N7 72 B3
Heddon Cl TW7 131 A1
Heddon Court Ave EN4 14 D6
Heddon Court Par EN4 15 A6
Heddon Ct EN4 15 A6
Heddon Rd EN4 14 D6
Heddon St W1 249 A6
Hedge Hill EN2 4 D4
Hedge La N13 17 A1
Hedgeley IG4 56 B5
Hedgemans Rd RM9 81 A1
Hedgemans Way RM9 81 A2
Hedgemoor Ct 1 E4 36 B5
Hedgerley Gdns UB6 86 A5
Hedgerow La EN5 12 B6
Hedger's Gr E9 75 A2
Hedger St SE11 261 C4
Hedge Wlk SE6 185 D6
Hedgewood Gdns IG5 56 C4
Hedgewood Sch UB4 83 C4
Hedgley Mews SE12 164 D6
Hedgley St SE12 164 D6
Hedingham Cl 6 N1 73 A1
Hedingham Ho 7 KT2 176 A2
Hedingham Rd RM8 80 B3
Hedley Ct SW15 156 D5
Hedley Ho E14 120 A3
Hedley Rd TW4 151 C4
Hedley Row N5, N16 73 B3
Hedsor Ho E2 243 C6
Heenan Cl IG11 79 A2
Heene Rd EN2 5 B4
Heidegger Cres SW13 134 B5
Heigham Rd E6 78 A1
Heighton Gdns CR0 220 D3
Heights Cl SW20 178 B3
Heights The
Beckenham BR3 186 A3
Greenwich SE7 121 C1
Hampstead NW3 70 A4
Northolt UB5 63 C3
Stroud Green N4 50 C3
Heiron St SE17 138 D6
Helby Rd SW4 159 D5
Heldar Ct SE1 252 D1
Helder Gr SE12 164 D4
Helder St CR2 221 B2
Heldmann Cl TW7 130 B1
Helegan Cl BR6 227 D4
Helena Cl EN4 2 B5
Helena Ct W5 87 D2
Helena Pl 3 E9 96 C6
Helena Rd Ealing W5 87 D2
Newham E13 99 A5
Walthamstow E17 53 C4
Willesden NW10 68 B3
Helena Sq 12 SE16 119 A6
Helen Ave TW14 150 B4
Helen Cl
East Finchley N2 48 A6
East Molesey KT8 195 D5
Helen Clare Ct EN2 4 D2
Helen Ct N3 47 A6
Helen Gladstone Ho SE1 251 C2
Helen Ho 9 E2 96 B5
Helen Mackay Ho 10 E14 98 B1
Helen Peele Cotts 10 SE16 118 C3
Helenslea Ave NW11 47 C1
Helen's Pl E2 96 C4
Helen St SE18 122 D2
Helen Taylor Ho 5 SE16 118 A2
Helen Way WD19 22 D6
Helford Cl HA4 61 C6
Helgiford Gdns TW16 171 C3
Helios Rd CR4 203 A1
Heliport Ind Est SW11 136 B3
Helix Ct 17 W11 112 D5
Helix Gdns SW2 160 B5
Helix Ho TW7 131 B3
Helix Rd SW2 160 B5
Helix The SW19 156 D2
Hellings St E1 118 A5
Helme Cl SW19 179 B5
Helmet Row EC1 242 B6
Helmore Rd IG11 79 D1
Helmsdale Cl UB4 85 A3
Helmsdale Ho NW6 91 D5
Helmsdale Rd SW16 181 D2
Helmsley 11 E18 55 A6
Helmsley Pl E8 74 B1
Helmsley St 7 E8 74 B1
Helperby Rd NW10 67 C1
Helsby Ct NW8 236 C6
Helsinki Sq SE16 119 A3
Helston NW1 232 B4
Helston Cl HA5 23 B3
Helston Ct N15 51 C4
Helston Ho SE11 261 B2
Helvetia St SE6 163 B2
Helwys Ct E4 36 A4
Hemans Est SW8 137 D5 269 D3
Hemans St SW8 137 D5 269 D3
Hemberton Rd SW9 138 A2
Hemery Rd UB6 64 B3
Hemingford Cl N12 30 B5
Hemingford Rd
Cheam SM3 216 C4
Islington N1 94 B6 233 D6
Heming Rd HA8 26 D3
Hemington Ave N11 30 D5
Hemlock Cl SW16 181 D1
Hemlock Rd W12 111 D6
Hemmen La UB3 83 D1
Hemming Cl 6 TW12 173 C2
Hemmings Cl DA14 168 B2
Hemmings Ct HA8 27 A3
Hemmings Mead KT19 215 A2
Hemming St E1 96 A3
Hemmingway Cl NW5 71 A4
Hempstead Cl IG9 21 A2
Hempstead Rd E17 36 B1
Hemp Wlk SE17 262 D4

Hemsby Rd KT9 214 B2
Hemstal Rd NW6 69 C1
Hemswell Dr NW9 27 C2
Hemsworth Ct N1 95 C5
Hemsworth St N1 95 C5
Hemus Pl SW3 257 B1
Henchman St W12 89 D1
Hendale Ave NW4 46 B6
Hendale Ho 13 E5 74 B6
Henderson Cl NW10 67 A2
Henderson Ct
8 Deptford SE14 140 D6
Hampstead NW3 70 B3
Wandsworth SW18 158 C4
Woodside Pk N12 29 D6
Henderson Dr
NW8 92 B3 236 C6
Henderson Ho 7
RM10 81 C5
Henderson Rd
Edmonton N9 18 B3
Forest Gate E7 77 C2
Hayes UB4 84 A4
Thornton Heath CR0 205 B3
Wandsworth SW18 158 C4
Hendfield Ct 5 SM6 219 B2
Hendham Rd SW17 158 D2
HENDON 46 C3
Hendon Ave N3 29 A2
Hendon Central NW4 46 B4
Hendon Central Sta
NW4 46 B4
Hendon Hall Ct NW4 46 D6
Hendon Ho NW4 46 D4
Hendon La N3 29 B1
Hendon L Ctr NW2 46 D2
Hendon Lo NW4 46 B6
Hendon Park Mans
NW4 46 C4
Hendon Park Row
NW11 47 B3
Hendon Pk Cotts
NW7 11 D2
Hendon Prep Sch
NW4 46 D6
Hendon Rd N9 18 A2
Hendon Sch NW4 46 D4
Hendon Sta NW4 46 A3
Hendon Terr TW15 171 B4
Hendon Way NW2,
NW4 46 C3
Hendon Wood La
NW7 12 A3
Hendre Ho SE1 263 B3
Hendren Cl UB6 64 B3
Hendre Rd
SE1 117 C2 263 B3
Hendrick Ave SW12 158 D4
Heneage La EC3 243 B1
Heneage Pl EC3 243 B1
Heneage St
E1 95 D2 243 D4
Henfield Cl
London N19 49 C1
Old Bexley DA5 169 C5
Henfield Rd SW19 179 B2
Hengelo Gdns CR4 202 B5
Hengist Rd
Eltham SE12 165 B4
Erith DA8 147 D5
Hengist Way
Beckenham BR2,
BR3 208 C5
Wallington SM6 219 D1
Hengrave Rd SE23 162 D4
Hengrove Ct DA5 169 A3
Henley Ave SM3 217 A5
Henley Cl
Greenford UB6 86 A5
Hounslow TW7 130 D4
Rotherhithe SE16 118 C4
Henley Ct
Brondesbury NW2 68 D2
Hendon NW4 46 A6
Ilford IG1 78 D4
Mitcham CR4 203 A6
Oakwood N14 15 C4
Peckham SE15 140 A2
Sidcup DA5 169 B4
Henley Dr
Bermondsey
SE1 117 D2 263 D4
Kingston u T KT2 177 D3
Henley Gdns
Dagenham RM6 59 A4
Pinner HA5 40 B6
Henley Ho London N12 30 B5
Shoreditch E2 243 D6
Henley Lo
South Norwood
SE25 205 D5
Walthamstow E17 53 B4
Henley Prior N1 233 C3
Henley Rd
Edmonton N18 33 C6
Ilford IG1 79 B4
Newham E16 122 B4
Willesden NW10 90 C6
Henleys Cnr NW11 47 B5
Henleys Rdbt TW5 128 C3
Henley St SW11 137 A3
Henley Way TW13 172 D5
Henlow Pl TW10 153 D2
Hennel Cl SE23 162 C1
Hennessy Rd N9 18 C2
Henniker Gdns E6 100 A4
Henniker Mews SW3 266 C6
Henniker Point E15 76 C3
Henniker Rd E15 76 B3
Henningham Rd N17 33 B2
Henning St
SW11 136 C4 267 A1
Henrietta Barnett Sch
NW11 47 D3
Henrietta Cl SE8 141 C6
Henrietta Ho
11 Hammersmith
W6 112 C1
3 New Barnet EN5 2 A1
3 South Tottenham
N15 51 C3
Henrietta Mews
WC1 240 B6
Henrietta Pl
W1 93 B1 238 C2
Henrietta St
Strand
WC2 116 A6 250 B6
Stratford New Town
E15 76 A3
Henriques St E1 96 A1
Henry Addlington Cl
E6 100 D2
Henry Cavendish Prim
Sch 2 SW12 159 C3
Henry Cl EN2 5 C5
Henry Compton Sch
SW6 135 A4 264 A2
Henry Cooper Way
SE12 187 D6
Henry Darlot Dr NW7 29 A5
Henry Dent Cl SE5 139 B2
Henry Dickens Ct
W11 244 A4
Henry Doulton Dr
SW17 181 B6
Henry Fawcett Prim Sch
16 SE11 138 C6
Henry Green Prim Sch
RM8 80 D6
Henry Hatch Ct SM2 218 A1
Henry Ho
Lambeth SE1 251 B3
South Lambeth SW8 270 A4
St John's Wood NW8 230 A4
Henry Jackson Ho 4
SW15 134 D2
Henry Jackson Rd
SW15 134 D2
Henry Macaulay Ave 13
KT2 175 D2
Henry Maynard Inf Sch
E17 54 A4
Henry Maynard Jun Sch
E17 54 A4
Henry Peters Dr
TW11 174 C5
Henry Rd London N4 51 A1
New Barnet EN4 14 B6
Newham E6 100 A5
Henry's Ave IG8 36 D5
Henryson Rd SE4 163 C6
Henry St BR1 187 B2
Henry Tate Mews
SW16 182 C5
Henry Wise Ho SW1 259 B3
Henshall Point 19 E3 97 D4
Henshall St N1 73 B2
Henshawe Rd RM8 80 D5
Henshaw St
SE17 117 B2 262 C4
Hensley Point 28 E9 74 D2
Henslowe Rd SE22 162 A6
Henslow Ho 12 SE15 140 A5
Henson Ave NW2 68 C3
Henson Cl BR6 226 D6
Henson Ct 3 N5 73 A4
Henson Path HA3 43 D6
Henson Pl UB5 84 C6
Henstridge Pl NW8 230 A5
Henty Cl
SW11 136 C4 267 B2
Henty Wlk SW15 156 B6
Henville Rd BR1 187 B2
Henwick Prim Sch
SE9 144 A2
Henwick Rd SE9 144 A2
Hepburn Gdns BR2 208 D1
Hepburn Mews
SW11 158 D6
Hepple Cl TW7 131 B3
Hepplestone Cl
SW15 156 B5
Hepscott Rd E9 75 C1
Hepworth Ct
Barking IG11 80 A3
Cheam SM3 201 C1
Chelsea SW1 258 C1
Islington N1 234 C6
Hepworth Gdns IG11 80 A3
Hepworth Ho IG8 21 A1
Hepworth Rd SW16 182 A3
Hepworth Way KT12 193 D1
Heracles 30 NW9 27 D2
Heracles Cl SM6 220 A1
Hera Ct 15 E14 119 C2
Herald Gdns SM6 219 B5
Heralds Pl SE11 261 C4
Herald St 5 E2 96 B3
Herbal Hill EC1 241 B5
Herbert Chapman Ct
N5 72 D4
Herbert Cres SW1 257 D6
Herbert Ct 4 KT5 198 B3
Herbert Gdns
Chiswick W4 132 D6
Dagenham RM6 58 D2
Willesden Green NW10 90 B5
Herbert Ho E1 243 C2
Herbert Mews 15
SW2 160 C5
Herbert Morrison Ho
SW6 264 C5
Herbert Morrison Prim
Sch SW8 138 A5 270 A3
Herbert Pl
Hounslow TW3 130 B3
Shooters Hill SE18 144 D6
Herbert Rd
Bexleyheath DA7 147 A3
Bromley BR2 210 A4
Hendon NW9 46 A3
Ilford IG3 79 C6
Kingston u T KT1 198 B6
Manor Pk E12 78 A4
Merton SW19 179 B3
Shooters Hill SE18 144 D6
Southall UB1 107 B5
South Tottenham N15 51 D4
Walthamstow E17 53 B2
Wood Green N11 32 A3
Herbert St
Camden Town NW5 71 A2
Newham E13 99 A5
Herbrand Est
WC1 94 A3 240 A6
Herbrand St
WC1 94 A3 240 A6
Hercies Rd UB10 60 C2
Hercules Ct 7 SE14 141 A6
Hercules Pl N7 72 A5
Hercules Rd
SE1 116 B3 260 D5
Hercules St N7 72 A5
Hereford Ave EN4 14 D3
Hereford Bldgs SW3 266 D6
Hereford Ct
20 Belmont SM2 217 C1
6 Croydon CR0 205 D1
6 Ealing W7 86 D2
Harrow HA1 42 C6
Hereford Gdns
London SE13 164 C6
Pinner HA5 41 A4
Redbridge IG1 56 A2
Twickenham TW2 152 A3
Hereford Ho
7 Acton W3 88 C1
Hereford Ho *continued*
5 Brixton SW2 138 C1
25 Camberwell SE5 139 A3
Edgware HA8 26 B3
Knightsbridge SW3 257 B6
Walham Green SW10 265 D4
Hereford Mans 10
W2 91 C1
Hereford Mews 11
W2 91 C1
Hereford Pl SE14 141 B5
Hereford Rd
Acton W3 111 A6
Bayswater
W2 113 C6 245 B6
Ealing W5 109 C3
Feltham TW13 150 C3
Wanstead E11 55 B4
Hereford Retreat 5
SE15 140 A5
Hereford Sq
SW7 114 A2 256 B3
Hereford St E2 96 A3
Hereford Way KT9 213 D3
Herent Dr IG5 56 B6
Hereward Gdns N13 32 C5
Hereward House Sch
NW3 70 B2
Hereward Rd SW17 180 D6
Herga Ct HA1 64 C6
Herga Rd HA3 42 D5
Heriot Ave E4 19 C2
Heriot Rd NW4 46 C4
Heriots Cl HA7 25 A6
Heritage Ave NW9 27 D1
Heritage Cl
London SW9 138 D2
Sunbury TW16 172 A2
Heritage Ct SE8 118 D1
Heritage Hill BR2 225 C3
Heritage Ho
22 Putney SW19 156 D3
3 Twickenham TW1 153 A4
Heritage View HA1 64 D5
Herlwyn Ave HA4 61 C5
Herlwyn Gdns SW17 180 D6
Herm Cl TW7 130 A5
Hermes Cl 5 W9 91 C3
Hermes Ct 4 SW9 138 C4
Hermes Ho BR3 185 A2
Hermes St N1 234 A3
Hermes Wlk UB5 85 C5
Herm Ho EN3 6 D5
Hermiston Ave N8 50 A4
Hermiston Ct
3 Hornsey N8 50 A4
7 North Finchley N12 30 B5
Hermitage Cl
1 Abbey Wood
SE2 124 C3
Claygate KT10 213 A2
Enfield EN2 4 D3
Littleton TW17 192 C5
Snaresbrook E18 54 D5
Hermitage Ct
2 Child's Hill NW2 69 C5
Colney Hatch N11 30 D4
3 Wanstead E18 55 A5
13 Wapping E1 118 A5
Hermitage Gdns
Child's Hill NW2 69 C5
South Norwood SE19 183 A3
Hermitage La
Child's Hill NW2 69 C5
Croydon CR0 206 A3
South Norwood SW16 182 B3
Hermitage Prim Sch 19
E1 118 A5
Hermitage Rd
London N4, N15 51 A3
South Norwood SE19 183 B4
Hermitage Row 9
E8 74 A3
Hermitage St W2 236 C3
Hermitage The
Barnes SW13 133 D4
Feltham TW13 149 D1
Forest Hill SE23 162 C3
Kingston u T KT1 197 D5
Richmond TW10 154 A6
Uxbridge UB8 60 A2
Hermitage Villas
SW6 265 A6
Hermitage Wall E1 118 A5
Hermitage Way HA7 25 A2
Hermitage Wlk E18 54 D5
Hermit Pl NW6 91 D6
Hermit Rd E16 98 D3
Hermit St EC1 234 C2
Hermon Gr UB3 106 A5
Hermon Hill E11 55 A5
Herndon Rd SW18 158 A6
Herne Cl Hayes UB3 83 D1
Willesden NW10 67 B3
Herne Ct WD23 8 A4
HERNE HILL 161 A6
Herne Hill SE24 139 A1
Herne Hill Ho SE24 160 D5
Herne Hill Mans
SE24 161 A5
Herne Hill Rd SE24 139 A1
Herne Hill Sch SE24 161 A6
Herne Hill Sta SE24 160 D5
Herne Hill Velodrome
SE24 161 B5
Herne Mews N18 34 A6
Herne Pl SE24 160 D6
Herne Rd KT6 214 A6
Heron Cl
Buckhurst Hill IG9 21 A3
Cheam SM1 217 B3
Walthamstow E17 35 B1
Willesden NW10 67 C2
Heron Cres DA14 189 C6
Heron Ct
Bromley BR2 209 C5
16 Cubitt Town E14 120 A3
7 Dulwich SE21 161 B2
9 Forest Hill SE23 162 C3
Ilford IG1 78 D6
5 Kingston u T KT1 198 A6
Merton SW20 178 C1
Mitcham CR4 180 C2
Ruislip HA4 61 B6
Stanwell TW19 148 A3
Herondale Ave
SW18 158 C3
Heron Dr N4 73 A6
Herongate N1 235 B6
Herongate Rd E12 77 C6
Heron Hill DA17 125 B2
Heron Ho
Battersea SW11 267 B2
Ealing W13 87 A3
Peckham SE15 139 D4
Sidcup DA14 168 B1
St John's Wood NW8 230 A3
Teddington KT1 175 C2
Heron Mead EN3 7 C5
Heron Mews IG1 78 D6
Heron Pl
Marylebone W1 238 B2
Rotherhithe SE16 119 A5
Heron Quays E14 119 C5
Heron Quays Sta
E14 119 C5
Heron Rd
Croydon CR0 221 C6
Herne Hill SE24 139 A1
Isleworth TW1 131 B1
Heronsforde W13 87 C1
Heronsgate HA8 26 C5
Heronsgate Prim Sch
SE28 123 B3
Heron's Lea N6 48 D3
Heronslea Dr HA7 26 A5
Herons Pl TW7 131 B2
Heron Sq 27 TW10 153 D6
Herons Rise EN4 2 C1
Herons The E11 54 D3
Heron Trad Est W3 88 D2
Heronway IG8 37 C6
Heron Way
Hatton TW14 128 A1
Wallington SM6 219 D1
Herrick Ct 4 TW10 175 D6
Herrick Ho
18 Camberwell SE5 139 B5
17 Canonbury N16 73 B4
Herrick Rd N5 73 A5
Herrick St
SW1 115 D2 259 D3
Herries St W10 91 A5
Herringham Rd SE7 121 C3
Herrongate Cl EN1 5 D3
Hersant Cl NW10 90 A6
Herschell Rd SE23 163 A4
Herschell's Mews
SE5 139 A2

Hersham Cl SW15 156 A4
Hersham Rd KT12 194 A1
Hershell Ct 1 SW14 132 D1
Hertford Ave SW14 133 C1
Hertford Cl EN4 2 B2
Hertford Ct
16 London SW11 136 C2
Newham E6 100 B4
Palmers Green N13 16 C1
Hertford Ho 5 UB5 85 B3
Hertford Lo 10 SW19 157 A3
Hertford Pl W1 239 B5
Hertford Rd
Barking IG11 78 D1
Barnet EN4 2 A2
East Finchley N2 48 C6
Edmonton N9 18 B3
Enfield EN3 6 C5
Ilford IG2 57 C3
Shoreditch N1 95 C6
Hertford Rd High St EN3 18 C6
Hertford St W1 115 B5 248 C3
Hertford Way CR4 204 A5
Hertford Wlk 13 DA17 125 C1
Hertmitage The 5 SE13 142 A3
Hertslet Rd N7 72 B5
Hertsmere Rd E14 119 C6
Hertswood Ct 1 EN5 1 A1
Hervey Cl N3 29 C2
Hervey Park Rd E17 53 A5
Hervey Rd SE3 143 B4
Hesa Rd UB3 106 A6
Hesewall Cl SW4 137 C3
Hesketh Pl W11 244 A5
Hesketh Rd E7 77 A5
Heslop Ct 1 SW12 159 A3
Heslop Rd SW12 158 D3
Hesper Mews SW5 113 D2 255 C3
Hesperus Cres E14 119 D2
Hessel Rd W13 109 B4
Hessel St E1 96 B1
Hestercombe Ave SW6 135 A4 264 B1
Hester Ct SW16 181 C5
Hesterman Way CR0 204 B1
Hester Rd
Battersea SW11 136 C5 267 A3
Edmonton N18 34 A5
Hester Terr TW9 132 C2
Hestia Ho SE1 253 A1
HESTON 129 B5
Heston Ave TW5 129 A5
Heston Com Sch TW5 129 C5
Heston Ctr The TW5 106 C1
Heston Grange TW5 129 B6
Heston Grange La TW5 129 B6
Heston Ho
Gunnersbury W4 110 D1
5 St Johns SE8 141 C4
Heston Ind Mall TW5 129 B5
Heston Inf Sch TW5 129 C5
Heston Jun Sch TW5 129 C5
Heston Phoenix Distribution Pk TW5 128 C6
Heston Pool TW5 129 B6
Heston Rd TW5 129 C5
Heston St SE14 141 C4
Hetherington Rd
Charlton TW17 171 A1
Stockwell SW2, SW4 138 A1
Hetherington Way UB10 60 A4
Hethpool Ho W2 236 C5
Hetley Gdns 1 SE19 183 D3
Hetley Rd W12 112 B4
Heton Gdns NW4 46 A5
Hetty Rees Ct 6 N19 50 A2
Hevelius Cl SE10 120 D1
Hever Croft SE9 188 C6
Heverfield Ct CR4 180 D3
Hever Gdns BR1 188 C1
Heverham Rd SE18 123 C2
Hever Ho SE15 140 D6
Heversham Ho SE15 140 C6
Heversham Rd DA7 147 C4
Hevingham Dr RM6 58 C4
Heward Ct SE13 142 A3
Hewens Rd UB4 83 A3
Hewer Ho 6 SW4 159 C6
Hewer St W10 90 D2
Hewes Ho E17 52 D5
Hewett Cl HA7 25 B6
Hewett Ho
Putney SW15 134 C3
7 Woolwich SE18 122 D1
Hewett Rd RM8 80 D4
Hewetts Quay 6 IG11 101 A6
Hewett St EC2 95 C3 243 B5
Hewish Rd N18 33 C6
Hewison St E3 97 B5
Hewitt Ave N22 32 D1
Hewitt Cl CR0 223 C5
Hewitt Ho 2 E4 36 B5
Hewitt Rd N8 50 D4
Hewlett Rd E3 97 A5
Hewling Ho 1 N16 73 C3
Hexagon Bsns Ctr UB4 106 C6
Hexagon The N6 48 D1
Hexal Rd SE6 164 C1
Hexham Gdns TW7 131 A5
Hexham Rd Barnet EN5 1 D1
Cheam SM4 201 D1
West Norwood SE27 161 A2
Hexton Ct N4 73 A6
Heybourne Rd N17 34 B3
Heybridge 9 NW1 71 B2
Heybridge Ave SW16 182 B4
Heybridge Dr IG6 57 B6
Heybridge Way E10 53 B1
Heydon Ct BR4 224 C6
Heydon Ho 3 SE14 140 C4
Heyford Ave
Merton SW20 201 B6
South Lambeth SW8 138 A5 270 B4
Heyford Rd CR4 180 C1
Heyford Terr SW8 270 B4
Heygate St SE17 117 A2 262 B4
Heylyn Sq E3 97 B4
Heynes Rd RM8 80 C4
Heysham Dr WD19 22 D5
Heysham La NW3 69 D5
Heysham Rd N15 51 B3
Heythorp St SW18 157 B2
Heythrop Coll W8 113 D3 255 C6
Heythrop Dr UB10 60 B4
Heyward Ct SM2 217 C2
Heywood Ave NW9 27 C2
Heywood Ct 2 HA7 25 C5
Heywood Ho
11 Deptford SE14 140 D6
6 Tulse Hill SW2 160 C5
Heyworth Rd
Lower Clapton E5 74 B4
Stratford E15 76 D4
Hibbert Ho 13 E14 119 C3
Hibbert Rd
Harrow HA3 24 D1
Walthamstow E17 53 B2
Hibbert St SW11 136 B2
Hibernia Gdns TW3 151 C6
Hibernia Point 9 SE2 124 D4
Hibernia Rd TW3 129 C1
Hibiscus Cl 6 HA8 27 A6
Hibiscus Lo 5 E15 76 C1
Hichisson Rd SE15 162 C6
Hicken Rd SW2 160 B6
Hickes Ho 6 NW6 70 B1
Hickey's Almshouses 7 TW9 132 B1
Hickin Cl SE7 121 D2
Hickin St 2 E14 120 A3
Hickleton NW1 232 B5
Hickling Ho 10 SE16 118 B3
Hickling Rd IG1 78 D3
Hickman Ave E4 36 A4
Hickman Cl E16 99 D2
Hickman Rd RM6 58 C2
Hickmore Wlk SW4 137 C2
Hickory Cl N9 18 A4
Hicks Ave UB6 86 C4
Hicks Cl SW11 136 C2
Hicks Ct RM10 81 D5
Hicks St SE8 119 A1
Hidaburn Ct 7 SW16 181 C6
Hidcote Gdns SW20 200 B6
Hidcote Ho 11 SM2 218 A1
Hide E6 100 C1
Hide Pl SW1 115 D2 259 C3
Hider Ct SE3 143 C5
Hide Rd HA1 42 B5
Hide Twr SW1 259 C3
Hieover SE21 161 A2
Higgins Ho 7 N1 95 C6
Higginson Ho 2 NW3 70 D1
Higgins Wlk TW12 173 A4
Higgs Ind Est 9 SE24 138 D2
High Acre EN2 4 D2
Higham Ct 9 IG8 37 A4
HIGHAM HILL 35 A2
Higham Hill Ho E17 34 D2
Higham Hill Rd E17 35 A1
Higham Ho E4 35 C4
Higham Mews UB5 85 B3
Higham Pl E17 53 A6
Higham Rd
Tottenham N17 51 B6
Woodford IG8 37 A4
Highams Lodge Bsns Ctr E17 52 D6
HIGHAMS PARK 36 A3
Highams Park Sch E4 36 B4
Highams Park Sta E4 36 B4
Higham St E17 53 A6
Higham Station Ave E4 35 D4
Highams The E17 36 A2
High Ashton 11 KT2 176 D3
Highbanks Cl DA16 146 B5
Highbanks Rd HA5 23 D4
Highbank Way N8 50 C3
HIGH BARNET 1 B2
High Barnet Sta EN5 1 C1
Highbarrow Rd CR0 206 A1
High Beech
South Croydon CR2 221 C1
Southgate N21 16 B5
High Beeches DA14 191 A5
High Birch Ct 7 EN4 2 C1
Highbridge Ct 13 SE14 140 C5
Highbridge Rd IG11 100 D6
High Bridge Wharf SE10 120 B1
Highbrook Rd SE3 143 D2
High Broom Cres BR4 207 D2
Highburty Mans 24 N1 72 D1
HIGHBURY 72 D4
Highbury Ave CR7 182 D1
Highbury Cl
New Malden KT3 199 A4
West Wickham BR4 223 D6
Highbury Cnr N5 72 D2
Highbury Corner N5 72 D2
Highbury Cres N5 72 C3
Highbury Fields Sch 4 N5 72 D3
Highbury Gdns IG3 79 C6
Highbury Gr N5 72 D2
Highbury Grange N5 73 A4
Highbury Grove Ct N5 72 D2
Highbury Grove Sch 7 N5 73 A3
Highbury Hill N5 72 D4
Highbury & Islington Sta N1 72 D2
Highbury New Pk N5 73 A4
Highbury Pk N5 72 D4
Highbury Pl N5 72 D3
Highbury Pool N5 72 D2
Highbury Quadrant N5 73 A5
Highbury Quadrant Prim Sch N5 73 A4
Highbury Rd SW19 179 A5
Highbury Sq N14 15 C3
Highbury Station Rd N1 72 C2
Highbury Terr N5 72 D3
Highbury Terrace Mews N5 72 D3
High Cedar Dr SW20 178 B3
Highclears 6 IG9 21 B2
Highclere Rd KT3 199 B6
Highclere St SE26 185 A6
Highcliffe
Beckenham BR3 185 D2
Ealing W13 87 B2
Highcliffe Dr SW15 155 D5
Highcliffe Gdns IG4 56 A4
Highcombe SE7 143 B6
Highcombe Cl SE9 166 A3
High Coombe Pl KT2 177 B3
Highcroft Highgate N6 49 A3
Hyde The NW9 45 C4
2 Kingston u T KT5 198 B4
Highcroft Ave HA0 88 C6
Highcroft Gdns NW11 47 B3
Highcroft Point E17 35 D2
Highcroft Rd N19 50 A2
High Cross Ctr The N15 52 A5
High Cross Rd N17 52 A6
Highcross Way 4 SW15 156 A3
Highdaun Dr SW16 204 B5
High Dene EN2 4 D2
Highdown KT4 215 D6
Highdown Rd SW15 156 B5
High Dr KT2, KT3 177 A1
High Elms IG8 37 A5
High Elms Ctry Pk★ BR6 227 A1
High Elms Rd BR6 227 A1
Highfield WD23 8 C2
Highfield Ave
Erith DA8 147 D6
Greenford UB6 64 D3
Hendon NW11 47 A2
Kingsbury NW9 45 A4
Orpington BR6 227 D3
Pinner HA5 41 B4
Wembley HA9 66 B5
Highfield Cl
Hither Green SE13 164 B5
Kingsbury NW9 45 A4
Long Ditton KT6 197 C1
Wood Green N22 32 C2
Highfield Ct
7 Barnet EN5 1 D1
Hendon NW11 47 A3
Mitcham CR4 202 C5
Southgate N14 15 C5
Wanstead E12 77 C6
Highfield Dr
Beckenham BR2 208 D5
Ickenham UB10 60 A5
West Ewell KT19 215 D2
West Wickham BR4 224 A5
Highfield Gdns NW11 47 A3
Highfield Hill SE19 183 C3
Highfield Ho N21 16 D3
Highfield Inf Sch BR2 208 C5
Highfield Jun Sch BR2 208 C5
Highfield Mews NW6 69 D1
Highfield Prim Sch
Edmonton N21 17 A3
Hillingdon UB10 82 D4
Highfield Rd
Acton W3 89 A2
Bexley DA6 169 B6
Bromley BR1 210 B5
Carshalton SM1 218 C3
Edmonton N21 16 D2
Feltham TW13 150 A2
4 Feltham TW13 150 B3
Hendon NW11 47 A3
Hounslow TW7 130 D4
Orpington BR5, BR7 211 D6
St Paul's Cray BR5, BR7 211 D6
Tolworth KT5 199 A2
Upper Halliford TW16 193 D4
Walton-on-T KT12 194 A1
Highfields SM1 217 C6
Highfields Gr N6 48 D1
High Foleys KT10 213 B1
High Gables
Beckenham BR2 186 C1
Loughton IG10 21 D6
High Garth KT10 212 A2
HIGHGATE 49 A2
Highgate Archway N6 49 C1
Highgate Ave N6 49 B2
Highgate Cemetery★ N19 71 B6
Highgate Cl N6 49 A2
High Gate Edge N2 48 C4
Highgate High St N6 49 B1
Highgate Hill N19 49 C1
Highgate Ho 11 SE26 162 A1
Highgate Hts N6 49 C3
Highgate Pre-Prep & Jun Sch N6 48 D2
Highgate Prim Sch N6 48 D3
Highgate (Private) Hospl N6 48 D3
Highgate Rd NW5 71 B4
Highgate Sch N6 49 A2
Highgate Spinney N8 49 D3
Highgate Sta N6 49 B3
Highgate West Hill
Highgate N6 49 A1
London N6 71 A6
Highgate Wlk SE23 162 C2
Highgate Wood Sch N8 49 C4
High Gr Bromley BR1 187 D2
Woolwich SE18 145 B4
Highgrove Cl
London N11 31 A5
Widmore BR7 188 A2
Highgrove Ct BR3 185 C3
Highgrove Ho HA4 40 A3
Highgrove Mews SM5 218 D5
Highgrove Point 2 NW3 70 A4
Highgrove Rd RM8 80 C4
Highgrove Way HA4 40 A2
High Hill Ferry 3 E5 52 B1
High Holborn WC1 94 B2 240 C3
High Holborn Ho WC1 240 D3
High La W7 86 B1
Highland Ave W7 86 C1
Highland Cotts SM6 219 C4
Highland Croft BR3 185 D4
Highland Ct E18 37 B2
Highland Dr WD23 8 A4
Highland Lo 3 SE19 183 D3
Highland Pk TW13 171 D6
Highland Rd
Bexley DA6 147 C1
Bromley BR1 186 D2
Pinner HA6 22 A1
West Norwood SE19 183 C4
Highlands N20 14 B2
Highlands Ave
Acton W3 111 A6
Southgate N21 16 B6
Highlands Cl
Hornsey N4 50 A2
Hounslow TW3 129 D4
Highlands Ct SE19 183 C4
Highlands Gdns IG1 56 B1
Highlands Heath SW15 156 C4
Highlands Prim Sch IG1 56 B1
Highlands Rd EN5 13 C6
Highlands Sch N21 4 C1
Highlands The
Barnet EN5 1 D1
Edgware HA8 26 D1
Highlawn Hall HA1 64 C5
Highlea Cl NW9 27 C2
High Level Dr SE26 184 A6
Highlever Rd W10 90 C2
High Limes 2 SE19 183 C4
High London 5 N6 49 D2
Highmead
9 Edmonton N18 34 A5
Plumstead Comm SE18 145 D5
High Mead
Harrow HA1 42 D4
West Wickham BR4 224 C6
Highmead Cres HA0 66 B1
High Meadow Cl HA5 40 C5
High Meadow Cres NW9 45 B4
High Meads Rd E16 99 D1

Highmore Rd SE3 . . . . 142 C5
High Mount
Hendon NW4 . . . . 46 A3
11 Hornsey N4 . . . . 50 A2
High Oaks EN2 . . . . 4 B5
High Oaks Lo 9 E18 . . 37 A1
High Park Ave TW9 . . . 132 C4
High Park Rd TW9 . . . 132 C4
High Par The SW16 . . . 160 A1
High Path SW19 . . . . . 180 A2
Highpoint EN5 . . . . 14 A6
High Point
Chislehurst SE9 . . . . . 166 D1
Highgate N6 . . . . 49 A2
High Range SW20 . . . . 178 C3
High Rd
Buckhurst Hill IG9,
IG10 . . . . 21 C5
Bushey WD23 . . . . 8 B3
Chadwell Heath RM6 . . . 58 C2
East Finchley N2 . . . . . . 48 C6
Finchley N2, N12 . . . . . . 30 A3
Friern Barnet N11 . . . . . 31 B5
Harrow HA3 . . . . 24 C3
Ilford IG1 . . . . 78 D6
Leyton E10 . . . . 53 D3
Oakleigh Pk N20 . . . . 14 A4
Seven Kings IG1, IG3 . . . 79 C6
South Tottenham N15,
N17 . . . . 51 D5
Tottenham N17 . . . . 33 D2
Wembley HA0, HA9 . . . . 66 A3
Willesden NW10 . . . . . . 68 A2
Woodford E18 . . . . 37 A2
Wood Green N22 . . . . . . 32 B3
High Ridge N10 . . . . 31 B2
Highridge Pl EN2 . . . . . . 4 B5
High Road Buckhurst Hill
5 IG9 . . . . 21 B2
High Road Eastcote
HA5 . . . . 40 B4
High Road, Ickenham
UB10 . . . . 61 A6
High Road Leyton
E10 . . . . 75 D6
High Road Leytonstone
E11 . . . . 76 C6
High Road Woodford Gn
IG8 . . . . 37 A6
High St Mews SW19 . . 179 A5
High St N
Newham E6 . . . . 100 A6
Plashet E12 . . . . 78 A2
High St S E6 . . . . 100 B4
High Sheldon N6 . . . . . 48 D3
Highshore Rd SE15 . 139 D3
Highshore Sch 16
SE15 . . . . 139 D4
High Silver IG10 . . . . . . 21 D6
High St Acton W3 . . . . 110 D5
Barnet EN5 . . . . 1 B1
Beckenham BR3 . . . . . 185 C1
Brentford TW8 . . . . . . 132 A6
Bromley BR1 . . . . 187 A1
Cheam SM1, KT17 . . . 217 A2
Claygate KT10 . . . . . . 212 D2
Cranford TW5 . . . . 128 B5
Croydon CR0 . . . . 221 A5
Ealing W5 . . . . 109 D6
East Molesey KT8 . . . 195 C5
Edgware HA8 . . . . 26 C4
Elstree WD6 . . . . 9 D5
Farnborough BR6 . . . . 227 A3
Feltham TW13 . . . . . . 150 A2
Green Street Green
BR6 . . . . 227 D2
Hampton TW12 . . . . . 174 A4
Harlington UB3 . . . . . 127 B6
Harrow on t H HA1 . . . . 42 C1
Hornsey N8 . . . . 50 B5
Hounslow TW3 . . . . . . 129 D2
Ilford IG6 . . . . 57 A6
Kingston u T KT1 . . . . 175 D2
Kingston u T KT1 . . . . 197 D6
Mill Hill NW7 . . . . 28 B5
Newham E13 . . . . 99 A5
New Malden KT3 . . . . . 199 C5
Palmers Green N14 . . . . 15 D2
Penge SE20 . . . . 184 D3
Pinner HA5 . . . . 41 A6
Ruislip HA4 . . . . 39 C1
Shepperton TW17 . . . 193 A3
Sidcup DA14 . . . . 190 A6
Southall UB1 . . . . 107 B5
South Norwood CR7 . . . 205 B5
South Norwood SE25 . 206 A5
High St *continued*
Stratford Marsh E15 . . . 98 A6
Sutton SM1 . . . . 217 D4
Sutton SM1, SM2 . . . . 217 D3
Teddington TW11 . . . . 175 A5
Thames Ditton KT7 . . . 197 A3
Twickenham TW2 . . . . 152 A4
Wallington SM5 . . . . . 219 A4
Walthamstow E17 . . . . . 53 B5
Walton-on-T KT12 . . . 194 A1
Wanstead E11 . . . . 55 A4
Wealdstone HA3 . . . . . . 24 C1
Wealdstone HA3 . . . . . . 42 C6
Wembley HA9 . . . . 66 B4
West Wickham BR4 . . 207 D1
Wimbledon SW19 . . . 178 D5
Yiewsley UB7 . . . . 104 A6
Highstone Ave E11 . . . . 55 A3
Highstone Ct E11 . . . . . 54 D3
High Street Collier's
Wood SW17, SW19 . 180 B4
High Street Harlesden
NW10 . . . . 89 D5
High Street Harlington
TW6 . . . . 127 B5
High Street Kensington
Sta W8 . . . . 113 D4 245 C1
High The SW16 . . . . . . 160 A1
High Timber St EC4 . 252 A6
High Tor Cl BR1 . . . . . . 187 B3
High Tor View SE28 . . . 123 C5
High Trees
Cheam SM3 . . . . 201 B2
Croydon CR0 . . . . 207 A1
East Barnet EN4 . . . . . . 14 C6
Streatham SW2 . . . . . 160 C3
Uxbridge UB10 . . . . 61 A6
Whetstone N20 . . . . 14 A1
Hightrees Ct W7 . . . . . 108 C6
Hightrees Ho SW12 . . 159 A5
Highview
Crouch End N6 . . . . 49 C3
Hornsey N8 . . . . 50 A2
Northolt UB5 . . . . 85 A4
Woolwich SE18 . . . . . 144 D5
High View
6 Penge SE19 . . . . . 183 D3
Pinner HA5 . . . . 40 C6
Highview Ave HA8 . . . . 27 A6
High View Ave CR0,
SM6 . . . . 220 B3
High View Cl
Loughton IG10 . . . . 21 C6
South Norwood SE19 . 183 D1
Highview Ct 2
SW19 . . . . 157 A3
High View Ct HA3 . . . . . 24 C3
Highview Gdns
Edgware HA8 . . . . 27 A6
Hendon N3 . . . . 47 A6
New Southgate N11 . . . . 31 C5
Highview Ho
1 Buckhurst Hill
IG9 . . . . 21 D1
2 Buckhurst Hill IG9 . . 21 D1
High View Ho RM6 . . . . 59 A5
High View Par 1 IG4 . . 56 B4
High View Prim Sch
1 London SW11 . . . . . 136 B1
Wallington SM6 . . . . . 220 A3
Highview Rd
Ealing W13 . . . . 87 A1
Sidcup DA14 . . . . 190 B6
High View Rd
London N10 . . . . 30 D2
Snaresbrook E18 . . . . . . 54 D6
South Norwood SE19 . . 183 B4
Highway Bsns Pk The 7
E1 . . . . 118 D6
Highway The
Shadwell E1 . . . . 118 C6
Stanmore HA7 . . . . 25 A3
Highway Trad Ctr The 6
E1 . . . . 118 D6
High Wigsell TW11 . . . 175 A5
Highwood IG8 . . . . 36 D6
Highwood Ave N12 . . . 30 A6
Highwood Cl
Dulwich SE22 . . . . 162 A3
Orpington BR6 . . . . . . 227 A6
Highwood Ct
Barnet EN5 . . . . 13 C6
Whetstone N12 . . . . 14 A1
Highwood Dr BR6 . . . . 227 A6
Highwood Gdns IG5 . . 56 B5
Highwood Gr NW7 . . . . 27 B5
Highwood Hill NW7 . . . 11 D2
Highwood Rd N19 . . . . 72 A5
High Worple HA2 . . . . . 41 B1
Highworth Rd N11 . . . . 31 D5
Highworth St NW1 . . 237 B4
Hilary Ave CR4 . . . . . . 203 A6
Hilary Cl Bexley DA8 . 147 D4
Walham Green SW6 . . 265 C4
Hilary Ct N9 . . . . 18 D3
Hilary Rd W12 . . . . . . 111 D6
Hilbert Rd SM3 . . . . . . 216 D5
Hilborough Cl SW19 . 180 A3
Hilborough Ct 1 E8 . . 95 D6
Hilborough Rd 1 E8 . . 73 D1
Hilborough Way
BR6 . . . . 227 B3
Hilda Rd Newham E16 . . 98 C3
Upton Pk E6 . . . . 77 D1
Hilda Terr 2 SW9 . . . . 138 C3
Hilda Vale Cl BR6 . . . 226 D4
Hilda Vale Rd BR6 . . . 226 D4
Hildenborough Gdns
BR1 . . . . 186 D4
Hildenbrough Ho
BR3 . . . . 185 B3
Hildenlea Pl BR2 . . . . . 186 C1
Hilditch Ho 7 TW10 . 154 B5
Hildred Ho SW1 . . . . 258 C4
Hildreth St 6 SW12 . . 159 B3
Hildreth Street Mews 2
SW12 . . . . 159 B3
Hildyard Rd SW6 . . . . 265 B6
Hiley Rd NW10 . . . . 90 C4
Hilfield La WD23 . . . . . . 8 C6
Hilgrove Rd NW6 . . . . . 70 A1
Hiliary Gdns HA7 . . . . . 25 C1
Hillary Cres KT12 . . . . 194 C1
Hillary Ct
3 Chislehurst SE9 . . 166 A2
13 Shepherd's Bush
W12 . . . . 112 C4
Stanwell TW19 . . . . . . 148 A3
Hillary Dr TW7 . . . . . . 152 D6
Hillary Rd UB2 . . . . 107 C3
Hillary Rise EN5 . . . . 1 C1
Hillbeck Cl
Deptford SE15 . . . . . . 140 C5
Deptford SE15 . . . . . . 140 C6
Hillbeck Way UB6 . . . . . 86 B6
Hillborne Cl UB3 . . . . . 106 A1
Hillboro Ct
Leytonstone E11 . . . . . . 54 B2
1 Woodford E18 . . . . . 36 D2
Hillborough Ct HA1 . . . 42 C2
Hillbrook Prim Sch
SW17 . . . . 181 A6
Hillbrook Rd SW17 . . . 181 A6
Hillbrow
Kingston u T KT3 . . . . 199 D6
7 Richmond TW10 . . 154 A5
Hill Brow BR1 . . . . 187 D2
Hillbrow Ct KT10 . . . . . 212 A4
Hillbrow Rd
Catford BR1 . . . . 186 C4
Esher KT10 . . . . 212 A4
Hill Bunker's DA17 . . . 125 C2
Hillbury Ave HA3 . . . . . 43 B4
Hillbury Rd SW17 . . . . 159 B1
Hill Cl Barnet EN5 . . . . . . 12 C6
Chislehurst BR7 . . . . . 188 D5
Dollis Hill NW2 . . . . 68 B5
Hampstead Garden Suburb
NW11 . . . . 47 C3
Harrow HA1 . . . . 64 C5
Stanmore HA7 . . . . 25 B6
Hillcote Ave SW16 . . . 182 C3
Hillcourt N6 . . . . 49 C3
Hillcourt Ave N12 . . . . . 29 D4
Hillcourt Rd SE22 . . . . 162 B5
Hill Cres Harrow HA1 . . . 43 A4
Kingston u T KT5 . . . . . 198 B4
North Cheam KT4 . . . . 216 C6
Totteridge N20 . . . . 13 D2
Hillcrest
Camberwell SE24 . . . . . 139 B1
Highgate N6 . . . . 49 A2
Notting Hill W11 . . . . 244 C5
Southgate N21 . . . . 16 C4
Hill Crest DA15 . . . . . . 168 B4
Hillcrest Ave
Edgware HA8 . . . . 26 D6
Pinner HA5 . . . . 40 D5
Temple Fortune NW11 . . 47 B4
Hillcrest Cl
Beckenham BR3 . . . . . . 207 B3
Forest Hill SE26 . . . . . 184 A6
Hillcrest Ct
Brondesbury NW2 . . . . . 69 A3
8 Edgware HA8 . . . . . . 26 D5
Lewisham SE6 . . . . 164 B4
Sutton SM2 . . . . 218 B2
Hillcrest Gdns
Dollis Hill NW2 . . . . 68 A5
Hendon N3 . . . . 47 A5
Hinchley Wood KT10 . 212 D5
Hillcrest Hts W5 . . . . . . 88 A3
Hillcrest Rd
Acton W3 . . . . 110 D5
Chingford E17 . . . . 36 B1
Ealing W5 . . . . 88 A2
Grove Pk BR1 . . . . 187 A6
Loughton IG10 . . . . 21 D5
Woodford E18 . . . . 37 A1
Hillcrest View BR3 . . . 207 B3
Hillcroft Ave HA5 . . . . . 41 B3
Hillcroft Coll KT6 . . . 198 A3
Hillcroft Cres
Ealing W5 . . . . 87 D1
Ruislip HA4 . . . . 62 D5
Wembley HA9 . . . . 66 B4
Hillcroft Rd E6 . . . . . . 100 D2
Hillcroome Rd SM2 . . 218 B2
Hillcross Ave SM4 . . . . 201 A4
Hillcross Prim Sch
SM4 . . . . 201 B5
Hill Ct Barnet EN4 . . . . 2 C1
Ealing W5 . . . . 88 B3
Hampstead NW3 . . . . . . 70 C4
8 Norbiton KT2 . . . . 176 D3
Northolt UB5 . . . . 63 C3
Putney SW15 . . . . 156 D6
14 Surbiton KT6 . . . . . 198 A4
Wembley HA0 . . . . 65 A4
9 Wimbledon SW19 . . 179 A4
Hilldale Rd SM1 . . . . . 217 B4
Hilldown Ct SW16 . . . . 182 A3
Hilldown Rd
Hayes BR2 . . . . 208 D1
South Norwood SW16 182 B3
Hill Dr London NW9 . . . . 45 A1
Thornton Heath
SW16 . . . . 204 B6
Hilldrop Cres N7 . . . . . . 71 D3
Hilldrop La N7 . . . . 71 D3
Hilldrop Rd
Bromley BR1 . . . . 187 B4
Kentish Town N7 . . . . . . 71 D3
Hill End
Orpington BR6 . . . . . . 227 D6
Shooters Hill SE18 . . . 144 C4
Hillersdon Ave
Barnes SW13 . . . . 134 A3
Edgware HA8 . . . . 26 B5
Hillersdon Ho SW1 . . 258 C2
Hillery Cl SE17 . . . . . . 262 D3
Hill Farm Rd W10 . . . . . 90 D2
Hillfield Ave
Colindale NW9 . . . . 45 C5
Hornsey N8 . . . . 50 A5
Mitcham SM4 . . . . 202 C4
Wembley HA0 . . . . 66 B1
Hillfield Cl HA2 . . . . 42 A5
Hillfield Ct NW3 . . . . 70 C3
Hillfield Ho N5 . . . . 73 A3
Hillfield La S WD23 . . . . . 8 D5
Hillfield Lo SW17 . . . . 180 D5
Hillfield Mans NW3 . . . 70 C3
Hillfield Par SM4 . . . . . 202 B3
Hillfield Park Mews
N10 . . . . 49 B5
Hillfield Pk
London N10 . . . . 49 B5
Southgate N21 . . . . 16 C2
Hillfield Rd
Hampton TW12 . . . . . . 173 B2
West Hampstead NW6 . 69 C3
Hillgate Pl
Balham SW12 . . . . 159 B4
Kensington
W8 . . . . . . 113 C5 245 A4
Hillgate St W8 . . . . 245 A4
Hill Gate Wlk N6 . . . . . . 49 C3
Hill Gr TW13 . . . . 151 B2
Hill Ho Southall UB1 . . . . 85 C1
Stanmore HA7 . . . . 9 A1
Upper Clapton E5 . . . . . . 52 B1
Woolwich SE28 . . . . . . 123 C5
Hill House Ave HA7 . . . 24 D3
Hill House Cl N21 . . . . . 16 C4
Hill House Dr TW12 . . 173 C2
Hill House International
Jun Sch
SW1 . . . . 114 D3 257 D5
Hill House Rd SW16 . . 182 B5
Hilliard Ct SM6 . . . . . . 219 D2
Hilliard Ho 15 E1 . . . . . 118 B5
Hilliard's Ct E1 . . . . . . 118 C5
Hillier Cl EN5 . . . . 13 D5
Hillier Gdns CR0 . . . . . 220 C3
Hillier Ho 1 NW1 . . . . . 71 D1
Hillier Lo TW12 . . . . . . 174 B5
Hillier Pl KT9 . . . . 213 D2
Hillier Rd SW11 . . . . . 158 D5
Hilliers Ave UB8 . . . . . . 82 C4
Hillier's La CR0, SM6 . 220 A5
HILLINGDON 82 D5
Hillingdon Ave
TW19 . . . . 148 A3
Hillingdon Circus
UB10 . . . . 60 D2
HILLINGDON HEATH . 82 D2
Hillingdon Hill UB10 . . 82 B4
Hillingdon Hospl UB8 82 B2
Hillingdon Manor Sch
UB8 . . . . 82 D2
Hillingdon Manor Upper
Sch UB3 . . . . 83 D1
Hillingdon Par 6
UB10 . . . . 82 D3
Hillingdon Prim Sch
UB10 . . . . 82 D4
Hillingdon Rd UB10 . . . 82 A5
Hillingdon St SE17 . . . 138 D6
Hillingdon Sta UB10 . . . 60 D3
Hillington Gdns IG8 . . . 37 D1
Hill La HA4 . . . . 39 A1
Hill Lo SW11 . . . . 136 B1
Hillman Cl UB8 . . . . 60 A3
Hillman Dr 12 NW10 . . . 90 C3
Hillman St E8 . . . . 74 B2
Hillmarton Rd N7 . . . . . 72 A3
Hillmead Dr SW9 . . . 138 D1
Hill Mead Prim Sch 23
SW9 . . . . 138 D1
Hillmont Rd KT10 . . . . 212 C5
Hillmore Ct SE13 . . . . . 142 B2
Hillmore Gr SE26 . . . . 185 A5
Hill Rd
Carshalton SM5 . . . . . 218 C2
Finchley N10 . . . . 30 D2
Harrow HA1 . . . . 43 A4
Mitcham CR4 . . . . 181 B3
Pinner HA5 . . . . 41 A3
St John's Wood
NW8 . . . . 92 A5 229 B3
Sutton SM1 . . . . 217 D3
Wembley HA0 . . . . 65 B5
Hillreach SE7, SE18 . . . 122 B1
Hillrise KT12 . . . . 193 D2
Hill Rise
East Finchley NW11 . . . . 47 D5
Enfield N9 . . . . 18 B5
Forest Hill SE23 . . . . . . 162 B3
Greenford UB6 . . . . 86 A6
Hinchley Wood KT10 . . 213 B6
Richmond TW10 . . . . . 153 D6
Ruislip HA4 . . . . 39 B1
Hillrise Mans N19 . . . . . 50 A2
Hillrise Rd N19 . . . . 50 A2
Hillsboro Rd SE22 . . . . 161 C6
Hillsborough Ct 13
NW6 . . . . 91 D6
Hillsde 6 SM1 . . . . 218 B3
Hillsgrove Cl DA16 . . . 146 C5
Hillsgrove Prim Sch
DA16 . . . . 146 C5
Hillside Barnet EN5 . . . . 14 A6
Crouch End N8 . . . . 49 D3
Greenwich SE10 . . . . . . 142 B5
Kingsbury NW9 . . . . 45 B5
Stonebridge NW10 . . . . 89 B6
Wimbledon SW19 . . . 178 D4
Hill Side EN5 . . . . 14 A6
Hillside Ave
London N11 . . . . 30 D4
Wembley HA9 . . . . 66 B4
Woodford IG8 . . . . 37 C5
Hillside Cl
Merton SM4 . . . . 201 A5
St John's Wood NW8 . . . 91 D5
Woodford IG8 . . . . 37 C5
Hillside Cres
Enfield EN2 . . . . 5 B5

Hillside Cres *continued*
Harrow HA2 ... 42 A1
Northwood HA6 ... 22 A2
Hillside Ct
Hampstead NW3 ... 69 D3
7 Kingston u T KT2 ... 176 D3
Hillside Dr HA8 ... 26 C5
Hillside Gdns
Chipping Barnet EN5 ... 1 A1
Edgware HA8 ... 26 B6
Friern Barnet N11 ... 31 C4
Harrow HA3 ... 44 A2
Highgate N6 ... 49 B3
Northwood HA6 ... 22 B2
Streatham SW2 ... 160 C2
Wallington SM6 ... 219 C1
Walthamstow E17 ... 54 B6
Hillside Glen CR0 ... 220 D4
Hillside Gr
Hendon NW7 ... 28 A3
Southgate N14 ... 15 D4
Hillside Ho CR0 ... 220 D4
Hillside Jun & Inf Schs
HA6 ... 22 A3
Hillside La BR2 ... 224 D6
Hillside Mans EN5 ... 1 B1
Hillside Rd
Beckenham BR2 ... 208 D6
Belmont SM2 ... 217 B1
Croydon CR0 ... 220 D4
Ealing W5 ... 88 A2
Northwood HA6, HA5 ... 22 B3
Southall UB1 ... 85 C3
South Tottenham N15 ... 51 C3
Streatham SW2 ... 160 C2
Surbiton KT5 ... 198 C4
Hillside Rise HA6 ... 22 A3
Hillsleigh Rd
W14 ... 113 B5 244 D4
Hillsley DA14 ... 190 A6
Hills Mews 2 W5 ... 110 A6
Hills Pl W1 ... 239 A1
Hill's Rd IG9 ... 21 B3
Hill St
Mayfair W1 ... 115 B5 248 C4
Richmond TW10 ... 153 D6
Hillstone Ct 5 E3 ... 97 D3
Hillstowe St E5 ... 74 C5
Hilltop 7 E17 ... 53 D6
Hill Top Cheam SM3 ... 201 B2
East Finchley NW11 ... 47 D5
Hilltop Ave NW10 ... 67 A1
Hilltop Ct
12 London SW18 ... 136 B1
South Hampstead NW8 70 A1
South Norwood SE19 ... 183 B2
Hilltop Gdns
Hendon NW4 ... 28 B1
Orpington BR6 ... 227 C6
Hilltop Ho 7 N6 ... 49 D2
Hilltop Rd NW6 ... 69 C1
Hilltop Way HA7 ... 9 A1
Hillview SW20 ... 178 B3
Hill View
Mitcham CR4 ... 204 A5
Primrose Hill NW1 ... 230 D6
Hillview Ave HA3 ... 44 A4
Hillview Cl Pinner HA5 . 23 B4
Wembley HA9 ... 66 B6
Hillview Cres
Orpington BR6 ... 211 D1
Redbridge IG1 ... 56 B3
Hillview Ct SE19 ... 183 C6
Hill View Dr
Bexley DA16 ... 145 C3
Woolwich SE28 ... 123 C5
Hillview Gdns
Harrow HA2 ... 41 C5
Hendon NW4 ... 46 D5
Hill View Gdns NW9 ... 45 B4
Hillview Rd
Carshalton SM1 ... 218 B5
Chislehurst BR7 ... 188 D6
Mill Hill NW7 ... 28 D6
Pinner HA5 ... 23 B4
Hill View Rd
Claygate KT10 ... 213 A1
Orpington BR6 ... 227 D6
Twickenham TW1 ... 153 A5
Hillway Highgate N6 ... 71 A6
London NW9 ... 45 C1
Hill Wood Ho NW1 ... 232 C3
Hillworth 7 BR3 ... 185 D1
Hillworth Rd SW2 ... 160 C4
Hillyard Rd W7 ... 86 C2
Hillyard St SW9 ... 138 C4
Hillyfield E17 ... 35 A1
Hillyfield Cl E9 ... 75 A3
Hillyfield Prim Sch
E17 ... 53 A6
Hilly Fields Cres
SE4 ... 141 C2
Hilly Mead SW19 ... 179 A3
Hilsea Point 7
SW15 ... 156 B3
Hilsea St E5 ... 74 C4
Hilton Ave N12 ... 30 B5
Hilton Ho
4 Ealing W13 ... 87 C1
12 Finchley N2 ... 30 B1
Lower Holloway N7 ... 72 A4
9 Nunhead SE4 ... 140 D1
Hilversum Cres 10
SE22 ... 161 C6
Himley Rd SW17 ... 180 D4
Hinchlay Manor
KT10 ... 212 D5
Hinchley Cl KT10 ... 212 D5
Hinchley Dr KT10 ... 212 D5
Hinchley Way KT10 ... 213 A5
HINCHLEY WOOD ... 212 D6
Hinchley Wood Prim Sch
KT10 ... 213 A6
Hinchley Wood Sch
KT10 ... 213 A6
Hinchley Wood Sta
KT10 ... 212 D5
Hinckley Rd SE15 ... 140 A1
Hind Ct EC4 ... 241 B1
Hinde Mews W1 ... 238 B2
Hindes Rd HA1 ... 42 C4
Hinde St W1 ... 93 A1 238 B2
Hind Gr E14 ... 97 C1
Hindhead Cl UB8 ... 82 D2
Hindhead Gdns UB5 ... 85 A6
Hindhead Gn WD19 ... 22 C5
Hindhead Point 6
SW15 ... 156 B3
Hindhead Way SM6 ... 220 A3
Hind Ho
13 Deptford SE14 ... 140 D6
Islington N7 ... 72 C4
Hindhurst Ct NW9 ... 45 A5
Hindle Ho E8 ... 73 D3
Hindley Ho N7 ... 72 B5
Hindlip Ho SW8 ... 269 C1
Hindmans Rd SE22 ... 162 A6
Hindmans Way RM9 ... 103 B3
Hindmarsh Cl E1 ... 118 A6
Hindrey Rd E5 ... 74 B3
Hindsley's Pl SE23 ... 162 C2
Hines Ct HA1 ... 43 A4
Hinkler Rd HA3 ... 43 D6
Hinksey Path SE2 ... 124 D3
Hinstock NW6 ... 91 D6
Hinstock Rd SE18 ... 145 A5
Hinton Ave TW4 ... 128 D1
Hinton Cl SE9 ... 166 A3
Hinton Ct 3 E10 ... 75 D6
Hinton Rd
Brixton SE24 ... 138 D2
Edmonton N18 ... 33 C6
Wallington SM6 ... 219 C2
Hippisley Ct TW7 ... 130 D2
Hippodrome Mews
W11 ... 244 A5
Hippodrome Pl W11 244 B5
Hirst Cres HA9 ... 66 A5
Hirst Ct SW1 ... 258 C1
Hispano Mews 17 EN3 ... 7 C6
Hitcham Rd E17 ... 53 B2
Hitchcock Cl TW17 ... 192 B6
Hitchin Sq E3 ... 97 A5
Hithe Gr 15 SE16 ... 118 C3
Hitherbroom Rd
UB3 ... 106 A6
Hither Farm Rd SE3 ... 143 C2
Hitherfield Prim Sch
SW16 ... 160 C2
Hitherfield Rd
Dagenham RM8 ... 81 A6
Streatham SW16,
SW27 ... 160 C1
HITHER GREEN ... 164 C5
Hither Green La
SE13 ... 164 B5
Hither Green Prim Sch
SE13 ... 164 B5
Hither Green Sta
SE13 ... 164 C5
Hitherlands SW12 ... 159 B2
Hitherwell Dr HA3 ... 24 B2
Hitherwood Ct SE21 183 D6
Hitherwood Dr SE19 183 D6
Hive Cl WD23 ... 8 B2
Hive Rd WD23 ... 8 C2
Hive Wood Ho E7 ... 77 A2
HM Prison Wormwood
Scrubs W12 ... 90 A1
HMS Belfast★ SE1 ... 253 B4
Hoadly Rd SW16 ... 159 D2
Hobart Cl
East Barnet N20 ... 14 C2
Hayes UB4 ... 84 D3
Hobart Ct Harrow HA1 . 42 C2
Woodford IG8 ... 36 D6
Hobart Dr UB4 ... 84 D3
Hobart Gdns CR7 ... 205 B6
Hobart Ho 24 KT6 ... 198 A4
Hobart La UB4 ... 84 D3
Hobart Pl
Richmond TW10 ... 154 B4
Westminster
SW1 ... 115 B3 258 C6
Hobart Rd
Dagenham RM9 ... 80 D4
Hayes UB4 ... 84 D3
North Cheam KT4 ... 216 B5
Hobbayne Prim Sch
W7 ... 86 D1
Hobbayne Rd W7 ... 86 B1
Hobbes Wlk SW15 ... 156 B6
Hobb's Ct SE1 ... 253 D2
Hobbs Gn N2 ... 48 A6
Hobbs Mews IG3 ... 79 D6
Hobbs' Pl N1 ... 95 C6
Hobbs Rd 5 SE27 ... 183 A6
Hobby St EN3 ... 18 D6
Hobday St E14 ... 97 D1
Hobhouse Ct SW1 ... 249 D5
Hobill Wlk KT5 ... 198 B3
Hoblands End BR7 ... 189 C4
Hobsons Pl 7 E1 ... 96 A2
Hobury St
SW10 ... 136 B6 266 C5
Hockenden La BR5,
BR8 ... 191 D1
Hocker St 41 E2 ... 95 D4
Hockett Cl SE8 ... 119 B2
Hockington Ct 7
EN5 ... 13 D6
Hockley Ave E6 ... 100 A5
Hockley Ct 2 E18 ... 37 A2
Hockley Ho 4 E9 ... 74 C2
Hockley Mews IG11 ... 101 C5
Hockliffe Ho 5 W10 ... 90 C2
Hockney Ct 1 SE16 ... 118 B1
Hockworth Ho 7
N16 ... 51 C1
Hocroft Ave NW2 ... 69 B5
Hocroft Ct NW2 ... 69 B5
Hocroft Rd NW2 ... 69 B5
Hocroft Wlk NW2 ... 69 B5
Hodder Dr UB6 ... 86 D5
Hoddesdon Rd DA17 ... 125 C1
Hodford Lo NW11 ... 69 C6
Hodford Rd NW11 ... 47 B1
Hodgkins Cl SE28 ... 124 D6
Hodgkins Mews HA7 ... 25 B5
Hodister Cl 26 SE5 ... 139 A5
Hodnet Gr SE16 ... 118 C2
Hodson Cl HA2 ... 63 B5
Hodson Pl EN3 ... 7 C5
Hoecroft Ct EN3 ... 6 C5
Hoe La EN1 ... 6 B5
Hoe St E17 ... 53 C4
Hoffman Gdns CR2 ... 222 B1
Hoffman Sq N1 ... 235 D2
Hofland Rd
W14 ... 113 A3 254 A6
Hogan Mews W2 ... 236 C4
Hogan Way E5 ... 74 A6
Hogarth Ave TW15 ... 171 A4
Hogarth Bsns Pk
W4 ... 133 C6
Hogarth Cl Ealing W5 ... 88 A2
Newham E16 ... 99 D2
Hogarth Cres
Mitcham SW19 ... 180 B2
Thornton Heath CR0 ... 205 A2
Hogarth Ct
8 Camden Town
NW1 ... 71 C1
City of London EC3 ... 253 B6
Hogarth Ct *continued*
Dulwich SE19 ... 183 D6
Heston TW5 ... 129 A5
24 Whitechapel E1 ... 96 A1
Hogarth Gdns TW5 ... 129 C5
Hogarth Hill NW11 ... 47 B5
Hogarth Ho
Enfield EN1 ... 18 A6
12 Northolt UB5 ... 84 D5
1 Sutton SM1 ... 218 B3
Westminster SW1 ... 259 D3
6 West Norwood
SE27 ... 183 A6
Hogarth Ind Est
NW10 ... 90 A3
Hogarth La W4 ... 133 C6
Hogarth Pl SW5 ... 255 C3
Hogarth Rd
Barking RM8 ... 80 B3
Earl's Ct
SW5 ... 113 D2 255 C3
Edgware HA8 ... 26 C1
Hogarth Roundabout
W4 ... 133 C6
Hogarth's House★
W4 ... 133 C6
Hogarth Way TW12 ... 174 A2
Hogsmill Way KT19 ... 215 A4
Holbeach Cl 8 NW9 ... 27 C2
Holbeach Gdns
DA15 ... 167 D5
Holbeach Mews 1
SW12 ... 159 B3
Holbeach Prim Sch
SE6 ... 163 C4
Holbeach Rd SE6 ... 163 D4
Holbeck Row SE15 ... 140 A5
Holbein Ho
Chelsea SW1 ... 258 A2
10 Stanmore HA7 ... 25 C5
Holbein Mews
SW1 ... 115 A1 258 A2
Holbein Pl
SW1 ... 115 A2 258 A3
Holberry Ho 5
SE21 ... 183 C6
Holberton Gdns
NW10 ... 90 B4
HOLBORN ... 94 C2
Holborn EC1 ... 94 C2 241 B3
Holborn Cir
EC1 ... 94 C2 241 B3
Holborn Coll SE18 ... 121 D2
Holborn Ho 1 W12 ... 90 B1
Holborn Pl WC1 ... 240 C3
Holborn Rd E13 ... 99 B3
Holborn Sta
WC1 ... 94 B2 240 C3
Holborn Viaduct
EC1 ... 94 D2 241 C3
Holborn Way CR4 ... 180 D1
Holbrook Cl Enfield EN1 . 6 A5
Highgate N19 ... 49 B1
Holbrook Ct W7 ... 108 C6
Holbrooke Ct N7 ... 72 A4
Holbrooke Pl 25
TW10 ... 153 D6
Holbrook Ho
Acton W3 ... 89 B2
Chislehurst BR7 ... 189 B2
5 Streatham SW2 ... 160 B3
Holbrook La BR7 ... 189 B3
Holbrook Rd E15 ... 98 D5
Holbrook Way BR2 ... 210 B4
Holburne Cl SE3 ... 143 C4
Holburne Gdns SE3 ... 143 D4
Holburne Rd SE3 ... 143 D4
Holcombe Hill NW7 ... 12 A1
Holcombe Ho SW9 ... 138 A2
Holcombe Pl SE4 ... 141 A2
Holcombe Rd
Ilford IG1 ... 56 C2
Tottenham Hale N17 ... 52 A6
1 Tottenham N17 ... 51 D6
Holcombe St W6 ... 112 B2
Holcote Cl DA17 ... 125 A3
Holcroft Ct W1 ... 239 A4
Holcroft Ho
Battersea SW11 ... 136 B2
Lewisham SE10 ... 142 A4
Holcroft Rd E9 ... 74 C1
Holden Ave
North Finchley N12 ... 29 D5
Welsh Harp NW9 ... 45 A1
Holdenby Rd SE4 ... 163 A6
Holden Cl RM8 ... 80 B5
Holden Ho
12 Deptford SE8 ... 141 C5
Islington N1 ... 235 A5
Holden Hts N12 ... 13 D1
Holdenhurst Ave N12 . 30 A3
Holden Lo N11 ... 31 C5
Holden Point E15 ... 76 B2
Holden Rd
East Barnet N11 ... 15 B1
London N12 ... 29 D6
Holden St SW11 ... 137 A3
Holdernesse Rd
Isleworth TW7 ... 131 A4
6 Upper Tooting
SW17 ... 159 A2
Holderness Ho SE5 ... 139 C2
Holderness Way
SE27 ... 182 D5
Holders Hill Ave NW4 . 46 D6
Holders Hill Cres
NW4 ... 28 D1
Holders Hill Dr NW4 ... 28 D1
Holders Hill Gdns
NW4 ... 29 A1
Holders Hill Par NW7 . 29 A2
Holders Hill Rd
Church End NW4,
NW7 ... 29 A2
Hendon NW4 ... 28 D1
Holdsworth Ho 5
SW2 ... 160 C4
Holford Ho
6 Bermondsey
SE16 ... 118 B2
Finsbury WC1 ... 233 D2
Holford Pl WC1 ... 233 D2
Holford Rd NW3 ... 70 A5
Holford St WC1 ... 234 A2
Holford Yd WC1 ... 234 A3
Holgate Ave SW11 ... 136 B2
Holgate Ct HA8 ... 26 B6
Holgate Gdns RM10 ... 81 C2
Holgate Rd RM10 ... 81 C3
Holgate St SE7 ... 121 D3
Holkham Ho 6 EN5 ... 1 A2
Hollam Ho N8 ... 50 B5
Holland Ave
Belmont SM2 ... 217 C1
Wimbledon SW20 ... 177 D2
Holland Cl
Coney Hall BR2 ... 224 D6
New Barnet EN5 ... 14 B4
Stanmore HA7 ... 25 B5
Holland Ct
Ashford TW15 ... 170 B4
Hendon NW7 ... 28 A4
6 Walthamstow E17 ... 54 A5
Holland Dr SE23 ... 163 A1
Holland Gdns
Brentford TW8 ... 132 A6
Kensington W14 ... 254 B6
Holland Gr SW9 ... 138 C5
Holland Ho E4 ... 36 A6
Holland House Sch
HA8 ... 26 D6
Holland Park
W11 ... 113 B5 244 C3
Holland Park Ave
Ilford IG3 ... 57 D4
Notting Hill
W11 ... 113 A5 244 B3
Holland Park Ct W14 244 B2
Holland Park Gdns
W14 ... 113 A4 244 A2
Holland Park Mews
W11 ... 113 B5 244 C3
Holland Park Pre Prep
Sch W14 ... 113 B3 254 C5
Holland Park Rd
W14 ... 113 B3 254 D5
Holland Park Rdbt
W12 ... 112 D4
Holland Park Sch
W8 ... 113 B4 244 D2
Holland Park Sta
W11 ... 113 B5 244 C3
Holland Pas N1 ... 235 A6
Holland Pl W8 ... 245 C2
Holland Rd
Croydon SE25 ... 206 A4
Newham E15 ... 98 C4
Wallend E6 ... 78 C1
Wembley HA0 ... 65 D2
West Kensington
W14 ... 113 A3 254 B6
Willesden Green NW10 90 B5

Holland Rise Ho SW9 ... 270 D3
Holland St
Kensington W8 ... 113 C4 245 B2
Lambeth SE1 116 D5 251 D4
Hollands The
Feltham TW13 ... 172 D6
New Malden KT4 ... 199 D1
Holland Villas Rd W14 ... 113 A4 244 A1
Holland Way BR2 ... 224 D6
Holland Wlk
Kensington W14 ... 113 B4 244 D1
Stanmore HA7 ... 25 A5
Upper Holloway N19 ... 49 D1
Hollar Rd N16 ... 73 D5
Hollen St W1 ... 239 C2
Holles Cl TW12 ... 173 C5
Holles Ho 8 SW9 ... 138 C3
Holles St W1 .. 93 B1 238 D2
Holley Rd W3 ... 111 C4
Hollickwood Ave N12 . 30 D4
Hollickwood JMI Sch N10 ... 31 B3
Holliday Sq 6 SW11 . 136 B2
Hollidge Way RM10 ... 81 D1
Hollies Ave DA15 ... 167 D3
Hollies Cl
South Norwood SW16 ... 182 C4
Twickenham TW1 ... 152 D2
Hollies End NW7 ... 28 B5
Hollies Rd W5 ... 109 C2
Hollies The
Harrow HA3 ... 43 A5
Oakleigh Pk N20 ... 14 B3
Upper Tooting SW12 . 159 C2
9 Wanstead E11 ... 55 A4
Wood Green N11 ... 31 D4
Hollies Way 1 SW12 ... 159 A4
Holligrave Rd BR1 ... 187 A2
Hollingbourne Ave DA7 ... 147 B4
Hollingbourne Gdns W13 ... 87 B2
Hollingbourne Rd SE24 ... 161 A6
Hollingsworth Ct 7 KT6 ... 197 D2
Hollingsworth Rd CR0 ... 222 B2
Hollington Cres KT3 199 D3
Hollington Ct BR7 .. 188 D4
Hollington Rd
Newham E6 ... 100 B4
Tottenham N17 ... 34 A1
Hollingworth Cl KT8 . 195 B5
Hollingworth Rd BR2, BR5 ... 210 D2
Hollins Ho N7 ... 72 A4
Hollisfield WC1 ... 233 B1
Hollman Gdns SW16 182 D4
Holloway Cl UB7 ... 104 A1
Holloway La UB7 ... 104 B1
Holloway Rd
Leyton E11 ... 76 B5
Lower Holloway N7 ... 72 B4
Newham E6 ... 100 B4
Upper Holloway N19 ... 71 D6
Holloway Road Sta N7 ... 72 B3
Holloway Sch N7 ... 71 D3
Holloway St TW3 ... 129 D2
Hollow Combe SE20 . 184 B6
Hollowfield Wlk UB5 .. 63 A2
Hollow The IG8 ... 36 D6
Holly Ave London N2 ... 47 D6
Stanmore HA7 ... 26 A1
Walton-on-T KT12 ... 194 D1
Hollybank Cl TW12 ... 173 C5
Holly Berry La 8 NW3 ... 70 A4
Hollybrake Cl BR7 ... 189 B3
Hollybush Cl
Harrow HA3 ... 24 C2
Wanstead E11 ... 55 A4
Hollybush Gdns E2 ... 96 B4
Hollybush Hill E11 ... 54 D3
Holly Bush Hill 4 NW3 ... 70 A4
Hollybush Ho 23 E2 ... 96 B4
Holly Bush La TW12 .. 173 C3
Hollybush Pl E2 ... 96 B4
Hollybush Rd KT2 ... 176 A4
Hollybush St E13 ... 99 B4
Holly Bush Steps 6 NW3 ... 70 A4
Holly Bush Vale 10 NW3 ... 70 A4
Holly Cl
Beckenham BR3 ... 208 A5
Buckhurst Hill IG9 ... 21 D1
Feltham TW13 ... 173 A5
Wallington SM6 ... 219 B1
Willesden NW10 ... 67 C1
Holly Cottage Mews UB8 ... 82 C2
Holly Cotts KT7 ... 197 A1
Holly Cres
Beckenham BR3 ... 207 B4
Chingford IG8 ... 36 B3
Hollycroft Ave
Child's Hill NW3 ... 69 C5
Wembley HA9 ... 66 B5
Hollycroft Cl
Harmondsworth UB7 ... 126 C6
South Croydon CR2 .. 221 C3
Hollycroft Gdns UB7 . 126 C6
Holly Ct
16 Belmont SM2 ... 217 C1
Catford SE6 ... 164 A1
4 Sidcup DA14 ... 190 B6
South Tottenham N15 ... 51 C5
Hollydale Cl UB5 ... 63 D4
Hollydale Dr BR2 ... 226 B5
Hollydale Prim Sch 7 SE15 ... 140 C3
Hollydale Rd SE15 ... 140 C3
Hollydene
Bromley BR1 ... 186 D2
Hither Green SE13 ... 164 B5
5 Peckham SE15 ... 140 B4
Hollydown Way E11 ... 76 B5
Holly Dr E4 ... 19 D4
Holly Farm Rd UB2 ... 107 A1
Hollyfield Ave N11 ... 30 D5
Hollyfield Rd KT5 ... 198 B2
Hollyfield Sch & Sixth Form Ctr The KT6 . 198 A4
Holly Gdns UB7 ... 104 B4
Holly Gr
Kingsbury NW9 ... 45 A2
Peckham SE15 ... 140 A3
Pinner HA5 ... 23 A2
Hollygrove WD23 ... 8 B4
Hollygrove Cl TW3 ... 129 B1
Hollyhedge Ho SE3 ... 142 B3
Holly Hedge Terr SE13 ... 164 B6
Holly Hill
Hampstead NW3 ... 70 A4
Southgate N21 ... 16 B5
Holly Hill Rd DA8, DA17 ... 125 D1
Holly Ho
Brentford TW8 ... 131 C6
Ilford IG3 ... 58 A1
Holly House (Private) Hospl IG9 ... 21 B2
Holly Lo
Cottenham Pk SW20 ... 178 B1
Harrow HA1 ... 42 B4
Kensington W8 ... 245 A2
Southgate N21 ... 16 C3
4 Wimbledon SW19 . 179 A4
Holly Lodge
Lewisham SE13 ... 142 B1
Southall UB2 ... 107 B2
Holly Lodge Gdns N6 . 49 A1
Holly Lodge Mans N6 . 71 A6
Hollymead SM5 ... 218 D5
Holly Mews SW10 ... 256 B1
Holly Mount NW3 ... 70 A4
Hollymount Cl 9 SE10 ... 142 A4
Hollymount Sch SW20 ... 178 C2
Holly Park Est N4 ... 50 B2
Holly Park Gdns N3 ... 47 C6
Holly Park JMI Sch N11 ... 31 A5
Holly Park Rd
Ealing W7 ... 108 D5
Friern Barnet N11 ... 31 A5
Holly Pk
East Finchley N3 ... 47 C6
Hornsey N4 ... 50 B2
Holly Pl NW3 ... 70 A4
Holly Rd
6 Chiswick W4 ... 111 B2
Hampton TW12 ... 174 A4
Hounslow TW3 ... 129 D1
Leytonstone E11 ... 54 D2
Twickenham TW1 ... 153 A3
Holly St E8 ... 73 D1
Holly Terr N6 ... 49 A1
Hollytree Cl SW19 ... 156 D3
Holly Tree Ho SE4 ... 141 B2
Holly Tree Lo EN2 ... 4 D3
Hollyview Cl NW4 ... 46 A3
Holly Village N6 ... 71 B6
Holly Way CR4 ... 203 D6
Holly Wlk Enfield EN2 ... 5 B2
Hampstead NW3 ... 70 A4
Hollywood Ct W5 ... 110 B6
Hollywood Gdns UB4 .. 84 B1
Hollywood Lofts E1 . 243 C5
Hollywood Mews SW10 ... 266 A6
Hollywood Rd
Chelsea SW10 ... 136 A6 266 A6
Highams Pk E4 ... 35 A5
Hollywood Way IG8 ... 36 B4
Holman Ho 2 E2 ... 96 D4
Holman Hunt Ho W14 ... 254 A1
Holman Rd
London SW11 ... 136 B3
West Ewell KT19 ... 215 A3
Holmbank Dr TW17 .. 193 C5
Holmbridge Gdns EN3 . 6 D1
Holmbrook NW1 ... 232 B3
Holmbrook Dr NW4 ... 46 D4
Holmbury Cl WD23 ... 8 C2
Holmbury Ct
Mitcham SW19 ... 180 C3
Upper Tooting SW17 . 158 D1
Holmbury Gdns UB3 105 D5
Holmbury Gr CR0 ... 223 B1
Holmbury Ho SW9 ... 160 D6
Holmbury Manor 9 DA14 ... 190 A6
Holmbury Pk BR7 ... 188 A3
Holmbury View 2 E5 . 52 B1
Holmbush Ct NW4 ... 46 D4
Holmbush Rd SW15 .. 157 A5
Holmcote Gdns N5 ... 73 A3
Holmcroft Ho 10 E17 .. 53 D5
Holmcroft Way BR2 .. 210 B4
Holm Ct SE12 ... 165 B1
Holmdale Gdns NW4 .. 46 D4
Holmdale Rd
Chislehurst BR7 ... 189 A5
South Hampstead NW6 69 C3
Holmdale Terr N15 ... 51 C3
Holmdene N12 ... 29 D5
Holmdene Ave
Harrow HA2 ... 41 D6
Hendon NW7 ... 28 A4
Herne Hill SE24 ... 161 A6
Holmdene Cl BR3 ... 186 A1
Holmdene Ct BR1 ... 210 A6
Holmead Rd SW6 ... 135 D5 265 D3
Holme Ct 12 TW7 ... 131 A2
Holmefield Ct 4 NW3 ... 70 C2
Holmefield Ho W10 ... 91 A3
Holme Lacey Rd SE12 ... 164 D5
Holmeleigh Ct EN3 ... 6 C1
Holme Rd E6 ... 100 A6
Holmes Ave
Mill Hill NW7 ... 29 A5
Walthamstow E17 ... 53 B6
Holmes Cl SE22 ... 140 A1
Holmes Ct
Chingford E4 ... 20 B2
18 South Acton W4 .. 111 A3
18 South Lambeth SW4 ... 138 A3
Holmesdale Ave SW14 ... 132 D1
Holmesdale Cl SE25. 205 D6
Holmesdale Ho 12 NW6 ... 91 C6
Holmesdale Rd
Bexley DA7 ... 146 D3
Highgate N6 ... 49 B2
Richmond TW9 ... 132 B4
South Norwood SE25. 205 C5
Teddington TW11 ... 175 C4
Holmesdale Rd *continued*
Thornton Heath CR0 .. 205 B4
Holmesley Rd SE23 .. 163 A5
Holmes Pl SW10 ... 266 B6
Holmes Rd
Kentish Town NW5 ... 71 B3
Merton SW19 ... 180 A3
Twickenham TW1 ... 152 D2
Holmes Terr SE1 ... 251 A2
Holmeswood 1 SM2 ... 217 D1
Holmeswood Ct 3 N22 ... 32 C1
Holme Way HA7 ... 24 D4
Holmewood Gdns SW2 ... 160 B4
Holmewood Rd
South Norwood SE25 ... 205 C6
Streatham SW2 ... 160 B4
Holmfield Ave NW4 ... 46 D4
Holmfield Ho E17 ... 54 B5
Holm Gr UB10 ... 60 C1
Holmhurst
London SE13 ... 164 B5
Wimbledon SW19 ... 178 C3
Holmhurst Rd DA17 . 125 D1
Holmlea Ct CR0 ... 221 B4
Holmleigh Prim Sch N16 ... 51 C1
Holmleigh Rd N16 ... 51 C1
Holm Oak Cl SW15 ... 157 B5
Holmoaks Ho BR3 ... 186 A1
Holmsbury Ho 6 N7 ... 71 D3
Holmsdale Ho
6 London N11 ... 31 B6
24 Poplar E14 ... 119 D6
Holmshaw Cl SE26 ... 185 A6
Holmside Ct SW12 ... 159 A5
Holmside Rd SW12 ... 159 A5
Holmsley Cl KT3 ... 199 D2
Holmsley Ho SW15 .. 155 D4
Holmstall Ave HA8 ... 27 A1
Holmstall Par HA8 ... 27 A1
Holm Wlk SE3 ... 143 A3
Holmwood 2 KT5 ... 198 B3
Holmwood Cl
Cheam SM2 ... 216 D1
Harrow HA2 ... 42 A6
Northolt UB5 ... 63 D2
Holmwood Ct
Kingston u T KT3 ... 199 B6
Sidcup DA14 ... 189 D5
3 Stamford Hill N16 ... 51 D2
Holmwood Gdns
London N3 ... 29 C1
Wallington SM6 ... 219 B2
Holmwood Gr NW7 ... 27 B5
Holmwood Mans W3 ... 110 C5
Holmwood Rd
Chessington KT9 ... 214 A3
Ilford IG3 ... 79 C6
Holne Chase
London N2 ... 48 A3
Morden SM4 ... 201 C3
Holne Lo N6 ... 49 C3
Holness Rd E15 ... 76 D2
Holocaust Meml Gdn* W2 ... 114 D4 247 D2
Holroyd Rd SW15 ... 156 C6
Holsgrove Ct W3 ... 111 C5
Holstein Way 6 DA18 ... 125 A3
Holst Mans SW13 ... 134 C5
Holstock Rd IG1 ... 79 A6
Holsworth Cl HA2 ... 42 A4
Holsworthy Ho 49 E3 .. 97 D4
Holsworthy Sq WC1 . 240 D5
Holsworthy Way KT9 ... 213 C3
Holt Cl London N10 ... 49 A5
Sidcup DA14 ... 191 A6
Woolwich SE28 ... 124 C6
Holt Ct SE10 ... 142 A6
Holt Ho SW2 ... 160 C5
Holtoake Ct 1 W5 ... 87 C3
Holtoake Ho 3 W5 ... 87 C3
Holton St E1 ... 96 D3
Holt Rd Newham E16 .. 122 A5
Wembley HA0 ... 65 C5
Holt The
Morden SM4 ... 201 C5
Wallington SM6 ... 219 C4
Holtwhite Ave EN2 ... 5 A3
Holtwhite's Hill EN2 ... 4 D4
Holwell Pl HA5 ... 41 A5
Holwood Park Ave BR2, BR6 ... 226 B4
Holwood Pl 7 SW4 . 137 D1
Holybourne Ave SW15 ... 156 A4
Holy Cross Prep Sch KT2 ... 177 A3
Holy Cross Prim Sch SW6 ... 135 C4 265 A2
Holy Cross RC Prim Sch SE6 ... 164 A3
Holy Cross Sch The 4 KT3 ... 199 C4
Holy Family RC Prim Sch
Kidbrooke SE9 ... 143 C1
23 Poplar E14 ... 119 C6
Holy Family Tech Coll E17 ... 54 A5
Holy Ghost RC Prim Sch 4 SW12 ... 159 A4
Holyhead Cl Bow E3 ... 97 C4
3 Newham E6 ... 100 B2
Holyhead Ct KT1 ... 197 D5
Holy Innocents RC Prim Sch BR6 ... 227 D5
Holyoake Ct SE16 ... 119 B4
Holyoake Wlk
Ealing W5 ... 87 C3
East Finchley N2 ... 48 A6
Holyoak Rd SE11 ... 116 D2 261 D3
Holyport Rd SW6 ... 134 D5
Holyrood Ave HA2 ... 63 B4
Holyrood Gdns HA8 ... 26 D1
Holyrood Ho N4 ... 51 A1
Holyrood Mews
6 Greenwich SE7 ... 121 A1
10 Newham E16 ... 121 A5
Holyrood Rd EN5 ... 14 B5
Holyrood St SE1 ... 117 C5 253 A3
Holy Trinity CE Jun Sch 1 SM6 ... 219 C4
Holy Trinity CE Prim Sch
Belgravia SW1 ... 115 A2 258 A4
Dalston E8 ... 73 D2
East Finchley N2 ... 48 B6
10 Forest Hill SE26 .. 162 C2
10 Hampstead NW3 ... 70 A2
Richmond TW10 ... 132 C1
Streatham SW2 ... 160 B4
Wimbledon SW19 ... 179 D4
Holy Trinity Coll Prep Sch BR1 ... 187 C2
Holy Trinity Lamorbey CE Prim Sch DA15 ... 168 A3
Holy Trinity & Saint Silas CE Prim Sch 22 NW1 ... 71 B1
Holywell Cl
35 Bermondsey SE16 ... 118 B1
2 Greenwich SE3 ... 143 A6
Stanwell TW19 ... 148 A3
Holywell La EC2 ... 243 B6
Holywell Lo EN2 ... 4 B5
Holywell Row EC2 ... 95 C3 243 A5
Holywell Way TW19 .. 148 A3
Homan Ct N12 ... 30 A6
Homan Ho 6 SW4 .. 159 D4
Homebush Ho E4 ... 19 D4
Homecedars Ho WD23 . 8 B3
Homecherry Ho 3 IG10 ... 21 D6
Home Cl
Carshalton SM5 ... 218 D6
Northolt UB5 ... 85 B4
Homecoppice Ho 1 BR1 ... 186 D3
Homecroft Rd
Forest Hill SE26 ... 184 C5
Tottenham N22 ... 33 A2
Homecross Ho 7 W4 ... 111 B2
Home Ct KT6 ... 197 D4
Homedale Ho SM1 .. 217 D4

Home Farm Cl
Thames Ditton KT7 196 D2
Upper Halliford TW17 193 C5
Home Farm Cotts BR5 190 D2
Homefarm Rd W7 86 D1
Homefield SM4 201 C5
Home Field EN5 13 B6
Homefield Ave IG2 57 C4
Homefield Cl
Hayes UB4 84 D3
Willesden NW10 67 A2
Homefield Ct NW4 46 C5
Homefield Gdns
London N2 48 B6
Mitcham CR4, SW19 180 B1
Homefield Ho SE23 162 D1
Homefield Pk SM1, SM2 217 D2
Homefield Pl 4 SW19 178 D5
Homefield Prep Sch SM1 217 C3
Homefield Rd
Bromley BR1 187 C2
Burnt Oak HA8 27 B4
Chiswick W4 111 D1
Walton-on-T KT12 195 A2
Wembley HA0 65 B4
Wimbledon SW19 179 A4
Homefield St 14 N1 95 C5
Homefirs Ho HA9 66 B5
Homeheather Ho 5 IG4 56 B4
Homelands Dr SE19 183 C3
Home Lea BR6 227 D3
Homeleigh Ct 8 SW16 160 A1
Homeleigh Rd SE15 162 D6
Homemead SW12 159 B2
Home Mead HA7 25 C2
Homemead Rd
Bromley BR2 210 B4
Wallington CR0 203 C3
Home Office SW1 259 D5
Home Park Rd SW19 157 B1
Home Park Terr KT1 175 D1
Home Park Wlk KT1 197 D5
Home Rd SW11 136 C3
Homer Dr E14 119 C2
Homer Rd
Croydon CR0 206 D3
Homerton E9 75 A2
Homer Row W1 237 B3
Homersham Rd KT1 176 D1
Homer St W1 92 C2 237 B3
HOMERTON 74 D1
Homerton Ct 2 EN4 14 D3
Homerton Gr E9 74 D3
Homerton High St E9 74 D3
Homerton Rd E9 75 B3
Homerton Row E9 74 C3
Homerton Sta E9 74 D2
Homerton Terr E9 74 C2
Homerton University Hospl E9 74 D3
Homesdale Cl E11 55 A4
Homesdale Rd
Bromley BR1, BR2 209 C6
Orpington BR5 211 C2
Homesfield NW11 47 C4
Homes Of Rest (CE Temperance Society) IG1 79 B5
Homestall Rd SE22 162 C6
Homestead Ct EN5 13 C6
Homestead Gdns KT10 212 C3
Homestead Paddock N14 15 B6
Homestead Pk NW2 67 D5
Homestead Rd
Dagenham RM8 81 B6
Fulham SW6 135 B5 264 D3
Homesteads The BR3 185 D4
Homestead The N11 31 B6
Homewalk Ho 1 SE26 184 C6
Homewaters Ave TW16 171 D2
Homewillow Cl N21 16 D5
Homewood Cl TW12 173 B4
Homewood Cres BR7 189 C4
Homewood Gdns SE25 205 C4
Homewoods 2 SW12 159 C4
Homildon Ho 10 SE26 162 A1
Homington Ct KT2 176 A3
Honduras St EC1 242 A6
Honeybourne Rd NW6 69 D3
Honeybourne Way BR5 211 B1
Honeybrook Rd SW12, SW4 159 C4
Honey Cl RM10 81 D2
Honeycroft Hill UB10 60 A1
Honeyden Rd DA14 191 A4
Honeyfield N4 72 C6
Honey Hill UB10 60 B1
Honey La EC2 242 B1
Honey Lane Ho SW10 265 D6
Honeyman Cl NW6 68 D1
Honeypot Bsns Ctr HA7 26 A2
Honeypot Cl NW9 44 B5
Honeypot La
Stanmore HA3, HA7, NW9 44 B6
Stanmore HA7 25 D3
Honeysett Rd 3 N17 33 D1
Honeysuckle Cl UB1 107 A6
Honeysuckle Ct
Ilford IG1 78 D2
2 Lee SE12 165 A4
6 Sutton SM2 217 D2
Honeysuckle Gdns CR0 206 D1
Honeywell Jun & Inf Schs 3 SW11 158 D5
Honeywell Rd SW11 158 D5
Honeywood Ho 5 SE15 140 A4
Honeywood Mus★ SM5 218 D4
Honeywood Rd
Harlesden NW10 89 D5
Isleworth TW7 131 A1
Honeywood Wlk SM5 218 D4
Honister Cl HA7 25 B2
Honister Gdns HA7 25 B2
Honister Pl HA7 25 B2
Honiton Gdns
Edgware NW7 28 D3
1 Nunhead SE15 140 C3
Honiton Ho 29 SE5 139 A3
Honiton Rd
Bexley DA16 145 D3
Kilburn NW6 91 B5
Honley Rd SE6 163 D4
Honnor Gdns TW7 130 B3
HONOR OAK 162 C6
Honor Oak Park Sta SE23 162 D5
Honor Oak Pk SE23 162 D5
Honor Oak Rd SE23 162 C4
Honor Oak Rise SE23 162 C5
Honwell Ho 24 W2 91 C2
Hood Ave
East Barnet N14 15 B5
Mortlake SW14 155 A6
Hood Cl CR0 204 D1
Hoodcote Gdns N21 16 D4
Hood Ct N7 72 B5
Hood Ho 17 SE5 139 B5
Hood Lo E11 77 B6
Hood Rd SW20 177 D3
HOOK 214 A4
Hook KT6 214 A5
Hooke Ct SE10 142 A4
Hooke Ho 32 E3 97 A5
Hooker's Rd E17 52 D6
Hook Farm Rd BR2 209 D4
Hookham Ct SW8 269 C2
Hook Ho 9 SW27 182 D5
Hooking Gn HA2 41 D4
Hook La DA16 146 A1
Hook Lane Prim Sch DA16 146 A2
Hook Rd KT19, KT17 215 A1
Hook Rise N
Surbiton KT6 214 A5
Tolworth KT6 214 D6
Hook Rise S KT6, KT9 214 D6
Hook Rise S Ind Est KT6 214 C5
Hook Rise South KT6 214 A5
Hook Rise South Ind Pk KT6 214 C5
Hooks Cl SE15 140 B4
Hookstone Way IG8 37 D3
Hook The EN5 14 B5
Hook Underpass KT6 214 A5
Hook Wlk HA8 27 A4
Hooper Dr UB8 82 D2
Hooper Ho 9 SW18 157 B6
Hooper Rd E16 99 A1
Hooper's Ct SW1 247 C1
Hooper's Mews 4 W3 111 A5
Hooper St E1 96 A1
Hoop La NW11 47 C2
Hoover Ho 5 SE6 186 A6
Hope Cl
2 Brentford TW8 110 A1
Canonbury N1 73 A2
Dagenham RM6 58 D5
Grove Pk SE12 165 B1
Sutton SM1 218 A3
1 Woodford IG8 37 C4
Hope Ct 1 SE1 118 A1
Hopedale Rd SE7 143 B6
Hopefield 3 W7 108 D5
Hopefield Ave NW6 91 A5
Hope Gdns 10 W3 110 D4
Hope Pk BR1 186 D3
Hopes Cl TW5 129 C6
Hope St SW11 136 B2
Hopetown St E1 243 D3
Hopewell Sch IG11 79 B2
Hopewell St SE5 139 B5
Hop Gdns WC2 250 A5
Hopgood St 5 W12 112 C5
Hopkins Cl N10 31 A3
Hopkins Ho 17 E14 97 C1
Hopkins Mews E15 98 D6
Hopkinson Ho 1 SW11 137 A3
Hopkinson's Pl NW1 231 A6
Hopkins Rd E10 53 D2
Hopkins St W1 93 D1 239 C1
Hopley Ho W13 109 B6
Hoppers Rd N21 16 C2
Hoppett Rd E4 20 C2
Hopping La N1 72 D2
Hoppingwood Ave KT3 199 C6
Hoppner Rd UB4 83 B5
Hop St SE10 120 D2
Hopton Ct BR2 209 A1
Hopton Gdns KT3 200 A3
Hopton Ho 5 SW9 138 D3
Hopton Par 2 SW16 182 A5
Hopton Rd
Streatham SW16 182 A5
Woolwich SE18 122 D3
Hopton's Gdns SE1 251 D4
Hopton St SE1 116 D5 251 D4
Hoptree Cl N12 29 D6
Hopwood Cl SW17 158 A1
Hopwood Rd SE17 139 B6
Hopwood Wlk E8 74 A1
Horace Rd
Forest Gate E7 77 B4
Ilford IG6 57 A6
Kingston u T KT1 198 B6
Horatio Ho
13 Haggerston E2 95 D5
4 Merton SW19 179 D3
Horatio Pl
9 Canary Wharf E14 120 A5
Merton SW19 179 C2
Horatio St 11 E2 95 D5
Horatius Way CR0 220 B2
Horbury Cres W11 113 C6 245 A5
Horbury Lo TW12 173 C3
Horbury Mews W11 113 B6 244 D5
Horder Rd SW6 135 A4 264 B1
Hordle Prom E 15 SE15 139 D5
Hordle Prom N 4 SE15 139 D5
Hordle Prom S 7 SE15 139 D5
Horizon Bldg 22 E14 119 C6
Horizon Ind Est SE15 140 A5
Horizon Sch N16 73 C4
Horle Wlk SE5 138 D3
Horley Cl DA6 169 C6
Horley Rd SE9 188 A6
Hormead Rd W9 91 B3
Hornbeam Cl
Barking IG11 102 B3
Buckhurst Hill IG9 21 D1
Edgware NW7 11 D1
Ilford IG1 79 B3
Lambeth SE11 261 A4
Northolt UB5 63 B3
Hornbeam Cres TW8 131 B5
Hornbeam Gdns KT3 200 A3
Hornbeam Gr E4 20 D1
Hornbeam Ho
1 Buckhurst Hill IG9 21 D1
2 Maitland Pk NW3 70 D2
6 Penge SE20 184 D3
6 Sidcup DA15 168 A1
Hornbeam La E4 20 C6
Hornbeam Rd
Buckhurst Hill IG9 21 D1
Hayes UB4 84 C2
Hornbeam Sq 8 E3 97 B6
Hornbeams Rise N11 31 A4
Hornbeam Terr SM5 202 C1
Hornbeam Way BR2 210 C3
Hornblower Cl 2 SE16 119 A2
Hornbuckle Cl HA2 64 B6
Hornby Cl NW3 70 B1
Hornby Ho
6 Kennington SE11 138 C6
13 Richmond TW10 153 C1
Horncastle Cl SE12 165 A4
Horncastle Rd SE12 165 A4
Hornchurch N17 33 B1
Hornchurch Cl KT2 175 D6
Horndean Cl 3 SW15 156 A3
Horne Ho 4 SE18 144 A4
Horner Ct E11 76 B5
Horne Rd TW17 192 C5
Horner Hos 18 N1 95 C6
Horner La 3 CR4 180 B1
Horne Way SW15 134 C3
Hornfair Rd SE7 143 D5
Horniman Dr SE23 162 C4
Horniman Grange 7 SE23 162 C3
Horniman Mus & Gdns★ SE23 162 B3
Horniman Prim Sch SE23 162 B3
Horning Cl SE9 188 A6
Horn La Acton W3 89 A1
Greenwich SE10 121 A2
Woodford IG8 37 A3
Horn Link Way SE10 121 A2
Horn Park Cl SE12 165 B6
Horn Park La SE12 165 B5
Horn Park Prim Sch SE12 165 B4
Hornsby House Sch 7 SW12 159 A3
Horns Croft IG11 79 C1
Hornscroft Cl IG11 79 C1
Horns End Pl HA5 40 C4
HORNSEY 50 A5
Hornsey La N6 49 C2
Hornsey Lane Gdns N6 49 C2
Hornsey Park Rd N8 50 B6
Hornsey Rd N7, N19 72 B6
Hornsey Rise Gdns N19 50 A2
Hornsey Sch for Girls N8 50 B4
Hornsey St N7 72 B3
Hornsey Sta N8 50 B5
HORNSEY VALE 50 B4
Hornshay St SE15 140 C6
Horns Rd IG2, IG6 57 A4
Hornton Ct W8 245 B1
Hornton Pl W8 245 B1
Hornton St W8 113 C4 245 B2
Horrocks Ho SW15 156 B6
Horsa Rd
Eltham SE12 165 C4
Erith DA8 147 D5
Horsebridge Cl RM9 103 A6
Horsecroft Rd HA8 27 B3
Horse & Dolphin Yd W1 249 D6
Horse Fair KT1 175 D1
Horseferry Pl SE10 142 A6
Horseferry Rd
Limehouse E14 119 A6
Westminster SW1 115 D2 259 D4
Horseferry Rd Est SW1 259 C5
Horse Guards Ave SW1 116 A5 250 A3
Horse Guards Par★ SW1 115 D5 249 D3
Horse Guards Rd SW1 115 D4 249 D2
Horse Leaze E6 100 C1
Horsell Rd
Islington N5 72 C3
St Paul's Cray BR5 190 B2
Horselydown La SE1 117 D5 253 C3
Horselydown Mans SE1 253 C2
Horsemongers Mews SE1 252 B1
Horsenden Ave UB6 64 D3
Horsenden Cres UB6 64 D3
Horsenden La N UB6 64 D1
Horsenden La S UB6 87 A6
Horsenden Prim Sch UB6 64 C2
Horsendon Ho 11 N7 71 D3
Horseshoe Cl
Cubitt Town E14 120 A1
Dollis Hill NW2 68 B6
Horse Shoe Cres UB5 85 C5
Horseshoe Dr UB8 82 C1
Horse Shoe Gn SM1 217 D6
Horseshoe La
Barnet N20 12 D3
Enfield EN2 5 A2
Horse Yd N1 234 D6
Horsfeld Gdns 1 SE9 166 A6
Horsfeld Rd SE9 165 D6
Horsfield Ho 13 N1 73 A1
Horsford Rd SW2 160 B6
Horsham Ave N12 30 C5
Horsham Ct N17 34 A2
Horsham Rd
Bexley DA6 169 C6
East Bedfont TW14 149 A5
Horsley Ct SW1 259 D3
Horsley Dr
Kingston u T KT2 175 D5
New Addington CR0 224 A1
Horsley Ho 11 SE4 140 D1
Horsley Rd
Bromley BR1 187 B2
Chingford E4 20 A2
Horsley St 3 SE17 139 B6
Horsman Ho SE5 139 A6
Horsman St SE5 139 A6
Horsmonden Cl BR6 211 D2
Horsmonden Rd SE4 163 B5
Horston Ho N4 51 A2
Hortensia Ho SW10 266 A4
Hortensia Rd SW10 136 A5 266 A4
Horticultural Pl 6 W4 111 B1
Horton Ave NW2 69 A4
Horton Bridge Rd UB7 104 B5
Horton Cl UB7 104 B5
Horton Ctry Pk KT19 214 C1
Horton Ho
13 Deptford SE15 140 C6
South Lambeth SW8 270 C4
West Kensington W14 254 A1
Horton Ind Pk UB7 104 B5

Horton La KT19 . . . . . 215 A1
Horton Par UB7 . . . . . 104 A5
Horton Rd Hackney E8 . 74 B2
Yiewsley UB7 . . . . 104 B5
Horton Road Ind Est
UB7 . . . . 104 B5
Horton St SE13 . . . . . 141 D2
Horton Way CR0 . . . . 206 D4
Hortus Rd
Chingford E4 . . . . 20 A2
Southall UB2 . . . . 107 B4
Horwood Ho
24 Bethnal Green E2 . . . 96 B4
Marylebone NW8 . . . . 237 B6
Hosack Rd SW12,
SW17 . . . . 159 A2
Hoser Ave SE12 . . . . . . 165 A2
Hosier La EC1 . 94 D2 241 D3
Hoskins Cl UB3 . . . . . 105 D1
Hoskin's Cl E16 . . . . 99 C1
Hoskins St SE10 . . . . . 120 B1
Hospital Bridge Rd
TW2 . . . . 151 D3
Hospital Bridge Rdbt
TW2 . . . . 151 D2
Hospital of the Holy
Trinity (Almshouses) 5
CR0 . . . . 221 A6
Hospital Rd
Hounslow TW3 . . . . . . 129 C2
Leytonstone E10, E11 . . 54 B4
Hospital Way SE13 . . . 164 B4
Hospl for Tropical
Diseases
NW1 . . . . 93 C3 239 B5
Hospl of St John & St
Elizabeth
NW8 . . . . 92 B5 229 C3
Hotham Cl KT8 . . . . . . 195 C6
Hotham Prim Sch
SW15 . . . . 134 D1
Hotham Rd
Merton SW19 . . . . 180 A3
Putney SW15 . . . . 134 C2
Hotham Road Mews 12
SW19 . . . . 180 A3
Hotham St E15 . . . . 98 C6
Hothfield Pl SE16 . . . . 118 C3
Hotspur Ind Est N17 . . 34 B4
Hotspur Rd UB5 . . . . . . 85 C5
Hotspur St
SE11 . . . . 116 C1 261 A2
Houblon Rd TW10 . . . . 154 A6
Houghton Cl
10 Dalston E8 . . . . 73 D2
Hampton TW12 . . . . . . 173 A4
Houghton Rd N15 . . . . . 51 D5
Houghton Sq SW9 . . . 138 A2
Houghton St WC2 . . . 240 D1
Houlder Cres CR0 . . . 220 D2
Houndsden Rd N21 . . . 16 C5
Houndsditch
EC3 . . . . 95 C1 243 B2
Houndsfield Prim Sch
N9 . . . . 18 B4
Houndsfield Rd N9 . . . 18 B4
HOUNSLOW 129 C3
Hounslow Ave TW3 . 151 D6
Hounslow Bsns Pk
TW3 . . . . 129 D1
Hounslow Central Sta
TW3 . . . . 129 D2
Hounslow Ctr The
TW3 . . . . 129 D2
Hounslow East Sta
TW3 . . . . 130 A3
Hounslow Gdns
TW3 . . . . 151 D6
Hounslow Heath Jun &
Inf Schs TW4 . . . . . . 129 A2
Hounslow Heath Nature
Reserve TW4 . . . . . . 151 A5
Hounslow Manor Sch
TW3 . . . . 130 A2
Hounslow Rd
Feltham TW14 . . . . 150 B4
Hanworth TW13 . . . . . 151 A2
Twickenham TW2,
TW3 . . . . 152 A5
Hounslow Sta TW3 . . 151 D6
Hounslow Town Prim
Sch TW3 . . . . 130 B2
Hounslow Urban Farm★
TN14 . . . . 150 A6
HOUNSLOW WEST . 128 D2
Hounslow West Sta
TW3 . . . . 129 A3
Household Cavalry Mus★
SW1 . . . . 250 A3
Houseman Way 20
SE5 . . . . 139 B5
House Mill The★ E3 . . . 98 A4
Houses of Parliament★
SW1 . . . . 116 A3 260 B6
Houston Ct 3 CR0 . . . 205 C1
Houston Pl KT10 . . . . . 196 C1
Houston Rd
Forest Hill SE23 . . . . . 163 A1
Thames Ditton KT6 . . . . 197 B3
Houstoun Ct TW5 . . . . 129 B5
Hove Ave E17 . . . . 53 B4
Hoveden Rd NW2 . . . . . 69 A3
Hove Gdns SM1 . . . . . 201 D1
Hovenden Ho 6
SE21 . . . . 183 C6
Hoveton Rd SE28 . . . . 102 C1
Howard Ave DA5 . . . . . 168 C4
Howard Bldg SW8 . . . 268 C5
Howard Cl Acton W3 . . . 88 D1
Ashford TW16 . . . . . . 171 D4
Brunswick Pk N11 . . . . . 15 A2
Bushey WD23 . . . . 8 C4
Cricklewood NW2 . . . . 69 A4
Hampton TW12 . . . . . 174 A4
Howard Ct
12 Barking IG11 . . . . . 101 B6
Beckenham BR3 . . . . . 186 A1
Lewisham SE10 . . . . . 142 A4
Peckham SE15 . . . . . . 140 A2
Howard Ho
6 Brixton SW9 . . . . . 138 C2
14 Deptford SE8 . . . . . 141 B6
Fitzrovia W1 . . . . 238 D5
Penge SE20 . . . . 184 C2
6 Upper Clapton E5 . . . 74 C6
Howard Mans E17 . . . . . 53 D6
Howard Mews N5 . . . . . 72 D4
Howard Prim Sch
CR0 . . . . 221 A4
Howard Rd
Barking IG11 . . . . 101 B6
Canonbury N16 . . . . . . 73 B4
Cricklewood NW2 . . . . . 68 D4
Croydon SE25 . . . . 206 A3
Ilford IG1 . . . . 78 D4
Isleworth TW7 . . . . . . 130 D2
Leyton E11 . . . . 76 C5
Newham E6 . . . . 100 B5
New Malden KT3 . . . . 199 D5
Penge SE20 . . . . 184 C2
Plaistow BR1 . . . . 187 A3
Southall UB1 . . . . 85 D1
South Tottenham N15 . . . 51 C3
Surbiton KT5 . . . . 198 B3
Walthamstow E17 . . . . . 53 D6
Howards Cl HA5 . . . . . . 22 B1
Howards Crest Cl
BR3 . . . . 186 A1
Howard's La SW15 . . . 134 C1
Howard's Rd E13 . . . . . . 99 A4
Howard St KT7 . . . . . . 197 B3
Howard Way EN5 . . . . . 12 D6
Howard Wlk N2 . . . . 48 B5
Howarth Rd SE2 . . . . . 124 A2
Howberry Cl HA8 . . . . . 25 D4
Howberry Rd
South Norwood CR7 . . . 183 B1
Stanmore HA7, H8 . . . . . 25 D4
Howbury Rd SE15 . . . . 140 C2
Howcroft Cres N3 . . . . . 29 C3
Howcroft Ho 3 E3 . . . . . 97 B4
Howcroft La UB6 . . . . . . 86 B4
Howden Cl SE28 . . . . . 124 D6
Howden Ct SE25 . . . . . 183 D1
Howden Rd SE25 . . . . 183 D1
Howden St SE15 . . . . . 140 A2
Howell Cl RM6 . . . . 58 D4
Howell Ct 2 E10 . . . . . . 53 D2
Howell Ho 5 N7 . . . . 71 D3
Howell Wlk SE1 . . . . . 261 D3
Howe Lo TW1 . . . . 153 A4
Howerd Way SE18 . . . 144 A4
Howes Cl N3 . . . . 47 C6
Howeth Ct 7 N11 . . . . . 31 A4
Howfield Pl N17 . . . . . . 51 D6
Howgate Rd SW14 . . . 133 B2
Howick Mans SE18 . . . 122 A3
Howick Pl
SW1 . . . . 115 C3 259 B5
Howie St
SW11 . . . . . . 136 C5 267 A3
Howitt Cl
6 Maitland Pk NW3 . . . 70 C2
Stoke Newington N16 . . 73 C4
Howitt Rd NW3 . . . . 70 C2
Howland Ho 9
SW16 . . . . 160 A1
Howland Mews E
W1 . . . . 239 B4
Howland St
W1 . . . . 93 C2 239 B4
Howland Way SE16 . . 119 A4
Howletts La HA4 . . . . . . 39 A3
Howletts Rd SE24 . . . . 161 A5
Howley Pl W2 . 92 A2 236 B4
Howley Rd CR0 . . . . . . 221 A5
Howmic Ct 1 TW1 . . . 153 C5
Howsman Rd SW13 . . 134 A6
Howson Rd SE4 . . . . . . 141 A1
Howson Terr TW10 . . . 154 A5
How's St E2 . . . . 95 D5
Howton Pl WD23 . . . . 8 B3
HOXTON 95 C5
Hoxton Mkt 10 N1 . . . . . 95 C4
Hoxton Point EC1 . . . . . 95 C4
Hoxton Sq N1 . . . . 95 C4
Hoxton St N1 . . . . 95 C5
Hoxton Sta E2 . . . . 95 D5
Hoylake Cres UB10 . . . . 60 D6
Hoylake Gdns
Mitcham CR4 . . . . 203 C6
Ruislip HA4 . . . . 40 B1
South Oxhey WD19 . . . . 22 D6
Hoylake Rd W3 . . . . 89 C1
Hoyland Cl 4 SE15 . . . 140 B5
Hoyle Rd SW17 . . . . . . 180 C5
Hoy St E16 . . . . 98 D1
Hubbard Dr KT9 . . . . . 213 D2
Hubbard Rd SE27 . . . . 183 A6
Hubbards Cl UB8 . . . . . 82 D1
Hubbard St E15 . . . . 98 C6
Hub Buildings The 4
SW12 . . . . 159 B3
Hub E15 E15 . . . . 97 D5
Huberd Ho SE1 . . . . . 262 D6
Hubert Gr SW9 . . . . . . 138 A2
Hubert Ho NW8 . . . . . 237 A5
Hubert Rd E6 . . . . 99 D4
Hucknall Ct NW8 . . . 236 C6
Huddart St 6 E3 . . . . . . 97 B2
Huddleston Cl E2 . . . . . 96 C5
Huddlestone Rd
Forest Gate E7 . . . . 76 D4
Willesden NW2 . . . . 68 B2
Huddleston Rd N7 . . . . 71 C4
Hudson 27 NW9 . . . . . . 27 D2
Hudson Cl
Newham E15 . . . . 99 A6
15 Shepherd's Bush
W12 . . . . 112 B6
Hudson Ct
Croydon SE25 . . . . 206 A5
1 Isle Of Dogs E14 . . 119 C1
4 Merton SW19 . . . . . 179 D2
Hudson Ho
Chelsea SW10 . . . . . . 266 A4
5 Notting Hill W11 . . . . 91 A1
Hudson Pl SE18 . . . . . . 123 A1
Hudson Rd Erith DA7 . 147 B4
Harlington UB7 . . . . . 127 B6
Hudsons Ho N1 . . . . . 235 D1
Hudson's Pl
SW1 . . . . 115 C2 259 A4
Hudson Way N9 . . . . . . 18 C2
Huggin Ct EC4 . . . . . . 252 B6
Huggin Hill EC4 . . . . . 252 B6
Huggins Ho 9 E3 . . . . . 97 C4
Huggins Pl SW2 . . . . . 160 B3
Hughan Rd E15 . . . . 76 B3
Hugh Astor Ct SE1 . . . 261 D6
Hugh Clark Ho 13
W13 . . . . 109 A5
Hugh Dalton Ave
SW6 . . . . 264 C5
Hughenden Ave HA3 . . 43 B4
Hughenden Gdns
UB5 . . . . 84 C4
Hughenden Ho NW8 237 A6
Hughenden Rd KT4 . . 200 A2
Hughendon EN5 . . . . 1 D1
Hughendon Terr E15 . . 76 A4
Hughes Cl N12 . . . . 30 A5
Hughes Ho
26 Bethnal Green E2 . . . 96 C4
Camberwell SE5 . . . . . 139 A4
15 Deptford SE8 . . . . . 141 C6
Newington SE17 . . . . . 261 D3
Hughes Mans E1 . . . . . . 96 A3
Hughes Rd
Ashford TW15 . . . . . . 171 A4
Hayes UB3 . . . . 106 B6
Hughes Terr 6 E16 . . . 98 D2
Hughes Wlk CR0 . . . . . 205 A2
Hugh Gaitskell Cl
SW6 . . . . 264 C5
Hugh Gaitskell Ho
Stoke Newington N16 . . 73 D6
Willesden NW10 . . . . . . 67 D1
Hugh Herland KT1 . . . 198 A6
Hugh Mews SW1 . . . . 258 D3
Hugh Morgan Ho 5
SW4 . . . . 137 D2
Hugh Myddelton Prim
Sch EC1 . . . . . 94 C4 234 B1
Hugh Platt Ho 29 E2 . . 96 B5
Hugh St SW1 . 115 B2 258 D3
Hugo Ho SW1 . . . . . . 257 D6
Hugon Rd SW6 . . . . . . 135 D2
Hugo Rd N19 . . . . 71 C4
Huguenot Ct 9 E1 . . . . 96 A2
Huguenot Pl
London SW18 . . . . 158 A6
Spitalfields E1 . . . . . . 243 D4
Huguenot Sq SE15 . . . 140 B2
Hullbridge Mews N1 235 C6
Hull Cl SE16 . . . . 118 D5
Hull Ct SE5 . . . . 139 B3
Hull Pl E16 . . . . 123 A5
Hull St EC1 . . . . 235 A1
Hulme Pl SE1 . . . . 252 B1
Hulse Ave IG11 . . . . 79 C2
Humber Ct W7 . . . . 86 B1
Humber Dr W10 . . . . . . 90 D3
Humber Rd
Dollis Hill NW2 . . . . 68 B6
Greenwich SE3 . . . . . 142 D6
Humberstone Rd E13 . 99 C4
Humberton Cl E9 . . . . . 75 A3
Humber Trad Est
NW2 . . . . 68 B6
Humbolt Rd
W6 . . . . 135 A6 264 A5
Hume Ct N1 . . . . 72 D1
Hume Ho 14 W11 . . . 112 D5
Humes Ave W7 . . . . . 108 D4
Hume Terr E16 . . . . 99 B1
Hume Way HA4 . . . . 40 A3
Humphrey Ct SW11 . 266 D1
Humphrey St
SE1 . . . . 117 D1 263 C2
Humphries Cl RM9 . . . . 81 B4
Humphry Ho 10
SW15 . . . . 156 D6
Hundred Acre NW9 . . . 27 D1
Hungerdown E4 . . . . . . 20 A3
Hungerford Bridge
WC2 . . . . 250 C4
Hungerford Ho SW1 269 B6
Hungerford La WC2 . 250 B4
Hungerford Prim Sch 19
N7 . . . . 71 D2
Hungerford Rd
12 Camden Town N7 . . . 71 D2
Lower Holloway N7 . . . . 72 A3
Hungerford St 21 E1 . . . 96 B1
Hunsdon Cl RM9 . . . . . . 81 A2
Hunsdon Ho E5 . . . . 74 B5
Hunsdon Rd SE14 . . . 140 D5
Hunslett St 26 E2 . . . . . 96 C5
Hunstanton Ho NW1 237 B4
Hunston Rd SM4 . . . . 201 D1
Hunt Cl W11 . . . . 112 D5
Hunt Ct London N14 . . . . 15 B4
10 Northolt UB5 . . . . 84 D5
Hunter Cl
Borehamwood WD6 . . . . 11 A6
Borough The SE1 . . . . 262 D5
Upper Tooting SW12 . 159 A3
3 Wallington SM6 . . . 220 A1
Huntercombe-
Roehampton Hospl The
SW15 . . . . 156 A4
Huntercrombe Gdns
WD19 . . . . 22 C5
Hunter Ct
8 London SE5 . . . . 139 B1
27 Streatham SW2 . . . 160 C4
11 Wanstead E11 . . . . . 55 A4
Hunter Ho
Bloomsbury WC1 . . . . 240 B6
Feltham TW14 . . . . . . 150 A3
Lambeth SE1 . . . . 251 D1
South Lambeth SW8 . 269 D3
Hunter Ho *continued*
1 Tufnell Pk N19 . . . . . . 71 C5
West Brompton SW5 . 255 B1
Hunterian Mus★
WC2 . . . . 94 B1 240 D2
Hunter Lo 9 W9 . . . . . . 91 C2
Hunter Rd
South Norwood CR7 . . 205 B6
Wimbledon SW20 . . . 178 C2
Hunters Ct 5 TW9 . . 153 D6
Hunters Gr
Harrow HA3 . . . . 43 C5
Hayes UB3 . . . . 106 A4
Hunter's Gr BR6 . . . . . 227 A4
Hunters Hall Prim Sch
RM10 . . . . 81 D3
Hunters Hall Rd
RM10 . . . . 81 C3
Hunters Hill HA4 . . . . . . 62 D5
Hunters Lo
9 Edgware HA8 . . . . . . 26 D5
10 Sidcup DA15 . . . . . 168 A1
Hunters Mdw SE19 . . 183 C6
Hunters Rd
Chessington KT9 . . . . 214 A4
Ilford IG1 . . . . 78 D3
Hunters Sq RM10 . . . . . 81 C4
Hunter St
WC1 . . . . 94 A3 240 B6
Hunters The 2 BR3 . . . 186 A2
Hunters Way
Enfield EN2 . . . . 4 C4
South Croydon CR0 . . 221 C4
Hunter Wlk
Borehamwood WD6 . . . . 11 B6
Newham E13 . . . . 99 A5
Huntingdon Cl
Mitcham CR4,
SW16 . . . . 204 A5
Northolt UB5 . . . . 63 C2
Huntingdon Ct
3 Barnet EN5 . . . . 1 B2
Mortlake SW14 . . . . . 133 A2
Huntingdon Gdns
Chiswick W4 . . . . 133 A5
North Cheam KT4 . . . . 216 C5
Huntingdon Ho SW5 255 B4
Huntingdon Rd
East Finchley N2 . . . . . . 48 C6
Edmonton N9 . . . . 18 C3
Huntingdon St
Canning Town E16 . . . . . 98 D1
Islington N1 . . . . 72 B1
Huntingfield CR0 . . . . 223 B1
Huntingfield Rd
SW15 . . . . 156 A6
Huntingford Ho
SW15 . . . . 134 C3
Hunting Gate Cl EN2 . . . 4 C2
Hunting Gate Dr
KT9 . . . . 214 A1
Hunting Gate Mews
Sutton SM1 . . . . 217 D5
Twickenham TW2 . . . . 152 C3
Huntings Farm IG1 . . . 79 C6
Huntings Rd RM10 . . . . 81 C2
Huntington Ho NW2 . . 68 C2
Huntley Cl TW19 . . . . . 148 A4
Huntley Ho 7 SE21 . . . 183 C6
Huntley St
WC1 . . . . 93 D3 239 C5
Huntley Way SW20 . . . 178 A1
Huntly Dr N3 . . . . 29 C4
Huntly Rd SE25 . . . . . . 205 C5
Hunton St E1 . . . . 96 A2
Hunt Rd UB2 . . . . 107 C3
Hunts Cl SE3 . . . . 143 A3
Hunt's Ct WC2 . . . . . . 249 D5
Huntshaw Ho 37 E3 . . . 97 D4
Hunt's La E15 . . . . 98 A5
Huntsmans Cl TW13 . . 172 B6
Huntsman St SE17 . . 263 A3
Hunts Mead EN3 . . . . 6 D2
Hunts Medde Cl
BR7 . . . . 188 B3
Huntsmoor Rd KT19 . . 215 B3
Huntspill St SW17 . . . . 158 A1
Hunts Slip Rd SE21 . . . 161 C2
Huntsworth Ct SE6 . . . 163 C3
Huntsworth Mews
NW1 . . . . 92 D3 237 C5
Huon Ct N20 . . . . 14 C2
Hurdwick Ho NW1 . . 232 A4

Hurdwick Pl NW1 ... 232 A4
Hurleston Ho 11 SE8 ... 119 B1
Hurley Cres SE16 ... 118 D4
Hurley Ct 1 W5 ... 87 C1
Hurley Ho
Lambeth SE11 ... 261 B3
34 Shoreditch E2 ... 95 D4
Hurley Lo SE22 ... 162 C5
Hurley Rd UB6 ... 85 D2
Hurlingham Bsns Pk SW6 ... 135 C2
Hurlingham & Chelsea Sec Sch SW6 ... 135 C2
Hurlingham Court Mans SW6 ... 135 C3
Hurlingham Ct SW6 ... 135 B2
Hurlingham Gdns SW6 ... 135 B2
Hurlingham Rd
Erith DA7 ... 147 B5
Fulham SW6 ... 135 B3
Hurlingham Sch SW15 ... 135 B1
Hurlingham Sq SW6 135 D2
Hurlock Ho 1 N5 ... 72 D5
Hurlock St N5 ... 72 D5
Hurlstone Rd SE25 ... 205 C4
Hurn Court Rd TW5 . 128 D3
Hurn Ct TW5 ... 128 D3
Huron Cl 5 BR6 ... 227 D2
Huron Rd SW17 ... 159 A1
Huron Univ WC1 ... 94 A2 240 A4
Hurren Cl SE3 ... 142 C2
Hurricane Rd SM6 ... 220 B1
Hurricane Trad Ctr NW9 ... 28 A2
Hurry Cl E15 ... 76 C1
Hursley Ct 11 KT6 ... 197 D2
Hurst Ave
Chingford E4 ... 19 C1
Highgate N6 ... 49 C3
Hurstbourne KT10 . 212 D2
Hurstbourne Cotts DA5 ... 169 D4
Hurstbourne Gdns IG11 ... 79 C2
Hurstbourne Ho SW15 ... 155 D5
Hurstbourne Priors CR2 ... 221 C2
Hurstbourne Rd SE23 ... 163 A3
Hurst Cl
Chessington KT9 ... 214 C3
Chingford E4 ... 19 C1
Hampstead Garden Suburb NW11 ... 47 D3
Hayes BR2 ... 208 D1
Northolt UB5 ... 63 B3
Hurstcombe IG9 ... 21 A2
Hurstcourt Rd SM1 . 217 D6
Hurst Ct
Beckenham BR3 ... 185 C3
Newham E6 ... 99 D2
South Norwood SE25 . 205 D5
Woodford IG8 ... 37 B4
Hurstdene Ave BR2 . 208 D1
Hurstdene Gdns N15 .. 51 C2
Hurstfield BR2 ... 209 A4
Hurstfield Cres UB4 ... 83 C2
Hurstfield Rd KT8 ... 195 C6
Hurst Gr KT12 ... 193 D1
Hurst Ho
7 Penge SE26 ... 184 B5
Pentonville WC1 ... 233 D3
West Heath SE2 ... 124 D1
Hurst La
East Molesey KT8 ... 196 A6
West Heath SE2 ... 124 D1
Hurst Lo London N8 ... 49 D3
Wembley HA0 ... 66 B1
Hurstmead Ct HA8 ... 26 D6
Hurstmere Foundation Sch DA15 ... 168 C3
HURST PARK ... 174 A1
Hurst Park Prim Sch KT8 ... 195 C6
Hurst Pl Erith SE2 ... 146 D6
Woolwich SE2 ... 124 C1
Hurst Pool The KT8 . 195 D6
Hurst Prim Sch DA5 . 168 D3
Hurst Rd
Buckhurst Hill IG9 ... 21 D3
Croydon CR0 ... 221 B3
East Molesey KT8, KT12 ... 195 C6
Sidcup DA5, DA15 ... 168 C3
Southgate N21 ... 16 C3
Walthamstow E17 ... 53 D6
Walton-on-T KT8&KT12 ... 194 D5
Hurst Rise EN5 ... 1 C2
Hurst Springs DA5 ... 169 A3
Hurst St SE24 ... 160 D5
Hurst View Grange CR2 ... 220 D1
Hurst View Rd CR2 ... 221 C1
Hurst Way CR2 ... 221 C2
Hurstway Wlk 2 W11 ... 112 D6
Hurstwood Ave
Sidcup DA5 ... 169 A3
Wanstead E18 ... 55 B5
Hurstwood Ct
Colney Hatch N12 ... 30 C4
Temple Fortune NW11 .. 47 B5
Hurstwood Dr BR1 ... 210 B6
Hurstwood Rd NW11 .. 47 B5
Hurtwood Rd KT12 ... 195 B2
Husbourne Ho 8 SE8 ... 119 A2
Huson Cl NW3 ... 70 C1
Hussain Cl HA1 ... 64 D4
Hussars Cl TW4 ... 129 A2
Husseywell Cres BR2 ... 209 A1
Hutching's St E14 ... 119 C4
Hutching's Wharf 11 E14 ... 119 C4
Hutchings Wlk NW11 . 47 D5
Hutchins Cl E15 ... 76 A1
Hutchins Ho 8 SW4 ... 159 D4
Hutchinson Ct RM6 ... 58 D5
Hutchinson Ho 9 SE14 ... 140 C5
Hutchinson Terr HA9 .. 65 D5
Hutchins Rd SE28 ... 124 A5
Hutton Cl
Greenford UB6 ... 64 B3
Woodford IG8 ... 37 B4
Hutton Ct
1 Ealing W5 ... 87 C2
Edmonton N9 ... 18 C4
4 Finsbury Pk N4 ... 50 B1
Hutton Gdns HA3 ... 24 A3
Hutton Gr N12 ... 29 D5
Hutton Ho 19 E2 ... 96 A4
Hutton La HA3 ... 24 A3
Hutton Row 4 HA8 ... 27 A3
Hutton St EC4 ... 241 B1
Hutton Wlk HA3 ... 24 A3
Huxbear St SE4 ... 163 B6
Huxley Cl UB5 ... 85 A6
Huxley Dr RM6 ... 58 B2
Huxley Gdns NW10 ... 88 B5
Huxley Ho
4 London SW9 ... 138 B3
Paddington NW8 ... 236 D5
West Heath SE2 ... 124 D1
Huxley Par N18 ... 33 B5
Huxley Pl N13 ... 16 D1
Huxley Rd
Edmonton N18 ... 33 C6
Falconwood DA16 ... 145 D2
Leyton E10 ... 76 A6
Huxley Sayze N18 ... 33 B5
Huxley South N18 ... 33 B5
Huxley St W10 ... 91 A4
Hyacinth Cl
3 Hampton TW12 ... 173 C4
Ilford IG1 ... 78 D2
Hyacinth Ct 2 HA5 ... 40 C6
Hyacinth Dr UB10 ... 60 A1
Hyacinth Rd SW15 ... 156 A3
Hyde Cl
Ashford TW16 ... 171 C4
Barnet EN5 ... 1 B2
Newham E13 ... 99 A5
Hyde Cres NW9 ... 45 C4
Hyde Ct
Forest Hill SE23 ... 163 A2
Hounslow TW4 ... 151 B6
Kingsbury NW9 ... 45 B2
Whetstone N20 ... 14 B1
Hyde Estate Rd NW9 .. 45 D4
Hyde Farm Mews SW12 ... 159 D3
Hydefield Cl N21 ... 17 B3
Hydefield Ct N9 ... 17 C2
Hyde Ho
12 Ealing W13 ... 109 A5
Hounslow TW3 ... 130 A2
Hyde Ind Est The NW9 ... 45 D4
Hyde La SW11 ... 136 C4 267 A2
Hyde Park★ W2 ... 114 D5 247 C3
Hyde Park Ave N21 ... 17 B3
Hyde Park Cnr SW1 . 248 B2
Hyde Park Corner Sta SW1 ... 115 A4 248 B2
Hyde Park Cres W2 ... 92 C1 237 A1
Hyde Park Gate Mews SW7 ... 246 B1
Hyde Park Gdns
Bayswater W2 ... 114 B6 246 D6
Edmonton N21 ... 17 A3
Hyde Park Gdns Mews W2 ... 114 C6 247 A6
Hyde Park Mans NW1 ... 237 A3
Hyde Park Pl W2 ... 247 B6
Hyde Park Sq W2 ... 92 C1 237 A1
Hyde Park Square Mews W2 ... 237 A1
Hyde Park St W2 ... 92 C1 237 A1
Hyde Park Twrs W2 . 246 A5
Hyderabad Way E15 . 76 C1
Hyde Rd
Bexleyheath DA7 ... 147 B3
Richmond TW10 ... 154 B6
Shoreditch N1 ... 95 C6
Hyde Sch The NW9 ... 45 D4
Hydeside Gdns N9 ... 17 D2
Hyde's Pl 12 N1 ... 72 D1
Hyde St SE8 ... 141 C6
Hyde Terr TW15, TW16 ... 171 C4
HYDE THE ... 45 D4
Hydethorpe Ave N9 ... 17 D2
Hydethorpe Rd SW12 ... 159 C3
Hyde Vale SE10 ... 142 A5
Hyde Way
Edmonton N9 ... 17 D2
Hayes UB3 ... 105 D2
Hyde Wlk SM4 ... 201 C2
Hydon Ct N11 ... 30 D5
Hyh Ho E17 ... 35 D2
Hyland House Sch E17 ... 36 B1
Hylands Rd E17 ... 36 B1
Hylda Ct NW5 ... 71 A5
Hylton St SE18 ... 123 D2
Hyndewood 14 SE23 162 D1
Hyndman Ho
5 Dagenham RM10 ... 81 C5
4 Tufnell Pk N19 ... 71 D4
Hyndman St SE15 ... 140 B6
Hynton Rd RM8 ... 80 C6
Hyperion Ho
27 Bow E3 ... 97 A5
Streatham SW2 ... 160 B4
Hyrstdene CR0 ... 220 D4
Hyrst The CR0 ... 207 A1
Hyson Rd SE16 ... 118 B1
Hythe Ave DA7 ... 147 B5
Hythe Cl N18 ... 34 A6
Hythe Ho 14 SE16 ... 118 C4
Hythe Rd
College Pk NW10 ... 90 A3
South Norwood CR7 ... 183 B1
Hythe Road Ind Est NW10 ... 90 A3
Hyver Hill NW7 ... 11 B4

I

Ian Ct SE23 ... 162 C2
Ian Hamilton Ho NW1 ... 232 C2
Ian Mikardo Sch 52 E3 ... 97 D4
Ian Sq EN3 ... 6 D4
Ibberton Ho
Kensington W14 ... 254 B5
South Lambeth SW8 . 270 C4
Ibbotson Ave E16 ... 98 D1
Ibbott St 22 E1 ... 96 C3
Iberia Ho 17 N19 ... 49 D2
Iberian Ave CR0, SM6 ... 220 A4
Ibex Ho E15 ... 76 C3
Ibis Ct 16 SE8 ... 141 B6
Ibis Ho E12 ... 78 B4
Ibis La W4 ... 133 A4
Ibis Way UB4 ... 84 D1
Ibrox Ct 3 IG9 ... 21 C2
Ibsley Gdns SW15 ... 156 A3
Ibsley Way EN4 ... 2 C1
Ibstock Place Sch SW15 ... 155 C5
Icarus Ho 21 E3 ... 97 B4
Iceland Rd E3 ... 97 C6
Iceland Wharf SE16 . 119 A2
Iceni Ct 23 Bow E3 ... 97 B6
Buckhurst Hill IG9 ... 21 B3
Ice Wharf NW1 ... 233 B4
Ickburgh Est E5 ... 74 B6
Ickburgh Rd E5 ... 74 B5
Ickburgh Sch E5 ... 74 B5
ICKENHAM ... 60 C4
Ickenham Cl HA4 ... 61 B6
Ickenham Rd HA4 ... 39 B1
Ickenham Sta UB10 ... 61 A4
Ickleton Rd SE9 ... 188 A6
Icknield Dr IG2 ... 56 D4
Ickworth Park Rd E17 ... 53 A5
Icough Ct SE3 ... 143 B5
Idaho Bldg 7 SE13 . 141 D4
Ida Rd N15 ... 51 B5
Ida St E14 ... 98 A1
Iden Cl BR2 ... 208 C6
Identity & Passport Office SW1 115 B2 258 D4
Idlecombe Rd SW17 . 181 A4
Idmiston Rd
New Malden KT4 ... 199 D2
Stratford E15 ... 76 D3
West Norwood SE21, SE27 ... 161 A2
Idmiston Sq KT4 ... 199 D2
Idol La EC3 ... 117 C6 253 A5
Idonia St SE8 ... 141 C5
Iffley Ho 47 E2 ... 95 D4
Iffley Rd W6 ... 112 B3
Ifield Ho SE17 ... 263 B2
Ifield Rd SW10 ... 135 D6 265 D6
Ifor Evans Pl E1 ... 96 D3
Ightham Ho
Beckenham BR3 ... 185 B3
Walworth SE17 ... 263 A3
Ightham Rd DA8 ... 147 C5
Ikon Ho 21 E1 ... 118 C6
Ilbert St W10 ... 91 A4
Ilchester Gdns W2 .. 245 C6
Ilchester Mans W8 .. 255 A6
Ilchester Pl W14 ... 113 B3 254 D6
Ilchester Rd RM8 ... 80 C3
Ildersly Gr SE21 ... 161 B2
Ilderton Prim Sch 16 SE16 ... 118 C1
Ilderton Rd SE15, SE16 ... 140 C6
Ilex Cl TW16 ... 172 C1
Ilex Rd NW10 ... 67 D2
Ilex Way SW16 ... 182 C5
ILFORD ... 78 D6
Ilford Chambers 10 IG1 ... 78 D5
Ilford Hill IG1 ... 78 C5
Ilford Ho 14 N1 ... 73 B2
Ilford Interchange IG1 ... 78 C5
Ilford Jewish Prim Sch IG6 ... 57 B6
Ilford La IG1 ... 78 D4
Ilford Mus★ IG1 ... 78 D5
Ilford Prep Sch IG3 ... 58 A1
Ilford Ret Pk IG1 ... 79 A6
Ilford Sta IG1 ... 78 D6
Ilford Ursuline High Sch IG1 ... 78 D6
Ilford Ursuline Prep Sch 7 IG1 ... 78 D6
Ilfracombe Flats SE1 252 B2
Ilfracombe Gdns RM6 58 B2
Ilfracombe Rd BR1 ... 164 D1
Iliffe St SE17 . 116 D1 261 D2
Iliffe Yd SE17 ... 116 D1 261 D2
Ilkeston Ct 7 E5 ... 74 D4
Ilkley Cl SE19 ... 183 B4
Ilkley Ct N11 ... 31 A4
Ilkley Rd Newham E16 .. 99 C2
South Oxhey WD19 ... 22 D5
Illingworth Cl CR4 ... 202 B6
Illingworth Way EN1 .. 17 C6
Ilmington Rd HA3 ... 43 D3
Ilminster Gdns SW11 ... 136 C1
Ilsley Ct 8 SW8 ... 137 C3
Iman Zakaria Acad 2 E7 ... 77 C3
Imber Cl London N14 ... 15 C4
Thames Ditton KT7 ... 196 B1
Imber Court Trad Est KT8 ... 196 B3
Imber Cross KT7 ... 196 D3
Imber Ct 4 SE9 ... 166 C5
Imber Gr KT10 ... 196 B2
Imber Park Rd KT10 .. 196 B1
Imber St N1 ... 235 C5
Immanuel CE Prim Sch SW16 ... 182 A4
Immanuel Coll WD23 ... 8 C4
Impact Ct SE20 ... 184 B1
Imperial Ave 5 N16 ... 73 C4
Imperial Cl
Harrow HA2 ... 41 C3
Willesden NW2 ... 68 B3
Imperial College London (Charing Cross) W6 ... 112 D1
Imperial College London (Chelsea & Westminster) SW10 ... 136 A6 266 B5
Imperial College London (Hammersmith) W12 ... 90 B1
Imperial College London (Northwick Park) HA1 ... 43 A1
Imperial College London (Royal Brompton) SW3 ... 114 C1 257 A2
Imperial College London (South Kensington) SW7 ... 114 B3 256 C6
Imperial College London (St Mary's) W2 ... 92 B1 236 D2
Imperial College Rd SW7 ... 114 B3 256 C6
Imperial Cres SW6 ... 136 A3
Imperial Ct
Chislehurst BR7 ... 188 D4
Harrow HA2 ... 41 C2
St John's Wood NW8 . 230 B4
Wembley HA9 ... 66 C5
Whetstone N20 ... 14 A1
Imperial Dr HA2 ... 41 C3
Imperial Gdns CR4 ... 203 B6
Imperial Ho
1 Bow E3 ... 97 A4
2 Poplar E14 ... 119 B6
Strand WC2 ... 240 C1
Imperial Mews 5 E6 . 99 D5
Imperial Pl BR7 ... 188 C2
Imperial Rd
East Bedfont TW14 .. 149 C4
Walham Green SW6 .. 265 D1
Wood Green N22 ... 32 A2
Imperial Sq SW6 ... 265 D2
Imperial St E3 ... 98 A4
Imperial Twrs 3 NW3 ... 70 A2
Imperial War Mus★ SE1, SE11 ... 116 C3 261 B5
Imperial Way
Croydon CR0, CR9 ... 220 C2
Harrow HA3 ... 44 A3
Longlands BR7 ... 167 A1
Imperial Wharf Sta SW10 ... 136 A4 266 B1
Impington 19 KT1 ... 176 C1
Imre Cl W12 ... 112 B5
Inca Dr SE9 ... 166 D4
Ince Terr 3 N15 ... 50 D6
Inchbald Sch of Design (Garden Design) SW1 ... 115 B2 258 D3

Inchbald Sch of Design (Interior Design) SW1 .... 115 A2 258 A4
Inchmery Rd SE6 .... 164 A3
Inchwood BR4, CR0 .. 223 D4
Independant Jewish Day Sch 2 NW4 .... 46 D4
Independence Ho 4 SW19 .... 180 B2
Independent Ind Est UB7 .... 104 C5
Independent Pl E8 .... 73 D3
Independents Rd SE3 .... 142 D2
Inderwick Rd N8 ...... 50 B4
Indescon Ct E14 .... 119 D4
Indiana Bldg 7 SE8 .. 141 C4
India St EC3 .... 243 C1
India Way W12 ...... 112 B6
Indigo Ct TW13 ..... 149 D1
Indigo Mews N16 ..... 73 B5
Indoor Go Karting Arena (The Raceway) SE7 .... 121 C3
Indoor Sports Arena E14 .... 120 A5
Indus Ct 16 SE15 .... 139 D5
Indus Rd SE7 .... 143 C5
Ingal Rd E13 .... 99 A3
Ingate Pl SW8 .... 137 B4 268 D1
Ingatestone Rd
Croydon SE25 .... 206 B5
Wanstead E12 .... 55 C1
Woodford IG8 .... 37 B3
Ingelow Ho W8 ..... 245 C2
Ingelow Rd SW8 ..... 137 B3
Ingersoll Rd
Enfield EN3 .... 6 C5
Shepherd's Bush W12 . 112 B5
Ingestre Pl W1 ...... 239 B1
Ingestre Rd
Forest Gate E7 .... 77 A4
Gospel Oak NW5 ...... 71 B4
Ingham Rd NW6 ...... 69 C4
Inglebert St EC1 .... 94 C4 234 A2
Ingleborough EN2 ..... 4 C3
Ingleborough St SW9 .... 138 C3
Ingleby Ct N21 .... 16 D3
Ingleby Dr HA1 .... 64 B5
Ingleby Rd
Dagenham RM10 ...... 81 D2
Ilford IG1 .... 56 D1
Lower Holloway N7 .... 72 A5
Ingleby Way
Chislehurst West BR7 .... 188 C5
Wallington SM6 ..... 219 D1
Ingle Cl HA5 .... 41 B6
Ingledew Rd SE18 .... 123 B1
Inglefield Sq 12 E1 ... 118 B5
Ingle Ho 3 SW12 .... 159 D3
Inglehurst Gdns IG4 .. 56 B4
Inglemere Ct CR4, SW17 .... 180 D3
Inglemere Rd
Forest Hill SE23 ..... 162 D1
Mitcham CR4, SW17 . 180 D3
Inglesham Wlk E9 .... 75 B2
Ingleside Cl BR3 ..... 185 C3
Ingleside Gr SE3 .... 142 D6
Inglethorpe Ho 6 E5 . 74 A6
Inglethorpe St SW6 . 134 D4
Ingleton Ave DA16 ... 168 A6
Ingleton Rd N18 ...... 34 A4
Ingleton St SW9 ..... 138 C3
Ingleway N12 .... 30 C4
Inglewood BR7 ...... 189 B4
Inglewood Cl E14 .... 119 C2
Inglewood Copse BR1 .... 188 B1
Inglewood Ct 4 BR1 .... 186 D3
Inglewood Mans 11 NW6 .... 69 C3
Inglewood Mews KT6 .... 198 C1
Inglewood Rd NW6 ... 69 C3
Inglis Ct W5 .... 110 B6
Inglis Ho 1 SW15 .... 156 C6
Inglis Rd
Croydon CR0 .... 205 D1
Ealing W5 .... 110 B6
Inglis St SE5 .... 138 D4
Ingram Ave NW11 ..... 48 A2
Ingram Cl
Lambeth SE11 .... 260 D4
Stanmore HA7 .... 25 C5
Ingram Ct EN1 .... 17 D5
Ingram Ho
7 Harrow HA1 .... 42 D4
Old Ford E3 .... 97 A6
Teddington KT8 ..... 175 C2
Ingram Lo 8 SW4 .. 159 D5
Ingram Rd London N2 .. 48 C5
South Norwood CR7 .. 183 A2
Ingram Way UB6 ...... 86 B6
Ingrave Ho RM9 ..... 102 B6
Ingrave St SW11 ..... 136 C2
Ingrebourne Ct E4 .... 19 D2
Ingrebourne Ho
2 Catford BR1 ...... 186 B5
Lisson Gr NW8 ...... 236 D4
Ingress St 4 W4 ..... 111 C1
Inigo Jones Rd SE7 .. 144 A5
Inigo Pl WC2 .... 250 A6
Inkerman Rd NW5 .... 71 B2
Inkerman Terr W8 ... 255 B5
Inks Gn E4 .... 36 A5
Inkster Ho 8 SW11 .. 136 C2
Inkwell Cl N12 .... 14 A1
Inman Rd
Harlesden NW10 ...... 89 C6
Wandsworth SW18 .. 158 A4
Inmans Row IG8 ...... 37 A6
Innellan House Sch HA5 .... 41 A6
Inner Circ NW1 .... 93 A4 231 A2
Inner Park Rd SW19 . 156 D2
Inner Ring E TW6 ... 126 D2
Inner Ring W TW6 ... 126 C2
Inner Temple★ EC4 . 251 A6
Inner Temple La EC4 241 A1
Innes Cl SW20 ...... 179 A1
Innes Gdns SW15 .... 156 B5
Innes Lo SE23 ...... 162 D1
Innes Yd CR0 .... 221 A5
Innisfree Ho NW2 ..... 68 D2
Innis Ho SE17 ...... 263 A2
Inniskilling Rd E13 .... 99 C5
Innova Bsns Pk EN3 .... 7 B3
Innovation Cl HA0 .... 88 A6
Inskip Cl E10 .... 75 D6
Inskip Rd RM8 .... 58 D1
Insley Ho 13 E3 ...... 97 D4
Institute of Cancer Research The SW7 .... 114 A1 256 B2
Institute Pl 31 E8 ..... 74 B3
Institute The N2 ..... 48 C5
Inst of Child Health WC1 .... 94 B3 240 C5
Inst of Neurology
Bloomsbury WC1 .... 94 A2 240 B4
St Pancras WC1 .... 94 A3 240 B5
Int Coll of Accountancy The SW17 .... 158 D1
Integer Gdns E11 ..... 54 B2
Interchange The
Kentish Town NW5 ..... 71 B3
Thornton Heath CR0 . 204 D2
International Ave TW5 .... 106 C1
International Com Sch W1 .... 93 A3 238 B5
International House Language Sch WC2 .... 94 A1 240 B2
International Sch of Bsns Studies HA2 .... 41 C2
International Sch of London W3 .... 110 C2
International Trad Est UB2 .... 106 B3
International Univ of America (London Campus) 15 SE18 .. 122 D2
International Way TW16 .... 171 C2
Inverary Pl SE18 ..... 145 B6
Inver Cl E5 .... 74 C6
Inverclyde Gdns RM6 . 58 D5
Inver Ct
11 Bayswater W2 ..... 91 D1
4 Hammersmith W6 112 A3
Inveresk Gdns KT4 ... 216 A5
Inverey Ho 2 N12 .... 29 D5
Inverforth Cl NW3 .... 70 A6
Inverforth Ho NW3 .... 70 A6
Inverforth Rd N11 .... 31 B5
Invergarry Ct 11 EN5 .. 13 D6
Invergarry Ho NW6 ... 91 D5
Inverine Rd SE7 ...... 121 B1
Invermead Cl W6 .... 112 A2
Invermore Pl SE18 ... 123 A2
Inverness Ave EN1 ..... 5 C4
Inverness Ct
8 Acton W3 .... 88 C1
10 Catford SE6 ..... 164 D3
Inverness Gdns W8 . 245 C3
Inverness Mews
Bayswater W2 ...... 245 D6
Newham E16 .... 122 D5
North Woolwich E16 . 123 A5
Inverness Pl W2 .... 245 D6
Inverness Rd
Edmonton N18 .... 34 B5
Hounslow TW3 ...... 129 C1
North Cheam KT4 .... 200 D1
Southall UB2 .... 107 A2
Inverness St NW1 ... 231 D6
Inverness Terr W2 .... 113 D6 245 D6
Inverton Rd SE15 ... 140 D1
Invicta Cl
Chislehurst West BR7 .... 188 C5
East Bedfont TW14 .. 149 D3
21 Tower Hamlets E3 ... 97 C2
Invicta Ct KT9 .... 214 B3
Invicta Ctr The IG11 . 102 A6
Invicta Gr UB5 .... 85 B4
Invicta Plaza SE1 ... 251 C4
Invicta Prim Sch SE3 .... 143 A5
Invicta Rd SE3, SE7 ... 143 A6
Inville Rd SE17 .... 117 B1 262 D1
Inwen Ct SE8 .... 119 A1
Inwood Ave TW3 ..... 130 A2
Inwood Bsns Pk TW3 .... 129 D1
Inwood Cl CR0 ...... 223 A6
Inwood Ct 12 NW1 .... 71 C1
Inwood Ho 19 SE22 .. 139 C2
Inwood Rd TW3 ...... 130 A1
Inworth St SW11 .... 136 C3
Inworth Wlk N1 ..... 235 A6
Io Ctr Barking IG11 ... 101 D3
Woolwich SE18 ..... 123 A3
Iona Cl Catford SE6 ... 163 C4
Morden SM4 .... 201 D2
Ion Ct 8 E2 .... 96 A5
Ionian Bldg 19 E14 ... 119 A6
Ionian Ho 22 E1 ...... 96 D3
Ipsden Bldgs SE1 ... 251 B2
Ipswich Ho SE4 ..... 162 D6
Ipswich Rd SW17 .... 181 A4
Iqra Ind Sch SW9 ... 138 C2
Irby Ho SW2 .... 160 C5
Ireland Cl E6 .... 100 B2
Ireland Pl N22 .... 32 A3
Ireland Yd EC4 ...... 241 D1
Irene Rd
Broom Hill BR6 ...... 211 D2
Parsons Green SW6 .... 135 C4 265 B1
Ireton Cl N10 .... 31 A3
Ireton Ho 22 SW9 .... 138 C3
Ireton St 12 E3 .... 97 C3
Iris Ave DA5 .... 169 A5
Iris Cl Croydon CR0 .... 206 D1
Newham E6 .... 100 A3
Surbiton KT6 .... 198 B2
Iris Cres DA7 .... 147 B6
Iris Ct Dagenham IG11 .. 80 B1
8 Peckham SE15 .... 140 B3
4 Pinner HA5 .... 40 C6
Iris Rd KT19 .... 214 D3
Iris Way E4 .... 35 B4
Iris Wlk 1 HA8 .... 27 A6
Irkdale Ave EN1 .... 5 D4
Iroko Ho 7 NW3 ...... 69 D2
Iron Bridge Cl
Southall UB2 .... 108 A5
Willesden NW10 ...... 67 C3
Iron Bridge Ho NW3 ... 70 D1
Iron Bridge Rd N UB11 .... 104 C5
Iron Bridge Rd S UB7 .... 104 C4
Irongate Ho EC3 .... 243 B2
Iron Mill Pl SW18 ... 157 D5
Iron Mill Rd SW18 ... 157 D5
Ironmonger La EC2 .... 95 B1 242 C1
Ironmonger Pas EC1 235 B1
Ironmonger Row EC1 .... 95 A4 235 B1
Ironmonger Row Baths EC1 .... 235 B1
Ironmongers Pl E14 . 119 C2
Ironmonger's Pl 22 E14 .... 119 C2
Ironside Cl SE16 .... 118 D4
Ironside Ho E9 .... 75 A4
Ironworks 1 E3 ...... 97 C6
Irvine Ave HA3 .... 43 B6
Irvine Cl N20 .... 14 C2
Irvine Ct
Marylebone W1 .... 239 B5
Thornton Heath CR7 . 204 C3
Irvine Ho N7 .... 72 B2
Irvine Way BR6 ..... 211 D2
Irving Ave UB5 .... 84 D6
Irving Ct N22 .... 32 D2
Irving Gr SW9 ...... 138 B3
Irving Ho SE17 ...... 261 C1
Irving Mews N1 .... 73 A2
Irving Rd W14 ...... 112 D3
Irving St WC2 .... 249 D5
Irwell Ct W7 .... 86 B1
Irwell Est 31 SE16 .... 118 C4
Irwin Ave SE18 ...... 145 C5
Irwin Cl UB10 .... 60 C5
Irwin Gdns NW10 ..... 90 B6
Isabel Hill Cl TW12 ... 173 C2
Isabella Cl N14 .... 15 C4
Isabella Ct 8 TW10 .. 154 B5
Isabella Dr BR6 ..... 227 A4
Isabella Ho
19 Hammersmith W6 .... 112 C1
Kennington SE11 .... 261 C2
Isabella Mews 11 E8 .. 73 C2
Isabella Pl KT2 ...... 176 B5
Isabella Rd E9 .... 74 C3
Isabel St SW9 .... 270 D2
Isambard Mews E14 . 120 A3
Isambard Pl SE16 .... 118 C5
Iseldon Ct N7 .... 72 A4
Isel Way 4 SE22 .... 161 C6
Isham Rd SW16 ..... 182 A1
Isis Cl Putney SW15 .. 134 C1
Ruislip HA4 .... 39 A3
Isis Ct W4 .... 132 D5
Isis Ho
2 Edmonton N18 ..... 33 D4
Paddington NW8 .... 236 D5
Isis St SW18 .... 158 A2
Islamia Girls' High Sch NW6 .... 91 A6
Islamia Prim Sch NW6 .... 91 A6
Islamic Coll for Advanced Studies 2 NW10 .... 68 B2
Islamic Shaksiyah Foundation Sch N15 .... 51 B4
Island Centre Way 16 EN3 .... 7 C6
Island Farm Ave KT8 .... 195 B4
Island Farm Rd KT8 .. 195 C4
Island Gardens Sta E14 .... 120 A1
Island Ho Bromley E14 . 98 A4
Morden SW19 ...... 202 A5
Island Rd
Deptford SE16 ...... 118 D2
Mitcham CR4 .... 180 D3
Island Row E14 .... 97 B1
Isla Rd SE18 .... 145 A6
Islay Gdns TW4 ..... 150 D6
Islay Wlk 17 N1 ...... 73 A2
Isleden Ho N1 ...... 235 A6
Isledon Rd N4, N7 .... 72 C5
Islehurst Cl BR7 ..... 188 C2
ISLE OF DOGS 120 A2
ISLEWORTH 131 B2
Isleworth Bsns Complex TW7 .... 130 D3
Isleworth Sta TW7 .. 130 D3
Isleworth & Syon Sch for Boys TW7 .... 130 C5
Isleworth Town Prim Sch TW7 .... 131 A3
ISLINGTON 72 D2
Islington Arts & Media Sch 6 N4 .... 50 B1
Islington Bsns Ctr N1 .... 235 B6
Islington Est N1 .... 95 A6 235 A6
Islington Gn N1 .... 94 D6 234 C5
Islington High St N1 .... 94 D5 234 C4
Islington Mus★ WC1 .... 94 D4 234 C1
Islington Park Mews 1 N1 .... 72 D1
Islington Park St N1 .. 72 D1
Islington Tennis Ctr N7 .... 72 A2
Islip Gdns
Burnt Oak HA8 .... 27 B3
Northolt UB5 .... 63 A1
Islip Manor Rd UB5 ... 63 A1
Islip St NW5 .... 71 C3
Ismailia Rd E7 .... 77 B1
Isobel Ho
10 Ashford TW16 .... 171 D3
Harrow HA1 .... 42 D4
Isokon Flats 3 NW3 .. 70 D3
Isom Cl E13 .... 99 B4
Issac Way SE1 ...... 252 B2
Issa Rd TW3 .... 129 B1
Italia Conti Acad of Theatre Arts EC1 .. 242 A5
Ithell Ct HA0 .... 65 D3
Ivanhoe Dr HA3 .... 25 B1
Ivanhoe Ho
11 Balham SW12 ..... 159 B4
34 Bow E3 .... 97 A5
Ivanhoe Rd
Hounslow TW4 ...... 128 D2
Peckham SE5 .... 139 D2
Ivatt Pl W14 .. 113 B1 254 D1
Ivatt Way N17 .... 50 D6
Ivax Quays E16 ...... 123 A6
Iveagh Ave NW10 ..... 88 C5
Iveagh Cl Ealing NW10 . 88 C5
South Hackney E9 ..... 96 D6
Iveagh Ct
4 Beckenham BR3 .. 207 D6
Whitechapel EC3 .... 243 C1
Iveagh Ho
2 Brixton SW9 ..... 138 D3
Chelsea SW10 ...... 266 B4
Ivebury Ct 9 W10 .... 90 C1
Ivedon Rd DA16 ...... 146 C3
Ive Farm Cl E10 .... 75 C6
Ive Farm La E10 .... 75 C6
Iveley Rd SW4 .... 137 C3
Iver Ct N1 .... 73 A2
Ivere Dr EN5 .... 13 D5
Iverhurst Cl DA6 .... 168 D6
Iverna Ct W8 .... 255 B6
Iverna Gdns
Hatton TW14 .... 149 B6
Kensington W8 .... 113 C3 255 B6
Iverson Rd NW6 ...... 69 C2
Ivers Way CR0 ...... 223 D1
Ives Rd E16 .... 98 C2
Ives St SW3 ... 114 C2 257 B4
Ivestor Terr SE23 ..... 162 C4
Ivimey St E2 .... 96 A4
Ivinghoe Cl EN1 .... 5 C4
Ivinghoe Ho 14 N7 ..... 71 D3
Ivinghoe Rd
Barking RM8 .... 80 B3
Bushey WD23 .... 8 B4
Ivor Ct Hendon N3 ..... 47 A6
Hornsey N8 .... 50 A3
Lisson Gr NW1 ...... 237 C6
Ivor Gr SE9 .... 166 D3
Ivor Ho DA14 .... 190 C5
Ivories The N1 .... 73 A1
Ivor Mayor Lo SW12 .. 159 A5
Ivor Pl NW1 ... 92 D3 237 C5
Ivor St NW1 .... 71 C1
Ivory Ct TW13 .... 150 A3
Ivorydown BR1 ...... 187 A6
Ivory Ho
9 London SW11 .... 136 A2
St George in t East E1 253 D4
Ivory Sq 15 SW18 .... 136 A2

Ivybridge Cl
2 Twickenham TW1 ... 153 A4
Uxbridge UB8 ... 82 A4
Ivybridge Ct 1 BR7 ... 188 C2
Ivybridge Ho 18 SE22 ... 139 C2
Ivybridge La WC2 ... 250 B5
Ivybridge Prim Sch TW1 ... 152 D5
Ivybridge Ret Pk TW7 ... 152 D6
Ivychurch Cl SE20 ... 184 C3
Ivy Church La SE1, SE17 ... 263 C2
Ivy Cl Harrow HA2 ... 63 B4
Pinner HA5 ... 40 C2
Sunbury TW16 ... 172 C1
Ivy Cotts UB10 ... 82 C4
Ivy Cres W4 ... 111 A2
Ivy Ct
19 Bermondsey SE16 ... 118 A1
Lewisham SE3 ... 142 D1
Ivydale Prim Sch SE15 ... 140 D1
Ivydale Rd
Carshalton SM5 ... 218 D6
Nunhead SE15 ... 140 D1
Ivyday Gr SW16 ... 160 B1
Ivydene KT12, KT8 ... 195 B4
Ivydene Cl SM1 ... 218 A4
Ivy Gdns London N8 ... 50 A3
Mitcham CR4 ... 203 D6
Ivy Ho Croydon CR0 ... 206 D1
6 Upper Clapton E5 ... 52 B1
Ivyhouse Rd RM9 ... 81 A2
Ivy House Rd UB10 ... 60 D5
Ivy La TW4 ... 129 B1
Ivy Lo W8 ... 245 A4
Ivymount Rd SE27 ... 160 C1
Ivy Rd Brockley SE4 ... 141 C1
Cricklewood NW2 ... 68 C4
Hounslow TW3 ... 129 D1
Newham E16 ... 99 A1
Southgate N14 ... 15 D4
Tolworth KT6 ... 198 C1
Upper Tooting SW17 ... 180 C5
Walthamstow E17 ... 53 C3
Ivy St N1 ... 95 C5
Ivy Terr 2 IG2 ... 57 A3
Ivy Wlk RM9 ... 81 A2
Ixworth Pl SW3 ... 114 C2 257 A3
Izane Rd DA6 ... 147 B1

J

Jacaranda Cl KT3 ... 199 C6
Jacaranda Gr E8 ... 73 D1
Jack Ashley Ct 5 NW9 ... 27 C2
Jackass La BR2 ... 225 C2
Jack Barnett Way N22 ... 32 B1
Jack Clow Rd E15 ... 98 C5
Jack Cook Ho 9 IG11 ... 78 D1
Jack Cornwell St E12 ... 78 C4
Jack Dash Gdns E6 ... 100 A3
Jack Goodchild Way KT3 ... 198 D6
Jack & Jill Sch
Hampton TW12 ... 173 C4
1 Twickenham TW2 ... 152 C2
Jack Jones Way RM9 ... 103 B5
Jacklin Gn IG8 ... 37 A6
Jackman Ho 24 E1 ... 118 B5
Jackman Mews NW2 ... 67 C5
Jackman St E8 ... 96 B6
Jackson Cl
Hackney E9 ... 74 D1
Uxbridge UB10 ... 60 A1
Jackson Ct
Forest Gate E7 ... 77 B2
Wanstead E11 ... 55 B1
Jackson Ho
15 London SW11 ... 136 B2
13 New Southgate N11 ... 31 C5
Jackson Rd
Barking IG11 ... 101 B6
Jackson Rd *continued*
Bromley BR2 ... 226 B6
East Barnet EN4 ... 14 C5
Lower Holloway N7 ... 72 B4
Uxbridge UB10 ... 60 A1
Jackson's La N6 ... 49 B2
Jackson's Pl CR0 ... 205 C1
Jackson St SE18 ... 144 C6
Jackson's Way CR0 ... 223 C5
Jackson Way UB2 ... 107 D4
Jack Taylor Sch NW8 ... 92 A6 229 A6
Jack Tizard Sch W12 ... 112 B5
Jack Walker Ct N5 ... 72 D4
Jacob Ct 24 EN3 ... 7 C6
Jacob Ho 14 DA18 ... 124 D4
Jacobin Lo N7 ... 72 A3
Jacob Mans 15 E1 ... 96 B1
Jacobs Cl RM10 ... 81 D4
Jacobs Ho E13 ... 99 C4
Jacobson Ct SW11 ... 267 B1
Jacobson Ho E1 ... 243 C2
Jacob St SE1 ... 118 A4
Jacob's Well Mews W1 ... 238 B2
Jacotts Ho W10 ... 90 C3
Jacqueline Cl UB5 ... 85 A6
Jacqueline Ho 8 E1 ... 96 D2
Jacques Prevert Sch 3 W6 ... 112 D2
Jade Cl
Dagenham RM8 ... 58 C1
Hendon NW2 ... 46 D2
Newham E16 ... 99 D1
Jaffe Rd IG1 ... 57 B1
Jaffray Rd BR2 ... 209 D5
Jaggard Way SW12 ... 158 D4
Jagger Ho SW11 ... 267 C2
Jago Cl SE18 ... 145 A6
Jago Wlk SE5 ... 139 B5
Jamahirya Sch SW3 ... 136 C6 267 A6
Jamaica Rd
Bermondsey SE1 ... 253 D1
Bermondsey SE16 ... 118 B3
Thornton Heath CR7 ... 204 D3
Jamaica St E1 ... 96 C2
James Allen's Girls' Sch 12 SE22 ... 161 C6
James Allen's Pre-Prep Sch SE21 ... 161 B5
James Allen's Prep Sch 13 SE22 ... 161 C6
James Anderson Ct 29 E2 ... 95 C5
James Ave
Cricklewood NW2 ... 68 C3
Dagenham RM8 ... 59 B1
James Bedford Cl HA5 ... 22 C1
James Boswell Cl 1 SW16 ... 182 C6
James Brine Ho 6 E2 ... 95 D4
James Campbell Ho 2 E2 ... 96 C5
James Cl
London NW11 ... 47 A3
8 Newham E13 ... 99 A5
James Collins Cl W9 ... 91 B3
James Ct Chingford E4 ... 20 B2
Finchley N12 ... 30 C3
Hendon NW9 ... 27 C1
Northolt UB5 ... 85 A5
3 Woodford E18 ... 37 B1
James Dixon Prim Sch SE20 ... 184 A2
James Docherty Ho 4 E2 ... 96 C5
James Dudson Ct NW10 ... 67 A1
James Est CR4 ... 180 D1
James Gdns N22 ... 32 D3
James Hammett Ho 9 E2 ... 95 D5
James Ho Mile End E1 ... 97 A3
33 Rotherhithe SE16 ... 118 D4
James Joyce Wlk 7 SE24 ... 138 D1
James La E10, E11 ... 54 B3
James Lee Sq EN3 ... 7 C5
James Leicester Hall of Residence N7 ... 72 A2
James Lind Ho 6 SE8 ... 119 B2
James Middleton Ho 20 E2 ... 96 B4
James Newman Ct SE9 ... 166 C1
Jameson Ct 6 E2 ... 96 C5
Jameson Ho SE11 ... 260 C2
Jameson Lo N6 ... 49 C3
Jameson Pl 11 W3 ... 111 A4
Jameson St W8 ... 245 B4
James Pl N17 ... 33 D2
James's Cotts TW9 ... 132 C5
James St Barking IG11 ... 79 A1
Enfield EN1 ... 17 D6
Hounslow TW3 ... 130 B2
Marylebone W1 ... 93 A1 238 B1
Strand WC2 ... 116 A6 250 B6
James Stewart Ho NW6 ... 69 B1
James Stroud Ho SE17 ... 262 B1
Jamestown Rd NW1 ... 93 B6 231 C6
Jamestown Way E14 ... 120 B6
James Voller Way 30 E1 ... 96 C1
James Way WD19 ... 22 D6
James Wolfe Prim Sch 16 SE10 ... 142 A5
Jamiatul Ummah Sch 40 E1 ... 96 B1
Jamieson Ho TW4 ... 151 B5
Jamuna Cl E14 ... 97 A2
Jane Austen Hall 14 E16 ... 121 B5
Jane St E1 ... 96 B1
Janet Ct
4 Bexleyheath DA7 ... 147 C1
Wood Green N22 ... 32 B2
Janet St E14 ... 119 C3
Janeway Pl 2 SE16 ... 118 B4
Janeway St SE16 ... 118 A4
Janice Mews 3 IG1 ... 78 D5
Jansen Ho 5 SW15 ... 156 A6
Jansen Wlk SW11 ... 136 B1
Janson Cl
Stratford E15 ... 76 C3
Willesden NW10 ... 67 C5
Janson Rd E15 ... 76 C3
Jansons Rd N15 ... 51 C6
Japan Cres N4 ... 50 B1
Japanese Sch The W3 ... 110 C6
Japan Rd RM6 ... 58 D3
Jaquets Ct DA5 ... 169 C2
Jardine Ho HA1 ... 42 C2
Jardine Rd E1 ... 118 D6
Jarman Ho
Bermondsey SE16 ... 118 D2
16 Stepney E1 ... 96 C2
Jarrett Cl SW2 ... 160 D3
Jarrow Cl SM4 ... 201 D4
Jarrow Rd
Bermondsey SE16 ... 118 C1
Dagenham RM6 ... 58 C3
Tottenham Hale N17 ... 52 B5
Jarrow Way E9 ... 75 A4
Jarvis Cl
1 Barking IG11 ... 101 B6
Barnet EN5 ... 12 D6
Jarvis Ho 3 SE15 ... 140 A4
Jarvis Rd
London SE22 ... 139 C1
South Croydon CR2 ... 221 B2
Jasmin SE1 ... 253 D3
Jasmine Cl Ilford IG1 ... 78 D3
Orpington BR6 ... 226 D6
Southall UB1 ... 107 A6
Jasmine Ct Lee SE12 ... 165 A5
11 Wallington SM6 ... 219 B2
Wimbledon SW19 ... 179 C5
Jasmine Gdns
Harrow HA2 ... 63 C6
West Wickham CR0 ... 223 D5
Jasmine Gr SE20 ... 184 B2
Jasmine Sq 15 E3 ... 97 B6
Jasmine Terr UB7 ... 104 C4
Jasmine Way KT7 ... 196 C5
Jasmin Ho SE4 ... 141 B2
Jasmin Lo 17 SE16 ... 118 B1
Jasmin Rd KT19 ... 214 D3
Jason Ct
2 London SW9 ... 138 C4
Marylebone W1 ... 238 B2
Jason Ho UB5 ... 84 B4
Jason Wlk SE9 ... 188 C6
Jasper Cl EN3 ... 6 C5
Jasper Ho KT4 ... 199 B1
Jasper Rd
Newham E16 ... 99 D1
Penge SE19 ... 183 D4
Jasper Wlk N1 ... 235 C2
Java Wharf SE1 ... 253 D2
Javelin Ct HA7 ... 25 B5
Javelin Way UB5 ... 84 D4
Jawahar Bagh SW16 ... 182 D4
Jaycroft EN2 ... 4 C4
Jay Gdns BR7 ... 188 B6
Jay Ho SW15 ... 134 C3
Jay Mews SW7 ... 114 A4 246 B1
Jayson Ct 7 CR0 ... 206 A1
Jazzfern Terr HA0 ... 65 A3
Jean Batten Cl SM6 ... 220 B1
Jean Darling Ho SW10 ... 266 C5
Jean Ho 3 SW17 ... 180 C5
Jean Humbert Ho 2 SE27 ... 183 B6
Jean Pardies Ho 23 E1 ... 96 C2
Jebb Ave SW2 ... 160 A5
Jebb St E3 ... 97 C5
Jedburgh Rd E13 ... 99 C4
Jedburgh St SW11 ... 137 A1
Jeddo Mews W12 ... 111 D4
Jeddo Rd W12 ... 111 D4
Jefferies Ho 13 NW10 ... 67 B1
Jefferson Bldg 3 E14 ... 119 C4
Jefferson Cl
Ealing W13 ... 109 B3
Ilford IG2 ... 56 D4
Jefferson Wlk 13 SE18 ... 144 C6
Jeffrey Row SE12 ... 165 B6
Jeffrey's Ct 2 SW4 ... 138 A3
Jeffrey's Pl NW1 ... 71 C1
Jeffreys Rd EN3 ... 7 B1
Jeffrey's Rd SW4 ... 138 A3
Jeffrey's St NW1 ... 71 C1
Jeffs Cl TW12 ... 173 D4
Jeffs Rd SM1 ... 217 B4
Jeff Wooller Coll WC1 ... 94 A2 240 B4
Jefton Ct SM6 ... 219 C3
Jeger Ave E2 ... 95 D6
Jeken Rd SE9 ... 143 C1
Jelf Rd SW2 ... 160 C6
Jellicoe Ct E4 ... 36 B4
Jellicoe Gdns HA7 ... 25 A4
Jellicoe Ho
5 Bethnal Green E2 ... 96 A5
Fitzrovia NW1 ... 238 D5
11 Putney SW15 ... 156 D6
Jellicoe Rd
4 Newham E13 ... 99 A3
Tottenham N17 ... 33 B3
Jemmett Cl KT2 ... 176 D2
Jemotts Ct 9 SE14 ... 140 D6
Jem Paterson Ct HA1 ... 64 C4
Jengar Cl SM1 ... 217 D4
Jenkins Ho SW8 ... 269 C2
Jenkins La IG11 ... 101 A4
Jenkinson Ho 12 E2 ... 96 D4
Jenkins Rd E13 ... 99 B3
Jenner Ave W3 ... 89 B2
Jenner Cl DA14 ... 190 A6
Jenner Ct N21 ... 16 A6
Jenner Ho
5 Belvedere DA17 ... 125 C3
Greenwich SE3 ... 142 C6
Jenner Pl SW13 ... 134 B6
Jenner Rd N16 ... 73 D5
Jennett Rd CR0 ... 220 C5
Jennifer Ho SE11 ... 261 B3
Jennifer Rd BR1 ... 164 D1
Jennings Cl KT6 ... 197 C2
Jennings Ho SE10 ... 120 B1
Jennings Rd SE22 ... 161 D5
Jenny Hammond Cl E11 ... 76 D5
Jenny Hammond Prim Sch E11 ... 76 C4
Jensen Ho 10 E3 ... 97 C3
Jenson Way SE19 ... 183 D3
Jenton Ave DA7 ... 147 A3
Jephson Ct 17 SW4 ... 138 A3
Jephson Ho 6 SE17 ... 138 D6
Jephson Rd E7 ... 77 C1
Jephson St SE5 ... 139 B4
Jephtha Rd SW18 ... 157 C5
Jeppo's La CR4 ... 202 D5
Jerdan Pl SW6 ... 265 A4
Jeremiah St 11 E14 ... 97 D1
Jeremy Bentham Ho 24 E2 ... 96 A4
Jeremy's Gn N18 ... 34 C6
Jermyn St SW1 ... 115 C5 249 B4
Jerningham Ct SE14 ... 141 A4
Jerningham Rd SE14 ... 141 A4
Jerome Cres NW8 ... 92 C3 237 A6
Jerome Ct 2 N11 ... 31 C5
Jerome Ho
Kingston u T KT1 ... 175 D1
Lisson Gr NW1 ... 237 B4
Jerome Pl KT1 ... 175 D1
Jerome St E1 ... 95 D3 243 C5
Jerome Twr 5 W3 ... 110 D4
Jerrard St SE13 ... 141 D2
Jerrold Lo SW15 ... 134 C2
Jerrold St 24 N1 ... 95 C5
Jersey Ave HA7 ... 25 C1
Jersey Ct UB2 ... 107 B3
Jersey Dr BR5 ... 211 B3
Jersey Ho
15 Canonbury N1 ... 73 A2
Enfield EN3 ... 6 D5
Jersey Rd
Canonbury N1 ... 73 A2
Ealing W7 ... 109 A4
Hounslow TW5, TW7 ... 130 B5
Ilford IG1 ... 78 D4
Leytonstone E11 ... 54 B1
Mitcham SW17 ... 181 B4
Newham E16 ... 99 C1
Jersey St E2 ... 96 B4
Jerusalem Pas EC1 ... 241 C5
Jervis Bay Ho 9 E14 ... 98 B1
Jervis Ct
9 Dagenham RM10 ... 81 D2
2 Greenwich SE10 ... 142 A4
Marylebone W1 ... 238 D1
Jerviston Gdns SW16 ... 182 C4
Jesmond Ave HA9 ... 66 B2
Jesmond Cl CR4 ... 203 B6
Jesmond Ct HA9 ... 66 C2
Jesmond Rd CR0 ... 205 D2
Jesmond Way HA7 ... 26 A5
Jessam Ave E5 ... 52 B1
Jessamine Rd W7 ... 108 D5
Jessel Ho
St Pancras WC1 ... 233 A1
Westminster SW1 ... 259 D4
Jesse Rd E10 ... 54 A1
Jessica Rd SW18 ... 158 A6
Jessie Blythe La 4 N19 ... 50 A2
Jessie Duffett Ho 11 SE5 ... 139 A5
Jessie's Cotts E17 ... 53 A3
Jessiman Terr TW17 ... 192 C4
Jesson Ho SE17 ... 262 C3
Jessop Ave UB2 ... 107 B2
Jessop Ct N1 ... 234 D3
Jessop Ho 9 W4 ... 111 B2
Jessop Pl CR4 ... 202 C5
Jessop Sq E14 ... 119 C5
Jessops Way CR0 ... 203 C3
Jessops Wharf 4 TW8 ... 131 C5
Jessup Cl SE18 ... 123 A2
Jeston Ho 10 SE27 ... 160 D1
Jethou Ho 16 N1 ... 73 A2
Jetstar Way UB5 ... 85 A4
Jevington Way SE12 ... 165 B3
Jevons Ho 9 NW8 ... 70 B1
Jewell Ho 3 SW12 ... 159 C4
Jewel Rd E17 ... 53 C6
Jewish Free Sch HA3 ... 44 C3
Jewish Mus The★ NW1 ... 93 B6 231 D5
Jewry St EC3 ... 95 D1 243 C1
Jews Row SW18 ... 136 A1
Jews Wlk SE26 ... 184 B6
Jeymer Ave NW2 ... 68 C3
Jeymer Dr UB6 ... 86 A6
Jeypore Rd SW18 ... 158 A5
Jillian Cl TW12 ... 173 C3

Jim Bradley Cl 10 SE18 122 C2
Jim Griffiths Ho SW6 264 D5
Jimis Coll HA9 65 C5
Jim Veal Dr 3 N17 72 A2
Joan Cres SE9 165 D4
Joan Gdns RM8 81 A6
Joanna Ho 7 W6 112 C1
Joanne Ct EN1 17 C5
Joan Player Ho EN3 6 D6
Joan Rd RM8 81 A6
Joan St SE1 116 D5 251 C3
Joan Villas IG2 57 A2
Jocelin Ho N1 233 D5
Jocelyn Rd TW9 132 A2
Jocelyn St SE15 140 A4
Jockey's Fields WC1 94 B2 240 D4
Jodane Rd SE8 119 B2
Jodrell Cl TW7 131 A4
Jodrell Rd E3 75 B1
Joe Hunte Ct 2 SW27 182 D5
Joel St HA5, HA6 40 A5
Johanna Prim Sch SE1 116 C4 251 A1
Johanna St SE1 251 A1
John Adam St WC2 116 A6 250 B5
John Aird Ct W2 92 A2 236 B4
John Aldis Ho N22 32 B1
John Archer Way SW18 158 B5
John Ashby Cl SW2 160 A5
John Austin Cl KT2 176 B2
John Baird Ct SE26 184 D6
John Baird Ho 11 SE20 184 C3
John Ball Prim Sch SE3 142 C3
John Barker Ct NW6 69 A1
John Barker Ho IG1 79 B6
John Barnes Wlk E15 76 D2
John Barter Ho TW3 129 B3
John Betts' Ho W12 112 A3
John Betts Prim Sch W6 112 B3
John Bond Ho 2 E3 97 B5
John Bradshaw Rd N14 15 D3
John Brent Ho 8 SE8 118 D2
John Buck Ho NW10 89 D6
John Burns Dr IG11 79 C1
John Burns Prim Sch 17 SW11 137 A3
Johnby Cl EN3 7 A6
John Campbell Rd 26 N16 73 C3
John Carpenter St EC4 251 C6
John Cartwright Ho 7 E2 96 B4
John Chilton Sch UB5 63 A1
John Clifford Ho N8 50 A3
John Clynes Ct SW15 134 B1
John Conwey Ho 23 SW2 160 C5
John Cornwell VC Ho 6 E12 78 C4
John Day Ho TW7 131 B2
John Dee Ho 3 SW14 133 B2
John Donne Prim Sch 13 SE15 140 B4
John Drinkwater Cl E11 54 D2
John Dwight Ho SW6 135 D2
John Fearon Wlk 5 W10 91 A4
John Felton Rd 19 SE16 118 A4
John Fielden Ho 10 E2 96 B4
John Fisher St E1 118 A6
John F Kennedy Specl Sch 6 E15 98 B6
John Gooch Dr EN2 4 D4
John Harris Ho SE15 140 A2
John Harrison Way SE10 120 D3
John Hunt Ct 5 SE9 166 A2
John Islip St SW1 116 A2 260 A3
John Kaye Ct TW17 192 C4
John Keall Ho 3 SW15 134 D2
John Keats Ho N22 32 B2
John Keats Lo EN2 5 B4
John Keble CE Prim Sch NW10 89 D6
John Kelly Tech Colls NW2 67 D5
John Kennedy Ct 1 N1 73 B2
John Kennedy Ho 1 SE16 118 D2
John Kennedy Lo 2 N1 73 B2
John King Ct 5 N19 71 D6
John Kirk Ho
21 Battersea SW11 136 B2
Beckenham BR3 207 A5
5 Streatham SW16 160 A1
John Knight Lo SW6 265 B4
John Lamb Ct HA3 24 C2
John Loughborough Sch 9 N17 33 D1
John Lyon Sch The HA2 42 B1
John McDonald Ho 3 E14 120 A3
John McKenna Wlk 17 SE16 118 A3
John Masefield Ho N15 51 B3
John Maurice Cl SE17 117 B2 262 C4
John Nettleford Ho 14 E2 96 B4
John Newton Ct DA16 146 B2
John Orwell Sports Ctr E1 118 B5
John Parker Cl RM10 81 D1
John Parker Sq 7 SW11 136 B2
John Parry Ct 28 N1 95 C5
John Paul II Sch 9 SW19 156 D4
John Penn Ho SE8 141 B5
John Penn St SE13 141 D4
John Perrin Pl HA3 44 A2
John Perryn Prim Sch W3 89 C1
John Prince's St W1 238 D2
John Pritchard Ho 16 E1 96 A3
John Ratcliffe Ho 8 NW6 91 C4
John Rennie Wlk 1 E1 118 C5
John Roan Sch SE3 142 C5
John Roll Way SE16 118 A3
John Ruskin Coll CR2 223 A1
John Ruskin Prim Sch SE5 139 A6
John Ruskin St SE5 139 A6
John's Ave NW4 46 C5
Johns Cl TW15 171 A6
John Scurr Ho 18 E14 97 A1
John Scurr Prim Sch 46 E1 96 C3
John Silkin La SE8 118 D1
Johns La SM4 202 A4
John's Mews WC1 94 B3 240 D5
John Smith Ave SW6 135 B5 264 C4
John Smith Mews E14 120 B6
Johnson Cl E8 96 A6
Johnson Ct
Hendon NW4 46 A6
10 Wandsworth SW18 136 B1
Johnson Ho
Belgravia SW1 258 B3
23 Bethnal Green E2 96 A4
Somers Town NW1 232 B3
South Lambeth SW8 269 D3
Johnson Lo 12 W9 91 C2
Johnson Rd
Bromley Comm BR2 209 D4
Heston TW5 128 C5
Stonebridge NW10 89 B6
Thornton Heath CR0 205 B2
Johnson's Cl SM5 218 D5
Johnsons Ct EC4 241 B1
Johnsons Dr TW12 174 A2
Johnson's Ind Est UB3 106 A3
Johnson's Pl SW1 115 C1 259 A1
Johnson St
Southall UB2 106 D3
Stepney E1 96 C1
Johnsons Way NW10 88 D3
John Spencer Sq N1 72 D2
John's Pl E1 96 B1
John St
Croydon SE25 206 A5
Enfield EN1 17 D6
Finsbury WC1 94 B3 240 D5
Hounslow TW3, TW5 129 A3
West Ham E15 98 D6
John Stainer Prim Sch SE4 141 A2
John's Terr CR0 205 C1
Johnston Cl SW9 270 D1
Johnstone Ho SE13 142 B2
Johnstone Rd E6 100 B4
Johnston Rd IG8 37 A5
John Strachey Ho SW6 264 D5
John Strype Ct E10 53 D1
John Trundle Ct EC4 242 A4
John Tucker Ho 3 E14 119 C3
John Walsh Twr E11 76 D6
John Wesley Cl 4 E6 100 B4
John Wesley Ct 6 TW1 153 A3
John Wesley's House & Mus of Methodism* EC1 242 D6
John Wheatley Ho
14 London N19 49 D2
West Brompton SW6 264 D5
John William Cl 12 KT2 175 D2
John Williams Cl SE14 140 D6
John Wilson St SE18 122 C2
John Wooley Cl SE13 142 C1
Joiners Arms Yd 1 SE5 139 B4
Joiners Ct 5 N20 14 D1
Joiner St SE1 252 D3
Joiners Yd N1 233 B3
Joint Rd N10 30 C2
Jolles Ho 9 E3 97 D4
Jollys La Harrow HA2 42 B1
Hayes UB4 84 D2
Jonathan Ct 9 W4 111 C2
Jonathan St SE11 116 B1 260 C2
Jones Ho
4 South Bromley E14 98 B1
Stamford Hill N16 51 C1
Jones Rd E13 99 B3
Jones St W1 248 C5
Jones Wlk 6 TW10 154 B5
Jonquil Gdns 5 TW12 173 C4
Jonson Cl Hayes UB4 84 A2
Mitcham CR4 203 B6
Jonson Ho
Borough The SE1 262 D5
16 Canonbury N16 73 B4
Jordan Cl HA2 63 B5
Jordan Ct SW15 134 D1
Jordan Hill N10 30 C2
Jordan Ho
12 London SE4 140 D1
Shoreditch N1 235 D5
Jordan Lo SW17 180 C5
Jordan Rd UB6 87 C6
Jordans Cl
Dagenham RM10 81 D4
Hounslow TW7 130 C4
Jordans Ho NW8 237 A5
Jordans Mews TW11 152 C2
Jo Richardson Com Sch RM9 102 D6
Joscoyne Ho 5 E1 96 B1
Josef Perrin Ho 1 SE27 183 B6
Joseph Ave W3 89 B1
Joseph Clarke Specl Sch E4 36 B4
Joseph Conrad Ho SW1 259 B3
Joseph Ct N16 51 C2
Joseph Hardcastle Cl SE14 140 D5
Joseph Hood Prim Sch SW20 201 A6
Josephine Ave SW2 160 B6
Joseph Irwin Ho 11 E14 119 B6
Joseph Lister Ct E7 77 A1
Joseph Lister Lo E11 55 B1
Joseph Powell Cl 1 SW12 159 C5
Joseph Priestley Ho 12 E2 96 B4
Joseph Ray Rd E11 76 C6
Joseph St E3 97 B3
Joseph Trotter Cl EC1 234 B1
Joshua Cl
Croydon CR2 220 D1
Muswell Hill N10 31 B3
Joshua St E14 98 A1
Joslings Cl W12 112 A6
Joslyn Cl EN3 7 C5
Josseline Ct 9 E3 97 A5
Joubert Mans SW3 257 B2
Joubert St SW11 136 D3
Jowett Ho 27 SW9 138 A3
Jowett St SE15 139 D5
Joyce Ave N18 33 D5
Joyce Butler Ho N22 32 B2
Joyce Dawson Way SE28 124 A6
Joyce Lattimore Ct N9 18 B1
Joyce Page Cl SE7 143 D6
Joy Ct NW2 68 D5
Joydon Dr RM6 58 B3
Joyner Ct UB1 107 B6
Joyners Cl RM9 81 B4
Joystone Ct 8 EN4 2 C1
Jubb Powell Ho N15 51 C3
Jubet Ho 9 N16 73 B4
Jubilee Ave
Chingford E4 36 A4
Romford RM7 59 D4
Twickenham TW2 152 A3
Jubilee Bldgs NW8 229 C4
Jubilee Cl
4 Harlesden NW10 89 D5
Kingsbury NW9 45 B3
Pinner HA5 22 C1
Romford RM7 59 D4
Teddington KT1 175 C2
Jubilee Cres
Cubitt Town E14 120 A3
Edmonton N9 18 A3
Jubilee Ct
Harrow HA3 44 A2
Hounslow TW3 129 D2
Islington N1 233 B6
Muswell Hill N10 49 A6
12 Sutton SM2 218 A2
Thornton Heath CR7 204 C5
Jubilee Dr HA4 63 A4
Jubilee Gdns UB1 85 C1
Jubilee Hall Mkt* WC2 250 B6
Jubilee Ho
3 Hampton TW12 173 C2
Lambeth SE11 261 B3
Jubilee Hts NW2 69 B2
Jubilee JMI Sch N16 52 A1
Jubilee Lo HA7 25 A5
Jubilee Mans 10 E1 96 C1
Jubilee Par IG8 37 C4
Jubilee Park Ctry Pk BR2 210 C4
Jubilee Pl SW3 114 C1 257 B2
Jubilee Prim Sch
London SW2 160 C5
Woolwich SE28 124 C6
Jubilee Rd
Cheam SM3 216 D1
Wembley UB6 87 B6
Jubilee St E1 96 C2
Jubilee The 2 SE10 141 D5
Jubilee Villas KT10 196 C1
Jubilee Way
East Bedfont TW14 150 A3
Merton SW19 179 D2
Sidcup DA14 168 A2
Tolworth KT4, KT9 214 D5
Jubilee Wks SW19 180 A1
Jubilee Wlk WD19 22 B6
Jubilee Yd SE1 253 C2
Judd St WC1 94 A4 233 A1
Jude St E16 98 D1
Judge Heath La UB3 83 B1
Judges' Wlk NW3 70 A5
Judge Wlk KT10 212 C2
Juer St SW11 136 C5 267 B3
Jules Thorn Ave EN1 6 A1
Julia Ct E17 53 D4
Julia Garfield Mews 4 E16 121 B5
Julia Gdns IG11 102 D5
Juliana Cl N2 48 A6
Julian Ave W3 110 D6
Julian Cl EN5 1 D2
Julian Ct SW13 133 D4
Julian Hill HA1 64 C6
Julian Ho SE21 183 C6
Julian Pl E14 119 D1
Julian's Prim Sch SW16 182 C6
Julian Taylor Path 7 SE23 162 B2
Julia St NW5 71 A3
Julien Rd W5 109 C3
Juliet Ho 11 N1 95 C5
Juliette Rd E13 99 A5
Julius Caesar Way HA7 9 D1
Julius Ct TW8 132 A5
Julius Ho 8 E14 98 B1
Julius Nyerere Cl N1 233 C5
Junction App
Battersea SW11 136 C2
Lewisham SE13 142 A2
Junction Mews W2 237 A2
Junction Pl W2 236 D2
Junction Rd
Ashford TW15 171 B5
Brentford TW8 109 D2
Croydon CR2 221 B3
Dartmouth Pk N19 71 C5
Edmonton N9 18 A3
Harrow HA1 42 C3
Newham E13 99 B5
Tottenham Hale N17 52 A6
Junction Rd E RM6 59 A2
Junction Rd W RM6 59 A2
Junction Wembley Ret Pk The HA9 66 D4
Juniper Cl Barnet EN5 12 D6
Chessington KT9 214 B3
Wembley HA9 66 C3
Juniper Cres NW1 71 A1
Juniper Ct
Dagenham RM6 58 C3
Harrow HA3 24 D2
Hounslow TW3 129 D1
Stoke Newington N16 73 B6
Thornton Heath CR0 204 C3
Juniper Dr SW18 136 A1
Juniper Gdns
Ashford TW16 171 D4
Streatham CR4 181 C2
Juniper Ho
12 Ealing W5 87 C2
6 Peckham SE14, SE15 140 C5
9 Richmond TW9 132 D4
Juniper La E6 100 A2
Juniper Rd IG1 78 D4
Juniper St 16 E1 118 C6
Juniper Way UB3 105 C6
Juno Ct 11 SW9 138 C5
Juno Ho 2 E3 97 C6
Juno Way SE14 140 D6
Juno Way Ind Est SE14 140 D6
Jupiter Ct
10 Brixton SW9 138 C5
8 Northolt UB5 84 D4
Jupiter Hts UB10 82 B6
Jupiter Way N7 72 B2

Jupp Rd E15 76 B1
Jupp Rd W E15 98 B6
Jura Ho SE16 119 A2
Jurston Ct SE1 251 B1
Justice Wlk SW3 267 A5
Justin Cl TW8 131 D5
Justin Ct 3 CR7 204 C4
Justines Pl E2 96 D4
Justin Plaza CR4 202 C5
Justin Rd E4 35 B4
Jute La EN3 7 A2
Jutland Cl N19 50 A1
Jutland Ho
4 London SE5 139 A3
10 Woolwich SE7 122 A2
Jutland Rd
Catford SE6 164 A4
Newham E13 99 A3
Jutsums Ave RM7 59 D3
Jutsums Ct RM7 59 D3
Jutsums La RM7 59 D2
Juxon Cl HA3 23 D2
Juxon St
SE11 116 B2 260 D4
JVC Bsns Pk NW2 46 A1

K

Kaduna Cl HA5 40 B4
Kaine Pl CR0 207 A2
Kaizen Prim Sch E13 99 B3
Kale Rd DA18 125 A4
Kambala Rd SW11 136 B2
Kangley Bridge Ctr
SE26 185 B5
Kangley Bridge Rd
SE26 185 B5
Kaplan Dr N21 16 B6
Karachi Ho E15 76 C2
Kara Way NW2 68 D4
Karen Ct
Bromley BR1 186 D2
2 Camberwell SE5 139 C2
Forest Hill SE23 163 A5
Karen Ho 7 N16 73 B4
Karens Ct EN3 6 D6
Karen Terr Ilford IG2 57 B4
Leyton E11 76 D6
Karenza Ct HA9 43 C2
Kariba Cl N9 18 C1
Karman Ct HA3 42 C6
Karma Way HA2 41 C1
Karoline Gdns UB6 86 B5
Karyatis Ct EN1 17 D6
Kashgar Rd SE18 123 D2
Kashmir Rd SE7 143 D5
Kasmin Ct NW10 68 A1
Kassala Rd
SW11 136 D4 267 D1
Katella Trad Est
IG11 101 C4
Kates Cl EN5 12 A6
Katharine Rd 1
TW1 153 A3
Katharine St CR0 221 A5
Katherine Cl 3
SE16 118 D5
Katherine Ct
10 Forest Hill SE23 162 C3
Penge SE20 184 C2
Katherine Gdns SE9 143 D1
Katherine Ho
15 Kensal Town W10 91 A3
6 South Croydon
CR0 221 A5
South Norwood SE19 183 C4
Katherine Rd E6, E7 77 C1
Katherine Sq W11 244 A4
Kathleen Ave
Acton W3 89 A2
Wembley HA0 66 A1
Kathleen Ferrier Ct 4
N17 33 D3
Kathleen Godfree Ct
SW19 179 C5
Kathleen Moore Ct
BR4 224 A6
Kathleen Rd SW11 136 D2
Katrine Ct NW2 68 C5
Kayemoor Rd SM2 218 C2
Kay Rd SW9 138 B3
Kays Ct EN3 6 D1
Kay St E2 96 A5
Keadby Ho 2 UB5 85 B4
Kean Ho 5 SE17 138 D6
Kean St WC2 94 B1 240 C1
Keates Est N16 73 D6
Keatley Gn E4 35 B4
Keats Ave E16 121 B5
Keats Cl
Bermondsey SE1 263 C3
Enfield EN3 18 D6
Hampstead NW3 70 C4
Hayes UB4 84 A2
Mitcham SW19 180 B4
Wanstead E11 55 B4
Keats Ct HA0 65 C5
Keats Gr NW3 70 C4
Keats Ho
7 Beckenham BR3 185 D4
22 Bethnal Green E2 96 C4
30 Camberwell SE5 139 A5
Chelsea SW1 269 B6
Harrow HA2 64 C6
Keats House Mus★
NW3 70 C4
Keats Par 3 N9 18 A2
Keats Pl EC2 242 C3
Keats Rd DA16 145 D4
Keats Way
Croydon CR0 206 C3
Southall UB6 85 D2
West Drayton UB7 104 B2
Kebbell Terr E7 77 B3
Keble Cl
New Malden KT4 199 D1
Northolt UB5 64 A3
Keble Ct SW19 179 C4
Keble Ho 4 SW15 156 D5
Keble Pl SW13 134 B6
Keble Prep Sch N21 16 C4
Keble St SW17 180 A6
Kechill Gdns BR2 209 A2
Kedelston Ct E5 75 A4
Kedeston Ct SM1 201 D1
Kedge Ho 16 E14 119 C3
Kedleston Dr BR5 211 D4
Kedleston Wlk 21 E2 96 B4
Kedyngton Ho 5
HA8 27 A1
Keeble Cl SE18 144 D6
Keedonwood Rd
BR1 186 D5
Keel Cl Barking IG11 102 C5
Rotherhithe SE16 118 D5
Keel Ct 8 E14 120 B6
Keeley Rd CR0 221 A6
Keeley St WC2 94 B1 240 C1
Keeling 2 TW11 174 C5
Keeling Ct CR0 220 D4
Keeling Ho 4 E2 96 B5
Keeling Rd SE9 165 D6
Keelson Ho 9 E14 119 C3
Keely Cl EN4 14 C6
Keemor Cl SE18 144 C5
Keens Cl SW16 181 D5
Keen's Rd CR0 221 A4
Keen's Yd N1 72 D2
Keepers Ct 4 CR2 221 A3
Keepers Mews
TW11 175 C4
Keeper Wharf E1 118 D6
Keepier Wharf 15
E1 118 D6
Keep The
Forest Hill SE6 163 C3
Kidbrooke SE3 143 A3
Kingston u T KT2 176 B3
Keeton's Rd SE16 118 B3
Keevil Dr SW19 157 A4
Keighley Cl N7 72 A4
Keightley Dr SE9 167 A3
Keilder Cl UB10 82 C5
Keildon Rd SW11 136 D1
Keir Hardie Est E5 52 B1
Keir Hardie Ho
6 Belvedere DA17 125 C3
Fulham W6 134 D6
15 Upper Holloway
N19 49 D2
Willesden NW10 67 D1
Keir Hardie Way
Barking IG11 80 A1
Hayes UB4 84 A4
Keir Hardy Prim Sch 13
E16 99 A2
Keir The SW19 178 C5
Keith Connor Cl 5
SW8 137 B2
Keith Gr W12 112 A5
Keith Ho NW6 91 D5
Keith Park Rd UB10 60 B1
Keith Rd
Barking IG11 101 B5
Hayes UB3 105 C3
Walthamstow E17 35 B2
Keith Sutton Ho 3
SE9 167 A2
Kelbrook Rd SE3 144 A2
Kelby Ho N7 72 B2
Kelceda Cl NW2 68 A6
Kelf Gr UB3 83 D1
Kelfield Ct 1 W10 90 D1
Kelfield Gdns W10 90 D1
Kelfield Mews W10 90 D1
Kelham Ho 10 SE18 144 D6
Kelland Cl 1 N8 49 D4
Kelland Rd E13 99 A3
Kellaway Rd SE3 143 D3
Keller Cres E12 77 D4
Kellerton Rd SE13 164 C6
Kellett Ho N1 235 D5
Kellett Rd SW2 138 C1
Kelling Gdns CR0 204 D2
Kellino St SW17 180 D6
Kellner Rd SE28 123 D3
Kellow Ho SE1 252 C2
Kell St SE1 116 D3 261 D6
Kelly Ave SE15 139 D4
Kelly Cl
Upper Halliford
TW17 171 C1
Willesden NW10 67 B5
Kelly Ct 18 E14 119 C6
Kelly Mews 4 W9 91 B3
Kelly Rd NW7 29 A4
Kelly St NW1 71 B2
Kelly Way RM6 59 A3
Kelman Cl SW4 137 D3
Kelmore Gr SE22 140 A1
Kelmscott 5 SE23 162 D1
Kelmscott Cl E17 35 B2
Kelmscott Ct 2 HA7 25 C6
Kelmscott Gdns
W12 112 A3
Kelmscott House★
W6 112 B2
Kelmscott L Ctr E17 53 B3
Kelmscott Rd SW11 158 D6
Kelmscott Sch E17 53 B3
Kelross Rd N5 73 A4
Kelsall Cl SE3 143 B3
Kelsall Mews TW9 132 D4
Kelsey Gate 8 BR3 185 D1
Kelsey La BR3 207 C6
Kelsey Park Ave
BR3 185 D1
Kelsey Park Man
BR3 207 D6
Kelsey Park Rd BR3 185 C1
Kelsey Park Sp Coll
BR3 207 C6
Kelsey Rd BR5 190 B1
Kelsey Sq BR3 185 C1
Kelsey St E2 96 A3
Kelsey Way BR3 207 C6
Kelshall Ct N4 73 A6
Kelso Ct SE20 184 B3
Kelso Lo E18 37 B1
Kelson Ho E14 120 A3
Kelso Pl W8 113 D3 255 D6
Kelso Rd SM5 202 A2
Kelvedon Cl KT2 176 C4
Kelvedon Ct HA4 62 C4
Kelvedon Ho SW8 270 B2
Kelvedon Rd
SW6 135 B5 264 D3
Kelvin Ave N13 32 B4
Kelvinbrook KT8 195 D6
Kelvin Cl KT19 214 C2
Kelvin Cres HA3 24 C3
Kelvin Ct
Chiswick W4 133 A5
Harrow HA2 42 A1
Isleworth TW7 130 C3
Notting Hill W11 245 A5
7 Penge SE20 184 B2
8 Twickenham TW1 153 B5
Kelvin Dr TW1 153 B5
Kelvin Gdns
Southall UB1 85 C1
Thornton Heath CR0 204 A2
Kelvin Gr
Forest Hill SE26 162 B1
Surbiton KT6 214 A5
Kelvin Grove Prim Sch 7
SE26 162 B1
Kelvington Cl CR0 207 A2
Kelvington Rd SE15 162 D6
Kelvin Ho 3 DA17 125 C3
Kelvin Ind Est UB6 85 D6
Kelvin Par BR6 211 C1
Kelvin Rd Highbury N5 73 A4
Welling DA16 146 A2
Kelyway Ho 20 SW2 160 C4
Kember St N1 72 B1
Kemble Dr BR2 226 A5
Kemble Ho
London SW9 138 D2
Stanmore HA7 24 D5
Kemble Rd
Croydon CR0 220 D5
Forest Hill SE23 162 D3
Tottenham N17 34 A2
Kemble St
WC2 94 B1 240 C1
Kemerton Rd
Beckenham BR3 185 D1
Camberwell SE5 139 A2
Croydon CR0 205 D2
Kemey's St E9 75 A3
Kemnal Rd BR7 189 B5
Longlands BR7, SE9 167 B1
Kemnal Tech Coll
DA14 190 B3
Kemnal Warren BR7 189 B4
Kemp 24 NW9 27 D2
Kemp Ct SW8 270 A3
Kempe Ho SE1 262 D5
Kempe Rd NW6 90 D5
Kemp Gdns CR0 205 A3
Kemp Ho
Finsbury EC1 235 C1
1 Globe Town E2 96 D5
Wallend E6 78 C2
Kempis Way 5
SE22 161 C6
Kemplay Rd NW3 70 B4
Kemp Rd RM8 58 D1
Kemps Ct NW2 68 D5
Kemp's Ct W1 239 C1
Kemps Dr E14 119 C6
Kempsford Gdns
SW5 113 C1 255 B1
Kempsford Rd
Lambeth SE11 261 B3
Newington SE11 261 C3
Kemps Gdns SE13 164 A6
Kempshott Rd SW16 182 A3
Kempson Rd
SW6 135 C5 265 B3
Kempthorne Rd SE8 119 B2
Kempton Ave
Northolt UB5 63 C3
Sunbury TW16 172 B2
Kempton Cl UB10 61 A4
Kempton Ct
Stepney E1 96 B2
Sunbury TW16 172 B2
Kempton Ho 13 N1 95 C6
Kempton Lo 3 SM6 219 D5
Kempton Park Race
Course TW16 172 C3
Kempton Park Sta
TW16 172 B3
Kempton Rd E6 100 B6
Kempton Wlk CR0 207 A3
Kempt St SE18 144 C6
Kemsing Cl
Coney Hall BR2 224 D6
Sidcup DA5 169 A4
South Norwood CR7 205 A5
Kemsing Ho SE1 252 D1
Kemsing Rd SE10 121 A1
Kemsley SE13 163 D6
Kemsley Ct
Ealing W13 109 C5
St Paul's Cray BR5 190 B2
Kenbrook Ho
Kensington W14 254 D5
5 Kentish Town NW5 71 C3
Kenbury Cl UB10 60 C5
Kenbury Gdns 10
SE5 139 A3
Kenbury Mans 18
SE5 139 A3
Kenbury St SE5 139 A3
Kenchester Cl
SW8 138 A5 270 B3
Kencot Cl DA18 125 B4
Kencot Way DA18 125 B4
Kendal NW1 231 D2
Kendal Ave Acton W3 88 D2
Barking IG11 101 C6
Edmonton N18 33 B6
Kendal Cl
Camberwell SE5 138 D5
East Barnet N20 14 C2
East Bedfont TW14 149 D3
Hayes UB4 83 C5
Woodford IG8 20 D2
Kendal Ct Acton W3 88 C2
Brondesbury NW2 69 A3
9 Chingford E4 20 A3
Kendale Rd BR1 186 C5
Kendal Gdns
Edmonton N18 33 B6
Sutton SM1 218 A6
Kendal Ho
Edgware HA8 27 A6
Forest Hill SE23 163 B3
32 Hackney E9 74 C1
Islington N1 233 D4
Penge SE20 184 B1
Kendall Ave BR3 185 A1
Kendall Ct
3 London SE22 162 A6
Mitcham SW19 180 B4
5 Penge SE19 183 D3
Sidcup DA15 168 A1
Kendall Ho SE12 164 D4
Kendall Lo 5 BR1 187 B2
Kendall Pl W1 238 A3
Kendall Rd
Beckenham BR3 185 A1
Isleworth TW7 131 A3
Kidbrooke SE18 144 A4
Kendalmere Cl N10 31 B2
Kendal Par N18 33 B6
Kendal Pl SW15 157 B6
Kendal Rd NW10 68 A4
Kendal St W2 92 C1 237 B1
Kendal Stps W2 237 B1
Kender Prim Sch
SE14 140 C4
Kender St SE14 140 C4
Kendoa Rd 1 SW4 137 D1
Kendon Cl E11 55 B4
Kendon Ho E15 76 B1
Kendra Ct CR2 220 D1
Kendra Hall Rd CR2 220 D1
Kendrey Gdns TW2 152 C4
Kendrick Ct 12 SE15 140 B4
Kendrick Mews SW7 256 C3
Kendrick Pl SW7 256 C3
Kenelm Cl HA1 65 A5
Kenerne Dr EN5 13 A6
Kenilford Rd SW12 159 B4
Kenilworth Ave
Harrow HA2 63 B4
Walthamstow E17 53 C6
Wimbledon SW19 179 C6
Kenilworth Cres EN1 5 C4
Kenilworth Ct
7 Chingford E4 20 A2
Fulham SW6 135 A2
Twickenham TW2 152 C2
Kenilworth Gdns
Hayes UB4 83 D2
Ilford IG3 79 D6
Southall UB1 85 B4
South Oxhey WD19 22 C5
Woolwich SE18 144 D3
Kenilworth Ho HA7 25 B3
Kenilworth Rd
Ashford TW15,
TW19 148 A1
Bow E3 97 A5
Ealing W5 110 A5
Edgware HA8 11 A1
Kilburn NW6 91 B6
Orpington BR5 211 A3
Penge SE20 184 D2
Stoneleigh KT17 216 A3
Kenilworth Terr 3
SM2 217 C1
Kenley N17 33 B1
Kenley Ave NW9 27 C2
Kenley Cl Barnet EN4 2 C1
Sidcup DA5 169 C4
St Paul's Cray BR7 211 C6
Kenley Gdns CR7 204 D5

Kenley Ho
5 Croydon CR0 ..... 206 A1
6 St Paul's Cray BR5 . 190 B1
Kenley Rd
Kingston u T KT1,
KT3 ..... 176 D1
Merton SW19 ..... 201 C6
Twickenham TW1 ..... 153 B5
Kenley Wlk
Cheam SM3 ..... 216 D4
Notting Hill W11 ..... 244 A5
Kenlor Ct 6 HA8 ..... 26 D5
Kenlor Rd SW17 ..... 180 B5
Kenmare Ct 5 HA7 ... 25 C6
Kenmare Dr
Mitcham CR4 ..... 180 D3
1 Tottenham N17 ..... 33 D1
Kenmare Gdns N13 ... 33 A6
Kenmare Rd CR7 ..... 204 C3
Kenmere Gdns HA0 ... 88 C6
Kenmere Rd DA16 ... 146 C3
Kenmont Gdns NW10 . 90 B4
Kenmont Prim Sch
NW10 ..... 90 B4
Kenmore Ave HA3 ... 43 A6
Kenmore Cl TW9 ..... 132 C5
Kenmore Cres UB4 ... 83 D4
Kenmore Ct NW6 ..... 69 C1
Kenmore Gdns HA8 ... 26 D1
Kenmore Park Fst & Mid
Schs HA3 ..... 44 A6
Kenmore Rd HA3 ..... 43 D5
Kenmure Mans W5 ... 87 C3
Kenmure Rd E8 ..... 74 B3
Kenmure Yd E8 ..... 74 B3
Kennacraig Cl 6
E16 ..... 121 A5
Kennard Ho 12
SW11 ..... 137 A3
Kennard Mans 6
N11 ..... 30 D5
Kennard Rd
London N11 ..... 30 D5
Stratford E15 ..... 76 B1
Kennard St
9 London SW11 ..... 137 A3
Newham E16 ..... 122 B5
Kennedy Ave EN3 ..... 18 C5
Kennedy Cl
Crofton BR5 ..... 211 B1
1 Mitcham CR4 ..... 181 A1
Newham E13 ..... 99 A5
Pinner HA5 ..... 23 B4
Kennedy Cox Ho 9
E16 ..... 98 D2
Kennedy Ct
Ashford TW15 ..... 171 A5
Bushey WD23 ..... 8 B2
Kennedy Ho SE11 ... 260 C2
Kennedy Path W7 ..... 86 D3
Kennedy Rd
Barking IG11 ..... 101 C6
Ealing W7 ..... 86 C2
Kennedy Wlk SE17 .. 262 D3
Kennet Cl SW11 ..... 136 B1
Kennet Ct 47 W2 ..... 91 C2
Kennet Dr UB4 ..... 85 A2
Kenneth Ave IG1 ..... 78 D4
Kenneth Campbell Ho
NW8 ..... 236 D6
Kenneth Cres NW2 ... 68 B3
Kenneth Ct SE11 ..... 261 B4
Kenneth Gdns HA7 ... 25 A4
Kenneth More Rd 4
IG1 ..... 78 D5
Kennet Ho NW8 ..... 236 D5
Kenneth Rd RM6 ..... 59 A2
Kenneth Robbins Ho 1
N17 ..... 34 B3
Kenneth Younger Ho
SW6 ..... 264 D5
Kennet Rd
Isleworth TW7 ..... 130 D2
West Kilburn W9 ..... 91 B3
Kennet Sq CR4 ..... 180 C2
Kennet St E1 ..... 118 A5
Kennett Ho HA1 ..... 64 D6
Kennett Wharf La
EC4 ..... 252 B6
Kenninghall N18 ..... 34 C5
Kenninghall Rd
London N18 ..... 34 C5
Lower Clapton E5 ..... 74 B5
Kenning Ho 6 N1 ..... 95 C6
Kenning St 18 SE16 .. 118 C4
Kennings Way
SE11 ..... 116 C1 261 B2
KENNINGTON 116 C1
Kennington Ent Ctr
SE17 ..... 261 C1
Kennington La
SE11 ..... 116 B1 260 D1
Kennington Oval
SE11 ..... 138 B6 270 D5
Kennington Palace Ct
SE11 ..... 261 A2
Kennington Park Gdns
SE17 ..... 138 D6
Kennington Park Ho
SE11 ..... 261 B1
Kennington Park Pl
SE11 ..... 138 D6
Kennington Park Rd
SE11 ..... 116 D1 261 C2
Kennington Rd
SE11 ..... 116 C2 261 A3
Kennington Sta
SE17 ..... 116 D1 261 C2
Kennoldes SE21 ..... 161 B2
Kennyland Ct NW4 ... 46 B3
Kenrick Pl W1 ..... 238 A3
KENSAL GREEN 90 C4
Kensal Green Cemy (All
Souls)* NW10 ..... 90 C4
Kensal Green Sta
NW10 ..... 90 C4
Kensal Ho W10 ..... 90 D3
Kensal Rd W10 ..... 91 A3
KENSAL RISE 90 D5
Kensal Rise Prim Sch
NW6 ..... 90 D5
Kensal Rise Sta
NW10 ..... 90 D5
KENSAL TOWN 91 A3
KENSINGTON 113 C4
Kensington Acad
SW6 ..... 256 C3
Kensington Ave
Plashet E12 ..... 78 B2
South Norwood CR7 .. 182 C2
Kensington Avenue Prim
Sch CR7 ..... 182 C2
Kensington & Chelsea
Coll
Chelsea
SW10 ..... 136 A5 266 A4
14 Kensal Town W10 ... 91 A2
Kensington Church Ct
W8 ..... 245 C1
Kensington Church St
W8 ..... 113 C5 245 B3
Kensington Church Wlk
W8 ..... 245 C1
Kensington Cl N11 ... 31 A4
Kensington Court Mans
W8 ..... 245 D1
Kensington Court Mews
W8 ..... 255 D6
Kensington Court Pl
W8 ..... 113 D3 255 D6
Kensington Ct
2 Burnt Oak NW7 ..... 27 B5
Enfield EN2 ..... 5 C5
Hendon NW4 ..... 28 C1
Kensington
W8 ..... 113 D4 245 D1
Kensington Ct Gdns
W8 ..... 255 D6
Kensington Dr IG8 ... 37 D1
Kensington Gardens*
W2 ..... 114 A5 246 B3
Kensington Gate
W8 ..... 114 A3 256 A6
Kensington Gdns
Kingston u T KT1 ..... 197 D6
Redbridge IG1 ..... 56 B1
Kensington Gdns Sq
W2 ..... 91 D1
Kensington Gore
SW7 ..... 114 B4 246 C1
Kensington Hall Gdns
W14 ..... 254 C2
Kensington High St
W8 ..... 113 C3 255 B6
Kensington Ho 3
NW5 ..... 71 C3
Kensington Hts
Harrow HA1 ..... 42 D3
Kensington W8 ..... 245 A3
Kensington L Ctr
W11 ..... 113 A6 244 A6
Kensington Lodge
UB5 ..... 85 C5
Kensington Mall W8 245 B4
Kensington Mans
SW5 ..... 255 B2
Kensington Olympia Sta
W14 ..... 113 A3 254 A6
Kensington Pal*
W8 ..... 113 D5 245 D3
Kensington Palace Gdns
W8 ..... 113 D5 245 C4
Kensington Park Gdns
W11 ..... 113 B6 244 D5
Kensington Park Mews
W11 ..... 91 B1
Kensington Park Rd
W11 ..... 113 B6 244 D6
Kensington Pl
W8 ..... 113 C5 245 A4
Kensington Prep Sch
SW6 ..... 135 B4 264 D2
Kensington Prim Sch
E12 ..... 78 B2
Kensington Rd
Kensington
SW7 ..... 114 A4 246 B1
Northolt UB5 ..... 85 C5
Kensington Sq
W8 ..... 113 D4 245 C1
Kensington Terr
CR2 ..... 221 B1
Kensington Village
W14 ..... 113 B2 254 D3
Kensington W W14 .. 254 A4
Kensit Meml Coll N3 .. 29 A1
Kensworth Ho EC1 .. 235 D1
Kent Ave
Bexley DA16 ..... 167 D6
Dagenham RM9 ..... 103 C3
Ealing W13 ..... 87 B2
Kent Cl
Mitcham CR4,
SW16 ..... 204 A5
Orpington BR6 ..... 227 C2
Kent Ct Acton W3 ..... 88 B1
3 Haggerston E2 ..... 95 D5
Hendon NW9 ..... 27 C1
Kent Dr
Cockfosters EN4 ..... 15 A6
Teddington TW11 ..... 174 C5
Kentford Way UB5 ... 85 A6
Kent Gate Way CR0 . 223 D3
Kent Gdns Ealing W13 .. 87 B2
Ruislip HA4 ..... 40 B3
Kent Ho
Camberwell SE1 ..... 263 D1
13 Chiswick W4 ..... 111 C1
Edgware HA8 ..... 26 B3
Marylebone W1 ..... 239 A2
Pimlico SW1 ..... 259 C1
Richmond TW10 ..... 154 C6
Kent House La BR3 .. 185 A5
Kent House Rd BR3 . 185 A4
Kent House Sta BR3 . 185 A2
Kent House Station App
BR3 ..... 184 D2
Kentish Bldgs SE1 .. 252 C3
Kentish Rd DA17 ..... 125 C2
KENTISH TOWN 71 C3
Kentish Town CE Prim
Sch 13 NW5 ..... 71 C3
Kentish Town City
Farm* NW5 ..... 71 A3
Kentish Town Rd
NW1 ..... 71 B2
Kentish Town Sta
NW5 ..... 71 C3
Kentish Town West Sta
NW5 ..... 71 B2
Kentish Way BR1,
BR2 ..... 209 B6
Kentlea Rd SE28 ..... 123 C4
Kent Lo 9 SW19 ..... 156 D3
Kentmere Ho SE15 ... 140 C6
Kentmere Rd SE18 ... 123 C2
KENTON 43 C3
Kenton Ave
Harrow HA1 ..... 42 D2
Southall UB1 ..... 107 C6
Sunbury TW16 ..... 173 A1
Kenton Ct
2 Forest Hill SE26 .. 185 A6
Harrow HA3 ..... 43 B3
3 Richmond TW10 .. 153 D5
Kenton Ct *continued*
West Kensington W14 254 C5
Kenton Gdns HA3 ..... 43 C4
Kenton Grove Ho
HA3 ..... 44 B4
Kenton Ho
20 Globe Town E1 ..... 96 C3
Highbury N5 ..... 72 C5
Kenton La
Harrow HA3 ..... 24 D3
Kenton HA3 ..... 43 C6
Kenton Park Ave HA3 . 43 D5
Kenton Park Cl HA3 ... 43 C4
Kenton Park Cres
HA3 ..... 43 D5
Kenton Park Mans
HA3 ..... 43 C4
Kenton Park Par HA3 . 43 D4
Kenton Park Rd HA3 .. 43 C5
Kenton Rd
Harrow HA3 ..... 43 C4
Homerton E9 ..... 74 D2
Kenton St WC1 ..... 240 A6
Kenton Sta HA3 ..... 43 B3
Kenton Way UB4 ..... 83 C4
Kent Pas NW1 ..... 237 C6
Kent Pk Ind Est
SE15 ..... 140 B6
Kent Rd
Dagenham RM10 ..... 81 D3
East Molesey KT8 ... 196 A5
Kingston u T KT1 ... 197 D6
Richmond TW9 ..... 132 C5
South Acton W4 ..... 111 A3
Southgate N21 ..... 17 B4
West Wickham BR4 .. 207 D1
Kent St Haggerston E2 .. 95 D5
Newham E13 ..... 99 B4
Kent Terr
NW1 ..... 92 C4 230 B1
Kent Twr SE20 ..... 184 B3
Kent View Gdns IG3 ... 79 C6
Kent Way KT6 ..... 214 B6
Kentwell Cl SE4 ..... 141 A1
Kentwins N14 ..... 15 B6
Kentwode Gn SW13 . 134 A5
Kent Yard SW7 ..... 247 B1
Kenver Ave N12 ..... 30 B4
Kenward Rd SE9 ..... 165 D6
Ken Way HA9 ..... 67 A5
Kenway Rd
SW5 ..... 113 D2 255 C3
Ken Wilson Ho 19 E2 .. 96 A5
Kenwood Ave N14 ... 15 D6
Kenwood Cl
North End NW3 ..... 48 B1
Sipson UB7 ..... 126 C6
Kenwood Ct NW9 ..... 45 A5
Kenwood Dr BR3 ... 208 A6
Kenwood Gdns
Ilford IG2 ..... 56 C4
2 Wanstead E18 ..... 55 B6
Kenwood Ho
15 Brixton SW9 ..... 138 D1
Enfield EN1 ..... 17 C5
Kenwood Ho* NW3 ... 48 C1
Kenwood Rd
Edmonton N9 ..... 18 A3
Highgate N6 ..... 48 D3
Kenworthy Rd E9 ..... 75 A2
Kenwrick Ho N1 ..... 233 D5
Kenwyn Dr NW2 ..... 67 D5
Kenwyn Rd
Clapham SW4 ..... 137 D1
Wimbledon SW20 ..... 178 C2
Kenya Rd SE7 ..... 143 D5
Kenyngton Dr TW16 .. 172 A5
Kenyngton Manor Prim
Sch TW16 ..... 172 A4
Kenyngton Pl HA3 ... 43 C4
Kenyon Ho 31 SE5 ... 139 A5
Kenyon St SW6 ..... 134 D4
Keogh Rd E15 ..... 76 D2
Kepler Ho 9 SE10 ... 120 D1
Kepler Rd SW2, SW4 . 138 A1
Keppel Ho
Brompton SW3 ..... 257 A3
5 Deptford SE8 ..... 119 B1
Keppel Rd
Dagenham RM9 ..... 81 A4
Newham E6 ..... 100 B6
Keppel Row SE1 ..... 252 A3
Keppel St WC1 ..... 239 D4
Kerala Ct N17 ..... 33 D2
Kerbela St 3 E2 ..... 96 A3
Kerbey St E14 ..... 97 D1
Kerem Sch N2 ..... 48 B4
Kerfield Cres SE5 ... 139 B4
Kerfield Pl SE5 ..... 139 B4
Kerridge Ct 10 N1 ..... 73 C2
Kerrier Ho SW10 ..... 266 B3
Kerrington Ct 7
W12 ..... 112 C4
Kerrison Pl W5 ..... 109 D5
Kerrison Rd
Battersea SW11 ..... 136 C2
Ealing W5 ..... 109 D5
Mill Meads E15 ..... 98 B6
Kerrison Villas W5 .. 109 D5
Kerry N7 ..... 72 A2
Kerry Ave HA7 ..... 25 D6
Kerry Cl Newham E16 .. 99 B1
Palmers Green N13 ..... 16 B2
Kerry Ct HA7 ..... 25 D6
Kerry Ho 5 E1 ..... 96 C1
Kerry Path SE8 ..... 141 B6
Kerry Rd SE8 ..... 141 B6
Kerscott Ho 30 E3 ..... 97 D4
Kersey Gdns SE9 ..... 188 A6
Kersfield Ho SW15 .. 156 D5
Kersfield Rd SW15 .. 156 D5
Kershaw Cl SW18 ..... 158 B5
Kershaw Ho 7
SE27 ..... 160 D1
Kershaw Rd RM10 ..... 81 C5
Kersley Mews SW11 . 267 C1
Kersley Rd N16 ..... 73 C5
Kersley St SW11 ..... 136 D3
Kerstin Cl UB3 ..... 105 D6
Kerswell Cl N15 ..... 51 C4
Kerwick Cl 1 N7 ..... 72 B1
Keslake Mans NW10 .. 90 D5
Keslake Rd NW6 ..... 90 D5
Kessock Cl N17 ..... 52 B4
Kestlake Rd DA5 ..... 168 C5
KESTON 225 D4
Keston Ave BR2 ..... 225 C3
Keston CE Prim Sch
BR2 ..... 225 D3
Keston Cl
Bexley DA16 ..... 146 C5
Edmonton N18 ..... 17 B1
Keston Ct DA5 ..... 169 B4
Keston Gdns BR2 ... 225 C4
Keston Ho SE17 ..... 263 B2
KESTON MARK 225 D6
Keston Mark BR2 ..... 226 A5
Keston Park Cl BR2 .. 226 B5
Keston Rd
East Dulwich SE15 ... 140 A2
Thornton Heath CR7 . 204 C3
West Green N17 ..... 51 B5
Kestrel Ave
East Ham E6 ..... 100 A2
Herne Hill SE24 ..... 161 A6
Kestrel Cl
Grahame Pk NW9 ..... 27 C1
Kingston u T KT2 ..... 175 D6
Neasden NW10 ..... 67 B3
Kestrel Ct
Higham Hill E17 ..... 34 D1
Ruislip HA4 ..... 61 B6
South Croydon CR2 .. 221 A2
Wallington SM6 ..... 219 C3
Kestrel Ho
4 Battersea SW11 .. 136 C2
Enfield EN3 ..... 19 A6
Finsbury EC1 ..... 235 A2
Kestrel Pl SE14 ..... 141 A6
Kestrel Way UB3 ..... 105 B4
Keswick Apartments 4
N17 ..... 51 D6
Keswick Ave
Kingston u T KT2,
SW15 ..... 177 C5
Merton SW19 ..... 179 C1
Upper Halliford TW17 193 C6
Keswick Broadway 1
SW15 ..... 157 B6
Keswick Cl SM1 ..... 218 A4
Keswick Ct
13 Catford SE6 ..... 164 D3
2 East Dulwich SE22 162 A6
Keswick Dr EN3 ..... 6 C6
Keswick Gdns
Redbridge IG4 ..... 56 A5
Ruislip HA4 ..... 39 B3
Wembley HA9 ..... 66 A4
Keswick Ho 8 SE5 ... 139 A4

Keswick Hts 9 SW15 157 A6
Keswick Lo E8 73 D2
Keswick Mews W5 110 A5
Keswick Rd
Bexleyheath DA7 147 C4
Broom Hill BR6 211 D1
Putney SW15 157 A6
Twickenham TW2 152 A5
West Wickham BR4 224 C6
Kettering Ct CR7 205 A5
Kettering Rd EN3 6 D6
Kettering St SW16 181 C4
Kett Gdns SW2 160 B6
Kettlebaston Rd E10 53 B1
Kettleby Ho SW9 138 D2
Kettlewell Cl N11 31 A4
Ketton Ho 11 W10 90 C3
Kevan Ct 6 E17 53 D5
Kevan Ho SE5 139 A5
Kevelioc Rd N17 33 A2
Kevin Cl TW4 128 D3
Kevington Cl BR5 211 D5
Kevington Dr BR5, BR7 211 D5
KEW 132 C6
Kew Bridge TW8 110 B1
Kew Bridge Ct W4 110 C1
Kew Bridge Distribution Ctr TW8 110 B1
Kew Bridge Rd TW8 110 B1
Kew Bridge Sta TW8 110 B1
Kew Bridge Steam Mus★ TW8 110 B1
Kew Coll TW9 132 C5
Kew Cres SM3 217 B5
Kew Ct KT2 176 A2
Kew Foot Rd TW9 132 A2
Kew Gardens Rd TW9 132 C4
Kew Gardens (Royal Botanic)★ TW9 132 A4
Kew Gardens Sta TW9 132 C4
Kew Gn TW9 132 B6
Kew Green TW9 132 C6
Kew Green Prep Sch TW9 132 B6
Kew Lo 11 TW9 132 B4
Kew Obsy★ TW9 131 C2
Kew Pal★ TW9 132 A5
Kew Pier TW9 132 C6
Kew Rd Finchley N2 30 C2
Richmond TW9, W4 132 B4
Kew Ret Pk TW9 132 D4
Kew Riverside Prim Sch TW9 132 D3
Key Cl E1 96 B3
Keyes Ct SE22 162 A6
Keyes Rd NW2 68 D3
Keyham Ho 31 W2 91 C2
Key Ho 9 SE11 138 C6
Keymer Rd SW2 160 B2
Keynes Cl N2 48 D6
Keynes Ct 9 SE28 124 B6
Keynsham Ave IG8 36 C6
Keynsham Gdns SE9 166 A6
Keynsham Ho 2 N4 51 A2
Keynsham Rd
Cheam SM4 201 D1
Eltham SE9 166 A6
Keynsham Wlk SM4 201 D1
Keysham Ave TW5 128 A4
Keysham Ct HA9 66 A6
Keystone Cres N1 233 B3
Keywood Dr TW16 172 A4
Keyworth Cl E5 75 A4
Keyworth Pl SE1 261 D6
Keyworth Prim Sch SE17 116 D1 261 C2
Keyworth St SE1 116 D3 261 D6
Kezia St SE8 119 A1
Khalsa Coll London HA1 42 B3
Khalsa Ct N22 32 D2
Khama Rd SW17 180 C6
Khartoum Rd
Ilford IG1 78 D3
Newham E13 99 B4
Upper Tooting SW17 180 B6
Khyber Rd SW11 136 C3
Kibworth St SW8 138 B5 270 C3
KIDBROOKE 143 C3
Kidbrooke Gdns SE3 143 A4
Kidbrooke Gr SE3 143 B4
Kidbrooke Interchange SE3 143 C2
Kidbrooke La SE9 144 A1
Kidbrooke Park Cl SE3 143 B4
Kidbrooke Park Prim Sch SE3 143 C4
Kidbrooke Park Rd SE12, SE3 143 B2
Kidbrooke Sch SE3 143 D3
Kidbrooke Sta SE3 143 B2
Kidbrooke Way SE3 143 B3
Kiddens BR8 191 D1
Kidderminster Pl CR0 204 D1
Kidderminster Rd CR0 205 A2
Kidderpore Ave NW3 69 C4
Kidderpore Gdns NW3 69 C4
Kidd Ho RM9 81 B4
Kidd Pl SE7 122 A1
Kidlington Way NW9 27 C2
Kidspace Indoor Adventure Pk★ CR0 220 C2
Kierbeck Bsns Complex E16 121 B4
Kiffen St EC2 242 D6
Kilberry Cl TW7 130 B4
Kilbrennan Ho 9 E14 98 A1
KILBURN 91 C6
Kilburn Bridge 14 NW6 91 C6
Kilburn Gate NW6 91 D5
Kilburn High Rd NW6 91 C6
Kilburn High Road Sta NW6 91 D6
Kilburn Ho 11 W9 91 B4
Kilburn La W10 91 A5
Kilburn Park Rd NW6 91 C4
Kilburn Park Sch 10 NW6 91 B5
Kilburn Park Sta NW6 91 C5
Kilburn Pl NW6 91 C6
Kilburn Priory NW6 91 D6
Kilburn Sq NW6 91 C6
Kilburn Sta NW2 69 B2
Kilburn Vale NW6 91 D6
Kilburn Vale Est 13 NW6 91 C6
Kilby Ct SE10 120 D3
Kildare Cl HA4 40 C1
Kildare Ct W2 91 C1
Kildare Gdns W2 91 C1
Kildare Rd E16 99 A2
Kildare Terr W2 91 C1
Kildare Wlk E14 97 C1
Kildoran Rd SW2 160 A6
Kildowan Rd IG3 58 A1
Kilgour Rd SE23 163 A5
Kilkie St SW6 136 A3
Killarney Rd SW18 158 A5
Killburns Mill Cl SM6 219 B6
Killearn Rd SE6 164 B3
Killester Gdns KT17, KT4 216 B4
Killick Ho SM1 217 D4
Killick Mews 6 SM3 217 A2
Killick St N1 94 B5 233 C3
Killieser Ave SW2 160 A2
Killigrew Ho TW16 171 C3
Killip Cl E16 98 D1
Killoran Ho 9 E14 120 A3
Killowen Ave UB5 64 A3
Killowen Rd E9 74 D2
Killyon Rd SW8 137 C3
Kilmaine Rd SW6 135 A5 264 B3
Kilmarnock Gdns RM8 80 C5
Kilmarnock Rd WD19 22 D6
Kilmarsh Rd W6 112 C2
Kilmartin Ave SW16 204 C6
Kilmartin Rd IG3 80 A6
Kilmington Rd SW13 134 A6
Kilmiston Ave TW17 193 A3
Kilmiston Ho TW17 193 A3
Kilmore Ho 17 E14 97 D1
Kilmorey Gdns TW1 131 B1
Kilmorey Rd TW1 131 B1
Kilmorie Prim Sch SE23 163 A2
Kilmorie Rd SE23 163 A2
Kilmuir Ho SW1 258 B3
Kiln Cl UB3 127 B6
Kiln Ct E14 119 B6
Kilner Ho 3 SE11 138 C6
Kilner St E14 97 C2
Kiln Mews SW17 180 B5
Kiln Pl NW5 71 A3
Kilnsey Ct 8 N11 31 A4
Kilnside KT10 213 A1
Kiloh Ct 1 SW11 136 C2
Kilpatrick Ct N16 51 D1
Kilpatrick Way UB4 85 A2
Kilpeck Ho 3 N4 51 A2
Kilravock Ho SE25 205 C6
Kilravock St W10 91 A4
Kilronan 5 W3 89 B1
Kilross Rd TW14 149 C3
Kilsby Wlk RM9 80 B2
Kilsha Rd KT12 194 C3
Kilvinton Dr EN2 5 B5
Kimbell Gdns SW6 135 A4 264 A1
Kimbell Pl SE9 143 C1
Kimber Ctr The SW18 157 C4
Kimber Ho 11 SE18 144 D6
Kimberley Ave
Ilford IG2 57 C2
Newham E6 100 A5
Nunhead SE15 140 C2
Kimberley Ct
Belvedere DA17 125 B2
Kilburn NW6 91 A6
Kimberley Dr DA14 168 D2
Kimberley Gate 3 BR1 186 D3
Kimberley Gdns
Enfield EN1 5 D2
Harringay N4 50 D4
Kimberley Ho 7 E14 120 A3
Kimberley Ind Est E17 35 B2
Kimberley Rd
Chingford E4 20 C3
Edmonton N18 34 B4
Kilburn NW6 91 A6
Leyton E11 76 B6
Newham E16 98 D3
Penge BR3 184 D1
Stockwell SW9 138 A2
Thornton Heath CR0 204 D3
Tottenham N17 34 A1
Walthamstow E17 35 B2
Kimberley Way E4 20 C3
Kimberley Wlk KT12 194 B2
Kimber Pl TW4 151 C4
Kimber Rd SW18 157 D4
Kimble Cres WD23 8 A4
Kimble Ho
Lisson Gr NW8 237 B6
1 Lower Holloway N7 72 A3
Kimble Rd SW17 180 B4
Kimbolton Cl SE12 164 D5
Kimbolton Row SW3 257 A3
Kimmeridge Gdns 3 SE9 188 A6
Kimmeridge Rd SE9 188 A6
Kimm Ho 16 E17 53 D6
Kimpton Ct 12 SE5 139 B4
Kimpton Ho SW15 156 A4
Kimpton Link Bsns Ctr SM3 217 B6
Kimpton Park Way SM3 217 B6
Kimpton Rd
Camberwell SE5 139 B4
Cheam SM3 217 B6
Kimpton Trade & Bsns Ctr SM3 217 B6
Kinburn St SE16 118 D4
Kincaid Rd SE15 140 B5
Kincardine Gdns W9 91 C3
Kinch Gr HA3, HA9 44 B2
Kincraig BR7 188 C2
Kindell Ho 4 SW14 133 B2
Kinder Cl SE28 124 D6
Kinder Ho N1 235 D4
Kindersley Ho 33 E1 96 A1
Kinder St 19 E1 96 B1
Kinderton Cl N14 15 C3
Kinefold Ho N7 72 A2
Kinfauns Rd Ilford IG3 58 B1
Streatham SW2 160 C2
King Alfred Ave
Catford SE6 163 C1
Catford SE6 185 C6
King Alfred Sch NW11 47 D1
King Arthur Cl SE15 140 C5
King Athelstan Prim Sch KT1 198 B6
King Charles Cres KT5 198 B2
King Charles Ct 16 SE17 138 D6
King Charles Ho SW6 265 D4
King Charles' Rd KT5, KT6 198 B3
King Charles St SW1 116 A4 250 A2
King Charles Terr 11 E1 118 B6
King Charles Wlk 6 SW19 157 A3
King Ct 16 E10 53 D2
Kingcup Cl CR0 206 D1
King David La E1 118 C6
Kingdom St W2 92 A2 236 A3
Kingdon Ho 8 E14 120 A3
Kingdon Rd NW6 69 C2
Kingdown Cl W10 90 D1
King Edward Dr KT6 214 A5
King Edward Mans 12 E8 96 B6
King Edward Mews SW13 134 A4
King Edward Rd
Barnet EN5 1 D1
Leytonstone E10 54 A1
Walthamstow E17 53 A6
King Edward's Gdns W3 110 C5
King Edward's Gr TW11 175 C4
King Edwards Mans SW6 265 A3
King Edwards Pl 5 W3 110 C5
King Edwards Rd HA4 39 B1
King Edward's Rd
Barking IG11 101 B5
Edmonton N9 18 B4
Enfield EN3 6 D1
South Hackney E9 96 C6
King Edward St EC1 242 A2
King Edward The Third Mews 11 SE16 118 B4
King Edward VII Hospl for Officers W1 93 A2 238 B4
King Edward Wlk SE1 116 C3 261 B6
King Fahad Acad The W5 109 C2
King Fahed Acad W3 111 D6
Kingfield Rd W5 87 D3
Kingfield St E14 120 A2
Kingfisher Ave E11 55 B3
Kingfisher Cl
Harrow HA3 24 D3
Woolwich SE28 124 C6
Kingfisher Ct
11 Battersea SW11 136 C2
Cheam SM1 217 B3
17 Cubitt Town E14 120 A4
East Molesey KT8 196 C5
Enfield EN2 4 B5
Hounslow TW3 151 D6
Merton SW19 179 B3
Putney SW19 157 A2
Spring Gr TW3 130 B3
Kingfisher Dr TW10 175 B6
Kingfisher Ho
16 Battersea SW18 136 A2
Peckham SE15 139 D4
West Kensington W14 254 C6
Kingfisher L Ctr KT1 176 A1
Kingfisher Lo TW11 175 A
Kingfisher Mews SE13 163 D6
Kingfisher Sq 19 SE8 141 B6
Kingfisher St E6 100 A
Kingfisher Way
Croydon CR0 206 D4
Neasden NW10 67 B3
Kingfisher Wlk NW9 27 C
King Frederick IX Twr SE16 119 B3
King Garth Mews SE23 162 C2
King Gdns CR0 220 D
King George Ave
Ilford IG2 57 B3
Newham E16 99 D1
Walton-on-T KT12 194 D1
King George Cl TW16 171 C5
King George Hospl IG3 58 A4
King George Sq TW10 154 B5
King George St SE10 142 A5
King George's Trad Est KT9 214 C4
King George VI Ave CR4 202 D5
King George V Sta E16 122 C5
Kingham Cl
3 Shepherd's Bush W11 112 D4
Wandsworth SW18 158 A4
Kingham Ind Est NW10 89 B4
King Harolds Way DA7 147 A5
King Henry Mews
Harrow HA2 42 C1
7 Orpington BR6 227 D3
King Henry's Mews EN3 7 C6
King Henry's Rd
Kingston u T KT1, KT3 198 D6
Primrose Hill NW3 70 C1
King Henry's Reach W6 134 C6
King Henry St N16 73 C3
King Henry's Wlk N1 73 C2
King Henry's Yd 5 N16 73 C3
King Henry Terr 10 E1 118 B6
King Ho 5 W12 90 B1
Kinghorn St EC1 242 A3
King James Ct SE1 251 D1
King James St SE1 116 D4 251 D1
King John Ct EC2 243 B6
King John St E1 96 D2
King John's Wlk SE9 166 A5
Kinglake St SE17 117 C1 263 B2
Kinglet Cl E7 77 A2
Kingly Ct W1 249 B6
Kingly St W1 115 C6 249 A6
King & Queen Cl 4 SE9 188 A6
King & Queen St SE17 117 A1 262 B2
Kingsand Rd SE12 165 A2
Kings Arbour UB2 107 A1
King's Arms Ct E1 96 A2
King's Arms Yd EC2 242 C2
Kingsash Dr UB4 85 A3
Kings Ave
Bromley BR1 186 D4
Clapham Pk SW4 160 A5
Dagenham RM6 59 B3
Ealing W5 87 D1
Muswell Hill N10 49 A6
New Malden KT3 199 D5
Wallington SM5 218 D1
King's Ave
Ashford TW16 171 D4
Buckhurst Hill IG9 21 D2
Hounslow TW3, TW5 129 D4
Southall UB1 85 D1
Southgate N21 16 D3
Woodford IG8 37 C5

Kings Avenue Sch SW4 160 A6
King's Bench St SE1 116 D4 251 D2
King's Bench Wlk EC4 241 B1
Kingsbridge N16 51 B1
Kingsbridge Ave W3 110 B4
Kingsbridge Cres UB1 85 B2
Kingsbridge Ct
Edmonton N21 16 D2
Millwall E14 119 C2
Kingsbridge Dr NW7 28 D3
Kingsbridge Ho 10 SE20 184 B2
Kingsbridge Ind Est IG11 101 C4
Kingsbridge Rd
Barking IG11 101 B5
North Kensington W10 90 C1
Southall UB2 107 B2
Walton-on-T KT12 194 B2
West Barnes SM4 200 D2
Kingsbridge Way UB4 83 C4
KINGSBURY 45 B3
Kingsbury Green Prim Sch NW9 44 D4
Kingsbury High Sch (Lower Sch) NW9 45 A5
Kingsbury High Sch (Upper Sch) NW9 44 D5
Kingsbury Rd
Kingsbury NW9 44 D4
Kingsland N1 73 C2
Kingsbury Sta NW9 44 C4
Kingsbury Terr N1 73 C2
Kingsbury Trad Est NW9 45 B3
Kings Chase KT8 196 A6
Kings Chase View EN2 4 C3
Kings Cl Hendon NW4 46 D5
Walthamstow E10 53 D2
Walton-on-T KT12 194 B1
King's Cl KT7 197 A2
Kingsclere Cl SW15 156 A4
Kingsclere Ct
Colney Hatch N12 30 C5
New Barnet EN5 14 A6
Kingsclere Pl EN2 5 A3
Kingscliffe Gdns SW19 157 B3
King's Coll SE24 161 B5
Kings College Ct NW3 70 C1
King's College Hospl SE5 139 B3
Kings College Rd
Primrose Hill NW3 70 B1
Ruislip HA4 39 D3
King's Coll Jun Sch SW19 178 D4
King's Coll London (Denmark Hill Campus) SE5 139 A2
King's Coll London School of Medicine SE1 117 B5 252 D3
King's Coll London (Strand Campus) WC2 116 B6 250 D6
King's Coll London (St Thomas' Campus) SE1 116 B3 260 C5
King's Coll London (Waterloo Campus) SE1 116 C5 251 A3
King's Coll Sch SW19 178 D4
Kingscote NW11 47 B1
Kingscote Rd
Bedford Pk W4 111 B3
Croydon CR0 206 B2
Kingston u T KT3 199 B6
Kingscote St EC4 251 C6
Kings Court Mews KT8 196 B4
King's Court N SW3 257 A1
Kingscourt Rd SW16 160 A1
King's Court S SW3 257 A1
King's Cres N4, N5 73 A5
Kingscroft SW4 160 A5
Kingscroft Rd NW2 69 B2
KING'S CROSS 94 A5
King's Cross WC1 94 A4 233 B2
King's Cross Bridge WC1 233 B2
King's Cross Rd WC1 94 B4 233 D1
King's Cross, St Pancras N1 94 A4 233 A2
King's Cross Sta N1 94 A5 233 B3
Kings Ct
6 Barnsbury N7 72 B1
2 Buckhurst Hill IG9 21 D2
Chiswick W6 112 A2
East Dulwich SE22 140 A1
16 Kingston u T KT2 176 C3
Newham E13 99 B6
Primrose Hill NW8 230 C5
10 Putney SW15 156 A4
3 Wallington SM6 219 B2
Wembley Pk HA9 66 D6
King's Ct
Beckenham BR3 207 D6
9 Ealing W5 87 C2
Wimbledon SW19 179 C4
Kingsdale Ct EN4 2 D3
Kingsdale Gdns W11 112 D5
Kingsdale Rd
Penge SE20 184 D3
Plumstead Comm SE18 145 D6
Kingsdale Sch SE21 161 C1
Kingsdown SW19 178 D3
Kingsdown Ave
East Acton W3 111 C6
West Ealing W13 109 B4
Kingsdown Cl
26 Deptford SE16 118 B1
8 Notting Hill W11 91 A1
Kingsdown Ct SW11 158 C5
Kingsdowne Rd KT6 198 B2
Kingsdown Ho 1 E8 74 A3
Kingsdown Rd
Cheam SM3 217 A3
Leyton E11 76 C5
4 Upper Holloway N19 72 A6
Kingsdown Way BR2 209 A3
Kings Dr Edgware HA8 26 B6
Surbiton KT5 198 C3
Wembley Pk HA9 66 D6
King's Dr KT7 197 B2
Kingsend HA4 39 C1
Kingsend Ct HA4 39 C1
Kings Farm E17 35 D2
Kings Farm Ave TW10 132 C1
Kingsfield Ave HA1, HA2 42 A4
Kingsfield Ct HA1 42 B2
Kingsfield Ho
Mottingham SE9 165 D1
7 Muswell Hill N10 31 A3
18 Stoke Newington N16 73 C5
Kingsfield Rd HA1 42 B2
Kingsford Com Sch E6 100 B1
Kingsford St NW5 70 D3
Kingsford Way E6 100 B2
Kingsgate HA9 67 A5
Kingsgate Ave N3 47 C6
Kingsgate Bsns Ctr KT2 176 A2
Kingsgate Cl
Erith DA7 147 A4
Sidcup BR5 190 C1
Kingsgate Est N1 73 C2
Kingsgate Ho 29 SW9 138 C4
Kingsgate Par SW1 259 B5
Kingsgate Pl NW6 69 C1
Kingsgate Prim Sch NW6 69 C1
Kingsgate Rd
Hampstead NW6 69 C1
Kingston u T KT2 176 A2
Kings Gdns IG1 57 B1
King's Gdns 6 NW6 69 C1
King's Gr
Peckham SE15 140 B4
Peckham SE15 140 B5
Kings Grange HA4 39 D1
Kingsground SE9 166 A5
Kingshall Mews SE13 142 A2
Kings Hall Rd BR3 185 A2
Kings Head Hill E4 19 D4
King's Head Yd SE1 252 C3
King's Highway SE18 145 D6
Kingshill SE17 262 B4
Kingshill Ave
Harrow HA3 43 B5
Hayes UB4 83 D4
New Malden KT4 200 B2
Northolt UB5 84 B4
Kingshill Cl UB4, UB5 84 A4
Kingshill Ct 8 EN5 1 A1
Kingshill Dr HA3 43 B6
Kings Ho
19 Limehouse E14 119 B6
South Lambeth SW8 270 B4
Kingshold Rd E9 74 C1
Kingsholm Gdns SE9 144 A1
King's House Sch TW10 154 B6
King's House Sch (Jun) TW10 154 B6
Kingshurst Rd SE12 165 A4
Kings Keep KT6 198 A5
King's Keep 6 SW15 156 D6
King's La SM1 218 B3
KINGSLAND 73 C2
Kingsland NW8 92 C6 230 B5
Kingsland Gn 1 E8, N1 73 C2
Kingsland High St E8 73 D3
Kingsland Pas 2 E8 73 C2
Kingsland Rd
Hoxton E2 95 C5
Newham E13 99 C4
Kingsland Sh Ctr 12 E8 73 D2
Kingslawn Cl SW15 156 B6
Kingslee Ct 4 SM2 217 D1
Kingsleigh Cl TW8 131 D6
Kingsleigh Pl CR4 202 D6
Kingsleigh Wlk BR2 208 D5
Kingsley Ave
Ealing W13 87 A1
Hounslow TW3 130 A3
Southall UB1 107 C6
Sutton SM1 218 B4
Kingsley Cl
Dagenham RM10 81 D4
East Finchley N2 48 A4
Kingsley Ct
Bexley DA6 147 C1
Edgware HA8 10 D2
Snaresbrook E11 54 D3
1 Thamesmead SE28 124 C5
Willesden NW2 68 B2
Wood Green N22 32 B3
Worcester Pk KT4 215 D6
Kingsley Dr KT4 215 D6
Kingsley Flats SE1 263 B3
Kingsley Gdns E4 35 C5
Kingsley Grange 1 E11 55 A4
Kingsley High Sch HA3 24 A3
Kingsley Ho
Chelsea SW3 266 D5
3 Clapham SW4 137 D3
East Finchley NW11 48 A3
8 Kingston u T KT6 198 A4
Kingsley Mews
Chislehurst West BR7 188 D4
Dagenham RM9 80 D4
4 Ilford IG1 78 D6
Kensington W8 255 D5
15 St George in t East E1 118 B6
Kingsley Pl N6 49 A2
Kingsley Prim Sch CR9 204 C1
Kingsley Rd
Chingford E17 36 A1
Edmonton N13 32 D6
Harrow HA2 64 A5
Hounslow TW3 130 A3
Kilburn NW6 91 B6
Orpington BR6 227 D1
Pinner HA5 41 B5
Kingsley Rd *continued*
Thornton Heath CR0 204 C1
Upton E7 77 A1
Wimbledon SW19 179 D5
Kingsley St SW11 136 D2
Kingsley Way N2 48 A4
Kingsley Wood Dr SE9 166 B1
Kings Lo HA4 39 C1
Kingslyn Cres SE19 183 C2
Kings Mall Sh Ctr W6 112 C2
Kingsman Par SE18 122 B3
King's Mans SW3 267 A5
Kingsman St SE18 122 B2
Kingsmead Barnet EN5 1 C1
Richmond TW10 154 B5
Kingsmead Ave
Edmonton N9 18 B3
Kingsbury NW9 45 B2
Mitcham CR4 203 C6
North Cheam KT4 216 B5
Sunbury TW16 172 C1
Tolworth KT6 214 C6
Kingsmead Cl
Sidcup DA15 168 A2
Teddington TW11 175 B4
West Ewell KT19 215 B1
Kingsmead Cotts BR2 210 A1
Kingsmead Ct
Bromley BR1 186 D3
Crouch End N6 49 D2
Kingsmead Dr UB5 63 B1
Kingsmead Ho E9 75 A4
Kingsmead Lo
9 Chingford E4 20 A2
Sutton SM2 218 B2
Kings Mead Pk KT10 212 C1
Kingsmead Prim Sch E9 75 A4
Kingsmead Rd SW2 160 C2
Kingsmead Sch EN1 6 A2
King's Mead Way E5, E9 75 A4
Kingsmere
Catford SE6 163 D3
Widmore BR7 188 A2
Kingsmere Cl 13 SW15 134 D2
Kingsmere Ct NW9 44 D1
Kingsmere Pk NW9 45 A1
Kingsmere Pl N16 51 B1
Kingsmere Rd SW19 156 D2
King's Mews
1 Clapham Pk SW4 160 A6
Gray's Inn WC1 94 B3 240 D5
Kingsmill NW8 92 B5 229 D4
Kingsmill Bsns Pk KT1 198 B6
Kingsmill Gdns RM9 81 B3
Kingsmill Rd RM9 81 B3
Kingsmill Terr NW8 92 B5 229 D4
Kingsmount Ct SM1 217 D4
Kingsnorth Ho 12 W10 90 D1
Kingsnympton Pk KT2 176 D4
Kings Oak RM7 59 C6
Kings Oak Hospl (Private) The EN2 4 C5
King Solomon Acad NW1 92 C2 237 A4
King's Orch SE9 166 A5
King's Paddock TW12 174 A2
King's Par
3 Hammersmith W12 112 A3
Willesden NW10 90 C6
Kingspark Bsns Ctr KT3 199 A6
Kingspark Ct E18 55 A6
King's Penny Ho 4 KT2 176 A3
Kings Pl
Acton Green W4 111 A2
Buckhurst Hill IG9 21 D2
Kings Pl★ N1 94 A5 233 B4
Kings Pl IG10 21 D4
King's Pl SE1 252 A1
King Sq EC1 95 A4 235 A1
King's Quay SW10 266 B2
Kings Rd Ealing W5 87 D2
Feltham TW13 150 C3
Harrow HA2 63 B6
Mitcham CR4 203 A6
Orpington BR6 227 D4
Richmond TW10, TW9 154 B6
Walton-on-T KT12 194 B1
West Drayton UB7 104 B4
Willesden NW10 68 B1
Wood Green N22 32 B2
King's Rd Barking IG11 79 A1
Chelsea SW3 257 B1
Chelsea SW10 136 B6 266 C5
Chingford E4 20 B3
Edmonton N18 34 A6
Kingston u T KT2 176 B3
Leytonstone E11 54 C2
Long Ditton KT6 197 C1
Mortlake SW14 133 B2
Newham E6 99 C6
South Norwood SE25 206 A6
Teddington TW11, TW12 174 B5
Tottenham N17 33 D2
Twickenham TW1 153 B5
Wimbledon SW19 179 C4
Kings Ride Gate TW10 132 C1
Kingsridge SW19 157 A2
Kings Road Bglws HA2 63 B5
King's Scholars' Pas SW1 259 A4
King St Acton W3 111 A5
East Finchley N2 48 B6
Hammersmith W6 112 A2
Newham E13 98 D3
Newham E13 99 A3
Richmond TW9 153 D6
Southall UB2 107 A3
St James SW1 115 C5 249 B4
Strand WC2 250 A6
Tottenham N17 33 D2
Twickenham TW1 153 A3
Whitechapel EC2 95 A1 242 B1
King Stairs Cl SE16 118 B4
King's Terr
Camden Town NW1 93 C6 232 A5
10 Isleworth TW7 131 A2
Kingsthorpe Rd SE26 184 D6
Kingston Ave
Cheam SM3 217 A5
Feltham TW14 149 D5
Yiewsley UB7 104 B6
Kingston Bsns Ctr KT9 214 B5
Kingston By-Pass KT6, KT7, KT9 213 C5
Kingston Cl
Dagenham RM6 59 A6
Northolt UB5 85 B6
Teddington TW11 175 B4
Kingston Coll
Kingston u T KT1 197 D6
Kingston u T KT2 176 A2
Kingston Cres BR3 185 B2
Kingston Ct HA3 44 B4
Kingston Gdns CR0 220 A5
Kingston Gram Sch KT2 176 B1
Kingston Hall Rd KT1 197 D6
Kingston Hill KT2 177 A5
Kingston Hill Ave RM6 59 A6
Kingston Hill Pl KT2, TW10 177 A6
Kingston Ho 4 NW6 69 A1
Kingston Ho E SW7 247 A1
Kingston Ho N SW7 247 A1
Kingston Ho S SW7 247 A1
Kingston Hospl KT2 176 D2
Kingston House Est KT6 197 B3
Kingston La
Teddington TW11 175 B4

Kingston La *continued*
Uxbridge UB8. . . . . .82 A4
West Drayton UB7. . . .104 B4
Kingston Lo 2 KT3 . .199 C5
Kingston Mus★ KT1 .176 A1
Kingston Pl HA3 . . . . . .24 D3
Kingston Rd
Ashford TW15 . . . . . . 170 A4
Ashford TW15 . . . . . . .170 B4
Edmonton N9. . . . . .18 A2
Ewell KT17. . . . . 215 D1
Ilford IG1. . . . . .79 A4
Kingston u T KT1, KT3. 199 A5
Merton SW19, SW20. . .179 B1
New Barnet EN4 . . . . . .14 B6
Roehampton SW15,
SW19 . . . . .156 B3
Southall UB2 . . . . .107 B4
Teddington TW11. . . . .175 B4
Kingston Sq SE19. . . .183 B5
Kingston Sta KT2 . . . 176 A2
Kingston Univ (Kingston Hill) KT2. . . . . .177 B5
Kingston Univ (Knights Park) KT1. . . . . 198 A6
Kingston Univ (Penrhyn Road) KT1 . . . . 198 A6
Kingston Univ (Roehampton Vale)
SW15. . . . . 155 D1
KINGSTON UPON THAMES 197 C6
KINGSTON VALE. 177 B6
Kingston Vale SW15. .155 C1
Kingstown St
NW1. . . . . . . .93 A6 231 A6
King Street Cloisters 8
W6 . . . . .112 B2
King Street Coll 10
W12. . . . . 112 C2
King Street Par 7
TW1 . . . . .153 A3
Kings View Ct 1
SW20 . . . . 178 D3
Kingswater Pl SW11 267 A3
Kingsway
Coney Hall BR4 . . . . . 224 D5
Enfield EN3 . . . . .18 B6
Hayes UB3 . . . . .83 A2
Mortlake SW14, TW9. 132 D2
North Finchley N12 . . . .30 A4
Petts Wood BR5. . . . . .211 B4
Stanwell TW19. . . . . . . 148 A3
St Giles WC2 . . 94 B1 240 C2
Wembley HA9 . . . . .66 A4
West Barnes KT3. . . . 200 C4
Woodford IG8 . . . . .37 C5
Kings Way
Croydon CR0 . . . . .220 B3
Harrow HA1. . . . . .42 C5
Kingsway Bsns Pk
TW12. . . . . .173 B2
Kingsway Coll 12
NW5. . . . . .71 B2
Kingsway Cres HA2 . . .42 A5
Kingsway Est N18. . . . .34 D4
Kingsway Mans WC1 240 C4
Kingsway Pl EC1. . . . 241 C6
Kingsway Rd SM3. . . .217 A1
Kingswear Ho 5
SE23. . . . . .162 C2
Kingswear Rd
Dartmouth Pk NW5 . . . .71 B5
Ruislip HA4 . . . . .62 A6
Kings Well 25 NW3. . . .70 A4
Kings Wlk Sh Mall
SW3. . . . . . . 114 D1 257 C2
Kingswood 31 E2 . . . . .96 C5
Kingswood Ave
Beckenham BR2,
BR3. . . . . 208 C5
Belvedere DA17. . . . . .125 B2
Hampton TW12 . . . . . . 173 D4
Hounslow TW3, TW5 . .129 B3
Kensal Rise NW6. . . . . . .91 A5
Thornton Heath CR7 . 204 C4
Kingswood Cl
Ashford TW15 . . . . . . .171 B5
Crofton BR6. . . . . .211 B2
East Barnet N20. . . . . . .14 A4
Enfield EN1 . . . . .17 D6
New Malden KT3 . . . . 199 D3
South Lambeth SW8 . 270 B3
Kingswood Cl *continued*
Surbiton KT6 . . . . 198 A2
Kingswood Ct
Chingford E4 . . . . .35 C5
Hither Green SE13. . . .164 B5
7 Richmond TW10 . . .154 B6
Kings Wood Ct 4
NW6. . . . . .69 C1
Kingswood Dr
Carshalton SM5. . . . . 202 D1
Dulwich SE19, SE21. . 183 D6
Kingswood Ho 3
KT2. . . . . 176 D4
Kingswood Mans 14
SM2 . . . . .217 C1
Kingswood Pk N3. . . . .29 B1
Kingswood Pl SE13 . .142 C1
Kingswood Prim Sch
SE27. . . . . .183 B5
Kingswood Rd
Beckenham BR2. . . . . 208 C6
Ilford IG3. . . . . .58 A2
Leytonstone E11 . . . . . .54 C2
Merton SW19. . . . . . . .179 B2
Penge SE20 . . . . 184 C4
South Acton W4 . . . . . 111 A3
Streatham SW2 . . . . . 160 A4
Wembley HA9 . . . . .66 C5
Kingswood Terr W4 . .111 A3
Kingswood Way
SM6 . . . . .220 A3
Kingsworth Cl BR3. . . .207 A4
Kingsworthy Cl KT1. .198 B6
Kings Yd E15 . . . . .75 C2
Kingthorpe Rd NW10. . 67 B1
Kingthorpe Terr 2
NW10. . . . . .67 B1
Kington Ho 18 NW6. . . 91 D6
Kingward Ho E1 . . . . . .96 A2
Kingwell Rd EN4. . . . . . . 2 B5
Kingweston Cl NW2. . . 69 A5
King William IV Gdns
SE20. . . . . .184 C4
King William La 3
SE10. . . . . .120 C1
King William St
EC4. . . . . . . .117 B6 252 D6
King William Wlk
SE10. . . . . .142 A6
Kingwood Rd
SW6 . . . . . . .135 A5 264 A3
Kinlet Rd SE18. . . . . . .145 A4
Kinloch Dr NW9 . . . . . .45 C2
Kinloch St N7 . . . . .72 B5
Kinloss Ct NW3. . . . . . .47 B5
Kinloss Gdns NW3 . . . .47 B5
Kinloss Rd SM5. . . . . .202 A2
Kinnaird Ave
Bromley BR1 . . . . 186 D4
Chiswick W4 . . . . 133 A5
Kinnaird Cl BR1. . . . . . 186 D4
Kinnear Ct 2 SW20. 178 D2
Kinnear Rd W12 . . . . . 111 D4
Kinnerton Pl N SW1. 247 D1
Kinnerton Pl S SW1. 247 D1
Kinnerton St
SW1 . . . . . . .115 A4 248 A1
Kinnerton Yd SW1 . . 248 A1
Kinnoull Mans 10 E5 . .74 B4
Kinnoul Rd
W6 . . . . .135 A6 264 A6
Kinross Ave KT4 . . . . .216 A6
Kinross Cl
Ashford TW16 . . . . . . 171 D5
Edgware HA8. . . . . .10 D2
Harrow HA3. . . . . .44 B4
Kinross Ct 1 SE6 . . . 164 D2
Kinross Dr TW16 . . . . 171 D5
Kinross Ho N1. . . . . . 233 C6
Kinross Terr E17 . . . . . .35 B1
Kinsale Grange 10
SM2 . . . . .218 A2
Kinsale Rd SE15 . . . . .140 A2
Kinsella Gdns SW19. .178 B5
Kinsey Ho SE21 . . . . . .183 C6
Kinsham Ho 5 E2 . . . .96 A3
Kintore Way SE1. . . . 263 C4
Kintyre Cl SW16 . . . . .204 B6
Kintyre Ct 17 SW2. . . .160 A4
Kintyre Ho 6 E14. . . .120 A5
Kinveachy Gdns SE7 .122 A1
Kinver Ho N4. . . . . .51 B2
Kinver Rd SE26 . . . . . .184 C6
Kipling Ct W7. . . . . . . .108 D6
Kipling Dr SW17 . . . . .180 B4
Kipling Ho 29 SE5. . . .139 A5
Kipling Pl HA7. . . . . . . .24 D4
Kipling Rd DA7 . . . . . .147 A4
Kipling St
SE1. . . . . . . .117 B4 252 D2
Kipling Terr N9 . . . . . . .17 B2
Kipling Twr 3 W3. . . .111 A3
Kippington Dr SE9. . 165 D3
Kirby Cl KT19 . . . . . . .215 D3
Kirby Est SE16 . . . . . . .118 B3
Kirby Gr SE1. . .117 C4 253 A2
Kirby St EC1 . . . 94 C2 241 B4
Kirby Way
Hillingdon UB8. . . . . . . .82 B3
Walton-on-T KT12 . . . 194 C3
Kirchen Rd W13 . . . . .109 B6
Kirkby Cl N11. . . . . .31 A4
Kirkdale SE26 . . . . . . .162 B1
Kirkdale Rd E11 . . . . . .54 C2
Kirkeby Bldg EC1 . . . 241 A4
Kirkfield Cl W13 . . . . .109 B5
Kirkham Rd E6 . . . . . .100 A1
Kirkham St SE18. . . . .145 C6
Kirk Ho HA9 . . . . .66 A5
Kirk La SE18. . . . . .145 A6
Kirkland Cl DA15. . . . .167 C5
Kirkland Dr EN2 . . . . 5 A4
Kirkland Terr BR3. . . .185 C4
Kirkland Wlk 4 E8 . . .73 D2
Kirkleas Rd KT6. . . . . .198 A1
Kirklees Rd
Dagenham RM8. . . . . . .80 C3
Thornton Heath CR7 . 204 C4
Kirkley Ho N16 . . . . . . .51 C1
Kirkley Rd SW19. . . . .179 C2
Kirkman Ho W1. . . . . 239 C3
Kirkman Pl W1 . . . . . 239 C3
Kirkmichael Rd E14. . . .98 A1
Kirk Rd E17. . . . . .53 B3
Kirk Rise SM1 . . . . . . 217 D5
Kirkside Rd SE3 . . . . .143 A6
Kirk St WC1 . . . . 240 D5
Kirkstall Ave N17 . . . . .51 B5
Kirkstall Gdns SW2 . .160 A3
Kirkstall Ho SW1. . . . 258 C2
Kirkstall Rd SW2. . . . .160 A3
Kirkstead Ct E5. . . . . . .75 A4
Kirksted Rd SM4. . . . .201 D1
Kirkstone NW1 . . . . . . 232 A2
Kirkstone Way BR1 . .186 C3
Kirkton Rd N15 . . . . . . .51 C5
Kirkwall Pl E2 . . . . .96 C4
Kirkwood Rd SE15 . . .140 B3
Kirn Rd W13 . . . . .109 B6
Kirrane Cl KT3. . . . . . . 199 D4
Kirtley Ho SW8 . . . . . 269 B2
Kirtley Rd SE26 . . . . . .185 A6
Kirtling St
SW8 . . . . . . .137 C5 269 A4
Kirton Cl W4. . . . . .111 B2
Kirton Gdns 23 E2 . . . .95 D4
Kirton Rd E13. . . . . .99 C5
Kirton Wlk HA8. . . . . . . .27 A3
Kirwin Way SE5. . . . . .138 D5
Kisharon Sch NW11. . . 47 B3
Kismul Sch KT6. . . . . 213 C6
Kitcat Terr E3. . . . . .97 C4
Kitchener Rd
Dagenham RM10. . . . . . .81 D2
East Finchley N2 . . . . . .48 C6
South Norwood CR7. . .205 B6
Tottenham N17 . . . . . . .51 C6
Upton E7 . . . . .77 B2
Walthamstow E17 . . . . .35 D2
Kite Ho 5 SW11 . . . . .136 C2
Kite Pl 9 E2. . . . . .96 A4
Kitley Gdns SE19. . . . 183 D2
Kitson Rd
Barnes SW13. . . . . 134 A4
Camberwell SE5. . . . . 139 A5
Kittiwake Ct 26 SE8 . .141 B6
Kittiwake Pl SM1 . . . .217 B3
Kittiwake Rd UB5 . . . . .84 D4
Kittiwake Way UB4. . . .84 D2
Kitto Rd SE14. . . . . . . 140 D3
KITTS END. 1 A5
Kitt's End Rd EN5 . . . . . . 1 A6
Kiver Rd N19 . . . . .72 A6
Klea Ave SW4. . . . . . . .159 C5
Kleffens Ct 2 SE3 . . . 142 D5
Kleine Wharf 30 N1. . . .95 C6
Knaggs Ho 1 TW11. .174 C5
Knapdale Cl SE23 . . . .162 B2
Knapmill Rd SE6. . . . 163 D2
Knapmill Way SE6 . . 163 D2
Knapp Cl NW10. . . . . . .67 C2
Knapp Rd
Ashford TW15 . . . . . . .170 B6
Bow E3. . . . . .97 C3
Knapton Mews
SW17 . . . . .181 A4
Knaresborough Dr
SW18 . . . . 157 D3
Knaresborough Ho 4
N4. . . . . .51 A2
Knaresborough Pl
SW5 . . . . . . 113 D2 255 C4
Knatchbull Rd
Brixton SE5 . . . . 138 D4
Stonebridge NW10 . . . .89 B6
Knebworth Ave E17 . . .35 C2
Knebworth Cl EN5 . . . . . 1 D1
Knebworth Ho
South Lambeth SW8 . 269 D1
2 Stoke Newington
N16. . . . . .73 C4
Walthamstow E17 . . . . .35 C2
Knebworth Rd 3
N16. . . . . .73 C4
Knee Hill SE2. . . . . .124 C1
Knee Hill Cres SE2 . . .124 C2
Kneller Gdns TW7. . . . .152 B5
Kneller Ho 9 SW8. . . 137 D3
Kneller Rd
Brockley SE4 . . . . 141 A1
Isleworth TW2. . . . . . . .152 B5
New Malden KT3 . . . . 199 C2
Knevett Terr TW3 . . . .129 C1
Knight Cl RM8 . . . . .80 C6
Knight Ct N15 . . . . .51 C4
Knighten St E1 . . . . . .118 B5
Knighthead Point 26
E14. . . . . .119 C4
Knight Ho
Walworth SE17 . . . . . . 263 A3
Worcester Pk KT4 . . . 216 A6
Knightland Ho E5. . . . .74 B6
Knightland Rd E5. . . . . .74 B6
Knightleas Ct NW2. . . .68 C2
Knightleys Ct E10. . . . .53 A1
Knighton Cl
Croydon CR2 . . . . 220 D1
Woodford IG8 . . . . .37 B6
Knighton Dr IG8. . . . . . .37 B6
Knighton Gn IG9. . . . . . 21 B2
Knighton La IG9 . . . . . . 21 B2
Knighton Park Rd
SE26. . . . . 184 D5
Knighton Rd E7. . . . . . .77 A4
Knightrider Ct EC4. . . 252 A6
Knightrider St EC4. . . 251 D6
Knights Arc SW1. . . . . 247 C1
Knight's Ave W5 . . . . .110 A4
KNIGHTSBRIDGE . . .114 C4
Knightsbridge SW1,
SW7 . . . . . . 114 D4 247 C1
Knightsbridge Ct
SW1 . . . . 247 D1
Knightsbridge Gn
SW1 . . . . 247 C1
Knightsbridge Mews
BR7. . . . . .188 B3
Knightsbridge Sch
SW11. . . . . . 114 D3 257 C5
Knightsbridge Sta
SW1. . . . . . . 114 D4 247 C1
Knightsbridge Under Sch
SW7. . . . . 256 B3
Knights Cl
East Molesey KT8 . . . .195 B4
Lower Clapton E9. . . . . .74 C3
Knights Ct
Bushey WD23. . . . . .8 B3
11 Friern Barnet N11. . .30 D5
Kingston u T KT1 . . . . 198 A6
Penge BR3. . . . . 185 A2
Knight's Ct BR1. . . . . . 164 D1
Knightshayes Ho 8
NW4. . . . . .28 D1
Knight's Hill SE19,
SE27 . . . . 182 D6
Knight's Hill Sq
SE27. . . . . 182 D6
Knights Ho
Bermondsey SE1 . . . . 253 C2
South Lambeth SW8 . 270 B3
West Kensington SW5 254 C2
Knight's Ho SW10. . . . 266 A4
Knight's Pk KT1 . . . . .198 A6
Knight's Pl TW2. . . . . .152 C3
Knights Rd
Newham E16 . . . . 121 A4
Knights Rd *continued*
Stanmore HA7 . . . . .25 C6
Knight's Wlk SE11 . . 261 C3
Knightswood Cl HA8. . 11 A2
Knightswood Ct N6. . .49 D2
Knightswood Ho N12 . 30 A4
Knightwood Cres
KT3. . . . . .199 C3
Knivet Rd
SW6 . . . . . . .135 C6 265 A5
Knockholt Rd SE9. . . . 165 D6
Knole Cl CR0 . . . . .206 C3
Knole Ct UB5 . . . . .84 C4
Knole Gate DA15. . . . .167 C1
Knole The SE9 . . . . . . .188 C6
Knoll Ct
Dulwich SE19. . . . . . . 183 D5
Orpington BR6. . . . . . . 227 D6
Knoll Dr N14 . . . . .15 A4
Knoll Ho NW8 . . . . 229 A4
Knoll Lo EN5 . . . . .14 A6
Knollmead KT4, KT5. .199 A1
Knollmead Prim Sch
KT5 . . . . 215 A6
Knoll Rd Bexley DA5 . .169 C5
Sidcup DA14. . . . . .190 B6
Wandsworth SW18 . . 158 A6
Knoll Rise BR6. . . . . . 211 D1
Knolls Cl KT4 . . . . .216 B5
Knoll The
Beckenham BR3. . . . . 185 D2
Ealing W13. . . . . .87 C2
Hayes BR2 . . . . 209 A1
Knolly's Cl SE27,
SW16 . . . . .160 C1
Knolly's Rd SE27,
SW16 . . . . .160 C1
Knot Ho SE1. . . . . 253 C3
Knottisford St E2 . . . . .96 C4
Knotts Green Mews
E10. . . . . .54 A3
Knotts Green Rd E10. . 54 A3
Knowlden Ho 5 E1 . .118 C6
Knowle Ave DA7 . . . . .147 B5
Knowle Cl SW9 . . . . . .138 C2
Knowledge Point Sch 6
N7 . . . . .72 B2
Knowle Lo BR7 . . . . . .188 B4
Knowle Rd
Bromley BR2 . . . . 226 A6
Twickenham TW2. . . . . 152 C3
Knowles Cl UB7. . . . . .104 A5
Knowles Ct 7 HA1. . . .42 D3
Knowles Hill Cres
SE13. . . . . .164 B6
Knowles Ho
Wandsworth SW18 . . 157 D5
Willesden Green NW10 90 A6
Knowles Wlk SW4 . . .137 C2
Knowl Pk WD6. . . . . . . .10 A6
Knowlton Gn 1
BR2. . . . . 208 D4
Knowlton Ho 32
SW9 . . . . .138 C4
Knowl Way WD6 . . . . . .10 B6
Knowsley Ave UB1 . . 107 D5
Knowsley Rd SW11. . 136 D3
Knox Ct 16 SW4. . . . . .138 A3
Knox Ho SW15. . . . . . .134 C3
Knox Rd E7. . . . . .77 A2
Knox St W1. . . . 92 D2 237 C4
Knoyle Ho W14 . . . . . 254 B6
Knoyle St SE14. . . . . . .141 A6
Kobi Nazrul Prim Sch 43
E1. . . . . .96 A1
Koblenz Ho N8 . . . . . . .50 A6
Kohat Rd SW19. . . . . . 179 D5
Korda Cl TW17. . . . . . .192 B6
Kossuth St SE10 . . . . .120 C1
Kotree Way 16 SE1. . . .118 A2
Kramer Mews SW5 . . 255 C1
Kreedman Wlk 8 E8. .74 A3
Kreisel Wlk TW9 . . . . .132 B6
Krishna Avanti Prim Sch
HA8. . . . . .26 C2
Kristina Ct 5 SM2 . . .217 C2
Kuala Gdns SW16. . . .182 B2
Kubrick Bsns Est E7 . .77 B4
Kuhn Way E7 . . . . .77 A3
Kwesi Johnson Ct 4
N22. . . . . .32 C1
Kydbrook Cl BR5. . . . .211 A2
Kyle Ho TW12. . . . . . . .174 A2
Kylemore Cl 3 E6 . . . .99 D5
Kylemore Ct 4 W12 .112 A4
Kylemore Rd NW6 . . . .69 C1

Kylestrome Ho SW1. 258 B3
Kymberley Rd HA1 42 C3
Kynance Gdns HA7 25 C2
Kynance Mews
SW7 113 D3 255 D5
Kynance Pl SW7 256 A5
Kynaston Ave CR7 205 A4
Kynaston Cl HA3 24 B3
Kynaston Cres CR7 205 A4
Kynaston Ho 7
SW2 160 B3
Kynaston Rd
Enfield EN2 5 B4
Plaistow BR1 187 A5
Stoke Newington N16 73 C5
Thornton Heath CR7 205 A4
Kynaston Wood HA3 24 B3
Kynersley Cl 1 SM5 218 D5
Kynoch Rd N18 34 D6
Kyrle Rd SW11 159 A5
Kyverdale Rd N16 51 D1

L

Laburnam Ct 12
SW16 182 C5
Laburnham Ct
Child's Hill NW2 69 B6
Sutton SM1 217 C3
Laburnham Pl SE9 166 C6
Laburnum Ave
Carshalton SM1 218 C5
Edmonton N9 17 D2
Tottenham N17 33 B3
Yiewsley UB7 104 B6
Laburnum Cl
Friern Barnet N11 31 A4
5 Nunhead SE15 140 C5
Walthamstow E4 35 B4
Wembley HA0 88 C6
Laburnum Cres
TW16 172 B2
Laburnum Ct
26 Haggerston E2 95 D6
Harrow HA1 41 D3
5 Mitcham CR4 181 A1
Stanmore HA7 25 C6
Laburnum Gdns
Croydon CR0 206 D1
Edmonton N21 17 A2
Laburnum Gr
Edmonton N21 17 A2
Hounslow TW3 129 B1
Kingsbury NW9 45 A2
Kingston u T KT3 177 B1
Ruislip HA4 39 B3
Southall UB1 85 B3
Laburnum Ho
Dagenham RM10 81 C6
New Cross SE4 141 B3
6 Stoke Newington
N16 73 B6
Laburnum Lo 2 N3 29 B1
Laburnum Rd
Hayes UB3 105 D2
Merton SW19 180 A3
Mitcham CR4 181 A1
Laburnum St E2 95 D6
Laburnums The E6 100 A3
Laburnum Way
Southborough BR2 210 D2
Stanwell TW19 148 B3
Lacebark Cl DA15 167 D4
Lacewing Cl E13 99 A4
Lacey Cl N9 18 A2
Lacey Dr
Dagenham RM8 80 C5
Edgware HA8 26 B6
Hampton TW12 173 B2
Lacey Ho 7 SE13 142 A3
Lacey Mews 9 E3 97 C5
Lacine Ct 12 SE16 118 D4
Lackington St EC2 242 D4
Lackland Ho SE1 263 D2
Lacland Ho SW10 266 C4
Lacock Cl SW19 180 A4
Lacock Ct 3 W13 109 A5
Lacon Rd SE22 140 A1
Lacrosse Way SW16. 181 D2
Lacy Rd SW15 134 D1
Ladas Rd SE27 183 A5
Ladbroke Cres W11 91 A1
Ladbroke Gdns
W11 113 B6 244 C6
Ladbroke Gr
Kensal Town W10 91 A2
Notting Hill
W11 113 B6 244 C6
Ladbroke Grove Ho
W11 244 C6
Ladbroke Grove Sta
W10 91 A1
Ladbroke Ho E1 243 D3
Ladbroke Mews W11 244 B3
Ladbroke Rd
Enfield EN1 17 D5
Notting Hill
W11 113 B5 244 C4
Ladbroke Sq
W11 113 B6 244 D5
Ladbroke Terr
W11 113 B5 244 D4
Ladbroke Wlk
W11 113 B5 244 D4
Ladbrook Cl HA5 41 B4
Ladbrooke Cres
DA14 168 D1
Ladbrook Rd SE25 205 B5
Ladderstile Ride KT2,
TW10 176 D5
Ladderswood Way
N11 31 C5
Ladlands SE22 162 A4
Lady Alesford Ave
HA7 25 B5
Lady Bankes Jun & Inf
Schs HA4 62 A6
Lady Booth Rd 7
KT1 176 A1
Ladybower Ct 6 E5 74 D4
Ladycroft Gdns 6
BR6 227 A3
Ladycroft Rd SE13 141 D2
Ladycroft Way BR6 227 A3
Ladycroft Wlk HA7 25 D1
Lady Eleanor Holles Sch
(Jun Girls) The
TW12 173 D5
Lady Eleanor Holles Sch
(Senior Girls) The
TW12 173 D5
Lady Elizabeth Ho
SW14 133 A2
Ladyfern Ho 19 E3 97 C2
Lady Florence Ctyd 15
SE8 141 C5
Ladygate La HA4 39 A3
Lady Hay KT4 215 D6
Lady Helen Seymour Ho
14 E13 99 A5
Lady Margaret Prim Sch
UB1 85 B2
Lady Margaret Rd
Kentish Town NW5 71 C3
Southall UB1 85 B2
Lady Margaret Sch
SW6 135 C4 265 A1
Lady Shaw Ct N13 16 B1
Ladysmith Ave
Ilford IG2 57 C2
Newham E6 100 A5
Ladysmith Cl NW7 28 A3
Ladysmith Rd
Edmonton N18 34 B5
Eltham SE9 166 C5
Enfield EN1 5 D3
Harrrow HA3 24 C1
Newham E16 98 D4
Tottenham N17 34 A1
Lady Somerset Rd
NW5 71 B4
LADYWELL 163 C6
Ladywell Arena
SE13 163 D5
Ladywell Cl SE4 141 C1
Ladywell Ho 7 BR5 190 B1
Ladywell Hts SE4 163 B5
Ladywell Rd SE13 163 D6
Ladywell St 4 E15 98 D6
Ladywell Sta SE13 163 D6
Ladywell Water Twr
SE4 163 C6
Ladywood Ave BR5 211 C4
Ladywood Rd KT6 214 C6
Lafitte Ho 22 N19 49 D2
Lafone Ave TW13 150 C2
Lafone Ho 11 SW2 160 A4
Lafone St
SE1 117 D4 253 C2
Lagado Mews SE16 118 D5
Lagonda Ho 11 E3 97 C3
Lagonier Ho EC1 235 B1
Laidlaw Dr N21 16 B6
Laindon Ho 6 N16 51 D1
Laing Dean UB5 84 C6
Laing Ho SE5 139 A5
Laings Ave CR4 180 D1
Laings Cnr CR4 180 D2
Lainlock Pl TW3 129 D4
Lainson St SW18 157 C4
Lairdale Cl SE21 161 A4
Laird Ho SE5 139 A5
Lairs Cl N7 72 A2
Lait Ho 3 BR3 185 D2
Laitwood Rd SW12 159 B3
Lakanal 14 SE5 139 C4
Lake Ave BR1 187 A4
Lake Bsns Ctr N17 34 A3
Lake Cl
Dagenham RM8 80 D5
6 Wimbledon SW19 179 B5
Lakedale Ct IG11 102 A3
Lakedale Rd SE18 123 C1
Lake Dr WD23 8 B2
Lake Farm Ctry Pk
UB3 105 C5
Lakefield Cl SE20 184 B3
Lakefield Rd N22 32 D1
Lake Gdns
Dagenham RM10 81 C3
Hackbridge SM6 219 B5
Richmond TW10 153 B2
Lakehall Gdns CR7 204 D4
Lakehall Rd CR7 204 D4
Lake Ho
Borough The SE1 252 A1
4 West Norwood
SW27 182 D5
Lake House Rd E11 77 A6
Lakehurst Rd KT19 215 C3
Lakeland Cl HA3 24 B4
Lakeman Ct CR7 183 A1
Lakenheath N14 15 D6
Laker Ct SW4 138 A3
Lake Rd Croydon CR0 223 B6
Dagenham RM6 58 D5
Wimbledon SW19 179 B5
Laker Pl SW15 157 A5
Lakeside
Beckenham BR3 207 D6
Deacons Hill WD6 10 C6
Ealing W13 87 C1
Enfield EN2 3 D1
Finchley N3 29 D1
10 Kingston u T KT2 176 D3
Wallington SM6 219 B4
West Ewell KT19 215 C2
Lakeside Ave
Redbridge IG4 55 D5
Thamesmead SE28 124 A5
Lakeside Cl
Ruislip HA4 39 B5
Sidcup DA15 168 C6
South Norwood SE25 184 A1
Lakeside Complex The
SE2 124 D5
Lakeside Cres EN4 14 D6
Lakeside Ct N4 51 A1
Lakeside Dr
Acton NW10 88 B4
Esher KT10 212 A2
Keston Mark BR2 226 A5
Lakeside Lo NW4 47 A5
Lakeside Rd
Brook Green W14 112 D3
Palmers Green N13 16 B1
Lakeside Way HA9 66 C4
Lakes Rd BR2 225 C3
Lakeswood Rd BR5 211 A3
Lake The WD23 8 B3
Lakeview 23 E3 96 D5
Lake View HA8 26 B5
Lakeview Ct E4 36 B4
Lake View Ct SW1 258 D6
Lakeview Rd
Bexley DA16 146 B1
West Norwood SE27 182 D5
Lake View Terr N18 33 D6
Lakis Cl NW3 70 A4
Laleham Ave NW7 11 B1
Laleham Ho E2 243 C6
Laleham Rd
Catford SE6 164 A4
Littleton TW17 192 C4
Lalor St SW6 135 A3
Lambarde Ave SE9 188 C6
Lambard Ho 4
SE10 142 A5
Lamb Cl UB5 85 A4
Lamb Ct 16 E14 119 A6
Lamberhurst Ho 14
SE15 140 C6
Lamberhurst Rd
Dagenham RM8 59 B1
West Norwood SE27 182 C5
Lambert Ave TW9 132 D2
Lambert Ho
16 Brixton SW9 138 C3
19 Crouch End N19 49 D2
Lambert Lo TW8 109 D1
Lambert Rd
Clapham Pk SW2 160 B6
Newham E16 99 B1
North Finchley N12 30 B5
Lambert's Pl CR0 205 B1
Lambert's Rd KT6 198 B4
Lambert St N1 72 C1
Lambert Way N12 30 A5
Lambert Wlk HA9 65 D5
LAMBETH 116 B4
Lambeth Acad SW4. 159 C6
Lambeth Coll SW16. 160 A1
Lambeth Coll (Brixton
Ctr) SW2 160 B6
Lambeth Coll (Clapham
Ctr) SW4 159 C6
Lambeth Coll (Vauxhall
Ctr) SW8 137 D4 269 C2
Lambeth Ct 8
SW18 157 C6
Lambeth High St
SE1 116 B2 260 C4
Lambeth Hill EC4 252 A6
Lambeth Hospl SW9 138 B2
Lambeth North Sta
SE1 116 C3 261 A6
Lambeth Pal*
SE1 116 B3 260 C5
Lambeth Palace Rd
SE1 116 B3 260 C6
Lambeth Pier SE1 260 B5
Lambeth Prospect
SE19 183 B4
Lambeth Rd
Lambeth
SE1 116 C3 261 B5
Thornton Heath CR0 204 D1
Lambeth Twrs SE11 261 A5
Lambeth Wlk
SE11 116 B2 260 D4
Lambfold Ho N7 72 A2
Lamb Ho
28 Camberwell SE5 139 A5
11 Camberwell SE5 139 B4
Greenwich SE10 142 A6
Lamb La E8 74 B1
Lamble St NW5 71 A4
Lambley Rd RM9 80 B2
Lamb Office Ct WC1 240 C4
Lambolle Pl NW3 70 C2
Lambolle Rd NW3 70 C2
Lambourn Cl
Hanwell W7 108 D4
9 Kentish Town NW5 71 C4
Lambourne Ave
SW19 179 B6
Lambourne Ct 5 IG8 37 C3
Lambourne Gdns
5 Barking IG11 79 D1
Chingford E4 19 C2
Enfield EN1 5 D3
Lambourne Gr
Deptford SE16 118 D1
Kingston u T KT1 176 D1
Lambourne Ho NW8 236 D4
Lambourne Pl SE3 143 B4
Lambourne Rd
Barking IG11 79 D1
Ilford IG3 79 C6
Leytonstone E11 54 A2
Lambourn Ho BR1 188 A3
Lambourn Rd SW4 137 B2
Lambrook Ho 13
SE15 140 A4
Lambrook Terr
SW6 135 A4 264 A2
Lamb's Bldgs EC1 242 C5
Lamb's Cl N9 18 A2
Lamb's Conduit Pas
WC1 240 C4
Lamb's Conduit St
WC1 94 B3 240 C5
Lambscroft Ave SE9,
SE12 165 D1
Lambs Mdw IG8 37 D1
Lamb's Mews N1 234 C5
Lamb's Pas
EC1 95 B3 242 C5
Lamb St E1 95 D2 243 C4
Lamb's Terr N9 17 B2
Lambs Wlk EN2 5 A3
Lambton Ct 2 N19 50 A1
Lambton Mews 4
N19 50 A1
Lambton Pl W11 244 D6
Lambton Rd
Finsbury Pk N19 50 A1
Wimbledon SW20 178 C2
Lamb Wlk SE1 253 A1
Lamerock Rd BR1 186 D6
Lamerton Lo 10
TW9 132 B4
Lamerton St 8 SE8 141 C6
Lamford Cl N17 33 B3
Lamington St 3 W6 112 B2
Lamlash St SE11 261 C4
Lamley Ho SE10 141 D5
Lammas Ave CR4 181 A1
Lammas Gn SE26 162 B1
Lammas Park Gdns
W5 109 C5
Lammas Park Rd
W5 109 D4
Lammas Rd
Homerton E9 74 D1
Richmond TW10 175 C6
Walthamstow E10 53 A1
Lammas Sch E10 53 B1
Lammermoor Rd
SW12 159 B4
Lamont Rd
SW10 136 B6 266 C5
Lamont Rd Pas
SW10 266 C5
Lamorbey Cl DA15 167 D2
Lamorna Cl E17 36 A2
Lamorna Gr HA7 25 D1
Lampard Gr N16 51 D1
Lampern Sq 8 E2 96 A4
Lampeter Cl NW9 45 C3
Lampeter Sq W6 264 A5
Lamplighter Cl 34 E1 96 C3
Lampmead Rd SE12 142 D1
Lamport Cl SE18 122 B2
Lampson Ho 6 N19 71 C4
LAMPTON 129 D4
Lampton Ave TW5 129 D4
Lampton Ct TW5 129 D4
Lampton House Cl
SW19 178 D6
Lampton Park Rd
TW3 129 D3
Lampton Rd TW3,
TW5 129 D3
Lampton Sch TW5 129 C4
Lampton Sp Ctr
TW5 129 C4
Lanacre Ave NW9 27 C2
Lanadron Cl 5 TW7 130 D3
Lanain Ct SE12 164 D4
Lanark Cl W5 87 C2
Lanark Ct UB5 63 C3
Lanark Ho 12 SE1 118 A1
Lanark Mans
Paddington W9 236 B6
15 Shepherd's Bush
W12 112 C4
Lanark Mews NW8 229 B1
Lanark Pl W9 92 A3 236 B6
Lanark Rd W9 92 A4 229 A1
Lanark Sq E14 119 D3
Lanata Wlk UB4 84 D3
Lanbury Rd SE15 140 D1
Lancashire Ct W1 248 D6
Lancaster Ave
Barking IG11 101 C6
Croydon CR4 204 A5
Hadley Wood EN4 2 B5
Wanstead E18 55 B5
West Norwood SE21,
SE27 161 A2
Wimbledon SW19 178 D5
Lancaster Cl
Ashford TW15 170 A6
Beckenham BR2 208 D5

Lancaster Cl *continued*
10 De Beauvoir Town N1 73 C1
Grahame Pk NW9 27 D3
Kensington W2 245 C5
Kingston u T KT2 175 D5
New Malden KT4 200 B2
Stanwell TW19 148 A5
Tottenham N17 34 A3
Lancaster Cotts 1 TW10 154 A5
Lancaster Ct
Bayswater W2 246 B6
1 Belmont SM2 217 C1
Parsons Green SW6 264 D3
Stanwell TW19 148 A3
Walton-on-T KT12 194 B2
West Norwood SE27 160 D2
Lancaster Dr
Canary Wharf E14 120 A5
Maitland Pk NW3 70 C2
Lancaster Gate W2 114 A6 246 B6
Lancaster Gate Sta W2 114 B6 246 C6
Lancaster Gdns
Bromley BR1 210 A4
Kingston u T KT2 175 D5
West Ealing W13 109 B4
Wimbledon SW19 179 A5
Lancaster Gr NW3 70 C2
Lancaster hall 14 E16 121 A5
Lancaster Ho
Enfield EN2 5 B4
Putney SW15 134 C3
Stanmore HA7 9 A1
Lancaster Ho SW1 249 A2
Lancaster Ho SW18 157 D4
Lancasterian Prim Sch N17 33 D2
Lancaster Lo 2 W11 91 A1
Lancaster Mews
Bayswater W2 114 A6 246 B6
2 Richmond TW10 154 A5
3 Wandsworth SW18 157 D6
Lancaster Pk TW10 154 A6
Lancaster Pl
Hounslow TW5 128 D3
Ilford IG1 79 A4
Strand WC2 116 B6 250 C5
Twickenham TW1 153 A4
1 Wimbledon SW19 178 D5
Lancaster Rd
Bowes Pk N11 31 D4
Dudden Hill NW10 68 A3
Edmonton N18 33 D5
Enfield EN2 5 B4
Finsbury Pk N4 50 C2
Harrow HA2 41 C4
Higham Hill E17 34 D1
Leytonstone E11 76 C6
New Barnet EN4 14 B6
Northolt UB5 64 A2
Notting Hill W11 91 A1
Southall UB1 107 A6
South Norwood SE25 206 A6
Upton E7 77 A1
Wimbledon SW19 178 D5
Lancaster Road Ind Est 2 EN4 14 B6
Lancaster St SE1 116 D4 251 D1
Lancaster Stables 10 NW3 70 C2
Lancaster Terr W2 114 B6 246 C6
Lancaster Wlk
Hayes UB3 83 A1
Knightsbridge W2 114 A5 246 B4
Lancastrian Rd SM6 220 B1
Lancefield Ho SE15 140 B2
Lancefield St W10 91 B4
Lancell St N16 73 C6
Lancelot Ave HA0 65 D4
Lancelot Cres HA0 65 D4
Lancelot Gdns EN4 15 A4
Lancelot Ho SM5 202 C1
Lancelot Pl SW7 114 D4 247 C1
Lancelot Rd
Welling DA16 146 A2
Wembley HA0 65 D3
Lance Rd HA1 42 A2
Lancer Sq W8 245 C2
Lancey Cl SE7 122 A2
Lanchester Ct W2 237 C1
Lanchester Rd N6 48 D4
Lanchester Way SE14 140 D4
Lancing Gdns N9 17 D3
Lancing Rd
Ealing W13 109 B6
Feltham TW13 149 D2
Ilford IG2 57 B2
Thornton Heath CR0 204 B2
Lancing St NW1 232 C1
Lancresse Ct N1 95 C6
Landale Ct SE10 142 A4
Landale Ho 13 SE16 118 C3
Landau Ct 11 CR2 221 A3
Landcroft Rd SE22 161 D5
Landells Rd SE22 162 A5
Lander Ct EN5 14 A6
Landford Rd SW15 134 C2
Landgrove Rd SW19 179 C5
Landin Ho 1 E14 97 C1
Landleys Field 21 N7 71 D3
Landmann Ho 16 SE16 118 B2
Landmann Way SE14 118 D1
Landmark Commercial Ctr N18 33 C4
Landmark Hts E5 75 A4
Landon Pl SW1 257 C6
Landons Cl E14 120 A5
Landon Way TW15 170 D4
Landon Wlk 16 E14 119 D6
Landor Ct N16 73 C3
Landor Ho 7 SE5 139 B5
Landor Rd SW9 138 A2
Landor Wlk 11 W12 112 A4
Landra Gdns N21 16 D5
Landrake NW1 232 B5
Landridge Dr EN1 6 B5
Landridge Rd SW6 135 B3
Landrock Rd N8 50 B3
Landscape Rd IG8 37 B3
Landsdown Cl 9 EN5 2 A1
Landseer Ave E12 78 C3
Landseer Cl
Edgware HA8 26 C1
Mitcham SW19 180 B2
Landseer Ct
Hayes UB4 83 B5
10 Upper Holloway N19 72 A6
Landseer Ho
Battersea SW11 268 B1
16 Northolt UB5 84 D5
Paddington NW8 236 D6
Westminster SW1 259 D3
Landseer Rd
Cheam SM1 217 C2
Enfield EN1 18 A6
New Malden KT3 199 B2
Upper Holloway N19 72 A6
Lands' End WD6 9 D5
Landstead Rd SE18 145 B5
Landulph Ho SE11 261 B2
Landward Ct W1 237 B2
Lane Cl NW2 68 B5
Lane Ct SW11 158 D4
Lane End DA7 147 D2
Lane Gdns
Bushey Heath WD23 8 C4
Claygate KT10 212 D1
Lane Mews E12 78 B5
Lanercost Cl SW2 160 C2
Lanercost Gdns N14 16 A4
Lanercost Rd SW2 160 C2
Laneside
Chislehurst BR7 189 A5
Edgware HA8 27 A5
Laneside Ave RM8 59 B2
Lane The
Blackheath Pk SE3 143 A2
St John's Wood NW8 92 A5 229 A3
Laneway SW15 156 B6
Laney Bldg EC1 241 A4
Lanfranc Ct HA1 64 D5
Lanfranc Rd E3 97 A5
Lanfrey Pl W14 254 C1
Langbourn Ct E17 53 A3
Langbourne Ave N6 71 A6
Langbourne Ho 7 SW2 160 C6
Langbourne Mans N6 71 A6
Langbourne Pl E14 119 D1
Langbourne Prim Sch SE21 161 C1
Langbourne Way KT10 213 A2
Langbrook Rd SE3 143 D3
Langcroft Cl SM5 218 D5
Langdale NW1 232 A2
Langdale Ave CR4 202 D6
Langdale Cl
Camberwell SE17 139 A6
Dagenham RM8 58 C1
Locksbottom BR6 226 D5
Mortlake SW14 132 D1
Langdale Cres DA7 147 C4
Langdale Ct
3 Ealing W5 87 C2
9 Ilford IG1 78 D5
Ruislip HA4 62 B3
Langdale Dr UB4 83 C5
Langdale Gdns UB6 87 B4
Langdale Ho SW1 259 A1
Langdale Par 8 CR4 202 D6
Langdale Rd
Greenwich SE10 142 A5
Thornton Heath CR7 204 C5
Langdale St 25 E1 96 B1
Langdon Cres E6 100 C5
Langdon Ct
Finsbury EC1 234 D3
Harlesden NW10 89 C6
Langdon Dr NW9 45 A1
Langdon Ho 3 E14 98 A1
Langdon Park Rd N6 49 C2
Langdon Park Sch E14 98 A1
Langdon Park Sta E14 97 D1
Langdon Pk TW11 175 C3
Langdon Pk L Ctr E14 98 A1
Langdon Pk Sta E3 97 D2
Langdon Pl SW14 133 A2
Langdon Rd
Barking E6 100 C6
Bromley BR2 209 B6
Morden SM4 202 A4
Langdon Sch E6 100 D6
Langdons Ct UB2 107 C3
Langdon Shaw DA14 189 D5
Langdon Way 18 SE1 118 A2
Langdon Wlk SM4 202 A4
Langford Cl
Shacklewell E8 74 A3
7 South Tottenham N15 51 C3
St John's Wood NW8 229 B4
Langford Cres EN4 2 D1
Langford Ct NW8 229 B3
Langford Gn SE5 139 C2
Langford Ho 5 SE8 141 C6
Langford Pl
Sidcup DA14 168 A1
St John's Wood NW8 92 A5 229 B4
Langford Prim Sch SW6 135 D3
Langford Rd
Cockfosters EN4 2 D1
4 Sands End SW6 135 D3
Woodford IG8 37 C4
Langfords IG9 21 D2
Langham Cl 1 N15 50 D6
Langham Ct
Hendon NW4 46 D4
Merton SW20 178 C1
4 Putney SW15 156 D6
Ruislip HA4 62 B3
12 Twickenham TW1 153 C5
Langham Dr RM6 58 B3
Langham Gdns
Burnt Oak HA8 27 A3
Ealing W13 109 B6
Richmond TW10 175 C6
Southgate N21 16 D6
Wembley HA0 65 C6
Langham Ho
Clapham Pk SW4 159 C6
3 Wanstead E11 55 B5
Langham House Cl TW10 175 D6
Langham Mans SW5 255 C1
Langham Park Pl BR2 208 D5
Langham Pl
Chiswick W4 133 C6
Fitzrovia W1 93 B2 238 D3
Noel Pk N15 50 D6
Langham Rd
Burnt Oak HA8 27 A4
Teddington TW11 175 B4
West Green N15 51 A6
Wimbledon SW20 178 C2
Langham St W1 93 B2 238 D3
Langhedge Cl N18 33 D4
Langhedge La N18 33 D4
Langhedge Lane Ind Est N18 33 D4
Lang Ho
South Lambeth SW8 270 A3
Stanwell TW19 148 A3
3 Tufnell Pk N19 71 C5
Langholm Cl SW12 159 D4
Langholme WD23 8 A3
Langhorn Dr TW2 152 C4
Langhorne Ct 10 NW8 70 B1
Langhorne Ho 5 SE7 143 C6
Langhorne Rd RM10 81 C1
Langhurst Ho 10 SW11 137 A3
Langland Cres HA7 25 D1
Langland Dr HA5 23 A3
Langland Gdns
Croydon CR0 223 B6
West Hampstead NW3 69 D3
Langland Ho 10 SE5 139 B5
Upper Tooting SW17 180 B5
Langland Mans NW3 69 D3
Langler Rd NW10 90 C5
Langley Ave
North Cheam KT4, SM3 216 D6
Ruislip HA4 62 B6
Surbiton KT6 198 A1
Langley Cres
Dagenham RM9 80 D1
Edgware HA8 11 A1
Harlington UB3 127 D5
Wanstead E11 55 C2
Langley Ct
South Lambeth SW8 270 A2
Strand WC2 250 A6
13 Sutton SM2 218 A2
Langley Dr
South Acton W3 110 D4
Wanstead E11 55 B2
Langley Gdns
Bromley BR2 209 C5
Dagenham RM9 80 D1
Southborough BR5 210 D3
Langley Gr KT3 177 C1
Langley Ho
11 Lower Clapton E5 74 B3
36 Paddington W2 91 C2
Langley La SW8 138 A6 270 B6
Langley Lawns SM2 218 B1
Langley Manor BR3 208 A4
Langley Mans SW8 270 B6
Langley Park Rd SM1, SM2 218 A1
Langley Park Sch for Boys BR3 207 D3
Langley Park Sch for Girls BR3 208 A3
Langley Pk NW7 27 C4
Langley Pl 4 KT4 216 D6
Langley Rd
Beckenham BR3 207 A5
Isleworth TW7 130 D3
Merton SW19 179 C2
Surbiton KT6 198 A2
West Heath DA16 146 C6
Langley Row EN5 1 B4
Langley St WC2 94 A1 240 A1
Langley Way BR4 208 C2
Langmead Dr WD23 8 B3
Langmead Ho 34 E3 97 D4
Langmead St SE27 183 A6
Langmore Ct DA6 146 D2
Langmore Ho 39 E1 96 A1
Langport Ct KT12 194 C1
Langport Ho 1 SW9 138 D3
Langridge 15 NW5 71 A2
Langridge Mews TW12 173 B4
Langroyd Rd SW17 158 D2
Langside Ave SW15 134 A1
Langside Cres N14 15 D1
Lang St E1 96 C3
Langstone Way NW7 28 D3
Langston Hughes Cl 5 SE24 138 D1
Langthorn Ct EC2 242 D2
Langthorne Ct 3 SE6 186 A6
Langthorne Ho UB3 105 C2
Langthorne Lo 30 SW2 160 C4
Langthorne Rd E11 76 B5
Langthorne St SW6 134 D5
Langton Ave
Oakleigh Pk N20 14 B4
Wallend E6 100 C4
Langton Cl WC1 94 B3 240 D6
Langton Ct SW15 157 B5
Langton Ho
Harrow HA2 64 C6
Lambeth SE11 260 D4
5 Streatham SW16 181 C6
Langton Pl SW18 157 C3
Langton Rd
Camberwell SW9 138 D5
Cricklewood NW2 68 C5
East Molesey KT8 196 A5
Harrow Weald HA3 24 A3
Langton Rise SE22, SE23 162 B4
Langton St SW10 136 A6 266 B5
Langton Way
Greenwich SE3 143 A5
South Croydon CR0 221 C4
Langtry Ho BR1 187 B3
Langtry Pl SW6 265 B6
Langtry Rd
Northolt UB5 84 D5
Paddington NW8 91 D6
Langtry Wlk NW8 92 A6 229 A6
Langwood Chase TW11 175 C4
Langworth Dr UB4 84 B1
Langworthy HA5 23 C4
Lanherne Ho 7 SW19 178 D3
Lanhill Rd W9 91 C3
Lanier Rd SE13 164 B5
Lanigan Dr TW3 151 D6
Lankaster Gdns N2 30 B2
Lankers Dr HA2 41 B3
Lankton Cl BR3 186 A2
Lanner Ho 2 SW11 136 C2
Lannock Ct 2 SW17 180 C4
Lannock Rd UB3 105 D5
Lannoy Point SW6 264 B4
Lannoy Rd SE9 167 A3
Lanrick Rd E14 98 C1
Lanridge Rd SE2 124 D3
Lansan Ct E11 76 D6
Lansbury Ave
Barking IG11 80 A1
Dagenham RM6 59 A4
Edmonton N18 33 C5
Feltham TW14 150 B5
Lansbury Cl NW10 67 A3
Lansbury Ct 4 SE28 124 B6
Lansbury Dr UB4 83 D3
Lansbury Gdns 1 E14 98 B1
Lansbury Ho 5 DA17 125 B1
Lansbury Lawrence Prim Sch 20 E14 97 D1
Lansbury Rd EN3 6 D4
Lansbury Way N18 33 C5
Lanscombe Wlk SW8 270 A3
Lansdell Ho 9 SW2 160 C5
Lansdell Rd CR4 181 A1
Lansdown Cl KT12 194 C1
Lansdowne Ave
Orpington BR6 210 D1

Lansdowne Ave *continued*
West Heath DA7 .... 146 D5
Lansdowne Cl
Tolworth KT5 .... 214 D6
Twickenham TW1 .... 152 D3
Wimbledon SW20 .... 178 D3
Lansdowne Coll W2. 245 C5
Lansdowne Copse [1]
KT4 .... 216 A6
Lansdowne Cres
W11 .... 113 A6 244 B5
Lansdowne Ct
Redbridge IG5 .... 56 A6
[2] Worcester Pk KT4. 216 A6
Lansdowne Dr E8 .... 74 A1
Lansdowne Gdns
SW8 .... 138 A4 270 A2
Lansdowne Gr NW10 .. 67 C4
Lansdowne Hill
SE27 .... 160 D1
Lansdowne Ho
[19] Belmont SM2 .... 217 D1
Enfield EN2 .... 4 C3
Notting Hill W11 .... 244 C4
Lansdowne La SE7 .. 121 D1
Lansdowne Mews
Greenwich SE7 .... 121 D1
Notting Hill W11 .... 244 C4
Lansdowne Pl
Borough The SE1 .... 262 D6
Penge SE19 .... 183 D3
Lansdowne Rd
Chingford E4 .... 19 C2
Croydon CR0 .... 205 B1
Finchley N3 .... 29 C3
Harrow HA1 .... 42 C2
Hayes UB8 .... 83 A1
Hounslow TW3 .... 129 D2
Ilford IG3 .... 57 D2
Leytonstone E11 .... 76 D6
Muswell Hill N10 .... 31 C1
Notting Hill
W11 .... 113 A6 244 B5
Stanmore HA7 .... 25 C4
Sundridge BR1 .... 187 B3
Tottenham N17 .... 34 A2
Walthamstow E17 .... 53 C3
Wanstead E18 .... 55 A6
West Ewell KT19 .... 215 B1
Wimbledon SW19,
SW20 .... 178 C3
Lansdowne Rise
W11 .... 113 A6 244 B5
Lansdowne Row W1 248 D4
Lansdowne Sch [5]
SW9 .... 138 B2
Lansdowne Terr
WC1 .... 240 B5
Lansdowne Way SW4,
SW8 .... 138 A4 270 B1
Lansdowne Wlk
W11 .... 113 B5 244 C4
Lansdowne Wood Cl [11]
SE27 .... 160 D1
Lansdowne Workshops
SE7 .... 121 D1
Lansdown Ho [28]
SE5 .... 139 A3
Lansdown Rd
Sidcup DA14 .... 168 B1
Upton E7 .... 77 C1
Lansfield Ave N18 .... 34 A6
Lanson Ho HA8 .... 26 C4
Lantern Cl
Orpington BR6 .... 226 D4
Putney SW15 .... 134 A1
Wembley HA0 .... 65 D3
Lantern Ct
Southgate N14 .... 15 D3
[4] Wimbledon SW20. 178 D2
Lantern Ho
Millwall E14 .... 119 C4
Woolwich SE18 .... 122 C1
Lantern of Knowledge
Boys Sec Sch [1]
E10 .... 76 A6
Lanterns Ct E14 .... 119 C3
Lanterns The N12 .... 29 D4
Lantern Way UB7 .... 104 B4
Lant Ho SE1 .... 252 A1
Lantry Ct [1] W3 .... 110 D5
Lant St SE1 .... 117 A4 252 B1
Lanvanor Rd SE15 .... 140 C3
Lanyard Ho [4] SE8 .... 119 B2
Lapford Cl W9 .... 91 B3
Lapponum Wlk UB4 ... 84 D2
Lapsang SE1 .... 253 D3
Lapse Wood Wlk
SE22 .... 162 B3
Lapstone Gdns HA3 .... 43 C3
Lapwing Ct
Grahame Pk NW9 .... 27 C1
Tolworth KT6 .... 214 C5
Lapwing Terr E7 .... 77 D3
Lapwing Twr [31] SE8 .. 141 B6
Lapwing Way UB4 .... 84 D1
Lapworth [2] N11 .... 31 B6
Lapworth Ct W2 .... 91 D2
Lara Cl
Chessington KT9 .... 214 A1
Lewisham SE13 .... 164 A5
Lara Lo SM1 .... 217 C3
Larbert Rd SW16 .... 181 C3
Larch Ave W3 .... 111 C5
Larch Cl
Balham SW12 .... 159 B2
Colney Hatch N11 .... 31 A3
[15] Deptford SE8 .... 141 B6
Newham E13 .... 99 C3
[10] Upper Holloway
N19 .... 71 C6
Larch Cres Hayes UB4. . 84 D2
West Ewell KT19 .... 214 D2
Larch Ct [41] W2 .... 91 C2
Larch Dene BR6 .... 226 C6
Larches Ave SW14 .... 133 B1
Larches The
Edmonton N13 .... 17 A1
Hillingdon UB10 .... 82 D5
Larchfield Ho [2] N5 ... 73 A3
Larch Gn NW9 .... 27 C2
Larch Gr DA15 .... 167 D3
Larch Ho Hayes UB4 ... 84 C2
[23] Rotherhithe SE16. 118 C4
Larchmont HA4 .... 39 B2
Larchmore Ct N19 .... 72 A6
Larch Rd
Cricklewood NW2 .... 68 C4
Leyton E10 .... 75 C6
Larch Tree Way CR0 . 223 C5
Larchvale Ct [20]
SM2 .... 217 D1
Larch Way BR2 .... 210 C2
Larchwood Rd SE9 ... 166 D2
Larcombe Cl CR0 ... 221 D4
Larcom St
SE17 .... 117 A2 262 B3
Larden Rd W3 .... 111 C4
La Retraite RC Girls Sch
SW12 .... 159 C4
Largewood Ave KT6. 214 C6
Larissa St SE17 .... 262 D3
Larix Ct NW10 .... 90 A6
Larkbere Rd SE26 .... 185 A6
Larken Cl WD23 .... 8 A3
Larken Dr WD23 .... 8 A3
Larkfield Ave HA3 .... 43 B6
Larkfield Cl BR2 .... 225 A6
Larkfield Rd
Longlands DA14 .... 167 D1
Richmond TW9 .... 132 A1
Larkhall La
SW4 .... 138 A4 270 A1
Lark Hall Prim Sch
SW4 .... 137 D3
Larkhall Rise SW4 .. 137 D3
Larkham Cl TW13 .... 149 C1
Lark Row E2 .... 96 C6
Larksfield Gr EN1 .... 6 B4
Larks Gr IG11 .... 79 C1
Larkshall Bsns Ctr E4 . 20 B2
Larkshall Cres E4 .... 36 A6
Larkshall Ct E4 .... 36 A5
Larkshall Rd E4 .... 36 B6
Larkspur Cl
Kingsbury NW9 .... 44 D4
[4] Newham E6 .... 100 A2
Ruislip HA4 .... 39 A2
Tottenham N17 .... 33 B3
Larkspur Ct SM6 .... 219 B1
Larkspur Gr HA8 .... 27 A6
Larkspur Way KT19 . 215 A3
Larkswood Ct E4 .... 36 B5
Larkswood L Ctr E4 ... 36 A6
Larkswood Prim Sch
E4 .... 35 D6
Larkswood Rd E4 .... 35 D6
Larkswood Rise HA5 .. 40 C5
Lark Way SM5 .... 202 C2
Larkway Cl NW9 .... 45 B5
Larmenier & Sacred
Heart RC Prim Sch [4]
W6 .... 112 D2
Larnaca Ho SE1 .... 263 C6
Larnach Rd W6 .... 134 D6
Larne Rd HA4 .... 39 D2
Larpent Ave SW15 ... 156 C6
Larwood Cl UB6 .... 64 B3
La Saint Union RC Sec
Sch NW5 .... 71 A5
Lascelles Ave HA1 .... 42 B2
Lascelles Cl E11 .... 76 B6
Lascelles Ho NW1 .. 237 B5
Lascott's Rd N22 .... 32 B4
Laseron Ho [1] N15 .... 51 D5
Lashford Ho HA8 .... 27 A4
Lassa Rd SE9 .... 166 B6
Lassell St SE10 .... 120 B1
Lasseter Pl SE3 .... 142 D6
Latchett Rd E18 .... 37 B2
Latchingdon Ct E17 ... 52 D5
Latchmere Cl KT2,
TW10 .... 176 A5
Latchmere La KT2,
TW10 .... 176 B5
Latchmere L Ctr
SW11 .... 136 D3
Latchmere Prim Sch
KT2 .... 176 B4
Latchmere Rd
Battersea SW11 .... 136 D3
Kingston u T KT2 .... 176 B4
Latchmere St [5]
SW11 .... 136 D3
Lateward Rd TW8 ... 131 D6
Latham Cl
Newham E6 .... 100 A1
[6] Twickenham TW1 . 153 A4
Latham Ct
[3] Bowes Pk N11 .... 32 A4
[7] Northolt UB5 .... 84 D4
Latham Ho Stepney E1 . 96 D1
[18] Walthamstow E17 ... 53 D6
Latham Rd
Bexleyheath DA6 .... 169 C6
Twickenham TW1 .... 152 D4
Latham's Way CR0 ... 220 B6
Lathkill Cl EN1 .... 18 A4
Lathkill Ct BR3 .... 185 B2
Lathom Jun Sch E6 ... 78 A1
Lathom Rd E6 .... 78 B1
Lathwood Ho [6]
SE26 .... 184 B5
Latimer SE17 .... 263 A1
Latimer Ave E6 .... 100 B6
Latimer Cl
North Cheam KT4 .... 216 B4
Pinner Green HA5 .... 22 C2
Latimer Gdns HA5 .... 22 C2
Latimer Ho
[11] Homerton E9 .... 74 D2
Notting Hill W11 .... 244 D5
Latimer Ind Est [1]
NW10 .... 90 C1
Latimer Pl W10 .... 90 C1
Latimer Rd Barnet EN5 .. 1 D2
[1] Croydon CR0 .... 220 D5
Forest Gate E7 .... 77 B4
North Kensington W10 .. 90 C1
South Tottenham N15 ... 51 C3
Teddington TW11 .... 174 D5
Wimbledon SW19 .... 179 D4
Latimer Road Sta
W10 .... 112 D6
Latitude Ct E16 .... 123 A6
Latitude Ho NW1 .... 231 C5
Latona Rd SE15 .... 140 A6
La Tourne Gdns
BR6 .... 227 A5
Lattimer Pl W4 .... 133 C6
Latton Cl KT12 .... 195 A2
Latvia Ct SE17 .... 262 B1
Latymer All Saints CE
Prim Sch N9 .... 17 D2
Latymer Ct W6 .... 112 D2
Latymer Rd N9 .... 17 D3
Latymer Sch The N9 .. 17 C2
Latymer Upper Sch [14]
W6 .... 112 A2
Latymer Way N9 .... 17 C2
Laubin Cl TW1 .... 131 B1
Lauder Cl UB5 .... 84 D5
Lauder Ct N14 .... 16 A4
Lauderdale Dr
TW10 .... 153 D1
Lauderdale Mans W9 . 91 D4
Lauderdale Rd W9 .... 91 D4
Lauderdale Twr EC2. 242 A4
Laud St Croydon CR0 .. 221 A5
Vauxhall
SE11 .... 116 B1 260 C2
Laughton Ho [11]
SW2 .... 160 C5
Laughton Rd UB5 .... 84 D6
Launcelot Prim Sch
BR1 .... 187 A6
Launcelot Rd BR1,
SE12 .... 187 A6
Launcelot St SE1 .... 251 A1
Launceston Ct CR7 .. 204 C3
Launceston Gdns
UB6 .... 65 C1
Launceston Pl
W8 .... 114 A3 256 A5
Launceston Rd UB6 ... 87 C6
Launch St E14 .... 120 A3
Laundress La N16 .... 74 A5
Laundry La [7] N1 .... 73 A1
Laundry Mews SE23. 162 D4
Laundry Rd
W6 .... 135 A6 264 A5
Launton Dr DA6 .... 146 D1
Laura Cl Enfield EN1 ... 17 C6
Wanstead E11 .... 55 C4
Laura Ct HA2 .... 24 A1
Lauradale Rd N2 .... 48 D5
Laura Pl E5 .... 74 C4
Laurel Ave TW1 .... 152 D3
Laurel Bank Gdns [3]
SW6 .... 135 B3
Laurel Bank Rd EN2 .... 5 B4
Laurel Cl
Sidcup DA14 .... 168 A1
[8] Upper Holloway
N19 .... 71 C6
Upper Tooting SW17 . 180 C5
Laurel Cres CR0 .... 223 C5
Laurel Ct Dalston E8 ... 73 D1
[2] Putney SW15 .... 156 D6
[9] Rotherhithe SE16 . 119 A5
South Norwood SE25. 205 C4
[8] Wembley HA0 .... 88 A5
Laurel Dr N21 .... 16 C4
Laurel Gdns
Bromley BR1 .... 210 A5
Chingford E4 .... 19 D4
Ealing W7 .... 108 C5
Edgware NW7 .... 11 B1
Hounslow TW4 .... 129 A1
Laurel Gr
Forest Hill SE26 .... 185 A6
Penge SE20 .... 184 C3
Laurel Ho
Brentford W5 .... 109 C2
[9] Deptford SE8 .... 141 B6
[5] Hamstead NW3 .... 69 D2
Morden SM4 .... 201 D4
Laurel La UB7 .... 104 A2
Laurel Manor SM2 ... 218 A1
Laurel Mead Ct [8]
E18 .... 37 A2
Laurel Pk HA3 .... 24 D3
Laurel Rd
Barnes SW13 .... 134 A3
Teddington TW12 .... 174 B5
Wimbledon SW20 .... 178 B2
Laurel St E8 .... 73 D2
Laurels The
[8] Belvedere DA17 .. 125 C1
[2] Buckhurst Hill IG9 .. 21 C3
Bushey WD23 .... 8 C2
Finchley N3 .... 29 D4
Shortlands BR2 .... 209 A5
[9] Sundridge BR1 .... 187 B2
Laurel View N12 .... 13 D1
Laurel Way
Snaresbrook E18 .... 54 D5
Woodside Pk N20 .... 13 C1
Laurence Ct E10 .... 53 D2
Laurence Mews [12]
W12 .... 112 A4
Laurence Pountney Hill
EC4 .... 252 C6
Laurence Pountney La
EC4 .... 252 D6
Laurie Gr SE14 .... 141 A4
Laurie Ho
Newington SE1 .... 261 D5
Notting Hill
W8 .... 113 C5 245 A3
Laurie Rd W7 .... 86 C2
Laurier Rd
Croydon CR0 .... 205 D2
Dartmouth Pk NW5 .... 71 B5
Laurimel Cl HA7 .... 25 B4
Laurino Pl WD23 .... 8 A2
Lauriston Apartments [6]
N17 .... 51 D6
Lauriston Ho [6] E9 .... 74 D1
Lauriston Lo NW6 .... 69 B2
Lauriston Prim Sch [6]
E9 .... 96 D6
Lauriston Rd
Homerton E9 .... 74 D1
Wimbledon SW19 .... 178 D4
Lausanne Rd
Hornsey N8 .... 50 C5
St Johns SE15 .... 140 C4
Lavehham Ho E17 .... 35 D2
Lavell St N16 .... 73 B4
Lavender Ave
Mitcham CR4 .... 180 D2
North Cheam KT4,
SM3 .... 216 C5
Welsh Harp NW9 .... 45 A1
Lavender Cl
Bromley Comm BR2 .. 210 A3
Chingford E4 .... 35 C6
South Kensington
SW3 .... 266 D5
Wallington SM5 .... 219 B4
Lavender Ct
Colney Hatch N12 .... 30 C4
East Molesey KT8 .... 195 D6
Edgware HA8 .... 27 A5
Feltham TW14 .... 150 B5
South Lambeth SW4 . 270 B1
Sutton SM2 .... 218 A1
Lavender Gdns
Clapham SW11 .... 136 D1
Enfield EN2 .... 4 D4
Stanmore HA3 .... 24 C4
Lavender Gr
Dalston E8 .... 74 A1
Mitcham CR4 .... 180 C2
Lavender Hill
Clapham SW11 .... 137 A2
Enfield EN2 .... 4 D4
Lavender Ho
[8] Richmond TW9 ... 132 D4
[14] Rotherhithe SE16 . 118 D5
Lavender Pl IG1 .... 78 D3
Lavender Prim Sch
EN2 .... 5 C5
Lavender Rd
Battersea SW11 .... 136 B2
Enfield EN2 .... 5 B4
Hillingdon UB8 .... 82 B2
Rotherhithe SE16 .... 119 A5
Sutton SM1 .... 218 B4
Thornton Heath CR0 .. 204 B3
Wallington SM5 .... 219 A4
West Ewell KT19 .... 214 D2
Lavender Rise UB7 ... 104 C4
Lavender St E15 .... 76 C2
Lavender Sweep
SW11 .... 136 D1
Lavender Terr [12]
SW11 .... 136 C2
Lavender Vale SM6 .. 219 D2
Lavender Way CR0 .. 206 D3
Lavender Wlk SW11. 136 D1
Lavendon Ho NW8 .. 237 B6
Lavengro Rd SE27 ... 161 A2
Lavenham Rd SW18 .. 157 C3
Lavernock Rd DA7 ... 147 C3
Lavers Rd N16 .... 73 C5
Laverstoke Gdns
SW15 .... 156 A4
Laverton Mews SW5 255 D3
Laverton Pl SW5 .... 255 D3
Lavidge Rd SE9 .... 166 B2
Lavina Gr N1 .... 233 C4
Lavington Cl E9 .... 75 B2
Lavington Rd
Ealing W13 .... 109 B5
Wallington CR0 .... 220 B4
Lavington St
SE1 .... 116 D5 251 D3
Lavinia Ct BR1 .... 186 C3
Lavisham Ho BR1 .... 187 B5
Lawdale Jun Sch [32]
E2 .... 96 A4
Lawdon Gdns CR0 .. 220 D4

Lawford Rd
Chiswick W4 ... 133 A5
De Beauvoir Town N1 ... 73 C1
Kentish Town NW5 ... 71 C2
Lawfords Wharf 18
NW1 ... 71 C1
Law Ho IG11 ... 102 A5
Lawless Ho 5 E14 ... 120 A6
Lawless St 12 E14 ... 119 D6
Lawley Ho 11 TW1 ... 153 D5
Lawley Rd N14 ... 15 B4
Lawley St E5 ... 74 C4
Lawman Ct 2 TW9 ... 132 B4
Lawn Cl Edmonton N9 ... 17 D4
Kingston u T KT3 ... 177 C1
Ruislip HA4 ... 61 D5
Sundridge BR1 ... 187 B3
Lawn Cres TW9 ... 132 C3
Lawn Farm Gr RM6 ... 59 A5
Lawnfield Ct NW6 ... 68 D1
Lawn Gdns W7 ... 108 C5
Lawn House Cl E14 ... 120 A4
Lawn La SW8 138 B6 270 C6
Lawn Mans EN5 ... 1 B1
Lawn Rd
Beckenham BR3 ... 185 B3
Maitland Pk NW3 ... 70 D3
Lawns Ct HA9 ... 66 C6
Lawnside SE3 ... 142 D1
Lawns The
Belmont SM2 ... 217 A1
Blackheath SE3 ... 142 D2
Chingford E4 ... 35 C5
Harrow HA5 ... 23 D3
Sidcup DA14 ... 190 B6
South Norwood SE19 ... 183 B2
Stoke Newington N16 ... 73 C3
1 Wimbledon SW19 ... 179 B5
Lawn Terr SE3 ... 142 C2
Lawn The UB2 ... 107 C1
Lawn Vale HA5 ... 23 A1
Lawrence Ave
Edmonton N13 ... 32 D6
Higham Hill E17 ... 34 D2
Little Ilford E12 ... 78 C4
Mill Hill NW7 ... 27 D6
New Malden KT3 ... 199 C2
Stonebridge NW10 ... 89 B6
Lawrence Bldgs 1
N16 ... 73 D5
Lawrence Camp Cl
N20 ... 14 B1
Lawrence Cl Bow E3 ... 97 C5
6 Shepherd's Bush
W12 ... 112 B6
West Green N15 ... 51 C5
Lawrence Cres
Dagenham RM10 ... 81 D5
Edgware HA8 ... 26 C1
Lawrence Ct
Hornsey N10 ... 49 C6
Mill Hill NW7 ... 27 C5
4 South Acton W3 ... 111 A3
Stoke Newington N16 ... 73 D5
5 Woodford IG8 ... 37 C4
Lawrence Dr UB10 ... 61 A4
Lawrence Est TW4 ... 128 C1
Lawrence Gdns NW7 ... 11 D1
Lawrence Hall E13 ... 99 B3
Lawrence Hill E4 ... 19 C2
Lawrence Ho
Bowes Pk N22 ... 32 B4
20 Camden Town NW1 ... 71 B1
Westminster SW1 ... 259 D3
Lawrence La EC2 ... 242 B2
Lawrence Mans SW3 267 A5
Lawrence Pl N1 ... 233 B6
Lawrence Rd
Coney Hall BR4 ... 225 A4
Ealing W5 ... 109 D2
Edmonton N18 ... 34 B6
Erith DA8 ... 147 D5
Hampton TW12 ... 173 B3
Hillingdon UB4 ... 83 A5
Hounslow TW4 ... 128 C1
Pinner HA5 ... 40 D4
Richmond TW10 ... 175 C6
South Norwood SE25 ... 205 D5
Tottenham N15 ... 51 C5
Upton Pk E6 ... 100 A6
West Ham E13 ... 99 B6
Lawrence St
Canning Town E16 ... 98 D2

Lawrence St *continued*
Chelsea SW3 136 C6 267 A5
Mill Hill NW7 ... 27 D6
Lawrence Trad Est
SE10 ... 120 C2
Lawrence Univ SW7 ... 256 B3
Lawrence Way NW10 ... 67 B5
Lawrence Weaver Cl
SM4 ... 201 C3
Lawrence Yd N15 ... 51 C5
Lawrie Ct HA3 ... 24 D3
Lawrie Park Ave
SE26 ... 184 B5
Lawrie Park Cres
SE26 ... 184 B5
Lawrie Park Gdns
SE26 ... 184 B5
Lawrie Park Rd
SE26 ... 184 C5
Laws Cl SE25 ... 205 B5
Lawson Cl Ilford IG1 ... 79 B3
Newham E16 ... 99 C2
Wimbledon SW19 ... 156 D1
Lawson Ct
1 Finsbury Pk N4 ... 50 B1
13 Surbiton KT6 ... 197 D2
Lawson Gdns HA5 ... 40 B6
Lawson Ho
17 Shepherd's Bush
W12 ... 112 B6
1 Woolwich SE18 ... 144 C6
Lawson Rd Enfield EN3 ... 6 C4
Southall UB1 ... 85 C3
Law St SE1 ... 117 B3 262 D6
Lawton Rd Barnet EN4 ... 2 B2
Bow E3 ... 97 A4
Leytonstone E10 ... 54 A1
Laxcon Cl NW10 ... 67 B3
Laxey Rd BR6 ... 227 D2
Laxfield Ct E8 ... 96 A6
Laxley Cl SE5 ... 138 D5
Laxmi Ct N3 ... 29 B2
Laxton Ct CR7 ... 205 A5
Laxton Path 1 SE4 ... 140 D1
Laxton Pl NW1 ... 238 D6
Layard Rd Enfield EN1 ... 5 D4
Rotherhithe SE16 ... 118 B2
South Norwood CR7 ... 183 B1
Layard Sq SE16 ... 118 B2
Laybourne Ho 18
E14 ... 119 C4
Laycock Prim Sch 5
N1 ... 72 D2
Laycock St N1 ... 72 C2
Layer Gdns W3 ... 110 C6
Layfield Cl NW4 ... 46 B2
Layfield Cres NW4 ... 46 B2
Layfield Ho 1 SE10 ... 121 A1
Layfield Rd NW4 ... 46 B2
Laymarsh Cl DA17 ... 125 B3
Laymead Cl UB5 ... 63 A2
Laystall Ct EC1 ... 241 A5
Laystall St EC1 ... 241 A5
Layton Cres CR0 ... 220 D3
Layton Ct TW8 ... 109 D1
Layton Pl TW9 ... 132 C4
Layton Rd
Brentford TW8 ... 109 D1
Hounslow TW3 ... 129 D1
Layton's La TW16 ... 171 D1
Layzell Wlk SE9 ... 165 D3
Lazar Wlk 2 N7 ... 72 B6
Leabank Cl HA1 ... 64 C5
Leabank Sq E9 ... 75 C2
Leabank View N15 ... 52 A3
Leabourne Rd N16 ... 52 A2
LEA BRIDGE ... 74 D5
Lea Bridge Rd E10 ... 53 C2
Lea Cl TW2 ... 151 B4
Lea Cotts 10 CR4 ... 181 A1
Lea Cres HA4 ... 61 D4
Leacroft Ave SW12 ... 158 D4
Leacroft Cl
Southgate N21 ... 16 D2
3 Yiewsley UB7 ... 104 A6
Lea Ct
3 Bedford Pk W12 ... 111 C4
1 Chingford E4 ... 20 A2
3 Hillingdon UB10 ... 82 D3
2 Newham E13 ... 99 A4
Leadale Ave E4 ... 19 C2
Leadale Rd N16 ... 52 A3
Leadbeaters Cl 8
N11 ... 30 D5
Leadbetter Ct 12
NW10 ... 67 B1

Leadenhall Mkt*
EC3 ... 243 A1
Leadenhall Pl EC3 ... 243 A1
Leadenhall St
EC3 ... 95 C1 243 A1
Leadenham Ct 15 E3 ... 97 C3
Leader Ave E12 ... 78 C3
Leadings The HA9 ... 67 A5
Leaf Cl KT7, KT8 ... 196 C4
Leaf Gr SE27 ... 182 C5
Leaf Ho Barnet EN5 ... 1 D1
9 Harrow HA1 ... 42 D4
Leafield Cl SW16 ... 182 D4
Leafield La DA14 ... 169 B1
Leafield Rd
Merton SW19,
SW20 ... 201 B6
Sutton SM1 ... 217 C6
Leafy Gr BR2 ... 225 C3
Leafy Oak Rd SE12 ... 165 C1
Leafy Way CR0 ... 221 D6
Lea Gdns HA9 ... 66 B4
Leagrave St E5 ... 74 C5
Lea Hall Gdns E10 ... 53 C1
Lea Hall Rd E10 ... 53 C1
Lea Ho
2 Edmonton N9 ... 18 A1
Lisson Gr NW8 ... 237 A5
Upper Clapton E5 ... 52 C1
Leaholme Waye HA4 ... 39 A3
Leahurst Rd SE13 ... 164 B6
Lea Int E9 ... 75 C3
Leake St Lambeth SE1 251 A1
South Bank
SE1 ... 116 B4 250 D2
Lealand Rd N15 ... 51 D3
Leamington Ave
Bromley BR1 ... 187 C5
Farnborough BR6 ... 227 C4
Merton SM4 ... 201 B5
Walthamstow E17 ... 53 C4
Leamington Cl
Bromley BR1 ... 187 C5
Hounslow TW3 ... 152 A6
Plashet E12 ... 78 A3
Leamington Cres HA2 63 B5
Leamington Ct
4 Forest Hill SE26 ... 162 A1
North Acton W3 ... 89 B2
Leamington Gdns
IG3 ... 79 D6
Leamington Ho
Edgware HA8 ... 26 B5
4 Kensal Town W11 ... 91 B2
Leamington Pk W3 ... 89 B2
Leamington Pl UB4 ... 83 D3
Leamington Rd UB2 ... 106 D2
Leamington Rd Villas
W11 ... 91 B2
Leamington Villas
SE13 ... 164 C6
Leamore St W6 ... 112 C2
Leamouth Rd
Newham E6 ... 100 A2
South Bromley E14 ... 98 B1
Leander Ct
11 Edgware NW9 ... 27 C2
27 Hackney E9 ... 74 C1
St Johns SE8 ... 141 C4
5 Surbiton KT6 ... 197 D2
Leander Rd
Northolt UB5 ... 85 C5
Thornton Heath CR7 ... 204 B5
Tulse Hill SW2 ... 160 C5
Lea Park Trad Est
E10 ... 53 B1
Lea Rd
2 Beckenham BR3 ... 185 C1
Enfield EN2 ... 5 B4
Southall UB2 ... 107 A2
Learner Dr HA2 ... 63 C6
Learoyd Gdns E6 ... 122 C6
Leary Ho SE11 ... 260 D1
Leas Cl KT9 ... 214 B1
Leas Dale SE9 ... 166 C1
Leas Gn BR7 ... 189 D4
Leaside Ave N10 ... 49 A5
Leaside Bsns Ctr EN3 ... 7 B3
Leaside Ct UB10 ... 82 D4
Leaside Ho 4 E5 ... 52 B1
Leaside Mans N10 ... 49 A6
Leaside Rd E5 ... 52 C1
Leasowes Rd E10 ... 53 C1
Lea Sq 22 E3 ... 97 B6
Leas The SE18 ... 144 D4

Leatherbottle Gn
DA18 ... 125 B3
Leather Cl CR4 ... 181 A1
Leatherdale St
32 Bethnal Green E1 ... 96 C3
19 Globe Town E1 ... 96 D4
Leather Gdns E15 ... 98 C6
Leatherhead Cl N16 ... 51 D1
Leatherhead Rd
KT9 ... 213 D1
Leather La
EC1 ... 94 C2 241 B4
Leather La Mkt*
EC1 ... 94 C2 241 B4
Leathermarket Ct
SE1 ... 253 A1
Leathermarket St
SE1 ... 117 C4 253 A1
Leather Rd SE16 ... 118 D2
Leathersellers Cl 5
EN5 ... 1 A2
Leathsale Rd HA2 ... 63 D5
Leathwaite Rd
SW11 ... 158 D6
Leathwell Rd SE8 ... 141 D3
Lea Valley Athletics Stad
N9 ... 18 D3
Lea Valley Prim Sch
N17 ... 34 A3
Lea Valley Rd EN3 ... 19 B5
Lea Valley Technopark
N17 ... 52 A6
Lea Valley Trad Est
N18 ... 34 D5
Leaveland Cl BR3 ... 207 C5
Leaver Gdns UB6 ... 86 C5
Leavesden Rd HA7 ... 25 A4
Lea View Ho E5 ... 52 B1
Lebanon Ave TW13 ... 172 D5
Lebanon Ct 10 TW1 ... 153 B4
Lebanon Gdns
SW18 ... 157 C5
Lebanon Park Mans
TW1 ... 153 B4
Lebanon Pk TW1 ... 153 B4
Lebanon Rd
Croydon CR0 ... 205 C1
Wandsworth SW18 ... 157 C6
Lebanon Road Sta
CR0 ... 221 C6
Lebrun Sq SE3 ... 143 B2
Lebus Ho NW8 ... 230 A3
Le Chateau CR0 ... 221 B5
Lechmere App IG8 ... 37 D1
Lechmere Ave IG8 ... 37 D1
Lechmere Rd NW2 ... 68 B2
Leckford Rd SW18 ... 158 A3
Leckhampton Pl 23
SW2 ... 160 C4
Leckwith Ave DA7 ... 147 A6
Lecky Ho NW2 ... 68 B4
Lecky St
SW7 ... 114 B1 256 C2
Leclair Ho SE3 ... 143 B2
L'Ecole des Petits Sch
SW6 ... 135 D3
Leconfield Ave SW13,
SW15 ... 133 D2
Leconfield Ho SE5 ... 139 C2
Leconfield Rd N5 ... 73 B4
Lector Ct EC1 ... 241 B5
Leda Ave EN3 ... 6 D5
Leda Ct 9 SW9 ... 138 C5
Ledalle Ho NW2 ... 68 B5
Ledam Bldg EC1 ... 241 A4
Leda Rd SE18 ... 122 B3
Ledbury Ho 12 SE22 ... 139 C2
Ledbury Mews N
W11 ... 91 C1
Ledbury Mews W
W11 ... 245 A6
Ledbury Pl 10 CR0 ... 221 A4
Ledbury Rd
Croydon CR0 ... 221 B4
Kensington W11 ... 91 C1
Ledbury St SE15 ... 140 A5
Ledo Ho 1 N16 ... 73 B4
Ledrington Rd SE19 ... 184 A4
Ledway Dr HA9 ... 44 B2
LEE ... 164 D5
Lee Ave RM6 ... 59 A3
Leechcroft Ave
DA15 ... 167 D6
Leechcroft Rd SM6 ... 219 A5
Lee Church St SE13 ... 142 C1
Lee Cl Higham Hill E17 ... 34 D2

Lee Cl *continued*
New Barnet EN5 ... 2 A1
Lee Conservancy Rd
E9 ... 75 B3
Leecroft Rd EN5 ... 1 A1
Lee Ct SE13 ... 142 B1
Leeds Ct
7 Carshalton SM5 ... 218 D5
Catford SE6 ... 163 D1
Clerkenwell EC1 ... 241 C6
Leeds Rd IG1 ... 57 B1
Leeds St N18 ... 34 A5
Leegate SE12 ... 164 D6
Leegate Sh Ctr SE12 164 D6
Lee Green SE12 ... 142 D1
Lee High Rd SE12,
SE13 ... 142 C1
Lee Ho
3 Kentish Town N19 ... 71 D3
Wimbledon SW19 ... 179 D4
Leeke St WC1 ... 94 B4 233 C2
Leeland Mans 15
W13 ... 109 A5
Leeland Rd W13 ... 109 A5
Leeland Terr W13 ... 109 A5
Leeland Way NW10 ... 67 D4
Lee Manor Prim Sch
SE13 ... 164 C5
Lee Mews BR3 ... 207 A6
Lee Park Way N9, N18 ... 19 A1
Lee Pk SE3 ... 142 D2
Lee Rd Enfield EN1 ... 18 A5
Lewisham SE3 ... 142 D1
Merton SW19 ... 179 D2
Mill Hill NW7 ... 28 D3
Wembley UB6 ... 87 C6
Leerdam Dr E14 ... 120 A3
Lees Ct W1 ... 248 A6
Lees Ho SE17 ... 262 D1
Leeside EN5 ... 13 A5
Leeside Cres NW11 ... 47 C3
Leeside Ind Est N17 ... 34 B3
Leeside Rd N17 ... 34 B4
Leeside Trad Est N17 ... 34 C3
Leeside Works N17 ... 34 C3
Leeson Ho 7 TW1 ... 153 B4
Leeson Rd 12 SE24 ... 138 C1
Leesons Hill BR5,
BR7 ... 211 D6
Leesons Way BR5 ... 189 D1
Lees Par UB10 ... 82 D3
Lees Pl W1 ... 115 A6 248 A6
Lees Rd UB8 ... 82 D3
Lee St E8 ... 95 D6
Lee Sta SE12 ... 165 A5
Lees The CR0 ... 223 B6
Leet Ct N16 ... 73 B4
Lee Terr SE3 ... 142 C2
Lee Valley Athletics Ctr
N9 ... 18 D3
Lee Valley Country Pk
EN3 ... 7 C4
Lee Valley Ice Ctr
E10 ... 74 D6
Lee Valley Leisure
Complex N9 ... 19 A3
Lee Valley Riding Ctr
E10 ... 52 D1
Leeve Ho 7 W9 ... 91 B4
Lee View EN2 ... 4 D4
Leeview Ct 5 E4 ... 20 A3
Leeward Ct 3 E1 ... 118 A5
Leeward Gdns SW19 ... 179 B5
Leeway SE8 ... 119 B1
Leeway Cl HA5 ... 23 B3
Leewood Cl SE12 ... 165 A5
Lefevre Wlk E3 ... 97 C6
Leffern Rd W12 ... 112 A4
Leff Ho 9 NW6 ... 69 A1
Lefroy Ho SE1 ... 252 A1
Lefroy Rd W12 ... 111 D4
Legard Rd N5 ... 72 D5
Legat Ct N4 ... 51 A4
Legatt Rd SE9 ... 165 D6
Leggatt Rd E15 ... 98 A5
Legge St SE13 ... 164 A6
Leghorn Rd
Plumstead SE18 ... 123 B1
Willesden Green NW10 90 A5
Legion Cl N1 ... 72 C1
Legion Ct SM4 ... 201 C3
Legion Rd UB6 ... 86 A5
Legion Terr E3 ... 97 C6
Legion Way N12 ... 30 C3
Legrace Ave TW4,
TW5 ... 128 D3

Leicester Ave CR4 ... 204 A5
Leicester Cl KT4 ... 216 C4
Leicester Ct
46 Paddington W2 ... 91 C2
St James WC2 ... 249 D6
5 Twickenham TW1 ... 153 D5
Leicester Gdns IG3 ... 57 C2
Leicester Ho
4 Brixton SW9 ... 138 D2
Carshalton SM5 ... 218 C5
5 Putney SW15 ... 156 C4
2 Thames Ditton KT7 ... 197 A2
Leicester Mews N2 ... 48 C6
Leicester Pl WC2 ... 249 D6
Leicester Rd
Barnet EN5 ... 1 D1
Croydon CR0 ... 205 C2
East Finchley N2 ... 48 C6
Stonebridge NW10 ... 67 B1
Wanstead E11 ... 55 B4
Leicester Sq★ WC2 ... 115 D6 249 D5
Leicester Square Sta WC2 ... 115 D6 249 D6
Leicester St WC2 ... 249 D6
Leigham Ave SW16 ... 160 A1
Leigham Cl
5 Streatham SW16 ... 160 B1
Streatham SW16 ... 182 B6
9 Wallington SM6 ... 219 C2
Leigham Court Rd SW16 ... 182 C6
Leigham Dr TW7 ... 130 C5
Leigham Hall 3 SW16 ... 160 A1
Leigham Hall Par 2 SW16 ... 160 A1
Leigham Vale SE27, SW16, SW2 ... 160 C2
Leigh Ave IG4 ... 55 D5
Leigh Cl KT3 ... 199 B5
Leigh Cl Ind Est KT3 ... 199 B5
Leigh Close Ind Est KT3 ... 199 B5
Leigh Cres CR0 ... 223 D1
Leigh Ct Harrow HA2 ... 42 C1
22 Tulse Hill SW2 ... 160 C5
3 Woodford E18 ... 37 A1
Leighfield Ho 5 N4 ... 51 A2
Leigh Gdns NW10 ... 90 C5
Leigh Ho
4 Kingston u T KT2 ... 176 D4
9 Putney SW15 ... 156 A6
Leigh Hunt Dr N14 ... 15 D3
Leigh Orchard Cl SW16 ... 160 B1
Leigh Pl
Feltham TW13 ... 150 C3
Holborn EC1 ... 241 A4
Welling DA16 ... 146 A3
Leigh Rd Highbury N5 ... 72 D4
Isleworth TW3 ... 130 B1
Leytonstone E10 ... 54 A2
Wallend E6 ... 78 C2
Leigh St WC1 ... 94 A4 233 A1
Leigh The KT2 ... 177 C3
Leighton Ave
Little Ilford E12 ... 78 C3
Pinner HA5 ... 41 A6
Leighton Cl HA8 ... 26 C1
Leighton Cres NW5 ... 71 C3
Leighton Ct NW7 ... 28 D3
Leighton Gdns
Thornton Heath CR0 ... 204 D1
Willesden Green NW10 ... 90 C5
Leighton Gr NW5 ... 71 C3
Leighton Ho 7 KT6 ... 198 A3
Leighton House (Art Gall & Mus)★ W14 ... 254 D6
Leighton Pl NW5 ... 71 C3
Leighton Rd
Ealing W13 ... 109 A4
Enfield EN1 ... 18 A6
Harrow HA3 ... 24 B1
Kentish Town NW5 ... 71 C3
Leighton St CR0 ... 204 D1
Leila Parnell Pl 14 SE7 ... 143 C6
Leinster Ave SW14 ... 133 A1
Leinster Gdns W2 ... 114 A6 246 A6
Leinster Mews
7 Barnet EN5 ... 1 A2
Bayswater W2 ... 246 A6
Leinster Pl W2 ... 236 A1
Leinster Rd N10 ... 49 B5
Leinster Sq W2 ... 91 D1
Leinster Terr W2 ... 246 A6
Leisure Way N12 ... 30 B3
Leitch Ho 8 NW8 ... 70 B1
Leith Cl NW9 ... 45 B1
Leithcote Gdns SW16 ... 182 B6
Leithcote Path SW16 ... 160 B1
Leith Hill BR5 ... 190 A2
Leith Hill Gn BR5 ... 190 A2
Leith Ho
7 Kentish Town N7 ... 71 D3
13 Streatham SW2 ... 160 B4
Leith Mans W9 ... 91 D4
Leith Rd N22 ... 32 D2
Leith Towers 7 SM2 ... 217 D1
Leith Yd 3 NW6 ... 91 C6
Lela Ave TW4, TW5 ... 128 C3
Lelitia Cl E8 ... 96 A6
Lely Ho 3 UB5 ... 84 D5
Leman St E1 ... 96 A1
Lemark Cl HA7 ... 25 C4
Le May Ave SE12 ... 165 B1
Lemmon Rd SE10 ... 142 C6
Lemna Ct E11 ... 54 C2
Lemna Rd E11 ... 54 C2
Le Moal Ho 28 E1 ... 96 C2
Lemon Gr TW14 ... 150 A3
Lemonwell Ct SE9 ... 167 A6
Lemonwell Dr SE9 ... 167 A6
Lemsford Cl N15 ... 52 A4
Lemsford Ct N4 ... 73 A6
Lena Cres N9 ... 18 C2
Lena Gardens Prim Sch W6 ... 112 C3
Lena Gdns W6 ... 112 C3
Lena Kennedy Cl E4 ... 36 A4
Lenan Ct W13 ... 109 C5
Len Clifton Ho 12 SE18 ... 122 B2
Lendal Terr 7 SW4 ... 137 D2
Lenelby Rd KT6 ... 198 C1
Len Freeman Pl SW6 ... 264 C5
Lenham 11 NW5 ... 71 A2
Lenham Ho SE1 ... 252 D1
Lenham Rd Erith DA7 ... 147 B6
Lewisham SE12 ... 142 D1
South Norwood CR7 ... 183 B1
Sutton SM1 ... 218 A3
Lennard Ave BR4 ... 224 C6
Lennard Cl BR4 ... 224 C6
Lennard Rd
Bromley BR2 ... 210 B1
Croydon CR0 ... 205 A1
Penge BR3 ... 185 A4
Lennon Rd NW2 ... 68 C2
Lennox Gdns
Croydon CR0 ... 220 D4
Knightsbridge SW1 ... 114 D3 257 C5
Redbridge IG1 ... 56 B1
Willesden NW10 ... 67 D4
Lennox Gdns Mews SW1 ... 257 C4
Lennox Ho
7 Belvedere DA17 ... 125 C3
10 Hackney E9 ... 74 C2
4 Twickenham TW1 ... 153 D5
Lennox Rd
Finsbury Pk N4, N7 ... 72 C6
Walthamstow E17 ... 53 C3
Lenor Cl DA6 ... 147 A1
Lensbury Way SE2 ... 124 D3
Lens Rd E7 ... 77 C1
Lenthall Ho SW1 ... 259 B1
Lenthall Rd E8 ... 74 A1
Lenthorp Rd SE10 ... 120 D2
Lentmead Rd BR1 ... 164 D1
Lenton Rise TW9 ... 132 A2
Lenton St SE18 ... 123 B2
Len Williams Ct NW6 ... 91 C5
Leo Ct 4 TW8 ... 131 D5
Leof Cres SE6 ... 185 D5
Leominster Rd SM4 ... 202 A3
Leominster Wlk SM4 ... 202 A3
Leonard Ave SM4 ... 202 A4
Leonard Ct
Bloomsbury WC1 ... 240 A6
Leonard Ct *continued*
Harrow HA3 ... 24 C3
Kensington W8 ... 255 A6
Leonard Day Ho 3 NW5 ... 71 B2
Leonard Ho 10 E17 ... 54 A5
Leonard Pl 6 N16 ... 73 C4
Leonard Rd
Chingford E4 ... 35 C4
Edmonton N9 ... 18 A1
Forest Gate E7 ... 77 A4
Mitcham CR4, SW16 ... 181 C2
Southall UB2 ... 106 D2
Leonard Robbins Path 3 SE28 ... 124 B6
Leonard St
Broadgate EC2 ... 95 B3 242 D6
Newham E16 ... 122 A5
Leonora Ho W9 ... 236 A6
Leontine Cl SE15 ... 140 A5
Leopards Ct EC1 ... 241 A4
Leopold Ave SW19 ... 179 B5
Leopold Bldgs 14 E2 ... 95 D4
Leopold Ct 12 SW19 ... 179 B5
Leopold Mews E9 ... 96 C6
Leopold Prim Sch NW10 ... 67 D1
Leopold Rd
Ealing W5 ... 110 B5
East Finchley N2 ... 48 B6
Edmonton N18 ... 34 B5
Walthamstow E17 ... 53 C4
Willesden NW10 ... 67 C1
Wimbledon SW19 ... 179 B5
Leopold St E3 ... 97 B2
Leopold Terr SW19 ... 179 C5
Leopold Wlk SE11 ... 260 C1
Leo St SE15 ... 140 B5
Leo Yd EC1 ... 241 D5
Leppoc Rd SW4 ... 159 D6
Leroy St SE1 ... 117 C2 263 A4
Lerry Cl W14 ... 264 D6
Lerwick Ct 4 EN1 ... 17 C6
Lerwick Ho SW18 ... 136 A1
Lescombe Cl SE23 ... 163 A1
Lescombe Rd SE23, SE6 ... 163 A1
Lesley Cl DA5 ... 169 D4
Lesley Ct
8 Wallington SM6 ... 219 B4
Westminster SW1 ... 259 C5
Leslie Gdns SM2 ... 217 C1
Leslie Gr CR0 ... 205 C1
Leslie Grove Pl CR0 ... 205 C1
Leslie Park Rd CR0 ... 205 C1
Leslie Prince Ct 8 SE5 ... 139 B5
Leslie Rd
East Finchley N2 ... 48 B6
Leyton E11 ... 76 B4
Newham E16 ... 99 B1
Leslie Smith Sq 7 SE18 ... 144 C6
Lessar Ave SW4 ... 159 C5
Lessar Ct SW4 ... 159 C5
Lessingham Ave
Ilford IG5 ... 56 C6
Upper Tooting SW17 ... 181 A6
Lessing St SE23 ... 163 A4
Lessness Ave DA7 ... 146 D5
LESSNESS HEATH ... 125 D1
Lessness Heath Prim Sch DA17 ... 125 C1
Lessness Pk DA17 ... 125 C1
Lessness Rd
Belvedere DA17 ... 125 C1
Morden SM4 ... 202 A4
Lester Ave E16 ... 98 C3
Lester Ct 42 E3 ... 97 D4
Lester Ho IG8 ... 36 B3
Lestock Cl 2 SE25 ... 206 A6
Lestock Ho SE3 ... 143 D4
Lestor Ct TW7 ... 130 D2
Leswin Pl N16 ... 73 D5
Leswin Rd N16 ... 73 D5
Letchford Gdns NW10 ... 90 A4
Letchford Mews NW10 ... 90 A4
Letchmore Ho 7 W10 ... 90 C3
Letchworth Ave TW14 ... 149 D4
Letchworth Cl
Bromley BR2 ... 209 A4
Letchworth Cl *continued*
South Oxhey WD19 ... 22 D5
Letchworth Dr BR2 ... 209 A4
Letchworth St SW17 ... 180 D6
Lethaby Ho 15 SW4 ... 138 B1
Lethbridge Cl SE13 ... 142 A3
Letterstone Rd SW6 ... 264 C3
Lettice St SW6 ... 135 B4 264 D1
Lett Rd E15 ... 76 B1
Lettsom St SE5 ... 139 C3
Lettsom Wlk 1 E13 ... 99 A5
Leucha Rd E17 ... 53 A4
Levana Cl SW19 ... 157 A3
Levant Ho 17 E1 ... 96 D3
Levehurst Ho SE27 ... 183 A5
Levehurst Way SW4, SW9 ... 138 A3
Leven Cl WD19 ... 22 D5
Levendale Rd SE23 ... 163 B2
Leven Rd E14 ... 98 B1
Leven Way UB3 ... 83 C1
Lever Ct 15 E9 ... 74 D2
Leverett St SW3 ... 257 B4
Leverholme Gdns SE9 ... 188 C6
Leverington Pl N1 ... 235 D1
Leverson St SW16 ... 181 C4
Lever St EC1 ... 95 A4 235 A1
Leverstock Ho SW3 ... 257 B2
Leverton Pl NW5 ... 71 C3
Leverton St NW5 ... 71 C3
Levett Gdns IG3 ... 80 A5
Levett Ho 8 SW16 ... 181 C5
Levett Rd IG11 ... 79 C2
Levine Gdns IG11 ... 102 D5
Levison Way 2 N19 ... 49 D1
Levita Ho NW1 ... 232 D2
Levyne Ct EC1 ... 241 A6
Lewes Cl UB5 ... 63 C2
Lewes Ct 3 CR4 ... 202 D6
Lewesdon Cl 13 SW19 ... 156 D3
Lewes Ho
Bermondsey SE1 ... 253 B2
Peckham SE15 ... 140 A6
Lewes Rd
Bromley BR1 ... 187 D1
Colney Hatch N12 ... 30 C5
Leweston Pl N16 ... 51 D2
Lewey Ho E3 ... 97 B3
Lewgars Ave NW9 ... 45 A3
Lewin Ct
4 Plumstead SE18 ... 123 C2
Streatham SW16 ... 182 A4
Lewing Cl BR6 ... 211 C1
Lewington Ct EN3 ... 6 D6
Lewin Rd Bexley DA6 ... 147 A1
Mortlake SW14 ... 133 B2
Streatham SW16 ... 181 D4
Lewin Terr TW14 ... 149 B4
Lewis Ave E17 ... 35 C2
Lewis Cl N14 ... 15 C4
Lewis Cres NW10 ... 67 B3
Lewis Ct 5 SE16 ... 118 B1
Lewis Gdns London N2 ... 30 B1
South Tottenham N15, N16 ... 51 D3
Lewis Gr SE13 ... 142 A2
LEWISHAM ... 142 A1
Lewisham Bridge Prim Sch 3 SE13 ... 141 D2
Lewisham Bsns Ctr SE14 ... 140 D6
Lewisham Coll (Deptford Campus) 12 SE8 ... 141 C4
Lewisham Coll (Lewisham Way Campus) SE4 ... 141 C3
Lewisham Ct EN3 ... 7 C5
Lewisham Ctr SE13 ... 142 A2
Lewisham High St SE13 ... 163 D6
Lewisham Hill SE13 ... 142 A3
Lewisham Hospl SE13 ... 163 D6
Lewisham Pk SE13 ... 164 A5
Lewisham Rd SE13 ... 142 A3
Lewisham St SW1 ... 249 D1
Lewisham Sta SE13 ... 142 A2
Lewisham Way SE4, SE14 ... 141 B4
Lewis Ho 2 E4 ... 35 C5
Lewis King Ho BR1 ... 187 B3
Lewis Pl E8 ... 74 A3
Lewis Rd
Bexley DA16 ... 146 C2
Mitcham CR4 ... 180 C1
19 Richmond TW10 ... 153 D6
Sidcup DA14 ... 168 C1
Southall UB1 ... 107 A4
Sutton SM1 ... 217 D4
Lewis Silkin Ho 9 SE15 ... 140 C6
Lewis Sports & L Ctr SE19 ... 183 D2
Lewis St NW1 ... 71 B2
Lewiston Cl KT4 ... 200 B2
Lewis Way RM10 ... 81 D2
Lexden Dr RM6 ... 58 B3
Lexden Rd Acton W3 ... 110 D5
Mitcham CR4 ... 203 D5
Lexdon Ct RM6 ... 58 B3
Lexfield Ho N5 ... 73 A4
Lexham Ct UB6 ... 86 B6
Lexham Gardens Mews W8 ... 255 D5
Lexham Gdns W8 ... 113 D2 255 C4
Lexham Ho 9 IG11 ... 101 B6
Lexham Mews W8 ... 113 C2 255 B4
Lexham Wlk W8 ... 255 D5
Lexington Pl KT1 ... 175 D2
Lexington St W1 ... 115 C6 249 B6
Lexton Gdns SW12 ... 159 D3
Leyborne Ave W13 ... 109 C4
Leyborne Pk TW9 ... 132 C4
Leybourne Cl BR2 ... 209 A3
Leybourne Ct 1 SE25 ... 206 A6
Leybourne Ho 20 SE15 ... 140 C6
Leybourne Rd
17 Camden Town NW1 ... 71 B1
Hillingdon UB10 ... 83 A6
Leytonstone E11 ... 54 D1
Queensbury NW9 ... 44 C4
Leybourne St 5 NW1 ... 71 B1
Leybridge Ct SE12 ... 165 A6
Leyburn Cl E17 ... 53 D5
Leyburn Gdns CR0 ... 221 C6
Leyburn Gr N18 ... 34 A4
Leyburn Rd N18 ... 34 B4
Leyden Mans 7 N19 ... 50 A2
Leyden St E1 ... 95 D2 243 C3
Leydon Cl
Rotherhithe SE16 ... 118 D5
SE16 ... 118 D5
Leyes Rd E16 ... 99 D1
Leyfield KT4 ... 199 D1
Ley Ho SE1 ... 252 A1
Leyland Ave EN3 ... 7 A3
Leyland Ct 8 N11 ... 31 B6
Leyland Gdns IG8 ... 37 C5
Leyland Ho
6 Canary Wharf E14 ... 119 D6
12 Richmond TW10 ... 153 C1
Leyland Rd SE12 ... 165 A6
Leylands SW18 ... 157 B5
Leylang Rd SE14 ... 140 D5
Leys Cl Finchley N12 ... 30 C3
Harrow HA1 ... 42 B4
Leys Ct 9 SW9 ... 138 C3
Leysdown 9 NW5 ... 71 A2
Leysdown Ho SE17 ... 263 B2
Leysdown Rd SE9 ... 166 B2
Leysfield Rd W12 ... 112 A4
Leys Gdns EN4 ... 15 A6
Leyspring Rd E11 ... 54 D1
Leys Rd E EN3 ... 7 A4
Leys Rd W EN3 ... 7 A4
Ley St Ilford IG1 ... 78 D6
Newbury Pk IG1, IG2 ... 57 B1
Leys The
East Finchley N2 ... 48 A5
Harrow HA3 ... 44 B3
Leyswood Dr IG2 ... 57 C4
Leythe Rd W3 ... 111 A4
LEYTON ... 76 B5
Leyton Bsns Ctr E10 ... 75 C6
Leyton Ct SE23 ... 162 C3
Leyton Grange E10 ... 53 C1
Leyton Green Rd E10 ... 54 A3

Leyton Green Twrs
E10 ... 54 A3
Leyton Ind Village
E10 ... 52 D2
Leyton Leisure Lagoon
E10 ... 54 A2
Leyton Link Est E10 ... 53 A2
Leyton Midland Road Sta
E10 ... 54 A1
Leyton Mill Ret Pk
E10 ... 76 A4
Leyton Mills E10 ... 76 A4
Leyton Park Rd E10 ... 76 A5
Leyton Rd
Merton SW19 ... 180 A3
Stratford E15 ... 76 B2
Leyton Sixth Form Coll
E10 ... 54 B3
Leyton Sta E11 ... 76 A5
LEYTONSTONE ... 54 D1
Leytonstone High Road
Sta E11 ... 76 C6
Leytonstone Rd E15 ... 76 C3
Leytonstone Sch E11 ... 54 C3
Leytonstone Sta E11 ... 54 C1
Leyton Town Ctr E10 ... 76 A5
Leywick St E15 ... 98 C5
Lezayre Rd BR6 ... 227 D2
Liardet St SE14 ... 141 A6
Liberia Rd N5 ... 72 D2
Libert Cl N18 ... 33 D6
Liberty Ave SW19 ... 180 B2
Liberty Cl KT4 ... 200 C1
Liberty Ct IG11 ... 102 C5
Liberty Ctr HA0 ... 88 B6
Liberty Ho 11 E1 ... 118 A6
Liberty Mews
Balham SW12 ... 159 B5
Orpington BR6 ... 227 D6
Wood Green N22 ... 32 D2
Liberty Sch CR4 ... 180 C1
Liberty St
SW9 ... 138 B4 270 D2
Libra Rd 7 Bow E3 ... 97 B5
Newham E13 ... 99 A5
Library Ct N17 ... 51 D6
Library Mans 4
W12 ... 112 C4
Library Par NW10 ... 89 C6
Library Pl E1 ... 118 B6
Library St
SE1 ... 116 D4 251 D1
Library Way 1 TW2 ... 152 A4
Libro Ct E4 ... 35 C6
Lichen Ct IG6 ... 56 D6
Lichfield Cl EN4 ... 2 D2
Lichfield Ct
Kingston u T KT6 ... 198 A4
Richmond TW9 ... 132 A1
Lichfield Gdns TW10,
TW9 ... 154 A6
Lichfield Gr N3 ... 29 C1
Lichfield Ho 27 SE5 ... 139 A3
Lichfield Rd
Dagenham RM8 ... 80 C5
Edmonton N9 ... 18 A2
Hounslow TW4 ... 128 C2
Mile End E3 ... 97 A4
Newham E6 ... 99 D4
Northwood HA6 ... 40 A6
Richmond TW9 ... 132 B4
West Hampstead NW2 ... 69 A4
Woodford IG8 ... 36 C6
Lichfield Terr 1
TW9 ... 154 A6
Lichlade Cl 7 BR6 ... 227 D4
Lickey Ho W14 ... 264 D6
Lidbury Rd NW7 ... 29 A4
Lidcote Gdns 22
SW9 ... 138 B3
Liddall Way UB7 ... 104 B5
Liddell Cl HA3 ... 43 D6
Liddell Gdns NW10 ... 90 C5
Liddell Rd NW6 ... 69 C2
Lidding Rd HA3 ... 43 D4
Liddington Rd E15 ... 98 D6
Liddlesdale Ho E 6
KT2 ... 176 D2
Liddlesdale Ho W 5
KT2 ... 176 D2
Liddon Rd
Bromley BR1 ... 209 D6
Newham E13 ... 99 B4
Liden Cl E10, E17 ... 53 B1
Lidfield Rd N16 ... 73 B4
Lidgate Rd 22 SE15 ... 139 D5
Lidiard Rd SW18 ... 158 A2
Lidlington Pl NW1 ... 232 B3
Lido Sq N17 ... 33 B1
Lido The★
W2 ... 114 A4 247 A3
Lidyard Rd N19 ... 49 C1
Liffey Ct Edmonton N9 ... 18 C1
Willesden NW10 ... 68 A1
Liffler Rd SE18 ... 123 C1
Liffords Pl SW13 ... 133 D3
Lifford St SW15 ... 134 D1
Lightcliffe Rd N13 ... 16 C1
Lighted Lady★ IG11 ... 78 D1
Lighter Cl 16 SE16 ... 119 A2
Lighterman Mews 15
E1 ... 96 D1
Lighterman's Rd
E14 ... 119 D4
Lighterman's Wlk
SW18 ... 135 C1
Lightfoot Rd N8 ... 50 A4
Light Horse Ct SW1 ... 258 A1
Lightley Cl
Wembley HA0 ... 66 B1
Wembley HA0 ... 88 B6
Ligonier St E2 ... 243 C6
Lilac Cl E4 ... 35 B4
Lilac Ct
Colney Hatch N12 ... 30 C4
3 Newham E13 ... 99 C6
Teddington TW11 ... 174 D6
Lilac Gdns
Croydon CR0 ... 223 C5
Ealing W5 ... 109 D3
Hayes UB3 ... 83 C1
Lilac Ho SE4 ... 141 B2
Lilac Pl
Vauxhall
SE11 ... 116 B2 260 C3
Yiewsley UB7 ... 104 B6
Lilac St W12 ... 112 A6
Lilah Mews BR2 ... 186 D1
Lilburne Gdns SE9 ... 166 A6
Lilburne Rd SE9 ... 166 A6
Lilburne Wlk NW10 ... 67 A2
Lile Cres W7 ... 86 C2
Lilestone Est NW8 ... 236 D5
Lilestone Ho NW8 ... 236 D6
Lilestone St
NW8 ... 92 C3 237 A6
Lilford Ho 21 SE5 ... 139 A3
Lilford Rd SE5 ... 138 D3
Lilian Barker Cl
SE12 ... 165 A6
Lilian Baylis Ho N1 ... 73 A2
Lilian Baylis Tech Sch
SE11 ... 116 B1 260 D1
Lilian Board Way UB6 ... 64 B3
Lilian Gdns IG8 ... 37 B2
Lilian Rd SW16 ... 181 C2
Lilian Rolfe Ho 5
SE27 ... 183 B6
Lillechurch Rd RM8 ... 80 C2
Lilleshall Rd SM4 ... 202 B3
Lilley Cl E1 ... 118 A5
Lillian Ave W3 ... 110 C4
Lillian Cl 14 N16 ... 73 C5
Lillian Rd SW13 ... 134 B6
Lillie Ho N5 ... 72 C3
Lillie Rd SW6 135 B6 264 C5
Lillie Road Mans
SW6 ... 264 B5
Lillieshall Rd SW4 ... 137 C2
Lillie Yd SW6 ... 135 C6 265 A6
Lillington Ho N7 ... 72 C4
Lilliput Ave UB5 ... 85 B6
Lillywhite 21 NW9 ... 27 D2
Lily Albon Ct RM9 ... 81 B4
Lily Cl W14 ... 112 D2
Lily Gdns HA0 ... 87 C5
Lily Ho 7 HA9 ... 66 A3
Lily Pl EC1 ... 241 B4
Lily Rd E17 ... 53 C3
Lilyville Rd
SW6 ... 135 B4 264 C2
Limavady Ho 12
SE18 ... 122 C2
Limborough Ho 5
E14 ... 97 C2
Limbourne Ave RM8 ... 59 B2
Limburg Rd SW11 ... 136 C1
Lime Ave UB7 ... 104 B6
Limeburner La
EC4 ... 94 D1 241 C2
Lime Cl Bromley BR1 ... 210 A5
Buckhurst Hill IG9 ... 21 D2
Carshalton SM5 ... 218 D6
Harrow HA3 ... 25 A1
Pinner HA5 ... 39 D6
Wapping E1 ... 118 A5
Lime Cres TW16 ... 172 C1
Limecroft Cl KT19 ... 215 B1
Lime Ct
9 Harrow HA1 ... 42 D3
Hendon NW4 ... 28 C1
Kingston u T KT3 ... 198 D6
9 Leyton E11 ... 76 C6
Mitcham CR4 ... 180 B1
Putney SW15 ... 134 B2
Limedene Cl HA5 ... 22 D2
Lime Gr Barnet N20 ... 13 B3
Blackfen DA15 ... 167 D5
Hayes UB3 ... 105 B6
Kingston u T KT3 ... 199 C6
Orpington BR6 ... 226 D6
Ruislip HA4 ... 40 B2
Shepherd's Bush W12 ... 112 C4
Twickenham TW1 ... 153 A5
Walthamstow E4 ... 35 B4
Limeharbour E14 ... 119 D4
Lime Ho 7 TW9 ... 132 D4
LIMEHOUSE ... 119 A6
Limehouse Cswy
E14 ... 119 B6
Limehouse Ct 5 E14 ... 97 C1
Lime House Ct 23
E14 ... 97 B1
Limehouse Cut 4
E14 ... 97 D2
Limehouse Fields Est 14
E14 ... 97 A2
Limehouse Link (Tunnel)
E14 ... 119 B6
Limehouse Sta E14 ... 97 A1
Lime Kiln Dr SE7 ... 143 B6
Limekiln Pl SE19 ... 183 D3
Limekiln Wharf 21
E14 ... 119 B6
Limeleaf Ct HA8 ... 27 A6
Lime Lo 3 TW16 ... 171 D3
Limerick Cl SW12 ... 159 C4
Limerick Ct 1
SW12 ... 159 C4
Lime Row DA18 ... 125 B3
Limerston St
SW10 ... 136 A6 266 B5
Lime St Pas EC3 ... 253 A6
Limes Ave
Barnes SW13 ... 133 D3
Carshalton SM5 ... 202 D1
Croydon CR0 ... 220 C5
Edgware NW7 ... 27 C4
Golders Green NW11 ... 47 A2
North Finchley N12 ... 30 A6
Penge SE20 ... 184 B3
Wanstead E11 ... 55 B5
Limes Ave The N11 ... 31 C5
Limes Cl
Ashford TW15 ... 170 C5
3 Friern Barnet N11 ... 31 C5
Limes Ct
Beckenham BR3 ... 185 D1
Willesden NW6 ... 68 D1
Limesdale Gdns HA8 ... 27 A1
Limes Field Rd
SW14 ... 133 C2
Limesford Rd SE15 ... 140 D1
Limes Gdns SW18 ... 157 C5
Limes Gr SE13 ... 142 A1
Limes Rd
Beckenham BR3 ... 185 D1
Thornton Heath CR0 ... 205 B2
Limes Row BR6 ... 226 D3
Lime St
Walthamstow E17 ... 53 A5
Whitechapel
EC3 ... 95 C1 243 A1
Limes The
Camberwell SE5 ... 139 C2
3 Cheam SM2 ... 217 C2
East Molesey KT8 ... 195 D5
Kensington W2 ... 245 B5
Keston Mark BR2 ... 226 A6
Stanmore HA7 ... 9 B2
Limestone Wlk 12
DA18 ... 124 D4
Limes Wlk Ealing W5 ... 109 D4
Nunhead SE15 ... 140 C1
Lime Terr W7 ... 108 C6
Lime Tree Ave KT10,
KT7 ... 196 C1
Limetree Cl SW2 ... 160 B3
Lime Tree Cl E11 ... 55 C5
Limetree Ct HA5 ... 23 C3
Lime Tree Ct
East Barnet EN4 ... 14 C6
East Finchley N2 ... 47 D6
14 Poplar E3 ... 97 C2
South Croydon CR2 ... 221 A2
Lime Tree Gr CR0 ... 223 B5
Limetree Pl CR4 ... 181 B2
Lime Tree Rd TW5 ... 129 D4
Limetree Wlk 2
SW17 ... 181 A5
Lime Tree Wlk
Bushey WD23 ... 8 C2
Coney Hall BR4 ... 224 D4
Enfield EN2 ... 5 A5
Lime Wlk 11 E15 ... 98 C6
Limewood Cl
Beckenham BR3 ... 208 A4
Ealing W13 ... 87 B1
Walthamstow E17 ... 53 B5
Limewood Ct IG4 ... 56 B4
Limpsfield Ave
Putney SW19 ... 156 D2
Thornton Heath CR7 ... 204 B4
Limscott Ho 35 E3 ... 97 D4
Linacre Cl SE15 ... 140 B2
Linacre Ct W6 ... 112 D1
Linacre Rd NW2 ... 68 B2
Linale Ho N1 ... 235 C3
Linberry Wlk 3 SE8 ... 119 B2
Linchmere Rd SE12 ... 164 D4
Lincoln Ave
Osidge N14 ... 15 C2
Twickenham TW2 ... 152 A2
Wimbledon SW19 ... 156 D1
Lincoln Cl
Croydon SE25 ... 206 B3
Greenford UB6 ... 86 A6
Harrow HA2 ... 41 B4
Lincoln Cres EN1 ... 17 D6
Lincoln Ct
Borehamwood WD6 ... 11 B6
Enfield EN2 ... 5 B1
Grove Pk SE12 ... 165 C1
Hampton TW12 ... 173 B5
Hendon NW4 ... 46 B5
Mitcham CR4 ... 204 A4
Redbridge IG1 ... 56 B2
5 South Croydon
CR2 ... 221 A3
Stoke Newington N16 ... 51 B2
Lincoln Gdns IG1 ... 56 A2
Lincoln Green Rd
BR5 ... 211 D4
Lincoln Ho
Bloomsbury WC1 ... 240 D3
9 Dartmouth Pk NW5 ... 71 C5
2 Islington N1 ... 73 A1
Knightsbridge SW1 ... 247 C1
Lincoln Lo 10 BR3 ... 185 D1
Lincoln Mews NW6 ... 91 B6
Lincoln Rd
Croydon SE25 ... 206 B6
East Finchley N2 ... 48 C6
Enfield EN1, EN3 ... 17 D6
Harrow HA2, HA5 ... 41 B4
Kingston u T KT3 ... 199 A6
Mitcham CR4 ... 204 A4
Newham E13 ... 99 B3
North Cheam KT4 ... 200 B1
Northwood HA6 ... 39 D6
Plashet E7 ... 77 D2
Sidcup DA14 ... 190 B5
Twickenham TW13 ... 151 B1
Wembley HA0 ... 65 D2
Woodford E18 ... 37 A2
Lincoln's Inn★
WC2 ... 94 B1 240 D2
Lincoln's Inn Fields
WC2 ... 94 B1 240 D2
Lincoln St
Chelsea SW3 ... 257 C3
Leyton E11 ... 76 C6
Lincolns The NW7 ... 11 D1
Lincoln Terr 4 SM2 ... 217 C1
Lincoln Way
Charlton TW16 ... 171 C2
Enfield EN1 ... 18 B6
Lincombe Rd BR1 ... 164 D1
Linda Ct KT9 ... 213 D4
Lindal Cres EN2 ... 4 B1
Lindal Ct 1 E18 ... 37 A2
Lindale SW19 ... 157 A2
Lindales The N17 ... 33 D4
Lindal Rd SE4 ... 163 B6
Lindbergh Rd SM6 ... 220 A1
Linden Ave Enfield EN1 ... 6 A4
Hounslow TW3 ... 151 D6
Kensal Rise NW10 ... 90 D5
Ruislip HA4 ... 40 A1
Thornton Heath CR7 ... 204 D5
Wembley HA9 ... 66 B3
Linden Bridge Sch
KT4 ... 215 C5
Linden Cl Ruislip HA4 ... 40 A1
Southgate N14 ... 15 C5
Stanmore HA7 ... 25 B5
Thames Ditton KT7 ... 197 A2
Linden Cotts 6
SW19 ... 179 A4
Linden Cres
Kingston u T KT1 ... 176 B1
Wembley UB6 ... 64 D2
Woodford IG8 ... 37 B4
Linden Ct
8 Battersea SW18 ... 136 B1
1 Beckenham BR3 ... 207 D6
2 Bromley BR1 ... 186 D3
Edgware NW7 ... 27 B5
Penge SE20 ... 184 B3
1 Shepherd's Bush
W12 ... 112 C5
Sidcup DA14 ... 189 C6
11 Sutton SM2 ... 218 A2
Lindenfield BR7 ... 188 D1
Linden Gate SW20 ... 200 C6
Linden Gdns
Chiswick W4 ... 111 B1
Enfield EN1 ... 6 A4
Notting Hill
W2 ... 113 C6 245 B5
Linden Gr
Kingston u T KT3 ... 199 C6
Nunhead SE15 ... 140 C2
Penge SE20 ... 184 C4
Teddington TW11 ... 174 D5
Linden Ho
Bromley BR1 ... 187 B3
10 Deptford SE8 ... 141 B6
Hampton TW12 ... 173 D4
Walthamstow E17 ... 35 B1
Linden Lawns HA9 ... 66 B4
Linden Lea N2 ... 48 A4
Lindenlea Ct E17 ... 53 B5
Linden Leas BR4 ... 224 B6
Linden Lo N21 ... 16 B4
Linden Lodge Sch
SW19 ... 157 A3
Linden Mans N6 ... 49 B1
Linden Mews
Kensington W2 ... 245 B5
Stoke Newington N1 ... 73 B3
Linden Pl CR4 ... 202 C5
Linden Rd
Brunswick Pk N11 ... 15 A2
Cranley Gdns N10 ... 49 B5
Hampton TW12 ... 173 C2
Tottenham N15 ... 51 A5
Lindens The
Chiswick W4 ... 133 A4
New Addington CR0 ... 224 A2
North Finchley N12 ... 30 B5
5 Walthamstow E17 ... 53 D5
Linden Way
Shepperton TW17 ... 193 A4
Southgate N14 ... 15 C5
Lindeth Cl HA7 ... 25 B4
Lindfield Gdns NW3 ... 70 A3
Lindfield Hts NW3 ... 70 A3
Lindfield Rd
Croydon CR0 ... 205 D3
Ealing W5 ... 87 C3
Lindfield St E14 ... 97 C1
Lindhill Cl EN3 ... 6 D3
Lindholme Ct 3
NW9 ... 27 C2
Lindisfarne Rd
Dagenham RM8 ... 80 C5
Wimbledon SW20 ... 178 A3
Lindisfarne Way E9 ... 75 A4
Lindley Ct KT1 ... 175 C2
Lindley Ho
13 Peckham SE15 ... 140 A5
9 Stepney E1 ... 96 C2
Lindley Pl TW9 ... 132 C4
Lindley Rd E10 ... 76 A6
Lindley St E1 ... 96 C2

Lindon Bennett Sch The TW13 172 D5
Lindop Ho 8 E1 97 A3
Lindore Rd SW11 136 D1
Lindores Rd SM5 202 A1
Lindo St SE15 140 C3
Lind Rd SM1 218 A3
Lindrop St SW6 136 A3
Lindsay Cl KT9 214 A1
Lindsay Ct
Battersea SW11 266 D1
Sutton SM1 217 C3
Lindsay Dr
Harrow HA3 44 B4
Shepperton TW17 193 B3
Lindsay Ho 2 SE18 122 C2
Lindsay Rd
Hampton TW12 173 D6
North Cheam KT4 216 B6
Lindsay Sq
SW1 115 D1 259 D2
Lindsell St 6 SE10 142 A4
Lindsey Cl
Bickley BR1 210 A6
Mitcham CR4, SW16 204 A5
Lindsey Ct N13 16 C1
Lindsey Gdns TW14 149 B4
Lindsey Ho W5 109 D2
Lindsey Ho★ SW10 266 D4
Lindsey Mews 18 N1 73 A1
Lindsey Rd RM8 80 C5
Lindsey St
EC1 94 D2 241 D4
Lind St SE8 141 D3
Lindum Rd TW11 175 C3
Lindums The BR3 185 B4
Lindway SE27 182 D5
Lindwood Cl 8 E6 100 B2
Linear View HA9 66 D6
Linfield WC1 233 C1
Linfield Cl NW4 46 C5
Linford Christie Stadium The W12 90 B2
Linford Ct 1 CR4 180 C2
Linford Ho 17 E2 96 A6
Linford Rd E17 54 A6
Linford St
SW8 137 C4 269 A1
Linford Street Bsns Est
SW8 269 A2
Lingard Ho 11 E14 120 A3
Lingards Rd SE13 142 A1
Lingey Cl DA15 167 D2
Lingfield Ave KT1, KT5 198 A5
Lingfield Cl EN1 17 C5
Lingfield Cres SE9 145 B1
Lingfield Ct
Northolt UB5 85 C5
Wimbledon SW19 178 D4
Lingfield Gdns N9 18 B4
Lingfield Ho
5 Acton Green W4 111 A1
Lambeth SE1 251 D1
Penge SE26 184 B4
Lingfield Rd
North Cheam KT4 216 C5
Wimbledon SW19 178 D4
Lingham St SW9 138 B3
Lingholm Way EN5 12 D6
Ling Rd E16 99 A2
Lingrove Gdns IG9 21 B2
Ling's Coppice SE21 161 B2
Lingwell Rd SW17 158 C1
Lingwood DA7 147 D3
Lingwood Gdns
TW7 130 C5
Lingwood Rd E5 52 A2
Linhope St
NW1 92 D3 237 C5
Link Day Prim Sch The
CR0 220 A4
Linkenholt Mans 3
W6 111 D2
Linkfield KT8 195 D6
Link Field BR2 209 A3
Linkfield Rd TW7 130 D3
Link La SM6 220 A2
Linklea Cl NW9 27 C3
Link Rd
Dagenham RM9 103 D5
East Bedfont TW14 149 D4
Friern Barnet N11 31 A6
Hackbridge SM6 203 A1
Links Ave SM4 201 C5
Linkscroft Ave
TW15 170 D4
Links Ct N20 14 B1
Links Dr N20 13 D3
Link Sec Sch The
CR0 220 B4
Links Gdns SW16 182 C3
Linkside Finchley N12 29 C4
Kingston u T KT3 177 C1
Linkside Cl EN2 4 C2
Linkside Gdns EN2 4 B2
Links Ind Est TW13 151 A1
Links Prim Sch
SW17 181 A4
Links Rd Acton W3 88 C1
Ashford TW15 170 A5
Mitcham SW16, SW17 181 A4
West Wickham BR4 208 A1
Willesden NW2 67 D6
Woodford IG8 37 A5
Links Side EN2 4 C2
Link St E9 74 C3
Links The E17 53 A5
Linksview N2 48 D4
Links View Finchley N3 29 B3
Shooters Hill SE18 144 D4
Links View Cl HA7 25 A4
Links View Rd
Croydon CR0 223 C5
Hampton TW12 174 A6
Linksway NW4 28 D1
Links Way
Beckenham BR3 207 C3
Streatham SW17 181 A4
Links Yd
10 Spitalfields E1 96 A2
Spitalfields E1 243 D4
Link The Acton W3 88 D1
Chislehurst SE9 166 C1
Enfield EN3 7 A4
Hendon NW2 46 A1
Northolt UB5 63 B3
Pinner HA5 40 C2
Teddington TW11 174 D4
Wembley HA0 43 C1
Linkway
Dagenham RM8 80 C4
Pinner HA5 22 D2
Stoke Newington N4 51 A2
West Barnes SW20 200 B5
Link Way
Bromley BR2 210 A2
Richmond TW10 153 B2
Linkway The EN5 13 D5
Linkwood Wlk NW1 71 D1
Linley Cres RM7 59 D6
Linley Ct
1 Dulwich SE21 183 C6
Sutton SM1 218 A4
Linley House Sch
KT5 198 B3
Linley Rd N17 33 C1
Linnell Cl NW11 47 D3
Linnell Dr NW11 47 D3
Linnell Ho
Spitalfields E1 243 C4
St John's Wood NW8 229 A6
Linnell Rd
Camberwell SE5 139 C3
Edmonton N18 34 A5
Linnet Cl Bushey WD23 8 A3
Lower Edmonton N9 18 D3
Woolwich SE28 124 C6
Linnet Ct CR4 180 C2
Linnet Mews SW12 159 A4
Linnett Cl E4 36 A6
Linom Rd SW4 138 A1
Linscott Rd E5 74 C4
Linsdell Rd IG11 101 A6
Linsey St
Bermondsey SE16 118 A2
Bermondsey SE16 118 A3
Linslade Cl
Hounslow TW4 151 A6
Pinner HA5 40 B6
Linslade Ho
10 Hackney E2 96 A6
Marylebone NW8 237 B6
Linstead St 1 NW6 69 C1
Linstead Way SW18,
SW19 157 A4
Linsted Ct SE9 167 C5
Linster Gr WD6 11 A6
Lintaine Cl W6 264 B5
Linthorpe Ave HA0 65 C2
Linthorpe Rd
Cockfosters EN4 2 C2
Stamford Hill N16 51 C2
Linton Cl
Carshalton CR4 202 D2
2 Greenwich SE7 121 C1
Welling DA16 146 B4
Linton Gdns E6 100 A1
Linton Gr SE27 183 A5
Linton Ho
Lower Holloway N7 72 B4
2 Tower Hamlets E3 97 C2
Linton Mead Prim Sch
SE28 124 B6
Linton Rd IG11 79 A1
Linton St N1 95 A6 235 B5
Lintons The
Barking IG11 79 A1
Finchley N3 29 B2
Linver Rd SW6 135 C3
Linwood Cl SE5 139 D3
Linwood Cres EN1 6 A4
Linzee Rd N8 50 A5
Lion Ave TW1 152 D3
Lion Cl Ladywell SE4 163 C5
Littleton TW17 192 A6
Lion Ct 12 NW9 46 A5
Lion Ctr The TW13 151 A1
Lionel Gdns SE9 165 D6
Lionel Ho
Bowes Pk N22 32 B4
5 Kensal Town W10 91 A2
Lionel Mans 14 W14 112 D3
Lionel Mews 13 W10 91 A2
Lionel Rd SE9 165 D6
Lionel Road N TW8 110 A2
Lionel Road Prim Sch
TW8 110 A2
Lionel Road S TW8 110 B1
Lion Gate Gdns TW9 132 B2
Lion Gate Mews
SW18 157 C4
Lion House Sch
SW15 134 D1
Lion Mills 36 E2 96 A5
Lion Park Ave KT9 214 C4
Lion Rd
Bexleyheath DA6 147 B1
Edmonton N9 18 A2
Newham E6 100 B2
Thornton Heath CR0 205 A4
Twickenham TW1,
TW2 152 D3
Lions Cl SE12 165 D1
Lion Way TW8 131 D5
Lion Wharf Rd TW7 131 B2
Lion Yd SW4 137 D1
Liphook Cres SE23 162 C4
Liphook Rd WD19 22 D6
Lipton Cl SE28 124 C6
Lipton Ct N14 15 C4
Lipton Rd 9 E1 96 D1
Lisa Lo 5 EN5 13 D6
Lisbon Ave TW2 152 A2
Lisbon Cl E17 35 B1
Lisburne Rd NW3 70 D4
Lisford St SE15 139 D4
Lisgar Terr
W14 113 B2 254 C4
Liskeard Cl BR7 189 A4
Liskeard Gdns SE3 143 A4
Liskeard Ho SE11 261 B2
Lisle Cl SW17 181 B6
Lisle Ct NW2 69 A5
Lisle St WC2 115 D6 249 D6
Lismirrane Ind Pk
WD6 9 B5
Lismore 9 SW19 179 B5
Lismore Cir NW5 71 A3
Lismore Cl TW7 131 A3
Lismore Rd
South Croydon CR2 221 C2
Tottenham N17 51 B6
Lismore Wlk 4 N1 73 A2
Lissant Cl KT6 197 D2
Lisselton Ho 3 NW4 46 D5
Lissenden Gdns NW5 71 A4
Lissenden Mans NW5 71 A4
Lisson Cotts NW1 237 B4
Lisson Gr NW1,
NW8 92 C3 237 A6
LISSON GROVE 92 B3
Lisson Ho NW1 237 A4
Lisson St NW1 92 C2 237 A4
Lister Cl
Dagenham W3 89 B2
Lister Cl *continued*
Mitcham SW19 180 C2
Lister Com Sch 1
E13 99 B5
Lister Cotts WD6 9 A6
Lister Ct Hendon NW9 27 C1
Stoke Newington N16 73 C6
Lister Gdns N18 33 A5
Lister Ho
Greenwich SE3 142 C6
Hayes UB3 105 C2
Marylebone W1 238 C2
Spitalfields E1 96 A2
6 Wembley HA9 67 A5
West Heath SE2 124 D1
Lister Hospl
SW1 115 B1 258 C1
Lister Mews N7 72 B4
Lister Rd E11 54 D1
Lister Wlk SE28 124 D6
Liston Ho N21 16 B6
Liston Rd
Clapham SW4 137 C2
Tottenham N17 34 A2
Liston Way 1 IG8 37 C3
Listowel Cl 2 SW9 138 C5
Listowel Rd RM10 81 C5
Listria Lo N16 73 D6
Listria Pk N16 73 D6
Litcham Ho 23 E1 96 D4
Litchfield Ave
Morden SM4 201 B2
Stratford E15 76 C2
Litchfield Ct E17 53 C3
Litchfield Gdns NW10 68 A2
Litchfield Rd SM1 218 A4
Litchfield St WC2 249 D6
Litchfield Way NW11 48 A4
Lithgow's Rd TW14,
TW6 127 D1
Lithos Rd NW3 70 A2
Little Acre BR3 207 C6
Little Albany St NW1 238 D6
Little Argyll St W1 239 A1
Littleberry Ct NW7 28 C6
Little Birches DA15 167 C2
Little Boltons The
SW10 255 D1
Little Bornes SE21 183 C6
Littlebourne 2
SE13 164 C4
Little Britain EC1 242 A3
Littlebrook Cl CR0 206 D3
Little Brownings
SE23 162 B2
Littlebury Rd SW4 137 D2
Little Bury St N9 17 C4
Little Bushey La WD23 8 B5
Little Cedars N12 30 A6
Little Chelsea Ho
SW10 266 B5
Little Chester St
SW1 258 C6
Little Cloisters SW1 260 A6
Little College St
SW1 260 A6
Littlecombe SE7 143 B6
Little Combe Cl 13
SW15 156 D5
Little Common HA7 9 A1
Littlecote Cl SW19 157 A4
Littlecote Pl HA5 23 B2
Little Cottage Pl
SE10 141 D5
Littlecroft SE9 144 C2
Little Ct Harrow HA1 42 C2
West Wickham BR4 224 C6
Littledale SE2 146 A6
Little David's Sch
CR0 223 D2
Little Deans Yd SW1 260 A6
Little Dell Lo 8 N3 29 B1
Little Dimocks
SW12 159 B2
Little Dorrit Ct SE1 252 B2
Little Ealing La W5 109 C2
Little Ealing Prim Sch 2
W5 109 C3
Little Edward St
NW1 231 D2
Little Elms UB3 127 B5
Little Essex St WC2 251 A6
Little Ferry Rd TW1 153 B3
Littlefield Cl
9 Kingston u T
KT1 176 A1
Littlefield Cl *continued*
Tufnell Pk N19 71 C4
Littlefield Ct UB7 126 A5
Littlefield Ho KT1 176 A1
Littlefield Rd HA8 27 A3
Little Friday Rd E4 20 C2
Little Gearies IG6 56 D5
Little George St SW1 250 A1
Little Gn TW9 131 D1
Little Grange UB6 87 A4
Little Green St NW5 71 B4
Littlegrove EN4 14 C5
Littlegrove Ct 3 EN4 14 C5
Little Halliards KT12 194 A3
LITTLE HEATH 58 B5
Little Heath
Ilford RM6 58 B5
Woolwich SE7 122 A1
Littleheath Rd CR2 222 B1
Little Heath Rd DA7 147 B5
Little Heath Sch RM6 58 B5
Little Holt 10 E11 55 A4
LITTLE ILFORD 78 C3
Little Ilford La E12 78 B4
Little Ilford Sch E12 78 B3
Littlejohn Rd W7 86 D1
Little Larkins EN5 13 A5
Little London Cl UB8 82 D2
Little Marlborough St
W1 239 A1
Littlemead KT10 212 B4
Littlemede SE9 166 B1
Littlemoor Rd IG1 79 B5
Littlemore Rd SE2 124 A4
Little Moss La HA5 23 A1
Little Newport St
WC2 249 D6
Little New St EC4 241 B2
Little Oak Cl TW17 192 B5
Little Orchard Cl
Esher KT10 212 A5
Pnr HA5 23 A1
Little Oxhey La WD19 23 A6
Little Park Dr TW13 151 A2
Little Park Gdns EN2 5 B2
Little Pluckett's Way
IG9 21 D3
Little Portland St
W1 239 A2
Little Potters WD23 8 C4
Little Queens Rd
TW11 174 D4
Little Rd UB3 105 D4
Little Redlands BR1 188 A1
Littlers Cl SW19 180 B2
Little Russell St WC1 240 A3
Little St James's St
SW1 249 A3
Little St Leonards
SW14 133 A2
Little Sanctuary SW1 250 A1
Little Smith St SW1 259 D6
Little Somerset St
E1 243 C1
LITTLE STANMORE 26 B2
Little Stanmore Fst &
Mid Sch HA8 26 B2
Littlestone Cl BR3 185 C4
Little Strand NW9 27 D1
Little Thrift BR5 211 A5
Little Titchfield St
W1 239 A3
LITTLETON 192 C6
Littleton Ave E4 20 D3
Littleton CE Inf Sch
TW17 192 C6
LITTLETON
COMMON 171 B3
Littleton Cres HA1 64 D6
Littleton Ho TW15 171 A3
Littleton La TW17,
TW18 192 A4
Littleton Rd
Harrow HA1 64 D6
Littleton TW15, TW17 171 A3
Littleton St SW18 158 A2
Little Trinity La EC4 252 B6
Little Turnstile WC1 240 C3
LITTLE VENICE 92 A2
Little Venice★
W9 92 A2 236 A4
Littlewood SE13 164 A5
Littlewood Cl W13 109 B3

Little Wood Cl BR5. . .190 A2
Littleworth Ave
KT10. . . . . .212 B3
Littleworth Common Rd
KT10. . . . . .212 B5
Littleworth La KT10. .212 B4
Littleworth Pl KT10. .212 B4
Littleworth Rd KT10. .212 C5
Livermere Ct 3 E8. . . .95 D6
Livermere Rd E8. . . . . .95 D6
Liverpool Gr
SE17. . . . . . .117 B1 262 C1
Liverpool Ho N7. . . . . .72 C2
Liverpool Rd
Ealing W5. . . . . .109 D4
Islington N1. . . . . 234 B5
Islington N1, N7. . . . . . .72 C1
Kingston u T KT2 . . . . 176 C3
Leytonstone E10 . . . . . .54 A3
Newham E16 . . . . .98 C2
South Norwood CR7. . 205 A6
Liverpool St
EC2. . . . . . . .95 C2 243 A3
Liverpool Street Sta
EC2 . . . . .95 C2 243 A3
Livesey Cl
Kingston u T KT1 . . . . .198 B6
Woolwich SE28 . . . . . 123 A3
Livesey Pl SE15 . . . . . .140 A6
Livingstone Ct
Barnet EN5 . . . . .1 A3
Leytonstone E10 . . . . . .54 A3
Stanwell TW19. . . . . . . 148 A3
Livingstone Ho 16
SE5. . . . . .139 A5
Livingstone Lo
13 Paddington W9. . . . .91 C2
Walthamstow E17 . . . . . .35 C1
Livingstone Pl E14. . .120 A1
Livingstone Prim Sch
EN4 . . . . .2 B2
Livingstone Rd
13 Battersea SW11. . .136 B2
Bowes Pk N13 . . . . .32 A5
Isleworth TW3. . . . . . 130 A1
Mill Meads E15 . . . . . . .98 A6
Southall UB1 . . . . 106 D6
South Norwood CR7. . .183 B1
Walthamstow E17 . . . . .53 D3
Livity Sch The SW2. . 160 A6
Livonia St W1. . . . . . . 239 B1
Lizard St EC1 . . 95 A4 235 B1
Lizban St SE3. . . . . . . .143 B5
Llandovery Ho 1
E14. . . . . .120 A4
Llanelly Rd NW2. . . . . . .69 B6
Llanover Rd
Shooters Hill SE18. . . 144 C5
Wembley HA9 . . . . .65 D4
Llanthony Rd SM4 . . . .202 B4
Llanvanor Rd NW2. . . . .69 B6
Llewellyn Ct SE20. . . .184 C2
Llewellyn Ho 10 N19 . .71 C5
Llewellyn St SE16. . . .118 A4
L'Ile aux Enfants NW5 71 A3
Lloyd Ave SW16. . . . . .182 A2
Lloyd Baker St
WC1. . . . . . . .94 C4 234 A1
Lloyd Ct
Ladywell SE13 . . . . . . 163 D6
Pinner HA5. . . . . .40 D4
6 West Norwood
SE27 . . . . 160 D1
Lloyd Ho
3 Beckenham BR3 . . 185 D4
Bromley BR1 . . . . .187 B5
Stoke Newington N16 . .73 B5
Lloyd Mews EN3. . . . . . .7 C5
Lloyd Park Ave CR0 . . 221 D4
Lloyd Park Ho E17 . . . .53 C6
Lloyd Park Sta CR0. . 221 D4
Lloyd Rd
Dagenham RM9. . . . . . . .81 B1
Newham E6. . . . . .100 B6
North Cheam KT4,
SM3. . . . . 216 D5
Walthamstow E17 . . . . .52 D5
Lloyd's Ave EC3. . . . . 243 B1
Lloyd's Bldg★
EC3 . . . . .95 C1 243 A1
Lloyd's Pl SE3 . . . . . . .142 C3
Lloyd Sq WC1. . 94 C4 234 A2
Lloyd's Row
EC1. . . . . .94 D4 234 C1
Lloyd St WC1 . . 94 C4 234 A2
Lloyds Way BR3. . . . . . .207 B4
Lloyd Villas SE4 . . . . . .141 C3
Lloyd Williamson Sch 17
W10. . . . . .91 A2
Loampit Hill SE13. . . 141 D3
Loampit Vale SE13 . . . 142 A2
Loanda Cl 17 E8 . . . . . .95 D6
Loats Rd SW2. . . . . . . .160 A5
Lobelia Cl 5 E6 . . . . . .100 A2
Locarno Cl 15 SW16. .181 C5
Locarno Rd
6 Acton W3 . . . . 111 A5
Greenford UB6. . . . . .86 B3
Lochaber Rd SE13 . . . .142 C1
Lochaline St W6 . . . . . .134 C6
Lochan Cl UB4. . . . . .85 A3
Lochbie 9 N4. . . . . .50 A2
Lochinvar St SW12. . . .159 B4
Lochleven Ho 9 N2. . .30 B1
Lochmere Cl DA8 . . . . . 147 D6
Lochmore Ho SW1. . 258 B3
Lochnagar St E14. . . . .98 A2
Lockbridge Ct 3 W9. . .91 C2
Lock Chase SE3. . . . . . 142 C2
Lock Cl UB2 . . . . .108 A4
Locke Ho
Nine Elms SW8 . . . . . 269 A2
Stamford Hill N16 . . . . .51 D1
Lockesfield Pl E14 . . 119 D1
Lockesley Dr BR5 . . . 211 D3
Lockesley Sq KT6 . . . 197 D3
Locket Rd HA3. . . . . . . .24 D1
Locket Rd Ms HA3 . . . .42 C6
Lockfield Ave EN3 . . . . .7 B4
Lockgate Cl E9 . . . . . . .75 B3
Lockhart Cl
Barnsbury N7. . . . . .72 B2
Enfield EN3 . . . . .18 B6
Lockhart Lo 4 E4 . . . .20 C4
Lockhart St E3. . . . . . . .97 B3
Lockhurst St E5 . . . . . .74 D4
Lockier Wlk HA9. . . . . .65 D5
Lockington Rd
SW8 . . . . .137 B4 268 D2
Lockmead Rd
Lewisham SE13 . . . . . 142 A2
South Tottenham N15. . .52 A3
Lock Mews 9 NW1 . . .71 D2
Lock Rd TW10 . . . . . . .175 C6
LOCKSBOTTOM. . . . 226 D5
Lockside 17 E14 . . . . .119 A6
Lock's La CR4 . . . . . . .181 A1
Locksley St E14. . . . . . . 97 B2
Locksmeade Rd
TW10 . . . . .175 C6
Lock View Ct 9 E14. .119 A6
Lockwell Rd RM10 . . . .81 C5
Lockwood Cl
Barnet EN4 . . . . .2 D1
Forest Hill SE26 . . . . . 184 D6
Lockwood Ct KT3. . . . .199 A5
Lockwood Ho 10
SE11. . . . . .138 C6
Lockwood Ind Pk
N17 . . . . .52 B6
Lockwood Pl E4 . . . . . . .35 C4
Lockwood Sq SE16. . .118 B3
Lockwood Way
Chessington KT9 . . . . 214 C3
Higham Hill E17 . . . . . . .34 D1
Lockyer Cl EN3 . . . . .7 D5
Lockyer Est SE1 . . . . 252 D1
Lockyer Ho
7 Greenwich SE10. . . 120 D1
10 Putney SW15 . . . . . 134 D2
South Lambeth SW8 . 270 A4
Lockyer St SE1 . . . . . 252 D1
Locomotive Dr
TW14 . . . . .150 A3
Locton Gn 4 E3. . . . . . .97 B6
Lodden Lo 13 SM2 . . .218 A1
Loddiges Ho 5 E9. . . .74 C1
Loddiges Rd E9. . . . . . .74 C1
Loddon Ho NW8 . . . . 236 D5
Loder St SE15. . . . . . . .140 C5
Lodge Ave
Borehamwood WD6. . . . .10 B6
Croydon CR0 . . . . 220 C5
Dagenham RM8, RM9,
IG11 . . . . .80 B3
Harrow HA3. . . . . .44 A5
Mortlake SW14 . . . . . . 133 C2
Lodge Cl Edgware HA8 . 26 C4
Lodge Cl *continued*
Edmonton N18. . . . . .33 A5
Hackbridge SM6 . . . . 203 A1
Isleworth TW7. . . . . . .131 B4
Lodge Ct 3 HA0. . . . . . .66 A3
Lodge Dr N13. . . . . .32 C6
Lodge Gdns BR3 . . . . .207 B4
Lodge Hill
East Wickham DA16. . .146 B5
Redbridge IG4 . . . . .56 A5
Lodgehill Park Cl
HA2. . . . . .63 D6
Lodge La Bexley DA5. 168 D5
New Addington CR0 . . 223 D1
North Finchley N12 . . . .30 A5
Lodge Mead Ct 5
N3. . . . . .29 D3
Lodge Pl SM1. . . . . . . 217 D3
Lodge Rd
Bromley BR1 . . . . 187 C3
Hendon NW4 . . . . .46 C5
Lisson Gr NW8 92 C4 230 A1
Sutton SM1 . . . . 217 D3
Thornton Heath CR0 . 204 D2
Wallington SM6 . . . . . .219 B3
Lodge The
9 Chiswick W4. . . . . 111 C3
1 Sutton SM1. . . . . . 218 A4
Lodge Villas IG8 . . . . . .36 D4
Lodge Way
Charlton TW17. . . . . . 171 A1
Stanwell TW15. . . . . . 148 A2
Lodore Gdns NW9 . . . .45 C4
Lodore Gn UB10 . . . . . .60 A5
Lodore St E14 . . . . .98 A1
Lodsworth Ho SW11 268 A1
Lofthouse Pl KT9 . . . 213 C2
Loftie St SE16. . . . . . .118 A4
Lofting Ho 8 N1. . . . . .72 C1
Lofting Rd N1 . . . . .72 C1
Lofts on the Park 24
E9. . . . . .74 D2
Loftus Rd
Barking IG11 . . . . .79 A2
Shepherd's Bush W12 .112 B5
Loftus Rd (Queens Park
Rangers FC) W12. . .112 B5
Logan Cl Enfield EN3 . . . .6 D4
Hounslow TW4. . . . . . .129 B2
Logan Mews W8. . . . . 255 A4
Logan Pl W8. . 113 C2 255 A4
Logan Rd
Edmonton N9. . . . . .18 B2
Wembley HA9 . . . . .66 A6
Loggetts SE21 . . . . . . .161 C2
Logs Hill BR1, BR7 . . . .188 A2
Logs Hill Cl BR7. . . . .188 A2
Lohmann Ho 5
SE11. . . . . .138 C6
Lois Dr TW17 . . . . 192 D4
Lolesworth Cl E1 . . . 243 D3
Lolland Ho 8 SE7 . . .122 A2
Lollard St
SE11. . . . . . . .116 C2 261 A3
Lollards Twr SE1 . . . . 260 C5
Loman St
SE1. . . . . . . 116 D4 251 D2
Lomas Cl CR0. . . . . . . 224 A1
Lomas Dr 10 E8. . . . . . .73 D1
Lomas St E1. . . . . .96 A2
Lombard Ave
Enfield EN3 . . . . .6 C4
Ilford IG3. . . . . .57 C1
Lombard Bsns Pk
Merton SW19. . . . . . . 179 D1
Thornton Heath CR0 . .204 B2
Lombard Ct
14 Acton W3 . . . . 110 D5
City of London EC3. . . 252 D6
Lombard La EC4 . . . . 241 B1
Lombard Rd
Battersea SW11 . . . . .136 B3
Friern Barnet N11 . . . . . .31 B5
Merton SW19. . . . . . . 179 D1
Lombard Rdbt CR0. . .204 B2
Lombard St
EC3. . . . . .95 B1 242 D1
Lombard Trad Est
SE7. . . . . .121 B2
Lombard Wall SE7 . . . .121 B2
Lombardy Pl W2. . . . 245 D5
Lombardy Ret Pk
UB3 . . . . .106 B6
Lomley Ho 10 SW2. . .160 C5
Lomond Cl
Tottenham N15 . . . . . . .51 C4
Lomond Cl *continued*
Wembley HA0 . . . . .66 B1
Lomond Ct HA3. . . . . . .42 D6
Lomond Gdns CR2 . . .223 A1
Lomond Gr SE5 . . . . . .139 B5
Lomond Ho 10 SE5. . .139 B4
Loncroft Rd SE5 . . . . .139 C6
Londesborough Ho 1
N16. . . . . .73 C4
Londesborough Rd
N16. . . . . .73 C4
London Acadamy
HA8 . . . . .26 B6
London Acad for Higher
Education The E15 . . 98 B6
London Acad of
Computing &
Electronics SW17 . 158 D1
London Bridge EC4,
SE1. . . . . . . .117 B6 252 D5
London Bridge City Pier
SE1. . . . . . . 117 C5 253 A4
London Bridge
Experience The
SE1. . . . . 252 D4
London Bridge Hospl
SE1. . . . . 117 B5 252 D4
London Bridge St
SE1. . . . . . . .117 B5 252 D3
London Bridge Sta
SE1. . . . . . . 117 B5 252 D3
London Bridge Wlk
SE1. . . . . 252 D4
London Britannia Coll
N1. . . . . .95 B4 235 C2
London Business Sch
NW1. . . . . .92 D3 237 C6
London Canal Mus★
N1 . . . . .94 A5 233 B4
London Central
Mosque★
NW8. . . . . .92 C4 230 B1
London Chest Hospl
E2. . . . . .96 C5
London Christian Sch
SE16. . . . . 118 C3
London City Airport
E16. . . . . .122 B5
London City Airport Sta
E16. . . . . 122 A5
London City Sh Ctr
EC1 . . . . 242 B5
London Clinic (Hospl)
NW1. . . . . .93 A3 238 B5
London Coll of Advanced
Studies SE1. . . . . . . 252 C3
London Coll of Beauty
Therapy W1. . 93 C1 239 B1
London Coll of Bsns &
Computer Studies 12
SW4. . . . . 137 D1
London Coll of
Communication (Sch of
Printing & Publishing)
SE11. . . . . . . 116 D3 261 D5
London Coll of
Economics & Science
NW10. . . . . .89 A3
London Coll of Fashion
(Curtain Rd)
EC2 . . . . .95 C3 243 B6
London Coll of Fashion
(Davies St) W1. . . . 238 C1
London Coll of Fashion
(Golden La)
EC1 . . . . .95 A3 242 A5
London Coll of Fashion
(John Prince's St)
W1. . . . . 238 D2
London Coll of Fashion
(Lime Grove) 18
W6. . . . . 112 C4
London Coll of Fashion
(Mare St) E8. . . . . .74 C1
London Coll of
International Business
Studies WC1 . . . . . . 240 B3
London Coll of Tech
IG2. . . . . .56 C3
London Ct 3 SW18 . .157 C6
London Dungeon The★
SE1. . . . . .117 B5 252 D4
London Electronics Coll
SW5. . . . . . . 113 D1 255 C2
London Eye (Millennium
Wheel)★
SE1. . . . . . . .116 B4 250 C2
London Fields East Side
E8. . . . . .74 B1
London Fields Prim Sch
15 E8. . . . . .96 B6
London Fields Sta E8 . 74 B1
London Fields West Side
E8. . . . . .74 A1
London Fire Brigade
Mus★ SE1 . . . . 252 A2
London Glassblowing
Workshop SE1. . . . 253 A1
London Group Bsns Pk
NW2. . . . . .46 A1
London Ho
Edgware HA8. . . . . .26 A6
13 Hammersmith W6 112 A2
London Ho TW9. . . . . . .132 B2
London Ho NW8 . . . . 230 B4
London Hospital Dental
Inst 5 E1. . . . . .96 B2
London Independent
Hospl The E1. . . . . .96 D2
London Inst The
SW17. . . . . .181 B5
London International
Film Sch
WC2. . . . . .94 A1 240 A1
London Irish Rifles
Mus★ SW9 . . . . . . .139 A4
London Jewish Girls
High Sch NW4 . . . . . .46 C4
London La
Bromley BR1 . . . . 186 D3
Hackney E8 . . . . .74 B1
London Meridian Coll 2
N7 . . . . .72 B5
London Metrocity Coll 21
E3. . . . . .97 E3
London Metropolitan
Univ
Islington N7. . . . . .72 C3
Whitechapel
E1 . . . . .95 D1 243 C1
Whitechapel
E1 . . . . .95 D1 243 C2
London Metropolitan
Univ (Central Ho) 44
E1. . . . . .96 A1
London Metropolitan
Univ (Commercial Rd)
42 E1. . . . . .96 A1
London Metropolitan
Univ (Ladbrook Ho) 5
N5 . . . . .72 D3
London Metropolitan
Univ (Moorgate)
EC2 . . . . .95 B2 242 D3
London Metropolitan
Univ (Tower Hill)
EC3 . . . . 253 C6
London Metropolitian
Univ (Spring Ho) 1
N7 . . . . .72 C2
London Mews W2. . . 236 D2
London Motorcycle
Mus★ UB6. . . . . .86 A4
London Nautical Sch
SE1. . . . . . . .116 C5 251 B4
London Oratory Sch The
SW6. . . . . . . .135 C5 265 B4
London Oratory The★
SW7. . . . . . . .114 C3 257 A5
London Rd
Ashford TW15, TW18,
TW19, TW14 . . . . . . .148 B2
Brentford TW7, TW8 . .131 B4
Bromley BR1 . . . . 186 D3
Carshalton CR4 . . . . . 203 A2
Enfield EN2 . . . . .5 B1
Forest Hill SE22,
SE23 . . . . 162 C3
Hackbridge SM6, CR4 .219 B6
Harrow HA1. . . . . .64 C6
Hounslow TW3, TW7, TW1,
TW8 . . . . .130 B3
Kingston u T KT1, KT2. .176 B1
Lambeth SE1 116 D3 261 D6
Mitcham CR4 . . . . 180 D2
Morden SM4 . . . . 201 C5
Newham E13 . . . . .99 A5
Romford RM7, RM8 . . . .59 C5
Stanmore HA7 . . . . .25 D6

London Rd *continued*
Stoneleigh KT17, KT4, SM3 216 B3
Thornton Heath CR0, CR7, SW16 204 C3
Twickenham TW1 153 A4
Wembley HA9 66 A2
London Road Rdbt TW1 153 A5
London Sch of Economics & Political Science WC2 94 B1 240 D1
London Sch of Jewish Studies 5 NW4 46 D5
London South Bank Univ SE1 116 D3 261 D6
London St
City of London EC3 253 B6
Paddington W2 92 B1 236 C1
London Stile 5 W4 110 C1
London Stock Exchange★ EC2 242 A2
London Stone Bsns Est 15 SW11 137 A3
London Terr 1 E2 96 A5
London Tottenham Coll 12 N17 33 D3
London Transport Mus★ WC2 250 B6
London Trocadero★ W1 249 C5
London Wall EC2 95 B2 242 D3
London Wall Bldgs EC2 242 D3
London Wetland Ctr★ SW13 134 B5
London Wetland Visitor Ctr★ SW13 134 B4
London Wharf 4 E2 96 B6
London Zoo★ NW1 93 A5 231 A4
Lonesome Prim Sch CR4 181 B1
Lonesome Way CR4 181 C2
Long Acre WC2 94 A1 240 B1
Long Acre Ct W13 87 A2
Longacre Pl SM5 219 A2
Longacre Rd E17 36 B2
Longbeach Rd SW11 136 D2
Longberrys NW2 69 B5
Longboat Row UB1 85 B1
Longbridge Ho RM8 80 B4
Longbridge Rd
Barking IG11 79 C3
Dagenham RM8 80 B4
Longbridge Way SE13 164 A6
Longbury Dr BR5 190 B1
Longchamp Ct 13 HA7 25 C5
Longcliffe Ho SW18 157 D6
Longcroft SE9 166 C1
Longcrofte Rd HA8 25 D3
Long Deacon Rd E4 20 C3
LONG DITTON 197 C1
Long Ditton City Inf Sch KT6 197 C1
Longdon Wood BR2 226 A4
Longdown Rd SE6 185 C6
Long Dr Dagenham W3 89 C1
Greenford UB6 85 D6
Ruislip HA4 62 D4
Long Elmes HA3 24 A2
Longfellow Rd
North Cheam KT4 200 B1
Walthamstow E17 53 B3
Longfellow Way SE1 263 D3
Longfield
3 Bromley BR1 186 D2
Loughton IG10 21 C6
Long Field NW9 27 D3
Longfield Ave
Ealing W5 109 C6
Enfield EN3 6 C5
Hackbridge SM6 203 A1
Hendon NW7 28 A3
Walthamstow E17 53 A5
Wembley HA9 44 A1
Longfield Cres SE23, SE26 162 C1
Longfield Ct 4 N2 48 A6
Longfield Dr
Mitcham SW19 180 C2
Mortlake SW14 154 D6
Longfield Est SE1 263 D3
Longfield Fst & Mid Schs HA2 41 C3
Longfield Ho
Ealing W5 109 C6
Walthamstow E17 53 B4
Longfield Rd W5 87 C1
Longfield St SW18 157 C4
Longford Ave
Feltham TW14 149 D5
Southall UB1 107 D6
Stanwell TW19 148 A3
Longford Cl
Feltham TW13 151 A1
Hampton TW12 173 C6
Hayes UB4 106 D6
Longford Com Sch TW14 149 D4
Longford Ct
1 Bedford Pk W12 111 C4
2 Clapton Pk E5 74 D4
Hampton TW12 173 D4
9 Hendon NW4 46 C5
Southall UB1 107 C5
West Ewell KT19 215 A4
Longford Gdns
Hayes UB4 106 D6
Sutton SM1 218 A6
Longford Ho
1 Catford BR1 186 B5
Hampton TW12 173 C6
7 Stepney E1 96 C1
Longford Ind Est TW12 173 D4
Longford Rd TW2 151 D3
Longford St NW1 93 B3 238 D6
Longford Way TW19 148 A3
Longford Wlk 9 SW2 160 C4
Longhayes Ave RM6 58 D5
Longhayes Ct RM6 58 D5
Longheath Gdns CR0 206 C4
Longhedge Ho SE26 184 A6
Longhedge St SW11 137 A3
Longhill Rd SE6 164 B1
Long Ho SM5 218 C6
Longhook Gdns UB5 84 B4
Longhope Cl SE15 139 D6
Longhurst Ho 8 W9 91 B4
Longhurst Rd
Croydon CR0 206 B3
Lewisham SE13 164 C6
Long La
Bermondsey SE1 117 B4 252 D1
Croydon CR0 206 C3
East Finchley N2 48 B6
Erith DA7 147 B4
Finchley N3 29 D2
Hillingdon UB10 82 D6
Holborn EC1 94 D2 241 D4
Stanwell TW15, TW19 148 B3
Longland Ct
Bermondsey SE1 118 A1
Hackney E9 75 A3
Longland Dr N20 13 D2
LONGLANDS 167 B1
Longlands Ct
Higham Hill E17 35 A2
Mitcham CR4 181 A2
Notting Hill W11 244 D6
Sidcup DA15 167 D1
Longlands Park Cres DA15 167 C2
Longlands Prim Sch DA15 167 C1
Longlands Rd DA15 167 D1
Longleat Ct 3 DA6 147 A1
Longleat Ho SW1 259 C2
Longleat Rd EN1 17 C6
Longleat Way TW14 149 B4
Longleigh Ho 8 SE5 139 C4
Longleigh La SE2, DA7 146 C6
Longlents Ho 3 NW10 89 B6
Longley Ave HA0 88 B6
Longley Ho 5 N19 71 C4
Longley Rd
Harrow HA1 42 B5
Longley Rd *continued*
Thornton Heath CR0 204 D2
Upper Tooting SW17 180 D4
Long Leys E4 36 A4
Longley St SE1 118 A2
Longley Way NW2 68 C5
Longman Ho
9 Globe Town E2 96 D5
10 Shoreditch E8 95 D6
Long Mark Rd 5 E16 99 D2
Longmarsh La SE28 123 C5
Longmead BR7 188 C1
Long Mead NW9 27 D2
Longmead Dr DA14 168 D2
Longmead Ho SE27 183 A5
Long Meadow 20 N7 71 D3
Long Meadow Cl BR3, BR4 208 A2
Longmeadow Rd DA15 167 C3
Longmead Prim Sch UB7 104 A2
Longmead Rd
Hayes UB3 105 D6
Thames Ditton KT7 196 D2
Upper Tooting SW17 180 D5
Longmoor Point 14 SW15 156 B3
Longmore Ave EN4, EN5 14 B5
Longmore St SW1 115 C2 259 A3
Longnor Rd E1 96 D4
Long Pond Rd SE3 142 C4
Long Rd SW4 137 C1
Longreach Ct IG11 101 B5
Long Reach Rd IG11 101 D3
Longridge Ho SE1 262 B5
Longridge La UB1 85 D1
Longridge Rd SW5 113 C2 255 B3
Long Ridges N2 49 A6
Longs Ct 2 TW9 132 B1
Long's Ct W1 249 D5
Longshaw Prim Sch E4 20 B1
Longshaw Rd E4 20 B1
Longshore SE8 119 B2
Long St E2 95 D4
Longstaff Cres SW18 157 C4
Longstaff Rd SW18 157 C5
Longstone Ave NW10 89 D6
Longstone Rd SW17 181 B5
Longthorne Ho 18 E3 97 B4
Longthornton Rd SW16 181 D1
Longthorpe Ct 9 W6 112 A2
Longton Ave SE26 184 A6
Longton Gr SE26 184 B6
Longville Rd SE11 261 D4
Longwalk Rd UB11 104 D5
Long Wlk
Bermondsey SE1 263 B6
Kingston u T KT3 199 A6
Shooters Hill SE18 144 D6
Longwood Bsns Pk TW16 193 D4
Longwood Dr SW15 156 A5
Longwood Gdns IG2, IG6, IG5 56 C6
Longwood Par IG6 56 D6
Longworth Cl SE28 102 D1
Long Yd WC1 94 B3 240 C5
Loning The Enfield EN3 6 C5
Hyde The NW9 45 D5
Lonsdale Ave
Newham E6 100 A3
Wembley HA9 66 A3
Lonsdale Cl
Edgware HA8 26 B5
Hillingdon UB8 83 A2
Mottingham SE12 165 D1
Newham E6 100 A3
Pinner HA5 23 A2
Lonsdale Cres IG2 56 D3
Lonsdale Dr EN2 16 A6
Lonsdale Dr N EN2 4 A1
Lonsdale Gdns CR7, SW16 204 B5
Lonsdale Ho
Fulham SW6 135 C2
6 Stoke Newington N4 51 A2
Lonsdale Mews
Notting Hill W11 91 B1
4 Richmond TW9 132 C4
Lonsdale Pl N1 72 C1
Lonsdale Rd
Barnes SW13 133 D5
Bexley DA7 147 B3
Chiswick W4 111 D2
Croydon SE25 206 B5
Kilburn NW6 91 B6
Leytonstone E11 54 D2
Notting Hill W11 91 B1
Southall UB2 106 D3
Lonsdale Sq
Islington N1 72 C1
Islington N1 234 B6
Loobert Rd N15 51 C6
Looe Gdns IG6 56 D6
Loop Rd BR7 189 A4
Lopen Rd N18 33 C6
Lopen Works N18 33 C6
Lopez Ho 4 SW9 138 A2
Lorac Ct 13 SM2 217 C1
Loraine Cl EN3 18 C6
Loraine Ct BR7 188 D5
Loraine Ho 1 SM5 219 B4
Loraine Rd
Chiswick W4 132 D6
Islington N7 72 B4
Lord Ave IG5 56 B6
Lord Chancellor Wlk KT2 177 A2
Lord David Pitt Ho 8 SE24 138 C1
Lordell Pl SW19 178 C4
Lorden Wlk 13 E2 96 A4
Lord Gdns IG5 56 B5
Lord Hills Rd W2 91 D2
Lord Holland La 5 SW9 138 C3
Lord Knyvetts Ct 3 TW19 148 A5
Lord Napier Pl W6 112 A1
Lord North St SW1 260 A5
Lord Roberts Mews SW6 265 C3
Lord Roberts Terr SE18 122 C1
Lords Cl
Feltham TW13 151 A2
West Norwood SE21 161 A2
Lord's Cricket Mus★ NW8 92 B4 229 D1
Lords Ct 3 HA8 27 A3
Lordship Gr N16 73 B6
Lordship Ho 3 N16 73 B6
Lordship La
Dulwich Village SE22 161 D5
Tottenham N22 33 B2
Lordship Lane Prim Sch 1 N22 33 A2
Lordship Park Mews N16 73 A6
Lordship Pk N16 73 B6
Lordship Pl SW3 267 A5
Lordship Rd
Northolt UB5 63 A1
Stoke Newington N16 73 B6
Lordship Terr N16 73 B6
Lord's Indoor Cricket Sch NW8 230 A2
Lord's (MCC & Middlesex Cty Cricket Ground)★ NW8 92 B4 229 D2
Lordsmead Rd N17 33 C1
Lord St E16 122 A5
Lord's View NW8 229 D1
Lord Warwick St SE18 122 B3
Loreburn Ho 2 N7 72 B4
Lorenzo St N1, WC1 233 C2
Loretto Gdns HA3 44 A5
Lorian Cl N12 29 D6
Loring Rd
East Barnet N20 14 C2
Isleworth TW7 130 D3
Loris Rd W6 112 C3
Lorn Ct SW9 138 C3
Lorne Ave CR0 206 D2
Lorne Cl NW8 92 C4 230 B1
Lorne Ct Harrow HA1 42 C2
Putney SW15 156 D5
Lorne Gdns
Croydon CR0 206 D2
Lorne Gdns *continued*
5 Hammersmith W11 112 D4
Wanstead E11 55 C5
Lorne Ho
Friern Barnet N11 31 B5
Hornsey N4 50 B2
7 Tower Hamlets E1 97 A2
Lorne Rd
Finsbury Pk N4 50 B1
Forest Gate E7 77 C4
Harrow HA3 24 D1
3 Richmond TW10 154 B6
Walthamstow E17 53 C4
Lorn Rd SW9 138 C3
Lorraine Ct
Beckenham BR3 186 A2
9 Belmont SM2 217 C1
10 Camden Town NW1 71 B1
Lorraine Pk HA3 24 C3
Lorrimore Rd SE17 138 D6
Lorrimore Sq SE17 138 D6
Lorton Ho 9 NW6 91 C6
Loseberry Rd KT10 212 B3
Lostock Ho 10 SW8 137 D3
Lothair Rd W5 109 D4
Lothair Rd N N4 50 D3
Lothair Rd S N4 50 D2
Lothbury EC2 95 B1 242 C2
Lothian Ave UB4 84 B2
Lothian Cl HA0 65 A5
Lothian Rd SW9 138 D4
Lothrop St W10 91 A4
Lots Rd SW10 136 A5 266 B3
Loubet St SW17 180 D4
Loudoun Ave IG6 56 D4
Loudoun Rd NW8 92 A6 229 B5
Loudwater Cl TW16 194 A5
Loudwater Rd TW16 194 A5
Loughborough Ct 7 SW9 138 D2
Loughborough Junction Sta SW9 138 D2
Loughborough Pk SW9 138 D1
Loughborough Prim Sch SW9 138 D3
Loughborough Rd SE5, SW9 138 D3
Loughborough St SE11 116 B1 260 D1
Lough Rd N7 72 B2
LOUGHTON 21 D5
Loughton Way IG9 21 D3
Louie Black Ho 4 SW19 179 A3
Louisa Cl E9 96 D6
Louisa Ct
Twickenham TW2 152 C2
Wood Green N11 31 D3
Louisa Gdns E1 96 D3
Louisa Ho SW15 133 D1
Louisa St E1 96 D3
Louis Ct 3 RM10 81 D2
Louise Bennett Cl 9 SE24 138 D1
Louise Ct
7 Bexley DA6 147 A1
4 Wanstead E11 55 B4
Wood Green N22 32 C2
Louise De Marillac Ho 26 E1 96 C2
Louise Graham Ho 5 IG11 101 B6
Louise Rd E15 76 C2
Louise White Ho 1 N19 49 D1
Louis Gdns BR7 188 B6
Louis Mews N10 31 B2
Louisville Rd SW17 159 A1
Lousada Lo N14 15 C5
Louvaine Rd SW11 136 B1
Lovage App E6 100 A2
Lovat Cl NW2 67 D5
Lovat La EC3 253 A5
Lovatt Cl HA8 26 D4
Lovatt Ct SW12 159 B3
Lovatt Dr HA4 39 D4
Lovat Wlk TW5 129 A5
Loveday Ho 2 SW2 160 C3
Loveday Rd W13 109 B5

Lovegrove St SE1 . . . 140 A6
Lovegrove Wlk E14 . . . 120 A5
Lovekyn Cl KT2 . . . 176 B1
Love La Cheam SM3 . . . 217 A2
City of London
EC2 . . . 95 A1 242 B2
Croydon SE25 . . . 206 B6
Long Ditton KT6 . . . 213 D6
Mitcham CR4 . . . 202 C6
Morden SM4 . . . 201 D2
Old Bexley DA5 . . . 169 C5
Pinner HA5 . . . 41 A6
Tottenham N17 . . . 33 D3
Woolwich SE18 . . . 122 D2
Lovelace Ave BR2 . . . 210 C3
Lovelace Gdns
Barking IG11 . . . 80 A4
Surbiton KT6 . . . 197 D2
Lovelace Gn SE9 . . . 144 B2
Lovelace Ho 12 E8 . . . 95 D6
Lovelace Prim Sch
KT9 . . . 213 C3
Lovelace Rd
East Barnet EN4 . . . 14 C4
Surbiton KT6 . . . 197 D2
West Norwood SE21 . . . 161 A3
Loveland Mans 7
IG11 . . . 79 D1
Lovel Ave DA16 . . . 146 A3
Lovelinch Cl SE15 . . . 140 C6
Lovell Ho Hackney E8 . . . 96 A6
4 Merton SW19 . . . 180 A2
Lovell Pl SE16 . . . 119 A3
Lovell Rd
Richmond TW10 . . . 153 C1
Southall UB1 . . . 85 D1
Loveridge Mews NW6 69 B2
Loveridge Rd NW6 . . . 69 B2
Lover's Wlk
W1 . . . 115 A5 248 A3
Lovett Dr SM5 . . . 202 B2
Lovette Ho 4 E3 . . . 97 C4
Lovetts Pl SW18 . . . 135 D1
Lovett Way NW10 . . . 67 A3
Love Wlk SE5 . . . 139 B3
Lovibonds Ave
Hillingdon UB7 . . . 82 B1
Locksbottom BR6 . . . 226 D5
Lowbrook Rd IG1 . . . 78 D4
Low Cross Wood La
SE21 . . . 161 D1
Lowdell Cl UB7 . . . 82 A1
Lowden Rd
Edmonton N9 . . . 18 B3
Herne Hill SE24 . . . 139 A1
Southall UB1 . . . 107 A6
Lowder Ho 6 E1 . . . 118 B5
Lowe Ave E16 . . . 99 A2
Lowell Ho 10 SE5 . . . 139 A5
Lowell St E14 . . . 97 A1
Lower Addiscombe Rd
CR0 . . . 205 C1
Lower Addison Gdns
W14 . . . 113 A4 244 A1
Lower Belgrave St
SW1 . . . 115 B3 258 C5
Lower Boston Rd
W7 . . . 108 C4
Lower Broad St
RM10 . . . 103 C6
Lower Camden BR7 . . . 188 B2
Lower Church St
CR0 . . . 220 D6
LOWER CLAPTON . . . 74 C4
Lower Clapton Rd E5 . . 74 C4
Lower Clarendon Wlk 9
W11 . . . 91 A1
Lower Comm S
SW15 . . . 134 B2
Lower Coombe St
CR0 . . . 221 A4
Lower Downs Rd
SW20 . . . 178 D2
LOWER EDMONTON . . 18 B1
LOWER FELTHAM . . 149 D1
Lower Fosters NW4 . . 46 C4
Lower George St 13
TW10 . . . 153 D6
Lower Gn W CR4 . . . 202 C6
Lower Gravel Rd
BR2 . . . 210 B1
LOWER GREEN . . . 195 C1
Lower Green Gdns
KT4 . . . 200 A1
Lower Green Rd
KT10 . . . 212 A6
Lower Grosvenor Pl
SW1 . . . 115 B3 258 D6
Lower Grove Rd
TW10 . . . 154 B6
LOWER HALLIFORD 193 C3
Lower Hall La E4 . . . 35 A6
Lower Hampton Rd TW12,
TW16 . . . 172 D1
Lower Ham Rd KT2 . 175 D4
LOWER HOLLOWAY . 72 A3
Lower James St W1 . 249 B6
Lower John St W1 . . 249 B6
Lower Kenwood Ave
EN2 . . . 16 A6
Lower Kings Rd KT2 . 176 A3
Lower Lea Crossing E14,
E16 . . . 120 C6
Lower Maidstone Rd
N11 . . . 31 C4
Lower Mall W6 . . . 112 B1
Lower Marsh
SE1 . . . 116 C4 251 A1
Lower Marsh La KT1,
KT5 . . . 198 C5
Lower Merton Rise
NW3 . . . 70 C1
LOWER MORDEN . . . 201 A2
Lower Morden La
SM4 . . . 201 A3
Lower Mortlake Rd
TW9 . . . 132 B2
Lower Park Rd
Belvedere DA17 . . . 125 C2
Friern Barnet N11 . . . 31 C5
2 Loughton IG10 . . . 21 D6
Lower Pk Acton W3 . . . 89 A3
5 Putney SW15 . . . 156 D6
LOWER PLACE . . . 89 A5
Lower Place Bsns Ctr
NW10 . . . 89 A5
Lower Queen's Rd
IG9 . . . 21 D2
Lower Rd
Belvedere DA17 . . . 125 D3
Finchley N2 . . . 30 B2
Harrow HA2 . . . 42 B1
Rotherhithe SE16 . . . 118 C4
Sutton SM1 . . . 218 A4
Lower Richmond Rd
Mortlake SW14,
TW9 . . . 132 D2
Putney SW15 . . . 134 C2
Lower Robert St
WC2 . . . 250 B5
Lower Sand Hills
KT6 . . . 197 C2
Lower Sloane St
SW1 . . . 115 A1 258 A2
Lower Sq TW7 . . . 131 B2
Lower Strand NW9 . . . 27 D1
Lower Sunbury Rd
TW12 . . . 173 C1
LOWER
SYDENHAM . . . 185 A6
Lower Sydenham Sta
SE26 . . . 185 B5
Lower Teddington Rd
KT1 . . . 175 D2
Lower Terr NW3 . . . 70 A5
Lower Thames St
EC3 . . . 117 C6 253 A5
Lower Tub WD23 . . . 8 B4
Lowerwood Ct W11 . . . 91 A1
Lower Wood Rd
KT10 . . . 213 B2
Lowestoft Cl 5 E5 . . . 74 C6
Lowestoft Mews
E16 . . . 122 D4
Loweswater Cl HA9 . . . 65 D6
Loweswater Ho E3 . . . 97 B3
Lowfield Rd
Dagenham W3 . . . 89 A1
Hampstead NW6 . . . 69 C1
Low Hall Cl E4 . . . 19 D4
Low Hall La E17 . . . 53 A3
Lowick Rd HA1 . . . 42 C4
Lowland Gdns RM7 . . . 59 D3
Lowlands NW3 . . . 70 C2
Lowlands Ct NW7 . . . 27 D5
Lowlands Rd
Harrow HA1 . . . 42 C2
Pinner HA5 . . . 40 C3
Lowman Rd N7 . . . 72 B4
Lowndes Cl SW1 . . . 258 B5
Lowndes Ct
Knightsbridge SW1 . . 257 D6
Marylebone W1 . . . 239 A1
Lowndes Lo Barnet EN5 1 D2
SW1 . . . 257 D6
Lowndes Pl
SW1 . . . 115 A3 258 A5
Lowndes Sq
SW1 . . . 114 D4 247 D1
Lowndes St
SW1 . . . 115 A3 258 A6
Lownds Ct BR1 . . . 187 A1
Lowood Ct SE19 . . . 183 D5
Lowood Ho 12 E1 . . . 118 C6
Lowood St E1 . . . 118 B6
Lowry Cres CR4 . . . 180 C1
Lowry Ct 3 SE16 . . . 118 B1
Lowry Ho N17 . . . 33 D2
Lowry Lo 1 HA0 . . . 65 D3
Lowry Rd RM8 . . . 80 B3
Lowther Cl WD6 . . . 10 B6
Lowther Dr EN2 . . . 4 A1
Lowther Hill SE23 . . . 163 A4
Lowther Ho
Pimlico SW1 . . . 259 B1
11 Shoreditch E8 . . . 95 D6
Lowther Prim Sch
SW13 . . . 134 A6
Lowther Rd
Barnes SW13 . . . 133 D4
Higham Hill E17 . . . 35 A1
Islington N7 . . . 72 C3
Kingston u T KT2 . . . 176 B2
Stanmore HA7 . . . 44 B6
Lowth Rd SE5 . . . 139 A3
Lowton Lo E17 . . . 53 A6
LOXFORD . . . 79 A3
Loxford Ave E6 . . . 99 D5
Loxford Ho SW1 . . . 258 B3
Loxford La IG1 . . . 79 B3
Loxford Rd IG11 . . . 78 D2
Loxford Sch of Science &
Tech IG1 . . . 79 B3
Loxham Rd E4 . . . 35 D3
Loxham St WC1 . . . 233 B1
Loxley Cl SE26 . . . 184 D5
Loxley Hall E11 . . . 54 C2
Loxley Ho HA9 . . . 66 A5
Loxley Rd
Feltham TW12 . . . 173 B6
Wandsworth SW18 . . . 158 B3
Loxton Rd SE23 . . . 163 A3
Loxwood Cl TW14 . . . 149 B3
Loxwood Rd N17 . . . 51 C6
Loyola Prep Sch IG9 . . 21 C3
LTC Coll London W1 239 A2
Lubavitch Boys Prim Sch
6 E5 . . . 51 D2
Lubavitch Girls Prim Sch
8 N16 . . . 51 D2
Lubavitch House Sch
(Jun Boys) 9 E5 . . . 51 D2
Lubbock Ct BR7 . . . 188 B3
Lubbock Ho
21 Canary Wharf
E14 . . . 119 D6
Orpington BR6 . . . 227 C6
Lubbock Rd BR7 . . . 188 B3
Lubbock St SE14 . . . 140 C5
Lucan Ho N1 . . . 235 D5
Lucan Pl
SW3 . . . 114 C2 257 B3
Lucan Rd EN5 . . . 1 A2
Lucas Ave Harrow HA2 . 63 C6
Newham E13 . . . 99 B6
Lucas Ct
Battersea SW11 . . . 268 B1
Forest Hill SE26 . . . 185 A5
Lucas Gdns N2 . . . 30 A1
Lucas Ho
2 Clapham SW8 . . . 137 C3
Walham Green SW10 . 265 D4
Lucas Rd SE20 . . . 184 C4
Lucas Sq NW11 . . . 47 C3
Lucas St SE4, SE8 . . . 141 C4
Lucas Vale Prim Sch 10
SE8 . . . 141 C4
Lucerne Cl N14 . . . 16 A1
Lucerne Ct
5 Abbey Wood
DA18 . . . 125 A3
8 Beckenham BR3 . . . 185 C3
Lucerne Gr E17 . . . 54 B5
Lucerne Mews W8 . . . 245 B4
Lucerne Rd
Highbury N5 . . . 72 D4
Orpington BR6 . . . 211 D1
South Norwood CR7 . . 205 A5
Lucey Rd SE16 . . . 118 A3
Lucey Way SE16 . . . 118 A2
Lucie Ave TW15 . . . 170 D4
Lucien Rd
Upper Tooting
SW17 . . . 181 A6
Wandsworth SW18 . . 157 D2
Lucille Ho SE26 . . . 184 B4
Lucknow St SE18 . . . 145 C5
Lucorn Cl SE12 . . . 164 D5
Lucraft Ho 12 SW2 . . . 160 A4
Luctons Ave IG9 . . . 21 C3
Lucy Ashe Ho SE17 . . 261 D3
Lucy Brown Ho SE1 . . 252 B3
Lucy Cres W3 . . . 89 A3
Lucy Gdns RM8 . . . 81 A5
Luddesdon Rd DA8 . . 147 C5
Ludford Cl
Croydon CR0 . . . 220 D4
Edgware NW9 . . . 27 C1
Ludgate Broadway
EC4 . . . 241 D1
Ludgate Cir
EC4 . . . 94 D1 241 C1
Ludgate Hill
EC4 . . . 94 D1 241 D1
Ludgate Ho EC4 . . . 241 C1
Ludgate Sq EC4 . . . 241 D1
Ludgrove Ct EN4 . . . 2 C1
Ludgrove Hall EN4 . . . 2 C2
Ludham NW5 . . . 70 D3
Ludham Cl SE28 . . . 102 C1
Lud Lo TW15 . . . 148 A2
Ludlow Cl
Bromley BR2 . . . 209 A6
Harrow HA2 . . . 63 B4
Ludlow Ct Acton W3 . . 111 A4
East Barnet EN4 . . . 14 C6
Ludlow Rd Ealing W5 . . 87 C3
Feltham TW13 . . . 172 A6
Ludlow St EC1 . . . 242 A6
Ludlow Way N2 . . . 48 A5
Ludovick Wlk SW15 . . 133 C1
Ludwell Ho W14 . . . 254 B6
Ludwick Mews SE14 . 141 A5
Luffield Rd SE2 . . . 124 B3
Luffman Rd SE12 . . . 165 B1
Lugard Ho 2 W12 . . . 112 B5
Lugard Rd SE15 . . . 140 B4
Lugg App E12 . . . 78 C5
Luke Ho 32 E1 . . . 96 B1
Lukes Ct N3 . . . 47 C6
Luke St EC2 . . . 95 C3 243 A6
Lukin Cres E4 . . . 20 B1
Lukin St E1 . . . 96 C1
Lullingstone Cl BR5 . . 190 B3
Lullingstone Cres
BR5 . . . 190 B3
Lullingstone Ho 21
SE15 . . . 140 C6
Lullingstone La
SE13 . . . 164 B5
Lullingstone Rd 3
DA17 . . . 147 B6
Lullington Garth
Borehamwood WD6 . . 10 D6
Bromley BR1 . . . 186 C3
Finchley N12 . . . 29 B5
Lullington Rd
Dagenham RM9 . . . 81 A1
Penge SE20 . . . 184 A3
Lulot Gdns N19 . . . 71 B6
Lulworth
Camden Town NW1 . . . 71 D1
Walworth SE17 . . . 262 C2
Lulworth Ave
Hounslow TW5,
TW7 . . . 130 A5
Wembley HA9 . . . 43 C2
Lulworth Cl HA2 . . . 63 B5
Lulworth Cres CR4 . . 180 C1
Lulworth Ct N14 . . . 16 A1
Lulworth Dr HA5 . . . 41 A2
Lulworth Gdns HA2 . . . 63 B6
Lulworth Ho SW8 . . . 270 C3
Lulworth Rd
Bexley DA16 . . . 145 D3
Chislehurst SE9 . . . 166 A2
Peckham SE15 . . . 140 B3
Lulworth Waye UB4 . . . 84 B1
Lumen Rd HA9 . . . 65 D6
Lumiere Bldg The E7 . . 77 D3
Lumiere Ct 7 SW17 . . 159 A2
Lumina Bldg 1 E14 . . 120 A5
Lumley Cl DA17 . . . 125 C1
Lumley Ct WC2 . . . 250 B5
Lumley Flats SW1 . . . 258 A2
Lumley Gdns SM3 . . . 217 A3
Lumley Ho KT3 . . . 199 B1
Lumley Rd SM1, SM3 . 217 A3
Lumley St W1 . . . 238 B1
Lumsdon NW8 . . . 91 D6
Luna Ho 6 SE16 . . . 118 A4
Lunan Ho 14 E3 . . . 97 B5
Luna Rd CR7 . . . 205 A6
Lundin Wlk WD19 . . . 22 D6
Lund Point E15 . . . 98 A6
Lundy Dr UB3 . . . 105 C2
Lunham Rd SE19 . . . 183 C4
Luntley Pl E1 . . . 96 A2
Lupin Cl Croydon CR0 206 D1
Streatham SW2 . . . 160 D2
Lupin Cres IG11 . . . 78 D2
Lupino Ct SE11 . . . 260 D4
Lupin Point SE1 . . . 253 D1
Lupton Cl SE12 . . . 187 B6
Lupton St NW5 . . . 71 C4
Lupus Ct SE19 . . . 183 B2
Lupus St
SW1 . . . 115 C1 259 B1
Luralda Gdns E14 . . . 120 B1
Lurgan Ave W6 . . . 134 D6
Lurline Gdns
SW11 . . . 137 A4 268 B2
Luscombe Ct BR2 . . . 186 C1
Luscombe Ho SW18 . . 157 B6
Luscombe Way
SW8 . . . 138 A5 270 A4
Lusher Ho SW15 . . . 156 D5
Lushington Ho KT12 . 194 C3
Lushington Rd
Catford SE6 . . . 185 D5
Willesden Green NW10 90 B5
Lushington Terr 11
E8 . . . 74 A3
Lutea Ho SM2 . . . 218 A1
Luther Cl HA8 . . . 11 A2
Luther King Cl E17 . . . 53 A3
Luther Mews 2
TW11 . . . 174 D5
Luther Rd TW11 . . . 174 D5
Luton Pl SE10 . . . 142 A5
Luton Rd Newham E13 . 99 A3
Sidcup DA14 . . . 168 C1
Walthamstow E17 . . . 53 B6
Luton St NW8 . . 92 B3 236 D5
Luttrell Ave SW15 . . . 156 B6
Lutwyche Rd SE6 . . . 163 B2
Lutyens Ho SW1 . . . 259 A1
Luxborough Ho W1 . 238 A4
Luxborough St
W1 . . . 93 A2 238 A4
Luxborough Twr W1 . 238 A4
Luxembourg Mews 2
E15 . . . 76 C3
Luxemburg Gdns
W6 . . . 112 D2
Luxfield Rd SE9 . . . 166 A3
Luxford St SE16 . . . 118 D2
Luxmore St SE4 . . . 141 B4
Luxor St SE5 . . . 139 A2
Lyall Ave SE21 . . . 183 D6
Lyall Mews
SW1 . . . 115 A3 258 A5
Lyall Mews W SW1 . . 258 A5
Lyall St SW1 . 115 A3 258 A5
Lyal Rd E3 . . . 97 A5
Lycett Ho 10 SW2 . . . 160 A4
Lycett Pl 3 W12 . . . 112 A4
Lychgate Ct 4 N12 . . . 30 B5
Lychgate Manor HA1 . . 42 C2
Lych Gate Wlk UB3 . . 105 D6
Lyconby Gdns CR0 . . 207 A2
Lycott Gr SE22 . . . 161 D6
Lydd Cl DA14 . . . 167 C1
Lydden Ct SE9 . . . 167 C5
Lydden Gr SW18 . . . 157 D4
Lydden Rd SW18 . . . 157 D4
Lydd Rd DA7 . . . 147 B5
Lydeard Rd E6 . . . 78 B1
Lydford NW1 . . . 232 B5
Lydford Cl 22 N16 . . . 73 C3
Lydford Rd
Brondesbury NW2 . . . 68 D2
Paddington W9 . . . 91 B3
Tottenham N15 . . . 51 B4
Lydgate Ho 8 N16 . . . 73 C3
Lydhurst Ave SW2 . . . 160 B2

Lydia Ct 2 N12 ....30 A4
Lydia Lodge HA1......64 C4
Lydney Cl
Camberwell SE15.... 139 C5
Putney SW19....... 157 A2
Lydon Rd SW4.......137 C2
Lydstep Rd BR7......188 C6
Lydwell Ho 29 SW8.. 137 D3
Lyford Rd SW18......158 C3
Lyford St SE18.......122 A2
Lygoe Ho 18 N6.......49 D2
Lygoe Rd N2..........30 B2
Lygon Ho 2 E2.........96 A4
Lygon Pl SW1....... 258 C5
Lyham Cl SW2........160 A5
Lyham Rd SW2.......160 A5
Lyle Cl CR4..........203 A2
Lyle Ct SM4..........202 B3
Lyle Pk SW15....... 156 D5
Lyly Ho SE1......... 262 D5
Lyme Farm Rd SE12..143 B1
Lyme Gr E9...........74 C1
Lyme Grove Ho 2 E9 .74 C1
Lymer Ave SE19...... 183 D5
Lyme Rd DA16.......146 B4
Lymescote Gdns
SM1 ....217 C6
Lyme St NW1..93 C6 232 A6
Lyminge Cl DA14.... 189 D6
Lyminge Gdns SW17,
SW18 ....158 C3
Lymington Ave N22...32 D1
Lymington Cl
Mitcham SW16 ..... 181 D1
2 Newham E6 ......100 B2
Lymington Ct SM1...218 A5
Lymington Dr HA4....61 B6
Lymington Gdns
KT19........... 215 D3
Lymington Mans
NW6..............69 D2
Lymington Rd
Dagenham RM8.......58 D1
Hampstead NW6......69 D2
Lyminster Cl UB4 .....85 A2
Lympne N17..........33 B1
Lympstone Gdns
SE15.............140 A5
Lynbridge Gdns N13...32 D6
Lynbrook Gr SE15....139 C5
Lynchen Cl TW5 .....128 B4
Lynch Wlk 2 SE8.....141 B6
Lyncott Cres SW4....137 B1
Lyncourt SE3........142 B3
Lyncroft Ave HA5.....41 A4
Lyncroft Gdns
Ealing W13......... 109 C5
Hampstead NW6......69 C3
Hounslow TW3...... 152 A6
Lyncroft Mans 4
NW6..............69 C3
Lyndale NW2.........69 B5
Lyndale Ave NW2.....69 B5
Lyndale Cl SE3...... 142 D6
Lyndean Ind Est SE2 124 C3
Lynde Ho
2 Clapham SW4.... 137 D2
Walton-on-T KT12 ... 194 C3
Lynden Gate SW15...156 B4
Lyndenhurst SE3 .... 142 D2
Lynden Hyrst CR0... 221 D6
Lyndhurst BR7....... 188 D4
Lyndhurst Ave
Colney Hatch N12 .....30 D4
Edgware NW7 ....27 C4
Mitcham SW16 ..... 181 D1
Pinner HA5..........22 B2
Southall UB1 .... 107 D5
Sunbury TW16...... 194 A6
Tolworth KT5....... 198 D1
Twickenham TW2,
TW4 .... 151 C3
Lyndhurst Cl
Bexleyheath DA7.... 147 D2
Neasden NW10 ....67 B5
Orpington BR6....... 226 D4
South Croydon CR0 .. 221 D5
Lyndhurst Ct
8 Belmont SM2 .... 217 C1
11 Woodford E18......37 A2
Lyndhurst Dr
Leytonstone E10 ......54 A2
New Malden KT3 .... 199 D2
Lyndhurst Gdns
Barking IG11.........79 C2
Enfield EN1 ....5 C1
Lyndhurst Gdns *continued*
Hampstead NW3......70 B3
Hendon N3..........29 A2
Ilford IG2...........57 B3
Pinner HA5..........22 B2
Lyndhurst Gr SE5,
SE15 .... 139 D3
Lyndhurst Ho 2
SW15 ....156 A4
Lyndhurst House Prep
Sch NW3 ....70 B3
Lyndhurst Lo 3 E14 .120 B2
Lyndhurst Rd
Bexleyheath DA7.... 147 D2
Chingford E4 ....36 A3
Edmonton N18........34 A6
Greenford UB6........85 D3
Hampstead NW3.......70 B3
Thornton Heath CR7 . 204 C5
Tottenham N22 ....32 C4
Lyndhurst Sch SE5...139 B3
Lyndhurst Sq SE15... 139 D4
Lyndhurst Terr NW3...70 B3
Lyndhurst Way
Belmont SM2....... 217 C1
Camberwell SE15.... 139 D3
Lyndon Ave
Bexley DA15....... 167 D6
Hackbridge SM6 .... 219 A5
Pinner HA5...........23 A4
Lyndon Rd DA17 .....125 C2
Lyndon Yd SW17..... 179 D6
Lyndum Ct N22 ....32 C2
Lyne Cres E17 ....35 B2
Lyne Ct NW9..........45 B2
Lynegrove Ave
TW15 ....171 A5
Lyneham Wlk
Hackney E5 ....75 A3
Pinner HA5...........39 D6
Lynette Ave SW4.....159 C5
Lynfield Ct SE23 .... 162 D4
Lynford Cl
Barnet Gate EN5 ......11 D6
Burnt Oak HA8........27 A2
Lynford French Ho
SE17............. 262 A2
Lynford Gdns
Edgware HA8.........10 D1
Ilford IG3...........79 D6
Lynford Terr N9.......17 D3
Lyngham Ct 10 N4 ....50 A2
Lynhurst Cres UB10...61 B1
Lynhurst Ct NW8.... 229 C5
Lynhurst Rd UB10.....61 A1
Lynmere Rd DA16.....146 B3
Lyn Mews 12 E3 ......97 B4
Lynmouth Ave
Enfield EN1 ....17 D5
West Barnes SM4 ... 200 D2
Lynmouth Dr HA4.....62 B5
Lynmouth Gdns
Heston TW5........ 128 D4
Wembley UB6 ....65 B1
Lynmouth Rd
Fortis Green N2.......48 D5
Stamford Hill N16 .....51 D1
Walthamstow E17 .....53 A4
Wembley UB6 ....87 B6
Lynn Cl
Ashford TW15 ....171 B5
Harrow HA3..........24 B1
Lynn Ct SW16....... 181 D5
Lynne Cl 7 BR6 .... 227 D2
Lynne Ct
Forest Hill SE23.......163 B4
Hampstead NW6......69 D1
South Croydon CR2 .. 221 C4
Wimbledon SW20 .....178 B2
Lynnett Ct E9.........75 A2
Lynnett Rd RM8.......58 D1
Lynne Way UB5.......84 D5
Lynne Wlk KT10......212 A3
Lynn Ho SE15........140 A6
Lynn Mews E11.......76 C6
Lynn Rd
Balham SW12 ....159 B4
Ilford IG2............57 B2
Leyton E11 ....76 C5
Lynn St EN2 ....5 B4
Lynsted Cl
Bexley DA6......... 169 D6
Bromley BR1 .... 187 C1
Lynsted Ct 4 BR3....185 A1
Lynsted Gdns SE9... 143 D2
Lynton KT7..........197 A2
Lynton Ave
Ealing W13...........87 A1
Hyde The NW9 ....45 D5
North Finchley N12 ....30 B6
Lynton Cl
Chessington KT9 .... 214 A4
Isleworth TW7...... 130 D1
Willesden NW10 ......67 D3
Lynton Cres IG2 ......56 D3
Lynton Ct
Bowes Pk N13 ....32 A5
9 Dagenham W3 .....89 A1
Penge SE20 ....184 B2
Sutton SM2 .... 218 A2
Lynton Est SE1.......118 A2
Lynton Gdns
Enfield EN1 ....17 C4
Friern Barnet N11 .....31 D4
Lynton Grange N2.....48 D6
Lynton Ho 16 W2.....91 D1
Lynton Lo N5.........72 D3
Lynton Mans SE1 ... 261 A6
Lynton Mead N20.......13 D2
Lynton Rd Acton W3 . 110 D6
Bermondsey SE1 .... 117 D2
Chingford E4 ....35 D5
Harrow HA2..........63 A6
Hornsey N8 ....50 A4
New Malden KT3 ....199 B4
Paddington NW6 ......91 B5
Thornton Heath CR0 . 204 C3
Lynton Terr 4 W3.....89 A1
Lynton Wlk UB4 ......83 C4
Lynwood Cl
Harrow HA2..........63 A5
Woodford E18 ....37 C2
Lynwood Ct TW15.....170 B5
Lynwood Dr KT4.....216 A6
Lynwood Gdns
Southall UB1 ....85 B1
Wallington CR0 ......220 B4
Lynwood Gr
Orpington BR6....... 211 C1
Southgate N21........16 C3
Lynwood Rd
Ealing W5............88 A3
Thames Ditton KT7... 196 D1
Upper Tooting SW17 . 180 D6
Lynx Terr SW19 ......157 C1
Lynx Way E16........ 121 D6
Lyon Bsns Pk IG11... 101 C5
Lyon Ct HA4..........39 D1
Lyon Ho NW8........ 237 A5
Lyon Meade HA7......25 C2
Lyon Park Ave HA0... 66 B2
Lyon Park Jun & Inf Schs
HA0 ....66 B1
Lyon Rd Harrow HA1...42 D3
Merton SW19....... 180 A2
Lyonsdown Ave EN5 ..14 A5
Lyonsdown Ct EN5 ....14 A6
Lyonsdown Rd EN5 ...14 A6
Lyonsdown Sch EN5 ..14 A6
Lyons Pl NW8.. 92 B3 236 C5
Lyon St N1 ....72 B1
Lyons Wlk W14 ..... 254 A4
Lyon Way UB6 ....86 C6
Lyoth Rd BR5........227 A6
Lyric Dr UB6..........85 D3
Lyric Mews SE26.....184 C6
Lyric Rd SW13 ...... 133 D4
Lysander 20 NW9 .....27 D2
Lysander Ct 8 EN5 ...13 D6
Lysander Gdns KT5 ..198 B3
Lysander Gr N19.......49 D1
Lysander Ho 10 E2.....96 B5
Lysander Mews N19 ..49 C1
Lysander Rd
Ruislip HA4 ....61 B6
Wallington CR0 ......220 B2
Lysander Way BR6 ...227 A5
Lysia Ct SW6 .... 134 D5
Lysias Rd SW12......159 B5
Lysia St SW6........ 134 D5
Lysons Wlk SW15....156 A6
Lytchet Rd BR1.......187 B3
Lytchet Way EN3.......6 C4
Lytchgate Cl CR2 ....221 C1
Lytcott Dr KT8 ....195 B6
Lytham Ave WD19.....22 D5
Lytham Cl SE28 ......103 A1
Lytham Ct 5 UB1.....85 D1
Lytham Gr W5 ....88 B4
Lytham St
SE17 ......117 B1 262 C1
Lyttelton Cl NW3......70 C1
Lyttelton Ct N2 ....48 A4
Lyttelton Rd
Hampstead Garden Suburb
N2...............48 A4
Leyton E10..........76 A5
Lytten Ct 6 W12.....112 A4
Lyttleton Ct UB4 ......84 C3
Lyttleton Ho 10 E9 ....74 C1
Lyttleton Rd N8.......50 C6
Lytton Ave Enfield EN3 ..7 A5
Southgate N13........16 C2
Lytton Cl
Hampstead Garden Suburb
N2...............48 B4
Northolt UB5 ....63 B1
Lytton Ct WC1 ...... 240 B3
Lytton Gdns SM6.... 219 D4
Lytton Gr SW15......157 A5
Lytton Ho 3 TW12 .. 173 D4
Lytton Rd
Leytonstone E11 ......54 C2
New Barnet EN5 ....2 A1
Pinner HA5...........23 A3
Lytton Strachey Path 8
SE28.............124 B6
Lyveden Rd
Greenwich SE3 ......143 B5
Mitcham SW17,
SW19 .... 180 D4

M

Mabbett Ho 2 SE18..144 C6
Mabel Crout Ct SE9 ...145 B1
Mabel Evetts Ct UB3 .106 B6
Mabel Thornton Ho 12
N16...............73 B4
Maberley Cres SE19..184 A3
Maberley Ct SE19....184 A3
Maberley Rd SE19 ...182 C2
Mabledon Pl NW1,
WC1 .... 232 D1
Mablethorpe Rd
SW6 .... 264 A3
Mabley St E9 ....75 A3
Mablin Lo 3 IG9 ......21 C3
Mcadam Dr EN2 ....4 D3
Macallister Ho 8
SE18............ 144 D6
Macaret Cl N20.......14 A4
Macarthur Cl
London E7 ....77 A2
Wembley HA9 ....66 D2
MacArthur Ho 4
SW2 ....160 A4
Macartney Ho SE10 ..142 B5
Macaulay Ave KT10 ..212 C6
Macaulay CE Prim Sch
SW4...............137 B1
Macaulay Ct SW4....137 B2
Macaulay Ho
2 Kensal Town W10...91 A2
10 Stoke Newington
N16...............73 C5
Macaulay Rd
Clapham SW4 ....137 B2
Newham E6 ....99 D5
Macaulay Sq SW4....137 B1
Macaulay Way 2
SE28.............124 B5
McAuley Cl
Eltham SE9......... 166 C6
Lambeth SE1 116 C3 261 A6
Macauley Mews
SE13..............142 A3
McAusland Ho 5 E3..97 B5
Macbean St SE18 ... 122 D3
Macbeth Ho 4 N1.....95 C5
Macbeth St W6.......112 B1
McBride Ho 6 E3 ....97 B5
McCall Cl SW4.......138 A3
McCall Cres SE7 .....122 A1
McCall Ho N7 ....72 A4
Mccarthy Ct SW11 .. 267 B1
McCarthy Rd TW13.. 172 D5
Macclesfield Rd
Croydon SE25....... 206 C4
Shoreditch
EC1 ....95 A4 235 A2
Macclesfield St W1 . 249 D6
McClintock Pl EN3.....7 D6
McCoid Way SE1.... 252 A1
Mcconnell Ho SW8 . 269 C1
McCormick Ho 9
SW2 ....160 C3
McCrone Mews 3
NW3..............70 B2
McCullum Rd E3......97 B6
McDermott Cl SW11 .136 C2
McDermott Rd SE15 .140 A2
Macdonald Ave RM10 .81 D5
Macdonald Ct TW3...130 A1
McDonald Ho 1
KT2...............176 B3
Macdonald Ho 2
SW11 ....137 A3
Macdonald Rd
Chingford E17 ....36 A1
Dartmouth Pk N19.....71 C6
Forest Gate E7........77 A4
Friern Barnet N11 ......30 D5
McDonough Cl KT9 ..214 A4
McDougall Ct TW9...132 C3
Mcdougall Ho E2 ......96 A4
McDowall Cl E16 .....98 D2
McDowall Rd SE5....139 A4
Macduff Rd
SW11 ......137 A4 268 B2
Mace Cl E1..........118 B5
Mace Ho 2 E17 ....53 D6
McEntee Ave E17 .....35 A2
Mace St E2...........96 D5
McEwan Way E15.....98 B6
Macey Ho
Battersea SW11 .... 267 A1
10 Greenwich SE10.. 142 A6
Macfarlane La TW7 ..131 A6
Macfarlane Rd W12..112 C5
Macfarren Ho 7
W10 ....91 A4
MacFarren Pl NW1.. 238 B5
McGlashon Ho 15 E1..96 A3
McGrath Rd E15 ....76 D2
McGregor Ct 8 N1 ....95 C4
MacGregor Ho 2
SW12 .... 159 D3
McGregor Rd W11 ....91 B2
Macgregor Rd E16....99 C2
Mcguffie Ct E17 ......53 B6
Machell Rd SE15.....140 C2
McIndoe Ct N1 ..... 235 C6
McIntosh Cl SM6.....220 A1
McIntosh Ho 14
SE16..............118 C2
McIntyre Ct 19 SW4..138 A3
Mackay Ho 33 W12...112 B6
McKay Rd SW20 .....178 C4
Mackay Rd SW4 .....137 B2
McKellar Cl WD23.......8 A2
McKenna Ho 3 E3....97 B5
Mackennal St
NW8........92 C5 230 B4
Mackenzie Cl 7
W12 ....112 B6
Mackenzie Ho
5 Dollis Hill NW2.....68 A5
1 Hornsey N8........50 A5
Mackenzie Rd
Barnsbury N7.........72 B2
Penge BR3.......... 184 D1
Mackenzie Wlk E14..119 C5
McKerrell Rd SE15....140 A4
Mackeson Rd NW3.....70 D4
Mackie Ho 18 SW2...160 C4
Mackie Rd SW2.......160 C4
McKiernan Ct 2
SW11 ....136 C3
Mc Killop Way DA14..190 C3
McKinlay Ct
Beckenham BR3......185 B1
Bexley DA16........ 146 C2
McKinnon Wood Ho 16
E2.................96 A4
Mackintosh La E9.....74 D3
Macklin Ho SE23.....162 B2
Macklin St
WC2........94 A1 240 B2
Mackonochie Ho
EC1............. 241 A4
Mackrow Wlk 11
E14...............120 A6
Macks Rd SE16 ......118 A2
Mackworth Ho NW1 232 A2
Mackworth St NW1 . 232 A2
Mac Laren Mews
SW15 ....134 C1
Maclean Rd SE23 ....163 A5
Mcleod Ct SE21......162 A3

McLeod Ho 3 SE23 ... 162 C2
McLeod Rd SE2 ... 124 B2
Macleod Rd N21 ... 16 A6
McLeod's Mews
SW7 ... 113 D2 255 D4
Macleod St
SE17 ... 117 A1 262 B1
Maclise Rd
W14 ... 113 A3 254 A5
McManus Ho 2
SW11 ... 136 B2
McMillan Ct 2 SE6 . 164 D3
Macmillan Ct HA2 ... 41 C1
Mcmillan Ho SE4 ... 141 A2
Macmillan Ho
Cricklewood NW4 ... 68 B4
Lisson Gr NW8 ... 230 B1
McMillan St SE8 ... 141 C6
Macmillan Way
SW17 ... 181 B6
Mcmorran Ho 4 N7 ... 72 A4
McNair Rd UB2 ... 107 D3
Macnamara Ho
SW10 ... 266 C4
Mcneil Rd SE5 ... 139 C3
McNicol Dr NW10 ... 89 A5
Macoma Rd SE18 ... 145 B6
Macoma Terr SE18 ... 145 B6
Maconochies Rd 9
E14 ... 119 D1
Macquarie Way E14 . 119 D2
McRae La CR4 ... 202 D2
Macready Ho W1 ... 237 B3
Macready Pl 2 N7 ... 72 A4
Macroom Ho W9 ... 91 B4
Macroom Rd W9 ... 91 B4
Mac's Pl EC4 ... 241 B2
Madame Tussaud's★
NW1 ... 93 A3 238 A5
Madani Girls Sch 36
E1 ... 96 B1
Mada Rd BR6 ... 226 D5
Maddams St E3 ... 97 D3
Madderfields Ct N11 ... 31 D2
Maddison Cl
Finchley N2 ... 30 A1
Teddington TW11 ... 174 D4
Maddison Ct NW4 ... 28 C1
Maddocks Cl DA14 ... 191 A5
Maddocks Ho 3 E1 ... 118 B6
Maddock Way SE17 . 138 D6
Maddox Ct 1 E4 ... 20 B3
Maddox St W1 ... 248 D6
Madeira Ave BR1 ... 186 C3
Madeira Gr IG8 ... 37 C4
Madeira Rd
Edmonton N13 ... 16 D1
Leytonstone E11 ... 54 C1
Mitcham CR4 ... 202 D5
Streatham SW16 ... 182 A5
Madeleine Cl RM6 ... 58 C3
Madeleine Dr RM6 ... 58 C3
Madeley Ct W5 ... 88 A1
Madeley Rd W5 ... 88 A1
Madeline Gr IG1 ... 79 B3
Madeline Rd SE20 ... 184 A3
Madge Gill Way 4
E6 ... 100 A6
Madge Hill W7 ... 108 C6
Madinah Rd
7 Dalston E8 ... 74 A2
London E8 ... 74 A3
Madingley 11 KT1 ... 176 C1
Madingley Ct TW1 ... 153 C6
Madison Apartments
N11 ... 31 D3
Madison Cl SM2 ... 218 B1
Madison Cres DA7 ... 146 C5
Madison Ct 15 RM10 ... 81 D2
Madison Gdns
Beckenham BR2 ... 208 D6
Bexley DA7 ... 146 C5
Madison Ho E3 ... 98 A4
Madras Ho IG1 ... 78 D4
Madras Pl N7 ... 72 C2
Madras Rd IG1 ... 78 D4
Madrid Rd SW13 ... 134 A5
Madron St
SE17 ... 117 C1 263 B2
Mafeking Ave
Brentford TW8 ... 132 A6
Ilford IG2 ... 57 B2
Newham E6 ... 100 A5
Mafeking Rd
Enfield EN1 ... 5 D2
Newham E16 ... 98 D3
Tottenham N17 ... 34 A1
Magdala Ave N19 ... 71 C6
Magdala Rd
Isleworth TW7 ... 131 A2
South Croydon CR2 ... 221 B1
Magdalen Ct SE25 ... 206 A4
Magdalene Cl 7
SE15 ... 140 B3
Magdalene Gdns
7 East Barnet N11 ... 14 D3
Newham E6 ... 100 C3
Magdalene Ho 7
SW15 ... 156 D5
Magdalene Rd
TW17 ... 192 B6
Magdalen Pas E1 ... 253 D6
Magdalen Rd SW18 ... 158 B3
Magdalen St SE1 ... 253 A3
Magee St SE11 ... 138 C6
Magellan Bvd E16 ... 123 A6
Magellan Ct 11 NW10 . 67 B1
Magellan Ho 16 E1 ... 96 D3
Magellan Pl 25 E14 ... 119 C2
Magna Ct UB6 ... 86 B4
Magnaville Rd WD23 ... 8 D4
Magnetic Cres EN3 ... 7 B6
Magnet Rd HA9 ... 65 D6
Magnin Cl 5 E8 ... 96 A6
Magnolia Cl
Kingston u T KT2 ... 176 D4
Leyton E10 ... 75 C6
Magnolia Ct
13 Belmont SM2 ... 217 D1
Feltham TW14 ... 150 A3
2 Finchley N12 ... 29 D6
Forest Hill SE26 ... 184 C5
Harrow HA3 ... 44 B2
Hillingdon UB10 ... 60 D2
Northolt UB5 ... 85 A3
Richmond TW9 ... 132 D4
Wallington SM6 ... 219 B3
Wandsworth SW11 ... 158 D5
Magnolia Gdns HA8 ... 27 A6
Magnolia Ho 13 SE8 . 141 B6
Magnolia Lo E4 ... 19 D1
Magnolia Pl
Clapham Pk SW4 ... 160 A6
Ealing W5 ... 87 D2
Magnolia Rd W4 ... 132 D6
Magnolia Way KT19 . 215 A3
Magnolia Wharf W4 132 D6
Magpie Cl
Edgware NW9 ... 27 C1
Enfield EN1 ... 6 A4
Forest Gate E7 ... 76 D3
Magpie Hall Cl BR2 ... 210 A3
Magpie Hall La BR2 ... 210 B3
Magpie Hall Rd WD23 ... 8 C2
Magpie Ho 7 E3 ... 97 B6
Magpie Pl SE14 ... 141 A6
Magri Wlk 22 E1 ... 96 C2
Maguire Dr TW10 ... 175 C6
Maguire St
SE1 ... 117 D4 253 D2
Mahatma Gandhi Ind Est
1 SE24 ... 138 D1
Mahlon Ave HA4 ... 62 B2
Mahogany Cl SE16 ... 119 A5
Mahon Cl EN1 ... 5 D4
Mahoney Ho SE14 ... 141 B4
Maida Ave
Chingford E4 ... 19 D4
Little Venice
W2 ... 92 A3 236 B5
Maida Rd DA17 ... 125 C3
MAIDA VALE ... 91 D4
Maida Vale
W9 ... 92 A4 229 A1
Maida Vale Sta W9 ... 91 D4
Maida Way E4 ... 19 D4
Maiden Erlegh Ave
DA5 ... 169 A3
Maiden La
Borough The
SE1 ... 117 A5 252 B4
Camden Town NW1 ... 71 D1
Strand WC2 ... 116 A6 250 B6
Maiden Rd E15 ... 76 C1
Maidenstone Hill
SE10 ... 142 A4
Maids of Honour Row 4
TW9 ... 153 D6
Maidstone Bldgs
SE1 ... 252 C3
Maidstone Ct N11 ... 31 D4
Maidstone Ho 4 E14 . 97 D1
Maidstone Rd
Friern Barnet N11 ... 31 D4
Ruxley DA14 ... 191 C3
Mail Coach Yd 23 E2 ... 95 C4
Main Ave EN1 ... 17 D6
Main Dr HA9 ... 65 D5
Main Rd
Chislehurst BR5 ... 190 C1
Sidcup DA14 ... 167 C1
Mainridge Rd BR7,
SE9 ... 188 C6
Main St TW13 ... 172 D5
Mainwaring Ct 3
CR4 ... 181 A1
Main Yd E9 ... 75 C2
Mais Ho SE26 ... 162 B2
Maismore St SE15 ... 140 A6
Maison Alfort HA3 ... 24 C2
Maisonettes The
SM1 ... 217 B3
Maitland Cl
3 Greenwich SE10 ... 141 D5
Hounslow TW4 ... 129 B2
Maitland Ct W2 ... 246 C6
Maitland Ho
Chelsea SW1 ... 269 A6
16 South Hackney E2 ... 96 C5
MAITLAND PARK ... 70 D2
Maitland Park Rd
NW3 ... 70 D2
Maitland Park Villas
NW3 ... 70 D2
Maitland Pl E5 ... 74 C4
Maitland Rd
Penge SE26 ... 184 D4
Stratford E15 ... 76 D2
Majendie Rd SE18 ... 123 B1
Majestic Ct N4 ... 50 D1
Majestic Way CR4 ... 180 D1
Major Cl SW9 ... 138 D2
Majorie Mews 6 E1 ... 96 D1
Major Rd
22 Bermondsey
SE16 ... 118 A3
Stratford New Town
E15 ... 76 B3
Makepeace Ave N6 ... 71 A6
Makepeace Mans N6 ... 71 A6
Makepeace Rd
Northolt UB5 ... 85 A6
Wanstead E11 ... 55 A5
Makinen Ho 5 IG9 ... 21 C3
Makins St SW3 ... 257 B3
Malabar Ct 20 W12 ... 112 B6
Malabar St E14 ... 119 C4
Malam Ct SE11 ... 261 A3
Malam Gdns 3 E14 ... 119 D6
Malatia CR2 ... 221 A2
Malay Ho 2 E1 ... 118 C5
Malborough Ho 3
N20 ... 14 D1
Malbrook Rd SW15 ... 134 B1
Malbury Ct N22 ... 32 A3
Malcolm Cl SE20 ... 184 C3
Malcolm Cres NW4 ... 46 A3
Malcolm Ct Ealing W5 ... 88 B3
Hendon NW4 ... 46 A3
Stanmore HA7 ... 25 C5
Stratford E7 ... 76 D2
Malcolm Dr KT6 ... 198 A1
Malcolm Ho 13 N1 ... 95 C5
Malcolm Pl E2 ... 96 C3
Malcolm Prim Sch
SE20 ... 184 C3
Malcolm Rd
Bethnal Green E1 ... 96 C3
Croydon SE25 ... 206 A3
Ickenham UB10 ... 60 B4
Penge SE20 ... 184 C3
Wimbledon SW19 ... 179 A4
Malcolmson Ho SW1 259 D1
Malcolms Way N14 ... 15 C6
Malcolm Way E11 ... 55 A5
Malden Ave
Croydon SE25 ... 206 B6
Northolt UB6 ... 64 C2
Malden Cres NW1 ... 71 A2
Malden Ct
Stoke Newington N4 ... 51 A3
West Barnes KT3 ... 200 B6
Malden Ctr The KT3 . 199 D5
Malden Green Ave
KT4 ... 200 A1
Malden Hill KT3 ... 199 D6
Malden Hill Gdns
KT3 ... 199 D6
Malden Junc KT3 ... 199 D4
Malden Manor Prim Sch
KT3 ... 199 C2
Malden Manor Sta
KT3 ... 199 C2
Malden Parochial Prim
Sch KT4 ... 199 C1
Malden Pk KT3 ... 199 D3
Malden Pl NW5 ... 71 A3
Malden Rd
Camden Town NW5 ... 71 A2
Cheam KT4, SM3 ... 216 D4
New Malden KT3,
KT4 ... 199 D2
Malden Way KT3 ... 200 A5
Malden Way (Kingston
By-Pass) KT3, KT5 . 199 C4
Maldon Cl
Camberwell SE5 ... 139 C2
Shoreditch N1 ... 235 B6
Stratford New Town
E15 ... 76 B3
Maldon Ct
Barking E6 ... 100 C6
Wallington SM6 ... 219 C3
Maldon Rd Acton W3 . 111 A6
Edmonton N9 ... 17 D1
Wallington SM6 ... 219 B3
Maldon Wlk IG8 ... 37 C4
Malet Pl WC1 ... 239 C5
Malet St WC1 ... 93 D2 239 D4
Maley Ave SE27 ... 160 D2
Malford Ct E18 ... 37 A1
Malford Gr E18 ... 54 D6
Malfort Rd SE5 ... 139 C2
Malham Cl N11 ... 31 A4
Malham Rd SE23 ... 162 D3
Malham Road Ind Est
SE23 ... 162 D3
Malindi Ct N8 ... 49 D4
Malins Cl EN5 ... 12 C6
Malins Ct SW12 ... 159 A5
Mallaig Ct HA8 ... 10 D2
Mallams Mews 1
SW9 ... 138 D2
Mallard Cl
1 Hackney E9 ... 75 B2
Hanwell W7 ... 108 C4
Kilburn NW6 ... 91 C6
New Barnet EN5 ... 14 B5
Twickenham TW4 ... 151 C4
Mallard Ct
Chingford E4 ... 20 B4
Ilford IG1 ... 79 A6
Kingsbury NW9 ... 45 A2
Little Ilford E12 ... 78 B3
16 Richmond TW10 ... 153 D5
Walthamstow E17 ... 54 B6
Mallard Ho
8 Camberwell
SE15 ... 139 D4
St John's Wood NW8 . 230 A3
Mallard Path 3
SE28 ... 123 B3
Mallard Pl TW1 ... 153 A1
Mallard Point 6 E3 ... 97 C4
Mallards E11 ... 55 A2
Mallards Rd
Barking IG11 ... 102 A3
Woodford IG8 ... 37 B3
Mallard Way NW9 ... 45 A2
Mallard Wlk
Beckenham BR3 ... 206 D4
Sidcup DA14 ... 190 C4
Mall Ct W5 ... 110 A6
Mallet Dr UB5 ... 63 B3
Mallet Ho 11 SW15 ... 156 A6
Mallet Rd SE13 ... 164 B5
Mall Galleries★ SW1 249 D4
Malling SE13 ... 163 D6
Malling Cl CR0 ... 206 C3
Malling Gdns SM4 ... 202 A3
Malling Ho 9 BR3 ... 185 C3
Malling Way BR2 ... 208 D2
Mallinson Ct 2 E11 ... 76 C6
Mallinson Rd
Wallington SM6 ... 219 D5
Wandsworth SW11 ... 158 D6
Mallinson Sp Ctr N6 ... 48 D2
Mallon Gdns E1 ... 243 D3
Mallord St
SW3 ... 136 B6 266 D6
Mallory Bldgs EC1 ... 241 C5
Mallory Cl
London SE4 ... 141 A1
South Bromley E14 ... 98 C3
Mallory Gdns EN4 ... 15 A4
Mallory St
NW8 ... 92 C3 237 B6
Mallow Cl CR0 ... 206 D1
Mallow Ct
Colney Hatch N12 ... 30 C4
Lewisham SE13 ... 142 A3
Mallow Mead NW7 ... 29 A3
Mallow St EC1 ... 242 C6
Mallows The UB10 ... 60 D5
Mall Rd W6 ... 112 B1
Mall Sh Ctr The RM10 . 81 C2
Mall Studios 9 NW3 ... 70 D3
Mall The
6 Bexley DA6 ... 147 C1
Brentford TW8 ... 131 D6
4 Bromley BR1 ... 209 A6
Ealing W5 ... 110 A6
Harrow HA3 ... 44 B3
Kingston u T KT6 ... 197 D4
Mortlake SW14 ... 155 A6
Palmers Green N14 ... 16 A1
St James
SW1 ... 115 D5 249 C3
Mall The N22 ... 32 C1
Mall The (Sch) TW2 ... 152 B1
Malmains Cl BR3 ... 208 B5
Malmains Way BR3 ... 208 B5
Malmesbury 30 E2 ... 96 C5
Malmesbury Cl HA5 ... 40 A5
Malmesbury Prim Sch
Morden SM4 ... 202 A3
25 Tower Hamlets E3 ... 97 B4
Malmesbury Rd
Bow E3 ... 97 B5
Morden SM4 ... 202 A3
Newham E16 ... 98 C2
Woodford E18 ... 36 D2
Malmesbury Terr E16 . 98 D2
Malmsey Ho SE11 ... 260 D2
Malmsmead Ho E9 ... 75 A3
Malorees Jun & Inf Schs
NW6 ... 68 D1
Malory Cl BR3 ... 185 A1
Malpas Dr HA5 ... 40 D4
Malpas Rd
Dagenham RM9 ... 80 D2
Hackney E8 ... 74 B2
New Cross SE4 ... 141 B3
Malta Rd E10 ... 53 C2
Malta St EC1 ... 241 D6
Maltby Dr EN1 ... 6 B5
Maltby Rd KT9 ... 214 C2
Maltby St
SE1 ... 117 D3 263 C6
Maltham Terr N18 ... 34 B4
Malthouse Dr
Chiswick W4 ... 133 D6
Feltham TW13 ... 172 D5
Malthouse Pas
SW13 ... 133 C3
Malthus Path 7
SE28 ... 124 C5
Malting Ho E14 ... 119 B6
Maltings W4 ... 110 C1
Maltings Cl
Barnes SW13 ... 133 C3
South Bromley E3 ... 98 C3
Maltings Lo W4 ... 133 C5
Maltings Pl
Bermondsey SE1 ... 253 B2
Parsons Green SW6 . 265 D1
Maltings The BR6 ... 211 D1
Malting Way TW7 ... 130 D2
Malt Mill SE1 ... 253 C3
Malton Ho SE25 ... 205 C5
Malton Mews
1 Notting Hill W10 ... 91 A1
Plumstead Comm
SE18 ... 145 C6
Malton Rd W10 ... 91 A1
Malton St SE18 ... 145 C6
Maltravers St WC2 ... 251 A6
Malt St SE1 ... 140 A6
Malva Cl SW18 ... 157 D6
Malvern Ave
Chingford E4 ... 36 B3
Erith DA7 ... 147 A5
Harrow HA2 ... 63 B5

Malvern Cl
Bushey WD23 8 A5
Ickenham UB10 60 C6
Mitcham CR4 203 C6
Notting Hill W10 91 B2
Penge SE20 184 A1
Surbiton KT6 198 A1
Malvern Ct
Belmont SM2 217 C1
5 East Barnet N20 14 C2
15 Shepherd's Bush W12 112 A4
South Kensington SW7 256 D4
3 Surbiton KT6 198 A1
Malvern Dr
Feltham TW13 172 D5
Ilford IG3 79 D4
Woodford IG8 37 C6
Malvern Gdns
Cricklewood NW2 69 A6
Harrow HA3 44 A5
Malvern Ho
London N16 51 D1
SE17 262 B1
Malvern Lo N12 30 B6
Malvern Mews NW6 91 C4
Malvern Pl NW6 91 B4
Malvern Rd
Dalston E8 74 A1
Enfield EN3 7 A6
Hampton TW12 173 C3
Harlington UB3 127 C5
Hornsey N8 50 C6
Leytonstone E11 76 D6
Maida Vale NW6 91 C4
Newham E6 100 A6
Surbiton KT6 198 A1
Thornton Heath CR7 204 C5
Tottenham Hale N17 52 A6
Upper Holloway N19 49 D1
Malvern Terr
Edmonton N9 17 D3
Islington N1 234 A6
Malvern Way W13 87 B2
Malwood Rd SW12 159 B5
Malyons Rd SE13 163 D6
Malyons Terr SE13 163 D6
Malyons The TW17 193 B3
Managers St 8 E14 120 A5
Manatee Pl SM6 219 D5
Manaton Cl SE15 140 B2
Manaton Cres UB1 85 C1
Manbey Gr E15 76 C2
Manbey Park Rd E15 76 C2
Manbey Rd E15 76 C2
Manbey St E15 76 C2
Manbre Rd W6 134 C6
Manbrough Ave E6 100 C4
Manchester Ct E16 99 B1
Manchester Dr W10 91 A3
Manchester Gr E14 120 A1
Manchester Ho SE17 262 B2
Manchester Mans N19 49 D2
Manchester Mews W1 238 A3
Manchester Rd
Cubitt Town E14 120 A3
South Norwood CR7 205 A6
Tottenham N15 51 B3
Manchester Sq W1 93 A1 238 B2
Manchester St W1 93 A2 238 A3
Manchester Way RM10 81 D4
Manchuria Rd SW11 159 A5
Manciple St SE1 117 B3 262 D6
Mandalay Ho 6 N16 73 B4
Mandalay Rd SW4 159 C6
Mandarin Ct
6 Deptford SE8 141 C6
Willesden NW10 67 B2
Mandarin Way UB4 84 D1
Mandela Cl
36 Shepherd's Bush W12 112 B6
Stonebridge NW10 67 A1
Mandela Ho
Plumstead Comm SE18 145 B6
18 Spitalfields E2 95 D4
Mandela Rd E16 99 A1
Mandela St
Camden Town NW1 93 C6 232 B6
Kennington SW9 138 C5
Mandela Way SE1 117 C2 263 B4
Manderville Ho SE1 263 D2
Mandeville Cl
5 Greenwich SE3 142 D5
Merton SW19 179 A2
Mandeville Ct
Hampstead NW3 69 D3
Highams Pk E4 35 A6
Mandeville Ctyd SW11 268 A1
Mandeville Dr KT6 197 D1
Mandeville Ho 8 SW4 159 C6
Mandeville Pl W1 238 B2
Mandeville Prim Sch E5 74 D5
Mandeville Rd
Enfield EN3 7 A6
Isleworth TW7 131 A3
Littleton TW17 192 C4
Northolt UB5 63 C1
Osidge N14 15 C2
Mandeville Sch UB5 63 B2
Mandeville St E5 75 A5
Mandrake Rd SW17 158 D1
Mandrake Way 3 E15 76 C1
Mandrell Rd SW2 160 A6
Manesty Ct N14 15 D4
Manette St W1 239 D1
Manfred Ct 7 SW15 157 B6
Manfred Rd SW15 157 B6
Manger Rd N7 72 A2
Mangold Way 4 DA18 125 A3
Manilla Ct RM6 58 B3
Manilla St E14 119 C4
Manister Rd SE2 124 A3
Manitoba Ct 29 SE16 118 C4
Manitoba Gdns 6 BR6 227 D2
Manley Ct N16 73 D5
Manley Ho SE11 261 A2
Manley St NW1 231 A6
Manly Dixon Dr EN3 7 A6
Mann Cl 3 CR0 221 A5
Manneby Prior N1 233 D3
Mannering Ho 16 SW2 160 B6
Manning Ct 3 SE28 124 B5
Manningford Cl EC1 234 C2
Manning Gdns
Croydon CR0 206 B2
Harrow HA3 43 D2
Manning Ho
3 Notting Hill W11 91 A1
6 Walthamstow E17 54 A6
Manning Pl TW10 154 B5
Manning Rd
Dagenham RM10 81 C1
Walthamstow E17 53 A4
Manningtree Cl SW19 157 A3
Manningtree Rd HA4 62 B4
Manningtree St 2 E1 96 A1
Mannin Rd RM6 58 B2
Mannock Cl NW9 45 B6
Mannock Mews IG8 37 B2
Mannock Rd N22 50 D6
Mann's Cl TW7 152 D6
Manns Rd HA8 26 C4
Manny Shinwell Ho SW6 264 D5
Manoel Rd TW2 152 A2
Manor Ave
Hounslow TW4 128 D3
New Cross SE4 141 B3
Northolt UB5 63 B1
Manorbrook SE12, SE3 143 A1
Manor Circus TW9 132 C2
Manor Cl Barnet EN5 1 A1
Edgware NW7 27 B5
Higham Hill E17 35 A1
Kingsbury NW9 44 D4
New Malden KT4 199 C1
Ruislip HA4 39 D1
Thamesmead SE28 102 C1
Manor Cottages App N2 30 A1
Manor Cotts N2 30 A1
Manor Court Lo 12 E18 37 A2
Manor Court Rd W7 108 C6
Manor Cres KT5 198 C3
Manor Croft HA8 26 C4
Manor Ct
4 Barking IG11 79 D1
7 Brixton SW2 160 B6
Camberwell SE15 139 D4
Chingford E4 20 C3
Fortis Green N2 48 D4
Friern Barnet N20 14 D1
Gunnersbury W3 110 C2
5 Hackbridge SM6 219 A5
Harrow HA1 42 D3
Kingston u T KT2 176 C2
Osidge N14 15 D2
Parsons Green SW6 265 D1
Streatham SW16 160 A1
Surbiton KT5 198 C3
8 Sutton SM1 218 A4
Twickenham TW2 152 A2
Walthamstow E10 53 D1
5 Wembley HA9 66 A3
Manordene Cl KT7 197 A1
Manordene Rd SE28 102 D1
Manor Dr
East Barnet N14 15 B3
Edgware NW7 27 B5
Feltham TW13 172 D5
Friern Barnet N20 14 D1
Hinchley Wood KT10 213 A5
Sunbury TW16 172 A1
Surbiton KT5 198 C3
Wembley HA9 66 B4
West Ewell KT19 215 C2
Manor Dr N KT3, KT4 199 B2
Manor Dr The KT4 199 D1
Manor Farm Ave TW17 192 D3
Manor Farm Cl KT4 199 C1
Manor Farm Ct E6 100 B4
Manor Farm Dr E4 20 C1
Manor Farm Rd
Thornton Heath CR7, SW16 182 C1
Wembley HA0 87 D5
Manorfield Cl 3 N19 71 C4
Manorfield Prim Sch 8 E14 97 D2
Manorfields Cl BR7 211 D6
Manor Gate UB5 63 A1
Manorgate Rd KT2 176 C2
Manor Gdns
8 Chiswick W4 111 C1
Clapham SW4 137 C3
Gunnersbury W3 110 C2
Hampton TW12 174 A3
Merton SW20 179 B1
Richmond TW10, TW9 132 B1
Ruislip HA4 62 C3
South Croydon CR2 221 D2
Sunbury TW16 172 A1
Upper Holloway N7 72 A5
Manor Gr
Beckenham BR3 185 D1
Deptford SE15 140 C6
Richmond TW9 132 C2
Manor Gt SW15 157 A6
Manor Hall Ave NW4 28 D1
Manor Hall Dr NW4 28 D1
Manor Hall Gdns E10 53 C1
Manor Ho
Brentford TW8 109 C1
Manor Pk E12 77 D4
Osidge N14 15 D3
Paddington NW1 237 B4
Twickenham TW2 152 C2
Wallington SM6 219 B3
Manor Ho The
Bexley DA5 169 D3
Chislehurst SE9 188 A5
Manor House Ct
Lower Halliford TW17 192 D2
Paddington W9 236 A5
Manor House Dr NW6 68 D1
Manor House Est HA7 25 B5
Manor House Gdns E11 55 B3
Manor House Sta N4 50 D1
Manor House Way TW7 131 B2
Manor Jun & Inf Schs IG11 79 D2
Manor La
Feltham TW13 150 A2
Harlington UB3 127 B6
Hither Green SE12 164 C5
Sunbury TW16 172 B1
Sutton SM1 218 A3
Manor Lane Terr SE13 164 C6
Manor Lo NW2 68 D2
Manor Mans
7 Hampstead NW3 70 C2
Tufnell Pk N7 72 A5
Manor Mead Sch TW17 192 D4
Manor Mews
New Cross SE4 141 B3
Paddington NW6 91 C5
Manor Mount SE23 162 C3
Manor Oak Mans SE22 162 B5
Manor Par
Harrow HA1 42 D3
Stoke Newington N16 73 D6
MANOR PARK 78 A4
Manor Park Cl BR4 207 D1
Manor Park Cres HA8 26 C4
Manor Park Dr HA2 41 D6
Manor Park Gdns HA8 26 C4
Manor Park Par SE13 142 B1
Manor Park Prim Sch 8 SM1 218 A3
Manor Park Rd
Chislehurst BR7 189 B2
Dagenham NW10 89 D6
East Finchley N2 48 B6
Manor Pk E12 77 D4
Sutton SM1 218 A3
West Wickham BR4 207 D1
Manor Park Sta E12 77 D4
Manor Pk
Chislehurst BR7 189 B2
Lewisham SE13 164 C6
Richmond TW9 132 B1
Manor Pl
Chislehurst BR7 189 B1
East Bedfont TW14 150 A3
Mitcham CR4 203 C6
Newington SE17 117 A1 262 A2
Sutton SM1 217 D4
Walton-on-T KT12 194 A2
Manor Prim Sch E15 98 C5
Manor Rd
Ashford TW15 170 C5
Barking IG11 79 D2
Barnet EN5 1 A1
Beckenham BR3 185 D1
Belmont SM2 217 B1
Bowes Pk N22 32 A4
Dagenham RM6 58 D3
Ealing W13 109 A6
East Molesey KT8 196 B5
Enfield EN2 5 B3
Harrow HA1 43 A3
Hayes UB3 84 A1
Higham Hill E17 35 A1
Loughton IG10 21 B5
Merton SW20 179 B1
Mitcham CR4 203 C6
Newham E15, E16 98 C4
Old Bexley DA5 169 D3
Richmond TW10, TW9 132 B1
Ruislip HA4 39 B1
Sidcup DA15 168 A1
South Norwood SE25 206 A6
Stamford Hill N16 51 C1
Teddington TW11 175 B5
Tottenham N17 34 B2
Twickenham TW2 152 B2
Wallington SM5, SM6 219 B3
Walthamstow E10 53 C2
Walton-on-T KT12 193 D2
West Wickham BR4 223 D6
Manor Rd N
Hinchley Wood KT7 213 A6
Wallington SM5, SM6 219 B4
Manor Rd S KT10 212 C4
Manor Road Ho HA1 43 A3
Manorside EN5 1 A1
Manorside Cl SE2 124 D2
Manorside Prim Sch N3 30 A2
Manor Specl Sch NW10 90 C6
Manor Sq RM8 80 C6
Manor Street Est SW3 267 B6
Manor The
Dulwich SE23 162 C4
Mayfair W1 248 C5
Manor Vale TW8 109 C1
Manor View N3 29 D1
Manorway Enfield EN1 17 C4
Woodford IG8 37 C5
Manor Way
Beckenham BR3 207 C6
Bromley BR2 210 A3
Chingford E4 36 B6
Colindale NW9 45 C5
Greenwich SE3 143 A1
Gunnersbury W3 110 C2
Harrow HA2 41 D5
Mitcham CR4 203 C6
New Malden KT4 199 D1
Orpington BR5 211 A5
Ruislip HA4 39 D1
Sidcup DA5 169 C3
Southall UB2 106 D2
South Croydon CR2 221 D2
Manor Waye UB8 82 A6
Manor Way The SM6 219 B4
Manpreet Ct E12 78 B3
Manray Ct 2 N8 50 A4
Manresa Rd SW3 114 C1 257 A1
Mansard Beeches SW17 181 A5
Mansard Cl HA5 40 D6
Mansard Manor 4 SM2 218 A1
Manse Cl UB3 127 B6
Manse Ct DA14 190 C5
Mansel Ct SW11 267 B1
Mansel Gr E17 35 C2
Mansell Ho SW8 269 B2
Mansell Rd
Acton W3 111 B4
Southall UB6 85 D2
Mansell St E1 95 D1 243 D1
Mansel Rd SW19 179 B4
Manse Rd N16 73 D5
Mansergh Cl SE18 144 A5
Mansfield Ave
East Barnet EN4 15 A5
Ruislip HA4 40 B1
Tottenham N15 51 B5
Mansfield Cl N9 18 A5
Mansfield Ct 27 E2 95 D6
Mansfield Dr UB4 83 C3
Mansfield Hill E4 19 D3
Mansfield Ho SW15 156 D5
Mansfield Hts N2 48 D4
Mansfield Mews W1 238 C3
Mansfield Pl 28 NW3 70 A4
Mansfield Rd
Acton W3 88 D3
Chessington KT9 213 D3
Ilford IG1 78 C6
Maitland Pk NW3 70 D4
South Croydon CR2 221 B2
Walthamstow E17 53 B5
Wanstead E11 55 B3
Mansfield St W1 93 B2 238 C3
Mansford St E2 96 A5
Manship Rd CR4 181 A2
Mansion Cl SW9 138 C4
Mansion Gdns NW3 69 D5
Mansion Ho* EC4 242 C1
Mansion House Pl EC3, EC4 242 C1
Mansion House St EC2 242 C1
Mansion House Sta EC4 117 A6 252 B6
Mansions The NW6 69 B3
Manson Mews SW7 114 B2 256 C3
Manson Pl SW7 114 B2 256 C3
Manstead Gdns RM6 58 C2

Manston
Camden Town NW1 71 C1
Tottenham N17 33 B1
Manston Ave UB2 107 C2
Manston Cl SE20 184 C2
Manstone Rd NW2 69 A3
Manston Gr KT2 175 D5
Manston Ho W14 254 B5
Mantell Ho SW4 159 C6
Manthorpe Rd SE18 123 A1
Mantilla Rd SW17 181 A6
Mantle Rd SE4 141 A2
Mantlet Cl SW16 181 C3
Mantle Way E15 76 C1
Manton Ave W7 109 A4
Manton Cl UB3 105 C6
Manton Ho N16 73 B5
Manton Rd
Holdbrook EN3 7 C5
Plumstead SE2 124 A2
Mantua St 22 SW11 136 B2
Mantus Cl
Bethnal Green E1 96 C3
19 Stepney E1 96 C3
Mantus Rd E1 96 C3
Manus Way N20 14 A3
Manville Gdns SW17 159 B1
Manville Rd SW17 159 B1
Manwood Rd SE4 163 B5
Manwood St E16 122 B5
Manygate La TW17 193 A3
Many Gates SW12 159 B2
Mapesbury Ct NW2 69 A3
Mapesbury Mews 1 NW9 46 A3
Mapesbury Rd NW2 69 A2
Mapeshill Pl NW2 68 C2
Mapes Ho 7 NW6 69 A1
Mape St E2 96 B3
Maple Ave
East Acton W3 111 C5
Harrow HA2 63 D6
Walthamstow E4 35 B4
Yiewsley UB7 104 B6
Maple Cl
Buckhurst Hill IG9 21 D1
Clapham Pk SW4 159 D5
Finchley N3 29 C4
Hampton TW12 173 B4
Hayes UB4 84 D4
Mitcham CR4 181 B2
Petts Wood BR5 211 B4
Ruislip HA4 40 B3
South Tottenham N16 52 A3
Maple Cres DA15 168 A5
Maplecroft Cl E6 100 A1
Maple Ct
Ashford TW15 171 B3
Catford SE6 163 D3
2 Croydon CR0 221 A4
7 Dagenham RM8 58 D2
Kingston u T KT3 199 B6
Newham E6 100 C2
6 Pinner HA5 22 C1
Sidcup DA14 190 B5
11 West Norwood SW16 182 C5
3 Willesden NW2 68 D4
Mapledale Ave CR0 222 A5
Mapledene BR7 189 A5
Mapledene Est E8 74 A1
Mapledene Rd E8 74 A1
Mapledown Sch NW2 46 C2
Mapledurham Ct 3 N13 32 C6
Maple Gdns
Grahame Pk HA8 27 C3
Stanwell TW19 148 A2
Maple Gr
Brentford TW8 131 B5
Ealing W5 109 D3
Kingsbury NW9 45 A2
Southall UB1 85 B2
Maple Gr Bsns Ctr TW4 128 C1
Maple Ho
2 Kingston u T KT6 198 A4
11 Maitland Pk NW3 70 D2
5 New Cross SE8 141 B5
4 Richmond TW9 132 D4
Teddington KT1 175 C3
13 Walthamstow E17 53 D6
Maple House Ind Montessori Sch 3 CR7 205 A6
Maplehurst 2 BR2 186 C1
Maplehurst Cl KT1 198 A5
Maple Ind Est TW13 150 A1
Maple Inf Sch KT6 197 D4
Maple Leaf Dr DA15 167 D3
Mapleleafe Gdns IG6 56 D6
Maple Leaf Sq 27 SE16 118 D4
Maple Lo
Buckhurst Hill IG9 21 D3
Putney SW15 157 A5
Welsh Harp NW9 67 B6
Maple Mews
Paddington NW6 91 D5
Streatham SW16 182 B5
Maple Pl
Marylebone W1 239 B5
3 Tottenham N17 34 A3
Yiewsley UB7 104 B6
Maple Rd Hayes UB4 84 D4
Kingston u T KT6 197 D4
Leytonstone E11 54 C3
Penge SE20 184 C2
Maples Pl E1 96 B2
Maple St
5 Bethnal Green E2 96 B5
Fitzrovia W1 93 C3 239 B5
Maplestead Rd
Dagenham RM9 102 B6
Streatham SW2 160 B4
Maples The 4 KT1 175 C3
Maplethorpe Rd CR7 204 D5
Mapleton Cl BR2 209 A3
Mapleton Cres
Enfield EN3 6 C5
Wandsworth SW18 157 D5
Mapleton Rd
Chingford E4 20 A1
Enfield EN1 6 B3
Wandsworth SW18 157 D5
Maple Tree Pl 7 SE3 144 A4
Maple Way TW13 150 B1
Maple Wlk W10 90 D3
Maplin Cl N21 16 B5
Maplin Ho 7 SE2 124 D4
Maplin Rd E16 99 B1
Maplin St E3 97 B4
Mapperley Cl 3 E11 55 A3
Mapperley Dr IG8 36 C3
Marabou Cl E12 78 A3
Marada Ho NW6 69 A1
Marais W4 133 A5
Maran Way DA18 124 D3
Marathon Way SE28 123 D4
Marban Rd W9 91 B4
Marble Arch★ W1 114 D6 247 D6
Marble Arch Sta W1 92 D1 237 D1
Marble Cl W3 110 D5
Marble Dr NW2 46 D2
Marbleford Ct 4 N6 49 D2
Marble Hill Cl TW1 153 B4
Marble Hill Gdns TW1 153 B4
Marble Hill House★ TW1 153 C4
Marble Ho
Paddington W9 91 B3
Plumstead Comm SE18 123 D1
Marble Quay SE1 118 A5
Marbrook Ct SE12 165 C1
Marcella Rd SW9 138 C3
Marcellina Way BR6 227 D5
March 23 NW9 27 D2
Marchant Cl NW7 27 C3
Marchant Ho 13 SW2 160 B6
Marchant Rd E11 76 B6
Marchant St SE14 141 A6
Marchbank Rd W14 135 B6 264 D6
March Ct SW15 134 B1
Marchmont Ho 10 SW16 181 C5
Marchmont Rd
Richmond TW10 154 B6
Wallington SM6 219 C1
Marchmont St WC1 94 A3 240 A6
March Rd 7 TW1 153 A4
Marchside Cl TW5 128 D4
Marchwood Cl 9 SE5 139 C5
Marchwood Cres W5 87 D1
Marcia Rd SE1 117 C2 263 B3
Marcilly Rd SW18 158 B6
Marcol Ho W1 238 D2
Marcon Ct 29 E8 74 B3
Marconi Pl N11 31 B6
Marconi Rd E10 53 C1
Marconi Way UB1 85 D1
Marcon Pl E8 74 B3
Marco Rd W6 112 C3
Marcourt Lawns W5 88 A3
Marcus Ct
Brentford TW8 132 A5
Newham E15 98 C6
Marcus Garvey Mews SE22 162 B6
Marcus Garvey Way 9 SE24 138 C1
Marcus Ho 14 SE15 139 D4
Marcus St
Wandsworth SW18 157 D5
West Ham E15 98 D6
Marcus Terr SW18 157 D5
Mardale Ct NW7 28 A3
Mardale Dr NW9 45 B4
Mardell Rd CR0 206 D4
Marden Ave BR2 209 A3
Marden Cres CR0 204 B3
Marden Ho 6 E8 74 B3
Marden Rd
Thornton Heath CR0 204 B3
Tottenham N17 33 C1
Marden Sq SE16 118 B3
Marder Rd W13 109 A4
Mardon HA5 23 B3
Mardyke Ho SE17 262 D4
Marechal Niel Ave DA15 167 B1
Marechal Niel Par DA15 167 B1
Maresby Ho E4 19 D2
Maresfield CR0 221 C5
Maresfield Gdns NW3 70 A2
Mare St E8 74 B1
Marey Ct 10 CR2 221 A3
Marfleet Cl SM5 218 C6
Margaret Ave E4 19 D5
Margaret Bondfield Ave IG11 80 A1
Margaret Bondfield Ho
5 Bow E3 97 A5
22 Kentish Town N7 71 D3
Margaret Ct Barnet EN4 2 B1
Marylebone W1 239 A2
Margaret Gardner Dr SE9 166 B2
Margaret Herbison Ho SW6 264 D5
Margaret Hill Ho 1 N8 50 A4
Margaret Ho
16 Hammersmith W6 112 C1
2 Sutton SM1 217 D5
Margaret Ingram Cl SW6 264 C5
Margaret Lockwood Cl KT5 198 B5
Margaret Mcmillan Ho 10 N19 49 D2
Margaret Rd
Barnet EN4 2 B1
Bexley DA5 168 D5
Stamford Hill N16 51 D1
Margaret Rutherford Pl 3 SW12 159 C3
Margarets Ct HA8 26 D5
Margaret's Ct E11 54 B2
Margaret St W1 93 C1 239 A2
Margaretta Terr SW3 136 C6 267 B6
Margaretting Rd E12 55 C1
Margaret Way IG4 56 A3
Margaret White Ho NW1 232 C2
Margate Rd SW2 160 A6
Margery Fry Ct N7 72 A5
Margery Park Rd E7 77 A2
Margery Rd RM8 80 D5
Margery St WC1 94 C4 234 A1
Margin Dr SW19 178 D6
Margravine Gdns
Hammersmith W6 112 D1
West Kensington W14 254 A2
Margravine Rd W6 135 A6 264 A6
Marham Dr 17 NW9 27 C2
Marham Gdns
Morden SM4 202 A3
Wandsworth SW17, SW18 158 C3
Mar Ho 4 SE7 143 C6
Maria Cl 13 SE1 118 A2
Maria Fidelis Convent Sch (Lower) NW1 93 C4 232 B1
Maria Fidelis Convent Sch (Upper) NW1 93 D4 232 C2
Marian Cl UB4 84 D3
Marian Ct Hackney E9 74 C3
1 Sutton SM1 217 D3
Marian Lo 5 SW20 178 D3
Marian Pl E2 96 B5
Marian Rd SW16 181 C2
Marian Sq E2 96 B5
Marian St 2 E2 96 B5
Marian Vian Prim Sch BR3 207 A4
Marian Way NW10 67 D1
Maria Terr E1 96 D3
Maria Theresa Cl KT3 199 B4
Maribor 13 SE10 142 A5
Maricas Ave HA3 24 B2
Marie Curie SE5 139 C4
Marie Lloyd Ct 13 SW9 138 B1
Marie Lloyd Gdns 1 N19 50 A2
Marie Lloyd Ho N1 235 C3
Marien Ct E4 36 B5
Marie Stopes Ct 3 N19 50 A2
Marigold Cl UB1 107 A6
Marigold Rd N17 34 C3
Marigold St SE16 118 B4
Marigold Way CR0 206 D1
Marilea Ct W5 109 D4
Marillic Ho NW7 28 C6
Marina App UB4 85 A2
Marina Ave KT3 200 B4
Marina Cl 1 BR2 209 A6
Marina Ct 12 Bow E3 97 C4
Greenford UB6 85 D5
Marina Dr DA16 145 C3
Marina Gdns RM7 59 D4
Marina Pl KT1 175 D2
Marina Point 4 E14 119 D3
Marina Way TW11 175 D3
Marine Dr
Barking IG11 102 B4
5 Woolwich SE18 122 B2
Marinefield Rd SW6 135 D3
Marinel Ho 25 SE5 139 A5
Mariner Gdns TW10 153 C1
Mariner Rd E12 78 C4
Mariners Mews E14 120 B2
Marine St SE16 118 A3
Marine Twr 20 SE8 141 B6
Marion Ave TW17 192 D4
Marion Ct 4 SW17 180 C5
Marion Gr IG8 36 C6
Marion Rd
Mill Hill NW7 28 A5
Thornton Heath CR0 205 B4
Marion Richardson Prim Sch 17 E1 96 D1
Marischal Rd SE13 142 B2
Maritime Greenwich Coll 18 SE8 141 C5
Maritime Ho
5 Clapham SW4 137 C2
14 Woolwich SE18 122 D2
Maritime Ind Est SE7 121 B2
Maritime Quay 5 E14 119 C1
Maritime St E3 97 B3
Marius Mans 3 SW17 159 A2
Marius Rd SW17 159 A2
Marjorie Gr SW11 136 D1
Marjorie McClure Sch BR7 189 A2
Marjory Kinnon Sch TW14 149 C6
Markab Rd HA6 22 A5
Mark Ave E4 19 D5
Mark Cl
Bexleyheath DA7 147 A4
Keston Mark BR2 226 A4
Southall UB1 107 D5
Markeston Gn WD19 22 D6
Market Ct W1 239 A2
Market Ctr The UB2 106 B2
Market La
Burnt Oak HA8 27 A2
Shepherd's Bush W12 112 C4
Market Mews W1 115 B5 248 C3
Market Par
Croydon SE25 206 A5
1 Edmonton N9 18 A2
Feltham TW13 151 A2
Leyton E10 53 D3
Walthamstow E17 53 B6
Market Pavilion E10 75 C5
Market Pl
3 Acton W3 111 A5
1 Bermondsey SE16 118 B2
2 Bexleyheath DA6 147 C1
Brentford TW8 131 C5
East Finchley N2 48 C6
Enfield EN2 5 B2
Kingston u T KT1 175 D1
Marylebone W1 239 A2
Market Pl The NW11 47 D5
Market Rd
Barnsbury N7 72 A2
Richmond TW9 132 C2
Market Sq
Bromley BR1 187 A1
Poplar E14 97 D1
Market Sq The N9 18 B2
Market St
Spitalfields E1 243 C4
Wallend E6 100 C5
Woolwich SE18 122 C2
Market Studios 14 W12 112 C4
Market The SM1, SM5 202 A1
Market Way
Poplar E14 97 D1
2 Wembley HA0 66 A3
Market Yd Mews SE1 263 A6
Markfield Beam Engine & Mus★ N15 52 A4
Markfield Gdns E4 19 D4
Markfield Ho N15 52 A4
Markfield Rd N15 52 A4
Markham Ct NW4 46 C6
Markham Ho
1 Dagenham RM10 81 C5
9 Dulwich SE21 183 C6
Markham Pl SW3 257 C2
Markham Sq SW3 114 D1 257 C2
Markham St SW3 114 C1 257 B2
Mark Ho 3 E2 96 D5
Markhole Cl TW12 173 B3
Markhouse Ave E17 53 A3
Markhouse Pas E17 53 B3
Markhouse Rd E17 53 B3
Mark La EC3 117 C6 253 B6
Markland Ho W10 112 D6
Mark Lo 9 EN4 2 C1
Markmanor Ave E17 53 B2
Mark Mans W12 112 A4
Mark Rd N22 32 D1
Marksbury Ave TW9 132 C2
Marks Gate Jun & Inf Schs RM6 59 A6
Mark Sq EC2 243 A6
Mark St
Broadgate EC2 243 A6
Stratford E15 76 C1
Markstone Ho SE1 251 C1
Mark Wade Cl E12 55 D1
Markway The TW16 172 C1
Markwell Cl SE26 184 B6
Markyate Ho 6 W10 90 C3
Markyate Rd RM8 80 B3
Marland Ho SW1 257 D6
Marlands Rd IG5 56 B6
Marlang Ct BR3 186 B2

Marlborough
11 Putney SW19 .... 156 D3
St John's Wood W9 .. 229 A2
Marlborough Ave
Edgware HA8 .... 10 D1
3 Hackney E8 .... 96 A6
New Southgate N14 .... 15 C1
Ruislip HA4 .... 39 B3
Marlborough Cl
Broom Hill BR6 ...... 211 D3
Friern Barnet N20 ..... 14 D1
Mitcham SW19 ..... 180 C4
Newington SE17 .... 261 D3
Marlborough Cres
Bedford Pk W4 ...... 111 C3
Harlington UB3 ...... 127 B5
Marlborough Ct
6 Beckenham BR3 .. 185 C2
7 Bromley BR1 ...... 186 D3
7 Buckhurst Hill IG9 .. 21 C2
Harrow HA1 .... 42 B5
Kensington W8 ...... 255 A4
Marylebone W1 ..... 239 A1
Wallington SM6 ..... 219 C1
Marlborough Dr IG5 .. 56 A6
Marlborough Flats
SW3 .... 257 B4
Marlborough Fst & Mid Sch HA1 .... 42 C5
Marlborough Gdns
Friern Barnet N20 ..... 14 D1
Surbiton KT6 .... 197 D2
Marlborough Gr
SE1 .... 118 A1
Marlborough Hill
Harrow HA1 .... 42 C5
St John's Wood NW8 .... 92 A6 229 B5
Marlborough Ho
Marylebone NW1 .... 238 D6
Richmond TW10 ..... 154 C6
Stoke Newington N4 ... 51 A1
Marlborough Ho SW1 .... 249 B3
Marlborough Ho
SW19 .... 156 D1
Marlborough La
SE7 .... 143 C5
Marlborough Lo
36 Stepney E1 .... 96 C3
St John's Wood NW8 . 229 A3
Marlborough Mans 5
NW6 .... 69 C3
Marlborough Mews 18
SW2 .... 138 B1
Marlborough Par 1
UB10 .... 82 D3
Marlborough Park Ave
DA15 .... 168 A3
Marlborough Pl
NW8 .... 92 A5 229 B4
Marlborough Prim Sch
Chelsea
SW3 ...... 114 C2 257 B3
Isleworth TW7 ...... 131 A4
Marlborough Rd
Acton Green W4 ..... 111 A1
Ashford TW15 ...... 170 A5
Bexley DA7 .... 146 D2
Bowes Pk N22 .... 32 B4
Brentford TW7 ...... 131 B5
Bromley BR2 .... 209 C5
Chingford E4 .... 35 D4
Dagenham RM8 .... 80 C4
Ealing W5 .... 109 D4
Edmonton N9 .... 18 A3
Feltham TW13 ...... 150 D2
Hampton TW12 ..... 173 C4
Hillingdon UB10 .... 82 D4
Leyton E15 .... 76 C4
Mitcham SW19 ..... 180 C4
Richmond TW10 ..... 154 B5
Romford RM7 .... 59 D5
Southall UB2 .... 106 C3
South Croydon CR2 .. 221 A1
St James
SW1 ...... 115 C5 249 B3
Sutton SM1 .... 217 C6
Upper Holloway N19 ... 72 A6
Upton E7 .... 77 C1
Wanstead E18 .... 55 A6
Woolwich SE18 ..... 123 A3
Marlborough Sch
DA15 .... 168 A4
Marlborough St
SW3 .... 114 C2 257 B3
Marlborough Trad Est
TW9 .... 132 D4
Marlborough Yd N19 .. 71 D6
Marlbury NW8 .... 91 D6
Marler Rd SE23 ...... 163 B3
Marlesford Ct SM6 ... 219 C4
Marlex Lo N3 .... 29 D2
Marley Ave DA7 ..... 146 D6
Marley Cl
Harringay N15 .... 50 D5
Southall UB6 .... 85 C4
Marley Ho 14 W11 .. 112 D6
Marley Wlk NW2 ...... 68 C3
Marlfield Cl KT4 ..... 200 A1
Marlfield Ct KT3 .... 199 D2
Marlin Cl TW16 ...... 171 C4
Marlin Ct 5 DA14 .... 190 A6
Marling Ct TW12 ..... 173 B4
Marlingdene Cl
TW12 .... 173 C4
Marlings Cl BR7 ..... 211 C5
Marlings Park Ave
BR7 .... 211 C6
Marlin Ho SW15 ..... 157 A6
Marlins Cl 3 SM1 .... 218 A3
Marloes Cl HA0 .... 65 D4
Marloes Rd
W8 .... 113 D3 255 C5
Marlow Cl SE20 ...... 206 B6
Marlow Cres TW1 ... 152 D5
Marlow Ct
Colindale NW9 .... 45 D6
1 Ealing W7 .... 108 C5
6 Finchley N3 .... 29 C2
Harrow HA1 .... 42 A3
Osidge N14 .... 15 C4
Willesden NW6 .... 68 D1
Marlow Dr SM3 ..... 216 D5
Marlowe Bsns Ctr 2
SE14 .... 141 A5
Marlowe Cl BR7 ..... 189 B4
Marlowe Ct
Chelsea SW3 .... 257 B3
2 Dulwich SE19 .... 183 D5
6 Kingston u T KT2 .. 175 D6
Marlowe Gdns SE9 ... 166 C5
Marlowe Ho
Kingston u T KT1 .... 197 D5
15 Stoke Newington
N16 .... 73 C4
Marlowe Lo CR0 ..... 223 A6
Marlowe Rd E17 ...... 54 A5
Marlowe Sq CR4 ..... 203 C5
Marlowes The
NW8 .... 92 B6 229 C6
Marlowe Way CR0 ... 220 A6
Marlow Gdns UB3 ... 105 B3
Marlow Ho
Bermondsey SE1 .... 263 C6
15 Kensington W2 ..... 91 D1
44 Spitalfields E2 ..... 95 D4
Teddington TW11 ..... 175 A6
Wallington CR0 ..... 220 A5
Marlow Rd
Newham E6 .... 100 B4
Penge SE20 .... 184 B1
Southall UB2 .... 107 B3
Marlow Studio Workshops 43 E2 ... 95 D4
Marlow Way SE16 ... 118 D4
Marl Rd SW18 ...... 136 A1
Marlston NW1 ...... 231 D1
Marlton St SE10 .... 120 D1
Marlwood Cl DA15 ... 167 C2
Marmadon Rd SE18,
SE2 .... 123 D2
Marmara Apts 4
E16 .... 121 A6
Marmion App E4 ..... 35 C6
Marmion Ave E4 ...... 35 B6
Marmion Cl E4 .... 35 B6
Marmion Ho 13
SW12 .... 159 B4
Marmion Mews 4
SW11 .... 137 A2
Marmion Rd SW11 ... 137 A1
Marmont Rd SE15 .... 140 A5
Marmora Ho E1 ...... 97 A2
Marmora Rd SE22 ... 162 C5
Marmot Rd TW4 .... 128 D2
Marncrest Ct KT5 ... 198 B4
Marne Ave
Friern Barnet N11 ..... 31 B6
Welling DA16 .... 146 A2
Marnell Way TW4 ... 128 D2
Marner Prim Sch 6
E3 .... 97 D3
Marne St W10 .... 91 A4
Marney Rd SW11 .... 137 A1
Marnfield Cres SW2 .. 160 B3
Marnham Ave NW2 ... 69 A4
Marnham Cres UB6 ... 85 D5
Marnham Ct HA0 ..... 65 C3
Marnie Ct 11 E11 ..... 76 C6
Marnock Ho SE17 ... 262 C2
Marnock Rd SE4 ..... 163 B6
Maroon St E14 .... 97 A2
Maroons Way SE6 ... 185 C5
Marqueen Twrs 1
SW16 .... 182 B3
Marquess Rd N1 ...... 73 B2
Marquis Cl HA0 .... 66 B1
Marquis Ct
Barking IG11 .... 79 C3
Finsbury Pk N4 .... 50 B1
1 Kingston u T KT1 .. 198 A5
Stanwell TW19 ...... 148 A3
Marquis Rd
Bowes Pk N22 .... 32 B4
Finsbury Pk N4 .... 50 C1
Kentish Town NW1 .... 71 D2
Marrabon Cl DA15 ... 168 A3
Marrick Cl SW15 .... 134 A1
Marrick Ho 19 NW6 ... 91 D6
Marrilyne Ave EN3 ..... 7 B5
Marriner Ct UB3 ..... 105 C6
Marriott Cl TW14 .... 149 B5
Marriott Ho 8 SE6 ... 186 A6
Marriott Rd
Finsbury Pk N4 .... 50 B1
Muswell Hill N10 ...... 30 D2
Newham E15 .... 98 C6
Marriotts Cl NW9 ..... 45 D3
Marryat Cl TW3 ...... 129 B1
Marryat Ct 12 W6 ... 112 B2
Marryat Ho SW1 .... 259 A1
Marryat Pl SW19 .... 179 A6
Marryat Rd SW19 .... 179 A6
Marryat Sq SW6 .... 264 A2
Marryatt Ct W5 .... 88 B1
Marryfields Way
SE6 .... 163 D4
Marsala Rd SE13 .... 141 D1
Marsalis Ho 3 E3 .... 97 C4
Marsden Rd
Camberwell SE15 .... 139 D2
Edmonton N9 .... 18 B2
Marsden St NW5 ...... 71 A2
Marsden Way 2
BR6 .... 227 D4
Marshall Cl
Brunswick Pk N11 ..... 15 B1
Harrow HA1 .... 42 B2
Hounslow TW4 ...... 151 B6
Wandsworth SW18 .. 158 A5
Marshall Ct SW4 .... 270 B1
Marshall Dr UB4 ...... 83 D2
Marshall Ho
5 New Malden
KT3 .... 199 C5
Paddington NW6 ...... 91 B5
Shoreditch N1 ...... 235 D4
Walworth SE17 ..... 262 C2
Marshall Path 10
SE28 .... 124 B6
Marshall Rd
Leyton E10 .... 75 D4
Tottenham N17 .... 33 B2
Marshall St L Ctr
W1 .... 93 C1 239 B1
Marshalls Gr SE18 ... 122 A2
Marshall's Pl SE16 .. 263 D5
Marshall's Rd SM1 .. 217 D4
Marshall St
W1 .... 93 C1 239 B1
Marshalsea Rd
SE1 .... 117 A4 252 B2
Marsham Cl BR7 .... 188 D5
Marsham Ct
19 Putney SW19 .... 156 D3
Westminster SW1 ... 259 D4
Marsham St
SW1 .... 115 D2 259 D4
Marsh Ave CR4 ..... 181 A1
Marshbrook Cl SE3 . 143 D2
Marsh Cl NW7 .... 11 D1
Marsh Ct Dalston E8 ... 74 A2
3 Merton SW19 .... 180 A2
Marsh Dr NW9 .... 45 D3
Marsh Farm Rd
TW2 .... 152 D3
Marshfield St E14 .... 120 A3
Marsh Gate Bsns Ctr
E15 .... 98 A5
Marshgate Sch
TW10 .... 154 B6
Marsh Green Prim Sch
RM10 .... 103 C5
Marsh Green Rd
RM10 .... 103 C6
Marsh Hall HA9 .... 66 B5
Marsh Hill E9 .... 75 A3
Marsh Ho
Nine Elms SW8 ..... 269 B2
Pimlico SW1 .... 259 D1
Marsh La
Edgware NW7 .... 11 C1
Leyton E10 .... 75 C6
Stanmore HA7 .... 25 C4
Tottenham N17 .... 34 B2
Marsh Point HA5 ..... 41 B5
Marsh Rd Pinner HA5 .. 41 A5
Wembley HA0 .... 87 D5
Marshside Cl N9 ...... 18 C3
Marsh St E14 .... 119 D2
Marsh Wall E14 ..... 119 D4
Marshwood Ho 10
NW6 .... 91 C6
Marsland Cl SE17 ... 261 D1
Marsom Ho N1 ..... 235 C3
Marston SE17 ...... 262 B4
Marston Ave
Chessington KT9 .... 214 A2
Dagenham RM10 ...... 81 C5
Marston Cl
Dagenham RM10 ...... 81 C5
South Hampstead NW6 70 A1
Marston Ct
Barnet EN5 .... 13 C6
Sidcup DA14 .... 189 D6
Walton-on-T KT12 .... 194 C1
Marston Ho 23 SW9 .. 138 C3
Marston Rd TW11 .... 175 B5
Marston Way SE19 ... 183 A3
Marsworth Ave HA5 ... 22 D2
Marsworth Cl UB4 .... 85 A2
Marsworth Ho 8 E2 .. 96 A6
Martaban Rd N16 ..... 73 D6
Martello St E8 .... 74 B1
Martello Terr E8 ...... 74 B1
Martell Rd SE21 ..... 161 B1
Martel Pl E8 .... 73 D2
Marten Rd E17 .... 35 C1
Martens Ave DA7 ... 147 D1
Martham Cl SE28 ... 124 D6
Martha Rd E15 .... 76 C2
Martha's Bldgs EC1 . 242 C6
Martha St E1 .... 96 C1
Marthorne Cres HA3 .. 24 B1
Martin Bowes Rd
SE9 .... 144 B2
Martinbridge Trad Est
EN1 .... 18 A6
Martin Cl
Lower Edmonton N9 ... 18 D3
Uxbridge UB10 .... 82 A5
Martin Cres CR0 ..... 204 C1
Martin Ct
15 Cubitt Town E14 .. 120 A4
Lewisham SE12 ..... 164 D4
Merton SW19 .... 179 C3
Southall UB2 .... 107 B4
Martindale SW14 .... 155 A6
Martindale Ave 2
E16 .... 121 A6
Martindale Ho 23
E14 .... 119 D6
Martindale Rd
Balham SW12 .... 159 B4
Hounslow TW4 ...... 129 A2
Martin Dene DA6 .... 169 B6
Martin Dr UB5 .... 63 B3
Martineau Cl KT10 ... 212 B4
Martineau Dr TW1 ... 131 B1
Martineau Ho SW1 .. 259 A1
Martineau Mews N5 .. 72 D4
Martineau Rd N5 ..... 72 D4
Martingale Cl TW16 .. 194 A5
Martingales Cl
TW10 .... 153 D1
Martin Gdns RM8 ..... 80 D4
Martin Gr SM4 ...... 201 C6
Martin Ho
Newington SE1 ..... 262 B5
7 New Malden KT3 .. 199 C5
South Lambeth SW8 . 270 A4
Martini Dr EN3 .... 7 C6
Martin La EC4 ...... 252 D6
Martin Prim Sch N2 ... 30 C1
Martin Rd RM8 .... 80 D4
Martin Rise DA6 .... 169 B6
Martins Cl BR4 ..... 224 B6
Martins Mount EN5 .... 1 D1
Martins Pl SE28 ..... 123 C5
Martin's Rd BR2 .... 186 D1
Martin St SE28 ...... 123 C5
Martins The
Penge SE26 .... 184 B5
Wembley HA9 .... 66 B5
Martins Wlk
Muswell Hill N10 ...... 31 A2
Woolwich SE28 ..... 123 C5
Martin Way SW20,
SM4 .... 201 B6
Martlesham N17 ...... 33 C1
Martlesham Wlk
NW9 .... 27 C2
Martlet Gr 5 UB5 ..... 84 D4
Martlett Ct WC2 .... 240 B1
Martlett Lo NW3 ...... 69 D4
Martley Dr IG2 .... 56 D4
Martley Ho SW8 .... 269 B2
Martock Cl HA3 ...... 43 A5
Martock Ct 10 SE15 .. 140 B4
Martock Gdns N11 .... 31 A5
Marton Cl SE6 ...... 163 C1
Marton Rd 2 N16 ..... 73 C5
Martyn Ct HA8 .... 26 B6
Martyn Ho SE2 ..... 146 D6
Martynside 22 NW9 ... 27 D2
Marvel Ho 5 SE5 .... 139 B5
Marvell Ave UB4 ..... 84 A2
Marvels Cl SE12 .... 165 B2
Marvels La SE12 .... 165 C1
Marvels Lane Prim Sch
SE12 .... 187 C6
Marville Rd
SW6 .... 135 B5 264 C3
Marvin Ho 9 SE18 .. 144 D6
Marvin St 3 E8 .... 74 B2
Marwell Cl BR4 ..... 224 D6
Marwell Ct SE3 ..... 142 B3
Marwick Rd UB7 .... 104 B4
Marwood Cl DA16 ... 146 B2
Marwood Ct N3 ...... 29 D3
Marwood Dr NW7 ..... 28 D3
Mary Adelaide Cl
Kingston u T SW15 ... 155 C1
Kingston u T SW15 ... 177 C6
Mary Adelaide Ho
W2 .... 236 D4
Mary Ann Bldgs SE8 . 141 C6
Maryatt Ave HA2 ..... 63 D6
Marybank SE18 ..... 122 B2
Mary Cl HA7 .... 44 B5
Mary Datchelor Cl
SE5 .... 139 B4
Mary Dine Ct SW8 .. 270 D3
Mary Gn NW8 .... 91 D6
Marygold Ho TW3 .... 130 A4
Mary Ho
8 Hammersmith
W6 .... 112 C1
6 Stockwell SW9 .... 138 B3
Mary James Ho 32
E2 .... 96 A5
Mary Jones Ho 20
E14 .... 119 C6
Maryland Ct KT1 .... 176 D1
Maryland Pk E15 ..... 76 C3
Maryland Point E15 ... 76 C2
Maryland Prim Sch
E15 .... 76 C3
Maryland Rd
Paddington W9 .... 91 C3
South Norwood CR7 .. 182 D2
Stratford New Town
E15 .... 76 B3
Tottenham N22 .... 32 C4
Marylands Ind Est
E15 .... 76 C3
Maryland Sq E15 ..... 76 C3
Marylands Rd W9 ..... 91 D3
Maryland St E15 ..... 76 C3
Maryland Sta E15 ..... 76 C2
Maryland Way TW16 . 172 A1
Maryland Wlk N1 ... 235 A6
Mary Lawrenson Pl 1
SE3 .... 143 A5
MARYLEBONE 93 B1

Marylebone Ct 3 HA0 66 A2
Marylebone Flyover NW1 92 C2 237 A3
Marylebone High St W1 93 A2 238 B4
Marylebone La W1 93 A1 238 B2
Marylebone Mews W1 238 C3
Marylebone Pas W1 239 B2
Marylebone Rd NW1 92 D2 237 D4
Marylebone St W1 93 A2 238 B3
Marylebone Sta NW1 92 D3 237 C5
Marylee Way SE11 116 B2 260 D3
Mary McArthur Ho 12 N19 49 D2
Mary Macarthur Ho
8 Belvedere DA17 125 C3
11 Dagenham RM10 81 C5
15 Globe Town E2 96 D4
W14 264 A6
Marymount International Sch KT2 177 A3
Maryon Gr SE7 122 A2
Maryon Mews NW3 70 C4
Maryon Rd SE7 122 A2
Mary Peters Dr UB6 64 B3
Mary Pl W11 113 A6 244 A5
Mary Rose Cl TW12 173 C2
Mary Rose Mall E6 100 B2
Maryrose Way N20 14 B3
Mary's Ct NW8 237 B6
Mary Seacole Villas 19 NW10 67 B1
Mary Secole Cl 21 E8 95 D6
Mary Smith Ct SW5 255 B3
Mary St
5 Canning Town E16 98 D2
Shoreditch N1 95 A6 235 B5
Mary's Terr TW1 153 A4
Mary Tates Cotts CR4 202 D5
Mary Terr NW1 232 A5
Maryville DA16 145 D3
Mary Way WD19 22 C6
Mary Wharrie Ho 4 NW3 70 D1
Marzena Ct TW2 152 A6
Masbro' Rd W14 112 D3
Mascalls Ct 13 SE7 143 C6
Mascalls Rd SE7 143 C6
Mascotte Rd 2 SW15 134 D1
Mascotts Cl NW2 68 B5
Masefield Ave
Borehamwood WD6 10 D6
Southall UB1 107 C6
Stanmore HA7 24 D5
Masefield Cres N14 15 C5
Masefield Ct
New Barnet EN5 2 A1
Stoke Newington N5 73 B3
19 Surbiton KT6 197 D2
Masefield Gdns E6 100 C3
Masefield Ho 4 NW6 91 C4
Masefield La UB4 84 C3
Masefield Rd TW13 173 B6
Masefield View BR6 227 A5
Masefield Way TW19 148 B3
Masham Ho 13 DA18 124 D4
Mashie Rd W3 89 C1
Maskall Cl SW2 160 C3
Maskani Wlk SW16 181 C3
Maskell Rd SW17 158 A1
Maskelyne Cl SW11 136 C4 267 B2
Mason Cl
Bermondsey SE16 118 A1
Bexleyheath DA7 147 D2
Hampton TW12 173 B2
Newham E16 121 A6
Wimbledon SW20 178 D2
Mason Ct
4 Penge SE19 183 D3
Wembley HA9 66 C6
Mason Ho
15 Bermondsey SE1 118 A2
8 Friern Barnet N11 31 C5
16 Hackney E9 74 C1
Mason Rd
Sutton SM1 217 D3
Woodford IG8 36 C6
Mason's Arms Mews W1 248 D6
Masons Ave HA3 42 D5
Mason's Ave
City of London EC2 242 C2
Croydon CR0 221 A5
Masons Hill
Bromley BR2 209 B5
13 Woolwich SE18 122 D2
Masons Ho NW9 44 D4
Mason's Pl
Finsbury EC1 235 A2
Mitcham CR4 180 D2
Mason St SE17 117 B2 262 D4
Mason's Yd
Finsbury EC1 234 D2
St James SW1 249 B4
Wimbledon SW19 178 D5
Massey Cl N11 31 B5
Massey Ct 6 E6 99 C6
Massie Rd E8 74 A2
Massingberd Way SW17 181 B6
Massinger St SE1, SE17 263 A3
Massingham St E1 96 D3
Masson Ave HA4 62 C2
Mast Ct 17 SE16 119 A2
Master Gunner's Pl 1 SE18 144 A4
Masterman Ho 1 SE5 139 B5
Masterman Rd E6 100 A4
Masters Cl SW16 181 C4
Masters Ct HA4 61 C6
Masters Dr SE16 118 B1
Masters Lo 24 E1 96 C1
Master's St 16 E1 96 D2
Mast House Terr E14 119 C2
Mastin Ho SW18 157 C3
Mastmaker Rd E14 119 C4
Maswell Park Cres TW3 152 A6
Maswell Park Rd TW3 130 A1
Matara Mews SE17 262 A1
Matcham Rd E11 76 D5
Matching Ct 14 E3 97 C4
Matchless Dr SE18 144 C5
Matchroom Stadium (Brisbane Rd) (Leyton Orient FC) E10 75 D5
Matfield Cl BR2 209 A4
Matfield Rd DA17 147 C6
Matham Gr SE22 139 D1
Matham Rd KT8 196 B4
Mathart Ct E4 36 B4
Matheson Lang Ho SE1 251 A1
Matheson Rd W14 113 B2 254 C3
Mathews Ave E6 100 C5
Mathews Park Ave E15 76 D2
Mathews Yd WC2 240 A1
Mathieson Ct SE1 251 D1
Mathieson Ho 10 E4 20 C4
Mathilda Marks-Kennedy Jewish Prim Sch 5 NW7 27 B5
Mathison Ho SW10 266 A4
Matilda Cl SE19 183 B3
Matilda Gdns 10 E3 97 C5
Matilda Ho E1 118 A5
Matilda St N1 94 B6 233 D6
Matlock Cl Barnet EN5 12 D6
Herne Hill SE24 139 A1
Matlock Cres SM3 217 A4
Matlock Ct
7 Herne Hill SE5 139 B1
St John's Wood NW8 229 A4
Woodford IG8 36 D2
Matlock Gdns SM1, SM3 217 A4
Matlock Pl SM1, SM3 217 A4
Matlock Rd E10 54 A3
Matlock St E14 97 A1
Matlock Way KT3 177 B2
Maton Ho SW6 264 C4
Matson Ct IG8 36 C3
Matson Ho
9 Bermondsey SE16 118 B3
16 Homerton E9 74 D2
Matthew Cl W10 90 D3
Matthew Ct
Mitcham CR4 203 D4
4 Walthamstow E17 54 A6
Matthew Parker St SW1 249 D1
Matthews Ct N5 73 A4
Matthews Ho 8 E14 97 C2
Matthews Rd UB6 64 B3
Matthews St SW11 136 D3
Matthias Ct 12 TW10 154 A5
Matthias Ho 2 N16 73 C3
Matthias Rd N16 73 C3
Mattingly Way 8 SE15 139 D5
Mattison Rd N4 50 D3
Mattock La W5, W13 109 C5
Maud Cashmore Way SE18 122 B3
Maude Ho 3 E2 96 A5
Maude Rd
Camberwell SE5 139 C4
Walthamstow E17 53 A4
Maudesville Cotts W7 108 C5
Maude Terr E17 53 A5
Maud Gdns
Barking IG11 101 D5
Newham E13 98 D5
Maudlins Gn E1 118 A5
Maud Rd Leyton E10 76 A5
Newham E13 98 D5
Maudslay Rd SE9 144 B2
Maudsley Ho TW8 110 A1
Maudsley Hospl SE5 139 B3
Maud St E16 98 D2
Maud Wilkes Cl 10 NW5 71 C3
Maugham Ct 5 W3 111 A3
Mauleverer Rd SW2 160 A6
Maultway Ct KT19 215 B3
Maundeby Wlk NW10 67 C2
Maunder Rd 4 W7 108 D5
Maunsel St SW1 115 D2 259 C4
Maureen Campbell Ct TW17 192 D4
Maurer Ct 2 SE10 120 D3
Mauretania Bldg 11 E1 118 D6
Maurice Ave N22 32 D1
Maurice Browne Cl NW7 28 D4
Maurice Ct
3 Brentford TW8 131 D5
4 Mile End E1 97 A4
Wood Green N22 32 C2
Maurice Ho
Hither Green SE12 164 D5
1 Stockwell SW9 138 B3
Maurice St W12 90 B1
Maurice Wlk NW11 48 A5
Maurier Cl UB5 84 C6
Mauritius Rd SE10 120 C2
Maury Rd N16 74 A5
Mausoleum Rd N2 30 C2
Mauveine Gdns TW3 129 C1
Mavelstone Cl BR1 188 A2
Mavelstone Rd BR1 188 A2
Maverton Rd E3 97 C6
Mavery Ct 5 BR1 186 D3
Mavis Ave KT19 215 C3
Mavis Cl KT19 215 C3
Mavis Ct 33 NW9 27 D1
Mavis Wlk 9 E6 100 A2
Mavor Ho N1 233 D5
Mawbey Ho SE1 263 D1
Mawbey Pl SE1 117 D1 263 D1
Mawbey Rd SE1 263 D1
Mawbey St SW8 270 A3
Mawdley Ho SE1 251 B1
Mawney Cl RM7 59 D6
Mawney Rd RM7 59 D6
Mawson Cl SW20 179 A1
Mawson Ct N1 235 D5
Mawson Ho EC1 241 A4
Mawson La W4 133 D6
Maxden Ct SE15 140 A2
Maxey Gdns RM9 81 A4
Maxey Rd
Dagenham RM9 81 A4
Plumstead SE18 123 A2
Maxfield Cl N20 14 A4
Maxim Apartments 3 BR2 209 B5
Maxim Rd N21 16 C5
Maxted Pk HA1 42 C2
Maxted Rd SE15 139 D2
Maxwell Cl
Croydon CR0 204 A1
Hayes UB3 106 A6
Maxwell Ct SE21 162 A3
Maxwell Gdns BR6 227 D5
Maxwell Ho
Bowes Pk N22 32 B4
Chislehurst BR7 188 D3
12 Shooters Hill SE18 144 D6
Maxwell Rd
Ashford TW15 171 A4
Fulham SW6 135 D5 265 D3
Welling DA16 146 A2
West Drayton UB7 104 B2
Maxwelton Ave NW7 27 B5
Maxwelton Cl NW7 27 B5
Maya Angelou Ct E4 36 A6
Maya Cl SE15 140 B3
Mayall Cl EN3 7 C5
Mayall Rd SE24 160 D6
Maya Pl N11 31 D3
Maya Rd N2 48 A5
Maybank Ave
Wembley HA0 65 A3
Woodford E18 37 B1
Maybank Gdns HA5 40 A4
Maybank Rd E18 37 C2
May Bate Ave KT2 175 D2
Maybells Commercial Est IG11 102 D5
Mayberry Pl KT5 198 B2
Maybourne Cl SE26 184 B5
Maybourne Grange CR0 221 C6
Maybrook Ct E11 77 B6
Maybury Cl Enfield EN1 6 B5
Petts Wood BR5 210 D4
Maybury Ct
Beckenham BR3 185 B3
Croydon CR2 220 D3
Harrow HA1 42 B3
Marylebone W1 238 B3
Maybury Gdns NW10 68 B2
Maybury Mews N6 49 C2
Maybury Rd
Barking IG11 102 A5
Newham E13 99 C3
Maybury St SW17 180 C5
Maychurch Cl HA7 25 D3
May Cl KT9 214 B2
Maycroft
2 Hayes BR2 208 D1
Pinner HA5 22 B1
Maycross Ave SM4 201 C5
May Ct 2 SW19 180 A2
Mayday Gdns SE3 144 A3
Mayday Rd CR0, CR7 204 D3
Mayday University Hospl CR7 204 D3
Maydeb Ct RM6 59 B3
Maydew Ho SE16 118 C2
Maydwell Ho 6 E14 97 C2
Mayerne Rd SE9 165 D6
Mayesbrook Rd
Barking IG11 101 D6
Dagenham RM8, IG3 80 B5
Mayesford Rd RM6 58 C2
Mayespark Prim Sch IG3 80 A5
Mayes Rd N22 32 B1
Mayeswood Rd SE12 187 C6
MAYFAIR 115 B6
Mayfair Ave
Bexley DA7 146 D4
Dagenham RM6 58 D3
Ilford IG1 56 C1
New Malden KT4 200 A1
Twickenham TW2 152 A4
Mayfair Cl
Beckenham BR3 185 D2
Surbiton KT6 198 A1
Mayfair Ct
2 Beckenham BR3 185 D2
7 Croydon CR0 221 D6
Edgware HA8 26 B5
13 Wimbledon SW19 179 A3
Mayfair Gdns
Tottenham N17 33 B4
Woodford IG8 37 A3
Mayfair Ho 11 SE1 118 A2
Mayfair Pl W1 248 D4
Mayfair Terr N14 15 D4
Mayfield DA7 147 B2
Mayfield Ave
Broom Hill BR6 211 D2
Chiswick W4 111 C2
Harrow HA3 43 B4
North Finchley N12 30 B6
Osidge N14 15 D2
West Ealing W13 109 B4
Woodford IG8 37 A4
Mayfield Cl
Ashford TW15 170 D4
Clapham Pk SW4 159 D6
Dalston E8 73 D2
Hillingdon UB10 82 D4
Long Ditton KT7 197 B1
Penge SE20 184 B2
Mayfield Cres
Enfield N9 18 B5
Thornton Heath CR7 204 B4
Mayfield Ct SM2 218 A1
Mayfield Dr HA5 41 B5
Mayfield Gdns
Ealing W7 86 C2
Hendon NW4 46 D3
Mayfield Ho
31 Bethnal Green E2 96 B5
Stamford Hill N16 51 C2
Mayfield Mans SW15 157 B6
Mayfield Prim Sch W7 86 B1
Mayfield Rd
Acton W3 110 D6
Bedford Pk W12 111 C4
Bromley BR1 210 A4
Chingford E4 20 B2
Dagenham RM8 58 C1
Dalston E8 73 D1
Enfield EN3 6 D3
Higham Hill E17 35 A1
Hornsey Vale N8 50 B3
Merton SW19 179 B2
Newham E13 98 D3
South Croydon CR2 221 B1
Sutton SM2 218 B2
Thornton Heath CR7 204 B4
Mayfields HA9 66 C6
Mayfield Sch & Coll RM8 58 C1
Mayfields Cl HA9 66 C6
Mayfield Villas DA14 190 C4
Mayflower Cl
Bermondsey SE16 118 D2
Ruislip HA4 39 A3
Mayflower Ho 2 IG11 101 B6
Mayflower Lo
Hendon N3 47 B6
Muswell Hill N10 31 A2
Mayflower Prim Sch 22 E14 97 D1
Mayflower Rd SW9 138 A2
Mayflower St 1 SE16 118 C4
Mayfly Cl HA5 40 C2
Mayfly Gdns 12 UB5 84 D4
Mayford NW1 232 B4
Mayford Cl
Balham SW12 158 D4
Penge BR3 206 D6
Mayford Rd SW12 159 A4
May Gdns Elstree WD6 9 D5
Wembley HA0 87 C4
Maygood Ho N1 234 A4
Maygood St N1 94 C5 234 A4
Maygrove Rd NW6 69 B2
Mayhew Cl E4 19 C1
Mayhew Ct 2 SE5 139 B1
Mayhill Rd Barnet EN5 13 A5
Greenwich SE7 143 B6
Mayland Mans 4 IG11 78 D1
Maylands Dr DA14 168 D1

Maylands Ho SW3 .. 257 B3
Maylands Rd WD19 ... 22 C6
Maylie Ho 4 SE16 ... 118 B4
Maynard Cl
Fulham
SW6 ..... 135 D5 265 D3
Tottenham N15 .... 51 C4
Maynard Ct EN3 .... 7 C5
Maynard Ho
Mile End E1 .... 97 A4
2 Plumstead SE18 .. 123 A2
Maynard Rd E17 ...... 54 A4
Maynards Quay E1 ... 118 C6
Mayne Ct E8 .... 74 A4
Maynooth Gdns CR4 202 D2
Mayo Ct W13 .... 109 B3
Mayo Ho 10 E1 .... 96 C2
Mayola Rd E5 .... 74 C4
Mayo Rd
Thornton Heath CR0 .. 205 B4
Walton-on-T KT12 ... 194 A2
Willesden NW10 ...... 67 C2
Mayow Rd SE23,
SE26 .... 184 D6
Mayplace Cl DA7 ... 147 D2
Mayplace La SE18 ... 144 D6
Mayplace Rd W DA7 .147 C1
Maypole Ct UB2 .... 107 B4
May Rd Chingford E4 ... 35 C4
Newham E13 .... 99 A5
Twickenham TW2 .... 152 C3
Mayroyd Ave KT6 ... 214 C6
May's Buildings Mews
SE10 .... 142 B5
Mays Ct WC2 .... 250 A5
May's Ct SE10 ...... 142 B5
May's Hill Rd BR2 ... 208 C6
May's La EN5 .... 12 C5
Maysoule Rd SW11 .. 136 B1
Mays Rd TW11, TW12 .. 174 B5
May St W14 .... 254 D1
Maystocks E18 .... 55 C6
Mayston Mews 3
SE10 .... 121 A1
May Terr IG1 .... 78 D4
Maythorne Cotts
SE13 .... 164 B5
Mayton St N7 .... 72 B5
Maytree Cl HA8 .... 11 A1
Maytree Ct
Mitcham CR4 .... 203 A6
Northolt UB5 .... 85 A4
May Tree Ho SE4 ..... 141 B2
Maytree La HA7 .... 24 D3
Maytree Wlk SW2 .... 160 C2
Mayville Prim Sch
E11 .... 76 C6
Mayville Rd Ilford IG1 . 78 D3
Leyton E11 .... 76 C6
Mayward Ho 7 SE5 .. 139 C4
May Wlk E13 .... 99 B5
Maywood Cl BR3 .... 185 D3
May Wynne Ho E16 ... 99 B1
Maze Hill SE10, SE3 .. 142 C6
Maze Hill Lodge 7
SE10 .... 142 B6
Maze Hill Sta SE10 .. 142 C6
Mazenod Ave NW6 .... 69 C1
Maze Rd TW9 .... 132 C5
Mead Cl
3 Camden Town
NW1 .... 71 A1
Harrow HA3 .... 24 B2
Mead Cres
Carshalton SM1 ..... 218 C4
Chingford E4 .... 36 A6
Meadcroft Ho 4
KT3 .... 199 C2
Meadcroft Rd SE17 . 138 D6
Mead Ct NW9 .... 45 B4
Meade Cl W4 .... 132 C6
Meader Ct SE14 ..... 140 D5
Meadfield HA8 .... 10 D2
Mead Field HA2 ...... 63 B5
Meadfield Gn HA8 .... 10 D2
Meadfoot Rd SW16 .. 181 C2
Mead Gr RM6 .... 58 D6
Mead Ho W11 ...... 244 C4
Mead House La UB4 ... 83 B3
Meadhurst Club
TW16 .... 171 D5
Meadhurst Pk TW16 .171 C4
Mead Inf Sch The
KT19 .... 215 D4
Meadlands Dr TW10. 153 D2
Meadlands Prim Sch
TW10 .... 175 C6
Mead Lo W4 .... 111 B4
Meadow Ave CR0 ... 206 D3
Meadowbank
Lewisham SE3 ...... 142 D2
Primrose Hill NW3 ..... 70 D1
Southgate N21 .... 16 B5
Surbiton KT5 .... 198 B3
Meadow Bank 8
SW15 .... 157 B6
Meadowbank Cl
SW6 .... 134 C5
Meadowbank Gdns
TW5 .... 128 B4
Meadowbank Rd
NW9 .... 45 B2
Meadowbanks EN5 ... 12 A6
Meadowbrook Ct
TW7 .... 130 D2
Meadow Cl
Barking IG11 .... 80 A1
Barnet EN5 .... 13 B5
Bexley DA6 .... 169 B6
Catford SE6 .... 185 C5
Chingford E4 .... 19 D3
Chislehurst BR7 ..... 188 D5
Enfield EN3 .... 7 A5
Hackney E9 .... 75 B3
Hinchley Wood KT10 . 212 D5
Hounslow TW4 ...... 151 C5
Northolt UB5 .... 85 C5
Richmond TW10 ..... 154 A3
Ruislip HA4 .... 39 D3
Sutton SM1 .... 218 A6
West Barnes SW20 .. 200 C5
Meadowcourt Rd
SE3 .... 142 D1
Meadowcroft 8 W4 .110 C1
Meadow Croft BR1 ... 210 B6
Meadowcroft Rd N13 .16 C2
Meadow Dr
Hendon NW4 .... 28 C1
Muswell Hill N10 ...... 49 B6
Meadowford Cl
SE28 .... 124 A6
Meadow Garth NW10 . 67 B2
Meadow Gate HA2 .... 63 D5
Meadowgate Cl NW7 .. 27 D5
Meadowgate Sch
SE4 .... 141 A2
Meadow Gdns HA8 ... 27 A4
Meadow High Sch
UB8 .... 82 A2
Meadow Hill KT3 .... 199 C3
Meadow La SE12 .... 165 B1
Meadow Mews SW8 270 C5
Meadow Pl
Chiswick W4 .... 133 C5
South Lambeth
SW8 ...... 138 A5 270 B4
Meadow Rd
Ashford TW15 .... 171 B5
Barking IG11 .... 80 A1
Beckenham BR2 ..... 186 C1
Carshalton SM1 ..... 218 C3
Claygate KT10 ...... 212 C2
Dagenham RM9 .... 81 B2
Feltham TW13 ...... 151 A2
Merton SW19 .... 180 A3
Pinner HA5 .... 41 A5
Southall UB1 .... 107 B6
South Lambeth
SW8 ...... 138 B5 270 C4
Meadow Row SE1 ... 262 A5
Meadows Cl E10 ...... 75 C6
Meadows Ct DA14 ... 190 B4
Meadows End TW16 . 172 A2
Meadowside
Eltham SE9 .... 143 C1
Twickenham TW1 .... 153 D4
Meadow Stile CR0 ... 221 A5
Meadowsweet Cl
3 Newham E16 ...... 99 D2
West Barnes KT3 .... 200 C5
Meadow The BR7 .... 189 A4
Meadowview TW17 .. 193 A2
Meadow View
Blackfen DA15 ...... 168 B4
Harrow HA1 .... 42 C1
Meadowview Rd
Catford SE6 .... 185 C5
Sidcup DA5 .... 169 B5
West Ewell KT19 .... 215 C1
Meadow View Rd
Hayes UB4 .... 83 B3
Meadow View Rd
continued
Thornton Heath CR7 . 204 D4
Meadow Way
Kingsbury NW9 .... 45 B4
Locksbottom BR6 .... 226 C5
Ruislip HA4 .... 40 B3
Wembley HA9 .... 65 D4
Meadow Waye TW5 .. 129 A5
Meadow Way The
HA3 .... 24 C2
Meadow Wlk
Dagenham RM9 .... 81 B2
Hackbridge SM6 ..... 219 B5
Wanstead E18 .... 55 A5
West Ewell KT17,
KT19 .... 215 D1
Meadow Wood Sch
WD23 .... 8 A6
Mead Pl Croydon CR0 .205 A1
Hackney E9 .... 74 C2
Mead Plat NW10 ...... 67 A2
Mead Rd
Chislehurst BR7 ..... 189 A4
Edgware HA8 .... 26 C4
Richmond TW10 ..... 153 C1
Mead Road Inf Sch
BR7 .... 189 A4
Mead Row
SE1 .... 116 C3 261 A6
Meads Ct E15 .... 76 D2
Meadside Cl BR3 .... 185 A2
Meads La IG3 .... 57 D2
Meads Rd Enfield EN3 ... 7 A4
Tottenham N22 .... 32 D1
Meads The
Cheam SM3 .... 217 A5
Edgware HA8 .... 27 B4
Hillingdon UB8 .... 82 A3
Mead The
Beckenham BR3 ..... 186 A2
Ealing W13 .... 87 B2
Finchley N2 .... 30 A1
Ickenham UB10 .... 60 C6
Wallington SM6 ..... 219 D2
West Wickham BR4 ... 208 B1
Meadvale Rd
Croydon CR0 .... 206 A3
Ealing W5 .... 87 C3
Meadway
Ashford TW15 ...... 170 C6
Barnet EN5 .... 1 C1
Beckenham BR3 ..... 186 A2
Enfield EN3 .... 6 D6
Esher KT10 .... 212 A1
Hampstead Garden Suburb
NW11 .... 47 D3
Ilford IG3 .... 79 C4
Palmers Green N14 .... 16 A2
Tolworth KT5 .... 199 A1
Twickenham TW2 .... 152 B3
West Barnes SW20 .. 200 C5
Woodford IG8 .... 37 C5
Mead Way
Croydon CR0 .... 223 A6
Hayes BR2 .... 209 A3
Ruislip HA4 .... 39 B3
Meadway Cl
Barnet EN5 .... 1 C1
Hampstead Garden Suburb
NW11 .... 47 D3
Pinner HA5 .... 23 D4
Meadway Ct
Dagenham RM8 .... 81 B6
Ealing W5 .... 88 B2
Hampstead Garden Suburb
NW11 .... 47 D3
Meadway Gate NW11 . 47 C3
Meadway Gdns HA4 ... 39 B3
Meadway The
Buckhurst Hill IG9 ..... 21 D3
Lewisham SE3 .... 142 B3
Meaford Way SE20 ... 184 B3
Meakin Est SE1 ..... 263 A6
Meakin Ho N7 .... 72 B3
Meanley Rd E12 ...... 78 A3
Meard St W1 .... 239 C1
Meath Cres E1, E2 ..... 96 D4
Meath Ho SE24 ..... 160 D5
Meath Rd Ilford IG1 ... 79 A5
Newham E15 .... 98 D5
Meath St
SW11 ...... 137 B4 268 C2
Mecklenburgh Pl
WC1 .... 240 C6
Mecklenburgh Sq
WC1 .... 94 B3 240 C6
Mecklenburgh St
WC1 .... 240 C6
Medburn St NW1 ... 232 C4
Medcalf Rd EN3 .... 7 B6
Medcroft Gdns
SW14 .... 133 A1
Medebourne Cl SE3 .. 143 A2
Mede Ho BR1 .... 187 B5
Medesenge Way N13 .. 32 D4
Medfield St SW15 ... 156 B4
Medhurst Cl 19 E3 .... 97 A5
Medhurst Dr BR1 ... 186 C5
Median Rd E5 .... 74 C3
Medici Cl IG3 .... 58 A3
Medina Ave KT10 ... 212 C5
Medina Ct N7 .... 72 C5
Medina Gr N7 .... 72 C5
Medina Ho SE15 .... 140 C1
Medina Rd N7 .... 72 C5
Medlar Cl 1 UB5 ..... 84 D5
Medlar Ho 3 DA15 .. 168 A1
Medlar St SE5 ...... 139 A4
Medley Rd NW6 .... 69 C2
Medora Rd SW2 ..... 160 B4
Medresco Ho NW3 .... 70 B3
Medusa Rd SE6,
SE13 .... 163 D5
Medway Bldgs E3 ..... 97 A5
Medway Cl
Croydon CR0 .... 206 C3
Ilford IG1 .... 79 A3
Medway Ct
South Norwood
SE25 .... 205 C4
St Pancras WC1 .... 233 A1
Medway Dr UB6 ...... 86 D5
Medway Gdns HA0 .... 65 A4
Medway Ho
Bermondsey SE1 .... 252 D1
6 Kingston u T KT2 .. 175 D2
Paddington NW8 .... 237 A4
Stoke Newington N16 .. 73 B4
Medway Mews 35 E3 .. 97 A5
Medway Par 1 UB6 ... 86 D5
Medway Rd E3 .... 97 A5
Medway St
SW1 ...... 115 D3 259 D5
Medwin St SW4 ..... 138 B1
Meecham Ct 1
SW11 .... 136 C3
Meerbrook Rd SE3 .. 143 C2
Meers Ct SW20 ...... 178 C2
Meeson Rd E15 .... 76 D1
Meeson St E5 .... 75 A4
Meeting House Alley 7
E1 .... 118 B5
Meeting House La
SE15 .... 140 B5
Mehetabel Rd E9 ..... 74 C3
Meister Cl IG1 .... 57 B1
Melanda Cl BR7 ..... 188 B5
Melanie Cl DA7 ..... 147 A4
Melba Way SE13 .... 141 D4
Melbourne Ave
Bowes Pk N13 .... 32 B4
Ealing W13 .... 109 A5
Pinner HA2, HA5 ...... 41 D6
Melbourne Cl
Broom Hill BR6 ..... 211 C2
Ickenham UB10 .... 60 C4
Wallington SM6 ..... 219 C3
Melbourne Ct
Hackney E5 .... 75 A4
Muswell Hill N10 ...... 31 B3
Paddington W9 ..... 236 B6
Penge SE20 .... 184 A3
Twickenham TW2 .... 152 B3
Melbourne Gdns RM6 59 A4
Melbourne Gr SE22 . 139 D1
Melbourne Ho
Hayes UB4 .... 84 C3
Kensington W8 ..... 245 A3
South Norwood SE25 . 205 D5
Melbourne Mews
Brixton SW9 .... 138 C4
Catford SE6 .... 164 A4
Melbourne Pl WC2 .. 240 D1
Melbourne Rd
Ilford IG1 .... 56 D1
Leyton E10 .... 53 D2
Merton SW19 .... 179 C2
Newham E6 .... 100 B5
Teddington TW11 .... 175 C4
Wallington SM6 ..... 219 C3
Melbourne Rd continued
Walthamstow E17 ..... 53 A5
Melbourne Sq 21
SW9 .... 138 C4
Melbourne Way EN1 .. 17 D5
Melbray Mews 11
SW6 .... 135 B3
Melbreak Ho 11
SE22 .... 139 C2
Melbury Ave UB2 ... 107 D3
Melbury Cl
Claygate KT10 ...... 213 B2
Elmstead BR7 ...... 188 B4
Melbury Ct
W8 .... 113 B3 254 D6
Melbury Dr SE5 ..... 139 C5
Melbury Gdns SW20 . 178 B2
Melbury Grange
BR1 .... 188 A2
Melbury Ho
South Lambeth SW8 . 270 C4
Twickenham TW2 .... 152 B2
Melbury Rd
Harrow HA3 .... 44 B4
Kensington
W14 ..... 113 B3 254 D6
Melchester 5 W11 ... 91 B1
Melchester Ho 1
N19 .... 71 D5
Melcombe Ct NW1 .. 237 C4
Melcombe Gdns HA3 .. 44 B3
Melcombe Ho SW8 .. 270 C3
Melcombe Pl NW1 .. 237 C4
Melcombe Prim Sch 6
W6 .... 134 D6
Melcombe St
NW1 .... 92 D3 237 D5
Meldex Cl NW7 .... 28 C4
Meldon Cl SW6 ..... 265 D2
Meldone KT3 .... 199 B1
Meldone Cl KT5 ..... 198 D3
Meldrum Rd IG3 ...... 80 A6
Melfield Gdns SE6 .. 186 A5
Melford Ave IG11 ..... 79 D2
Melford Cl KT9 ..... 214 B3
Melford Ct
Bermondsey SE1 .... 263 B6
Dulwich SE22 .... 162 A4
Hackney E5 .... 74 B5
2 Sutton SM2 ...... 218 A1
Melford Rd
Dulwich SE21, SE22 .. 162 A3
Ilford IG1 .... 79 B6
Leyton E11 .... 76 C6
Newham E6 .... 100 B4
Walthamstow E17 ..... 53 B5
Melfort Ave CR7 .... 204 D6
Melfort Rd CR7 ..... 204 D6
Melgund Rd N5 .... 72 C3
Melina Cl UB3 .... 83 B2
Melina Ct
Putney SW15 .... 134 A2
St John's Wood NW8 . 229 C1
Melina Pl
NW8 .... 92 B4 229 C1
Melina Rd W12 ...... 112 B4
Melior Ct N6 .... 49 C3
Melior Pl SE1 ...... 253 A2
Melior St
SE1 .... 117 C4 253 A2
Meliot Rd SE6 ...... 164 B2
Melisa Ct N6 .... 49 D2
Meller Cl SM6 ...... 220 A5
Mellifont Cl SM5 .... 202 B2
Melling Dr EN1 .... 6 A4
Melling St SE18 .... 145 C6
Mellington Ct 2 N16 . 74 A5
Mellis Ave TW9 ..... 132 D4
Mellish Cl IG11 ..... 101 D6
Mellish Ct KT6 ..... 198 A3
Mellish Flats E10 ..... 53 C2
Mellish Gdns IG8 ..... 37 A5
Mellish Ho 2 E1 ...... 96 B1
Mellish Ind Est SE18 121 D3
Mellish St E14 ...... 119 C3
Mellison Rd SW17 ... 180 C5
Mellitus St W12 ...... 89 D1
Mellor Cl KT12 ..... 195 B2
Mellor Ct 2 SW19 ... 180 A3
Mellor Ho 2 SE21 ... 183 C6
Mellow La E UB4 ..... 83 A3
Mellow Lane Sch
UB4 .... 83 A3

Mellow La W UB10 83 A4
Mellows Rd
Redbridge IG5 56 B6
Wallington SM6 219 D3
Mells Cres SE9 188 B6
Mell St 6 SE10 120 C1
Melody La N5 73 A3
Melody Rd SW18 158 A6
Melon Pl W8 245 B2
Melon Rd Leyton E11 76 C5
Peckham SE15 140 A4
Melrose Ave
Borehamwood WD6 10 D6
Cricklewood NW2 68 C3
Greenford UB6 85 D5
Mitcham CR4 181 B3
Thornton Heath SW16 204 C6
Tottenham N22 32 D2
Twickenham TW2 151 D4
Wimbledon SW19 157 C1
Melrose Cl
Greenford UB6 85 D5
Grove Pk SE12 165 B3
Hayes UB4 84 A2
Melrose Cres BR6 227 B3
Melrose Ct
5 Ealing W13 109 A5
Wandsworth SW18 157 B5
Melrose Dr UB1 107 C5
Melrose Gdns
Edgware HA8 26 D1
Hammersmith W6 112 C3
Kingston u T KT3 199 B6
Melrose Ho
Maida Vale NW6 91 C4
Pimlico SW1 258 D2
Melrose Rd
1 Barnes SW13 133 D3
Merton SW19 179 C2
Pinner HA5 41 B5
Wandsworth SW18 157 B5
Melrose Specl Sch 2 CR4 202 C6
Melrose Terr W6 112 C3
Melrose Tudor SM6 220 A3
Melsa Rd SM4 202 A3
Melthorne Dr HA4 62 C5
Melthorpe Gdns SE3 144 A4
Melton Cl HA4 40 C1
Melton Ct
11 Croydon CR0 221 D6
South Kensington SW7 256 D3
Sutton SM2 218 A1
1 Twickenham TW1 153 B4
Melton Ho E5 74 A6
Melton St NW1 93 D4 232 C1
Melville Ave
Greenford UB6 64 D3
South Croydon CR2 221 D3
Wimbledon SW20 178 A3
Melville Cl UB10 61 B5
Melville Court Flats 8 W12 112 B4
Melville Ct
4 Brentford W4 110 C1
Rotherhithe SE8 119 A2
Melville Gdns N13 32 D5
Melville Ho
Lewisham SE10 142 A4
New Barnet EN5 14 B5
Melville Pl 4 N1 73 A1
Melville Rd
Barnes SW13 134 A4
Sidcup DA14 168 C2
Stonebridge NW10 67 B1
Walthamstow E17 53 B6
Melville Villas Rd W3 111 B5
Melvin Ct 11 TW9 132 C4
Melvin Rd SE20 184 C2
Melwood Ho 23 E1 96 B1
Melyn Cl N7 71 C4
Memel Ct EC1 242 A5
Memel St EC1 242 A5
Memess Path 4 SE18 144 C6
Memorial Ave E15 98 C4
Memorial Cl TW5 129 B6
Memorial Hospl SE18 144 C3
Memorial Hts IG2 57 B3
Menai Pl 2 E3 97 C5
Menard Ct EC1 235 B1
Mendham Ho SE1 263 A6
Mendip Cl
Forest Hill SE26 184 C6
Harlington UB3 127 B5
North Cheam KT4 216 C6
Mendip Ct
12 Battersea SW11 136 A2
Deptford SE14 140 C6
1 East Barnet N20 14 C2
Mendip Dr NW2, NW11 69 A6
Mendip Ho
Harrow HA3 43 A3
2 Stoke Newington N4 51 B2
Mendip Hos 12 E2 96 C4
Mendip Rd
Battersea SW11 136 A2
Bushey WD23 8 A5
Ilford IG2 57 C4
Mendora Rd SW6 135 B5 264 C4
Menelik Rd NW2 69 B4
Menin Wks CR4 180 D1
Menlo Gdns SE19 183 B3
Mennie Ho SE18 144 B4
Mennis Ho SM5 218 C6
Menon Dr N9 18 B1
Menorah Foundation Sch 8 HA8 27 A3
Menorah Gram Sch HA8 27 A3
Menorah High Sch for Girls NW2 68 A5
Menorah Prim Sch NW11 47 A2
Menotti St 6 E2 96 A3
Menteath Ho 9 E14 97 C1
Mentmore Cl HA3 43 C3
Mentmore Terr E8 74 B1
Mentone Ct SW8 270 B2
Meon Ct TW7 130 C3
Meon Rd W3 111 A4
Meopham Rd CR4, SW16 181 C2
Mepham Cres HA3 24 A3
Mepham Gdns HA3 24 A3
Mepham St SE1 116 C5 251 A3
Mera Dr DA7 147 D1
Merantun Way SW19 180 A2
Merbury Cl
Lewisham SE13 164 B6
Woolwich SE28 123 B5
Merbury Rd SE28 123 C4
Mercator Pl 4 E14 119 C1
Mercator Rd SE13 142 B1
Mercer Cl KT7 196 D2
Merceron Ho 3 E2 96 C4
Merceron St E1 96 B3
Mercer Pl HA5 22 C1
Mercers Cl SE10 120 D2
Mercer's Cotts 3 E3 97 A1
Mercers Mews N7 71 D4
Mercers Pl W6 112 D2
Mercers Rd N19 71 D5
Mercer St WC2 94 A1 240 A1
Merchant Ct E1 118 C5
Merchants Cl SE25 206 A5
Merchants Ho SE10 120 B1
Merchants Lo 5 E17 53 C5
Merchant Sq W2 236 C3
Merchant St E3 97 B4
Merchant Taylors' Almshouses SE13 142 C1
Merchant Taylors Hall* EC3 242 D1
Merchiston Rd SE6 164 B2
Merchland Rd SE9 167 A3
Merchon Ho N7 71 C4
Mercia Gr SE13 142 A1
Mercia Ho
9 Camberwell SE5 139 A3
Charlton TW15 171 A2
Mercie Ct SE22 162 A3
Mercier Rd SW15 157 A6
Mercury 25 NW9 27 D2
Mercury Ct
8 Brixton SW9 138 C4
Mercury Ct *continued*
10 Millwall E14 119 C2
Mercury Ctr TW14 150 A6
Mercury Ho
Brentford TW8 109 D1
6 Old Ford E3 97 C6
Mercury Rd 2 TW8 109 C1
Mercury Way SE14 140 D6
Mercy Terr SE13 163 D6
Merebank La CR0, SM6 220 B3
Mere Cl
Orpington BR6 226 D6
Putney SW15, SW19 156 D4
Meredith Ave NW2 68 C3
Meredith Cl HA5 22 D3
Meredith Ho 17 N16 73 C3
Meredith Mews SE4 141 B1
Meredith St
Finsbury EC1 234 C1
Newham E13 99 A4
Meredith Twr W3 110 D3
Meredyth Rd SW13 134 A3
Mere End CR0 206 D2
Mere Rd TW17 192 D3
Mereside BR6 226 C6
Mereside Pk TW15 171 A6
Meretone Cl SE4 141 A1
Mereton Mans 6 SE8 141 C4
Meretune Ct SM4 201 B6
Merevale Cres SM4 202 A3
Mereway Industry TW2 152 C4
Mereway Rd TW2 152 C3
Merewood Cl BR1 188 C1
Merewood Gdns CR0 206 D2
Mereworth Cl BR2 208 D4
Mereworth Dr SE18 145 A5
Mereworth Ho 3 SE15 140 C6
Merganser Ct 17 SE8 141 B6
Merganser Gdns SE28 123 B3
Meridan Ct SE13 142 B1
Meriden Cl BR1 187 D3
Meriden Ct SW3 257 A1
Meriden Ho
4 Barnet EN5 1 A1
25 Hoxton N1 95 C6
Meridian Building* SE10 142 B5
Meridian Cl NW7 27 B6
Meridian Ct
4 Bermondsey SE16 118 A4
4 Catford SE6 164 D3
Croydon CR0 220 C4
Meridian Ho SE10 120 C2
Meridian Pl E14 120 A4
Meridian Prim Sch 9 SE10 142 B6
Meridian Rd SE7 143 D5
Meridian Sq E15 76 B1
Meridian Trad Est SE7 121 B2
Meridian Way
Enfield EN3 19 A5
Lower Edmonton N9, N18 18 D1
Meridian Wlk N17 33 C4
Merifield Rd SE9 143 C1
Merino Cl E11 55 C5
Merino Pl DA15 168 A6
Merioneth Ct 7 W7 86 D2
Merivale Rd
Harrow HA1 42 A2
Putney SW15 135 A1
Merlewood Dr BR7 188 B2
Merley Ct NW9 45 A1
Merlin 26 NW9 27 D2
Merlin Cl
Mitcham CR4 202 C6
4 Northolt UB5 84 C4
South Croydon CR0 221 C4
Wallington SM6 220 B2
Merlin Cres HA8 26 B2
Merlin Ct
Beckenham BR2 208 D5
6 Ealing W7 86 D3
Mitcham CR4 180 C2
Ruislip HA4 61 B6
Stanmore HA7 25 B5
Wood Green N22 32 C2
Merling Cl KT9 213 D3
Merlin Gdns BR1 165 A1
Merlin Gr BR3 207 C4
Merlin Ho
7 Chiswick W4 111 B1
Enfield EN3 18 D6
West Hampstead NW3 69 D4
Merlin Prim Sch BR1 165 A1
Merlin Rd
Bexley DA16 146 A1
Wanstead E12 77 D6
Merlin Rd N DA16 146 A1
Merlins Ave HA2 63 B5
Merlin Sch The 11 SW15 157 A6
Merlins Ct WC1 234 A1
Merlin St EC1 94 C4 234 A1
Mermaid Ct
Bermondsey SE1 117 B4 252 C2
Rotherhithe SE16 119 B5
Stroud Green N4 50 C3
Mermaid Ho 8 E14 120 A6
Mermaid Twr 22 SE8 141 B6
Meroe Ct N16 73 C6
Merredene St SW2 160 B5
Merriam Ave 2 E9 75 B2
Merriam Cl E4 36 A5
Merrick Rd UB2 107 B3
Merricks Ct 5 SW14 132 D1
Merrick Sq SE1 117 B3 262 C6
Merridale SE12 164 D6
Merridene N21 16 D5
Merrielands Cres RM9 103 B5
Merrielands Ret Pk RM9 103 B5
Merrilands Rd KT4 200 C1
Merrilees Rd DA15 167 C4
Merrilyn Cl KT10 213 A2
Merriman Rd SE3 143 C4
Merrington Rd SW6 265 B6
Merrion Ave HA7 25 D5
Merritt Gdns KT9 213 C2
Merritt Rd SE4 163 B6
Merrivale
Camden Town NW1 232 B5
Southgate N14 15 D6
Merrivale Ave IG4 55 D5
Merrow Ct CR4 180 B1
Merrow St SE17 117 B1 262 C1
Merrow Way CR0 224 A2
Merrow Wlk SE17 262 D2
Merrydown Way BR7 188 B2
Merry Fiddlers RM8 81 B6
Merryfield SE3 142 D3
Merryfield Gdns HA7 25 C5
Merryfield Ho SE12 165 C1
Merryhill Cl E4 19 D4
Merry Hill Rd WD23 8 A3
Merryhills Ct N14 15 C6
Merryhills Dr EN2 4 A1
Merryhills Prim Sch EN2 4 B1
Merryweather Ct
13 Dartmouth Pk N19 71 C5
1 New Malden KT3 199 C4
Mersea Ho IG11 78 D2
Mersey Ct 10 KT2 175 D2
Mersey Ho 10 N7 72 C3
Mersey Rd E17 53 B6
Mersey Wlk UB5 85 C5
Mersham Dr NW9 44 D4
Mersham Pl
Penge SE20 184 B2
South Norwood CR7 183 B1
Mersham Rd CR7 183 B1
Merstone Ho SW18 157 D5
Merten Rd RM6 59 A2
Merthyr Terr SW13 134 B6
MERTON 179 C2
Merton Abbey Mills Mkt* SW19 180 A2
Merton Abbey Prim Sch SW19 179 D2
Merton Ave
Chiswick W4 111 D2
Hillingdon UB10 60 D1
Northolt UB5 64 A3
Merton Coll SM4 201 B4
Merton Court Prep Sch DA14 190 C6
Merton Ct Barnet EN5 1 D1
Welling DA16 146 B3
Merton Gdns BR5 210 D4
Merton Hall Gdns SW20 179 A2
Merton Hall Rd SW19 179 A2
Merton High St SW19 180 A3
Merton Ho SW18 157 C3
Merton Ind Pk SW19 180 A2
Merton La N6 70 D6
Merton Lo
New Barnet EN5 14 A6
3 Streatham SW16 182 A5
Merton Mans SW20 178 D1
MERTON PARK 179 C1
Merton Park Par SW19 179 B2
Merton Park Prim Sch SW19 179 C1
Merton Park Sta SW19 179 C2
Merton Pl 9 SW19 180 A3
Merton Rd
Barking IG11 79 D1
Croydon CR0 205 D3
Croydon SE25 206 A4
Enfield EN2 5 B5
Harrow HA2 42 A1
Ilford IG3 57 D2
Leytonstone E17 54 A3
Merton SW19 179 D3
Wandsworth SW18 157 C4
Merton Rise NW3 70 C1
Merton Road Ind Est SW18 157 C4
Merton Way
East Molesey KT8 196 A6
Hillingdon UB10 60 D1
Merttins Rd SE15 162 D6
Meru Cl NW5 71 A3
Mervan Rd SW2 138 C1
Mervyn Ave SE9 167 A2
Mervyn Ct SE18 145 C6
Mervyn Rd
Brentford W13 109 A3
Shepperton TW17 193 A2
Mervyn Stockwood Ho 1 SE9 167 A2
Messaline Ave W3 89 A1
Messent Rd SE9 165 D6
Messer Ct CR0 220 D4
Messeter Pl SE9 166 C5
Messina Ave NW6 69 C1
Messiter Ho N1 233 D5
Met Appts The SE12 164 D6
Metcalfe Ho 28 SW8 137 D3
Metcalfe Wlk 2 TW13 173 A6
Metcalf Rd TW15 170 D5
Meteor St SW11 137 A1
Meteor Way SM6 220 A1
Metford Cres EN3 7 C5
Metherell Ho N21 17 B5
Metheringham Way NW9 27 C2
Methley Ho 8 N7 72 B6
Methley St SE11 116 C1 261 B1
Methodist Central Hall* SW1 115 D4 249 D1
Methuen Cl HA8 26 C3
Methuen Pk N10 49 B6
Methuen Rd
Belvedere DA17 125 D2
Bexleyheath DA6 147 B1
Edgware HA8 26 C3
Methwold Rd W10 90 D2
Metro Bsns Ctr The SE26 185 B5
Metro Ctr UB4 106 C6
Metro Ho E7 77 B2
Metro Ind Ctr TW7 130 C3
Metropolis Apartments 5 SW12 159 B3
Metropolitan Benefit Societies Almshouses 3 N1 73 C2
Metropolitan Bsns Ctr 9 N1 73 C1

Metropolitan Cl 23 E14 ... 97 C2
Metropolitan Ctr The UB6 ... 85 D6
Metro Trad Ctr HA9 ... 66 D4
Meudon Ct KT6 ... 197 D4
Mews Pl IG8 ... 37 A6
Mews St E1 ... 118 A5
Mews The
Beckenham BR3 ... 185 C2
Hampton TW12 ... 174 A4
Hornsey N8 ... 50 C5
Redbridge IG4 ... 55 D4
Shoreditch N1 ... 235 B6
Thornton Heath SW16 ... 182 B2
Tottenham N15 ... 51 C5
5 Upper Holloway N19 ... 50 A1
Woolwich SE18 ... 122 D1
Mexborough NW1 ... 232 A5
Mexfield Rd SW15 ... 157 B6
Meyer Gn EN1 ... 6 A5
Meyer Ho 1 SW12 ... 159 B4
Meymott St SE1 ... 116 D5 251 C3
Meynell Cres E9 ... 74 D1
Meynell Gdns E9 ... 74 D1
Meynell Rd E9 ... 74 D1
Meyrick Ct CR7 ... 204 C3
Meyrick Ho 8 E14 ... 97 C2
Meyrick Rd
Battersea SW11 ... 136 C2
Willesden NW10 ... 68 A2
Miah Terr 9 E1 ... 118 A5
Miall Wlk SE26 ... 185 A6
Micawber Ave UB8 ... 82 C3
Micawber Ct N1 ... 235 B2
Micawber Ho 27 SE16 ... 118 A4
Micawber St N1 ... 95 A4 235 B2
Michael Cliffe Ho EC1 ... 234 B1
Michael Faraday Ho SE17 ... 262 D1
Michael Faraday Prim Sch SE17 ... 117 B1 262 D1
Michael Gaynor Cl W7 ... 108 D5
Michael Manley Ind Est 12 SW8 ... 137 C3
Michael Marshall Ho 2 SE9 ... 167 A2
Michaelmas Cl SW20 ... 200 C6
Michael Rd
Leytonstone E11 ... 54 D1
Parsons Green SW6 ... 135 D4 265 D2
South Norwood SE25 ... 205 C6
Michaels Cl SE13 ... 142 C1
Michael Sobell Sinai Sch HA3 ... 44 C3
Michaelson Ho 4 SE21 ... 183 C6
Michael Tippett Sch The SE24 ... 139 A1
Michelangelo Ct 14 SE16 ... 118 B1
Micheldever Rd SE12 ... 164 D5
Michelham Gdns TW1 ... 152 D1
Michelle Ct
Acton W3 ... 111 B6
North Finchley N12 ... 30 A5
Michell Ho TW1 ... 152 D3
Michels Almshouses 11 TW10 ... 154 A6
Michelsdale Dr 3 TW9 ... 132 A1
Michelson Ho SE11 ... 260 D3
Michel's Row 2 TW9 ... 132 A1
Michel Wlk SE18 ... 122 D1
Michigan Ave E12 ... 78 B4
Michigan Ho E14 ... 119 C3
Michleham Down N12 ... 29 B6
Mickledore NW1 ... 232 B3
Micklefield Ct CR0 ... 204 D3
Mickleham Cl BR5 ... 190 A1
Mickleham Gdns SM3 ... 217 A2
Mickleham Rd BR5 ... 190 A1
Mickleham Way CR0 ... 224 B1
Micklethwaite Rd SW6 ... 135 C6 265 B5
Mickleton Ho 30 W2 ... 91 C2
Midas Bsns Ctr RM10 ... 81 D4
Midas Metro Ctr SM4 ... 200 D2
Midcroft HA4 ... 39 C1
Middle Dene NW7 ... 11 B1
Middlefield NW8 ... 92 B6 229 C6
Middlefielde W13 ... 87 B2
Middlefield Gdns IG2 ... 56 D3
Middle Green Cl 3 KT5 ... 198 B3
Middleham Gdns N18 ... 34 A4
Middleham Rd N18 ... 34 A4
Middle La Hornsey N8 ... 50 A4
Teddington TW11 ... 174 D4
Middle Lane Mews N8 ... 50 A4
Middle Mill KT5 ... 198 B6
Middle Park Ave SE9 ... 165 D4
Middle Park Prim Sch SE9 ... 165 D4
Middle Rd
East Barnet EN4 ... 14 C5
Finchley N10 ... 30 C2
Harrow HA2 ... 42 B1
Mitcham SW16 ... 181 D1
12 Newham E13 ... 99 A5
Middle Row W10 ... 91 A3
Middle Row Prim Sch 21 W10 ... 91 A3
Middlesborough Rd N18 ... 34 A4
Middlesex Bsns Ctr UB2 ... 107 B4
Middlesex Cl UB6 ... 85 D3
Middlesex Ct
5 Chiswick W4 ... 111 D2
6 Harrow HA1 ... 42 D4
Middlesex Cty Cricket Sch N3 ... 29 D1
Middlesex Ho
Marylebone W1 ... 239 B4
4 Penge SE20 ... 184 C3
Wembley HA0 ... 87 D6
Middlesex Pas EC1 ... 241 D3
Middlesex Pl 13 E9 ... 74 C2
Middlesex Rd CR4 ... 204 A4
Middlesex Sch of Complementary Medicine HA7 ... 26 A1
Middlesex St E1 ... 95 D1 243 C2
Middlesex Univ (Archway Campus) 15 N19 ... 71 C6
Middlesex Univ (Cat Hill) EN4 ... 15 A6
Middlesex Univ (Chase Farm Hospl) EN2 ... 4 C5
Middlesex Univ (Hendon Campus) NW4 ... 46 B5
Middlesex Univ (Trent Park) EN4 ... 3 C3
Middle St
Croydon CR0 ... 221 A5
Holborn EC1 ... 242 A4
Middle Temple★ EC4 ... 251 A6
Middle Temple La EC4 ... 116 C6 251 A6
Middleton Ave
Chingford Green E4 ... 19 B1
Greenford UB5 ... 86 B5
Sidcup DA14 ... 190 C5
Middleton Cl E4 ... 19 B1
Middleton Ct
Bromley BR1 ... 187 B3
New Barnet EN5 ... 2 A1
Middleton Dr
Bermondsey SE16 ... 118 D4
Pinner HA5 ... 40 A6
Middleton Gdns IG2 ... 56 D3
Middleton Gr N7 ... 72 A3
Middleton Ho
Dalston E8 ... 73 D1
Newington SE1 ... 262 C5
Middleton Mews N7 ... 72 A3
Middleton Pl W1 ... 239 A3
Middleton Rd
Carshalton CR4, SM5 ... 202 B2
Dalston E8 ... 73 D1
Middleton Rd *continued*
Golders Green NW11 ... 47 C2
Hayes UB3 ... 83 B2
Middleton St E2 ... 96 B4
Middleton Way SE13 ... 142 B1
Middleway NW11 ... 47 D4
Middle Way
Hayes UB4 ... 84 C3
Mitcham SW16 ... 181 D1
Middle Way The HA3 ... 24 D1
Middlewich Ho 7 UB5 ... 85 B3
Middle Yd SE1 ... 253 A4
Midfield Prim Sch BR5 ... 190 A3
Midfield Way BR5 ... 190 B2
Midford Ho 1 NW4 ... 46 D5
Midford Pl W1 ... 239 B5
Midholm
East Finchley NW11 ... 47 D5
Wembley HA9 ... 44 C1
Midholm Cl NW11 ... 47 D5
Midholm Rd CR0 ... 223 A6
Midhope Ho WC1 ... 233 B1
Midhope St WC1 ... 233 B1
Midhurst 1 SE26 ... 184 C4
Midhurst Ave
Muswell Hill N10 ... 49 A6
Thornton Heath CR0 ... 204 C2
Midhurst Ct N8 ... 50 A2
Midhurst Gdns UB10 ... 61 A1
Midhurst Hill DA6 ... 169 C6
Midhurst Ho 6 E14 ... 97 B1
Midhurst Par N10 ... 49 A6
Midhurst Rd W13 ... 109 A3
Midhurst Way E5 ... 74 A4
Midland Pl E14 ... 120 A1
Midland Rd
Leytonstone E10 ... 54 A2
St Pancras NW1 ... 94 A4 233 A2
Midland Terr NW10 ... 89 C3
Midlea Ho EN3 ... 6 C4
Midleton Rd KT3 ... 177 A1
Midlothian Ho NW2 ... 68 B4
Midlothian Rd E3 ... 97 B3
Midmoor Rd
Merton SW19 ... 179 A2
Streatham SW12 ... 159 C3
Midship Cl SE16 ... 118 D5
Midship Point E14 ... 119 C4
Midstrath Rd NW10 ... 67 C4
Midsummer Apartments 7 SM2 ... 217 C1
Midsummer Ave TW4 ... 129 B1
Midsummer Ct
Blackheath Pk SE12 ... 143 A1
Edgware HA8 ... 10 D1
Harrow HA1 ... 42 B4
Midway SM3 ... 201 B2
Midway Ho EC1 ... 234 D2
Midwinter Cl 3 DA16 ... 146 A2
Midwood Cl NW2 ... 68 B5
Mighell Ave IG4 ... 55 D4
Milan Ct N11 ... 31 D2
Milan Rd UB1 ... 107 B4
Milborne Gr SW10 ... 256 B1
Milborne Ho 11 E9 ... 74 C2
Milborne St E9 ... 74 C2
Milborough Cres SE12 ... 164 C5
Milbourne La KT10 ... 212 A3
Milbourne Lodge Jun Sch KT10 ... 212 A2
Milbourne Lodge Sch KT10 ... 212 B2
Milbrook KT10 ... 212 A2
Milbrook Ct NW3 ... 48 A1
Milburn Dr 1 UB7 ... 104 A6
Milburn Ho SW20 ... 178 B1
Milcote St SE1 ... 251 D1
Mildenhall Rd E5 ... 74 C5
Mildmay Ave N1 ... 73 B2
Mildmay Ct N1 ... 73 B3
Mildmay Gr N N1 ... 73 B3
Mildmay Gr S N1 ... 73 B3
Mildmay Ho 6 SW15 ... 156 C6
Mildmay Mission Hospl E2 ... 95 D4
Mildmay Pk N1 ... 73 B3
Mildmay Rd Ilford IG1 ... 78 D5
Stoke Newington N1 ... 73 C3
Mildmay St N1 ... 73 B2
Mildon Ho EN3 ... 6 C3
Mildred Ave
Hayes UB3 ... 105 B3
Northolt UB5 ... 63 D3
Mildura Ct N8 ... 50 B5
MILE END ... 97 A3
Mile End Hospl E2 ... 96 D4
Mile End Park L Ctr & Stad E3 ... 97 B2
Mile End Pl E1 ... 96 D3
Mile End Rd E1, E3 ... 96 D3
Mile End Sta E3 ... 97 B4
Mile End The E17 ... 34 D2
Mile Rd
Hackbridge SM6 ... 203 A1
Wallington CR0, CR4, CR9 ... 203 D1
Miles Bldgs NW1 ... 237 A4
Miles Cl SE28 ... 123 B5
Miles Coverdale Prim Sch 16 W12 ... 112 C4
Miles Ct Croydon CR0 ... 220 D6
Stepney E1 ... 96 B1
Miles Dr SE28 ... 123 C5
Miles Ho 5 SE10 ... 120 C1
Miles Lo Harrow HA1 ... 42 B4
Stratford New Town E15 ... 76 B3
Milespit Hill NW7 ... 28 C5
Miles Pl NW8 ... 236 D4
Miles Rd Hornsey N8 ... 50 A6
Mitcham CR4 ... 202 C6
Miles St SW8 ... 138 A6 270 B5
Milestone Cl
Edmonton N9 ... 18 A2
Sutton SM2 ... 218 B1
Milestone Ct TW7 ... 131 A4
Milestone Green SW14 ... 133 B1
Milestone Ho KT1 ... 197 D5
Milestone Rd SE19 ... 183 D4
Miles Way N20 ... 14 C2
Milfoil St W12 ... 112 A6
Milford Cl SE2 ... 147 A6
Milford Ct
Southall UB1 ... 107 C5
3 Stamford Hill N16 ... 51 C1
Milford Gdns
Croydon CR0 ... 206 D4
Edgware HA8 ... 26 C3
Wembley HA0 ... 65 D3
Milford Gr SM1 ... 218 A4
Milford La WC2 ... 116 C6 251 A6
Milford Mews SW16 ... 160 B1
Milford Rd
Ealing W13 ... 109 B5
Southall UB1 ... 107 C6
Milk St Bromley BR1 ... 187 B4
City of London EC2 ... 95 A1 242 B2
Newham E16 ... 122 D5
Milkwell Gdns IG8 ... 37 B3
Milkwell Yd 7 SE5 ... 139 A4
Milkwood Rd SE24 ... 138 D1
Milk Yd E1 ... 118 C6
Millais Ave E12 ... 78 C3
Millais Cres KT19 ... 215 C3
Millais Ct 9 UB5 ... 84 D5
Millais Gdns HA8 ... 26 C1
Millais Rd Enfield EN1 ... 17 D6
Leyton E11 ... 76 B4
New Malden KT3 ... 199 C2
Millais Way KT19 ... 215 A4
Milland Ho 11 SW15 ... 156 A3
Millard Cl 21 N16 ... 73 C3
Millard Rd SE8 ... 119 B1
Millard Terr RM10 ... 81 C2
Millars Meadow Cl SE12 ... 165 A6
Millbank
Wallington SM6 ... 219 D3
Westminster SW1 ... 116 A2 260 A3
Millbank Ho KT6 ... 198 B2
Millbank Prim Sch SW1 ... 115 D2 259 D3
Millbank Way SE12 ... 165 A6
Millbourne Rd TW13 ... 173 A6
Mill Bridge EN5 ... 13 B5
Millbrook 1 E18 ... 55 A6
Millbrook Ave DA16 ... 145 B1
Millbrooke Ct 7 SW15 ... 157 A6
Millbrook Gdns RM6 ... 59 A3
Millbrook Ho 4 SE15 ... 140 A6
Millbrook Pl NW1 ... 232 A4
Millbrook Rd
Brixton SW9 ... 138 D2
Edmonton N9 ... 18 B3
Mill Cl SM5 ... 219 A6
Mill Cnr EN5 ... 1 B4
Millcroft Ho SE6 ... 185 D6
Mill Ct Hendon NW7 ... 29 A2
Leyton E10 ... 76 A5
14 Thamesmead SE28 ... 124 B6
Millender Wlk SE16 ... 118 C2
Millennium Bridge★ SE1, EC4 ... 252 A5
Millennium Bsns Ctr NW2 ... 68 B6
Millennium City Acad W1 ... 238 D3
Millennium Cl E16 ... 99 B1
Millennium Dr E14 ... 120 B2
Millennium Harbour E14 ... 119 C4
Millennium Ho E17 ... 52 D4
Millennium Pl 27 E2 ... 96 B5
Millennium Prim Sch The SE10 ... 120 D3
Millennium Sq SE1 ... 253 D2
Millennium Way SE10 ... 120 C3
Miller Ave EN3 ... 7 C5
Miller Cl
Bromley BR1 ... 187 B5
Carshalton CR4 ... 202 D2
Pinner HA5 ... 22 C1
Miller Ct
Bexleyheath DA7 ... 147 D2
8 Hendon NW9 ... 46 A5
Miller Ho
Harringay N15 ... 50 D5
9 Streatham SW2 ... 160 A4
Miller Rd
Mitcham SW19 ... 180 B4
Thornton Heath CR0 ... 204 C1
Miller's Ave E8, N16 ... 73 D3
Millers Cl NW7 ... 28 A6
Millers Ct 3 HA0 ... 88 A5
Miller's Ct 1 W4 ... 111 D1
Millers Green Cl EN2 ... 4 D2
Millers Mead Ct SW19 ... 180 B3
Miller St NW1 ... 232 A4
Miller's Terr 1 E8 ... 73 D3
Miller's Way W6 ... 112 C4
Millers Wharf Ho E1 ... 118 A5
Millers Yd N3 ... 29 D3
Miller Wlk SE1 ... 251 B3
Millet Rd UB6 ... 85 D5
Mill Farm Ave TW16 ... 171 C3
Millfarm Bsns Pk TW4 ... 151 A4
Mill Farm Cl HA5 ... 22 C1
Mill Farm Cres TW4 ... 151 A3
Millfield
Charlton TW16 ... 171 B2
Finsbury Pk N4 ... 72 C6
Kingston u T KT1 ... 198 B6
Millfield Ave E17 ... 35 B2
Millfield La N6 ... 70 D6
Millfield Pl N6 ... 71 A6
Millfield Rd
Hendon HA8 ... 27 A1
Twickenham TW4 ... 151 B3
Millfields Com Sch E5 ... 74 C4
Millfields Rd E5 ... 74 C5
Mill Gdns SE26 ... 162 B1
Mill Gn CR4 ... 203 A2
Mill Green Bsns Pk CR4 ... 203 A2
Mill Green Rd CR4 ... 203 A2
Millgrove St 6 SW11 ... 137 A3
Millharbour E14 ... 119 D4
Millhaven Cl RM6 ... 58 B3
MILL HILL ... 28 B5
Mill Hill SW13 ... 134 A2
Mill Hill Broadway Sta NW7 ... 27 C4
Mill Hill Circus NW7 ... 27 D5

Mill Hill Cty High Sch NW7 11 C2
Mill Hill East Sta NW7 29 A3
Mill Hill Gr [11] W3 110 D5
Mill Hill Ind Est NW7 27 D4
Mill Hill Rd
Barnes SW13 134 A3
South Acton W3 110 D4
Mill Hill Sch NW7 28 B6
Mill Hill Terr [9] W3 110 D5
Mill Ho
[4] Lewisham SE13 142 A2
Morden SM4 202 A5
Woodford IG8 36 D5
Millhouse Pl SE27 182 D6
Millicent Fawcett Ct N17 33 D2
Millicent Gr N13 32 D5
Millicent Preston Ho [4] IG11 101 B6
Millicent Rd E10 53 B1
Milligan Ho SE23 163 B3
Milligan St E14 119 B6
Milliners Ho SW18 135 C1
Milling Rd HA8 27 B3
Millington Ho N16 73 B5
Millington Rd UB3 105 C3
Mill La
Brondesbury NW6 69 B3
Carshalton SM5 219 A5
Croydon CR0 220 C5
Dagenham RM6 59 A3
Sewardstone E4 7 D2
Woodford IG8 36 D5
Woolwich SE18 122 C1
Mill Lane Trad Est CR0 220 B5
Millman Ct
Bloomsbury WC1 240 C5
Greenwich SE3 143 B5
Millman Mews WC1 240 C5
Millman Pl WC1 240 D5
Millman St WC1 94 B3 240 C5
Millmark Gr SE14 141 A3
Millmarsh La EN3 7 B3
Millmead Bsns Ctr N17 52 B6
Millmead Ind Ctr N17 52 B6
Mill Mead Rd N17 52 B6
MILL MEADS 98 B5
Millner Ct SE4 141 B3
Mill Pl
Chislehurst BR7 188 D2
Kingston u T KT1 198 B6
Limehouse E14 97 A1
Mill Plat TW7 131 A3
Mill Plat Ave TW7 131 A3
Mill Pond Cl SW8 137 D5 269 D3
Millpond Est SE16 118 B4
Millpond Pl [2] SM6 219 A5
Mill Rd Ilford IG1 78 C5
Merton SW19 180 A3
Newham E16 121 B5
Twickenham TW2 152 A2
Mill Ridge HA8 26 C5
Mill River Trad Est EN3 7 A1
Mill Row N1 95 C6
Mills Cl UB10 82 C5
Mills Ct [9] Leyton E11 76 C5
Shoreditch EC2 95 C4
Mills Gr Hendon NW4 46 D6
[1] South Bromley E14 98 A2
Mills Ho
Nine Elms SW8 269 B2
Walthamstow E17 54 B6
Millshott Cl SW6 134 C4
Millside SM5 218 D6
Millside Pl TW7 131 B3
Millson Cl N20 14 B2
Mills Row W4 111 B2
Mill St
Bermondsey SE1 117 D4 253 D2
Kingston u T KT1 198 A6
Mayfair W1 249 A6
Millstone Cl E15 76 B2
Millstream Cl N13 32 C5
Millstream Ho [14] SE16 118 B4
Millstream Rd SE1 117 D4 253 C1
Mill Trad Est The NW10 89 A4
Mill Vale BR2 186 D1
Mill View Cl KT17 215 D1
Mill View Gdns CR0 222 D5
MILLWALL 119 C3
Millwall Dock Rd E14 119 C3
Mill Way
Edgware NW7 27 C5
Feltham TW14 150 B6
Millway Gdns UB5 63 B2
Millwood Rd TW3, TW7 152 A6
Millwood St [10] W10 91 A2
Mill Yd E1 118 A6
Milman Cl HA5 40 D6
Milman Rd NW6 91 A5
Milman's Ho SW10 266 C5
Milman's St SW10 136 B6 266 C5
Milne Ct Enfield EN2 4 C3
[4] Woodford E18 37 A2
Milne Field HA5 23 C3
Milne Gdns SE9 166 A6
Milne Ho [18] SE18 122 B2
Milner Bldg N16 73 B5
Milner Dr TW2 152 B4
Milner Ho
[1] Battersea SW11 136 B2
Hayes UB4 84 B4
Milner Pl N1 94 C6 234 B6
Milner Rd
Dagenham RM8 80 C6
Kingston u T KT1 197 D6
Merton SW19 179 D2
Morden SM4 202 B4
Newham E15 98 C4
South Norwood CR7 205 B6
Milner Sq N1 72 D1
Milner St SW3 114 D2 257 C4
Milner Wlk SE9 167 B3
Milnthorpe Rd W4 133 B6
Milo Rd SE22 161 D5
Milrood Ho [5] E1 96 D2
Milroy Wlk SE1 251 C4
Milson Rd W14 113 A3 254 A6
Milsted Ho [23] E5 74 B3
Milton Ave Barnet EN5 13 B6
Becontree NW10 89 B6
Carshalton SM1 218 C4
Crouch End N6 49 C2
Kingsbury NW9 45 A6
Plashet E6 78 A1
Stonebridge NW10 89 A6
Thornton Heath CR0 205 B2
Milton Cl
Bermondsey SE1 117 D2 263 C3
Carshalton SM1 218 B5
Hampstead Garden Suburb N2 48 A3
Hayes UB4 84 A1
Milton Court Rd SE14 141 A6
Milton Cres IG2 57 A3
Milton Ct
Fulham SW6 135 A2
Ilford RM6 58 C2
Kingston u T KT2 176 A6
St Luke's EC2 242 C4
Twickenham TW2 152 C1
Uxbridge UB10 60 D5
[9] Wandsworth SW18 157 C6
Milton Dr
Borehamwood WD6 10 D6
Littleton TW17 192 A5
Milton Gdns TW19 148 B3
Milton Gr
Friern Barnet N11 31 D5
Stoke Newington N16 73 C4
Milton Ho
[12] Beckenham BR3 185 C3
[19] Bethnal Green E2 96 C4
[2] Camberwell SE5 139 B5
[5] Kingston u T KT2 176 D4
Sutton SM1 217 C5
Milton House Mans E8 73 D4
Milton Lo
[4] Sidcup DA14 190 A6
Milton Lo *continued*
Southgate N21 16 D3
Twickenham TW1 152 D4
Milton Pk N6 49 C2
Milton Pl [3] N7 72 C3
Milton Rd Acton W3 111 B5
Belvedere DA17 125 C2
Bexley DA16 145 D4
Crouch End N6 49 C2
Ealing W7 108 D6
Hampton TW12 173 C3
Harrow HA1 42 C5
[1] Hendon NW9 46 A2
Mill Hill NW7 28 A5
Mitcham CR4 181 A3
Mortlake SW14 133 B2
Sutton SM1 217 C4
Thornton Heath CR0 205 B2
Tottenham N15 50 D6
Tulse Hill SE24 160 D6
Uxbridge UB10 60 D4
Wallington SM6 219 D2
Walthamstow E17 53 C5
Wimbledon SW19 180 A4
Milton St EC1, EC2 95 B2 242 C4
Milton Way UB7 104 B2
Milverton NW5 71 A3
Milverton Dr UB10 61 A4
Milverton Gdns IG3 79 D6
Milverton Ho SE23 163 A1
Milverton Rd NW6 68 C1
Milverton St SE11 116 C1 261 B1
Milverton Way SE9 188 C6
Milward St E1 96 B2
Milward Wlk [14] SE18 144 C6
Mimosa N15 51 B4
Mimosa Ct
Colney Hatch N12 30 C4
South Lambeth SW4 270 B1
Mimosa Ho UB4 84 C2
Mimosa Rd UB4 84 C2
Mimosa St SW6 135 B4 264 D1
Mina Rd
Merton SW19 179 C2
Walworth SE17 117 C1 263 B2
Minard Rd SE6 164 C3
Minchenden Cres N14 15 D1
Minchenden Ct N14 15 D2
Minchin Ho [10] E14 97 C1
Mincing La EC3 117 C6 253 A6
Minden Rd
Cheam SM3 217 B6
Penge SE20 184 B2
Minehead Ct HA2 63 C6
Minehead Rd
Harrow HA2 63 C5
Streatham SW16 182 B5
Mineral Cl EN5 12 C6
Mineral St SE18 123 C2
Minera Mews SW1 258 B4
Minerva Cl
Kennington SW9 138 C5
Sidcup DA14 189 C6
Minerva Rd
Becontree NW10 89 B4
Chingford E4 35 D3
Kingston u T KT1 176 B1
Minerva St E2 96 B5
Minerva Wlk EC1 241 D2
Minet Ave NW10 89 C5
Minet Ctry Pk UB2, UB3, UB4 106 C5
Minet Dr UB3 106 A5
Minet Gdns
Dagenham NW10 89 C5
Hayes UB3 106 B5
Minet Ho [20] E1 96 A1
Minet Jun & Inf Schs UB3 106 B5
Minet Rd SE5, SW9 138 D3
Minetta Ct [19] EN5 13 D6
Minford Gdns W14 112 D4
Mingard Wlk N7 72 B5
Ming St E14 119 C6
Minimax Cl TW14 150 A5
Ministry Way SE9 166 B2
Mink Ct TW4 128 C3
Minnie Bennett Ho SE3 143 C5
Minniedale KT5 198 B4
Minnow Wlk SE17 263 B3
Minories EC3 117 D6 253 C6
Minshaw Ct DA14 189 D6
Minshull Pl [23] BR3 185 C3
Minshull St SW8 269 C1
Minson Rd E9 96 D6
Minstead Gdns SW15 155 D4
Minstead Way KT3 199 C3
Minster Ave SM1 217 C6
Minster Ct EC3 253 B6
Minster Dr CR0 221 C4
Minster Gdns KT8 195 B5
Minsterley Ave TW16, TW17 193 C5
Minster Rd
Bromley BR1 187 B3
Brondesbury NW2 69 A3
Minster Wlk N8 50 A5
Minstrel Ct HA3 24 C1
Minstrel Gdns KT5 198 B5
Mint Bsns Pk [12] E16 99 A2
Mint Cl UB10 82 D4
Mintern Cl N13 16 D1
Minterne Ave UB2 107 C2
Minterne Rd HA3 44 B4
Minterne Waye UB4 84 C1
Mintern St N1 95 B5 235 D4
Minton Ho SE11 261 A4
Minton Mews [3] NW6 69 D2
Mint Rd SM5, SM6 219 B4
Mint St SE1 252 B2
Mint Wlk CR0 221 A5
Mirabel Rd SW6 135 B5 264 D4
Mirage Ctr The HA9 66 D4
Miranda Cl [19] E1 96 C2
Miranda Ct W3 88 B1
Miranda Ho
[6] Belvedere DA17 125 C1
[17] Hoxton N1 95 C5
Miranda Rd N19 49 C1
Mirfield Ct SE20 184 A1
Mirfield St SE7 121 D3
Miriam Ct DA14 190 B6
Miriam Rd SE18 123 C1
Mirravale Ct [11] IG9 21 C2
Mirravale Trad Est RM8 59 A2
Mirren Cl HA2 63 B5
Mirror Path SE12 165 C1
Misbourne Rd UB10 82 C6
Missenden SE17 262 D1
Missenden Cl TW14 149 D3
Missenden Gdns SM4 202 A3
Missenden Ho NW8 237 A6
Mission Gr E17 53 A4
Mission Grove Prim Sch E17 53 B5
Mission Pl SE15 140 A4
Mission Sq [13] TW8 132 A6
Mission The
[13] Bermondsey SE16 118 B4
[14] Poplar E14 97 B1
Missouri Ct HA5 40 C3
Misterton Ct SW11 266 D2
Mistletoe Cl CR0 206 D1
Mistley Thorn IG1 56 C2
Mistral SE5 139 C4
Mistral Ct E4 19 D1
Mistys Field KT12 194 C1
Mitali Pas [21] E1 96 A1
MITCHAM 202 D5
Mitcham Eastfields Sta CR4 181 A1
Mitcham Garden Village CR4 203 A4
Mitcham Ho [9] SE5 139 A4
Mitcham Ind Est CR4 181 A2
Mitcham Junction Sta CR4 203 A4
Mitcham La SW16 181 C5
Mitcham Pk CR4 202 C5
Mitcham Rd
Ilford IG3 57 D2
Newham E6 100 A4
Upper Tooting SW17 180 D5
Mitcham Sta CR4 202 C5
Mitchell [19] NW9 27 D2
Mitchell Brook Prim Sch NW10 67 C2
Mitchellbrook Way NW10 67 B2
Mitchell Cl
Abbey Wood SE2 124 C2
Belvedere DA17 125 D3
Mitchell Ct SW14 133 C1
Mitchell Ho
Gunnersbury W4 110 D1
[6] Islington N1 72 C1
[31] Shepherd's Bush W12 112 B6
Mitchell Rd
Edmonton N13 33 A5
Orpington BR6 227 D4
Mitchell's Pl SE21 161 C4
Mitchell St EC1 95 A3 242 B6
Mitchell Way
[1] Bromley BR1 187 A2
Tokyngton NW10 67 A2
Mitchell Wlk E6 100 B2
Mitchison Rd N1 73 B2
Mitchley Rd N17 52 A6
Mitford Cl KT9 213 C2
Mitford Rd N19 72 A6
Mitre Bridge Ind Pk W10 90 B3
Mitre Cl
Shepperton TW17 193 B3
Sutton SM2 218 B1
Mitre Ct
Belvedere DA17 125 C1
[1] Ilford RM6 58 B2
[9] Woodford E18 37 A2
Mitre Ho RM7 59 D5
Mitre Rd
Lambeth SE1 116 C4 251 B2
Newham E15 98 C5
Mitre Sq EC3 243 B1
Mitre St EC3 95 C1 243 B1
Mitre The [9] E14 119 B6
Mitre Way W10 90 B2
Mizzen Ct E14 119 C4
Moatbridge Sch SE9 165 D5
Moat Cl BR6 227 D2
Moat Cres N3 47 D6
Moat Croft DA16 146 C2
Moat Ct Eltham SE9 166 B5
Sidcup DA15 167 D1
Moat Dr Harrow HA1 42 B5
[5] Newham E13 99 C5
Ruislip HA4 39 C2
Moat Farm Rd UB5 63 B1
Moatfield NW6 69 A1
Moat Lodge The HA1 64 C6
Moat Pl Acton W3 88 D1
Stockwell SW9 138 B2
Moat Sch The [7] SW6 135 A3
Moat Side Enfield EN3 6 D1
Feltham TW13 172 C6
Moat The KT3 177 C2
Moberly Rd SW4 159 D4
Mobey Ct SW4 270 A1
Moby Dick RM6 59 B5
Mocatta Ho [9] E1 96 B3
Modbury Gdns NW5 71 A2
Modder Pl SW15 134 D1
Model Cotts SW14 133 A2
Model Farm Cl SE9 166 A1
Modling Ho [8] E2 96 D5
Modoc Ho EN3 18 D6
Moelwyn Hughes Ct N7 71 D3
Moelyn Mews HA1 43 A4
Moffat Ct
Upper Tooting SW17 180 C6
Wimbledon SW19 179 C5
Moffat Ho [24] SE5 139 A5
Moffat Rd
Bowes Pk N13 32 A4
South Norwood CR7 183 B1
Upper Tooting SW17 180 D6
Mogden La TW7 152 D6
Mohammedi Pk Complex UB5 85 C6
Mohawk Ho [33] E3 97 A5
Mohmmad Khan Rd E11 54 D1
Mohr Ct N22 32 B3
Moidart Ct HA8 10 D2
Moineau [18] NW9 27 D2
Moira Cl N17 33 C1

Moira Ct SW17 159 A2
Moira Ho 13 SW9 138 C4
Moira Rd SE9 144 B1
Molasses Ho 1 SW11 136 A2
Molasses Row 2 SW11 136 A2
Mole Abbey Gdns KT8 195 D6
Mole Ct
2 Bedford Pk W12 111 C4
West Ewell KT19 215 A4
Mole Ho NW8 236 D5
Molember Ct KT7 196 C5
Molember Rd KT8 196 C4
Molescroft SE9 167 A1
Molesey Ave KT12, KT8 195 B4
Molesey Bsns Ctr KT8 195 B4
Molesey Dr SM3 217 A5
Molesey Ho E2 243 C6
Molesey Hospl KT8 195 C4
Molesey Park Ave KT8 195 D4
Molesey Park Cl KT8 196 A4
Molesey Park Rd KT8 196 A4
Molesey Rd KT12 195 A2
Molesford Rd SW6 265 A1
Molesham Cl KT8 195 D6
Molesham Way KT8 195 D6
Molesworth Ho 9 SE17 138 D6
Molesworth St SE13 142 A2
Moliner Ct 4 BR3 185 C3
Mollie Davis Ct SE19 183 D4
Mollison Ave EN3 7 B5
Mollison Dr SM6 220 A1
Mollison Sq SM6 219 D1
Mollison Way HA8 26 C1
Molly Huggins Cl SW12 159 C4
Molton Ho N1 233 D5
Molvic Ct BR3 185 B1
Molyneux Dr SW17 181 B6
Molyneux Ho W1 237 B2
Molyneux St W1 92 C2 237 B3
Monarch Cl
Coney Hall BR4 224 D4
East Bedfont TW14 149 C4
Monarch Ct Ealing W5 87 C2
Hampstead Garden Suburb N2 48 A4
Monarch Dr E16 99 D2
Monarch Mews
Walthamstow E17 53 D3
West Norwood SW16 182 C5
Monarch Par CR4 180 D1
Monarch Pl
Buckhurst Hill IG9 21 C2
Sutton SM1 218 B3
Monarch Rd DA17 125 C3
Monarchs Ct
1 Edgware NW7 27 B5
Harrow HA2 41 C2
Monarchs Way HA4 39 C1
Monarch Way IG2 57 B3
Mona Rd SE15 140 C3
Mona St E16 98 D2
Monastery Gdns EN2 5 B3
Monaveen Gdns KT8 195 D6
Monck's Row SW18 157 B5
Monck St SW1 115 D3 259 D5
Monckton Ct W14 254 C6
Monclar Rd SE5 139 B1
Moncorvo Cl SW7 114 C4 247 A1
Moncrieff Cl 4 E6 100 A1
Moncrieff St SE15 140 A3
Mondial Way UB7 127 A5
Mondragon Ho SW8 270 B2
Monega Prim Sch E12 77 D2
Monega Rd E7, E12 77 D2
Monet Ct 15 SE16 118 B1
Moneyer Ho N1 235 C2
Monica Ct SW16 181 D4
Monica James Ho 12 DA14 168 A1
Monica Shaw Ct NW1 232 D3
Monier Rd E3 75 C1
Monivea Rd BR3 185 B3
Monkbretton Ho E2 96 A4
Monk Ct W12 112 A5
Monk Dr E16 121 A6
MONKEN HADLEY 1 A3
Monken Hadley CE Prim Sch EN4 1 C4
Monkfrith Ave N14 15 B5
Monkfrith Cl N14 15 B4
Monkfrith Prim Sch N14 15 A4
Monkfrith Way N14 15 B4
Monkham's Ave IG8 37 B5
Monkham's Dr IG8 37 B5
Monkham's La IG8 37 B6
Monkleigh Rd SM4, SW20 201 A5
Monkridge 3 N8 49 D2
Monks Ave
East Molesey KT8 195 B4
New Barnet EN5 14 A5
Monks Cl
Abbey Wood SE2 124 D2
Enfield EN2 5 A3
Harrow HA2 63 D6
Ruislip HA4 62 D4
Monks Cres KT12 194 B1
Monksdene Gdns SM1 217 D5
Monks Dr W3 88 C1
Monksfield N4 72 C6
Monks Hill Sp Ctr CR2 222 D1
MONKS ORCHARD 207 A3
Monks Orchard Rd BR3, CR0 207 C2
Monks Orchard Sch CR0 206 D4
Monks Park Gdns HA9 66 D1
Monks Pk HA9 67 A2
Monks Rd EN2 5 A3
Monk St SE18 122 C2
Monks Way
Beckenham BR3 207 C3
Crofton BR5 211 B1
Harmondsworth UB7 126 A6
Temple Fortune NW11 47 B5
Monkswell Ct N10 31 A2
Monkswell Ho E2 96 A4
Monkswood Gdns
Borehamwood WD6 11 B6
Ilford IG5 56 C6
Monk Terr SE23 163 B2
Monkton Ho
32 Bermondsey SE16 118 D4
22 Hackney E5 74 B3
Monkton Rd DA16 145 D3
Monkton St SE11 116 C2 261 B4
Monkville Ave NW11 47 B5
Monkville Par 1 NW11 47 B5
Monkwell Sq EC2 242 B3
Monmouth Ave
Teddington KT1 175 C3
Wanstead E18 55 B6
Monmouth Cl
Bedford Pk W4 111 B3
Bexley DA16 146 A1
Mitcham CR4, SW16 204 A5
Monmouth Ct 9 W7 86 D2
Monmouth Gr TW8 110 A2
Monmouth Ho
5 Camden Town NW5 71 B2
Wandsworth SW18 157 C5
Monmouth Pl W2 91 D1
Monmouth Rd
Dagenham RM9 81 B3
Hayes UB3 105 D2
Lower Edmonton N9 18 C2
Newham E6 100 B4
Notting Hill W2 91 C1
Monmouth St WC2 94 A1 240 A1
Monnery Rd N19 71 C5
Monnow Rd SE1 118 A2
Mono La TW13 150 B2
Monoux Almshouses E17 53 D5
Monoux Gr E17 35 C2
Monroe Cres EN1 6 B4
Monroe Dr SW14 154 D6
Monroe Ho
16 Crouch End N19 49 D2
Lisson Gr NW8 230 B1
Monro Gdns HA3 24 C3
Monro Ho
16 Hampstead NW3 70 A4
Putney SW15 156 B6
Monro Way E5 74 A4
Monsal Ct E5 75 A4
Monsell Ct 4 N4 72 D5
Monsell Rd N4, N5 72 D5
Monson Rd
Deptford SE14 140 D5
Willesden Green NW10 90 B5
Mons Way BR2 210 A3
Montacute Rd
Bushey WD23 8 C4
Carshalton SM4 202 B3
Forest Hill SE6 163 B4
Montagu Cres N18 34 B6
Montagu Ct W1 237 D3
Montague Ave
Brockley SE4 141 C1
Ealing W7 108 D5
Montague Cl
4 Barnet EN5 1 B1
Borough The SE1 252 C4
Walton-on-T KT12 194 A2
Montague Fell HA0 64 D4
Montague Gdns W3 110 C6
Montague Pl WC1 93 D2 239 D4
Montague Rd
Ealing W13 87 B1
Hanwell W7 108 D4
Hornsey Vale N8 50 B4
Hounslow TW3 129 D2
Leytonstone E11 76 D6
Merton SW19 179 D3
Richmond TW10 154 A5
Shacklewell E8 74 A3
Southall UB2 107 A2
Thornton Heath CR0 204 D1
Tottenham Hale N15 52 A5
Uxbridge UB8 60 A1
Montague Sq SE15 140 C5
Montague St
Bloomsbury WC1 94 A2 240 A4
City of London EC1 242 A3
Montague Terr 1 BR2 209 A5
Montague Waye UB2 107 A3
Montague Works HA0 88 B5
Montagu Gdns
Edmonton N18 34 B6
Wallington SM6 219 C4
Montagu Ind Est N18 34 C6
Montagu Mans W1 92 D2 237 D3
Montagu Mews N W1 237 D3
Montagu Mews S W1 237 D2
Montagu Mews W W1 237 D2
Montagu Pl W1 92 D2 237 D3
Montagu Rd
Hendon NW4 46 A3
Lower Edmonton N9, N18 18 C1
Montagu Row W1 237 D3
Montagu Sq W1 92 D1 237 D2
Montagu St W1 92 D1 237 D2
Montaigne Cl SW1 259 D3
Montalt Ho IG8 36 D6
Montalt Rd IG8 36 D5
Montana Bldg 4 SE13 141 D4
Montana Gdns
Penge SE26 185 B5
5 Sutton SM1 218 A3
Montana Rd
Upper Tooting SW17 159 A1
Wimbledon SW20 178 C2
Montbelle Prim Sch SE9 188 C6
Montbelle Rd SE9 166 D1
Montcalm Cl
Hayes BR2 209 A3
Yeading UB4 84 B4
Montcalm Ho E14 119 C3
Montcalm Rd SE7 143 D5
Montclair Ct 21 N12 29 D6
Montclare St E2 95 D3 243 C6
Monteagle Ave IG11 79 A2
Monteagle Ct
Barking IG11 79 A1
27 Hoxton N1 95 C5
Monteagle Prim Sch RM9 102 B6
Monteagle Way
Nunhead SE15 140 B2
Shacklewell E5 74 A5
Montefiore Ct 2 N16 51 D1
Montefiore St 2 SW8 137 B3
Montego Cl 10 SW2 138 C1
Montem Prim Sch 5 N7 72 B5
Montem Rd
Forest Hill SE23 163 B4
New Malden KT3 199 C5
Montem St N4 50 B1
Montenotte Rd N8 49 C4
Monteray Studios W10 91 A5
Monterey Cl NW7 27 C5
Montesole Ct 7 HA5 22 C1
Montesquieu Terr 3 E16 98 D1
Montford Pl
Kennington SE11 138 C6
Kennington SE11 261 A1
Montford Rd TW16 194 A5
Montfort Ho
4 Bethnal Green E2 96 C4
Cubitt Town E14 120 A3
Montfort Pl SW19 156 D3
Montgolfier Wlk UB5 85 A4
Montgomerie Ct 2 BR3 185 C2
Montgomery Ave KT10 212 C6
Montgomery Cl
Blackfen DA15 167 D5
Mitcham CR4 204 A5
Montgomery Ct W4 133 A6
Montgomery Gdns SM2 218 B1
Montgomery Ho 5 SW14 133 B2
Montgomery Lo 38 E1 96 C3
Montgomery Rd
Acton W4 111 A2
Edgware HA8 26 B4
Montgomery St E14 119 D5
Montholme Rd SW11 158 D5
Monthope Rd 17 E1 96 A2
Montolieu Gdns SW15 156 B6
Montpelier Ave
Ealing W5 87 C2
Sidcup DA5 168 D4
Montpelier Cl UB10 82 C6
Montpelier Ct
5 Beckenham BR2 208 D5
Ealing W5 87 D2
Montpelier Gdns
Ilford RM6 58 C2
Newham E6 99 D4
Montpelier Gr NW5 71 C3
Montpelier Mews SW7 257 B6
Montpelier Pl
Knightsbridge SW7 257 B6
21 Stepney E1 96 C1
Montpelier Prim Sch W5 87 D2
Montpelier Rd
Ealing W5 87 D2
Finchley N3 30 A2
Peckham SE15 140 B4
Sutton SM1 218 A4
Montpelier Rise
Golders Green NW11 47 A2
Wembley HA9 43 D1
Montpelier Row
Blackheath Vale SE3 142 D3
Twickenham TW1 153 C4
Montpelier Sq SW7 114 C4 247 B1
Montpelier St SW7 114 C3 257 B6
Montpelier Terr SW7 247 B1
Montpelier Vale SE3 142 D3
Montpelier Way NW11 47 A2
Montpelier Wlk SW7 114 C3 257 B6
Montpellier Ct KT12 194 B3
Montrave Rd SE20 184 C3
Montreal Ho
Catford SE6 163 D3
Hayes UB4 84 B4
Montreal Pl WC2 250 C6
Montreal Rd IG1 57 A2
Montrell Rd SW2 160 A3
Montrose Ave
Falconwood DA16 145 C2
Hendon HA8 27 B2
Kensal Rise NW6 91 A5
Sidcup DA15 168 A4
Twickenham TW2 151 D4
Montrose Cl
Ashford TW15 171 A5
Falconwood DA16 145 D2
Woodford IG8 37 A6
Montrose Cres
Finchley N12 30 A4
1 Wembley HA0 66 A2
Montrose Ct
2 Catford SE6 164 D2
Hendon NW9 27 A1
Knightsbridge SW7 114 B4 246 D1
Temple Fortune NW11 47 B5
Montrose Gdns
Mitcham CR4 180 D1
Sutton SM1 217 D6
Montrose Ho
Belgravia SW1 248 B1
Millwall E14 119 C3
Twickenham TW2 151 D4
Montrose Pl SW1 115 A4 248 B1
Montrose Rd
East Bedfont TW14 149 B5
Harrow HA3 24 D1
Montrose Villas 5 W6 112 A1
Montrose Way SE23 162 D3
Montserrat Ave IG8 36 B3
Montserrat Cl SE19 183 B5
Montserrat Rd SW15 135 A1
Montway Hts SW19 179 D3
Monument* EC3 252 D6
Monument Gdns SE13 164 A6
Monument St EC3 117 B6 252 D6
Monument Sta EC3 117 B6 252 D6
Monument Way N17 51 D6
Monza Bldg The E1 118 C6
Monza St E1 118 C6
Moodkee St SE16 118 C3
Moody Rd SE15 139 D4
Moody St E1 96 D4
Moolintock Pl EN3 7 D6
Moon Ct SE12 143 A1
Moon Ho HA1 42 D5
Moon La EN5 1 B2
Moon St N1 94 D6 234 C6
Moorcroft HA8 26 D2
Moorcroft Ct 4 N3 29 B1
Moorcroft Gdns BR1 210 A4
Moorcroft La UB8 82 C2
Moorcroft Rd SW16 160 A1
Moorcroft Sch UB8 82 B1
Moorcroft Way HA5 41 A4
Moordown SE18 144 D4
Moore Cl
Mitcham CR4 181 B1
Mortlake SW14 133 A2
Wallington SM6 220 A1
Moore Cres RM9 102 B6
Moore Ct N1 234 C5
Moorefield Rd N17 33 D1

Moorehead Way SE3 143 B2
Moore Ho
16 Bethnal Green E2 96 C4
5 Greenwich SE10 120 D1
Hornsey N8 50 A5
7 Shadwell E1 118 C6
Wandsworth SW17 158 B1
1 West Norwood SE27 183 A6
Mooreland Rd BR1 187 A2
Moore Park Ct SW6 265 D4
Moore Park Rd SW6 135 D5 265 C3
Moore Rd SE19 183 A4
Moore St SW3 114 D2 257 C4
Moore Wlk E7 77 A4
Moorey Cl 2 E15 98 D6
Moorfield Ave W5 87 D3
Moorfield Rd
Chessington KT9 214 A3
Enfield EN3 6 C4
Moorfields EC2 95 B2 242 C3
Moorfields Ct 6 SW16 181 C6
Moorfields Eye Hospl EC1 95 B4 235 C1
Moorfields Highwalk EC2 242 C3
Moorgate EC2 95 B2 242 C3
Moorgate Pl EC2 242 C2
Moorgate Sta EC2 95 B2 242 C3
Moorgreen Ho EC1 234 C2
Moorhouse
Moorgate EC2 242 C3
17 NW9 27 D2
Moorhouse Rd
Harrow HA3 43 D6
Notting Hill W2 91 C1
Moorings Ho 3 TW8 131 C5
Moorings The 5 E16 99 C2
Moor La
Broadgate EC2 95 B2 242 C3
Chessington KT9 214 A3
Moorland Cl TW4 151 C4
Moorland Ct N21 16 B5
Moorland Rd SW9 138 D1
Moorlands
Chislehurst BR7 188 D3
Northolt UB5 85 A6
17 Wallington SM6 219 B2
Moorlands Ave NW7 28 B4
Moormead Dr KT19 215 C3
Moor Mead Rd TW1 153 A5
Moor Park Gdns KT2 177 C3
Moor Park Ho N21 16 D4
Moor Pl EC2 242 C3
Moorside Ct W13 109 C5
Moorside Rd BR1 186 D6
Moor St W1 239 D1
Moortown Rd WD19 22 C6
Moot Ct NW9 44 C4
Morant Ho SW9 138 B3
Morant Pl N22 32 B2
Morant St E14 119 C6
Mora Prim Sch NW2 68 C4
Mora Rd NW2 68 C4
Mora St EC1 95 A4 235 B1
Morat St SW9 138 B4 270 D2
Moravian Cl SW3 266 D5
Moravian Pl SW10 136 B6 266 D5
Moravian St 10 E2 96 C4
Moray Ave UB3 105 D5
Moray Cl HA8 10 D2
Moray Ho
11 Kingston u T KT6 198 A4
9 Mile End E1 97 A3
Moray Mews N4, N7 72 B6
Moray Rd N4, N7 72 B6
Mordaunt Gdns RM9 81 A1
Mordaunt Ho
4 Becontree NW10 89 B6
34 Clapham SW8 137 D3
Mordaunt Rd NW10 89 B6
Mordaunt St SW9 138 B2
MORDEN 201 D3
Morden Court Par SM4 201 D5
Morden Ct SM4 201 D5
Morden Gdns
Greenford UB6 64 D3
Mitcham CR4 202 B5
Morden Hall SW19 201 D6
Morden Hall Rd SM4 202 A5
Morden Hill SE13 142 A3
Morden Ho
Morden SM4 201 C5
19 Tulse Hill SW2 160 C5
Morden La SE13 142 A4
Morden Lo BR2 186 B1
Morden Mount Prim Sch 1 SE13 141 D3
MORDEN PARK 201 A3
Morden Park Pools SM4 201 B4
Morden Prim Sch SM4 201 C4
Morden Rd
Dagenham RM6 59 A2
Kidbrooke SE3 143 A3
Merton SW19 179 D1
Mitcham CR4, SM4 202 B5
Morden Road Mews SE3 143 A3
Morden Road Sta SW19 179 D1
Morden South Sta SM4 201 C4
Morden St SE13 141 D4
Morden Sta SW19 201 D6
Morden Way SM3 201 C2
Morden Wharf Rd SE10 120 C3
Mordern Ho NW1 237 B5
Mordon Rd IG3 57 D2
Mordred Rd SE6 164 C2
Morecambe Cl 3 E1 96 D2
Morecambe Gdns HA7 25 D6
Morecambe St SE17 117 A1 262 B2
Morecambe Terr N18 33 B6
More Cl
Canning Town E16 98 D1
West Kensington W14 113 A2 254 A3
Morecoombe Cl KT2 176 D3
Morecroft TW2 152 A2
Moredown Ho 3 E8 74 A3
Moree Way N18 34 A6
More House Sch SW1 114 D3 257 D5
Moreland Ct 3 NW2 69 C5
Moreland Prim Sch EC1 94 D4 234 D1
Moreland St EC1 94 D4 234 D2
Moreland Way E4 20 A1
Morella Rd SW11, SW12 158 D4
Morell Ho 5 SW9 138 B3
Morello Ave UB8 82 D2
Morello Ct HA9 66 B5
More London Pl SE1 253 A3
Moremead Rd SE6 185 C6
Morena St SE6 163 D4
Moresby Ave KT5 198 D2
Moresby Rd E5 52 B1
Moresby Wlk 6 SW8 137 B3
More's Gdn SW3 266 D5
Moreton Ave TW7 130 C4
Moreton Cl
Mill Hill NW7 28 C4
Tottenham N15 51 B3
Upper Clapton E5 52 C1
Moreton Ho
Bermondsey SE16 118 B3
Upper Tooting SW17 180 B6
Moreton Pl SW1 115 C1 259 B2
Moreton Rd
Croydon CR2 221 B3
North Cheam KT4 216 B6
Tottenham N15 51 B3
Moreton St SW1 115 D1 259 C2
Moreton Terr SW1 115 C1 259 B2
Moreton Terr Mews N SW1 259 B2
Moreton Terr Mews S SW1 259 B2
Moreton Twr 3 W3 110 D5
Morford Cl HA4 40 B2
Morford Way HA4 40 B2
Morgan Ave E17 54 B5
Morgan Cl RM10 81 C1
Morgan Ct
Ashford TW15 170 D5
5 Battersea SW11 136 B3
Carshalton SM5 218 D4
Morgan Ho
Nine Elms SW8 269 B2
Pimlico SW1 259 B3
Morgan Rd
Islington N7 72 C3
Notting Hill W10 91 B2
Plaistow BR1 187 A3
Morgans La SE1 253 A3
Morgan's La UB3 83 B2
Morgan St
Canning Town E16 98 D2
Globe Town E3 96 D4
Morgan's Wlk SW11 267 A3
Morgan Terr RM6 58 C4
Moriah Jewish Day Sch HA5 41 A1
Moriarty Cl BR1 210 D5
Moriatry Cl N7 72 A4
Morie St SW18 157 D6
Morieux Rd E10 53 B1
Moring Rd SW17 181 A6
Morkyns Wlk SE21 161 C1
Morland Ave CR0 205 C1
Morland Cl
Golders Green NW11 47 D1
Hampton TW12 173 B5
Mitcham CR4 202 C6
Morland Ct W12 112 B4
Morland Est E8 74 A1
Morland Gdns
Southall UB1 107 D5
Stonebridge NW10 67 B1
Morland Ho
Kilburn NW6 91 C6
Notting Hill W11 91 A1
Somers Town NW1 232 B3
Westminster SW1 260 A4
Morland Mews N1 72 C1
Morland Rd
Croydon CR0 205 D2
Dagenham RM10 81 C1
Harrow HA3 44 A5
Ilford IG1 78 D6
Penge SE20 184 D4
Sutton SM1 218 A3
Walthamstow E17 52 D4
Morley Ave
Chingford E4 36 B3
Edmonton N18 34 A6
Tottenham N22 32 D1
Morley Cl BR6 226 D6
Morley Coll SE1 116 C3 261 B6
Morley Cres
Edgware HA8 11 A2
Ruislip HA4 62 C6
Morley Cres E HA7 43 D6
Morley Cres W HA7 43 C6
Morley Ct
Bromley BR3 186 B2
Chingford Hatch E4 35 B5
Lewisham SE13 142 A1
Shortlands BR2 208 D5
Morley Hill EN2 5 B5
Morley Ho
Stoke Newington N16 74 A6
Streatham SW2 160 A4
W1 238 D2
Morley Rd
Barking IG11 101 B6
Cheam SM3 201 B1
Chislehurst BR7 189 A2
Dagenham RM6 59 A4
Lewisham SE13 142 A1
Leytonstone E10 54 A1
Newham E15 98 D5
Twickenham TW1 153 D5
Morley St SE1 116 C4 251 B1
Morna Rd SE5 139 A3
Morning La E9 74 C2
Morningside Prim Sch 17 E9 74 C2
Morningside Rd KT4 216 C6
Mornington Ave
Bromley BR1 209 D6
Ilford IG1 56 C2
West Kensington W14 113 B2 254 C3
Mornington Avenue Mans W14 254 C3
Mornington Cl IG8 37 A6
Mornington Cres
Camden Town NW1 93 C5 232 A4
Cranford TW5 128 B4
NW1 232 A4
Mornington Crescent Sta NW1 93 C5 232 A4
Mornington Ct NW1 232 A4
Mornington Gr E3 97 C4
Mornington Lo EN1 17 C6
Mornington Mews 2 SE5 139 A4
Mornington Pl
4 New Cross SE8 141 B5
Regent's Pk NW1 232 A4
Mornington Rd
Ashford TW15 171 A5
Chingford E4 20 B4
Greenford UB6 85 D3
Leytonstone E11 54 D1
New Cross SE14, SE8 141 B5
Woodford IG8 36 D6
Mornington St NW1 93 B5 231 D4
Mornington Terr NW1 93 B5 231 D4
Mornington Wlk TW10 175 C6
Morocco St SE1 117 C4 253 A1
Morpeth Gr E9 96 D6
Morpeth Rd E9 96 D6
Morpeth Sch E2 96 C4
Morpeth St E2 96 D4
Morpeth Terr SW1 115 C2 259 A4
Morpeth Wlk N17 34 B3
Morphou Rd NW7 29 A5
Morrab Gdns IG3 79 D5
Morrel Cl EN5 2 A2
Morrel Ct 11 E2 96 A5
Morris Ave E12 78 B3
Morris Blitz Ct 2 N16 73 D4
Morris Cl
Croydon CR0 207 A4
Orpington BR6 227 C5
Morris Ct Chingford E4 19 D1
Croydon CR0 220 D4
3 Herne Hill SE5 139 B1
Morris Gdns SW18 157 C4
Morris Ho
17 Bethnal Green E2 96 C4
Lisson Gr NW8 237 A5
1 Stockwell SW4 138 A1
10 Tufnell Pk N19 71 C4
Morrish Rd SW2 160 A4
Morrison Ave
Chingford E4 35 C4
Tottenham N17 51 C6
Morrison Bldgs 5 E1 96 A1
Morrison Ct
7 Barnet EN5 1 A1
Finchley N12 30 C3
Morrison Ho SW2 160 C3
Morrison Rd
Barking IG11 103 A5
24 Brixton SW9 138 C3
Hayes UB4 84 B4
Morrison St SW11 137 A2
Morrison Yd N17 33 D1
Morris Pl N4 72 C6
Morris Rd
Bow Comm E14 97 D2
Dagenham RM8 81 B6
Isleworth TW7 130 D2
Leyton E15 76 C4
Morriss Ho
9 Bermondsey SE16 118 B4
5 Upper Clapton E5 74 B6
Morris St E1 96 B1
Morris Stephany Ho 4 SE27 182 D6
Morriston Cl WD19 22 C5
Morritt Ho 2 HA0 65 D3
Morse Cl E13 99 A4
Morshead Mans W9 91 C4
Morshead Rd W9 91 C4
Morson Rd EN3 19 A5
Morston Gdns SE9 188 B6
Mortain Ho 9 SE16 118 B2
Morten Cl SW4 159 D5
Morteyne Rd N17 33 B2
Mortgramit Sq SE18 122 C3
Mortham St E15 98 C6
Mortimer Cl
1 Child's Hill NW2 69 B5
Streatham SW16 159 D2
Mortimer Cres
Paddington NW6 91 D6
Worcester Pk KT4 215 B5
Mortimer Ct
St John's Wood NW8 229 B3
4 Whetstone N20 14 A2
Mortimer Dr EN1 17 C6
Mortimer Est NW6 91 D6
Mortimer Ho
6 Shepherd's Bush W11 112 D5
West Kensington W14 254 B3
Mortimer Lo 11 SW19 157 A3
Mortimer Market WC1 239 B5
Mortimer Pl NW6 91 D6
Mortimer Rd
De Beauvoir Town N1 73 C1
Ealing W13 87 C1
Kensal Green NW10 90 C4
Mitcham CR4 180 D2
Newham E6 100 B4
Mortimer Sq W11 112 D6
Mortimer St W1 93 C2 239 B3
Mortimer Terr NW5 71 B4
MORTLAKE 133 A2
Mortlake Cl CR0 220 A5
Mortlake Dr CR4 180 C2
Mortlake High St SW14 133 B2
Mortlake Ho 7 W4 111 A2
Mortlake Rd
Ilford IG1 79 B4
Newham E16 99 B1
Richmond SW14, TW9 132 C4
Mortlake Sta SW14 133 A2
Mortlake Terr TW9 132 C5
Mortlock Cl SE15 140 B4
Mortlock Ct E12 77 D4
Morton Cl
Hillingdon UB8 82 B3
29 Stepney E1 96 C1
Wallington SM6 220 B1
Morton Cres N14 31 D6
Morton Ct UB5 64 A3
Morton Gdns SM6 219 C3
Morton Ho
Kennington SE17 138 D6
West Norwood SE27 183 B5
Morton Mews SW5 255 C3
Morton Pl SE1 261 A5
Morton Rd
Islington N1 73 A1
Morden SM4 202 B4
Stratford E15 76 D1
Morton Way N14 31 D6
Morvale Cl DA17 125 B2
Morval Rd SW2 160 C6
Morven Rd SW17 158 D1
Morville Ho SW18 158 B5
Morville St E3 97 C5
Morwell St WC1 239 D3
Moscow Pl W2 245 C6
Moscow Rd W2 113 D6 245 C6
Mosedale NW1 231 D1
Moseley Row SE10 120 D2
Moselle Ave N22 32 C1
Moselle Cl N8 50 B6
Moselle Ct N9 18 C1
Moselle Ho 2 N17 33 D3
Moselle Pl N17 33 D3
Moselle Sch (Upper) N17 51 A6
Moselle Specl Sch N17 33 C1
Moselle St N17 33 D3

Mosque Tower 26 E1 ..96 A2
Mosquito Cl 5 SM6 ..220 A1
Mossborough Cl N12 ..29 D4
Mossbourne Com Acad E8 ..74 A3
Mossbury Rd SW11 ..136 C2
Moss Cl Pinner HA5 ..23 A1
Spitalfields E1 ..96 A2
Mossdown Cl DA17 ..125 C2
Mossford Ct IG6 ..56 D6
Mossford Gn IG6 ..57 A6
Mossford St E3 ..97 B3
Moss Gdns
Feltham TW13 ..150 A2
South Croydon CR2 ..222 D1
Moss Hall Cres N12 ..30 A4
Moss Hall Ct N12 ..29 D4
Moss Hall Gr N12 ..29 D4
Moss Hall Inf Sch 1 N12 ..29 D4
Moss Hall Jun Sch N3 ..29 D4
Mossington Gdns SE16 ..118 C2
Moss La HA5 ..23 A1
Mosslea Rd
Bromley Comm BR2 ..209 D4
Orpington BR6 ..227 A5
Penge SE20 ..184 C4
Mossop St SW3 ..114 C2 257 B4
Moss Rd RM10 ..81 C1
Mossville Gdns SM4 ..201 B5
Mosswell Ho 4 N10 ..31 A3
Moston Cl UB3 ..105 D1
Mostyn Ave HA9 ..66 B3
Mostyn Gdns NW10 ..90 D5
Mostyn Gr E3 ..97 C5
Mostyn Lo N5 ..73 A4
Mostyn Rd
Brixton SW9 ..138 C4
Bushey WD23 ..8 A6
Grahame Pk HA8 ..27 C3
Merton SW19 ..179 B1
Mosul Way BR2 ..210 A3
Motcomb St SW1 ..115 A3 258 A6
Moth Cl SM6 ..220 A1
Mothers Sq The 13 E5 ..74 B4
Motley Ave EC2 ..243 A6
Motley St SW8 ..137 C3
MOTSPUR PARK ..200 A3
Motspur Park Sta KT3 ..200 B4
Motspur Pk KT3 ..200 A3
MOTTINGHAM ..165 D2
Mottingham Ct SE9 ..166 B3
Mottingham Gdns SE9 ..165 D3
Mottingham La SE9 ..165 C3
Mottingham Nature Reserve★ SE12 ..165 C3
Mottingham Prim Sch SE9 ..166 B1
Mottingham Rd
Chislehurst SE9 ..166 B1
Ponders End N9 ..18 D4
Mottingham Sta SE9 ..166 B3
Mottisfont Rd SE2 ..124 B2
Moules Ct SE5 ..139 A5
Moulins Rd E9 ..74 C1
Moulsford Ho
5 Lower Holloway N7 ..72 A3
32 Paddington W2 ..91 C2
Moulton Ave TW3, TW5 ..129 B3
Moundfield Rd N16 ..52 A3
Mound The SE9 ..166 C1
Mounsey Ho 13 W10 ..91 A4
Mountacre Cl SE26 ..183 D6
Mount Adon Pk SE21, SE22 ..162 A4
Mountague Pl 2 E14 ..120 A6
Mountain Ho SE11 ..260 C2
Mountaire Ct NW9 ..45 B4
Mount Angelus Rd SW15 ..155 D4
Mount Ararat Rd TW10 ..154 A6
Mount Arlington 3 BR2 ..186 C1
Mount Ash Rd SE26 ..162 B1
Mount Ave
Chingford E4 ..19 D1
Ealing W5 ..87 D2
Southall UB1 ..85 C1
Mountbatten Cl
Plumstead Comm SE18 ..145 C6
6 West Norwood SE19 ..183 C5
Mountbatten Ct 8 IG9 ..21 D2
Mountbatten Gdns BR3 ..207 A5
Mountbatten Ho N6 ..49 A2
Mountbatten Mews SW18 ..158 A3
Mountbel Rd HA7 ..25 A1
Mount Carmel 3 N7 ..72 B3
Mount Carmel RC Tech Coll for Girls 6 N19 ..49 D1
Mount Cl
Bromley BR1 ..188 A2
Cockfosters EN4 ..3 A1
Ealing W5 ..87 C2
Mountcombe Cl KT6 ..198 A2
Mountcombe Ho SW17 ..180 B5
Mount Ct
6 Kingston u T KT2 ..176 D3
West Wickham BR4 ..224 C6
Mount Culver Ave DA14 ..190 D4
Mount Dr Bexley DA6 ..169 A6
Harrow HA2, HA5 ..41 B4
Welsh Harp HA9 ..67 A6
Mountearl Gdns SW16, SW2 ..160 B1
Mount Eaton Ct W5 ..87 C2
Mount Echo Ave E4 ..19 D3
Mount Echo Dr E4 ..19 D3
Mount Ephraim La SW16 ..159 D1
Mount Ephraim Rd SW16 ..159 D1
Mount Felix KT12 ..193 D1
Mountfield NW2 ..69 B6
Mountfield Cl SE6 ..164 B4
Mountfield Ct SE13 ..164 B5
Mountfield Rd
Ealing W5 ..88 A1
East Finchley N3 ..47 C6
Wallend E6 ..100 C4
Mountford Ho EN2 ..4 D1
Mount Ford St E1 ..96 A1
Mountfort Cres N1 ..72 C1
Mountfort Terr 1 N1 ..72 C1
Mount Gdns SE26 ..162 B1
Mount Gr HA8 ..27 B6
Mountgrove Rd N5 ..73 A5
Mount Holme KT7 ..197 B2
Mounthurst Rd BR2 ..208 D2
Mountier Ct 12 E11 ..55 A4
Mountington Park Cl HA3 ..43 D3
Mountjoy Cl SE2 ..124 B4
Mountjoy Ho EC2 ..242 A3
Mount Lo N6 ..49 C3
Mount Lodge SW4 ..137 D1
Mount Mews TW12 ..173 D2
Mount Mills EC1 ..234 D1
Mount Nod Rd SW16, SW2 ..160 B1
Mount Olive Ct W7 ..108 C4
Mount Par EN4 ..2 C1
Mount Park Ave HA1 ..64 C6
Mount Park Cres W5 ..87 D1
Mount Park Rd
Ealing W5 ..87 D1
Harrow HA1 ..64 B5
Pinner HA5 ..40 A4
Mount Pk SM5 ..219 A1
Mount Pl 7 W3 ..110 D5
Mount Pleasant
Cockfosters EN4 ..2 D1
Finsbury WC1 ..94 C3 241 A5
Ilford IG1 ..79 A3
Ruislip HA4 ..62 D6
Wembley HA0 ..88 B6
West Norwood SE27 ..183 A6
Mount Pleasant Cotts
Osidge N14 ..15 D4
Southall UB1 ..85 C1
Mount Pleasant Cres N4 ..50 B2
Mount Pleasant Hill E5 ..74 C6
Mount Pleasant La E5 ..52 B1
Mount Pleasant Pl SE18 ..123 B2
Mount Pleasant Rd
Ealing W5 ..87 C3
Higham Hill E17 ..35 A1
Kingston u T KT3 ..199 A6
Lewisham SE13 ..164 A5
Tottenham N17 ..33 C1
Willesden NW10 ..90 C6
Mount Pleasant Villas N4 ..50 B2
Mount Prim Sch The KT3 ..199 A6
Mount Rd
Bexley DA6 ..169 A6
Chessington KT9 ..214 B3
Dagenham RM8 ..59 B1
Dollis Hill NW2 ..68 C5
East Barnet EN4 ..14 C6
Feltham TW13 ..151 A1
Hayes UB3 ..106 A4
Hendon NW4 ..46 A3
Kingston u T KT3 ..199 B6
Mitcham CR4 ..180 C1
South Norwood SE19 ..183 B4
Wimbledon SW18, SW19 ..157 D2
Mount Row W1 ..115 B6 248 C5
Mount Sch The NW7 ..28 C5
Mountside HA7 ..25 A2
Mounts Pond Rd SE3, SE13 ..142 B3
Mount Sq The 3 NW3 ..70 A5
Mount St W1 ..115 A6 248 B5
Mount Stewart Ave HA3 ..43 D2
Mount Stewart Jun & Inf Schs HA3 ..43 D2
Mount Terr E1 ..96 B2
Mount The
Bexley DA6 ..169 D6
Cheam SM1 ..217 C2
Chislehurst BR7 ..188 C2
Finchley N2 ..30 C1
Hampstead NW3 ..70 A5
Harrow HA1 ..64 C6
Kensington W8 ..245 A3
Kingston u T KT3 ..199 D6
North Cheam KT4 ..216 B4
Northolt UB5 ..63 D3
6 South Croydon CR2 ..221 A3
Upper Clapton E5 ..74 B6
Welsh Harp HA9 ..67 A6
Whetstone N20 ..14 A2
Mount Tyndal NW3 ..48 B1
Mount Vernon NW3 ..70 A4
Mountview
Edgware NW7 ..11 B1
Northwood HA6 ..22 A4
5 Streatham SW16 ..160 B1
Mount View
Ealing W5 ..87 D3
Enfield EN2 ..4 B5
Southall UB2 ..106 D2
Mountview Cl NW11 ..48 A1
Mountview Cotts EN5 ..11 D5
Mountview Ct
Harringay N8 ..50 D5
3 Whetstone N20 ..14 A2
Mount View Rd
Chingford E4 ..20 B4
Claygate KT10 ..213 B1
Hornsey Vale N4 ..50 B3
Kingsbury NW9 ..45 B4
Mount Villas SE27 ..160 D1
Mountwood KT8 ..195 D6
Mountwood Ho W5 ..87 D3
Mourne Ho NW3 ..70 A2
Movers La IG11 ..101 C6
Movers Lane (Flyover) IG11 ..101 C5
Movieum The★ SE1 ..250 C2
Mowat Ct KT4 ..215 D6
Mowatt Cl N19 ..49 D1
Mowbray Ct
South Norwood SE19 ..183 D2
Wood Green N22 ..32 C2
Mowbray Gdns UB5 ..85 C6
Mowbray Ho 5 N2 ..30 B1
Mowbray Rd
Brondesbury NW6 ..69 A1
Edgware HA8 ..26 C6
New Barnet EN5 ..14 A6
Richmond TW10 ..153 C1
South Norwood SE19 ..183 D2
Mowlem Prim Sch 36 E2 ..96 C5
Mowlem St E2 ..96 B5
Mowlem Trad Est N17 ..34 C3
Mowll St SW9 ..138 C5
Moxon Cl E13 ..98 D5
Moxon St Barnet EN5 ..1 B2
Marylebone W1 ..93 A2 238 A3
Moye Cl 10 E2 ..96 A5
Moyers Rd E10 ..54 A2
Moylan Rd W6 ..135 A6 264 B5
Moyle Ho SW1 ..269 B6
Moyne Ho 16 SW9 ..138 D1
Moyne Pl NW10 ..88 C5
Moynihan Dr N21 ..16 A6
Moys Cl CR0 ..204 A3
Moyser Rd SW16 ..181 B5
Mozart St W10 ..91 B4
Mt Carmel RC Prim Sch 1 W5 ..109 C3
Muchelney Rd SM4 ..202 A3
Mudchute Pk & Farm★ E14 ..120 A2
Mudchute Sta E14 ..119 D2
Mudie Ho 8 SW2 ..160 A4
Mudlarks Blvd 3 SE10 ..120 D3
Muggeridge Cl CR2 ..221 B3
Muggeridge Rd RM10 ..81 D4
Muirdown Ave SW14 ..133 B1
Muir Dr SW18 ..158 C5
Muirfield W3 ..89 C1
Muirfield Cl
23 Bermondsey SE16 ..118 B1
South Oxhey WD19 ..22 C6
Muirfield Cres E14 ..119 D3
Muirfield Gn WD19 ..22 C6
Muirfield Rd WD19 ..22 C6
Muirhead Quay IG11 ..101 A5
Muirkirk Rd SE6 ..164 A3
Muir Rd E5 ..74 A5
Muir St E16 ..122 A5
Mulbarton Ct BR7 ..189 B4
Mulberry Ave TW19 ..148 A3
Mulberry Bsns Ctr SE16 ..118 D4
Mulberry Cl Barnet EN4 ..2 B1
Charlton SE7 ..143 D6
Chelsea SW3 ..266 D5
Chingford E4 ..19 C2
East Dulwich SE22 ..162 A5
Hampstead NW3 ..70 B4
Hendon NW4 ..46 C6
Hornsey N8 ..50 A4
Northolt UB5 ..85 A5
Streatham SW16 ..181 C6
Mulberry Cres
Brentford TW8 ..131 C5
West Drayton UB7 ..104 C4
Mulberry Ct
Barking IG11 ..79 D1
Bexley DA16 ..145 D3
Finchley N2 ..48 C6
Finsbury EC1 ..234 D1
Islington N5 ..72 D3
1 Leyton E11 ..76 B4
10 Paddington W9 ..91 B4
4 Surbiton KT6 ..197 D2
Twickenham TW1 ..152 D1
Willesden NW10 ..67 B2
Mulberry Ho
1 Bethnal Green E2 ..96 C4
8 Deptford SE8 ..141 B6
Mulberry House Sch NW2 ..69 A3
Mulberry La CR0 ..205 D1
Mulberry Mews
New Cross SE14 ..141 B4
2 Wallington SM6 ..219 C2
Mulberry Par UB7 ..104 C4
Mulberry Pl
Chiswick W6 ..112 A1
Greenwich SE9 ..143 D1
Mulberry Prim Sch N17 ..34 A1
Mulberry Rd E8 ..73 D1
Mulberry Sch for Girls
39 Stepney E1 ..96 B1
16 St George in t East E1 ..118 B6
Mulberry St 7 E1 ..96 A1
Mulberry Trees TW17 ..193 B2
Mulberry Way
Ilford IG6 ..57 A5
Woodford E18 ..37 B1
Mulberry Wlk SW3 ..136 B6 266 D6
Mulgrave Chambers SM2 ..217 D2
Mulgrave Hall SM2 ..217 D2
Mulgrave Ho 19 SE18 ..122 B2
Mulgrave Manor SM2 ..217 D2
Mulgrave Prim Sch SE18 ..122 C2
Mulgrave Rd
Belmont SM2 ..217 C2
Ealing W5 ..87 D3
Harrow HA1 ..65 A6
South Croydon CR0 ..221 B5
West Kensington W14 ..264 C6
Willesden NW10 ..67 D4
Woolwich SE18 ..122 C2
Mulholland Cl CR4 ..181 B1
Mulkern Rd N19 ..49 D1
Mullard Ho WC1 ..239 C4
Mullards Cl CR4 ..202 D1
Mullens Ho 7 SW15 ..156 C6
Mullen Twr EC1 ..241 A5
Muller Ho SE18 ..122 C1
Muller Rd SW4 ..159 D5
Mullet Gdns 7 E2 ..96 A4
Mulletsfield WC1 ..233 B1
Mull Ho 17 E3 ..97 B5
Mullins Path SW14 ..133 B2
Mullion Cl HA3 ..23 D2
Mullion Wlk WD19 ..22 D6
Mulready St NW8 ..237 A5
Multi Way W3 ..111 C4
Multon Ho E9 ..74 C1
Multon Rd SW18 ..158 B4
Mulvaney Way SE1 ..252 D1
Mumford Rd SE24 ..160 D6
Muncaster Cl TW15 ..170 C6
Muncaster Rd
Ashford TW15 ..170 D5
Balham SW11 ..159 A6
Muncies Mews SE6 ..164 A2
Mundania Ct SE22 ..162 B5
Mundania Rd SE22 ..162 C5
Munday Ho SE1 ..262 C5
Munday Rd E16 ..121 A6
Munden Ho 5 E3 ..97 D4
Munden St W14 ..113 A2 254 A4
Mundford Rd E5 ..74 C6
Mundon Gdns IG1 ..57 B1
Mundsley Cl WD19 ..22 C6
Mund St W14 ..113 B1 254 D1
Mundy Ho 6 W10 ..91 A4
Mundy St N1 ..95 C4
Mungo-Park Cl WD23 ..8 A2
Munnery Way BR6 ..226 D6
Munning Ho 12 E16 ..121 B5
Munnings Gdns TW7 ..152 B6
Munro Dr N11 ..31 C4
Munro Ho
Bermondsey SE1 ..252 D1
Lambeth SE1 ..251 A1
Munro Mews W10 ..91 A2
Munro Rd WD23 ..8 A6
Munslow Gdns SM1 ..218 B4
Munstead Ct 12 SM2 ..218 A1
Munster Ave TW4 ..151 A6
Munster Ct
Fulham SW6 ..135 B3
Teddington TW11 ..175 C4
Munster Gdns N13 ..33 A6
Munster Ho N17 ..33 D2

Munster Rd
Fulham
SW6 135 A5 264 B4
Teddington TW11 175 C4
Munster Residences
SW6 264 B2
Munster Sq
NW1 93 B3 238 D6
Munton Rd SE1,
SE17 117 A2 262 B4
Murchison Ave DA5 169 A3
Murchison Ho 1
W10 91 A2
Murchison Rd E10 76 A6
Murdoch Ho 4
SE16 118 C3
Murdock Cl E16 98 D1
Murdock St SE15 140 B6
Murfett Cl SW19 157 A2
Muriel Ct 18 E10 53 D2
Muriel St N1 94 B6 233 D6
Murillo Rd SE13 142 C1
Murley Ct N21 17 A4
Murphy Ho SE1 261 D6
Murphy St
SE1 116 C4 251 A1
Murray Ave
Bromley BR1 187 B1
Hounslow TW3 151 D6
Murray Cl SE28 123 C5
Murray Cres HA5 22 D2
Murray Ct
5 Harrow HA1 42 D3
Southall TW7 108 C3
Twickenham TW2 152 A2
Murray Gr N1 95 B5 235 C3
Murray Grey Ho UB4 83 B2
Murray Ho
1 North Finchley
N12 30 B5
20 Woolwich SE18 122 B2
Murray Mews NW1 71 D1
Murray Rd
Brentford W5 109 C2
Richmond TW10 153 C2
Wimbledon SW19 178 D4
Murray Sq E16 121 B6
Murray St NW1 71 D1
Murray Terr NW3 70 B4
Musard Rd
W6 135 A6 264 B6
Musbury St E1 96 C1
Muscal W6 264 A6
Muscatel Pl SE5 139 C4
Muschamp Prim Sch
SM5 218 C6
Muschamp Rd
Camberwell SE15 139 D2
Carshalton SM5 218 C6
Muscott Ho 15 E2 96 A6
Muscovy Ho DA18 125 A4
Muscovy St EC3 253 B6
Museum & Galleries of Modern London★
EC2 242 A2
Museum Ho 7 E2 96 C4
Museum La SW7 256 C5
Museum Mans WC1 240 A3
Museum of Brands, Packaging & Advertising★ W11 91 B1
Museum of Childhood (V&A)★ E2 96 C4
Museum of Culinary History & Alimentation★
NW1 93 C5 232 B4
Museum of Domestic Design & Architecture (MoDA)★ EN4 15 A6
Museum of Instruments★
SW7 256 C6
Museum of London★
EC2 95 A2 242 A3
Museum of London Docklands★ E14 119 C6
Museum of Richmond★
TW10 153 D6
Museum of the Great Eastern Rly★ E16 122 C4
Museum of the Order of St John★
EC1 94 D3 241 C5
Museum St
WC1 94 A1 240 A2
Museum Way W3 110 C4
Musgrave Cl EN4 2 A4
Musgrave Cres
SW6 135 C4 265 B2
Musgrave Ct SW11 267 A2
Musgrave Rd TW7 130 D4
Musgrove Ho 1 E9 74 D2
Musgrove Rd SE14 141 A4
Musical Mus The★
TW8 132 B6
Musjid Rd 7 SW11 136 B3
Muslim Coll The
W5 110 C6
Mus of the Royal Pharmaceutical Society★ SE1 260 C4
Musquash Way TW4 128 C3
Muston Rd E5 74 B6
Mustow Pl 2 SW6 135 B3
Muswell Ave N10 31 B1
MUSWELL HILL 49 A6
Muswell Hill N10 49 C6
Muswell Hill Broadway
N10 49 B6
Muswell Hill Pl N10 49 B5
Muswell Hill Prim Sch
N10 49 B6
Muswell Hill Rd N10 49 A4
Muswell Mews N10 49 B6
Muswell Rd N10 31 B1
Mutrix Rd NW6 91 C6
Mutton Pl NW1 71 A2
Muybridge Rd KT3 177 A1
Myatt Garden Prim Sch
SE4 141 B3
Myatt Ho SE5 138 D3
Myatt Rd SW9 138 D4
Myatts Field Ct SE5 139 A4
Mycenae Rd SE3 143 A6
Mychell Ho 8 SW19 180 A3
Myddelton Ave EN1 5 C5
Myddelton Cl EN1 5 D4
Myddelton Gdns N21 17 A4
Myddelton Ho N8 50 A6
Myddelton Pas
EC1 94 C4 234 B2
Myddelton Pk N20 14 B2
Myddelton Rd N8 50 A5
Myddelton Sq
EC1 94 C4 234 B2
Myddelton St
EC1 94 C4 234 B1
Myddleton Ave N4 73 A6
Myddleton Cl HA7 9 A2
Myddleton Ho 14 N2 30 B1
Myddleton Mews
N22 32 A3
Myddleton Rd N22 32 B3
Myers Ho 5 SE5 139 A5
Myers La SE14 140 D6
Myherin Ct SE23 163 B2
Mylis Cl SE26 184 B6
Mylius Cl SE14 140 C4
Mylne Cl W6 112 A1
Mylne Ho N21 17 B5
Mylne St EC1 234 A3
Mynterne Ct 16
SW19 156 D3
Myra St SE2 124 A2
Myrdle Ct 14 E1 96 A1
Myrdle St E1 96 A1
Myrna Cl SW19 180 C3
Myron Pl SE13 142 A2
Myrtle Alley SE18 122 C3
Myrtle Ave
Hatton TW14 149 C6
Ruislip HA4 40 B2
Myrtle Cl Barnet EN4 14 D3
Hillingdon UB8 82 B2
West Drayton UB7 104 B3
Myrtledene Rd SE2 124 A1
Myrtle Gdns W7 108 C5
Myrtle Gr Enfield EN2 5 B5
Kingston u T KT3 177 A1
Myrtle Ho SE14 140 D4
Myrtle Rd Acton W3 111 A5
Croydon CR0 223 C5
Edmonton N13 17 B1
Hampton TW12 174 A4
Hounslow TW3 130 A3
Ilford IG1 78 D6
Myrtle Rd *continued*
Newham E6 100 A6
Sutton SM1 218 A3
Walthamstow E17 53 A3
Myrtle Wlk 20 N1 95 C5
Mysore Rd SW11 136 D1
Myton Rd SE21 161 B1
Mytton Ho SW8 270 C3

N

N1 Shopping Ctr
N1 94 C5 234 B4
Nacton Ct 2 RM6 58 C4
Nadine St SE7 121 C1
Nadir Ct E11 55 A2
Naffenton Rise IG10 21 D6
Nagle Cl E17 36 B1
Nags Head N7 72 B4
Nags Head Ct EC1 242 B5
Nag's Head La DA16 146 B2
Nags Head Rd EN3 6 D1
Nags Head Sh Ctr The
N7 72 B4
Naima Jewish Prep Sch
4 NW6 91 D5
Nainby Ho SE11 261 A3
Nairn Ct
3 Wallington SM6 219 C2
Wimbledon SW19 179 D4
Nairne Gr SE5, SE24 139 B1
Nairn Rd HA4 62 C2
Nairn St E14 98 A2
Naish Ho SW19 201 D6
Naldera Gdns SE3 143 A6
Nallhead Rd TW13 172 C5
Nalton Ho 4 NW6 70 A1
Namba Roy Cl SW16 182 B6
Namco Sta★ SE1 250 C2
Namton Dr CR7,
SW16 204 B5
Nan Clark's La NW7 11 D2
Nancy Reuben Prim Sch
8 NW4 46 D5
Nankin St E14 97 C1
Nansen Ct 1 E11 76 C6
Nansen Ho 8 NW10 67 B1
Nansen Rd SW11 137 A2
Nansen Village 5
N12 29 D6
Nant Ct NW2 69 B6
Nantes Cl SW18 136 A1
Nant Rd NW2 69 B6
Nant St E2 96 B4
Naomi Watts Ho 11
SW19 179 A3
Naoroji St WC1 234 A1
Napier 15 NW9 27 D2
Napier Ave
Deptford E14 119 C1
Fulham SW6 135 B2
Napier Cl
New Cross SE14,
SE8 141 B5
West Drayton UB7 104 B3
West Kensington W14 254 C6
Napier Ct
13 Croydon CR0 221 D6
Fulham SW6 135 B2
Grove Pk SE12 165 B1
Hayes UB4 84 C3
Shoreditch N1 235 C4
1 Surbiton KT6 197 D2
12 Wallington SM6 219 B2
Wembley HA0 65 D2
Napier Gr N1 95 A5 235 B4
Napier Ho
Eltham SE12 165 B1
Kennington SE17 138 D6
Napier Lo TW15 171 B4
Napier Pl
W14 113 B3 254 C5
Napier Rd
Ashford TW15 171 B3
Belvedere DA17 125 B2
Bromley BR2 209 B5
College Pk NW10 90 B4
Croydon SE25 206 B5
Enfield EN3 18 D6
Isleworth TW7 131 A1
Kensington
W14 113 B3 254 C5
Leyton E11 76 C5
Newham E15 98 C5
South Croydon CR2 221 B1
Napier Rd *continued*
Tottenham N17 51 C6
Wallend E6 100 C5
Wembley HA0 65 D2
Napier Terr N1 72 D1
Napier Wlk TW15 171 B3
Napoleon Rd
Hackney E5 74 B5
Twickenham TW1 153 B4
Napton Cl UB4 85 A3
Narbonne Ave SW4 159 C6
Narborough Cl UB10 61 A6
Narborough St SW6 135 D3
Narcissus Rd NW6 69 C3
Nardini 12 NW9 27 D2
Naresby Fold HA7 25 C4
Narford Rd E5 74 A6
Narrow Boat Cl
SE28 123 B4
Narrow St
6 Acton W3 110 D5
Limehouse E14 119 A6
Narrow Way BR2 210 A3
Nascot St W12 90 C1
Naseby Cl
Hounslow TW7 130 C4
South Hampstead NW6 70 A1
Naseby Ct DA14 189 D6
Naseby Rd
Dagenham RM10 81 C5
South Norwood SE19 183 B4
NASH 225 A2
Nash Cl SM1 218 B5
Nash Coll of FE BR4 224 D4
Nash Ct HA3 43 B3
Nashe Ho SE1 262 C5
Nash Gn BR1 187 A4
Nash Ho
5 Millwall E14 119 C3
Pimlico SW1 258 D1
1 Walthamstow E17 53 D5
Nash La BR2 225 A2
Nash Rd
Brockley SE4 163 A6
Dagenham RM6 58 D5
Lower Edmonton N9 18 C2
Nash St NW1 231 D2
Nash Way HA3 43 B3
Nasmyth St W6 112 B3
Nassau Path 6
SE28 124 C5
Nassau Rd SW13 133 D4
Nassau St W1 239 A3
Nassington Rd NW3 70 D4
Natalie Cl TW14 149 B4
Natalie Mews TW2 152 B1
Natal Rd
Bowes Pk N11 32 A4
Ilford IG1 78 D4
South Norwood CR7 205 B6
Streatham SW16 181 D4
Nathan Ct N9 18 C4
Nathan Ho SE11 261 B3
Nathaniel Cl E1 243 D3
Nathaniel Ct E17 53 A3
Nathans Rd HA0 65 C6
Nathan Way SE28,
SE18 123 D3
National Archives The
TW9 132 D5
National Army Mus★
SW3 136 D6 267 D6
National Construction Coll & National Skills Acad E16 123 A5
National Gallery★
W1 115 D6 249 D5
National Hospl for Neurology & Neurosurgery
WC1 94 A3 240 B5
National Maritime Mus★
SE10 142 B6
National Physical Laboratory TW11 174 C4
National Portrait Gallery★ W1 249 D5
National Portrait Gallery (Annexe)★ SW1 249 D4
National Theatre★
SE1 116 B5 250 D4
National Wks TW4 129 B2
Nation Way E4 20 A3
Natural History Mus★
SW7 114 B3 256 C5
Nautilus Bldg The
EC1 234 B2
Naval Row E14 120 A6
Navarino Gr E8 74 A2
Navarino Mans E8 74 A2
Navarino Rd E8 74 A2
Navarre Rd E6 100 A5
Navarre St E2 243 C6
Navenby Wlk 13 E3 97 C3
Navestock Cl E4 20 A1
Navestock Cres IG8 37 C3
Navestock Ho IG11 102 B5
Navigation Ct E16 123 A6
Navigator Dr UB2 108 A4
Navy St SW4 137 D2
Naxos Bldg 9 E14 119 C4
Nayland Ho SE6 186 A6
Naylor Bldg W 4 E1 96 A1
Naylor Gr EN3 18 D6
Naylor Ho
33 Clapham SW8 137 D3
Walworth SE17 262 D2
5 West Kilburn W10 91 B4
Naylor Rd
Peckham SE15 140 B5
Whetstone N20 14 A2
Nayor Bldg E 6 E1 96 A1
Nazareth Cl SE15 140 B3
Nazrul St E2 95 D4
Neal Ave UB1 85 B3
Neal Cl HA6 22 A2
Nealden St SW9 138 B2
Neale Cl N2 48 A6
Neale Ct
Dagenham RM9 80 B2
Muswell Hill N10 31 B3
Neal St WC2 94 A1 240 A1
Neal's Yd WC2 240 A1
Near Acre NW9 27 D2
NEASDEN 67 B4
Neasden Cl NW10 67 C3
Neasden Junc NW10 67 C4
Neasden La
Church End NW10 67 C3
Neasden NW10 67 B5
Neasden La N NW10 67 C5
Neasden Sta NW10 67 C3
Neasham Rd RM8 80 B3
Neath Gdns SM4 202 A3
Neathouse Pl SW1 259 A4
Neats Acre HA4 39 B2
Neatscourt Rd E16 99 D2
Nebraska Bldg 11
SE13 141 D4
Nebraska St
SE1 117 B4 252 C1
Neckinger
SE16 117 D3 263 D6
Neckinger Est SE16 263 D6
Neckinger St SE1 263 D6
Nectarine Way SE13 141 D3
Nedahall Ct 4 NW11 47 B2
Needham Ct 20 EN3 7 C6
Needham Ho SE11 261 A3
Needham Rd W11 91 C1
Needham Terr NW2 68 D5
Needleman St SE16 118 D4
Needwood Ho N4 51 A1
Neela Cl UB10 60 D4
Neeld Cres
Hendon NW4 46 B4
Wembley HA9 66 C3
Neeld Ct HA9 66 C3
Neeld Par HA9 66 B3
Neil Cl TW15 171 A5
Neilson-Terry Ct 9
SW9 138 B1
Neil Wates Cres 17
SW2 160 C3
Nelgarde Rd SE6 163 C4
Nella Rd W6 134 D6
Nelldale Rd SE16 118 C2
Nellgrove Rd UB10 82 D3
Nell Gwynn Ave
TW17 193 B3
Nell Gwynn Ho SW3 257 B3
Nello James Gdns
SE27 183 B6
Nelson Cl
East Bedfont TW14 149 D3
Hillingdon UB10 82 D4
2 Paddington NW6 91 C4
Thornton Heath CR0 204 D1
Walton-on-T KT12 194 B1
Nelson Ct
5 Carshalton SM5 218 D5

Nelson Ct *continued*
Rotherhithe SE16.....**119** B5
Nelson Docks SE16 ..**119** B5
Nelson Gdns
Bethnal Green E2......**96** A4
Twickenham TW3, TW4 .... **151** C5
Nelson Grove Rd
SW19 ....**180** A2
Nelson Ho 1 W5 ......**88** A4
Nelson Hospl SW20 ..**179** B1
Nelson La UB10.......**82** D4
Nelson Mandela Cl
N10................**31** A1
Nelson Mandela Rd
SE3...............**143** C2
Nelson Pas EC1..... **235** B2
Nelson Pl N1....... **234** D3
Nelson Prim Sch
Twickenham TW2.... **151** D5
Wallend E6......... **100** C5
Nelson Rd
Ashford TW15 ...... **170** A5
Bromley BR2 .... **209** C5
Chingford E4 ....**35** D4
Edmonton N9.........**18** B2
Enfield EN3 ....**18** D5
Erith DA17 ....**125** B1
Greenwich SE10 ..... **142** A6
Harmondsworth TW6 .**126** B4
Harrow HA1..........**42** C1
Hillingdon UB10.......**82** D4
Hornsey Vale N8 ......**50** B3
Merton SW19....... **180** A3
New Malden KT3 .....**199** B4
Sidcup DA14........ **190** A6
Stanmore HA7.........**25** C4
Tottenham N15 ....**51** C5
Twickenham TW2, TW4 .... **151** C5
Wanstead E11........**55** B5
Nelson's Monument★
WC2........**116** A5 **250** A4
Nelson Sq
SE1....... **116** D4 **251** C2
Nelsons Row SW4 .. **137** D1
Nelson St Barking E6..**100** C6
Canning Town E16 ... **120** D6
Newham E6 ....**100** B5
Stepney E1...........**96** B1
Nelsons Yd NW1.... **232** A4
Nelson Terr N1 ..... **234** D3
Nelson Trad Est
SW19.............. **179** D2
Nemoure Rd W3.....**111** A6
Nene Gdns TW13.....**151** B2
Nene Rd TW6, UB7... **126** D4
Nene Road Rdbt
TW6 .... **126** D4
Nepaul Rd 17 SW11 ..**136** C2
Nepean St SW15.....**156** A4
Neptune Ct
Dagenham IG11......**102** B4
13 Millwall E14 ..... **119** C2
Neptune Ho
2 Rotherhithe SE16 .... **118** C3
14 Stoke Newington N16...............**73** C3
Neptune Rd
Harlington TW6 ..... **127** A4
Harrow HA1...........**42** B3
Neptune St SE16.....**118** C3
Nero Ct 6 TW8 ..... **131** D5
Nesbit Cl SE3........**142** C2
Nesbit Rd SE9 ...... **143** D1
Nesbitt Ho DA6 ...... **169** D6
Nesbitt Sq SE19......**183** C3
Nesham Ho 14 N1.....**95** C6
Nesham St E1 ....**118** A5
Ness St 9 SE16.......**118** A3
Nesta Rd IG8 ....**36** D4
Nestle's Ave UB3.... **105** D3
Nestor Ave N21 ....**16** D5
Nestor Ho 13 E2 ......**96** B5
Netheravon Rd
Chiswick W4 .... **111** D1
Ealing W7.......... **108** D5
Netheravon Rd S
W4 .... **111** D1
Netherbury Rd W5.. **109** D3
Netherby Gdns EN2....**4** A1
Netherby Ho 23
SW8 .... **137** D3
Netherby Rd SE23....**162** C4
Nether Cl N3 ....**29** C3
Nethercombe Ho 1
SE3...............**143** A6
Nethercott Ho 27 E3 ..**97** D4
Nethercourt Ave N3...**29** C4
Netherfield Gdns
IG11................**79** B1
Netherfield Rd
Finchley N12 ....**29** D5
Upper Tooting SW17 . **159** A1
Netherford Rd SW4 ..**137** C3
Netherhall Gdns NW3 **70** A3
Netherhall Int Coll
NW3................**70** A2
Netherhall Way NW3..**70** A3
Netherlands Rd EN5 ..**14** B5
Netherleigh Cl N6 ....**49** B1
Nether St Finchley N3 ..**29** D4
North Finchley N12 ....**30** A5
Netherton Gr
SW10 ......**136** A6 **266** B5
Netherton Ho 1 UB5 .**85** B4
Netherton Rd
Isleworth TW1.......**153** B6
Tottenham N15 ....**51** B3
Netherwood 24 N2....**30** B1
Netherwood Rd
W14 .... **112** D4
Netherwood St NW6..**69** C2
Nethewode Ct DA17. **125** D3
Netley 13 SE5.......**139** C4
Netley Cl Cheam SM3 **216** D3
New Addington CR0... **224** A1
Netley Ct IG2.........**57** B4
Netley Dr KT12.......**195** B2
Netley Gdns SM4 ....**202** A2
Netley Prim Sch
NW1.........**93** C4 **232** A1
Netley Rd
Brentford TW8...... **132** A6
Cheam SM4 .... **202** A2
Ilford IG2............**57** B4
Walthamstow E17 .....**53** B4
Netley St NW1 **93** C4 **232** A1
Nettlecombe NW1 ....**71** D1
Nettleden Ave HA9....**66** C2
Nettleden Ho SW3... **257** B3
Nettlefold Pl SE27 ... **160** D1
Nettlestead Cl 16
BR3...............**185** C3
Nettleton Rd
Harlington TW6 ..... **126** D4
Ickenham UB10........**60** B4
New Cross Gate SE14 **140** D4
Nettlewood Rd
SW16.............. **181** D3
Neuchatel Rd SE6....**163** B2
Nevada Cl KT3.......**199** A5
Nevada St SE10......**142** A6
Nevena Ct 3 SW2 ...**160** C6
Nevern Mans SW5 .. **255** A2
Nevern Pl
SW5...........**113** C2 **255** B3
Nevern Rd SW5..... **255** A3
Nevern Sq
SW5.......**113** C2 **255** B3
Nevil Ho 7 SW9.... **138** D3
Nevill Ct SW10...... **266** A4
Neville Ave KT3......**177** B2
Neville Cl Acton W3...**111** A4
Hounslow TW3...... **129** D3
Leyton E11...........**76** D5
Paddington NW6 ......**91** B5
Peckham SE15....... **140** A4
Sidcup DA15........ **189** D6
Somers Town NW1... **232** D3
Neville Ct 10 SW12...**159** C4
Neville Dr N2.........**48** A3
Neville Gdns RM8.....**80** D5
Neville Gill Cl SW18. **157** D5
Neville Ho
Friern Barnet N11 .....**31** A6
5 Twickenham TW1 . **153** A4
Neville Pl N22 ....**32** B2
Neville Rd
Dagenham RM8.......**80** D5
Ealing W5............**87** D3
Forest Gate E7........**77** B1
Kingston u T KT1 .... **176** C1
Paddington NW6 ......**91** B5
Richmond TW10...... **153** C2
Thornton Heath CR0 ..**205** B2
Neville's Ct NW2......**68** A5
Neville St
SW7 ....**114** B1 **256** C2
Neville Terr SW7.... **256** C2
Neville Wlk SM5 .....**202** C2
Nevill Rd N16..........**73** C5
Nevin Dr E4 ....**19** D3
Nevin Ho UB3........**105** A3
Nevinson Cl SW18 ...**158** B5
Nevis Rd SW17.......**159** A2
Nevitt Ho N1 .... **235** D3
New Acres Rd SE28 . **123** C5
NEW ADDINGTON...**224** B1
Newall Ho SE1...... **262** B6
Newall Rd TW6 ......**127** A4
Newark Cres NW10 ...**89** B4
Newark Ct KT12......**194** C1
Newark Ho 3 SW9 . **138** D3
Newark Knok E6.....**100** C2
Newark Rd CR2.......**221** B2
Newark St E1.........**96** B2
Newark Way NW4.....**46** A6
New Ash Cl N2.........**48** B6
New Atlas Wharf
E14.................**119** C3
New Barn Cl SM6 ....**220** B2
NEW BARNET.........**14** A6
New Barnet Sta EN5 ..**14** B6
New Barns Ave CR4 . **203** D5
New Barn St E13.......**99** B3
NEW BECKENHAM ..**185** A4
New Beckenham Sta
BR3 ....**185** B3
New Belmont Ho 4
SE23.............. **162** C3
New Bentham Ct 10
N1...................**73** A1
Newbery Ho N1.......**73** A1
Newbiggin Path
WD19...............**22** C6
Newbold Cotts 4 E1..**96** C1
Newbolt Ave SM3... **216** D3
Newbolt Ho SE17 ... **262** C2
Newbolt Rd HA7 ......**24** D5
New Bond St
W1 ....**115** B6 **248** D6
Newborough Gn
KT3.................**199** B5
Newborough Ho
SW19 ....**180** B3
New Brent St NW4....**46** C4
Newbridge Ct SW17..**180** A6
Newbridge Point 3
SE23.............. **162** D1
Newbridge Sch RM6 ..**58** B4
New Bridge St
EC4.........**94** D1 **241** C1
New Broad St
EC2.........**95** C2 **243** A3
New Broadway
Ealing W5.......... **109** D6
7 Hillingdon UB10 ....**82** D3
Teddington TW12......**174** B5
New Bsns Ctr The
NW10...............**89** D4
Newburgh Rd W3.....**111** A5
Newburgh St W1 ... **239** B1
New Burlington Mews
W1 .... **249** A6
New Burlington Pl
W1 .... **249** A6
New Burlington St
W1 .... **249** A6
Newburn Ct N12.......**30** A3
Newburn Ho SE11 .. **260** D2
Newburn St
SE11.......**116** B1 **260** D2
Newbury Ave EN3.......**7** B6
Newbury Cl UB5 ......**63** B2
Newbury Cotts 3
IG2..................**57** A3
Newbury Ct
Hackney E5 ....**75** A3
Sidcup DA14........ **189** D6
7 Wanstead E11.......**55** A5
Newbury Gdns KT19 **215** D4
Newbury Ho
Barnet EN4 ....**2** B1
Brixton SW9........ **138** D3
14 Kensington W2......**91** D1
Wood Green N22 ......**32** A2
Newbury Mews NW5..**71** A2
NEWBURY PARK.....**57** B3
Newbury Park Prim Sch
IG2..................**57** B3
Newbury Park Sta
IG2..................**57** B3
Newbury Rd
Bromley BR2 .... **209** A6
Chingford E4 ....**36** A4
Harmondsworth TW6 .**126** B4
Newbury Rd *continued*
Ilford IG2.............**57** C3
Newbury St EC1 .... **242** A4
Newbury Way UB5 ....**63** B2
New Butt La SE8 .....**141** C5
Newby NW1 .... **232** A2
Newby Cl EN1 ....**5** C3
Newby Pl E14........**120** A6
Newby St SW8........**137** B2
New Caledonian Mkt★
SE1.........**117** C3 **263** B6
New Caledonian Wharf
SE16................**119** B3
New Campden Ct 9
NW3.................**70** A4
Newcastle Cl EC4... **241** C2
Newcastle Ct EC4... **252** B6
Newcastle Ho W1... **238** A4
Newcastle Pl
W2 ....**92** B2 **236** D4
Newcastle Row EC1. **241** B5
New Cavendish St
W1 ....**93** B2 **238** C3
New Change
EC4.........**95** A1 **242** A1
New Chapel Sq
TW13...............**150** B3
New Charles St EC1. **234** D2
NEW CHARLTON **121** C2
New Church Ct 3
SE19...............**184** A3
New Church Rd
32 Camberwell SE5.. **139** A5
Camberwell SE5......**139** B6
New City Prim Sch
E13..................**99** C4
New City Rd E13 ......**99** C4
New Cl
Feltham TW13 ...... **173** A5
Morden SW19 ...... **202** A6
New Colebrooke Ct
SM5 ....**219** A1
New College Ct 6
NW3.................**70** A2
New College Mews 7
N1...................**72** C1
New College Par 1
NW3.................**70** B1
Newcombe Gdns
TW3 ....**129** B1
Newcombe Ho N5 ....**73** A3
Newcombe Pk
Edgware NW7 ....**27** C5
Wembley HA0 ....**88** B6
Newcombe Rise UB7..**82** A1
Newcombe St W8... **245** B4
Newcome Gdns
SW16...............**182** A6
Newcome Ho E5......**74** B5
Newcomen Ho 5
NW5.................**71** B4
Newcomen Rd
Battersea SW11 .....**136** B2
Leyton E11...........**76** D5
Newcomen St
SE1........**117** B4 **252** C2
New Compton St
WC2........**94** A1 **240** A1
New Concordia Wharf
SE1............... **253** D2
Newcourt Ho 26 E2 ...**96** B4
Newcourt St
NW8........**92** C5 **230** A3
New Covent Garden Flower Market★
SW8........**138** A6 **270** A5
New Covent Garden Fruit & Vegetable Mkt★
SW8....... **137** D5 **269** C3
New Crane Pl E1.......**118** C5
New Crescent Yd 1
NW10...............**89** D5
Newcroft Cl UB8......**82** B2
Newcroft Ho 10
NW10...............**67** B1
NEW CROSS.........**141** B4
New Cross SE14 .....**141** B5
NEW CROSS GATE . **140** D4
New Cross Gate
SE14 .... **140** D4
New Cross Gate Sta
SE14............... **141** A5
New Cross Rd SE14 ..**141** A4
New Cross Sta SE14..**141** B5
New Ct
City of London EC4.... **241** A1
New Ct *continued*
26 Hampstead NW3 ...**70** A4
Northolt UB5 ....**63** D3
Stoke Newington N16 ..**51** B1
Newdales Cl N9 ......**18** A2
Newdene Ave UB5 ....**84** D5
New Den (Millwall FC)
The SE16 .... **118** C1
Newdigate Ho
6 Kingston u T KT2 .... **176** D4
5 Poplar E14 ....**97** B1
Newell St E14 ....**97** B1
NEW ELTHAM.........**167** A2
New Eltham Sta
SE9................**166** D3
New End NW3 ....**70** A5
New End Prim Sch 33
NW3.................**70** A4
New End Sq NW3 .....**70** B4
New England Est
IG11............... **101** A5
Newent Cl
Camberwell SE15.... **139** C5
Carshalton SM5...... **202** D1
New Farm Ave BR2...**209** A5
New Ferry App SE18 .**122** C3
New Fetter La
EC4.........**94** C1 **241** B2
Newfield Cl TW12....**173** C2
Newfield Prim Sch
NW10...............**67** D1
Newfield Rise NW2 ...**68** B5
Newgale Gdns HA8 ...**26** B2
New Garden Dr UB7..**104** A4
Newgate CR0.........**205** A1
Newgate Cl TW13....**151** A1
Newgate St
Chingford E4 ....**20** C1
Holborn EC1...**94** D1 **241** D2
New Globe Wlk SE1. **252** A4
New Goulston St E1. **243** C2
New Green Pl SE19...**183** C4
NEWHAM...............**98** D4
Newham Acad of Music
8 E6...............**100** A6
Newham City Farm★
E6...................**99** D1
Newham Coll of FE 3
E6..................**100** B5
Newham Coll of FE (Stratford Campus)
E15..................**76** C1
Newham Ctr for Mental Health E13..........**99** D3
Newham Gn N22......**32** C2
Newham L Ctr E13.....**99** C2
Newham Sixth Form Coll
E13..................**99** B3
Newham Sixth Form Coll (Stratford Ctr) 7
E15..................**76** B1
Newham's Row SE1. **253** B1
Newham Training & Ed Ctr E15 ....**76** C2
Newham University Hospl E13..........**99** C3
Newham Way
Beckton E6..........**100** B3
Canning Town E13 .....**99** B2
Newhaven Cl UB3... **105** D2
Newhaven Cres
TW15 ....**171** B5
Newhaven Gdns
SE9............... **143** D1
Newhaven La 3 E16 ..**99** A2
Newhaven Rd SE25 ..**205** B4
New Heston Rd TW5 .**129** B5
New Hope Christian Sch
1 SE22........... **139** D1
New Horizons Ct
TW8 ....**131** A6
Newhouse 5 KT3....**199** C2
Newhouse Ave RM6...**58** D6
Newhouse Cl KT3....**199** C2
Newhouse Wlk SM4. .**202** A2
Newick Cl DA5....... **169** D5
Newick Rd E5 ....**74** C5
Newing Gn BR1..... **187** D3
NEWINGTON....... **116** D2
Newington Barrow Way
N7..................**72** B5

Newington Butts SE1,
SE11 . . . . . . 116 D2 **261** D3
Newington Cswy
SE1 . . . . 117 A3 **262** A6
Newington Gn N16 . . . . .73 B3
Newington Green Mans
N16 . . . . .73 B3
Newington Green Prim
Sch N16 . . . . .73 B3
Newington Green Rd
N1 . . . . .73 B3
Newington Ind Est
SE17 . . . .**262** A3
New Inn Broadway
EC2 . . . .**243** B6
New Inn Ct The KT8 . .**196** B4
New Inn Sq EC2 . . . . .**243** B6
New Inn St EC2 . . . . .**243** B6
New Inn Yd
EC2 . . . . 95 C3 **243** B6
New James Ct SE15 . .140 B2
New Jubilee Ct **1** 37 A3
New Kelvin Ave
TW11 . . . . .174 C4
New Kent Rd
SE1 . . . . 117 A2 **262** D4
New King's Prim Sch **12**
SW6 . . . . .135 C4
New King's Rd
SW6 . . . . . .135 C4 **265** B1
New King St SE8 . . . . .141 C6
Newland Cl N18 . . . . . . .23 B4
Newland Ct
St Luke's EC1 . . . . . .**242** C6
Wembley HA9 . . . . . .66 C6
Newland Dr EN1 . . . . . . .6 B4
Newland Gdns W13 . .109 A4
Newland Ho
17 Deptford SE14 . . . .140 D6
Hornsey N8 . . . . .50 A6
Newland House Sch
TW1 . . . . .174 D6
Newland Rd N8 . . . . . . .50 A6
Newlands Ave W3 . . . . . .86 A4
Newlands Ave K17 . . . .196 C1
Newlands Cl
Edgware HA8 . . . . . . .10 A1
Southall UB2 . . . . . . .107 A1
Wembley HA0 . . . . . .65 C2
Newlands Croft
SE20 . . . . .184 D4
Newlands Ct
6 Eltham SE9 . . . . . .166 C5
6 Penge SE26 . . . . . .184 C4
Streatham SW16 . . . .182 A5
Newlands Pk SE26 . . .184 D5
Newlands Pl EN5 . . . . . .12 C6
Newlands Quay E1 . . . .118 C6
Newlands The
Thornton Heath
SW16 . . . . .182 A1
Woodford IG8 . . . . . . .20 D2
Newland St E16 . . . . . . .35 C1
Newlands The
Thames Ditton KT7 . .196 C1
Wallington SM6 . . . . .219 D1
Newlands Way KT9 . . .213 D3
New Life Christian Sch
CR0 . . . . .220 D6
Newling Ct E6 . . . . . . .100 B1
New London St EC3 . .**253** B6
New Lydenburg
Commercial Est
SE7 . . . . .121 C3
New Lydenburg St
SE7 . . . . .121 C3
Newlyn NW1 . . . .**232** B5
Newlyn Cl
Hillingdon UB8 . . . . . .82 C2
Orpington BR6 . . . . .227 D4
Newlyn Gdns HA2 . . . . .41 B2
Newlyn Ho
7 Pinner HA5 . . . . . . .23 B3
5 Sutton SM1 . . . . . .218 A4
Newlyn Rd Barnet EN5 . .1 B1
Bexley DA16 . . . . . . .145 D3
Tottenham N17 . . . . . .33 D2
NEW MALDEN 199 D5
New Malden Sta
KT3 . . . . .199 C6
Newman Ct
3 Bromley BR1 . . . . .187 A2

Newman Ct continued
8 Finchley N3 . . . . . . .29 C2
Newman Ho **11**
TW10 . . . . .153 C1
Newman Pas W1 . . . . **239** B3
Newman Rd
Bromley BR1 . . . . . . .187 A2
Harmondsworth UB7 .126 C4
Hayes UB3 . . . . .106 B6
Newham E13 . . . . .99 B4
Thornton Heath CR0 . .204 B1
Walthamstow E17 . . . . .52 D4
Newman's Ct EC3 . . . .**242** D1
Newmans La N16 KT6 . .198 A3
Newman's Row WC2 . .**240** D3
Newman St
W1 . . . . 93 C2 **239** B3
Newman's Way EN4 . . . .2 A4
Newman Terr **7**
CR4 . . . . .202 D6
Newmarket Ave UB5 . .63 D3
Newmarket Gn SE9 . . .165 D4
Newmarsh Rd SE28 . . .123 D5
Newmill Ho E3 . . . . .98 A3
New Mill Rd BR5 . . . .190 C2
Newminster Rd SM4 . .202 A3
Newmount NW3 . . . . . . .70 B3
New Mount St E15 . . . . .76 B4
Newnes Path SW15 . . .134 B1
Newnham Ave HA4 . . . .40 C1
Newnham Cl
Loughton IG10 . . . . . . .21 D5
Northolt UB5 . . . . . . .64 A2
South Norwood CR7 . .183 A1
Newnham Gdns UB5 . . .64 A2
Newnham Ho
Catford SE6 . . . . . . .164 A1
Loughton IG10 . . . . . . .21 D5
9 Putney SW15 . . . . .156 D5
Newnham Jun & Inf Schs
HA4 . . . . .40 C1
Newnham Lo **10**
DA17 . . . . .125 C1
Newnham Mews N22 . .32 C2
Newnham Rd N22 . . . . .32 C2
Newnhams Cl BR1 . . . .210 B6
Newnham Terr SE1 . . .**261** B6
Newnham Way HA3 . . .44 A4
New North Com Sch
N1 . . . . 95 A6 **235** A6
New North Pl EC2 . . . .**243** B6
New North Rd
N1 . . . . 95 B6 **235** D5
New North St
WC1 . . . . 94 B2 **240** C4
New Oak Rd N2 . . . . . . .30 A1
New Oxford St
WC1 . . . . 94 A1 **240** A2
New Palace Yd
SW1 . . . . . . .116 A4 **250** A1
New Par
Ashford TW15 . . . . . .170 B6
Yiewsley UB7 . . . . . .104 A5
New Park Ave N13 . . . .17 B1
New Park Cl UB5 . . . . . .63 A2
New Park Ct **26**
SW2 . . . . .160 A4
New Park Ho N13 . . . . . .32 B6
New Park Par **14**
SW2 . . . . .160 A4
New Park Rd
Ashford TW15 . . . . . .171 A5
Streatham SW2 . . . . .160 A4
New Pl CR0 . . . . .223 C2
New Place Sq SE16 . . .118 B3
New Plaistow Rd E15 . .98 C6
New Pond Par HA4 . . . .62 A5
Newport Ave
Blackwall E14 . . . . . .120 B6
Newham E13 . . . . .99 B3
Newport Cl EN3 . . . . .**249** D6
Newport Ct WC2 . . . . .**249** D6
Newport Ho **2** 97 A4
Newport Lo **2** EN1 . . . .17 C6
Newport Mead WD19 . .22 D6
Newport Pl WC2 . . . . .**249** D6
Newport Rd
Barnes SW13 . . . . . .147 A3
Harmondsworth TW6 .126 C4
Hayes UB4 . . . . .83 B4
Leyton E10 . . . . .76 B6
Walthamstow E17 . . . . .53 A5
Newport Sch E10, E11 .76 A6

Newport St
SE11 . . . . . . .116 B2 **260** D4
New Priory Ct **3**
NW6 . . . . .69 C1
New Providence Wharf
E14 . . . . .120 B5
Newquay Cres HA2 . . . .63 A6
Newquay Ho SE11 . . . .**261** A2
Newquay Rd SE6 . . . . .164 A2
New Quebec St W1 . . .**237** D1
New Rd
Brentford TW8 . . . . . .109 D1
Carshalton CR4 . . . . .203 A1
Chingford E4 . . . . .36 A6
Dagenham RM10 . . . .103 D5
East Bedfont TW14 . . .150 A6
East Molesey KT8 . . . .195 C6
Edmonton N9 . . . . . . .18 B2
Elstree WD6 . . . . .9 D5
Esher KT10 . . . . .212 A4
Feltham TW14 . . . . . .150 B3
Finchley N10 . . . . .30 D5
Hanworth TW13 . . . . .173 A5
Harlington TW6, UB7, UB3 127 A5
Harrow HA1 . . . . .64 D4
Hendon NW7 . . . . .29 A3
Hillingdon UB8 . . . . . .83 A2
Hornsey N8 . . . . .50 A4
Hounslow TW3 . . . . . .129 D1
Ilford IG3 . . . . .79 C5
Kingston u T KT2 . . . .176 C3
Littleton TW17 . . . . . .192 D6
Richmond TW10 . . . . .175 C6
Stepney E1 . . . . .96 B2
Tottenham N22 . . . . . .33 A2
Welling DA16 . . . . . . .146 B2
West Heath SE2 . . . . .124 D1
New River Ave N8 . . . . .50 B6
New River Cres N13 . . .32 C6
New River Ct N5 . . . . . .73 B4
New River Stad N22 . . .32 D3
New River Way N4 . . . . .51 B2
New Row
WC2 . . . . . . .116 A6 **250** A6
New Rush Hall Sch
IG1 . . . . .79 A6
Newry Rd TW1 . . . . . .153 C6
New Scotland Yard★
SW1 . . . . . . .115 D3 **259** C6
New Shepherd's Bush
Mkt★ **6** W12 . . . .112 C4
Newsholme Dr N21 . . .16 B6
NEW SOUTHGATE 31 C6
New Southgate Ind Est
N10 N11 . . . . .31 C5
New Southgate Sta
N11 . . . . .31 B5
New Spitalfields Mkt
E10 . . . . .97 C5
New Spring Gdns Wlk
SE11 . . . .**260** B1
New Sq
East Bedfont TW14 . . .149 A3
St Giles WC2 . . .94 B1 **240** D2
New Square Pas
WC2 . . . .**241** A2
New St EC2 . . . . 94 C2 **243** B3
Newstead Ave BR6 . . .227 C5
Newstead Cl N12 . . . . . .30 C4
Newstead Ct UB5 . . . . .85 A4
Newstead Ho
Edmonton N9 . . . . .17 D1
Islington N1 . . . . **234** B4
Newstead Rd SE12 . . .164 D4
Newstead Way
SW19 . . . . .178 D6
Newstead Wlk SM5 . . .202 A2
Newstead Wood Sch for
Girls BR6 . . . . .227 B5
New Street Hill BR1 . . .187 C5
Newton Ave
Acton W3 . . . . .111 A4
Muswell Hill N10 . . . . .31 B2
Newton Cl
Harrow HA2 . . . . .63 C6
Walthamstow E17 . . . . .53 A3
Newton Farm Ecology Pk
HA2 . . . . .63 C6
Newton Farm Fst & Mid
Sch HA2 . . . . .63 B6
Newton Gr W4 . . . . . .111 C2
Newton Ho
22 Clapham SW8 . . . .137 D3
Paddington NW8 . . . . .91 D6

Newton Ho continued
10 Stepney E1 . . . . . .118 B6
10 Walthamstow E17 . . .54 A6
Newton Ind Est RM6 . .58 D5
Newton Pl E14 . . . . . .119 C2
Newton Point **1** E16 . .98 D1
Newton Prep Sch
SW8 . . . . . . .137 B4 **268** D2
Newton Rd
Acton W3 . . . . .111 A4
Cricklewood NW2 . . . . .68 C5
Harmondsworth UB7 .126 B4
Harrow HA3 . . . . .24 C1
Isleworth TW7 . . . . . .130 D3
Kensington W2 . . . . . . .91 D1
South Tottenham N15 . .52 A4
Stratford New Town
E15 . . . . .76 A3
Welling DA16 . . . . . . .146 A2
Wembley HA0 . . . . . . .66 B1
Wimbledon SW19 . . . .179 A3
Newton St
WC2 . . . . . 94 A1 **240** B2
Newton's Yd **16**
SW18 . . . . .157 C6
Newton Terr BR2 . . . .209 D3
Newton Way N18 . . . . .33 A5
Newton Wlk HA8 . . . . . .26 D2
New Tower Bldgs **21**
E1 . . . . .118 B5
Newtown Ct
Battersea SW11 . . . .**268** C1
Clapham SW4 . . . . . .159 B6
New Trinity Rd **1** N2 . .30 B1
New Union Cl E14 . . . .120 A3
New Union St EC2 . . . .**242** C3
New Victoria Hospl
KT3 . . . . .177 C2
New Wanstead E11 . . . .55 A3
New Way Rd NW9 . . . . .45 C5
New Wharf Rd
N1 . . . . 94 A5 **233** B4
New Woodlands Sch
BR1 . . . . .186 C6
NEWYEARS GREEN 38 B3
Newyears Green La
UB9 . . . . .38 B3
New Zealand Ave
KT12 . . . . .193 D1
Nexus Ct SE11 . . . . . .**54** C2
Niagara Ave W5 . . . . .109 C2
Niagara Cl N1 . . . .**235** B4
Niagara Ct SE16 . . . . .118 C3
Niagara Ho W5 . . . . . .109 C2
Nibthwaite Rd HA1 . . .42 C4
Nicholas Cl UB6 . . . . . .85 D5
Nicholas Ct
Chiswick W4 . . . . . . .133 C5
Golders Green NW11 . .47 C2
Lewisham SE12 . . . . .165 A3
Newham E13 . . . . .99 B4
9 Shepherd's Bush
W11 . . . . .112 D6
Wallington CR0 . . . . .220 A4
Nicholas Stacey Ho **3**
SE7 . . . . .121 B1
Nicholay Rd N19 . . . . . .49 D1
Nichol Cl N14 . . . . .15 D3
Nicholes Rd TW3 . . . .129 C1
Nichol La BR1 . . . . . . .187 A3
Nichol Ho N4 . . . . .51 A1
Nicholl Ho N4 . . . . .51 A1
Nicholls Almshouses **4**
NW7 . . . . .28 B5
Nicholls Ave UB8 . . . . .82 C3
Nicholls Point **4** E15 .99 A6
Nicholl St E2 . . . . .96 A6
Nichols Cl
Chessington KT9 . . . .213 C2
Finsbury Pk N4 . . . . . .50 C1
Nichols Ct E2 . . . . .95 D5
Nichols Gn W5 . . . . . . .88 A4
Nicholson Ct **3** N17 . .51 D6
Nicholson Ho SE17 . . .**262** C2
Nicholson Mews
KT1 . . . . .198 A5

Nicholson Rd CR0 . . . .205 D1
Nicholson St SE1 . . . .**251** C3
Nickelby Cl SE28 . . . .102 C1
Nickleby Cl UB8 . . . . . .82 D1
Nickleby Ho
18 Bermondsey
SE1 . . . . .118 A4
7 Shepherd's Bush
W11 . . . . .112 D5
Nickols Wlk SW18 . . . .135 C1
Nicola Cl Harrow HA3 . .24 B1
South Croydon CR2 . .221 A2
Nicola Terr DA7 . . . . . .147 A4
Nicol Cl **6** TW1 . . . . .153 B5
Nicole Ho SE25 . . . . . .206 A6
Nicoll Ct
Dagenham NW10 . . . . .89 C6
Muswell Hill N10 . . . . . .31 B3
Nicoll Pl NW4 . . . . .46 B2
Nicoll Rd NW10 . . . . . .89 C6
Nicoll Way IG8 . . . . . . .11 B6
Nicolson **14** NW9 . . . .27 D2
Nicosia Rd SW18 . . . .158 C4
Niederwald Rd SE26 .185 A6
Nield Rd UB3 . . . . . . .105 D4
Nigel Bldg EC1 . . . . . .**241** A4
Nigel Cl UB5 . . . . .85 A6
Nigel Ct N3 . . . . .29 D3
Nigel Fisher Way
KT9 . . . . .213 D1
Nigel Mews IG1 . . . . . .78 D4
Nigel Playfair Ave
W6 . . . . .112 B1
Nigel Rd
Forest Gate E7 . . . . . . .77 C3
Peckham SE15 . . . . . .140 A2
Nigeria Rd SE7 . . . . . .143 D5
Nighthawk **16** NW9 . . .27 D2
Nightingale Ave
Chingford E4 . . . . .36 C5
Harrow HA1 . . . . .43 B1
Nightingale Cl
Carshalton SM5 . . . . .219 A6
Chingford E4 . . . . .36 C6
Chiswick W4 . . . . . . .133 A6
Pinner HA5 . . . . .40 C4
Nightingale Ct
1 Cubitt Town E14 . .120 A3
Finsbury Pk N4 . . . . . .72 B6
1 Harrow HA1 . . . . . .42 D3
1 Penge SE19 . . . . .183 D4
Sutton SM1 . . . . .218 A3
1 Wanstead E11 . . . . .55 B4
Nightingale Dr KT19 .214 D2
Nightingale Gr SE13 .164 B6
Nightingale Ho
Hayes UB3 . . . . .105 D2
2 Hoxton E1 . . . . . . .95 C6
4 North Kensington
W12 . . . . .90 C1
7 St George in East
E1 . . . . .118 A5
Woolwich SE18 . . . . .122 C1
Nightingale La
Balham SW11,
SW12 . . . . .159 A5
Bromley BR1 . . . . . . .187 B5
Hornsey N8 . . . . .50 A6
Richmond TW10 . . . . .154 A4
Wanstead E11 . . . . . . .55 B4
Nightingale Lo
Edgware HA8 . . . . . . .27 A4
5 Paddington W9 . . . .91 C2
Nightingale Mans **4**
SW12 . . . . .159 A5
Nightingale Mews
1 Bow E3 . . . . .97 A5
7 Newington SE11 . . .**261** C4
Nightingale Pl
Shooters Hill SE18 . . .144 D6
West Brompton
SW10 . . . . . .136 A6 **266** B6
Nightingale Prim Sch
Shacklewell E5 . . . . . .74 A4
Walthamstow E18 . . . . .55 C5
Wood Green N22 . . . . .32 B2
Woolwich SE18 . . . . .122 D1
Nightingale Rd
22 Canonbury N1 . . . .73 A2
Carshalton SM5 . . . . .219 A6
Dagenham NW10 . . . . .89 C5
Hanwell W7 . . . . .108 D5
East Molesey KT8 . . . .195 D4
Hackney E5 . . . . .74 B5

Nightingale Rd *continued*
Hampton TW12 ..... 173 C4
Orpington BR5 .... 211 A3
Ponders End N9 .... 18 C4
Walton-on-T KT12 ..... 194 B2
Wood Green N22 ...... 32 B3
Nightingale Sch
SW17 .... 158 C2
Nightingale Sq
SW12 .... 159 A4
Nightingales The
TW19 .... 148 B3
Nightingale Vale
SE18 .... 144 C6
Nightingale Way E6 .. 100 A2
Nightingale Wlk SW18,
SW4 .... 159 B5
Nile Cl N16 .... 73 D5
Nile Ct N12 .... 30 C4
Nile Dr N9 .... 18 C2
Nile Ho N1 .... 235 C2
Nile Path [6] SE18 .... 144 C6
Nile Rd E13 .... 99 C5
Nile St N1 ..... 95 B4 235 C2
Nile Terr SE1,
SE15 ...... 117 D1 263 D1
Nimegen Way [9]
SE22 ...... 161 C6
Nimmo Dr WD23 ..... 8 B4
Nimrod [12] NW9 .... 27 C2
Nimrod Cl UB5 ...... 84 D4
Nimrod Pas [4] N1 ..... 73 C2
Nimrod Rd SW16 .... 181 B5
Nina Mackay Cl [10]
E15 .... 98 C6
Nine Acres Cl
Hayes UB3 ...... 105 A3
London E12 ...... 78 A3
NINE ELMS 137 C5
Nine Elms Cl TW14 .. 149 D3
Nine Elms La
SW8 ...... 137 D6 269 C5
Nineteenth Rd CR4 .. 204 A5
Ninhams Wood BR6 .. 226 C4
Ninth Ave UB3 .... 106 A6
Nisbet [13] NW9 ...... 27 C2
Nisbet Ho E9 ...... 74 D3
Nisbett Wlk DA14 .... 190 A6
Nita Ct SE12 ...... 165 A3
Nithdale Rd SE18 .... 145 A5
Nithsdale Gr UB10 .... 61 A5
Niton Cl EN5 ...... 12 D5
Niton Rd TW9 ...... 132 C2
Niton St SW6 ...... 134 D5
No 1 St SE18 ...... 122 D3
No 2 Willow Rd*
NW3 ...... 70 C4
Noam Prim Sch HA9 .. 66 B5
Nobel Dr TW6 ...... 127 C5
Nobel Ho [8] SE5 ..... 139 A3
Nobel Rd N18 ...... 34 C6
Noble Cnr TW5 ..... 129 C4
Noble Ct
Mitcham CR4 .... 180 B1
Stepney E1 .... 118 B6
Noblefield Hts N2 .... 48 D4
Noble Ho [18] E1 ..... 118 A6
Noble St EC2 .. 95 A1 242 A2
Noel [13] NW9 ...... 27 D2
Noel Baker Ct [5] E11 .. 76 C6
Noel Coward Ho
SW1 .... 259 B3
Noel Ct TW4 ...... 129 B2
Noel Dene W5 ...... 109 C1
Noel Ho [3] NW3 ...... 70 B1
NOEL PARK 32 D1
Noel Park Prim Sch
N22 ...... 32 C1
Noel Park Rd N22 .... 32 C1
Noel Rd Acton W3 .... 88 D1
Islington N1 .. 94 D5 234 D4
Newham E6 ..... 100 A3
Noel Sq RM8 ...... 80 C4
Noel St W1 .... 93 C1 239 B1
Noel Terr
Forest Hill SE23 .... 162 C2
Sidcup DA14 ...... 190 B6
Noko NW10 ...... 90 D4
Nolan Way E5 ...... 74 A4
Noll Ho N7 ...... 72 B6
Nolton Pl HA8 ...... 26 B2
Nonsuch Ct SM3 .... 217 A2
Nonsuch High Sch for
Girls SM3 ...... 216 D1
Nonsuch Ho [5]
SW19 ...... 180 B2

Nonsuch Prim Sch
KT17 ...... 216 B3
Nook The SW19 ...... 180 A1
Noor Ul Islam Prim Sch
E10 ...... 76 A6
Nora Gdns NW4 ...... 46 D5
NORBITON 176 C1
Norbiton Ave KT1,
KT2 ...... 176 C1
Norbiton Common Rd KT1,
KT3 ...... 198 D6
Norbiton Hall KT2 ... 176 B1
Norbiton Rd E14 ...... 97 B1
Norbiton Sta KT1 ... 176 C2
Norbreck Gdns NW10 . 88 B4
Norbreck Par NW10 ... 88 B4
Norbroke St W12 ... 111 D6
Norburn St W10 ...... 91 A2
NORBURY 182 C2
Norbury Ave
Isleworth TW3 ...... 130 B1
Thornton Heath CR7,
SW16 ...... 182 C1
Norbury Cl SW16 ... 182 D2
Norbury Court Rd
SW16 ...... 182 A1
Norbury Cres SW16 .. 182 C1
Norbury Cross
SW16 ...... 204 A6
Norbury Ct N12 ...... 30 A6
Norbury Fst & Mid Sch
HA1 ...... 42 C4
Norbury Gdns RM6 ... 58 D4
Norbury Gr NW7 ...... 11 C1
Norbury Hill SW16 .. 182 D3
Norbury Manor Bsns &
Enterprise Coll For
Girls CR7 ...... 182 C2
Norbury Manor Prim Sch
SW16 ...... 182 A2
Norbury Rd
Chingford E4 ...... 35 C5
Feltham TW13 ...... 149 D1
South Norwood CR7 .. 205 A6
Norbury Rise SW16 .. 204 A6
Norbury Sta SW16 ... 182 B2
Norbury Trad Est
SW16 ...... 182 B1
Norcombe Gdns HA3 .. 43 C4
Norcombe Ho [2] N19 . 71 D5
Norcott Cl UB4 ...... 84 C3
Norcott Rd N16 ...... 74 A5
Norcroft Gdns SE22 .. 162 A4
Norcutt Rd TW2 ...... 152 C3
Norden Ho [25] E2 ...... 96 B4
Norden Point NW2 ... 46 C1
Nore Ct NW10 ...... 68 A1
Norfolk Ave
Edmonton N13 ...... 32 D4
South Tottenham N15 ... 51 D3
Norfolk Cl
Cockfosters EN4 ...... 3 A1
East Finchley N2 ...... 48 C6
Edmonton N13 ...... 32 D4
[5] Twickenham TW1 ... 153 B5
Norfolk Cres
Paddington
W2 ...... 92 C1 237 B2
Sidcup DA15 ...... 167 C4
Norfolk Ct
[5] Barnet EN5 ...... 1 A1
[4] Ilford RM6 ...... 58 B4
Surbiton KT5 ...... 198 B3
Wembley HA0 ...... 65 C2
Norfolk Gdns DA7 ... 147 B4
Norfolk Ho
[13] Acton W3 ...... 88 C1
Beckenham BR2 ...... 208 D5
City of London EC4 ... 252 A6
Edgware HA8 ...... 26 B3
Greenwich SE3 ...... 142 C6
[11] Merton SW19 ...... 180 A3
Penge SE20 ...... 184 C2
[4] Putney SW15 ...... 156 C4
Richmond TW10 ...... 154 C6
Shacklewell E8 ...... 73 D4
[2] South Croydon
CR0 ...... 221 B6
[3] Stanmore HA7 ...... 25 C5
St Johns SE8 ...... 141 C4
Westminster SW1 ... 259 D4
Norfolk House Rd
SW16 ...... 160 A1
Norfolk House Sch
N10 ...... 31 B1

Norfolk Mans
Battersea SW11 ...... 267 D1
[10] Wandsworth
SW18 ...... 157 C6
Norfolk Mews [12]
W10 ...... 91 A2
Norfolk Pl
Paddington
W2 ...... 92 B1 236 D2
Welling DA16 ...... 146 A3
Norfolk Rd
Barking IG11 ...... 79 C1
Barnet EN5 ...... 1 C2
Claygate KT10 ...... 212 C3
Dagenham RM10 ...... 81 D3
Enfield EN3 ...... 18 B6
Feltham TW13 ...... 150 C3
Harrow HA1 ...... 41 D4
Higham Hill E17 ...... 34 D1
Ilford IG3 ...... 57 C2
Mitcham SW19 ...... 180 C4
Newham E6 ...... 100 B6
South Norwood CR7 .. 205 A6
St John's Wood
NW8 ...... 92 B6 229 D5
Willesden NW10 ...... 67 C1
Norfolk Row SE1,
SE11 ...... 116 B2 260 C4
Norfolk Sq
W2 ...... 92 B1 236 D2
Norfolk Sq Mews
W2 ...... 236 D1
Norfolk St E7 ...... 77 A3
Norgrove St SW12 ... 159 A4
Norhyrst Ave SE25 .. 205 D6
Norland Ho [13] W11 . 112 D5
Norland Pl
W11 ...... 113 A5 244 B3
Norland Place Sch
W11 ...... 113 A5 244 A3
Norland Rd [16] W11 . 112 D5
Norlands Cres BR7 .. 188 D2
Norland Sq
W11 ...... 113 A5 244 B3
Norley Vale SW15 ... 156 A3
Norlington Rd E10,
E11 ...... 54 B1
Norlington Sch E10 ... 54 B1
Norman Ave
Feltham TW13 ...... 151 B2
Southall UB1 ...... 107 A6
Tottenham N22 ...... 33 A2
Twickenham TW1 ...... 153 C4
Norman Butler Ho [10]
W10 ...... 91 A3
Normanby Cl SW15 .. 157 B6
Normanby Rd NW10 .. 67 D4
Norman Cl
Orpington BR6 ...... 227 A5
Tottenham N22 ...... 33 A2
Norman Cres
Heston TW5 ...... 128 D5
Pinner HA5 ...... 22 C2
Norman Ct
Dulwich SE22 ...... 162 A4
[5] Finchley N3 ...... 29 C2
Finsbury Pk N4 ...... 50 C2
[8] Hampton TW12 ... 173 C2
Ilford IG2 ...... 57 B2
West Norwood SW16 182 C5
Willesden NW10 ...... 68 A1
Woodford IG8 ...... 37 B5
Normand Croft Com Sch
W14 ...... 135 B6 264 D6
Normand Mews W14 264 B6
Normand Rd
W14 ...... 135 B6 264 C6
Normandy Ave EN5 ... 1 B1
Normandy Cl SE26 .. 163 A1
Normandy Dr UB3 ... 83 A1
Normandy Ho
[8] Cubitt Town E14 .. 120 A4
[4] Hendon NW4 ...... 28 D1
Normandy Rd SW9 .. 138 C4
Normandy Terr E16 ... 99 B1
Norman Gr E3 ...... 97 A5
Norman Hay Trad Est
UB7 ...... 126 B4
Norman Ho
[1] Cheam SM1 ...... 217 C2
Feltham TW13 ...... 151 B2
[7] Leyton E11 ...... 76 C6
Lower Halliford TW17 192 C2
South Lambeth SW8 . 270 A4
Normanhurst TW15 .. 170 C5

Normanhurst Ave
DA7 ...... 146 D4
Normanhurst Dr
TW1 ...... 153 B6
Normanhurst Rd
St Paul's Cray BR5 ... 190 B1
Streatham SW2 ...... 160 B2
Walton-on-T KT12 ... 194 D1
Normanhurst Sch E4 . 20 B4
Norman Par DA14 ... 168 D2
Norman Rd
Ashford TW15 ...... 171 B4
Belvedere DA17 ...... 125 D3
Greenwich SE10 ...... 141 D5
Ilford IG1 ...... 78 D3
Leyton E11 ...... 76 C6
Merton SW19 ...... 180 A3
Newham E6 ...... 100 B3
South Tottenham N15 ... 51 D4
Sutton SM1 ...... 217 C3
Thornton Heath CR7 . 204 D4
Normans Cl
Hillingdon UB8 ...... 82 A2
Willesden NW10 ...... 67 B2
Normansfield Ave KT1,
KT8 ...... 175 C3
Normanshire Dr E4 ... 35 D6
Normans Mead NW10 67 B2
Norman St
EC1 ...... 95 A4 235 B1
Normanton Ave SW18,
SW19 ...... 157 C2
Normanton Ct CR2 .. 221 C3
Normanton Ho [6]
SW4 ...... 159 C5
Normanton Pk E4 ...... 20 C2
Normanton Rd CR2 .. 221 C2
Normanton St SE23 . 162 D2
Norman Way
Acton W3 ...... 88 D1
Palmers Green N14 ... 16 A2
Normington Cl
SW16 ...... 182 C5
Norrice Lea N2 ...... 48 B4
Norris [11] NW9 ...... 27 D2
Norris Ho
[12] Hoxton N1 ...... 95 C6
[15] South Hackney E9 ... 96 C6
Norris St SW1 ...... 249 C5
Norroy Rd SW15 ...... 134 D1
Norrys Cl EN4 ...... 2 D1
Norrys Rd EN4 ...... 2 D1
Norse Ho [13] SE5 ...... 139 A3
Norseman Cl [3] IG3 ... 58 B1
Norseman Way UB6 ... 85 D6
Norstead Pl SW15 ... 156 A2
North Access Rd E17 . 52 D3
North Acre NW9 ...... 27 C2
NORTH ACTON 89 B4
North Acton Rd
NW10 ...... 89 B4
North Acton Sta W3 ... 89 B2
Northala Fields UB5 .. 85 B6
Northampton Gr N1 .. 73 B3
Northampton Pk N1 .. 73 B2
Northampton Rd
Croydon CR0 ...... 222 A6
Enfield EN3 ...... 7 A1
Finsbury EC1 .. 94 C3 241 B6
Northampton Sq
EC1 ...... 94 D4 234 C1
Northampton St N1 ... 73 A1
Northanger Rd
SW16 ...... 182 A4
North Audley St
W1 ...... 115 A6 248 A6
North Ave Ealing W13 .. 87 B2
Edmonton N18 ...... 34 A6
Harrow HA2 ...... 41 D3
Hayes UB3 ...... 106 A6
[8] Richmond TW9 ... 132 C4
Southall UB1 ...... 107 B6
Wallington SM5 ...... 219 A1
Northaw Ho [4] W10 ... 90 C3
North Bank
NW8 ...... 92 C4 230 A1
Northbank Rd E17 ... 36 A1
North Beckton Prim Sch
E6 ...... 100 B2
North Birkbeck Rd
E11 ...... 76 B5
North Block [19] E1 ... 118 C6
Northborough Rd
SW16 ...... 182 A1
Northbourne BR2 ... 209 A2

Northbourne Ho
[21] Hackney E5 ...... 74 B3
Osidge N14 ...... 15 D4
Northbourne Rd
SW4 ...... 159 D6
North Bridge House Sch
[13] NW3 ...... 70 A2
North Bridge House
Senior Sch
NW1 ...... 93 B6 231 C5
Northbrook CE Sch
SE12 ...... 164 B6
Northbrook Rd
Barnet EN5 ...... 13 A5
Ilford IG1 ...... 78 C6
Lewisham SE13 ...... 164 C6
Thornton Heath CR0 .. 205 B4
Wood Green N22 ...... 32 A3
Northburgh St
EC1 ...... 94 D3 241 D6
Northbury Inf & Jun Schs
IG11 ...... 79 A2
North Carriage Dr
W2 ...... 114 C6 247 B6
NORTH CHEAM 216 C6
Northchurch SE17 .. 262 D2
Northchurch Ho [19]
E2 ...... 96 A6
Northchurch Rd
De Beauvoir Town N1 ... 73 B1
Wembley HA9 ...... 66 C2
Northchurch Terr N1 .. 73 C1
North Circular Rd
Edmonton N13 ...... 32 C5
Finchley N2 ...... 30 B2
Highams Pk E17 ...... 35 D2
Ilford IG1, E12 ...... 78 C4
Neasden NW2, NW10 .. 67 C3
Temple Fortune N3, NW2,
NW4 ...... 47 A4
Woodford E18 ...... 37 C1
North Cl Barnet EN5 ... 12 C6
Bexley DA6 ...... 146 D1
Dagenham RM10 ...... 103 C6
East Bedfont TW14 ... 149 B5
Merton SM4 ...... 201 A5
Northcliffe Cl KT4 ... 215 C5
Northcliffe Dr N20 ... 13 B3
North Colonnade The
E14 ...... 119 D5
North Common Rd
Ealing W5 ...... 110 A6
Uxbridge UB8 ...... 60 A3
Northcote [3] HA5 ...... 22 C1
Northcote Ave
Ealing W5 ...... 110 A6
Isleworth TW7 ...... 153 A6
Southall UB1 ...... 107 A6
Tolworth KT5 ...... 198 D2
Northcote Ho UB4 ... 84 D2
Northcote Lodge Sch
SW11 ...... 158 D5
Northcote Rd
Isleworth TW7 ...... 153 A6
Kingston u T KT3 ...... 199 B6
Sidcup DA14 ...... 189 C6
Thornton Heath CR0 .. 205 B3
Walthamstow E17 ...... 53 A5
Wandsworth SW11 .. 158 D6
Willesden NW10 ...... 67 C1
Northcott Ave N22 ... 32 A2
North Countess Rd
E17 ...... 35 B2
Northcourt W1 ...... 239 B4
NORTH CRAY 169 B1
North Cray Rd DA14 .. 191 A5
North Cres
Finchley N3 ...... 29 B1
Marylebone WC1 ...... 239 C4
Newham E16 ...... 98 B3
Northcroft Ct [3]
W12 ...... 112 A4
Northcroft Rd
Brentford W13 ...... 109 B3
West Ewell KT19 ...... 215 C1
North Crofts SE21 ... 162 B3
North Cross Rd
East Dulwich SE22 ... 162 A6
Ilford IG6 ...... 57 A5
North Ct SW1 ...... 260 A5
North Dene
Edgware NW7 ...... 11 B1
Hounslow TW5 ...... 129 D4

Northdene Gdns N15..51 D3
Northdown Cl HA4....61 D5
Northdown Gdns IG2 .57 C4
Northdown Rd DA16 .146 C3
Northdown St
N1..........94 B5 233 C3
North Dr
Beckenham BR3.....207 D5
Hounslow TW3, TW7 . 130 A3
Orpington BR6.......227 C4
Ruislip HA4 ....39 C2
Streatham SW16.... 181 C6
North Dulwich Sta
SE21..................161 B6
North Ealing Prim Sch
W5......................87 B3
North Ealing Sta W3 ..88 B1
NORTH END 70 A6
North End
Buckhurst Hill IG9 .....21 C4
Croydon CR0 .... 221 A6
North End NW3 ....70 A6
North End Ave NW3...70 A6
North End Cres
W14 ......113 B2 254 C3
North End Ho
W14.......113 A2 254 B3
North End La BR6.... 226 D1
Northend Lodge 2
HA5......................40 D6
North End Par W14 . 254 B3
North End Rd
Golders Green NW11...47 D1
Wembley HA9 ....66 D5
West Kensington
W14 ..... 113 B1 254 D1
North End Way NW3 ..70 A6
Northern Ave N9......17 D2
Northernhay Wlk
SM4 ....201 A5
Northern Hts N8......49 D2
Northern Perimeter Rd
TW6 ....127 C4
Northern Perimeter Rd (W) TW6 ....126 B4
Northern Rd E13......99 B5
Northern Relief Rd
IG11......................79 A2
Northern Star Ho
N11......................31 B5
Northesk Ho 6 E1.... 96 B3
North Eyot Gdns 5
W6 ....111 D1
Northey St E14 ......119 A6
NORTH FELTHAM ...150 B6
North Feltham Trad Est
TW14....................128 B1
Northfield IG10.......21 D6
Northfield Ave
Pinner HA5............40 D5
West Ealing W13, W5..109 B4
Northfield Cl
Bromley BR1 ....188 A2
Hayes UB3........ 105 D3
Northfield Cres SM3 .217 A4
Northfield Gdns RM9.. 81 B4
Northfield Hall N6....49 A2
Northfield Ho
2 Newham E13 ......99 C5
3 Peckham SE15 ... 140 A6
Northfield Ind Est
HA0 ....88 C6
Northfield Par UB3 . 105 D3
Northfield Path RM9 ..81 B4
Northfield Pk UB3 .. 105 D3
Northfield Rd
Cockfosters EN4 ....2 C2
Dagenham RM9 ....81 B4
Enfield EN3 ....18 B6
Heston TW5........ 128 D5
Plashet E6 ....78 B1
Stamford Hill N16 .....51 C2
West Ealing W13 .....109 B4
Northfields SW18....135 C1
Northfields Prospect
SW18...................135 C1
Northfields Rd W3....89 A2
Northfields Sta W5 . 109 C3
NORTH FINCHLEY....30 A6
Northfleet Ho SE1 .. 252 C2
North Flower Wlk
W2 ....114 B6 246 C5
North Gate
NW8.........92 C5 230 A3
Northgate Bsns Ctr
EN1 ....6 B1
Northgate Ct 14
SW9 ....138 C2
Northgate Dr NW9.....45 C3
North Gates N12.......30 A2
North Gdns SW19....180 B3
North Glade The
DA5......................169 B3
North Gn NW9..........27 C3
North Gower St
NW1 ....93 C4 232 B1
North Gr Highgate N6 ..49 A2
Tottenham N15 ....51 B4
North Greenwich Sta
SE10.....................120 C4
North Harringay Prim
Sch N8 ....50 C5
NORTH HARROW 41 D2
North Harrow Sta
HA2 ....41 D4
North Hill N6 ....49 A3
North Hill Ave N6 .....48 D3
North Hill Ct N6 ....49 A2
NORTH HILLINGDON .61 A2
North Ho 3 SE8 ......119 B1
NORTH HYDE 107 A1
North Hyde Gdns UB2,
UB3.......................106 A3
North Hyde La UB2....107 A1
North Hyde Rd UB3 . 105 D3
Northiam Finchley N12 .29 C6
St Pancras WC1...... 233 B1
Northiam St E9 ....96 B6
Northington St
WC1 ....94 B3 240 D5
NORTH KENSINGTON......90 D2
North Kingston Ctr
KT2 ....176 A4
North La TW11....... 174 D4
Northlands 4 BR1...187 C1
Northlands Ave BR6. 227 C4
Northlands St SE5 ...139 A3
Northleigh Ho 36 E3 ..97 D4
North Lo
Clapham SW4 ....137 B1
Muswell Hill N22 ....31 D1
New Barnet EN5 ......14 A6
North Lodge Cl
SW15 ....156 D6
North London Bsns Pk
N11 ....15 A1
North London Coll 13
N17 ....51 D6
North London Collegiate
Sch HA7, HA8...........26 A5
North London Int Sch (IB
Diploma Ctre) 15
N11 ....30 D5
North London Int Sch
(Lower Sch)
5 North Finchley
N12......................14 A1
24 North Finchley N12..29 D6
North London Int Sch
(Lower School) 24
N12........................29 D6
North London Int Sch
(Upper Sch) 14 N11 .30 D5
North London Rudolf
Steiner Sch 7 N8....50 A5
North London Science
Ctr 12 N1 ....72 C1
North Mall The N9 ....18 B2
North Mews
WC1 ....94 B3 240 D5
North Middlesex
University Hospl
N18 ....33 C5
Northmoor 4 SE23 . 162 D1
North Mount N20.....14 A2
Northolm HA8...........27 B6
Northolme Gdns HA8 .26 C2
Northolme Rd N5.....73 A4
Northolme Rise BR6 .227 C6
NORTHOLT 63 C1
Northolt N17 ....33 C1
Northolt Aerodrome
HA4 ....61 D3
Northolt Ave HA4 .....62 B3
Northolt Gdns UB6....64 D3
Northolt High Sch
UB5 ....63 B2
Northolt Park Sta
HA2.......................63 D4
Northolt Rd HA2 ......64 A5
Northolt Sta UB5 .....63 C2
Northolt Trad Est
UB5 ....63 D1
Northover BR1 ..... 164 D1
North Par
Chessington KT9 .....214 B3
Edgware HA8..........26 C1
Southall UB1 ....85 C1
North Pas SW18 ......157 C6
North Pk SE9 ....166 C5
North Pl
Mitcham SW19 ......180 D3
Teddington TW11.... 174 D4
Northpoint BR1......187 A2
North Point UB7.... 104 A5
Northpoint Cl SM1...218 A5
Northpoint Sq 8
NW1......................71 D2
North Pole La BR2 ..225 A2
North Pole Rd W10....90 C2
Northport St N1 .... 235 D5
North Prim Sch UB1 .107 B6
North Rd
Barnsbury N7...........72 A2
Brentford TW8...... 132 A6
Bromley BR1 ....187 B2
Dagenham RM6........59 A4
Ealing W5.............109 D3
East Bedfont TW14 ...149 B5
Edgware HA8..........26 D2
Edmonton N9 ....18 B3
Erith DA17 .... 125 D4
Finchley N2 ....30 C2
Hayes UB3.............83 B2
Highgate N6............49 A2
Ilford IG3...............79 C6
Plumstead SE18..... 123 C2
Richmond TW9...... 132 C3
Southall UB1 .... 107 C6
Surbiton KT6 .... 197 D3
West Drayton UB7....104 B3
1 West Wickham
BR4............... 207 D1
Wimbledon SW19 ... 180 A4
North Residence IG3 . 58 B4
North Ride
W2 ....114 C6 247 A5
North Rise W2...... 237 B1
Northrop Rd TW6 ....127 C4
North Row
W1 ....115 A6 248 A6
NORTH SHEEN......132 C3
North Sheen Sta
TW10............. 132 C1
Northside Prim Sch
N12 ....30 A5
Northside Rd BR1....187 A2
North Side Wandsworth Comm SW18 ......158 B6
Northspur Rd SM1...217 C5
North Sq Edmonton N9 . 18 B2
Hampstead Garden Suburb
NW11 ....47 C4
North St Barking IG11 ..79 A1
Bexleyheath DA7..... 147 C1
Bromley BR1 .... 187 A2
Carshalton SM5...... 218 D4
Clapham SW4 ...... 137 C2
Hendon NW4 ....46 C4
Isleworth TW7...... 131 A2
Newham E13 ....99 B5
Northstead Rd SW2..160 C2
North Tenter St E1 .. 243 D1
North Terr SW3...... 257 A5
Northumberland Alley
EC3.................... 243 B1
Northumberland Ave
Enfield EN1 ....6 B4
Falconwood DA16 .... 145 C2
Hounslow TW7...... 130 D4
Wanstead E12 ....55 C1
Westminster
WC2 ..... 116 A5 250 A4
Northumberland Cl
TW19..................148 A5
Northumberland Cres
TW14.................149 C5
Northumberland Ct
3 Hounslow TW3 ... 129 D1
South Croydon CR2 .. 221 C3
Northumberland Gdns
Brentford TW7...... 131 A5
Bromley BR1 .... 210 C5
Edmonton N9...........17 D1
Mitcham CR4 .... 203 D4
Northumberland Gr
N17.......................34 B3
Northumberland Heath
Prim Sch DA8...... 147 D5
Northumberland Ho
Finchley N12 ....29 D4
Kentish Town NW5....71 C2
Northumberland Mans
E5.........................74 C4
Northumberland Park
Com Sch 2 N17.....34 A3
Northumberland Park
Ind Est N17 ....34 B3
Northumberland Park
Resource Ctr N17 ...34 A3
Northumberland Park
Sta N17..................34 B3
Northumberland Pk
Erith DA8 .... 147 D5
Tottenham N17 ....34 A3
Northumberland Pl
Notting Hill W2........91 C1
26 Richmond TW10 .. 153 D6
Northumberland Rd
Harrow HA2..........41 C4
New Barnet EN5 ....14 A4
Newham E6 .... 100 A1
Walthamstow E17 ......53 C2
Northumberland St
WC2 .... 250 A4
Northumbria Ct 10
TW9 ....132 A1
Northumbria St E14.. 97 C1
North Verbena Gdns 2
W6 ....112 A1
Northview 1 N7.......72 A5
North View Ealing W5 ..87 C3
Pinner HA5...........40 C2
Wimbledon SW19 ... 178 C5
Northview Cres
NW10.....................67 D4
Northview Dr IG8......37 D1
Northview Prim Sch
NW10....................67 D4
North View Rd N8.....49 D6
North Villas NW1.......71 D2
Northway
Hampstead Garden Suburb
NW11 ....47 D4
Merton SM4......... 201 A5
Wallington SM6...... 219 C4
North Way
Friern Barnet N11 .....31 C4
Lower Edmonton N9 ...18 D2
Pinner HA5.............40 D5
Queensbury NW9 .....44 D6
Uxbridge UB10..........60 A1
Northway Cir NW7....27 B6
Northway Cres NW7 ..27 C6
Northway Ct NW7.....27 B6
Northway Rd
Camberwell SE5..... 139 A2
Croydon CR0 .... 205 D2
Northway Sch NW7 ...11 B1
Northways Par 2
NW3......................70 B1
North Weald La KT2. 175 D5
NORTH WEMBLEY ...65 C6
North Wembley Sta HA0,
HA9 ....65 D5
North Western Ave (Tylers Way) WD23... 8 C6
North Western Ave (Watford By-Pass)
WD6 ....9 B4
North West London
Jewish Day Sch
NW6......................69 A1
Northwest Pl N1.... 234 B4
North Wharf Rd
W2 ....92 B2 236 C3
Northwick Ave HA3 ...43 B3
Northwick Circ HA3...43 C3
Northwick Cl
Harrow HA1...........43 B1
Lisson Gr NW8 92 B3 236 C6
Northwick Ho NW8 . 236 B6
Northwick Park Hospl
HA1 ....43 A2
Northwick Park Rd
HA1.......................42 D3
Northwick Park Sta
HA3 ....43 B2
Northwick Rd
South Oxhey WD19 ....22 C6
Wembley HA0 ....87 D6
Northwick Terr
NW8.........92 B3 236 C6
North Wlk
Bayswater
W2 ...... 114 A6 246 A5
New Addington CR0.. 224 A3
Northwold Dr HA5 ....40 C6
Northwold Prim Sch
E5.........................74 A6
Northwold Rd E5, N16 .74 A6
NORTHWOOD 22 A3
Northwood Gdns
Greenford UB6........64 D3
Ilford IG5..............56 C5
North Finchley N12 .....30 B5
NORTHWOOD HILLS .22 A1
Northwood Hills Cir
HA6.......................22 A2
Northwood Hills Sta
HA6 ....22 A1
North Wood Lo NW3 ..69 D4
Northwood Pl DA18..125 B3
Northwood Prim Sch
DA18 ....125 B3
Northwood Rd
Forest Hill SE23......163 B3
Highgate N6............49 B2
South Norwood CR7... 183 A1
Wallington SM5...... 219 A2
Northwood Sch HA6 ..22 A2
Northwood Twr 1
E17........................54 A5
Northwood Way
Northwood HA6........22 A3
1 West Norwood
SE19 .... 183 C4
NORTH WOOLWICH 122 D4
North Woolwich Rd
E16.....................121 B5
North Woolwich Rdbt
E16.................. 121 D5
North Worple Way
SW14 ....133 B2
Norton Ave KT5..... 198 D2
Norton Cl Chingford E4 35 C5
Enfield EN1 ....6 B3
Norton Ct
Beckenham BR3......185 B2
Ilford IG2...............57 B3
Norton Folgate E1... 243 B4
Norton Gdns SW16...182 A1
Norton Ho
14 Globe Town E2 .....96 D5
6 New Malden KT3 199 C5
30 Stepney E1 ....96 B1
16 Stockwell SW9 ....138 B3
Norton Rd
Walthamstow E10 ......53 B1
Wembley HA0 ....65 D2
Norval Gn 1 SW9....138 C3
Norval Rd HA0.........43 B1
Norvic Ho 5 SE5 ....139 A3
Norway Gate SE16 ...119 A3
Norway Pl E14..........97 B1
Norway St SE10...... 141 D6
Norwegian Sch The 6
SW20............. 178 C3
Norwich Cres RM6.....58 B4
Norwich Ho 6 E14....97 D1
Norwich Mews IG3 ...58 A1
Norwich Rd
Forest Gate E7........77 A3
Greenford UB6.........85 D6
Northwood HA6.........39 D6
South Norwood CR7.. 205 A6
Norwich St
EC4.........94 C1 241 A2
Norwich Wlk HA8......27 A3
Norwood Ave HA0 ....88 B5
Norwood Cl
Cricklewood NW2 .....69 A5
Southall UB2 .... 107 C2
Twickenham TW2.....152 B2
Norwood Dr HA2 .....41 C3
Norwood Gdns
Hayes UB4............84 C3
Southall UB2 ....107 B2
NORWOOD GREEN. .107 C2
Norwood Green Inf Sch
UB2.....................107 B1

Norwood Green Jun Sch UB2 107 A1
Norwood Green Rd UB2 107 C2
Norwood Heights Sh Ctr 13 SE19 183 C4
Norwood High St SE27 183 A6
Norwood Ho 25 E14 119 D6
Norwood Junction Sta SE25 206 A5
NORWOOD NEW TOWN 183 A4
Norwood Park Rd SE27 183 A5
Norwood Rd
Southall UB2 107 C2
West Norwood SE24, SE27 160 D3
Norwood Sch SE19 183 A5
Norwood Terr UB2 107 D2
Notley St SE5 139 B5
Notre Dame RC Girls Sch SE1 116 D3 261 D5
Notre Dame RC Prim Sch SE18 144 D6
Notson Rd SE25 206 B5
Notting Barn Rd W10 90 D3
Nottingdale Sq W11 244 A4
Nottingham Ave E16 99 C1
Nottingham Ct WC2 240 A1
Nottingham Ho
33 Camberwell SE5 139 A3
Stoke Newington N4 51 A1
Nottingham Pl W1 93 A2 238 A4
Nottingham Rd
Croydon CR2 221 A3
Isleworth TW7 130 D3
Leytonstone E10 54 A3
Upper Tooting SW17 158 D3
Nottingham St W1 238 A4
Nottingham Terr NW1 238 A5
NOTTING HILL 113 B6
Notting Hill & Ealing High Sch W13 87 B2
Notting Hill Gate W11 113 C5 245 A4
Notting Hill Gate Sta W11 113 C5 245 A4
Notting Hill Prep Sch 17 W11 91 A1
Nottingwood Ho W11 244 A6
Nova Bldg 1 E14 119 C2
Nova Ct E 3 E14 120 A5
Nova Ct W 2 E14 120 A5
Nova Mews SM4 201 A2
Novar Cl BR6 211 D2
Nova Rd CR0 205 A2
Novar Rd SE9 167 A3
Novello St SW6 135 C4 265 A2
Nowell Rd SW13 134 A6
Nower Ct HA5 41 B5
NOWER HILL 41 B6
Nower Hill HA5 41 B5
Nower Hill High Sch HA5 41 C5
Noyna Rd SW17 158 D1
Nubia Way SE6 164 C1
Nucleus NW10 89 A4
Nuding Cl SE13 141 C2
Nuffield Ct TW5 129 B5
Nuffield Lo 14 W9 91 C2
Nugent Ct
Streatham SW16 181 C6
3 Upper Holloway N19 50 A1
Nugent Rd
Finsbury Pk N19 50 A1
South Norwood SE25 205 D6
Nugents Ct HA5 23 A2
Nugent's Pk HA5 23 B2
Nugent Terr NW8 92 A5 229 B3
Numa Ct TW8 131 D5
Nun Ct EC2 242 C2
Nuneaton Rd RM9 81 A1
Nuneham SW16 181 D6
NUNHEAD 140 C1
Nunhead Cres SE15 140 B2
Nunhead Gn SE15 140 B2
Nunhead Gr SE15 140 C2
Nunhead La SE15 140 B2
Nunhead Sta SE15 140 C3
Nunnington Cl SE9 166 A1
Nunn's Rd EN2 5 A3
Nupton Dr EN5 12 C5
Nurse Cl HA8 27 A2
Nursery Ave
Bexleyheath DA7 147 B2
Croydon CR0 222 D6
Finchley N3 30 A1
Nursery Cl
Broom Hill BR6 211 D2
Croydon CR0 222 D6
Dagenham RM6 58 D3
Enfield EN3 6 D4
Feltham TW14 150 B4
New Cross SE4 141 B3
Putney SW15 134 D1
Woodford IG8 37 B5
Nursery Ct Ealing W13 87 A2
8 Tottenham N17 33 D3
Nursery Gdns
Chislehurst BR7 188 D4
Enfield EN3 6 D4
Hampton TW13 173 B6
Hounslow TW4 151 B6
Sunbury TW16 171 D1
Nursery La
Forest Gate E7 77 A2
North Kensington W10 90 C2
Shoreditch E2 95 D6
Nurserymans Rd N11 15 A2
Nursery Rd
Finchley N2 30 B2
Hackney E9 74 C2
Loughton IG10 21 C6
Merton SW19 179 D1
Mitcham CR4 202 C6
Osidge N14 15 C4
Pinner HA5 40 C6
South Norwood CR7 205 B5
Stockwell SW9 138 B1
Sunbury TW16 171 D1
Sutton SM1 218 A4
Wimbledon SW19 179 A3
Nursery Row SE17 262 C3
Nursery St N17 33 D3
Nursery Walk Ct NW4 46 B6
Nursery Wlk NW4 46 C6
Nurstead Rd DA8 147 C5
Nutborn Ho SW19 178 D4
Nutbourne St W10 91 A4
Nutbrook St SE15 140 A2
Nutbrowne Rd RM9 103 B6
Nutchford EN1 17 C5
Nutcroft Rd SE15 140 B5
Nutfield Cl
Carshalton SM5 218 C5
Edmonton N18 34 A4
Nutfield Gdns
Ilford IG3 80 A6
Northolt UB5 84 C5
Nutfield Pl 1 CR7 204 D5
Nutfield Rd
Dollis Hill NW2 68 A5
East Dulwich SE22 139 D1
Leyton E15 76 A4
Thornton Heath CR7 204 D5
Nutfield Way BR6 226 D6
Nutford Pl W1 92 D1 237 C2
Nuthatch Cl TW19 148 B3
Nuthatch Gdns SE28 123 B4
Nuthurst Ave SW2 160 B2
Nutkin Wlk UB8 60 A1
Nutley Terr NW3 70 B2
Nutmeg Cl E16 98 C3
Nutmeg La E14 98 B1
Nuttall St N1 95 C5
Nutter La E11 55 C4
Nutt Gr HA8 9 D2
Nutt St SE15 139 D5
Nutty La TW17 193 A6
Nutwell St SW17 180 C5
Nuxley Rd DA17 125 C1
Nyanza St SE18 145 B6
Nye Bevan Est E5 74 D5
Nye Bevan Ho SW6 264 C4
Nye's Wharf SE1, SE15 140 A6
Nylands Ave TW9 132 C3
Nymans Gdns SW20 200 B6
Nynehead St SE14 141 A5
Nyon Gr SE6 163 B2
Nyton Cl N19 50 A1

O

O2 Ctr NW6 70 A2
O2 Millennium Dome The★ SE10 120 C5
Oak Apple Ct SE12 165 A3
Oak Ave Croydon CR0 223 D6
Enfield EN2 4 B5
Hampton TW12, TW13 173 A4
Heston TW5 129 A5
Hornsey N8 50 A5
Muswell Hill N10 31 B3
Tottenham N17 33 C3
Uxbridge UB10 60 D6
West Drayton UB7 104 C3
Oak Bank CR0 224 A2
Oakbank Ave KT12 195 B2
Oakbank Gr SE24 139 A1
Oakbark Ho 10 TW8 131 C5
Oakbrook 3 BR3 185 D1
Oakbrook Cl BR1 187 B6
Oakbury Rd SW6 135 D3
Oak Cl East Barnet N14 15 B4
Sutton SM1 218 A6
Oakcombe Cl KT3 177 C2
Oak Cottage Cl 11 SE6 164 D3
Oak Cotts W7 108 C4
Oakcourt 17 SE15 139 D5
Oak Cres E16 98 C2
Oakcroft SE12 165 B1
Oakcroft Bsns Ctr KT9 214 B4
Oakcroft Cl HA5 22 B1
Oakcroft Ct SE3 143 A4
Oakcroft Ho 3 KT3 199 C2
Oakcroft Rd
Chessington KT9 214 B4
Lewisham SE13 142 B3
Oakcroft Villas KT9 214 B4
Oak Ct Bickley BR1 188 B1
Chingford E4 35 D4
Oakdale
Beckenham BR3 186 A1
East Barnet N14 15 B3
Oakdale Ave
Harrow HA3 44 A4
Pinner HA6 22 A1
Oakdale Cl WD19 22 C6
Oakdale Ct
Chingford E4 36 A5
Upper Holloway N19 72 A6
Oakdale Gdns E4 36 A5
Oakdale Inf Sch E18 37 B1
Oakdale Jun Sch E18 37 B1
Oakdale Lo NW4 29 A2
Oakdale Rd
Leyton E11 76 B6
Nunhead SE15 140 C2
South Oxhey WD19 22 C6
Streatham SW16 182 A5
Tottenham N4 51 B3
Upton E7 77 B1
Woodford E18 37 B1
Oakdale Way CR4 203 A2
Oakdene Ealing W13 87 B2
3 Peckham SE15 140 B4
1 West Norwood SE19 183 C5
Oakdene Ave
Chislehurst West BR7 188 C5
Thames Ditton KT7 197 A1
Oakdene Cl HA5 23 B3
Oakdene Ct
Feltham TW12 173 B6
1 Streatham SW16 182 A5
Oakdene Dr KT5 199 A1
Oakdene Ho
Enfield EN2 4 D2
11 Stamford Hill N16 51 C1
Oakdene Lo 3 SE20 184 B3
Oakdene Mews SM3 201 B1
Oakdene Pk N3 29 B3
Oakdene Rd
Hillingdon UB10 82 D5
Orpington BR5 211 D4
Oakden St SE11 116 C2 261 B4
Oakeford Ho W14 254 B5
Oakend Ho 10 N4 51 B2
Oaken Dr KT10 212 D2
Oakenholt Ho 1 SE2 124 D4
Oaken La KT10 212 C3
Oakenshaw Cl KT6 198 A2
Oakes Cl E6 100 B1
Oakeshott Ave N6 71 A6
Oakey La SE1 261 A6
Oak Farm WD6 11 A6
Oak Farm Jun & Inf Schs UB10 82 D6
Oakfield E4 35 D5
Oakfield Ave HA3 43 B6
Oakfield Cl
New Malden KT3 199 D4
Ruislip HA4 39 D3
Oakfield Ct
Clapham Pk SW4 160 A5
2 Ealing W5 110 C5
Finchley N3 29 D2
Finsbury Pk N8 50 A2
Hendon NW2 46 D2
South Croydon CR2 221 A2
Oakfield Gdns
Beckenham BR3 207 C4
Carshalton SM5 202 D1
Edmonton N18 33 C6
Greenford UB6 86 B4
3 West Norwood SE19 183 C5
Oakfield Ho 2 IG1 78 D5
Oakfield La BR2 225 C4
Oakfield Lo 8 IG1 78 D5
Oakfield Prep Sch SE21 161 B3
Oakfield Rd
Ashford TW15 170 D5
Croydon CR0 205 A1
Finchley N3 29 D2
Finsbury Pk N4 50 C2
Higham Hill E17 35 A1
Ilford IG1 78 D5
Newham E6 100 A6
Palmers Green N14 16 A2
Penge SE20 184 B3
Wimbledon SW19 156 D1
Oakfield Road Ind Est 11 SE20 184 B3
Oakfields KT12 194 A1
Oakfields Rd NW11 47 A3
Oakfield St SW10 136 A6 266 A6
Oakford Rd NW5 71 C4
Oak Gdns
Croydon CR0 223 C6
Hendon HA8 27 A1
Oak Gr Ruislip HA4 40 B1
Sunbury TW16 172 B3
West Hampstead NW2 69 A4
West Wickham BR4 208 A1
Oak Grove Rd SE20 184 C1
Oakhall Ct
Ashford TW16 171 D5
Wanstead E11 55 B3
Oakhall Dr TW16 171 D5
Oak Hall Rd E11 55 B3
Oakham Cl
Cockfosters EN4 2 D2
Forest Hill SE6 163 B2
Oakham Dr BR2 208 D5
Oakham Ho 5 W10 90 C3
Oakhampton Rd NW7 28 D3
Oakhill KT10 213 A2
Oak Hill Chingford IG8 36 C3
Surbiton KT6 198 A2
Oakhill Ave
Pinner HA5 23 A1
West Hampstead NW3 69 D4
Oak Hill Cl IG8 36 B3
Oak Hill Cres
Chingford IG8 36 C3
Surbiton KT6 198 A2
Oakhill Ct
Honor Oak SE23 162 C5
Putney SW15 157 B6
8 Surbiton KT6 198 A3
Wimbledon SW19 178 D3
Oak Hill Ct IG8 36 C3
Oak Hill Gdns E4 36 C2
Oak Hill Gr KT6 198 A3
Oakhill Ho BR5 190 A2
Oak Hill Lo NW3 69 D4
Oakhill Mans EN4 14 C5
Oak Hill Park Mews NW3 70 A4
Oak Hill Pk NW3 69 D4
Oakhill Pl SW15 157 C6
Oakhill Prim Sch IG8 36 C4
Oakhill Rd
Beckenham BR3 186 A1
Orpington BR6 227 D6
Putney SW15 157 B6
Sutton SM1 218 A5
Thornton Heath SW16 182 B2
Oak Hill Rd KT6 198 A3
Oak Hill Theological Coll N14 15 A5
Oak Hill Way NW3 70 A4
Oak Ho
13 Cubitt Town E14 120 A4
11 Finchley N2 30 B1
8 Maitland Pk NW3 70 D2
Penge SE20 184 B1
2 Richmond TW9 132 D4
13 Sidcup DA15 168 A1
9 Stoke Newington N16 73 B6
Teddington TW11 175 C4
Wood Green N22 32 A3
Oakhouse Rd DA6 169 C6
Oak Hts Ind Sch 1 TW3 129 D2
Oakhurst Ave
East Barnet EN4 14 C4
Erith DA7 147 A5
Oakhurst Cl
Chislehurst BR7 188 B2
Snaresbrook E17 54 C5
4 Teddington TW11 174 C5
Oakhurst Ct E17 54 C5
Oakhurst Gdns
Chingford E4 20 D3
Erith DA7 147 A5
Snaresbrook E11, E17 54 C5
Oakhurst Gr SE22 140 A1
Oakhurst Rd KT19 215 B2
Oakington 14 KT1 176 C1
Oakington Ave
Harrow HA2 41 C2
Hayes UB3 105 B2
Wembley HA9 66 B5
Oakington Cl TW16 172 C1
Oakington Ct 1 EN2 4 D3
Oakington Dr TW16 172 C1
Oakington Manor Dr HA9 66 C3
Oakington Manor Sch HA9 66 D3
Oakington Rd W9 91 C3
Oakington Way N8 50 A2
Oak La Finchley N2 30 B1
Friern Barnet N11 31 D4
Isleworth TW7 130 C1
Limehouse E14 119 B6
Twickenham TW1 153 A4
Woodford IG8 36 D6
Oakland Pl IG9 21 A2
Oakland Rd E15 76 C4
Oaklands
Chislehurst BR7 189 B4
Croydon CR0 220 D3
Ealing W13 87 A2
Southgate N21 16 B2
Twickenham TW2 152 A4
Oaklands Ave
Enfield N9 18 B5
Hounslow TW7 130 D6
Sidcup DA15 167 D4
Thames Ditton KT10 196 B1
Thornton Heath CR7 204 C5
West Wickham BR4 223 D5
Oaklands Cl
Bexley DA6 169 B6
Chessington KT9 213 C4
Orpington BR5 211 C3
Oaklands Ct
Beckenham BR3 186 A1
Dagenham NW10 89 C6
Orpington BR6 227 A6
5 Shepherd's Bush W12 112 B5
Wembley HA0 65 D3
Oaklands Dr TW2 152 A4
Oaklands Gr W12 112 A5
Oaklands Ho SE4 141 B2
Oaklands Mews 1 NW2 68 D4
Oaklands Park Ave IG1 79 A6
Oaklands Pas NW2 68 D4

Oaklands Pl 8 SW4. 137 D1
Oaklands Prim Sch
W7 108 D4
Oaklands Rd
Barnet N20 13 B4
Bexley DA6 169 B6
Bromley BR1 186 C3
Cricklewood NW2 68 D4
Ealing W7 108 D4
Mortlake SW14 133 B2
West Ealing W7, W13. 109 A4
Oaklands Sch
Hounslow TW3 130 B2
Loughton IG10 21 D6
Oaklands Sec Sch 31
E2 96 B4
Oaklands Way SM6 219 D1
Oakland Way KT19 215 C2
Oaklawn Ct HA7 25 B4
Oakleafe Gdns IG6 56 D6
Oaklea Pas KT1 197 D6
Oakleigh Ave
East Barnet N20 14 C3
Edgware HA8 26 D2
Tolworth KT6 214 D6
Oakleigh Cl N20 14 D1
Oakleigh Cres N20 14 C1
Oakleigh Ct
East Barnet EN4 14 C5
Hendon HA8 27 A1
7 Penge SE20 184 B3
Southall UB1 107 B5
Surbiton KT6 214 B6
Oakleigh Gdns
Edgware HA8 26 B5
Oakleigh Pk N20 14 B3
Orpington BR6 227 C4
Oakleigh Lodge IG3 80 A5
Oakleigh Mews 2
N20 14 A2
OAKLEIGH PARK 14 B3
Oakleigh Park Ave
BR7 188 C2
Oakleigh Park Sta
EN4 14 C4
Oakleigh Pk N N20 14 B3
Oakleigh Pk S N20 14 C3
Oakleigh Rd
Hillingdon UB10 61 A1
Pinner HA5 23 B4
Oakleigh Rd N N20 14 C2
Oakleigh Rd S N11 31 A6
Oakleigh Sch N20 14 D1
Oakleigh Way
Mitcham CR4 181 B2
1 Tolworth KT6 198 D1
Oakley Ave
Barking IG11 79 D1
Ealing W5 110 C6
Wallington CR0 220 A4
Oakley Cl Chingford E4 20 A1
Ealing W7 108 C6
Hounslow TW7 130 B4
7 Newham E6 100 A1
Oakley Cres EC1 234 D3
Oakley Ct
Carshalton CR4 203 A2
Harlington UB7 127 A5
Wembley HA0 65 A4
Oakley Dr
Keston Mark BR2 226 A5
Lewisham SE13 164 B5
New Eltham SE9 167 B3
Oakley Gdns
Chelsea
SW3 136 C6 267 B6
Hornsey Vale N8 50 B4
Oakley Ho
Chelsea SW1 257 D4
Ealing W5 110 C6
Oakley Pk DA5 168 C4
Oakley Pl
SE1 117 D1 263 C1
Oakley Rd
Croydon SE25 206 B4
De Beauvoir Town N1 73 B1
Harrow HA1 42 C3
Keston Mark BR2 226 A6
Oakley Sq
NW1 93 C5 232 B4
Oakley St
SW3 136 C6 267 A6
Oakley Wlk W6 134 D6
Oak Lo
4 Ashford TW16 171 D3
Southgate N21 16 B5
10 Sutton SM1 218 A4
Wanstead E11 55 A2
6 Wembley HA0 65 D3
Oak Lodge 14 SE21 161 B2
Oak Lodge Cl HA7 25 C5
Oak Lodge Dr BR4 207 D2
Oak Lodge Prim Sch
BR4 207 D2
Oak Lodge Sch
Balham SW12 159 A4
East Finchley N2 48 A5
Oaklodge Way NW7 27 D4
Oakman Ho 29
SW19 156 D3
Oakmead HA1 64 B5
Oakmead Ave BR2 209 A3
Oakmead Ct HA7 25 C6
Oakmeade HA5 23 C4
Oakmead Gdns HA8 27 B6
Oakmead Pl CR4 180 C2
Oakmead Rd
Balham SW12 159 B3
Wallington CR0 203 D3
Oakmere Rd SE2 146 A6
Oakmont Pl 6 BR6 211 B1
Oak Park Gdns
SW19 156 D3
Oak Park Mews N16 73 D5
Oak Rd Ealing W5 109 D6
Kingston u T KT3 177 B1
Oakridge Dr N2 48 B6
Oakridge La BR1 186 B5
Oakridge Rd BR1 186 C6
Oak Rise IG9 21 D1
Oak Row CR4 181 C1
Oaks Ave
Feltham TW13 151 A2
North Cheam KT4 216 B4
West Norwood SE19 183 C5
Oaksford Ave SE26 162 B1
Oaks Gr E4 20 C2
Oakshade Rd BR1 186 B6
Oakshaw Rd SW18 157 D4
Oakshott Ct NW1 232 C3
Oaks La Ilford IG2 57 C5
South Croydon CR0 222 C5
Oaks Park High Sch
IG2 57 C4
Oaks Rd CR0 222 C4
Oaks Sh Ctr The W3 111 A5
Oaks The
Brondesbury Pk NW6 68 D1
Chingford IG8 36 C3
Enfield EN2 4 D2
Finchley N12 29 D6
Hayes UB4 83 A5
Long Ditton KT6 213 C5
Ruislip HA4 39 C2
Southborough BR2 210 C3
Wallington SM6 219 C4
Willesden NW10 68 B1
Wimbledon SW19 179 A4
Woolwich SE18 123 A1
Oaks Way
Surbiton KT6 197 D1
Wallington SM5 218 D1
Oakthorpe Ct N13 33 A5
Oakthorpe Prim Sch
N13 33 A5
Oakthorpe Rd N13 32 C5
Oaktree Ave N13 16 D1
Oak Tree Ave N2 47 D6
Oak Tree Cl Ealing W5 87 C1
Stanmore HA7 25 C3
Oak Tree Ct
Acton W3 110 D6
8 Clapham Pk SW4 160 A6
Elstree WD6 9 D5
Oak Tree Dell NW9 45 B4
Oak Tree Dr N20 13 D3
Oak Tree Gdns BR1 187 B5
Oaktree Gr IG1 79 B3
Oak Tree Ho W9 91 D3
Oak Tree Rd
NW8 92 C4 230 A1
Oaktree Sch EN4 15 A5
Oaktrees Hostel HA8 11 A2
Oakview Gdns N2 48 B5
Oakview Gr CR0 207 A1
Oakview Lo NW11 47 B2
Oakview Rd SE6 185 D5
Oak Village NW5 71 A4
Oakway
Beckenham BR2 186 B1
West Barnes SW20 200 C5
Oak Way
Croydon CR0 206 D3
East Acton W3 111 C5
East Barnet N14 15 B4
East Bedfont TW14 149 C3
Oakway Cl DA5 169 A5
Oakways SE9 166 D5
Oakwell Ho 24 SW8 137 D3
Oak Wlk CR4 203 A1
OAKWOOD 15 D6
Oakwood Ave
Beckenham BR2,
BR3 186 A1
Bromley BR2 209 B6
Chessington KT9 214 B1
Mitcham CR4 180 B1
Osidge N14 15 D4
Southall UB1 107 C6
Oakwood Cl
Chislehurst West
BR7 188 C4
Lewisham SE13 164 B5
Southgate N14 15 C5
Oakwood Cres
Southgate N21 16 B5
Wembley UB6 65 B2
Oakwood Ct
Beckenham BR3 186 A1
6 Chingford E4 20 C4
Kensington
W14 113 B3 254 C6
1 Newham E6 100 A6
17 Sutton SM1 218 A4
Oakwood Dr
Burnt Oak HA8 27 A4
West Norwood SE19 183 C4
Oakwood Gdns
Ilford IG3 79 D6
Orpington BR6 227 A6
Sutton SM1 217 C6
Oakwood La
W14 113 B3 254 C6
Oakwood Park Rd
N14 16 A5
Oakwood Pl CR0 204 C3
Oakwood Rd
Hampstead Garden Suburb
NW11 47 D4
Orpington BR6 227 A6
Pinner HA5 22 B1
Thornton Heath CR0 204 C3
Wimbledon SW20 178 A2
Oakwood Sta N14 15 C6
Oakwood View N14 15 D4
Oakworth Rd W10 90 D2
Oarsman Pl KT8 196 C5
Oasis The 6 BR1 187 C1
Oast Ct 8 E14 119 B6
Oast Lo W4 133 C5
Oates Cl BR2 208 B6
Oatfield Ho 1 N15 51 C3
Oatfield Rd BR6 211 D1
Oat La EC2 95 A1 242 B2
Oatland Rise E17 35 A1
Oatlands Ct 3
SW19 156 D3
Oatlands Dr KT13 193 C1
Oatlands Rd EN3 6 C4
Oatwell Ho SW3 257 B3
Oban Cl E13 99 C3
Oban Ct HA8 10 D2
Oban Ho
5 Barking IG11 101 B5
South Bromley E14 98 B1
Oban Rd Newham E13 99 C4
South Norwood SE25 205 B5
Oban St E14 98 B1
Oberon Ho 5 N1 95 C5
Oberon Way TW17 192 A6
Oberstein Rd 15
SW11 136 B1
Oborne Cl SE24 160 D6
O'Brian Ho 10 E1 96 D4
Observatory Gdns
W8 245 B2
Observatory Mews
E14 120 B2
Observatory Rd
Kensington SW7 256 C5
Mortlake SW14 133 A1
Occupation La
Brentford W5 109 D2
Shooters Hill SE18 144 D4
Occupation Rd
Newington
SE17 117 A1 262 A2
West Ealing W13 109 B4
Ocean St E1 96 D2
Ocean Wharf E14 119 C4
Ochre Ct TW13 149 D1
Ockbrook 3 E1 96 C2
Ockendon Rd N1 73 B2
Ockham Dr BR5 190 A3
Greenford UB6 64 B1
Ockley Ct
Sidcup DA14 167 C1
Sutton SM1 218 A4
Ockley Ho 8 KT2 176 D4
Ockley Rd
Streatham SW16 160 A1
Thornton Heath CR0 204 B2
Octagon Arc EC2 243 A3
Octagon The NW3 69 C4
Octavia Cl CR4 202 C4
Octavia Ho
Catford SE6 163 D4
Kensal Town W10 91 A3
Octavia Mews 1 W9 91 B3
Octavia Rd TW7 130 D2
Octavia St
SW11 136 C4 267 B1
Octavia Way 12
SE28 124 B6
Octavius St SE8 141 C5
October Ct BR2 208 D6
October Pl NW4 46 D6
Odard Rd KT8 195 C5
Odell Cl IG11 79 D1
Odell Wlk SE13 142 A2
Odeon Ct
Dagenham NW10 89 C6
1 Newham E16 99 A2
Odeon Par
Eltham SE9 144 A1
Wembley UB6 65 B2
Odeon The IG11 79 B1
Odessa Inf Sch E7 77 A3
Odessa Rd Leyton E7 76 D4
Willesden Green NW10 90 A5
Odessa St SE16 119 B3
Odette Ct N20 14 A1
Odette Duval Ho 29
E1 96 C2
Odette Ho 6 SE27 183 B6
Odger St SW11 136 D3
Odhams Wlk WC2 240 B1
Odin Ho 6 SE5 139 A3
O'Donnell Ct WC1 240 B6
O'Driscoll Ho 4 W12 90 B1
Odyssey Bsns Pk HA4 62 B3
Offa's Mead E9 75 A4
Offenbach Ho 12 E2 96 D5
Offenham Rd BR7,
SE9 188 B6
Offers Ct KT1 198 B6
Offerton Rd SW4 137 C2
Offham Ho SE17 263 A3
Offham Slope N12 29 B5
Offley Ho 10 E9 74 D2
Offley Pl TW7 130 B3
Offley Rd SW9 138 C5
Offord Cl N17 34 A4
Offord Rd N1 72 B1
Offord St N1 72 B1
Ogden Ho TW13 173 A6
Ogilby St SE18 122 B2
Ogilvie Ho 12 E1 96 D1
Oglander Rd SE15 139 D2
Ogle St W1 93 C2 239 A4
Oglethorpe Rd RM10 81 C5
O'Gorman Ho SW10 266 B4
O'Grady Ct 17 W13 109 A5
O'Grady Ho 17 E17 53 D6
Ohio Bldg 13 SE13 141 D4
Ohio Rd E13 98 D3
Oil Mill La W6 112 A1
Okeburn Rd SW17 181 A5
Okehampton Cl N12 30 B5
Okehampton Cres
DA16 146 C4
Okehampton Rd
NW10 90 D6
Okeover Manor
SW4 137 B1
Olaf Palme Ho
TW13 150 B1
Olaf St W11 112 D6
Old Bailey
EC4 94 D1 241 D1
Old Bailey (Central Criminal Court)★
EC4 94 D1 241 D2
Old Barn Cl SM2 217 A1
Old Barrack Yd SW1 248 A1
Old Barrowfield 7
E15 98 C6
Old Bellgate Wharf
E14 119 C3
Oldberry Rd HA8 27 B4
Old Bethnal Green Rd
E2 96 B4
OLD BEXLEY 169 D4
Old Bexley Bsns Pk
DA5 169 D4
Old Bexley CE Prim Sch
DA5 169 B3
Old Billingsgate Wlk
EC3 253 A5
Old Bldgs WC2 241 A2
Old Bond St
W1 115 C6 249 A5
Oldborough Rd HA0 65 C5
Old Brewery Mews
NW3 70 B4
Old Bridge Cl UB5 85 C5
Old Bridge St KT1 175 D1
Old Broad St
EC2 95 B1 242 D2
Old Bromley Rd BR1 186 B5
Old Brompton Rd SW5,
SW7 114 A2 256 B3
Old Burlington St
W1 115 C6 249 A5
Oldbury Ct E9 75 A3
Oldbury Pl W1 93 A2 238 B4
Oldbury Rd EN1 6 A3
Old Castle St
E1 95 D1 243 D2
Old Cavendish St
W1 238 C1
Old Change Ct EC4 242 A1
Old Chapel Pl 2 N10 49 B6
Old Charlton Rd
TW17 193 A4
Old Chiswick Yd W4 133 C6
Old Church Ct N11 31 B5
Old Church La
Ealing UB6 87 A4
Stanmore HA7 25 C4
Welsh Harp NW9 67 B6
Old Church Path
KT10 212 A4
Old Church Rd
Chingford E4 19 C1
Stepney E1 96 D1
Old Church St SW3 256 D1
Old Claygate La
KT10 213 A3
Old Clem Sq 12
SE18 144 C6
Old College Ct DA17 125 D1
Old Compton St
W1 93 D1 239 C1
Old Cople La SE26 184 A5
Old Cote Dr TW5 129 C6
Old Court Ho W8 245 C1
Old Court (Mus & Liby)★
HA0 65 C3
Old Court Pl
W8 113 D4 245 C1
Old Covent Gdn★
WC2 116 A6 250 B6
Old Ctyd The BR1 187 B2
Old Cty H★ SE1 250 C2
Old Dairy Mews
5 Balham SW12 159 A3
4 Camden Town NW5 71 B2
Old Dairy Sq The N21 16 C4
Old Deer Park Gdns
TW9 132 A2
Old Devonshire Rd
SW12 159 B4
Old Dock Cl TW9 132 C6
Old Dover Rd SE3 143 B5
Oldegate Ho 1 E6 99 D6
Old Farm Ave
Osidge N14 15 C4
Sidcup DA15 167 C2
Old Farm Cl TW4 129 B1
Old Farm Ct UB2 107 D2
Old Farm Rd
Hampton TW12 173 C4
London N2 30 B2
Old Farm Rd E DA15 168 A2

Old Farm Rd W DA15 167 D2
Oldfield Cl
Bromley BR1 210 B5
Greenford UB6 64 C2
Stanmore HA7 25 A5
Oldfield Farm Gdns UB6 86 B6
Oldfield Gr SE16 118 D2
Oldfield Ho
14 Chiswick W4 111 C1
Streatham SW16 181 B6
Oldfield House Specl Sch TW12 173 B2
Oldfield La N UB6 64 B1
Oldfield La S UB6 86 A4
Oldfield Mews N6 49 C2
Oldfield Prim Sch UB6 86 B5
Oldfield Rd
Bedford Pk W3, W12 111 D4
Bexleyheath DA7 147 A3
Bromley BR1 210 B5
Hampton TW12 173 B2
Stoke Newington N16 73 C5
Willesden NW10 67 D1
Wimbledon SW19 179 A4
Oldfields Cir UB5 64 A2
Oldfields Rd SM1, SM3 217 C6
Oldfields Trad Est SM1 217 C5
Old Fire Station The SE18 144 D5
Old Fish St Hill EC4 252 A6
Old Fleet La EC4 241 C2
Old Fold Cl EN5 1 B4
Old Fold La EN5 1 B4
OLD FORD 97 B6
Old Ford Ho CR0 220 A5
Old Ford Prim Sch 38 E3 97 B5
Old Ford Rd E2, E3 96 D5
Old Ford Trad Est E3 97 C6
Old Forge Cl HA7 25 A6
Old Forge Cres TW17 192 D3
Old Forge Mews W12 112 B4
Old Forge Rd
Enfield EN1 5 D5
Upper Holloway N19 71 D6
Old Forge Way DA14 190 B6
Old Gloucester St WC1 94 A2 240 B4
Old Hall Cl HA5 23 A2
Old Hall Dr HA5 23 A2
Oldham Ho 10 SE21 183 C6
Oldham Terr W3 111 A5
Old Hatch Manor HA4 40 A2
Old Hill
Chislehurst BR7 188 C2
Orpington BR6 227 C2
Oldhill St N16 52 A1
Old Homesdale Rd BR2 209 C5
Old Hospital Cl SW12, SW17 158 D3
Old Ho The BR7 189 B2
Old House Cl SW19 179 A5
Old House Gdns 9 TW1 153 C5
Old Howlett's La HA4 39 B3
Olding Ho 6 SW12 159 C4
Old Jamaica Bsns Est 23 SE16 118 A3
Old Jamaica Rd SE16 118 A3
Old James St SE15 140 B2
Old Jewry EC2 95 B1 242 C1
Old Kenton La NW9 44 D4
Old Kent Rd
Deptford SE1, SE15 140 B6
Walworth SE1 117 C1 263 B2
Old Kingston Rd KT4 215 A5
Old Laundry The 14 SW18 136 B1
Old Lodge Pl 7 TW1 153 B5
Old Lodge Way HA7 25 A5
Old London Rd KT2 176 A1
Old Maidstone Rd BR8, DA14 191 B3
OLD MALDEN 199 C1
Old Malden La KT4 215 C6
Oldman Ct SE12 165 B2
Old Manor Ct NW8 229 B4
Old Manor Dr TW7 152 A5
Old Manor House Mews TW17 192 C6
Old Manor Rd UB2 106 D2
Old Manor Way BR7, SE9 188 B5
Old Manor Yd SW5 255 C3
Old Market Ct SM1 217 D4
Old Market Sq 11 E2 95 D4
Old Marylebone Rd NW1 92 C2 237 B3
Oldmead Ho 8 RM10 81 D2
Old Mill Ct E18 55 C6
Old Mill Rd SE18 145 B6
Old Mitre Ct EC4 241 B1
Old Montague St E1 96 A2
Old Nichol St E2 95 D3 243 C6
Old North St WC1 240 C4
Old Nursery Pl TW15 170 D5
OLD OAK COMMON 89 D3
Old Oak Common La NW10 89 C3
Old Oak La NW10 89 D4
Old Oak Prim Sch W12 89 D1
Old Oak Rd W3 111 D6
Old Orch TW16 172 C1
Old Orchard Cl
Hadley Wood EN4 2 B5
Hillingdon UB8 82 C1
Old Orch The NW3 70 D4
Old Palace La TW9 153 C6
Old Palace of John Whitgift Sch (Juniors) CR2 221 D3
Old Palace of John Whitgift Sch (Seniors) 11 CR9 220 D5
Old Palace Prim Sch 51 E3 97 D4
Old Palace Rd CR0 221 A5
Old Palace Terr 8 TW9 153 D6
Old Palace Yd 2 TW9 153 D6
Old Paradise St SE11 116 B2 260 C4
Old Park Ave
Balham SW12 159 A5
Enfield EN2 5 A1
Old Park Gr EN2 5 A1
Old Park Ho N13 32 B6
Old Park La W1 115 B5 248 C3
Old Park Mews TW5 129 B5
Old Park Rd
Enfield EN2 4 D2
Palmers Green N13 32 B6
Plumstead Comm SE2 124 A1
Old Park Rd S EN2 4 D1
Old Park Ridings N21 17 A6
Old Park View EN2 4 D2
Old Pearson St SE10 141 D5
Old Perry St BR7 189 C3
Old Post Office La SE3 143 B2
Old Pound Cl TW7 131 A4
Old Priory UB9 38 D2
Old Pye St SW1 259 C6
Old Pye Street Est SW1 259 C5
Old Quebec St W1 237 D1
Old Queen St SW1 115 D4 249 D1
Old Rd Enfield EN3 6 C4
Lewisham SE13 142 C1
Old Rectory Gdns HA8 26 C4
Old Redding HA3 24 A6
Oldridge Rd SW12 159 B4
Old Royal Free Pl N1 234 B5
Old Royal Free Sq N1 94 C6 234 B5
Old Ruislip Rd UB5 84 C5
Old St Andrews Mans NW9 67 B6
Old School Cl
3 Beckenham BR3 185 A1
Merton SW19 179 C1
Old School Cres E7 77 A2
Old School Ct 8 N17 51 D6
Old School Ho CR4 202 C6
Old School Ho The EN2 4 D2
Old School Pl CR0 220 C4
Old School Rd UB8 82 B3
Old School Sq
12 Poplar E14 97 C1
Thames Ditton KT7 196 D3
Old School The
Bloomsbury WC1 240 D4
Merton SW19 179 C1
Old Seacoal La EC4 241 C1
Old South Cl HA5 22 D2
Old South Lambeth Rd SW8 138 A5 270 B4
Old Spitalfields Mkt* E1 95 D2 243 D4
Old Sq WC2 241 A2
Old St
Broadgate EC1 95 B3 242 D6
Newham E13 99 B5
Old Stable Mews N5 73 A5
Old Station Rd UB3 105 D3
Old Station Yard The 11 E17 54 A5
Oldstead Rd BR1 186 B6
Old Street Sta EC1 95 B3 242 D6
Old Studio Cl CR0 205 B2
Old Sun Wharf E14 119 A6
Old Swan Wharf SW11 266 D2
Old Swan Yd SM5 218 D4
Old Theatre Ct SE1 252 B4
Old Town
Clapham SW4 137 C2
Croydon CR0 220 D5
Old Tramyard SE18 123 C2
Old Twelve Cl W7 86 C3
Old Vicarage Sch 13 TW10 154 A5
Old Vicarage The CR4 202 C6
Old Woolwich Rd SE10 120 B1
Old York Rd SW18 157 D6
Oleander Cl BR6 227 B3
O'Leary Sq E1 96 C2
Oleastor Ct IG5 56 A6
Olga Prim Sch 37 E3 97 A5
Olga St 20 E3 97 A5
Olinda Rd N16 51 D3
Oliphant St W10 91 A4
Olive Blythe Ho 14 W10 91 A3
Oliver Ave SE25 205 D6
Oliver Bsns Pk NW10 89 A5
Oliver Cl W4 132 D6
Oliver Ct
Isleworth TW7 130 D2
2 Penge SE26 184 C4
Plumstead SE18 123 A2
Olive Rd
Cricklewood NW2 68 C4
Ealing W5 109 D3
3 Merton SW19 180 A3
Newham E13 99 C4
Oliver Gdns E6 100 A2
Oliver Goldsmith Prim Sch
18 Camberwell SE5 139 D4
Kingsbury NW9 45 B4
Oliver Gr SE25 205 D5
Oliver Ho
22 Bermondsey SE16 118 A4
Notting Hill W11 244 A5
South Lambeth SW8 270 A4
Oliver House Prep Sch 1 SW4 159 B5
Oliver Mews SE15 140 A3
Oliver Rd
Kingston u T KT3 177 A1
Leyton E10 75 D5
Sutton SM1 218 B4
Walthamstow E17 54 A4
Oliver's Yd EC1 242 D6
Olive Tree Ho
7 Deptford SE15 140 C6
Olive Tree Ho *continued*
Stroud Green N4 50 C3
Olive Tree Sch The SE13 163 D5
Olivette St 1 SW15 134 D1
Olive Waite Ho NW6 69 D1
Olivia Ct 1 EN5 1 B1
Ollard's Gr IG10 21 D6
Ollerton Gn E3 97 B6
Ollerton Rd N11 31 D5
Olley Cl SM6 220 A2
Ollgar Cl W12 111 D5
Olliffe St E14 120 A3
Olmar St SE1 140 A6
Olney Ho NW8 237 B6
Olney Rd SE17 139 A6
Olron Cres DA6 169 A6
Olven Rd SE18 145 A6
Olveston Wlk SM5 202 B3
Olwen Mews HA5 22 D1
Olyffe Ave DA16 146 A3
Olyffe Dr BR3 186 A2
Olympia Ex Ctr* W14 113 A3 254 B5
Olympia Ind Est N22 50 B6
Olympian Ct 8 E14 119 C2
Olympia Way W14 113 A3 254 B5
Olympia Yd W2 245 D5
Olympic Ho 10 W10 90 C1
Olympic Ret Pk HA9 66 D4
Olympic Way
Greenford UB6 85 D6
Wembley HA9 66 C4
Olympus Gr N22 32 C2
Olympus Sq E5 74 A5
Oman Ave NW2 68 C4
Oman Ct NW4 68 B4
Ombersley Ho N4 51 A2
Omeara St SE1 252 B3
Omega Cl E14 119 D3
Omega Ho SW10 266 B4
Omega Pl N1 233 B3
Omega St SE14 141 C4
Omega Works E3 75 C1
Ommaney Rd SE14 141 A4
Omnibus Bsns Ctr N7 72 A3
Omnibus Way E17 35 C1
Ondine Rd SE15 139 D1
Onedin Point 10 E1 118 A6
Onega Gate SE16 119 A3
O'Neill Ho NW8 229 D3
O'Neill Path 11 SE18 144 C6
One Tree Cl SE23 162 C5
Ongar Cl RM6 58 C4
Ongar Ho 15 N1 73 B2
Ongar Rd SW6 135 C6 265 B6
Onra Rd E17 53 C2
Onslow Ave TW10 154 A6
Onslow Avenue Mans 10 TW10 154 A6
Onslow Cl
Chingford E4 20 B2
Notting Hill W9 91 B4
Thames Ditton KT7 196 C1
Onslow Cres BR7 188 D2
Onslow Ct SW10 256 B1
Onslow Dr DA14 168 D2
Onslow Gdns
Chelsea SW7 114 B1 256 C2
Cranley Gdns N10 49 B4
Southgate N21 16 C6
Thames Ditton KT7 196 C1
Wallington SM6 219 C1
Wanstead E18 55 C6
Onslow Ho 1 KT2 176 B2
Onslow Lo 28 SW2 160 C4
Onslow Mews E SW7 256 C3
Onslow Mews W SW7 256 C3
Onslow Par N14 15 B3
Onslow Rd
Richmond TW10 154 A5
Thornton Heath CR0 204 C1
West Barnes KT3 200 A5
Onslow Sq SW7 114 B2 256 D3
Onslow St EC1 241 B5
Onslow Way KT7 196 C1
Ontario St SE1 116 D3 261 D6
Ontario Way E14 119 C6
Onyx Ct N11 31 D3
Onyx Ho KT4 199 B1
Onyx Mews 4 E15 76 D2
Opal Cl E16 99 D1
Opal Ct N11 31 D3
Opal Ho KT4 199 B1
Opal Mews 2 IG1 78 D6
Opal St SE11 116 D1 261 C2
Open Air Theatre, Regent's Pk* NW1 231 A1
Openshaw Rd SE2 124 B2
Openview SW17, SW18 158 B2
Opera Ct 7 N19 71 D5
Operating Theatre Mus & Herb Garret The* SE1 117 B5 252 D3
Ophelia Gdns NW2 69 A5
Ophir Terr SE15 140 A4
Opie Ho NW8 230 B4
Opossum Way TW4 128 C2
Oppenheim Rd SE13 142 A3
Oppidan Apartments NW6 69 C2
Oppidans Rd NW3 70 D1
Opus Studios E13 99 A5
Orange Gr E11 76 C5
Orange Hill Rd HA8 27 A3
Orange Pl SE16 118 C3
Orangery Gallery The* W8 113 B4 244 C1
Orangery La SE9 166 B6
Orangery The TW10 153 C2
Orange St WC2 115 D6 249 D5
Orange Yd WC2 239 D1
Oransay Rd 25 N1 73 A2
Oratory La SW3 256 D2
Oratory RC Prim Sch SW3 114 C1 257 A2
Orbain Rd SW6 135 A5 264 B3
Orbel St SW11 136 C4 267 A1
Orb St SE17 117 B2 262 C3
Orchard Ave
Ashford TW15 171 A4
Carshalton CR4 203 A1
Croydon CR0 207 A1
East Finchley N3 47 C6
Erith DA17 147 B6
Hatton TW14 149 B6
Heston TW5 129 A5
Hinchley Wood KT7 213 A6
Kingston u T KT3 199 C6
Osidge N14 15 C4
Southall UB1 107 B5
Whetstone N20 14 B2
Orchard Bsns Ctr SE26 185 B5
Orchard Cl
Ashford TW15 171 A4
Bexleyheath DA7 147 A4
Bushey WD23 8 B3
Chingford E4 35 C6
Dollis Hill NW2 68 A5
Edgware HA8 26 A4
Honor Oak SE23 162 C5
21 Islington N1 73 A1
Kensal Town W10 91 A2
Northolt UB5 64 A2
Ruislip HA4 39 A2
Thames Ditton KT7 197 B2
Walton-on-T KT12 194 B2
Wanstead E11 55 B5
Wembley HA0 88 A6
West Barnes SW20 200 C5
West Ewell KT19 214 D2
Orchard Cotts
Chislehurst BR7 189 C4
Hayes UB3 105 C4
Orchard Cres
Edgware HA8 27 A5
Enfield EN1 5 D4
Orchard Ct
Barnes SW13 133 D2
Barnet EN5 1 D2
Croydon BR3 207 C1
Edgware HA8 26 B5
Hounslow TW7 130 B5
Marylebone W1 238 A2
New Malden KT4 200 A1
Penge SE26 184 D5
Southgate N14 15 C5
Wallington SM6 219 B3

Orchard Ct *continued*
Walthamstow E10 53 D1
1 Walton-on-T KT12 193 D1
Wood Green N22 32 A3
Orchard Dr
Blackheath Vale
SE3 142 C3
Edgware HA8 26 B5
Upper Halliford TW17 193 C6
Orchard Gate
Colindale NW9 45 C5
Thames Ditton KT10 196 B1
Wembley UB6 65 B2
Orchard Gdns
Chessington KT9 214 A4
Sutton SM1 217 C3
Orchard Gn
Bromley BR1 187 C2
Orpington BR6 227 C6
Orchard Gr BR6 227 D6
Croydon CR0 207 A2
Edgware HA8 26 D2
Harrow HA3 44 B4
Orpington BR6 211 D1
Penge SE20 184 A3
Orchard Hill SE13 141 D4
Orchard Hill Coll 18
SM6 219 B2
Orchard Ho
Camberwell SE5 139 A4
11 Rotherhithe SE16 118 C3
Shepherd's Bush W12 112 A5
Orchard House Sch 15
W4 111 C2
Orchard La
Thames Ditton KT8 196 B3
Wimbledon SW20 178 B2
Woodford IG8 37 C6
Orchardleigh Ave EN3 6 C3
Orchard Lo N12 14 A1
Orchard Mead Ho
NW11 69 C6
Orchardmede N21 17 B5
Orchard Mews N1 73 B1
Orchard Pl
Canning Town E14 120 C6
Tottenham N17 33 D3
Orchard Prim Sch
DA14 190 B5
41 London E9 74 C1
Orchard Prim Sch The
TW3 151 C6
Orchard Rd Barnet EN5 1 B1
Belvedere DA17 125 C2
Brentford TW8 131 C6
Bromley BR1 187 C2
Carshalton CR4 203 A1
Chessington KT9 214 A4
Dagenham RM10 103 C6
Enfield EN3 18 C6
Farnborough BR6 226 D3
Feltham TW14 150 A3
Hampton TW12 173 B3
Hayes UB3 106 A6
Highgate N6 49 B2
Hounslow TW4 151 C6
Isleworth TW1 153 B6
Kingston u T KT1 176 A1
Richmond TW9 132 C2
Sidcup DA14 189 C6
Sunbury TW16 172 B3
Sutton SM1 217 C4
Welling DA16 146 B2
Orchard Rise
Croydon CR0 207 B1
Kingston u T KT2 177 A2
Mortlake TW10 132 D1
Pinner HA5 39 D6
Orchard Rise E
DA15 167 D6
Orchard Rise W
DA15 167 C6
Orchard Sch HA3 44 B4
Orchard Sch The
KT8 196 B5
Orchardson Ho NW8 236 D5
Orchardson St
NW8 92 B3 236 D5
Orchard Sq W14 254 C1
Orchard St
Marylebone W1 238 B2
Walthamstow E17 53 A5
Orchard Terr EN1 18 A5
Orchard The
Acton Green W4 111 B2
Ealing W5 87 D2
East Barnet N14 15 B6
Edgware HA8 26 C5
Enfield N21 17 B5
Ewell KT17 215 D1
Hampstead Garden Suburb
NW11 47 C4
Hounslow TW3 130 A3
Lewisham SE3 142 B3
Totteridge N20 13 D3
Orchard Villas BR7 189 C4
Orchard Way
Ashford TW15 148 B2
Croydon BR3, CR0 207 A3
Enfield EN1 5 C2
Esher KT10 212 A2
Sutton SM1 218 B4
Orchard Way Prim Sch
CR0 207 A2
Orchestra Ct HA8 26 D3
Orchid Cl
Chessington KT9 213 C1
Lewisham SE13 164 B6
1 Newham E6 100 A2
Southall UB1 85 A1
Orchid Ct
Catford BR1 164 B1
Harrow HA3 24 C2
Wembley HA9 66 A6
Orchid Gdns TW3 129 B1
Orchid Grange N14 15 C4
Orchid Lo N14 15 C4
Orchid Rd N14 15 C4
Orchid St W12 112 A6
Orch Sch The 15
SW2 160 B3
Orde 6 NW9 27 D2
Orde Hall St
WC1 94 B2 240 C4
Orde Ho 10 N16 73 B4
Ordell Ct 36 E3 97 B5
Ordell Rd E3 97 B5
Ordnance Cl TW13 150 A2
Ordnance Cres SE10 120 C4
Ordnance Hill
NW8 92 B6 229 D5
Ordnance Mews
NW8 229 D4
Ordnance Rd
Canning Town E16 98 D2
Enfield EN3 7 B6
Shooters Hill SE18 144 C6
Oregano Cl UB7 104 B6
Oregano Dr E14 98 B1
Oregon Ave E12 78 B4
Oregon Bldg 5
SE13 141 D4
Oregon Cl KT3 199 A5
Oregon Sq BR6 211 B1
Orestes Ct 9 E18 55 A6
Orestes Mews 1
NW6 69 C3
Orford Ct
Stanmore HA7 25 C4
Wallington SM6 219 C3
West Norwood SE27 160 D2
Orford Gdns TW1 152 D2
Orford Rd
Catford SE6 163 D1
Walthamstow E17 53 D4
Wanstead E18 55 B6
Organ Crossroads
KT17 216 A1
Oriana Ct CR0 221 B1
Oriana Ho 3 E14 119 B6
Oriel Cl CR4 203 D6
Oriel Ct
6 Croydon CR0 205 B1
Hampstead NW3 70 A4
Oriel Dr SW13 134 C6
Oriel Gdns IG5 56 B6
Oriel Prim Sch
TW13 151 A1
Oriel Rd Hackney E9 75 A2
Homerton E9 74 D2
Oriel Way UB5 63 D1
Oriental Rd E16 121 D5
Orient Ind Pk E10 75 C6
Orient St
SE11 116 D2 261 C4
Orient Way
Lea Bridge E5 74 D5
Leyton E10 75 B6
Oriole Way SE28 124 B6
Orion Bsns Ctr SE14 118 D1
Orion Ct 10 HA8 26 D5
Orion Ctr The CR0 220 A6
Orion Ho 20 E1 96 B3
Orion Mews SM4 201 C5
Orion Point 5 E14 119 C2
Orion Prim Sch The
NW9 27 D2
Orion Rd N11 31 A4
Orion Way HA6 22 A6
Orissa Rd SE18 123 C1
Orkney Ho N1 233 C6
Orkney St SW11 137 A3
Orlando Rd SW4 137 C2
Orleans Cl KT10 212 B6
Orleans Ct 9 TW1 153 B4
Orleans House Gallery*
TW1 153 B3
Orleans Inf Sch TW1 153 B4
Orleans Park Sch
TW1 153 B4
Orleans Rd
South Norwood
SE19 183 B4
Twickenham TW1 153 C4
Orleston Mews N7 72 C2
Orleston Rd N7 72 C2
Orley Farm Rd HA1 64 C5
Orley Farm Sch HA1 64 B5
Orlop St SE10 120 C1
Ormanton Rd SE26 184 A6
Orme Ct W2 113 D6 245 C5
Orme Ct Mews W2 245 D5
Orme Ho 8 E8 95 D6
Orme La W2 113 D6 245 C5
Ormeley Rd SW12 159 B3
Orme Rd
Kingston u T KT1,
KT3 176 D1
Sutton SM1 217 D2
Ormerod Gdns CR4 181 A2
Ormerod Ho 3
SW9 138 A2
Ormesby Cl SE28 124 D6
Ormesby Way HA3 44 B4
Orme Sq W2 245 C5
Ormiston Gr W12 112 B5
Ormiston Rd SE10 121 A1
Ormond Ave
Hampton TW12 173 D2
23 Richmond TW10 153 D6
Ormond Cl WC1 240 B4
Ormond Cres TW12 173 D2
Ormond Dr TW12 173 D3
Ormonde Ave BR6 227 A6
Ormonde Ct
Hendon NW4 46 D6
Putney SW15 134 C1
Ormonde Gate
SW3 114 D1 257 D1
Ormonde Mans WC1 240 B4
Ormonde Pl SW1 258 B3
Ormonde Rd SW14 133 A2
Ormonde Rise IG9 21 C3
Ormonde Terr
NW8 92 D6 230 C5
Ormond Ho 7 N16 73 B6
Ormond Mans WC1 240 C5
Ormond Mews WC1 240 B5
Ormond Rd
Finsbury Pk N4, N19 50 A1
Richmond TW10 153 D6
Ormond Yd SW1 249 B4
Ormrod Ct W11 91 B1
Ormsby SM2 217 D1
Ormsby Gdns UB6 86 A5
Ormsby Lo 7 W4 111 C3
Ormsby Pl N16 73 D5
Ormsby Point 6
SE18 122 D2
Ormsby St E2 95 D5
Ormside St SE15 140 C6
Ormskirk Rd WD19 22 D5
Ornan Rd NW3 70 C3
Orpen Ho SW5 255 B3
Orpen Wlk N16 73 C5
Orpheus Ho 25 N19 49 D2
Orpheus St SE5 139 B4
ORPINGTON 227 D6
Orpington Gdns N18 17 C1
Orpington Hospl
BR6 227 D4
Orpington Mans N21 16 C3
Orpington Rd
Southgate N21 16 D3
St Paul's Cray BR7 211 C6
Orpington Sta BR6 227 C6
Orpwood Cl TW12 173 B4
Orsett Mews
W2 92 A1 236 A2
Orsett St
SE11 116 B1 260 D2
Orsett Terr
Bayswater
W2 92 A1 236 A2
Woodford IG8 37 C3
Orsman Rd N1 95 C6
Orton Gr EN1 6 A4
Orton St E1 118 A5
Orville Rd SW11 136 B3
Orwell Cl UB3 105 C6
Orwell Ct Hackney E8 96 A6
Highbury N5 73 A4
Northolt UB5 85 A6
Orwell Ho W12 112 A6
Orwell Lo 2 E18 55 A5
Orwell Rd E13 99 C6
Osbaldeston Rd N16 52 A1
Osberton Rd SE12 165 A6
Osbert St SW1 259 C3
Osborn Cl E8 96 A6
Osborne Ave TW19 148 B3
Osborne Cl
Beckenham BR3 207 A5
Cockfosters EN4 2 D2
Feltham TW13 172 D5
Osborne Ct Ealing W5 88 A2
10 Surbiton KT6 198 A3
17 Walthamstow E10 53 D2
Osborne Gdns CR7 183 A1
Osborne Gr E17 53 B5
Osborne Mews E17 53 B5
Osborne Pl SM1 218 B3
Osborne Rd
Buckhurst Hill IG9 21 B3
Dagenham RM9 81 B3
Enfield EN3 7 A3
Erith DA17 147 B6
Finsbury Pk N4 50 C1
Forest Gate E7 77 B3
Hackney E9 75 B2
Hounslow TW3, TW4 129 B2
Kingston u T KT2 176 A3
Leyton E10 75 D6
Palmers Green N13 16 C1
South Acton W3 110 D4
Southall UB1 86 A1
South Norwood CR7 183 A1
Walton-on-T KT12 194 A1
Willesden NW2 68 B2
Osborne Sq RM9 81 B4
Osborne Terr 1
SW17 181 A5
Osborne Way KT9 214 B3
Osborn Gdns NW7 28 D3
Osborn La SE23 163 A4
Osborn St E1 95 D2 243 D4
Osborn Terr SE3 142 D1
Osbourne Ct HA2 41 D5
Osbourne Ho
Richmond TW10 154 C6
Twickenham TW2 152 A2
Oscar Faber Pl 8 N1 73 C1
Oscar St SE8 141 C3
Oseney Cres NW5 71 D2
Osgood Ave BR6 227 D3
Osgood Gdns 1
BR6 227 D3
OSIDGE 15 B2
Osidge Ct N14 15 B3
Osidge La N14 15 B3
Osidge Prim Sch N14 15 C3
Osier Cres N10 30 D2
Osier Ct E1 96 D3
Osier La SE10 120 D3
Osier Mews W4 133 D6
Osiers Ct 3 KT1 175 D2
Osiers Rd SW18 135 C1
Osier St E1 96 C3
Osier Way Leyton E10 75 D5
Mitcham CR4 202 D4
Oslac Rd SE6 185 D5
Oslo Ct
Mitcham SW19 180 B3
St John's Wood NW8 230 A3
Oslo Ho 2 SE5 139 A3
Oslo Sq SE16 119 A3
Oslow Cl W10 91 B4
Osman Cl N15 51 B3
Osmani Prim Sch E1 96 A2
Osman Rd
Edmonton N9 18 A1
Osman Rd *continued*
Hammersmith W6 112 C3
Osmington Ho SW8 270 D3
Osmond Cl HA2 64 A6
Osmond Gdns SM6 219 C3
Osmund St W12 89 D2
Osnaburgh St
NW1 93 B3 238 D6
Osnaburgh Terr
NW1 238 D6
Osney Ho 4 SE2 124 D4
Osney Wlk SM5 202 B3
Osprey 7 NW9 27 D2
Osprey Cl
Cheam SM1 217 B3
Higham Hill E17 35 A3
Keston Mark BR2 210 A1
Newham E6 100 A2
Wanstead E11 55 A5
West Drayton UB7 104 A4
Osprey Ct
7 Ealing W7 86 D3
Hampstead NW3 69 D3
Thornton Heath
SW16 182 B1
Osprey Ho
Camberwell SE15 139 D4
Isleworth TW7 131 B2
3 Limehouse E14 119 A6
Walthamstow E4 35 B4
Osprey Mews EN3 18 B6
Ospringe Cl 6 SE20 184 C3
Ospringe Ct SE9 167 B5
Ospringe Ho SE1 251 B3
Ospringe Rd NW5 71 C4
Osram Ct W6 112 C3
Osram Rd HA9 65 D5
Osric Path 8 N1 95 C5
Ossian Mews N4 50 B2
Ossian Rd N4 50 B2
Ossie Garvin Rdbt
UB4 106 C6
Ossington Bldgs W1 238 A3
Ossington Cl W2 245 B5
Ossington St
W2 113 D6 245 C5
Ossory Rd SE1 140 A6
Ossulston St
NW1 93 D5 232 D4
Ossultan Pl N2 48 A6
Ossulton Way N2 48 A5
Ostade Rd SW2 160 B4
Ostell Cres EN3 7 C5
Osten Mews
SW7 113 D3 255 D5
OSTERLEY 130 B5
Osterley Ave TW7 130 B5
Osterley Cl BR5 190 A2
Osterley Cres TW7 130 D4
Osterley Ct
Hounslow TW7 130 B4
7 Northolt UB5 84 C4
Osterley Gdns
Southall UB2 108 A4
South Norwood CR7 183 A1
Osterley Ho 5 E14 97 D1
Osterley La
Isleworth TW7 108 C1
Southall UB2, TW7 107 D1
Osterley Lo 1 TW7 130 C4
Osterley Park* TW7 108 B1
Osterley Park Rd
UB2 107 B3
Osterley Park View Rd
W7 108 C4
Osterley Rd
Hounslow TW7 130 C4
Stoke Newington N16 73 C4
Osterley Sta TW7 130 B5
Osterley Views UB2 108 B4
Osterly Lodge UB2 107 B3
Oster Terr E17 52 D4
Ostlers Dr TW15 171 A5
Ostliffe Rd N13 33 A5
Oswald Bldg SW8 268 C5
Oswald Rd UB1 107 A5
Oswald's Mead E9 75 A4
Oswald St E5 74 D5
Oswald Terr NW2 68 C5
Osward Pl N9 18 B2
Osward Rd SW12,
SW17 158 D2
Oswell Ho 9 E1 118 B5
Oswin St
SE11 116 D2 261 D4
Oswyth Rd SE5 139 C3

Otford Cl Bexley DA5 . 169 D5
Bromley BR1 . 210 C6
Penge SE20 . 184 C2
Otford Cres SE4 . 163 B5
Otford Ho
Bermondsey SE1 . 252 D1
6 Deptford SE15 . 140 C6
Otha Ho 18 SW9 . 138 A3
Othello Cl SE11 . 261 C2
Otho Ct 5 TW8 . 131 D5
Otis St E3 . 98 A4
Otley App IG2 . 56 D3
Otley Ct N11 . 31 A4
Otley Dr IG2 . 56 D3
Otley Ho N5 . 72 D5
Otley Rd E16 . 99 C1
Otley Terr E5 . 74 D5
Ottawa Ho 4 HA4 . 40 C1
Ottaway Ct E5 . 74 A5
Ottaway St E5 . 74 A5
Otterbourne Rd
Chingford E4 . 20 B1
1 Croydon CR0 . 221 A6
Otterburn Gdns
TW7 . 131 A5
Otterburn Ho 12
SE5 . 139 A5
Otterburn St SW17 . 180 D4
Otter Cl E15 . 98 A6
Otterden Cl BR6 . 227 C4
Otterden St SE6 . 185 C6
Otterfield Rd UB7 . 104 A6
Otter Rd UB6 . 86 A3
Ottershaw Ho BR5 . 190 B2
Otto Cl SE26 . 162 B1
Ottoman Ct W5 . 109 D2
Otto St SE17 . 138 D6
Otway Ct N4 . 50 B3
Otway Gdns WD23 . 8 C4
Oulton Cl Erith SE28 . 102 C1
Upper Clapton E5 . 74 C6
Oulton Cres IG11 . 79 D3
Oulton Rd N15 . 51 B4
Oulton Way WD19 . 23 B6
Oundle Ave WD23 . 8 A5
Our Lady Immaculate RC Prim Sch KT6 . 198 D1
Our Lady of Dolours RC Prim Sch 1 W2 . 91 D2
Our Lady of Grace RC Inf Sch NW2 . 68 C6
Our Lady of Grace RC Jun Sch NW2 . 68 B5
Our Lady of Grace RC Prim Sch 4 SE7 . 143 B6
Our Lady of Lourdes RC Prim Sch
1 Finchley N12 . 30 A2
Friern Barnet N11 . 31 C5
1 Lewisham SE13 . 142 B2
London NW10 . 89 A6
Our Lady of Lourds RC Prim Sch E11 . 55 A3
Our Lady of Muswell Prim Sch N10 . 49 A6
Our Lady of Muswell RC Prim Sch N10 . 31 A1
Our Lady of the Rosary RC Prim Sch DA15 . 167 C5
Our Lady of the Visitation RC Combined Prim Sch UB6 . 86 A3
Our Lady of Victories RC Prim Sch
7 Putney SW15 . 134 D1
South Kensington SW7 . 114 A2 256 B3
Our Lady Queen of Heaven RC Prim Sch 10 SW19 . 156 D4
Our Lady RC Prim Sch
Camden Town NW1 . 93 C6 232 B6
28 Poplar E14 . 97 B1
Our Lady & St John's RC Jun & Inf Sch 4 TW8 . 109 C1
Our Lady & St Joseph RC Prim Sch 14 N1 . 73 C2
Our Lady & St Philip Neri RC Infants Sch 16 SE23 . 162 D1
Our Lady & St Philip Neri RC Prim Sch 6 SE26 . 185 A6
Our Lady's Convent RC High Sch 3 N15 . 51 C2
Ouseley Rd SW12 . 158 D3
Outer Circ
NW8 . 92 D5 230 D3
Outgate Rd NW10 . 67 D1
Outram Pl N1 . 94 A6 233 B6
Outram Rd
Croydon CR0 . 221 D6
Muswell Hill N22 . 31 D2
Newham E6 . 100 A6
Outwich St EC3 . 243 B2
Outwood Ct CR2 . 221 A1
Outwood Ho 3
SW2 . 160 B4
Oval Ct Burnt Oak HA8 . 27 A3
8 Teddington TW11 . 174 D5
Oval Mans SE11 . 270 D6
Oval Pl SW8 . 138 B5 270 D4
Oval Prim Sch CR0 . 205 C1
Oval Rd
Camden Town NW1 . 93 B6 231 C6
Croydon CR0 . 205 C1
Oval Rd N RM10 . 103 D6
Oval Rd S RM10 . 103 D5
Oval Sta SE11 . 138 C6
Oval The Hackney E2 . 96 B5
Sidcup DA15 . 168 A4
Oval Way
SE11 . 116 B1 260 D1
Overbrae BR3 . 185 C5
Overbrook Wlk HA8 . 26 C3
Overbury 1 BR3 . 208 A6
Overbury Ave BR3 . 208 A6
Overbury Ho 3 E5 . 74 D4
Overbury Rd N4, N15 . 51 B3
Overbury St E5 . 74 D4
Overcliff Rd SE13 . 141 C2
Overcourt Cl DA15 . 168 B5
Overdale Ave KT3 . 177 B1
Overdale Rd W5 . 109 C3
Overdown Rd SE6 . 185 D6
Overhill Rd SE21, SE22 . 162 A4
Overhill Way BR3 . 208 B4
Overlea Rd E5 . 52 A2
Overmead DA15 . 167 B4
Oversley Ho 17 W2 . 91 C2
Overstand Cl BR3 . 207 C4
Overstone Gdns CR0 . 207 B2
Overstone Ho 19 E14 . 97 C1
Overstone Rd W6 . 112 C2
Overstrand Mans SW11 . 268 A1
Overton Cl
1 Hounslow TW7 . 130 D4
Tokyngton NW10 . 67 A2
Overton Ct E11 . 55 A2
Overton Dr Ilford RM6 . 58 C2
Wanstead E11 . 55 B2
Overton Grange Sch SM2 . 217 D1
Overton Ho SW15 . 155 D4
Overton Rd
Abbey Wood SE2 . 124 D3
Belmont SM2 . 217 C1
Brixton SW9 . 138 C3
Southgate N14 . 16 A6
Walthamstow E10 . 53 A1
Overton's Yd CR0 . 221 A5
Overy Ho SE1 . 251 C1
Ovesdon Ave HA2 . 41 B1
Ovett Cl SE19 . 183 C4
Ovex Cl E14 . 120 A4
Ovington Ct SW3 . 257 B5
Ovington Gdns SW3 . 257 B5
Ovington Mews SW3 . 257 B5
Ovington Sq
SW3 . 114 C3 257 B5
Ovington St
SW3 . 114 C2 257 B4
Owen Cl Hayes UB4 . 84 B4
Northolt UB5 . 63 A2
Thamesmead SE28 . 124 C5
Thornton Heath CR0 . 205 B3
Owen Ct UB4 . 84 B4
Owen Ho
Feltham TW14 . 150 A4
11 Tufnell Pk N19 . 71 C4
5 Twickenham TW1 . 153 B4
Owenite St SE2 . 124 B2
Owen Rd
Edmonton N13 . 33 A5
Hayes UB4 . 84 B4
Owen's Ct EC1 . 234 C2
Owens Mews 10 E11 . 76 C6
Owen's Row EC1 . 234 C2
Owen St EC1 . 234 C3
Owens Way SE23 . 163 A4
Owen Way NW10 . 67 A3
Owen Wlk 7 SE20 . 184 A3
Owgan Cl SE5 . 139 B5
Oxberry Ave SW6 . 135 A3
Oxbridge Ct 4 W4 . 110 D1
Oxendon St SW1, W1 . 115 D6 249 C5
Oxenford St SE15 . 139 D2
Oxenham Ho 13 SE8 . 141 C6
Oxenholme NW1 . 232 B3
Oxenpark Ave HA9 . 44 A2
Oxestalls Rd SE8 . 119 A1
Oxford Ave
Harlington TW6 . 127 D5
Hounslow TW5 . 107 C1
Merton SW20 . 179 A1
Southgate N14 . 15 C3
Oxford & Cambridge Mans NW1 . 237 B3
Oxford Cir W1 . 93 C1 239 A1
Oxford Circus Ave W1 . 239 A1
Oxford Circus Sta W1 . 93 C1 239 A1
Oxford Cl
Edmonton N9 . 18 B2
Littleton TW15, TW17 . 171 A3
Mitcham CR4 . 203 C6
Oxford Cres KT3 . 199 B3
Oxford Ct
16 Acton W3 . 88 C1
City of London EC4 . 252 C6
8 Ealing W7 . 86 D2
Gunnersbury W4 . 110 D1
17 Kingston u T KT6 . 198 A4
48 Paddington W2 . 91 C2
Sidcup DA14 . 189 D6
Oxford Dr
Bermondsey SE1 . 253 A3
Ruislip HA4 . 62 C6
Oxford Gardens Prim Sch 21 W10 . 90 D1
Oxford Gate W6 . 112 D2
Oxford Gdns
Brentford W4 . 132 C6
Edmonton N21 . 17 A4
North Kensington W10 . 90 D1
Oakleigh Pk N20 . 14 B3
Oxford Ho N4 . 50 C1
Oxford Mews DA5 . 169 C4
Oxford Rd
Carshalton SM5 . 218 C3
Ealing W5 . 109 D6
Edmonton N9 . 18 B2
Enfield EN3 . 18 B6
Finsbury Pk N4 . 50 C1
Harrow HA1 . 42 A3
Ilford IG1 . 79 A3
Paddington NW6 . 91 C5
Putney SW15 . 135 A1
Sidcup DA14 . 190 B5
South Norwood SE19 . 183 B4
Stratford E15 . 76 B2
Teddington TW11, TW12 . 174 B5
Wallington SM6 . 219 C3
Wealdstone HA3 . 42 D6
Woodford IG8 . 37 D5
Oxford Rd N W4 . 110 D1
Oxford Rd S W4 . 110 D1
Oxford Sq W2 . 92 C1 237 B1
Oxford St W1 . 93 B1 238 D1
Oxford Way TW13 . 172 D6
Oxford Wlk UB1 . 107 B5
Oxgate Ct NW2 . 68 A6
Oxgate Ct Par NW2 . 68 A6
Oxgate Ctr NW2 . 68 B6
Oxgate Gdns NW2 . 68 B6
Oxgate La NW2 . 68 B6
Oxhawth Cres BR2 . 210 D3
Oxhey Dr WD19 . 22 B6
Oxhey Dr S HA6 . 22 B5
Oxhey La HA5 . 23 C5
Oxhey Ridge Cl HA6 . 22 B5
Oxhey Wood Prim Sch WD19 . 22 C6
Oxleas E6 . 100 D1
Oxleas Cl DA16 . 145 B3
Oxleay Rd HA2 . 41 C1
Oxleigh Cl KT3 . 199 C4
Oxley Cl SE1 . 118 A1
Oxleys Rd NW2 . 68 B5
Oxlip Cl 2 CR0 . 206 D1
Oxlow La RM10 . 81 C4
Oxonian St SE22 . 139 D1
Oxo Tower Wharf SE1 . 251 B5
Oxo Twr* SE1 . 251 B5
Oxted Cl CR4 . 202 B6
Oxted Ct N16 . 51 C1
Oxtoby Way SW16 . 181 D2
Oyster Catchers Cl E16 . 99 B1
Oyster Catcher Terr IG5 . 56 C6
Oyster Row E1 . 96 C1
Ozolins Way E16 . 99 A1

P

Pablo Neruda Cl 4 SE24 . 138 D1
Pace Pl E1 . 96 B1
Pacific Cl TW14 . 149 D3
Pacific Ho 15 E1 . 96 D3
Pacific Hts BR3 . 185 C3
Pacific Rd E16 . 99 A1
Pacific Wharf IG11 . 78 D1
Pacific Wharf SE16 . 118 D5
Packenham Ho
24 Crouch End N19 . 49 D2
21 Spitalfields E2 . 95 D4
Packham Ct KT4 . 216 C5
Packington Sq N1 . 95 A6 235 A6
Packington St N1 . 94 D6 234 D5
Packmores Rd SE9 . 167 B6
Padbury SE17 . 263 B1
Padbury Cl TW14 . 149 B3
Padbury Ct E2 . 95 D4
Padbury Ho NW8 . 237 B6
Padden Ct NW7 . 28 D3
Paddenswick Ct 2 W6 . 112 B3
Paddenswick Rd W6 . 112 A3
PADDINGTON . 92 A2
Paddington Acad 7 W9 . 91 C3
Paddington Cl UB4 . 84 D3
Paddington Ct
10 Ealing W7 . 86 D2
7 Wembley HA0 . 66 A2
Paddington Gn W2 . 92 B2 236 C4
Paddington Green Prim Sch NW8 . 92 B3 236 C5
Paddington St W1 . 238 A4
Paddington Sta W2 . 92 B1 236 C2
Paddock Cl
Forest Hill SE26 . 184 D6
Kidbrooke SE3 . 143 A3
New Malden KT4 . 199 C1
Northolt UB5 . 85 C5
Orpington BR6 . 226 D4
Paddock Ct SW20 . 200 C5
Paddock Gdns SE19 . 183 C4
Paddock Lo 13 EN1 . 17 C6
Paddock Prim Sch SW11 . 137 A1
Paddock Rd
Bexley DA6 . 147 A1
Dollis Hill NW2 . 68 A6
Ruislip HA4 . 62 D5
Paddock Sch SW15 . 133 D1
Paddocks Cl HA2 . 63 D4
Paddocks Gn NW9 . 44 D1
Paddocks The
Addington CR0 . 223 C2
Cockfosters EN4 . 2 D2
Preston HA9 . 66 D6
Paddock The
Muswell Hill N10 . 49 B6
Uxbridge UB10 . 60 D4
Paddock Way
Chislehurst BR7 . 189 B3
11 Putney SW15 . 156 C4
Padelford La HA7 . 9 A2
Padfield Ct HA9 . 66 B5
Padfield Rd SE5 . 139 A2
Padley Cl KT9 . 214 B3
Padnall Ct RM6 . 58 D6
Padnall Rd RM6 . 58 D5
Padstone Ho 50 E3 . 97 D4
Padstow Cl BR6 . 227 D4
Padstow Ho 12 E14 . 119 B6
Padstow Rd EN2 . 4 D4
Padstow Wlk TW14 . 149 D3
Padua Rd SE20 . 184 C2
Pagden St SW8 . 268 D2
Pageant Ave NW9 . 27 C2
Pageant Cres SE16 . 119 B5
Pageantmaster Ct EC4 . 241 C1
Pageant Wlk CR0 . 221 C5
Page Cl
Dagenham RM9 . 81 A3
Hampton TW12 . 173 A4
Harrow HA3 . 44 B3
Page Cres CR0 . 220 D3
Page Ct NW7 . 28 A3
Page Green Rd N15 . 52 A4
Page Green Terr N15 . 51 D4
Page Heath La BR1 . 209 D6
Page Heath Villas BR1 . 209 D6
Page High N22 . 50 C6
Page Ho SE10 . 142 A6
Pagehurst Rd CR0 . 206 B2
Page Mdw NW7 . 28 A3
Page Rd TW14 . 149 B5
Page's Ct N10 . 31 A1
Page's Hill N10 . 31 A1
Page's La N10 . 31 A1
Page St Hendon NW7 . 28 A3
Westminster SW1 . 115 D2 259 D4
Page's Wlk SE1 . 117 C3 263 B5
Page's Yd W4 . 133 C6
Paget Ave SM1 . 218 B5
Paget Cl TW12 . 174 B6
Paget Ct UB7 . 104 A4
Paget Gdns BR7 . 188 D2
Paget Ho 15 E2 . 96 C5
Paget La TW7 . 130 C2
Paget Pl
Kingston u T KT2 . 177 A4
Thames Ditton KT7 . 196 D1
Paget Rd
Hillingdon UB10 . 83 A3
Ilford IG1 . 78 D4
Stoke Newington N16 . 51 B1
Paget Rise SE18 . 144 C5
Paget St EC1 . 234 C2
Paget Terr SE18 . 144 D6
Pagham Ho 8 W10 . 90 C3
Pagin Ho N15 . 51 C4
Pagitts Gr EN4 . 1 D4
Pagnell St SE14 . 141 B5
Pagoda Ave TW9 . 132 B2
Pagoda Gdns SE3 . 142 B3
Pagoda Gr SE27 . 161 A2
Paignton Rd
Ruislip HA4 . 62 A5
Tottenham N15 . 51 C3
Paine Ct SE3 . 142 D6
Paines Cl HA5 . 41 A6
Paine's La HA5 . 23 A1
Pain's Cl CR4 . 181 B1
Painsthorpe Rd 3 N16 . 73 C5
Painswick Ct 1 SE15 . 139 D5
Painters Mews SE16 . 118 A2
Painters Rd IG2, RM6 . 58 A6
Paisley Rd
Carshalton SM5 . 202 B1
Tottenham N22 . 32 D2
Paisley Terr SM5 . 202 B2
Pakeman Ho SE1 . 251 D2
Pakeman Prim Sch 1 N7 . 72 B5
Pakeman St N7 . 72 B5
Pakenham Cl SW12 . 159 A3
Pakenham St WC1 . 94 B3 240 D6
Pakington Ho 22 SW9 . 138 A3
Palace Ave W8 . 113 D4 245 D2
Palace Cl 4 E9 . 75 B2
Palace Court Gdns N10 . 49 C6

Palace Ct
- Bromley BR1 187 B2
- Eltham SE9 166 B5
- Hampstead NW3 69 D3
- Harrow HA3 44 A3
- Kensington W2 113 D6 245 C5
- 2 South Norwood CR7 205 B5
- Streatham SW2 160 C2

Palace Exchange EN2 5 B1
Palace Garden Mews W8 245 B4
Palace Gate
- Hampton KT8 196 C6
- Knightsbridge W8 114 A4 246 A1

Palace Gate Mews 4 N8 50 A5
Palace Gates Rd N22 31 D2
Palace Gdns IG9 21 D3
Palace Gdns Mews W8 113 D5 245 D3
Palace Gdns Sh Ctr EN2 5 B1
Palace Gn
- Kensington W8 113 D5 245 C3
- New Addington CR0 223 B1

Palace Gr
- Bromley BR1 187 B2
- Penge SE19 183 D3

Palace Mans W14 254 B4
Palace Mews
- Belgravia SW1 258 B3
- Fulham SW6 264 D4
- 1 Walthamstow E17 53 B5

Palace of Ind HA9 66 C4
Palace Par E17 53 C5
Palace Pl SW1 259 A6
Palace Rd
- Bromley BR1 187 B2
- East Molesey KT8 196 B6
- Hornsey N8 49 D4
- Kingston u T KT1 197 D5
- Penge SE19 183 D3
- Ruislip HA4 63 A4
- Streatham SE27, SW16, SW2 160 C2
- Wood Green N11 32 A3

Palace Sq SE19 183 D3
Palace St SW1 115 C3 259 A6
Palace View
- Bromley BR1 209 B6
- Croydon CR0 223 B4
- Grove Pk SE12 165 A2

Palace View Rd E4 35 D5
Palamos Rd E10 53 C1
Palatine Ave N16 73 C4
Palatine Rd N16 73 C4
Palazzo Apartments 11 N1 73 C1
Palemead Cl SW6 134 D4
Palermo Rd NW10 90 A5
Palestine Gr SW19 180 B2
Palewell Cl BR5 190 B1
Palewell Common Dr SW14 155 B6
Palewell Pk SW14 133 B1
Palfrey Pl SW8 138 B5 270 D4
Palgrave Ave UB1 107 C6
Palgrave Gdns NW1 92 C3 237 B6
Palgrave Ho
- 7 Camberwell SE5 139 A5
- 4 Maitland Pk NW3 70 D3
- Twickenham TW2 152 A4

Palgrave Rd W12 111 D3
Palissy St 35 E2 95 D4
Palladino Ho 6 SW17 180 C5
Pallant Ho SE1 262 D5
Pallant Way BR6 226 C5
Pallester Ct NW11 47 A1
Pallet Way SE18 144 A4
Palliser Ct W14 254 A1
Palliser Ho
- 3 Greenwich SE10 142 B6
- 21 Stepney E1 96 D3

Palliser Rd W14 113 A1 254 A1
Pallister Terr SW15 155 D2
Pall Mall SW1 115 D5 249 C3
Pall Mall E SW1 115 D5 249 D4
Pall Mall Pl SW1 249 B3
Palmar Cres DA7 147 C3
Palmar Rd DA7 147 C3
Palm Ave DA14 190 D4
Palm Cl E10 75 D5
Palm Ct
- Beckenham BR3 207 B6
- 18 Camberwell SE15 139 D5
- Stoke Newington N16 73 B6
- Wood Green N22 32 B3

Palmeira Rd DA7 146 D2
Palmer Ave KT4, SM3 216 C4
Palmer Cl
- Heston TW5 129 C4
- Northolt UB5 63 A2
- West Wickham BR4 224 B6

Palmer Cres KT1 198 A6
Palmer Gdns EN5 12 D6
Palmer Ho
- 6 Deptford SE14 140 D5
- 8 Kentish Town NW5 71 C4
- 5 Tufnell Pk N19 71 C5

Palmer Pl N7 72 C3
Palmer Rd
- Dagenham RM8 58 D1
- Newham E13 99 B3

Palmer's Ct 11 N11 31 C5
Palmers Gr KT8 195 C5
PALMERS GREEN 16 A1
Palmers Green High Sch N21 16 C2
Palmers Green Sta N13 32 B6
Palmers La EN3 6 C4
Palmers Rd
- Globe Town E2 96 D5
- Mortlake SW14 133 A2
- Thornton Heath SW16 182 B1

Palmer's Rd N11 31 C5
Palmer St SW1 259 C6
Palmerston Cres
- Bowes Pk N13 32 B5
- Woolwich SE18 145 A6

Palmerston Ct
- 2 Buckhurst Hill IG9 21 C2
- 22 Globe Town E3 96 D5
- 9 Surbiton KT6 197 D2
- 7 Sutton SM1 218 A3
- Walthamstow E17 53 B5

Palmerston Ctr HA3 42 D6
Palmerston Gr 11 SW19 179 C3
Palmerston Ho
- Battersea SW11 268 B1
- Kensington W8 245 A3

Palmerston Rd
- Acton Green W3 111 A3
- Bowes Pk N22 32 B4
- Brondesbury NW6 69 B1
- Buckhurst Hill IG9 21 C3
- Farnborough BR6 227 A3
- Hampstead NW6 69 C1
- Harrow HA3 42 D6
- Hounslow TW3 130 A4
- Merton SW19 179 C3
- Mortlake SW14 133 A1
- Sutton SM1 218 A3
- Thornton Heath CR0 205 B4
- Twickenham TW2 152 C5
- Upton E7 77 B2
- Wallington SM5 219 A4
- Walthamstow E17 53 B5

Palmerston Way SW8 268 D3
Palm Gr W5 110 A3
Palm Tree Ct 5 N17 33 D1
Palm Tree Ho 2 SE14 140 D5
Pamela Ct
- Finchley N12 29 D4
- Willesden NW10 68 A1

Pamela Gdns HA5 40 B4
Pamela Ho 14 E8 95 D6
Pamir Ct 10 SM2 217 D2
Pamlion Ct N4 50 A2
Pams Way KT19 215 B3
Panama Ho 6 E1 96 D2
Panbro Ho SE18 144 B4
Pancras La EC2 242 C1
Pancras Rd NW1 93 D5 232 D4
Pancras Way Bow E3 98 C5
- Old Ford E3 97 C5

Pandian Way 4 NW5 71 D2
Pandora Ct 4 KT6 198 A3
Pandora Rd NW6 69 C2
Panfield Mews IG2 56 C3
Panfield Rd SE2 124 A3
Pangbourne NW1 232 A1
Pangbourne Ave W10 90 C2
Pangbourne Ct
- Oakleigh Pk N20 14 A4
- Upper Tooting SW17 180 A6

Pangbourne Dr HA7 26 A5
Pangbourne Ho 4 N7 72 A3
Panhard Pl UB1 107 D6
Pank Ave EN5 14 A6
Pankhurst Ave 8 E16 121 B5
Pankhurst Cl
- 7 Deptford SE14 140 D5
- Isleworth TW7 130 D2

Pankhurst Ho
- 2 Kensington NW10 90 C1
- Streatham SW16 181 D5

Pankhurst Rd KT12 194 C2
Panmuir Rd SW20 178 B2
Panmure Cl N5 72 D4
Panmure Ct 11 UB1 86 A1
Panmure Rd SE26 162 B1
Panorama Ct N6 49 C3
Pan Penisula Sq E14 119 D4
Pansy Gdns W12 112 A6
Panther Dr NW10 67 B3
Pantiles Cl N13 32 D5
Pantiles The
- Bickley BR1 210 A6
- Bushey WD23 8 B3
- Erith DA7 147 B5
- Temple Fortune NW11 47 B4

Panton Cl CR0 204 D1
Panton St SW1 249 C5
Panyer Alley EC2 242 A2
Papermill Cl SM5 219 A4
Paper Mill Wharf E14 119 A6
Papillons Wlk SE3 143 A2
Papworth Gdns N7 72 B3
Papworth Way SW2 160 C4
Parade Mans
- 19 Camberwell SE5 139 A3
- 2 Hendon NW4 46 B4

Parade Mews SE27, SW2 160 D2
Parade The
- Ashford TW16 171 D3
- Battersea SW11 136 D5 267 D4
- Claygate KT10 212 C2
- Ilford IG2 57 B3
- Thornton Heath CR0 204 A3
- Thornton Heath CR7 204 C6
- Waddon CR0 220 B3
- Wembley UB6 65 B3

Paradise Pas N7 72 C3
Paradise Pl 15 SE7 122 A2
Paradise Rd
- Richmond TW10 154 A6
- South Lambeth SW4 138 A3

Paradise Row E2 96 B4
Paradise St SE16 118 B4
Paradise Wlk SW3 136 D6 267 D6
Paragon N8 50 C5
Paragon Christian Acad E5 74 D4
Paragon Cl E16 99 A1
Paragon Ct NW4 29 A2
Paragon Gr KT5 198 B3
Paragon Ho SE3 142 D3
Paragon Mews SE1 262 D4
Paragon Pl
- Blackheath Vale SE3 142 D3
- Surbiton KT5 198 B3

Paragon Rd E9 74 C2
Paragon The
- Kidbrooke SE3 143 A3
- Walworth SE17 262 D4

Paramount Bldg EC1 241 C6
Paramount Ct WC1 239 B5
Paramount Ho 10 E11 76 C5
Parbury Rd SE23 163 A5
Parbury Rise KT9 214 A2
Parchmore Rd CR7 205 A6
Parchmore Way CR7 182 D1
Pardes House Gram Sch 11 N3 29 B1
Pardes House Prim Sch 12 N3 29 B1
Pardoner St SE1 117 B3 262 D6
Pardon St EC1 241 D6
Parfett St E1 96 A1
Parfew Ct 2 SE22 162 B2
Parfitt Cl NW11 48 A1
Parfrey St W6 134 C6
Pargraves Ct HA9 66 C6
Parham Dr IG2 56 D4
Paris Gdn SE1 116 D5 251 C4
Parish CE Prim Sch BR1 187 A3
Parish Church CE Inf Sch 10 CR0 220 D5
Parish Church CE Jun Sch 9 CR0 220 D5
Parish Ct KT6 198 A3
Parish Gate Dr DA15 167 C5
Parish La SE20 184 D3
Paris Ho 12 E2 96 B5
Parish Wharf 6 SE7 122 A2
Park App DA16 146 B1
Park Ave Barking IG11 79 A2
- Bromley BR6 226 C6
- Edmonton N18 34 A6
- Enfield EN1 17 C5
- Finchley N3 29 D2
- Golders Green NW11 47 D1
- Ilford IG1 56 C1
- Mitcham CR4 181 B3
- Mortlake SW14 133 B1
- Palmers Green N13 16 C1
- Plaistow BR1 187 A4
- Ruislip HA4 39 C3
- Southall UB1 107 C5
- Stratford E15 76 C2
- Twickenham TW3 151 D5
- Upper Halliford TW17 193 C6
- Wallend E6 100 C5
- Wallington SM5 219 A2
- West Wickham BR4 224 A6
- Willesden NW2 68 C2
- Woodford IG8 37 B5
- Wood Green N22 32 B2

Park Ave E KT17 216 A2
Park Ave N
- Dudden Hill NW10 68 B3
- Hornsey N8 49 D5

Park Avenue Mews CR4 181 B3
Park Avenue Rd N17 34 B3
Park Ave S N8 49 D5
Park Ave W KT17 216 A2
Park Chase HA9 66 B4
Park Cl Dollis Hill NW2 68 B5
- Ealing NW10 88 B4
- Hampton TW12 174 A2
- Harrow HA3 24 C2
- Isleworth TW3, TW7 152 A6
- Kensington W14 113 B3 254 D6
- Kingston u T KT2 176 C2
- Knightsbridge SW1 247 C1
- North Finchley N12 30 B6
- 13 South Hackney E9 96 C6
- Wallington SM5 218 D2

Park Cotts 10 TW1 153 B5
Park Cres Enfield EN2 5 B1
- Finchley N3 30 A3
- Harrow HA3 24 C2
- Regent's Pk W1 93 B3 238 C5
- Twickenham TW2 152 B3

Park Crescent Mews E W1 238 D5
Park Crescent Mews W W1 238 C5
Park Croft HA8 27 A2
Parkcroft Rd SE12 164 D4
Park Ct
- Battersea SW11 268 C2
- 2 Beckenham BR3 207 D6

Park Ct *continued*
- 2 Chingford E4 20 A2
- Clapham Pk SW4 159 D6
- Dulwich SE21 161 B1
- 12 Hammersmith W6 112 A2
- New Barnet EN5 14 B4
- New Malden KT3 199 B5
- North Finchley N12 30 B5
- Teddington KT1 175 C2
- Twickenham TW4 151 D6
- Upper Tooting SW12 159 A3
- Wallington SM6 220 A3
- Walthamstow E17 53 D4
- Wembley HA9 66 A3
- Wood Green N11 31 D3

Parkdale N11 31 D4
Parkdale Cres KT4 215 B5
Parkdale Rd SE18 123 C1
Park Dr Acton W3 110 C3
- Enfield N21 17 A5
- Golders Green NW11 47 D1
- Harrow HA2 41 C2
- Mortlake SW14 133 B1
- Stanmore HA3 24 C4
- Woolwich SE7 144 A6

Park Dwellings 7 NW3 70 D3
Park End
- Bromley BR1 186 D2
- Hampstead NW3 70 C4

Parker Cl
- Newham E16 122 A5
- Wallington SM5 218 D2

Parker Ct
- Shoreditch N1 235 B6
- South Lambeth SW4 270 A1
- Wimbledon SW19 179 A3

Parke Rd
- Barnes SW13 134 A4
- Sunbury TW16 194 A5

Parker Ho 4 SE18 122 D1
Parker Mews WC2 240 B2
Parker Rd CR0 221 A4
Parkers Rd N10 30 C2
Parkers Row 15 SE16 118 A4
Parker's Row SE1 253 D1
Parker St
- Newham E16 122 A5
- St Giles WC2 94 A1 240 B2

Park Farm Cl
- East Finchley N2 48 A6
- Pinner HA5 40 B4

Park Farm Ct UB3 105 C6
Park Farm Rd
- Bromley BR1 187 D2
- Kingston u T KT2 176 A3

Parkfield 3 TW7 130 C4
Parkfield Ave
- Feltham TW13 150 A1
- Harrow HA2 24 A1
- Hillingdon UB10 82 D4
- Mortlake SW14 133 C1
- Northolt UB5 84 D5

Parkfield Cl
- Edgware HA8 26 D4
- Northolt UB5 85 A5

Parkfield Cres
- Feltham TW13 150 A1
- Harrow HA2 24 A1
- Ruislip HA4 63 A5

Parkfield Ct SE14 141 B4
Parkfield Dr UB5 84 D5
Parkfield Gdns HA2 41 D6
Parkfield Ho HA2 23 D2
Parkfield Ind Est SW11 137 A3
Parkfield Par TW13 150 A1
Parkfield Prim Sch NW4 46 B2
Parkfield Rd
- Feltham TW13 150 A1
- Harrow HA2 64 A5
- New Cross SE14 141 B4
- Northolt UB5 85 A5
- Uxbridge UB10 60 D6
- Willesden NW10 68 B1

Parkfields
- Croydon CR0 207 B1
- Putney SW15 134 C1

Parkfields Ave
- Welsh Harp NW9 45 B1
- Wimbledon SW20 178 B1

Parkfields Cl SM5 219 A4
Parkfields Rd KT2 176 B5

Parkfield St N1 . . . . 94 C5 234 B4
Parkfield Way BR2 . . . 210 B4
Park Flats N6 . . . . 48 C2
Parkgate SE3 . . . . 142 D2
Park Gate Ealing W5 . . . 87 D2
East Finchley N2 . . . . . . 48 B6
Southgate N21 . . . . 16 B4
Parkgate Ave EN4 . . . . . . 2 A4
Parkgate Cl KT2 . . . . 176 D4
Parkgate Cres EN4 . . . . 2 A4
Park Gate Ct TW12 . . . 174 A5
Parkgate Gdns SW14 . . . . 155 B6
Parkgate House Sch SW11 . . . . 137 A1
Parkgate Mews N6 . . . 49 C2
Parkgate Rd
Battersea SW11 . . . . . 136 C5 267 B3
Wallington SM5, SM6 . . 219 B3
Park Gates HA2 . . . . 63 C4
Park Gdns
Kingston u T KT2 . . . . . 176 B5
Queensbury NW9 . . . . . 44 D6
Park Gr Bromley BR1 . . . 187 B2
Edgware HA8 . . . . 26 B5
Newham E15 . . . . 99 A6
Wood Green N11 . . . . 31 D3
Park Grove Rd E11 . . . . 76 C6
Park Hall SE10 . . . . 142 B5
Park Hall Rd
Dulwich SE21 . . . . 161 B1
East Finchley N2 . . . . . . 48 C5
Park Hall Road Trad Est SE21 . . . . 161 B1
Parkham Ct BR2 . . . . . 186 C1
Parkham St SW11 . . . . . . 136 C4 267 A1
Parkham Way N10 . . . . 31 C1
Park Heights Ct 21 E14 . . . . 97 B1
Park High Sch HA7 . . . 25 D1
Park Hill
Bromley BR1 . . . . 210 B5
Clapham Pk SW4 . . . . 159 D6
Ealing W5 . . . . 87 D2
Forest Hill SE23 . . . . . . 162 C3
Loughton IG10 . . . . 21 D6
Richmond TW10 . . . . . . 154 B5
Wallington SM5 . . . . . 218 D2
Park Hill Cl SM5 . . . . . 218 C3
Park Hill Ct
Croydon CR0 . . . . 221 C6
Ealing W5 . . . . 87 D2
Upper Tooting SW17 . 158 D1
Parkhill Ho 1 SW16 . 182 C5
Parkhill Inf Sch IG5 . . . 56 C6
Park Hill Inf Sch CR0 . . . . 221 C5
Parkhill Jun Sch IG5 . . 56 C6
Park Hill Jun Sch CR0 . . . . 221 C5
Parkhill Rd
Chingford E4 . . . . 20 A4
Maitland Pk NW3 . . . . . 70 D3
Old Bexley DA5 . . . . . . 169 B4
Sidcup DA15 . . . . 167 C1
Park Hill Rd
Beckenham BR2 . . . . . 186 C1
South Croydon CR0 . . 221 C5
Wallington SM6 . . . . . . 219 B1
Park Hill Rise CR0 . . 221 D5
Park Hill Sch 17 KT2 . . . . 176 C3
Park Hill Wlk 10 NW3 . 70 D3
Park Ho
8 Camberwell SE5 . . . 139 B4
Finsbury Pk N4 . . . . 72 D6
Forest Hill SE26 . . . . . 184 A5
35 Hackney E9 . . . . 74 C1
Richmond TW10 . . . . . 154 A5
Sidcup DA14 . . . . 190 A5
Southgate N21 . . . . 16 B4
Parkholme Rd E8 . . . . . 74 A2
Park House Gdns TW1 . . . . 153 C6
Parkhouse St SE5 . . . . 139 B5
Park Hts NW4 . . . . 46 B6
Parkhurst Ct N7 . . . . . . 72 A4
Parkhurst Gdns 2 DA5 . . . . 169 C4
Parkhurst Rd
Bowes Pk N22 . . . . 32 B4
Friern Barnet N11 . . . . . 31 A5
Little Ilford E12 . . . . 78 C4
Parkhurst Rd *continued*
Lower Holloway N7 . . . . 72 A4
Sidcup DA5 . . . . 169 C4
Sutton SM1 . . . . 218 B4
Tottenham N17 . . . . 34 A1
Walthamstow E17 . . . . . 53 A5
Parkin Ho SE20 . . . . . 184 D3
Parkinson Ct
Finsbury N1 . . . . 235 C1
Shoreditch EC1 . . . . . 235 D2
Parkinson Ho 6 E9 . . . 74 C1
Park La Cheam SM3 . . . 217 A2
Cranford TW5 . . . . 128 A5
Dagenham RM6 . . . . 58 D3
Edmonton N9 . . . . 17 D1
Harrow HA2 . . . . 63 D5
Hayes UB4 . . . . 83 C3
Mayfair W1 . 115 A6 248 A5
Mill Meads E15 . . . . 98 B6
Richmond TW9 . . . . . . 131 D1
South Croydon CR0 . . . 221 B5
Stanmore HA7 . . . . 9 A1
Teddington TW11 . . . . . 174 D4
Tottenham N17 . . . . 34 A3
Wallington SM5, SM6 . 219 A3
Wembley HA9 . . . . 66 A4
Parkland Ct
Kensington W14 . . . . . 244 A2
Stratford E15 . . . . 76 C3
Parkland Gdns 12 SW19 . . . . 156 D3
Parkland Gr
Ashford TW15 . . . . 170 C6
Hounslow TW7 . . . . 130 D4
Parkland Mead BR1 . 210 D6
Parkland Rd
Ashford TW15 . . . . 170 C6
Woodford IG8 . . . . 37 B3
Wood Green N22 . . . . . . 32 B1
Parklands
Bushey WD23 . . . . 8 A5
East Dulwich SE22 . . . . 162 B6
Highgate N6 . . . . 49 B2
Kingston u T KT5 . . . . . 198 B4
5 Whetstone N20 . . . . . 14 A2
Parklands Cl
Hadley Wood EN4 . . . . . . 2 B5
Ilford IG2 . . . . 57 A2
Mortlake SW14 . . . . . . 155 A6
Parklands Ct TW5 . . . 128 D3
Parklands Dr N3 . . . . . . 47 A6
Parklands Par TW5 . . 128 D3
Parklands Pl HA8 . . . . . 26 B6
Parklands Rd SW16 . . 181 B5
Parklands Way KT4 . . 215 C6
Park Lane Cl N17 . . . . . 34 A3
Park Lane Mans CR0 . . . . 221 B5
Park Lane Prim Sch HA9 . . . . 66 A4
PARK LANGLEY 208 B4
Park Lawn CR7 . . . . . . 183 A1
Parklea Cl NW9 . . . . 27 C2
Park Lea Ct N16 . . . . . . 51 C2
Parkleigh Ct SW19 . . 179 D1
Parkleigh Rd SW19 . 179 D1
Parkleys KT2, TW10 . . 175 D6
Parklife Oxford St W1 . . . . 238 A1
Park Lo 3 Ealing W5 . . . 87 B3
North Finchley N12 . . . . 30 A5
11 South Hampstead NW8 . . . . 70 B1
10 Wapping E1 . . . . 118 B5
Willesden NW2 . . . . 68 C4
Park Lodge Ave UB7 . 104 B4
Park Lofts 9 SW4 . . . 160 A6
Park Lorne NW8 . . . . 230 B1
Park Mans
Battersea SW11 . . . . . 267 C1
Bedford Pk W6 . . . . . . 111 D3
Forest Hill SE26 . . . . . 162 C1
Fulham SW6 . . . . 264 B1
5 Hendon NW4 . . . . 46 B4
Knightsbridge SW1 . . . 247 C1
St John's Wood NW8 . 230 A3
Vauxhall SW8 . . . . 270 B6
Parkmead SW15 . . . . . 156 B5
Park Mead
Blackfen DA15 . . . . 168 B5
Harrow HA2 . . . . 63 D5
Parkmead Gdns NW7 . 27 D4
Park Mews
Chislehurst BR7 . . . . . 188 D4
Greenwich SE10 . . . . . 120 D1
Hornsey N8 . . . . 50 A3
Park Mews *continued*
Kensal Rise W10 . . . . . . 91 A5
Stanwell TW19 . . . . 148 B4
Parkmore BR7 . . . . 188 D3
Parkmore Cl IG8 . . . . . . 37 A6
Park Nook Gdns EN2 . . . 5 B6
Park Par Acton W3 . . . . 110 C3
Dagenham NW10 . . . . . . 89 D5
Hayes UB3 . . . . 83 C1
Kingsbury NW9 . . . . 45 B6
Park Piazza 3 SE13 . . 164 B5
Park Pl
Canary Wharf E14 . . . . 119 C5
Ealing W5 . . . . 109 D5
Gunnersbury W3 . . . . . 110 C2
Hampton TW12 . . . . . . 174 A4
Shoreditch N1 . . . . 235 D6
St James SW1 . . . . . 115 C5 249 A4
Wembley HA9 . . . . 66 B4
Park Place Dr W3 . . . . 110 C3
Park Place Ho 8 SE10 . . . . 142 B6
Park Place Villas W2 236 B4
Park Prim Sch E15 . . . . 76 D1
Park Rd
Ashford TW15 . . . . 170 D5
Beckenham BR3 . . . . . 185 C3
Bromley BR1 . . . . 187 B2
Cheam SM3 . . . . 217 A2
Chipping Barnet EN5 . . . . 1 B1
Chislehurst BR7 . . . . . 188 D4
Chiswick W4 . . . . 133 B6
Cockfosters EN4 . . . . 2 C1
Dagenham NW10 . . . . . . 89 C6
Ealing W7 . . . . 108 D6
East Finchley N2 . . . . . . 48 B6
East Molesey KT8 . . . 196 A5
Edmonton N18 . . . . 34 A6
Feltham TW13 . . . . 172 D6
Hackbridge SM6 . . . . . 219 B6
Hampton TW12 . . . . . . 174 A5
Hampton Wick KT1 . . . 175 C2
Harringay N8, N15 . . . . . 50 D5
Hayes UB4 . . . . 83 C2
Hendon NW4 . . . . 46 B3
Hornsey N8 . . . . 49 D4
Hounslow TW3, TW7 . 152 A6
Ilford IG1 . . . . 79 B5
Isleworth TW7 . . . . 131 B3
Kingsbury NW9 . . . . 45 B2
Kingston u T KT2, TW10 . . . . 176 C3
Leyton E10 . . . . 53 C1
Lisson Gr NW1, NW8 . . . . 92 C3 237 B6
Lower Halliford TW17 192 C1
Mitcham SW19 . . . . . 180 C4
Newham E15 . . . . 99 A6
New Malden KT3 . . . . . 199 B5
Osidge N14 . . . . 15 D4
Richmond TW10 . . . . . . 154 B5
South Norwood SE25 . 205 C5
Sunbury TW16 . . . . 172 B3
Teddington TW11 . . . . 174 D4
Twickenham TW1 . . . . 153 C5
Upton Pk E6 . . . . 99 C6
Uxbridge UB8 . . . . 60 A2
Wallington SM6 . . . . . . 219 B3
Walthamstow E17 . . . . . 53 B4
Wanstead E12 . . . . 77 B6
Wembley HA0 . . . . 66 A2
Wood Green N11 . . . . . . 31 D3
Park Rd E Acton W3 . . . 111 A4
Uxbridge UB10 . . . . 82 A5
Park Rd N
Chiswick W4 . . . . 111 B1
South Acton W3 . . . . . 110 D4
Park Ridings N8 . . . . . . 50 C6
Park Rise
Forest Hill SE23 . . . . . 163 A3
Harrow HA3 . . . . 24 C2
Park Rise Rd SE23 . . . 163 A3
Park Road E 11 W3 . . 110 D4
Park Road Ho 3 KT2 . . . . 176 C3
Park Row SE10 . . . . . . 142 B6
PARK ROYAL 88 D4
Park Royal NW10 . . . . . 88 D6
Park Royal Bsns Ctr NW10 . . . . 89 A3
Park Royal Metro Ctr NW10 . . . . 88 D3
Park Royal Rd NW10, W3 . . . . 89 A3
Park Royal Sta W5 . . . . 88 C3
Park S SW11 . . . . 268 A1
Park St James NW8 . 230 C5
Park Sch for Girls IG1 . . . . 56 D1
Park Sheen 3 SW14 . . . . 132 D1
Parkshot TW9 . . . . 132 A1
Parkside
1 Beckenham BR3 . . 185 D1
Cheam SM3 . . . . 217 A2
Ealing W5 . . . . 110 A6
East Acton W3 . . . . . . 111 C5
Finchley N3 . . . . 29 D3
Greenwich SE3 . . . . . . 142 D5
Hampton TW12 . . . . . . 174 A5
Hayes UB3 . . . . 105 C6
Hendon NW7 . . . . 28 A4
Sidcup DA14 . . . . 168 B2
Wimbledon SW19 . . . . 178 D6
Park Side Chigwell IG9 21 B2
Dollis Hill NW2 . . . . 68 B4
Parkside Ave
Bromley BR1 . . . . 210 A5
Wimbledon SW19 . . . 178 D5
Parkside Bsns Est SE8 . . . . 141 A6
Parkside Cl SE20 . . . . 184 C3
Parkside Cres
Highbury N7 . . . . 72 C5
Tolworth KT5 . . . . 199 A3
Parkside Ct
Bowes Pk N22 . . . . 32 B4
2 Wanstead E11 . . . . . . 55 A3
Parkside Dr HA8 . . . . . . 10 C1
Parkside Est E9 . . . . 96 D6
Parkside Gdns
East Barnet EN4 . . . . . . 15 A4
Wimbledon SW19 . . . 178 D6
Parkside Lo DA17 . . . 125 D1
Parkside Prep Sch 2 N17 . . . . 33 C2
Parkside (Private) Hospl SW19 . . . . 156 D1
Parkside Rd
Belvedere DA17 . . . . . 125 D2
Hounslow TW3 . . . . . . 151 D6
Parkside St SW11 . . . 268 A1
Parkside Terr N18 . . . . 33 B6
Parkside Way HA2 . . . . 42 A5
Park Sq E NW1 . . . . 93 B3 238 D6
Park Square Mews NW1 . . . . 238 C5
Park Sq W NW1 . . . . 93 B3 238 C5
Park St
Borough The SE1 . . . . 117 A5 252 B4
Croydon CR0 . . . . 221 A6
Mayfair W1 . 115 A6 248 A5
Teddington TW11 . . . . 174 C4
Parkstead Rd SW15 . . 156 B6
Parkstone Ave N18 . . . 33 D5
Parkstone Rd
5 Peckham SE15 . . . . 140 A3
Walthamstow E17 . . . . . 54 A6
Park Stps W2 . . . . 247 B6
Park Terr
Carshalton SM5 . . . . . 218 C5
Enfield EN3 . . . . 7 A5
New Malden KT4 . . . . . 200 A1
Park The Ealing W5 . . 109 D5
Forest Hill SE23 . . . . . 162 C3
Golders Green NW11 . . 47 D1
Highgate N6 . . . . 49 A3
Sidcup DA14 . . . . 190 A5
Wallington SM5 . . . . . 218 D3
Parkthorne Cl HA2 . . . . 41 D3
Parkthorne Dr HA2 . . . 41 D3
Parkthorne Rd SW12 . . . . 159 D4
Park Twrs W1 . . . . 248 C3
Parkview UB6 . . . . 87 A4
Park View
Dagenham W3 . . . . 89 A2
Highbury N5 . . . . 73 A4
Kingston u T KT3 . . . . 199 D6
Morden SM4 . . . . 202 B4
Pinner HA5 . . . . 23 B2
Southgate N21 . . . . 16 B4
Wembley HA9 . . . . 66 D3
Willesden NW2 . . . . 68 C4
Yiewsley UB7 . . . . 104 A6
Park View Acad N15 . . . 51 A5
Park View Cl SM5 . . . 219 A1
Parkview Cres KT4 . . 200 C1
Park View Cres N11 . . . 31 B6
Parkview Ct
Fulham SW6 . . . . 135 A3
Harrow HA3 . . . . 24 C3
Ilford IG2 . . . . 57 C3
Penge SE20 . . . . 184 B2
Twickenham TW1 . . . . 153 C4
Park View Ct
Colney Hatch N12 . . . . . 30 C6
Kingsbury NW9 . . . . 45 A5
Wandsworth SW18 . . 157 C5
Park View Dr CR4 . . . . 180 B1
Park View Gdns
Hendon NW4 . . . . 46 D4
Redbridge IG4 . . . . 56 B5
Wood Green N22 . . . . . . 32 C2
Park View Ho
Chingford E4 . . . . 35 C5
Hampton TW12 . . . . . . 174 A5
Streatham SE24 . . . . . 160 D5
Parkview Lo BR3 . . . . 207 D6
Park View Mans N4 . . . 50 D2
Park View Mews 24 SW9 . . . . 138 B3
Parkview Rd
Chislehurst SE9 . . . . . 166 D2
Croydon CR0 . . . . 206 A1
Park View Rd
Bexley DA16 . . . . 146 C2
Ealing W5 . . . . 88 A2
Finchley N3 . . . . 29 D2
Hillingdon UB8 . . . . 82 C1
Pinner HA5 . . . . 22 B3
Southall UB1 . . . . 107 C5
Tottenham N17 . . . . 34 A1
Tottenham N17 . . . . 34 B2
Willesden NW10 . . . . . . 67 D4
Park Village E NW1 . . . . 93 B5 231 D3
Park Village W NW1 . . . . 93 B5 231 C4
Park Villas RM6 . . . . 58 D3
Parkville Rd SW6 . . . . 135 B5 264 C3
Park Vista SE10 . . . . . . 142 B6
Park Vista Apartments E13 . . . . 98 D4
Park Walk Prim Sch SW10 . . . . 136 B6 266 C5
Parkwat Cres E15 . . . . . 76 A3
Parkway
Abbey Wood DA18 . . . 125 A3
Camden Town NW1 . . . . 93 B6 231 C5
Hillingdon UB10 . . . . 60 D1
Ilford IG3 . . . . 79 D5
Palmers Green N14 . . . . 16 A2
West Barnes SW20 . . . 200 D5
Woodford IG8 . . . . 37 C5
Park Way
East Molesey KT8 . . . 195 D6
Edgware HA8 . . . . 26 D2
Enfield EN2 . . . . 4 C3
Feltham TW14 . . . . 150 B4
Friern Barnet N20 . . . . . 30 D6
Gunnersbury W3 . . . . 110 C2
Ruislip HA4 . . . . 40 A1
Temple Fortune NW11 . . 47 A4
Park Way Ct HA4 . . . . . . 39 D1
Parkway Ho SW14 . . . 133 B1
Parkway Prim Sch DA18 . . . . 125 A3
Parkway The
Cranford TW5 . . . . 128 B5
Hayes UB2, UB3, UB4, TW5 . . . . 106 B3
Yeading UB4 . . . . 84 D2
Parkway Trad Est TW5 . . . . 128 C6
Park West W2 . 92 C1 237 B1
Park West Pl W1, W2 . . . . 92 C1 237 B2
Park Wlk
Chelsea SW10 . . . . . 136 B6 266 C6
Highgate N6 . . . . 49 A2
Parkwood
Beckenham BR3 . . . . . 185 C3
Primrose Hill NW8 . . . 230 C5
Parkwood Ave KT10 . . 196 A1
Parkwood Gr TW16 . . 194 A6
Parkwood Mews N6 . . 49 B3

Parkwood Prim Sch 1 N4 72 D6
Parkwood Rd
Hounslow TW7 130 D4
Old Bexley DA5 169 B4
Wimbledon SW19 179 B5
Parliament Ct NW3 70 C4
Parliament Hill NW3 70 C4
Parliament Hill Mans NW5 71 A4
Parliament Hill Sch NW5 71 A4
Parliament Mews SW14 133 A3
Parliament Sq★ SW1 116 A4 250 A1
Parliament St SW1 116 A4 250 A2
Parliament View Apartments SE11 260 C4
Parma Cres SW11 136 D1
Parminter Ind Est 24 E2 96 B5
Parmiter St E2 96 B5
Parmoor Ct EC1 242 A6
Parnall Ho 11 SE19 183 C6
Parnell Cl
Edgware HA8 27 A6
Hammersmith W12 112 B3
Parnell Ho WC1 239 D2
Parnell Rd E3 97 B6
Parnham Cl BR1 210 D6
Parnham St E14 97 A1
Parolles Rd N19 49 C1
Paroma Rd DA17 125 C3
Parr Cl N9 34 B6
Parr Ct
Feltham TW13 172 C6
Shoreditch N1 235 C4
Parrington Ho 1 SW4 159 D5
Parr Pl W4 111 D2
Parr Rd Newham E6 99 D6
Stanmore HA7 26 A2
Parr's Pl TW12 173 C3
Parr St N1 95 B5 235 C4
Parry Ave E6 100 B1
Parry Cl KT17 216 A1
Parry Ho 32 E1 118 B5
Parry Pl SE18 122 D2
Parry Rd
South Norwood SE25 205 C6
West Kilburn W10 91 A4
Parry St SW8 138 A6 270 B6
Parsifal Coll 1 NW3 69 C4
Parsifal Ho NW3 69 C4
Parsifal Rd NW6 69 C3
Parsley Gdns CR0 206 D1
Parsloes Ave RM9 81 A3
Parsloes Prim Sch RM9 81 B2
Parsonage Cl UB3 83 D1
Parsonage Ct WD6 11 A6
Parsonage Gdns EN2 5 A3
Parsonage La
Enfield EN2 5 B3
Sidcup DA14 191 B6
Parsonage Manorway DA17 147 C6
Parsonage St E14 120 A2
Parsons Cl SM1 217 D5
Parsons Cres HA8 10 C1
Parsons Gn SW6 135 C4 265 A1
PARSONS GREEN 135 C4
Parsons Green La SW6 135 C4 265 A2
Parsons Green Sta SW6 135 C4 265 A1
Parsons Hill SE18 122 C3
Parsons Ho
Paddington W2 236 C5
21 Streatham SW12 160 A4
Parsons Lo NW6 69 D1
Parsons Mead KT8 196 A6
Parson's Mead CR0 204 D1
Parsons Rd
Edgware HA8 10 C1
Newham E13 99 C5
Parson St NW4 46 C6
Parthenia Rd SW6 135 C4 265 B1
Partingdale La NW7 28 D5
Partington Cl N19 49 D1
Parton Lo 14 E8 73 D2
Partridge Cl
Barnet EN5 12 C5
Bushey WD23 8 A3
1 Newham E16 99 D2
Stanmore HA7 26 A6
Partridge Ct EC1 241 C6
Partridge Dr BR6 227 A5
Partridge Gn SE9 166 C1
Partridge Ho 22 E3 97 B5
Partridge Rd
8 Hampton TW12 173 C4
Sidcup DA14 189 C6
Partridge Sq 3 E6 100 A2
Partridge Way N22 32 A2
Pasadena Cl UB3 106 B4
Pascall Ho SE17 139 A6
Pascals Coll BR3 185 C1
Pascal St SW8 137 D5 269 D4
Pascoe Rd SE13 164 B6
Pasley Cl SE17 262 A1
Pasquier Rd E17 53 A6
Passey Pl SE9 166 B5
Passfield Dr E14 97 D2
Passfield Ho SE18 123 B2
Passfield Path 13 SE28 124 B6
Passfields
Catford SE6 164 A1
West Kensington W14 254 C1
Passing Alley EC1 241 D5
Passingham Ho TW5 129 C6
Passmore Edwards Ho N11 31 D3
Passmore Gdns N11 31 D4
Passmore Ho 12 N9 18 A1
Passmore St SW1 115 A1 258 A2
Pasters Ct EN1 17 D5
Pasteur Cl NW9 27 C1
Pasteur Gdns N18 33 A5
Paston Cl SM6 219 C5
Paston Cres SE12 165 B4
Pastor Ct N6 49 C3
Pastor St SE1, SE11 116 D2 261 D4
Pasture Cl
Bushey WD23 8 A4
Wembley HA0 65 B5
Pasture Rd
Catford SE6 164 D3
Dagenham RM9 81 B3
Wembley HA0 65 B5
Pastures Mead UB10 60 C2
Pastures Path E11 54 C1
Pastures The N20 13 B3
Patcham Terr SW8 268 D2
Patch Cl UB10 82 B6
Patching Way UB4 85 A2
Pat Drew Ho BR1 187 C2
Patent Ho E14 97 D2
Paternoster La EC4 94 D1 241 D2
Paternoster Sq EC4 94 D1 241 D2
Pater St W8 113 C3 255 A5
Pates Manor Dr TW14 149 B4
Pathfield Rd SW16 181 D4
Path The SW19 179 D2
Pathway Ho SW17 180 D4
Pathway Lo CR4 180 D2
Patience Rd SW11 136 C3
Patience Villas SE13 142 B2
Patio Cl SW4 159 D5
Patmore Ho 9 N16 73 C3
Patmore St SW8 137 C4 269 B2
Patmos Rd SW9 138 D4
Paton Cl E3 97 C4
Paton Ho 3 SW9 138 B3
Paton St EC1 235 A1
Patricia Ct
Chislehurst BR7 189 B2
Woolwich DA16 146 B5
Patrick Coman Ho EC1 234 C1
Patrick Connolly Gdns 41 E3 97 D4
Patrick Rd E13 99 C4
Patriot Sq E2 96 B5
Patrol Pl SE6 163 D5
Pat Shaw Ho 2 E1 96 D3
Patshull Pl NW5 71 C2
Patshull Rd NW5 71 C2
Patson Cl E5 74 D5
Pattenden Rd SE6 163 B3
Patten Ho N4 51 A1
Patten Rd SW18 158 C4
Patterdale NW1 231 D1
Patterdale Cl BR1 186 C4
Patterdale Rd SE15 140 C5
Patterson Ct SE19 183 D4
Patterson Rd SE19 183 D4
Pattina Wlk SE16 119 A5
Pattinson Point 10 E16 99 A2
Pattison Ho
Borough The SE1 252 B2
1 Stepney E1 96 D1
Pattison Rd NW2 69 C5
Pattison Wlk SE18 123 A1
Pat Williams Ho SE27 161 A1
Paul Byrne Ho 3 N2 48 A6
Paul Cl E15 76 C1
Paul Ct
7 Edmonton N18 34 A6
Hendon N3 29 A1
Paul Daisley Ct 2 NW6 69 A1
Paulet Rd SE5 138 D4
Paul Gdns CR0 221 D6
Paulhan Rd HA3 43 D5
Paul Ho 13 W10 91 A3
Paulin Dr N21 16 C4
Pauline Cres TW2 152 A3
Pauline Ho 21 E1 96 A2
Paulinus Cl BR5 190 C1
Paul Julius Cl E14 120 B6
Paul Robeson Cl E6 100 C4
Paulson Ho 7 IG11 78 D1
Paul St
Broadgate EC2 95 C3 243 A6
Newham E15 98 C6
Paultons Ho SW3 266 D6
Paultons Sq SW3 136 B6 266 D6
Paultons St SW3 136 B6 266 D5
Pauntley Ho 6 N19 49 C1
Pauntley St 4 N19 49 C1
Pavan Ct 29 E2 96 C4
Paved Ct 9 TW9 153 D6
Paveley Ct NW7 28 D3
Paveley Dr SW11 136 C5 267 A3
Paveley Ho N1 233 C3
Paveley St NW8 92 C3 237 B6
Pavement Mews 1 RM6 58 D2
Pavement Sq CR0 206 A1
Pavement The
Brentford W5 110 A3
Clapham SW4 137 C1
Leytonstone E11 54 A1
11 West Norwood SE27 183 A6
Pavet Cl RM10 81 D2
Pavilion Ct
Dagenham RM9 103 A6
7 Hampstead NW3 70 A4
Hampstead NW3 70 B3
3 Paddington NW6 91 C4
5 South Norwood SW16 182 B3
3 Wimbledon SW19 179 A3
Pavilion L Ctr The BR1 187 A1
Pavilion Lo HA2 42 B1
Pavilion Mans 10 SW9 138 B1
Pavilion Mews N3 29 C1
Pavilion Rd
Knightsbridge SW1 114 D3 257 D5
Redbridge IG1 56 B2
Pavilion Sq SW17 158 D1
Pavilion St SW1 257 D5
Pavilions The BR3 185 C4
Pavilion Terr
Ilford IG2 57 C4
8 North Kensington W12 90 C1
Pavilion Way
Burnt Oak HA8 27 A3
Pavilion Way *continued*
Ruislip HA4 62 C6
Pavillion Ct SW1 268 C6
Pavitt Ct NW10 68 A1
Pawleyne Cl SE20 184 C3
Pawsey Cl E13 99 A6
Pawson's Rd CR0 205 A4
Paxford Rd HA0 65 B6
Paxton Cl
Richmond TW9 132 B3
Walton-on-T KT12 194 C2
Paxton Ct
1 Forest Hill SE26 185 A6
Grove Pk SE9 165 C1
Mitcham CR4 180 D1
Paxton Ho SE17 262 B2
Paxton Pl SE27 183 C6
Paxton Prim Sch 14 SE19 183 C4
Paxton Rd
Chiswick W4 133 C6
Forest Hill SE23 163 A1
Plaistow BR1 187 A3
Tottenham N17 34 A3
Paxton Terr SW1 268 D6
Paymal Ho 33 E1 96 C2
Payne Cl IG11 79 D1
Payne Ho N1 233 D5
Paynell Ct SE3 142 C2
Payne Rd E3 97 D5
Paynesfield Ave SW14 133 B2
Paynesfield Rd WD23 8 D4
Payne St SE8 141 B6
Paynes Wlk W6 135 A6 264 A5
Payzes Gdns IG8 36 D5
Peabody Ave SW1 115 B1 258 D1
Peabody Bldgs
6 Camberwell SE5 139 B4
Walworth SE17 262 C3
Peabody Cl
Croydon CR0 206 C1
SW1 268 D6
Peabody Cotts N17 33 C2
Peabody Ct
9 Camberwell SE5 139 B4
25 Enfield EN3 7 C6
St Luke's EC1 242 B5
Peabody Est
18 Bethnal Green E2 96 B5
Borough The SE1 252 A3
Fulham SW6 135 B6 264 D6
17 Hammersmith W6 112 C1
Holborn EC1 241 B5
Lambeth SE1 251 B3
North Kensington W10 90 C2
4 Ratcliff E1 118 D6
7 St George in t East E1 118 A6
St Luke's EC1 242 B5
Strand WC2 240 C1
Streatham SE24 161 A4
Westminster SW1 259 B4
Peabody Hill SE21 161 A3
Peabody Sq SE1 251 C1
Peabody Twr EC1 242 B5
Peabody Yd N1 235 A6
Peace Cl
East Barnet N14 15 B6
Greenford UB6 86 B6
South Norwood SE25 205 C5
Peace Ct 10 NW9 46 A5
Peace Gr HA9 66 D5
Peacehaven Ct 8 N10 31 A3
Peace Pagoda★ SW3 267 D4
Peace St SE18 144 C6
Peach Ct E4 35 C6
Peaches Cl SM2 217 A1
Peaches Ct SM2 217 A1
Peach Gr E11 76 B5
Peach Rd
Feltham TW14 150 A3
London W10 91 A4
Peach Tree Ave UB7 82 B1
Peachum Rd SE3 142 D6
Peach Walk Mews 24 E3 96 D5
Peacock Ave TW14 149 B3
Peacock Cl
Dagenham RM8 80 C6
Finchley NW7 29 A5
Walthamstow E4 35 B3
Peacock Ct EN1 17 C5
Peacock Ind Est N17 33 D3
Peacock St SE17 116 D2 261 D3
Peacock Wlk E16 99 B1
Peacock Yd SE17 261 D3
Peaketon Ave IG4 55 D4
Peak Hill SE26 184 C6
Peak Hill Ave SE26 184 C6
Peak Hill Gdns SE26 184 C6
Peak Ho N4 51 A1
Peak The SE26 162 C1
Peal Gdns W13 87 A3
Peall Rd CR0 204 B3
Peall Rd Ind Est CR0 204 B3
Pearce Cl 2 CR4 181 A1
Pearcefield Ave 5 SE23 162 C3
Pearce Ho
Camden Town N19 71 C5
7 Streatham SW2 160 A4
Westminster SW1 259 D3
Pear Cl Kingsbury NW9 45 B5
New Cross Gate SE14 141 A5
Pearcroft Rd E11 76 B6
Pear Ct 21 SE15 139 D5
Peardon St SW8 137 B3
Peareswood Gdns HA7 25 D2
Pearfield Ho 1 N5 73 A3
Pearfield Rd SE23 163 A1
Pearing Cl 2 KT4 216 D6
Pearl Cl Hendon NW2 46 D2
Newham E6 100 C1
Pearl Ct 18 NW9 46 A5
Pearl Rd E17 53 C6
Pearl St E1 118 B5
Pearlstones Ct RM10 103 C6
Pearmain Cl TW17 192 D4
Pearmain Ho 9 SE13 142 A3
Pearman St SE1 116 C4 251 B1
Pear Pl SE1 251 A2
Pear Rd E11 76 C5
Pears Ave TW17 193 C6
Pearscroft Ct SW6 135 D4 265 D1
Pearscroft Rd SW6 135 D4 265 D1
Pearse St 3 SE15 139 C6
Pearson Cl Barnet EN5 1 D2
4 Camberwell SE5 139 A4
Pearson Ct SM4 201 D4
Pearson Ho SW15 134 C3
Pearson's Ave SE8, SE14 141 C4
Pearson St E2 95 D5
Pearson Way CR4 181 A2
Pears Rd TW3 130 A2
Peartree Ave SW17 158 A1
Pear Tree Ave UB7 82 B1
Peartree Cl BR2 209 D4
Pear Tree Cl
Chessington KT9 214 C3
Mitcham CR4 180 C1
23 Shoreditch E2 95 D6
Pear Tree Ct
Holborn EC1 241 B5
Putney SW15 134 B1
Woodford IG8 37 B2
Peartree Gdns RM8 80 B4
Pear Tree Ho
Brockley SE4 141 B1
Hayes UB8 83 A1
Peartree La E1 118 C6
Peartree Rd EN1 5 C2
Pear Tree Rd TW15 171 A5
Peartree St EC1 95 A3 242 A6
Peartree Way SE10 121 A2
Peary Ho 4 NW10 67 B1
Peary Pl E2 96 C4
Peaslake Ct SM2 218 A1
Peas Mead Terr E4 36 A6
Peatfield Cl DA15 167 C1
Pebworth Lo
2 Belmont SM2 217 D1
South Norwood SE25 205 D5
Pebworth Rd HA1 65 A6
Peckarmans Wood SE21, SE26 162 A1
Peckett Sq 3 N5 72 D4
Peckford Pl SW9 138 C3
PECKHAM 140 A4

Peckham Gr SE15 139 C5
Peckham High St
SE15 140 A4
Peckham Hill St
SE15 140 A5
Peckham Park Prim Sch
25 SE15 140 A5
Peckham Park Rd
SE15 140 A5
Peckham Rd SE5 139 C4
Peckham Rye
East Dulwich SE22 140 A1
Peckham SE15, SE22 140 B1
Peckham Rye Sta
SE15 140 A3
Peckwater Ho 2
NW5 71 D2
Peckwater St NW5 71 C3
Pedlars Wlk N7 72 A3
Pedley Rd RM8 58 C1
Pedley St E1 95 D3 243 D5
Pedro St E5 74 D4
Pedworth Gdns 4
SE16 118 C2
Peebles Ct UB1 86 A1
Peek Cres SW19 178 D5
Peel Centre (Metropoliton Police Training Establishment)
NW9 45 D6
Peel Cl Chingford E4 19 D2
Edmonton N9 18 A1
Peel Ct UB6 86 A4
Peel Dr Colindale NW9 45 D6
Redbridge IG5 56 A6
Peel Gr E2 96 C5
Peel Pass W8 245 A3
Peel Pl IG5 37 D1
Peel Prec NW6 91 C5
Peel Rd
Farnborough BR6 227 A3
Harrow HA3 42 D6
Wembley HA0, HA9 65 D5
Woodford E18 36 D2
Peel St W8 113 C5 245 A3
Peel Way UB8 82 A2
Peel Yates Ho 13
SE7 122 A2
Peerglow Est EN3 18 C6
Peerless St
EC1 95 B4 235 C1
Pegamoid Rd N18 18 C1
Pegasus Cl N16 73 B4
Pegasus Ct
11 Acton W3 89 A1
Brentford TW8 110 B1
6 Buckhurst Hill IG9 21 D2
College Pk NW10 90 B4
Edmonton N21 17 A4
Harrow HA3 43 D4
Kingston u T KT1 197 D6
Sutton SM1 217 D6
Pegasus Ho 9 E1 96 D3
Pegasus Lo N21 17 A4
Pegasus Pl 2 SE11 138 C6
Pegasus Rd CR0,
CR9 220 C2
Pegasus Way N11 31 B4
Peggotty Way UB8 82 D1
Pegg Rd TW5 128 D5
Peggy Quirke Ct 2
HA0 66 A2
Pegley Gdns SE12 165 A2
Pegwell Ho 19 E5 74 B3
Pegwell St SE18 145 C5
Pekin St E14 97 C1
Pekoe SE1 253 D3
Peldon Ct TW10 154 B6
Pele Ct N17 33 B3
Pelham Ave IG11 101 D6
Pelham Cl SE5 139 C2
Pelham Cotts DA5 169 D3
Pelham Cres SW7 257 A3
Pelham Ct SW3 257 A3
Pelham Ho W14 254 C3
Pelham Pl
Chelsea SW7 257 A3
8 Ealing W7 86 D3
Pelham Prim Sch
Bexleyheath DA7 147 C2
15 Merton SW19 179 C3
Pelham Rd
Bexleyheath DA7 147 C2
Ilford IG1 79 B6
Merton SW19 179 C3
Pelham Rd *continued*
Penge BR3, SE20 184 C1
Tottenham N15 51 D5
Wanstead E18 55 B6
Wood Green N22 32 C1
Pelham St
SW7 114 B2 256 D4
Pelican Ho 8 SE8 119 B2
Pelican Pas 3 E1 96 C3
Pelier St SE17 139 A6
Pelinore Rd SE6 164 C2
Pella Ho SE11 260 D2
Pellant Rd
SW6 135 A5 264 B4
Pellatt Gr N22 32 C2
Pellatt Rd
East Dulwich SE22 161 D6
Wembley HA9 66 A6
Pellerin Rd N16 73 C3
Pellew Ho 15 E1 96 B3
Pellings Cl BR2 208 C6
Pelling St E14 97 C1
Pellipar Cl N13 16 C1
Pellipar Gdns SE18 122 B1
Pellipar Rd SE18 122 B1
Pellow Cl EN5 13 B5
Pelly Ct 4 E17 54 A5
Pelly Rd E13 99 A5
Pelter St E2 95 D4
Pelton Ct CR2 221 A2
Pelton Rd SE10 120 C1
Pembar Ave E17 53 A6
Pemberley Chase
KT19 214 D3
Pemberley Cl KT19 214 D3
Pemberley Ho KT19 214 D3
Pember Rd NW10 90 D4
Pemberton Cl TW19 148 A3
Pemberton Ct 18 E1 96 D4
Pemberton Gdns
Camden Town N19 71 C5
Dagenham RM6 59 A4
Pemberton Ho SE26 184 A6
Pemberton Pl
Esher KT10 212 A5
2 Hackney E8 74 B1
Pemberton Rd
East Molesey KT8 196 A5
Harringay N4 50 D4
Pemberton Row EC4 241 B2
Pemberton Terr N19 71 C5
Pembridge Ave TW4 151 B3
Pembridge Cres
W11 113 C6 245 A6
Pembridge Gdns
W2 113 C6 245 A5
Pembridge Hall Prep Sch for Girls
W2 113 C6 245 B5
Pembridge Mews
W11 113 C6 245 A6
Pembridge Pl
Notting Hill
W2 113 C6 245 B6
1 Wandsworth
SW15 157 C6
Pembridge Rd
W11 113 C6 245 A5
Pembridge Sq
W2 113 C6 245 B5
Pembridge Villas
W11 113 C6 245 A6
Pembroke W14 254 D3
Pembroke Ave
Enfield EN1 6 B4
Harrow HA3 43 B6
Islington N1 94 A6 233 B6
Surbiton KT5 198 D4
Pembroke Bldgs
NW10 90 A4
Pembroke Cl SW1 248 B1
Pembroke Ct 11 W7 86 D2
Pembroke Gdns
Dagenham RM10 81 D5
West Kensington
W8 113 B2 254 D4
Pembroke Gdns Cl
W8 255 A5
Pembroke Hall NW4 46 C6
Pembroke Ho
Acton W3 111 A4
Chelsea SW1 258 A5
5 Clapham Pk SW2 160 A6
17 Kensington W2 91 D1
Putney SW15 156 A6
Upper Tooting SW17 180 B5
Pembroke Lo 2
SW16 160 B1
Pembroke Mews
8 Bow E3 97 A4
Kensington W8 255 A5
Muswell Hill N10 31 A2
Pembroke Pl
Edgware HA8 26 C3
Isleworth TW7 130 C3
Kensington W8 255 A5
Pembroke Rd
Bromley BR1 187 D1
Edmonton N13 17 A1
Greenford UB6 85 D3
Hornsey N8 50 A5
Ilford IG3 57 D2
Kensington
W8 113 C2 255 A4
Mitcham CR4 181 A1
Muswell Hill N10 31 A3
Newham E6 100 B2
Ruislip HA4 39 D1
South Norwood SE25 205 C5
South Tottenham N15 51 D4
Walthamstow E17 53 D4
Wembley HA9 65 D5
Pembroke Sq
W8 113 C3 255 A5
Pembroke St
N1 94 A6 233 B6
Pembroke Studios
W8 254 D5
Pembroke Terr NW8 229 C5
Pembroke Villas
Kensington W8 255 A4
Richmond TW9 131 D1
Pembroke Way UB3 105 A3
Pembroke Wlk W8 255 A4
Pembry Cl SW9 138 C4
Pembury Ave KT4 200 A2
Pembury Cl
Hackney E5 74 B3
Hayes BR2 208 D2
Pembury Cres DA14 169 A2
Pembury Ct UB3 127 B6
Pembury Ho
Camberwell SE5 139 C3
Keston Mark BR2 210 A1
Pembury Pl 15 E5, E8 74 B3
Pembury Rd
Croydon SE25 206 A5
Erith DA7 147 A6
Hackney E5 74 B3
Tottenham N17 33 D1
Pemdevon Rd CR0 204 C2
Pemell Cl 30 E1 96 C3
Pemell Ho 31 E1 96 C3
Pemerich Cl UB3 105 D1
Pempath Pl HA9 65 D6
Penair Lodge HA1 64 C5
Penally Pl N1 235 D6
Penang St E1 118 B5
Penard Rd UB2 107 D3
Penarth Ct SM2 218 A1
Penarth Ctr The
SE15 140 C6
Penarth St SE15 140 C6
Penates KT10 212 B4
Penberth Rd SE6 164 A3
Penbury Rd UB2 107 B1
Penceat Ct SE20 184 C1
Pencombe Mews
W11 244 D6
Pencraig Way SE15 140 B6
Pendall Cl EN4 2 C1
Penda Rd DA8 147 D5
Pendarves Rd SW20 178 C2
Penda's Mead E9 75 A4
Pendell Ave UB3 127 D5
Pendennis Ho 15
SE8 119 A2
Pendennis Rd
Streatham SW16 182 A6
Tottenham N17 51 B6
Penderel Rd TW3 151 C6
Penderry Rise SE6 164 B2
Penderyn Way N7 71 D4
Pendlebury Ho 5
SE18 144 A4
Pendle Ho 13 SE26 162 A1
Pendle Rd SW16 181 B5
Pendlestone Rd E17 53 D4
Pendlewood Cl 13
W5 87 C2
Pendley Ho 18 E2 96 A6
Pendolino Way NW10 66 D1
Pendragon Rd BR1 165 A1
Pendragon Sch BR1 165 A1
Pendragon Wlk NW9 45 C3
Pendrell Ho WC2 239 D1
Pendrell Rd SE4 141 A3
Pendrell St SE18 145 B6
Pendula Dr UB4 84 D3
Penelope Ho 20
SW9 138 C4
Penerley Rd SE6 163 D3
Penfield Lo 7 W9 91 C2
Penfields Ho N7 72 A2
Penfold Cl CR0 220 C5
Penfold Ct 7 CR4 181 A1
Penfold Ho 14 SE18 144 D6
Penfold La DA5 168 D3
Penfold Pl
NW1 92 C2 237 A4
Penfold Rd N9 18 D3
Penfold St
NW8 92 B3 236 D5
Penford Gdns SE9 143 D2
Penford St SE5 138 D3
Pengarth Rd DA5 168 D5
PENGE 184 D4
Penge East Sta
SE20 184 C4
Penge La SE20 184 D3
Penge Rd
Newham E13 99 C6
South Norwood SE25 206 A6
Penge West Sta
SE20 184 B4
Penhall Rd SE7 121 D2
Penhill Rd DA5 168 C4
Penhurst Mans SW6 264 C2
Penifather La UB6 86 B4
Peninsula Ct E14 119 D3
Peninsular Cl TW14 149 C5
Peninsular Park Rd
SE7 121 A2
Penistone Rd SW16 182 A3
Penketh Dr HA1 64 B5
Penmayne Ho SE11 261 B2
Penmon Rd SE2 124 A3
Pennack Rd SE15 139 D6
Penn Almshouses 1
SE10 142 A4
Pennant Mews
W8 113 D2 255 C4
Pennant Terr E17 35 B1
Pennard Mans 5
W12 112 C4
Pennard Rd W12 112 C4
Pennards The TW16 194 C6
Penn Cl
Greenford UB6 85 D5
Harrow HA3 43 C5
Penn Ct NW9 45 B6
Pennefather Ho N1 73 B2
Pennells Ct TW5 129 C6
Penner Cl SW19 157 A2
Penners Gdns KT6 198 A2
Pennethorne Cl E9 96 C6
Pennethorne Ho
SW11 136 B2
Pennethorne Rd
SE15 140 B5
Penn Gdns BR7 188 D1
Penn Ho
7 Edmonton N9 18 A1
Lisson Gr NW8 237 A5
Pennine Dr NW2 68 D6
Pennine La NW2 69 A6
Pennine Mans NW2 69 A6
Pennine Par NW2 69 A6
Pennine Way UB7 127 B5
Pennington Cl 10
SE27 183 B6
Pennington Ct
4 Rotherhithe
SE16 119 A5
23 St George in t East
E1 118 A6
Pennington Dr N21 16 A6
Pennington Lo 18
KT5 198 A4
Pennington St E1 118 B6
Pennington Way
SE12 165 B2
Penniston Cl N17 33 A1
Penniwell Cl HA8 26 B6
Penn La Bexley DA5 168 D5
Sidcup DA5 169 A5
Penn Rd N7 72 A4
Penn St N1 95 B6 235 D5
Penny Ct SW10 266 B6
Pennyfields E14 119 C6
Pennyford Ct NW8 236 C6
Penny La TW17 193 C2
Penny Mews SW12 159 B4
Pennymore Wlk W9 91 B3
Penny Rd NW10 88 D4
Penny Royal SM6 219 D2
Pennyroyal Ave E6 100 C1
Penpoll Rd E8 74 B2
Penpool La DA16 146 B2
Penray EN5 1 A2
Penrhyn Ave E17 35 C2
Penrhyn Cres
Mortlake SW14 133 A1
Walthamstow E17 35 C2
Penrhyn Gdns KT1 197 D5
Penrhyn Gr E17 35 C2
Penrhyn Rd KT1 198 A6
Penrith Cl
Beckenham BR3 185 D2
Putney SW15 157 A6
Penrith Pl SE27 160 D2
Penrith Rd
New Malden KT3 199 B5
South Norwood CR7 183 A1
Tottenham N15 51 B4
Penrith St SW16 181 C4
Penrose Gr
SE17 117 A1 262 A1
Penrose Ho
Camberwell SE17 262 A1
Southgate N21 16 B6
Penrose St
SE17 117 A1 262 A1
Penryn Ho SE11 261 C2
Penryn St
NW1 93 D5 232 C4
Penry St SE1 263 B3
Pensbury Pl SW8 137 C3
Pensbury St SW8 137 C3
Pensford Ave TW9 132 C3
Penshurst 2 NW5 71 A2
Penshurst Ave DA15 168 A5
Penshurst Ct
Croydon CR2 220 D1
1 Edgware HA8 26 D5
Penshurst Gdns HA8 26 D5
Penshurst Gn BR2 208 D4
Penshurst Ho 1
SE15 140 C6
Penshurst Rd
Erith DA7 147 B4
Homerton E9 74 D1
Thornton Heath CR7 204 D4
Tottenham N17 33 D3
Penshurst Way SM2 217 C1
Penshurst Wlk 4
BR2 208 D4
Pensilver Cl EN4 2 C1
Penstemon Cl N3 29 C4
Pentavia Retail Pk
NW7 27 D3
Pentelow Gdns
TW14 150 A5
Pentire Rd E17 36 B2
Pentland Ave
Edgware HA8 10 D2
Littleton TW17 192 C4
Pentland Cl
Cricklewood NW11 69 A6
Lower Edmonton N9 18 C2
Pentland Gdns
SW18 158 A5
Pentland Ho
17 Camden Town
NW5 71 A2
7 Stamford Hill N16 51 D1
Pentland Pl UB5 85 A6
Pentland Rd
Bushey WD23 8 A5
1 Maida Vale NW6 91 C4
Pentlands BR3 186 A2
Pentlands Cl CR4 203 B6
Pentland St SW18 158 A5
Pentland Way UB10 61 A5
Pentlow St SW15 134 C2
Pentney Rd
5 Chingford E4 20 B3
Merton SW19, SW20 179 A2
Streatham SW12 159 C3
Penton Gr N1 234 A3

Penton Ho
3 Abbey Wood SE2 124 D4
Islington N1 234 A3
Sutton SM2 218 A1
Penton Pl SE17 116 D1 261 D2
Penton Rise WC1 94 B4 233 D2
Penton St N1 94 C5 234 A3
PENTONVILLE 94 B5
Pentonville Rd WC1 94 B5 233 C3
Pentrich Ave EN1 6 A5
Pentridge St SE15 139 D5
Pentyre Ave N18 33 B5
Penwerris Ave TW5, TW7 130 A5
Penwerris Ct TW7 130 A5
Penwith Rd SW18 157 D2
Penwood Ct HA5 41 B5
Penwood Ho SW15 155 D5
Penwortham Ct 1 N22 32 C1
Penwortham Prim Sch SW17 181 B4
Penwortham Rd SW16 181 C4
Penylan Pl HA8 26 C3
Penywern Rd SW5 113 C1 255 B2
Penzance Ho SE11 261 B2
Penzance Pl W11 113 A5 244 B4
Penzance St W11 113 A5 244 A4
Peony Ct IG8 36 C3
Peony Gdns W12 112 A6
Peperfield WC1 233 C1
Pepler Ho 17 W10 91 A3
Pepler Mews SE1 263 C1
Peploe Rd NW6 90 D5
Pepper Cl E6 100 B2
Peppercorn Cl CR7 183 B1
Peppermead Sq SE13 163 C6
Peppermint Cl CR0 204 A2
Peppermint Pl 7 E11 76 C5
Pepper St
Borough The SE1 252 A2
Millwall E14 119 D3
Peppie Cl N16 73 C6
Pepys Cl UB10 60 D4
Pepys Cres
Barnet EN5 12 C6
2 Newham E16 121 A5
Pepys Ct SW20 178 C1
Pepys Ent Ctr 13 SE8 119 B2
Pepys Ho
14 Bethnal Green E2 96 C4
Clapham Pk SW4 159 D6
Pepys Rd
New Cross Gate SE14 140 D3
Wimbledon SW20 178 C2
Pepys Rise BR6 211 D1
Pepys St EC3 117 C6 253 B6
Perak Ct KT5 199 A2
Peralte Terr CR4 204 A5
Perceval Ave NW3 70 C3
Perceval Ct UB5 63 C3
Percheron Cl TW7 130 D2
Percheron Ct 3 SW9 138 B2
Percheron Rd WD6 11 B5
Perch St E8 73 D4
Percival Ct N17 33 D3
Percival Gdns RM6 58 C3
Percival Ho 3 IG8 37 A6
Percival Rd Enfield EN1 5 D1
Feltham TW13 149 D2
Mortlake SW14 133 A1
Orpington BR6 226 D6
Percival St EC1 94 D4 234 D1
Percival Way KT19 215 B4
Percy Ave TW15 170 C5
Percy Bilton Ct TW5 129 D4
Percy Bryant Rd TW16 171 C3
Percy Bush Rd UB7 104 B3
Percy Cir WC1 94 B4 233 D2
Percy Ct 1 KT5 198 B3
Percy Gdns
Enfield EN3 18 D6
Hayes UB4 83 C4
5 Isleworth TW7 131 A2
New Malden KT4 199 C1
Percy Ho 4 SW16 181 C6
Percy Laurie Ho 6 SW15 134 D1
Percy Mews W1 239 C3
Percy Pas W1 239 C3
Percy Rd
Bexleyheath DA7 147 A3
Carshalton CR4 203 A2
Croydon SE25 206 A4
Edmonton N21 17 A4
Hampton TW12 173 C3
Ilford IG3 58 A2
Isleworth TW7 131 A1
Leytonstone E11 54 C2
Newham E16 98 C2
North Finchley N12 30 A5
Penge SE20 184 D2
Romford RM7 59 D6
Shepherd's Bush W12 112 A4
Twickenham TW2 152 A3
Percy St W1 93 D2 239 C3
Percy Terr BR1 210 D6
Percy Way TW2 152 A3
Peregrine Cl NW10 67 B3
Peregrine Ct
Bexley DA16 145 D4
Streatham SW16 182 B6
Peregrine Gdns CR0 223 A6
Peregrine Ho
6 Battersea SW11 136 C2
Finsbury EC1 234 D2
Peregrine Rd
Sunbury TW16 171 D1
Tottenham N17 33 B3
Peregrine Way SW19, SW20 178 C3
Perham Rd W14 113 A1 254 B1
Peridot St E6 100 A2
Perifield SE21 161 A3
Perimeade Rd UB6 87 C5
Period Wks E10 53 A1
Periton Rd SE9 143 D1
PERIVALE 87 B5
Perivale UB6 86 D5
Perivale Gdns W13 87 B3
Perivale Grange UB6 87 A4
Perivale Ind Pk UB6 87 B5
Perivale La UB6 87 A4
Perivale Lo UB6 87 A4
Perivale New Bsns Ctr UB6 87 C5
Perivale Pk Athletics Tk UB6 86 C4
Perivale Prim Sch UB6 87 C5
Perivale Sta UB6 87 A5
Periwood Cres UB6 87 A6
Perkin Cl
Hounslow TW3 129 D1
Wembley HA0 65 B3
Perkins Ct TW15 170 B5
Perkins Ho 15 E14 97 B2
Perkins Rd IG2 57 B4
Perkins Rents SW1 259 C5
Perkins Sq SE1 252 B4
Perks Cl SE3 142 C2
Perley Ho 9 E3 97 B2
Perotti Ho SW6 135 D2
Perpins Rd SE9 167 C5
Perran Rd SE24, SW2 160 D2
Perren St NW5 71 B2
Perrers Rd W6 112 B2
Perrin Cl TW15 170 B5
Perrin Ct TW15 170 C6
Perring Est E3 97 C2
Perrin Grange HA9 66 B6
Perrin Rd HA0 65 B4
Perrins Ct HA3 44 B2
Perrin's Ct 20 NW3 70 A4
Perrin's La NW3 70 A4
Perrin's Wlk NW3 70 A4
Perronet Ho SE1 261 D5
Perry Ave W3 89 B1
Perry Cl UB8 82 D1
Perry Ct
6 Isle of Dogs E14 119 C1
2 Kingston u T KT2 176 A1
Perry Ct *continued*
Sutton SM1 217 C3
2 Tottenham N15 51 C3
Perryfield Way
Richmond TW10 153 B2
West Hendon NW9 45 D3
Perry Garth UB5 84 C6
Perry Gdns N9 17 C1
Perry Hall Prim Sch BR6 211 D3
Perry Hill SE6 163 B1
Perry Ho 24 SW2 160 A4
Perry How KT4 199 D1
Perryman Ho
Barking IG11 101 A6
Tottenham N17 34 B3
Perrymans Farm Rd IG2 57 B4
Perry Mead
Bushey WD23 8 A5
Enfield EN2 4 D3
Perrymead St SW6 135 D4 265 C1
Perrymount Prim Sch 5 SE23 162 D2
Perryn Ct 1 TW1 153 A4
Perryn Ho W3 111 C6
Perryn Rd Acton W3 111 B6
1 Bermondsey SE16 118 B3
Perry Rd RM9 103 B2
Perry Rise SE23 163 A1
Perry's Pl W1 239 C2
Perry St BR7 189 C4
Perry Street Gdns BR7 189 C4
Perry Vale SE23 162 D2
Perrywood Ho 17 E5 74 B3
Persant Rd SE6 164 C2
Perseverance Pl SW9 138 C5
Perseverance Works 17 E2 95 C4
Pershore Cl IG2 56 D4
Pershore Gr SM5 202 B3
Pershore Ho 11 W13 109 A5
Pert Cl N10 31 B4
Perth Ave Hayes UB4 84 C3
Kingsbury NW9 45 B2
Perth Cl Northolt UB5 63 C3
Wimbledon SW20 178 A1
Perth Ct 5 SE5 139 B1
Perth Ho 12 Acton W3 88 C1
Barnsbury N1 72 B1
Perth Rd
Barking IG11 101 B6
Beckenham BR3 186 A1
Finsbury Pk N4 50 C1
Ilford IG2 56 D3
Newham E13 99 B5
Tottenham N22 32 D2
Walthamstow E10 53 B1
Perth Terr IG2 57 A2
Perwell Ave HA2 41 B1
Perystreete SE23 162 C2
Petavel Rd TW11 174 C4
Petchey Acad The E8 73 D3
Peter Ave NW10 68 B1
Peter Best Ho 1 E1 96 B1
Peterboat Cl SE10 120 C2
Peterborough Ct EC4 241 B1
Peterborough Gdns IG1 56 A2
Peterborough Mews SW6 135 C3
Peterborough Rd
Carshalton SM5 202 C3
Fulham SW6 135 C2
Harrow HA1 42 D2
Leytonstone E10 54 B3
Peterborough & St Margarets High Sch HA7 8 C1
Peterborough Villas SW6 265 C2
Peter Bradley Ct RM9 81 B1
Peter Butler Ho 9 SE1 118 A4
Peterchurch Ho SE15 140 B6
Peter Fagan Ho UB3 105 C3
Petergate SW11 136 A1
Peterhead Ct 12 UB1 86 A1
Peter Heathfield Ho 4 E15 98 B6
Peter Hills Ho 6 SE16 118 A2
Peter Hills Sch 29 SE16 118 D5
Peter Ho SW8 270 A4
Peter James Bsns Ctr UB3 106 A4
Peter James Ent Ctr NW10 89 A4
Peter Kennedy Ct CR0 207 B3
Peterley Bsns Ctr 21 E2 96 B5
Peter Lyell Ct HA4 62 B6
Peters Cl
Bexley DA16 145 C3
Dagenham RM8 58 D1
Stanmore HA7 25 D4
Peters Ct 9 W2 91 D1
Peter's Ct SW4 160 A5
Petersfield Cl N18 33 A5
Petersfield Rd W3 111 A4
Petersfield Rise SW15 156 B3
PETERSHAM 154 A3
Petersham Cl
Richmond TW10 153 D2
Sutton SM1 217 C3
Petersham Dr BR5 190 A1
Petersham Gdns BR5 189 D1
Petersham Ho SW7 256 C4
Petersham La SW7 256 A6
Petersham Mews SW7 114 A3 256 B5
Petersham Pl SW7 114 A3 256 B6
Petersham Rd TW10 154 A3
Petersham Terr CR0 220 A5
Peter's La EC1 241 D4
Peter's Lo HA8 26 B4
Peter's Path SE26 184 B6
Peter St W1 115 D6 249 C6
Peterstone Rd SE2 124 B4
Peterstow Cl SW19 157 A2
Peterwood Pk CR9 220 B6
Peterwood Way CR0 220 B6
Petherton Ct
Brondesbury Pk NW10 90 D6
10 Harrow HA1 42 D3
Petherton Ho N4 51 A1
Petherton Rd N5 73 A3
Petiver Cl 26 E9 74 C1
Petley Rd W6 134 D5
Peto Pl NW1 238 D6
Peto St N E16 98 D1
Petrel Ct 8 SE21 161 B2
Petrie Cl NW2 69 A2
Petrie Ho 3 SE18 144 C6
Petrie Mus of Egyptian Archaeology★ WC1 93 D3 239 C5
Petros Gdns 1 NW3 70 A2
Pettacre Cl SE28 123 A3
Petticoat Lane Mkt★ EC2 95 D2 243 C3
Petticoat Sq E1 243 C2
Petticoat Twr E1 243 C2
Pettit's Pl RM10 81 C3
Pettit's Rd RM10 81 C3
Pettiward Cl SW15 134 C1
Pettman Cres SE18, SE28 123 B3
Pettsgrove Ave HA0 65 C3
Pett's Hill UB5 63 D3
Petts Hill Prim Sch UB5 63 D3
Petts La TW17 192 C5
Pett St SE18 122 A2
PETTS WOOD 211 B5
Petts Wood Rd BR5 211 B4
Petts Wood Sta BR5 211 A4
Petty France SW1 115 D3 259 C6
Petty Wales EC3 253 B5
Petworth Cl UB5 63 B1
Petworth Gdns
Hillingdon UB10 83 A6
West Barnes SW20 200 B6
Petworth Ho 16 SE22 139 C2
Petworth Rd
Bexley DA6 169 C6
Colney Hatch N12 30 C5
Petworth St SW11 136 C4 267 B2
Petyt Pl SW3 136 C6 267 A5
Petyward SW3 114 C2 257 B3
Pevensey Ave
Enfield EN1 5 C3
Friern Barnet N11 31 D5
Pevensey Cl TW7 130 A5
Pevensey Ct
4 South Acton W3 110 D4
West Norwood SW16 160 C1
10 Woodford E18 37 A2
Pevensey Ho 5 E1 97 A2
Pevensey Rd
Feltham TW13 151 A3
Forest Gate E7 77 A4
Upper Tooting SW17 180 B6
Peverel E6 100 C1
Peverel Ho RM10 81 C6
Peverett Cl N11 31 B5
Peveril Dr TW11 174 B5
Peveril Ho SE1 262 D5
Pewsey Cl E4 35 C5
Pewsham Ho N4 51 A1
Pewterers Ct N3 29 B2
Peyton Ho N11 31 A6
Peyton Pl SE10 142 A5
Pharamond NW2 68 D2
Pharaoh Cl CR4 202 D2
Pheasant Cl E16 99 B1
Phelps Ho 11 SW15 134 D2
Phelp St SE17 139 B6
Phelps Way UB3 105 D2
Phene St SW3 136 C6 267 B6
Philadelphia Ct SW10 266 B3
Philbeach Gdns SW5 113 C1 255 A2
Phil Brown Pl 3 SW8 137 B2
Philchurch Pl 36 E1 96 A1
Philia Ho 4 NW1 71 C1
Philimore Cl SE18 123 C1
Philip Blairman Ho E1 243 C5
Philip Ct Enfield EN2 5 B4
Paddington W2 236 C4
Philip Gdns CR0 223 B6
Philip Ho
East Barnet N20 14 D2
12 Paddington NW6 91 D6
Philip La N15 51 C6
Philipot Almshouse SE9 166 B5
Philipot Path SE9 166 B5
Philippa Gdns SE9 165 D6
Philips Cl CR4 203 A1
Philip St E13 99 A3
Philip Turner Est 28 E9 74 C1
Philip Wlk SE15 140 A2
Phillimore Ct W8 245 B1
Phillimore Gardens Cl W8 113 C3 255 A6
Phillimore Gdns
Kensington W8 113 C4 245 A1
Willesden NW10 90 C6
Phillimore Pl W8 113 C4 245 A1
Phillimore Terr W8 255 B6
Phillimore Wlk W8 113 C3 255 B6
Phillip Ho E1 243 D3
Phillipp St N1 95 C6
Phillips Ct
Edgware HA8 26 C4
Hayes UB4 84 B4
Phillipson Ho 6 N12 29 D5
Philpot La EC3 253 A6
Philpot Sq SW6 135 D2
Philpot St E1 96 B1
Philson Mans 13 E1 96 B1
Phineas Pett Rd SE9 144 A2
Phipp's Bridge Rd CR4, SW19 202 B6
Phipps Bridge Sta CR4 202 B6
Phipps Hatch La EN2 5 A5
Phipps Ho
1 Greenwich SE7 121 B1

Phipps Ho *continued*
16 Shepherd's Bush W12 . . . . . 112 B6
Phipp St EC2 . . 95 C3 243 A6
Phoebeth Rd SE4 . . . . 163 C6
Phoenix Acad 2 N9 . . 18 B3
Phoenix Bsns Ctr 22 E3 . . . . . 97 C2
Phoenix Cl
18 Shoreditch E8 . . . . . 95 D6
Walthamstow E17 . . . . . 35 B1
West Wickham BR4 . . 224 C6
Phoenix Ct
4 Brentford TW8 . . . 110 A1
Chingford E4 . . . . 19 D1
Croydon SE25 . . . . . . 206 A4
2 Deptford SE14 . . . 141 A6
Enfield EN3 . . . . 6 C5
Feltham TW13 . . . . . . 171 C6
Millwall E14 . . . . 119 C2
8 New Barnet EN5 . . . . . 2 A1
Phoenix Ctr The 1 SM6 . . . . 220 A1
Phoenix Dr BR2 . . . . 225 D5
Phoenix High Sch W12 . . . . 112 A6
Phoenix Ho
Chelsea SW1 . . . . . . 258 A4
Kingston u T KT3 . . . . 199 D6
Phoenix Ind Est HA1 . . 42 D5
Phoenix Lodge Mans 1 W6 . . . . 112 C2
Phoenix Pk NW2 . . . . . 68 A6
Phoenix Pl WC1 . . . . 94 B3 240 D6
Phoenix Rd
Penge SE20 . . . . 184 C4
Somers Town NW1 . . . . . . 93 D4 232 C2
Phoenix Sch The 12 NW3 . . . . 70 A2
Phoenix Sec & Prim Sch 26 E3 . . . . 97 B4
Phoenix St WC2 . . . . . . 239 D1
Phoenix Trad Est UB6 . . . . 87 D6
Phoenix Trad Pk TW8 . . . . 109 D1
Phoenix Way TW5 . . . 128 D6
Phoenix Wharf Rd SE1 . . . . 253 D1
Phyllis Ave KT3 . . . . . . 200 B4
Phyllis Ho CR0 . . . . . . 220 D4
Phyllis Hodges Ho NW1 . . . . 93 D5 232 C3
Physic Pl SW3 . . . . . . 136 D6 267 C6
Picador Ho 1 RM10 . . 81 D2
Picardy Manorway DA17 . . . . 125 D4
Picardy Rd DA17 . . . . . 125 C2
Picardy St DA17 . . . . . 125 C3
Piccadilly W1 . . . . 115 C5 249 A4
Piccadilly Arc SW1 . . 249 A4
Piccadilly Cir★ W1 . . . . . . 115 D6 249 C5
Piccadilly Circus Sta SW1 . . . . . . 115 D6 249 C5
Piccadilly Ct 5 N7 . . . . 72 B2
Piccadilly Pl W1 . . . . . 249 B5
Pickard Cl N14 . . . . 15 D3
Pickard St EC1 . . . . . . 234 D2
Pickering Ave E6 . . . . 100 C4
Pickering Cl E9 . . . . 74 D1
Pickering Ct N22 . . . . . 32 D2
Pickering Gdns
Croydon SE25 . . . . 205 D3
Friern Barnet N11 . . . . . 31 A4
Pickering Ho
Brentford W5 . . . . 109 C2
18 Kensington W2 . . . . . 91 D1
Stoke Newington N4 . . . 51 B2
4 Woolwich SE18 . . . 122 C2
Pickering Mews 9 W2 . . . . 91 D1
Pickering Pl SW1 . . . 249 B3
Pickering St N1 . . . . . 234 D6
Pickets Cl WD23 . . . . 8 C3
Pickets St SW12 . . . . . 159 B4
Pickett Croft HA7 . . . . . 25 D2
Pickett's Lock La N9 . . 18 D2
Pickford Cl DA7 . . . . . . 147 A3
Pickford La DA7 . . . . . . 147 A3
Pickford Rd DA7 . . . . . . 147 A2
Pickfords Wharf N1 . 235 A3
Pickhurst Gn BR2 . . . 208 D2
Pickhurst Inf Sch BR2 . . . . 208 D3
Pickhurst Jun Sch BR2 . . . . 208 D3
Pickhurst La BR2, BR3, BR4 . . . . 208 C2
Pickhurst Mead BR2 . . . . 208 D2
Pickhurst Pk BR2 . . . 208 D4
Pickhurst Rise BR4 . . 208 B1
Pickwick Cl TW4 . . . . . 151 A6
Pickwick Ct SE9 . . . . . 166 B3
Pickwick Ho
21 Bermondsey SE16 . . . . 118 A4
3 Shepherd's Bush W11 . . . . 112 D5
Pickwick Mews N18 . . 33 C5
Pickwick Pl HA1 . . . . . . 42 C2
Pickwick Rd SE21 . . . . 161 C4
Pickwick St SE1 . . . . . 252 A1
Pickwick Way BR7 . . . 189 A4
Pickworth Cl SW8 . . . 270 B3
Picton Ho 1 SW4 . . . . 160 A4
Picton Pl
Marylebone W1 . . . . . 238 B1
Tolworth KT6 . . . . 198 C1
Picton St SE5 . . . . 139 B5
Picture Ho 6 SW16 . . 160 A2
Pied Bull Ct WC1 . . . . 240 B3
Pied Bull Yd WC1 . . . . 240 B3
Piedmont Rd SE18 . . . 123 B1
Pield Heath Ave UB8 . . 82 C3
Pield Heath Rd UB8 . . . 82 B3
Pield Heath Sch UB8 . . 82 A3
Pier Head E1 . . . . 118 B5
Pierhead Wharf 37 E1 . . . . 118 B5
Pier Ho SW3 . . . . 267 B5
Piermont Pl BR1 . . . . . 188 A1
Piermont Rd SE22 . . . 162 B6
Pier Par 3 E16 . . . . . . 122 C5
Pierpoint Bldg 4 E14 . . . . 119 C4
Pier Rd
Feltham TW14 . . . . 150 B6
Newham E16 . . . . 122 C4
Pierrepoint SE25 . . . . 205 C6
Pierrepoint Rd W3 . . 110 D6
Pierrepoint Row N1 . 234 C4
Pierson Ho 12 SE19 . . 183 C6
Pier St E14 . . . . 120 A2
Pier Terr SW18 . . . . 136 A1
Pier Way SE18 . . . . 123 B3
Pigeon Ct E4 . . . . 36 A4
Pigeon La TW12 . . . . . 173 C6
Piggott Ho 2 E2 . . . . . . 96 D5
Pigott St E14 . . . . 97 C1
Pike Cl Bromley BR1 . . . 187 B5
Hillingdon UB10 . . . . 82 B6
Pike Rd NW7 . . . . 27 B6
Pike's End HA5 . . . . 40 B5
Pikestone Cl UB4 . . . . . 85 A3
Pikethorne 1 SE23 . . 162 D2
Pilgrimage St SE1 . . . . 117 B4 252 C1
Pilgrim Cl SM4 . . . . . . 201 D2
Pilgrim Hill SE27 . . . . . 183 A6
Pilgrim Ho SE1 . . . . . . 262 D5
Pilgrims Cl
Northolt UB5 . . . . 64 A3
Palmers Green N13 . . . . 32 B6
Pilgrims Cloisters 10 SE5 . . . . 139 C5
Pilgrims Ct Enfield EN1 . . 5 B3
Greenwich SE3 . . . . . 143 A4
Pilgrim's La NW3 . . . . . 70 B4
Pilgrims Mews 12 E14 . . . . 120 B6
Pilgrim's Pl 6 NW3 . . . 70 B4
Pilgrim's Rise EN4 . . . . 14 C6
Pilgrim St EC4 . . . . . . 241 C1
Pilgrims Way
5 Newham E6 . . . . . 100 A6
Upper Holloway N19 . . . 49 D1
Wembley HA9 . . . . 44 D1
Pilgrim's Way CR2 . . 221 D3
Pilgrims Way Prim Sch 22 SE15 . . . . 140 C6
Pilkington Ct 1 NW9 . 46 A5
Pilkington Rd
Orpington BR6 . . . . . . 227 A6
4 Peckham SE15 . . . . . 140 B3
Pillions La UB4 . . . . 83 B3
Pilot Ind Ctr NW10 . . . . 89 C3
Pilsden Cl SW19 . . . . 156 D3
Piltdown Rd WD19 . . . . 22 D6
Pilton Est The CR0 . . 220 D6
Pilton Pl SE17 . . . . . . 262 B2
Pimento Ct W5 . . . . . 109 D3
Pimlico Sta SW1 . . . . . . 115 D1 259 C2
PIMLICO 115 C1
Pimlico Acad SW1 . . . . 115 C1 259 B1
Pimlico Rd SW1 . . . . 115 A1 258 B2
Pimlico Wlk 1 N1 . . . . 95 C4
Pinchbeck Rd BR6 . . 227 D2
Pinchin St E1 . . . . 118 A6
Pincombe Ho SE17 . . 262 C2
Pincott Pl SE4 . . . . . . 140 D2
Pincott Rd
7 Bexley DA6 . . . . . . 147 C1
Merton SW19 . . . . 180 A2
Pindar St EC2 . . 95 C2 243 A4
Pindock Mews W9 . . . . 91 D3
Pine Apple Ct SW1 . . 259 A6
Pine Ave
Stratford New Town E15 . . . . 76 B3
West Wickham BR4 . . 207 D1
Pine Cl
11 Dartmouth Pk N19 . . . . 71 C6
London E10 . . . . 75 D6
Osidge N14 . . . . 15 C4
3 Penge SE20 . . . . . 184 C2
Stanmore HA7 . . . . 25 B6
Pine Coombe CR0 . . 222 D4
Pinecrest Gdns BR6 . 226 D4
Pinecroft
East Wickham DA16 . . 146 A5
Harrow HA3 . . . . 44 B4
Pinecroft Cres EN5 . . . . 1 A1
Pine Ct UB5 . . . . 85 A4
Pinedene 2 SE15 . . . . 140 B4
Pinefield Cl E14 . . . . . 119 C6
Pine Gdns Ruislip HA4 . . 62 B6
Surbiton KT5 . . . . 198 C3
Pine Glade BR6 . . . . . . 226 B4
Pine Gr
Finsbury Pk N4, N19 . . . . 72 B6
Totteridge N20 . . . . 13 C3
Wimbledon SW19 . . . . 179 B5
Pine Ho Bow E3 . . . . 97 A6
21 Rotherhithe SE16 . 118 C4
Pinehurst
Chislehurst BR7 . . . . . 188 D4
Stanmore HA7 . . . . 25 A5
Pinehurst Ct 6 W11 . . 91 B1
Pinehurst Wlk 4 BR6 . . . . 211 B1
Pinelands Cl 7 SE3 . 142 D5
Pine Lo SW15 . . . . 157 A5
Pinemartin Cl NW2 . . . 68 C5
Pine Pl UB4 . . . . 83 D3
Pine Rd
Brunswick Pk N11 . . . . . 15 A2
Cricklewood NW2 . . . . . . 68 D4
Pine Ridge SM5 . . . . . . 219 A1
Pines Ct 14 SW19 . . . 156 D3
Pines Rd BR1 . . . . 188 A1
Pine St EC1 . . . . 94 C3 241 A6
Pines The
Southgate N14 . . . . 15 C6
South Norwood SE19 . 182 D4
Sunbury TW16 . . . . . . 194 A6
Surbiton KT6 . . . . 214 A5
Woodford IG8 . . . . 21 A1
Pine Tree Cl TW5 . . . . 128 B4
Pine Tree Ho SE14 . . . 140 D5
Pine Tree Lo BR2 . . . . 208 D5
Pine Trees Dr UB10 . . . . 60 A4
Pine Tree Way 1 SE13 . . . . 141 D2
Pineview Ct 3 E4 . . . . 20 A3
Pine Wlk KT5 . . . . 198 C3
Pinewood BR7 . . . . . . 188 C4
Pine Wood TW16 . . . . 172 A2
Pinewood Ave
Hillingdon UB8 . . . . 82 B1
Pinner HA5 . . . . 23 D4
Sidcup DA15 . . . . 167 C3
Pinewood Cl
Crofton BR6 . . . . 211 B1
Croydon CR0 . . . . 223 A5
Pinner HA5 . . . . 23 D4
South Oxhey HA6 . . . . . . 22 B5
Pinewood Ct
Clapham Pk SW4 . . . . 159 D5
Pinewood Ct *continued*
Enfield EN2 . . . . 4 D2
Merton SW19 . . . . 179 D3
Pinewood Dr BR6 . . . . 227 C3
Pinewood Gr W5 . . . . . 87 C1
Pinewood Lo WD23 . . . . 8 B3
Pinewood Pl KT19 . . . 215 B4
Pinewood Rd
Bromley BR2 . . . . 209 A5
Feltham TW13 . . . . 150 B1
West Heath SE2 . . . . . 146 D6
Pinfold Rd SW16 . . . . . 182 A6
Pinglestone Cl UB7 . . 126 A5
Pinkcoat Cl TW13 . . . . 150 B1
Pinkerton Ct KT2 . . . 176 D1
Pinkerton Pl SW16 . . 181 D6
Pinkham Mans W4 . . . 110 C1
Pinkham Way (North Circular Rd) N12 . . . . 31 A4
Pinkwell Ave UB3 . . . . 105 B2
Pinkwell La UB3 . . . . . 105 B2
Pinkwell Prim Sch UB3 . . . . 105 A2
Pinley Gdns RM9 . . . . . 102 B6
Pinnace Ho E14 . . . . . . 120 A3
Pinnacle Hill DA7 . . . 147 D1
Pinnacle Hill N DA7 . 147 D1
Pinnacle Ho EC3 . . . . 253 A5
Pinnacle The
Dagenham RM6 . . . . 59 A3
7 Kingsland N1 . . . . . . 73 B2
Pinnata Cl EN2 . . . . 5 A4
Pinnell Rd SE9 . . . . . . 143 D1
PINNER 41 A6
Pinner Ct NW8 . . . . . . 236 C6
Pinner Gn HA5 . . . . 22 C1
Pinner Gr HA5 . . . . 41 A4
PINNER GREEN 22 C1
Pinner Hill HA5 . . . . 22 B3
Pinner Hill Rd HA5 . . . . 22 C1
Pinner Ho
30 Camberwell SE5 . . 139 A3
Pinner HA5 . . . . 41 A6
Pinner Park Ave HA2 . . 24 A1
Pinner Park Fst & Mid Schs HA5 . . . . 41 D6
Pinner Park Gdns HA2 . . . . 24 A1
Pinner Rd
Harrow HA1, HA2 . . . . . 42 A3
Northwood HA6 . . . . 22 A1
Pinner HA2, HA5 . . . . . . 41 C5
Pinner Sta HA5 . . . . 41 A5
Pinner View HA1, HA2 . . 42 A4
PINNERWOOD PARK . 22 C3
Pinner Wood Sch HA5 . . . . 22 C2
Pinn Way HA4 . . . . 39 C2
Pintail Cl E6 . . . . 100 A2
Pintail Ct 39 SE8 . . . . . 141 B6
Pintail Rd IG8 . . . . 37 B3
Pintail Way UB4 . . . . 84 D2
Pinter Ho 30 SW9 . . . . 138 A3
Pinto Cl WD6 . . . . 11 B5
Pinto Way SE3 . . . . 143 B1
Pioneer Cl
10 Bow Comm E14 . . . . . 97 D2
London W12 . . . . 90 B1
Pioneers Ind Pk CR0 . . . . 204 A1
Pioneer St SE15 . . . . . 140 A4
Pioneer Way W12 . . . . . 90 C1
Piper Cl N7 . . . . 72 B3
Piper Rd KT1 . . . . 198 C6
Pipers Gdns CR0 . . . . . 207 A2
Pipers Gn NW9 . . . . 45 A4
Pipers Green La HA8 . . 10 A1
Pipers Ho SE10 . . . . . . 120 B1
Piper Way IG1 . . . . 57 B1
Pipewell Rd SM5 . . . . . 202 C3
Pippenhall SE9 . . . . . . 166 D5
Pippin Cl
Croydon CR0 . . . . 207 B1
Dollis Hill NW2 . . . . 68 B5
Pippin Ct 5 EN4 . . . . 2 C1
Pippin Ho 17 W10 . . . . 112 D6
Pippins Ct TW15 . . . . . 170 D4
Piquet Rd SE20 . . . . . . 184 C1
Pirate Castle The★ NW1 . . . . 71 A1
Pirbright Cres CR0 . . . 224 A2
Pirbright Ho 11 KT2 . 176 D4
Pirbright Rd SW18 . . . 157 C3
Pirie St 6 E16 . . . . 121 B5
Pitcairn Cl RM7 . . . . . . 59 C5
Pitcairn Ct CR4 . . . . . 180 D3
Pitcairne Ct N21 . . . . . . 16 B6
Pitcairn Ho 1 E9 . . . . . 74 C1
Pitcairn Rd CR4 . . . . . 180 D3
Pitchford St E15 . . . . . . 76 C1
Pitfield Cres SE28 . . . 124 A5
Pitfield Ho N5 . . . . 73 A3
Pitfield St N1 . . . . 95 C5
Pitfield Way
Enfield EN3 . . . . 6 C4
Tokyngton NW10 . . . . . . 67 A2
Pitfold Cl SE12 . . . . . . 165 B5
Pitfold Rd SE12 . . . . . . 165 A4
Pit Ho NW10 . . . . 67 B5
Pitlake CR0 . . . . 220 D6
Pitman Ho
Southgate N21 . . . . 16 B6
4 St Johns SE8 . . . . . 141 C4
Pitman St SE5 . . . . 139 A5
Pitmaston Ho 2 SE13 . . . . 142 A3
Pitsea Pl E1 . . . . 96 D1
Pitsea St E1 . . . . 96 D1
Pitshanger Ct 2 W5 . . 87 C3
Pitshanger La W5 . . . . . 87 C3
Pitt Cres SW19 . . . . . . 179 D6
Pitt Ho 4 SW11 . . . . . . 136 B1
Pittman Gdns IG1 . . . . . 79 A3
Pitt Rd Harrow HA2 . . . . 64 A6
Orpington BR6 . . . . . . 227 A4
Thornton Heath CR0, CR7 . . . . 205 A4
Pitt's Head Mews W1 . . . . 248 B3
Pittsmead Ave BR2 . . 209 A2
Pitt St W8 . . . . 113 C4 245 B2
Pittville Gdns SE25 . . 206 A6
Pitzhanger Manor House & Gallery★ W5 . . . . 109 D5
Pixfield Ct BR2 . . . . . . 186 D1
Pixham Ct 5 SW19 . . 179 B5
Pixley St E14 . . . . 97 B1
Pixton 14 NW9 . . . . 27 C2
Pixton Way CR2 . . . . . 223 B1
Place Farm Ave BR5, BR6 . . . . 211 B1
Plains The 7 E4 . . . . . . 20 C4
PLAISTOW BR1 . . . . . . 187 A4
E13 . . . . 99 B4
Plaistow Gr
Bromley BR1 . . . . 187 B3
West Ham E15 . . . . 98 D6
Plaistow La BR1 . . . . . 187 C2
Plaistow Park Rd E13 . 99 B5
Plaistow Prim Sch E13 . . . . 99 B5
Plaistow Rd E13, E15 . . 98 D5
Plaistow Sta E13 . . . . . . 98 D5
Plane St SE26 . . . . 162 B1
Plane Tree Cres TW13 . . . . 150 B1
Planetree Ct W6 . . . . 112 D2
Plane Tree Ho
Deptford SE8 . . . . 141 A6
Greenwich SE7 . . . . . . 121 D1
Plane Tree Wlk 4 SE19 . . . . 183 C4
Plantagenet Cl KT19 . 215 B4
Plantagenet Gdns RM6 . . . . 58 D2
Plantagenet Ho SE18 . . . . 122 B3
Plantagenet Pl RM6 . . . 58 D2
Plantagenet Rd EN5 . . . 2 A1
Plantain Gdns E11 . . . . 76 B5
Plantain Pl SE1 . . . . . . 252 C2
Plantation La EC3 . . . . 253 A6
Plantation The SE3 . . . 143 A3
Plasel Ct E13 . . . . 99 B6
PLASHET 78 A2
Plashet Gr E6 . . . . 77 D1
Plashet Rd E13 . . . . 77 B1
Plashet Sch E6 . . . . 78 A1
Plassy Rd SE6 . . . . . . 163 D4
Platehouse The 3 E14 . . . . 119 D1
Platina St EC2 . . . . . . 242 D6
Platinum Ct RM7 . . . . . 59 D6
Plato Pl 1 SW6 . . . . . . 135 B3
Plato Rd SW2 . . . . 138 A1
Platt Halls (a) 35 NW9 . . . . 27 D1
Platt Halls (b) 37 NW9 . . . . 27 D1

Platt Halls (c) 38 NW9 27 D1
Platt's Eyot TW12 173 C1
Platt's La NW3 69 C5
Platts Rd EN3 6 C4
Platt St NW1 232 C4
Plaxdale Ho SE17 263 A3
Plaxtol Cl BR1 187 C2
Plaxtol Rd DA8 147 C5
Plaxton Ct E11 76 D5
Playfair St W6 112 C1
Playfield Cres SE22 161 D6
Playfield Rd HA8 27 A1
Playford Rd
Finsbury Pk N4 72 B6
Finsbury Pk N4 72 C6
Playgreen Way SE6 185 C6
Playground Cl BR3 184 D1
Playhouse Yd EC4 241 C1
Plaza Bsns Ctr EN3 7 B3
Plaza Hts E10 76 A5
Plaza Sh Ctr W1 93 C1 239 B2
Plaza Wlk NW9 45 A6
Pleasance Rd
Putney SW15 156 B6
St Paul's Cray BR5 190 B1
Pleasance The SW15 134 B1
Pleasant Gr CR0 223 B5
Pleasant Pl N1 72 D1
Pleasant Row NW1 231 D5
Pleasant View BR6 227 A3
Pleasant View Pl BR6 227 A3
Pleasant Way HA0 87 C5
Pleasaunce Ct SE9 144 B1
Plender Ct NW1 232 B5
Plender St NW1 93 C6 232 B5
Pleshey Rd N7 71 D4
Plevna Cres N15 51 C3
Plevna Ho 1 N9 18 A1
Plevna Rd
Edmonton N9 18 B1
Hampton TW12 173 D2
Plevna St E14 120 A3
Pleydell Ave
Chiswick W6 111 D2
Penge SE19 183 D3
Pleydell Ct EC4 241 B1
Pleydell Gdns SE19 183 D4
Pleydell St EC4 241 B1
Plimsoll Cl E14 97 D1
Plimsoll Rd N4 72 D5
Plough Ct EC3 252 D6
Plough Farm Cl HA4 39 B3
Plough La
Dulwich Village SE22 161 D5
7 Teddington TW11 175 A5
Wallington CR0, SM6 220 A3
Wimbledon SW17, SW19 180 A6
Plough Lane Cl CR0, SM6 220 A3
Ploughmans Cl NW1 232 C6
Ploughmans End TW7 152 B6
Plough Mews 19 SW11 136 B1
Plough Pl EC4 241 B2
Plough Rd
Battersea SW11 136 B1
West Ewell KT19 215 B1
Plough St 16 E1 96 A1
Plough Terr SW11 136 B1
Plough Way SE16 119 A2
Plough Yd EC2 243 B5
Plover Ho 4 SW9 138 C5
Plover Way
Hayes UB4 84 D2
Rotherhithe SE16 119 A3
Plowman Cl N18 33 B5
Plowman Ho SW19 156 D2
Plowman Way RM8 58 C1
Plumbers Row E1 96 A1
Plumbridge St 7 SE10 142 A4
Plum Cl TW14 150 A3
Plumcroft Prim Sch SE18 145 A6
Plume Ho SE10 141 D6
Plum Garth TW8 109 D2
Plum La SE18 145 A5
Plummer Ct SE13 163 D5
Plummer La CR4 180 D1
Plummer Rd SW4 159 D4
Plumpton Cl UB5 63 C2
Plumpton Ct SE23 163 A4
Plumpton Lo E5 74 D5
Plumpton Way SM5 218 C5
PLUMSTEAD 123 C2
PLUMSTEAD COMMON 145 D6
Plumstead Common Rd SE18 145 A6
Plumstead High St SE18, SE2 123 C2
Plumstead Manor Sch SE18 145 B6
Plumstead Rd SE18, SE28 123 A2
Plumstead Road Covered Mkt★ SE18 122 D2
Plumstead Sta SE18 123 B2
Plumtree Cl
Dagenham RM10 81 D2
Wallington SM6 219 D1
Plumtree Ct EC4 241 C2
Plymen Ho KT8 195 C4
Plymouth Ho
10 Barking IG11 80 A1
20 Lewisham SE10 141 D4
Plymouth Rd
Bromley BR1 187 B2
Newham E16 99 A2
Plymouth Wharf E14 120 B2
Plympton Ave NW6 69 B1
Plympton Cl 8 DA17 125 A3
Plympton Pl NW1 237 A5
Plympton Rd NW6 69 B1
Plympton St NW8 237 A5
Plymstock Rd DA16 146 C5
Pocklington Cl NW9 27 C1
Pocklington Ct SW15 156 A3
Pocklington Lo 6 W12 112 A3
Pocock Ave UB7 104 B3
Pocock St SE1 116 D4 251 D2
Podmore Rd SW18 136 A1
Poets Cnr★ SW1 260 A6
Poets Mews 3 SE24 160 D6
Poet's Rd N5 73 B3
Poets Way HA1 42 C5
Pointalls Cl N3 30 A1
Point Cl SE10 142 A4
Pointer Cl SE28 102 D1
Pointer Sch The SE3 143 A5
Pointers Cl E14 119 D1
Point Hill SE10 142 A4
Point Ho SE10 142 A4
Point Pl HA9 66 D1
Point Pleasant SW18 135 C1
Point Terr E7 77 B3
Point The HA4 62 A4
Point Wharf La TW8 132 A5
Poland Ho 3 E15 98 B6
Poland St W1 93 C1 239 B1
Polaris Ct EN4 14 B6
Polebrook Rd SE3 143 C2
Polecroft La SE6 163 B2
Polehamptons The TW12 174 A2
Pole Hill Rd
Chingford E4 20 A4
Hillingdon UB4 83 A4
Polesden Gdns SW20 178 B1
Polesworth Ho 16 W2 91 C2
Polesworth Rd RM9 80 D1
Polish Inst & Sikorski Mus★ SW7 246 D1
Polish Univ Abroad 16 W6 112 A2
Polish War Meml HA4 62 C2
Pollard Cl Islington N7 72 B4
Newham E16 121 A6
Pollard Ct SM4 202 C4
Pollard Ho
Cheam KT4 216 C4
Islington N1 233 C3
Pollard Rd
East Barnet N20 14 C2
Morden SM4 202 B4
Pollard Row E2 96 A4
Pollards Cl IG10 21 C6
Pollards Cres SW16 204 A6
Pollards Hill E SW16 204 B6
Pollards Hill N SW16 204 B6
Pollards Hill S SW16 204 B6
Pollards Hill W SW16 204 B6
Pollard St E2 96 A4
Pollards Wood Rd SW16 204 A6
Pollard Wlk DA14 190 C4
Pollen St W1 238 D1
Pollitt Dr NW8 92 B3 236 D6
Pollock Ho W10 91 A3
Pollock's Toy Mus★ W1 239 B4
Polperro Cl BR6 211 D3
Polperro Mans 3 NW6 69 C3
Polperro Mews SE11 261 C4
Polsted Rd SE6 163 B4
Polsten Mews 2 EN3 7 C6
Polthorne Gr SE18 123 B2
Polworth Rd SW16 182 A5
Polygon Rd NW1 93 D5 232 C3
Polygon The
1 Clapham SW4 137 C1
St John's Wood NW8 229 D6
Polytechnic St SE18 122 C2
Pomell Way E1 243 D2
Pomeroy Cl TW1 131 B1
Pomeroy Ct W11 91 A1
Pomeroy Ho 5 E2 96 D5
Pomeroy St SE14 140 C4
Pomfret Rd SE5 138 D2
Pomoja La N19 72 A6
Pomona Ho 10 SE8 119 A2
Pond Cl
Colney Hatch N12 30 C4
Kidbrooke SE3 143 A3
Pond Cottage La BR3, BR4 207 C1
Pond Cotts SE21 161 C3
PONDERS END 18 D6
Ponders End Ind Est EN3 19 A6
Ponders End Sta EN3 19 A6
Ponder St 5 N7 72 B1
Pond Farm Est E5 74 C5
Pondfield End IG10 21 C4
Pondfield Ho
4 Islington N5 73 A3
West Norwood SE27 183 A5
Pondfield Rd
Dagenham RM10 81 D3
Locksbottom BR6 226 D5
West Wickham BR2 208 C1
Pond Gn HA4 61 C6
Pond Hill Gdns SM3 217 A2
Pond Ho Chelsea SW3 257 A3
Stanmore HA7 25 B4
Pond Mead SE21 161 B5
Pond Path BR7 188 D4
Pond Pl SW3 114 C2 257 A3
Pond Rd
Blackheath Vale SE3 142 D3
Newham E15 98 C5
Pondside Ave KT4 200 C1
Pondside Cl UB3 127 B6
Pond Sq N6 49 A1
Pond St NW3 70 C3
Pond Way TW11 175 C4
Pondwood Rise BR6 211 C2
Ponler St E1 96 B1
Ponsard Rd NW10 90 B4
Ponsford St E9 74 C2
Ponsonby Ho 13 E2 96 C5
Ponsonby Pl SW1 115 D1 259 D2
Ponsonby Rd SW15 156 B4
Ponsonby Terr SW1 259 D2
Pontefract Ct UB5 63 D3
Pontefract Rd BR1 186 D5
Ponton Ho SW2 160 C3
Ponton Rd SW8 137 D6 269 D5
Pontoon Dock Sta E16 121 C5
Pont St Mews SW1 257 C5
Pont St SW1 114 D3 257 D5
Pontypool Pl SE1 251 C2
Pool Cl
Beckenham BR3 185 C5
East Molesey KT8 195 B4
Pool Ct SE6 163 C2
Poole Cl HA4 61 C6
Poole Court Rd TW5 129 A3
Poole Ct
De Beauvoir Town N1 73 C1
Hounslow TW5 129 A3
Poole Ho SE11 260 D5
Pool End Cl TW17 192 C4
Poole Rd Homerton E9 74 D2
West Ewell KT19 215 B2
Pooles Bldgs EC1 241 A5
Pooles Ct IG3 80 A5
Pooles La SW10 266 A3
Pooles Park Prim Sch 10 N4 72 B6
Pooles Pk N4 72 C6
Poole St N1 95 B6 235 C5
Poole Way UB4 83 C4
Pooley Ho E1 96 D4
Pool Ho NW8 236 D4
Poolmans St SE16 118 D4
Pool Rd
East Molesey KT12, KT8 195 B4
Harrow HA1 42 B2
Poolsford Rd NW9 45 C5
Poonah St E1 96 C1
Pope Cl
East Bedfont TW14 149 D3
Mitcham SW17, SW19 180 B4
Pope Ct 10 KT2 175 D6
Pope Ho
7 Bermondsey SE16 118 B2
3 Camberwell SE5 139 B5
Pope John Prim Sch W12 112 B6
Pope Rd BR2 209 D4
Pope's Ave TW2 152 C2
Popes Ct TW2 152 C2
Popes Dr N3 29 C2
Popes Gr CR0 223 B5
Pope's Gr TW1, TW2 152 D2
Pope's Head Alley EC3 242 D1
Pope's La W5 110 A3
Pope's Rd SW9 138 C2
Pope St SE1 253 B1
Pope Street Ct SE9 166 B3
Popham Cl TW13 151 B1
Popham Ct N16 73 C5
Popham Gdns TW9 132 D2
Popham Rd N1 95 A6 235 A6
Popham St
Islington N1 234 D6
Shoreditch N1 95 A6 235 A6
Pop In Bsns Ctr HA9 66 D3
POPLAR 97 C1
Poplar Ave
Mitcham CR4 180 D2
Orpington BR6 226 D6
Southall UB2 107 D3
Yiewsley UB7 104 B6
Poplar Bath St 11 E14 119 D6
Poplar Bsns Pk E14 120 A6
Poplar Cl Hackney E9 75 B3
Pinner HA5 22 D2
Poplar Cres KT19 215 A2
Poplar Ct Chingford E4 35 D4
Northolt UB5 84 C5
4 Streatham SW16 160 B1
13 Twickenham TW1 153 C5
Wimbledon SW19 179 C5
Poplar Farm Cl KT19 215 A2
Poplar Gdns KT3 177 B1
Poplar Gr
Friern Barnet N11 31 A4
Hammersmith W6 112 C4
Kingston u T KT3 199 B6
Wembley HA9 67 A5
Poplar High St E14 119 D6
Poplar Ho
Brockley SE4 141 B1
Poplar Ho *continued*
19 Rotherhithe SE16 118 D4
Poplar La BR3 207 D4
Poplar Mews 4 W12 112 C5
Poplar Mount DA17 125 D2
Poplar Pl Hayes UB3 106 A6
Kensington W2 113 D6 245 D6
Woolwich SE28 124 C6
Poplar Prim Sch SW19 201 C6
Poplar Rd
Ashford TW15 171 A5
Cheam SM3 201 B1
Herne Hill SE24 139 A1
Merton SW19 179 C1
Poplar Rd S SW19 201 C6
Poplars Cl HA4 39 C1
Poplars Ho 14 E17 53 D6
Poplars Rd E17 53 D3
Poplar Sta E14 119 D6
Poplars The
East Barnet N14 15 B6
Kentish Town NW5 71 C3
Poplar View HA9 65 D6
Poplar Way
Feltham TW13 150 B1
Ilford IG6 57 A5
Poplar Wlk
Croydon CR0 205 A1
Herne Hill SE24 139 A1
Poppins Ct EC4 241 C1
Poppleton Rd E11 54 C3
Poppy Cl
Belvedere DA17 125 D4
Hackbridge SM6 203 A1
Northolt UB5 63 B2
Poppy Ct HA3 42 C6
Poppy La CR0 206 C1
Porchester Ct W2 91 D1
Porchester Gate W2 246 A5
Porchester Gdn Mews W2 91 D1
Porchester Gdns W2 113 D6 245 D6
Porchester Ho 3 E1 96 B1
Porchester Mead BR3 185 D4
Porchester Mews W2 91 D1
Porchester Pl W2 237 B1
Porchester Rd
Kensington W2 91 D1
Kingston u T KT1 176 D1
Porchester Sq W2 91 D1
Porchester Terr W2 114 A6 246 A6
Porchester Terr N W2 91 D1
Porch Way N20 14 D1
Porcupine Cl SE9 166 A2
Porden Rd SW2 138 B1
Porland Ct SE1 262 C6
Porlock Ave HA1, HA2 42 A1
Porlock Ho 5 SE26 162 A1
Porlock Rd EN1 17 D4
Porlock St SE1 117 B4 252 D2
Porrington Cl BR7 188 C2
Porson Ct SE13 141 D2
Portal Cl
Hillingdon UB10 60 B1
Ruislip HA4 62 B4
West Norwood SE27 160 C1
Portal Way W3 89 B2
Portbury Cl 17 SE15 140 A4
Portchester Cl SE24 139 B1
Port Cres E13 99 B3
Portcullis Lodge Rd EN1 5 B2
Porte 10 NW9 27 D2
Portelet Ct 1 N1 95 C6
Portelet Rd E1 96 D4
Porten Hos W14 254 A5
Porten Rd W14 254 A5
Porter Rd E6 100 B1
Porters Ave RM8, RM9 80 C3
Porter Sq N19 50 A1
Porter St
Borough The SE1 117 A5 252 B4
Marylebone W1 237 D4
Porters & Walters Almshouses N22 32 B3
Porters Way UB7 104 B4

Porteus Rd W2 236 B4
Portfleet Pl 24 N1 95 C6
Portgate Cl W9 91 B3
Porthallow Cl BR6 227 D4
Porthcawe Rd SE26 185 B6
Porthkerry Ave DA16 146 A1
Port Ho 6 SW11 136 A2
Port House The 6 E14 119 D1
Portia Ct 12 IG11 80 A1
Portia Way E3 97 B3
Porticos The SW3 266 C5
Portinscale Rd SW15 157 B6
Portishead Ho 29 W2 91 C2
Portland Ave
Blackfen DA15 168 A5
New Malden KT3 199 D2
Stamford Hill N16 51 D2
Portland Cl
Dagenham RM6 59 A4
New Malden KT4 200 B2
Portland Commercial Est IG11 102 C5
Portland Cotts
Feltham TW13 173 A5
Wallington CR0 203 D2
Portland Cres
1 Chislehurst SE9 166 A2
Feltham TW13 171 B6
Southall UB6 86 A2
Stanmore HA7 25 D1
Portland Cres W HA7 43 D6
Portland Ct
7 De Beauvoir Town N1 73 C1
1 Deptford SE14 141 A6
1 Sutton SM2 217 D2
Portland Dr EN2 5 C5
Portland Gdns
Harringay N4 50 D3
Ilford RM6 58 D4
Portland Gr SW8 138 B4 270 C2
Portland Ho 19 SW2 160 C3
Portland Hospl for Women & Children The W1 238 D5
Portland Mans SE25 206 B4
Portland Mews W1 239 B1
Portland Pl
Croydon SE25 206 A5
Marylebone W1 93 B2 238 D3
Portland Place Sch W1 93 B2 238 D4
Portland Rd
Ashford TW15 148 A1
Bromley BR1 187 C5
Chislehurst SE9 166 A2
Croydon SE25 206 B4
Hayes UB4 83 C4
Kingston u T KT1 198 B5
Kingston u T KT1 198 B6
Mitcham CR4 180 C1
Notting Hill W11 113 A5 244 B4
Notting Hill W11 113 A6 244 A5
Southall UB2 107 B3
Tottenham N15 51 D5
Portland Rise N4 51 A1
Portland Sq 4 E1 118 B5
Portland St SE17 117 B1 262 C1
Portland Terr
Edgware HA8 26 C3
Richmond TW9 131 D1
Portland Village W6 112 C3
Portman Ave SW14 133 B2
Portman Cl
Bexley DA7 147 A2
Marylebone W1 93 A1 238 A2
Portman Dr IG8 37 D1
Portman Gate NW1 237 B5
Portman Gdns
Hendon NW9 27 B1
Hillingdon UB10 60 C1
Portman Hall HA3 24 B5
Portman Hts 1 NW3 69 C5
Portman Lo N21 16 D6
Portman Mews S W1 238 A1
Portman Pl E2 96 C4
Portman Rd KT1 176 B1
Portman Sq W1 93 A1 238 A2
Portman St W1 93 A1 238 A1
Portman The NW11 47 C2
Portman Twrs W1 237 D2
Portmeadow Wlk SE2 124 D4
Portmeers Cl E17 53 C3
Portnall Rd W9 91 B4
Portobello Ct Est W11 91 B1
Portobello Ho 6 SW27 182 D5
Portobello Mews W11 245 A5
Portobello Rd W11 113 B6 244 D6
Portobello Road Mkt* W10 91 A2
Porton Ct KT6 197 C3
Portpool La EC1 94 C2 241 A4
Portree Cl N22 32 B3
Portree St E14 98 B1
Port Royal Pl 3 N16 73 C3
Portrush Ct 9 UB1 86 A1
Portsdown HA8 26 C5
Portsdown Ave NW11 47 B3
Portsdown Mews NW11 47 B3
Portsea Hall W2 237 B1
Portsea Ho 3 SW15 156 B3
Portsea Mews W2 237 B1
Portsea Pl W2 237 B1
Portslade Rd SW8 137 C3
Portsmouth Ave KT7 197 A2
Portsmouth Mews 16 E16 121 B5
Portsmouth Rd
Esher KT10 212 A5
Putney SW15 156 C4
Thames Ditton KT6, KT7 197 C3
Portsmouth St WC2 240 D1
Portsoken St E1, EC3 253 C6
Portswood Pl SW15 155 D5
Portugal Gdns TW2 152 A2
Portugal St WC2 94 B1 240 D1
Portway E15 98 D6
Portway Gdns SE18 143 D5
Portway Prim Sch 7 E13 99 A6
Poseidon Ct
Dagenham IG11 102 B4
9 Millwall E14 119 C2
Postern Gn EN2 4 C2
Postern The EC2 242 B3
Post La TW2 152 B3
Postmasters Lodge HA5 41 A2
Postmill Cl CR0 222 D5
Post Office App E7 77 B3
Post Office Way SW8 137 D5 269 C4
Post Rd UB2 107 D3
Postway Mews 1 IG1 78 D5
Potier St SE1 262 D5
Potter Cl CR4 181 B1
Potteries The EN5 13 C6
Potterill Ct TW11 175 B3
Potterne Cl 5 SW19 156 D4
Potters Cl
5 Camberwell SE15 139 C5
Croydon CR0 207 A1
Pottersfield EN1 5 C1
Potters Fields SE1 117 C5 253 B3
Potters Gr KT3 199 A5
Potters Heights Cl HA5 22 B3
Potter's La Barnet EN5 1 C1
Streatham SW16 181 D4
Potters Lo E14 120 A1
Potters Mews WD6 9 D5
Potters Rd SW6 136 A3
Potter's Rd EN5 1 D1
Potter St HA5 22 B2
Potter Street Hill HA5 22 B3
Pottery La W11 113 A5 244 B4
Pottery Rd TW8 132 A6
Pottery St SE16 118 B4
Pott St E2 96 B4
Poulett Gdns TW1 153 A3
Poulett Rd E6 100 B5
Poullett Ho SW2 160 D3
Poulters Wood BR2 225 D3
Poulton Ave SM1 218 B5
Poulton Cl E8 74 B2
Poultry EC2 95 B1 242 C1
Pound Cl
Long Ditton KT6 197 C1
Orpington BR6 227 B6
Pound Court Dr BR6 227 B6
Pound Farm Cl KT10 196 B1
Pound Green Ct 4 DA5 169 C4
Pound La NW10 68 A2
Pound Park Rd SE7 121 D2
Pound Pl SE9 166 C5
Pound St SM5 218 D3
Pountney Rd SW11 137 A2
Poverest Rd BR5 211 D4
Povey Ho
Tulse Hill SW2 160 C5
Walworth SE17 263 A3
Powder Mill La TW2, TW4 151 C3
Powell Cl
Chessington KT9 213 D3
Edgware HA8 26 B4
Wallington SM6 220 A1
Powell Ct
Croydon CR2 221 A4
19 Walthamstow E17 53 D6
Powell Gdns RM10 81 C4
Powell Ho 10 SW19 179 A4
Powell Rd
Buckhurst Hill IG9 21 C4
Hackney E5 74 B5
Powell's Wlk W4 133 D6
Powell Terr CR4 204 A5
Powergate Bsns Pk NW10 89 B4
Power Ho 13 TW9 132 C4
Power Ho The W4 111 D2
Power Rd W4 110 C2
Powerscroft Rd
Lower Clapton E5 74 C4
Sidcup DA14 190 C4
Powers Ct TW1 153 D4
Powis Ct Bushey WD23 8 B3
Edgware HA8 26 B6
Powis Gdns
Golders Green NW11 47 B2
Notting Hill W11 91 B1
Powis Ho WC2 240 B2
Powis Mews W11 91 B1
Powis Pl WC1 94 A3 240 B5
Powis Rd E3 97 D4
Powis Sq W11 91 B1
Powis St SE18 122 D2
Powis Terr W11 91 B1
Powlesland Ct 21 E14 97 A1
Powle Terr IG1 79 B3
Powlett Ho NW1 71 B2
Powlett Pl NW1 71 B1
Pownall Gdns TW3 129 D1
Pownall Rd
Hackney E8 96 A6
Hounslow TW3 129 D1
Pownsett Terr IG1 79 A3
Powrie Ho 4 SW11 136 B3
Powster Rd BR1 187 B5
Powys Cl DA7 146 D6
Powys Ct N11 32 A5
Powys La
Bowes Pk N13 32 A5
Palmers Green N14 32 A6
Poynder Ct 3 N7 72 A3
Poynder Lo TW7 131 A4
Poynders Ct 9 SW4 159 C5
Poynders Gdns SW12 159 C4
Poynders Rd SW12, SW4 159 D4
Poynings Rd N19 71 C5
Poynings Way N12 29 C5
Poyntell Cres BR7 189 B2
Poynter Ct 11 UB5 84 D5
Poynter Ho
Paddington NW8 236 C6
10 Shepherd's Bush W11 112 D5
Poynter Rd EN1 18 A6
Poynton Rd N17 34 A1
Poyntz Rd SW11 136 D3
Poyser St E2 96 B5
Praed Mews W2 236 D2
Praed St W2 92 B1 236 D2
Pragel St E13 99 C5
Pragnell Rd SE12 165 B2
Prague Pl SW2 160 A6
Prah Rd N4 72 C6
Prairie St SW8 137 B3
Pratt Mews NW1 232 A5
Pratt St NW1 93 C6 232 A6
Pratt Wlk SE1, SE11 116 B2 260 D4
Prayle Gr NW2 46 D1
Preachers Ct EC1 241 D5
Prebend Gdns W4, W6 111 D2
Prebend Mans 4 W4 111 D2
Prebend St N1 95 A6 235 A6
Precinct Rd UB3 106 A6
Precincts The SM4 201 C3
Precinct The
Islington N1 235 A5
Islington N5 72 D3
Premier Corner NW6 91 B5
Premier Ct EN3 6 D5
Premier Ho 25 N1 72 D1
Premier Lo N3 29 C2
Premier Park Rd NW10 88 D5
Premier Pk NW10 88 D5
Premier Pl 17 E14 119 C6
Prendergast Ho 7 SW4 159 D4
Prendergast Ladywell Fields Coll SE4 163 C5
Prendergast Rd SE3 142 C2
Prendergast Sch SE4 141 C1
Prentice Ct 2 SW19 179 B5
Prentis Rd SW16 181 D6
Prentiss Ct SE7 121 D2
Presburg Rd KT3 199 C4
Prescelly Pl HA8 26 B2
Prescot St E1 117 D6 253 D6
Prescott Ave BR5 210 D3
Prescott Ho
Croydon CR0 220 C5
13 Kennington SE17 138 D6
Prescott Pl SW4 137 D1
Presentation Mews SW2 160 B3
Preshaw Cres CR4 202 C6
President Dr E1 118 B5
President Ho EC1 234 D1
President St EC1 235 A2
Prespa Cl N9 18 C2
Press Ho NW10 67 B5
Press Rd NW10 67 B5
Prestage Way 13 E14 120 A6
Prestbury Rd E7 77 C1
Prestbury Sq SE9 188 B6
Prested Rd SW11 136 C1
PRESTON 44 A1
Preston Ave E4 36 B4
Preston Cl
Twickenham TW2 152 C1
Walworth SE1 263 A4
Preston Ct
5 New Barnet EN5 2 A1
Northwood Hills HA6 22 A1
Sidcup DA14 189 D6
Walton-on-T KT12 194 C1
Preston Dr
Bexley DA7 146 D4
Wanstead E11 55 C4
West Ewell KT19 215 D2
Preston Gdns
Enfield EN3 7 A6
Redbridge IG1 56 A3
Willesden NW10 67 C2
Preston Hill HA3 44 B3
Preston Ho
Bermondsey SE1 263 C6
3 Dagenham RM10 81 C5
Walworth SE1 263 A4
1 Woolwich SE18 122 C2
Preston Manor High Sch HA9 66 B6
Preston Park Prim Sch HA9 43 D1
Preston Pl
Richmond TW10 154 A6
Willesden NW2 68 A2
Preston Rd
Leytonstone E11 54 C3
Littleton TW17 192 C4
South Norwood SE19 182 D4
Wembley HA3, HA9 66 A6
Wimbledon SW20 177 D3
Preston Road Sta HA3 44 A1
Prestons Rd BR2 225 A6
Preston's Rd E14 120 A5
Preston Waye HA3 44 A1
Prestwich Terr SW4 159 D6
Prestwick Cl UB2 107 A1
Prestwick Ct
Southall UB1 108 A6
Tottenham N17 34 A3
Prestwick Rd WD19 22 D6
Prestwood Ave HA3 43 B5
Prestwood Cl
East Wickham SE18 146 A6
Harrow HA3 43 B5
Prestwood Gdns CR0 205 A2
Prestwood Ho 3 SE16 118 B3
Prestwood St N1 235 B3
Pretoria Ave E17 53 A5
Pretoria Cres E4 20 A3
Pretoria Ho 3 HA4 40 C1
Pretoria Rd
Chingford E4 20 B3
Ilford IG1 78 D3
Leytonstone E11 54 B1
Newham E16 98 D3
Streatham SW16 181 C5
Tottenham N17 33 D4
Pretoria Rd N N18 33 D4
Pretty Cnr HA6 22 A5
Prevost Rd N11 15 A2
Priam Ho 17 E2 96 B5
Price Cl Finchley NW7 29 A4
Upper Tooting SW17 158 D1
Price Ct HA1 43 A4
Price Ho N1 235 A5
Price Rd CR0 220 D3
Prices Ct SW11 136 B2
Price's St SE1 251 D4
Price's Yd N1 233 D5
Price Way TW12 173 A4
Prichard Ct
Battersea SW11 266 D1
Islington N7 72 B3
Pricklers Hill EN5 13 D5
Prickley Wood BR2 208 D1
Priddy's Yd 4 CR0 221 A6
Prideaux Ho WC1 233 D2
Prideaux Pl
Acton W3 111 B6
St Pancras WC1 94 B4 233 D2
Prideaux Rd SW9 138 A2
Pride Ct N1 234 B4
Pridham Rd CR7 205 B5
Priestfield Rd SE23 163 A1
Priestlands Park Rd DA15 167 D1
Priestley Cl N16 51 D2
Priestley Gdns RM6 58 B3
Priestley Ho
2 Camden Town NW5 71 B2
St Luke's EC1 242 B6
3 Wembley HA9 67 A5
Priestley Rd CR4 181 A1
Priestley Way
Hendon NW2 46 A1
Walthamstow E17 52 D6
Priestman Point 25 E3 97 D4
Priestmead Fst & Mid Schs HA3 43 B6
Priest Park Ave HA2 63 C6
Priests Bridge SW14 133 C2
Priest's Ct EC2 242 A2
Prima Rd SW9 138 C5
Primrose Ave
Enfield EN2 5 C4
Ilford RM6 58 B2

Primrose Cl
6 Bow E3 97 C5
Catford SE6 186 A5
Finchley N3 29 D1
Hackbridge SM6 203 B1
Harrow HA2 63 B5
Primrose Ct
2 Child's Hill NW2 69 B5
New Malden KT4 200 A2
Primrose Hill NW8 230 C5
11 Streatham SW12 159 D4
Primrose Gdns
Hampstead NW3 70 C2
Ruislip HA4 62 C3
PRIMROSE HILL 70 D1
Primrose Hill EC4 241 B1
Primrose Hill Ct NW3 70 D1
Primrose Hill Rd
Primrose Hill NW1, NW3 70 D1
Primrose Hill NW1, NW3 230 C6
Primrose Hill Sch NW1 93 A6 231 B6
Primrose Hill Studios NW1 231 A6
Primrose Ho
7 Peckham SE15 140 A4
1 Richmond TW9 132 B4
Primrose La CR0 206 D1
Primrose Mans SW11 268 A2
Primrose Mews 9 NW1 70 D1
Primrose Pl 4 TW7 130 D3
Primrose Rd
Walthamstow E10 53 D1
Woodford E18 37 B1
Primrose Sq E9 96 C6
Primrose St EC2 95 C2 243 B4
Primrose Way HA0 87 D5
Primrose Wlk
Ewell KT17 215 D1
6 New Cross Gate SE14 141 A5
Primula St W12 90 A1
Prince Albert Ct
Primrose Hill NW8 230 C5
Sunbury TW16 171 C3
Prince Albert Rd NW8 92 D6 230 C5
Prince Arthur Ct 18 NW3 70 A4
Prince Arthur Mews 17 NW3 70 A4
Prince Arthur Rd NW3 70 A3
Prince Charles Dr NW2 46 C2
Prince Charles Rd SE3 142 D4
Prince Charles Way SM6 219 B5
Prince Consort Dr BR7 189 B2
Prince Consort Ho SE1 260 B2
Prince Consort Rd SW7 114 B3 256 C6
Princedale Rd W11 113 A5 244 B4
Prince Edward Mans W2 245 B6
Prince Edward Rd E9 75 B2
Prince George Ave N14 15 D6
Prince George Rd N16 73 C4
Prince George's Ave SW20 178 C1
Prince Georges Rd SW19 180 B2
Prince Henry Rd SE7 143 D5
Prince Imperial Rd
Chislehurst BR7 188 D3
Kidbrooke SE18 144 B4
Prince John Rd SE9 166 A6
Princelet St E1 95 D2 243 D4
Prince of Orange La 3 SE10 142 A5
Prince Of Wales Cl NW4 46 B5
Prince of Wales Dr SW11 137 A4 268 A2
Prince of Wales Mans
Battersea SW11 268 B2
Clapham SW4 159 B6
Prince of Wales Pas NW1 232 A1
Prince of Wales Prim Sch EN3 7 B6
Prince of Wales Rd
Blackheath Vale SE3 142 D4
Camden Town NW5 71 A2
Newham E16 99 C1
Prince Of Wales' Rd SM1 218 B6
Prince Of Wales Terr
Chiswick W4 111 C1
Kensington W8 245 D1
Prince Rd SE25 205 C4
Prince Regent E16 99 C2
Prince Regent Ct 2 SE16 119 A5
Prince Regent La E13 99 C3
Prince Regent Mews NW1 232 A1
Prince Regent Rd TW3 130 A2
Prince Regent Sta E16 121 C6
Prince Rupert Rd SE9 144 B1
Princes Arc SW1 249 B4
Princes Ave
Acton W3 110 C3
Edmonton N13 32 C5
Finchley N3 29 D2
Muswell Hill N10 49 B6
Orpington BR5 211 C4
Queensbury NW9 44 D5
Tolworth KT6 214 C6
Wallington SM5 218 D1
Woodford IG8 37 C6
Wood Green N22 31 D2
Prince's Ave UB1 85 D1
Princes Cir WC2 94 A1 240 A2
Princes Cl
Edgware HA8 26 C5
Finsbury Pk N4 50 D1
Queensbury NW9 44 C5
Sidcup DA14 168 D1
Prince's Cl TW11, TW12 174 B6
Princes Coll WC1 240 A2
Princes Court Bsns Ctr 14 E1 118 B6
Princes Ct
Brondesbury NW2 69 A3
Hampstead NW3 70 B4
Kingston u T KT3 199 D6
Stepney E1 118 B6
Wembley HA9 66 A3
Prince's Ct SE16 119 B3
Princes Dr HA1 42 C6
Princes Gate SW7 114 B4 246 D1
Prince's Gate SW7 114 C4 247 A1
Princes Gate Ct SW7 246 D1
Princes Gate Mews SW7 114 B3 256 D6
Princes Gdns
Acton W3 88 C2
Brompton SW7 114 B3 256 D6
Ealing W5 87 C3
Princes Ho W11 245 A5
Princes La N10 49 B6
Princes Mews TW3 129 C1
Prince's Mews
1 Hammersmith W6 112 B1
Kensington W2 113 D6 245 C6
Princes Par NW11 47 A3
Princes Park Ave
Hayes UB3 105 B6
Temple Fortune NW11 47 A4
Princes Park Circ UB3 105 B6
Princes Park Cl UB3 105 B6
Princes Park La UB3 105 B6
Princes Park Par UB3 105 B6
Princes Pl
Notting Hill W11 113 A5 244 A4
St James SW1 249 B4
Prince's Plain BR2 210 A1
Princes Plain Prim Sch BR2 210 A2
Princes Rd
Ashford TW15 170 B5
Buckhurst Hill IG9 21 C2
Ealing W13 109 B5
Edmonton N18 34 C6
Feltham TW13 149 D1
Ilford IG6 57 B5
Kew TW9 132 B4
Kingston u T KT2 176 C3
Penge SE20 184 D4
Richmond TW10 154 B6
Prince's Rd
Mortlake SW14 133 B2
Teddington TW11, TW12 174 B6
Wimbledon SW19 179 C4
Princes Rise SE13 142 A3
Princes Riverside Rd 7 SE16 118 D5
Princessa Ct EN2 17 B6
Princess Alexandra School of Nursing The 6 E1 96 B2
Princess Alice Ho 1 W10 90 C3
Princess Alice Way SE28 123 B4
Princess Ave HA9 66 A6
Princess Beatrice Ho SW10 255 C1
Princess Cl SE28 102 D1
Princess Cres N4 72 D6
Princess Ct
Catford BR1 186 C4
3 Croydon CR0 221 D6
Hampstead NW6 69 D1
Hounslow TW4 128 C2
Kensington W2 245 D6
Marylebone W1 237 C3
11 Wimbledon SW19 178 D3
Princess Frederica CE Jun & Inf Sch NW10 90 C5
Princess Grace Hospl The W1 93 A3 238 A5
Princess La HA4 39 C1
Princess Louise Cl W2 236 D4
Princess Mary Ho SW1 259 D3
Princess May Prim Sch 6 N16 73 D4
Princess May Rd N16 73 C4
Princess Mews
Hampstead NW3 70 B2
Kingston u T KT1 198 B6
Princess Par
Dagenham RM10 103 C5
Locksbottom BR6 226 C5
Princess Park Manor N11 31 A5
Prince's Sq W2 113 D6 245 C6
Princess Rd
Camden Town NW1 93 A6 231 B6
Paddington NW6 91 C5
Thornton Heath CR0 205 A3
Princess Royal University Hospl BR6 226 C5
Princess St
Bexley DA7 147 B2
Newington SE1 261 D5
Princes St
Bexleyheath DA7 147 B1
Marylebone W1 238 D1
Sutton SM1 218 B4
Tottenham N17 33 C4
Prince's St
City of London EC2 95 B1 242 C1
Richmond TW10, TW9 154 A6
Prince St SE8 141 B6
Prince's Terr E13 99 B6
Princes Way
Acton W3 110 C3
Buckhurst Hill IG9 21 C2
Princes Way *continued*
Coney Hall BR4 224 D5
Croydon CR0 220 B3
Putney SW15, SW19 157 A3
Ruislip HA4 63 A4
Princes Yd W11 244 B3
Princethorpe Ho W2 91 D2
Princethorpe Rd SE26 184 D6
Princeton Ct 12 SW15 134 D2
Princeton Mans WC1 240 C3
Princeton Mews 3 KT2 176 C2
Princeton St WC1 94 B2 240 C4
Prince William Ct TW15 170 B5
Principal Cl N14 15 C3
Principal Sq E9 74 D3
Pringle Gdns SW16 181 C6
Pringle Ho N21 16 B6
Printers Mews E3 97 A6
Printer St EC4 241 B2
Printinghouse La UB3 105 C4
Printing House Yd 16 E2 95 C4
Printon Ho 16 E3 97 B2
Print Village Ind Est SE15 139 D3
Priolo Rd SE7 121 C1
Prior Ave SM2, SM5 218 C1
Prior Bolton St N1 72 D2
Prioress Ho 2 E3 97 D4
Prioress Rd SE27 160 D1
Prioress St SE1 262 D5
Prior Rd IG1 78 C5
Priors Croft E17 35 B1
Priors Field UB5 63 A2
Priors Gdns HA4 62 C3
Priors Lo 4 TW10 154 A5
Priors Mead EN1 5 C4
Prior St SE10 142 A5
Priors Wood KT10 212 D6
Prior Weston Prim Sch EC1 95 B3 242 C6
Priory Ave
Bedford Pk W4 111 C3
Cheam SM3 216 D4
Chingford E4 19 C1
Hornsey N8 49 D5
Petts Wood BR5 211 B3
Walthamstow E17 53 C4
Wembley HA0 64 D4
Priory CE Prim Sch SW19 179 D5
Priory Cl
Ashford TW16 172 A3
Barnet N20 13 B4
Beckenham BR3 207 A6
Chingford Green E4 19 B1
Chislehurst BR7 188 B2
East Barnet N14 15 B6
Finchley N3 29 B2
Hampton TW12 173 B2
Hayes UB3 106 B6
3 Merton SW19 179 D2
Ruislip HA4 39 D1
Stanmore HA7 8 D1
Wembley HA0 64 D4
Woodford E18 37 A2
Priory Cres
Cheam SM3 216 D4
South Norwood SE19 183 A3
Wembley HA0 65 A5
Priory Ct Bushey WD23 8 A3
Cheam SM3 217 A4
City of London EC4 241 D1
Hampton TW12 173 C3
Highgate N6 49 B3
Homerton E9 74 D3
Hounslow TW3 129 D2
Ilford RM6 58 B3
Newham E6 99 D6
Nunhead SE15 140 C1
Roehampton SW15 133 D1
South Lambeth SW8 137 D4 269 D2
Walthamstow E17 35 B1
4 Wembley HA0 88 A5
Priory Dr Stanmore HA7 8 D1
West Heath SE2 124 D1
Priory Field Dr HA8 26 D6
Priory Gdns
Ashford TW15 171 B5
Priory Gdns *continued*
Barnes SW13 133 D2
6 Chiswick W4 111 C2
Ealing W5 88 A4
Hampton TW12 173 B2
Highgate N6 49 B3
South Norwood SE25 205 D5
Wembley HA0 65 A4
Priory Gn N1 233 C4
Priory Gr Barnet EN5 13 C6
South Lambeth SW8 138 A4 270 A1
Priory Grange N2 48 D6
Priory Hill HA0 65 A4
Priory Ho
3 Charlton SE7 143 C6
Clerkenwell EC1 241 C6
Pimlico SW1 259 C2
Spitalfields E1 243 C4
Priory Hospl Grange Roehampton SW15 133 D1
Priory Hospl Hayes Grove The BR2 225 A6
Priory Hospl North London The (Grovelands) N14 16 A3
Priory House Ct SE6 163 D3
Priory Hts N1 233 D4
Priory La
East Molesey KT8 195 D5
Roehampton SW15 155 D6
Priory Leas SE9 166 A3
Priory Lo
7 Brentford W4 110 C1
Coney Hall BR4 224 C5
Ealing W5 87 C1
Priory Mans
17 Maitland Pk NW3 70 D2
South Kensington SW10 256 B1
Priory Park Rd
Kilburn NW6 91 B6
Wembley HA0 65 A4
Priory Pk SE3 142 D2
Priory Rd Barking IG11 79 B1
Bedford Pk W4 111 B3
Cheam SM3 216 D4
Chessington KT9 214 A5
Hampstead NW6 69 D1
Hampton TW12 173 C3
Hornsey N8 49 D5
Hounslow TW3 152 A6
Mitcham SW19 180 B3
Newham E6 99 D5
Richmond TW9 132 C5
Thornton Heath CR0 204 C2
Priory Ret Pk SW19 180 B3
Priory Specl Sch SE25 205 D5
Priory St 16 E3 97 D4
Priory Terr NW6 91 D6
Priory The
Croydon CR0 220 C5
Hornsey N8 49 D5
21 Kingston u T KT6 198 A4
Lambeth SE1 251 C1
Lewisham SE3 142 D1
Priory View WD23 8 C4
Priory Villas N11 30 D5
Priory Way
Harmondsworth UB7 126 A6
Harrow HA2 41 D5
Southall UB2 106 D3
Priory Wlk
South Kensington SW10 114 A1 256 B1
Sunbury TW16 172 A3
Priscilla Cl N15 51 A4
Priscilla Ho 8 TW16 171 D3
Pritchard Ho 38 E2 96 A5
Pritchard's Rd E2 96 A5
Pritchett Cl 13 EN3 7 C6
Priter Rd SE16 118 A3
Priter Road Hostel 14 SE16 118 A3
Private Rd EN1 17 C6
Probert Rd SW2 160 C6
Probyn Ho SW1 259 D4
Probyn Rd SW2 160 D2
Procter Ho 12 SE5 139 B5
Procter St WC1 94 B2 240 C3

Proctor Cl CR4......181 A2
Proctor Ho 5 SE1......118 A1
Proctors Cl TW14......150 A3
Prodger 8 NW9......27 D2
Progress Bsns Pk
CR9......220 B6
Progress Way
Croydon CR0......220 B6
Enfield EN1......18 A6
Wood Green N22......32 C2
Prologis Pk
Hounslow TW4......128 C1
Wallington CR0......220 B6
Prome Ho 3 N16......73 B4
Promenade Approach Rd
W4......133 C5
Promenade Mans
*HA8......26 C5
Promenade The W4......133 C4
Pronto Trad Est UB4......83 C2
Prospect Cl
Belvedere DA17......125 C2
Bushey WD23......8 B4
Forest Hill SE26......184 B6
Hounslow TW5......129 B4
Ruislip HA4......40 D2
Prospect Cotts
SW18......135 C1
Prospect Cres TW2......152 A5
Prospect Ct E17......53 D5
Prospect Ho
1 Dalston E8......73 D2
Islington N1......234 A3
3 Mitcham SW19......180 B2
14 North Kensington
W10......90 D1
5 Walthamstow E17......54 A6
Prospect House Sch 11
SW15......156 A4
Prospect Pl
Bromley BR2......209 B6
5 Child's Hill NW2......69 B5
3 Chiswick W4......111 B1
6 Deptford SE8......141 B6
East Finchley N2......48 B5
12 Hampstead NW3......70 A4
7 Lower Holloway N7......72 A4
Tottenham N17......33 C3
Wapping E1......118 C5
Wimbledon SW20......178 B3
Prospect Quay
SW18......135 C1
Prospect Rd
Barnet EN5......1 D1
Child's Hill NW2......69 B5
Kingston u T KT6......197 C3
Woodford IG8......37 C5
Prospect Ring N2......48 B6
Prospect St SE16......118 B5
ProspectVale SE18......122 A2
Prospect Wharf E1......118 C6
Prospero Ho 7
DA17......125 C1
Prospero Rd N19......49 A1
Protea Cl E16......98 D3
Prothero Ho 1 N17......51 D6
Prothero Gdns NW4......46 B4
Prothero Ho 15 NW10......67 B1
Prothero Rd
SW6......135 B5 264 C4
Proud Ho 10 E1......96 B1
Prout Gr NW10......67 D4
Prout Rd E5......74 B5
Provence St N1......235 A4
Providence Ave HA2......41 C1
Providence Cl E9......96 D6
Providence Ct
Harlington UB3......127 B5
Islington N1......234 C5
Mayfair W1......248 B6
Providence La UB3......127 B5
Providence Pl N1......234 C5
Providence Rd UB7......104 B5
Providence Row N1......233 C3
Providence Row Cl 50
E1......96 B2
Providence Sq 36
SE1......118 A4
Providence Yd E1 2......96 A4
Provident Ind Est
UB3......106 A4
Provincial Terr 2
SE20......184 D3
Provost Ct NW3......70 D2

Provost Rd NW3......70 D1
Provost St N1......95 B4 235 C2
Prowse Ave WD23......8 A2
Prowse Pl NW1......71 C1
Prudence La BR6......226 C4
Pruden Cl N14......15 C4
Prudent Pas EC2......242 B1
Prusom's Island 8
E1......118 B5
Prusom St E1......118 B5
Pryors The NW3......70 B5
Puccinia Ct TW19......148 A3
Pudding La EC3......252 D6
Pudding Mill La E15......97 D6
Pudding Mill Lane Sta
E15......97 D6
Puddle Dock
EC4......116 D6 252 C6
Puffin Cl
Barking IG11......102 B4
Beckenham BR3......206 D4
Puffin Ct 1 SE21......86 D3
PuffinTerr IG5......56 C6
Puget Ct 11 E2......96 C4
Pugin Ct N1......85 A6
Pulborough Rd
SW18......157 B4
Pulborough Way
TW4......128 C1
Pulford Rd N15......51 B3
Pulham Ave N2......48 B5
Pulham Ho SW8......270 C3
Puller Rd EN5......100 A4
Pulleyns Ave E6......100 A4
Pullman Ct 2......160 B3
Pullman Gdns SW15......156 C5
Pullman Mews SE12......165 B1
Pullman Pl SE9......166 A6
Pulross Rd SW9......163 A4
Pulteney Cl
3 Isleworth TW7......131 A2
20 Old Ford E3......97 B6
Pulteney Gdns 2 E18......55 B6
Pulteney Rd E18......55 B6
Pulteney Terr
N1......84 B6 233 D6
Pulton Ho SE4......141 A4
Pulton Pl
SW6......135 C5 265 A3
Puma Trade Pk 284......202 B5
Pump Alley 6 TW8......131 D5
Pump Cl UB5......45 C5
Pump Ct EC4......241 A1
Pump House Cl
Bromley BR2......186 D1
Rotherhithe SE16......118 C5
Pumphouse Educational
Mus The* SE16......119 C4
Pump House Gall*
SW11......137 A3 268 A3
Pumping Ho 3 E14......120 B6
Pumping Station Rd
W4......133 C3
Pump La
Deptford SE14......140 C5
Hayes UB3......106 A5
Pump Pail N CR0......221 A5
Pump Pail S CR0......221 A5
Punchard Cres E14......121 D5
Punderson's Gdns E2......96 B4
Puran Ho E1......96 C5
Purbeck Ave KT3......199 D3
Purbeck Ct 2 N20......14 C2
Purbeck Dr NW2......68 D6
Purbeck Ho SW8......162 D6
Purbrook Est SE1......253 B1
Purbrook Ho 2
SW15......156 B3
Purbrook St SE1......253 B6
Purcell Cres
SW6......135 A5 264 A4
Purcell Ho
Chelsea SW10......266 C5
Isleworth TW2......152 B5
Southall UB1......85 C1
Purcell Mews 2
NW10......67 C1
Purcell Rd UB6......85 D2
Purcells Ave HA8......26 C5
Purcell St N1......95 C5
Purchese St
NW1......83 D2 234 A6
Purday Ho 4 W10......91 B4
Purdey Ct 3 KT4......200 A1
Purdon Ho 11 SE15......140 A4

Purdy St E3......97 D3
Purkis Cl UB3......105 A6
Purland Ct RM8......59 B1
Purland Rd SE28,
SE18......123 D4
Purley Ave NW2......69 A6
Purley Oaks Prim Sch
CR2......221 B1
Purley Pl N1......72 D1
PurleyView Terr
CR2......221 B1
Purley Rd
Edmonton N9......17 C1
South Croydon CR2......221 B1
Purley Way
Croydon CR0, CR9......220 C3
Thornton Heath CR0......204 B1
Purley Way Cres
CR0......204 B2
Purneys Rd SE9......143 D1
Purrett Rd SE18......123 D1
Purser Ho 3 SW2......160 C5
Pursers Cross Rd
SW6......135 B4 264 D2
Pursewardens Cl
W13......109 C5
Pursley Rd NW7......28 B3
Purves Rd NW10......90 C5
Purvis Ho CR0......205 B2
Pusey Ho 20 E14......97 C1
Puteaux Ho 6 E2......96 D5
PUTNEY......156 C6
Putney Bridge App
SW6......135 A2
Putney Bridge Rd
SW15......135 B1
Putney Bridge Sta
SW6......135 B2
Putney Comm SW15......134 C2
Putney Exchange
Shopping Ctr
SW15......134 D1
Putney Gdns RM6......58 B4
PUTNEY HEATH......156 C4
Putney Heath
SW15......156 C5
Putney Heath La
SW15......156 D5
Putney High Sch
SW15......156 D6
Putney High St
SW15......134 D1
Putney Hill
12 Putney SW15......156 C4
Putney SW15......156 D6
Putney L Ctr SW15......134 C1
Putney Park Ave
SW15......134 A1
Putney Park La
SW15......156 B6
Putney Park Sch
SW15......134 B1
Putney Pier SW15......135 A2
Putney School of Art &
Design SW15......135 A1
Putney Sta SW15......135 A1
PUTNEY VALE......156 A1
Putney Wharf Twr
SW15......135 A2
Pycombe Cnr N12......29 B6
Pycroft Way N9......34 A6
Pylbrook Rd SM1......217 D5
Pylon Trad Est E16......98 B2
Pym CI EN4......14 B6
Pymers Mead SE21......161 A3
Pymmes Brook Dr EN4......2 C1
Pymmes Brook Ho 3
N10......31 A3
Pymmes Cl
Bowes Pk N13......32 B5
Tottenham N17......34 B2
Pymmes Gdns N NW9......17 D1
Pymmes Gdns S N9......17 D1
Pymmes Green Rd
N11......16 A6
Pymmes Mews N13......32 A5
Pymmes Rd N13......32 A5
Pynchester Cl UB10......40 C6
Pyne Rd KT6......198 C1
Pynfolds SE16......118 B4
Pynham Cl SE2......124 B3
Pynnacles Cl HA7......25 B5
Pynnersmead SE24......161 A6
Pyramid Ho N10......31 D6
Pyrford Ho 12 SW9......138 D1

Pyrland Rd
Richmond TW10......154 B5
Stoke Newington N5......73 B3
Pyrmont Gr SE27......160 D1
Pyrmont Rd W4......132 C6
Pytchley Cres SE19......183 A4
Pytchley Rd SE22......139 C2

Q

Quadrangle Cl SE1......263 A4
Quadrangle HoThe
E15......76 C2
Quadrangle Lo
SW19......179 C4
QuadrangleThe
Chelsea SW10......266 B2
Fulham SW6......264 A3
Herne Hill SE24......161 A6
8 North Kensington
W12......90 C1
Paddington W2......237 A2
Stanmore HA7......25 C3
Walthamstow E17......35 B1
Quadrant Arc 5 E1......249 B5
Quadrant Bsns Ctr
NW6......46 B4
Quadrant Gr NW5......70 D3
Quadrant Ho E15......98 C4
Quadrant Rd
Finchley N2......30 C2
Richmond TW9......131 D1
Thornton Heath CR7......204 D5
QuadrantThe
4 Kensal Green
W10......90 D6
Richmond TW9......132 A1
Sutton SM2......218 A2
Walthamstow E17......35 B1
Wimbledon SW20......179 A2
Quaggy Wlk SE3......143 A1
Quainton Hall Sch
HA1......42 C3
Quainton St NW10......55 D2
Quaker Ct EC1......242 B6
Quaker La UB2......107 C3
Quakers CourseNW9......27 D2
Quakers LaTW7......131 A4
Quaker's Pl E7......77 D3
Quaker St E1......95 D3 243 C5
Quakers Wlk N21......17 B5
Quality Ct WC2......241 A2
Quantock Cl UB3......127 B5
Quantock Ct
4 East Barnet N20......14 C2
Greenford UB6......64 C3
Quantock Dr KT4......200 A1
Quantock Gdns NW2......68 D6
Quantock Ho N16......51 C1
Quantock Mews 3
SE15......140 A3
Quarles Park Rd RM6......58 C3
Quarrendon StSW6......135 C3
Quarr Rd SM1......217 B2
Quarry Park Rd SM1......217 B2
Quarry Rd SW18......158 A5
Quarry Rise SM1......217 B2
QuarterdeckThe
E14......119 C4
Quartermain Ho
SM4......202 A4
Quartermaine Ct
SM4......202 A4
Quayle Ct 3 E10......75 D4
Quayside Ct 8 SE16......118 C5
Quay West TW11......175 B5
Quebec & Crown
Wharves E14......97 B1
Quebec Ind Est
SE16......119 A4
Quebec Mews W1......237 A1
Quebec Rd Hayes UB4......84 C1
Ilford IG1......56 C3
Quebec Way SE16......119 A4
Quebec Wharf 8 E8......95 C6
QuedgeleyCt 3
SE15......139 C1
Queen Adelaide Ct
SE20......184 C4
Queen Adelaide Rd
SE20......184 C3
Queen Alexandra Mans
WC1......233 A1
Queen Alexandra's Ct
SW19......179 B5

Queen Anne Ave
BR2......208 D6
Queen Anne Dr
KT10......212 C1
Queen Anne Gate
DA7......146 D2
Queen Anne Mews
W1......238 D3
Queen Anne Rd E9......74 D2
Queen Annes Cl
TW2......152 B1
Queen Anne's Gate
SW1......115 D4 249 C1
Queen Anne's Gdns
Bedford Pk W4......111 C3
Ealing W5......110 A4
Enfield EN1......17 C5
Mitcham CR4......202 D6
Queen Anne's Gr
Bedford Pk W4......111 C3
Ealing W5......110 A4
Enfield EN1......17 C5
Queen Anne's Pl EN1......17 C5
Queen Anne's Sch 8
W1......93 B2 238 C3
Queen AnneTerr 9
E1......118 B6
Queenborough Gdns
Chislehurst BR7......189 B4
Ilford IG2......56 C5
Queen Caroline St
W6......112 C1
Queen Charlotte's &
Chelsea Hospl W12......90 A1
Queen Ct WC1......240 B5
Queen Elizabeth Ct
Barnet EN5......1 B1
5 Kingsland N1......73 B2
Queen Elizabeth Gdns
SM4......201 C5
Queen Elizabeth Hall &
Purcell Room*
SE1......250 D4
Queen Elizabeth Ho
SW12......159 A4
Queen Elizabeth Hospl
SE18......144 A5
Queen Elizabeth II Con
Ctr SW1......249 D1
Queen Elizabeth II
Jubilee Sch 8 NW9......91 B3
Queen Elizabeth II Pier
SE10......120 D5
Queen Elizabeth Rd
Kingston u T KT2......176 B1
Walthamstow E17......53 A6
Queen Elizabeth's Cl
N16......73 B6
Queen Elizabeth's Coll 18
SE10......142 A5
Queen Elizabeth's Dr
N14......16 A3
Queen Elizabeth's Girls
Sch EN5......1 B1
Queen Elizabeth's
Hunting Lodge Mus*
E4......20 D4
Queen Elizabeth St
SE1......117 D4 253 C2
Queen Elizabeth's Wlk
Stoke Newington N16......73 B6
Wallington SM6......219 D3
Queen Elizabeth Wlk
SW13......134 B4
Queenhithe EC4......252 B6
Queen Margaret Flats 22
E2......96 B4
Queen Margarets Ct
N1......73 C3
Queen Margaret's Gr
N1......73 C3
Queen Mary Ave
SM4......200 D4
Queen Mary Cl KT9......214 C5
Queen Mary Ct
TW19......148 A3
Queen Mary Rd
Charlton TW17......171 A1
South Norwood SE19......182 D4
Queen Mary's Ave
SM5......218 D1
Queen Mary's Gdns*
NW1......231 A1

Queen Mary's Hospl DA14 190 A4
Queen Mary's Univ Hospl SW15 156 A5
Queen Mary, Univ of London E1 97 A3
Queen Mother Sp Ctr SW1 259 A4
Queen of Denmark Ct SE16 119 B3
Queens Acre SM3 217 A1
Queen St Pl EC4 252 B6
Queens Ave
Feltham TW13 172 C6
Muswell Hill N10 49 B6
Stanmore HA7 25 C1
Whetstone N20 14 B2
Queen's Ave
Finchley N3 30 A2
Southall UB1 86 A1
Southgate N21 16 D3
Woodford IG8 37 B5
Queensberry Ho 6 TW9 153 D6
Queensberry Mews W SW7 256 C4
Queensberry Pl
Chelsea SW7 114 B2 256 C4
Plashet E12 78 A3
Queensberry Way SW7 256 C4
Queensborough Ct N3 47 B5
Queensborough Mews W2 246 A6
Queensborough Pas W2 246 A6
Queensborough Terr W2 113 D6 245 D6
Queensbridge Ct 1 E2 95 D5
Queensbridge Inf Sch 11 E8 73 D1
Queensbridge Pk TW7 152 C6
Queensbridge Rd
Dalston E8 73 D1
Shoreditch E2, E8 95 D6
QUEENSBURY 44 B6
Queensbury IG9 21 B3
Queensbury Circ Par HA3 44 A6
Queensbury Ct CR7 183 A1
Queensbury Rd
Kingsbury NW9 45 B2
Wembley HA0 88 B5
Queensbury St 22 N1 73 A1
Queensbury Sta HA7, HA8 44 B6
Queensbury Station Par HA8 44 B6
Queen's CE Prim Sch The TW9 132 C5
Queen's Cir SW11 137 B5 268 C3
Queen's Cl
Edgware HA8 26 C5
Wallington SM6 219 B3
Queen's Club Gdns W14 135 A6 264 B6
Queen's Club The W14 113 A1 254 B1
Queen's Coll W1 93 B2 238 C3
Queen's Coll Prep Sch W1 238 C4
Queenscourt HA9 66 A4
Queens Cres TW10 154 B6
Queen's Cres NW5 71 A2
Queenscroft Rd SE9 165 D5
Queens Ct
Battersea SW11 268 C2
Beckenham BR3 185 D3
Camberwell SE5 139 C3
Leyton E10 53 C2
4 Limehouse E14 119 B6
Sidcup DA14 190 A6
Stanmore HA7 25 B1
8 Temple Fortune NW11 47 B4
Walthamstow E17 53 C4
Queen's Ct
Barnes SW13 134 A2
Beckenham BR3 185 C2
Croydon CR2 221 A3
8 Ealing W5 87 C2
Hampstead Garden Suburb NW11 47 C4
Kensington W2 245 D5
1 Kingston u T KT2 176 C3
Leytonstone E11 54 C2
3 Richmond TW10 154 B5
St John's Wood NW8 229 C4
Thornton Heath CR7 204 C4
Queensdale W11 112 D5
Queensdale Cres W11 112 D5
Queensdale Pl W11 244 A3
Queensdale Rd
Notting Hill W11 112 D5
Notting Hill W11 113 A5 244 A3
Queensdale Wlk W11 244 A3
Queensdown Rd E5 74 B4
Queens Dr
Surbiton KT5 198 C3
Walthamstow E10 53 C2
Queen's Dr Acton W3 88 C1
Finsbury Pk N4 72 D6
Thames Ditton KT7 197 A3
Queen's Elm Par SW3 256 D2
Queen's Elm Sq SW3 256 D1
Queensferry Wlk N17 52 B5
Queensfield Ct SM3 216 C4
Queen's Gallery★ SW1 115 B4 248 D1
Queens Gate IG4 56 B5
Queen's Gate SW7 114 A3 256 B5
Queensgate Ct N12 29 D5
Queensgate Gdns SW15 134 B1
Queens Gate Gdns BR7 189 B2
Queen's Gate Gdns SW7 114 A3 256 B5
Queensgate Ho 34 E3 97 B5
Queen's Gate Jun Sch SW7 256 C4
Queen's Gate Mews SW7 114 A3 256 B6
Queensgate Pl 10 NW6 69 C1
Queen's Gate Pl SW7 114 A3 256 B5
Queen's Gate Pl Mews SW7 114 A3 256 B5
Queen's Gate Terr SW7 114 A3 256 B6
Queens Gate Villas E9 75 A1
Queens Gdns NW4 46 C4
Queen's Gdns
Bayswater W2 114 A6 246 A6
Ealing W5 87 C3
Heston TW5 129 A4
Queen's Gr NW8 92 B6 229 D5
Queen's Grove Rd E4 20 B3
Queen's Head Pas EC2 242 A2
Queen's Head St N1 94 D6 234 D5
Queen's Head Yd SE1 252 C3
Queens Ho 1 SE17 139 B6
Queen's Ho TW11 174 D4
Queen's House The★ SE10 142 B6
Queens Keep 10 TW1 153 C5
Queens La
2 Ashford TW15 170 B6
Muswell Hill N10 49 B6
Queensland Ave
Edmonton N18 33 A4
Merton SW19 179 D2
Queensland Cl E17 35 B1
Queensland Ct N10 31 B3
Queensland Ho 2 E16 122 C5
Queensland Rd N7 72 C4
Queens Lo HA7 25 A5
Queens Manor Sch SW6 134 D5
Queens Mans
Hampstead NW6 69 D3
Hendon NW4 46 B4
Queen's Mans
Brook Green W6 112 D2
Muswell Hill N10 49 A6
Queensmead
Ashford TW15 170 B5
St John's Wood NW8 92 B6 229 D6
Queens Mead HA8 26 B4
Queen's Mead Rd BR2 186 D1
Queensmead Sch HA4 62 D4
Queensmead Sp Ctr HA4 62 D3
Queensmere 4 SM1 217 D3
Queensmere Cl SW19 156 D2
Queensmere Ct SW13 134 A6
Queensmere Rd SW19 156 D2
Queens Mews 5 IG9 21 C2
Queen's Mews W2 113 D6 245 C6
Queensmill Rd SW6 134 D5
Queensmill Sch SW6 135 C3
Queen's Mkt★ E13 99 C6
Queens Par Ealing W5 88 B1
7 Hendon NW4 46 B4
3 Willesden NW2 68 C2
Queen's Par
3 Friern Barnet N11 30 D5
Wood Green N11 32 A3
Queens Parade Cl N11 30 D5
Queens Park Com Sch NW6 90 D6
Queens Park Ct 5 W10 90 D4
Queens Park Gdns TW13 149 D1
Queen's Park Prim Sch 20 W10 91 A3
Queen's Park Sta NW6 91 B5
Queen's Pas BR7 188 D4
Queen's Pl SM4 201 C5
Queen Sq WC1 94 A2 240 B4
Queen's Quay EC4 252 B6
Queens Rd Hayes UB3 83 C1
Morden SM4 201 C5
Twickenham TW1 153 A3
West Drayton UB7 104 B4
Queen's Rd
Barking IG11 79 A2
Beckenham BR3 185 A1
Bowes Pk N11 32 A4
Bromley BR1 187 A1
Buckhurst Hill IG9 21 C2
Chislehurst BR7 188 D4
Ealing W5 88 A1
Edmonton N9 18 B2
Enfield EN1 5 C1
Feltham TW13 150 B3
Finchley N3 30 A2
Hampton TW12 173 D6
Hendon NW4 46 C4
Hounslow TW3 129 D2
Kingston u T KT2 176 C3
Leytonstone E11 54 C2
Mitcham CR4 202 B6
Mortlake SW14 133 B2
New Cross Gate SE14, SE15 140 C4
Newham E13 99 C6
New Malden KT3 199 D4
Richmond KT2, TW10 176 C5
Richmond TW10 154 B5
Southall UB2 107 A4
Teddington TW11 174 D4
Thames Ditton KT7 196 D4
Thornton Heath CR0 205 A3
Wallington SM6 219 B3
Walthamstow E17 53 C3
Welling DA16 146 B3
Wimbledon SW19 179 C4
Queen's Rd W E13 99 B5
Queens Reach KT8 196 C5
Queen's Ride SW13 134 B2
Queen's Rise TW10 154 B5
Queen's Road Sta SE15 140 C4
Queen's Row SE17 139 B6
Queen St
Bexleyheath DA7 147 B2
City of London EC4 117 A6 252 B6
Croydon CR0 221 A4
Mayfair W1 115 B5 248 C4
Tottenham N17 33 C4
Queens Terr
Harrow HA3 24 C1
Newham E13 99 B6
St John's Wood NW8 92 B5 229 C4
Queen's Terr TW7 131 A1
Queens Terr Cotts W7 108 C4
Queensthorpe Rd SE26 184 D6
Queenstown Mews SW8 268 C1
Queenstown Rd SW8 137 B5 268 C4
Queenstown Road (Battersea) Sta SW8 137 B4 268 D2
Queensville Rd SW12, SW4 159 D4
Queens Walk Ho W5 87 C2
Queensway
Coney Hall BR4 224 D4
Croydon CR0 220 B3
Enfield EN3 6 C1
Kensington W2 113 D6 245 D6
Orpington BR5 211 A3
Sunbury TW16 172 B1
Queens Way
Feltham TW13 172 C6
Hendon NW4 46 C4
Queensway Bsns Ctr EN3 6 C1
Queensway Sta W2 113 D6 245 D5
Queens Well Ave N20 30 C6
Queenswell Jun & Inf Schs N20 14 B2
Queens Wlk
Ashford TW15 170 A6
Chingford E4 20 B3
Harrow HA1 42 C5
Ruislip HA4 62 C5
Welsh Harp NW9 67 A6
Queen's Wlk
Ealing W5 87 C2
St James SW1 115 C5 249 A3
Queenswood Ave
Chingford E17 36 A2
Hampton TW12 173 D4
Hounslow TW3, TW5 129 B3
Thornton Heath CR7 204 C4
Wallington CR0, SM6 219 D4
Queenswood Ct
7 Clapham Pk SW4 160 A6
11 West Norwood SE27 183 B6
Queenswood Gdns E11 55 B1
Queenswood Pk N3 29 A2
Queenswood Rd
Blackfen DA15 167 D5
Forest Hill SE23 163 A1
Queen's Wood Rd N6 49 B3
Queens Yd E9 75 C2
Queen's Yd W1 239 B5
Queen Victoria Ave HA0 65 D1
Queen Victoria Meml★ SW1 249 A2
Queen Victoria St EC4 117 A6 252 A6
Queen Victoria Terr 12 E1 118 B6
Quelch Ho 2 N19 71 D3
Quemerford Rd N7 72 B3
Quendon Ho 9 W10 90 C3
Quenington Ct 5 SE15 139 D6
Quenington Mans SW6 264 C2
Quennel Ho 7 SW12 159 C4
Quentin Pl SE13 142 C2
Quentin Rd SE13 142 C2
Quernmore Cl BR1 187 A4
Quernmore Rd
Plaistow BR1 187 A4
Stroud Green N4 50 C3
Querrin St SW6 136 A3
Quested Ct 27 E8 74 B3
Quex Mews NW6 91 C6
Quex Rd NW6 91 C6
Quick Rd W4 111 C1
Quicks Rd SW19 179 D3
Quick St N1 94 D5 234 D3
Quick Street Mews N1 234 C3
Quickswood NW3 70 C1
Quiet Nook BR2 225 D5
Quill La SW15 134 D1
Quill St Ealing W5 88 A5
Highbury N4 72 C5
Quilp St SE1 252 A2
Quilters Pl SE9 167 A3
Quilter St
Bethnal Green E2 96 A4
Plumstead Comm SE18 123 D1
Quilting Ct 23 SE16 118 D4
Quince Ho TW13 150 A3
Quince Rd SE13 141 D3
Quinnel Cl SE18 123 D1
Quinta Dr EN5 12 C6
Quintin Ave SW20 179 B2
Quintin Cl HA5 40 B4
Quintin Ct W4 133 A5
Quintin Kynaston Sch NW8 92 B6 229 C5
Quintock Ho 2 TW9 132 C4
Quinton Cl
Beckenham BR3 208 A6
Cranford TW5 128 B5
Wallington SM6 219 B4
Quinton Ho SW8 270 A4
Quinton Rd KT7 197 A1
Quinton St SW18 158 A2
Quixley St 1 E14 120 B6
Quorn Rd SE22 139 C2
Quwwatul Islam Girls Sch E7 77 B2

R

Rabbit Row W8 245 B4
Rabbits Rd E12 78 A4
Rabbs Farm Prim Sch UB7 104 A6
Rabinal Ho EN3 18 D6
Rabournmead Dr UB5 63 A3
Raby Rd KT3 199 B5
Raby St E14 97 A1
Raccoon Way TW4 128 C3
Rachel Cl IG6 57 B6
Rachel Ct SM2 218 B1
Racine 15 SE5 139 C4
Rackham Cl DA16 146 B3
Rackham Mews SW16 181 C4
Racs Flats 9 SE1 118 A2
Racton Rd SW6 135 C6 265 A5
Radbourne Ave W5 109 C2
Radbourne Cl E5 74 D4
Radbourne Cres E17 36 B1
Radbourne Ct HA3 43 B3
Radbourne Rd SW12 159 D3
Radcliff Bldg EC1 241 A4
Radcliffe Ave
Enfield EN2 5 A4
Willesden Green NW10 90 A5
Radcliffe Coll
Marylebone W1 93 C1 239 A1
Soho W1 93 D1 239 C2
Radcliffe Gdns SM5 218 C1
Radcliffe Ho 10 SE16 118 B2
Radcliffe Path 5 SW8 137 B3
Radcliffe Rd
Bermondsey SE1 263 B6
Harrow HA3 25 A1

Radcliffe Rd *continued*
South Croydon CR0 .. 221 D5
Southgate N21 .... 16 D3
Radcliffe Sq SW15 .. 156 D5
Radcliffe Way UB5 .... 84 D4
Radcliff Mews TW12 . 174 A5
Radcot Point 2
SE23 .... 162 D1
Radcot St SE11 ..... 261 B1
Raddington Rd W10... 91 A2
Radfield Way DA15... 167 B4
Radford Ho
7 Bow Comm E14..... 97 D2
Islington N7 .... 72 B3
Radford Rd SE13..... 164 A5
Radford Way IG11 .. 101 D4
Radipole Rd
SW6 .... 135 B4 264 C2
Radius Pk TW6 ..... 127 D1
Radland Rd E16...... 99 A1
Radlet Ave SE23 ..... 162 B2
Radlett Cl E7 .... 76 D2
Radlett Pl
NW8........ 92 C6 230 A6
Radley Ave IG3 .... 80 A4
Radley Cl TW14 ..... 149 D3
Radley Ct
4 Catford BR1 ..... 186 A6
25 Rotherhithe SE16 . 118 D4
Radley Gdns HA3 ..... 44 A5
Radley Ho
11 Abbey Wood
SE2 .... 124 D4
Marylebone NW1.... 237 C6
Radley Lo 30 SW19.. 156 D3
Radley Mews W8 ... 255 B5
Radley Rd N17 .... 33 C1
Radley's La E18........ 37 A1
Radleys Mead RM10... 81 D2
Radley Sq E5 .... 74 C6
Radley Terr 1 E16 .... 98 D2
Radlix Rd E10......... 53 C1
Radnor Ave
Bexley DA16......... 168 B6
Harrow HA1.......... 42 C4
Radnor Cl
Chislehurst BR7..... 189 C4
Mitcham CR4 .... 204 A5
Radnor Cres
Redbridge IG4......... 56 B4
Woolwich SE18 ..... 146 A5
Radnor Ct Ealing W7... 86 D1
6 Forest Hill SE23 .. 162 D1
Harrow HA3........... 24 D2
Radnor Gdns
Enfield EN1 .... 5 C4
Twickenham TW1.... 152 D2
Radnor Gr UB10 ...... 82 C5
Radnor Ho
East Molesey KT8 .... 196 B5
Thornton Heath
SW16 .... 182 B1
Radnor Lo W2 ...... 236 D1
Radnor Mews
W2 .... 92 B1 236 D1
Radnor Pl W2 . 92 C1 237 A1
Radnor Rd
Harrow HA1.......... 42 C4
Kensal Rise NW6...... 91 A6
Peckham SE15...... 140 A5
Twickenham TW1.... 152 D2
Radnor St EC1 95 A4 235 B1
Radnor Terr
W14 .... 113 B2 254 C4
Radnor Way NW10.... 88 D3
Radnor Wlk
Chelsea
SW3 ..... 114 D1 257 C1
Croydon CR0 .... 207 A3
21 Millwall E14 ..... 119 C2
Radstock Ave HA3 .... 43 B6
Radstock Cl N11....... 31 A4
Radstock St SW11 .. 267 A3
Radway Ho 38 W2..... 91 C2
Radwell Ho SW2...... 160 C6
Raebarn Ct 6 SW16 . 160 A1
Raebarn Gdns EN5.... 12 B6
Raeburn Ave KT5 ... 198 D3
Raeburn Cl
Hampstead Garden Suburb
NW11 .... 48 A3
Teddington KT1 ..... 175 D3
Raeburn Ho
5 Belmont SM2 .... 217 D1
6 Northolt UB5....... 84 D5
Raeburn Rd
Edgware HA8......... 26 C2
Hayes UB4........... 83 B5
Sidcup DA15......... 167 C5
Raeburn St SW2 ..... 138 A1
Raffles Ct HA8 .... 26 B6
Raffles Ho NW4....... 46 B5
Rafford Way BR1..... 209 B6
RAF Mus★ NW9 ...... 28 A1
Ragged School Mus★
E3................. 97 A2
Raggleswood BR7 ... 188 C2
Raglan Cl TW4 .... 151 B6
Raglan Ct
Brixton SW9........ 138 C2
Croydon CR0, CR2 ... 220 D3
Lee SE12 .... 165 A6
Wembley HA9 .... 66 C5
Raglan Jun & Inf Schs
EN1 .... 17 C4
Raglan Prim Sch
BR2 .... 209 D5
Raglan Rd
Belvedere DA17...... 125 B2
Bromley BR2 .... 209 C5
Enfield EN1 .... 17 D4
Walthamstow E17 ..... 54 B4
Woolwich SE18 ..... 123 A1
Raglan St NW5 .... 71 B2
Raglan Terr HA2 .... 63 D4
Raglan Way UB5 ...... 64 A2
Ragley Cl W3 .... 111 A4
Ragwort Ct 1 SE26 .. 184 B5
Rahere Ho EC1 ..... 235 A2
Railey Mews NW5..... 71 C3
Railshead Rd TW1,
TW7 .... 131 B1
Railton Rd SE24..... 160 D6
Railway App
Bermondsey SE1 .... 252 D4
Harrow HA1, HA3 ..... 42 D5
Stroud Green N4 ...... 50 C3
11 Twickenham TW1 . 153 A4
Wallington SM6 ..... 219 B3
Railway Ave SE16 .... 118 C4
Railway Cotts
Hammersmith W6 ... 112 C4
Ilford IG6............ 57 B6
Railway Gr SE14 ..... 141 B5
Railway Pl DA17 ..... 125 C3
Railway Rd TW11 ... 174 D6
Railway Rise SE22 .. 139 C1
Railway Side SW13 .. 133 C2
Railway St Ilford RM6 .. 58 C2
King's Cross N1 ..... 233 B3
Railway Terr
Chingford E17 .... 36 A2
Feltham TW13, TW14. 150 A3
Ladywell SE13 ...... 163 D6
Rainborough Cl
NW10.............. 67 A2
Rainbow Ave E14 .... 119 D1
Rainbow Ct 3 SE14 .. 141 A6
Rainbow Ind Est
SW20............. 178 B1
Rainbow Montessori Sch
NW6................ 69 D1
Rainbow Quay SE16.. 119 A3
Rainbow Sch 5
SW17............. 158 A2
Rainbow St SE5...... 139 C5
Rainbow Works N15 .. 52 A4
Raine Gdns 4 IG8 .... 37 A6
Raines Ct N16 .... 73 D6
Raine's Foundation
Lower Sch 32 E2 .... 96 B4
Raine's Foundation Sch
34 E2............... 96 C5
Raine St E1.......... 118 B5
Rainford Ho 9 N7 .... 72 B6
Rainham Cl
Sidcup SE9 .... 167 C5
Wandsworth SW11 ... 158 C5
Rainham Ho NW1 .... 232 B5
Rainham Rd NW10..... 90 C4
Rainham Rd N RM10 .. 81 D6
Rainham Rd S RM10... 81 D4
Rainhill Way E3....... 97 C4
Rainsborough Ave
SE8................ 119 A2
Rainsford Cl HA7 ..... 25 C5
Rainsford Ct NW10.... 88 D5
Rainsford Ho 14
SW2.............. 160 B6
Rainsford Rd NW10 ... 88 D5
Rainsford St W2 .... 237 A2
Rainstar Est N18...... 34 C6
Rainton Rd SE7 ...... 121 A1
Rainville Rd W6...... 134 C6
Raisins Hill HA5 ...... 40 C6
Raith Ave N14 .... 15 D1
Raleigh Ave
Hayes UB4........... 84 B2
Wallington SM6 ..... 219 D4
Raleigh Cl
Hendon NW4 .... 46 C4
Pinner HA5........... 40 D2
Ruislip HA4 .... 61 D6
Raleigh Ct
Beckenham BR3..... 185 D2
4 Dulwich SE19 .... 183 D5
Ealing W13........... 87 B2
7 Hammersmith
W12 .... 112 B4
2 Rotherhithe SE16. 118 D5
Wallington SM6...... 219 B2
Raleigh Dr
East Barnet N20....... 14 C1
Esher KT10 .... 212 B3
Tolworth KT5 .... 199 A1
Raleigh Gdns
Mitcham CR4 .... 202 D6
Tulse Hill SW2 .... 160 B5
Raleigh Ho
30 Clapham SW8.... 137 D3
Isle of Dogs E14..... 119 D4
1 Thames Ditton
KT7 .... 197 A2
Raleigh Mews
Islington N1........ 234 D5
6 Orpington BR6 ... 227 D3
Raleigh Rd Enfield EN2 .. 5 B1
Feltham TW13 ...... 149 D2
Finchley N10 .... 30 C2
Hornsey N8 .... 50 C5
Penge SE20 .... 184 D3
Richmond TW9 ...... 132 B2
Southall UB2 .... 107 A1
Raleigh St N1 .94 D6 234 D5
Raleigh Way
Feltham TW13 ...... 172 C5
Southgate N14........ 16 A3
Ralph Ct 8 W2 .... 91 D1
Ralph Perring Ct
BR3............... 207 C5
Ralston St SW3 ..... 257 C1
Ramac Ind Est SE7... 121 B1
Rama Cl SW16....... 182 A3
Rama Ct HA1 .... 64 C6
Ramac Way SE7 ..... 121 B1
Rama La SE19 .... 183 D3
Ramar Ho 12 E1 ...... 96 A2
Rambler Cl SW16 .... 181 C6
Rambler Ct 11 NW9 ... 46 A5
Rame Cl SW17....... 181 A5
Ramilles Cl SW2..... 160 A5
Ramilles Ho W1 .... 239 B1
Ramillies Pl
W1 .... 93 C1 239 A1
Ramillies Rd
Bedford Pk W4 ...... 111 B3
Blackfen DA15 ...... 168 B5
Edgware NW7 .... 11 C2
Ramillies St W1..... 239 A1
Ramney Dr EN3 .... 7 A6
Rampart St E1......... 96 B1
Ram Pas KT1 .... 175 D1
Rampayne St SW1 ... 259 C2
Rampton Cl E4 .... 19 C1
Ramsay Ho NW8 .... 230 A4
Ramsay Rd
Acton W3 .... 111 A4
Leyton E7 .... 76 D4
Ramscroft Cl N9 ...... 17 C4
Ramsdale Rd SW17 .. 181 A5
Ramsdean Ho 1
SW15............. 156 B3
Ramsden Rd
Balham SW12 ...... 159 A4
Friern Barnet N11 ..... 30 D5
Ramsey Cl
Greenford UB6........ 64 B3
West Hendon NW9 .... 45 D3
Ramsey Ct
Croydon CR0 .... 220 D6
Hornsey N8 .... 49 D4
Putney SW15........ 156 C5
6 Upper Holloway
N19 .... 71 D6
Ramsey Ho
5 Battersea SW11... 136 B1
14 Kennington SW9.. 138 C5
Ramsey Ho *continued*
7 Merton SW19 .... 179 D2
Ramsey Rd CR7...... 204 B3
Ramsey St E2......... 96 A3
Ramsey Way N14 ..... 15 C4
Ramsey Wlk N1....... 73 B2
Ramsfort Ho 4
SE16.............. 118 B2
Ramsgate Cl 10 E16.. 121 B5
Ramsgate St E8 ...... 73 D2
Ramsgill App IG2 ..... 57 D5
Ramsgill Dr IG2 ...... 57 D5
Rams Gr RM6......... 59 A5
Ram St SW18 .... 157 D6
Ramulis Dr UB4....... 84 D3
Ramus Wood Ave
BR6............... 227 C3
Rance Ho 12 SE7..... 122 A2
Rancliffe Gdns SE9 .. 144 A1
Rancliffe Rd E6...... 100 A5
Randal Cremer JMI Sch
16 E2............... 95 D5
Randall 9 NW9 .... 27 D2
Randall Ave NW2 ..... 67 D5
Randall Cl
SW11 ...... 136 C4 267 A2
Randall Ct NW7....... 28 A3
Randall Pl SE10...... 142 A5
Randall Rd
SE11 .... 116 B2 260 C3
Randall Row SE11... 260 C3
Randell's Rd
N1 .... 94 A6 233 B6
Randisbourne Gdns
SE6............... 163 D1
Randle Rd TW10 ..... 175 C6
Randlesdown Rd
SE6............... 163 D1
Randmore Ct 6
BR3............... 185 C3
Randolf Ct
Paddington NW6 ...... 91 D5
St John's Wood NW8 . 229 A5
Randolf Rd BR2...... 210 B1
Randolph App E16 .... 99 C1
Randolph Ave
W9 .... 92 A4 229 A1
Randolph Cl KT2..... 177 A5
Randolph Cres
W9 .... 92 A3 236 A6
Randolph Ct HA5 ..... 23 C3
Randolph Gdns NW6.. 91 D5
Randolph Gr RM6..... 58 C4
Randolph Mews
W9 .... 92 A3 236 B5
Randolph Rd
Paddington
W9 .... 92 A3 236 B5
Southall UB1 .... 107 B4
Walthamstow E17 ..... 53 D4
Randolph St NW1..... 71 C1
Randon Cl HA2 .... 23 D1
Ranelagh Ave
Barnes SW13....... 134 A3
Fulham SW6......... 135 B2
Ranelagh Cl HA8...... 26 C6
Ranelagh Ct HA8 ..... 26 C6
Ranelagh Dr
Edgware HA8......... 26 C6
Twickenham TW1.... 153 C6
Ranelagh Gardens Mans
SW6 .... 135 A2
Ranelagh Gardens (site
of Chelsea Flower
Show)★
SW1........ 115 A1 258 B1
Ranelagh Gdns
3 Bedford Pk W6 ... 111 D3
Chiswick W4 .... 133 A5
Fulham SW6......... 135 B2
Ilford IG1............ 56 C1
Wanstead E11 .... 55 C4
Ranelagh Gr
SW1....... 115 A1 258 B2
Ranelagh Ho SW3 .. 257 C2
Ranelagh Mans 4
SW6 .... 135 B3
Ranelagh Pl KT3..... 199 C4
Ranelagh Prim Sch
E15................. 98 C5
Ranelagh Rd
Dagenham NW10...... 89 D5
Ealing W5.......... 109 D4
Leyton E11........... 76 C4
Newham E15 .... 98 C5
Pimlico SW1. 115 C1 259 B1
Ranelagh Rd *continued*
Southall UB1 .... 106 D5
Tottenham N17 .... 51 C6
Wallend E6......... 100 C5
Wembley HA0 .... 65 D2
Wood Green N22 ...... 32 B2
Ranfurly Rd SM1..... 217 C6
Rangdon St EC3 .... 243 C1
Rangefield Prim Sch
BR1 .... 186 C5
Rangefield Rd BR1.. 186 D5
Rangemoor Rd N15 ... 51 D4
Ranger's House (The
Wernher Collection)★
SE10.............. 142 B4
Ranger's Rd
Buckhurst Hill IG9,
IG10 .... 21 A4
Chingford E4 .... 20 D4
Rangers Sq SE10..... 142 B4
Range Villas TW17 ... 192 A2
Range Way TW17 .... 192 C2
Rangeworth Pl
DA15.............. 167 D1
Rangoon Ho 5 N16... 73 B4
Rankin Cl NW9 .... 45 C6
Rankine Ho SE1 .... 262 A5
Ranleigh Gdns DA7 . 147 B5
Ranmere St SW12.... 159 B3
Ranmoor Cl HA1 ...... 42 B5
Ranmoor Gdns HA1... 42 C5
Ranmore Ave CR0... 221 D5
Ranmore Ct
Kingston u T KT6 .... 197 D4
3 Wimbledon SW20. 178 D2
Rann Ho 1 SW14.... 133 B2
Rannoch Cl HA8 ...... 10 D2
Rannoch Ct 9 KT6... 198 A4
Rannoch Rd W6 .... 134 D6
Rannock Ave NW9 .... 45 C2
Ransford Ho 16
SE21.............. 183 C6
Ransomes Dock Bsns Ctr
SW11 .... 267 B3
Ransomes Mews
SW11 .... 267 B4
Ransom Rd 1 SE7... 121 C1
Ranston St NW1 .... 237 A4
Ranulf Rd NW2 .... 69 B4
Ranwell Cl 18 E3 ..... 97 B6
Ranwell Ho 17 E3..... 97 B6
Ranworth Rd N9...... 18 C2
Ranyard Cl KT9...... 214 B5
Raphael Ct 9 SE16 .. 118 B1
Raphael Dr KT7 ..... 196 D2
Raphael St SW7 .... 247 C1
Rapide 15 NW9 .... 27 C2
Rapley Ho 14 E2 ...... 96 A4
Rashleigh Ct 8
SW8............... 137 B2
Rashleigh Ho WC1.. 233 A1
Rasper Rd N20........ 14 A2
Rastell Ave SW12 ... 159 D3
RATCLIFF........... 118 D6
Ratcliffe Cl SE12..... 165 A4
Ratcliffe Cross St E1 .. 96 D1
Ratcliffe Ho 10 E14 ... 97 A1
Ratcliffe La 16 E14 ... 97 A1
Ratcliffe Orch 9 E1. 118 D6
Ratcliff Rd E7 .... 77 C3
Rathbone Ho
5 Canning Town
E16 .... 98 D1
Kilburn NW6 .... 91 C6
10 Wimbledon SW19. 178 D3
Rathbone Mkt★ 3
E16................. 98 D2
Rathbone Pl
W1 .... 93 D1 239 C2
Rathbone St
Canning Town E16 ..... 98 D1
Fitzrovia W1... 93 C2 239 B3
Rathcoole Ave N8..... 50 B4
Rathcoole Gdns N8 ... 50 B4
Rathfern Prim Sch
SE6............... 163 B3
Rathfern Rd SE6 .... 163 B3
Rathgar Ave W13 .... 109 C5
Rathgar Cl N3 .... 29 B1
Rathgar Rd SW9 .... 138 D2
Rathmell Dr SW4 .... 159 D5
Rathmore Rd SE7.... 121 B1
Ratier 16 NW9 .... 27 C2

Rattray Ct 3 SE6 ... 164 D2
Rattray Rd SW2 ... 160 C6
Raul Rd SE15 ... 140 A4
Raveley St NW5 ... 71 C4
Raven Cl NW9 ... 27 C1
Ravendale Rd TW16 . 171 D1
Ravenet Ct
Battersea SW11 ... 268 C1
Clapham SW4 ... 159 B6
Ravenet St
SW11 ... 137 B4 268 C1
Ravenfield Rd SW17 158 D1
Ravenhill Rd E13 ... 99 C5
Raven Ho 10 SE16 ... 118 D2
Ravenings Par IG3 ... 58 A1
Ravenna Rd SW15 .. 156 D6
Ravenor Ct UB6 ... 85 D3
Ravenor Park Rd UB6 . 86 A4
Ravenor Prim Sch
UB6 ... 85 C4
Raven Rd E18 ... 37 C1
Raven Row E1 ... 96 B2
Ravensbourne Ave
Bromley BR2, BR3 .. 186 C2
Catford BR2 ... 186 B3
Stanwell TW19 ... 148 A3
Ravensbourne Bsns Ctr
BR2 ... 225 D4
Ravensbourne Coll of
Design &
Communication
BR7 ... 188 B5
Ravensbourne Ct
SE6 ... 163 C4
Ravensbourne Gdns
W13 ... 87 B2
Ravensbourne Ho
10 Catford BR1 ... 186 B5
Paddington NW8 ... 237 A4
3 Twickenham TW1 . 153 C5
Ravensbourne Mans 9
SE8 ... 141 C6
Ravensbourne Park Cres
SE6 ... 163 B4
Ravensbourne Pk
SE6 ... 163 C4
Ravensbourne Pl
SE13 ... 141 D3
Ravensbourne Rd
Bromley BR1, BR2 ... 209 A6
Forest Hill SE23 ... 163 B3
Twickenham TW1 ... 153 C5
Ravensbourne Sch The
BR2 ... 209 B5
Ravensbourne Sta
BR3 ... 186 B3
Ravensbury Ave
SM4 ... 202 A4
Ravensbury Ct CR4 .. 202 B5
Ravensbury Gr CR4 .. 202 B5
Ravensbury La CR4 .. 202 B5
Ravensbury Rd
Orpington BR5 ... 211 D5
Wandsworth SW18 .. 157 D2
Ravensbury Terr
SW18 ... 157 D2
Ravenscar NW1 ... 232 A5
Ravenscar Lo 14
SW19 ... 178 D3
Ravenscar Rd
Catford BR1 ... 186 C6
Surbiton KT6 ... 214 B6
Ravens Cl
Bromley BR2 ... 186 D1
Enfield EN1 ... 5 C3
Kingston u T KT1 ... 197 D5
Kingston u T KT6 ... 197 D3
Ravenscourt
1 Shacklewell N16 ... 74 A5
Sunbury TW16 ... 171 D2
Ravenscourt Ave
W6 ... 112 A2
Ravenscourt Cl HA4 .. 39 A2
Ravenscourt Gdns
W6 ... 112 A2
Ravenscourt Ho 13
W6 ... 112 B2
Ravenscourt Park Mans
1 W6 ... 112 B3
Ravenscourt Park Prep
Sch W6 ... 112 A2
Ravenscourt Park Sta
W6 ... 112 B2
Ravenscourt Pk W6 .. 112 A2
Ravenscourt Pl W6 .. 112 B2
Ravenscourt Rd
Hammersmith W6 ... 112 B2
St Paul's Cray BR5 ... 190 B1
Ravenscourt Sq W6 .. 112 A3
Ravenscourt Theatre Sch
14 W6 ... 112 B2
Ravenscraig Rd N11 .. 31 C6
Ravenscroft Ave
Golders Green NW11 .. 47 B2
Wembley HA9 ... 44 B2
Ravenscroft Cl 4
E16 ... 99 A2
Ravenscroft Cres
SE9 ... 166 B1
Ravenscroft Ct NW11 . 47 B2
Ravenscroft Pk EN5 ... 1 A1
Ravenscroft Point 26
E9 ... 74 D2
Ravenscroft Prim Sch 12
E16 ... 99 A3
Ravenscroft Rd
Acton W4 ... 111 A2
Newham E16 ... 99 A2
Penge BR3 ... 184 D1
Ravenscroft Sch N20 .. 13 B4
Ravenscroft St E2 ... 95 D4
Ravensdale Ave N12 .. 30 B6
Ravensdale Commercial
Est N16 ... 52 A3
Ravensdale Gdns
Hounslow TW4 ... 129 A2
South Norwood SE19 . 183 B3
Ravensdale Mans N8 . 50 A3
Ravensdale Rd
Hounslow TW4 ... 129 A2
South Tottenham N16 .. 51 D3
Ravensdon St
SE11 ... 116 C1 261 B1
Ravensfield Cl RM9 ... 80 D4
Ravensfield Gdns
KT19 ... 215 C4
Ravenshaw St NW6 ... 69 B3
Ravenshill BR7 ... 188 D2
Ravens Ho KT1 ... 175 D1
Ravenshurst Ave
NW4 ... 46 C5
Ravenside KT6 ... 197 D4
Ravenside Cl N18 ... 34 D5
Ravenside Ret Pk
N18 ... 34 D5
Ravenslea Rd SW11,
SW12 ... 158 D4
Ravensleigh Gdns
BR1 ... 187 B5
Ravensmead Rd
BR2 ... 186 B3
Ravensmede Way
W4 ... 111 D2
Ravensroost SE19 ... 183 B2
Ravenstone
SE17 ... 117 C1 263 B1
Ravenstone Prim Sch
SW12 ... 159 A2
Ravenstone Rd
Hornsey N8 ... 50 C6
West Hendon NW9 ... 45 D3
Ravenstone St
SW12 ... 159 A3
Ravensview Ct KT6 .. 197 D4
Ravens Way SE3,
SE12 ... 165 A6
Ravenswood
Bowes Pk N22 ... 32 B4
Sidcup DA5 ... 169 A3
Ravenswood Ave
Tolworth KT6 ... 214 C6
West Wickham BR4 .. 208 A1
Ravenswood Cres
Harrow HA2 ... 63 B6
West Wickham BR4 .. 208 A1
Ravenswood Gdns
TW7 ... 130 C4
Ravenswood Ind Est 5
E17 ... 54 A5
Ravenswood Pk HA6 .. 22 A4
Ravenswood Rd
Balham SW12 ... 159 B4
Croydon CR0 ... 220 D5
Walthamstow E17 ... 54 A5
Ravens Wood Sch
BR2 ... 225 D5
Ravensworth Ct SW6 265 A3
Ravensworth Rd
Chislehurst SE9 ... 188 B6
Ravensworth Rd *continued*
College Pk NW10 ... 90 B4
Raven Wharf SE1 ... 253 C2
Ravey St EC2 ... 95 C3 243 A6
Ravine Gr SE18 ... 145 C6
Rav Pinter Cl N16 ... 51 C2
Rawlings Cl
Beckenham BR3 ... 208 A4
3 Orpington BR6 ... 227 D3
Rawlings Cres HA9 ... 66 D5
Rawlings St
SW3 ... 114 D2 257 C4
Rawlins Cl Hendon N3 .. 47 A6
South Croydon CR2 ... 223 B1
Rawlinson Ct NW2 ... 46 C2
Rawlinson Ho SE13 .. 142 B1
Rawlinson Point 8
E16 ... 98 D2
Rawnsley Ave CR4 ... 202 C4
Rawreth Wlk N1 ... 235 B6
Rawson Ct SW11 ... 268 B1
Rawson St
SW11 ... 137 B4 268 C1
Rawsthorne Cl E16 .. 122 B5
Rawstone Wlk 5 E13 . 99 A5
Rawstorne Pl EC1 ... 234 C2
Rawstorne St
EC1 ... 94 D4 234 C2
Raybell Ct TW7 ... 130 D3
Rayburne Ct
1 Buckhurst Hill IG9 .. 21 C3
West Kensington W14 254 A6
Ray Cl KT9 ... 213 C2
Ray Ct Ealing W13 ... 109 B5
Stanmore HA7 ... 25 B5
Woodford IG8 ... 37 D4
Raydean Rd EN5 ... 13 D6
Raydons Gdns RM9 ... 81 A3
Raydons Rd RM9 ... 81 A3
Raydon St N19 ... 71 B6
Rayfield Cl BR2 ... 210 A3
Rayford Ave SE12 ... 164 D4
Ray Gdns
Barking IG11 ... 102 A5
Stanmore HA7 ... 25 B5
Ray Ho
7 North Kensington
W10 ... 90 D1
Shoreditch N1 ... 235 D5
Rayleas Cl SE18 ... 144 D4
Rayleigh Ave TW11 ... 174 C4
Rayleigh Cl N13 ... 17 B1
Rayleigh Ct
2 Kingston u T KT1 ... 176 B1
Tottenham N22 ... 33 A2
Rayleigh Rd
Edmonton N13 ... 17 B1
Merton SW19 ... 179 B2
5 Newham E16 ... 121 B5
Woodford IG8 ... 37 C3
Rayleigh Rise CR2 ... 221 C2
Ray Lodge Prim Sch
IG8 ... 37 D4
Ray Lodge Rd IG8 ... 37 D4
Ray Massey Way 3
E6 ... 100 A6
Raymead Ave CR7 ... 204 C4
Raymede Twr 2
W10 ... 90 D2
Raymere Gdns SE18 . 145 C5
Raymond Ave
Brentford W13 ... 109 A3
Woodford E18 ... 36 D1
Raymond Bldgs WC1 240 D4
Raymond Cl SE26 ... 184 C5
Raymond Ct N10 ... 31 A3
Raymond Postgate Ct 5
SE28 ... 124 B6
Raymond Rd
Beckenham BR3 ... 207 A5
Ilford IG2 ... 57 B2
Newham E13 ... 99 C6
Wimbledon SW19 ... 179 A4
Raymond Way KT10 .. 213 A2
Raymouth Rd SE16 ... 118 B2
Raynald Ho 15
SW16 ... 160 A1
Rayne Ct
Bermondsey SE1 ... 253 C2
Snaresbrook E18 ... 54 D5
Rayne Ho
1 Balham SW12 ... 159 A5
Paddington W9 ... 91 D3
Rayner Ct 10 W12 ... 112 C4
Rayners Cl HA0 ... 65 D3
Rayners Cres UB5 ... 84 B4
Rayners Gdns UB5 ... 84 B4
Rayners La
Harrow HA2 ... 63 D6
Pinner HA5 ... 41 B3
RAYNERS LANE ... 41 B1
Rayners Lane Sta
HA5 ... 41 B2
Rayner's Rd SW15 ... 157 A6
Rayner Twrs E10 ... 53 C2
Raynes Ave E11 ... 55 C2
Raynes Ct NW2 ... 69 A4
Raynesfield SW20 ... 200 C6
RAYNES PARK ... 200 C6
Raynes Park High Sch
SW20 ... 200 B6
Raynes Park Sta
SW20 ... 178 C1
Raynham W2 ... 237 A2
Raynham Ave N18 ... 34 A5
Raynham Ho 1 E1 ... 96 D3
Raynham Prim Sch
N18 ... 34 A5
Raynham Rd
Edmonton N18 ... 34 A5
Hammersmith W6 ... 112 B2
Raynham Terr N18 ... 34 A5
Raynor Cl UB1 ... 107 B5
Raynor Pl
23 Canonbury N1 ... 73 A1
N1 ... 235 B6
Raynton Cl
Harrow HA2 ... 41 A2
Hayes UB4 ... 83 D3
Raynton Dr
Hayes UB4 ... 83 C5
Hayes UB4 ... 83 D3
Raynton Rd EN3 ... 6 D6
Ray Rd KT8 ... 195 D4
Rays Ave N18 ... 34 C6
Rays Rd Edmonton N18 . 34 C6
West Wickham BR4 .. 208 A2
Ray St EC1 ... 241 B5
Ray Wlk N7 ... 72 B6
Raywood Cl UB7 ... 127 A5
Reachview Cl 17
NW1 ... 71 C1
Read Cl KT7 ... 197 A2
Read Ct E17 ... 53 D3
Reade Ct 6 W3 ... 111 A3
Reade Wlk 5 NW10 ... 67 C1
Read Ho
Friern Barnet N11 ... 30 D6
4 Kennington SE11 . 138 C6
Reading Ho
Paddington W2 ... 236 A1
Peckham SE15 ... 140 A6
Reading La E8 ... 74 B2
Reading Rd
Northolt UB5 ... 64 A3
Sutton SM1 ... 218 A3
Reading Way NW7 ... 29 A5
Readman Ct 8 SE20 . 184 B2
Reads Cl IG1 ... 78 D5
Reapers Cl NW1 ... 232 C6
Reapers Way TW7 ... 152 B6
Reardon Ho 5 E1 ... 118 B5
Reardon Path 31 E1 .. 118 B5
Reardon St E1 ... 118 B5
Reaston St SE14 ... 140 D5
Reay Prim Sch
SW9 ... 138 B5 270 D3
Rebecca Ct
3 Beckenham BR3 .. 185 C2
Sidcup DA14 ... 190 B6
Rebecca Ho 12 N12 ... 29 D6
Reckitt Rd W4 ... 111 C1
Record St SE16 ... 140 C6
Recovery St SW17 ... 180 C5
Recreation Rd
Bromley BR2 ... 186 D1
Forest Hill SE26 ... 184 D6
Southall UB2 ... 107 A2
Recreation Way CR4,
SW16 ... 204 A6
Rector St N1 .. 95 A6 235 A5
Rectory Bsns Ctr 5
DA14 ... 190 B6
Rectory Cl
Chingford E4 ... 19 C1
Finchley N3 ... 29 B2
Littleton TW17 ... 192 C6
Long Ditton KT6 ... 197 C1
Sidcup DA14 ... 190 B6
Stanmore HA7 ... 25 B5
West Barnes SW20 .. 200 C6
Rectory Cres E11 ... 55 C3
Rectory Ct
Cranford TW5 ... 128 C3
Feltham TW13 ... 172 C6
Leyton E11 ... 76 D5
Wallington SM6 ... 219 C4
West Drayton UB7 ... 104 A4
Woodford E18 ... 36 D2
Rectory Field Cres
SE7 ... 143 C5
Rectory Gdns
Beckenham BR3 ... 185 C2
6 Clapham SW4 ... 137 C2
Hornsey N8 ... 50 A5
Northolt UB5 ... 85 B6
Rectory Gn BR3 ... 185 B2
Rectory Gr
Clapham SW4 ... 137 C2
Croydon CR0 ... 220 D6
Hampton TW12,
TW13 ... 173 B6
Rectory La
Edgware HA8 ... 26 C4
Long Ditton KT6 ... 197 C1
Sidcup DA14 ... 190 C6
Stanmore HA7 ... 25 B5
Upper Tooting SW17 . 181 A5
Wallington SM6 ... 219 C4
Rectory Orch SW19 .. 179 A6
Rectory Park Ave
UB5 ... 85 B4
Rectory Pl SE18 ... 122 C2
Rectory Rd
Barnes SW13 ... 134 A3
Beckenham BR3 ... 185 C2
Cranford TW5 ... 128 C3
Dagenham RM10 ... 81 D1
Hayes UB3 ... 84 A1
Keston BR2 ... 225 D1
Little Ilford E12 ... 78 B3
1 London W3 ... 111 A5
Shacklewell N16 ... 73 D5
Southall UB2 ... 107 B3
Sutton SM1 ... 217 D5
Walthamstow E17 ... 53 D5
Rectory Road Sta
N16 ... 73 D5
Rectory Sq E1 ... 96 D2
Rectory Way UB10 ... 60 D5
Reculver Ho 2
SE15 ... 140 C6
Reculver Mews N18 ... 34 A6
Reculver Rd SE16 ... 118 D1
Red Anchor Cl SW3 . 267 A5
Redan Pl W2 ... 91 D1
Redan St W14 ... 112 D3
Redan Terr SE5 ... 138 D3
Red Barracks Rd 4
SE18 ... 122 B2
Redberry Gr SE23,
SE26 ... 162 C1
Redbourne Ave N3 ... 29 C2
Redbourne Dr SE28 . 102 D1
Redbourne Ho
Finchley N3 ... 29 C2
7 Poplar E14 ... 97 B1
Redbourn Ho 10 W10 . 90 C3
REDBRIDGE ... 55 C3
Redbridge Coll RM6 .. 58 B4
Redbridge Ct IG1 ... 55 D3
Redbridge Ent Ctr
IG1 ... 79 A6
Redbridge Foyer IG1 . 79 A6
Redbridge Gdns
SE5 ... 139 C5
Redbridge La E IG4 ... 56 A4
Redbridge La W E11 .. 55 C3
Redbridge Prim Sch
IG4 ... 56 A4
Redbridge Rdbt IG4 .. 55 D3
Redbridge Sta IG4 ... 55 D3
Redburn St
SW3 ... 136 D6 267 C6
Redburn Trad Est
EN3 ... 18 D5
Redcar Cl UB5 ... 63 D2
Redcar Ho SE26 ... 184 B4
Redcar St SE5 ... 139 A5
Redcastle Cl E1 ... 118 C6
Red Cedars Rd BR6 .. 211 C2
Redchurch St
E2 ... 95 D3 243 C6
Redcliffe Cl SW5 ... 255 C1
Redcliffe Ct 2 E5 ... 74 B5
Redcliffe Gdns
Chiswick W4 ... 132 D5

Redcliffe Gdns *continued*
Fulham
SW10 .... 135 D6 265 D6
Ilford IG1 ... 56 C1
Redcliffe Mews
SW10 ... 255 D1
Redcliffe Pl SW10 ... 266 A5
Redcliffe Rd
SW10 ... 136 A6 266 B6
Redcliffe Sch
SW10 ... 136 A6 266 A6
Redcliffe Sq
SW10 ... 113 D1 255 D1
Redcliffe St SW10 ... 265 D6
Redclose Ave SM4 ... 201 C4
Redclyffe Rd E6 ... 99 C6
Redclyffe Terr 2
SM2 ... 217 C1
Redclyf Ho 13 E1 ... 96 C3
Redcroft 5 NW6 ... 69 C2
Redcroft Rd UB1 ... 86 A1
Red Cross Cotts SE1 252 B2
Redcross Way
SE1 ... 117 A5 252 B3
Reddiford Sch HA5 ... 41 A5
Redding Ho SE18 ... 122 A3
Reddings Ave WD23 ... 8 A6
Reddings Cl NW7 ... 27 D6
Reddings The NW7 ... 11 D1
Reddins Rd SE15 ... 140 A6
Reddons Rd BR3 ... 185 A3
Rede Pl W2 ... 113 C6 245 B6
Redesdale Gdns
TW7 ... 131 A5
Redesdale St SW3 ... 267 C6
Redfern Ave TW2,
TW4 ... 151 C4
Redfern Ho 6 E13 ... 98 D6
Redfern Rd
Catford SE6 ... 164 A4
Willesden NW10 ... 67 C1
Redfield La
SW5 ... 113 D2 255 C4
Redfield Mews SW5. 255 B4
Redfiff Est SE16 ... 119 B3
Redford Ave
Thornton Heath CR7 ... 204 B5
Wallington SM6 ... 220 A2
Redford Cl TW13 ... 149 D2
Redford Wlk N1 ... 235 A6
Redgate Dr BR2 ... 225 B6
Red Gates Sch CR9 ... 220 C3
Redgate Terr SW15 ... 156 D5
Redgrave Cl SE25 ... 205 D3
Redgrave Rd SW15 ... 134 D2
Red Hill BR7 ... 188 D5
Redhill Ct SW2 ... 160 C2
Redhill Dr HA8 ... 27 A1
Red Hill Prim Sch
BR7 ... 188 D5
Redhill St
NW1 ... 93 B4 231 D2
Red House★ DA6 ... 147 A1
Red House La DA6 ... 147 A1
Red House Rd CR0 ... 203 D3
Red House Sq 20 N1 ... 73 A1
Redif Ho RM10 ... 81 D4
Redington Gdns NW3 . 69 D4
Redington Ho N1 ... 233 D4
Redington Rd NW3 ... 69 D4
Redknap Ho TW10 ... 153 C1
Red La KT10 ... 213 A2
Redland Gdns KT8 ... 195 B5
Redlands
Teddington TW11 ... 175 A4
Tottenham N15 ... 51 B5
Redlands Ct BR1 ... 186 D3
Redlands Prim Sch 35
E1 ... 96 C2
Redlands Rd EN3 ... 7 A4
Redlands The 5
BR3 ... 185 D1
Redlands Way SW2 ... 160 B4
Redleaf Cl DA17 ... 147 C6
Redleaves Ave
TW15 ... 170 D4
Redlees Cl TW7 ... 131 A1
Red Leys UB8 ... 60 A1
Red Lion Bsns Ctr
KT6 ... 214 B5
Red Lion Cl 9 SE17 ... 139 B6
Red Lion Ct
Holborn EC4 ... 241 B1
Hounslow TW3 ... 129 D2
Red Lion Hill N2 ... 30 B1
Red Lion La SE18 ... 144 C4
Red Lion Pl SE18 ... 144 C4
Red Lion Rd KT6 ... 214 C6
Red Lion Row SE17 ... 139 A6
Red Lion Sq
WC1 ... 94 B2 240 C3
Red Lion St
Gray's Inn
WC1 ... 94 B2 240 C3
Richmond TW10 ... 153 D6
Red Lion Yd W1 ... 248 B4
Red Lo Ealing W5 ... 88 A2
West Wickham BR4 ... 208 A2
Red Lodge Rd BR3,
BR4 ... 208 B2
Redlynch Ct
W14 ... 113 A4 244 B1
Redlynch Ho 27
SW9 ... 138 C4
Redman Bldg EC1 ... 241 A4
Redman Cl UB5 ... 84 C5
Redman Ho SE1 ... 252 B1
Redman's Rd E1 ... 96 C2
Redmayne Ho 15
SW9 ... 138 B3
Redmead La E1 ... 118 A5
Redmead Rd UB3 ... 105 C2
Redmill Ho 24 E1 ... 96 B3
Redmond Ho N1 ... 233 D5
Redmore Rd W6 ... 112 B2
Red Oak Cl BR6 ... 226 D6
Redo Ho 3 E12 ... 78 C3
Red Pl W1 ... 248 A6
Redpoll Way DA18 ... 124 D3
Red Post Hill SE21,
SE24 ... 161 B6
Red Post Ho E6 ... 77 D1
Redriffe Rd E13 ... 98 D6
Redriff Prim Sch
SE16 ... 119 A4
Redriff Rd SE16 ... 119 A3
Redroofs Cl BR3 ... 185 D2
Redrose Trad Ctr 1
EN4 ... 14 B6
Red Rover SW13 ... 134 A2
Redrup Ho 21 SE14 ... 140 D6
Redruth Cl N22 ... 32 B3
Redruth Gdns KT10 . 212 D1
Redruth Ho SM2 ... 217 D1
Redruth Rd E9 ... 96 C6
Red Sq The N16 ... 73 B5
Redstart Cl
New Cross Gate
SE14 ... 141 A5
Newham E6 ... 100 A2
Redston Rd N8 ... 49 D5
Redvers Rd N22 ... 32 C1
Redvers St E2 ... 95 C4
Redwald Rd E5 ... 74 D4
Redway Dr TW2 ... 152 A4
Redwing Path SE28 ... 123 B4
Redwing Rd SM6 ... 220 B1
Redwood Cl
4 Bow E3 ... 97 C5
Chigwell IG9 ... 21 B2
Hillingdon UB10 ... 82 D5
Osidge N14 ... 15 D4
Rotherhithe SE16 ... 119 A5
Sidcup DA15 ... 168 A3
South Oxhey WD19 ... 22 D6
Redwood Ct
Brondesbury NW6 ... 69 A1
Crouch End N19 ... 49 D2
Northolt UB5 ... 85 A4
10 Surbiton KT6 ... 197 D2
Redwood Est TW5 ... 128 B6
Redwood Gdns E4 ... 19 D5
Redwood Gr W5 ... 109 B2
Redwood Mews
Ashford TW15 ... 171 B3
2 Clapham SW4 ... 137 B2
Redwoods SW15 ... 156 A3
Redwood Way EN5 ... 12 D6
Redwood Wlk KT6 ... 197 D1
Reece Mews SW7 ... 256 C4
Reed Ave BR6 ... 227 C5
Reed Cl Lee SE12 ... 165 A6
Newham E16 ... 99 A2
Reede Gdns RM10 ... 81 D3
Reede Rd RM10 ... 81 D2
Reede Way RM10 ... 81 D2
Reedham Cl N17 ... 52 B5
Reedham St SE15 ... 140 A2
Reed Ho SW15 ... 156 A5
Reedholm Villas N16 ... 73 B4
Reed Mans 6 E11 ... 55 A3
Reed Pl
Battersea SW11 ... 136 C1
Clapham SW4 ... 137 D1
Lower Halliford TW17 . 192 B1
Reed Rd N17 ... 33 D1
Reedsfield Cl TW15 . 148 D1
Reedsfield Rd TW15 . 170 D6
Reed's Pl NW1 ... 71 C1
Reedworth St
SE11 ... 116 C2 261 B3
Reef Ho E14 ... 120 A3
Reenglass Rd HA7 ... 25 D6
Rees Dr HA7 ... 26 A6
Rees Gdns CR0 ... 205 D3
Rees Ho 6 N17 ... 33 D3
Reesland Cl E12 ... 78 C2
Rees St N1 ... 95 A6 235 B5
Reets Farm Cl NW9 ... 45 C3
Reeves Ave NW9 ... 45 B2
Reeves Cnr CR0 ... 220 D6
Reeves Cnr Sta CR0 . 220 D6
Reeves Ho
Lambeth SE1 ... 251 A1
Mayfair W1 ... 248 A5
Reeves Mews
W1 ... 115 A6 248 B5
Reeves Rd Bromley E3 . 97 D3
Shooters Hill SE18 ... 144 D6
Reflection Ho 9 E2 ... 96 A3
Reflection The E16 .. 122 D4
Reflex Apartments 1
BR2 ... 209 B5
Reform Row N17 ... 33 D1
Reform St SW11 ... 136 D3
Regal Cl Ealing W5 ... 87 D2
Spitalfields E1 ... 96 A2
Regal Cres SM6 ... 219 B5
Regal Ct
Edmonton N18 ... 33 D5
2 Mitcham CR4 ... 202 D6
Wembley HA0 ... 65 D4
Regal Dr N11 ... 31 B5
Regal Ho IG2 ... 57 B3
Regal Int Coll HA9 ... 66 A3
Regal La NW1 ... 231 B5
Regal Pl
8 Tower Hamlets E3 ... 97 B4
Walham Green SW6 .. 265 D3
Regal Way HA3 ... 44 A3
Regan Ho 1 N18 ... 33 D4
Regan Way N1 ... 95 C5
Regatta Ho TW11 ... 175 A6
Regatta Point TW8 ... 132 B6
Regel Ct NW7 ... 29 A2
Regency Cl Ealing W5 .. 88 A1
Hampton TW12 ... 173 B5
Regency Cres 3
NW4 ... 28 D1
Regency Ct 9 Bow E3 . 97 B5
Enfield EN1 ... 17 B6
4 Kingston u T KT5 ... 198 B4
4 Penge SE19 ... 184 A3
14 South Hackney E9 ... 96 C6
Sutton SM1 ... 217 D5
Wimbledon SW19 ... 179 B3
7 Woodford E18 ... 37 A1
Regency Dr HA4 ... 39 C1
Regency Gdns KT12 . 194 C1
Regency Ho
Finchley N3 ... 29 B1
Marylebone NW1 ... 238 D6
Regency Lo
1 Buckhurst Hill
IG9 ... 21 D2
Harrow HA3 ... 42 C6
South Hampstead NW3 70 B1
Regency Mews
Beckenham BR3 ... 186 A2
Camberwell SW9 ... 138 D5
Isleworth TW7 ... 152 C6
1 Willesden NW10 ... 68 A2
Regency Pl SW1 ... 259 D4
Regency St
SW1 ... 115 D2 259 D3
Regency Terr SW7 ... 256 C2
Regency Way DA6 ... 147 A2
Regency Wlk
Croydon CR0 ... 207 B3
8 Richmond TW10 ... 154 A6
Regeneration Rd
SE16 ... 118 D1
Regent Ave UB10 ... 60 D1
Regent Bsns Ctr
UB3 ... 106 A4
Regent Cl
Cranford TW4 ... 128 B4
Regent Cl *continued*
Harrow HA3 ... 44 A3
North Finchley N12 ... 30 A5
Regent Ct
4 Finchley N3 ... 29 D3
Lisson Gr NW8 ... 230 A1
South Norwood SE19 . 182 D4
1 Stamford Hill N16 ... 51 D2
Regent Gdns IG3 ... 58 A2
Regent Ho W14 ... 254 A4
Regent Pl
Croydon CR0 ... 205 D1
St James W1 ... 249 B6
Wimbledon SW19 ... 180 A5
Regent Rd
Surbiton KT5 ... 198 C4
Tulse Hill SE24 ... 160 D6
Regents Ave N13 ... 32 C5
Regents Bridge Gdns
SW8 ... 270 B4
Regents Canal Ho 19
E14 ... 97 A1
Regents Cl Hayes UB4 . 83 C2
South Croydon CR2 .. 221 C2
Regent's Coll
NW1 ... 93 A3 238 A6
Regents Ct
22 Beckenham BR3 .. 185 C3
Bromley BR1 ... 186 D3
Edgware HA8 ... 26 A6
Hackney E8 ... 96 A6
1 Kingston u T KT2 ... 176 A2
Regent's Ct HA5 ... 22 D1
Regents Dr BR2 ... 225 D3
Regents Gate Ho 20
E14 ... 119 A6
Regents Lo 9 SW2 ... 160 B3
Regents Mews
NW8 ... 92 A5 229 B4
REGENT'S PARK ... 93 B4
Regent's Park★
NW1 ... 93 A5 231 A3
Regent's Park Barracks
NW1 ... 231 D3
Regent's Park Rd
Camden Town
NW1 ... 93 A6 231 A6
Hendon N3 ... 47 B6
Primrose Hill NW3 ... 71 A1
Regent's Park Sta
NW1 ... 93 B3 238 C5
Regent's Park Terr
NW1 ... 231 C6
Regents Pl IG10 ... 21 D4
Regent's Pl SE3 ... 143 A3
Regents Plaza 2
NW6 ... 91 D5
Regent Sq
Belvedere DA17 ... 125 D2
23 Bromley E3 ... 97 D4
St Pancras
WC1 ... 94 A4 233 B1
Regent's Row E8 ... 96 A6
Regent St
Brentford W4 ... 110 C1
7 Kensal Green
NW10 ... 90 D4
Mayfair W1 . 115 C6 249 A6
Regents Wharf
3 Hackney E2 ... 96 B6
Islington N1 ... 233 C4
Regina Coeli RC Prim
Sch CR2 ... 220 D1
Regina Ct TW11 ... 174 C5
Reginald Ct BR3 ... 186 A2
Reginald Pl 6 SE8 ... 141 C5
Reginald Rd
Deptford SE8 ... 141 C5
Forest Gate E7 ... 77 A2
Reginald Sorenson Ho
E11 ... 54 B2
Reginald Sq SE8 ... 141 C5
Regina Point SE16 ... 118 C3
Regina Rd
Ealing W13 ... 109 A5
Finsbury Pk N4 ... 50 B1
Southall UB2 ... 107 A2
South Norwood SE25 . 206 A6
Regina Terr W13 ... 109 B5
Regis Ct
East Bedfont TW14 ... 149 B5
Hornsey N8 ... 50 B5
Marylebone NW1 ... 237 C4
Mitcham SW19 ... 180 C2
Regis Pl 17 SW2 ... 138 B1
Regis Rd NW5 ... 71 B3
Regnart Bldgs NW1 . 232 B1
Regnolruf Ct KT12 ... 194 A2
Reid Cl Hayes UB3 ... 83 C1
Pinner HA5 ... 40 A5
Reid Ct SW14 ... 133 A3
Reidhaven Rd SE18 .. 123 C2
Reigate Ave SM1 ... 201 D1
Reigate Rd
Catford BR1 ... 164 D1
Grove Pk BR1, SE12 .. 165 A2
Ilford IG3 ... 79 D6
Reigate Way SM6 ... 220 A3
Reighton Rd E5 ... 74 A6
Reinckendorf Ave
SE9 ... 167 A5
Reindeer Cl 5 E13 ... 99 A6
Reizel Cl N16 ... 51 D1
Relay Rd W12 ... 112 C5
Relf Rd SE15 ... 140 A2
Reliance Sq E2 ... 243 B6
Relko Gdns SM1 ... 218 B3
Relton Ct W3 ... 110 C4
Relton Mews SW7 .. 257 B6
Rembrandt Cl E14 ... 120 B3
Rembrandt Ct
10 Bermondsey
SE16 ... 118 B1
Harrow HA3 ... 43 A3
West Ewell KT19 ... 215 D2
Rembrandt Rd
Edgware HA8 ... 26 C1
Lewisham SE13 ... 142 C1
Rembrant Cl SW1 ... 258 A3
Remembrance Ave
N2 ... 47 D6
Remington Rd
Newham E6 ... 100 A1
Tottenham N15 ... 51 B3
Remington St
N1 ... 94 D5 234 D3
Remnant St WC2 ... 240 C2
Remsted Ho 7 NW6 ... 91 D6
Remus Rd E3 ... 75 C1
Renaissance Ct SM1 . 202 A1
Renaissance Wlk 4
SE10 ... 120 D3
Renbold Ho 5 SE10 .. 142 A4
Rendlebury Ho 17
SE18 ... 122 B2
Rendle Cl CR0 ... 206 A4
Rendlesham Ho 3 E5,
N16 ... 74 A5
Rendlesham Rd
Enfield EN2 ... 4 D4
Shacklewell E5 ... 74 A5
Renforth St SE16 ... 118 C4
Renfree Way TW17 ... 192 C2
Renfrew Cl E6 ... 122 C6
Renfrew Ct TW5 ... 129 A3
Renfrew Ho
Paddington NW6 ... 91 D5
Walthamstow E17 ... 35 B1
Renfrew Rd
Hounslow TW5 ... 129 A3
Kingston u T KT2 ... 177 A3
Newington
SE11 ... 116 D2 261 C3
Renmuir St SW17 ... 180 D4
Rennell Ho 18 E9 ... 74 D2
Rennell St SE13 ... 142 A2
Renness Rd E17 ... 53 A6
Rennets Cl SE9 ... 167 C6
Rennets Wood Ho
SE9 ... 167 B6
Rennets Wood Rd
SE9 ... 167 B6
Rennie Cotts 29 E1 ... 96 C3
Rennie Ct
Holdbrook EN3 ... 7 C5
Lambeth SE1 ... 251 C4
Rennie Ho SE1 ... 262 A5
Rennie St
SE1 ... 116 D5 251 C4
Renoir Ct 7 SE16 ... 118 B1
Renovation The E16 . 122 D4
Renown Cl CR0 ... 204 D1
Rensburg Rd E17 ... 52 D3
Rensburg Villas E17 ... 52 D4
Renshaw Cl 7 DA17 . 147 B6
Renshaw Cnr CR4 ... 181 A2
Renshaw Ct SW19 ... 179 A6
Renshaw Ho 11
SW27 ... 182 D5

Renters Ave NW4 . . . . .46 C3
Renton Cl SW2 . . . . . . .160 B5
Renwick Rd IG11 . . . .102 B4
Repens Way UB4. . . . . .84 D3
Rephidim St SE1. . . . 263 A5
Replingham Rd
SW18. . . . . .157 C3
Reporton Rd
SW6. . . . . . . .135 A5 264 B3
Repository Rd SE7,
SE18. . . . . .122 B1
Repton Ave
Hayes UB3. . . . . .105 B2
Wembley HA0 . . . . .65 C4
Repton Cl SM5. . . . . . .218 C3
Repton Ct
Beckenham BR3. . . . . 185 D2
Southgate N21. . . . . . . .16 C3
Repton Ho SW1. . . . . 259 B3
Repton Rd
Harrow HA3. . . . . .44 B5
Orpington BR6. . . . . . 227 D5
Repton St E14 . . . . .97 A1
Reserve Rd N2. . . . . . . .30 C2
Reservoir Cl 3 CR7 . .205 B5
Reservoir Rd
New Cross Gate
SE4. . . . . 141 A3
Ruislip HA4 . . . . .39 B5
Southgate N14. . . . . . . .15 C6
Reservoir Studios 14
E1. . . . . .96 D1
Resham Cl UB2 . . . . . .106 C3
Resolution Way 14
SE8. . . . . .141 C5
Resolution Wlk
SE18. . . . . .122 B3
Restell Cl SE3 . . . . . . .142 C6
Restmor Way SM5,
SM6 . . . . .219 A6
Reston Pl SW7. . . . . . 246 A1
Restons Cres DA15,
SE9. . . . . .167 C5
Restoration Sq
SW11 . . . . 266 D1
Restormel Cl TW3. . . .151 C6
Retcar Pl N19. . . . . .71 B6
Retford St E2. . . . . .95 C5
Retingham Way E4 . . .19 D2
Retlas Ct HA1. . . . . .42 B2
Retreat Cl HA3. . . . . . . .43 C4
Retreat Cvn Site The
IG9. . . . . .21 A3
Retreat Ho 5 E9. . . . . .74 C2
Retreat Pl E9 . . . . .74 C2
Retreat Rd TW9. . . . . 153 D6
Retreat The
Harrow HA2. . . . . .41 C2
Kingsbury NW9 . . . . . . .45 B4
Mortlake SW14 . . . . . 133 C2
North Cheam KT4. . . . .216 B6
South Norwood CR7. . .205 B5
Surbiton KT5 . . . . .198 B3
Reunion Row E1. . . . . .118 B6
Reveley Sq SE16 . . . . .119 A4
Revell Rd
Cheam SM1. . . . . .217 B2
Kingston u T KT1 . . . . 176 D2
Revell Rise SE18 . . . . 145 D6
Revelon Rd SE4. . . . . .141 A2
Revelstoke Rd SW18,
SW19. . . . . .157 C2
Reventlow Rd SE9 . . .167 A3
Reverdy Rd SE1. . . . . .118 A2
Reverend Cl HA2. . . . . .63 D5
Revesby Rd SM5 . . . .202 C3
Review Lo RM10. . . . 103 D5
Review Rd
Dagenham RM10. . . . 103 D6
Willesden NW2 . . . . . . .67 D6
Rewell St
SW6. . . . . . . .136 A5 266 A3
Rewley Rd SM4 . . . . . .202 B3
Rew Lo 25 N2. . . . . . . .30 B1
Rex Ave TW15. . . . . . .170 C5
Rex Ho TW13 . . . . . . .151 A1
Rex Par 2 IG8. . . . . . . .37 C4
Rex Pl W1 . . . .115 A5 248 B4
Reydon Ave E11 . . . . . .55 C3
Reygate Ct N4. . . . . . . .51 A3
Reynard Cl
Brockley SE4 . . . . 141 A2
Bromley BR1 . . . . 210 C6
Reynard Dr SE19. . . . 183 D3
Reynard Mills Trad Est
TW8. . . . . .109 C1
Reynard Pl SE14 . . . . .141 A6
Reynardson Rd N17. . .33 A3
Reynardson's Ct 10
N17. . . . . .51 D6
Reynola Gdns SE7 . . .121 B1
Reynolds Ave
Chessington KT9 . . . . 214 A1
Ilford RM6. . . . . .58 C2
Little Ilford E12 . . . . . . .78 C3
Reynolds Cl
Carshalton SM5 . . . . . 202 D1
Golders Green NW11. . .47 D2
Mitcham SW19 . . . . . .180 B2
Reynolds Ct
Ilford RM6. . . . . .58 D6
Leyton E11. . . . . .76 D5
Reynolds Dr HA8. . . . . .44 B6
Reynolds Ho
Enfield EN1 . . . . .18 A6
Finsbury Pk N4. . . . . . . .50 A1
18 South Hackney E2. . .96 C5
St John's Wood NW8 . 229 D3
Westminster SW1 . . . 259 D3
Reynolds Pl
Greenwich SE3 . . . . . .143 B5
12 Richmond TW10 . . .154 B5
Reynolds Rd
Acton Green W4. . . . . 111 A3
Hayes UB4. . . . . .84 C3
New Malden KT3 . . . . .199 B2
Nunhead SE15. . . . . . 140 C1
Reynolds Sp Ctr W3. 110 C4
Reynolds Way CR0 . . .221 C4
Rffra Rd Ret Pk
SW2. . . . . 160 C6
Rheidol Mews N1 . . . 235 A4
Rheidol Terr
N1. . . . . .95 A6 235 A5
Rhein Ho N8. . . . . .50 A6
Rheola Cl N17 . . . . .33 D2
Rhizotron & Xstrata
Treetop Walkway★
TW9. . . . . .132 A4
Rhoda St E2 . . .95 D3 243 D6
Rhodes Ave N22 . . . . . .31 C2
Rhodes Avenue Prim Sch
N22 . . . . .31 C2
Rhodes Ho
Shepherd's Bush
W12 . . . . .112 B5
Shoreditch N1 . . . . . . 235 C2
Rhodesia Rd
Leyton E11. . . . . .76 B6
Stockwell SW9. . . . . . 138 A3
Rhodes-Moorhouse Ct
SM4 . . . . .201 C3
Rhodes St N7. . . . . .72 B3
Rhodeswell Rd E14 . . . .97 B1
Rhodrons Ave KT9 . . .214 A3
Rhondda Gr E3 . . . . . . .97 B4
Rhyl Prim Sch 21
NW5. . . . . .71 A2
Rhyl Rd UB6 . . . . .86 D5
Rhyl St NW5. . . . . .71 A2
Rhys Ave N11. . . . . .31 D3
Rialto Rd CR4. . . . . . . .181 A1
Ribble Cl IG8 . . . . .37 C4
Ribblesdale Ave
Friern Barnet N11 . . . . .31 A4
Northolt UB5 . . . . .63 D2
Ribblesdale Ho 11
NW6. . . . . .91 C6
Ribblesdale Rd
Hornsey N8 . . . . .50 B5
Streatham SW16 . . . . .181 B5
Ribbon Dance Mews
SE5. . . . . .139 B4
Ribchester Ave UB6. . .86 D4
Ribston Cl BR2 . . . . . .210 B1
Ribstone Ho 12 E9 . . . .74 D2
Ricardo Path 5
SE28. . . . . .124 C5
Ricardo St E14. . . . . . . .97 D1
Ricards Lodge High Sch
SW19. . . . . .179 B5
Ricards Rd SW19 . . . .179 B5
Riccall Ct 2 NW9. . . . .27 C2
Riceyman Ho WC1 . . 234 A1
Richard Alibon Prim Sch
RM10. . . . . .81 C3
Richard Anderson Ct 1
SE14. . . . . 140 D5
Richard Atkins Prim Sch
29 SW2 . . . . 160 A4
Richard Burbidge Mans
SW13. . . . . .134 C6
Richard Burton Ct 4
IG9. . . . . .21 C2
Richard Challoner Sch
KT3 . . . . .199 B2
Richard Cl SE18. . . . . .122 A2
Richard Cloudesley Sch
(Prim Dept)
EC1 . . . . .95 A3 242 B5
Richard Cloudesley Sch
(Secondary Dept)
EC1 . . . . .95 A3 242 A5
Richard Cobden Prim
Sch NW1 . . . . 93 C6 232 B5
Richard Ct
Ashford TW15 . . . . . . .170 B5
1 Barnet EN5 . . . . 1 A2
Richard Fell Ho 3
E12. . . . . .78 C4
Richard Fox Ho N4. . . .73 A5
Richard Ho 10 SE16 . .118 C2
Richard House Dr
E16. . . . . .100 A1
Richard Knight Ho
SW6. . . . . 265 B2
Richard Neale Ho 2
E1. . . . . .118 B6
Richard Neve Ho 2
SE18. . . . . .123 C2
Richards Cl
Bushey WD23. . . . . 8 B4
Harlington UB3 . . . . . .127 B6
Harrow HA1. . . . . .43 A4
Hillingdon UB10. . . . . . .82 C6
Richards Ct BR3 . . . . 184 D2
Richard Sharples Ct 16
SM2 . . . . .218 A1
Richardson Cl 19 E8 . . .95 D6
Richardson Ct 20
SW4 . . . . .138 A3
Richardson Gdns 12
RM10 . . . . .81 D2
Richardson Ho
Isleworth TW7. . . . . . . 130 D2
10 Poplar E14 . . . . .97 C2
Richardson Rd E15. . . . .98 C5
Richardson's Mews
W1. . . . . 239 A5
Richards Pl E17. . . . . . . .53 C6
Richard's Pl SW3 . . . . 257 B4
Richard St 20 E1. . . . . . .96 B1
Richbell WC1. . . . . 240 B4
Richbell Pl WC1 . . . . . 240 C4
Richborne Terr
SW8 . . . . .138 B5 270 D4
Richborough Ho
10 Deptford SE15 . . . 140 C6
14 Hackney E5. . . . . .74 B4
Richborough Rd NW2 69 A4
Richbourne Ct W1 . . . 237 B2
Richens Cl TW3. . . . . . .130 B3
Riches Rd IG1 . . . . .79 A6
Richfield Ct
4 Beckenham BR3. . .185 B2
Wembley HA0 . . . . .66 A2
Richfield Rd WD23. . . . . 8 A4
Richford Gate W6. . . . .112 C3
Richford Rd E15 . . . . . .98 D6
Richford St W6 . . . . . .112 C3
Richill Lodge TW2 . . . .151 C5
Rich Ind Est SE15 . . . .140 B6
Richings Ho BR5. . . . . .190 A2
Rich La SW5. . . . . 255 C2
Richland Ho 4
SE15. . . . . .140 A4
Richlands Ave KT17 . .216 A4
Richman Ho 10 SE8 . . .119 B1
RICHMOND. 131 C1
Richmond Adult Com
Coll TW9. . . . . 131 D1
Richmond American Int
Univ in London
TW10. . . . . 154 A4
Richmond Ave
Chingford E4 . . . . .36 B5
Feltham TW14 . . . . . . 149 C5
Hillingdon UB10. . . . . . .60 D2
Islington N1 . . .94 B6 233 D6
Willesden NW10 . . . . . .68 C2
Wimbledon SW20 . . . 179 A2
Richmond Bldgs W1 239 C1
Richmond Bridge
TW1. . . . . 153 D5
Richmond Bridge Mans
1 TW1. . . . . 153 D5
Richmond Circus
TW9. . . . . .132 A1
Richmond Cl
Borehamwood WD6. . . .11 B6
Walthamstow E17 . . . . .53 B3
Richmond Coll
W8. . . . . 113 D3 255 D6
Richmond Cres
Chingford E4 . . . . .36 B5
Edmonton N9. . . . . .18 A3
Islington N1. . .94 C6 234 A6
Richmond Ct
Bromley BR1 . . . . .187 B3
12 Kingston u T KT2. . 176 C3
Knightsbridge SW1 . . 247 D1
Mitcham CR4 . . . . .202 B6
4 New Southgate N11 31 A4
Wembley HA9 . . . . .66 B6
Wimbledon SW20 . . . .178 B1
Richmond Dr TW17 . .193 B3
Richmond Gate
TW10. . . . . .154 B4
Richmond Gdns
Harrow HA3. . . . . .24 D3
Hendon NW4 . . . . .46 A4
Richmond Gn CR0 . . .220 A5
Richmond Gr
Islington N1. . . . . .72 D1
Surbiton KT5 . . . . .198 B3
Richmond Healthcare
Hamlet Hospl TW9 132 A2
RICHMOND HILL. 154 A5
Richmond Hill TW10 .154 A5
Richmond Hill Ct 5
TW10 . . . . .154 A5
Richmond Ho
12 Forest Hill SE26 . . 162 A1
Regent's Pk NW1. . . . 231 D3
Walworth SE17 . . . . . 262 C2
Richmond Ho (Hampton
Com Coll) TW12. . . . .173 B5
Richmond International
Bsns Ctr 9 TW9. . . .132 B1
Richmond Mans
Earl's Ct SW5. . . . . . . 255 C2
Putney SW15. . . . . 135 A2
13 Twickenham TW1 . 153 D5
Richmond Mews W1 239 C1
Richmond Park★
TW10. . . . . .155 A3
Richmond Park Rd
Kingston u T KT2 . . . . 176 A3
Mortlake SW14 . . . . . .133 B1
Richmond Pk IG10. . . .21 D4
Richmond Pl SE18 . . .123 A2
Richmond Rd
Bowes Pk N11 . . . . .32 A4
Chingford E4 . . . . .20 B3
Dalston E8 . . . . .74 A1
Ealing W5. . . . . 110 A4
Finchley N2 . . . . .30 A1
Forest Gate E7. . . . . . . .77 B3
Ilford IG1. . . . . .79 A5
Isleworth TW7. . . . . . . 131 A2
Kingston u T KT2 . . . . 176 A4
Leyton E11. . . . . .76 B6
New Barnet EN5 . . . . . .14 A6
Thornton Heath CR7 . 204 D5
Tottenham N15 . . . . . . .51 C3
Twickenham TW1. . . . 153 C4
Wallington CR0 . . . . . 220 A5
Wimbledon SW20 . . . .178 B2
Richmond St E13 . . . . . .99 A5
Richmond Sta TW9 . 132 A1
Richmond Terr
SW1 . . . . . . .116 A4 250 A2
Richmond upon Thames
Coll TW2. . . . . 152 C4
Richmond Way
Hammersmith W12,
W14 . . . . 112 D4
Wanstead E11 . . . . .77 A6
Richmount Gdns
SE3. . . . . .143 A2
Rich St E14. . . . . .119 B6
Rickard Cl
Hendon NW4 . . . . .46 A5
Streatham SW2. . . . . . 160 C3
Rickards Cl KT6. . . . . .214 A6
Rickett St SW6. . . . . . 265 B6
Rickman Ho 23 E2 . . . . .96 C3
Rickman St 24 E1. . . . .96 C3
Rickmansworth Rd
HA5. . . . . .22 C1
Rick Roberts Way
E15. . . . . .98 B5
Rickthorne Rd 7
N19. . . . . .72 A6
Rickyard Path SE9 . . .144 A1
Riddell Ct SE1 . . . . . . 263 C2
Riddell Lo EN2. . . . . 4 D3
Ridding La UB6 . . . . . . .64 D3
Riddons Rd SE12. . . . .187 C6
Rideout St SE18. . . . . .122 B2
Rider Cl DA15. . . . . . . .167 C5
Ride The
Brentford TW8. . . . . . 109 C1
Enfield EN3 . . . . 6 D2
Ridgdale St E3 . . . . . . .97 D5
Ridge Ave N21. . . . . . . .17 B4
Ridgebrook Rd SE3,
SE9. . . . . 143 D2
Ridge Cl Hendon NW4 . .28 D1
Kingsbury NW9 . . . . . . .45 B5
Plumstead SE28. . . . . .123 B4
Ridge Crest EN2 . . . . 4 B4
Ridge Hill NW11. . . . . . .47 A1
Ridge Ho 4 KT2. . . . . 176 D3
Ridgeleigh Ct 3 EN5. . . 1 A2
Ridgemead Cl N13,
N14. . . . . .16 A2
Ridgemont Gdns HA8 .27 A6
Ridgemount Ave
CR0. . . . . 222 D6
Ridgemount Cl 4
SE20. . . . . .184 B3
Ridgemount Gdns EN2 4 D3
Ridgeon Ct N22. . . . . . .32 B4
Ridge Rd Cheam SM3 .201 B1
Child's Hill NW2. . . . . . .69 B5
Edmonton N21. . . . . . . .17 B3
Hornsey Vale N8 . . . . . .50 B3
Mitcham CR4 . . . . .181 B3
Ridges The E4 . . . . .35 C6
Ridge's Yd 8 CR0. . . 220 D5
Ridge Terr N21. . . . . . . .17 A4
Ridge The Barnet EN5 . .13 B6
Old Bexley DA5 . . . . . .169 B4
Orpington BR6. . . . . . .227 B6
Surbiton KT5 . . . . 198 C4
Twickenham TW2. . . . .152 B4
Ridgeview Cl EN5. . . . .12 D5
Ridgeview Ct EN4. . . . .15 C6
Ridgeview Rd N20 . . . .14 A1
Ridgeway Hayes BR2 .225 A6
11 Richmond TW10 . . . 154 A5
Walton-on-T KT12 . . . 193 D1
Woodford IG8 . . . . .37 C6
Ridge Way
Feltham TW13 . . . . . . 151 A1
7 West Norwood
SE19. . . . . 183 C4
Ridgeway Ave EN4 . . . .14 D5
Ridgeway Cres BR6 . .227 C5
Ridgeway Crescent Gdns
BR6. . . . . .227 C5
Ridgeway Dr
Acton W3. . . . . 110 C3
Grove Pk BR1. . . . . . . .187 B6
Ridgeway E DA15 . . . 167 D6
Ridgeway Gdns
Crouch End N6. . . . . . . .49 C2
Redbridge IG4. . . . . . . .56 A4
Ridgeway Rd TW7. . . .130 C4
Ridgeway Rd N TW7. .130 C5
Ridgeway The
Acton W3. . . . . 110 C3
Chingford E4 . . . . .20 A3
1 Chingford E4. . . . . . . .20 A3
Enfield EN2 . . . . 4 B5
Finchley N3 . . . . .29 D3
Friern Barnet N11 . . . . .30 D6
Golders Green NW11. . .47 B1
Kenton HA3 . . . . .43 C3
Kingsbury NW9 . . . . . . .45 B5
Mill Hill NW7 . . . . .28 B6
North Harrow HA2. . . . .41 D3
Palmers Green N14. . . .16 A2
Pinner HA2. . . . . .41 B4
Ruislip HA4 . . . . .40 A2
Stanmore HA7 . . . . .25 C4
Wallington CR0 . . . . . .220 B5
Ridgeway W DA15 . . .167 C6
Ridgeway Wlk UB5. . . .63 A2
Ridgewell Cl
Dagenham RM10. . . . 103 D6
Forest Hill SE26. . . . . .185 B6
Shoreditch N1 . . . . . . 235 B6

Ridgmount Gdns WC1 93 D2 239 C4
Ridgmount Pl WC1 239 C4
Ridgmount Rd SW18 157 D6
Ridgmount St WC1 93 D2 239 C4
Ridgway SW19, SW20 178 D4
Ridgway Ct SW19 178 D4
Ridgway Gdns SW19 178 D3
Ridgway Pl SW19 179 A4
Ridgway Rd SW9 138 D2
Ridgway The SM2 218 B1
Ridgwell Rd E16 99 C2
Riding House St W1 93 C2 239 A3
Ridings Ave N21 17 A6
Ridings Cl N6 49 C2
Ridings The Ealing W5 88 B3
Oakleigh Pk EN4 14 B4
Sunbury TW16 172 A2
Surbiton KT5 198 C4
Riding The NW11 47 B2
Ridler Rd EN1 5 C5
Ridley Ave W13 109 B3
Ridley Cl IG11 79 D1
Ridley Ct
Orpington BR6 227 A4
Streatham SW16 182 A4
Ridley Ho 14 SW11 136 C2
Ridley Rd
Beckenham BR2 208 D6
Dalston E8 73 D3
Forest Gate E7 77 C4
Merton SW19 179 D3
Welling DA16 146 B4
Willesden Green NW10 90 A5
Ridley Road Mkt★ E8 73 D3
Ridsdale Rd SE20 184 B2
Riefield Rd SE9 167 A6
Riesco Dr CR0 222 C2
Riffel Rd NW2 68 C3
Rifle Ct SE11 138 C6
Rifle Pl W11 112 D5
Rifle St E14 97 D2
Riga Ho 12 E1 96 D2
Rigault Rd SW6 135 A3
Rigby Cl CR0 220 C5
Rigby Ho 2 N17 51 D6
Rigby La UB3 105 A4
Rigby Mews IG1 78 C6
Rigby Pl 8 EN3 7 C6
Rigden St E14 97 D1
Rigeley Rd NW10 90 A4
Rigg App E10 53 A1
Rigge Pl SW4 137 D1
Rigg Ho 2 SW4 160 A4
Riggindale Rd SW16 181 D6
Rignold Ho 6 SE5 139 C3
Riley Ho 9 Bow E3 97 C3
Chelsea SW10 266 C5
1 Streatham SW4 159 D4
Riley Rd
Bermondsey SE1 117 D3 263 C6
Enfield EN3 6 C5
Riley St SW10 136 B5 266 C4
Rill Ho 16 SE5 139 C5
Rimini Ct SW12 158 D3
Rinaldo Rd SW12 159 B4
Ring Cl BR1 187 B3
Ringcroft St N7 72 C3
Ringer's Rd BR1 209 A6
Ringford Ho SW18 157 B6
Ringford Rd SW18 157 C5
Ring Ho 15 E1 118 C6
Ringlet Cl E16 99 B2
Ringlewell Cl EN1 6 B3
Ringmer Ave SW6 135 A4 264 B1
Ringmer Gdns 3 N19 72 A6
Ringmer Ho 15 SE22 139 C2
Ringmer Pl N21 17 B6
Ringmer Way BR1 210 B4
Ringmore Rise SE23 162 B4
Ring Rd W12 112 C5
Ringsfield Ho SE17 262 B1
Ringslade Rd N22 32 B1
Ringstead Bldgs SE6 163 D4
Ringstead Ct SM1 218 B3
Ringstead Rd
Catford SE6 163 D4
Sutton SM1 218 B3
Ringway UB2 107 A1
Ring Way N11 31 C4
Ringwold Cl BR3 185 A3
Ringwood Ave
Muswell Hill N2 48 D6
Thornton Heath CR0 204 A2
Ringwood Cl HA5 40 C6
Ringwood Gdns
17 Millwall E14 119 C2
Roehampton SW15 156 A3
Ringwood Rd E17 53 B3
Ringwood Way
Hampton TW12 173 C6
Southgate N21 16 D4
Ripley Cl
Bromley BR1 210 B4
New Addington CR0 224 A2
Ripley Ct 1 CR4 180 B1
Ripley Gdns
Mortlake SW14 133 B2
Sutton SM1 218 A4
Ripley Ho
13 Kingston u T KT2 176 D4
Mortlake SW14 133 C2
Nine Elms SW1 269 A6
5 Penge SE26 184 B5
Ripley Mews E11 54 C3
Ripley Rd
Belvedere DA17 125 C2
Enfield EN2 5 A4
Hampton TW12 173 C3
Ilford IG3 79 D6
Newham E16 99 C1
Ripley's Believe It or Not!★ SW1 249 C5
Riplington Ct SW15 156 B4
Ripon Cl UB5 63 C2
Ripon Ct 10 N11 31 A4
Ripon Gdns
Chessington KT9 213 D3
Redbridge IG1 56 A2
Ripon Rd Edmonton N9 18 B4
Shooters Hill SE18 144 D6
Tottenham N17 51 B6
Ripon Way WD6 11 B6
Rippersley Rd DA16 146 A4
Ripple Ct 10 IG11 101 B6
Ripple Jun & Inf Schs IG11 79 C1
Ripple Rd
Barking IG11 79 A1
Barking IG11 101 C6
Castle Green RM9 102 A6
Rippleside Commercial Est IG11 102 C5
Ripplevale Gr N1 72 B1
Rippolson Rd SE18 123 D1
Ripston Rd TW15 171 B5
Risborough SE17 262 A4
Risborough Cl 4 N10 49 B6
Risborough Ct 5 N10 49 B6
Risborough Dr KT4 200 A2
Risborough Ho NW8 237 B6
Risborough St SE1 251 D2
Risdon Ho 26 SE16 118 C4
Risdon St 27 SE16 118 C4
Risedale Rd DA7 147 D2
Riseholme Ct E9 75 B2
Riseholme Ho 14 SE22 139 C2
Riseldine Rd SE23 163 A5
Rise The
Borehamwood WD6 10 B6
Buckhurst Hill IG9 21 D4
Chingford E4 20 C3
Edgware HA8 26 D5
Edmonton N13 32 C6
Harrow HA2 24 A1
Hendon NW7 27 D4
Hillingdon UB10 82 B5
Neasden NW10 67 B5
Sidcup DA5 168 C4
Wanstead E11 55 A4
Wembley HA0, UB6 65 A3
Risinghill St N1 234 A4
Risingholme Cl HA3 24 C2
Risingholme Rd HA3 24 C1
Risings The E17 54 B5
Rising Sun Ct EC1 241 D3
Risley Ave N17 33 B2
Risley Avenue Prim Sch 1 N17 33 C2
Risley Ho 7 E9 74 D2
Rita Rd SW8 138 B5 270 C4
Ritches Rd N15 51 A4
Ritchie Ho
Crouch End N19 49 D2
8 Rotherhithe SE16 118 C3
12 South Bromley E14 98 B1
Ritchie Rd CR0 206 B3
Ritchie St N1 94 C5 234 B4
Ritchings Ave E17 53 A5
Ritherdon Rd SW17 159 B2
Ritson Ho N1 233 C5
Ritson Rd E8 74 A2
Ritter St SE18 144 C6
Ritz Par W5 88 B3
Rivaz Pl E9 74 C2
Riven Ct 10 W2 91 D1
Rivenhall Gdns E11, E18 54 D5
Riverains The SW11 266 C1
River Ave
Southgate N13 16 D1
Thames Ditton KT7 197 A2
Riverbank KT8 196 C5
River Bank
Edmonton N21 17 A4
Thames Ditton KT7 196 D4
Riverbank Rd BR1 165 A1
Riverbank Way TW8 131 C6
River Barge Cl E14 120 A4
River Brent Bsns Pk W7 108 C3
River Cl Ruislip HA4 39 D3
Southall UB2 108 A4
Wanstead E11 55 C3
River Cotts BR5 190 C1
Rivercourt Rd W6 112 B1
River Crane Way TW13 151 B2
River Ct
Kingston u T KT6 197 D4
Lambeth SE1 251 C5
Shepperton TW17 193 A2
Wanstead E11 55 C3
Riverdale Cl IG11 102 B3
Riverdale Ct N21 17 B6
Riverdale Dr SW18 157 D3
Riverdale Gdns TW1 153 C6
Riverdale Rd
Erith DA8 125 D1
Feltham TW13 173 B6
Plumstead Comm SE18 123 D1
Sidcup DA5 169 B5
Twickenham TW1 153 C5
Riverdene HA8 11 A1
Riverdene Rd IG1 78 D5
Riverfleet WC1 233 B2
Riverford Ho 28 W2 91 C2
River Front EN1 5 C2
River Gdns
Carshalton SM5 219 A5
Feltham TW14 150 B6
River Gdns Bsns Ctr TW14 128 B1
River Grove Pk BR3 185 B2
Riverhead Cl E17 34 D1
Riverhill Mews KT4 215 B5
River Ho
Barnes SW13 133 C3
1 Forest Hill SE26 162 B1
Riverholme KT8 196 C6
Riverhope Mans SE18 122 A3
River House Montessori Sch E14 119 D4
Riverine Lo HA7 25 A5
River La TW10 153 D3
Riverleigh Ct E4 35 A5
Riverly Prim Sch E10 53 C1
Rivermead
East Molesey KT8 196 A6
Kingston u T KT6 197 D4
Rivermead Cl TW11 175 B5
Rivermead Ct
Ealing UB6 87 A4
Fulham SW6 135 B2
Rivermead Ho
Hackney E9 75 A3
Sunbury TW16 194 C6
River Meads Ave TW13, TW2 151 D1
River Mole Bsns Pk KT10 195 C1
River Mount KT12 193 D2
Rivernook Cl KT12 194 C4
River Park Gdns BR2 186 B3
River Park Rd N22 32 B1
River Pl N1 73 A1
River Plate Ho EC2 242 D3
River Rd
Barking IG11 101 D3
Buckhurst Hill IG9 21 D3
River Reach TW11 175 C5
River Road Bsns Pk IG11 101 D4
Riversdale Gdns N22 32 C2
Riversdale Prim Sch SW18 157 C3
Riversdale Rd
Highbury N5 73 A5
Thames Ditton KT7 197 A3
Riversdene N5 73 A5
Riversfield Rd EN1 5 C2
Rivers Ho 10 TW8 110 C1
Riverside
Battersea SW11 267 B4
Forest Hill SE6 185 B6
Greenwich SE7 121 B3
Hendon NW4 46 B2
Oatlands Pk TW17 193 C2
Richmond TW9 153 D6
11 Rotherhithe SE16 118 C4
St Pancras WC1 233 B2
Sunbury TW16 172 D1
Twickenham TW1 153 B3
Riverside Apartments N13 32 B5
Riverside Ave KT8 196 B4
Riverside Bsns Ctr SW18 157 D3
Riverside Bsns Pk SW19 180 A2
Riverside Cl
Chislehurst BR5 190 C1
Ealing W7 86 C3
Hackbridge SM6 219 B5
Kingston u T KT1 197 D5
Upper Clapton E5 74 C6
Riverside Ct
Chingford E4 19 D5
Lewisham SE12 142 D1
Nine Elms SW8 269 D6
Richmond TW11 175 C5
Riverside Dr
Chiswick W4 133 C4
Mitcham CR4 202 C4
Richmond TW10 153 B1
Temple Fortune NW11 47 A3
Riverside Est EN3 19 A5
Riverside Gdns
Enfield EN2 5 A3
Hammersmith W6 112 B1
Hendon N3 47 A6
Wembley HA0 88 A5
Riverside Health & Racquets Club Chiswick The W4 133 C4
Riverside Ho
Finchley N12 29 D6
14 Islington N1 73 A1
Morden SW19 202 A5
30 Richmond TW10 153 D6
Riverside Ind Est IG11 102 A4
Riverside Mans 4 E1 118 C5
Riverside Pl
New Southgate N11 15 C1
Stanwell TW19 148 A5
Riverside Prim Sch 37 SE16 118 A4
Riverside Rd
Mill Meads E15 98 A5
Sidcup DA14 169 A2
South Tottenham N15 52 A3
Stanwell TW19 148 A5
Wandsworth SW17, SW19 158 A1
Riverside Sch BR5 190 C1
Riverside The KT8 196 B6
Riverside Wlk
Isleworth TW7 130 C2
3 West Wickham BR4 207 D1
Riverside Wlk Mkt★ WC2 116 B5 250 D4
Riverside Works IG11 78 D1
Riverside Workshops SE1 252 B4
River St EC1 94 C4 234 A2
Riverstone Cl HA2 64 B6
Riverstone Ct KT2 176 B2
Riverston Sch SE12 165 A6
River Terr
London W6 112 C1
St James SW1 250 C5
Riverton Cl W9 91 B4
Riverview TW17 193 B2
River View EN2 5 A2
Riverview CE Prim Sch KT19 215 B4
Riverview Ct 14 DA17 125 C1
Riverview Gdns SW13 134 B6
River View Gdns TW1 152 D2
Riverview Gr W4 132 D6
Riverview Hts SE18 144 D5
Riverview Lo NW9 67 B6
Riverview Pk SE6 163 C2
Riverview Rd
Chiswick W4 132 D6
West Ewell KT19 215 B4
Riverway N13 32 C6
River Way
Canning Town SE10 120 D3
Twickenham TW13, TW2 151 D2
West Ewell KT19 215 C3
River Wlk KT12 194 A3
Riverwood La BR7 189 B2
Rivet Ho SE1 263 D2
Rivington Ave IG8 37 D1
Rivington Cres NW7 27 D3
Rivington Ct
17 Dagenham RM10 81 D2
Willesden Green NW10 90 A6
Rivington Pl EC2 95 C4
Rivington St EC2 95 C4
Rivington Wlk 4 E8 96 A6
Rivulet Rd N17 33 A3
Rixon Ho SE18 144 D6
Rixon St N7 72 C5
Rixsen Rd E12 78 A3
Roach Rd E3 75 C1
Roads Pl N19 72 A6
Roan Ind Est CR4 180 D2
Roan St SE10 142 A6
Robart Ho 2 N12 30 A5
Robarts Cl HA5 40 B4
Robbins Hall EN3 18 D5
Robb Rd HA7 25 A4
Robert Adam St W1 238 A2
Roberta St E2 96 A4
Robert Bell Ho 2 SE16 118 A2
Robert Blair Prim Sch N7 72 A2
Robert Browning Prim Sch SE17 117 B1 262 C2
Robert Burns Ho N17 34 B3
Robert Cl
Barking IG11 79 A2
Paddington W9 236 B5
Robert Clack Sch
Dagenham RM8 59 C1
Dagenham RM8 81 B6
Robert Dashwood Way SE17 262 A3
Robert Gentry Ho W14 254 B1
Robert Gerard Ho 7 SE27 183 B6
Robert Ho 12 HA1 42 D4
Robert Jones Ho 3 SE16 118 A2
Robert Keen Cl 18 SE15 140 A4
Robert Lowe Cl SE14 140 D5
Roberton Dr BR1 187 C2
Robert Owen Ho
Fulham SW6 134 D4
8 Spitalfields E2 95 D4
Robert Owen Lo 4 E5 74 B4
Robertsbridge Rd SM5 202 B2

Roberts Cl
Cheam SM3 .... 216 D1
Dagenham RM10 ......81 C2
New Eltham SE9......167 B3
South Norwood CR7...205 B6
Yiewsley UB7....... 104 A5
Roberts Ct
Chessington KT9 .... 213 D3
Ealing W5............88 A1
Islington N1........ 234 D5
Penge SE20 .... 184 C2
Willesden NW10 ......67 C2
Roberts Ho
Dagenham RM10......81 D1
Friern Barnet N11 .....31 B5
6 Kidbrooke SE18 .. 144 A4
5 West Norwood SE27 .... 160 D1
Roberts Mews SW1 . 258 A5
Robertson Ho
Kidbrooke SE18......144 B4
11 Lewisham SE10 .. 142 A4
1 Upper Tooting SW17 .... 180 C5
Robertson St SW8 ...137 B3
Robert's Pl EC1..... 241 B6
Roberts Rd
Belvedere DA17..... 125 C1
Finchley NW7.........29 A4
Highams Pk E17.......35 D2
Robert St
Croydon CR0 .... 221 A5
Newham E16 .... 122 D5
Plumstead SE18......123 B2
Regent's Pk NW1 ....93 B4 231 D1
Strand WC2 .... 250 B5
Robert Sutton Ho 20 E1..........96 C1
Robeson St 7 E3......97 B2
Robina Cl DA6....... 146 D1
Northwood HA6.......22 A2
Robin Cl
Edgware NW7 ....11 C1
Hampton TW12 ..... 173 A5
Robin Cres E16 ....99 D2
Robin Ct
15 Cubitt Town E14 .. 120 A3
Wallington SM6..... 219 C2
Wood Green N22......32 B3
Robin Gr
Brentford TW8...... 131 C6
Dartmouth Pk N6 ......71 A6
Harrow HA3..........44 B3
Highgate N6..........71 A6
Robin Hill Dr BR7 ....188 A4
Robin Ho NW8...... 230 A3
Robin Hood SW15 ....155 C1
Robinhood Cl CR4 ...203 C6
Robin Hood Ct 2 SM1 .... 217 D3
Robin Hood Dr HA3....24 D3
Robin Hood Gdns 12 E14..........120 A6
Robin Hood Jun Sch 8 SM1 .... 217 D3
Robinhood La CR4 ...203 C6
Robin Hood La
Bexley DA6.......... 169 A6
Blackwall E14........ 120 A6
Kingston u T SW15... 177 C6
Sutton SM1 .... 217 D3
Robin Hood Prim Sch
Kingston u T SW15.... 177 C5
Sutton SM1 .... 217 C3
Robin Hood Way
Kingston u T SW15.... 177 C5
Wembley UB6 ....64 D2
Robin Hood Way (Kingston By-Pass) KT2, SW15, SW20 ....177 C5
Robinia Cl SE20.......184 A2
Robinia Cres E10 .....75 D6
Robin La NW4 ....46 D6
Robinscroft Mews 18 SE10 .... 141 D4
Robins Ct
Grove Pk SE12...... 165 C1
Richmond TW10..... 154 A5
South Croydon CR2 .. 221 C4
Robin's Ct
Beckenham BR3......186 B1
Clapham Pk SW4.... 160 A5
Robinsfield Inf Sch NW8.........92 C5 230 A4
Robins Gr BR4........225 A5
Robinson Cl Enfield EN2.. 5 A2
11 Leyton E11 ....76 C5
Robinson Cres WD23... 8 A3
Robinson Ct
5 Barnet EN4........14 D3
Islington N1.......... 234 D6
4 Richmond TW9 ....132 B1
Thornton Heath CR0 . 204 D3
Robinson Ho
4 North Kensington W10 ....90 D1
12 Tower Hamlets E14.. 97 C2
Robinson Rd
Dagenham RM10......81 C4
Mitcham SW19 ..... 180 C4
South Hackney E2 .....96 C5
Robinson's Cl W13....87 A2
Robinson St SW3 ... 267 C6
Robinswood Mews 6 N5...............72 D3
Robinwood Gr UB8 ...82 B3
Robinwood Pl SW15 .177 B6
Rob Pascoe La RM9 ..103 A4
Robsart St SW9......138 C3
Robson Ave NW10 ....68 A1
Robson Cl Enfield EN2... 4 D3
Newham E6 .... 100 A1
Robson Ct N12 ....30 A5
Robson Rd SE21, SE27...............161 A1
Roby Ho EC1........ 242 A6
Roch Ave HA8 ....26 B1
Rochdale 8 SE19....183 C4
Rochdale Rd
Abbey Wood SE2 .....124 B2
Walthamstow E17 .....53 C2
Rochdale Way 4 SE8...............141 C5
Roche Ho 15 E14.....119 B6
Rochelle Cl SW11....136 B1
Rochelle Ct
Beckenham BR3..... 185 D3
14 Stepney E1 ....96 C1
Rochelle St 31 E2.....95 D4
Rochemont Wlk 2 E8.................96 A6
Roche Rd SW16......182 B2
Roche Sch The 15 SW18............. 157 C6
Rochester Ave
Bromley BR1 ....187 B1
Feltham TW13 ...... 149 D2
Newham E13 ....99 C6
Rochester Cl
1 Blackfen DA15 ....168 B5
Enfield EN1 ....5 C4
Streatham SW16 .... 182 A3
Rochester Ct
1 Bethnal Green E2 ... 96 B3
9 Camden Town NW1. .71 C1
Finchley N3 ....29 A1
Kingsbury NW9 ....45 B4
South Norwood SE25. 184 A1
Rochester Dr
Old Bexley DA5 ...... 169 C5
Pinner HA5............40 D4
Rochester Gdns
Redbridge IG1........56 B2
South Croydon CR0 .. 221 C5
Rochester Ho
Bermondsey SE1 .... 252 D1
18 Deptford SE15 ... 140 C6
Rochester Mews NW1.................71 C1
Rochester Par TW13 .150 A1
Rochester Pl NW1 ....71 C1
Rochester Rd
Carshalton SM5...... 218 D4
Kentish Town NW1.....71 C2
Northwood HA6........39 D6
Rochester Row SW1 ....115 C2 259 B4
Rochester Sq NW1....71 C1
Rochester St SW1 ... 259 C5
Rochester Terr NW1...71 C2
Rochester Way
Eltham SE9.......... 144 C2
Kidbrooke SE3, SE9 .. 143 D2
Rochester Wlk SE1 . 252 C4
Roche Wlk SM5......202 B3
Rochford N17 ....33 C1
Rochford Ave RM6 ....58 C4
Rochford Cl 2 E6.....99 D5
Rochford Way CR0...204 A3
Rochford Wlk 3 E8...74 A1
Rochfort Ho 4 SE8 ..119 B1
Rock Ave 13 SW14 ...133 B2
Rockbourne Rd SE23............. 162 D3
Rock Cl CR4 ....180 B1
Rockell's Pl SE22 ....162 B5
Rockfield Ho
Greenwich SE10 .... 142 A6
2 Hendon NW4 ....46 D5
Rockford Ave UB6 ....87 B5
Rock Gdns RM10......81 D3
Rock Grove Way SE16..............118 A2
Rockhall Rd NW2 .....68 D4
Rockhampton Cl 4 SE27..............182 C6
Rockhampton Rd
South Croydon CR2 .. 221 C2
West Norwood SE27, SW16 .... 182 C6
Rock Hill SE19...... 183 D6
Rockingham Cl SW15............. 133 D1
Rockingham Ct 19 BR3...............185 C3
Rockingham Gate WD23.................8 A5
Rockingham St SE1........117 A3 262 A5
Rockland Rd SW15...135 A1
Rocklands N3 ....29 B3
Rocklands Dr HA7 ....25 C1
Rockley Ct 9 W14 .. 112 D4
Rockley Rd W14 .... 112 D4
Rockliffe Manor Prim Sch SE18 .... 145 D6
Rockmount Prim Sch SE19...............183 B4
Rockmount Rd
Plumstead Comm SE18, SE2 .... 123 D1
South Norwood SE19..183 B4
Rocks La SW13 ......134 A2
Rock St N4 ....72 C6
Rockstraw Ho 5 NW3.................70 D1
Rockware Ave UB6....86 C6
Rockware Bsns Ctr UB6 ....86 B6
Rockways EN5.........11 D5
Rockwell Gdns SE19 .183 C6
Rockwell Rd RM10....81 D3
Rockwood Ct N16.....52 A2
Rocliffe St N1 .94 D5 234 D3
Rocombe Cres SE23..162 C4
Rocque Ho SW6 .... 264 C4
Rocque La SE3 ..... 142 D2
Rodborough Rd NW11..............47 C1
Rodd Est TW17.......193 B4
Roden Gdns CR0.....205 C3
Rodenhurst Ct SW4. 159 D6
Rodenhurst Rd SW4 159 D5
Roden St Ilford IG1.....78 C5
Upper Holloway N7 ....72 B5
Roderick Ho 3 SE16...............118 C2
Roderick Rd NW3.....70 D4
Rodgers Cl WD6 ....9 D5
Rodgers Ho 4 SW4. 159 D4
Rodin Ct N1 .... 234 C5
Roding Ct 6 W12.....111 C4
Roding Ho N1 ...... 234 A5
Roding La IG9 ....21 D3
Roding La N IG8 ......37 D1
Roding La S IG4 ......55 D5
Roding Lo IG1 ....55 D3
Roding Mews E1.....118 A5
Roding Prim Sch RM8.................80 C3
Roding Rd Hackney E5 .75 A3
Newham E6 .... 100 D2
Rodings Ct E4 ....36 B5
Rodings Row EN5......1 A1
Rodings The 4 IG8 ...37 C4
Roding Valley Sta IG9.................37 D6
Roding View IG9......21 D3
Rodmarton St W1.........92 D2 237 D3
Rodmell WC1........ 233 B1
Rodmell Cl UB4.......85 A3
Rodmell Slope N12 ...29 B5
Rodmere St SE10 ....120 C1
Rodney Cl
New Malden KT3 .... 199 C4
Pinner HA5............41 A2
Thornton Heath CR0 . 204 D1
Walton-on-T KT12 ... 194 C1
Rodney Ct NW8..... 236 B6
Rodney Gdns
Hayes BR4 .... 225 A4
Pinner HA5...........40 C4
Rodney Ho
4 Cubitt Town E14 .. 119 D2
Islington N1........ 233 D3
Notting Hill W11..... 245 A6
Rodney Pl
Merton SW19....... 180 A2
Newington SE17 ......117 A2 262 B4
Walthamstow E17 .....35 B1
Rodney Rd
Mitcham CR4 .... 202 C6
New Malden KT3 .... 199 C4
Twickenham TW4.... 151 C4
Walton-on-T KT12 ... 194 C1
Walworth SE17 ......117 B2 262 C3
Wanstead E11 ....55 B5
Rodney St N1. .94 B5 233 D3
Rodwall Pl HA8.......26 C3
Rodway Rd
Bromley BR1 ....187 B2
Putney SW15........ 156 A4
Rodwell Cl 2 HA4 ....40 C1
Rodwell Rd SE22.... 161 D5
Roe 5 NW9 ....27 D2
Roebourne Way E16 .122 C4
Roebuck Cl
Feltham TW13 ....172 B6
Tottenham N17 ....33 D4
Roebuck Ct
Chingford E4 ....36 A3
2 New Malden KT3 . 199 C4
Roebuck Hts IG10 ....21 C4
Roebuck La IG9 ....21 C3
Roebuck Rd KT9.....214 C3
Roedean Ave EN3......6 C5
Roedean Cl EN3 ....6 C4
Roedean Cres SW15 .155 C6
Roe End NW9.........45 A5
Roe Gn NW9..........45 A4
Roe Green Jun & Inf Schs NW9 ....44 D5
ROEHAMPTON......155 C4
Roehampton Church Sch SW15.............156 B4
Roehampton Cl SW15 ....134 A1
Roehampton Ct SW13 ....134 A2
Roehampton Dr BR7..................189 A4
Roehampton Gate SW15 ....155 C5
Roehampton High St SW15..............156 A4
Roehampton La
Putney SW15....... 156 A5
Roehampton SW15 ....156 B3
Roehampton Univ (Digby Stuart Coll) SW15 . 156 A6
Roehampton Univ (Froebel Coll) SW15............. 155 D5
Roehampton Univ (Southlands Coll) SW15............. 156 A6
Roehampton Univ (Whitelands Coll) SW15............. 156 A4
Roehampton Vale SW15 .... 155 D2
Roe La NW9 ....45 A5
Roe Rd SM6 ....220 A1
Roe Way SM6........220 A2
Roffey Ct 9 NW9 .....46 A5
Roffey St E14 ....120 A4
Rogate Ho E5..........74 A5
Roger Ascham Prim Sch E17...................35 B2
Roger Dowley Ct 8 E2...................96 C5
Roger's Almshouses 2 SW9 ....138 B1
Rogers Ct 16 E14 ....119 C6
Rogers Est 28 E2......96 C4
Rogers Gdns RM10....81 C3
Rogers Ho
9 Dagenham RM10 ...81 C5
Westminster SW1.... 259 D4
Rogers Rd
Canning Town E16 .....98 D1
Dagenham RM10.......81 C3
Upper Tooting SW17 . 180 C6
Roger St WC1. .94 B3 240 D5
Roger Stone Ct NW10 67 B6
Rogers Wlk N12 ......13 D1
Rohan Pl 4 IG4 ......56 B4
Rojack Rd SE23..... 162 D3
Rokeby Gdns IG8 .....37 A2
Rokeby Ho
9 Balham SW12......159 B4
Bloomsbury WC1.... 240 C5
Rokeby Pl SW20 .....178 B3
Rokeby Rd SE4 ......141 B3
Rokeby Sch
Kingston u T KT2 .... 177 A3
Stratford E15.........76 B1
Rokeby St E15.........98 C6
Rokeland Ho SE4 ....141 A1
Rokell Ho BR3 ...... 185 D5
Roker Park Ave UB10. .60 A4
Rokesby Cl DA16.....145 B3
Rokesby Pl HA0.......65 D3
Rokesly Ave N8 ....50 A4
Rokesly Jun & Inf Schs 5 N8...............50 A4
Roland Ct SE19 ..... 183 D2
Roland Gdns SW7 ....114 A1 256 B2
Roland Ho SW7...... 256 B2
Roland Mews 1 E1....96 D2
Roland Rd E17.........54 B5
Roland Way
South Kensington SW7 ......114 A1 256 B2
Walworth SE17 ..... 262 D1
Worcester Pk KT4 ... 215 D6
Roles Gr RM6.........59 A5
Rolfe Cl EN4...........2 C1
Rolfe Ho N11 ....30 D6
Rolinsden Way BR2 . 225 D4
Rolland Ho W7 ....86 C2
Rollesby Rd KT19, KT9..................214 C2
Rollesby Way SE28....102 C1
Rolleston Ave BR5 .. 210 D3
Rolleston Cl BR5... 210 D2
Rolleston Rd CR2 ....221 B1
Roll Gdns IG2 ....56 C4
Rollins St SE15 ......140 C6
Rollit Cres TW3 ......151 C6
Rollit Ho N7 ....72 C3
Rollit St N7............72 C3
Rollo Ct SW11 ...... 268 C1
Rolls Bldgs EC4..... 241 B2
Rollscourt Ave SE24 ..161 A6
Rolls Ct The E4 ....36 A5
Rolls Park Ave E4......35 D5
Rolls Park Rd E4......35 D5
Rolls Pas EC4....... 241 A2
Rolls Rd SE1. 117 D1 263 D2
Rolt St SE8 ....141 A6
Rolvenden Gdns BR1............. 187 D3
Rolvenden Pl N17.....34 A2
Roman Cl
Feltham TW14 ...... 150 C6
South Acton W3 ..... 110 D4
Roman Ct 4 N7 ....72 B2
Romanfield Rd SW2..160 B4
Romanhurst Ave BR2...............208 C5
Romanhurst Gdns BR2, BR3...............208 C5
Roman Ind Est CR0 . 205 C2
Roman Lo 6 IG9 .....21 C3
Roman Rd
Chiswick W4 .... 111 D2
Elstree WD6...........9 D5
Finchley N12 ....30 C2
Globe Town E2, E3 .....96 D5
Ilford IG1..............78 D2
Muswell Hill N10 ......31 B3
Newham E6 .... 100 A3
25 Old Ford E3........97 B6
Willesden NW2 ....68 C5
Roman Rise SE19....183 B4
Roman Road Mkt* 1 E3...................97 B5
Roman Road Prim Sch E6....................99 D3

Roman Sq SE28 124 A5
Roman Way
Barnsbury N7 72 B2
Croydon CR0 220 D6
4 Deptford SE15 140 C5
Enfield EN1 17 D6
Romany Gdns
Cheam SM3 201 C2
1 Higham Hill E17 35 A2
Romany Ho 8 N9 18 A1
Romany Prospect
SE19 183 B4
Romany Rise BR5 211 A1
Roma Rd E17 53 A6
Roma Read Cl SW15 156 B4
Romayne Ho SW4 137 D2
Romberg Rd SW17 159 A1
Romborough Gdns
SE13 164 A6
Romborough Way
SE13 164 A6
Romeland WD6 9 D5
Romeland Ct WD6 9 D5
Romer Ho 9 SW2 160 B6
Romero Cl SW9 138 B2
Romero Sq SE9 143 C1
Romeyn Rd SW16 160 B1
ROMFORD 59 D4
Romford Ho 17 N1 73 B2
Romford Rd
Forest Gate E7, E12 77 C3
Stratford E15 76 D2
Romford St E1 96 B2
Romilly Dr WD19 23 A6
Romilly Rd N4 72 D6
Romilly St W1 249 D6
Romily Ct 2 SW6 135 A3
Rommany Ct SE27 183 B6
Rommany Rd SE27 183 B6
Romney Cl
Ashford TW15 171 A5
Chessington KT9 214 A4
7 Deptford SE14 140 C5
Harrow HA2 41 C2
North End NW11 48 A1
Tottenham N17 34 B2
Romney Ct
9 Hammersmith
W12 112 C4
9 Hampstead NW3 70 C2
15 Northolt UB5 84 D5
Romney Dr
Bromley BR1 187 D3
Harrow HA2 41 C2
Romney Gdns DA7 147 B4
Romney Ho
2 Blackwall E14 120 B6
Enfield EN1 18 A6
Sutton SM2 217 D2
Romney Mews W1 238 A4
Romney Par UB4 83 B5
Romney Rd
Greenwich SE10 142 B6
Hayes UB4 83 B5
New Malden KT3 199 B3
10 Woolwich SE18 123 A3
Romney Row NW2 68 D6
Romney St
SW1 116 A3 260 A5
Romola Rd SE24,
SW2 160 D3
Romsey Cl BR6 226 D4
Romsey Gdns RM9 102 D6
Romsey Rd
Dagenham RM9 102 D6
Ealing W13 109 A6
Romulus Ct 7 TW8 131 D5
Ronald Ave E15 98 C4
Ronald Cl BR3 207 B4
Ronald Ct EN5 1 D2
Ronald Ho
Eltham SE9 143 C1
4 Sutton SM1 218 B3
Ronald Ross Prim Sch 6
SW19 157 A4
Ronaldshay N4 50 C1
Ronalds Rd
Bromley BR1 187 A2
Islington N5 72 C3
Ronald St E1 96 C1
Ronaldstone Rd
DA15 167 C5
Rona Rd NW3 71 A4
Ronart St HA3 42 D6
Rona Wlk 20 N1 73 B2
Rondu Rd NW2 69 A3
Ronelean Rd KT6 214 B5
Ron Leighton Way
E6 100 A6
Ronnie La E12 78 C4
Ron Todd Cl RM10 103 C6
Ronver Lo E4 20 C1
Ronver Rd SE12 164 D3
Rood La EC3 117 C6 253 A6
Rookby Ct N21 16 D2
Rook Cl HA9 66 D5
Rookeries Cl TW13 150 C1
Rookery Cl NW9 45 D4
Rookery Cotts EN4 3 B2
Rookery Cres RM10 81 D1
Rookery Dr BR7 188 C2
Rookery La BR2 209 D3
Rookery Rd SW4 137 C1
Rookery Way NW9 45 D4
Rooke Way SE10 120 D1
Rookfield Ave N10 49 C5
Rookfield Cl N10 49 C5
Rook Lo IG1 55 D3
Rooks Heath Coll Bsns &
Enterprise HA2 63 C5
Rooksmead Rd
TW16 172 A1
Rooks Terr UB7 104 A4
Rookstone Rd SW17 180 D5
Rook Wlk E6 100 A1
Rookwood Ave
Wallington SM6 219 D4
West Barnes KT3 200 A5
Rookwood Gdns E4 20 D2
Rookwood Ho 2
IG11 101 B5
Rookwood Rd N16 52 A2
Roosevelt Ct 15
SW19 157 A3
Rootes Dr W10 90 D2
Ropemaker Rd SE16 119 A3
Ropemaker's Fields 7
E14 119 B6
Ropemaker St
EC2 95 B2 242 C4
Roper Ho 13 SE21 183 C6
Roper La SE1 117 C4 253 B1
Ropers Ave E4 36 A5
Roper's Orch SW3 267 A5
Roper St 1 SE9 166 C5
Ropers Wlk 13 SE24 160 C4
Roper Way CR4 181 A1
Ropery Bsns Pk SE7 121 C2
Ropery St E3 97 B3
Rope St SE16 119 A3
Ropewalk Gdns 18
E1 96 A1
Rope Yard Rails
SE18 122 D3
Ropley St 6 E2 96 A5
Rosa Alba Mews N5 73 A4
Rosa Ave TW15 170 C6
Rosa Freedman Ctr
NW2 46 C1
Rosalind Ct 6 IG11 80 A1
Rosalind Ho 25 N1 95 C5
Rosaline Rd
SW6 135 A5 264 B3
Rosaline Terr SW6 264 B3
Rosamond St SE26 162 B1
Rosamund Cl CR2 221 B4
Rosamun St UB2 107 A2
Rosa Parks Ho 8
SW9 138 B3
Rosary Cl TW3, TW5 129 A3
Rosary Ct 17 E1 96 D2
Rosary Gdns
Ashford TW15 170 D6
Bushey WD23 8 C4
South Kensington
SW7 114 A2 256 B3
Rosary RC Inf Sch
TW5 129 C6
Rosary RC Jun Sch
TW5 129 C6
Rosary RC Prim Sch
NW3 70 C3
Rosaville Rd
SW6 135 B5 264 C3
Rosbury SW15 157 A5
Roscastle Rd SE4 163 A6
Roscoe St EC1 95 A3 242 B5
Roscoff Cl HA8 27 A2
Roscommon Ho 2
NW3 70 B3
Roseacre Cl
Ealing W13 87 B2
Roseacre Cl *continued*
Littleton TW17 192 C4
Roseacre Lo EN3 6 C1
Roseacre Rd DA16 146 B2
Rose Alley
Borough The SE1 252 B4
Broadgate EC2 243 B3
Rose Ave
Mitcham CR4 180 D2
Morden SM4 202 A4
Woodford E18 37 B1
Rosebank
2 Dagenham W3 89 B1
Fulham SW6 134 C5
Penge SE20 184 B3
Rosebank Ave HA0 64 D4
Rosebank Cl
Colney Hatch N12 30 C5
Teddington TW11 175 A4
Rosebank Gdns
Bow E3 97 B5
1 Dagenham W3 89 B1
Rosebank Gr E17 53 B6
Rosebank Rd
Hanwell W7 108 C4
Walthamstow E17 53 D3
Rosebank Villas E17 53 C5
Rosebank Way W3 89 B1
Rosebank Wlk
Camden Town NW1 71 D1
14 Woolwich SE7 122 A2
Rose Bates Dr NW9 44 C5
Rosebay Ho 20 E3 97 C2
Roseberry Gdns
Harringay N4 50 D3
Orpington BR6 227 C5
Roseberry Pl E8 73 D2
Roseberry St SE16 118 B2
Rosebery Ave
Finsbury EC1 94 C4 234 B1
Harrow HA2 63 B4
Kingston u T KT3 199 D6
Plashet E12 78 B2
Sidcup DA15 167 C4
South Norwood CR7 183 A1
Tottenham N17 34 A1
Rosebery Cl SM4 200 D3
Rosebery Ct
Chessington KT9 214 B3
Holborn EC1 241 A6
Mayfair W1 248 C4
Rosebery Gdns
Ealing W13 87 A1
Hornsey N8 50 A4
Sutton SM1 217 D4
Rosebery Ho 21 E2 96 C5
Rosebery Ind Pk N17 34 B1
Rosebery Mews N10 31 C1
Rosebery Rd
Cheam SM1, SM2 217 B2
Clapham Pk SW2 160 A5
Isleworth TW3, TW7 152 A6
Kingston u T KT1 176 D1
Muswell Hill N10 31 C1
Rosebery Sq
Holborn EC1 241 A5
Kingston u T KT1 176 D1
Rosebine Ave TW2 152 B4
Rosebriars KT10 212 A3
Rose Bruford Coll
DA15 168 B3
Rosebury Ct SW16 182 B2
Rosebury Rd SW6 135 D3
Rosebury Vale HA4 62 A6
Rose Bush Ct NW3 70 D3
Rose Cotts KT10 212 B3
Rosecourt Rd CR0 204 B3
Rosecroft N22 32 B2
Rosecroft Ave NW3 69 C5
Rosecroft Gdns
Dollis Hill NW2 68 A5
Twickenham TW2 152 B3
Rosecroft Rd UB1 85 C3
Rosecroft Wlk
Pinner HA5 40 D4
Wembley HA0 65 D3
Rose & Crown Ct
EC2 242 A2
Rose & Crown Yd
SW1 249 B3
Rose Ct 7 Dalston E8 73 D1
Harrow HA2 64 A6
Ilford IG1 78 D2
Islington N1 234 C5
Muswell Hill N10 31 B3
3 Pinner HA5 40 C6
Rose Ct *continued*
Spitalfields E1 243 D3
7 Wembley HA0 88 A5
10 Wimbledon SW19 179 B5
Rose Dale BR6 226 D6
Rosedale Ave UB3 83 B2
Rosedale Cl
Abbey Wood SE2 124 B3
Hanwell W7 108 D4
Stanmore HA7 25 B4
Rosedale Cnr BR7 188 B2
Rosedale Coll UB3 83 C1
Rosedale Ct N5 72 D4
Rosedale Dr RM9 80 B1
Rosedale Gdns RM9 80 B1
Rosedale Ho N16 51 B1
Rosedale Lo N14 15 B4
Rosedale Pl CR0 206 D2
Rosedale Rd
Dagenham RM9 80 B1
Forest Gate E7 77 C3
Richmond TW9 132 A1
Stoneleigh KT17 216 A3
Rosedale Terr W6 112 B3
Rosedene NW6 90 D6
Rosedene Ave
Morden SM4 201 C4
Southall UB6 85 C4
Streatham SW16 160 B1
Thornton Heath CR0 204 A2
Rosedene Ct HA4 39 C1
Rosedene Gdns IG2 56 C5
Rosedene Terr E10 75 D6
Rosedew Rd W6 134 D6
Rose End KT4 200 D1
Rosefield Cl SM5 218 C3
Rosefield Ct EN4 2 D1
Rosefield Gdns E14 119 C6
Roseford Ct 16 W12 112 D4
Rose Garden Cl HA8 26 A4
Rosegate Ho 32 E3 97 B5
Rose Gdns
Ealing W5 109 D3
Feltham TW13 150 A2
Southall UB1 85 C3
Rose Glen NW9 45 B5
Rosehart Mews 8
W11 91 C1
Rosehatch Ave RM6 58 D6
Roseheath Rd TW4 151 B6
ROSEHILL 202 A1
Rosehill
Claygate KT10 213 A2
Hampton TW12 173 C2
Rose Hill
Carshalton SM4,
SM5 202 A2
Cheam SM1 201 D1
Rosehill Ave SM1,
SM5 202 A1
Rosehill Ct SM4 202 A2
Rosehill Gdns
Greenford UB6 64 D3
Sutton SM1 218 A6
Rose Hill Park W
SM1 218 A6
Rosehill Rd SW18 158 A6
Rose Joan Mews
NW6 69 C4
Rose La RM6 59 A5
Roseland Cl N17 33 B3
Roseland Ho SW6 135 A2
Rose Lawn WD23 8 A3
Roseleigh Ave N5 72 D4
Roseleigh Cl 15
TW1 153 D5
Roselle Ct W5 88 A1
Rosemary Ave
East Finchley NW2 47 D5
East Molesey KT8 195 C5
Edmonton N9 18 B3
Enfield EN2 5 C4
Finchley N3 29 D1
Hounslow TW4 128 D3
Rosemary Branch Bridge
N1 235 D6
Rosemary Cl
Hillingdon UB8 82 C2
Thornton Heath CR0 204 A3
Rosemary Cotts 4
SW19 178 C3
Rosemary Ct 35 SE8 141 B6
Rosemary Dr
Redbridge IG4 55 D4
16 South Bromley E14 98 B1
Rosemary Gdns
Chessington KT9 214 A4
Dagenham RM8 59 B1
Mortlake SW14 133 A2
Rosemary Ho
Shoreditch N1 235 D5
Willesden NW10 90 B6
Rosemary La SW14 133 A2
Rosemary Rd
Bexley DA16 145 D4
Camberwell SE15 139 D5
Wandsworth SW17 158 A1
Rosemary St N1 235 D6
Rosemary Works Sch
N1 95 B6 235 D5
Rosemead NW9 46 A2
Rosemead Ave
Feltham TW13 149 D2
Mitcham CR4 181 C1
Wembley HA9 66 A3
Rosemead Prep Sch
SE27 161 A2
Rose Mews N18 34 B6
Rosemont Ave N12 30 A4
Rosemont Mans 11
NW3 69 D2
Rosemont Rd
Acton W3 110 D6
Kingston u T KT3 199 A6
Richmond TW10 154 A5
South Hampstead NW3 70 A2
Wembley HA0 88 A6
Rosemoor Ho 14
W13 109 A5
Rosemoor St
SW3 114 D2 257 C3
Rosemount Ct
2 Acton W3 110 D5
South Norwood SE25 205 C6
Rosemount Dr BR1 210 B5
Rosemount Lo W3 110 D6
Rosemount Point 10
SE23 162 D1
Rosemount Rd W13 87 A1
Rosemount Twrs 5
SM6 219 C2
Rosenau Cres SW11 267 C1
Rosenau Rd
SW11 136 D4 267 C2
Rosendale Prim Sch
SE21 161 A4
Rosendale Rd SE21,
SE24 161 A3
Roseneath Ave N21 16 D3
Roseneath Pl 2
SW16 182 B6
Roseneath Rd SW11 159 A5
Roseneath Wlk EN1 5 C1
Rosens Wlk HA8 10 D1
Rosenthal Ho SE6 163 D5
Rosenthal Rd SE6 164 A5
Rosenthorpe Rd
SE15 162 D6
Roserton St E14 120 A4
Rosery The CR0 206 D3
Rose Sq SW7 256 D2
Rose St Holborn EC4 241 D2
Strand WC2 116 A6 250 A6
Roses The IG8 36 D3
Rose Theatre SE1 252 A4
Rosethorn Cl SW12 159 D4
Rosetree Pl TW12 173 C4
Rosetta Cl SW8 270 B3
Rosetta Ct SE19 183 C3
Rosetta Prim Sch E16 99 B2
Rosetti Terr RM8 80 B4
Roseveare Rd SE12 187 C6
Roseville N21 16 C3
Roseville Ave TW3,
TW4 151 C6
Roseville Rd UB3 106 A2
Rosevine Rd SW20 178 C2
Rosewall Ct SW19 179 D5
Roseway
7 Edgware HA8 27 A6
London SE21 161 B5
Rose Way
Edgware HA8 27 A6
Lee SE12 165 A6
Rosewell Cl SE20 184 B3
Rose Wlk
Surbiton KT5 198 D4
West Wickham BR4 224 B6

Rosewood Ave UB6 ... 65 A2
Rosewood Cl DA14 ... 168 C1
Rosewood Ct
Bromley BR1 ... 187 D2
Dagenham RM6 ... 58 C4
Kingston u T KT2 ... 176 C3
2 Leyton E11 ... 76 B4
Rosewood Dr TW17 ... 192 B4
Rosewood Gdns
SE13 ... 142 A3
Rosewood Gr SM1 ... 218 A6
Rosewood Ho 9
NW3 ... 69 D2
Rosewood Sq W12 ... 90 A1
Rosher Cl E15 ... 76 B1
Roshni Ho SW17 ... 180 C4
Rosh Pinah Prim Sch
HA8 ... 10 D1
Rosina Ct SW17 ... 180 C5
Rosina St E9 ... 74 D2
Roskeen Ct 1
SW19 ... 178 C3
Roskell Rd SW15 ... 134 D2
Roskild Ct HA9 ... 66 B4
Roslin Ho 2 E1 ... 118 D6
Roslin Rd W3 ... 110 D3
Roslin Way BR1 ... 187 A5
Roslyn Cl CR4 ... 180 B1
Roslyn Rd N15 ... 51 C4
Rosmead Rd
W11 ... 113 A6 244 B6
Rosoman Pl EC1 ... 241 B6
Rosoman St EC1 ... 234 B1
Rossal Ct 2 SE20 ... 184 B3
Rossall Cres NW10 ... 88 B4
Rossanne Ho N3 ... 29 D3
Ross Ave RM8 ... 59 B1
Ross Cl Harrow HA3 ... 24 A3
Hayes UB3 ... 105 B2
Northolt UB5 ... 64 B4
Ross Ct
Chislehurst BR7 ... 188 B3
Colindale NW9 ... 45 C6
Ealing W13 ... 87 B2
Edgware HA8 ... 10 D2
1 Hackney E5 ... 74 B4
4 Putney SW15 ... 156 D4
South Croydon CR2 ... 221 A2
Rossdale SM1 ... 218 C3
Rossdale Dr
Ponders End N9 ... 18 C5
Welsh Harp NW9 ... 45 A1
Rossdale Rd SW15 ... 134 C1
Rosse Gdns SE13 ... 164 B5
Rosse Mews SE3 ... 143 B4
Rossendale Cl EN2 ... 4 D6
Rossendale Ho 7 E5 ... 74 B6
Rossendale St E5 ... 74 B6
Rossendale Way
NW1 ... 93 C6 232 B6
Rossendon Ct 1
SM6 ... 219 C2
Rossetti Ct WC1 ... 239 C4
Rossetti Gdns Mans
SW3 ... 267 C6
Rossetti Ho SW1 ... 259 D3
Rossetti Mews NW8 ... 229 D5
Rossetti Rd SE16 ... 118 B1
Rossetti Studios
SW3 ... 267 B6
Ross Ho
2 Kidbrooke SE18 ... 144 A4
Twickenham TW2 ... 151 D2
18 Wapping E1 ... 118 B5
Rossignol Gdns SM5 ... 219 A6
Rossindel Rd TW3 ... 151 C6
Rossington Cl EN1 ... 6 B5
Rossington St E5 ... 74 A6
Rossiter Cl SE19 ... 183 A3
Rossiter Fields EN5 ... 13 B5
Rossiter Rd SW12 ... 159 B3
Rossland Cl DA6 ... 169 D6
Rosslyn Ave
Barnes SW13 ... 133 D2
Chingford E4 ... 20 D2
Dagenham RM8 ... 59 C2
East Barnet EN4 ... 14 C5
Feltham TW14 ... 150 A5
Rosslyn Cl
Ashford TW16 ... 171 C4
Coney Hall BR4 ... 224 D5
Hayes UB3 ... 83 B2
Rosslyn Cres
Harrow HA1 ... 42 D5
Wembley HA9 ... 66 A4
Rosslyn Ct NW3 ... 70 C3
Rosslyn Hill NW3 ... 70 B3
Rosslyn Ho 8 TW9 ... 132 B4
Rosslyn Mans
8 Hampstead NW3 ... 70 A2
South Hampstead NW6 70 A2
Rosslyn Mews 7
NW3 ... 70 B4
Rosslyn Park Mews
NW3 ... 70 B3
Rosslyn Rd
Barking IG11 ... 79 B1
Twickenham TW1 ... 153 C5
Walthamstow E17 ... 54 A5
Rossmore Cl EN3 ... 6 D1
Rossmore Ct NW1 ... 237 C6
Rossmore Rd
NW1 ... 92 C3 237 B6
Ross Par SM6 ... 219 B2
Ross Rd
South Norwood
SE25 ... 205 C6
Twickenham TW2 ... 152 A3
Wallington SM6 ... 219 C3
Ross Way SE9 ... 144 A2
Rossway Dr WD23 ... 8 B6
Rosswood Gdns
SM6 ... 219 C2
Rosswood Ho 13
SM6 ... 219 B2
Rosswood Lo CR0 ... 222 D6
Rostella Rd SW17 ... 180 B6
Rostrever Gdns UB3 ... 105 C5
Rostrevor Ave N15 ... 51 D3
Rostrevor Gdns UB2 ... 107 A1
Rostrevor Mans SW6 264 C2
Rostrevor Mews
SW6 ... 264 C1
Rostrevor Rd
Fulham
SW6 ... 135 B4 264 C2
Wimbledon SW19 ... 179 C5
Rotary Ct KT8 ... 196 C6
Rotary Lo 12 SE27 ... 160 D1
Rotary St SE1 ... 261 D6
Rothay NW1 ... 231 D2
Rothbury Gdns TW7 ... 131 A5
Rothbury Rd E9 ... 75 C1
Rothbury Wlk N17 ... 34 A3
Rotheley Ho 39 E9 ... 74 C1
Rotherfield Ct
De Beauvoir Town N1 ... 73 B1
Shoreditch N1 ... 95 B6 235 C6
Rotherfield Prim Sch
N1 ... 95 A6 235 B6
Rotherfield Rd
Enfield EN3 ... 6 D6
Wallington SM5 ... 219 A3
Rotherfield St
Islington N1 ... 73 A1
Shoreditch N1 ... 95 A6 235 B6
Rotherham Wlk SE1 251 C3
Rotherhill Ave
SW16 ... 181 D4
ROTHERHITHE ... 118 D3
Rotherhithe Bsns Est 6
SE16 ... 118 C2
Rotherhithe New Rd
SE16 ... 118 B1
Rotherhithe Old Rd
SE16 ... 118 D2
Rotherhithe Prim Sch 24
SE16 ... 118 D2
Rotherhithe St SE16 ... 118 C4
Rotherhithe Sta
SE16 ... 118 C4
Rotherhithe Tunnel
SE16 ... 118 D5
Rother Ho SE15 ... 140 B1
Rotherwick Hill W5 ... 88 B3
Rotherwick Rd NW11 ... 47 C2
Rotherwood Cl
SW20 ... 179 A2
Rotherwood Rd
SW15 ... 134 D2
Rothery St N1 ... 234 D6
Rothesay Ave
Merton SW20 ... 179 A1
Mortlake SW14,
TW10 ... 132 D1
Northolt UB6 ... 64 B2
Rothesay Ct
4 Catford SE6 ... 164 D2
Rothesay Ct *continued*
Grove Pk SE12 ... 165 B1
13 Kennington SE11 ... 138 C6
Rothesay Rd SE25 ... 205 C5
Rothley Ct NW8 ... 236 C6
Rothsay Rd E7 ... 77 C2
Rothsay St
SE1 ... 117 C3 263 A5
Rothsay Wlk 19 E14 ... 119 C2
Rothschild Rd W4 ... 111 A3
Rothschild St SE27 ... 182 D6
Rothwell Ct
2 Bromley BR1 ... 187 B2
4 Harrow HA1 ... 42 D4
Rothwell Gdns RM9 ... 102 C6
Rothwell Ho TW5 ... 129 C6
Rothwell Rd RM9 ... 102 C6
Rothwell St
10 Hampstead NW1 ... 70 D1
Primrose Hill NW1 ... 230 D6
Roth Wlk N7 ... 72 B6
Rotten Row
SW1 ... 114 D4 247 C2
Rotterdam Dr E14 ... 120 A3
Rouel Rd
Bermondsey SE16 ... 118 A2
Bermondsey SE16 ... 118 A3
Rougemont Ave
SM4 ... 201 C3
Roundabout Ho HA6 ... 22 A2
Roundacre SW19 ... 156 D2
Roundel Cl SE4 ... 141 B1
Roundell Ho 14
SE21 ... 183 C6
Rounders Ct 7 RM10 ... 81 D2
Round Gr CR0 ... 206 D2
Roundhay Cl SE23 ... 162 D2
Roundhedge Way EN2 ... 4 B5
Round Hill SE23 ... 162 C1
Roundhill Dr EN2 ... 4 B1
ROUNDSHAW ... 220 B1
Roundshaw Ctr SM6 ... 220 A1
Roundtable Rd BR1 ... 164 D1
Roundtree Rd HA0 ... 65 B3
Roundways HA4 ... 61 D5
Roundway The
Claygate KT10 ... 212 D2
Tottenham N17 ... 33 B2
Roundwood BR7 ... 188 D1
Roundwood Ave
UB11 ... 105 A5
Roundwood Cl HA4 ... 39 B2
Roundwood Rd
NW10 ... 67 D1
Rounton Rd E3 ... 97 C3
Rountree Ct 9 UB1 ... 85 D1
Roupell Ho 7 KT2 ... 176 B3
Roupell Rd SW2 ... 160 B3
Roupell St
SE1 ... 116 C5 251 B3
Rousden St NW1 ... 71 C1
Rouse Gdns SE21 ... 183 C6
Routemaster Cl E13 ... 99 B4
Routh Ct TW14 ... 149 B3
Routh Rd SW18 ... 158 C4
Routh St E6 ... 100 B2
Rover Ho 26 N1 ... 95 C6
Rowallan Ct 3 SE6 ... 164 D3
Rowallan Rd
SW6 ... 135 A5 264 A3
Rowallen Par RM8 ... 58 C1
Rowan N10 ... 31 B1
Rowan Ave E4 ... 35 B4
Rowan Cl Ealing W5 ... 110 A4
Harrow HA7 ... 24 D4
Ilford IG1 ... 79 B3
Kingston u T KT3 ... 177 C1
Streatham SW16 ... 181 C2
Wembley HA0 ... 65 A5
Rowan Cres SW16 ... 181 C2
Rowan Ct
19 Camberwell
SE15 ... 139 D5
Forest Hill SE26 ... 184 C6
11 Kingston u T KT2 ... 176 C3
Newham E13 ... 99 B5
Twickenham TW4 ... 151 D6
Wandsworth SW11 ... 158 D5
Wimbledon SW20 ... 178 B1
Rowan Dr NW9 ... 46 A6
Rowan Gdns CR0 ... 221 D5
Rowan Ho 9 Bow E3 ... 97 B6
Dagenham NW10 ... 89 C3
East Bedfont TW14 ... 149 B5
Ilford IG1 ... 79 B3
5 Maitland Pk NW3 ... 70 D2
Rowan Ho *continued*
Sidcup DA14 ... 167 D1
Rowan Pl UB3 ... 105 D6
Rowan Pre Prep Sch
KT10 ... 212 C1
Rowan Prep Sch
KT10 ... 212 D1
Rowan Rd
Brentford TW8 ... 131 B5
Brook Green W6 ... 112 D2
DA7 ... 147 A2
Mitcham SW16 ... 181 C1
West Drayton UB7 ... 104 A2
Rowans Sch The
SW20 ... 178 A3
Rowans The
Ashford TW16 ... 171 D5
Edmonton N13 ... 17 A1
7 Sutton SM2 ... 217 D2
Rowan Terr W6 ... 112 D2
Rowantree Cl N21 ... 17 B3
Rowantree Rd
Edmonton N21 ... 17 B3
Enfield EN2 ... 4 D3
Rowan Way RM6 ... 58 C6
Rowan Wlk BR2 ... 226 B5
7 Dartmouth Pk N19 ... 71 C6
Hampstead Garden Suburb
N2 ... 48 A4
Kensal Town W10 ... 91 A3
1 New Barnet EN5 ... 13 D6
Rowanwood Ave
DA15 ... 168 A3
Rowanwood Mews
EN2 ... 4 D3
Rowben Cl N20 ... 13 D3
Rowberry Cl SW6 ... 134 C5
Rowcross St
SE1 ... 117 D1 263 D2
Rowdell Rd UB5 ... 85 C6
Rowden Par E4 ... 35 C4
Rowden Park Gdns
E4 ... 35 C4
Rowden Rd
Beckenham BR3 ... 185 B2
Chingford E4 ... 35 D4
West Ewell KT19 ... 215 A4
Rowditch La SW11 ... 137 A3
Rowdon Ave NW10 ... 68 B1
Rowdowns Rd RM9 ... 81 B1
Rowe Gdns IG11 ... 102 A5
Rowe Ho E9 ... 74 C2
Rowe La E9 ... 74 C3
Rowena Cres SW11 ... 136 C3
Rowe Wlk HA2 ... 63 C5
Rowfant Rd SW12,
SW17 ... 159 A2
Rowhill Mans 11 E5 ... 74 B4
Rowhill Rd E5 ... 74 B4
Rowington Cl W2 ... 91 D2
Rowland Ave HA3 ... 43 C6
Rowland Ct E16 ... 98 D3
South Croydon CR0 ... 221 C6
Rowland Gr SE26 ... 162 B1
Rowland Hill Almshouses
7 TW15 ... 170 C5
Rowland Hill Ave N17 ... 33 B4
Rowland Hill Ho SE1 251 C2
Rowland Hill St NW3 ... 70 C3
Rowlands Ave HA5 ... 23 D4
Rowlands Cl
Hendon NW7 ... 28 A3
Highgate N6 ... 49 A3
Rowlands Rd RM8 ... 81 B6
Rowland Way
Ashford TW15 ... 171 B3
Merton SW19 ... 179 D2
Rowley Ave DA15 ... 168 B4
Rowley Cl HA0 ... 66 B1
Rowley Ct EN1 ... 17 C6
Rowley Gdns N4 ... 51 A2
Rowley Green Rd
EN5 ... 12 A6
Rowley Ho SE8 ... 141 C6
Rowley Ind Pk W3 ... 110 D3
Rowley La EN5 ... 11 D6
Rowley Rd N15 ... 51 A4
Rowley Way NW8 ... 229 A6
Rowlheys Pl UB7 ... 104 A3
Rowlls Rd KT1 ... 198 B6
Rowney Gdns RM9 ... 80 C2
Rowney Rd RM9 ... 80 B2
Rowntree Cl NW6 ... 69 C2
Rowntree Clifford Cl 7
E13 ... 99 B4
Rowntree Path 1
SE28 ... 124 B5
Rowntree Rd TW2 ... 152 C3
Rowse Cl E15 ... 98 A6
Rowsham Ct HA1 ... 64 C5
Rowsley Ave NW4 ... 46 C6
Rowstock 1 NW5 ... 71 D2
Rowstock Gdns N7 ... 71 D3
Rowton Rd SE18 ... 145 A5
Roxborough Ave
Harrow HA1 ... 42 C2
Hounslow TW7 ... 130 D5
Roxborough Pk HA1 ... 42 C2
Roxborough Rd HA1 ... 42 B3
Roxbourne Cl UB5 ... 62 D2
Roxbourne Fst & Mid
Schs HA2 ... 63 A6
Roxburgh Rd SE27 ... 182 D5
Roxburn Way HA4 ... 61 D5
Roxby Pl
SW6 ... 135 C6 265 B6
ROXETH ... 64 A6
Roxeth Ct 6 TW15 ... 170 C5
Roxeth Fst & Mid Sch
HA2 ... 64 B6
Roxeth Gr HA2 ... 63 D4
Roxeth Green Ave
HA2 ... 63 D6
Roxeth Hill HA2 ... 64 C6
Roxeth Manor Fst & Mid
Schs HA2 ... 63 C5
Roxeth Mead Sch
HA2 ... 64 B6
Roxford Cl TW17 ... 193 C4
Roxford Ho 2 E3 ... 97 D3
Roxley Rd SE13 ... 163 D5
Roxton Gdns CR0 ... 223 C3
Roxwell 10 NW1 ... 71 B2
Roxwell Rd
Barking IG11 ... 102 A5
Shepherd's Bush W12 112 A4
Roxwell Trad Pk E10 ... 53 A2
Roxwell Way IG8 ... 37 C3
Roxy Ave RM6 ... 58 C2
Royal Academy of
Dramatic Art★
WC1 ... 93 D2 239 C4
Royal Acad of Arts★
W1 ... 115 C6 249 A5
Royal Acad of Dance
SW11 ... 266 D1
Royal Acad of Music
NW1 ... 238 B5
Royal Albert Hall★
SW7 ... 114 B4 246 C1
Royal Albert Sta
E16 ... 122 A6
Royal Albert Way
E6 ... 122 B6
Royal Arc W1 ... 249 A5
Royal Armouries The★
E1 ... 253 C5
Royal Ave
SW3 ... 114 D1 257 C2
Worcester Pk KT4 ... 215 C6
Royal Avenue Ho
SW3 ... 257 C2
Royal Ballet Sch (White
Lodge) The TW10 ... 155 B3
Royal Ballet Upper Sch
The WC2 ... 94 A1 240 B1
Royal Brompton Hospl
Chelsea
SW3 ... 114 B1 256 C2
Chelsea SW3 114 C1 257 A2
Royal Cir SE27 ... 160 D1
Royal Cl Deptford SE8 ... 141 B6
Hillingdon UB7 ... 82 B1
Ilford IG3 ... 58 A2
Locksbottom BR6 ... 226 D4
Putney SW19 ... 156 D2
Stamford Hill N16 ... 51 C1
Worcester Pk KT4 ... 215 C6
Royal College of
Physicians Liby
NW1 ... 93 B3 238 D6
Royal College St
NW1 ... 93 C6 232 B6
Royal Coll of
Anaesthetists WC1 240 C3
Royal Coll of Art
SW7 ... 114 B4 246 C1
Royal Coll of Art
Sculpture Sch
SW11 ... 136 C5 267 A3

Royal Coll of Midwives W1 93 B2 238 C3
Royal Coll of Music SW7 114 B3 256 C6
Royal Coll of Obstetricians & Gynaecologists NW1 92 D3 230 C1
Royal Coll of Ophthalmologists NW1 238 A5
Royal Coll of Paediatrics & Child Health W1 240 D4
Royal Coll of Pathologists SW1 115 D5 249 C3
Royal Coll of Physicians NW1 93 B3 238 D6
Royal Coll of Radiologists W1 238 D4
Royal Coll of Science SW7 114 B3 256 C6
Royal Coll of Speech Language Therapists SE1 252 C3
Royal Coll of Surgeons WC2 94 B1 240 D2
Royal Coll of Veterinary Surgeons SW1 116 A3 260 A5
Royal Connaught Apts E16 121 D5
Royal Courts of Justice WC2 94 C1 241 A1
Royal Cres Ilford IG2 57 B3
Ruislip HA4 63 A5
W11 113 A5 244 A3
Royal Crescent Mews W11 112 D5
Royal Crest Ho SM2 217 A1
Royal Ct
City of London EC3 242 D1
Enfield EN1 17 C5
9 Kingston u T KT2 176 D3
Mottingham SE9 166 B3
Rotherhithe SE16 119 B3
Ruislip HA4 40 A2
Royal Dock Com Sch The E16 99 C1
Royal Docks Rd E6 100 D2
Royal Dr N11 31 A5
Royal Duchess Mews 16 SW12 159 B4
Royal Exchange* EC3 242 D1
Royal Exchange Bldgs EC3 242 D1
Royal Festival Hall* SE1 116 B5 250 D3
Royal Free Hospl NW3 70 C3
Royal Fusiliers Mus* E1 253 C5
Royal Gdns W7 109 A3
Royal Geographical Society SW7 246 D1
Royal Hill SE10 142 A5
Royal Hill Ct 2 SE10 142 A5
Royal Horticultural Society (Lawrence Hall & Conf Ctr) SW1 259 C5
Royal Horticultural Society (Lindley Hall) SW1 259 C4
Royal Hospital Chelsea The* SW1 115 A1 258 A1
Royal Hospital Rd SW3 114 D1 257 D1
Royal Hospl for Neuro-Disability The SW15 157 A5
Royal Hospl Mus* SW3 257 D1
Royal Institute of British Architects W1 93 B2 238 D4
Royal Institution Mus The* SW1 249 A5
Royal La
Hillingdon UB7 82 B1
Hillingdon UB8 82 B3
Royal Langford Apartments 3 NW6 91 D5
Royal London Est N17 34 B4
Royal London Est The NW10 89 B5
Royal London Homeopathic Hospl WC1 94 A2 240 B4
Royal London Hospl Mus* E1 96 B2
Royal London Hospl (Whitechapel) The E1 96 B2
Royal Marsden Hospl SW3 114 B1 256 D2
Royal Mews KT8 196 C6
Royal Mews The* SW1 115 B3 258 D6
Royal Military Sch of Music (Kneller Hall) TW2 152 B5
Royal Mint Pl 6 E1 118 A6
Royal Mint St E1 117 D6 253 D6
Royal National Orthopaedic Hospl
Regent's Pk W1 93 B3 238 D5
Stanmore HA7 9 C2
Royal National TNE Hospl The WC1 94 B4 233 C2
Royal Naval Pl SE14 141 B5
Royal Oak Ct
Dagenham RM8 80 C6
9 Shoreditch N1 95 C4
Royal Oak Mews 9 TW11 175 A5
Royal Oak Pl SE22 162 B5
Royal Oak Rd
Bexley DA6 147 C1
DA6 169 B6
5 Hackney E8 74 B2
Royal Oak Sta W2 91 D2
Royal Oak Yd SE1 253 A1
Royal Observatory The* SE10 142 B5
Royal Opera Arc SW1 249 C4
Royal Orchard Cl SW18 157 A4
Royal Par
Blackheath Vale SE3 142 D3
Chislehurst BR7 189 A3
11 Dagenham RM10 81 D2
Ealing W5 88 A4
Fulham SW6 264 A4
12 Richmond TW9 132 C4
Royal Park Prim Sch DA14 169 A1
Royal Pl 11 SE10 142 A5
Royal Rd
Kennington SE17 138 D6
Newham E16 99 D1
Sidcup DA14 168 D1
Teddington TW11 174 B5
Royal Route HA9 66 B4
Royal Russell Sch CR0 222 B3
Royal Sch Hampstead The 8 NW3 70 B4
Royal St SE1 116 B3 260 D6
Royal Tower Lo 3 E1 118 A6
Royalty Ho W1 239 C1
Royalty Mews W1 239 C1
Royalty Studios W11 91 A1
Royal United Services Mus* SW1 250 A3
Royal Veterinary Coll NW1 93 D6 232 C5
Royal Victoria Pl 7 E16 121 B5
Royal Victoria Sq E16 121 B6
Royal Victoria Sta E16 121 A6
Royal Victor Pl E3 96 D5
Royal Wlk SM6 219 B5
Roycraft Ave IG11 101 D5
Roycroft Cl
Streatham SW2 160 C3
Woodford E18 37 B2
Roydene Rd SE18 123 C1
Roydon Cl 7 SW11 136 D3
Roy Gdns IG2 57 D4
Roy Gr TW12 173 D4
Royle Cres W13 87 A3
Roymount Ct TW2 152 C1
Roy Ridley Ho 6 SW4 137 D2
Roy Sq E14 119 A6
Royston Ave
Carshalton SM1 218 B5
Chingford E4 35 D5
Wallington SM6 219 D4
Royston Cl
Cranford TW5 128 B4
Walton-on-T KT12 194 A1
Royston Ct
Hinchley Wood KT10 212 D6
New Cross SE4 141 B3
1 Newham E13 99 A6
Redbridge IG1 55 D3
3 Richmond TW9 132 B4
Ruislip HA5 40 C2
Tolworth KT6 214 C6
Royston Gdns IG1 55 D3
Royston Gr HA5 23 C4
Royston Ho
Friern Barnet N11 31 A6
14 SE15 140 A6
Royston Lo SW19 180 A4
Royston Par IG1 55 D3
Royston Park Rd HA5 23 C5
Royston Prim Sch SE20 184 D2
Royston Rd
Penge SE20 184 D2
Richmond TW10 154 A6
Royston St 24 E2 96 C5
Roystons The KT5 198 D4
Rozel Ct 3 N1 95 C6
Rozelle Ct 1 CR7 204 C3
Rozel Rd SW4 137 C2
Rubastic Rd UB2 106 C3
Rubens Rd UB5 84 D5
Rubens St SE6 163 B2
Rubin Pl 14 EN3 7 C6
Ruby Ct TW13 149 D1
Ruby Rd E17 53 C6
Ruby St SE15 140 B6
Stonebridge NW10 67 A1
Ruby Triangle SE15 140 B6
Ruckholt Cl E10 75 D5
Ruckholt Rd
London E10 75 D5
Temple Mills E9, E10 75 C4
Rucklidge Ave NW10 90 A5
Rudall Cres NW3 70 B4
Rudbeck Ho 11 SE15 140 A5
Ruddington Cl E5 75 A4
Ruddock Cl HA8 27 A3
Ruddstreet Cl SE18 123 A2
Rudge Ho 1 SE16 118 A3
Rudgwick Terr NW8 92 C6 230 B5
Rudhall Ho 4 SW2 160 C5
Rudland Rd DA7 147 D2
Rudloe Rd SW12 159 C4
Rudolf Pl SW8 270 B5
Rudolph Ct SE22 162 B4
Rudolph Rd E13 98 D5
Paddington NW6 91 C5
Rudstone Ho 10 E3 97 D4
Rudyard Ct SE1 252 D1
Rudyard Gr NW7 27 A4
Ruegg Ho 5 SE18 144 C6
Ruffetts Cl CR2 222 B1
Ruffetts The CR2 222 B1
Ruffle Cl UB7 104 B4
Rufford Cl HA3 43 A3
Rufford St N1 94 A6 233 B6
Rufford Street Mews N1 72 A1
Rufford Twr 5 W3 110 D5
Rufforth Ct 1 NW9 27 C2
Rufus Bsns Ctr SW18 157 D2
Rufus Cl HA4 63 A5
Rufus Ho SE1 263 D6
Rufus St N1 95 C4
Rugby Ave
Edmonton N9 17 D3
Northolt UB6 64 B2
Wembley HA0 65 C4
Rugby Cl HA1 42 C5
Rugby Gdns RM9 80 C2
Rugby Mans W14 254 B4
Rugby Rd
Bedford Pk W4 111 C4
Dagenham RM9 80 C2
Queensbury NW9 44 D5
Twickenham TW1, TW2, TW7 152 C5
Rugby St WC1 94 B3 240 C5
Rugg St E14 119 C6
Rugless Ho 2 E14 120 A4
Rugmere 4 NW1 71 A1
RUISLIP 39 B2
Ruislip Cl UB6 85 D3
RUISLIP COMMON 39 B4
Ruislip Ct HA4 61 D6
RUISLIP GARDENS 61 D5
Ruislip Gardens Prim Sch HA4 61 D4
Ruislip Gardens Sta HA4 62 A4
Ruislip High Sch HA4 62 A5
Ruislip Lido* HA4, HA5 39 B5
Ruislip Lido Rly* HA4 39 B5
RUISLIP MANOR 40 A1
Ruislip Manor Sta HA4 40 A1
Ruislip Rd UB6, UB5 85 C4
Ruislip Rd E
Ealing UB6, W7 86 D3
Greenford UB6 86 B3
Ruislip St SW17 180 D6
Ruislip Sta HA4 39 D1
Rumball Ho 14 SE5 139 C5
Rumbold Rd SW6 135 D5 265 D3
Rum Cl E1 118 C6
Rumford Ho SE1 262 A5
Rumsey Cl TW12 173 B4
Rumsey Rd SW9 138 B2
Runacres Ct SE17 262 A1
Runbury Circ NW9 67 B6
Runcorn Cl N17 52 B5
Runcorn Pl W11 244 A6
Rundell Cres NW4 46 B4
Rundell Twr SW8 270 C2
Runes Cl CR4 202 C5
Runnelfield HA1 64 C5
Running Horse Yd 12 TW8 132 A6
Runnymede SW19 180 B2
Runnymede Cl TW2 151 D4
Runnymede Cres SW16 182 A2
Runnymede Ct
Roehampton SW15 156 A3
1 Wallington SM6 219 B2
Runnymede Gdns
Greenford UB6 86 C5
Twickenham TW2 151 D4
Runnymede Ho
Hackney E9 75 A4
Richmond TW10 154 C6
Runnymede Rd TW2 151 D5
Runway The HA4 62 C3
Rupack St 3 SE16 118 C4
Rupert Ave 6 HA9 66 A3
Rupert Ct W1 249 C6
Rupert Gdns SW9 138 D3
Rupert Ho SE11 261 B3
8 Upper Holloway N19 71 D5
Rupert Rd
Bedford Pk W4 111 C3
Paddington NW6 91 B5
Upper Holloway N19 71 D6
Rupert St W1 115 D6 249 C6
Rural Way SW16 181 B3
Rusbridge Cl E8 74 A3
Ruscoe Ho 12 SW27 182 D5
Ruscoe Rd E16 98 D1
Ruscombe Way TW14 149 D4
Rusham Rd SW12 158 D4
Rushbridge Cl CR0 205 A3
Rushbrook Cres E17 35 B2
Rushbrook Ho 20 SW8 137 D3
Rushbrook Rd SE9 167 A2
Rushbury Ct 4 TW12 173 C2
Rushby Ct SW4 270 A1
Rush Common Mews 18 SW2 160 B4
Rushcroft Rd
Brixton SW2, SW9 138 C1
Chingford E4 35 D3
Rush Croft Sch E4 35 D3
Rushcutters Ct 18 SE16 119 A2
Rushden Cl SE19 183 B3
Rushdene SE2 124 D3
Rushdene Ave EN4 14 C4
Rushdene Cl UB5 84 C5
Rushdene Cres UB5 84 C4
Rushdene Rd HA5 40 D3
Rushden Gdns
Ilford IG5 56 C6
Mill Hill NW7 28 C4
Rushen Wlk SM5 202 B1
Rushet Rd BR5 190 A1
Rushett Cl KT7 197 B1
Rushett Rd KT7 197 B2
Rushey Cl KT3 199 B5
Rushey Gn SE6 163 D4
Rushey Green Prim Sch SE6 163 D3
Rushey Hill EN2 4 B1
Rushey Mead SE4 163 C6
Rushford Rd SE4 163 B5
Rush Green Rd RM7, RM8, RM10 59 D1
Rushgrove Ave NW9 45 D5
Rushgrove Ct NW9 45 C4
Rushgrove St SE18 122 B2
Rush Hill Mews 3 SW11 137 A2
Rush Hill Rd SW11 137 A2
Rushlake Ho 3 SW11 137 A3
Rushley Cl BR2 226 A4
Rushman Villas KT3 199 D5
Rushmead
5 Bethnal Green E2 96 B4
Richmond TW10 153 B1
Rushmead Cl CR0 221 D4
Rushmere Ct KT4 216 A6
Rushmere Ho 2 SW15 156 A3
Rushmere Pl SW19 178 D5
Rushmon Pl SM3 217 A2
Rushmoor Cl HA5 40 B5
Rushmore Cl BR1 210 A6
Rushmore Cres 9 E5 74 D4
Rushmore Ho
9 Kentish Town N7 71 D3
W14 254 B5
Rushmore Prim Sch 12 E5 74 D4
Rushmore Rd
Clapton Pk E5 74 D4
Hackney E5 75 A4
Rusholme Ave RM10 81 C5
Rusholme Gr SE19 183 C5
Rusholme Rd SW15 157 A5
Rushout Ave HA3 43 B3
Rush The SW20 179 B2
Rushton Ho 26 SW8 137 D3
Rushton St N1 95 B5 235 D4
Rushworth St SE1 116 D4 251 D1
Rushy Meadow La SM5 218 C5
Rushy Meadow Prim Sch SM5 218 C5
Ruskin Ave DA16 146 A3
Feltham TW14 149 D5
Plashet E12 78 A2
Richmond TW9 132 C5
Ruskin Cl NW11 47 D3
Ruskin Ct
Herne Hill SE5 139 B2
SE9 166 B5
Southgate N21 16 B4
Ruskin Dr
North Cheam KT4 216 C6
Orpington BR6 227 C5
Welling DA16 146 A2
Ruskin Gdns
Ealing W5 87 D3
Harrow HA3 44 B5
Ruskin Gr DA16 146 A3
Ruskin Ho SW1 259 D3
Ruskin Par CR0 221 B3
Ruskin Park Ho SE5 139 B2

Ruskin Rd
Belvedere DA17 125 C2
Croydon CR0 220 D6
Isleworth TW7 130 D2
Southall UB1 107 A6
Tottenham N17 33 D2
Wallington SM5 219 A3
Ruskin Way SW19 180 B2
Ruskin Wlk BR2 210 B3
Edmonton N9 18 A2
Herne Hill SE24 161 A6
Rusland Ave BR6 227 B5
Rusland Hts HA1 42 C5
Rusland Park Rd HA1 42 C5
Rusper Cl
Cricklewood NW2 68 C5
Stanmore HA7 25 C6
Rusper Ct SW9 138 A3
Rusper Rd
Dagenham RM9 80 C2
Tottenham N17, N22 51 A6
Russel Cl BR3 208 A6
Russel Ct N14 15 D6
Russell Ave N22 32 D1
Russell Cl
Bexleyheath DA7 147 C1
Chiswick W4 133 D6
Greenwich SE7 143 C5
Ruislip HA4 62 C6
Stonebridge NW10 67 A1
Russell Ct
Battersea SW11 268 B1
Bloomsbury WC1 240 A5
Bromley BR1 186 D3
12 New Barnet EN5 2 A1
5 Peckham SE15 140 B3
St James SW1 249 B3
Streatham SW16 182 B5
Surbiton KT6 198 A2
Wallington SM6 219 C3
4 Walthamstow E10 53 D2
Wembley HA0 66 A1
Russell Gdns
East Barnet N20 14 C2
Ilford IG2 57 B2
Richmond TW10 153 C2
Temple Fortune NW11 47 A3
W14 113 A3 254 A6
West Drayton UB7 104 C1
Russell Gdns Mews
W14 113 A3 254 A6
Russell Gr
33 Brixton SW9 138 C4
Edgware NW7 27 C6
Russell Ho
21 Poplar E14 97 C1
SW1 259 A2
Russell Kerr Cl W4 133 A5
Russell La N20 14 D2
Russell Lo
5 Chingford E4 20 A2
SE1 262 C6
Russell Mans WC1 240 B4
Russell Mead HA3 24 D2
Russell Par NW11 47 A3
Russell Pickering Ho 2
SW4 138 A2
Russell Pl
Hampstead NW3 70 C3
Rotherhithe SE16 119 A3
Russell Prim Sch The
TW10 153 D3
Russell Rd
Bowes Pk N13 32 B4
Buckhurst Hill IG9 21 C3
Chingford Hatch E4 35 B6
Crouch End N8 49 D3
East Barnet N20 14 C2
Enfield EN1 5 D5
Leyton E10 53 D3
Merton SW19 179 C3
Mitcham CR4 202 C6
Newham E16 99 B1
Northolt UB5 64 A3
Shepperton TW17 193 A2
Tottenham N15 51 C4
Twickenham TW1, TW2 152 D5
W14 113 A3 254 B5
Walthamstow E17 53 B6
Walton-on-T KT12 194 A3
West Hendon NW9 45 D3
Russell Sq
WC1 94 A3 240 A5
Russell Square Ho
WC1 240 A5
Russell Square Mans
WC1 240 B4
Russell Square Sta
WC1 94 A3 240 A5
Russell St
WC2 116 A6 250 B6
Russell's Wharf 2
W9 91 B3
Russell Way SM1 217 D3
Russell Wlk 4
TW10 154 B5
Russell Yd SW15 135 A1
Russet Ave TW16, TW17 193 C6
Russet Cl UB10 83 A3
Russet Cres N7 72 B3
Russet Ct
6 Barnet EN4 2 C1
Dollis Hill NW2 68 B5
Feltham TW13 149 C1
Russet Dr CR0 207 A1
Russet Ho TW3 129 B1
Russet House Sch EN1 6 B4
Russets Cl E4 36 B6
Russettings 1 HA5 23 B3
Russett Way SE13 141 D3
Russia Dock Rd
SE16 119 A5
Russia La E2 96 C5
Russia Row EC2 242 B1
Russington Rd
TW17 193 B3
Rusthall Ave W4 111 B3
Rusthall Cl CR0 206 C3
Rusthall Mans 3
W4 111 B2
Rustic Ave SW16 181 B3
Rustic Pl HA0 65 D4
Rustic Wlk E16 99 B1
Rustington Wlk SM4 201 B2
Ruston Ave KT5 198 D2
Ruston Gdns N14 15 A5
Ruston Mews W11 91 A1
Ruston Rd SE18 122 A3
Ruston St E3 97 B6
Rust Sq SE5 139 B5
Rutford Rd SW16 182 A5
Ruth Cl HA7 44 B5
Ruth Ct 16 E3 97 A5
Rutherford Cl
Hillingdon UB8 82 B3
Sutton SM2 218 B2
Rutherford Ct
Mitcham SW19 180 B3
Southgate N21 16 B6
Rutherford Ho
12 Bethnal Green E1 96 B3
Teddington TW11 174 D5
4 Wembley HA9 67 A5
Rutherford Sch CR2 221 D3
Rutherford St
SW1 115 D2 259 C4
Rutherford Twr 8
UB1 85 D1
Rutherford Way
Bushey WD23 8 C3
Wembley HA9 66 C4
Rutherglen Rd SE2 146 A6
Rutherwyke Cl KT17 216 A2
Ruth Ho W10 91 A3
Ruthin Cl NW9 45 C3
Ruthin Rd SE3 143 A6
Ruthven St E9 96 D6
Rutland Ave DA15 168 A4
Rutland Cl
Chessington KT9 214 B2
DA5 168 D3
Mitcham SW19 180 C3
Mortlake SW14 133 A2
Rutland Ct
15 Acton W3 88 C1
Chislehurst BR7 188 C2
Enfield EN3 18 B6
Herne Hill SE5 139 B1
Sidcup SE9 167 A2
SW7 247 B1
Twickenham TW2 152 C1
Rutland Dr
Morden SM4 201 C2
Richmond TW10 154 A3
Rutland Gate
Beckenham BR2 208 D5
Rutland Gate *continued*
Belvedere DA17 125 D1
SW7 114 C4 247 B1
Rutland Gate Mews
SW7 247 A1
Rutland Gdns
Dagenham RM8 80 C3
Ealing W13 87 A2
South Croydon CR0 221 C4
Stoke Newington N4 51 A3
SW7 114 C4 247 B1
Rutland Gdns Mews
SW7 247 B1
Rutland Gr W6 112 B1
Rutland Ho
Edgware HA8 26 B4
6 Northolt UB5 63 C2
2 Penge SE20 184 C2
10 Putney SW15 156 C4
Tolworth KT6 198 C1
W8 255 C5
15 Woolwich SE18 122 B2
Rutland Lo
Forest Hill SE6 163 B2
Teddington TW11 174 C5
Rutland Mews 21
NW8 91 D6
Rutland Mews E
SW7 257 B6
Rutland Mews S
SW7 257 A6
Rutland Mews W
SW7 257 A6
Rutland Park Gdns 1
NW2 68 C2
Rutland Park Mans 2
NW2 68 C2
Rutland Pk
Forest Hill SE6 163 B2
Willesden NW2 68 C2
Rutland Pl
Bushey WD23 8 B3
EC1 241 D4
Rutland Rd
Forest Gate E7 77 D1
Harrow HA1 42 A3
Hayes UB3 105 B2
Ilford IG1 78 D5
Mitcham SW19 180 C3
Southall UB1 85 C2
South Hackney E9 96 D6
Twickenham TW2 152 B2
Walthamstow E17 53 C3
Wanstead E11 55 B4
Rutland St SW7 257 B6
Rutland Studios
NW10 90 A4
Rutland Wlk SE6 163 B2
Rutley Cl SE11 138 D6
Rutlish Rd SW19 179 C2
Rutlish Sch SW20 179 B1
Rutter Gdns CR4 202 B5
Rutters Cl UB7 104 C4
Rutt's Terr SE14 140 D4
Rutts The WD23 8 B3
Ruvigny Gdns SW15 134 D2
Ruvigny Mans 7
SW15 134 D2
Ruxbury Ct TW15 148 A1
RUXLEY 191 A3
Ruxley Cl
Chessington KT19 214 D3
Sidcup DA14 191 A4
Ruxley Cnr DA14 191 A4
Ruxley Corner Ind Est
DA14 190 D4
Ruxley Cres KT10 213 B1
Ruxley Ct KT19 215 A3
Ruxley Gdns TW17 193 A4
Ruxley La KT19 215 B3
Ruxley Mews KT19 214 D3
Ruxley Ridge KT10 213 A1
Ryall's Ct N20 14 D1
Ryan Cl Ruislip HA4 40 B1
SE9 143 C1
Ryan Ct SW16 182 A3
Ryan Dr TW8 131 A6
Ryan Ho 3 HA1 42 D4
Ryarsh Cres BR6 227 C4
Rycott Path SE22 162 A4
Rycroft Way N17 51 D6
Ryculff Sq SE3 142 D3
Rydal Cl NW4 29 A2
Rydal Cres UB6 87 C5
Rydal Ct Edgware HA8 26 B5
Wembley HA9 44 A2
Rydal Dr DA7 147 C4
West Wickham BR4 224 C6
Rydal Gdns
Kingsbury NW9 45 C4
Kingston u T SW15 177 C5
Twickenham TW2, TW3 151 D5
Wembley HA9 43 C1
Rydal Ho 25 SW8 137 D3
Rydal Lo N17 34 A3
Rydal Rd SW16 181 D6
Rydal Water NW1 232 A1
Rydal Way Enfield EN3 18 C5
Ruislip HA4 62 C4
Ryde Ho 1 NW6 91 C6
Rydens Ho SE9 165 C1
Rydens Rd KT12 194 D1
Ryde Pl TW1 153 D5
Ryder Cl BR1 187 B5
Ryder Ct Leyton E10 75 D6
SW1 249 B4
Ryder Dr SE16 118 B1
Ryder Ho
18 Bethnal Green E1 96 C3
5 Merton SW19 179 D2
Ryder St SW1 249 B4
Ryder's Terr
NW8 92 A5 229 A4
Ryder Yd SW1 249 B4
Ryde Vale Rd SW12 159 C2
Rydon Mews SW19 178 C3
Rydons Cl SE9 144 A2
Rydon St N1 235 B6
Rydston Cl 2 N7 72 B1
Rye Cl DA5 169 D5
Ryecotes Mead
SE21 161 C3
Ryecroft Ave TW2 151 D3
Ryecroft Cres EN5 12 B6
Ryecroft Rd BR5 211 B3
Lewisham SE13 164 A6
South Norwood SW16 182 C4
Ryecroft St
SW6 135 D4 265 C1
Rye Ct BR3 185 B2
Ryedale SE22 162 B5
Ryedale Ct 7 TW12 173 C2
Ryefield Ave UB10 60 D1
Ryefield Cres HA5, HA6 22 A1
Ryefield Ct HA6 22 A1
Ryefield Jun & Inf Sch
UB10 83 B6
Ryefield Path 7
SW15 156 A3
Ryefield Rd SE19 183 A4
Ryegates 2 SE15 140 B3
Ryehill Ct KT3 199 D2
Rye Hill Pk SE15 140 C1
Rye Ho 17 SE16 118 C4
Rye La SE15 140 A3
Ryeland Cl UB7 82 A1
Ryelands Cres SE12 165 C5
Ryelands Prim Sch
SE25 206 B4
Rye Lane Mkt★
SE15 140 A3
Rye Oak Sch 7
SE15 140 B2
Rye Rd SE15 140 D1
Rye The N14 15 C4
Rye Way HA8 26 B4
Rye Wlk SW15 156 D6
Ryfold Rd SW19 157 C1
Ryhope Rd N11 31 B6
Ryland Cl TW13 171 D6
Rylandes Rd NW2 68 A5
Ryland Ho 11 SW16 181 C5
Ryland Rd NW5 71 B2
Rylett Cres W12 111 D3
Rylett Rd W12 111 D3
Rylston Rd
Edmonton N13 17 B1
SW6 135 B6 264 C5
Rylton Ho KT12 194 A1
Rymer Rd CR0 205 C2
Rymer St SE24 160 D5
Rymill St E16 122 C5
Rysbrack St SW1 257 C6
Rythe Cl
Chessington KT9 213 C1
Claygate KT10 212 C3
Rythe Ct KT7 197 A2
Rythe Ho 7 BR1 186 B5
Rythe Rd KT10 212 C3

S

Saatchi Gallery Duke of York's HQ★
SW3 114 D1 257 D2
Sabah Ct TW15 170 C6
Sabbarton St 9 E16 98 D1
Sabella Ct E3 97 B5
Sabine Rd SW11 137 A2
Sable Cl TW4 128 C2
Sable Ct 3 KT3 199 C4
Sable St N1 72 D1
Sach Rd E5 74 B6
Sacketts Ho 24 SW9 138 C4
Sackville Ave BR2 209 A1
Sackville Cl HA2 64 B5
Sackville Gdns IG1 56 B1
Sackville Ho
Hornsey N8 50 A5
16 Streatham SW16 160 A1
Sackville Rd SM2 217 C1
Sackville St
W1 115 C6 249 B5
Sacred Heart High Sch
9 W6 112 C2
Sacred Heart Language Coll HA3 24 C1
Sacred Heart Prim Sch, Battersea SW11 136 C3
Sacred Heart RC Prim Sch
East Barnet N20 14 C2
Putney SW15 156 A6
Ruislip HA4 61 C6
Teddington TW11 175 B3
West Barnes KT3 200 A5
Sacred Heart RC Sec Sch
10 SE5 139 A4
Sacred Heart Sch N7 72 B3
Saddlebrook Pk
TW16 171 C3
Saddlers Cl
Barnet EN5 12 B6
Borehamwood WD6 11 B5
Pinner HA5 23 C5
Saddlers Mews SW8 270 B2
Teddington KT1 175 C2
Wembley HA0 64 D4
Saddlers Path WD6 11 B6
Saddlescombe Way
N12 29 C5
Sadler Cl CR4 180 D1
Sadler Ho
17 Bromley E3 97 D4
EC1 234 C2
Sadlers Ho EN1 17 C6
Sadlers Ride KT8 174 A1
Saffron Ave E14 120 B6
Saffron Cl
Temple Fortune NW11 47 B3
Thornton Heath CR0 204 A3
Saffron Ct
East Bedfont TW14 149 A4
10 Kingsland N1 73 B2
Stratford E15 76 C3
Saffron Hill
EC1 94 C2 241 B4
Saffron Ho 6 TW9 132 D4
Saffron St EC1 241 B4
Saffron Way KT6 197 D1
Saffron Wharf SE1 253 D2
Sage Cl 7 E6 100 B2
Sage Mews SE22 161 D6
Sage St E1 118 C6
Sage Way WC1 233 C1
Sage Yd KT6 198 B1
Sahara Ct UB1 107 A6
Saigasso Cl E16 99 D1
Sailacre Ho 10 SE10 120 D1
Sail Ct 10 E14 120 B6
Sailmakers Ct SW6 136 A2
Sail St SE11 116 B2 260 D4
Saimet 3 NW9 27 D2
Sainfoin Rd SW17 159 A2
Sainsbury Rd SE19 183 C5
St Agatha's Dr KT2 176 B4
St Agatha's Gr SM5 202 D1
St Agatha's RC Prim Sch
KT2 176 B4
St Agnes Cl E9 96 C6
St Agnes Pl SE11 138 D6
St Agnes RC Prim Sch
15 E3 97 D4
London NW2 69 A5

St Aidans Ct IG11 ... 102 B5
St Aidan's Prim Sch N4 ... 50 C2
St Aidan's RC Prim Sch IG1 ... 57 B1
St Aidan's Rd
East Dulwich SE22 ... 162 B6
West Ealing W13 ... 109 B4
St Aiden's Ct W13 ... 109 C4
St Albans Ave
Bedford Pk W4 ... 111 B3
Feltham TW13 ... 172 D5
St Alban's Ave E6 ... 100 C4
St Alban's CE Prim Sch EC1 ... 94 C2 241 A4
St Alban's Cl NW11 ... 47 C1
St Albans Cres N22 ... 32 C2
St Alban's Cres IG8 ... 37 A2
St Alban's Gdns TW11 ... 175 A5
St Alban's Gr
Carshalton SM5 ... 202 C2
W8 ... 113 D3 255 D6
St Albans Ho 2 SW16 ... 182 C6
St Albans La NW11 ... 47 C1
St Albans Mans W8 . 255 D6
St Alban's Pl N1 ... 94 D6 234 C5
St Alban's RC Aided Prim Sch KT8 ... 196 A4
St Albans Rd
Barnet EN5 ... 1 A3
Cheam SM1 ... 217 B4
Ilford IG3 ... 57 D2
Kingston u T KT2 ... 176 A4
St Alban's Rd
Dagenham NW10 ... 89 C6
Dartmouth Pk NW5 ... 71 B5
Woodford IG8 ... 37 A3
St Alban's St SW1 ... 249 C5
St Albans Studios W8 ... 255 D6
St Albans Terr W6 ... 264 A6
St Alban's Villas NW5 . 71 A5
St Alfege Pas SE10 ... 142 A6
St Alfege Rd SE7 ... 143 D6
St Alfege with St Peter's CE Prim Sch SE10 . 142 A6
St Aloysius Convent NW1 ... 93 D4 232 C2
St Aloysius RC Coll 9 N19 ... 49 C1
St Aloysius RC Inf Sch NW1 ... 93 D4 232 C2
St Aloysius RC Jun Sch NW1 ... 93 D5 232 C3
St Alphage Ct NW9 ... 45 B6
St Alphage Gdn EC2 . 242 B3
St Alphage Highwalk EC2 ... 242 B3
St Alphage Wlk HA8 ... 27 A1
St Alphege Rd N9 ... 18 C4
St Alphonsus Rd SW4 ... 137 D1
St Amunds Cl SE6 ... 185 C6
St Andrew & St Francis CE Prim Sch 6 NW2 ... 68 A2
St Andrews Ave HA0 ... 65 A4
St Andrew's (Barnsbury) Prim Sch N1 94 B6 233 D6
St Andrew's CE Prim Sch
Enfield EN1 ... 5 C3
Osidge N14 ... 15 D3
St Andrew's CE VA Prim Sch N20 ... 13 B2
St Andrews Chambers W1 ... 239 B2
St Andrews Cl
25 Bermondsey SE16 ... 118 B1
Erith SE28 ... 102 D1
Long Ditton KT7 ... 197 B1
Ruislip HA4 ... 62 D6
Stanmore HA7 ... 25 C1
Wimbledon SW19 ... 179 D4
St Andrew's Cl
Dollis Hill NW2 ... 68 B5
2 Hounslow TW7 ... 130 C4
North Finchley N12 ... 30 A6
Upper Halliford TW17 . 193 B5
St Andrews Ct W4 ... 133 A4
St Andrew's Ct
Carshalton SM5 ... 218 C5
St Andrew's Ct *continued*
2 Higham Hill E17 ... 35 A1
Kingston u T KT3 ... 199 D6
2 Wandsworth SW18 ... 158 A2
St Andrews Dr HA7 ... 25 C2
St Andrew's Gr N16 ... 51 B1
St Andrew's Greek Sch NW1 ... 71 C2
St Andrew's High Sch CR0 ... 220 D4
St Andrew's Hill EC4 ... 94 D1 241 D1
St Andrews Ho
11 Bermondsey SE16 ... 118 B3
Bromley BR1 ... 187 B4
St Andrews Mans 9 E5 ... 74 B4
St Andrew's Mans W1 ... 238 A3
St Andrews Mews
Greenwich SE3 ... 143 A5
4 Streatham SW12 ... 159 D3
St Andrew's Mews N16 ... 51 C1
St Andrew's Pl NW1 . 238 D6
St Andrew's Prim Sch 33 SW9 ... 138 A3
St Andrews RC Prim Sch SW16 ... 182 A5
St Andrews Rd
Carshalton SM5 ... 218 C5
DA14 ... 168 D1
Dagenham W3 ... 89 C1
Higham Hill E17 ... 35 A1
Ponders End N9 ... 18 C4
Uxbridge UB10 ... 60 B1
Welsh Harp NW9 ... 45 B1
St Andrew's Rd
3 Croydon CR0 ... 221 A4
Enfield EN1 ... 5 B2
Hanwell W7 ... 108 C4
Hillingdon UB10 ... 82 B6
Leytonstone E11 ... 54 C3
Newham E13 ... 99 B4
Redbridge IG1 ... 56 B2
Surbiton KT6 ... 197 D3
Temple Fortune NW11 .. 47 B3
W14 ... 264 B6
Willesden NW2 ... 68 B2
St Andrew's & St Mark's CE Jun Sch KT6 ... 197 D4
St Andrew's Sq
Notting Hill W11 ... 91 A1
Surbiton KT6 ... 197 D3
St Andrew St EC4 ... 241 B3
St Andrews Terr WD19 ... 22 C5
St Andrew's Twr UB1 ... 108 A6
St Andrews Way E3 ... 97 D3
St Andrew's Wharf SE1 ... 253 D2
St Angela's & St Bonaventure's Sixth Form Ctr E7 ... 77 B2
St Angela's Ursuline Sch E7 ... 77 B2
St Anna Rd EN5 ... 12 D6
St Anne RC Prim Sch 18 E1 ... 96 A3
St Annes Catholic High Sch N13 ... 32 C6
St Anne's CE Prim Sch 6 SW18 ... 157 D6
St Annes Cl WD19 ... 22 C6
St Anne's Cl N6 ... 71 A5
St Annes Ct 8 SM2 . 217 D2
St Anne's Ct
Kensal Rise NW6 ... 91 A6
W1 ... 239 C1
St Anne's Flats NW1 232 C2
St Annes Gdns NW10 .. 88 B4
St Anne's Independent PRU CR0 ... 205 B3
St Anne's Pas E14 ... 97 B1
St Anne's RC High Sch for Girls EN2 ... 5 B1
St Anne's RC Prim Sch SE11 ... 138 B6 270 C6
St Anne's Rd
Leyton E11 ... 76 B6
Wembley HA0 ... 65 D3
St Anne's Row E14 ... 97 B1
St Anne St E14 ... 97 B1
St Anne's Trad Est 25 E14 ... 97 B1
St Ann's IG11 ... 101 A6
St Ann's CE Prim Sch N15 ... 51 B4
St Ann's Cres SW18 .. 158 A5
St Ann's Ct NW4 ... 46 B6
St Ann's Ctr HA1 ... 42 C3
St Ann's Gdns NW5 ... 71 A2
St Ann's Hill SW18 ... 158 A5
St Ann's Ho WC1 ... 234 A1
St Ann's Hospl N4, N15 ... 51 A4
St Ann's La SW1 ... 259 D5
St Ann's Park Rd SW18 ... 158 A5
St Anns Rd
Barnes SW13 ... 133 D4
Shepherd's Bush W11 ... 112 D6
St Ann's Rd
1 Barking IG11 ... 101 A6
Edmonton N9 ... 17 D3
Harrow HA1 ... 42 C3
Tottenham N15 ... 51 B4
St Ann's Sch 9 W7 . 108 C5
St Ann's Specl Sch SM4 ... 201 D4
St Ann's St SW1 ... 115 D3 259 D6
St Ann's Terr NW8 ... 92 B5 229 D4
St Ann's Villas W11 ... 113 A5 244 A3
St Ann's Way CR2 ... 220 D2
St Anselm RC Prim Sch UB2 ... 107 B3
St Anselm's Ct SW16 ... 182 A5
St Anselm's Pl W1 ... 248 C6
St Anselm's RC Prim Sch
Harrow HA1 ... 42 C2
Upper Tooting SW17 . 159 A1
St Anselms Rd UB3 . 105 D4
St Anthony's Ave IG8 .. 37 C3
St Anthonys Cl 5 SW17 ... 158 C2
St Anthony's Cl
8 E1 ... 118 A5
5 Hackney Wick E9 ... 75 B2
St Anthony's Ct
2 Balham SW12 ... 159 A5
Orpington BR6 ... 226 D6
Upper Tooting SW17 . 159 A2
St Anthony's Flats NW1 ... 232 C3
St Anthony's Hospl SM3 ... 200 D1
St Anthony's RC Prim Sch
East Dulwich SE22 ... 162 A5
4 Penge SE20 ... 184 C2
Upton E7 ... 77 B1
St Anthony's Sch 8 NW3 ... 70 B3
St Anthony's Way TW14 ... 127 D1
St Antony's RC Prim Sch IG8 ... 37 A6
St Antony's Rd E7 ... 77 B1
St Arvans Cl CR0 ... 221 C5
St Asaph Ct SE4 ... 140 D2
St Asaph Rd SE4 ... 140 D2
St Aubins Ct N1 ... 235 D6
St Aubyns E18 ... 54 D5
St Aubyn's Ave
Hounslow TW3, TW4 ... 151 C6
Wimbledon SW19 ... 179 B5
St Aubyns Cl BR6 ... 227 D5
St Aubyn's Ct SW19 ... 179 A4
St Aubyns Gdns BR6 227 D6
St Aubyn's Rd SE19 . 183 D4
St Aubyn's Sch IG8 ... 36 D3
St Audrey Ave DA7 ... 147 C3
St Augustine's Ave
BR1, BR2 ... 210 A4
Ealing W5 ... 88 A4
South Croydon CR2 .. 221 A1
Wembley HA9 ... 66 A5
St Augustine's CE High Sch 5 NW6 ... 91 C5
St Augustine's CE Prim Sch DA17 ... 125 B2
St Augustines Ct
Beckenham BR3 ... 185 A1
4 New Barnet EN5 ... 14 A6
St Augustine's Ct E11 . 54 D1
St Augustine's Ho
NW1 ... 232 C2
Upper Tooting SW17 . 180 D6
St Augustine's Prim Sch 5 NW6 ... 91 D5
St Augustines Priory Sch W5 ... 88 B2
St Augustine's RC Prim Sch
Catford SE6 ... 186 A5
1 Ilford IG2 ... 56 D4
W6 ... 135 A6 264 B5
St Augustine's Rd
Camden Town NW1 ... 71 D1
DA17 ... 125 B2
St Austell Cl HA8 ... 26 B1
St Austell Rd SE13 ... 142 B3
St Awdry's Rd IG11 ... 79 B1
St Barnabas CE Prim Sch SW1 ... 115 A1 258 B2
St Barnabas Cl
Beckenham BR3 ... 186 A1
11 Dulwich Village SE22 ... 161 C6
St Barnabas Ct HA3 ... 24 A2
St Barnabas' Gdns KT8 ... 195 C4
St Barnabas Ho CR4 . 181 A3
St Barnabas Rd
Mitcham CR4 ... 181 A3
Sutton SM1 ... 218 B3
Walthamstow E17 ... 53 C3
Woodford IG8 ... 37 C3
St Barnabas & St Philip CE Prim Sch W8 ... 113 C3 255 A5
St Barnabas St SW1 . 258 B2
St Barnabas Terr E9 ... 74 D3
St Barnabas Villas SW8 ... 138 A4 270 B2
St Bartholomew's CE Prim Sch SE26 ... 184 C6
St Bartholomew's Cl SE26 ... 184 C6
St Bartholomews Ct 6 E6 ... 100 A6
St Bartholomew's Hospl EC1 ... 94 D2 241 D3
St Bartholomew's Mus* EC1 ... 241 D3
St Bartholomew's Rd E6 ... 100 B5
St Bede's RC Inf Sch SW12 ... 159 D3
St Bede's RC Prim Sch RM6 ... 58 C4
St Benedict's Cl SW17 ... 181 A5
St Benedict's Jun Sch 15 W5 ... 87 C2
St Benedict's Sch W5 87 D2
St Benets Cl 6 SW17 ... 158 C2
St Benet's Gr SM5 ... 202 A2
St Benet's Pl EC3 ... 252 D6
St Bernadette RC Jun Sch 12 SW12 ... 159 C4
St Bernadette's Fst & Mid Sch HA3 ... 44 B5
St Bernadette's RC Prim Sch UB10 ... 82 D6
St Bernard Ho 6 E14 ... 120 A3
St Bernards CR0 ... 221 C5
St Bernards Cl 8 SE27 ... 183 B6
St Bernards Ho 1 KT6 ... 214 A6
St Bernard's Rd E6 ... 99 D6
St Blaise Ave BR1 ... 187 B1
St Bonaventure's Sch E7 ... 77 A1
St Boniface RC Prim Sch 1 SW17 ... 180 D5
St Botolph St E1, EC3 ... 95 D1 243 C2
St Brelades Ct N1 ... 235 D6
St Bride's EC4 ... 241 C1
St Bride's Ave EC4 .. 241 C1
Edgware HA8 ... 26 B2
St Brides Cl DA18 ... 124 D4
St Bride's Pas EC4 .. 241 C1
St Bride St EC4 ... 94 D1 241 C2
St Catherines Cl
Chessington KT9 ... 213 D2
7 Upper Tooting SW17 ... 158 C2
St Catherines Ct TW13 ... 150 A3
St Catherine's Ct 8 W4 ... 111 C3
St Catherine's Dr SE14 ... 140 D3
St Catherines Farm Ct HA4 ... 39 A3
St Catherines Mews SW3 ... 257 C4
St Catherine's RC Sch EN5 ... 1 C1
St Catherine's RC Sch for Girls DA6 ... 169 D6
St Catherines Rd
Chingford E4 ... 19 C2
Ruislip HA4 ... 39 B3
St Catherine's Sch TW1 ... 153 A2
St Catherines Twr 5 E10 ... 53 D2
St Cecilia's CE Sch SW18 ... 157 B3
St Cecilia's Cl SM3 ... 201 A1
St Cecilia's RC Prim Sch SM3 ... 216 D6
St Chads Cl KT6 ... 197 C2
St Chad's Gdns RM6 ... 59 A2
St Chad's Pl WC1 ... 233 C2
St Chad's RC Prim Sch SE25 ... 205 C4
St Chad's Rd RM6 ... 59 A2
St Chad's St WC1 ... 233 B2
St Charles' Hospl W10 ... 90 D2
St Charles Pl W10 ... 91 A2
St Charles RC Prim Sch 7 W10 ... 90 D2
St Charles RC Sixth Form Coll 8 W10 ... 90 D2
St Charles Sq W10 ... 90 D2
St Christina's RC Prep Sch NW8 ... 92 C5 230 B4
St Christopher's Cl TW7 ... 130 C4
St Christophers Ct 15 N19 ... 71 C5
St Christophers Dr UB3 ... 106 B6
St Christophers Gdns CR7 ... 204 C6
St Christopher's Ho NW1 ... 232 C3
St Christopher's Mews SM6 ... 219 C3
St Christopher's Pl W1 ... 238 B2
St Christopher's Sch
Beckenham BR3 ... 186 A1
5 Hampstead NW3 ... 70 B3
Wembley HA9 ... 66 B5
St Clair Dr KT4 ... 216 B4
St Clair Ho 17 E3 ... 97 B4
St Clair Rd E13 ... 99 B5
St Clair's Rd CR0 ... 221 C6
St Clare Bsns Pk TW12 ... 174 A4
St Clare St EC3 ... 243 C1
St Clement Danes CE Prim Sch WC2 ... 94 B1 240 C1
St Clement & St James CE Prim Sch W11 ... 113 A5 244 A4
St Clements Ct
Barnsbury N7 ... 72 B2
7 SE14 ... 140 D6
8 Shepherd's Bush W11 ... 112 D6
St Clement's Ct EC3 . 252 D6
St Clements Ho E1 .. 243 C3
Walton-on-T KT12 ... 194 A2
St Clement's Hts SE26 ... 184 A6
St Clement's La WC2 240 D1
St Clements Mans 3 SW6 ... 134 D6

St Clements St N7 . . . 72 C1
St Cloud Rd SE27 . . . 183 B6
St Columba's Ct E15 . . 76 C4
St Columbas Ho 2 E17 . . . 53 D5
St Columba's RC Boys Sch DA6 . . . 169 D6
St Columb's Ho 11 W10 . . . 91 A2
St Crispins Cl NW3 . . . 70 C4
St Crispin's Cl UB1 . . . 85 B1
St Crispins Ct 1 UB1 . . 85 B1
St Cross St EC1 . . . 94 C2 241 B4
St Cuthberts Gdns 2 HA5 . . . 23 B3
St Cuthberts Rd N13 . . 32 C4
St Cuthbert's Rd NW2 69 B2
St Cuthbert with St Matthias CE Prim Sch SW5 . . . 113 D1 255 C2
St Cyprian's Greek Orthodox Prim Sch CR7 . . . 183 A2
St Cyprian's St SW17 . . . 180 D6
St Davids Cl
27 Bermondsey SE16 . . . 118 B1
Wembley HA9 . . . 67 A5
St David's Cl BR4 . . . 207 D2
St David's Coll BR4 . 207 D2
St Davids Ct 5 E11 . . 55 B4
St David's Ct
Bromley BR1 . . . 210 D6
8 Southall UB1 . . . 86 A1
1 Walthamstow E17 . . 54 A6
St David's Dr HA8 . . . 26 B2
St David's Pl NW4 . . . 46 B2
St David's Sch TW15 . 148 B1
St David's Sq E14 . . . 119 D1
St Denis Rd SE27 . . . 183 B6
St Dionis Rd
Fulham SW6 . . . 135 B3
Wanstead E12 . . . 78 A5
St Domingo Ho SE18 . . . 122 B3
St Dominic RC Prim Sch 14 NW5 . . . 70 D3
St Dominics RC Prim Sch 6 E9 . . . 75 A2
St Dominic's Sixth Form Coll HA1 . . . 64 C6
St Donatt's Rd
London SE14 . . . 141 B4
New Cross Gate SE4 . . 141 B3
St Dunstan Ave W3 . . . 111 B6
St Dunstan Gdns W3 . . . 111 B6
St Dunstans SM1 . . . 217 B2
St Dunstan's Alley EC3 . . . 253 A5
St Dunstan's CE Prim Sch 2 SM3 . . . 217 A1
St Dunstans Cl UB3 . 105 D2
St Dunstan's Coll SE6 . . . 163 C3
St Dunstan's Ct EC4 . 241 B1
St Dunstan's Hill
Cheam SM1, SM3 . . . 217 A3
EC3 . . . 253 A5
St Dunstan's La
Beckenham BR3 . . . 208 A4
EC3 . . . 253 A5
St Dunstans Rd E7 . . . 77 C2
St Dunstan's Rd
Cranford TW5 . . . 128 B3
Feltham TW13 . . . 149 D1
Hammersmith W6 . . . 112 D1
Hanwell W7 . . . 108 C4
South Norwood SE25 . 205 D5
St Edmunds Ave HA4 . . 39 B3
St Edmunds Cl
DA18 . . . 124 D4
3 Upper Tooting SW17 . . . 158 C2
St Edmund's Cl NW8 230 C5
St Edmund's Ct NW8 230 C5
St Edmunds Dr HA7 . . . 25 A2
St Edmund's La TW2 . . . 151 D4
St Edmunds RC Prim Sch E14 . . . 119 C2
St Edmund's RC Prim Sch
1 Edmonton N9 . . . 18 B3
Twickenham TW2 . . . 151 D4
St Edmunds Rd N9 . . . 18 A4
St Edmund's Rd IG1 . . 56 B3
St Edmund's Sq SW13 . . . 134 C6
St Edmund's Terr NW8 . . . 92 D6 230 C5
St Edward's CE Comp Sch RM7 . . . 59 C3
St Edward's Cl NW11 . . 47 C3
St Edwards Ct 3 E10 . . 54 A2
St Edward's Ct NW11 . . 47 C3
St Edwards RC Prim Sch 10 E6 . . . 99 C6
St Edward's RC Prim Sch NW1 . . . 92 C3 237 B5
St Egberts Way E4 . . . 20 A3
St Elizabeth Ct
North Finchley N12 . . . 30 A6
9 Walthamstow E10 . . . 53 D2
St Elizabeth RC Prim Sch 33 E2 . . . 96 C5
St Elizabeth's RC Prim Sch TW10 . . . 154 B5
St Elmo Rd W12 . . . 111 D4
St Elmos Rd SE16 . . . 119 A4
St Elphege's RC Sch SM6 . . . 220 A2
SS Peter & Paul's Prim Sch CR4 . . . 202 D5
SS Peter & Paul's RC Prim Sch IG1 . . . 79 B5
St Erkenwald Mews IG11 . . . 101 B6
St Erkenwald Rd IG11 . . . 101 B6
St Ermin's Hill SW1 . 259 C6
St Ervan's Rd W10 . . . 91 B2
St Eugene de Mazenod RC Prim Sch 12 NW6 . . . 69 C1
St Faith's CE Prim Sch 1 SW18 . . . 158 A6
St Faith's Cl EN2 . . . 5 A4
St Faith's Rd SE24 . . 160 D3
St Fillans Rd SE6 . . . 164 A4
St Francesca Cabrini RC Prim Sch SE23 . . . 162 C5
St Francis Cl BR5 . . . 211 C3
St Francis de Sales RC Jun & Inf Sch 12 N17 . . . 33 D3
St Francis' Ho NW1 . 232 C3
St Francis Lodge HA0 . . . 64 D5
St Francis of Assisi Prim Sch 19 W11 . . . 112 D6
St Francis Pl SW12 . . . 159 B5
St Francis RC Prim Sch
26 SE15 . . . 140 A5
Stratford E15 . . . 76 C3
St Francis Rd SE22 . . . 139 C1
St Francis Way IG1 . . . 79 B4
St Francis Xavier Coll SW12 . . . 159 B5
St Frideswides Mews 5 E14 . . . 98 A1
St Gabriel's CE Prim Sch SW1 . . . 115 C1 259 A1
St Gabriels Cl 3 E14 . 97 D2
St Gabriel's Cl E11 . . . 55 B1
St Gabriels Ct N11 . . . 31 D3
St Gabriel's Rd NW2 . . 68 D3
St George Ho SW11 . 268 B1
ST GEORGE IN THE EAST . . . 118 A6
St George's Ave
Ealing W5 . . . 109 D4
Kingsbury NW9 . . . 45 B5
Southall UB1 . . . 107 B6
Tufnell Pk N7 . . . 71 D4
Upton E7 . . . 77 B1
St George's Bldgs SE11 . . . 261 D5
St George's Cath NW1 . . . 231 D2
St George's Cath RC Prim Sch SE1 . . . 116 D3 261 C6
St George's CE Prim Sch
BR1 . . . 187 D1
18 SE5 . . . 139 C5
St George's CE Prim Sch *continued*
SW8 . . . 137 C5 269 B3
St George's Circ SE1 . . . 116 D3 261 C6
St Georges Cl
Erith SE28 . . . 102 D1
Nine Elms SW8 . . . 269 B2
Wembley HA0 . . . 65 A5
St George's Cl NW11 . . 47 B3
St Georges Coll N7 . . . 72 C5
St Georges Ct
Harrow HA3 . . . 43 A3
Newham E6 . . . 100 B3
Penge SE20 . . . 184 B2
Putney SW15 . . . 135 B1
Walthamstow E17 . . . 54 B4
St George's Ct
Brompton SW3 . . . 257 A4
Kensington SW7 . . . 256 A5
Newington SE1 . . . 261 C5
St George's Dr
Ickenham UB10 . . . 60 B6
South Oxhey WD19 . . . 23 A6
SW1 . . . 115 C1 259 A2
St George's Field W2 . . . 92 C1 237 B1
St George's Gdns KT6 . . . 214 D6
St George's Gr SW17 . . . 158 B1
St Georges Hanover Sq Sch W1 . . . 115 A6 248 B5
St George's Ho NW1 232 B3
St George's Hospl SW17 . . . 180 B5
St Georges Ind Est N22 . . . 32 D3
St George's Ind Est KT2 . . . 175 D5
St George's La EC3 . . 253 A6
St Georges Lo N10 . . . 49 C5
St Georges Mews 11 NW1 . . . 70 D1
St George's Mews
2 Rotherhithe SE8 . . . 119 B2
SE1 . . . 261 B6
St Georges Pl N7 . . . 71 D4
St George's Pools E1 . . . 118 B6
St George's RC Cath SE1 . . . 116 C3 261 B6
St George's RC Prim Sch
Enfield EN2 . . . 5 B3
Harrow HA1 . . . 64 D5
St George's RC Sec Sch W9 . . . 91 D5
St Georges Rd
Acton W4 . . . 111 B4
Bickley BR1 . . . 210 B6
Dagenham RM9 . . . 81 A4
Petts Wood BR5 . . . 211 B3
St George's Rd
Beckenham BR3 . . . 185 D2
Ealing W7 . . . 108 D5
Enfield EN1 . . . 5 D5
Feltham TW13 . . . 172 D6
Isleworth TW1 . . . 153 B6
2 Kingston u T KT2 . . . 176 C3
Leyton E10 . . . 76 A5
Mitcham CR4 . . . 203 B6
Newington SE1 . . . 116 D3 261 C5
Palmers Green N13 . . . 16 B2
Redbridge IG1 . . . 56 B2
Richmond TW9 . . . 132 B2
Sidcup DA14 . . . 190 D4
Temple Fortune NW11 . . 47 B3
Upton E7 . . . 77 B2
Wallington SM6 . . . 219 B3
Wimbledon SW19 . . . 179 B4
St Georges Rd Ctr RM9 . . . 81 B4
St Georges Rd W BR1 . . . 188 A1
St George's Residences 4 SW2 . . . 160 C6
St Georges's Ct EC4 . 241 C2
St George's Sh Ctr HA1 . . . 42 C3
St Georges Sq 1 E14 . . . 119 A6
St George's Sq
Kingston u T KT3 . . . 199 C6
Rotherhithe SE8 . . . 119 B2
St George's Sq *continued*
SW1 . . . 115 D1 259 C1
Upton E7 . . . 77 B1
St George's Square Mews SW1 . . . 259 C1
St George St W1 . . . 115 B6 248 D6
St Georges Terr
Hampstead NW1 . . . 70 D1
NW1 . . . 230 D6
St Georges Univ of London SW17 . . . 180 B5
St George's Way SE15 . . . 139 C6
St George's Wlk CR0 . . . 221 A5
St George the Martyr CE Prim Sch WC1 . . . 94 B3 240 D5
St George Wharf SW8 . . . 270 A6
St Gerards Cl SW4 . . . 159 C6
St German's Pl SE3 . . 143 A4
St German's Rd SE23 . . . 163 A3
St Gildas' RC Jun Sch 13 N8 . . . 50 A2
ST GILES . . . 94 A1
St Giles Ave
Dagenham RM10 . . . 81 D1
Uxbridge UB10 . . . 61 A4
St Giles Cir WC1 . . . 93 D1 239 D2
St Giles Cl BR6 . . . 227 B3
Dagenham RM10 . . . 81 D1
Heston TW3 . . . 129 A5
St Giles Coll
Highgate N6 . . . 49 C3
WC1 . . . 94 A2 240 B4
St Giles Ct
Ealing W13 . . . 109 C5
WC2 . . . 240 A2
St Giles High St WC2 . . . 93 D1 239 D2
St Giles Ho
2 New Barnet EN5 . . . 2 A1
Streatham SW16 . . . 160 A1
St Giles Pas WC2 . . . 239 D1
St Giles Rd SE5 . . . 139 C4
St Giles' Specl Sch CR2 . . . 220 D2
St Giles Terr EC1 . . . 242 B3
St Giles Twr 3 SE5 . . 139 C4
St Gilles Ho 15 E2 . . . 96 D5
St Gothard Rd SE21, SE27 . . . 183 B6
St Gregor High Sch HA3 . . . 43 D4
St Gregory Cl HA4 . . . 62 C4
St Gregory's RC Prim Sch 14 W5 . . . 87 D2
St Helena Ho WC1 . . 234 A1
St Helena Pier TW9 153 D6
St Helena Rd SE16 . . 118 D2
St Helena St WC1 . . . 234 A1
St Helena Terr 31 TW9 . . . 153 D6
St Helens KT7 . . . 196 D2
St Helens Coll UB10 . . . 60 C1
St Helen's Cres SW16 . . . 182 B2
St Helens Gdns W10 . . 90 D1
St Helens Pl E10 . . . 53 A2
St Helen's Pl EC3 . . 243 A2
St Helen's RC Inf Sch E17 . . . 54 A4
St Helen's RC Prim Sch E13 . . . 99 A3
St Helen's RC Sch 17 SW9 . . . 138 C2
St Helens Rd 5 DA18 . . . 124 D4
St Helen's Rd
Ealing W13 . . . 109 C5
Redbridge IG1 . . . 56 B3
Thornton Heath SW16 . . . 182 B2
ST HELIER . . . 202 B2
St Helier Ave SM4 . . . 202 A3
St Helier Ct 4 N1 . . . 95 C6
St Helier Hospl SM5 202 A1
St Heliers Ave TW3, TW4 . . . 151 C6
St Helier's Rd E10 . . . 54 A3
St Helier Sta SM4 . . . 201 C3
St Hilary's Ct BR1 . . . 210 D6
St Hilda's Ave TW15 . . 170 A5
St Hildas Cl 2 SW17 . . . 158 C2
St Hilda's Cl NW6 . . . 68 D1
St Hilda's Rd SW13 . . 134 B6
St Hildas Wharf E1 . . 118 C5
St Hubert's Ho 2 E14 . . . 119 C3
St Hughes Cl 4 SW17 . . . 158 C2
St Hugh's Rd SE20 . . . 184 B3
St Ignatius Coll EN1 . . . 6 B6
St Ignatius RC Prim Sch TW16 . . . 172 A2
St Ignatius' RC Prim Sch N15 . . . 51 D3
St Ives Ct NW2 . . . 69 A2
St Ivian Ct 3 N10 . . . 31 B1
ST JAMES . . . 115 C5
St James Apartments 2 E17 . . . 53 A4
St James Ave
East Barnet N20 . . . 14 C1
Sutton SM1 . . . 217 C3
St James' Ave W13 . . 109 A5
St James' CE Jun & Inf Sch 24 SE16 . . . 118 A3
St James CE Jun Sch E7 . . . 77 A3
St James CE Prim Sch EN3 . . . 6 C3
St James Cl Barnet EN4 . 2 B1
East Barnet N20 . . . 14 C1
St James' Cl
New Malden KT3 . . . 199 D4
Ruislip HA4 . . . 62 C6
St James Ct
26 Bethnal Green E2 . . . 96 A4
9 Brentford W4 . . . 110 C1
1 Bromley BR2 . . . 187 A1
Forest Hill SE23 . . . 163 A3
SE3 . . . 143 B4
Thornton Heath CR0 . 204 D2
Wanstead E12 . . . 77 C6
St James' Ct
Bedford Pk W4 . . . 111 B3
7 Kingston u T KT1 . . . 198 A6
SW1 . . . 259 B6
St James Gate IG9 . . . 21 B3
St James Gdns IG6 . . . 58 B5
St James' Gdns HA0 . . . 66 A1
St James Ho N5 . . . 72 C3
St James Hts 3 SE18 . . . 123 A1
St James Independent Schs W14 . . . 113 A2 254 B4
St James Ind Mews 16 SE1 . . . 118 A1
St James Ind Sch for Boys TW1 . . . 153 A2
St James' Mans NW6 . . 69 C1
St James Mews E14 . . 120 A3
St James' RC High Sch NW9 . . . 27 D2
St James RC Prim Sch BR5 . . . 210 D4
St James Rd
Carshalton SM5 . . . 218 C5
Kingston u T KT1 . . . 175 D1
Sutton SM1, SM2 . . . 217 C3
St James' Rd
Edmonton N9 . . . 18 B2
Forest Gate E15 . . . 76 D3
Mitcham CR4 . . . 181 A3
Surbiton KT6 . . . 197 D3
Sutton SM1 . . . 217 C2
St James's SE14 . . . 141 A4
St James & St Michael's CE Prim Sch W2 . . . 114 A6 246 B6
St James's App EC2 . 243 A5
St James's Ave
Beckenham BR3 . . . 207 A6
Hampton TW12 . . . 174 A5
South Hackney E2 . . . 96 C5
St James's CE Prim Sch
Cranley Gdns N10 . . . 49 A5
London SE14 . . . 141 A4
St James School Flats 5 N7 . . . 72 C3
St James's Cl NW8 . . 230 C5
Upper Tooting SW17 . 158 D2
Woolwich SE18 . . . 123 A1
St James's Cloisters 2 SE22 . . . 139 D1

St James's Cotts [14] TW10 ... 153 D6
St James's Cres SW9 ... 138 C2
St James's Ct
[8] Edmonton N18 ... 34 A5
Harrow HA1 ... 43 A3
St James's Dr
Balham SW12, SW17 ... 158 D4
Upper Tooting SW17 . 158 D3
St James's Gdns W11 ... 113 A5 244 A4
St James's Gr SW11. 136 D3
St James's La N10 ... 49 B5
St James's Market SW1 ... 249 C5
St James's Mews E17 . 53 A4
St James's Pal★ SW1 ... 115 C5 249 B3
St James's Park Sta SW1 ... 115 D3 259 C6
St James's Pas EC3 . 243 B1
St James's Pk★ SW1 249 C2
St James's Pk CR0 ... 205 A2
St James's Pl SW1 ... 115 C5 249 A3
St James's RC Prim Sch TW2 ... 152 C1
St James's Rd
Bermondsey SE1, SE16 ... 118 A2
Hampton TW12 ... 173 D5
Peckham SE1 ... 140 A6
Thornton Heath CR0 .. 205 B2
St James's Sq SW1 ... 115 C5 249 B4
St James's St SW1 ... 115 C5 249 A4
Walthamstow E17 ... 53 A4
St James St W6 ... 112 C1
St James's Terr NW8 230 C6
[2] Upper Tooting SW12 ... 159 A3
St James's Terrace Mews NW8 ... 230 C5
St James Street Sta E17 ... 53 A4
St James The Great RC Prim Sch
[17] Camberwell SE15 ... 139 D4
South Norwood CR7.. 182 D1
St James Way DA14 .. 191 A5
St James Wlk EC1... 241 C6
St Jerome's Gr UB3 ... 83 A1
St Joachim's RC Prim Sch [1] E16 ... 99 C1
St Joan of Arc RC Prim Sch N5 ... 73 A4
St Joan's Rd N9 ... 17 D2
St John Baptist CE Prim Sch BR1 ... 186 A6
St John Fisher RC Fst & Mid Sch HA5 ... 41 C5
St John Fisher RC Prim Sch
DA18 ... 125 A3
Wembley UB6 ... 87 C5
West Barnes SW20 .. 200 D4
St John of Jerusalem CE Prim Sch [42] E9 ... 74 C1
ST JOHN'S ... 141 C3
St John & St James CE Prim Sch
Edmonton N18 ... 33 D5
[1] Hackney E9 ... 74 C3
St John's Angell Town CE Prim Sch [28] SW9 ... 138 C3
St John's Ave
Dagenham NW10 ... 89 D6
Friern Barnet N11 ... 30 D5
Putney SW15 ... 156 D6
St John's CE First Sch HA7 ... 25 A6
St John's CE Prim Sch
Buckhurst Hill IG9 ... 21 B3
Croydon CR0 ... 222 D5
Enfield EN2 ... 4 D6
Kingston u T KT1 ... 198 A6
London N11 ... 30 D6
[12] Penge SE20 ... 184 C3
[35] South Hackney E2... 96 C5
St John's CE Prim Sch continued
Whetstone N20 ... 14 A2
St John's CE Sch HA7 25 A6
St John's CE Walham Green Prim Sch SW6 ... 135 A4 264 B2
St John's Church Rd E9 ... 74 C3
St Johns Cl N14 ... 15 C5
St John's Cl SW6 ... 265 A4
Wembley HA9 ... 66 A3
St John's Concert Hall★ SW1 ... 260 A5
St John's Cotts [2] SE20 ... 184 C3
St John's Cres SW9 .. 138 C2
St Johns Ct [39] E1 ... 118 B5
St John's Ct
Buckhurst Hill IG9 ... 21 B3
Finsbury Pk N4 ... 72 D6
Hammersmith W6 ... 112 B2
[2] Harrow HA1 ... 42 D3
Isleworth TW7 ... 130 D3
Kingston u T KT1 ... 198 A5
Lewisham SE13 ... 142 A3
Leytonstone E11 ... 54 D1
[5] South Hampstead NW3 ... 70 A2
Saint John's Ct N5 ... 72 D4
St Johns Dr KT12 ... 194 C1
St John's Dr SW18 .. 157 D3
St John's Est SE1 .. 253 C1
St John's Gdns W11 ... 113 B6 244 C5
St John's Gr
[3] Barnes SW13 ... 133 D3
[1] Richmond TW9 ... 132 A1
Upper Holloway N19 ... 71 C6
St John's Highbury Vale CE Prim Sch N5 ... 72 D5
St John's Hill SW11 .. 136 B1
St John's Hill Gr SW11 ... 136 B1
St Johns Ho [5] SE17 . 139 B6
Streatham SW16 ... 182 A4
St John's Ho [1] E14 .. 120 A2
St John's La EC1 ... 94 D2 241 D4
St John's Lodge [8] SE8 ... 141 C4
St John's Mans E5 ... 74 C3
St John's Par
Ealing W13 ... 109 B5
[3] Sidcup DA14 ... 190 B6
St John's Park Mans N19 ... 71 C5
St John's Path EC1.. 241 C5
St John's Pk SE3 ... 143 A5
St John's Pl EC1 ... 241 C5
St John's Prim Sch W13 ... 109 A6
St John's RC Prim Sch SE16 ... 119 A4
St Johns Rd Ilford IG2 . 57 C2
Kingston u T KT3 ... 199 A6
St John's Rd
Barking IG11 ... 101 C6
Battersea SW11 ... 136 C1
Canning Town E16 ... 99 A1
Carshalton SM5 ... 218 C5
Chingford E4 ... 35 D6
Croydon CR0 ... 220 D5
DA16 ... 146 B2
East Ham E6 ... 100 A6
East Molesey KT8 ... 196 B5
Feltham TW13 ... 173 B6
Harrow HA1 ... 42 D3
Isleworth TW7 ... 130 D3
Orpington BR5 ... 211 C3
Penge SE20 ... 184 C4
Richmond TW9 ... 132 A1
Sidcup DA14 ... 190 B6
Southall UB2 ... 107 A3
Sutton SM1 ... 217 D6
Teddington KT1 ... 175 C1
Temple Fortune NW11 .. 47 B3
Tottenham N15 ... 51 C3
Walthamstow E17 ... 36 A1
Wembley HA9 ... 66 A3
Wimbledon SW19 ... 179 A4
St John's & St Clements CE Jun & Inf Sch [4] SE15 ... 140 A2
St John's Sch HA6 ... 22 B4
St John's Sq EC1 ... 94 D3 241 C5
St Johns Sta SE8 ... 141 C3
St John St EC1 ... 94 D3 241 C6
St John's Terr
Enfield EN2 ... 5 B6
North Kensington W10 .. 90 D3
SE18 ... 145 B6
Upton E7 ... 77 B2
St John's Therapy Ctr SW11 ... 136 B1
St Johnstone Ho [17] N12 ... 29 D6
St John's Upper Holloway CE Prim Sch [7] N19 ... 71 D6
St John's Vale SE8 ... 141 C3
St John's Villas
[4] Friern Barnet N11 .. 30 D5
Upper Holloway N19 ... 71 D6
W8 ... 255 D5
St John's Walworth CE Prim Sch SE17 ... 117 A2 262 B3
St John's Way N19 ... 49 D1
ST JOHN'S WOOD ... 92 B5
St John's Wood Ct NW8 ... 229 D1
St John's Wood High St NW8 ... 92 C5 230 A3
St John's Wood Park NW8 ... 92 B6 229 C6
St John's Wood Pre-Prep Sch NW8 ... 92 C4 230 A2
St John's Wood Rd NW8 ... 92 B4 229 D1
St John's Wood Sta NW8 ... 92 B5 229 C4
St John's Wood Terr NW8 ... 92 C5 230 A4
St John the Baptist CE Jun Sch KT1 ... 175 D3
St John the Baptist VA CE Prim Sch N1 ... 95 B5 235 D3
St John the Divine CE Jun & Inf Sch SE5 . 138 D5
St John the Evangelist RC Prim Sch N1 ... 94 D5 234 C4
St John Vianney RC Prim Sch [4] N8 ... 50 D5
St Josephs Cl BR6 . 227 D4
St Joseph's Cl W10 ... 91 A2
St Joseph's Convent Sch [9] E11 ... 55 A3
St Josephs Ct
[3] Dagenham NW10 ... 89 D5
[20] Walthamstow E10 ... 53 D2
St Joseph's Ct E4 ... 20 B4
St Joseph's Dr UB1 ... 107 B5
St Joseph's Flats NW1 ... 232 C2
St Josephs Gr NW4 ... 46 B5
St Joseph's Ho W6 .. 112 D2
St Joseph's Hospice E9, E8 ... 96 B6
St Joseph's RC Coll SW16 ... 182 D4
St Joseph's RC Fst & Mid Sch HA3 ... 25 A1
St Joseph's RC Inf & Jun Schs
Hendon NW4 ... 46 B5
[36] SE5 ... 139 A5
St Joseph's RC Inf Sch
Leyton E10 ... 75 C6
South Norwood SE19. 183 A4
St Joseph's RC Jun & Inf Schs HA9 ... 66 B3
St Joseph's RC Jun Sch
South Norwood SE19 ... 183 A4
Walthamstow E10 ... 53 D1
St Josephs RC Prim Sch
[10] W7 ... 108 C5
St Joseph's RC Prim Sch
Barking IG11 ... 101 A6
[39] Bermondsey SE16 118 A4
Bromley BR1 ... 187 B3
Chelsea SW3 114 D2 257 C3
Dagenham RM9 ... 81 B4
[19] Deptford SE8 ... 141 C5
St Joseph's RC Prim Sch continued
[11] Greenwich SE10 .. 120 C1
Kingston u T KT1 ... 176 B1
Paddington W9 ... 92 A4 229 A1
Rotherhithe SE16 ... 118 C3
St Giles WC2 .. 94 A1 240 B2
Upper Holloway N19 ... 49 B1
[16] Wandsworth SW18 ... 157 C6
[8] Willesden NW10 ... 67 C1
St Joseph's Rd N9 ... 18 C3
St Joseph's St SW8 . 268 D2
St Joseph's Vale SE3 ... 142 B2
St Jude & St Paul's CE Prim Sch [12] N1 ... 73 C2
St Jude's CE Prim Sch
[4] London SE24 ... 160 D6
SE1 ... 116 D3 261 C5
St Judes Ho [6] W10 ... 91 B4
St Jude's Rd E2 ... 96 B5
St Jude St N16 ... 73 C3
St Julian's Cl SW16 .. 182 C6
St Julian's Farm Rd SE27, SW16 ... 182 D6
St Julian's Rd NW6 ... 91 C6
St Katharine's Ho N1 234 A4
St Katharine's Prec NW1 ... 231 C4
St Katharine's Way E1 ... 117 D5 253 D4
St Katherines Rd DA18 ... 124 D4
St Katherine's Row EC3 ... 243 B1
St Katherine's Wlk [1] W11 ... 112 D5
St Keverne Rd SE9 ... 188 A6
St Kilda Rd BR6 ... 211 D1
Ealing W13 ... 109 A4
St Kilda's Rd
Harrow HA1 ... 42 C3
Stamford Hill N16 ... 51 C1
St Kitts Terr SE19 ... 183 C5
St Laurence's Cl NW6 90 D6
St Lawrence Bsns Ctr TW13 ... 150 B2
St Lawrence Cl HA8 ... 26 B3
St Lawrence Ct N1 .. 235 D6
St Lawrence Dr HA5 ... 40 B4
St Lawrence Ho SE1 263 B6
St Lawrence Jun Sch KT8 ... 196 B5
St Lawrence RC Prim Sch TW13 ... 150 B2
St Lawrence St E14 .. 120 A5
St Lawrence Terr W10 ... 91 A2
St Lawrence Way SW9 ... 138 C3
St Leonards Ave HA3 .. 43 C4
St Leonard's Ave E4 ... 36 B4
St Leonard's CE Prim Sch SW16 ... 181 D5
St Leonards Cl [4] DA16 ... 146 A2
St Leonards Ct SW14 ... 133 A2
St Leonard's Ct N1 .. 235 D2
St Leonards Gdns IG1 ... 79 A3
St Leonard's Gdns TW5 ... 129 A4
St Leonard's Hospl N1 ... 95 C5
St Leonards Rd SW14 ... 133 A2
St Leonard's Rd
Becontree NW10 ... 89 B3
Claygate KT10 ... 212 D2
Croydon CR0 ... 220 D5
Ealing W13 ... 109 C6
Kingston u T KT6 ... 197 D4
South Bromley E14 ... 98 A2
Thames Ditton KT7 ... 197 A2
St Leonards Rise BR6 ... 227 C4
St Leonard's Sq
Camden Town NW5 ... 71 A2
Kingston u T KT6 ... 197 D4
St Leonard's St E3 ... 97 D4
St Leonard's Terr SW3 ... 114 D1 257 D1
St Leonard's Wlk SW16 ... 182 B3
St Loo Ave SW3 ... 136 C6 267 B6
St Loo Ct SW3 ... 267 C6
St Louis Rd SE27 ... 183 B6
St Loy's Rd N17 ... 51 D6
St Lucia Dr E15 ... 98 D6
St Luke Prim CE Sch [9] E16 ... 98 D1
ST LUKE'S ... 95 A3
St Luke's Ave
Clapham SW4 ... 137 D1
Enfield EN2 ... 5 B5
Ilford IG1 ... 78 D3
St Luke's CE Prim Sch
[7] Cubitt Town E14 ... 120 B2
Kingston u T KT2 ... 176 B2
Paddington W9 ... 91 B4
Shoreditch EC1 95 A4 235 B1
West Norwood SE27 . 183 A5
St Luke's Cl
Croydon SE25 ... 206 B3
St Luke's EC1 .. 95 A3 242 B6
St Lukes Ct [6] E10 ... 53 D2
St Luke's Ct W11 ... 91 B1
St Luke's Mews W11 .. 91 B1
St Luke's Path [1] IG1 . 78 D3
St Luke's RC Sixth Form Coll DA14 ... 189 D5
St Luke's Rd
Notting Hill W11 ... 91 B2
Uxbridge UB10 ... 60 A1
St Luke's Sq E16 ... 98 D1
St Luke's St SW3 ... 257 B2
St Luke's Woodside Hospl N10 ... 49 A5
St Malo Ave N9 ... 18 C1
St Margaret Clitherow RC Prim Sch
Neasden NW10 ... 67 B4
Woolwich SE28 ... 124 B5
St Margaret Lee CE Prim Sch SE13 ... 142 C1
ST MARGARETS ... 153 A5
St Margarets IG11 ... 101 B6
St Margarets Ave
Ashford TW15 ... 170 D5
DA15 ... 167 B1
Hillingdon UB8 ... 82 C3
Whetstone N20 ... 14 A3
St Margaret's Ave
Cheam SM3 ... 217 A5
Harringay N8, N15 ... 50 D5
Harrow HA2 ... 64 A5
St Margarets Bsns Ctr [11] TW1 ... 153 B5
St Margaret's CE Prim Sch
Barking IG11 ... 79 A1
Woolwich SE18 ... 123 A1
St Margaret's Cres SW15 ... 156 B6
St Margaret's Ct
Leyton E15 ... 76 C4
Putney SW15 ... 134 B1
SE1 ... 252 C3
[9] Twickenham TW1 .. 153 B5
St Margaret's Dr TW1 ... 153 B6
St Margaret's Gr
Leyton E11 ... 76 D5
SE18 ... 145 A6
Twickenham TW1 ... 153 A5
St Margaret's La W8 ... 113 D3 255 C5
St Margarets Lo W3. 110 D4
St Margaret's Pass SE13 ... 142 C2
St Margaret's Path [4] SE18 ... 123 A1
St Margarets Rd
Edgware HA8 ... 26 D5
Ruislip HA4 ... 39 B3
St Margaret's Rd
Brockley SE4 ... 141 B1
Hanwell W7 ... 108 C4
Isleworth TW1 ... 153 B6
Kensal Green NW10 ... 90 C4
Tottenham N17 ... 51 C6
Wanstead E12 ... 77 C6

St Margarets Rdbt TW1 153 B6
St Margaret's Sch NW3 69 D4
St Margaret's Sta TW1 153 B5
St Margaret St SW1 250 A1
St Margaret's Terr SE18 123 A1
St Margret's Ct N11 31 A6
St Mark's CE Acad CR4 181 B1
St Mark's CE Prim Sch
Bromley BR2 209 A6
3 Croydon SE25 206 A5
Kennington SE11 138 B6 270 D6
St Marks Cl 5 SE10 142 A5
St Mark's Cl Barnet EN5 1 D2
Harrow HA1 43 B1
St Mark's Cres NW1 93 A6 231 B6
St Mark's Ct
Hanwell W7 108 C4
8 Walthamstow E10 53 D2
St Marks Gate E9 75 B1
St Mark's Gr SW10 135 D5 265 D4
St Mark's Hill KT6 198 A3
St Marks Ho 6 SE17 139 B6
St Mark's Ho 8 E17 54 A5
St Mark's Hospl HA1 43 B2
St Mark's Hts 25 KT6 198 A4
St Marks Ind Est E16 121 D5
St Mark's Mans 14 N4 72 B6
St Marks Pl RM10 81 D2
St Mark's Pl
Notting Hill W11 91 A1
Wimbledon SW19 179 B4
St Mark's Prim Sch
Hanwell W7 108 C4
8 Mitcham CR4 180 D1
11 Upper Holloway N19 72 A6
St Mark's RC Sch TW3 129 C2
St Marks Rd
15 North Kensington NW10 90 D1
North Kensington W10 90 D2
St Mark's Rd
Bromley BR2 209 B6
Croydon SE25 206 A5
Ealing W5 110 A5
Enfield EN1 17 D6
Hanwell W7 108 C4
Mitcham CR4 181 A1
Notting Hill W11 91 A1
Teddington TW11 175 B3
St Mark's Rise E8 73 D3
St Mark's Sq NW1 231 A5
St Mark St E1 95 D1 243 D1
St Martha's Convent Jun Sch 11 EN5 1 A1
St Martha's Senior Sch EN4 1 C4
St Martin-in-the-Fields High Sch 21 SW2 160 C3
St Martin of Porres Prim Sch N11 31 C4
St Martin's Almshouses NW1 232 A6
St Martins App HA4 39 C2
St Martin's Ave E6 99 D5
St Martins Cl DA18 124 D4
South Oxhey WD19 22 C6
St Martin's Cl
Enfield EN1 6 B4
NW1 232 A6
St Martins Ct N1 95 C6
St Martin's Ct WC2 250 A6
West Norwood SE27 160 D2
St Martins La BR3 207 D4
St Martin's La WC2 116 A6 250 A5
St Martin's Le Grand EC1 242 A2
St Martin's Pl WC2 250 A5
St Martin's Rd
Edmonton N9 18 B2
St Martin's Rd *continued*
Finchley N2 30 B2
Stockwell SW9 138 B3
St Martin's Sch NW7 27 B5
St Martin's St WC2 249 D5
St Martin's Way SW17 158 A1
St Mary Abbots CE Prim Sch W8 113 D4 245 C1
St Mary Abbot's Ct W14 254 C5
St Mary Abbot's Pl W8 254 D5
St Mary Abbots Terr W14 254 D5
St Mary at Hill EC3 117 C6 253 A5
St Mary Ave SM6 219 B5
St Mary Axe EC3 95 C1 243 B2
St Marychurch St SE16 118 C4
St Mary Graces Ct E1 253 D5
St Marylebone CE Sch The W1 93 A2 238 B4
St Mary le Bow Church* EC2 242 B1
St Mary- le-Park Ct SW11 267 B3
St Mary Magdalene Acad N7 72 C2
St Mary Magdalene CE Prim Sch
3 Paddington W2 91 D2
10 Peckham SE15 140 B3
16 Woolwich SE18 122 C2
St Mary Magdalen's RC Prim Sch
Brockley SE4 141 A1
14 Mortlake SW14 133 B2
St Mary Magdelen's RC Jun Sch 1 NW2 68 B2
St Mary Newington Cl SE17 263 B2
St Mary of the Angels RC Prim Sch 12 W2 91 C1
St Mary RC Prim Sch 22 W10 91 A3
St Mary Rd E17 53 D5
St Marys IG11 101 B6
St Mary & St Michael Prim Sch 27 E1 96 C1
St Mary & St Pancras CE Prim Sch NW1 93 D5 232 C3
St Mary's App E12 78 B3
St Marys Ave UB2 107 D2
St Mary's Ave
Beckenham BR2 208 C6
Finchley N3 29 B1
Teddington TW11 174 D4
Wanstead E11 55 B2
St Mary's Bryanston Square CE Sch W1 92 D2 237 C3
St Mary's CE High Sch NW4 46 C6
St Mary's CE Inf Sch 3 N8 50 B5
St Mary's CE Jun Sch 5 N8 50 A5
St Mary's CE Prim Sch
Chessington KT9 214 B2
East Barnet EN4 14 C5
Finchley N3 29 B3
Islington N1 94 D6 234 D6
London SE13 163 D6
Long Ditton KT7 197 B1
15 Putney SW15 134 D2
Walthamstow E17 53 D5
Willesden NW10 67 C2
St Mary's CE Prim Sch (Inf) 12 TW1 153 A4
St Mary's CE Prim Sch (Jun) TW1 153 B4
St Mary's Church Ho 11 E17 53 D5
St Mary's Cl BR5 190 B1
Chessington KT9 214 B1
Ewell KT17 215 D1
Sunbury TW16 194 A5
Tottenham N17 34 A2
St Mary's Coll TW1 152 D1
St Mary's Cres
Hayes UB3 105 D6
Hendon NW4 46 B6
Hounslow TW7 130 C5
St Marys Ct
Abbey Wood SE2 124 D2
Newham E6 100 B3
SE7 143 D5
St Mary's Ct
Bedford Pk W6 111 D3
Ealing W5 109 D4
Finchley N12 30 A3
Kingston u T KT3 199 C6
Leytonstone E11 54 D1
Wallington SM6 219 C4
St Mary's Dr TW14 149 A4
St Mary's Est 2 SE16 118 C4
St Mary's Flats NW1 232 C2
St Mary's Gate W8 255 C5
St Mary's Gdns SE11 261 B4
St Mary's Gn 1 N2 48 A6
St Mary's Gr
Barnes SW13 134 B2
Chiswick W4 132 D6
Islington N1 72 D2
Richmond TW10, TW9 132 B1
St Mary's Ho
Ealing W5 109 D3
N1 234 D6
St Mary's Hospl W2 92 B1 236 D2
St Mary's Hospl Medical Sch W2 92 B1 236 D2
St Mary's Kilburn CE Prim Sch 16 NW6 91 C6
St Mary's Lo E11 55 B3
St Mary's Mans
Dagenham NW10 89 C6
Paddington W2 92 B2 236 C4
St Mary's Mews NW6 69 D1
St Mary's Path N1 234 D6
St Mary's Pl
Ealing W5 109 D4
Eltham SE9 166 C5
Kensington W8 113 D3 255 C5
St Mary's RC High Sch CR0 205 A1
St Mary's RC Inf Sch SM5 218 D4
St Mary's RC Jun & Inf Schs
Croydon CR0 205 B1
London N15 51 B4
St Mary's RC Jun Sch
Wallington SM5 218 D3
Walthamstow E17 54 A6
St Mary's RC Prim Sch
Beckenham BR3 186 A3
8 Chingford E4 20 B3
Chiswick W4 133 C6
10 Clapham Pk SW4 159 C6
Clapham SW8 137 B4 268 D2
Enfield EN3 6 D1
Hammersmith W14 112 D3
13 Isleworth TW7 131 A2
Merton SW19 179 C3
Paddington NW6 91 C5
SE9 166 C6
St Marys Rd IG1 79 B6
St Mary's Rd
Ealing W5 109 D5
East Barnet EN4 14 D4
East Molesey KT8 196 B4
Finchley N2 30 B2
Golders Green NW11 47 A2
Harlesdon NW10 89 C6
Hayes UB3 105 D6
Hornsey N8 50 A5
Leyton E10 76 A6
Long Ditton KT6 197 C1
Lower Edmonton N9 18 C3
Newham E13 99 B5
Nunhead SE15 140 C3
South Norwood SE25 205 C6
Surbiton KT6 197 D3
Wimbledon SW19 179 B5
Worcester Pk KT4 215 C6
St Mary's & St John's CE Prim Sch NW4 46 B4
St Mary's & St Peter's CE Prim Sch 12 TW11 174 D5
St Mary's Sch Hampstead NW3 70 B3
St Mary's Sq
Ealing W5 109 D4
W2 236 C4
St Mary's Stoke Newington CE Prim Sch 2 N16 73 C6
St Mary St SE18 122 C2
St Mary's Terr W2 236 C4
St Mary's Twr EC1 242 B5
St Marys View HA3 43 C4
St Mary's Wlk
Hayes UB3 105 D6
SE11 261 B4
St Matthew Acad SE3 142 C2
St Matthew's Ave KT6 198 B1
St Matthew's CE Prim Sch
Enfield EN3 18 C6
Surbiton KT6 198 A2
Wimbledon SW20 178 A2
Yiewsley UB7 104 A5
St Matthews CE Sch SW1 115 D3 259 D6
St Matthews Ct
Muswell Hill N10 31 A1
SE1 262 A5
2 Stratford E15 76 D1
7 Walthamstow E10 53 D2
St Matthew's Ct 1 TW15 170 C5
St Matthews Dr BR1 210 B6
St Matthew's Ho 8 SE17 139 B6
St Matthew's Lo NW1 232 B4
St Matthew's Rd
Clapham Pk SW2 160 B6
Ealing W5 110 A5
St Matthew's Row E2 96 A3
St Matthew St SW1 259 C5
St Matthias CE Prim Sch E2 95 D3 243 D6
St Matthias Cl NW9 45 D4
St Matthias's CE Prim Sch 32 N16 73 C4
St Mauritius Ho SE13 164 A6
St Maur Rd SW6 135 B4 264 D1
St Mellion Cl SE28 102 D1
St Merryn Cl SE18 145 B5
St Merryn Ct BR3 185 C3
St Michael & All Angels CE Acad 35 SE5 139 A5
St Michael-at-Bowes CE Jun Sch N13 32 C4
St Michael & St Martin RC Prim Sch 1 TW4 129 B2
St Michael's Alley EC3 242 D1
St Michaels Ave N9 18 C4
St Michael's Ave HA9 66 C2
St Michael's CE Prim Sch
Camden Town NW1 93 C6 232 A6
DA16 146 C4
Enfield EN2 5 A4
5 Forest Hill SE26 185 A6
Highgate N6 49 A2
Wandsworth SW18 157 B4
Wood Green N22 32 B2
St Michaels Cl BR1 210 A6
4 Newham E16 99 D2
Worcester Pk KT4 215 D6
St Michael's Cl
Colney Hatch N12 30 C5
DA18 124 D4
Finchley N3 29 B1
St Michael's Cres HA5 41 A3
St Michaels Ct 2 E14 98 A2
St Michael's Ct
Brunswick Pk N11 15 A1
Golders Green NW11 47 B2
St Michael's Flats NW1 232 C3
St Michael's Gdns W10 91 A2
St Michaels Ho SE26 185 B6
St Michael's Hospl EN2 5 B4
St Michael's RC Gram Sch 8 N12 30 A5
St Michaels RC Prim Sch TW15 170 C5
St Michael's RC Prim Sch 4 E6 100 B5
St Michael's RC Sec Sch 38 SE16 118 A4
St Michaels Rd TW15 170 C5
St Michael's Rd
Cricklewood NW2 68 C4
Croydon CR0 205 A1
DA16 146 B2
Stockwell SW9 138 B3
Wallington SM6 219 C2
St Michael's Rise DA16 146 B4
St Michael's St W2 92 C1 237 A2
St Michael Steiner Sch The 18 SW18 157 C6
St Michael's Terr N22 32 A2
St Mildred's Ct EC2 242 C1
St Mildreds Rd SE12, SE6 164 D4
St Mirren Ct 8 EN5 14 A6
St Monica's RC Prim Sch
Palmers Green N14 16 A1
24 Shoreditch N1 95 C4
St Nicholas CE Prim Sch TW17 192 D3
St Nicholas Cl WD6 9 D5
St Nicholas Ct E4 36 A4
St Nicholas Ctr 7 SM1 217 D3
St Nicholas Dr TW17 192 C2
St Nicholas' Flats NW1 232 C3
St Nicholas Glebe SW17 181 A4
St Nicholas Ho SE8 141 C6
St Nicholas Mans SW17 158 D2
St Nicholas Rd
Plumstead SE18 123 D2
Sutton SM1 217 D3
Thames Ditton KT7 196 D3
St Nicholas Sch
Elst WD6 9 D5
London NW9 67 A6
St Nicholas St SE8 141 C4
St Nicholas Way SM1 217 D3
St Nicolas La BR7 188 A2
St Ninian's Ct N20 14 D1
St Norbert Gn SE4 141 A1
St Norbert Rd SE4 141 A1
St Olaf's Rd SW6 135 A5 264 B3
St Olaves Ct W2 245 C5
St Olave's Ct EC2 242 C1
St Olave's Est SE1 253 B2
St Olave's Gdns SE11 261 A4
St Olave's Mans SE11 261 A4
St Olaves Prep Sch SE9 166 D2
St Olave's Rd E6 100 C6
St Olave's Wlk SW16 181 D1
St Olav's Sq 32 SE16 118 C4
St Osmund's RC Prim Sch SW13 133 D4
St Oswald's Pl SE11 116 B1 260 C1
St Oswald's Rd SW16 182 D2
St Oswulf St SW1 259 D3
St Owen Ho SE1 263 B6
ST PANCRAS 94 A4
St Pancras Almshouses 13 NW5 70 D3
St Pancras Commercial Ctr NW1 232 B6
St Pancras Ct
Finchley N2 30 B1
6 Wembley HA0 66 A2
St Pancras Hospl NW1 93 D6 232 C5
St Pancras International Sta WC1 94 A4 233 A2

St Pancras Way NW1 ....93 D6 232 C6
St Patrick's Coll W1 ....93 D1 239 C2
St Patricks Ct IG8 ....36 C3
St Patrick's RC Prim Sch
Camden Town NW5 ....71 B3
Plumstead SE18 ....123 B2
6 Walthamstow E17 ...53 A5
St Paul's Acad SE2 .. 146 A6
St Paul's & All Hallows CE Jun & Inf Schs 1 N17 ....34 A3
St Paul's Ave
Harrow HA3 ....44 B5
Rotherhithe SE16 .... 118 D5
Willesden NW2 ....68 C2
St Paul's Cath★ EC4 ....95 A1 242 A1
St Paul's Cath Sch EC4 ....95 A1 242 A1
St Paul's CE Jun Sch 18 KT2 .... 176 C3
St Pauls CE Prim Sch
14 Brentford TW8 ... 131 D6
1 Friern Barnet N11 ...31 B5
St Paul's CE Prim Sch
Chessington KT9 .... 214 A4
24 E1 .... 118 A6
1 Friern Barnet N11 ...31 B5
23 Hammersmith W6 112 C1
Hampstead NW3 ....70 D1
Mill Hill NW7 ....28 B6
SE17 .... 117 A1 262 A2
Southgate N21 ....16 D4
St Paul's Church Yd EC4 ....95 A1 242 A1
St Pauls Cl
Ealing W5 ....110 B4
Hayes UB3 ....105 B1
St Paul's Cl
Ashford TW15 .... 171 A5
Borehamwood WD6 ....11 A6
Carshalton SM5 .... 202 C1
Chessington KT9 .... 213 D4
Greenwich SE7 .... 121 D1
Hounslow TW3, TW4 . 129 A3
ST PAUL'S CRAY 190 A1
St Paul's Cray Rd BR7 ....189 B2
St Pauls Cres NW1 ....71 D1
St Paul's Ct
Clapham SW4 .... 137 D1
Hounslow TW4 .... 129 A2
6 Upper Holloway N19 ....72 A6
St Paul's Dr E15 ....76 B3
St Paul's Girls' Sch 1 W6 .... 112 D2
St Pauls Ho N17 ....34 A3
St Pauls Mews NW1 ...71 D1
St Paul's Pl N1 ....73 B2
St Paul's RC Coll TW16 .... 172 A2
St Paul's RC Prim Sch
Thames Ditton KT7 ... 196 C2
2 Wood Green N22 ...32 B1
St Pauls Rd
Barking IG11 .... 101 A6
Richmond TW9 ....132 B2
St Paul's Rd
Brentford TW8 .... 131 D6
Canonbury N1 ....73 A2
South Norwood CR7 .. 205 A6
Tottenham N17 ....34 A2
St Pauls Rise N13 ....32 D4
St Paul's Sch SW13 . 112 A1
St Paul's Sq BR2 ....187 A1
St Paul's Sta EC2 ....95 A1 242 A2
St Pauls Steiner Sch 22 N1 ....73 B2
St Paul St N1 .... 235 B5
St Paul's Terr SE17 .. 138 D6
St Paul's Twr 14 E10 ...53 D2
St Pauls View WC1 .. 234 A1
St Paul's Way
Finchley N3 ....29 D3
Tower Hamlets E3 ....97 C2
St Paul's Way Com Sch 25 E3 ....97 C2
St Paul's with St Michael's Prim Sch 24 E8 ....96 A6
St Paul's Wood Hill BR5 ....189 D1
St Paul with St Luke CE Prim Sch 18 E3 ....97 B2
St Peter Chanel RC Prim Sch DA14 .... 190 C5
St Peter in Chains RC Inf Sch N8 ....50 A3
St Peter & Paul RC Prim Sch BR5 .... 189 C1
St Peter & St Paul RC Prim Sch EC1 ....94 D3 241 D6
St Peter & St Paul RC Sch CR4 .... 202 D5
St Peter's Alley EC3 . 242 D1
St Peters Ave N12 ....30 C3
St Peter's Ave
Edmonton N18 ....34 A6
37 Hackney E2 ....96 A5
Walthamstow E17 ....54 C5
St Petersburgh Mews W2 .... 245 C6
St Petersburgh Pl W2 .... 113 D6 245 C5
St Peter's CE Prim Sch
15 Chiswick W6 .... 112 A2
9 E1 .... 118 C5
6 Paddington W9 ....91 C3
SE17 ....117 B1 262 C1
SW1 .... 115 B3 258 D5
St Peter's Church Ct N1 .... 234 D5
St Peters Cl BR7 ....189 B3
Ilford IG2 ....57 D5
1 Upper Tooting SW17 .... 158 C2
St Peter's Cl
Barnet EN5 ....12 B6
Bushey WD23 ....8 B3
Hackney E2 ....96 A5
Ruislip HA4 ....62 D6
St Peters Ct
East Molesey KT8 ... 195 C5
New Cross SE4 ....141 B3
28 Stepney E1 ....96 C3
St Peter's Ct
Hendon NW4 ....46 C4
Lewisham SE12 .... 164 D6
St Peter's Gdns SE27 ....160 C1
St Peter's Gr W6 ....112 A2
St Peters Ho
Tottenham Hale N15 ...52 A5
WC1 .... 233 B1
St Peter's Ho
4 SE17 ....139 B6
Stamford Hill N16 ....51 C2
St Peters La BR5 ....190 A1
St Peters Mews N4 ...50 D4
St Peter's Pl W9 ....91 D3
St Peter's Prim Sch CR2 .... 221 C2
St Peter's RC Prim Sch
Dagenham RM9 ....103 B6
Woolwich SE18 .... 122 D2
St Peters Rd KT1 ....176 C1
St Peter's Rd
Chiswick W6 .... 112 A1
Croydon CR0 ....221 B4
East Molesey KT8 ... 195 C5
Edmonton N9 ....18 B3
Isleworth TW1 ....153 B6
Southall UB1 ....85 C2
St Peter's Sq
Chiswick W6 .... 111 D1
Hackney E2 ....96 A5
St Peter's St
Croydon CR2 ....221 B3
Islington N1 ...94 D6 234 D5
St Peter's Street Mews N1 .... 234 D4
St Peter's Terr SW6 . 264 B3
St Peter's Villas 5 W6 ....112 A2
St Peters Way UB3 ...105 B1
St Peter's Way
De Beauvoir Town N1 ...73 C1
Ealing W5 ....87 D2
St Peter's Wharf 8 W6 ....112 A1
St Philip Ho WC1 .... 234 A1
St Philip's Ave KT4 ..216 B6
St Philips Gate KT4 ..216 B6
St Philip Sq 1 SW8 ..137 B3
St Philip's Rd
Dalston E8 ....74 A2
Surbiton KT6 .... 197 D3
St Philip's Sch
Chessington KT9 .... 213 D2
SW7 ....114 A2 256 B3
St Philip St SW8 ....137 B3
St Philip's Way N1 .. 235 B5
St Philomena's RC High Sch SM5 .... 218 C3
St Quentin Ho SW18 .158 B5
St Quentin Rd DA16 . 145 D2
St Quintin Ave W10 ...90 B2
St Quintin Gdns 21 W10 ....90 C2
St Quintin Rd E13 ....99 B5
St Raphaels Ho W13 .109 C5
St Raphael's RC Prim Sch UB5 ....84 B5
St Raphael's Way NW10 ....67 A3
St Regis Cl N10 ....31 B1
St Regis Hts NW3 ....69 D5
St Richards Ct TW10 .153 B1
St Richard's Ho NW1 232 C2
St Richard's with St Andrew's CE Prim Sch TW10 ....153 B1
St Robert Southwell RC Prim Sch NW9 ....45 A3
St Ronan's 2 N3 ....29 C2
St Ronans Cl EN4 .... 2 B5
St Ronans Cres IG8 ...37 A3
St Rule St SW8 ....137 C3
St Savior's CE Inf Sch 3 W5 .... 109 D6
St Saviours SW4 ....137 B1
St Saviour & St Olaves CE Sch SE1 117 B3 262 D5
St Saviour's CE Prim Sch
9 Bow Comm E14 ....97 D2
Camberwell SE24 .... 139 A2
26 Paddington W9 ....91 D3
Walthamstow E17 ....53 B2
St Saviour's Coll SE27 ....183 B6
St Saviours Ct
Harrow HA1 ....42 C4
Muswell Hill N22 ....31 D1
St Saviours Ho 35 SE1 ....118 A4
St Saviour's RC Prim Sch SE13 .... 142 A1
St Saviour's Rd
Clapham Pk SW2 ....160 B6
Thornton Heath CR0 . 205 A3
St Saviour's Wharf SE1 .... 253 D2
St Scholastica's RC Prim Sch 6 E5 ....74 A5
Saints Cl SE27 .... 182 D6
Saints Dr E7 ....77 D3
St Silas Pl NW5 ....71 A2
St Simon's Ave SW15 ....156 C6
St Stephens Ave E17 ..54 A4
St Stephen's Ave
Ealing W13 ....87 B1
Shepherd's Bush W12 .112 B4
St Stephen's CE Jun Sch TW1 ....153 B5
St Stephen's CE Prim Sch
Paddington W2 ....91 C2
17 Shepherd's Bush W12 .... 112 C4
2 St Johns SE8 .... 141 C3
SW8 ....138 B5 270 C4
St Stephens Cl E17 ...53 D4
St Stephen's Cl
Maitland Pk NW5 ....70 D3
NW8 .... 230 B5
Southall UB1 ....85 C2
St Stephen's Cres
Notting Hill W2 ....91 C1
Thornton Heath CR7 . 204 C6
St Stephens Ct
Ealing W13 ....87 B1
Enfield EN1 ....17 C5
Hornsey Vale N8 ....50 B3
St Stephen's Gdns
Notting Hill W2 ....91 C1
4 Putney SW15 ....157 B6
Twickenham TW1 .... 153 C5
St Stephen's Gr SE13 ....142 A2
St Stephens Ho 7 SE17 ....139 B6
St Stephen's Mews 34 W2 ....91 C2
St Stephens Par E6 ...77 C1
St Stephens Prim Sch E6 ....77 C1
St Stephen's RC Prim Sch DA16 .... 146 A3
St Stephens Rd
Barnet EN5 ....12 D6
Upton E6 ....77 C1
Walthamstow E17 ....53 D4
St Stephen's Rd
Bow E3 ....97 B5
Ealing W13 ....87 C1
Enfield EN3 ....6 D6
Hounslow TW3, TW4 . 151 C6
Yiewsley UB7 .... 104 A5
St Stephen's Row EC4 .... 242 C1
St Stephen's Terr SW8 .... 270 C3
St Stephen's Wlk SW7 .... 256 A4
St Swithin's La EC4 ....117 B6 252 C6
St Swithun's Rd SE13 ....164 B6
St Swithun Wells RC Prim Sch HA4 ....62 D5
St Teresa's RC Fst & Mid Sch HA3 ....24 A2
St Teresa's RC Prim Sch SM4 ....202 B3
St Teresa's RC Prim Sch The RM8 ....80 C4
St Theresa Ct E4 ....20 B4
St Theresas Cl E9 ....75 C4
St Theresa's RC Prim Sch N3 ....47 D6
St Theresa's Rd TW14 .... 127 D1
St Thomas a Beckett RC Prim Sch SE2 .... 124 A3
St Thomas Becket RC Prim Sch 4 SE25 .. 206 A3
St Thomas' CE Prim Sch 23 W10 ....91 A3
St Thomas' Cl KT6 ....198 B1
St Thomas Ct
14 Camden Town NW1 ....71 C1
Sidcup DA5 .... 169 C4
11 Walthamstow E10 ...53 D2
St Thomas' Ct HA5 ....23 A2
St Thomas' Dr BR5 ...211 A1
Pinner HA5 ....23 A2
St Thomas Gdns IG1 ...79 A2
St Thomas Ho 2 E1 ...96 D1
St Thomas More Language Coll SW3 .... 114 D2 257 C3
St Thomas More RC Prim Sch
Bexley DA7 ....147 B3
SE9 .... 144 A2
St Thomas More RC Sch
SE9 .... 166 C5
Wood Green N22 ....32 C3
St Thomas of Canterbury RC Prim Sch
Mitcham CR4 .... 203 A6
SW6 ....135 B5 264 C4
St Thomas Rd
Newham E16 ....99 A1
Osidge N14 ....15 D4
St Thomas' Rd W4 ...133 A6
St Thomas's Gdns NW5 ....71 A2
St Thomas's Hospl SE1 ....116 B3 260 C6
St Thomas's Pl 20 E9 ..74 C1
St Thomas's Rd
Dagenham NW10 ....89 C6
Highbury N4, N5 ....72 C5
St Thomas's Sq E9 ....74 C1
St Thomas St SE1 ....117 B5 252 D3
St Thomas's Way SW6 ....135 B5 264 D4
St Thomas the Apostle Coll SE15 .... 140 C4
St Timothy's Mews 3 BR1 ....187 B2
St Ursula Gr HA5 ....41 A4
St Ursula Rd UB1 ....85 C1
St Ursula's Convent Sch SE10 ....142 B5
St Vincent Cl SE27 ... 182 D5
St Vincent De Paul Ho 24 E1 ....96 C2
St Vincent De Paul RC Prim Sch SW1 ....115 C3 259 B6
St Vincent Ho SE1 ... 263 C6
St Vincent Rd TW2 ...152 A5
St Vincents La NW7 ...28 C6
St Vincent's Nursing Home HA5 ....39 D6
St Vincents RC Prim Sch SE9 .... 188 A6
St Vincent's RC Prim Sch
Acton W3 .... 110 D6
Dagenham RM8 ....80 C6
London NW7 ....28 C5
Marylebone W1 ....93 A2 238 B3
St Vincent St W1 .... 238 B3
St Wilfrid's Cl EN4 ....14 C6
St Wilfrid's Rd EN4 ....14 C6
St William of York Prim Sch SE23 .... 163 A3
St Winefride's Ave E12 ....78 B3
St Winefride's RC Prim Sch E12 ....78 B3
St Winifred's RC Inf Sch SE12 .... 164 C6
St Winifred's RC Jun Sch SE12 .... 164 D4
St Winifred's Rd TW11 ....175 B4
Sakura Dr N22 ....31 D2
Sala Ho SE3 ....143 B1
Salamanca Pl SE1 .. 260 C3
Salamanca St SE1, SE11 ....116 B2 260 C3
Salamander Cl KT2 ..175 C5
Salamander Quay KT1 .... 175 D2
Salcombe Dr
Dagenham RM6 ....59 B3
North Cheam SM4 ... 200 D1
Salcombe Gdns
Clapham SW4 ....137 B1
Mill Hill NW7 ....28 C4
Salcombe Ho 6 SE23 ....162 C2
Salcombe Lo NW5 ....71 A4
Salcombe Pk IG10 ....21 D6
Salcombe Prep Sch (Infant Dept) N14 ...15 B6
Salcombe Prep Sch (Junior Dept) 1 N14 ....15 B4
Salcombe Rd
Ashford TW15 .... 148 A1
23 Stoke Newington N16 ....73 C3
Walthamstow E17 ....53 B2
Salcombe Villas 13 TW10 ....154 A6
Salcombe Way
Hayes UB4 ....83 C4
Ruislip HA4 ....62 A6
Salcot N4 ....72 B6
Salcott Rd
Wallington CR0 ....220 B4
Wandsworth SW11 .. 158 D6
Salehurst Cl HA3 ....44 A4
Salehurst Rd SE4 ....163 B5
Salem Ho 13 E9 ....74 D2
Salem Pl CR0 ....221 A5
Salem Rd W2 .... 113 D6 245 D6
Sale Pl W2 ....92 C1 237 A2
Salesian Coll SW11 .... 136 C4 267 A1
Sale St E2 ....96 A3
Salford Ho 5 E14 ....120 A2
Salford Rd SW12, SW2 .... 159 D3

Salhouse CI SE28 . . . . . . .102 C1
Salisbury Ave
 Barking IG11 . . . . .79 C1
 Cheam SM1, SM2. . . . .217 B2
 Hendon N3. . . . . .47 B6
Salisbury CI 2 . . . . . . .262 C4
 Worcester Pk KT4 . . . .215 D5
Salisbury Ct
16 Bermondsey
  SE16 . . . . .118 A3
 Chiswick W4 . . . . .111 C2
 EC4. . . . . .241 C1
 Edgware HA8. . . . . .26 B6
 Enfield EN2 . . . . .5 B1
 Finchley N3 . . . . .29 B1
 Hackney E9 . . . . .75 A3
 Northolt UB5 . . . . .63 D3
Salisbury Gdns
5 Buckhurst Hill
  IG9 . . . . .21 D2
 Wimbledon SW19 . . . .179 A3
Salisbury Hall Gdns
 E4 . . . . .35 C4
Salisbury Ho
2 Islington N1 . . . . .72 D2
 Islington N1. . . . . . . .234 C6
3 Poplar E14 . . . . .97 D1
2 Ruislip HA4 . . . . .40 C1
 Stanmore HA7 . . . . .25 A4
8 Wallington SM6 . . . .219 B3
 Westminster SW1 . . . .259 D2
 Wimbledon SW19 . . . .156 D1
Salisbury Lower Sch
 N9 . . . . .18 C4
Salisbury Mans
 Edmonton N9 . . . . .18 A1
 Harringay N4, N15. . . . .50 D4
Salisbury Mews
 Bromley Comm BR2. . . .210 A4
 Fulham SW6. . . . . . . .264 C3
Salisbury PI
 Camberwell SW9 . . . . .138 D5
 Marylebone W1 . . . . . .237 C4
Salisbury Prim Sch 1
 E12. . . . . .78 A3
Salisbury Rd
 Barnet EN5 . . . . .1 A2
 Bromley Comm BR2 . . . .210 A4
 Chingford E4 . . . . .19 C1
 Croydon SE25. . . . . . . .206 A3
 Dagenham RM10. . . . . . .81 D2
 East Bedfont TW14 . . . .149 A5
 Enfield EN3 . . . . .7 B6
 Feltham TW13 . . . . . . .150 C3
 Forest Gate E7 . . . . .77 A2
 Harringay N4 . . . . .50 D4
 Harrow HA1 . . . . .42 B4
 Hounslow TW4 . . . . . . .128 C2
 Ilford IG3. . . . . .79 C6
 Kingston u T KT3 . . . . .199 B6
 Leyton E10 . . . . .76 A6
 Old Bexley DA5 . . . . . .169 C3
 Pinner HA5 . . . . .40 A5
 Plashet E12 . . . . .78 A3
 Richmond TW9 . . . . . . .132 A1
 Southall UB2 . . . . .107 A2
 Tottenham N22 . . . . . . .32 D1
 Wallington SM5. . . . . .218 D2
 Walthamstow E17 . . . . .54 A4
 West Ealing W13 . . . . .109 B4
 Wimbledon SW19 . . . .179 A3
 Worcester Pk KT4 . . . .215 C5
Salisbury Sq EC4 . . . . . .241 B1
Salisbury St
10 Acton W3 . . . . .111 A4
 NW8. . . . . .237 A5
Salisbury Terr SE15 . . . .140 C2
Salisbury Upper Sch
 N9 . . . . .18 C4
Salisbury Wlk N19 . . . . . .71 C6
Salix CI TW16 . . . . .172 B3
Salix Ct N3 . . . . .29 C4
Salliesfield TW2 . . . . . . .152 B5
Sally Murray CI E12 . . . . .78 C4
Salmen Rd E13 . . . . .98 D5
Salmond CI HA7 . . . . .25 A4
Salmon La E14 . . . . .97 A1
Salmon Rd DA17 . . . . . . .125 C1
Salmons Brook Ho
 EN2 . . . . .4 D2
Salmons Rd
 Chessington KT9 . . . . .214 A2
 Edmonton N9. . . . . .18 A3

Salmon St
 Kingsbury NW9 . . . . . . .45 A2
13 Poplar E14 . . . . .97 B1
Salomons Rd 2 E13 . . .99 C2
Salop Rd E17 . . . . .52 D3
Saltash CI SM1 . . . . . . .217 A3
Saltash Rd DA16 . . . . . .146 C4
Saltcoats Rd W4 . . . . . .111 C4
Saltcroft CI HA9 . . . . . . .44 D1
Saltdene N4 . . . . .50 B1
Salter CI HA2 . . . . .63 A8
Salterford Rd SW17 . . .181 A4
Salter Ho 8 SW16 . . .181 D6
Saltern Ct IG11 . . . . . . .102 B4
Salter Rd
 Rotherhithe SE16. . . . .118 D5
 SE16. . . . . .119 C6
Salters' Hall Ct EC4 . . .252 C6
Salter's Hill SE19 . . . . .183 B5
Salters Rd
 North Kensington
  W10 . . . . .90 D3
 Walthamstow E17 . . . . .54 C2
Salter St
 College Pk NW10. . . . . .90 A4
 Poplar E14 . . . . .119 C6
Salterton Rd N7 . . . . . . .72 B5
Salt Hill CI UB8 . . . . .24 A1
Saltley CI E6. . . . . .100 A1
Saltoun Rd SW2,
SW9. . . . . .138 C1
Saltram CI N15 . . . . .51 D5
Saltram Cres W9 . . . . . . .91 C4
Saltwell St E14 . . . . .119 C6
Saltwood Gr SE17 . . . . .262 C1
Saltwood Ho 19
 SE15. . . . . .140 C6
Salusbury Prim Sch
 NW6. . . . . .91 A6
Salusbury Rd NW6 . . . . .91 A6
Salutation Rd SE10 . . . .120 C2
Salvador SW17 . . . . . . .180 D5
Salvia Gdns UB6 . . . . . . .87 A5
Salvin Rd SW15 . . . . . .134 D2
Salway CI IG8 . . . . .37 A3
Salway Ho E10 . . . . .75 D6
Salway PI E15 . . . . .76 C2
Salway Rd E15. . . . . .76 B2
Salween Ho 2 N16 . . . .73 B4
Samantha CI E17 . . . . . . .53 B2
Samantha Ct E11 . . . . . . .54 C2
Sam Bartram CI SE7 . . .121 C1
Sambrooke Ct EN1. . . . . .17 D6
Sambrook Ho E21 . . . . . . .96 C2
Sambruck Mews
 SE6. . . . . .163 D3
Samels Ct W6 . . . . .112 A1
Samford Ho N1. . . . . . . .234 A4
Samford St NW8 . . . . . .237 A5
Samira Ct 1 E17 . . . . . . .53 C3
Sam Manners Ho 7
 SE10. . . . . .120 C1
Sam March Ho 5
 E14. . . . . .98 B1
Samos Rd SE20 . . . . . . .184 B1
Sampson Ave EN5 . . . . .12 D6
Sampson CI DA17 . . . . .125 A3
Sampson Ct TW17 . . . . .193 A4
Sampson St E1. . . . . . . .118 A5
Samson Ct 5 DA17 . . .125 C2
Samson Ho SE18. . . . . .123 A2
Samson St E13 . . . . .99 C5
Samuel CI Bushey HA7 . . .25 A4
 SE14. . . . . .140 D6
 Shoreditch E8 . . . . .95 D6
 Woolwich SE18 . . . . . .122 A2
Samuel Ct
 Beckenham BR3. . . . . .207 D6
 Shoreditch N1 . . . . .95 C4
Samuel Gray Gdns
 KT2 . . . . .175 D2
Samuel Ho
15 Shoreditch E8. . . . . . .95 D6
3 West Norwood
  SE27 . . . . .182 D6
Samuel Johnson CI
 SW16. . . . . .182 B6
Samuel Jones Ind Est 1
 SE15. . . . . .139 C5
Samuel Lewis Bldgs
 N1. . . . . .72 C2
Samuel Lewis Trust
Dwellings
6 Camberwell SE5. . . . .139 A4

Samuel Lewis Trust
Dwellings continued
 Chelsea SW3 . . . . .257 A3
 Walham Green
  SW6 . . . . .135 C5 265 B4
 West Kensington W14 254 B4
Samuel Lewis Trust Est
 N15. . . . . .51 C3
Samuel Lo N3 . . . . .29 B1
Samuel Rhodes Sch
 N1 . . . . .94 C1 234 A6
Samuel Richardson Ho
 W14 . . . . .254 C3
Samuel's CI 2 W6. . . . .112 C2
Samuel St SE15 . . . . . . .139 D5
 Woolwich SE18 . . . . . .122 B2
Sancroft CI NW2 . . . . . . .68 B5
Sancroft Ho SE11. . . . . .260 D2
Sancroft Rd HA3. . . . . . .25 A1
Sancroft St
 SE11. . . . . . . .149 B1 260 D2
Sanctuary Mews 18
 E8. . . . . .73 D2
Sanctuary Rd TW6 . . . . .148 C5
Sanctuary St SE1 . . . . . .252 B2
Sanctuary The
 Morden SM4 . . . . .201 C3
 Sidcup DA5. . . . . .168 D5
35 Wapping E1. . . . . . .118 B5
 Westminster
  SW1 . . . . . . .115 D3 259 D6
Sandale CI N16 . . . . .73 B5
Sandall CI W5 . . . . .88 A3
Sandall Ho 7 E3 . . . . . . .97 A5
Sandall Rd Ealing W5. . . .88 A3
 Kentish Town NW5. . . . .71 C2
Sandal Rd
 Edmonton N18. . . . . . . .34 A5
 New Malden KT3 . . . . .199 C5
Sandal St E15 . . . . .98 C6
Sandalwood CI
 Borehamwood EN5 . . . .11 D6
 1 E1 . . . . .97 A3
Sandalwood Dr HA4 . . . .39 A2
Sandalwood Ho
 DA15 . . . . .167 D1
6 Hampstead NW3 . . . .69 D2
Sandalwood Rd
 TW13 . . . . .150 B1
Sandbach PI SE18 . . . . .123 A1
Sandbourne
4 Kensington W11. . . . . .91 C1
17 Paddington NW8. . . . .91 D6
Sandbourne Ave
 SW19 . . . . .179 C4
Sandbourne Rd SE4. .141 A3
Sandbrook CI NW7 . . . . .27 B4
Sandbrook Rd N16 . . . . .73 C5
Sandby Ct BR3. . . . . . . .185 B2
Sandby Gn SE9 . . . . . . .144 A2
Sandby Ho
 6 Camberwell SE5. . . .139 C4
 6 Kilburn NW6 . . . . . . .91 C6
Sandcroft CI N13 . . . . . . .32 D4
Sandells Ave
 Ashford TW15 . . . . . . .171 A6
 Ashford TW15 . . . . . . .171 A6
Sandell St SE1. . . . . . . .251 A2
Sanderling Ct
20 SE8 . . . . .141 B6
 Woolwich SE28 . . . . . .124 C6
Sanders CI TW12 . . . . . .174 A5
Sanders Ho
 Streatham SW16 . . . . .182 A4
 WC1 . . . . .234 A2
Sanders La NW7 . . . . . . .28 C3
Sanderson CI NW5 . . . . .71 B4
Sanderson Ho 7
 SE8 . . . . .119 B1
Sanderson Sq BR1 . . . . .210 C6
Sanderstead Ave
 NW2 . . . . .69 A6
Sanderstead CI
 SW12 . . . . .159 C4
Sanderstead Rd
 South Croydon CR2 . . . .221 B1
 Walthamstow E10. . . . . .53 A1
Sanders Way 3 N19 . . . .49 D1
Sandfield WC1. . . . . . . .233 B1
Sandfield Gdns CR7. .204 D6
Sandfield PI CR7 . . . . . .205 A6
Sandfield Rd CR7 . . . . . .204 D6
Sandford Ave N22. . . . . .33 A2
Sandford CI E6 . . . . .100 B3

Sandford Ct Barnet EN5 1 D2
 Stamford Hill N16 . . . . .51 C1
Sandford Rd
 Bexley DA7. . . . . .147 A2
 BR2 . . . . .209 A5
 Newham E6. . . . . .100 B3
Sandford Row SE17 . . .262 D2
Sandford St SW6 . . . . . .265 D3
Sandgate Ho
14 Beckenham BR3 . .185 C3
 Ealing W5. . . . . .87 C2
10 Hackney E5. . . . . . . .74 B4
Sandgate La SW17,
 SW18 . . . . .158 C3
Sandgate Rd DA16 . . . .146 C5
Sandgate St SE15 . . . . .140 B6
Sandgate Trad Est
 SE15. . . . . .140 B6
Sandham Point 10
 SE18 . . . . .122 D2
Sandhills CRO, SM6. . .219 D4
Sandhills Mdw
 TW17 . . . . .193 A2
Sandhills The SW10 . .266 B6
Sandhurst Ave
 Harrow HA2. . . . . .41 D3
 Tolworth KT5 . . . . .198 D2
Sandhurst CI
 Queensbury NW9 . . . . . .44 C5
 South Croydon CR2 . . . .221 C1
Sandhurst Ct SW2 . . . . .138 A1
Sandhurst Dr IG3. . . . . . .79 D4
Sandhurst Ho 13
 SE6. . . . . .164 C3
Sandhurst Mkt SE6 . . .164 A3
Sandhurst Rd
 Bexley DA5. . . . . .168 D6
 Catford SE6 . . . . .164 B3
 DA15 . . . . .168 A1
 Ponders End N9 . . . . . . .18 D5
 Queensbury HA8, NW9 .44 C6
Sandhurst Way CR2. .221 C1
Sandifer Dr NW2 . . . . . . .68 D5
Sandiford Rd SM3 . . . . .217 B6
Sandiland Cres BR2 . . .224 D6
Sandilands CRO. 222 A5
Sandilands Rd
 SW6 . . . . .135 D4 265 D2
Sandilands Sta CRO. .221 D6
Sandison St SE15 . . . . .140 A2
Sandland St WC1. . . . . .240 D3
Sandling Rise SE9 . . . . .166 C5
Sandlings CI SE15. . . . .140 B3
Sandlings The
 Tottenham N22 . . . . . . .50 D6
8 Wood Green N22 . . . .32 C1
Sandmartin Way
 CR4. . . . . .203 A1
Sandmere Rd SW4 . . . . .138 A1
Sandon CI KT10. . . . . . .196 B1
Sandon Rd IG3. . . . . .80 A5
Sandow Commercial Est
 UB3 . . . . .105 D3
Sandow Cres UB3 . . . . .105 D3
Sandown Ave KT10. . . .212 A3
Sandown CI TW5. . . . . .128 A4
Sandown Gate KT10. .212 B5
Sandown Ho
2 Acton Green W4 . . . .111 A1
 Ealing W5. . . . . .87 C2
 Penge SE26 . . . . .184 B4
Sandown Rd
 Croydon SE25. . . . . . . .206 B4
 Esher KT10 . . . . .212 A4
Sandown Way UB5. . . . . .63 B3
Sandpiper CI
 Rotherhithe SE16. . . . .119 B4
Sandpiper Ct
10 Cubitt Town E14 . . .120 A3
 1 SE8 . . . . .141 C5
Sandpiper Rd SM1 . . . . .217 B2
Sandpiper Terr IG5 . . . . .56 D6
Sandpit PI SE7 . . . . .122 A1
Sandpit Rd BR1. . . . . . .186 C5
Sandpits Rd
 Richmond TW10. . . . . . .153 D2
 South Croydon CRO 222 D4
Sandra Cl
 Hounslow TW3. . . . . . .151 D6
 Tottenham N17 . . . . . . .33 A2

Sandra Ho KT8. . . . . . . .196 B4
Sandridge CI
 Hadley Wood EN4. . . . . .2 C6
 Harrow HA1. . . . . .42 C5
Sandridge St 3 N19 . .71 C6
Sandringham Ave
 SW20 . . . . .179 A1
Sandringham CI
 Enfield EN1 . . . . .5 C3
 Ilford IG6. . . . . .57 A6
 1 Putney SW19 . . . . . .156 D3
Sandringham Cres
 HA2. . . . . .63 D6
Sandringham Ct
3 Beckenham BR3 . .186 A2
6 Edgware HA8. . . . . . .26 D6
 Hillingdon UB10. . . . . . .83 A3
 Kingston u T KT2 . . . . .176 A2
 Marylebone W1 . . . . . .239 B1
 Putney SW15. . . . . . . .156 D5
5 Rotherhithe SE16. . .118 D5
 St John's Wood W9 . . . .229 B1
 2 Twickenham TW1 . . .153 A3
Sandringham Dr
 Ashford TW15 . . . . . . .170 A6
 DA16 . . . . .145 C3
Sandringham Flats
 WC2 . . . . .249 D6
Sandringham Gdns
 Cranford TW5 . . . . . . .128 A4
 East Molesey KT8 . . . .195 C5
 Finchley N12 . . . . .30 B4
 Hornsey Vale N8 . . . . . .50 A3
 Ilford IG6. . . . . .57 A6
Sandringham Ho
 Richmond TW10. . . . . . .154 A6
 W14 . . . . .254 A4
Sandringham Lo
 BR6. . . . . .226 C4
Sandringham Mews
 8 Ealing W5. . . . . . . .109 D6
 Hampton TW12 . . . . . .173 B2
Sandringham Prim Sch
 1 E7 . . . . .77 C3
Sandringham Rd
 Barking IG11 . . . . .79 D2
 BR1 . . . . .187 A5
 Dalston E8 . . . . .73 D3
 Forest Gate E7. . . . . . . .77 C3
 Golders Green NW11. . . .47 A2
 Leytonstone E10 . . . . . .54 B3
 Northolt UB5 . . . . .63 C1
 Stanwell TW19, TW6 . .148 A6
 Thornton Heath CR0 . . .205 A4
 Tottenham N22 . . . . . . .33 A1
 Willesden NW2 . . . . . . .68 B2
 Worcester Pk KT4 . . . .216 A5
Sandrock PI CR0. . . . . .222 D4
Sandrock Rd SE13 . . . .141 C2
SANDS END 136 A2
Sands End La
 SW6 . . . . .135 D4 265 D2
Sandstone TW9. . . . . . .132 C5
Sandstone La E11 . . . . . .76 D6
Sandstone PI N19. . . . . .71 B6
Sandtoft Rd SE7 . . . . . .143 B6
Sandways 2 TW9 . . . . .132 C4
Sandwell Cres 2
 NW6. . . . . .69 C2
Sandwell Mans 3
 NW6. . . . . .69 C2
Sandwich Ho
15 Rotherhithe
  SE16 . . . . .118 C4
 WC1. . . . . .233 A1
Sandwich St
 WC1 . . . . .94 A4 233 A1
Sandwick CI NW7. . . . . . .28 A3
Sandy Bury BR6 . . . . . .227 B5
Sandycombe Ctr
 TW9 . . . . .132 C2
Sandycombe Rd
 East Bedfont TW14 . . . .150 A3
 Richmond TW9 . . . . . . .132 C3
Sandycoombe Rd
 TW1 . . . . .153 C5
Sandycroft SE2. . . . . . .146 A6
Sandy Dr TW14 . . . . . . .149 C3
Sandy Hill Ave SE18 . . .122 D1
Sandy Hill La SE18 . . . .122 D2
Sandyhill Rd IG1. . . . . . .78 B4
Sandy Hill Rd SE18 . . . .122 D1
Sandy La
 Belmont SM2 . . . . . . .217 A1
 BR5 . . . . .190 D2

Sandy La *continued*
Eastbury HA6 ... 22 A6
Harrow HA3 ... 44 C3
Mitcham CR4 ... 181 A2
Richmond TW10 ... 153 D2
Teddington KT8, TW11 ... 175 B3
Walton-on-T KT12 ... 194 C3
Sandy Lane N SM6 ... 219 D3
Sandy Lane S SM6 ... 219 C1
Sandy Lo N6 ... 49 C2
Sandymount Ave HA7 25 D5
Sandy Rd NW3 ... 69 D6
Sandy Ridge BR7 ... 188 C4
Sandy's Row E1 ... 243 B3
Sandy Way
Croydon CR0 ... 223 B5
Walton-on-T KT12 ... 193 D1
Sanford La 3 N16 ... 73 D6
Sanford St SE14, SE8 ... 141 A6
Sanford Terr N16 ... 73 D5
Sanford Wlk SE14 ... 141 A6
4 Stoke Newington N16 ... 73 D6
Sangam Cl UB2 ... 107 A3
Sanger Ave KT9 ... 214 B4
Sangley Rd
Catford SE6 ... 164 A3
South Norwood SE25 . 205 C5
Sangora Rd 17 SW11 ... 136 B1
San Ho 29 E9 ... 74 D2
Sankey Ho 22 E2 ... 96 C5
Sansom Rd E11 ... 76 D6
Sansom St
Camberwell SE5 ... 139 B4
SE5 ... 139 B5
Sans Wlk EC1 .. 94 D3 241 C6
Santana SE18 ... 144 D5
Santley Ho SE1 ... 251 B1
Santley St SW4 ... 138 B1
Santos Rd SW18 ... 157 C6
Sapcote Trad Ctr NW10 ... 67 D2
Saperton Wlk SE11 . 260 D4
Saphora Cl BR6 ... 227 B3
Sapperton Ct EC1 ... 242 A6
Sapphire Cl
Dagenham RM8 ... 58 C1
Newham E6 ... 100 C1
Sapphire Ct 13 E1 ... 118 A6
Sapphire Rd
Rotherhithe SE8 ... 119 A2
Willesden NW10 ... 67 A1
Saracen Cl CR0 ... 205 B3
Saracen's Head Yd EC2 ... 243 B1
Saracen St E14 ... 97 C1
Sarah Bonnell Sch E15 ... 76 C2
Sarah Ct UB5 ... 85 B6
Sarah Ho
Roehampton SW15 ... 133 D1
8 Stepney E1 ... 96 B1
Sarah Swift Ho SE1 . 252 D2
Sarah Turnbull Ho 2 SE18 ... 122 B2
Sara Lane Ct 31 N1 ... 95 C5
Saratoga Rd E5 ... 74 C4
Sardeson Ho 13 SW27 ... 182 D5
Sardinia Ho WC2 ... 240 C1
Sardinia St WC2 ... 240 C2
Sargents Hill N2 ... 30 C2
Sarita Cl HA3 ... 24 B1
Sarjant Path SW19 ... 156 D2
Sark Cl TW5 ... 129 C5
Sark Ho
9 Canonbury N1 ... 73 A2
Enfield EN3 ... 6 D5
Sark Twr SE28 ... 123 A4
Sark Wlk E16 ... 99 B1
Sarnersfield Ho SE15 ... 140 B6
Sarnes Ct 4 N11 ... 31 B6
Sarnesfield Rd EN2 ... 5 B2
Sarratt Ho 6 W10 ... 90 C2
Sarre Rd NW2 ... 69 B3
Sarsden Bldgs W1 ... 238 B1
Sarsen Ave TW3 ... 129 C3
Sarsfeld Rd SW12, SW17 ... 158 D3
Sarsfield Rd UB6 ... 87 C5
Sartor Rd SE15 ... 140 D1
Sarum Hall Sch NW3 ... 70 C1
Sarum Ho W11 ... 244 D5
Sarwan Ho 1 E7 ... 77 C1
Sassoon 4 NW9 ... 27 D2
Sassoon Ho SE15 ... 140 C3
Satanita Cl E16 ... 99 D1
Satchell Mead NW9 ... 27 D2
Satchwell Rd 17 E2 ... 96 A4
Satin Ct NW9 ... 45 D5
Saturn Ho 4 E3 ... 97 C6
Saul Ct 4 SE15 ... 139 D6
Sauls Gn E11 ... 76 C5
Saunders Cl Ilford IG1 57 B1
14 Limehouse E14 ... 119 B6
Saunders Ho 11 SW2 ... 160 C3
Saunders Ness Rd E14 ... 120 B2
Saunders Rd
Hillingdon UB10 ... 82 B6
Plumstead Comm SE18 ... 123 D1
Saunders St SE11 ... 261 A4
Saunders Way SE28 ... 124 B6
Saunderton Rd HA0 ... 65 B3
Saunton Ave UB3 ... 127 D5
Saunton Cl UB1 ... 108 A6
Savage Gdns EC3 ... 253 B6
Newham E6 ... 100 B1
Savana N16 ... 73 C6
Savannah Cl 9 SE15 ... 139 D5
Savera Cl UB2 ... 106 C3
Savernake Ct HA7 ... 25 B4
Savernake Ho N4 ... 51 B2
Savernake Rd
Enfield N9 ... 18 A5
Maitland Pk NW3 ... 70 D4
Savery Dr KT6 ... 197 C2
Savile Cl
New Malden KT3 ... 199 C4
Thames Ditton KT7 ... 197 A1
Savile Gdns CR0 ... 221 D6
Savill Ct IG8 ... 36 D4
Saville Cres TW15 ... 171 B4
Saville Ho E16 ... 122 D5
Saville Rd
Bedford Pk W4 ... 111 B3
Dagenham RM6 ... 59 B2
Newham E16 ... 122 A5
Twickenham TW1 ... 152 D3
Saville Row Enfield EN3 . 6 D3
Hayes BR2 ... 208 D1
W1 ... 115 C6 249 A6
Savill Gdns SW20 ... 200 A6
Savill Ho 2 SW4 ... 159 D5
Savill Row IG8 ... 36 D4
Savin Lo 7 SM2 ... 218 A1
Savona Cl 16 SW19 ... 178 D3
Savona Ct SW20 ... 178 D2
Savona St SW8 ... 137 C5 269 A3
Savoy Ave UB3 ... 105 C1
Savoy Circus W3 ... 111 D6
Savoy Cl Edgware HA8 ... 26 C5
Newham E15 ... 98 C6
Savoy Ct
Earl's Ct SW5 ... 255 B4
Strand WC2 ... 250 B5
Savoy Hill WC2 ... 250 C5
Savoy Mews SW9 ... 138 A2
Savoy Par EN1 ... 5 C2
Savoy Pier WC2 ... 250 C5
Savoy Pl WC2 ... 116 B6 250 C5
Savoy Row WC2 ... 250 C6
Savoy St WC2 ... 116 B6 250 C5
Savoy Stps WC2 ... 250 C5
Savoy Way WC2 ... 250 C5
Sawbill Cl UB4 ... 84 D2
Sawkins Cl SW19 ... 157 A2
Sawley Rd W12 ... 112 A5
Sawmill Yd E3 ... 97 A6
Sawtry Cl SM5 ... 202 C2
Sawyer Cl N9 ... 18 A2
Sawyer Ho 15 SE21 ... 183 C6
Sawyer's Hill TW10 ... 154 B4
Sawyers Lawn W13 ... 87 A1
Sawyer St SE1 ... 117 A4 252 A2
Saxby Rd SW2 ... 160 A4
Saxham Rd IG11 ... 101 D5
Saxlingham Rd E4 ... 20 B1
Saxon Ave TW13 ... 151 B2
Saxon Bsns Ctr SW19 ... 180 A2
Saxonbury Ave TW16 ... 172 B1
Saxonbury Cl CR4 ... 202 B6
Saxonbury Ct
16 Kentish Town N7 ... 71 D3
2 Lower Holloway N7 ... 72 A3
Saxonbury Gdns KT6 ... 197 C1
Saxon Cl
Hillingdon UB8 ... 82 A2
Surbiton KT6 ... 197 D3
Walthamstow E17 ... 53 C2
Saxoncroft Ho SW16 ... 159 D1
Saxon Ct
Colney Hatch N12 ... 30 C5
4 Edgware HA8 ... 26 D5
Saxon Dr W3 ... 88 D2
Saxonfield Cl SW2 ... 160 B4
Saxon Gdns UB1 ... 107 A6
Saxon Hall W2 ... 245 C5
Saxon Ho
4 Clapham SW4 ... 137 D1
Feltham TW13 ... 151 B2
Saxon Prim Sch TW17 ... 192 C4
Saxon Rd
Ashford TW15 ... 171 B4
Bow E3 ... 97 B5
Bromley BR1 ... 186 D3
Ilford IG1 ... 78 D3
Kingston u T KT2 ... 176 A2
Newham E6 ... 100 B3
Southall UB1 ... 107 A6
South Norwood SE25 ... 205 B4
Tottenham N22 ... 32 D2
Wembley HA9 ... 67 A5
Saxon Terr SE6 ... 163 B2
Saxon Way N14 ... 15 D5
Saxon Wlk DA14 ... 190 C4
Saxony Par UB3 ... 83 A2
Saxton Cl SE13 ... 142 B2
Saxville Rd BR5 ... 190 B1
Sayer Ho SE4 ... 141 A1
Sayers Ho 4 N2 ... 30 B1
Sayer's Wlk TW10 ... 154 B4
Sayesbury La N18 ... 34 A5
Sayes Court St SE8 ... 141 B6
Sayes Ct SE8 ... 141 B6
Sayline Ct CR0 ... 221 B5
Scadbury Gdns BR5 ... 190 A1
Scadbury Park★ BR7 ... 189 D4
Scads Hill Cl BR6 ... 211 D3
Scafell NW1 ... 232 A2
Scala St W1 ... 239 B4
Scales Rd N17 ... 52 A6
Scampston Mews 5 W10 ... 90 D1
Scandrett St 38 E1 ... 118 B5
Scarba Wlk N1 ... 73 B2
Scarborough Rd
East Bedfont TW6 ... 149 A5
Finsbury Pk N4 ... 50 C1
Leytonstone E11 ... 54 B1
Ponders End N9 ... 18 C4
Scarborough St E1 . 243 D1
Scarbrook Rd CR0 ... 221 A5
Scardale Ho 12 E5 ... 74 B6
Scarle Rd HA0 ... 65 D2
Scarlet Rd SE6 ... 164 C1
Scarlette Manor Wlk 10 SE24 ... 160 C4
Scarsbrook Ho 2 SW2 ... 160 C5
Scarsbrook Rd SE3 . 143 D2
Scarsdale Pl W8 ... 255 C6
Scarsdale Rd HA2 ... 64 A5
Scarsdale Villas W8 ... 113 C3 255 B5
Scarth Rd SW13 ... 133 D2
Scawen Cl SM5 ... 219 A4
Scawen Rd SE8 ... 119 A1
Scawfell St E2 ... 95 D5
Scaynes Link N12 ... 29 C6
Sceptre Ho 10 E1 ... 96 C3
Sceptre Rd E2 ... 96 C4
Schiller International Univ SE1 ... 116 C5 251 A3
Schofield Wlk SE3 ... 143 A5
Sch of Pharmacy WC1 ... 94 A3 240 B6
Sch of the Islamic Republic of Iran The 6 NW6 ... 91 C5
Scholars Cl EN5 ... 1 A1
Scholars Ct 5 N19 ... 49 D1
Scholars Ho 6 E4 ... 20 B3
Scholars Rd
Chingford E4 ... 20 B3
Streatham SW12 ... 159 C3
Scholefield Rd N19 ... 71 D6
Scholey Ho SW11 ... 136 C2
Schomberg Ho SW1 259 D4
Schonfeld Sq N16 ... 51 B1
School App 21 E2 ... 95 C4
Schoolbank Rd SE10 ... 120 D2
School Bell Cloisters 17 E3 ... 97 A5
Schoolbell Mews 18 E3 ... 97 A5
School Cotts
Bromley BR1 ... 187 A3
Sidcup DA14 ... 190 C5
School Flats SW8 ... 270 A1
School Ho SE1 ... 263 A4
Schoolhouse La E1 . 118 D6
School House La TW11 ... 175 C3
Schoolhouse Yd 9 SE18 ... 122 D1
School La
Lower Halliford TW17 ... 192 D2
Pinner HA5 ... 41 A5
Surbiton KT6 ... 198 B1
Teddington KT1 ... 175 C2
School Pas
3 Kingston u T KT1 ... 176 B1
Southall UB1 ... 107 B6
School Rd
Ashford TW15 ... 170 D4
Becontree NW10 ... 89 B3
BR7 ... 189 A3
Dagenham RM10 ... 103 D6
East Molesey KT8 ... 196 B5
Hampton TW12 ... 174 A4
Hounslow TW3 ... 130 A2
Ilford E12 ... 78 B4
Littleton TW15 ... 170 D3
Teddington KT1 ... 175 C2
School Road Ave TW12 ... 174 A4
School Sq SE10 ... 120 D3
Schoolway N12 ... 30 B4
School Way RM8 ... 80 C5
School Wlk TW16 ... 193 D6
Schooner Cl
Barking IG11 ... 102 B4
Cubitt Town E14 ... 120 B3
1 Rotherhithe SE16 . 118 D4
Schubert Rd
Elstree WD6 ... 9 D5
Putney SW15 ... 157 B6
Science Mus★ SW7 ... 114 B3 256 C5
Scilly Isles KT10 ... 212 C6
Sclater St E1 ... 243 D6
Scoles Cres SW2 ... 160 C3
Scope Way KT1 ... 198 A5
Scoresby St SE1 ... 251 C3
Scoresdale SE19 ... 183 C2
Scorton Ave UB6 ... 87 A5
Scorton Ho 2 N1 ... 95 C5
Scotch Comm W13 ... 87 B2
Scotch Ho SW1 ... 114 D4 247 C1
Scoter Cl IG8 ... 37 B3
Scoter Ct 23 SE8 ... 141 B6
Scot Gr HA5 ... 22 D3
Scotia Bldg 10 E1 ... 118 D6
Scotia Ct 3 SE16 ... 118 C3
Scotia Rd 24 SW2 ... 160 C4
Scotland Gn N17 ... 33 D1
Scotland Green Rd EN3 ... 18 D6
Scotland Green Rd N EN3 ... 7 A1
Scotland Pl SW1 ... 250 A3
Scotland Rd IG9 ... 21 C3
Scotney Cl BR6 ... 226 C4
Scotney Ho E9 ... 74 C2
Scots Cl TW19 ... 148 A3
Scotsdale Cl
Belmont SM3 ... 217 A1
BR5 ... 211 C5
Scotsdale Rd SE12 ... 165 B6
Scotson Ho SE11 ... 261 A3
Scotswood St EC1 ... 94 C3 241 B6
Scotswood Wlk N17 ... 34 A3
Scott Ave SW15, SW18 ... 157 A5
Scott Cl
Thornton Heath SW16 ... 182 B2
West Drayton UB7 ... 104 B2
West Ewell KT19 ... 215 A3
Scott Ct Acton W4 ... 111 B4
4 Clapham SW11 ... 137 B3
17 Stoke Newington N16 ... 73 C5
Scott Ellis Gdns NW8 ... 92 B4 229 C1
Scottes La RM8 ... 58 D1
Scott Farm Cl KT7 ... 197 B1
Scott Gdns TW5 ... 128 D5
Scott Ho
2 Barnsbury N7 ... 72 B2
3 Edmonton N18 ... 34 A5
4 Erith DA17 ... 125 B1
Islington N1 ... 235 C6
Lisson Gr NW8 ... 237 A5
17 Millwall E14 ... 119 C4
6 Newham E13 ... 99 A5
Richmond TW10 ... 153 C2
3 Stonebridge NW10 ... 67 B1
Scott Lidgett Cres SE16 ... 118 A4
Scott Rd HA8 ... 26 D1
Scott's Ave
Ashford TW16 ... 171 C3
Beckenham BR2 ... 186 B1
Scotts Ct 6 W12 ... 112 B4
Scotts Dr TW12 ... 173 D3
Scotts Farm Rd KT19 ... 215 A2
Scotts Ho DA16 ... 146 C4
Scott's La BR2, BR3 ... 186 B1
Scotts Park Prim Sch BR1 ... 187 C2
Scotts Rd BR1 ... 187 A3
Southall UB2 ... 106 D3
Scott's Rd
Leytonstone E10 ... 54 A1
Shepherd's Bush W12 ... 112 B4
Scott's Sufferance Wharf SE1 ... 253 D1
Scott St E1 ... 96 B3
Scott's Way TW16 ... 171 C3
Scott's Yd EC4 ... 252 C6
Scott Trimmer Way TW3 ... 129 A3
Scottwell Dr NW9 ... 45 D4
Scott Wilkie Prim Sch E16 ... 99 C1
Scoulding Ho 12 E14 ... 119 C3
Scoulding Rd E16 ... 99 A1
Scouler St E14 ... 120 B6
Scout App NW10 ... 67 C4
Scout La SW4 ... 137 C2
Scout Way NW7 ... 27 B6
Scovell Cres SE1 ... 252 A1
Scovell Rd SE1 ... 252 A1
Scratchwood Nature Trail★ NW7 ... 11 B4
Scrattons Terr IG11 ... 103 A5
Scriven Ct 2 E8 ... 95 D6
Scriven St E8 ... 95 D6
Scrooby St SE6 ... 163 D5
Scrope Bldg EC1 ... 241 A4
Scrubs La NW10, W10, W12 ... 90 B3
Scrutton Cl SW12 ... 159 D4
Scrutton St EC2 ... 95 C3 243 A5
Scudamore La NW9 ... 45 A5
Scutari Rd SE22 ... 162 C6
Scylla Cres TW6&TW14 ... 148 D4
Scylla Rd
East Bedfont TW14, TW6 ... 148 D5
Nunhead SE15 ... 140 B2
Seabright St 27 E2 ... 96 B4
Seabrook Dr BR4 ... 224 C6
Seabrook Gdns RM7 ... 59 C2
Seabrook Rd RM8 ... 80 D5
Seacole Cl W3 ... 89 B2
Seacole Ct N15 ... 51 D4
Seacole Lo N21 ... 16 B6
Seacon Twr 8 E14 ... 119 C4
Seacourt Rd SE2 ... 124 D4

Seacroft Gdns WD19 22 D6
Seafield Rd N11 31 D6
Seaford Cl HA4 61 B6
Seaford Ho 13 SE16 118 C4
Seaford Rd
Ealing W13 109 B5
Enfield EN1 5 C1
Tottenham N15 51 C4
Walthamstow E17 53 D6
Seaford St WC1 233 B1
Seaforth Ave KT3 200 B5
Seaforth Cres N5 73 A3
Seaforth Gdns
Southgate N21 16 C3
Woodford IG8 37 C5
Worcester Pk KT19 215 D3
Seaforth Lo 2 SW13 133 D3
Seaforth Pl SW1 259 B6
Seagrave Lo SW6 265 B6
Seagrave Rd SW6 135 C6 265 B6
Seagrove Cl E1 96 D2
Seagry Rd E11 55 B2
Seagull Cl IG11 102 A4
Seagull La E16 121 A6
Sealand Rd TW6 148 C5
Sealand Wlk UB5 85 A4
Seal Ho SE1 262 D6
Sea Life London Aquarium★ SE1 250 C1
Seal St E8 73 D4
Searle Ct 2 CR4 180 C2
Searle Pl N4 50 B1
Searles Cl SW11 136 C5 267 B3
Searles Dr E6 100 D2
Searles Rd SE1 262 D4
Searson Ho SE17 261 D3
Sears Ret Pk UB6 86 C6
Sears St SE5 139 B5
Seasalter Ho 10 SW9 138 C4
Seasprite Cl 10 UB5 84 D4
Seath Ho 4 SE26 184 B5
Seaton Ave IG3 79 D3
Seaton Cl
Isleworth TW2 152 B5
6 Newham E13 99 A3
Roehampton SW15 156 B4
Seaton Dr TW15 148 A2
Seaton Gdns HA4 62 A6
Seaton Point E5 74 A4
Seaton Rd
Bexley DA16 146 C5
Hayes UB3 105 B3
Mitcham CR4 180 C1
Twickenham TW2 152 A5
Wembley HA0 88 A5
Seaton Sq NW7 28 D3
Seaton St N18 34 A5
Seavington Ho 3 SE5 139 C2
Sebastian Ct 11 IG11 79 D1
Sebastian Ho 22 N1 95 C5
Sebastian St EC1 94 D4 234 D1
Sebastopol Rd N9 34 A6
Sebbon St N1 72 D1
Sebergham Gr NW7 28 A3
Sebert Rd E7 77 B4
Sebright Ho 22 E2 96 A5
Sebright Pas 29 E2 96 A5
Sebright Rd EN5 1 A2
Sebright Sch 39 E2 96 A5
Secker Cres HA3 24 A2
Secker Ho SW9 138 D3
Secker St SE1 251 A3
Second Ave
Chadwell Heath RM6 58 C4
Dagenham RM10 103 D5
East Acton W3 111 D5
Edmonton N18 34 C6
Enfield EN1 17 D6
Hayes UB3 105 D5
Hendon NW4 46 D5
Kensal Town W10 91 A3
Manor Pk E12 78 A3
Mortlake SW14 133 C2
Newham E13 99 A4
Walthamstow E17 53 C4
Walton-on-T KT12 194 B3
Wembley HA9 65 D6
Second Cl KT8 196 A5
Second Cross Rd TW2 152 C2
Second Way HA9 66 D4
Secrett Ho 6 TW10 153 C1
Sedan Way SE17 117 C1 263 A2
Sedcombe Cl DA14 190 C6
Sedcote Rd EN3 18 D6
Sedding St SW1 258 A4
Seddon Ho EC2 242 A4
Seddon Rd SM4 202 B4
Seddon St WC1 94 B4 233 D1
Sedgebrook Rd SE3 143 D2
Sedgecombe Ave HA3 43 C4
Sedgefield Ct UB5 63 D3
Sedgeford Rd W12 111 D5
Sedgehill Rd SE6 185 D5
Sedgehill Sch SE6 185 D5
Sedgemere Ave N2 48 A6
Sedgemere Rd SE2 124 C3
Sedgemoor Dr RM10 81 C4
Sedge Rd N17 34 C3
Sedgeway SE6 164 D3
Sedgewick Ho SW19 156 D2
Sedgewood Cl BR2 208 D2
Sedgley Ho N4 72 B6
Sedgmoor Pl SE5 139 C5
Sedgwick Ave UB10 60 D1
Sedgwick Rd E10 76 A6
Sedgwick St E9 74 D3
Sedleigh Rd SW18 157 B5
Sedlescombe Rd SW6 135 C6 265 A6
Sedley Cl EN1 6 B5
Sedley Ct SE26 162 B2
Sedley Ho SE11 260 D2
Sedley Pl W1 238 C1
Sedum Cl NW9 44 D4
Seeley Dr SE21 183 C6
Seelig Ave NW9 46 A2
Seely Rd SW17 181 A4
Seething La EC3 117 C6 253 B6
SEETHING WELLS 197 D3
Seething Wells Halls of Residence KT6 197 C3
Seething Wells La KT6 197 C3
Sefton Ave
Edgware NW7 27 B5
Harrow HA3 24 B2
Sefton Cl BR5 211 D5
Sefton Ct TW5 129 D4
Sefton Lo 2 TW1 153 C5
Sefton Rd
Croydon CR0 206 A1
Orpington BR5 211 D5
Sefton St SW15 134 C2
Segal Cl SE23 163 A4
Sekforde St EC1 94 D3 241 C6
Sekhon Terr TW13 151 C1
Selan Gdns UB4 84 B2
Selbie Ave NW10 67 D3
Selborne 2 SW11 137 A2
Selborne Ave DA5 169 A3
Little Ilford E12 78 C4
Walthamstow E17 53 B5
Selborne Gdns
Hendon NW4 46 A5
Wembley UB6 87 A5
Selborne Ho SE1 252 C1
Selborne Prim Sch UB6 86 D5
Selborne Rd
1 Camberwell SE5 139 B3
Ilford IG1 78 C6
Kingston u T KT3 177 C1
Palmers Green N14 16 A1
Sidcup DA14 190 B6
South Croydon CR0 221 D5
Walthamstow E17 53 C4
Wood Green N22 32 B2
Selborne Wlk E17 53 B5
Selborne Wlk Sh Ctr E17 53 B5
Selbourne Ave KT6 214 C5
Selbridge Ct SW19 179 C4
Selby Chase HA4 62 B6
Selby Cl BR7 188 C4
Chessington KT9 214 A1
14 Newham E6 100 A2
Selby Ct TW2 152 B2
Selby Gdns UB1 85 C3
Selby Gn SM5 202 C2
Selby Ho 10 SW4 159 C5
Selby Rd
Ashford TW15 171 A4
Carshalton SM5 202 C2
Ealing W5 87 C3
Leyton E11 76 C5
Newham E13 99 B2
Penge SE20 184 A1
Tottenham N17 33 C4
Selby Sq 1 W10 91 A4
Selby St E1 96 A3
Selden Ho 2 SE15 140 C3
Selden Rd SE15 140 C3
Selden Wlk N7 72 B6
Seldon Ho
Nine Elms SW8 269 A3
Pimlico SW1 259 A1
Selena Ct N20 14 D1
SELHURST 205 B4
Selhurst Cl SW19 156 D3
Selhurst New Ct SE25 205 C3
Selhurst New Rd SE25 205 C3
Selhurst Park (Crystal Palace FC) SE25 205 C5
Selhurst Pl SE25 205 C3
Selhurst Rd
Edmonton N9 17 C1
South Norwood SE25 205 C5
Selhurst Sta SE25 205 C4
Selina Ho NW8 236 D6
Selinas La RM8 59 B2
Selkirk Ct N17 33 C1
Selkirk Ho N1 233 C6
4 Stoke Newington N16 73 C5
Selkirk Rd
Twickenham TW2 152 A3
Upper Tooting SW17 180 C6
Sellers Hall Cl N3 29 C3
Sellincourt Prim Sch SW17 180 C4
Sellincourt Rd SW17 180 C4
Sellindge Cl BR3 185 B3
Sellons Ave NW10 89 D6
Sellsby Ct N11 31 B5
Sellwood Dr EN5 12 D6
Selma Ho 7 W12 90 B1
Selman Ho 3 E9 75 A2
SELSDON 223 A1
Selsdon Ave CR2 221 B2
Selsdon Cl KT6 198 A4
Selsdon High Sch CR2 222 D1
Selsdon Park Rd CR0, CR2 223 B1
Selsdon Rd
Newham E13 99 C5
South Croydon CR2 221 B2
Wanstead E11 55 A2
West Norwood SE27 182 D6
Willesden NW2 67 D6
Selsdon Road Ind Est CR2 221 B2
Selsdon Way E14 119 D3
Selsea Pl N16 73 C3
Selsey Cres DA16 146 D4
Selsey St E14 97 C2
Selvage La NW7 27 B6
Selway Cl HA5 40 B6
Selway Ho SW8 270 B2
Selwood Ho
Chislehurst BR7 189 A4
1 Stoke Newington N4 51 B2
Selwood Pl SW7 114 B1 256 C2
Selwood Rd
Cheam SM3 201 B1
Chessington KT9 213 D4
Croydon CR0 206 B1
Selwood Terr SW7 256 C2
Selworthy Cl E11 55 A4
Selworthy Ho SW11 266 D2
Selworthy Rd SE6 163 B1
Selwyn Ave
Chingford E4 36 A4
Ilford IG3 57 D3
Richmond TW9 132 B2
Selwyn Cl TW4 129 A1
Selwyn Cres DA16 146 B1
Selwyn Ct
Edgware HA8 26 D3
Lewisham SE3 142 D2
8 Richmond TW10 154 B6
Walthamstow E17 53 C4
Wembley HA9 67 A5
Selwyn Ho 3 SW15 156 D5
Selwyn Prim Sch
Chingford E4 36 A4
6 Newham E13 99 A6
Selwyn Rd Bow E3 97 B5
Newham E13 99 B6
New Malden KT3 199 B4
Willesden NW10 67 C1
Semley Gate E9 75 B2
Semley Ho SW1 258 C3
Semley Pl SW1 115 B2 258 C3
Thornton Heath SW16 182 B1
Semley Rd SW16 182 A1
Senate St SE15 140 C3
Senators Lo 31 E3 97 A5
Senator Wlk 2 SE28 123 B3
Sencler Ho SE2 146 D6
Sendall Ct 12 SW11 136 B2
Seneca Rd CR7 205 A5
Senga Rd SM6 203 A1
Senhouse Rd SM3 216 D5
Senior St W2 91 D2
Senlac Rd SE12 165 B3
Sennen Rd EN1 17 D4
Sennen Wlk SE9 166 A1
Senrab St E1 96 D1
Sentinel Cl UB5 85 A3
Sentinel Ho NW4 46 C5
Sentinel Sq NW4 46 C5
September Ct UB1 107 D5
September Way HA7 25 B4
Sequoia Cl WD23 8 B3
Sequoia Gdns BR6 211 D2
Sequoia Pk HA5 23 D4
Seraph Ct EC1 95 A4 235 A2
Serbin Cl E10 54 A2
Serenaders Rd 20 SW9 138 C3
Sergeant Ind Est The SW18 157 D5
Serica Ct 14 SE10 142 A5
Serjeants' Inn EC4 241 B1
Serlby Ct W14 254 C6
Serle St WC2 94 B1 240 D2
Sermon La EC4 242 A1
Serpentine Ct 10 SE16 118 D4
Serpentine Gallery★ W2 114 B4 246 D2
Serpentine Rd W2 114 D5 247 C3
Serpentine The★ W2 114 C5 247 B3
Service Route No 1 E15 76 B1
Service Route No 2 1 E15 76 B1
Service Route No 3 2 E15 76 B1
Serviden Dr BR1 187 D2
Servite Ho
Beckenham BR3 185 B2
Bromley BR1 188 B1
East Barnet N14 15 B6
Lewisham SE13 141 D4
Penge SE26 184 C4
Worcester Pk KT4 215 D6
Servite RC Prim Sch SW10 136 A6 266 A6
Servius Ct 2 TW8 131 D5
Sessions Terr CR4 180 D2
Setchell Rd SE1 117 D2 263 C4
Setchell Way SE1 263 C4
Seth St 25 SE16 118 C4
Seton Ct 3 NW9 46 A5
Seton Gdns RM9 80 C1
Settle Point 11 E13 99 A5
Settlers Ct 11 E14 120 B6
Settles St E1 96 A1
Settrington Rd SW6 135 D3
Seven Acres
Carshalton SM5 218 C6
Northwood HA6 22 A4
Seven Dials WC2 94 A1 240 A1
Seven Islands L Ctr SE16 118 C3
SEVEN KINGS 57 D2
Seven Kings High Sch IG2 57 B2
Seven Kings Rd IG3 79 D6
Seven Kings Sta IG3 57 C1
Seven Kings Way KT2 176 A2
Seven Mills Prim Sch 27 E14 119 C4
Sevenoaks Cl DA7 147 D1
Sevenoaks Rd BR6 227 D4
Catford SE4 163 B5
Sevenoaks Way BR5 190 C1
Seven Seas Rd TW6 149 A5
Seven Sisters N15 51 D4
Seven Sisters Prim Sch N15 51 B4
Seven Sisters Rd
Finsbury Pk N4 72 D6
Stoke Newington N4, N7, N15 51 A2
Seven Sisters Sta N15 51 C4
Seven Stars Cnr W12 112 A3
Seven Stars Yd E1 243 D4
Seventh Ave
Hayes UB3 106 A5
Ilford E12 78 B4
Seven Ways Par IG2 56 C4
Severnake Cl E14 119 C2
Severn Ave 2 W10 91 A4
Severn Ct 11 KT2 175 D2
Severn Dr Enfield EN1 6 A5
Hinchley Wood KT10 213 A6
Severn Way NW10 67 D3
Severus Rd SW11 136 C1
Seville Ho 10 E1 118 A5
Seville Mews N1 73 C1
Seville St SW1 247 D1
Sevington Rd NW4 46 B3
Sevington St W9 91 D3
Seward Rd
Penge BR3 184 D1
West Ealing W7 109 A4
Seward St EC1 95 A4 235 A1
SEWARDSTONEBURY 20 C6
Sewardstone Gdns E4 19 D6
Sewardstone Rd
Chingford E4 19 D6
South Hackney E2 96 C5
Sewdley St E5 74 D5
Sewell Ho 7 N16 73 C3
Sewell Rd SE2 124 B4
Sewell St E13 99 A4
Sextant Ave E14 120 B2
Sexton Ct 7 E14 120 B6
Sexton's Ho 5 SE13 142 A6
Seychelle Ct BR3 185 D3
Seymour Ave
Tottenham N17 34 A1
West Barnes SM4 200 D2
Seymour Cl
East Molesey KT8 196 A4
Pinner HA5 23 B2
Seymour Ct
Chingford E4 20 D2
Dollis Hill NW2 68 B6
Muswell Hill N10 31 A1
Putney SW15 134 B1
Southgate N21 16 B5
Upper Clapton N16 52 A1
Seymour Dr BR2 210 B1
Seymour Gdns
Brockley SE4 141 A2
Feltham TW13 172 C6
Kingston u T KT5 198 B4
Redbridge IG1 56 B1
Ruislip HA4 40 D1
Twickenham TW1 153 B4
Seymour Ho
Bloomsbury WC1 240 A6
1 Clapham SW8 137 C3
Ruislip HA4 40 A5
Somers Town NW1 232 D1
Seymour Lo 14 KT1 175 D2
Seymour Mews W1 238 A2
Seymour Pl
Croydon SE25 206 B5
Paddington W1 92 D1 237 C2

Seymour Rd
Acton W4 111 A2
Carshalton CR4 203 A2
Chingford E4 19 D3
East Molesey KT8 196 A4
Edmonton N9 18 B2
Finchley N3 29 D3
Hampton TW12 174 A5
Harringay N8 50 D4
Newham E6 99 D6
Teddington KT1 175 D2
Wallington SM5 219 A3
Walthamstow E10 53 B1
Wandsworth SW18 157 B5
Wimbledon SW19 156 D1
Seymour St
Paddington W1 92 D1 237 D1
Woolwich SE18 123 A3
Seymour Terr SE20 184 B2
Seymour Villas SE20 184 A2
Seymour Way TW16 171 C3
Seymour Wlk SW10 136 A6 266 A6
Seyssel St E14 120 A2
Shaa Rd W3 111 B6
Shabana Ct 3 W12 112 B5
Shacklegate La TW11 174 C6
Shackleton Cl SE23 162 B2
Shackleton Ct
3 Dulwich SE21 161 B2
2 Isle of Dogs E14 119 C1
4 Shepherd's Bush W12 112 B4
7 Stanwell TW19 148 A5
Shackleton Ho
5 Stonebridge NW10 67 B1
5 Wapping E1 118 C5
Shackleton Lo SW16 181 D5
Shackleton Rd UB1 107 B6
SHACKLEWELL 73 D4
Shacklewell Ho 3 E8 73 D4
Shacklewell La E8 73 D3
Shacklewell Prim Sch 5 E8 73 D4
Shacklewell Rd N16 73 D4
Shacklewell Row E8 73 D4
Shacklewell St 30 E2 95 D4
Shadbolt Ave E4 35 A5
Shadbolt Cl KT4 215 D6
Shad Thames SE1 117 D4 253 D2
SHADWELL 118 C6
Shadwell Ct UB5 85 B5
Shadwell Dr UB5 85 B4
Shadwell Gdns E1 118 C6
Shadwell Pierhead E1 118 C6
Shadwell Pl 1 E1 118 C6
Shadwell Sta E1 118 B6
Shady Bush Cl WD23 8 A4
Shaef Way TW11 175 A3
Shaftesbury Ave
Enfield EN3 6 D3
Feltham TW14 150 A5
Kenton HA3 44 A3
New Barnet EN5 2 A1
Southall UB2 107 C3
W1 115 D6 249 D6
West Harrow HA1, HA2 42 A1
Shaftesbury Circ HA2 42 A1
Shaftesbury Ct
Borough The SE1 262 C6
1 Herne Hill SE5 139 B1
Ilford RM6 58 C2
Newham E6 100 C1
Shoreditch N1 235 C3
Streatham SW16 159 D1
3 Thamesmead SE28 124 C5
Shaftesbury Ctr NW10 90 D3
Shaftesbury Gdns NW10 89 C3
Shaftesbury High Sch HA3 23 D2
Shaftesbury Ho
11 Canning Town E16 98 D1
Croydon SE25 206 A3

Shaftesbury Ho *continued*
13 Stoke Newington N16 73 C5
Upper Tooting SW17 180 B6
W2 245 D6
Shaftesbury Lo 9 E14 97 D1
Shaftesbury Mews
2 Clapham Pk SW4 159 C6
W8 255 B5
Shaftesbury Park Chambers 1 SW11 137 A2
Shaftesbury Point E13 99 B5
Shaftesbury Prim Sch E7 77 C1
Shaftesbury Rd
Beckenham BR3 185 B1
Carshalton SM5 202 C2
Chingford E4 20 B3
Edmonton N18 33 D4
Finsbury Pk N4, N19 50 A1
Leyton E10 53 C1
Richmond TW9 132 A2
Upton E7 77 C1
Walthamstow E17 53 D3
Shaftesbury St N1 235 C3
Shaftesburys The IG11 101 A5
Shaftesbury Way TW2 152 B1
Shaftesbury Waye UB4 84 C1
Shafteswood Ct SW17 158 D1
Shafto Mews SW1 257 D5
Shafton Rd E9 96 D6
Shaftsbury Park Prim Sch 16 SW11 137 A3
Shafts Ct EC3 243 A1
Shahjalal Ho 18 E2 96 A5
Shakespeare Ave
7 Becontree NW10 89 B6
Feltham TW14 150 A5
Friern Barnet N11 31 C5
Hayes UB4 84 B2
Shakespeare Cl HA3 44 C2
Shakespeare Cres E12 78 B2
Shakespeare Ct EN5 1 D2
Shakespeare Dr HA3 44 B3
Shakespeare Gdns N2 48 D5
Shakespeare Ho
1 Erith DA17 125 B1
3 Hackney E9 74 C1
Osidge N14 15 D2
Shakespeare Rd
Acton W3 111 A5
Brixton SE24 138 D1
DA7 147 A4
Ealing W7 108 D6
Finchley N3 29 C2
Higham Hill E17 34 D1
Mill Hill NW7 28 A6
Stonebridge NW10 89 B6
Shakespeare's Globe Theatre (site of)★ SE1 252 B4
Shakespeare Twr EC2 242 B4
Shakespeare Way TW13 172 C6
Shakspeare Mews 7 N16 73 C4
Shakspeare Wlk N16 73 C4
Shalbourne Sq E9 75 B2
Shalcomb St SW10 136 A6 266 B5
Shalden Ho SW15 155 D5
Shaldon Dr
Ruislip HA4 62 C5
West Barnes SM4 201 A4
Shaldon Rd HA8 26 B1
Shalfleet Dr W10 112 D6
Shalford
Willesden Green NW10 90 A6
3 Woodford IG8 37 C4
Shalford Cl BR6 227 A4
Shalford Ct N1 234 C4
Shalford Ho SE1 262 D6
Shalimar Gdns W3 111 A6
Shalimar Lo W3 111 A6

Shalimar Rd W3 111 A6
Shallons Rd SE9 188 D6
Shalstone Rd SW14, TW9 132 D2
Shalston Villas KT5, KT6 198 B3
Shamrock Ct E7 77 D3
Shamrock Ho
East Barnet N14 15 B4
Forest Hill SE26 184 A6
Shamrock Rd CR0 204 B3
Shamrock St SW4 137 D2
Shamrock Way N14 15 B3
Shandon Ct SE4 141 A3
Shandon Rd SW4 159 C5
Shand St SE1 117 C4 253 B2
Shandy St E1 96 D3
Shane Ct EN2 5 A3
Shan Ho WC1 240 C5
Shanklin Gdns WD19 22 C6
Shanklin Ho E17 35 B1
Shanklin Rd
Hornsey N8 49 D4
Tottenham Hale N15 52 A5
Shannon Cl UB2 106 D1
Shannon Cnr KT3 200 A5
Shannon Cnr Ret Pk KT3 200 A5
Shannon Commercial Ctr KT3 200 A5
Shannon Ct
Croydon CR0 205 A1
11 Peckham SE15 139 D5
Stoke Newington N16 73 C5
Willesden NW10 68 A2
Shannon Gr SW9 138 B1
Shannon Pl NW8 92 C5 230 B4
Shannon Way BR3 185 D4
Shanti Ct SW18 157 C3
Shap Cres SM5 202 D1
Shapland Way N13 32 B5
Shapla Prim Sch 25 E1 118 A6
Shapwick Cl N11 30 D5
Shardcroft Ave SE24 160 D6
Shardeloes Rd SE14 141 B3
Shard's Sq SE15 140 A6
Sharebourne Ho SW2 160 C6
Sharland Cl CR7 204 C3
Sharman Ct DA14 190 A6
Sharman Ho 13 E14 98 A1
Sharnbrooke Cl DA16 146 C2
Sharnbrook Ho W6 265 A6
Sharon Cl KT6 197 C1
Sharon Ct 1 N12 30 A4
Sharon Gdns E9 96 C6
Sharon Rd
Chiswick W4 111 B1
Enfield EN3 7 A3
Sharpe Cl W7 86 D2
Sharp Ho SW8 137 B2
Sharples Hall St 8 NW1 70 D1
Sharpness Cl UB4 85 A2
Sharpness Ct 2 SE15 139 D5
Sharps La HA4 39 B2
Sharratt St SE15 140 C6
Sharsted St SE17 116 D1 261 C1
Sharvel La UB5 84 B6
Sharwood WC1 233 D3
Shaver's Pl SW1 249 C5
Shaw Ave IG11 103 A5
Shawbrooke Rd SE9 143 D1
Shawbury Cl 9 NW9 27 C2
Shawbury Ct SE22 161 D6
Shawbury Rd SE22 161 D6
Shaw Cl Bushey WD23 8 C2
Woolwich SE28 124 B5
Shaw Cotts SE23 163 A1
Shaw Cres 6 E14 97 A1
Shaw Ct
8 Acton Green W3 111 A3
11 Battersea SW11 136 B2
Cheam SM4 202 A2
Upper Holloway N19 72 A6
Shaw Dr KT12 194 C2
Shawfield Ct UB7 104 A3
Shawfield Pk BR1 187 D1
Shawfield St SW3 114 C1 257 B1

Shawford Ct 8 SW15 156 A4
Shawford Rd KT19 215 B2
Shaw Gdns IG11 103 A5
Shaw Ho
6 Erith DA17 125 B1
5 Newham E16 122 C5
Shaw Path BR1 164 D1
Shaw Rd
Camberwell SE22 139 C1
Catford BR1 164 D1
Enfield EN3 6 D4
Shaw Sq E17 35 A2
Shaws Wood Cotts EN4 3 C3
Shaw Way SM6 220 A1
Shearing Dr SM4 202 A2
Shearling Way N7 72 A2
Shearman Rd SE3 142 D2
Shears Ct TW16 171 C3
Shearsmith Ho 19 E1 118 A6
Shears The TW16 171 C3
Shears Way TW16 171 C2
Shearwater Cl IG11 102 A4
Shearwater Ct 24 SE8 141 B6
Shearwater Rd SM1 217 B3
Shearwater Way UB4 84 D1
Sheaveshill Ave NW9 45 C5
Sheaveshill Ct NW9 45 C5
Sheaveshill Par NW9 45 C5
Sheba Ct N17 34 A4
Sheba Pl E1 243 D5
Sheen Common Dr SW14, TW10 154 C6
Sheen Court Rd TW10 132 C1
Sheen Ct TW10 132 C1
Sheendale Rd TW9 132 B1
Sheenewood SE26 184 B6
Sheen Gate Gdns SW14 133 A1
Sheengate Mans SW14 133 B1
Sheen Gr N1 94 C6 234 A6
Sheen La SW14 133 A1
Sheen Mount Prim Sch SW14 154 D6
Sheen Pk TW10, TW9 132 A1
Sheen Rd
Orpington BR5 211 D5
Richmond TW10, TW9 132 B1
Sheen Way SM6 220 B3
Sheen Wood SW14 155 A6
Sheepcote Cl TW5 128 A5
Sheepcote La SW11 136 D3
Sheepcote Rd HA1 42 D3
Sheepcotes Rd RM6 59 A5
Sheephouse Way KT3 199 C2
Sheep La E8 96 B6
Sheepwalk TW17 192 B3
Sheep Walk Mews 7 SW19 179 A4
Sheerness Mews E16 122 D4
Sheerwater Rd E16 99 D2
Sheffield Ho 15 SE15 139 D4
Sheffield Rd TW14, TW6 149 A6
Sheffield Sq 2 E3 97 B4
Sheffield St WC2 240 C1
Sheffield Terr W8 113 C5 245 B3
Sheffield Way TW14, TW6 149 B6
Shefton Rise HA6 22 A3
Shelbey Ct BR1 186 D2
Shelbourne Cl HA5 41 B6
Shelbourne Ho 20 N19 49 D2
Shelbourne Rd N17 34 B2
Shelburne Ct SW15 156 D6
Shelburne Dr TW4 151 C5
Shelburne Ho 9 SW16 181 C5
Shelburne Rd N7 72 B4
Shelbury Cl DA14 168 A1
Shelbury Rd SE22 162 B6
Sheldon Ave N6 48 D3
Sheldon Cl
Penge SE20 184 B2
SE12 165 B6

Sheldon Ct Barnet EN5 1 D1
SW8 270 A3
Sheldon Ho
Chingford E4 36 C4
9 Homerton E9 74 D2
Teddington TW11 175 A4
Sheldon Pl E2 96 B5
Sheldon Rd
Cricklewood NW2 68 D4
DA7 147 B4
Dagenham RM9 81 A1
Edmonton N18 33 C6
Sheldon Sq W2 236 B3
Sheldon St CR0 221 A5
Sheldrake Cl E16 122 B5
Sheldrake Ho 15 SE16 118 D2
Sheldrake Pl W8 113 C4 245 A2
Sheldrick Cl CR4 180 B1
Shelduck Cl E15 76 D3
Shelduck Ct 37 SE8 141 B6
Sheldwich Terr BR2 210 A3
Shelford 20 KT1 176 C1
Shelford Ct 7 E5 52 B1
Shelford Pl N16 73 B5
Shelford Rd EN5 12 C5
Shelford Rise SE19 183 D3
Shelgate Rd SW11 158 D6
Shell Cl BR2 210 A3
Shell Ctr SE1 250 D3
Shellduck Cl NW9 27 C1
Shelley N8 50 A6
Shelley Ave
Greenford UB6 86 B4
Plashet E12 78 A2
Shelley Cl BR6 227 C5
Edgware HA8 26 C6
Greenford UB6 86 B4
Hayes UB4 84 A2
Peckham SE15 140 B3
Shelley Cres
Heston TW5 128 D4
Southall UB1 85 B1
Shelley Ct
Finsbury Pk N4 50 B1
9 Kingston u T KT2 175 D6
SW3 267 D6
13 Walthamstow E10 53 D2
8 Wanstead E11 55 A5
Wembley HA0 65 C4
West Barnes KT3 200 A4
Shelley Dr DA16 145 C4
Shelley Gdns HA0 65 C6
Shelley Ho
21 Bethnal Green E2 96 C4
Chelsea SW1 269 A6
9 Stoke Newington N16 73 C4
Walworth SE17 262 B2
Shelley Rd NW10 89 B6
Shelley Way SW17 180 B4
Shellgrove Rd 31 N16 73 C3
Shellness Rd E5 74 B3
Shell Rd SE13 141 D2
Shellwood Rd SW11 136 D3
Shelly Lo EN2 5 B4
Shelmerdine Cl E3 97 C2
Shelson Ave TW13 171 D6
Shelton Ct N21 16 C4
Shelton Rd SW19 179 C2
Shelton St WC2 94 A1 240 A1
Shene Bldg EC1 241 A4
Shene Sch SW14 133 C1
Shenfield Ho 3 SE18 143 D5
Shenfield Rd IG8 37 B3
Shenfield St N1 95 C5
Shenley Ave HA4 39 D1
Shenley Ho 3 SW16 182 B6
Shenley Rd
Camberwell SE5 139 C4
Heston TW5 129 A4
Shenstone W13 109 C5
Shenstone Gdns IG2 57 D4
Shenstone Ho SW16 181 C5
Shepard Ho 17 SW11 136 B2
Sheperdess Pl N1 235 B2
Shepherd Cl
Feltham TW13 173 A6
W1 248 A6

Shepherdess Wlk
N1 . . . . 95 A5 235 B3
Shepherd Ho
Barnsbury N7 . . . . 72 A2
10 Poplar E14 . . . . 97 D1
Shepherd Mkt W1 . . 248 C3
SHEPHERD'S BUSH 112 B5
Shepherd's Bush Gn
W12 . . . . 112 C4
Shepherd's Bush Market
W12 . . . . 112 C4
Shepherd's Bush Mkt Sta
W12 . . . . 112 C5
Shepherd's Bush Overground Sta
W12 . . . . 112 D4
Shepherd's Bush Pl
W12 . . . . 112 D4
Shepherd's Bush Rd
W6 . . . . 112 C3
Shepherd's Bush Sta
W12 . . . . 112 D4
Shepherds Cl
Dagenham RM6 . . . . 58 D5
Orpington BR6 . . . . . . 227 D5
Shepperton TW17 . . . 192 D3
Stanmore HA7 . . . . 25 A5
Shepherd's Cl N6 . . . . . 49 B3
Shepherds Ct
8 Hammersmith W12 . . . . 112 D4
13 Harrow HA1 . . . . 42 D3
Shepherds Gn BR7 . . . 189 B3
Shepherd's Hill N6 . . . 49 C3
Shepherds La SE28 . . 123 C5
Shepherd's La E9 . . . . . 74 D2
Shepherds Leas SE9 . 145 B1
Shepherds Path UB5 . . 63 A2
Shepherds Pl W1 . . . 248 A6
Shepherd St
W1 . . . . 115 B5 248 C3
Shepherds Way CR2 222 D1
Shepherds Wlk
Bushey WD23 . . . . 8 B2
Dollis Hill NW2 . . . . 68 A6
Shepherd's Wlk NW3 . 70 B4
Shepiston La UB3 . . . . 105 A1
Shepley Cl SM5 . . . . . 219 A5
Shepley Ct SW16 . . . . 181 C6
Shepley Mews EN3 . . . . . 7 C6
Sheppard Cl
Enfield EN1 . . . . 6 B5
Kingston u T KT6 . . . . 198 A5
Sheppard Dr SE16 . . . 118 B1
Sheppard Ho
31 Hackney E2 . . . . 96 A5
8 Streatham SW2 . . 160 C3
Sheppard's Ct
Harrow HA1 . . . . 42 C2
Wembley UB6 . . . . 64 D2
Sheppard St E16 . . . . . . 98 D3
SHEPPERTON 193 A3
Shepperton Bsns Park
TW17 . . . . 193 A4
Shepperton Court Dr
TW17 . . . . 192 D4
Shepperton Ct
TW17 . . . . 192 D3
SHEPPERTON GREEN 192 D5
Shepperton Rd
Littleton TW17, TW18 . . . . 192 A5
Orpington BR5 . . . . . . 211 A3
Shoreditch N1 . 95 B6 235 C6
Shepperton Sta
TW17 . . . . 193 A4
Shepperton Studios
TW17 . . . . 192 B6
Sheppey Gdns RM9 . . . 80 C1
Sheppey Ho 16 E5 . . . . 74 B4
Sheppey Rd RM9 . . . . . . 80 C1
Shepton Ct SW11 . . . 266 D2
Shepton Hos 11 E2 . . . . 96 C4
Sherard Ct N19 . . . . . . 72 A5
Sherard Ho 24 E9 . . . . . 74 C1
Sherard Rd SE9 . . . . . . 166 A6
Sheraton Bsns Ctr
UB6 . . . . 87 C5
Sheraton Cl WD6 . . . . . 10 B6
Sheraton Ho SW1 . . . 268 D6
Sheraton Lo HA3 . . . . . 42 C6
Sheraton St W1 . . . . . 239 C1
Sheraton The 22
KT6 . . . . 198 A4
Sherborne Ave
Enfield EN3 . . . . 6 C3
Southall UB2 . . . . 107 C2
Sherborne Cl UB4 . . . . 84 C1
Sherborne Cres
SM5 . . . . 202 C2
Sherborne Ct SE20 . . . 184 C1
Sherborne Gdns
Ealing W13 . . . . 87 B2
Queensbury NW9 . . . . . 44 C6
Sherborne Ho
Pimlico SW1 . . . . 258 D2
South Lambeth SW8 . 270 C3
Sherborne La EC4 . . 252 D6
Sherborne Rd BR5 . . 211 D4
Cheam SM3 . . . . 201 C1
Chessington KT9 . . . . 214 A3
East Bedfont TW14 . . . 149 B3
Sherborne St
N1 . . . . 95 B6 235 C6
Sherboro Rd 1 N15 . . . 51 D3
Sherbourne Ct
1 Hampton TW12 . . . 173 C2
9 Sutton SM2 . . . . . . 218 A2
SW5 . . . . 255 C4
Sherbourne Gdns
TW17 . . . . 193 C2
Sherbourne Pl HA7 . . . 25 A4
Sherbrooke Cl DA7 . . 147 C1
Sherbrooke Ho 9 E2 . 96 C5
Sherbrooke Rd
SW6 . . . . 135 A5 264 B3
Sherbrooke Terr
SW6 . . . . 264 B3
Sherbrooke Way
KT4 . . . . 200 B2
Sherbrook Gdns N21 . 16 D4
Sherbrook Ho 2 N3 . . 29 D3
Shere Cl KT9 . . . . 213 D3
Sheredan Rd E4 . . . . . . 36 C5
Shere Ho SE1 . . . . 262 C6
Shere Lo 1 SW19 . . . 180 C3
Shere Rd IG2 . . . . 56 C4
Sherfield Cl KT3 . . . . 198 D5
Sherfield Gdns
SW15 . . . . 155 D5
Sheridan N8 . . . . 50 C5
Sheridan Bldgs WC2 240 B1
Sheridan Cl UB10 . . . . . 83 A3
Sheridan Cres BR7 . . 188 D1
Sheridan Ct
Ealing W7 . . . . 108 D6
Earl's Ct SW5 . . . . 255 C3
Harrow HA1 . . . . 42 B3
Hounslow TW4 . . . . . . 151 A6
South Hampstead NW6 70 A1
South Lambeth SW9 . 270 D1
Sheridan Gdns HA3 . . . 43 D3
Sheridan Ho SE11 . . 261 B3
7 Stoke Newington N16 . . . . 73 C5
Sheridan Lo
Barnet EN5 . . . . 1 D1
Bromley BR2 . . . . 209 C5
East Barnet N14 . . . . . . 15 B4
Sheridan Mews E11 . . . 55 B3
Sheridan Pl
Barnes SW13 . . . . 133 D2
Bromley BR1 . . . . 187 D1
Hampton TW12 . . . . . 174 A2
Harrow HA1 . . . . 42 C2
Sheridan Rd
Belvedere DA17 . . . . . 125 C2
DA7 . . . . 147 A2
Leyton E7 . . . . 76 D5
Little Ilford E12 . . . . 78 B3
Merton SW19 . . . . 179 B2
Richmond TW10 . . . . . . 153 C1
Sheridan St 34 E1 . . . . . 96 B1
Sheridan Terr UB5 . . . . 63 D3
Sheridan Way 5
BR3 . . . . 185 B2
Sheridan Wlk
Golders Green NW11 . . . 47 C3
Wallington SM5 . . . . . 218 D3
Sheringdale Prim Sch
SW18 . . . . 157 B3
Sheringham NW8 . . . 229 D6
Sheringham Ave
Feltham TW13 . . . . . . 150 A1
Little Ilford E12 . . . . 78 B3
Southgate N14 . . . . 15 D5
Twickenham TW2 . . . . 151 C3
Sheringham Ct 1 N3 . 29 C2
Sheringham Dr IG11 . . 80 A3
Sheringham Ho NW1 237 B4
Sheringham Jun Sch
E12 . . . . 78 B4
Sheringham Mews 4
SW18 . . . . 158 A2
Sheringham Rd
Islington N7 . . . . 72 C2
Penge SE20 . . . . 206 C6
Sheringham Twr
UB1 . . . . 107 D6
Sherington Ave HA5 . . 23 C3
Sherington Prim Sch 3
SE7 . . . . 143 B6
Sherington Rd SE7 . . . 143 B6
Sheriton Ct SM1 . . . . 217 C5
Sherland Rd TW1 . . . 152 D3
Sherleys Ct HA4 . . . . . . 61 C6
Sherlies Ave BR6 . . . . 227 C6
Sherlock Ct NW8 . . . 229 C6
Sherlock Holmes Mus*
NW1 . . . . 92 D3 237 D5
Sherlock Mews W1 . 238 A4
Sherman Gdns RM6 . . . 58 C3
Sherman Rd BR1 . . . . 187 A2
Shernhall St E17 . . . . . 54 A5
Shernwood Ho 1
E18 . . . . 55 A5
Sherrard Rd E7, E12 . . . 77 D2
Sherrards Way EN5 . . . 13 D5
Sherren Ho 35 E1 . . . . . 96 C3
Sherrick Green Rd
NW10 . . . . 68 B3
Sherriff Ct NW6 . . . . . . 69 C2
Sherriff Rd NW6 . . . . . . 69 C2
Sherringham Ave
N17 . . . . 34 A1
Sherrin Rd E10 . . . . 75 D4
Sherrock Gdns NW4 . . 46 A5
Sherry Mews IG11 . . . . 79 B1
Sherston Ct
Finsbury WC1 . . . . 234 A1
Newington SE1 . . . . . 261 D4
Sherwin Ho 1 SE11 . . 138 C6
Sherwin Rd SE14 . . . . 140 D4
Sherwood
3 Barnet EN5 . . . . 1 D1
Brondesbury NW6 . . . . . 69 A1
Long Ditton KT6 . . . . . 213 D6
Sherwood Ave
Greenford UB6 . . . . 64 C3
Hayes UB4 . . . . 84 B3
Mitcham SW16 . . . . . 181 D2
Ruislip HA4 . . . . 39 C3
Wanstead E18 . . . . 55 B6
Sherwood Cl
Barnes SW13 . . . . 134 B2
DA5 . . . . 168 C5
Ealing W13 . . . . 109 B5
Walthamstow E17 . . . . . 35 B1
Sherwood Ct
11 Battersea SW11 . . 136 A2
Colney Hatch N12 . . . . . 30 C5
2 South Croydon CR2 . . . . 221 A3
St Johns SE13 . . . . . . 141 D3
Sutton SM1 . . . . 217 C3
W1 . . . . 237 C3
6 West Wickham BR4 . . . . 207 D1
Sherwood Gdns
Barking IG11 . . . . 79 B1
Bermondsey SE16 . . . . 118 B1
Millwall E14 . . . . 119 C2
Sherwood Hall 7 N2 . 48 A6
Sherwood Ho N4 . . . . . 51 A2
Sherwood Park Ave
DA15 . . . . 168 B5
Sherwood Park Prim Sch
DA15 . . . . 168 B5
Sherwood Park Rd
Mitcham CR4 . . . . 203 D5
Sutton SM1 . . . . 217 C3
Sherwood Park Sch
SM6 . . . . 219 D5
Sherwood Rd
Croydon CR0 . . . . 206 B1
DA16 . . . . 145 C2
Hampton TW12 . . . . . 174 A5
Harrow HA2 . . . . 64 A6
Hendon NW4 . . . . 46 C6
Ilford IG6 . . . . 57 B5
Merton SW19 . . . . 179 B3
Sherwood Sch CR4 . 203 C5
Sherwood St W1 . . . 249 B6
Whetstone N20 . . . . 14 B1
Sherwood Terr N20 . . . 14 B1
Sherwood Way BR4 . . 224 A6
Shetland Cl WD6 . . . . . . 11 B5
Shetland Rd Bow E3 . . . 97 B5
East Bedfont TW6 . . . 149 A5
Shield Dr TW8 . . . . . . 131 A6
Shieldhall St SE2 . . . 124 C2
Shield Rd TW15 . . . . . 171 B6
Shifford Path SE23 . . 162 D1
Shillaker Ct W3 . . . . . 111 D5
Shillibeer Ct N18 . . . . . 34 B5
Shillibeer Pl W1 . . . . 237 B3
Shillingford Cl NW7 . . . 28 D3
Shillingford Ho 40 E3 . 97 D4
Shillingford St 23 N1 . . 72 D1
Shilling Pl TW8 . . . . . 109 A5
Shillingstone Ho
W14 . . . . 254 B5
Shine Ho 3 N3 . . . . 29 D3
Shinfield St W12 . . . . . 90 C1
Shinglewell Rd DA8 . . 147 C5
Shinners Cl SE25 . . . 206 A4
Shipka Rd SW12 . . . . . 159 B3
Ship La SW14 . . . . 133 A3
Shiplake Ct SW17 . . . 180 B6
Shiplake Ho 45 E2 . . . . 95 D4
Shipley Ct SE20 . . . . . 184 A1
Shipley Ho 32 SW8 . . 137 D3
Shipman Rd
Forest Hill SE23 . . . . . 162 D2
Newham E16 . . . . 99 C1
Ship & Mermaid Row
SE1 . . . . 253 A2
Ship St SE8 . . . . 141 C4
Ship Tavern Pas EC3 253 A6
Shipton Cl RM8 . . . . . . 80 D5
Shipton Ho
7 Camden Town NW5 . . . . 71 A2
14 Haggerston E2 . . . . 95 D5
Shipton Rd UB8 . . . . . . 60 B4
Shipton St E2 . . . . 95 D4
Shipwright Rd SE16 . 119 A4
Shipwright Yd SE1 . . 253 A3
Shirburn Cl SE23 . . . . 162 C4
Shirbutt St E14 . . . . . 119 D6
Shirebrook Rd SE3 . . 143 D2
Shire Ct DA18 . . . . . . 124 D3
Ewell KT17 . . . . 215 D1
Shirehall Cl NW4 . . . . . 46 D3
Shirehall Gdns NW4 . . 46 D3
Shirehall La NW4 . . . . . 46 D3
Shirehall Pk NW4 . . . . . 46 D3
Shire Ho E11 . . . . 76 D5
Shire Horse Way
TW7 . . . . 130 D2
Shire La BR6 . . . . 227 B2
Shiremeade WD6 . . . . . 10 B6
Shire Mews TW2 . . . . 152 A5
Shire Pl
12 Brentford TW8 . . . 131 C5
Wandsworth SW18 . . 158 A4
Shires The TW10 . . . . 176 A6
Shirland Mews W9 . . . . 91 B4
Shirland Rd W9 . . . . . . 91 C3
SHIRLEY 206 C1
Shirley Ave
Carshalton SM1 . . . . . 218 C4
Croydon CR0 . . . . 206 D1
DA5 . . . . 168 D3
Shirley Church Rd
CR0 . . . . 223 A5
Shirley Cl
Hounslow TW3 . . . . . . 152 A6
Walthamstow E17 . . . . . 53 D4
Shirley Cres BR3 . . . . 207 A5
Shirley Ct
8 Ealing W13 . . . . . . 109 A5
Ilford IG2 . . . . 57 B4
Kingsbury NW9 . . . . 45 B4
2 South Norwood SW16 . . . . 182 B3
Thornton Heath SW16 . . . . 204 B6
Shirley Dr TW3 . . . . . 152 A6
Shirley Gdns
Barking IG11 . . . . 79 C2
Ealing W7 . . . . 108 D5
Shirley Gr
Clapham SW11 . . . . . 137 A2
Ponders End N9 . . . . . . 18 D4
Shirley High Sch
CR0 . . . . 222 D5
Shirley Hills Rd CR0 . 222 D3
Shirley Ho 13 SE5 . . . . 139 B5
Shirley House Dr
SE7 . . . . 143 C5
Shirley Hts 6 DA6 . . . 147 A1
Shirley Lo 4 SE26 . . . 185 A6
SHIRLEY OAKS 207 A1
Shirley Oaks Hospl
CR0 . . . . 206 C2
Shirley Oaks Rd
CR0 . . . . 222 D6
Shirley Park Rd CR0 . 206 C1
Shirley Rd Acton W4 . . 111 B4
Croydon CR0 . . . . 206 B1
Enfield EN2 . . . . 5 A2
Sidcup DA15 . . . . 167 C1
Stratford E15 . . . . 76 C1
Shirley St E16 . . . . 98 D1
Shirley Way CR0 . . . . 223 B5
Shirlock Rd NW3 . . . . . 70 D4
Shirwell Cl NW7 . . . . . . 28 D3
Shobden Rd N17 . . . . . . 33 B2
Shobroke Cl NW2 . . . . . 68 C5
Shoebury Rd E6 . . . . . . 78 B1
Shoe La EC4 . . . 94 C1 241 B2
Shoelands Ct NW9 . . . . 45 B6
Shona Ho E16 . . . . 99 C2
Shooters Ave HA3 . . . . 43 C5
SHOOTERS HILL . . . 145 A4
Shooters Hill SE18 . . . 144 B4
Shooters Hill Post 16 Campus SE18 . . . . . 144 C4
Shooters Hill Rd
Blackheath Vale SE3, SE10 . . . . 142 C4
SE18, SE3, SE7 . . . . . . 143 D5
Shooters Rd EN2 . . . . 4 D4
Shoot-Up Hill NW2 . . . 69 A2
Shopstop SW11 . . . . . 136 C1
Shore Bsns Ctr 31 E9 . . 74 C1
Shore Cl
Feltham TW14 . . . . . . 150 A4
Hampton TW12 . . . . . 173 A5
Shorediche Cl UB10 . . . 60 B5
SHOREDITCH 95 B5
Shoreditch Ct 2 E8 . . . 73 D1
Shoreditch High St Sta
E2 . . . . 95 D3 243 C5
Shoreditch High St
E2 . . . . 95 C3 243 B6
Shoreditch Ho N1 . . 235 D1
Shore Gr TW13 . . . . . 151 C2
Shoreham Cl
Croydon CR0 . . . . 206 C3
DA5 . . . . 168 D3
Wandsworth SW18 . . 157 D6
Shoreham Rd BR5 . . . 190 B1
Shoreham Rd (E)
TW6 . . . . 148 A6
Shoreham Rd (W)
TW6 . . . . 148 A6
Shoreham Way BR2 . 209 A3
Shore Ho SW8 . . . . . . 137 B2
Shore Mews 30 E9 . . . . 74 C1
Shore Pl E9 . . . . 74 C1
Shore Point 2 IG9 . . . . 21 B2
Shore Rd E9 . . . . 74 C1
Shore Way 26 SW9 . . 138 C3
Shorncliffe Rd
SE1 . . . . 117 D1 263 C2
Shorndean St SE6 . . . 164 A3
Shorne Cl 3 DA15 . . . 168 B5
Shornefield Cl BR1 . . . 210 C6
Shornells Way SE2 . . 124 C1
Shorrolds Rd
SW6 . . . . 135 B5 264 D4
Shortcroft Mead Ct
NW10 . . . . 68 A3
Shortcroft Rd KT17 . . 215 D1
Shortcrofts Rd RM9 . . . 81 B2
Shorter St
EC3 . . . . 117 D6 253 D6
Shortgate N12 . . . . 29 B6
Short La TW15, TW19 . . 148 B3
SHORTLANDS 208 C6
Shortlands
Brook Green W6 . . . . . 112 D2
Harlington UB3 . . . . . . 127 B6
Shortlands Cl DA17 . . 125 B3
Edmonton N18 . . . . 17 B1
Shortlands Gdns
BR2 . . . . 186 C1
Shortlands Gr BR2 . . . 208 B6
Shortlands Rd
Beckenham BR2, BR3 . . . . 208 C6
Kingston u T KT2 . . . . . 176 B3

Shortlands Rd *continued*
Walthamstow E10 .....53 D2
Shortlands Sta BR2. 186 C1
Short Path SE18 .... 144 D6
Short Rd
Chiswick W4 .... 133 C6
Leyton E11...........76 C6
Stanwell TW19........ 148 A5
Shorts Croft NW9.....44 D5
Shorts Gdns
WC2........94 A1 240 A1
Shorts Rd SM5.......218 C3
Short St
7 Hendon NW4 ......46 C5
SE1............... 251 B2
Shortway SE9 ....144 A2
Short Way
Colney Hatch N12 .....30 C4
Twickenham TW2..... 152 A4
Shotfield SM6 ....219 B2
Shott Cl SM1 ....218 A3
Shottendane Rd
SW6.......135 C4 265 A2
Shottery Cl SE9.......166 A1
Shottfield Ave SW14 .133 C1
Shottsford 1 W11....91 C1
Shoulder of Mutton Alley
10 E14 ....119 A6
Shouldham St
W1.........92 C2 237 B3
Showers Way UB3 ...106 A5
Shrapnel Cl SE18 ....144 A5
Shrapnel Rd SE9.....144 B2
Shreveport Ho 23
N19...............49 D2
Shrewsbury Ave
Harrow HA3..........44 A5
Mortlake SW14 ....133 B1
Shrewsbury Cl KT6...214 A6
Shrewsbury Cres
NW10...............89 B6
Shrewsbury Ho
Chelsea SW3....... 267 A5
Kennington SE11.... 270 D5
Shrewsbury House Sch
KT6 .... 214 A6
Shrewsbury La SE18 144 D4
Shrewsbury Mews 33
W2.................91 C2
Shrewsbury Rd
Beckenham BR3..... 207 A6
Carshalton SM5..... 202 C2
Friern Barnet N11 .....31 D4
Harlington TW14,
TW6 ....149 B5
Notting Hill W2........91 C1
Plashet E7 ....77 D2
Shrewsbury St W10...90 C3
Shrewsbury Wlk 9
TW7 ....131 A2
Shrewton Rd SW17 . 180 D3
Shri Swaminarayan
Mandir★ NW10 .....67 B2
Shroffold Rd BR1... 164 D1
Shropshire Cl CR4...204 A5
Shropshire Ct W7.....86 D1
Shropshire Ho WC1. 239 B5
Shropshire Rd N22....32 B3
Shroton St
NW1........92 C2 237 B4
Shrubberies The
Ilford IG2............57 D4
Woodford E18 ....37 A1
Shrubbery Cl N1.... 235 B5
Shrubbery Gdns N21...16 D4
Shrubbery Rd
Edmonton N9.........18 A1
Southall UB1 .... 107 C5
Streatham SW16.... 182 A6
Shrubbery The
2 Surbiton KT6..... 198 A1
7 Wanstead E11......55 B4
Shrub Ct 5 SM2.....218 A2
Shrubland Gr KT4....216 C5
Shrubland Rd
Hackney E8 ....96 A6
Leyton E10...........53 C2
Walthamstow E17 .....53 C4
Shrublands Ave CR0 .223 C4
Shrublands Cl
Forest Hill SE26..... 162 C1
Whetstone N20 ....14 B2
Shrubsall Cl SE9.....166 A3
Shrubs Ho SW1...... 259 D3
Shurland Ave EN4.....14 B5
Shurland Gdns SE15 139 D5
Shurlock Dr BR6.....227 A4
Shuters Sq W14 .... 254 C1
Shuttle Cl DA15...... 167 D4
Shuttlemead DA5....169 B4
Shuttle St E1.........96 A3
Shuttleworth Rd
SW11..............136 C3
Siamese Mews 11 N3 .29 C2
Sibella Rd SW4 ...... 137 D3
Sibford Ct 5 CR4 ... 202 D6
Sibley Cl Bexley DA6 ..169 A6
Bromley BR1 .... 210 A4
Sibley Ct
Beckenham BR3...... 186 C1
Hillingdon UB8........83 A2
Sibley Gr E12.........78 A1
Sibthorpe Rd SE12...165 C4
Sibthorp Rd 2 CR4 . 180 D1
Sibton Rd SM5.......202 C2
Sicilian Ave WC1.... 240 B3
Sidbury St
SW6.......135 A4 264 A2
SIDCUP 190 A5
Sidcup By-Pass Rd
Sidcup DA14........ 189 C6
St Paul's Cray BR5, BR7,
DA14..............190 B3
Sidcup Hill DA14.....190 B5
Sidcup Hill Gdns
DA14..............190 C5
Sidcup Pl DA14 ......190 A5
Sidcup Rd SE9.......166 A3
Sidcup Sta DA15.... 168 A2
Sidcup Tech Ctr
DA14.............. 190 D4
Siddeley Dr TW4.....129 A3
Siddons Ct WC2..... 240 C1
Siddons Ho 8 NW3...70 D3
Siddons La
NW1........92 D3 237 D5
Siddons Rd
Croydon CR0 .... 220 D5
Forest Hill SE23..... 163 A2
Tottenham N17........34 A2
Side Rd E17 ....53 B4
Sidewood Rd SE9....167 B3
Sidford Ho SE1 ..... 260 D5
Sidford Pl
SE1........116 B3 260 D5
Sidgwick Ho 26
SW9..............138 A3
Sidi Ct 2 N15 ....50 D6
Sidings Mews N7 .....72 C4
Sidings The E11.......54 A1
Sidlaw Ho N16.........51 D1
Sidmouth Ave TW7...130 C3
Sidmouth Dr HA4.....62 A5
Sidmouth Ho
18 Camberwell
SE15 .... 140 A5
Marylebone W1 ..... 237 B2
26 Streatham SW2 .. 160 C4
Sidmouth Mews
WC1.............. 233 C1
Sidmouth Par NW2 ...68 C1
Sidmouth Rd
Bexley DA16......... 146 C5
Leyton E10...........76 A5
Willesden NW2 ....68 C1
Sidmouth St
WC1........94 B4 233 C1
Sidney Ave N13 ....32 B5
Sidney Boyd Ct NW6 ..69 C1
Sidney Elson Way
E6................100 C5
Sidney Gdns TW8 ... 131 D6
Sidney Godley (VC) Ho
31 E2 ....96 C4
Sidney Gr EC1 ...... 234 C3
Sidney Ho
4 Globe Town E2 .....96 D5
SE18...............144 B4
Sidney Miller Ct 8
W3 .... 110 D5
Sidney Rd
Beckenham BR3..... 185 A1
Croydon SE25....... 206 A4
Harrow HA2...........42 A6
Stockwell SW9.......138 B3
Twickenham TW1.....153 B5
Walton-on-T KT12 ...194 B1
Wanstead E7 ....77 A5
Wood Green N22 .....32 B3
Sidney Sq E1.........96 C2
Sidney St E1..........96 C2
Sidworth St 6 E8.....74 B1
Siebert Rd SE3 ......143 A6
Siedle Ho 9 SE18....144 C6
Siege Ho 14 E1 ....96 B1
Siemens Rd SE18 ... 121 D3
Sienna SE28........ 123 D3
Sienna Cl KT9 ...... 213 D2
Sienna Ct TW13...... 149 D1
Sierra Dr RM9, RM10. 103 D5
Sigdon Rd E8.........74 A3
Sigers The HA5 ....40 B3
Signal Ho
9 London E8..........74 B1
SE1................ 252 A1
Signmakers Yd NW1 231 D5
Sigrist Sq 4 KT2.....176 A2
Silbury Ave CR4......180 C2
Silbury Ho 9 SE26...162 A1
Silbury St N1....... 235 C2
Silchester Ct
Stanwell TW15...... 148 A2
Thornton Heath CR7 . 204 C5
Silchester Rd W10....90 D1
Silecroft Rd DA7.....147 C4
Silesia Bldgs E8 ......74 B1
Silex St SE1 . 116 D4 251 D1
Silicone Bsns Ctr
UB6 ....87 C5
Silk Cl SE12.........165 A5
Silkfield Rd NW9......45 C4
Silk Ho NW9..........45 B6
Silkin Mews 24
SE15..............140 A5
Silk Mews SE11..... 261 B1
Silk Mills Path SE13..142 A2
Silk Mills Sq E9.......75 B2
Silks Ct E11 ....54 C1
Silk St EC2 .....95 A2 242 B4
Silkstream Par HA8....27 A2
Silkstream Rd HA8....27 A2
Sillitoe Ho N1 ...... 235 D5
Silsoe Ho NW1...... 231 D3
Silsoe Rd N22 ....50 B6
Silverbell Ct 1 N12...29 D5
Silver Birch Ave E4 ...35 B4
Silver Birch Cl
Forest Hill SE6.......163 B1
Friern Barnet N11 .....31 A4
Ickenham UB10.......60 A4
SE28............... 124 A5
Silver Birch Ct EN3....18 D6
Silver Birch Gdns
E6................100 B3
Silverbirch Wlk 1
NW3...............71 A2
Silverburn Ho 4
SW9 .... 138 D4
Silver Cl Harrow HA3...24 B3
SE14.............. 141 A5
Silvercliffe Gdns EN4 ..2 C1
Silver Cres W4....... 110 D2
Silver Ct N19 ....71 C5
Silverdale Enfield EN2...4 A1
Forest Hill SE26..... 184 C6
NW1............. 232 A2
Silverdale Ave IG3....57 D4
Silverdale Cl
Cheam SM1 ....217 B4
1 Ealing W7 .... 108 D5
Northolt UB5 ....63 B3
Silverdale Ct EC1 ... 241 D6
Silverdale Dr
Chislehurst SE9..... 166 A2
Sunbury TW16 ....172 B1
Silverdale Factory Ctr
UB3 .... 106 A3
Silverdale Gdns UB3 .106 A4
Silverdale Ind Est
UB3 .... 106 A4
Silverdale Par IG3....57 D4
Silverdale Rd
Bexleyheath DA7.... 147 D3
Chingford E4 ....36 B4
Hayes UB3......... 106 A4
Petts Wood BR5..... 211 A5
Silverhall St TW7 ....131 A2
Silverholme Cl HA3 ...44 A2
Silver Ind Est N17.....33 D1
Silver Jubilee Way
TW4 ....128 B3
Silver La BR4........224 B6
Silverland St E16 ....122 B5
Silverleigh Rd CR7...204 B4
Silvermead 7 E18....37 A2
Silvermere Rd SE6 .. 163 D5
Silver Pl W1........ 249 B6
Silver Rd
Shepherd's Bush
W12 .... 112 D6
St Johns SE13 ...... 141 D2
Silvers 4 IG9 ....21 C3
Silver Spring Cl
DA8............. 147 D6
Silver St
Edmonton N18........33 C6
Enfield EN1 .... 5 B2
Silverstone Ct 8
BR1...............187 C1
Silverston Way HA7...25 C4
Silver Street Sta N18..33 D5
Silverthorn 17 NW6...91 D6
Silverthorne Lo EN1 ..17 C6
Silverthorne Rd
SW8...............137 B3
Silverthorn Gdns E4 ..19 C2
Silverton Lo SE19....183 C3
Silverton Rd W6 .... 134 D6
SILVERTOWN 121 B4
Silvertown Way E16..121 A5
Silvertree La UB6 .....86 B4
Silver Way
Hillingdon UB10.......82 D5
Romford RM7..........59 D6
Silver Wing Ind Est
CR0 ....220 B2
Silver Wlk SE16......119 B5
Silverwood Cl BR3 ...185 C3
Silvester Ho
27 Bethnal Green E2 ...96 C4
1 Notting Hill W11....91 B1
Pinner HA5...........40 A5
6 Stepney E1 ....96 B1
Silvester Rd SE22 ... 161 D6
Silvester St SE1..... 252 C1
Silwex Ho E1 .... 243 C5
Silwood St SE16 .....118 C1
Simba Ct TW1 ...... 152 D3
Simla Ho SE1....... 252 D1
Simmil Rd KT10......212 C3
Simmonds Ct SW5.. 255 C3
Simmons Cl
Chessington KT9 .... 213 C2
East Barnet N20.......14 C3
Simmons Dr RM8.....81 A5
Simmons Gate KT10 .212 A3
Simmons Ho
20 Bethnal Green E2...96 A4
Finsbury Pk N7........72 B6
Simmons La E4.......20 B2
Simmons Rd SE18 .. 122 D1
Simmons' Way N20 ...14 C2
Simms Cl SM5 ....218 C6
Simms Ct SW6........135 A2
Simms Gdns N2 ......30 A1
Simms Rd SE1.......118 A2
Simnel Rd SE12......165 B4
Simon Cl
W11.......113 B6 244 D6
Simon Ct
Paddington W9 ....91 C4
5 Woolwich SE28....124 B5
Simonds Rd E10 ......75 C6
Simone Cl BR1...... 187 D2
Simon Lo 31 SW19 .. 156 D3
Simon Marks Jewish
Prim Sch 8 N16 ....73 D6
Simons Wlk E15 ......76 B3
Simpson Cl
Southgate N21........16 B6
Thornton Heath CR0 . 205 A3
Simpson Dr W3.......89 B1
Simpson Ho
Lisson Gr NW8...... 230 A1
Vauxhall SE11 ...... 260 C1
Wembley HA9 ....65 D6
Simpson Rd
Hounslow TW4.......151 B5
Richmond TW10...... 175 C6
Simpson's Rd BR2 ...209 A6
Poplar E14 .... 119 D6
Simpson St SW11....136 C3
Simpson Way KT6....197 C3
Sim's Cotts KT10.... 212 D2
Sims Wlk SE3....... 142 D1
Sinclair Ct
21 Beckenham BR3.. 185 C3
Canonbury N5 ....73 A2
5 Croydon CR0..... 221 D6
Sinclair Gdns W14 .. 112 D4
Sinclair Gr NW11 .....46 D3
Sinclair Ho
Harrow HA7..........24 D4
Sinclair Ho *continued*
3 South Norwood
SW16 ....182 B3
1 Streatham SW12 . 159 D3
Sinclair Mans 13
W12 .... 112 D4
Sinclair Pl SE4.......163 C5
Sinclair Rd
Chingford Hatch E4 ....35 B5
W14.......113 A3 254 A6
Sinclairs Ho 18 E3 ....97 B5
Sinclare Cl EN1.........5 D4
Singapore Rd W13...109 A5
Singer St EC2...... 235 D1
Singlegate Prim Sch
SW19..............180 B3
Singleton Cl
Mitcham SW17 ..... 180 D3
Thornton Heath CR0 . 205 A2
Singleton Rd RM9 ....81 B3
Singleton Scarp N12..29 C5
Sinnott Rd E17 ....34 D2
Sion Ct TW1 ....153 B3
Sion Ho SE13 ....142 A1
Sion-Manning RC Sch
for Girls
16 Kensal Town W10...91 A2
6 North Kensington
W10 ....90 D2
Sion Rd TW1.........153 B3
Sippetts Ct IG1 ....57 B1
SIPSON 126 C6
Sipson Cl UB7 ....126 C6
Sipson La UB3, UB7.. 126 D6
Sipson Rd
Harmondsworth
UB7............. 126 C6
West Drayton UB7....104 B2
West Drayton UB7.... 104 C1
Sipson Way UB7 .....126 C5
Sir Abraham Dawes
Cotts SW15........135 A1
Sir Alexander Cl
W3 .... 111 D5
Sir Alexander Rd
W3 .... 111 D5
Sir Arthur Bliss Ct 4
SW19 .... 180 D1
Sir Cyril Black Way 2
SW19 ....179 C3
Sirdar Rd
Mitcham CR4 .... 181 A4
Tottenham N22 ....33 A1
W11....... 113 A6 244 A5
Sir Francis Drake Prim
Sch 1 SE8........ 119 A1
Sir George Monoux Coll
E17...............35 D1
Sir Henry Floyd Ct HA7. 9 B2
Sirinham Point SW8 270 D5
Sirius Bldg 13 E1 ... 118 D6
Sir James Barrie Prim
Sch SW8....137 C4 269 B1
Sir John Cass
Foundation & Redcoat
CE Sec Sch 19 E1....96 D2
Sir John Cass's
Foundation Prim Sch
EC3 ....95 C1 243 B1
Sir John Heron Prim Sch
E12...............78 B4
Sir John Kirk Cl 33
SE5...............139 A5
Sir John Lillie Prim Sch
SW6........135 A6 264 B5
Sir John Soane's Mus★
WC2........94 B1 240 C2
Sir Martin Bowes Ho 9
SE18..............122 C2
Sir Oswald Stoll
Foundation The
SW6 .... 265 C4
Sir Thomas Abney Prim
Sch N16 ....51 B1
Sir Thomas More Est
SW3 ....136 B6 266 D5
Sirus Rd HA6 ....22 A5
Sir William Burrough
Prim Sch 27 E14.....97 B1
Sir William Powell's
Almshos SW6 .....135 A2
Sise La EC4......... 242 C1

Siskin Ho
Edmonton N9 18 D3
14 Rotherhithe SE16 118 D2
Sisley Rd IG11 101 D6
Sispara Gdns SW18 157 B5
Sissinghurst Cl BR1 186 C5
Sissinghurst Ho 17 SE15 140 C6
Sissinghurst Rd CR0 206 A2
Sissulu Ct 8 E6 99 C6
Sister Mabel's Way 15 SE15 140 A5
Sisters Ave SW11 136 D1
Sisters of St Marcellina Sch 34 NW3 70 A4
Sistova Rd SW12 159 B3
Sisulu Pl SW9 138 C2
Sitarey Ct 4 W12 112 B5
Site of Changing of the Guard★ SW1 249 A1
Sittingbourne Ave EN1 17 B5
Sitwell Gr HA7 24 D5
Siverst Cl UB5 63 D2
Sivill Ho 9 E2 95 D4
Siviter Way RM10 81 D1
Siward Rd
Bromley BR2 209 C6
Tottenham N17 33 B2
Wandsworth SW17 158 A1
Six Bridges Ind Est 15 SE1 118 A1
Sixpenny Ct IG11 79 A2
Sixth Ave Hayes UB3 105 D5
Ilford E12 78 B4
West Kilburn W10 91 A4
Sixth Cross Rd TW2 152 A1
Skardu Rd NW2 69 A3
Skeena Hill SW18, SW19 157 A4
Skeffington Rd E6 100 B6
Skeffington St SE18 123 A3
Skeggs Ho 5 E14 120 A3
Skegness Ho 3 N7 72 B1
Skelbrook St SW18 158 A2
Skelgill Rd SW15 135 B1
Skelley Rd E15 76 D1
Skelton Cl 7 E8 73 D2
Skelton Ho N16 73 C3
Skelton Rd E7 77 A2
Skeltons La E10 53 D2
Skelwith Rd W6 134 C6
Skenfrith Ho SE15 140 B6
Skerne Rd KT2 175 D2
Skerne Wlk KT2 175 D2
Sketchley Gdns SE16 118 D1
Sketty Rd EN1 5 D2
Skiers St E15 98 C6
Skiffington Cl SW2 160 C3
Skillen Lodge HA5 22 D2
Skinner Ct E17 53 C4
Skinner Pl SW1 258 A3
Skinners Almshouses N13 16 C1
Skinners Company Sch (Upper) 10 N16 51 D2
Skinner's Company's Lower Sch 8 E5 52 B1
Skinners La EC4 252 B6
Hounslow TW5 129 D4
Skinner St EC1 94 C3 241 B6
Skip La UB9 38 A1
Skipper Ct 5 IG11 101 A6
Skipsea Ho SW18 158 B5
Skipsey Ave E6 100 B4
Skipton Cl N11 31 A4
Skipton Dr UB3 105 A3
Skipton Ho SE4 141 A1
Skipwith Bldg EC1 241 A4
Skipworth Rd E9 96 C6
Skua Ct 33 SE8 141 B6
Skyline Ct SE1 263 C5
Skyline Plaza Bldg 19 E1 96 A1
Skylines E14 120 A4
Sky Peals Rd IG8 36 B3
Sky Studios E16 122 C4
Sladebrook Rd SE3 143 D2
Slade Ct Barnet EN5 1 D2
Brondesbury NW2 69 A3
Muswell Hill N10 31 B3
Sladedale Rd SE18 123 C1
Slade Ho TW4 151 B5
Sladen Pl 12 E5 74 B4
Slades Cl EN2 4 C2
Slades Dr BR7 189 A6
Slades Gdns EN2 4 C2
Slades Hill EN2 4 C2
Slades Rise EN2 4 C2
Slade The SE18 145 C6
Slade Twr E10 75 C6
Slade Way CR4 181 A2
Slagrove Pl SE13 163 D6
Slaidburn St SW10 136 A6 266 B5
Slaithwaite Rd SE13 142 A1
Slaney Ct NW10 68 C1
Slaney Pl 1 N7 72 C3
Slater Cl 13 SE18 122 C2
Slatter 1 NW9 27 D2
Slattery Rd TW13 150 C3
Sleaford Ho 16 E3 97 C3
Sleaford Ind Est SW8 137 C5 269 B3
Sleaford St SW8 137 C5 269 B3
Sleat Ho 11 E3 97 B5
Sledmere Ct TW14 149 C3
Slievemore Cl 8 SW4 137 D2
Sligo Ho 8 E1 96 D3
Slingsby Pl WC2 250 A6
Slippers Pl SE16 118 B3
Slipway Ho 1 E14 119 D1
Sloane Ave SW3 114 C2 257 B3
Sloane Avenue Mans SW3 257 C3
Sloane Ct E SW3 258 A2
Sloane Ct W SW3 258 A2
Sloane Gate Mans SW1 258 A4
Sloane Gdns
Belgravia SW1 115 A2 258 A3
Orpington BR6 227 A5
Sloane Ho 7 E9 74 C1
Sloane Hospl BR3 186 B2
Sloane Sq SW1 257 D3
Sloane Square Sta SW1 115 A2 258 A3
Sloane St SW1 114 D3 257 D5
Sloane Terr SW1 258 A4
Sloane Terr Mans SW1 258 A4
Sloane Wlk CR0 207 B3
Sloan Ho RM10 81 D1
Slocum Cl SE28 124 C6
Slough La NW9 45 A3
Sly St 17 E1 96 B1
Smaldon Cl UB7 104 C3
Smallberry Ave TW7 130 D3
Smallberry Green Prim Sch TW7 131 A3
Smallbrook Mews W2 236 C1
Smallbugh Mans HA0 65 B4
Smalley Cl N16 73 D5
Smallwood Prim Sch SW17 180 B6
Smallwood Rd SW17 180 B6
Smarden Cl DA17 125 C1
Smarden Gr SE9 188 B6
Smart's Pl
Edmonton N18 34 A5
WC1, WC2 240 B2
Smart St E2 96 D4
Smeaton Cl KT9 213 D2
Smeaton Ct SE1 262 A5
Smeaton Rd
Holdbrook EN3 7 C6
Wandsworth SW18 157 C4
Smeaton St E1 118 B5
Smedley St SW4 137 D3
Smeed Rd E3 75 C1
Smiles Pl SE13 142 A3
Smith Cl SE16 118 D5
Smithers Ho 3 SE20 184 D3
Smithfield Mkt★ EC1 94 D2 241 D3
Smithfield St EC1 94 D2 241 C3
Smithies Rd SE2 124 B2
Smith's Ct W1 249 C6
Smithson Rd N17 33 B2
Smiths Point E13 99 A6
Smith Sq SW1 116 A3 260 A5
Smith St
Surbiton KT5 198 B3
SW3 114 D1 257 C1
Smith's Yd
7 Croydon CR0 221 A5
Wandsworth SW18 158 A2
Smith Terr SW3 114 D1 257 C1
Smithwood Cl SW19 157 A2
Smithy St E1 96 C2
Smithy Street Sch 34 E1 96 C2
Smock Wlk CR0 205 A3
Smoothfield TW3 129 C1
Smtyhe Cl N9 18 A2
Smugglers Way SW18 135 D1
Smyrk's Rd SE17 117 C1 263 B1
Smyrna Mans 8 NW6 69 C1
Smyrna Rd NW6 69 C1
Smythe St E14 119 D6
Snakes La EN4, N14 3 C1
Snakes La E IG8 37 C4
Snakes La W IG8 37 B4
Snakey La TW13 172 B6
SNARESBROOK 54 D6
Snaresbrook Coll Prep Sch 10 E18 37 A1
Snaresbrook Dr HA7 26 A6
Snaresbrook Hall 12 E18 55 A6
Snaresbrook Ho E18 54 D5
Snaresbrook Prim Sch E18 55 A5
Snaresbrook Rd E11 54 D5
Snaresbrook Sta E11 55 A4
Snarsgate St W10 90 C2
Sneath Ave NW11 47 B2
Snell's Pk N18 33 D4
Sneyd Rd NW2 68 C4
Snowberry Cl E11 76 B4
Snowbury Rd 6 SW6 135 D3
Snow Ct 4 HA0 65 D3
Snowden Ave UB10 82 D5
Snowden St EC2 95 C3 243 A5
Snowdon Cres UB3 105 A3
Snowdon Dr NW9 45 C3
Snowdon Rd TW6 149 A5
Snowdown Cl SE20 184 D2
Snowdrop Cl 2 TW12 173 C4
Snowe Ho SE27 160 D1
Snow Hill EC1 94 D2 241 C3
Snowman Ho NW6 91 D6
Snowsfields SE1 117 B4 252 D2
Snowsfields Prim Sch SE1 117 C4 253 A2
Snowshill Rd E12 78 A3
Snowy Fielder Waye TW7 131 B3
Soames St SE15 139 D2
Soames Wlk KT3 177 C2
Soane Cl W5 109 D4
Soane Ct 10 NW1 71 C1
Soane Ho SE17 262 D1
Soaphouse La TW8 132 A5
Sobell L Ctr N7 72 B5
Soham Rd EN3 7 B6
SOHO 93 D1
Soho★ W1 93 D1 239 C2
Soho Mills SM6 203 B1
Soho Parish CE Prim Sch W1 115 D6 249 C6
Soho Sq W1 93 D1 239 C2
Soho St W1 239 C2
Sojourner-Truth Cl 11 E8 74 B2
Sola Ct 8 CR0 205 B1
Solander Gdns
13 Shadwell E1 118 C6
Stepney E1 118 B6
Solar Ct N3 29 D3
Soldene Ct N7 72 B2
Solebay St E1 97 A3
Solent Ct SW16 182 B1
Solent Ho 6 E1 97 A2
Solent Rd NW6 69 C3
Solent Rise E13 99 A4
Soley Mews WC1 234 A2
Solidarity Ho 5 NW10 68 C2
Solna Ave SW15 156 C6
Solna Rd N21 17 B4
Solomon Ave N9 34 A6
Solomons Ct N12 30 A3
Solomon's Pas SE15 140 B1
Solon New Rd SW4 138 A1
Solon Rd SW2 138 A1
Solway Cl TW4 129 A2
Solway Ho 12 E1 96 D3
Solway Rd
East Dulwich SE22 140 A1
Tottenham N22 32 D2
Somaford Gr EN4 14 B5
Somali Rd NW2 69 B3
Somborne Ho 11 SW15 156 A4
Sombrook Ho SE11 261 A3
Somerby Rd IG11 79 B1
Somercoates Cl EN4 2 C2
Somer Ct SW6 265 A5
Somerfield Rd N4 72 D6
Somerfield St SE16 118 D1
Somerford Cl HA5 40 A5
Somerford Gr
Shacklewell N16 73 D4
Tottenham N17 34 A3
Somerford Grove Est N16 73 D4
Somerford St E1 96 B3
Somerford Way SE16 119 A4
Somerhill Ave DA15 168 B4
Somerhill Rd DA16 146 B3
Somerleyton Rd SW9 138 C1
Somersby Est SE20 184 C3
Somersby Gdns IG4 56 B4
Somers Cl NW1 232 C4
Somers Cres W2 237 A1
Somerset Ave
Chessington KT9 213 D4
DA16 145 D1
Wimbledon SW20 178 B1
Somerset Cl
New Malden KT3 199 C3
North Cheam KT4 216 C5
Tottenham N17 33 B1
Woodford IG8 37 A2
Somerset Ct
10 Buckhurst Hill IG9 21 C2
Ealing W7 86 D1
2 Hampton TW12 173 C2
Somerset Gdns
Highgate N6 49 A2
St Johns SE13 141 D3
Teddington TW11 174 C5
Thornton Heath SW16 204 B6
Tottenham N17 33 C3
Somerset Hall N17 33 C3
Somerset Ho WC2 116 B6 250 D6
Somerset Ho SW19 157 A1
Somerset Lo
9 Brentford TW8 131 D6
5 New Barnet EN5 14 A6
Putney SW15 134 B1
Somerset Rd
Bedford Pk W4 111 B3
Brentford TW8 131 C6
Ealing W13 109 C5
Edmonton N18 33 D5
Harrow HA1 42 A4
Hendon NW4 46 C5
Holdbrook EN3 7 C5
Kingston u T KT1 176 B1
New Barnet EN5 14 A6
Southall UB1 85 C2
Teddington TW11 174 C5
Tottenham N17 51 D6
Walthamstow E17 53 C3
Wimbledon SW19 157 A1
Somerset Sq W14 113 B4 244 C1
Somerset Waye TW5 129 A5
Somersham Rd DA7 147 A3
Somers Pl SW2 160 B4
Somers Rd
Tulse Hill SW2 160 B5
Walthamstow E17 53 B5
SOMERS TOWN 93 D4
Somers Town Est NW1 93 C5 232 B3
Somers Way WD23 8 A4
Somerton Ave TW9 132 D2
Somerton Rd
Cricklewood NW2 69 A5
Nunhead SE15 140 B1
Somertrees Ave SE12 165 B2
Somervell Rd HA2 63 C3
Somerville Ave SW13 134 C6
Somerville Cl SW9 138 B3
Somerville Ct SW16 181 D4
Somerville Ho 10 SW15 156 D5
Somerville Point SE16 119 B4
Somerville Rd
Dagenham RM6 58 C4
Penge SE20 184 D3
Sonderburg Rd 13 N7 72 B6
Sondes St SE17 139 B6
Songhurst Cl CR0 204 B3
Sonia Ct Edgware HA8 26 B3
North Finchley N12 30 A6
Sonia Gdns
Heston TW5 129 C5
North Finchley N12 30 A6
Willesden NW10 67 D4
Sonning Ct CR0 222 A6
Sonning Gdns TW12 173 A4
Sonning Ho 32 E2 95 D4
Sonning Rd CR0 206 A3
Soper Cl
Chingford Hatch E4 35 B5
4 Forest Hill SE23 162 D2
Soper Mews EN3 7 C5
Sophia Cl N7 72 B2
Sophia Ho
10 Hammersmith W6 112 C1
Tottenham N15 51 D5
Sophia Rd
Newham E13 99 B2
Walthamstow E10 53 D1
Sophia Sq 14 SE16 119 A6
Sopwith 2 NW9 27 D2
Sopwith Ave KT9 214 A3
Sopwith Cl KT2 176 B5
Sopwith Rd TW5 128 C5
Sopwith Way
Battersea SW8 137 B5 268 C4
Kingston u T KT2 176 A2
Sorbus Ct EN2 4 D3
Sorensen Ct 2 E10 75 D6
Sorrel Cl SE28 124 A5
Sorrel Gdns E6 100 A2
Sorrel Ho TW3 130 A4
Sorrel La 17 E14 98 B1
Sorrell Cl
6 Brixton SW9 138 C3
SE14 141 A5
Sorrento Rd SM1 217 D5
Soseki Mus★ SW4 137 B2
Sotheby Rd N5 73 A4
Sotheran Cl E8 96 A6
Sotheron Pl SW6 265 D3
Soudan Rd SW11 136 D4 267 C1
Souldern Rd 10 W14 112 D3
South Access Rd E17 53 A3
South Acre NW9 27 D1
Southacre Way HA5 22 C2
SOUTH ACTON 110 D3
South Acton Sta W3, W4 111 A3
South Africa Rd W12 112 B6
SOUTHALL 107 A5
Southall Ct UB1 107 B6
Southall Ent Ctr UB2 107 C4
Southall La TW5 106 B1
Southall Norwood Hospl UB2 107 B3
Southall Pl SE1 252 C1
Southall Sp Ctr UB1 107 B5
Southall Sta UB1 107 B4
Southall & West London Coll UB1 107 A5
Southam Ho 9 W10 91 A3

Southampton Bldgs WC2 ... 241 A3
Southampton Gdns CR4 ... 204 A4
Southampton Mews E16 ... 121 B5
Southampton Pl WC1 ... 240 B3
Southampton Rd
Maitland Pk NW5 ... 70 D3
Stanwell TW19, TW6 . 148 A5
Southampton Rd E TW6 ... 148 B5
Southampton Rd W TW6 ... 148 B5
Southampton Row WC1 ... 94 A2 240 B4
Southampton St WC2 ... 250 B6
Southampton Way SE5 ... 139 C5
Southam St W10 ... 91 A3
South Audley St W1 ... 115 A5 248 B4
South Ave
Chingford E4 ... 20 A4
East Finchley NW11 ... 47 D5
Richmond TW9 ... 132 C3
Southall UB1 ... 107 B6
Wallington SM5 ... 219 A1
South Avenue Gdns UB1 ... 107 B6
Southbank KT7 ... 197 B2
SOUTH BANK ... 116 B4
South Bank KT6 ... 198 A3
South Bank Bsns Ctr SW8 ... 137 D6 269 D5
Southbank International Sch 14 NW3 ... 70 A2
Southbank International Sch (Westminster Campus) W1 93 B2 238 C4
Southbank Int Sch W11 ... 113 C6 245 A5
South Bank Lo 2 KT6 ... 198 A3
South Bank Terr KT6 ... 198 A3
South Bank Univ SW8 ... 137 D4 269 D2
South Bank University (Erlang House) SE1 ... 116 D4 251 C1
SOUTH BEDDINGTON ... 219 C2
South Bermondsey Sta SE16 ... 118 C1
South Birkbeck Rd E11 ... 76 B5
South Black Lion La 7 W6 ... 112 A1
South Bldg SW1 ... 259 B6
South Block 20 E1 ... 118 C6
South Bolton Gdns SW10 ... 255 D2
SOUTHBOROUGH
BR2 ... 210 B3
KT6 ... 197 D1
Southborough Cl KT6 ... 197 D1
Southborough Ho SE17 ... 263 B2
Southborough La BR1, BR2 ... 210 B4
Southborough Prim Sch BR2 ... 210 C4
Southborough Rd
Bromley BR1, BR2 ... 210 A5
South Hackney E9 ... 96 D6
Surbiton KT6 ... 198 A1
Southborough Rd (The Lane) KT6 ... 198 A1
Southborough Sch KT6 ... 214 A5
Southbourne BR2 ... 209 A2
Southbourne Ave NW9 ... 27 B1
Southbourne Cl HA5 .. 41 A2
Southbourne Cres NW4 ... 47 A5
Southbourne Ct NW9 . 27 A1
Southbourne Gdns
Ilford IG1 ... 79 A3
Ruislip HA4 ... 40 B1
SE12 ... 165 B6
Southbridge Pl CR0 .. 221 A4
Southbridge Rd CR0 . 221 A4
Southbridge Way UB2 ... 107 A4
SOUTH BROMLEY ... 98 B2
Southbrook Mews SE12 ... 164 D5
Southbrook Rd
Hither Green SE12 ... 164 D5
Thornton Heath SW16 ... 182 A2
South Building★ SE10 ... 142 B5
Southbury NW8 ... 229 B6
Southbury Ave EN1 ... 6 A1
Southbury Prim Sch EN3 ... 6 C1
Southbury Rd
Enfield EN1 ... 5 D2
Enfield EN1, EN3 ... 6 B1
Southbury Sta EN3 ... 6 B1
South Camden Com Sch NW1 ... 93 D5 232 C4
South Carriage Dr SW1, SW7 ... 114 D4 247 C2
South Chelsea Coll 22 SW9 ... 138 B1
Southchurch Ct
Bowes Pk N13 ... 32 B5
Newham E6 ... 100 B5
Southchurch Rd E6 .. 100 B5
South Cl Barnet EN5 ... 1 B2
DA6 ... 146 D1
Dagenham RM10 ... 103 C6
Highgate N6 ... 49 B3
Morden SM4 ... 201 C3
Pinner HA5 ... 41 B2
Twickenham TW2 ... 151 C1
West Drayton UB7 ... 104 C3
South Colonnade The E14 ... 119 D5
Southcombe St W14 254 A4
South Common Rd UB8 ... 60 A2
Southcote Ave
Feltham TW13 ... 150 A2
Tolworth KT5 ... 198 D2
Southcote Rd
Croydon SE25 ... 206 B3
Tufnell Pk N19 ... 71 C4
Walthamstow E17 ... 53 A4
Southcote Rise HA4 ... 39 B2
Southcott Ho
31 Bromley E3 ... 97 D4
W9 ... 236 B5
South Countess Rd E17 ... 53 B6
South Cres
Newham E16 ... 98 B3
WC1 ... 239 C3
Southcroft
Carshalton SM1 ... 218 C3
8 Stonebridge NW10 .. 89 B6
Southcroft Ave
DA16 ... 145 C2
West Wickham BR4 .. 224 A6
Southcroft Rd BR6 ... 227 C5
Streatham SW17 ... 181 A4
South Cross Rd IG6 ... 57 A4
South Croxted Rd SE21 ... 183 B6
SOUTH CROYDON ... 221 B1
South Croydon Sta CR2 ... 221 B3
South Ct 17 SW15 ... 156 D5
Southdean Gdns SW19 ... 157 B2
South Dene NW7 ... 11 B1
Southdene Ct N11 ... 15 C1
Southdown N7 ... 72 A2
Southdown Ave W7 .. 109 A3
Southdown Cres
Harrow HA2 ... 42 A1
Ilford IG2 ... 57 C4
Southdown Dr SW20 ... 178 D3
Southdown Rd SW20 ... 178 D2
South Dr
Orpington BR6 ... 227 C3
Ruislip HA4 ... 39 C1
South Ealing Cemy W5 ... 109 D2
South Ealing Rd W5 . 109 D3
South Ealing Sta W5 ... 109 D3
South Eastern Ave N9 ... 17 D1
South Eastern Univ 3 N7 ... 72 B5
South Eaton Pl SW1 ... 115 A2 258 B4
South Eden Park Rd BR3 ... 207 D4
South Edwardes Sq W8 ... 255 A5
SOUTHEND ... 186 B6
South End
Croydon CR0 ... 221 A4
W8 ... 113 D3 255 D6
Southend Cl SE9 ... 166 D5
South End Cl NW3 ... 70 C4
Southend Cres SE9 . 166 D5
South End Gn NW3 ... 70 C4
Southend Ho SE9 ... 166 C4
Southend La SE6 ... 185 C6
Southend Rd
Beckenham BR3 ... 185 C2
Plashet E6 ... 78 B1
Woodford IG8 ... 37 D1
South End Rd NW3 ... 70 C4
Southend Road (North Circular Rd) E17, E18 ... 36 B2
South End Row W8 ... 113 D3 255 D6
Southern Ave
East Bedfont TW14 .. 150 A3
South Norwood SE25 . 205 D6
Southerngate Way SE14 ... 141 A5
Southern Gr E3 ... 97 B3
Southernhay IG10 ... 21 D6
Southern Perimeter Rd
Hatton TW14, TW6 ... 149 B6
West Bedfont TW19, TW6 ... 148 C5
Southern Rd
Fortis Green N2 ... 48 D5
Newham E13 ... 99 B5
Southern Road Prim Sch E13 ... 99 B5
Southern Row W10 ... 91 A3
Southern St N1 ... 233 C4
Southern Way
Greenwich SE10 ... 120 D3
Romford RM7 ... 59 C3
Southerton Rd W6 .. 112 C2
South Esk Rd E7 ... 77 C2
Southey Ho SE17 ... 262 B2
Southey Mews E16 .. 121 A5
Southey Rd
Brixton SW9 ... 138 C4
Merton SW19 ... 179 C3
Tottenham N15 ... 51 C4
Southey St SE20 ... 184 D3
Southfield EN5 ... 12 D5
Southfield Cl UB8 ... 82 C4
Southfield Cotts W7 ... 108 D4
Southfield Ct E11 ... 76 D5
Southfield Gdns TW1, TW2 ... 174 D6
Southfield Lo W4 ... 111 B4
Southfield Pk HA2 ... 41 D5
Southfield Prim Sch W4 ... 111 C4
Southfield Rd
Acton W4 ... 111 B4
Enfield EN3 ... 18 C5
St Paul's Cray BR7 ... 211 D6
SOUTHFIELDS ... 157 D3
Southfields
Hendon NW4 ... 46 B6
Thames Ditton KT8 ... 196 C3
Southfields Ave TW15 ... 170 D4
Southfields Com Coll SW18 ... 157 C3
Southfields Ct SM3 .. 217 C6
Southfields Rd SW18 ... 157 C5
Southfields Sta SW18 ... 157 B3
Southfleet Rd BR6 ... 227 C4
SOUTHGATE ... 16 B4
South Gate Ave TW13 ... 171 B6
Southgate Cir 3 N14 . 15 D3
Southgate Coll N14 ... 15 D2
Southgate Ct N1 ... 73 B1
Southgate Gr N1 ... 73 B1
Southgate Ho 7 E17 .. 54 A6
Southgate Rd N1 ... 95 B6 235 D6
South Gate Rd E12 ... 77 D5
Southgate Sch EN4 ... 15 B6
Southgate Sta N14 ... 15 D3
Southgate Way N2 ... 30 C2
South Gdns
Mitcham SW19 ... 180 B3
Wembley HA9 ... 66 C6
South Gipsy Rd DA16 ... 146 D2
South Glade The DA5 ... 169 B3
South Gn NW9 ... 27 C2
South Gr Highgate N6 .. 49 A1
Tottenham N15 ... 51 B4
Walthamstow E17 ... 53 B4
South Greenford Sta UB6 ... 86 C4
South Grove Ho N6 ... 49 A1
South Grove Prim Sch E17 ... 53 B3
SOUTH HACKNEY ... 96 C6
SOUTH HAMPSTEAD 70 A1
South Hampstead High Sch 11 NW3 ... 70 B2
South Hampstead Sta NW8 ... 70 A1
South Harringay Jun & Inf Schs 1 N4 ... 50 D4
SOUTH HARROW ... 63 D5
South Harrow Sta HA2 ... 64 A5
South Hill BR7 ... 188 B4
South Hill Ave HA1, HA2 ... 64 B5
South Hill Gr HA1 ... 64 C4
South Hill Pk NW3 ... 70 C4
South Hill Pk Gdns NW3 ... 70 C4
South Hill Rd
Beckenham BR2 ... 208 C5
6 Beckenham BR2 .. 208 D5
Southholme Cl SE19 . 183 C2
Southill La HA5 ... 40 B5
Southill Rd BR7 ... 188 B3
Southill St E14 ... 97 D1
South Island Pl SW9 . 138 C5
SOUTH KENSINGTON ... 114 A1
South Kensington Sta SW7 ... 114 B2 256 D4
South Kensington Station Arc SW7 .. 256 D4
South Kenton Sta HA9 ... 43 C1
South La
Kingston u T KT1 ... 197 D6
New Malden KT3 ... 199 B3
SOUTH LAMBETH ... 138 A4
South Lambeth Pl SW8 ... 270 B6
South Lambeth Rd SW8 ... 138 A5 270 B4
Southland Rd SE18 .. 145 D5
Southlands Ave BR6 . 227 C3
Southlands Ct BR2 .. 209 D5
Southlands Dr SW19 ... 156 D2
Southlands Gr BR1 .. 210 A6
Southlands Rd BR1, BR2 ... 209 D5
Southland Way TW7 . 152 B6
South La W KT3 ... 199 B5
South Lo
6 New Barnet EN5 ... 13 D6
NW8 ... 229 C2
Twickenham TW2 ... 152 A5
South Lodge Ave CR4, CR7, SW16 ... 204 A5
South Lodge Cres EN2 . 3 D1
South Lodge Dr N14 .. 15 D6
South London Gall★ SE5 ... 139 C4
South London Montessori Sch SW11 ... 267 A1
South Mall The N9 ... 18 A1
South Mead
Grahame Pk NW9 ... 27 D2
West Ewell KT19 ... 215 D1
Southmead Prim Sch 16 SW19 ... 157 A3
Southmead Rd SW19 ... 157 A3
South Merton Sta SW20 ... 201 B6
South Molton La W1 ... 93 B1 238 C1
South Molton Rd E16 . 99 A1
South Molton St W1 ... 93 B1 238 C1
Southmont Rd KT10 .. 212 C5
Southmoor Way E9 ... 75 B3
South Mount N20 ... 14 A2
SOUTH NORWOOD .. 205 C6
South Norwood Ctry Pk★ SE25 ... 206 C5
South Norwood Hill SE19, SE25 ... 183 D1
South Norwood Pools & L Ctr SE25 ... 206 B4
South Norwood Prim Sch SE25 ... 206 A5
South Oak Rd SW16 .. 182 B6
Southold Rise SE9 ... 166 B1
Southolm St SW11 ... 137 B4 268 D1
South Ordnance Rd EN3 ... 7 C5
Southover BR1 ... 187 A5
Finchley N12 ... 29 C6
SOUTH OXHEY ... 22 B6
South Par
Acton Green W4 ... 111 B2
Edgware HA8 ... 26 C1
Wallington SM6 ... 219 C2
South Parade SW3 ... 114 B1 256 D2
South Park Bsns Ctr IG3 ... 79 C6
South Park Cres
Catford SE6 ... 164 D3
Ilford IG1 ... 79 C5
Southpark Ct SW19 .. 179 C4
South Park Ct 24 BR3 ... 185 C3
South Park Dr IG3 ... 79 C4
South Park Gr KT3 ... 199 A5
South Park Hill Rd CR2 ... 221 B4
South Park Mews SW6 ... 135 D2
South Park Prim Sch IG3 ... 79 C5
South Park Rd
Ilford IG1 ... 79 B5
Wimbledon SW19 ... 179 D4
South Park Terr IG1 ... 79 C5
South Park Villas IG3 . 79 C4
South Park Way HA4 .. 62 C3
South Pl
Broadgate EC2 ... 95 B2 242 D3
Enfield EN3 ... 18 C6
Surbiton KT5 ... 198 B2
South Pl Mews EC2 . 242 D3
Southport Rd SE18 ... 123 B2
South Quay Plaza E14 ... 119 D4
South Quay Sta E14 . 119 D4
South Rd
Brentford W5 ... 109 D2
Edgware HA8 ... 26 D2
Edmonton N9 ... 18 A3
Feltham TW13 ... 172 D5
Forest Hill SE23 ... 162 D2
Hampton TW12 ... 173 B4
Heston TW5 ... 128 D6
Mitcham SW19 ... 180 B4
Southall UB1 ... 107 B5
Twickenham TW2 ... 152 B1
West Drayton UB7 ... 104 C3
South Residence IG3 . 58 B4
South Ridge BR2 ... 209 C5
Southridge Pl SW20 178 D3
South Rise W2 ... 247 B6
South Rise Prim Sch 3 SE18 ... 123 B1
South Rise Way SE18 ... 123 B2
South Row SE3 ... 142 D3
SOUTH RUISLIP ... 62 D4
South Ruislip Sta HA4 ... 62 C3
Southsea Rd KT1 ... 198 A5
South Sea St SE16 ... 119 B3
Southside N7 ... 71 D4

South Side W6 111 D3
Southside Comm SW19 178 D4
Southside Ind Est SW8 269 A2
Southside Quarter 4 SW11 136 D3
Southside Sh Ctr SW18 157 D5
Southspring DA15 167 B4
South Sq
Hampstead Garden Suburb NW11 47 D3
WC1 241 A3
South St
Bromley BR1 187 A1
Enfield EN3 18 D6
Isleworth TW7 131 A2
Mayfair W1 115 A5 248 B4
South Tenter St E1 95 D1 243 D1
South Terr
Muswell Hill N22 31 D1
Surbiton KT6 198 A3
SW7 114 C2 257 A4
South Thames Coll (Putney Ctr) 12 SW15 156 D6
South Thames Coll (Roehampton Ctr) SW15 156 A5
South Thames Coll (Tooting Ctr) 7 SW17 180 C5
South Thames Coll (Wandsworth Ctr) 7 SW18 157 D6
SOUTH TOTTENHAM 51 D3
South Tottenham Sta N15 51 D4
South Vale
Harrow HA1 64 C4
West Norwood SE19 183 C4
Southvale Rd SE3 142 C3
South View BR1 187 C1
Wimbledon SW19 178 D4
Southview Ave NW10 67 D3
Southview Cl SW17 181 A5
South View Cl DA5 169 B5
South View Cres IG2 56 D3
South View Ct
8 Forest Hill SE23 162 C3
South Norwood SE19 183 A3
Southview Dr E18 55 B6
Southview Gdns SM6 219 C1
Southview Rd BR1 186 B6
South View Rd
Hornsey N8 50 A6
Pinner HA5 22 B4
South Villas NW1 71 D2
Southville
London SW8 137 D4 269 D1
South Lambeth SW8 137 A4
Southville Cl
East Bedfont TW14 149 C3
West Ewell KT19 215 B1
Southville Cres TW14 149 C3
Southville Jun & Inf Schs TW14 149 D3
Southville Rd
East Bedfont TW14 149 C4
Thames Ditton KT7 197 B2
SOUTHWARK 117 B5
Southwark Bridge SE1, EC4 117 A6 252 B5
Southwark Bridge Rd SE1 117 A5 252 B3
Southwark Cath★ SE1 117 B5 252 C4
Southwark Coll SE1 116 D4 251 C2
Southwark Coll (Blackfriars Ctr) SE1 251 C3
Southwark Coll (Camberwell Ctr) 17 SE5 139 C5
Southwark Coll (Grange Ctr) SE1 263 B5
Southwark Coll (Surrey Docks Ctr) 12 SE16 118 B3
Southwark Park Est 11 SE16 118 B2
Southwark Park Prim Sch 19 SE16 118 B2
Southwark Park Rd SE16 118 A2
Southwark Pk Sports Complex SE16 118 C2
Southwark Pl BR1 210 B6
Southwark St SE1 117 A5 252 A3
Southwark Sta SE1 116 D5 251 C3
Southwater Cl
Beckenham BR3 185 D3
8 Poplar E14 97 B1
Southway
Hampstead Garden Suburb NW11 47 D4
Hayes BR2 209 A2
Totteridge N20 13 C2
Wallington SM6 219 C4
West Barnes SW20 200 D5
South Way
Croydon CR0 223 A5
Friern Barnet N11 31 C4
Harrow HA2 41 C5
Lower Edmonton N9 18 C2
Wembley HA9 66 C3
Southway Cl 9 W12 112 B4
Southwell Ave UB5 63 C2
Southwell Gdns SW7 256 A3
Southwell Grove Rd E11 76 C6
Southwell Ho
8 Bermondsey SE16 118 B2
13 Stoke Newington N16 73 C3
Southwell Rd
Camberwell SE5 139 A2
Harrow HA3 43 D3
Thornton Heath CR0 204 C3
South Western Rd TW1 153 B5
Southwest Rd E11 54 B1
South Wharf Rd W2 92 B1 236 D2
Southwick Mews W2 236 D2
Southwick Pl W2 237 A1
Southwick St W2 92 C1 237 A2
Southwick Yd W2 237 A1
SOUTH WIMBLEDON 179 D4
South Wimbledon Sta SW19 179 D3
South Wlk
Coney Hall BR4 224 C5
Hayes UB3 83 B2
Southwold Dr IG11 80 A3
Southwold Mans W9 91 C4
Southwold Prim Sch E5 74 B6
Southwold Rd DA5 169 D5
Upper Clapton E5 74 C6
Southwood Ave
Highgate N6 49 B2
Kingston u T KT2, KT3 177 A2
Southwood Cl BR1 210 B5
North Cheam KT4 200 D1
Southwood Ct EC1 234 C1
Hampstead Garden Suburb NW11 47 D4
Southwood Dr KT5 199 A1
South Woodford 10 E18 37 A1
South Woodford Sta E18 37 B1
Southwood Gdns
Hinchley Wood KT10 213 A5
Ilford IG2 56 D5
Southwood Hall N6 49 B3
Southwood Ho
New Eltham SE9 166 D2
Notting Hill W11 244 A6
Southwood Hts N6 49 B2
Southwood La N6 49 A2
Southwood Lawn Rd N6 49 B2
Southwood Mans N6 49 B3
Southwood Park N6 49 A2
Southwood Prim Sch RM9 81 A4
Southwood Rd SE9 166 D2
Woolwich SE28 124 B5
Southwood Smith Ho 4 E2 96 B4
Southwood Smith St N1 234 C5
South Worple Ave SW14 133 C2
Southwyck Ho SW9 138 C1
South Yd EC1 242 C4
Sovereign Bsns Ctr EN3 7 B2
Sovereign Cl
Ealing W5 87 C2
Ruislip HA4 39 C1
Stepney E1 118 B6
Sovereign Cres SE16 119 A6
Sovereign Ct BR2 210 B3
East Molesey KT8 195 B5
Harlington UB7 126 D5
3 Richmond TW9 132 B1
13 Stepney E1 118 B6
Sovereign Gr HA0 65 D5
Sovereign Ho
Ashford TW15 170 A6
23 Bethnal Green E1 96 B3
Chislehurst BR7 189 B3
Edgware NW7 27 B6
3 Wimbledon SW19 179 A4
Woolwich SE18 122 B3
Sovereign Mews
Barnet EN4 2 D2
6 Haggerston E2 95 D5
Sovereign Pk NW10 88 D3
Sovereign Pl HA1 42 D4
Sovereign Rd IG11 102 C4
Sovreign Ct HA6 22 A2
Sowerby Cl SE9 166 B6
Spa at Beckenham The BR3 185 A2
Space Apartments N22 32 B3
Space Bsns Pk NW10 88 D4
Spa Central 1 SW16 182 A3
Space Waye TW14 150 B6
Spa Cl SE19 183 C2
Spa Ct
12 Bermondsey SE16 118 A3
Streatham SW16 182 B6
Spafield St EC1 241 A6
Spa Hill CR7, SE19 183 B2
Spalding Cl HA8 27 C3
Spalding Ct HA8 26 B6
Spalding Ho SE4 163 A6
Spalding Rd
Hendon NW4 46 C3
Streatham SW17 181 B5
Spanby Rd E3 97 C3
Spangate SE3 142 D2
Spaniards Cl NW11 48 B1
Spaniards End NW3 48 B1
Spaniards Rd NW3 70 A6
Spanish Billingual Sch W10 91 A2
Spanish Pl W1 238 B2
Spanish Rd SW18 158 A6
Spanswick Lo 2 N15 50 D5
Spa Rd SE16 117 D3 263 D5
Sparkbridge Rd HA1 42 C5
Sparkes Cl BR2 209 B5
Sparke Terr 2 E16 98 D1
Sparkford Gdns N11 31 A5
Sparkford Ho SW11 266 D2
Sparks Cl Acton W3 89 B1
Dagenham RM8 80 D6
Hampton TW12 173 A4
Sparrow Cl TW12 173 A4
Sparrow Ct E4 36 A4
Sparrow Dr BR5 211 B1
Sparrow Farm Com Jun Sch KT17 216 B4
Sparrow Farm Dr TW14 150 D4
Sparrow Farm Inf Sch TW14 150 C4
Sparrow Farm Jun Sch TW14 150 C4
Sparrow Farm Rd KT17, KT4 216 B4
Sparrow Gn RM10 81 D5
Sparrows Herne WD23 8 A4
Sparrows La SE9 167 A3
Sparrows Way WD23 8 A4
Sparsholt Rd
Barking IG11 101 C6
Finsbury Pk N19 50 B1
Sparta St SE10 142 A4
Spa Sch SE1 118 A2
Spa View 6 SW16 160 B1
Speakers' Corner★ W1 114 D6 247 D6
Speaker's Ct 3 CR0 205 B1
Speakman Ho SE4 141 A2
Spearman St 8 SE18 144 C6
Spear Mews SW5 113 C2 255 B3
Spearpoint Gdns IG2 57 D5
Spears Rd N19 50 A1
Speart La TW5 129 A5
Spectacle Works E13 99 C4
Spectrum Ho NW5 71 A4
Spectrum Twr 1 IG1 79 A6
Spedan Cl NW3 70 A5
Speechly Mews E8 73 D3
Speed Ho EC2 242 C4
Speedwell Ct 9 N12 29 D6
Speedwell Ho 11 N12 29 D6
Speedwell St 5 SE8 141 C5
Speedy Pl WC1 233 A1
Speer Rd KT7 196 D3
Speirs Cl KT3 199 D3
Spekehill SE9 166 B1
Speke Rd CR7 183 B1
Speldhurst Cl 2 BR2 208 D4
Speldhurst Rd
Bedford Pk W4 111 B3
Homerton E9 74 D1
Spellbrook Wlk N1 235 B6
Spelman Ho 15 E1 96 A2
Spelman St E1 96 A2
Spelthorne Gr TW16 171 D3
Spelthorne Inf Sch TW15 171 B4
Spelthorne Jun Sch TW15 171 B4
Spelthorne La TW15, TW17 171 A2
Spelthorne Sports Club TW16 171 B3
Spence Cl SE16 119 B4
Spencer Ave
Bowes Pk N13 32 B4
Hayes UB4 84 A2
Spencer Cl BR6 227 D6
Church End N3 29 C1
Ealing NW10 88 B4
Woodford IG8 37 C5
Spencer Ct 5 BR6 227 A3
6 Finchley N3 29 D3
Wimbledon SW20 178 B2
Spencer Dr N2 48 A3
Spencer Gdns SW14 155 A6
Spencer Hill SW19 179 A3
Spencer Hill Rd SW19 179 A3
Spencer Ho
31 Clapham SW8 137 D3
Hendon NW4 46 B4
24 Putney SW19 156 D3
Vale of Health NW3 70 B5
Wimbledon SW19 156 D1
Spencer House Mus★ SW1 115 C5 249 A3
Spencer Mews
Fulham W6 264 A6
South Lambeth SW9 270 C1
Spencer Park Ct SW18 158 B6
Spencer Pk
East Molesey KT8 196 A4
Wandsworth SW18 158 B6
Spencer Pl
16 Islington N1 72 D1
SW1 259 B5
Thornton Heath CR0 205 B2
Spencer Rd
Acton W3 111 A5
Bromley BR1 186 D3
Carshalton CR4 203 A2
Chingford E17 36 A1
Chiswick W4 133 A5
East Molesey KT8 196 A4
Friern Barnet N11 31 B6
Harrow HA3 24 C1
Spencer Rd *continued*
Hornsey Vale N8 50 B4
Hounslow TW3, TW5, TW7 130 A4
Ilford IG3 57 D1
Mitcham CR4 203 A6
Newham E6 99 D6
South Croydon CR2 221 C3
Tottenham N17 34 A2
Twickenham TW2 152 C2
Wandsworth SW18 158 B6
Wembley HA0 65 C6
Wimbledon SW20 178 B2
Spencer Rise NW5 71 B5
Spencer St
Finsbury EC1 94 D4 234 C1
Southall UB2 106 D4
Spencer Way 35 E1 96 B1
Spencer Wlk
23 Hampstead NW3 70 A4
Putney SW15 134 D1
Spencer Yd SE3 142 D3
Spenlow Ho 2 SE16 118 A3
Spenser Ct 5 TW10 175 D6
Spenser Gr N16 73 C4
Spenser Mews SE21 161 B3
Spenser Rd SE24 160 D6
Spenser St SW1 259 B6
Spens Ho WC1 240 C5
Spensley Wlk N16 73 B5
Speranza St SE18 123 D1
Sperling Rd N17 33 C1
Spert St E14 119 A6
Speyside N14 15 C5
Spey St E14 98 A2
Spezia Rd NW10 90 A5
Spice Ct
10 Battersea SW11 136 A2
2 St George in t East E1 118 A5
Spice Quay Hts SE1 253 D3
Spicer Cl
Brixton SE5, SW9 138 D3
Walton-on-T KT12 194 C3
Spicer Ct EN1 5 C2
Spicer Ho E2 96 A4
Spices Yd CR0 221 A4
Spigurnell Rd N17 33 B2
Spikes Bridge Rd UB1 107 A6
Spilsby Cl NW9 27 C1
Spindle Cl SE18 122 A3
Spindle Ho 8 DA15 168 A1
Spindlewood Gdns CR0 221 C4
Spindrift Ave E14 119 D2
Spinel Cl SE18 123 D1
Spinnaker Cl IG11 102 B4
Spinnaker Ct 2 KT1 175 D2
Spinnaker Ho 21 E14 119 C4
Spinnells Rd HA2 41 B1
Spinney Cl
Beckenham BR3 207 D5
New Malden KT3 199 C4
Worcester Pk KT4 215 D6
Yiewsley UB7 104 A6
Spinney Dr TW14 149 A4
Spinney Gdns
Dagenham RM9 81 A3
Dulwich SE19 183 D5
Spinney Oak BR1 188 A1
Spinneys The BR1 188 B1
Spinney The
Barnes SW13 134 B6
Barnet EN5 1 D3
Cheam SM3 216 C4
DA14 191 A5
Edgware HA7 26 A6
Southgate N21 16 C4
Streatham SW16 159 D1
Sunbury TW16 172 A2
Wembley HA0 65 A5
Spire Bushey Hospl WD23 8 D3
Spire Ct 10 TW10 154 A5
Spire Ho W2 246 B6
Spire Roding Hospl IG4 55 D6
Spires The EN5 1 A2
Spirit Quay E1 118 B5
SPITALFIELDS 95 D2
Spital Sq E1 95 C2 243 B4
Spital St E1 96 A2
Spital Yd E1 243 B4

Spitfire Bsns Pk CR0 220 C2
Spitfire Est The TW5 106 C1
Spitfire Rd SM6 220 A1
Spitfire Way TW5 106 C1
Splendour Wlk SE16 118 C1
Spode Ho SE11 261 A5
Spode Wlk NW3 69 D3
Spondon Rd N15 52 A5
Spoonbill Way UB4 84 D2
Spooner 8 NW9 27 D3
Spooner Ho TW5 129 C6
Spooner Wlk SM6 219 D3
Sporle Ct 5 SW11 136 B2
Sportsbank St SE6 164 A4
Spottons Gr N17 33 A2
Spout Hill CR0 223 C3
Spratt Hall Rd E11 55 A3
Spray St SE18 122 D2
Spreighton Rd KT8 195 D5
Sprewell SW15 157 A5
Spriggs Ho 14 N1 72 D1
Sprimont Pl SW3 114 D1 257 C2
Springall St 9 SE15 140 B5
Springalls Wharf 2 SE16 118 A4
Springbank N21 16 B5
Springbank Rd SE13 164 C5
Springbank Wlk NW1 71 D1
Springbourne Ct BR3 186 A2
Spring Bridge Rd W5 109 D6
Spring Cl Barnet EN5 12 D6
Dagenham RM8 58 D1
Springclose La SM3 217 A2
Spring Cnr TW13 149 D1
Spring Cott 10 W12 112 A4
Spring Cotts KT6 197 D4
Spring Court Rd EN2 4 C5
Springcroft Ave N2 48 D5
Spring Ct
Brondesbury NW2 69 B2
Ealing W7 108 B6
Edgware HA8 26 B5
10 Wanstead E18 55 B6
Spring Ct Rd EN2 4 B5
Springdale Rd N16 73 B4
Spring Dr HA5 40 A3
Springett Ho 15 SW2 160 B6
Springfield
Bushey WD23 8 B3
South Norwood SE25 206 A6
Upper Clapton E5 52 B1
Springfield Ave
Hampton TW12 173 D4
Hornsey N10 49 C6
Merton SW20 201 B6
Springfield Christian Sch SE6 163 B1
Springfield Cl
Finchley N12 29 D5
Stanmore HA7 9 A1
Springfield Com Prim Sch N16 52 A3
Springfield Ct
7 Dagenham W3 89 A1
1 Friern Barnet N20 14 D1
Hampstead NW3 70 C1
2 Ilford IG1 78 D3
9 Kingston u T KT1 198 A6
Upper Clapton E5 52 B1
Wallington SM6 219 B3
Springfield Dr IG2 57 A3
Springfield Gdns
BR1 210 B5
Kingsbury NW9 45 B4
Ruislip HA4 40 B1
Upper Clapton E5 52 B1
West Wickham BR4 223 D6
Woodford IG8 37 C3
Springfield Gr SE7 143 C6
Sunbury TW16 172 A2
Springfield Ho
Acton W3 111 A5
1 Camberwell SE5 139 C3
13 Dalston E8 73 D2
Springfield La NW6 91 D6
Springfield Mount NW9 45 C4
Springfield Par Mews 4 N13 32 C6
Springfield Pl KT3 199 A5
Springfield Prim Sch TW16 171 D1
Springfield Rd
Ashford TW15 170 B5
Bexleyheath DA7 147 D1
Bromley BR1 210 B5
Chingford E4 20 C4
Ealing W7 108 C5
Friern Barnet N11 31 C5
Harrow HA1 42 C3
Hayes UB4 106 C5
Kingston u T KT1 198 A6
Newham E15 98 C4
Penge SE26 184 B5
Plashet E6 78 B1
South Norwood CR7 183 A2
St John's Wood NW8 92 A6 229 B5
8 Teddington TW11 175 A5
Tottenham Hale N15 52 A5
Twickenham TW2 151 C3
Wallington SM6 219 B3
Walthamstow E17 53 B3
Welling DA16 146 B2
Wimbledon SW19 179 B5
Springfield Rise SE26 162 B1
Springfields 16 EN5 13 D6
Springfield University Hospl SW17 158 C1
Springfield Wlk
3 BR6 211 B1
Paddington NW6 91 D6
Spring Gdns
East Molesey KT8 196 A5
Islington N5 73 A3
SW1 116 A5 250 A4
Wallington SM6 219 C3
Woodford IG8 37 C3
Spring Gr
Brentford W4 132 C6
Hampton TW12 173 D2
Loughton IG10 21 D5
Mitcham CR4 181 A2
SPRING GROVE 130 C3
Spring Grove Cres TW3, TW5 130 A4
Spring Grove Prim Sch TW7 130 B3
Spring Grove Rd
Hounslow TW3, TW5, TW7 130 A4
Richmond TW10 154 B6
Springhallow Sch W13 87 A1
Spring Hill
Forest Hill SE26 184 C6
Upper Clapton E5 52 A2
Springhill Cl SE5 139 B2
Spring Ho
Merton SW19 179 B2
WC1 234 A1
Springhurst Cl CR0 223 B4
Spring La
Croydon SE25 206 B3
Muswell Hill N10 49 A6
Upper Clapton E5 52 B1
Spring Lake HA7 25 B6
Spring Mews W1 237 D4
SPRING PARK 223 B5
Spring Park Ave CR0 222 D6
Springpark Dr
Beckenham BR3 208 A6
Stoke Newington N4 51 A1
Spring Park Prim Sch CR0 223 C5
Spring Park Rd CR0 222 D6
Spring Pl
Barking IG11 101 A5
Camden Town NW5 71 B3
Church End N3 29 C1
Springpond Rd RM9 81 A3
Spring Rd TW13 149 D1
Springrice Rd SE13 164 B5
Spring Shaw Rd BR5 190 A2
Spring St W2 92 B1 236 C1
Spring Terr TW10 154 A6
Springtide Cl 10 SE15 140 A4
Spring Vale DA7 147 D1
Springvale Ave TW8 110 A1
Springvale Ct SE12 143 A1
Springvale Terr 5 W14 112 D3
Spring Villa Rd HA8 26 C3
Springwater WC1 240 C4
Springwater Cl SE18 144 C4
Springway HA1 42 B2
Springwell Ave NW10 89 D6
Springwell Cl SW16 182 B6
Springwell Ct TW5 128 D3
Springwell Jun & Inf Schs TW5 129 A5
Springwell Rd
Heston TW5 128 D4
West Norwood SW16 182 C5
Spring Wlk E1 96 A2
Springwood Cl 8 E3 97 C5
Springwood Cres HA8 11 A2
Springwood Ct CR2 221 C4
Sproggit Ind Est TW19 148 B5
Sprowston Mews E7 77 A3
Sprowston Rd E7 77 A3
Spruce Ct W5 110 A3
Sprucedale Gdns CR0 222 D4
Spruce Hills Rd E17 36 A1
Spruce Ho
2 Brentford TW8 131 C5
15 Rotherhithe SE16 118 D4
Spruce Pk BR2 208 D5
Sprules Rd SE4 141 A3
Spurfield KT8 195 D6
Spurgeon Ave SE19 183 B2
Spurgeon Rd SE19 183 B3
Spurgeon's Coll SE25 183 C1
Spurgeon St SE1 117 B3 262 C6
Spur Ho 10 SW19 179 D2
Spurling Rd
Dagenham RM9 81 B2
East Dulwich SE22 139 D1
Spur Rd
Brentford TW7 131 B5
Edgware HA8 26 A6
Feltham TW14 128 B1
SE1 116 C4 251 A2
Tottenham N15 51 B5
Wallend IG11 101 A4
Spurstowe Rd E8 74 B2
Spurstowe Terr E8 74 B3
Spurway Par 2 IG2 56 B4
Square Rigger Row 7 SW11 136 A2
Square The
Hammersmith W6 112 C1
Hayes UB11 105 B5
Ilford IG1 56 C2
Leyton E10 76 A5
12 Richmond TW10 153 D6
SW6 265 A1
Wallington SM5 219 A3
Woodford IG8 37 A5
Squarey St SW17 158 A1
Squire Ct 2 CR0 205 C1
Squire Gdns NW8 229 C1
Squire's Almshouses 7 E17 53 D5
Squires Bridge Rd KT17 192 B5
Squires Ct Finchley N3 30 A2
SW4 270 B1
Wimbledon SW19 179 C6
Squires Ho 3 SE18 144 D6
Squires La N3 30 A2
Squire's Mount NW3 70 B5
Squire's Rd TW17 192 C5
Squires The RM7 59 D3
Squires Wlk TW15 171 B3
Squires Wood Dr BR7 188 B3
Squirrel Cl TW4 128 C2
Squirrel Mews W13 109 A6
Squirrels Cl
Hillingdon UB10 60 C1
North Finchley N12 30 A6
Orpington BR6 211 C1
Squirrels Ct KT4 215 D6
Squirrels Gn KT4 216 A6
Squirrel's La IG9 21 D1
Squirrels The
Bushey WD23 8 B5
Lewisham SE13 142 B2
Pinner HA5 41 B6
Squirrels Trad Est UB3 105 D3
Squirries St E2 96 A4
Stable Cl
Kingston u T KT2 176 B4
Northolt UB5 85 C5
Stable Ct 4 SM6 219 A5
Stable Ho 9 SE16 118 C4
Stable La DA5 169 D2
Stable Mews
Twickenham TW1 152 D3
West Norwood SE27 183 A5
Stables End BR6 227 A5
Stables The IG9 21 C4
Stables Way SE11 116 C1 261 A2
Stable Way W10 90 C1
Stable Wlk N2 30 B2
Stable Yd Rd SW1 115 C4 249 B2
Staburn Ct HA8 27 A1
Stacey Ave N18 34 C6
Stacey Cl E10 54 B4
Stacey St Highbury N7 72 C5
Soho WC2 93 D1 239 D1
Stack Ho SW1 258 B3
Stackhouse St SW1 257 C6
Stacy Path 13 SE5 139 C5
Staddon Cl BR3 207 A5
Stadium Bsns Ctr HA9 66 D5
Stadium Rd
Hendon NW2 46 C2
SE7, SE18 144 B6
Stadium Rd E NW2 46 C2
Stadium Ret Pk HA9 66 C5
Stadium St SW10 136 A5 266 B3
Stadium Way HA9 66 C4
Staffa Rd E10 53 A1
Stafford Cl
Cheam SM3 217 A2
Maida Vale NW6 91 C4
Southgate N14 15 C6
Walthamstow E17 53 B3
Stafford Cripps Ho
30 Bethnal Green E2 96 C4
SW6 264 D5
Stafford Cross CR0 220 B3
Stafford Cross Bsns Pk CR0 220 B3
Stafford Ct
Croydon CR0 220 C4
Ealing W7 86 D1
Kensington W8 255 B6
South Lambeth SW8 270 A2
Stafford Gdns CR0 220 B3
Stafford Ho SE1 263 D2
Stafford Mans
13 Hammersmith W14 112 D3
14 Stockwell SW4 138 A1
SW11 267 C3
Stafford Morris Ho 9 E15 98 C6
Stafford Pl
Richmond TW10 154 B4
SW1 115 C3 259 A6
Stafford Rd Bow E3 97 B5
Harrow HA3 24 A3
Kingston u T KT3 199 A6
Maida Vale NW6 91 C4
Plashet E7 77 D2
Ruislip HA4 61 D4
Sidcup DA14 189 C6
Wallington CR0, SM6 220 A3
Staffordshire Ho N3 47 A6
Staffordshire St
Peckham SE15 140 A4
Peckham SE15 140 B4
Stafford St W1 249 A4
Stafford Terr W8 113 C3 255 A6
Stag Cl HA8 27 A1
Stag Ct 16 SM6 219 B2
Stagg Hill EN4 2 C6
Stag Hts 1 IG9 21 B2
Stag La Chigwell IG9 21 B2
Edgware HA8, NW9 45 A6
Roehampton SW15 155 D2
Stag Lane Fst & Mid Schs HA8 26 C1
Stags Ct KT7 197 A2
Stagshaw Ho 17 SE22 139 C2
Stags Way TW7 130 D6
Stainbank Rd CR4 203 B6
Stainby Cl UB7 104 A3
Stainby Rd N15 51 D5
Staincliffe Ho 5 SM1 218 A4
Stainer Ho SE9 143 C1
Stainer St SE1 252 D3
Staines Ave SM3 216 D6
Staines By-Pass TW15 170 A4
Staines Rd
East Bedfont TW14 149 B4
Feltham TW14, TW3 150 C6
Hounslow TW3 129 C1
Ilford IG1 79 B4
Twickenham TW2 152 A1
Twickenham TW13, TW2 151 D1
Staines Rd E TW12, TW16 172 C2
Staines Rd W TW15 171 B3
Staines Wlk DA14 190 C4
Stainford Cl TW15 171 B5
Stainforth Rd
Ilford IG2 57 B2
Walthamstow E17 53 C5
Staining La EC2 242 B2
Stainmore Cl BR7 189 B2
Stainsbury St 25 E2 96 C5
Stainsby Rd E14 97 C1
Stainton Rd Enfield EN3 6 C4
Lewisham SE13 164 B4
Stalbridge Flats W1 238 B1
Stalbridge Ho NW1 232 A3
Stalbridge St NW1 237 B4
Stalham St SE16 118 B3
Stambourne Ho SW8 270 B2
Stambourne Way
Penge SE19 183 D3
West Wickham BR4 224 A5
Stambourne Woodland Wlk 7 SE19 183 D3
Stamford Bridge Stadium (Chelsea FC) SW6 135 D5 265 C4
Stamford Brook Ave W6 111 D3
Stamford Brook Gdns 1 W6 111 D3
Stamford Brook Mans 2 W6 111 D2
Stamford Brook Rd W6 111 D3
Stamford Brook Sta W6 111 D2
Stamford Cl
Harrow HA3 24 C3
2 London NW3 70 A5
Southall UB1 107 C6
Tottenham Hale N15 52 A5
Stamford Cotts SW10 265 D4
Stamford Ct
Chiswick W6 112 A2
Edgware HA8 26 B6
Stamford Dr BR2 208 D5
Stamford Gdns RM9 80 C1
Stamford Gr E 1 N16 52 A1
Stamford Gr W 4 N16 52 A1
STAMFORD HILL 51 C1
Stamford Hill N16 51 D1
Stamford Hill Mans 1 N16 51 D1
Stamford Hill Prim Sch N15 51 B3
Stamford Hill Sta N16 51 C2
Stamford Ho N15 52 A4
Stamford Lo 2 N16 51 D2
Stamford Mans 2 N16 52 A1
Stamford Rd
Dagenham RM9 80 C1
Kingsland N1 73 C2
Newham E6 100 A6
South Tottenham N15 52 A4
Stamford St SE1 116 C5 251 B4
Stamp Pl E2 95 D4
Stanard Cl N16 51 C2
Stanborough Cl TW12 173 B4

Stanborough Ho 4
E3 . . . . 97 D3
Stanborough Pas E8 . . 73 D2
Stanborough Rd TW3,
. . . . 130 B2
Stanbridge Mans
SW15 . . . . 134 C2
Stanbridge Pl N21 . . . . 16 D2
Stanbridge Rd
SW15 . . . . 134 C2
Stanbrook Ct W1 . . . 249 A4
Stanbrook Rd SE2 . . 124 B4
Stanburn Fst & Mid Schs
HA7 . . . . 25 C3
Stanbury Ct 18 NW3 . 70 D2
Stanbury Rd
Nunhead SE15 . . . . . . 140 B3
Peckham SE15 . . . . . . 140 B3
Stancroft NW9 . . . . . . 45 C4
Standale Gr HA4 . . . . 39 A4
Standard Ind Est
E16 . . . . 122 B4
Standard Pl 13 EC2 . . 95 C4
Standard Rd
Beckontree NW10 . . . . 89 B3
Belvedere DA17 . . . . 125 C1
DA6 . . . . 147 A1
Enfield EN3 . . . . 7 A6
Hounslow TW4 . . . . . 129 A2
Standen Rd SW18 . . 157 C4
Standfield Gdns
RM10 . . . . 81 C2
Standfield Rd RM10 . . 81 C3
Standish Ho
6 Chiswick W6 . . . . . 112 A2
SE9 . . . . 143 B1
Standish Rd W6 . . . . 112 A2
Standlake Point 11
SE23 . . . . 162 D1
Standor Ho 7 SE4 . . 202 D6
Stane Cl SW19 . . . . . 179 D3
Stanedge Ct SW4 . . 182 A5
Stane Gr SW4 . . . . . . 138 A3
Stanesgate Ho 20
SE15 . . . . 140 A5
Stanetta Ct 18 RM6 . 58 B2
Stane Way SE18 . . . . 144 A5
Stanfield Ho
8 Northolt UB5 . . . . . . 84 D5
NW8 . . . . 236 D6
Stanfield Rd 14 E3 . . 97 A5
Stanford Cl
Hampton TW12 . . . . . 173 B4
Romford RM7 . . . . 59 D3
Ruislip HA4 . . . . 39 A3
Stanford Ct
Friern Barnet N11 . . . . 31 A5
Kensington W8 . . . . . 255 D5
Walham Green SW6 . . 265 D1
Stanford Ho 11 E1 . . 102 B5
Stanford Pl
SE1 . . . . 117 C2 263 A3
Stanford Prim Sch
SW16 . . . . 181 D2
Stanford Rd
Friern Barnet N11 . . . . 30 D5
Thornton Heath
SW16 . . . . 182 A1
W8 . . . . 113 D3 255 D6
Stanford St SW1 . . . . 259 C3
Stanford Way SW16 . 181 D1
Stangate SE1 . . . . . . 260 D6
Stangate Cres WD6 . . 11 C6
Stangate Gdns HA7 . . 25 B4
Stangate Lo N21 . . . . 16 B4
Stangate Mansi
TW1 . . . . 152 D1
Stanger Rd SE25 . . . 206 A5
Stanhope Ave
Harrow HA3 . . . . 24 B2
Hayes BR2 . . . . 209 A1
Hendon N3 . . . . 47 B6
Stanhope Cl 28
SE16 . . . . 118 D4
Stanhope Ct N3 . . . . 29 B1
Stanhope Gate W1 . . 248 B4
Stanhope Gdns
Crouch End N6 . . . . . . 49 C3
Dagenham RM8 . . . . . 81 B5
Edgware NW7 . . . . . . 27 D5
Redbridge IG1 . . . . . . 56 B1
Stoke Newington N4 . . 51 A4
SW7 . . . . 114 A2 256 B4

Stanhope Gr BR3 . . . 207 B5
Stanhope Ho
Crouch End N6 . . . . . . 49 C3
5 Friern Barnet N11 . . 31 B6
6 Putney SW15 . . . . 156 C6
SE8 . . . . 141 B5
Stanhope Mews E
SW7 . . . . 114 A2 256 B4
Stanhope Mews S
SW7 . . . . 256 B4
Stanhope Mews W
SW7 . . . . 114 A2 256 B4
Stanhope Par NW1 . . 232 A2
Stanhope Park Rd
UB6 . . . . 86 A3
Stanhope Pl W2 . . . . 237 C1
Stanhope Prim Sch
UB6 . . . . 86 A3
Stanhope Rd
Barnet EN5 . . . . 12 C2
Crouch End N6 . . . . . . 49 C2
Dagenham RM8 . . . . . 81 B5
North Finchley N12 . . . 30 A5
Sidcup DA15 . . . . . . 190 A6
Southall UB6 . . . . 86 A3
South Croydon CR0 . . 221 C5
Wallington SM5 . . . . 219 A1
Walthamstow E17 . . . 53 D4
Stanhope Row 4 . . . 248 C3
Stanhope St
NW1 . . . . 94 A3 232 A1
Stanhope Terr
W2 . . . . 114 B6 246 D6
Stanier Cl SW5 . . . . 254 D1
Stanlake Mews 7
W12 . . . . 112 C5
Stanlake Rd W12 . . . 112 C5
Stanlake Villas 8
W12 . . . . 112 C5
Stanley Ave
Barking IG11 . . . . 101 D5
Beckenham BR2, BR3 . 208 A6
Dagenham RM8 . . . . . 59 B2
Greenford UB6 . . . . . . 86 A6
Wembley HA0 . . . . 66 A3
West Barnes KT3 . . . 200 A4
Stanley Cl
Eltham SE9 . . . . 167 A3
SW8 . . . . 270 C5
Wembley HA0 . . . . 66 A1
Stanley Cohen Ho
EC1 . . . . 242 A5
Stanley Cres
W11 . . . . 113 B6 244 B6
Stanleycroft Cl TW7 . 130 C4
Stanley Ct
Belmont SM2 . . . . . . 217 D1
11 Ealing W5 . . . . 87 C2
Wallington SM5 . . . . 219 A1
Wimbledon SW19 . . . 179 C4
Stanley Gardens Rd
TW11 . . . . 174 C5
Stanley Gdns
Bedford Pk W3 . . . . . 111 C4
Cricklewood NW2 . . . . 68 C3
Mitcham CR4 . . . . . . 181 A4
W11 . . . . 244 C6
Wallington SM6 . . . . 219 B2
Stanley Glynn Ct
BR7 . . . . 188 C5
Stanley Gr
Clapham SW11 . . . . . 137 A3
Thornton Heath CR0 . 204 C3
Stanley Ho
32 Clapham SW10 . . 266 B6
Leytonstone E11 . . . . 54 C3
2 Poplar E14 . . . . 97 B2
Wembley HA0 . . . . 66 A1
Stanley Holloway Ct
E16 . . . . 99 A1
Stanley Inf Sch
KT11 . . . . 174 C6
Stanley Jun Sch
KT11 . . . . 174 C6
Stanley Mans SW10 . 266 B6
Upper Tooting SW17 . 158 D2
Stanley Park Dr HA0 . 88 B6
Stanley Park High Sch
SM5 . . . . 219 A1
Stanley Park Inf Sch
SM5 . . . . 218 D1
Stanley Park Jun Sch
SM5 . . . . 218 D1
Stanley Park Rd SM5,
SM6 . . . . 219 A1

Stanley Rd
Acton Green W3 . . . . . 111 A3
Ashford TW15 . . . . . . 170 A5
Belmont SM2 . . . . . . 217 D1
BR6 . . . . 211 D1
Bromley BR2 . . . . 209 C5
Chingford E4 . . . . 20 B3
East Finchley N2 . . . . . 48 B6
Edmonton N9 . . . . 17 D2
Enfield EN1 . . . . 5 C2
Friern Barnet N11 . . . . 31 D5
Harringay N15 . . . . . . 50 D5
Harrow HA2 . . . . 64 A6
2 Hendon NW9 . . . . . . 46 A2
Ilford IG1 . . . . 79 B6
Isleworth TW3 . . . . . 130 A1
Mill Meads E15 . . . . . 98 B6
Mitcham CR4 . . . . . . 181 A3
Morden SM4 . . . . . . 201 C5
Mortlake SW14 . . . . . 132 D1
Muswell Hill N10 . . . . 31 B3
Northwood HA6 . . . . . . 22 A2
Plashet E12 . . . . 78 A3
Sidcup DA14 . . . . . . 168 A1
Southall UB1 . . . . . . 107 A6
Teddington TW11,
TW2 . . . . 174 C5
Thornton Heath CR0 . 204 C3
Twickenham TW2 . . . 152 B1
Wallington SM5 . . . . 219 A1
Walthamstow E10 . . . 53 D3
Wembley HA9 . . . . 66 B2
Wimbledon SW19 . . . 179 C4
Woodford E18 . . . . . . 36 D2
Stanley St SE14, SE8 . 141 B5
Stanley Studios
SW10 . . . . 266 B6
Stanley Terr 8 N19 . . 72 B4
Stanliff Ho 8 E14 . . . 119 C3
Stanmer St SW11 . . . 136 C3
STANMORE 25 A5
Stanmore Coll HA7 . . 25 C4
Stanmore Gdns
Richmond TW9 . . . . . 132 B2
Sutton SM1 . . . . 218 A5
Stanmore Hill HA7 . . 25 A6
Stanmore Ho 21
SW8 . . . . 137 D3
Stanmore Lo HA7 . . . 25 B6
Stanmore Pl NW1 . . 231 D6
Stanmore Rd
Harringay N15 . . . . . . 50 D5
Leytonstone E11 . . . . 54 D1
Richmond TW9 . . . . . 132 B2
Stanmore St
N1 . . . . 94 B6 233 C6
Stanmore Sta HA7 . . 25 D6
Stanmore Terr 8
BR3 . . . . 185 C1
Stanmuir Lo NW7 . . . . 27 C6
Stannard Cotts 27 E1 . 96 C3
Stannard Ct SE6 . . . 163 D3
Stannard Mews E8 . . 74 A2
Stannard Rd E8 . . . . 74 A2
Stannary Pl SE11 . . . 261 B1
Stannary St
SE11 . . . . . . 116 C1 261 B1
Stannet Way SM6 . . 219 C4
Stansbury Sq 3 W10 . 91 A4
Stansfeld Ho SE1 . . . 263 D3
Stansfield Rd E6 . . . . 99 D1
Stansfield Rd
Cranford TW4, TW5 . . 128 B3
Stockwell SW9 . . . . . 138 B2
Stansgate Rd RM10 . . 81 C5
Stanstead Cl BR2 . . . 208 D3
Stanstead Gr SE23 . . 163 B3
Stanstead Ho E3 . . . . 98 A3
Stanstead Manor
SM1 . . . . 217 C2
Stanstead Rd
Forest Hill SE23,
SE6 . . . . 163 A3
Wanstead E11 . . . . . . 55 B4
Stanstead Rd DA15 . 168 D3
Stansted Express
Terminal EC2 . . . . . 243 A4
Stansted Rd TW6 . . 148 B5
Stanswood Gdns
SE5 . . . . 139 C5
Stanthorpe Cl SW16 . 182 A5
Stanthorpe Rd
SW16 . . . . 182 A5
Stanton Ave TW11 . . 174 C4
Stanton Cl
Chessington KT19 . . . 214 D3

Stanton Cl continued
North Cheam KT4 . . . 200 D1
Stanton Ct 3 DA15 . 168 A1
Finchley N3 . . . . 29 C2
Stoke Newington N16 . 51 B2
Stanton Ho 9 SE10 . 142 A6
Stanton Rd
Barnes SW13 . . . . . . 133 D3
Thornton Heath CR0 . 205 A2
Wimbledon SW20 . . . 178 D2
Stanton Sq SE26 . . . 185 B6
Stanton Way SE26 . . 185 B6
Stanway Ct 23 N1 . . . 95 C5
Stanway Gdns
Acton W3 . . . . 110 C5
Edgware HA8 . . . . 27 A5
Stanway St N1 . . . . . . 95 C5
STANWELL 148 A4
Stanwell Fields CE Prim
Sch TW19 . . . . 148 A4
Stanwell Rd
Ashford TW15 . . . . . . 170 A6
East Bedfont TW14, TW19,
. . . . 148 B4
Stanwell TW15 . . . . . 148 A1
Stanwick Rd
W14 . . . . 113 B2 254 C3
Stanworth Ct TW5 . . 129 C5
Stanworth St SE1 . . 253 D6
Stanyhurst SE23 . . . 163 A3
Stapenhill Rd HA0 . . 65 B5
Staplefield Cl
Pinner HA5 . . . . 23 A3
3 Streatham SW2 . . 160 A3
Stapleford N17 . . . . . 33 C1
Stapleford Ave IG2 . . 57 C4
Stapleford Cl
Chingford E4 . . . . 20 A1
Kingston u T KT1 . . . 198 C6
Putney SW19 . . . . . . 157 A4
Stapleford Rd HA0 . . 65 B5
Stapleford Way
IG11 . . . . 102 B4
Staplehurst Ct 1
SW11 . . . . 158 D5
Staplehurst Ho 18 E5 . 74 B3
Staplehurst Rd
Lewisham SE13 . . . . . 164 C6
Sutton SM5 . . . . 218 C1
Staple Inn WC2 . . . . 241 A3
Staple Inn Bldgs
WC2 . . . . 241 A3
Staples Cl SE16 . . . . 119 A5
Staples Corner Bsns Pk
NW2 . . . . 46 B1
Staples Corner (East)
NW2 . . . . 46 B1
Staples Corner Ret Pk
NW2 . . . . 46 B1
Staples Corner (West)
NW2 . . . . 46 B1
Staple St SE1 117 B4 252 D1
Stapleton Gdns CR0 . 220 C3
Stapleton Hall N4 . . . 50 D2
Stapleton Hall Rd N4 . 50 B2
Stapleton Ho 10 E2 . . 96 B4
Stapleton Rd
DA7, BR6 . . . . 147 B6
Orpington BR6 . . . . . 227 D5
Upper Tooting SW17 . 159 A1
Stapley Rd DA17 . . . 125 C1
Stapylton Rd EN5 . . . 1 A2
Star Alley EC3 . . . . . 253 B6
Star and Garter Hill
TW10 . . . . 154 A4
Starboard Way E14 . 119 C3
Starbuck Cl SE9 . . . . 166 C4
Star Cl EN3 . . . . 18 C5
Starcross St
NW1 . . . . 93 C4 232 B1
Star Ct UB10 . . . . 83 A3
Stardome* NW1 . . . 238 A5
Starfield Rd W12 . . . 112 A4
Star & Garter Mans 8
SW15 . . . . 134 D2
Starks Field Prim Sch
N9 . . . . 17 C2
Star La E13 . . . . 98 C3
Starliner Ct N7 . . . . . 72 C2
Starling Cl
Beckenham BR3 . . . . 207 A3
Buckhurst Hill IG9 . . . 21 A3
Pinner HA5 . . . . 40 C6
Starling Ct E13 . . . . . 99 B6
Starling Ho NW8 . . . 230 A4
Starling Wlk TW12 . . 173 A5
Starmans Ct RM9 . . 100 A2

Star Path UB5 . . . . 85 C5
Star Pl E1 . . . . 118 A6
Star Prim Sch E16 . . . 98 C3
Star Rd
Hillingdon UB10 . . . . . 83 A3
Hounslow TW7 . . . . . 130 B3
W14 . . . . 113 B1 254 C1
Star St W2 . . . . 92 C1 237 A2
Starts Cl BR6 . . . . . . 226 C5
Starts Hill Ave BR6 . . 226 C4
Starts Hill Rd BR6 . . 226 B4
Starveall Cl UB7 . . . . 104 B3
Star Works NW10 . . . . 90 A4
Star Yd WC2 . . 94 C1 241 A2
State Farm Ave BR6 . 227 A4
Stateland Ct 10 N11 . 31 B6
Staten Gdns TW1 . . 152 D2
Statham Ct N7 . . . . . . 72 A5
Statham Gr
Edmonton N18 . . . . . . 33 C5
Stoke Newington N16 . 73 B5
Statham Ho SW8 . . . 269 A2
Station App
Ashford TW15 . . . . . . 170 B6
Belmont SM2 . . . . . . 217 A1
Bexleyheath DA7 . . . 147 A3
Chislehurst BR7 . . . . 188 C1
Dagenham NW10 . . . . 89 D4
Elmstead BR7 . . . . . 188 A4
2 Finchley N12 . . . . . 29 D6
Forest Gate E7 . . . . . . 77 B4
Friern Barnet N11 . . . . 31 B5
Fulham SW6 . . . . . . 135 A2
Greenford UB6 . . . . . . 64 B1
Hampton TW12 . . . . . 173 C2
Harrow HA1 . . . . 42 C2
Hayes BR2 . . . . 209 A1
Hayes Town UB3 . . . 105 D3
Hinchley Wood KT10 . 212 D5
4 Kingston u T KT1,
KT2 . . . . 176 C2
Lewisham SE3 . . . . . 143 B2
Mottingham SE9 . . . . 166 D3
New Barnet EN5 . . . . . 2 A2
6 New Malden KT4 . . 200 A1
Orpington BR6 . . . . . 227 D6
Penge SE26 . . . . 185 B5
Pinner HA5 . . . . 41 A6
Richmond TW9 . . . . . 132 C4
Ruislip HA4 . . . . 39 D1
Shepperton TW17 . . . 193 A4
7 South Croydon
CR0 . . . . 221 B6
South Ruislip HA4 . . . 62 B3
Streatham SW16 . . . 181 D5
Sunbury TW16 . . . . . 172 A2
1 Surbiton KT6 . . . . 198 A3
Walthamstow E17 . . . 53 C4
Wanstead E11 . . . . . . 55 A4
Welling DA16 . . . . . . 146 A3
Wembley HA0 . . . . 65 B2
2 Woodford E18 . . . . 37 B1
Woodford IG8 . . . . 37 B4
Woodford IG8 . . . . 37 B4
Worcester Pk KT19 . . 216 A3
Yiewsley UB7 . . . . . . 104 A5
Station Approach Rd
W4 . . . . 133 C6
Station Ave
5 Brixton SW9 . . . . . 138 D2
Kingston u T KT3 . . . 199 C6
10 Richmond TW9 . . 132 C4
West Ewell KT19 . . . 215 D1
Station Bldgs
Catford SE6 . . . . 163 C4
Merton SW20 . . . . . . 178 C1
Station Blgs W5 . . . . 110 B5
Station Cl Finchley N3 . 29 C2
Hampton TW12 . . . . . 173 C2
Station Cres
Ashford TW15 . . . . . . 170 A6
Greenwich SE3 . . . . . 121 A1
Tottenham N15 . . . . . . 51 B5
Wembley HA0 . . . . 65 B2
Station Ct
Mitcham CR4 . . . . . . 202 C5
6 Nunhead SE15 . . . 140 C3
South Tottenham N15 . 51 D4
Wembley HA9 . . . . 43 C1
Stationers Hall Ct
EC4 . . . . 241 D1
Station Est BR3 . . . . 206 D5
Station Est 8 E18 . . . . 37 B1
Station Estate Rd
TW14 . . . . 150 B3
Station Gdns W4 . . . 133 A5

Station Gr HA0 ... 66 A2
Station Hill BR2 ... 225 A6
Station House Mews N9 ... 34 A6
Station Mans 9 N3 ... 29 C2
Station Mews Terr 4 SE3 ... 121 A1
Station Par Acton W3 ... 88 C1
1 Ashford TW15 ... 170 B6
Barking IG11 ... 79 A1
Belmont HA3 ... 25 A1
Cockfosters EN4 ... 3 A1
Cricklewood NW2 ... 68 C2
Dagenham RM10 ... 81 C2
Ealing W5 ... 110 B5
Edgware HA8 ... 26 A3
Feltham TW14 ... 150 B4
Northolt UB5 ... 63 D4
4 Osidge N14 ... 15 D3
Richmond TW9 ... 132 C4
Ruislip HA4 ... 61 B6
South Harrow HA2 ... 63 D4
4 Upper Tooting SW12 ... 159 A3
2 Wanstead E11 ... 55 A4
Woodford IG9 ... 37 D6
Station Pas
New Cross Gate SE15 ... 140 C4
Woodford E18 ... 37 B1
Station Pl N4 ... 72 C6
Station Rd
Ashford TW15 ... 170 B6
Barkingside IG6 ... 57 B6
Barnes SW13 ... 133 D3
Beckenham BR2 ... 186 C1
Belvedere DA17 ... 125 C3
Bexleyheath DA7 ... 147 A2
Bromley BR1 ... 187 A2
Camden Town N19 ... 71 C5
Carshalton SM5 ... 218 D4
Chadwell Heath RM6 ... 58 D2
Chessington KT9 ... 214 A3
Chingford E4 ... 20 B3
Church End N3 ... 29 C1
Claygate KT10 ... 212 C3
Croydon CR0 ... 205 A1
Edgware HA8 ... 26 C4
Edgware NW7 ... 27 C4
Esher KT10 ... 212 B6
Forest Gate E7 ... 77 A4
Friern Barnet N11 ... 31 B5
Greenhill HA1 ... 42 D4
Hampton TW12 ... 173 D2
Hampton Wick KT1 ... 175 D2
Hanwell W7 ... 108 C5
Harlesden NW10 ... 89 D5
Hayes UB3 ... 105 C2
Hendon NW4 ... 46 A4
Hounslow TW3 ... 129 D1
Ilford IG1 ... 78 D5
Kingston u T KT2 ... 176 C2
Lewisham SE13 ... 142 A2
Leyton E10 ... 76 A5
Manor Pk E12 ... 78 A4
Merton SW19 ... 180 A2
New Barnet EN5 ... 13 D6
North Harrow HA1, HA2 ... 41 D4
Orpington BR6 ... 227 D6
Penge SE20 ... 184 C4
Shepperton TW17 ... 193 A4
Sidcup DA14, DA15 ... 168 A1
Southgate N21 ... 16 D3
South Norwood SE25 ... 205 D5
Sunbury TW16 ... 172 A3
Teddington TW11 ... 175 A4
Thames Ditton KT7 ... 196 D2
Tottenham Hale N17 ... 52 A6
Twickenham TW1 ... 152 D4
Walthamstow E17 ... 53 A4
West Acton W5 ... 88 B1
West Barnes KT3 ... 200 B4
West Drayton UB7 ... 104 A4
West Wickham BR4 ... 208 A1
Wood Green N22 ... 32 B1
Station Rd N DA17 ... 125 D3
Station Rise SE27 ... 160 D2
Station Sq BR5 ... 211 A4
Station St
Newham E16 ... 122 D5
Stratford E15 ... 76 B1
Station Terr
Camberwell SE5 ... 139 A4
Kensal Rise NW10 ... 90 D5
Station View UB6 ... 86 B6
Station Way
Cheam SM2, SM3 ... 217 A1
Claygate KT10 ... 212 C2
Woodford IG9 ... 37 D6
Station Yd TW1 ... 153 A4
Staton Ct 1 E10 ... 53 D2
Staunton Ho SE17 ... 263 A3
Staunton Rd KT2 ... 176 B3
Staunton St SE8 ... 141 B6
Staveley NW1 ... 232 A2
Staveley Cl
Hackney E9 ... 74 C3
Lower Holloway N7 ... 72 A4
New Cross Gate SE15 ... 140 C4
8 Peckham SE15 ... 140 B4
Staveley Ct 4 E11 ... 55 A4
Staveley Gdns W4 ... 133 B4
Staveley Ho SE4 ... 163 A6
Staveley Rd
Ashford TW15 ... 171 B4
Chiswick W4 ... 133 B5
Stavers Ho 31 E3 ... 97 B5
Staverton Rd NW2 ... 68 C1
Stave Yard Rd SE16 ... 119 A5
Stavordale Lo W14 ... 254 D6
Stavordale Rd
Carshalton SM5 ... 202 A2
Highbury N5 ... 72 D4
Stayner's Rd E1 ... 96 D3
Stayton Rd SM1 ... 217 C5
Steadfast Rd KT1 ... 175 D2
Steadman Ct EC1 ... 242 B6
Steadman Ho 4 RM10 ... 81 C5
Stead St SE17 ... 117 B2 262 C3
Steam Farm La TW14 ... 127 D1
Stean St E8 ... 95 D6
Stebbing Ho 8 W11 ... 112 D5
Stebbing Way IG11 ... 102 A5
Stebondale St E14 ... 120 A2
Stebon Prim Sch 26 E14 ... 97 C2
Stedham Pl WC1 ... 240 A2
Stedman Cl UB10 ... 60 C5
Steedman St SE17 ... 117 A2 262 A3
Steeds Rd N10 ... 30 D2
Steel App IG11 ... 102 B5
Steele Rd
Acton Green W4 ... 111 A3
Becontree NW10 ... 89 A5
Isleworth TW7 ... 131 A1
Leyton E11 ... 76 C4
Tottenham N17 ... 51 C6
Steele's Mews N NW3 ... 70 D2
Steele's Mews S NW3 ... 70 D2
Steele's Rd NW3 ... 70 D2
Steele Wlk DA8 ... 147 D5
Steel's La 23 E1 ... 96 C1
Steen Way 7 SE22 ... 161 C6
Steep Cl BR6 ... 227 D2
Steep Hill
South Croydon CR0 ... 221 C4
Streatham SW16 ... 159 D1
Steeple Cl
Fulham SW6 ... 135 A3
Wimbledon SW19 ... 179 A5
Steeple Ct
19 Bethnal Green E1 ... 96 B3
Wimbledon SW19 ... 179 A5
Steeplestone Cl N18 ... 33 A5
Steepleton Ct E11 ... 54 A1
Steeple Wlk N1 ... 235 B6
Steerforth St SW18 ... 158 A2
Steering Cl N9 ... 18 C3
Steers Mead CR4 ... 180 D2
Steers Way SE16 ... 119 A4
Steetley Ct 14 SM2 ... 218 A1
Steinman Ct TW7 ... 130 D2
Stelfax Ho WC1 ... 233 D2
Stella Cl UB8 ... 82 D2
Stella Rd SW17 ... 180 D4
Stellar Ho 4 N17 ... 33 D4
Stellman Cl E5 ... 74 A5
Stembridge Rd SE20 ... 184 B1
Sten Cl 12 EN3 ... 7 C6
Stephan Cl E8 ... 96 A6
Stephen Cl BR6 ... 227 D5
Stephen Ct 18 SW19 ... 156 D3
Stephendale Rd SW6 ... 136 A3
Stephen Fox Ho 7 W4 ... 111 C1
Stephen Hawking Sch 23 E14 ... 97 A1
Stephen Mews W1 ... 239 C3
Stephen Pl SW4 ... 137 C2
Stephen Saunders Ct SW11 ... 158 C6
Stephens Collection The★ N3 ... 29 C1
Stephens Ct
Brockley SE4 ... 141 A2
E16 ... 98 D3
Stephens Lo N12 ... 14 A1
Stephenson Ct SM2 ... 217 B1
Stephenson Ho
2 Gospel Oak NW5 ... 71 B4
6 Maitland Pk NW3 ... 70 D3
Newington SE1 ... 262 A6
West Heath SE2 ... 124 D1
Stephenson Rd
Ealing W7 ... 86 D1
Twickenham TW4 ... 151 C4
Walthamstow E17 ... 53 A4
Stephenson St
Dagenham NW10 ... 89 D4
Newham E16 ... 98 C2
Stephenson Way NW1 ... 93 C3 239 B6
Stephen's Rd E15 ... 98 C6
Stephen St W1 ... 239 C3
STEPNEY ... 96 D2
Stepney City E1 ... 96 C2
Stepney Cswy E1 ... 96 D1
Stepney Gn E1 ... 96 D2
Stepney Greencoat CE Prim Sch The 26 E14 ... 97 B1
Stepney Green Ct 4 E1 ... 96 D2
Stepney Green Maths & Computing Coll 18 E1 ... 96 D2
Stepney Green Sta E1 ... 96 D3
Stepney High St E1 ... 96 D2
Stepney Way
Mitcham CR4 ... 181 A2
Stepney E1 ... 96 C2
Stepping Stones Farm★ E1 ... 96 D2
Sterling Ave HA8 ... 26 B6
Sterling Cl NW10 ... 68 A1
Sterling Gdns SE14 ... 141 A6
Sterling Ho SE9 ... 143 B1
Sterling Ind Est RM10 ... 81 D4
Sterling Pl W5 ... 110 A2
Sterling Rd EN2 ... 5 B5
Sterling St SW7 ... 257 B6
Sterling Way (North Circular Rd) N18 ... 33 C5
Stern Cl IG11 ... 102 C5
Sterndale Rd W14 ... 112 D3
Sterne St W12 ... 112 D4
Sternhall La SE15 ... 140 A2
Sternhold Ave SW12, SW2 ... 159 D2
Sterry Cres RM10 ... 81 C3
Sterry Dr
Thames Ditton KT7 ... 196 C3
Worcester Pk KT19 ... 215 C4
Sterry Gdns RM10 ... 81 C2
Sterry Rd
Barking IG11 ... 101 D6
Dagenham RM10 ... 81 D3
Sterry St SE1 ... 252 C1
Steucers La SE23 ... 163 A3
Stevanne Ct 1 DA17 ... 125 C1
Steve Biko Ct W10 ... 90 D3
Steve Biko La SE6 ... 185 C6
Steve Biko Lodge 13 E13 ... 99 A5
Steve Biko Rd N7 ... 72 C5
Steve Biko Way TW3 ... 129 C2
Stevedale Rd DA16 ... 146 C3
Stevedore St 3 E1 ... 118 B5
Stevenage Rd
Fulham SW6 ... 134 D4
Wallend E6 ... 78 C2
Stevens Ave E9 ... 74 C2
Stevens Cl
Beckenham BR3 ... 185 C4
Hampton TW12 ... 173 B4
Pinner HA5 ... 40 C4
Stevens Ct BR3 ... 185 C4
Stevens Gn WD23 ... 8 A3
Stevens Ho KT1 ... 175 D1
Stevens' La KT10 ... 213 A2
Stevenson Cl EN5 ... 14 B4
Stevenson Cres SE16 ... 118 B1
Stevenson Ho
1 Battersea SW11 ... 136 D3
6 Clapham Pk SW2 ... 160 A6
NW8 ... 229 A6
Wembley HA9 ... 65 D6
Stevens Rd RM8 ... 80 C5
Stevens St SE1 ... 263 B6
Steventon Rd W12 ... 111 D6
Stewards Holte Wlk 3 N11 ... 31 B6
Stewart Ave TW17 ... 192 C5
Stewart Cl BR7 ... 188 D6
Hampton TW12 ... 173 A4
Kingsbury NW9 ... 45 A3
Stewart Fleming Prim Sch SE20 ... 206 C6
Stewart Headlam Prim Sch 28 E1 ... 96 B3
Stewart Ho SE1 ... 263 A5
Stanmore HA7 ... 25 B5
Stewart Quay UB3 ... 105 C4
Stewart Rainbird Ho 1 E12 ... 78 C3
Stewart Rd E15 ... 76 B4
Stewartsby Cl N18 ... 33 A5
Stewart's Gr SW3 ... 114 C1 257 A2
Stewart's Rd SW8 ... 137 C4 269 A2
Stewart St E14 ... 120 A4
Stew La EC4 ... 252 A6
Steyne Ho
15 Acton W3 ... 110 D5
11 Acton W3 ... 111 A5
Steyne Rd W3 ... 110 D5
Steyning Gr SE9 ... 188 B6
Steynings Way N12 ... 29 C5
Steyning Way TW4 ... 128 C1
Steynton Ave DA5 ... 168 D2
Stickland Rd DA17 ... 125 C2
Stickleton Cl UB6 ... 85 D4
Stifford Ho E1 ... 96 C2
Stilecroft Gdns HA0 ... 65 B5
Stile Hall Gdns W4 ... 110 C1
Stile Hall Par 6 W4 ... 110 C1
Stileman Ho 4 E3 ... 97 B2
Stile Path TW16 ... 194 A5
Stiles Cl BR2 ... 210 B3
Erith DA8 ... 125 D1
Stillingfleet Rd SW13 ... 134 A6
Stillington St SW1 ... 115 C2 259 B4
Stillness Jun & Inf Schs SE23 ... 163 A5
Stillness Rd SE23 ... 163 B5
Stilwell Dr UB8 ... 82 B3
Stilwell Rdbt UB8 ... 104 D6
Stipularis Dr UB4 ... 84 D3
Stirling Ave
Pinner HA5 ... 41 A2
Upper Halliford TW17 ... 193 C6
Wallington SM6 ... 220 A1
Stirling Cl
Sidcup DA14 ... 189 D6
Streatham SW16 ... 181 C2
Stirling Cnr EN5, WD6 ... 11 B5
Stirling Ct
Clerkenwell EC1 ... 241 C6
Ealing W13 ... 109 B6
Strand WC2 ... 240 C1
Stirling Gr TW3 ... 130 A3
Stirling Ho 5 SE18 ... 122 D1
Stirling Ind Ctr WD6 ... 11 B6
Stirling Lo 7 EN5 ... 14 A6
Stirling Mans NW6 ... 70 A2
Stirling Rd
Harrow HA3 ... 42 D6
Hayes UB3 ... 106 B6
Newham E13 ... 99 B5
South Acton W3 ... 110 D3
Stanwell TW19, TW6 ... 148 B5
Stockwell SW9 ... 138 A3
Tottenham N17 ... 34 A2
Twickenham TW2 ... 151 D4
Walthamstow E17 ... 53 A6
Wood Green N22 ... 32 D2
Stirling Ret Pk WD6 ... 11 B5
Stirling Way
Borehamwood WD6 ... 11 B6
Thornton Heath CR0 ... 204 A2
Stiven Cres HA2 ... 63 B5
Stoatley Ho 10 SW15 ... 156 A3
Stockbeck NW1 ... 232 B3
Stockbridge Ho EN2 ... 4 D3
Stockbury Rd CR0 ... 206 C3
Stockdale Rd RM8 ... 81 B6
Stockdove Way UB6 ... 86 D4
Stocker Gdns RM9 ... 80 C1
Stockfield Rd
Claygate KT10 ... 212 C3
Streatham SW16 ... 160 B1
Stockford Ave NW7 ... 28 D3
Stockholm Ho E1 ... 118 A6
Stockholm Rd SE16 ... 118 C1
Stockholm Way E1 ... 118 A5
Stockhurst Cl SW15 ... 134 D3
Stockingswater La EN3 ... 7 B2
Stockleigh Hall NW8 ... 230 B4
Stockley Acad UB8 ... 82 B1
Stockley Cl UB7 ... 104 D4
Stockley Ctry Pk UB7 ... 104 C6
Stockley Farm Rd UB7 ... 104 D3
Stockley Park Bsns Pk UB11 ... 105 A5
Stockley Rd UB7, UB8, UB11 ... 104 D4
Stock Orchard Cres N7 ... 72 B3
Stock Orchard St N7 ... 72 B3
Stockport Rd SW16 ... 181 D2
Stocks Ct 5 E1 ... 96 D3
Stocksfield Rd E17 ... 54 A6
Stocks Pl
Hillingdon UB10 ... 82 C6
16 Limehouse E14 ... 119 B6
Stock St E13 ... 99 A5
Stockton Cl EN5 ... 2 A1
Stockton Gdns
Edgware NW7 ... 11 C1
Tottenham N17 ... 33 A3
Stockton Ho 16 E2 ... 96 B4
Harrow HA2 ... 41 C1
Stockton Rd
Edmonton N18 ... 34 B4
Tottenham N17 ... 33 A3
STOCKWELL ... 138 A2
Stockwell Ave SW9 ... 138 B2
Stockwell Cl BR1 ... 187 B1
Stockwell Gdns SW9 ... 138 B4 270 C1
Stockwell Gn SW9 ... 138 B3
Stockwell La SW9 ... 138 B3
Stockwell Park Cres SW9 ... 138 B3
Stockwell Park Rd SW9 ... 138 B4 270 D1
Stockwell Park Sch SW9 ... 138 B4 270 C1
Stockwell Park Wlk SW9 ... 138 C2
Stockwell Prim Sch 6 SW9 ... 138 B2
Stockwell Rd SW9 ... 138 B3
Stockwell St SE10 ... 142 A6
Stockwell Sta SW4 ... 138 A3
Stockwell Terr SW9 ... 270 C1
Stodart Rd SE20 ... 184 C2
Stoddart Ho SW8 ... 270 D5
Stodmarsh Ho 28 SW9 ... 138 C4
Stofield Gdns SE9 ... 165 D1
Stoford Cl 4 SW19 ... 157 A4
Stokenchurch St SW6 ... 135 D4 265 C1
STOKE NEWINGTON ... 73 C6
Stoke Newington Church St N16 ... 73 C6
Stoke Newington Comm N16 ... 73 D6
Stoke Newington High St N16 ... 73 D5
Stoke Newington Rd N16 ... 73 D4
Stoke Newington Sch N16 ... 73 B5

Stoke Newington Sta N16 73 D6
Stoke Pl NW10 89 D4
Stoke Rd KT2 177 A3
Stokesby Rd KT9 214 B2
Stokes Ct N2 48 C5
Stokesley St W12 89 D1
Stokes Rd
Croydon CR0 206 D3
Newham E6 100 A3
Stokley Ct N8 50 A5
Stoll Cl NW2 68 C5
Stoms Path SE6 185 C5
Stonard Rd
Dagenham RM8 80 B4
Palmers Green N13 16 C1
Stondon Pk SE23 163 A5
Stondon Wlk 4 E6 99 D5
Stonebanks KT12 194 A2
Stone Bldgs WC2 94 B2 240 D3
STONEBRIDGE 89 A6
Stonebridge Ct 9 NW10 67 B1
Stonebridge Ctr 6 NW10 89 B6
Stonebridge Ctr The N15 52 A4
Stonebridge Park HA9 66 D1
Stonebridge Park Sta NW10 66 D1
Stonebridge Pk NW10 67 B1
Stonebridge Prim Sch NW10 89 B6
Stonebridge Rd N15 51 D4
Stonebridge Way HA9 66 D2
Stonechat Sq 6 E6 100 A2
Stone Cl
Clapham SW4 137 C3
Dagenham RM8 81 B6
Yiewsley UB7 104 B5
Stonecot Cl SM3 201 A1
Stonecot Hill SM3 201 A1
Stone Cres TW14 149 D4
Stonecroft Way CR0 204 A2
Stonecrop Cl NW9 45 B6
Stone Ct
Southgate N21 16 B6
4 Stratford E15 76 D1
Stonecutter St EC4 241 C2
Stonefield N4 72 B6
Stonefield Cl DA7 147 C2
Ruislip HA4 63 A3
Stonefield Mans N1 234 A5
Stonefield St N1 94 C6 234 B6
Stonefield Way
Ruislip HA4 63 A3
SE7 143 D5
Stonegate 8 NW5 71 A2
Stone Gr HA8 26 B5
Stone Grove Ct HA8 26 B5
Stonegrove Gdns HA8 26 A5
Stonegrove Ho HA8 26 B5
Stonehall Ave IG1 56 A3
Stone Hall Rd N21 16 C4
Stoneham Rd N11 31 C5
Stonehaven BR3 185 D1
Stonehill Bsns Pk N18 34 D5
Stonehill Cl SW14 155 B6
Stonehill Ct E4 19 D4
Stonehill Rd
Brentford W4 110 C1
Mortlake SW14 155 B6
Stonehills Ct SE21 161 C1
Stonehill's Mans 3 SW16 160 A2
Stonehill Woods Pk DA14 191 D4
Stonehorse Rd EN3 18 C6
Stonehouse NW1 232 B5
Stonehouse Ct EC2 243 B2
Stonehouse Ho 27 W2 91 C2
Stone Lake Ind Pk SE7 121 C2
Stone Lake Ret Pk SE7 121 C2
STONELEIGH 216 A3
Stoneleigh Ave
Enfield EN1 6 B4
North Cheam KT17, KT4 216 A5
Stoneleigh Broadway KT17 216 A3
Stoneleigh Cres KT19 215 D3
Stoneleigh Ct
Redbridge IG5 56 A6
6 Tottenham N17 33 D1
Stoneleigh Fst Sch KT17 216 B4
Stoneleigh Lo 13 TW9 132 B4
Stoneleigh Mews 15 E3 97 A5
Stoneleigh Park Ave CR0 206 D3
Stoneleigh Park Rd KT19, KT4 216 A3
Stoneleigh Pl W11 112 D6
Stoneleigh Rd
Bromley BR1 210 D6
Carshalton SM5 202 C2
Redbridge IG5 56 B6
Tottenham N17 33 D1
Stoneleigh St W11 112 D6
Stoneleigh Sta KT19 216 A3
Stoneleigh Terr N19 71 B6
Stonell's Rd SW11 158 D6
Stonemasons Cl N15 51 B5
Stonenest St N4 50 B1
Stone Park Ave BR3 207 D5
Stone Pl KT4 216 A6
Stone Rd BR2 208 D4
Stones End St SE1 252 A1
Stonewall E6 100 C2
Stoneworth Ct SE25 206 A3
Stoneyard La E14 119 D6
Stoneycroft Cl SE12 164 D4
Stoney Deep TW11 175 A6
Stoneydown E17 53 A5
Stoneydown Ave E17 53 A5
Stoneydown Ho 2 E17 53 A5
Stoneydown Park Sch 5 E17 53 A5
Stoneyfields Gdns HA8 27 A6
Stoneyfields La HA8 27 A6
Stoney La EC3 243 B2
Penge SE19 183 D4
Stoney St SE1 117 B5 252 C4
Stonhouse St SW4 137 D1
Stonor Rd W14 113 B2 254 C3
Stonycroft Cl EN3 7 A3
Stopes St SE15 139 D5
Stopford Rd
Newham E13 99 A6
SE17 261 D1
Stopher Ho SE1 251 D1
Storace Ho 6 SW4 138 A1
Store Rd E16 122 C4
Storers Quay E14 120 B2
Store St
Bloomsbury WC1 93 D2 239 C4
Stratford New Town E15 76 B3
Storey Ct NW8 229 C1
Storey Ctr The E16 122 C5
Storey Ho 13 E14 119 D6
Storey Rd Highgate N6 48 D3
Walthamstow E17 53 B5
Storey's Gate SW1 115 D4 249 D1
Storey St E16 122 C4
Stories Rd SE5 139 C2
Stork Rd E7 77 A2
Storksmead Rd HA8 27 C3
Storks Rd SE16 118 A3
Stormont House Sch E5 74 B4
Stormont Rd
Clapham SW11 137 A1
Highgate N6 48 D2
Stormont Way KT9 213 C3
Stormount Dr UB3 105 A4
Storrington WC1 233 B1
Storrington Rd CR0 205 D1
Story St N1 72 B1
Stotfold BR1 188 A2
Stothard Ho 25 E1 96 C3
Stothard Pl E2 243 B4
Stothard St 12 E1 96 C3
Stott Cl SW18 158 B5
Stoughton Ave SM3 217 A3
Stoughton Cl
Roehampton SW15 156 A3
SE11 260 D3
Stour Ave UB2 107 C3
Stourbridge Ho 8 UB5 85 B3
Stour Cl BR2 225 C4
Stourcliffe Cl W1 237 C2
Stourcliffe St W1 237 C1
Stour Ct UB1 86 B1
Stourhead Cl 6 SW19 156 D4
Stourhead Gdns SW20 200 A6
Stour Rd
Dagenham RM10 81 C6
Hackney Wick E3 75 C1
Stourton Ave TW13 173 B6
Stowage SE8 141 D6
Stow Cres E17 35 A3
Stowe Cres HA4 39 A3
Stowe Gdns N9 17 D3
Stowe Ho
Hampstead Garden Suburb NW11 48 A3
11 Stoke Newington N16 73 C5
Stowell Ho 2 N8 50 A5
Stowe Rd W12 112 B4
Stowford Coll SM2 218 A1
Stowting Rd BR6 227 C4
Stox Mead HA3 24 B2
Stracey Rd
Becontree NW10 89 B6
Forest Gate E7 77 A4
Strachan Pl SW19, SW20 178 C4
Stradbroke Gr
Buckhurst Hill IG9 21 D3
Redbridge IG5 56 C6
Stradbroke Rd N5 73 A4
Stradbrook Cl HA2 63 B5
Stradella Rd SE24 161 A5
Straffan Lo 8 NW3 70 C2
Strafford Ho 9 SE8 119 B1
Strafford Rd
Acton W3 111 A4
Barnet EN5 1 A2
Hounslow TW3 129 B2
Twickenham TW1 153 A4
Strafford St E14 119 C4
Strahan Rd E3 97 A4
Straightsmouth SE10 142 A5
Straight The UB2 107 A4
Strait Rd E6 122 B6
Straker's Rd SE15 140 B1
Strale Ho 17 N1 95 C6
STRAND 116 B6
Strand
Strand WC2 116 B6 250 C6
Strand WC2 240 D1
Strand Ct SE18 123 D1
Strand Dr TW9 132 D5
Strandfield Cl SE18 123 C1
Strand Ho SE28 123 B5
Strand La WC2 250 D6
STRAND ON THE GREEN 132 C6
Strand-on-the-Green W4 132 C6
Strand-on-the-Green Schs 5 W4 132 C6
Strand Pl N18 33 C6
Strang Ho N1 235 A5
Strangways Terr W14 254 C5
Stranraer Way
Barnsbury N1 72 A1
1 Stanwell TW6 148 A5
Strasburg Rd SW11 137 B4 268 C1
Stratfield Ho SE12 165 A2
Stratfield Park Cl N21 16 D4
STRATFORD 76 A2
Stratford Ave UB10 82 B5
Stratford Bus Sta E15 76 B1
Stratford Cl IG11 80 A1
Stratford Coll (Newham 6th Form Coll) E15 76 B2
Stratford Ct KT3 199 B5
Stratford Gr SW15 134 D1
Stratford House Ave BR1 210 A6
Stratford International Sta E15 76 A2
STRATFORD MARSH 97 D6
STRATFORD NEW TOWN 76 A3
Stratford Office Village The 1 E15 76 C1
Stratford Pl W1 238 C1
Stratford Rd
Harlington TW6 149 A6
Hayes UB4 84 B3
Hendon NW4 46 D5
Newham E13 99 A6
Southall UB2 107 A2
Thornton Heath CR7 204 D6
W8 113 C3 255 B5
Stratford Sch E7 77 A1
Stratford Sh Ctr E15 76 B1
Stratford Sta E15 76 B1
Stratford Studios W8 255 C5
Stratford Villas NW1 71 D1
Stratford Workshops E15 98 B6
Strathan Cl SW18 157 A5
Strathaven Rd SE12 165 B5
Strathblaine Rd SW11 136 B1
Strathbrook Rd SW16 182 B3
Strathcona Rd HA9 65 D6
Strathdale SW16 182 B5
Strathdon Dr SW17 158 B1
Strathearn Ave
Harlington UB3 127 D5
Twickenham TW2 152 A3
Strathearn Ho W2 247 A6
Strathearn Pl W2 114 C6 247 A6
Strathearn Rd
Sutton SM1 217 C3
Wimbledon SW19 179 C6
Stratheden Par SE3 143 A5
Stratheden Rd SE3 143 A5
Strathfield Gdns IG11 79 B2
Strathleven Rd SW2 160 A6
Strathmore Ct NW8 230 A2
Strathmore Gdns
Edgware HA8 26 D1
Finchley N3 29 D2
W8 245 B4
Strathmore Rd
Teddington TW11, TW2 174 C6
Thornton Heath CR0 205 B2
Wimbledon SW19 157 C1
Strathmore Sch TW10 153 D2
Strathnairn St SE1 118 A2
Strathray Gdns NW3 70 C2
Strath Terr SW11 136 C1
Strathville Rd SW18 157 D2
Strathyre Ave SW16 204 C6
Stratton Ave EN2 5 B6
Stratton Cl DA7 147 A2
Edgware HA8 26 B4
Heston TW5 129 C4
Merton SW19 179 C1
Walton-on-T KT12 194 C1
Stratton Ct
4 De Beauvoir Town N1 73 C1
10 Kingston u T KT6 198 A4
10 Pinner HA5 23 B3
Strattondale St E14 120 A3
Stratton Dr IG11 79 D2
Stratton Gdns UB1 85 C1
Stratton Ho HA8 26 B6
Stratton Lo 10 EN5 1 D1
Stratton Rd DA7 147 A2
Merton SW19 179 C1
Sunbury TW16 171 D1
Stratton St W1 115 B5 248 D4
Strauss Rd W4 111 B4
Strawberry Fields BR6 226 D3
STRAWBERRY HILL 152 D1
Strawberry Hill Cl TW1 152 D1
Strawberry Hill Rd TW1 152 D1
Strawberry Hill Sta TW2 152 D1
Strawberry La SM5 219 A5
Strawberry Terr N10 30 D2
Strawberry Vale
Finchley N2 30 B2
Twickenham TW1 153 A1
Strayfield Rd EN2 4 D6
Streakes Field Rd NW2 68 A6
Streamdale SE2 146 B6
Stream La HA8 26 D5
Streamline Mews SE22 162 A3
Streamside Cl BR2 209 A5
Edmonton N9 17 D3
Stream Way DA17 147 C6
Streatfeild Ave E6 100 B6
Streatfield Rd HA3, HA7 43 D6
STREATHAM 182 A4
Streatham Cl SW16 160 A2
Streatham & Clapham High Sch SW16 159 D1
Streatham Common N SW16 182 B5
Streatham Common S SW16 182 B4
Streatham Common Sta SW16 181 D3
Streatham Ct SW16 160 A1
Streatham High Rd SW16, SW2 182 A5
STREATHAM HILL 160 A3
Streatham Hill SW2 160 A3
Streatham Hill & Clapham High Sch 14 SW2 160 B3
Streatham Hill Sta SW2 160 A2
Streatham L Ctr & Ice Arena SW16 181 D5
STREATHAM PARK 181 C6
Streatham Pl SW2 160 A4
Streatham Rd CR4 181 A2
Streatham St WC1 240 A2
Streatham Sta SW16 181 D5
STREATHAM VALE 181 D3
Streatham Vale SW16 181 D3
Streathbourne Rd SW17 159 A1
Streathem Wells Prim Sch SW2 160 C2
Streatleigh Par 4 SW16 160 A2
Streatley Pl
27 Hampstead NW3 70 A4
Hampstead NW3 70 B4
Streatley Rd NW6 69 B1
Streeters La SM6 219 D5
Streetfield Mews SE3 143 A2
Streimer Rd E15 98 A5
Strelley Way W3 111 C6
Stretford Ct 1 SW19 179 A3
Stretton Lo W13 109 B6
Stretton Mans 16 SE8 141 C6
Stretton Rd
Croydon CR0 205 C2
Richmond TW10 153 C2
Strickland Ct SE15 140 A2
Strickland Ho 26 E2 95 D4
Strickland Row SW18 158 B4
Strickland St SE8 141 C4
Strickland Way 4 BR6 227 D4
Stride Rd E13 98 D5
Strimon Cl N9 18 C2
Stringer Hos 19 N1 95 C6
Strode Cl N10 31 A3
Strode Ho 3 SW2 160 C3
Strode Rd
Forest Gate E7 77 A4
SW6 135 A5 264 A4
Tottenham N17 33 C1
Willesden NW10 68 A2
Strome Ho NW6 91 D5
Strone Rd E7, E12 77 D2
Strone Way UB4 85 A3

Strongbow Cres SE9 . 166 B6
Strongbow Rd SE9 ... 166 B6
Strongbridge Cl HA2 .. 41 C1
Stronsa Rd W12 .... 111 D4
Strood Ho
9 Penge SE20 ..... 184 C3
SE1 ... 252 D1
Stroud Cres SW15 ... 156 A1
Stroudes Cl KT4 .... 199 D2
Stroud Field UB5 ..... 63 A2
Stroud Gate HA2 ..... 63 D4
STROUD GREEN 50 C3
Stroud Green Gdns CR0 ... 206 C2
Stroud Green Prim Sch N4 ... 50 C1
Stroud Green Rd N4 .. 50 C1
Stroud Green Way CR0 ... 206 C3
Stroudley Ho SW8 .. 269 B2
Stroudley Wlk E3 ..... 97 D4
Stroud Rd
Croydon SE25 ... 206 A3
Wimbledon SW19 ... 157 C1
Strouds Cl RM6 ... 58 B4
Stroud Way TW15 ... 171 A4
Strout's Pl 2 E2 ... 95 D4
Struan Ho 15 E11 ... 55 A4
Strudwick Ct SW4 .. 270 B1
Strutton Ground SW1 ... 115 D3 259 C5
Strype St E1 ... 243 C3
Stuart Ave Ealing W5 .. 110 B4
Harrow HA2 ... 63 B5
Hayes BR2 ... 209 A1
Hendon NW9 ... 46 A2
Walton-on-T KT12 ... 194 B1
Stuart Cl UB10 ... 60 C2
Stuart Cres
Croydon CR0 ... 223 B5
Hayes UB3 ... 83 A1
Wood Green N22 ... 32 B2
Stuart Ct Chingford E4 .. 20 D2
6 Croydon CR0 ... 220 D5
2 Elstree WD6 ... 9 D5
Stuart Evans Cl DA16 ... 146 C2
Stuart Gr TW11 ... 174 C5
Stuart Ho
Hammersmith W6 ... 112 C3
1 Homerton E9 ... 74 D1
Queensbury NW9 ... 44 C5
5 Stockwell SW4 ... 138 A1
W14 ... 254 A4
Stuart Lo SE25 ... 183 C1
Stuart Mill Ho N1 ... 233 C3
Stuart Pl CR4 ... 180 D2
Stuart Rd Acton W3 ... 111 A5
Barking IG11 ... 79 D1
DA16 ... 146 B4
East Barnet EN4 ... 14 D4
Harrow HA3 ... 42 D6
Maida Vale NW6 ... 91 C4
Nunhead SE15 ... 140 C1
Richmond TW10 ... 153 B1
South Norwood CR7 .. 205 A5
Wimbledon SW19 ... 157 C1
Stubbs Cl NW9 ... 45 A4
Stubbs Dr SE16 ... 118 B1
Stubbs Ho
Finsbury Pk N4 ... 50 B1
1 Globe Town E2 ... 96 D4
Stubbs Mews RM8 ... 80 B4
Stubbs Point E13 ... 99 B3
Stubbs Way SW19 ... 180 B2
Stucley Pl 19 NW1 ... 71 B1
Stucley Rd TW5, TW7 ... 130 A5
Studdridge St SW6 .. 135 C3
Studd St N1 ... 94 D6 234 C6
Studholme Ct NW3 ... 69 C4
Studholme St SE15 .. 140 B5
Studio Mews 5 NW4 . 46 C5
Studio Pl SW1 ... 247 D1
Studios NW8 ... 229 A4
Studios Rd TW17 ... 192 B6
Studios The
4 Clapham SW4 ... 137 C1
SW8 ... 269 D1
Studland SE17 ... 262 C2
Studland Cl DA15 ... 167 D1
Studland Ho E14 ... 97 A1
Studland Rd
Ealing W7 ... 86 C1
Forest Hill SE26 ... 184 D5
Kingston u T KT2 ... 176 A4
Studland St W6 ... 112 B2
Studley Ave E4 ... 36 B3
Studley Cl E5 ... 75 A3
Studley Ct
13 Blackwall E14 ... 120 B6
DA14 ... 190 B5
Redbridge IG4 ... 55 D3
Studley Dr IG4 ... 55 D3
Studley Grange Rd W7 ... 108 D4
Studley Rd
Dagenham RM9 ... 80 D1
South Lambeth SW4 . 138 A3
Upton E7 ... 77 B2
Study Prep Sch The (Spencer House) SW19 ... 178 D5
Study Prep Sch The (Wilberforce House) SW19 ... 178 C5
Study Sch The KT3 .. 199 C4
Stukeley Rd E7 ... 77 B1
Stukeley St WC2 ... 94 A1 240 B2
Stumps Hill La BR3 .. 185 C4
Stunell Ho 23 SE14 .. 140 D6
Sturdee Ho 2 E2 ... 96 A5
Sturdy Ho 28 E3 ... 97 A5
Sturdy Rd SE15 ... 140 B3
Sturge Ave E17 ... 35 D1
Sturgeon Rd SE17 ... 117 A1 262 A1
Sturges Field BR7 ... 189 B4
Sturgess Ave NW4 ... 46 B2
Sturge St SE1 ... 117 A4 252 A2
Sturmer Way N7 ... 72 B3
Sturminster Cl UB4 ... 84 C1
Sturminster Ho SW8 270 D3
Sturrock Cl N15 ... 51 B5
Sturry St E14 ... 97 D1
Sturt St N1 ... 235 B3
Stutfield St E1 ... 96 A1
Stuttle Ho 14 E1 ... 96 A3
Styles Gdns SW9 ... 138 D2
Styles Ho SE1 ... 251 C3
Styles Way BR3 ... 208 A5
Stylus Apartments 25 E1 ... 96 C1
Sudbourne Prim Sch 18 SW2 ... 160 B6
Sudbourne Rd SW2 .. 160 B6
Sudbrooke Rd SW12 . 159 A5
Sudbrook Gdns TW10 ... 154 A1
Sudbrook La TW10 ... 154 A2
SUDBURY ... 65 A4
Sudbury E6 ... 100 C1
Sudbury Ave HA0 ... 65 D4
Sudbury Court Dr HA1 ... 65 A5
Sudbury Court Rd HA1 ... 65 A5
Sudbury Cres BR1 ... 187 A5
Wembley HA0 ... 65 B3
Sudbury Croft HA0 ... 64 D4
Sudbury Ct
1 Ilford RM6 ... 58 B4
SW8 ... 269 D2
Sudbury Gdns CR0 ... 221 C4
Sudbury & Harrow Road Sta HA0 ... 65 B3
Sudbury Heights Ave UB6 ... 65 A3
Sudbury Hill HA1 ... 64 C5
Sudbury Hill Cl HA0 ... 64 D5
Sudbury Hill Harrow Sta HA1 ... 64 C4
Sudbury Hill Sta HA1 .. 64 C4
Sudbury Ho SW18 ... 157 D6
Sudbury Prim Sch HA0 ... 65 B4
Sudbury Rd IG11 ... 79 D3
Sudbury Town Sta UB6 ... 65 B2
Sudeley St N1 . 94 D5 234 D3
Sudlow Rd SW18 ... 157 C6
Sudrey St SE1 ... 252 A1
Suez Ave UB6 ... 86 D5
Suez Rd EN3 ... 7 A2
Suffah Prim Sch TW3 ... 129 B1
Suffield Ho SE17 ... 261 D2
Suffield Rd
Chingford E4 ... 35 D6
Penge SE20 ... 184 C1
Suffield Rd *continued*
2 South Tottenham N15 ... 51 D4
Suffolk Cl WD6 ... 11 B6
Suffolk Ct
3 Dagenham RM6 ... 58 C4
Ilford IG3 ... 57 C3
Walthamstow E17 ... 53 C2
3 West Norwood SW16 ... 182 C6
Suffolk Ho
11 Acton W3 ... 88 C1
Beckenham BR2 ... 208 D5
8 Dartmouth Pk NW5 .. 71 C5
Edgware HA8 ... 26 B4
Penge SE20 ... 184 C2
4 South Croydon CR0 ... 221 B6
Suffolk La EC4 ... 252 C6
Suffolk Park Rd E17 ... 53 A5
Suffolk Pl SW1 ... 249 D4
Suffolk Rd
Barking IG11 ... 79 B1
Barnes SW13 ... 134 A5
Dagenham RM10 ... 81 D3
Enfield EN3 ... 18 B6
Harrow HA2 ... 41 C4
Ilford IG3 ... 57 C3
4 Newham E13 ... 99 A4
Sidcup DA14 ... 190 C4
South Norwood SE25 . 205 D5
Tottenham N15 ... 51 B3
Willesden NW10 ... 67 C1
Worcester Pk KT4 ... 215 D6
Suffolks Prim Sch EN1 . 6 B3
Suffolk St
Forest Gate E7 ... 77 A4
SW1 ... 115 D5 249 D4
Sugar House La E15 ... 98 A5
Sugar Loaf Wlk 6 E2 . 96 C4
Sugden Rd
Clapham SW11 ... 137 A1
Long Ditton KT7 ... 197 B1
Sugden Way IG11 ... 101 D5
Sulby Ho SE4 ... 141 A1
Sulgrave Gdns 11 W6 ... 112 C4
Sulgrave Rd W6 ... 112 C3
Sulina Rd SW2 ... 160 A4
Sulivan Ct SW6 ... 135 C3
Sulivan Ent Ctr SW6 135 C2
Sulivan Prim Sch SW6 ... 135 C3
Sulivan Rd SW6 ... 135 C2
Sulkin Ho 11 E2 ... 96 D4
Sullivan Ave E16 ... 99 D2
Sullivan Cl
Battersea SW11 ... 136 C2
Hayes UB4 ... 84 C2
Sullivan Ct
4 Croydon CR0 ... 206 A1
Stamford Hill N16 ... 51 D1
SW5 ... 255 B4
Sullivan Ho
Chelsea SW1 ... 268 D6
Isleworth TW2 ... 152 B5
Vauxhall SE11 ... 260 D3
Sullivan Rd SE11 ... 116 C2 261 B4
Sullivans Reach KT12 ... 193 D2
Sullivan Way WD6 ... 9 C5
Sultan Ho SE1 ... 118 A1
Sultan Rd E11 ... 55 B5
Sultan St Penge BR3 . 184 D1
SE5 ... 139 A5
Sumal Ct E9 ... 76 B6
Sumatra Rd NW6 ... 69 C2
Sumburgh Rd SW12 .. 159 A5
Summer Ave KT8 ... 196 C4
Summercourt Rd E1 .. 96 C1
Summer Crossing KT7 ... 196 C4
Summerene Cl SW16 ... 181 C3
Summerfield 6 BR1 187 B2
Summerfield Ave
Colney Hatch N12 ... 30 C4
Kensal Rise NW6 ... 91 A5
Summerfield Ho RM9 . 80 D4
Summerfield La KT6 ... 213 D6
Summerfield Rd
Ealing W5 ... 87 B3
Loughton IG10 ... 21 D5
Summerfield St SE12 ... 164 D4
Summer Gdns KT8 ... 196 C4
Summer Gr WD6 ... 9 D5
Summer Hill
Borehamwood WD6 ... 10 C6
BR7 ... 188 C1
Summerhill Cl BR6 ... 227 C5
Summerhill Gr EN1 ... 17 C5
Summerhill Rd N15 ... 51 B5
Summerhill Villas BR7 ... 188 D2
Summerhill Way CR4 ... 181 A2
Summer Ho SE13 ... 142 B1
Summerhouse Ave TW5 ... 129 A4
Summerhouse Rd N16 ... 73 C6
Summerland Gdns N10 ... 49 B6
Summerland Grange N10 ... 49 B6
Summerlands Ave W3 ... 111 A6
Summerlands Lo BR6 ... 226 C4
Summerlee Ave N2 ... 48 D5
Summerlee Gdns N2 .. 48 D5
Summerley St SW18 157 D2
Summer Rd
East Molesey KT8 ... 196 B4
Thames Ditton KT7, KT8 ... 196 D4
Summersby Rd N6 ... 49 B3
Summers Cl
Belmont SM2 ... 217 C1
Wembley HA9 ... 44 D1
Summersell Ho SE27 ... 183 B5
Summerside Prim Sch N12 ... 30 B4
Summerskille Cl N9 .. 18 B2
Summers La N12 ... 30 B3
Summers Row N12 ... 30 C4
Summers St EC1 ... 241 A5
SUMMERSTOWN ... 158 A1
Summerstown SW17 ... 180 A6
Summerswood Prim Sch WD6 ... 10 D6
Summerton Way SE28 ... 102 D1
Summer Trees TW16 ... 172 B2
Summerville Gdns SM1 ... 217 B2
Summerwood Rd TW1, TW7 ... 152 D5
Summit Ave NW9 ... 45 B4
Summit Bsns Pk TW16 ... 172 A3
Summit Cl
Edgware HA8 ... 26 C3
Kingsbury NW9 ... 45 B5
Osidge N14 ... 15 C2
Summit Ct
5 Barnet EN5 ... 1 B2
Brondesbury NW2 ... 69 A3
Summit Dr IG8 ... 37 D1
Summit Est N16 ... 52 A2
Summit Rd
Northolt UB5 ... 63 C1
Walthamstow E17 ... 53 D5
Summit Way
Brunswick Pk N14 ... 15 B2
South Norwood SE19 . 183 C3
Sumner Ave SE15 ... 139 D4
Sumner Bldgs SE1 .. 252 A4
Sumner Cl BR6 ... 227 A4
Sumner Ct SW8 ... 270 A2
Sumner Gdns CR0 ... 204 C1
Sumner Ho 1 E3 ... 97 D2
Sumner Pl SW7 ... 114 B2 256 D3
Sumner Place Mews SW7 ... 256 D3
Sumner Rd
Harrow HA1 ... 42 A2
SE15 ... 139 D5
Thornton Heath CR0 . 204 D1
Sumner Rd S CR0 ... 204 C1
Sumner St SE1 ... 117 A5 252 A4
Sumpter Cl NW3 ... 70 A2
Sun Alley 6 TW9 ... 132 A1
Sun Alliance Ho WC2 ... 241 A2
Sunbeam Cres W10 ... 90 C3
Sunbeam Rd NW10 ... 89 B3
SUNBURY ... 194 B6
Sunbury Ave
Edgware NW7 ... 27 B6
Mortlake SW14 ... 133 B1
Sunbury Cl KT12 ... 194 A3
SUNBURY COMMON ... 171 D3
Sunbury Court Island TW16 ... 194 D6
Sunbury Court Mews TW16 ... 172 D1
Sunbury Court Rd TW16 ... 172 C1
Sunbury Cres TW13 . 171 D6
Sunbury Cross TW16 ... 172 A3
Sunbury Cross Ctr 9 TW16 ... 171 D3
Sunbury Ct
3 Barnet EN5 ... 1 A1
3 SE14 ... 140 D6
Sunbury TW16 ... 172 D1
Sunbury Ct (Con Ctr) TW16 ... 172 D1
Sunbury Gdns NW7 ... 27 B5
Sunbury Ho 38 E2 ... 95 D4
Sunbury Int Bsns Ctr TW16 ... 171 C2
Sunbury La
Battersea SW11 ... 136 B4 266 D2
Walton-on-T KT12 ... 194 A3
Sunbury L Ctr TW16 . 171 D2
Sunbury Manor Sch TW16 ... 171 D2
Sunbury Rd
Cheam SM3 ... 217 A5
Feltham TW13 ... 171 D6
Sunbury St SE18 ... 122 B3
Sunbury Sta TW16 .. 172 A2
Sunbury Walled Gdn★ TW16 ... 194 B6
Sunbury Way TW13 .. 172 C5
Sunbury Workshops 39 E2 ... 95 D4
Suncroft Pl SE26 ... 162 C1
Sun Ct EC3 ... 242 D1
Sundeala Cl TW16 ... 172 A3
Sunderland Ct
Dulwich SE22 ... 162 A4
12 Stanwell TW19 ... 148 A5
Sunderland Ho 26 W2 ... 91 C2
Sunderland Mount SE23 ... 162 D2
Sunderland Point E16 ... 123 A5
Sunderland Rd
Ealing W5 ... 109 D3
Forest Hill SE23 ... 162 D2
Sunderland Terr W2 ... 91 D1
Sunderland Way E12 .. 77 D6
Sundew Ave W12 ... 112 A6
Sundew Ct 9 HA0 ... 88 A5
Sundial Ave SE25 ... 205 D6
Sundial Ct KT5 ... 214 D6
Sundorne Rd SE7 ... 121 C1
Sundown Rd TW15 ... 171 A5
Sundra Wlk 26 E1 ... 96 D3
SUNDRIDGE ... 187 C4
Sundridge Ave
Bromley BR1, BR7 ... 188 A3
DA16 ... 145 B2
Sundridge Ho
Bromley BR1 ... 187 B5
4 Homerton E9 ... 74 D1
Sundridge Par BR1 ... 187 B3
Sundridge Park Sta BR1 ... 187 B3
Sundridge Pl 8 CR0 ... 206 A1
Sundridge Rd CR0 ... 206 A1
Sunfields Pl SE3 ... 143 B5
Sun in the Sands SE3 ... 143 B5
Sunken Rd CR0 ... 222 C3
Sun La SE3 ... 143 B5
Sunland Ave DA6 ... 147 A1
Sunleigh Ct HA0 ... 88 A6

Sunleigh Rd HA0 88 A6
Sunley Gdns UB6 87 A6
Sunley Ho E1 243 D3
Sun Life Trad Est TW14 128 A2
Sunlight Cl SW19 180 A4
Sunlight Sq [29] E2 96 B4
Sunmead Rd TW16 194 A6
Sunna Gdns TW16 172 B1
Sunna Lo TW16 171 D3
Sunniholme Ct CR2 221 A3
Sunningdale
Ealing W13 87 B2
Friern Barnet N14 31 D5
Sunningdale Ave
Barking IG11 79 B1
East Acton W3 111 C6
Feltham TW13 151 A2
Ruislip HA4 40 C1
Sunningdale Cl
[22] Bermondsey SE16 118 B1
Erith SE28 103 A1
[3] Newham E6 100 B4
Stanmore HA7 25 A3
[3] Surbiton KT6 214 A6
Sunningdale Ct
[13] Kingston u T KT2 176 C3
[13] Southall UB1 86 A1
Sunningdale Gdns
Kingsbury NW9 45 A4
W8 255 B5
Sunningdale Lo HA8 26 B5
Sunningdale Rd
BR1, BR2 210 A4
Cheam SM1 217 B4
Sunningfields Cres NW4 28 B1
Sunningfields Rd NW4 46 B6
Sunninghill Ct [9] W3 111 A4
Sunninghill Gdns IG2 57 D4
Sunninghill Rd SE13 141 D3
Sunny Bank SE25 206 A6
Sunny Cres NW10 67 A1
Sunnycroft Rd
Hounslow TW3 129 D3
Southall UB1 85 C2
South Norwood SE25 206 A6
Sunnydale BR6 226 C6
Sunnydale Gdns NW7 27 C4
Sunnydale Rd SE12 165 B6
Sunnydene Ave
Chingford E4 36 B5
Ruislip HA4 62 A6
Sunnydene Gdns HA0 65 C2
Sunnydene St SE26 185 A6
Sunnyfield NW7 27 D6
Sunnyfields Prim Sch NW4 46 B6
Sunny Gardens Par NW4 28 B1
Sunny Gardens Rd NW4 46 C6
Sunny Hill NW4 46 B6
Sunnyhill Cl E5 75 A4
Sunny Hill Ct NW4 28 B1
Sunnyhill Prim Sch SW16 182 B6
Sunnyhill Rd SW16 182 A6
Sunnyhurst Cl SM1 217 C5
Sunnymead Ave CR4 203 D6
Sunnymead Ct W5 109 D6
Sunnymead Rd
Kingsbury NW9 45 B2
Putney SW15 156 B6
Sunnymede Ave KT19 215 C1
Sunnymede Dr IG6 56 D5
Sunny Nook Gdns CR2 221 B2
Sunny Pl NW4 46 C5
Sunny Rd The EN3 6 D4
Sunnyside
[4] Child's Hill NW2 69 B5
Walton-on-T KT12 194 C4
Wimbledon SW19 179 A4
Sunnyside Dr E4 20 A4
Sunnyside Ho [3] NW2 69 B5
Sunnyside Pl SW19 179 A4
Sunnyside Rd
Crouch End N19 49 D2
Ealing W5 109 D5
Ilford IG1 79 B5
Teddington TW11 174 B6
Walthamstow E10 53 C1
Sunnyside Rd E N9 18 A1
Sunnyside Rd N N9 18 A1
Sunnyside Rd S N9 18 A1
Sunny View NW9 45 B4
Sunny Way N12 30 C3
Sun Pas [8] SE16 118 A3
Sunray Ave BR2 210 B3
Herne Hill SE5, SE24 139 B1
Tolworth KT5 214 D6
Sun Rd W14 113 B1 254 C1
Sunrise Cl TW13 151 B1
Sunrise Sch N17 34 A4
Sunrise View NW7 27 D4
Sun St Pas EC2 95 C2 243 A3
Sunset Ave
Chingford E4 19 D3
Woodford IG8 36 D6
Sunset Ct [4] IG8 37 C3
Sunset Gdns SE25 183 D1
Sunset Ho HA3 42 C6
Sunset Rd
Herne Hill SE5 139 B1
SE28 124 A5
Wimbledon SW19 178 B5
Sunset View EN5 1 A3
Sunshine Way CR4 180 D1
Sun St EC2 95 B2 242 D4
Sunwell Cl SE15 140 B4
Superior Dr [4] BR6 227 D2
Suraj Ho [6] N22 32 C1
SURBITON 198 A2
Surbiton Boys Prep Sch [26] KT6 198 A4
Surbiton Cres KT1, KT6 198 A5
Surbiton Ct KT6 197 D3
Surbiton Ct Mews KT6 197 D3
Surbiton Hall Cl KT1 198 A5
Surbiton High Sch Jun Girls Sch [3] KT1 198 A5
Surbiton High Senior Sch [4] KT1 198 A5
Surbiton Hill Pk KT5 198 C4
Surbiton Hill Rd KT6 198 A4
Surbiton Hospl KT6 198 A3
Surbiton Par [11] KT6 198 A3
Surbiton Rd KT1 198 A5
Surbiton Sta KT6 198 A3
Surcot Ho [2] SW4 137 D3
Surlingham Cl SE28 124 D6
Surma Cl E1 96 A3
Surmans Cl RM9 102 C6
Surrendale Pl W9 91 C3
Surrey Canal Rd SE14, SE8 140 D6
Surrey Cl N3 47 A6
Surrey Cres [1] W4 110 C1
Surrey Ct [15] SM6 219 B2
Surrey Docks Farm★ SE16 119 B4
Surrey Docks Watersports Ctr SE8 119 B2
Surrey Gdns N4 51 A3
Surrey Gr
Carshalton SM1 218 B5
SE17 263 A1
Surrey Ho
Edgware HA8 26 B4
[8] Rotherhithe SE16 118 D5
Surrey La SW11 136 C4 267 B1
Surrey Lo SW20 178 C1
Surrey Mews SE27 183 C6
Surrey Mount SE23 162 B3
Surrey Quays Rd SE16 118 D4
Surrey Quays Sh Ctr SE16 118 D3
Surrey Quays Sta SE16 118 D2
Surrey Rd
Barking IG11 79 C1
Dagenham RM10 81 D3
Harrow HA1 42 A4
Honor Oak SE15 162 D6
Surrey Rd *continued*
West Wickham BR4 207 D1
Surrey Row SE1 116 D4 251 D2
Surrey Sq SE17 117 C1 263 B2
Surrey Square Inf Sch SE17 117 C1 263 A2
Surrey Square Jun Sch SE17 117 C1 263 A2
Surrey St
Croydon CR0 221 A5
[4] Newham E13 99 B4
WC2 116 B6 250 D6
Surrey Terr SE17 263 B2
Surrey Water Rd SE16 118 D5
Surrey Wharf SE1 140 A6
Surridge Ct [15] SW9 138 A3
Surridge Gdns SE19 183 B4
Surr St N7 72 A3
Sury Basin KT2 176 A2
Susan Constant Ct [18] E14 120 B6
Susan Lawrence Ho [4] E12 78 C4
Susannah St E14 98 A1
Susan Rd SE3 143 B3
Susan Wood BR7 188 C2
Sussex Ave TW7 130 C2
Sussex Cl
New Malden KT3 199 C5
Redbridge IG4 56 B4
[4] Twickenham TW1 153 B5
Upper Holloway N19 72 A6
Sussex Cres UB5 63 C2
Sussex Ct
[4] Barnes SW13 133 D3
Greenwich SE10 142 A6
Mitcham CR4 204 A4
Paddington W2 236 C1
Sussex Gate N6 48 D4
Sussex Gdns
Chessington KT9 213 D2
Fortis Green N6 48 D4
Harringay N4 51 A4
Paddington W2 92 B1 236 D1
Sussex Ho
Edgware HA8 26 B4
Hampstead NW3 70 C2
Richmond TW9 132 B3
Sussex House Sch SW3 114 D2 257 C4
Sussex Lo W2 236 D1
Sussex Mans
South Kensington SW7 256 C3
Strand WC2 250 B6
Sussex Mews SE6 163 C3
Sussex Mews E W2 236 D1
Sussex Mews W W2 246 D6
Sussex Pl
[22] Hammersmith W6 112 C1
Lisson Gr NW1 92 D3 237 C6
New Malden KT3 199 C5
Paddington W2 92 B1 236 D1
Sussex Rd
Barking E6 100 C6
Erith DA8 147 D5
Harrow HA1 42 A4
Mitcham CR4 204 A4
New Malden KT3 199 C5
Sidcup DA14 190 B5
Southall UB2 106 D3
South Croydon CR2 221 B2
Uxbridge UB10 61 A3
Wallington SM5 218 D2
[2] West Wickham BR4 207 D1
Sussex Ring N12 29 C5
Sussex Sq W2 114 B6 246 D6
Sussex St Newham E13 99 B4
SW1 258 D2
Sussex Way
Cockfosters EN4 15 B6
Upper Holloway N7 72 B5
Upper Holloway N7, N19 72 A6
Upper Holloway N19 49 D1
Sutcliffe Cl NW11 47 D4
Sutcliffe Ho UB3 84 A1
Sutcliffe Rd
Bexley DA16 146 C3
SE18 145 C6
Sutherland Ave
Ealing W13 87 B1
Falconwood DA16 145 C1
Hayes UB3 106 A2
Orpington BR5 211 D4
Paddington W9 92 A3 236 A6
Sunbury TW16 171 D1
Sutherland Cl EN5 1 A1
Sutherland Ct
Kingsbury NW9 44 D4
[3] Paddington W9 91 C3
Stoke Newington N16 73 B5
Sutherland Dr SW19 180 B2
Sutherland Gdns
Mortlake SW14 133 C2
North Cheam KT4 200 B1
Sunbury TW16 171 D1
Sutherland Gr
Putney SW18, SW19 157 B4
Teddington TW11 174 C5
Sutherland Ho
Ealing W13 109 A6
Kensington W8 255 C5
Kidbrooke SE18 144 B4
[7] Putney SW15 156 C4
Richmond TW10 153 C2
[9] South Hampstead NW6 70 A2
Sutherland Pl W2 91 C1
Sutherland Rd
Belvedere DA17 125 C3
Chiswick W4 133 C6
Ealing W13 87 A1
Edmonton N9 18 B3
Enfield EN3 18 D6
Southall UB1 85 B1
Thornton Heath CR0 204 C2
Tottenham N17 34 A2
Walthamstow E17 53 A6
Sutherland Row SW1 258 D2
Sutherland Sq SE17 117 A1 262 A1
Sutherland St SW1 115 B1 258 D2
Sutherland Wlk SE17 262 B1
Sutlej Rd SE7 143 C5
Sutterton St N7 72 B2
SUTTON 218 A2
Sutton Arena L Ctr SM5 202 B2
Sutton Cl
Beckenham BR3 185 D2
Pinner HA5 40 A4
Sutton Coll of Learning for Adults [10] SM1 217 D3
Sutton Common Rd
Cheam SM3 201 C1
Sutton SM1, SM3 217 D6
Sutton Common Sta SM1 217 D6
Sutton Courtenay Ho SW17 180 B6
Sutton Court Mans W4 133 A6
Sutton Court Rd
Chiswick W4 133 A6
Hillingdon UB10 82 D6
Newham E13 99 C4
Sutton SM1 218 A2
Sutton Cres EN5 12 D6
Sutton Ct
Chiswick W4 133 A6
Ealing W5 110 A5
East Molesey KT8 195 B4
[8] Hackney E5 74 B4
Penge SE19 183 D3
Sutton SM2 218 A2
Sutton Dene TW3 129 D4
Sutton Est
SW3 114 C1 257 B2
Sutton Est The [8] W10 90 C2
Sutton Gdns
Barking IG11 101 C5
Croydon CR0 205 D4
Sutton Gn IG11 101 C6
Sutton Gr SM1 218 B3
Sutton Gram Sch For Boys [8] SM1 218 A3
Sutton Hall Rd TW5 129 C5
Sutton High Sch SM1 217 D2
Sutton Ho N21 16 B6
Sutton House★ E9 74 C3
Sutton Hts SM2 218 B1
Sutton La EC1 241 D5
Hounslow TW3, TW4, TW5 129 B3
Sutton La N W4 111 A1
Sutton La S W4 133 A6
Sutton Par NW4 46 C5
Sutton Park Rd SM1, SM2 217 D2
Sutton Pl E9 74 C3
Sutton Rd
Barking IG11 101 C6
E13 98 D3
Heston TW5 129 C4
Higham Hill E17 34 D2
Muswell Hill N10 31 A2
Sutton Row W1 239 D2
Sutton Sq Hackney E9 74 C3
Hounslow TW5 129 B4
Sutton St E1 96 C1
Sutton Sta SM2 218 A2
Suttons Way EC1 242 B5
Sutton Way
Hounslow TW5 129 B4
North Kensington W10 90 C2
Sutton Wlk SE1 116 B5 250 D3
Swaby Rd SW17, SW18 158 A2
Swaffham Ct [1] RM6 58 C4
Swaffield Prim Sch SW18 158 A4
Swaffield Rd SW18 158 A4
Swain Cl SW16 181 B4
Swain Ho CR4 180 D3
Swain Rd CR7 205 A4
Swains Cl UB7 104 A4
Swain's La N6 71 B6
Swainson Ho N7 72 C4
Swainson Rd W3 111 D4
Swains Rd CR4, SW17 180 D3
Swain St NW8 92 C3 237 A6
Swakeleys Dr UB10 60 C3
Swakeleys Rd UB10 60 C5
Swakeleys Rdbt UB8, UB10 60 A4
Swakeleys Sch UB10 82 D5
Swaledale Cl N11 31 A4
Swallands Rd SE6 163 C1
Swallowbrook Bsns Ctr UB4 106 D5
Swallow Cl
Bushey WD23 8 A3
New Cross Gate SE14 140 D4
Swallow Ct
Chingford IG8 36 B3
Ilford IG2 56 D4
[4] Paddington W9 91 C2
[5] Ruislip HA4 40 C1
[1] SE12 165 A4
Swallow Dr
Northolt UB5 85 C5
Willesden NW10 67 B2
Swallowfield NW1 231 D1
Swallowfield Rd SE7 121 B1
Swallowfield Way UB3 105 B4
Swallow Gdns SW16 181 D5
Swallow Ho
Hornsey N8 50 B6
NW8 230 A4
Swallow Pk KT6 214 B5
Swallow Pl
[24] Poplar E14 97 B1
W1 238 D1
Swallows Ct [5] SE20 184 D3
Swallow St
Newham E6 100 A2
W1 115 C6 249 B5
Swaminarayan Sch The NW10 67 B2
Swanage Ct [5] N1 73 C1
Swanage Ho SW8 270 C3
Swanage Rd
Chingford E4 36 A3
Wandsworth SW18 158 A5
Swanage Waye UB4 84 C1
Swan And Pike Rd EN3 7 C5

Swan App E6 ....100 A2
Swanbourne SE17 .. 262 A3
Swanbourne Ho
NW8 .... 237 A6
Swanbridge Rd DA7 .147 C4
Swan Bsns Ctr 8
W4 ....111 B2
Swan Cl Croydon CR0. .205 C2
Feltham TW13 ...... 173 A6
Higham Hill E17 ....35 A3
Swan Ct Chelsea SW3 257 B1
Parsons Green SW6 . 265 A3
Poplar E14 ......97 B1
Whetstone N20 ......14 A2
Swan Ctr SW17 ..... 158 A1
Swandon Way SW18 135 D1
Swan Dr NW9 ......27 C1
Swanfield St E2 ......95 D4
Swan Ho
De Beauvoir Town N1...73 B1
Enfield EN3 ....18 C6
Swan La EC4 .117 B6 252 D5
Loughton IG10 ....21 C4
Whetstone N20 ....14 A1
Swan Lane Pier
EC4 ....117 B6 252 C5
Swanlea Sch E1 ......96 B3
Swanley Ho SE17 ... 263 B2
Swanley Rd DA16 ....146 C4
Swan Mead
SE1 ....117 C3 263 A5
Swan Mews
Stockwell SW9 ....138 B3
SW6 .... 265 A2
Swanmore Ct SW18 . 158 A5
Swann Ct 8 TW7 ....131 A2
Swanne Ho 12 SE10 ..142 A5
Swan Pas 5 E1 ......118 A6
Swan Pl SW13 ...... 133 D3
Swan Rd
Feltham TW13 ...... 173 A6
Greenwich SE18 ..... 121 D3
Rotherhithe SE16 .... 118 C4
Southall UB1 ....85 D1
West Drayton UB7 ... 104 A4
Swanscombe Ho
1 BR5 ....190 B1
11 Shepherd's Bush
W11 .... 112 D5
Swanscombe Point 7
E16 ....98 D2
Swanscombe Rd
5 Chiswick W4 ..... 111 C1
Shepherd's Bush
W11 .... 112 D5
Swansea Ct E16 .... 122 D5
Swansea Rd
Enfield EN3 ....6 C1
Harlington TW14,
TW6 ....149 B5
Swansland Gdns 2
E17 ....35 A2
Swan St
Isleworth TW7 ....131 B2
SE1 ......117 A4 252 B1
Swanston Ct TW1 ... 152 D4
Swan The BR4 ....224 A6
Swanton Gdns
SW19 .... 156 D3
Swanton Rd DA8 .... 147 D5
Swan Way EN3 ....6 D3
Swanwick Cl SW15 .. 155 D4
Swan Wlk
Oatlands Pk TW17 ... 193 C2
SW3 .... 136 D6 267 C6
Swan Yd N1 ....72 D2
Swaton Rd E3 ....97 C3
Swaylands Rd DA17 . 147 C6
Swaythling Cl N18 ....34 B6
Swaythling Ho
SW15 .... 155 D5
Swedenborg Gdns
E1 ....118 B6
Sweden Gate SE16 ...119 A2
Swedish Quays
SE16 ....119 A3
Swedish Sch The
SW13 .... 134 A6
Sweeney Cres SE1 .. 253 D1
Sweet Briar Gn N9 ...17 D1
Sweet Briar Gr N9 ....17 D1
Sweet Briar Wlk N18 ..33 D6
Sweetcroft La UB10 ...60 C1
Sweetmans Ave HA5 ..40 D6
Sweets Way N20 ......14 B2
Swell Ct E17 ....53 D3
Swetenham Wlk
SE18 ....123 A1
Swete St E13 ....99 A5
Sweyn Pl SE3 ....143 A3
Swift Cl Harrow HA2 ...63 D6
Hayes UB3 ....83 D1
Higham Hill E17 ....35 A3
Thamesmead SE28 ...124 B6
Swift Ct SM2 .... 217 D1
Swift Ctr CR0 ....220 B1
Swift Ho
16 Stepney E1 ....96 C1
15 Stoke Newington
N16 ....73 C5
1 SW9 .... 138 C5
8 Wanstead E18 ......55 B6
Swift Rd
Feltham TW13 ...... 173 A6
Southall UB2 ....107 B3
Swiftsden Way BR1 ..186 C4
Swift St SW6 .135 B4 264 C2
Swinbrook Rd W10 ...91 A2
Swinburne Cres
CR0 ....206 C3
Swinburne Ct 4
SE5 ....139 B1
Swinburne Ho 15 E2 ..96 C4
Swinburne Rd SW15 .134 A1
Swinderby Rd HA0 ....66 A2
Swindon Cl IG3 ....57 C1
Swindon Rd TW6 ....149 A6
Swindon St W12 .....112 C5
Swinfield Cl TW13 ...173 A6
Swinford Gdns SW9 . 138 D2
Swingate La SE18 ....145 C5
Swingfield Ct BR2 .. 209 D4
Swingfield Ho 4 E9 ..96 C6
Swinley Ho NW1 .... 231 D2
Swinnerton St E9 .....75 A3
Swinson Ho 12 N11 ...31 C5
Swinton Cl HA9 ....44 D1
Swinton Ho 21 E2 .....96 A4
Swinton Pl WC1 .... 233 C2
Swinton St
WC1 ....94 B4 233 C2
Swires Shaw BR2 ... 225 D4
Swiss Cottage NW3 ...70 B1
Swiss Cottage L Ctr
NW3 ....70 B1
Swiss Cottage Sch
14 South Hampstead
NW3 ....70 B1
St John's Wood
NW8 ....92 B6 229 D6
Swiss Cottage Sta
NW3 ....70 B1
Swiss Ct SW1 .... 249 D5
Swiss Re Building★
EC2 ....95 C1 243 B2
Swiss Terr 7 NW3 ....70 B1
Switch Ho 4 E14 ....120 B6
Swithland Gdns SE9 .188 C6
Swyncombe Ave W5 .109 B2
Swynford Gdns 7
NW4 ....46 A5
Sybil Elgar Sch UB2 ..107 B3
Sybil Mews N4 ....50 D3
Sybil Phoenix Cl
SE8 .... 118 D1
Sybil Thorndike Casson
Ho SW5 .... 255 B1
Sybil Thorndike Ho 12
N1 ....73 A2
Sybourn Inf Sch E17 ..53 B2
Sybourn Inf Sch
(Annexe) E10 ....53 A1
Sybourn St E17 ....53 B2
Sycamore Ave DA15 . 167 D5
Ealing W5 .... 109 D3
East Finchley N3 ......47 D6
Hayes UB3 .... 105 C6
Old Ford E3 ....97 B6
Sycamore Cl
Carshalton SM5 ..... 218 D4
Chislehurst SE9 ..... 166 A2
East Acton W3 ...... 111 C5
2 Edgware HA8 ......27 A6
Edmonton N9 ....34 A6
Feltham TW13 ...... 150 A1
New Barnet EN4 ......14 B5
Newham E16 ....98 C3
Northolt UB5 ....85 A6
South Croydon CR2 .. 221 C3
Yiewsley UB7 ....104 B6
Sycamore Ct
4 Beckenham BR3 .. 185 C2
Sycamore Ct *continued*
Forest Gate E7 ....77 A2
3 Forest Hill SE26 .. 184 C6
Golders Green NW11 ...47 A3
Hendon NW4 ....28 C1
Hillingdon UB8 ....82 C3
Hounslow TW4 ...... 129 A1
Kilburn NW6 ....91 C6
Surbiton KT6 .... 198 A2
Tufnell Pk N19 ....71 D5
10 West Norwood
SW16 .... 182 C5
Sycamore Gdns
Hammersmith W6,
W12 ....112 B3
Mitcham CR4 ....180 B1
Tottenham N15 ....51 D5
Sycamore Gr
Kingsbury NW9 ....45 A2
Kingston u T KT3 .... 199 C6
Lewisham SE6 ...... 164 A5
Penge SE20 .... 184 A2
Sycamore Hill N11 ....31 A4
Sycamore Ho
4 Buckhurst Hill
IG9 ....21 D2
23 Finchley N2 ....30 B1
10 Maitland Pk NW3 ...70 D2
Penge SE20 .... 184 D4
17 Rotherhithe SE16 . 118 D4
3 Shepherd's Bush
W6 ....112 B4
2 Stoke Newington
N16 ....73 B6
Teddington TW11 .... 175 C3
Twickenham TW1 .... 152 D2
Sycamore Lo
7 Ashford TW16 .... 171 D3
Putney SW15 ....134 B2
Sycamore Lodge HA2 . 64 B6
Sycamore Mews 4
SW4 ....137 C2
Sycamore Rd SW19,
SW20 ....178 C4
Sycamore St EC1 ... 242 A5
Sycamore Way
TW11 ....175 C4
Sycamore Wlk
Ilford IG6 ....57 A5
1 Kensal Town W10 ...91 A3
Sydcote SE21 ....161 A3
Sydenham Ave
Penge SE26 ....184 B5
Southgate N21 ....16 B6
Sydenham Girls Sch
SE26 ....162 B1
Sydenham High Sch Jun
Dept SE26 ....184 B6
Sydenham High Sch
(Sec) 13 SE26 ......184 B5
Sydenham Hill SE21, SE22,
SE23, SE26, SE19 ....162 A1
Sydenham Hill Sta
SE21 .... 161 D1
Sydenham Hill Wood
Nature Reserve
SE26 .... 162 A1
Sydenham Ho 16
KT6 .... 197 D2
Sydenham Ind Est
SE26 ....185 B5
Sydenham Park Mans 2
SE26 ....162 C1
Sydenham Park Rd SE23,
SE26 ....162 C1
Sydenham Pk SE26 ..162 C1
Sydenham Rd
Forest Hill SE26 ..... 185 A6
Thornton Heath CR0 ..205 B2
Sydenham Rise
SE23 ....162 B2
Sydenham Sta SE26 . 184 C6
Sydenham Station App
4 SE26 ....184 C6
Sydmons Ct SE23 ....162 C4
Sydner Mews N16 ....73 D4
Sydner Rd N16 ......73 D4
Sydney Chapman Way
EN5 ....1 B3
Sydney Cl SW3 ..... 256 D3
Sydney Cotts KT10 .. 212 D2
Sydney Cres TW15 .. 170 D4
Sydney Ct Hayes UB4 ..84 C3
Surbiton KT6 .... 214 A6
Sydney Gr NW4 ....46 C4
Sydney Ho
4 Chiswick W4 ..... 111 C2
Muswell Hill N10 ......31 B3
Sydney Mews SW3 .. 256 D3
Sydney Pl SW7 ..... 257 A3
Sydney Rd
Abbey Wood SE2 .... 124 D3
Bexley DA6 .... 146 D1
Ealing W13 .... 109 A4
East Bedfont TW14 .. 150 A3
Hornsey N8 ....50 C5
Muswell Hill N10 ......31 B3
Richmond TW10,
TW9 .... 132 A1
Sidcup DA14 .... 189 C6
Sutton SM1 .... 217 C4
Teddington TW11 .... 174 D5
Wanstead E11 ....55 B3
West Barnes SW20 .. 178 D1
Woodford IG8 ....37 A6
Sydney Russell Sch The
RM9 ....80 D3
Sydney St
SW3 ....114 C1 257 A2
Sydney Terr KT10 ... 212 D2
Sylva Cotts 3 SE8 ...141 C4
Sylva Ct 3 SW15 .... 156 D4
Sylvana Cl UB10 ......82 B6
Sylvan Ave
Church End N3 ....29 C1
Dagenham RM6 ....59 B3
Edgware NW7 ....27 D4
Wood Green N22 ......32 C3
Sylvan Ct Finchley N12 .29 D6
1 Kilburn NW6 ....91 D6
South Croydon CR2 .. 221 A2
Sylvan Gdns KT6 .... 197 D2
Sylvan Gr
Hampstead NW2 ......68 D4
SE15 ....140 B6
Sylvan Hill SE19 .....183 C2
Sylvan Ho N21 ....16 B6
Sylvan Rd Ilford IG1 ...79 A6
South Norwood SE19 . 183 D2
Upton E7 ....77 B2
Walthamstow E17 .....53 C4
Wanstead E11 ....55 A4
Sylvan Way
Coney Hall BR4 ..... 224 C4
Dagenham RM8 ....80 B5
Sylvan Wlk BR1 ......210 B6
Sylverdale Rd CR0 .. 220 D5
Sylvester Ave BR7 ....188 B4
Sylvester Ct HA0 ......65 D3
Sylvester Ho 7 E8 ....74 B2
Sylvester Path 8 E8 ..74 B2
Sylvester Rd
Finchley N2 ....30 B1
Hackney E8 ....74 B2
Walthamstow E17 .....53 B2
Wembley HA0 ....65 C3
Sylvestrus Cl KT1 ....176 C1
Sylvia Ave HA5 ....23 B4
Sylvia Ct N1 .... 235 C3
Wembley HA9 ....66 D1
Sylvia Gdns HA9 .....66 D1
Sylvia Lawla Ct N22 ..32 B1
Sylvia Pankhurst Ho
10 Dagenham RM10 ...81 C5
14 Globe Town E2 .....96 D4
Sylvia Young Theatre
Sch NW1 ....92 C3 237 B5
Symes Mews NW1 .. 232 A4
Symington Ho SE1 .. 262 C5
Symington Mews E9 ..74 D3
Symister Mews N1 .....95 C4
25 Shoreditch N1 .....95 C4
Symons Cl 6 SE15 ...140 C3
Symons St
SW3 ...... 114 D2 257 D3
Symphony Cl HA8 .....26 D3
Symphony Mews 15
W10 ....91 A4
Syon Gate Way TW7,
TW8 ....131 B5
Syon Ho & Pk★
TW8 ....131 C4
Syon La
Brentford TW7,
TW8 ....131 B5
Hounslow TW7 ...... 130 D6
Syon Lane Sta TW7 . 131 A5
Syon Lo 6 SE12 .....165 A4
Syon Park Cotts
TW8 ....131 C4
Syon Park Gdns
TW7 .... 130 D5
Syracuse Univ
W11 ....113 B6 244 C5
Syringa Ho SE4 ......141 B2

T

Tabard Ct 6 E14 ......98 A1
Tabard Ho SE1 .... 262 D6
Teddington KT1 ..... 175 C2
Tabard St
SE1 ....117 B3 262 C6
Tabernacle Ave 7
E13 ....99 A3
Tabernacle St
EC2 ....95 B3 242 D6
Tableer Ave SW4 .... 159 D6
Tabley Rd N7 ....72 A4
Tabor Ct 3 SM3 .....217 A2
Tabor Gdns SM2,
SM3 ....217 B1
Tabor Gr SW19 ....179 B3
Tabor Rd W6 ....112 B3
Tachbrook Est
SW1 ...... 115 D1 259 D1
Tachbrook Mews
SW1 .... 259 A4
Tachbrook Rd
East Bedfont TW14 .. 149 D4
Southall UB2 .... 106 D2
Tachbrook St
SW1 ....115 C2 259 B3
Tack Mews SE4 .....141 C2
Tadbourne Ct 1 HA8 . 27 A3
Tadema Ho NW8 .... 236 D5
Tadema Rd
SW10 ......136 A5 266 B3
Tadlow KT1 ....198 C6
Tadmor Cl TW16 .... 193 D5
Tadmor St W12 ..... 112 D5
Tadworth Ave KT3 .. 199 D4
Tadworth Ct 5 N11 ...31 A4
Tadworth Ho SE1 ... 251 C1
Tadworth Rd NW2 ....68 A6
Taeping St E14 ..... 119 D2
Taffrail Ho 2 E14 .... 119 D1
Taffy's How CR4 .....202 C6
Taft Way 44 E3 ....97 D4
Taggs Ho KT1 .... 175 D1
Tailors Ct 9 SW16 ...181 C6
Tailworth St 16 E1 ....96 A2
Tait 7 NW9 ....27 D3
Tait Ct 16 Old Ford E3 .. 97 B6
SW8 .... 269 D2
Tait Ho SE1 .... 251 B3
2 Tufnell Pk N19 ......71 C4
Tait Rd CR0 ....205 C2
Tait Rd Ind Est CR0 .. 205 C2
Takhar Mews SW11 ..136 C3
Talacre Com Sp Ctr
NW5 ....71 B2
Talacre Rd NW5 ......71 A2
Talbot Ave N2 ....48 B6
Talbot Cl N15 ....51 D5
Talbot Cres NW4 ......46 A4
Talbot Ct EC3 .... 252 D6
Neasden NW9 ....67 B5
Talbot Gdns IG3 ......80 A6
Talbot Grove Ho 10
W11 ....91 A1
Talbot Ho Highbury N7 .72 C5
Poplar E14 ....97 D1
Talbot Pl SE3 ....142 C3
Talbot Rd
Ashford TW15 ...... 170 A5
Camberwell SE22 .... 139 C1
Dagenham RM9 ....81 B1
Ealing W13 .... 109 A5
Forest Gate E7 ....77 A4
Harrow HA3 ....24 D1
Highgate N6 ....49 A3
Isleworth TW1, TW7 . 131 A1
Notting Hill W2 ....91 C1
Notting Hill W11 ....91 B1
Southall UB2 .... 107 A2
South Norwood CR7 ..205 B5
Tottenham N15 ....51 D5
Twickenham TW2 .... 152 D3
Wallend E6 .... 100 C5
Wallington SM5 ..... 219 A3
Wembley HA0 ....65 D2

Talbot Rd *continued*
Wood Green N22 ....31 C2
Talbot Sq W2 ..92 B1 236 C1
Talbot Wlk
Notting Hill W11 ....91 A1
Willesden NW10 ....67 C2
Talbot Yd SE1 .... 252 C3
Talcott Path 12 SW2 ..160 C3
Talehangers Cl DA6 . 146 D1
Talfourd Pl SE15 .... 139 D4
Talfourd Rd SE15 ... 139 D4
Talgarth Rd
Hammersmith W6 ... 112 C1
W14 ....113 A1 254 B2
Talgarth Wlk NW9 ....45 C4
Talia Ho E14 ....120 A3
Talisman Cl 2 IG3 ....58 B1
Talisman Sq SE26 ....184 A6
Talisman Way HA9 ....66 B5
Tallack Cl HA3 ....24 C3
Tallack Rd E10 ....53 B1
Tall Elms Cl BR2 ....208 D4
Talleyrand Ho SE5 ...139 A3
Tallis Cl E16 ....99 B1
Tallis Gr SE7 ....143 B6
Tallis St EC4 .... 251 B6
Tallis View NW10 ....67 B2
Tallow Cl RM9 ....81 A2
Tallow Rd TW8 ....131 C5
Tall Trees SW16 ....204 B6
Talma Gdns TW2 ....152 C4
Talmage Cl SE23 ....162 C4
Talman Gr HA7 ....25 D4
Talma Rd SW2 ....138 C1
Talmud Torah Machzikei Hadass Sch E5 ....52 A2
Talmud Torah Tiferes Shlomo 1 NW11 ....47 A2
Talmud-Torah Yetev-Lev 6 N16 ....52 A1
Talwin St E3 ....97 D4
Tamar Cl 24 E3 ....97 B6
Tamar Ho
10 Cubitt Town E14 .. 120 A4
SE11 .... 261 B2
Tamarind Ct 8 W3 ....89 A1
Tamarind Ho 4
SE15 ....140 A5
Tamarind Yd 5 E1 ...118 A5
Tamarisk Sq W12 ... 111 D6
Tamar Sq IG8 ....37 B4
Tamar St SE7 ....122 A2
Tamar Way N17 ....52 A6
Tame Ho 3 UB5 ....85 B4
Tamesa Ho TW17 ....192 C2
Tamesis Gdns KT4 ...215 C6
Tamian Ind Est TW4 . 128 C1
Tamian Way TW4 ...128 C1
Tamil Ho SE6 ....163 C2
Tamworth N7 ....72 A2
Tamworth Ave IG8 ....36 C4
Tamworth La CR4 ....203 B6
Tamworth Pk CR4 ....203 B6
Tamworth Pl 3 CR0 .221 A6
Tamworth Rd CR0 ....221 A6
Tamworth St
SW6 ....135 C6 265 A5
Tancred Rd N4 ....50 D3
Tandem Ctr SW19 ...180 B2
Tandridge Ct SM2 ... 217 D2
Tandridge Dr BR6 ....211 B1
Tandridge Pl 2 BR6 .211 B1
Tanfield Ave NW2 ....67 D5
Tanfield Rd CR0 ....221 A6
Tangier Rd TW10 .... 132 D2
Tangleberry Cl BR1 ..210 B5
Tangle Tree Cl N3 ....29 D1
Tanglewood Cl
Hillingdon UB10 ....82 C3
South Croydon CR0 .. 222 C5
Stanmore HA7 ....8 C2
Tanglewood Lo HA8 ...27 A4
Tanglewood Way
TW13 ....150 B1
Tangley Gr SW15 .... 155 D4
Tangley Park Rd
TW12 ....173 B4
Tanglyn Ave TW17 ... 192 D4
Tangmere
Tottenham N17 ....33 B1
WC1 .... 233 C1
Tangmere Gdns UB5 ..84 C5
Tangmere Gr KT2 ... 175 D5
Tangmere Way NW9 ..27 C1
Tanhurst Ho 27
SW2 ....160 A4
Tanhurst Wlk SE2 ... 124 D3
Tankerton Rd KT6 ....214 B6
Tankerton St WC1 ... 233 B1
Tankerton Terr CR0 ..204 B3
Tankerville Rd
SW16 ....182 A3
Tankridge Rd NW2 ....68 B6
Tanner Ho
1 Merton SW19 .... 180 A2
SE1 .... 253 B1
Tanner Point 3 E13 ...99 A6
Tanners Cl KT12 ....194 B3
Tanners End La N18 ...33 C5
Tanner's Hill SE8 ....141 C4
Tanners La IG6 ....57 A6
Tanners Mews SE8 ...141 B4
Tanner St
Barking IG11 ....79 A2
SE1 ....117 C4 253 B1
Tanners Yd 33 E2 ....96 B5
Tannery Cl
Beckenham BR3,
CR0 .... 206 D4
Dagenham RM10 ....81 D5
Tannery Ho 22 E1 ....96 A2
Tannington Terr N5 ...72 C5
Tannsfeld Rd SE26 .. 184 D5
Tansley Cl N7 ....71 D3
Tanswell St SE1 .... 251 A1
Tansy Cl E6 ....100 C1
Tantallon Rd SW12 ...159 A3
Tant Ave E16 ....98 D1
Tantony Gr RM6 ....58 D6
Tanworth Gdns HA5 ...22 C1
Tanyard Ho 8 TW8 ...131 C5
Tan Yard La DA5 ....169 C4
Tanza Rd NW3 ....70 D4
Tapestry Cl SM2 .... 217 D1
Tapley Ho 11 SE1 ....118 A4
Taplow NW3 ....70 B1
Taplow Ct CR4 ....202 C5
Taplow Ho 36 E2 ....95 D4
Taplow Rd N13 ....33 A6
Taplow St N1 ... 95 A5 235 B3
Tappesfield Rd
SE15 ....140 C2
Tapping Cl 5 KT2 ....176 C3
Tapp St E1 ....96 B3
Tapster St EN5 ....1 B2
Tara Ct 4 BR3 .... 185 D1
Tara Mews N8 ....50 A3
Taranto Ho 14 E1 ....96 D2
Tarati Ct HA0 ....65 D1
Tarbert Rd SE22 ....161 C6
Tarbert Wlk E1 ....118 C6
Target Cl TW14 ....149 C5
Target Ho W13 ....109 B5
Target Rdbt UB5 ....85 B6
Tariff Rd N17 ....34 A4
Tarleton Ct 2 N22 ....32 C1
Tarleton Gdns SE23 ..162 B3
Tarling Cl DA14 ....168 B1
Tarling Rd
Canning Town E16 ....98 D1
Finchley N2 ....30 A1
Tarling St E1 ....96 C1
Tarnbank EN2 ....16 A6
Tarnbrook Ct SW1 .. 258 A3
Tarn St SE1 ...117 A3 262 A5
Tarns The NW1 .... 232 A2
Tarnwood Pk SE9 ....166 B3
Tarplett Ho 22 SE14 . 140 D6
Tarquin Ho SE26 ....184 A6
Tarragon Cl SE14 ....141 A5
Tarragon Gr SE26 ... 184 D4
Tarranbrae NW6 ....69 A1
Tarrant Ho E2 ....96 C4
Tarrant Pl W1 .... 237 C3
Tarrantt Ho W14 .... 254 A6
Tarriff Cres SE8 ....119 B2
Tarrington Cl SW16 . 159 D1
Tartan Ho 12 E14 ....98 A1
Tarver Rd
SE17 .... 116 D1 261 D2
Tarves Way SE10 .... 141 D5
Tashbar of Edgware Prim Sch HA8 ....26 C6
Tash Pl N11 ....31 B5
Tasker Cl UB7 ....127 A5
Tasker Ho
3 Barking IG11 .... 101 B5
17 Poplar E14 ....97 B2
Tasker Lo W8 .... 245 A2
Tasker Rd NW3 ....70 D3
Tasman Ct
Ashford TW16 .... 171 C3
9 Cubitt Town E14 .. 119 D2
Tasman Ho 17 E1 ....118 B5
Tasmania Terr N18 ....33 A4
Tasman Rd SW9 ....138 A2
Tasman Wlk E16 ....99 D1
Tasso Rd W6 ..135 A6 264 A6
Tasso Yd W6 .... 264 A5
Tatam Rd NW10 ....67 B1
Tatchbury Ho SW15 . 155 D5
Tate Britain★
SW1 ....116 A2 260 A3
Tate Gdns WD23 ....8 C4
Tate Ho 13 E2 ....96 D5
Tate Modern★
EC4 .... 116 D5 251 D4
Tate Rd Newham E16 ..122 B5
Sutton SM1 .... 217 C3
Tatham Pl
NW8 ....92 B5 229 D4
Tatnell Rd SE23 ....163 A5
Tattersall Cl SE9 ....166 A6
Tatton Cres E5, N16 ....51 D2
Tatum St
SE17 ....117 B2 262 D3
Tauheed Cl N4 ....73 A6
Taunton Ave
Hounslow TW3 .... 130 A3
Wimbledon SW20 ....178 B1
Taunton Cl SM3 ....201 C1
Taunton Dr Enfield EN2 ..4 C2
Finchley N2 ....30 A1
Taunton Ho W2 .... 236 A1
Taunton Mews NW1 . 237 C5
Taunton Pl
NW1 ....92 D3 237 C6
Taunton Rd
Greenford UB6 ....85 D6
Lewisham SE12 .... 164 D6
Taunton Way HA7 ....26 A1
Tavern Cl SM5 ....202 C2
Tavern Ct SE1 .... 262 B5
Taverner Ho N16 ....73 B5
Taverners Cl W11 .... 244 A3
Taverners Ct HA9 ....66 B6
Taverners Lo EN4 ....15 A6
Taverner Sq 4 N5 ....73 A4
Taverners Way E4 ....20 C3
Tavern La SW9 ....138 C3
Tavistock Ave
Mill Hill NW7 ....28 D3
Walthamstow E17 ....53 A6
Wembley UB6 ....87 A5
Tavistock Cl N16 ....73 C3
Tavistock Cres
Mitcham CR4 .... 204 A5
Notting Hill W11 ....91 B2
Tavistock Ct
1 Croydon CR0 ....205 B1
WC1 .... 239 D6
Tavistock Gdns IG3 ...79 C4
Tavistock Gr CR0 ....205 B2
Tavistock Ho 3 W11 ..91 B2
Tavistock Mews 3
W11 ....91 B1
Tavistock Pl
Bloomsbury
WC1 ....94 A3 240 A6
East Barnet N14 ....15 B5
Tavistock Rd
4 Beckenham BR2 .. 208 D5
Carshalton SM5 ....202 B1
Croydon CR0 ....205 B1
DA16 .... 146 C4
Dagenham NW10 ....89 D5
Edgware HA8 ....26 C2
Leyton E7 ....76 D4
Notting Hill W11 ....91 B2
Stratford E15 ....76 D2
Tottenham N4, N15 ....51 B3
Uxbridge UB10 ....61 A3
Wanstead E18 ....55 A6
Tavistock Sq
WC1 ....93 D3 239 D6
Tavistock St
WC2 ....116 A6 250 B6
Tavistock Terr N19 ....71 D5
Tavistock Twr SE16 ...119 A3
Tavistock Wlk SM5 ...202 B1
Taviton St
WC1 ....93 D3 239 C6
Tavy Bridge SE2 ....124 C4
Tavy Cl SE11 .... 261 B2
Tawhid Boys Sch
N16 ....73 D6
Tawney Rd SE28 ....124 B6
Tawny Cl Ealing W13 ..109 B5
Feltham TW13 .... 150 A1
Tawny Way SE16 .... 118 D2
Tayben Ave TW2 ....152 C5
Taybridge Rd SW11 ..137 A1
Tayburn Cl E14 ....98 A1
Tayfield Cl UB10 ....61 A5
Tay Ho 10 E3 ....97 B5
Tayler Ct NW8 .... 229 C6
Taylor Ave TW9 .... 132 D3
Taylor Cl
Deptford SE8 ....141 B6
Hampton TW12 .... 174 A5
Hounslow TW3 .... 130 A4
3 Orpington BR6 .... 227 D4
Tottenham N17 ....34 A3
Taylor Ct Ealing W13 ..109 C5
Penge SE20 .... 184 C1
Taylor Ho
Carshalton SM5 .... 218 C6
10 Streatham SW2 .. 160 C3
Taylor Rd
Mitcham CR4 .... 180 C3
Wallington SM6 ....219 B3
Taylor's Bldgs SE18 . 122 D2
Taylors Cl DA14 .... 167 D1
Taylors Ct TW13 ....150 A2
Taylor's Gn W3 ....89 C1
Taylor's La Barnet EN5 .. 1 B4
Forest Hill SE26 ....184 B6
Willesden NW10 ....67 C1
Taylorsmead NW7 ....28 A5
Taymount Grange 2
SE23 ....162 C2
Taymount Ri SE23 ....162 B2
Taymount Rise SE23 .162 C2
Tayport Cl N1 ....72 A1
Tayside Ct 6 SE5 ....139 B1
Tayside Dr HA8 ....10 D2
Taywood Rd UB5 ....85 B3
Tayyibah Girls Sch 5
E5 ....52 B1
Teak Cl SE16 ....119 A5
Tealby Ct N7 ....72 B2
Teal Cl Enfield EN3 ....6 C6
Newham E16 ....99 D2
Teal Ct 30 SE8 ....141 B6
Wallington SM6 .... 219 C3
Willesden NW10 ....67 B2
Teale St E2 ....96 A5
Tealing Dr KT19 ....215 B4
Teal Pl SM1 ....217 B3
Teal St 1 SE10 .... 120 D3
Teasel Cl CR0 .... 206 D1
Teasel Cres SE28 ....123 C5
Teasel Way E15 ....98 C4
Teather St 12 SE5 ....139 C5
Tebbs Ho 14 SW2 ....160 C4
Tebworth Rd N17 ....33 D3
Technology Pk NW9 ..45 C6
Teck Cl TW7 ....131 A3
Tedder 5 NW9 ....27 D3
Tedder Cl
Chessington KT9 .... 213 C3
Hillingdon UB10 ....60 B1
Ruislip HA4 ....62 B3
Tedder Rd CR2 .... 222 D1
TEDDINGTON 175 C5
Teddington Bsns Pk
TW11 .... 174 D4
Teddington Meml Hospl
TW11 .... 174 C4
Teddington Park Rd
TW11 .... 174 D6
Teddington Pk
TW11 .... 174 D5
Teddington Sch
TW11 .... 175 C4
Teddington Sta
TW11 .... 175 A4
Ted Hennem Ho
RM10 ....81 D5
Tedman Ct SE13 ....142 A1
Ted Roberts Ho 25
E2 ....96 B5
Tedworth Gdns SW3 257 C1
Tedworth Sq
SW3 .... 114 D1 257 C1
Tees Ave UB6 ....86 D5
Tees Ct W7 ....86 B1
Teesdale Ave TW7 ....131 A4
Teesdale Cl E2 ....96 B5
Teesdale Gdns
Isleworth TW7 .... 131 A4
South Norwood SE25 . 183 C1
Teesdale Rd E11 ....54 D2
Teesdale St E2 ....96 B5
Teesdale Yd 34 E2 ....96 B5
Teeswater Ct DA18 .. 124 D3
Tee The W3 ....89 C1
Teevan Cl CR0 ....206 A2
Teevan Rd CR0 ....206 A2
Tegan Cl SM2 ....217 C1
Teign Mews SE9 ....166 A2
Teignmouth Cl
6 Clapham SW4 .... 137 D1
Edgware HA8 ....26 B1
Teignmouth Gdns
UB6 ....87 A4
Teignmouth Par UB6 ..87 B5
Teignmouth Rd
Bexley DA16 .... 146 C3
Brondesbury NW2 ....68 D2
Tejas Ct N3 ....47 A5
Tej Ct E7 ....77 D3
Telcote Way HA4 ....40 C2
Telegraph Hill NW3 ..69 D5
Telegraph La KT10 .. 212 D3
Telegraph Mews IG3 ..58 A1
Telegraph Pl E14 .... 119 D2
Telegraph Rd SW15 ..156 C4
Telegraph St EC2 .... 242 C2
Telemann Sq SE3 ....143 B2
Telephone Pl SW6 .. 264 D6
Telfer Cl 4 W3 ....111 A4
Telfer Ho
8 Dulwich SE21 .... 183 C6
EC1 .... 234 D1
Telferscot Prim Sch 5
SW12 .... 159 D3
Telferscot Rd SW12 . 159 D3
Telford Ave SW12,
SW2 ....160 A3
Telford Avenue Mans 7
SW2 ....160 A3
Telford Cl
Penge SE19 .... 183 D4
Walthamstow E17 ....53 A2
Telford Ct EN5 ....13 C6
Telford Dr KT12 ....194 C2
Telford Ho
2 Belvedere DA17 .. 125 C3
8 Kensal Town W10 ...91 A2
SE1 .... 262 A6
Telford Parade Mans 8
SW2 ....160 A3
Telford Rd
3 Hendon NW9 ....46 A3
Kensal Town W10 ....91 A2
Sidcup SE9 ....167 B2
Southall UB1 ....85 D1
Twickenham TW4 .... 151 C4
Telford Rd (North Circular Rd) N11 ....31 C5
Telford's Yd 21 SE1 ...118 A6
Telford Terr SW1 .... 269 A6
Telford Way
Dagenham W3 ....89 C2
Hayes UB4 ....85 A2
Telham Rd E6 ....100 C5
Tell Gr SE22 .... 139 D1
Tellson Ave SE18 ....144 A4
Telscombe Cl BR6 ...227 C6
Telscombe Ho SW11 268 A1
Temair Ho 1 SE10 ...142 A5
Temeraire Pl TW8 ....110 B1
Temeraire St SE16 ...118 C4
Tempelhof Ave NW2 ..46 C2
Temperley Rd SW12 .159 A4
Templar Ct RM7 ....59 D5
Templar Dr SE28 .... 102 D1
Templar Ho
Hampstead NW2 ....69 B2
7 Upper Clapton E5 ..74 C6
Templar Pl TW12 ....173 C3
Templars Ave NW11 ...47 B3
Templars Cres N3 ....29 C1
Templars Dr HA3 ....24 B4
Templar St SE5 .... 138 D3
Temple Ave
Croydon CR0 ....223 B5
Dagenham RM8 ....59 C1
EC4 ....116 C6 251 B6
Oakleigh Pk N20 ....14 B4
Temple Bar★ EC4 ... 241 D1
Temple Cl Finchley N3 ..29 B1
Leytonstone E11 ....54 C2
Woolwich SE18 .... 123 A3

Templecombe Rd E9 96 C6
Templecombe Way
SM4 201 A4
Templecroft TW15 171 B4
Temple Ct Stepney E1 96 D2
SW8 270 A3
Templedene BR2 186 B1
Temple Dwellings 7
E2 96 B5
TEMPLE FORTUNE 47 A4
Temple Fortune Ct 9
NW11 47 B4
Temple Fortune Hill
NW11 47 C4
Temple Fortune Ho 3
NW11 47 B4
Temple Fortune La
NW11 47 C3
Temple Fortune Par 5
NW11 47 B4
Temple Gdns
Dagenham RM8 80 D5
Edmonton N21 16 D2
Temple Fortune NW11 47 B3
Temple Gr Enfield EN2 4 D2
Golders Green NW11 47 C3
Temple Gr Hatcham Sch
SE14 141 A3
Temple Hall Ct E4 20 B2
Temple Ho
13 Battersea SW11 136 C2
4 Tufnell Pk N7 71 C5
11 Walthamstow E17 53 D6
Temple La
EC4 94 C1 241 B1
Temple Lo EN5 14 B4
Templeman Rd W7 86 D2
Templemead Cl W3 89 C1
Temple Mead Cl HA7 25 B4
Templemead Ho E9 75 A4
TEMPLE MILLS 75 D3
Temple Mills La
London E10, E15 76 A4
Stratford E15 75 D4
Temple Mills Rd E9 75 C4
Templemore DA14 190 B5
Temple Par EN5 14 B4
Temple Pk UB8 82 C4
Temple Pl
WC2 116 B6 250 D6
Temple Rd
Acton Green W4 111 A3
Cricklewood NW2 68 C5
Croydon CR0 221 B4
Ealing W5 109 D3
Hornsey N8 50 B5
Isleworth TW3 130 A1
Newham E6 100 A6
Richmond TW9 132 B2
Temple Sheen
SW14 155 A6
Temple Sheen Rd
SW14 133 A1
Temple St E2 96 B5
Temple Sta
WC2 116 C6 251 A6
Temple Terr N22 32 C1
Templeton Ave E4 35 D6
Templeton Cl
South Norwood
SE19 183 B2
25 Stoke Newington
N16 73 C3
Templeton Ct
Enfield EN3 6 C5
Walthamstow E10 53 D1
Templeton Pl
SW5 113 C2 255 B3
Templeton Rd N4,
N15 51 B3
Temple Way SM1 218 B5
Temple West Mews
SE11 261 C5
Templewood W13 87 B2
Templewood Ave
NW3 69 D5
Templewood Gdns
NW3 69 D5
Templewood Point
NW2 69 B6
Tempsford Cl EN2 5 A2
Tempsford Ct HA1 42 D3
Temsford Cl HA2 24 A1
Ten Acre Wood Nature
Reserve UB4 83 D6
Tenbury Cl E7 77 D3
Tenbury Ct SW12 159 D3
Tenby Ave HA3 25 B1
Tenby Cl
Dagenham RM6 59 A3
Tottenham N15 51 D5
Tenby Ct E17 53 A4
Tenby Gdns UB5 63 C2
Tenby Ho Hayes UB3 105 A3
Islington N7 72 C4
W2 236 A1
Tenby Rd DA16 146 D4
Dagenham RM6 59 A3
Edgware HA8 26 B1
Enfield EN3 6 C1
Walthamstow E17 53 A4
Tench St E1 118 B5
Tenda Rd SE16 118 B2
Tendring Ho SW2 160 C5
Tendring Way RM6 58 C4
Tenham Ave SW2 159 D2
Tenison Ct W1 249 A6
Tenison Way SE1 251 A3
Tenniel Cl W2 245 D6
Tennison Ave WD6 10 D6
Tennison Rd SE25 205 D4
Tennis St
SE1 117 B4 252 C2
Tenniswood Rd EN1 5 C4
Tennyson Ave
Kingsbury NW9 45 A6
Plashet E12 78 A1
Twickenham TW1 152 D3
Wanstead E11 55 A2
West Barnes KT3 200 B4
Tennyson Cl DA16 145 D4
Enfield EN3 18 D6
Feltham TW14 150 A5
Tennyson Ct 3
TW10 175 D6
Tennyson Ho
2 Erith DA17 125 B1
SE17 262 B2
Southall UB1 85 C1
Tennyson Rd
Ashford TW15 170 A5
Ealing W7 108 D6
Hounslow TW3 130 A3
Kilburn NW6 91 B6
Leyton E10 75 D6
Mill Hill NW7 28 A5
Penge SE20 184 D3
Stratford E15 76 C1
Walthamstow E17 53 B3
Wimbledon SW19 180 A4
Tennyson St SW8 137 B3
Tensing Ct TW19 148 A3
Tensing Ho N1 72 D2
Tensing Rd UB2 107 C3
Tentelow La UB2 107 D3
Tenterden Cl
Hendon NW4 46 D6
SE9 188 B6
Tenterden Dr NW4 46 D6
Tenterden Gdns
Croydon CR0 206 A2
Hendon NW4 46 D6
Tenterden Gr NW4 46 D6
Tenterden Ho SE17 263 B2
Tenterden Rd
Croydon CR0 206 A2
Dagenham RM8 81 B6
Tottenham N17 33 D3
Tenterden St W1 238 D1
Tenter Ground E1 243 C3
Tent Peg La BR5 211 A4
Tent St E1 96 B3
Tenzing Ct 4 SE9 166 A2
Tequila Wharf E14 97 A1
Terborch Way 6
SE22 161 C6
Tercelet Terr NW3 70 A4
Teredo St SE16 118 D3
Terence Ct 6 DA17 147 B6
Teresa Mews E17 53 C5
Teresa Wlk N10 49 B4
Terling Cl E11 76 D5
Terling Ho 9 W10 90 C2
Terling Rd RM8 81 C6
Terling Wlk N1 235 A6
Terminal Four Rdbt
TW6 149 A5
Terminus Pl SW1 258 D5
Tern Ho 9 SE15 139 D4
Terrace Gdns SW13 133 D3
Terrace Ho 2 N20 14 A1
Terrace La TW10 154 A5
Terrace Rd
Hackney E9 74 C1
Newham E13 99 B6
Walton-on-T KT12 194 B3
Terraces The 6
SW20 178 D3
Terrace The
Barnes SW13,
SW14 133 C3
Chingford E4 20 C1
Cranley Gdns N2 49 A5
EC4 241 B1
Kilburn NW6 91 C6
10 Rotherhithe SE8 119 B2
1 Woodford IG8 37 A4
Terrace Wlk RM9 81 A3
Terrall Apartments 7
N17 51 D6
Terrano Ho 1 TW9 132 D4
Terrapin Ct SW17 159 B1
Terrapin Rd SW17 159 B1
Terrapins KT6 197 D2
Terrence McMillan Stad
E13 99 C3
Terrick Rd N22 32 A2
Terrick St W12 90 B1
Terrilands HA5 41 B6
Territorial Ho SE11 261 B3
Terront Rd N15 51 A5
Terry Ct 8 SM6 219 C2
Terry Ho SW2 160 C3
Terry Lodge 2 CR7 204 C4
Tersha St TW9 132 B1
Tessa Sanderson Pl 6
SW8 137 B2
Tessa Sanderson Way
UB6 64 B3
Testerton Wlk 3
W11 112 D6
Testwood Ct W7 108 C6
Tetcott Rd
SW10 136 A5 266 A3
Tetherdown N10 49 A6
Tetherdown Prim Sch
N10 49 A5
Tetty Way BR1, BR2 187 A1
Teversham La
SW8 138 A4 270 B2
Teviot Cl DA16 146 B4
Teviot St E14 98 A2
Tewkesbury Ave
Forest Hill SE23 162 B4
Pinner HA5 41 A4
Tewkesbury Cl
Barnet EN4 2 B1
Tottenham N15 51 B3
Tewkesbury Ct N11 31 D4
Tewkesbury Gdns
NW9 44 D6
Tewkesbury Rd
Carshalton SM5 202 B1
Ealing W13 109 A6
Tottenham N15 51 B3
Tewkesbury Terr N11 31 D4
Tewson Rd SE18 123 C1
Teyham Ct 2 SW11 158 D5
Teynham Ave EN1 17 B5
Teynham Ct N12 30 A6
Teynham Gn BR2 209 A4
Teynham Ho SE9 167 B5
Teynton Terr N17 33 A2
Thackeray Ave N17 34 A1
Thackeray Cl
Hayes UB8 82 D1
Isleworth TW7 131 A3
Wimbledon SW19 178 D3
Thackeray Ct
Chelsea SW3 257 C2
Ealing W5 88 B1
West Kensington W14 254 A5
Thackeray Dr RM6 58 B2
Thackeray Ho
College Pk NW10 90 A4
WC1 240 A6
Thackeray Manor
SM1 218 A3
Thackeray Mews 6
E8 74 A2
Thackeray Rd
Clapham SW8 137 B3
Newham E6 99 D5
Thackeray's Almshouses
SE6 163 D5
Thackeray St W8 255 D6
Thackery Lo TW14 149 B5
Thackrah Cl N2 30 A1
Thakeham Cl SE26 184 B5
Thalia Cl SE10 142 B6
Tham Cl 10 SE24 138 D2
Thame Rd SE16 118 D4
Thames Ave
Dagenham RM9 103 D3
North Cheam KT4 200 C1
Sands End
SW10 136 A4 266 B2
Wembley UB6 86 D5
Thames Bank SW14 133 A3
Thamesbank Pl
SE28 102 C1
Thames Barrier Visitor
Ctr* SE18 121 D3
Thames Christian Coll 25
SW11 136 B2
Thames Circ E14 119 C2
Thames Cl TW12 173 D1
Thames Cnr TW16 194 C6
Thames Cres W4 133 C5
Thames Ct Ealing W7 86 C1
Edmonton N9 18 C1
10 SE15 139 D5
West Molesey KT8 173 D1
THAMES DITTON 197 B2
Thames Ditton Inf Sch
KT7 196 D3
Thames Ditton Island
KT7 197 A3
Thames Ditton Jun Sch
KT7 196 D2
Thames Ditton Sta
KT7 196 D2
Thames Dr HA4 39 A3
Thames Eyot 8
TW1 153 A3
Thamesfield Ct
TW17 193 A2
Thamesfield Ho
TW17 193 A2
Thamesfield Mews
TW17 193 A2
Thamesgate Cl
TW10 175 B6
Thames Gateway Pk
RM9 103 B4
Thames Haven KT6 197 D4
Thames Hts SE1 253 C2
Thameside TW11 175 D3
Thameside Ctr TW8 132 B6
Thameside Ind Est
E16 121 D4
Thameside Pl KT1 175 D2
Thames Link Ho 7
TW9 132 A1
Thames Mdw KT12,
TW17 193 C1
THAMESMEAD 124 A5
Thames Mead KT12 194 A3
Thames Meadow
KT8 195 C6
Thamesmead Sch
TW17 193 B3
Thamesmead Sh Ctr
SE28 124 A6
Thamesmere Dr
SE28 124 A6
Thames Pl SW15 134 D2
Thamespoint TW11 175 D3
Thames Quay
Millwall E14 119 D4
SW10 266 B1
Thames Rd
Barking IG11 102 A4
Chiswick W4 132 D6
Newham E16 121 D5
Thames Reach
Fulham W6 134 C6
Woolwich SE28 123 C4
Thames Road Ind Est
E16 121 D4
Thames Row TW9 132 B6
Thames Side
Teddington KT1 175 D2
Thames Ditton KT7 197 B3
Thames St
Hampton TW12 173 D1
Kingston u T KT1, KT2 175 D1
SE10 141 D6
Sunbury TW16 194 B6
Walton-on-T KT12 193 D2
Thamesvale Cl TW3 129 C3
Thames Valley Univ
W5 109 D5
Thames Valley Univ
(Ealing Campus)
W5 109 D5
Thames Valley Univ
(Walpole House)
W5 109 C6
Thames View 2 IG1 79 A6
Thames View Ho
TW12 194 A3
Thames View Inf Sch
IG11 102 A5
Thames View Jun Sch
IG11 101 D5
Thames View Lo
IG11 101 C4
Thames Village W4 133 A4
Thames Wlk
SW11 136 C5 267 A4
Thane Mans N7 72 B5
Thanescroft Gdns
CR0 221 C5
Thanet Ct 14 W3 88 C1
Thanet Dr BR2 225 D5
Thanet Ho WC1 233 A1
1 West Norwood
SE27 160 D1
Thanet Lo NW2 69 A2
Thanet Pl CR0 221 A4
Thanet Rd DA5 169 C4
Thanet St
WC1 94 A4 233 A1
Thane Villas N7 72 B5
Thane Works N7 72 B5
Thanington Ct DA15 167 C5
Thant Cl E10 75 D5
Tharp Rd SM6 219 D3
Thatcham Ct N20 14 A4
Thatcham Gdns N20 14 A4
Thatcher Cl UB7 104 A4
Thatchers Way TW7 152 B6
Thatches Gr RM6 59 A5
Thavies Inn EC4 241 B2
Thaxted Ct N1 235 D3
Thaxted Ho
Bermondsey SE16 118 C2
Dagenham RM10 81 D1
Thaxted Lo 3 E18 55 B6
Thaxted Pl 9 SW20 178 D3
Thaxted Rd
Buckhurst Hill IG9 21 D4
SE9 167 A2
Thaxton Rd
W14 135 B6 264 D6
Thayers Farm Rd
BR3 185 A2
Thayer St W1 93 A1 238 B2
Theatre Royal* E10 76 B2
Theatre Sq E15 76 B2
Theatre St SW11 136 D2
Theberton St
N1 94 D6 234 C6
Theed St SE1 116 C5 251 B3
Thelbridge Ho 28 E3 97 D4
Thelma Gdns SE3 144 A4
Thelma Gr TW11 175 A4
Theobald Cres HA3 24 A2
Theobald Rd
Croydon CR0 220 D6
Walthamstow E17 53 C2
Theobalds Ave N12 30 A6
Theobalds Ct N4 73 A6
Theobalds Park Rd
EN2 4 D6
Theobald's Rd
WC1 94 B2 240 C4
Theobald St SE1 262 C5
Theodora Way HA5 39 D6
Theodore Ct SE13 164 B5
Theodore Ho 1
SW15 156 A6
Theodore Rd SE13 164 B5
Therapia La
Thornton Heath
CR0 204 A2
Thornton Heath CR0 204 A3
Wallington CR0 203 D2
Therapia Lane Sta
CR0 204 A2
Therapia Rd SE22 162 C5
Theresa Rd W6 112 A2
Therfield Ct N4 73 A6
Thermopylae Gate
E14 119 D2

Theseus Ho
[2] South Bromley
E14 ... 98 B1
2 E14 ... 98 B1
Theseus Wlk N1 ... 234 D3
Thesiger Rd SE20 ... 184 D3
Thessaly Ho SW8 ... 269 A3
Thessaly Rd
SW8 ... 137 C4 269 B2
Thetford Cl N13 ... 32 D4
Thetford Ct
[3] Dulwich SE21 ... 162 B2
New Malden KT3 ... 199 C4
Thetford Gdns RM9 ... 103 A6
Thetford Ho SE1 ... 263 C6
Thetford Rd
Ashford TW15 ... 148 A1
Dagenham RM9 ... 80 D1
New Malden KT3 ... 199 C4
Thetis Terr TW9 ... 132 C6
Theydon Gr IG8 ... 37 C4
Theydon Rd E5 ... 74 C6
Theydon St E17 ... 53 B2
Thicket Cres SM1 ... 218 A4
Thicket Ct [14] SM1 ... 218 A4
Thicket Gr
Dagenham RM9 ... 80 C2
Penge SE20 ... 184 A3
Thicket Rd
Penge SE20 ... 184 B3
Sutton SM1 ... 218 A4
Thicket The UB7 ... 82 A1
Third Ave
Chadwell Heath RM6 ... 58 C3
Dagenham RM10 ... 103 D5
East Acton W3 ... 111 D5
Enfield EN1 ... 17 D6
Hayes UB3 ... 105 D5
Little Ilford E12 ... 78 B3
[3] Newham E13 ... 99 A4
Walthamstow E17 ... 53 C4
Wembley HA9 ... 65 D6
West Kilburn W10 ... 91 A4
Third Cl KT8 ... 196 A5
Third Cross Rd TW2 ... 152 B2
Thirleby Rd
Hendon HA8 ... 27 B2
SW1 ... 115 C3 259 B5
Thirlestane Ct N10 ... 31 A1
Thirlestane Ho
TW12 ... 173 D6
Thirlmere NW1 ... 231 D2
Thirlmere Ave UB6 ... 87 C4
Thirlmere Gdns HA9 ... 43 D1
Thirlmere Ho
Isleworth TW1 ... 152 D6
[19] Stoke Newington
N16 ... 73 B4
Thirlmere Rd
Muswell Hill N10 ... 31 B2
Streatham SW16 ... 181 D6
Thirlmere Rise BR1 ... 186 D4
Thirsk Cl UB5 ... 63 C2
Thirsk Rd
Clapham SW11 ... 137 A1
Mitcham CR4 ... 181 A3
South Norwood SE25 ... 205 B5
Thistlebrook SE2 ... 124 C3
Thistlebrook Ind Est
SE2 ... 124 C4
Thistlecroft Gdns
HA7 ... 25 D1
Thistle Ct N17 ... 52 B5
Thistledene KT7 ... 196 C3
Thistledene Ave HA2 ... 63 A5
Thistledown Ct
SE25 ... 205 C6
Thistlefield Cl DA5 ... 168 D3
Thistle Gr SW7 ... 256 B1
Thistle Ho [10] E14 ... 98 A1
Thistlemead BR7 ... 188 D1
Thistlewaite Rd E5 ... 74 B5
Thistlewood Cl [3] N7 ... 72 B6
Thistleworth Cl TW7 ... 130 B5
Thistley Cl N12 ... 30 C4
Thistly Ct SE8 ... 141 D6
Thomas a' Beckett Cl
HA0 ... 64 D4
Thomas Arnold Prim Sch
RM9 ... 81 B1
Thomas Baines Rd
SW11 ... 136 B2
Thomas Burt Ho [9]
E2 ... 96 B4
Thomas Buxton Jun & Inf
Sch [17] E1 ... 96 A3
Thomas Cribb Mews
E6 ... 100 B1
Thomas Crowell Ct [29]
N1 ... 73 C3
Thomas Ct RM8 ... 80 C6
Thomas Dean Rd
SE26 ... 185 B6
Thomas Dinwiddy Rd
SE12 ... 165 B2
Thomas Doyle St
SE1 ... 261 D6
Thomas Fairchild Com
Sch N1 ... 95 A5 235 B4
Thomas Gamuel Prim
Sch E17 ... 53 C3
Thomas Hardy Ho
N22 ... 32 B2
Thomas Hewlett Ho
HA1 ... 64 C4
Thomas Ho
[9] Belmont SM2 ... 217 D1
[3] Hackney E9 ... 74 C2
[4] Stockwell SW4 ... 138 A1
Thomas Hollywood Ho [3]
E2 ... 96 C5
Thomas Jacomb Pl [2]
E17 ... 53 B5
Thomas Jones Prim Sch
[16] W11 ... 91 A1
Thomas Knyvett Coll
TW15 ... 148 A1
Thomas' La SE6 ... 163 C4
Thomas Lo E17 ... 53 D4
Thomas London Ind Day
Sch W8 ... 113 D3 255 D6
Thomas Milner Ho [8]
SE15 ... 140 A5
Thomas More Bldg The
HA4 ... 39 C1
Thomas More Ho
EC2 ... 242 A3
Thomas More Sq E1 ... 118 A6
Thomas More St E1 ... 118 A5
Thomas More Way
N2 ... 48 A6
Thomas Neal's Ctr
WC1 ... 94 A1 240 A1
Thomas North Terr [4]
E16 ... 98 D2
Thomas Pl W8 ... 255 C5
Thomas Pooley Ct
KT6 ... 198 A2
Thomas Rd E14 ... 97 C2
Thomas Road Ind Est [2]
E14 ... 97 C1
Thomas Shearley Ct
DA5 ... 169 D4
Thomas's Prep Sch
Clapham SW11 ... 158 D6
Thomas's Prep Schs
SW11 ... 136 B4 266 D1
Thomas St SE18 ... 122 D2
Thomas Tallis Sch
SE3 ... 143 B2
Thomas Wall Cl
SM1 ... 217 D3
Thomas Watson Cottage
Homes The EN5 ... 13 A6
Thompson Ave
Richmond TW9 ... 132 C2
[6] SE5 ... 139 A5
Thompson Cl
Ilford IG1 ... 79 A6
Morden SM3 ... 201 C1
Thompson Ho
[11] Kensal Town W10 ... 91 A3
SE14 ... 140 D6
Southall UB1 ... 107 A6
Thompson Rd
Dagenham RM9 ... 81 B5
Dulwich Village SE22 ... 161 D5
Hounslow TW3 ... 129 D1
Uxbridge UB10 ... 60 A1
Thomson Cres CR0 ... 204 C1
Thomson Ct [4] E8 ... 74 A2
Thomson Ho
Pimlico SW1 ... 259 D1
Walworth SE17 ... 263 A3
Thomson Rd HA3 ... 42 C6
Thorburn Ho SW1 ... 248 A1
Thorburn Sq SE1 ... 118 A2
Thorburn Way SW19 ... 180 B2
Thoresby Ho N16 ... 73 B5
Thoresby St
N1 ... 95 A4 235 B2
Thorkhill Gdns KT7 ... 197 B1
Thorkhill Rd KT7 ... 197 B2
Thornaby Gdns N18 ... 34 B5
Thornaby Ho [15] E2 ... 96 B4
Thorn Ave WD23 ... 8 A3
Thornbill Ho [1]
SE15 ... 140 A5
Thornbridge Ct [10]
EN5 ... 13 D6
Thornbury [3] NW4 ... 46 C5
Thornbury Ave TW7 ... 130 B5
Thornbury Cl
Edgware NW7 ... 28 D3
Stoke Newington N16 ... 73 C3
Thornbury Ct
Croydon CR2 ... 221 B3
Hounslow TW7 ... 130 C5
W11 ... 245 A6
Thornbury Ho N6 ... 49 C1
Thornbury Lo EN2 ... 4 D2
Thornbury Rd
Clapham Pk SW2 ... 160 A5
Hounslow TW7 ... 130 B4
Thornbury Sq N6 ... 49 C1
Thornby Rd E5 ... 74 C5
Thorn Cl BR2 ... 210 C3
Northolt UB5 ... 85 B4
Thorncliffe Ct SW2 ... 160 A5
Thorncliffe Rd
Clapham Pk SW2 ... 160 A5
Southall UB2 ... 107 B1
Thorncombe Rd
SE22 ... 161 C6
Thorncroft HA2 ... 64 A5
Thorncroft Rd SM1 ... 217 D4
Thorncroft St
SW8 ... 138 A5 270 A3
Thorndale BR7 ... 188 B3
Thorndale Ho [10] N16 ... 51 C1
Thorndean St SW18 ... 158 A2
Thorndene Ave N11 ... 15 A3
Thorndike Ave UB5 ... 84 D6
Thorndike Cl
SW10 ... 136 A5 266 A4
Thorndike Ho SW1 ... 259 C2
Thorndike Rd [21] N1 ... 73 B2
Thorndike St
SW1 ... 115 D2 259 C3
Thorndon Cl BR5 ... 189 D1
Thorndon Gdns
KT19 ... 215 C4
Thorndon Rd BR5 ... 189 D1
Thorndyke Ct HA5 ... 23 B3
Thorne Cl
Claygate KT10 ... 213 A1
DA8 ... 147 D6
Leyton E11 ... 76 C4
Littleton TW15 ... 171 A3
Newham E16 ... 99 A1
Thorne Ho
[34] Bethnal Green E2 ... 96 C4
[4] Cubitt Town E14 ... 120 A3
Thorneloe Gdns CR0,
CR9 ... 220 D3
Thorne Pas [7]
SW13 ... 133 D3
Thorne Rd
SW8 ... 138 A5 270 B3
Thorne's Cl BR3 ... 208 A6
Thorness Ct SW18 ... 158 A5
Thorne St SW13,
SW14 ... 133 C2
Thornet Wood Rd
BR1 ... 210 C6
Thornewill Ho [8]
E1 ... 118 C6
Thorney Cres
SW11 ... 136 B5 266 D3
Thorneycroft Cl
KT12 ... 194 C3
Thorneycroft Dr EN3 ... 7 C6
Thorneycroft Ho [11]
W4 ... 111 C1
Thorney Ct W8 ... 246 A1
Thorney Hedge Rd
W4 ... 110 D2
Thorney St
SW1 ... 116 A2 260 A4
Thornfield Ave NW7 ... 29 A2
Thornfield Ct NW7 ... 29 A2
Thornfield Ho [5]
E14 ... 119 C6
Thornfield Par NW7 ... 29 A3
Thornfield Rd W12 ... 112 B4
Thornford Rd SE13 ... 164 A6
Thorngate Rd W9 ... 91 C3
Thorngrove Rd E13 ... 99 B6
Thornham Gr E15 ... 76 B3
Thorn Ham Ho SE1 ... 262 D6
Thornham St SE10 ... 141 D6
Thornhaugh St WC1 ... 239 D5
Thornhill Ave SE18 ... 145 C5
Surbiton KT6 ... 214 A6
Thornhill Bridge Wharf
N1 ... 233 C5
Thornhill Cres N1 ... 72 B1
Thornhill Ct N8 ... 49 D3
Thornhill Gdns
Barking IG11 ... 79 C1
Leyton E10 ... 75 D6
Thornhill Gr N1 ... 72 C1
Thornhill Ho
[12] Chiswick W4 ... 111 C1
Islington N1 ... 72 C1
Thornhill Mews
SW15 ... 135 B1
Thornhill Prim Sch [11]
N1 ... 72 C1
Thornhill Rd
Ickenham UB10 ... 60 C4
Islington N1 ... 94 C6 234 A6
Leyton E10 ... 75 D6
Surbiton KT6 ... 214 B6
Thornton Heath CR0 ... 205 A2
Thornhill Sq N1 ... 72 B1
Thornhill Way TW17 ... 192 C4
Thornicroft Ho [12]
SW9 ... 138 B3
Thornlaw Rd SE27 ... 182 D6
Thornley Cl N17 ... 34 A3
Thornley Dr HA2 ... 63 D6
Thornley Pl [2] SE10 ... 120 C1
Thornsbeach Rd
SE6 ... 164 A2
Thornsett Pl SE20 ... 184 B1
Thornsett Rd
Penge SE20 ... 184 B1
Wandsworth SW18 ... 157 D3
Thornsett Terr SE20 ... 184 B1
Thornton Ave
Chiswick W4 ... 111 C2
Streatham SW2 ... 159 D3
Thornton Heath CR0 ... 204 B3
West Drayton UB7 ... 104 B3
Thornton Cl UB7 ... 104 B3
Thornton Ct
Lower Holloway N7 ... 72 A3
West Barnes SW20 ... 200 D4
Thornton Dene BR3 ... 185 C1
Thornton Gdns
SW12 ... 159 D3
Thornton Gr HA5 ... 23 C4
THORNTON HEATH ... 204 D3
Thornton Heath L Ctr
CR7 ... 205 A5
Thornton Heath Pond
CR7 ... 204 C4
Thornton Heath Sta
CR7 ... 205 A5
Thornton Hill SW19 ... 179 A3
Thornton Ho SE17 ... 263 A3
[7] Wanstead E11 ... 55 A3
Thornton Lo
South Norwood CR7 ... 205 A6
[8] Wimbledon SW19 ... 179 A3
Thornton Pl W1 ... 237 D4
Thornton Rd
Barnet EN5 ... 1 A2
Belvedere DA17 ... 125 D2
BR1 ... 187 A5
Carshalton SM5 ... 202 B1
Ilford IG1 ... 78 D4
Leyton E11 ... 76 B6
Lower Edmonton N18 ... 18 C1
Mortlake SW14 ... 133 B2
Streatham SW12,
SW2 ... 159 D3
Thornton Heath CR0,
CR7 ... 204 B3
Wimbledon SW19 ... 178 D3
Thornton Rd E
SW19 ... 178 D4
Thornton Rd Ind Est
CR0 ... 204 B3
Thornton Row CR7 ... 204 C4
Thornton St SW9 ... 138 C3
Thornton Way NW11 ... 47 D4
Thorntree Ct W5 ... 88 A2
Thorntree Prim Sch
SE7 ... 121 D1
Thorntree Rd SE7 ... 121 D1
Thornville Gr CR4 ... 180 B1
Thornville St SE8 ... 141 C4
Thornwell Ct W7 ... 108 C4
Thornwood Cl E18 ... 37 B1
Thornwood Gdns
W8 ... 245 A2
Thornwood Lo W8 ... 245 A2
Thornwood Rd SE13 ... 164 C6
Thornycroft Ct TW9 ... 132 B3
Thorogood Gdns E15 ... 76 C3
Thorold Ho SE1 ... 252 A2
[6] Streatham SW2 ... 160 A4
Thorold Rd Ilford IG1 ... 57 A1
Wood Green N22 ... 32 A3
Thorparch Rd
SW8 ... 137 D5 269 D3
Thorpebank Rd
W12 ... 112 A5
Thorpe Cl BR6 ... 227 C6
Forest Hill SE26 ... 184 D6
Notting Hill W10 ... 91 A1
Thorpe Coombe Hospl
E17 ... 54 A6
Thorpe Cres E17 ... 35 B1
Thorpe Ct Enfield EN2 ... 4 D2
Upper Tooting SW17 ... 180 C6
Thorpedale Gdns IG6 ... 56 D5
Thorpedale Rd N4 ... 50 B1
Thorpe Hall W5 ... 87 D2
Thorpe Hall Prim Sch
E17 ... 36 B2
Thorpe Hall Rd E17 ... 36 A2
Thorpe Ho N1 ... 233 D5
Thorpe Rd
Barking IG11 ... 79 B1
Chingford E17 ... 36 A1
Kingston u T KT2 ... 176 A3
Leyton E7 ... 76 D4
Newham E6 ... 100 B6
Tottenham N15 ... 51 C3
Thorpewood Ave SE23,
SE26 ... 162 B2
Thorpland Ave UB10 ... 61 A5
Thorsden Way [2]
SE19 ... 183 C5
Thorverton Rd NW2 ... 69 A5
Thoydon Rd E3 ... 97 A5
Thrale Almshouses
SW16 ... 182 A5
Thrale Rd SW16 ... 181 C5
Thrale St SE1 ... 252 B3
Thrasher Cl [20] E8 ... 95 D6
Thrawl St E1 ... 95 D2 243 D3
Thrayle Ho [2] SW9 ... 138 B2
Threadgold Ho [8] N1 ... 73 B2
Threadneedle St EC2,
EC3 ... 95 B1 242 D1
Three Bridges Bsns Ctr
UB2 ... 108 A4
Three Bridges Prim Sch
UB2 ... 107 D3
Three Colts La E2 ... 96 B3
Three Colt St E14 ... 119 B6
Three Corners DA7 ... 147 D3
Three Cups Yd WC1 ... 240 D3
Three Kings Yd W1 ... 248 C6
Three Meadows Mews
HA7 ... 24 D2
Three Mill La E3 ... 98 A4
Three Mills Studios★
E14 ... 98 A4
Three Nun Ct EC2 ... 242 B2
Three Oak La SE1 ... 253 C2
Three Oaks Cl UB10 ... 60 B5
Threshers Pl W11 ... 244 A6
Thriffwood SE23,
SE26 ... 162 D1
Thrigby Rd KT9 ... 214 B2
Thring Ho [2] SW9 ... 138 B3
Throckmorten Rd
E16 ... 99 B1
Throgmorton Ave
EC2 ... 95 B1 242 D2
Throgmorton St
EC2 ... 95 B1 242 D2
Throwley Cl SE2 ... 124 C3
Throwley Rd SM1 ... 217 D3
Throwley Way SM1 ... 217 D3
Thrupp Cl CR4 ... 181 B1
Thrush Gn HA2 ... 41 C5
Thrush St SE17 ... 262 A2
Thunderer Rd RM9 ... 103 B3
Thurbarn Rd SE6 ... 185 D5

Thurbin Ho UB4 83 B2
Thurland Ho 3
SE16 118 B2
Thurland Rd SE16 118 A3
Thurlby Cl HA1 43 A3
Thurlby Croft NW4 46 C6
Thurlby Rd
Wembley HA0 65 D2
West Norwood SE27 182 C6
Thurleigh Ave SW12 159 A5
Thurleigh Ct SW12 159 A5
Thurleigh Rd SW12 159 A5
Thurleston Ave SM4 201 A4
Thurlestone Ave
Colney Hatch N12 30 D4
Ilford IG3 79 D4
Thurlestone Cl
TW17 193 A3
Thurlestone Ct 1
UB1 85 D1
Thurlestone Par
TW17 193 A3
Thurlestone Rd
SE27 182 C6
Thurloe Cl SW7 257 A4
Thurloe Ct SW3 257 A3
Thurloe Pl
SW7 114 B2 256 D4
Thurloe Place Mews
SW7 256 D4
Thurloe Sq
SW7 114 C2 257 A4
Thurloe St
SW7 114 B2 256 D4
Thurlow Cl E4 35 D4
Thurlow Ct 5 E11 55 A4
Thurlow Gdns HA0 65 D3
Thurlow Hill SE21 161 A2
Thurlow Ho 17
SW16 160 A1
Thurlow Park Rd SE21,
SE24 161 A2
Thurlow Rd
Hampstead NW3 70 B3
West Ealing W7 109 A4
Thurlow St
SE17 117 C1 263 A1
Thurlow Terr NW5 71 A3
Thurlow Twrs SE27 160 C1
Thurlow Wlk SE17 263 A1
Thurlston Rd HA4 62 A5
Thurnby Ct TW2 152 C1
Thurnscoe NW1 232 A5
Thursland Rd DA14 191 A5
Thursley Cres CR0 224 B1
Thursley Gdns
SW19 156 D2
Thursley Ho
3 Kingston u T
KT2 176 D3
10 Streatham SW2 160 B4
Thursley Rd SE9 166 B1
Thurso Ho NW6 91 D5
Thurso St SW17 180 B6
Thurstan Rd SW20 178 B3
Thurston Ho 4 BR3 185 D4
Thurston Ind Est
SE13 141 D2
Thurston Rd
Southall UB1 85 B1
St Johns SE8, SE13 141 D3
Thurtle Rd E2 95 D5
Thurza Ct 3 TW7 130 D3
Thyer Cl BR6 227 A4
Thyme Cl SE3 143 C2
Thyme Ct NW7 29 A3
Thyra Gr N12 29 D4
Tibbatt's Rd E3 97 D3
Tibbenham Pl SE6 163 C2
Tibbenham Wlk E13 98 D5
Tibberton Sq N1 235 A6
Tibbets Cl SW19 156 D3
Tibbet's Corner
SW19 156 D4
Tibbet's Ride SW19 156 D4
Tiber Cl 10 E3 97 C6
Tiber Gdns N1 233 B5
Ticehurst Cl BR5 190 A3
Ticehurst Rd SE23 163 A2
Tickford Cl SE2 124 C4
Tickford Ho NW8 230 A1
Tidal Basin Rd E16 120 D6
Tidbury Ct SW8 269 A3
Tide Cl 3 CR4 181 A2
Tideham Ho SE28 123 B5
Tidelock Ho SE28 123 B4
Tidemill Prim Sch 20
SE8 141 C5
Tidenham Gdns CR0 221 C5
Tideside Ct SE18 122 A3
Tideslea Path SE28 123 B5
Tideslea Twr SE28 123 A4
Tideswell 10 NW5 71 B4
Tideswell Rd
Croydon CR0 223 C5
Putney SW15 134 C1
Tideway Cl TW10 175 C6
Tideway Ct 9 SE16 118 D5
Tideway Ho E14 119 C4
Tideway Ind Est
SW8 137 C6 269 B5
Tideway Wharf
SW13 133 C3
Tideway Yd SW13 133 C3
Tidey St E3 97 C2
Tidford Rd DA16 145 D3
Tidworth Ho 13
SE22 139 C2
Tidworth Rd E3 97 C3
Tiepigs La BR2, BR4 208 D1
Tierney Ct 4 CR0 221 D6
Tierney Rd SW2 160 A3
Tierney Terr SW2 160 A3
Tiffin Girls' Sch KT2 176 A4
Tiffin Sch KT2 176 B1
Tiger Ho WC1 232 D1
Tiger La BR2 209 B5
Tiger Way E5 74 B4
Tignel Ct W3 110 C4
Tigris Cl N9 18 C2
Tilbrook Rd SE3 143 C2
Tilbury Cl
14 Camberwell
SE15 139 D5
12 Pinner HA5 23 B3
St Paul's Cray BR5 190 B1
Tilbury Ho 4 SE14 140 D6
Tilbury Rd
Leytonstone E10 54 A2
Newham E6 100 B5
Tildesley Rd SW15 156 C5
Tile Farm Rd BR6 227 B5
Tilehurst NW1 231 D1
Tilehurst Point 2
SE2 124 C4
Tilehurst Rd
Cheam SM3 217 A3
Wandsworth SW17,
SW18 158 B3
Tile Kiln La
Edmonton N13 33 A5
Harefield UB9 38 D2
Upper Holloway N6 49 C1
Tileyard Rd N7 72 A1
Tilford Ave CR0 224 A1
Tilford Gdns SW19 156 D3
Tilford Ho 8 SW2 160 B4
Tilia Cl SM1 217 B3
Tilia Rd E5 74 B4
Tilia Wlk 21 SW9 138 D1
Tiller Ho 28 N1 95 C6
Tiller L Ctr E14 119 C3
Tiller Rd E14 119 C3
Tillet Sq SE16 119 A4
Tillett Cl NW10 67 A2
Tillet Way 6 E2 96 A4
Tilley Rd TW14 150 A3
Tillingbourne Gdns
N3 47 B6
Tillingbourne Way
N3 47 B5
Tillingham Way N12 29 D6
Tilling Ho 1 SE15 140 B2
Tilling Rd NW2 46 C2
Tilling Way HA9 65 D6
Tillman Ho 8 SW2 160 B3
Tillman St E1 96 B1
Tilloch St 9 N1 72 B1
Tillotson Ct SW8 269 D3
Tillotson Rd
Edmonton N9 17 D2
Harrow HA3 23 D3
Ilford IG1 56 C2
Tilney Ct EC1 242 B6
Kingston u T KT6 197 D4
Woodford IG9 21 A2
Tilney Dr IG9 21 A2
Tilney Gdns 12 N1 73 B2
Tilney Rd
Dagenham RM9 81 B2
Southall UB2 106 C2
Woodford IG9 21 A2
Tilney St W1 248 B4
Tilson Cl 2 SE15 139 C5
Tilson Gdns SW2,
SW4 160 A4
Tilson Ho SW2 160 A4
Tilson Rd N17 34 A2
Tilston Cl E11 76 D5
Tilton St SW6 264 B5
Tiltwood The W3 111 A6
Tilt Yard App SE9 166 B5
Timber Cl BR7 188 C1
Timbercroft KT19 215 C4
Timbercroft La SE18 145 C5
Timbercroft Prim Sch
SE18 145 C5
Timberdene NW4 28 D1
Timberland Cl 16
SE15 140 A5
Timberland Rd E1 96 B1
Timber Mill Way
SW4 137 D2
Timber Pond Rd
SE16 118 D4
Timber St EC1 242 A6
Timberwharf Rd N16 52 A3
Time Sq E8 73 D3
Times Sq SM1 217 D3
Times Sq Sh Ctr
SM1 217 D3
Timms Cl BR1 210 B5
Timor Ct UB1 107 D5
Timothy Cl
Bexley DA6 169 A6
1 Clapham Pk SW4 159 C6
Timothy Ho DA18 125 A4
Timsbury Wlk 5
SW15 156 A3
Tina Ct
Forest Hill SE6 163 B4
West Norwood SW16 160 C1
Tindal St SW9 138 D4
Tinniswood Cl N5 72 C3
Tinsley Cl SE25 206 B6
Tinsley Rd E1 96 C2
Tintagel Cres SE22 139 D1
Tintagel Ct EC1 241 C6
Tintagel Dr HA7 25 D6
Tintagel Ho SE20 184 A3
Tintern Ave NW9 44 D6
Tintern Cl
Putney SW15 157 A6
Wimbledon SW19 180 A4
Tintern Ct W13 109 A6
Tintern Gdns N14 16 A4
Tintern Ho
Belgravia SW1 258 C3
Regent's Pk NW1 231 D3
Tintern Path NW9 45 C3
Tintern Rd
Carshalton SM5 202 B1
Tottenham N22 33 A2
Tintern St SW4 138 A1
Tintern Way HA2 41 D1
Tinto Rd E16 99 A3
Tinwell Mews WD6 11 B6
Tinworth St
SE11 116 A1 260 B2
Tippett Ct 2 E6 100 B5
Tippetts Cl EN2 5 A4
Tipthorpe Rd SW11 137 A2
Tipton Dr CR0 221 C4
Tiptree 7 NW1 71 B1
Tiptree Cl E4 20 A1
Tiptree Cres IG5 56 C6
Tiptree Ct EN2 5 B1
Tiptree Dr EN2 5 B1
Tiptree Rd HA4 62 B4
Tirlemont Rd CR2 221 A1
Tirrell Rd CR0 205 A3
Tisbury Ct W1 249 C6
Tisbury Rd SW16 182 A1
Tisdall Pl
SE17 117 B2 262 D3
Tissington Ct 4
SE16 118 D2
Titan Bsns Est 3
SE8 141 C5
Titan Ct TW8 110 B1
Titchborne Row W2 237 B1
Titchfield Rd
Carshalton SM5 202 B1
Enfield EN3 7 A6
Paddington
NW8 92 D6 230 C6
Titchfield Wlk SM5 202 B2
Titchwell Rd SW18 158 B3
Tite St SW3 136 D6 267 C6
Tithe Barn Cl KT2 176 B2
Tithe Barn Way UB5 84 B5
Tithe Cl Hayes UB4 83 D2
Hendon NW7 28 A2
Walton-on-T KT12 194 B3
Tithe Ct NW4 28 A2
Tithe Farm Ave HA2 63 C5
Tithe Farm Cl HA2 63 C5
Tithe Wlk NW7 28 A2
Titian Ave WD23 8 C4
Titley Cl E4 35 C5
Titmus Cl UB8 83 A1
Titmuss Ave SE28 124 B6
Titmuss St W12 112 C4
Tivendale N8 50 A6
Tiverton Ave IG5 56 C6
Tiverton Cl CR0 205 D2
Tiverton Dr SE9 167 A3
Tiverton Prim Sch
N15 51 B3
Tiverton Rd
Brondesbury Pk NW6,
NW10 90 D6
Edgware HA8 26 B1
Edmonton N18 33 C5
Hounslow TW3 130 A3
Ruislip HA4 62 A5
Tottenham N4, N15 51 B3
Wembley HA0 88 A5
Tiverton St
SE1 117 A3 262 A6
Tiverton Way
Chessington KT9 213 D3
Edgware NW7 28 D3
Tivoli Ct SE16 119 B5
Tivoli Gdns 11 SE18 122 A2
Tivoli Rd Hornsey N8 49 D4
Hounslow TW4 129 A1
West Norwood SE27 183 A5
Toad La TW4 129 B1
Tobago St 12 E14 119 C4
Tobin Cl NW3 70 C1
Toby Ct N9 18 C4
Toby La E1 97 A3
Toby Way KT5, KT6 214 D6
Todber Ho W14 254 A6
Todd Ho 3 N2 30 B1
Todds Wlk N7 72 B6
Tokenhouse Yd EC2 242 C2
Token Yd SW15 135 A1
TOKYNGTON 66 D2
Tokyngton Ave HA9 66 C2
Toland Sq SW15 156 A6
Tolcairn Ct 2 DA17 125 C1
Tolcarne Dr HA5 40 B6
Tolchurch 2 W11 91 C1
Toldos Sch N16 51 C1
Toley Ave HA3, HA9 44 A2
Tolhurst Dr 4 W10 91 A4
Tollbridge Cl W10 91 A3
Tollesbury Gdns IG6 57 B6
Tollet St E1 96 D3
Tollgate Dr
Dulwich SE21 161 C2
Hayes UB4 106 D6
Tollgate Ho 1 NW6 91 D5
Tollgate Prim Sch
E13 99 C3
Tollgate Rd E6 100 A2
Tollhouse Way N19 71 C6
Tollington Ct N4 72 B6
Tollington Ho 4 N19 72 A5
Tollington Pk N4 72 B6
Tollington Pl N4 72 B6
Tollington Rd N7 72 B4
Tollington Way N7 72 A5
Tolmers Sq
NW1 93 C3 239 B6
Tolpaide Ho SE11 261 A3
Tolpuddle Ave 1 E13 99 C6
Tolpuddle St
N1 94 C5 234 A4
Tolsford Rd E5 74 B3
Tolson Ho 4 TW7 131 A2
Tolson Rd TW7 131 A2
Tolverne Rd SW20 178 C2
TOLWORTH 214 C6
Tolworth Cl KT6 198 D1
Tolworth Gdns RM6 58 D4
Tolworth Girls' Sch
KT6 214 B5
Tolworth Hospl KT6 214 C6
Tolworth Inf Sch
KT6 198 B1
Tolworth Junc KT6 214 D6
Tolworth Jun Sch
KT6 198 B1
Tolworth Par RM6 59 A4
Tolworth Park Rd
KT6 214 B6
Tolworth Rd KT6 214 A6
Tolworth Recn Ctr
KT6 214 B5
Tolworth Rise N
KT5 198 D1
Tolworth Rise S
KT5 198 D1
Tolworth Sta KT5 214 D6
Tolworth Underpass KT5,
KT6 214 D6
Tomahawk Gdns 4
UB5 84 D4
Tom Blau Gallery★
SE1 250 C2
Tom Coombs Cl SE9 144 A1
Tom Cribb Rd SE18,
SE28 123 B3
Tom Groves Cl E15 76 B3
Tom Hood Cl E15 76 B3
Tom Hood Sch E11 76 D5
Tom Jenkinson Rd 5
E16 121 A5
Tomkyns Ho SE11 261 A3
Tomline Ho SE1 252 A3
Tomlin's Gr E3 97 C4
Tomlinson Cl
5 Gunnersbury
W4 110 D1
Spitalfields E2 95 D4
Tomlins Orch IG11 101 A6
Tomlin's Terr E14 97 A1
Tomlins Wlk 4 N7 72 B6
Tom Mann Cl IG11 101 C6
Tom Nolan Cl E15 98 C5
Tompion Ho EC1 241 D6
Tompion St EC1 234 D1
Tom Smith Cl SE10 142 C6
Tom Smith Ho 3 E17 54 A4
Tomson Ho SE1 263 C6
Tom Williams Ho
SW6 264 C5
Tonbridge Cres HA3 44 A5
Tonbridge Hos WC1 233 A1
Tonbridge Rd KT12,
KT8 195 B5
Tonbridge St
WC1 94 A4 233 A1
Toneborough 16
NW8 91 D6
Tonfield Rd SM3 201 B1
Tonge Cl BR3 207 C4
Tonsley Hill SW18 157 D6
Tonsley Pl SW18 157 D6
Tonsley Rd SW18 157 D6
Tonsley St SW18 157 D6
Tonstall Rd CR4 181 A1
Tony Law Ho SE12 165 A6
Tooke Cl HA5 23 A2
Tookey Cl HA3 44 B2
Took's Ct EC4 241 A2
Tooley St
SE1 117 C5 253 A3
Toorack Rd HA3 24 B1
Tooting Bec Gdns
SW16 181 D6
Tooting Bec Lido
SW16 181 C6
Tooting Bec Rd
Furzedown SW17 181 B6
Streatham SW16 181 C5
Tooting Bec Sta
SW17 159 A1
Tooting Broadway
SW17 180 D5
Tooting Broadway Sta
SW17 180 C5
Tooting Gr SW17 180 C5
TOOTING
GRAVENEY 180 B5
Tooting High St SW17,
SW19 180 C5
Tooting L Ctr SW17 180 B6
Tooting Mkts★
SW17 180 D6
Tooting Sta SW17 180 D4
Tootswood Rd BR2,
BR3 208 C5
Topaz Ct TW13 149 D1

Topaz Ho KT4 ... 199 B1
Topaz Wlk NW2 ... 46 D2
Topcliffe Dr BR6 ... 227 B4
Topham Ho 8 SE10 ... 142 A5
Topham Sq N17 ... 33 A2
Topham St EC1 ... 241 A6
Top House Rise E4 ... 20 A4
Topiary Sq TW9 ... 132 B2
Topley St SE9 ... 143 D1
Topmast Point 23 E14 ... 119 C4
Top Pk BR3 ... 208 C4
Topsfield Cl N8 ... 49 D4
Topsfield Par N8 ... 50 A3
Topsfield Rd N8 ... 50 A4
Topsham Rd SW17 ... 181 A6
Tora Ct 9 IG9 ... 21 C2
Torah Vodaas NW11 ... 47 B1
Tora Temimah Prim Sch NW2 ... 68 B4
Torbay Ct 13 NW1 ... 71 B1
Torbay Mans NW6 ... 91 B6
Torbay Rd
Brondesbury NW6 ... 69 B1
Harrow HA2 ... 63 A6
Torbay St 15 NW1 ... 71 B1
Torbitt Way IG2 ... 57 D4
Torbridge Cl HA8 ... 26 A3
Torbrook Cl DA5 ... 169 A5
Torcross Dr SE23 ... 162 C2
Torcross Rd HA4 ... 62 C5
Tor Ct W8 ... 245 B2
Torfell 5 E18 ... 36 D1
Tor Gdns W8 ... 113 C4 245 A2
Tor Gr SE28 ... 123 C5
Tor Ho N6 ... 49 B3
Tormead Cl SM1 ... 217 C2
Tormount Rd SE18 ... 145 C6
Tornay Ho Hackney E9 ... 74 C1
N1 ... 233 C4
Toronto Ave E12 ... 78 B4
Toronto Rd IG1 ... 57 A1
Torquay Gdns IG4 ... 55 D5
Torquay Ho 1 SM6 ... 219 D3
Torquay St W2 ... 91 D2
Tor Rd DA16 ... 146 C4
Torrence Ho 6 N19 ... 71 C6
Torrens Ct SE5 ... 139 B2
Torrens Rd
Clapham Pk SW2 ... 160 B6
Stratford E15 ... 76 D2
Torrens Sq E15 ... 76 D2
Torrens St
EC1 ... 94 D5 234 C3
Torres Sq E14 ... 119 C1
Torre Wlk SM5 ... 202 C1
Torrey Dr SW9 ... 138 C3
Torriano Ave NW5 ... 71 D3
Torriano Cotts NW5 ... 71 C3
Torriano Jun & Inf Schs 24 NW5 ... 71 D3
Torriano Mews NW5 ... 71 C3
Torridge Gdns SE15 ... 140 C1
Torridge Rd CR7 ... 204 D4
Torridon Ct HA8 ... 10 D2
Torridon Ho NW6 ... 91 D5
Torridon Jun & Inf Schs SE6 ... 164 B2
Torridon Rd SE13, SE6 ... 164 B3
Torrington Ave N12 ... 30 B5
Torrington Cl
Claygate KT10 ... 212 C2
North Finchley N12 ... 30 B6
Torrington Ct
Forest Hill SE26 ... 184 A5
Harrow HA2 ... 63 D5
North Finchley N12 ... 30 B6
Torrington Dr HA2 ... 63 D5
Torrington Gdns
Friern Barnet N11 ... 31 C4
Wembley UB6 ... 65 C1
Torrington Gr N12 ... 30 C5
Torrington Pk N12 ... 30 B6
Torrington Pl
Bloomsbury WC1 ... 93 D2 239 C4
St George in t East E1 ... 118 A5
Torrington Rd
Claygate KT10 ... 212 C2
Dagenham RM8 ... 59 B1
Ruislip HA4 ... 62 A5
Wanstead E18 ... 55 A6
Torrington Rd *continued*
Wembley UB6 ... 87 C6
Torrington Sq
Bloomsbury WC1 ... 93 D3 239 D5
Thornton Heath CR0 ... 205 B2
Torrington Way SM4 ... 201 C3
Torr Rd SE20 ... 184 D3
Tortington Ho 1 SE15 ... 140 B5
Torver Rd HA1 ... 42 C5
Torver Way BR6 ... 227 B5
Torwood Rd SW15 ... 156 A6
Totham Lo SW20 ... 178 B2
Tothill Ho SW1 ... 259 D4
Tothill St SW1 ... 115 D4 249 D1
Totland Ho SW18 ... 157 D5
Totnes Rd DA16 ... 146 C5
Totnes Villas N11 ... 31 C5
Totnes Wlk N2 ... 48 B5
Tottan Terr E1 ... 96 D1
Tottenhall 5 NW1 ... 71 A1
Tottenhall Inf Sch N13 ... 32 C4
Tottenhall Rd N13 ... 32 D4
TOTTENHAM ... 33 D1
Tottenham Court Rd W1 ... 93 C2 239 B4
Tottenham Court Road Sta W1 ... 93 D1 239 D2
Tottenham Gn E 3 N15 ... 51 D5
Tottenham Gn E South Side 4 N15 ... 51 D5
Tottenham Gn L Ctr N17 ... 51 B5
TOTTENHAM HALE ... 52 A6
Tottenham Hale N15 ... 52 A5
Tottenham Hale Ret Pk N15 ... 52 A5
Tottenham Hale Sta N17 ... 52 B6
Tottenham La N8 ... 50 B4
Tottenham Mews W1 ... 239 B4
Tottenham Rd N1 ... 73 C2
Tottenham St W1 ... 93 C2 239 B4
Totterdown St SW17 ... 180 D5
TOTTERIDGE ... 13 C3
Totteridge Comm N20 ... 12 C3
Totteridge Gn N20 ... 13 C2
Totteridge Ho
Barnet N20 ... 13 B3
Battersea SW11 ... 136 B3
Totteridge La N20 ... 13 D3
Totteridge Pk N20 ... 12 D3
Totteridge Rd EN3 ... 6 D6
Totteridge Village N20 ... 13 B3
Totteridge & Whetstone Sta N20 ... 14 A2
Totternhoe Cl HA3 ... 43 C4
Totton Rd CR7 ... 204 C6
Toucan Cl NW10 ... 88 C4
Touchard Ho N1 ... 235 D1
Toulmin St SE1 ... 117 A4 252 A1
Toulon St SE5 ... 139 A5
Toulouse Ct 2 SE16 ... 118 B1
Tounson Ct SW1 ... 259 D3
Tournay Rd SW6 ... 135 B5 264 D4
Toussaint Wlk 18 SE16 ... 118 A3
Tovil Cl SE20 ... 184 B1
Tovy Ho 6 SE1 ... 118 A1
Towcester Rd E3 ... 98 A3
Tower 42★ EC2 ... 95 C1 243 A2
Tower Bldgs 22 E1 ... 118 B5
Tower Br App E1, EC3 ... 253 C5
Tower Bridge★ E1, EC3, SE1 ... 117 D5 253 C4
Tower Bridge Bsns Complex SE16 ... 118 B3
Tower Bridge Bsns Sq SE16 ... 118 B2
Tower Bridge Ex★ E1 ... 253 C4
Tower Bridge Mews HA0 ... 64 D4
Tower Bridge Piazza SE1 ... 253 C3
Tower Bridge Prim Sch SE1 ... 117 D4 253 C2
Tower Bridge Rd SE1 ... 117 C4 253 A1
Tower Bridge Sq SE1 ... 253 C2
Tower Bridge Wharf SE1 ... 118 A5
Tower Cl
Hampstead NW3 ... 70 B3
Orpington BR6 ... 227 D5
Penge SE20 ... 184 B3
Tower Ct
Brockley SE4 ... 141 A1
Stamford Hill E5 ... 51 D2
St Giles WC2 ... 240 A1
St John's Wood NW8 ... 230 B4
Tower Gardens Rd N17 ... 33 B2
Towergate SE1 ... 263 A4
Towergate Cl UB8 ... 60 A3
Towergate Ho 35 E3 ... 97 B5
Tower Gateway Sta EC3 ... 117 D6 253 C6
Tower Gdns KT10 ... 213 A1
Tower Gr KT13 ... 193 C1
TOWER HAMLETS ... 97 B2
Tower Hamlets Coll
25 Poplar E14 ... 97 D1
27 Poplar E14 ... 119 D6
16 Stepney E1 ... 96 D1
Tower Hamlets Rd
Forest Gate E7 ... 76 D3
Walthamstow E17 ... 53 C6
Tower Hill EC3 ... 117 D6 253 D5
Tower Hill Sta EC3 ... 117 D6 253 C6
Tower House Sch SW14 ... 133 A1
Tower La HA9 ... 65 D5
Tower Mans SE1 ... 263 C5
Tower Mews
Hackney E5 ... 75 A3
Walthamstow E17 ... 53 C5
Tower Millennium Pier EC3 ... 117 C5 253 B4
Tower Mill Rd
7 Camberwell SE15 ... 139 C6
1 SE15 ... 139 C5
Tower Pl E EC3 ... 253 B5
Tower Pl W EC3 ... 253 B5
Tower Rd DA7 ... 147 D1
Orpington BR6 ... 227 D5
Twickenham TW1, TW2 ... 152 D1
Willesden NW10 ... 68 A1
Tower Rise TW9 ... 132 A2
Tower Royal EC4 ... 252 C6
Towers Ave UB10 ... 83 A4
Towers Bsns Pk HA9 ... 66 D4
Towers Ct UB10 ... 83 A4
Towers Pl TW10 ... 154 A6
Towers Rd Pinner HA5 ... 23 A2
Southall UB1 ... 85 C3
Tower St WC2 ... 240 A1
Towers The
Dartmouth Pk NW5 ... 71 B5
1 Richmond TW9 ... 132 B1
Tower Terr
Brockley SE4 ... 141 A1
Wood Green N22 ... 32 B1
Tower The★ EC3 ... 117 D6 253 C5
Towerview SE13 ... 163 C6
Tower View
Bushey WD23 ... 8 C4
Croydon CR0 ... 207 A2
Tower Wharf SE1 ... 253 C2
Tower Wlk SE1 ... 263 A4
Towfield Ct TW13 ... 151 B2
Towfield Rd TW13 ... 151 B2
Towncourt Cres BR5 ... 211 B5
Towncourt La BR5 ... 211 B2
Towncourt Path N4 ... 51 A1
Townend Ct 6 BR1 ... 186 D2
Towney Mead UB5 ... 85 B5
Towney Mead Ct UB5 ... 85 B5
Townfield Rd UB3 ... 105 D5
Townfield Sq UB3 ... 105 D6
Town Field Way TW7 ... 131 A3
Town Hall Approach Rd N15 ... 51 D5
Townhall Ave 3 W4 ... 111 B1
Town Hall Rd SW11 ... 136 D2
Townholm Cres W7 ... 108 D3
Town Hos EC1 ... 241 D5
Town La TW19 ... 148 A2
Townley Ct E15 ... 76 D2
Townley Gram Sch for Girls DA6 ... 169 B6
Townley Rd DA6 ... 169 B6
Dulwich Village SE22 ... 161 C6
Townley St SE17 ... 117 B1 262 C2
Townmead Bsns Ctr SW6 ... 136 A2
Town Meadow TW8 ... 131 D5
Townmead Rd
Richmond TW9 ... 132 D3
Sands End SW6 ... 136 A3
Town Quay IG11 ... 100 D6
Town Quay Wharf IG11 ... 100 D6
Town Rd N9 ... 18 B2
Townsend Ave N14 ... 31 D6
Townsend Ct NW9 ... 45 B2
Townsend Ho 14 SE1 ... 118 A2
Townsend Ind Est NW10 ... 89 A5
Townsend La NW9 ... 45 B3
Townsend Mews 3 SW18 ... 158 A2
Townsend Prim Sch SE17 ... 117 C2 263 A4
Townsend Rd
Ashford TW15 ... 170 A5
Regents Park NW8 ... 92 C5 230 B4
Southall UB1 ... 107 A5
South Tottenham N15 ... 51 D4
Townsend St SE1, SE17 ... 117 C2 263 A4
Townsend Way HA6 ... 22 A3
Townsend Yd N6 ... 49 B1
Townshend Cl DA14 ... 190 C4
Townshend Ct NW8 ... 230 B4
Townshend Est NW8 ... 92 C5 230 A4
Townshend Ho 16 SE18 ... 122 B2
Townshend Rd
Chislehurst BR7 ... 188 D5
Primrose Hill NW8 ... 92 C6 230 A5
Richmond TW9 ... 132 B1
Townshend Terr TW9 ... 132 B1
Towns Ho 4 SW4 ... 137 D2
Townson Ave UB5 ... 84 B5
Townson Way UB5 ... 84 A5
Town The EN2 ... 5 B2
Town Tree Rd TW15 ... 170 C5
Towpath TW17 ... 192 B1
Towpath Way CR0 ... 205 D4
Towpath Wlk E9 ... 75 B3
Towton Rd SE27 ... 161 A2
Toxteth Ho N4 ... 51 A2
Toynbec Cl BR7 ... 188 D6
Toynbee Rd SW19, SW20 ... 179 A2
Toynbee St E1 ... 95 D2 243 C3
Toynbee Studios★ E1 ... 243 D3
Toyne Way N6 ... 48 D3
Tracey Ave NW2 ... 68 C3
Tracy Ct HA7 ... 25 C3
Tracy Ho 15 E3 ... 97 B4
Trade Cl N13 ... 32 C6
Trader Rd E6 ... 100 D1
Tradescant Ho 15 E9 ... 74 C1
Tradescant Rd SW8 ... 138 A5 270 B3
Trade Twr 8 SW11 ... 136 A2
Trade Winds Ct 1 E1 ... 118 A5
Trading Estate Rd NW10 ... 89 A3
Traemore Ct SW16 ... 160 C1
Trafalgar Ave
North Cheam KT4, SM3, SM4 ... 200 D1
SE15 ... 139 D6
Tottenham N17 ... 33 C4
Trafalgar Bsns Ctr IG11 ... 101 D3
Trafalgar Cl 1 SE16 ... 119 A2
Trafalgar Ct
Barking E6 ... 100 C6
Hounslow TW3 ... 129 B2
West Barnes KT3 ... 200 B6
Trafalgar Gdns
Stepney E1 ... 96 D2
W8 ... 255 D6
Trafalgar Gr SE10 ... 142 B6
Trafalgar Ho
Barking IG11 ... 102 B4
SE17 ... 262 B2
Trafalgar Inf Sch TW2 ... 152 B2
Trafalgar Jun Sch TW2 ... 152 B2
Trafalgar Mews E9 ... 75 B2
Trafalgar Pl
Edmonton N18 ... 34 A5
Wanstead E11 ... 55 A5
Trafalgar Point 2 N1 ... 73 B1
Trafalgar Rd
Greenwich SE10 ... 120 C1
Merton SW19 ... 180 A3
Twickenham TW2 ... 152 B2
Trafalgar Sq★ SW1 ... 115 D5 249 D4
Trafalgar St SE17 ... 117 B1 262 D2
Trafalgar Terr HA1 ... 42 C1
Trafalgar Trad Est EN3 ... 7 A1
Trafalgar Way
Canary Wharf E14 ... 120 A5
Croydon CR0 ... 220 C6
Trafford Ho N1 ... 235 D4
Trafford Rd CR7 ... 204 B4
Trafford Villas CR0 ... 204 B4
Tragail SW15 ... 157 A6
Traherne Lo 5 TW11 ... 174 D5
Trahorn Cl E1 ... 96 B3
Traitors Gate★ EC3 ... 117 D5 253 C4
Tralee Ct 31 SE16 ... 118 B1
Tramsheds Ind Est The CR0, CR4 ... 203 D2
Tramway Ave
Ponders End N9 ... 18 C4
Stratford E15 ... 76 B1
Tramway Cl SE20 ... 184 C2
Tramway Path CR4 ... 202 C5
Trance Way W3 ... 110 C3
Tranmere Ct 5 SM2 ... 218 A1
Tranmere Ho 7 N7 ... 72 C3
Tranmere Rd
Edmonton N9 ... 17 D4
Twickenham TW2 ... 151 D4
Wandsworth SW17, SW18 ... 158 A2
Tranquil Pas SE3 ... 142 D3
Tranquil Vale SE3 ... 142 C3
Transept St NW1 ... 237 B3
Transmere Cl BR5 ... 211 A3
Transmere Rd BR5 ... 211 A3
Transom Cl SE16 ... 119 A2
Transom Sq E14 ... 119 D1
Transport Ave TW8 ... 131 B6
Tranton Rd SE16 ... 118 B3
Trappes Ho 2 SE16 ... 118 B2
Traps La KT2, KT3 ... 177 C2
Travellers Way TW5 ... 128 C3
Travers Cl E17 ... 34 D2
Travers Ho 6 SE10 ... 142 B6
Travers Rd N7 ... 72 C5
Travis Ho SE10 ... 142 A4
Treacy Cl WD23 ... 8 A2
Treadgold Ho 7 W11 ... 112 D6
Treadgold St W11 ... 112 D6
Treadway St E2 ... 96 B5
Treasury Bldgs SW1 ... 250 A2
Treasury Cl SM6 ... 219 D3
Treaty Ctr TW3 ... 129 D2
Treaty St N1 ... 94 B6 233 C5
Trebeck St W1 ... 248 C3
Treborough Ho W1 ... 238 A4
Trebovir Rd SW5 ... 113 C2 255 B3
Treby St E3 ... 97 B3
Trecastle Way 2 N7 ... 71 D4
Tredegar Mews 10 E3 ... 97 B4
Tredegar Rd Bow E3 ... 97 B5

Tredegar Rd *continued*
Wood Green N11 ... 31 D3
Tredegar Sq E3 ... 97 B4
Tredegar Terr E3 ... 97 B4
Trederwen Rd E8 ... 96 A6
Tredown Rd SE26 ... 184 C5
Tredwell Cl BR2 ... 210 A5
Tredwell Rd SE27 ... 182 D6
Tree Cl TW10 ... 153 D3
Treehouse Sch N10 ... 49 A5
Treen Ave SW13 ... 133 D2
Tree Rd E16 ... 99 C1
Trees The N16 ... 51 B2
Tree Tops 1 IG8 ... 37 A6
Treetops Cl SE2 ... 125 A1
Treetops Ct CR7 ... 205 A4
Treetops View IG10 ... 21 D4
Treeview Cl SE19 ... 183 C2
Treewall Gdns BR1 ... 187 B6
Trefgarne Rd RM10 ... 81 C6
Trefil Wlk N7 ... 72 A4
Trefoil Ho DA18 ... 125 A4
Trefoil Rd SW18 ... 158 A6
Trefusis Ct TW5 ... 128 B4
Tregaron Ave N8 ... 50 A3
Tregaron Gdns KT3 ... 199 C5
Tregarvon Rd SW11 ... 137 A1
Tregenna Ave HA2 ... 63 C4
Tregenna Cl 1 N14 ... 15 C6
Tregenna Ct HA2 ... 63 C4
Trego Rd E9 ... 75 C1
Tregothnan Rd SW9 ... 138 A2
Tregunter Rd
SW10 ... 114 A1 256 A1
Treherne Ct
Brixton SW9 ... 138 D4
Upper Tooting SW17 ... 181 A6
Trehern Rd 12 SW14 ... 133 B2
Trehurst St E5 ... 75 A3
Trelawney Cl E17 ... 53 D5
Trelawney Est E9 ... 74 C2
Trelawney Ho SE1 ... 252 A2
Trelawn Rd
Leyton E10 ... 76 A5
Tulse Hill SW2 ... 160 C6
Trellis Ho SW19 ... 180 A3
Trellis Sq 1 E3 ... 97 B4
Treloar Gdns SE19 ... 183 B4
Tremadoc Rd SW4 ... 137 D1
Tremaine Cl SE4 ... 141 C3
Tremaine Rd SE20 ... 184 B1
Trematon Ho SE11 ... 261 B2
Trematon Pl TW11 ... 175 C3
Tremlett Gr N19 ... 71 C5
Tremlett Mews 17
N19 ... 71 C5
Trenance Gdns IG3 ... 80 A5
Trenchard Ave HA4 ... 62 B4
Trenchard Cl
Grahame Pk NW9 ... 27 C2
Stanmore HA7 ... 25 B4
Trenchard Ct SM4 ... 201 C3
Trenchard St SE10 ... 120 B1
Trenchold St
SW8 ... 138 A6 270 A5
Trend Ct W13 ... 109 B5
Trendell Ho 8 E14 ... 97 C1
Trenholme Cl 6
SE20 ... 184 B3
Trenholme Rd SE20 ... 184 B3
Trenholme Terr
SE20 ... 184 B3
Trenmar Gdns NW10 ... 90 B4
Trent Ave W5 ... 109 C3
Trent CE Prim Sch
EN4 ... 2 D1
Trent Ct
1 South Croydon
CR2 ... 221 A3
Wanstead E11 ... 55 A4
Trent Ctry Pk* EN4 ... 3 A3
Trent Gdns N14 ... 15 B5
Trentham Ct W3 ... 89 B2
Trentham Lo 8 EN1 ... 17 C6
Trentham St SW18 ... 157 C3
Trent Ho
4 Kingston u T
KT2 ... 175 D2
Nunhead SE15 ... 140 C1
Trent Rd
Buckhurst Hill IG9 ... 21 B3
Clapham Pk SW2 ... 160 B6
Trent Way Hayes UB4 ... 83 C4
North Cheam KT4 ... 216 C5
Trentwood Side EN2 ... 4 B2
Treport St SW18 ... 157 D4
Tresco Cl BR1 ... 186 C4
Trescoe Gdns HA2 ... 41 A2
Tresco Gdns IG3 ... 80 A6
Tresco Ho SE11 ... 261 A2
Tresco Rd SE15 ... 140 B1
Tresham Cres
NW8 ... 92 C3 237 A6
Tresham Rd IG11 ... 79 D1
Tresham Wlk E9 ... 74 C3
Tresidder Ho 10
SW4 ... 159 D4
Tresilian Ave N21 ... 16 B6
Tressel Cl 20 N1 ... 72 D1
Tressillian Cres SE4 ... 141 C2
Tressillian Rd SE4 ... 141 C2
Trestis Cl UB4 ... 84 D2
Treswell Rd RM9 ... 103 A6
Tretawn Gdns NW7 ... 11 C1
Tretawn Pk NW7 ... 27 C6
Trevallyn Lo 1 KT2 ... 176 D2
Trevanion Rd W14 ... 254 B2
Treve Ave HA1 ... 42 B2
Trevelyan Ave E12 ... 78 B4
Trevelyan Cres HA3 ... 43 D2
Trevelyan Ct KT3 ... 199 D2
Trevelyan Gdns
NW10 ... 90 C6
Trevelyan Ho
16 Globe Town E2 ... 96 D4
SE5 ... 138 D5
6 Twickenham TW1 ... 153 C5
Trevelyan Rd
Leyton E15 ... 76 D4
Upper Tooting SW17 ... 180 D4
Trevenna Ho 13
SE23 ... 162 D1
Trevera Ct EN3 ... 19 A6
Treveris St SE1 ... 251 D3
Treversh Ct 7 BR1 ... 186 D2
Treverton St W10 ... 90 D3
Treverton Twr 1
W10 ... 90 D2
Treves Cl N21 ... 16 B6
Treves Ho E1 ... 96 A3
Treville St SW15 ... 156 B4
Treviso Rd SE23 ... 163 A2
Trevithick Cl TW14 ... 149 D3
Trevithick Ho
13 Bermondsey
SE16 ... 118 B2
3 Gospel Oak NW5 ... 71 B4
SW8 ... 269 C2
Trevithick St SE8 ... 141 C6
Trevone Gdns HA5 ... 41 A3
Trevor Cl Harrow HA3 ... 24 D3
Hayes BR2 ... 209 A2
Isleworth TW7 ... 152 D6
New Barnet EN4 ... 14 B5
Northolt UB5 ... 84 C5
Trevor Cres HA4 ... 61 D4
Trevor Gdns
Hendon HA8 ... 27 B2
Northolt UB5 ... 84 C5
Ruislip HA4 ... 62 A4
Trevor Pl
SW7 ... 114 C4 247 B1
Trevor Rd Hayes UB3 ... 105 C4
Hendon HA8 ... 27 B2
Wimbledon SW19 ... 179 A3
Woodford IG8 ... 37 A3
Trevor Roberts Sch
NW8 ... 70 B1
Trevor Sq
SW7 ... 114 C4 247 B1
Trevor St
SW7 ... 114 C4 247 B1
Trevose Ho SE11 ... 260 D2
Trevose Rd E17 ... 36 B2
Trewenna Dr KT9 ... 213 D3
Trewince Rd SW20 ... 178 C2
Trewint St SW18 ... 158 A2
Trewsbury Ho 2
SE2 ... 124 D4
Trewsbury Rd SE26 ... 184 D5
Triandra Way UB4 ... 84 D2
Triangle Ct
4 Newham E16 ... 99 C2
SE1 ... 252 B3
Triangle Ctr UB1 ... 108 B5
Triangle Est The
SE11 ... 261 A1
Triangle Ho SE1 ... 253 C2
Triangle Pl SW4 ... 137 D1
Triangle Rd 7 E8 ... 96 B6
Triangle The
Barking IG11 ... 79 A2
Triangle The *continued*
Crouch End N19 ... 49 D2
EC1 ... 241 D6
16 Hackney E8 ... 96 B6
Kingston u T KT3 ... 177 A1
Tribune Ct 16 NW9 ... 46 A5
Tricorn Ho SE28 ... 123 B5
Trident Bsns Ctr
SW17 ... 180 D5
Trident Gdns 6 UB5 ... 84 D4
Trident Ho
14 South Bromley
E14 ... 98 A1
Woolwich SE28 ... 123 B5
Trident St SE16 ... 118 D2
Trident Way UB2 ... 106 B3
Trieste Ct SW12 ... 158 D3
Trig La EC4 ... 252 A6
Trigon Rd
SW8 ... 138 B5 270 D4
Trilby Rd SE23 ... 162 D2
Trillington Ho W12 ... 112 A5
Trillo Ct IG1 ... 57 C2
Trimdon NW1 ... 232 B5
Trimmer Ct TW7 ... 130 D2
Trimmer Wlk 11
TW8 ... 132 A6
Trim St SE8 ... 141 B6
Trinder Gdns N19 ... 50 A1
Trinder Mews 10
TW11 ... 175 A5
Trinder Rd Barnet EN5 ... 12 C6
Finsbury Pk N4, N19 ... 50 A1
Tring Ave Ealing W5 ... 110 B5
Southall UB1 ... 85 B1
Wembley HA9 ... 66 C2
Tring Cl IG2 ... 57 B4
Tring Ct TW1 ... 175 A6
Trinidad Ho 17 E14 ... 119 B6
Trinidad St E14 ... 119 B6
Trinity Ave
East Finchley N2 ... 48 B6
Enfield EN1 ... 17 D5
Trinity Church Rd
SW13 ... 134 B6
Trinity Church Sq
SE1 ... 117 A3 262 B6
Trinity Cl
3 Clapham SW4 ... 137 C1
Hounslow TW4 ... 129 A1
Keston Mark BR2 ... 210 A1
Lewisham SE13 ... 142 B1
Leyton E11 ... 76 C6
Trinity Coll London
SE1 ... 116 A1 260 B1
Trinity Coll of Music
SE10 ... 142 B6
Trinity Cotts TW9 ... 132 B2
Trinity Cres SW17 ... 159 A2
Trinity Ct
8 Chingford E4 ... 20 A2
Edmonton N18 ... 33 D4
Eltham SE9 ... 166 D5
Finsbury WC1 ... 240 C6
Forest Hill SE23 ... 162 C1
Greenwich SE7 ... 121 D2
2 Hoxton N1 ... 95 C6
Rotherhithe SE16 ... 119 A4
Southgate N21 ... 16 D3
Thornton Heath SE25 ... 205 C3
Twickenham TW2 ... 152 C2
Wallington SM6 ... 219 C1
Willesden NW2 ... 68 C3
Wimbledon SW19 ... 179 C4
Trinity Dr UB8 ... 83 A1
Trinity Gdns E16 ... 98 D2
Stockwell SW2, SW9 ... 138 B1
11 Wanstead E18 ... 55 B6
Trinity Gn E1 ... 96 C2
Trinity Gr 8 SE10 ... 142 A4
Trinity Ho SE1 ... 262 B6
5 Walthamstow E17 ... 53 D6
Trinity Homes 14
SW2 ... 138 B1
Trinity Mews
Penge SE20 ... 184 B2
SE9 ... 167 B5
Wandsworth SW18 ... 157 C3
Trinity Par TW3 ... 129 D2
Trinity Pl
Bexleyheath DA6 ... 147 B1
City of London EC3 ... 253 C5
Trinity RC High Sch
(Lower) IG8 ... 37 A6
Trinity RC High Sch
(Upper) IG8 ... 37 A6
Trinity RC High Sch
(Upper Sch) IG8 ... 36 D6
Trinity Rd
East Finchley N2 ... 48 B6
Ilford IG6 ... 57 A6
Richmond TW9 ... 132 B2
Southall UB1 ... 107 A5
Wandsworth SW17,
SW18 ... 158 C4
Wimbledon SW19 ... 179 C4
Wood Green N22 ... 32 A3
Wood Green N22 ... 32 B2
Trinity Rise SE24,
SW2 ... 160 D4
Trinity St Mary's Prim
Sch 8 SW12 ... 159 A3
Trinity Sch
Croydon CR0 ... 222 C6
Dagenham RM10 ... 81 C4
Trinity Sq
EC3 ... 117 C6 253 B6
Trinity St Enfield EN2 ... 5 A3
9 Newham E16 ... 99 A2
SE1 ... 117 B3 262 C6
Trinity Terr IG9 ... 21 B4
Trinity Way
East Acton W3 ... 111 D6
Walthamstow E4 ... 35 B4
Trio Pl SE1 ... 117 A4 252 B1
Triscott Ho UB3 ... 106 A5
Tristan Ct 34 SE8 ... 141 B6
Tristan Sq SE3 ... 142 C2
Tristram Cl E17 ... 54 B6
Tristram Dr N9 ... 18 A1
Tristram Rd BR1 ... 186 D6
Triton Ct EC2 ... 242 D5
Woodford IG9 ... 21 A2
Triton Ho 2 E14 ... 119 D2
Tritton Ave CR0 ... 220 A4
Tritton Ho N21 ... 17 B5
Tritton Rd SE21,
SE27 ... 161 B1
Triumph Cl UB7 ... 127 A4
Triumph Ho IG11 ... 102 A4
Triumph Rd E6 ... 100 B1
Triumph Trad Est
N17 ... 34 A4
Trocette Mans SE1 ... 263 B6
Trojan Ct
Brondesbury NW6 ... 69 A1
9 Ealing W7 ... 109 A5
Trojan Ind Est NW10 ... 67 D2
Trojan Way CR0 ... 220 B5
Troon Cl
34 Bermondsey
SE16 ... 118 B1
Erith SE28 ... 102 D1
Troon Ct UB1 ... 108 A6
Troon Ho 9 E14 ... 97 A1
Troon St E1 ... 97 A1
Tropical Ct 2 W10 ... 90 D4
Trosley Rd DA17 ... 147 C6
Trossachs Rd SE22 ... 161 C6
Trothy Rd SE1 ... 118 A2
Trotman Ho 1 SE14 ... 140 C4
Trott Rd N10 ... 31 A3
Trott St
SW11 ... 136 C4 267 A1
Trotwood Ho 3
SE16 ... 118 B4
Troubridge Ct 12
W4 ... 111 A1
Troughton Rd SE7 ... 121 B1
Troutbeck NW1 ... 231 D1
Troutbeck Rd SE14 ... 141 A4
Trouville Rd SW4 ... 159 C5
Trowbridge Est 6
E15 ... 75 B2
Trowbridge Rd E9 ... 75 B2
Trower Ho 5 E9 ... 75 A2
Trowlock Ave TW11 ... 175 C4
Trowlock Island
TW11 ... 175 D4
Trowlock Way
TW11 ... 175 D4
Troy Ct W8 ... 255 A6
5 Woolwich SE18 ... 122 D2
Troyes Ho NW3 ... 70 D3
Troy Rd SE19 ... 183 B4
Troy Town SE15 ... 140 A2
Troy Town Flats
SE15 ... 140 A2
Trubshaw Rd UB2 ... 107 D3
Trulock Ct N17 ... 34 A3
Trulock Rd N17 ... 34 A3
Truman Cl 2 HA8 ... 27 A3
Truman's Rd 24 N16 ... 73 C3
Trumpers Way W7 ... 108 D3
Trumpeters Inn
TW9 ... 153 C6
Trumpington Rd E7 ... 76 D4
Trump St EC2 ... 242 B1
Trundlers Way WD23 ... 8 C3
Trundle St SE1 ... 252 A2
Trundleys Rd SE8 ... 141 A6
Trundley's Rd SE8 ... 118 D1
Trundley's Terr SE8 ... 118 D2
Truro Ct 2 N8 ... 49 D4
Truro Gdns IG1 ... 56 A2
Truro Ho
25 Paddington W2 ... 91 C2
Pinner HA5 ... 23 B2
Truro Rd
Walthamstow E17 ... 53 B5
Wood Green N22 ... 32 B3
Truro St NW5 ... 71 A2
Truro Way UB4 ... 83 C4
Truscott Ho 3 CR7 ... 204 C3
Trusedale Rd E6 ... 100 B1
Truslove Rd SE27 ... 182 D5
Trussley Rd W6 ... 112 C3
Trust Wlk SE21 ... 160 D3
Tryfan Cl IG4 ... 55 D4
Tryon Cres E9 ... 96 C6
Tryon St
SW3 ... 114 D1 257 C2
Trystings Cl KT10 ... 213 A2
Tuam Rd SE18 ... 145 B6
Tubbenden Cl BR6 ... 227 C5
Tubbenden Dr BR6 ... 227 B4
Tubbenden Jun & Inf
Schs BR6 ... 227 B4
Tubbenden La BR6 ... 227 C5
Tubbenden La S
BR6 ... 227 B3
Tubbs Rd NW10 ... 89 D5
Tudor Ave
Hampton TW12 ... 173 C3
North Cheam KT4 ... 216 B4
Tudor Cl
Ashford TW15 ... 170 A6
BR7 ... 188 B2
Cheam SM3 ... 217 A2
Chessington KT9 ... 214 A3
Crouch End N6 ... 49 C2
Hampstead NW3 ... 70 C2
Hampton TW12 ... 174 A5
Hendon NW7 ... 28 A4
Pinner HA5 ... 40 A4
Tulse Hill SW2 ... 160 B5
Wallington SM6 ... 219 C1
Welsh Harp NW9 ... 67 A6
Woodford IG8 ... 37 B5
Tudor Coll WC1 ... 233 A1
Tudor Court N HA9 ... 66 C3
Tudor Court S HA9 ... 66 C3
Tudor Cres EN2 ... 5 A4
Tudor Ct 2 Barnet EN5 ... 1 B1
3 Ealing W13 ... 87 C1
Feltham TW13 ... 172 C6
Kingsland N1 ... 73 C2
5 Rotherhithe SE16 ... 118 D5
Sidcup DA14 ... 168 A1
South Acton W5 ... 110 C4
4 Stanwell TW19 ... 148 A5
Teddington TW11 ... 174 D4
Walthamstow E17 ... 53 B2
Tudor Dr
Kingston u T KT2 ... 176 A5
Walton-on-T KT12 ... 194 D1
West Barnes SM4 ... 201 A3
Tudor Ent Pk HA3 ... 42 B6
Tudor Est NW10 ... 88 D5
Tudor Gables NW7 ... 27 D6
Tudor Gdns Acton W3 ... 88 C1
Harrow HA3 ... 24 B1
Mortlake SW14 ... 133 C2
Twickenham TW1 ... 152 D3
Welsh Harp NW9 ... 67 A6
West Wickham BR4 ... 224 A5
Tudor Gr E9 ... 74 C1
Tudor Ho
Brook Green W14 ... 112 D2
Feltham TW13 ... 172 C6
34 Hackney E9 ... 74 C1
Mitcham CR4 ... 181 A2
6 Muswell Hill N10 ... 31 A3
Queensbury NW9 ... 44 C5
Tolworth KT6 ... 198 C1

Tudor Lo 4 N12 29 D5
Tudor Mews
Walthamstow E17 53 B5
2 Willesden NW10 68 A2
Tudor Par
Dagenham RM6 58 D2
SE9 144 A1
Tudor Pl SW19 180 C3
Tudor Prim Sch
Finchley N3 30 A2
Southall UB1 107 A6
Tudor Rd
Ashford TW15 171 B4
Barking IG11 101 D6
Barnet EN5 1 D2
Beckenham BR3 208 A6
Chingford E4 35 D4
Croydon SE25 206 B4
Hackney E9 96 B6
Hampton TW12 173 C3
Harrow HA3 24 B1
Hayes UB3 83 B1
Isleworth TW3 130 B1
Kingston u T KT2 176 C3
Newham E6 99 C6
Penge SE19 183 D3
Pinner HA5 22 C1
Ponders End N9 18 C4
Southall UB1 107 A6
Tudor Sq UB3 83 B2
Tudor St EC4 116 C6 251 B6
Tudors The 2 BR3 185 D1
Tudor Way BR5 211 B3
Hillingdon UB10 60 C2
Osidge N14 15 D3
South Acton W3 110 C4
Tudor Well Cl HA7 25 B5
Tudor Wlk DA5 169 A5
Tudway Rd SE3, SE9 143 C1
Tufnell Ct 19 E3 97 B6
Tufnell Mans 7 N7 71 D4
TUFNELL PARK 71 D4
Tufnell Park Mans 2
N7 72 A5
Tufnell Park Prim Sch
N7 71 D4
Tufnell Park Rd N19,
N7 71 D4
Tufnell Park Sta N19 71 C4
Tufton Ct SW1 260 A5
Tufton Gdns KT8 173 D1
Tufton Rd E4 35 C6
Tufton St
SW1 116 A3 260 A5
Tugboat St SE28 123 C4
Tugela Rd CR0 205 B3
Tugela St SE6 163 B2
Tugmutton Cl BR6 226 D4
Tuke Sch SE15 140 B4
Tulip Cl Croydon CR0 206 D1
Hampton TW12 173 B4
5 Newham E6 100 B2
Southall UB2 108 A4
Tulip Ct 1 HA5 40 C6
Tulip Gdns
Chingford E4 20 B1
Ilford IG1 78 D2
Tullis Ho 12 E9 74 C1
Tull St CR4 202 D2
Tulse Cl BR3 208 A6
TULSE HILL 160 D4
Tulse Hill
Tulse Hill SW2 160 C4
Tulse Hill SW27 160 D2
Tulse Hill Sta SE27 160 D2
Tulse Ho SW2 160 C5
Tulsemere Rd SE21,
SE27 161 A2
Tumbling Bay KT12 194 A3
Tummons Gdns
SE25 183 C1
Tump Ho SE28 123 C5
Tunbridge Ct 1
SE26 162 A1
Tunbridge Ho EC1 234 C2
Tuncombe Rd N18 33 C6
Tunis Rd W12 112 B5
Tunley Gn 12 E14 97 B2
Tunley Rd
Dagenham NW10 89 C6
Upper Tooting SW12,
SW17 159 A2
Tunmarsh La E13 99 C4
Tunnan Leys E6 100 C1
Tunnel Avenue Trad Est
SE10 120 B4
Tunnel Gdns N11 31 C3
Tunnel Link Rd TW6 148 C5
Tunnel Rd SE16 118 C4
Tunnel Rd E TW6 126 D3
Tunnel Rd W TW6 126 D4
Tunstall Cl BR6 227 C4
Tunstall Ct 14 TW9 132 B4
Tunstall Rd
Croydon CR0 205 C1
Stockwell SW9 138 B1
Tunstall Wlk 10
TW8 132 A6
Tunstock Way DA17 125 A3
Tunworth Cl NW9 45 A3
Tunworth Cres
SW15 155 D5
Tun Yd SW8 137 B2
Tupelo Rd E10 75 D6
Tupman Ho 26 SE16 118 A4
Tuppy St SE28 123 A3
Turberville Ho 1
SW9 138 B2
Turenne Cl SW18 136 A1
Turin Gr Sch N9 18 C4
Turin Rd N9 18 C4
Turin St E2 96 A4
Turkey Oak Cl SE19 183 C2
Turkey St EN1, EN3 6 C6
Turkey Street Sta EN3 6 C6
Turks Cl UB8 82 C4
Turk's Head Yd EC1 241 C4
Turks Row
SW3 114 D1 257 D2
Turle Rd
Finsbury Pk N4 72 B6
Thornton Heath
SW16 182 A1
Turlewray Cl N4 50 B1
Turley Cl E15 98 C6
Turnagain La EC4 241 C2
Turnage Rd RM8 59 A1
Turnant Rd N17 33 A2
Turnberry Cl
24 Bermondsey
SE16 118 B1
Hendon NW4 28 D1
Turnberry Quay 1
E14 119 D3
Turnberry Way BR6 211 B1
Turnbull Ho N1 234 D6
Turnbury Cl SE28 102 D1
Turnchapel Mews 1
SW4 137 B2
Turner Ave
Mitcham CR4 180 D2
Tottenham N15 51 C5
Twickenham TW2 152 A1
Turner Cl
7 Brixton SW9 138 D4
Hampstead Garden Suburb
NW11 47 D3
Hillingdon UB4 83 A4
Wembley HA0 65 D2
Turner Cres CR7 205 A3
Turner Ct
9 Herne Hill SE5 139 B1
24 Rotherhithe SE16 118 C4
Turner Dr NW11 47 D3
Turner Ho
Finsbury Pk N4 50 B1
24 Millwall E14 119 C4
St John's Wood NW8 230 A4
Strand WC2 250 B5
6 Twickenham TW1 153 D5
Westminster SW1 259 D3
Turner Lo 10 SW19 156 D3
Turner Mews SM2 217 D1
Turner Pl SW11 158 C6
Turner Rd
Edgware HA8 26 B1
New Malden KT3 199 B2
Walthamstow E17 54 A6
Turners Cl N20 14 D1
Turners Ct Leyton E15 76 A4
New Barnet EN5 13 D5
Tottenham N15 51 B4
Turners Meadow Way
BR3 185 B2
Turner's Rd E3 97 B2
Turner St
Canning Town E16 98 D1
Stepney E1 96 B2
Turners Way CR0 220 C6
Turneville Rd
W14 135 B6 264 C6
Turney Rd SE21 161 B4
Turney Sch SE21 161 A4
Turnham Green Sta
W4 111 C2
Turnham Green Terr
W4 111 C2
Turnham Ho SE4 141 A1
Turnham Prim Sch 1
SE4 141 A1
Turnham Rd SE4 141 A1
Turnmill Ho 8 SW2 160 C6
Turnmill St
EC1 94 D2 241 C4
Turnour Ho 31 E1 96 B1
Turnpike Cl SE8 141 B5
Turnpike Ct DA6 146 D1
Turnpike Ho EC1 234 D1
Turnpike La
Hornsey N8 50 C6
Sutton SM1 218 A3
Uxbridge UB10 82 A5
Turnpike Lane Sta
N15 50 D6
Turnpike Link CR0 221 C6
Turnpike Mews N8 50 C6
Turnpike Way TW7 131 A4
Turnpin La 3 SE10 142 A6
Turnstone Cl
Edgware NW9 27 C1
Newham E13 99 A4
Uxbridge UB10 60 D3
Turnstone Terr 11
W13 86 D3
Turpentine La
SW1 115 B1 258 D1
Turpin Cl 15 EN3 7 C6
Turpington Cl BR2 210 A2
Turpington La BR2 210 A3
Turpin Ho SW11 268 C2
Turpin Rd TW14 149 D5
Turpin Way
Upper Holloway N19 49 D1
Wallington SM6 219 B1
Turquand St SE17 262 B3
Turret Gr SW4 137 C2
Turret Ho KT2 176 A4
Turton Ho 5 SE18 144 D6
Turton Rd HA0 66 A3
Turville Ho NW8 237 A6
Turville St E2 243 C6
Tuscan Ho 36 E2 96 C4
Tuscan Rd SE18 123 B1
Tuscany Ho E17 35 B1
Tuskar St SE10 120 C1
Tuttlebee La IG9 21 A2
Tuttle Ho SW1 259 D1
Tweed Ct W7 86 C1
Tweeddale Gr UB10 61 A5
Tweeddale Prim Sch
SM5 202 B2
Tweeddale Rd SM5 202 B1
Tweed Ho E14 98 A3
Tweedmouth Rd E13 99 B5
Tweedy Cl EN1 17 D6
Tweedy Rd BR1 187 A2
Tweezer's Alley WC2 251 A6
Twelve Acre Ho 5
E12 78 C5
Twelvetrees Bsns Pk
E16 98 B3
Twelvetrees Cres E3 98 A3
Twentyman Cl IG8 37 A5
TWICKENHAM 152 D4
Twickenham Bridge
TW9 153 C6
Twickenham Cl CR0 220 B5
Twickenham Gdns
Harrow HA3 24 C3
Wembley UB6 65 A3
Twickenham Mus The★
TW1 153 A3
Twickenham Pl KT7 212 D6
Twickenham Prep Sch
TW12 174 A2
Twickenham Rd
Isleworth TW1,
TW7 131 A2
Leyton E11 76 B6
Richmond TW1, TW9 131 C1
Teddington TW11 175 A6
Twickenham TW13 151 B1
Twickenham Sta
TW1 153 A4
Twickenham Stad
(Rugby Football Union)
TW2 152 C5
Twickenham Stoop
Stadium TW2 152 D4
Twickenham Trad Ctr
TW1 152 D5
Twickenham Trad Est
TW1 152 D5
Twig Folly Cl 21 E2 96 D5
Twilley St SW18 157 D4
Twine Cl IG11 102 B4
Twine Ct E1 118 C6
Twineham Gn N12 29 C6
Twining Ave TW2 152 B1
Twinings Mus★ WC2 241 A1
Twinn Rd NW7 29 A4
Twin Tumps Way
SE28 124 A6
Twisden Rd NW5 71 B4
Twiss Ho 6 SE18 122 D1
Twist Ho E10 75 D6
Two Bridges Ind Est
CR0 221 B2
Twybridge Way
NW10 67 A1
Twycross Mews
SE10 120 C2
Twyford Abbey Rd
NW10 88 B4
Twyford Ave
Acton W3 110 C6
Muswell Hill N2 48 D6
Twyford CE High Sch
W3 110 D5
Twyford Cres W3 110 C5
Twyford Ct
Acton W3 110 C6
Muswell Hill N10 49 A6
6 Wembley HA0 88 A5
Twyford Ho
Highbury N5 72 D5
6 Tottenham N15 51 C3
Twyford Par KT6 198 C1
Twyford Rd
Carshalton SM5 202 B1
Harrow HA2 41 D2
Ilford IG1 79 A3
Twyford Sp Ctr W3 110 D5
Twyford St N1 94 B6 233 C6
Twynholm Mans
SW6 264 A4
Tyas Rd E16 98 D3
Tybenham Rd SW19 201 C6
Tyberry Rd EN3 6 C2
Tyburn La HA1 42 D2
Tyburn Tree (site of)★
W2 247 C6
Tyburn Way W1 247 D6
Tye La BR6 227 A3
Tyer's Est SE1 253 A2
Tyers Gate
SE1 117 C4 253 A1
Tyers Ho 1 SW16 181 C5
Tyers St SE11 116 B1 260 C2
Tyers Terr
SE11 116 B1 260 D1
Tyeshurst Cl SE2 125 A1
Tylecroft Rd SW16 182 A1
Tylehurst Gdns IG1 79 A3
Tyler Cl Erith DA8 147 D5
Haggerston E2 95 D5
Tyler Ho SE3 142 B3
Tyler Rd UB2 107 D3
Tylers Ct
4 Walthamstow E17 53 C5
5 Wembley HA0 88 A5
Tylers Gate HA3 44 A3
Tylers Path SM5 218 D4
Tyler St
Greenwich SE10 120 C1
SE10 142 C6
Tylney Ave SE19 183 D5
Tylney Ho 10 E1 96 B1
Tylney Rd BR1 187 D1
Forest Gate E7 77 C4
Tymperley Ct SW19 157 A3
Tynamara KT1 197 D5
Tynan Cl TW14 150 A3
Tyndale La N1 72 D1
Tyndale Mans N1 72 D1
Tyndale Terr 13 N1 72 D1
Tyndall Gdns E10 76 A6
Tyndall Rd DA16 145 D2
Leyton E10 76 A6
Tyne Ct W7 86 C1
Tyneham Cl 10
SW11 137 A2
Tyneham Rd SW11 137 A2
Tyne Ho 8 KT2 175 D2
Tynemouth Cl E6 100 D1
Tynemouth Dr EN1 6 A5
Tynemouth Rd
Mitcham CR4 181 A3
Plumstead Comm
SE18 123 C1
Tottenham N15 51 D5
Tynemouth St SW6 136 A3
Tynemouth Terr 9
N15 51 D5
Tyne St E1 243 D2
Tynsdale Rd NW10 67 C2
Tynte Ct E9 75 A3
Tynwald Ho 14 SE26 162 A1
Type St E2 96 D5
Tyrawley Rd SW6 265 C2
Tyrell Cl HA1 64 C4
Tyrell Ct SM5 218 D4
Tyrells Ct 3 SE15 140 B2
Tyrols Rd SE23 162 D3
Tyrone Ct SW16 181 D5
Tyrone Rd E6 100 B4
Tyron Way DA14 189 D5
Tyrrell Ave DA16 168 B6
Tyrrell Ho
Catford BR3 185 D5
SW1 269 B6
Tyrrell Rd SE22 140 A1
Tyrrell Sq CR4 180 C2
Tyrrel Way NW9 46 A2
Tyrwhitt Rd SE4 141 C2
Tysoe Ave EN3 7 B6
Tysoe St EC1 234 B1
Tyson Rd SE23 162 C4
Tyssen Com Prim Sch
N16 52 A1
Tyssen Rd N16 73 D5
Tyssen St Dalston E8 73 D2
Hoxton N1 95 C5
Tysson Ho E9 75 A1
Tytherton 29 E2 96 C5
Tytherton Rd N19 71 D5

U

Uamvar St E14 97 D2
Uckfield Gr CR4 181 A2
Uckfield Rd EN3 6 D6
Udall St SW1 259 B3
Udimore Ho 11 W10 90 C2
Udney Park Rd
TW11 175 A4
Uffington Rd
West Norwood
SE27 182 C6
Willesden Green NW10 90 B6
Ufford Cl HA3 23 D3
Ufford Rd HA3 23 D3
Ufford St SE1 116 C4 251 B2
Ufton Ct UB5 84 D4
Ufton Gr N1 73 B1
Ufton Rd N1 73 C1
Uhura Sq 19 N16 73 C5
Ujima Ct
Finsbury Pk N19 50 A1
Streatham SW16 182 A6
Ujima Ho SW16 182 A6
UK Coll of Bsns &
Computing IG2 56 C3
Uk Cotts UB3 105 B4
Ullathorne Rd SW16 181 C6
Ulleswater Rd N14 16 B1
Ullin St E14 98 A2
Ullswater SW15 156 D5
Ullswater Cl
Bromley BR1 186 C3
Hayes UB4 83 C5
Kingston u T KT2,
SW15 177 B6
Ullswater Cres
SW15 177 B6
Ullswater Ct
Harrow HA2 41 C2
2 Woodford E18 37 A1
Ullswater Ho SE15 140 C6
Ullswater Rd
Barnes SW13 134 A5
West Norwood SE27,
SW16 160 D2
Ulster Ct KT2 175 D4
Ulster Gdns N13 33 A6

Ulster Pl NW1 238 C5
Ulster Terr NW1 238 C6
Ulundi Rd SE3 142 C6
Ulva Rd SW15 134 D1
Ulverscroft Rd SE22 162 A6
Ulverstone Rd SE27 160 D2
Ulverston Rd E17 36 B1
Ulysses Rd NW6 69 B3
Umberston St E1 96 B1
Umbria St SW15 156 A5
Umfreville Rd N4 50 D3
Umoja Ho N22 32 B1
Una Ho 7 NW5 71 B2
Undercliff SE10 142 A4
Undercliff Rd SE13 141 D2
UNDERHILL 13 C6
Underhill EN5 13 C6
Underhill Ct EN5 13 C6
Underhill Ho 7 E14 97 C2
Underhill Jun & Inf Schs EN5 13 A6
Underhill Pas NW1 231 D6
Underhill Rd SE21, SE22 162 B4
Underhill St NW1 231 D5
Underne Ave N14 15 B2
Undershaft EC3 95 C1 243 A1
Undershaw Rd BR1 164 D1
Underwood CR0 224 A3
Underwood Ct 3 E10 53 D1
Underwood Ho
East Molesey KT8 195 C4
Hammersmith W6 112 B3
Underwood Rd
Bethnal Green E1 96 A3
Chingford E4 35 D5
Woodford IG8 37 D3
Underwood Row N1 235 B2
Underwood St N1 95 A4 235 B2
Underwood The SE9 166 B2
Undine Rd E14 119 D2
Undine St SW17 180 D5
Uneeda Dr UB6 86 B6
Unicorn Bldg 14 E1 118 D6
Unicorn Prim Sch BR3 207 D4
Unicorn Sch TW9 132 B4
Unicorn Works N17 34 C3
Union Cl E11 76 B4
Union Ct
45 Paddington W2 91 C2
2 Richmond TW10 154 A6
South Lambeth SW4 138 A3
Whitechapel EC2 243 A2
Union Dr E1 97 A3
Union Gr SW8 137 D3
Union Mews 32 SW9 138 A3
Union Pk 11 SE10 120 D1
Union Rd BR2 209 D4
Clapham SW8 137 D3
Friern Barnet N11 31 D4
Northolt UB5 85 C5
Thornton Heath CR0 205 A2
Wembley HA0 66 A2
Union Sq N1 95 A6 235 B5
Union St Barnet EN5 1 A2
Kingston u T KT1 175 D1
Mill Meads E15 98 B6
SE1 117 A5 252 A3
Union Terr HA2 41 C1
Union Wharf N1 235 B4
Union Wlk E2 95 C4
Union Yd W1 238 D1
United International Coll W1 238 D3
Unity Cl
West Norwood SE19 183 A5
Willesden NW10 68 A2
Unity Mews NW1 232 C4
Unity Rd EN3 6 C6
Unity Terr HA2 63 D6
Unity Way SE18 121 D3
Univ Coll Jun Sch 31 NW3 70 A4
Univ Coll London
Bloomsbury WC1 93 D3 239 C6
Bloomsbury WC1 94 A3 240 B6
Univ Coll London (Windeyer Inst) W1 93 C2 239 B4
Univ Coll London (Wolfson Ho) NW1 93 C4 232 B1
University Cl NW7 27 D3
University Coll Hospl WC1 93 C3 239 B6
University Coll Sch NW3 70 A3
University Gdns DA5 169 B4
University Mans 9 SW15 134 D2
University Pl DA8 147 D5
University Rd SW19 180 B4
University St WC1 93 C3 239 B5
University Way E16 122 D6
Univ of California WC1 93 D2 239 D3
Univ of East London
Barking RM8 80 A4
Newham E16 122 C6
Stratford E15 76 C2
Univ of East London (Duncan Ho) 7 E15 98 B6
Univ of East London (Holbrook Ctr) E15 98 D5
Univ of Greenwich SE10 142 B6
Univ of Greenwich Avery Hill Campus Mansion Site SE9 167 A5
Univ of Greenwich Avery Hill Campus Southwood Site SE9 167 B4
Univ of London WC1 93 D3 239 D5
Univ of London (King's Coll Hall) SE5 139 B2
Univ of London Obsy NW7 27 D4
Univ of London (Queen Mary & Westfield Coll) E1 97 A3
Univ of Notre Dame SW1 115 D6 249 D5
Univ of Notre Dame SW1 249 D4
Univ of Westminster (Cavendish Campus) W1 93 C2 239 A4
Univ of Westminster (Harrow Campus) HA1 43 A2
Univ of Westminster (Marylebone Campus) W1 93 A2 238 A4
Univ of Westminster (Regent Campus) W1 93 C2 239 A3
Univ of Westminster (Regent Campus, Univ HQ) W1 93 B1 238 D2
Univ of Westminster (Wigram House Halls of Residence) SW1 115 C3 259 B5
Uno Apartments 4 BR1 187 A2
Unwin Ave TW14 149 B6
Unwin Cl SE15 140 A6
Unwin Rd
Isleworth TW7 130 C2
SW7 114 B3 256 D6
Upbrook Mews W2 92 A1 236 B1
Upcerne Rd SW10 136 A5 266 B3
Upchurch Cl 8 SE20 184 B3
Upcott Ho
33 Bromley E3 97 D4
4 Hackney E9 74 C1
Upcroft Ave HA8 27 A6
Updale Rd DA14 189 D6
Upfield CR0 222 B5
Upfield Rd W7 86 D2
Upgrove Manor Way 12 SE24 160 C4
Uphall Prim Sch IG1 78 D3
Uphall Rd IG1 78 D3
Upham Park Rd W4 111 C2
Uphill Dr
Edgware NW7 27 C5
Kingsbury NW9 45 A4
Uphill Gr NW7 27 C6
Uphill Rd NW7 27 C6
Upland Ct SE23 162 C2
Upland Prim Sch DA7 147 B2
Upland Rd
Croydon CR2 221 B3
DA7 147 B2
East Dulwich SE22 162 A5
8 Newham E13 99 A3
Sutton SM2 218 B1
Uplands
Beckenham BR3 185 C1
Woolwich SE18 122 D1
Uplands Ave E17 34 D1
Uplands Bsns Pk E17 52 D6
Uplands Cl SW14 154 D6
Uplands Ct N21 16 C4
Uplands Park Rd EN2 4 C3
Uplands Rd
East Barnet EN4 15 A3
Hornsey Vale N8 50 B4
Ilford RM6 58 D6
Woodford IG8 37 D3
Uplands The HA4 40 A1
Uplands Way N21 16 C6
Upnall Ho 16 SE15 140 C6
Upney Ct 2 IG11 79 D1
Upney La IG11 79 D1
Upney Sta IG11 79 D1
Upnor Way SE17 263 B2
Uppark Dr IG2 57 A3
Upper Abbey Rd DA17 125 C2
Upper Addison Gdns W14 113 A4 244 A2
Upper Bank St E14 119 D5
Upper Bardsey Wlk 7 N1 73 A2
Upper Belgrave St SW1 115 A3 258 B6
Upper Berkeley St W1 92 D1 237 D1
Upper Beulah Hill SE19 183 C2
Upper Brighton Rd KT6 198 A2
Upper Brockley Rd SE4 141 B3
Upper Brook St W1 115 A6 248 A6
Upper Butts TW8 131 C6
Upper Caldy Wlk 18 N1 73 A2
Upper Camelford Wlk 14 W10 91 A1
Upper Cavendish Ave N3 47 C6
Upper Cheyne Row SW3 136 C6 267 A6
UPPER CLAPTON 52 B1
Upper Clapton Rd E5 74 B6
Upper Clarendon Wlk 12 W11 91 A1
Upper Dengie Wlk N1 235 A6
UPPER EDMONTON 34 B5
UPPER ELMERS END 207 B3
Upper Elmers End Rd BR3 207 A4
Upper Farm Rd KT8 195 B5
Upper Fosters NW4 46 C5
Upper Gn W CR4 180 D1
Upper Gr SE25 205 D5
Upper Grosvenor St W1 115 A6 248 A5
Upper Grotto Rd TW1 152 D2
Upper Ground SE1 116 C5 251 A4
Upper Grove Rd DA17 147 B6
Upper Gulland Wlk 23 N1 73 A2
UPPER HALLIFORD 193 B5
Upper Halliford Rd TW17 193 C6
Upper Halliford Sta TW16 171 C1
Upper Hampstead Wlk 29 NW3 70 A4
Upper Ham Rd KT2, TW10 175 D6
Upper Handa Wlk 2 N1 73 A2
Upper Harley St NW1 238 B5
Upper Hawkwell Wlk N1 235 B6
UPPER HOLLOWAY 71 D6
Upper Holloway Sta N19 71 D6
Upper Holly Hill Rd DA17 125 D1
Upper James St W1 249 B6
Upper John St W1 249 B6
Upper Lismore Wlk 8 N1 73 A2
Upper Lodge Mews TW12 174 A4
Upper Mall W6 112 B1
Upper Marsh SE1 116 B3 260 D6
Upper Montague St W1 92 D2 237 C3
Upper Mulgrave Rd SM2 217 A1
Upper North St E3, E14 97 C2
UPPER NORWOOD 183 C3
Upper Park Rd
Belvedere DA17 125 D2
BR1 187 C2
Friern Barnet N11 31 C5
Kingston u T KT2 176 C4
Maitland Pk NW3 70 D3
Upper Phillimore Gdns W8 113 C4 245 A1
Upper Pk IG10 21 D6
Upper Ramsey Wlk 19 N1 73 B2
Upper Rawreth Wlk N1 235 B6
Upper Rd Finchley N2 30 C2
Newham E13 99 A4
Wallington SM6 219 D3
Upper Richmond Rd SW15 134 C1
Upper Richmond Rd W TW10, SW14, SW15 133 A1
UPPER RUXLEY 191 C3
Upper St Martin's La WC2 250 A6
Upper Selsdon Rd CR2 221 D1
Upper Sheridan Rd 3 DA17 125 C2
UPPER SHIRLEY 222 D4
Upper Shirley Rd CR0 222 D5
Upper Sq TW7 131 A2
Upper St N1 94 D6 234 C5
Upper Sunbury Rd TW12 173 C2
Upper Sutton La TW5 129 C4
UPPER SYDENHAM 184 A6
Upper Tachbrook St SW1 259 B4
Upper Talbot Wlk 7 W10 91 A1
Upper Teddington Rd KT1, KT8 175 C2
Upper Terr NW3 70 A5
Upper Thames St EC4 117 A6 252 B6
Upper Tollington Pk N4 50 C1
Upperton Rd DA14 189 D5
Upperton Rd E E13 99 C4
Upperton Rd W E13 99 C4
UPPER TOOTING 158 D1
Upper Tooting Park Mans 1 SW17 159 A2
Upper Tooting Pk SW17 158 D2
Upper Tooting Rd SW17 158 D1
Upper Town Rd UB6 85 D3
Upper Tulse Hill SW2 160 B3
Upper Vernon Rd SM1 218 B3
UPPER WALTHAMSTOW 54 C6
Upper Walthamstow Rd E17 54 B6
Upper Wickham La DA16 146 B4
Upper Wimpole St W1 93 A2 238 B4
Upper Woburn Pl NW1, WC1 93 D4 232 D1
Uppingham Ave HA7 25 C1
Upsdell Ave N13 32 C4
Upshire Ho E17 35 B1
Upstall St SE5 138 D4
UPTON 77 B1
Upton Ave E7 77 A1
Upton Cl
Cricklewood NW2 69 A5
Sidcup DA5 169 B5
Upton Cross E13 99 A6
Upton Cross Prim Sch E13 99 B6
Upton Ct Penge SE20 184 C3
Southall UB1 107 D5
4 Wimbledon SW19 178 D3
Upton Day Hospl DA6 147 A1
Upton Dene SM2 217 D1
Upton Gdns HA3 43 C3
Upton Hts E7 77 A1
Upton La E7 77 A1
Upton Lo E7 77 A2
Upton Lodge Cl WD23 8 A4
UPTON PARK 99 D6
Upton Park Rd E7 77 B1
Upton Park Sta E13 99 C6
Upton Prim Sch DA5 169 B6
Upton Rd Bexley DA6 169 A6
Edmonton N18 34 A5
Hounslow TW3 129 C2
SE18 145 A6
South Norwood CR7 183 B1
Upton Rd S DA5 169 B5
Upton Villas 4 DA6 147 A1
Upway N12 30 C4
Upwood Rd SE12 165 A5
Thornton Heath SW16 182 A2
Urban Mews N4 50 D2
Urlwin St SE5 139 A6
Urlwin Wlk SW9 138 D4
Urmston Dr SW19 157 A3
Urmston Ho 4 E14 120 A2
Urquhart Ct BR3 185 B3
Ursula Lo DA14 190 B5
Ursula Mews N4 51 A1
Ursula St SW11 136 C4 267 A1
Ursuline High Sch SW20 178 D2
Ursuline Prep Sch 20 SW19 178 D3
Urswick Gdns RM9 81 A1
Urswick Rd
Dagenham RM9 81 A1
Hackney E5, E9 74 C3
Usborne Mews SW8 270 D4
Usher Hall NW4 46 B5
Usher Rd E3 97 B5
Usk Rd SW11 136 A1
Usk St E2 96 D4
Utah Bldg 3 SE13 141 D4
Utopia Ho 3 NW2 68 A2
Utopia Village NW1 93 A6 231 A6
Uvedale Rd
Dagenham RM10 81 C5
Enfield EN2 17 B6
Uverdale Rd SW10 136 A5 266 B3
UXBRIDGE 82 A6
Uxbridge Coll
Hayes UB3 106 A6
Uxbridge UB8 60 A2
Uxbridge High Sch UB8 82 A5
Uxbridge Rd
Acton W3, W5 110 C5
Ealing W13 109 C6
Feltham TW13 150 D2
Hampton TW12, TW13 173 D5
Hayes UB4 106 C6
Hillingdon UB10, UB4 83 C2
Kingston u T KT1, KT6 197 D4
Shepherd's Bush W12 112 B5

Uxbridge Rd *continued*
Southall UB1, UB2, W5, W7 .... 108 B5
Stanmore HA7 .... 25 A5
Uxbridge Road (Harrow Weald) HA3 .... 24 B3
Uxbridge Road (Hatch End) HA5 .... 23 B3
Uxbridge Road (Pinner) HA5 .... 22 D1
Uxbridge St W8 .... 113 C5 245 A4
Uxendon Cres HA3, HA9 .... 44 A1
Uxendon Hill HA9 .... 44 B2
Uxendon Manor JMI Sch HA3 .... 44 A4

V

Vadnie Bish Ho NW5 .. 71 C2
Vaine Ho 4 E9 .... 75 A2
Valance Ave E4 .... 20 D3
Valan Leas BR2 .... 208 C6
Vale Ave WD6 .... 10 D6
Vale Cl Muswell Hill N2 .. 48 D6
Orpington BR6 .... 226 C4
St John's Wood W9 .... 92 A4 229 A1
Twickenham TW1 .... 153 A1
Vale Cres SW15 .... 177 C6
Vale Croft
Claygate KT10 .... 212 D1
Pinner HA5 .... 41 A4
Vale Ct Barnet EN5 .... 1 D1
East Acton W3 .... 111 D5
St John's Wood W9 .... 92 A4 229 A1
Wembley HA0 .... 65 C5
Vale Dr EN5 .... 13 C6
Vale End SE22 .... 139 D1
Vale Est The W3 .... 111 C5
Vale Farm Sports Ctr HA0 .... 65 B4
Vale Gr Acton W3 .... 111 B5
Stoke Newington N4 .... 51 A2
Vale La W3 .... 88 C2
Vale Lo SE23 .... 162 C2
Valence Ave RM8 .... 80 D6
Valence Cir RM8 .... 81 A5
Valence House Mus★ RM8 .... 81 A6
Valence Prim Sch RM8 .... 80 D6
Valence Wood Rd RM8 .... 81 A5
Valencia Rd HA7 .... 25 C6
Valens Ho 1 SW2 .... 160 C3
Valentia Pl SW9 .... 138 C1
Valentine Ave DA5 .... 169 A3
Valentine Ct
Elstree WD6 .... 9 D5
3 Forest Hill SE23 .... 162 D2
Valentine Ho
11 Clapham Pk SW4 .... 159 C5
26 Old Ford E3 .... 97 B6
Valentine Pl SE1 .... 116 D4 251 C2
Valentine Rd
Harrow HA2 .... 64 A5
Homerton E9 .... 74 D2
Valentine Row SE1 .. 251 C1
Valentines High Sch IG2 .... 56 C3
Valentines Rd IG1 .... 56 D1
VALE OF HEALTH 70 B5
Vale of Health NW3 .... 70 B5
Vale Rd BR1 .... 188 C1
Claygate KT10 .... 212 D1
Mitcham CR4 .... 203 D5
Stoke Newington N4 .... 51 A2
Sutton SM1 .... 217 D4
Upton E7 .... 77 B2
Worcester Pk KT19, KT4 .... 215 D5
Vale Rd N KT6 .... 214 A6
Vale Rd S KT6 .... 214 A6
Valerian Way E15 .... 98 C4
Valerian Wlk N11 .... 15 A2
Valerie Ct
Belmont SM2 .... 217 D1
Valerie Ct *continued*
Bushey WD23 .... 8 A4
Vale Rise NW11 .... 47 B1
Vale Row N5 .... 72 D5
Vale Royal N7 .... 72 A1
Valery Pl TW12 .... 173 C3
Vale Sch The SW7 .... 256 A5
Valeside Ct 2 EN5 .... 1 D1
Valeswood Rd BR1 .. 186 D5
Vale Terr N4 .... 51 A3
Vale The
Ashford TW16 .... 172 A4
Cricklewood NW11 .... 69 A6
Croydon CR0 .... 222 D6
East Acton W3 .... 111 C5
Feltham TW14 .... 150 B5
Heston TW5 .... 129 A6
Muswell Hill N10 .... 31 A2
Ruislip HA4 .... 62 C4
Southgate N14 .... 16 A4
SW3 .... 136 B6 266 D6
Woodford IG8 .... 37 A3
Valetta Gr E13 .... 99 A5
Valetta Rd W3 .... 111 D4
Valette Ct N10 .... 49 B5
Valette Ho E9 .... 74 C2
Valette St E8 .... 74 B2
Valiant Cl 13 UB5 .... 84 D4
Valiant Ho
9 Cubitt Town E14 .. 120 A4
5 Greenwich SE7 .... 121 C1
SW11 .... 266 D1
Valiant Way E6 .... 100 B2
Vallance Rd
Bethnal Green E1 .... 96 A3
Muswell Hill N22 .... 31 C1
Vallentin Rd E17 .... 54 A5
Valley Ave N12 .... 30 B6
Valley (Charlton Athletic FC) The SE7 .... 121 C1
Valley Cl HA5 .... 22 B1
Valley Ct IG8 .... 37 B3
Valley Dr NW9 .... 44 D3
Valleyfield Rd SW16 .. 182 B5
Valley Fields Cres EN2 . 4 C3
Valley Gdns
Mitcham SW19 .... 180 B3
Wembley HA0 .... 66 B1
Valley Gr SE7 .... 121 C1
Valley Ho
4 Edmonton N9 .... 18 A1
Upper Clapton E5 .... 52 C1
Valleylink Est EN3 .... 19 A5
Valley Mews TW1 .... 153 A2
Valley Pl KT6 .... 198 A3
Valley Point Ind Est CR0 .... 204 A2
Valley Prim Sch BR2 .... 186 D1
Valley Prospect 3 SE19 .... 183 C4
Valley Rd
Beckenham BR2 .... 186 C1
BR5 .... 190 B2
Streatham SW16 .... 182 B6
Uxbridge UB10 .... 82 A5
Valleyside SE7 .... 121 D1
Valley Side E4 .... 19 C3
Valley Side Par E4 .... 19 C2
Valley View EN5 .... 13 A5
Valley Wlk CR0 .... 222 C6
Valliere Rd NW10 .... 90 A4
Valliers Wood Rd DA15 .... 167 C3
Vallis Way
Chessington KT9 .... 213 D4
Ealing W13 .... 87 A2
Val McKenzie Ave N7 .. 72 C5
Valmar Rd SE5 .... 139 A4
Valmar Trad Est SE5 .... 139 A4
Valnay St SW17 .... 180 D5
Valognes Ave E17 .... 35 A2
Valois Ho SE1 .... 263 C6
Valonia Gdns SW18 .. 157 B5
Vambery Rd SE18 .. 145 A6
Vanbern Ho NW5 .... 71 A2
Vanborough Ct 4 SM2 .... 218 A2
Vanbrough Cres UB5 .. 84 C6
Vanbrugh Ct SE11 .... 261 B3
Vanbrugh Dr KT12 .... 194 C3
Vanbrugh Fields SE3 .... 142 D5
Vanbrugh Hill SE10, SE3 .... 142 D6
Vanbrugh Ho 8 E9 .... 74 C1
Vanbrugh Mews KT12 .... 194 C2
Vanbrugh Park Rd SE3 .... 142 D5
Vanbrugh Park Rd W SE3 .... 142 D5
Vanbrugh Pk SE3 .... 142 D5
Vanbrugh Rd W4 .... 111 B3
Vanbrugh Terr SE3 .. 142 D4
Vanburgh Cl
2 Newham E16 .... 99 D2
Orpington BR6 .... 211 C1
Vanburgh Ct 6 EN5 .... 1 A1
Vanburgh Ho E1 .... 243 C4
Vancouver Rd
Edgware HA8 .... 26 D2
Forest Hill SE23 .... 163 B2
Hayes UB4 .... 84 B3
Richmond TW10 .... 175 C6
Vancover Ho 33 E1 .... 118 B5
Vanderbilt Rd SW18 .. 158 A3
Vanderbilt Villas 1 W12 .... 112 D4
Vanderville Gdns N2 .. 30 B1
Vandome Cl E16 .... 99 B1
Vandon Ct SW1 .... 259 B6
Vandon Pas SW1 .... 259 B6
Vandon St SW1 .... 259 B6
Van Dyck Ave KT3 .... 199 B2
Vandyke Cl SW15 .... 156 D5
Vandyke Cross SE9 .. 166 A6
Vandy St EC2 .... 243 A5
Vane Cl
Hampstead NW3 .... 70 B4
Harrow HA3 .... 44 B3
Vane Ho 18 N2 .... 30 B1
Vanessa Cl DA17 .... 125 C1
Vane St SW1 .... 259 B4
Vanfame Ct KT3 .... 199 D6
Vange Ho 12 W10 .... 90 C2
Van Gogh Cl 11 TW7 .... 131 A2
Van Gogh Ct E14 .... 120 B3
Vanguard Bldg 6 E14 .... 119 C4
Vanguard Cl
Newham E16 .... 99 B2
Thornton Heath CR0 . 204 D1
Vanguard Ho
11 Hackney E8 .... 74 B1
7 Merton SW19 .... 180 A3
6 Stanwell TW19 .... 148 A5
Vanguard St SE8 .... 141 C4
Vanguard Way
Hatton TW6 .... 127 C3
Wallington SM6 .... 220 A1
Van Lang Ho EN3 .... 18 D6
Vanneck Sq SW15 .... 156 A6
Vanner Point 27 E9 .... 74 D2
Vanoc Gdns BR1 .... 187 A6
Vanquish Cl TW2 .... 151 C4
Vansittart Rd E7 .... 77 A4
Vansittart St 7 SE14 .... 141 A5
Vanston Pl SW6 .... 135 C5 265 B4
Vantage Ct
Harlington UB3 .... 127 C5
4 South Norwood SW16 .... 182 B3
Vantage Mews 7 E14 .... 120 A5
Vantage Pl W8 .... 255 B5
Vant Rd SW17 .... 180 D5
Vantrey Ho SE11 .... 261 A3
Varcoe Rd SE16 .... 118 C1
Vardens Rd SW11 .... 136 B1
Varden St E1 .... 96 B1
Vardon Cl W3 .... 89 B1
Vardon Ho SE10 .... 142 A4
Vardy Ho HA7 .... 25 B5
Varey Ho E1 .... 97 A4
Varley Ho 5 NW6 .... 91 C6
Varley Par NW9 .... 45 C5
Varley Rd E16 .... 99 B1
Varley Way CR4 .... 180 B1
Varma Ct SE3 .... 143 A4
Varna Rd
Hampton TW12 .... 173 D2
SW6 .... 135 B5 264 C3
Varndell St NW1 .... 93 C4 232 A2
Varnishers Yard N1 . 233 B3
Varsity Dr TW1, TW7 . 152 D5
Varsity Row SW14 .... 133 A3
Vartry Rd N15 .... 51 C3
Vascroft Est NW10 .... 88 D3
Vassall Ho 3 E3 .... 97 A4
Vassall Rd SW9 .... 138 C5
Vat Ho SW8 .... 270 B4
Vauban Est SE16 .... 263 D5
Vauban St SE16 .... 117 D3 263 D5
Vaudeville Ct N4 .... 72 C6
Vaughan Almshouses TW15 .... 170 D5
Vaughan Ave
Chiswick W6 .... 111 D2
Hendon NW4 .... 46 A4
Vaughan Cl TW12 .... 173 A4
Vaughan Est 3 E2 .... 95 D4
Vaughan Fst & Mid Sch HA1 .... 42 A3
Vaughan Gdns IG1 .... 56 B2
Vaughan Ho SE1 .... 251 C2
Vaughan Rd
Camberwell SE5 .... 139 A2
DA16 .... 145 D3
Harrow HA1 .... 42 B3
Stratford E15 .... 76 D2
Thames Ditton KT7 .... 197 B2
Vaughan St SE16 .... 119 B4
Vaughan Way E1 .... 118 A5
Vaughan Williams Cl SE8 .... 141 C5
VAUXHALL 116 A1
Vauxhall Bridge Rd SW1 .... 115 C2 259 B3
Vauxhall City Farm★ SE1 .... 260 C1
Vauxhall Cross SE1, SW8 .... 116 A1 260 B1
Vauxhall Gdns CR2 .. 221 A2
Vauxhall Gr SW8 .... 138 B6 270 C6
Vauxhall Prim Sch SE11 .... 116 B1 260 D2
Vauxhall St SE11 .... 116 B1 260 D2
Vauxhall Sta SE11 .... 116 A1 260 B1
Vauxhall Wlk SE11 .. 260 C2
Vawdrey Cl E1 .... 96 C3
Vaynor Ho N7 .... 72 A4
Veals Mead CR4 .... 180 C2
Vectis Ct SW18 .... 157 D5
Vectis Gdns SW17 .... 181 B4
Vectis Rd SW17 .... 181 B4
Veda Rd SE13 .... 141 C1
Vega Cres HA6 .... 22 A5
Vega Rd WD23 .... 8 A4
Veitch Cl TW14 .... 149 D4
Veldene Way HA2 .... 63 B5
Velde Way 1 SE22 .. 161 C6
Vellacott Ho 3 W12 .... 90 B1
Velletri Ho 17 E2 .... 96 D5
Vellum Dr SM5 .... 219 A5
Velocity Way EN3 .... 7 B6
Venables Cl RM10 .... 81 D4
Venables St NW8 .... 92 B2 236 D4
Vencourt Pl W6 .... 112 A2
Venetian Rd SE5 .... 139 A3
Venetia Rd
Ealing W5 .... 109 D4
Harringay N4 .... 50 D3
Venice Ct 14 SE5 .... 139 A5
Venita Manor SE27 .. 182 C5
Venmead Ct 7 DA17 .... 125 C2
Venner Rd SE26 .... 184 C5
Venn Ho N1 .... 233 D5
Venn St SW4 .... 137 C1
Ventnor Ave HA7 .... 25 B1
Ventnor Dr N20 .... 13 D2
Ventnor Gdns IG11 .... 79 C2
Ventnor Mans IG11 .... 79 C2
Ventnor Rd
Belmont SM2 .... 217 D1
SE14 .... 140 D5
Ventnor Terr N15 .... 52 A5
Ventura Ho 12 SW2 .. 138 A1
Venture Cl DA5 .... 169 A4
Venture Ct 3 SE12 .... 165 A4
Venue St E14 .... 98 A2
Venus Ho
7 Millwall E14 .... 119 C2
8 Old Ford E3 .... 97 C6
Venus Mews CR4 .... 202 C6
Venus Rd SE18 .... 122 B3
Vera Ave N21 .... 16 C6
Vera Ct
1 Kensington W2 .... 91 D1
Tottenham N22 .... 32 D2
Vera Lynn Cl 5 E7 .... 77 A4
Vera Rd SW6 . 135 A4 264 B2
Verbena Cl E16 .... 98 D3
Verbena Gdns 4 W6 .... 112 A1
Verdant Ct 3 SE6 .... 164 C4
Verdant La SE6 .... 164 C3
Verdayne Ave CR0 .. 222 D6
Verdun Rd
Barnes SW13 .... 134 A5
SE18 .... 146 A6
Vere Bank SW19 .... 157 B3
Vereker Dr TW16 .... 194 A6
Vereker Rd W14 .... 254 B1
Vere St W1 .... 93 B1 238 C1
Verity Cl W11 .... 91 A1
Verity Ct N9 .... 18 D3
Verity Ho 20 E3 .... 97 B4
Vermeer Ct E14 .... 120 B3
Vermillion Ct TW13 . 149 D1
Vermont Cl EN2 .... 4 D1
Vermont Ho E17 .... 35 B1
Vermont Rd
Sutton SM1 .... 217 D5
Wandsworth SW18 .. 157 D5
West Norwood SE19 . 183 C4
Verne Ct 9 W3 .... 111 A3
Verneer Gdns SE15 .. 140 C1
Verney Gdns RM9 .... 81 A4
Verney Ho
Isleworth TW3 .... 130 A1
Lisson Gr NW8 .... 237 A6
South Kensington SW10 .... 266 A6
Verney Rd
Bermondsey SE16 .... 118 B1
Dagenham RM9 .... 81 A4
Verney St NW10 .... 67 B5
Verney Way SE16 .... 118 B1
Vernham Rd SE18 .... 145 A6
Vernon Ave Ilford E12 .. 78 B4
West Barnes SW20 .. 178 D1
Woodford IG8 .... 37 B3
Vernon Cl
Stanwell TW19 .... 148 A3
West Ewell KT19 .... 215 A2
Vernon Cres EN4 .... 15 A5
Vernon Ct
Child's Hill NW2 .... 69 B5
Ealing W5 .... 109 C6
Stanmore HA7 .... 25 B2
Vernon Dr HA7 .... 25 A2
Vernon Ho
Hyde The NW9 .... 45 D4
SE11 .... 260 D1
Vernon House Specl Sch NW10 .... 67 B3
Vernon Mews W14 .. 254 B3
Vernon Pl WC1 .... 240 B3
Vernon Rd Bow E3 .... 97 B5
Feltham TW13 .... 149 D2
Hornsey N8 .... 50 C6
Ilford IG3 .... 57 D1
Leytonstone E11 .... 54 C1
Mortlake SW14 .... 133 B2
Stratford E15 .... 76 C1
Sutton SM1 .... 218 B3
Walthamstow E17 .... 53 B4
Vernon Rise
Greenford UB6 .... 64 B3
WC1 .... 233 D2
Vernon Sq WC1 .... 233 D2
Vernon St W14 .... 113 A2 254 B3
Vernon Yd W11 .... 113 B6 244 C6
Veroan Rd DA7 .... 147 A3
Verona Ct
Chiswick W4 .... 111 C1
10 SE14 .... 140 D6
Verona Dr KT6 .... 214 A6
Verona Rd E7 .... 77 A1
Veronica Gdns CR4, SW16 .... 181 C2
Veronica Ho
Brockley SE4 .... 141 B2
46 Bromley E3 .... 97 D4
Veronica Rd SW17 .... 159 B2
Veronique Gdns IG6 .. 57 A4
Verran Rd SW12 .... 159 B4
Versailles Rd SE20 .... 184 A3
Verulam Ave E17 .... 53 B2
Verulam Bldgs WC1 . 240 D4

Verulam Ct
Hendon NW9 ... 46 A2
4 Southall UB1 ... 86 A1
Verulam Ho 1 W6 ... 112 C4
Verulam Rd UB6 ... 85 C3
Verulam St
EC1 ... 94 C2 241 A4
Vervain Ho 2 SE15 ... 140 A5
Verwood Dr EN4 ... 2 D2
Verwood Ho SW8 ... 270 D3
Verwood Lo 1 E14 ... 120 B2
Verwood Rd HA2 ... 24 A1
Veryan Ct 3 N8 ... 49 D4
Vesage Ct EC1 ... 241 B3
Vesey Path 15 E14 ... 97 D1
Vespan Rd W12 ... 112 A4
Vesta Ct SE1 ... 253 A1
Vesta Ho 9 E3 ... 97 C6
Vesta Rd SE4, SE14 ... 141 A3
Vestris Rd SE23 ... 162 D2
Vestry House (Mus)★
E17 ... 53 D5
Vestry Mews 12 SE5 ... 139 C4
Vestry Rd
Camberwell SE5 ... 139 C4
Walthamstow E17 ... 53 D5
Vestry St N1 ... 95 B4 235 C2
Vevey St SE23, SE6 ... 163 B2
Veysey Gdns RM10 ... 81 C5
Viaduct Pl 28 E2 ... 96 B4
Viaduct Rd N2 ... 30 C1
Viaduct St E2 ... 96 B4
Viaduct The
Harrow HA2 ... 64 A5
Woodford E18 ... 37 B1
Vian St SE13 ... 141 D2
Vibart Gdns SW2 ... 160 B4
Vibart Wlk N1 ... 233 B6
Vicarage Ave SE3 ... 143 A5
Vicarage Cl
New Malden KT4 ... 199 C1
Northolt UB5 ... 63 B1
Ruislip HA4 ... 39 B2
Vicarage Cres
SW11 ... 136 B4 266 C1
Vicarage Ct
Beckenham BR3 ... 207 A6
East Bedfont TW14 ... 149 A4
Finchley N12 ... 29 D5
7 Putney SW15 ... 156 A4
W8 ... 245 C2
Vicarage Dr
Barking IG11 ... 79 A1
Beckenham BR3 ... 185 C2
Mortlake SW14 ... 155 B6
Vicarage Farm Ct
TW5 ... 129 B5
Vicarage Farm Rd TW3,
TW4, TW5 ... 129 A4
Vicarage Fields
KT12 ... 194 C3
Vicarage Field Sh Ctr
The IG11 ... 79 A1
Vicarage Gate
W8 ... 113 D5 245 C3
Vicarage Gdns
Mitcham CR4 ... 202 C6
Mortlake SW14 ... 155 B6
W8 ... 245 B3
Vicarage Gr SE5 ... 139 B4
Vicarage Ho 1 KT1 ... 176 B1
Vicarage La Ilford IG1 ... 57 B1
Stratford E15 ... 76 D1
Wallend E6 ... 100 C4
Vicarage Mans N15 ... 51 A5
Vicarage Pk SE18 ... 123 A1
Vicarage Prim Sch 5
E6 ... 100 B4
Vicarage Rd
Ashford TW16 ... 171 D4
Croydon CR0 ... 220 C5
DA5 ... 169 D3
Dagenham RM10 ... 81 D1
Hampton Wick KT1 ... 175 C2
Hendon NW4 ... 46 A3
Kingston u T KT1 ... 175 D1
Mortlake SW14 ... 155 B6
Old Bexley DA5 ... 169 D2
Stratford E15 ... 76 D1
Sutton SM1 ... 217 D5
Teddington TW11 ... 175 A5
Tottenham N17 ... 34 A2
Walthamstow E10 ... 53 D1
Woolwich SE18 ... 123 A1
Vicarage The N8 ... 50 B3
Vicarage Way
Harrow HA2 ... 41 C2
Neasden NW10 ... 67 B5
Vicarage Wlk
SW11 ... 136 B4 266 D2
Vicars Bridge Cl HA0 ... 88 A5
Vicar's Cl Enfield EN1 ... 5 C3
Newham E15 ... 99 A6
South Hackney E9 ... 96 C6
Vicar's Green Prim Sch
HA0 ... 87 C5
Vicars Hill SE13 ... 141 D1
Vicar's Moor La N21 ... 16 D4
Vicars Oak Rd SE19 ... 183 C4
Vicar's Rd NW5 ... 71 A3
Vicar's Wlk RM8 ... 80 B5
Viceroy Cl N2 ... 48 C6
Viceroy Ct
5 Croydon CR0 ... 205 B1
NW8 ... 230 B4
Viceroy Lo 6 KT6 ... 198 A4
Viceroy Par N2 ... 48 C6
Viceroy Rd
SW8 ... 138 A4 270 A2
Vic Johnson Ho 21
E3 ... 97 B6
Vickers Cl SM6 ... 220 B1
Vickers Ct 10 TW19 ... 148 A5
Vickery Ct EC1 ... 242 B6
Vickery Ho 13 SW4 ... 138 A1
Vickery's Wharf 3
E14 ... 97 C1
Victor Cazalet Ho N1 234 C6
Victor Gr HA0 ... 66 A1
Victor Ho 2 N20 ... 14 D1
Victoria & Albert Mus★
SW7 ... 114 B3 256 D5
Victoria Arc SW1 ... 258 D5
Victoria Ave Barnet EN4 ... 2 B1
East Molesey KT8 ... 195 D6
EC2 ... 243 B3
Finchley N3 ... 29 B2
Hackbridge SM5, SM6 219 A5
Hillingdon UB10 ... 60 D1
Hounslow TW3, TW4 ... 151 C6
Newham E6 ... 99 D6
Surbiton KT6 ... 197 D3
Wembley HA9 ... 66 D2
Victoria Bglws DA14 ... 191 B3
Victoria Bldgs 13 E8 ... 96 B6
Victoria Bsns Ctr
DA16 ... 146 B3
Victoria Chambers
EC2 ... 243 A6
Victoria Cl Barnet EN4 ... 2 B1
East Molesey KT8 ... 195 C6
Harrow HA1 ... 42 D3
Hayes UB3 ... 83 B1
Victoria Coach Sta
SW1 ... 115 B2 258 C3
Victoria Coll WC2 ... 241 A2
Victoria Cotts
Ilford IG6 ... 57 A4
Muswell Hill N10 ... 31 A1
7 Richmond TW9 ... 132 C4
3 Spitalfields E1 ... 96 A2
Victoria Cres
Tottenham N15 ... 51 C4
West Norwood SE19 ... 183 C4
Victoria Ct
5 Clapham Pk
SW4 ... 159 D5
3 Penge SE26 ... 184 C4
South Acton W3 ... 110 C4
4 St George in t East
E1 ... 118 A6
1 Wanstead E18 ... 55 B6
Wembley HA9 ... 66 C2
Victoria Dock Rd
E16 ... 121 B6
Victoria Dr SW19 ... 156 D3
Victoria Emb
WC2 ... 116 C6 251 A5
Victoria Gdns
Heston TW5 ... 129 A4
W11 ... 113 C5 245 A4
Victoria Gr
North Finchley N12 ... 30 B5
W8 ... 114 A3 256 A6
Victoria Gr Mews
W2 ... 245 C5
Victoria Hall 15 E16 ... 121 A5
Victoria Ho
6 Clapham Pk
SW4 ... 159 D5
Edgware HA8 ... 26 D4
Victoria Ho *continued*
2 Shepherd's Bush
W12 ... 112 A4
SW1 ... 258 C2
Victoria Ind Est W3 ... 89 C2
Victoria Jun Sch
TW13 ... 150 B3
Victoria La Barnet EN5 ... 1 B1
Hayes UB3 ... 105 B1
Victoria Lo 5 SW19 ... 178 C3
Victoria Mans
8 Islington N7 ... 72 C3
Willesden NW10 ... 68 B1
Victoria Mews
Kilburn NW6 ... 91 C6
Wandsworth SW18 ... 158 A3
Victoria Mills 1 E15 ... 98 B6
Victorian Gr N16 ... 73 C5
Victorian Hts 7
SW8 ... 137 B3
Victorian Rd N16 ... 73 D5
Victoria Park Ct 11
E9 ... 74 C1
Victoria Park Ind Ctr
E9 ... 75 B1
Victoria Park Lofts
E9 ... 96 D6
Victoria Park Rd E9 ... 74 D1
Victoria Park Sq E2 ... 96 C4
Victoria Pas NW8 ... 236 C6
Victoria Pl 17 TW10 ... 153 D6
Victoria Place Sh Ctr
SW1 ... 115 B2 258 D4
Victoria Point 10 E13 ... 99 A5
Victoria Rd
Barking IG11 ... 78 D2
Barnet EN4 ... 2 B1
Bexley DA6 ... 147 C1
Bromley Comm BR2 ... 209 D4
Buckhurst Hill IG9 ... 21 D2
Chingford E4 ... 20 C3
Chislehurst West BR7 188 C5
Dagenham RM10 ... 81 D3
Ealing W5 ... 87 B2
Edgware NW7 ... 27 D5
Edmonton N9 ... 17 D1
Feltham TW13 ... 150 B3
Finsbury Pk N4 ... 50 B1
Hendon NW4 ... 46 D5
Kensington
W8 ... 114 A3 256 A6
Kilburn NW6 ... 91 B6
Kingston u T KT1 ... 176 B1
Leyton E11 ... 76 C4
Mitcham CR4 ... 180 D3
Mortlake SW14 ... 133 B2
Muswell Hill N22 ... 31 D2
Newham E13 ... 99 A5
North Acton NW10 ... 89 C3
Ruislip HA4 ... 62 B4
Sidcup DA15 ... 168 A1
Southall UB2 ... 107 B3
Surbiton KT6 ... 197 D3
Sutton SM1 ... 218 B3
Teddington TW11 ... 175 A4
Tottenham Hale N15 ... 52 A5
Twickenham TW1 ... 153 B4
Walthamstow E17 ... 36 A1
Wanstead E18 ... 55 B6
Victoria Ret Pk HA4 ... 62 D3
Victoria Rise SW4 ... 137 B2
Victoria Sq SW1 ... 258 D6
Victoria St
Erith DA17 ... 125 B1
Stratford E15 ... 76 C1
SW1 ... 115 C3 259 B5
Victoria Sta
SW1 ... 115 B2 258 D4
Victoria Terr
Dagenham NW10 ... 89 C3
Finsbury Pk N4 ... 50 C1
Harrow HA1 ... 42 C1
Victoria (Underground)
SW1 ... 115 B3 258 D5
Victoria Villas TW9 ... 132 B1
Victoria Way SE7 ... 143 C6
Victoria Wharf E14 ... 119 A6
Victoria Yd 28 E1 ... 96 A1
Victor Mills Cotts
BR8 ... 191 C3
Victor Rd
College Pk NW10 ... 90 B4
Harrow HA2 ... 42 A6
Penge SE20 ... 184 D3
Teddington TW11 ... 174 C6
Victors Dr TW12 ... 173 A4
Victor Seymour Inf Sch
6 SM5 ... 219 A5
Victors Way EN5 ... 1 B2
Victor Villas N9 ... 17 B1
Victory Ave SM4 ... 202 A4
Victory Bsns Ctr
TW7 ... 130 D1
Victory Cl TW19 ... 148 A3
Victory Ct IG11 ... 102 B4
Victory Pl
6 Limehouse E14 ... 119 A6
SE17 ... 117 B2 262 C4
West Norwood SE19 ... 183 C4
Victory Prim Sch
SE17 ... 117 A2 262 B4
Victory Rd
Merton SW19 ... 180 A3
Wanstead E11 ... 55 B5
Victory Road Mews 5
SW19 ... 180 A3
Victory Way
Hounslow TW5 ... 106 C1
Rotherhithe SE16 ... 119 A4
Victory Wlk SE8 ... 141 C4
Video Ct N4 ... 50 A2
Vidler Cl KT9 ... 213 C2
Vienna Cl IG5 ... 37 D1
Victory Day Sch 3
CR7 ... 205 A6
View Cl Harrow HA1 ... 42 B5
Highgate N6 ... 48 D2
View Cres N8 ... 49 D4
Viewfield Cl HA3 ... 44 A2
Viewfield Rd DA5 ... 168 C3
Wandsworth SW18 ... 157 B5
Viewland Rd SE18 ... 123 D1
Viewpoint Ealing W5 ... 110 B6
3 Islington N5 ... 72 D3
View Point N20 ... 14 A4
Viewpoint Ct 8 HA5 ... 22 C1
View Rd N6 ... 48 D3
Viewside Lo N6 ... 49 C3
View The SE2 ... 125 A1
Viga Rd N21 ... 16 C5
Vigilant Cl SE26 ... 184 A6
Vignoles Rd RM7 ... 59 C2
Vigo St W1 ... 115 C6 249 A5
Vi & John Rubens Ho
IG2 ... 56 C3
Viking Cl 13 E3 ... 97 A5
Viking Ct
Hampton TW12 ... 173 D2
New Barnet EN4 ... 14 B6
Viking Gdns E6 ... 100 A3
Viking Ho
3 Camberwell SE5 ... 139 A3
3 Woolwich SE18 ... 122 A2
Viking Pl E10 ... 53 B1
Viking Prim Sch UB5 ... 84 D4
Viking Rd UB1 ... 107 A6
Villacourt Rd SE18 ... 146 A6
Village Arc The 2 E4 ... 20 B3
Village Cl Chingford E4 ... 36 A5
Hampstead NW3 ... 70 B3
Village Ct
Blackheath SE3 ... 142 C2
Walthamstow E17 ... 53 D4
Village Gate TW17 ... 192 D4
Village Home The
IG6 ... 57 A6
Village Hts IG8 ... 36 D5
Village Inf Sch RM10 ... 81 C1
Village Mount 19
NW3 ... 70 A4
Village Park Cl EN1 ... 17 C5
Village Rd Enfield EN1 ... 17 C6
Hendon N3 ... 29 A1
Village Row SM2 ... 217 C1
Village Sch The NW3 ... 70 D2
Village The
Battersea SW11 ... 136 D2
SE7 ... 143 D6
Village Way
Ashford TW15 ... 170 C6
Beckenham BR3 ... 207 C6
Dulwich Village SE21 ... 161 B5
Ilford IG6 ... 57 A6
Pinner HA5 ... 41 B2
Willesden NW10 ... 67 B4
Village Way E HA2 ... 41 C2
Villa Rd SW9 ... 138 C2
Villas On The Heath
NW3 ... 70 A5
Villas Rd SE18 ... 123 A2
Villa St SE17 ... 117 B1 262 D1
Villiers Ave
Kingston u T KT5 ... 198 B5
Twickenham TW2 ... 151 B3
Villiers Cl
Kingston u T KT5 ... 198 B5
Leyton E10 ... 75 C6
Villiers Ct
Oakleigh Pk N20 ... 14 A4
SW11 ... 267 B2
Villiers High Sch
UB1 ... 107 B5
Villiers Ho W5 ... 109 D6
Villiers Rd
Isleworth TW7 ... 130 C3
Kingston u T KT1 ... 198 B6
Penge BR3 ... 184 D1
Southall UB1 ... 107 B5
Willesden NW2 ... 68 A2
Villiers St WC2 ... 250 B4
Vimy Cl TW4 ... 151 B6
Vincam Cl TW2 ... 151 C4
Vince Ct N1 ... 235 D1
Vincent Ave KT5 ... 215 A6
Vincent Cl
Avery Hill DA15 ... 167 C3
Barnet EN5 ... 1 D2
Bromley BR2 ... 209 B5
Harmondsworth UB7 ... 126 C6
Vincent Ct
Finsbury Pk N4 ... 50 A1
Hendon NW4 ... 46 D5
Marylebone W1 ... 237 C2
Ruislip HA4 ... 62 B3
South Lambeth SW9 ... 270 D1
Vincent Dr
Hillingdon UB10 ... 82 B6
Upper Halliford TW17 193 C6
Vincent Gdns NW2 ... 67 D5
Vincent Ho KT3 ... 199 D5
Vincent Mews 1 E3 ... 97 C5
Vincent Rd
Acton Green W3 ... 111 A3
Chingford E4 ... 36 B4
Croydon CR0 ... 205 C2
Dagenham RM9 ... 81 A1
Hounslow West TW4 ... 128 D2
Kingston u T KT1 ... 198 C6
Osterley TW7 ... 130 B4
Tottenham N15 ... 51 A5
Wembley HA0 ... 66 B1
Wood Green N22 ... 32 C1
Woolwich SE18 ... 122 D2
Vincent Row TW12 ... 174 A5
Vincents Cl SE16 ... 119 A4
Vincents Path UB5 ... 63 A2
Vincent Sq
SW1 ... 115 D2 259 C4
Wood Green N22 ... 32 C1
Vincent St
Canning Town E16 ... 98 D2
Westminster
SW1 ... 115 D2 259 D4
Vincent Terr
N1 ... 94 D5 234 D4
Vince St EC1 ... 95 B4 235 D1
Vine Cl Shacklewell E5 ... 74 A4
Surbiton KT5 ... 198 B3
Sutton SM1 ... 218 A5
West Drayton UB7 ... 104 C2
Vine Cotts
3 Ealing W7 ... 108 C5
Southall UB2 ... 107 D2
Vine Ct Harrow HA3 ... 44 A3
Spitalfields E1 ... 96 A2
Vinegar St E1 ... 118 B5
Vinegar Yd SE1 ... 253 A2
Vine Gdns IG1 ... 79 A3
Vine Gr UB10 ... 60 C1
Vine Hill EC1 ... 241 A5
Vine La
Hillingdon UB10 ... 82 B6
SE1 ... 117 C5 253 B3
Uxbridge UB10 ... 60 B1
Vine Lo N12 ... 30 A4
Vine Pl Ealing W5 ... 110 A5
Hounslow TW3 ... 129 D1
Vine Rd
Barnes SW13 ... 133 D2
BR6 ... 227 D2
East Molesey KT8 ... 196 A5
Stratford E15 ... 76 D1
Vineries Bank NW7 ... 28 B5

Vineries Cl
Dagenham RM9 ... 81 B2
Harmondsworth UB7. 126 C6
Vineries The
Enfield EN1 ... 5 C2
Southgate N14 ... 15 C5
Viners Cl KT12 ... 194 C3
Vine St Bridge EC1.. 241 B5
Vines Ave N3 ... 29 D2
Vine Sq W14 ... 254 D1
Vine St W1 ... 249 B5
Whitechapel EC3 ... 95 D1 243 C1
Vinewood Ct E17 ... 54 B4
Vineyard Ave NW7 ... 29 A3
Vineyard Cl
Forest Hill SE6 ... 163 C3
Kingston u T KT1 ... 198 B6
Vineyard Gr N3 ... 29 D2
Vineyard Hill Rd SW19 ... 179 C6
Vineyard Path SW14 . 133 B2
Vineyard Prim Sch The TW10 ... 154 A5
Vineyard Rd TW13 ... 150 A1
Vineyard Row KT1, KT8 ... 175 C2
Vineyards The TW13. . 150 A1
Vineyard Studios 3 E7 ... 77 C1
Vineyard The TW10 ... 154 A6
Vineyard Wlk EC1 ... 241 A6
Viney Ct 9 SW4 ... 159 D5
Vine Yd SE1 ... 252 B2
Viney Rd SE13 ... 141 D2
Vining St SW2, SW9 ... 138 C1
Vinlake Ave UB10 ... 60 C5
Vinson Ho N1 ... 235 D3
Vinter Ct TW17 ... 192 C4
Vintners Ct EC4 ... 252 B6
Vintry Mews 3 E17 ... 53 C5
Viola Ave
Feltham TW14 ... 150 C5
SE2 ... 124 B1
Stanwell TW19 ... 148 A3
Viola Ct HA8 ... 26 D3
Viola Sq W12 ... 111 D6
Violet Ave Enfield EN2 ... 5 B5
Hillingdon UB8 ... 82 B2
Violet Cl Cheam SM3 .. 201 A1
Hackbridge SM6 ... 203 A1
Newham E16 ... 98 C3
32 SE8 ... 141 B6
Violet Ct 2 E15 ... 76 C1
Violet Gdns CR0 ... 220 D3
Violet Hill NW8 ... 92 A5 229 A3
Violet Hill Ho NW8 .. 229 A3
Violet La CR0 ... 220 D3
Violet Rd Bromley E3 ... 97 D3
Walthamstow E17 ... 53 C3
Woodford E18 ... 37 B1
Violet St E2 ... 96 B3
Violet Terr UB8 ... 82 C2
Violette Szabo Ho 4 SE27 ... 183 B6
VIP Trad Est SE7 ... 121 C2
Virgil Pl W1 ... 237 C3
Virgil St SE1 .. 116 B3 260 D6
Virginia Cl
Beckenham BR2 ... 208 C6
New Malden KT3 ... 199 A5
Virginia Ct
Ashford TW15 ... 170 A6
7 Rotherhithe SE16. 118 D4
Virginia Ho
3 Blackwall E14 ... 120 A6
Teddington TW11 ... 175 A5
Virginia Prim Sch 48 E2 ... 95 D4
Virginia Rd
South Norwood CR7 .. 182 D2
19 Spitalfields E2 ... 95 D4
Virginia St E1 ... 118 A6
Virginia Wlk SW2 ... 160 B5
Virgo Fidelis Convent Senior Sch SE19 ... 183 B4
Virgo Fidelis Prep Sch SE19 ... 183 B4
Viridian Ct TW13 ... 149 D1
Viscount Cl N11 ... 31 B5
Viscount Ct
9 Kensington W11 ... 91 C1
Viscount Ct *continued*
1 Littleton TW15 ... 171 A3
Viscount Dr E6 ... 100 B2
Viscount Gr 3 UB5 ... 84 D4
Viscount Point 6 SW19 ... 179 C3
Viscount Rd TW19 ... 148 A3
Viscount St EC1 ... 242 A4
Viscount Way TW6 ... 127 C1
Vision Coll of Theology E9 ... 75 C2
Vista Ave EN3 ... 6 D3
Vista Bldgs 19 E3 ... 97 B4
Vista Bldg The 14 SE18 ... 122 C2
Vista Dr IG4 ... 55 D4
Vista Ho 2 SW19 ... 180 B2
Vista Hts SE23 ... 163 A4
Vista The Chingford E4 ... 20 B4
SE9 ... 165 D4
Sidcup DA14 ... 189 D5
Vista Way HA3 ... 44 A3
Vitae Apartments 7 W6 ... 112 A3
Vita Et Pax Sch N14 ... 15 B6
Vittoria Ho N1 ... 233 D5
Vittoria Prim Sch N1 ... 94 C5 234 A4
Viveash Cl UB3 ... 105 D3
Vivian Ave
Hendon NW4 ... 46 B4
Wembley HA9 ... 66 C2
Vivian Comma Cl 3 N4 ... 72 D5
Vivian Ct Finchley N12 .. 29 D5
Paddington NW6 ... 91 D5
Vivian Gdns HA9 ... 66 C3
Vivian Ho N4 ... 51 B2
Vivian Mans 1 NW4 ... 46 B4
Vivian Rd E3 ... 97 A5
Vivian Sq SE15 ... 140 B2
Vivian Way N2 ... 48 B4
Vivien Cl KT9 ... 214 A1
Vivienne Cl TW1 ... 153 D5
Voce Rd SE18 ... 145 B5
Voewood Cl KT3 ... 199 D3
Vogans Mill SE1 ... 253 D2
Vogler Ho 3 E1 ... 118 C6
Vogue Ct 8 BR1 ... 187 B2
Vollasky Ho 5 E1 ... 96 A2
Volta Cl N9 ... 18 C1
Voltaire
2 Camberwell SE5 .. 139 D4
15 Richmond TW9 ... 132 B4
Voltaire Ct 13 SW11 .. 137 A3
Voltaire Rd SW4 ... 137 D2
Voltaire Way UB3 ... 105 C6
Volt Ave NW10 ... 89 C4
Volta Way CR0 ... 204 B1
Voluntary Pl E11 ... 55 A3
Vora Ho HA0 ... 65 D2
Vorley Rd N19 ... 71 C6
Voss Ct SW16 ... 182 A4
Voss St E2 ... 96 A4
Voyager Bsns Est 10 SE16 ... 118 A3
Voyagers Cl IG11 ... 102 C1
Voysey Cl N3 ... 47 A6
Vulcan Cl E6 ... 100 C1
Vulcan Gate EN2 ... 4 C3
Vulcan Rd SE4 ... 141 B3
Vulcan Sq E14 ... 119 C2
Vulcan Terr SE4 ... 141 B3
Vulcan Way N7 ... 72 B2
Vyne Ho SM5 ... 218 D2
Vyner Ct E5 ... 74 A6
Vyner Rd W3 ... 111 B6
Vyners Sch UB10 ... 60 B4
Vyner St E2 ... 96 B6
Vyners Way UB10 ... 60 C3
Vyne The DA7 ... 147 D2
Vyvyan Ho SE18 ... 144 C4

W

Wadbrook St KT1 ... 175 D1
Wadcroft Ct SE4 ... 141 B2
Waddesdon Lo HA3 ... 43 A3
Wadding St SE17 ... 117 B2 262 C3
Waddington Cl EN1 ... 5 C1
Waddington Rd E15 ... 76 B2
Waddington St E15 ... 76 B2
Waddington Way SE19 ... 183 B2
WADDON ... 220 C4
Waddon Cl CR0 ... 220 C5
Waddon Court Rd CR0 ... 220 C5
Waddon Inf Sch CR9 ... 220 C3
Waddon Marsh Sta CR0 ... 220 C6
Waddon Marsh Way CR0 ... 204 B1
Waddon New Rd CR0 ... 220 D6
Waddon Park Ave CR0 ... 220 C5
Waddon Rd CR0 ... 220 D5
Waddon Sta CR0 ... 220 C4
Waddon Way CR0, CR2, CR9 ... 220 D2
Wade Ct
Muswell Hill N10 ... 31 B3
Wembley HA0 ... 65 D5
Wade Ho
16 Bermondsey SE1 ... 118 A4
1 Enfield EN1 ... 17 C6
Wade's Gr N21 ... 16 C4
Wade's Hill N21 ... 16 C4
Wade's La TW11 ... 175 A5
Wadeson St E2 ... 96 B5
Wade's Pl E14 ... 119 D6
Wadeville Ave RM6 ... 59 B2
Wadeville Cl DA17 ... 125 C1
Wadham Ave E17 ... 35 D3
Wadham Cl TW17 ... 193 A2
Wadham Gdns
Greenford UB6 ... 64 B2
Primrose Hill NW3 ... 92 C6 230 A6
Wadham Ho N18 ... 33 D5
Wadham Rd
Chingford E4 ... 36 A2
Highams Pk E17 ... 35 D2
Putney SW15 ... 135 A1
Wadhurst Cl SE20 ... 184 B1
Wadhurst Ct E6 ... 100 C5
Wadhurst Rd W4 ... 111 B3
Wadley Rd E11 ... 54 C2
Wadsworth Bsns Ctr UB6 ... 87 C5
Wadsworth Cl
Enfield EN3 ... 18 D6
Wembley UB6 ... 87 C5
Wadsworth Ct E10 ... 54 A3
Wadsworth Rd UB6 ... 87 C5
Wager St E3 ... 97 B3
Waggoners Rdbt TW5 ... 128 B4
Waggon Mews N14 ... 15 C3
Waggon Rd EN4 ... 2 B6
Waghorn Rd
Harrow HA3 ... 43 D6
Newham E13 ... 99 C6
Waghorn St SE15 ... 140 A2
Wagner St SE15 ... 140 C5
Wagon Rd EN4, EN5 ... 1 D6
Wagstaff Gdns RM9 ... 80 C1
Wagtail Cl Enfield EN1 ... 6 B4
NW9 ... 27 C1
Wagtail Wlk BR3 ... 208 A4
Waights Ct KT2 ... 176 A2
Waikato Lo IG9 ... 21 C3
Wainford Cl SW19 ... 156 D3
Wainwright Gr TW7 .. 130 B1
Wainwright Ho 3 E1 ... 118 C5
Waite Davies Rd SE12 ... 164 D4
Waitelands Ho KT3 .. 199 B5
Waite St SE15 ... 139 D6
Waithman St EC4 ... 241 C1
Wakefield Ct 4 SE26 ... 184 C4
Wakefield Gdns
Redbridge IG1 ... 56 A3
South Norwood SE19. 183 C3
Wakefield Ho
Dulwich SE22 ... 162 B3
6 Peckham SE15 ... 140 A4
Wakefield Mews WC1 ... 233 B1
Wakefield Rd
Friern Barnet N11 ... 31 D5
20 Richmond TW10 .. 153 D6
South Tottenham N15 ... 51 D4
Wakefield St
Edmonton N18 ... 34 A5
Wakefield St *continued*
Newham E6 ... 100 A6
St Pancras WC1 ... 94 A4 233 B1
Wakeford Cl
London SW4 ... 159 C6
Sidcup OP5 ... 168 D3
Wakehams Hill HA5 ... 41 B6
Wakeham St 9 N1 ... 73 B2
Wakehurst Rd SW11 158 D6
Wakeling Ct E7 ... 77 C2
Wakeling Ho 8 SE27 ... 160 D1
Wakeling La HA0 ... 65 B5
Wakeling Rd W7 ... 86 D2
Wakeling St 11 E14 ... 97 A1
Wakelin Ho
Forest Hill SE23 ... 163 A4
19 Islington N1 ... 72 D1
Wakelin Rd E15 ... 98 C5
Wakeman Ho HA8 ... 26 A6
Wakeman Rd NW10 ... 90 D4
Wakemans Hill Ave NW9 ... 45 B4
Wakering Rd IG11 ... 79 A1
Wakerley Cl 6 E6 ... 100 B1
Wakley St EC1 . 94 D4 234 C2
Walberswick St SW8 270 B3
Walbrook EC4 ... 252 C6
10 Wanstead E18 ... 55 A6
Walbrook Ct 32 N1 ... 95 C5
Walbrook Ho N9 ... 18 C2
Walbrook Wharf EC4 252 C6
Walburgh St E1 ... 96 B1
Walcorde Ave SE17 . 262 B3
Walcot Ct CR0 ... 222 A6
Walcot Gdns SE11 .. 261 A4
Walcot Ho 9 SE22 ... 139 C2
Walcot Rd EN3 ... 7 B3
Walcot Sq SE11 ... 116 C2 261 B4
Walcott St SW1 ... 259 B4
Waldair Ct E16 ... 122 D4
Waldeck Gr SE27 ... 160 D1
Waldeck Rd
Brentford W4 ... 132 C6
Ealing W13 ... 87 B1
Mortlake SW14 ... 133 A2
Tottenham N15 ... 50 D6
Waldeck Terr SW14 .. 133 A2
Waldegrave Ct
11 Barking IG11 ... 101 B6
1 Teddington TW11 .. 174 D5
Waldegrave Gdns TW1 ... 152 D1
Waldegrave Girls Sch TW2 ... 152 B1
Waldegrave Ho 5 SW15 ... 156 C6
Waldegrave Pk TW1. 174 D6
Waldegrave Rd BR1. . 210 B5
Dagenham RM8 ... 80 C6
Ealing W5 ... 110 B6
Hornsey N8 ... 50 C6
Penge SE19 ... 183 D3
Teddington TW11 ... 174 D6
Waldegrove CR0 ... 221 D5
Waldemar Ave
Ealing W13 ... 109 C5
Fulham SW6 ... 135 A3
Waldemar Avenue Mans SW6 ... 264 A1
Waldemar Rd SW19 .. 179 C5
Walden Ave BR7 ... 188 B6
Edmonton N13 ... 33 A6
Walden Cl DA17 ... 125 B1
Walden Ct SW8 ... 269 D2
Walden Gdns CR7, SW16 ... 204 B5
Walden Ho Barnet EN4 .. 2 C1
8 Clapham SW11 ... 137 A3
SW1 ... 258 B3
Walden Rd BR7 ... 188 B4
Tottenham N17 ... 33 B2
Waldenshaw Rd SE23 ... 162 C3
Walden St E1 ... 96 B1
Walden Way NW7 ... 28 D4
Waldo Cl SW4 ... 159 C6
Waldo Ind Est BR1 .. 209 D6
Waldo Pl SW19 ... 180 C3
Waldo Rd BR1 ... 209 D6
College Pk NW10 ... 90 B4
Waldorf Cl CR2 ... 220 D1
Waldorf Sch of S W London SW16 ... 159 D2
Waldram Cres SE23 .. 162 C3
Waldram Park Rd SE23 ... 162 D3
Waldram Pl 6 SE23 .. 162 C3
Waldrist Way DA18 ... 125 B4
Waldron Gdns BR2 ... 208 B6
Waldron Ho 17 SW2 .. 160 B6
Waldronhyrst CR0, CR2 ... 220 D4
Waldron Mews SW3 266 D6
Waldron Rd
Harrow HA1, HA2 ... 42 C1
Wandsworth SW18 .. 158 A1
Waldrons The CR0 ... 221 A4
Waldron's Yd HA2 ... 64 B6
Waldstock Rd SE28 .. 124 A6
Waleran Cl HA7 ... 24 D4
Walerand Rd SE13 ... 142 A3
Waleran Flats SE1 ... 263 A4
Wales Ave SM5 ... 218 C3
Wales Cl SE15 ... 140 B6
Wales Farm Rd W3 ... 89 B2
Waleton Acres SM6 .. 219 C2
Waley St 1 E1 ... 97 A2
Walfield Ave N20 ... 13 D4
Walfield Ho N20 ... 14 A4
Walford Ho 28 E1 ... 96 B1
Walford Rd N16 ... 73 C4
Walfrey Gdns RM9 ... 81 A1
Walham Ct 15 NW3 ... 70 D2
Walham Gr SW6 ... 135 C5 265 A4
WALHAM GREEN ... 135 D5
Walham Green Arc SW6 ... 265 B4
Walham Rise 1 SW19 ... 179 A4
Walham Yd SW6 ... 265 A4
Walkden Rd BR7 ... 188 C5
Walker Cl Ealing W7 ... 108 C5
East Bedfont TW14 .. 149 D4
Friern Barnet N11 ... 31 C6
Hampton TW12 ... 173 B4
Plumstead SE18 ... 123 A2
Walker Ho NW1 ... 232 C3
Walker Mews 9 SW2 ... 160 C6
Walker Prim Sch N14 . 15 D2
Walkerscroft Mead SE21 ... 161 A3
Walker's Ct W1 ... 249 C6
Walkers Lo 18 E14 ... 120 A4
Walker's Pl SW15 ... 135 A1
Walkinshaw Ct 9 N1 . 73 A1
Walks The N2 ... 48 B6
Walk The
Ashford TW16 ... 171 D3
Palmers Green N13 ... 16 C1
Walkynscroft 1 SE15 ... 140 B3
Wallace Cl SE28 ... 124 D6
Upper Halliford TW17 . 193 B5
Uxbridge UB10 ... 82 A5
Wallace Collection* W1 ... 238 A2
Wallace Cres SM5 ... 218 D3
Wallace Ct
19 Enfield EN3 ... 7 C6
NW1 ... 237 B3
Wallace Ho N7 ... 72 B2
Wallace Lo N4 ... 50 C1
Wallace Rd N1, N5 ... 73 A2
Wallasey Cres UB10 ... 60 C5
Wallbrook Bsns Ctr TW4 ... 128 B2
Wallbutton Rd SE4 ... 141 A3
Wallcote Ave NW2 ... 46 D1
Wall Ct N4 ... 50 B1
Walled Garden Cl BR3 ... 207 D5
WALLEND ... 100 C6
Wall End Ct E6 ... 100 C6
Wall End Rd E6 ... 78 C1
Waller Dr HA6 ... 22 A2
Waller Rd SE14 ... 140 D3
Wallers Cl RM9 ... 103 B6
Wallett Ct 11 NW1 ... 71 C1
Wallflower St W12 ... 111 D6
Wallgrave Rd SW5 .. 255 C3
Wallingford Ave W10 .. 90 D1
WALLINGTON ... 219 A2
Wallington Cl HA4 ... 39 A3
Wallington Ct 10 SM6 ... 219 B2
Wallington Cty Gram Sch SM6 ... 219 B5

Wallington Green SM6 219 B4
Wallington Rd IG3 57 D2
Wallington Sq [4] SM6 219 C2
Wallington Sta SM6 219 B2
Wallis Alley SE1 252 B2
Wallis Cl SW11 136 B2
Wallis Ho
[5] New Cross Gate SE14 141 A4
Ruislip HA4 39 A1
Ruislip HA4 39 B1
Wallis Rd
Hackney Wick E9 75 C2
Southall UB1 85 D1
Wallman Pl N22 32 B2
Wallorton Gdns SW14 133 B1
Wallside EC2 242 B3
Wall St N1 73 B2
Wallwood Rd E11 54 B2
Wallwood St E14 97 B2
Walmar Cl EN4 2 B4
Walmer Cl BR6 227 B4
Chingford E4 19 D2
Walmer Gdns W13 109 A4
Walmer Ho
[8] North Kensington W10 90 D1
[8] Penge SE20 184 C3
Walmer Pl W1 237 C4
Walmer Rd
North Kensington W10 90 C1
W11 113 A6 244 A5
Walmer Terr SE18 123 B2
Walmgate Rd UB6 87 B6
Walmington Fold N12 29 C4
Walm La NW2 68 C2
Walmsley Ho [1] SW16 181 C6
Walney Wlk [6] N1 73 A2
Walnut Ave UB7 104 C3
Walnut Cl Hayes UB3 105 C6
Ilford IG6 57 A5
SE8 141 B6
Wallington SM5 218 D3
Walnut Ct [2] E17 54 A5
Walnut Gdns E15 76 C3
Walnut Gr EN1 17 B6
Walnut Ho [11] E3 97 B6
Walnut Mews SM2 218 A1
Walnut Rd E10 75 D6
Walnut Tree Ave CR4 202 C6
Walnut Tree Cl
Barnes SW13 133 D4
Chislehurst BR7 189 A2
Walnut Tree Cotts SW19 179 A5
Walnut Tree Ho SW10 265 D6
Walnut Tree Rd
Brentford TW8 132 A6
Charlton TW17 171 A1
Dagenham RM8 81 A6
Greenwich SE10 120 C1
Heston TW5 129 B6
Walnut Tree Walk Prim Sch SE11 116 C2 261 A4
Walnut Tree Wlk SE11 116 C2 261 A4
Walnut Way
Buckhurst Hill IG9 21 D1
Ruislip HA4 62 C2
Walpole Ave TW9 132 B3
Walpole Cl Pinner HA5 23 C4
West Ealing W13 109 C4
Walpole Cres [10] TW11 174 D5
Walpole Ct
Ealing W5 109 D5
[7] Hammersmith W14 112 D3
South Hampstead NW6 70 A1
Twickenham TW2 152 C2
[2] Wallington SM6 219 B3
Walpole Gdns
Acton Green W4 111 A1
Twickenham TW2 152 C1
Walpole Ho
Chislehurst BR7 189 B2
East Molesey KT8 195 C4
Walpole Lo W13 109 C5
Walpole Mews NW8 229 C5
Walpole Pl
[9] Teddington TW11 174 D5
[3] Woolwich SE18 122 D2
Walpole Rd BR2 209 D4
Mitcham SW19 180 B4
South Croydon CR0 221 B6
Surbiton KT6 198 A3
Teddington TW11 174 D5
Tottenham N17 33 A1
Tottenham N17 51 A6
Twickenham TW2 152 C2
Upton E6 77 C1
Walthamstow E17 53 A5
Woodford E18 36 D2
Walpole St SW3 114 D1 257 D2
Walrond Ave HA9 66 A3
Walsham Cl SE28 124 D6
Upper Clapton N16 52 A1
Walsham Ho
New Cross Gate SE14 140 D3
SE17 262 C2
Walsham Rd
Feltham TW14 150 B4
New Cross Gate SE14 140 D3
Walsh Lodge HA4 40 B3
Walsingham NW8 229 D6
Walsingham Gdns KT19 215 D3
Walsingham Ho
Chingford E4 20 B4
Twickenham TW2 152 B2
Walsingham Lo SW13 134 A4
Walsingham Mans SW6 265 D4
Walsingham Pk BR7 189 B1
Walsingham Pl SW4, SW11 159 A5
Walsingham Rd BR5 190 B2
Ealing W13 109 A5
Enfield EN2 17 B6
Mitcham CR4 202 D4
Shacklewell E5 74 A5
Walsingham Wlk DA17 147 C6
Walter Besant Ho [20] E1 96 D4
Walter Ct [3] W3 89 A1
Walter Green Ho SE15 140 C4
Walter Ho SW10 266 C4
Walter Hurford Par [5] E12 78 C4
Walter Northcott Ho [2] NW6 69 C3
Walter Rodney Cl E12 78 B2
Walter Savill Twr [2] E17 53 C3
Walters Cl
Hayes UB3 105 D4
SE17 262 B3
Walters Ho
[3] Camberwell SE5 139 C3
Islington N1 234 D6
[10] Kennington SE17 138 D6
Walter Sickert Hall N1 235 A3
Walters Rd EN3 6 C1
Walter's Rd SE25 205 C5
Walter St
Globe Town E2 96 D4
[2] Kingston u T KT2 176 A2
Walters Way SE23 162 D5
Walters Yd BR1 187 A1
Walter Taylor Ct SE4 141 B1
Walter Terr E1 96 D1
Walterton Rd W9 91 C3
Walter Wlk HA8 27 A4
Waltham Ave
Hayes UB3 105 B3
Preston NW9 44 C3
Waltham Ct
Chingford E17 36 A2
Whetstone N20 14 B1
Waltham Dr HA8 44 C6
Waltham Forest Coll E17 35 D1
Waltham Forest Pool & Tk E17 35 D1
Waltham Gdns EN3 6 C6
Waltham Green Ct SW6 265 C3
Waltham Ho NW8 229 A6
[10] Stockwell SW9 138 B3
Waltham Park Way E17 35 C3
Waltham Pk E17 35 C2
Waltham Rd
Carshalton SM5 202 C1
Southall UB2 107 A3
WALTHAMSTOW 53 D6
Walthamstow Acad E17 35 B2
Walthamstow Ave E4 35 C3
Walthamstow Ave (North Circular Rd) E4 35 B4
Walthamstow Bsns Ctr E17 36 A1
Walthamstow Central Sta E17 53 C4
Walthamstow Marshes Country Pk E10 52 C1
Walthamstow Mkt* E17 53 C5
Walthamstow Queens Road Sta E17 53 C4
Walthamstow Sch for Girls E17 53 D5
Waltham Way E4 19 C2
Waltheof Ave N17 33 B2
Waltheof Gdns N17 33 B2
Walton Ave
Cheam SM3 217 B5
Harrow HA2 63 B4
New Malden KT3 199 D5
Wembley HA9 66 D5
Walton Bridge Rd KT12, TW17 193 C2
Walton Cl
Dollis Hill NW2 68 B6
Harrow HA1 42 B5
Lea Bridge E5 74 D5
SW8 138 A5 270 B4
Walton Croft HA1 64 C4
Walton Ct EN5 14 A6
Walton Dr
Harrow HA1 42 B5
Willesden NW10 67 B2
Walton Gdns
Acton W3 88 D2
Feltham TW13 171 D6
Wembley HA9 66 A6
Walton Gn CR0 224 A1
Walton Ho E2 243 D6
Ealing W5 109 D2
[1] Edmonton N9 34 A6
[1] Kingston u T KT2 176 A3
Upper Holloway N7 72 B5
[10] Walthamstow E17 53 D6
Wandsworth SW18 157 C5
Walton La
Oatlands Pk KT13, TW17 193 B1
Shepperton TW17 193 B2
Walton Oak Sch KT12 194 C1
WALTON-ON-THAMES 194 C2
Walton Pl SW3 257 C6
Walton Rd
East Molesey KT8, KT12 195 C5
Harrow HA1 42 B5
Little Ilford E12 78 C4
Newham E13 99 C5
Sidcup DA14 168 C1
Tottenham N15 51 D5
Walton-on-T KT12&KT8 194 D4
Walton St Enfield EN2 5 B4
SW3 114 C3 257 B5
Walton Way Acton W3 88 D2
Mitcham CR4 203 C5
Walt Whitman Cl [6] SE24 138 D1
WALWORTH 117 B1
Walworth Acad (Lower School) SE17 117 B1 262 D2
Walworth Acad (Upper School) SE17 117 C1 263 B1
Walworth Pl SE17 117 A1 262 B1
Walworth Rd SE17 117 A1 262 B2
Walwyn Ave BR1 209 D6
Wanborough Dr SW15 156 B3
Wanderer Dr IG11 102 C4
Wandle Bank
Mitcham SW19 180 B3
Wallington CR0 220 A5
Wandle Court Gdns CR0 220 A5
Wandle Ct
[4] Bedford Pk W12 111 C4
Wallington CR0 220 A5
West Ewell KT19 215 A4
Wandle Ho
[6] Catford BR1 186 B5
NW8 237 A4
Wandsworth SW18 157 D4
Wandle Ind Mus* CR4 202 D6
Wandle Lo CR0 220 A5
Wandle Lodge SM6 219 B6
Wandle Pk Sta CR0 220 C6
Wandle Rd
Croydon CR0 221 A5
Hackbridge SM6 219 B6
Morden SM4 202 B4
Upper Tooting SW17 158 C2
Wallington CR0 220 A5
Wandle Side
Hackbridge SM6 219 B5
Wallington CR0 220 B5
Wandle Tech Pk CR4 202 D2
Wandle Trad Est CR4 202 D2
Wandle Valley Sch SM5 202 C2
Wandle Way
Mitcham CR4 202 D4
Wandsworth SW18 157 D3
Wandon Rd SW6 135 D5 265 D3
WANDSWORTH 157 C5
Wandsworth Bridge Rd SW6 135 D4 265 C1
Wandsworth Common Sta SW12 158 D4
Wandsworth Common West Side SW18 158 A6
Wandsworth Gyratory SW18 157 D6
Wandsworth High St SW18 157 D6
Wandsworth Plain SW18 157 D6
Wandsworth Rd SW8 138 A5 270 A3
Wandsworth Road Sta SW4 137 C3
Wandsworth Town Sta SW18 135 D1
Wangey Rd RM6 58 D2
Wangford Ho [13] SW9 138 D1
Wanless Rd SE24 139 A2
Wanley Rd SE5 139 B1
Wanlip Rd E13 99 B3
Wansbeck Ct EN2 4 D2
Wansbeck Rd E3, E9 75 B1
Wansdown Pl SW6 135 D5 265 C4
Wansdworth Riverside Quarter Pier SW6 135 C2
Wansey St SE17 117 A2 262 B3
Wansford Rd IG8 37 C2
WANSTEAD 55 C3
Wanstead CE Prim Sch E11 55 A4
Wanstead Cl BR1 187 C1
Wanstead High Sch E11 55 C3
Wanstead Hts [8] E11 55 A4
Wanstead La IG1 56 A3
Wanstead L Ctr E11 55 C3
Wanstead Park Ave E12 77 D6
Wanstead Park Rd IG1 56 A1
Wanstead Park Sta E7 77 B4
Wanstead Pl E11 55 A4
Wanstead Rd BR1 187 C1
Wanstead Sta E11 55 B3
Wantage Rd SE12 164 D6
Wantz Rd RM10 81 D3
WAPPING 118 B5
Wapping Dock St [19] E1 118 B5
Wapping High St E1 118 B5
Wapping La E1 118 B5
Wapping Sta E1 118 C5
Wapping Wall E1 118 C5
Warbank La KT2 177 D3
Warbeck Rd W12 112 B4
Warberry Rd N22 32 B1
Warboys App KT2 176 D4
Warboys Cres E4 36 A5
Warboys Rd KT2 176 D4
Warburg Ho E2 96 A4
Warburton Cl
[6] Kingsland N1 73 C2
Stanmore HA3 24 B4
Warburton Ct
Peckham SE15 140 A2
Ruislip HA4 62 A6
Warburton Ho [5] E8 96 B6
Warburton Rd
[8] Hackney E8 96 B6
Twickenham TW2 151 D3
Warburton St [6] E8 96 B6
Warburton Terr E17 35 D1
Wardalls Ho [12] SE8 141 B6
Ward Cl CR2 221 C3
Wardell Cl NW7 27 C3
Wardell Ct N2 48 B6
Wardell Field [18] NW9 27 C2
Wardell Ho [7] SE10 142 A6
Warden Ave HA2 41 B1
Warden Rd NW5 71 A2
Wardens Field Cl [2] BR6 227 D2
Wardens Gr SE1 252 A3
Wardle St E9 74 D3
Wardley Lo E11 54 D3
Wardley St SW18 157 D4
Wardlow [8] NW5 71 B4
Wardo Ave SW6 135 A4 264 A2
Wardour Mews W1 239 B1
Wardour St W1 93 D1 239 C1
Ward Point SE11 261 A3
Ward Rd
Camden Town N19 71 C5
Mill Meads E15 98 B6
Wardrew Ct [9] EN5 14 A6
Wardrobe Pl EC4 241 D1
Wardrobe Terr EC4 251 D6
Wardrobe The [3] TW9 153 D6
Wards Cotts TW19 148 B4
Wards Rd IG2 57 B2
Wards Wharf App E16 121 D4
Ware Ct Cheam SM1 217 B4
Edgware HA8 26 A6
Wareham Cl TW3 129 D1
Wareham Ct [2] N1 73 C1
Wareham Ho SW8 270 C4
Warehouse W E16 121 B6
Waremead Rd IG2 56 D4
Ware Point Dr SE28 123 B4
Warfield Rd
East Bedfont TW14 149 C4
Hampton TW12 173 D2
Kensal Green NW10 90 D4
Warfield Yd [6] NW10 90 D4
Wargrave Ave N15 51 D3
Wargrave Ho [46] E2 95 D4
Wargrave Rd HA2 64 A5
Warham Rd
Croydon CR2 221 A3
Harringay N4 50 D4
Harrow HA3 24 D1
Warham St SE5 138 D5
Waring Cl BR6 227 D2
Waring Dr BR6 227 D2
Waring Ho [25] E2 96 A4
Waring Rd DA14 190 C4
Waring St SE27 183 A6
Warkworth Gdns TW7 131 A5
Warkworth Rd N17 33 B3
Warland Rd SE18 145 C5
Warley Ave
Dagenham RM8 59 B2
Hayes UB4 84 A1

Warley Cl E10 ... 53 B1
Warley Ho N1 ... 73 B2
Warley Rd Hayes UB4 ... 84 A2
Lower Edmonton N9 ... 18 C2
Woodford IG8 ... 37 B3
Warley St E2 ... 96 D4
Warlingham Rd CR7 204 D5
Warlock Rd W9 ... 91 C3
Warlow Cl 6 EN3 ... 7 C6
Warlters Cl N7 ... 72 A4
Warlters Rd N7 ... 72 A4
Warltersville Mans N19 ... 50 A2
Warltersville Rd N4, N8, N19 ... 50 A2
War Meml Homes W4 ... 133 B5
Warming Cl E5 ... 74 D5
Warmington Rd SE24 ... 161 A5
Warmington St 3 E13 ... 99 A3
Warminster Gdns SE25 ... 184 A1
Warminster Rd SE25 ... 184 A1
Warminster Sq SE25 . 184 A1
Warminster Way CR4 ... 181 B1
Warmsworth NW1 .. 232 A6
Warmwell Ave NW9 ... 27 C2
Warndon St SE16 ... 118 C2
Warneford Rd HA3 ... 44 A6
Warneford St E9 ... 96 B6
Warne Pl 4 DA15 ... 168 B5
Warner Ave SM3 ... 217 A6
Warner Cl
Hadley Wood EN4 ... 2 C6
Hampton TW12 ... 173 B5
Harlington UB3 ... 127 B5
Hendon NW9 ... 46 A2
Stratford E15 ... 76 C3
Warner Ct SM3 ... 217 A6
Warner Ho
1 Beckenham BR3 .. 185 D4
Harrow HA1 ... 42 B2
4 Homerton E9 ... 74 D2
Lewisham SE13 ... 141 D3
NW8 ... 229 A2
Warner Pl E2 ... 96 A4
Warner Rd
Bromley BR1 ... 186 D3
Camberwell SE5 ... 139 A4
Hornsey N8 ... 49 D5
Walthamstow E17 ... 53 A5
Warners Cl IG8 ... 37 A5
Warner St EC1 94 C3 241 A5
Warner Yd EC1 ... 241 A5
Warnford Ho SW15 .. 155 C5
Warnford Ind Est UB3 ... 105 C4
Warnford Rd BR6 ... 227 D3
Warnham WC1 ... 233 C1
Warnham Court Rd SM5 ... 218 D1
Warnham Ho 6 SW2 ... 160 B4
Warnham Rd N12 ... 30 C5
Warple Mews W3 ... 111 C4
Warple Way W3, W12 ... 111 C4
Warren Ave
Bromley BR1 ... 186 C3
Leyton E11 ... 76 B5
Mortlake SW14, TW10 ... 132 D1
Orpington BR6 ... 227 D3
South Croydon CR2 .. 222 D1
Warren Cl DA6 ... 169 C6
Esher KT10 ... 212 A4
Hayes UB4 ... 84 C2
Ponders End N9 ... 18 D4
Wembley HA9 ... 65 D6
West Norwood SE21 . 161 A4
Warren Comp Sch RM6 ... 59 B4
Warren Cres N9 ... 17 D4
Warren Ct
17 Beckenham BR3 .. 185 C3
6 Croydon CR0 ... 205 C1
6 Ealing W5 ... 87 C2
Greenwich SE7 ... 143 C6
N1 ... 234 A4

Warren Ct *continued*
Tottenham Hale N17 ... 52 A6
Warren Cutting KT2 .. 177 B3
Warrender Prim Sch HA4 ... 39 D2
Warrender Rd N19 ... 71 C4
Warrender Way HA4 .. 40 A2
Warren Dr
Greenford UB6 ... 86 A3
Ruislip HA4 ... 40 D2
Warren Dr N KT5, KT6 ... 198 D1
Warren Dr S KT5 ... 199 A1
Warren Dr The E11 ... 55 C2
Warren Farm Cotts RM6 ... 59 B5
Warren Fields HA7 ... 25 C6
Warren Gdns E15 ... 76 B3
Warren Hill IG10 ... 21 C6
Warren Ho 21 E3 ... 97 D4
Warren Jun Sch RM6 .. 59 B4
Warren La
Stanmore HA7 ... 9 A2
Woolwich SE18 ... 122 D3
Warren La Gate SE18 ... 122 D3
Warren Mews W1 ... 239 A5
Warren Park Rd SM1 ... 218 C2
Warren Pk KT2 ... 177 A4
Warren Pond Rd E4 ... 20 D4
Warren Rd
Ashford TW15 ... 171 C3
Bexleyheath DA6 ... 169 C6
Bushey WD23 ... 8 B3
Chingford E4 ... 20 A2
Croydon CR0 ... 205 D1
Hayes BR2 ... 225 A6
Ickenham UB10 ... 60 B4
Ilford IG6 ... 57 B4
Isleworth TW2 ... 152 B5
Kingston u T KT2 ... 177 A4
Leyton E10 ... 76 A5
Mitcham SW19 ... 180 C4
Sidcup DA14 ... 168 C1
Wanstead E11 ... 55 C2
Willesden NW2 ... 67 D6
Warren Rise KT3 ... 177 B2
Warren Road Prim Sch BR6 ... 227 D4
Warrens Shawe La HA8 ... 10 D2
Warren St W1 . 93 C3 239 A5
Warren Street Sta NW1 ... 93 C3 239 B6
Warren Terr RM6 ... 58 D5
Warren The
Hayes UB4 ... 84 A1
Heston TW5 ... 129 B5
Manor Pk E12 ... 78 A4
Worcester Pk KT19 .. 215 B5
Warren Way HA8 ... 26 D1
Warren Wlk 1 SE7 ... 143 C6
Warren Wood Cl BR2 ... 225 A6
Warriner Dr N9 ... 18 A1
Warriner Gdns SW11 ... 137 A4 268 A1
Warrington Cres W9 ... 92 A3 236 A6
Warrington Ct
4 Croydon CR0 ... 220 D5
13 Merton SW19 ... 179 C3
Warrington Gdns W9 ... 236 A5
Warrington Rd
Croydon CR0 ... 220 D5
Dagenham RM8 ... 81 A6
Harrow HA1 ... 42 C4
22 Richmond TW10 .. 153 D6
Warrington Sq RM8 ... 80 D6
Warrior Cl SE28 ... 123 C5
Warrior Sq E12 ... 78 C4
Warsaw Cl HA4 ... 62 B2
Warspite Ho 3 E14 . 119 D2
Warspite Rd SE18 ... 122 A3
Warton Rd E15 ... 98 A6
Warwall E6 ... 100 D1
Warwick W14 ... 113 B2 254 D3
Warwick Ave
Edgware HA8 ... 11 A1
Harrow HA2 ... 63 B4
Paddington W9 ... 92 A3 236 A5

Warwick Avenue Sta W9 ... 92 A3 236 A5
Warwick Bldg SW8 . 268 C5
Warwick Chambers W8 ... 255 A6
Warwick Cl
Bushey WD23 ... 8 C4
DA5 ... 169 B4
Hampton TW12 ... 174 A3
New Barnet EN4 ... 14 B6
Warwick Cres
Hayes UB4 ... 83 D3
Little Venice W2 ... 92 A2 236 A4
Warwick Ct
1 Beckenham BR2 .. 186 C1
Ealing W7 ... 86 D1
5 East Finchley N2 ... 48 A6
Friern Barnet N11 ... 31 D4
Harrow HA1 ... 42 C6
Merton SW19 ... 179 B2
13 New Barnet EN5 ... 13 D6
Northolt UB5 ... 63 C3
Surbiton KT6 ... 214 A6
3 Upper Clapton E5 ... 74 B6
WC1 ... 240 D3
Warwick Dene W5 ... 110 A5
Warwick Dr SW15 ... 134 B2
Warwick Gdns
Harringay N4 ... 51 A4
Ilford IG1 ... 56 D1
Thames Ditton KT7 ... 196 D4
Thornton Heath CR7 . 204 C5
W14 ... 113 B2 254 D4
Warwick Gr
Surbiton KT5 ... 198 B2
Upper Clapton E5 ... 52 B1
Warwick Ho
9 Acton W3 ... 88 C1
10 Brixton SW9 ... 138 C3
6 Kingston u T KT2 .. 176 A2
6 Putney SW15 ... 156 C4
Stoke Newington N4 ... 51 A1
5 Wimbledon SW19 . 179 A3
Warwick House St SW1 ... 249 D4
Warwick La EC4 ... 94 D1 241 D1
Warwick Lo
Brondesbury NW2 ... 69 A3
Cheam SM1 ... 217 B4
Twickenham TW2 ... 151 D1
Warwick Mans SW5 . 255 A4
Warwick Par HA7 ... 25 B1
Warwick Pas EC4 ... 241 D2
Warwick Pl
Ealing W5 ... 109 D4
Little Venice W9 ... 92 A2 236 A4
Warwick Pl N SW1 .. 259 A3
Warwick Rd
Ashford TW15 ... 170 A5
Barnet EN5 ... 1 D1
Bexley DA16 ... 146 C2
Chingford E4 ... 35 C5
Ealing W5 ... 110 A5
Edmonton N18 ... 33 D6
Enfield EN3 ... 7 B6
Friern Barnet N11 ... 31 D4
Hounslow TW4 ... 128 B2
Kingston u T KT3 ... 199 A6
Penge SE20 ... 206 B6
Plashet E12 ... 78 A3
Sidcup DA14 ... 190 B5
Southall UB2 ... 107 B3
Stratford E15 ... 76 D2
Sutton SM1 ... 218 A3
Teddington KT1 ... 175 C2
Thames Ditton KT7 ... 196 D4
Thornton Heath CR7 . 204 C6
Twickenham TW2 ... 152 C3
Walthamstow E17 ... 35 B1
Wanstead E11 ... 55 B4
West Kensington W14, SW5 ... 113 B2 254 D4
Yiewsley UB7 ... 104 A5
Warwick Row SW1 ... 115 B3 258 D6
Warwick Sch for Boys E17 ... 54 A5
Warwickshire Path SE8 ... 141 B5
Warwick Sq
Holborn EC4 ... 241 D2
Pimlico SW1. 115 C1 259 A2

Warwick Sq Mews SW1 ... 259 A3
Warwick St W1 ... 115 C6 249 B6
Warwick Terr
Leytonstone E17 ... 54 B4
SE18 ... 145 B6
Warwick Way SW1 ... 115 B2 258 D4
Warwick Yd EC1 ... 242 B5
Wasdale NW1 ... 231 D1
Washbourne Ct N9 ... 18 A2
Washbrook Ho SW2 .. 160 C5
Washington Ave E12 .. 78 B4
Washington Bldg 1 SE13 ... 141 D4
Washington Cl 45 E3 .. 97 D4
Washington Ct SW17 ... 180 D4
Washington Ho SW1 247 C1
Walthamstow E17 ... 35 B1
Washington Rd
Barnes SW13 ... 134 A5
Kingston u T KT1 ... 176 C1
North Cheam KT4 ... 200 B1
Upton E6 ... 77 C1
2 Woodford E18 ... 36 D1
Wastdale Rd SE23 ... 162 D3
Watchfield Ct 7 W4 ... 111 A1
Watcombe Cotts TW9 ... 132 C6
Watcombe Rd SE25 .. 206 B4
Waterbank Rd SE6 ... 186 A6
Waterbeach Rd RM9 .. 80 C2
Water Brook La NW4 ... 46 C4
Watercress Pl 12 N1 .. 73 C1
Waterdale Rd SE2 ... 146 A6
Waterden Rd E15 ... 75 C2
Waterer Ho 7 SE6 ... 186 A6
Waterer Rise SM6 ... 219 D2
Waterfall Cl N14 ... 15 C1
Waterfall Cotts SW19 ... 180 B4
Waterfall Rd
Mitcham SW19 ... 180 B4
New Southgate N11, N14 ... 15 C1
Waterfall Terr SW17 .. 180 C4
Waterfield Cl
Belvedere DA17 ... 125 C3
Woolwich SE28 ... 124 B5
Waterfield Gdns SE25 ... 205 C4
Waterford Ct 16 W13 ... 109 A5
Waterford Rd SW6 ... 135 D5 265 C3
Waterford Way NW10 . 68 A3
Watergardens The
Kingston u T KT2 ... 177 A4
Woodford IG8 ... 37 A5
Water Gardens The W2 ... 92 C1 237 B2
Watergate EC4 ... 251 C6
Watergate Ho 5 SE18 ... 122 C2
Watergate Sch SE6 . 185 D5
Watergate St SE8 ... 141 C6
Watergate Wlk WC2. 250 B4
Water Gdns HA7 ... 25 B4
Waterglade Ctr The W5 ... 109 D6
Waterhall Ave E4 ... 36 C6
Waterhall Cl E17 ... 34 D2
Waterhead NW1 ... 232 A2
Waterhedge Mews EN1 ... 17 D6
Waterhouse Cl
Hammersmith W6 ... 112 D1
Hampstead NW3 ... 70 B3
Newham E16 ... 99 D2
Waterhouse Ct 7 TW11 ... 174 D5
Waterhouse Sq EC1. 241 A3
Wateridge Cl E14 ... 119 C3
Wateringbury Cl BR5 ... 190 B1
Water La
16 Camden Town NW1 ... 71 B1
Edmonton N9 ... 18 B4
Ilford IG3 ... 79 D5
Richmond TW10, TW9 ... 153 D6
SE14 ... 140 C5

Water La *continued*
Sidcup DA14 ... 169 B2
Stratford E15 ... 76 C2
Teddington KT1 ... 175 D2
Twickenham TW1 ... 153 A3
Water Lane Ho 29 TW10 ... 153 D6
Water Lily Cl UB2 ... 108 A4
Waterloo Bridge SE1, WC2 ... 116 B6 250 D5
Waterloo Cl
East Bedfont TW14 .. 149 D3
Hackney E9 ... 74 C3
Waterloo Ct 4 HA0 ... 66 A2
Waterloo East Sta SE1 ... 116 C5 251 B3
Waterloo Gdns
26 Islington N1 ... 72 D1
South Hackney E2 ... 96 C5
Waterloo Millennium Pier SE1 ... 250 C2
Waterloo Pl
Kew TW9 ... 132 C6
9 Richmond TW9 ... 132 A1
SW1 ... 115 D5 249 C4
Waterloo Rd
Dollis Hill NW2 ... 68 A6
Forest Gate E7 ... 76 D3
SE1 ... 116 C4 251 B2
Sutton SM1 ... 218 B3
Upton E6 ... 77 C1
Walthamstow E10 ... 53 C2
Waterloo Sta SE1 ... 116 C4 251 A2
Waterloo Terr N1 ... 72 D1
Waterlow Ct NW11 ... 47 D2
Waterlow Rd N19 ... 49 C1
Waterman Bldg 2 E14 ... 119 C4
Watermans Arts Ctr* TW8 ... 132 A6
Watermans Ct
12 Brentford TW8 ... 131 D6
2 Brentford TW8 ... 132 A6
Watermans Mews 1 W5 ... 110 A6
Waterman St SW15 . 134 D2
Waterman Way E1 ... 118 B5
Watermark Ct RM6 ... 58 B3
Watermead TW14 ... 149 C3
Watermead Ho E9 ... 75 B3
Watermead La CR4 . 202 D2
Watermeadow La SW6 ... 136 A3
Watermead Rd SE6 .. 186 A6
Watermead Way N17 .. 34 B1
Watermen's Sq 1 SE20 ... 184 C3
Water Mews SE15 ... 140 C1
Watermill Bsns Ctr EN3 ... 7 B3
Watermill Cl TW10 ... 153 C1
Watermill Ct SE13 .. 141 D2
Watermill La N18 ... 33 C5
Watermill Way SW19 ... 180 A2
Water Mill Way TW13 ... 151 C2
Watermint Quay N16 .. 52 A2
Water Rd HA0 ... 88 B6
Watersedge KT19 ... 215 A4
Water's Edge SW6 ... 134 C4
Watersfield Way HA8 . 26 A3
Waters Gdns RM10 ... 81 C3
Watershipdown Ho 4 E11 ... 54 D2
Waterside
11 Beckenham BR3 .. 185 C2
N1 ... 235 A3
Walthamstow E17 ... 52 C3
Waterside Ave BR3 .. 207 D4
Waterside Bsns Ctr TW7 ... 131 B1
Waterside Cl
Barking IG11 ... 80 A4
30 Bermondsey SE16 118 A4
Northolt UB5 ... 85 B4
Old Ford E3 ... 97 B6
Surbiton KT6 ... 214 A6
Woolwich SE28 ... 123 D5
Waterside Ct
3 Hackbridge SM6 .. 219 A5
Lewisham SE13 ... 142 B1
Waterside Dr KT12 ... 194 B4
Waterside Pl NW1 .. 231 B6

Waterside Point SW11 . . . . 267 B4
Waterside Prim Sch SE18. . . . . .123 B1
Waterside Rd UB2 . . .107 C3
Waterside Trad Ctr W7. . . . . 108 C3
Waterside Way SW17 . . . . .180 A5
Watersmeet Way SE28. . . . . 102 D1
Waterson St E2. . . . . . .95 D4
Waters Pl SW15. . . . . . .134 C3
Watersplash Cl KT1. .198 A6
Watersplash La
Hayes UB3. . . . . 106 A2
Southall TW5 . . . . .106 B1
Watersplash Rd
Littleton TW17 . . . . . . 192 C5
Littleton TW17 . . . . . . 192 C6
Waters Rd
Catford SE6 . . . . 164 C1
Kingston u T KT1 . . . . 176 D1
Waters Sq KT1. . . . . . 198 D6
Water St WC2. . . . . . . 251 A6
Water Tower Cl UB8. . .60 A3
Water Tower Hill CR0. . . . . .221 B4
Water Tower Pl N1 . . 234 C5
Water View Cl DA6 . . 168 D6
Waterview Ho 13 E14 .97 A2
Waterville Lo 6 N12. .30 A5
Waterway Ave 2 SE13. . . . . 141 D2
Waterways Bsns Ctr EN3 . . . . .7 C5
Waterworks Cnr E17. .36 C1
Waterworks Ctr★ E10. . . . . .75 A6
Waterworks La E5 . . . .74 D6
Waterworks Nature Reserve E10 . . . . .75 A6
Waterworks Rd SW2. . . . . .160 B5
Waterworks Yd 4 CR0. . . . . .221 A5
Watery La DA14. . . . . .190 B4
Hayes UB3. . . . . .105 B1
Merton SW19, SW20. .179 B1
Northolt UB5 . . . . .84 C5
Wates Way CR4 . . . . . 202 D3
Wateville Rd N17 . . . . .33 A2
Watford Cl SW11. . . . . 267 B2
Watford Rd
Elstree WD6. . . . . .9 C5
Harrow HA1. . . . . .43 A1
Newham E16 . . . . .99 A2
Northwood HA6. . . . . . .22 A4
Sudbury HA0, HA1 . . . . .65 B4
Watford Way NW4 . . . .46 A5
Watford Way (Barnet By-Pass) NW9 . . . . .27 D3
Watkin Mews 18 EN3. . .7 C6
Watkin Rd HA9 . . . . . . .66 D5
Watkins Ho
11 Cubitt Town E14 . . 120 A4
Harrow HA1. . . . . .42 D4
Watkinson Rd N7 . . . . .72 B2
Watling Ave HA8. . . . . .27 B2
Watling Ct EC4 . . . . . 242 B1
1 Elstree WD6 . . . . .9 D5
Watling Farm Cl HA7, WD6. . . . . .9 C3
Watling Gate NW9. . . . .45 C5
Watling Gdns NW2. . . . .69 A2
Watling Ho 10 SE18 . .144 C6
Watlings Cl CR0 . . . . .207 A3
Watling St
Bexleyheath DA7. . . . 147 D1
4 Camberwell SE15 . 139 C6
City of London EC4 . . . . .95 A1 242 B1
Elstree WD6. . . . . .9 D6
Watlington Gr SE26 . .185 A5
Watney Cotts SW14 . .133 A2
Watney Mkt★ E1 . . . . .96 B1
Watney Rd SW14. . . . .133 A2
Watneys Rd CR4 . . . . 203 D4
Watney St E1. . . . . .96 B1
Watson Ave
Cheam SM3 . . . . 217 A6
Wallend E6. . . . . .78 C1
Watson Cl
Mitcham SW19 . . . . . 180 C3
Stoke Newington N16 . .73 B3
Watson Ho 3 SW2. . .160 A4
Watsons Lo 4 RM10 . .81 D2
Watsons Mews W1. . 237 B3
Watsons Rd N22 . . . . . .32 B2
Watson's St SE8 . . . . .141 C5
Watson St E13. . . . . . . .99 B5
Wattisfield Rd E5 . . . . .74 C5
Watts Cl N15 . . . . .51 C4
Wattsdown Cl E13 . . . .99 A6
Watts Gr E3 . . . . .97 D2
Watts Ho 6 W10. . . . . . .91 A2
Watt's La
Chislehurst BR7. . . . . 189 A2
Teddington TW11. . . . . 175 A5
Watts Rd KT7. . . . . . . .197 A2
Watts St SE15. . . . . . . 139 D4
Wapping E1 . . . . .118 B5
Wat Tyler Ho N8 . . . . . .50 A6
Wat Tyler Rd SE10. . . .142 B4
Wauthier Cl N13. . . . . .32 D5
Wavel Ct
7 Streatham SW16 . . . . 160 A1
7 Wapping E1. . . . . . . 118 C5
Wavell Dr DA15 . . . . . .167 C5
Wavell Ho N6. . . . . .49 A3
Wavel Mews
Hampstead NW6. . . . . .69 D1
Hornsey N8 . . . . .49 D5
Wavel Pl SE26 . . . . . . 183 D6
Wavendon Ave W4. . .111 B1
Waveney Ave SE15. . .140 B1
Waveney Cl 20 E1. . . .118 A5
Waveney Ho SE15. . . .140 B1
Waverley Ave
Chingford Hatch E4 . . . .35 B6
Sutton SM1 . . . . 217 D6
Tolworth KT5. . . . . . . 199 A3
Twickenham TW2, TW4 . . . . 151 C3
Walthamstow E17 . . . . .54 B6
Wembley HA9 . . . . .66 B3
Waverley Cl BR2. . . . . 209 D4
East Molesey KT8 . . . 195 C4
Hayes UB3. . . . . .105 B2
Woodford E18 . . . . .37 C1
Waverley Cres SE18. .123 B1
Waverley Ct
5 Brondesbury NW6. . . . . .69 A1
Enfield EN2 . . . . .5 A2
North Finchley N12 . . . .30 B6
W1. . . . . 238 B4
Waverley Gdns
Barking IG11 . . . . 101 C5
Ealing NW10 . . . . .88 B5
Ilford IG6. . . . . .57 B6
Newham E6 . . . . 100 A2
Northwood HA6. . . . . . .22 A2
Waverley Gr N3. . . . . . .47 A6
Waverley Ind Pk HA1. . 42 B6
Waverley Pl
Finsbury Pk N4. . . . . . . .50 D1
St John's Wood NW8 . . . . . . 92 B5 229 C4
Waverley Rd
Croydon SE25. . . . . . . .206 B6
Enfield EN2 . . . . .4 D2
Finsbury Pk N8. . . . . . . .50 A2
Harrow HA2. . . . . .41 A1
Plumstead SE18. . . . . .123 B1
Southall UB1 . . . . 107 C6
Stoneleigh KT17, KT4. .216 B3
Tottenham N17 . . . . . . .34 B3
Walthamstow E17 . . . . .54 A6
Woodford E18 . . . . .37 C2
Waverley Sch EN3 . . . . .6 C1
Waverley Way SM5. . .218 C2
Waverly Ct NW3 . . . . . .70 D2
Waverton Ho 2 E3 . . . .97 B6
Waverton Rd SW18 . .158 A4
Waverton St W1 . . . . .115 B5 248 C4
Wavertree Ct 9 SW2. . . . . .160 A3
Wavertree Rd
Streatham SW2. . . . . . .160 B3
Woodford E18 . . . . .37 A1
Waxham NW5 . . . . .70 D3
Waxlow Cres UB1. . . . .85 C1
Waxlow Ho UB4. . . . . . .84 C2
Waxlow Rd NW10. . . . . .89 B5
Waxlow Way UB5 . . . . .85 B3
Waxwell Cl HA5. . . . . . .22 D1
Waxwell La HA5 . . . . . .22 D1
Wayatt Point 1 SE28. . . . . .123 A3
Wayborne Gr HA4. . . . .39 A3
Waye Ave TW5. . . . . . .128 A4
Wayfarer Rd UB5 . . . . .85 A4
Wayfield Link SE9. . . .167 B5
Wayford St SW11 . . . .136 C3
Wayland Ave E8 . . . . . .74 A3
Wayland Ho 12 SW9. .138 C3
Waylands UB3 . . . . .83 B2
Waylands Ct IG1. . . . . .79 B4
Waylands Mead BR3. . . . . 185 D2
Waylett Ho SE11 . . . . 261 A1
Waylett Pl
Wembley HA0 . . . . .65 D4
West Norwood SE27 . 160 D1
Wayman Ct E8. . . . . . . .74 B2
Wayne Cl BR6 . . . . . . 227 D5
Waynflete Ave CR0. . 220 D5
Waynflete Sq
18 North Kensington W10 . . . . .90 D1
16 Shepherd's Bush W10 . . . . 112 D6
Waynflete St SW18. . .158 A2
Wayside
Chislehurst BR7. . . . . .189 B2
Golders Green NW11. . .47 A1
Mortlake SW14 . . . . . 155 A6
New Addington CR0. . 223 D2
Wayside Ave WD23. . . . . 8 B5
Wayside Cl N14. . . . . . .15 C5
Wayside Commercial Est IG11. . . . . 102 A5
Wayside Ct
Isleworth TW7. . . . . . 130 C3
Twickenham TW1. . . . . 153 C5
Wembley HA9 . . . . .66 C5
Wayside Gdns RM10 . .81 C3
Wayside Gr BR7, SE9. .188 B6
Wayside Mews IG2 . . .56 C4
Weald Cl
16 Bermondsey SE16 . . . . .118 B1
BR2 . . . . 226 A6
Weald Fst & Mid Schs HA3 . . . . .24 D3
Weald La HA3. . . . . . . .24 B2
Weald Rd UB10 . . . . . . .82 C5
Weald Rise HA3. . . . . . .24 D2
Weald Sq E5. . . . . .74 B6
WEALDSTONE 42 D6
Wealdstone Rd SM3. .217 B6
Weald The BR7 . . . . . .188 B4
Weald Way Hayes UB4 .83 C4
Romford RM7. . . . . .59 D3
Wealdwood Gdns HA5. . . . . .23 D4
Weale Rd E4. . . . . .20 B1
Weall Ct HA5 . . . . .41 A5
Weardale Ct EN5. . . . . . .12 C6
Weardale Gdns EN2. . . . 5 B4
Weardale Ho N4 . . . . . .51 A2
Weardale Rd SE13 . . .142 B1
Wearmouth Ho 1 E3 . .97 B2
Wear Pl 13 E2 . . . . .96 B4
Wearside Rd SE13 . . 141 D1
Weatherbury 6 W2. . . .91 C1
Weatherbury Ho 3 N19. . . . . .71 D5
Weatherill Ct SE25. . .206 B3
Weatherley Cl E3 . . . . .97 B2
Weathersfield Ct SE9. . . . . .166 B5
Weaver Cl
Newham E16 . . . . 122 D6
South Croydon CR0 . . 221 D4
Weaver Ct 2 E2 . . . . . .96 B3
Weaver Ho
12 Bethnal Green E1 . . .96 A3
1 Northolt UB5. . . . . . . .85 B3
Weavers Cl TW7 . . . . .130 C1
Weavers Ho 4 E11 . . . .55 A3
Weaver's La SE1. . . . . . . .117 C5 253 B3
Weaver St E1. . . . . .96 A3
Weavers Way
6 Camden Town NW1 . . . . .71 D1
NW1. . . . . 232 C6
Weaver Wlk SE27 . . . 182 D6
Webb Cl NW10. . . . . . . .90 C3
Webb Ct 6 SE28. . . . . .124 B6
South Acton W3 . . . . . 110 D4
Webber Cl WD6. . . . . 9 D5
Webber Ho 6 IG11 . . .78 D1
Webber Row SE1. . . . . . . 116 D4 251 C1
Webber St SE1. . . . . . . 116 D4 251 C1
Webb Est E5. . . . . .52 A2
Webb Gdns 1 E13 . . . .99 A3
Webb Ho
2 Dagenham RM10 . . .81 C5
Feltham TW13 . . . . . . 151 A1
SW8. . . . . 269 D3
Webb Pl NW10. . . . . . . .89 D4
Webb Rd SE3 . . . . 142 D6
Webbscroft Rd RM10. .81 D4
Webbs Rd UB4 . . . . .84 B4
Webb's Rd SW11. . . . . . 158 D6
Webb St SE1. . .117 C3 263 A5
Webheath 6 NW6 . . . . .69 B1
Webley Ct 22 EN3. . . . . .7 C6
Webster Gdns W5. . . 109 D5
Webster Ho 16 N16 . . .73 C3
Webster Rd
Bermondsey SE16 . . . 118 A3
Leyton E11. . . . . .76 A5
Weddell Ho 23 E1. . . . .96 D3
Wedderburn Rd
Barking IG11 . . . . 101 C6
Hampstead NW3 . . . . . .70 B3
Wedgewood Ct
1 Beckenham BR2 . . 208 D5
DA5 . . . . .169 B4
Wedgewood Ho SW1. . . . . 259 A1
Thames Ditton KT7. . . 196 D1
Wedgewood Mews W1 . . . . 239 D1
Wedgewood Wlk NW3 . . . . .69 D3
Wedgwood Ho
17 Globe Town E2 . . . . .96 D4
SE11. . . . . 261 A5
Wedgwood Way SE19. . . . . .183 A3
Wedlake St W10 . . . . . .91 A3
Wedmore Gdns N19. . .71 D6
Wedmore Mews N19. . .71 D5
Wedmore Rd UB6. . . . . .86 B4
Wedmore St N19. . . . . .71 D5
Weech Rd NW6 . . . . . . .69 C4
Weedington Rd NW5. . .71 A3
Weedon Ho W12. . . . . . .90 A1
Weekley Sq SW11. . . . .136 B2
Weeks Ho TW10. . . . . . .175 C6
Weigall Rd SE12, SE3 .143 A1
Weighhouse St W1 . . 238 B1
Weighton Rd
Harrow HA3. . . . . .24 B2
Penge SE20 . . . . .184 B1
Weihurst Ct SM1. . . . .218 C3
Weihurst Gdns SM1. . .218 B3
Weimar St SW15. . . . . .135 A2
Weirdale Ave N20. . . . .14 D2
Weir Hall Ave N18. . . . .33 B4
Weir Hall Gdns N18 . . . .33 B5
Weir Hall Rd N18 . . . . .33 B4
Weir Ho 8 SW12 . . . . .159 C4
Weir Rd Sidcup DA5 . . 169 D4
Streatham SW12. . . . . . 159 C4
Walton-on-T KT12 . . . 194 A3
Wimbledon SW18, SW19 . . . . 157 D1
Weiss Rd SW15 . . . . . 134 D2
Welbeck Ave
Grove Pk BR1. . . . . . . .187 B6
Hayes UB4. . . . . .84 B3
Sidcup DA15. . . . . 168 A3
Welbeck Cl
New Malden KT3 . . . . 199 D4
North Finchley N12 . . . .30 B5
Stoneleigh KT17. . . . . 216 A1
Welbeck Ct
Hayes UB4 . . . . .84 B3
W14. . . . . 254 C4
Welbeck Mans 10 NW6. . . . . .69 C3
Welbeck Rd
Carshalton SM1. . . . . .218 B6
Carshalton SM5. . . . . 202 C1
East Barnet EN4. . . . . . .14 C5
Harrow HA2. . . . . .41 D1
Newham E6 . . . . .99 D4
Welbeck St W1 . . . . .93 B1 238 C2
Welbeck Villas N21. . . .17 A3
Welbeck Way W1 . . . . 238 C2
Welbeck Wlk SM5. . . .202 B1
Welbourne Prim Sch 2 N17 . . . . .52 A6
Welbury Ct E8 . . . . .73 C1
Welby Ho N19 . . . . .49 D2
Welby St SE5 . . . . 138 D4
Welch Pl HA5. . . . . .22 C2
Welcome Ct E17 . . . . . .53 C2
Weldon Cl HA4 . . . . . . .62 B2
Weldon Ct
Southgate N21. . . . . . . .16 B6
St Johns SE8 . . . . 141 C3
7 Sutton SM1. . . . . . . .218 B3
Thornton Heath CR7 . 204 D4
Weldon Dr KT8 . . . . . .195 B5
Weld Pl N11. . . . . .31 B5
Welfare Rd E15 . . . . . . .76 C1
Welford Cl E5. . . . . .74 D5
Welford Ct
12 Camden Town NW1 . . . . .71 B1
7 Clapham SW8. . . . 137 C3
Welford Ho 4 UB5. . . .85 B3
Welford Pl SW19. . . . .179 A6
Welham Rd SW16, SW17 . . . . .181 B4
Welhouse Rd SM5 . . . .202 C1
Wellacre Rd HA3. . . . . .43 B3
Wellan Cl DA15, DA16. . . . . .168 B6
Welland Ct SE6 . . . . . .163 B2
Welland Gdns UB6 . . . .86 D5
Welland Ho SE15. . . . .140 C1
Welland Mews 21 E1. . . . . .118 A5
Wellands Cl BR1. . . . . .188 B1
Welland St SE10 . . . . .142 A6
Well App EN5. . . . . .12 C6
Wellbrook Rd BR6 . . .226 C4
Wellby Cl N9 . . . . .18 A3
Wellby Ct 1 E13. . . . . .99 C5
Well Cl Ruislip HA4. . . . .63 A5
Streatham SW16. . . . . .182 B6
Wellclose Sq E1 . . . . .118 A6
Wellclose St 20 E1 . . .118 A6
Well Cottage Cl E11. . .55 C2
Well Ct EC4. . . . . 242 B1
Wellday Ho 2 E9 . . . . .75 A2
Welldon Cres HA1 . . . .42 C3
Welldon Ct
Harrow HA1. . . . . .42 C4
1 West Dulwich SE21 . . . . .161 B2
Welldon Park Fst Sch HA2 . . . . .64 A4
Welldon Park Mid Sch HA2 . . . . .64 A4
Weller Ho 23 SE16 . . .118 A4
Weller Mews 6 BR2. . . . . .209 B5
Weller St SE1. . . . . . . 252 A2
Welles Ct 15 E14. . . . .119 C6
Wellesley Ave W6. . . . .112 B3
Wellesley Cl 8 SE7 . .121 C1
Wellesley Court Rd 1 CR0. . . . . .221 B6
Wellesley Cres TW2. . .152 C1
Wellesley Ct
Cheam SM3 . . . . 201 A1
St John's Wood W9 . . . . .92 A4 229 A2
Twickenham TW2. . . . 152 C1
Wellesley Gr CR0 . . . .221 B6
Wellesley Ho NW1 . . 232 C1
12 Wimbledon SW19. 179 A3
Wellesley Park Mews EN2. . . . . .4 D3
Wellesley Pl
Camden Town NW5 . . . .71 A3
NW1. . . . . 232 C1
Wellesley Rd
Croydon CR0 . . . . 205 A1
Gospel Oak NW5 . . . . . .71 A3
Gunnersbury W4 . . . . 110 D1
Harrow HA1. . . . . .42 C4
Ilford IG1. . . . . .57 A1
Sutton SM2 . . . . 218 A2
Twickenham TW2. . . . 152 C1
Walthamstow E17 . . . . .53 C3
Wanstead E11 . . . . .55 A4
Wood Green N22 . . . . . .32 C1
Wellesley Road Sta CR0 . . . . .221 B6
Wellesley St E1. . . . . . .96 D2

Wellesley Terr
N1 95 A4 235 B2
Wellfield Ave N10 49 B6
Wellfield Rd SW16 182 B6
Wellfit St 6 SE24 138 D2
Wellgarth UB6 65 B2
Wellgarth Rd NW11 47 D1
Well Gr N20 14 B3
Wellgrove Sch N20 14 B3
Well Hall Par SE9 144 B1
Well Hall Pleasaunce★
SE9 144 A1
Well Hall Rd SE9 144 B1
Well Ho 11 N9 18 A1
Wellhouse Rd BR3 207 C5
Wellhurst Cl BR6 227 D1
WELLING 146 B2
Wellingfield Ct 1
DA16 146 A2
Welling High St
DA16 146 B2
Welling Sch DA16 146 B4
Wellings Ho UB3 106 B5
Welling Sta DA16 146 A3
Wellington
1 Grahame Pk NW9 27 D3
Hornsey N8 50 A5
Wellington Arch★
SW1 248 B2
Wellington Ave
Chingford E4 19 D2
DA15 168 A5
Edmonton N9 18 B1
Hounslow TW3, TW4 151 C6
North Cheam KT4 216 C5
Pinner HA5 23 B2
South Tottenham N15 52 A3
Wellington Bldgs
15 Bow E3 97 C4
SW1 258 B1
Wellington Cl
Kensington W11 91 C1
New Cross Gate SE14 140 D4
Walton-on-T KT12 193 D1
Wellington Cres
KT3 199 A6
Wellington Ct
Ashford TW15 170 A6
Knightsbridge SW1 247 C1
Stanwell TW19 148 A4
St John's Wood NW8 229 D3
Strand WC2 250 A6
5 Surbiton KT6 198 A3
Teddington TW12 174 B5
4 Upper Tooting
SW17 180 C4
Wandsworth SW18 158 C6
Wellington Gdns
Greenwich SE7 121 C1
Teddington TW12,
TW2 174 B6
Wellington Gr SE10 142 B5
Wellington Ho
4 Ealing W5 88 A4
18 Maitland Pk NW3 70 D2
Northolt UB5 63 C1
6 Ruislip HA4 40 C1
Stanmore HA7 9 A1
Wellington Hospl The
NW8 92 B5 229 D3
Wellington Mans
Shacklewell N16 73 D4
1 Walthamstow E10 53 C1
Wellington Mews
East Dulwich SE22 140 A1
3 Islington N7 72 B2
SE7 143 C6
Streatham SW16 159 D1
Wellington Par
DA15 168 A6
Wellington Park Est
NW2 68 A6
Wellington Pas 7
E11 55 A4
Wellington Pl
East Finchley N2 48 C4
St John's Wood
NW8 92 B4 229 D2
Wellington Prim Sch
20 Bow E3 97 C4
Chingford E4 19 D2
Hounslow TW3 129 B3

Wellington Rd
Ashford TW15 170 A5
Bexley DA5 168 D6
Brentford W5 109 C3
Bromley BR2 209 C5
Enfield EN1 17 C6
Erith DA17 125 B1
Harrow HA3 42 C6
Hatton TW14 149 C6
Kensal Green NW10 90 D4
Leyton E7 76 D4
Newham E6 100 B5
Pinner HA5 23 B2
St John's Wood
NW8 92 B5 229 D3
Teddington TW12,
TW2 174 B6
Thornton Heath CR0 204 D2
Walthamstow E10 53 A1
Walthamstow E17 53 A5
Wanstead E11 55 A4
Wimbledon SW19 157 C2
Wellington Rd N
TW4 129 B2
Wellington Rd S
TW4 151 B6
Wellington Row E2 96 A4
Wellington Sq
Islington N1 233 B6
SW3 114 D1 257 C2
Wellington St
WC2 116 B6 250 C6
Woolwich SE18 122 C2
Wellington Terr
Harrow HA1 42 B1
2 Wapping E1 118 B5
Wellington Way E3 97 C4
Welling Way DA16 145 B2
Well La SW14 155 A6
Wellmead IG3 58 A2
Wellmeadow Rd
Brentford W7 109 A2
Catford SE13, SE6 164 C3
Wellow Wlk SM5 202 B1
Well Rd Barnet EN5 12 C6
Vale of Health NW3 70 B5
Wells Cl
2 Northolt UB5 84 C4
South Croydon CR2 221 C3
Wells Ct
21 Hampstead NW3 70 A4
4 Mitcham CR4 180 C2
1 Paddington NW6 91 C5
Stoke Newington N1 73 C3
Wells Dr NW9 45 B1
Wells Gdns
Dagenham RM10 81 D3
Redbridge IG1 56 A2
Wells Ho
4 Barking IG11 80 A1
Ealing W5 109 D6
Finsbury EC1 234 C2
12 Kensal Town W10 91 A3
New Cross Gate SE4 141 A3
Plaistow BR1 187 B5
9 Rotherhithe SE16 118 C3
Wells Ho The 2 NW3 70 B4
Wells House Rd
NW10 89 C2
Wellside Gdns
SW14 155 A6
Wells Mews W1 239 B2
Wellsmoor Gdns
BR1 210 C6
Wells Park Ct SE26 184 B6
Wells Park Rd SE26 184 B6
Wells Pl SW18 158 A4
Wells Prim Sch IG8 37 A6
Wellspring Cres HA9 66 D5
Wells Rd BR1 188 B1
Hammersmith W12 112 C4
Wells Rise
NW8 92 D6 230 C5
Wells Sq WC1 233 D1
Wells St W1 93 C1 239 B2
Well St Hackney E9 74 C1
Stratford E15 76 C2
Wellstead Ave N9 18 D4
Wellstead Rd E6 100 C5
Wells Terr N4 72 C6
Wells The N14 15 D4
Wells Way
Brompton
SW7 114 B3 256 C6
Camberwell SE5 139 C6
Well Wlk NW3 70 B5

Wellwood Ct SW15 134 C1
Wellwood Rd IG3 58 A2
Welmar Works SW4 137 D1
Welsby Ct W5 87 C2
Welsford St SE1 118 A2
Welsh Cl E13 99 A4
Welsh Harp Field Centre
NW9 45 B1
Welsh Ho 14 E1 118 B5
Welshpool Ho 22 E8 96 A6
Welshpool St 1 E8 96 B6
Welshside NW9 45 C3
Welshside Wlk NW9 45 C3
Welstead Ho 29 E1 96 B1
Welstead Way W4 111 D2
Weltje Rd W6 112 A1
Welton Ct SE5 139 C4
Welton Ho E1 96 D2
Welton Rd SE18 145 C5
Welwyn Ave TW14 149 D5
Welwyn St E2 96 C4
Welwyn Way UB4 83 C3
WEMBLEY 65 D2
Wembley HA0 65 D2
Wembley Arena HA9 66 C4
Wembley Central Sta
HA9 66 A3
Wembley Commercial
Ctr HA9 65 D6
Wembley Conference Ctr
HA9 66 C4
Wembley Exhibition
Halls HA9 66 C4
Wembley High Tech Coll
HA0 65 C5
Wembley Hill Rd HA9 66 B4
Wembley Mkt
1 Wembley HA0 66 A3
1 Wembley Pk HA9 66 C4
WEMBLEY PARK 66 C5
Wembley Park Bsns Ctr
Wembley HA9 66 C5
Wembley HA9 66 D5
Wembley Park Dr
HA9 66 B5
Wembley Park Sta
HA9 66 C5
Wembley Prim Sch
HA9 66 A5
Wembley Rd TW12 173 C2
Wembley Stadium
HA9 66 C3
Wembley Stadium Ind
Est HA9 66 D4
Wembley Stadium Sta
HA9 66 B3
Wembley Way HA9 66 D2
Wemborough Rd
HA7 25 C3
Wembury Mews N6 49 C2
Wembury Rd N6 49 B2
Wemyss Rd SE3 142 D3
Wendela Ct HA1 64 C6
Wendell Park Prim Sch
W12 111 D4
Wendell Rd W12 111 D4
Wenderholme CR2 221 B3
Wendle Ct SW8 270 A5
Wendling NW5 70 D3
Wendling Rd SM1 218 B6
Wendon Ct 13 SM6 219 C2
Wendon St E3 97 B6
Wendover
SE17 117 C1 263 A1
Wendover Cl UB4 85 A3
Wendover Ct
Acton W3 88 D3
Becontree W3 89 A3
Bromley BR2 209 B6
4 Child's Hill NW2 69 C5
W1 238 A3
Wendover Dr KT3 199 D3
Wendover Ho
Bowes Pk N22 32 B5
W1 238 A3
Wendover Lo NW9 45 D3
Wendover Rd
Blackheath SE9 143 D2
Bromley BR1, BR2 209 B6
Dagenham NW10 89 D5
Wendover Way
Bexley DA16 146 A1
Bushey WD23 8 A5
Wendy Cl EN1 17 D5
Wendy Ho 3 N12 30 B5
Wendy Way HA0 88 A6

Wengham Ho W12 112 A6
Wenham Ho SW8 269 A3
Wenlake Ho EC1 242 A6
Wenlock Ct N1 235 D3
Wenlock Gdns 13
NW4 46 A5
Wenlock Rd
Burnt Oak HA8 27 A4
Shoreditch N1 95 A5 235 B3
Wenlock St
N1 95 B5 235 C3
Wennington Rd E3 96 D5
Wensdale Ho E5 74 A6
Wensley Ave IG8 37 A3
Wensley Cl
6 Barnet N11 31 A4
SE9 166 B5
Wensleydale Gdns
TW12 173 D3
Wensleydale Ho 8
N4 51 A2
Wensleydale Rd
TW12 173 D3
Wensley Rd N18 34 B4
Wentland Cl SE6 164 B2
Wentland Rd SE6 164 B2
Wentway Ct W13 87 A3
Wentwood Ho 1 E5 74 B6
Wentworth Ave
Borehamwood WD6 10 B6
Finchley N3 29 C3
Wentworth Cl
Ashford TW15 170 D6
Finchley N3 29 D3
Hayes BR2 225 A6
Long Ditton KT6 213 D6
Morden SM4 201 C2
Orpington BR6 227 C3
Thamesmead SE28 102 D1
Wentworth Cres
Hayes UB3 105 B3
SE15 140 A5
Wentworth Ct
Barnet EN5 1 A2
7 Chingford E4 36 B5
20 Kingston u T KT6 198 A4
Southall UB2 106 C2
2 Surbiton KT6 214 A6
Twickenham TW2 152 C1
W6 264 A5
Wandsworth SW18 157 D5
Wentworth Dr
Pinner HA5 40 A4
South Oxhey WD19 22 D5
Wentworth Dwellings
E1 243 C2
Wentworth Gdns N13 16 D1
Wentworth Hall NW7 28 C5
Wentworth Hill HA9 44 B1
Wentworth Ho
Enfield EN1 17 C5
4 Greenwich SE3 143 A5
Wentworth Lo N3 29 D3
Wentworth Mews E3 97 B4
Wentworth Pk N3 29 D3
Wentworth Pl HA7 25 B4
Wentworth Rd
Manor Pk E12 77 D4
Southall UB2 106 D2
Temple Fortune NW11 47 B3
Thornton Heath CR0 204 C2
Wentworth St
E1 95 D2 243 D3
Wentworth Tutorial Coll
NW11 46 D3
Wentworth Way HA5 41 A5
Wenvoe Ave DA7 147 D3
Wepham Cl UB4 84 D2
Wernbrook St SE18 145 A6
Werndee Rd SE25 206 A5
Werneth Hall Rd IG5 56 C6
Werrington St
NW1 93 C5 232 B3
Werter Rd SW15 135 A1
Wesleyan Pl NW5 71 B4
Wesley Ave
Becontree NW10 89 B4
Hounslow TW3 129 B3
Newham E16 121 B5
Wesley Cl
Finsbury Pk N7 72 B6
Harrow HA2 64 A6
SE17 261 D3
Wesley Ct W1 238 B3
Wesley Ho SE24 161 B5

Wesley Rd
Becontree NW10 89 A6
Finchley N10 30 C2
Hayes UB3 84 A1
Leytonstone E10 54 A2
Wesley Sq W11 91 A1
Wesley St W1 238 B3
Wessex Ave SW19 201 C6
Wessex Cl
Hinchley Wood KT10,
KT7 212 D6
Ilford IG3 57 C3
Kingston u T KT1, KT2 176 D2
Wessex Ct
Putney SW15 156 D6
5 Stanwell TW19 148 A5
Wembley HA9 66 B6
Wessex Dr HA5 23 A3
Wessex Gardens Prim
Sch NW11 47 A1
Wessex Gdns NW11 47 A1
Wessex Ho SE1 263 D1
4 Tufnell Pk N19 71 D5
Wessex La UB6 86 B5
Wessex St E2 96 C4
Wessex Way NW11 47 A1
Wesson Ho 3 CR0 206 A1
West 12 Sh Ctr W12 112 D4
Westacott UB4 83 C2
Westacott Cl N19 49 D1
WEST ACTON 88 C1
West Acton Prim Sch
W3 88 D1
West Acton Sta W3 88 C1
West App BR5 211 A4
West Arbour St E1 96 D1
West Ave
East Finchley N2 47 D6
Finchley N3 29 C4
Hayes UB3 105 D6
Hendon NW4 46 D4
Pinner HA5 41 B2
Southall UB1 107 B6
Wallington SM6 220 A3
Walthamstow E17 53 D4
West Avenue Rd E17 53 D5
West Bank
Barking IG11 100 D6
Enfield EN2 5 A3
Stamford Hill N16 51 C2
Westbank Rd TW12 174 A4
WEST BARNES 200 C4
West Barnes La KT3,
SW20 200 B5
WEST BEDFONT 148 B4
Westbeech Rd N22 50 C6
Westbere Ct HA7 25 D5
Westbere Dr HA7 25 D5
Westbere Rd NW2 69 A3
West Block 18 E1 118 C6
Westbourne Ave
Cheam SM3 217 A6
Dagenham W3 89 B1
Westbourne Cl UB4 84 C3
Westbourne Cres
W2 246 C6
Westbourne Ct
Cheam SM3 217 A6
W2 236 A2
Westbourne Dr
SE23 162 D2
Westbourne Gdns
W2 91 D1
Westbourne Gr
Notting Hill W2, W11 91 C1
W11 113 B6 244 D6
WESTBOURNE
GREEN 91 D3
Westbourne Gr Mews 7
W11 91 C1
Westbourne Gr Terr
W2 91 D1
Westbourne Ho
Heston TW5 129 C6
SW1 258 C2
8 Twickenham TW1 153 B4
Westbourne Par 4
UB10 82 D3
Westbourne Park Rd
Notting Hill W2 91 C1
Notting Hill W11 91 B1
Westbourne Park Sta
W11 91 B2
Westbourne Park Villas
W2 91 D2
Westbourne Pl N9 18 B1

Westbourne Prim Sch
SM1 . . . . **217** C5
Westbourne Rd
Barnsbury N7 . . . . **72** B2
Croydon CR0 . . . . **205** D3
DA7 . . . . **147** A5
Feltham TW13 . . . . . . **149** D1
Hillingdon UB8 . . . . **82** D3
Penge SE20 . . . . **184** D4
Westbourne St
W2 . . . . **114** B6 **246** C6
Westbourne Terr
W2 . . . . **92** A1 **236** B2
Westbourne Terrace
Mews W2 . . . . **236** A2
Westbourne Terrace Rd
W2 . . . . **92** A2 **236** A3
Westbridge Cl W12 . . **112** A5
Westbridge Prim Sch
SW11 . . . . **267** A2
Westbridge Rd
SW11 . . . . . . **136** C4 **267** A2
WEST BROMPTON . **135** D6
West Brompton Sta
SW5 . . . . **113** C1 **255** B1
Westbrook Ave
TW12 . . . . **173** B3
Westbrook Cl EN4 . . . . . **2** B2
Westbrook Cres EN4 . . . **2** B2
Westbrook Ct SE3 . . . **143** B4
Westbrooke Cres
DA16 . . . . **146** C2
Westbrooke Rd
Bexley DA16 . . . . **146** C2
DA15 . . . . **167** B2
Westbrooke Sch
DA16 . . . . **146** D2
Westbrook Ho
5 Bethnal Green E2 . . **96** C4
5 Clapham Pk SW4 . . **159** C4
Westbrook Rd
Heston TW5 . . . . **129** B5
SE3 . . . . **143** B4
South Norwood CR7 . . **183** B1
Westbrook Sq EN4 . . . . **2** B2
West Brow BR7 . . . . . **188** D5
Westbury Ave
Claygate KT10 . . . . . . **212** D2
Southall UB1 . . . . **85** C3
Tottenham N22 . . . . **32** D1
Wembley HA0 . . . . **66** A1
Westbury Cl
Ruislip HA4 . . . . **40** A2
Shepperton TW17 . . . **192** D3
Westbury Ct
1 Barking IG11 . . . . . **101** B6
Beckenham BR3 . . . . . **185** D2
1 Buckhurst Hill IG9 . . **21** C2
Clapham SW4 . . . . . . **159** B5
11 New Barnet EN5 . . . **14** A6
Tottenham N22 . . . . **33** A1
Westbury Gr N12 . . . . . **29** C4
Westbury Ho
2 Walthamstow E17 . . **53** C5
6 Willesden NW10 . . . . **67** C1
Westbury House Sch
KT3 . . . . **199** B4
Westbury La IG9 . . . . . . **21** C2
Westbury Lodge Cl
HA5 . . . . **40** D6
Westbury Pl **2** TW8 . **131** D6
Westbury Rd
Barking IG11 . . . . **101** B6
Beckenham BR3 . . . . . **207** A6
Bowes Pk N11 . . . . **32** A4
Bromley BR1 . . . . **187** D2
Buckhurst Hill IG9 . . . . **21** C2
Ealing W5 . . . . **88** A1
Feltham TW13 . . . . . . **150** D3
Finchley N12 . . . . **29** D5
Ilford IG1 . . . . **78** C6
New Malden KT3 . . . . **199** B4
Penge SE20 . . . . **184** D2
Thornton Heath CR0 . . **205** B3
Upton E7 . . . . **77** B2
Walthamstow E17 . . . . **53** C5
Wembley HA0 . . . . **66** A1
Westbury Terr E7 . . . . . **77** B2
Westbush Ct **1**
W12 . . . . **112** B4
West Carriage Dr
W2 . . . . **114** C5 **247** A6
West Central St WC1 . **240** A2
West Chantry HA3 . . . . **23** D2
Westchester Dr NW4 . . **46** D6
Westchester Dr NW4 . . **46** D6

Westchester Ho W2 . **237** C1
West Cl
Ashford TW15 . . . . . . **170** A6
Barnet EN5 . . . . **12** B6
Cockfosters EN4 . . . . . . **3** A1
Edmonton N9 . . . . **17** D1
Greenford UB6 . . . . **86** A5
Hampton TW12 . . . . . **173** A4
Wembley HA9 . . . . **44** B1
Westcliff Ho **13** N1 . . . . **73** B2
Westcombe Ave
CR0 . . . . **204** B2
Westcombe Ct **1**
SE3 . . . . **142** D5
Westcombe Dr EN5 . . **13** C6
Westcombe Hill SE3,
SE10 . . . . **143** A6
Westcombe Lodge Dr
UB4 . . . . **83** B2
Westcombe Park Rd
SE3 . . . . **142** D5
Westcombe Park Sta
SE3 . . . . **121** A1
West Common Rd
BR2 . . . . **225** B5
Westcoombe Ave
SW20 . . . . **177** D2
Westcote Rd SW16 . . **181** C5
Westcote Rise HA4 . . . **39** A2
Westcott **2** BR1 . . . . **210** A4
2 South Tottenham
N15 . . . . **51** D3
Westcott Cres W7 . . . . **86** C2
Westcott Ho **1** E14 . **119** D6
Westcott Rd SE17 . . . **138** C6
West Cotts NW6 . . . . . **69** C3
Westcroft **1** SM5 . . **219** A4
Westcroft Cl
Enfield EN3 . . . . **7** A1
West Hampstead NW2 . **69** A4
Westcroft Ct
3 Chiswick W6 . . . . **112** A2
Kingsbury NW9 . . . . . . **44** D4
Westcroft Gdns SM4 . **201** B5
Westcroft Ho **2**
SM5 . . . . **219** A4
Westcroft L Ctr SM5 . **219** A4
Westcroft Rd SM5,
SM6 . . . . **219** A4
Westcroft Way NW2 . . **69** A4
West Cromwell Rd
W14 . . . . . **113** B1 **254** D2
West Cross Ctr TW8 . **131** B6
West Cross Route W10,
W11 . . . . **112** D6
West Cross Way
TW8 . . . . **131** B6
West Croydon Sta
CR9 . . . . **205** A1
West Ct
Hounslow TW7 . . . . . . **130** A5
Sunbury TW16 . . . . . . **172** B1
1 Walthamstow E17 . . **53** D5
Wembley HA0 . . . . **65** C6
Westdale Rd SE18 . . . **144** D6
Westdean Ave SE12 . **165** C3
Westdean Cl SW18 . . **157** D5
Westdown Rd
Catford SE6 . . . . **163** C4
Leyton E15 . . . . **76** A4
West Dr Stanmore HA3 . **24** B4
Streatham SW16 . . . . **181** C6
WEST DRAYTON **104** B4
West Drayton Park Sta
UB7 . . . . **104** A4
West Drayton Prim Sch
UB8 . . . . **82** D1
West Drayton Rd
UB8 . . . . **82** D1
West Drive Gdns HA3 . **24** B4
WEST DULWICH **161** A2
West Dulwich Sta
SE21 . . . . **161** B3
West Eaton Pl SW1L . **258** A4
West Eaton Pl Mews
SW1 . . . . **258** A4
West Ella Rd NW10 . . **67** C1

West End Ave
Leytonstone E10 . . . . . . **54** B4
Pinner HA5 . . . . **40** D5
West End Cl
Stonebridge NW10 . . . . **67** A1
Willesden NW10 . . . . . . **67** A1
West End Ct
Hampstead NW6 . . . . . . **69** D1
Pinner HA5 . . . . **40** D5
West End Gdns UB5 . . **84** C5
West End La
Hampstead NW6 . . . . . . **69** D2
Harlington UB7 . . . . . **127** A5
Pinner HA5 . . . . **40** D5
West End Rd
Ruislip HA4, UB5 . . . . . **62** C5
Ruislip UB5 . . . . **62** C1
Southall UB1 . . . . **85** D5
Westerdale Ct N5 . . . . **72** D4
Westerdale Rd **2**
SE10 . . . . **121** A1
Westerfield Rd **1**
N15 . . . . **51** D4
Westergate W5 . . . . . . **88** A2
Westergate Rd SE2 . **147** A6
Westerham
13 Kingston u T
KT1 . . . . **198** A4
NW1 . . . . **232** A5
Westerham Ave N9 . . . **17** B1
Westerham Dr DA15 . **168** C5
Westerham Ho SE1 . . **263** B3
Westerham Lo **10**
BR3 . . . . **185** C3
Westerham Rd
Keston BR2 . . . . **225** D2
Walthamstow E10 . . . . **53** D2
Westerley Cres
SE26 . . . . **185** A6
Westerley Ct HA4 . . . . **62** B3
Western Ave
Hendon NW11 . . . . **46** D3
Hendon NW11 . . . . **89** B1
Hillingdon HA4, UB4, UB5,
UB10 . . . . **61** C1
Northolt UB5, UB6 . . . . **85** A6
Ruislip UB8, UB9, UB10 **60** B3
Wembley UB6 . . . . **87** C4
Western Avenue Bsns Pk
W3 . . . . **88** D2
Western Beach Apts
E16 . . . . **121** A5
Western Ct
4 Dagenham W3 . . . **89** B1
Finchley N3 . . . . **29** C4
3 Kilburn W9 . . . . . . **91** B5
Southall UB2 . . . . **107** A3
Western Dr TW17 . . . **193** B3
Western Eye Hospl TW
NW1 . . . . . . **92** D2 **237** C4
Western Gateway
E16 . . . . **121** A6
Western Gdns W5 . . . **110** C6
Western Ho **8** W9 . . . **91** B3
Western Hts SM1 . . . **217** C3
Western International
Market UB2 . . . . **106** B2
Western La SW12 . . . **159** A4
Western Mews W9 . . . **91** B3
Western Par EN5 . . . . **13** D6
Western Pl **7** SE16 . **118** C4
Western Rd
Becontree NW10 . . . . . **89** A3
Brixton SW9 . . . . **138** C2
Ealing W5 . . . . **109** D6
Fortis Green N2 . . . . . . **48** D5
Mitcham CR4, SW19 . . **180** C1
Newham E13 . . . . **99** C5
Southall UB2 . . . . **106** D2
Sutton SM1 . . . . **217** C3
Walthamstow E17 . . . . **54** A4
Wood Green N22 . . . . . **32** B1
Western Terr **1**
W6 . . . . **112** A1
WesternView UB3 . . . **105** A4
Westernville Gdns
IG2 . . . . **57** A2
Western Way
New Barnet EN5 . . . . . . **13** D5
Plumstead SE28 . . . . . **123** C4
West Ewell **2**
SE15 . . . . **140** A4
WEST EWELL **215** C1
West Ewell Inf Sch
KT19 . . . . **215** B3
West Farm Ct EN4 . . . . **2** D2
Westferry Cir E14 . . . **119** C5

Westferry Rd E14 . . . **119** C3
Westferry Sta E14 . . . **119** C6
Westfield **1** BR6 . . . **227** A3
Loughton IG10 . . . . **21** C4
West Hampstead NW3 . **69** C4
Westfield Cl
Cheam SM1 . . . . **217** B4
Enfield EN3 . . . . **7** A2
Kingsbury NW9 . . . . . . **45** A6
SW10 . . . . **266** A3
Westfield Ct
1 Kensal Green
W10 . . . . **90** D4
Kingston u T KT6 . . . **197** D4
Westfield Dr HA3 . . . . . **43** D5
Westfield Gdns
Harrow HA3 . . . . **43** D5
Ilford RM6 . . . . **58** C3
Westfield Ho **6**
SE16 . . . . **118** D2
Westfield La HA3 . . . . **43** D5
Westfield London Sh Ctr
W12 . . . . **112** D5
Westfield Pk HA5 . . . . **23** B3
Westfield Rd
Beckenham BR3 . . . . . **185** B1
Cheam SM1 . . . . **217** B4
Croydon CR0 . . . . **205** A1
Dagenham RM9 . . . . . . **81** A4
Ealing W13 . . . . **109** A5
Edgware NW7 . . . . **11** C1
Kingston u T KT6 . . . **197** D4
Mitcham CR4 . . . . **180** D1
Walton-on-T KT12 . . . **195** A2
Westfields SW13 . . . . **133** D2
Westfields Ave
SW13 . . . . **133** C2
Westfields Rd W3 . . . . **88** D2
Westfield St SE18 . . . **121** D3
Westfield Way
Mile End E1 . . . . **97** A3
Ruislip HA4 . . . . **61** D5
West Finchley Sta N3 . **29** C4
West Garden Pl W2 . **237** B1
West Gate **8** **88** A4
Westgate Bsns Ctr
2 Kensal Town W10 . **91** A3
North Kensington W10 . **90** D3
Westgate Ct
8 Beckenham BR3 . **186** A2
15 Brixton SW9 . . . . **138** C2
Lewisham SE12 . . . . . **165** A3
Westgate EstTW14 . . **148** D3
Westgate Rd
Beckenham BR3 . . . . . **186** A2
Croydon SE25 . . . . . . **206** B5
Westgate St E8 . . . . . . **96** A6
Westgate Terr
SW10 . . . . . **135** D6 **265** D6
West Gdns
Mitcham SW19 . . . . . . **180** C4
Stepney E1 . . . . **118** B6
Westglade Ct HA3 . . . **43** D4
West Gr
Lewisham SE10 . . . . . **142** B4
Woodford IG8 . . . . **37** C5
WEST GREEN **51** A5
West Green Pl UB6 . . **86** B6
West Green Prim Sch
N15 . . . . **51** A5
West Green Rd N15 . . **51** B5
Westgrove La SE10 . . **142** A4
West Grove Prim Sch
N14 . . . . **15** D4
West Halkin St
SW1 . . . . . **115** A3 **258** A6
West Hallowes SE9 . **166** A3
West Hall Rd TW9 . . . **132** D4
WEST HAM **99** B6
West Ham Church Prim
Sch **1** E15 . . . . **98** D6
West Ham La E15 . . . . **76** C1
WEST HAMPSTEAD . . **69** C4
West Hampstead Mews
NW6 . . . . **69** D2
West Hampstead Sta
NW6 . . . . **69** C2
West Hampstead
Thameslink Sta
NW6 . . . . **69** C2
West Ham Sta E15 . . . . **98** B2
West Harding St EC4 . **241** B2
WEST HARROW **42** A2
West Harrow Sta
HA1 . . . . **42** A3

West Hatch Manor
HA4 . . . . **39** D2
Westhaven Sm1 . . . . **217** C3
Westhay Gdns
SW14 . . . . **154** D6
WEST HEATH **146** D6
West Heath Ave
NW11 . . . . **47** C1
West Heath Cl NW3 . . **69** C5
West Heath Cl NW11 . **47** C1
West Heath Dr NW11 . **47** C1
West Heath Gdns
NW3 . . . . **69** C5
West Heath Rd
SE2, DA7 . . . . **146** D6
West Hampstead NW3 . **45** D3
WEST HILL **157** B5
West Hill Harrow HA2 . **64** C6
Putney SW15 . . . . **157** A5
South Croydon CR2 . . **221** C1
Wembley HA9 . . . . **44** B1
Westhill Ct W11 . . . . . **244** B6
West Hill Ct N6 . . . . . . **71** A5
West Hill Hall HA2 . . . **64** C6
West Hill Pk
Dartmouth Pk N6 . . . . . **71** A6
Highgate N6 . . . . **70** D6
West Hill Prim Sch **17**
SW18 . . . . **157** C6
West Hill Rd SW18 . . **157** B5
West Hill Way N20 . . . . **13** D3
West Ho Barking IG11 . **78** D2
4 Penge SE20 . . . . . **184** D3
9 Streatham SW12 . **159** C4
Westholm NW11 . . . . . **47** D5
Westholme BR6 . . . . . **211** D2
Westholme Gdns
HA4 . . . . **40** A1
Westhope Ho **20** E2 . . **96** A4
Westhorne Ave SE9,
SE12 . . . . **165** C5
Westhorpe Gdns
NW4 . . . . **46** C6
Westhorpe Rd SW15 . **134** C2
West House Cl
SW19 . . . . **157** A3
Westhurst Dr BR7 . . . **188** D5
West India Ave E14 . **119** C5
West India Dock Rd
E14 . . . . **119** C6
West India Ho **1**
E14 . . . . **119** C6
West India Quay Sta
E14 . . . . **119** C6
WEST
KENSINGTON **113** A2
West Kensington Ct
W14 . . . . **254** C2
West Kensington Mans
W14 . . . . **254** C1
West Kensington Sta
W14 . . . . **113** B1 **254** C2
WEST KILBURN **91** A4
West La SE16 . . . . **118** B4
Westlake **12** SE16 . . . **118** C2
Westland Ct **9** UB5 . . **84** A4
Westland Dr BR2,
BR4 . . . . **224** D6
Westland Ho **1** E16 . **122** C5
Westland Lo **1** BR1 . **187** C1
Westland Pl N1 . . . . . **235** C2
Westlands Cl UB3 . . . **106** A2
Westlands Ct KT8 . . . **196** C5
Westlands Terr **5**
SW12 . . . . **159** C5
Westlea Rd W7 . . . . . . **109** A3
West Lea Sch N9 . . . . . **17** C1
Westleigh Ave
SW15 . . . . **156** C6
Westleigh Ct
7 Finchley N12 . . . . . **29** D4
2 Wanstead E11 . . . . **55** A4
Westleigh Dr BR1 . . . **188** A2
Westleigh Gdns HA8 . **26** C1
West Links HA0 . . . . . . **87** D4
Westlinton Cl NW7 . . . **29** A4
West Lodge Ave W3 . . **110** C5

West Lodge Ct W3 110 C5
West Lodge Fst & Mid Schs HA5 40 D5
West Lodge Sch DA15 168 A1
West London Acad
Northolt UB5 63 A1
Northolt UB5 85 A6
West London Shooting Sch UB5 84 B6
Westly Ct NW2 68 D2
Westly Ho N9 18 B3
Westmacott Dr TW14 149 D3
Westmacott Ho NW8 236 D5
West Mall W11 245 B4
Westmark Point 13 SW15 156 B3
Westmead SW15 156 B5
West Mead
Ruislip HA4 62 C4
West Ewell KT19 215 C2
Westmead Cnr SM5 218 C4
Westmead Rd SM1 218 B4
Westmeath Ho NW2 68 A5
Westmere Dr NW7 11 B1
West Mersea Cl 9 E16 121 B5
West Mews SW1 259 A3
West Middlesex Univ Hosp TW7 131 A3
Westmill Ct N4 73 A6
WESTMINSTER 115 C4
Westminster Abbey★ SW1 116 A3 260 A6
Westminster Abbey Choir Sch SW1 115 D3 259 D6
Westminster Acad W2 91 C2
Westminster Acad (Sch of English) W1 93 C1 239 B2
Westminster Ave CR7 182 D1
Westminster Boating Base SW1 269 C6
Westminster Bridge SE1, SW1 116 A4 250 B1
Westminster Bridge Rd SE1 116 B4 250 C1
Westminster Cath★ SW1 115 C3 259 A5
Westminster Cath Choir Sch SW1 115 C2 259 B4
Westminster Cath RC Prim Sch SW1 115 D1 259 D2
Westminster City Hall SW1 259 B6
Westminster City Sch SW1 259 B6
Westminster Cl
East Bedfont TW14 150 A3
Teddington TW11 175 A5
Westminster Coll W1 115 D6 249 C6
Westminster Ct
22 Rotherhithe SE16 118 D5
South Norwood CR7 183 A1
5 Wandsworth SW18 157 C6
Wanstead E11 55 B3
Westminster Dr N13 32 A5
Westminster Dragoons Mus★ SW6 135 A2
Westminster Gdns
Barking IG11 101 C5
Chingford E4 20 C3
SW1 260 A4
Westminster Ind Est SE18 121 D3
Westminster Kingsway Coll (King's Cross Centre) WC1 94 B4 233 C1
Westminster Kingsway Coll (Regent's Park Ctr) NW1 93 C3 239 A6
Westminster Kingsway Coll (Victoria Centre) SW1 115 D2 259 C4
Westminster Pier SW1 250 B1
Westminster Rd
Carshalton SM1 218 B6
Ealing W7 108 C5
Edmonton N9 18 B3
Westminster Sch SW1 116 A3 260 A6
Westminster Sta SW1 116 A4 250 B1
Westminster Under Sch SW1 115 D2 259 C3
Westmoat Cl BR3 186 A3
WEST MOLESEY 195 C5
Westmont Rd KT10 212 C6
Westmoor Gdns EN3 6 D3
Westmoor Rd EN3 6 D3
Westmoor St SE7 121 D3
Westmore Ct SW15 157 A6
Westmoreland Ave DA16 145 C1
Westmoreland Dr SM2 217 D1
Westmoreland Ho NW10 90 A4
Westmoreland Pl
5 Bromley BR1 209 A6
Ealing W5 87 D2
Pimlico SW1 258 D1
Westmoreland Rd
Barnes SW13 134 A4
Beckenham BR2, BR3 208 D5
Bromley BR2 209 A5
Camberwell SE17 139 B6
Queensbury NW9 44 B5
Westmoreland St W1 238 B3
Westmoreland Terr
10 Penge SE20 184 B3
SW1 115 B1 258 D1
Westmorland Cl
3 Twickenham TW1 153 B5
Wanstead E12 77 D6
Westmorland Ct
12 Surbiton KT6 197 D2
Sutton SM1 218 A5
Westmorland Rd
BR2 209 A5
Harrow HA1 41 D4
Walthamstow E17 53 C3
Westmorland Way CR4 203 D4
Westmount Ct W5 88 B2
Westmount Rd SE9 144 C1
WEST NORWOOD 161 A1
West Norwood Sta SE27 160 D1
West Oak BR3 186 B2
Westoe Rd N9 18 B2
Weston A?e
East Molesey KT8 195 B5
Thames Ditton KT10, KT7 196 C2
Westonbirt Ct 6 SE15 139 D6
Weston Ct
Highbury N4 73 A5
3 Kingston u T KT1 198 A6
Oakleigh Pk N20 14 A4
Weston Dr HA7 25 B2
West One Ho W1 239 A3
Westone Mans 6 IG11 79 D1
West One Sh Ctr W1 93 B1 238 C1
Weston Gdns TW7 130 C4
Weston Gn
Dagenham RM9 81 B4
Thames Ditton KT7 196 C1
Weston Gr 1 BR1 186 D2
WESTON GREEN 196 D1
Weston Green Rd KT7 196 C2
Weston Green Sch KT7 196 C1
Weston Ho
6 Brondesbury NW6 69 A1
8 South Hackney E9 96 C6
Weston Lo KT7 196 D1
Weston Park Cl KT7 196 C1
Weston Park Prim Sch N8 50 B4
Weston Pk
Hornsey Vale N8 50 B3
Weston Pk *continued*
Kingston u T KT1 176 A1
Thames Ditton KT10, KT7 196 C1
Weston Rd
Acton Green W4 111 A3
Bromley BR1 186 D3
Dagenham RM9 81 A4
Enfield EN2 5 B3
Thames Ditton KT7 196 C1
Weston Rise N1, WC1 94 B4 233 D2
Weston St SE1 117 B4 252 D2
Weston Wlk 3 E8, E9 74 B1
Westover Hill NW3 69 C6
Westover Rd SW18 158 A5
Westow Hill SE19 183 D4
Westow St SE19 183 C4
Westpark W5 87 D1
West Park Ave TW9 132 D4
West Park Cl
Heston TW5 129 B6
Ilford RM6 58 D4
West Park Rd
Richmond TW9 132 C4
Southall UB2 108 B5
West Parkside
Greenwich SE10 120 D3
Greenwich SE10 121 A2
West Pk SE9 166 A3
West Pl SW19 178 C5
West Plaza E14 119 D5
Westpoint
Beckenham BR2 208 B6
Putney SW15 156 D5
West Point 2 SE1 118 A1
Westpoint Apartments N8 50 B5
Westpoint Trad Est W3 88 D2
Westpole Ave EN4 3 B1
Westport Ct UB4 84 C3
Westport Rd E13 99 B3
Westport St E1 96 D1
West Poultry Ave EC1 241 C3
West Quarters W12 90 A1
West Quay Dr UB4 85 A2
West Ramp TW6 126 C4
West Rd
Chelsea SW3 136 D6 267 D6
Clapham Pk SW4 159 D6
Dagenham RM6 59 A3
Ealing W5 88 A2
East Barnet EN4 15 A3
East Bedfont TW14 149 B4
Finchley N2 30 B2
Kingston u T KT2, KT3 177 A2
Tottenham N17 34 B4
West Drayton UB7 104 B3
West Ham E15 98 D6
West Ridge Gdns UB6 86 A5
Westrow SW15 156 C5
West Row W10 91 A3
Westrow Dr IG11 80 A2
Westrow Gdns IG3 79 D5
WEST RUISLIP 61 B6
West Ruislip Ct HA4 61 B6
West Ruislip Elementary Sch UB10 61 A5
West Ruislip Sta HA4 61 A6
West Sheen Vale TW9 132 B1
Westside
11 Hammersmith W6 112 A2
Hendon NW4 28 B1
Muswell Hill N2 48 D6
West Side Comm SW19 178 C5
Westside Ct 1 W9 91 C3
West Silvertown Sta E16 121 A5
West Smithfield EC1 94 D2 241 D3
West Sq SE11 116 D3 261 C5
West St
30 Bethnal Green E2 96 B5
Bexleyheath DA7 147 B2
Bromley BR1 187 A1
Carshalton SM5 218 D4
Croydon CR0 221 A4
West St *continued*
Harrow HA1 42 C1
Leyton E11 76 C5
Soho WC2 93 D1 239 D1
Sutton SM1 217 D3
Walthamstow E17 53 D4
West Street La SM5 218 D4
West Street Pl 1 CR0 221 A4
West Surrey Est TW15 171 A2
West Sutton Sta SM1 217 C4
West Temple Sheen SW14 154 D6
West Tenter St E1 95 D1 243 D1
West Terr DA15 167 C3
West Thames Coll TW7 130 C4
West Thamesmead Bsns Pk SE28 123 D3
West Thornton Prim Sch CR0 204 B3
West Towers HA5 40 D3
West Twyford Prim Sch NW10 88 C5
Westvale Mews W3 111 C4
Westview W7 86 C1
West View
Dagenham RM6 58 C4
East Bedfont TW14 149 A4
Westview Cl
North Kensington W10 90 C1
Willesden NW10 67 D3
Westview Cres N9 17 C4
Westview Ct
3 Elstree WD6 9 D5
1 Whetstone N20 14 A2
Westview Dr IG8 37 D1
West View Gdns WD6 9 D5
Westville Rd
Shepherd's Bush W12 112 A4
Thames Ditton KT7 197 A2
Westward Rd E4 35 B5
Westward Way HA3 44 A3
West Warwick Pl SW1 259 A3
Westway
Shepherd's Bush W10, W12 112 A6
West Barnes SW20 200 C5
West Way BR5 211 B4
Burnt Oak HA8 27 A4
Croydon CR0 223 A5
Edmonton N18 33 B6
Hounslow TW5 129 B4
Neasden NW10 67 B5
Pinner HA5 40 D5
Ruislip HA4 39 D1
Shepperton TW17 193 B3
West Wickham BR4 208 C3
Westway Cl SW20 200 B6
Westway Ct UB5 85 C6
Westway (Elevated Rd) W10 91 B2
West Way Gdns CR0 222 D6
Westway Lo 35 W2 91 C2
Westways KT19 215 D4
West Ways HA6 22 A1
Westwell 4 NW5 71 A2
Westwell Rd SW16 182 A4
Westwell Road App SW16 182 A4
Westwick 7 KT1 176 C1
Westwick Gdns
Cranford TW4, TW5 128 B3
Hammersmith W14 112 D4
WEST WICKHAM 224 C6
West Wickham Sta BR3 208 A2
West Wimbledon Prim Sch SW20 200 B6
West Wlk
East Barnet EN4 15 A3
Hayes UB3 106 A5
Westwood Ave
Harrow HA2 63 D4
South Norwood SE19 183 A2
Westwood Bsns Ctr NW10 89 C3
Westwood Cl BR1 209 D6
Esher KT10 212 A5
Ruislip HA4 38 D3
Westwood Ct
Enfield EN1 17 C5
8 Forest Hill SE23 162 C3
7 Wimbledon SW19 179 B5
Westwood Gdns SW13 133 D2
Westwood Hill SE26 184 B6
Westwood Ho
6 Shepherd's Bush W12 112 C5
5 Stoke Newington N4 51 B2
Westwood La DA16 145 D1
Westwood Language College for Girls SE19 183 B3
Westwood Lo N12 30 C5
Westwood Park Trad Est W3 88 D3
Westwood Pk SE23 162 B4
Westwood Pl SE26 184 A6
Westwood Rd
Barnes SW13 133 D2
Ilford IG3 58 A2
Westwood Sch WD23 8 B2
West Woodside DA5 169 A3
Wetheral Ct SW17 180 B6
Wetheral Dr HA7 25 C1
Wetherby Cl UB5 63 D2
Wetherby Ct SE25 183 C1
Wetherby Gdns SW5 114 A2 256 A3
Wetherby Mans SW5 255 C2
Wetherby Mews SW5 255 D2
Wetherby Pl SW7 114 A2 256 B3
Wetherby Prep Sch W11 113 C6 245 A6
Wetherby Rd EN2 5 A4
Wetherby Way KT9 214 A1
Wetherden St E17 53 B2
Wetherell Rd E9 96 D6
Wetherill Rd N10 31 A2
Wevco Wharf SE15 140 B6
Wexford Ho 11 E1 96 C2
Wexford Rd SW12 158 D4
Weybourne St SW18 158 A2
Weybridge Ct 19 SE16 118 B1
Weybridge Ho N4 51 A2
Weybridge Point 11 SW11 136 D3
Weybridge Rd CR7 204 C5
Wey Ct KT19 215 A4
Weydown Cl SW19 157 A3
Weyhill Ho 26 SE5 139 A3
Weyhill Rd 11 E1 96 A1
Wey Ho
6 Northolt UB5 85 B3
NW8 236 D5
Weylands Cl KT12 195 B1
Weylond Rd RM8 81 B5
Weyman Rd SE3 143 C4
Weymarks The N17 33 B4
Weymouth Ave
Brentford W5 109 C3
Edgware NW7 27 C5
Weymouth Cl 1 E6 100 D1
Weymouth Ct
Belmont SM2 217 C1
5 Haggerston E2 95 D5
15 Streatham SW2 160 B4
Weymouth Ho
Bromley BR2 186 D1
Edgware HA8 26 B4
Fitzrovia W1 238 D4
South Lambeth SW8 270 C3
Weymouth Mews W1 93 B2 238 C4
Weymouth Rd UB4 83 C4
Weymouth St W1 93 B2 238 C4
Weymouth Terr E2 95 D5
Weymouth Wlk HA7 25 A4
Whadcoat St N4 72 C6
Whaddon Ho
10 Camberwell SE5 139 C2
SW1 247 D1
Whalebone Ave RM6 59 B3
Whalebone Gr RM6 59 B3
Whalebone La E15 76 C1
Whalebone Lane N RM6 59 A6
Whalebone Lane S RM6, RM8 59 B2

Whales Yd E15........76 C1
Wharfdale Cl N11.....31 A4
Wharfdale Rd
N1........94 A5 233 B4
Wharfedale Ct 5 E5..74 D4
Wharfedale Gdns CR7,
SW16............204 B6
Wharfedale St SW10 255 C1
Wharf La
19 Poplar E14........97 B1
Twickenham TW1.... 153 A3
Wharf Pl E2..........96 B6
Wharf Rd Enfield EN3..19 A5
King's Cross
NW1.......93 D6 232 D5
Shoreditch N1 .95 A5 235 A3
Wharf Road
NW1.........94 A5 233 A4
Wharfside HA0.......88 A6
Wharfside Rd E16.....98 C2
Wharf St E16.........98 C2
Wharf View Ct 15
E14...............98 A1
Wharncliffe Dr UB1...108 B5
Wharncliffe Gdns
SE25..............183 C1
Wharncliffe Ho 3
SW15..............156 C6
Wharncliffe Rd
SE25..............183 C1
Wharton Cl NW10.....67 C2
Wharton Ho SE1.... 263 C6
Wharton Rd BR1.....187 B2
Wharton St
WC1.........94 B4 233 D1
Whateley Rd
East Dulwich SE22... 161 D6
Penge SE20........ 184 D3
Whatley Ave SW20...201 A6
Whatman Ho 10 E14..97 B1
Whatman Rd SE23... 162 D4
Wheatcroft Ct SM1.. 201 D1
Wheatfields Enfield EN3. 7 A3
Newham E6........ 100 D1
Wheatfield Way KT1 .176 A1
Wheathill Ho SE20...184 B1
Wheathill Rd SE20...206 B6
Wheat Ho TW19......148 A3
Wheatland Ho 7
SE22..............139 C2
Wheatlands TW5....129 C6
Wheatlands Rd
SW17..............159 A1
Wheatley Cl NW4.....28 A1
Wheatley Cres UB3..106 A6
Wheatley Gdns N9....17 C2
Wheatley Ho
Gospel Oak NW5......71 B4
3 Putney SW15.... 156 A4
Wheatley Mans 8
IG11..............80 A1
Wheatley Rd TW7... 130 D2
Wheatley St W1.... 238 B3
Wheatsheaf Cl UB5...63 A3
Wheat Sheaf Cl E14. 119 D2
Wheatsheaf La
Fulham SW6........ 134 C5
SW8.............. 270 B4
Wheatsheaf Par 7
BR4.............. 207 D1
Wheatsheaf Terr
SW6.............. 264 D3
Wheatstone Cl
SW19..............180 C2
Wheatstone Ho 7
W10...............91 A2
Wheatstone Rd W10..91 A2
Wheeler 2 NW9......27 D3
Wheeler Ct 4 SW11 .136 B2
Wheeler Gdns N1... 233 B6
Wheeler La E1...... 243 C4
Wheeler Pl 2 BR2...209 B5
Wheelers Cross
IG11..............101 B5
Wheelers Dr HA4.....39 A3
Wheeler's St SM1....217 C5
Wheelhouse The 4
E14.............. 119 D1
Wheelock Cl DA8... 147 D5
Wheelwright St N7...72 B1
Whelan Way SM6... 219 D5
Wheldon Ct SE1.... 253 C2
Wheler Ho E1...... 243 C5
Wheler St E1...95 D3 243 C5
Whellock Rd W4.....111 C3
Whernside Cl SE28...124 C6
WHETSTONE........14 A2
Whetstone Cl N20....14 B2
Whetstone Park
WC2........94 B1 240 C2
Whetstone Rd SE3.. 143 D4
Whewell Rd N19......72 A6
Whichcote St SE1... 251 A3
Whidborne Bldgs
WC1.............. 233 A1
Whidborne Cl SE8...141 C3
Whidborne St WC1.. 233 B1
Whimbrel Cl SE28....124 C6
Whimbrel Way UB4...84 D2
Whinchat Rd SE18,
SE28..............123 B3
Whinfell Cl SW16... 181 D5
Whinyates Rd SE9...144 A2
Whippendell Cl BR5 .190 B2
Whippendell Way
BR5...............190 B1
Whippingham Ho 22
E3................97 B4
Whipps Cross E17...54 B4
Whipps Cross Ho E17 .54 B4
Whipps Cross Hospl E10,
E11...............54 B3
Whipps Cross Rd E11 .54 C3
Whiskin St
EC1.........94 D4 234 C1
Whisperwood Cl HA3 .24 C3
Whistler Gdns HA8....26 B1
Whistler Mews
Dagenham RM8.......80 B3
23 SE15........... 139 D5
Whistlers Ave
SW11.......136 B5 266 D3
Whistler St N5........72 D3
Whistler Twr SW10.. 266 A3
Whistler Wlk SW10 . 266 B4
Whiston Ho 18 N1....72 D1
Whiston Rd E2.......96 A6
Whitakers Lo EN2......5 B4
Whitbread Cl N17.....34 A2
Whitbread Ctr EC1.. 242 C5
Whitbread Rd SE4...141 B1
Whitburn Rd SE13...142 A1
Whitby Ave NW10.....88 D4
Whitby Ct
6 Lower Holloway
N7................72 A4
3 New Southgate N11 31 A4
Whitby Gdns
Carshalton SM1......218 B6
Queensbury NW9.....44 C6
Whitby Ho NW8...... 229 A5
Whitby Par HA4......62 C6
Whitby Rd
Carshalton SM1......218 B6
Harrow HA2..........64 A5
Ruislip HA4.........62 C6
Woolwich SE18......122 B2
Whitby St E1....... 243 C6
Whitcher Cl SE14....141 A6
Whitcher Pl NW1.....71 C2
Whitchurch Ave HA8..26 B3
Whitchurch Cl HA8...26 B4
Whitchurch Ct
SW17..............180 B6
Whitchurch Fst Sch
HA7...............25 D3
Whitchurch Gdns
HA8...............26 B4
Whitchurch Ho
Catford SE6........ 164 A1
16 North Kensington
W10...............90 D1
Whitchurch La HA8...26 B3
Whitchurch Par HA8..26 C3
Whitchurch Rd W11. 112 D6
Whitcomb Ct W1... 249 D5
Whitcomb St
WC2...... 115 D6 249 D5
Whitcome Mews
TW9.............. 132 D4
Whiteacre Mews
SE11.............. 261 B1
Whiteadder Way
E14.............. 119 D2
Whitear Wlk E15......76 B2
Whitebarn La RM10..103 C6
Whitebeam Ave BR2 .210 C3
Whitebeam Cl SW9 . 270 D3
Whitebeam Ho 3
NW3...............70 D2
White Bear Pl 1
NW3...............70 B4
White Bear Yd EC1.. 241 A5
White Bridge Ave
CR4...............202 B6
White Bridge Cl
TW14............ 149 D5
White Butts Rd HA4...62 D5
WHITECHAPEL......95 D1
Whitechapel Bell
Foundry★ E1.......96 A2
Whitechapel Gall★
E1............... 243 D2
Whitechapel High St
E1..........95 D1 243 D2
Whitechapel Mkt★
E1................96 A2
Whitechapel Rd E1...96 B2
Whitechapel Sta E1...96 B2
Whitechurch La 3
E1................96 A1
Whitechurch Pas 1
E1................96 A1
White City W10.......90 C1
White City Cl W12...112 C6
White City Est W12...112 B6
White City Rd W12...112 C6
White City Sta W12 . 112 C6
Whitecliff Ho SW18. 157 D5
White Conduit St N1 234 B4
Whitecote Rd UB1....86 A1
White Craig Cl HA5...23 C5
Whitecroft Cl BR3...208 B5
Whitecroft Way BR3 .208 B5
Whitecross Pl EC2.. 242 D4
Whitecross St
EC1.........95 A3 242 B5
White Cube The, Art
Gallery★ N1........95 C4
Whitefield Ave NW2...46 C1
Whitefield Cl SW15..157 A5
Whitefield Sch NW2...46 D2
Whitefield Sch & Ctr
E17...............36 A1
Whitefoot La BR1....164 B1
Whitefoot Terr BR1 . 164 D1
Whitefriars Ave HA3..24 C1
Whitefriars Ct 9 N12 .30 B5
Whitefriars Dr HA3...24 C1
Whitefriars Fst & Mid
Sch HA3............24 C1
Whitefriars St
EC4.........94 C1 241 B1
Whitefriars Trad Est
HA3...............24 B1
White Gate Gdns
HA3...............24 D3
Whitegates 4 EN5....13 D6
White Gates 5 KT7..197 A2
White Gdns RM10.....81 C2
Whitehall SW1..... 250 A2
Whitehall Cres KT9 . 213 D3
Whitehall Ct
SW1.......116 A5 250 B3
Whitehall Gdns
Acton W3.......... 110 C5
Chingford E4.........20 C3
Chiswick W4....... 132 D6
SW1.............. 250 A3
Whitehall La IG9......21 A2
Whitehall Lo
Muswell Hill N10......49 A6
Woodford IG8........21 A1
Whitehall Mans 3
N19...............49 C1
Whitehall Park Rd
W4............... 132 D6
Whitehall Pk N19.....49 C1
Whitehall Pl
Wallington SM5......219 B4
WC2, SW1.. 116 A5 250 A3
Whitehall Prim Sch
E4................20 C2
Whitehall Rd
Bromley BR2....... 209 D5
Chingford E4.........20 C2
Harrow HA1.........42 C2
Thornton Heath CR7 . 204 C4
West Ealing W7..... 109 A4
Woodford IG8........21 A1
Whitehall St N17.....33 D3
White Hart Ave SE28,
SE18.............. 123 D3
White Hart Ct EC2.. 243 A3
White Hart La
Mortlake SW13..... 133 C2
Willesden NW10.....67 D2
White Hart Lane Sta
N17...............33 D3
White Hart Lane
(Tottenham Hotspur
FC) N17............34 A3
Whitehart Lo SW19..180 A4
White Hart Rd SE18..123 C2
White Hart Rdbt UB5..84 D5
White Hart St
Holborn EC4........ 241 D2
Kennington
SE11......116 C1 261 B2
White Hart Terr N17...33 D3
White Hart Yd SE1... 252 C3
Whitehaven Cl BR2..209 A5
Whitehaven Ct 5
DA6...............147 A1
Whitehaven St NW8. 237 A5
Whitehead Cl
Edmonton N18........33 B5
Wandsworth SW18.. 158 A4
Whitehead Ct
Muswell Hill N10......31 A2
Twickenham TW1.... 152 D4
Whitehead Ho 8
SW15............ 156 D6
Whitehead's Gr
SW3.......114 C2 257 B3
White Heart Ave UB8..83 A2
Whiteheath Ave HA4..39 A2
Whiteheath Inf Sch
HA4...............39 A3
Whiteheath Jun Sch
HA4...............39 A2
White Heron Mews
TW11............ 174 D4
White Ho
2 Battersea SW11...136 B3
Lower Edmonton N9...18 C2
3 Streatham SW4... 159 D4
Whitehorn Ho 6 E1 .118 C5
White Horse Hill BR7,
SE9...............188 C6
Whitehorse La SE25. .205 C5
White Horse La E1....96 D2
Whitehorse Manor Inf
Sch 6 CR7.........205 B5
Whitehorse Manor Jun
Sch 5 CR7.........205 B5
Whitehorse Mews
SE1.............. 261 C6
Whitehorse Rd
South Norwood CR0,
CR7...............205 B3
Tower Hamlets E1.....97 A2
White Horse Rd
Limehouse E1........97 A1
Newham E6.........100 B4
White Horse St
W1........115 B5 248 D3
White Horse Yd EC2. 242 C2
White Ho The NW1.. 238 D6
Tottenham N17.......51 C6
Upper Tooting SW17 . 180 D5
White House Ct
1 Beckenham BR3.. 186 A2
Osidge N14..........15 D2
White House Dr HA7..25 C6
Whitehouse Est E10..54 A3
White House La EN2...5 A4
White House Prep Sch
SW12............. 159 D3
Whitehouse Way N14 .15 B1
White Kennett St E1 243 B2
Whitelands Cres
SW18..............157 A4
Whitelands Ho SW3. 257 D2
Whiteledges W13.....87 C1
Whitelegg Rd E13.....98 D5
Whiteley Ho 9 SW4 159 D4
Whiteley Rd SE19....183 B5
Whiteleys Ctr 19 W2..91 D1
Whiteleys Ho TW13..151 C1
Whiteleys Par 5
UB10..............82 D3
Whiteleys Way
TW13..............151 C1
White Lion Ct EC3... 243 A1
White Lion Hill
EC4....... 116 D6 251 D6
White Lion St
N1.........94 C5 234 B3
White Lo 7 Ealing W5 .87 C2
Golders Green NW11...47 B1
South Norwood SE19. 182 D3
Whitelock Ho 21 E9...74 D2
White Lodge Cl
Hampstead Garden Suburb
N2................48 B3
Isleworth TW7...... 131 A3
Sutton SM2........ 218 A1
White Lodge Ct
TW16..............172 C2
Whitely Ct TW13.....151 B1
White Lyon Ct EC2... 242 A4
Whiteness Ho 18
SW9...............138 C4
White Oak Dr BR3....186 A1
White Oak Gdns
DA15.............. 167 D4
Whiteoak Ho SE19...183 A3
Whiteoaks La UB6....86 B5
White Orchards
Barnet N20..........13 B3
Stanmore HA7........25 A5
White Post La E9.....75 C2
White Post St SE14,
SE15..............140 C5
White Rd
Broadgate EC2...... 243 A3
London E15..........76 C1
Whites Ave IG2.......57 C3
Whites Dr BR2...... 208 D2
White's Grounds
SE1........117 C4 253 B2
White's Grounds Est
SE1.............. 253 B2
White's Mdw BR1....210 C5
Whitespar DA14.... 189 D6
White's Row
E1.........95 D2 243 C3
White's Sq SW4.... 137 D1
White St UB1....... 106 D4
Whitestile Rd TW8... 109 D1
Whitestone La NW3...70 A5
Whitestone Wlk NW3 .70 A5
Whitethorn Ave UB7 .104 B6
Whitethorn Gdns
Croydon CR0........222 B6
Enfield EN2..........17 B6
Whitethorn Pl UB7...104 B5
Whitethorn St E3.....97 C2
White Twr Way E1....97 A2
Whiteways NW4......46 D5
Whitewebbs Way
BR5.............. 189 D2
Whitfield Ct
3 Dulwich SE21.... 183 C6
Redbridge IG1........56 B2
SW4.............. 270 A1
West Barnes SW20.. 178 D1
Whitfield Gdns W1.. 239 B4
Whitfield Ho NW8... 237 A5
Whitfield Pl W1.... 239 B5
Whitfield Rd DA7....147 B5
Upton E6............77 C1
Whitfield St
W1.........93 C2 239 B4
Whitford Gdns CR4. 202 D6
Whitgift Ave CR2.....221 A3
Whitgift Ct CR2......221 A3
Whitgift Ctr CR0.... 221 A6
Whitgift Ho
Battersea SW11.... 267 A2
Croydon CR2....... 221 A3
Lambeth SE11...... 260 C4
Whitgift Sch CR2... 221 A3
Whitgift St
Croydon CR0....... 221 A5
SE11.......116 B2 260 C4
Whiting Ave IG11.....78 D1
Whitings Hill Prim Sch
EN5...............12 C6
Whitings Rd EN5.....12 C6
Whitings The IG2.....57 C4
Whitings Way E6....100 C2
Whitington Ave EC3. 243 A1
Whitland Rd SM5....202 B1
Whitley Cl TW19.....148 A5
Whitley Ho SW1.... 269 B6
Whitley Rd N17.......33 C1
Whitlock Dr SW19...157 A3
Whitman Ho 20 E2...96 C4
Whitman Rd E3.......97 A3
Whitmead Cl CR2....221 C2
Whitmore Cl N11.....31 B5
Whitmore Gdns
NW10..............90 C5

Whitmore High Sch HA1, HA2 42 A1
Whitmore Ho
Friern Barnet N11 30 D6
20 Hoxton E1 95 C6
Whitmore Prim Sch N1 95 B6 235 D5
Whitmore Rd
Beckenham BR3 207 B6
Harrow HA1 42 A2
Hoxton N1 95 C6
Whitnell Ct 7 SW15 156 D6
Whitnell Way SW15 156 D6
Whitney Ave IG4 55 D5
Whitney Ho 6 SE22 139 C2
Whitney Rd E10 53 D2
Whitney Wlk DA14 191 A4
Whitstable Cl
Beckenham BR3 185 B2
Ruislip HA4 61 C6
Whitstable Ho 11 W10 90 D1
Whitstable Pl 9 CR0 221 A4
Whitsters Ho SE1 253 C2
Whitstone La BR3 207 D4
Whittaker 3 NW9 27 D3
Whittaker Ave TW10, TW9 153 D6
Whittaker Ct SW4 270 B1
Whittaker Pl 28 TW10 153 D6
Whittaker Rd
Cheam SM3 217 B5
Forest Gate E6 77 D1
Whittaker St SW1 258 A3
Whittaker Way 19 SE1 118 A2
Whittam Ho SE27 183 A5
Whitta Rd E12 77 D4
Whittell Gdns SE26 162 C1
Whitten Lo N12 30 C6
Whittingham 6 N17 34 B3
Whittingham Com Prim Sch E17 35 A2
Whittingham Ct W4 133 C5
Whittingstall Mans SW6 264 D1
Whittingstall Rd SW6 135 B4 264 D1
Whittington Ave UB4 83 D2
Whittington Ct
Fortis Green N2 48 D4
Penge SE20 184 B1
Whittington Hospl The N19 71 C6
Whittington Mews N12 30 A6
Whittington Rd N22 32 A3
Whittington Way HA5 41 A4
Whittle 4 NW9 27 D3
Whittlebury Cl SM5 218 D1
Whittlebury Ho N4 51 A2
Whittle Cl
Southall UB1 85 D1
Walthamstow E17 53 A2
Whittle Rd
Heston TW5 128 C5
Southall UB2 107 D4
Whittlesea Cl HA3 24 A3
Whittlesea Path HA3 24 A2
Whittlesea Rd HA3 24 A2
Whittlesey St SE1 116 C5 251 B3
WHITTON 152 A4
Whitton NW3 70 D1
Whitton Ave W UB5, UB6 64 B3
Whitton Cl UB6 65 B2
Whitton Dene TW3, TW7 152 B6
Whitton Dr UB6 65 A2
Whitton Manor Rd TW7 152 A5
Whitton Rd
Hounslow TW3 151 D6
Twickenham TW1 153 A4
Whitton Road Rdbt TW1 152 D5
Whitton Sch TW2 151 D2
Whitton Sta TW2 152 A4
Whitton Waye TW2, TW3 151 C5
Whitton Wlk E3 97 C4
Whitwell Ho 11 E5 74 B6
Whitwell Rd E13 99 A4
Whitworth Cres 1 EN3 7 C6
Whitworth Ho SE1 262 B5
Whitworth Rd SE18 144 C5
South Norwood SE25 205 D5
Whitworth St SE10 120 C1
Whorlton Rd SE15 140 B2
Whychcote Point NW2 46 C2
Whymark Ave N22 50 D6
Whytecroft TW5 128 D5
Whyte Mews 5 SM3 217 A2
Whyteville Ho E7 77 B2
Whyteville Rd E7 77 B2
Whytlaw Ho 10 E3 97 B2
Wickersley Rd SW11 137 A3
Wickers Oake SE19 183 D6
Wicker St 24 E1 96 B1
Wicket Rd UB6 87 A4
Wickets The TW15 170 A6
Wicket The CR0 223 C3
Wickfield Ho 32 SE16 118 A4
Wickford Ho 5 E1 96 C3
Wickford St E1 96 C3
Wickford Way E17 52 D5
Wickham Ave
Cheam KT4, SM3 216 C3
Croydon CR0 207 A1
Wickham Chase BR4 208 C2
Wickham Cl Enfield EN3 6 C2
New Malden KT3 199 D4
Stepney E1 96 C2
Wickham Common Prim Sch BR4 225 A4
Wickham Court Rd BR4 224 A6
Wickham Court Sch BR4 224 B4
Wickham Cres BR4 224 A6
Wickham Ct DA16 145 C3
Wickham Gdns SE4 141 B2
Wickham Ho SW15 156 D5
Wickham La SE2 146 A6
Wickham Mews SE4 141 B3
Wickham Rd
Beckenham BR3 207 D6
Brockley SE4 141 B2
Chingford E4 36 A3
Croydon CR0 207 B1
Harrow HA3 24 B1
Wickham St
Bexley DA16 145 C3
Vauxhall SE11 116 B1 260 C2
Welling DA16 146 A4
Wickham Way BR3 208 A4
Wick Ho 1 KT1 175 D2
Wick La Hackney E3 75 B1
Stratford Marsh E3 97 C6
Wickliffe Ave N3 29 A1
Wickliffe Gdns HA9 66 D6
Wicklow Ct SE26 184 C5
Wicklow Ho N16 51 D1
Wicklow St WC1 94 B4 233 C2
Wick Rd Hackney E9 74 D2
Hackney E9 75 A2
Teddington TW11 175 C3
Wicks Cl SE12 187 D6
Wickstead Ho TW8 110 B1
Wicksteed Ho SE1 262 B5
Wick Village 7 E15 75 B2
Wickway Ct 7 SE15 139 D6
Wickwood St SE5 138 D3
Widdenham Rd N7 72 B4
Widdicombe Ave HA2 63 A6
Widdin St E15 76 C1
Widecombe Ct N2 48 B4
Widecombe Gdns IG4 56 A5
Widecombe Ho 32 SE5 139 A3
Widecombe Rd SE9 166 A1
Widecombe Way N2 48 B5
Widegate St E1 243 B3
Widenham Cl HA5 40 C4
Wide Way CR4 203 D6
Widewing Cl TW11 175 B3
Widford 8 NW1 71 B2
Widford Ho N1 234 C3
Widgeon Cl E16 99 B1
Widgeon Path SE28 123 B3
Widley Rd W9 91 C3
Widmer Ct TW5 129 A3
WIDMORE 188 A1
Widmore Lodge Rd BR1 187 D1
Widmore Rd BR1 187 C1
Hillingdon UB8 82 D3
Widnes Ho 6 N7 72 C3
Wieland Rd HA6 22 A3
Wigeon Way UB4 84 D1
Wiggins La TW10 153 C2
Wiggins Mead NW9 27 D3
Wigginton Ave HA9 66 D2
Wigham Ho IG11 79 A1
Wightman Rd N4, N8 50 C4
Wighton Mews TW7 130 C3
Wigley Rd TW13 150 D3
Wigmore Ct 4 W13 109 A5
Wigmore Hall★ W1 238 C2
Wigmore Pl W1 93 B1 238 C2
Wigmore Rd SM5 202 C1
Wigmore St W1 93 A1 238 B2
Wigmore Wlk SM5 218 B6
Wigram Ct SW11 267 A2
Wigram Ho 7 E14 119 D6
Wigram Rd E11 55 C3
Wigram Sq E17 54 A6
Wigston Cl N18 33 C5
Wigston Rd E13 99 B3
Wigton Gdns HA7 26 A2
Wigton Pl SE11 261 B1
Wigton Rd E17 35 B2
Wilberforce Ct
Edgware HA8 26 B6
2 SE28 124 C5
Wilberforce Ho 3 SW11 136 B2
Wilberforce Mews 9 SW4 137 D1
Wilberforce Prim Sch W10 91 A4
Wilberforce Rd
Finsbury Pk N4 72 D6
Hendon NW9 46 A3
Highbury N4, N5 73 A5
Wilberforce Way SW19 178 D4
Wilbraham Ho SW8 270 A3
Wilbraham Pl SW1 258 A4
Wilbury Prim Sch N18 33 B5
Wilbury Way N18 33 B5
Wilby Mews W11 113 B5 244 D4
Wilcox Cl SW8 270 B4
Wilcox Gdns TW17 192 B6
Wilcox Ho 5 E3 97 B2
Wilcox Pl SW1 259 B5
Wilcox Rd
Sutton SM1 217 D4
SW8 138 A5 270 A4
Teddington TW11 174 B6
Wildcroft Gdns HA8 25 D4
Wildcroft Manor SW15 156 C4
Wildcroft Rd SW15 156 C4
Wild Ct WC2 94 B1 240 C2
Wilde Cl E8 96 A6
Wilde Pl
Edmonton N13 32 D4
Wandsworth SW18 158 B4
Wilder Cl HA4 40 B1
Wilde Rd DA8 147 D5
Wilderness Mews SW4 137 B1
Wilderness Rd BR7 188 D3
Wilderness The
East Molesey KT8 196 A4
Hampton TW12 173 D6
Wilderton Rd N16 51 C2
Wildes Cotts SM3 217 A2
Wildfell Rd SE6 163 D4
Wild Goose Dr SE14 140 C4
Wild Hatch NW11 47 C3
Wilding Ho 17 E9 74 D2
Wild Marsh Ct EN3 7 A6
Wild's Rents SE1 117 C3 263 A6
Wild St WC2 94 B1 240 C1
Wildwood Cl SE12 164 D4
Wildwood Gr NW3 48 A1
Wildwood Rd NW11 48 A1
Wildwood Rise NW11 48 A1
Wildwood Terr NW3, NW11 48 A1
Wilford Cl EN2 5 B2
Wilford Ho 3 SE18 122 D1
Wilford Rd CR0 205 A2
Wilfred Fienburgh Ho N7 71 D4
Wilfred Owen Cl SW19 180 A4
Wilfred St SW1 115 C3 259 A6
Wilfrid Gdns W3 89 A2
Wilkes Rd 3 TW8 132 A6
Wilkes St E1 95 D2 243 D4
Wilkie Ho SW1 259 D2
Wilkin St Mews NW1 71 B2
Wilkins Cl
Hayes UB3 105 D1
Mitcham CR4 180 C2
Wilkins Ho SW1 269 A6
Wilkinson Cl UB10 83 A6
Wilkinson Ct SW17 180 B6
Wilkinson Gdns CR7 183 C2
Wilkinson Ho
Isleworth TW7 130 D2
N1 235 D3
Twickenham TW2 152 B2
Wilkinson Rd E16 99 C1
Wilkinson St SW8 138 B5 270 C3
Wilkinson Way W4 111 B4
Wilkin St NW5 71 B2
Wilks Gdns CR0 207 A1
Wilks Pl N1 95 C5
Willan Rd N17 33 C1
Willan Wall E16 120 D6
Willard St SW8 137 B2
Willbury Ho 4 N7 71 D3
Willcocks Cl KT9 214 A5
Willcott Rd W3 110 D5
Will Crooks Gdns SE9 143 D1
Willenfield Rd NW10 89 A5
Willenhall Ave EN5 14 A5
Willenhall Ct EN5 14 A5
Willenhall Dr UB3 105 C6
Willenhall Rd SE18 122 D1
Willersley Ave
Blackfen DA15 167 D4
Orpington BR6 227 B5
Willersley Cl DA15 167 D3
WILLESDEN 67 D1
Willesden Community Hospl The NW10 68 A1
WILLESDEN GREEN 90 B6
Willesden Green Sta NW2 68 C2
Willesden Junction Sta NW10 89 D4
Willesden La NW2, NW6 68 D2
Willesden Sports Ctr W10 90 B6
Willes Rd NW5 71 B2
Willett Cl BR5 211 C3
3 Northolt UB5 84 C4
Willett Ho
7 Newham E13 99 A5
Stockwell SW9 138 A2
Willett Pl CR7 204 C4
Willett Rd CR7 204 C4
Willett Way BR5 211 C3
William Allen Ho HA8 26 B3
William Ash Cl RM9 80 B2
William Atkinson Ho N17 33 C3
William Banfield Ho 10 SW6 135 B3
William Barefoot Dr SE9 166 C1
William Bellamy Jun & Inf Schs RM10 81 C6
William Blake Ho 2 SE15 140 A3
William Bonney Est 10 SW4 137 D1
William Booth Meml Training Coll SE5 139 B3
William Booth Rd SE20 184 A2
William Brown Ct SE27 160 D2
William Byrd Sch UB3 127 A6
William Carey Way HA1 42 C3
William Caslon Ho 28 E2 96 B5
William Channing Ho 6 E2 96 B4
William C Harvey Specl Sch N17 33 B1
William Cl
26 Finchley N2 30 B1
Lewisham SE13 142 A2
Southall UB2 108 A4
William Covell Cl EN2 4 B5
William Ct
4 Belvedere DA17 125 C2
4 Ealing W5 87 C2
Ilford IG6 57 B5
William Davies Prim Sch E7 77 D2
William Davis Prim Sch 19 E2 96 A3
William Dr HA7 25 B5
William Dromey Ct NW6 69 B1
William Dunbar Ho NW6 91 B5
William Dyce Mews 1 SW16 181 D6
William Ellis Sch NW5 71 A5
William Ellis Way 16 SE16 118 A3
William Evans Ho 9 SE8 118 D2
William Ford CE Jun Sch RM10 81 C1
William Foster La DA16 146 A3
William Gdns SW15 156 B6
William Guy Gdns 47 E3 97 D4
William Harvey Ho 1 SW19 157 A3
William Ho N13 32 D4
William Hogarth Sch The 15 W4 111 C1
William Hunt Mans SW13 134 C6
William IV St WC2 116 A6 250 A5
William Margrie Cl 1 SE15 140 A3
William Marsden Ho 2 SE27 182 D6
William Mews SW1 114 D4 247 D1
William Morley Cl E6 99 D6
William Morris Acad W6 112 D1
William Morris Cl E17 53 B6
William Morris Gallery★ E17 53 C6
William Morris Ho W6 134 D6
William Morris Prim Sch CR4 203 D6
William Morris Sch E17 35 A2
William Morris Way SW6 136 A3
William Patten Prim Sch 9 N16 73 D6
William Perkin Ct UB6 64 C2
William Pl 37 E3 97 B5
William Rainbird Ho 9 N17 33 D3
William Rathbone Ho 3 E2 96 B4
William Rd
Regent's Pk NW1 93 C4 232 A1
Sutton SM1 218 A3
Wimbledon SW19 179 A3
William Rushbrooke Ho 4 SE16 118 A2
Williams Ave E17 35 B2
William Saville Ho 2 NW6 91 B5
William's Bldgs 1 E2 96 C3
Williams Cl SW6 135 A5 264 B4
Williams Coll EC1 241 B3

Williams Dr TW3 129 C1
Williams Gr
Kingston u T KT6 197 C3
Wood Green N22 32 C2
Williams Ho
10 Bow E3 97 C4
9 Hackney E9 96 B6
14 Streatham SW2 160 C3
7 Tottenham N17 33 D3
Willesden NW2 68 C5
Williams La
Morden SM4 202 A4
Mortlake SW14 133 A3
William Smith Ho 10
DA17 125 C3
Williamson Cl SE10 120 D1
Williamson Ct SE17 262 A1
Williamson Rd N4 50 D3
Williamson St N7 72 A4
William Sq 15 SE16 119 A6
Williams Rd UB2 107 A2
William's Rd W13 109 A5
William St
Barking IG11 79 A1
Carshalton SM5 218 D5
SW1 114 D4 247 D1
Tottenham N17 33 D3
Walthamstow E10 53 D3
Williams Terr CR0 220 C2
William Torbitt Prim Sch
IG2 57 D4
William Tyndale Prim
Sch 27 N1 72 D1
William Wilberforce Ho
1 SE27 182 D6
William Winter Ct 29
SW2 160 C4
William Wood Ho 3
SE26 162 C1
Willifield Way NW11 47 C4
Willingale Cl IG8 37 C4
Willingdon Rd N22 32 D1
Willingham Cl 4
NW5 71 C3
Willingham Terr
NW5 71 C3
Willingham Way
KT1 176 C1
Willington Ct E5 75 A5
Willington Rd SW9 138 A2
Willington Sch 13
SW19 179 B5
Willis Ave SM2, SM5 218 C2
Willis Ct CR7 204 C3
Willis Ho 2 Ilford E12 78 C5
8 Poplar E14 119 D6
Willis Rd E15 98 D5
Thornton Heath CR0 205 A2
Willis St E14 97 D1
Willis Yd N14 15 D4
Willows The CR0 223 A6
Will Miles Ct 6
SW19 180 A3
Willmore End SW19 179 D1
Willoughby Ave CR0 220 B4
Willoughby Gr N17 34 B3
Willoughby Ho EC2 242 C3
34 Wapping E1 118 B5
Willoughby La N17 34 B3
Willoughby Mews
N17 34 B3
Willoughby Park Rd
N17 34 B3
Willoughby Rd
Hampstead NW3 70 B4
Hornsey N8 50 C5
Kingston u T KT2 176 B2
Twickenham TW1 153 D6
Willoughby St WC1 240 A3
Willoughbys The
SW14 133 C1
Willoughby Way
SE7 121 B2
Willow Ave
Barnes SW13 133 D3
DA15 168 A5
Yiewsley UB7 104 B6
Willowbank SW6 135 A2
Willow Bank TW10 153 B1
Willowbank Rd
SE15 139 D6
Willowbay Cl EN5 12 D5
Willow Bridge Rd N1 73 A2
Willow Brook Prim Sch
E10 53 C1
Willowbrook Rd
Southall UB2 107 C3
Stanwell TW19 148 A2
Willow Bsns Ctr
CR4 202 D3
Willow Bsns Pk
SE26 162 C1
Willow Cl BR2 210 B4
Brentford TW8 131 C6
Buckhurst Hill IG9 21 D1
12 Catford SE6 164 D3
Sidcup DA5 169 B5
Willow Cotts
Carshalton CR4 202 D2
Feltham TW13 151 A1
Richmond TW9 132 C6
Willowcourt Ave HA3 43 B4
Willowcroft SE3 142 D1
Willow Ct
Ashford TW16 171 C3
5 Beckenham BR3 185 C2
Brixton SW9 138 C4
Chiswick W4 133 C5
8 Dagenham RM8 58 D2
EC2 243 A6
Edgware HA8 26 A6
6 Finchley N12 29 D6
Harrow HA3 24 D2
Headstone HA2 24 A1
Ilford IG1 79 A3
Islington N7 72 B3
Kingston u T KT3 198 D6
8 London E11 76 C6
Mitcham CR4 202 C5
40 Paddington W2 91 C2
3 Streatham SW16 160 B1
Thornton Heath CR7 205 B4
Willow Ctr The CR4 202 D3
Willow Dean HA5 22 D1
Willowdene
Highgate N6 48 D2
1 Peckham SE15 140 B4
5 SE15 140 B5
Willow Dene WD23 8 C4
Willowdene Cl TW2 152 A4
Willowdene Ct N20 14 A4
Willow Dene Sch
SE18 145 C4
Willow Dr EN5 1 A1
Willow End
Northwood HA6 22 A4
Surbiton KT6 198 A1
Totteridge N20 13 C2
Willow Farm La
SW15 134 B2
Willowfield Sch E17 52 D6
Willowfields Cl
SE18 123 C1
Willow Gdns
Heston TW5 129 C4
Ruislip HA4 61 D6
Willow Gn
Borehamwood WD6 11 B6
Grahame Pk NW9 27 C2
Willow Gr BR7 188 D4
Newham E13 99 A5
Ruislip HA4 39 D1
Willow Hall NW3 70 B4
Willowhayne Dr
KT12 194 B2
Willowhayne Gdns
KT4 216 C4
Willow Ho TW14 150 B6
Willow Ho
17 Finchley N2 30 B1
9 Maitland Pk NW3 70 D2
North Kensington W10 90 D3
Teddington TW11 175 C3
Willow La
Mitcham CR4 202 D3
Woolwich SE18 122 C2
Willow Lo
6 Ashford TW16 171 D3
Fulham SW6 134 D4
New Barnet EN5 14 A6
Putney SW15 134 B2
Willow Lodge 10
SW8 137 B2
Willow Manor SM1 217 B4
Willowmead Cl W5 87 D2
Willowmere
Esher KT10 212 A4
Ladywell SE13 163 D6
Willow Mount CR0 221 C5
Willow Pl
SW1 115 C2 259 B4
Willow Rd
Dagenham RM6 59 A3
Ealing W5 110 A4
Enfield EN1 5 C3
Hampstead NW3 70 B4
New Malden KT3 199 A5
Wallington SM6 219 B1
Willows Ave SM4 201 D4
Willows Cl HA5 22 C1
Willows Ct 3 SW19 179 C3
Willows Sch The UB4 84 D3
Willow St
Broadgate
EC2 95 C3 243 A6
Chingford E4 20 B4
Willows Terr NW10 89 D5
Willows The
Beckenham BR3 185 C2
Claygate KT10 212 C2
Loughton IG10 21 D6
Wallend E12 78 C1
Whetstone N20 14 A1
Willowtree Cl UB10 61 A5
Willow Tree Cl
Hayes UB4 84 C3
Northolt UB5 63 A2
14 Old Ford E3 97 B6
Wandsworth SW18 157 D3
Willow Tree Ct
DA14 189 D5
5 Wembley HA0 65 D3
Willow Tree La UB4 84 C3
Willow Tree Prim Sch
UB5 63 A2
Willow Tree Rd UB4 84 D2
Willowtree Way
SW16 182 C2
Willow Tree Wlk
BR1 187 B2
Willow Vale BR7 188 D4
Shepherd's Bush W12 112 A5
Willow View SW19 180 B2
Willow Way
Finchley N3 29 D3
Forest Hill SE26 162 C1
9 Shepherd's Bush
W11 112 D6
Sunbury TW16 194 A5
Twickenham TW2 151 D2
Wembley HA0 65 A5
West Ewell KT19 215 B2
Willow Wlk
Bermondsey
SE1 117 D2 263 C4
Cheam SM1, SM3 217 B5
15 Finchley N2 30 B1
Harringay N15 50 D5
Locksbottom BR6 226 D5
Southgate N21 16 B5
Walthamstow E17 53 B4
Willow Wood Cres
SE25 205 C3
Willridge Ct E11 54 B2
Willrose Cres SE2 124 B1
Willsbridge Ct 1
SE15 139 D6
Wills Cres TW3 151 D5
Wills Gr NW7 28 B5
Will Thorne Pav The
E16 100 A1
Wilman Gr E8 74 A1
Wilmar Cl UB4 83 B3
Wilmar Gdns BR4 207 D1
Wilmcote Ho W2 91 D2
Wilment Ct NW2 68 C5
Wilmer Cl KT2 176 B5
Wilmer Cres KT2 176 B5
Wilmer Gdns 22 N1 95 C6
Wilmer Ho 6 E3 97 A5
Wilmer Lea Cl E15 76 B1
Wilmer Pl N16 73 D6
Wilmers Ct 5 NW10 89 B6
Wilmer Way N14 31 D5
Wilmington Ave W4 133 B5
Wilmington Ct
SW16 182 A3
Wilmington Gdns
IG11 79 C1
Wilmington Sq
WC1 94 C4 234 A1
Wilmington St WC1 234 A1
Wilmot Cl Finchley N2 30 A1
SE15 140 A5
Wilmot Ho 14 SM2 218 A2
Wilmot Pl
Camden Town NW1 71 C1
Wilmot Pl *continued*
Ealing W7 108 C5
Wilmot Rd Leyton E10 75 D6
Tottenham N17 51 B6
Wallington SM5 218 D3
Wilmot St E2 96 B3
Wilmount St SE18 122 D2
Wilna Rd SW18 158 A4
Wilnett Ct 4 RM6 58 B2
Wilnett Villas 5 RM6 58 B2
Wilsham St
W11 113 A5 244 A4
Wilshaw Cl NW4 46 A6
Wilshaw Ho 10 SE8 141 C5
Wilshaw St SE14 141 C4
Wilsmere Dr
Harrow HA3 24 C3
Northolt UB5 63 A3
Wilson Ave CR4 180 C2
Wilson Cl
Croydon CR2 221 B3
Wembley HA9 44 B2
Wilson Ct 9 SE28 123 A3
Wilson Dr HA9 44 B2
Wilson Gdns HA1 42 A2
Wilson Gr SE16 118 B4
Wilson Ho
39 Clapham SW8 137 D3
2 SE7 143 C6
South Hampstead NW6 70 A1
Wilson Rd
Camberwell SE5 139 C4
Chessington KT9 214 B2
Newham E6 99 D4
Redbridge IG1 56 B2
Wilson's Ave 4 N17 33 D1
Wilson's Pl E14 97 B1
Wilson's Rd W6 112 D1
Wilson's Sch SM6 220 A2
Wilson St
Broadgate
EC2 95 B2 242 D4
Southgate N21 16 C4
Walthamstow E17 54 A4
Wilstone Cl UB4 85 A3
Wiltern Ct NW2 69 A2
Wilthorne Gdns
RM10 81 D1
Wilton Ave W4 111 C1
Wilton Cres
Merton SW19 179 B2
SW1 115 A4 248 A1
Wilton Ct
3 Edgware HA8 26 D5
Muswell Hill N10 31 A1
4 Richmond TW10 154 A6
7 Stepney E1 96 B1
7 Woodford IG8 37 A4
Wilton Est E8 74 A2
Wilton Gdns
East Molesey KT8 195 C6
Walton-on-T KT12 194 D1
Wilton Gr
Merton SW19 179 B2
New Malden KT3 199 D3
Wilton Ho
8 Camberwell
SE22 139 C2
Chislehurst BR7 189 B2
Ealing W13 109 B6
Wilton Mews
SW1 115 A3 258 B6
Wilton Par TW13 150 B2
Wilton Pl
2 Beckenham BR3 208 A6
4 Harrow HA1 42 D3
SW1 115 A4 248 A1
Wilton Rd
Abbey Wood SE2 124 C2
Cockfosters EN4 2 D1
Hounslow TW4 128 D2
Mitcham SW19 180 C3
Muswell Hill N10 31 A1
Westminster
SW1 115 C2 259 A4
Wilton Row SW1 248 A1
Wilton Sq N1 95 B6 235 C6
Wilton St
SW1 115 B3 258 C6
Wilton Terr SW1 258 A6
Wilton Villas N1 235 C5
Wilton Way E8 74 A2
Wiltshire Cl
Edgware NW7 27 D5
SW3 257 C3
Wiltshire Ct
Barking IG11 79 A2
2 Finsbury Pk N4 50 B1
Wiltshire Gdns
Stoke Newington N4 51 A3
Twickenham TW2 152 A3
Wiltshire La
Pinner HA5 40 A5
Ruislip HA4 39 D6
Wiltshire Rd
Brixton SW9 138 C2
Thornton Heath CR7 204 C6
Wiltshire Row
N1 95 B6 235 D5
Wilverley Cres KT3 199 C3
Wimbart Rd SW2 160 B4
WIMBLEDON 179 B4
Wimbledon Bridge
SW19 179 B4
Wimbledon Central
SW19 179 B4
Wimbledon Chase Prim
Sch 2 SW20 179 A2
Wimbledon Chase Sta
SW20 179 A1
Wimbledon Cl 2
SW20 178 D3
Wimbledon Coll
SW19 178 D3
Wimbledon Common★
SW19 178 B6
Wimbledon Common
Prep Sch SW19 178 D3
Wimbledon High Sch
SW19 179 A4
Wimbledon Hill Rd
SW19 179 B4
Wimbledon Lawn Tennis
Mus★ SW19 157 A1
Wimbledon L Ctr
SW19 179 D4
Wimbledon Mus★
SW19 179 A4
Wimbledon Park Ct
SW19 157 B3
Wimbledon Park
Montessori Sch
SW18 157 C2
Wimbledon Park Prim
Sch SW19 157 D2
Wimbledon Park Rd SW18,
SW19 157 B3
Wimbledon Park Side
SW19 156 D3
Wimbledon Park Sta
SW19 157 C1
Wimbledon Rd
SW17 180 A6
Wimbledon Sch of Art 1
SW19 179 A2
Wimbledon Sch of Art
Annexe 14 SW19 179 C3
Wimbledon Sta
SW19 179 B4
Wimbledon Stad
SW17 180 A6
Wimbledon Stadium
Bsns Ctr SW17 157 D1
Wimbledon Windmill
Mus★ SW19 156 C1
Wimbolt St E2 96 A4
Wimborne 2 DA14 190 B6
Wimborne Ave
Hayes UB4 84 B1
Southall UB2 107 C2
St Paul's Cray BR5,
BR7 211 D5
Wimborne Cl
Buckhurst Hill IG9 21 C2
Lewisham SE12 164 D6
North Cheam KT4 200 C1
Wimborne Ct 1 UB5 63 C2
Wimborne Dr
Pinner HA5 41 A2
Queensbury NW9 44 C6
Wimborne Gdns W13 87 B2
Wimborne Ho
Canning Town E16 120 D6
Croydon CR0 206 C4
Marylebone NW1 237 B5
South Lambeth SW8 270 D3
Upper Tooting SW12 159 C1

Wimborne Rd
Edmonton N9 18 A2
Tottenham N17 33 C1
Wimborne Way BR3 207 A5
Wimbourne Ct
Mitcham SW19 180 B3
N1 235 C4
South Croydon CR2 221 C2
Wimbourne St
N1 95 B5 235 C4
Wimbush Ho 3 N12 29 D5
Wimpole Cl
Bromley BR2 209 C5
1 Kingston u T KT1 176 C1
Wimpole Mews
W1 93 B2 238 C3
Wimpole St
W1 93 B1 238 C2
Wimshurst Cl CR0 204 A1
Winans Wlk SW9 138 C3
Winant Ho 19 E14 119 D6
Wincanton Cres UB5 63 C3
Wincanton Ct 2 N11 31 A4
Wincanton Gdns IG6 56 D6
Wincanton Rd SW18 157 B4
Winchcombe Rd
SM5 202 C1
Winchcomb Gdns
SE9 143 D2
Winchelsea Ave
DA7 147 B5
Winchelsea Cl
SW15 156 D6
Winchelsea Ho 16
SE16 118 C4
Winchelsea Rd
Becontree NW10 89 B6
Forest Gate E7 77 A4
Tottenham N17 51 C6
Winchelsey Rise
CR2 221 D2
Winchendon Rd
Fulham
SW6 135 B4 264 D2
Teddington TW11,
TW12 174 B6
Winchester Ave
Brondesbury NW6 69 A1
Heston TW5 129 B6
Queensbury NW9 44 C6
Winchester Cl
Beckenham BR2 208 D6
Enfield EN1 17 C6
Kingston u T KT2 176 D3
11 Newham E6 100 B1
SE17 261 D3
Winchester Ct
15 Belvedere DA17 125 C1
5 Higham Hill E17 35 A2
Richmond TW9 132 B2
W8 245 C2
Winchester Dr HA5 40 D4
Winchester Ho
5 Barking IG11 80 A1
Bayswater W2 236 A1
Chelsea SW3 266 D5
1 Greenwich SE18 143 D5
24 Tower Hamlets E3 97 B4
Twickenham TW1 153 C4
Winchester Mews
KT4 216 D6
Winchester Pal★
SE1 252 C4
Winchester Pk BR2 208 D6
Winchester Pl
6 Dalston E8 73 D3
Highgate N6 49 B1
Winchester Rd
Beckenham BR2 208 D6
Bexley DA7 146 D3
Chingford E4 36 A3
Edmonton N9 18 A3
Harlington UB3 127 C5
Harrow HA3 44 A5
Highgate N6 49 B1
Ilford IG1 79 B5
Northwood HA6 40 A6
South Hampstead NW3 70 B1
St Margarets TW1 153 B5
Twickenham TW13 151 B1
Walton-on-T KT12 194 A1
Winchester Sq SE1 252 C4
Winchester St
Acton W3 111 A4
SW1 115 B1 258 D2
Winchester Wlk SE1 252 C4
Winchet Wlk CR0 206 C3
Winchfield Cl HA3 43 C3
Winchfield Ho
SW15 155 D5
Winchfield Rd SE26 185 A5
Winch Ho
Isle of Dogs E14 119 D3
SW10 266 B4
Winchilsea Cres
KT8 174 A1
Winchilsea Ho NW8 229 D1
WINCHMORE HILL 16 D4
Winchmore Hill Rd N14,
N21 16 A4
Winchmore Hill Sta
N21 16 D4
Winchmore Sch N21 17 A2
Winchmore Villas
N21 16 B4
Winchstone Cl
TW17 192 B5
Winckley Cl HA3 44 B4
Wincott St
SE11 116 C2 261 B3
Wincrofts Dr SE9 145 B1
Windall Cl SE20 184 A2
Windborough Rd
SM5 219 A1
Windcott Ct HA3 43 C2
Windermere NW1 231 D2
12 Putney SW15 156 D5
Windermere Ave
Golders Green N3 47 C6
Kensal Rise NW6 91 A6
Merton SW19 201 D6
Ruislip HA4 40 D2
Wembley HA9 43 C1
Windermere Cl BR6 226 D5
East Bedfont TW14 149 D3
Stanwell TW19 148 A2
Windermere Ct
Barnes SW13 133 D6
Barnet EN5 1 D1
Carshalton SM5 219 A5
Wembley HA9 43 C2
Windermere Gdns
IG4 56 A4
Windermere Gr HA9 43 C1
Windermere Hall
HA8 26 B5
Windermere Ho
Isleworth TW1 152 D6
Tower Hamlets E3 97 B3
Windermere Point 3
SE15 140 C5
Windermere Rd
Brentford W5 109 C3
Croydon CR0 205 D1
Kingston u T SW15 177 C5
Mitcham SW16 181 D1
Muswell Hill N10 31 B2
Southall UB1 85 B2
Upper Holloway N19 71 C6
West Wickham BR4 224 C6
Windermere Way
UB7 104 B5
Winders Rd SW11 136 C3
Windfield Cl SE26 184 D6
Windham Rd TW9 132 B2
Winding Way RM8 80 C5
Windlass Pl SE8 119 A2
Windlesham Gr
SW19 156 D3
Windley Cl SE23 162 C2
Windmill WC1 240 C4
Windmill Alley 7
W4 111 C2
Windmill Ave UB2 108 A4
Windmill Bridge Ho 1
CR0 205 C1
Windmill Bsns Ctr
UB2 108 A5
Windmill Bsns Village
TW16 171 C2
Windmill Cl
Ashford TW16 171 C3
12 Bermondsey SE1 118 A2
Kingston u T KT6 197 C2
4 Lewisham SE13 142 A3
Windmill Ct
Brentford W5 109 C2
Brondesbury NW2 69 A2
Windmill Ct *continued*
Bushey WD23 8 B3
Windmill Dr
Clapham SW4 159 B6
Cricklewood NW2 69 A5
Windmill Gdns
Brixton SW2 160 B5
Enfield EN2 4 C2
Windmill Gr CR0 205 A3
Windmill Hill
Enfield EN2 5 A2
1 Hampstead NW3 70 A4
Hampstead NW3 70 A5
Ruislip HA4 39 D1
Windmill Ho
4 Millwall E14 119 C2
SE1 251 B3
Windmill La
Barnet Gate EN5 11 D5
BR2 225 C4
Bushey WD23 8 C3
Greenford UB6 86 A2
Isleworth TW7, UB2,
W7 108 C2
Southall UB2 108 A4
Stratford E15 76 B2
Thames Ditton KT7 197 B2
Windmill Lo TW16 171 C2
Windmill Pas 10 W4 111 C2
Windmill Pl UB1 108 A5
Windmill Rd
Brentford TW8, W5 109 C1
Charlton TW16 171 C2
Chiswick W4 111 C2
Edmonton N18 33 B6
Hampton TW12 174 A5
Mitcham CR4 203 C5
Roehampton SW19 156 B1
Thornton Heath CR0 205 A2
Wandsworth SW18 158 B5
Windmill Rd W
TW16 171 C1
Windmill Rise KT2 176 D3
Windmill Row SE11 261 A1
Windmill St
Bloomsbury
W1 93 D2 239 C3
Bushey WD23 8 C3
Windmill Terr TW17 193 C2
Windmill Trad Est
CR4 203 C5
Windmill Way HA4 39 D1
Windmill Wlk SE1 251 B2
Windmore Cl HA0 65 A3
Windover Ave NW9 45 B5
Windrose Cl SE16 118 D4
Windrush KT3 199 A5
Windrush Cl
Battersea SW11 136 B1
Chiswick W4 133 A5
4 Hackney E8 74 A1
Ickenham UB10 60 B4
Tottenham N17 33 C2
Windrush Ho NW8 236 D4
Windrush La SE23 162 D1
Windrush Prim Sch
SE28 124 B5
Windrush Rd NW10 89 B6
Windrush Sq SW9 138 C1
Windsock Cl 1
SE16 119 B2
Windsor Ave
Cheam SM3 217 A5
East Molesey KT8 195 C6
Edgware HA8 10 D1
Higham Hill E17 35 A1
Hillingdon UB10 60 D1
Merton SW19 180 A2
New Malden KT3 199 A4
Windsor Cl
Brentford TW8 131 B6
Chislehurst BR7 188 D5
Harrow HA2 63 C5
Hendon N3 29 A1
Pinner HA6 22 A1
West Norwood SE27 183 A6
Windsor Cres
Harrow HA2 63 C5
Wembley HA9 66 D5
Windsor Ct
Battersea SW11 136 B3
Bayswater W2 245 C6
Bickley BR1 210 A6
Bushey WD23 8 A4
Chelsea SW3 257 B2
2 Clapham SW4 137 C1
Windsor Ct *continued*
Edgware HA8 26 B3
Friern Barnet N11 30 D5
Fulham SW6 135 A2
Northolt UB5 63 B3
Osidge N14 15 C4
20 Rotherhithe SE16 118 D5
South Norwood SE19 183 C2
Sunbury TW16 172 A3
Temple Fortune NW11 47 A3
Walthamstow E17 53 B6
4 Wandsworth
SW18 157 C6
West Hampstead NW3 69 C4
5 West Wickham
BR4 207 D1
Windsor Ctr The
SE27 183 A6
Windsor Dr EN4 14 D5
Windsor Gdns
Hayes UB3 105 B3
Paddington W9 91 C3
Wallington CR0 220 A5
Windsor Gr SE27 183 A6
Windsor Hall 11 E16 121 B5
Windsor Ho
4 Acton Green W4 111 A1
Brondesbury NW2 69 A2
4 Globe Town E2 96 D4
2 Hendon NW4 28 D1
7 Northolt UB5 63 C2
Queensbury NW9 44 C5
Regent's Pk NW1 231 D2
Shoreditch N1 235 B4
Stanmore HA7 25 B5
Stoke Newington N4 51 A1
Windsor Lo KT3 199 A4
Windsor Mews
Catford SE6 164 A3
Forest Hill SE23 163 A3
Windsor Park Rd
UB3 127 D5
Windsor Pk SW19 180 A2
Windsor Pl SW1 259 B4
Windsor Rd
Ashford TW16 172 A4
Barnet EN5 12 D5
Chingford E4 35 D6
Cranford TW4, TW5 128 C3
DA6 147 A1
Dagenham RM8 81 A5
Ealing W5 110 A6
Forest Gate E7 77 C3
Harrow HA3 24 B2
Hendon N3 29 A1
Ilford IG1 79 A4
Kingston u T KT2 176 A3
Leyton E10 75 D6
Palmers Green N13 16 C1
Richmond TW9 132 B3
Southall UB2 107 B3
South Norwood CR7 182 D1
Teddington TW11 174 B5
Tottenham N17 34 A1
Upper Holloway N7 72 A5
Wanstead E11 77 A6
Willesden NW2 68 B2
Worcester Pk KT4 216 A6
Windsor St
N1 94 D6 234 D6
Windsor Terr
N1 95 A4 235 B2
Windsor Way
W14 113 A2 254 A4
Windsor Wharf E9 75 B3
Windsor Wlk
Camberwell SE5 139 B3
Walton-on-T KT12 194 D1
Windspoint Dr SE15 140 B6
Windus Rd N16 51 D1
Windus Wlk N16 51 D1
Windy Ridge BR1 188 A2
Windy Ridge Cl
SW19 178 D5
Wine Cl E1 118 C6
Wine Office Ct EC4 241 B2
Winery La KT1 198 B6
Winey Cl KT9 213 C1
Winfield Ho 3
SW11 136 B3
Winford Ct 16 SE15 140 A4
Winford Ho E3 75 B1
Winford Par 6 UB1 85 D1
Winforton St SE10 142 A4
Winfrith Rd SW18 158 A3
Wingate Cres CR0 204 A3
Wingate Ho
26 Bromley E3 97 D4
8 Stoke Newington
N16 73 B4
Wingate Rd
Hammersmith W6 112 B3
Ilford IG1 78 D3
Sidcup DA14 190 C4
Wingate Trad Est 11
N17 33 D3
Wingfield Ct
5 Blackwall E14 120 B6
Sidcup DA15 167 D3
Wingfield Ho
Paddington NW6 91 D5
16 Spitalfields E2 95 D4
Wingfield Mews
SE15 140 A2
Wingfield Prim Sch
SE3 143 B2
Wingfield Rd
Kingston u T KT2 176 C4
Leyton E15 76 C4
Walthamstow E17 53 D4
Wingfield St SE15 140 A2
Wingfield Way HA4 62 B2
Wingford Rd SW2 160 A5
Wingham 3 NW5 71 A2
Wingham Ho 3
SE26 184 B5
Wingmore Rd SE24 139 A2
Wingrad Ho 18 E1 96 C2
Wingrave SE17 262 C3
Wingrave Rd W6 134 C6
Wingreen 15 NW8 91 D6
Wingrove Ho E4 19 D4
Wingrove Rd SE6 164 C2
Wings Cl SM1 217 C4
Winicotte Ho W2 236 D4
Winifred Cl EN5 11 D5
Winifrede Paul Ho 7
NW5 71 B4
Winifred Pl N12 30 A5
Winifred Rd
Dagenham RM8 59 A1
Hampton TW12 173 C6
Merton SW19 179 C2
Winifred St E16 122 B5
Winifred Terr
Enfield EN1 17 D4
15 Newham E13 99 A5
Winkfield Rd
Newham E13 99 B5
Wood Green N22 32 C2
Winkley Ct
Cranley Gdns N10 49 B5
Harrow HA2 63 C5
Winkley St 6 E2 96 B5
Winkworth Cotts 14
E1 96 C3
Winlaton Rd BR1 186 B6
Winmill Rd RM8 81 B5
Winn Bridge Cl IG8 37 D2
Winn Common Rd
SE18 145 C6
Winnett St W1 249 C6
Winningales Ct IG5 56 A6
Winnings Wlk UB5 63 A2
Winnington Cl N2 48 B3
Winnington Ho
19 Kensal Town W10 91 A3
8 SE5 139 A5
Winnington Rd
Enfield EN3 6 C6
Hampstead Garden Suburb
N2 48 B3
Winnipeg Dr 3 BR6 227 D2
Winnipeg Ho UB4 84 B3
Winn Rd SE12 165 B3
Winns Ave E17 53 B6
Winns Mews N15 51 C5
Winns Prim Sch E17 35 B1
Winns Terr E17 53 C6
Winsbeach E17 36 B1
Winscombe Cres W5 87 D3
Winscombe Ct W5 87 D3
Winscombe St N19 71 B6
Winscombe Way HA7 25 A5
Winsford Rd SE6 163 B1
Winsford Terr N18 33 B5
Winsham Gr SW11 159 A6
Winsham Ho NW1 232 D2
Winslade Ho 4 E5 74 B6
Winslade Rd SW2 160 A6
Winslade Way SE6 163 D4
Winsland Mews W2 236 C2

Winsland St
W2 .... 92 B1 236 C2
Winsley St W1 .... 239 B2
Winslow SE17 .... 263 A1
Winslow Cl
2 Neasden NW10 .... 67 C5
Pinner HA5 .... 40 B3
Winslow Gr E4 .... 20 C2
Winslow Rd W6 ...... 134 C6
Winslow Way TW13 .. 151 A1
Winsmoor Ct EN2 ...... 4 D2
Winsor Prim Sch E6 100 C1
Winsor Terr E6 .... 100 C2
Winstanley Rd SW11 . 136 B2
Winston Ave NW9 ..... 45 C2
Winston Churchill Britain at War Experience★
SE1 .... 253 A3
Winston Cl
Harrow HA3 .... 24 D4
Romford RM7 .... 59 D5
Winston Ct 7 BR1 ... 187 B2
Harrow HA3 .... 23 D3
Winston Ho WC1 .... 239 D6
Winston House Prep Sch
E18 .... 37 A1
Winston Rd N16 ...... 73 B4
Winston Way IG1 ..... 79 A5
Winston Way Prim Sch
IG1 .... 78 D5
Winston Wlk 2 W4 .. 111 B2
Winter Ave E6 .... 100 A6
Winterberry Ct 22
N12 .... 29 D6
Winterborne Ave
BR6 .... 227 B5
Winterbourne Ho
W11 .... 244 A5
Winterbourne Inf Sch
CR7 .... 204 C5
Winterbourne Jun Boys' Sch CR7 .... 204 C5
Winterbourne Jun Girls' Sch CR7 .... 204 C5
Winterbourne Rd
Dagenham RM8 .... 80 C6
Forest Hill SE6 .... 163 B3
Thornton Heath CR7 . 204 C5
Winter Box Wlk
TW10 .... 154 B6
Winterbrook Rd
SE24 .... 161 A5
Winterburn Cl N11 .... 31 A4
Winterfold Cl SW19 .. 157 A2
Wintergreen Cl 7
E6 .... 100 A2
Winterleys 7 NW6 .... 91 B5
Winter Lo 17 SE16 .... 118 A1
Winter's Ct E4 .... 19 D1
Winterslow Ho 20
SE5 .... 139 A3
Winters Rd KT7 ...... 197 B2
Winterstoke Gdns
NW7 .... 28 A5
Winterstoke Rd SE6 .. 163 B3
Winterton Ct KT1 ... 175 D2
Winterton Ho 15 E1 ... 96 C1
Winterton Pl SW10 .. 266 B6
Winterwell Rd SW2 .. 160 A6
Winthorpe Rd SW15 . 135 A1
Winthrop Ho 10
W12 .... 112 B6
Winthrop St E1 .... 96 B2
Winthrop Wlk HA9 .... 66 A5
Winton Ave N11 ...... 31 C3
Winton Cl N9 .... 18 D4
Winton Ct 15 KT6 ... 197 D2
Winton Gdns HA8 ..... 26 B3
Winton Prim Sch
N1 .... 94 B5 233 C3
Winton Rd BR6 ...... 226 D4
Winton Way SW16 ... 182 C5
Wintour Ho HA9 ...... 65 D6
Wirrall Ho 15 SE26 ... 162 A1
Wirral Wood Cl BR7 . 188 C4
Wisbeach Rd CR0 ... 205 B4
Wisbech 5 N4 .... 50 B1
Wisden Ho SW8 .... 270 D5
Wisdom Ct 7 TW7 ... 131 A2
Wisdom Sch 1 N15 ... 51 B5
Wisdons Cl RM7, RM9 .. 59 D1
Wise La NW7 .... 28 A4
Wiseman Ct 12 SE19 . 183 C5
Wiseman Rd E10 ...... 75 C6
Wise Rd E15 .... 98 B6
Wiseton Rd SW17 ... 158 D3
Wishart Rd SE3 ..... 143 D3
Wishaw Wlk N13 ...... 32 A4
Wisley Ho SW1 ..... 259 C2
Wisley Rd
Balham SW11 ...... 159 A6
St Paul's Cray BR5 ... 190 B3
Wistaria Cl BR6 ..... 226 D6
Wisteria Cl
Edgware NW7 .... 27 D4
Ilford IG1 .... 78 D3
Wisteria Ho SE4 ..... 141 A2
Wisteria Rd SE13 .... 142 B1
Wistow Ho 14 E2 ...... 96 A6
Witanhurst La N6 ..... 49 A1
Witan St E2 .... 96 B4
Witchwood Ho 10
SW9 .... 138 C2
Witcombe Point 14
SE15 .... 140 A4
Witechapel Sp Ctr E1 . 96 C2
Witham Ct Leyton E10 . 75 D5
Upper Tooting SW17 . 158 D1
Witham Ho 34 SE5 ... 139 A3
Witham Rd
Dagenham RM10 ...... 81 C3
Ealing W13 .... 109 B5
Hounslow TW7 .... 130 B4
Penge SE20 .... 206 C6
Witherby Cl CR0 ..... 221 C4
Witherington Rd N5 .. 72 C3
Withers Cl KT9 ...... 213 C2
Withers Mead NW9 ... 27 D2
Withers Pl EC1 ...... 242 B6
Witherston Way SE9 . 166 C1
Withington Rd N2 .... 30 C2
Withycombe Rd
SW19 .... 156 D4
Withy Ho 4 E1 .... 96 D3
Withy La HA4 .... 39 A4
Withy Mead E4 .... 20 B1
Witley Cres CR0 ..... 224 A2
Witley Ct
Southall UB2 .... 107 B2
WC1 .... 240 A5
Witley Gdns UB2 .... 107 B2
Witley Ho 2 SW2 .... 160 B4
Witley Ind Est UB2 ... 107 B2
Witley Point 8
SW15 .... 156 B3
Witley Rd N19 .... 71 C6
Witney Cl
Ickenham UB10 ...... 60 B4
Pinner HA5 .... 23 B4
Witney Path SE23 ... 162 D1
Wittenham Way E4 ... 20 B1
Witten Ho KT3 ...... 199 B1
Wittering Cl KT2 .... 175 D5
Wittering Ho 9
SW11 .... 136 D3
Wittersham Rd BR1 . 186 D5
Witts Ho KT2 .... 198 B6
Wivenhoe Cl SE15 ... 140 B2
Wivenhoe Ct TW4 ... 129 B1
Wivenhoe Rd IG11 ... 102 B5
Wiverton Rd SE26 ... 184 C5
Wixom Ho SE9 .... 143 C1
Wix Prim Sch SW4 ... 137 B1
Wix Rd RM9 .... 102 D6
Wix's La SW4 .... 137 B1
Woburn W13 .... 87 B2
Woburn Cl
Bushey WD23 .... 8 A5
SE28 .... 102 D1
Wimbledon SW19 ... 180 A4
Woburn Ct
32 Bermondsey
SE16 .... 118 B1
Croydon CR0 .... 205 A1
1 DA6 .... 147 A1
Richmond TW9 ...... 132 B2
4 Woodford E18 ...... 37 A1
Woburn Pl
WC1 .... 94 A3 240 A5
Woburn Rd
Carshalton SM5 ..... 202 C1
Croydon CR0 .... 205 A1
Woburn Sq
WC1 .... 93 D3 239 D5
Woburn Twr 14 UB5 ... 84 D4
Woburn Wlk WC1 ... 232 D1
Wodeham Gdns 1
E1 .... 96 B2
Wodehouse Ave
SE15 .... 139 D4
Wodehouse Ct 10
W3 .... 111 A3
Woffington Cl KT1,
KT8 .... 175 C2
Woking Cl SW15 .... 133 D1
Wolcot Ho NW1 ..... 232 B3
Woldham Pl BR2 .... 209 C5
Woldham Rd BR2 .... 209 C5
Wolds Dr BR6 .... 226 C4
Wolfe Cl Hayes BR2 .. 209 A3
Yeading UB4 .... 84 B4
Wolfe Cres
Greenwich SE7 ..... 121 D1
34 Rotherhithe SE16 . 118 D4
Wolfe Ho 19 W12 .... 112 B6
Wolferton Rd E12 .... 78 B4
Wolffe Gdns 2 E15 ... 76 D2
Wolf Fields Prim Sch
UB2 .... 107 B2
Wolfington Rd SE27 . 182 D6
Wolfram Cl SE13 .... 164 C6
Wolfson Ct
4 Barnet EN4 .... 14 D3
Golders Green NW11 .. 47 A2
SE1 .... 253 D2
Wolfson Hillel Prim Sch
N14 .... 15 D5
Wolftencroft Cl
SW11 .... 136 B2
Wollaston Cl SE1 ... 262 A4
Wollotan Ho N1 .... 234 B4
Wolmer Cl HA8 .... 26 D6
Wolmer Gdns HA8 .... 10 C1
Wolmer Rd HA8 ...... 26 D6
Wolseley Ave SW18,
SW19 .... 157 C2
Wolseley Gdns W4 .. 132 D6
Wolseley Rd
Acton W4 .... 111 A2
Carshalton CR4 ..... 203 A2
Harrow HA3 .... 42 C6
Hornsey N8 .... 49 D4
Upton E7 .... 77 B1
Wood Green N22 ...... 32 B2
Wolseley St
SE1 .... 117 D4 253 D1
Wolsey Ave
Thames Ditton KT7 ... 196 D4
Wallend E6 .... 100 C4
Walthamstow E17 ..... 53 B6
Wolsey Cl
Isleworth TW3 ...... 130 A1
Kingston u T KT2 .... 176 D2
Southall UB2 .... 108 A3
Wimbledon SW20 .... 178 B3
Worcester Pk KT19,
KT4 .... 216 A4
Wolsey Cres SM4 .... 201 B2
Wolsey Ct
Bromley BR1 .... 186 D3
SE9 .... 166 B5
South Hampstead NW6 70 A1
Wolsey Dr
Kingston u T KT2 .... 176 A4
Walton-on-T KT12 ... 194 D1
Wolsey Gr HA8 .... 27 B3
Wolsey Ho
2 Hampton TW12 ... 173 D4
3 Kentish Town NW5 .. 71 D2
Wolsey Inf Sch CR0 . 224 A1
Wolsey Jun Sch
CR0 .... 224 A1
Wolsey Mews
Kentish Town NW5 .... 71 C2
Orpington BR6 ...... 227 D3
Wolsey Rd
Ashford TW15 .... 170 B6
East Molesey KT8 ... 196 B5
Enfield EN1 .... 6 B3
Hampton TW12 ..... 174 A4
Stoke Newington N1 .. 73 B3
Sunbury Comm TW16 . 171 D4
Wolsey St E1 .... 96 C2
Wolsey Way KT9 .... 214 C3
Wolstenholme HA7 ... 25 B5
Wolstonbury N12 ..... 29 C5
Wolvercote Rd SE2 . 124 D4
Wolverley St E2 ...... 96 B4
Wolverton SE17 ..... 263 A2
Wolverton Ave KT2 .. 176 C2
Wolverton Gdns
Brook Green W6 .... 112 D2
Ealing W5 .... 110 B6
Wolverton Mans W5 . 110 B5
Wolverton Rd HA7 .... 25 B3
Wolverton Way N14 ... 15 C6
Wolves La N22 .... 32 C4
Woman's Liby The★
EC2 .... 243 C2
Womersley Rd N4, N8 . 50 B3
Wonford Cl KT2, KT3 . 177 C2
Wontner Cl 5 N1 ..... 73 A1
Wontner Rd SW12,
SW17 .... 158 D2
Wooburn Cl UB8 ...... 82 D3
Wooburn Ct N14 ...... 15 D3
Woodall Cl
Chessington KT9 .... 213 D2
15 Poplar E14 ...... 119 D6
Woodall Ho TW7 .... 130 D2
Woodall Rd EN3 ...... 18 D5
Woodbank Rd BR1 .. 164 D1
Woodbastwick Rd
SE26 .... 185 A5
Woodberry Ave
Edmonton N21 .... 16 D2
Harrow HA2 .... 42 A5
Woodberry Cl
Ashford TW16 ...... 172 A4
Mill Hill NW7 .... 28 D3
Woodberry Cres N10 .. 49 B6
Woodberry Down N4 . 51 A2
Woodberry Down Com Prim Sch N4 .... 51 A2
Woodberry Gdns N12 . 30 A4
Woodberry Gr
Finchley N12 .... 30 A4
Stoke Newington N4 ... 51 A2
Woodberry View N6 ... 49 A3
Woodberry Way
Chingford E4 .... 20 A4
Finchley N12 .... 30 A4
Woodbine Cl TW2 .... 152 B2
Woodbine Gr
Enfield EN2 .... 5 B5
Penge SE20 .... 184 B3
Woodbine La KT4 .... 216 C5
Woodbine Pl E11 ..... 55 A3
Woodbine Rd DA15 .. 167 C3
Woodbines Ave KT1 . 197 D6
Woodbine Terr E9 ..... 74 C2
Woodborough Rd
SW15 .... 134 B1
Woodbourne Ave
SW16 .... 159 D1
Woodbourne Cl
SW16 .... 160 A1
Woodbourne Dr
KT10 .... 212 D2
Woodbourne Gdns
SM6 .... 219 B1
Woodbridge Cl
4 Dollis Hill NW2 ..... 68 A5
10 Finsbury Pk N7 .... 72 B6
Woodbridge Ct
Forest Gate E7 .... 77 D3
Stoke Newington N16 .. 73 B5
Woodbridge High Sch
IG8 .... 37 B3
Woodbridge Ho E11 .. 54 D1
Woodbridge Rd IG11 . 79 D3
Woodbridge St
EC1 .... 94 D3 241 C6
Woodbrook Rd SE2 .. 146 B6
Woodburn Cl NW4 .... 46 D4
Woodbury Cl
Croydon CR0 .... 221 D6
Wanstead E11 .... 55 B5
Woodbury Ct 1 W13 .. 87 B3
Woodbury Gdns
Bromley SE12 .... 187 B6
Eltham SE12 .... 165 B1
Woodbury Ho 4
SE26 .... 162 B1
Woodbury Park Rd
W13 .... 87 B3
Woodbury Rd E17 ..... 53 D5
Woodbury St SW17 .. 180 C5
Woodchester Sq W2 .. 91 D2
Woodchurch Cl
DA14 .... 167 B1
Woodchurch Dr
BR1 .... 187 D3
Woodchurch Ho 15
SW9 .... 138 C4
Woodchurch Rd NW6 . 69 D1
Wood Cl
Bethnal Green E2 ..... 96 A3
Harrow HA1 .... 42 B2
Kingsbury NW9 .... 45 B2
Woodclyffe Dr BR7 .. 188 C1
Woodcock Ct HA3 .... 44 A2
Woodcock Dell Ave
HA3 .... 43 D2
Woodcock Hill HA3 ... 43 C3
Woodcock Ho 4 E14 . 97 C2
Woodcocks E16 .... 99 D2
Woodcombe Cres
SE23 .... 162 C3
Woodcote Ave
Mill Hill NW7 .... 28 C4
Thornton Heath CR7 . 204 D5
Wallington SM6 ..... 219 B1
Woodcote Cl
Enfield N9 .... 18 C5
Kingston u T KT2 .... 176 B5
Woodcote Ct 14
SM6 .... 219 B2
Woodcote Dr BR6 ... 211 B2
Woodcote Ho 4
SE8 .... 141 B6
Woodcote Mews
Loughton IG10 .... 21 D4
Wallington SM6 ..... 219 B2
Woodcote Pl 1
SE27 .... 182 D5
Woodcote Rd
Wallington SM6 ..... 219 C1
Wanstead E11 .... 55 A2
Woodcott Ho 1
SW15 .... 156 A4
Woodcroft SE9 ...... 166 B1
South Croydon CR0 .. 221 C5
Southgate N21 .... 16 C3
17 Stanmore HA7 ..... 25 C5
Wembley UB6 .... 65 A2
Woodcroft Ave
Edgware NW7 .... 27 C4
Stanmore HA7 .... 25 A2
Woodcroft Cres UB10 . 82 D6
Woodcroft Mews
SE8 .... 119 A2
Woodcroft Prim Sch
HA8 .... 27 C3
Woodcroft Rd CR7 .. 204 D3
Wood Dene 6 SE15 .. 140 B4
Wood Dr BR7 .... 188 A4
Woodedge Cl E4 ...... 20 D3
Woodend
South Norwood
SE19 .... 183 A4
Sutton SM1 .... 218 A6
Thames Ditton KT10 .. 212 A6
WOOD END 83 D1
Wood End UB3 .... 83 C1
Wood End Ave HA2 ... 64 A4
Wood End Cl UB5 ..... 64 B3
Woodend Gdns EN2 .... 4 A1
Wood End Gdns UB5 .. 64 A3
WOOD END GREEN ... 83 C2
Wood End Green Rd
UB3 .... 83 C1
Wood End Inf Sch
UB5 .... 64 B3
Wood End Jun Sch
UB6 .... 64 B3
Wood End La UB5 ..... 63 D3
Wood End Park Com Sch
UB3 .... 105 A6
Woodend Rd E17 ..... 36 A1
Wood End Rd HA1,
UB5 .... 64 B4
Wood End Way UB5 ... 64 A3
Wooder Gdns E7 ...... 77 A4
Wooderson Cl SE25 .. 205 C5
Wooderson Ct 9
BR3 .... 185 C2
Woodfall Ave EN5 ..... 13 B6
Woodfall Rd N4 .... 72 C6
Woodfall St SW3 .... 257 C1
Woodfarrs SE5 ...... 139 B1
Woodfield SW16 ..... 182 B2
Wood Field NW3 ...... 70 D3
Woodfield Ave
Colindale NW9 .... 45 C5
Ealing W5 .... 87 C3
Streatham SW16 .... 159 D1
Wallington SM5 ..... 219 A1
Wembley HA0 .... 65 C5
Woodfield Cl
1 Enfield EN1 .... 5 C1
South Norwood SE19 . 183 A3
Woodfield Cres W5 ... 87 D3
Woodfield Ct SW16 . 159 D1
Woodfield Dr EN4 ..... 15 A3

Woodfield Gdns KT3 ... 199 D4
Woodfield Gr SW16 ... 159 D1
Woodfield Ho
11 Forest Hill SE23 ... 162 D1
Hinchley Wood KT7 ... 212 D6
New Malden KT3 ... 199 D4
6 Upper Clapton E5 ... 74 B6
Wood Green N11 ... 31 D4
Woodfield La SW16 ... 159 D1
Woodfield Pl W9 ... 91 B3
Woodfield Rd
Cranford TW4, TW5 ... 128 B3
Ealing W5 ... 87 C3
Hinchley Wood KT10, KT7 ... 212 D6
Kensal Town W9 ... 91 B2
Woodfield Rise WD23 ... 8 B4
Woodfield Sch NW9 ... 45 C1
Woodfields Ct SM1 ... 218 A5
Woodfield Way N11 ... 31 D3
WOODFORD ... 37 D5
Woodford Ave IG2, IG4, IG5, IG8 ... 56 B5
Woodford Bridge Rd IG4 ... 56 A5
Woodford Cres HA5 ... 22 B1
Woodford Ct 15 W12 ... 112 D4
Woodford Cty High Sch for Girls IG8 ... 36 D4
Woodforde Ct UB3 ... 105 B1
WOODFORD GREEN ... 37 B3
Woodford Green Prep Sch IG8 ... 37 A4
Woodford Green Sch IG8 ... 36 D5
Woodford Ho
13 SE18 ... 144 D6
5 Wanstead E18 ... 55 A5
Woodford New Rd
Upper Walthamstow E17 ... 54 C6
Woodford E18 ... 36 D3
Woodford Pl HA9 ... 44 A1
Woodford Rd
Forest Gate E7 ... 77 B4
Wanstead E18 ... 55 A6
Woodford Sta IG8 ... 37 B4
Woodford Trad Est IG8 ... 37 D1
WOODFORD WELLS ... 21 B1
Woodgate Ave KT9 ... 213 D3
Woodgate Cres HA6 ... 22 A4
Woodgate Dr SW16 ... 181 D3
Woodgate Ho 12 KT6 ... 198 A3
Woodger Rd W12 ... 112 C4
Woodget Cl E6 ... 100 A1
Woodglen SM4 ... 202 C4
Woodgrange Ave
Ealing W5 ... 110 C5
Enfield EN1 ... 18 A5
Finchley N12 ... 30 B4
Harrow HA3 ... 43 D4
Woodgrange Cl HA3 ... 43 D4
Woodgrange Ct 1 BR2 ... 208 D1
Woodgrange Gdns EN1 ... 18 A5
Woodgrange Ho W5 ... 110 B5
Woodgrange Inf Sch E7 ... 77 B4
Woodgrange Mans HA3 ... 43 C4
Woodgrange Park Sta E12 ... 77 D3
Woodgrange Rd E7 ... 77 A3
Woodgrange Terr EN1 ... 18 A5
WOOD GREEN ... 32 B2
Wood Green Sh City N22 ... 32 C1
Wood Green Sta N22 ... 32 C1
Woodhall NW1 ... 232 A1
Woodhall Ave
Dulwich SE21 ... 161 D1
Pinner HA5 ... 23 A2
Woodhall Dr
Dulwich SE21 ... 161 D1
Pinner HA5 ... 23 A2
Woodhall Gate HA5 ... 22 D3
Woodhall Ho SW18 ... 158 B5
Woodhall La WD19 ... 23 A6
Woodhall Rd HA5 ... 22 D4
Woodhall Sch WD19 ... 23 A6
Woodham Ct E11 ... 54 D5
Woodham Rd SE6 ... 164 A1
Woodhatch Cl 16 E6 ... 100 A2
Woodhaven Gdns IG6 ... 57 A5
Woodhayes BR7 ... 188 D4
Woodhayes Rd SW19, SW20 ... 178 C4
Woodhead Dr BR6 ... 227 C6
Woodheyes Rd NW10 ... 67 C3
Woodhill SE7, SE18 ... 122 A2
Woodhill Cres HA3 ... 43 D3
Woodhill Prim Sch SE18 ... 122 A2
Wood Ho
4 Clapham SW4 ... 137 D3
6 Paddington NW6 ... 91 B5
Woodhouse Ave UB6 ... 86 D5
Woodhouse Cl
Hayes UB3 ... 105 C3
Wembley UB6 ... 86 D5
Woodhouse Coll N12 ... 30 B4
Woodhouse Eaves HA6 ... 22 A5
Woodhouse Gr E12 ... 78 A2
Woodhouse Rd
Colney Hatch N12 ... 30 C4
Leyton E11 ... 76 D5
Woodhurst Ave BR5 ... 211 A3
Woodhurst Rd
Acton W3 ... 111 A6
SE2 ... 124 A2
Woodington Cl SE9 ... 166 C5
Woodison St E3 ... 97 A3
Woodknoll Dr BR7 ... 188 B2
Wood La
Dagenham RM10 ... 81 A5
Highgate N6 ... 49 B3
Hounslow TW7 ... 130 D5
Kingsbury NW9 ... 45 B2
Ruislip HA4 ... 61 C6
Shepherd's Bush W12 ... 112 C6
Stanmore HA7 ... 9 B2
Woodford IG8 ... 36 D5
Woodland App UB6 ... 65 A2
Woodland Cl
Kingsbury NW9 ... 45 A3
Uxbridge UB10 ... 60 D6
West Ewell KT19 ... 215 C2
West Norwood SE19 ... 183 C4
Woodford IG8 ... 21 B1
Woodland Cres
18 Rotherhithe SE16 ... 118 D4
SE10 ... 142 C6
Woodland Ct
Cheam SM1 ... 217 C2
Temple Fortune NW4 ... 47 A4
13 Wanstead E11 ... 55 A4
Woodland Gdns
Cranley Gdns N10 ... 49 B4
Isleworth TW7 ... 130 C2
Woodland Gr SE10 ... 120 C1
Woodland Hill SE19 ... 183 C4
Woodland Hts SE3 ... 142 C6
Woodland Mews SW16 ... 160 A1
Woodland Rd
Chingford E4 ... 20 A3
Friern Barnet N11 ... 31 B5
Penge SE19 ... 183 D4
Thornton Heath CR7 ... 204 C5
Woodland Rise
Cranley Gdns N10 ... 49 B5
Wembley UB6 ... 65 A2
WOODLANDS ... 130 C2
Woodlands
Beckenham BR3 ... 185 D3
Bexley DA6 ... 169 D6
Clapham SW4 ... 137 B1
Finchley N12 ... 30 A4
Harrow HA2 ... 41 C5
Temple Fortune NW11 ... 47 A4
Walthamstow E11 ... 54 B2
West Barnes SW20 ... 200 D5
Woodlands Ave
Acton W3 ... 110 D5
DA15 ... 167 C3
Dagenham RM6 ... 59 A2
Finchley N3 ... 30 A2
Kingston u T KT3 ... 177 B2
Ruislip HA4 ... 40 D2
Wanstead E11 ... 55 B1
Woodlands Ave *continued*
Worcester Pk KT4 ... 216 A6
Woodlands Cl BR1 ... 188 B1
Claygate KT10 ... 212 D1
Temple Fortune NW11 ... 47 A4
Woodlands Ct
9 Bromley BR1 ... 186 D2
Brondesbury Pk NW10 ... 90 D6
Dulwich SE22 ... 162 B4
Southall UB1 ... 107 C6
Woodlands Dr
Harrow HA7 ... 24 D4
Sunbury TW16 ... 172 C1
Woodlands Fst & Mid Sch HA8 ... 26 B2
Woodlands Gdns E17 ... 54 C5
Woodlands Gr TW7 ... 130 C3
Woodlands Gt SW15 ... 157 B6
Woodlands Jun & Inf Schs IG1 ... 79 B3
Woodlands Par TW15 ... 171 A4
Woodlands Park Rd
SE10 ... 142 C6
Tottenham N15 ... 51 A4
Woodlands Rd
Barnes SW13 ... 133 D2
Bexleyheath DA7 ... 147 A2
Bickley BR1 ... 188 B1
Enfield EN2 ... 5 B4
Harrow HA1 ... 42 D4
Ilford IG1 ... 79 A5
Isleworth TW7 ... 130 C3
Lower Edmonton N9 ... 18 C3
Southall UB1 ... 106 D5
Surbiton KT6 ... 197 D2
Walthamstow E17 ... 54 A6
Woodlands St SE13 ... 164 B4
Woodland St 2 E8 ... 73 D2
Woodlands The
East Barnet N14 ... 15 B3
Harrow HA1 ... 64 C6
Highbury N5 ... 73 A4
12 Hornsey N8 ... 50 A2
Isleworth TW7 ... 130 D3
Lewisham SE13 ... 164 B4
Mitcham CR4 ... 203 A6
South Norwood SE19 ... 183 A3
Stanmore HA7 ... 25 B5
Thames Ditton KT10 ... 212 A6
Woodlands Way SW15 ... 157 B6
Woodland Terr SE7 ... 122 A2
Woodland Way
Abbey Wood SE2 ... 124 D2
Croydon CR0 ... 207 A1
Edgware NW7 ... 27 D4
Merton SM4 ... 201 B5
Mitcham CR4 ... 181 A3
Petts Wood BR5 ... 211 A4
Southgate N21 ... 16 C2
Tolworth KT5 ... 214 D6
West Wickham BR4 ... 224 A5
Woodford IG8 ... 21 B1
Woodland Wlk
Chessington KT19 ... 214 C2
9 Greenwich SE10 ... 120 C1
Hampstead NW3 ... 70 C3
Wood Lane High Sch W12 ... 90 B1
Wood Lane Sta W12 ... 112 C6
Wood La Sp Ctr RM8 ... 59 D1
Wood La Sta W12 ... 112 C6
Woodlawn Cl SW15 ... 157 B6
Woodlawn Cres TW2 ... 151 D2
Woodlawn Dr TW13 ... 150 D2
Woodlawn Rd SW6 ... 134 D4
Woodlea Dr BR2 ... 208 C4
Woodlea Lo EN1 ... 17 C5
Woodlea Rd N16 ... 73 C5
Woodleigh
1 Kingston u T KT5 ... 198 B4
3 Woodford E18 ... 37 A2
Woodleigh Ave N12 ... 30 C4
Woodleigh Ct N22 ... 32 B2
Woodleigh Gdns SW16 ... 160 A1
Woodley Cl SW17 ... 180 D3
Woodley La SM1, SM5 ... 218 C5
Woodlodge 4 SW19 ... 179 B5
Wood Lodge Gdns BR1 ... 188 A3
Wood Lodge La BR4 ... 224 A5
Woodman La E4 ... 20 C6
Woodman Mews TW9 ... 132 D4
Woodman Par 4 E16 ... 122 C5
Woodmans Ct HA7 ... 44 A6
Woodmans Gr NW10 ... 67 D3
Woodmans Mews W12 ... 90 B2
Woodman St E16 ... 122 C5
Woodmansterne Prim Sch SW16 ... 181 D2
Woodmansterne Rd
Mitcham SW16 ... 181 D2
Sutton SM5 ... 218 C1
Wood Mead N17 ... 34 A4
Woodmere SE9 ... 166 B3
Woodmere Ave CR0 ... 206 D2
Woodmere Cl
11 Clapham SW11 ... 137 A2
Croydon CR0 ... 206 D2
Woodmere Ct N14 ... 15 B4
Woodmere Gdns CR0 ... 206 D2
Woodmere Way BR3 ... 208 B4
Woodmill Rd E5 ... 74 C6
Woodnook Rd SW16 ... 181 B5
Woodpecker Cl
Bushey WD23 ... 8 A3
Enfield N9 ... 18 B5
Harrow HA3 ... 24 D2
Woodpecker Ct TW2 ... 151 D4
Woodpecker Ho E17 ... 53 C6
Woodpecker Mews SE13 ... 142 B1
Woodpecker Rd
6 SE14 ... 141 A6
Woolwich SE28 ... 124 C6
Wood Point 8 E16 ... 99 A2
Woodquest Ave SE24 ... 161 A6
Wood Rd
Littleton TW17 ... 192 C5
Willesden NW10 ... 67 A1
Wood Retreat SE18 ... 145 B5
Wood Ride Barnet EN4 ... 2 B4
Orpington BR5 ... 211 C5
Woodridge Cl EN2 ... 4 C4
Woodridge Prim Sch N12 ... 13 C1
Woodridings Ave HA5 ... 23 B2
Woodridings Cl HA5 ... 23 B3
Woodridings Ct N22 ... 31 D2
Woodriffe Rd E11 ... 54 B2
Wood Rise HA5 ... 40 A4
Woodrow SE18 ... 122 B2
Woodrow Ave UB4 ... 83 D3
Woodrow Cl UB6 ... 65 B1
Woodrow Ct 3 N17 ... 34 B3
Woodruff Ho 12 SW2 ... 160 C5
Woodrush Cl 4 SE14 ... 141 A5
Woodrush Way RM6 ... 58 D5
Woodseer St E1 ... 96 A2
Woodsford SE17 ... 262 C1
Woodsford Sq W14 ... 113 A4 244 B2
Woodshire Rd RM10 ... 81 D5
Woods Ho SW8 ... 269 A2
WOODSIDE ... 206 A4
Woodside
Buckhurst Hill IG9 ... 21 C2
Hampstead Garden Suburb NW11 ... 47 C4
Muswell Hill N10 ... 49 A6
Walton-on-T KT12 ... 194 A1
Wimbledon SW19 ... 179 B5
Woodside Ave
Chislehurst BR7 ... 189 A5
Croydon SE25 ... 206 B4
Fortis Green N6 ... 48 D5
North Finchley N12 ... 30 A6
Thames Ditton KT10 ... 196 C2
Wembley HA0 ... 88 A6
Woodside Cl
Ruislip HA4 ... 39 B3
Stanmore HA7 ... 25 B5
Tolworth KT5 ... 199 A2
Wembley HA0 ... 88 A6
Woodside Court Rd CR0 ... 206 A2
Woodside Cres DA15 ... 167 C1
Woodside Ct
Ealing W5 ... 110 A5
Enfield EN2 ... 4 D4
10 Finchley N12 ... 29 D6
Palmers Green N13 ... 16 C1
Wanstead E12 ... 55 C1
Woodside End HA0 ... 88 A6
Woodside Gdns
Chingford E4 ... 35 D4
Tottenham N17 ... 33 D1
Woodside Gn SE25 ... 206 A3
Woodside Gr N12 ... 14 A1
Woodside Grange Rd N12 ... 29 D6
Woodside High Sch N22 ... 32 D3
Woodside Ho SW19 ... 179 B4
Woodside Jun & Inf Sch CR0 ... 206 A2
Woodside La DA5 ... 168 D5
Whetstone N12 ... 14 A1
WOODSIDE PARK ... 29 C6
Woodside Park Ave E17 ... 54 B5
Woodside Park Rd N12 ... 30 A6
Woodside Pk SE25 ... 206 B3
Woodside Pk Sta N12 ... 29 D6
Woodside Pl HA0 ... 88 A6
Woodside Prim Sch E17 ... 54 A6
Woodside Rd BR1 ... 210 A4
Coombe KT3 ... 177 C1
Croydon SE25 ... 206 B3
Kingston u T KT2 ... 176 A3
Newham E13 ... 99 C3
Northwood HA6 ... 22 A3
Sidcup DA15 ... 167 C1
Sutton SM1 ... 218 A5
Woodford IG8 ... 37 A6
Wood Green N22 ... 32 C3
Woodside Sch DA17 ... 125 D2
Woodside Sta SE25 ... 206 B3
Woodside Way
Croydon CR0 ... 206 C3
Streatham CR4 ... 181 C2
Wood's Mews W1 ... 115 A6 248 A6
Woodsome Rd NW5 ... 71 B5
Wood's Pl SE1 ... 263 B5
Woodspring Rd SW19 ... 157 A2
Wood's Rd SE15 ... 140 B4
Wood St Barnet EN5 ... 1 A1
Carshalton CR4 ... 203 A2
Chiswick W4 ... 111 C1
City of London EC2 ... 95 A1 242 B2
Custom Ho E16 ... 121 B6
Kingston u T KT1 ... 175 D1
Kingston u T KT2 ... 176 A2
Walthamstow E17 ... 54 B5
Woodstar Ho 3 SE15 ... 140 A5
Woodstead Gr HA8 ... 26 A4
Woods The
Eastbury HA6 ... 22 A5
Uxbridge UB10 ... 60 D4
Woodstock Ave
Brentford W13 ... 109 A3
Cheam SM3 ... 201 B2
Golders Green NW11 ... 47 A2
Isleworth TW7 ... 153 A6
Southall UB1 ... 85 B4
Woodstock Cl DA5 ... 169 B3
Stanmore HA7 ... 26 A1
Woodstock Cres N9 ... 18 B5
Woodstock Ct
Kingston u T KT2 ... 176 D1
Lee SE12 ... 165 A5
Vauxhall SE11 ... 260 D2
Woodstock Dr UB10 ... 60 B4
Woodstock Gdns
Beckenham BR3 ... 185 D3
Hayes UB4 ... 83 D2
Ilford IG3 ... 80 A6
Woodstock Gr W12 ... 112 D4
Woodstock Grange W5 ... 110 A5
Woodstock Ho
Hayes UB3 ... 83 B2
2 Highbury N5 ... 73 A4

Woodstock Lane N KT6 213 C6
Woodstock Lane S KT6, KT9, KT10 213 C4
Woodstock Mews W1 238 B3
Woodstock Rd
Bedford Pk W4 111 C3
Bushey WD23 8 D4
Chingford E17 36 B1
Finsbury Pk N4 50 C1
Golders Green NW11 47 B1
South Croydon CR0 221 B5
Upton E7 77 C1
Wallington SM5, SM6 219 A3
Wembley HA0 66 B1
Woodstock Rise SM3 201 B2
Woodstock St W1 238 C1
Woodstock Studios 17 W12 112 D4
Woodstock Terr E14 119 D6
Woodstock The SM3 201 B2
Woodstock Way CR4 181 C1
Woodstone Ave KT17, KT4 216 A3
Wood Street Sta E17 54 B5
Woodsyre SE26 183 D6
Woodthorpe Rd
Ashford TW15 170 A6
Putney SW15 134 B1
Woodtree Cl NW4 28 C1
Wood Vale
Cranley Gdns N10 49 C4
Dulwich SE22 162 B4
Woodvale Ave SE25 183 D1
Woodvale Ct BR1 187 B1
South Norwood SE25 205 D6
Woodvale Way NW11 68 D5
Woodvale Wlk SE27 183 A5
Woodview Ave E4 36 A6
Woodview Cl
Finsbury Pk N4 50 D2
Kingston u T SW15 177 B6
Orpington BR6 227 A6
Woodville SE3 143 B4
Woodville Cl SE12 165 A6
Teddington TW11 175 A6
Woodville Ct
3 Lewisham SE10 142 A4
Southgate N14 15 C6
Woodville Gdns
Ealing W5 88 A1
Hendon NW11 46 D2
Ilford IG6 56 D5
Ruislip HA4 39 A2
Surbiton KT6 197 D2
Woodville Gr 2 DA16 146 A2
Woodville Ho SE1 263 C6
Sutton SM1 217 D4
Woodville Rd
Barnet EN5 1 D2
Ealing W5 87 D1
Golders Green NW11 47 A2
Leytonstone E11 54 D1
Morden SM4 201 C5
Paddington NW6 91 B5
Richmond TW10 153 C1
South Norwood CR7 205 B6
Stoke Newington N16 73 C3
Walthamstow E17 53 B5
Woodford E18 37 B1
Woodville St 16 SE18 122 A2
Woodville The W5 87 D1
Woodward Ave NW4 46 A4
Woodward Cl KT10 212 D2
Woodwarde Rd SE22 161 C5
Woodward Gdns
Dagenham RM9 80 C1
Harrow HA7 24 D3
Woodward Rd RM9 80 C1
Wood Way BR6 226 C6
Woodway Cres HA1 43 A3
Woodwell St SW18 158 A6
Wood Wharf SE10 142 A6
Woodyard Cl NW5 71 A3
Woodyard La SE21 161 C4
Woodyates Rd SE12 165 B4
Woolacombe Rd SE3 143 C3
Woolacombe Way UB3 105 C2
Woolands Rd E11 76 C6
Woolcombes Ct 4 SE16 118 D5
Woolden Ho 2 E4 20 C4
Wooler St SE17 117 B1 262 D2
Woolf Cl SE28 124 B5
Woolf Ct 7 W3 111 A3
Woolf Mews WC1 240 A6
Woollaston Rd N4 50 D3
Woolley Ho SW9 138 D2
Woollon Ho 1 E1 96 C1
Woolmead Ave NW9 46 A2
Woolmer Gdns N18 34 A5
Woolmer Ho 2 E5 74 B6
Woolmer Rd N18 34 A5
Woolmore Prim Sch 14 E14 120 A6
Woolmore St E14 120 A6
Woolneigh St SW6 135 D3
Woolpack Ho 1 E9 74 C2
Wool Rd SW20 178 B4
Woolridge Cl TW14 149 A3
Woolridge Way E9 74 C1
Woolstaplers Way SE16 118 A2
Woolston Cl E17 34 D1
Woolstone Ho 7 E2 96 A6
Woolstone Rd SE23 163 A2
Woolven Ho SE3 142 D6
WOOLWICH 122 D3
Woolwich Arsenal Sta SE18 122 D2
Woolwich Church St SE7, SE18 122 A3
Woolwich Comm SE18 144 C6
Woolwich Ct EN3 7 C5
Woolwich Dockyard Ind Est SE18 122 A3
Woolwich Dockyard Sta SE18 122 B2
Woolwich High St SE18 122 C3
Woolwich Manorway E16 122 D4
Woolwich Manor Way
Beckton E6 100 C1
North Woolwich E16 122 D5
Woolwich New Rd SE18 122 D2
Woolwich Poly Sch SE28 124 A5
Woolwich Rd
Belvedere DA17 125 C1
DA7 147 C2
Erith SE2 125 B1
Greenwich SE7, SE10 121 C2
Woolwich Tramshed The★ 16 SE18 122 D2
Wooster Gdns E14 98 B1
Wooster Mews HA2 42 A6
Wooster Pl SE1 262 D4
Wootton KT10 212 A4
Wootton Gr N3 29 C2
Wootton Ho SE9 167 B5
Wootton St SE1 116 C5 251 B3
Worbeck Rd SE20 184 C1
Worcester Ave N17 34 A3
Worcester Cl
Croydon CR0 223 C6
Dollis Hill NW2 68 B5
Mitcham CR4 181 A1
Worcester Cres
Edgware NW7 11 C1
Woodford IG8 37 C6
Worcester Ct
Ashford TW15 170 D5
Ealing W7 86 D1
Finchley N12 29 D5
Harrow HA1 42 C6
44 Paddington W2 91 C2
12 Sutton SM2 217 D2
Walton-on-T KT12 194 C1
Worcester Pk KT4 215 C5
Worcester Dr
Ashford TW15 170 D5
Bedford Pk W4 111 C4
Worcester Gdns
Northolt UB6 64 B2
Redbridge IG1 56 A2
Wandsworth SW11 158 D6
Worcester Pk KT4 215 C5
Worcester Ho
Bayswater W2 236 A1
3 Islington N1 73 A1
Lambeth SE11 261 A5
9 Putney SW15 156 C4
Worcester Mews 2 NW6 69 D2
WORCESTER PARK 215 C4
Worcester Park Rd KT4 215 B5
Worcester Park Sta KT4 200 A1
Worcester Rd
Belmont SM2 217 D1
Higham Hill E17 34 D1
Ilford E12 78 B4
11 Wimbledon SW19 179 B5
Worcesters Ave EN1 6 A5
Worcesters Prim Sch EN1 5 D5
Wordsworth N8 50 C5
Wordsworth Ave
Greenford UB6 86 B5
Plashet E12 78 A1
Snaresbrook E18 54 D6
Wordsworth Ct
Harrow HA1 42 B2
New Barnet EN5 14 A6
Wordsworth Dr KT4, SM3 216 C4
Wordsworth Gdns WD6 10 C6
Wordsworth Ho
Maida Vale NW6 91 C4
15 SE18 144 C6
Wordsworth Par 1 N15 50 D5
Wordsworth Pl 11 NW5 70 D3
Wordsworth Rd
Bermondsey SE1 263 D3
Bexley DA16 145 C4
Hampton TW12, TW13 173 B6
Penge SE20 184 D3
Stoke Newington N16 73 C4
Wallington SM6 219 D2
Wordsworth Way UB7 104 B2
Wordsworth Wlk NW11 47 C5
Worfield St SW11 136 C5 267 B3
Worgan St
Rotherhithe SE16 118 D2
SE11 116 B1 260 C2
Working Men's Coll The NW1 93 C5 232 B4
Worland Rd E15 76 C1
World Bsns Ctr TW6 127 A4
World Rugby Mus★ TW1 152 C5
WORLD'S END 4 C1
Worlds End La BR6 227 D1
World's End La EN2 4 B1
World's End Pas SW10 266 C4
World's End Pl SW10 266 B4
World Trade Ctr London E14 119 D4
Worley Ct NW2 68 D5
Worleys Dr BR6 227 B4
Worlidge St W6 112 C1
Worlingham Rd SE22 139 D1
Wormholt Park Prim Sch W12 112 A6
Wormholt Rd W12 112 A5
Wormwood St EC2 243 A2
Wornington Rd W10 91 A2
Woronzow Rd NW8 92 C6 230 A5
Worple Ave
Isleworth TW7 153 A6
Wimbledon SW19 178 D3
Worple Cl HA2 41 B1
Worple Ct SW19 179 A4
Worple Prim Sch TW7 131 A1
Worple Rd
Isleworth TW7 131 A1
Wimbledon SW19, SW20 178 D2
Worple Road Mews SW19 179 B4
Worple St SW14 133 B2
Worple Way
Harrow HA2 41 B1
Richmond TW10 132 A1
Worship St EC2 95 C3 243 A5
Worslade Rd SW17 180 B6
Worsley Bridge Jun Sch 25 BR3 185 C3
Worsley Bridge Rd BR3, SE6 185 C5
Worsley Ct N3 29 D4
Worsley Gr E5 74 A4
Worsley Grange BR7 189 A4
Worsley Ho 9 SE23 162 B2
Worsley Rd E11 76 C4
Worsopp Dr SW4 159 C6
Worth Cl BR6 227 C4
Worthfield Cl KT19 215 B1
Worth Gr SE17 262 C1
Worthing Cl 5 E15 98 C6
Worthing Rd TW5 129 B6
Worthington Cl CR4 203 B6
Worthington Ho EC1 234 B2
16 Streatham SW2 160 C4
Worthington Rd KT6 198 B1
Wortley Rd
Forest Gate E6 77 D1
Thornton Heath CR0 204 C2
Worton Ct TW7 130 C1
Worton Gdns TW7 130 B3
Worton Hall Ind Est TW7 130 C1
Worton Rd TW7 130 C2
Worton Way TW3, TW7 130 B3
Wotton Ct 14 E14 120 B6
Wotton Rd
Cricklewood NW2 68 C5
18 SE8 141 B6
Wouldham Rd E16 98 D1
Wragby Rd E11 76 C5
Wrampling Pl N9 18 A3
Wrangthorne Wlk CR0 220 C4
Wray Ave IG5 56 C6
Wrayburn Ho 28 SE16 118 A4
Wray Cres N4 72 B6
Wray Ct N4 72 B6
Wrayfield Rd SM3 216 D5
Wray Ho 11 SW2 160 A3
Wraysbury Cl TW4 151 A6
Wrays Way UB4 83 C3
Wrekin Rd SE18 145 A5
Wren Acad N12 30 B5
Wren Ave
Cricklewood NW2 68 C4
Southall UB2 107 B2
Wren Cl E16 98 D1
Lower Edmonton N9 18 D3
Wren Cres WD23 8 A3
Wren Ct
1 Barnet EN4 14 D3
Croydon CR0 221 B4
Wren Gdns RM9 80 D3
Wren Ho 29 Bow E3 97 A5
4 Hampton TW12 173 D4
SW1 259 C1
Wren Landing E14 119 C5
Wrenn Ho SW13 134 C6
Wren Path SE28 123 B4
Wren Rd
Camberwell SE5 139 B4
Dagenham RM9 80 D3
Sidcup DA14 168 C1
Wrens Ave TW15 171 A6
Wren's Park Ho E5 74 B6
Wren St WC1 94 B3 240 D6
Wrentham Ave NW10 90 D5
Wrenthorpe Rd BR1 186 C6
Wren View N6 49 C1
Wrenwood Way HA5 40 B5
Wrestlers Ct EC3 243 A2
Wrexham Rd E3 97 C5
Wricklemarsh Rd SE3 143 D4
Wrigglesworth St SE14 140 D5
Wright Cl SE13 142 B1
Wright Gdns TW17 192 C4
Wright Ho SW15 156 B6
Wrighton Ct SM1 217 B2
Wright Rd TW5 128 C5
Wrights Cl RM10 81 D4
Wright's Gn SW4 137 D1
Wright's La W8 113 D3 255 C6
Wrights Pl NW10 67 A2
Wrights Rd SE25 205 C6
Wright's Rd E3 97 B5
Wright's Row SM5 219 B4
Wrights Wlk SW14 133 B2
Writtle Ho 36 NW9 27 D1
Wrotham Ho
Beckenham BR3 185 B3
SE1 262 D6
Wrotham Rd
Barnet EN5 1 A3
13 Camden Town NW1 71 C1
DA16 146 C4
Ealing W13 109 C5
Wrottesley Rd SE18 145 A6
Willesden Green NW10 90 A5
Wroughton Rd SW11 158 D5
Wroughton Terr NW4 46 B5
Wroxall Rd RM9 80 C2
Wroxham Gdns N11 31 D3
Wroxham Rd SE28 124 D6
Wroxton Rd SE15 140 C3
Wrythe Gn 2 SM5 218 D5
Wrythe Green Rd SM5 218 D5
Wrythe La SM1, SM5, SM4 218 C5
WRYTHE THE 218 D6
Wulfstan St W12 89 D1
Wyatt Cl Bushey WD23 8 C4
Feltham TW13 150 D3
Hayes UB4 84 A2
Rotherhithe SE16 119 B4
Wyatt Ct HA0 66 A1
Wyatt Dr SW13 134 B5
Wyatt Ho
Blackheath Vale SE3 142 D3
NW8 236 D5
Wyatt Park Mans 1 SW2 160 A2
Wyatt Park Rd SW2 160 B2
Wyatt Rd
Forest Gate E7 77 A2
Highbury N5 73 A5
Wyatt's La E17 54 A6
Wybert St NW1 239 A6
Wyborne Ho NW10 67 A1
Wyborne Prim Sch SE9 166 D3
Wyborne Way NW10 67 A1
Wyburn Ave EN5 1 B2
Wyche Gr CR2 221 A1
Wycherley Cl SE3 142 D5
Wycherley Cres EN5 13 D5
Wychwood Ave
Edgware HA8 25 D4
South Norwood CR7 205 A6
Wychwood Cl
Ashford TW16 172 A4
Edgware HA8 25 D4
Wychwood End N6 49 C2
Wychwood Gdns IG5 56 C5
Wychwood Ho N4 51 A2
Wychwood Way SE19 183 B4
Wyclif Ct EC1 234 C1
Wycliffe Cl DA16 145 D4
Wycliffe Ho 13 N16 73 C4
Wycliffe Rd
Battersea SW11 137 A3
Wimbledon SW19 179 D4
Wyclif St EC1 234 C1
Wycombe Ct SE3 143 A5
Wycombe Gdns NW11 69 C6
Wycombe Ho NW8 237 A6
Wycombe Pl SW18 158 A5
Wycombe Rd
Redbridge IG2 56 B4
Tottenham N17 34 A2
Wembley HA0 88 C6
Wycombe Sq W8 245 A3
Wydehurst Rd CR0 206 B2
Wydell Cl SM4 200 D3
Wydeville Manor Rd SE12 187 B6
Wye Cl Ashford TW15 170 D6
BR6 211 D2
Ruislip HA4 39 A3

Wye Ct W13 . . . . .87 B2
Wyemead Cres E4 . . . . . . .20 C2
Wyersdale Ho N4 . . . . . .51 A2
Wye St SW11 . . . . .136 B3
Wyevale Cl HA5 . . . . .40 A6
Wyfold Ho ⑧ SE2 . . . .124 D4
Wyfold Rd
SW6 . . . . . .135 A5 264 A3
Wyke Cl TW7 . . . . .130 D6
Wyke Gdns W7 . . . . .109 A3
Wykeham Ave RM9 . . . . .80 C2
Wykeham Cl UB7 . . . .126 C6
Wykeham Ct
Chislehurst BR7 . . . . .189 C4
Hendon NW4 . . . . .46 C4
Wykeham Gn RM9 . . . . .80 C2
Wykeham Hill HA9 . . . . .44 B1
Wykeham Ho SW19 . .179 C2
Wykeham Prim Sch
NW10 . . . . .67 C5
Wykeham Rd
Harrow HA3 . . . . .43 B5
Hendon NW4 . . . . .46 C4
Wykeham Rise N20 . . . .13 A3
Wykehurst Rd SW17 .180 B5
Wyke Rd
Hackney Wick E3 . . . . .75 C1
Merton SW20 . . . . . . .178 C1
Wylchin Cl HA5 . . . . . . .39 A6
Wyldes Cl NW11 . . . . . . .48 A1
Wyldfield Gdns N9 . . . . .17 D2
Wyld Way HA9 . . . . .66 D2
Wyleu St SE23 . . . . . . .163 A4
Wylie Rd UB2 . . . . .107 C3
Wyllen Cl E1 . . . . .96 C3
Wylo Dr EN5 . . . . .12 A5
Wymering Mans
W9 . . . . .91 C4
Wymering Rd W9 . . . . . .91 C4
Wymondham Ct
NW8 . . . . .229 D6
Wymond St SW15 . . . .134 C2
Wynan Rd E14 . . . . .119 D1
Wynash Gdns SM5 . . . .218 C3
Wynaud Ct N22 . . . . .32 A4
Wynbourne St SE20 .184 B1
Wyncham Ave DA15 . .167 C3
Wynchgate
Harrow HA3 . . . . .24 C3
Southgate N14 . . . . . . .16 A4
Wyncroft Cl BR1 . . . . . .210 B6
Wyndale Ave NW9 . . . . .44 C3
Wyndcliff Rd SE7 . . . .143 B6
Wyndcroft Cl EN2 . . . . . .4 A2
Wyndham Cl
Belmont SM2 . . . . . . .217 C1
Orpington BR6 . . . . . .211 A1
Wyndham Cres
Camden Town N19 . . . .71 C5
Hounslow TW4 . . . . . .151 C5
Wyndham Ct
Brentford W7 . . . . . . .109 A2
❶ Thornton Heath
CR0 . . . . .204 D3
Wyndham Deedes Ho ❷
E2 . . . . .96 A5
Wyndham Ho SW1 . . .258 A3
Wyndham Lo TW7 . . . .130 C4
Wyndham Mews W1 .237 C3
Wyndham Pl W1 . . . . .237 C3
Wyndham Rd
Barnet EN4 . . . . .14 D3
Brentford W7 . . . . .77 D1
Forest Gate E6 . . . . . . .77 D1
Kingston u T KT2 . . . .176 B3
SE5 . . . . .139 A5
Wyndhams Ct ❽ E8 . . .73 D1
Wyndham St
W1 . . . . . . .92 D2 237 C4
Wyndham Yd W1 . . . .237 C3
Wyndhurst Cl CR2 . . . .220 D1
Wyneham Rd SE24 . .161 B6
Wynell Rd SE23 . . . . . .162 D1
Wynford Rd DA17 . . . .147 C6
Wynford
N1 . . . . .94 B5 233 D6
Wynford Way SE9 . . . .166 B1

Wynlie Gdns HA5 . . . . . .22 B1
Wynndale Rd E18 . . . . . .37 B2
Wynne Ct ⑩ TW7 . . . .131 A2
Wynne Ho SE14 . . . . . .140 D4
Wynne Rd SW9 . . . . . .138 C3
Wynn's Ave DA15 . . . .168 A6
Wynnstay Gdns
W8 . . . . . . .113 C3 255 B6
Wynter Ho ⑳ SW9 . .138 B3
Wynter St SW11 . . . . .136 A1
Wynton Gdns SE25 . .205 D4
Wynton Pl W3 . . . . .88 D1
Wynyard Ho SE11 . . . .260 D2
Wynyard Terr SE11 . . .260 D2
Wynyatt Ho EC1 . . . . .234 C3
Wynyatt St
EC1 . . . . . . .94 D4 234 C2
Wyre Gr Edgware HA8 . .10 C1
Hayes UB3 . . . . .106 A2
Wyresdale Cres UB6 . .86 D4
Wyteleaf Cl HA4 . . . . . . .39 A3
Wytham Ho NW8 . . . .236 D5
Wythburn Ct W1 . . . . .237 C2
Wythburn Pl W1 . . . . .237 C2
Wythenshawe Rd
RM10 . . . . .81 C5
Wythens Wlk SE9 . . . .166 D6
Wythes Cl BR1 . . . . . . .188 B1
Wythes Rd E16 . . . . . .122 A5
Wythfield Rd SE9 . . . .166 B5
Wyvenhoe Rd HA2 . . . .64 A5
Wyvern Est The KT3. .200 A5
Wyvil Prim Sch
SW8 . . . . . . .138 A5 270 A4
Wyvil Rd
SW8 . . . . . . .138 A5 270 A4
Wyvis St E14 . . . . .97 D2

X

Xavier Ho E17 . . . . .35 B1

Y

Yabsley St E14 . . . . .120 A5
Yaldam Ho SE1 . . . . . .263 A3
Yalding Ho ⑳ E5 . . . . . .74 B3
Yalding Rd SE16 . . . . .118 A2
Yale Cl TW4 . . . . .151 B2
Yale Ct NW6 . . . . .69 D3
Yarborough Rd ❶
SW19 . . . . .180 B2
Yardley Cl E4 . . . . .19 D6
Yardley Ct SM3 . . . . . .216 D4
Yardley La E4 . . . . .19 D6
Yardley Prim Sch E4 . .20 A5
Yardley St WC1 . . . . . .234 A1
Yard The N1 . . . . .233 B3
Yarlington Ct N11 . . . . .31 A5
Yarmouth Cres N17 . . .52 B4
Yarmouth Pl W1 . . . . .248 C3
Yarnfield Sq ⑮
SE15 . . . . .140 A4
Yarnton Way DA17, . . .
. . . . .148 B3
Yarrow Cres E6 . . . . . .100 A2
Yarrow Ho
⑫ Cubitt Town E14 . .120 A3
⑯ North Kensington
W10 . . . . .90 C2
Yateley St SE18 . . . . . .121 D3
Yatesbury Ct E5 . . . . . .75 A3
Yates Ct NW2 . . . . .68 D2
Yates Ho ㉒ E2 . . . . .96 A4
Yatton Ho ⑲ W10 . . . .90 C2
YEADING 84 D3
Yeading Ave HA2 . . . . . .41 A1
Yeading Ct UB4 . . . . . . .84 D3
Yeading Fork UB4 . . . . .84 C3
Yeading Gdns UB4 . . . .84 B2
Yeading Ho UB4 . . . . . .84 D2
Yeading Jun & Inf Schs
UB4 . . . . .84 C2
Yeading La Hayes UB4 .84 B2
Northolt UB4, UB5 . . . .84 C4
Yeadon Ho ⑰ W10 . . . .90 C2
Yeames Cl W13 . . . . . . .87 A1
Yearby Ho W10 . . . . . . .90 C3

Yeate St N1 . . . . .73 B1
Yeatman Rd N6 . . . . . . .48 D3
Yeats Cl Ealing W7 . . .108 D6
London NW10 . . . . .67 C2
Yeend Cl KT8 . . . . .195 C5
Yeldham Ho W6 . . . . . .112 D1
Yeldham Rd W6 . . . . . .112 D1
Yellowhammer Ct
NW9 . . . . .27 C1
Yelverton Lo TW1 . . . .153 C4
Yelverton Rd SW11. .136 B3
Ye Market CR0 . . . . . . .221 B3
Yenston Cl SM4 . . . . . .201 C3
Yeoman Cl
Newham E16 . . . . . . .122 D6
West Norwood SE27 .160 D1
Yeoman Ct
Heston TW5 . . . . .129 B5
❸ Sutton SM1 . . . . . .218 B3
Yeoman Dr TW19 . . . .148 A3
Yeoman Rd UB5 . . . . . .63 A1
Yeomans Acre HA4 . . .40 A3
Yeomans Mews
TW7 . . . . .152 B6
Yeoman's Row
SW3 . . . . . . .114 C3 257 B5
Yeoman St SE8 . . . . . .119 A2
Yeomans Way E3 . . . . .6 C3
Yeoman's Yd E1 . . . . . .253 D6
Yeo St E3 . . . . .97 D2
Yeovil Cl BR6 . . . . .227 C6
Yeovil Ho
Finsbury Pk N7 . . . . . . .72 B6
North Kensington W10. .90 C3
Yeovilton Pl KT2 . . . . .175 C5
Yerbury Prim Sch
N19 . . . . .71 D5
Yerbury Rd N19 . . . . . . .71 D5
Yeshivo Horomo
Talmudical Coll N16 .51 B1
Yesodey Hatorah Jun
Sch for Girls ❼ N16 .51 D2
Yesodey Hatorah Sec
Sch for Girls N16 . .51 D2
Yester Dr BR7 . . . . .188 A3
Yester Pk BR7 . . . . . . .188 B4
Yester Rd BR7 . . . . . . .188 B3
Yew Lev Ct E5 . . . . .52 A1
Yew Ave UB7 . . . . .104 A6
Yew Cl IG9 . . . . .21 D2
Yewdale Cl BR1 . . . . . .186 C4
Yewfield Rd NW10 . . . .67 D2
Yew Gr NW2 . . . . .68 D4
Yew Ho SE14 . . . . .141 B3
Yews The TW15 . . . . . .170 D6
Yew Tree Ave N2 . . . . . .47 D6
Yew Tree Cl
Harrow HA2 . . . . .41 D5
Wood Green N22 . . . . .31 C2
Yew Tree Cl DA16 . . . .146 A4
❸ Lewisham SE13 . . .142 A2
New Malden KT4 . . . .199 C1
Southgate N21 . . . . . .16 C4
Yew Tree Cotts
KT10 . . . . .212 B6
Yew Tree Ct
Elstree WD6 . . . . .9 D5
❸ Stoke Newington
N16 . . . . .73 B6
❸ Sutton SM2 . . . . . .218 A1
❹ Temple Fortune
NW11 . . . . .47 B4
Yew Tree Gdns RM6 . .59 A4
Yew Tree Grange ❷
W5 . . . . .109 C6
Yew Tree Ho
New Malden KT4 . . . .199 C1
❺ Surbiton KT6 . . . . .198 A1
Yew Tree Lo
SW16 . . . . .181 C6
Yewtree Rd BR3 . . . . .207 B6
Yew Tree Rd
East Acton W12 . . . . .111 D6
Hillingdon UB10 . . . . . .82 B6
Yew Trees TW17 . . . . .192 B5
Yew Tree Wlk TW4 . . .151 C1
Yew Wlk HA1 . . . . .42 C1
YIEWSLEY 104 A6
Yiewsley Ct UB7 . . . . .104 A5
Yoakley Rd N16 . . . . . . .73 C6

Yoke Cl N7 . . . . .72 A2
Yolande Gdns SE9 . . .166 A6
Yonge Pk N4, N7 . . . . . .72 C5
York Ave Ealing W7 . . .108 C5
Hayes UB3 . . . . .83 A1
Mortlake SW14 . . . . . .155 A6
Sidcup DA15 . . . . .167 D2
Stanmore HA7 . . . . . . .25 B1
Walworth SE17 . . . . . .262 B2
York Bldgs
WC2 . . . . . . .116 A6 250 B5
York Bridge
NW1 . . . . . . .93 A3 238 A6
York Cl
❶❼ Camberwell SE5 .139 A3
Ealing W7 . . . . .108 C5
Morden SM4 . . . . .201 D5
Newham E6 . . . . .100 B1
York Ct
Beckenham BR3 . . . .186 B2
Kingston u T KT2 . . . .175 D4
Palmers Green N13 . . .16 A1
Wallington SM6 . . . . .219 C3
York Gate NW1 . . . . . .238 B5
Southgate N14 . . . . . . .15 D6
York Gr SE15 . . . . .140 C4
York Hall L Ctr E2 . . . .96 C5
York Hill SE27, SW16. .160 D1
York Ho Acton W3 . . . .111 A6
Chelsea SW3 . . . . . . .257 D2
Chingford E4 . . . . .20 C4
Edgware HA8 . . . . .26 B4
Enfield EN2 . . . . .5 B4
Forest Hill SE26 . . . .184 C5
❶ Hendon NW4 . . . . .28 D1
❶ Ilford IG1 . . . . .78 D6
Islington N5 . . . . .72 C4
Kensington W8 . . . . .245 C2
❸ Kentish Town N7 . .71 D2
Kew TW9 . . . . .132 C4
❹ Kingston u T KT2 . .175 D4
Lambeth SE1 116 B3 260 D5
Marylebone W1 . . . . .237 C4
Richmond TW10 . . . . .154 C6
South Norwood SE25 .205 C5
❶❶ West Acton W3 . . .88 C1
York House Pl
W8 . . . . . .113 D4 245 C2
Yorkland Ave DA16. .145 D1
Yorkley Ho ❸ W10 . . .90 C3
York Mans
Battersea SW11 . . . . .268 B2
❷ Hendon NW4 . . . . .46 A3
Marylebone W1 . . . . .238 A4
Walworth SE17 . . . . . .262 B2
York Mews
Camden Town NW5 . .71 B3
❷ Ilford IG1 . . . . .78 C5
York Par
Brentford TW8 . . . . . .109 D1
Hendon NW9 . . . . .46 A6
York Pl
Battersea SW11 . . . .136 B2
❷ Ilford IG1 . . . . .78 C6
❸ Ilford IG1 . . . . .78 C6
York Place Mans
NW1 . . . . .237 D4
York Rd
Battersea SW11,
SW18 . . . . .136 B2
Belmont SM1, SM2 . .217 C1
Brentford TW8 . . . . . .109 D1
Chingford E4 . . . . .35 C5
Dagenham W3 . . . . . . .89 B1
Ealing W5 . . . . .109 C3
Edmonton N18 . . . . . . .34 B5
Forest Gate E7 . . . . . . .77 A4
Friern Barnet N11 . . . .31 D4
Hounslow TW3 . . . . .129 D2
❸ Ilford IG1 . . . . .78 C6
Kingston u T KT2 . . . .176 B3
Leyton E10 . . . . .54 B6
New Barnet EN5 . . . . .14 B6
Pinner HA6 . . . . .22 C2
❹ Richmond TW10 . .154 B6
SE1 . . . . . . .116 B4 250 D2
Southgate N21 . . . . . .17 B4
Teddington TW11 . . . .174 C6
Thornton Heath CR0 .204 C2

York Rd continued
Walthamstow E17 . . . .52 D4
Wimbledon SW19 . . . .180 A4
York Rise BR6 . . . . .227 C6
Dartmouth Pk NW5 . . . .71 B5
York Road Bsns Ctr
SW11 . . . . .136 B3
York St Chambers
W1 . . . . .237 C4
Yorkshire Cl N16 . . . . . .73 C5
Yorkshire Gdns N18 . . .34 B5
Yorkshire Grey SE9 . .165 D6
Yorkshire Grey Pl ⑬
NW3 . . . . .70 A4
Yorkshire Grey Yd
WCL 240 C3
Yorkshire Rd
Limehouse E14 . . . . . .97 A1
Mitcham CR4 . . . . . . .204 A5
York Sq ⑫ E14 . . . . . . .97 A1
York St
Carshalton CR4 . . . . .203 A2
Paddington
W1 . . . . . . .92 D2 237 D4
Twickenham TW1. . . .153 A3
York Terr EN2 . . . . .5 A5
York Terr E
NW1 . . . . . . .93 A3 238 B5
York Terr W
NW1 . . . . . . .93 A3 238 A5
Yorkton St E2 . . . . .96 A5
York Way
Barnsbury N1, N7,
NW1 . . . . .72 A1
Chessington KT9 . . . .214 A1
Friern Barnet N20 . . . .14 D1
N1 . . . . .233 B5
Twickenham TW13. . .151 B1
York Way Ct
Islington N1 . . . . .233 C5
Islington N1 . . . . .233 B5
York Wr Gate * SW1 .250 B4
Youngmans Cl EN2. . . . .5 A4
Young Rd E16 . . . . .99 C1
Young's Bldgs EC1 . .242 B6
Young's Brewery Visitor
Ctr ⁂ SW18 . . . . . . .157 D6
Youngs Ct SW11 . . . . .268 B1
Young St W8 .113 D4 245 C1
Young St W8 113 D4 245 C1
Youngs Rd IG2 . . . . . . .57 B4
Yoxall Ho ❸ W10 . . . . .90 C3
Yoxford Ct ❹ RM6 . . . .58 B4
Yoxley App IG2 . . . . . . .57 A3
Yoxley Dr IG2 . . . . .57 A3
Yukon Rd SW12 . . . . . .159 B4
Yunus Khan Cl E17 . . .53 C4

Z

Zambezie Dr N9 . . . . . . .18 C1
Zampa Rd SE16 . . . . . .118 C1
Zander Ct E2 . . . . .96 A4
Zangwill Ho NW6 . . . . . .91 B5
Zangwill Rd SE18,
SE3 . . . . .143 D4
Zaskin Coll ⑱ HA1 . . . .42 D3
Zealand Ave UB7 . . . .126 A5
Zealand Ho
❶ Camberwell SE5 . .139 A3
❹ Woolwich SE18 . . .122 A2
Zealand Rd E3 . . . . .97 A5
Zenith Lo ⑦ N3 . . . . . .29 D3
Zennor Rd SW12 . . . .159 C3
Zenoria St SE22 . . . . .139 D1
Zermatt Rd CR7 . . . . . .205 A5
Zetland Ho ❽ W8 . . . .255 C6
Zetland St E14 . . . . .98 A2
Zeus Ho N1 . . . . .235 C1
Zion Ho ❻ E1 . . . . .96 C1
Zion Pl CR7 . . . . .205 B5
Zion Rd CR7 . . . . .205 B5
Zircon Ct N11 . . . . .31 D3
ZK Pk CR0 . . . . .220 B5
Zoar St SE1 . . . . . . .117 A5 252 A4
Zodiac Ct CR0 . . . . . . .204 D1
Zodiac Ho ⑧ E3 . . . . . .97 C3
Zoffany St N19 . . . . .71 D6

List of numbered locations

In some busy areas of the maps it is not always possible to show the name of every place.

Where not all names will fit, some smaller places are shown by a number. If you wish to find out the name associated with a number, use this listing.

Page number	10
Grid square	C1 2 Sunset Square
Location number	
Place name	

The places in this list are also listed conventionally in the Index.

478 27 A6

3 Aster Ct
4 Firethorn Cl
6 Berberry Cl
6 Hibiscus Cl
7 Roseway
B5 1 Monarchs Ct
2 Kensington Ct
3 Grosvenor Ct
4 Chaswood Ct
5 Mathilda Marks-Kennedy Jewish Prim Sch
C2 1 Rufforth Ct
2 Riccall Ct
3 Lindholme Ct
4 Driffield Ct
5 Jack Ashley Ct
6 Folkingham La
7 Debden Ct
8 Holbeach Ct
9 Shawbury Cl
10 Daniel Ct
11 Leander Ct
12 Nimrod
13 Nisbet
14 Pixton
15 Rapide
16 Ratier
17 Marham Dr
18 Wardell Field
D1 1 Gauntlet
2 Guilfoyle
3 Grebe
4 Gates
5 Galy
6 Folland
7 Firefly
8 Halifax
9 Debussy
10 Crosbie
11 Grant Ct
12 Ham Ct
13 Deal Ct
14 Ember Ct
15 Canterbury Ct
16 Beaumont Ct
17 Cirrus
18 Defiant
19 Dessouter
20 Douglas
21 Cobham
22 Clayton
23 Camm
24 Bradon
25 Boarhound
26 Bodmin
27 Bleriot
28 Blackburn
29 Audax
30 Anson
31 Albatross
32 Arran Ct
33 Mavis Ct
34 Goosander Ct
35 Platt Halls (a)
36 Writtle Ho
37 Platt Halls (b)
38 Platt Halls (c)
D2 1 Slatter
2 Sopwith
3 Saimet
4 Sassoon
5 Roe
6 Orde
7 Osprey
8 Prodger
9 Randall
10 Porte
11 Norris
12 Nardini
13 Noel
14 Nicolson
15 Napier
16 Nighthawk
17 Moorhouse
18 Moineau
19 Mitchell
20 Lysander
21 Lillywhite
22 Martynside
23 March
24 Kemp
25 Mercury

26 Merlin
27 Hudson
28 Hawker
29 Hawfinch
30 Heracles
31 Hector
32 Concourse The
D3 1 Wellington
2 Wheeler
3 Whittaker
4 Whittle
5 Tedder
6 Cranwell Ct
7 Tait
8 Spooner

28
D1 1 York Ho
2 Windsor Ho
3 Regency Cres
4 Normandy Ho
5 Allerton Ct
6 Beaulieu Ho
7 Dewlands Ct
8 Knightshayes Ho

29
A3 2 Frances & Dick James Ct
3 Farthing Ct
4 Coniston Ct
B1 1 Carlisle Ct
2 Laburnum Lo
3 Eden Ct
4 Moorcroft Ct
5 Clifford Lo
6 Acacia Lo
7 Cumberland Ct
8 Little Dell Lo
9 Cyprus Ct
10 Cyprus Ho
11 Pardes House Gram Sch
12 Pardes House Prim Sch
C2 1 Sheringham Ct
2 St Ronan's Ct
3 Crescent Rise
4 Elm Ct
5 Norman Ct
6 Marlow Ct
7 Dancastle Ct
8 Newman Ct
9 Station Mans
10 Alice Ct
11 Siamese Mews
D3 1 Hadley Ct
2 Sherbrook Ho
3 Shine Ho
4 Regent Ct
5 Lodge Mead Ct
6 Spencer Ct
7 Zenith Lo
8 Burberry Ct
D4 1 Moss Hall Inf Sch
D5 1 Silverbell Ct
2 Inverey Ho
3 Wimbush Ho
4 Tudor Lo
5 Duncan Ct
6 Phillipson Ho
D6 1 Brookfield Ct
2 Magnolia Ct
3 Dunbar Ct
4 Haughmond
5 Nansen Village
6 Willow Ct
7 Birch Ct
8 Beechcroft Ct
9 Speedwell Ct
10 Woodside Ct
11 Speedwell Ho
12 Rebecca Ho
13 Ashbourne Ct
14 Forest Ct
15 Beecholme
16 Greville Lo
17 St Johnstone Ho
18 Ashbourne Ct
19 Clements Ct
20 Station App
21 Montclair Ct
22 Winterberry Ct
23 Caroline Ct

24 North London Int Sch (Lower Sch)
24 North London Int Sch (Lower School)

30
A2 1 Our Lady of Lourdes RC Prim Sch
A4 1 Sharon Ct
2 Lydia Ct
3 Beatrice Lo
4 Grange Ct
5 Blissland Ct
A5 1 Archgate Bsns Ctr
2 Robart Ho
3 Danescroft
4 Cornelius Ct
5 Gable Lo
6 Waterville Lo
7 Chand Ho
8 St Michael's RC Gram Sch
B1 1 New Trinity Rd
2 Garden Ho
3 Todd Ho
4 Sayers Ho
5 Mowbray Ho
6 Bouchier Ho
7 Cleveland Ho
8 Goodyear Ho
9 Lochleven Ho
10 Berwick Ho
11 Oak Ho
12 Hilton Ho
13 East View Ho
14 Myddleton Ho
15 Willow Wlk
16 Craven Ho
17 Willow Ho
18 Vane Ho
19 Adelphi Ct
20 Annette White Lo
21 Foskett Ho
22 Elmfield Ho
23 Sycamore Ho
24 Netherwood
25 Rew Lo
26 William Cl
B5 1 Damon Ho
2 Wendy Ho
3 Lychgate Ct
4 Clarence Ct
5 Carley Ct
6 Hermiston Ct
7 Cardewe Ct
8 Whitefriars Ct
D5 1 Halliwick Ct
2 Halliwick Court Par
3 Queen's Par
4 St Andrew's Villas
5 Hartland Ct
6 Kennard Mans
7 Bensley Ct
8 Leadbeaters Cl
9 Gibson Ct
10 Burton Ct
11 Knights Ct
12 Constable Cl
13 Alderman Ct
14 North London Int Sch (Upper Sch)
15 North London Int Sch (IB Diploma Ctre)

31
A3 1 Campe Ho
2 Betstyle Ho
3 Pymmes Brook Ho
4 Mosswell Ho
5 Cavendish Ho
6 Tudor Ho
7 Kingsfield Ho
8 Peacehaven Ct
9 Hatch Ho
10 Hampden Ct
11 Crown Ct

A4 1 Cheddar Cl
2 Wincanton Ct
3 Whitby Ct
4 Richmond Ct
5 Tadworth Ct
6 Wensley Cl
7 Howeth Ct
8 Kilnsey Ct
9 Harrogate Ct
10 Ripon Ct
B1 1 Cedar Ct
2 Carisbrook
3 St Ivian Ct
4 Barrington Ct
5 Essex Lo
B5 1 St Pauls CE Prim Sch
1 St Paul's CE Prim Sch
B6 1 Grovefield
2 Lapworth
3 Stewards Holte Wlk
4 Sarnes Ct
5 Stanhope Ho
6 Holmsdale Ho
7 Crosby Ct
8 Leyland Ct
9 Boundary Ct
10 Stateland Ct
C5 1 Barbara Martin Ho
2 Jerome Ct
3 Limes Cl
4 Arnos Grove Ct
5 Cedar Ct
6 Betspath Ho
7 Curtis Ho
8 Mason Ho
9 New Southgate Ind Est
10 Palmer's Ct
11 Swinson Ho
12 Jackson Ho

32
A4 1 Brownlow Lo
2 Brownlow Ho
3 Latham Ct
4 Fairlawns
5 Beaumaris
B1 2 St Paul's RC Prim Sch
C1 1 Penwortham Ct
2 Tarleton Ct
3 Holmeswood Ct
4 Kwesi Johnson Ct
5 Sandlings The
6 Suraj Ho
C6 1 Hazelwood Ct
2 Ashbourne Lo
3 Mapledurham Ct
4 Springfield Par Mews

33
A2 1 Lordship Lane Prim Sch
C2 1 Risley Avenue Prim Sch
2 Parkside Prep Sch
D1 1 Kenmare Dr
2 Ashling Ho
3 Honeysett Ho
4 Wilson's Ave
5 Palm Tree Ct
6 Stoneleigh Ct
7 Brook St
8 Assunah Sch
9 John Loughborough Sch
D3 1 Charles Ho
2 Moselle Ho
3 Ermine Ho
4 Kathleen Ferrier Ct
5 Concord Ho
6 Rees Ho
7 Williams Ho
8 Nursery Ct
9 William Rainbird Ho
10 Gibson Bsns Ctr

11 Wingate Trad Est
12 London Tottenham Coll
13 St Francis de Sales RC Jun & Inf Sch
D4 1 Regan Ho
2 Isis Ho
3 Boundary Ct
4 Stellar Ho
5 Cooperage Cl

34
A3 1 St Paul's & All Hallows CE Jun & Inf Schs
2 Northumberland Park Com Sch
3 Maple Pl
A5 1 Angel Pl
2 Cross St
3 Scott Ho
4 Beck Ho
5 Booker Rd
6 Bridport Ho
7 Cordwain Ho
8 St James's Ct
9 Highmead
A6 1 Walton Ho
2 Alma Ho
3 Brompton Ho
4 Field Ho
5 Bradwell Mews
6 Angel Corner Par
7 Paul Ct
8 Cuthbert Rd
9 Brockenhurst Mews
10 Brettenham Prim Sch
B3 1 Kenneth Robbins Ho
2 Charles Bradlaugh Ho
3 Woodrow Ct
4 Cheviot
5 Corbridge
6 Whittingham
7 Eastwood Cl
8 Alnwick
9 Bamburgh
10 Bellingham
11 Briaris Cl

35
A1 1 Clayton Ct
2 St Andrew's Ct
3 Aranya Ct
4 Fitzwilliam Ho
A2 1 Romany Gdns
2 Swansland Gdns
3 Garnett Way
4 Claymore Ct
5 Winchester Ct
C5 1 Ainslie Ho
2 Lewis Ho

36
B5 1 Hedgemoor Ct
2 Hewitt Ho
3 Castle Ho
4 Bailey Ct
5 Harcourt Ho
6 Gerboa Ct
7 Wentworth Ct
D1 1 Chatham Rd
2 Washington Rd
3 Cherry Tree Ct
4 Grosvenor Lo
5 Torfell
D2 1 Hillboro Ct
2 Dorchester Ct

37
A1 1 Chiltons The
2 Ullswater Ct
3 Leigh Ct
4 Woburn Ct
5 Alveston Sq
6 Eaton Ct
7 Regency Ct
8 Cowley Ct
9 High Oaks Lo

10 Snaresbrook Coll Prep Sch
10 South Woodford
A2 1 Lindal Ct
2 Hockley Ct
3 Woodleigh
4 Milne Ct
5 Cedar Ct
6 Elizabeth Ct
7 Silvermead
8 Laurel Mead Ct
9 Mitre Ct
10 Pevensey Ct
11 Lyndhurst Ct
12 Manor Court Lo
A3 1 New Jubilee Ct
2 Chartwell Ct
3 Greenwood
4 Clementine Wlk
A4 1 Terrace The
2 Broomhill Ct
3 Clifton Ct
4 Fairstead Lo
5 Hadleigh Ct
6 Broadmead Ct
7 Wilton Ct
8 Fairfield Ct
9 Higham Ct
10 Aston Ct
A6 1 Tree Tops
2 Cranfield Ct
3 Percival Ho
4 Raine Gdns
B1 1 Station East
2 Station App
3 James Ct
C3 1 Liston Way
2 Elizabeth Ct
3 Coopersale Ct
4 Sunset Ct
5 Lambourne Ct
C4 1 Hope Cl
2 Rex Par
3 Shalford
4 Rodings The
5 Lawrence Ct
6 Cowan Lo

40
C1 1 Salisbury Ho
2 Rodwell Ct
3 Pretoria Ho
4 Ottawa Ho
5 Swallow Ct
6 Wellington Ho
7 Canberra Ho
C6 1 Tulip Ct
2 Hyacinth Ct
3 Rose Ct
4 Iris Ct
D6 1 Ashburton Ct
2 Northend Lodge

41
C2 1 Buckingham College Prep Sch

42
C2 1 Harrovian Bsns Village
D3 1 Nightingale Ct
2 St John's Ct
3 Gayton Ct
4 Wilton Pl
5 Murray Ct
6 Cymbeline Ct
7 Knowles Ct
8 Charville Ct
9 Lime Ct
10 Petherton Ct
11 Garth Ct
12 Chalfont Ct
13 Shepherds Ct
14 Zaskin Coll
D4 1 Crystal Cctr The
2 Blue Point Ct
3 Ryan Ho
4 Rothwell Ct
5 Bruce Ho
6 Middlesex Ct
7 Ingram Ho
8 Arless Ho
9 Leaf Ho
10 Becket Fold
11 Brandan Ho
12 Robert Ho

46

A2 1 Milton Rd
2 Stanley Rd
A3 1 Mapesbury Mews
2 York Mans
3 Telford Rd
4 Beis Soroh Schneirer (Sch)
A5 1 Pilkington Ct
2 Cousins Ct
3 Seton Ct
4 Frensham Ct
5 Chatton Ct
6 Geraldine Ct
7 Swynford Gdns
8 Miller Ct
9 Roffey Ct
10 Peace Ct
11 Rambler Ct
12 Lion Ct
13 Wenlock Gdns
14 Dogrose Ct
15 Harry Ct
16 Tribune Ct
17 Bonville Gdns
18 Pearl Ct
B4 1 Vivian Mans
2 Parade Mans
3 Georgian Ct
4 Florence Mans
5 Park Mans
6 Cheyne Cl
7 Queens Par
8 Central Mans
C5 1 Courtney Ho
2 Golderton
3 Thornbury
4 Ferrydale Lo
5 Studio Mews
6 Brampton La
7 Short St
8 Belle Vue Rd
9 Longford Ct
10 Ashwood Ho
D4 1 Hasmonean Prim Sch
2 Independant Jewish Day Sch
D5 1 Midford Ho
2 Rockfield Ho
3 Lisselton Ho
4 Acrefield Ho
5 London Sch of Jewish Studies
6 Beth Jacob Gram Sch
7 Bell Lane Prim Sch
8 Nancy Reuben Prim Sch

47

A2 1 Talmud Torah Tiferes Shlomo
B2 1 Berkeley Ct
2 Exchange Mans
3 Beechcroft Ct
4 Nedahall Ct
B3 1 Charlton Lo
2 Clifton Gdns
B4 1 Hallswelle Par
2 Belmont Par
3 Temple Fortune Ho
4 Yew Tree Ct
5 Temple Fortune Par
6 Courtleigh
7 Arcade Ho
8 Queens Ct
9 Temple Fortune Ct
10 Crispin Mews
B5 1 Monkville Par
2 Ashbourne Par

48

A6 1 St Mary's Gn
2 Dunstan Cl
3 Paul Byrne Ho
4 Longfield Ct
5 Warwick Ct
6 Branksome Ct
7 Sherwood Hall

49

B6 1 Dorchester Ct
2 Old Chapel Pl
3 Athenaeum Pl
4 Risborough Cl
5 Risborough Ct
C1 1 Calvert Ct
2 Academy The
3 Whitehall Mans
4 Pauntley St
5 Archway Hts
6 Pauntley Ho
9 St Aloysius RC Coll
D1 1 Louise White Ho
2 Levison Way
3 Sanders Way
4 Birbeck Ho
5 Scholars Ct
6 Mount Carmel RC Tech Coll for Girls
D2 1 Eleanor Rathbone Ho
2 Christopher Lo
3 Monkridge
4 Marbleford Ct
5 High London
6 Garton Ho
7 Hilltop Ho
8 Caroline Martyn Ho
9 Arthur Henderson Ho
10 Margaret Mcmillan Ho
11 Enid Stacy Ho
12 Mary McArthur Ho
13 Bruce Glasier Ho
14 John Wheatley Ho
15 Keir Hardie Ho
16 Monroe Ho
17 Iberia Ho
18 Lygoe Ho
19 Lambert Ho
20 Shelbourne Ho
21 Arkansas Ho
22 Lafitte Ho
23 Shreveport Ho
24 Packenham Ho
25 Orpheus Ho
26 Fayetville Ho
27 Bayon Ho
D4 1 Kelland Cl
2 Truro Ct
3 Veryan Ct
4 Coulsdon Ct

50

A1 1 Beeches The
2 Lambton Ct
3 Nugent Ct
4 Lambton Mews
5 Mews The
A2 1 Marie Lloyd Gdns
2 Edith Cavell Cl
3 Marie Stopes Ct
4 Jessie Blythe La
5 Barbara Rudolph Ct
6 Hetty Rees Ct
7 Leyden Mans
8 Brambledown
9 Lochbie
10 Lyngham Ct
11 High Mount
12 Woodlands The
13 St Gildas' RC Jun Sch
A4 1 Margaret Hill Ho
2 Manray Ct
3 Hermiston Ct
4 Carleton Ho
5 Rokesly Jun & Inf Schs
A5 1 Mackenzie Ho
2 Stowell Ho
3 Campsbourne Ho
4 Palace Gate Mews
5 St Mary's CE Jun Sch
6 Greig City Acad
7 North London Rudolf Steiner Sch
B1 1 Lawson Ct
2 Wiltshire Ct
3 Fenstanton
4 Hutton Ct
5 Wisbech
6 Islington Arts & Media Sch
B5 3 St Mary's CE Inf Sch
D4 1 South Harringay Jun & Inf Schs
D5 1 Wordsworth Par
2 Spanswick Lo
3 Barker Ho
4 St John Vianney RC Prim Sch
D6 1 Langham Cl
2 Sidi Ct
3 Ince Terr

51

A2 1 Finmere Ho
2 Keynsham Ho
3 Kilpeck Ho
4 Knaresborough Ho
5 Leighfield Ho
6 Lonsdale Ho
7 Groveley Ho
8 Wensleydale Ho
9 Badminton Ct
B2 1 Selwood Ho
2 Bnois Jerusalem Girls Sch
2 Mendip Ho
3 Ennerdale Ho
3 Getters Talmud Torah
4 Delamere Ho
5 Westwood Ho
6 Bernwood Ho
7 Allerdale Ho
8 Chattenden Ho
9 Farningham Ho
10 Oakend Ho
B5 1 Wisdom Sch
C1 1 Godstone Ct
2 Farnham Ct
3 Milford Ct
4 Cranleigh Ct
5 Haslemere Ct
6 Belmont Ct
7 Hockworth Ho
8 Garratt Ho
9 Fairburn Ho
10 Thorndale Ho
11 Oakdene Ho
12 Briardale Ho
C2 1 Beis Rochel d'Satmar Girls Sch
3 Our Lady's Convent RC High Sch
C3 1 Oatfield Ho
2 Perry Ct
3 Henrietta Ho
4 Bournes Ho
5 Chisley Rd
6 Twyford Ho
7 Langford Cl
8 Hatchfield Ho
D1 1 Stamford Hill Mans
2 Montefiore Ct
3 Berwyn Ho
4 Clent Ho
5 Chiltern Ho
6 Laindon Ho
7 Pentland Ho
D2 1 Regent Ct
2 Stamford Lo
3 Holmwood Ct
4 Bobov Foundation Sch
5 Yesodey Hatorah Sec Sch for Girls
6 Lubavitch Boys Prim Sch
7 Yesodey Hatorah Jun Sch for Girls
8 Lubavitch Girls Prim Sch
9 Lubavitch House Sch (Jun Boys)
10 Skinners Company Sch (Upper)
D3 1 Sherboro Rd
2 Westcott Cl
3 Cadoxton Ave
D4 1 Westerfield Rd
2 Suffield Rd
D5 1 Laseron Ho
2 Greenway Cl
3 Earlsmead Prim Sch
3 Tottenham Gn E
4 Tottenham Gn E South Side
5 Deaconess Ct
6 Elliot Ct
7 Bushmead Cl
8 Beaufort Ho
9 Tynemouth Terr
10 Green CE Sch Holy Trinity (Inf Annexe) The
D6 1 Holcombe Rd
2 Rigby Ho
3 Chaplin Rd
4 Keswick Apartments
5 Ambleside Cl
6 Lauriston Apartments
7 Terrall Apartments
8 Old School Ct
9 Nicholson Ct
10 Reynardson's Ct
11 Protheroe Ho
13 North London Coll
14 Green CE Prim Sch The

52

A1 1 Stamford Gr E
2 Stamford Mans
3 Grove Mans
4 Stamford Gr W
6 Talmud-Torah Yetev-Lev
A6 2 Welbourne Prim Sch
B1 1 Hawkwood Mount
2 Holmbury View
3 High Hill Ferry
4 Leaside Ho
5 Courtlands
5 Tayyibah Girls Sch
6 Ivy Ho
7 Shelford Ct
8 Skinner's Company's Lower Sch

53

A4 1 Hammond Ct
2 St James Apartments
3 Grange The
A5 1 Bristol Park Rd
2 Stoneydown Ho
3 Callonfield
4 Hardyng Ho
5 Stoneydown Park Sch
6 St Patrick's RC Prim Sch
B5 1 Palace Mews
2 Thomas Jacomb Pl
C1 1 Wellington Mans
2 Clewer Ct
3 Cochrane Ct
C3 1 Samira Cl
2 Walter Savill Twr
3 Boston Rd
C5 1 Westbury Ho
2 Hatherley Ho
3 Vintry Mews
4 Tylers Ct
5 Merchants Lo
6 Gillards Mews
7 Blacksmiths Ho
8 Central Par
D1 1 Fitzgerald Ct
2 Bechervaise Ct
3 Underwood Ct
D2 1 Staton Ct
2 Howell Ct
3 Atkinson Ct
4 Russell Ct
5 St Catherines Twr
6 St Lukes Ct
7 St Matthews Ct
8 St Mark's Ct
9 St Elizabeth Ct
10 Emanuel Ct
11 St Thomas Ct
12 Beaumont Ho
13 Shelley Ct
14 St Paul's Twr
15 Flack Ct
16 King Ct
17 Osborne Ct
18 Muriel Ct
19 All Saints Twr
20 St Josephs Ct
D4 1 Harriet Ho
2 Eastbank Cl
D5 1 Nash Ho
2 St Columbas Ho
3 Attlee Terr
4 Astins Ho
5 Lindens The
6 Kevan Ct
7 Squire's Almshouses
8 Berry Field Cl
9 Connaught Ct
10 Holmcroft Ho
11 St Mary's Church Ho
D6 1 Hallingbury Ct
2 Mace Ho
3 Gaitskell Ho
4 Hancocke Ho
5 Trinity Ho
6 Fanshaw Ho
7 Hilltop
8 Batten Ho
9 Bradwell Ho
10 Walton Ho
11 Temple Ho
12 Gower Ho
13 Maple Ho
14 Poplars Ho
15 Cedars Ho
16 Kimm Ho
17 O'Grady Ho
18 Latham Ho
19 Powell Ct
20 Crosbie Ho

54

A2 1 Ayerst Ct
2 Dare Ct
3 St Edwards Ct
A4 1 Collard's Almshouses
2 Ellen Miller Ho
3 Tom Smith Ho
A5 1 Northwood Twr
2 Walnut Ct
3 Albert Whicher Ho
4 Pelly Ct
5 Ravenswood Ind Est
6 Holland Ct
7 Emberson Ho
8 St Mark's Ho
9 Alfred Villas
10 Leonard Ho
11 Old Station Yard The
A6 1 St David's Ct
2 Golden Par
3 Chestnuts Ct
4 Matthew Ct
5 Gilbert Ho
6 Manning Ho
7 Southgate Ho
8 Boyden Ho
9 Prospect Ho
10 Newton Ho
C1 2 Connaught Sch for Girls
D2 1 Buxton Ct
2 Hanbury Dr
3 Forest Lea
4 Watershipdown Ho

55

A3 1 Aldham Hall
2 Parkside Ct
3 Mapperley Cl
4 Weavers Ho
5 Cyna Ct
6 Reed Mans
7 Thornton Ho
8 Hardwick Ct
9 St Joseph's Convent Sch
A4 1 Kingsley Grange
2 Station Par
3 Gwynne Ho
4 Staveley Ct
5 Thurlow Ct
6 Devon Ho
7 Wellington Pas
8 Wanstead Hts
9 Hollies The
10 Little Holt
11 Hunter Ct
12 Mountier Ct
13 Woodland Ct
14 Dudley Ct
15 Struan Ho
16 Westleigh Ct
A5 1 Shernwood Ho
2 Orwell Lo
3 Hermitage Ct
4 Gowan Lea
5 Woodford Ho
6 Eagle Ct
7 Newbury Ct
8 Shelley Ct
9 Hardy Ct
10 Dickens Ct
11 Byron Ct
A6 1 Millbrook
2 Half Acre
3 Elmbrook
4 Grange The
5 Glenavon Lo
6 Glenwood Ct
7 Ferndown
8 Embassy Ct
9 Orestes Ct
10 Walbrook
11 Helmsley
12 Snaresbrook Hall
B4 1 Nightingale Ct
2 Chelston Ct
3 Grosvenor Ct
4 Louise Ct
5 St Davids Ct
6 Cedar Ct
7 Shrubbery The
8 Nightingale Mews
B5 1 Great Hall The
2 Clock Ct
3 Langham Ho
B6 1 Victoria Ct
2 Kenwood Gdns
3 Thaxted Lo
4 Albert Rd
5 Albert Ho
6 Falcon Ct
7 Deborah Ct
8 Swift Ho
9 Pulteney Gdns
10 Spring Ct
11 Trinity Gdns
12 Foxdene Cl

56

B4 1 High View Par
2 Spurway Par
3 Florence Root Ho
4 Rohan Pl
5 Homeheather Ho
D4 1 St Augustine's RC Prim Sch

57

A3 1 Catherine Ct
2 Ivy Terr
3 Newbury Cotts

3 Cobham Mews
4 Bergholt Mews
5 Blakeney Cl
6 Weavers Way
7 Allensbury Pl
D2 1 Rowstock
2 Peckwater Ho
3 Wolsey Ho
4 Pandian Way
5 Busby Mews
6 Caledonian Rd
7 Canal Bvd
8 Northpoint Sq
9 Lock Mews
10 Carters Cl
11 York Ho
12 Hungerford Rd
13 Cliff Road Studios
14 Cliff Ct
15 Camelot Ho
16 Church Studios
17 Camden Terr
18 Brecknock Prim Sch
19 Hungerford Prim Sch
D3 1 Blake Ho
2 Quelch Ho
3 Lee Ho
4 Willbury Ho
5 Howell Ho
6 Holmsbury Ho
7 Leith Ho
8 Betchworth Ho
9 Rushmore Ho
10 Dugdale Ho
11 Horsendon Ho
12 Colley Ho
13 Coombe Ho
14 Ivinghoe Ho
15 Buckhurst Ho
16 Saxonbury Ct
17 Charlton Ct
18 Apollo Studios
19 Barn Cl
20 Long Meadow
21 Landleys Field
22 Margaret Bondfield Ho
23 Haywood Lo
24 Torriano Jun & Inf Schs
D4 1 Fairlie Ct
2 Trecastle Way
3 Dalmeny Avenue Est
4 Hyndman Ho
5 Carpenter Ho
6 Graham Ho
7 Tufnell Mans
D5 1 Melchester Ho
2 Norcombe Ho
3 Weatherbury Ho
4 Wessex Ho
5 Archway Bsns Ctr
6 Harford Mews
7 Opera Ct
8 Rupert Ho
9 All Saints Church
D6 1 Bowerman Ho
2 Gresham Ho
3 Hargrave Mans
4 Church Garth
5 John King Ct
6 Ramsey Ct
7 St John's Upper Holloway CE Prim Sch
8 Byam Shaw Sch of Art

72
A2 1 Clock Tower Pl
2 Clock View Cres
3 Jim Veal Dr
4 Gower Sch The
A3 1 Kimble Ho
2 Saxonbury Ct
3 Poynder Ct
4 Pangbourne Ho
5 Moulsford Ho
A4 1 Arcade The
2 Macready Pl
3 Cardwell Rd
4 Mcmorran Ho

5 Crayford Ho
6 Whitby Cl
7 Prospect Pl
8 City & Islington Coll (Ctr for Bsns, Arts & Technology)
A5 1 Northview
2 Tufnell Park Mans
3 Fulford Mans
4 Tollington Ho
5 Grafton Prim Sch
A6 1 Bracey Mews
2 Christie Ct
3 Ringmer Gdns
4 Kingsdown Rd
5 Cottenham Ho
6 St Paul's Ct
7 Rickthorne Rd
8 Stanley Terr
9 Arundel Lo
10 Landseer Ct
11 St Mark's Prim Sch
B1 1 Kerwick Cl
2 Rydston Cl
3 Skegness Ho
4 Frederica St
5 Ponder St
6 Kings Ct
7 Freeling St
8 Coatbridge Ho
9 Tilloch St
B2 1 Burns Ho
2 Scott Ho
3 Wellington Mews
4 Roman Ct
5 Piccadilly Ct
6 Knowledge Point Sch
B3 1 Culverin Ct
2 Garand Ct
3 Mount Carmel
B4 1 Buckmaster Ho
2 Loreburn Ho
3 Cairns Ho
4 Halsbury Ho
5 Chelmsford Ho
6 Cranworth Ho
7 City & Islington Coll (Ctr for Health, Social & Child Care)
B5 1 Pakeman Prim Sch
2 London Meridian Coll
3 American Univ in London The
4 South Eastern Univ
5 Dean Coll of London
6 Montem Prim Sch
B6 1 Berkeley Ho
2 Lazar Wlk
3 Thistlewood Cl
4 Tomlins Wlk
5 Andover Ho
6 Barmouth Ho
7 Chard Ho
8 Christ the King RC Prim Sch
9 Methley Ho
10 Rainford Ho
11 Woodbridge Cl
12 Allerton Wlk
13 Falconer Wlk
14 Sonderburg Rd
15 St Mark's Mans
16 Athol Ct
17 Pooles Park Prim Sch
C1 1 Mountfort Terr
2 Avon Ho
3 Buckland Ho
4 Dovey Lo
5 Carfree Cl
6 Mitchell Ho
7 New College Mews
8 Lofting Ho
9 Brooksby Ho
10 Cara Ho
11 Thornhill Prim Sch

12 North London Science Ctr
C2 1 London Metropolitan Univ (Spring Ho)
C3 1 Slaney Pl
2 Eastwood Cl
3 Milton Pl
4 Hartnoll Ho
5 St James School Flats
6 Widnes Ho
7 Tranmere Ho
8 Victoria Mans
9 Formby Ct
10 Mersey Ho
11 Birkenhead Ho
12 Drayton Park Mews
C6 1 Brookfield
2 Churnfield
3 Cornwallis Sq
D1 1 Islington Park Mews
2 Evelyn Denington Ct
3 Bassingbourn Ho
4 Cadmore Ho
5 Adstock Ho
6 Garston Ho
7 Flitton Ho
8 Datchworth Ho
9 Battishill St
10 Almeida St
11 Edward's Cotts
12 Hyde's Pl
13 Tyndale Terr
14 Spriggs Ho
15 Barratt Ho
16 Spencer Pl
17 Chadston Ho
18 Whiston Ho
19 Wakelin Ho
20 Tressel Ct
21 Canonbury Ct
22 Halton Ho
23 Shillingford St
24 Highbury Mans
25 Premier Ho
26 Waterloo Gdns
27 William Tyndale Prim Sch
D2 1 Hampton Ct
2 Salisbury Ho
3 Canonbury Prim Sch
4 Laycock Prim Sch
D3 1 De Barowe Mews
2 Fieldview Ct
3 Ashurst Lo
4 Highbury Fields Sch
5 London Metropolitan Univ (Ladbrook Ho)
6 Robinswood Mews
D4 1 Chestnuts The
2 Bowen Ct
3 Peckett Sq
4 De Barowe Mews
D5 1 Hurlock Ho
2 Blackstock Ho
3 Vivian Comma Cl
4 Monsell Ct
D6 1 Parkwood Prim Sch
2 Ambler Prim Sch
3 City & Islington Coll (Ctr for Lifelong Learning)

73
A1 1 Astey's Row
2 Lincoln Ho
3 Worcester Ho
4 Melville Pl
5 Wontner Cl
6 Hedingham Cl
7 Laundry La
8 Base Apartments
9 Walkinshaw Ct
10 New Bentham Ct

11 Bentham Ct
12 Haslam Ho
13 Horsfield Ho
14 Riverside Ho
15 Eric Fletcher Ct
16 Annette Cres
17 Ashby Ho
18 Lindsey Mews
19 Cardigan Wlk
20 Red House Sq
21 Orchard Cl
22 Queensbury St
A2 1 Cruden Wlk
2 Upper Handa Wlk
3 Handa Wlk
4 Lismore Wlk
5 Bardsey Wlk
6 Walney Wlk
7 Upper Bardsey Wlk
8 Upper Lismore Wlk
9 Sark Ho
10 Guernsey Ho
11 Guernsey Rd
12 Sybil Thorndike Ho
13 Clephane Rd
14 Florence Nightingale Ho
15 Jersey Ho
16 Jethou Ho
17 Islay Wlk
18 Upper Caldy Wlk
19 Caldy Wlk
20 Alderney Ho
21 Gulland Wlk
22 Nightingale Rd
23 Upper Gulland Wlk
24 Church Rd
25 Oransay Rd
26 Canonbury Yd E
A3 1 Pearfield Ho
2 Larchfield Ho
3 Beresford Terr
4 Pondfield Ho
5 Ashfield Ho
6 Elmfield Ho
7 Highbury Grove Sch
A4 1 Fountain Mews
2 Woodstock Ho
3 Henson Ct
4 Taverner Sq
B1 1 Downham Ct
2 Trafalgar Point
B2 1 John Kennedy Ct
2 John Kennedy Lo
3 Ball's Pond Pl
4 Haliday Wlk
5 Queen Elizabeth Ct
6 Canonbury Hts
7 Pinnacle The
8 Threadgold Ho
9 Wakeham St
10 Saffron Ct
11 Callaby Terr
12 Tilney Gdns
13 Westcliff Ho
14 Ilford Ho
15 Ongar Ho
16 Greenhills Terr
17 Romford Ho
18 Bute Wlk
19 Upper Ramsey Wlk
20 Rona Wlk
21 Thorndike Rd
22 St Pauls Steiner Sch
B3 1 Newington Green Prim Sch
B4 1 Ledo Ho
2 Salween Ho
3 Prome Ho
4 Arakan Ho
5 Rangoon Ho
6 Mandalay Ho
7 Karen Ho
8 Wingate Ho
9 Jubet Ho
10 Orde Ho
11 Chindit Ho

12 Mabel Thornton Ho
13 Crawshay Ho
14 Avon Ho
15 Connaught Mans
16 Jonson Ho
17 Herrick Ho
18 Donne Ho
19 Thirlmere Ho
20 Grasmere Ho
B5 1 Betty Layward Prim Sch
B6 1 Chestnut Cl
2 Sycamore Ho
3 Lordship Ho
4 Clissold Ho
5 Beech Ho
6 Laburnum Ho
7 Ormond Ho
8 Yew Tree Ct
9 Oak Ho
C1 1 Dorchester Ct
2 Wareham Ct
3 Dorset Ct
4 Stratton Ct
5 Swanage Ct
6 Blandford Ct
7 Portland Ct
8 Oscar Faber Pl
9 Metropolitan Bsns Ctr
10 Lancaster Cl
11 Palazzo Apartments
12 Watercress Pl
C2 1 Kingsland Gn
2 Kingsland Pas
3 Metropolitan Benefit Societies Almshouses
4 Nimrod Pas
5 De Beauvoir Pl
6 Warburton Ct
7 Buckingham Mews
8 Aztec Ct
9 Kerridge Ct
10 Isabella Mews
11 St Jude & St Paul's CE Prim Sch
12 De Beauvoir Prim Sch
13 Our Lady & St Joseph RC Prim Sch
14 Childrens House Upper Sch
C3 1 Hewling Ho
2 Matthias Ho
3 Port Royal Pl
4 Cressington Cl
5 King Henry's Yd
6 Bronte Ho
7 Sewell Ho
8 Lydgate Ho
9 Patmore Ho
10 Congreve Ho
11 Elton St
12 Conrad Ho
13 Southwell Ho
14 Neptune Ho
15 Campion Ho
16 Webster Ho
17 Meredith Ho
18 Beckford Ho
19 Ashley Ct
20 Hayling Cl
21 Millard Cl
22 Lydford Cl
23 Salcombe Rd
24 Truman's Rd
25 Templeton Cl
26 John Campbell Rd
27 Gillett Pl
28 Bradbury St
29 Thomas Crowell Ct
C4 1 Londesborough Ho
2 Knebworth Ho
3 Knebworth Rd
4 Bransby Ct
5 Imperial Ave
6 Leonard Pl

7 Shakspeare Mews
8 Binyon Ho
9 Shelley Ho
10 Browning Ho
11 Burns Ho
12 Andrew Marvell Ho
13 Wycliffe Ho
14 Blake Ho
15 Marlowe Ho
16 Fletcher Ho
17 Chaucer Ct
32 St Matthias's CE Prim Sch
C5 1 Gujarat Ho
2 Marton Rd
3 Painsthorpe Rd
4 Selkirk Ho
5 Defoe Ho
6 Edward Friend Ho
7 Sheridan Ho
8 Barrie Ho
9 Arnold Ho
10 Macaulay Ho
11 Stowe Ho
12 Carlyle Ho
13 Shaftesbury Ho
14 Lillian Cl
15 Swift Ho
16 Dryden Ho
17 Scott Ct
18 Kingsfield Ho
19 Uhura Sq
20 Hartopp Ct
C6 1 Denman Ho
2 St Mary's Stoke Newington CE Prim Sch
D1 1 Hilborough Rd
2 Shoreditch Ct
3 Evergreen Sq
4 Wyndhams Ct
5 Festival Ct
6 Fortune Ct
7 Rose Ct
8 Ability Plaza
9 Briar Ct
10 Lomas Dr
11 Queensbridge Inf Sch
D2 1 Prospect Ho
2 Woodland St
3 Crosby Wlk
4 Kirkland Wlk
5 Bowness Cl
6 Carlisle Wlk
7 Skelton Cl
8 Camerton Cl
9 Buttermere Wlk
10 Houghton Cl
11 Hayton Ct
12 Kingsland Sh Ctr
13 Springfield Ho
14 Parton Lo
15 Sanctuary Mews
16 Fenton Cl
D3 1 Miller's Terr
2 Chow Sq
3 Drysdale Flats
4 Gateway Mews
5 Birkbeck Mews
6 Winchester Pl
D4 1 Coronation Ave
2 Morris Blitz Ct
3 Shacklewell Ho
4 Alexandra Ct
5 Shacklewell Prim Sch
6 Princess May Prim Sch
D5 1 Lawrence Bldgs
2 Cottage Wlk
3 Batley Pl
D6 1 Garnham St
2 Garnham Cl
3 Sanford La
4 Sanford Wlk
5 Abney Gdns
6 Fleet Wood
7 Simon Marks Jewish Prim Sch

482 **73 D6**

9 William Patten
Prim Sch

74

A1 1 Aldington Ct
2 Bayton Ct
3 Rochford Wlk
4 Windrush Cl
5 Gayhurst Prim
Sch
A2 1 Burdon Ct
2 Thomson Ct
3 Bruno Ct
4 Thackeray Mews
5 Madinah Rd
A3 1 Kingsdown Ho
2 Glendown Ho
3 Moredown Ho
4 Blakeney Cl
5 Beeston Cl
6 Benabo Ct
7 David Devine Ho
8 Kreedman Wlk
9 Hermitage Row
10 Grafton Ct
11 Lushington Terr
12 Aspen Ct
13 Pykewell Lo
14 Albion Works
Studios
A5 1 Ravenscourt
2 Mellington Ct
3 Rendlesham Ho
4 Carroll Ct
5 St Scholastica's
RC Prim Sch
A6 1 Cazenove Mans
2 Chedworth Ho
3 Alderprove Ho
4 Abbotstone Ho
5 Briggeford Cl
6 Inglethorpe Ho
7 Ashdown Ho
8 Epping Ho
9 Cypress Cl
B1 1 Fortescue Ave
2 Pemberton Pl
3 Weston Wlk
4 Bayford St Ind
Ctr
5 Bayford St
6 Sidworth St
7 Helmsley St
8 Cyntra Pl
9 Signal Ho
10 All Nations Ho
11 Vanguard Ho
12 Hacon Sq
B2 1 Bohemia Pl
2 Graham Mans
3 Marvin St
4 Boscobel Ho
5 Royal Oak Rd
6 Colonnades The
7 Sylvester Ho
8 Sylvester Path
9 Doctor
Spurstowe
Almshouses
10 Great Eastern
Bldgs
11 Sojourner-Truth
Cl
B3 1 Birchington Ho
2 Bicknor Ho
3 Boxley Ho
4 Adisham Ho
5 Cranbrook Ho
6 Marden Ho
7 Broome Ho
8 Crandale Ho
9 Cheriton Ho
10 Ditton Ho
11 Langley Ho
12 Dymchurch Ho
13 Elham Ho
14 Davina Ho
15 Pembury Ho
16 Downs Ct
17 Perrywood Ho
18 Staplehurst Ho
19 Pegwell Ho
20 Yalding Ho

21 Northbourne Ho
22 Monkton Ho
23 Milsted Ho
24 Athlone Cl
25 Clarence Pl
26 Gould Terr
27 Quested Ct
28 Brett Pas
29 Marcon Ct
30 Appleton Ho
31 Institute Pl
B4 1 Ross Ct
2 Downs La
3 Gaviller Pl
4 Robert Owen Lo
5 Apprentice Way
6 Arrowe Ct
7 Gilwell Ct
8 Sutton Ct
9 St Andrews Mans
10 Kinnoull Mans
11 Rowhill Mans
12 Sladen Pl
13 Mothers Sq The
14 Richborough Ho
15 Sandgate Ho
16 Sheppey Ho
B5 1 De Vere Ct
2 Redcliffe Ct
3 Greville Ct
4 Anthony Kendal
Ho
5 Brook House
Sixth Form Coll
6 Al Falah Sch
7 Baden Powell
Sch
B6 1 Wentwood Ho
2 Woolmer Ho
3 Warwick Ct
4 Winslade Ho
5 Morriss Ho
6 Woodfield Ho
7 Rossendale Ho
8 Ettrick Ho
9 Charnwood Ho
10 Boyne Ho
11 Whitwell Ho
12 Scardale Ho
13 Hendale Ho
14 Brampton Cl
15 Aveley Ho
16 Aldeburgh Cl
17 Dennington Cl
18 Chiltern Pl
C1 1 Pitcairn Ho
2 Lyme Grove Ho
3 Shakespeare Ho
4 Upcott Ho
5 Loddiges Ho
6 Parkinson Ho
7 Sloane Ho
8 Vanbrugh Ho
9 Cambridge Pas
10 Lyttleton Ho
11 Victoria Park Ct
12 Tullis Ho
13 Fairchild Ho
14 Forsyth Ho
15 Tradescant Ho
16 Mason Ho
17 Capel Ho
18 Cordwainers Ct
19 Bridgeman Ho
20 St Thomas's Pl
21 Barclay Ho
22 Clayton Ho
23 Danby Ho
24 Sherard Ho
25 Catesby Ho
26 Petiver Cl
27 Leander Ct
28 Philip Turner Est
29 Grendon Ho
30 Shore Mews
31 Shore Bsns Ctr
32 Kendal Ho
33 Classic Mans
34 Tudor Ho
35 Park Ho
36 Enterprise Ho
37 Alpine Gr
38 Clarendon Cl
39 Rotheley Ho
40 Bernie Grant Ho
41 Orchard Prim Sch

42 St John of
Jerusalem CE Prim
Sch
C2 1 Woolpack Ho
2 Elvin Ho
3 Thomas Ho
4 Hockley Ho
5 Retreat Ho
6 Butfield Ho
7 Brooksbank Ho
8 Cresset Ho
9 Brooksbank St
10 Lennox Ho
11 Milborne Ho
12 Collent Ho
13 Middlesex Pl
14 Elsdale Ho
15 Devonshire Hall
16 Brent Ho
17 Morningside
Prim Sch
18 Hackney Free &
Parochial CE Sec
Sch
C3 1 St John & St
James CE Prim Sch
C6 1 Haybridge Ho
2 Framlingham Ct
3 Halesworth Cl
4 Harleston Cl
5 Lowestoft Cl
6 Howard Ho
7 Templar Ho
D1 1 Stuart Ho
2 Gascoyne Ho
3 Chelsfield Point
4 Sundridge Ho
5 Banbury Ho
6 Lauriston Ho
D2 1 Musgrove Ho
2 Cheyne Ho
3 Haynes Ho
4 Warner Ho
5 Gilby Ho
6 Gadsden Ho
7 Risley Ho
8 Baycliffe Ho
9 Sheldon Ho
10 Offley Ho
11 Latimer Ho
12 Ribstone Ho
13 Salem Ho
14 Fieldwick Ho
15 Lever Ct
16 Matson Ho
17 Wilding Ho
18 Rennell Ho
19 Dycer Ho
20 Granard Ho
21 Whitelock Ho
22 Harrowgate Ho
23 Cass Ho
24 Lofts on the Park
25 Heathcote Point
26 Ravenscroft
Point
27 Vanner Point
28 Hensley Point
29 San Ho
30 Berger Prim Sch
D4 1 Cromford Path
2 Longford Ct
3 Overbury Ho
4 Heanor Ct
5 Wharfedale Ct
6 Ladybower Ct
7 Ilkeston Ct
8 Derby Ct
9 Rushmore Cres
10 Blackwell Cl
11 Belper Ct
12 Rushmore Prim
Sch

75

A2 1 Chigwell Ct
2 Wellday Ho
3 Selman Ho
4 Vaine Ho
5 Trower Ho
6 St Dominics RC
Prim Sch
B2 1 Mallard Cl
2 Merriam Ave
3 Gainsborough St
4 Palace Ct

5 St Anthony's Cl
6 Trowbridge Est
7 Wick Village
D6 1 Hammond Ct
2 Sorensen Ct
3 Hinton Ct

76

A6 1 Lantern of
Knowledge Boys
Sec Sch
B1 1 Service Route No
2
2 Service Route No
3
3 Newham Sixth
Form Coll (Stratford
Ctr)
B4 1 Mulberry Ct
2 Rosewood Ct
3 Gean Ct
4 Blackthorn Ct
5 Cypress Ct
C1 1 Stratford Office
Village The
2 Violet Ct
3 Mandrake Way
4 Brimstone Ho
5 Hibiscus Lo
6 Glasier Ct
C2 1 Christ the
Redeemer Bible Coll
C3 1 Bordeaux Ho
2 Luxembourg
Mews
3 Basle Ho
C5 1 Acacia Bsns Ctr
2 Brook Ct
3 Gainsfield Ct
4 Artesian Wlk
5 Doreen Capstan
Ho
6 Apollo Ho
7 Peppermint Pl
8 Denmark St
9 Mills Ct
10 Paramount Ho
11 Robinson Ct
C6 1 Nansen Ct
2 Mallinson Ct
3 Barbara Ward Ct
4 Caradon Ct
5 Noel Baker Ct
6 Corigan Ct
7 Norman Ho
8 Willow Ct
9 Lime Ct
10 Owens Mews
11 Marnie Ct
12 Cotton Cl
13 Connaught Sch
for Girls (Annexe)
14 East London Coll
D1 1 Flint Cl
2 St Matthews Ct
3 Ammonite Ho
4 Stone Ct
D2 1 Common The
2 Wolffe Gdns
3 Onyx Mews
4 Candlelight Ct
5 Boltons The

77

A4 1 Bronte Ct
2 Anna Neagle Cl
3 Brownlow Rd
4 Carrington Gdns
5 Vera Lynn Cl
C1 1 Sarwan Ho
2 Bridgepoint Lofts
3 Vineyard Studios
C3 1 Sandringham
Prim Sch
2 Iman Zakaria
Acad

78

A3 1 Salisbury Prim
Sch
C3 1 Stewart Rainbird
Ho
2 Abraham Fisher
Ho
3 Redo Ho

4 George
Comberton Wlk
C4 1 Cardamom Ct
2 Annie Taylor Ho
3 Richard Fell Ho
4 Susan Lawrence
Ho
5 Walter Hurford
Par
6 John Cornwell VC
Ho
7 Alfred Prior Ho
C5 1 Willis Ho
2 Arthur Walls Ho
3 Blakesley Ho
4 Twelve Acre Ho
5 Beech Ct
6 Golding Ct
7 Golding Ct
D1 1 Aveley Mans
2 Harlow Mans
3 Danbury Mans
4 Mayland Mans
5 Bowers Ho
6 Webber Ho
7 Paulson Ho
8 Collins Ho
9 Jack Cook Ho
D3 1 St Luke's Path
2 Springfield Ct
D5 1 Postway Mews
2 Oakfield Ho
3 Janice Mews
4 Kenneth More Rd
5 Clements Ct
6 Handforth Rd
7 Churchill Ct
8 Oakfield Lo
9 Langdale Ct
10 Ilford Chambers
D6 1 York Ho
2 Opal Mews
3 Florentine Ho
4 Kingsley Mews
5 Hainault Bridge
Par
6 Ilford Ursuline
Prep Sch

79

A1 1 Harvey Ho
2 Gower Ho
3 Apex Prim Sch
A6 1 Spectrum Twr
2 Thames View
3 City View
4 Centreway
5 Axon Pl
D1 1 Gibbards Cott
2 Upney Ct
3 Edgefield Ct
4 Manor Ct
5 Lambourne Gdns
6 Westone Mans
7 Loveland Mans
8 Edward Mans
9 Clarke Mans
10 Dawson Gdns
11 Sebastian Ct

80

A1 1 Bristol Ho
2 Canterbury Ho
3 Durham Ho
4 Wells Ho
5 Winchester Ho
6 Rosalind Ct
7 Exeter Ho
8 Wheatley Mans
9 Greenwood Mans
10 Plymouth Ho
11 Graham Mans
12 Portia Ct

81

C5 1 Markham Ho
2 Webb Ho
3 Preston Ho
4 Steadman Ho
5 Hyndman Ho
6 Clynes Ho
7 Henderson Ho
8 Blatchford Ho
9 Rogers Ho
10 Sylvia Pankhurst
Ho

11 Mary Macarthur
Ho
12 Ellen Wilkinson
Ho
D2 1 Picador Ho
2 Centurion Lodge
3 Louis Ct
4 Watsons Lo
5 Carpenters Ct
6 Bell Ho
7 Rounders Ct
8 Oldmead Ho
9 Jervis Ct
10 Bartletts Ho
11 Royal Par
12 Richardson Gdns
13 Forsyth Ct
14 Eldridge Ct
15 Madison Ct
16 Bowery Ct
17 Rivington Ct

82

D3 1 Marlborough Par
2 Blenheim Par
3 Lea Ct
4 Westbourne Par
5 Whiteleys Par
6 Hillingdon Par
7 New Broadway

84

C4 1 Dilston Cl
2 Wells Cl
3 Willett Cl
4 Merlin Cl
5 Glyndebourne Ct
6 Albury Ct
7 Osterley Ct
8 Hatfield Ct
9 Gayhurst Ct
D4 1 Caravelle Gdns
2 Farman Gr
3 Viscount Gr
4 Tomahawk Gdns
5 Martlet Gr
6 Trident Gdns
7 Latham Ct
8 Jupiter Ct
9 Westland Ct
10 Seasprite Ct
11 Convair Wlk
12 Mayfly Gdns
13 Valiant Ct
14 Woburn Twr
15 Brett Ct
16 Friars Ct
D5 1 Medlar Ct
2 Cranberry Cl
3 Lely Ho
4 Girtin Ho
5 Cotman Ho
6 Raeburn Ho
7 Gainsborough
Twr
8 Stanfield Ho
9 Millais Ct
10 Hunt Ct
11 Poynter Ct
12 Hogarth Ho
13 Constable Ho
14 Bonnington Ct
15 Romney Ct
16 Landseer Ho

85

B1 1 St Crispins Ct
B3 1 Weaver Ho
2 Caldon Ho
3 Ashby Ho
4 Welford Ho
5 Hertford Ho
6 Wey Ho
7 Middlewich Ho
8 Stourbridge Ho
B4 1 Netherton Ho
2 Keadby Ho
3 Tame Ho
4 Dorset Ct
D1 1 Thurlestone Ct
2 Disley Ho
3 Burgess Ct
4 Bayliss Ct
5 Lytham Ct
6 Winford Par
7 Brunel Pl

8 Rutherford Twr
9 Rountree Ct

86

A1 1 Farnham Ct
2 Gleneagles Twr
3 Birkdale Ct
5 Hartsbourne Ct
6 Ferndown Ct
7 Deal Ct
8 St David's Ct
9 Portrush Ct
10 Alnmouth Ct
11 Panmure Ct
12 Peterhead Ct
13 Sunningdale Ct
D2 1 Denbigh Ct
2 Devon Ct
3 Dorset Ct
4 Glamorgan Ct
5 Gloucester Ct
6 Hereford Ct
7 Merioneth Ct
8 Oxford Ct
9 Monmouth Ct
10 Paddington Ct
11 Pembroke Ct
12 Chadwick Cl
13 Cotts Cl
D3 1 Berkshire Ct
2 Buckingham Ct
3 Cardigan Ct
4 Carmarthen Ct
5 Cornwall Ct
6 Merlin Ct
7 Osprey Ct
8 Pelham Pl
9 Puffin Ct
10 Fulmar Ct
11 Turnstone Terr
D5 1 Medway Par
2 Brabstone Ho
3 Cotswold Ct

87

B1 1 Ealing Coll
2 Avenue House
B3 1 Woodbury Ct
2 Edward Ct
3 Park Lo
C1 1 Hurley Ct
2 Amherst Gdns
3 Tudor Ct
4 Hilton Ho
C2 1 Hutton Ct
2 Cain Ct
3 Langdale Ct
4 William Ct
5 Castlebar Ct
6 Warren Ct
7 White Lo
8 Queen's Ct
9 King's Ct
10 Cheriton Cl
11 Stanley Ct
12 Juniper Ho
13 Pendlewood Cl
14 St Benedict's Jun Sch
C3 1 Holtoake Ct
2 Pitshanger Ct
3 Holtoake Ho
D2 14 St Gregory's RC Prim Sch

88

A4 1 Nelson Ho
2 Gordon Ho
3 Frobisher Ho
4 Wellington Ho
5 Fairfax Ho
A5 1 Carlyon Mans
2 Ainslie Ct
3 Millers Ct
4 Priory Ct
5 Tylers Ct
6 Twyford Ct
7 Rose Ct
8 Laurel Ct
9 Sundew Ct
10 Campion Ct
11 Foxglove Ct
C1 1 Buckingham Ho
2 Chester Ct

3 Devon Ct
4 Essex Ho
5 Fife Ct
6 Gloucester Ho
7 Hereford Ho
8 Inverness Ct
9 Warwick Ho
10 York Ho
11 Suffolk Ho
12 Perth Ho
13 Norfolk Ho
D1 1 Kelfield Ct
2 Downing Ho
3 Crosfield Ct
4 Robinson Ho
5 Scampston Mews
6 Girton Villas
7 Ray Ho
8 Walmer Ho
9 Goodrich Ct
10 Arthur Ct
11 Whitstable Ho
12 Kingsnorth Ho
13 Bridge Ct
14 Prospect Ho
15 St Marks Rd
16 Whitchurch Ho
17 Blechynden Ho
18 Waynflete Sq
19 Bramley Ho
20 Dixon Ho
21 Oxford Gardens Prim Sch
22 Bassett House Sch
D2 1 Treverton Twr
2 Raymede Twr
3 Bruce Ho
4 Balfour Ho
5 Burleigh Ho
6 Sion-Manning RC Sch for Girls
7 St Charles RC Prim Sch
8 St Charles RC Sixth Form Coll
D4 1 Westfield Ct
2 Tropical Ct
3 Chamberlayne Mans
4 Quadrant The
5 Queens Park Ct
6 Warfield Yd
7 Regent St
8 Cherrytree Ho
9 Artisan Mews
10 Artisan Quarter

89

A1 1 Avon Ct
2 Bromley Lo
3 Walter Ct
4 Lynton Terr
5 Acton Ho
6 Fells Haugh
7 Springfield Ct
8 Tamarind Ct
9 Lynton Ct
10 Aspen Ct
11 Pegasus Ct
12 Friary Park Ct
B1 1 Rosebank Gdns
2 Rosebank
3 Edinburgh Ho
4 Western Ct
5 Kilronan
B6 1 Carlyle Rd
2 Bernard Shaw Ho
3 Longlents Ho
4 Mordaunt Ho
5 Wilmers Ct
6 Stonebridge Ctr
7 Shakespeare Ave
8 Southcroft
9 Brent Adult Comm Education Service Coll
C5 1 Futters Ct
2 Barrett Ct
3 Elms The
4 Fairlight Ct
D5 1 New Crescent Yd
2 Harlesden Plaza
3 St Josephs Ct
4 Jubilee Ct
5 Ellery Ct

90

B1 1 Holborn Ho
2 Clement Danes Ho
3 Vellacott Ho
4 O'Driscoll Ho
5 King Ho
6 Daley Ho
7 Selma Ho
8 Garrett Ho
C1 1 Latimer Ind Est
2 Pankhurst Ho
3 Quadrangle The
4 Nightingale Ho
5 Gordon Ct
6 Ducane Cl
7 Browning Ho
8 Pavilion Terr
9 Ivebury Ct
10 Olympic Ho
C2 1 Galleywood Ho
2 Edgcott Ho
3 Cuffley Ho
4 Addlestone Ho
5 Hocklliffe Ho
6 Sarratt Ho
7 Firle Ho
8 Sutton Est The
9 Terling Ho
10 Danes Ho
11 Udimore Ho
12 Vange Ho
13 Binbrook Ho
14 Yeadon Ho
15 Yatton Ho
16 Yarrow Ho
17 Clement Ho
18 Danebury
19 Coronation Ct
20 Calderon Pl
21 St Quintin Gdns
C3 1 Princess Alice Ho

1 Yoxall Ho
2 Yorkley Ho
3 Northaw Ho
4 Oakham Ho
5 Markyate Ho
6 Letchmore Ho
7 Pagham Ho
8 Quendon Ho
9 Redbourn Ho
10 Ketton Ho
11 Hillman Dr
D1 1 Kelfield Ct
2 Downing Ho
(continues)

91

A1 1 Malton Mews
2 Lancaster Lo
3 Manning Ho
4 Galsworthy Ho
5 Hudson Ho
6 Cambourne Mews
7 Upper Talbot Wlk
8 Kingsdown Cl
9 Lower Clarendon Wlk
10 Talbot Grove Ho
11 Clarendon Wlk
12 Upper Clarendon Wlk
13 Camelford Wlk
14 Upper Camelford Wlk
15 Camelford Ct
16 Thomas Jones Prim Sch
17 Notting Hill Prep Sch
A2 1 Murchison Ho
2 Macaulay Ho
3 Chesterton Ho
4 Chiltern Ho
5 Lionel Ho
6 Watts Ho
7 Wheatstone Ho
8 Telford Ho
9 Golborne Mews
10 Millwood St
11 St Columb's Ho
12 Norfolk Mews
13 Lionel Mews

14 Kensington & Chelsea Coll
15 Bevington Prim Sch
16 Sion-Manning RC Sch for Girls
17 Lloyd Williamson Sch
A3 1 Sycamore Wlk
2 Westgate Bsns Ctr
3 Buspace Studios
4 Bosworth Ho
5 Golborne Gdns
6 Appleford Ho
7 Adair Twr
8 Gadsden Ho
9 Southam Ho
10 Norman Butler Ho
11 Thompson Ho
12 Wells Ho
13 Paul Ho
14 Olive Blythe Ho
15 Katherine Ho
16 Breakwell Ct
17 Pepler Ho
18 Edward Kennedy Ho
19 Winnington Ho
20 Queen's Park Prim Sch
21 Middle Row Prim Sch
22 St Mary RC Prim Sch
23 St Thomas' CE Prim Sch
A4 1 Selby Sq
2 Severn Ave
3 Tolhurst Dr
4 John Fearon Wlk
5 Mundy Ho
6 Macfarren Ho
7 Bantock Ho
8 Banister Ho
9 Batten Ho
10 Croft Ho
11 Courtville Ho
12 Mounsey Ho
13 Bliss Mews
14 Symphony Mews
B1 1 Silvester Ho
2 Golden Cross Mews
3 Tavistock Mews
4 Clydesdale Ho
5 Colville Prim Sch
6 Melchester
7 Pinehurst Ct
8 Denbigh Ho
B2 1 Blagrove Rd
2 All Saints Ho
3 Tavistock Ho
4 Leamington Ho
B3 1 Octavia Mews
2 Russell's Wharf
3 Kelly Mews
4 Queen Elizabeth II Jubilee Sch
B4 1 Boyce Ho
2 Farnaby Ho
3 Danby Ho
4 Purday Ho
5 Naylor Ho
6 St Judes Ho
7 Leeve Ho
8 Longhurst Ho
9 Harrington Ct
10 Mulberry Ct
11 Kelfield Ct
12 Carlton Vale Inf Sch
B5 1 Claremont Ct
2 William Saville Ho
3 Western Ct
4 Bond Ho
5 Crone Ct
6 Wood Ho
7 Winterleys
8 Carlton Ho
9 Fiona Ct
10 Kilburn Park Sch

C1 1 Shottsford
2 Tolchurch
3 Casterbridge
4 Sandbourne
5 Anglebury
6 Weatherbury
7 Westbourne Gr Mews
8 Rosehart Mews
9 Viscount Ct
10 Hereford Mans
11 Hereford Mews
12 St Mary of the Angels RC Prim Sch
C2 1 Ascot Ho
2 Ashgrove Ct
3 Lockbridge Ct
4 Swallow Ct
5 Nightingale Lo
6 Hammond Lo
7 Penfield Lo
8 Harvey Lo
9 Hunter Lo
10 Barnard Lo
11 Falcon Lo
12 Johnson Lo
13 Livingstone Lo
14 Nuffield Lo
15 Finch Lo
16 Polesworth Ho
17 Oversley Ho
18 Derrycombe Ho
19 Buckshead Ho
20 Combe Ho
21 Culham Ho
22 Dainton Ho
23 Devonport Ho
24 Honwell Ho
25 Truro Ho
26 Sunderland Ho
27 Stonehouse Ho
28 Riverford Ho
29 Portishead Ho
30 Mickleton Ho
31 Keyham Ho
32 Moulsford Ho
33 Shrewsbury Mews
34 St Stephen's Mews
35 Westway Lo
36 Langley Ho
37 Brindley Ho
38 Radway Ho
39 Astley Ho
40 Willow Ct
41 Larch Ct
42 Elm Ct
43 Beech Ct
44 Worcester Ct
45 Union Ct
46 Leicester Ct
47 Kennet Ct
48 Oxford Ct
49 Fazerley Ct
C3 1 Westside Ct
2 Byron Mews
3 Sutherland Ct
4 Fleming Cl
5 Hermes Cl
6 St Peter's CE Prim Sch
7 Paddington Acad
C4 1 Pentland Rd
2 Nelson Cl
3 Pavilion Ct
4 Masefield Ho
5 Austen Ho
6 Fielding Ho
7 Argo Bsns Ctr
8 John Ratcliffe Ho
9 Wymering Mans
10 City of Westminster Coll, Queens Park Ctr
11 Essendine Prim Sch
C5 1 Wells Ct
2 Cambridge Ct
3 Ely Ct
4 Durham Ct
5 St Augustine's CE High Sch
6 Sch of the Islamic Republic of Iran The
C6 1 Ryde Ho

95 C4 483

2 Glengall Pass
3 Leith Yd
4 Daynor Ho
5 Varley Ho
6 Sandby Ho
7 Colas Mews
8 Bishopsdale Ho
9 Lorton Ho
10 Marshwood Ho
11 Ribblesdale Ho
12 Holmesdale Ho
13 Kilburn Vale Est
14 Kilburn Bridge
15 Coll of NW London
16 St Mary's Kilburn CE Prim Sch
D1 1 Vera Ct
2 Alexander Mews
3 Gurney Ho
4 Burdett Mews
5 Greville Lo
6 Hatherley Ct
7 Bridge Field Ho
8 Ralph Ct
9 Peters Ct
10 Pickering Mews
11 Riven Ct
12 Inver Ct
13 Cervantes Ct
14 Bishops Ct
15 Newbury Ho
16 Marlow Ho
17 Lynton Ho
18 Pembroke Ho
19 Pickering Ho
20 Whiteleys Ctr
21 College Park Ct
22 Halfield Jun & Inf Schs
D2 1 Our Lady of Dolours RC Prim Sch
2 Edward Wilson Prim Sch
3 St Mary Magdalene CE Prim Sch
D3 1 Ellwood Ct
26 St Saviour's CE Prim Sch
D4 1 City of Westminster Coll, Maida Vale Ctr
D5 1 Tollgate Ho
2 Regents Plaza
3 Royal Langford Apartments
4 Naima Jewish Prep Sch
5 St Augustine's Prim Sch
D6 1 Sylvan Ct
2 Birchington Ct
3 Farndale Ho
4 Greville Mews
5 Goldsmith's Pl
6 Remsted Ho
7 Bradwell Ho
8 Cheshunt Ho
9 Haliwell Ho
10 Broadoak Ho
11 Philip Ho
12 Hillsborough Ct
13 Sandbourne
14 Wingreen
15 Toneborough
16 Silverthorn
17 Kington Ho
18 Marrick Ho
19 Rutland Mews

95

C4 1 Pimlico Wlk
2 Aske Ho
3 Hathaway Ho
4 Haberdasher Pl
5 Fairchild Ho
6 Burtt Ho
7 Enfield Cloisters
8 McGregor Ct
9 Royal Oak Ct
10 Hoxton Mkt

1 Bath Pl
2 Chapel Pl
3 Standard Pl
4 Cleeve Workshops
5 Cleeve Ho
6 Printing House Yd
7 Perseverance Works
8 Crooked Billet Yd
9 Drysdale Ho
10 Castlefrank Ho
11 School App
12 Basing House Yd
13 Mail Coach Yd
14 St Monica's RC Prim Sch
15 Symister Mews
16 Hackney Com Coll

C5
1 Bracer Ho
2 Scorton Ho
3 Fern Cl
4 Macbeth Ho
5 Oberon Ho
6 Buckland Ct
7 Osric Path
8 Crondall Ct
9 Caliban Twr
10 Celia Ho
11 Juliet Ho
12 Bacchus Wlk
13 Malcolm Ho
14 Homefield St
15 Crondall Pl
16 Blanca Ho
17 Miranda Ho
18 Falstaff Ho
19 Charmian Ho
20 Myrtle Wlk
21 Arden Ho
22 Sebastian Ho
23 Stanway Ct
24 Jerrold St
25 Rosalind Ho
26 Cordelia Ho
27 Monteagle Ct
28 John Parry Ct
29 James Anderson Ct
30 Ben Jonson Ct
31 Sara Lane Ct
32 Walbrook Ct
33 Burbage Ct

C6
1 Portelet Ct
2 Trinity Ct
3 Rozel Ct
4 St Helier Ct
5 Corbiere Ho
6 Kenning Ho
7 Higgins Ho
8 Cavell Ho
9 Girling Ho
10 Fulcher Ho
11 Francis Ho
12 Norris Ho
13 Kempton Ho
14 Nesham Ho
15 Crossbow Ho
16 Catherine Ho
17 Strale Ho
18 Horner Hos
19 Stringer Hos
20 Whitmore Ho
21 Nightingale Ho
22 Wilmer Gdns
23 Arrow Ho
24 Archer Ho
25 Meriden Ho
26 Rover Ho
27 Bowyer Ho
28 Tiller Ho
29 Canalside Studios
30 Kleine Wharf
31 Benyon Wharf
32 Quebec Wharf
33 Belvedere Ct
34 Portfleet Pl

D4
1 Gorsuch Pl
2 Strout's Pl
3 Vaughan Est

4 George Loveless Ho
5 Baroness Rd
6 James Brine Ho
7 Arthur Wade Ho
8 Robert Owen Ho
9 Sivill Ho
10 Georgina Gdns
11 Old Market Sq
12 Cuff Point
13 Bakers Rents
14 Leopold Bldgs
15 Dunmore Point
16 Wingfield Ho
17 Gascoigne Pl
18 Mandela Ho
19 Virginia Rd
20 Briggs Ho
21 Packenham Ho
22 Gowan Ho
23 Kirton Gdns
24 Chambord Ho
25 Ducal St
26 Strickland Ho
27 Alliston Ho
28 Gibraltar Wlk
29 Equity Sq
30 Shacklewell St
31 Rochelle St
32 Sonning Ho
33 Culham Ho
34 Hurley Ho
35 Palissy St
36 Taplow Ho
37 Chertsey Ho
38 Sunbury Ho
39 Sunbury Workshops
40 Datchett Ho
41 Hocker St
42 Coll Sharp Ct
43 Marlow Studio Workshops
44 Marlow Ho
45 Shiplake Ho
46 Wargrave Ho
47 Iffley Ho
48 Virginia Prim Sch
49 Bethnal Green Tech Coll
50 Columbia Prim Sch

D5
1 Queensbridge Ct
2 Godwin Ho
3 Kent Ct
4 Brunswick Ho
5 Weymouth Ct
6 Sovereign Mews
7 Dunloe Ct
8 Cremer Bsns Ctr
9 James Hammett Ho
10 Allgood St
11 Horatio St
12 Cadell Ho
13 Horatio Ho
14 Shipton Ho
15 Haggerston Sch
16 Randal Cremer JMI Sch

D6
1 Hilborough Ct
2 Scriven Ct
3 Livermere Ct
4 Angrave Ct
5 Angrave Pas
6 Benfleet Ct
7 Belford Ho
8 Orme Ho
9 Clemson Ho
10 Longman Ho
11 Lowther Ho
12 Lovelace Ho
13 Harlowe Ho
14 Pamela Ho
15 Samuel Ho
16 Acton Ho
17 Loanda Cl
18 Phoenix Cl
19 Richardson Cl
20 Thrasher Cl
21 Mary Secole Cl
22 Canal Path
23 Pear Tree Cl
24 Hebden Ct
25 Charlton Ct
26 Laburnum Ct

27 Mansfield Ct
28 Garden Pl
29 Amber Wharf
30 Haggerston Studios

96

A1
1 Whitechurch Pas
2 Manningtree St
3 Whitechurch La
4 Naylor Bldg W
5 Morrison Bldgs
6 Naylor Bldg E
7 Mulberry St
8 Albany Ct
9 Cornell Bldg
10 Dryden Bldg
11 Weyhill Rd
12 Colefax Bldg
13 Fordham St
14 Myrdle Ct
15 Buckle St
16 Plough St
17 Goodman's Stile
18 Ropewalk Gdns
19 Skyline Plaza
20 Minet Ho
21 Mitali Pas
22 Basil Ho
23 Bernhard Baron Ho
24 Hogarth Ct
25 Delafield Ho
26 Chandlery Ho
27 Berner Terr
28 Victoria Yd
29 Batson Ho
30 Harkness Ho
31 Drewett Ho
32 Dowler Ho
33 Everard Ho
34 Bicknell Ho
35 Danvers Ho
36 Philchurch Pl
37 Hadfield Ho
38 Kindersley Ho
39 Langmore Ho
40 Halliday Ho
41 Harry Gosling Prim Sch
42 London Metropolitan Univ (Commercial Rd)
43 Kobi Nazrul Prim Sch
44 London Metropolitan Univ (Central Ho)
45 European Coll

A2
1 Arthur Deakin Ho
2 Albert Cotts
3 Victoria Cotts
4 Boden Ho
5 Vollasky Ho
6 Daplyn St
7 Hobsons Pl
8 Hanbury Ho
9 Huguenot Ct
10 Links Yd
11 Casson Ho
12 Ramar Ho
13 Greatorex Ho
14 Chicksand Ho
15 Spelman Ho
16 Tailworth St
17 Monthope Rd
18 Evelyn Ho
19 Bloomfield Ho
20 Davenant Ho
21 Pauline Ho
22 Tannery Ho
23 Don Gratton Ho
24 Green Dragon Yd
25 Fieldgate Mans
26 Mosque Tower

A3
1 Bentworth Ct
2 Hawksmoor Pl
3 Kerbela St
4 Fuller Ct
5 Kinsham Ho
6 Menotti St
7 Barwell Ho
8 Grimsby St
9 Reflection Ho
10 Fleet Street Hill

11 Bratley St
12 Weaver Ho
13 Cornerstone Ct
14 Stuttle Ho
15 McGlashon Ho
16 John Pritchard Ho
17 Thomas Buxton Jun & Inf Sch
18 St Anne RC Prim Sch
19 William Davis Prim Sch

A4
1 Providence Yd
2 Lygon Ho
3 Brabner Ho
4 Delta St
5 Delta Point
6 Tillet Way
7 Mullet Gdns
8 Lampern Sq
9 Kite Pl
10 Elver Gdns
11 Cobden Ho
12 Eversley Ho
13 Lorden Wlk
14 Rapley Ho
15 Dence Ho
16 McKinnon Wood Ho
17 Satchwell Rd
18 Dickinson Ho
19 Hutton Ho
20 Simmons Ho
21 Swinton Ho
22 Yates Ho
23 Johnson Ho
24 Jeremy Bentham Ho
25 Waring Ho
26 St James Ct
27 Ebony Ho
28 Azure Ho
29 Westhope Ho
30 Hague St
31 Elizabeth Selby Inf Sch
32 Lawdale Jun Sch

A5
1 London Terr
2 Sturdee Ho
3 Maude Ho
4 Haig Ho
5 Jellicoe Ho
6 Ropley St
7 Guinness Trust Bldgs
8 Ion Ct
9 Columbia Rd
10 Moye Cl
11 Morrel Ct
12 Courtauld Ho
13 Drummond Ho
14 Gurney Ho
15 Atkinson Ho
16 Halley Ho
17 Goldsmith's Sq
18 Shahjalal Ho
19 Ken Wilson Ho
20 April Ct
21 Crofts Ho
22 Sebright Ho
23 Beechwood Ho
24 Gillman Ho
25 Cheverell Ho
26 Besford Ho
27 Dinmont Ho
28 Elizabeth Mews
29 Sebright Pas
30 Wyndham Deedes Ho
31 Sheppard Ho
32 Mary James Ho
33 Hadrian Est
34 Blythendale Ho
35 George Vale Ho
36 Lion Mills
37 St Peter's Ave
38 Pritchard Ho
39 Sebright Sch

A6
1 Broke Wlk
2 Rochemont Wlk
3 Marlborough Ave
4 Rivington Wlk
5 Magnin Cl
6 Gloucester Sq
7 Woolstone Ho

8 Marsworth Ho
9 Cheddington Ho
10 Linslade Ho
11 Cosgrove Ho
12 Blisworth Ho
13 Eleanor Ct
14 Wistow Ho
15 Muscott Ho
16 Boxmoor Ho
17 Linford Ho
18 Pendley Ho
19 Northchurch Ho
20 Debdale Ho
21 Broadway Market Mews
22 Welshpool Ho
23 Ada Ho
24 St Paul's with St Michael's Prim Sch

B1
1 Peter Best Ho
2 Mellish Ho
3 Porchester Ho
4 Dickson Ho
5 Joscoyne Ho
6 Silvester Ho
7 Wilton Ct
8 Sarah Ho
9 Bridgen Ho
10 Tylney Ho
11 Greenwich Ct
12 Damien Ct
13 Philson Mans
14 Siege Ho
15 Jacob Mans
16 Proud Ho
17 Sly St
18 Barnett St
19 Kinder St
20 Richard St
21 Hungerford St
22 Colstead Ho
23 Melwood Ho
24 Wicker St
25 Langdale St
26 Chapman Ho
27 Burwell Cl
28 Walford Ho
29 Welstead Ho
30 Norton Ho
31 Turnour Ho
32 Luke Ho
33 Dunch St
34 Sheridan St
35 Brinsley St
36 Spencer Way
37 Madani Girls Sch
38 East End Computing & Bsns Coll
39 Mulberry Sch for Girls
40 Jamiatul Ummah Sch
41 Bigland Green Prim Sch

B2
1 Wodeham Gdns
2 Castlemaine St
3 Court St
4 Ashfield St
5 London Hospital Dental Inst
6 Princess Alexandra School of Nursing The

B3
1 Rochester Ct
2 Weaver Ct
3 Greenheath Bsns Ctr
4 Glass St
5 Herald St
6 Northesk Ho
7 Codrington Ho
8 Heathpool Ct
9 Mocatta Ho
10 Harvey Ho
11 Blackwood Ho
12 Rutherford Ho
13 Bullen Ho
14 Fremantle Ho
15 Pellew Ho
16 Ashington Ho
17 Dinnington Ho
18 Bartholomew Sq
19 Steeple Ct
20 Orion Ho
21 Fellbrigg St

22 Hague Prim Sch
23 Eagle Ho
24 Sovereign Ho
25 Redmill Ho
26 Berry Ho
27 Grindall Ho
28 Collingwood Ho
29 Stewart Headlam Prim Sch

B4
1 Charles Dickens Ho
2 Adrian Bolt Ho
3 William Rathbone Ho
4 Southwood Smith Ho
5 Rushmead
6 William Channing Ho
7 John Cartwright Ho
8 Charles Darwin Ho
9 Thomas Burt Ho
10 John Fielden Ho
11 Gwilym Maries Ho
12 Joseph Priestley Ho
13 Wear Pl
14 John Nettleford Ho
15 Thornaby Ho
16 Stockton Ho
17 Barnard Ho
18 Gainford Ho
19 Stapleton Ho
20 James Middleton Ho
21 Kedleston Wlk
22 Queen Margaret Flats
23 Hollybush Ho
24 Horwood Ho
25 Norden Ho
26 Newcourt Ho
27 Seabright St
28 Viaduct Pl
29 Sunlight Sq
30 Providence Row Cl
31 Oaklands Sec Sch
32 Raine's Foundation Lower Sch
33 Beatrice Tate Sch

B5
1 Dinmont St
2 Marian St
3 Claredale Ho
4 Keeling Ho
5 Maple St
6 Winkley St
7 Temple Dwellings
8 Argos Ho
9 Helen Ho
10 Lysander Ho
11 Antenor Ho
12 Paris Ho
13 Nestor Ho
14 Hector Ho
15 Ajax Ho
16 Achilles Ho
17 Priam Ho
18 Peabody Est
19 Felix St
20 Cambridge Cres
21 Peterley Bsns Ctr
22 Beckwith Ho
23 Brookfield Ho
24 Parminter Ind Est
25 Ted Roberts Ho
26 Cambridge Ct
27 Millennium Pl
28 William Caslon Ho
29 Hugh Platt Ho
30 West St
31 Mayfield Ho
32 Apollo Ho
33 Tanners Yd
34 Teesdale St

B6
1 Welshpool St
2 Broadway Ho
3 Regents Wharf
4 London Wharf
5 Warburton Ho
6 Warburton St

7 Triangle Rd
8 Warburton Rd
9 Williams Ho
10 Booth Cl
11 Albert Cl
12 King Edward Mans
13 Victoria Bldgs
14 Andrews Wharf
15 London Fields Prim Sch
16 Triangle The
17 Com Coll Hackney The
C1 1 Woollon Ho
2 Dundalk Ho
3 Anne Goodman Ho
4 Newbold Cotts
5 Kerry Ho
6 Zion Ho
7 Longford Ho
8 Bromehead St
9 Athlone Ho
10 Jubilee Mans
11 Harriott Ho
12 Brayford Sq
13 Clearbrook Way
14 Rochelle Ct
15 Winterton Ho
16 Swift Ho
17 Brinsley Ho
18 Dean Ho
19 Foley Ho
20 Robert Sutton Ho
21 Montpelier Pl
22 Glastonbury Pl
23 Steel's La
24 Masters Lo
25 Stylus Apartments
26 Arta Ho
27 St Mary & St Michael Prim Sch
28 Bishop Challoner Collegiate Sch
29 Morton Cl
30 James Voller Way
C2 1 Fulneck
2 Gracehill
3 Ockbrook
4 Fairfield
5 Dunstan Hos
6 Cressy Ct
7 Cressy Hos
8 Callahan Cotts
9 Lindley Ho
10 Mayo Ho
11 Wexford Ho
12 Sandhurst Ho
13 Addis Ho
14 Colverson Ho
15 Beckett Ho
16 Jarman Ho
17 Armsby Ho
18 Wingrad Ho
19 Miranda Cl
20 Drake Ho
21 Ashfield Yd
22 Magri Wlk
23 Jean Pardies Ho
24 St Vincent De Paul Ho
25 Sambrook Ho
26 Louise De Marillac Ho
27 Dagobert Ho
28 Le Moal Ho
29 Odette Duval Ho
30 Charles Auffray Ho
31 Boisseau Ho
32 Clichy Ho
33 Paymal Ho
34 Smithy Street Sch
35 Redlands Prim Sch
36 Cressy Ct
C3 1 William's Bldgs
2 Donegal Ho
3 Pelican Pas
4 Frederick Charrington Ho
5 Wickford Ho
6 Braintree Ho
7 Doveton Ho
8 Doveton St
9 Cephas Ho
10 Sceptre Ho
11 Bancroft Ho
12 Stothard St
13 Redclyf Ho
14 Winkworth Cotts
15 Amiel St
16 Hadleigh Ho
17 Hadleigh Cl
18 Ryder Ho
19 Mantus Cl
20 Kenton Ho
21 Colebert Ho
22 Ibbott St
23 Rickman Ho
24 Rickman St
25 Stothard Ho
26 Barbanel Ho
27 Stannard Cotts
28 St Peters Ct
29 Rennie Cotts
30 Pemell Cl
31 Pemell Ho
32 Leatherdale St
33 Gouldman Ho
34 Lamplighter Cl
35 Sherren Ho
36 Marlborough Lo
37 Hamilton Lo
38 Montgomery Lo
39 Cleveland Gr
40 Cromwell Lo
41 Bardsey Pl
42 Charrington Ho
43 Hayfield Yd
44 Allport Mews
45 Colin Winter Ho
46 John Scurr Prim Sch
C4 1 Mulberry Ho
2 Gretton Ho
3 Merceron Ho
4 Montfort Ho
5 Westbrook Ho
6 Sugar Loaf Wlk
7 Museum Ho
8 Burnham Est
9 Globe Terr
10 Moravian St
11 Shepton Hos
12 Mendip Hos
13 Academy Ct
14 Pepys Ho
15 Swinburne Ho
16 Moore Ho
17 Morris Ho
18 Burns Ho
19 Milton Ho
20 Whitman Ho
21 Shelley Ho
22 Keats Ho
23 Dawson Ho
24 Bradbeer Ho
25 Forber Ho
26 Hughes Ho
27 Silvester Ho
28 Rogers Est
29 Pavan Ct
30 Stafford Cripps Ho
31 Sidney Godley (VC) Ho
32 Butler Ho
33 Butler St
34 Thorne Ho
35 Bevin Ho
36 Tuscan Ho
37 Globe Prim Sch
38 Bangabandhu Prim Sch
39 Bonner Prim Sch
C5 1 Evesham Ho
2 James Campbell Ho
3 Thomas Hollywood Ho
4 James Docherty Ho
5 Ebenezer Mussel Ho
6 Jameson Ct
7 Edinburgh Cl
8 Roger Dowley Ct
9 Sherbrooke Ho
10 Calcraft Ho
11 Burrard Ho
12 Dundas Ho
13 Ponsonby Ho
14 Barnes Ho
15 Paget Ho
16 Maitland Ho
17 Chesil Ct
18 Reynolds Ho
19 Cleland Ho
20 Goodrich Ho
21 Rosebery Ho
22 Sankey Ho
23 Cyprus Pl
24 Royston St
25 Stainsbury St
26 Hunslett St
27 Baildon
28 Brockweir
29 Tytherton
30 Malmesbury
31 Kingswood
32 Colville Ho
33 St Elizabeth RC Prim Sch
34 Raine's Foundation Sch
35 St John's CE Prim Sch
36 Mowlem Prim Sch
C6 1 Halkett Ho
2 Christchurch Sq
3 Helena Pl
4 Swingfield Ho
5 Greenham Ho
6 Dinmore Ho
7 Anstey Ho
8 Weston Ho
9 Carbroke Ho
10 Bluebell Cl
11 Cherry Tree Cl
12 Georgian Ct
13 Park Cl
14 Regency Ct
15 Norris Ho
D1 1 Pattison Ho
2 St Thomas Ho
3 Arbour Ho
4 Bladen Ho
5 Antill Terr
6 Majorie Mews
7 Billing Ho
8 Dowson Ho
9 Lipton Rd
10 Chalkwell Ho
11 Corringham Ho
12 Ogilvie Ho
13 Edward Mann Cl
14 Reservoir Studios
15 Lighterman Mews
16 Tower Hamlets Coll
17 Marion Richardson Prim Sch
D2 1 Roland Mews
2 Beatrice Ho
3 Morecambe Cl
4 Stepney Green Ct
5 Milrood Ho
6 Panama Ho
7 Galway Ho
8 Jacqueline Ho
9 Crown Mews
10 Caspian Ho
11 Darien Ho
12 Riga Ho
13 Flores Ho
14 Taranto Ho
15 Aden Ho
16 Master's St
17 Rosary Ct
18 Stepney Green Maths & Computing Coll
19 Sir John Cass Foundation & Redcoat CE Sec Sch
D3 1 Raynham Ho
2 Pat Shaw Ho
3 Colmar Cl
4 Withy Ho
5 Stocks Ct
6 Downey Ho
7 Bay Ct
8 Sligo Ho
9 Pegasus Ho
10 Barents Ho
11 Biscay Ho
12 Solway Ho
13 Bantry Ho
14 Aral Ho
15 Pacific Ho
16 Magellan Ho
17 Levant Ho
18 Adriatic Ho
19 Genoa Ho
20 Hawke Ho
21 Palliser Ho
22 Ionian Ho
23 Weddell Ho
24 Carlyle Mews
25 Greencourt Ho
26 Sundra Wlk
D4 1 Stubbs Ho
2 Holman Ho
3 Clynes Ho
4 Windsor Ho
5 Gilbert Ho
6 Chater Ho
7 Ellen Wilkinson Ho
8 George Belt Ho
9 Ayrton Gould Ho
10 O'Brian Ho
11 Sulkin Ho
12 Jenkinson Ho
13 Bullards Pl
14 Sylvia Pankhurst Ho
15 Mary Macarthur Ho
16 Trevelyan Ho
17 Wedgwood Ho
18 Pemberton Ct
19 Leatherdale St
20 Walter Besant Ho
21 Barber Beaumont Ho
22 Brancaster Ho
23 Litcham Ho
24 Bradwell St
D5 1 Kemp Ho
2 Piggott Ho
3 Mark Ho
4 Sidney Ho
5 Pomeroy Ho
6 Puteaux Ho
7 Doric Ho
8 Modling Ho
9 Longman Ho
10 Ames Ho
11 Alzette Ho
12 Offenbach Ho
13 Tate Ho
14 Norton Ho
15 St Gilles Ho
16 Harold Ho
17 Velletri Ho
18 Bridge Wharf
19 Gathorne St
20 Bow Brook The
21 Twig Folly Cl
22 Palmerston Ct
23 Lakeview
24 Peach Walk Mews
25 Caesar Ct
26 Gatehouse Sch
D6 6 Lauriston Prim Sch

97

A1 1 Hearnshaw St
2 Berry Cotts
3 Causton Cotts
4 Elizabeth Blount Ct
5 Carr St
6 Shaw Cres
7 Darnley Ho
8 Mercer's Cotts
9 Troon Ho
10 Ratcliffe Ho
11 Wakeling St
12 York Sq
13 Anglia Ho
14 Cambria Ho
15 Caledonia Ho
16 Ratcliffe La
17 Bekesbourne St
18 John Scurr Ho
19 Regents Canal Ho
20 Basin App
21 Powlesland Ct
22 Cayley Prim Sch
23 Stephen Hawking Sch
A2 1 Waley St
2 Edith Ramsay Ho
3 Andaman Ho
4 Atlantic Ho
5 Pevensey Ho
6 Solent Ho
7 Lorne Ho
8 Cromarty Ho
9 Dakin Pl
10 Greaves Cotts
11 Donaghue Cotts
12 Ames Cotts
13 Waterview Ho
14 Limehouse Fields Est
A3 1 Formosa Ho
2 Galveston Ho
3 Arabian Ho
4 Greenland Ho
5 Coral Ho
6 Anson Ho
7 Cambay Ho
8 Lindop Ho
9 Moray Ho
10 Azov Ho
11 Sandalwood Cl
12 Broadford Ho
A4 1 Imperial Ho
2 Newport Ho
3 Vassall Ho
4 Maurice Ct
5 Creed Ct
6 Christopher France Ho
7 Beaumont Ct
8 Pembroke Mews
9 Guardian Angels RC Prim Sch
10 Central Foundation Lower Girls Sch The
A5 1 Nightingale Mews
2 Bunsen Ho
3 Bunsen St
4 Beatrice Webb Ho
5 Margaret Bondfield Ho
6 Wilmer Ho
7 Sandall Ho
8 Butley Ct
9 Josseline Ct
10 Dalton Ho
11 Brine Ho
12 Ford Cl
13 Viking Cl
14 Stanfield Rd
15 Stoneleigh Mews
16 Ruth Ct
17 School Bell Cloisters
18 Schoolbell Mews
19 Medhurst Cl
20 Olga St
21 Conyer St
22 Diamond Ho
23 Daring Ho
24 Crane Ho
25 Exmoor Ho
26 Grenville Ho
27 Hyperion Ho
28 Sturdy Ho
29 Wren Ho
30 Ardent Ho
31 Senators Lo
32 Hooke Ho
33 Mohawk Ho
34 Ivanhoe Ho
35 Medway Mews
36 Chisenhale Prim Sch
37 Olga Prim Sch
B1 1 Dora Ho
2 Flansham Ho
3 Gatwick Ho
4 Ashpark Ho
5 Newdigate Ho
6 Midhurst Ho
7 Redbourne Ho
8 Southwater Cl
9 Andersens Wharf
10 Whatman Ho
11 Butler Ho
12 Fitzroy Ho
13 Salmon St
14 Mission The
15 Aithan Ho
16 Britley Ho
17 Cheadle Ho
18 Elland Ho
19 Wharf La
20 Docklands Ct
21 Park Heights Ct
22 Grosvenor Ct
23 Lime House Ct
24 Swallow Pl
25 St Anne's Trad Est
26 Stepney Greencoat CE Prim Sch The
27 Sir William Burrough Prim Sch
28 Our Lady RC Prim Sch
B2 1 Wearmouth Ho
2 Elmslie Point
3 Grindley Ho
4 Stileman Ho
5 Wilcox Ho
6 Huddart St
7 Robeson St
8 Couzens Ho
9 Perley Ho
10 Whytlaw Ho
11 Booker Cl
12 Tunley Gn
13 Callingham Cl
14 Bowry Ho
15 Perkins Ho
16 Printon Ho
17 Tasker Ho
18 St Paul with St Luke CE Prim Sch
B4 1 Trellis Sq
2 Sheffield Sq
3 Howcroft Ho
4 Astra Ho
5 Frye Ct
6 Byas Ho
7 George Lansbury Ho
8 Regal Pl
9 Coborn Mews
10 Tredegar Mews
11 Cavendish Terr
12 Lyn Mews
13 Buttermere Ho
14 Coniston Ho
15 Tracy Ho
16 Hanover Pl
17 St Clair Ho
18 Longthorne Ho
19 Vista Bldgs
20 Verity Ho
21 Icarus Ho
22 Whippingham Ho
23 Hamilton Ho
24 Winchester Ho
25 Malmesbury Prim Sch
26 Phoenix Sec & Prim Sch
27 Central Foundation Upper Girls Sch The
B5 1 Roman Road Mkt
2 John Bond Ho
3 McKenna Ho
4 Dennis Ho
5 McAusland Ho
6 McBride Ho
7 Libra Rd
8 Dave Adams Ho
9 Regency Ct
10 Tay Ho
11 Sleat Ho
12 Brodick Ho
13 Ewart Pl
14 Lunan Ho
15 Cruden Ho

486 97 B5

Anglo Rd
Mull Ho
Sinclairs Ho
Driftway Ho
Clayhall Ct
Berebinder Ho
Partridge Ho
Barford Ho
Gullane Ho
Gosford Ho
Dornoch Ho
Dunnet Ho
Enard Ho
Fraserburgh Ho
Forth Ho
Stavers Ho
Rosegate Ho
Crowngate Ho
Queensgate Ho
Towergate Ho
Ordell Ct
William Ho
Old Ford Prim Sch

B6 Hampstead Wlk
Waverton Ho
Elton Ho
Locton Gn
Birtwhistle Ho
Clare Ho
Magpie Ho
Hornbeam Sq
Rowan Ho
Barge La
Walnut Ho
Birdsfield La
Atkins Ct
Willow Tree Cl
Jasmine Sq
Tait Ct
Ranwell Ho
Ranwell Cl
Tufnell Ct
Pulteney Cl
Vic Johnson Ho
Lea Sq
Iceni Ct
Tamar Cl
Roman Rd
Valentine Ho

C1 Landin Ho
Thomas Road Ind Est
Vickery's Wharf
Abbotts Wharf
Limehouse Ct
Charlesworth Ho
Gurdon Ho
Trendell Ho
Menteath Ho
Minchin Ho
Donne Ho
Old School Sq
Anglesey Ho
Gough Wlk
Baring Ho
Gladstone Ho
Hopkins Ho
Granville Ho
Overstone Ho
Pusey Ho
Russell Ho
Stanley Ho

C2 Bredel Ho
Linton Ho
Matthews Ho
Woodcock Ho
Limborough Ho
Maydwell Ho
Underhill Ho
Meyrick Ho
Ambrose Ho
Richardson Ho
Carpenter Ho
Robinson Ho
Bellmaker Ct
Lime Tree Ct
Bracken Ho
Bramble Ho
Berberis Ho
Bilberry Ho
Mayflower Ho
Rosebay Ho

Invicta Cl
Phoenix Bsns Ctr
Metropolitan Cl
Busbridge Ho
St Paul's Way Com Sch

C3 Fairmont Ho
Healy Ho
Zodiac Ho
Buick Ho
Consul Ho
Bentley Ho
Cresta Ho
Daimler Ho
Riley Ho
Jensen Ho
Lagonda Ho
Ireton St
Navenby Wlk
Burwell Wlk
Leadenham Ct
Sleaford Ho
Bow Triangle Bsns Ctr
Clara Grant Prim Sch The

C4 Bow Ho
Denmark Pl
Marsalis Ho
Lovette Ho
Drapers Almshouses
Mallard Point
Creswick Wlk
Bevin Ho
Huggins Ho
Williams Ho
Harris Ho
Marina Ct
Electric Ho
Matching Ct
Wellington Bldgs
Grafton Ho
Berkeley Ho
Columbia Ho
Bow Sec Sch
Wellington Prim Sch
Cherry Trees Sch The

C5 Vincent Mews
Menai Pl
Heathfield Ct
Redwood Cl
Acorn Ct
Primrose Cl
Briar Ct
Springwood Cl
Lacey Mews
Matilda Gdns

C6 Ironworks
Juno Ho
Chariot Cl
Saturn Ho
Hadrian Cl
Mercury Ho
Forum Cl
Venus Ho
Vesta Ho
Tiber Cl
Gemini Ho
Crown Close Bsns Ctr

D1 Colebrook Ho
Essex Ho
Salisbury Ho
Maidstone Ho
Osterley Ho
Norwich Ho
Clarissa Ho
Elgin Ho
Shaftesbury Ho
Shepherd Ho
Jeremiah St
Elizabeth Cl
Chilcot Cl
Fitzgerald Ho
Vesey Path
Ennis Ho
Kilmore Ho
Cygnet House N
Cygnet House S
Lansbury
Lawrence Prim Sch
Bygrove Prim Sch

Mayflower Prim Sch
Tower Hamlets Coll

D2 Sumner Ho
David Hewitt Ho
St Gabriels Ct
Limehouse Cut
Colmans Wharf
Foundary Ho
Radford Ho
Manorfield Prim Sch
St Saviour's CE Prim Sch
Pioneer Ct

D3 Broxbourne Ho
Roxford Ho
Biscott Ho
Stanborough Ho
Hillstone Ct
Marner Prim Sch

D4 Bradley Ho
Prioress Ho
Alton Ho
Foxley Ho
Munden Ho
Canterbury Ho
Corbin Ho
Barton Ho
Jolles Ho
Rudstone Ho
Baxter Ho
Baker Ho
Insley Ho
Hardwicke Ho
St Agnes RC Prim Sch
Priory St
Sadler Ho
Ballinger Point
Henshall Point
Dorrington Point
Warren Ho
Fairlie Ct
Regent Sq
Hackworth Point
Priestman Point
Wingate Ho
Nethercott Ho
Thelbridge Ho
Bowden Ho
Kerscott Ho
Southcott Ho
Birchdown Ho
Upcott Ho
Langmead Ho
Limscott Ho
Northleigh Ho
Huntshaw Ho
Chagford Ho
Ashcombe Ho
Shillingford Ho
Patrick Connolly Gdns
Lester Ct
Franklin St
Taft Way
Washington Cl
Veronica Ho
William Guy Gdns
Denbury Ho
Holsworthy Ho
Padstone Ho
Old Palace Prim Sch
Ian Mikardo Sch

E3 London Metrocity Coll

98

A1 Glenkerry Ho
Carradale Ho
Langdon Ho
Balfron Twr
St Frideswides Mews
Tabard Ct
Delta Bldg
Findhorn St
Kilbrennan Ho
Thistle Ho
Heather Ho
Tartan Ho
Sharman Ho
Trident Ho

Wharf View Ct
Culloden Prim Sch

A21 Mills Gr
St Michaels Cl
Duncan Ct

B1 Lansbury Gdns
Theseus Ho
Adams Ho
Jones Ho
Sam March Ho
Arapiles Ho
Athenia Ho
Julius Ho
Jervis Bay Ho
Helen Mackay Ho
Gaze Ho
Ritchie Ho
Blairgowrie Ct
Circle Ho
Dunkeld Ho
Rosemary Dr
Sorrel La
East India Dock Road Tunnel

B3 Crescent Court Bsns Ctr
Ashmead Bsns Ctr
Forward Bsns Ctr The

B6 Victoria Mills
Hallings Wharf Studios
Poland Ho
Peter Heathfield Ho
Burford Rd
John F Kennedy Specl Sch
Univ of East London (Duncan Ho)

C5 Abbey Lane Commercial Est
Greenway Ct

C6 Barnby Sq
Barnby St
Brassett Point
David Lee Point
Worthing Cl
Bexhill Wlk
Old Barrowfield
Elmgreen Cl
Stafford Morris Ho
Nina Mackay Cl
Lime Wlk

D1 Newton Point
Sparke Terr
Montesquieu Terr
Crawford Point
Rathbone Ho
George St
Emily St
Sabbarton St
St Luke Prim Sch
Briary Ct
Shaftesbury Ho

D2 Radley Terr
Bernard Cassidy St
Rathbone Mkt
Thomas North Terr
Mary St
Hughes Terr
Swanscombe Point
Rawlinson Point
Kennedy Cox Ho
Cooper St

D6 Harris Cotts
Moorey Cl
Euro Bsns Ctr
Ladywell St
Caistor Ho
Redfern Ho
West Ham Church Prim Sch

99

A2 Odeon Ct
Edward Ct

Newhaven La
Ravenscroft Cl
Douglas Rd
Ferrier Point
Harvey Point
Wood Point
Trinity St
Pattinson Point
Clinch Ct
Mint Bsns Pk
Keir Hardy Prim Sch

A3 Webb Gdns
Eric Shipman Terr
Warmington St
Jellicoe Rd
Frank St
Seaton Cl
Tabernacle Ave
Upland Rd
Clove St
Edward St
Ravenscroft Prim Sch

A4 Bob Anker Cl
Lea Ct
Third Ave
Suffolk Rd

A5 Lettsom Wlk
Ashburton Terr
Grasmere Rd
Dimsdale Wlk
Rawstone Wlk
Scott Ho
Willett Ho
James Cl
Cordwainers Wlk
Victoria Point
Settle Point
Middle Rd
Steve Biko Lodge
Lady Helen Seymour Ho
Winifred Terr

A6 Royston Ct
Chadd Gn
Tanner Point
Nicholls Point
Reindeer Cl
Selwyn Prim Sch
Portway Prim Sch

B4 Barbers Alley
Grengate Lodge
Augurs La
Surrey St
Dongola Rd W
Bemersyde Point
Rowntree Clifford Cl

B5 Lister Com Sch
Eleanor Smith Sch

C1 St Joachim's RC Prim Sch

C2 Alliance Rd
Salomons Rd
Barnes Ct
Triangle Ct
Moorings The

C5 Wellby Ct
Northfield Ho
Bishop Wilfred Wood Ct
Castle Point
Moat Dr

C6 Tolpuddle Ave
Crown Mews
Lilac Ct
Hamara Ghar
Greenleaf Rd
Massey Ct
Florence Rd
Sissulu Ct
Austin Ct
St Edwards RC Prim Sch

D2 Partridge Cl
Vanburgh Cl
Meadowsweet Cl
St Michaels Cl
Long Mark Rd
Congreve Wlk

D5 Foxcombe Cl
Rochford Cl

Kylemore Cl
Stondon Wlk
Imperial Mews
Dominica Cl
Central Park Prim Sch

D6 Oldegate Ho
Gaitskell Ho
Cabot Way

100

A1 Hadleigh Wlk
Hawksmoor Cl
Fraser Cl
Moncrieff Cl
Burlington Cl
Dundonald Cl
Oakley Cl
Ashwell Cl

A2 Orchid Cl
Bellflower Cl
Partridge Sq
Larkspur Cl
Lobelia Cl
Stonechat Sq
Wintergreen Cl
Garnet Wlk
Mavis Wlk
Beacons Cl
Abbess Cl
Elmley Cl
Selby Cl
Denny Cl
Woodhatch Cl

A6 Oakwood Ct
Harrow Rd
Ray Massey Way
Madge Gill Way
Pilgrims Way
St Bartholomews Ct
Hartley Prim Sch
Newham Acad of Music

B1 Bowers Wlk
Barton Cl
Clayton Cl
Dixon Cl
Gautrey Sq
Wakerley Cl
Canterbury Cl
Goose Sq
Coventry Cl
Butterfield Sq
Winchester Cl

B2 Fleetwood Cl
Lymington Cl
Holyhead Cl
Bondfield Rd
Tulip Cl
Ambrose Cl
Sage Cl
Lindwood Cl

B4 Butterfly Cl
Cricket Ct
Sunningdale Cl
John Wesley Cl
Vicarage Prim Sch

B5 Hastingwood Ct
Tippett Ct
Newham Coll of FE
St Michael's RC Prim Sch

D1 Weymouth Cl
Founder Ct
Admirals Ct

101

A6 St Ann's Rd
Cooke St
Gateway Ho
Ardleigh Ho
Skipper Ct
Hewetts Quay

B5 Anderson Ho
Rookwood Ho
Tasker Ho
Crispe Ho
Oban Ho
Earlsdown Ho

B6 Jarvis Ho
Mayflower Ho
Westbury Ct

4 Millicent Preston Ho
5 Louise Graham Ho
6 Grange Ho
7 Basing Ho
8 Barnes Ho
9 Lexham Ho
10 Ripple Ct
11 Waldegrave Ct
12 Howard Ct

104
A6 1 Milburn Dr
2 Cousins Cl
3 Leacroft Cl

107
C4 1 Decimal Ctr
2 Bridge Bsns Ctr The

108
C5 1 Marlow Ct
2 Andrewes Ct
3 Vine Cotts
4 Benjamin Ct
5 Broadway Bldgs
6 Clocktower Mews
7 Amberley Ho
8 Diamond Ct
9 St Ann's Sch
10 St Josephs RC Prim Sch
D5 1 Silverdale Ct
2 Burdett Cl
3 Hopefield
4 Maunder Rd
5 Clare Ho

109
A5 1 Glastonbury Ct
2 Evesham Ct
3 Lacock Ct
4 Wigmore Ct
5 Melrose Ct
6 Brownlow Rd
7 Chignell Pl
8 Shirley Ct
9 Trojan Ct
10 Hatfield Rd
11 Pershore Ho
12 Hyde Ho
13 Hugh Clark Ho
14 Rosemoor Ho
15 Leeland Mans
16 Waterford Ct
17 O'Grady Ct
C1 1 Barrow Wlk
2 Mercury Rd
3 Our Lady & St John's RC Jun & Inf Sch
C3 1 Mt Carmel RC Prim Sch
2 Little Ealing Prim Sch
C6 1 Abbey Lo
2 New Tree Grange
3 Abinger Ct
D6 1 Sandringham Mews
2 St Savior's CE Inf Sch

110
A1 1 Burford Ho
2 Hope Cl
3 Centaur Ct
4 Phoenix Ct
A6 1 Watermans Mews
2 Hills Mews
3 Grosvenor Ct
4 Elton Lo
5 Hambledon Ct
6 Edwards Language Sch
C1 1 Surrey Cres
2 Forbes Ho
3 Haining Cl
4 Melville Ct
5 London Stile
6 Stile Hall Par
7 Priory Lo
8 Meadowcroft
9 St James Ct

10 Rivers Ho
C5 1 Grosvenor Par
2 Oakfield Ct
3 Hart Grove Ct
4 Grosvenor Ct
5 King Edwards Pl
D1 1 Churchdale Ct
2 Cambridge Rd S
3 Oxbridge Ct
4 Cromwell Cl
5 Tomlinson Cl
6 Gunnersbury Mews
7 Grange The
8 Gunnersbury Ct
9 Bellgrave Lo
D4 1 Cheltenham Pl
2 Beaumaris Twr
3 Arundel Ho
4 Pevensey Ct
5 Jerome Twr
6 Anstey Ct
7 Bennett Ct
8 Gunnersbury Ct
9 Barrington Ct
10 Hope Gdns
11 Park Road E
D5 1 Lantry Ct
2 Rosemount Ct
3 Moreton Twr
4 Acton Central Ind Est
5 Rufford Twr
6 Narrow St
7 Mount Pl
8 Sidney Miller Ct
9 Mill Hill Terr
10 Cheltenham Pl
11 Mill Hill Gr
12 Benjamin Ho
13 Arlington Ct
14 Lombard Ct
15 Steyne Ho
16 Acton & West London Coll

111
A1 1 Arlington Park Mans
2 Sandown Ho
3 Goodwood Ho
4 Windsor Ho
5 Lingfield Ho
6 Ascot Ho
7 Watchfield Ct
8 Belgrave Ct
9 Beverley Ct
10 Beaumont Ct
11 Harvard Rd
12 Troubridge Ct
13 Branden Lo
14 Fromow's Cnr
15 Heathfield House Sch
A2 1 Chiswick Green Studios
2 Bell Ind Est
3 Fairlawn Ct
4 Dukes Gate
5 Dewsbury Ct
6 Chiswick Terr
7 Mortlake Ho
A3 1 Blackmore Twr
2 Bollo Ct
3 Kipling Twr
4 Lawrence Ct
5 Maugham Ct
6 Reade Ct
7 Woolf Ct
8 Shaw Ct
9 Verne Ct
10 Wodehouse Ct
11 Greenock Rd
12 Garden Ct
13 Barons Gate
14 Cleveland Rd
15 Carver Ct
16 Chapter Ct
17 Beauchamp Cl
18 Copper Mews
A4 1 Belgrave Ct
2 Buckland Wlk
3 Frampton Ct
4 Telfer Ct
5 Harlech Twr

6 Corfe Twr
7 Barwick Ho
8 Charles Hocking Ho
9 Sunninghill Ct
10 Salisbury St
11 Jameson Pl
12 Castle Cl
A5 1 Rectory Rd
2 Derwentwater Mans
3 Market Pl
4 Hooper's Mews
5 Cromwell Pl
6 Locarno Rd
7 Edgecote Cl
8 Harleyford Manor
9 Coopers Ct
10 Avingdor Ct
11 Steyne Ho
B1 1 Chatsworth Ct
2 Prospect Pl
3 Townhall Ave
4 Devonhurst Pl
5 Heathfield Ct
6 Horticultural Pl
7 Merlin Ho
8 Garth Rd
9 Autumn Rise
B2 1 Disraeli Ct
2 Winston Wlk
3 Rusthall Mans
4 Bedford Park Mans
5 Essex Place Sq
6 Holly Rd
7 Homecross Ho
8 Swan Bsns Ctr
9 Jessop Ho
10 Belmont Prim Sch
C1 1 Glebe Cl
2 Devonshire Mews
3 Binns Terr
4 Ingress St
5 Swanscombe Rd
6 Brackley Terr
7 Stephen Fox Ho
8 Manor Gdns
9 Coram Ho
10 Flaxman Ho
11 Thorneycroft Ho
12 Thornhill Ho
13 Kent Ho
14 Oldfield Ho
15 William Hogarth Sch The
C2 1 Chestnut Ho
2 Bedford Ho
3 Bedford Cnr
4 Sydney Ho
5 Bedford Park Cnr
6 Priory Gdns
7 Windmill Alley
8 Castle Pl
9 Jonathan Ct
10 Windmill Pas
11 Chardin Rd
12 Gable Ho
13 St Catherine's Ct
14 Arts Educational Sch The
15 Orchard House Sch
C3 1 Fleet Ct
2 Ember Ct
3 Emlyn Gdns
4 Clone Ct
5 Brent Ct
6 Abbey Ct
7 Ormsby Lo
8 St Catherine's Ct
9 Lodge The
C4 1 Longford Ct
2 Mole Ct
3 Lea Ct
4 Wandle Ct
5 Beverley Ct
6 Roding Ct
7 Crane Ct
D1 1 Miller's Ct
2 British Grove Pas
3 British Grove S
4 Berestede Rd

5 North Eyot Gdns
D2 1 Flanders Mans
2 Stamford Brook Mans
3 Linkenholt Mans
4 Prebend Mans
5 Middlesex Ct
D3 1 Stamford Brook Gdns
2 Hauteville Court Gdns
3 Ranelagh Gdns

112
A1 1 Chisholm Ct
2 North Verbena Gdns
3 Western Terr
4 Verbena Gdns
5 Montrose Villas
6 Hammersmith Terr
7 South Black Lion La
8 St Peter's Wharf
9 Eden High Sch
A2 1 Hamlet Ct
2 Derwent Ct
3 Westcroft Ct
4 Black Lion Mews
5 St Peter's Villas
6 Standish Ho
7 Chambon Pl
8 Court Mans
9 Longthorpe Ct
10 Charlotte Ct
11 Westside
12 Park Ct
13 London Ho
14 Latymer Upper Sch
15 St Peter's CE Prim Sch
16 Polish Univ Abroad
A3 1 Elizabeth Finn Ho
2 Ashchurch Ct
3 King's Par
4 Inver Ct
5 Ariel Ct
6 Pocklington Lo
7 Vitae Apartments
A4 1 Becklow Gdns
2 Victoria Ho
3 Lycett Pl
4 Kylemore Ct
5 Alexandra Ct
6 Lytten Ct
7 Becklow Mews
8 Northcroft Ct
9 Bailey Ct
10 Spring Cott
11 Landor Wlk
12 Laurence Mews
13 Hadyn Park Ct
14 Askew Mans
15 Malvern Ct
B1 1 Prince's Mews
2 Aspen Gdns
3 Hampshire Hog La
4 Blades Ct
B2 1 Albion Gdns
2 Flora Gdns
3 Lamington St
4 Felgate Mews
5 Galena Ho
6 Albion Mews
7 Albion Ct
8 King Street Cloisters
9 Dimes Pl
10 Clarence Ct
11 Hampshire Hog La
12 Marryat Ct
13 Ravenscourt Ho
14 Ravenscourt Theatre Sch
15 Cambridge Sch
16 Godolphin & Latymer Sch
17 Flora Gardens Prim Sch
B3 1 Ravenscourt Park Mans

2 Paddenswick Rd
3 Ashbridge Ct
4 Brackenbury Prim Sch
B4 1 Westbush Ct
2 Goldhawk Mews
3 Sycamore Ho
4 Shackleton Ct
5 Drake Ct
6 Scotts Ct
7 Raleigh Ct
8 Melville Court Flats
9 Southway Cl
B5 1 Arlington Ho
2 Lugard Ho
3 Shabana Ct
4 Sitarey Ct
5 Oaklands Ct
6 Davenport Mews
B6 1 Abercrombie Ho
2 Bathurst Ho
3 Brisbane Ho
4 Bentinck Ho
5 Ellenborough Ho
6 Lawrence Cl
7 Mackenzie Cl
8 Carteret Ho
9 Calvert Ho
10 Winthrop Ho
11 Auckland Ho
12 Blaxland Ho
13 Havelock Cl
14 Hargraves Ho
15 Hudson Cl
16 Phipps Ho
17 Lawson Ho
18 Hastings Ho
19 Wolfe Ho
20 Malabar Ct
21 Commonwealth Ave
22 Charnock Ho
23 Canning Ho
24 Cornwallis Ho
25 Commonwealth Ave
26 Champlain Ho
27 Grey Ho
28 Durban Ho
29 Baird Ho
30 Campbell Ho
31 Mitchell Ho
32 Denham Ho
33 Mackay Ho
34 Evans Ho
35 Davis Ho
36 Mandela Cl
C1 1 Bridge Avenue Mans
2 Bridgeview
3 College Ct
4 Beatrice Ho
5 Amelia Ho
6 Edith Ho
7 Joanna Ho
8 Mary Ho
9 Adela Ho
10 Sophia Ho
11 Henrietta Ho
12 Charlotte Ho
13 Alexandra Ho
14 Bath Pl
15 Elizabeth Ho
16 Margaret Ho
17 Peabody Est
18 Eleanor Ho
19 Isabella Ho
20 Caroline Ho
21 Chancellors Wharf
22 Sussex Pl
23 St Paul's CE Prim Sch
C2 1 Phoenix Lodge Mans
2 Samuel's Cl
3 Broadway Arc
4 Brook Ho
5 Hammersmith Broadway
6 Broadway Ctr The
7 Cambridge Ct
8 Ashcroft Sq
9 Sacred Heart High Sch

112 D5   487
10 King Street Coll
C4 1 Verulam Ho
2 Grove Mans
3 Frobisher Ct
4 Library Mans
5 Pennard Mans
6 New Shepherd's Bush Mkt
7 Kerrington Ct
8 Granville Mans
9 Romney Ct
10 Rayner Ct
11 Sulgrave Gdns
12 Bamborough Gdns
13 Hillary Ct
14 Market Studios
15 Lanark Mans
16 Miles Coverdale Prim Sch
17 St Stephen's CE Prim Sch
18 London Coll of Fashion (Lime Grove)
C5 1 Linden Ct
2 Frithville Ct
3 Blomfield Mans
4 Poplar Mews
5 Hopgood St
6 Westwood Ho
7 Stanlake Mews
8 Stanlake Villas
9 Alexandra Mans
D2 1 St Paul's Girls' Sch
2 Bute House Prep Sch
3 Jacques Prevert
4 Larmenier & Sacred Heart RC Sch
D3 1 Grosvenor Residences
2 Blythe Mews
3 Burnand Ho
4 Bradford Ho
5 Springvale Terr
6 Ceylon Rd
7 Walpole Ct
8 Bronte Ct
9 Boswell Ct
10 Souldern Rd
11 Brook Green Flats
12 Haarlem Rd
13 Stafford Mans
14 Lionel Mans
15 Barradell Ho
D4 1 Vanderbilt Villas
2 Bodington Ct
3 Kingham Cl
4 Clearwater Terr
5 Lorne Gdns
6 Cameret Ct
7 Rush Ct
8 Shepherds Ct
9 Rockley Ct
10 Grampians The
11 Charcroft Ct
12 Addison Park Mans
13 Sinclair Mans
14 Fountain Ct
15 Woodford Ct
16 Roseford Ct
17 Woodstock Studios
D5 1 St Katherine's Wlk
2 Dorrit Ho
3 Pickwick Ho
4 Dombey Ho
5 Caraday Villas
6 Mortimer Ho
7 Nickleby Ho
8 Stebbing Ho
9 Boxmoor Ho
10 Poynter Ho
11 Swanscombe Ho
12 Darnley Terr
13 Norland Ho

14 Hume Ho
15 Boundary Ho
16 Norland Ho
17 Helix Ct
D6 1 Frinstead Ho
2 Hurstway Wlk
3 Testerton Wlk
4 Grenfell Wlk
5 Grenfell Twr
6 Barandon Wlk
7 Treadgold Ho
8 St Clements Ct
9 Willow Way
10 Florence Ho
11 Dora Ho
12 Carton Ho
13 Agnes Ho
14 Marley Ho
15 Estella Ho
16 Waynflete Sq
17 Pippin Ho
18 Baseline Business Studios
19 St Francis of Assisi Prim Sch
20 Nicholas Rd

118
A1 1 Hope Ct
2 West Point
3 Centre Point
4 East Point
5 Proctor Ho
6 Tovy Ho
7 Avondale Pavement
8 Brettinghurst
9 Colehurch Ho
10 Harman Cl
11 Avondale Ho
12 Lanark Ho
13 George Elliston Ho
14 Eric Wilkins Ho
15 Six Bridges Ind Est
16 St James Ind Mews
17 Winter Lo
18 Fern Wlk
19 Ivy Ct
20 Fallow Ct
21 Culloden Ct
22 Archers Lo
23 Eveline Lowe Prim Sch
A2 1 Cadbury Way
2 Robert Bell Ho
3 Robert Jones Ho
4 William Rushbrooke Ho
5 Helen Taylor Ho
6 Peter Hills Ho
7 Charles Mackenzie Ho
8 Drappers Way
9 Racs Flats
10 Abbey Gdns
11 Mayfair Ho
12 Windmill Cl
13 Maria Cl
14 Townsend Ho
15 Mason Ho
16 Kotree Way
17 Hannah Mary Way
18 Langdon Way
19 Whittaker Way
20 Cherry Garden Sch
21 Alma Prim Sch
A3 1 Rudge Ho
2 Spenlow Ho
3 Darnay Ho
4 Carton Ho
5 Giles Ho
6 Bowley Ho
7 Casby Ho
8 Sun Pas
9 Ness St
10 Voyager Bsns Est
11 Dockley Road Ind Est

12 Spa Ct
13 Discovery Bsns Pk
14 Priter Road Hostel
15 Salisbury Ct
16 William Ellis Way
17 John McKenna Wlk
18 Toussaint Wlk
19 Gillison Wlk
20 Bromfield Ct
21 Ben Smith Way
22 Major Rd
23 Old Jamaica Bsns Est
24 St James' CE Jun & Inf Sch
A4 1 Providence
2 Springalls Wharf
3 Flockton St
4 Meridian Ct
5 East La
6 Luna Ho
7 Axis Ct
8 Farthing Alley
9 Peter Butler Ho
10 Brownlow Ho
11 Tapley Ho
12 Copperfield Ho
13 Dombey Ho
14 Fleming Ho
15 Parkers Row
16 Wade Ho
17 Bardell Ho
18 Nickleby Ho
19 John Felton Rd
20 Flockton St
21 Pickwick Ho
22 Oliver Ho
23 Weller Ho
24 Haredale Ho
25 Havisham Ho
26 Tupman Ho
27 Micawber Ho
28 Wrayburn Ho
29 Dartle Ct
30 Waterside Cl
31 Burnaby Ct
32 Wickfield Ho
33 Fountain Ho
34 Fountain Green Sq
35 St Saviours Ho
36 Providence Sq
37 Riverside Prim Sch
38 St Michael's RC Sec Sch
39 St Joseph's RC Prim Sch
A5 1 Trade Winds Ct
2 Spice Ct
3 Leeward Ct
4 Bridgeport Pl
5 Tamarind Yd
6 Cape Yd
7 Nightingale Ho
8 St Anthony's Cl
9 Miah Terr
10 Seville Ho
11 Douthwaite Sq
12 Codling Ct
13 Hermitage Ct
14 Capital Wharf
15 Cinnabar Wharf East
16 Cinnabar Wharf Central
17 Cinnabar Wharf West
18 Bushell St
19 Hermitage Prim Sch
20 Waveney Cl
21 Welland Mews
22 Conant Mews
23 Hanson Ho
24 Royal Tower Lo
25 Victoria Ct
26 Swan Pas
27 Royal Mint Pl
28 Peabody Est
29 Florin Ct
30 Flank St
31 Onedin Point

11 Liberty Ho
12 Ensign Ct
13 Sapphire Ct
14 Graces Alley
15 George Leybourne Ho
16 Fletcher St
17 Hatton Ho
18 Noble Ho
19 Shearsmith Ho
20 Wellclose St
21 Telford's Yd
22 Breezer's Ct
23 Pennington Ct
24 St Paul's CE Prim Sch
25 Shapla Prim Sch
B1 1 Hockney Ct
2 Toulouse Ct
3 Lowry Ct
4 Barry Ho
5 Lewis Ct
6 Gainsborough Ct
7 Renoir Ct
8 Blake Ct
9 Raphael Ct
10 Rembrandt Ct
11 Constable Ct
12 Da Vinci Ct
13 Gaugin Ct
14 Michelangelo Ct
15 Monet Ct
16 Weald Cl
17 Jasmin Lo
18 Birchmere Lo
19 Weybridge Ct
20 Florence Ho
21 Gleneagles Cl
22 Sunningdale Cl
23 Muirfield Cl
24 Turnberry Cl
25 St Andrews Cl
26 Kingsdown Cl
27 St Davids Cl
28 Galway Cl
29 Edenbridge Cl
30 Birkdale Cl
31 Tralee Ct
32 Woburn Ct
33 Belfry Ct
34 Troon Ct
35 Holywell Cl
B2 1 Market Pl
2 Trappes Ho
3 Thurland Ho
4 Ramsfort Ho
5 Hambley Ho
6 Holford Ho
7 Pope Ho
8 Southwell Ho
9 Mortain Ho
10 Radcliffe Ho
11 Southwark Park Est
12 Galleywall Road Trad Est
13 Trevithick Ho
14 Barlow Ho
15 Donkin Ho
16 Landmann Ho
17 Fitzmaurice Ho
18 Dodd Ho
19 Southwark Park Prim Sch
B3 1 Perryn Rd
2 Chalfont Ho
3 Prestwood Ho
4 Farmer Ho
5 Gataker St
6 Gataker St
7 Cornick Ho
8 Glebe Ho
9 Matson Ho
10 Hickling Ho
11 St Andrews Ho
12 Southwark Coll (Surrey Docks Ctr)
B4 1 Butterfield Cl
2 Janeway Pl
3 Trotwood Ho
4 Maylie Ho
5 Cranbourn Pas
6 Cranbourn Ho
7 Cherry Garden Ho
8 Burton Ho

6 Morriss Ho
7 Dixon's Alley
8 King Edward The Third Mews
9 Cathay St
10 Mission The
11 Millstream Ho
B5 1 China St
2 Wellington Terr
3 Stevedore St
4 Portland St
5 Reardon Ho
6 Lowder Ho
7 Meeting House Alley
8 Farthing Fields
9 Oswell Ho
10 Park Lo
11 Doughty Ct
12 Inglefield Sq
13 Chopin's Ct
14 Welsh Ho
15 Hilliard Ho
16 Clegg St
17 Tasman Ho
18 Ross Ho
19 Wapping Dock St
20 Bridewell Pl
21 New Tower Bldgs
22 Tower Bldgs
23 Chimney Ct
24 Jackman Ho
25 Fenner Ho
26 Franklin Ho
27 Frobisher Ho
28 Flinders Ho
29 Chancellor Ho
30 Beechey Ho
31 Reardon Path
32 Parry Ho
33 Vancover Ho
34 Willoughby Ho
35 Sanctuary The
36 Dundee Ct
37 Pierhead Wharf
38 Scandrett St
39 St Johns Ct
B6 1 Newton Ho
2 Richard Neale Ho
3 Maddocks Ho
4 Cornwall St
5 Brockmer Ho
6 Dellow Ho
7 Bewley Ho
8 Artichoke Hill
9 Queen Anne Terr
10 King Henry Terr
11 King Charles Terr
12 Queen Victoria Terr
13 Sovereign Ct
14 Princes Court Bsns Ctr
15 Kingsley Mews
16 Mulberry Sch for Girls
C1 10 Ilderton Prim Sch
C2 1 Damory Ho
2 Antony Ho
3 Roderick Ho
4 Pedworth Gdns
5 Banner Ct
6 Rotherhithe Bsns Est
7 Beamish Ho
8 Corbetts Pas
9 Gillam Ho
10 Richard Ho
11 George Walter Ho
12 Westlake
13 Adron Ho
14 Cavendish Sch
15 McIntosh Ho
C3 1 Blick Ho
2 Neptune Ho
3 Scotia Ct
4 Murdoch Ho
5 Edmonton Ct
6 Niagara Ct
7 Columbia Point
8 Ritchie Ho
9 Wells Ho
10 Helen Peele Cotts
11 Orchard Ho

12 Dock Offices
13 Landale Ho
14 Courthope Ho
15 Hithe Gr
16 China Hall Mews
C4 1 Mayflower St
2 St Mary's Est
3 Rupack St
4 Frank Whymark Ho
5 Adams Gardens Est
6 Hatteraick St
7 East India Ct
8 Bombay Ct
9 Stable Ho
10 Grannary The
11 Riverside
12 Cumberland Wharf
13 Seaford Ho
14 Hythe Ho
15 Sandwich Ho
16 Winchelsea Ho
17 Rye Ho
18 Kenning St
19 Western Pl
20 Ainsty St
21 Pine Ho
22 Beech Ho
23 Larch Ho
24 Turner Ct
25 Seth St
26 Risdon Ho
27 Risdon St
28 Aylton Est
29 Manitoba Ct
30 Calgary Ct
31 Irwell Est
32 St Olav's Sq
33 City Bsns Ctr
C5 1 Albion Prim Sch
2 John Rennie Wlk
3 Malay Ho
4 Wainwright Ho
5 Riverside Mans
6 Shackleton Ho
7 Whitehorn Ho
8 Wavel Ct
9 Prusom's Island
10 St Peter's CE Prim Sch
C6 1 Shadwell Pl
2 Gosling Ho
3 Vogler Ho
4 Donovan Ho
5 Knowlden Ho
6 Chamberlain Ho
7 Moore Ho
8 Thornewill Ho
9 Fisher Ho
10 All Saints Ct
11 Coburg Dwellings
12 Lowood Ho
13 Solander Gdns
14 Chancery Bldgs
15 Ring Ho
16 Juniper St
17 Gordon Ho
18 West Block
19 North Block
20 South Block
21 Ikon Ho
22 Blue Gate Fields Jun & Inf Schs
D2 1 John Kennedy Ho
2 Brydale Ho
3 Balman Ho
4 Tissington Ct
5 Harbord Ho
6 Westfield Ho
7 Albert Starr Ho
8 John Brent Ho
9 William Evans Ho
10 Raven Ho
11 Egret Ho
12 Fulmar Ho
13 Dunlin Ho
14 Siskin Ho
15 Sheldrake Ho
16 Buchanan Ct
17 Burrage Ct
18 Biddenham Ho
19 Ayston Ho
20 Empingham Ho
21 Deanshanger Ho

23 Codicote Ho
22 Buryfield Ct
24 Rotherhithe Prim Sch
D4 1 Schooner Cl
2 Dolphin Cl
3 Clipper Cl
4 Deauville Ct
5 Colette Ct
6 Coniston Ct
7 Virginia Ct
8 Derwent Ct
9 Grantham Ct
10 Serpentine Ct
11 Career Ct
12 Lacine Ct
13 Fairway Ct
14 Harold Ct
15 Spruce Ho
16 Cedar Ho
17 Sycamore Ho
18 Woodland Cres
19 Poplar Ho
20 Adelphi Ct
21 Basque Ct
22 Aberdale Ct
23 Quilting Ct
24 Chargrove Ct
25 Radley Ct
26 Greenacre Sq
27 Maple Leaf Sq
28 Stanhope Ct
29 Hawke Pl
30 Drake Cl
31 Brass Talley Alley
32 Monkton Ho
33 James Ho
34 Wolfe Cres
D5 1 Clarence Mews
2 Raleigh Ct
3 Katherine Ct
4 Woolcombes Ct
5 Tudor Ct
6 Quayside Ho
7 Princes Riverside Rd
8 Surrey Ho
9 Tideway Ct
10 Edinburgh Ct
11 Falkirk Ct
12 Byelands Cl
13 Gwent Ct
14 Lavender Ho
15 Abbotshade Rd
16 Bellamy's Ct
17 Blenheim Ct
18 Sandringham Ct
19 Hampton Ct
20 Windsor Ct
21 Balmoral Ct
22 Westminster Ct
23 Beatson Wlk
24 Peter Hills Sch
D6 1 Barnardo Gdns
2 Roslin Ho
3 Glamis Est
4 Peabody Est
5 East Block
6 Highway Trad Ctr The
7 Highway Bsns Pk The
8 Cranford Cotts
9 Ratcliffe Orch
10 Scotia Bldg
11 Mauretania Bldg
12 Compania Bldg
13 Sirius Bldg
14 Unicorn Bldg
15 Keeper Wharf

119
A1 1 Sir Francis Drake Prim Sch
2 Deptford Park Prim Sch
A2 1 Trafalgar Cl
2 Hornblower Cl
3 Cunard Wlk
4 Caronia Ct
5 Carinthia Ct
6 Freswick Ho
7 Graveley Ho
8 Husbourne Ho
9 Crofters Ct
10 Pomona Ho

11 Hazelwood Ho
12 Cannon Wharf Bsns Ctr
13 Bence Ho
14 Clement Ho
15 Pendennis Ho
16 Lighter Cl
17 Mast Ct
18 Rushcutters Ct
19 Boat Lifter Way
A5 1 Edward Sq
2 Prince Regent Ct
3 Codrington Ct
4 Pennington Ct
5 Cherry Ct
6 Ash Ct
7 Beech Ct
8 Hazel Ct
9 Laurel Ct
A6 1 St Georges Sq
2 Drake Ho
3 Osprey Ho
4 Fleet Ho
5 Gainsborough Ho
6 Victory Pl
7 Challenger Ho
8 Conrad Ho
9 Lock View Ct
10 Shoulder of Mutton Alley
11 Frederick Sq
12 Helena Sq
13 Elizabeth Sq
14 Sophia Sq
15 William Sq
16 Lamb Ct
17 Lockside
18 Adriatic Bldg
19 Ionian Bldg
20 Regents Gate Ho
B1 1 Gransden Ho
2 Daubeney Twr
3 North Ho
4 Rochfort Ho
5 Keppel Ho
6 Camden Ho
7 Sanderson Ho
8 Berkeley Ho
9 Strafford Ho
10 Richman Ho
11 Hurleston Ho
12 Grafton Ho
13 Fulcher Ho
14 Citrus Ho
B2 1 Windsock Cl
2 St George's Mews
3 Linberry Wlk
4 Lanyard Ho
5 Golden Hind Pl
6 James Lind Ho
7 Harmon Ho
8 Pelican Ho
9 Bembridge Ho
10 Terrace The
11 George Beard Rd
12 Colonnade The
13 Pepys Ent Ctr
B6 1 Hamilton Ho
2 Imperial Ho
3 Oriana Ho
4 Queens Ct
5 Brightlingsea Pl
6 Faraday Ho
7 Ropemaker's Fields
8 Oast Ct
9 Mitre The
10 Bate St
11 Joseph Irwin Ho
12 Padstow Ho
13 Bethlehem Ho
14 Saunders Cl
15 Roche Ho
16 Stocks Pl
17 Trinidad Ho
18 Grenada Ho
19 Kings Ho
20 Dunbar Wharf
21 Limekiln Wharf
22 Belgrave Ct
23 Eaton Ho
24 Cyril Jackson Prim Sch (North Bldg)
25 Cyril Jackson Prim Sch (South Bldg)
C1 1 Hudson Ct
2 Shackleton Ct
3 De Gama Pl
4 Mercator Pl
5 Maritime Quay
6 Perry Ct
7 Amundsen Ct
C2 1 Nova Bldg
2 Apollo Bldg
3 Gaverick Mews
4 Windmill Ho
5 Orion Point
6 Galaxy Bldg
7 Venus Ho
8 Olympian Ct
9 Poseidon Ct
10 Mercury Ct
11 Aphrodite Ct
12 Cyclops Mews
13 Neptune Ct
14 Artemis Ct
15 Hera Ct
16 Ares Ct
17 Ringwood Gdns
18 Dartmoor Wlk
19 Rothsay Wlk
20 Ashdown Wlk
21 Radnor Wlk
22 Ironmonger's Pl
23 Britannia Rd
24 Deptford Ferry Rd
25 Magellan Pl
26 Dockers Tanner Rd
C3 1 Bowsprit Point
2 St Hubert's Ho
3 John Tucker Ho
4 Broadway Wlk
5 Nash Ho
6 Fairlead Ho
7 Crosstrees Ho
8 Stanliff Ho
9 Keelson Ho
10 Clara Grant Ho
11 Gilbertson Ho
12 Scoulding Ho
13 Hibbert Ho
14 Cressall Ho
15 Alexander Ho
16 Kedge Ho
C4 1 Anchorage Point
2 Waterman Bldg
3 Jefferson Bldg
4 Pierpoint Bldg
5 Franklin Bldg
6 Vanguard Bldg
7 Edison Bldg
8 Seacon Twr
9 Naxos Bldg
10 Express Wharf
11 Hutching's Wharf
12 Tobago St
13 Bellamy Cl
14 Dowlen Ct
15 Cochrane Ho
16 Beatty Ho
17 Scott Ho
18 Laybourne Ho
19 Ensign Ho
20 Beaufort Ho
21 Spinnaker Ho
22 Bosun Cl
23 Topmast Point
24 Turner Ho
25 Constable Ho
26 Knighthead Point
27 Seven Mills Prim Sch
C6 1 West India Ho
2 Berber Pl
3 Birchfield Ho
4 Elderfield Ho
5 Thornfield Ho
6 Gorsefield Ho
7 Arborfield Ho
8 Colborne Ho
9 East India Bldgs
10 Compass Point
11 Salter St
12 Garland Ct
13 Bogart Ct
14 Fonda Ct
15 Welles Ct
16 Rogers Ct
17 Premier Pl
18 Kelly Ct
19 Flynn Ct
20 Mary Jones Ho
21 Cannon Dr
22 Horizon Bldg
23 Holy Family RC Prim Sch
D1 1 Slipway Ho
2 Taffrail Ho
3 Platehouse The
4 Wheelhouse The
5 Chart House The
6 Port House The
7 Beacon Ho
8 Blasker Wlk
9 Maconochies Rd
D2 1 Brassey Ho
2 Triton Ho
3 Warspite Ho
4 Rodney Ho
5 Conway Ho
6 Exmouth Ho
7 Akbar Ho
8 Arethusa Ho
9 Tasman Ct
10 Cutty Sark Ho
11 Harbinger Prim Sch
D3 1 Turnberry Quay
2 Balmoral Ho
3 Aegon Ho
4 Marina Point
D6 1 Westcott Ho
2 Corry Ho
3 Malam Gdns
4 Blomfield Ho
5 Devitt Ho
6 Leyland Ho
7 Wigram Ho
8 Willis Ho
9 Balsam Ho
10 Finch's Ct
11 Poplar Bath St
12 Lawless St
13 Storey Ho
14 Abbot Ho
15 Woodall Cl
16 Landon Wlk
17 Goodhope Ho
18 Goodfaith Ho
19 Winant Ho
20 Goodspeed Ho
21 Lubbock Ho
22 Goodwill Ho
23 Martindale Ho
24 Holmsdale Ho
25 Norwood Ho
26 Constant Ho
27 Tower Hamlets Coll

120

A2 1 St John's Ho
2 Betty May Gray Ho
3 Castleton Ho
4 Urmston Ho
5 Salford Ho
6 Capstan Ho
7 Frigate Ho
8 Galleon Ho
9 Barons Lo
A3 1 Cardale St
2 Hickin St
3 John McDonald Ho
4 Thorne Ho
5 Skeggs Ho
6 St Bernard Ho
7 Kimberley Ho
8 Kingdon Ho
9 Killoran Ho
10 Alastor Ho
11 Lingard Ho
12 Yarrow Ho
13 Sandpiper Ct
14 Nightingale Ct
15 Robin Ct
16 Heron Ct
17 Ferndown Lo
18 Crosby Ho
A4 1 Llandovery Ho
2 Rugless Ho
3 Ash Ho
4 Elm Ho
5 Cedar Ho
6 Castalia Sq
7 Aspect Ho
8 Normandy Ho
9 Valiant Ho
10 Tamar Ho
11 Watkins Ho
12 Alice Shepherd Ho
13 Oak Ho
14 Ballin Ct
15 Martin Ct
16 Grebe Ct
17 Kingfisher Ct
18 Walkers Lo
19 Antilles Bay
A5 1 Lumina Bldg
2 Nova Ct W
3 Nova Ct E
4 Aurora Bldg
5 Arran Ho
6 Kintyre Ho
7 Vantage Mews
8 Managers St
9 Horatio Pl
10 Concordia Wharf
A6 1 Discovery Ho
2 Mountague Pl
3 Virginia Ho
4 Collins Ho
5 Lawless Ho
6 Carmichael Ho
7 Commodore Ho
8 Mermaid Ho
9 Bullivant St
10 Anderson Ho
11 Mackrow Wlk
12 Robin Hood Gdns
13 Prestage Way
14 Woolmore Prim Sch
B2 1 Verwood Lo
2 Fawley Lo
3 Lyndhurst Lo
4 Blyth Cl
5 Farnworth Ho
6 Francis Cl
7 St Luke's CE Prim Sch
B6 1 Quixley St
2 Romney Ho
3 Pumping Ho
4 Switch Ho
5 Wingfield Ct
6 Explorers Ct
7 Sexton Ct
8 Keel Ct
9 Bridge Ct
10 Sail Ct
11 Settlers Ct
12 Pilgrims Mews
13 Studley Ct
14 Wotton Ct
15 Cape Henry Ct
16 Bartholomew Ct
17 Adventurers Ct
18 Susan Constant Ct
19 Atlantic Ct
C1 1 Bellot Gdns
2 Thornley Pl
3 King William La
4 Bolton Ho
5 Miles Ho
6 Mell St
7 Sam Manners Ho
8 Hatcliffe Almshouses
9 Woodland Wlk
10 Earlswood Cl
11 St Joseph's RC Prim Sch
D1 1 Baldrey Ho
2 Christie Ho
3 Dyson Ho
4 Cliffe Ho
5 Moore Ho
6 Collins Ho
7 Lockyer Ho
8 Halley Ho
9 Kepler Ho
10 Sailacre Ho
11 Union Pk
D3 1 Teal St
2 Maurer Ct
3 Mudlarks Blvd
4 Renaissance Wlk
5 Alamaro Lo

121

A1 1 Layfield Ho
2 Westerdale Rd
3 Mayston Mews
4 Station Mews Terr
5 Halstow Prim Sch
6 Holyrood Mews
A5 1 Capulet Mews
2 Pepys Cres
3 De Quincey Mews
4 Hardy Ave
5 Tom Jenkinson Rd
6 Kennacraig Cl
7 Charles Flemwell Mews
8 Gatcombe Rd
9 Badminton Mews
10 Holyrood Mews
11 Britannia Gate
12 Dalemain Mews
13 Bowes-Lyon Hall
14 Lancaster hall
15 Victoria Hall
A6 1 Clements Ave
2 Martindale Ave
3 Balearic Apts
4 Marmara Apts
5 Baltic Apts
6 Coral Apts
7 Aegean Apts
8 Capital East Apts
B1 1 Phipps Ho
2 Hartwell Ho
3 Nicholas Stacey Ho
4 Fossdene Prim Sch
5 Frank Burton Cl
B5 1 Beaulieu Ave
2 Charles Whincup Rd
3 Audley Dr
4 Julia Garfield Mews
5 Rayleigh Rd
6 Pirie St
7 Royal Victoria Pl
8 Pankhurst Ave
9 West Mersea Cl
10 Ramsgate Cl
11 Windsor Hall
12 Munning Ho
13 Drake Hall
14 Jane Austen Hall
15 Eastern Quay
16 Portsmouth Mews
17 Britannia Village Prim Sch
C1 1 Ransom Rd
2 Linton Cl
3 Cedar Pl
4 Gooding Ho
5 Valiant Ho
6 Chaffey Ho
7 Benn Ho
8 Wellesley Cl
9 Gollogly Terr

122

A2 1 Harden Ct
2 Albion Ct
3 Viking Ho
4 Zealand Ho
5 Glenalvon Way
6 Parish Wharf
7 Elsinore Ho
8 Lolland Ho
9 Denmark Ho
10 Jutland Ho
11 Tivoli Gdns
12 Rance Ho
13 Peel Yates Ho
14 Rosebank Wlk
15 Paradise Pl
16 Woodville St
B2 1 Bowling Green Row
2 Sarah Turnbull Ho
3 Brewhouse Rd
4 Red Barracks Rd
5 Marine Dr
6 Hastings Ho
7 Centurion Ct
8 Cambridge Ho
9 Churchill Ct
10 Elizabeth Ct
11 Cambridge Barracks Rd
12 Len Clifton Ho
13 Granby Ho
14 Harding Ho
15 Rutland Ho
16 Townshend Ho
17 Rendlebury Ho
18 Milne Ho
19 Mulgrave Ho
20 Murray Ho
21 Chatham Ho
22 Biddulph Ho
23 Carew Ho
24 Eleanor Wlk
25 Cardwell Prim Sch
C2 1 Preston Ho
2 Lindsay Ho
3 Fraser Ho
4 Pickering Ho
5 Watergate Ho
6 Grinling Ho
7 Glebe Ho
8 Elliston Ho
9 Sir Martin Bowes Ho
10 Jim Bradley Cl
11 Bathway
12 Limavady Ho
13 Slater Cl
14 Vista Bldg The
15 Greenwich London Coll
16 St Mary Magdalene CE Prim Sch
C5 1 Westland Ho
2 Queensland Ho
3 Pier Par
4 Woodman Par
5 Shaw Ho
6 Glen Ho
7 Brocklebank Ho
D1 1 Branham Ho
2 Ford Ho
3 Wilford Ho
4 Parker Ho
5 Stirling Ho
6 Twiss Ho
7 Hewett Ho
8 De Haviland Dr
9 Schoolhouse Yd
D2 1 Beresford Sq
2 Central Ct
3 Walpole Pl
4 Anglesea Ave
5 Troy Ct
6 Ormsby Point
7 Haven Lo
8 Green Lawns
9 Eardley Point
10 Sandham Point
11 Bingham Point
12 Anglesea Mews
13 Masons Hill
14 Maritime Ho
15 International Univ of America (London Campus)
16 Woolwich Tramshed The

123

A1 1 Glenmount Path
2 Claymill Ho
3 St James Hts
4 St Margaret's Path
5 George Akass Ho
A2 1 Abel Ho
2 Maynard Ho
3 Crown Ho

490 123 A3

A3
1 Wayatt Point
2 Albert Ho
3 Building 50
4 Building 49
5 Building 48
6 Building 47
7 Building 36
8 Blenheim Ho
9 Wilson Ct
10 Romney Rd
B1
1 Bert Reilly Ho
2 Heavitree Rd
3 South Rise Prim Sch
B3
1 Apollo Way
2 Senator Wlk
3 Mallard Path
4 Fortune Wlk
C1
1 Fox Hollow Cl
2 Goldsmid St
C2
1 Gavin Ho
2 Richard Neve Ho
3 Bateson St
4 Lewin Ct
5 Conway Prim Sch

124

B5
1 Rowntree Path
2 Macaulay Way
3 Manning Ct
4 Chadwick Ct
5 Simon Ct
B6
1 Beveridge Ct
2 Hammond Way
3 Leonard Robbins Path
4 Lansbury Ct
5 Raymond Postgate Ct
6 Webb Ct
7 Curtis Way
8 Lytton Strachey Path
9 Keynes Ct
10 Marshall Path
11 Cross Ct
12 Octavia Way
13 Passfield Path
14 Mill Ct
15 Besant Ct
C3
1 Hermitage Ct
2 Chantry Cl
C4
1 Binsey Wlk
2 Tilehurst Point
3 Blewbury Ho
4 Coralline Wlk
5 Evenlode Ho
C5
1 Kingsley Ct
2 Wilberforce Ct
3 Shaftesbury Ct
4 Hazlitt Cl
5 Ricardo Path
6 Nassau Path
7 Malthus Path
8 Bright Ct
9 Cobden Ct
D4
1 Oakenhelt Ho
2 Trewsbury Ho
3 Penton Ho
4 Osney Ho
5 St Helens Rd
6 Clewer Ho
7 Maplin Ho
8 Wyfold Ho
9 Hibernia Point
10 Duxford Ho
11 Radley Ho
12 Limestone Wlk
13 Masham Ho
14 Jacob Ho

125

A3
1 Harlequin Ho
2 Dexter Ho
3 Argali Ho
4 Mangold Way
5 Lucerne Ct
6 Holstein Way
7 Abbotswood Cl
8 Plympton Cl
9 Benedict Cl
B1
1 Shakespeare Ho
2 Tennyson Ho
3 Dickens Ho
4 Scott Ho
5 Lansbury Ho
6 Shaw Ho
7 Chestnuts The
C1
1 Stevanne Ct
2 Tolcairn Ct
3 Chalfont Ct
4 Alonso Ho
5 Ariel Ct
6 Miranda Ho
7 Prospero Ho
8 Laurels The
9 Camden Ct
10 Newnham Lo
11 Court Lo
12 Flaxman Ct
13 Hertford Wlk
14 Riverview Ct
15 Winchester Ct
C2
1 Brushwood Lo
2 Bletchington Ct
3 Upper Sheridan Rd
4 William Ct
5 Samson Ct
6 Cowper Rd
7 Venmead Ct
C3
1 Cressingham Ct
2 Telford Ho
3 Kelvin Ho
4 Faraday Ho
5 Jenner Ho
6 Keir Hardie Ho
7 Lennox Ho
8 Mary Macarthur Ho
9 Elizabeth Garrett Anderson Ho
10 William Smith Ho
11 Baden Powell Ho
12 Baird Ho
13 Boyle Ho

129

B2
1 St Michael & St Martin RC Prim Sch
D1
1 Bellview Ct
2 Heathwood Ct
3 Aldermead
4 Northumberland Ct
D2
1 Oak Hts Ind Sch

130

C4
1 Osterley Lo
2 St Andrew's Ct
3 Parkfield
4 Fairways
5 Granwood Ct
6 Growewood Ct
D3
2 Beechen Cliff Way
3 Thurza Ct
4 Primrose Pl
5 Lanadron Cl
D4
1 Overton Cl

131

A2
1 Brewery Mews Bsns Ctr
2 Forge Lo
3 Pulteney Ct
4 Tolson Ho
5 Percy Gdns
6 Wynne Ct
7 Wisdom Ct
8 Swann Ct
9 Shrewsbury Wlk
10 King's Terr
11 Van Gogh Ct
12 Holme Ct
13 St Mary's RC Prim Sch
C5
1 Canute Ho
2 Spruce Ho
3 Moorings Ho
4 Jessops Wharf
5 Corsell Ho
6 Barnes Qtr
7 Dorey Ho
8 Tanyard Ho
9 Booth Ho
10 Oakbark Ho
11 Bordeston Ho
12 Shire Pl
D5
1 Galba Ct
2 Servius Ct
3 Maurice Ct
4 Leo Ct
5 Otho Ct
6 Nero Ct
7 Romulus Ct
8 Pump Alley
9 Caxton Mews
D6
1 Brockshott Cl
2 Westbury Pl
3 Brook La N
4 Braemar Ct
5 Brook Ct
6 Clifden Ho
7 Cedar Ct
8 Cranbrook Ct
9 Somerset Lo
10 Alexandra Rd
11 Berkeley Ho
12 Watermans Ct
13 Ferry Quays Ctyd
14 St Pauls CE Prim Sch

132

A1
1 St John's Gr
2 Michel's Row
3 Michelsdale Dr
4 Blue Anchor Alley
5 Clarence St
6 Sun Alley
7 Thames Link Ho
8 Benns Wlk
9 Waterloo Pl
10 Northumbria Ct
A6
1 Ferry Sq
2 Watermans Ct
3 Wilkes Rd
4 Albany Par
5 Charlton Ho
6 Albany Mews
7 Alma Ho
8 Griffin Ct
9 Cressage Ho
10 Tunstall Wlk
11 Trimmer Wlk
12 Running Horse Yd
13 Mission Sq
14 Distillery Wlk
B1
1 Towers The
2 Longs Ct
3 Sovereign Ct
4 Robinson Ct
5 Calvert Ct
6 Bedford Ct
7 Hickey's Almshouses
8 Church Estate Almshouses
9 Richmond International Bsns Ctr
10 Abercorn Mews
B4
1 Primrose Ho
2 Lawman Ct
3 Royston Ct
4 Garden Ct
5 Capel Lo
6 Devonshire Ct
7 Celia Ct
8 Rosslyn Ho
9 Branstone Ct
10 Lamerton Lo
11 Kew Lo
12 Dunraven Ho
13 Stoneleigh Lo
14 Tunstall St
15 Voltaire
C4
1 Clarendon Ct
2 Quintock Ho
3 Broome Ct
4 Lonsdale Mews
5 Elizabeth Cotts
6 Sandways
7 Victoria Cotts
8 North Ave
9 Grovewood
10 Hamilton Ho
11 Melvin Ct
12 Royal Par
13 Power Ho
14 Station Ave
15 Blake Mews
C6
5 Strand-on-the-Green Schs
D1
1 Hershell Ct
2 Deanhill Ct
3 Park Sheen
4 Furness Lo
5 Merricks Ct
D4
1 Terrano Ho
2 Oak Ho
3 Aura Ho
4 Maple Ho
5 Cedar Ho
6 Saffron Ho
7 Lime Ho
8 Lavender Ho
9 Juniper Ho
D6
1 Falcons Pre Prep school The

133

B2
1 Rann Ho
2 Craven Ho
3 John Dee Ho
4 Kindell Ho
5 Montgomery Ho
6 Avondale Ho
7 Addington Ct
8 Dovecote Gdns
9 Firmston Ho
10 Glendower Gdns
11 Chestnut Ave
12 Trehern Rd
13 Rock Ave
14 St Mary Magdalen's RC Prim Sch
D3
1 Melrose Rd
2 Seaforth Lo
3 St John's Gr
4 Sussex Ct
5 Carmichael Ct
6 Hampshire Ct
7 Thorne Pas
8 Brunel Ct
9 Beverley Path

134

D1
1 Olivette St
2 Mascotte Rd
3 Glegg Pl
4 Crown Ct
5 Charlwood Terr
6 Percy Laurie Ho
7 Our Lady of Victories RC Prim Sch
D2
1 Griffin Gate
2 Darfur St
3 John Keall Ho
4 Henry Jackson Ho
5 Felsham Ho
6 Ardshiel Cl
7 Ruvigny Mans
8 Star & Garter Mans
9 University Mans
10 Lockyer Ho
11 Phelps Ho
12 Princeton Ct
13 Kingsmere Cl
14 Felsham Mews
15 St Mary's CE Prim Sch
D6
1 Cobb's Hall
2 Dorset Mans
3 St Clements Mans
4 Bothwell St
5 Hawksmoor St
6 Melcombe Prim Sch

135

A3
1 Drive Mans
2 Romily Ct
3 Dwight Ct
4 Burlington Gdns
5 Fulham Prep Sch
6 Moat Sch The
7 All Saints CE Prim Sch
B3
1 Plato Pl
2 Mustow Pl
3 Laurel Bank Gdns
4 Ranelagh Mans
5 Churchfield Mans
6 Bear Croft Ho
7 Elysium Gate
8 Ethel Rankin Ct
9 Arthur Henderson Ho
10 William Banfield Ho
11 Melbray Mews
12 New King's Prim Sch
13 Eridge House Sch
D3
1 Brightwells
2 Broughton Road App
3 Bulow Ct
4 Langford Rd
5 Elizabeth Barnes Ct
6 Snowbury Rd

136

A2
1 Molasses Ho
2 Molasses Row
3 Cinnamon Row
4 Calico Ho
5 Calico Row
6 Port Ho
7 Square Rigger Row
8 Trade Twr
9 Ivory Ho
10 Spice Ct
11 Sherwood Ct
12 Mendip Ct
13 Chalmers Ho
14 Coral Row
15 Ivory Sq
16 Kingfisher Ho
B1
1 Burke Ho
2 High View Prim Sch
3 Centre Acad
4 Fox Ho
5 Buxton Ho
6 Pitt Ho
7 Ramsey Ho
8 Beverley Cl
9 Florence Ho
10 Linden Ct
11 Dorcas Ct
12 Johnson Ct
13 Agnes Ct
14 Hilltop Ct
15 Courtyard The
16 Old Laundry The
17 Oberstein Rd
18 Fineran Ct
19 Sangora Rd
20 Harvard Mans
21 Plough Mews
B2
1 Milner Ho
2 McManus Ho
3 Wilberforce Ho
4 Wheeler Ct
5 Sporle Ct
6 Holliday Sq
7 John Parker Sq
8 Carmichael Ct
9 Fenner Sq
10 Clark Lawrence Ct
11 Shaw Ct
12 Sendall Ct
13 Livingstone Rd
14 Farrant Ho
15 Jackson Ho
16 Darien Ho
17 Shepard Ho
18 Ganley Ct
19 Arthur Newton Ho
20 Chesterton Ho
21 John Kirk Ho
22 Mantua St
23 Heaver Rd
24 Candlemakers
25 Thames Christian Coll
26 Falconbrook Prim Sch
B3
1 Archer Ho
2 White Ho
3 Winfield Ho
4 Powrie Ho
5 Morgan Ct
6 Fairchild Ct
7 Musjid Rd
C2
1 Kiloh Ct
2 Lanner Ho
3 Griffon Ho
4 Kestrel Ho
5 Kite Ho
6 Peregrine Ho
7 Hawk Ho
8 Inkster Ho
9 Harrier Ho
10 Eagle Hts
11 Kingfisher Ct
12 Lavender Terr
13 Temple Ho
14 Ridley Ho
15 Eden Ho
16 Hertford Ct
17 Nepaul Rd
C3
1 Meecham Ct
2 McKiernan Ct
3 Banbury St
4 Colestown St
5 Crombie Mews
6 Frere St
D3
1 Stevenson Ho
2 Ambrose Mews
3 Harling Ct
4 Southside Quarter
5 Latchmere St
6 Dovedale Cotts
7 Roydon Ct
8 Castlemaine
9 Wittering Ho
10 Berry Ho
11 Weybridge Point

137

A2
1 Shaftesbury Park Chambers
2 Selborne
3 Rush Hill Mews
4 Marmion Mews
5 Crosland Pl
6 Craven Mews
7 Garfield Mews
8 Audley Cl
9 Basnett Rd
10 Tyneham Cl
11 Woodmere Cl
A3
1 Hopkinson Ho
2 Macdonald Ho
3 Rushlake Ho
4 Bishopstone Ho
5 Dresden Ho
6 Millgrove St
7 Farnhurst Ho
8 Walden Ho
9 Kennard St
10 Langhurst Ho
11 Atkinson Ho
12 Kennard Ho
13 Voltaire Ct
14 Barloch Ho
15 London Stone Bsns Est
16 Shaftesbury Park Prim Sch
17 John Burns Prim Sch
B2
1 Turnchapel Mews
2 Redwood Mews
3 Phil Brown Pl
4 Bev Callender Cl
5 Keith Connor Cl
6 Tessa Sanderson Pl
7 Daley Thompson Way
8 Rashleigh Ct
9 Abberley Mews
10 Willow Lodge
11 Beaufoy Rd
B3
1 St Philip Sq
2 Montefiore St
3 Gambetta St
4 Scott Ct
5 Radcliffe Path
6 Moresby Wlk
7 Victorian Hts
C1
1 Polygon The
2 Windsor Ct
3 Trinity Cl
4 Studios The
5 Bourne Ho
C2
1 Clapham Manor Ct

14 Riseholme Ho
15 Ringmer Ho
16 Petworth Ho
17 Stagshaw Ho
18 Ivybridge Ho
19 Inwood Ho
20 Gatcombe Ho
21 Felbridge Ho
22 Cowdray Ho
23 Dog Kennel Hill Sch
C3 1 Springfield Ho
2 Craston Ho
3 Walters Ho
4 Edgecombe Ho
5 Fowler Ho
6 Rignold Ho
7 Chatham Ho
C4 1 Barnwell Ho
2 Brunswick Villas
3 St Giles Twr
4 Bentley Ho
5 Dawson Ho
6 Dryden Ho
7 Mayward Ho
8 Longleigh Ho
9 Fairwall Ho
10 Bodeney Ho
11 Sandby Ho
12 Vestry Mews
13 Netley
14 Lakanal
15 Racine
16 Camberwell Coll of Arts
C5 1 Tower Mill Rd
2 Tilson Cl
3 Granville Sq
4 Edgar Wallace Cl
5 Potters Cl
6 Dorton Cl
7 Samuel Jones Ind Est
8 Dibden Ho
9 Marchwood Cl
10 Pilgrims Cloisters
11 Beacon Ho
12 Teather St
13 Stacy Path
14 Rumball Ho
15 Ballow Cl
16 Rill Ho
17 Southwark Coll (Camberwell Ctr)
18 St George's CE Prim Sch
C6 1 Downend Ct
2 Andoversford Ct
3 Pearse St
4 Watling St
5 Gandolfi St
6 Comfort St
7 Tower Mill Rd
D1 1 Dulwich Mews
2 New Hope Christian Sch
3 St James's Cloisters
D4 1 Colbert
2 Voltaire
3 Finch Mews
4 Charles Coveney Rd
5 Bamber Rd
6 Crane St
7 Curlew Ho
8 Mallard Ho
9 Tern Ho
10 Crane Ho
11 Falcon Ho
12 Bryanston Ho
13 Basing Ct
14 Marcus Ho
15 Sheffield Ho
16 Highshore Sch
17 St James The Great RC Prim Sch
18 Oliver Goldsmith Prim Sch
D5 1 Painswick Ct
2 Sharpness Ct
3 Mattingly Way
4 Hordle Prom N

5 Burcher Gale Gr
6 Calypso Cres
7 Hordle Prom S
8 Cinnamon Cl
9 Savannah Cl
10 Thames Ct
11 Shannon Ct
12 Amstel Ct
13 Danube Ct
14 Tilbury Cl
15 Hordle Prom E
16 Indus Ct
17 Oakcourt
18 Palm Ct
19 Rowan Ct
20 Blackthorn Ct
21 Pear Ct
22 Lidgate Ho
23 Whistler Mews
24 Boathouse Wlk
25 Camberwell Coll of Arts
D6 1 Millsbridge Ct
2 Cam Ct
3 Quedgeley Ct
4 Saul Ct
5 Quenington Ct
6 Westonbirt Ct
7 Wickway Ct

140
A2 4 St John's & St Clements CE Jun & Inf Sch
5 Bellenden Prim Sch
A3 1 William Margrie Cl
2 William Blake Ho
3 Quantock Mews
4 Choumert Sq
5 Parkstone Rd
6 Atwell Rd
A4 1 Canal Head Public Sq
2 Angelina Ho
3 Jarvis Ho
4 Richland Ho
5 Honeywood Ho
6 Wakefield Ho
7 Primrose Ho
8 Hardcastle Ho
9 Dunstall Ho
10 Springtide Cl
11 Purdon Ho
12 Flamborough Ho
13 Lambrook Ho
14 Witcombe Point
15 Yarnfield Sq
16 Winford Ct
17 Portbury Cl
18 Robert Keen Cl
A5 1 Thornhill Ho
2 Vervain Ho
3 Woodstar Ho
4 Tamarind Ho
5 Hereford Retreat
6 Haymerle Ho
7 Furley Ho
8 Thomas Milner Ho
9 Applegarth Ho
10 Freda Corbett Cl
11 Rudbeck Ho
12 Henslow Ho
13 Lindley Ho
14 Collinson Ho
15 Sister Mabel's Way
16 Timberland Cl
17 Hastings Cl
18 Sidmouth Ho
19 Budleigh Ho
20 Stanesgate Ho
21 Breamore Ho
22 Ely Ho
23 Gisburn Ho
24 Silkin Mews
25 Peckham Park Prim Sch
26 St Francis RC Prim Sch
A6 1 Bowles Rd
2 Western Wharf
3 Northfield Ho
4 Millbrook Ho

5 Denstone Ho
6 Deerhurst Ho
7 Caversham Ho
8 Battle Ho
9 Cardiff Ho
10 Bridgnorth Ho
11 Exeter Ho
12 Grantham Ho
13 Aylesbury Ho
14 Royston Ho
15 Haymerle Sch
B2 1 Tilling Ho
2 Goodwin Ho
3 Tyrells Ct
4 Citron Terr
5 Basswood Cl
6 Cheam St
7 Rye Oak Sch
B3 1 Walkynscroft
2 Ryegates
3 Hathorne Cl
4 Pilkington Rd
5 Russell Ct
6 Heaton Ho
7 Magdalene Cl
8 Iris Ct
9 St Mary Magdalene CE Prim Sch
B4 1 Willowdene
2 Pinedene
3 Oakdene
4 Beechdene
5 Hollydene
6 Wood Dene
7 Staveley Cl
8 Carnicot Ho
9 Martock Ct
10 Cherry Tree Ct
11 Kendrick Ct
12 John Donne Prim Sch
B5 1 Tortington Ho
2 Credenhill Ho
3 Bromyard Ho
4 Hoyland Cl
5 Willowdene
6 Ashdene
7 Acorn Par
8 Havelock Ct
9 Springall St
10 Harry Lambourn Ho
11 Grenier Apartments
C3 1 Honiton Gdns
2 Selden Ho
3 Hathway Ho
4 Hathway St
5 Station Ct
6 Symons Cl
7 Hollydale Prim Sch
C4 1 Trotman Ho
2 Boddington Ho
3 Heydon Ho
4 Boulter Ho
5 Astbury Bsns Pk
C5 1 Ambleside Point
2 Grasmere Point
3 Windermere Point
4 Roman Way
5 Laburnum Cl
6 Juniper Ho
7 Romney Cl
8 Hammersley Ho
9 Hutchinson Ho
10 Hammond Ho
11 Fir Tree Ho
12 Glastonbury Ct
13 Highbridge Ct
14 Filton Ct
15 Chiltern Ct
16 Cheviot Ct
C6 1 Penshurst Ho
2 Reculver Ho
3 Mereworth Ho
4 Camber Ho
5 Chiham Ho
6 Otford Ho
7 Olive Tree Ho
8 Aspen Ho
9 Lewis Silkin Ho
10 Richborough Ho
11 Dover Ho

12 Eynsford Ho
13 Horton Ho
14 Lamberhurst Ho
15 Canterbury Ind Pk
16 Upnall Ho
17 Sissinghurst Ho
18 Rochester Ho
19 Saltwood Ho
20 Leybourne Ho
21 Lullingstone Ho
22 Pilgrims Way Prim Sch
D1 1 Laxton Path
2 Barlings Ho
3 Bayfield Ho
4 Coston Wlk
5 Coverham Ho
6 Gateley Ho
7 Dereham Ho
8 Greenwood Ho
9 Hilton Ho
10 Goodall Ho
11 Horsley Ho
12 Jordan Ho
D5 1 Richard Anderson Ct
2 Palm Tree Ho
3 Edward Robinson Ho
4 Antony Ho
5 Gerrard Ho
6 Palmer Ho
7 Pankhurst Cl
D6 1 Harrisons Ct
2 Grantley Ho
3 Sunbury Ct
4 Tilbury Ho
5 Graham Ct
6 Connell Ct
7 St Clements Ct
8 Henderson Ct
9 Jemotts Ct
10 Verona Ct
11 Heywood Ho
12 Francis Ct
13 Hind Ho
14 Donne Ho
15 Carew Ct
16 Burbage Ho
17 Newland Ho
18 Dobson Ho
19 Dalton Ho
20 Greene Ct
21 Redrup Ho
22 Tarplett Ho
23 Stunell Ho
24 Gasson Ho
25 Bryce Ho
26 Barnes Ho
27 Barkwith Ho
28 Bannister Ho
29 Apollo Ind Bsns Ctr

141
C1 1 Turnham Prim Sch
A4 1 Archer Ho
2 Browning Ho
3 Hardcastle Ho
4 Brooke Ho
5 Wallis Ho
A5 1 Batavia Ho
2 Marlowe Bsns Ctr
3 Batavia Mews
4 Woodrush Cl
5 Alexandra St
6 Primrose Wlk
7 Vansittart St
8 Granville Ct
9 Cottesbrook St
10 Ewen Henderson Ct
11 Fordham Ho
12 Deptford Green Sch (Annex)
A6 1 Portland Ct
2 Phoenix Ct
3 Rainbow Ct
4 Hawke Twr
5 Chubworthy St
6 Woodpecker Rd
B5 1 Austin Ho
2 Exeter Way

3 Crossleigh Ct
4 Mornington Pl
5 Maple Ho
B6 1 Chester Ho
2 Lynch Wlk
3 Arlington Ho
4 Woodcote Ho
5 Cornbury Ho
6 Prospect Pl
7 Akintaro Ho
8 Mulberry Ho
9 Laurel Ho
10 Linden Ho
11 Ashford Ho
12 Wardalls Ho
13 Magnolia Ho
14 Howard Ho
15 Larch Cl
16 Ibis Ct
17 Merganser Ct
18 Wotton Rd
19 Kingfisher Sq
20 Sanderling Ct
21 Dolphin Twr
22 Mermaid Twr
23 Scoter Ct
24 Shearwater Ct
25 Brambling Ct
26 Kittiwake Ct
27 Guillemot Ct
28 Marine Twr
29 Teal Ct
30 Lapwing Twr
31 Violet Cl
32 Skua Ct
33 Tristan Ct
34 Rosemary Ct
35 Cormorant Ct
36 Shelduck Ct
37 Eider Ct
38 Pintail Ct
39 Fulcher Ct
40 Grinling Gibbons Prim Sch
C3 1 Ashmead Mews
2 St Stephen's CE Prim Sch
C4 1 Admiralty Cl
2 Harton Lodge
3 Sylva Cotts
4 Pitman Ho
5 Heston Ho
6 Mereton Mans
7 Indiana Bldg
8 St John's Lodge
9 Dean's Gateway
10 Lucas Vale Prim Sch
11 Addey & Stanhope Sch
12 Lewisham Coll (Deptford Campus)
C5 1 Sandpiper Ct
2 Flamingo Ct
3 Titan Bsns Est
4 Rochdale Way
5 Speedwell St
6 Reginald Pl
7 Fletcher Path
8 Frankham Ho
9 Cremer Ho
10 Wilshaw Ho
11 Castell Ho
12 Holden Ho
13 Browne Ho
14 Resolution Way
15 Lady Florence Ctyd
16 Covell Ct
17 Albion Ho
18 Maritime Greenwich Coll
19 St Joseph's RC Prim Sch
20 Tidemill Prim Sch
C6 1 Dryfield Wlk
2 Blake Ho
3 Hawkins Ho
4 Grenville Ho
5 Langford Ho
6 Mandarin Ct
7 Bittern Ct
8 Lamerton St
9 Ravensbourne Mans

10 Armada St
11 Armada Ct
12 Benbow Ho
13 Oxenham Ho
14 Caravel Mews
15 Hughes Ho
16 Stretton Mans
D21 1 Pine Tree Way
2 Waterway Ave
3 Lewisham Bridge Prim Sch
D3 1 Morden Mount Prim Sch
D4 1 Washington Bldg
2 California Bldg
3 Utah Bldg
4 Montana Bldg
5 Oregon Bldg
6 Dakota bldg
7 Idaho Bldg
8 Atlanta Bldg
9 Colorado Bldg
10 Arizona Bldg
11 Nebraska Bldg
12 Alaska Bldg
13 Ohio Bldg
14 Charter Bldgs
15 Flamsteed Ct
16 Friendly Pl
17 Dover Ct
18 Robinscroft Mews
19 Doleman Ho
20 Plymouth Ho
D5 1 Finch Ho
2 Jubilee The
3 Maitland Cl
4 Ashburnham Retreat

142
A2 1 Bankside Ave
2 Elder Wlk
3 Yew Tree Cl
4 Mill Ho
A3 1 Ellison Ho
2 Pitmaston Ho
3 Aster Ho
4 Windmill Ct
5 Hertmitage The
6 Burnett Ho
7 Lacey Ho
8 Darwin Ho
9 Pearmain Ho
A4 1 Penn Almshouses
2 Jervis Ct
3 Woodville Ct
4 Darnall Ho
5 Renbold Ho
6 Lindsell St
7 Plumbridge St
8 Trinity Gr
9 Hollymount Cl
10 Cade Tyler Ho
11 Robertson Ho
A5 1 Temair Ho
2 Royal Hill Ct
3 Prince of Orange La
4 Lambard Ho
5 St Marks Cl
6 Ada Kennedy Ct
7 Arlington Pl
8 Topham Ho
9 Darnell Ho
10 Hawks Mews
11 Royal Pl
12 Swanne Ho
13 Maribor
14 Serica Ct
15 Queen Elizabeth's Coll
16 James Wolfe Prim Sch
17 Greenwich Coll
A6 1 Crescent Arc
2 Greenwich Mkt
3 Turpin La
4 Durnford St
5 Sexton's Ho
6 Bardsley Ho
7 Wardell Ho
8 Clavell St
9 Stanton Ho
10 Macey Ho
11 Boreman Ho

12 Clipper Appts
B2 1 Our Lady of Lourdes RC Prim Sch
B6 1 Frobisher Ct
2 Hardy Cotts
3 Palliser Ho
4 Bernard Angell Ho
5 Corvette Sq
6 Travers Ho
7 Maze Hill Lodge
8 Park Place Ho
9 Meridian Prim Sch
D3 1 Heath House Prep Sch
D5 1 Westcombe Ct
2 Kleffens Ct
3 Ferndale Ct
4 Combe Mews
5 Mandeville Ct
6 Pinelands Cl

143

A5 1 Mary Lawrenson Pl
2 Bradbury Ct
3 Dunstable Ct
4 Wentworth Ho
A6 1 Nethercombe Ho
2 Holywell Ct
B6 1 Capella Ho
2 Collington Ho
3 Sherington Prim Sch
4 Our Lady of Grace RC Prim Sch
C6 1 Warren Wlk
2 Wilson Ho
3 Priory Ho
4 Mar Ho
5 Langhorne Ho
6 Games Ho
7 Erskine Ho
8 Ducie Ho
9 Downe Ho
10 Bayeux Ho
11 Elliscombe Mount
12 Harold Gibbons Ct
13 Mascalls Ct
14 Leila Parnell Pl
15 East Mascalls
16 Birch Tree Ho
17 Cherry Tree Ct
18 Elm Tree Ct
19 Cedar Ct
D5 1 Winchester Ho
2 Brentwood Ho
3 Shenfield Ho
4 Chesterford Ho

144

A4 1 Master Gunner's Pl
2 Ross Ho
3 Dickson Ho
4 Horne Ho
5 Pendlebury Ho
6 Roberts Ho
7 Maple Tree Pl
8 Berber Par
9 Centurian Sq
C6 1 Lawson Ho
2 Mabbett Ho
3 Petrie Ho
4 Memess Path
5 Ruegg Ho
6 Nile Path
7 Leslie Smith Sq
8 Spearman St
9 Siedle Ho
10 Watling Ho
11 O'Neill Path
12 Old Clem Sq
13 Jefferson Wlk
14 Milward Wlk
15 Wordsworth Ho
16 Fenwick Ct
D6 1 Acworth Ho
2 Griffiths Ho
3 Squires Ho
4 Cowen Ho
5 Turton Ho

6 Alford Ho
7 Boxshall Ho
8 Macallister Ho
9 Marvin Ho
10 Kelham Ho
11 Kimber Ho
12 Maxwell Ho
13 Woodford Ho
14 Penfold Ho
15 Butterfield Mews

146

A2 1 Wellingfield Ct
2 Woodville Gr
3 Midwinter Ct
4 St Leonards Cl

147

A1 1 Woburn Ct
2 Arundel Ct
3 Longleat Ct
4 Upton Villas
5 Whitehaven Ct
6 Shirley Hts
7 Louise Ct
8 Bethany Ct
B6 1 Bevercote Wlk
2 Lullingstone Rd
3 Benjamin Ct
4 Charton Ct
5 Terence Ct
6 Renshaw Ct
C1 1 Grove Rd
2 Friswell Pl
3 Market Pl
4 Geddes Pl
5 Janet Ct
6 Broadway Sh Ctr
7 Mall The
8 Pincott Rd

148

A5 1 Stranraer Way
2 Deri Dene Cl
3 Lord Knyvetts Ct
4 Tudor Ct
5 Wessex Ct
6 Vanguard Ho
7 Shackleton Ct
8 Fleetwood Ct
9 Clifton Ct
10 Vickers Ct
11 Bristol Ct
12 Sunderland Ct

150

B3 1 Bergenia Ho
2 Azalea Ho
3 Hamlyn Ho
4 Highfield Rd
5 Cardinal Road Inf Sch

152

A4 1 Library Way
C2 1 Jack & Jill Sch
2 Archdeacon Cambridge's CE Prim Sch

153

A3 1 Katharine Rd
2 Sandringham Ct
3 Garfield Rd
4 Arragon Rd
5 Flood La
6 John Wesley Ct
7 King Street Par
8 Thames Eyot
A4 1 Perryn Ct
2 Ivybridge Cl
3 Heritage Ho
4 Brook Ho
5 Neville Ho
6 Latham Ct
7 March Rd
8 Berkley Ct
9 Cole Court Lo
10 Cheltenham Ave
11 Railway App
12 St Mary's CE Prim Sch (Inf)
A5 1 Greenways The
2 Cole Park View
B4 1 Melton Ct

2 Amyand Park Gdns
3 Crown Ct
4 Burrell Ho
5 Owen Ho
6 Brentford Ho
7 Leeson Ho
8 Westbourne Ho
9 Orleans Ct
10 Lebanon Ct
B5 1 Grove The
2 Cumberland Cl
3 Westmorland Ct
4 Sussex Ct
5 Norfolk Cl
6 Nicol Cl
7 Old Lodge Pl
8 Kelvin Ct
9 St Margaret's Ct
10 Park Conts
11 St Margarets Bsns Ctr
12 Amyand Cotts
C1 1 Benson Ho
2 Bowes Lyon Ho
3 Cavendish Ho
4 Bentinck Ho
5 Clarke Ho
6 Secrett Ho
7 Edwards Ho
8 Field Ho
9 Greig Ho
10 Hawkins Ho
11 Newman Ho
12 Leyland Ho
13 Hornby Ho
14 Hatch Ho
C5 1 Howmic Ct
2 Sefton Lo
3 Ravensbourne Ho
4 Arlington Ct
5 Georgina Ct
6 Trevelyan Ho
7 Caradon Ct
8 Green Hedges
9 Old House Gdns
10 Queens Keep
11 Beresford Ct
12 Langham Ct
13 Poplar Ct
D5 1 Richmond Bridge Mans
2 Heatherdene Mans
3 Kenton Ct
4 Lennox Ho
5 Leicester Ct
6 Turner Ho
7 Blanchard Ho
8 Arosa Rd.
9 Ashe Ho
10 Bevan Ct
11 Lawley Ho
12 Darling Ho
13 Richmond Mans
14 Beaulieu Cl
15 Roseleigh Cl
16 Mallard Ct
D6 1 Garrick Cl
2 Old Palace Yd
3 Wardrobe The
4 Maids of Honour Row
5 Hunters Ct
6 Queensberry Ho
7 Old Palace Terr
8 Paved Ct
9 Golden Ct
10 Brewers La
11 Square The
12 Lower George St
13 St James's Cotts
14 Church Wlk
15 Church Ct
16 Victoria Pl
17 Castle Yd
18 Lewis Rd
19 Wakefield Rd
20 Church Terr
21 Warrington Rd
22 Ormond Ave
23 Glovers Lo
24 Holbrooke Pl
25 Northumberland Pl

27 Heron Sq
28 Whittaker Pl
29 Water Lane Ho
30 Riverside Ho
31 St Helena Terr

154

A5 1 Lancaster Cotts
2 Lancaster Mews
3 Bromwich Ho
4 Priors Lo
5 Richmond Hill Ct
6 Glenmore Ho
7 Hillbrow
8 Heathshott
9 Friars Stile Pl
10 Spire Ct
11 Ridgeway
12 Matthias Ct
13 Old Vicarage Sch
A6 1 Lichfield Terr
2 Union Ct
3 Carrington Lo
4 Wilton Ct
5 Egerton Ct
6 Beverley Lo
7 Bishop Duppa's Almshouses
8 Regency Wlk
9 Clear Water Ho
10 Onslow Avenue Mans
11 Michels Almshouses
12 Albany Pas
13 Salcombe Villas
B5 1 Chester Cl
2 Evesham Ct
3 Queen's Ct
4 Russell Wlk
5 Charlotte Sq
6 Jones Wlk
7 Hilditch Ho
8 Isabella Ct
9 Damer Ho
10 Eliot Ho
11 Fitzherbert Ho
12 Reynolds Pl
13 Chisholm Rd
B6 1 Alberta Ct
2 Beatrice Rd
3 Lorne Rd
4 York Rd
5 Connaught Rd
6 Albany Terr
7 Kingswood Ct
8 Selwyn Ct
9 Broadhurst Cl

156

A3 1 Farnborough Ho
2 Rushmere Ho
3 Horndean Cl
4 Highcross Way
5 Timsbury Wlk
6 Foxcombe Rd
7 Ryefield Path
8 Greatham Wlk
9 Gosport Ho
10 Stoatley Ho
11 Milland Ho
12 Clanfield Ho
13 Fareham Ho
14 Grayswood Point
A4 1 Woodcott Ho
2 Lyndhurst Ho
3 Wheatley Ho
4 Allbrook Ho
5 Bordon Wlk
6 Chilcombe Ho
7 Vicarage Ct
8 Shawford Ct
9 Eastleigh Wlk
10 Kings Ct
11 Somborne Ho
A6 1 Theodore Ho
2 Nicholas Ho
3 Bonner Ho
4 Downing Ho
5 Jansen Ho
6 Fairfax Ho
7 Devereux Ho
8 David Ho
9 Leigh Ho
10 Clipstone Ho
11 Mallet Ho

12 Arton Wilson Ho
B3 1 Ramsdean Ho
2 Purbrook Ho
3 Portsea Ho
4 Blendworth Point
5 Eashing Point
6 Hindhead Point
7 Hilsea Point
8 Witley Point
9 Buriton Ho
10 Grateley Ho
11 Hascombe Ho
12 Dunhill Point
13 Westmark Point
14 Longmoor Point
15 Cadnam Point
C4 1 Cumberland Ho
2 Devonshire Ho
3 Cornwall Ho
4 Norfolk Ho
5 Leicester Ho
6 Warwick Ho
7 Sutherland Ho
8 Carmarthen Ho
9 Worcester Ho
10 Rutland Ho
11 Paddock Way
12 Putney Hill
C6 1 Inglis Ho
2 Ducie Ho
3 Wharncliffe Ho
4 Stanhope Ho
5 Waldegrave Ho
6 Mildmay Ho
7 Mullens Ho
D3 1 Sandringham Cl
2 Eastwick Ct
3 Oatlands Ct
4 Banning Ho
5 Grantley Ho
6 Caryl Ho
7 Duncombe Ho
8 Chilworth Ct
9 Kent Lo
10 Turner Lo
11 Marlborough
12 Parkland Gdns
13 Lewesdon Cl
14 Pines Ct
15 Ashtead Ct
16 Mynterne Ct
17 Arden
18 Stephen Ct
19 Marsham Ct
20 Doradus Ct
21 Acorns The
22 Heritage Ho
23 Conifer Ct
24 Spencer Ho
25 Chartwell
26 Blenheim
27 Chivelston
28 Greenfield Ho
29 Oakman Ho
30 Radley Lo
31 Simon Lo
32 Admirals Ct
33 Augustus Rd
D4 1 Brett Ho
2 Brett House Cl
3 Sylva Ct
4 Ross Ct
5 Potterne Cl
6 Stourhead Cl
7 Fleur Gates
8 Greenwood
9 John Paul II Sch
10 Our Lady Queen of Heaven RC Prim Sch
11 Prospect House Sch
D5 1 Balmoral Ho
2 Glenalmond Ho
3 Selwyn Ho
4 Keble Ho
5 Bede Ho
6 Gonville Ho
7 Magdalene Ho
8 Armstrong Ho
9 Newnham Ho
10 Somerville Ho
11 Balliol Ho
12 Windermere
13 Little Combe Cl
14 Classinghall Ho

12 Chalford Ct
13 Garden Royal
14 South Ct
15 Anne Kerr Ct
16 Ewhurst
D6 1 Geneva Ct
2 Laurel Ct
3 Cambalt Ho
4 Langham Ct
5 Lower Pk
6 King's Keep
7 Whitnell Ct
8 Whitehead Ho
9 Halford Ho
10 Humphry Ho
11 Jellicoe Ho
12 South Thames Coll (Putney Ctr)

157

A3 1 William Harvey Ho
2 Highview Ct
3 Cameron Ct
4 Galgate Ct
5 Green Ho The
6 King Charles Wlk
7 Florys Ct
8 Augustus Ct
9 Albert Ct
10 Hertford Lo
11 Mortimer Lo
12 Allenswood
13 Ambleside
14 Hansler Ct
15 Roosevelt Ct
16 Southmead Prim Sch
A4 1 Douglas Gracey Ho
2 Aman Dalvi Ho
3 Andrew Reed Ho
4 Stoford Cl
5 Ronald Ross Prim Sch
A6 1 Claremont
2 Downside
3 Cavendish Cl
4 Ashcombe Ct
5 Carltons The
6 Espirit Ho
7 Millbrooke Ct
8 Coysh Ct
9 Keswick Hts
10 Avon Ct
11 Merlin Sch The
B6 1 Keswick Broadway
2 Burlington Mews
3 Cambria Ho
4 St Stephen's Gdns
5 Atlantic Ho
6 Burton Lo
7 Manfred Ct
8 Meadow Bank
9 Hooper Ho
10 Aspire Bld
C6 1 Pembridge Pl
2 Adelaide Rd
3 London Ct
4 Windsor Ct
5 Westminster Ct
6 Fullers Ho
7 Bridge Pk
8 Lambeth Ct
9 Milton Ct
10 Norfolk Mans
11 Francis Snary Lo
12 Bush Cotts
13 Downbury Mews
14 Newton's Yd
15 Roche Sch The
16 St Joseph's RC Prim Sch
17 West Hill Prim Sch
18 St Michael Steiner Sch The
D6 1 Fairfield Ct
2 Blackmore Ho
3 Lancaster Mews
4 Cricketers Mews

157 D6
5 College Mews
6 Arndale Wlk
6 St Anne's CE Prim Sch
7 South Thames Coll (Wandsworth Ctr)

158
A2 1 Bremans Row
2 St Andrew's Ct
3 Townsend Mews
4 Sheringham Mews
5 Rainbow Sch
6 Garratt Park Sec Specl Sch
A6 1 St Faith's CE Prim Sch
C2 1 St Peters Cl
2 St Hildas Cl
3 St Edmunds Cl
4 St Hughes Cl
5 St Anthonys Cl
6 St Benets Cl
7 St Catherines Cl
8 Elsley Sch
D5 1 Staplehurst Ct
2 Teyham Ct
3 Honeywell Jun & Inf Schs
D6 1 Clapham Computer & Secretarial Coll

159
A2 1 Upper Tooting Park Mans
2 Cecil Mans
3 Marius Mans
4 Boulevard The
5 Elmfield Mans
6 Holdernesse Rd
7 Lumiere Ct
A3 1 Heslop Ct
2 St James's Terr
3 Boundaries Mans
4 Station Par
5 Old Dairy Mews
6 Chestnut Grove Sch
7 Hornsby House Sch
8 Trinity St Mary's Prim Sch
A4 1 Hollies Way
2 Endlesham Ct
3 Broomwood Hall Sch (Upper Sch)
4 Holy Ghost RC Prim Sch
A5 1 Rayne Ho
2 St Anthony's Ct
3 Earlsthorpe Mews
4 Nightingale Mans
5 Broomwood Hall (Lower Sch)
B3 1 Holbeach Mews
2 Hildreth Street Mews
3 Coalbrook Mans
4 Hub Buildings The
5 Metropolis Apartments
6 Hildreth St
B4 1 Meyer Ho
2 Faraday Ho
3 Hales Ho
4 Frankland Ho
5 Graham Ho
6 Gibbs Ho
7 Dalton Ho
8 Ainslie Wlk
9 Rokeby Ho
10 Caistor Ho
11 Ivanhoe Ho
12 Catherine Baird Ct
13 Marmion Ho
14 Devonshire Ct
15 Blueprint Apartments
16 Royal Duchess Mews
17 Alderbrook Prim Sch
B5 1 Oliver House Prep Sch
C3 2 Henry Cavendish Prim Sch
3 Margaret Rutherford Pl
C4 1 Limerick Ct
2 Homewoods
3 Jewell Ho
4 Glanville Ho
5 Dan Bryant Ho
6 Olding Ho
7 Quennel Ho
8 Weir Ho
9 West Ho
10 Neville Ct
11 Friday Grove Mews
12 St Bernadette RC Jun Sch
C5 1 Joseph Powell Cl
2 Cavendish Mans
3 Westlands Terr
4 Cubitt Ho
5 Hawkesworth Ho
6 Normanton Ho
7 Eastman Ho
8 Couchman Ho
9 Poynders Ct
10 Selby Ho
11 Valentine Ho
12 Gorham Ho
13 Deauville Mans
14 Deauville Ct
C6 1 Timothy Cl
2 Shaftesbury Mews
3 Brook Ho
4 Grover Ho
5 Westbrook Ho
6 Hewer Ho
7 Batten Ho
8 Mandeville Ho
9 George Beare Lo
10 St Mary's RC Prim Sch
D3 1 Sinclair Ho
2 MacGregor Ho
3 Ingle Ho
4 St Andrews Mews
5 Telferscot Prim Sch
D4 1 Riley Ho
2 Bennett Ho
3 White Ho
4 Rodgers Ho
5 Dumphreys Ho
6 Homan Ho
7 Prendergast Ho
8 Hutchins Ho
9 Whiteley Ho
10 Tresidder Ho
11 Primrose Ct
12 Angus Ho
13 Currie Ho
D5 1 Parrington Ho
2 Savill Ho
3 Blackwell Ho
4 Bruce Ho
5 Victoria Ct
6 Victoria Ho
7 Belvedere Ct
8 Ingram Lo
9 Viney Ct
10 Bloomsbury Ho
11 Belgravia Ho
12 Barnsbury Ho

160
A1 1 De Montfort Ct
2 Leigham Hall Par
3 Leigham Hall
4 Endsleigh Mans
5 John Kirk Ho
6 Raebarn Ct
7 Wavel Ct
8 Homeleigh Ct
9 Howland Ho
10 Beauclerk Ho
11 Bertrand Ho
12 Drew Ho
13 Dowes Ho
14 Dunton Ho
15 Raynald Ho
16 Sackville Ho
17 Thurlow Ho
18 Astoria Mans
A2 1 Wyatt Park Mans
2 Broadlands Mans
3 Stonehill's Mans
4 Streatleigh Par
5 Dorchester Ct
6 Picture Ho
A3 1 Beaumont Ho
2 Christchurch Ho
3 Staplefield Cl
4 Chipstead Ho
5 Coulsdon Ho
6 Conway Ho
7 Telford Avenue Mans
8 Telford Parade Mans
9 Wavertree Ct
10 Hartswood Ho
11 Wray Ho
A4 1 Picton Ho
2 Rigg Ho
3 Watson Ho
4 MacArthur Ho
5 Sandon Ho
6 Thorold Ho
7 Pearce Ho
8 Mudie Ho
9 Miller Ho
10 Lycett Ho
11 Lafone Ho
12 Lucraft Ho
13 Freeman Ho
14 New Park Par
15 Argyll Ct
16 Dumbarton Ct
17 Kintyre Ct
18 Cotton Ho
19 Crossman Hos
20 Cameford Ct
21 Parsons Ho
22 Brindley Ho
23 Arkwright Ho
24 Perry Ho
25 Brunel Ho
26 New Park Ct
27 Tanhurst Ho
28 Hawkshaw Cl
29 Richard Atkins Prim Sch
A6 1 King's Mews
2 Clapham Court Terr
3 Clapham Ct
4 Clapham Park Terr
5 Pembroke Ho
6 Stevenson Ho
7 Queenswood Ct
8 Oak Tree Ct
9 Park Lofts
10 Ashby Mews
B1 1 Carisbrooke Ct
2 Pembroke Lo
3 Willow Ct
4 Poplar Ct
5 Leigham Cl
6 Mountview
6 Spa View
B3 1 Charlwood Ho
2 Earlswood Ho
3 Balcombe Ho
4 Claremont Cl
5 Holbrook Ho
6 Gwynne Ho
7 Kynaston Ho
8 Tillman Ho
9 Regents Lo
10 Hazelmere Ct
11 Dykes Ct
12 Hartwell Cl
13 Christ Church Streatham CE Prim Sch
14 Streatham Hill & Clapham High Sch
15 Orch Sch The
B4 1 Archbishop's Pl
2 Witley Ho
3 Outwood Ho
4 Dunsfold Ho
5 Deepdene Lo
6 Warnham Ho
7 Albury Lo
8 Tilford Ho
9 Elstead Ho
10 Thursley Ho
11 Brockham Ho
12 Capel Lo
13 Leith Ho
14 Fairview Ho
15 Weymouth Ct
16 Ascalon Ct
17 China Mews
18 Rush Common Mews
B6 1 Beatrice Ho
2 Florence Ho
3 Evelyn Ho
4 Diana Ho
5 Brixton Hill Ct
6 Austin Ho
7 Manor Ct
8 Camsey Ho
9 Romer Ho
10 Gale Ho
11 Byrne Ho
12 Farnfield Ho
13 Marchant Ho
14 Rainsford Ho
15 Springett Ho
16 Mannering Ho
17 Waldron Ho
18 Sudbourne Prim Sch
19 Corpus Christi RC Prim Sch
C3 1 Valens Ho
2 Loveday Ho
3 Strode Ho
4 Ethelworth Ct
5 Harbin Ho
6 Brooks Ho
7 Godolphin Ho
8 Sheppard Ho
9 McCormick Ho
10 Taylor Ho
11 Saunders Ho
12 Talcott Path
13 Derrick Ho
14 Williams Ho
15 Baldwin Ho
16 Churston Cl
17 Neil Wates Cres
18 Burnell Ho
19 Portland Ho
20 Fenstanton Prim Sch
21 St Martin-in-the-Fields High Sch
C4 1 Ellacombe Ho
2 Booth Ho
3 Hathersley Ho
4 Brereton Ho
5 Holdsworth Ho
6 Dearmer Ho
7 Cherry Cl
8 Greenleaf Cl
9 Longford Wlk
10 Scarlette Manor Wlk
11 Chandlers Way
12 Upgrove Manor Way
13 Ropers Wlk
14 Tebbs Ho
15 Bell Ho
16 Worthington Ho
17 Courier Ho
18 Mackie Ho
19 Hamers Ho
20 Kelyway Ho
21 Harriet Tubman Cl
22 Estoria Cl
23 Leckhampton Pl
24 Scotia Rd
25 Charles Haller St
26 Sidmouth Ho
27 Hunter Ct
28 Onslow Lo
29 William Winter Ct
30 Langthorne Lo
C5 1 Eccleston Ho
2 Scarsbrook Ho
3 Purser Ho
4 Rudhall Ho
5 Hardham Ho
6 Heywood Ho
7 Haworth Ho
8 Birch Ho
9 Lansdell Ho
10 Lomley Ho
11 Laughton Ho
12 Woodruff Ho
13 Bascome St
14 Dudley Mews
15 Herbert Mews
16 Blades Lo
17 Dick Shepherd Ct
18 Charman Ho
19 Morden Ho
20 Bishop Ct
21 Blackburn Ct
22 Leigh Ct
23 John Conwey Ho
24 Bristowe Cl
C6 1 Crownstone Ct
2 Brockwell Ct
3 Nevena Ct
4 St George's Residences
5 Hanover Mans
6 Fleet Ho
7 Langbourne Ho
8 Turnmill Ho
9 Walker Mews
10 Cossar Mews
11 Carter Ho
12 Arungford Mews
D1 1 Thanet Ho
2 Chapman Ho
3 Beaufoy Ho
4 Easton Ho
5 Roberts Ho
6 Lloyd Ct
7 Kershaw Ho
8 Wakeling Ho
9 Edridge Ho
10 Jeston Ho
11 Lansdowne Wood Cl
12 Rotary Lo
D6 3 Poets Mews
4 St Jude's CE Prim Sch

161
B2 1 Welldon Ct
2 Coppedhall
3 Shackleton Ct
4 Bullfinch Ct
5 Gannet Ct
6 Fulmar Ct
7 Heron Ct
8 Petrel Ct
9 Falcon Ct
10 Eagle Ct
11 Dunnock Ct
12 Dunlin Ct
13 Cormorant Ct
14 Oak Lodge
15 Corfe Lodge
C6 1 Velde Way
2 Delft Way
3 Arnhem Way
4 Isel Way
5 Kempis Way
6 Terborch Way
7 Steen Way
8 Deventer Cres
9 Nimegen Way
10 Hilversum Cres
11 St Barnabas Cl
12 James Allen's Girls' Sch
13 James Allen's Prep Sch

162
A1 1 Tunbridge Ct
2 Harrogate Ct
3 Bath Ct
4 Leamington Ct
5 Porlock Ho
6 Cissbury Ho
7 Eddisbury Ho
8 Dundry Ho
9 Silbury Ho
10 Homildon Ho
11 Highgate Ho
12 Richmond Ho
13 Pendle Ho
14 Tynwald Ho
15 Wirrall Ho
16 Greyfriars
A6 1 Dorothy Charrington Ho
2 Keswick Ct
3 Kendall Ct
4 Halliwell Ct
B1 1 River Ho
2 Fordington Ho
3 Arbury Terr
4 Woodbury Ho
5 Gainsborough Mews
6 Forest Hill Ct
7 Kelvin Grove Prim Sch
B2 1 Bromleigh Ct
2 Parfew Ct
3 Thetford Ct
4 Attleborough Ct
5 Dunton Ct
6 Frobisher Ct
7 Julian Taylor Path
8 Grizedale Terr
9 Worsley Ho
C1 1 Forest Lo
2 Sydenham Park Mans
3 William Wood Ho
C2 1 Fitzwilliam Hts
2 Taymount Grange
3 McLeod Ho
4 Featherstone Ave
5 Kingswear Ho
6 Salcombe Ho
7 Glynwood Ct
10 Holy Trinity CE Prim Sch
C3 1 Harlech Ct
2 Angela Ct
3 Westwood Ct
4 New Belmont Ho
5 Pearcefield Ave
6 Waldram Pl
7 Horniman Grange
8 South View Ct
9 Heron Ct
10 Katherine Ct
D1 1 Standlake Point
2 Radcot Point
3 Newbridge Point
4 Northmoor
5 Kelmscott
6 Radnor Ct
7 Heathwood Point
8 Ashleigh Point
9 Deepdene Point
10 Rosemount Point
11 Woodfield Ho
12 Clairville Point
13 Trevenna Ho
14 Hyndewood
15 Brent Knoll Sch
16 Our Lady & St Philip Neri RC Infants Sch
D2 1 Pikethorne
2 Andrew Ct
3 Valentine Ct
4 Soper Cl
5 Perrymount Prim Sch
6 Christ Church CE Prim Sch

164
B5 3 Park Piazza
4 Birdwood Ave
C4 1 Beaumont Terr
2 Littlebourne
3 Verdant Ct
D2 1 Kinross Ct
2 Montrose Ct
3 Rattray Ct
4 Rothesay Ct
D3 1 Edinburgh Ct
2 McMillan Ct
3 Rowallan Ct
4 Meridian Ct
5 Braemar Ct
6 Barrow Ct
7 Blair Ct
8 Darlington Ct

496 182 B6

4 Blytheswood Pl
C5 1 Parkhill Ho
2 Ash Ct
3 Alder Ct
4 Beech Ct
5 Acacia Ct
6 Blackthorn Ct
7 Cypress Ct
8 Hawthorn Ct
9 Hazel Ct
10 Sycamore Ct
11 Maple Ct
12 Laburnam Ct
13 Fern Lo
14 Colyton La
C6 1 James Boswell Cl
2 St Albans Ho
3 Suffolk Ct
4 Rockhampton Cl
5 Delphian Ct
6 Heather Ct
D5 1 Woodcote Pl
2 Joe Hunte Ct
3 Cork Tree Ho
4 Lake Ho
5 Cedars Ho
6 Portobello Ho
7 Cooper Ho
8 Farnsworth Ho
9 Hook Ho
10 Crest The
11 Renshaw Ho
12 Ruscoe Ho
13 Sardeson Ho
D6 1 William
   Wilberforce Ho
2 William Marsden
   Ho
3 Samuel Ho
4 Morris Stephany
   Ho
5 Church Ct

183

A6 1 Moore Ho
2 Chaucer Ho
3 Bushell Ho
4 Bligh Ho
5 Hobbs Rd
6 Hogarth Ho
7 Goodbehere Ho
8 Astley Ho
9 Elder Gdns
10 Elderberry Gr
11 Pavement The
12 Dunkirk St
B6 1 Josef Perrin Ho
2 Jean Humbert Ho
3 Charles Staunton
   Ho
4 Violette Szabo
   Ho
5 Lilian Rolfe Ho
6 Odette Ho
7 Robert Gerard Ho
8 St Bernards Cl
9 Champness Cl
10 Pennington Cl
11 Queenswood Ct
C4 1 Northwood Way
2 High Limes
3 Valley Prospect
4 Plane Tree Wlk
5 City Prospect
6 Bankside Way
7 Ridge Way
8 Rochdale
9 Barrington Wlk
10 Gatestone Ct
11 Childs La
12 Carberry Rd
13 Norwood Heights
   Sh Ctr
14 Paxton Prim Sch
C5 1 Oakdene
2 Thorsden Way
3 Oakfield Gdns
4 Georgetown Cl
5 Bridgetown Cl
6 Mountbatten Cl
7 Brabourne Cl
8 Alexandra Wlk
9 Compton Ct

184

10 Battenburg Wlk
11 Burma Terr
12 Wiseman Ct
C6 1 Linley Ct
2 Mellor Ho
3 Whitfield Ct
4 Michaelson Ho
5 Holberry Ho
6 Hovenden Ho
7 Huntley Ho
8 Telfer Ho
9 Markham Ho
10 Oldham Ho
11 Parnall Ho
12 Pierson Ho
13 Roper Ho
14 Roundell Ho
15 Sawyer Ho
16 Ransford Ho
17 Carmichael Ho
18 Bonne Marche
   Terr Mews
D3 1 Hetley Gdns
2 Claybourne Mews
3 Highland Lo
4 Mason Ct
5 Kendall Ct
6 High View
7 Stambourne
   Woodland Wlk
D5 1 Glenhurst Cl
2 Marlowe Ct
3 Grenville Ct
4 Raleigh Ct
5 Beechwoods Ct
6 Burntwood View

184

A3 1 Hanover Ct
2 Brunswick Ct
3 New Church Ct
4 Regency Ct
5 Owen Wlk
6 Bargrove Ct
7 Beaver Cl
B2 1 Dorset Ho
2 Collingwood Cl
3 Chartwell Way
4 Essex Twr
5 Appletree Cl
6 Ditton Pl
7 Kelvin Ct
8 Readman Ct
9 Glen Ct
10 Kingsbridge Ho
11 Carlton Ct
12 Benhurst Ct
13 Carole Ho
14 Dover Ho
15 Bettswood Ct
B3 1 Avery Ct
2 Rossal Ct
3 Oakdene Lo
4 Ridgemount Cl
5 Blakewood Ct
6 Trenholme Ct
7 Oakleigh Ct
8 Upchurch Ct
9 Devon Ho
10 Westmoreland
   Terr
11 Oakfield Road Ind
   Est
B5 1 Ragwort Ct
2 Firs The
3 Wingham Ho
4 Seath Ho
5 Ripley Ho
6 Lathwood Ho
7 Hurst Ho
8 George Ho
9 Browne Ho
10 Beacon Ho
11 Bailey Ho
12 Agate Ho
13 Sydenham High
   Sch (Sec)
C2 1 Challin St
2 Rutland Ho
3 Pine Ct
4 St Anthony's RC
   Prim Sch
C3 1 Watermen's Sq
2 St John's Cotts
3 Gladstone Mews
4 Middlesex Ho

5 Bethesda Ct
6 Ospringe Cl
7 Goudhurst Ho
8 Walmer Ho
9 Strood Ho
10 Greatstone Ho
11 John Baird Ho
12 St John's CE Prim
   Sch
C4 1 Midhurst
2 Oliver Ct
3 Victoria Ct
4 Wakefield Ct
5 Fountain Ct
6 Newlands Ct
C6 1 Homewalk Ho
2 Grace Path
3 Sycamore Ct
4 Sydenham
   Station App
5 Greenways
6 Faircroft
D3 1 Grombridge Ho
2 Provincial Terr
3 Smithers Ho
4 West Ho
5 Swallows Ct
6 Hornbeam Ho
7 Blenheim Centre

185

A1 1 Clock House Ct
2 Blandford Ave
3 Old School Cl
4 Lynsted Ct
5 Florence Rd
A6 1 Paxton Ct
2 Kenton Ct
3 Grove Ct
4 Shirley Lo
5 St Michael's CE
   Prim Sch
6 Our Lady & St
   Philip Neri RC Prim
   Sch
B2 1 Ashton Ct
2 Coombe Ct
3 Fontaine Ct
4 Richfield Ct
5 Sheridan Way
C1 1 Christ Church Rd
2 Lea Rd
3 Stanmore Terr
C2 1 Erindale Ct
2 Montgomerie Ct
3 Rebecca Ct
4 Sycamore Ct
5 Willow Ct
6 Marlborough Ct
7 Bearsted Terr
8 Berwick Ct
9 Wooderson Ct
10 Beck River Pk
C3 1 Gardenia Ct
2 Brackendale Ct
3 Daniel Ct
4 Moliner Ct
5 Chartwell Lo
6 Randmore Ct
7 Dover Ho
8 Lucerne Ct
9 Malling Ho
10 Westerham Lo
11 Brasted Lo
12 Milton Ho
13 Bradsole Ho
14 Sandgate Ho
15 Adelaide Ct
16 Nettlesteed Ct
17 Warren Ct
18 Alton Ct
19 Rockingham Ct
20 Camellia Ct
21 Sinclair Ct
22 Regents Ct
23 Minshull Pl
24 South Park Ct
25 Worsley Bridge
   Jun Sch
D1 1 Parkside
2 Tudors The
3 Oakbrook
4 Tara Ct
5 Redlands The
6 Cambria

7 Hillworth
8 Kelsey Gate
9 Burrells
10 Lincoln Lo
11 Courtlands
12 Fairleas
13 Ashdown Ct
14 Barons
D21 1 Clifton Ct
2 Mayfair Ct
3 Lait Ho
4 Fire Station
   Mews
5 Bromley Road Inf
   Sch
D41 1 Warner Ho
2 Clifford Ho
3 Lloyd Ho
4 Thurston Ho
5 Byron Ho
6 Blake Ho
7 Keats Ho

186

A21 1 White House Ct
2 Hunters The
3 Sandringham Ct
4 Glenhurst
5 Copperfields
6 Westgate Ct
A6 1 Dedham Ho
2 Flatford Ho
3 Langthorne Ct
4 Radley Ct
5 Hoover Ho
6 Brunner Ho
7 Waterer Ho
8 Marriott Ho
9 Bourbon Ho
B5 1 Longford Ho
2 Ingrebourne Ho
3 Brent Ho
4 Darent Ho
5 Beverley Ho
6 Wandle Ho
7 Rythe Ho
8 Ember Ho
9 Crane Ho
10 Ravensbourne Ho
C1 1 Warwick Ct
2 Maplehurst
3 Mount Arlington
4 Arundel Ct
D21 1 Weston Gr
2 Gibbs Ho
3 Longfield
4 Hammelton Ct
5 Bracken Hill Ct
6 Townend Ct
7 Treversh Ct
8 Cameron Ho
9 Woodlands Ct
10 Blythwood Pk
11 Bromley Pk
D31 1 Homecoppice Ho
2 Linden Ct
3 Kimberley Gate
4 Inglewood Ct
5 Mavery Ct
6 Glen Ct
7 Marlborough Ct
8 Cawston Ct
9 Blendon Path

187

A1 1 St James Ct
2 Court St
A21 1 Mitchell Way
2 Harrington Ho
3 Newman Ct
4 Uno Apartments
5 Bromley Ho
B21 1 Dainton Ct
2 Rothwell Ct
3 St Timothy's
   Mews
4 Andrignham Lo
5 Kendall Lo
6 Summerfield
7 Winston Ct
8 Vogue Ct
9 Laurels The
C1 1 Westland Lo
2 Eastland Ct
3 Dairsie Ct
4 Northlands

5 Beechfield Cotts
6 Oasis The
7 Cromarty Ct
8 Silverstone Ct

188

A61 1 Beaconsfield Par
2 Cranley Par
3 Kimmeridge Gdns
4 King & Queen Cl
5 Ballantyne Cl
C21 1 Ivybridge Ct
2 Greenbank Lo

190

A62 1 Cyril Lo
2 Hazlemere
3 Milton Lo
4 Marlin Ct
5 Conroy Ct
6 Glenwood Ct
7 Culverton Ct
8 Holmbury Manor
B11 1 Swanscombe Ho
2 Haverstock Ct
3 Arrandene Ho
4 Broomfield Ho
5 Headley Ho
6 Kenley Ho
7 Ladywell Ho
B61 1 Chudleigh
2 Wimborne
3 St John's Par
4 Holly Ct
5 Rectory Bsns Ctr

193

D11 1 Orchard Ct
2 Bridge Ct

197

A21 1 Raleigh Ho
2 Leicester Ho
3 Gresham Ho
4 White Gates
D21 1 Napier Ct
2 Darlington Ho
3 Charminster Ct
4 Mulberry Ct
5 Leander Ct
6 Clinton Ho
7 Hollingsworth Ct
8 Gloucester Ct
9 Palmerston Ct
10 Redwood Ct
11 Hursley Ct
12 Westmorland Ct
13 Lawson Ct
14 Alexander Ct
15 Winton Ct
16 Sydenham Ho
17 Caroline Ct
18 Ellswood Ct
19 Masefield Ct

198

A1 1 Ash Tree Cl
2 Shrubbery The
3 Malvern Ct
4 Gate Ho
5 Yew Tree Ho
A31 1 Station App
2 South Bank Lo
3 Bramshott Ct
4 Pandora Ct
5 Wellington Ct
6 Glenbuck Ct
7 Leighton Ho
8 Oakhill Ct
9 Downs View Lo
10 Osborne Ct
11 Surbiton Par
12 Woodgate Ho
13 Godwyn Ho
14 Ashby Ho
15 Newmans La
A41 1 Effingham Lo
2 Maple Ho
3 Channon Ct
4 Falconhurst
5 Ferndown
6 Viceroy Lo
7 Frensham Ho
8 Kingsley Ho
9 Rannoch Ct
10 Stratton Ct

11 Moray Ho
12 Dulverton Ct
13 Westerham
14 Hill Ct
15 Assheton-
   Bennett Ho
16 Hatfield Ho
17 Oxford Ct
18 Pennington Lo
19 Austin Ho
20 Wentworth Ct
21 Priory The
22 Sheraton The
23 Christopher Ct
24 Hobart Ho
25 St Mark's Hts
26 Surbiton Boys
   Prep Sch
A51 1 Marquis Ct
2 Garrick Ho
3 Surbiton High
   Sch Jun Girls Sch
4 Surbiton High
   Senior Sch
A61 1 College Rdbt
2 Edinburgh Ct
3 Weston Ct
4 Grebe Terr
5 Heron Ct
6 Agar Ho
7 St James' Ct
8 Grove Ct
9 Springfield Ct
10 College Wlk
B31 1 Percy Ct
2 Holmwood
3 Middle Green Cl
4 Herbert Ct
5 Alfriston Ct
B41 1 Woodleigh
2 Highcroft
3 Caernarvon Ct
4 Regency Ct
D11 1 Oakleigh Way
2 Chandler Ct

199

C21 1 Goodland Ho
2 Furzeland Ho
3 Oakcroft Ho
4 Meadcroft Ho
5 Newhouse
C41 1 Merryweather Ct
2 Roebuck Ct
3 Sable Ct
4 Holy Cross Sch
C51 1 Acacia Ho
2 Kingston Lo
3 Carrington Ct
4 Fairholme Ho
5 Marshall Ho
6 Norton Ho
7 Martin Ho

200

A1 1 Brookside Cres
2 Beverley Gdns
3 Purdey Ct
4 Avenue The
5 Briarwood Ct
6 Station App

202

C61 1 Cricket Green
   Specl Sch
2 Melrose Specl
   Sch
D61 1 Fair Green Ct
2 Regal Ct
3 Lewes Ct
4 Esher Mews
5 Sibford Ct
6 Deseret Ho
7 Standor Ho
8 Langdale Par
9 Newman Terr

204

A21 1 Barcom Trad Est
2 Croydon Valley
   Trade Pk
C31 1 Rozelle Ct
2 Dunheved Ct
3 Truscott Ho
C41 1 Brigstock Par

2 Terry Lodge
3 Justin Ct
D3 1 Wyndham Ct
2 Byrne Cl
D5 1 Nutfield Pl
2 Braidwood Ho
3 Elliott Ho

205

A6 1 Beulah Jun Sch
2 Beulah Inf Sch
3 Maple House Ind Montessori Sch
3 Vietory Day Sch
B1 1 Tavistock Ct
2 Chartwell Cl
3 Speaker's Ct
4 Cumberland Ct
5 Viceroy Ct
6 Oriel Ct
7 Cherry Orchard Gdns
8 Sola Ct
9 Gamma Ct
10 Croydon Coll Annexe
10 Edwin Pl
B5 1 Decimus Cl
2 Palace Ct
3 Reservoir Cl
4 Broxholme Cl
5 Whitehorse Manor Jun Sch
6 Whitehorse Manor Inf Sch
C1 1 Windmill Bridge Ho
2 Squire Ct
3 Houston Ct
5 Warren Ct
6 Freemasons Pl
7 Al Khair Prim & Sec Sch
8 Croydon Prim Independant Sch
D1 1 Hastings Pl
2 Grant Pl
3 Clive Ho
4 Havelock Ho
5 Bellmore Ct
6 Hereford Ct
7 Chequers Ct
8 Havelock Hall

206

A1 1 Farleycroft
2 Edgecumbe Ct
3 Wesson Ho
4 Sullivan Ct
5 Kenley Ho
6 Christopher Ct
7 Jayson Ct
8 Sundridge Pl
A3 4 St Thomas Becket RC Prim Sch
A5 3 St Mark's CE Prim Sch
A6 1 Leybourne Ct
2 Lestock Cl
3 Croftside The
D1 1 Cottongrass Cl
2 Oxlip Cl
3 Eyebright Cl

207

D1 1 North Rd
2 Sussex Rd
3 Riverside Wlk
4 Christie Ho
5 Windsor Ct
6 Sherwood Ct
7 Wheatsheaf Par
D6 1 Linden Ct
2 Park Ct
3 Chilchester Ct
4 Iveagh Ct

208

A6 1 Overbury
2 Wilton Pl
D1 1 Woodgrange Ct
2 Maycroft
3 Farnborough Cres
D4 1 Knowlton Gn
2 Speldhurst Cl
3 Bidborough Cl
4 Penshurst Wlk
D5 1 Wedgewood Ct
2 Birches The
3 Eccleshill
4 Tavistock Rd
5 Montpelier Ct
6 South Hill Rd

209

A5 1 Montague Terr
2 Chatsworth Ho
A6 1 Marina Cl
2 Cheveney Wlk
3 Bromley Manor Mans
4 Mall The
5 Westmoreland Pl
B5 1 Reflex Apartments
2 Wheeler Pl
3 Maxim Apartments
4 Exchange Apartments
5 Axiom Apartments
6 Weller Mews

211

B1 1 Gleneagles Gn
2 Tandridge Pl
3 Springfield Wlk
4 Pinehurst Wlk
5 Cromer Pl
6 Oakmont Pl

214

A6 1 St Bernards Ho
2 Wentworth Ct
3 Sunningdale Cl
4 Arklow Mews
5 Edward Pinner Ct

216

A6 1 Lansdowne Copse
2 Lansdowne Ct
D6 1 Edwards Cl
2 Pearing Cl
3 Churchlands Way
4 Langley Pl

217

A1 2 St Dunstan's CE Prim Sch
A2 1 Cheam Court Flats
2 Farnham Ct
3 Tabor Ct
5 Whyte Mews
6 Killick Mews
C1 1 Lancaster Ct
2 Redclyffe Terr
3 Kenilworth Terr
4 Lincoln Terr
5 Garden Ct
6 Ashwood Pk
7 Midsummer Apartments
8 Lyndhurst Ct
9 Lorraine Ct
10 Gloucester Ct
11 Banbury Ct
12 Camilla Ct
13 Lorac Ct
14 Kingswood Mans
15 Claremont Ho
16 Holly Ct
17 Castle Ho
18 Balmoral Ct
19 Davington Ct
20 Hereford Ct
C2 1 Norman Ho
2 Hawthorns The
3 Limes The
4 Alexa Ct
5 Kristina Ct
6 Beverley Ct
7 Chestnut Ct
D1 1 Holmeswood
2 Pebworth Lo
3 Addison Ct
4 Kingslee Ct
5 Raeburn Ho
6 Girtin Ho
7 Leith Towers
8 Courtlands
9 Thomas Ho
10 Grayshott Ct
11 Hadrian Ct
12 Sandown Ct
13 Magnolia Ct
14 Dunsfold Ct
15 Camberley Ct
16 Berrylands Ct
17 Brockham Ct
18 Alford Ct
19 Lansdowne Ho
20 Larchvale Ct
D2 1 Portland Ct
2 Durnston Ct
3 Barton Ct
4 Aplin Ct
5 Hannah Ct
6 Honeysuckle Ct
7 Rowans The
8 St Annes Ct
9 Bonnington Ho
10 Pamir Ct
11 Bradbourne Ct
12 Worcester Ct
D3 1 Marian Ct
2 Robin Hood Ct
3 Distin Ct
4 Queensmere
5 Grosvenor Ho
6 Cromer Mans
7 St Nicholas Ctr
8 Robin Hood Jun Sch
10 Sutton Coll of Learning for Adults
D5 1 Dorothy Pettingel Ho
2 Margaret Ho
3 All Saints' Benhilton CE Prim Sch

218

A1 1 Beauclere Ho
2 Melford Ct
3 Elmhurst Lo
4 Mansard Manor
5 Tranmere Ct
6 Beechcroft Lo
7 Savin Lo
8 Yew Tree Ct
9 Avondale Ct
10 Devonshire Ho
11 Hidcote Ho
12 Munstead Ct
13 Lodden Lo
14 Steetley Ct
15 Grampian Cl
16 Richard Sharples Ct
18 Devonshire Prim Sch
A2 1 Grosvenor Ct
2 Forest Dene Ct
3 Cedar Ct
4 Vanborough Ct
5 Shrub Ct
6 Evergreen Ct
7 Grasmere Ct
8 Heathfield Ct
9 Sherbourne Ct
10 Kinsale Grange
11 Linden Ct
12 Jubilee Ct
13 Langley Ct
14 Wilmot Ho
15 Farendon Ho
16 Alexander Ho
A3 1 Goossens Cl
2 Cliffe Wlk
3 Marlins Cl
4 Clowser Cl
5 Montana Gdns
6 Bournemouth Ct
7 Palmerston Ct
8 Manor Park Prim Sch
8 Sutton Gram Sch For Boys
A4 1 Lodge The
2 Hazelwood Ho
3 Chesterton Ho
4 Clevedon Ho
5 Staincliffe Ho
6 Denewood Ho
7 Newlyn Ho
8 Manor Ct
9 Glenrose Ho
10 Oak Lo
11 Briar The
12 Fernhead
13 Branch Ho
14 Thicket Ct
15 Adam Ct
16 Arndell Ho
17 Oakwood Ct
B3 1 Hogarth Ho
2 Gillray Ho
3 Cramhurst Ho
4 Ronald Ho
5 Blythewood
6 Hillsde
7 Weldon Ct
8 Yeoman Ct
D5 1 Kynersley Cl
2 Wrythe Gn
3 Bedford Villas
4 Chateau The
5 Nelson Ct
6 Errington Manor
7 Leeds Ct
8 Blair Ct

219

A4 1 Westcroft
2 Westcroft Ho
A5 1 Burnside Ct
2 Millpond Pl
3 Waterside Ct
4 Stable Ct
5 Manor Ct
6 Victor Seymour Inf Sch
B2 1 Runnymede Ct
2 Dolphin Ct
3 Kings Ct
4 Cheyne Ct
5 Hendfield Ct
6 Ellerslie Ct
7 Embassy Ct
8 Chandler Ct
9 Hambledon Ct
10 Wallington Ct
11 Jasmine Ct
12 Napier Ct
13 Rosswood Ho
14 Woodcote Ct
15 Surrey Ct
16 Stag Ct
17 Moorlands
18 Orchard Hill Coll
B3 1 Cornelion Cotts
2 Walpole Ct
3 Farmstead Ct
4 Derby Ho
5 Salisbury Ho
6 Chatham Ho
7 Collingwood Sch
B4 1 Loraine Ho
2 Harcourt Lo
3 Coniston Ct
4 Alcester Ct
5 Friars Ct
6 Campbell Ho
7 Brodie Ho
8 Lesley Ct
9 Birch Ct
10 Airborne Ho
C2 1 Rossendon Ct
2 Mulberry Mews
3 Nairn Ct
4 Wallington Sq
5 Rosemount Twrs
6 Connell Ho
7 Ashby Grange
8 Terry Ct
9 Leigham Cl
10 Clyde Works
11 Chandos Bsns Ctr
12 Beech Ho
13 Wendon Ct
C4 1 Holy Trinity CE Jun Sch
D3 1 Torquay Ho
2 Ashburton Ho
D5 1 Goodwood Lo
2 Haydock Lo
3 Kempton Lo

220

A1 1 Phoenix Ctr The
2 Ensign Way
3 Hunter Cl
4 Cirrus Cl
5 Mosquito Cl
D5 1 Latimer Rd
2 Cromwell Ho
3 Arundel Ct
4 Warrington Ct
5 Grace Ct
6 Stuart Ct
7 Bridge Par
8 Ridge's Yd
9 Parish Church CE Jun Sch
10 Parish Church CE Inf Sch
11 Old Palace of John Whitgift Sch (Seniors)

221

A3 1 Trent Ct
2 Sherwood Ct
3 Archers Ct
4 Keepers Ct
5 Lincoln Ct
6 Mount The
7 Fairhaven Ct
8 Brockham Ct
9 Chelwood Ct
10 Marey Ct
11 Landau Ct
A4 1 West Street Pl
2 Maple Ct
3 St Andrew's Rd
4 Albury Ct
5 Chestnut Ct
6 Elgin Ct
7 Beechfield Ct
8 Barham Ct
9 Whitstable Pl
10 Ledbury Pl
A5 1 Fellmongers Yd
2 Halstead Cl
3 Mann Cl
4 Waterworks Yd
5 Chanderia Ct
6 Katherine Ho
7 Smith's Yd
A6 1 Otterbourne Rd
2 Charrington Rd
3 Tamworth Pl
4 Priddy's Yd
5 Hospital of the Holy Trinity (Almshouses)
B6 1 Wellesley Court Rd
2 Norfolk Ho
3 Station App
4 Suffolk Ho
5 Cherry Orchard Gdns
6 Harrington Ct
D6 1 Cheyne Ct
2 Fourways
3 Princess Ct
4 Tierney Ct
5 Sinclair Ct
6 Guinness Ct
7 Mayfair Ct
8 Bishopscourt
9 Gloucester Lo
10 Beverley Hyrst
11 Melton Ct
12 Cecil Ct
13 Napier Ct

227

A3 1 Westfield
2 Farnborough Ct
3 Fern Hill Pl
4 Churchill Ct
5 Spencer Ct
6 Ladycroft Gdns
7 Crabbs Croft Cl
8 Clifton Cl
D2 1 Brittenden Cl
2 Wardens Field Cl
3 Winnipeg Dr
4 Superior Dr
5 Huron Cl
6 Manitoba Gdns
7 Lynne Cl
8 Flint Cl
9 Bakers Mews
D3 1 Osgood Gdns
2 Amberley Cl
3 Rawlings Cl
4 Beblets Cl
5 Fir Tree Cl
6 Raleigh Mews
7 King Henry Mews
D4 1 Healy Dr
2 Marsden Way
3 Taylor Cl
4 Strickland Way
5 Dryland Ave
6 Adcot Wlk
7 Lichlade Cl

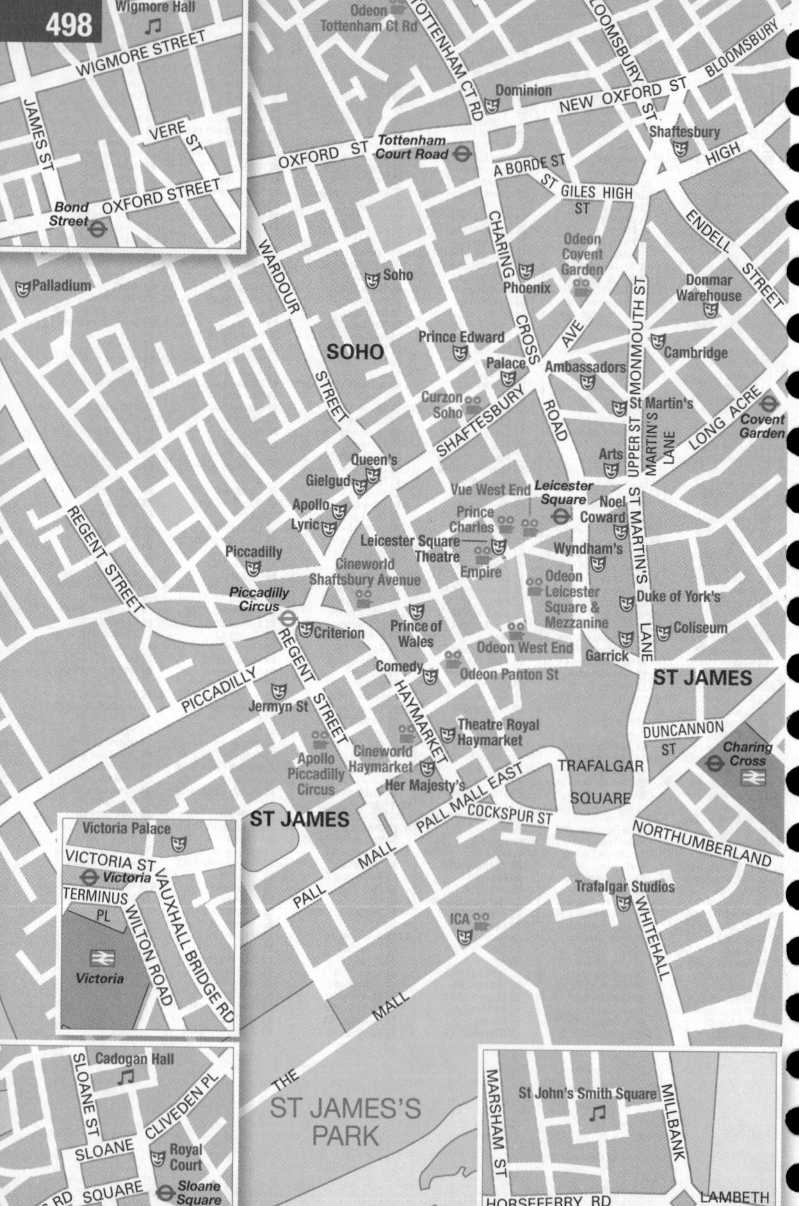

Wigmore Hall
WIGMORE STREET
JAMES ST
VERE ST
OXFORD STREET
Bond Street
Odeon Tottenham Ct Rd
TOTTENHAM CT RD
Dominion
BLOOMSBURY ST
NEW OXFORD ST
BLOOMSBURY
Shaftesbury
HIGH
OXFORD ST
Tottenham Court Road
A BORDE ST
ST GILES HIGH ST
ENDELL STREET
WARDOUR STREET
Palladium
Soho
CHARING CROSS ROAD
Phoenix
Odeon Covent Garden
Donmar Warehouse
SOHO
Prince Edward
AVE
MONMOUTH ST
Cambridge
Palace
Ambassadors
Curzon Soho
SHAFTESBURY
St Martin's
LONG ACRE
Covent Garden
UPPER ST MARTIN'S LANE
Arts
Queen's
Gielgud
Vue West End
Leicester Square
Apollo
Lyric
Prince Charles
Noel Coward
REGENT STREET
Leicester Square Theatre
Wyndham's
Piccadilly
Cineworld Shaftsbury Avenue
Empire
Odeon Leicester Square & Mezzanine
Piccadilly Circus
Duke of York's
ST MARTIN'S LANE
Criterion
Prince of Wales
Coliseum
Odeon West End
Garrick
Comedy
Odeon Panton St
ST JAMES
PICCADILLY
HAYMARKET
Jermyn St
Theatre Royal Haymarket
DUNCANNON ST
Charing Cross
Apollo Piccadilly Circus
Cineworld Haymarket
TRAFALGAR SQUARE
Her Majesty's
PALL MALL EAST
ST JAMES
COCKSPUR ST
NORTHUMBERLAND
Victoria Palace
VICTORIA ST
Victoria
TERMINUS PL
VAUXHALL BRIDGE RD
WILTON ROAD
PALL MALL
Trafalgar Studios
WHITEHALL
ICA
THE MALL
Cadogan Hall
SLOANE ST
CLIVEDEN PL
SLOANE SQUARE
Royal Court
Sloane Square
KING'S RD
ST JAMES'S PARK
MARSHAM ST
St John's Smith Square
MILLBANK
HORSEFERRY RD
LAMBETH BRIDGE

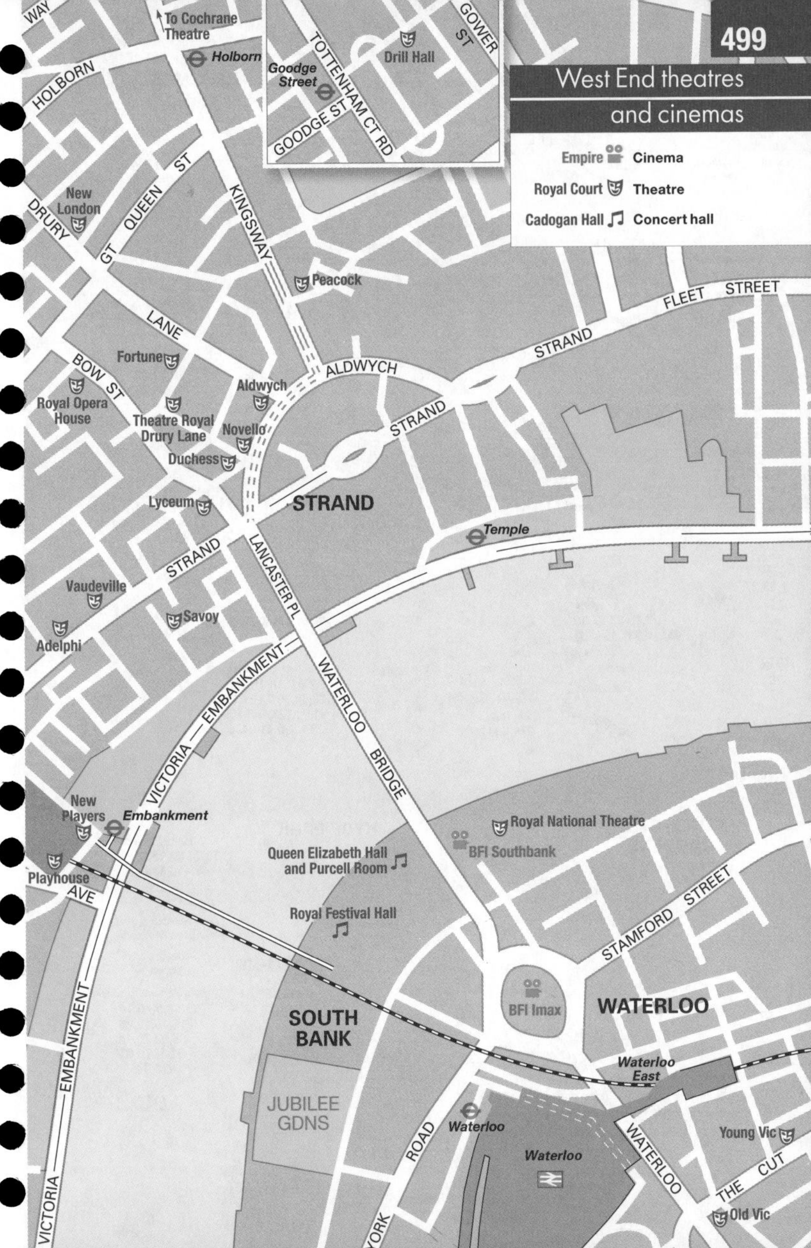

West End theatres
and cinemas

Empire 📽️ Cinema
Royal Court 🎭 Theatre
Cadogan Hall 🎵 Concert hall

To Cochrane
Theatre
Holborn
Goodge
Street
Drill Hall
GOWER ST
TOTTENHAM CT RD
GOODGE ST
KINGSWAY
HOLBORN
WAY
New
London
DRURY
GT QUEEN ST
LANE
BOW ST
Fortune
Royal Opera
House
Theatre Royal
Drury Lane
Novello
Duchess
Lyceum
Peacock
Aldwych
ALDWYCH
STRAND
FLEET STREET
STRAND
STRAND
STRAND
LANCASTER PL
Vaudeville
Savoy
Adelphi
Temple
WATERLOO BRIDGE
VICTORIA EMBANKMENT
WATERLOO
New
Players
Embankment
Playhouse
AVE
EMBANKMENT
VICTORIA
Royal National Theatre
BFI Southbank
Queen Elizabeth Hall
and Purcell Room
Royal Festival Hall
STAMFORD STREET
SOUTH
BANK
BFI Imax
WATERLOO
JUBILEE
GDNS
Waterloo
East
YORK ROAD
Waterloo
Waterloo
WATERLOO
Young Vic
THE CUT
Old Vic

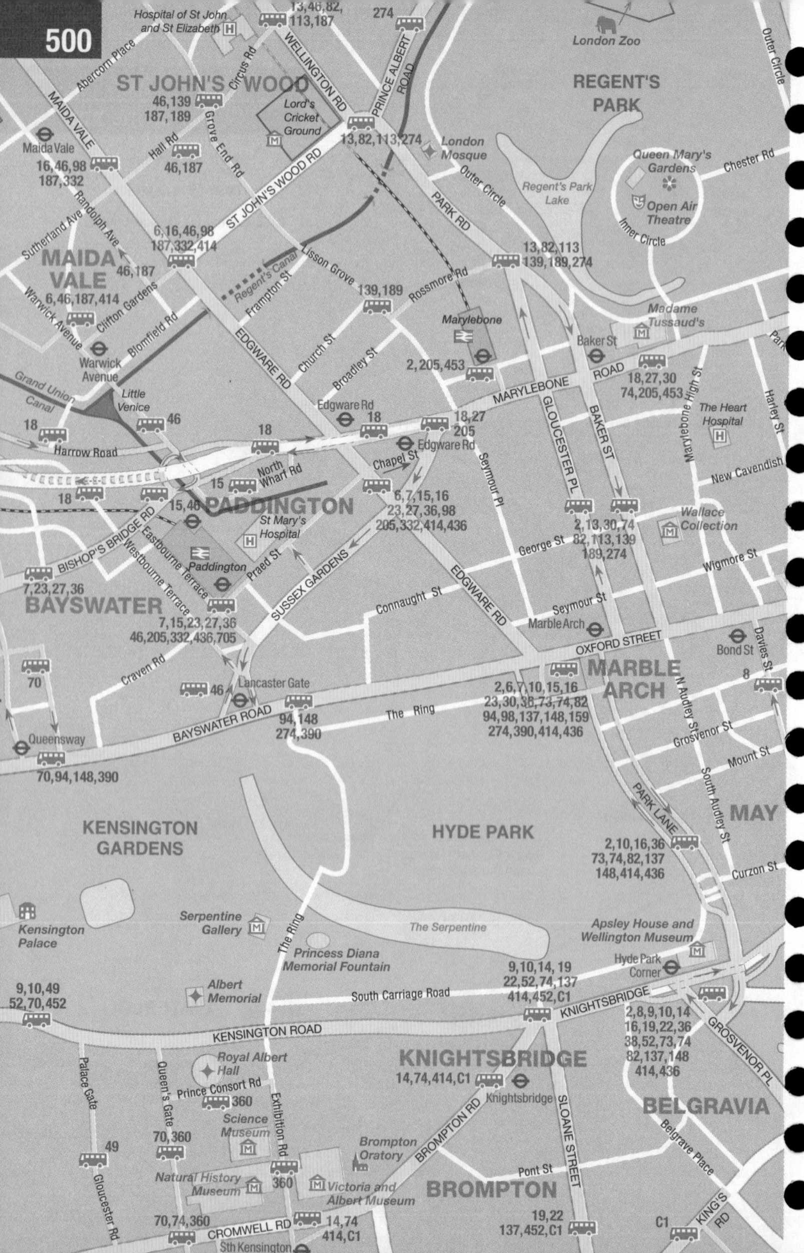

Hospital of St John and St Elizabeth
13,46,82, 113,187
274

London Zoo

ST JOHN'S WOOD
46,139
187,189

Abercorn Place

MAIDA VALE

Maida Vale
16,46,98
187,332

Grove End Rd

Circus Rd

WELLINGTON RD

Hall Rd
46,187

Lord's Cricket Ground

13,82,113,274

PRINCE ALBERT ROAD

London Mosque

REGENT'S PARK

Queen Mary's Gardens

Chester Rd

6,16,46,98
187,332,414

ST JOHN'S WOOD RD

Outer Circle

Regent's Park Lake

Open Air Theatre

Inner Circle

Lisson Grove

Sutherland Ave

Randolph Ave

46,187

Warwick Ave
6,46,187,414

Clifton Gardens

Blomfield Rd

Warwick Avenue

PARK RD

139,189

Rossmore Rd

Madame Tussaud's

Regent's Canal

Frampton St

Church St

Broadley St

Marylebone

Baker St

18,27,30
74,205,453

The Heart Hospital

Grand Union Canal

Little Venice

46

Edgware Rd

MARYLEBONE

New Cavendish

18
Harrow Road

18

Edgware Rd
18

18,27
205

GLOUCESTER PL

BAKER ST

2,13,30,74
82,113,139
189,274

Marylebone High St

Harley St

18
North Wharf Rd

Chapel St

15

Edgware Rd

Seymour Pl

Wallace Collection

Wigmore St

15,46

PADDINGTON
St Mary's Hospital

6,7,15,16
23,27,36,98
205,332,414,436

George St

Seymour St

Davies St

BISHOP'S BRIDGE RD

Eastbourne Terrace

Westbourne Terrace

Paddington

Praed St

EDGWARE RD

Marble Arch

OXFORD STREET

Bond St

7,23,27,36

BAYSWATER

7,15,23,27,36
46,205,332,436,705

SUSSEX GARDENS

Connaught St

Craven Rd

MARBLE ARCH

N Audley St

70

Lancaster Gate

46

The Ring

2,6,7,10,15,16
23,30,38,73,74,82
94,98,137,148,159
274,390,414,436

Grosvenor St

Queensway

BAYSWATER ROAD

94,148
274,390

Mount St

South Audley St

70,94,148,390

KENSINGTON GARDENS

HYDE PARK

PARK LANE

2,10,16,36
73,74,82,137
148,414,436

MAY

Curzon St

Kensington Palace

Serpentine Gallery

The Ring

The Serpentine

Apsley House and Wellington Museum

9,10,49
52,70,452

Albert Memorial

Princess Diana Memorial Fountain

South Carriage Road

9,10,14,19
22,52,74,137
414,452,C1

Hyde Park Corner

2,8,9,10,14
16,19,22,36
38,52,73,74
82,137,148
414,436

GROSVENOR PL

KENSINGTON ROAD

KNIGHTSBRIDGE

BELGRAVIA

Royal Albert Hall

KNIGHTSBRIDGE

14,74,414,C1

Knightsbridge

Belgrave Place

Queen's Gate

Prince Consort Rd

360

Exhibition Rd

BROMPTON RD

SLOANE STREET

Palace Gate

70,360

Science Museum

49

Natural History Museum

360

Brompton Oratory

Pont St

C1

KING'S RD

Gloucester Rd

70,74,360

CROMWELL RD

14,74
414,C1

Sth Kensington

Victoria and Albert Museum

BROMPTON

19,22
137,452,C1

Central London buses

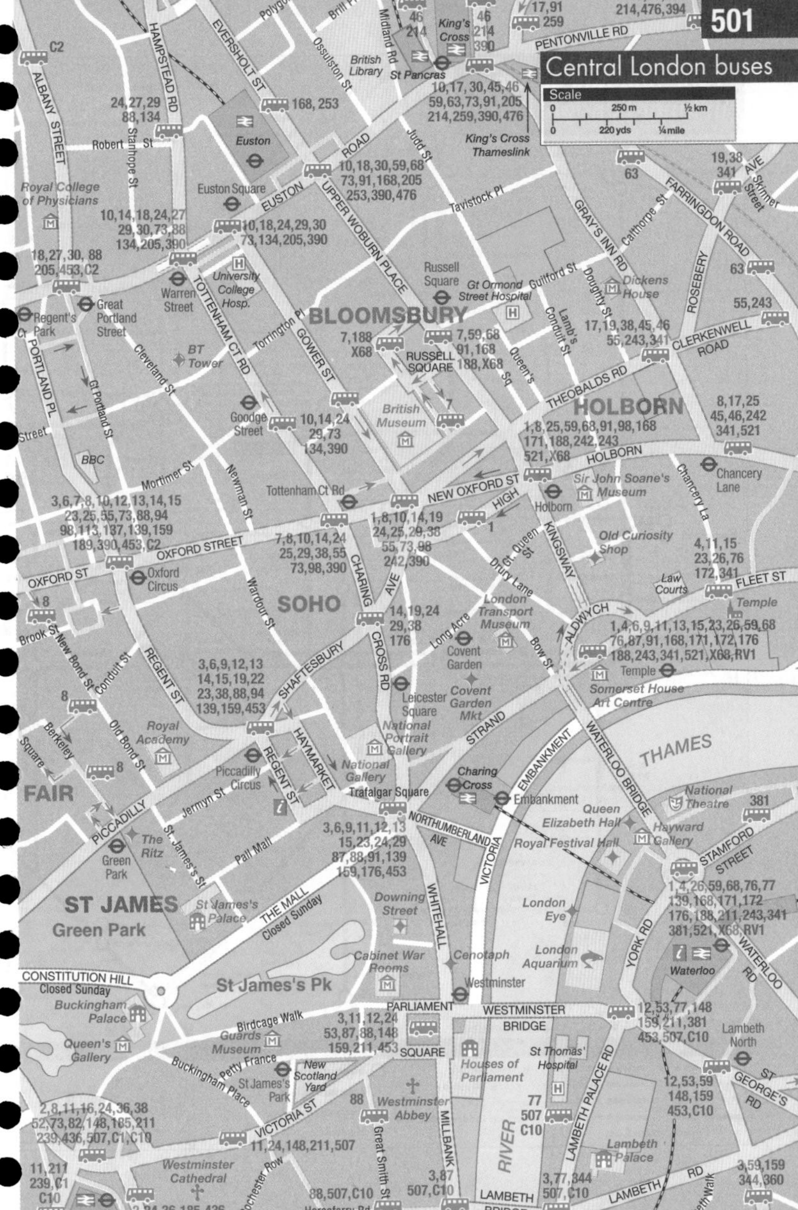
Scale
0
250 m
½ km
0
220 yds
¼ mile
PENTONVILLE RD
King's Cross
St Pancras
British Library
King's Cross Thameslink
Euston
Euston Square
Warren Street
Great Portland Street
Regent's Park
Goodge Street
Tottenham Ct Rd
Oxford Circus
Russell Square
Holborn
Chancery Lane
Covent Garden
Leicester Square
Piccadilly Circus
Green Park
Charing Cross
Embankment
Temple
Westminster
St James's Park
Victoria
Waterloo
Lambeth North
ALBANY STREET
HAMPSTEAD RD
EVERSHOLT ST
Polygon Rd
Brill Pl
Midland Rd
Ossulston St
Judd St
Robert St
Stanhope St
EUSTON ROAD
UPPER WOBURN PLACE
Tavistock Pl
GRAY'S INN RD
Calthorpe St
FARRINGDON ROAD
ROSEBERY AVE
Skinner Street
Royal College of Physicians
University College Hosp.
Gt Ormond Street Hospital
Guilford St
Doughty St
Lamb's Conduit St
Dickens House
CLERKENWELL ROAD
BLOOMSBURY
RUSSELL SQUARE
Queen's Sq
THEOBALDS RD
HOLBORN
TOTTENHAM CT RD
GOWER ST
Torrington Pl
BT Tower
Cleveland St
Gt Portland St
PORTLAND PL
British Museum
BBC
Mortimer St
Newman St
NEW OXFORD ST
HIGH HOLBORN
Sir John Soane's Museum
Chancery La
OXFORD STREET
OXFORD ST
Wardour St
CHARING CROSS RD
SOHO
Gt Queen St
Drury Lane
KINGSWAY
Old Curiosity Shop
Law Courts
FLEET ST
London Transport Museum
Long Acre
ALDWYCH
Bow St
Brook St
New Bond St
Conduit St
REGENT ST
SHAFTESBURY AVE
Covent Garden Mkt
Somerset House Art Centre
Berkeley Square
Old Bond St
Royal Academy
HAYMARKET
National Portrait Gallery
STRAND
EMBANKMENT
WATERLOO BRIDGE
THAMES
FAIR
Jermyn St
National Gallery
Trafalgar Square
NORTHUMBERLAND AVE
National Theatre
Queen Elizabeth Hall
Hayward Gallery
Royal Festival Hall
PICCADILLY
The Ritz
St James's St
Pall Mall
VICTORIA EMBANKMENT
STAMFORD STREET
ST JAMES
St James's Palace
THE MALL
Closed Sunday
Downing Street
WHITEHALL
London Eye
YORK RD
WATERLOO RD
Green Park
Cabinet War Rooms
Cenotaph
London Aquarium
CONSTITUTION HILL
Closed Sunday
Buckingham Palace
St James's Pk
PARLIAMENT SQUARE
WESTMINSTER BRIDGE
Birdcage Walk
Guards Museum
Queen's Gallery
Houses of Parliament
St Thomas' Hospital
Buckingham Place
Petty France
New Scotland Yard
LAMBETH PALACE RD
ST GEORGE'S RD
Westminster Abbey
VICTORIA ST
Great Smith St
MILLBANK
RIVER
Lambeth Palace
Westminster Cathedral
Rochester Row
Horseferry Rd
LAMBETH BRIDGE
LAMBETH RD
Lambeth Walk
C2
24,27,29
88,134
46
214
46
214
390
17,91
259
30,73,205
214,476,394
168, 253
10,17,30,45,46
59,63,73,91,205
214,259,390,476
10,18,30,59,68
73,91,168,205
253,390,476
63
19,38
341
10,14,18,24,27
29,30,73,88
134,205,390
10,18,24,29,30
73,134,205,390
18,27,30, 88
205,453,C2
63
55,243
17,19,38,45,46
55,243,341
7,188
X68
7,59,68
91,168
188,X68
7
10,14,24
29,73
134,390
8,17,25
45,46,242
341,521
1,8,25,59,68,91,98,168
171,188,242,243
521,X68
3,6,7,8,10,12,13,14,15
23,25,55,73,88,94
98,113,137,139,159
189,390,453,C2
7,8,10,14,24
25,29,38,55
73,98,390
1,8,10,14,19
24,25,29,38
55,73,98
242,390
1
4,11,15
23,26,76
172,341
8
14,19,24
29,38
176
1,4,6,9,11,13,15,23,26,59,68
76,87,91,168,171,172,176
188,243,341,521,X68,RV1
3,6,9,12,13
14,15,19,22
23,38,88,94
139,159,453
8
8
381
3,6,9,11,12,13
15,23,24,29
87,88,91,139
159,176,453
1,4,26,59,68,76,77
139,168,171,172
176,188,211,243,341
381,521,X68,RV1
3,11,12,24
53,87,88,148
159,211,453
12,53,77,148
159,211,381
453,507,C10
12,53,59
148,159
453,C10
77
507
C10
88
2,8,11,16,24,36,38
52,73,82,148,185,211
239,436,507,C1,C10
11,24,148,211,507
11,211
239,C1
C10
2,24,36,185,436
88,507,C10
3,87
507,C10
3,77,344
507,C10
3,59,159
344,360

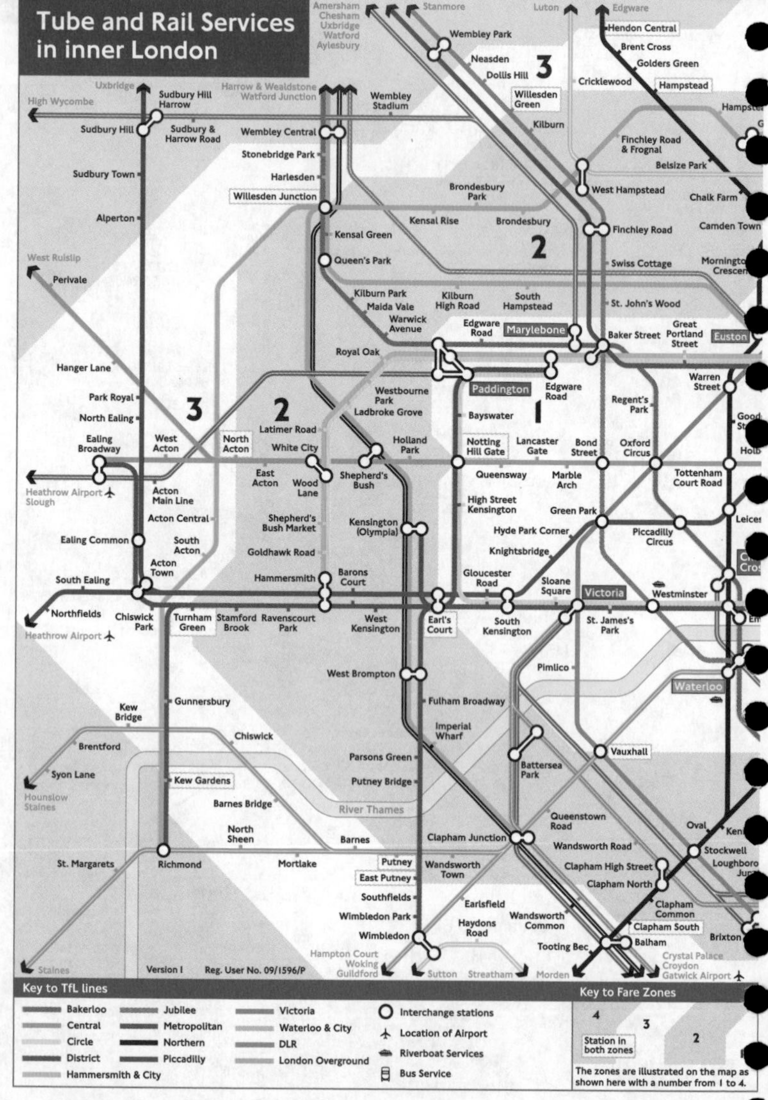
Tube and Rail Services in inner London
Amersham Chesham Uxbridge Watford Aylesbury
Stanmore
Luton
Edgware
Hendon Central
Brent Cross
Golders Green
Hampstead
Wembley Park
Neasden
Dollis Hill
Willesden Green
Kilburn
Cricklewood
Uxbridge
High Wycombe
Sudbury Hill Harrow
Sudbury Hill
Sudbury & Harrow Road
Harrow & Wealdstone Watford Junction
Wembley Stadium
Wembley Central
Stonebridge Park
Harlesden
Willesden Junction
Sudbury Town
Alperton
Finchley Road & Frognal
Belsize Park
West Hampstead
Chalk Farm
Brondesbury Park
Kensal Rise
Brondesbury
Kensal Green
Queen's Park
Finchley Road
Camden Town
Swiss Cottage
West Ruislip
Perivale
Kilburn Park
Maida Vale
Warwick Avenue
Kilburn High Road
South Hampstead
St. John's Wood
Edgware Road
Marylebone
Baker Street
Great Portland Street
Euston
Royal Oak
Paddington
Edgware Road
Warren Street
Hanger Lane
Park Royal
North Ealing
Westbourne Park
Ladbroke Grove
Bayswater
Regent's Park
Latimer Road
Ealing Broadway
West Acton
North Acton
White City
Holland Park
Notting Hill Gate
Lancaster Gate
Bond Street
Oxford Circus
East Acton
Wood Lane
Shepherd's Bush
Queensway
Marble Arch
Tottenham Court Road
Heathrow Airport
Slough
Acton Main Line
High Street Kensington
Green Park
Acton Central
Shepherd's Bush Market
Kensington (Olympia)
Hyde Park Corner
Piccadilly Circus
Ealing Common
South Acton
Goldhawk Road
Knightsbridge
Acton Town
Gloucester Road
Sloane Square
Victoria
Westminster
South Ealing
Hammersmith
Barons Court
Northfields
Chiswick Park
Turnham Green
Stamford Brook
Ravenscourt Park
West Kensington
Earl's Court
South Kensington
St. James's Park
Heathrow Airport
Pimlico
West Brompton
Waterloo
Gunnersbury
Fulham Broadway
Kew Bridge
Imperial Wharf
Chiswick
Brentford
Parsons Green
Battersea Park
Vauxhall
Syon Lane
Kew Gardens
Putney Bridge
Hounslow Staines
Barnes Bridge
River Thames
Queenstown Road
Oval
North Sheen
Barnes
Clapham Junction
Wandsworth Road
Stockwell
St. Margarets
Richmond
Mortlake
Putney
East Putney
Wandsworth Town
Clapham High Street
Clapham North
Southfields
Earlsfield
Clapham Common
Wimbledon Park
Haydons Road
Wandsworth Common
Clapham South
Wimbledon
Tooting Bec
Balham
Brixton
Hampton Court Woking Guildford
Crystal Palace Croydon Gatwick Airport
Staines
Sutton
Streatham
Morden
Version I
Reg. User No. 09/1596/P
Key to TfL lines
Bakerloo
Central
Circle
District
Hammersmith & City
Jubilee
Metropolitan
Northern
Piccadilly
Victoria
Waterloo & City
DLR
London Overground
Interchange stations
Location of Airport
Riverboat Services
Bus Service
Key to Fare Zones
Station in both zones
The zones are illustrated on the map as shown here with a number from 1 to 4.

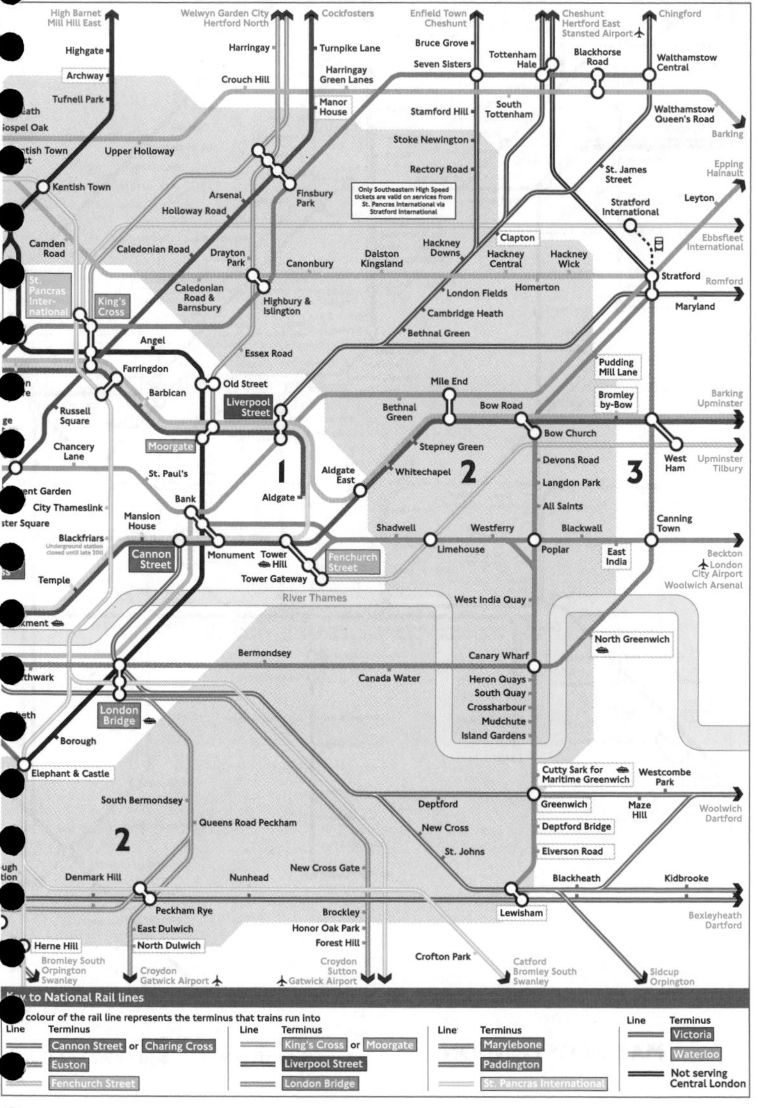

High Barnet, Mill Hill East · Welwyn Garden City, Hertford North · Cockfosters · Enfield Town, Cheshunt · Cheshunt, Hertford East, Stansted Airport ✈ · Chingford

Highgate · Harringay · Turnpike Lane · Bruce Grove · Seven Sisters · Tottenham Hale · Blackhorse Road · Walthamstow Central

Archway · Harringay Green Lanes · Stamford Hill · South Tottenham · Walthamstow Queen's Road

Tufnell Park · Crouch Hill · Manor House · Barking

Gospel Oak · Upper Holloway · Stoke Newington · St. James Street · Epping, Hainault

Kentish Town West · Rectory Road · Stratford International · Leyton · Ebbsfleet International

Camden Road · Arsenal · Holloway Road · Finsbury Park · Clapton · Stratford · Romford

Caledonian Road · Drayton Park · Canonbury · Dalston Kingsland · Hackney Downs · Hackney Central · Hackney Wick · Homerton · Maryland

St. Pancras International · King's Cross · Caledonian Road & Barnsbury · Highbury & Islington · London Fields · Cambridge Heath · Bethnal Green

Only Southeastern High Speed tickets are valid on services from St. Pancras International via Stratford International

Angel · Essex Road

Farringdon · Old Street · Pudding Mill Lane · Barking, Upminster

Russell Square · Barbican · Liverpool Street · Mile End · Bow Road · Bow Church · Bromley by-Bow

Chancery Lane · Moorgate · Bethnal Green · Stepney Green · Devons Road · West Ham · Upminster, Tilbury

St. Paul's · Aldgate East · Whitechapel · Langdon Park

Covent Garden · Bank · Aldgate · All Saints · Canning Town

City Thameslink · Mansion House · Shadwell · Westferry · Blackwall · Beckton, London City Airport ✈, Woolwich Arsenal

Leicester Square · Blackfriars · Underground station closed until late 2011 · Monument · Tower Hill · Limehouse · Poplar · East India

Temple · Cannon Street · Tower Gateway · Fenchurch Street

Embankment · River Thames · West India Quay

Bermondsey · North Greenwich

Southwark · Canada Water · Canary Wharf · Heron Quays, South Quay, Crossharbour, Mudchute, Island Gardens

Heath · London Bridge · Cutty Sark for Maritime Greenwich · Westcombe Park

Borough · Greenwich · Maze Hill · Woolwich, Dartford

Elephant & Castle · Deptford Bridge · Elverson Road

South Bermondsey · Queens Road Peckham · Deptford · New Cross · Blackheath · Kidbrooke

Denmark Hill · Nunhead · New Cross Gate · St. Johns · Bexleyheath, Dartford

Peckham Rye · Brockley · Lewisham

East Dulwich · Honor Oak Park · Forest Hill · Crofton Park · Catford, Bromley South, Swanley · Sidcup, Orpington

North Dulwich · Croydon, Sutton, Gatwick Airport ✈ · Gatwick Airport ✈

Herne Hill · Bromley South, Orpington, Swanley

Key to National Rail lines
colour of the rail line represents the terminus that trains run into

Line	Terminus	Line	Terminus	Line	Terminus	Line	Terminus
	Cannon Street or Charing Cross		King's Cross or Moorgate		Marylebone		Victoria
	Euston		Liverpool Street		Paddington		Waterloo
	Fenchurch Street		London Bridge		St. Pancras International		Not serving Central London

504

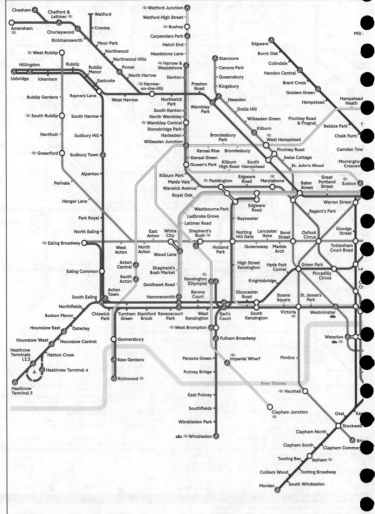

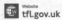